DRUG INFORMATION HANDBOOK for ONCOLOGY

A Complete Guide to Combination Chemotherapy Regimens

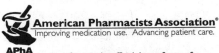

American Pharmacists Association®
Improving medication use. Advancing patient care.

APhA

Lexi-Comp is the official drug reference for the American Pharmacists Association

7th Edition

LEXI-COMP

Dominic A. Solimando, Jr., MA, BCOP
Senior Editor

DRUG INFORMATION HANDBOOK for ONCOLOGY

A Complete Guide to Combination Chemotherapy Regimens

Dominic A. Solimando, Jr, MA, FAPhA, FASHP, BCOP
Senior Editor

Oncology Pharmacist
President, Oncology Pharmacy Services, Inc.
Arlington, VA

LEXI-COMP, INC

NOTICE

This data is intended to serve the user as a handy reference and not as a complete drug information resource. It does not include information on every therapeutic agent available. The publication covers over 250 commonly used drugs and is specifically designed to present important aspects of drug data in a more concise format than is typically found in medical literature or product material supplied by manufacturers.

The nature of drug information is that it is constantly evolving because of ongoing research and clinical experience and is often subject to interpretation. While great care has been taken to ensure the accuracy of the information and recommendations presented, the reader is advised that the authors, editors, reviewers, contributors, and publishers cannot be responsible for the continued currency of the information or for any errors, omissions, or the application of this information, or for any consequences arising therefrom. Therefore, the author(s) and/or the publisher shall have no liability to any person or entity with regard to claims, loss, or damage caused, or alleged to be caused, directly or indirectly, by the use of information contained herein. Because of the dynamic nature of drug information, readers are advised that decisions regarding drug therapy must be based on the independent judgment of the clinician, changing information about a drug (eg, as reflected in the literature and manufacturer's most current product information), and changing medical practices. Therefore, this data is designed to be used in conjunction with other necessary information and is not designed to be solely relied upon by any user. The user of this data hereby and forever releases the authors and publishers of this data from any and all liability of any kind that might arise out of the use of this data. The editors are not responsible for any inaccuracy of quotation or for any false or misleading implication that may arise due to the text or formulas as used or due to the quotation of revisions no longer official.

Certain of the authors, editors, and contributors have written this book in their private capacities. No official support or endorsement by any federal or state agency or pharmaceutical company is intended or inferred.

The publishers have made every effort to trace any third party copyright holders, if any, for borrowed material. If they have inadvertently overlooked any, they will be pleased to make the necessary arrangements at the first opportunity.

If you have any suggestions or questions regarding any information presented in this data, please contact our drug information pharmacists at (330) 650-6506.

This manual was produced using Lexi-Comp's Information Management System™ (LIMS) — A complete publishing service of Lexi-Comp Inc.

LEXI-COMP

1100 Terex Road
Hudson, Ohio 44236
(330) 650-6506

ISBN 978-1-59195-228-2

TABLE OF CONTENTS

TABLE OF CONTENTS *(Continued)*

ABOUT THE AUTHOR

Dominic A. Solimando, Jr, MA, FAPhA, FASHP, BCOP

Dominic Solimando is President of Oncology Pharmacy Services, Inc. He received a Bachelor of Science in Pharmacy from the Philadelphia College of Pharmacy and Science, and a Master of Arts in Management and Supervision, specializing in Health Care Administration, from Central Michigan University. Dominic is a Board Certified Oncology Pharmacist. He has practiced as an oncology pharmacist at Georgetown University Medical Center, Washington, DC; Thomas Jefferson University Hospital, Philadelphia; Walter Reed Army Medical Center, Washington, DC; Letterman Army Medical Center, San Francisco; and Tripler Army Medical Center, Honolulu.

Mr Solimando is a contributing editor for *Hospital Pharmacy*, and on the editorial advisory board of *Pharmacy Today*. He served on the Editorial Board for *Drug Intelligence and Clinical Pharmacy* from 1984-1988, and the Journal of the American Pharmacists Association from 2000-2003. In addition to APhA and ASHP, Dominic is a member of the American College of Clinical Pharmacy, International Pharmaceutical Federation, International Society of Oncology Pharmacy Practitioners, Hematology/Oncology Pharmacists Association, American Institute of the History of Pharmacy, the Virginia Pharmacists Association, and the Washington Metropolitan Area Society of Health-System Pharmacists. His interests include safety precautions in handling parenteral medications, drug preparation and administration procedures, pain control, antiemetic therapy, and manangement of drug-induced toxicities.

EDITORIAL ADVISORY PANEL

4

Michael S. Edwards, PharmD, MBA
Chief, Oncology Pharmacy
Director, Oncology Pharmacy Residency
Program
Walter Reed Army Medical Center
Washington, D.C.

Vicki L. Ellingrod, PharmD, BCPP
Associate Professor
University of Iowa
Iowa City, Iowa

Kelley K. Engle, BSPharm
Pharmacotherapy Specialist
Lexi-Comp, Inc
Hudson, Ohio

Erin Fabian, PharmD, RPh
Pharmacotherapy Specialist
Lexi-Comp, Inc
Hudson, Ohio

Margaret A. Fitzgerald, MS, APRN, BC, NP-C, FAANP
President
Fitzgerald Health Education Associates, Inc.
North Andover, Massachusetts
Family Nurse Practitioner
Greater Lawrence Family Health Center
Lawrence, Massachusetts

Lawrence A. Frazee, PharmD
Pharmacotherapy Specialist in Internal Medicine
Akron General Medical Center
Akron, Ohio

Matthew A. Fuller, PharmD, BCPS, BCPP, FASHP
Clinical Pharmacy Specialist, Psychiatry
Cleveland Department of Veterans Affairs Medical Center
Brecksville, Ohio
Associate Clinical Professor of Psychiatry
Clinical Instructor of Psychology
Case Western Reserve University
Cleveland, Ohio
Adjunct Associate Professor of Clinical Pharmacy
University of Toledo
Toledo, Ohio

Morton P. Goldman, PharmD
Director of Pharmacotherapy Services
The Cleveland Clinic Foundation
Cleveland, Ohio

Julie A. Golembiewski, PharmD
Clinical Associate Professor
Colleges of Pharmacy and Medicine
Clinical Pharmacist, Anesthesia/Pain
University of Illinois
Chicago, Illinois

Jeffrey P. Gonzales, PharmD, BCPS
Critical Care Clinical Pharmacy Specialist
University of Maryland Medical Center
Baltimore, Maryland

Roland Grad, MDCM, MSc, CCFP, FCFP
Department of Family Medicine
McGill University
Montreal, Quebec, Canada

Larry D. Gray, PhD, ABMM
Director of Clinical Microbiology
TriHealth
Bethesda and Good Samaritan Hospitals
Cincinnati, Ohio

Tracey Hagemann, PharmD
Associate Professor
College of Pharmacy
The University of Oklahoma
Oklahoma City, Oklahoma

Martin D. Higbee, PharmD
Associate Professor
Department of Pharmacy Practice and Science
The University of Arizona
Tucson, Arizona

Jane Hurlburt Hodding, PharmD
Director, Pharmacy
Miller Children's Hospital
Long Beach, California

Collin A. Hovinga, PharmD
Assistant Professor of Pharmacy and Pediatrics
College of Pharmacy
University of Tennessee Health Science Center
Memphis, Tennessee

Darrell T. Hulisz, PharmD
Department of Family Medicine
Case Western Reserve University
Cleveland, Ohio

EDITORIAL ADVISORY PANEL *(Continued)*

PREFACE

The *Drug Information Handbook for Oncology* was designed to meet the needs of all oncology professionals involved in prescribing, preparing, and administering therapy. Presented in a concise and uniform format, this book contains monographs with information pertaining to both antineoplastic agents and ancillary medications. This handbook serves as a portable quick reference while providing comprehensive oncology-related drug information. Organized like a dictionary for ease-of-use, a drug can be quickly located by generic name and cross-referenced by brand name.

The Chemotherapy Regimen section provides a comprehensive presentation of cancer chemotherapy regimens. The regimens are listed alphabetically by regimen name (acronym). An index lists regimens by indication. In addition, a special Combination Chemotherapy Regimen field in each drug monograph will link you to the applicable regimens.

A special topics section addresses issues regarding Cancer Treatment-Related Complications (eg, fertility and cancer therapy, management of nausea and vomiting, management of infections); Cancer-Related Complications (eg, hypercalcemia, pain); Bone Marrow Transplantation; Drug Development, Approval, and Distribution; Investigational Drug Service; and Safe Handling of Hazardous Drugs.

The appendix section includes information related to conversions, renal function, and adult reference values. A pharmacologic category index provides a practical approach to categorizing drugs by their respective therapeutic classification.

We know you will find this handbook to be a valuable source of information and we welcome comments or suggestions to further improve future editions.

ACKNOWLEDGMENTS

The *Drug Information Handbook for Oncology* exists in its present form as the result of the concerted efforts of the following individuals: Robert D. Kerscher, publisher and chief executive officer of Lexi-Comp, Inc; Steven Kerscher, president and chief operating officer; Mark F. Bonfiglio, BS, PharmD, RPh, chief content officer; Stacy S. Robinson, editorial manager; Diedra L. Bragalone, pharmacotherapy specialist; Sherry L. Lyons, project manager; David C. Marcus, chief information officer; Leslie Jo Hoppes, pharmacology database manager; Tracey J. Henterly, senior graphic designer; Robin L. Farabee and Alexandra Hart, composition specialists; Katie Seabeck, product manager; and Julian I. Graubart, American Pharmacists Association (APhA), Director of Books and Electronic Products.

Special acknowledgement to all Lexi-Comp staff for their contributions on this handbook.

Much of the material contained in this book was a result of pharmacy contributors throughout the United States and Canada. Lexi-Comp has assisted many medical institutions to develop hospital-specific formulary manuals that contain clinical drug information as well as dosing. Working with these clinical pharmacists, hospital pharmacy and therapeutics committees, and hospital drug information centers, Lexi-Comp has developed an evolutionary drug database that reflects the practice of pharmacy in these major institutions.

USE OF THE DRUG INFORMATION HANDBOOK FOR ONCOLOGY

The *Drug Information Handbook for Oncology* is divided into six sections.

The first section is a compilation of introductory text pertinent to the use of this book.

The drug information section of the handbook, in which all drugs are listed alphabetically, details information pertinent to each drug. Extensive cross-referencing is provided by U.S. brand names, Canadian brand names, and index terms.

The Chemotherapy Regimen section provides a comprehensive presentation of cancer chemotherapy regimens. The regimens are listed alphabetically by regimen name (acronym). An index lists regimens by indications. In addition, a special Combination Chemotherapy Regimen field in each drug monograph will link you to the applicable regimens.

The Special Topics section contains important cancer-related issues (ie, pain management, bone marrow transplantation, and safe handling of hazardous drugs). These issues are discussed in detail.

The fifth section is an appendix section.

The last section of this handbook is an index listing drugs in their unique pharmacologic category.

Alphabetical Listing of Drugs

Drug information is presented in a consistent format and provides the following:

Generic Name	U.S. adopted name
Pronunciation Guide	Phonetic pronunciation
Medication Safety Issues	In an effort to promote the safe use of medications, this field is intended to highlight possible sources of medication errors such as look-alike/sound-alike drugs or highly concentrated formulations which require vigilance on the part of healthcare professionals. In addition, medications which have been associated with severe consequences in the event of a medication error are also identified in this field.
Related Information	Cross-reference to other pertinent drug information found elsewhere in this handbook
U.S. Brand Names	Trade names (manufacturer-specific) found in the United States. The symbol [DSC] appears after trade names that have been recently discontinued.
Index Terms	Includes names or accepted abbreviations of the generic drug; may include common brand names no longer available; this field is used to create cross-references to monographs
Generic Available	Specifies whether a generic equivalent is available
Canadian Brand Names	Trade names found in Canada
Pharmacologic Category	Unique systematic classification of medications
Use	Information pertaining to appropriate FDA-approved indications of the drug
Unlabeled/Investigational Use	Information pertaining to non-FDA approved and investigational indications of the drug

USE OF THE DRUG INFORMATION HANDBOOK FOR ONCOLOGY *(Continued)*

Restrictions	The controlled substance classification from the Drug Enforcement Agency (DEA). U.S. schedules are I-V. Schedules vary by country and sometimes state (ie, Massachusetts uses I-VI). May also include restricted availability information.
Pregnancy Risk Factor	Five categories established by the FDA to indicate the potential of a systemically absorbed drug for causing birth defects
Lactation	Information describing characteristics of using the drug while breast-feeding
Labeled Contraindications	Information pertaining to inappropriate use of the drug
Warnings/Precautions	Precautionary considerations, hazardous conditions related to use of the drug, and disease states or patient populations in which the drug should be cautiously used
Adverse Reactions	Side effects are grouped by percentage of incidence (if known) and/or body system
Overdosage/Toxicology	Comments and/or considerations are offered when appropriate and include signs or symptoms of excess drug and suggested management of the patient
Drug Interactions	
Cytochrome P450 Effect	Describes which cytochrome P450 enzymes are responsible for metabolizing the drug and/or which enzymes might be induced or inhibited by the drug.
Increased Effect/Toxicity	Drug combinations that result in an increased or toxic therapeutic effect between the drug listed in the monograph and other drugs or drug classes
Decreased Effect	Drug combinations that result in a decreased therapeutic effect between the drug listed in the monograph and other drugs or drug classes.
Ethanol/Nutrition/Herb Interactions	Information regarding potential interactions with food, nutritionals, herbal products, vitamins, or ethanol
Storage/Stability	Information regarding storage of product. Provides the time and conditions for which a solution or mixture will maintain full potency. For example, some solutions may require refrigeration after reconstitution while stored at room temperature prior to preparation.
Reconstitution	Includes comments on solution choice with time or conditions for the mixture to maintain full potency before administration
Compatibility	Whether drug is compatible, Y-site compatible, or incompatible with other drugs
Mechanism of Action	How the drug works in the body to elicit a response
Pharmacodynamics/ Kinetics	The magnitude of a drug's effect depends on the drug concentration at the site of action. The pharmacodynamics are expressed in terms of onset of action and duration of action. Pharmacokinetics are expressed in terms of absorption, distribution (including appearance in breast milk and crossing of the placenta), protein binding, metabolism, bioavailability, half-life, time to peak serum concentration, and elimination.
Dosage	The amount of the drug to be typically given or taken during therapy for children and adults; also includes any dosing adjustment for renal impairment or hepatic failure
Combination Regimens	List of combination chemotherapy regimens in which the drug is a component

Administration	Information regarding the recommended final concentrations, rates of administration for parenteral drugs, or other guidelines when giving the medication
Monitoring Parameters	Suggested monitoring parameters are listed
Test Interactions	Listing of assay interferences when relevant; (B) = Blood; (S) = Serum; (U) = Urine
Dietary Considerations	Specific dietary modifications and/or restrictions
Patient Information	Specific information pertinent for the patient
Special Geriatric Considerations	Pertinent information specific to the elderly population
Additional Information	Pertinent information about specific brands
Emetic Potential	Likelihood that the drug will cause nausea or vomiting
Vesicant	Indicates whether the drug is considered to be a vesicant and likely to cause significant morbidity if the infusion infiltrates soft tissues
High Dose Considerations	Special information regarding high dose chemotherapy use, such as transplantation of autologous or allogeneic bone marrow or peripheral blood cells to facilitate hematopoietic recovery after myeloablative chemotherapy (autologous, allogeneic), and replace a diseased hematopoietic system (allogeneic)
Comments	Additional information
High Dose	Chemotherapy doses 1.5- to 30-fold greater than standard dosages. Nonhematologic adverse reactions are dose-limiting.
Unique Toxicities	Nonhematologic adverse reactions that occur commonly with, or are unique to, high-dose chemotherapy administration
Dosage Forms	Information with regard to form, strength, and availability of the drug. **Note:** Additional formulation information (eg, excipients, preservatives) is included when available. Please consult product labeling for further information.
Extemporaneous Preparations	Directions for preparing oral or rectal suppositories or liquid formulations from solid drug products. May include stability information and references.
References	Recommended for additional information

Chemotherapy Regimens

The Chemotherapy Regimen section provides a comprehensive presentation of cancer chemotherapy regimens. The regimens are listed alphabetically by regimen name (acronym). An index lists regimens by indications. In addition, a special Combination Chemotherapy Regimen field in each drug monograph will link you to the applicable regimens.

Special Topics

Important cancer-related issues (ie, pain management, bone marrow transplantation, managing infections, safe handling of hazardous drugs) are discussed in detail.

Appendix

The appendix offers a compilation of tables, guidelines, nomograms, algorithms, and conversion information which can often be helpful when considering patient care.

Pharmacologic Category Index

This index provides a useful listing of drugs by their pharmacologic classification.

FDA PREGNANCY CATEGORIES

Throughout this book, there is a field labeled Pregnancy Risk Factor and the letter A, B, C, D, or X immediately following the field name which signifies a category. The FDA has established these five categories to indicate the potential of a systemically absorbed drug for causing birth defects. The key differentiation among the categories rests upon the reliability of documentation and the risk:benefit ratio. Pregnancy Category X is particularly notable in that if any data exists that may implicate a drug as a teratogen and the risk:benefit ratio is clearly negative, the drug is contraindicated during pregnancy.

These categories are summarized as follows:

A   Controlled studies in pregnant women fail to demonstrate a risk to the fetus in the first trimester with no evidence of risk in later trimesters. The possibility of fetal harm appears remote.

B   Either animal-reproduction studies have not demonstrated a fetal risk but there are no controlled studies in pregnant women, or animal-reproduction studies have shown an adverse effect (other than a decrease in fertility) that was not confirmed in controlled studies in women in the first trimester and there is no evidence of a risk in later trimesters.

C   Either studies in animals have revealed adverse effects on the fetus (teratogenic or embryocidal effects or other) and there are no controlled studies in women, or studies in women and animals are not available. Drugs should be given only if the potential benefits justify the potential risk to the fetus.

D   There is positive evidence of human fetal risk, but the benefits from use in pregnant women may be acceptable despite the risk (eg, if the drug is needed in a life-threatening situation or for a serious disease for which safer drugs cannot be used or are ineffective).

X   Studies in animals or human beings have demonstrated fetal abnormalities or there is evidence of fetal risk based on human experience, or both, and the risk of the use of the drug in pregnant women clearly outweighs any possible benefit. The drug is contraindicated in women who are or may become pregnant.

REDUCING PRESCRIBING ERRORS

Antineoplastic drugs have a low therapeutic index and therefore carry a high risk for toxicity. Even modest deviations in dosage can produce under- or over-dosage. Medication errors often occur during prescribing or order writing. The field of oncology is filled with acronyms that may serve as a source of medication error. While acronyms are useful and convenient, they may prove to be an obstacle to those less familiar with antineoplastic therapy, leading to possible misinterpretation. The newspapers have been quick to report fatal antineoplastic orders that resulted from poor prescribing habits and misinterpretation. Standardizing prescribing vocabulary in your institution is one way of reducing the risk for error. The following guidelines outline strategies for error reduction in medication prescribing. These guidelines can be applied to either written treatment protocols or treatment plans as well as written medication orders.

DRUG NAME

Use only approved generic names (United States Adopted Names [USAN]). The use of abbreviations is a source of potential error. This is especially true because abbreviations may stand for more than one drug. Common abbreviations such as "MTX", "CTX", "HN₂", "VCR", and "CDDP" can easily be misinterpreted and should be avoided. Even using terms such as "platinum" may cause confusion between cisplatin, carboplatin, or oxaliplatin. Drugs with similar names and actions, but different toxicities and dosage requirements, have been involved in medication errors. Continuing the use of drug name abbreviations that were once utilized when the drug product was investigational is also a problem. Abbreviations such as "VP-16", "VM-26", "CBDCA", "2-Cda", and "FK506" should no longer be used. Abbreviations for current investigational drugs should also be avoided. If your institution utilizes some abbreviations, they should be listed so that everyone has access to them and they are applied consistently.

NUMBERS AND DOSAGE UNITS

The use of zeros in drug doses is a source of error, especially with regard to the use of decimal points. Leading zeros should **always** be used before a decimal point (eg, 0.4 mg) but trailing zeros should **never** be used (eg, 7 mg **NOT** 7.0 mg). The word "units" should always be spelled out rather than abbreviated as "U". A "U" can be mistaken for a zero. The Greek letter mu (μ) should not be used; use "mcg" instead. The use of numbers within drug names should also be avoided. For example, fluorouracil instead of 5-fluorouracil, thioguanine instead of 6-thioguanine, mercaptopurine instead of 6-mercaptopurine.

DOSE, TOTAL DOSE, AND DURATION

The description of dose and duration is complicated and often left to interpretation because of nonstandard language in treatment plans and protocols. For example, "cisplatin 100 mg/m² continuously infused days 1-4" has been misinterpreted as cisplatin 100 mg/m²/day for 4 days, dispensed and administered, resulting in the death of the patient. Providing clear dose and duration instructions will prevent errors that occur due to interpretation of the author's meaning. Treatment plans and medication orders should include the dose based on patient parameters (body surface area, body weight, pharmacokinetic parameters), the calculated dose with any dosage reduction, how many hours or days the dose is to be administered, which specific days the dose should be administered, and the total dose per treatment course or cycle.

REDUCING PRESCRIBING ERRORS *(Continued)*

Example: Patient is 1.8 m². ABC 50 mg/m²/day I.V. push for 3 days = 90 mg
I.V. push on days 3, 4, and 5
(total dose per cycle = 270 mg).

Some would argue that each institution should standardize the calculations for body surface area and creatinine clearance.

VERIFYING DOSES/PROTOCOLS

Each institution should develop policies for as many independent dose checks as possible. The pharmacist should review the treatment protocol. If there is no treatment protocol, or the treatment plan is from a published article, the pharmacist should verify the doses from additional sources due to the possibility of errors in the literature.

STANDARDIZED ORDER FORMS

Many prescribing errors can be eliminated by the use of preprinted order forms. Pharmacists should be involved in the development of a form in their institution. The format of the form can vary. Three common formats have been suggested. First, a blank form that includes preprinted areas for premedications, antineoplastic drugs with doses in mg/m² or mg/kg, an area for the duration and dates of therapy, and an area for post-treatment drugs. Second, a preprinted form that is specific to a treatment protocol and contains preprinted drug doses. Third, a form that includes preprinted names of all antineoplastic drugs with check-off boxes and fill-ins for doses and routes. Whichever form is adapted for use, it is important that the form is easily distinguished from other order forms and is readily available at the point when and where antineoplastic orders are written.

COMMUNICATION

Communication is an important part of preventing medication errors from occurring. Pharmacists should be involved in writing or editing treatment protocols within institutions along with other healthcare providers. Pharmacists may participate in national study group committees that review dosing guidelines in protocols. Educating patients and families on their antineoplastic therapy will encourage them to question healthcare providers and become part of the error prevention process.

CONCLUSION

It is possible for anyone to make a mistake. A systematic method for preventing medication prescribing errors includes policies on drug names, use of abbreviations, stating duration and days of therapy, and total dose per cycle. The addition of preprinted order forms and communication among all disciplines during the protocol development process provides additional tools for preventing errors. It is important to remember that this is only one part of an entire process that contributes to potential medication errors.

Selected Readings

"ASHP Guidelines on Preventing Medication Errors in Hospitals," *Am J Hosp Pharm*, 1993, 50(2):305-14.

Attilio RM, "Strategies for Reducing Chemotherapy-Related Medication Errors: Improving the Chemotherapy Prescribing, Dispensing, and Administration Process, and the Patient's Role in Ensuring Safety," *Hosp Pharm*, 1997, 32(Suppl 1):S14-20.

Cohen MR, Anderson RW, Attilio RM, et al, "Preventing Medication Errors in Cancer Chemotherapy," *Am J Health Syst Pharm*, 1996, 53(7):737-46.

Kohler DR, Montello MJ, Green L, et al, "Standardizing the Expression and Nomenclature of Cancer Treatment Regimens," *Am J Health Syst Pharm*, 1998; 55(2):137-44.

ALPHABETICAL LISTING OF DRUGS

Abarelix (a ba REL iks)

U.S. Brand Names Plenaxis™ [DSC]

Index Terms PPI-149; R-3827

Generic Available No

Pharmacologic Category Gonadotropin Releasing Hormone Antagonist

Use Palliative treatment of advanced prostate cancer; treatment is limited to men who are not candidates for LHRH therapy, refuse surgical castration, and have one or more of the following complications due to metastases or local encroachment: 1) risk of neurological compromise, 2) ureteral or bladder outlet obstruction, or 3) severe bone pain (persisting despite narcotic analgesia)

Restrictions Abarelix is not distributed through retail pharmacies. Prior to its discontinuation, prescribing and distribution of abarelix was limited to physicians and hospital pharmacies participating in the Plenaxis™ PLUS program. Additional information may be obtained by calling 1-877-772-3247 or 1-866-753-2947.

Pregnancy Risk Factor X

Lactation Excretion in breast milk unknown/not indicated in women

Labeled Contraindications Hypersensitivity to abarelix or any component of the formulation

Warnings/Precautions Hazardous agent - use appropriate precautions for handling and disposal. **[U.S. Boxed Warning]: Has been associated with immediate-onset allergic reactions; may occur with initial dose and risk increases with duration of treatment. Observe for signs/symptoms of allergic reactions (which may include hypotension and/or syncope) for at least 30 minutes following each injection.** Abarelix may cause prolongation of the QT interval; consider risk:benefit in patients with baseline QT_c values >450 msec or patients receiving concurrent medications which prolong the QT_c interval (class Ia and class III antiarrhythmics). **[U.S. Boxed Warning]: Efficacy may diminish during prolonged treatment,** particularly in patients weighing >225 pounds; monitor serum testosterone levels to identify treatment failures. Monitor transaminase levels and hepatic function during therapy. Extended treatment may result in a decrease in bone mineral density. **[U.S. Boxed Warning]: May only be prescribed by physicians enrolled in the Plenaxis™ Plus Program.**

Adverse Reactions

>10%:

Cardiovascular: Hot flushes (79%), peripheral edema (15%)

Central nervous system: Sleep disturbance (44%), pain (31%), dizziness (12%), headache (12%)

Endocrine & metabolic: Breast enlargement (30%), nipple discharge/tenderness (20%)

Gastrointestinal: Constipation (15%), diarrhea (11%)

Neuromuscular & skeletal: Back pain (17%)

Respiratory: Upper respiratory infection (12%)

1% to 10%:

Central nervous system: Fatigue (10%)

Endocrine & metabolic: Serum triglycerides increased (10%)

Gastrointestinal: Nausea (10%)

Genitourinary: Dysuria (10%), micturition frequency (10%), urinary retention (10%), urinary tract infection (10%)

Hepatic: Transaminases increased (2% to 8%)

Miscellaneous: Allergic reactions (urticaria, pruritus, syncope, hypotension); risk increases with prolonged treatment

Overdosage/Toxicology No experience in overdose. Treatment is symptomatic and supportive.

Drug Interactions

Increased Effect/Toxicity: When used with other QT_c-prolonging agents, additive QT_c prolongation may occur. Life-threatening ventricular arrhythmias may result; example drugs include class Ia and class III antiarrhythmics, cisapride, selected quinolones, erythromycin, pimozide, mesoridazine, and thioridazine.

Storage/Stability Store at room temperature: 25°C (77°F); excursions permitted to 15°C to 30°C (58°F to 86°F). Reconstituted solution is stable for at least 8 hours at 30°C.

Reconstitution Reconstitute vial with 2.2 mL of NS; reconstituted solutions contain abarelix 50 mg/mL.

Mechanism of Action Competes with naturally-occurring GnRH for binding on receptors of the pituitary. Suppresses LH and FSH, resulting in decreased testosterone.

Pharmacodynamics/Kinetics
Distribution: V_d: 4040 L (± 1607)
Metabolism: Hepatic, via peptide hydrolysis
Half-life elimination: 13 days
Time to peak, serum: 3 days (following I.M. administration)
Excretion: Urine (13% as unchanged drug)

Dosage I.M.: Male prostate cancer: 100 mg administered on days 1, 15, 29 (week 4), then every 4 weeks

Administration Administer intramuscularly (to the buttock).

Monitoring Parameters Signs/symptoms of allergic reaction (for at least 30 minutes after each injection). Obtain transaminase levels at baseline and periodically during treatment. Serum testosterone (to identify treatment failure) just prior to abarelix administration, beginning on day 29 and every 8 weeks thereafter. PSA and bone mineral density may be monitored as needed.

Additional Information Prior to distribution, Praecis Pharmaceuticals must enroll prescribing physicians and/or hospital pharmacies in the Plenaxis™ user safety program (Plenaxis™ PLUS). A Physician Attestation form must be used to document the physician's qualifications and acceptance of responsibilities concerning patient education and adverse effect reporting. Physicians must obtain the patient's signature and personally cosign the two-part Plenaxis™ Patient Information leaflet. The original signed copy should be retained in the patient's medical record while the other copy should be given to the patient. Hospital pharmacies must submit a hospital pharmacy agreement form to allow dispensing, which will be limited to physicians enrolled in the prescriber's registry. Confirmation of physician enrollment may be obtained by calling 1-866-753-6294. All doses must be dispensed with a Patient Information leaflet. Distributors must restrict shipment to physicians or hospital pharmacies enrolled in the Plenaxis™ prescribing program. Additional details may be obtained by calling 1-877-772-3247 or 1-866-753-2947.

Emetic Potential Low (10%)

Vesicant No

Dosage Forms Excipient information presented when available (limited, particularly for generics); consult specific product labeling. [DSC] = Discontinued product.
Injection, powder for reconstitution [preservative free]: 113 mg [provides 100 mg/2 mL depot suspension when reconstituted; packaged with diluent and syringe] [DSC]
(Continued)

Abarelix *(Continued)*

References

"Abarelix: Abarelix-depot-F, Abarelix-depot-M, Abarelix-L, PPI 149, R 3827," *Drugs R D*, 2003, 4(3):161-6.

McLeod D, Zinner N, Tomera K, et al, "A Phase 3, Multicenter, Open-Label, Randomized Study of Abarelix Versus Leuprolide Acetate in Men With Prostate Cancer," *Urology*, 2001, 58(5):756-61.

Trachtenberg J, Gittleman M, Steidle C, et al, "A Phase 3, Multicenter, Open Label, Randomized Study of Abarelix Versus Leuprolide Plus Daily Antiandrogen in Men With Prostate Cancer," *J Urol*, 2002, 167(4):1670-4.

Wong SL, Lau DR, Baughman SA, et al, "Pharmacokinetics and Pharmacodynamics of Abarelix, a Gonadotropin-Releasing Hormone Antagonist, After Subcutaneous Continuous Infusion in Patients With Prostate Cancer," *Clin Pharmacol Ther*, 2003, 73(4):304-11.

- ◆ **Abbott-43818** *see* Leuprolide *on page 672*
- ◆ **ABCD** *see* Amphotericin B Cholesteryl Sulfate Complex *on page 68*
- ◆ **Abelcet®** *see* Amphotericin B (Lipid Complex) *on page 77*
- ◆ **ABI-007** *see* Paclitaxel (Protein Bound) *on page 865*
- ◆ **ABLC** *see* Amphotericin B (Lipid Complex) *on page 77*
- ◆ **Abraxane®** *see* Paclitaxel (Protein Bound) *on page 865*
- ◆ **ABX-EGF** *see* Panitumumab *on page 876*
- ◆ **9-AC** *see* Aminocamptothecin *on page 61*
- ◆ **Acetoxymethylprogesterone** *see* MedroxyPROGESTERone *on page 703*
- ◆ **Aciclovir** *see* Acyclovir *on page 22*
- ◆ **Aclasta®** *(Can) see* Zoledronic Acid *on page 1122*
- ◆ **4-(9-Acridinylamino) Methanesulfon-m-Anisidide** *see* Amsacrine *on page 85*
- ◆ **Acridinyl Anisidide** *see* Amsacrine *on page 85*
- ◆ **ACT** *see* Dactinomycin *on page 287*
- ◆ **Act-D** *see* Dactinomycin *on page 287*
- ◆ **Actimmune®** *see* Interferon Gamma-1b *on page 624*
- ◆ **Actinomycin** *see* Dactinomycin *on page 287*
- ◆ **Actinomycin D** *see* Dactinomycin *on page 287*
- ◆ **Actinomycin Cl** *see* Dactinomycin *on page 287*
- ◆ **Actiq®** *see* Fentanyl *on page 426*
- ◆ **Activase®** *see* Alteplase *on page 45*
- ◆ **Activase® rt-PA** *(Can) see* Alteplase *on page 45*
- ◆ **ACV** *see* Acyclovir *on page 22*
- ◆ **Acycloguanosine** *see* Acyclovir *on page 22*

Acyclovir *(ay SYE kloe veer)*

Medication Safety Issues

Sound-alike/look-alike issues:

Zovirax® may be confused with Zostrix®, Zyvox®

International issues:

Opthavir® [Mexico] may be confused with Optivar® which is a brand name for azelastine in the U.S.

U.S. Brand Names Zovirax®

Index Terms Aciclovir; ACV; Acycloguanosine

Generic Available Yes: Excludes cream, ointment

Canadian Brand Names Apo-Acyclovir®; Gen-Acyclovir; Nu-Acyclovir; ratio-Acyclovir; Zovirax®

Pharmacologic Category Antiviral Agent

Use Treatment of genital herpes simplex virus (HSV), herpes labialis (cold sores), herpes zoster (shingles), HSV encephalitis, neonatal HSV, mucocutaneous HSV in immunocompromised patients, varicella-zoster (chickenpox)

Unlabeled/Investigational Use Prevention of HSV reactivation in HIV-positive patients; prevention of HSV reactivation in hematopoietic stem-cell transplant (HSCT); prevention of HSV reactivation during periods of neutropenia in patients with acute leukemia

Pregnancy Risk Factor B

Lactation Enters breast milk/use with caution (AAP rates "compatible")

Labeled Contraindications Hypersensitivity to acyclovir, valacyclovir, or any component of the formulation

Warnings/Precautions Use with caution in immunocompromised patients; thrombocytopenic purpura/hemolytic uremic syndrome (TTP/HUS) has been reported. Use caution in the elderly, pre-existing renal disease, or in those receiving other nephrotoxic drugs. Renal failure (sometimes fatal) has been reported. Maintain adequate hydration during oral or intravenous therapy. Use I.V. preparation with caution in patients with underlying neurologic abnormalities, serious hepatic or electrolyte abnormalities, or substantial hypoxia.

Safety and efficacy of oral formulations have not been established in pediatric patients <2 years of age.

Chickenpox: Treatment should begin within 24 hours of appearance of rash; oral route not recommended for routine use in otherwise healthy children with varicella, but may be effective in patients at increased risk of moderate to severe infection (>12 years of age, chronic cutaneous or pulmonary disorders, long-term salicylate therapy, corticosteroid therapy).

Genital herpes: Physical contact should be avoided when lesions are present; transmission may also occur in the absence of symptoms. Treatment should begin with the first signs or symptoms.

Herpes labialis: For external use only to the lips and face; do not apply to eye or inside the mouth or nose. Treatment should begin with the first signs or symptoms.

Herpes zoster: Acyclovir should be started within 72 hours of appearance of rash to be effective.

Adverse Reactions

Systemic: Oral:
>10%: Central nervous system: Malaise (12%)
1% to 10%:
  Central nervous system: Headache (2%)
  Gastrointestinal: Nausea (2% to 5%), vomiting (3%), diarrhea (2% to 3%)

Systemic: Parenteral:
1% to 10%:
  Dermatologic: Hives (2%), itching (2%), rash (2%)
  Gastrointestinal: Nausea/vomiting (7%)
  Hepatic: Liver function tests increased (1% to 2%)
  Local: Inflammation at injection site or phlebitis (9%)
  Renal: BUN increased (5% to 10%), creatinine increased (5% to 10%), acute renal failure

Topical:
>10%: Dermatologic: Mild pain, burning, or stinging (ointment 30%)
1% to 10%: Dermatologic: Pruritus (ointment 4%), itching

All forms: <1%, postmarketing, and/or case reports: Abdominal pain, aggression, agitation, alopecia, anaphylaxis, anemia, angioedema, (Continued)

Acyclovir *(Continued)*

anorexia, ataxia, coma, confusion, consciousness decreased, delirium, desquamation, diarrhea, disseminated intravascular coagulopathy (DIC), dizziness, dry lips, dysarthria, encephalopathy, erythema multiforme, fatigue, fever, gastrointestinal distress, hallucinations, hematuria, hemolysis, hepatitis, hyperbilirubinemia, hypotension, insomnia, jaundice, leukocytoclastic vasculitis, leukocytosis, leukopenia, local tissue necrosis (following extravasation), lymphadenopathy, mental depression, myalgia, neutrophilia, paresthesia, peripheral edema, photosensitization, pruritus, psychosis, renal failure, seizure, somnolence, sore throat, Stevens-Johnson syndrome, thrombocytopenia, thrombocytopenic purpura/hemolytic uremic syndrome (TTP/HUS), thrombocytosis, toxic epidermal necrolysis, tremor, urticaria, visual disturbances

Overdosage/Toxicology Overdoses of up to 20 g have been reported. Symptoms of overdose include agitation, seizures, somnolence, confusion, elevated serum creatinine, and renal failure. In the event of overdose, sufficient urine flow must be maintained to avoid drug precipitation within renal tubules. Hemodialysis has resulted in up to 60% reduction in serum acyclovir levels.

Ethanol/Nutrition/Herb Interactions Food: Does not affect absorption of oral acyclovir.

Storage/Stability

Capsule, tablet: Store at controlled room temperature of 15°C to 25°C (59°F to 77°F); protect from moisture.

Cream, suspension: Store at controlled room temperature of 15°C to 25°C (59°F to 77°F).

Ointment: Store at controlled room temperature of 15°C to 25°C (59°F to 77°F) in a dry place.

Injection: Store powder at controlled room temperature of 15°C to 25°C (59°F to 77°F). Reconstituted solutions remain stable for 12 hours at room temperature. Do not refrigerate reconstituted solutions as they may precipitate. Once diluted for infusion, use within 24 hours.

Reconstitution Powder for injection: Reconstitute acyclovir 500 mg with SWFI 10 mL; do not use bacteriostatic water containing benzyl alcohol or parabens. For intravenous infusion, dilute to a final concentration ≤7 mg/mL. Concentrations >10 mg/mL increase the risk of phlebitis.

Compatibility Stable in D_5W, D_5NS, $D_5^{1}/_4NS$, $D_5^{1}/_2NS$, LR, NS.

Incompatible with blood products and protein-containing solutions.

Y-site administration: Compatible: Allopurinol, amikacin, amphotericin B cholesteryl sulfate complex, ampicillin, cefamandole, cefazolin, cefoperazone, cefotaxime, cefoxitin, ceftazidime, ceftizoxime, ceftriaxone, cefuroxime, chloramphenicol, cimetidine, clindamycin, co-trimoxazole, dexamethasone, dimenhydrinate, diphenhydramine, docetaxel, doxorubicin liposome, doxycycline, erythromycin lactobionate, etoposide, famotidine, filgrastim, fluconazole, gatifloxacin, gentamicin, granisetron, heparin, hydrocortisone sodium succinate, hydromorphone, imipenem/cilastatin, linezolid, lorazepam, magnesium sulfate, melphalan, methylprednisolone sodium succinate, metoclopramide, metronidazole, multivitamins, nafcillin, oxacillin, paclitaxel, penicillin G potassium, pentobarbital, perphenazine, piperacillin, potassium chloride, propofol, ranitidine, remifentanil, sodium bicarbonate, tacrolimus, teniposide, theophylline, thiotepa, ticarcillin, tobramycin, vancomycin, zidovudine. **Incompatible:** Amifostine, amsacrine, aztreonam, cefepime, dobutamine, dopamine, fludarabine, foscarnet, gemcitabine, idarubicin, levofloxacin, ondansetron, piperacillin/

tazobactam, sargramostim, vinorelbine. **Variable (consult detailed reference):** Cisatracurium, diltiazem, meperidine, meropenem, morphine, TPN.
Compatibility when admixed: Compatible: Fluconazole. **Incompatible:** Dobutamine, dopamine. **Variable (consult detailed reference):** Meropenem.

Mechanism of Action Acyclovir is converted to acyclovir monophosphate by virus-specific thymidine kinase then further converted to acyclovir triphosphate by other cellular enzymes. Acyclovir triphosphate inhibits DNA synthesis and viral replication by competing with deoxyguanosine triphosphate for viral DNA polymerase and being incorporated into viral DNA.

Pharmacodynamics/Kinetics

Absorption: Oral: 15% to 30%

Distribution: V_d: 0.8 L/kg (63.6 L): Widely (eg, brain, kidney, lungs, liver, spleen, muscle, uterus, vagina, CSF)

Protein binding: 9% to 33%

Metabolism: Converted by viral enzymes to acyclovir monophosphate, and further converted to diphosphate then triphosphate (active form) by cellular enzymes

Bioavailability: Oral: 10% to 20% with normal renal function (bioavailability decreases with increased dose)

Half-life elimination: Terminal: Neonates: 4 hours; Children 1-12 years: 2-3 hours; Adults: 3 hours

Time to peak, serum: Oral: Within 1.5-2 hours

Excretion: Urine (62% to 90% as unchanged drug and metabolite)

Dosage Note: Obese patients should be dosed using ideal body weight

Genital HSV:

I.V.: Children ≥12 years and Adults (immunocompetent): Initial episode, severe: 5 mg/kg every 8 hours for 5-7 days

Oral:

Children:

Initial episode (unlabeled use): 40-80 mg/kg/day divided into 3-4 doses for 5-10 days (maximum: 1 g/day)

Chronic suppression (unlabeled use; limited data): 80 mg/kg/day in 3 divided doses (maximum: 1 g/day), re-evaluate after 12 months of treatment

Adults:

Initial episode: 200 mg every 4 hours while awake (5 times/day) for 10 days (per manufacturer's labeling); 400 mg 3 times/day for 5-10 days has also been reported

Recurrence: 200 mg every 4 hours while awake (5 times/day) for 5 days (per manufacturer's labeling); begin at earliest signs of disease; 400 mg 3 times/day for 5 days has also been reported

Chronic suppression: 400 mg twice daily or 200 mg 3-5 times/day, for up to 12 months followed by re-evaluation (per manufacturer's labeling); 400-1200 mg/day in 2-3 divided doses has also been reported

Topical: Adults (immunocompromised): Ointment: Initial episode: ½" ribbon of ointment for a 4" square surface area every 3 hours (6 times/day) for 7 days

Herpes labialis (cold sores): Topical: Children ≥12 years and Adults: Cream: Apply 5 times/day for 4 days

Herpes zoster (shingles):

Oral: Adults (immunocompetent): 800 mg every 4 hours (5 times/day) for 7-10 days

(Continued)

Acyclovir *(Continued)*

I.V.:
   Children <12 years (immunocompromised): 20 mg/kg/dose every 8 hours for 7 days
   Children ≥12 years and Adults (immunocompromised): 10 mg/kg/dose or 500 mg/m²/dose every 8 hours for 7 days

HSV encephalitis: I.V.:
   Children 3 months to 12 years: 20 mg/kg/dose every 8 hours for 10 days (per manufacturer's labeling); dosing for 14-21 days also reported
   Children ≥12 years and Adults: 10 mg/kg/dose every 8 hours for 10 days (per manufacturer's labeling); 10-15 mg/kg/dose every 8 hours for 14-21 days also reported

Mucocutaneous HSV:
I.V.:
   Children <12 years (immunocompromised): 10 mg/kg/dose every 8 hours for 7 days
   Children ≥12 years and Adults (immunocompromised): 5 mg/kg/dose every 8 hours for 7 days (per manufacturer's labeling); dosing for up to 14 days also reported
Oral: Adults (immunocompromised, unlabeled use): 400 mg 5 times a day for 7-14 days
Topical: Ointment: Adults (nonlife-threatening, immunocompromised): ½" ribbon of ointment for a 4" square surface area every 3 hours (6 times/day) for 7 days

Neonatal HSV: I.V.: Neonate: Birth to 3 months: 10 mg/kg/dose every 8 hours for 10 days (manufacturer's labeling); 15 mg/kg/dose or 20 mg/kg/dose every 8 hours for 14-21 days has also been reported

Varicella-zoster (chickenpox): Begin treatment within the first 24 hours of rash onset:
Oral:
   Children ≥2 years and ≤40 kg (immunocompetent): 20 mg/kg/dose (up to 800 mg/dose) 4 times/day for 5 days
   Children >40 kg and Adults (immunocompetent): 800 mg/dose 4 times a day for 5 days
I.V.:
   Children <1 year (immunocompromised, unlabeled use): 10 mg/kg/dose every 8 hours for 7-10 days
   Children ≥1 year and Adults (immunocompromised, unlabeled use): 1500 mg/m²/day divided every 8 hours or 10 mg/kg/dose every 8 hours for 7-10 days

Prevention of HSV reactivation in HIV-positive patients, for use only when recurrences are frequent or severe (unlabeled use): Oral:
   Children: 80 mg/kg/day in 3-4 divided doses
   Adults: 200 mg 3 times/day or 400 mg 2 times/day

Prevention of HSV reactivation in HSCT (unlabeled use): Note: Start at the beginning of conditioning therapy and continue until engraftment or until mucositis resolves (~30 days)
Oral: Adults: 200 mg 3 times/day
I.V.:
   Children: 250 mg/m²/dose every 8 hours or 125 mg/m²/dose every 6 hours
   Adults: 250 mg/m²/dose every 12 hours

Bone marrow transplant recipients (unlabeled use): I.V.: Children and

Adults: Allogeneic patients who are HSV and CMV seropositive: 500 mg/m^2/dose (10 mg/kg) every 8 hours; for clinically-symptomatic CMV infection, consider replacing acyclovir with ganciclovir

Dosing adjustment in renal impairment:

Oral:

Cl_{cr} 10-25 mL/minute/1.73 m^2: Normal dosing regimen 800 mg every 4 hours: Administer 800 mg every 8 hours

Cl_{cr} <10 mL/minute/1.73 m^2:

Normal dosing regimen 200 mg every 4 hours, 200 mg every 8 hours, or 400 mg every 12 hours: Administer 200 mg every 12 hours

Normal dosing regimen 800 mg every 4 hours: Administer 800 mg every 12 hours

I.V.:

Cl_{cr} 25-50 mL/minute/1.73 m^2: Administer recommended dose every 12 hours

Cl_{cr} 10-25 mL/minute/1.73 m^2: Administer recommended dose every 24 hours

Cl_{cr} <10 mL/minute/1.73 m^2: Administer 50% of recommended dose every 24 hours

Hemodialysis: Administer dose after dialysis

Continuous ambulatory peritoneal dialysis (CAPD): Administer 50% of normal dose once daily; no supplemental dose needed

Continuous renal replacement therapy (CRRT): Drug clearance is highly dependent on the method of renal replacement, filter type, and flow rate. Appropriate dosing requires close monitoring of pharmacologic response, signs of adverse reactions due to drug accumulation, as well as drug levels in relation to target trough (if appropriate). The following are general recommendations only (based on dialysate flow/ultrafiltration rates of 1 L/hour) and should not supersede clinical judgment:

CVVH or CVVHD/CVVHDF: 5-7.5 mg/kg every 24 hours

Note: The higher dose of 7.5 mg/kg is recommended for infections with CNS involvement (Trotman, 2005).

Administration

Oral: May be administered with or without food.

I.V.: Avoid rapid infusion; infuse over 1 hour to prevent renal damage; maintain adequate hydration of patient; check for phlebitis and rotate infusion sites

Topical: Not for use in the eye. Apply using a finger cot or rubber glove to avoid transmission to other parts of the body or to other persons.

Monitoring Parameters Urinalysis, BUN, serum creatinine, liver enzymes, CBC

Dietary Considerations May be taken with or without food. Acyclovir 500 mg injection contains sodium ~50 mg (~2 mEq).

Patient Information This is not a cure for herpes (recurrences tend to continually reappear every 3-6 months after original infection), nor will this medication reduce the risk of transmission to others when lesions are present; avoid sexual intercourse when visible lesions are present. Take as directed for full course of therapy; do not discontinue even if feeling better. Oral doses may be taken with food.

Special Geriatric Considerations For herpes zoster, acyclovir should be started within 72 hours of the appearance of the rash to be effective. Dose adjustment may be necessary depending on creatinine clearance.

Emetic Potential Very low (<10%)

Vesicant No

(Continued)

Acyclovir *(Continued)*

Dosage Forms Excipient information presented when available (limited, particularly for generics); consult specific product labeling. [DSC] = Discontinued product

Capsule: 200 mg
    Zovirax®: 200 mg

Cream, topical:
    Zovirax®: 5% (2 g, 5 g)

Injection, powder for reconstitution, as sodium: 500 mg, 1000 mg
    Zovirax®: 500 mg [DSC]

Injection, solution, as sodium [preservative free]: 25 mg/mL (20 mL, 40 mL); 50 mg/mL (10 mL, 20 mL)

Ointment, topical:
    Zovirax®: 5% (15 g)

Suspension, oral: 200 mg/5 mL (480 mL)
    Zovirax®: 200 mg/5 mL (480 mL) [banana flavor]

Tablet: 400 mg, 800 mg
    Zovirax®: 400 mg, 800 mg

References

American Academy of Pediatrics Committee on Infectious Diseases, "The Use of Oral Acyclovir in Otherwise Healthy Children With Varicella," *Pediatrics*, 1993, 91(3):674-6.

American Academy of Pediatrics Committee on Drugs, "The Transfer of Drugs and Other Chemicals Into Human Breast Milk," *Pediatrics*, 2001, 108:776-89.

Aronoff GR, Bennett WM, Berns JS, et al, *Drug Prescribing in Renal Failure: Dosing Guidelines for Adults and Children*, 5th ed. Philadelphia, PA: American College of Physicians; 2007.

Centers for Disease Control and Prevention, "Treating Opportunistic Infections Among HIV-Infected Adults and Adolescents: Recommendations From CDC, the National Institutes of Health, and the HIV Medicine Association/Infectious Diseases Society of America," *MMWR Recomm Rep*, 2004, 53(RR-15):1-112. Available at: http://www.cdc.gov/mmwr/preview/mmwrhtml/rr5315a1.htm. Accessed January 9, 2006.

Centers for Disease Control and Prevention, "Treating Opportunistic Infections Among HIV-Exposed and Infected Children: Recommendations from CDC, the National Institutes of Health, and the Infectious Diseases Society of America," *MMWR Recomm Rep*, 2004, 53(RR-14):1-63. Available at: http://www.cdc.gov/mmwr/preview/mmwrhtml/rr5314a1.htm. Accessed January 9, 2006.

Centers for Disease Control and Prevention, "Guidelines for Preventing Opportunistic Infections Among HIV-Infected Persons. 2002 Recommendations of the U.S. Public Health Service and the Infectious Diseases Society of America," *MMWR Recomm Rep*, 2002, 51(RR-8):1-46. Available at: http://www.cdc.gov/mmwr/preview/mmwrhtml/rr5108a1.htm. Accessed January 26, 2004.

Centers for Disease Control and Prevention, "Guidelines for Preventing Opportunistic Infections Among Hematopoietic Stem Cell Transplant Recipients: Recommendations of CDC, the Infectious Disease Society of America, and the American Society of Blood and Marrow Transplantation," *MMWR Recomm Rep*, 2000, 49(RR-10):1-112. Available at: http://www.cdc.gov/mmwr/preview/mmwrhtml/rr4910a1.htm. Accessed January 26, 2004.

Dunkle LM, Arvin AM, Whitley RJ, et al, "A Controlled Trial of Acyclovir for Chickenpox in Normal Children," *N Engl J Med*, 1991, 325(22):1539-44.

Eck P, Silver SM, and Clark EC, "Acute Renal Failure and Coma After a High Dose of Oral Acyclovir," *N Engl J Med*, 1991, 325(16):1178-9.

Eisen D, Essell J, Broun ER, et al, "Clinical Utility of Oral Valacyclovir Compared With Oral Acyclovir for the Prevention of Herpes Simplex Virus Mucositis Following Autologous Bone Marrow Transplantation or Stem Cell Rescue Therapy," *Bone Marrow Transplant*, 2003, 31(1):51-5.

Englund JA, Fletcher CV, and Balfour HH Jr, "Acyclovir Therapy in Neonates," *J Pediatr*, 1991, 119(1 Pt 1):129-35.

National Comprehensive Cancer Network, "Clinical Practice Guidelines in Oncology," Version 1, 2005. Available at: http://www.nccn.org/professionals/physician_gls/PDF/fever.pdf. Accessed January 20, 2006.

Novelli VM, Marshall WC, Yeo J, et al, "High-Dose Oral Acyclovir for Children at Risk of Disseminated Herpesvirus Infections," *J Infect Dis*, 1985, 151(2):372.

Rayani SA, Nimmo CJ, Frighetto L, et al, "Implementation and Evaluation of a Standardized Herpes Simplex Virus Prophylaxis Protocol on a Leukemia/Bone Marrow Transplant Unit," *Ann Pharmacother*, 1994, 28(7-8):852-6.

Trotman RL, Williamson JC, Shoemaker DM, et al, "Antibiotic Dosing in Critically Ill Adult Patients Receiving Continuous Renal Replacement Therapy," *Clin Infect Dis*, 2005, 41(8):1159-66.

Wade JC, Newton B, Flournoy N, et al, "Oral Acyclovir for Prevention of Herpes Simplex Virus Reactivation After Marrow Transplantation," *Ann Intern Med*, 1984, 100(6):823-8.

Wood MJ, Johnson RW, McKendrick MW, et al, "A Randomized Trial of Acyclovir for 7 Days or 21 Days With and Without Prednisolone for Treatment of Acute Herpes Zoster," *N Engl J Med*, 1994, 330(13):896-900.

♦ **AD3L** *see* Valrubicin *on page 1086*

♦ **ADR (error-prone abbreviation)** *see* DOXOrubicin *on page 352*

♦ **Adria** *see* DOXOrubicin *on page 352*

♦ **Adriamycin®** *see* DOXOrubicin *on page 352*

♦ **Adrucil®** *see* Fluorouracil *on page 462*

♦ **Advate** *see* Antihemophilic Factor (Recombinant) *on page 95*

♦ **AG** *see* Aminoglutethimide *on page 65*

♦ **Agrylin®** *see* Anagrelide *on page 87*

♦ **AGT** *see* Aminoglutethimide *on page 65*

♦ **AHF (Human)** *see* Antihemophilic Factor (Human) *on page 92*

♦ **AHF (Recombinant)** *see* Antihemophilic Factor (Recombinant) *on page 95*

♦ **A-hydroCort** *see* Hydrocortisone *on page 545*

♦ **AKTob®** *see* Tobramycin *on page 1041*

♦ **Albumin-Bound Paclitaxel** *see* Paclitaxel (Protein Bound) *on page 865*

♦ **Alcomicin® (Can)** *see* Gentamicin *on page 512*

Aldesleukin (al des LOO kin)

Medication Safety Issues

Sound-alike/look-alike issues:

Aldesleukin may be confused with oprelvekin

Proleukin® may be confused with oprelvekin

High alert medication: The Institute for Safe Medication Practices (ISMP) includes this medication among its list of classes of drugs which have a heightened risk of causing significant patient harm when used in error.

Related Information

Safe Handling of Hazardous Drugs *on page 1382*

U.S. Brand Names Proleukin®

Index Terms Epidermal Thymocyte Activating Factor; IL-2; Interleukin-2; Lymphocyte Mitogenic Factor; NSC-373364; T-Cell Growth Factor; TCGF; Thymocyte Stimulating Factor

Generic Available No

Canadian Brand Names Proleukin®

Pharmacologic Category Antineoplastic Agent, Miscellaneous; Biological Response Modulator

Use Treatment of metastatic renal cell cancer, metastatic melanoma

Unlabeled/Investigational Use HIV infection, and AIDS; non-Hodgkin's lymphoma

Pregnancy Risk Factor C

Lactation Excretion unknown/not recommended

Labeled Contraindications Hypersensitivity to aldesleukin or any component of the formulation; patients with abnormal thallium stress or pulmonary function tests; patients who have had an organ allograft; retreatment in patients who have experienced sustained ventricular tachycardia (≥5 beats), refractory cardiac rhythm disturbances, recurrent chest pain with ECG changes consistent with angina or myocardial infarction, intubation ≥72 (Continued)

Aldesleukin *(Continued)*

hours, pericardial tamponade, renal dialysis for ≥72 hours, coma or toxic psychosis lasting ≥48 hours, repetitive or refractory seizures, bowel ischemia/perforation, GI bleeding requiring surgery

Warnings/Precautions Hazardous agent - use appropriate precautions for handling and disposal. **[U.S. Boxed Warning]: High-dose aldesleukin therapy has been associated with capillary leak syndrome (CLS) resulting in hypotension and reduced organ perfusion which may be severe and can result in death. Therapy should be restricted to patients with normal cardiac and pulmonary functions as defined by thallium stress and formal pulmonary function testing.** Extreme caution should be used in patients with a history of prior cardiac or pulmonary disease. Patients must have a serum creatinine ≤1.5 mg/dL prior to treatment.

[U.S. Boxed Warning]: Should be administered under the supervision of an experienced cancer chemotherapy physician in a facility with cardiopulmonary or intensive specialists and intensive care facilities available. Adverse effects are frequent and sometimes fatal. May exacerbate pre-existing or initial presentation of autoimmune diseases and inflammatory disorders. Patients should be evaluated and treated for CNS metastases and have a negative scan prior to treatment. Mental status changes (irritability, confusion, depression) can occur and may indicate bacteremia, hypoperfusion, CNS malignancy, or CNS toxicity.

[U.S. Boxed Warning]: Impaired neutrophil function is associated with treatment; patients are at risk for sepsis, bacterial endocarditis, and central line-related gram-positive infections. Antibiotic prophylaxis which has been associated with a reduced incidence of staphylococcal infections in aldesleukin studies includes the use of oxacillin, nafcillin, ciprofloxacin, or vancomycin.

[U.S. Boxed Warning]: Withhold treatment for patients developing moderate-to-severe lethargy or somnolence; continued treatment may result in coma. Standard prophylactic supportive care during high-dose aldesleukin treatment includes acetaminophen to relieve constitutional symptoms and an H_2 antagonist to reduce the risk of GI ulceration and/or bleeding. Safety and efficacy have not been established in children.

Adverse Reactions

>10%:

Cardiovascular: Hypotension (71%; grade 4: 3%), peripheral edema (28%), tachycardia (23%), edema (15%), vasodilation (13%), cardiovascular disorder (11%; includes blood pressure changes, CHF and ECG changes)

Central nervous system: Chills (52%), confusion (34%), fever (29%; grade 4: 1%), malaise (27%), somnolence (22%), anxiety (12%), pain (12%), dizziness (11%)

Dermatologic: Rash (42%), pruritus (24%), exfoliative dermatitis (18%)

Endocrine & metabolic: Acidosis (12%), hypomagnesemia (12%), hypocalcemia (11%)

Gastrointestinal: Diarrhea (67%), vomiting (19% to 50%), nausea (19% to 35%), stomatitis (22%), anorexia (20%), weight gain (18%), abdominal pain (11%)

Hematologic: Thrombocytopenia (37%; grade 4: 1%), anemia (29%), leukopenia (16%)

Hepatic: Hyperbilirubinemia (40%), AST increased (23%)

Neuromuscular & skeletal: Weakness (23%)

Renal: Oliguria (63%; grade 4: 6%), creatinine increased (33%)

Respiratory: Dyspnea (43%), lung disorder (24%; includes pulmonary congestion, rales, and rhonchi), cough (11%), respiratory disorder (11%; includes acute respiratory distress syndrome, infiltrates and pulmonary changes)

Miscellaneous: Infection (13%; grade 4: 1%)

1% to 10%:

Cardiovascular: Arrhythmia (10%), cardiac arrest (grade 4: 1%), MI (grade 4: 1%), supraventricular tachycardia (grade 4: 1%), ventricular tachycardia (grade 4: 1%)

Gastrointestinal: Abdomen enlarged (10%)

Hematologic: Coagulation disorder (grade 4: 1%)

Hepatic: Alkaline phosphatase increased (10%)

Renal: Anuria (grade 4: 5%), acute renal failure (grade 4: 1%)

Respiratory: Rhinitis (10%), apnea (grade 4: 1%)

Miscellaneous: Sepsis (grade 4: 1%)

<1%, postmarketing, and/or case reports (limited to important or life threatening): Acute tubular necrosis, allergic interstitial nephritis, allergic reactions, anaphylaxis, atrial arrhythmia, AV block, blindness (transient or permanent), bowel necrosis, bradycardia, bullous pemphigoid, BUN increased, cardiomyopathy, cellulitis, cerebral edema, cerebral lesions, cerebral vasculitis, CHF, cholecystitis, colitis, coma, crescentic IgA glomuleronephritis, Crohn's disease exacerbation, depression (severe; leading to suicide), diabetes mellitus, duodenal ulcer, encephalitis, endocarditis, extrapyramidal syndrome, gastrointestinal hemorrhage, hematemesis, hemoptysis, hemorrhage, hepatic failure, hepatitis, hepatosplenomegaly, hypertension, hyperuricemia, hyperventilation, hypothermia, hyperthyroidism, hypoventilation, hypoxia, inflammatory arthritis, injection site necrosis, intestinal obstruction, intestinal perforation, leukocytosis, malignant hyperthermia, meningitis, myocardial ischemia, myocarditis, myopathy, myositis, neuritis, neuropathy, neutropenia, oculobulbar myasthenia gravis, optic neuritis, pancreatitis, pericardial effusion, pericarditis, peripheral gangrene, phlebitis, pneumonia, pneumothorax, pulmonary edema, pulmonary embolus, renal failure, respiratory acidosis, respiratory arrest, respiratory failure, retroperitoneal hemorrhage, rhabdomyolysis, scleroderma, seizure (including grand mal), shock, Stevens-Johnson syndrome, stroke, syncope, thrombosis, thyroiditis, tracheoesophageal fistula, transient ischemic attack, urticaria, ventricular extrasystoles

Overdosage/Toxicology Side effects following the use of aldesleukin are dose related. Administration of more than the recommended dose has been associated with a more rapid onset of expected dose-limiting toxicities. Adverse reactions generally will reverse when the drug is stopped, particularly because of its short serum half-life. Provide supportive treatment of any continuing symptoms. Life-threatening toxicities have been ameliorated by the I.V. administration of dexamethasone, but may decrease the therapeutic effect of aldesleukin.

Management of vascular leak syndrome: If actual body weight increases >10% above baseline, or rales or rhonchi are audible administer furosemide; administer dopamine (1-5 mcg/kg/minute) to maintain renal blood flow and urine output. If patient has dyspnea at rest, give supplemental oxygen by facemask. If patient has severe respiratory distress, intubate and provide mechanical ventilation. Administer ranitidine hydrochloride 50 mg I.V. every 8-12 hours as prophylaxis against stress ulcers.
(Continued)

Aldesleukin *(Continued)*

Drug Interactions

Increased Effect/Toxicity: Aldesleukin may affect central nervous function; therefore, interactions could occur following concomitant administration of psychotropic drugs (eg, narcotics, analgesics, antiemetics, sedatives, tranquilizers). Concomitant administration of drugs possessing nephrotoxic (eg, aminoglycosides, indomethacin), myelotoxic (eg, cytotoxic chemotherapy), cardiotoxic (eg, doxorubicin), or hepatotoxic effects with aldesleukin may increase toxicity in these organ systems. Beta-blockers and other antihypertensives may potentiate the hypotension seen with aldesleukin. Contrast media (nonionic) may enhance the potential for allergic or hypersensitivity reactions to aldesleukin

Decreased Effect: Corticosteroids have been shown to decrease toxicity of aldesleukin, but may reduce the efficacy of the lymphokine.

Ethanol/Nutrition/Herb Interactions Ethanol: May increase CNS adverse effects.

Storage/Stability Store vials of lyophilized injection in a refrigerator at 2°C to 8°C (36°F to 46°F). Reconstituted vials and solutions diluted for infusion are stable for 48 hours at room temperature or refrigerated, per the manufacturer. Solution diluted with D_5W to a concentration of 220 mg/mL and repackaged into tuberculin syringes was reported to be stable for 14 days refrigerated.

Reconstitution Reconstitute vials with 1.2 mL SWFI to a concentration of 18 million units/1 mL (sterile water should be injected towards the side of the vial). Gently swirl; do not shake. Further dilute with 50 mL of D_5W. Smaller volumes of D_5W should be used for doses <1.5 mg; avoid concentrations <30 mcg/mL and >70 mcg/mL (an increased variability in drug delivery has been seen).

Note: Filtration will result in significant loss of bioactivity.

Final Dilution Concentration (mcg/mL)	Final Dilution Concentration (10^6 int. units/mL)	Stability
<30	<0.49	Albumin must be added to bag **prior to addition** of aldesleukin at a final concentration of 0.1% (1 mg/mL) albumin; stable at room temperature or at ≥32°C (89°F) for 6 days[1,2]
≥30 to ≤70	≥0.49 to ≤1.1	Stable at room temperature at 6 days without albumin added or at ≥32°C (89°F) for 6 days only if albumin is added (0.1%)[1,2]
70-100	1.2-1.6	Unstable; avoid use
>100-500	1.7-8.2	Stable at room temperature and at ≥32°C (89°F) for 6 days[1,2]

[1]These solutions do not contain a preservative; use for more than 24 hours may not be advisable.

[2]Continuous infusion via ambulatory infusion device raises aldesleukin to this temperature.

Compatibility Stable in D_5W.

Y-site administration: Compatible: Amikacin, amphotericin B, calcium gluconate, co-trimoxazole, diphenhydramine, dopamine, fat emulsion 10%, fluconazole, foscarnet, gentamicin, heparin, magnesium sulfate, metoclopramide, morphine, ondansetron, piperacillin, potassium chloride, ranitidine, thiethylperazine, ticarcillin, tobramycin. **Incompatible:** Ganciclovir, lorazepam, NS, pentamidine, prochlorperazine edisylate, promethazine.

Compatibility when admixed: Incompatible with NS.

Mechanism of Action Aldesleukin promotes proliferation, differentiation, and recruitment of T and B cells, natural killer (NK) cells, and thymocytes; causes cytolytic activity in a subset of lymphocytes and subsequent interactions between the immune system and malignant cells; can stimulate lymphokine-activated killer (LAK) cells and tumor-infiltrating lymphocytes (TIL) cells.

Pharmacodynamics/Kinetics

Distribution: V_d: 4-7 L; primarily in plasma and then in the lymphocytes

Half-life elimination: I.V.: Initial: 6-13 minutes; Terminal: 80-120 minutes

Dosage Refer to individual protocols.

I.V.:

Renal cell carcinoma: 600,000 int. units/kg every 8 hours for a maximum of 14 doses; repeat after 9 days for a total of 28 doses per course. Retreat if needed 7 weeks after previous course.

Melanoma:

Single-agent use: 600,000 int. units/kg every 8 hours for a maximum of 14 doses; repeat after 9 days for a total of 28 doses per course. Retreat if needed 7 weeks after previous course.

In combination with cytotoxic agents (unlabeled use): 24 million int. units/m^2 days 12-16 and 19-23

SubQ (unlabeled route):

Single-agent doses: 3-18 million int. units/day for 5 days each week, up to 6 weeks

In combination with interferon:

5 million int. units/m^2 3 times/week

1.8 million int. units/m^2 twice daily 5 days/week for 6 weeks

Investigational regimen: SubQ: 11 million int. units (flat dose) daily for 4 days per week for 4 consecutive weeks; repeat every 6 weeks

Dosage adjustment in renal impairment: No specific recommendations by manufacturer. Use with caution.

Combination Regimens

Melanoma:

Dacarbazine-Carboplatin-Aldesleukin-Interferon *on page 1187*

IL-2 + IFN *on page 1240*

Renal cell cancer:

Interleukin 2-Interferon Alfa-2 *on page 1240*

Interleukin 2-Interferon Alfa-2-Fluorouracil *on page 1241*

Administration Administer as I.V. infusion over 15 minutes (do not administer with an inline filter); may also be administered by SubQ injection (unlabeled route)

Management of symptoms related to vascular leak syndrome:

If actual body weight increases >10% above baseline, or rales or rhonchi are audible:

Administer furosemide at dosage determined by patient response

Administer dopamine hydrochloride 1-5 mcg/kg/minute to maintain renal blood flow and urine output

If patient has dyspnea at rest: Administer supplemental oxygen by face mask

If patient has severe respiratory distress: Intubate patient and provide mechanical ventilation; administer ranitidine (as the hydrochloride salt) 50 mg I.V. every 8-12 hours as prophylaxis against stress ulcers

(Continued)

Aldesleukin (Continued)

Monitoring Parameters

The following clinical evaluations are recommended for all patients prior to beginning treatment and then frequently during drug administration:

CBC with differential, blood chemistries including electrolytes, renal and hepatic function tests

Chest x-rays

Monitoring during therapy should include vital signs (temperature, pulse, blood pressure, and respiration rate) and weight; in a patient with a decreased blood pressure, especially <90 mm Hg, cardiac monitoring for rhythm should be conducted. If an abnormal complex or rhythm is seen, an ECG should be performed; vital signs in these hypotension patients should be taken hourly and central venous pressure (CVP) checked; monitor for change in mental status.

Pulmonary function (baseline and periodic) basis.

Additional Information

1 Cetus unit = 6 int. units

1.1 mg = 18×10^6 int. units (or 3×10^6 Cetus units)

1 Roche unit (Teceleukin) = 3 int. units

Emetic Potential Highly emetogenic (60% to 90%, dose related)

Vesicant No

Dosage Forms Excipient information presented when available (limited, particularly for generics); consult specific product labeling.

Injection, powder for reconstitution:

Proleukin®: 22×10^6 int. units [18 million int. units/mL = 1.1 mg/mL when reconstituted]

References

Atkins MB, Lotze MT, Dutcher JP, et al, "High-Dose Recombinant Interleukin 2 Therapy for Patients With Metastatic Melanoma: Analysis of 270 Patients Treated Between 1985 and 1993," *J Clin Oncol*, 1999, 17(7):2105-16.

Foa R, "Interleukin 2 in the Management of Acute Leukaemia," *Br J Haematol*, 1996, 92(1):1-8.

Kintzel PE and Calis KA, "Recombinant Interleukin-2: Biological Response Modifier," *Clin Pharm*, 1991, 10(2):110-28.

Sundin DJ and Wolin MJ, "Toxicity Management in Patients Receiving Low-Dose Aldesleukin Therapy," *Ann Pharmacother*, 1998, 32(12):1344-52.

Whittington R and Faulds D, "Interleukin-2: A Review of Its Pharmacological Properties and Therapeutic Use in Patients With Cancer," *Drugs*, 1993, 46(3):446-514.

Yang JC, Topalian SL, Parkinson D, et al, "Randomized Comparison of High-Dose and Low-Dose Intravenous Interleukin-2 for the Therapy of Metastatic Renal Cell Carcinoma: An Interim Report," *J Clin Oncol*, 1994, 12(8):1572-6.

Alemtuzumab (ay lem TU zoo mab)

Medication Safety Issues

High alert medication: The Institute for Safe Medication Practices (ISMP) includes this medication among its list of drugs which have a heightened risk of causing significant patient harm when used in error.

Related Information

Safe Handling of Hazardous Drugs *on page 1382*

U.S. Brand Names Campath®

Index Terms C1H; Campath-1H; Humanized IgG1 Anti-CD52 Monoclonal Antibody; NSC-715969

Generic Available No

Canadian Brand Names MabCampath®

Pharmacologic Category Antineoplastic Agent, Monoclonal Antibody

Use Treatment of B-cell chronic lymphocytic leukemia (B-CLL)

Unlabeled/Investigational Use Treatment of refractory T-cell prolymphocytic leukemia (T-PLL); rheumatoid arthritis; graft-versus-host disease; multiple myeloma; preconditioning regimen for stem-cell transplantation and renal and liver transplantation; post-transplant rejection (renal); treatment of autoimmune cytopenias

Pregnancy Risk Factor C

Lactation Excretion in breast milk unknown/not recommended

Labeled Contraindications There are no contraindications listed in the manufacturer's labeling

Warnings/Precautions Hazardous agent - use appropriate precautions for handling and disposal. **[U.S. Boxed Warning]: Serious infections (bacterial, viral, fungal, and protozoan) have been reported. Prophylactic therapy against PCP pneumonia and herpes viral infections is recommended upon initiation of therapy** and for at least 2 months following last dose or until CD4+ counts are ≥200 cells/μL (whichever is later). CD4+ and CD8+ lymphocyte counts may not return to baseline levels for more than 1 year. Withhold treatment during serious infections; may be reinitiated upon resolution of infection.

[U.S. Boxed Warning]: Serious and potentially fatal infusion-related reactions (acute respiratory distress syndrome, bronchospasm, cardiac arrest, cardiac arrhythmias, chills, fever, hypotension, myocardial infarction, pulmonary infiltrates, rash, rigors, shortness of breath, syncope) may occur, especially during the first week of treatment. Premedication with acetaminophen and an oral antihistamine is recommended. Withhold infusion for grade 3 or 4 infusion reaction. Use caution and carefully monitor blood pressure in patients with ischemic heart disease and patients on antihypertensive therapy. Gradual escalation to the recommended maintenance dose is required at initiation and after interruption of therapy for ≥7 days to minimize infusion-related reactions.

[U.S. Boxed Warning]: Severe, prolonged myelosuppression, autoimmune anemia, and autoimmune thrombocytopenia have occurred. Single doses >30 mg and cumulative weekly doses >90 mg are associated with an increased incidence of pancytopenia and should not be administered. Hemolytic anemia, pure red cell aplasia, bone marrow aplasia, and hypoplasia have also been reported. Median duration of neutropenia is 21 days; median duration of thrombocytopenia is 21 days. Discontinue therapy during serious hematologic or other serious toxicity (except lymphopenia) until the event resolves. Permanently discontinue if autoimmune anemia or autoimmune thrombocytopenia occurs. Patients receiving blood products should only receive irradiated blood products due to the potential for GVHD during lymphopenia.

Patients should not be immunized with live, viral vaccines during or recently after treatment. The ability to respond to any vaccine following therapy is unknown. Women of childbearing potential and men of reproductive potential should use effective contraceptive methods during treatment and for a minimum of 6 months following therapy. Safety and efficacy have not been established in pediatric patients.

Adverse Reactions

>10%:

  Cardiovascular: Hypotension (15% to 32%), peripheral edema (13%), hypertension (11% to 15%), dysrhythmia/tachycardia/SVT (10% to 14%)

  Central nervous system: Fever (69% to 85%), chills (53%), fatigue (22% to 34%), headache (13% to 24%), dysthesias (15%), dizziness (12%)

(Continued)

Alemtuzumab *(Continued)*

Dermatologic: Rash (13% to 40%), urticaria (16% to 30%), pruritus (14% to 24%)

Gastrointestinal: Nausea (47% to 54%), vomiting (33% to 41%), anorexia (20%), diarrhea (10% to 22%), stomatitis/mucositis (14%), abdominal pain (11%)

Hematologic: Lymphopenia (grades 3/4: 97%), neutropenia (77% to 85%; grade 3/4: 42% to 70%; median duration: 28 days), anemia (76% to 80%; grade 3/4: 13% to 47%), thrombocytopenia (71% to 72%; grade 3/4: 13% to 52%; median duration: 21 days)

Local: Injection site reaction (SubQ administration: 90%)

Neuromuscular & skeletal: Rigors (86% to 89%), skeletal pain (24%), weakness (13%), myalgia (11%)

Respiratory: Dyspnea (14% to 26%), cough (25%), bronchitis/pneumonitis (21%), pneumonia (16%), pharyngitis (12%)

Miscellaneous: Infection (43% to 74%; grades 3/4: 21% to 37%; incidence is lower if prophylactic anti-infectives are utilized), CMV viremia (55%), infusion reactions (grades 3/4: 10% to 35%), diaphoresis (19%), CMV infection (16%), sepsis (15%), herpes viral infections (1% to 11%)

1% to 10%:

Cardiovascular: Chest pain (10%)

Central nervous system: Insomnia (10%), malaise (9%), anxiety (8%), depression (7%), temperature change sensation (5%), somnolence (5%)

Dermatologic: Purpura (8%), erythema (4%)

Gastrointestinal: Dyspepsia (10%), constipation (9%)

Hematologic: Neutropenic fever (10%), pancytopenia/marrow hypoplasia (5% to 6%; grade 3/4: 3%), positive Coombs' test without hemolysis (2%), autoimmune thrombocytopenia (2%), autoimmune hemolytic anemia (1%)

Neuromuscular & skeletal: Back pain (10%), tremor (3% to 7%)

Respiratory: Bronchospasm (9%), epistaxis (7%), rhinitis (7%)

Miscellaneous: Moniliasis (8%)

<1%, postmarketing, and/or case reports (limited to important or life-threatening): Acidosis, acute renal failure, acute respiratory distress syndrome, agranulocytosis, alkaline phosphatase increased, allergic reactions, anaphylactoid reactions, angina pectoris, angioedema, anuria, aphasia, aplastic anemia, arrhythmia, ascites, asthma, atrial fibrillation, bacterial infection, biliary pain, bone marrow aplasia, bullous eruption, capillary fragility, cardiac arrest, cardiac failure, cardiac insufficiency, cardiomyopathy, cellulitis, cerebral hemorrhage, cerebrovascular disorder, chronic inflammatory demyelinating polyradiculoneuropathy, coagulation abnormality, colitis, coma, COPD, coronary artery disorder, cyanosis, deep vein thrombosis, dehydration, diabetes mellitus exacerbation, disseminated intravascular coagulation (DIC), duodenal ulcer, ejection fraction decreased, endophthalmitis, Epstein-Barr virus, esophagitis, fluid overload, flu-like syndrome, gastrointestinal hemorrhage, Goodpasture's syndrome, Graves' disease, Guillain-Barré syndrome, hallucinations, hematemesis, hematoma, hematuria, hemolysis, hemolytic anemia, hemoptysis, hepatic failure, hepatocellular damage, hyperbilirubinemia, hyper-/hypoglycemia, hyper-/hypokalemia, hyperthyroidism, hypoalbuminemia, hyponatremia, hypovolemia, hypoxia, idiopathic thrombocytopenic purpura (ITP), interstitial pneumonitis, intestinal obstruction, intestinal perforation, intracranial hemorrhage, lymphadenopathy, marrow depression, melena, meningitis, MI, mouth edema, myositis, optic neuropathy, osteomyelitis, pancreatitis, paralysis, paralytic ileus, paroxysmal nocturnal

hemoglobinuria-like monocytes, peptic ulcer, pericarditis, peritonitis, plasma cell dyscrasia, phlebitis, pleural effusion, pleurisy, *Pneumocystis jiroveci* pneumonia, pneumothorax, polymyositis, progressive multifocal leukoencephalopathy, pseudomembranous colitis, pulmonary edema, pulmonary embolism, pulmonary fibrosis, pulmonary infiltration, pure red cell aplasia, purpuric rash, renal dysfunction, respiratory alkalosis, respiratory arrest, respiratory depression, respiratory insufficiency, seizure (grand mal), serum sickness, splenic infarction, splenomegaly, stridor, subarachnoid hemorrhage, syncope, toxic nephropathy, thrombocythemia, thrombophlebitis, throat tightness, tuberculosis, tumor lysis syndrome, ureteric obstruction, urinary retention, urinary tract infection, ventricular arrhythmia, ventricular tachycardia, viral infection

Overdosage/Toxicology Symptoms are likely to be extensions of adverse events (may include hematologic toxicity, respiratory distress, bronchospasm, anuria, tumor lysis syndrome). Single doses >30 mg or cumulative doses >90 mg/week have been associated with pancytopenia and severe (and occasionally fatal) ITP. Treatment is symptom-directed and supportive.

Drug Interactions

Increased Effect/Toxicity: Monoclonal antibodies (eg, abciximab, infliximab, and rituximab) may increase the risk for allergic reactions to alemtuzumab due to the presence of HACA antibodies. Alemtuzumab may enhance the adverse/toxic effects of vaccines (live organisms); vaccinal infections may develop.

Decreased Effect:

Alemtuzumab may decrease the effect of vaccines (dead organisms).

Ethanol/Nutrition/Herb Interactions Herb/Nutraceutical: Echinacea may diminish the therapeutic effect of alemtuzumab.

Storage/Stability Prior to dilution, store at 2°C to 8°C (36°F to 46°F); do not freeze (if accidentally frozen, thaw in refrigerator prior to administration). Do not shake; protect from light. Following dilution, store at room temperature or refrigerate; protect from light; use within 8 hours.

Reconstitution Dilute with 100 mL NS or D_5W. Gently invert the bag to mix the solution. Do not shake prior to use.

Compatibility Medications should not be added to the solution or simultaneously infused through the same I.V. line.

Mechanism of Action Binds to CD52, a nonmodulating antigen present on the surface of B and T lymphocytes, a majority of monocytes, macrophages, NK cells, and a subpopulation of granulocytes. After binding to $CD52^+$ cells, an antibody-dependent lysis of leukemic cells occurs.

Pharmacodynamics/Kinetics

Distribution: V_d: 0.1-0.4 L/kg

Metabolism: Clearance decreases with repeated dosing (due to loss of CD52 receptors in periphery), resulting in a sevenfold increase in AUC.

Half-life elimination: 11 hours (following first 30 mg dose; range: 2-32 hours); 6 days (following the last 30 mg dose; range: 1-14 days)

Dosage Note: **Dose escalation is required;** usually accomplished in 3-7 days. Do not exceed single doses >30 mg or cumulative doses >90 mg/week. Pretreatment (with acetaminophen and an oral antihistamine) is recommended prior to the first dose, with dose escalations, and as clinically indicated; I.V. hydrocortisone may be used for severe infusion-related reactions.

I.V. infusion, SubQ (unlabeled route): Adults: B-CLL:

Initial: 3 mg/day beginning on day 1; when tolerated (no grade 3 or 4 (Continued)

Alemtuzumab *(Continued)*

infusion reactions), increase to maintenance dose of 30 mg/dose 3 times/week on alternate days for a total duration of therapy of up to 12 weeks

Maximum dose/day: 30 mg; maximum cumulative dose/week: 90 mg

Dosage adjustment for hematologic toxicity (severe neutropenia or thrombocytopenia, not autoimmune): Note: If delay between dosing is ≥7 days, restart at 3 mg/day and escalate as tolerated.

First occurrence: ANC <250/μL and/or platelet count ≤25,000/μL: Hold therapy; resume at 30 mg/dose when ANC ≥500/μL and platelet count ≥50,000/μL

Second occurrence: ANC <250/μL and/or platelet count ≤25,000/μL: Hold therapy; resume at 10 mg/dose when ANC ≥500/μL and platelet count ≥50,000/μL

Third occurrence: ANC <250/μL and/or platelet count ≤25,000/μL: Permanently discontinue therapy

Patients with a baseline ANC ≤250/μL and/or a baseline platelet count ≤25,000/μL at initiation of therapy: If ANC and/or platelet counts decrease to ≤50% of the baseline value, hold therapy

First occurrence: When ANC and/or platelet count return to baseline, resume therapy at 30 mg/dose

Second occurrence: When ANC and/or platelet count return to baseline, resume therapy at 10 mg/dose

Third occurrence: Permanently discontinue therapy

Administration Administer by I.V. infusion over 2 hours. Consider premedicating with diphenhydramine 50 mg and acetaminophen 500-1000 mg 30 minutes before initiation of infusion. Hydrocortisone 200 mg has been effective in decreasing severe infusion-related events. Start anti-infective prophylaxis. Other drugs should not be added to or simultaneously infused through the same I.V. line. Do not give I.V. push.

SubQ (unlabeled route): A longer dose escalation time (1-2 weeks) may be needed due to injection site reactions. Premedication and anti-infective prophylaxis regimens should be given as are recommended with I.V. administration.

Monitoring Parameters Vital signs; carefully monitor BP especially in patient with ischemic heart disease or on antihypertensive medications; CBC with differential and platelets (weekly); signs and symptoms of infection; CD4+ lymphocyte counts (after treatment until recovery). Monitor closely for infusion reactions (including hypotension, rigors, fever, shortness of breath, bronchospasm, chills, and/or rash).

Test Interactions May interfere with diagnostic serum tests that utilize antibodies.

Patient Information You will need frequent laboratory tests during course of therapy. Do not use any prescription or OTC medications unless approved by your prescriber. Maintain adequate hydration (2-3 L/day unless otherwise instructed) and nutrition (frequent small meals will help). You may experience abdominal pain, mouth sores, nausea, or vomiting (small frequent meals, good mouth care with soft toothbrush or swabs, sucking lozenges or chewing gum, and avoidance of spicy or salty foods may help). Report unresolved gastrointestinal problems, persistent fever, chills, muscle pain, skin rash, unusual bleeding or bruising, signs of infection (mouth sores, sore throat, white plaques in mouth or perianal area, burning on urination); swelling of extremities; difficulty breathing; chest pain or palpitations; or other persistent adverse reactions.

Emetic Potential Moderate (30% to 60%)

Vesicant No

Dosage Forms Excipient information presented when available (limited, particularly for generics); consult specific product labeling.

Injection, solution [vial; preservative free]:

Campath®: 30 mg/mL (1 mL) [contains polysorbate 80; disodium edetate dihydrate]

References

Basu A, Ramkumar M, Tan HP, et al, "Reversal of Acute Cellular Rejection After Renal Transplantation With Campath-1H," *Transplant Proc*, 2005, 37(2):923-6.

Ciancio G, Burke GW, Gaynor JJ, et al, "A Randomized Trial of Three Renal Transplant Induction Antibodies: Early Comparison of Tacrolimus, Mycophenolate Mofetil, and Steroid Dosing, and Newer Immune-Monitoring," *Transplantation*, 2005, 80(4):457-65.

Hillmen P, Skotnicki A, Robak T, et al,"Preliminary Phase III Efficacy and Safety of Alemtuzumab vs Chlorambucil as Front-Line Therapy for Patients With Progressive B-Cell Chronic Lymphocytic Leukemia (BCLL)," *J Clin Oncol*, 2006, 24(18S):6511 [abstract from ASCO Annual Meeting Proceedings, Part I].

Keating MJ, Flinn I, Jain V, et al, "Therapeutic Role of Alemtuzumab (Campath-1H) in Patients Who Have Failed Fludarabine: Results of a Large International Study," *Blood*, 2002, 99(10):3554-61.

Kennedy B and Hillmen P, "Immunological Effects and Safe Administration of Alemtuzumab (MabCampath) in Advanced B-cLL," *Med Oncol*, 2002, 19(Suppl):49-55.

Lundin J, Kimby E, Bjorkholm M, et al, "Phase II Trial of Subcutaneous Anti-CD52 Monoclonal Antibody Alemtuzumab (Campath-1H) as First-Line Treatment for Patients With B-Cell Chronic Lymphocytic Leukemia (B-CLL)," *Blood*, 2002, 100(3):768-73.

Lundin J, Osterborg A, Brittinger G, et al, "CAMPATH-1H Monoclonal Antibody in Therapy for Previously Treated Low-Grade Non-Hodgkin's Lymphomas: A Phase II Multicenter Study. European Study Group of CAMPATH-1H Treatment in Low-Grade Non-Hodgkin's Lymphoma," *J Clin Oncol*, 1998, 16(10):3257-63.

Marcos A, Eghtesad B, Fung JJ, et al, "Use of Alemtuzumab and Tacrolimus Monotherapy for Cadaveric Liver Transplantation: With Particular Reference to Hepatitis C Virus," *Transplantation*, 2004, 78(7):966-71.

Osterborg A, Dyer MJ, Bunjes D, et al, "Phase II Multicenter Study of Human CD52 Antibody in Previously Treated Chronic Lymphocytic Leukemia. European Study Group of CAMPATH-1H Treatment in Chronic Lymphocytic Leukemia," *J Clin Oncol*, 1997, 15(4):1567-74.

Osterborg A, Fassas AS, Anagnostopoulos A, et al, "Humanifed CD52 Monoclonal Antibody Campath-1H as First-Line Treatment in Chronic Lymphocytic Leukaemia," *Br J Haematol*, 1996, 93(1):151-3.

Rai KR, Freter CE, Mercier RJ, et al, "Alemtuzumab in Previously Treated Chronic Lymphocytic Leukemia Patients Who Also Had Received Fludarabine," *J Clin Oncol*, 2002, 20(18):3891-7.

Ru X and Liebman HA, "Successful Treatment of Refractory Pure Red Cell Aplasia Associated With Lymphoproliferative Disorders With the Anti-CD52 Monoclonal Antibody Alemtuzumab (Campath-1H)," *Br J Haematol*, 2003, 123(2):278-81.

van Besien K, Artz A, Smith S, et al, "Fludarabine, Melphalan, and Alemtuzumab Conditioning in Adults With Standard-Risk Advanced Acute Myeloid Leukemia and Myelodysplastic Syndrome," *J Clin Oncol*, 2005, 23(24):5728-38.

Willis F, Marsh JC, Bevan DH, et al, "The Effect of Treatment With Campath-1H in Patients With Autoimmune Cytopenias," *Br J Haematol*, 2001, 114(4):891-8.

♦ **Alimta®** see Pemetrexed on page 884

Alitretinoin (a li TRET i noyn)

Medication Safety Issues

Sound-alike/look-alike issues:

Panretin® may be confused with pancreatin

High alert medication: The Institute for Safe Medication Practices (ISMP) includes this medication among its list of drugs which have a heightened risk of causing significant patient harm when used in error.

Related Information

Safe Handling of Hazardous Drugs on page 1382

U.S. Brand Names Panretin®

Generic Available No

(Continued)

Alitretinoin *(Continued)*

Canadian Brand Names Panretin®
Pharmacologic Category Antineoplastic Agent, Miscellaneous
Use Orphan drug: Topical treatment of cutaneous lesions in AIDS-related Kaposi's sarcoma
Unlabeled/Investigational Use Cutaneous T-cell lymphomas
Pregnancy Risk Factor D
Lactation Excretion in breast milk unknown/not recommended
Labeled Contraindications Hypersensitivity to alitretinoin, other retinoids, or any component of the formulation; pregnancy
Warnings/Precautions Hazardous agent - use appropriate precautions for handling and disposal. May cause fetal harm if absorbed by a woman who is pregnant. Do not use concurrently with topical products containing DEET (a common component of insect repellent products). Safety in pediatric patients or geriatric patients has not been established.
Adverse Reactions
>10%:
    Central nervous system: Pain (0% to 34%)
    Dermatologic: Rash (25% to 77%), pruritus (8% to 11%)
    Neuromuscular & skeletal: Paresthesia (3% to 22%)
5% to 10%:
    Cardiovascular: Edema (3% to 8%)
    Dermatologic: Exfoliative dermatitis (3% to 9%), skin disorder (0% to 8%)
Overdosage/Toxicology There has been no experience with human overdosage of alitretinoin, and overdose is unlikely following topical application. Treatment is symptomatic and supportive.
Drug Interactions
    Increased Effect/Toxicity: Increased toxicity of DEET may occur if products containing this compound are used concurrently with alitretinoin. Due to limited absorption after topical application, interaction with systemic medications is unlikely.
Storage/Stability Store at room temperature.
Mechanism of Action Binds to retinoid receptors to inhibit growth of Kaposi's sarcoma
Pharmacodynamics/Kinetics Absorption: Not extensive
Dosage Topical: Apply gel twice daily to cutaneous lesions
Administration Do not use occlusive dressings.
Patient Information For external use only; avoid UV light exposure (sun or sunlamps) of treated areas; avoid DEET-containing products
Emetic Potential Very low (<10%)
Dosage Forms Excipient information presented when available (limited, particularly for generics); consult specific product labeling.
    Gel: 0.1% (60 g tube)

♦ **Alkeran**® *see* Melphalan *on page 710*
♦ **Alloprin**® **(Can)** *see* Allopurinol *on page 40*

Allopurinol *(al oh PURE i nole)*
Medication Safety Issues
    Sound-alike/look-alike issues:
        Allopurinol may be confused with Apresoline
        Zyloprim® may be confused with Xylo-Pfan®, ZORprin®
Related Information
    Investigational Drug Service *on page 1379*

Tumor Lysis Syndrome *on page 1340*

U.S. Brand Names Aloprim™; Zyloprim®

Index Terms Allopurinol Sodium

Generic Available Yes

Canadian Brand Names Alloprin®; Apo-Allopurinol®; Novo-Purol; Zyloprim®

Pharmacologic Category Xanthine Oxidase Inhibitor

Use

> Oral: Prevention of attack of gouty arthritis and nephropathy; treatment of secondary hyperuricemia which may occur during treatment of tumors or leukemia; prevention of recurrent calcium oxalate calculi
>
> I.V.: Treatment of elevated serum and urinary uric acid levels when oral therapy is not tolerated in patients with leukemia, lymphoma, and solid tumor malignancies who are receiving cancer chemotherapy

Pregnancy Risk Factor C

Lactation Enters breast milk/use caution (AAP rates "compatible")

Labeled Contraindications Hypersensitivity to allopurinol or any component of the formulation

Warnings/Precautions Do not use to treat asymptomatic hyperuricemia. Has been associated with a number of hypersensitivity reactions, including severe reactions (vasculitis and Stevens-Johnson syndrome); discontinue at first sign of rash. Reversible hepatotoxicity has been reported; use with caution in patients with pre-existing hepatic impairment. Bone marrow suppression has been reported; use caution with other drugs causing myelosuppression. Caution in renal impairment, dosage adjustments needed. Use with caution in patients taking diuretics concurrently. Risk of skin rash may be increased in patients receiving amoxicillin or ampicillin. The risk of hypersensitivity may be increased in patients receiving thiazides, and possibly ACE inhibitors. Use caution with mercaptopurine or azathioprine; dosage adjustment necessary.

Adverse Reactions

> >1%:
>
> > Dermatologic: Rash (increased with ampicillin or amoxicillin use, 1.5% per manufacturer, >10% in some reports)
> >
> > Gastrointestinal: Nausea (1.3%), vomiting (1.2%)
> >
> > Renal: Renal failure/impairment (1.2%)
>
> <1%: Hypersensitivity syndrome, alkaline phosphatase or hepatic transaminases increased, granulomatous hepatitis, dyspepsia, pancreatitis, gynecomastia, agranulocytosis, aplastic anemia, acute tubular necrosis, interstitial nephritis, nephrolithiasis, vasculitis, toxic epidermal necrolysis, exfoliative dermatitis, Stevens-Johnson syndrome, granuloma annulare, toxic pustuloderma, peripheral neuropathy, neuritis, paresthesia, bronchospasm, cataracts, macular retinitis, angioedema, epistaxis

Overdosage/Toxicology If significant amounts of allopurinol have been absorbed, it is theoretically possible that oxypurinol stones could form, but no record of such occurrence exists. Alkalinization of urine and forced diuresis can help prevent potential xanthine stone formation.

Drug Interactions

> **Increased Effect/Toxicity:** Allopurinol may increase the effects of azathioprine, chlorpropamide, mercaptopurine, theophylline, and oral anticoagulants. An increased risk of bone marrow suppression may occur when given with myelosuppressive agents (cyclophosphamide, possibly other alkylating agents). Amoxicillin/ampicillin, ACE inhibitors, and thiazide diuretics have been associated with hypersensitivity reactions when combined with allopurinol (rare), and the incidence of rash may be

(Continued)

Allopurinol *(Continued)*

increased with penicillins (ampicillin, amoxicillin). Urinary acidification with large amounts of vitamin C may increase kidney stone formation.

Decreased Effect: Ethanol decreases effectiveness.

Ethanol/Nutrition/Herb Interactions

Ethanol: May decrease effectiveness.

Iron supplements: Hepatic iron uptake may be increased.

Vitamin C: Large amounts of vitamin C may acidify urine and increase kidney stone formation.

Storage/Stability

Powder for injection: Store at controlled room temperature of 15°C to 30°C (59°F to 86°F). Following reconstitution, intravenous solutions should be stored at 20°C to 25°C. Do not refrigerate reconstituted and/or diluted product. Must be administered within 10 hours of solution preparation.

Tablet: Store at controlled room temperature of 15°C to 25°C (59°F to 77°F).

Reconstitution Further dilution with NS or D_5W (50-100 mL) to ≤6 mg/mL is recommended.

Compatibility Stable in D_5W, NS, sterile water for injection.

Y-site administration: Compatible: Acyclovir, aminophylline, aztreonam, bleomycin, bumetanide, buprenorphine, butorphanol, calcium gluconate, carboplatin, cefazolin, cefoperazone, cefotetan, ceftazidime, ceftizoxime, ceftriaxone, cefuroxime, cisplatin, co-trimoxazole, cyclophosphamide, dactinomycin, dexamethasone sodium phosphate, doxorubicin liposome, enalaprilat, etoposide, famotidine, fluconazole, fludarabine, fluorouracil, furosemide, ganciclovir, heparin, hydrocortisone sodium phosphate, hydrocortisone sodium succinate, hydromorphone, ifosfamide, lorazepam, mannitol, mesna, methotrexate, metronidazole, mitoxantrone, morphine, piperacillin, plicamycin, potassium chloride, ranitidine, thiotepa, ticarcillin, ticarcillin/clavulanate, vancomycin, vinblastine, vincristine, zidovudine.

Incompatible: Amikacin, amphotericin B, carmustine, cefotaxime, chlorpromazine, cimetidine, clindamycin, cytarabine, dacarbazine, daunorubicin, diphenhydramine, doxorubicin, doxycycline, droperidol, floxuridine, gentamicin, haloperidol, hydroxyzine, idarubicin, imipenem/cilastatin, mechlorethamine, meperidine, methylprednisolone sodium succinate, metoclopramide, minocycline, nalbuphine, netilmicin, ondansetron, prochlorperazine edisylate, promethazine, sodium bicarbonate, streptozocin, tobramycin, vinorelbine.

Mechanism of Action Allopurinol inhibits xanthine oxidase, the enzyme responsible for the conversion of hypoxanthine to xanthine to uric acid. Allopurinol is metabolized to oxypurinol which is also an inhibitor of xanthine oxidase; allopurinol acts on purine catabolism, reducing the production of uric acid without disrupting the biosynthesis of vital purines.

Pharmacodynamics/Kinetics

Onset of action: Peak effect: 1-2 weeks

Absorption: Oral: ~80%; Rectal: Poor and erratic

Distribution: V_d: ~1.6 L/kg; V_{ss}: 0.84-0.87 L/kg; enters breast milk

Protein binding: <1%

Metabolism: ~75% to active metabolites, chiefly oxypurinol

Bioavailability: 49% to 53%

Half-life elimination:

Normal renal function: Parent drug: 1-3 hours; Oxypurinol: 18-30 hours

End-stage renal disease: Prolonged

Time to peak, plasma: Oral: 30-120 minutes

Excretion: Urine (76% as oxypurinol, 12% as unchanged drug)

Allopurinol and oxypurinol are dialyzable

Dosage

Oral: Doses >300 mg should be given in divided doses.

Children ≤10 years: Secondary hyperuricemia associated with chemo-therapy: 10 mg/kg/day in 2-3 divided doses **or** 200-300 mg/m^2/day in 2-4 divided doses, maximum: 800 mg/24 hours

Alternative (manufacturer labeling): <6 years: 150 mg/day in 3 divided doses; 6-10 years: 300 mg/day in 2-3 divided doses

Children >10 years and Adults:

Secondary hyperuricemia associated with chemotherapy: 600-800 mg/day in 2-3 divided doses for prevention of acute uric acid nephropathy for 2-3 days starting 1-2 days before chemotherapy

Gout: Mild: 200-300 mg/day; Severe: 400-600 mg/day; to reduce the possibility of acute gouty attacks, initiate dose at 100 mg/day and increase weekly to recommended dosage.

Recurrent calcium oxalate stones: 200-300 mg/day in single or divided doses

Elderly: Initial: 100 mg/day, increase until desired uric acid level is obtained

I.V.: Hyperuricemia secondary to chemotherapy: Intravenous daily dose can be given as a single infusion or in equally divided doses at 6-, 8-, or 12-hour intervals. A fluid intake sufficient to yield a daily urinary output of at least 2 L in adults and the maintenance of a neutral or, preferably, slightly alkaline urine are desirable.

Children ≤10 years: Starting dose: 200 mg/m^2/day

Children >10 years and Adults: 200-400 mg/m^2/day (maximum: 600 mg/day)

Dosing adjustment in renal impairment: Must be adjusted due to accumulation of allopurinol and metabolites:

Oral: Removed by hemodialysis; adult maintenance doses of allopurinol (mg) based on creatinine clearance (mL/minute): See table.

Adult Maintenance Doses of Allopurinol[1]

Creatinine Clearance (mL/min)	Maintenance Dose of Allopurinol (mg)
140	400 daily
120	350 daily
100	300 daily
80	250 daily
60	200 daily
40	150 daily
20	100 daily
10	100 every 2 days
0	100 every 3 days

[1]This table is based on a standard maintenance dose of 300 mg of allopurinol per day for a patient with a creatinine clearance of 100 mL/min.

Hemodialysis: Administer dose posthemodialysis or administer 50% supplemental dose

I.V.:

Cl_{cr} 10-20 mL/minute: 200 mg/day

Cl_{cr} 3-10 mL/minute: 100 mg/day

Cl_{cr} <3 mL/minute: 100 mg/day at extended intervals

Administration

Oral: Should administer oral forms after meals with plenty of fluid.

(Continued)

Allopurinol *(Continued)*

I.V.: Infuse over 15-60 minutes. The rate of infusion depends on the volume of the infusion. Whenever possible, therapy should be initiated at 24-48 hours before the start of chemotherapy known to cause tumor lysis (including adrenocorticosteroids). I.V. daily dose can be administered as a single infusion or in equally divided doses at 6-, 8-, or 12-hour interval.

Monitoring Parameters CBC, serum uric acid levels, I & O, hepatic and renal function, especially at start of therapy

Dietary Considerations Should administer oral forms after meals with plenty of fluid. Fluid intake should be administered to yield neutral or slightly alkaline urine and an output of ~2 L (in adults).

Patient Information Take after meals with plenty of fluid (at least 10-12 glasses of fluids per day); discontinue the drug and contact prescriber at first sign of rash, painful urination, blood in urine, irritation of the eyes, or swelling of the lips or mouth; may cause drowsiness; alcohol decreases effectiveness

Special Geriatric Considerations Adjust dose based on renal function.

Emetic Potential Very low (<10%)

Vesicant No

Dosage Forms Excipient information presented when available (limited, particularly for generics); consult specific product labeling.

Injection, powder for reconstitution, as sodium (Aloprim™): 500 mg

Tablet (Zyloprim®): 100 mg, 300 mg

Extemporaneous Preparations Crush tablets to make a 5 mg/mL suspension in simple syrup; stable 14 days under refrigeration

Nahata MC and Hipple TF, *Pediatric Drug Formulations*, 1st ed, Harvey Whitney Books Co, 1990.

References

Allen LV and Erickson MA 3d, "Stability of Acetazolamide, Allopurinol, Azathioprine, Clonazepam, and Flucytosine in Extemporaneously Compounded Oral Liquids," *Am J Health Syst Pharm*, 1996, 53(16):1944-9.

"American Academy of Pediatrics Committee on Drugs. The Transfer of Drugs and Other Chemicals Into Human Milk," *Pediatrics*, 2001, 108(3):776-89.

Appelbaum SJ, Mayersohn M, Dorr RT, et al, "Allopurinol Kinetics and Bioavailability. Intravenous, Oral and Rectal Administration," *Cancer Chemother Pharmacol*, 1982, 8(1):93-8.

Bennett WM, Aronoff GR, Golper TA, et al, *Drug Prescribing in Renal Failure*, Philadelphia, PA: American College of Physicians, 1987.

Day RO, Birkett DJ, Hicks M, et al, "New Uses for Allopurinol," *Drugs*, 1994, 48(3):399-44.

Elasy T, Kaminsky D, Tracy M, et al, "Allopurinol Hypersensitivity Syndrome Revisited," *West J Med*, 1995, 162(4):360-1.

Emmerson BT, "The Management of Gout," *N Engl J Med*, 1996, 334(7):445-51.

Ferner RE, Simmonds HA, and Bateman DN, "Allopurinol Kinetics After Massive Overdose," *Hum Toxicol*, 1988, 7(3):293-4.

Hande KR and Garrow GC, "Acute Tumor Lysis Syndrome in Patients With High-Grade Non-Hodgkin's Lymphoma," *Am J Med*, 1993, 94(2):133-9.

Krakoff IH and Murphy ML, "Hyperuricemia in Neoplastic Disease in Children: Prevention With Allopurinol, A Xanthine Oxidase Inhibitor," *Pediatrics*, 1968, 41(1):52-6.

McInnes GT, Lawson DH, and Jick H, "Acute Adverse Reactions Attributed to Allopurinol in Hospitalized Patients," *Ann Rheum Dis*, 1981, 40(3):245-9.

Murrell GA and Rapeport WG, "Clinical Pharmacokinetics of Allopurinol," *Clin Pharmacokinet*, 1986, 11(5):343-53.

Parra E, Gota R, Gamen A, et al, "Granulomatous Interstitial Nephritis Secondary to Allopurinol Treatment," *Clin Nephrol*, 1995, 43(5):350.

Vinciullo C, "Allopurinol Hypersensitivity," *Med J Aust*, 1984, 141(7):449-50.

◆ **Allopurinol Sodium** *see Allopurinol on page 40*

◆ **All-*trans*-Retinoic Acid** *see Tretinoin (Oral) on page 1069*

◆ **Alophen® [OTC]** *see Bisacodyl on page 144*

◆ **Aloprim™** *see Allopurinol on page 40*

◆ **Aloxi®** *see Palonosetron on page 869*

◆ **AlphaNine® SD** *see* Factor IX *on page 418*

Alteplase (AL te plase)

Medication Safety Issues

Sound-alike/look-alike issues:

Alteplase may be confused with Altace®

"tPA" abbreviation should not be used when writing orders for this medication; has been misread as TNKase (tenecteplase)

High alert medication: The Institute for Safe Medication Practices (ISMP) includes this medication (I.V.) among its list of drugs which have a heightened risk of causing significant patient harm when used in error.

U.S. Brand Names Activase®; Cathflo® Activase®

Index Terms Alteplase, Recombinant; Alteplase, Tissue Plasminogen Activator, Recombinant; tPA

Generic Available No

Canadian Brand Names Activase® rt-PA; Cathflo® Activase®

Pharmacologic Category Thrombolytic Agent

Use Management of acute myocardial infarction for the lysis of thrombi in coronary arteries; management of acute ischemic stroke

Acute myocardial infarction (AMI): Chest pain ≥20 minutes, ≤12-24 hours; S-T elevation ≥0.1 mV in at least two ECG leads

Acute pulmonary embolism (APE): Age ≤75 years: Documented massive pulmonary embolism by pulmonary angiography or echocardiography or high probability lung scan with clinical shock

Cathflo® Activase®: Restoration of central venous catheter function

Unlabeled/Investigational Use Acute peripheral arterial occlusive disease

Pregnancy Risk Factor C

Lactation Excretion in breast milk unknown/use caution

Labeled Contraindications Hypersensitivity to alteplase or any component of the formulation

Treatment of acute MI or PE: Active internal bleeding; history of CVA; recent intracranial or intraspinal surgery or trauma; intracranial neoplasm; arteriovenous malformation or aneurysm; known bleeding diathesis; severe uncontrolled hypertension

Treatment of acute ischemic stroke: Evidence of intracranial hemorrhage or suspicion of subarachnoid hemorrhage on pretreatment evaluation; recent (within 3 months) intracranial or intraspinal surgery; prolonged external cardiac massage; suspected aortic dissection; serious head trauma or previous stroke; history of intracranial hemorrhage; uncontrolled hypertension at time of treatment (eg, >185 mm Hg systolic or >110 mm Hg diastolic); seizure at the onset of stroke; active internal bleeding; intracranial neoplasm; arteriovenous malformation or aneurysm; known bleeding diathesis including but not limited to: current use of anticoagulants or an INR >1.7, administration of heparin within 48 hours preceding the onset of stroke and an elevated aPTT at presentation, platelet count <100,000/mm³.

Other exclusion criteria (NINDS recombinant tPA study): Stroke or serious head injury within 3 months, major surgery or serious trauma within 2 weeks, GI or urinary tract hemorrhage within 3 weeks, aggressive treatment required to lower blood pressure, glucose level <50 mg/dL or >400 mg/dL, arterial puncture at a noncompressible site or lumbar puncture within 1 week, clinical presentation suggesting post-MI pericarditis, pregnancy, breast-feeding.
(Continued)

Alteplase *(Continued)*

Warnings/Precautions Concurrent heparin anticoagulation may contribute to bleeding. Monitor all potential bleeding sites. Doses >150 mg are associated with increased risk of intracranial hemorrhage. Intramuscular injections and nonessential handling of the patient should be avoided. Venipunctures should be performed carefully and only when necessary. If arterial puncture is necessary, use an upper extremity vessel that can be manually compressed. If serious bleeding occurs, the infusion of alteplase and heparin should be stopped.

For the following conditions, the risk of bleeding is higher with use of alteplase and should be weighed against the benefits of therapy: Recent major surgery (eg, CABG, obstetrical delivery, organ biopsy, previous puncture of noncompressible vessels), cerebrovascular disease, recent gastrointestinal or genitourinary bleeding, recent trauma, hypertension (systolic BP >175 mm Hg and/or diastolic BP >110 mm Hg), high likelihood of left heart thrombus (eg, mitral stenosis with atrial fibrillation), acute pericarditis, subacute bacterial endocarditis, hemostatic defects including ones caused by severe renal or hepatic dysfunction, significant hepatic dysfunction, pregnancy, diabetic hemorrhagic retinopathy or other hemorrhagic ophthalmic conditions, septic thrombophlebitis or occluded AV cannula at seriously infected site, advanced age (eg, >75 years), patients receiving oral anticoagulants, any other condition in which bleeding constitutes a significant hazard or would be particularly difficult to manage because of location.

Coronary thrombolysis may result in reperfusion arrhythmias. Treatment of patients with acute ischemic stroke more than 3 hours after symptom onset is not recommended. Treatment of patients with minor neurological deficit or with rapidly improving symptoms is not recommended. Follow standard management for MI while infusing alteplase.

Cathflo® Activase®: When used to restore catheter function, use Cathflo® cautiously in those patients with known or suspected catheter infections. Evaluate catheter for other causes of dysfunction before use. Avoid excessive pressure when instilling into catheter.

Adverse Reactions As with all drugs which may affect hemostasis, bleeding is the major adverse effect associated with alteplase. Hemorrhage may occur at virtually any site. Risk is dependent on multiple variables, including the dosage administered, concurrent use of multiple agents which alter hemostasis, and patient predisposition. Rapid lysis of coronary artery thrombi by thrombolytic agents may be associated with reperfusion-related atrial and/or ventricular arrhythmia. **Note:** Lowest rate of bleeding complications expected with dose used to restore catheter function.

1% to 10%:
   Cardiovascular: Hypotension
   Central nervous system: Fever
   Dermatologic: Bruising (1%)
   Gastrointestinal: GI hemorrhage (5%), nausea, vomiting
   Genitourinary: GU hemorrhage (4%)
   Hematologic: Bleeding (0.5% major, 7% minor: GUSTO trial)
   Local: Bleeding at catheter puncture site (15.3%, accelerated administration)
<1% (Limited to important or life-threatening): Intracranial hemorrhage (0.4% to 0.87% when dose is ≤100 mg), retroperitoneal hemorrhage, pericardial hemorrhage, gingival hemorrhage, epistaxis, allergic reactions: anaphylaxis, anaphylactoid reactions, laryngeal edema, rash, and urticaria (<0.02%).

Additional cardiovascular events associated **with use in MI:** AV block, cardiogenic shock, heart failure, cardiac arrest, recurrent ischemia/infarction, myocardial rupture, electromechanical dissociation, pericardial effusion, pericarditis, mitral regurgitation, cardiac tamponade, thromboembolism, pulmonary edema, asystole, ventricular tachycardia, bradycardia, ruptured intracranial AV malformation, seizure, hemorrhagic bursitis, cholesterol crystal embolization

Additional events associated **with use in pulmonary embolism:** Pulmonary re-embolization, pulmonary edema, pleural effusion, thromboembolism

Additional events associated **with use in stroke:** Cerebral edema, cerebral herniation, seizure, new ischemic stroke

Overdosage/Toxicology Symptoms of overdose include increased incidence of intracranial bleeding.

Drug Interactions

Increased Effect/Toxicity: The potential for hemorrhage with alteplase is increased by oral anticoagulants (warfarin), heparin, low molecular weight heparins, and drugs which affect platelet function (eg, NSAIDs, dipyridamole, ticlopidine, clopidogrel, IIb/IIIa antagonists). Concurrent use with aspirin and heparin may increase the risk of bleeding. However, aspirin and heparin were used concomitantly with alteplase in the majority of patients in clinical studies.

Decreased Effect: Aminocaproic acid (an antifibrinolytic agent) may decrease the effectiveness of thrombolytic therapy. Nitroglycerin may increase the hepatic clearance of alteplase, potentially reducing lytic activity (limited clinical information).

Ethanol/Nutrition/Herb Interactions Herb/Nutraceutical: Avoid cat's claw, dong quai, evening primrose, feverfew, red clover, horse chestnut, garlic, green tea, ginseng, ginkgo (all have additional antiplatelet activity).

Storage/Stability

Activase®: The lyophilized product may be stored at room temperature (not to exceed 30°C/86°F), or under refrigeration. Once reconstituted it should be used within 8 hours.

Cathflo® Activase®: Store lyophilized product in refrigerated. Once reconstituted, store at 2°C to 30°C (36°F to 86°F) and use within 8 hours.

Reconstitution

Activase®:

50 mg vial: Use accompanying diluent (50 mL sterile water for injection); do not shake. Final concentration: 1 mg/mL.

100 mg vial: Use transfer set with accompanying diluent (100 mL vial of sterile water for injection); no vacuum is present in 100 mg vial. Final concentration: 1 mg/mL.

Cathflo® Activase®: Add 2.2 mL SWFI to vial; do not shake. Final concentration: 1 mg/mL.

Compatibility Stable in NS, sterile water for injection; **incompatible** with bacteriostatic water; **variable stability (consult detailed reference)** in D_5W.

Y-site administration: Compatible: Lidocaine, metoprolol, propranolol. **Incompatible:** Dobutamine, dopamine, heparin, nitroglycerin.

Compatibility when admixed: Compatible: Lidocaine, morphine, nitroglycerin. **Incompatible:** Dobutamine, dopamine, heparin.

Mechanism of Action Initiates local fibrinolysis by binding to fibrin in a thrombus (clot) and converts entrapped plasminogen to plasmin

Pharmacodynamics/Kinetics

Duration: >50% present in plasma cleared ~5 minutes after infusion terminated, ~80% cleared within 10 minutes

(Continued)

Alteplase *(Continued)*

Excretion: Clearance: Rapidly from circulating plasma (550-650 mL/minute), primarily hepatic; >50% present in plasma is cleared within 5 minutes after the infusion is terminated, ~80% cleared within 10 minutes

Dosage

I.V.:

Coronary artery thrombi: Front loading dose (weight-based):

Patients >67 kg: Total dose: 100 mg over 1.5 hours; infuse 15 mg over 1-2 minutes. Infuse 50 mg over 30 minutes. Infuse remaining 35 mg of alteplase over the next hour. See "Note."

Patients ≤67 kg: Infuse 15 mg I.V. bolus over 1-2 minutes, then infuse 0.75 mg/kg (not to exceed 50 mg) over next 30 minutes, followed by 0.5 mg/kg over next 60 minutes (not to exceed 35 mg). See "Note."

Note: Concurrently, begin heparin 60 units/kg bolus (maximum: 4000 units) followed by continuous infusion of 12 units/kg/hour (maximum: 1000 units/hour) and adjust to aPTT target of 1.5-2 times the upper limit of control.

Acute pulmonary embolism: 100 mg over 2 hours.

Acute ischemic stroke: Doses should be given within the first 3 hours of the onset of symptoms; recommended total dose: 0.9 mg/kg (maximum dose should not exceed 90 mg) infused over 60 minutes.

Load with 0.09 mg/kg (10% of the 0.9 mg/kg dose) as an I.V. bolus over 1 minute, followed by 0.81 mg/kg (90% of the 0.9 mg/kg dose) as a continuous infusion over 60 minutes. Heparin should not be started for 24 hours or more after starting alteplase for stroke.

Intracatheter: Central venous catheter clearance: Cathflo® Activase® 1 mg/mL:

Patients <30 kg: 110% of the internal lumen volume of the catheter, not to exceed 2 mg/2 mL; retain in catheter for 0.5-2 hours; may instill a second dose if catheter remains occluded

Patients ≥30 kg: 2 mg (2 mL); retain in catheter for 0.5-2 hours; may instill a second dose if catheter remains occluded

Intra-arterial: Acute peripheral arterial occlusive disease (unlabeled use): 0.02-0.1 mg/kg/hour for up to 36 hours

Advisory Panel to the Society for Cardiovascular and Interventional Radiology on Thrombolytic Therapy recommendation: ≤2 mg/hour and subtherapeutic heparin (aPTT <1.5 times baseline)

Administration

Activase®: Acute MI: Accelerated infusion:

Bolus dose may be prepared by one of three methods:

1) removal of 15 mL reconstituted (1 mg/mL) solution from vial

2) removal of 15 mL from a port on the infusion line after priming

3) programming an infusion pump to deliver a 15 mL bolus at the initiation of infusion

Remaining dose may be administered as follows:

50 mg vial: Either PVC bag or glass vial and infusion set

100 mg vial: Insert spike end of the infusion set through the same puncture site created by transfer device and infuse from vial

If further dilution is desired, may be diluted in equal volume of 0.9% sodium chloride or D_5W to yield a final concentration of 0.5 mg/mL AD

Cathflo® Activase®: Intracatheter: Instill dose into occluded catheter. Do not force solution into catheter. After a 30-minute dwell time, assess catheter function by attempting to aspirate blood. If catheter is functional, aspirate 4-5 mL of blood in patients ≥10 kg or 3 mL in patients <10 kg to remove Cathflo® Activase® and residual clots. Gently irrigate the catheter with NS.

If catheter remains nonfunctional, let Cathflo® Activase® dwell for another 90 minutes (total dwell time: 120 minutes) and reassess function. If catheter function is not restored, a second dose may be instilled.

Monitoring Parameters

When using for central venous catheter clearance: Assess catheter function by attempting to aspirate blood.

When using for management of acute myocardial infarction: Assess for evidence of cardiac reperfusion through resolution of chest pain, resolution of baseline ECG changes, preserved left ventricular function, cardiac enzyme washout phenomenon, and/or the appearance of reperfusion arrhythmias; assess for bleeding potential through clinical evidence of GI bleeding, hematuria, gingival bleeding, fibrinogen levels, fibrinogen degradation products, prothrombin times, and partial thromboplastin times.

Test Interactions Altered results of coagulation and fibrinolytic agents

Special Geriatric Considerations No specific changes in use in elderly patients are necessary.

Dosage Forms Excipient information presented when available (limited, particularly for generics); consult specific product labeling.

Injection, powder for reconstitution, recombinant:

Activase®: 50 mg [29 million int. units; contains polysorbate 80; packaged with diluent]; 100 mg [58 million int. units; contains polysorbate 80; packaged with diluent and transfer device]

Cathflo® Activase®: 2 mg [contains polysorbate 80]

References

"A Comparison of Continuous Infusion of Alteplase With Double-Bolus Administration for Acute Myocardial Infarction. The Continuous Infusion Versus Double-Bolus Administration of Alteplase (COBALT) Investigators," *N Engl J Med*, 1997, 337(16):1124-30.

"A Comparison of Reteplase With Alteplase for Acute Myocardial Infarction. The Global Use of Strategies to Open Occluded Coronary Arteries (GUSTO III) Investigators," *N Engl J Med*, 1997, 337(16):1118-23.

Albers GW, Bates VE, Clark WM, et al, "Intravenous Tissue-Type Plasminogen Activator for Treatment of Acute Stroke: The Standard Treatment With Alteplase to Reverse Stroke (STARS) Study," *JAMA*, 2000, 283(9):1145-50.

Antman EM, Anbe SC, Alpert JS, et al, "ACC/AHA Guidelines for the Management of Patients With ST-Elevation Myocardial Infarction - Executive Summary: A Report of the American College of Cardiology/American Heart Association Task Force on Practice Guidelines (Writing Committee to Revise the 1999 Guidelines for the Management of Patients With Acute Myocardial Infarction)," *Circulation*, 2004, 110(5):588-636. Available at: http://www.circulationaha.org/cgi/content/full/110/5/588. Last accessed October 26, 2004.

Antman EM, Giugliano RP, Gibson CM, et al, "Abciximab Facilitates the Rate and Extent of Thrombolysis: Results of the Thrombolysis in Myocardial Infarction (TIMI) 14 Trial. The TIMI 14 Investigators," *Circulation*, 1999, 99(21):2720-32.

Broderick J, Connolly S, Feldmann E, et al, "Guidelines for the Management of Spontaneous Intracerebral Hemorrhage in Adults: 2007 Update: A Guideline From the American Heart Association/American Stroke Association Stroke Council, High Blood Pressure Research Council, and the Quality of Care and Outcomes in Research Interdisciplinary Working Group," *Stroke*, 2007, 38(6):2001-23. Available at http://stroke.ahajournals.org/cgi/content/short/STROKEAHA.107.183689.

Clark WM, Wissman S, Albers GW, et al, "Recombinant Tissue-Type Plasminogen Activator (Alteplase) for Ischemic Stroke 3 to 5 Hours After Symptom Onset: The ATLANTIS Study: A Randomized Controlled Trial," *JAMA*, 1999, 282(21):2019-26.

Comerota AJ and Schmieder FA, "Intraoperative Lytic Therapy: Agents and Methods of Administration," *Semin Vasc Surg*, 2001, 14(2):132-42.

Gerlach AT and Pickworth KK, "Use of Alteplase in Peripheral Arterial Occlusions: Outcomes and Complications," Abstracts of the American College of Clinical Pharmacy Annual Meeting, Los Angeles, 2000, November 5-8; Abs No 47.

Kwiatkowski TG, Libman RB, Frankel M, et al, "Effects of Tissue Plasminogen Activator for Acute Ischemic Stroke at One Year. National Institute of Neurological Disorders and Stroke Recombinant Tissue Plasminogen Activator Stroke Study Group," *N Engl J Med*, 1999, 340(23):1781-7.

Leonard MC and Shermock KM, "Using Efficacy, Safety, and Cost Data to Support a Formulary Decision Regarding Thrombolytic Therapy," *Semin Vasc Surg*, 2001, 14(2):150-5.

(Continued)

Alteplase *(Continued)*

Lincoff AM, Califf RM, Van de Werf F, et al, "Mortality at 1 Year With Combination Platelet Glycoprotein IIb/IIIa Inhibition and Reduced-Dose Fibrinolytic Therapy vs Conventional Fibrinolytic Therapy for Acute Myocardial Infarction: GUSTO V Randomized Trial," *JAMA*, 2002, 288(17):2130-5.

Lundergan CF, Reiner JS, McCarthy WF, et al, "Clinical Predictors of Early Infarct-Related Artery Patency Following Thrombolytic Therapy: Importance of Body Weight, Smoking History, Infarct-Related Artery and Choice of Thrombolytic Regimen: The GUSTO-I Experience. Global Utilization of Streptokinase and t-PA for Occluded Coronary Arteries," *J Am Coll Cardiol*, 1998, 32(3):641-7.

"NINDS tPA Stroke Study Group. Generalized Efficacy for Acute Stroke: Subgroup Analysis of the NINDS tPA Stroke Study Group," *Stroke*, 1997, 28(11):2119-25.

Ouriel K, "Current Status of Thrombolysis for Peripheral Arterial Occlusive Disease," *Ann Vasc Surg*, 2002, 16(6):797-804.

Ponec D, Irwin D, Haire WD, et al, "Recombinant Tissue Plasminogen Activator (Alteplase) for Restoration of Flow in Occluded Central Venous Access Devices: A Double-Blind Placebo-Controlled Trial - The Cardiovascular Thrombolytic to Open Occluded Lines (COOL) Efficacy Trial," *J Vasc Interv Radiol*, 2001, 12(8):951-5.

"Results of a Prospective, Randomised Trial Evaluating Surgery Versus Thrombolysis for Ischemia of the Lower Extremity. The STILE Trial," *Ann Surg*, 1994, 220(3):251-66; discussion 266-8.

Semba CP, Murphy TP, Bakal CW, et al, "Thrombolytic Therapy With Use of Alteplase (rtPA) in Peripheral Arterial Occlusive Disease: Review of the Clinical Literature. The Advisory Panel," *J Vasc Interv Radiol*, 2000, 11(2 Pt 1):149-61.

Sugimoto K, Hofmann LV, Razavi MK, et al, "The Safety, Efficacy, and Pharmacoeconomics of Low-Dose Alteplase Compared With Urokinase for Catheter-Directed Thrombolysis of Arterial and Venous Occlusions," *J Vasc Surg*, 2003, 37(3):512-7.

The Gusto Angiographic Investigators, "The Effects of Tissue Plasminogen Activator, Streptokinase, or Both on Coronary-Artery Patency, Ventricular Function, and Survival After Acute Myocardial Infarction," *N Engl J Med*, 1993, 329(22):1615-22.

"The NINDS tPA Stroke Study Group. Intracerebral Hemorrhage After Intravenous tPA Therapy for Ischemic Stroke," *Stroke*, 1997, 28:2109-18.

"The Seventh ACCP Conference on Antithrombotic and Thrombolytic Therapy: Evidence-Based Guidelines," *Chest*, 2004, 126(3 Suppl):163-703.

"Thrombolysis in the Management of Lower Limb Peripheral Arterial Occlusion - A Consensus Document. Working Party on Thrombolysis in the Management of Limb Ischemia," *Am J Cardiol*, 1998, 81(2):207-18.

"Tissue Plasminogen Activator for Acute Ischemic Stroke. The National Institute of Neurological Disorders and Stroke rt-PA Stroke Study Group," *N Engl J Med*, 1995, 333(24):1581-7.

Topol EJ, "Reperfusion Therapy for Acute Myocardial Infarction With Fibrinolytic Therapy or Combination Reduced Fibrinolytic Therapy and Platelet Glycoprotein IIb/IIIa Inhibition: The GUSTO V Randomized Trial. GUSTO V Investigators," *Lancet*, 2001, 357(9272):1905-14.

Valji K, "Evolving Strategies for Thrombolytic Therapy of Peripheral Vascular Occlusion," *J Vasc Interv Radiol*, 2000, 11(4):411-20.

Zacharias JM, Weatherston CP, Spewak CR, et al, "Alteplase Versus Urokinase for Occluded Hemodialysis Catheters," *Ann Pharmacother*, 2003, 37(1):27-33.

♦ **Alteplase, Recombinant** *see* Alteplase *on page 45*

♦ **Alteplase, Tissue Plasminogen Activator, Recombinant** *see* Alteplase *on page 45*

♦ **Alti-MPA (Can)** *see* MedroxyPROGESTERone *on page 703*

Altretamine *(al TRET a meen)*

Medication Safety Issues

High alert medication: The Institute for Safe Medication Practices (ISMP) includes this medication among its list of drugs which have a heightened risk of causing significant patient harm when used in error.

International issues:

Hexalen®: Brand name for hexetidine in Greece

Related Information

Safe Handling of Hazardous Drugs *on page 1382*

U.S. Brand Names Hexalen®
Index Terms Hexamethylmelamine; HEXM; HMM; HXM; NSC-13875
Generic Available No
Canadian Brand Names Hexalen®
Pharmacologic Category Antineoplastic Agent, Miscellaneous
Use Palliative treatment of persistent or recurrent ovarian cancer
Pregnancy Risk Factor D
Lactation Excretion in breast milk unknown/not recommended
Labeled Contraindications Hypersensitivity to altretamine or any component of the formulation; pre-existing severe bone marrow suppression or severe neurologic toxicity; pregnancy
Warnings/Precautions Hazardous agent - use appropriate precautions for handling and disposal. **[U.S. Boxed Warning]: Peripheral blood counts and neurologic examinations should be done routinely before and after drug therapy.** Myelosuppression and neurotoxicity are common; use with caution in patients previously treated with other myelosuppressive drugs or with pre-existing neurotoxicity. Use with caution in patients with renal or hepatic dysfunction. **[U.S. Boxed Warning]: Should be administered under the supervision of an experienced cancer chemotherapy physician.** Safety and efficacy in children have not been established.

Adverse Reactions
>10%:
  Central nervous system: Peripheral sensory neuropathy (31%; moderate-to-severe 9%), neurotoxicity (21%; may be progressive and dose-limiting)
  Gastrointestinal: Nausea/vomiting (33% to 70%; severe 1%), diarrhea (48%)
  Hematologic: Anemia (33%), leukopenia (5% to 15%; grade 4: 1%), neutropenia
1% to 10%:
  Central nervous system: Fatigue (1%), seizure (1%)
  Gastrointestinal: Stomach cramps, anorexia (1%)
  Hematologic: Thrombocytopenia (9%)
  Hepatic: Alkaline phosphatase increased (9%)
<1%: Alopecia, ataxia, depression, dizziness, hepatotoxicity, mood disorders, pruritus, rash, tremor, vertigo

Overdosage/Toxicology Symptoms of overdose include nausea, vomiting, peripheral neuropathy, severe bone marrow suppression. Treatment is symptom-directed and supportive.

Drug Interactions
  Increased Effect/Toxicity: Altretamine may enhance the hypotensive effects of MAO inhibitors and tricyclic antidepressants.
  Decreased Effect: Pyridoxine may diminish the effect of altretamine.

Storage/Stability Store at 15°C to 30°C (59°F to 86°F).
Mechanism of Action Although altretamine's clinical antitumor spectrum resembles that of alkylating agents, the drug has demonstrated activity in alkylator-resistant patients. The drug selectively inhibits the incorporation of radioactive thymidine and uridine into DNA and RNA, inhibiting DNA and RNA synthesis; reactive intermediates covalently bind to microsomal proteins and DNA; can spontaneously degrade to demethylated melamines and formaldehyde which are also cytotoxic.

Pharmacodynamics/Kinetics
  Absorption: Well absorbed (75% to 89%)
  Distribution: Highly concentrated hepatically and renally; low in other organs
  Protein binding: 50% to 94%
  (Continued)

Altretamine *(Continued)*

Metabolism: Hepatic; rapid and extensive demethylation to active metabolites (pentamethylmelamine and tetramethylmelamine)

Half-life elimination: 13 hours

Time to peak, plasma: 0.5-3 hours

Excretion: Urine (90%, <1% as unchanged drug)

Dosage Refer to individual protocols. Oral: Adults:

Ovarian cancer: 260 mg/m^2/day in 4 divided doses for 14 or 21 days of a 28-day cycle

Alternatively (unlabeled use): 4-12 mg/kg/day in 3-4 divided doses for 21-90 days

Alternatively (unlabeled use): 240-320 mg/m^2/day in 3-4 divided doses for 21 days, repeated every 6 weeks

Alternatively (unlabeled use): 150 mg/m^2/day in 3-4 divided doses for 14 days of a 28-day cycle

Dosage adjustment for toxicity: Temporarily withhold for 14 days or longer, and resume dose at 200 mg/m^2/day for any of the following:

Platelet count <75,000/mm^3

White blood cell count <2000/mm^3 or granulocyte count <1000/mm^3

Progressive neurotoxicity

Gastrointestinal intolerance not responsive to antiemetic regimens

Administration Administer total daily dose as 3-4 divided doses after meals and at bedtime.

Monitoring Parameters CBC with differential, liver function tests; neurologic examination

Dietary Considerations Should be taken after meals at bedtime.

Patient Information Report any numbness or tingling in extremities. Nausea and vomiting may occur.

Emetic Potential Moderate (30% to 60%)

Dosage Forms Excipient information presented when available (limited, particularly for generics); consult specific product labeling.

Gelcap:

Hexalen®: 50 mg

References

Ames MM, "Hexamethylmelamine: Pharmacology and Mechanism of Action," *Cancer Treat Rev*, 1991, 18(Suppl A):3-14.

Bruckner HW and Schleifer SJ, "Orthostatic Hypotension as a Complication of Hexamethylmelamine Antidepressant Interaction," *Cancer Treat Rep*, 1983, 67:516.

Damia G and D'Incalci M, "Clinical Pharmacokinetics of Altretamine," *Clin Pharmacokinet*, 1995, 28(6):439-48.

Hahn DA and Black C, "Hexamethylamine: A Review," *Drug Intell Clin Pharm*, 1980, 14:541-7.

Hansen LA and Hughes TE, "Altretamine," *DICP*, 1991, 25(2):146-52.

Lee CR and Faulds D, "Altretamine. A Review of Its Pharmacodynamic and Pharmacokinetic Properties, and Therapeutic Potential in Cancer Chemotherapy," *Drugs*, 1995, 49(6):932-53.

Manetta A, Mac Neill C, Lyter JA, et al, "Hexamethylmelamine as a Single Second-Line Agent in Ovarian Cancer," *Gynecol Oncol*, 1990, 36(1):93-6.

Sutton GP, "Secondary Therapy for Epithelial Ovarian Cancer - 1994," *Semin Oncol*, 1994, 21(4 Suppl 7):32-6.

Thigpen JT, Vance RB, and Khansur T, "Second-Line Chemotherapy for Recurrent Carcinoma of the Ovary," *Cancer*, 1993, 71(4 Suppl):1559-64.

Amifostine (am i FOS teen)

Medication Safety Issues
Sound-alike/look-alike issues:
Ethyol® may be confused with ethanol

Related Information
Safe Handling of Hazardous Drugs *on page 1382*

U.S. Brand Names Ethyol®

Index Terms Ethiofos; Gammaphos; WR-2721; YM-08310

Generic Available No

Canadian Brand Names Ethyol®

Pharmacologic Category Adjuvant, Chemoprotective Agent (Cytoprotective); Antidote

Use Reduce the incidence of moderate to severe xerostomia in patients undergoing postoperative radiation treatment for head and neck cancer, where the radiation port includes a substantial portion of the parotid glands; reduce the cumulative renal toxicity associated with repeated administration of cisplatin

Pregnancy Risk Factor C

Lactation Excretion in breast milk unknown/not recommended

Labeled Contraindications Hypersensitivity to amifostine, aminothiol compounds, or any component of the formulation

Warnings/Precautions Patients who are hypotensive or dehydrated should not receive amifostine. Interrupt antihypertensive therapy for 24 hours before amifostine. Patients who cannot safely stop their antihypertensives 24 hours before amifostine, should not receive it.

It is recommended that antiemetic medication, including dexamethasone 20 mg I.V. and a serotonin 5-HT$_3$ receptor antagonist be administered prior to and in conjunction with amifostine. Rare hypersensitivity reactions, including anaphylaxis and severe cutaneous reaction, have been reported with a higher frequency in patients receiving amifostine as a radioprotectant. Discontinue if allergic reaction occurs; do not rechallenge.

Reports of clinically-relevant hypocalcemia are rare, but serum calcium levels should be monitored in patients at risk of hypocalcemia, such as those with nephrotic syndrome. Safety and efficacy in children have not been established.

Adverse Reactions
>10%:
Cardiovascular: Hypotension (15% to 62%; grades 3/4: 3% to 8%; dose dependent)

Gastrointestinal: Nausea/vomiting (53% to 96%; grades 3/4: 8% to 30%; dose dependent)

<1%, postmarketing, and/or case reports: Apnea, anaphylactoid reactions, anaphylaxis, arrhythmia, atrial fibrillation, atrial flutter, back pain, bradycardia, cardiac arrest, chest pain, chest tightness, chills, cutaneous eruptions, dizziness, erythema multiforme, exfoliative dermatitis, extrasystoles, dyspnea, fever, flushing, hiccups, hypersensitivity reactions (fever, rash, hypoxia, dyspnea, laryngeal edema), hypertension (transient), hypocalcemia, hypoxia, myocardial ischemia, pruritus, rash (mild), renal failure, respiratory arrest, rigors, seizure, sneezing, somnolence, Stevens-Johnson syndrome, supraventricular tachycardia, syncope, tachycardia, toxic epidermal necrolysis, toxoderma, urticaria

Overdosage/Toxicology Symptoms of overdose include hypotension, nausea, vomiting, anxiety and reversible urinary retention. Treatment
(Continued)

Amifostine *(Continued)*

includes infusion of normal saline for hypotension and supportive measures as clinically indicated.

Drug Interactions

Increased Effect/Toxicity: Antihypertensives may potentiate the hypotensive effects of amifostine.

Storage/Stability Store intact vials of lyophilized powder at room temperature of 20°C to 25°C (68°F to 77°F). Reconstituted solutions (500 mg/10 mL) and solutions for infusion are chemically stable for up to 5 hours at room temperature (25°C) or up to 24 hours under refrigeration (2°C to 8°C).

Reconstitution For I.V. infusion, reconstitute intact vials with 9.7 mL 0.9% sodium chloride injection and dilute in 0.9% sodium chloride to a final concentration of 5-40 mg/mL. For SubQ administration, reconstitute with 2.5 mL NS or SWFI.

Compatibility Stable in NS.

Y-site administration: Compatible: Amikacin, aminophylline, ampicillin, ampicillin/sulbactam, aztreonam, bleomycin, bumetanide, buprenorphine, butorphanol, calcium gluconate, carboplatin, carmustine, cefazolin, cefotaxime, cefotetan, cefoxitin, ceftazidime, ceftizoxime, ceftriaxone, cefuroxime, cimetidine, ciprofloxacin, clindamycin, co-trimoxazole, cyclophosphamide, cytarabine, dacarbazine, dactinomycin, daunorubicin, dexamethasone sodium phosphate, diphenhydramine, dobutamine, docetaxel, dopamine, doxorubicin, doxycycline, droperidol, enalaprilat, etoposide, famotidine, floxuridine, fluconazole, fludarabine, fluorouracil, furosemide, gemcitabine, gentamicin, granisetron, haloperidol, heparin, hydrocortisone sodium phosphate, hydrocortisone sodium succinate, hydromorphone, idarubicin, ifosfamide, imipenem/cilastatin, leucovorin, lorazepam, magnesium sulfate, mannitol, mechlorethamine, meperidine, mesna, methotrexate, methylprednisolone sodium succinate, metoclopramide, metronidazole, mitomycin, mitoxantrone, morphine, nalbuphine, netilmicin, ondansetron, piperacillin, plicamycin, potassium chloride, promethazine, ranitidine, sodium bicarbonate, streptozocin, teniposide, thiotepa, ticarcillin, ticarcillin/clavulanate, tobramycin, vancomycin, vinblastine, vincristine, zidovudine. **Incompatible:** Acyclovir, amphotericin B, cefoperazone, chlorpromazine, cisplatin, ganciclovir, hydroxyzine, minocycline, prochlorperazine edisylate.

Mechanism of Action Prodrug that is dephosphorylated by alkaline phosphatase in tissues to a pharmacologically-active free thiol metabolite. The free thiol is available to bind to, and detoxify, reactive metabolites of cisplatin; and can also act as a scavenger of free radicals that may be generated in tissues.

Pharmacodynamics/Kinetics

Distribution: V_d: 3.5 L

Metabolism: Hepatic dephosphorylation to two metabolites (active-free thiol and disulfide)

Half-life elimination: 8-9 minutes

Excretion: Urine

Clearance, plasma: 2.17 L/minute

Dosage Note: Antiemetic medication, including dexamethasone 20 mg I.V. and a serotonin 5-HT$_3$ receptor antagonist, is recommended prior to and in conjunction with amifostine.

Adults:

Cisplatin-induced renal toxicity, reduction: I.V.: 740-910 mg/m^2 over 15 minutes once daily 30 minutes prior to cytotoxic therapy

Note: Doses >740 mg/m^2 are associated with a higher incidence of hypotension and may require interruption of therapy or dose modification for subsequent cycles. For 910 mg/m^2 doses, the manufacturer suggests the following blood pressure-based adjustment schedule:

The infusion of amifostine should be interrupted if the systolic blood pressure decreases significantly from baseline, as defined below:

Decrease of 20 mm Hg if baseline systolic blood pressure <100
Decrease of 25 mm Hg if baseline systolic blood pressure 100-119
Decrease of 30 mm Hg if baseline systolic blood pressure 120-139
Decrease of 40 mm Hg if baseline systolic blood pressure 140-179
Decrease of 50 mm Hg if baseline systolic blood pressure ≥180

If blood pressure returns to normal within 5 minutes (assisted by fluid administration and postural management) and the patient is asymptomatic, the infusion may be restarted so that the full dose of amifostine may be administered. If the full dose of amifostine cannot be administered, the dose of amifostine for subsequent cycles should be 740 mg/m^2.

Xerostomia from head and neck cancer, reduction:

I.V.: 200 mg/m^2/day over 3 minutes 15-30 minutes prior to radiation therapy **or**

SubQ (unlabeled route): 500 mg/day prior to radiation therapy

Administration I.V.: Administer over 3-15 minutes; administration as a longer infusion is associated with a higher incidence of side effects. Patients should be kept in supine position during infusion. **Note:** SubQ administration has been used.

Monitoring Parameters Blood pressure should be monitored every 5 minutes during the infusion and after administration if clinically indicated; serum calcium levels (in patients at risk for hypocalcemia)

Patient Information This medication is given to help reduce side effects of your cancer therapy. Report immediately lightheadedness, dizziness, fainting, or any nausea; you will be given medication. Report chills, severe dizziness, tremors or shaking, or sudden onset of hiccups.

Additional Information Mean onset of hypotension is 14 minutes into the 15-minute infusion and the mean duration 6 minutes.

Emetic Potential High (60% to 90%)

Vesicant No

Dosage Forms Excipient information presented when available (limited, particularly for generics); consult specific product labeling.

Injection, powder for reconstitution:

Ethyol®: 500 mg

References

Anne PR and Curran WJ Jr, "A Phase II Trial of Subcutaneous Amifostine and Radiation Therapy in Patients With Head and Neck Cancer," *Semin Radiat Oncol*, 2002, 12(1 Suppl 1):18-9.

Bonner HS and Shaw LM, "New Dosing Regimens for Amifostine: A Pilot Study to Compare the Relative Bioavailability of Oral and Subcutaneous Administration With Intravenous Infusion," *J Clin Pharmacol*, 2002, 42(2):166-74.

Capizzi RL and Oster W, "Chemoprotective and Radioprotective Effects of Amifostine: An Update of Clinical Trials," *Int J Hematol*, 2000, 72(4):425-35.

Culy CR and Spencer CM, "Amifostine: An Update on Its Clinical Status as a Cytoprotectant in Patients With Cancer Receiving Chemotherapy or Radiotherapy and Its Potential Therapeutic Application in Myelodysplastic Syndrome," *Drugs*, 2001, 61(5):641-84.

Koukourakis MI, "Amifostine in Clinical Oncology: Current Use and Future Applications," *Anticancer Drugs*, 2002, 13(3):181-209.

Koukourakis MI, Kyrias G, and Kakolyris S, "Subcutaneous Administration of Amifostine During Fractionated Radiotherapy: A Randomized Phase II Study," *J Clin Oncol*, 2000, 18(11):2226-33.

Norales G, Maria V, de Guzman A, et al, "Amifostine-Induced Back Pain: a Case Report," *Am J Health-Syst Pharm*, 2006, 63(4): 381-2.

(Continued)

Amifostine (Continued)

Samuels MA, Chico IM, Hirsch RL, et al, "Ongoing Prospective Multicenter Safety Study of the Cytoprotectant Amifostine Given Subcutaneously: Overview of Trial Design," *Semin Oncol*, 2003, 30(6 Suppl 18):94-5.

Schuchter LM, Hensley ML, Meropol NJ, et al, "2002 Update of Recommendationsfor the Use of Chemotherapy and Radiotherapy Protectants: Clinical Practice Guidelines of the American Society of Clinical Oncology," *J Clin Oncol*, 2002, 20(12): 2895-903 .

Spencer CM and Goa KL, "Amifostine. A Review of Its Pharmacodynamic and Pharmacokinetic Properties, and Therapeutic Potential as a Radioprotector and Cytotoxic Chemoprotector," *Drugs*, 1995, 50(6):1001-31.

Wasserman TH and Brizel DM, "The Role of Amifostine as a Radioprotector," *Oncology (Hunt-ingt)*, 2001, 15(10):1349-54.

Amikacin (am i KAY sin)

Medication Safety Issues

Sound-alike/look-alike issues:

Amikacin may be confused with Amicar®, anakinra

Amikin® may be confused with Amicar®

U.S. Brand Names Amikin®

Index Terms Amikacin Sulfate

Generic Available Yes

Canadian Brand Names Amikacin Sulfate Injection, USP; Amikin®

Pharmacologic Category Antibiotic, Aminoglycoside

Use Treatment of serious infections (bone infections, respiratory tract infections, endocarditis, and septicemia) due to organisms resistant to gentamicin and tobramycin, including *Pseudomonas*, *Proteus*, *Serratia*, and other gram-negative bacilli; documented infection of mycobacterial organisms susceptible to amikacin

Unlabeled/Investigational Use Bacterial endophthalmitis

Pregnancy Risk Factor D

Lactation Enters breast milk/compatible

Labeled Contraindications Hypersensitivity to amikacin sulfate or any component of the formulation; cross-sensitivity may exist with other aminoglycosides

Warnings/Precautions [U.S. Boxed Warning]: Amikacin may cause neurotoxicity, nephrotoxicity, and/or neuromuscular blockade and respiratory paralysis; usual risk factors include pre-existing renal impairment, concomitant neuro-/nephrotoxic medications, advanced age and dehydration. Dose and/or frequency of administration must be monitored and modified in patients with renal impairment. Drug should be discontinued if signs of ototoxicity, nephrotoxicity, or hypersensitivity occur. Ototoxicity is proportional to the amount of drug given and the duration of treatment. Tinnitus or vertigo may be indications of vestibular injury and impending bilateral irreversible damage. Renal damage is usually reversible. Use with caution in patients with neuromuscular disorders, hearing loss and hypocalcemia. Prolonged use may result in fungal or bacterial superinfection, including *C. difficile*-associated diarrhea (CDAD) and pseudomembranous colitis; CDAD has been observed >2 months postantibiotic treatment. Solution contains sodium metabisulfate; use caution in patients with sulfite allergy.

Adverse Reactions

1% to 10%:

Central nervous system: Neurotoxicity

Otic: Ototoxicity (auditory), ototoxicity (vestibular)

Renal: Nephrotoxicity

<1%: Hypotension, headache, drowsiness, drug fever, rash, nausea, vomiting, eosinophilia, paresthesia, tremor, arthralgia, weakness, dyspnea, allergic reaction

Overdosage/Toxicology Symptoms of overdose include ototoxicity, nephrotoxicity, and neuromuscular toxicity. Treatment of choice, following a single acute overdose, appears to be maintenance of urine output of at least 3 mL/kg/hour during the acute treatment phase. Dialysis is of questionable value in enhancing aminoglycoside elimination. If required, hemodialysis is preferred over peritoneal dialysis in patients with normal renal function.

Drug Interactions

Increased Effect/Toxicity: Amikacin may increase or prolong the effect of neuromuscular blocking agents. Concurrent use of amphotericin (or other nephrotoxic drugs) may increase the risk of amikacin-induced nephrotoxicity. The risk of ototoxicity from amikacin may be increased with other ototoxic drugs.

Storage/Stability Store at controlled room temperature. Following admixture at concentrations of 0.25-5 mg/mL, amikacin is stable for 24 hours at room temperature and 2 days at refrigeration when mixed in D_5W, NS, and LR.

Compatibility Stable in dextran 75 6% in NS, D_5LR, $D_5^1/_4NS$, $D_5^1/_3NS$, $D_5^1/_2NS$, D_5NS, $D_{10}NS$, D_5W, $D_{10}W$, $D_{20}W$, mannitol 20%, $^1/_4NS$, $^1/_2NS$, NS; **variable stability (consult detailed reference)** in peritoneal dialysis solutions.

Y-site administration: Compatible: Acyclovir, alatrofloxacin, amifostine, amiodarone, amsacrine, aztreonam, cefpirome, cisatracurium, cyclophosphamide, dexamethasone sodium phosphate, diltiazem, docetaxel, enalaprilat, esmolol, etoposide, filgrastim, fluconazole, fludarabine, foscarnet, furosemide, gatifloxacin, gemcitabine, granisetron, idarubicin, IL-2, labetalol, levofloxacin, linezolid, lorazepam, magnesium sulfate, melphalan, midazolam, morphine, ondansetron, paclitaxel, perphenazine, remifentanil, sargramostim, teniposide, thiotepa, vinorelbine, warfarin, zidovudine. **Incompatible:** Allopurinol, amphotericin B cholesteryl sulfate complex, hetastarch, propofol.

Compatibility in syringe: Compatible: Clindamycin, doxapram. **Incompatible:** Heparin.

Compatibility when admixed: Compatible: Amobarbital, ascorbic acid injection, bleomycin, calcium chloride, calcium gluconate, cefepime, cefoxitin, chloramphenicol, chlorpheniramine, cimetidine, ciprofloxacin, clindamycin, colistimethate, dimenhydrinate, diphenhydramine, epinephrine, ergonovine, fluconazole, furosemide, hyaluronidase, hydrocortisone sodium phosphate, hydrocortisone sodium succinate, lincomycin, metaraminol, metronidazole, metronidazole with sodium bicarbonate, norepinephrine, pentobarbital, phenobarbital, phytonadione, polymyxin B sulfate, prochlorperazine edisylate, promethazine, ranitidine, sodium bicarbonate, succinylcholine, vancomycin, verapamil. **Incompatible:** Amphotericin B, ampicillin, cefazolin, chlorothiazide, heparin, phenytoin, thiopental, vitamin B complex with C. **Variable (consult detailed reference):** Aminophylline, dexamethasone sodium phosphate, oxacillin, penicillin G potassium, potassium chloride.

Mechanism of Action Inhibits protein synthesis in susceptible bacteria by binding to 30S ribosomal subunits

Pharmacodynamics/Kinetics

Absorption:

I.M.: Rapid

Oral: Poorly absorbed

(Continued)

Amikacin *(Continued)*

Distribution: Primarily into extracellular fluid (highly hydrophilic); penetrates blood-brain barrier when meninges inflamed

Relative diffusion of antimicrobial agents from blood into CSF: Good only with inflammation (exceeds usual MICs)

CSF:blood level ratio: Normal meninges: 10% to 20%; Inflamed meninges: 15% to 24%

Protein-binding: 0% to 11%

Half-life elimination (renal function and age dependent):

Infants: Low birth weight (1-3 days): 7-9 hours; Full-term >7 days: 4-5 hours

Children: 1.6-2.5 hours

Adults: Normal renal function: 1.4-2.3 hours; Anuria/end-stage renal disease: 28-86 hours

Time to peak, serum: I.M.: 45-120 minutes

Excretion: Urine (94% to 98%)

Dosage Note: Individualization is critical because of the low therapeutic index

Use of ideal body weight (IBW) for determining the mg/kg/dose appears to be more accurate than dosing on the basis of total body weight (TBW)

In morbid obesity, dosage requirement may best be estimated using a dosing weight of IBW + 0.4 (TBW - IBW)

Initial and periodic peak and trough plasma drug levels should be determined, particularly in critically-ill patients with serious infections or in disease states known to significantly alter aminoglycoside pharmacokinetics (eg, cystic fibrosis, burns, or major surgery)

Usual dosage range:

Infants and Children: I.M., I.V.: 5-7.5 mg/kg/dose every 8 hours

Adults: I.M., I.V.: 5-7.5 mg/kg/dose every 8 hours

Note: Some clinicians suggest a daily dose of 15-20 mg/kg for all patients with normal renal function. This dose is at least as efficacious with similar, if not less, toxicity than conventional dosing.

Indication-specific dosing:

Adults:

Endophthalmitis, bacterial (unlabeled use): Intravitreal: 0.4 mg/0.1 mL NS in combination with vancomycin

Hospital-acquired pneumonia (HAP): I.V.: 20 mg/kg/day with antipseudomonal beta-lactam or carbapenem (American Thoracic Society/ ATS guidelines)

Meningitis *(Pseudomonas aeruginosa):* I.V.: 5 mg/kg every 8 hours (administered with another bacteriocidal drug)

Mycobacterium fortuitum, M. chelonae, or M. abscessus: I.V.: 10-15 mg/kg daily for at least 2 weeks with high dose cefoxitin

Dosing interval in renal impairment: Some patients may require larger or more frequent doses if serum levels document the need (ie, cystic fibrosis or febrile granulocytopenic patients).

Cl_{cr} ≥60 mL/minute: Administer every 8 hours

Cl_{cr} 40-60 mL/minute: Administer every 12 hours

Cl_{cr} 20-40 mL/minute: Administer every 24 hours

Cl_{cr} <20 mL/minute: Loading dose, then monitor levels

Hemodialysis: Dialyzable (50% to 100%); administer dose postdialysis or administer ⅔ normal dose as a supplemental dose postdialysis and follow levels

Peritoneal dialysis: Dose as Cl_{cr} <20 mL/minute: Follow levels

Continuous arteriovenous or venovenous hemodiafiltration effects: Dose as for Cl_{cr} 10-40 mL/minute and follow levels

Administration Administer around-the-clock to promote less variation in peak and trough serum levels. Do not mix with other drugs, administer separately.

I.M.: Administer I.M. injection in large muscle mass.

I.V.: Infuse over 30-60 minutes.

Some penicillins (eg, carbenicillin, ticarcillin, and piperacillin) have been shown to inactivate *in vitro*. This has been observed to a greater extent with tobramycin and gentamicin, while amikacin has shown greater stability against inactivation. Concurrent use of these agents may pose a risk of reduced antibacterial efficacy *in vivo*, particularly in the setting of profound renal impairment. However, definitive clinical evidence is lacking. If combination penicillin/aminoglycoside therapy is desired in a patient with renal dysfunction, separation of doses (if feasible), and routine monitoring of aminoglycoside levels, CBC, and clinical response should be considered.

Monitoring Parameters Urinalysis, BUN, serum creatinine, appropriately timed peak and trough concentrations, vital signs, temperature, weight, I & O, hearing parameters

Some penicillin derivatives may accelerate the degradation of aminoglycosides *in vitro*. This may be clinically-significant for certain penicillin (ticarcillin, piperacillin, carbenicillin) and aminoglycoside (gentamicin, tobramycin) combination therapy in patients with significant renal impairment. Close monitoring of aminoglycoside levels is warranted.

Test Interactions Some penicillin derivatives may accelerate the degradation of aminoglycosides *in vitro*, leading to a potential underestimation of aminoglycoside serum concentration.

Dietary Considerations Sodium content of 1 g: 29.9 mg (1.3 mEq)

Patient Information Report loss of hearing, ringing or roaring in the ears, or feeling of fullness in head.

Special Geriatric Considerations The aminoglycosides are important therapeutic interventions for infections due to susceptible organisms and as empiric therapy in seriously ill patients. Their use is not without risk of toxicity, however, these risks can be minimized if initial dosing is adjusted for estimated renal function and appropriate monitoring performed. High dose, once daily aminoglycosides have been advocated as an alternative to traditional dosing regimens. Once daily or extended interval dosing is as effective and may be safer than traditional dosing. Interval must be adjusted for renal function.

Additional Information Aminoglycoside levels measured from blood taken from Silastic® central catheters can sometimes give falsely high readings (draw levels from alternate lumen or peripheral stick, if possible).

Emetic Potential Very low (<10%)

Vesicant No

Dosage Forms Excipient information presented when available (limited, particularly for generics); consult specific product labeling. [DSC] = Discontinued product

Injection, solution, as sulfate: 50 mg/mL (2 mL, 4 mL); 62.5 mg/mL (8 mL) [DSC]; 250 mg/mL (2 mL, 4 mL)

Amikin®: 50 mg/mL (2 mL); 250 mg/mL (2 mL, 4 mL) [contains metabisulfite]

References
American Thoracic Society and Infectious Diseases Society of America, "Guidelines for the Management of Adults With Hospital-Acquired, Ventilator-Associated, and Healthcare-Associated Pneumonia," *Am J Respir Crit Care Med*, 2005, 171(4):388-416.

(Continued)

Amikacin *(Continued)*

Bauer LA and Blouin RA, "Influence of Age on Amikacin Pharmacokinetics in Patients Without Renal Disease. Comparison With Gentamicin and Tobramycin," *Eur J Clin Pharmacol*, 1983, 24(5):639-42.

Begg EJ and Barclay ML, "Aminoglycosides - 50 Years On," *Br J Clin Pharmacol*, 1995, 39(6):597-603.

Chow MS, Quintiliani R, and Nightingale CH, "*In Vivo* Inactivation of Tobramycin by Ticarcillin. A Case Report," *JAMA*, 1982, 247(5):658-9.

Cunha BA, "Aminoglycosides: Current Role in Antimicrobial Therapy," *Pharmacotherapy*, 1988, 8(6):334-50.

Daly JS, Dodge RA, Glew RH, et al, "Effect of Time and Temperature on Inactivation of Aminoglycosides by Ampicillin at Neonatal Dosages," *J Perinatol*, 1997, 17(1):42-5.

Dowell JA, Korth-Bradley J, Milisci M, et al, "Evaluating Possible Pharmacokinetic Interactions Between Tobramycin, Piperacillin, and a Combination of Piperacillin and Tazobactam in Patients With Various Degrees of Renal Impairment," *J Clin Pharmacol*, 2001, 41:979-86.

Edson RS and Terrell CL, "The Aminoglycosides," *Mayo Clin Proc*, 1999, 74(5):519-28.

Farchione LA, "Inactivation of Aminoglycosides by Penicillins," *J Antimicrob Chemother*, 1982, 8(Suppl A):27-36.

Flandrois JP, Bouletreau P, Auboyer R, et al, "Accidental Amikacin Overdose in Man: Emergency Therapy by Extrarenal Dialysis," *Infection*, 1979, 7:190-1.

Fuchs PC, Stickel S, Anderson PH, et al, "*In Vitro* Inactivation of Aminoglycosides by Sulbactam, Other Beta-Lactams, and Sulbactam-Beta-Lactam Combinations," *Antimicrob Agents Chemother*, 1991, 35(1):182-4.

Gilbert DN, "Once-Daily Aminoglycoside Therapy," *Antimicrob Agents Chemother*, 1991, 35(3):399-405.

Green FJ, Lavelle KJ, and Arnoff GR, "Management of Amikacin Overdose," *Am J Kidney Dis*, 1981, 1:110-2.

Halstenson CE, Wong MO, Herman CS, et al, "Effect of Concomitant Administration of Piperacillin on the Dispositions on Isepamicin and Gentamicin in Patients With End-Stage Renal Disease," *Antimicrob Agents Chemother*, 1992, 36(9):1832-36.

Hitt CM, Patel KB, Nicolau DP, et al, "Influence of Piperacillin-Tazobactam on Pharmacokinetics of Gentamicin Given Once Daily," *Am J Health Syst Pharm*, 1997, 54(23):2704-8.

Ho PW, Pien FD, and Kominami N, "Massive Amikacin Overdose," *Ann Intern Med*, 1979, 91:227-8.

Iseman MD, "Treatment of Multidrug-Resistant Tuberculosis," *N Engl J Med*, 1993, 329(11):784-91.

Kenyon CF, Knoppert DC, Lee SK, et al, "Amikacin Pharmacokinetics and Suggested Dosage Modifications for the Preterm Infant," *Antimicrob Agents Chemother*, 1990, 34(2):265-8.

Konishi H, Goto M, Nakamoto Y, et al, "Tobramycin Inactivation by Carbenicillin, Ticarcillin, and Piperacillin," *Antimicrob Agents Chemother*, 1983, 23(5):653-57.

Lau A, Lee M, Flascha S, et al, "Effect of Piperacillin on Tobramycin Pharmacokinetics in Patients With Normal Renal Function," *Antimicrob Agents Chemother*, 1983, 24(4):533-37.

Lortholary O, Tod M, Cohen Y, et al, "Aminoglycosides," *Med Clin North Am*, 1995, 79(4):761-87.

McCormack JP and Jewesson PJ, "A Critical Re-evaluation of the "Therapeutic Range" of Aminoglycosides," *Clin Infect Dis*, 1992, 14(1):320-39

Nicolau DP, Freeman CD, Belliveau PP, et al, "Experience With a Once-Daily Aminoglycoside Program Administered to 2184 Adult Patients," *Antimicrob Agents Chemother*, 1995, 39(3):650-5.

Preston SL and Briceland LL, "Single Daily Dosing of Aminoglycosides," *Pharmacotherapy*, 1995, 15(3):297-316.

Public Health Service Task Force on Prophylaxis and Therapy for *Mycobacterium avium* Complex, "Recommendations on Prophylaxis and Therapy for Disseminated *Mycobacterium avium* Complex Disease in Patients Infected With the Human Immunodeficiency Virus," *N Engl J Med*, 1993, 329(12):898-904.

"Results of the Endophthalmitis Vitrectomy Study. A Randomized Trial of Immediate Vitrectomy and of Intravenous Antibiotics for the Treatment of Postoperative Bacterial Endophthalmitis. Endophthalmitis Vitrectomy Study Group," *Arch Ophthalmol*, 1995, 113(12):1479-96.

Roth DB and Flynn HW Jr, "Antibiotic Selection in the Treatment of Endophthalmitis: The Significance of Drug Combinations and Synergy," *Surv Ophthalmol*, 1997, 41(5):395-401.

Russoe ME and Atkins-Thor E, "Gentamicin and Ticarcillin in Subjects With End-Stage Renal Disease. Comparison of Two Assay Methods and Evaluation of Inactivation Rate," *Clin Nephrol*, 1981, 15(4):175-80.

Starke JR and Correa AG, "Management of Mycobacterial Infection and Disease in Children," *Pediatr Infect Dis J*, 1995, 14(6):455-69.

Thompson MIB, Russo ME, Saxon BJ, et al, "Gentamicin Inactivation by Piperacillin or Carbenicillin in Patients With End-Stage Renal Disease," *Antimicrob Agents Chemother*, 1982, 21(2):268-73.

Tunkel AR, Hartman BJ, Kaplan SL, et al, "Practice Guidelines for the Management of Bacterial Meningitis," *Clin Infect Dis*, 2004, 39(9):1267-84.

Van der Auwera P, "Pharmacokinetic Evaluation of Single Daily Dose Amikacin," *J Antimicrob Chemother*, 1991, 27(Suppl C):63-71.

Vanhaeverbeek M, Siska G, Douchamps J, et al, "Comparison of the Efficacy and Safety of Amikacin Once or Twice-a-Day in the Treatment of Severe Gram-Negative Infections in the Elderly," *Int J Clin Pharmacol Ther Toxicol*, 1993, 31(3):153-6.

Viollier AF, Standiford HC, Drusano GL, et al, "Comparative Pharmacokinetics and Serum Bactericidal Activity of Mezlocillin, Ticarcillin and Piperacillin, With and Without Gentamicin," *J Antimicrob Chemother*, 1985, 15(5):597-606.

Vogelstein B, Kowarski A, and Lietman PS, "The Pharmacokinetics of Amikacin in Children," *J Pediatr*, 1977, 91(2):333-9.

Walterspiel JN, Feldman S, Van R, et al, "Comparative Inactivation of Isepamicin, Amikacin, and Gentamicin by Nine Beta-Lactams and Two Beta-Lactamase Inhibitors, Cilastatin and Heparin," *Antimicrob Agents Chemother*, 1991, 35(9):1875-8.

Wilson W, Taubert KA, Gewitz M, et al, "Prevention of Infective Endocarditis. Guidelines From the American Heart Association. A Guideline From the American Heart Association Rheumatic Fever, Endocarditis, and Kawasaki Disease Committee, Council on Cardiovascular Disease in the Young, and the Council on Clinical Cardiology, Council on Cardiovascular Surgery and Anesthesia, and the Quality of Care and Outcomes Research Interdisciplinary Working Group," *Circulation*, 2007, 115. Available at http://circ.ahajournals.org/cgi/reprint/CIRCULATIONAHA.106.183095v1; last accessed July 26, 2007.

Yasuhara H, Kobayashi S, Sakamoto K, et al, "Pharmacokinetics of Amikacin and Cephalothin in Bedridden Elderly Patients," *J Clin Pharmacol*, 1982, 22(8-9):403-9.

♦ **Amikacin Sulfate** *see* Amikacin *on page 56*

♦ **Amikacin Sulfate Injection, USP (Can)** *see* Amikacin *on page 56*

♦ **Amikin**® *see* Amikacin *on page 56*

♦ **2-Amino-6-Mercaptopurine** *see* Thioguanine *on page 1030*

♦ **2-Amino-6-Methoxypurine Arabinoside** *see* Nelarabine *on page 804*

Aminocamptothecin (a min o camp to THE sin)

Related Information
Investigational Drug Service *on page 1379*
Safe Handling of Hazardous Drugs *on page 1382*

Index Terms 9-AC; 9-Aminocamptothecin; NSC-603071

Generic Available No

Pharmacologic Category Antineoplastic Agent, DNA Binding Agent; Enzyme Inhibitor, Topoisomerase I Inhibitor

Unlabeled/Investigational Use Phase II trials: Relapsed lymphoma, refractory breast cancer, nonsmall cell lung cancer, untreated colorectal carcinoma

Restrictions Not available in U.S./Investigational

Labeled Contraindications Hypersensitivity to aminocamptothecin or any component of the formulation

Warnings/Precautions Hazardous agent - use appropriate precautions for handling and disposal.

Adverse Reactions Frequency not defined.
Central nervous system: Fatigue
Dermatologic: Alopecia
Gastrointestinal: Nausea, vomiting, diarrhea, mucositis, anorexia
Hematologic: Neutropenia (may be dose limiting), thrombocytopenia (reversible, but may be dose limiting), anemia

Drug Interactions
Decreased Effect: Anticonvulsants may decrease aminocamptothecin levels.
(Continued)

Aminocamptothecin *(Continued)*

Storage/Stability Store ampuls at room temperature. Diluted solutions are stable for 28 hours at room temperature. Undiluted aminocamptothecin should not contact plastic items.

Reconstitution Contents of ampul are added to vial (supplied) containing 24.5 mL of special diluent. Resulting aminocamptothecin concentration is 100 mcg/mL. Further dilutions with special diluent for administration via syringe pump is acceptable. May further dilute with NS if resulting concentration is <1 mcg/mL.

Mechanism of Action Aminocamptothecin binds to topoisomerase I, stabilizing the cleavable DNA-topoisomerase I complex, resulting in arrest of the replication fork and inhibition of DNA synthesis.

Pharmacodynamics/Kinetics Ratio of lactone to total drug is 8.7% ± 4.7% because of instability of aminocamptothecin lactone in plasma.

Distribution: V_d: 46-92 L
Metabolism: None identified
Half-life elimination: Terminal: 8-17 hours for total aminocamptothecin
Excretion: Urine (32% of total drug delivered)

Dosage I.V.: Adults: 45-59 mcg/m^2/hour for 72 hours as a continuous infusion; repeat every 2 weeks **or** 35 mcg/m^2/hour as a 72-hour continuous infusion

Administration Administer by continuous I.V. infusion.

Monitoring Parameters WBC with differential, platelet count

Emetic Potential Moderate (30% to 60%)

Vesicant No

Dosage Forms Excipient information presented when available (limited, particularly for generics); consult specific product labeling.
Injection: 5 mg ampul

References

Grossman SA, Hochberg F, Fisher J, et al, "Increased 9-Aminocamptothecin Dose Requirements in Patients on Oral Anticonvulsants. NAPTT CNS Consortium. The New Approaches to Brain Tumor Therapy," *Cancer Chemother Pharmacol*, 1998, 42(2):118-26.

Iyer L and Ratain MJ, "Clinical Pharmacology of Camptothecins," *Cancer Chemother Pharmacol*, 1998, 42(Suppl):31-43.

Potmesil M, Arbuck SG, Takimoto CH, et al, "9-Aminocamptothecin and Beyond. Preclinical and Clinical Studies," *Ann N Y Acad Sci*, 1996, 803:231-46.

Takimota CH, Wright J, and Arbuck SG, "Clinical Applications of the Camptothecins," *Biochim Biophys Acta*, 1998, 1400(1-3):107-19.

♦ **9-Aminocamptothecin** *see* Aminocamptothecin *on page 61*

Aminocaproic Acid *(a mee noe ka PROE ik AS id)*

Medication Safety Issues
Sound-alike/look-alike issues:
Amicar® may be confused with amikacin, Amikin®, Omacor®

U.S. Brand Names Amicar®

Index Terms Epsilon Aminocaproic Acid

Generic Available Yes

Pharmacologic Category Hemostatic Agent

Use Treatment of excessive bleeding from fibrinolysis

Unlabeled/Investigational Use Treatment of traumatic hyphema; control bleeding in thrombocytopenia; control oral bleeding in congenital and acquired coagulation disorders

Pregnancy Risk Factor C

Lactation Excretion in breast milk unknown/use caution

Labeled Contraindications Hypersensitivity to aminocaproic acid or any component of the formulation; disseminated intravascular coagulation (without heparin); evidence of an intravascular clotting process

Warnings/Precautions Avoid rapid I.V. administration; may induce hypotension, bradycardia, or arrhythmia. Aminocaproic acid may accumulate in patients with decreased renal function. Intrarenal obstruction may occur secondary to glomerular capillary thrombosis or clots in the renal pelvis and ureters. Do not use in hematuria of upper urinary tract origin unless possible benefits outweigh risks. Use with caution in patients with cardiac, renal, or hepatic disease. Do not administer without a definite diagnosis of laboratory findings indicative of hyperfibrinolysis. Inhibition of fibrinolysis may promote clotting or thrombosis; more likely due to the presence of DIC. Subsequently, use with great caution in patients with, or at risk for, veno-occlusive disease of the liver. Skeletal muscle weakness ranging from mild myalgias and fatigue to severe myopathy with rhabdomyolysis and acute renal failure has been reported with prolonged use. Monitor CPK; discontinue treatment with a rise in CPK. Benzyl alcohol is used as a preservative in the injection, therefore, these products should not be used in the neonate. Do not administer with factor IX complex concentrates or anti-inhibitor coagulant complexes.

Adverse Reactions Frequency not defined.

Cardiovascular: Arrhythmia, bradycardia, hypotension, peripheral ischemia, syncope, thrombosis

Central nervous system: Confusion, delirium, dizziness, fatigue, hallucinations, headache, intracranial hypertension, malaise, seizure, stroke

Dermatologic: Rash, pruritus

Gastrointestinal: Abdominal pain, anorexia, cramps, diarrhea, GI irritation, nausea

Genitourinary: Dry ejaculation

Hematologic: Agranulocytosis, bleeding time increased, leukopenia, thrombocytopenia

Neuromuscular & skeletal: CPK increased, myalgia, myositis, myopathy, rhabdomyolysis (rare), weakness

Ophthalmic: Watery eyes, vision decreased

Otic: Tinnitus

Renal: Failure (rare), myoglobinuria (rare)

Respiratory: Dyspnea, nasal congestion, pulmonary embolism

Overdosage/Toxicology Symptoms of overdose include acute renal failure, delirium, diarrhea, hepatic necrosis, nausea, seizures, transient hypotension, and thromboembolism. Aminocaproic acid may be removed by hemodialysis.

Drug Interactions

Increased Effect/Toxicity: Increased risk of hypercoagulability with oral contraceptives, estrogens. Should not be administered with factor IX complex concentrate or anti-inhibitor complex concentrates due to an increased risk of thrombosis.

Storage/Stability Store at 15°C to 30°C (59°F to 86°F).

Reconstitution Dilute I.V. solution (1 g/50 mL of diluent) with D_5W, 0.9% sodium chloride, or lactated Ringer's.

Compatibility Stable in D_5W, NS.

Compatibility when admixed: Compatible: Netilmicin.

Mechanism of Action Competitively inhibits activation of plasminogen to plasmin, also, a lesser antiplasmin effect

Pharmacodynamics/Kinetics

Onset of action: ~1-72 hours

(Continued)

Aminocaproic Acid *(Continued)*

Distribution: Widely through intravascular and extravascular compartments

V_d: Oral: 23 L, I.V.: 30 L

Metabolism: Minimally hepatic

Half-life elimination: 2 hours

Time to peak: Oral: Within 2 hours

Excretion: Urine (65% as unchanged drug, 11% as metabolite)

Dosage

Acute bleeding syndrome:

Children (unlabeled use): Oral, I.V.: 100-200 mg/kg during the first hour, followed by continuous infusion at 33.3 mg/kg/hour or 100 mg/kg (oral or I.V.) every 6 hours

Adults: Oral, I.V.: 4-5 g during the first hour, followed by 1 g/hour for 8 hours or until bleeding controlled (maximum daily dose: 30 g)

Control bleeding in thrombocytopenia (unlabeled use): Adults:

Initial: I.V.: 0.1 g/kg over 30-60 minutes

Maintenance: Oral: 1-3 g every 6 hours

Control oral bleeding in congenital and acquired coagulation disorder (unlabeled use): Adults: Oral: 50-60 mg/kg every 4 hours

Traumatic hyphema (unlabeled use): Children and Adults: Oral: 100 mg/kg/dose every 4 hours (maximum daily dose: 30 g)

Dosing adjustment in renal impairment: May accumulate in patients with decreased renal function.

Administration I.V.: May be administered over 30-60 minutes or by continuous infusion; rapid I.V. injection (IVP) should be avoided due to possible hypotension, bradycardia, and arrhythmia.

Monitoring Parameters Fibrinogen, fibrin split products, creatine phosphokinase (with long-term therapy)

Test Interactions Increased potassium, creatine phosphokinase [CPK] (S)

Patient Information Report any signs of bleeding; change positions slowly to minimize dizziness

Emetic Potential Very low (<10%)

Vesicant No

Dosage Forms Excipient information presented when available (limited, particularly for generics); consult specific product labeling.

Injection, solution: 250 mg/mL (20 mL)

Amicar®: 250 mg/mL (20 mL) [contains benzyl alcohol]

Solution, oral: 1.25 g/5 mL (240 mL, 480 mL)

Syrup:

Amicar®: 1.25 g/5 mL (480 mL) [raspberry flavor]

Tablet [scored]: 500 mg, 1000 mg

Amicar®: 500 mg, 1000 mg

References

Bartholomew JR, Salgia R, and Bell WR, "Control of Bleeding in Patients With Immune and Nonimmune Thrombocytopenia With Aminocaproic Acid," *Arch Intern Med*, 1989, 149(9):1959-61.

Crouch ER Jr, Williams PB, Gray MK, et al, "Topical Aminocaproic Acid in the Treatment of Traumatic Hyphema," *Arch Ophthalmol*, 1997, 115(9):1106-12.

Gardner FH and Helmer RE 3rd, "Aminocaproic Acid. Use in Control of Hemorrhage in Patients With Amegakaryocytic Thrombocytopenia," *JAMA*, 1980, 243(1):35-7.

Haut MT, Mauro VF, and Davis HH, "Effect of Renal Failure and Hemodialysis on Aminocaproic Acid Plasma Concentrations," *DICP*, 1989, 23(11):922-3.

Mannucci P, "Hemostatic Drugs," *N Engl J Med*, 1998, 339(4):245-53.

McGetrick JJ, Jampol LM, Goldberg MP, et al, "Aminocaproic Acid Decreases Secondary Hemorrhage After Traumatic Hyphema," *Arch Ophthalmol*, 1983, 101(7):1031-3.

Pieramici DJ, Goldberg MF, Melia M, et al, "A Phase III, Multicenter, Randomized, Placebo-Controlled Clinical Trial of Topical Aminocaproic Acid (Caprogel) in the Management of Traumatic Hyphema," *Ophthalmology*, 2003, 110(11):2106-12.

Sane DC, Califf RM, Topol EJ, et al, " Bleeding During Thrombolytic Therapy for Acute Myocardial Infarction: Mechanisms and Management," *Ann Intern Med*, 1989, 111(12):1010-22.

Teboul BK, Jacob JL, Barsoum-Homsy M, et al, "Clinical Evaluation of Aminocaproic Acid for Managing Traumatic Hyphema in Children," *Ophthalmology*, 1995, 102(11):1646-53.

Walton W, Von Hagen S, Grigorian R, et al, "Management of Traumatic Hyphema," *Surv Ophthalmol*, 2002, 47(4):297-334.

Aminoglutethimide (a mee noe gloo TETH i mide)

Medication Safety Issues
Sound-alike/look-alike issues:
Cytadren® may be confused with cytarabine

U.S. Brand Names Cytadren®

Index Terms AG; AGT; BA-16038; Elipten

Generic Available No

Pharmacologic Category Antineoplastic Agent, Aromatase Inhibitor; Enzyme Inhibitor; Hormone Antagonist, Anti-Adrenal; Nonsteroidal Aromatase Inhibitor

Use Suppression of adrenal function in selected patients with Cushing's syndrome

Unlabeled/Investigational Use Treatment of breast and prostate cancer (androgen synthesis inhibitor)

Pregnancy Risk Factor D

Lactation Excretion in breast milk unknown/contraindicated

Labeled Contraindications Hypersensitivity to aminoglutethimide, glutethimide, or any component of the formulation; pregnancy

Warnings/Precautions Monitor blood pressure in all patients at appropriate intervals. Hypothyroidism may occur. **Mineralocorticoid replacement is necessary in up to 50% of patients**. Glucocorticoid replacement is necessary in most patients.

Adverse Reactions Most adverse effects will diminish in incidence and severity after the first 2-6 weeks
>10%:
Central nervous system: Headache, dizziness, drowsiness, lethargy, clumsiness
Dermatologic: Skin rash
Gastrointestinal: Nausea, anorexia
Hepatic: Cholestatic jaundice
Neuromuscular & skeletal: Myalgia
Renal: Nephrotoxicity
Respiratory: Pulmonary alveolar damage
1% to 10%:
Cardiovascular: Hypotension, tachycardia, orthostasis
Dermatologic: Hirsutism, pruritus
Endocrine & metabolic: Adrenocortical insufficiency
Gastrointestinal: Vomiting
<1%: Adrenal suppression, hepatotoxicity, hypercholesterolemia, hyperkalemia, hypothyroidism, goiter, masculinization of females, pulmonary hypersensitivity, urticaria; rare cases of neutropenia, leukopenia, thrombocytopenia, pancytopenia, agranulocytosis have been reported

Overdosage/Toxicology Symptoms of overdose include ataxia, somnolence, lethargy, dizziness, distress, fatigue, coma, hyperventilation, respiratory depression, hypovolemia, and shock. Treatment is supportive.
(Continued)

Aminoglutethimide *(Continued)*

Drug Interactions

Cytochrome P450 Effect: Induces CYP1A2 (strong), 2C19 (strong), 3A4 (strong)

Decreased Effect: Aminoglutethimide may decrease therapeutic effect of dexamethasone, warfarin, medroxyprogesterone, megestrol, and tamoxifen. Aminoglutethimide may decrease the levels/effects of aminophylline, benzodiazepines, calcium channel blockers, citalopram, clarithromycin, cyclosporine, diazepam, erythromycin, estrogens, fluvoxamine, methsuximide, mirtazapine, nateglinide, nefazodone, nevirapine, phenytoin, proton pump inhibitors, protease inhibitors, ropinirole, sertraline, tacrolimus, theophylline, venlafaxine, voriconazole, and other drugs metabolized by CYP1A2, 2C19, or 3A4.

Storage/Stability Store at controlled room temperature not >30°C (86°F).

Mechanism of Action Blocks the enzymatic conversion of cholesterol to delta-5-pregnenolone, thereby reducing the synthesis of adrenal glucocorticoids, mineralocorticoids, estrogens, aldosterone, and androgens

Pharmacodynamics/Kinetics

Onset of action: Adrenal suppression: 3-5 days; following withdrawal of therapy, adrenal function returns within 72 hours

Absorption: 90%

Protein binding, plasma: 20% to 25%

Metabolism: Major metabolite is N-acetylaminoglutethimide; induces its own metabolism

Half-life elimination: 7-15 hours; shorter following multiple doses

Excretion: Urine (34% to 50% as unchanged drug, 25% as metabolites)

Dosage Oral: Adults:

Adrenal suppression: 250 mg every 6 hours may be increased at 1- to 2-week intervals to a total of 2 g/day

Breast cancer, prostate cancer (unlabeled use): 250 mg 4 times/day

Dosing adjustment in renal impairment: Dose reduction may be necessary.

Administration Administer every 6 hours to reduce incidence of nausea and vomiting.

Monitoring Parameters Follow adrenal cortical response by careful monitoring of plasma cortisol until the desired level of suppression is achieved. Mineralocorticoid (fludrocortisone) replacement therapy may be necessary in up to 50% of patients. If glucocorticoid replacement therapy is necessary, 20-30 mg hydrocortisone orally in the morning will replace endogenous secretion.

Test Interactions Increased alkaline phosphatase (S), AST, TSH; decreased plasma cortisol, thyroxine (S), and urinary aldosterone

Emetic Potential Very low (<10%)

Dosage Forms Excipient information presented when available (limited, particularly for generics); consult specific product labeling.

Tablet [scored]: 250 mg

References

Lonning PE and Kvinnsland S, "Mechanisms of Action of Aminoglutethimide as Endocrine Therapy of Breast Cancer," *Drugs*, 1988, 35(6):685-710.

Robinson MR, "Aminoglutethimide: Medical Adrenalectomy in the Management of Carcinoma of the Prostate. A Review After 6 Years," *Br J Urol*, 1980, 52(4):328-9.

Roseman BJ, Budzdar AU, and Singletary SE, "Use of Aromatase Inhibitors in Postmenopausal Women With Advanced Breast Cancer," *J Surg Oncol*, 1997, 66(3):215-20.

Russell CA, Green SJ, O'Sullivan J, et al, "Megestrol Acetate and Aminoglutethimide/Hydrocortisone in Sequence or in Combination as Second-Line Endocrine Therapy of Estrogen

Receptor-Positive Metastatic Breast Cancer: A Southwest Oncology Group Phase III Trial," *J Clin Oncol*, 1997, 15(7):2494-501.

Sanford EJ, Drago JR, Rohner TJ Jr, et al, "Aminoglutethimide Medical Adrenalectomy for Advanced Prostatic Carcinoma," *J Urol*, 1976, 115(2):170-4.

Santen RJ and Misbin RI, "Aminoglutethimide: Review of Pharmacology and Clinical Use," *Pharmacotherapy*, 1981, 1(2):95-120.

♦ **AMJ 9701** *see* Palifermin *on page 868*

♦ **AMN107** *see* Nilotinib *on page 807*

Amonafide (a MON a fide)

Related Information

Investigational Drug Service *on page 1379*
Safe Handling of Hazardous Drugs *on page 1382*

Index Terms Amonafide Hydrochloride; Benzisoquinolinedione; BIDA; M-FA-142; Nafidimide; NSC-308847

Generic Available No

Pharmacologic Category Antineoplastic Agent, DNA Binding Agent; Enzyme Inhibitor, Topoisomerase II Inhibitor

Unlabeled/Investigational Use Investigational: Breast, prostate, renal cell, ovarian, pancreatic, and nonsmall cell lung cancers

Labeled Contraindications Hypersensitivity to amonafide or any component of the formulation; pregnancy

Warnings/Precautions Hazardous agent - use appropriate precautions for handling and disposal. Amonafide should be used cautiously in bone marrow transplant patients and patients with existing bone marrow suppression, hepatic dysfunction, arrhythmias, conduction problems, congestive heart failure, or seizures or other neurological disorders. Amonafide toxicity, particularly hematologic, correlates with the patient's acetylator status. If possible, determination of acetylator type (fast vs slow) should be considered prior to beginning therapy.

Adverse Reactions

>10%:
  Gastrointestinal: Nausea and vomiting (mild)
  Hematologic: Granulocytopenia, possibly dose-limiting; nadir occurs at days 12-15, recovery by day 21

1% to 10%:
  Cardiovascular: Chest pain
  Central nervous system: Dizziness, fatigue, headache
  Dermatologic: Skin rash, exfoliative dermatitis, alopecia
  Local: Inflammatory reactions
  Otic: Tinnitus
  Neuromuscular & skeletal: Myoclonic jerking, weakness

<1%: CHF, hypotension, taste alteration, thrombocytopenia

Storage/Stability Store intact vials under refrigeration at 2°C to 8°C (36°F to 46°F). Reconstituted vials and solutions for infusion are stable for up to 14 days at room temperature or under refrigeration.

Reconstitution Vials may be reconstituted with SWFI or 0.9% sodium chloride.

Compatibility Incompatible with dextrose solutions.

Mechanism of Action Amonafide acts as a DNA intercalator, stabilizing DNA to thermal denaturation and producing single-strand DNA breaks.

Pharmacodynamics/Kinetics

Distribution: V_d: 370-530 L/m^2
Protein binding: High
Half-life:
  Elimination: 3.5-11 hours
(Continued)

Amonafide *(Continued)*

Terminal: 3-6 hours

Metabolism: Hepatic, primarily by oxidation and N-acetylation. N-acetylamonafide (active) and amonafide-N'-oxide are the major metabolites. Clearance depends on whether the patient is a fast or slow acetylator. Fast acetylators may experience greater toxicity from the drug.

Excretion: Urine (3% to 22% as unchanged drug)

Dosage Adults (refer to individual protocols):

Breast cancer: 800 mg/m^2 over 3 hours every 28 days

Renal cell, ovarian, pancreatic cancer: Up to 450 mg/m^2 over 1 hour on days 1-5 every 21 days

Nonsmall cell lung cancer: 1600 mg/m^2 by continuous infusion over 24 hours every 21 days

Dosage adjustment in hepatic impairment: May be required but specific guidelines have not been established.

Administration May be administered by short (1-3 hours) infusion or continuous (24-hour) infusion.

Emetic Potential Moderate (30% to 60%)

Vesicant No

Dosage Forms Excipient information presented when available (limited, particularly for generics); consult specific product labeling.

Powder for injection, lyophilized: 500 mg

References

Kornek G, Raderer M, Depisch D, et al, "Amonafide as First-Line Chemotherapy for Metastatic Breast Cancer," *Eur J Cancer*, 1994, 30A(3):398-400.

Kreis W, Chan K, Budman DR, et al, "Clinical Pharmacokinetics of Amonafide (NSC-308847) in 62 Patients," *Cancer Invest*, 1996, 14(4):320-7.

Leaf AN, Neuberg D, Schwartz EL, et al, "An ECOG Phase II Study of Amonafide in Unresectable or Recurrent Carcinoma of the Head and Neck (PB390). Eastern Cooperative Oncology Group," *Invest New Drugs*, 1997, 15(2):165-72.

Marshall ME, Blumenstein B, Crawford ED, et al, "Phase II Trial of Amonafide for the Treatment of Advanced, Hormonally Refractory Carcinoma of the Prostate," *Am J Clin Oncol*, 1994, 17(6):514-5.

Ratain MJ, Rosner G, Allen SL, et al, "Population Pharmacodynamic Study of Amonafide: A Cancer and Leukemia Group B Study," *J Clin Oncol*, 1995, 13(3):741-7.

♦ **Amonafide Hydrochloride** *see* Amonafide *on page 67*

♦ **Amphadase**™ *see* Hyaluronidase *on page 543*

♦ **Amphocin**® **[DSC]** *see* Amphotericin B (Conventional) *on page 71*

♦ **Amphotec**® *see* Amphotericin B Cholesteryl Sulfate Complex *on page 68*

♦ **Amphotec**® **(Can)** *see* Amphotericin B (Lipid Complex) *on page 77*

Amphotericin B Cholesteryl Sulfate Complex

(am foe TER i sin bee kole LES te ril SUL fate KOM plecks)

Medication Safety Issues

Safety issues:

Lipid-based amphotericin formulations (Amphotec®) may be confused with conventional formulations (Amphocin®, Fungizone®)

Large overdoses have occurred when conventional formulations were dispensed inadvertently for lipid-based products. Single daily doses of conventional amphotericin formulation never exceed 1.5 mg/kg.

High alert medication: The Institute for Safe Medication Practices (ISMP) includes this medication among its list of drugs which have a heightened risk of causing significant patient harm when used in error.

U.S. Brand Names Amphotec®

Index Terms ABCD; Amphotericin B Colloidal Dispersion

Generic Available No

Canadian Brand Names Amphotec®

Pharmacologic Category Antifungal Agent, Parenteral

Use Treatment of invasive aspergillosis in patients who have failed amphotericin B deoxycholate treatment, or who have renal impairment or experience unacceptable toxicity which precludes treatment with amphotericin B deoxycholate in effective doses.

Unlabeled/Investigational Use Effective in patients with serious *Candida* species infections

Pregnancy Risk Factor B

Lactation Excretion in breast milk unknown/contraindicated

Labeled Contraindications Hypersensitivity to amphotericin B or any component of the formulation

Warnings/Precautions Anaphylaxis has been reported. Facilities for cardio-pulmonary resuscitation should be available. Infusion reactions, sometimes severe, usually subside with continued therapy.

Adverse Reactions
>10%: Central nervous system: Chills, fever
1% to 10%:
  Cardiovascular: Hypotension, tachycardia
  Central nervous system: Headache
  Dermatologic: Rash
  Endocrine & metabolic: Hypokalemia, hypomagnesemia
  Gastrointestinal: Nausea, diarrhea, abdominal pain
  Hematologic: Thrombocytopenia
  Hepatic: LFT change
  Neuromuscular & skeletal: Rigors
  Renal: Creatinine increased
  Respiratory: Dyspnea
Note: Amphotericin B colloidal dispersion has an improved therapeutic index compared to conventional amphotericin B, and has been used safely in patients with amphotericin B-related nephrotoxicity; however, continued decline of renal function has occurred in some patients.

Overdosage/Toxicology Symptoms of overdose include renal dysfunction, anemia, thrombocytopenia, granulocytopenia, fever, nausea, and vomiting. Treatment is supportive.

Drug Interactions
Increased Effect/Toxicity: Toxic effect with other nephrotoxic drugs (eg, cyclosporine, aminoglycosides) may be additive. Corticosteroids may increase potassium depletion caused by amphotericin. Amphotericin B may predispose patients receiving digitalis glycosides or neuromuscular blocking agents to toxicity secondary to hypokalemia.

Decreased Effect: Pharmacologic antagonism may occur with azole antifungals (eg, ketoconazole, miconazole).

Storage/Stability Store intact vials under refrigeration. After reconstitution, the solution should be refrigerated at 2°C to 8°C (36°F to 46°F) and used within 24 hours. Concentrations of 0.1-2 mg/mL in dextrose 5% in water are stable for 14 days at 4°C and 23°C if protected from light, however, due to the occasional formation of subvisual particles, solutions should be used within 48 hours.

Reconstitution Reconstitute 50 mg and 100 mg vials with 10 mL and 20 mL of SWI, respectively. The reconstituted vials contain 5 mg/mL of amphotericin B. Shake the vial gently by hand until all solid particles have dissolved. Further dilute amphotericin B colloidal dispersion with dextrose 5% in water.

Compatibility Stable in D$_5$W; **incompatible** with NS.
(Continued)

Amphotericin B Cholesteryl Sulfate Complex
(Continued)

Y-site administration: Compatible: Acyclovir, aminophylline, cefoxitin, ceftizoxime, clindamycin, dexamethasone sodium phosphate, fentanyl, furosemide, ganciclovir, granisetron, hydrocortisone sodium succinate, ifosfamide, lorazepam, mannitol, methotrexate, methylprednisolone sodium succinate, nitroglycerin, sufentanil, trimethoprim/sulfamethoxazole, vinblastine, vincristine, zidovudine. **Incompatible:** Alfentanil, amikacin, ampicillin, ampicillin/sulbactam, atenolol, aztreonam, bretylium, buprenorphine, butorphanol, calcium chloride, calcium gluconate, carboplatin, cefazolin, cefepime, cefoperazone, ceftazidime, ceftriaxone, chlorpromazine, cimetidine, cisatracurium, cisplatin, cyclophosphamide, cyclosporine, cytarabine, diazepam, digoxin, diphenhydramine, dobutamine, dopamine, doxorubicin, doxorubicin liposome, droperidol, enalaprilat, esmolol, famotidine, fluconazole, fluorouracil, gatifloxacin, gentamicin, haloperidol, heparin, hydromorphone, hydroxyzine, imipenem/cilastatin, labetalol, leucovorin, lidocaine, magnesium sulfate, meperidine, mesna, metoclopramide, metoprolol, metronidazole, midazolam, mitoxantrone, morphine, nalbuphine, naloxone, ofloxacin, ondansetron, paclitaxel, pentobarbital, phenobarbital, phenytoin, piperacillin, piperacillin/tazobactam, potassium chloride, prochlorperazine, promethazine, propranolol, ranitidine, remifentanil, sodium bicarbonate, ticarcillin, ticarcillin/clavulanate, tobramycin, vancomycin, vecuronium, verapamil, vinorelbine.

Mechanism of Action Binds to ergosterol altering cell membrane permeability in susceptible fungi and causing leakage of cell components with subsequent cell death. Proposed mechanism suggests that amphotericin causes an oxidation-dependent stimulation of macrophages (Lyman, 1992).

Pharmacodynamics/Kinetics

Distribution: V_d: Total volume increases with higher doses, reflects increasing uptake by tissues (with 4 mg/kg/day = 4 L/kg); predominantly distributed in the liver; concentrations in kidneys and other tissues are lower than observed with conventional amphotericin B

Half-life elimination: 28-29 hours; prolonged with higher doses

Dosage Children and Adults: I.V.:

Premedication: For patients who experience chills, fever, hypotension, nausea, or other nonanaphylactic infusion-related immediate reactions, premedicate with the following drugs 30-60 minutes prior to drug administration: A nonsteroidal (eg, ibuprofen, choline magnesium trisalicylate) with or without diphenhydramine **or** acetaminophen with diphenhydramine **or** hydrocortisone 50-100 mg. If the patient experiences rigors during the infusion, meperidine may be administered.

Range: 3-4 mg/kg/day (infusion of 1 mg/kg/hour); maximum: 7.5 mg/kg/day

Administration Avoid injection faster than 1 mg/kg/hour. For a patient who experiences chills, fever, hypotension, nausea, or other nonanaphylactic infusion-related reactions, premedicate with the following drugs 30-60 minutes prior to drug administration: A nonsteroidal (eg, ibuprofen, choline magnesium trisalicylate) with or without diphenhydramine **or** acetaminophen with diphenhydramine **or** hydrocortisone 50-100 mg. If the patient experiences rigors during the infusion, meperidine may be administered. If severe respiratory distress occurs, the infusion should be immediately discontinued.

Monitoring Parameters Liver function tests, electrolytes, BUN, Cr, temperature, CBC, I/O, signs of hypokalemia (muscle weakness, cramping, drowsiness, ECG changes)

Special Geriatric Considerations The pharmacokinetics and dosing of amphotericin have not been studied in the elderly. It appears that use is similar to young adults. Caution should be exercised and renal function and desired effect monitored closely.

Additional Information Controlled trials which compare the original formulation of amphotericin B to the newer liposomal formulations (ie, Amphotec®) are lacking. Thus, comparative data discussing differences among the formulations should be interpreted cautiously. Although the risk of nephrotoxicity and infusion-related adverse effects may be less with Amphotec®, the efficacy profiles of Amphotec® and the original amphotericin formulation are comparable. Consequently, Amphotec® should be restricted to those patients who cannot tolerate or fail a standard amphotericin B formulation.

Dosage Forms Excipient information presented when available (limited, particularly for generics); consult specific product labeling.

Injection, powder for reconstitution: 50 mg, 100 mg

References

Edwards JE Jr, Bodey GP, Bowden RA, et al, "International Conference for the Development of a Consensus on the Management and Prevention of Severe Candidal Infections," *Clin Infect Dis*, 1997, 25(1):43-59.

Eggimann P, Francioli P, Bille J, et al, "Fluconazole Prophylaxis Prevents Intra-abdominal Candidiasis in High-Risk Surgical Patients," *Crit Care Med*, 1999, 27(6):1066-72.

Fichtenbaum CJ, Zackin R, Rajicic N, et al, "Amphotericin B Oral Suspension for Fluconazole-Refractory Oral Candidiasis in Persons With HIV Infection. Adult AIDS Clinical Trials Group Study Team 295," *AIDS*, 2000, 14(7):845-52.

Hiemenz JW and Walsh TJ, "Lipid Formulations of Amphotericin B: Recent Progress and Future Directions," *Clin Infect Dis*, 1996, 22(Suppl 2):133-44.

Lister J, "Amphotericin B Lipid Complex (Abelcet®) in the Treatment of Invasive Mycoses: The North American Experience," *Eur J Haematol Suppl*, 1996, 57:18-23.

Lyman CA and Walsh TJ, "Systemically Administered Antifungal Agents. A Review of Their Clinical Pharmacology and Therapeutic Applications," *Drugs*, 1992, 44(1):9-35.

Mora-Duarte J, Betts R, Rotstein C, et al, "Comparison of Caspofungin and Amphotericin B for Invasive Candidiasis," *N Engl J Med*, 2002, 347(25):2020-9.

Patel R, "Antifungal Agents. Part I. Amphotericin B Preparations and Flucytosine," *Mayo Clin Proc*, 1998, 73(12):1205-25.

Prentice HG, Hann IM, Herbrecht R, et al, "A Randomized Comparison of Liposomal Versus Conventional Amphotericin B for the Treatment of Pyrexia of Unknown Origin in Neutropenic Patients," *Br J Haematol*, 1997, 98(3):711-8.

Rex JH, Bennett JE, and Sugar AM, "A Randomized Trial Comparing Fluconazole With Amphotericin B for the Treatment of Candidemia in Patients Without Neutropenia. Candidemia Study Group and the National Institute," *N Engl J Med*, 1994, 331(20):1325-30.

Rex JH, Pappas PG, Karchmer AW, et al, "A Randomized and Blinded Multicenter Trial of High-Dose Fluconazole Plus Placebo Versus Fluconazole Plus Amphotericin B as Therapy for Candidemia and Its Consequences in Nonneutropenic Subjects," *Clin Infect Dis*, 2003, 36(10):1221-8.

Rex JH, Walsh TJ, Sobel JD, et al, "Practice Guidelines for the Treatment of Candidiasis. Infectious Diseases Society of America," *Clin Infect Dis*, 2000, 30(4):662-78.

Slain D, "Lipid-Based Amphotericin B for the Treatment of Fungal Infections," *Pharmacotherapy*, 1999, 19(3):306-23.

♦ **Amphotericin B Colloidal Dispersion** *see* Amphotericin B Cholesteryl Sulfate Complex *on page 68*

Amphotericin B (Conventional)
(am foe TER i sin bee con VEN sha nal)

Medication Safety Issues

Safety issues:

Conventional amphotericin formulations (Amphocin®, Fungizone®) may be confused with lipid-based formulations (AmBisome®, Abelcet®, Amphotec®).

Large overdoses have occurred when conventional formulations were dispensed inadvertently for lipid-based products. Single daily doses of conventional amphotericin formulation never exceed 1.5 mg/kg.

(Continued)

Amphotericin B (Conventional) *(Continued)*

High alert medication: The Institute for Safe Medication Practices (ISMP) includes this medication among its list of drugs which have a heightened risk of causing significant patient harm when used in error.

U.S. Brand Names Amphocin® [DSC]

Index Terms Amphotericin B Desoxycholate

Generic Available Yes

Canadian Brand Names Fungizone®

Pharmacologic Category Antifungal Agent, Parenteral

Use Treatment of severe systemic and central nervous system infections caused by susceptible fungi such as *Candida* species, *Histoplasma capsulatum*, *Cryptococcus neoformans*, *Aspergillus* species, *Blastomyces dermatitidis*, *Torulopsis glabrata*, and *Coccidioides immitis*; fungal peritonitis; irrigant for bladder fungal infections; used in fungal infection in patients with bone marrow transplantation, amebic meningoencephalitis, ocular aspergillosis (intraocular injection), candidal cystitis (bladder irrigation), chemoprophylaxis (low-dose I.V.), immunocompromised patients at risk of aspergillosis (intranasal/nebulized), refractory meningitis (intrathecal), coccidioidal arthritis (intra-articular/I.M.).

Low-dose amphotericin B has been administered after bone marrow transplantation to reduce the risk of invasive fungal disease.

Pregnancy Risk Factor B

Lactation Excretion in breast milk unknown/contraindicated

Labeled Contraindications Hypersensitivity to amphotericin or any component of the formulation

Warnings/Precautions Avoid use with other nephrotoxic drugs. Monitor BUN and serum creatinine, potassium, and magnesium levels every 2-4 days, and daily in patients at risk for acute renal dysfunction. The standard dosage of lipid-based amphotericin B formulations, including amphotericin B cholesteryl sulfate (Amphotec®), amphotericin B lipid complex (Abelcet®), and liposomal amphotericin B (AmBisome®) is many fold greater than the dosage of conventional amphotericin B. To prevent inadvertent overdose, the product name and dosage must be verified for any amphotericin B dosage exceeding 1.5 mg/kg. Amphotericin B has been administered to pregnant women without obvious deleterious effects to the fetus, but the number of cases reported is small. Use during pregnancy only if absolutely necessary.

Adverse Reactions

Systemic:

>10%:

Cardiovascular: Hypotension, tachypnea

Central nervous system: Fever, chills, headache (less frequent with I.T.), malaise

Endocrine & metabolic: Hypokalemia, hypomagnesemia

Gastrointestinal: Anorexia, nausea (less frequent with I.T.), vomiting (less frequent with I.T.), diarrhea, heartburn, cramping epigastric pain

Hematologic: Normochromic-normocytic anemia

Local: Pain at injection site with or without phlebitis or thrombophlebitis (incidence may increase with peripheral infusion of admixtures)

Neuromuscular & skeletal: Generalized pain, including muscle and joint pains (less frequent with I.T.)

Renal: Decreased renal function and renal function abnormalities including azotemia, renal tubular acidosis, nephrocalcinosis (>0.1 mg/mL)

1% to 10%:

Cardiovascular: Hypertension, flushing

Central nervous system: Delirium, arachnoiditis, pain along lumbar nerves (especially I.T. therapy)

Genitourinary: Urinary retention

Hematologic: Leukocytosis

Neuromuscular & skeletal: Paresthesia (especially with I.T. therapy)

<1% (Limited to important or life-threatening): Acute liver failure, agranulocytosis, anuria, bone marrow suppression, cardiac arrest, coagulation defects, convulsions, dyspnea, hearing loss, leukopenia, maculopapular rash, renal failure, renal tubular acidosis, thrombocytopenia, vision changes

Overdosage/Toxicology Symptoms of overdose include renal dysfunction, cardiac arrest, anemia, thrombocytopenia, granulocytopenia, fever, nausea, and vomiting. Treatment is supportive.

Drug Interactions

Increased Effect/Toxicity: Use of amphotericin with other nephrotoxic drugs (eg, cyclosporine and aminoglycosides) may result in additive toxicity. Amphotericin may increase the toxicity of flucytosine. Antineoplastic agents may increase the risk of amphotericin-induced nephrotoxicity, bronchospasms, and hypotension. Corticosteroids may increase potassium depletion caused by amphotericin. Amphotericin B may predispose patients receiving digitalis glycosides or neuromuscular-blocking agents to toxicity secondary to hypokalemia.

Decreased Effect: Pharmacologic antagonism may occur with azole antifungal agents (ketoconazole, miconazole).

Storage/Stability Store intact vials under refrigeration; protect from light. Reconstituted vials are stable, protected from light, for 24 hours at room temperature and 1 week when refrigerated. Parenteral admixtures are stable, protected from light, for 24 hours at room temperature and 2 days under refrigeration. Short-term exposure (<24 hours) to light during I.V. infusion does **not** appreciably affect potency.

Reconstitution Add 10 mL of SWFI (without a bacteriostatic agent) to each vial of amphotericin B. Further dilute with 250-500 mL D_5W; final concentration should not exceed 0.1 mg/mL (peripheral infusion) or 0.25 mg/mL (central infusion).

Compatibility

Solution compatibility:

Compatible: Heparin sodium, hydrocortisone, sodium bicarbonate.

Incompatible: Ampicillin, calcium gluconate, carbenicillin, cimetidine, dopamine, gentamicin, lidocaine, potassium chloride, sodium chloride, tetracycline, verapamil.

Mechanism of Action Binds to ergosterol altering cell membrane permeability in susceptible fungi and causing leakage of cell components with subsequent cell death. Proposed mechanism suggests that amphotericin causes an oxidation-dependent stimulation of macrophages (Lyman, 1992).

Pharmacodynamics/Kinetics

Distribution: Minimal amounts enter the aqueous humor, bile, CSF (inflamed or noninflamed meninges), amniotic fluid, pericardial fluid, pleural fluid, and synovial fluid

Protein binding, plasma: 90%

Half-life elimination: Biphasic: Initial: 15-48 hours; Terminal: 15 days

Time to peak: Within 1 hour following a 4- to 6-hour dose

(Continued)

Amphotericin B (Conventional) *(Continued)*

Excretion: Urine (2% to 5% as biologically active form); ~40% eliminated over a 7-day period and may be detected in urine for at least 7 weeks after discontinued use

Dosage

Premedication: For patients who experience infusion-related immediate reactions, premedicate with the following drugs 30-60 minutes prior to drug administration: NSAID (with or without diphenhydramine) **or** acetaminophen with diphenhydramine **or** hydrocortisone 50-100 mg. If the patient experiences rigors during the infusion, meperidine may be administered.

Usual dosage ranges:

Infants and Children:

Test dose: I.V.: 0.1 mg/kg/dose to a maximum of 1 mg; infuse over 30-60 minutes. Many clinicians believe a test dose is unnecessary.

Maintenance dose: 0.25-1 mg/kg/day given once daily; infuse over 2-6 hours. Once therapy has been established, amphotericin B can be administered on an every-other-day basis at 1-1.5 mg/kg/dose; cumulative dose: 1.5-2 g over 6-10 weeks.

Duration of therapy: Varies with nature of infection, usual duration is 4-12 weeks or cumulative dose of 1-4 g

Adults:

Test dose: 1 mg infused over 20-30 minutes. Many clinicians believe a test dose is unnecessary.

Maintenance dose: Usual: 0.05-1.5 mg/kg/day; 1-1.5 mg/kg over 4-6 hours every other day may be given once therapy is established; aspergillosis, rhinocerebral mucormycosis, often require 1-1.5 mg/kg/day; do not exceed 1.5 mg/kg/day

Indication-specific dosing:

Children: Meningitis, coccidioidal or cryptococcal: I.T.: 25-100 mcg every 48-72 hours; increase to 500 mcg as tolerated

Adults:

Aspergillosis, disseminated: I.V.: 0.6-0.7 mg/kg/day for 3-6 months

Bone marrow transplantation (prophylaxis): I.V.: Low-dose amphotericin B 0.1-0.25 mg/kg/day has been administered after bone marrow transplantation to reduce the risk of invasive fungal disease.

Candidemia (neutropenic or non-neutropenic): I.V.: 0.6-1 mg/kg/day until 14 days after last positive blood culture and resolution of signs and symptoms

Candidiasis, chronic, disseminated: I.V.: 0.6-0.7 mg/kg/day for 3-6 months and resolution of radiologic lesions

Cystitis: Candidal: Bladder irrigation: Irrigate with 50 mcg/mL solution instilled periodically or continuously for 5-10 days or until cultures are clear

Dematiaceous fungi: I.V.: 0.7 mg/kg/day in combination with an azole

Endocarditis: I.V.: 0.6-1 mg/kg/day (with or without flucytosine) for 1 week, then 0.8 mg/kg/day every other day for 6-8 weeks postoperatively

Endophthalmitis, fungal:

Intravitreal (unlabeled use): 10 mcg in 0.1 mL (in conjunction with systemic therapy)

I.V.: 0.7-1 mg/kg/day (with or without flucytosine) for at least 4 weeks

Esophagitis: I.V.: 0.3-0.7 mg/kg/day for 14-21 after clinical improvement

Histoplasmosis: Chronic, severe pulmonary or disseminated: I.V.: 0.5-1 mg/kg/day for 7 days, then 0.8 mg/kg every other day (or 3 times/week)

until total dose of 10-15 mg/kg; may continue itraconazole as suppressive therapy (lifelong for immunocompromised patients)

Meningitis:

Candidal: I.V.: 0.7-1 mg/kg/day (with or without flucytosine) for at least 4 weeks

Cryptococcal or *Coccidioides*: I.T.: Initial: 25-300 mcg every 48-72 hours; increase to 500 mcg to 1 mg as tolerated; maximum total dose: 15 mg has been suggested

Histoplasma: I.V.: 0.5-1 mg/kg/day for 7 days, then 0.8 mg/kg every other day (or 3 times/week) for 3 months total duration; follow with fluconazole suppressive therapy for up to 12 months

Meningoencephalitis, cryptococcal: I.V.:

HIV positive: 0.7-1 mg/kg/day (plus flucytosine 100 mg/kg/day) for 2 weeks, then change to oral fluconazole for at least 10 weeks; alternatively, amphotericin and flucytosine may be continued uninterrupted for 6-10 weeks

HIV negative: 0.5-0.7 mg/kg/day (plus flucytosine) for 2 weeks

Osteomyelitis: Candidal: I.V.: 0.5-1 mg/kg/day for 6-10 weeks

Penicillium marneffei: I.V.: 0.6 mg/kg/day for 2 weeks

Pneumonia: Cryptococcal (mild to moderate): I.V.:

HIV positive: 0.5-1 mg/kg/day

HIV negative: 0.5-0.7 mg/kg/day (plus flucytosine) for 2 weeks

Sporotrichosis: Pulmonary, meningeal, osteoarticular, or disseminated: I.V.: Total dose of 1-2 g, then change to oral itraconazole or fluconazole for suppressive therapy

Dosing adjustment in renal impairment: If renal dysfunction is due to the drug, the daily total can be decreased by 50% or the dose can be given every other day; I.V. therapy may take several months

Dialysis: Poorly dialyzed; no supplemental dosage necessary when using hemo- or peritoneal dialysis or continuous renal replacement therapy (CRRT)

Administration in dialysate: Children and Adults: 1-2 mg/L of peritoneal dialysis fluid either with or without low-dose I.V. amphotericin B (a total dose of 2-10 mg/kg given over 7-14 days). Precipitate may form in ionic dialysate solutions.

Administration May be infused over 4-6 hours. For a patient who experiences chills, fever, hypotension, nausea, or other nonanaphylactic infusion-related reactions, premedicate with the following drugs 30-60 minutes prior to drug administration: A nonsteroidal (eg, ibuprofen, choline magnesium trisalicylate) with or without diphenhydramine **or** acetaminophen with diphenhydramine **or** hydrocortisone 50-100 mg. If the patient experiences rigors during the infusion, meperidine may be administered. Bolus infusion of normal saline immediately preceding, or immediately preceding and following amphotericin B may reduce drug-induced nephrotoxicity. Risk of nephrotoxicity increases with amphotericin B doses >1 mg/kg/day. Infusion of admixtures more concentrated than 0.25 mg/mL should be limited to patients absolutely requiring volume contraction.

Monitoring Parameters Renal function (monitor frequently during therapy), electrolytes (especially potassium and magnesium), liver function tests, temperature, PT/PTT, CBC; monitor input and output; monitor for signs of hypokalemia (muscle weakness, cramping, drowsiness, ECG changes, etc)

Test Interactions Increased BUN (S), serum creatinine, alkaline phosphate, bilirubin; decreased magnesium, potassium (S)

Special Geriatric Considerations The pharmacokinetics and dosing of amphotericin have not been studied in elderly. It appears that use is similar (Continued)

Amphotericin B (Conventional) *(Continued)*

to young adults; caution should be exercised and renal function and desired effect monitored closely.

Additional Information Premedication with diphenhydramine and acetaminophen may reduce the severity of acute infusion-related reactions. Meperidine reduces the duration of amphotericin B-induced rigors and chilling. Hydrocortisone may be used in patients with severe or refractory infusion-related reactions. Bolus infusion of normal saline immediately preceding, or immediately preceding and following amphotericin B may reduce drug-induced nephrotoxicity. Risk of nephrotoxicity increases with amphotericin B doses >1 mg/kg/day. Infusion of admixtures more concentrated than 0.25 mg/mL should be limited to patients absolutely requiring volume restriction. Amphotericin B does not have a bacteriostatic constituent, subsequently admixture expiration is determined by sterility more than chemical stability.

Emetic Potential Very low (<10%)

Vesicant No

Dosage Forms Excipient information presented when available (limited, particularly for generics); consult specific product labeling. [DSC] = Discontinued product

Injection, powder for reconstitution, as desoxycholate: 50 mg

Amphocin®: 50 mg [DSC]

References

Anderson RP and Clark DA, "Amphotericin B Toxicity Reduced by Administration in Fat Emulsion," *Ann Pharmacother*, 1995, 29(5):496-500.

Arning M, Heer-Sonderhoff A, and Schneider W, "Cardiopulmonary Toxicity After Liposomal Amphotericin B (AmBisome®) in Neutropenic Patients With Acute Leukemia," *Onkologie*, 1994, 17:4.

Arsura EL, Ismail Y, Freedman S, et al, "Amphotericin B-Induced Dilated Cardiomyopathy," *Am J Med*, 1994, 97(6):560-2.

Benson JM and Nahata MC, "Clinical Use of Systemic Antifungal Agents," *Clin Pharm*, 1988, 7(6):424-38.

Benson JM and Nahata MC, "Pharmacokinetics of Amphotericin B in Children," *Antimicrob Agents Chemother*, 1989, 33(11):1989-93.

Bianco JA, Almgren J, Kern DL, et al, "Evidence That Oral Pentoxifylline Reverses Acute Renal Dysfunction in Bone Marrow Transplant Recipients Receiving Amphotericin B and Cyclosporine," *Transplantation*, 1991, 51(4):925-7.

Branch RA, "Prevention of Amphotericin B-Induced Renal Impairment. A Review on the Use of Sodium Supplementation," *Arch Intern Med*, 1988, 148(11):2389-94.

Brent J, Hunt M, Kulig K, et al, "Amphotericin B Overdoses in Infants: Is There a Role for Exchange Transfusion?" *Vet Hum Toxicol*, 1990, 32(2):124-5.

Cruz JM, Peacock JE Jr, Loomer L, et al, "Rapid Intravenous Infusion of Amphotericin B: A Pilot Study," *Am J Med*, 1992, 93:123-30.

Devuyst O, Goffin E, and Van Ypersele de Strihou C, "Recurrent Hemiparesis Under Amphotericin B for *Candida albicans* Peritonitis," *Nephrol Dial Transplant*, 1995, 10(5):699-701.

Edwards JE Jr, Bodey GP, Bowden RA, et al, "International Conference for the Development of a Consensus on the Management and Prevention of Severe Candidal Infections," *Clin Infect Dis*, 1997, 25(1):43-59.

Eggimann P, Francioli P, Bille J, et al, "Fluconazole Prophylaxis Prevents Intra-Abdominal Candidiasis in High-Risk Surgical Patients," *Crit Care Med*, 1999, 27(6):1066-72.

Gales MA and Gales BJ, "Rapid Infusion of Amphotericin B in Dextrose," *Ann Pharmacother*, 1995, 29(5):523-9.

Gallis HA, Drew RH, and Pickard WW, "Amphotericin B: 30 Years of Clinical Experience," *Rev Infect Dis*, 1990, 12(2):308-29.

Goodwin SD, Cleary JD, Walawander CA, et al, "Pretreatment Regimens for Adverse Events Related to Infusion of Amphotericin B," *Clin Infect Dis*, 1995, 20(4):755-61.

Jeffery GM, Beard ME, Ikram RB, et al, "Intranasal Amphotericin B Reduces the Frequency of Invasive Aspergillosis in Neutropenic Patients," *Am J Med*, 1991, 90(6):685-92.

Jones RS, Barman A, Suh B, et al, "Successful Treatment of *Aspergillus vertebral* Osteomyelitis With Amphotericin B Lipid Complex," *Infect Dis Clin Pract*, 1995, 4:237-9.

Kauffman CA and Carver PL, "Antifungal Agents in the 1990s. Current Status and Future Developments," *Drugs*, 1997, 53(4):539-49.

Kintzel PE and Smith GH, "Practical Guidelines for Preparing and Administering Amphotericin B," *Am J Hosp Pharm*, 1992, 49(5):1156-64.

Koren G, Lau A, Klein J, et al, "Pharmacokinetics and Adverse Effects of Amphotericin B in Infants and Children," *J Pediatr*, 1988, 113(3):559-63.

Levy M, Domaratzki J, and Koren G, "Amphotericin-Induced Heart Rate Decrease in Children," *Clin Pediatr (Phila)*, 1995, 34(7):358-64.

Lyman CA and Walsh TJ, "Systemically Administered Antifungal Agents. A Review of Their Clinical Pharmacology and Therapeutic Applications," *Drugs*, 1992, 44(1):9-35.

Patel R, "Antifungal Agents. Part I. Amphotericin B Preparations and Flucytosine," *Mayo Clin Proc*, 1998, 73(12):1205-25.

Rex JH, Bennett JE, Sugar AM, "A Randomized Trial Comparing Fluconazole With Amphotericin B for the Treatment of Candidemia in Patients Without Neutropenia. Candidemia Study Group and the National Institute," *N Engl J Med*, 1994, 331(20):1325-30.

Rex JH, Walsh TJ, Sobel JD, et al, "Practice Guidelines for the Treatment of Candidiasis. Infectious Diseases Society of America," *Clin Infect Dis*, 2000, 30(4):662-78.

Slain D, "Lipid-Based Amphotericin B for the Treatment of Fungal Infections," *Pharmacotherapy*, 1999, 19(3):306-23.

The Ad Hoc Advisory Panel on Peritonitis Management. "Continuous Ambulatory Peritoneal Dialysis (CAPD) Peritonitis Treatment Recommendations: 1989 Update," *Perit Dial Int*, 1989, 9(4):247-56.

Wong-Beringer A, Beringer PM, and Rho JP, "Focus on Amphotericin B Lipid Complex," *Formulary*, 1996, 13(3):169-85.

♦ **Amphotericin B Desoxycholate** see Amphotericin B (Conventional) on page 71

Amphotericin B (Lipid Complex)
(am foe TER i sin bee LIP id KOM pleks)

Medication Safety Issues
Safety issues:

Lipid-based amphotericin formulations (Abelcet®) may be confused with conventional formulations (Amphocin®, Fungizone®)

Large overdoses have occurred when conventional formulations were dispensed inadvertently for lipid-based products. Single daily doses of conventional amphotericin formulation never exceed 1.5 mg/kg.

High alert medication: The Institute for Safe Medication Practices (ISMP) includes this medication among its list of drugs which have a heightened risk of causing significant patient harm when used in error.

U.S. Brand Names Abelcet®

Index Terms ABLC

Generic Available No

Canadian Brand Names Abelcet®; Amphotec®

Pharmacologic Category Antifungal Agent, Parenteral

Use Treatment of aspergillosis or any type of progressive fungal infection in patients who are refractory to or intolerant of conventional amphotericin B therapy

Unlabeled/Investigational Use Effective in patients with serious *Candida* species infections

Pregnancy Risk Factor B

Lactation Enters breast milk/contraindicated

Labeled Contraindications Hypersensitivity to amphotericin or any component of the formulation

Warnings/Precautions Anaphylaxis has been reported with amphotericin B-containing drugs. If severe respiratory distress occurs, the infusion should be immediately discontinued. During the initial dosing, the drug should be administered under close clinical observation. Acute reactions (including fever and chills) may occur 1-2 hours after starting an intravenous infusion. These reactions are usually more common with the first few doses and generally diminish with subsequent doses.
(Continued)

Amphotericin B (Lipid Complex) *(Continued)*

Adverse Reactions Nephrotoxicity and infusion-related hyperpyrexia, rigor, and chilling are reduced relative to amphotericin deoxycholate.

>10%:
 Central nervous system: Chills, fever
 Renal: Serum creatinine increased
 Miscellaneous: Multiple organ failure

1% to 10%:
 Cardiovascular: Hypotension, cardiac arrest
 Central nervous system: Headache, pain
 Dermatologic: Rash
 Endocrine & metabolic: Bilirubinemia, hypokalemia, acidosis
 Gastrointestinal: Nausea, vomiting, diarrhea, gastrointestinal hemorrhage, abdominal pain
 Renal: Renal failure
 Respiratory: Respiratory failure, dyspnea, pneumonia

Drug Interactions
 Increased Effect/Toxicity: See Drug Interactions - Increased Effect/Toxicity in Amphotericin B (Conventional).
 Decreased Effect: See Drug Interactions - Decreased Effect in Amphotericin B (Conventional).

Storage/Stability Intact vials should be stored at 2°C to 8°C (35°F to 46°F) and protected from exposure to light; do not freeze intact vials. Solutions for infusion are stable for 48 hours under refrigeration and 6 hours at room temperature. Protect from light. Following reconstitution, protect from light.

Reconstitution Shake vial gently to disperse yellow sediment at bottom of container. Dilute with D_5W to 1-2 mg/mL.

Compatibility
 Incompatible with any blood products, intravenous drugs, or intravenous fluids other than D_5W when admixed or as Y-site administration.

Mechanism of Action Binds to ergosterol altering cell membrane permeability in susceptible fungi and causing leakage of cell components with subsequent cell death. Proposed mechanism suggests that amphotericin causes an oxidation-dependent stimulation of macrophages.

Pharmacodynamics/Kinetics
 Distribution: V_d: Increases with higher doses; reflects increased uptake by tissues (131 L/kg with 5 mg/kg/day)
 Half-life elimination: ~24 hours
 Excretion: Clearance: Increases with higher doses (5 mg/kg/day): 400 mL/hour/kg

Dosage Children and Adults: I.V.:
 Premedication: For patients who experience infusion-related immediate reactions, premedicate with the following drugs 30-60 minutes prior to drug administration: A nonsteroidal anti-inflammatory agent ± diphenhydramine **or** acetaminophen with diphenhydramine **or** hydrocortisone 50-100 mg. If the patient experiences rigors during the infusion, meperidine may be administered.
 Range: 2.5-5 mg/kg/day as a single infusion
 Dosing adjustment in renal impairment: None necessary; effects of renal impairment are not currently known
 Hemodialysis: No supplemental dosage necessary
 Peritoneal dialysis: No supplemental dosage necessary
 Continuous renal replacement therapy (CRRT): No supplemental dosage necessary

Administration For patients who experience nonanaphylactic infusion-related reactions, premedicate 30-60 minutes prior to drug administration with a nonsteroidal anti-inflammatory agent ± diphenhydramine **or** acetaminophen with diphenhydramine **or** hydrocortisone 50-100 mg. If the patient experiences rigors during the infusion, meperidine may be administered.

Invert infusion container several times prior to administration and every 2 hours during infusion.

Monitoring Parameters Renal function (monitor frequently during therapy), electrolytes (especially potassium and magnesium), liver function tests, temperature, PT/PTT, CBC; monitor input and output; monitor for signs of hypokalemia (muscle weakness, cramping, drowsiness, ECG changes, etc)

Test Interactions Increased BUN (S), serum creatinine, alkaline phosphate, bilirubin; decreased magnesium, potassium (S)

Special Geriatric Considerations The pharmacokinetics and dosing of amphotericin have not been studied in elderly. It appears that use is similar to young adults; caution should be exercised and renal function and desired effect monitored closely.

Additional Information As a modification of dimyristoyl phosphatidylcholine:dimyristoyl phosphatidylglycerol 7:3 (DMPC:DMPG) liposome, amphotericin B lipid-complex has a higher drug to lipid ratio and the concentration of amphotericin B is 33 M. ABLC is a ribbon-like structure, not a liposome.

Controlled trials which compare the original formulation of amphotericin B to the newer liposomal formulations (ie, Abelcet®) are lacking. Thus, comparative data discussing differences among the formulations should be interpreted cautiously. Although the risk of nephrotoxicity and infusion-related adverse effects may be less with Abelcet®, the efficacy profiles of Abelcet® and the original amphotericin formulation are comparable. Consequently, Abelcet® should be restricted to those patients who cannot tolerate or fail a standard amphotericin B formulation.

Emetic Potential Very low (<10%)

Vesicant No

Dosage Forms Excipient information presented when available (limited, particularly for generics); consult specific product labeling.

Injection, suspension [preservative free]: 5 mg/mL (20 mL)

References

De Marie S, "Clinical Use of Liposomal and Lipid-Complexed Amphotericin B," *J Antimicrob Chemother*, 1994, 33(5):907-16.

Edwards JE Jr, Bodey GP, Bowden RA, et al, "International Conference for the Development of a Consensus on the Management and Prevention of Severe Candidal Infections," *Clin Infect Dis*, 1997, 25(1):43-59.

Eggimann P, Francioli P, Bille J, et al, "Fluconazole Prophylaxis Prevents Intra-abdominal Candidiasis in High-Risk Surgical Patients," *Crit Care Med*, 1999, 27(6):1066-72.

Fichtenbaum CJ, Zackin R, Rajicic N, et al, "Amphotericin B Oral Suspension for Fluconazole-Refractory Oral Candidiasis in Persons With HIV Infection. Adult AIDS Clinical Trials Group Study Team 295," *AIDS*, 2000, 14(7):845-52.

Hiemenz JW and Walsh TJ, "Lipid Formulations of Amphotericin B: Recent Progress and Future Directions," *Clin Infect Dis*, 1996, 22(Suppl 2):133-44.

Kline S, Larsen TA, Fieber L, et al, "Limited Toxicity of Prolonged Therapy With High Doses of Amphotericin B Lipid Complex," *Clin Infect Dis*, 1995, 21(5):1154-8.

Lyman CA and Walsh TJ, "Systemically Administered Antifungal Agents. A Review of Their Clinical Pharmacology and Therapeutic Applications," *Drugs*, 1992, 44(1):9-35.

Mora-Duarte J, Betts R, Rotstein C, et al, "Comparison of Caspofungin and Amphotericin B for Invasive Candidiasis," *N Engl J Med*, 2002, 347(25):2020-9.

Patel R, "Antifungal Agents. Part I. Amphotericin B Preparations and Flucytosine," *Mayo Clin Proc*, 1998, 73(12):1205-25.

Rapp RP, Gubbins PO, and Evans ME, "Amphotericin B Lipid Complex," *Ann Pharmacother*, 1997, 31(10):1174-86.

(Continued)

Amphotericin B (Lipid Complex) *(Continued)*

Rex JH, Bennett JE, and Sugar AM, "A Randomized Trial Comparing Fluconazole With Amphotericin B for the Treatment of Candidemia in Patients Without Neutropenia. Candidemia Study Group and the National Institute," *N Engl J Med*, 1994, 331(20):1325-30.

Rex JH, Pappas PG, Karchmer AW, et al, "A Randomized and Blinded Multicenter Trial of High-Dose Fluconazole Plus Placebo Versus Fluconazole Plus Amphotericin B as Therapy for Candidemia and Its Consequences in Nonneutropenic Subjects," *Clin Infect Dis*, 2003, 36(10):1221-8.

Rex JH, Walsh TJ, Sobel JD, et al, "Practice Guidelines for the Treatment of Candidiasis. Infectious Diseases Society of America," *Clin Infect Dis*, 2000, 30(4):662-78.

Slain D, "Lipid-Based Amphotericin B for the Treatment of Fungal Infections," *Pharmacotherapy*, 1999, 19(3):306-23.

Amphotericin B (Liposomal)
(am foe TER i sin bee lye po SO mal)

Medication Safety Issues

Safety issues:

Lipid-based amphotericin formulations (AmBisome®) may be confused with conventional formulations (Amphocin®, Fungizone®)

Large overdoses have occurred when conventional formulations were dispensed inadvertently for lipid-based products. Single daily doses of conventional amphotericin formulation never exceed 1.5 mg/kg.

High alert medication: The Institute for Safe Medication Practices (ISMP) includes this medication among its list of drugs which have a heightened risk of causing significant patient harm when used in error.

U.S. Brand Names AmBisome®

Index Terms L-AmB

Generic Available No

Canadian Brand Names AmBisome®

Pharmacologic Category Antifungal Agent, Parenteral

Use Empirical therapy for presumed fungal infection in febrile, neutropenic patients; treatment of patients with *Aspergillus* species, *Candida* species, and/or *Cryptococcus* species infections refractory to amphotericin B desoxycholate, or in patients where renal impairment or unacceptable toxicity precludes the use of amphotericin B desoxycholate; treatment of cryptococcal meningitis in HIV-infected patients; treatment of visceral leishmaniasis

Unlabeled/Investigational Use Effective in patients with serious *Candida* species infections

Pregnancy Risk Factor B

Lactation Excretion in breast milk unknown/contraindicated

Labeled Contraindications Hypersensitivity to amphotericin B or any component of the formulation

Warnings/Precautions Patients should be under close clinical observation during initial dosing. As with other amphotericin B-containing products, anaphylaxis has been reported. Facilities for cardiopulmonary resuscitation should be available during administration. Acute reactions (including fever and chills) may occur 1-2 hours after starting infusions; reactions are more common with the first few doses and generally diminish with subsequent doses. Immediately discontinue infusion if severe respiratory distress occurs; the patient should not receive further infusions. Safety and efficacy have not been established in patients <1 month of age.

Adverse Reactions Percentage of adverse reactions is dependent upon population studied and may vary with respect to premedications and underlying illness. Incidence of decreased renal function and infusion-related events are lower than rates observed with amphotericin B desoxycholate.

>10%:

Cardiovascular: Peripheral edema (15%), edema (12% to 14%), tachycardia (9% to 18%), hypotension (7% to 14%), hypertension (8% to 20%), chest pain (8% to 12%), hypervolemia (8% to 12%)

Central nervous system: Chills (29% to 48%), insomnia (17% to 22%), headache (9% to 20%), anxiety (7% to 14%), pain (14%), confusion (9% to 13%)

Dermatologic: Rash (5% to 25%), pruritus (11%)

Endocrine & metabolic: Hypokalemia (31% to 51%), hypomagnesemia (15% to 50%), hyperglycemia (8% to 23%), hypocalcemia (5% to 18%), hyponatremia (8% to 12%)

Gastrointestinal: Nausea (16% to 40%), vomiting (10% to 32%), diarrhea (11% to 30%), abdominal pain (7% to 20%), constipation (15%), anorexia (10% to 14%)

Hematologic: Anemia (27% to 48%), blood transfusion reaction (9% to 18%), leukopenia (15% to 17%), thrombocytopenia (6% to 13%)

Hepatic: Alkaline phosphatase increased (7% to 22%), BUN increased (7% to 21%), bilirubinemia (9% to 18%), ALT (15%) increased, AST increased (13%), liver function tests abnormal (not specified) (4% to 13%)

Local: Phlebitis (9% to 11%)

Neuromuscular & skeletal: Weakness (6% to 13%), back pain (12%)

Renal: Creatinine increased (18% to 40%), hematuria (14%)

Respiratory: Dyspnea (18% to 23%), lung disorder (14% to 18%), cough increased (2% to 18%), epistaxis (8% to 15%), pleural effusion (12%), rhinitis (11%)

Miscellaneous: Sepsis (7% to 14%), infection (11% to 12%)

2% to 10%:

Cardiovascular: Arrhythmia, atrial fibrillation, bradycardia, cardiac arrest, cardiomegaly, facial swelling, flushing, postural hypotension, valvular heart disease, vascular disorder

Central nervous system: Agitation, abnormal thinking, coma, convulsion, depression, dysesthesia, dizziness (7% to 8%), hallucinations, malaise, nervousness, somnolence

Dermatologic: Alopecia, bruising, cellulitis, dry skin, maculopapular rash, petechia, purpura, skin discoloration, skin disorder, skin ulcer, urticaria, vesiculobullous rash

Endocrine & metabolic: Acidosis, fluid overload, hypernatremia (4%), hyperchloremia, hyperkalemia, hypermagnesemia, hyperphosphatemia, hypophosphatemia, hypoproteinemia, lactate dehydrogenase increased, nonprotein nitrogen increased

Gastrointestinal: Constipation, dry mouth, dyspepsia, abdomen enlarged, amylase increased, eructation, fecal incontinence, flatulence, gastrointestinal hemorrhage (10%), hematemesis, hemorrhoids, gum/oral hemorrhage, ileus, mucositis, rectal disorder, stomatitis, ulcerative stomatitis

Genitourinary: Vaginal hemorrhage

Hematologic: Coagulation disorder, hemorrhage, prothrombin decreased, thrombocytopenia

Hepatic: Hepatocellular damage, hepatomegaly, veno-occlusive liver disease

Local: Injection site inflammation

Neuromuscular & skeletal: Arthralgia, bone pain, dystonia, myalgia, neck pain, paresthesia, rigors, tremor

Ocular: Conjunctivitis, dry eyes, eye hemorrhage

(Continued)

Amphotericin B (Liposomal) *(Continued)*

Renal: Abnormal renal function, acute kidney failure, dysuria, kidney failure, toxic nephropathy, urinary incontinence

Respiratory: Asthma, atelectasis, cough, dry nose, hemoptysis, hyperventilation, lung edema, pharyngitis, pneumonia, respiratory alkalosis, respiratory insufficiency, respiratory failure, sinusitis, hypoxia (6% to 8%)

Miscellaneous: Allergic reaction, cell-mediated immunological reaction, flu-like syndrome, graft-versus-host disease, herpes simplex, hiccup, procedural complication (8% to 10%), diaphoresis (7%)

Postmarketing and/or case reports: Angioedema, erythema, urticaria, cyanosis/hypoventilation, pulmonary edema, agranulocytosis, hemorrhagic cystitis

Overdosage/Toxicology The toxicity due to overdose has not been defined. Repeated daily doses up to 7.5 mg/kg have been administered in clinical trials with no reported dose-related toxicity. If overdosage should occur, cease administration immediately. Symptomatic supportive measures should be instituted. Particular attention should be given to monitoring renal function.

Drug Interactions

Increased Effect/Toxicity: Drug interactions have not been studied in a controlled manner; however, drugs that interact with conventional amphotericin B may also interact with amphotericin B liposome for injection. See Drug Interactions - Increased Effect/Toxicity in Amphotericin B (Conventional) monograph.

Storage/Stability Unopened vials should be refrigerated at 2°C to 8°C (36°F to 46°F). Vials reconstituted with SWFI are stable for 24 hours under refrigeration. Infusion should begin within 6 hours of dilution with D5W.

Reconstitution Add 12 mL SWFI to vial. The use of any solution other than those recommended, or the presence of a bacteriostatic agent in the solution, may cause precipitation. **Shake the vial vigorously** for 30 seconds.

Filtration and dilution: The 5-micron filter should be on the syringe used to remove the reconstituted AmBisome®. Dilute to a final concentration of 1-2 mg/mL (0.2-0.5 mg/mL for infants and small children).

Compatibility Stable in D_5W; **incompatible** with NS, $^1/_2$NS, other saline-containing solutions, or preservatives.

Mechanism of Action Binds to ergosterol altering cell membrane permeability in susceptible fungi and causing leakage of cell components with subsequent cell death. Proposed mechanism suggests that amphotericin causes an oxidation-dependent stimulation of macrophages (Lyman, 1992).

Pharmacodynamics/Kinetics

Distribution: V_d: 131 L/kg

Half-life elimination: Terminal: 174 hours

Dosage

Usual dosage range:

Children ≥1 month: I.V.: 3-5 mg/kg/day

Adults: I.V.: 2-6 mg/kg/day; **Note:** Higher doses (15 mg/kg/day) have been used clinically.

Note: Premedication: For patients who experience nonanaphylactic infusion-related immediate reactions, premedicate with the following drugs 30-60 minutes prior to drug administration: A nonsteroidal anti-inflammatory agent ± diphenhydramine; **or** acetaminophen with diphenhydramine; **or** hydrocortisone 50-100 mg. If the patient experiences rigors during the infusion, meperidine may be administered.

Indication-specific dosing:
Children ≥1 month: I.V.:
  Candidal infection:
    Endocarditis: 3-6 mg/kg/day with flucytosine 25-37.5 mg/kg 4 times daily
    Meningitis: 5 mg/kg/day with flucytosine 100 mg/kg/day
  Cryptococcal meningitis (HIV-positive): 6 mg/kg/day
    Note: IDSA guidelines (April, 2000) report doses of 3-6 mg/kg/day, noting that 4 mg/kg/day was effective in a small, open-label trial. The manufacturer's labeled dose of 6 mg/kg/day was approved in June, 2000.
  Empiric therapy: 3 mg/kg/day
  Systemic fungal infections *(Aspergillus, Candida, Cryptococcus)*: 3-5 mg/kg/day
  Visceral leishmaniasis:
    Immunocompetent: 3 mg/kg/day on days 1-5, and 3 mg/kg/day on days 14 and 21; a repeat course may be given in patients who do not achieve parasitic clearance
    Note: Alternate regimen of 10 mg/kg/day for 2 days has been reportedly effective.
    Immunocompromised: 4 mg/kg/day on days 1-5, and 4 mg/kg/day on days 10, 17, 24, 31, and 38
Adults: I.V.:
  Candidal infection:
    Endocarditis: 3-6 mg/kg/day with flucytosine 25-37.5 mg/kg 4 times daily
    Meningitis: 5 mg/kg/day with flucytosine 100 mg/kg/day
  Cryptococcal meningitis (HIV-positive): 6 mg/kg/day
    Note: IDSA guidelines (April, 2000) report doses of 3-6 mg/kg/day, noting that 4 mg/kg/day was effective in a small, open-label trial. The manufacturer's labeled dose of 6 mg/kg/day was approved in June, 2000.
  Empiric therapy: 3 mg/kg/day
  Fungal sinusitis: 5-7.5 mg/kg/day
    Note: Use azole antifungal if causative organism is *Pseudallescheria boydii* (*Scedosporium* sp).
  Systemic fungal infections *(Aspergillus, Candida, Cryptococcus)*: 3-5 mg/kg/day
  Visceral leishmaniasis:
    Immunocompetent: 3 mg/kg/day on days 1-5, and 3 mg/kg/day on days 14 and 21; a repeat course may be given in patients who do not achieve parasitic clearance
    Note: Alternate regimen of 2 mg/kg/day for 5 days has been reportedly effective.
    Immunocompromised: 4 mg/kg/day on days 1-5, and 4 mg/kg/day on days 10, 17, 24, 31, and 38

Dosing adjustment in renal impairment: None necessary; effects of renal impairment are not currently known
Hemodialysis: No supplemental dosage necessary
Peritoneal dialysis effects: No supplemental dosage necessary
Continuous renal replacement therapy (CRRT): No supplemental dosage necessary

Administration Administer via intravenous infusion, over a period of approximately 2 hours. Infusion time may be reduced to approximately 1 hour in patients in whom the treatment is well-tolerated. If the patient experiences
(Continued)

Amphotericin B (Liposomal) *(Continued)*

discomfort during infusion, the duration of infusion may be increased. Administer at a rate of 2.5 mg/kg/hour. Existing intravenous line should be flushed with D_5W prior to infusion (if not feasible, administer through a separate line). An in-line membrane filter (not less than 1 micron) may be used.

For a patient who experiences chills, fever, hypotension, nausea, or other nonanaphylactic infusion-related reactions, premedicate with the following drugs, 30-60 minutes prior to drug administration: A nonsteroidal (eg, ibuprofen, choline magnesium trisalicylate) with or without diphenhydramine **or** acetaminophen with diphenhydramine **or** hydrocortisone 50-100 mg. If the patient experiences rigors during the infusion, meperidine may be administered.

Monitoring Parameters Renal function (monitor frequently during therapy), electrolytes (especially potassium and magnesium), liver function tests, temperature, PT/PTT, CBC; monitor input and output; monitor for signs of hypokalemia (muscle weakness, cramping, drowsiness, ECG changes, etc)

Additional Information Amphotericin B (liposomal) is a true single bilayer liposomal drug delivery system. Liposomes are closed, spherical vesicles created by mixing specific proportions of amphophilic substances such as phospholipids and cholesterol so that they arrange themselves into multiple concentric bilayer membranes when hydrated in aqueous solutions. Single bilayer liposomes are then formed by microemulsification of multilamellar vesicles using a homogenizer. Amphotericin B (liposomal) consists of these unilamellar bilayer liposomes with amphotericin B intercalated within the membrane. Due to the nature and quantity of amphophilic substances used, and the lipophilic moiety in the amphotericin B molecule, the drug is an integral part of the overall structure of the amphotericin B liposomal liposomes. Amphotericin B (liposomal) contains true liposomes that are <100 nm in diameter.

Dosage Forms Excipient information presented when available (limited, particularly for generics); consult specific product labeling.

Injection, powder for reconstitution:

AmBisome®: 50 mg [contains soy and sucrose]

References

Edwards JE Jr, Bodey GP, Bowden RA, et al, "International Conference for the Development of a Consensus on the Management and Prevention of Severe Candidal Infections," *Clin Infect Dis*, 1997, 25(1):43-59.

Eggimann P, Francioli P, Bille J, et al, "Fluconazole Prophylaxis Prevents Intra-abdominal Candidiasis in High-Risk Surgical Patients," *Crit Care Med*, 1999, 27(6):1066-72.

Emminger W, Graninger W, Emminger-Schmidmeir W, et al, "Tolerance of High Doses of Amphotericin B by Infusion of a Liposomal Formulation in Children With Cancer," *Ann Hematol*, 1994, 68:27-31.

Fichtenbaum CJ, Zackin R, Rajicic N, et al, "Amphotericin B Oral Suspension for Fluconazole-Refractory Oral Candidiasis in Persons With HIV Infection. Adult AIDS Clinical Trials Group Study Team 295," *AIDS*, 2000, 14(7):845-52.

Hiemenz JW and Walsh TJ, "Lipid Formulations of Amphotericin B: Recent Progress and Future Directions," *Clin Infect Dis*, 1996, 22(Suppl 2):133-44.

Lyman CA and Walsh TJ, "Systemically Administered Antifungal Agents. A Review of Their Clinical Pharmacology and Therapeutic Applications," *Drugs*, 1992, 44(1):9-35.

Mora-Duarte J, Betts R, Rotstein C, et al, "Comparison of Caspofungin and Amphotericin B for Invasive Candidiasis," *N Engl J Med*, 2002, 347(25):2020-9.

Patel R, "Antifungal Agents. Part I. Amphotericin B Preparations and Flucytosine," *Mayo Clin Proc*, 1998, 73(12):1205-25.

Rex JH, Bennett JE, and Sugar AM, "A Randomized Trial Comparing Fluconazole With Amphotericin B for the Treatment of Candidemia in Patients Without Neutropenia. Candidemia Study Group and the National Institute," *N Engl J Med*, 1994, 331(20):1325-30.

Rex JH, Pappas PG, Karchmer AW, et al, "A Randomized and Blinded Multicenter Trial of High-Dose Fluconazole Plus Placebo Versus Fluconazole Plus Amphotericin B as Therapy for

Candidemia and Its Consequences in Nonneutropenic Subjects," *Clin Infect Dis*, 2003, 36(10):1221-8.

Rex JH, Walsh TJ, Sobel JD, et al, "Practice Guidelines for the Treatment of Candidiasis. Infectious Diseases Society of America," *Clin Infect Dis*, 2000, 30(4):662-78.

Ringden O, Andstrom E, Remberger M, et al, "Safety of Liposomal Amphotericin B (AmBisome®) in 187 Transplant Recipients Treated With Cyclosporin," *Bone Marrow Transplant*, 1994, 14(Suppl 5):10-4.

Slain D, "Lipid-Based Amphotericin B for the Treatment of Fungal Infections," *Pharmacotherapy*, 1999, 19(3):306-23.

Walsh TJ, Finberg RW, Arndt C, et al, "Liposomal Amphotericin B for Empirical Therapy in Patients With Persistent Fever and Neutropenia," *N Engl J Med*, 1999, 340:764-71.

♦ **AMSA** see Amsacrine on page 85

Amsacrine (AM sah kreen)

Related Information
Investigational Drug Service *on page 1379*
Management of Drug Extravasations *on page 1301*
Safe Handling of Hazardous Drugs *on page 1382*

Index Terms 4-(9-Acridinylamino) Methanesulfon-m-Anisidide; Acridinyl Anisidide; AMSA; m-AMSA; NSC-249992

Generic Available No

Canadian Brand Names Amsa P-D

Pharmacologic Category Antineoplastic Agent

Unlabeled/Investigational Use Investigational: Refractory acute lymphocytic and nonlymphocytic leukemias, Hodgkin's disease, and non-Hodgkin's lymphomas; head and neck tumors

Restrictions Not available in U.S./Investigational

Labeled Contraindications Hypersensitivity to amsacrine or any component of the formulation; hypokalemia

Warnings/Precautions Hazardous agent - use appropriate precautions for handling and disposal. The drug should be used cautiously in patients who have underlying cardiac disease, severe renal or hepatic dysfunction, or who have received high cumulative doses of anthracyclines. **Do not administer amsacrine if serum potassium <4 mEq/L.**

Adverse Reactions
>10%:
  Cardiovascular: ECG changes (T-wave flattening, S-T wave alterations) consistent with anterolateral ischemia, ventricular fibrillation, ventricular extrasystoles, atrial tachycardia and fibrillation, CHF, cardiac arrest. Patients with hypokalemia, who have received >400 mg/m^2 of doxorubicin or daunorubicin (or the equivalent), >200 mg/m^2 of amsacrine within 48 hours, or a total dose of anthracycline + amsacrine >900 mg/m^2 have an increased risk of cardiac toxicity.
  Dermatologic: Alopecia
  Gastrointestinal: Nausea and vomiting (30%), diarrhea (30%), stomatitis (dose-limiting - 32%), oral ulceration (10%)
  Genitourinary: Orange-red discoloration of the urine
  Hematologic: Leukopenia (nadir at 10 days); thrombocytopenia (nadir at 12-14 days), with recovery at 21-25 days
  Hepatic: Hyperbilirubinemia (30%), liver enzymes increased (10%)
  Local: Phlebitis
1% to 10%:
  Central nervous system: Confusion, convulsions, dizziness, headache
  Hematologic: Anemia
  Neuromuscular & skeletal: Paresthesia
  Ocular: Blurred vision
<1%: Allergic reactions (0.4%), sperm production decreased
(Continued)

Amsacrine (Continued)

Storage/Stability Intact vials are stored at controlled room temperature 15°C to 30°C (59°F to 86°F). Reconstituted vials may be stored at room temperature for up to 48 hours. Solutions diluted for administration are stable for up to 48 hours at room temperature. The addition of 1 mEq/L of sodium bicarbonate increases the stability to 96 hours.

Note: Use of glass syringes and avoidance of plastic filters to draw up undiluted amsacrine solutions is recommended since the N,N-dimethylacetamide solvent has been reported to dissolve plastic syringes and filters. The solution may be mixed in plastic bags when diluted for infusion.

Reconstitution Reconstitute 1.5 mL of solution by adding 13.5 mL of lactic acid diluent (provided with the drug) to form a 5 mg/mL solution.

Compatibility Stable in D_5W; **incompatible** with BNS, D_5NS, $D_5^1/_4NS$, $D_5^1/_2NS$, D_5LR, $D_{10}NS$, NSS, LR, chloride ion. Amsacrine forms an immediate precipitate in the presence of chloride ion; do not mix with drugs that are chloride or hydrochloride salts.

Y-site administration: Compatible: Amikacin, chlorpromazine, clindamycin, cytarabine, dexamethasone, diphenhydramine, famotidine, fludarabine, gentamicin, granisetron, haloperidol, hydrocortisone sodium succinate, hydromorphone, lorazepam, morphine, prochlorperazine, promethazine, ranitidine, sodium bicarbonate, tobramycin, vancomycin. **Incompatible:** Acyclovir, amphotericin, aztreonam, calcium chloride, ceftazidime, ceftriaxone, cephalothin, cimetidine, cisplatin, filgrastim, furosemide, ganciclovir, heparin, methylprednisolone, metoclopramide, ondansetron, potassium chloride, sargramostim.

Compatibility when admixed: Compatible: Sodium bicarbonate, bleomycin

Mechanism of Action Amsacrine has been shown to inhibit DNA synthesis by binding to, and intercalating with, DNA; inhibits topoisomerase II activity.

Pharmacodynamics/Kinetics

Distribution: V_d: 1.67 L/kg; minimal CNS penetration

Protein binding: 96% to 98%

Metabolism: Hepatic, to inactive metabolites (major metabolite is 5' glutathione conjugate)

Half-life elimination: 1.4-5 hours; Terminal: 5.6-7.8 hours

Excretion: Bile; urine (2% to 10% as unchanged drug)

Dosage Refer to individual protocols. I.V.:

Children: 125-150 mg/m²/day for 5 days

Adults: 60-160 mg/m²/day every 3-4 weeks; 5- to 7-day I.V. infusions of 40-120 mg/m²/day every 3-4 weeks have also been reported.

Dosage adjustment in renal impairment: BUN >20 or S_{cr} >1.5: Administer 25% of normal dose.

Dosage adjustment in hepatic impairment: Bilirubin >2 mg/dL: Administer 75% of normal dose.

Administration I.V.: Administer as a 30- to 90-minute infusion or a 24-hour continuous infusion. Use of glass syringes and avoidance of plastic filters to draw up undiluted amsacrine solutions is recommended since the N,N-dimethylacetamide solvent has been reported to dissolve plastic syringes and filters. The solution can be placed in plastic bags when diluted for I.V. infusion.

Patient Information This drug may cause darkening or discoloration of the urine for 24-48 hours. Watch for fever, malaise, bleeding, bruising, sore throat or mouth, difficulty swallowing, or for pain, redness, or swelling at the injection site.

Emetic Potential Moderate (30% to 60%)

Vesicant Yes; see Management of Drug Extravasations *on page 1301.*

Dosage Forms Excipient information presented when available (limited, particularly for generics); consult specific product labeling.

Injection, solution [preservative free]: 50 mg/1.5 mL (supplied with L-lactic acid 0.0353 M 13.5 mL)

References

Arlin ZA, "A Special Role for Amsacrine in the Treatment of Acute Leukemia," *Cancer Invest,* 1989, 7(6):607-9.

Hornedo J and Van Echo DA, "Amsacrine (m-AMSA): A New Antineoplastic Agent. Pharmacology, Clinical Activity and Toxicity," *Pharmacotherapy,* 1985, 5(2):78-90.

Louie AC and Issell BF, "Amsacrine (AMSA) - A Clinical Review," *J Clin Oncol,* 1985, 3(4):562-92.

Van Mouwerik TJ, Caines PM, and Ballentine R, "Amsacrine Evaluation," *Drug Intell Clin Pharm,* 1987, 21(4):330-4.

♦ **Amsa P-D (Can)** *see* Amsacrine *on page 85*

Anagrelide (an AG gre lide)

Related Information

Safe Handling of Hazardous Drugs *on page 1382*

U.S. Brand Names Agrylin®

Index Terms Anagrelide Hydrochloride; BL4162A; NSC-724577

Generic Available Yes

Canadian Brand Names Agrylin®; Gen-Anagrelide; PMS-Anagrelide; Rhoxal-anagrelide; Sandoz-Anagrelide

Pharmacologic Category Phospholipase A_2 Inhibitor

Use Treatment of essential thrombocythemia (ET) and thrombocythemia associated with myeloproliferative disorders

Pregnancy Risk Factor C

Lactation Excretion in breast milk unknown/not recommended

Labeled Contraindications Hypersensitivity to anagrelide or any component of the formulation; severe hepatic impairment

Warnings/Precautions Use caution in patients with known or suspected heart disease; tachycardia, orthostatic hypotension, and CHF; a pretreatment cardiovascular evaluation is recommended. Use caution in patients with renal dysfunction (serum creatinine ≥2 mg/dL) or hepatic dysfunction (measures of liver function >1.5 times ULN); dosage reduction and careful monitoring is required for moderate hepatic impairment; has not been studied in severe hepatic impairment.

Adverse Reactions

>10%:

Cardiovascular: Palpitation (26%), edema (21%)

Central nervous system: Headache (44%), dizziness (15%), pain (15%)

Gastrointestinal: Diarrhea (26%), nausea (17%), abdominal pain (16%)

Neuromuscular & skeletal: Weakness (23%)

Respiratory: Dyspnea (12%)

1% to 10%:

Cardiovascular: Angina, arrhythmias, cardiovascular disease, chest pain (8%), CHF, hypertension, orthostatic hypotension, peripheral edema (9%), syncope, tachycardia (8%), thrombosis, vasodilatation

Central nervous system: Amnesia, chills, confusion, depression, fever (9%), insomnia, malaise (6%), migraine, nervousness, somnolence

Dermatologic: Alopecia, bruising, photosensitivity, pruritus (6%), rash (8%), urticaria

(Continued)

Anagrelide *(Continued)*

Endocrine & skeletal: Dehydration

Gastrointestinal: Anorexia (8%), aphthous stomatitis, constipation, dyspepsia (5%), eructation, flatulence (10%), gastritis, GI distress, GI hemorrhage, melena, vomiting (10%)

Hematologic: Anemia, hemorrhage, thrombocytopenia (grades 3/4: 5%)

Hepatic: Liver enzymes increased

Neuromuscular & skeletal: Arthralgia, back pain (6%), leg cramps, myalgia, paresthesia (6%)

Ocular: Amblyopia, diplopia, visual field abnormality

Otic: Tinnitus

Renal: Dysuria, hematuria, renal failure

Respiratory: Asthma, bronchitis, cough (6%), epistaxis, pharyngitis (7%), pneumonia, rhinitis, sinusitis

Miscellaneous: Flu-like syndrome, lymphadenopathy

Frequency not defined: Atrial fibrillation, cardiomegaly, cardiomyopathy, cerebrovascular accident, complete heart block, deep vein thrombosis, gastric/duodenal ulceration, leukocyte count increased, MI, myelofibrosis, pancreatitis, pericarditis, pericardial effusion, pleural effusion, polycythemia, pulmonary fibrosis, pulmonary infiltrates, pulmonary hypertension, seizure, stroke, transient ischemic attack

Overdosage/Toxicology There are no reports of human overdosage with anagrelide. Thrombocytopenia may occur in overdose; cardiac and central nervous systems adverse effects may also occur. Dosage should be decreased or stopped, as appropriate, until the platelet count returns to within the normal range. Treatment is otherwise symptom-directed and supportive.

Drug Interactions

Cytochrome P450 Effect: Substrate of CYP1A2 (minor)

Increased Effect/Toxicity: Antiplatelet agents may enhance the adverse/toxic effects of drotrecogin alfa. Concurrent use of anticoagulants, other antiplatelet agents, dasatinib, NSAIDs, salicylates, or treprostinil may enhance the adverse/toxic effects of antiplatelet agents.

Ethanol/Nutrition/Herb Interactions

Ethanol: May increase CNS adverse effects.

Food: No clinically significant effect on absorption.

Herb/Nutraceutical: Avoid herbs with anticoagulant/antiplatelet properties (alfalfa, anise, bilberry, bladderwrack, bromelain, cat's claw, celery, chamomile, coleus, cordyceps, dong quai, evening primrose oil, fenugreek, feverfew, garlic, ginger, ginkgo biloba, ginseng [American], ginseng [Panax], ginseng [Siberian], grape seed, green tea, guggul, horse chestnut seed, horseradish, licorice, prickly ash, red clover, reishi, SAMe [S-adenosylmethionine], sweet clover, turmeric, white willow); may enhance the adverse effect of antiplatelets agents.

Storage/Stability Store at 15°C to 30°C (59°F to 86°F). Protect from light.

Mechanism of Action Anagrelide appears to inhibit cyclic nucleotide phosphodiesterase and the release of arachidonic acid from phospholipase, possibly by inhibiting phospholipase A_2. It also causes a dose-related reduction in platelet production, which results from decreased megakaryocyte hypermaturation. The drug disrupts the postmitotic phase of maturation.

Pharmacodynamics/Kinetics

Onset: Initial: Within 7-14 days; complete response (platelets ≤600,000/mm^3): 4-12 weeks

Duration: 6-24 hours; upon discontinuation, platelet count begins to rise within 4 days

Metabolism: Hepatic; to RL603 and 3-hydroxy anagrelide

Half-life elimination, plasma: 1.3 hours

Time to peak, serum: 1 hour

Excretion: Urine (<1% as unchanged drug)

Dosage Note: Maintain for ≥1 week, then adjust to the lowest effective dose to reduce and maintain platelet count <600,000/μL ideally to the normal range; the dose must not be increased by >0.5 mg/day in any 1 week; maximum dose: 10 mg/day or 2.5 mg/dose

Oral: Thrombocythemia:

Children: Initial: 0.5 mg/day (range: 0.5 mg 1-4 times/day)

Adults: 0.5 mg 4 times/day or 1 mg twice daily (most patients will experience adequate response at dose ranges of 1.5-3 mg/day)

Elderly: There are no special requirements for dosing in the elderly

Dosage adjustment in hepatic impairment:

Moderate impairment: Initial: 0.5 mg once daily; maintain for at least 1 week with careful monitoring of cardiovascular status; the dose must not be increased by >0.5 mg/day in any 1 week.

Severe impairment: Contraindicated

Administration Administer 2-4 times/day. May be taken without regard to food.

Monitoring Parameters Platelet count (every 2 days during the first week of treatment and at least weekly until the maintenance dose is reached); CBC with differential, ALT, AST, BUN, and serum creatinine (monitor closely during first weeks of treatment); blood pressure; cardiovascular exam (pretreatment; monitor during therapy). Monitor for thrombosis or bleeding.

Dietary Considerations May be taken without regard to food.

Emetic Potential Low (10% to 30%)

Dosage Forms Excipient information presented when available (limited, particularly for generics); consult specific product labeling.

Capsule: 0.5 mg, 1 mg

Agrylin®: 0.5 mg, 1 mg

References

Anagrelide Study Group, "Anagrelide, a Therapy for Thrombocythemic States: Experience in 577 Patients," *Am J Med*, 1992, 92:69-76.

Brooks WG, Stanley DD, and Goode JV, "Role of Anagrelide in the Treatment of Thrombocytosis," *Ann Pharmacother*, 1999, 33(10):1116-8, 1121.

Dingli D and Tefferi A, "Anagrelide: An Update on its Mechanisms of Action and Therapeutic Potential," *Expert Rev Anticancer Ther*, 2004, 4(4):533-41.

Doubek M, Brychtova Y, Doubek R, et al, "Anagrelide Therapy in Pregnancy: Report of a Case of Essential Thrombocythemia," *Ann Hematol*, 2004, 83(11):726-7.

Harrison CN, Campbell PJ, Buck G, et al, "Hydroxyurea Compared With Anagrelide in High-Risk Essential Thrombocythemia," *N Engl J Med*, 2005, 353(1):33-45.

Pescatore SL and Lindley C, "Anagrelide: A Novel Agent for the Treatment of Myeloproliferative Disorders," *Expert Opin Pharmacother*, 2000, 1(3):537-46.

Petitt RM, Silverstein MN, and Petrone ME, "Anagrelide for Control of Thrombocythemia in Polycythemia and Other Myeloproliferative Disorders," *Semin Hematol*, 1997, 34(1):51-4.

Spencer CM and Brogden RN, "Anagrelide. A Review of Its Pharmacodynamic and Pharmacokinetic Properties, and Therapeutic Potential in the Treatment of Thrombocythaemia," *Drugs*, 1994, 47(5):809-22.

Steurer M, Gastl G, Jedrzejczak WW, et al, Anagrelide for Thrombocytosis in Myeloproliferative Disorders: A Prospective Study to Assess Efficacy and Adverse Event Profile," *Cancer*, 2004, 101(10):2239-46.

♦ **Anagrelide Hydrochloride** *see* Anagrelide *on page 87*

♦ **Anandron® (Can)** *see* Nilutamide *on page 812*

Anastrozole *(an AS troe zole)*

Related Information

Safe Handling of Hazardous Drugs *on page 1382*

(Continued)

Anastrozole *(Continued)*

U.S. Brand Names Arimidex®

Index Terms ICI-D1033; NSC-719344; ZD1033

Generic Available No

Canadian Brand Names Arimidex®

Pharmacologic Category Antineoplastic Agent, Aromatase Inhibitor

Use Treatment of locally-advanced or metastatic breast cancer (ER-positive or hormone receptor unknown) in postmenopausal women; treatment of advanced breast cancer in postmenopausal women with disease progression following tamoxifen therapy; adjuvant treatment of early ER-positive breast cancer in postmenopausal women

Pregnancy Risk Factor D

Lactation Excretion in breast milk unknown/use caution

Labeled Contraindications Hypersensitivity to anastrozole or any component of the formulation; pregnancy

Warnings/Precautions Hazardous agent - use appropriate precautions for handling and disposal. Use with caution in patients with hyperlipidemias; total cholesterol and LDL-cholesterol increase in patients receiving anastrozole. Exclude pregnancy before initiating therapy. Anastrozole may be associated with a reduction in bone mineral density. Safety and efficacy in premenopausal women or pediatric patients have not been established.

Adverse Reactions

>10%:

Cardiovascular: Vasodilatation (25% to 36%), hypertension (2% to 13%)

Central nervous system: Mood disturbance (19%), fatigue (19%), pain (11% to 17%), headache (9% to 13%), depression (5% to 13%)

Dermatologic: Rash (6% to 11%)

Endocrine & metabolic: Hot flashes (12% to 36%)

Gastrointestinal: Nausea (11% to 19%), vomiting (8% to 13%)

Neuromuscular & skeletal: Weakness (16% to 19%), arthritis (17%), arthralgia (2% to 15%), back pain (10% to 12%), bone pain (6% to 11%), osteoporosis (11%)

Respiratory: Pharyngitis (6% to 14%), cough increased (8% to 11%)

1% to 10%:

Cardiovascular: Peripheral edema (5% to 10%), chest pain (5% to 7%), ischemic cardiovascular disease (4%), venous thromboembolic events (3% to 4%), ischemic cerebrovascular events (2%), angina (2%)

Central nervous system: Insomnia (2% to 10%), dizziness (6% to 8%), anxiety (2% to 6%), fever (2% to 5%), malaise (2% to 5%), confusion (2% to 5%), nervousness (2% to 5%), somnolence (2% to 5%), lethargy (1%)

Dermatologic: Alopecia (2% to 5%), pruritus (2% to 5%)

Endocrine & metabolic: Hypercholesterolemia (9%), breast pain (2% to 8%)

Gastrointestinal: Constipation (7% to 9%), abdominal pain (7% to 9%), diarrhea (8% to 9%), anorexia (5% to 7%), xerostomia (6%), dyspepsia (7%), weight gain (2% to 9%), weight loss (2% to 5%)

Genitourinary: Urinary tract infection (2% to 8%), vulvovaginitis (6%), pelvic pain (5%), vaginal bleeding (1% to 5%), vaginitis (4%), vaginal discharge (4%), vaginal hemorrhage (2% to 4%), leukorrhea (2% to 3%), vaginal dryness (2%)

Hematologic: Anemia (2% to 5%), leukopenia (2% to 5%)

Hepatic: Liver function tests increased (2% to 5%), alkaline phosphatase increased (2% to 5%), gamma GT increased (2% to 5%)

Local: Thrombophlebitis (2% to 5%)

Neuromuscular & skeletal: Fracture (2% to 10%), arthrosis (7%), paresthesia (5% to 7%), joint disorder (6%), myalgia (2% to 6%), neck pain (2% to 5%), hypertonia (3%)

Ocular: Cataracts (6%)

Respiratory: Dyspnea (8% to 10%), sinusitis (2% to 6%), bronchitis (2% to 5%), rhinitis (2% to 5%)

Miscellaneous: Lymph edema (10%), infection (2% to 9%), flu-like syndrome (2% to 7%), diaphoresis (2% to 5%), cyst (5%), tumor flare (3%)

<1%, postmarketing, and/or case reports: Anaphylaxis, angioedema, CVA, cerebral ischemia, cerebral infarct, endometrial cancer, erythema multiforme, joint pain, joint stiffness, MI, myocardial ischemia, pulmonary embolus, retinal vein thrombosis, Stevens-Johnson syndrome, urticaria

Overdosage/Toxicology Symptoms of overdose include severe irritation to the stomach (necrosis, gastritis, ulceration, and hemorrhage). Treatment is symptom-directed and supportive. Dialysis may be helpful because anastrozole is not highly protein bound.

Drug Interactions

Cytochrome P450 Effect: Inhibits CYP1A2 (weak), 2C8 (weak), 2C9 (weak), 3A4 (weak)

Decreased Effect: Estrogen derivatives and tamoxifen may decrease the levels/effects of anastrozole.

Ethanol/Nutrition/Herb Interactions Herb/Nutraceutical: Avoid black cohosh, hops, licorice, red clover, thyme, and dong quai.

Storage/Stability Store at 20°C to 25°C (68°F to 77°F).

Mechanism of Action Potent and selective nonsteroidal aromatase inhibitor. By inhibiting aromatase, the conversion of androstenedione to estrone, and testosterone to estradiol, is prevented. Anastrozole causes an 85% decrease in estrone sulfate levels.

Pharmacodynamics/Kinetics

Onset of estradiol reduction: 70% reduction after 24 hours; 80% after 2 weeks therapy

Duration of estradiol reduction: 6 days

Absorption: Well absorbed; not affected by food

Protein binding, plasma: 40%

Metabolism: Extensively hepatic (~85%) via N-dealkylation, hydroxylation, and glucuronidation; primary metabolite inactive

Half-life elimination: ~50 hours

Excretion: Urine (10% as unchanged drug; 60% as metabolites)

Dosage Breast cancer: Adults: Oral (refer to individual protocols): 1 mg once daily

Dosage adjustment in renal impairment: Dosage adjustment not necessary

Dosage adjustment in hepatic impairment: Mild-to-moderate impairment: Plasma concentrations in subjects with stable hepatic cirrhosis were within the range concentrations in normal subjects across all clinical trials; therefore, no dosage adjustment required; however, patients should be monitored for side effects. Safety and efficacy in severe hepatic impairment have not been established.

Monitoring Parameters Bone mineral density; total cholesterol and LDL

Test Interactions Lab test abnormalities: GGT, AST, ALT, alkaline phosphatase, total cholesterol, and LDL increased; threefold elevations of mean serum GGT levels have been observed among patients with liver metastases. These changes were likely related to the progression of liver metastases in these patients, although other contributing factors could not be ruled

(Continued)

Anastrozole *(Continued)*

out. Mean serum total cholesterol levels increased by 0.5 mmol/L among patients.

Special Geriatric Considerations No age-related changes in pharmacokinetics were noted in clinical trials.

Emetic Potential Very low (<10%)

Dosage Forms Excipient information presented when available (limited, particularly for generics); consult specific product labeling.

Tablet:

Arimidex®: 1 mg

References

Boeddinghaus IM and Dowsett M, "Comparative Clinical Pharmacology and Pharmacokinetic Interactions of Aromatase Inhibitors," *J Steroid Biochem Mol Biol*, 2001, 79(1-5):85-91.

Buzdar AU, Robertson JF, Eiermann W, et al, "An Overview of the Pharmacology and Pharmacokinetics of the Newer Generation Aromatase Inhibitors Anastrozole, Letrozole, and Exemestane," *Cancer*, 2002, 95(9):2006-16.

Higa GM and AlKhouri N, "Anastrozole: A Selective Aromatase Inhibitor for the Treatment of Breast Cancer," *Am J Health Syst Pharm*, 1998, 55(5):445-52.

Kendall A, Dowsett M, Folkerd E, et al, "Caution: Vaginal Estradiol Appears to be Contraindicated in Postmenopausal Women on Adjuvant Aromatase Inhibitors," *Ann Oncol*, 2006, 17(4):584-7.

Koberle D and Thurlimann B, "Anastrozole: Pharmacological and Clinical Profile in Postmenopausal Women With Breast Cancer," *Expert Rev Anticancer Ther*, 2001, 1(2):169-76.

Lonning PE, Geisler J, and Dowsett M, "Pharmacological and Clinical Profile of Anastrozole," *Breast Cancer Res Treat*, 1998, 49(Suppl 1):53-7.

Njar VC and Brodie AM, "Comprehensive Pharmacology and Clinical Efficacy of Aromatase Inhibitors," *Drugs*, 1999, 58(2):233-55.

- ◆ **Ancobon®** *see Flucytosine on page 454*
- ◆ **Androcur® (Can)** *see Cyproterone on page 267*
- ◆ **Androcur® Depot (Can)** *see Cyproterone on page 267*
- ◆ **131 I Anti-B1 Antibody** *see Tositumomab and Iodine I 131 Tositumomab on page 1056*
- ◆ **131 I-Anti-B1 Monoclonal Antibody** *see Tositumomab and Iodine I 131 Tositumomab on page 1056*
- ◆ **Anti-CD20 Monoclonal Antibody** *see Rituximab on page 953*
- ◆ **Anti-CD20-Murine Monoclonal Antibody I-131** *see Tositumomab and Iodine I 131 Tositumomab on page 1056*

Antihemophilic Factor (Human)

(an tee hee moe FIL ik FAK tor HYU man)

U.S. Brand Names Hemofil M; Koāte®-DVI; Monarc-M™; Monoclate-P®

Index Terms AHF (Human); Factor VIII (Human)

Generic Available Yes

Canadian Brand Names Hemofil M

Pharmacologic Category Antihemophilic Agent; Blood Product Derivative

Use Prevention and treatment of hemorrhagic episodes in patients with hemophilia A (classic hemophilia); perioperative management of hemophilia A; can be of significant therapeutic value in patients with acquired factor VIII inhibitors not exceeding 10 Bethesda units/mL

Pregnancy Risk Factor C

Lactation Excretion in breast milk unknown/use caution

Labeled Contraindications Hypersensitivity to any component of the formulation

Warnings/Precautions [U.S. Boxed Warning]: Risk of viral transmission is not totally eradicated. Because antihemophilic factor is prepared

from pooled plasma, it may contain the causative agent of viral hepatitis and other viral diseases. Hepatitis B vaccination is recommended for all patients. Hepatitis A vaccination is also recommended for seronegative patients. Antihemophilic factor contains trace amounts of blood groups A and B isohemagglutinins and when large or frequently repeated doses are given to individuals with blood groups A, B, and AB, the patient should be monitored for signs of progressive anemia and the possibility of intravascular hemolysis should be considered. The dosage requirement will vary in patients with factor VIII inhibitors; optimal treatment should be determined by clinical response. Natural rubber latex is a component of Hemofil M and Monarc-M™ packaging. Hemofil M, Monoclate-P®, and Monarc-M™ contain trace amounts of mouse protein. Products contain naturally-occurring von Willebrand factor for stabilization, however efficacy has not been established for the treatment of von Willebrand disease. Products vary by preparation method; final formulations contain human albumin.

Adverse Reactions <1%: Acute hemolytic anemia, AHF inhibitor development, allergic reactions (rare), anaphylaxis (rare), bleeding tendency increased, blurred vision, chest tightness, chills, fever, headache, hyperfibrinogenemia, jittery feeling, lethargy, nausea, somnolence, stinging at the infusion site, stomach discomfort, tingling, urticaria, vasomotor reactions with rapid infusion, vomiting

Overdosage/Toxicology Massive doses have been reported to cause acute hemolytic anemia, increased bleeding tendency, or hyperfibrinogenemia. Occurrence is rare.

Storage/Stability Store under refrigeration, 2°C to 8°C (36°F to 46°F); avoid freezing. Use within 3 hours of reconstitution. Do not refrigerate after reconstitution, precipitation may occur.

Hemofil M, Monarc-M™: May also be stored at room temperature not to exceed 30°C (86°F).

Koāte®-DVI; Monoclate-P®: May also be stored at room temperature of 25°C (77°F) for ≤6 months.

Reconstitution If refrigerated, the dried concentrate and diluent should be warmed to room temperature before reconstitution. Gently swirl or rotate vial after adding diluent; do not shake vigorously.

Mechanism of Action Protein (factor VIII) in normal plasma which is necessary for clot formation and maintenance of hemostasis; activates factor X in conjunction with activated factor IX; activated factor X converts prothrombin to thrombin, which converts fibrinogen to fibrin, and with factor XIII forms a stable clot

Pharmacodynamics/Kinetics Half-life elimination: Mean: 8-27 hours

Dosage Children and Adults: I.V.: Individualize dosage based on coagulation studies performed prior to treatment and at regular intervals during treatment. In general, administration of factor VIII 1 int. unit/kg will increase circulating factor VIII levels by ~2 int. units/dL. (General guidelines presented; consult individual product labeling for specific dosing recommendations.)

Dosage based on desired factor VIII increase (%):

To calculate dosage needed based on desired factor VIII increase (%):

Body weight (kg) x 0.5 int. units/kg x desired factor VIII increase (%) = int. units factor VIII required

For example:

50 kg x 0.5 int. units/kg x 30 (% increase) = 750 int. units factor VIII (Continued)

Antihemophilic Factor (Human) *(Continued)*

Dosage based on expected factor VIII increase (%):

It is also possible to calculate the **expected** % factor VIII increase:

(# int. units administered x 2%/int. units/kg) divided by body weight (kg) = expected % factor VIII increase

For example:

(1400 int. units x 2%/int. units/kg) divided by 70 kg = 40%

General guidelines:

Minor hemorrhage: 10-20 int. units/kg as a single dose to achieve FVIII plasma level ~20% to 40% of normal. Mild superficial or early hemorrhages may respond to a single dose; may repeat dose every 12-24 hours for 1-3 days until bleeding is resolved or healing achieved.

Moderate hemorrhage/minor surgery: 15-25 int. units/kg to achieve FVIII plasma level 30% to 50% of normal. If needed, may continue with a maintenance dose of 10-15 int. units/kg every 8-12 hours.

Major to life-threatening hemorrhage: Initial dose 40-50 int. units/kg, followed by a maintenance dose of 20-25 int. units/kg every 8-12 hours until threat is resolved, to achieve FVIII plasma level 80% to 100% of normal.

Major surgery: 50 int. units/kg given preoperatively to raise factor VIII level to 100% before surgery begins. May repeat as necessary after 6-12 hours initially and for a total of 10-14 days until healing is complete. Intensity of therapy may depend on type of surgery and postoperative regimen.

Bleeding prophylaxis: May be administered on a regular basis for bleeding prophylaxis. Doses of 24-40 int. units/kg 3 times/week have been reported in patients with severe hemophilia to prevent joint bleeding.

If bleeding is not controlled with adequate dose, test for presence of inhibitor. It may not be possible or practical to control bleeding if inhibitor titers are >10 Bethesda units/mL.

Elderly: Response in the elderly is not expected to differ from that of younger patients; dosage should be individualized

Administration Administer I.V. over 5-10 minutes (maximum: 10 mL/minute). Infuse Monoclate-P® at 2 mL/minute.

Monitoring Parameters Heart rate and blood pressure (before and during I.V. administration); AHF levels prior to and during treatment; in patients with circulating inhibitors, the inhibitor level should be monitored; hematocrit; monitor for signs and symptoms of intravascular hemolysis; bleeding

Patient Information This medication can only be given intravenously. Report sudden-onset headache, rash, chest or back pain, wheezing, or respiratory difficulties, hives, itching, low grade fever, nausea, vomiting, tiredness, or decreased appetite to prescriber. Wear identification indicating that you have a hemophilic condition.

Special Geriatric Considerations Response in the elderly is not expected to differ from that of younger patients; dosage should be individualized.

Dosage Forms Excipient information presented when available (limited, particularly for generics); consult specific product labeling.

Injection, powder for reconstitution:

Hemofil M: Vial labeled with international units [contains albumin; derived from mouse proteins; packaging may contain natural rubber latex]

Koate®-DVI: ~250 int. units, ~500 int. units, ~1000 int. units [contains albumin]

Monarc-M™: Vial labeled with international units [contains albumin; derived from mouse proteins; packaging may contain natural rubber latex]

Monoclate-P®: ~250 int. units, ~500 int. units, ~1000 int. units, ~1500 int. units [contains albumin; derived from mouse proteins]

References

Abildgaard CF, Simone JV, Corrigan JJ, et al, "Treatment of Hemophilia With Glycine-Precipitated Factor VIII," N Engl J Med, 1966, 275(9):471-5.

Berntorp E, "Impact of Replacement Therapy on the Evolution of HIV Infection in Hemophiliacs," Thromb Haemost, 1994, 71(6):678-83.

Lusher JM, "Transfusion Therapy in Congenital Coagulopathies," Hematol Oncol Clin North Am, 1994, 8(6):1167-80.

Manucci PM, "Impact of Recombinant Factor VIII on Hemophilia Care," Vox Sang, 1994, 67(Suppl 3):49-52.

Nilsson IM, Berntorp E, Lofqvist T, et al, "Twenty-five Years' Experience of Prophylactic Treatment in Severe Haemophilia A and B," J Intern Med, 1992, 232(1):25-32.

Peterson CW, "Treating Hemophilia," Am Pharm, 1994, NS34(8):57-67.

White GC, Rosendaal F, Aledort LM, et al, "Definitions in Hemophilia. Recommendation of the Scientific Subcommittee on Factor VIII and Factor IX of the Scientific and Standardization Committee of the International Society on Thrombosis and Haemostasis," Thromb Haemost, 2001, 85(3):560.

Antihemophilic Factor (Recombinant)

(an tee hee moe FIL ik FAK tor ree KOM be nant)

U.S. Brand Names Advate; Helixate® FS; Kogenate® FS; Recombinate; ReFacto®

Index Terms AHF (Recombinant); Factor VIII (Recombinant); rAHF

Generic Available No

Canadian Brand Names Helixate® FS; Kogenate®; Kogenate® FS; Recombinate; ReFacto®

Pharmacologic Category Antihemophilic Agent

Use Prevention and treatment of hemorrhagic episodes in patients with hemophilia A (classic hemophilia); perioperative management of hemophilia A; can be of significant therapeutic value in patients with acquired factor VIII inhibitors ≤10 Bethesda units/mL

Pregnancy Risk Factor C

Lactation Excretion in breast milk unknown/use caution

Labeled Contraindications Hypersensitivity to any component of the formulation

Warnings/Precautions Monitor for signs of formation of antibodies to factor VIII; may occur at anytime but more common in young children with severe hemophilia. The dosage requirement will vary in patients with factor VIII inhibitors; optimal treatment should be determined by clinical response. Monitor for allergic hypersensitivity reactions. Products vary by preparation method. Recombinate is stabilized using human albumin. Helixate® FS and Kogenate® FS are stabilized with sucrose. Advate, Helixate® FS, Kogenate® FS and ReFacto® may contain trace amounts of mouse or hamster protein. Recombinate may contain mouse, hamster or bovine protein. Products may contain von Willebrand factor for stabilization; however, efficacy has not been established for the treatment of von Willebrand's disease.

Adverse Reactions Actual frequency may vary by product.

>1%:

Central nervous system: Chills, dizziness, fever, headache, pain

Dermatologic: Pruritus

Gastrointestinal: Nausea, taste perversion

Hematologic: Hemorrhage

Local: Injection site pain

Neuromuscular & skeletal: Arthralgia, weakness

Respiratory: Cough, dyspnea, nasopharyngitis, pharyngolaryngeal pain

Miscellaneous: Catheter thrombosis, factor VIII inhibitor formation

(Continued)

Antihemophilic Factor (Recombinant) *(Continued)*

≤1%, postmarketing, and/or case reports: Abdominal pain, adenopathy, allergic reactions, anaphylaxis, anemia, anorexia, arthralgia, AST increased, chest discomfort, chest pain, constipation, depersonalization, diaphoresis, diarrhea, edema, epistaxis, facial flushing, factor VIII decreased, fatigue, fever, GI hemorrhage, hot flashes, hyper-/hypotension (slight), infection, injection site reactions, joint swelling, lethargy, otitis media, pallor, rash, rhinitis, rigors, somnolence, urinary tract infection, urticaria, vasodilation, venous catheter access complications, vomiting

Overdosage/Toxicology Massive doses of antihemophilic factor (human) have been reported to cause acute hemolytic anemia, increased bleeding tendency, or hyperfibrinogenemia. Occurrence is rare.

Storage/Stability Store under refrigeration, 2°C to 8°C (36°F to 46°F); avoid freezing. Use within 3 hours of reconstitution. Do not refrigerate after reconstitution, a precipitation may occur.

  Advate: May also be stored at room temperature for up to 6 months.

  Helixate® FS, Kogenate® FS, ReFacto®: May also be stored at room temperature for up to 3 months; avoid prolonged exposure to light during storage.

  Recombinate: May also be stored at room temperature, not to exceed 30°C (86°F).

Reconstitution If refrigerated, the dried concentrate and diluent should be warmed to room temperature before reconstitution. Gently swirl or rotate vial after adding diluent, do not shake vigorously.

Mechanism of Action Factor VIII replacement, necessary for clot formation and maintenance of hemostasis. It activates factor X in conjunction with activated factor IX; activated factor X converts prothrombin to thrombin, which converts fibrinogen to fibrin, and with factor XIII forms a stable clot.

Pharmacodynamics/Kinetics

  Distribution: V_{ss}: 0.36-0.57 dL/kg

  Half-life elimination: Mean: 8-19 hours

Dosage Children and Adults: I.V.: Individualize dosage based on coagulation studies performed prior to treatment and at regular intervals during treatment. In general, administration of factor VIII 1 int. unit/kg will increase circulating factor VIII levels by ~2 int. units/dL. (General guidelines presented; consult individual product labeling for specific dosing recommendations.)

Dosage based on desired factor VIII increase (%):

  To calculate dosage needed based on desired factor VIII increase (%):

   [Body weight (kg) x desired factor VIII increase (%)] divided by 2%/int. units/kg = int. units factor VIII required

  For example:

   50 kg x 30 (% increase) divided by 2%/int. units/kg = 750 int. units factor VIII

Dosage based on expected factor VIII increase (%):

  It is also possible to calculate the **expected** % factor VIII increase:

   (# int. units administered x 2%/int. units/kg) divided by body weight (kg) = expected % factor VIII increase

  For example:

   (1400 int. units x 2%/int. units/kg) divided by 70 kg = 40%

General guidelines:

Minor hemorrhage: 10-20 int. units/kg as a single dose to achieve FVIII plasma level ~20% to 40% of normal. Mild superficial or early hemorrhages may respond to a single dose; may repeat dose every 12-24 hours for 1-3 days until bleeding is resolved or healing achieved.

Moderate hemorrhage/minor surgery: 15-30 int. units/kg to achieve FVIII plasma level 30% to 60% of normal. May repeat 1 dose at 12-24 hours if needed. Some products suggest continuing for ≥3 days until pain and disability are resolved

Major to life-threatening hemorrhage: Initial dose 40-50 int. units/kg followed by a maintenance dose of 20-25 int. units/kg every 8-24 hours until threat is resolved, to achieve FVIII plasma level 60% to 100% of normal.

Major surgery: 50 int. units/kg given preoperatively to raise factor VIII level to 100% before surgery begins. May repeat as necessary after 6-12 hours initially and for a total of 10-14 days until healing is complete. Intensity of therapy may depend on type of surgery and postoperative regimen.

Bleeding prophylaxis: May be administered on a regular basis for bleeding prophylaxis. Doses of 24-40 int. units/kg 3 times/week have been reported in patients with severe hemophilia to prevent joint bleeding.

If bleeding is not controlled with adequate dose, test for presence of inhibitor. It may not be possible or practical to control bleeding if inhibitor titers >10 Bethesda units/mL.

Elderly: Response in the elderly is not expected to differ from that of younger patients; dosage should be individualized

Administration I.V. infusion over 5-10 minutes (maximum: 10 mL/minute). Advate: Infuse over ≤5 minutes (maximum: 10 mL/minute).

Monitoring Parameters Heart rate and blood pressure (before and during I.V. administration); AHF levels prior to and during treatment; development of factor VIII inhibitors; bleeding

Dietary Considerations Advate contains sodium 108 mEq/L; Helixate® FS and Kogenate® FS contain sodium 27-36 mEq/L; Recombinate contains sodium 180 mEq/L

Patient Information This medication can only be given intravenously. Report hives, itching, wheezing, sudden-onset headache, rash, chest or back pain, or other respiratory difficulties to prescriber. Wear identification indicating that you have a hemophilic condition.

Special Geriatric Considerations Response in the elderly is not expected to differ from that of younger patients; dosage should be individualized.

Dosage Forms Excipient information presented when available (limited, particularly for generics); consult specific product labeling.

Injection, powder for reconstitution, recombinant [preservative free]:

Advate: 250 int. units, 500 int. units, 1000 int. units, 1500 int. units, 2000 int. units, 3000 int. units [plasma/albumin free; contains sodium 108 mEq/L, mannitol; derived from hamster or mouse proteins]

Helixate® FS: 250 int. units, 500 int. units, 1000 int. units [albumin free; contains sucrose 28 mg/vial, sodium 27-36 mEq/L; derived from hamster or mouse protein]

Kogenate® FS: 250 int. units, 500 int. units, 1000 int. units, 2000 int. units [albumin free; contains sucrose 28-56 mg/vial, sodium 27-36 mEq/L; derived from hamster or mouse protein]

Recombinate: 250 int. units, 500 units, 1000 int. units [contains human albumin, sodium 180 mEq/L; derived from bovine, hamster or mouse proteins; packaging contains natural rubber latex]

(Continued)

Antihemophilic Factor (Recombinant) *(Continued)*

ReFacto®: 250 int. units, 500 units, 1000 int. units, 2000 int. units [contains sucrose; derived from hamster or mouse proteins]

References

Abildgaard CF, Simone JV, Corrigan JJ, et al, "Treatment of Hemophilia With Glycine-Precipitated Factor VIII," *N Engl J Med*, 1966, 275(9):471-5.

Berntorp E, "Impact of Replacement Therapy on the Evolution of HIV Infection in Hemophiliacs," *Thromb Haemost*, 1994, 71(6):678-83.

Lusher JM, "Transfusion Therapy in Congenital Coagulopathies," *Hematol Oncol Clin North Am*, 1994, 8(6):1167-80.

Manucci PM, "Impact of Recombinant Factor VIII on Hemophilia Care," *Vox Sang*, 1994, 67(Suppl 3):49-52.

Nilsson IM, Berntorp E, Lofqvist T, et al, "Twenty-five Years' Experience of Prophylactic Treatment in Severe Haemophilia A and B," *J Intern Med*, 1992, 232(1):25-32.

Peterson CW, "Treating Hemophilia," *Am Pharm*, 1994, NS34(8):57-67.

White GC, Rosendaal F, Aledort LM, et al, "Definitions in Hemophilia. Recommendation of the Scientific Subcommittee on Factor VIII and Factor IX of the Scientific and Standardization Committee of the International Society on Thrombosis and Haemostasis," *Thromb Haemost*, 2001, 85(3):560.

Antithrombin III *(an tee THROM bin three)*

U.S. Brand Names Thrombate III®

Index Terms AT-III; Heparin Cofactor I

Generic Available No

Canadian Brand Names Thrombate III®

Pharmacologic Category Anticoagulant; Blood Product Derivative

Use Treatment of hereditary antithrombin III deficiency in connection with surgical procedures, obstetrical procedures, or thromboembolism

Unlabeled/Investigational Use Acquired antithrombin III deficiencies related to disseminated intravascular coagulation (DIC)

Pregnancy Risk Factor B

Lactation Excretion in breast milk unknown/use caution

Labeled Contraindications Hypersensitivity to any component of the formulation

Warnings/Precautions Product of human plasma; may potentially contain infectious agents which could transmit disease; screening of donors, as well as testing and/or inactivation or removal of certain viruses, reduces this risk. Infections thought to be transmitted by this product should be reported to Talecris Biotherapeutics at 1-800-520-2807. Safety and efficacy in children have not been established.

Adverse Reactions

1% to 10%: Central nervous system: Dizziness (2%)

<1%: Bowel fullness, chest pain, chest tightness, chills, cramps, dyspnea, fever, film over eye, foul taste, hematoma, hives, lightheadedness, nausea

Drug Interactions

Increased Effect/Toxicity: Heparin's anticoagulant effects are potentiated by antithrombin III (half-life of antithrombin III is decreased by heparin). Risk of hemorrhage with antithrombin III may be increased by drotrecogin alfa, thrombolytic agents, oral anticoagulants (warfarin), treprostinil, and drugs which affect platelet function (eg, aspirin, NSAIDs, dipyridamole, ticlopidine, clopidogrel, and IIb/IIIa antagonists).

Ethanol/Nutrition/Herb Interactions Herb/Nutraceutical: Recent use/intake of herbs with anticoagulant or antiplatelet activity (including cat's claw, dong quai, evening primrose, garlic, ginkgo and ginseng) may increase the risk of bleeding.

Storage/Stability Store vials under refrigeration at 2°C to 8°C (36°F to 46°F); avoid freezing. Bring drug and diluent to room temperature prior to reconstitution. Administer within 3 hours of mixing.

Reconstitution Reconstitute with sterile water for injection. Do not shake; swirl to mix to avoid foaming. Filter through sterile filter needle provided prior to administration.

Mechanism of Action Antithrombin III is the primary physiologic inhibitor of *in vivo* coagulation. It is an alpha₂-globulin. Its principal actions are the inactivation of thrombin, plasmin, and other active serine proteases of coagulation, including factors IXa, Xa, XIa, and XIIa. The inactivation of proteases is a major step in the normal clotting process. The strong activation of clotting enzymes at the site of every bleeding injury facilitates fibrin formation and maintains normal hemostasis. Thrombosis in the circulation would be caused by active serine proteases if they were not inhibited by antithrombin III after the localized clotting process.

Pharmacodynamics/Kinetics Half-life elimination: Biologic: 2.5 days (immunologic assay); 3.8 days (functional AT-III assay). Half-life may be decreased following surgery, with hemorrhage, acute thrombosis, and/or during heparin administration.

Dosage Adults:

Initial dose: Dosing is individualized based on pretherapy AT-III levels. The initial dose should raise antithrombin III levels (AT-III) to 120% and may be calculated based on the following formula:

[desired AT-III level % - baseline AT-III level %] x body weight (kg) divided by 1.4%/int. units/kg

For example, if a 70 kg adult patient had a baseline AT-III level of 57%, the initial dose would be

[(120% - 57%) x 70] divided by 1.4 = 3150 int. units

Maintenance dose: Subsequent dosing should be targeted to keep levels between 80% to 120% which may be achieved by administering 60% of the initial dose every 24 hours. Adjustments may be made by adjusting dose or interval. Maintain level within normal range for 2-8 days depending on type of procedure.

Administration I.V.: Infuse over 10-20 minutes.

Monitoring Parameters Monitor antithrombin III peak and trough levels (preinfusion and 20 minutes postinfusion) for each dose and monitor levels 12 hours after initial loading dose; liver function tests; monitor antithrombin III levels in neonates of parents with hereditary antithrombin III deficiency immediately after birth

Dietary Considerations Contains sodium 110-210 mEq/L

Additional Information Thromboembolism has been reported in children of women with hereditary antithrombin III (AT-III) deficiency; AT-III levels in neonates of parents with hereditary AT-III deficiency should be measured immediately after birth. Plasma AT-III levels are typically lower in neonates and infants than in adults. Low plasma AT-III levels in neonates may not be indicative of deficiency; consultation with a coagulation expert is recommended.

Dosage Forms Excipient information presented when available (limited, particularly for generics); consult specific product labeling.

Injection, powder for reconstitution [preservative free]: 500 int. units, 1000 int. units [contains heparin, sodium chloride 110-210 mEq/L; packaged with diluent]

(Continued)

Antithrombin III (Continued)

References
Schwartz RS, Bauer KA, Rosenberg RD, et al, "Clinical Experience With Antithrombin III Concentrate in Treatment of Congenital and Acquired Deficiency of Antithrombin. The Antithrombin III Study Group," *Am J Med*, 1989, 87(3B):53S-60S.

Antithymocyte Globulin (Equine)
(an te THY moe site GLOB yu lin, E kwine)

Medication Safety Issues

Sound-alike/look-alike issues:

Atgam® may be confused with Ativan®

U.S. Brand Names Atgam®

Index Terms Antithymocyte Immunoglobulin; ATG; Horse Antihuman Thymocyte Gamma Globulin; Lymphocyte Immune Globulin

Generic Available No

Canadian Brand Names Atgam®

Pharmacologic Category Immune Globulin; Immunosuppressant Agent

Use Prevention and treatment of acute renal allograft rejection; treatment of moderate to severe aplastic anemia in patients not considered suitable candidates for bone marrow transplantation

Unlabeled/Investigational Use Prevention and treatment of other solid organ allograft rejection; prevention of graft-versus-host disease following bone marrow transplantation

Pregnancy Risk Factor C

Lactation Excretion in breast milk unknown/use caution

Labeled Contraindications Hypersensitivity to lymphocytic immune globulin, any component of the formulation, or other equine gamma globulins

Warnings/Precautions For I.V. use only. Must be administered via central line due to chemical phlebitis. **[U.S. Boxed Warning]: Should only be used by physicians experienced in immunosuppressive therapy or management of solid organ or bone marrow transplant patients. Adequate laboratory and supportive medical resources must be readily available in the facility for patient management.** Hypersensitivity and anaphylactic reactions can occur; immediate treatment (including epinephrine 1:1000) should be available. Rash, dyspnea, hypotension, or anaphylaxis precludes further administration of the drug. Discontinue if severe and unremitting thrombocytopenia and/or leukopenia occur. Dose must be administered over at least 4 hours. Patient may need to be pretreated with an antipyretic, antihistamine, and/or corticosteroid.

Adverse Reactions

>10%:

Central nervous system: Fever, chills

Dermatologic: Pruritus, rash, urticaria

Hematologic: Leukopenia, thrombocytopenia

1% to 10%:

Cardiovascular: Bradycardia, chest pain, CHF, edema, encephalitis, hyper-/hypotension, myocarditis, tachycardia

Central nervous system: Agitation, headache, lethargy, lightheadedness, listlessness, seizure

Gastrointestinal: Diarrhea, nausea, stomatitis, vomiting

Hepatic: Hepatosplenomegaly, liver function tests abnormal

Local: Pain at injection site, phlebitis, thrombophlebitis, burning soles/palms

Neuromuscular & skeletal: Myalgia, back pain, arthralgia

Ocular: Periorbital edema

Renal: Abnormal renal function tests

Respiratory: Dyspnea, respiratory distress

Miscellaneous: Anaphylaxis, serum sickness, viral infection, night sweats, diaphoresis, lymphadenopathy

<1%: Dizziness, epigastric pain, faintness, herpes simplex reactivation, hiccups, hyperglycemia, iliac vein obstruction, infection, laryngospasm, malaise, paresthesia, pulmonary edema, renal artery thrombosis, serum sickness, toxic epidermal necrosis, weakness, wound dehiscence

Postmarketing and/or case reports: Acute renal failure, anemia, aplasia, confusion, cough, deep vein thrombosis, disorientation, GI bleeding, granulocytopenia, hemolysis, kidney enlarged, neutropenia, nosebleed, pancytopenia, vasculitis

Storage/Stability Ampuls must be refrigerated; do not freeze. Diluted solution is stable for 24 hours (including infusion time) at refrigeration.

Reconstitution Dilute into inverted bottle of sterile vehicle to ensure that undiluted lymphocyte immune globulin does not contact air. Gently rotate or swirl to mix. Final concentration should be 4 mg/mL. May be diluted in NS, $D_5$1/4NS, $D_5$1/2NS.

Mechanism of Action May involve elimination of antigen-reactive T lymphocytes (killer cells) in peripheral blood or alteration of T-cell function

Pharmacodynamics/Kinetics

Distribution: Poorly into lymphoid tissues; binds to circulating lymphocytes, granulocytes, platelets, bone marrow cells

Half-life elimination, plasma: 1.5-12 days

Excretion: Urine ($\sim$1%)

Dosage An intradermal skin test is recommended prior to administration of the initial dose of ATG; use 0.1 mL of a 1:1000 dilution of ATG in normal saline. A positive skin reaction consists of a wheal ≥10 mm in diameter. If a positive skin test occurs, the first infusion should be administered in a controlled environment with intensive life support immediately available. A systemic reaction precludes further administration of the drug. The absence of a reaction does **not** preclude the possibility of an immediate sensitivity reaction.

Premedication with diphenhydramine, hydrocortisone, and acetaminophen is recommended prior to first dose.

Children: I.V.:

Aplastic anemia protocol: 10-20 mg/kg/day for 8-14 days; then administer every other day for 7 more doses; addition doses may be given every other day for 21 total doses in 28 days

Renal allograft: 5-25 mg/kg/day

Adults: I.V.:

Aplastic anemia protocol: 10-20 mg/kg/day for 8-14 days, then administer every other day for 7 more doses, for a total of 21 doses in 28 days

Renal allograft:

Rejection prophylaxis: 15 mg/kg/day for 14 days followed by 14 days of alternative day therapy at the same dose; the first dose should be administered within 24 hours before or after transplantation

Rejection treatment: 10-15 mg/kg/day for 14 days, then administer every other day for 10-14 days up to 21 doses in 28 days

Administration Infuse dose over at least 4 hours. Any severe systemic reaction to the skin test, such as generalized rash, tachycardia, dyspnea, hypotension, or anaphylaxis, should preclude further therapy. Epinephrine and resuscitative equipment should be nearby. Patient may need to be pretreated with an antipyretic, antihistamine, and/or corticosteroid. Mild itching and erythema can be treated with antihistamines. Infuse into a (Continued)

Antithymocyte Globulin (Equine) *(Continued)*

vascular shunt, arterial venous fistula, or high-flow central vein through a 0.2-1 micron in-line filter.

First dose: Premedicate with diphenhydramine orally 30 minutes prior to and hydrocortisone I.V. 15 minutes prior to infusion and acetaminophen 2 hours after start of infusion.

Monitoring Parameters Lymphocyte profile, CBC with differential and platelet count, vital signs during administration

Emetic Potential Very low (<10%)

Vesicant No

Dosage Forms Excipient information presented when available (limited, particularly for generics); consult specific product labeling.

Injection, solution:

Atgam®: 50 mg/mL (5 mL)

References

Rosenfeld SJ, Kimball J, Vining D, et al, "Intensive Immunosuppression With Antithymocyte Globulin and Cyclosporine as Treatment for Severe Acquired Aplastic Anemia," *Blood*, 1995, 85(11):3058-65.

Whitehead B, James I, Helms P, et al, "Intensive Care Management of Children Following Heart and Heart-Lung Transplantation," *Intensive Care Med*, 1990, 16(7):426-30.

Antithymocyte Globulin (Rabbit)

(an te THY moe site GLOB yu lin RAB bit)

Related Information

Hematopoietic Stem Cell Transplantation *on page 1366*

U.S. Brand Names Thymoglobulin®

Index Terms Antithymocyte Immunoglobulin; rATG

Generic Available No

Pharmacologic Category Immune Globulin; Immunosuppressant Agent

Use Treatment of acute rejection of renal transplant; used in conjunction with concomitant immunosuppression

Unlabeled/Investigational Use Induction therapy in renal transplant

Pregnancy Risk Factor C

Lactation Excretion in breast milk unknown/use caution

Labeled Contraindications Hypersensitivity to antithymocyte globulin, rabbit proteins, or any component of the formulation; acute viral illness

Warnings/Precautions [U.S. Boxed Warning]: Should only be used by physicians experienced in immunosuppressive therapy for the treatment of renal transplant patients. Medical surveillance is required during the infusion. Initial dose must be administered over at least 6 hours into a high flow vein; patient may need pretreatment with an antipyretic, antihistamine, and/or corticosteroid. Hypersensitivity and anaphylactic reactions can occur; immediate treatment (including epinephrine 1:1000) should be available. An increased incidence of lymphoma, post-transplant lymphoproliferative disease (PTLD), other malignancies, or severe infections may develop following concomitant use of immunosuppressants and prolonged use or overdose of antithymocyte globulin. Appropriate antiviral, antibacterial, antiprotozoal, and/or antifungal prophylaxis is recommended. Reversible neutropenia or thrombocytopenia may result from the development of cross-reactive antibodies.

Adverse Reactions

>10%:

Cardiovascular: Hypertension, peripheral edema, tachycardia

Central nervous system: Chills, fever, headache, pain, malaise

Endocrine & metabolic: Hyperkalemia

Gastrointestinal: Abdominal pain, diarrhea, nausea
Genitourinary: Urinary tract infection
Hematologic: Leukopenia, thrombocytopenia
Neuromuscular & skeletal: Weakness
Respiratory: Dyspnea
Miscellaneous: Antirabbit antibody development, sepsis, systemic infection
1% to 10%:
Central nervous system: Dizziness
Gastrointestinal: Gastritis, gastrointestinal moniliasis
Miscellaneous: Herpes simplex infection, moniliasis
Postmarketing and/or case reports: Anaphylaxis, cytokine release syndrome, PTLD, neutropenia, serum sickness (delayed)

Storage/Stability Store powder under refrigeration at 2°C to 8°C (36°F to 46°F); do not freeze. Protect from light. Use immediately following reconstitution.

Reconstitution Allow vials to reach room temperature, then reconstitute each vial with SWFI 5 mL. Rotate vial gently until dissolved. Prior to administration, further dilute one vial in 50 mL saline or dextrose (total volume is usually 50-500 mL depending on total number of vials needed per dose). Mix by gently inverting infusion bag once or twice.

Mechanism of Action Polyclonal antibody which appears to cause immunosuppression by acting on T-cell surface antigens and depleting CD4 lymphocytes

Pharmacodynamics/Kinetics
Duration of action: Lymphopenia may persist ≥1 year
Half-life elimination, plasma: 2-3 days

Dosage I.V.: Children and Adults: Treatment of acute rejection: 1.5 mg/kg/day for 7-14 days
Dosage adjustment for toxicity:
WBC count 2000-3000 cells/mm^3 or platelet count 50,000-75,000 cells/mm^3: Reduce dose by 50%
WBC count <2000 cells/mm^3 or platelet count <50,000 cells/mm^3: Consider discontinuing treatment

Administration The first dose should be infused over at least 6 hours through a high-flow vein. Subsequent doses should be administered over at least 4 hours. Administer through an in-line 0.22 micron filter. Premedication with corticosteroids, acetaminophen, and/or an antihistamine may reduce infusion-related reactions.

Monitoring Parameters Lymphocyte profile, CBC with differential and platelet count; vital signs during administration; signs and symptoms of infection

Emetic Potential Very low (<10%)

Vesicant No

Dosage Forms Excipient information presented when available (limited, particularly for generics); consult specific product labeling.
Injection, powder for reconstitution:
Thymoglobulin®: 25 mg

References
Hardinger KL, "Rabbit Antithymocyte Globulin Induction Therapy in Adult Renal Transplantation," *Pharmacotherapy*, 2006, 26(12):1771-83.

♦ **Antithymocyte Immunoglobulin** *see* Antithymocyte Globulin (Equine) *on page 100*

♦ **Antithymocyte Immunoglobulin** *see* Antithymocyte Globulin (Rabbit) *on page 102*

♦ **Anti-VEGF Monoclonal Antibody** *see* Bevacizumab *on page 133*

- ◆ **Antrypol** *see* Suramin *on page 991*
- ◆ **Anucort-HC**® *see* Hydrocortisone *on page 545*
- ◆ **Anusol-HC**® *see* Hydrocortisone *on page 545*
- ◆ **Anusol**® **HC-1 [OTC]** *see* Hydrocortisone *on page 545*
- ◆ **Anzemet**® *see* Dolasetron *on page 348*
- ◆ **Apo-Acyclovir**® **(Can)** *see* Acyclovir *on page 22*
- ◆ **Apo-Allopurinol**® **(Can)** *see* Allopurinol *on page 40*
- ◆ **Apo-Benzydamine**® **(Can)** *see* Benzydamine *on page 132*
- ◆ **Apo-Bisacodyl**® **(Can)** *see* Bisacodyl *on page 144*
- ◆ **Apo-Calcitonin**® **(Can)** *see* Calcitonin *on page 160*
- ◆ **Apo-Ciproflox**® **(Can)** *see* Ciprofloxacin *on page 213*
- ◆ **Apo-Cyproterone**® **(Can)** *see* Cyproterone *on page 267*
- ◆ **Apo-Desmopressin**® **(Can)** *see* Desmopressin *on page 326*
- ◆ **Apo-Dexamethasone**® **(Can)** *see* Dexamethasone *on page 330*
- ◆ **Apo-Famciclovir (Can)** *see* Famciclovir *on page 423*
- ◆ **Apo-Fluconazole**® **(Can)** *see* Fluconazole *on page 449*
- ◆ **Apo-Flutamide**® **(Can)** *see* Flutamide *on page 470*
- ◆ **Apo-Furosemide**® **(Can)** *see* Furosemide *on page 483*
- ◆ **Apo-Haloperidol**® **(Can)** *see* Haloperidol *on page 526*
- ◆ **Apo-Haloperidol LA**® **(Can)** *see* Haloperidol *on page 526*
- ◆ **Apo-Hydroxyurea**® **(Can)** *see* Hydroxyurea *on page 559*
- ◆ **Apo-Hydroxyzine**® **(Can)** *see* HydrOXYzine *on page 564*
- ◆ **Apo-Ketoconazole**® **(Can)** *see* Ketoconazole *on page 649*
- ◆ **Apo-Lorazepam**® **(Can)** *see* Lorazepam *on page 693*
- ◆ **Apo-Medroxy**® **(Can)** *see* MedroxyPROGESTERone *on page 703*
- ◆ **Apo-Megestrol**® **(Can)** *see* Megestrol *on page 707*
- ◆ **Apo-Methotrexate**® **(Can)** *see* Methotrexate *on page 733*
- ◆ **Apo-Metoclop**® **(Can)** *see* Metoclopramide *on page 751*
- ◆ **Apo-Metronidazole**® **(Can)** *see* Metronidazole *on page 755*
- ◆ **Apo-Oflox**® **(Can)** *see* Ofloxacin *on page 825*
- ◆ **Apo-Ofloxacin**® **(Can)** *see* Ofloxacin *on page 825*
- ◆ **Apo-Ondansetron**® **(Can)** *see* Ondansetron *on page 837*
- ◆ **Apo-Paclitaxel**® **(Can)** *see* Paclitaxel *on page 858*
- ◆ **Apo-Prednisone**® **(Can)** *see* PredniSONE *on page 919*
- ◆ **Apo-Prochlorperazine**® **(Can)** *see* Prochlorperazine *on page 929*
- ◆ **Apo-Sulfatrim**® **(Can)** *see* Sulfamethoxazole and Trimethoprim *on page 982*
- ◆ **Apo-Sulfatrim**® **DS (Can)** *see* Sulfamethoxazole and Trimethoprim *on page 982*
- ◆ **Apo-Sulfatrim**® **Pediatric (Can)** *see* Sulfamethoxazole and Trimethoprim *on page 982*
- ◆ **Apo-Tamox**® **(Can)** *see* Tamoxifen *on page 1002*
- ◆ **Apo-Trimethoprim**® **(Can)** *see* Trimethoprim *on page 1075*

Aprepitant (ap RE pi tant)

U.S. Brand Names Emend®
Index Terms L 754030; MK 869
Generic Available No
Canadian Brand Names Emend®
Pharmacologic Category Antiemetic; Substance P/Neurokinin 1 Receptor Antagonist

Use Prevention of acute and delayed nausea and vomiting associated with moderately- and highly-emetogenic chemotherapy in combination with a corticosteroid and 5-HT$_3$ receptor antagonist; prevention of postoperative nausea and vomiting (PONV)

Pregnancy Risk Factor B

Lactation Excretion in breast milk unknown/not recommended

Labeled Contraindications Hypersensitivity to aprepitant or any component of the formulation; use with cisapride or pimozide

Warnings/Precautions Use caution with agents primarily metabolized via CYP3A4; aprepitant is a 3A4 inhibitor. Effect on orally administered 3A4 substrates is greater than those administered intravenously. Use caution with hepatic impairment. Not intended for treatment of existing nausea and vomiting or for chronic continuous therapy. Safety and efficacy in pediatric patients have not been established.

Adverse Reactions Note: Adverse reactions reported as part of a combination chemotherapy regimen or with general anesthesia.

>10%:
  Central nervous system: Fatigue (18% to 22%)
  Gastrointestinal: Nausea (7% to 13%), constipation (9% to 12%)
  Neuromuscular & skeletal: Weakness (3% to 18%)
  Miscellaneous: Hiccups (11%)
1% to 10%:
  Cardiovascular: Hypotension (6%), bradycardia (4%)
  Central nervous system: Dizziness (>0.5% to 7%)
  Endocrine & metabolic: Dehydration (6%), hot flushing (3%)
  Gastrointestinal: Diarrhea (6% to 10%), dyspepsia (8%), abdominal pain (5%), stomatitis (5%), epigastric discomfort (4%), gastritis (4%), mucous membrane disorder (3%), throat pain (3%), vomiting (3%)
  Hematologic: Neutropenia (3% to 9%), leukopenia (9%), hemoglobin decreased (2% to 5%)
  Hepatic: ALT increased (1% to 6%), AST increased (3%)
  Renal: BUN increased (5%), proteinuria (7%), serum creatinine increased (4%)
>0.5%: Acid reflux, acne, albumin decreased, alkaline phosphatase increased, anemia, anxiety, appetite decreased, back pain, bilirubin increased, candidiasis, confusion, conjunctivitis, cough, deglutition disorder, depression, diabetes mellitus, diaphoresis, dry mouth, DVT, dysgeusia, dysphagia, dyspnea, dysuria, edema, eructation, erythrocyturia, flatulence, flushing, hyperglycemia, hyper-/hypotension, hypokalemia, hyponatremia, hypovolemia, hypoxia, glucosuria, leukocytes increased, leukocyturia, malaise, MI, muscular weakness, musculoskeletal pain, myalgia, nasal secretion, obstipation, pelvic pain, peripheral neuropathy, pharyngitis, pneumonitis, pulmonary embolism, rash, renal insufficiency, respiratory infection, respiratory insufficiency, rigors, salivation, sensory neuropathy, septic shock, syncope, tachycardia, taste disturbance, thrombocytopenia, tremor, urinary tract infection, vocal disturbance, weight loss
Postmarketing and/or case reports: Angioedema, bradycardia, disorientation, duodenal ulcer (perforating), enterocolitis, febrile neutropenia, hypoesthesia, neutropenic sepsis, pneumonia, sinus tachycardia, Stevens-Johnson syndrome, urticaria

Overdosage/Toxicology Single doses up to 600 mg and daily doses of 375 mg for up to 42 days were well-tolerated in healthy subjects; drowsiness and headache were noted at a dose of 1440 mg. In cancer patients, a single dose of 375 mg followed by 250 mg on days 2 to 5 was well tolerated. In (Continued)

Aprepitant *(Continued)*

case of overdose, treatment should be symptom-directed and supportive. Not removed by hemodialysis.

Drug Interactions

Cytochrome P450 Effect: Substrate of CYP1A2 (minor), 2C19 (minor), 3A4 (major); **Inhibits** CYP2C9 (weak), 2C19 (weak), 3A4 (moderate); **Induces** CYP2C9 (weak), 3A4 (weak)

Increased Effect/Toxicity: Use with cisapride or pimozide is contraindicated. CYP3A4 inhibitors may increase the levels/effects of aprepitant; example inhibitors include azole antifungals, clarithromycin, diclofenac, diltiazem, doxycycline, erythromycin, imatinib, isoniazid, nefazodone, nicardipine, propofol, protease inhibitors, quinidine, telithromycin, and verapamil. Aprepitant may increase the bioavailability of corticosteroids; dose adjustment of dexamethasone and methylprednisolone is needed. Aprepitant may increase the levels/effects of CYP3A4 substrates; example substrates include benzodiazepines, calcium channel blockers, ergot derivatives, mirtazapine, nateglinide, nefazodone, tacrolimus, and venlafaxine. Aprepitant may increase the levels/effects of pimecrolimus.

Decreased Effect: CYP3A4 inducers may decrease the levels/effects of aprepitant; example inducers include aminoglutethimide, carbamazepine, nafcillin, nevirapine, phenobarbital, phenytoin, and rifamycins. Metabolism of warfarin may be induced; monitor INR following the start of each cycle. Efficacy of hormone-containing contraceptives (estrogens) may be decreased (plasma levels of ethinyl estradiol and norethindrone decreased with concomitant use).

Ethanol/Nutrition/Herb Interactions

Food: Aprepitant serum concentration may be increased when taken with grapefruit juice; avoid concurrent use.

Herb/Nutraceutical: St John's wort may decrease aprepitant levels.

Storage/Stability Store at controlled room temperature of 20°C to 25°C (68°F to 77°F).

Mechanism of Action Prevents acute and delayed vomiting at the substance P/neurokinin 1 (NK_1) receptor; augments the antiemetic activity of the $5\text{-}HT_3$ receptor antagonist and corticosteroid activity and inhibits both acute and delayed phases of cisplatin-induced emesis.

Pharmacodynamics/Kinetics

Distribution: V_d: 70 L; crosses the blood brain barrier

Protein binding: >95%

Metabolism: Extensively hepatic via CYP3A4 (major); CYP1A2 and CYP2C19 (minor); forms seven metabolites (weakly active)

Bioavailability: 60% to 65%

Half-life elimination: Terminal: 9-13 hours

Time to peak, plasma: 4 hours

Dosage Oral: Adults:

Prevention of chemotherapy induced nausea/vomiting: 125 mg on day 1, followed by 80 mg on days 2 and 3 in combination with a corticosteroid and $5\text{-}HT_3$ receptor antagonist

Prevention of PONV: 40 mg within 3 hours prior to induction

Dosage adjustment in renal impairment: No dose adjustment necessary in patients with renal disease or end-stage renal disease maintained on hemodialysis.

Dosage adjustment in hepatic impairment:

Mild-to-moderate impairment (Child-Pugh score 5-9): No adjustment necessary

Severe impairment (Child-Pugh score >9): No data available

Administration Administer with or without food.

Chemotherapy induced nausea/vomiting: First dose should be given 1 hour prior to antineoplastic therapy; subsequent doses should be given in the morning.

PONV: Administer within 3 hours of induction

Dietary Considerations May be taken with or without food.

Patient Information May be taken with or without food depending on reason for use. Common side effects include diarrhea, hiccups, loss of appetite, tiredness, or weakness. This medicine may not mix well with other medicines; check medicines with prescriber.

Special Geriatric Considerations In two studies by the manufacturer, with a total of 544 patients, 31% were >65 years of age, while 5% were >75 years. No differences in safety and efficacy were noted between elderly subjects and younger adults. No dosing adjustment is necessary.

Dosage Forms Excipient information presented when available (limited, particularly for generics); consult specific product labeling.

Capsule:

Emend®: 40 mg, 80 mg, 125 mg

Combination package: Capsule 80 mg (2s), capsule 125 mg (1s)

References

Kris MG, Hesketh PJ, Somerfield MR, et al, "American Society of Clinical Oncology Guideline for Antiemetics in Oncology: Update 2006," *J Clin Oncol*, 2006, 24(18):2932-47.

NCCN (National Comprehensive Cancer Network) "Practice Guidelines in Oncology: Antiemesis Version 2.2006." Available at http://www.nccn.org/professionals/physician_gls/PDF/antiemesis.pdf. Last accessed August 15, 2006.

- ◆ **Aquacort® (Can)** *see* Hydrocortisone *on page 545*
- ◆ **AquaMEPHYTON® (Can)** *see* Phytonadione *on page 895*
- ◆ **Aquanil™ HC [OTC]** *see* Hydrocortisone *on page 545*
- ◆ **Aquoral™** *see* Saliva Substitute *on page 960*
- ◆ **Ara-C** *see* Cytarabine *on page 269*
- ◆ **Arabinosylcytosine** *see* Cytarabine *on page 269*
- ◆ **Aranesp®** *see* Darbepoetin Alfa *on page 295*
- ◆ **Aredia®** *see* Pamidronate *on page 872*
- ◆ **Arimidex®** *see* Anastrozole *on page 89*
- ◆ **Arixtra®** *see* Fondaparinux *on page 473*
- ◆ **Aromasin®** *see* Exemestane *on page 414*
- ◆ **Arranon®** *see* Nelarabine *on page 804*

Arsenic Trioxide (AR se nik tri OKS id)

Medication Safety Issues

High alert medication: The Institute for Safe Medication Practices (ISMP) includes this medication among its list of drugs which have a heightened risk of causing significant patient harm when used in error.

Related Information

Management of Drug Extravasations *on page 1301*
Safe Handling of Hazardous Drugs *on page 1382*

U.S. Brand Names Trisenox®

Index Terms As$_2$O$_3$; NSC-706363

Generic Available No

Pharmacologic Category Antineoplastic Agent, Miscellaneous

Use Induction of remission and consolidation in patients with relapsed or refractory acute promyelocytic leukemia (APL) which is specifically characterized by t(15;17) translocation or PML/RAR-alpha gene expression

(Continued)

Arsenic Trioxide *(Continued)*

Unlabeled/Investigational Use Treatment of myelodysplastic syndrome (MDS), multiple myeloma

Pregnancy Risk Factor D

Lactation Enters breast milk/not recommended

Labeled Contraindications Hypersensitivity to arsenic or any component of the formulation

Warnings/Precautions Hazardous agent - use appropriate precautions for handling and disposal. **[U.S. Boxed Warnings]: May prolong the QT interval. May lead to torsade de pointes or complete AV block.** Risk factors for torsade de pointes include CHF, a history of torsade de pointes, pre-existing QT interval prolongation, patients taking potassium-wasting diuretics, and conditions which cause hypokalemia or hypomagnesemia. If possible, discontinue all medications known to prolong the QT interval. **[U.S. Boxed Warning]: A baseline 12-lead ECG, serum electrolytes (potassium, calcium, magnesium), and creatinine should be obtained prior to treatment.** Correct electrolyte abnormalities prior to treatment and monitor potassium and magnesium levels during therapy (potassium should stay >4 mEq/dL and magnesium >1.8 mg/dL). Correct QT_c >500 msec prior to treatment. Discontinue therapy and hospitalize patient if QT_c >500 msec, syncope, or irregular heartbeats develop during therapy; do not reinitiate until QT_c <460 msec.

[U.S. Boxed Warning]: May cause retinoic-acid-acute promyelocytic leukemia (RA-APL) syndrome or APL differentiation syndrome (dyspnea, fever, weight gain, pulmonary infiltrates, and pleural or pericardial effusions) in patients with APL. High-dose steroids have been used for treatment. May lead to the development of hyperleukocytosis (leukocytes ≥10,000/mm^3). Use with caution in renal impairment; arsenic is eliminated renally. **[U.S. Boxed Warning]: Should be administered under the supervision of an experienced cancer chemotherapy physician.** Safety and efficacy in children <5 years of age have not been established (limited experience with children 5-16 years of age).

Adverse Reactions

>10%:

Cardiovascular: Tachycardia (55%), edema (40%), QT interval >500 msec (40%), chest pain (25%; grades 3/4: 5%), hypotension (25%; grades 3/4: 5%)

Central nervous system: Fatigue (63%), fever (63%), headache (60%), insomnia (43%), anxiety (30%), dizziness (23%), depression (20%), pain (15%)

Dermatologic: Dermatitis (43%), pruritus (33%), bruising (20%), dry skin (13%)

Endocrine & metabolic: Hypokalemia (50%; grades 3/4: 13%), hyperglycemia (45%; grades 3/4: 13%), hypomagnesemia (45%; grades 3/4: 13%), hyperkalemia (18%; grades 3/4: 5%)

Gastrointestinal: Nausea (58%), abdominal pain (58%), vomiting (58%), diarrhea (53%), sore throat (35% to 40%), constipation (28%), anorexia (23%), appetite decreased (15%), weight gain (13%)

Genitourinary: Vaginal hemorrhage (13%)

Hematologic: Leukocytosis (50%; grades 3/4: 3%), APL differentiation syndrome (23%), anemia (20%; grades 3/4: 5%), thrombocytopenia (18%; grades 3/4: 13%), febrile neutropenia (13%; grades 3/4: 8%)

Hepatic: ALT increased (20%; grades 3/4: 5%), AST increased (13%; grades 3/4: 3%)

Local: Injection site: Pain (20%), erythema (13%)

Neuromuscular & skeletal: Neuropathy (43%), rigors (38%), arthralgia (33%), paresthesia (33%), myalgia (25%), bone pain (23%), back pain (18%), limb pain (13%), neck pain (13%), tremor (13%)

Respiratory: Cough (65%), dyspnea (38% to 53%; grades 3/4: 10%), epistaxis (25%), hypoxia (23%), pleural effusion (20%), sinusitis (20%), postnasal drip (13%), upper respiratory tract infection (13%), wheezing (13%)

Miscellaneous: Herpes simplex (13%)

1% to 10%:

Cardiovascular: Hypertension (10%), flushing (10%), pallor (10%), palpitation (10%), facial edema (8%), abnormal ECG (not QT prolongation) (7%)

Central nervous system: Convulsion (8%; grades 3/4: 5%), somnolence (8%), agitation (5%), coma (5%), confusion (5%)

Dermatologic: Erythema (10%), hyperpigmentation (8%), petechia (8%), skin lesions (8%), urticaria (8%), local exfoliation (5%)

Endocrine & metabolic: Hypocalcemia (10%), hypoglycemia (8%), acidosis (5%)

Gastrointestinal: Dyspepsia (10%), loose stools (10%), abdominal distension (8%), abdominal tenderness (8%), xerostomia (8%), fecal incontinence (8%), gastrointestinal hemorrhage (8%), hemorrhagic diarrhea (8%), oral blistering (8%), weight loss (8%), oral candidiasis (5%)

Genitourinary: Intermenstrual bleeding (8%), incontinence (5%)

Hematologic: Neutropenia (10%; grades 3/4: 10%), DIC (8%), hemorrhage (8%), lymphadenopathy (8%)

Local: Injection site edema (10%)

Neuromuscular & skeletal: Weakness (10%)

Ocular: Blurred vision (10%), eye irritation (10%), dry eye (8%), eyelid edema (5%), painful eye (5%)

Otic: Earache (8%), tinnitus (5%)

Renal: Renal failure (8%; grades 3/4: 3%), renal impairment (8%), oliguria (5%)

Respiratory: Crepitations (10%), breath sounds decreased (10%), rales (10%), hemoptysis (8%), rhonchi (8%), tachypnea (8%), nasopharyngitis (5%)

Miscellaneous: Diaphoresis increased (10%), APL differentiation syndrome (8%), bacterial infection (8%), herpes zoster (8%), night sweats (8%), hypersensitivity (5%), sepsis (5%; grades 3/4: 5%)

Postmarketing and/or case reports: Atrial dysrhythmia, AV block, torsade de pointes

Overdosage/Toxicology Symptoms of arsenic toxicity include convulsions, muscle weakness, and confusion. Discontinue treatment and consider chelation therapy. One suggested adult protocol: Dimercaprol 3 mg/kg I.M. every 4 hours; continue until life-threatening toxicity has subsided. Follow with penicillamine 250 mg orally up to 4 times/day (total daily dose ≤1 g).

Drug Interactions

Increased Effect/Toxicity: Concurrent use of arsenic trioxide with other drugs which may prolong QT_c interval may increase the risk of potentially-fatal arrhythmias; includes type Ia and type III antiarrhythmic agents, selected quinolones including ciprofloxacin and moxifloxacin; cisapride, dolasetron, thioridazine, and other agents

Ethanol/Nutrition/Herb Interactions Herb/Nutraceutical: Avoid homeopathic products (arsenic is present in some homeopathic medications). Avoid hypoglycemic herbs, including alfalfa, aloe, bilberry, bitter melon, burdock, celery, damiana, fenugreek, garcinia, garlic, ginger, ginseng, gymnema, (Continued)

Arsenic Trioxide *(Continued)*

marshmallow, and stinging nettle (may enhance the hypoglycemic effect of arsenic trioxide).

Storage/Stability Store at room temperature of 15°C to 30°C (59°F to 86°F); do not freeze. Following dilution, stable for 24 hours at room temperature or 48 hours when refrigerated.

Reconstitution Dilute in 100-250 mL D_5W or 0.9% NaCl. Discard unused portion.

Mechanism of Action Not fully understood; causes *in vitro* morphological changes and DNA fragmentation to NB4 human promyelocytic leukemia cells; also damages or degrades the fusion protein PML-RAR alpha

Pharmacodynamics/Kinetics

Distribution: V_d: ~4 L

Metabolism: Hepatic; pentavalent arsenic is reduced to trivalent arsenic (active) by arsenate reductase; trivalent arsenic is methylated to monomethylarsinic acid, which is then converted to dimethylarsinic acid via methyltransferases

Half-life elimination: Initial: 0.6-1.2 hours; Elimination: 9-15 hours

Excretion: Urine (as methylated metabolite)

Dosage I.V.:

APL: Children ≥5 years and Adults:

Induction: 0.15 mg/kg/day; administer daily until bone marrow remission; maximum induction: 60 doses

Consolidation: 0.15 mg/kg/day starting 3-6 weeks after completion of induction therapy; maximum consolidation: 25 doses over 5 weeks

MDS, multiple myeloma (unlabeled uses): Adults: 0.25 mg/kg/day 5 consecutive days/week for 2 weeks, followed by a 2-week rest period

Elderly: Safety and efficacy have not been established; clinical trials included patients ≤72 years of age; use with caution due to the increased risk of renal impairment in the elderly

Dosage adjustment in renal impairment: Safety and efficacy have not been established; use with caution due to renal elimination

Dosage adjustment in hepatic impairment: Safety and efficacy have not been established

Administration Administer as I.V. infusion over 1-2 hours. If acute vasomotor reactions occur, infuse over a maximum of 4 hours. Does not require administration via a central venous catheter.

Monitoring Parameters Baseline then weekly 12-lead ECG, baseline then twice weekly serum electrolytes, hematologic and coagulation profiles at least twice weekly during induction and at least weekly during consolidation; more frequent monitoring may be necessary in unstable patients

Patient Information Check other medications with physician. Some medications may not mix well. Avoid homeopathic, herbal, or over-the-counter medications during treatment without approval of physician. You may not be alert. Avoid driving, doing other tasks or hobbies until response to drug is known. May cause fatigue, fever, nausea, vomiting, diarrhea, cough, or headache. Contact physician immediately for unexplained fever, shortness of breath, lightheadedness, passing out, rapid heartbeats, or weight gain. ECG and blood tests will be performed regularly during treatment.

Additional Information Arsenic is stored in liver, kidney, heart, lung, hair, and nails. Arsenic trioxide is a human carcinogen.

Oncology Comment: Arsenic trioxide is listed within National Comprehensive Cancer Network (NCCN) guidelines for the treatment of acute myeloid leukemia as the recommended salvage therapy for relapsed or persistent

APL. For patients with APL in their second complete response, who are not candidates for stem cell transplant, in the absence of an appropriate clinical trial, maintenance therapy with arsenic trioxide is an option.

Emetic Potential High (60% to 90%)

Vesicant No

Dosage Forms Excipient information presented when available (limited, particularly for generics); consult specific product labeling.
Injection, solution [preservative free]:
Trisenox®: 1 mg/mL (10 mL)

References

Barbey JT, Pezzullo JC, and Soignet SL, "Effect of Arsenic Trioxide on QT Interval in Patients With Advanced Malignancies," *J Clin Oncol*, 2003, 21(19):3609-15.

Chen Z, Chen GQ, Shen ZX, et al, "Expanding the Use of Arsenic Trioxide: Leukemias and Beyond," *Semin Hematol*, 2002, 39(2 Suppl 1):22-6.

Concha G, Vogler G, Lezcano D, et al, "Exposure to Inorganic Arsenic Metabolites During Early Human Development," *Toxicol Sci*, 1998, 44(2):185-90.

Davison K, Mann KK, and Miller WH, "Arsenic Trioxide: Mechanisms of Action," *Semin Hematol*, 2002, 39(2 Suppl 1):3-7.

"Dietary Reference Intakes for Vitamin A, Vitamin K, Arsenic, Boron, Chromium, Copper, Iodine, Iron, Manganese, Molybdenum, Nickel, Silicon, Vanadium, and Zinc," Food and Nutrition Board, Institute of Medicine. National Academy of Sciences, Washington, DC: National Academy Press, 2001, 162-84.

Evens AM, Tallman MS, and Gartenhaus RB, "The Potential of Arsenic Trioxide in the Treatment of Malignant Disease: Past, Present, and Future," *Leuk Res*, 2004, 28(9):891-900.

Hussein MA, "Arsenic Trioxide: A New Immunomodulatory Agent in the Management of Multiple Myeloma," *Med Oncol*, 2001 18(4):239-42.

Hussein MA, Saleh M, Ravandi F, et al, "Phase 2 Study of Arsenic Trioxide in Patients With Relapsed or Refractory Multiple Myeloma," *Br J Haematol*, 2004, 125(4):470-6.

Liu P and Han ZC, "Treatment of Acute Promyelocytic Leukemia and Other Hematologic Malignancies With Arsenic Trioxide: Review of Clinical and Basic Studies," *Int J Hematol*, 2003, 78(1):32-9.

Miller WH, Schipper HM, Lee JS, et al, "Mechanisms of Action of Arsenic Trioxide," *Cancer Res*, 2002, 62(14):3893-903.

NCCN (National Comprehensive Cancer Network), "Practice Guidelines in Oncology: Acute Myeloid Leukemia, Version 1.2006." Accessible at http://www.nccn.org/professionals/physician_gls/PDF/aml.pdf

Schiller GJ, Slack J, Hainsworth JD, et al, "Phase II Multicenter Study of Arsenic Trioxide in Patients With Myelodysplastic Syndromes," *J Clin Oncol*, 2006, 24(16):2456-64.

Shen ZX, Chen GQ, Ni JH, et al, "Use of Arsenic Trioxide (As2O3) in the Treatment of Acute Promyelocytic Leukemia (APL): II. Clinical Efficacy and Pharmacokinetics in Relapsed Patients," *Blood*, 1997, 89(9):3354-60.

Soignet SL, Frankel SR, Douer D, et al, "United States Multicenter Study of Arsenic Trioxide in Relapsed Acute Promyelocytic Leukemia," *J Clin Oncol*, 2001, 19(18):3852-60.

Vey N, "Arsenic Trioxide for the Treatment of Myelodysplastic Syndromes," *Expert Opin Pharmacother*, 2004, 5(3):613-21.

Von Ehrenstein OS, Guha Mazumder DN, Hira-Smith M, et al, "Pregnancy Outcomes, Infant Mortality, and Arsenic in Drinking Water in West Bengal, India," *Am J Epidemiol*, 2006 Apr 1;163(7):662-9.

Yang CY, Chang CC, Tsai SS, et al, "Arsenic in Drinking Water and Adverse Pregnancy Outcome in an Arseniasis-Endemic Area in Northeastern Taiwan," *Environ Res*, 2003, 91(1):29-34.

◆ **Artificial Saliva** see Saliva Substitute *on page 960*

◆ **As₂O₃** see Arsenic Trioxide *on page 107*

Asparaginase (a SPEAR a ji nase)

Medication Safety Issues

Sound-alike/look-alike issues:

Asparaginase may be confused with pegaspargase

Elspar® may be confused with Elaprase™

High alert medication: The Institute for Safe Medication Practices (ISMP) includes this medication among its list of classes of drugs which have a heightened risk of causing significant patient harm when used in error.
(Continued)

Asparaginase *(Continued)*

Related Information
Safe Handling of Hazardous Drugs *on page 1382*

U.S. Brand Names Elspar®

Index Terms *E. coli* Asparaginase; *Erwinia* Asparaginase; L-asparaginase; NSC-106977 (*Erwinia*); NSC-109229 (*E. coli*)

Generic Available No

Canadian Brand Names Elspar®; Kidrolase®

Pharmacologic Category Antineoplastic Agent, Miscellaneous

Use Treatment of acute lymphocytic leukemia (ALL)

Unlabeled/Investigational Use Treatment of lymphoma

Pregnancy Risk Factor C

Lactation Excretion in breast milk unknown/not recommended

Labeled Contraindications History of serious allergic reaction to asparaginase or any *E. coli*-derived asparaginase; history of serious thrombosis with prior asparaginase treatment; history of pancreatitis with prior asparaginase treatment; serious hemorrhagic events with prior asparaginase treatment

Warnings/Precautions Hazardous agent - use appropriate precautions for handling and disposal. Monitor for severe allergic reactions; immediate treatment for hypersensitivity reactions should be available during administration. May alter hepatic function; use caution with pre-existing liver impairment. Serious thrombosis, including sagittal sinus thrombosis may occur; discontinue with serious thrombotic events. Increased prothrombin time, partial thromboplastin time and hypofibrinogenemia may occur; cerebrovascular hemorrhage has been reported; monitor coagulation parameters; use cautiously in patients with an underlying coagulopathy. Monitor blood glucose; may cause hyperglycemia/glucose intolerance (possibly irreversible). May cause serious and possibly fatal pancreatitis; promptly evaluate patients with abdominal pain; discontinue permanently if pancreatitis develops. Appropriate measures must be taken to prevent tumor lysis syndrome and subsequent hyperuricemia and uric acid nephropathy; monitor, consider allopurinol, hydration and urinary alkalization.

Severe allergic reactions may occur; monitor; immediate treatment for hypersensitivity reactions should be available during administration. Risk factors for allergic reactions include: I.V. administration, doses >6000-12,000 units/m², patients who have received previous cycles of asparaginase, and intervals of even a few days between doses. Up to 33% of patients who have an allergic reaction to *E. coli* asparaginase will also react to the *Erwinia* form or pegaspargase. A test dose may be administered prior to the first dose of asparaginase, or prior to restarting therapy after a hiatus of several days. **False-negative rates of up to 80% to test doses of 2-50 units are reported.** Desensitization may be performed in patients found to be hypersensitive by the intradermal test dose or who have received previous courses of therapy with the drug.

Adverse Reactions Note: Immediate effects: Fever, chills, nausea, and vomiting occur in 50% to 60% of patients.

>10%:
  Central nervous system: Fatigue, fever, chills, depression, agitation, seizure (10% to 60%), somnolence, stupor, confusion, coma (25%)

  Endocrine & metabolic: Hyperglycemia/glucose intolerance (10%)

  Gastrointestinal: Nausea, vomiting (50% to 60%), anorexia, abdominal cramps (70%), acute pancreatitis (15%, may be severe in some patients)

Hematologic: Hypofibrinogenemia and depression of clotting factors V and VIII, variable decrease in factors VII and IX, severe protein C deficiency and decrease in antithrombin III (may be dose limiting or fatal)

Hepatic: Transaminases, bilirubin, and alkaline phosphatase increased (transient)

Hypersensitivity: Acute allergic reactions (fever, rash, urticaria, arthralgia, hypotension, angioedema, bronchospasm, respiratory distress, anaphylaxis (15% to 35%); may be dose limiting in some patients, may be fatal)

Renal: Azotemia (66%)

1% to 10%:

Endocrine & metabolic: Hyperuricemia

Gastrointestinal: Stomatitis

Miscellaneous: Allergic reaction (including anaphylaxis), antibody formation/immunogenicity (~25%)

<1%, postmarketing case reports, and/or frequency not defined: Acute renal failure, albumin decreased, cerebrovascular hemorrhage, cerebrovascular thrombosis, cough, disorientation, drowsiness, fatty liver, fibrinogen decreased, glucosuria, hallucinations, headache, hemorrhagic pancreatitis, hyper-/hypolipidemia, hyperthermia, hypocholesterolemia, hypotension, insulin-dependent diabetes, intracranial hemorrhage, irritability, ketoacidosis, laryngospasm, malabsorption syndrome, pancreatic pseudocyst, Parkinsonian symptoms (including tremor and increased muscle tone), partial thromboplastin time increased, peripheral edema, polyuria, proteinuria, prothrombin time increased, pruritus, rash, renal insufficiency, serum ammonia increased, serum cholesterol decreased, sagittal sinus thrombosis, thrombosis, urticaria, venous thrombosis, weight loss; mild-to-moderate myelosuppression, leukopenia, anemia, thrombocytopenia (onset: 7 days, nadir: 14 days, recovery: 21 days)

Overdosage/Toxicology Symptoms of overdose include nausea and diarrhea. Treatment is symptom-directed and supportive.

Drug Interactions

Increased Effect/Toxicity: Asparaginase (I.V.) may increase the toxicity of vincristine and prednisone.

Decreased Effect: Asparaginase may diminish the effects of methotrexate.

Storage/Stability Intact vials of powder should be refrigerated at 2°C to 8°C (36°F to 48°F). Reconstituted solutions are stable 1 week refrigerated at 8°C (Stecher, 1999), although the manufacturer recommends use within 8 hours. Solutions for I.V. infusion are stable for 8 hours at room temperature or under refrigeration.

Reconstitution Lyophilized powder should be reconstituted with 1-5 mL sterile water for injection or NS for I.V. administration; NS for I.M. use. Shake well, but not too vigorously. A 5 micron filter may be used to remove fiber-like particles in the solution (do not use a 0.2 micron filter; has been associated with loss of potency).

Standard I.M. dilution: 2000, 5000, or 10,000 int. units/mL

Standard I.V. dilution: Dilute in 50-250 mL NS or D_5W

Test dose preparation: Reconstitute a 10,000 unit vial with 5 mL NS or SWFI (concentration = 2000 units/mL); withdraw 0.1 mL and add to 9.9 mL NS (concentration = 20 units/mL); test dose is 0.1 mL (2 units)

Compatibility Stable in D_5W, NS.

Y-site administration: Compatible: Methotrexate, sodium bicarbonate

Mechanism of Action Asparaginase inhibits protein synthesis by hydrolyzing asparagine to aspartic acid and ammonia. Leukemia cells, especially lymphoblasts, require exogenous asparagine; normal cells can synthesize asparagine. Asparaginase is cycle-specific for the G_1 phase.

(Continued)

Asparaginase *(Continued)*

Pharmacodynamics/Kinetics

Absorption: I.M.: Produces peak blood levels 50% lower than those from I.V. administration

Distribution: V_d: 4-5 L/kg; 70% to 80% of plasma volume; <1% CSF penetration

Metabolism: Systemically degraded

Half-life elimination: I.M.: 39-49 hours; I.V.: 8-30 hours

Time to peak, plasma: I.M.: 14-24 hours

Dosage Refer to individual protocols. **Note:** Dose, frequency, number of doses, and start date may vary by protocol and treatment phase.

Children:

I.V.:

6000 units/m^2/dose 3 times/week for ~6-9 doses **or**

1000 units/kg/day for 10 days **or**

High-dose therapy (unlabeled dose): 10,000 units/m^2/dose every ~3 days for ~4-8 doses

I.M.:

6000 units/m^2/dose 3 times/week **or** 6000 units/m^2/dose every ~3 days for ~6-9 doses

High-dose therapy (unlabeled dose): 10,000 units/m^2/dose every ~3 days for ~4-8 doses **or** 25,000 units/m^2/dose weekly for ~9 doses (generally used in high-risk continuation therapy)

Adults:

I.V.:

6000 units/m^2/dose 3 times/week for ~6-9 doses **or**

1000 units/kg/day for 10 days **or**

High-dose therapy (unlabeled dose): 10,000 units/m^2/day for ~3-12 doses

Single agent therapy (rare): 200 units/kg/day for 28 days

Asparaginase Desensitization

Injection No.	Elspar Dose (int. units)	Accumulated Total Dose
1	1	1
2	2	3
3	4	7
4	8	15
5	16	31
6	32	63
7	64	127
8	128	255
9	256	511
10	512	1023
11	1024	2047
12	2048	4095
13	4096	8191
14	8192	16,383
15	16,384	32,767
16	32,768	65,535
17	65,536	131,071
18	131,072	262,143

I.M.:

6000 units/m²/dose 3 times/week for ~6-9 doses **or** 6000 units/m²/dose every ~3 days for ~6-9 doses

High-dose therapy (unlabeled dose): 10,000 units/m²/day for ~3-12 doses

Test dose: A test dose is often recommended prior to the first dose of asparaginase, or prior to restarting therapy after a hiatus of several days. Most commonly, 0.1 mL of a 20 units/mL (2 units) asparaginase dilution is injected intradermally, and the patient observed for at least 1 hour. False-negative rates of up to 80% to test doses of 2-50 units are reported.

Some practitioners recommend an asparaginase desensitization regimen for patients who react to a test dose, or are being retreated following a break in therapy. Doses are doubled and given every 10 minutes until the total daily dose for that day has been administered. One schedule begins with a total of 1 unit given I.V. and doubles the dose every 10 minutes until the total amount given is the planned dose for that day. For example, if a patient was to receive a total dose of 4000 units, he/she would receive injections 1 through 12 during the desensitization. See table on previous page.

Combination Regimens

Leukemia, acute lymphocytic:

Hyper-CVAD (Leukemia, Acute Lymphocytic) *on page 1231*
Larson Regimen *on page 1242*
Linker Protocol *on page 1243*
PVA (POG 8602) *on page 1273*
PVDA *on page 1276*

Leukemia, acute myeloid: CA *on page 1156*

Administration May be administered I.M., I.V., or intradermal (skin test only); has been administered SubQ in specific protocols

I.M.: Doses should be given as a deep intramuscular injection into a large muscle; volumes >2 mL should be divided and administered in 2 separate sites

Note: I.V. administration greatly increases the risk of allergic reactions and should be avoided if possible.

I.V.: I.V. infusion in 50-250 mL of D₅W or NS over at least 30-60 minutes. The manufacturer recommends a test dose (0.1 mL of a dilute 20 unit/mL solution) prior to initial administration and when given after an interval of 7 days or more. Institutional policies vary. The skin test site should be observed for at least 1 hour for a wheal or erythema. Note that a negative skin test does not preclude the possibility of an allergic reaction. Desensitization may be performed in patients who have been found to be hypersensitive by the intradermal skin test or who have received previous courses of therapy with the drug. Have epinephrine, diphenhydramine, and hydrocortisone at the bedside. Have a running I.V. in place. A physician should be readily accessible.

Gelatinous fiber-like particles may develop on standing. Filtration through a 5-micron filter during administration will remove the particles with no loss of potency.

Monitoring Parameters Vital signs during administration; CBC with differential, urinalysis, amylase, liver enzymes, coagulation parameters (baseline and periodic), renal function tests, urine dipstick for glucose, blood glucose, uric acid. Monitor for allergic reaction, be prepared to treat anaphylaxis at each administration; monitor for onset of abdominal pain and mental status changes.

(Continued)

Asparaginase *(Continued)*

Test Interactions Decreased thyroxine and thyroxine-binding globulin

Patient Information This medication can be given I.M., I.V., or subcutaneously. It is vital to maintain good hydration (2-3 L/day of fluids unless instructed to restrict fluid intake) and good nutritional status (small frequent meals may help). You may experience acute gastric disturbances (eg, nausea or vomiting); frequent mouth care or lozenges may help or antiemetic may be prescribed. Report any respiratory difficulty, skin rash, or acute anxiety immediately. Report unusual fever or chills, confusion, agitation, depression, yellowing of skin or eyes, unusual bleeding or bruising, unhealed sores, or vaginal discharge. Contraceptive measures are recommended during therapy.

Additional Information Some institutions recommended the following precautions for asparaginase administration: Parenteral epinephrine, diphenhydramine, and hydrocortisone available at bedside; freely running I.V. in place; physician readily accessible; monitor the patient closely for 30-60 minutes; avoid administering at night.

The *E. coli* and the *Erwinia* strains of asparaginase differ slightly in their gene sequencing, and have slight differences in their enzyme characteristics. Both are highly specific for asparagine and have <10% activity for the D-isomer. The *E. coli* form is more commonly used. The *Erwinia* variety is no longer commercially available in the U.S., although may be obtained through clinical trials or on a compassionate use basis.

Emetic Potential Moderate (30% to 60%)

Vesicant No

Dosage Forms Excipient information presented when available (limited, particularly for generics); consult specific product labeling.

Injection, powder for reconstitution:

Elspar®: 10,000 units

References

Avramis VI, Sencer S, Periclou AP, et al, "A Randomized Comparison of Native Escherichia Coli Asparaginase and Polyethylene Glycol Conjugated Asparaginase for Treatment of Children With Newly Diagnosed Standard-Risk Acute Lymphoblastic Leukemia: A Children's Cancer Group Study," *Blood*, 2002, 99(6):1986-94.

Capizzi RL, "Asparaginase Revisited," *Leukemia & Lymphoma*, 1993, 10(Suppl):147-50.

Duval M, Suciu S, Ferster A, et al, "Comparison of *Escherichia Coli* -Asparaginase With *Erwinia*-Asparaginase in the Treatment of Childhood Lymphoid Malignancies: Results of a Randomized European Organisation for Research and Treatment of Cancer — Children's Leukemia Group Phase 3 Trial," *Blood*, 2002, 99(8):2734-9.

Ettinger LJ, Ettinger AG, Avramis VI, et al, "Acute Lymphoblastic Leukemia: A Guide to Asparaginase and Pegaspargase Therapy," *BioDrugs*, 1997, 7:30-9.

Gallagher MP, Marshall RD, and Wilson R, "Asparaginase as a Drug for Treatment of Acute Lymphoblastic Leukemia," *Essays Biochem*, 1989, 24:1-40.

Keating MJ, Holmes R, Lerner S, et al, "L-Asparaginase and PEG Asparaginase - Past, Present, and Future," *Leukemia & Lymphoma*, 1993, 10(Suppl):153-7.

Larson RA, Dodge RK, Burns P, et al, "A Five-Drug Remission Induction Regimen With Intensive Consolidation for Adults With Acute Lymphoblastic Leukemia: Cancer and Leukemia Group B Study 8811," *Blood*, 1995, 85(8):2025-37.

Lazarus HM, Richards SM, Chopra R, et al, "Central Nervous System Involvement in Adult Acute Lymphoblastic Leukemia at Diagnosis: Results from the International ALL Trial MRC UKALL XII/ECOG E2993," *Blood*, 2006, 108(2):465-72.

Muller HJ and Boos J, "Use of L-Asparaginase in Childhood ALL," *Crit Rev Oncol Hematol*, 1998, 28(2):97-113.

Pession A, Valsecchi MG, Masera G, et al, "Long-Term Results of a Randomized Trial on Extended Use of High Dose L-Asparaginase for Standard Risk Childhood Acute Lymphoblastic Leukemia," *J Clin Oncol*, 2005, 23(28):7161-7.

Stecher AL, de Deus PM, Polikarpov I, et al, "Stability of L-Asparaginase: An Enzyme Used in Leukemia Treatment," *Pharm Acta Helv*, 1999, 74(1):1-9.

◆ **Astramorph/PF**™ *see* Morphine Sulfate *on page 779*

- ◆ **AT-III** *see* Antithrombin III *on page 98*
- ◆ **Atarax® (Can)** *see* HydrOXYzine *on page 564*
- ◆ **ATG** *see* Antithymocyte Globulin (Equine) *on page 100*
- ◆ **Atgam®** *see* Antithymocyte Globulin (Equine) *on page 100*
- ◆ **Ativan®** *see* Lorazepam *on page 693*
- ◆ **ATRA** *see* Tretinoin (Oral) *on page 1069*
- ◆ **Atriance™ (Can)** *see* Nelarabine *on page 804*
- ◆ **Avastin®** *see* Bevacizumab *on page 133*
- ◆ **Avinza®** *see* Morphine Sulfate *on page 779*
- ◆ **AY-25650** *see* Triptorelin *on page 1077*
- ◆ **5-Aza-2'-deoxycytidine** *see* Decitabine *on page 313*
- ◆ **5-AzaC** *see* Decitabine *on page 313*

Azacitidine (ay za SYE ti deen)

Medication Safety Issues

High alert medication: The Institute for Safe Medication Practices (ISMP) includes this medication among its list of drugs which have a heightened risk of causing significant patient harm when used in error.

Related Information

Investigational Drug Service *on page 1379*
Safe Handling of Hazardous Drugs *on page 1382*

U.S. Brand Names Vidaza®

Index Terms AZA-CR; Azacytidine; 5-Azacytidine; 5-AZC; Ladakamycin; NSC-102816

Generic Available No

Pharmacologic Category Antineoplastic Agent, DNA Methylation Inhibitor

Use Treatment of myelodysplastic syndrome (MDS)

Unlabeled/Investigational Use Investigational: Refractory acute lymphocytic and myelogenous leukemia

Pregnancy Risk Factor D

Lactation Excretion in breast milk unknown/not recommended

Labeled Contraindications Hypersensitivity to azacitidine, mannitol, or any component of the formulation; advanced malignant hepatic tumors

Warnings/Precautions Hazardous agent - use appropriate precautions for handling and disposal. Azacitidine may be hepatotoxic, use caution with hepatic impairment. Progressive hepatic coma leading to death has been reported (rare) in patients with extensive tumor burden, especially those with a baseline albumin <30 g/L. Use caution with renal impairment; dose adjustment may be required. Serum creatinine elevations, renal tubular acidosis, and renal failure have been reported with combination chemotherapy; decrease or withhold dose for unexplained elevations in BUN or serum creatinine or reductions in serum bicarbonate to <20 mEq/L. Patients with renal and hepatic impairment were excluded from clinical studies. Neutropenia and thrombocytopenia are common. Safety and efficacy in children have not been established.

Adverse Reactions

>10%:

Cardiovascular: Peripheral edema (7% to 19%), chest pain (16%), pallor (16%), pitting edema (15%)

Central nervous system: Fever (52%), fatigue (13% to 36%), headache (22%), dizziness (19%), anxiety (13%), depression (12%), insomnia (11%), malaise (11%), pain (11%)

Dermatologic: Bruising (19% to 31%), petechiae (24%), erythema (17%), skin lesion (15%), rash (14%), pruritus (12%)

(Continued)

Azacitidine *(Continued)*

Endocrine & metabolic: Hypokalemia (13%)

Gastrointestinal: Nausea (71%), vomiting (54%), diarrhea (36%), constipation (34%), anorexia (13% to 21%), weight loss (16%), abdominal pain (11% to 16%), abdominal tenderness (12%)

Hematologic: Anemia (70%), thrombocytopenia (66%), leukopenia (48%), neutropenia (32%), febrile neutropenia (16%), myelosuppression (nadir: days 10-17; recovery: days 28-31)

Local: Injection site: Erythema (35%; more common with I.V. administration), pain (23%; more common with I.V. administration), bruising (14%)

Neuromuscular & skeletal: Weakness (29%), rigors (26%), arthralgia (22%), limb pain (20%), back pain (19%), myalgia (16%)

Respiratory: Cough (11% to 30%), dyspnea (5% to 29%), pharyngitis (20%), epistaxis (16%), nasopharyngitis (15%), upper respiratory tract infection (13%), pneumonia (11%), crackles (11%)

Miscellaneous: Diaphoresis (11%)

5% to 10%:

Cardiovascular: Cardiac murmur (10%), tachycardia (9%), hypotension (7%), syncope (6%), chest wall pain (5%)

Central nervous system: Lethargy (8%), hypoesthesia (5%), post-procedural pain (5%)

Dermatologic: Cellulitis (8%), urticaria (6%), dry skin (5%), skin nodule (5%)

Gastrointestinal: Gingival bleeding (10%), oral mucosal petechiae (8%), stomatitis (8%), dyspepsia (7%), hemorrhoids (7%), abdominal distension (6%), loose stools (6%), dysphagia (5%), oral hemorrhage (5%), tongue ulceration (5%)

Genitourinary: Dysuria (8%), urinary tract infection (8%)

Hematologic: Hematoma (9%), postprocedural hemorrhage (6%)

Local: Injection site: Pruritus (7%), granuloma (5%), pigmentation change (5%), swelling (5%)

Neuromuscular & skeletal: Muscle cramps (6%)

Respiratory: Rhinorrhea (10%), rales (9%), wheezing (9%), breath sounds decreased (8%), pleural effusion (6%), postnasal drip (6%), rhonchi (6%), nasal congestion (6%), atelectasis (5%), sinusitis (5%)

Miscellaneous: Lymphadenopathy (10%), herpes simplex (9%), night sweats (9%), transfusion reaction (7%), mouth hemorrhage (5%)

<5%, postmarketing, and/or case reports (limited to important or life-threatening): Abscess (limb), agranulocytosis, anaphylactic shock, atrial fibrillation, azotemia, bone marrow depression, cardiac failure, cardiorespiratory arrest, CHF, congestive cardiomyopathy, catheter site hemorrhage, cholecystitis, dehydration, diverticulitis, fibrosis (interstitial and alveolar), gastrointestinal hemorrhage, glycosuria, hematuria, hemoptysis, hepatic coma, hypersensitivity reaction, hypophosphatemia, infection, injection site infection, intracranial hemorrhage, lung infiltration, orthostatic hypotension, pneumonitis, polyuria, pyoderma gangrenosum, renal failure, renal tubular acidosis, seizure, respiratory distress, sepsis, serum bicarbonate levels decreased, serum creatinine increased, splenomegaly, systemic inflammatory response syndrome

Overdosage/Toxicology Diarrhea, nausea, and vomiting were reported following a single I.V. dose of 290 mg/m^2. Treatment is symptom-directed and supportive.

Storage/Stability Prior to reconstitution, store powder at room temperature of 15°C to 30°C (59°F to 86°F).

SubQ: Following reconstitution, suspension may be stored at room temperature for up to 1 hour, or immediately refrigerated at 2°C to 8°C (36°F to 46°F) and stored for up to 8 hours.

I.V.: **Solutions for I.V. administration have very limited stability and must be prepared immediately prior to each dose.** Administration must be completed within 1 hour of (vial) reconstitution.

Reconstitution

SubQ: To prepare a 25 mg/mL suspension, slowly add 4 mL SWFI to each vial. Vigorously shake or roll vial until a suspension is formed (suspension will be cloudy).

I.V.: Reconstitute vial with 10 mL SWFI to form a 10 mg/mL solution; vigorously shake until solution is clear. Mix in 50-100 mL of NS or lactated Ringer's injection for infusion.

Compatibility Stable in LR, NS

Compatibility when admixed: Incompatible with D_5W, hetastarch, or solutions containing bicarbonate

Mechanism of Action Antineoplastic effects may be a result of azacitidine's ability to promote hypomethylation of DNA leading to direct toxicity of abnormal hematopoietic cells in the bone marrow.

Pharmacodynamics/Kinetics

Absorption: SubQ: Rapid and complete

Distribution: V_d: I.V.: 76 ± 26 L; does not cross blood-brain barrier

Metabolism: Hepatic; hydrolysis to several metabolites

Bioavailability: SubQ: 89%

Half-life elimination: I.V., SubQ: ~4 hours

Time to peak, plasma: SubQ: 30 minutes

Excretion: Urine (50% to 85%); feces (minor)

Dosage

I.V., SubQ: Adults: MDS: 75 mg/m²/day for 7 days repeated every 4 weeks. Dose may be increased to 100 mg/m2/day if no benefit is observed after 2 cycles and no toxicity other than nausea and vomiting have occurred. Treatment is recommended for at least 4 cycles; treatment may be continued as long as patient continues to benefit.

I.V.:

Children:

Pediatric AML and ANLL (unlabeled uses): 250 mg/m² days 4 and 5 every 4 weeks

Pediatric AML induction (unlabeled use): 300 mg/m² days 5 and 6

Adults:

Acute leukemia (unlabeled use):

50-150 mg/m² days 1 through 5 of induction

200 mg/m² CIVI days 7 through 9 of induction

CML (accelerated phase and blast crisis; unlabeled use): 50-150 mg/m² days 1 through 5 of induction

AML (unlabeled use):

Induction: 150 mg/m² days 3 through 5 and 8 through 10, **then** 150 mg/m² days 1 through 5 and 8 through 10 (cycle 2 consolidation)

Consolidation: 150 mg/m² CIVI days 1 through 7 for 3 cycles

Maintenance: 150 mg/m² days 1 through 3 every 6 weeks

Elderly: Refer to adult dosing; due to the potential for decreased renal function in the elderly, select dose carefully and closely monitor renal function

(Continued)

Azacitidine *(Continued)*

Dosage adjustment based on hematology: I.V., SubQ: MDS:

For baseline WBC $\geq 3.0 \times 10^9$/L, ANC $\geq 1.5 \times 10^9$/L, and platelets $\geq 75 \times 10^9$/L:

Nadir count: ANC <0.5 x 10^9/L or platelets <25 x 10^9/L: Administer 50% of dose during next treatment course

Nadir count: ANC 0.5-1.5 x 10^9/L or platelets 25-50 x 10^9/L: Administer 67% of dose during next treatment course

Nadir count: ANC >1.5 x 10^9/L or platelets >50 x 10^9/L: Administer 100% of dose during next treatment course

For baseline WBC <3 x 10^9/L, ANC 1.5 x 10^9/L, or platelets <75 x 10^9/L: Adjust dose as follows based on nadir counts and bone marrow biopsy cellularity at the time of nadir, unless clear improvement in differentiation at the time of the next cycle:

WBC or platelet nadir decreased 50% to 75% from baseline and bone marrow biopsy cellularity at time of nadir 30% to 60%: Administer 100% of dose during next treatment course

WBC or platelet nadir decreased 50% to 75% from baseline and bone marrow biopsy cellularity at time of nadir 15% to 30%: Administer 50% of dose during next treatment course

WBC or platelet nadir decreased 50% to 75% from baseline and bone marrow biopsy cellularity at time of nadir <15%: Administer 33% of dose during next treatment course

WBC or platelet nadir decreased >75% from baseline and bone marrow biopsy cellularity at time of nadir 30% to 60%: Administer 75% of dose during next treatment course

WBC or platelet nadir decreased >75% from baseline and bone marrow biopsy cellularity at time of nadir 15% to 30%: Administer 50% of dose during next treatment course

WBC or platelet nadir decreased >75% from baseline and bone marrow biopsy cellularity at time of nadir <15%: Administer 33% of dose during next treatment course

Note: If a nadir defined above occurs, administer the next treatment course 28 days after the start of the preceding course as long as WBC and platelet counts are >25% above the nadir and rising. If a >25% increase above the nadir is not seen by day 28, reassess counts every 7 days. If a 25% increase is not seen by day 42, administer 50% of the scheduled dose.

Dosage adjustment based on serum electrolytes: The manufacturer recommends that if serum bicarbonate falls to <20 mEq/L (unexplained decrease): Reduce dose by 50% for next treatment course

Dosage adjustment based on renal toxicity: If increases in BUN or serum creatinine (unexplained) occur, delay next cycle until values reach baseline or normal, then reduce dose by 50% for next treatment course.

Dosage adjustment in renal impairment: Not studied in patients with renal impairment; select dose carefully (excretion is primarily renal; consider dose reduction); monitor closely for toxicity

Dosage adjustment in hepatic impairment: Not studied in patients with hepatic impairment; use caution. Contraindicated in patients with advanced malignant hepatic tumors.

Administration

SubQ: Premedication for nausea and vomiting is recommended. Volumes >2 mL may be divided into two syringes and injected into two separate sites. Administer subsequent injections at least 1 inch from previous injection sites. Allow refrigerated suspensions to come to room temperature (up to

30 minutes) prior to administration. Resuspend by inverting the syringe 2-3 times and then rolling the syringe between the palms for 30 seconds. If azacitidine suspension comes in contact with the skin, immediately wash with soap and water.

I.V.: Premedication for nausea and vomiting is recommended. Infuse over 10-40 minutes; infusion must be completed within 1 hour of (vial) reconstitution.

Monitoring Parameters Liver function tests, electrolytes, CBC, renal function tests (BUN and serum creatinine) should be obtained prior to initiation of therapy. Electrolytes, renal function (BUN and creatinine), CBC should be monitored periodically to monitor response and toxicity. At a minimum, CBC should be repeated prior to each cycle.

Emetic Potential Moderate (30% to 60%)

Vesicant No. Subcutaneous injection of undissolved crystals may cause localized reactions.

Dosage Forms Excipient information presented when available (limited, particularly for generics); consult specific product labeling.

Injection, powder for suspension [preservative free]:

Vidaza®: 100 mg [contains mannitol 100 mg]

References

Adams CD, Szumita PM, Baroletti SA, et al, "Azacitidine-Induced Interstitial and Alveolar Fibrosis in a Patient With Myelodysplastic Syndrome," *Pharmacother*, 2006, 25(5):765-8.

Aparicio A and Weber JS, "Review of the Clinical Experience With 5-Azacytidine and 5-Aza-2'-deoxycytidine in Solid Tumors," *Curr Opin Investig Drugs*, 2002, 3(4):627-33.

Beran M, "Intensive Chemotherapy for Patients With High-Risk Myelodysplastic Syndrome," *Int J Hematol*, 2000, 72(2):139-50.

Cheson BD, Zwiebel JA, Dancey J, et al, "Novel Therapeutic Agents for the Treatment of Myelodysplastic Syndromes," *Semin Oncol*, 2000, 27(5):560-77.

Christman JK, "5-Azacytidine and 5-aza-2'-deoxycytidine as Inhibitors of DNA Methylation: Mechanistic Studies and Their Implications for Cancer Therapy," *Oncogene*, 2002, 21(35):5483-95.

Dutcher JP, Eudey L, Wiernik PH, et al, "Phase II Study of Mitoxantrone and 5-Azacytidine for Accelerated and Blast Crisis of Chronic Myelogenous Leukemia: A Study of the Eastern Cooperative Oncology Group," *Leukemia*, 1992, 6(8):770-5.

Goldberg J, Gryn J, Raza A, et al, "Mitoxantrone and 5-Azacytidine for Refractory/Relapsed ANLL or CML in Blast Crisis: A Leukemia Intergroup Study," *Am J Hematol*, 1993, 43(4):286-90.

Holcombe E, Grier HE, Gelber RD, et al, "Intensive Sequential Chemotherapy for Children With Acute Myelogenous Leukemia: VAPA, 80-035, and HI-C-Daze," *Leukemia*, 1992, (6 Suppl 2):48-51.

Hurwitz CA, Krance R, Schell MJ, et al, "Current Strategies for Treatment of Acute Myeloid Leukemia at St Jude Children's Research Hospital," *Leukemia*, 1992, (6 Suppl 2):39-43.

Jehn U, "Long-Term Outcome of Postremission Chemotherapy for Adults With Acute Myeloid Leukemia Using Different Dose-Intensities," *Leuk Lymphoma*, 1994, 15(1-2):99-112.

Jehn U, Zittoun R, Suciu S, et al, "A Randomized Comparison of Intensive Maintenance Treatment for Adult Acute Myelogenous Leukemia Using Either Cyclic Alternating Drugs or Repeated Courses of the Induction-Type Chemotherapy: AML-6 Trial of the EORTC Leukemia Cooperative Group," *Haematol Blood Transfus*, 1990, 33:277-84.

Kornblith AB, Herndon JE 2nd, Silverman LR, et al, "Impact of Azacytidine on the Quality of Life of Patients With Myelodysplastic Syndrome Treated in a Randomized Phase III Trial: A Cancer and Leukemia Group B Study," *J Clin Oncol*, 2002, 20(10):2441-52.

Kritz AD, Raptis G, Menendez-Botet C, et al, "Pilot Study of 5-Azacytidine (5-AZA) and Carboplatin (CBDCA) in Patients With Relapsed/Refractory Leukemia," *Am J Hematol*, 1996, 51(2):117-21.

NCCN (National Comprehensive Cancer Network), "Practice Guidelines in Oncology: Myelodysplastic Syndromes Version 1.2007" (available at http://www.nccn.org/professionals/physician_gls/PDF/mds.pdf)

Peterson BA, Collins AJ, Vogelzang NJ, et al, "5-Azacytidine and Renal Tubular Dysfunction," *Blood*, 1981, 57(1):182-5.

Rees JK, Gray RG, and Wheatley K, "Dose Intensification in Acute Myeloid Leukaemia: Greater Effectiveness at Lower Cost. Principal Report of the Medical Research Council's AML9 Study. MRC Leukaemia in Adults Working Party," *Br J Haematol*, 1996, 94(1):89-98.

(Continued)

Azacitidine *(Continued)*

Silverman LR, Demakos EP, Peterson BL, et al, "Randomized Controlled Trial of Azacitidine in Patients With the Myelodysplastic Syndrome: A Study of the Cancer and Leukemia Group B," *J Clin Oncol*, 2002, 20(10):2429-40.

Silverman LR, Holland JF, Weinberg RS, et al, "Effects of Treatment With 5-Azacytidine on the *in vivo* and *in vitro* Hematopoiesis in Patients With Myelodysplastic Syndromes," *Leukemia*, 1993, 7(Suppl 1):21-9.

Silverman LR, McKenzie DR, Peterson BL, et al,"Further Analysis of Trials With Azacitidine in Patients With Myelodysplastic Syndrome: Studies 8421, 8921, and 9221 by the Cancer and Leukemia Group B," *J Clin Oncol*, 2006, 24(24):3895-903.

Steuber CP, Krischer J, Holbrook T, et al, "Therapy of Refractory or Recurrent Childhood Acute Myeloid Leukemia Using Amsacrine and Etoposide With or Without Azacitidine: A Pediatric Oncology Group Randomized Phase II Study," *J Clin Oncol*, 1996, 14(5):1521-5.

Steuber CP, Holbrook T, Camitta B, et al, "Toxicity Trials of Amsacrine (AMSA) and Etoposide ± Azacitidine (AZ) in Childhood Acute Nonlymphocytic Leukemia (ANLL): A Pilot Study," *Invest New Drugs*, 1991, 9(2):181-4.

Volger WR, Weiner RS, Moore JO, et al, "Long-Term Follow-up of a Randomized Postinduction Therapy Trial in Acute Myelogenous Leukemia (A Southeastern Cancer Study Group Trial)," *Leukemia*, 1995, 9(9):1456-60.

Aztreonam *(AZ tree oh nam)*

Medication Safety Issues
Sound-alike/look-alike issues:
Aztreonam may be confused with azidothymidine

U.S. Brand Names Azactam®

Index Terms Azthreonam

Generic Available No

Canadian Brand Names Azactam®

Pharmacologic Category Antibiotic, Miscellaneous

Use Treatment of patients with urinary tract infections, lower respiratory tract infections, septicemia, skin/skin structure infections, intra-abdominal infections, and gynecological infections caused by susceptible gram-negative bacilli

Pregnancy Risk Factor B

Lactation Enters breast milk/not recommended (AAP rates "compatible")

Labeled Contraindications Hypersensitivity to aztreonam or any component of the formulation

Warnings/Precautions Rare cross-allergenicity to penicillins and cephalosporins has been reported. Use caution in renal impairment; dosing adjustment required. Prolonged use may result in fungal or bacterial superinfection, including *C. difficile*-associated diarrhea (CDAD) and pseudomembranous colitis; CDAD has been observed >2 months postantibiotic treatment.

Adverse Reactions As reported in adults:
1% to 10%:
Dermatologic: Rash
Gastrointestinal: Diarrhea, nausea, vomiting
Local: Thrombophlebitis, pain at injection site
<1%: Abdominal cramps, abnormal taste, anaphylaxis, anemia, angioedema, aphthous ulcer, breast tenderness, bronchospasm, *C. difficile*-associated diarrhea, chest pain, confusion, diaphoresis, diplopia,

dizziness, dyspnea, eosinophilia, erythema multiforme, exfoliative dermatitis, fever, flushing, halitosis, headache, hepatitis, hypotension, insomnia,
jaundice, leukopenia, liver enzymes increased, muscular aches myalgia,
neutropenia, numb tongue, pancytopenia, paresthesia, petechiae, pruritus,
pseudomembranous colitis, purpura, seizure, sneezing, thrombocytopenia,
tinnitus, toxic epidermal necrolysis, urticaria, vaginitis, vertigo, weakness,
wheezing

Overdosage/Toxicology Symptoms of overdose include seizures. Treatment is supportive. If necessary, dialysis can reduce the drug concentration
in the blood.

Drug Interactions

Decreased Effect: Avoid antibiotics that induce beta-lactamase production
(cefoxitin, imipenem).

Storage/Stability Prior to reconstitution, store at room temperature; avoid
excessive heat. Reconstituted solutions are colorless to light yellow straw
and may turn pink upon standing without affecting potency. Use reconstituted solutions and I.V. solutions (in NS and D_5W) within 48 hours if kept at
room temperature (25°C) or 7 days under refrigeration (4°C).

Infusion: Solution for infusion may be frozen at less than -2°C (less than
-4°F) for up to 3 months. Thawed solution should be used within 24 hours if
thawed at room temperature or within 72 hours if thawed under refrigeration. **Do not refreeze.**

Reconstitution

I.M.: Reconstitute with at least 3 mL SWFI, sterile bacteriostatic water for
injection, NS, or bacteriostatic sodium chloride.

I.V.:

Bolus injection: Reconstitute with 6-10 mL SWFI.

Infusion: Reconstitute to a final concentration ≤2%; the final concentration
should not exceed 20 mg/mL.

Compatibility Solution for infusion: Stable in D_5LR, $D_5^1/_4NS$, $D_5^1/_2NS$, D_5NS,
D_5W, $D_{10}W$, mannitol 5%, mannitol 10%, LR, NS; **variable stability (consult
detailed reference)** in peritoneal dialysis solution.

Y-site administration: Compatible: Allopurinol, amifostine, amikacin,
aminophylline, ampicillin, ampicillin/sulbactam, bleomycin, bumetanide,
buprenorphine, butorphanol, calcium gluconate, carboplatin, carmustine,
cefazolin, cefepime, cefoperazone, cefotaxime, cefotetan, cefoxitin, ceftazidime, ceftizoxime, ceftriaxone, cefuroxime, cimetidine, ciprofloxacin, cisatracurium, cisplatin, clindamycin, co-trimoxazole, cyclophosphamide,
cytarabine, dacarbazine, dactinomycin, dexamethasone sodium phosphate, diltiazem, diphenhydramine, dobutamine, docetaxel, dopamine,
doxorubicin, doxorubicin liposome, doxycycline, droperidol, enalaprilat,
etoposide, etoposide phosphate, famotidine, filgrastim, floxuridine,
fluconazole, fludarabine, fluorouracil, foscarnet, furosemide, gatifloxacin,
gemcitabine, gentamicin, granisetron, haloperidol, heparin, hydrocortisone
sodium phosphate, hydrocortisone sodium succinate, hydromorphone,
hydroxyzine, idarubicin, ifosfamide, imipenem/cilastatin, insulin (regular),
leucovorin, linezolid, magnesium sulfate, mannitol, mechlorethamine,
melphalan, meperidine, mesna, methotrexate, methylprednisolone sodium
succinate, metoclopramide, minocycline, morphine, nalbuphine, netilmicin,
ondansetron, piperacillin, piperacillin/tazobactam, plicamycin, potassium
chloride, promethazine, propofol, ranitidine, remifentanil, sargramostim,
sodium bicarbonate, teniposide, theophylline, thiotepa, ticarcillin, ticarcillin/
clavulanate, tobramycin, vinblastine, vincristine, vinorelbine, zidovudine.
Incompatible: Acyclovir, alatrofloxacin, amphotericin B, amphotericin B
cholesteryl sulfate complex, amsacrine, chlorpromazine, daunorubicin,
(Continued)

Aztreonam *(Continued)*

ganciclovir, lorazepam, metronidazole, mitomycin, mitoxantrone, prochlor-perazine edisylate, streptozocin. **Variable (consult detailed reference):** Vancomycin.

Compatibility in syringe: Compatible: Clindamycin.

Compatibility when admixed: Compatible: Ampicillin/sulbactam, cefaz-olin, ciprofloxacin, clindamycin, gentamicin, linezolid, tobramycin. **Incompatible:** Metronidazole, nafcillin. **Variable (consult detailed reference):** Ampicillin, cefoxitin, vancomycin.

Mechanism of Action Inhibits bacterial cell wall synthesis by binding to one or more of the penicillin binding proteins (PBPs) which in turn inhibits the final transpeptidation step of peptidoglycan synthesis in bacterial cell walls, thus inhibiting cell wall biosynthesis. Bacteria eventually lyse due to ongoing activity of cell wall autolytic enzymes (autolysins and murein hydrolases) while cell wall assembly is arrested. Monobactam structure makes cross-allergenicity with beta-lactams unlikely.

Pharmacodynamics/Kinetics

Absorption: I.M.: Well absorbed; I.M. and I.V. doses produce comparable serum concentrations

Distribution: Widely to most body fluids and tissues; crosses placenta; enters breast milk

V_d: Children: 0.2-0.29 L/kg; Adults: 0.2 L/kg

Relative diffusion of antimicrobial agents from blood into CSF: Good only with inflammation (exceeds usual MICs)

CSF:blood level ratio: Meninges: Inflamed: 8% to 40%; Normal: ~1%

Protein binding: 56%

Metabolism: Hepatic (minor %)

Half-life elimination:

Children 2 months to 12 years: 1.7 hours

Adults: Normal renal function: 1.7-2.9 hours

End-stage renal disease: 6-8 hours

Time to peak: I.M., I.V. push: Within 60 minutes; I.V. infusion: 1.5 hours

Excretion: Urine (60% to 70% as unchanged drug); feces (~13% to 15%)

Dosage

Children >1 month: I.M., I.V.:

Mild-to-moderate infections: I.M., I.V.: 30 mg/kg every 8 hours

Moderate-to-severe infections: I.M., I.V.: 30 mg/kg every 6-8 hours; maximum: 120 mg/kg/day (8 g/day)

Cystic fibrosis: I.V.: 50 mg/kg/dose every 6-8 hours (ie, up to 200 mg/kg/day); maximum: 8 g/day

Adults:

Urinary tract infection: I.M., I.V.: 500 mg to 1 g every 8-12 hours

Moderately-severe systemic infections: 1 g I.V. or I.M. or 2 g I.V. every 8-12 hours

Severe systemic or life-threatening infections (especially caused by *Pseudomonas aeruginosa*): I.V.: 2 g every 6-8 hours; maximum: 8 g/day

Meningitis (gram-negative): I.V.: 2 g every 6-8 hours

Dosing adjustment in renal impairment: Adults: Following initial dose, maintenance doses should be given as follows:

Cl_{cr} 10-30 mL/minute: 50% of usual dose at the usual interval

Cl_{cr} <10 mL/minute: 25% of usual dosage at the usual interval

Hemodialysis: Moderately dialyzable (20% to 50%); Loading dose of 500 mg, 1 g, or 2 g, followed by 25% of initial dose at usual interval; for serious/life-threatening infections, administer 1/8 of initial dose after each hemodialysis session (given in addition to the maintenance doses)

Continuous ambulatory peritoneal dialysis (CAPD): Administer as for Cl_{cr} <10 mL/minute

Continuous renal replacement therapy (CRRT): Drug clearance is highly dependent on the method of renal replacement, filter type, and flow rate. Appropriate dosing requires close monitoring of pharmacologic response, signs of adverse reactions due to drug accumulation, as well as drug levels in relation to target trough (if appropriate). The following are general recommendations only (based on dialysate flow/ultrafiltration rates of 1 L/hour) and should not supersede clinical judgment:

CVVH: 1-2 g every 12 hours

CVVHD/CVVHDF: 2 g every 12 hours

Administration Doses >1 g should be administered I.V.

I.M.: Administer by deep injection into large muscle mass, such as upper outer quadrant of gluteus maximus or the lateral part of the thigh

I.V.: Administer by slow I.V. push over 3-5 minutes or by intermittent infusion over 20-60 minutes.

Monitoring Parameters Periodic liver function test; monitor for signs of anaphylaxis during first dose

Test Interactions May interfere with urine glucose tests containing cupric sulfate (Benedict's solution, Clinitest®); positive Coombs' test

Special Geriatric Considerations Adjust dose relative to renal function.

Additional Information Although marketed as an agent similar to aminoglycosides, aztreonam is a monobactam antimicrobial with almost pure gram-negative aerobic activity. It cannot be used for gram-positive infections. Aminoglycosides are often used for synergy in gram-positive infections.

Emetic Potential Very low (<10%)

Vesicant No

Dosage Forms Excipient information presented when available (limited, particularly for generics); consult specific product labeling.

Infusion [premixed]: 1 g (50 mL); 2 g (50 mL)

Injection, powder for reconstitution: 500 mg, 1 g, 2 g

References

Bosso JA and Black PG, "The Use of Aztreonam in Pediatric Patients: A Review," *Pharmacotherapy*, 1991, 11(1):20-5.

Brogden RN and Heel RC, "Aztreonam. A Review of Its Antibacterial Activity, Pharmacokinetic Properties and Therapeutic Use," *Drugs*, 1986, 31(2):96-130.

Creasey WA, Platt TB, Frantz M, et al, "Pharmacokinetics of Aztreonam in Elderly Male Volunteers," *Br J Clin Pharmacol*, 1985, 19:233-7.

Donowitz GR and Mandell GL, "Beta-Lactam Antibiotics," *N Engl J Med*, 1988, 318(7):419-26 and 318(8):490-500.

Hellinger WC and Brewer NS, "Carbapenems and Monobactams: Imipenem, Meropenem, and Aztreonam," *Mayo Clin Proc*, 1999, 74(4):420-34.

Johnson DH and Cunha BA, "Aztreonam," *Med Clin North Am*, 1995, 79(4):733-43.

Settler FR, Schramm M, and Swabb EA, "Safety of Aztreonam and SQ 26,992 in Elderly Patients With Renal Insufficiency," *Rev Infect Dis*, 1985, (Suppl 4):S622.

Stutman HR, Chartrand SA, Tolentino T, et al, "Aztreonam Therapy for Serious Gram-Negative Infections in Children," *Am J Dis Child*, 1986, 140(11):1147-51.

Trotman RL, Williamson JC, Shoemaker DM, et al, "Antibiotic Dosing in Critically Ill Adult Patients Receiving Continuous Renal Replacement Therapy," *Clin Infect Dis*, 2005, 41(8):1159-66.

Tunkel AR, Hartman BJ, Kaplan SL, et al, "Practice Guidelines for the Management of Bacterial Meningitis," *Clin Infect Dis*, 2004, 39(9):1267-84.

♦ **B1** *see* Tositumomab and Iodine I 131 Tositumomab *on page 1056*

♦ **B1 Antibody** *see* Tositumomab and Iodine I 131 Tositumomab *on page 1056*

♦ **BA-16038** *see* Aminoglutethimide *on page 65*

♦ **Bacillus Calmette-Guérin (BCG) Live** *see* BCG Vaccine *on page 128*

♦ **Bactrim™** *see* Sulfamethoxazole and Trimethoprim *on page 982*

♦ **Bactrim™ DS** *see* Sulfamethoxazole and Trimethoprim *on page 982*

Basiliximab (ba si LIK si mab)

U.S. Brand Names Simulect®

Generic Available No

Canadian Brand Names Simulect®

Pharmacologic Category Monoclonal Antibody

Use Prophylaxis of acute organ rejection in renal transplantation

Pregnancy Risk Factor B (manufacturer)

Lactation Excretion in breast milk unknown/not recommended

Labeled Contraindications Hypersensitivity to basiliximab, murine proteins, or any component of the formulation

Warnings/Precautions To be used as a component of immunosuppressive regimen which includes cyclosporine and corticosteroids. The incidence of lymphoproliferative disorders and/or opportunistic infections may be increased by immunosuppressive therapy. Severe hypersensitivity reactions, occurring within 24 hours, have been reported. Reactions, including anaphylaxis, have occurred both with the initial exposure and/or following re-exposure after several months. Use caution during re-exposure to a subsequent course of therapy in a patient who has previously received basiliximab. Discontinue the drug permanently if a reaction occurs. Medications for the treatment of hypersensitivity reactions should be available for immediate use. Treatment may result in the development of human antimurine antibodies (HAMA); however, limited evidence suggesting the use of muromonab-CD3 or other murine products is not precluded. **[U.S. Boxed Warning]: Should be administered under the supervision of a physician experienced in immunosuppression therapy.**

Adverse Reactions Administration of basiliximab did not appear to increase the incidence or severity of adverse effects in clinical trials. Adverse events were reported in 96% of both the placebo and basiliximab groups.

>10%:

Cardiovascular: Hypertension, peripheral edema

Central nervous system: Fever, headache, insomnia, pain

Dermatologic: Acne, wound complications

Endocrine & metabolic: Hypercholesterolemia, hyperglycemia, hyper-/hypokalemia, hyperuricemia, hypophosphatemia

Gastrointestinal: Abdominal pain, constipation, diarrhea, dyspepsia, nausea, vomiting

Genitourinary: Urinary tract infection

Hematologic: Anemia

Neuromuscular & skeletal: Tremor

Respiratory: Dyspnea, infection (upper respiratory)

Miscellaneous: Viral infection

3% to 10%:

Cardiovascular: Abnormal heart sounds, angina pectoris, arrhythmia, atrial fibrillation, cardiac failure, chest pain, generalized edema, hypotension, tachycardia

Central nervous system: Agitation, anxiety, depression, dizziness, fatigue, hypoesthesia, malaise, neuropathy, rigors

Dermatologic: Cyst, hypertrichosis, pruritus, rash, skin disorder, skin ulceration

Endocrine & metabolic: Acidosis, dehydration, diabetes mellitus, fluid overload, hyper-/hypocalcemia, hyperlipidemia, hypertriglyceridemia, hypoglycemia, hypomagnesemia, hyponatremia

Gastrointestinal: Abdomen enlarged, esophagitis, flatulence, gastroenteritis, GI hemorrhage, gingival hyperplasia, melena, moniliasis, stomatitis (including ulcerative), weight gain

Genitourinary: Albuminuria, bladder disorder, dysuria, genital edema, hematuria, impotence, oliguria, renal function abnormal, renal tubular necrosis, ureteral disorder, urinary frequency, urinary retention

Hematologic: Hematoma, hemorrhage, leukopenia, polycythemia, purpura, thrombocytopenia, thrombosis

Neuromuscular & skeletal: Arthralgia, arthropathy, back pain, cramps, fracture, hernia, leg pain, myalgia, paresthesia, weakness

Ocular: Abnormal vision, cataract, conjunctivitis

Respiratory: Bronchitis, bronchospasm, cough, pharyngitis, pneumonia, pulmonary edema, sinusitis, rhinitis

Miscellaneous: Accidental trauma, facial edema, glucocorticoids increased, herpes infection, sepsis

Postmarketing and/or case reports: Capillary leak syndrome, cytokine release syndrome; severe hypersensitivity reactions, including anaphylaxis, have been reported (symptoms may include hypotension, tachycardia, cardiac failure, dyspnea, bronchospasm, pulmonary edema, urticaria, rash, pruritus, sneezing, and respiratory failure)

Overdosage/Toxicology The maximum tolerated dose has not been determined. Single doses up to 60 mg and divided doses up to 120 mg were administered without adverse event in clinical trials; a pediatric patient received a single 20 mg dose without adverse event. Treatment is symptom-directed and supportive.

Drug Interactions

Increased Effect/Toxicity: Allergic reactions may be increased in patients who have received diagnostic or therapeutic monoclonal antibodies due to the presence of human antichimeric antibody (HACA). Basiliximab may increase the risk of vaccinial infection with live organism vaccine administration.

Decreased Effect: Basiliximab may decrease the effect of vaccines (dead organisms).

Ethanol/Nutrition/Herb Interactions Herb/Nutraceutical: Echinacea may diminish the therapeutic effect of basiliximab. Avoid hypoglycemic herbs, including alfalfa, bilberry, bitter melon, burdock, celery, damiana, fenugreek, garcinia, garlic, ginger, ginseng, gymnema, marshmallow, and stinging nettle (may enhance the hypoglycemic effect of basiliximab).

Storage/Stability Store intact vials under refrigeration 2°C to 8°C (36°F to 46°F). It is recommended that after reconstitution, the solution should be used immediately. If not used immediately, it can be stored at 2°C to 8°C for up to 24 hours or at room temperature for up to 4 hours. Discard the reconstituted solution within 24 hours.

Reconstitution Reconstitute vials with sterile water for injection, USP. Shake the vial gently to dissolve. Further dilute reconstituted solution with 25-50 mL 0.9% sodium chloride or dextrose 5% in water. When mixing the solution, gently invert the bag to avoid foaming. Do not shake.

Mechanism of Action Chimeric (murine/human) monoclonal antibody which blocks the alpha-chain of the interleukin-2 (IL-2) receptor complex; this receptor is expressed on activated T lymphocytes and is a critical pathway for activating cell-mediated allograft rejection

Pharmacodynamics/Kinetics

Duration: Mean: 36 days (determined by IL-2R alpha saturation)

Distribution: Mean: V_d: Children 1-11 years: 4.8 ± 2.1 L; Adolescents 12-16 years: 7.8 ± 5.1 L; Adults: 8.6 ± 4.1 L

(Continued)

Basiliximab *(Continued)*

Half-life elimination: Children 1-11 years: 9.5 days; Adolescents 12-16 years: 9.1 days; Adults: Mean: 7.2 days

Excretion: Clearance: Children 1-11 years: 17 mL/hour; Adolescents 12-16 years: 31 mL/hour; Adults: Mean: 41 mL/hour

Dosage Note: Patients previously administered basiliximab should only be re-exposed to a subsequent course of therapy with extreme caution.

I.V.:

Children <35 kg: Renal transplantation: 10 mg within 2 hours prior to transplant surgery, followed by a second 10 mg dose 4 days after transplantation; the second dose should be withheld if complications occur (including severe hypersensitivity reactions or graft loss)

Children ≥35 kg and Adults: Renal transplantation: 20 mg within 2 hours prior to transplant surgery, followed by a second 20 mg dose 4 days after transplantation; the second dose should be withheld if complications occur (including severe hypersensitivity reactions or graft loss)

Dosing adjustment/comments in renal or hepatic impairment: No specific dosing adjustment recommended

Administration For intravenous administration only. Infuse as a bolus or I.V. infusion over 20-30 minutes. (Bolus dosing is associated with nausea, vomiting, and local pain at the injection site.)

Monitoring Parameters Signs and symptoms of acute rejection

Emetic Potential Very low (<10%)

Vesicant No

Dosage Forms Excipient information presented when available (limited, particularly for generics); consult specific product labeling.

Injection, powder for reconstitution [preservative free]:

Simulect®: 10 mg, 20 mg

♦ **BAY 43-9006** *see* Sorafenib *on page 974*

♦ **Bayer 205** *see* Suramin *on page 991*

♦ **BCG, Live** *see* BCG Vaccine *on page 128*

BCG Vaccine *(bee see jee vak SEEN)*

Medication Safety Issues

High alert medication: The Institute for Safe Medication Practices (ISMP) includes this medication among its list of drugs which have a heightened risk of causing significant patient harm when used in error.

Related Information

Safe Handling of Hazardous Drugs *on page 1382*

U.S. Brand Names TheraCys®; TICE® BCG

Index Terms Bacillus Calmette-Guérin (BCG) Live; BCG, Live; BCG Vaccine U.S.P. *(percutaneous use product)*

Generic Available No

Canadian Brand Names ImmuCyst®; Oncotice™; Pacis™

Pharmacologic Category Biological Response Modulator; Vaccine

Use Immunization against tuberculosis and immunotherapy for cancer; treatment and prophylaxis of carcinoma *in situ* of the bladder; prophylaxis of primary or recurrent superficial papillary tumors following transurethral resection

Pregnancy Risk Factor C

Lactation Excretion in breast milk unknown/not recommended

Labeled Contraindications Hypersensitivity to BCG vaccine or any component of the formulation; immunocompromised state, HIV-infected, and burn patients; active tuberculosis; intravesicular BCG is contraindicated in febrile illness, urinary tract infection, gross hematuria and recent (<7-14 days) biopsy, transurethral resection (TUR), or traumatic catheterization

Warnings/Precautions [U.S. Boxed Warnings]: Hazardous agent - use appropriate precautions for handling and disposal. BCG is a biohazardous agent; proper technique and disposal of all equipment in contact with BCG vaccine as a biohazardous material is recommended. BCG infections have been reported in healthcare workers due to accidental exposure (needlestick, skin laceration); nosocomial infections have been reported in patients receiving parenteral medications prepared in areas where BCG vaccine was prepared. To avoid cross contamination, do not prepare parenteral medications in an area where BCG vaccine has been prepared. Systemic reactions have been reported in patients treated as immunotherapy for bladder cancer.

BCG should be administered with caution to persons in groups at high risk for HIV infection or persons known to be severely immunocompromised (including leukemia or lymphoma patients), patients undergoing chemotherapy, or patients on immunosuppressive therapy. Safety and efficacy of intravesicular BCG in children have not been established.

Although limited data suggest that the vaccine may be safe for use in asymptomatic children infected with HIV, BCG vaccination is not recommended for HIV-infected adults or for persons with a positive PPD reaction. Until further research can clearly define the risks and benefits of BCG vaccination for this population, vaccination should be restricted to persons at exceptionally high risk for tuberculosis infection. HIV-infected persons thought to be infected with *Mycobacterium tuberculosis* should be strongly recommended for tuberculosis preventive therapy.

Adverse Reactions All serious adverse reactions must be reported to the U.S. Department of Health and Human Services (DHHS) Vaccine Adverse Event Reporting System (VAERS) 1-800-822-7967.

Adverse reactions associated with **intravesicular administration**:
>10%:
  Central nervous system: Malaise (7% to 40%), fever (20% to 38%), chills (34%)
  Gastrointestinal: Nausea/vomiting (3% to 16%), anorexia/weight loss (2% to 11%)
  Genitourinary: Dysuria (52% to 60%), bladder irritation (50% to 60%), polyuria (40% to 42%), hematuria (26% to 39%), cystitis (6% to 29%), urinary urgency (6% to 18%), urinary tract infection (2% to 18%)
  Hematological: Anemia (<1% to 21%)
  Miscellaneous: Flu-like syndrome (33%)
1% to 10%:
  Central nervous system: Fatigue (7%), headache/dizziness (2%)
  Dermatologic: Rash (2%)
  Gastrointestinal: Diarrhea (6%), abdominal pain (2% to 3%)
  Genitourinary: Genital pain (10%), bladder cramps/pain (6%), urinary incontinence (2% to 6%), bladder spasm (5%), nocturia (5%), urinary debris (2%), genital inflammation/abscess (2%)
  Hematological: Leukopenia (5%), coagulopathy (3%)
  Neuromuscular & skeletal: Arthralgia/myalgia (3% to 7%), cramps/pain (4% to 6%), rigors (3%)
  Renal: Renal toxicity (10%)
  Respiratory: Pulmonary infection (3%)
  Miscellaneous: Infection (3%), allergy (2%)
<1%: Abscesses, conjunctivitis, constipation, disseminated sepsis, epididymitis, granulomatous chorioretinitis, hepatitis, hepatic granuloma, keratitis,
(Continued)

BCG Vaccine *(Continued)*

M. bovis infection (lung, liver, bone, bone marrow, kidney, lymph nodes, prostate), orchitis, pneumonitis, prostatitis, skin ulceration, thrombocytopenia, urethritis, urinary obstruction, uveitis

Adverse reactions associated with **BCG vaccination**: Axillary lymphadenopathy, cervical lymphadenopathy, disseminated BCG infection (BCG osteomyelitis), local reactions (induration, itching, lesions, lymphadenitis, pustule, tenderness, ulceration). Local reactions may persist for up to 3 months; more severe manifestations may occur up to 5 months after vaccination and persist for several weeks.

Overdosage/Toxicology Closely monitor for sign of active local or systemic infection. Consult with an infectious disease specialist for any suspected active infection.

Drug Interactions

Increased Effect/Toxicity: The following agents may decrease the effectiveness of BCG vaccine: Antimicrobials, immune globulins, immunosuppressants, and other live organism vaccines. Antimicrobials may interfere with the effectiveness of intravesicular BCG.

Decreased Effect: Immunosuppressants may increase the risk of vaccinal infections. BCG vaccination results in a reactive tuberculin skin test.

Storage/Stability Store vials under refrigeration at 2°C to 8°C (36°F to 46°F); protect from light. Use within 2 hours of mixing.

Reconstitution

TheraCys®: Reconstitute with 3 mL of diluent provided and shake gently. Withdraw contents and add 50 mL of 0.9% NaCl (preservative free).

TICE® BCG: Reconstitute with 1 mL 0.9% NaCl (preservative free) using a 3 mL syringe. Mix by drawing and expelling solution into ampul three times. Add to a catheter tip syringe containing 49 mL of 0.9% NaCl (preservative free).

BCG Vaccine U.S.P.: Reconstitute with 1 mL of SWFI; swirl gently, do not vigorously shake. For children <1 month, reconstitute with 2 mL SWFI.

Mechanism of Action BCG live is an attenuated strain of bacillus Calmette-Guérin (*Mycobacterium bovis*) used as a biological response modifier. BCG live, when used intravesically for treatment of bladder carcinoma *in situ*, is thought to cause a local, chronic inflammatory response involving macrophage and leukocyte infiltration of the bladder. By a mechanism not fully understood, this local inflammatory response leads to destruction of superficial tumor cells of the urothelium. BCG is active immunotherapy which stimulates the host's immune mechanism to reject the tumor. Evidence of systemic immune response is also commonly seen, manifested by a positive PPD tuberculin skin test reaction, however, its relationship to clinical efficacy is not well-established.

Dosage

Immunization against tuberculosis: Percutaneous: **Note:** Initial lesion usually appears after 10-14 days consisting of small, red papule at injection site and reaches maximum diameter of 3 mm in 4-6 weeks.

Children <1 month: 0.2-0.3 mL (half-strength dilution). Administer tuberculin test (5 TU) after 2-3 months; repeat vaccination after 1 year of age for negative tuberculin test if indications persist.

Children >1 month and Adults: 0.2-0.3 mL (full strength dilution); conduct postvaccinal tuberculin test (5 TU of PPD) in 2-3 months; if test is negative, repeat vaccination.

Immunotherapy for bladder cancer: Intravesicular: Adults:

TheraCys®: One dose instilled into bladder (for 2 hours) once weekly for 6 weeks followed by one treatment at 3, 6, 12, 18, and 24 months after initial treatment

TICE® BCG: One dose instilled into the bladder (for 2 hours) once weekly for 6 weeks followed by once monthly for 6-12 months

Administration Should only be given intravesicularly (bladder irrigation) or percutaneously; **do not administer I.V., SubQ, or intradermally**.

Intravesicular: Empty or drain bladder. Instill BCG vaccine; retain for up to 2 hours. Patient should lie prone, rotating positions every 15 minutes to maximize bladder surface exposure.

Percutaneous: Apply vaccine with syringe and needle by dropping onto 1-2 inch area of horizontally positioned surface of cleansed, dry site (deltoid region of arm preferred); pulling skin tight, puncture skin with multiple puncture device centered over the vaccine; apply pressure for 5 seconds; spread vaccine evenly over puncture area. Apply loose covering and keep dry for 24 hours.

Test Interactions PPD intradermal test; BCG vaccination results in reactive tuberculin skin test; rule out active tuberculosis prior to initiating intravesicular BCG treatment

Additional Information When used for immunization against tuberculosis, Federal law requires that the date of administration, the vaccine manufacturer, lot number of vaccine, and the administering person's name, title, and address be entered into the patient's permanent medical record. Multiple puncture device for vaccination available from Organon Tenika (1-800-662-6842).

BCG vaccination is not recommended by the CDC for general use in the U.S. for prevention of tuberculosis (TB).

BCG vaccination is recommended for infants and children with negative tuberculin skin tests who:
- are at high risk of intimate and prolonged exposure to persistently untreated or ineffectively treated patients with infectious pulmonary tuberculosis
- cannot be removed from the source of exposure
- cannot be placed on long-term preventive therapy
- are continuously exposed with tuberculosis who have bacilli resistant to isoniazid and rifampin

BCG vaccination is recommended for healthcare workers (HCW) in high-risk settings where:
- a high percentage of TB patients are infected with *M. tuberculosis* strains resistant to both isoniazid and rifampin
- transmission of drug-resistant *M. tuberculosis* strains and subsequent infection are likely
- comprehensive TB infection control precautions have been implemented yet have not been successful

BCG vaccination in not recommended for HCWs in low-risk settings.

Emetic Potential Low (10% to 30%)

Vesicant No

Dosage Forms Excipient information presented when available (limited, particularly for generics); consult specific product labeling.

Injection, powder for reconstitution, intravesical [preservative free]:
TheraCys®: 81 mg [with diluent]
TICE® BCG: 50 mg

Injection, powder for reconstitution, percutaneous [preservative free]:
BCG Vaccine U.S.P.: 50 mg

(Continued)

BCG Vaccine *(Continued)*

References

Alexandroff AB, Jackson AM, O'Donnell MA, et al, "BCG Immunotherapy of Bladder Cancer: 20 Years On," *Lancet*, 1999, 353(9165):1689-94.

Badalament RA and Farah RN, "Treatment of Superficial Bladder Cancer With Intravesicle Chemotherapy," *Semin Surg Oncol*, 1997, 13(5):335-41.

Bassi P, "BCG (Bacillus of Calmette Guerin) Therapy of High-Risk Superficial Bladder Cancer," *Surg Oncol*, 2002, 11(1-2):77-83.

Centers for Disease Control, "Recommendations of the Advisory Committee on Immunization Practices (ACIP): General Recommendations on Immunization," *MMWR Recomm Rep*, 2002, 51(RR-2):1-36.

Centers for Disease Control and Prevention,"TB Elimination: BCG Vaccine," Document 250120, January, 2005; available at http://www.cdc.gov/nchstp/tb/pubs/tbfactsheets/250120.pdf

Lamm DL, Steg A, Boccon-Gibod L, et al, "Complications of Bacillus Calmette-Guérin Immuno-therapy: Review of 2602 Patients and Comparison of Chemotherapy Complications," *Prog Clin Biol Res*, 1989, 310:335-55.

Martinez-Pineiro JA and Martinez-Pineiro L, "BCG Update: Intravesical Therapy," *Eur Urol*, 1997, 31(Suppl 1):31-41.

Meyer JP, Persad R, and Gillatt DA, "Use of Bacille Calmette-Guerin in Superficial Bladder Cancer," *Postgrad Med J*, 2002, 78(922):449-54.

Nathanson L, "Use of BCG in the Treatment of Human Neoplasms: A Review," *Semin Oncol*, 1974, 1(4):337-50.

Nseyo UO and Lamm DL, "Immunotherapy of Bladder Cancer," *Semin Surg Oncol*, 1997, 13(5):342-9.

Rischmann P, Desgrandchamps F, Malavaud B, et al, "BCG Intravesical Instillations: Recom-mendations for Side-Effects Management," *Eur Urol*, 2000, 37(Suppl 1):33-6.

♦ **BCG Vaccine U.S.P.** *(percutaneous use product)* see BCG Vaccine on page 128

♦ **BCNU** see Carmustine on page 178

♦ **Bebulin® VH** see Factor IX Complex (Human) on page 421

♦ **BeneFix®** see Factor IX on page 418

♦ **Beneflur® (Can)** see Fludarabine on page 457

♦ **Benzisoquinolinedione** see Amonafide on page 67

♦ **Benzmethyzin** see Procarbazine on page 926

Benzydamine (ben ZID a meen)

Index Terms Benzydamine Hydrochloride

Generic Available Yes

Canadian Brand Names Apo-Benzydamine®; Dom-Benzydamine; Novo-Benzydamine; PMS-Benzydamine; ratio-Benzydamine; Sun-Benz®; Tantum®

Pharmacologic Category Local Anesthetic, Oral

Use Symptomatic treatment of pain associated with acute pharyngitis; treat-ment of pain associated with radiation-induced oropharyngeal mucositis

Restrictions Not available in U.S.

Lactation Excretion in breast milk unknown/use caution

Labeled Contraindications Hypersensitivity to benzydamine or any compo-nent of the formulation

Warnings/Precautions May cause local irritation and/or burning sensation in patients with altered mucosal integrity. Dilution (1:1 in warm water) may attenuate this effect. Use caution in renal impairment. Safety and efficacy have not been established in children ≤5 years of age.

Adverse Reactions

Central nervous system: Drowsiness, headache

Gastrointestinal: Nausea and/or vomiting (2%), dry mouth

Local: Numbness (10%), burning/stinging sensation (8%)

Respiratory: Pharyngeal irritation, cough

Drug Interactions
Cytochrome P450 Effect: Substrate (minor) of CYP1A2, 2C19, 2D6, 3A4
Increased Effect/Toxicity: No interactions established.
Decreased Effect: No interactions established.
Storage/Stability Store at 15°C to 30°C. Protect from freezing.
Mechanism of Action Local anesthetic and anti-inflammatory, reduces local pain and inflammation. Does not interfere with arachidonic acid metabolism.

Pharmacodynamics/Kinetics
Absorption: Oral rinse may be absorbed, at least in part, through the oral mucosa

Excretion: Urine (primarily as unchanged drug)

Dosage Oral rinse: Adults:
Acute pharyngitis: Gargle with 15 mL of undiluted solution every 1½-3 hours until symptoms resolve. Patient should expel solution from mouth following use; solution should not be swallowed.

Mucositis: 15 mL of undiluted solution as a gargle or rinse 3-4 times/day; contact should be maintained for at least 30 seconds, followed by expulsion from the mouth. Clinical studies maintained contact for ~2 minutes, up to 8 times/day. Patient should not swallow the liquid. Begin treatment 1day prior to initiation of radiation therapy and continue daily during treatment. Continue oral rinse treatments after the completion of radiation therapy until desired result/healing is achieved.

Dosage adjustment in renal impairment: No adjustment required.

Dosage Forms Excipient information presented when available (limited, particularly for generics); consult specific product labeling. [CAN] = Canadian brand name

Oral rinse: 0.15% (100 mL, 250 mL) [not available in the U.S.]

References
Epstein JB, Silverman S Jr, Paggiarino DA, et al, "Benzydamine HCl for Prophylaxis of Radiation-Induced Oral Mucositis: Results From a Multicenter, Randomized, Double-Blind, Placebo-Controlled Clinical Trial," *Cancer*, 2001, 92(4):875-85.

Henschel R, Agathos M, and Breit R, "Photocontact Dermatitis After Gargling With a Solution Containing Benzydamine," *Contact Dermatitis*, 2002, 47(1):53.

Lang DH and Rettie AE, "*In vitro* Evaluation of Potential *in vivo* Probes for Human Flavin-Containing Monooxygenase (FMO): Metabolism of Benzydamine and Caffeine by FMO and P450 Isoforms," *Br J Clin Pharmacol*, 2000, 50(4):311-4.

Ribldi E, Frascaroli G, Transidico P, "Benzydamine Inhibits Monocyte Migration and MAPK Activation Induced by Chemotactic Agonists," *Br J Pharmacol*, 2003, 140(2):377-83.

♦ **Benzydamine Hydrochloride** *see* Benzydamine *on page 132*
♦ **Beta-HC**® *see* Hydrocortisone *on page 545*

Bevacizumab (be vuh SIZ uh mab)
Medication Safety Issues
Sound-alike/look-alike issues:
Bevacizumab may be confused with cetuximab

High alert medication: The Institute for Safe Medication Practices (ISMP) includes this medication among its list of classes of drugs which have a heightened risk of causing significant patient harm when used in error.

U.S. Brand Names Avastin®
Index Terms Anti-VEGF Monoclonal Antibody; NSC-704865; rhuMAb-VEGF
Generic Available No
Canadian Brand Names Avastin®
Pharmacologic Category Antineoplastic Agent, Monoclonal Antibody; Vascular Endothelial Growth Factor (VEGF) Inhibitor
Use Treatment of metastatic colorectal cancer; treatment of nonsquamous, nonsmall cell lung cancer
(Continued)

Bevacizumab *(Continued)*

Unlabeled/Investigational Use Breast cancer, ovarian cancer (early stage), renal cell cancer, age-related macular degeneration (AMD)

Pregnancy Risk Factor C

Lactation Excretion in breast milk unknown/not recommended

Labeled Contraindications There are no contraindications listed in the manufacturer's labeling.

Warnings/Precautions [U.S. Boxed Warning]: Gastrointestinal perforation, fistula (including gastrointestinal, enterocutaneous, esophageal, duodenal, and rectal fistulas), intra-abdominal abscess, and wound dehiscence/wound healing complications have been reported in patients receiving bevacizumab (not related to treatment duration); monitor patients for signs/symptoms of abdominal pain, constipation, or vomiting. Permanently discontinue in patients who develop these complications. Nongastrointestinal fistula formation (including tracheoesophageal, bronchopleural, biliary, vaginal, and bladder fistulas) has been observed, most commonly within the first 6 months of treatment; permanently discontinue in patients who develop fistulas. The appropriate intervals between administration of bevacizumab and surgical procedures to avoid impairment in wound healing has not been established. Do not initiate therapy within 28 days of major surgery and only following complete healing of the incision. Bevacizumab should be discontinued prior to elective surgery and the estimated half-life (20 days) should be considered.

Use with caution in patients with cardiovascular disease; patients with significant recent cardiovascular disease were excluded from clinical trials. An increased risk for arterial thromboembolic events (eg, stroke, MI, TIA, angina) is associated with bevacizumab use in combination with chemotherapy. History of arterial thromboembolism or ≥65 years of age may present an even greater risk; permanently discontinue if serious arterial thromboembolic events occur.

May cause CHF and/or potentiate cardiotoxic effects of anthracyclines. CHF is more common with prior anthracycline exposure and/or left chest wall irradiation. Bevacizumab may cause and/or worsen hypertension significantly; use caution in patients with pre-existing hypertension and monitor BP closely in all patients. Permanent discontinuation is recommended in patients who experience a hypertensive crisis or encephalopathy. Temporarily discontinue in patients who develop uncontrolled hypertension. Cases of reversible posterior leukoencephalopathy syndrome (RPLS) have been reported. Symptoms (which include headache, seizure, confusion, lethargy, blindness and/or other vision, or neurologic disturbances) may occur from 16 hours to 1 year after treatment initiation. RPLS may be associated with hypertension; discontinue bevacizumab and begin management of hypertension, if present.

[U.S. Boxed Warning]: Avoid use in patients with recent hemoptysis (>2.5 mL blood); significant pulmonary bleeding has been reported in patients receiving bevacizumab (primarily in patients with nonsmall cell lung cancer with squamous cell histology [not an FDA-approved indication]). Avoid use in patients with CNS metastases; patients with CNS metastases were excluded from clinical trials due to concerns for bleeding. Other serious bleeding events may occur, but with a lower frequency; discontinuation of treatment is recommended in all patients with serious hemorrhage.

Interrupt therapy in patients experiencing severe infusion reactions; there are no data to address reinstitution of therapy in patients who experience CHF and/or severe infusion reactions. Proteinuria and/or nephrotic syndrome has been associated with bevacizumab; discontinue in patients with nephrotic syndrome. Elderly patients (≥65 years of age) are at higher risk for proteinuria. When used in combination with myelosuppressive chemotherapy, increased rates of severe or febrile neutropenia and neutropenic infection were reported. Safety and efficacy in children have not been established.

Adverse Reactions Percentages reported as part of combination chemotherapy regimens.

>10%:

Cardiovascular: Hypertension (8% to 67%; grades 3/4: 8% to 18%), thromboembolism (18%); hypotension (7% to 15%)

Central nervous system: Pain (61% to 62%), headache (2% to 26%), dizziness (19% to 26%), fatigue (5% to 19%), sensory neuropathy (1% to 17%)

Dermatologic: Alopecia (6% to 32%), dry skin (7% to 20%), exfoliative dermatitis (3% to 19%), skin discoloration (2% to 16%)

Endocrine & metabolic: Weight loss (15% to 16%), hypokalemia (12% to 16%)

Gastrointestinal: Abdominal pain (8% to 61%), diarrhea (2% to 18%; grades 3/4: 34%), vomiting (6% to 52%), anorexia (35% to 43%), constipation (29% to 40%), stomatitis (30% to 32%), gastrointestinal hemorrhage (19% to 24%), dyspepsia (17% to 24%), taste disorder (14% to 21%), flatulence (11% to 19%), nausea (6% to 12%)

Hematologic: Leukopenia (grades 3/4: 37%), neutropenia (grades 3/4: 21% to 27%)

Neuromuscular & skeletal: Weakness (73% to 74%), myalgia (8% to 15%)

Ocular: Tearing increased (6% to 18%)

Renal: Proteinuria (36%)

Respiratory: Upper respiratory infection (40% to 47%), epistaxis (32% to 35%), dyspnea (25% to 26%)

Miscellaneous: Infection (serious: 14%; pneumonia, catheter, or wound infections)

1% to 10%:

Cardiovascular: DVT (6% to 9%; grades 3/4: 9%); arterial thrombosis (3% to 4%), syncope (grades 3/4: 3%), intra-abdominal venous thrombosis (grades 3/4: 3%), cardio-/cerebrovascular arterial thrombotic event (2% to 4%), CHF (2%)

Central nervous system: Confusion (1% to 6%), abnormal gait (1% to 5%)

Dermatologic: Nail disorder (2% to 8%), skin ulcer (6%), wound dehiscence (1%)

Endocrine & metabolic: Dehydration (6% to 10%)

Gastrointestinal: Xerostomia (4% to 7%), colitis (1% to 6%), ileus (4% to 5%), gingival bleeding (2%), fistula (1%), gastrointestinal perforation (<1% to 4%), intra-abdominal abscess (1%)

Genitourinary: Polyuria/urgency (3% to 6%), vaginal hemorrhage (4%)

Hematologic: Neutropenic fever (5%), thrombocytopenia (5%), hemorrhage (4% to 5%)

Hepatic: Bilirubinemia (1% to 6%)

Respiratory: Voice alteration (6% to 9%), hemoptysis (nonsquamous histology 2%)

Miscellaneous: Infusion reactions (<3%)

<1%, postmarketing, and/or case reports (limited to important or life-threatening): Anastomotic ulceration, angina, cerebral infarction; fistula (biliary, bladder, bronchopleural, duodenal, enterocutaneous, esophageal, (Continued)

Bevacizumab *(Continued)*

gastrointestinal, rectal, tracheoesophageal [TE] and vaginal); hemorrhagic stroke, hypertensive crises, hypertensive encephalopathy, hyponatremia, intestinal necrosis, intestinal obstruction, mesenteric venous occlusion, MI, nasal septum perforation, nephrotic syndrome, pancytopenia, polyserositis, pulmonary embolism, pulmonary hemorrhage, reversible posterior leukoencephalopathy syndrome (RPLS), subarachnoid hemorrhage, transient ischemic attack, ureteral stricture, wound healing complications

Overdosage/Toxicology No information available on overdoses. Doses up to 20 mg/kg have been used in clinical trials. Treatment is symptom-directed and supportive.

Drug Interactions

Increased Effect/Toxicity: Bevacizumab may potentiate the cardiotoxic effects of anthracyclines. Serum concentrations of irinotecan's active metabolite may be increased by bevacizumab; an approximate 33% increase has been observed.

Storage/Stability Store vials at 2°C to 8°C (36°F to 46°F). Protect from light; do not freeze or shake. Diluted solutions are stable for up to 8 hours under refrigeration.

Reconstitution Prior to infusion, dilute prescribed dose of bevacizumab in 100 mL NS. Do not mix with dextrose-containing solutions.

Mechanism of Action Bevacizumab is a recombinant, humanized monoclonal antibody which binds to, and neutralizes, vascular endothelial growth factor (VEGF), preventing its association with endothelial receptors. VEGF binding initiates angiogenesis (endothelial proliferation and the formation of new blood vessels). The inhibition of microvascular growth is believed to retard the growth of all tissues (including metastatic tissue).

Pharmacodynamics/Kinetics

Distribution: V_d: 46 mL/kg

Half-life elimination: 20 days (range: 11-50 days)

Excretion: Clearance: 2.75-5 mL/kg/day

Dosage Adults: Refer to individual protocols.

I.V.:

Colorectal cancer: 5 or 10 mg/kg every 2 weeks

Lung cancer, nonsquamous cell nonsmall cell: 15 mg/kg every 3 weeks

Breast cancer (unlabeled use): 10 mg/kg every 2 weeks

Renal cell cancer (unlabeled use): 10 mg/kg every 2 weeks

Intravitreal: AMD (unlabeled use): 1.25 mg (0.05 mL) monthly until improvement/resolution, usually ~1-3 injections (Avery, 2006) or 2.5 mg (0.1 mL) every 4 weeks for 3 doses (Bashshur, 2006)

Dosage adjustment for toxicity: I.V. administration (systemic): Temporary suspension is recommended in moderate-to-severe proteinuria or in patients with severe hypertension which is not controlled with medical management. Permanent discontinuation is recommended (by the manufacturer) in patients who develop wound dehiscence requiring intervention, gastrointestinal perforation, hypertensive crisis, serious bleeding, severe arterial thrombotic event, nephrotic syndrome, or reversible posterior leukoencephalopathy syndrome.

Combination Regimens

Brain tumors: Bevacizumab-Irinotecan (Glioblastoma) *on page 1151*

Breast cancer:

Bevacizumab-Capecitabine *on page 1150*

Paclitaxel-Bevacizumab *on page 1263*

Colorectal cancer:

Bevacizumab-Fluorouracil-Leucovorin *on page 1151*

Bevacizumab-Irinotecan-Fluorouracil-Leucovorin *on page 1151*

Bevacizumab-Oxaliplatin-Fluorouracil-Leucovorin *on page 1152*

Lung cancer (nonsmall cell): Paclitaxel-Carboplatin-Bevacizumab *on page 1263*

Renal cell cancer: Bevacizumab-Interferon Alfa-2a *on page 1151*

Administration

I.V. infusion, usually after the other antineoplastic agents. Infuse the initial dose over 90 minutes. Infusion may be shortened to 60 minutes if the initial infusion is well tolerated. The third and subsequent infusions may be shortened to 30 minutes if the 60-minute infusion is well tolerated. Monitor closely during the infusion for signs/symptoms of an infusion reaction. Some institutions use a 10-minute infusion (0.5 mg/kg/minute) for bevacizumab dosed at 5 mg/kg (Reidy, 2007).

Intravitreal injection (unlabeled use): Adequate anesthesia and a broad-spectrum antimicrobial agent should be administered prior to the procedure; administer topical antibiotics for 3 days after procedure.

Monitoring Parameters Monitor closely during the infusion for signs/symptoms of an infusion reaction. Monitor CBC with differential; signs/symptoms of gastrointestinal perforation, fistula, or abscess (including abdominal pain, constipation, vomiting, and fever); signs/symptoms of bleeding, including hemoptysis, gastrointestinal, and/or CNS bleeding, and/or epistaxis. Monitor blood pressure every 2-3 weeks; more frequently if hypertension develops during therapy. Continue to monitor blood pressure after discontinuing due to bevacizumab-induced hypertension. Monitor for proteinuria/nephrotic syndrome.

AMD: Monitor intraocular pressure and retinal artery perfusion

Patient Information Report any signs and symptoms of abdominal pain, unusual bleeding, or delayed wound healing.

Special Geriatric Considerations Elderly patients ≥65 years of age had an increased incidence of arterial thromboembolic events; an increased risk for proteinuria; other serious adverse events occurring often include weakness, sepsis, hyper-/hypotension, CHF, constipation, anorexia, anemia, hyper-/hypokalemia, and diarrhea.

Emetic Potential Very low <10%

Vesicant No

Dosage Forms Excipient information presented when available (limited, particularly for generics); consult specific product labeling.

Injection, solution [preservative free]:

Avastin®: 25 mg/mL (4 mL, 16 mL)

References

Avery RL, Pieramici DJ, Rabena MD, et al, "Intravitreal Bevacizumab (Avastin) for Neovascular Age-Related Macular Degeneration," *Ophthalmology*, 2006, 113(3):363-72.

Bashshur AF, Bazarbachi A, Schakal A, et al, "Intravitreal Bevacizumab for the Management of Choroidal Neovascularization in Age-Related Macular Degeneration," *Am J Ophthalmol*, 2006, 142(1):1-9.

Glusker P, Recht L, and Lane B, "Reversible Posterior Leukoencephalopathy Syndrome and Bevacizumab," *N Engl J Med*, 2006, 354(9):980-1.

Herbst RS, Johnson DH, Mininberg E, et al, "Phase I/II Trial Evaluating the Antivascular Endothelial Growth Factor Monoclonal Antibody Bevacizumab in Combination With the HER-1/Epidermal Growth Factor Receptor Tyrosine Kinase Inhibitor Erlotinib for Patients With Recurrent Non-Small-Cell Lung Cancer," *J Clin Oncol*, 2005, 23(11):2544-55.

Johnson DH, Fehrenbacher L, Novotny WF, et al, "Randomized Phase II Trial Comparing Bevacizumab Plus Carboplatin and Paclitaxel With Carboplatin and Paclitaxel Alone in Previously Untreated Locally Advanced or Metastatic Non-Small-Cell Lung Cancer," *J Clin Oncol*, 2004, 22(11):2184-91.

(Continued)

Bevacizumab *(Continued)*

Mauer AM, Cohen EE, Wong SJ, et al, "Phase I Study of Epidermal Growth Factor Receptor (EGFR) Inhibitor, Erlotinib, and Vascular Endothelial Growth Factor Monoclonal Antibody, Bevacizumab, in Recurrent and/or Metastatic Squamous Cell Carcinoma of the Head and Neck (SCCHN)," *J Clin Oncol*, 2004, 22(14S):5539.

Miller KD, "E2100: A Phase III Trial of Paclitaxel Versus Paclitaxel/Bevacizumab for Metastatic Breast Cancer," *Clin Breast Cancer*, 2003, 3(6):421-2.

Monk BJ, Choi DC, Pugmire G, et al, "Activity of Bevacizumab (rhuMAB VEGF) in Advanced Refractory Epithelial Ovarian Cancer," *Gynecol Oncol*, 2005, 96(3):902-5.

Ozcan C, Wong SJ, and Hari P, "Reversible Posterior Leukoencephalopathy Syndrome and Bevacizumab," *N Engl J Med*, 2006, 354(9):981-2.

Reidy DL, Chung KY, Timoney JP, et al, "Bevacizumab 5 mg/kg Can be Infused Safely over 10 minutes," *J Clin Oncol*, 2007, 25(19):2691-5.

Sandler A, Gray R, Perry MC, et al, "Paclitaxel-Carboplatin Alone or With Bevacizumab for Non-Small-Cell Lung Cancer," *N Engl J Med*, 2006, 355(24):2542-50.

Sane DC, Anton L, and Brosnihan KB, "Angiogenic Growth Factors and Hypertension," *Angengenesis*, 2004, 7(3):193-201.

Scappaticci FA, Skillings JR, Holden SN, et al, "Arterial Thromboembolic Events in Patients with Metastatic Carcinoma Treated With Chemotherapy and Bevacizumab," *J Natl Cancer Inst*, 2007, 99(16):1232-9.

Yang JC, Haworth L, Sherry RM, et al, "A Randomized Trial of Bevacizumab, An Antivascular Endothelial Growth Factor Antibody, for Metastatic Renal Cancer," *N Engl J Med*, 2003, 349(5):427-34.

Bexarotene (beks AIR oh teen)

Medication Safety Issues

High alert medication: The Institute for Safe Medication Practices (ISMP) includes this medication among its list of drugs which have a heightened risk of causing significant patient harm when used in error.

Related Information

Safe Handling of Hazardous Drugs *on page 1382*

U.S. Brand Names Targretin®

Generic Available No

Canadian Brand Names Targretin®

Pharmacologic Category Antineoplastic Agent, Miscellaneous

Use

Oral: Treatment of cutaneous manifestations of cutaneous T-cell lymphoma in patients who are refractory to at least one prior systemic therapy

Topical: Treatment of cutaneous lesions in patients with refractory cutaneous T-cell lymphoma (stage 1A and 1B) or who have not tolerated other therapies

Pregnancy Risk Factor X

Lactation Excretion in breast milk unknown/contraindicated

Labeled Contraindications Hypersensitivity to bexarotene or any component of the formulation; pregnancy

Warnings/Precautions Hazardous agent - use appropriate precautions for handling and disposal. **[U.S. Boxed Warning]: Bexarotene is a retinoid, a drug class associated with birth defects in humans; do not administer during pregnancy.** Pregnancy test needed 1 week before initiation and every month thereafter. Effective contraception must be in place 1 month before initiation, during therapy, and for at least 1 month after discontinuation. Male patients with sexual partners who are pregnant, possibly pregnant, or who could become pregnant, must use condoms during sexual intercourse during treatment and for 1 month after last dose. Induces significant lipid abnormalities in a majority of patients (triglyceride, total cholesterol, and HDL); reversible on discontinuation. Use extreme caution in patients with underlying hypertriglyceridemia. Pancreatitis secondary to hypertriglyceridemia has been reported. Monitor for liver function test abnormalities and discontinue drug if tests are three times the upper limit of normal values for

AST, ALT, or bilirubin. Hypothyroidism occurs in about a third of patients. Monitor for signs and symptoms of infection about 4-8 weeks after initiation (leukopenia may occur). Any new visual abnormalities experienced by the patient should be evaluated by an ophthalmologist (cataracts can form, or worsen, especially in the geriatric population). May cause photosensitization. Safety and efficacy are not established in the pediatric population. Avoid use in hepatically-impaired patients. Limit additional vitamin A intake to <15,000 int. units/day. Use caution with diabetic patients.

Adverse Reactions First percentage is at a dose of 300 mg/m²/day; the second percentage is at a dose >300 mg/m²/day.

Oral:

>10%:

    Cardiovascular: Peripheral edema (13% to 11%)

    Central nervous system: Headache (30% to 42%), chills (10% to 13%)

    Dermatologic: Rash (17% to 23%), exfoliative dermatitis (10% to 28%)

    Endocrine & metabolic: Hyperlipidemia (about 79% in both dosing ranges), hypercholesteremia (32% to 62%), hypothyroidism (29% to 53%)

    Hematologic: Leukopenia (17% to 47%)

    Neuromuscular & skeletal: Weakness (20% to 45%)

    Miscellaneous: Infection (13% to 23%)

<10%:

    Cardiovascular: Hemorrhage, hypertension, angina pectoris, right heart failure, tachycardia, cerebrovascular accident, syncope

    Central nervous system: Fever (5% to 17%), insomnia (5% to 11%), subdural hematoma, depression, agitation, ataxia, confusion, dizziness, hyperesthesia

    Dermatologic: Dry skin (about 10% for both dosing ranges), alopecia (4% to 11%), skin ulceration, acne, skin nodule, maculopapular rash, serous drainage, vesicular bullous rash, cheilitis

    Endocrine & metabolic: Hypoproteinemia, hyperglycemia, weight loss/gain, breast pain

    Gastrointestinal: Abdominal pain (11% to 4%), nausea (16% to 8%), diarrhea (7% to 42%), vomiting (4% to 13%), anorexia (2% to 23%), constipation, xerostomia, flatulence, colitis, dyspepsia, gastroenteritis, gingivitis, melena, pancreatitis, serum amylase increased

    Genitourinary: Albuminuria, hematuria, urinary incontinence, urinary tract infection, urinary urgency, dysuria, kidney function abnormality

    Hematologic: Hypochromic anemia (4% to 13%), anemia (6% to 25%), eosinophilia, thrombocythemia, coagulation time increased, lymphocytosis, thrombocytopenia

    Hepatic: LDH increased (7% to 13%), hepatic failure

    Neuromuscular & skeletal: Back pain (2% to 11%), arthralgia, myalgia, bone pain, myasthenia, arthrosis, neuropathy

    Ocular: Dry eyes, conjunctivitis, blepharitis, corneal lesion, visual field defects, keratitis

    Otic: Ear pain, otitis externa

    Renal: Creatinine increased

    Respiratory: Pharyngitis, rhinitis, dyspnea, pleural effusion, bronchitis, cough increased, lung edema, hemoptysis, hypoxia

    Miscellaneous: Flu-like syndrome (4% to 13%), bacterial infection (1% to 13%)

Topical:

    Cardiovascular: Edema (10%)

    Central nervous system: Headache (14%), weakness (6%), pain (30%)

(Continued)

Bexarotene *(Continued)*

Dermatologic: Rash (14% to 72%), pruritus (6% to 40%), contact dermatitis (14%), exfoliative dermatitis (6%)

Hematologic: Leukopenia (6%), lymphadenopathy (6%)

Neuromuscular & skeletal: Paresthesia (6%)

Respiratory: Cough (6%), pharyngitis (6%)

Miscellaneous: Diaphoresis (6%), infection (18%)

Overdosage/Toxicology Doses up to 1000 mg/m^2/day have been used in humans without acute toxic effects. Any overdose should be treated with supportive care focused on the symptoms exhibited.

Drug Interactions

Cytochrome P450 Effect: Substrate of CYP3A4 (minor); **Induces** CYP3A4 (weak)

Increased Effect/Toxicity: Bexarotene plasma concentrations may be increased by gemfibrozil. Bexarotene may increase the toxicity of DEET.

Decreased Effect: Bexarotene may decrease the plasma levels of hormonal contraceptives and tamoxifen.

Ethanol/Nutrition/Herb Interactions

Food: Take with a fat-containing meal. Bexarotene serum levels may be increased by grapefruit juice; avoid concurrent use.

Herb/Nutraceutical: Avoid dong quai, St John's wort (may also cause photosensitization). St John's wort may decrease bexarotene levels. Additional vitamin A supplements may lead to vitamin A toxicity (dry skin, irritation, arthralgias, myalgias, abdominal pain, hepatic changes).

Storage/Stability Store at 2°C to 25°C (36°F to 77°F). Protect from light.

Mechanism of Action The exact mechanism is unknown. Binds and activates retinoid X receptor subtypes. Once activated, these receptors function as transcription factors that regulate the expression of genes which control cellular differentiation and proliferation. Bexarotene inhibits the growth *in vitro* of some tumor cell lines of hematopoietic and squamous cell origin.

Pharmacodynamics/Kinetics

Absorption: Significantly improved by a fat-containing meal

Protein binding: >99%

Metabolism: Hepatic via CYP3A4 isoenzyme; four metabolites identified; further metabolized by glucuronidation

Half-life elimination: 7 hours

Time to peak: 2 hours

Excretion: Primarily feces; urine (<1% as unchanged drug and metabolites)

Dosage Adults:

Oral: 300-400 mg/m^2/day taken as a single daily dose.

Topical: Apply once every other day for first week, then increase on a weekly basis to once daily, 2 times/day, 3 times/day, and finally 4 times/day, according to tolerance

Dosing adjustment in renal impairment: No studies have been conducted; however, renal insufficiency may result in significant protein binding changes and alter pharmacokinetics of bexarotene

Dosing adjustment in hepatic impairment: No studies have been conducted; however, hepatic impairment would be expected to result in decreased clearance of bexarotene due to the extensive hepatic contribution to elimination

Administration

Oral: Administer capsule following a fat-containing meal.

Topical: Allow gel to dry before covering with clothing. Avoid application to normal skin. Use of occlusive dressings is not recommended.

Monitoring Parameters If female, pregnancy test 1 week before initiation then monthly while on bexarotene; lipid panel before initiation, then weekly until lipid response established and then at 8-week intervals thereafter; baseline LFTs, repeat at 1, 2, and 4 weeks after initiation then at 8-week intervals thereafter if stable; baseline and periodic thyroid function tests; baseline CBC with periodic monitoring

Dietary Considerations It is preferable to take the oral capsule following a fat-containing meal.

Patient Information Oral: Take with a fat-containing meal. Do not get pregnant while taking this medicine. Get pregnancy test before starting therapy and then every month thereafter while on the medicine. Use two forms of birth control 1 month before, during, and for at least a month after completion of therapy. For male patients, protect your partner against pregnancy by wearing a condom. Continue using protection for 1 month after last dose. Take at a similar time daily. You are at risk of infections; stay away from crowds and people with viruses. Wash your hands frequently. Call your prescriber if you have a fever, chills, or any signs of infection. Check vitamin A intake with your prescriber. You should avoid large amounts of vitamin A.

Topical gel: Allow gel to dry before covering. Avoid applying to normal skin or mucous membranes. Do not use occlusive dressings.

Emetic Potential Low (10% to 30%)

Dosage Forms Excipient information presented when available (limited, particularly for generics); consult specific product labeling.
Capsule:
Targretin®: 75 mg
Gel: 1% (60 g)
Targretin®: 1% (60 g) [contains dehydrated alcohol]

References
Duvic M, "Bexarotene and DAB(389)IL-2 (denileukin diftitox, ONTAK) in Treatment of Cutaneous T-cell Lymphomas: Algorithms," *Clin Lymphoma*, 2000, 1(Suppl 1):51-5.
Farol LT and Hymes KB, "Bexarotene: A Clinical Review," *Expert Rev Anticancer Ther*, 2004, 4(2):180-8.
Hurst RE, "Bexarotene Ligand Pharmaceuticals," *Curr Opin Investig Drugs*, 2000, 1(4):514-23.
Lowe MN and Plosker GL, "Bexarotene," *Am J Clin Dermatol*, 1(4):245-50.
Martin AG, "Bexarotene Gel: A New Skin-Directed Treatment Option for Cutaneous T-Cell Lymphomas," *J Drugs Dermatol*, 2003, 2(2):155-67.

♦ **Bexxar®** see Tositumomab and Iodine I 131 Tositumomab *on page 1056*

Bicalutamide (bye ka LOO ta mide)

Related Information
Safe Handling of Hazardous Drugs *on page 1382*

U.S. Brand Names Casodex®

Index Terms CDX; ICI-176334; NC-722665

Generic Available No

Canadian Brand Names Casodex®; CO Bicalutamide; Novo-Bicalutamide; PHL-Bicalutamide; PMS-Bicalutamide; ratio-Bicalutamide; Sandoz-Bicalutamide

Pharmacologic Category Antineoplastic Agent, Antiandrogen

Use In combination therapy with LHRH agonist analogues in treatment of metastatic prostate cancer

Unlabeled/Investigational Use Monotherapy for locally-advanced prostate cancer

Pregnancy Risk Factor X

Lactation Excretion in breast milk unknown/contraindicated

Labeled Contraindications Hypersensitivity to bicalutamide or any component of the formulation; female patients; pregnancy
(Continued)

Bicalutamide *(Continued)*

Warnings/Precautions Hazardous agent - use appropriate precautions for handling and disposal. Rare cases of death or hospitalization due to hepatitis have been reported postmarketing. Use with caution in moderate-to-severe hepatic dysfunction. Hepatotoxicity generally occurs within the first 3-4 months of use; patients should be monitored for signs and symptoms of liver dysfunction. Bicalutamide should be discontinued if patients have jaundice or ALT is >2 times the upper limit of normal. May cause gynecomastia, breast pain, or lead to spermatogenesis inhibition.

Adverse Reactions Adverse reaction percentages reported as part of combination regimen with an LHRH analogue.

>10%:
  Cardiovascular: Peripheral edema (13%)
  Central nervous system: Pain (35%)
  Endocrine & metabolic: Hot flashes (53%)
  Gastrointestinal: Constipation (22%), nausea (15%), diarrhea (12%), abdominal pain (11%)
  Genitourinary: Pelvic pain (21%), nocturia (12%), hematuria (12%)
  Hematologic: Anemia (11%)
  Neuromuscular & skeletal: Back pain (25%), weakness (22%)
  Respiratory: Dyspnea (13%)
  Miscellaneous: Infection (18%)

≥2% to 10%:
  Cardiovascular: Chest pain (8%), hypertension (8%), angina pectoris (2% to <5%), CHF (2% to <5%), edema (2% to <5%), MI (2% to <5%), coronary artery disorder (2% to <5%), syncope (2% to <5%)
  Central nervous system: Dizziness (10%), headache (7%), insomnia (7%), anxiety (5%), depression (4%), chills (2% to <5%), confusion (2% to <5%), fever (2% to <5%), nervousness (2% to <5%), somnolence (2% to <5%)
  Dermatologic: Rash (9%), alopecia (2% to <5%), dry skin (2% to <5%), pruritus (2% to <5%), skin carcinoma (2% to <5%)
  Endocrine & metabolic: Gynecomastia (9%), breast pain (6%; up to 39% as monotherapy), hyperglycemia (6%), dehydration (2% to <5%), gout (2% to <5%), hypercholesterolemia (2% to <5%), libido decreased (2% to <5%)
  Gastrointestinal: Dyspepsia (7%), weight loss (7%), anorexia (6%), flatulence (6%), vomiting (6%), weight gain (5%), dysphagia (2% to <5%), gastrointestinal carcinoma (2% to <5%), melena (2% to <5%), periodontal abscess (2% to <5%), rectal hemorrhage (2% to <5%), xerostomia (2% to <5%)
  Genitourinary: Urinary tract infection (9%), impotence (7%), polyuria (6%), urinary retention (5%), urinary impairment (5%), urinary incontinence (4%), dysuria (2% to <5%), urinary urgency (2% to <5%)
  Hepatic: LFTs increased (7%), alkaline phosphatase increased (5%)
  Neuromuscular & skeletal: Bone pain (9%), paresthesia (8%), myasthenia (7%), arthritis (5%), pathological fracture (4%), hypertonia (2% to <5%), leg cramps (2% to <5%), myalgia (2% to <5%), neck pain (2% to <5%), neuropathy (2% to <5%)
  Ocular: Cataract (2% to <5%)
  Renal: BUN increased, creatinine increased, hydronephrosis
  Respiratory: Cough (8%), pharyngitis (8%), bronchitis (6%), pneumonia (4%), rhinitis (4%), asthma (2% to <5%), epistaxis (2% to <5%), sinusitis (2% to <5%)

Miscellaneous: Flu syndrome (7%), diaphoresis (6%), cyst (2% to <5%), hernia (2% to <5%), herpes zoster (2% to <5%), sepsis (2% to <5%)

Postmarketing and/or case reports: Bilirubin increased, hemoglobin decreased, hepatitis, hypersensitivity reactions (including angioneurotic edema and urticaria), interstitial pneumonitis, pulmonary fibrosis, WBC decreased

Overdosage/Toxicology Doses up to 200 mg daily have been well tolerated in long term clinical trials. Symptoms of overdose may include hypoactivity, ataxia, anorexia, vomiting, slow respiration, and lacrimation. Vomiting may be induced if the patient is alert. Vital signs should be monitored frequently. Treatment is symptom-directed and supportive. Dialysis is of no benefit.

Storage/Stability Store at room temperature of 20°C to 25°C (68°F to 77°F).

Mechanism of Action Pure nonsteroidal antiandrogen that binds to androgen receptors; specifically a competitive inhibitor for the binding of dihydrotestosterone and testosterone; prevents testosterone stimulation of cell growth in prostate cancer

Pharmacodynamics/Kinetics

Absorption: Rapid and complete

Protein binding: 96%

Metabolism: Extensively hepatic; glucuronidation and oxidation of the R (active) enantiomer to inactive metabolites

Half-life elimination: Active enantiomer ~6 days, ~10 days in severe liver disease

Time to peak, plasma: 31 hours

Excretion: Urine (36%, as inactive metabolites); feces (42%, as unchanged drug and inactive metabolites)

Dosage Adults: Oral:

Metastatic prostate cancer: 50 mg once daily (in combination with an LHRH analogue)

Locally-advanced prostate cancer (unlabeled use): Oral: 150 mg once daily (as monotherapy)

Dosage adjustment in renal impairment: No adjustment required

Dosage adjustment in hepatic impairment: No adjustment required for mild, moderate, or severe hepatic impairment; use caution with moderate-to-severe impairment. Discontinue if ALT >2 times ULN or patient develops jaundice.

Combination Regimens

Prostate cancer: Bicalutamide + LHRH-A *on page 1152*

Administration Dose should be taken at the same time each day with or without food. Treatment should be started concomitantly with an LHRH analogue.

Monitoring Parameters Periodically monitor CBC, ECG, echocardiograms, serum testosterone, luteinizing hormone, and prostate specific antigen. Liver function tests should be obtained at baseline and repeated regularly during the first 4 months of treatment, and periodically thereafter; monitor for signs and symptoms of liver dysfunction (discontinue if jaundice is noted or ALT is >2 times the upper limit of normal).

Dietary Considerations May be taken with or without food.

Patient Information Take as directed and do not alter dose or discontinue this medicine without consulting prescriber. Take at the same time each day with or without food. Diabetics should monitor serum glucose closely and notify prescriber of changes; this medication can alter hypoglycemic requirements. You may lose your hair and experience impotency. May cause dizziness, confusion, or drowsiness (use caution when driving or engaging in tasks that require alertness until response to drug is known); nausea or (Continued)

Bicalutamide *(Continued)*

vomiting (small frequent meals, frequent mouth care, sucking lozenges, or chewing gum may help); or constipation (increased dietary fiber, fruit, or fluid and increased exercise may help). Report easy bruising or bleeding; yellowing of skin or eyes; change in color of urine or stool; unresolved CNS changes (nervousness, chills, insomnia, somnolence); skin rash, redness, or irritation; chest pain or palpitations; difficulty breathing; urinary retention or inability to void; muscle weakness, tremors, or pain; persistent nausea, vomiting, diarrhea, or constipation; or other unusual signs or adverse reactions.

Special Geriatric Considerations Renal impairment has no clinically-significant changes in elimination of the parent compound or active metabolite; therefore, no dosage adjustment is needed in the elderly. In dosage studies, no difference was found between young adults and elderly with regard to steady-state serum concentrations for bicalutamide and its active R-enantiomer metabolite.

Emetic Potential Very low (<10%)

Dosage Forms Excipient information presented when available (limited, particularly for generics); consult specific product labeling.

Tablet: 50 mg

References

Blackledge GR, Cockshott ID, and Furr BJ, "Casodex (Bicalutamide): Overview of a New Antiandrogen Developed for the Treatment of Prostate Cancer," *Eur Urol*, 1997, 31(Suppl 2):30-9.

Cockshott ID, "Bicalutamide: Clinical Pharmacokinetics and Metabolism," *Clin Pharmacokinet*, 2004, 43(13):855-78.

Goa KL and Spencer CM, "Bicalutamide in Advanced Prostate Cancer. A Review," *Drugs Aging*, 1998, 12(5):401-22

Iversen P, "Bicalutamide Monotherapy for Early Stage Prostate Cancer: An Update," J Urol, 2003, 170(6 Pt 2):S48-52.

Kennealey GT and Furr BJ, "Use of the Nonsteroidal Antiandrogen Casodex in Advanced Prostatic Carcinoma," *Urol Clin North Am*, 1991, 18(1):99-110.

Kolvenbag GJ and Blackledge GR, "Worldwide Activity and Safety of Bicalutamide: A Summary Review," *Urology*, 1996, 47(1A Suppl):70-9.

Kolvenbag GJ and Nash A, "Bicalutamide Dosages Used in the Treatment of Prostate Cancer," *Prostate*, 1999, 39(1):47-53.

Kolvenbag GJ, Blackledge GR, and Gotting-Smith K, "Bicalutamide (Casodex) in the Treatment of Prostate Cancer: History of Clinical Development," *Prostate*, 1998, 34(1):61-72.

Mahler C, Verhelst J, and Denis L, "Clinical Pharmacokinetics of the Antiandrogens and Their Efficacy in Prostate Cancer," *Clin Pharmacokinet*, 1998, 34(5):405-17.

Migliari R, Muscas G, Murru M, et al, "Antiandrogens: A Summary Review of Pharmacodynamic Properties and Tolerability in Prostate Cancer Therapy," *Arch Ital Urol Androl*, 1999, 71(5):293-302.

Schellhammer PF, "An Evaluation of Bicalutamide in the Treatment of Prostate Cancer," *Expert Opin Pharmacother*, 2002, 3(9):1313-28.

Schellhammer PF and Davis JW, "An Evaluation of Bicalutamide in the Treatment of Prostate Cancer," 2004, 2(4):213-9.

Tyrrell CJ, "Casodex: A Pure Nonsteroidal Antiandrogen Used as Monotherapy in Advanced Prostate Cancer," *Prostate Suppl*, 1992, 4:97-104.

♦ **BiCNU**® *see Carmustine on page 178*
♦ **BIDA** *see Amonafide on page 67*
♦ **Bio-Statin**® *see Nystatin on page 817*
♦ **Bisac-Evac**™ **[OTC]** *see Bisacodyl on page 144*

Bisacodyl *(bis a KOE dil)*

Medication Safety Issues

Sound-alike/look-alike issues:

Doxidan® may be confused with doxepin

Modane® may be confused with Matulane®, Moban®

U.S. Brand Names Alophen® [OTC]; Bisac-Evac™ [OTC]; Bisacodyl Uniserts® [OTC] [DSC]; Bisolax™ [OTC]; Correctol® Tablets [OTC]; Dacodyl™ [OTC]; Doxidan® [OTC]; Dulcolax® [OTC]; ex-lax® Ultra [OTC]; Fematrol [OTC]; Femilax™ [OTC]; Fleet® Bisacodyl [OTC]; Fleet® Stimulant Laxative [OTC]; Veracolate [OTC]

Generic Available Yes: Excludes enema

Canadian Brand Names Apo-Bisacodyl®; Carter's Little Pills®; Dulcolax®; Gentlax®

Pharmacologic Category Laxative, Stimulant

Use Treatment of constipation; colonic evacuation prior to procedures or examination

Pregnancy Risk Factor C

Labeled Contraindications Hypersensitivity to bisacodyl or any component of the formulation; abdominal pain or obstruction, nausea, or vomiting

Adverse Reactions <1%:

Central nervous system: Vertigo

Endocrine & metabolic: Electrolyte and fluid imbalance (metabolic acidosis or alkalosis, hypocalcemia)

Gastrointestinal: Mild abdominal cramps, nausea, vomiting, rectal burning

Drug Interactions

Decreased Effect: Milk or antacids may decrease the effect of bisacodyl. Bisacodyl may decrease the effect of warfarin.

Ethanol/Nutrition/Herb Interactions Food: Milk or dairy products may disrupt enteric coating, increasing stomach irritation.

Mechanism of Action Stimulates peristalsis by directly irritating the smooth muscle of the intestine, possibly the colonic intramural plexus; alters water and electrolyte secretion producing net intestinal fluid accumulation and laxation

Pharmacodynamics/Kinetics

Onset of action: Oral: 6-10 hours; Rectal: 0.25-1 hour

Absorption: Oral, rectal: Systemic, <5%

Dosage

Children:

Oral: >6 years: 5-10 mg (0.3 mg/kg) at bedtime or before breakfast

Rectal suppository:

<2 years: 5 mg as a single dose

>2 years: 10 mg

Adults:

Oral: 5-15 mg as single dose (up to 30 mg when complete evacuation of bowel is required)

Rectal suppository: 10 mg as single dose

Administration Administer with a glass of water on an empty stomach for rapid effect. Do not administer within 1 hour of milk, any dairy products, or taking an antacid, to protect the coating.

Dietary Considerations Should not be administered within 1 hour of milk, any dairy products, or taking an antacid, to protect the coating. Should be administered with a glass of water on an empty stomach for rapid effect.

Special Geriatric Considerations The chronic use of stimulant cathartics is inappropriate and should be avoided; although constipation is a common complaint from elderly, such complaints require evaluation; elderly are often predisposed to constipation due to disease, drugs, immobility, and a decreased fluid intake, partially because they have a blunted "thirst reflex" with aging; short-term use of stimulants is best; if prophylaxis is desired, this
(Continued)

Bisacodyl (Continued)

can be accomplished with bulk agents (psyllium), stool softeners, and hyper-osmotic agents (sorbitol 70%); stool softeners are unnecessary if stools are well hydrated, soft, or "mushy".

Emetic Potential Very low (<10%)

Dosage Forms Excipient information presented when available (limited, particularly for generics); consult specific product labeling. [DSC] = Discontinued product

Solution, rectal [enema]:
Fleet® Bisacodyl: 10 mg/30 mL (37 mL)

Suppository, rectal: 10 mg
Bisac-Evac™, Bisacodyl Uniserts® [DSC], Bisolax™, Dulcolax®: 10 mg

Tablet [enteric coated]: 5 mg
Alophen®, Bisac-Evac™, Correctol®, Dacodyl™, Dulcolax®, ex-lax® Ultra, Fematrol, Femilax™, Veracolate: 5 mg

Tablet, delayed release: 5 mg
Doxidan®, Fleet® Stimulant Laxative: 5 mg

+ **Bisacodyl Uniserts®** [OTC] [DSC] see Bisacodyl on page 144
+ **bis-chloronitrosourea** see Carmustine on page 178
+ **Bisolax™** [OTC] see Bisacodyl on page 144
+ **BL4162A** see Anagrelide on page 87
+ **Blenoxane®** see Bleomycin on page 146
+ **Bleo** see Bleomycin on page 146

Bleomycin (blee oh MYE sin)

Medication Safety Issues
Sound-alike/look-alike issues:
Bleomycin may be confused with Cleocin®

High alert medication: The Institute for Safe Medication Practices (ISMP) includes this medication among its list of drugs which have a heightened risk of causing significant patient harm when used in error.

Related Information
Fertility and Cancer Therapy on page 1298
Management of Drug Extravasations on page 1301
Safe Handling of Hazardous Drugs on page 1382

U.S. Brand Names Blenoxane®

Index Terms Bleo; Bleomycin Sulfate; BLM; NSC-125066

Generic Available Yes

Canadian Brand Names Blenoxane®; Bleomycin Injection, USP

Pharmacologic Category Antineoplastic Agent, Antibiotic

Use Treatment of squamous cell carcinomas, melanomas, sarcomas, testicular carcinoma, Hodgkin's lymphoma, and non-Hodgkin's lymphoma; sclerosing agent for malignant pleural effusion

Pregnancy Risk Factor D

Lactation Excretion in breast milk unknown/not recommended

Labeled Contraindications Hypersensitivity to bleomycin or any component of the formulation; severe pulmonary disease; pregnancy

Warnings/Precautions Hazardous agent - use appropriate precautions for handling and disposal. **[U.S. Boxed Warnings]: Occurrence of pulmonary fibrosis (commonly presenting as pneumonitis) is higher in elderly patients, patients receiving >400 units total, smokers, and patients with prior radiation therapy. A severe idiosyncratic reaction consisting of hypotension, mental confusion, fever, chills, and wheezing is possible.**

Use caution when administering O_2 during surgery to patients who have received bleomycin. Use caution with renal impairment, may require dose adjustment. May cause renal or hepatic toxicity. **[U.S. Boxed Warning]: Should be administered under the supervision of an experienced cancer chemotherapy physician.**

Adverse Reactions

>10%:

Dermatologic: Pain at the tumor site, phlebitis. About 50% of patients develop erythema, rash, striae, induration, hyperkeratosis, vesiculation, and peeling of the skin, particularly on the palmar and plantar surfaces of the hands and feet. Hyperpigmentation (50%), alopecia, nailbed changes may also occur. These effects appear dose related and reversible with discontinuation.

Gastrointestinal: Stomatitis and mucositis (30%), anorexia, weight loss

Respiratory: Tachypnea, rales, acute or chronic interstitial pneumonitis, and pulmonary fibrosis (5% to 10%); hypoxia and death (1%). Symptoms include cough, dyspnea, and bilateral pulmonary infiltrates. The pathogenesis is not certain, but may be due to damage of pulmonary, vascular, or connective tissue. Response to steroid therapy is variable and somewhat controversial.

Miscellaneous: Acute febrile reactions (25% to 50%)

1% to 10%:

Dermatologic: Skin thickening, diffuse scleroderma, onycholysis, pruritus

Miscellaneous: Anaphylactoid-like reactions (characterized by hypotension, confusion, fever, chills, and wheezing; onset may be immediate or delayed for several hours); idiosyncratic reactions (1% in lymphoma patients)

<1%: Angioedema, cerebrovascular accident, cerebral arteritis, hepatotoxicity, malaise, MI, nausea, Raynaud's phenomenon, renal toxicity, scleroderma-like skin changes, thrombotic microangiopathy, vomiting; Myelosuppression (rare); Onset: 7 days, Nadir: 14 days, Recovery: 21 days

Overdosage/Toxicology Symptoms of overdose include chills, fever, pulmonary fibrosis, and hyperpigmentation. Treatment is symptom-directed and supportive.

Drug Interactions

Increased Effect/Toxicity: Cisplatin may decrease bleomycin elimination.

Decreased Effect: Bleomycin may decrease plasma levels of digoxin. Concomitant therapy with phenytoin results in decreased phenytoin levels.

Storage/Stability Refrigerate intact vials of powder. Intact vials are stable for up to 1 month at 45°C. Solutions for infusion are stable for 96 hours at room temperature and 14 days under refrigeration.

Reconstitution Reconstitute powder with 1-5 mL BWFI or BNS which is stable at room temperature or under refrigeration for 28 days.

Standard I.V. dilution: Dose/50-1000 mL NS.

Compatibility Stable in NS; **variable stability (consult detailed reference)** in D_5W.

Y-site administration: Compatible: Allopurinol, amifostine, aztreonam, cefepime, cisplatin, cyclophosphamide, doxorubicin, doxorubicin liposome, droperidol, etoposide phosphate, filgrastim, fludarabine, fluorouracil, gemcitabine, granisetron, heparin, leucovorin, melphalan, methotrexate, metoclopramide, mitomycin, ondansetron, paclitaxel, piperacillin/tazobactam, sargramostim, teniposide, thiotepa, vinblastine, vincristine, vinorelbine.

(Continued)

Bleomycin (Continued)

Compatibility in syringe: Compatible: Cisplatin, cyclophosphamide, doxorubicin, droperidol, fluorouracil, furosemide, heparin, leucovorin, methotrexate, metoclopramide, mitomycin, vinblastine, vincristine.

Compatibility when admixed: Compatible: Amikacin, dexamethasone sodium phosphate, diphenhydramine, fluorouracil, gentamicin, heparin, hydrocortisone sodium phosphate, phenytoin, streptomycin, tobramycin, vinblastine, vincristine. **Incompatible:** Aminophylline, ascorbic acid injection, cefazolin, diazepam, hydrocortisone sodium succinate, methotrexate, mitomycin, nafcillin, penicillin G sodium, terbutaline.

Mechanism of Action Inhibits synthesis of DNA; binds to DNA leading to single- and double-strand breaks

Pharmacodynamics/Kinetics

Absorption: I.M. and intrapleural administration: 30% to 50% of I.V. serum concentrations; intraperitoneal and SubQ routes produce serum concentrations equal to those of I.V.

Distribution: V_d: 22 L/m²; highest concentrations in skin, kidney, lung, heart tissues; lowest in testes and GI tract; does not cross blood-brain barrier

Protein binding: 1%

Metabolism: Via several tissues including hepatic, GI tract, skin, pulmonary, renal, and serum

Half-life elimination: Biphasic (renal function dependent):
  Normal renal function: Initial: 1.3 hours; Terminal: 9 hours
  End-stage renal disease: Initial: 2 hours; Terminal: 30 hours

Time to peak, serum: I.M.: Within 30 minutes

Excretion: Urine (50% to 70% as active drug)

Dosage Maximum cumulative lifetime dose: 400 units; refer to individual protocols; 1 unit = 1 mg

May be administered I.M., I.V., SubQ, or intracavitary

Children and Adults:

Test dose for lymphoma patients: I.M., I.V., SubQ: Because of the possibility of an anaphylactoid reaction, administer 1-2 units of bleomycin before the first 1-2 doses; monitor vital signs every 15 minutes; wait a minimum of 1 hour before administering remainder of dose; if no acute reaction occurs, then the regular dosage schedule may be followed. **Note:** Test doses may produce false-negative results.

Single-agent therapy:
  I.M./I.V./SubQ: Squamous cell carcinoma, lymphoma, testicular carcinoma: 0.25-0.5 units/kg (10-20 units/m²) 1-2 times/week
  CIV: 15 units/m² over 24 hours daily for 4 days

Pleural sclerosing: Intrapleural: 60 units as a single instillation (some recommend limiting the dose in the elderly to 40 units/m²; usual maximum: 60 units). Dose may be repeated at intervals of several days if fluid continues to accumulate (mix in 50-100 mL of NS); may add lidocaine 100-200 mg to reduce local discomfort.

Dosing adjustment in renal impairment:

The FDA-approved labeling recommends the following adjustments:
  Cl_{cr} 40-50 mL/minute: Administer 70% of normal dose
  Cl_{cr} 30-40 mL/minute: Administer 60% of normal dose
  Cl_{cr} 20-30 mL/minute: Administer 55% of normal dose
  Cl_{cr} 10-20 mL/minute: Administer 45% of normal dose
  Cl_{cr} 5-10 mL/minute: Administer 40% of normal dose

The following guidelines have been used by some clinicians:
  Aronoff, 2007: Adults: Continuous renal replacement therapy (CRRT): Administer 75% of dose

Kintzel, 1995:

Cl$_{cr}$ 46-60 mL/minute: Administer 70% of dose

Cl$_{cr}$ 31-45 mL/minute: Administer 60% of dose

Cl$_{cr}$ <30 mL/minute: Consider use of alternative drug

Dosing adjustment in hepatic impairment: Not studied in patients with hepatic impairment; adjustment for hepatic impairment may be needed.

Combination Regimens

Cervical cancer: BIP *on page 1152*

Head and neck cancer: CABO *on page 1157*

Lymphoma, Hodgkin's:

ABVD *on page 1142*

BEACOPP *on page 1148*

CAD/MOPP/ABV *on page 1157*

MOPP/ABV Hybrid *on page 1251*

MOPP/ABVD *on page 1249*

Stanford V *on page 1278*

Lymphoma, non-Hodgkin's:

CEPP(B) *on page 1167*

COP-BLAM *on page 1182*

MACOP-B *on page 1245*

m-BACOD *on page 1246*

Pro-MACE-CytaBOM *on page 1273*

Melanoma:

BOLD *on page 1153*

BOLD + Interferon *on page 1153*

BOLD (Melanoma) *on page 1154*

Osteosarcoma: POG-8651 *on page 1272*

Ovarian cancer:

BEP (Ovarian Cancer) *on page 1149*

BEP (Ovarian Cancer, Testicular Cancer) *on page 1149*

Testicular cancer:

BEP (Ovarian Cancer, Testicular Cancer) *on page 1149*

BEP (Testicular Cancer) *on page 1149*

PVB *on page 1275*

VBP *on page 1288*

Administration

I.V. doses should be administered slowly (over 10-60 minutes).

I.M. or SubQ: May cause pain at injection site

Intrapleural: 60 units in 50-100 mL NS; use of topical anesthetics or narcotic analgesia is usually not necessary

Monitoring Parameters Pulmonary function tests (total lung volume, forced vital capacity, carbon monoxide diffusion), renal function, liver function, chest x-ray, temperature initially; check body weight at regular intervals

Patient Information You may experience loss of appetite, nausea, vomiting, mouth sores; small frequent meals, frequent mouth care with soft swab, frequent mouth rinses, sucking lozenges, or chewing gum may help; if unresolved, notify physician. You may experience fever or chills (will usually resolve); redness, peeling, or increased color of skin, or loss of hair (reversible after cessation of therapy). Report any change in respiratory status; difficulty breathing; wheezing; air hunger; increased secretions; difficulty expectorating secretions; confusion; unresolved fever or chills; sores in mouth; vaginal itching, burning, or discharge; sudden onset of dizziness; or acute headache. Contraceptive measures are recommended during therapy.

Special Geriatric Considerations Pulmonary toxicity has been reported more frequently in geriatric patients (>70 years of age).

(Continued)

Bleomycin *(Continued)*

Emetic Potential Very low (<10%)

Vesicant No

Dosage Forms Excipient information presented when available (limited, particularly for generics); consult specific product labeling.

Injection, powder for reconstitution, as sulfate: 15 units, 30 units

References

Aronoff GR, Bennett WM, Berns JS, et al, *Drug Prescribing in Renal Failure: Dosing Guidelines for Adults and Children*, 5th ed. Philadelphia, PA: American College of Physicians; 2007, p 97.

Kintzel PE and Dorr RT, "Anticancer Drug Renal Toxicity and Elimination: Dosing Guidelines for Altered Renal Function," *Cancer Treat Rev*, 1995, 21(1):33-64.

Lamey PJ and Lewis MAO, "Oral Medicine in Practice: White Patches," *Br Dent J*, 1990, 168(4):147-52.

Lazo JS and Sebti SM, "Bleomycin," *Cancer Chemother Biol Response Modif*, 1994, 15:44-50.

Lazo JS, Sebti SM, and Schellens JH, "Bleomycin," *Cancer Chemother Biol Response Modif*, 1996, 16:39-47.

Mir LM, Tounekti O, and Orlowski S, "Bleomycin: Revival of an Old Drug," *Gen Pharmacol*, 1996, 27(5):745-8.

♦ **Bleomycin Injection, USP (Can)** *see* Bleomycin *on page 146*
♦ **Bleomycin Sulfate** *see* Bleomycin *on page 146*
♦ **BLM** *see* Bleomycin *on page 146*
♦ **BMS-247550** *see* Ixabepilone *on page 644*
♦ **BMS-354825** *see* Dasatinib *on page 301*
♦ **Bondronat® (Can)** *see* Ibandronate *on page 567*
♦ **Bonefos® (Can)** *see* Clodronate *on page 234*
♦ **Boniva®** *see* Ibandronate *on page 567*

Bortezomib *(bore TEZ oh mib)*

Medication Safety Issues

High alert medication: The Institute for Safe Medication Practices (ISMP) includes this medication among its list of drugs which have a heightened risk of causing significant patient harm when used in error.

Related Information

Safe Handling of Hazardous Drugs *on page 1382*

U.S. Brand Names Velcade®

Index Terms LDP-341; MLN341; NSC-681239; PS-341

Generic Available No

Canadian Brand Names Velcade®

Pharmacologic Category Antineoplastic Agent; Proteasome Inhibitor

Use Treatment of relapsed or refractory multiple myeloma; relapsed or refractory mantle cell lymphoma

Unlabeled/Investigational Use Treatment of non-Hodgkin's lymphomas (other than mantle cell lymphoma)

Pregnancy Risk Factor D

Lactation Excretion in breast milk unknown/not recommended

Labeled Contraindications Hypersensitivity to bortezomib, boron, mannitol, or any component of the formulation

Warnings/Precautions Hazardous agent - use appropriate precautions for handling and disposal. May cause peripheral neuropathy (usually sensory but may be mixed sensorimotor); risk may be increased with previous use of neurotoxic agents or pre-existing peripheral neuropathy; adjustment of dose and schedule may be required. May cause hypotension; use caution with dehydration, history of syncope, or medications associated with hypotension. Has been associated with the development or exacerbation of congestive heart failure and decreased left ventricular ejection fraction; use caution in patients with risk factors or existing heart disease. Has also been associated with QT_c prolongation.

Pulmonary disorders including pneumonitis, interstitial pneumonia, lung infiltrates, and acute respiratory distress syndrome (ARDS) have been reported. Pulmonary hypertension (without left heart failure or significant pulmonary disease has been reported rarely). May cause tumor lysis syndrome; risk is increased in patients with large tumor burden prior to treatment. Reversible posterior leukoencephalopathy syndrome (RPLS) has been reported (rarely). Symptoms of RPLS include confusion, headache, hypertension, lethargy, seizure, blindness and/or other vision, or neurologic disturbances; discontinue if RPLS occurs. Hematologic toxicity, including neutropenia and severe thrombocytopenia, may occur; risk is increased in patients with pretreatment platelet counts <75,000/µL; frequent monitoring is required throughout treatment; may require dosage adjustments; withhold treatment for platelets <25,000/µL. Acute liver failure has been reported (rarely) in patients receiving multiple concomitant medications; hepatitis, transaminase increases, and hyperbilirubinemia have also been reported. Use caution in patients with hepatic dysfunction; toxicities may be increased. Hyper- and hypoglycemia may occur in diabetic patients receiving oral hypoglycemics; may require adjustment of diabetes medications. Safety and efficacy have not been established in pediatric patients.

Adverse Reactions

>10%:

Cardiovascular: Edema (11% to 28%), hypotension (12% to 15%; grades 3/4: 3%)

Central nervous system: Fever (19% to 37%), psychiatric disturbance (35%), headache (17% to 26%), dysesthesia (9% to 27%), insomnia (18% to 21%), dizziness (14% to 23%; excludes vertigo), anxiety (5% to 11%)

Dermatologic: Rash (17% to 28%), pruritus (11%)

Endocrine & metabolic: Dehydration (7% to 11%)

Gastrointestinal: Diarrhea (47% to 57%), nausea (44% to 57%), constipation (40% to 50%), anorexia (34% to 39%), vomiting (27% to 35%), abdominal pain (14% to 16%), abnormal taste (13%), dyspepsia (13%)

Hematologic: Thrombocytopenia (21% to 38%; grade 4: 4% to 5%; nadir: day 11; recovery: by day 21), anemia (17% to 30%; grade 4: <1%), neutropenia (6% to 19%; grade 4: 2% to 3%; nadir: day 11; recovery: by day 21)

Neuromuscular & skeletal: Weakness (61% to 72%; grades 3/4: 12% to 19%), peripheral neuropathy (36% to 55%; grade 3: 7% to 11%; grade 4: <1%), paresthesia (9% to 27%), arthralgia (13% to 18%), limb pain (5% to 17%), bone pain (2% to 16%), back pain (<1 % to 15%), myalgia (10% to 12%), muscle cramps (5% to 12%), rigors (11%)

Ocular: Blurred vision (11%)

Respiratory: Dyspnea (20% to 23%), cough (19% to 21%), lower respiratory infection (15%), upper respiratory tract infection (11% to 15%), nasopharyngitis (8% to 14%), pneumonia (9% to 12%)

Miscellaneous: Herpesvirus infections (7% to 13%)

1% to 10%:

Cardiovascular: Syncope (2%)

Endocrine & metabolic: Hypercalcemia (grade 4: 2%)

Frequency not defined (including postmarketing and/or case reports; limited to important or life-threatening): Acute diffuse infiltrative pulmonary

(Continued)

Bortezomib *(Continued)*

disease, acute respiratory distress syndrome, allergic reaction, anaphylaxis, angina, angioedema, ascites, aspergillosis, atelectasis, atrial fibrillation, atrial flutter, AV block, bacteremia, bradycardia, cardiac amyloidosis, cardiac arrest, cardiac tamponade, cardiogenic shock, cerebral hemorrhage, cerebrovascular accident, CHF, cholestasis, coma, confusion, cranial palsy, deafness, deep venous thrombosis, diplopia, disseminated intravascular coagulation (DIC), duodenitis (hemorrhagic), dysautonomia, dysphagia, edema (facial), encephalopathy, embolism, epistaxis, fecal impaction, fracture, gastritis (hemorrhagic), gastroenteritis, glomerular nephritis, hematemesis, hematuria, hemoptysis, hemorrhagic cystitis, hepatic failure, hepatic hemorrhage, hepatitis, herpes meningoencephalitis, hyperbilirubinemia, hyper-/hypoglycemia, hyper-/hypokalemia, hyper-/hyponatremia, hypersensitivity, hyperuricemia, hypocalcemia, hypoxia, immune complex hypersensitivity, injection site reaction, intestinal obstruction, intestinal perforation, ischemic colitis, laryngeal edema, leukocytoclastic vasculitis, leukopenia, listeriosis, lymphopenia, melena, MI, myocardial ischemia, neuralgia, neutropenic fever, ophthalmic herpes, oral candidiasis, pancreatitis, paralytic ileus, paraplegia, pericardial effusion, pericarditis, peritonitis, pleural effusion, pneumonia, pneumonitis, portal vein thrombosis, proliferative glomerular nephritis, pulmonary edema, pulmonary embolism, pulmonary hypertension, psychosis, QT_c prolongation, renal calculus, renal failure, respiratory failure, respiratory insufficiency, reversible posterior leukoencephalopathy syndrome (RPLS), seizure, septic shock, sepsis, sinus arrest, spinal cord compression, stomatitis, stroke (hemorrhagic), stroke, subdural hematoma, suicidal ideation, torsade de pointes, toxic epidermal necrolysis, toxoplasmosis, transient ischemic attack, tumor lysis syndrome, urinary incontinence, urinary retention, urinary tract infection, urticaria, ventricular tachycardia

Overdosage/Toxicology Doses of 2.6 mg/m^2 have been associated with fatal hypotension and thrombocytopenia. In case of overdose, monitor vital signs, maintain blood pressure and body temperature; treatment is otherwise symptom-directed and supportive.

Drug Interactions

Cytochrome P450 Effect: Substrate of CYP1A2 (minor), 2C9 (minor), 2C19 (major), 2D6 (minor), 3A4 (major); **Inhibits** CYP1A2 (weak), 2C9 (weak), 2C19 (moderate), 2D6 (weak), 3A4 (weak)

Increased Effect/Toxicity: Bortezomib may increase the levels/effects citalopram, diazepam, methsuximide, phenytoin, propranolol, sertraline, and other CYP2C19 substrates. Levels/effects of bortezomib may be increased by azole antifungals, clarithromycin, delavirdine, diclofenac, doxycycline, erythromycin, fluconazole, fluvoxamine, gemfibrozil, imatinib, isoniazid, nefazodone, nicardipine, omeprazole, propofol, protease inhibitors, quinidine, telithromycin, ticlopidine, verapamil, and other CYP2C19 and CYP3A4 inhibitors.

Decreased Effect: Levels/effects of bortezomib may be decreased by aminoglutethimide, carbamazepine, nafcillin, nevirapine, phenobarbital, phenytoin, rifamycins, rifapentine, and other CYP2C19 and CYP3A4 inducers.

Ethanol/Nutrition/Herb Interactions Herb/Nutraceutical: St John's wort may decrease bortezomib levels.

Storage/Stability Prior to reconstitution, store at room temperature, 15°C to 30°C (59°F to 86°F). Protect from light. Once reconstituted, although the manufacturer recommends use within 8 hours, solution may be stored at room temperature for up to 3 days, or under refrigeration for up to 5 days, in vial or syringe; protect from light.

Reconstitution Dilute each 3.5 mg vial with 3.5 mL NS.

Mechanism of Action Bortezomib inhibits proteasomes, enzyme complexes which regulate protein homeostasis within the cell. Specifically, it reversibly inhibits chymotrypsin-like activity at the 26S proteasome, leading to activation of signaling cascades, cell-cycle arrest, and apoptosis.

Pharmacodynamics/Kinetics

Distribution: 498-1884 L/m^2

Protein binding: ~83%

Metabolism: Hepatic primarily via CYP2C19 and 3A4 and to a lesser extent CYP1A2; forms metabolites (inactive) via deboronization followed by hydroxylation

Half-life elimination: Single dose: 9-15 hours; multiple dosing: 1 mg/m^2: 40-193 hours; 1.3 mg/m^2: 76-108 hours

Dosage I.V.: Adults:

Multiple myeloma, mantle cell lymphoma: 1.3 mg/m^2 twice weekly for 2 weeks on days 1, 4, 8, and 11 of a 21-day treatment cycle. Consecutive doses should be separated by at least 72 hours. Therapy extending beyond 8 cycles may be given once weekly for 4 weeks (days 1, 8, 15, and 22), followed by a 13-day rest (days 23 through 35).

Non-Hodgkin's lymphoma, other than mantle cell (unlabeled use): 1.3-1.5 mg/m^2 twice weekly for 2 weeks on days 1, 4, 8, and 11 of a 21-day treatment cycle.

Dosage adjustment in renal impairment: Dosage adjustment not necessary. **Note:** Dialysis may reduce bortezomib concentrations; administer post-dialysis.

Dosage adjustment in hepatic impairment: Specific guidelines are not available; clearance may be decreased; monitor closely for toxicity

Dosage adjustment for toxicity:

Grade 3 nonhematological (excluding neuropathy) or Grade 4 hematological toxicity: Withhold until toxicity resolved; may reinitiate with a 25% dose reduction (1.3 mg/m^2/dose reduced to 1 mg/m^2/dose; 1 mg/m^2/dose reduced to 0.7 mg/m^2/dose)

Neuropathic pain and/or peripheral sensory neuropathy:

Grade 1 without pain or loss of function: No action needed

Grade 1 with pain or Grade 2 interfering with function but not activities of daily living: Reduce dose to 1 mg/m^2

Grade 2 with pain or Grade 3 interfering with activities of daily living: Withhold until toxicity resolved, may reinitiate at 0.7 mg/m^2 once weekly

Grade 4: Discontinue therapy

Combination Regimens

Multiple myeloma:

Bortezomib-Doxorubicin (Liposomal) *on page 1155*

Bortezomib-Melphalan-Prednisone *on page 1156*

Bortezomib-Melphalan-Prednisone-Thalidomide *on page 1156*

Administration Administer via rapid I.V. push (3-5 seconds)

Monitoring Parameters Signs/symptoms of peripheral neuropathy, dehydration, or hypotension; CBC with differential and platelets (monitor frequently throughout therapy); renal function, pulmonary function (with new or worsening pulmonary symptoms), liver function tests (in patients with existing hepatic impairment)

Emetic Potential Moderate (30% to 60%)

Vesicant No

(Continued)

Bortezomib *(Continued)*

Dosage Forms Excipient information presented when available (limited, particularly for generics); consult specific product labeling.

Injection, powder for reconstitution [preservative free]:

Velcade®: 3.5 mg [contains mannitol 35 mg]

References

Adams J, "Proteasome Inhibition in Cancer: Development of PS-341," *Semin Oncol*, 2001, 28(6):613-9.

Aghajanian C, Soignet S, Dizon DS, et al, "A Phase I Trial of the Novel Proteasome Inhibitor PS341 in Advanced Solid Tumor Malignancies," *Clin Cancer Res*, 2002, 8(8):2505-11.

Andre P, Cisternino S, Chiadmi F, et al, "Stability of Bortezomib 1-mg/mL Solution in Plastic Syringe and Glass Vial," *Ann Pharmacother*, 2005, 39(9):1462-6.

Chanan-Khan AA, Kaufman JL, Mehta J, et al, "Activity and Safety of Bortezomib in Multiple Myeloma Patients With Advanced Renal Failure: A Multicenter Retrospective Study," *Blood*, 2006, 109(9):2604-6.

Fisher RI, Bernstein SH, Kahl BS, et al, "Multicenter Phase II Study of Bortezomib in Patients With Relapsed or Refractory Mantle Cell Lymphoma," *J Clin Oncol*, 2006, 24(30):4867-74.

Goy A, Younes A, McLaughlin P, et al, "Phase II Study of Proteasome Inhibitor Bortezomib in Relapsed or Refractory B-cell Non-Hodgkin's Lymphoma," *J Clin Oncol*, 2005, 23(4):667-75.

Jagannath S, Barlogie B, Berenson JR, et al, "Bortezomib in Recurrent and/or Refractory Multiple Myeloma; Initial Clinical Experience in Patients With Impaired Renal Function," *Cancer*, 2005, 103(6):1195-200.

Kastritis E, Anagnostopoulos A, Bamias A, et al, "Reversibility of Renal Failure in Newly Diagnosed Patients With Multiple Myeloma Treated With High-Dose Dexamethasone Containing Regimens and the Impact of Novel Agents," *Blood*, 2006, 108(11):3586. Abstract from ASH Annual Meeting.

Mulkerin D, Remick S, Ramanathan R, et al, "A Dose-Escalating and Pharmacologic Study of Bortezomib in Adult Cancer Patients With Impaired Renal Function," *J Clin Oncol*, ASCO Annual Meeting Proceedings, 2006, Part I, 24(18S):2032.

O'Connor OA, Wright J, Moskowitz C, et al "Phase II Clinical Experience With the Novel Proteasome Inhibitor Bortezomib in Patients With Indolent Non-Hodgkin's Lymphoma and Mantle Cell Lymphoma," *J Clin Oncol*, 2005, 23(4):676-84.

Orlowski RZ, Stinchcombe TE, Mitchell BS, et al, "Phase I Trial of the Proteasome Inhibitor PS-341 in Patients With Refractory Hematologic Malignancies," *J Clin Oncol*, 2002, 20(22):4420-7.

Pekol T, Daniels JS, Labutti J, et al, "Human Metabolism of the Proteasome Inhibitor Bortezomib: Identification of Circulating Metabolites," *Drug Metab Dispos*, 2005, 33(6):771-7.

Richardson PG, Sonneveld P, Schuster MW, et al, "Bortezomib or High-Dose Dexamethasone for Relapsed Multiple Myeloma," *N Engl J Med*, 2005, 352(24):2487-98.

Teicher BA, Ara G, Herbst R, et al, "The Proteasome Inhibitor PS-341 in Cancer Therapy," *Clin Cancer Res*, 1999, 5(9):2638-45.

Terpos E, Politou M, and Rahemtulla A, "Tumour Lysis Syndrome in Multiple Myeloma After Bortezomib (VELCADE) Administration," *J Cancer Res Clin Oncol*, 2004, 130(10):623-5.

Uttamsingh V, Lu C, Miwa G, et al, "Relative Contributions of the Five Major Hyman Cytochromes P450, 1A2, 2C9, 2C19, and 3A4, to the Hepatic Metabolism of the Proteosome Inhibitor Bortezomib," *Drug Metab Dispos*, 2005, 33(11):1723-8.

♦ **BRL 43694** *see* Granisetron *on page 522*

Busulfan *(byoo SUL fan)*

Medication Safety Issues

Sound-alike/look-alike issues:

Busulfan may be confused with Butalan®

Myleran® may be confused with Leukeran®, melphalan, Mylicon®

High alert medication: The Institute for Safe Medication Practices (ISMP) includes this medication among its list of drugs which have a heightened risk of causing significant patient harm when used in error.

Related Information

Fertility and Cancer Therapy *on page 1298*

Hematopoietic Stem Cell Transplantation *on page 1366*

Safe Handling of Hazardous Drugs *on page 1382*

U.S. Brand Names Busulfex®; Myleran®
Index Terms NSC-750
Generic Available No
Canadian Brand Names Busulfex®; Myleran®
Pharmacologic Category Antineoplastic Agent, Alkylating Agent
Use

Oral: Chronic myelogenous leukemia (CML); conditioning regimens for bone marrow transplantation

I.V.: Combination therapy with cyclophosphamide as a conditioning regimen prior to allogeneic hematopoietic progenitor cell transplantation for chronic myelogenous leukemia

Unlabeled/Investigational Use Oral: Bone marrow disorders, such as polycythemia vera and myeloid metaplasia; thrombocytosis

Pregnancy Risk Factor D

Lactation Excretion in breast milk unknown/not recommended

Labeled Contraindications Hypersensitivity to busulfan or any component of the formulation; oral busulfan is contraindicated in patients without a definitive diagnosis of CML

Warnings/Precautions Hazardous agent - use appropriate precautions for handling and disposal. **[U.S. Boxed Warning]: May induce severe bone marrow suppression.** May result in severe neutropenia, thrombocytopenia and/or anemia. Seizures have been reported with use; use caution in patients predisposed to seizures; initiate prophylactic anticonvulsant therapy (eg, phenytoin) prior to treatment; use caution with history of seizures or head trauma. May cause delayed pulmonary toxicity (known as "busulfan lung" - bronchopulmonary dysplasia with pulmonary fibrosis); the average onset is 4 years (range: 4 months to 10 years). Cardiac tamponade as been reported in children with thalassemia treated with high-dose oral busulfan in combination with cyclophosphamide. Busulfan has been causally related to the development of secondary malignancies (tumors and acute leukemias). Busulfan has been associated with ovarian failure (including failure to achieve puberty).

High busulfan area under the concentration versus time curve (AUC) values (>1500 µM/minute) are associated with increased risk of hepatic veno-occlusive disease during conditioning for allogenic BMT; patients with of history of radiation therapy, prior chemotherapy (≥3 cycles) and prior stem cell transplantation are at increased risk. Oral busulfan doses above 16 mg/kg (based on IBW) and concurrent use with alkylating agents may also increase the risk for hepatic VOD. The solvent in I.V. busulfan, DMA, may impair fertility. DMA may also be associated with hepatotoxicity, hallucinations, somnolence, lethargy, and confusion. **[U.S. Boxed Warning]: Should be administered under the supervision of an experienced cancer chemotherapy physician.**

Adverse Reactions

I.V.:
>10%

Cardiovascular: Tachycardia (44%), hypertension (36%; grades 3/4: 7%), edema (28% to 79%), thrombosis (33%), chest pain (26%), vasodilation (25%), hypotension (11%; grades 3/4: 3%)

Central nervous system: Insomnia (84%), fever (80%), anxiety (72% to 75%), headache (69%), chills (46%), pain (44%), dizziness (30%), depression (23%), confusion (11%)

Dermatologic: Rash (57%), pruritus (28%), alopecia (2% to 15%)

Endocrine & metabolic: Hypomagnesemia (77%), hyperglycemia (66%; grades 3/4: 15%), hypokalemia (64%), hypocalcemia (49%), hypophosphatemia (17%)

(Continued)

Busulfan (Continued)

Gastrointestinal: Nausea (98%), mucositis/stomatitis (97%; grades 3/4: 26%), vomiting (43% to 95%), anorexia (85%), diarrhea (84%; grades 3/4: 5%), abdominal pain (72%), dyspepsia (44%), constipation (38%), xerostomia (26%), rectal disorder (25%), abdominal fullness (23%)

Hematologic: Myelosuppression (≤100%), neutropenia (100%; median recovery: 13 days), thrombocytopenia (98%; median onset: 5-6 days), lymphopenia (children: 79%), anemia (69%)

Hepatic: Hyperbilirubinemia (49%; grades 3/4: 30%), ALT increased (31%; grades 3/4: 7%), veno-occlusive disease (adults: 8% to 12%; children: 21%), jaundice (12%)

Local: Injection site inflammation (25%), injection site pain (15%)

Neuromuscular & skeletal: Weakness (51%), back pain (23%), myalgia (16%), arthralgia (13%)

Renal: Creatinine increased (21%), oliguria (15%)

Respiratory: Rhinitis (44%), lung disorder (34%), cough (28%), epistaxis (25%), dyspnea (25%), pneumonia (children: 21%), hiccup (18%), pharyngitis (18%)

Miscellaneous: Infection (51%), allergic reaction (26%)

1% to 10%:

Cardiovascular: Arrhythmia (5%), cardiomegaly (5%), atrial fibrillation (2%), ECG abnormal (2%), heart block (2%), heart failure (grade 3/4: 2%), pericardial effusion (2%), tamponade (children with thalassemia: 2%), ventricular extrasystoles (2%), hypervolemia

Central nervous system: Lethargy (7%), hallucination (5%), agitation (2%), delirium (2%), encephalopathy (2%), seizure (2%), somnolence (2%), cerebral hemorrhage (1%)

Dermatologic: Vesicular rash (10%), vesiculobullous rash (10%), skin discoloration (8%), maculopapular rash (8%), acne (7%), exfoliative dermatitis (5%), erythema nodosum (2%)

Endocrine & metabolic: Hyponatremia (2%)

Gastrointestinal: Ileus (8%), weight gain (8%), hematemesis (2%), pancreatitis (2%)

Hematologic: Prothrombin time increased (2%)

Hepatic: Hepatomegaly (6%)

Renal: Hematuria (8%), dysuria (7%), hemorrhagic cystitis (grade 3/4: 7%), BUN increased (3%)

Respiratory: Asthma (8%), alveolar hemorrhage (5%), hyperventilation (5%), hemoptysis (3%), pleural effusion (3%), sinusitis (3%), atelectasis (2%), hypoxia (2%)

Oral: Frequency not defined:

Central nervous system: Seizure

Dermatologic: Hyperpigmentation of skin (busulfan tan 5% to 10%), alopecia, rash, urticaria

Endocrine & metabolic: Amenorrhea, ovarian suppression

Hematologic: Myelosuppression (anemia, leukopenia, thrombocytopenia), pancytopenia

I.V. and/or Oral: Infrequent, postmarketing, and/or case reports: Acute leukemias, adrenal suppression, alopecia (permanent), aplastic anemia (may be irreversible), azoospermia, blurred vision, cataracts, cheilosis, cholestatic jaundice, corneal thinning, dry skin, endocardial fibrosis, erythema multiforme, erythema nodosum, esophageal varices, gynecomastia, hemorrhagic cystitis, hepatic dysfunction, hepatocellular atrophy, hyperuricemia, hyperuricosuria, interstitial pulmonary fibrosis (busulfan lung; manifested by a diffuse interstitial pulmonary fibrosis and persistent cough, fever, rales, and dyspnea; may be relieved by corticosteroids); malignant tumors, myasthenia gravis, ocular (lens) changes, ovarian failure, porphyria cutanea tarda, radiation myelopathy, radiation recall (skin rash), sepsis, sterility, testicular atrophy

Overdosage/Toxicology Symptoms of overdose include bone marrow suppression and pancytopenia. Administration of the recommended dose of busulfan I.V. without a stem cell transplant is considered an overdose; profound bone marrow suppression, CNS, liver, lung and gastrointestinal toxicity may occur. Busulfan is dialyzable; dialysis may be considered for overdose. Induction of vomiting or gastric lavage with charcoal is indicated for recent ingestion. Treatment is otherwise symptom-directed and supportive.

Drug Interactions

Cytochrome P450 Effect: Substrate of CYP3A4 (major)

Increased Effect/Toxicity: CYP3A4 inhibitors may increase the levels/effects of busulfan; example inhibitors include azole antifungals, clarithromycin, diclofenac, doxycycline, erythromycin, imatinib, isoniazid, nefazodone, nicardipine, propofol, protease inhibitors, quinidine, telithromycin, and verapamil. Metronidazole may increase busulfan plasma levels. Pulmonary toxicity of other cytotoxic agents may be additive.

Decreased Effect: CYP3A4 inducers may decrease the levels/effects of busulfan; example inducers include aminoglutethimide, carbamazepine, nafcillin, nevirapine, phenobarbital, phenytoin, and rifamycins.

Ethanol/Nutrition/Herb Interactions

Ethanol: Avoid ethanol due to GI irritation.

Food: No clear or firm data on the effect of food on busulfan bioavailability.

Herb/Nutraceutical: Avoid St John's wort (may decrease busulfan levels).

Storage/Stability

Injection: Store unopened ampuls and vials under refrigeration (2°C to 8°C). Final solution is stable for up to 8 hours at room temperature (25°C); the infusion must be completed within that 8-hour timeframe. Dilution of busulfan injection in 0.9% sodium chloride is stable for up to 12 hours at refrigeration (2°C to 8°C); the infusion must be completed within that 12-hour timeframe.

Tablet: Store at room temperature at 15°C to 30°C (59°F to 86°F).

Reconstitution Injection: Dilute (using manufacturer provided 5-micron filters for ampuls) in 0.9% sodium chloride injection or dextrose 5% in water. The dilution volume of busulfan injection, ensuring that the final concentration of busulfan is 0.5 mg/mL.

Compatibility Variable stability (consult detailed reference) in D_5W, NS.

Mechanism of Action Busulfan is an alkylating agent which reacts with the N-7 position of guanosine and interferes with DNA replication and transcription of RNA. Busulfan has a more marked effect on myeloid cells than on lymphoid cells and is also very toxic to hematopoietic stem cells. Busulfan exhibits little immunosuppressive activity. Interferes with the normal function of DNA by alkylation and cross-linking the strands of DNA.

Pharmacodynamics/Kinetics

Duration: 28 days

Absorption: Rapid and complete

Distribution: V_d: ~1 L/kg; into CSF and saliva with levels similar to plasma

Protein binding: 32% to plasma proteins and 47% to red blood cells

Metabolism: Extensively hepatic (may increase with multiple doses); gluta-thione conjugation followed by oxidation

Half-life elimination: After first dose: 3.4 hours; After last dose: 2.3 hours

(Continued)

Busulfan *(Continued)*

Time to peak, serum: Oral: Within 4 hours; I.V.: Within 5 minutes

Excretion: Urine (10% to 50% as metabolites) within 24 hours (<2% as unchanged drug)

Dosage Note: Premedicate with prophylactic anticonvulsant therapy (eg, phenytoin) prior to high-dose busulfan treatment.

Children:

CML, remission induction: Oral: 0.06-0.12 mg/kg/day **or** 1.8-4.6 mg/m²/day; titrate dosage to maintain the leukocyte count above 40,000/mm³; reduce dosage by 50% if the leukocyte count reaches 30,000-40,000/mm³; discontinue drug if counts fall to ≤20,000/mm³

BMT marrow-ablative conditioning regimen:

Oral: 1 mg/kg/dose (ideal body weight) every 6 hours for 16 doses

I.V.:

≤12 kg: 1.1 mg/kg/dose (ideal body weight) every 6 hours for 16 doses

>12 kg: 0.8 mg/kg/dose (ideal body weight) every 6 hours for 16 doses

Adjust dose to desired AUC [1125 µmol(min)] using the following formula:

Adjusted dose (mg) = Actual dose (mg) x [target AUC µmol(min) / actual AUC µmol(min)]

Adults:

CML, remission induction: Oral: 60 mcg/kg/day or 1.8 mg/m²/day; usual range: 4-8 mg/day (may be as high as 12 mg/day); Maintenance doses: 1-4 mg/day to 2 mg/week to maintain WBC 10,000-20,000 cells/mm³

BMT marrow-ablative conditioning regimen:

Oral: 1 mg/kg/dose (ideal body weight) every 6 hours for 16 doses

I.V.: 0.8 mg/kg (ideal body weight or actual body weight, whichever is lower); for obese or severely-obese patients adjusted ideal body weight is recommended) every 6 hours for 4 days (a total of 16 doses)

Polycythemia vera (unlabeled use): Oral: 2-6 mg/day

Thrombocytosis (unlabeled use): Oral: 4-6 mg/day

Dosing adjustment in renal impairment: I.V.: Has not been studied in patients with renal impairment per the FDA-approved labeling. Some clinicians suggest adjustment is not necessary (Aronoff, 2007).

Dosing adjustment in hepatic impairment: I.V.: Has not been administered in clinical studies in patients with hepatic impairment per the FDA-approved labeling. Busulfan has extensive hepatic metabolism and risk of hepatic veno-occlusive disease with high doses; dosage adjustment may be needed.

Administration Intravenous busulfan should be administered as a 2-hour via central line.

BMT only: To facilitate ingestion of high oral doses, insert multiple tablets into gelatin capsules.

Monitoring Parameters CBC with differential and platelet count, liver function tests (evaluate transaminases, alkaline phosphatase, and bilirubin daily for at least 28 days post transplant)

Patient Information Take oral medication as directed with chilled liquids. Maintain adequate hydration (2-3 L/day of fluids unless instructed to restrict fluid intake) to help prevent kidney complications. Avoid alcohol, acidic or spicy foods, aspirin, or OTC medications unless approved by physician. Brush teeth with soft toothbrush or cotton swab. You may lose head hair or experience darkening of skin color (reversible when medication is discontinued), amenorrhea, sterility, or skin rash. You may experience nausea, vomiting, anorexia, or constipation (small frequent meals, increased exercise, and increased dietary fruit or fiber may help). You will be more susceptible to infection (avoid crowds or contagious persons, and do not receive any vaccinations unless approved by physician). Report palpitations or chest pain, excessive dizziness, confusion, respiratory difficulty, numbness or tingling of extremities, unusual bruising or bleeding, pain or changes in urination, or other adverse effects. Contraceptive measures are recommended during therapy.

Special Geriatric Considerations Toxicity to immunosuppressives is increased in the elderly. Start with lowest recommended adult doses. Signs of infection, such as fever and rise in WBCs, may not occur. Lethargy and confusion may be more prominent signs of infection.

Additional Information Oncology Comment: Low-dose monotherapy with oral busulfan for the palliative treatment of CML is no longer common. Treatment with imatinib or hematopoietic stem cell transplant (HSCT) are considered the primary treatments for CML (NCCN v1.2008).

Emetic Potential
Low-dose: Low (<10%)
High-dose: High (60% to 90%)

Vesicant No

High Dose Considerations
Comments: Phenytoin or clonazepam should be administered prophylactically during and for at least 48 hours following completion of busulfan. Risk of seizures is increased in patients with sickle cell disease. Increased risk of VOD when busulfan AUC >3000 μmol(min)/L (mean AUC, 2012 μmol(min)/L). Increased risk of failure to engraft for allogeneic BMT patients when AUC is <900 μmol (min)/L. To facilitate ingestion of high doses, multiple tablets may be inserted into gelatin capsules. Ursodiol 9-12 mg/kg/day may reduce the risk of hepatotoxicity.

High Dose: Note: Generally combined with other high-dose chemotherapeutic drugs or total body irradiation.
Oral:
0.875-1 mg/kg/dose every 6 hours for 16 doses; total dose: 12-16 mg/kg
37.5 mg/m^2 every 6 hours for 16 doses; total dose: 600 mg/m^2 (studied primarily in pediatric patients)
150 mg/m^2 daily for 4 days; total dose: 600 mg/m^2 (studied primarily in pediatric patients)
I.V.: 0.8 mg/kg every 6 hours for 16 doses (4 days)

Unique Toxicities:
Central nervous system: Generalized or myoclonic seizures and loss of consciousness, abnormal electroencephalographic findings
Gastrointestinal: Mucositis, anorexia, moderately emetogenic
Hepatic: Veno-occlusive disease (VOD), hyperbilirubinemia
Respiratory: Idiopathic pneumonia syndrome
Miscellaneous: Transient pain at tumor sites, transient autoimmune disorders

Dosage Forms Excipient information presented when available (limited, particularly for generics); consult specific product labeling.
Injection, solution:
Busulfex®: 6 mg/mL (10 mL) [contains N,N-dimethylacetamide (DMA), polyethylene glycol]
Tablet:
Myleran®: 2 mg

References
Aronoff GR, Bennett WM, Berns JS, et al, *Drug Prescribing in Renal Failure: Dosing Guidelines for Adults and Children*, 5th ed. Philadelphia, PA: American College of Physicians; 2007, p 97.
(Continued)

Busulfan (Continued)

Booth BP, Rahman A, Dagher R, et al, "Population Pharmacokinetic-Based Dosing of Intravenous Busulfan in Pediatric Patients," *J Clin Pharmacol*, 2007, 47(1):101-11.

Buggia I, Locatelli F, Regazzi MB, et al, "Busulphan," *Ann Pharmacother*, 1994, 28(9):1055-62.

Heard BE and Cooke RA, "Busulphan Lung," *Thorax*, 1968, 23(2):187-93.

NCCN (National Comprehensive Cancer Network) "Practice Guidelines in Oncology: Antiemesis Version 1.2007." Available at http://www.nccn.org/professionals/physician_gls/PDF/antiemesis.pdf

NCCN (National Comprehensive Cancer Network) "Practice Guidelines in Oncology: Chronic Myelogenous Leukemia Version 1.2008." Available at http://www.nccn.org/professionals/physician_gls/PDF/cml.pdf

Regazzi MB, Locatelli F, Buggia I, et al, "Disposition of High-Dose Busulfan in Pediatric Patients Undergoing Bone Marrow Transplantation," *Clin Pharmacol Ther*, 1993, 54(1):45-52.

Seddon BM, Cassoni AM, Galloway MJ, et al, "Fatal Radiation Myelopathy After High-Dose Busulfan and Melphalan Chemotherapy and Radiotherapy for Ewing's Sarcoma: A Review of the Literature and Implications for Practice," *Clin Oncol (R Coll Radiol)*, 2005, 17(5):385-90.

Shaw PJ, Nath C, Berry A, et al, "Busulphan Given as Four Single Daily Doses of 150 mg/m² Is Safe and Effective in Children of All Ages," *Bone Marrow Transplant*, 2004, 34(3):197-205.

Tosti A, Piraccini BM, Vincenzi C, et al, "Permanent Alopecia After Busulfan Chemotherapy," *Br J Dermatol*, 2005, 152(5):1056-8.

Vassal G, Gouyette A, Hartmann O, et al, "Pharmacokinetics of High-Dose Busulfan in Children," *Cancer Chemother Pharmacol*, 1989, 24(6):386-90.

♦ **Busulfex®** *see* Busulfan *on page 154*

♦ **C1H** *see* Alemtuzumab *on page 34*

♦ **C2B8 Monoclonal Antibody** *see* Rituximab *on page 953*

♦ **C225** *see* Cetuximab *on page 201*

♦ **Caelyx® (Can)** *see* DOXOrubicin (Liposomal) *on page 359*

♦ **Calcijex®** *see* Calcitriol *on page 163*

♦ **Calcimar® (Can)** *see* Calcitonin *on page 160*

Calcitonin (kal si TOE nin)

Medication Safety Issues

Sound-alike/look-alike issues:

Calcitonin may be confused with calcitriol

Miacalcin® may be confused with Micatin®

Calcitonin nasal spray is administered as a single spray into **one** nostril daily, using alternate nostrils each day.

U.S. Brand Names Fortical®; Miacalcin®

Index Terms Calcitonin (Salmon)

Generic Available No

Canadian Brand Names Apo-Calcitonin®; Calcimar®; Caltine®; Miacalcin® NS

Pharmacologic Category Antidote; Hormone

Use Calcitonin (salmon): Treatment of Paget's disease of bone (osteitis deformans); adjunctive therapy for hypercalcemia; treatment of osteoporosis in women >5 years postmenopause

Pregnancy Risk Factor C

Lactation Excretion in breast milk unknown/not recommended

Labeled Contraindications Hypersensitivity to calcitonin salmon or any component of the formulation

Warnings/Precautions A skin test should be performed prior to initiating therapy of calcitonin salmon in patients with suspected sensitivity. Have epinephrine immediately available for a possible hypersensitivity reaction. A detailed skin testing protocol is available from the manufacturers. Temporarily withdraw use of nasal spray if ulceration of nasal mucosa occurs. Patients >65 years of age may experience a higher incidence of nasal adverse events with calcitonin nasal spray. Safety and efficacy have not been established in pediatric patients.

Adverse Reactions Unless otherwise noted, frequencies reported are with nasal spray.

>10%: Respiratory: Rhinitis (12%)

1% to 10%:

Cardiovascular: Flushing (nasal spray: <1%; injection: 2% to 5%), angina (1% to 3%), hypertension (1% to 3%)

Central nervous system: Depression (1% to 3%), dizziness (1% to 3%), fatigue (1% to 3%)

Dermatologic: Erythematous rash (1% to 3%)

Gastrointestinal: Abdominal pain (1% to 3%), constipation (1% to 3%), diarrhea (1% to 3%), dyspepsia (1% to 3%), nausea (injection: 10%; nasal spray: 1% to 3%)

Genitourinary: Cystitis (1% to 3%)

Local: Injection site reactions (injection: 10%)

Neuromuscular & skeletal: Back pain (5%), arthrosis (1% to 3%), myalgia (1% to 3%), paresthesia (1% to 3%)

Ocular: Conjunctivitis (1% to 3%), lacrimation abnormality (1% to 3%)

Respiratory: Bronchospasm (1% to 3%), sinusitis (1% to 3%), upper respiratory tract infection (1% to 3%)

Miscellaneous: Flu-like syndrome (1% to 3%), infection (1% to 3%), lymphadenopathy (1% to 3%)

<1%: Agitation, allergic reactions, alopecia, anaphylaxis, anemia, anorexia, anxiety, appetite increased, arthritis, blurred vision, bronchitis, bundle branch block, cerebrovascular accident, cholelithiasis, cough, diaphoresis, dyspnea, earache, eczema, fever, flatulence, gastritis, goiter, hearing loss, hematuria, hepatitis, hyperthyroidism, insomnia, migraine, myocardial infarction, neuralgia, nocturia, palpitation, parosmia, periorbital edema, pharyngitis, pneumonia, polymyalgia rheumatica, pruritus, pyelonephritis, rash, renal calculus, skin ulceration, stiffness, tachycardia, taste perversion, thirst, thrombophlebitis, tinnitus, vertigo, vitreous floater, vomiting, weight gain, xerostomia

Overdosage/Toxicology Symptoms of overdose include nausea, vomiting, hypocalcemia, and hypocalcemic tetany. Administer parenteral calcium for hypocalcemia and hypocalcemic tetany. Treatment is otherwise symptom-directed and supportive.

Ethanol/Nutrition/Herb Interactions Ethanol: Avoid ethanol (may increase risk of osteoporosis).

Storage/Stability

Injection: Store under refrigeration at 2°C to 8°C (36°F to 46°F); protect from freezing.

Nasal: Store unopened bottle under refrigeration at 2°C to 8°C (36°F to 46°F); do not freeze.

Fortical®: After opening, store for up to 30 days at 20°C to 25°C (68°F to 77°F); excursions permitted to 15°C to 30°C (59°F to 86°F). Store in upright position.

Miacalcin®: After opening, store for up to 35 days at room temperature of 15°C to 30°C (59°F to 86°F). Store in upright position.

Reconstitution Injection: NS has been recommended for the dilution to prepare a skin test in patients with suspected sensitivity.

Mechanism of Action Peptide sequence similar to human calcitonin; functionally antagonizes the effects of parathyroid hormone. Directly inhibits (Continued)

Calcitonin *(Continued)*

osteoclastic bone resorption; promotes the renal excretion of calcium, phosphate, sodium, magnesium, and potassium by decreasing tubular reabsorption; increases the jejunal secretion of water, sodium, potassium, and chloride

Pharmacodynamics/Kinetics

Hypercalcemia: I.M. or SubQ:
Onset of action: ~2 hours
Duration: 6-8 hours
Absorption: Nasal: ~3% of I.M. level (range: 0.3% to 31%)
Distribution: Does not cross placenta
Half-life elimination: SubQ: 1.2 hours; Nasal: 43 minutes
Time to peak: Nasal: ~30-40 minutes
Excretion: Urine (as inactive metabolites)

Dosage

Children: Dosage not established
Adults:
Paget's disease (Miacalcin®): I.M., SubQ: Initial: 100 units/day; maintenance: 50 units/day or 50-100 units every 1-3 days
Hypercalcemia (Miacalcin®): Initial: I.M., SubQ: 4 units/kg every 12 hours; may increase up to 8 units/kg every 12 hours to a maximum of every 6 hours
Postmenopausal osteoporosis:
I.M., SubQ: Miacalcin®: 100 units/every other day
Intranasal: Fortical®, Miacalcin®: 200 units (1 spray) in one nostril daily

Administration

Injection solution: Administer I.M. or SubQ; intramuscular route is recommended over the subcutaneous route when the volume of calcitonin to be injected exceeds 2 mL.
Nasal spray: Before first use, allow bottle to reach room temperature, then prime pump by releasing at least 5 sprays until full spray is produced. To administer, place nozzle into nostril with head in upright position. Alternate nostrils daily. Do not prime pump before each daily use. Discard after 30 doses.

Monitoring Parameters Serum electrolytes and calcium; alkaline phosphatase and 24-hour urine collection for hydroxyproline excretion (Paget's disease), urinalysis (urine sediment); bone mineral density
Nasal formulation: Visualization of nasal mucosa, turbinate, septum, and mucosal blood vessels)

Dietary Considerations Adequate vitamin D and calcium intake is essential for preventing/treating osteoporosis. Patients with Paget's disease and hypercalcemia should follow a low calcium diet as prescribed.

Patient Information Nasal spray: Notify prescriber if you develop significant nasal irritation. To activate the pump, hold the bottle upright and depress the two white side arms toward the bottle six times until a faint spray is emitted. The pump is activated once this first faint spray has been emitted; at this point, firmly place the nozzle into the bottle. It is not necessary to reactivate the pump before each daily use. Alternate nostrils with the spray formulation.

Special Geriatric Considerations Studies have shown calcitonin's effects on bone density and fracture rates are beneficial, particularly in women unable to tolerate estrogens. Calcium and vitamin D supplements should also be given. Calcitonin may also be effective in steroid-induced osteoporosis and other states associated with high bone turnover. Nasal spray may provide faster onset of analgesic effects than I.M.

Emetic Potential Moderate (30% to 60%); nausea and vomiting are generally mild

Vesicant No

Dosage Forms Excipient information presented when available (limited, particularly for generics); consult specific product labeling.

Injection, solution [calcitonin-salmon]:

Miacalcin®: 200 int. units/mL (2 mL)

Solution, intranasal [spray, calcitonin-salmon]:

Fortical®: 200 int. units/0.09 mL (3.7 mL) [rDNA origin; contains benzyl alcohol; delivers 30 doses, 200 units/actuation]

Miacalcin®: 200 int. units/0.09 mL (3.7 mL) [contains benzalkonium chloride; delivers 30 doses, 200 units/actuation]

References

Bauwens SF, "Osteomalacia and Osteoporosis," *Pharmacotherapy: A Pathophysiologic Approach*, 2nd ed, DiPiro JT, Talbert RL, Hayes PE, et al, eds, New York, NY, 1992, 1293-312.

Bergqvist E, Sjoberg HE, Hjern B, et al, "Calcitonin in the Treatment of Hypercalcaemic Crisis," *Acta Med Scand*, 1972, 192(5):385-9.

Lyritis GP, Tsakalakos N, Magiasis B, et al, "Analgesic Effect of Salmon Calcitonin in Osteoporotic Vertebral Fractures: A Double-Blind, Placebo-Controlled Clinical Study," *Calcif Tissue Int*, 1991, 49(6):369-72.

Pontiroli AE, Pajetta E, Scaglia L, et al, "Analgesic Effect of Intranasal and Intramuscular Salmon Calcitonin in Postmenopausal Osteoporosis: A Double-Blind, Double-Placebo Study," *Aging (Milano)*, 1994, 6(6):459-63.

Reginster JY, Deroisy R, Lecart MP, et al, "A Double-Blind, Placebo-Controlled, Dose-Finding Trial of Intermittent Nasal Salmon Calcitonin for Prevention of Postmenopausal Lumbar Spine Bone Loss," *Am J Med*, 1995, 98(5):452-8.

Reginster JY, "Calcitonin for Prevention and Treatment of Osteoporosis," *Am J Med*, 1993, 95(5A):44S-47S.

Stevenson JC, "Current Management of Malignant Hypercalcemia," *Drugs*, 1988, 36(2):229-30.

♦ **Calcitonin (Salmon)** *see* Calcitonin *on page 160*

Calcitriol (kal si TRYE ole)

Medication Safety Issues

Sound-alike/look-alike issues:

Calcitriol may be confused with calcifediol, Calciferol®, calcitonin

Dosage is expressed in mcg (micrograms), **not** mg (milligrams); rare cases of acute overdose have been reported

U.S. Brand Names Calcijex®; Rocaltrol®

Index Terms 1,25 Dihydroxycholecalciferol

Generic Available Yes

Canadian Brand Names Calcijex®; Rocaltrol®

Pharmacologic Category Vitamin D Analog

Use Management of hypocalcemia in patients on chronic renal dialysis; management of secondary hyperparathyroidism in patients with chronic kidney disease (CKD); management of hypocalcemia in hypoparathyroidism and pseudohypoparathyroidism

Unlabeled/Investigational Use Decrease severity of psoriatic lesions in psoriatic vulgaris; vitamin D-dependent rickets

Pregnancy Risk Factor C (manufacturer); A/D (dose exceeding RDA recommendation) (expert analysis)

Lactation Enters breast milk/not recommended

Labeled Contraindications Hypersensitivity to calcitriol or any component of the formulation; hypercalcemia, vitamin D toxicity

Warnings/Precautions Adequate dietary (supplemental) calcium is necessary for clinical response to vitamin D. Excessive vitamin D may cause severe hypercalcemia, hypercalciuria, and hyperphosphatemia; calcium-phosphate product (serum calcium times phosphorus) must not

(Continued)

Calcitriol *(Continued)*

exceed 70 mg^2/dL^2. Other forms of vitamin D should be withheld during therapy. Immobilization may increase risk of hypercalcemia and/or hypercalciuria. Maintain adequate hydration. Use caution in patients with malabsorption syndromes (efficacy may be limited and/or response may be unpredictable). Use of calcitriol for the treatment of secondary hyperparathyroidism associated with CKD is not recommended in patients with rapidly worsening kidney function or in noncompliant patients. Increased serum phosphate levels in patients with renal failure may lead to calcification; the use of an aluminum-containing phosphate binder is recommended along with a low phosphate diet in these patients. Products may contain coconut or palm seed oil.

Adverse Reactions Frequency not defined.

Cardiovascular: Cardiac arrhythmia, hypertension

Central nervous system: Apathy, headache, hypothermia, psychosis, sensory disturbances, somnolence

Dermatologic: Erythema multiforme, pruritus

Endocrine & metabolic: Dehydration, growth suppression, hypercalcemia, hypercholesterolemia, hypermagnesemia, hyperphosphatemia, libido decreased, polydipsia

Gastrointestinal: Abdominal pain, anorexia, constipation, metallic taste, nausea, pancreatitis, stomach ache, vomiting, weight loss, xerostomia

Genitourinary: Urinary tract infection

Hepatic: ALT/AST increased

Local: Injection site pain (mild)

Neuromuscular & skeletal: Bone pain, myalgia, dystrophy, soft tissue calcification, weakness

Ocular: Conjunctivitis, photophobia

Renal: Albuminuria, BUN increased, creatinine increased, hypercalciuri-anephrocalcinosis, nocturia, polyuria

Respiratory: Rhinorrhea

Miscellaneous: Allergic reaction

Overdosage/Toxicology Toxicity rarely occurs from acute overdose. Symptoms of chronic overdose include hypercalcemia, hyperphosphatemia, hypercalciuria with weakness, altered mental status, GI upset, renal tubular injury, and occasionally cardiac arrhythmias. Following withdrawal of the drug, treatment consists of bedrest, liberal fluid intake, reduced calcium intake, and cathartic administration. Severe hypercalcemia requires I.V. hydration and forced diuresis. I.V. saline may increase excretion of calcium. Calcitonin, cholestyramine, prednisone, sodium EDTA, and bisphosphonates have all been used successfully to treat the more resistant cases of vitamin D-induced hypercalcemia. Use of peritoneal dialysis against a calcium-free dialysate has been reported.

Drug Interactions

Cytochrome P450 Effect: Induces CYP3A4 (weak)

Increased Effect/Toxicity: Risk of digoxin toxicity may be increased (if hypercalcemia occurs). Thiazide diuretics may decrease renal calcium excretion and increase risk of hypercalcemia. Magnesium containing antacids may increase the risk of hypermagnesemia in patients on renal dialysis.

Decreased Effect: Cholestyramine and colestipol decrease absorption/effect of calcitriol. Corticosteroids may reduce the effect of calcitriol. Phenobarbital and phenytoin may decrease endogenous levels of vitamin D.

Storage/Stability Store at room temperature of 15°C to 30°C (59°F to 86°F). Protect from light.

Compatibility Stable in D_5W, NS, sterile water for injection.

Mechanism of Action Calcitriol is a potent active metabolite of vitamin D. Vitamin D promotes absorption of calcium in the intestines and retention at the kidneys thereby increasing calcium levels in the serum; decreases excessive serum phosphatase levels, parathyroid hormone levels, and decreases bone resorption; increases renal tubule phosphate resorption

Pharmacodynamics/Kinetics

Onset of action: ~2-6 hours

Duration: 3-5 days

Absorption: Oral: Rapid

Protein binding: 99.9%

Metabolism: Primarily to 1,24,25-trihydroxycholecalciferol and 1,24,25-trihydroxy ergocalciferol

Half-life elimination: Children ~27 hours; Normal adults: 5-8 hours; Hemodialysis: 16-22 hours

Time to peak, serum: Oral: 3-6 hours; Hemodialysis: 8-12 hours

Excretion: Primarily feces; urine

Dosage

Hypocalcemia in patients on chronic renal dialysis (manufacturer labeling): *Adults:*

Oral: 0.25 mcg/day or every other day (may require 0.5-1 mcg/day); increases should be made at 4- to 8-week intervals

I.V.: Initial: 1-2 mcg 3 times/week (0.02 mcg/kg) approximately every other day. Adjust dose at 2-4 week intervals; dosing range: 0.5-4 mcg 3 times/week

Hypocalcemia in hypoparathyroidism/pseudohypoparathyroidism (manufacturers labeling): Oral (evaluate dosage at 2- to 4-week intervals):

Children <1 year (unlabeled use): 0.04-0.08 mcg/kg once daily

Children 1-5 years: 0.25-0.75 mcg once daily

Children ≥6 years and Adults: Initial: 0.25 mcg/day, range: 0.5-2 mcg once daily

Secondary hyperparathyroidism associated with moderate-to-severe CKD in patients not on dialysis (manufacturer labeling): Oral:

Children <3 years: Initial dose: 0.01-0.015 mcg/kg/day

Children ≥3 years and Adults: 0.25 mcg/day; may increase to 0.5 mcg/day

K/DOQI guidelines for vitamin D therapy in CKD:

Children:

CKD stage 2, 3: Oral:

<10 kg: 0.05 mcg every other day

10-20 kg: 0.1-0.15 mcg/day

>20 kg: 0.25 mcg/day

Note: Treatment should only be started with serum 25(OH) D >30 ng/mL, serum iPTH >70 pg/mL, serum calcium <10 mg/dL and serum phosphorus less than or equal to the age appropriate level.

CKD stage 4: Oral:

<10 kg: 0.05 mcg every other day

10-20 kg: 0.1-0.15 mcg/day

>20 kg: 0.25 mcg/day

Note: Treatment should only be started with serum 25(OH) D >30 ng/mL, serum iPTH >110 pg/mL, serum calcium <10 mg/dL and serum phosphorus less than or equal to the age appropriate level.

(Continued)

Calcitriol *(Continued)*

CKD stage 5: Oral, I.V.: **Note:** The following initial doses are based on plasma PTH and serum calcium levels for patients with serum phosphorus <5.5 mg/dL in adolescents or <6.5 in infants and children, and Ca-P product <55 in adolescents or <65 in infants and children <12 years. Adjust dose based on serum phosphate, calcium and PTH levels. Administer dose with each dialysis session (3 times/week). Intermittent I.V./oral administration is more effective than daily oral dosing.

Plasma PTH 300-500 pg/mL and serum Ca <10 mg/dL: 0.0075 mcg/kg (maximum: 0.25 mcg/day)

Plasma PTH >500-1000 pg/mL and serum Ca <10 mg/dL: 0.015 mcg/kg (maximum: 0.5 mcg/day)

Plasma PTH >1000 pg/mL and serum Ca <10.5 mg/dL: 0.025 mcg/kg (maximum: 1 mcg/day)

Adults:

CKD stage 3: Oral: 0.25 mcg/day. Treatment should only be started with serum 25(OH) D >30 ng/mL, serum iPTH >70 pg/mL, serum calcium <9.5 mg/dL and serum phosphorus <4.6 mg/dL

CKD stage 4: Oral: 0.25 mcg/day. Treatment should only be started with serum 25(OH) D >30 ng/mL, serum iPTH >110 pg/mL, serum calcium <9.5 mg/dL and serum phosphorus <4.6 mg/dL

CKD stage 5:

Peritoneal dialysis: Oral: Initial: 0.5-1 mcg 2-3 times/week or 0.25 mcg/day

Hemodialysis: **Note:** The following initial doses are based on plasma PTH and serum calcium levels for patients with serum phosphorus <5.5 mg/dL and Ca-P product <55. Adjust dose based on serum phosphate, calcium, and PTH levels. Intermittent I.V. administration may be more effective than daily oral dosing.

Plasma PTH 300-600 pg/mL and serum Ca <9.5 mg/dL: Oral, I.V.: 0.5-1.5 mcg

Plasma PTH 600-1000 pg/mL and serum Ca <9.5 mg/dL:

Oral: 1-4 mcg

I.V.: 1-3 mcg

Plasma PTH >1000 pg/mL and serum Ca <10 mg/dL:

Oral: 3-7 mcg

I.V.: 3-5 mcg

Vitamin D-dependent rickets (unlabeled use): Children and Adults: Oral: 1 mcg once daily

Elderly: No dosage recommendations, but start at the lower end of the dosage range

Dosage adjustment for toxicity: K/DOQI guidelines: Children and Adults: CKD stage 3 and 4:

iPTH below target: Hold calcitriol until levels rise then resume treatment at half the previous dose. If the lowest dose was being used, switch to alternate day therapy.

Corrected total calcium >9.5 mg/dL (adults) or 10.2 mg/dL (children): Hold calcitriol until serum calcium returns to <9.5 mg/dL (adults) or <9.8 mg/dL (children) then resume treatment at half the previous dose. If the lowest dose was being used, switch to alternate day therapy.

Serum phosphorus >4.6 mg/dL (adults) or greater than the age appropriate limits in children: Hold calcitriol (or add/increase dose of phosphate binder) until levels of phosphorous decrease, then resume at half the prior dose.

Combination Regimens

Prostate cancer: Estramustine + Docetaxel + Calcitriol *on page 1207*

Administration May be administered without regard to food. Give with meals to reduce GI problems. May be administered as a bolus dose I.V. through the catheter at the end of hemodialysis.

Monitoring Parameters Signs and symptoms of vitamin D intoxication; alkaline phosphatase, serum creatinine

Serum calcium and phosphorus:
    CKD stage 2-4: Every month for the first 3 months, then every 3 months
    CKD stage 5: Every 2 weeks for 1 month, then monthly
Serum or plasma intact PTH (iPTH):
    CKD stage 3 and 4: Every 3 months for 6 months, then every 3 months
    CKD stage 5: Monthly for 3 months, then every 3 months

Dietary Considerations May be taken without regard to food. Give with meals to reduce GI problems. Adequate calcium intake should be maintained during therapy; dietary phosphorous may need to be restricted. Rocaltrol® capsules contain coconut oil; Rocaltrol® solution contains palm seed oil.

Patient Information Compliance with dose, diet, and calcium supplementation is essential. Report weakness, lethargy, headache, or decreased appetite. Avoid taking magnesium supplements or magnesium-containing antacids.

Special Geriatric Considerations Recommended daily allowances (RDA) have not been developed for persons >65 years of age; vitamin D, folate, and B_{12} (cyanocobalamin) have decreased absorption with age, but the clinical significance is yet unknown. Calorie requirements decrease with age and therefore, nutrient density must be increased to ensure adequate nutrient intake, including vitamins and minerals. Therefore, the use of a daily supplement with a multiple vitamin with minerals is recommended. Elderly consume less vitamin D, absorption may be decreased, and many elderly have decreased sun exposure; therefore, elderly should receive supplementation with 800 units of vitamin D (20 mcg)/day. This is a recommendation of particular need to those with high risk for osteoporosis.

Dosage Forms Excipient information presented when available (limited, particularly for generics); consult specific product labeling.

Capsule, softgel: 0.25 mcg, 0.5 mcg
    Rocaltrol®: 0.25 mcg [contains coconut oil]; 0.5 mcg [contains coconut oil]
Injection, solution: 1 mcg/mL (1 mL)
    Calcijex®: 1 mcg/mL (1 mL) [contains aluminum]
Solution, oral: 1 mcg/mL (15 mL)
    Rocaltrol®: 1 mcg/mL (15 mL) [contains palm seed oil]

References

Callies F, Arlt W, Scholz HJ, et al, "Management of Hypoparathyroidism During Pregnancy -- Report of Twelve Cases," *Eur J Endocrinol,* 1998, 139(3):284-9.

"K/DOQI Clinical Practice Guidelines for Bone Metabolism and Disease in Children With Chronic Kidney Disease," *Am J Kidney Dis,* 2005, 46(4 Suppl 1):1-121.

"K/DOQI Clinical Practice Guidelines for Bone Metabolism and Disease in Chronic Kidney Disease. Guideline 1. Evaluation of Calcium and Phosphorus Metabolism," *Am J Kidney Dis,* 2003, 42(4 Suppl 3):52-7.

"K/DOQI Clinical Practice Guidelines for Chronic Kidney Disease: Evaluation, Classification, and Stratification, Part 4. Definition and Classification of Stages of Chronic Kidney Disease," *Am J Kidney Dis,* 2002, 39(2 Suppl 1):46-75.

"K/DOQI Clinical Practice Guidelines for Bone Metabolism and Disease in Chronic Kidney Disease. Guideline 3. Evaluation of Serum Phosphorus Levels," *Am J Kidney Dis,* 2003, 42(4 Suppl 3):62-3.

"K/DOQI Clinical Practice Guidelines for Chronic Kidney Disease: Evaluation, Classification, and Stratification, Part 6. Serum Calcium and Calcium-Phosphorus Product," *Am J Kidney Dis,* 2003, 42(4 Suppl 3):77-84.

(Continued)

Calcitriol *(Continued)*

"K/DOQI Clinical Practice Guidelines for Bone Metabolism and Disease in Chronic Kidney Disease. Guideline 8A. Active Vitamin D Therapy in Patients With Stages 3 and 4 CKD," *Am J Kidney Dis*, 2003, 42(4 Suppl 3):89-92.

"K/DOQI Clinical Practice Guidelines for Bone Metabolism and Disease in Chronic Kidney Disease. Guideline 8B. Vitamin D Therapy in Patients on Dialysis (CKD Stage 5)," *Am J Kidney Dis*, 2003, 42(4 Suppl 3):92-98.

Letsou AP and Price LS, "Health Aging and Nutrition: An Overview," *Clin Geriatr Med*, 1987, 3(2):253-60.

Myrianthopoulos M, "Dietary Treatment of Hyperlipidemia in the Elderly," *Clin Geriatr Med*, 1987, 3(2):343-59.

Capecitabine (ka pe SITE a been)

Medication Safety Issues

Sound-alike/look-alike issues:

Xeloda® may be confused with Xenical®

High alert medication: The Institute for Safe Medication Practices (ISMP) includes this medication among its list of drugs which have a heightened risk of causing significant patient harm when used in error.

Related Information

Safe Handling of Hazardous Drugs *on page 1382*

U.S. Brand Names Xeloda®

Index Terms NSC-712807

Generic Available No

Canadian Brand Names Xeloda®

Pharmacologic Category Antineoplastic Agent, Antimetabolite; Antineoplastic Agent, Antimetabolite (Pyrimidine Analog)

Use Treatment of metastatic colorectal cancer; adjuvant therapy of Dukes' C colon cancer; treatment of metastatic breast cancer

Pregnancy Risk Factor D

Lactation Excretion in breast milk unknown/not recommended

Labeled Contraindications Hypersensitivity to capecitabine, fluorouracil, or any component of the formulation; known deficiency of dihydropyrimidine dehydrogenase (DPD); severe renal impairment (Cl_{cr} <30 mL/minute); pregnancy

Warnings/Precautions Hazardous agent - use appropriate precautions for handling and disposal. Use with caution in patients with bone marrow suppression, ≥80 years of age, or renal or hepatic dysfunction. Patients with baseline moderate renal impairment require dose reduction. Patients with mild-to-moderate renal impairment require careful monitoring and subsequent dose reduction with any grade 2 or higher adverse event. Use with caution in patients who have received extensive pelvic radiation or alkylating therapy. Use cautiously with warfarin. Rare and unexpected severe toxicity may be attributed to dihydropyrimidine dehydrogenase (DPD) deficiency. Necrotizing enterocolitis (typhlitis) has been reported.

Capecitabine can cause severe diarrhea; median time to first occurrence is 34 days. Subsequent doses should be reduced after grade 3 or 4 diarrhea or recurrence of grade 2 diarrhea.

Hand-and-foot syndrome is characterized by numbness, dysesthesia/paresthesia, tingling, painless or painful swelling, erythema, desquamation, blistering, and severe pain. If grade 2 or 3 hand-and-foot syndrome occurs, interrupt administration of capecitabine until decreases to grade 1. Following grade 3 hand-and-foot syndrome, decrease subsequent doses of capecitabine.

There has been cardiotoxicity associated with fluorinated pyrimidine therapy. May be more common in patients with a history of coronary artery disease.
[U.S. Boxed Warning]: Capecitabine may increase the anticoagulant effects of warfarin; monitor closely.

Safety and efficacy in children <18 years of age have not been established.

Adverse Reactions Frequency listed derived from monotherapy trials.

>10%:

Cardiovascular: Edema (9% to 15%)

Central nervous system: Fatigue (16% to 42%), fever (7% to 18%), pain (12%)

Dermatologic: Palmar-plantar erythrodysesthesia (hand-and-foot syndrome) (54% to 60%; grade 3: 11% to 17%; may be dose limiting), dermatitis (27% to 37%)

Gastrointestinal: Diarrhea (47% to 57%; may be dose limiting; grade 3: 12% to 13%; grade 4: 2% to 3%), nausea (34% to 53%), vomiting (15% to 37%), abdominal pain (7% to 35%), stomatitis (22% to 25%), appetite decreased (26%), anorexia (9% to 23%), constipation (9% to 15%)

Hematologic: Lymphopenia (94%; grade 4: 14%), anemia (72% to 80%; grade 4: <1% to 1%), neutropenia (2% to 26%; grade 4: 2%), thrombocytopenia (24%; grade 4: 1%)

Hepatic: Bilirubin increased (22% to 48%; grades 3/4: 11% to 23%)

Neuromuscular & skeletal: Paresthesia (21%)

Ocular: Eye irritation (13% to 15%)

Respiratory: Dyspnea (14%)

5% to 10%:

Cardiovascular: Venous thrombosis (8%), chest pain (6%)

Central nervous system: Headache (5% to 10%), lethargy (10%), dizziness (6% to 8%), insomnia (7% to 8%), mood alteration (5%), depression (5%)

Dermatologic: Nail disorder (7%), rash (7%), skin discoloration (7%), alopecia (6%), erythema (6%)

Endocrine & metabolic: Dehydration (7%)

Gastrointestinal: Motility disorder (10%), oral discomfort (10%), dyspepsia (6% to 8%), upper GI inflammatory disorders (colorectal cancer: 8%), hemorrhage (6%), ileus (6%), taste perversion (colorectal cancer: 6%)

Neuromuscular & skeletal: Back pain (10%), weakness (10%), neuropathy (10%), myalgia (9%), arthralgia (8%), limb pain (6%)

Ocular: Abnormal vision (colorectal cancer: 5%), conjunctivitis (5%)

Respiratory: Cough (7%)

Miscellaneous: Viral infection (colorectal cancer: 5%)

(Continued)

Capecitabine *(Continued)*

<5%: Abdominal distension, angina, appetite increased, arthritis, ascites, asthma, ataxia, atrial fibrillation, bone pain, bradycardia, bronchitis, bronchopneumonia, bronchospasm, cachexia, cardiac arrest, cardiac failure, cardiomyopathy, cerebral vascular accident, cholestasis, coagulation disorder, colitis, confusion, deep vein thrombosis, diaphoresis, duodenitis, dysarthria, dysphagia, dysrhythmia, ecchymoses, ECG changes, encephalopathy, epistaxis, esophagitis, fibrosis, fungal infection, gastric ulcer, gastritis, gastroenteritis, hematemesis, hemoptysis, hepatic fibrosis, hepatitis, hoarseness, hot flushes, hypokalemia, hypomagnesemia, hyper-/hypotension, hypersensitivity, hypertriglyceridemia, idiopathic thrombocytopenia purpura, ileus, impaired balance, infection, influenza-like illness, intestinal obstruction (~1%), irritability, joint stiffness, keratoconjunctivitis, laryngitis, leukopenia, loss of consciousness, lymphedema, MI, myocardial ischemia, myocarditis, necrotizing enterocolitis, nocturia, oral candidiasis, pericardial effusion, thrombocytopenic purpura, pancytopenia, photosensitivity reaction, pneumonia, proctalgia, pruritus, pulmonary embolism, radiation recall syndrome, renal impairment, respiratory distress, sedation, sepsis, skin ulceration, sore throat, tachycardia, thirst, thrombophlebitis, toxic megacolon, tremor, ventricular extrasystoles, vertigo, weight gain

Postmarketing and/or case reports: Hepatic failure, lacrimal duct stenosis

Overdosage/Toxicology Symptoms of overdose include myelosuppression, nausea, vomiting, diarrhea, and gastrointestinal irritation/bleeding. No specific antidote exists. Monitor hematologically for at least 4 weeks. Dialysis may be of benefit in reducing levels of the metabolite 5'-DFUR. Treatment is symptom-directed and supportive.

Drug Interactions

Increased Effect/Toxicity: Phenytoin and warfarin levels or effects may be increased.

Ethanol/Nutrition/Herb Interactions Food: Food reduced the rate and extent of absorption of capecitabine.

Storage/Stability Store at room temperature between 15°C and 30°C (59°F and 86°F).

Mechanism of Action Capecitabine is a prodrug of fluorouracil. It undergoes hydrolysis in the liver and tissues to form fluorouracil which is the active moiety. Fluorouracil is a fluorinated pyrimidine antimetabolite that inhibits thymidylate synthetase, blocking the methylation of deoxyuridylic acid to thymidylic acid, interfering with DNA, and to a lesser degree, RNA synthesis. Fluorouracil appears to be phase specific for the G_1 and S phases of the cell cycle.

Pharmacodynamics/Kinetics

Absorption: Rapid and extensive

Protein binding: <60%; ~35% to albumin

Metabolism:

Hepatic: Inactive metabolites: 5'-deoxy-5-fluorocytidine, 5'-deoxy-5-fluorouridine

Tissue: Active metabolite: Fluorouracil

Half-life elimination: 0.5-1 hour

Time to peak: 1.5 hours; Fluorouracil: 2 hours

Excretion: Urine (96%, 57% as α-fluoro-β-alanine); feces (<3%)

Dosage Oral:

Adults: 1250 mg/m^2 twice daily (morning and evening) for 2 weeks, every 21-28 days

Adjuvant therapy of Dukes' C colon cancer: Recommended for a total of 24 weeks (8 cycles of 2 weeks of drug administration and 1 week rest period).

Elderly: The elderly may be more sensitive to the toxic effects of fluorouracil. Insufficient data are available to provide dosage modifications.

Dosing adjustment in renal impairment:
Cl$_{cr}$ 51-80 mL/minute: No adjustment of initial dose
Cl$_{cr}$ 30-50 mL/minute: Administer 75% of normal dose
Cl$_{cr}$ <30 mL/minute: Use is contraindicated

Dosing adjustment in hepatic impairment:
Mild-to-moderate impairment: No starting dose adjustment is necessary; however, carefully monitor patients
Severe hepatic impairment: Patients have not been studied

Dosage modification guidelines: See table.
Refer to package labeling for modifications when administered in combination with docetaxel.

Recommended Dose Modifications

Toxicity NCI Grades	During a Course of Therapy (Monotherapy)	Dose Adjustment for Next Cycle (% of starting dose)
Grade 1	Maintain dose level	Maintain dose level
Grade 2		
1st appearance	Interrupt until resolved to grade 0-1	100%
2nd appearance	Interrupt until resolved to grade 0-1	75%
3rd appearance	Interrupt until resolved to grade 0-1	50%
4th appearance	Discontinue treatment permanently	
Grade 3		
1st appearance	Interrupt until resolved to grade 0-1	75%
2nd appearance	Interrupt until resolved to grade 0-1	50%
3rd appearance	Discontinue treatment permanently	
Grade 4		
1st appearance	Discontinue permanently **or** If physician deems it to be in the patient's best interest to continue, interrupt until resolved to grade 0-1	50%

Dosage adjustments for hematologic toxicity in combination therapy with ixabepilone:
Neutrophils <500/mm^3 for ≥7 days or neutropenic fever: Hold for concurrent diarrhea or stomatitis until neutrophils recover to >1000/mm3, then continue at same dose
Platelets <25,000/mm^3 (or <50,000/mm^3 with bleeding): Hold for concurrent diarrhea or stomatitis until platelets recover to >50,000/mm^3, then continue at same dose

Combination Regimens
Biliary Adenocarcinoma: Gemcitabine-Capecitabine *on page 1225*
(Continued)

Capecitabine *(Continued)*

Breast cancer:

Bevacizumab-Capecitabine *on page 1150*
Capecitabine + Docetaxel (Breast Cancer) *on page 1158*
Capecitabine + Lapatinib *on page 1160*
Capecitabine-Trastuzumab *on page 1160*
Ixabepilone-Capecitabine *on page 1242*
TEX (Capecitabine + Docetaxel + Epirubicin) *on page 1280*
Colorectal cancer: XelOx *on page 1293*
Gastric cancer: Capecitabine + Docetaxel (Gastric Cancer) *on page 1159*
Lung cancer (nonsmall cell): Capecitabine + Docetaxel (Nonsmall Cell Lung Cancer) *on page 1159*
Pancreatic cancer: Gemcitabine-Capecitabine *on page 1225*

Administration Usually administered in 2 divided doses taken 12 hours apart. Doses should be taken with water within 30 minutes after a meal.

Monitoring Parameters Renal function should be estimated at baseline to determine initial dose. During therapy, CBC with differential, hepatic function, and renal function should be monitored.

Dietary Considerations Because current safety and efficacy data are based upon administration with food, it is recommended that capecitabine be administered with food. In all clinical trials, patients were instructed to take with water within 30 minutes after a meal.

Patient Information Take with water within 30 minutes after meal. Avoid use of antacids within 2 hours of taking capecitabine. Do not crush, chew, or dissolve tablets. You will need frequent blood tests while taking this medication. Maintain adequate hydration (2-3 L/day of fluids unless instructed to restrict fluid intake). You may experience lethargy, dizziness, visual changes, confusion, anxiety (avoid driving or engaging in tasks requiring alertness until response to drug is known). For nausea, vomiting, loss of appetite, or dry mouth, small, frequent meals, chewing gum, or sucking lozenges may help. You may experience loss of hair (will grow back when treatment is discontinued). You may experience photosensitivity (use sunscreen, wear protective clothing and eyewear, and avoid direct sunlight). You may experience dry, itchy, skin, and dry or irritated eyes (avoid contact lenses). You will be more susceptible to infection; avoid crowds or infected persons. Report chills or fever, confusion, persistent or violent vomiting or stomach pain, persistent diarrhea, respiratory difficulty, chest pain or palpitations, unusual bleeding or bruising, bone pain, muscle spasms/tremors, or vision changes immediately.

Special Geriatric Considerations Patients ≥80 years of age may experience a greater incidence of grade 3 or 4 adverse events (diarrhea, hand-and-foot syndrome, nausea/vomiting).

Emetic Potential Moderate (30% to 60%)

Dosage Forms Excipient information presented when available (limited, particularly for generics); consult specific product labeling.

Tablet: 150 mg, 500 mg

References

Budman DR, "Capecitabine," *Invest New Drugs*, 2000, 18(4):355-63.
Dooley M and Goa KL, "Capecitabine," *Drugs*, 1999, 58(1):69-76.
Ishitsuka H, "Capecitabine: Preclinical Pharmacology Studies," *Invest New Drugs*, 2000, 18(4):343-54.
Johnston PG and Kaye S, "Capecitabine: A Novel Agent for the Treatment of Solid Tumors," *Anticancer Drugs*, 2001, 12(8):639-46.
McGavin JK and Goa KL, "Capecitabine: A Review of Its Use in the Treatment of Advanced or Metastatic Colorectal Cancer," *Drugs*, 2001, 61(15):2309-26.

Schilsky RL, "Pharmacology and Clinical Status of Capecitabine," *Oncology*, 2000, 14(9):1297-306.

♦ **Caphosol**® *see* Saliva Substitute *on page 960*
♦ **Carac**™ *see* Fluorouracil *on page 462*

Carboplatin (KAR boe pla tin)

Medication Safety Issues
Sound-alike/look-alike issues:
Carboplatin may be confused with cisplatin, oxaliplatin
Paraplatin® may be confused with Platinol®

High alert medication: The Institute for Safe Medication Practices (ISMP) includes this medication among its list of drugs which have a heightened risk of causing significant patient harm when used in error.

Related Information
Hematopoietic Stem Cell Transplantation *on page 1366*
Management of Drug Extravasations *on page 1301*
Management of Nausea and Vomiting *on page 1319*
Safe Handling of Hazardous Drugs *on page 1382*

U.S. Brand Names Paraplatin® [DSC]

Index Terms CBDCA; NSC-241240

Generic Available Yes

Canadian Brand Names Paraplatin-AQ

Pharmacologic Category Antineoplastic Agent, Alkylating Agent; Antineoplastic Agent, Platinum Analog

Use Treatment of ovarian cancer

Unlabeled/Investigational Use Lung cancer, head and neck cancer, endometrial cancer, esophageal cancer, bladder cancer, breast cancer, cervical cancer, CNS tumors, germ cell tumors, osteogenic sarcoma, and high-dose therapy with stem cell/bone marrow support

Pregnancy Risk Factor D

Lactation Excretion in breast milk unknown/contraindicated

Labeled Contraindications History of severe allergic reaction to cisplatin, carboplatin, other platinum-containing formulations, or any component of the formulation; pregnancy; breast-feeding

Warnings/Precautions Hazardous agent - use appropriate precautions for handling and disposal. High doses have resulted in severe abnormalities of liver function tests. **[U.S. Boxed Warning]: Bone marrow suppression, which may be severe, and vomiting are dose related;** reduce dosage in patients with bone marrow suppression and impaired renal function. Anemia is cumulative. Clinically significant hearing loss has been reported to occur in pediatric patients when carboplatin was administered at higher than recommended doses in combination with other ototoxic agents.

[U.S. Boxed Warning]: Increased risk of allergic reactions in patients previously exposed to platinum therapy. When administered as sequential infusions, taxane derivatives (docetaxel, paclitaxel) should be administered before the platinum derivatives (carboplatin, cisplatin) to limit myelosuppression and to enhance efficacy. Loss of vision (reversible) has been reported with higher than recommended doses. The elderly (≥65 years) and patients who have previously received cisplatin have an increased incidence of peripheral neuropathy. **[U.S. Boxed Warning]: Should be administered under the supervision of an experienced cancer chemotherapy physician.**

Adverse Reactions Percentages reported with single-agent therapy.
(Continued)

Carboplatin *(Continued)*

>10%:
Central nervous system: Pain (23%)
Endocrine & metabolic: Hyponatremia (29% to 47%), hypomagnesemia (29% to 43%), hypocalcemia (22% to 31%), hypokalemia (20% to 28%)
Gastrointestinal: Vomiting (65% to 81%), abdominal pain (17%), nausea (10% to 15%)
Hematologic: Myelosuppression (dose related and dose limiting; nadir at ~21 days; recovery by ~28 days), leukopenia (85%; grades 3/4: 15% to 26%), anemia (71% to 90%; grades 3/4: 21%), neutropenia (67%; grades 3/4: 16% to 21%), thrombocytopenia (62%; grades 3/4: 25% to 35%)
Hepatic: Alkaline phosphatase increased (24% to 37%), AST increased (15% to 19%)
Neuromuscular & skeletal: Weakness (11%)
Renal: Creatinine clearance decreased (27%), BUN increased (14% to 22%)
1% to 10%:
Central nervous system: Neurotoxicity (5%)
Dermatologic: Alopecia (2% to 3%)
Gastrointestinal: Constipation (5%), diarrhea (6%), stomatitis/mucositis (1%), taste dysgeusia (1%)
Hematologic: Hemorrhagic complications (5%)
Hepatic: Bilirubin increased (5%)
Local: Pain at injection site
Neuromuscular & skeletal: Peripheral neuropathy (4% to 6%; up to 10% in older and/or previously-treated patients)
Ocular: Visual disturbance (1%)
Otic: Ototoxicity (1%)
Renal: Creatinine increased (6% to 10%)
Miscellaneous: Infection (5%), hypersensitivity (2%)
<1%, postmarketing, and/or case reports (limited to important or life-threatening): Anaphylaxis, anorexia, bronchospasm, cardiac failure, cerebrovascular accident, embolism, erythema, fever, hemolytic uremic syndrome (HUS), hyper-/hypotension, malaise, necrosis (associated with extravasation), nephrotoxicity, neurotoxicity, pruritus, rash, secondary malignancies, urticaria, vision loss

Overdosage/Toxicology Symptoms of overdose include bone marrow suppression and hepatic toxicity. Treatment is symptom-directed and supportive.

Drug Interactions
Increased Effect/Toxicity: Aminoglycosides increase risk of ototoxicity and/or nephrotoxicity. When administered as sequential infusions, observational studies indicate a potential for increased toxicity when platinum derivatives (carboplatin, cisplatin) are administered before taxane derivatives (docetaxel, paclitaxel).

Ethanol/Nutrition/Herb Interactions Herb/Nutraceutical: Avoid black cohosh, dong quai in estrogen-dependent tumors.

Storage/Stability Store intact vials at room temperature of 15°C to 30°C (59°F to 86°F); protect from light. Further dilution to a concentration as low as 0.5 mg/mL is stable at room temperature (25°C) for 8 hours in NS; stable at room temperature or under refrigeration for at least 9 days in D_5W, although the manufacturer states to use within 8 hours due to lack of preservative.

Powder for reconstitution: Reconstituted to a final concentration of 10 mg/mL is stable for 5 days at room temperature (25°C).

Solution for injection: Multidose vials are stable for up to 14 days after opening when stored at room temperature.

Reconstitution Reconstitute powder to yield a final concentration of 10 mg/mL. Reconstituted carboplatin 10 mg/mL should be further diluted to a final concentration of 0.5-2 mg/mL with D_5W or NS for administration.

Compatibility Stable in $D_5^1/_4NS$, $D_5^1/_2NS$, D_5NS, D_5W, NS.

Y-site administration: Compatible: Allopurinol, amifostine, aztreonam, cefepime, cladribine, doxorubicin liposome, etoposide phosphate, filgrastim, fludarabine, gatifloxacin, gemcitabine, granisetron, linezolid, melphalan, ondansetron, paclitaxel, piperacillin/tazobactam, propofol, sargramostim, teniposide, thiotepa, topotecan, vinorelbine. **Incompatible:** Amphotericin B cholesteryl sulfate complex.

Compatibility when admixed: Compatible: Cisplatin, etoposide, floxuridine, ifosfamide, ifosfamide with etoposide, paclitaxel. **Incompatible:** Fluorouracil, mesna.

Mechanism of Action Carboplatin is an alkylating agent which covalently binds to DNA; possible cross-linking and interference with the function of DNA

Pharmacodynamics/Kinetics

Distribution: V_d: 16 L/kg; into liver, kidney, skin, and tumor tissue

Protein binding: 0%; platinum is 30% irreversibly bound

Metabolism: Minimally hepatic to aquated and hydroxylated compounds

Half-life elimination: Terminal: 22-40 hours; Cl_{cr} >60 mL/minute: 2.5-5.9 hours

Excretion: Urine (~60% to 90%) within 24 hours

Dosage Refer to individual protocols: **Note:** Doses for adults are usually determined by the AUC using the Calvert formula.

IVPB, I.V. infusion:

Children:

Solid tumor (unlabeled use): 300-600 mg/m² once every 4 weeks

Brain tumor (unlabeled use): 175 mg/m² weekly for 4 weeks every 6 weeks, with a 2-week recovery period between courses

Adults:

Ovarian cancer: 300-360 mg/m² every 4 weeks

Autologous BMT (unlabeled use): 1600 mg/m² (total dose) divided over 4 days

In adults, dosing is commonly calculated using the Calvert formula:

Total dose (mg) = Target AUC x (GFR+ 25)

Usual target AUCs:

Previously untreated patients: 6-8

Previously treated patients: 4-6

Elderly: The Calvert formula should be used to calculate dosing for elderly patients.

Intraperitoneal (unlabeled use): Adults: 200-650 mg/m² in 2 L of dialysis fluid have been administered into the peritoneum of ovarian cancer patients **or** target AUC: 5-7

Dosage adjustment for toxicity: Platelets <50,000 cells/mm³ or ANC <500 cells/mm³: Administer 75% of dose

Dosing adjustment in renal impairment: Note: Dose determination with Calvert formula uses GFR and, therefore, inherently adjusts for renal dysfunction.

(Continued)

Carboplatin *(Continued)*

The FDA-approved labeling recommends the following dosage adjustment guidelines:

Baseline Cl_{cr} 41-59 mL/minute: Initiate at 250 mg/m^2 and adjust subsequent doses based on bone marrow toxicity

Baseline Cl_{cr} 16-40 mL/minute: Initiate at 200 mg/m^2 and adjust subsequent doses based on bone marrow toxicity

Baseline Cl_{cr} ≤15 mL/minute: No guidelines are available.

The following dosage adjustments have been used by some clinicians (Aronoff, 2007): Adults (for dosing based on mg/m^2):

Hemodialysis: Administer 50% of dose

Continuous ambulatory peritoneal dialysis (CAPD): Administer 25% of dose

Continuous renal replacement therapy (CRRT): 200 mg/m^2

Dosing adjustment in hepatic impairment: Minimal hepatic metabolism; dosage adjustment may not be needed. No specific dosage adjustment guidelines are available.

Combination Regimens

Adenocarcinoma, unknown primary:
Carbo-Tax (Adenocarcinoma) *on page 1161*
Paclitaxel-Carboplatin-Etoposide *on page 1264*
PCE *on page 1266*

Bladder cancer:
Gemcitabine-Carboplatin (Bladder Cancer) *on page 1225*
Paclitaxel-Carboplatin (Bladder Cancer) *on page 1264*
Paclitaxel-Carboplatin-Gemcitabine *on page 1264*

Breast cancer:
Docetaxel-Trastuzumab-Carboplatin *on page 1192*
ICE-T *on page 1238*

Head and neck cancer:
Carboplatin-Cetuximab *on page 1161*
Fluorouracil + Carboplatin *on page 1217*

Lung cancer (nonsmall cell):
Carbo-Tax (Nonsmall Cell Lung Cancer) *on page 1161*
CaT (Nonsmall Cell Lung Cancer) *on page 1162*
EC (Nonsmall Cell Lung Cancer) *on page 1197*
Gemcitabine-Carboplatin (Nonsmall Cell Lung Cancer) *on page 1226*
Paclitaxel-Carboplatin-Bevacizumab *on page 1263*
PC (Nonsmall Cell Lung Cancer) *on page 1267*

Lung cancer (small cell): EC (Small Cell Lung Cancer) *on page 1198*

Lymphoma, non-Hodgkin's:
ICE (Lymphoma, non-Hodgkin's) *on page 1238*
RICE *on page 1277*

Melanoma: Dacarbazine-Carboplatin-Aldesleukin-Interferon *on page 1187*

Neuroblastoma:
CE (Neuroblastoma) *on page 1166*
CE-CAdO *on page 1166*
CI (Neuroblastoma) *on page 1174*

Osteosarcoma: ICE (Sarcoma) *on page 1238*

Ovarian cancer:
Carbo-Tax (Ovarian Cancer) *on page 1162*
CaT (Ovarian Cancer) *on page 1163*
CC *on page 1164*
Gemcitabine-Carboplatin (Ovarian Cancer) *on page 1226*

Prostate cancer:
  Estramustine + Docetaxel + Carboplatin *on page 1208*
  Paclitaxel + Estramustine + Carboplatin *on page 1265*
Retinoblastoma: CE (Retinoblastoma) *on page 1167*
Rhabdomyosarcoma: CEV *on page 1168*
Soft tissue sarcoma:
  ICE (Sarcoma) *on page 1238*
  ICE-T *on page 1238*

Administration Infuse over 15 minutes to 24 hours. May also be administered intraperitoneally. When administered as sequential infusions, taxane derivatives (docetaxel, paclitaxel) should be administered before platinum derivatives to limit myelosuppression and to enhance efficacy.

Monitoring Parameters CBC (with differential and platelet count), serum electrolytes, creatinine clearance, liver function tests, BUN, creatinine

Patient Information Maintain adequate nutrition (frequent small meals may help) and adequate hydration (2-3 L/day of fluids unless instructed to restrict fluid intake). Nausea and vomiting may be severe; request antiemetic. You will be susceptible to infection; avoid crowds or exposure to infection. Report sore throat, fever, chills, unusual fatigue or unusual bruising/bleeding, difficulty breathing, muscle cramps or twitching, or change in hearing acuity. Contraceptive measures are recommended during therapy.

Special Geriatric Considerations Peripheral neuropathy is more frequent in patients >65 years of age.

Emetic Potential Moderate (30% to 60%)

Vesicant No

High Dose Considerations
  Comments: Observe serum creatinine. Carboplatin is nephrotoxic and drug accumulation occurs with decreased creatinine clearance.
  High Dose: I.V.: 1.2-2.4 g/m^2 administered as 3-4 divided doses every 24-48 hours; generally infused over at least 60 minutes; 400 mg/m^2 has been infused over 15-30 minutes; generally combined with other high-dose chemotherapeutic drugs.

Unique Toxicities:
  Dermatologic: Alopecia
  Endocrine & metabolic: Hypokalemia, hypomagnesemia
  Gastrointestinal: Nausea, vomiting, mucositis
  Hepatic: Liver function tests elevated
  Renal: Nephrotoxicity

Dosage Forms Excipient information presented when available (limited, particularly for generics); consult specific product labeling. [DSC] = Discontinued product
Injection, powder for reconstitution: 50 mg, 150 mg, 450 mg
  Paraplatin®: 50 mg, 150 mg, 450 mg [DSC]
Injection, solution: 10 mg/mL (5 mL, 15 mL, 45 mL, 60 mL)
  Paraplatin®: 10 mg/mL (5 mL, 15 mL, 45 mL, 60 mL) [DSC]

References
Aronoff GR, Bennett WM, Berns JS, et al, *Drug Prescribing in Renal Failure: Dosing Guidelines for Adults and Children*, 5th ed. Philadelphia, PA: American College of Physicians; 2007, p 97, 169.
Benaji B, Dine T, Luyckx M, et al, "Stability and Compatibility of Cisplatin and Carboplatin With PVC Infusion Bags," *J Clin Pharm Ther*, 1994, 19(2):95-100.
Calvert AH, Newell DR, Grumbell LA, et al, "Carboplatin Dosage: Prospective Evaluation of a Simple Formula Based on Renal Function," *J Clin Oncol*, 1989, 7(11):1748-56.
Cheung Y-W, Cradock JC, Vishnuvajjala BR, et al, "Stability of Cisplatin, Iproplatin, Carboplatin, and Tetraplatin in Commonly Used Intravenous Solutions," *Am J Hosp Pharm*, 1987, 44:124-30.
(Continued)

Carboplatin *(Continued)*

Duffull SB and Robinson BA, "Clinical Pharmacokinetics and Dose Optimisation of Carboplatin," *Clin Pharmacokinet*, 1997, 33(3):161-83.

Fujiwara K, Markman M, Morgan M, et al, "Intraperitoneal Carboplatin-Based Chemotherapy for Epithelial Ovarian Cancer," *Gynecol Oncol*, 2005, 97(1):10-5.

Lokich J, "What Is the "Best" Platinum: Cisplatin, Carboplatin, or Oxaliplatin," *Cancer Invest*, 2001, 19(7):756-60.

Lokich J and Anderson N, "Carboplatin Versus Cisplatin in Solid Tumors: An Analysis of the Literature," *Ann Oncol*, 1998, 9(1):13-21.

Lovett D, Kelsen D, Eisenberger M, et al, "A Phase II Trial of Carboplatin and Vinblastine in the Treatment of Advanced Squamous Cell Carcinoma of the Esophagus," *Cancer*, 1991, 67(2):354-6.

Markman M and Walker JL, "Intraperitoneal Chemotherapy of Ovarian Cancer: a Review, With a Focus on Practical Aspects of Treatment," *J Clin Oncol*, 2006, 24(6):988-94.

Murry DJ, "Comparative Clinical Pharmacology of Cisplatin and Carboplatin," *Pharmacotherapy*, 1997, 17(5 Pt 2):140S-145S.

Oguri S, Sakakibara T, Mase H, et al, "Clinical Pharmacokinetics of Carboplatin," *J Clin Pharmacol*, 1988, 28(3):208-15.

Polyzos A, Tsavaris N, Kosmas C, et al, "A Comparative Study of Intraperitoneal Carboplatin versus Intravenous Carboplatin With Intravenous Cyclophosphamide in Both Arms as Initial Chemotherapy for Stage III Ovarian Cancer," *Oncology*, 1999, 56(4):291-6.

Reece PA, Stafford I, Abbott RI, et al, "Two- Versus 24-Hour Infusion of Cisplatin: Pharmacokinetic Considerations," *J Clin Oncol*, 1989, 7(2):270-5.

Zeltzer PM, Epport K, Nelson MD Jr, et al, "Prolonged Response to Carboplatin in an Infant With Brain Stem Glioma," *Cancer*, 1991, 67(1):43-7.

♦ **Carimune® NF** *see* Immune Globulin (Intravenous) *on page 597*

Carmustine *(kar MUS teen)*

Medication Safety Issues
Sound-alike/look-alike issues:
Carmustine may be confused with lomustine

High alert medication: The Institute for Safe Medication Practices (ISMP) includes this medication among its list of drugs which have a heightened risk of causing significant patient harm when used in error.

Related Information
Hematopoietic Stem Cell Transplantation *on page 1366*
Management of Drug Extravasations *on page 1301*
Safe Handling of Hazardous Drugs *on page 1382*

U.S. Brand Names BiCNU®; Gliadel®

Index Terms BCNU; bis-chloronitrosourea; Carmustinum; NSC-409962; WR-139021

Generic Available No

Canadian Brand Names BiCNU®; Gliadel Wafer®

Pharmacologic Category Antineoplastic Agent; Antineoplastic Agent, Alkylating Agent (Nitrosourea); Antineoplastic Agent, DNA Adduct-Forming Agent; Antineoplastic Agent, DNA Binding Agent

Use
Injection: Treatment of brain tumors (glioblastoma, brainstem glioma, medulloblastoma, astrocytoma, ependymoma, and metastatic brain tumors), multiple myeloma, Hodgkin's disease (relapsed or refractory), non-Hodgkin's lymphomas (relapsed or refractory),

Wafer (implant): Adjunct to surgery in patients with recurrent glioblastoma multiforme; adjunct to surgery and radiation in patients with high-grade malignant glioma

Unlabeled/Investigational Use Melanoma

Pregnancy Risk Factor D

Lactation Excretion in breast milk unknown/not recommended

Labeled Contraindications Hypersensitivity to carmustine or any component of the formulation

Warnings/Precautions Hazardous agent - use appropriate precautions for handling and disposal. **[U.S. Boxed Warning]: Bone marrow suppression (thrombocytopenia, leukopenia) is the major toxicity and may be delayed; monitor blood counts weekly for at least 6 weeks after administration. Myelosuppression is cumulative; consider nadir blood counts from prior dose for dosage adjustment. May cause bleeding (due to thrombocytopenia) or infections (due to neutropenia); monitor closely.** Administer with caution to patients with depressed platelet, leukocyte, or erythrocyte counts; renal or hepatic impairment. Diluent contains significant amounts of ethanol; use caution with aldehyde dehydrogenase-2 deficiency or history of "alcohol-flushing syndrome."

[U.S. Boxed Warning]: Dose-related pulmonary toxicity may occur; patients receiving cumulative doses >1400 mg/m² are at higher risk. Baseline pulmonary function tests are recommended. **[U.S. Boxed Warning]: Delayed onset of pulmonary fibrosis has occurred up to 17 years after treatment** in children (1-16 years) who received carmustine in cumulative doses ranging from 770-1800 mg/m² combined with cranial radiotherapy for intracranial tumors. **[U.S. Boxed Warning]: Should be administered under the supervision of an experienced cancer chemotherapy physician.** Long-term use may be associated with the development of secondary malignancies. Safety and efficacy in children have not been established.

Adverse Reactions

>10%:

Cardiovascular: Hypotension (with high-dose I.V. therapy, due to the alcohol content of the diluent)

Central nervous system: Ataxia, dizziness

Postoperatively: Seizure (wafer 5% to 54%), brain edema (wafer 4% to 23%)

Dermatologic: Burning (with skin contact), hyperpigmentation of skin (with skin contact)

Gastrointestinal: Severe nausea and vomiting, usually begins within 2-4 hours of drug administration and lasts for 4-6 hours; dose related. Patients should receive a prophylactic antiemetic regimen.

Hematologic: Myelosuppression (cumulative, dose related, delayed, and dose limiting), thrombocytopenia (onset: 28 days; recovery: 35-42 days), leukopenia (onset: 35-42 days; recovery: 42-56 days)

Hepatic: Reversible increases in bilirubin, alkaline phosphatase, and AST occur in 20% to 25% of patients

Local: Pain and burning at injection site, phlebitis

Neuromuscular & skeletal: Weakness (wafer 22%)

Ocular: Ocular toxicities (transient conjunctival flushing and blurred vision), retinal hemorrhages

Respiratory: Interstitial fibrosis occurs in up to 50% of patients receiving a cumulative dose >1400 mg/m², or bone marrow transplantation doses; may be delayed up to 3 years; rare in patients receiving lower doses. A history of lung disease or concomitant bleomycin therapy may increase the risk of this reaction. Patients with forced vital capacity (FVC) or carbon monoxide diffusing capacity of the lungs (DLCO) <70% of predicted are at higher risk.

Miscellaneous: Disease progression/performance deterioration (wafer 82%)

(Continued)

Carmustine *(Continued)*

1% to 10%:

Cardiovascular: Chest pain, deep thrombophlebitis (wafer), facial edema (wafer), peripheral edema (wafer)

Central nervous system: Wafer: Amnesia, anxiety, aphasia, ataxia, brain abscess, confusion, convulsion, CSF leaks, depression, diplopia, dizziness, facial paralysis, headache, hemiplegia, hydrocephalus, hypoesthesia, insomnia, intracranial hypertension, meningitis, somnolence, speech disorder, stupor

Dermatologic: Facial flushing, probably due to the alcohol diluent; alopecia, rash (wafer), wound healing abnormal (wafer)

Gastrointestinal: Abdominal pain, anorexia, constipation, diarrhea, stomatitis

Hematologic: Anemia, hemorrhage (wafer)

Local: Abscess (wafer)

Neuromuscular & skeletal: Back pain

<1%: Allergic reaction, azotemia (progressive), cerebral hemorrhage infarction (wafer), cyst formation (wafer), dermatitis, hepatic coma, hyperpigmentation, hypotension, kidney size decreased, neuroretinitis, painless jaundice, renal failure, subacute hepatitis, tachycardia, thrombosis

Overdosage/Toxicology Symptoms of overdose include nausea, vomiting, thrombocytopenia, and leukopenia. Treatment is symptom-directed and supportive. Because myelosuppression is delayed, blood counts should be monitored for at least 6 weeks.

Drug Interactions

Increased Effect/Toxicity: Cimetidine may increase the bone marrow toxicity of carmustine

Decreased Effect: Carmustine may decrease the absorption of digoxin tablets.

Ethanol/Nutrition/Herb Interactions Ethanol: Diluent for infusion contains ethanol; avoid concurrent use of medications that inhibit aldehyde dehydrogenase-2 or cause disulfiram-like reactions.

Storage/Stability

Injection: Store intact vials under refrigeration at 2°C to 8°C (36°F to 46°F); vials are stable for 36 days at room temperature. Reconstituted solutions are stable for 8 hours at room temperature (25°C) and 24 hours under refrigeration (2°C to 8°C) and protected from light. Further dilution in D_5W or NS is stable for 8 hours at room temperature (25°C) and 48 hours under refrigeration (4°C) in glass or polyolefin containers and protected from light.

Wafer: Store at or below -20°C (-4°F). Unopened foil pouches may be kept at room temperature for up to 6 hours.

Reconstitution Injection: Initially, dilute with 3 mL of absolute alcohol. Further dilute with SWFI (27 mL) to a concentration of 3.3 mg/mL; protect from light; may further dilute with D_5W or NS, using a non-PVC container.

Compatibility Compatible with D_5W, NS, SWFI, dacarbazine.

Y-site administration: Compatible: Amifostine, aztreonam, cefepime, filgrastim, fludarabine, gemcitabine, granisetron, ondansetron, piperacillin/tazobactam, sargramostim, teniposide, thiotepa, vinorelbine. **Incompatible:** Allopurinol, sodium bicarbonate.

Compatibility when admixed: Incompatible with sodium bicarbonate.

Mechanism of Action Interferes with the normal function of DNA and RNA by alkylation and cross-linking the strands of DNA and RNA, and by possible protein modification; may also inhibit enzyme processes by carbamylation of amino acids in protein

Pharmacodynamics/Kinetics

Distribution: 3.3 L/kg; readily crosses blood-brain barrier producing CSF levels equal to >50% of blood plasma levels; highly lipid soluble

Metabolism: Rapidly hepatic; forms active metabolites

Half-life elimination: Biphasic: Initial: 1.4 minutes; Secondary: 20 minutes (active metabolites: plasma half-life of 67 hours)

Excretion: Urine (~60% to 70%) within 96 hours; lungs (6% to 10% as CO_2)

Dosage

I.V. (refer to individual protocols):

Children (unlabeled use): 200-250 mg/m² every 4-6 weeks as a single dose

Adults: Usual dosage (per manufacturer labeling): 150-200 mg/m² every 6 weeks **or** 75-100 mg/m²/day for 2 days every 6 weeks

Alternative regimens (unlabeled):
75-120 mg/m² days 1 and 2 every 6-8 weeks **or**
50-80 mg/m² days 1,2,3 every 6-8 weeks

Primary brain cancer:
150-200 mg/m² every 6-8 weeks as a single dose **or**
75-120 mg/m² days 1 and 2 every 6-8 weeks **or**
20-65 mg/m² every 4-6 weeks **or**
0.5-1 mg/kg every 4-6 weeks **or**
40-80 mg/m²/day for 3 days every 6-8 weeks

Autologous BMT: ALL OF THE FOLLOWING DOSES ARE FATAL WITHOUT BMT

Combination therapy: Up to 300-900 mg/m²

Single-agent therapy: Up to 1200 mg/m² (fatal necrosis is associated with doses >2 g/m²)

Implantation (wafer): Adults: Recurrent glioblastoma multiforme, malignant glioma: Up to 8 wafers may be placed in the resection cavity (total dose 62.6 mg); should the size and shape not accommodate 8 wafers, the maximum number of wafers allowed should be placed

Dosing adjustment in renal impairment: I.V.: The FDA-approved labeling does not contain renal dosing adjustment guidelines. The following dosage adjustments have been used by some clinicians (Kintzel, 1995):

Cl_{cr} 46-60 mL/minute: Administer 80% of dose

Cl_{cr} 31-45 mL/minute: Administer 75% of dose

Cl_{cr} ≤30 mL/minute: Consider use of alternative drug

Dosing adjustment in hepatic impairment: Dosage adjustment may be necessary; however, no specific guidelines are available.

Combination Regimens

Lymphoma, Hodgkin's disease: mini-BEAM *on page 1248*

Melanoma:
CCDT (Melanoma) *on page 1165*
Dartmouth Regimen *on page 1187*

Multiple myeloma:
M-2 *on page 1245*
VBAP *on page 1287*
VBMCP *on page 1288*

Administration

Injection: Significant absorption to PVC containers - should be administered in either glass or polyolefin containers. I.V. infusion over 1-2 hours is recommended; infusion through a free-flowing saline or dextrose infusion, or administration through a central catheter can alleviate venous pain/irritation.

High-dose carmustine: Maximum rate of infusion of ≤3 mg/m²/minute to avoid excessive flushing, agitation, and hypotension; infusions should

(Continued)

Carmustine *(Continued)*

run over at least 2 hours; some investigational protocols dictate shorter infusions. **(High-dose carmustine is fatal if not followed by bone marrow or peripheral stem cell infusions.)**

Extravasation management: Elevate extremity. Inject long-acting dexamethasone (Decadron® LA) or by hyaluronidase throughout tissue with a 25- to 37-gauge needle. Apply warm, moist compresses.

Implant: Use appropriate precautions for handling and disposal; double glove before handling; outer gloves should be discarded as chemotherapy waste after handling wafers. Any wafer or remnant that is removed upon repeat surgery should be discarded as chemotherapy waste. The outer surface of the external foil pouch is not sterile. Open pouch gently; avoid pressure on the wafers to prevent breakage. Wafer that are broken in half may be used, however, wafers broken into more than 2 pieces should be discarded. Oxidized regenerated cellulose (Surgicel®) may be placed over the wafer to secure; irrigate cavity prior to closure.

Monitoring Parameters CBC with differential and platelet count, pulmonary function, liver function, and renal function tests; monitor blood pressure during administration

Wafer: Complications of craniotomy (seizures, intracranial infection, brain edema)

Patient Information Limit oral intake for 4-6 hours before therapy. Do not use alcohol, aspirin-containing products, or OTC medications without consulting prescriber. You may experience nausea or vomiting (frequent small meals, frequent mouth care, sucking lozenges, or chewing gum may help). If this is ineffective, consult prescriber for antiemetic medication. You may experience loss of hair (reversible). You will be more susceptible to infection (avoid crowds and exposure to infection as much as possible). You will be more sensitive to sunlight; use sunblock, wear protective clothing and dark glasses, or avoid direct exposure to sunlight. Frequent mouth care with soft toothbrush or cotton swabs and frequent mouth rinses may help relieve mouth sores. Report fever, chills, unusual bruising or bleeding, signs of infection, excessive fatigue, yellowing of eyes or skin, or change in color of urine or stool. Contraceptive measures are recommended during therapy.

Additional Information Accidental skin contact may cause transient burning and brown discoloration of the skin. Delayed onset pulmonary fibrosis occurring up to 17 years after treatment has been reported in patients who received cumulative doses >1400 mg/m^2.

Emetic Potential Very high (>90%)

Vesicant No; the alcohol-based diluent may be an irritant, especially with high doses.

High Dose Considerations

Comments: Due to risk of hypotension, patients receiving high-dose carmustine must be supine and may require the Trendelenburg position, fluid support, and vasopressor support. Vital signs must be monitored frequently during the infusion of high-dose carmustine.

Infusion-related cardiovascular effects are primarily due to concomitant ethanol and acetaldehyde. Use with great caution in patients with aldehyde dehydrogenase-2 deficiency or history of "alcohol flushing syndrome". Avoid concurrent use of medications that inhibit aldehyde dehydrogenase-2 or cause disulfiram-like reactions. Acute lung injury tends to occur 1-3 months following carmustine infusion. Patients must be counseled to contact their BMT physician for dyspnea, cough, or fever following carmustine. Acute lung injury is managed with a course of corticosteroids.

High Dose: I.V.: 300-800 mg/m² infused over at least 2 hours; may be divided into two doses administered every 12 hours; generally combined with other high-dose chemotherapeutic drugs. **(High-dose carmustine is fatal if not followed by bone marrow or peripheral stem cell infusions.)**

Unique Toxicities:

Cardiovascular: Hypotension (infusion related), arrhythmias (infusion related)

Central nervous system: Encephalopathy, ethanol intoxication, seizures, fever

Endocrine & metabolic: Hyperprolactinemia and hypothyroidism in patients with brain tumors treated with radiation

Gastrointestinal: Severe nausea and vomiting

Hepatic: Hepatitis, hepatic veno-occlusive disease

Pulmonary: Dyspnea

Dosage Forms Excipient information presented when available (limited, particularly for generics); consult specific product labeling.

Injection, powder for reconstitution:

BiCNU®: 100 mg [packaged with 3 mL of absolute alcohol as diluent]

Implant:

Gliadel®: 7.7 mg (8s)

References

Buzaid AC and Murren J, "Chemotherapy for Advanced Malignant Melanoma," *Int J Clin Lab Res*, 1992, 21(3):205-9.

Durando X, Lemaire JJ, Tortochaux J, et al, "High-Dose BCNU Followed by Autologous Hematopoietic Stem Cell Transplantation in Supratentorial High-Grade Malignant Gliomas: A Retrospective Analysis of 114 Patients," *Bone Marrow Transplant*, 2003, 31(7):559-64.

Fleming AB and Saltzman WM, "Pharmacokinetics of the Carmustine Implant," *Clin Pharmacokinet*, 2002, 41(6):403-19.

Kintzel PE and Dorr RT, "Anticancer Drug Renal Toxicity and Elimination: Dosing Guidelines for Altered Renal Function," *Cancer Treat Rev*, 1995, 21(1):33-64.

Lesser GJ and Grossman SA, "The Chemotherapy of Adult Primary Brain Tumors," *Cancer Treat Rev*, 1993, 19(3):261-81.

Mahendra P, Johnson D, Scott MA, et al, "Peripheral Blood Progenitor Cell Transplantation: A Single Centre Experience Comparing Two Mobilisation Regimens in 67 Patients," *Bone Marrow Transplant*, 1996, 17(4):503-7.

Trissel LA, Xu QA, and Baker M, "Drug Compatability With New Polyolefin Infusion Solution Containers," *Am J Health-Syst Pharm*, 2006, 63(23):2379-82.

Weingart JD and Brem H, "Carmustine Implants: Potential in the Treatment of Brain Tumors," *CNS Drugs*, 1996, 4:263-9.

Weiss RB and Issell BF, "The Nitrosoureas: Carmustine (BCNU) and Lomustine (CCNU)," *Cancer Treat Rev*, 1982, 9(4):313-30.

♦ **Carmustinum** see Carmustine on page 178

♦ **Carter's Little Pills® (Can)** see Bisacodyl on page 144

♦ **Casodex®** see Bicalutamide on page 141

Caspofungin (kas poe FUN jin)

U.S. Brand Names Cancidas®

Index Terms Caspofungin Acetate

Generic Available No

Canadian Brand Names Cancidas®

Pharmacologic Category Antifungal Agent, Parenteral; Echinocandin

Use Treatment of invasive *Aspergillus* infections in patients who are refractory or intolerant of other therapy; treatment of candidemia and other *Candida* infections (intra-abdominal abscesses, esophageal, peritonitis, pleural space); empirical treatment for presumed fungal infections in febrile neutropenic patient

Pregnancy Risk Factor C

(Continued)

Caspofungin *(Continued)*

Lactation Excretion in breast milk unknown/use caution

Labeled Contraindications Hypersensitivity to caspofungin or any component of the formulation

Warnings/Precautions Concurrent use of cyclosporine should be limited to patients for whom benefit outweighs risk, due to a high frequency of hepatic transaminase elevations observed during concurrent use. Limited data are available concerning treatment durations longer than 4 weeks; however, treatment appears to be well tolerated. Use caution in hepatic impairment; dosage reduction required in moderate impairment. Safety and efficacy in pediatric patients have not been established.

Adverse Reactions

>10%:

Central nervous system: Headache (up to 11%), fever (3% to 26%), chills (up to 14%)

Endocrine & metabolic: Hypokalemia (4% to 11%)

Hematologic: Hemoglobin decreased (1% to 12%)

Hepatic: Serum alkaline phosphatase increased (3% to 11%), transaminases increased (up to 13%)

Local: Infusion site reactions (2% to 12%), phlebitis/thrombophlebitis (up to 16%)

1% to 10%:

Cardiovascular: Flushing (2% to 3%), facial edema (up to 3%), hypertension (1% to 2%), tachycardia (1% to 2%), hypotension (1%)

Central nervous system: Dizziness (2%), pain (1% to 5%), insomnia (1%)

Dermatologic: Rash (<1% to 6%), pruritus (1% to 3%), erythema (1% to 2%)

Gastrointestinal: Nausea (2% to 6%), vomiting (1% to 4%), abdominal pain (1% to 4%), diarrhea (1% to 4%), anorexia (1%)

Hematologic: Eosinophils increased (3%), neutrophils decreased (2% to 3%), WBC decreased (5% to 6%), anemia (up to 4%), platelet count decreased (2% to 3%)

Hepatic: Bilirubin increased (3%)

Local: Induration (up to 3%)

Neuromuscular & skeletal: Myalgia (up to 3%), paresthesia (1% to 3%), tremor (≤2%)

Renal: Nephrotoxicity (8%)*, proteinuria (5%), hematuria (2%), serum creatinine increased (<1% to 4%), urinary WBCs increased (up to 8%), urinary RBCs increased (1% to 4%), blood urea nitrogen increased (1%)

*Nephrotoxicity defined as serum creatinine ≥2x baseline value or ≥1 mg/dL in patients with serum creatinine above ULN range (patients with Cl_{cr} <30 mL/minute were excluded)

Miscellaneous: Flu-like syndrome (3%), diaphoresis (up to 3%)

<1%: Adult respiratory distress syndrome (ARDS), jaundice, pulmonary edema, renal insufficiency, serum bicarbonate decreased, tachypnea; histamine-mediated reactions (including facial swelling, bronchospasm, sensation of warmth) have been reported

Postmarketing and/or case reports: Anaphylaxis, dyspnea, dystonia, hepatic dysfunction, hypercalcemia, peripheral edema, swelling, stridor

Overdosage/Toxicology No experience with overdosage has been reported. Caspofungin is not dialyzable. Treatment is symptomatic and supportive.

Drug Interactions

Increased Effect/Toxicity: Concurrent administration of cyclosporine may increase caspofungin concentrations; hepatic serum transaminases may be observed.

Decreased Effect: Caspofungin may decrease blood concentrations of tacrolimus. Dosage adjustment of caspofungin to 70 mg is required for patients on rifampin.

Storage/Stability Store vials at 2°C to 8°C (36°F to 46°F). Reconstituted solution may be stored at less than 25°C (77°F) for 1 hour prior to preparation of infusion solution. Infusion solutions may be stored at less than 25°C (77°F) and should be used within 24 hours; up to 48 hours if stored at 2°C to 8°C (36°F to 46°F).

Reconstitution Bring refrigerated vial to room temperature. Reconstitute vials using 0.9% sodium chloride for injection, SWFI, or bacteriostatic water for injection. Mix gently until clear solution is formed; do not use if cloudy or contains particles. Solution should be further diluted with 0.9%, 0.45%, or 0.225% sodium chloride or LR.

Compatibility Stable in NS, 1/2NS, 1/4NS, LR. Do not mix with dextrose-containing solutions. Do not coadminister with other medications.

Mechanism of Action Inhibits synthesis of β(1,3)-D-glucan, an essential component of the cell wall of susceptible fungi. Highest activity in regions of active cell growth. Mammalian cells do not require β(1,3)-D-glucan, limiting potential toxicity.

Pharmacodynamics/Kinetics

Protein binding: 97% to albumin

Metabolism: Slowly, via hydrolysis and *N*-acetylation as well as by spontaneous degradation, with subsequent metabolism to component amino acids. Overall metabolism is extensive.

Half-life elimination: Beta (distribution): 9-11 hours; Terminal: 40-50 hours

Excretion: Urine (41% as metabolites, 1% to 9% unchanged) and feces (35% as metabolites)

Dosage I.V.:

Children: Safety and efficacy in pediatric patients have not been established

Adults: **Note:** Duration of caspofungin treatment should be determined by patient status and clinical response. Empiric therapy should be given until neutropenia resolves. In patients with positive cultures, treatment should continue until 14 days after last positive culture. In neutropenic patients, treatment should be given at least 7 days after both signs and symptoms of infection **and** neutropenia resolve.

Empiric therapy: Initial dose: 70 mg on day 1; subsequent dosing: 50 mg/day; may increase up to 70 mg/day if tolerated, but clinical response is inadequate

Invasive *Aspergillus*, candidiasis: Initial dose: 70 mg on day 1; subsequent dosing: 50 mg/day

Esophageal candidiasis: 50 mg/day; **Note:** The majority of patients studied for this indication also had oropharyngeal involvement.

Concomitant use of an enzyme inducer:

Patients receiving rifampin: 70 mg caspofungin daily

Patients receiving carbamazepine, dexamethasone, efavirenz, nevirapine, **or** phenytoin (and possibly other enzyme inducers) may require an increased daily dose of caspofungin (70 mg/day).

Elderly: The number of patients >65 years of age in clinical studies was not sufficient to establish whether a difference in response may be anticipated.

Dosage adjustment in renal impairment: No specific dosage adjustment is required; supplemental dose is not required following dialysis

(Continued)

Caspofungin *(Continued)*

Dosage adjustment in hepatic impairment:

Mild hepatic insufficiency (Child-Pugh score 5-6): No adjustment necessary

Moderate hepatic insufficiency (Child-Pugh score 7-9): 35 mg/day; initial 70 mg loading dose should still be administered in treatment of invasive infections

Severe hepatic insufficiency (Child-Pugh score >9): No clinical experience

Administration Infuse slowly, over 1 hour; monitor during infusion. Isolated cases of possible histamine-related reactions have occurred during clinical trials (rash, flushing, pruritus, facial edema).

Patient Information Report immediately any pain, burning, or swelling at infusion site, or any signs of allergic reaction (eg, difficulty breathing or swallowing, back pain, chest tightness, rash, hives, or swelling of lips or mouth). Report nausea, vomiting, abdominal pain, or diarrhea.

Special Geriatric Considerations The number of patients >65 years of age in clinical studies was not sufficient to establish whether a difference in response may be anticipated.

Dosage Forms Excipient information presented when available (limited, particularly for generics); consult specific product labeling.

Injection, powder for reconstitution, as acetate: 50 mg [contains sucrose 39 mg], 70 mg [contains sucrose 54 mg]

References

Mora-Duarte J, Betts R, Rotstein C, et al, "Comparison of Caspofungin and Amphotericin B for Invasive Candidiasis," *N Engl J Med*, 2002, 347(25):2020-9.

Pappas PG, Rex JH, Sobel JD, et al, "Guidelines for Treatment of Candidiasis," *Clin Infect Dis*, 2004, 38:161-89.

Stone EA, Fung HB, and Kirschenbaum HL, "Caspofungin: An Echinocandin Antifungal Agent," *Clin Ther*, 2002, 24(3):351-77.

- ♦ **Caspofungin Acetate** *see* Caspofungin *on page 183*
- ♦ **Cathflo® Activase®** *see* Alteplase *on page 45*
- ♦ **CB-1348** *see* Chlorambucil *on page 205*
- ♦ **CBDCA** *see* Carboplatin *on page 173*
- ♦ **CC-5013** *see* Lenalidomide *on page 659*
- ♦ **CCI-779** *see* Temsirolimus *on page 1014*
- ♦ **CCNU** *see* Lomustine *on page 690*
- ♦ **2-CdA** *see* Cladribine *on page 231*
- ♦ **CDDP** *see* Cisplatin *on page 224*
- ♦ **CDX** *see* Bicalutamide *on page 141*
- ♦ **CeeNU®** *see* Lomustine *on page 690*

Cefepime *(SEF e pim)*

U.S. Brand Names Maxipime®

Index Terms Cefepime Hydrochloride

Generic Available Yes

Canadian Brand Names Maxipime®

Pharmacologic Category Antibiotic, Cephalosporin (Fourth Generation)

Use Treatment of uncomplicated and complicated urinary tract infections, including pyelonephritis caused by typical urinary tract pathogens; monotherapy for febrile neutropenia; uncomplicated skin and skin structure infections caused by *Streptococcus pyogenes*; moderate-to-severe pneumonia caused by pneumococcus, *Pseudomonas aeruginosa*, and other gram-negative organisms; complicated intra-abdominal infections (in combination with metronidazole). Also active against methicillin-susceptible staphylococci, *Enterobacter* sp, and many other gram-negative bacilli.

Children 2 months to 16 years: Empiric therapy of febrile neutropenia patients, uncomplicated skin/soft tissue infections, pneumonia, and uncomplicated/complicated urinary tract infections.

Pregnancy Risk Factor B

Lactation Enters breast milk/use caution

Labeled Contraindications Hypersensitivity to cefepime, any component of the formulation, or other cephalosporins

Warnings/Precautions Modify dosage in patients with severe renal impairment; use with caution in patients with a history of penicillin or cephalosporin allergy, especially IgE-mediated reactions (eg, anaphylaxis, urticaria). Prolonged use may result in fungal or bacterial superinfection, including *C. difficile*-associated diarrhea (CDAD) and pseudomembranous colitis; CDAD has been observed <2 months postantibiotic treatment. Use in patients <2 months of age has not been established. May be associated with increased INR, especially in nutritionally-deficient patients, prolonged treatment, hepatic or renal disease. Use with caution in patients with a history of seizure disorder; high levels, particularly in the presence of renal impairment, may increase risk of seizures.

Adverse Reactions

>10%: Hematologic: Positive Coombs' test without hemolysis

1% to 10%:

Central nervous system: Fever (1%), headache (1%)

Dermatologic: Rash, pruritus

Gastrointestinal: Diarrhea, nausea, vomiting

Local: Pain, erythema at injection site

<1%, postmarketing, and/or case reports: Agranulocytosis, anaphylactic shock, anaphylaxis, coma, encephalopathy, hallucinations, leukopenia, myoclonus, neuromuscular excitability, neutropenia, seizure, status epilepticus (nonconvulsive), thrombocytopenia

Reactions reported with other cephalosporins: Aplastic anemia, erythema multiforme, hemolytic anemia, hemorrhage, pancytopenia, PT prolonged, renal dysfunction, Stevens-Johnson syndrome, superinfection, toxic epidermal necrolysis, toxic nephropathy, vaginitis

Overdosage/Toxicology Symptoms of overdose include neuromuscular hypersensitivity and CNS toxicity (including hallucinations, confusion, seizures, and coma). Many beta-lactam containing antibiotics have the potential to cause neuromuscular hyperirritability or convulsive seizures. Hemodialysis may be helpful to aid in removal of the drug from blood; otherwise, treatment is supportive and symptom-directed.

Drug Interactions

Increased Effect/Toxicity: High-dose probenecid decreases clearance and increases effect of cefepime. Aminoglycosides increase nephrotoxic potential when taken with cefepime.

Storage/Stability Stable with normal saline, D$_5$W, and a variety of other solutions for 24 hours at room temperature and 7 days refrigerated.

Compatibility Stable in D$_5$LR, D$_5$NS, D$_5$W, D$_{10}$W, NS, bacteriostatic water, sterile water for injection; **variable stability (consult detailed reference)** in peritoneal dialysis solutions.

Y-site administration: Compatible: Ampicillin/sulbactam, aztreonam, bleomycin, bumetanide, buprenorphine, butorphanol, calcium gluconate, carboplatin, carmustine, co-trimoxazole, cyclophosphamide, cytarabine, dactinomycin, dexamethasone sodium phosphate, docetaxel, doxorubicin

(Continued)

Cefepime *(Continued)*

liposome, fluconazole, fludarabine, fluorouracil, furosemide, granisetron, hydrocortisone sodium phosphate, hydrocortisone sodium succinate, hydromorphone, imipenem/cilastatin, leucovorin, lorazepam, melphalan, mesna, methotrexate, methylprednisolone sodium succinate, metronidazole, paclitaxel, piperacillin/tazobactam, ranitidine, sargramostim, sodium bicarbonate, thiotepa, ticarcillin/clavulanate, zidovudine. **Incompatible:** Acyclovir, amphotericin B, amphotericin B cholesteryl sulfate complex, chlordiazepoxide, chlorpromazine, cimetidine, ciprofloxacin, cisplatin, dacarbazine, daunorubicin, diazepam, diphenhydramine, dobutamine, dopamine, doxorubicin, droperidol, enalaprilat, etoposide, etoposide phosphate, famotidine, filgrastim, floxuridine, ganciclovir, haloperidol, hydroxyzine, idarubicin, ifosfamide, magnesium sulfate, mannitol, mechlorethamine, meperidine, metoclopramide, mitomycin, mitoxantrone, morphine, nalbuphine, ofloxacin, ondansetron, plicamycin, prochlorperazine edisylate, promethazine, streptozocin, vancomycin, vinblastine, vincristine.

Compatibility when admixed: Compatible: Amikacin, clindamycin, heparin, potassium chloride, theophylline, vancomycin. **Incompatible:** Aminophylline, gentamicin, netilmicin, tobramycin. **Variable (consult detailed reference):** Ampicillin, metronidazole.

Mechanism of Action Inhibits bacterial cell wall synthesis by binding to one or more of the penicillin-binding proteins (PBPs) which in turn inhibits the final transpeptidation step of peptidoglycan synthesis in bacterial cell walls, thus inhibiting cell wall biosynthesis. Bacteria eventually lyse due to ongoing activity of cell wall autolytic enzymes (autolysis and murein hydrolases) while cell wall assembly is arrested.

Pharmacodynamics/Kinetics

Absorption: I.M.: Rapid and complete

Distribution: V_d: Adults: 14-20 L; penetrates into inflammatory fluid at concentrations ~80% of serum levels and into bronchial mucosa at levels ~60% of those reached in the plasma; crosses blood-brain barrier

Protein binding, plasma: 16% to 19%

Metabolism: Minimally hepatic

Half-life elimination: 2 hours

Time to peak: 0.5-1.5 hours

Excretion: Urine (85% as unchanged drug)

Dosage

Usual dosage range:

Children: I.M., I.V.: 50 mg/kg every 8-12 hours (maximum not to exceed adult dosing)

Adults: I.V.: 1-2 g every 8-12 hours; I.M.: 500-1000 mg every 12 hours

Indication-specific dosing:

Children ≥2 months to 16 years (<40 kg):

Febrile neutropenia: I.V.: 50 mg/kg every 8 hours for 7 days or until neutropenia resolves

Skin and skin structure infections (uncomplicated) and pneumonia: I.V.: 50 mg/kg every 12 hours for 10 days

Urinary tract infections, complicated and uncomplicated: I.M., I.V.: 50 mg/kg every 12 hours for 7-10 days; **Note:** I.M. may be considered for mild-to-moderate infection only

Adults:

Brain abscess, postneurosurgical prevention (unlabeled use): I.V.: 2 g every 8 hours with vancomycin

Febrile neutropenia, monotherapy: I.V.: 2 g every 8 hours for 7 days or until the neutropenia resolves

Intra-abdominal infections, complicated: I.V.: 2 g every 12 hours for 7-10 days with metronidazole

Otitis externa, malignant (unlabeled use): I.V.: 2 g every 12 hours

Pneumonia: I.V.:

Nosocomial (HAP/VAP): 1-2 g every 8-12 hours; **Note:** Duration of therapy may vary considerably (7-21 days); usually longer courses are required if *Pseudomonas*. In absence of *Pseudomonas*, and if appropriate empiric treatment used and patient responsive, it may be clinically appropriate to reduce duration of therapy to 7-10 days (American Thoracic Society Guidelines, 2005).

Community-acquired (including pseudomonal): 1-2 g every 12 hours for 10 days

Septic lateral/cavernous sinus thrombosis (unlabeled use): I.V.: 2 g every 8-12 hours; with metronidazole for lateral

Skin and skin structure, uncomplicated: I.V.: 2 g every 12 hours for 10 days

Urinary tract infections, complicated and uncomplicated:

Mild-to-moderate: I.M., I.V.: 500-1000 mg every 12 hours for 7-10 days

Severe: I.V.: 2 g every 12 hours for 10 days

Dosing adjustment in renal impairment: Adults: Recommended maintenance schedule based on creatinine clearance (mL/minute), compared to normal dosing schedule: See table.

Cefepime Hydrochloride

Creatinine Clearance (mL/minute)	Recommended Maintenance Schedule			
>60 Normal recommended dosing schedule	500 mg every 12 hours	1 g every 12 hours	2 g every 12 hours	2 g every 8 hours
30-60	500 mg every 24 hours	1 g every 24 hours	2 g every 24 hours	2 g every 12 hours
11-29	500 mg every 24 hours	500 mg every 24 hours	1 g every 24 hours	2 g every 24 hours
<11	250 mg every 24 hours	250 mg every 24 hours	500 mg every 24 hours	1 g every 24 hours

Hemodialysis: Initial: 1 g (single dose) on day 1. Maintenance: 500 mg once daily (1 g once daily in febrile neutropenic patients). Dosage should be administered after dialysis on dialysis days.

Continuous ambulatory peritoneal dialysis (CAPD): Removed to a lesser extent than hemodialysis; administer normal recommended dose every 48 hours

Continuous renal replacement therapy (CRRT) (Trotman, 2005): Drug clearance is highly dependent on the method of renal replacement, filter type, and flow rate. Appropriate dosing requires close monitoring of pharmacologic response, signs of adverse reactions due to drug accumulation, as well as drug levels in relation to target trough (if appropriate). The following are general recommendations only (based on dialysate flow/ultrafiltration rates of 1 L/hour) and should not supersede clinical judgment:

CVVH: 1-2 g every 12 hours

CVVHDF: 2 g every 12 hours

(Continued)

Cefepime *(Continued)*

Note: Consider higher dosage of 4 g/day if treating *Pseudomonas* or life-threatening infections in order to maximize time above MIC.

Administration May be administered either I.M. or I.V.

Monitoring Parameters Obtain specimen for culture and sensitivity prior to the first dose. Monitor for signs of anaphylaxis during first dose.

Test Interactions Positive direct Coombs', false-positive urinary glucose test using cupric sulfate (Benedict's solution, Clinitest®, Fehling's solution), false-positive serum or urine creatinine with Jaffé reaction, false-positive urinary proteins and steroids

Patient Information Report side effects such as diarrhea, dyspepsia, headache, blurred vision, and lightheadedness.

Special Geriatric Considerations Adjust dose for changes in renal function.

Dosage Forms Excipient information presented when available (limited, particularly for generics); consult specific product labeling.

Injection, powder for reconstitution, as hydrochloride: 1 g, 2 g

Maxipime®: 500 mg, 1 g, 2 g

References

Allaouchiche B, Breilh D, Jaumain H, et al, "Pharmacokinetics of Cefepime During Continuous Veno-Venous Hemodiafiltration," *Antimicrob Agents Chemother*, 1997, 41(11):2424-7.

American Thoracic Society and Infectious Diseases Society of America, "Guidelines for the Management of Adults With Hospital-Acquired, Ventilator-Associated, and Health-care-Associated Pneumonia," *Am J Respir Crit Care Med*, 2005, 171(4):388-416.

Arguedas AG, Stutman HR, Zaleska M, et al, "Cefepime. Pharmacokinetics and Clinical Response in Patients With Cystic Fibrosis," *Am J Dis Child*, 1992, 146(7):797-802.

Barbhaiya RH, Knupp CA, and Pittman KA, "Effects of Age and Gender on Pharmacokinetics of Cefepime," *J Antimicrob Chemother*, 1992, 36(6):1181-5.

Barradell LB and Bryson HM, "Cefepime. A Review of Its Antibacterial Activity, Pharmacokinetic Properties, and Therapeutic Use," *Drugs*, 1994, 47(3):471-505.

Blumer JL, Reed MD, Lemon E, et al, "Pharmacokinetics (PK) of Cefepime in Pediatric Patients Administered Single and Multiple 50 mg/kg Doses Every 8 Hours by the Intravenous (I.V.) or Intramuscular (I.M.) Route," 34th Interscience Conference on Antimicrobial Agents and Chemotherapy, 1994, Orlando, Fl. Abs. A69.

Cunha BA and Gill MV, "Cefepime," *Med Clin North Am*, 1995, 79(4):721-32.

Marshall WF and Blair JE, "The Cephalosporins," *Mayo Clin Proc*, 1999, 74(2):187-95.

Malone RS, Fish DN, Abraham E, et al, "Pharmacokinetics of Cefepime During Continuous Renal Replacement Therapy in Critically Ill Patients," *Antimicrob Agents Chemother*, 2001, 45(11):3148-55.

Okamoto MP, Nakahiro RK, Chin A, et al, "Cefepime: A New Fourth-Generation Cephalosporin," *Am J Hosp Pharm*, 1994, 51(4):463-77.

Saez-Llorens X, Castano E, Garcia R, et al, "Prospective Randomized Comparison of Cefepime and Cefotaxime for Treatment of Bacterial Meningitis in Infants and Children," *Antimicrob Agents Chemother*, 1995, 39(4):937-40.

Sanders CC, "Cefepime: The Next Generation?" *Clin Infect Dis*, 1993, 17(3):369-79.

Trotman RL, Williamson JC, Shoemaker DM, et al, "Antibiotic Dosing in Critically Ill Adult Patients Receiving Continuous Renal Replacement Therapy," *Clin Infect Dis*, 2005, 41(8):1159-66.

Tunkel AR, Hartman BJ, Kaplan SL, et al, "Practice Guidelines for the Management of Bacterial Meningitis," *Clin Infect Dis*, 2004, 39(9):1267-84.

Wynd MA and Paladino JA, "Cefepime: A Fourth-Generation Parenteral Cephalosporin," *Ann Pharmacother*, 1996, 30(12):1414-24.

Yahav D, Paul M, Fraser A, et al, "Efficacy and Safety of Cefepime: A Systematic Review and Meta-Analysis," *Lancet Infect Dis*, 2007, 7(5):338-48.

♦ **Cefepime Hydrochloride** *see* Cefepime *on page 186*

Ceftazidime *(SEF tay zi deem)*

Medication Safety Issues

Sound-alike/look-alike issues:

Ceftazidime may be confused with ceftizoxime

Ceptaz® may be confused with Septra®

Tazicef® may be confused with Tazidime®
Tazidime® may be confused with Tazicef®

International issues:

Ceftim® [Italy] may be confused with Ceftin® which is a brand name for cefuroxime in the U.S.

Ceftim® [Italy] may be confused with Cefiton® which is a brand name for cefixime in Portugal

Ceftim® [Italy] may be confused with Ceftina® which is a brand name for cefalotin in Mexico

U.S. Brand Names Fortaz®; Tazicef®

Generic Available No

Canadian Brand Names Fortaz®

Pharmacologic Category Antibiotic, Cephalosporin (Third Generation)

Use Treatment of documented susceptible *Pseudomonas aeruginosa* infection and infections due to other susceptible aerobic gram-negative organisms; empiric therapy of a febrile, granulocytopenic patient

Unlabeled/Investigational Use Bacterial endophthalmitis

Pregnancy Risk Factor B

Lactation Enters breast milk (small amounts)/use caution (AAP rates "compatible")

Labeled Contraindications Hypersensitivity to ceftazidime, any component of the formulation, or other cephalosporins

Warnings/Precautions Modify dosage in patients with severe renal impairment. Use with caution in patients with a history of penicillin allergy, especially IgE-mediated reactions (eg, anaphylaxis, urticaria). Prolonged use may result in fungal or bacterial superinfection, including *C.difficile*-associated diarrhea (CDAD) and pseudomembranous colitis; CDAD has been observed <2 months postantibiotic treatment. May be associated with increased INR, especially in nutritionally-deficient patients, prolonged treatment, hepatic or renal disease. Use with caution in patients with a history of seizure disorder; high levels, particularly in the presence of renal impairment, may increase risk of seizures.

Adverse Reactions

1% to 10%:

Gastrointestinal: Diarrhea (1%)

Local: Pain at injection site (1%)

Miscellaneous: Hypersensitivity reactions (2%)

<1%: Anaphylaxis, angioedema, asterixis, BUN increased, candidiasis, creatinine increased, dizziness, encephalopathy, eosinophilia, erythema multiforme, fever, headache, hemolytic anemia, hyperbilirubinemia, jaundice, leukopenia, myoclonus, nausea, neuromuscular excitability, paresthesia, phlebitis, pruritus, pseudomembranous colitis, rash, Stevens-Johnson syndrome, thrombocytosis, toxic epidermal necrolysis, transaminases increased, vaginitis, vomiting

Reactions reported with other cephalosporins: Seizure, urticaria, serum-sickness reactions, renal dysfunction, interstitial nephritis, toxic nephropathy, elevated BUN, elevated creatinine, cholestasis, aplastic anemia, hemolytic anemia, pancytopenia, agranulocytosis, colitis, prolonged PT, hemorrhage, superinfection

Overdosage/Toxicology Symptoms of overdose include neuromuscular hypersensitivity and convulsions. Many beta-lactam containing antibiotics have the potential to cause neuromuscular hyperirritability or convulsive seizures. Hemodialysis may be helpful to aid in removal of the drug from blood; otherwise, treatment is supportive or symptom-directed.

(Continued)

Ceftazidime *(Continued)*

Drug Interactions

Increased Effect/Toxicity: Probenecid may decrease cephalosporin elimination. Cephalosporins may increase the anticoagulant effect of coumarin derivatives. When combined with aminoglycosides, *in vitro* studies indicate additive or synergistic effect against some strains of Enterobacteriaceae and *Pseudomonas aeruginosa*.

Storage/Stability Reconstituted solution and I.V. infusion in NS or D_5W solution are stable for 24 hours at room temperature, 10 days when refrigerated, or 12 weeks when frozen. After freezing, thawed solution is stable for 24 hours at room temperature or 4 days when refrigerated. After mixing for 96 hours refrigerated.

Compatibility Stable in D_5NS, D_5W, NS, sterile water for injection; **variable stability (consult detailed reference)** in peritoneal dialysis solutions.

Y-site administration: Compatible: Acyclovir, allopurinol, amifostine, aminophylline, aztreonam, ciprofloxacin, diltiazem, docetaxel, enalaprilat, esmolol, etoposide phosphate, famotidine, filgrastim, fludarabine, foscarnet, gatifloxacin, gemcitabine, granisetron, heparin, hydromorphone, labetalol, linezolid, melphalan, meperidine, morphine, ondansetron, paclitaxel, propofol, ranitidine, remifentanil, tacrolimus, teniposide, theophylline, thiotepa, vinorelbine, zidovudine. **Incompatible:** Alatrofloxacin, amphotericin B cholesteryl sulfate complex, amsacrine, doxorubicin liposome, fluconazole, idarubicin, midazolam, pentamidine, warfarin. **Variable (consult detailed reference):** Cisatracurium, sargramostim, vancomycin.

Compatibility in syringe: Compatible: Hydromorphone.

Compatibility when admixed: Compatible: Ciprofloxacin, clindamycin, fluconazole, linezolid, metronidazole, ofloxacin. **Incompatible:** Aminoglycosides (in same bottle/bag), aminophylline, ranitidine. **Variable (consult detailed reference):** Vancomycin.

Mechanism of Action Inhibits bacterial cell wall synthesis by binding to one or more of the penicillin-binding proteins (PBPs) which in turn inhibits the final transpeptidation step of peptidoglycan synthesis in bacterial cell walls, thus inhibiting cell wall biosynthesis. Bacteria eventually lyse due to ongoing activity of cell wall autolytic enzymes (autolysins and murein hydrolases) while cell wall assembly is arrested.

Pharmacodynamics/Kinetics

Distribution: Widely throughout the body including bone, bile, skin, CSF (higher concentrations achieved when meninges are inflamed), endometrium, heart, pleural and lymphatic fluids

Protein binding: 17%

Half-life elimination: 1-2 hours, prolonged with renal impairment; Neonates <23 days: 2.2-4.7 hours

Time to peak, serum: I.M.: ~1 hour

Excretion: Urine (80% to 90% as unchanged drug)

Dosage

Usual dosage range:

Infants and Children 1 month to 12 years: I.V.: 30-50 mg/kg/dose every 8 hours (maximum dose: 6 g/day)

Adults: I.M., I.V.: 500 mg to 2 g every 8-12 hours

Indication-specific dosing:

Bacterial arthritis (gram-negative bacilli): I.V.: 1-2 g every 8 hours

Cystic fibrosis: I.V.: 30-50 mg/kg every 8 hours (maximum: 6 g/day)

Endophthalmitis, bacterial (unlabeled use): Intravitreal: 2.25 mg/0.1 mL NS in combination with vancomycin

Melioidosis: I.V.: 40 mg/kg every 8 hours for 10 days, followed by oral therapy with doxycycline or TMP/SMX

Otitis externa: I.V.: 2 g every 8 hours

Peritonitis (CAPD):

Anuric, intermittent: 1000-1500 mg/day

Anuric, continuous (per liter exchange): Loading dose: 250 mg; maintenance dose: 125 mg

Severe infections, including meningitis, complicated pneumonia, endophthalmitis, CNS infection, osteomyelitis, intra-abdominal and gynecological, skin and soft tissue: I.V.: 2 g every 8 hours

Dosing interval in renal impairment:

Cl_{cr} 30-50 mL/minute: Administer every 12 hours

Cl_{cr} 10-30 mL/minute: Administer every 24 hours

Cl_{cr} <10 mL/minute: Administer every 48-72 hours

Hemodialysis: Dialyzable (50% to 100%)

Continuous renal replacement therapy (CRRT): Drug clearance is highly dependent on the method of renal replacement, filter type, and flow rate. Appropriate dosing requires close monitoring of pharmacologic response, signs of adverse reactions due to drug accumulation, as well as drug levels in relation to target trough (if appropriate). The following are general recommendations only (based on dialysate flow/ultrafiltration rates of 1 L/ hour) and should not supersede clinical judgment:

CVVH: 1-2 g every 12 hours

CVVHD/CVVHDF: 2 g every 12 hours

Administration Any carbon dioxide bubbles that may be present in the withdrawn solution should be expelled prior to injection. Administer around-the-clock to promote less variation in peak and trough serum levels. Ceftazidime can be administered deep I.M. into large mass muscle, IVP over 3-5 minutes, or I.V. intermittent infusion over 15-30 minutes. Do not admix with aminoglycosides in same bottle/bag. Final concentration for I.V. administration should not exceed 100 mg/mL.

Monitoring Parameters Observe for signs and symptoms of anaphylaxis during first dose

Test Interactions Positive direct Coombs', false-positive urinary glucose test using cupric sulfate (Benedict's solution, Clinitest®, Fehling's solution), false-positive serum or urine creatinine with Jaffé reaction

Dietary Considerations Sodium content of 1 g: 2.3 mEq

Special Geriatric Considerations Changes in renal function associated with aging and corresponding alterations in pharmacokinetics result in every 12-hour dosing being an adequate dosing interval. Adjust dose based on renal function.

Additional Information With some organisms, resistance may develop during treatment (including *Enterobacter* spp and *Serratia* spp). Consider combination therapy or periodic susceptibility testing for organisms with inducible resistance.

Emetic Potential Very low (<10%)

Vesicant No

Dosage Forms Excipient information presented when available (limited, particularly for generics); consult specific product labeling.

Infusion [premixed iso-osmotic solution]:

Fortaz®: 1 g (50 mL) [contains sodium carbonate, sodium 54 mg (2.3 mEq)/g]; 2 g (50 mL) [contains sodium carbonate, sodium 54 mg (2.3 mEq)/g]

(Continued)

Ceftazidime *(Continued)*

Injection, powder for reconstitution:

Fortaz®: 500 mg, 1 g, 2 g, 6 g [contains sodium carbonate, sodium 54 mg (2.3 mEq)/g]

Tazicef®: 1 g, 2 g, 6 g [contains sodium carbonate, sodium 54 mg (2.3 mEq)/g]

References

American Thoracic Society and Infectious Diseases Society of America, "Guidelines for the Management of Adults With Hospital-Acquired, Ventilator-Associated, and Health-care-Associated Pneumonia," *Am J Respir Crit Care Med*, 2005, 171(4):388-416.

Davies SP, Lacey LF, Kox WJ, et al, "Pharmacokinetics of Cefuroxime and Ceftazidime in Patients With Acute Renal Failure Treated by Continuous Arteriovenous Haemodialysis," *Nephrology, Dialysis, Transplantation*, 1991, 6(120):971-6.

Donowitz GR and Mandell GL, "Beta-Lactam Antibiotics," *N Engl J Med*, 1988, 318(7):419-26 and 318(8):490-500.

Klein NC and Cunha BA, "Third-Generation Cephalosporins," *Med Clin North Am*, 1995, 79(4):705-19.

Marshall WF and Blair JE, "The Cephalosporins," *Mayo Clin Proc*, 1999, 74(2):187-95.

McCracken GH Jr, Threlkeld N, and Thomas ML, "Pharmacokinetics of Ceftazidime in Newborn Infants," *Antimicrob Agents Chemother*, 1984, 26(4):583-4.

Rains CP, Bryson HM, and Peters DH, "Ceftazidime. An Update of Its Antibacterial Activity, Pharmacokinetic Properties and Therapeutic Efficacy," *Drugs*, 1995, 49(4):577-617.

"Results of the Endophthalmitis Vitrectomy Study. A Randomized Trial of Immediate Vitrectomy and of Intravenous Antibiotics for the Treatment of Postoperative Bacterial Endophthalmitis. Endophthalmitis Vitrectomy Study Group," *Arch Ophthalmol*, 1995, 113(12):1479-96.

Robinson DG, Cookson TL, and Frisafe JA, "Concentration Guidelines for Parenteral Antibiotics in Fluid-Restricted Patients," *Drug Intell Clin Pharm*, 1987, 21(12):985-9.

Roth DB and Flynn HW Jr, "Antibiotic Selection in the Treatment of Endophthalmitis: The Significance of Drug Combinations and Synergy," *Surv Ophthalmol*, 1997, 41(5):395-401.

Sirgo MA and Norris S, "Ceftazidime in the Elderly: Appropriateness of Twice-Daily Dosing," *DICP Ann Pharmacother*, 1991, 25(3):284-8.

Slaker RA and Danielson B, "Neurotoxicity Associated With Ceftazidime Therapy in Geriatric Patients With Renal Dysfunction," *Pharmacotherapy*, 1991, 11(4):351-2.

Stea S, Bachelor T, Cooper M, et al, "Disposition and Bioavailability of Ceftazidime After Intraperitoneal Administration in Patients Receiving Continuous Ambulatory Peritoneal Dialysis," *J Am Soc Nephrol*, 1996, 7(11):2399-402.

Trotman RL, Williamson JC, Shoemaker DM, et al, "Antibiotic Dosing in Critically Ill Adult Patients Receiving Continuous Renal Replacement Therapy," *Clin Infect Dis*, 2005, 41(8):1159-66.

Tunkel AR, Hartman BJ, Kaplan SL, et al, "Practice Guidelines for the Management of Bacterial Meningitis," *Clin Infect Dis*, 2004, 39(9):1267-84.

Vlasses PH, Bastion WA, Behal R, et al, "Ceftazidime Dosing in the Elderly: Economic Implications," *Ann Pharmacother*, 1993, 27(7-8):967-71.

Wilson W, Taubert KA, Gewitz M, et al, "Prevention of Infective Endocarditis. Guidelines From the American Heart Association. A Guideline From the American Heart Association Rheumatic Fever, Endocarditis, and Kawasaki Disease Committee, Council on Cardiovascular Disease in the Young, and the Council on Clinical Cardiology, Council on Cardiovascular Surgery and Anesthesia, and the Quality of Care and Outcomes Research Interdisciplinary Working Group," *Circulation*, 2007, 115:[epub April 19, 2007].

Ceftriaxone *(sef trye AKS one)*

Medication Safety Issues

Sound-alike/look-alike issues:

Rocephin® may be confused with Roferon®

U.S. Brand Names Rocephin®

Index Terms Ceftriaxone Sodium

Generic Available Yes

Canadian Brand Names Rocephin®

Pharmacologic Category Antibiotic, Cephalosporin (Third Generation)

Use Treatment of lower respiratory tract infections, acute bacterial otitis media, skin and skin structure infections, bone and joint infections, intra-abdominal and urinary tract infections, pelvic inflammatory disease

(PID), uncomplicated gonorrhea, bacterial septicemia, and meningitis; used in surgical prophylaxis

Unlabeled/Investigational Use Treatment of chancroid, epididymitis, complicated gonococcal infections; sexually-transmitted diseases (STD); periorbital or buccal cellulitis; salmonellosis or shigellosis; atypical community-acquired pneumonia; Lyme disease; used in chemoprophylaxis for high-risk contacts and persons with invasive meningococcal disease; sexual assault

Pregnancy Risk Factor B

Lactation Enters breast milk/use caution (AAP rates "compatible")

Labeled Contraindications Hypersensitivity to ceftriaxone sodium, any component of the formulation, or other cephalosporins; **do not use in hyperbilirubinemic neonates**, particularly those who are premature since ceftriaxone is reported to displace bilirubin from albumin binding sites; concomitant use with calcium-containing solutions or products in neonates (≤28 days)

Warnings/Precautions Modify dosage in patients with severe renal impairment. Prolonged use may result in fungal or bacterial superinfection, including *C. difficile*-associated diarrhea (CDAD) and pseudomembranous colitis; CDAD has been observed <2 months postantibiotic treatment. Use with caution in patients with a history of penicillin allergy, especially IgE-mediated reactions (eg, anaphylaxis, urticaria). Discontinue in patients with signs and symptoms of gallbladder disease. May be associated with increased INR, especially in nutritionally-deficient patients, prolonged treatment, hepatic or renal disease. Ceftriaxone may complex with calcium causing precipitation. Fatal lung and kidney damage associated with calcium-ceftriaxone precipitates has been observed in premature and term neonates. Do not reconstitute, admix, or coadminister with calcium-containing solutions, even via separate infusion lines/sites or at different times in any patient, regardless of age, due to concerns of potential precipitation reactions (contraindicated in neonates). Further recommendations include avoiding intravenous calcium-containing solutions within 48 hours of the last ceftriaxone dose in all patients. However, extending these recommendations to all patients is based solely on theoretical data, as there have been no reports of precipitant-induced adverse effects in non-neonatal patients.

Adverse Reactions

>10%: Local: Warmth, tightness, induration (5% to 17%) following I.M. injection

1% to 10%:

Dermatologic: Rash (2%)

Gastrointestinal: Diarrhea (3%)

Hematologic: Eosinophilia (6%), thrombocytosis (5%), leukopenia (2%)

Hepatic: Transaminases increased (3%)

Local: Pain, induration, tenderness at injection site (I.V. 1%)

Renal: BUN increased (1%)

<1%: Abdominal pain, agranulocytosis, alkaline phosphatase increased, allergic pneumonitis, anaphylaxis, anemia, basophilia, biliary lithiasis, bilirubin increased, bronchospasm, candidiasis, chills, colitis, creatinine increased, diaphoresis, dizziness, dysgeusia, dyspepsia, epistaxis, fever, flatulence, flushing, gallbladder sludge, gallstones, glycosuria, headache, hematuria, hemolytic anemia, jaundice, leukocytosis, lymphocytosis, (Continued)

Ceftriaxone *(Continued)*

lymphopenia, monocytosis, moniliasis, nausea, nephrolithiasis, neutropenia, palpitation, phlebitis, prolonged or decreased PT, pruritus, pseudomembranous colitis, renal stones, seizure, serum sickness, thrombocytopenia, urinary casts, vaginitis, vomiting

Postmarketing and/or case reports: Renal and pulmonary ceftriaxone-calcium precipitations (neonates; including some fatalities)

Reactions reported with other cephalosporins: Angioedema, aplastic anemia, asterixis, cholestasis, encephalopathy, erythema multiforme, hemorrhage, interstitial nephritis, neuromuscular excitability, pancytopenia, paresthesia, renal dysfunction, Stevens-Johnson syndrome, superinfection, toxic epidermal necrolysis, toxic nephropathy

Overdosage/Toxicology Symptoms of overdose include neuromuscular hypersensitivity and convulsions. Many beta-lactam containing antibiotics have the potential to cause neuromuscular hyperirritability or convulsive seizures. Hemodialysis may be helpful to aid in removal of the drug from blood; otherwise, treatment is supportive or symptom-directed.

Drug Interactions

Increased Effect/Toxicity: Cephalosporins may increase the anticoagulant effect of coumarin derivatives (eg, dicumarol, warfarin).

Decreased Effect: Uricosuric agents (eg, probenecid, sulfinpyrazone) may decrease the excretion of cephalosporin; monitor for toxic effects.

Storage/Stability

Powder for injection: Prior to reconstitution, store at room temperature of 25°C (77°F); protect from light.

Premixed solution (manufacturer premixed): Store at -20°C; once thawed, solutions are stable for 3 days at room temperature of 25°C (77°F) or for 21 days refrigerated at 5°C (41°F). Do not refreeze.

Stability of reconstituted solutions:

10-40 mg/mL: Reconstituted in D_5W or NS: Stable for 2 days at room temperature of 25°C (77°F) or for 10 days when refrigerated at 5°C (41°F).

100 mg/mL:

Reconstituted in D_5W or NS: Stable for 2 days at room temperature of 25°C (77°F) or for 10 days when refrigerated at 5°C (41°F). Stable for 26 weeks when frozen at -20°C. Once thawed, solutions are stable for 2 days at room temperature of 25°C (77°F) or for 10 days when refrigerated at 5°C (41°F); does not apply to manufacturer's premixed bags. Do not refreeze.

Reconstituted in lidocaine 1% solution: Stable for 24 hours at room temperature of 25°C (77°F) or for 10 days when refrigerated at 5°C (41°F).

250-350 mg/mL: Reconstituted in D_5W, NS, lidocaine 1% solution, or SWFI: Stable for 24 hours at room temperature of 25°C (77°F) or for 3 days when refrigerated at 5°C (41°F).

Reconstitution

I.M. injection: Vials should be reconstituted with appropriate volume of diluent (including D_5W, NS, or 1% lidocaine) to make a final concentration of 250 mg/mL or 350 mg/mL.

Volume to add to create a **250 mg/mL** solution:

250 mg vial: 0.9 mL
500 mg vial: 1.8 mL
1 g vial: 3.6 mL
2 g vial: 7.2 mL

Volume to add to create a **350 mg/mL** solution:
500 mg vial: 1.0 mL
1 g vial: 2.1 mL
2 g vial: 4.2 mL

I.V. infusion: Infusion is prepared in two stages: Initial reconstitution of powder, followed by dilution to final infusion solution.

Vials: Reconstitute powder with appropriate I.V. diluent (including SWFI, D_5W, NS) to create an initial solution of ~100 mg/mL. Recommended volume to add:
250 mg vial: 2.4 mL
500 mg vial: 4.8 mL
1 g vial: 9.6 mL
2 g vial: 19.2 mL

Note: After reconstitution of powder, further dilution into a volume of compatible solution (eg, 50-100 mL of D_5W or NS) is recommended.

Piggyback bottle: Reconstitute powder with appropriate I.V. diluent (D_5W or NS) to create a resulting solution of ~100 mg/mL. Recommended initial volume to add:
1 g bottle: 10 mL
2 g bottle: 20 mL

Note: After reconstitution, to prepare the final infusion solution, further dilution to 50 mL or 100 mL volumes with the appropriate I.V. diluent (including D_5W or NS) is recommended.

Compatibility Stable in D_5W with KCl 10 mEq, $D_5^{1}/_4$NS with KCl 20 mEq, $D_5^{1}/_2$ NS, D_5W, $D_{10}W$, NS, mannitol 5%, mannitol 10%, sodium bicarbonate 5%, bacteriostatic water, sterile water for injection. **Incompatible** with calcium-containing solutions (eg, LR, Hartmann's solution, parenteral nutrition solutions). **Variable stability (consult detailed reference)** in peritoneal dialysis solutions.

Y-site administration: Compatible: Acyclovir, allopurinol, amifostine, aztreonam, cisatracurium, diltiazem, docetaxel, doxorubicin liposome, etoposide phosphate, famotidine, fludarabine, foscarnet, gatifloxacin, gemcitabine, granisetron, heparin, linezolid, melphalan, meperidine, methotrexate, morphine, paclitaxel, propofol, remifentanil, sargramostim, sodium bicarbonate, tacrolimus, teniposide, theophylline, thiotepa, warfarin, zidovudine. **Incompatible:** Alatrofloxacin, amphotericin B cholesteryl sulfate complex, amsacrine, calcium, filgrastim, fluconazole, Hartmann's solution, labetalol, LR, pentamidine, parenteral nutrition solutions (containing calcium), vinorelbine. **Variable (consult detailed reference):** Vancomycin.

Compatibility in syringe: Variable (consult detailed reference): Lidocaine.

Compatibility when admixed: Compatible: Metronidazole. **Incompatible:** Aminophylline, calcium, clindamycin, linezolid, theophylline. **Variable (consult detailed reference):** Metronidazole, vancomycin.

Mechanism of Action Inhibits bacterial cell wall synthesis by binding to one or more of the penicillin-binding proteins (PBPs) which in turn inhibits the final transpeptidation step of peptidoglycan synthesis in bacterial cell walls, thus inhibiting cell wall biosynthesis. Bacteria eventually lyse due to ongoing activity of cell wall autolytic enzymes (autolysins and murein hydrolases) while cell wall assembly is arrested.

Pharmacodynamics/Kinetics

Absorption: I.M.: Well absorbed

Distribution: Widely throughout the body including gallbladder, lungs, bone, bile, CSF (higher concentrations achieved when meninges are inflamed); crosses placenta; enters amniotic fluid and breast milk

(Continued)

Ceftriaxone *(Continued)*

Protein binding: 85% to 95%

Half-life elimination: Normal renal and hepatic function: 5-9 hours

Time to peak, serum: I.M.: 2-3 hours

Excretion: Urine (33% to 67% as unchanged drug); feces

Dosage

Usual dosage range:

Infants and Children: I.M., I.V.: 50-100 mg/kg/day in 1-2 divided doses (maximum: 4 g/day)

Adults: I.M., I.V.: 1-2 g every 12-24 hours

Indication-specific dosing:

Infants and Children:

Epiglottitis: I.M., I.V.: 50-100 mg/kg once daily for 7-10 days with clindamycin

Gonococcal infections:

Conjunctivitis, complicated (unlabeled use): I.M.:

<45 kg: 50 mg/kg in a single dose (maximum: 1 g)

>45 kg: 1 g in a single dose

Disseminated (unlabeled use): I.M., I.V.:

<45 kg: 25-50 mg/kg once daily (maximum: 1 g)

>45 kg: 1 g once daily for 7 days

Endocarditis (unlabeled use):

<45 kg: I.M., I.V.: 50 mg/kg/day every 12 hours (maximum: 2 g/day) for at least 28 days

>45 kg: I.V.: 1-2 g every 12 hours, for at least 28 days

Uncomplicated: I.M.: 125 mg in a single dose

Mild-to-moderate infections: I.M., I.V.: 50-75 mg/kg/day in 1-2 divided doses every 12-24 hours (maximum: 2 g/day); continue until at least 2 days after signs and symptoms of infection have resolved

Meningitis:

Gonococcal, complicated:

<45 kg: I.V.: 50 mg/kg/day given every 12 hours (maximum: 2 g/day); usual duration of treatment is 10-14 days

>45 kg: I.V.: 1-2 g every 12 hours; usual duration of treatment is 10-14 days

Uncomplicated: I.M., I.V.: Loading dose of 100 mg/kg (maximum: 4 g), followed by 100 mg/kg/day divided every 12-24 hours (maximum: 4 g/day); usual duration of treatment is 7-14 days

Otitis media:

Acute: I.M.: 50 mg/kg in a single dose (maximum: 1 g)

Persistent or relapsing (unlabeled use): I.M., I.V.: 50 mg/kg once daily for 3 days

Pneumonia: I.V.: 50-75 mg/kg once daily

Prophylaxis against infective endocarditis: I.M., I.V.: 50 mg/kg 30-60 minutes before procedure; maximum dose: 1 g. Intramuscular injections should be avoided in patients who are receiving anticoagulant therapy. In these circumstances, orally administered regimens should be given whenever possible. Intravenously administered antibiotics should be used for patients who are unable to tolerate or absorb oral medications.

Note: American Heart Association (AHA) guidelines now recommend prophylaxis only in patients undergoing invasive procedures and in whom underlying cardiac conditions may predispose to a higher risk of adverse outcomes should infection occur. As of April 2007, routine prophylaxis for GI/GU procedures is no longer recommended by the AHA.

Serious infections: I.V.: 80-100 mg/kg/day in 1-2 divided doses (maximum: 4 g/day)

STD, sexual assault (unlabeled use): I.M.: 125 mg in a single dose

Typhoid fever: I.V.: 100 mg/kg once daily (maximum 4 g)

Children >8 years (≥45 kg) and Adolescents:

Epididymitis, acute (unlabeled use): I.M.: 125 mg in a single dose

Children ≤15 years:

Chemoprophylaxis for high-risk contacts and persons with invasive meningococcal disease (unlabeled use): I.M.: 125 mg in a single dose. Children >15 years: Refer to adult dosing.

Adults:

Arthritis (septic): I.V.: 1-2 g once daily

Brain abscess and necrotizing fasciitis: I.V.: 2 g every 12 hours

Cavernous sinus thrombosis: I.V.: 1 g every 12 hours with vancomycin or linezolid

Chancroid (unlabeled use): I.M.: 250 mg as single dose

Chemoprophylaxis for high-risk contacts and persons with invasive meningococcal disease (unlabeled use): I.M.: 250 mg in a single dose

Endocarditis, native valve: I.M., I.V.: 2 g once daily for 2-4 weeks

Epididymitis, acute (unlabeled use) and prostatitis: I.M.: 250 mg in a single dose with doxycycline

Gonococcal infections:

Conjunctivitis, complicated (unlabeled use): I.M., I.V.: 1 g in a single dose

Disseminated (unlabeled use): I.M., I.V.: 1 g once daily for 7 days

Endocarditis (unlabeled use): I.M., I.V.: 1-2 g every 12 hours for at least 28 days

Uncomplicated: I.M.: 125-250 mg in a single dose

Lyme disease: I.V.: 2 g once daily for 14-28 days

Mastoiditis (hospitalized): I.V.: 2 g once daily; >60 years old: 1 g once daily

Meningitis: I.V.: 2 g every 12 hours for 7-14 days (longer courses may be necessary for selected organisms)

Orbital cellulitis (unlabeled use) and endophthalmitis: I.V.: 2 g once daily

Pelvic inflammatory disease: I.M.: 250 mg in a single dose

Pneumonia, community-acquired: I.V.: 2 g once daily; >65 years of age: 1 g once daily

Prophylaxis against infective endocarditis: I.M., I.V.: 1 g 30-60 minutes before procedure. Intramuscular injections should be avoided in patients who are receiving anticoagulant therapy. In these circumstances, orally administered regimens should be given whenever possible. Intravenously administered antibiotics should be used for patients who are unable to tolerate or absorb oral medications.

Note: American Heart Association (AHA) guidelines now recommend prophylaxis only in patients undergoing invasive procedures and in whom underlying cardiac conditions may predispose to a higher risk of adverse outcomes should infection occur. As of April 2007, routine prophylaxis for GI/GU procedures is no longer recommended by the AHA.

Septic/toxic shock: I.V.: 2 g once daily; with clindamycin for toxic shock

Surgical prophylaxis: I.V.: 1 g 30 minutes to 2 hours before surgery

Syphilis: I.M., I.V.: 1 g once daily for 8-10 days

(Continued)

Ceftriaxone (Continued)

Typhoid fever: I.V.: 2-3 g once daily for 7-14 days

Dosage adjustment in renal/hepatic impairment: No adjustment necessary

Hemodialysis: Not dialyzable (0% to 5%); administer dose postdialysis

Continuous ambulatory peritoneal dialysis (CAPD): Administer 1 g every 12 hours

Continuous renal replacement therapy (CRRT): Drug clearance is highly dependent on the method of renal replacement, filter type, and flow rate. Appropriate dosing requires close monitoring of pharmacologic response, signs of adverse reactions due to drug accumulation, as well as drug levels in relation to target trough (if appropriate). The following are general recommendations only (based on dialysate flow/ultrafiltration rates of 1 L/hour) and should not supersede clinical judgment:

CVVH or CVVHD/CVVHDF: 2 g every 12-24 hours

Administration Do not admix with aminoglycosides in same bottle/bag. Do not reconstitute, admix, or coadminister with calcium-containing solutions. Infuse intermittent infusion over 30 minutes.

I.M.: Inject deep I.M. into large muscle mass; a concentration of 250 mg/mL or 350 mg/mL is recommended for all vial sizes except the 250 mg size (250 mg/mL is suggested); can be diluted with 1:1 water and 1% lidocaine for I.M. administration.

I.V.: Infuse intermittent infusion over 30 minutes.

Monitoring Parameters Observe for signs and symptoms of anaphylaxis

Test Interactions Positive direct Coombs', false-positive urinary glucose test using cupric sulfate (Benedict's solution, Clinitest®, Fehling's solution), false-positive serum or urine creatinine with Jaffé reaction

Dietary Considerations Sodium contents: 83 mg (3.6 mEq) per ceftriaxone 1 g

Special Geriatric Considerations No adjustment for changes in renal function necessary.

Emetic Potential Very low (<10%)

Vesicant No

Dosage Forms Excipient information presented when available (limited, particularly for generics); consult specific product labeling.

Infusion [premixed in dextrose]: 1 g (50 mL); 2 g (50 mL)

Injection, powder for reconstitution: 250 mg, 500 mg, 1 g, 2 g, 10 g

Rocephin®: 250 mg, 500 mg, 1 g, 2 g, 10 g [contains sodium 83 mg (3.6 mEq) per ceftriaxone 1 g]

References

American Academy of Family Physicians and American Academy of Pediatrics, Clinical Care and Research, "Diagnosis and Management of Acute Otitis Media: Clinical Recommendations," available at: http://www.aafp.org/x26481.xml. Accessed March 19, 2004.

Baddour LM, Wilson WR, Bayer AS, et al, "Infective Endocarditis. Diagnosis, Antimicrobial Therapy, and Management of Complications. A Statement for Healthcare Professionals from the Committee on Rheumatic Fever, Endocarditis, and Kawasaki Disease, Council on Cardiovascular Disease in the Young, and the Councils on Clinical Cardiology, Stroke, and Cardiovascular Surgery and Anesthesia, American Heart Association," *Circulation*, 2005, 111(23):e394-434.

Bradley JS, Compogiannis LS, Murray WE, et al, "Pharmacokinetics and Safety of Intramuscular Injection of Concentrated Ceftriaxone in Children," *Clin Pharm*, 1992, 11(11):961-4.

Centers for Disease Control and Prevention, "Sexually Transmitted Diseases Treatment Guidelines - 2002," *MMWR Recomm Rep*, 2002, 51(RR-6):1-78. Available at: http://www.cdc.gov/mmwr/preview/mmwrhtml/rr5106a1.htm. Accessed August 13, 2003.

Committee on Adolescence, AAP, "Sexual Assault and the Adolescent," *Pediatrics*, 1994, 94(5):761-5.

Deeter RG, Weinstein MP, Swanson KA, et al, "Crossover Assessment of Serum Bactericidal Activity and Pharmacokinetics of Five Broad-Spectrum Cephalosporins in the Elderly," *Antimicrob Agents Chemother*, 1990, 34(6):1007-13.

Dowell SF, Butler JC, Giebink GS, et al, "Acute Otitis Media: Management and Surveillance in an Era of Pneumococcal Resistance - A Report From the Drug-Resistant *Streptococcus pneumoniae* Therapeutic Working Group," *Pediatr Infect Dis J*, 1999, 18(1):1-9.

Hayton WL and Stoeckel K, "Age-Associated Changes in Ceftriaxone Pharmacokinetics," *Clin Pharmacokinet*, 1986, 11(1):76-82.

Kroh UF, Lennartz H, Edwards DJ, et al, "Pharmacokinetics of Ceftriaxone in Patients Undergoing Continuous Veno-Venous Hemofiltration," *J Clin Pharmacol*, 1996, 36(12):1114-9.

Marshall WF and Blair JE, "The Cephalosporins," *Mayo Clin Proc*, 1999, 74(2):187-95.

Schaad UB, Suter S, Gianella-Borradori A, et al, "A Comparison of Ceftriaxone and Cefuroxime for the Treatment of Bacterial Meningitis in Children," *N Engl J Med*, 1990, 322(3):141-7.

Trotman RL, Williamson JC, Shoemaker DM, et al, "Antibiotic Dosing in Critically Ill Adult Patients Receiving Continuous Renal Replacement Therapy," *Clin Infect Dis*, 2005, 41(8):1159-66.

Tunkel AR, Hartman BJ, Kaplan SL, et al, "Practice Guidelines for the Management of Bacterial Meningitis," *Clin Infect Dis*, 2004, 39(9):1267-84.

Wilson W, Taubert KA, Gewitz M, et al, "Prevention of Infective Endocarditis. Guidelines From the American Heart Association. A Guideline From the American Heart Association Rheumatic Fever, Endocarditis, and Kawasaki Disease Committee, Council on Cardiovascular Disease in the Young, and the Council on Clinical Cardiology, Council on Cardiovascular Surgery and Anesthesia, and the Quality of Care and Outcomes Research Interdisciplinary Working Group," *Circulation*, 2007, 115. Available at http://circ.ahajournals.org/cgi/reprint/CIRCULATIONAHA.106.183095v1; last accessed July 26, 2007.

♦ **Ceftriaxone Sodium** *see* Ceftriaxone *on page 194*

♦ **CellCept®** *see* Mycophenolate *on page 791*

♦ **Cerubidine®** *see* DAUNOrubicin Hydrochloride *on page 308*

♦ **Cesamet™** *see* Nabilone *on page 798*

♦ **Cetacort® [DSC]** *see* Hydrocortisone *on page 545*

Cetuximab (se TUK see mab)

Medication Safety Issues
Sound-alike/look-alike issues:
Cetuximab may be confused with bevacizumab

U.S. Brand Names Erbitux®

Index Terms C225; IMC-C225; NSC-714692

Generic Available No

Canadian Brand Names Erbitux®

Pharmacologic Category Antineoplastic Agent, Monoclonal Antibody; Epidermal Growth Factor Receptor (EGFR) Inhibitor

Use Treatment of metastatic colorectal cancer; treatment of squamous cell cancer of the head and neck

Unlabeled/Investigational Use Breast cancer, tumors overexpressing EGFR

Pregnancy Risk Factor C

Lactation Excretion in breast milk is unknown/not recommended

Labeled Contraindications There are no contraindications listed in the manufacturer's labeling

Warnings/Precautions [U.S. Boxed Warning]: Severe infusion reactions have been reported in 2% to 5% of patients (~90% with the first infusion despite the use of prophylactic antihistamines). Note: Although a 20 mg test dose was used in some studies, it did not reliably predict the risk of an infusion reaction, and is not recommended. In case of severe reaction, treatment should be stopped and permanently discontinued. Immediate treatment for anaphylactic/anaphylactoid reactions should be available during administration. Patients should be monitored for at least 1 hour following completion of infusion, or longer if a reaction occurs. (Continued)

Cetuximab *(Continued)*

Mild-to-moderate infusion reactions are managed by slowing the infusion rate (by 50%) and administering antihistamines.

[U.S. Boxed Warning]: Cardiopulmonary arrest has been reported in patients receiving radiation therapy in combination with cetuximab; use caution with history of coronary artery disease, CHF, and arrhythmias. Closely monitor serum electrolytes during and after (for at least 8 weeks) cetuximab therapy. Interstitial lung disease (ILD) has been reported; use caution with pre-existing lung disease; permanently discontinue with confirmed ILD. Dermatologic toxicities have been reported, including a 76% to 88% incidence of acneform rash (may require dose modification); sunlight may exacerbate skin reactions. Dermatologic toxicities should be treated with topical and/or oral antibiotics; topical corticosteroids are not recommended. Non-neutralizing anticetuximab antibodies were detected in 5% of evaluable patients. Safety and efficacy have not been established when used in combination with radiation therapy and cisplatin. Safety and efficacy in children have not been established.

Adverse Reactions Except where noted, percentages reported for cetuximab monotherapy.

>10%:
Central nervous system: Fatigue (89%), pain (17% to 51%), headache (26% to 33%), insomnia (10% to 30%), fever (27% to 30%), confusion (15%), anxiety (14%), chills/rigors (13%), depression (7% to 13%)
Dermatologic: Acneform rash (76% to 90%; grades 3/4: 1% to 17%), rash (89%), dry skin (49%), pruritus (11% to 40%), nail changes/disorder (16% to 21%)
Endocrine & metabolic: Hypomagnesemia (55%; grades 3/4: 6% to 17%)
Gastrointestinal: Abdominal pain (26% to 59%), constipation (26% to 46%), diarrhea (25% to 39%), vomiting (25% to 37%), nausea (mild-to-moderate 29%), weight loss (7% to 27%), anorexia (23%), stomatitis (10% to 25%), xerostomia (11%)
Neuromuscular & skeletal: Weakness (45% to 48%), bone pain (15%)
Respiratory: Dyspnea (17% to 48%), cough (11% to 29%)
Miscellaneous: Infection (13% to 35%), infusion reaction (15% to 21%; grades 3/4: 2% to 5%; 90% with first infusion)
1% to 10%:
Cardiovascular: Peripheral edema (10%), cardiopulmonary arrest (2%; with radiation therapy)
Dermatologic: Alopecia (4%), skin disorder (4%)
Endocrine & metabolic: Dehydration (2% to 10%)
Gastrointestinal: Dyspepsia (6%)
Hematologic: Anemia (9%)
Hepatic: Alkaline phosphatase increased (5% to 10%), transaminases increased (5% to 10%)
Neuromuscular & skeletal: Back pain (10%)
Ocular: Conjunctivitis (7%)
Renal: Renal failure (1%)
Respiratory: Pulmonary embolus (1%)
Miscellaneous: Sepsis (1% to 4%)
<1%: Arrhythmia, interstitial lung disease (occurred between the fourth and eleventh doses), leukopenia, MI

Overdosage/Toxicology Single doses >500 mg/m^2 have not been tested. A dose of 1000 mg/m^2 was administered in one patient without reports of adverse events. Treatment is symptom-directed and supportive.

Drug Interactions
Increased Effect/Toxicity: Interactions have not been evaluated in clinical trials.

Storage/Stability Store unopened vials under refrigeration at 2°C to 8°C (36°F to 46°F). Do not freeze. Preparations in infusion containers are stable for up to 12 hours under refrigeration at 2°C to 8°C (36°F to 46°F) and up to 8 hours at room temperature of 20°C to 25°C (68°F to 77°F).

Reconstitution Reconstitution is not required. Appropriate dose should be added to empty sterile container; do not shake or dilute.

Mechanism of Action Recombinant human/mouse chimeric monoclonal antibody which binds specifically to the epidermal growth factor receptor (EGFR, HER1, c-ErbB-1) and competitively inhibits the binding of epidermal growth factor (EGF) and other ligands. Binding to the EGFR blocks phosphorylation and activation of receptor-associated kinases, resulting in inhibition of cell growth, induction of apoptosis, and decreased matrix metalloproteinase and vascular endothelial growth factor production.

Pharmacodynamics/Kinetics
Distribution: V_d: ~2-3 L/m^2
Half-life elimination: ~112 hours (range: 63-230 hours)

Dosage I.V.: Adults: **Note:** Premedicate with an antihistamine (eg, diphenhydramine) I.V. 30-60 minutes prior to the first dose; premedication for subsequent doses is based on clinical judgement.
Colorectal cancer:
  Initial loading dose: 400 mg/m^2 infused over 120 minutes
  Maintenance dose: 250 mg/m^2 infused over 60 minutes weekly
Head and neck cancer:
  Initial loading dose: 400 mg/m^2 infused over 120 minutes
  Maintenance dose: 250 mg/m^2 infused over 60 minutes weekly
  Note: If given in combination with radiation therapy, administer loading dose 1 week prior to initiation of radiation course. Weekly maintenance dose should be completed 1 hour prior to radiation for the duration of radiation therapy (6-7 weeks).
Breast cancer (unlabeled use): 50-200 mg/m^2 weekly for 6 weeks
Tumors overexpressing EGFR (unlabeled use): 5-100 mg/m^2 weekly
  or
Loading dose: 100-500 mg/m^2
Maintenance dose: 5-400 mg/m^2 weekly

Dosage adjustment for toxicity:
Infusion reactions, grade 1 or 2 and nonserious grades 3 or 4: Reduce the infusion rate by 50% and continue to use prophylactic antihistamines
Infusion reactions, severe: Immediately and permanently discontinue treatment
Skin toxicity, mild to moderate: No dosage modification required
Acneform rash, severe (grade 3 or 4):
  First occurrence: Delay cetuximab infusion 1-2 weeks
    If improvement, continue at 250 mg/m^2
    If no improvement, discontinue therapy
  Second occurrence: Delay cetuximab infusion 1-2 weeks
    If improvement, continue at reduced dose of 200 mg/m^2
    If no improvement, discontinue therapy
  Third occurrence: Delay cetuximab infusion 1-2 weeks
    If improvement, continue at reduced dose of 150 mg/m^2
    If no improvement, discontinue therapy
  Fourth occurrence: Discontinue therapy
(Continued)

Cetuximab *(Continued)*

Note: Dose adjustments are not recommended for severe **radiation** dermatitis.

Dosage adjustment for renal/hepatic impairment: No adjustment required.

Combination Regimens

Colorectal cancer: Cetuximab-Irinotecan *on page 1167*

Head and neck cancer:

Carboplatin-Cetuximab *on page 1161*

Cisplatin-Cetuximab *on page 1175*

Administration Administer via I.V. infusion; loading dose over 2 hours, weekly maintenance dose over 1 hour. Do not administer as I.V. push or bolus. Do not shake or dilute. Administer via infusion pump or syringe pump. Following the infusion, an observation period (1 hour) is recommended; longer observation time (following an infusion reaction) may be required. Premedication with antihistamines is recommended. The maximum infusion rate is 10 mg/minute. Administer through a low protein-binding 0.22 micrometer in-line filter. Use 0.9% NaCl to flush line at the end of infusion.

Monitoring Parameters EGF receptor expression testing should be completed prior to treatment (for colorectal cancer). Vital signs during infusion and observe for at least 1 hour postinfusion. Patients developing dermatologic toxicities should be monitored for the development of complications. Periodic monitoring of serum magnesium, calcium, and potassium are recommended to continue over an interval consistent with the half-life (8 weeks); monitor closely (during and after treatment) for cetuximab plus radiation therapy.

Patient Information Patients should wear sunscreen and limit sun exposure as sunlight can exacerbate skin reactions.

Additional Information EGFR expression is detected in nearly all patients with head and neck cancer; laboratory evidence of EGFR expression is not necessary for head and neck cancers.

Emetic Potential Low (10% to 30%)

Vesicant No

Dosage Forms Excipient information presented when available (limited, particularly for generics); consult specific product labeling.

Injection, solution [preservative free]:

Erbitux®: 2 mg/mL (50 mL, 100 mL)

References

Baselga J, "The EGFR as a Target for Anticancer Therapy - Focus on Cetuximab," *Eur J Cancer*, 2001, 37(Suppl 4):16-22.

Bonner JA, Harari PM, Giralt J, et al, "Radiotherapy Plus Cetuximab for Squamous-Cell Carcinoma of the Head and Neck," *N Engl J Med*, 2006, 354(6):567-78.

Cunningham D, Humblet Y, Siena S, et al, "Cetuximab Monotherapy and Cetuximab Plus Irinotecan in Irinotecan-Refractory Metastatic Colorectal Cancer," *N Engl J Med*, 2004, 351(4):337-45.

Kies MS and Harari PM, "Cetuximab (Imclone/Merck/Bristol-Myers Squibb)," *Curr Opin Investig Drugs*, 2002, 3(7):1092-100.

Reynolds NA and Wagstaff AJ, "Cetuximab: In the Treatment of Metastatic Colorectal Cancer," *Drugs*, 2004, 64(1):109-18.

♦ **CGP-42446** *see* Zoledronic Acid *on page 1122*

♦ **CGP-57148B** *see* Imatinib *on page 583*

♦ **CGS-20267** *see* Letrozole *on page 665*

Chlorambucil (klor AM byoo sil)

Medication Safety Issues

Sound-alike/look-alike issues:

Chlorambucil may be confused with Chloromycetin®

Leukeran® may be confused with Alkeran®, leucovorin, Leukine®, Myleran®

High alert medication: The Institute for Safe Medication Practices (ISMP) includes this medication among its list of drugs which have a heightened risk of causing significant patient harm when used in error.

Related Information

Fertility and Cancer Therapy *on page 1298*

Safe Handling of Hazardous Drugs *on page 1382*

U.S. Brand Names Leukeran®

Index Terms CB-1348; Chlorambucilum; Chloraminophene; Chlorbutinum; NSC-3088; WR-139013

Generic Available No

Canadian Brand Names Leukeran®

Pharmacologic Category Antineoplastic Agent, Alkylating Agent

Use Management of chronic lymphocytic leukemia (CLL), Hodgkin's lymphoma, non-Hodgkin's lymphoma (NHL)

Unlabeled/Investigational Use Nephrotic syndrome, Waldenström's macroglobulinemia

Pregnancy Risk Factor D

Lactation Excretion in breast milk unknown/not recommended

Labeled Contraindications Hypersensitivity to chlorambucil or any component of the formulation; hypersensitivity to other alkylating agents (may have cross-hypersensitivity); pregnancy

Warnings/Precautions Hazardous agent - use appropriate precautions for handling and disposal. Seizures have been observed; use with caution in patients with seizure disorder or head trauma; history of nephrotic syndrome and high pulse doses are at higher risk of seizures. **[U.S. Boxed Warning]: May cause bone marrow suppression;** reduce initial dosage if patient has received myelosuppressive or radiation therapy, or has a depressed baseline leukocyte or platelet count within the previous 4 weeks. Lymphopenia may occur. Avoid administration of live vaccines to immunocompromised patients. Rare instances of severe skin reactions (eg, erythema multiforme, Stevens-Johnson syndrome) have been reported; discontinue if a reaction occurs.

[U.S. Boxed Warning]: Affects human fertility; carcinogenic in humans and probably mutagenic and teratogenic as well; chromosomal damage has been documented. Fertility effects (reversible and irreversible sterility) include azoospermia (when administered to prepubertal and pubertal males) and amenorrhea. Secondary malignancies and acute myelocytic leukemia may be associated with chronic therapy. Safety and efficacy in pediatric patients have not been established.

Adverse Reactions Frequency not always defined.

Central nervous system: Agitation (rare), ataxia (rare), confusion (rare), drug fever, focal/generalized seizure (rare), hallucinations (rare)

Dermatologic: Angioneurotic edema, erythema multiforme (rare), rash, skin hypersensitivity, Stevens-Johnson syndrome (rare), toxic epidermal necrolysis (rare), urticaria

Endocrine & metabolic: Amenorrhea, infertility, SIADH (rare)

Gastrointestinal: Diarrhea (infrequent), nausea (infrequent), oral ulceration (infrequent), vomiting (infrequent)

(Continued)

Chlorambucil *(Continued)*

Genitourinary: Azoospermia, cystitis (sterile)

Hematologic: Neutropenia (25%; dose- and duration-related; onset: 3 weeks; recovery: 10 days after last dose), bone marrow failure (irreversible), bone marrow suppression, anemia, leukemia (secondary), leukopenia, lymphopenia, pancytopenia, thrombocytopenia

Hepatic: Hepatotoxicity, jaundice

Neuromuscular & skeletal: Flaccid paresis (rare), muscular twitching (rare), myoclonia (rare), peripheral neuropathy, tremor (rare)

Respiratory: Interstitial pneumonia, pulmonary fibrosis

Miscellaneous: Allergic reactions, malignancies (secondary)

Overdosage/Toxicology Symptoms of overdose include vomiting, agitation, ataxia, coma, seizures, and pancytopenia. There are no known antidotes for chlorambucil intoxication. Treatment is symptom-directed and supportive. Monitor CBC closely; consider transfusion support. Chlorambucil is not dialyzable.

Drug Interactions

Increased Effect/Toxicity: Vaccines (live organism): Avoid the administration of live vaccines during chlorambucil treatment.

Storage/Stability Store in refrigerator at 2°C to 8°C (36°F to 46°F). Protect from light.

Mechanism of Action Interferes with DNA replication and RNA transcription by alkylation and cross-linking the strands of DNA

Pharmacodynamics/Kinetics

Absorption: Rapid and complete

Distribution: V_d: 0.14-0.24 L/kg

Protein binding: ~99%

Metabolism: Hepatic; forms a major active metabolite (phenylacetic acid mustard) and inactive metabolites

Bioavailability: Reduced 10% to 20% with food

Half-life elimination: ~1.5 hours; Phenylacetic acid mustard: ~1.8 hours

Time to peak, plasma: Within 1 hour; Phenylacetic acid mustard: 1.2-2.6 hours

Excretion: Urine (15% to 60% primarily as inactive metabolites, <1% as unchanged drug or phenylacetic acid mustard)

Dosage Oral (refer to individual protocols):

Children (unlabeled uses):

General short courses: 0.1-0.2 mg/kg/day for 3-6 weeks **or** maintenance therapy: 0.03-0.1 mg/kg/day

Nephrotic syndrome: 0.1-0.2 mg/kg/day every day for ~8-12 weeks with low-dose prednisone

Chronic lymphocytic leukemia (CLL):

Biweekly regimen: Initial: 0.4 mg/kg/dose every 2 weeks; increase dose by 0.1 mg/kg every 2 weeks until a response occurs and/or myelosuppression occurs

Monthly regimen: Initial: 0.4 mg/kg, increase dose by 0.1 mg/kg every 4 weeks until a response occurs and/or myelosuppression occurs

Malignant lymphomas:

Non-Hodgkin's lymphoma: 0.1 mg/kg/day

Hodgkin's lymphoma: 0.2 mg/kg/day

Adults:

CLL, NHL: 0.1 mg/kg/day for 3-6 weeks **or** 0.4 mg/kg (increased by 0.1mg/kg/dose until response/toxicity observed) biweekly **or** 0.4 mg/kg (increased by 0.1mg/kg/dose until response/toxicity observed) monthly **or** 0.03-0.1 mg/kg/day continuously

Hodgkin's lymphoma: 0.2 mg/kg/day for 3-6 weeks **or** 0.4 mg/kg (increased by 0.1mg/kg/dose until response/toxicity observed) biweekly **or** 0.4 mg/kg (increased by 0.1mg/kg/dose until response/toxicity observed) monthly **or** 0.03-0.1 mg/kg/day continuously

Waldenström's macroglobulinemia (unlabeled use): 0.1 mg/kg/day (continuously) for at least 6 months **or** 0.3 mg/kg/day for 7 days every 6 weeks for at least 6 months

Elderly: Refer to adult dosing; begin at the lower end of dosing range(s)

Dosage adjustment for toxicity:

Skin reactions: Discontinue treatment

Hematologic: Persistent neutropenia, thrombocytopenia, and/or lymphocytosis: Do not exceed 0.1 mg/kg/day

Concurrent or within 4 weeks of chemotherapy/radiotherapy: Initiate treatment cautiously; reduce dose; monitor closely. (May use the usual dose if radiation therapy is small doses of palliative radiation over isolated foci remote from bone marrow.)

Dosing adjustment in renal impairment: The FDA-appproved labeling does not contain renal dosing adjustment guidelines. The following guidelines have been used by some clinicians (Aronoff, 2007): Adults:

Cl_{cr} 10-50 mL/minute: Administer 75% of dose

Cl_{cr} <10 mL/minute: Administer 50% of dose

Continuous ambulatory peritoneal dialysis (CAPD): Administer 50% of dose

Dosing adjustment in hepatic impairment: The FDA-approved labeling does not contain hepatic dosing adjustment guidelines. Chlorambucil is hepatically metabolized into active and inactive metabolites; dosage adjustment may be needed in patients with hepatic impairment.

Combination Regimens

Leukemia, chronic lymphocytic:

CHL + PRED *on page 1173*

CP (Leukemia) *on page 1183*

Lymphoma, Hodgkin's disease:

ChIVPP *on page 1173*

LOPP *on page 1244*

Administration Usually administered as a single dose; preferably on an empty stomach.

Monitoring Parameters Liver function tests, CBC with differential and platelets (weekly, with WBC monitored twice weekly during the first 3-6 weeks of treatment), serum uric acid

Patient Information Take as directed. Maintain adequate hydration (2-3 L/day of fluids unless instructed to restrict fluid intake). Avoid OTC medications unless approved by prescriber. Hair may be lost during treatment (reversible). You may experience menstrual irregularities and/or sterility. You will be more susceptible to infection; avoid crowds and exposure to infection. Frequent mouth care with a soft toothbrush or cotton swab may reduce occurrence of mouth sores. Report easy bruising or bleeding; fever or chills; numbness, pain, or tingling of extremities; muscle cramping or weakness; unusual swelling of extremities; menstrual irregularities; or any difficulty breathing. Contraceptive measures are recommended during therapy.

Special Geriatric Considerations Toxicity to immunosuppressives is increased in the elderly. Start with lowest recommended adult doses. Signs of infection, such as fever and rise in WBCs, may not occur. Lethargy and confusion may be more prominent signs of infection.

Emetic Potential Very low (<10%)

(Continued)

Chlorambucil *(Continued)*

Dosage Forms Excipient information presented when available (limited, particularly for generics); consult specific product labeling.

Tablet:

Leukeran®: 2 mg

Extemporaneous Preparations A 2 mg/mL oral suspension can be prepared by crushing sixty 2 mg tablets in a mortar and then mixing in small amounts of methylcellulose (mix in a total of 30 mL of methylcellulose). Next, add a sufficient quantity of syrup to make 60 mL of final product. Transfer to amber container. Label "shake well," "refrigerate," and "protect from light." Refrigerated stability is 7 days.

Nahata MC and Hipple TF, *Pediatric Drug Formulations*, 4th ed, Cincinnati, OH: Harvey Whitney Books Co, 2000.

Dressman JB and Poust RI, "Stability of Allopurinol and of Five Antine-oplastics in Suspension," *Am J Hosp Pharm*, 1983, 40(4):616-8.

References

Aronoff GR, Bennett WM, Berns JS, et al, *Drug Prescribing in Renal Failure: Dosing Guidelines for Adults and Children*, 5th ed. Philadelphia, PA: American College of Physicians; 2007, p 98.

Begleiter A, Mowat M, Israels LG, et al, "Chlorambucil in Chronic Lymphocytic Leukemia: Mechanism of Action," *Leuk Lymphoma*, 1996, 23(3-4):187-201.

Brittinger G, Hellriegel KP, and Hiddemann W, "Chronic Lymphocytic Leukemia and Hairy-Cell Leukemia-Diagnosis and Treatment: Results of a Consensus Meeting of the German CLL Cooperative Group," *Ann Hematol*, 1997, 74(6):291-4.

Hogg RH, Portman RJ, Milliner D, et al, "Evaluation and Management of Proteinuria and Nephrotic Syndrome in Children: Recommendations From a Pediatric Nephrology Panel Established at the National Kidney Foundation Conference on Proteinuria, Albuminuria, Risk, Assessment, Detection, and Elimination (PARADE)," *Pediatrics*, 2000, 105(6):1242-9.

Kyle RA, Greipp PR, Gertz MA, et al, "Waldenström's Macroglobulinemia: A Prospective Study Comparing Daily With Intermittent Oral Chlorambucil," *Br J Haematol*, 2000, 108(4):737-42.

Robinson RF, Nahata MC, Mahan JD, "Management of Nephrotic Syndrome in Children," *Pharmacotherapy*, 2003, 23(8):1021-36.

Rozman C and Montserrat E, "Chronic Lymphocytic Leukemia," *N Engl J Med*, 1995, 333(16):1052-7.

Vandenberg SA, Kulig K, Spoerke DG, et al, "Chlorambucil Overdose: Accidental Ingestion of an Antineoplastic Drug," *J Emerg Med*, 1988, 6(6):495-8.

Wagner AM, Brunet S, Puig J, et al, " Chlorambucil-Induced Inappropriate Antidiuresis in Man With Chronic Lymphocytic Leukemia," *Ann Hemat*, 1999, 78(1):37-8.

♦ **Chlorambucilum** *see* Chlorambucil *on page 205*

♦ **Chloraminophene** *see* Chlorambucil *on page 205*

♦ **Chlorbutinum** *see* Chlorambucil *on page 205*

♦ **Chlorethazine** *see* Mechlorethamine *on page 700*

♦ **Chlorethazine Mustard** *see* Mechlorethamine *on page 700*

♦ **Chlormeprazine** *see* Prochlorperazine *on page 929*

♦ **2-Chlorodeoxyadenosine** *see* Cladribine *on page 231*

ChlorproMAZINE (klor PROE ma zeen)

Medication Safety Issues

Sound-alike/look-alike issues:

ChlorproMAZINE may be confused with chlorproPAMIDE, clomiPRAMINE, prochlorperazine, promethazine

Thorazine® may be confused with thiamine, thioridazine

Index Terms Chlorpromazine Hydrochloride; CPZ

Generic Available Yes

Canadian Brand Names Largactil®; Novo-Chlorpromazine

Pharmacologic Category Antipsychotic Agent, Typical, Phenothiazine

Use Control of mania; treatment of schizophrenia; control of nausea and vomiting; relief of restlessness and apprehension before surgery; acute intermittent porphyria; adjunct in the treatment of tetanus; intractable hiccups; combativeness and/or explosive hyperexcitable behavior in children 1-12 years of age and in short-term treatment of hyperactive children

Unlabeled/Investigational Use Management of psychotic disorders; behavioral symptoms associated with dementia (elderly)

Pregnancy Risk Factor C

Lactation Enters breast milk/not recommended (AAP rates "of concern")

Labeled Contraindications Hypersensitivity to chlorpromazine or any component of the formulation (cross-reactivity between phenothiazines may occur); severe CNS depression; coma

Warnings/Precautions Highly sedating, use with caution in disorders where CNS depression is a feature and in patients with Parkinson's disease. Use with caution in patients with hemodynamic instability, bone marrow suppression, predisposition to seizures, subcortical brain damage, severe cardiac, hepatic, renal, or respiratory disease. Esophageal dysmotility and aspiration have been associated with antipsychotic use - use with caution in patients at risk of aspiration pneumonia (ie, Alzheimer's disease). Caution in breast cancer or other prolactin-dependent tumors (may elevate prolactin levels). May alter temperature regulation or mask toxicity of other drugs due to antiemetic effects. May alter cardiac conduction - life-threatening arrhythmias have occurred with therapeutic doses of neuroleptics.

Use with caution in patients at risk of hypotension (orthostasis is common) or those who would tolerate transient hypotensive episodes (cerebrovascular disease, cardiovascular disease, or other medications which may predispose). Significant hypotension may occur, particularly with parenteral administration. Injection contains sulfites.

Use with caution in patients with decreased gastrointestinal motility, urinary retention, BPH, xerostomia, or visual problems (ie, narrow-angle glaucoma - screening is recommended) and myasthenia gravis. Relative to other neuroleptics, chlorpromazine has a moderate potency of cholinergic blockade.

May cause extrapyramidal symptoms, neuroleptic malignant syndrome (NMS) or pigmentary retinopathy.

Adverse Reactions Frequency not defined.

Cardiovascular: Postural hypotension, tachycardia, dizziness, nonspecific QT changes

Central nervous system: Drowsiness, dystonias, akathisia, pseudoparkinsonism, tardive dyskinesia, neuroleptic malignant syndrome, seizure

Dermatologic: Photosensitivity, dermatitis, skin pigmentation (slate gray)

Endocrine & metabolic: Lactation, breast engorgement, false-positive pregnancy test, amenorrhea, gynecomastia, hyper- or hypoglycemia

Gastrointestinal: Xerostomia, constipation, nausea

Genitourinary: Urinary retention, ejaculatory disorder, impotence

Hematologic: Agranulocytosis, eosinophilia, leukopenia, hemolytic anemia, aplastic anemia, thrombocytopenic purpura

Hepatic: Jaundice

Ocular: Blurred vision, corneal and lenticular changes, epithelial keratopathy, pigmentary retinopathy

Overdosage/Toxicology Symptoms of overdose include deep sleep, coma, extrapyramidal symptoms, abnormal involuntary muscle movements, and hypotension. Following initiation of essential overdose management, toxic
(Continued)

ChlorproMAZINE *(Continued)*

symptom treatment and supportive treatment should be initiated. Neuroleptics often cause extrapyramidal symptoms (eg, dystonic reactions) requiring management with anticholinergic agents such as benztropine mesylate 1-2 mg for adult patients (oral, I.M., I.V.) or diphenhydramine 25-50 mg (oral, I.M., I.V.) may be effective.

Drug Interactions

Cytochrome P450 Effect: Substrate of CYP1A2 (minor), 2D6 (major), 3A4 (minor); **Inhibits** CYP2D6 (strong), 2E1 (weak)

Increased Effect/Toxicity: The levels/effects of chlorpromazine may be increased by delavirdine, fluoxetine, miconazole, paroxetine, pergolide, quinidine, quinine, ritonavir, ropinirole, and other CYP2D6 inhibitors. Effects on CNS depression may be additive when chlorpromazine is combined with CNS depressants (opioid analgesics, ethanol, barbiturates, cyclic antidepressants, antihistamines, or sedative-hypnotics). Chlorpromazine may increase the levels/effects of amphetamines, selected beta-blockers, dextromethorphan, fluoxetine, lidocaine, mirtazapine, nefazodone, paroxetine, risperidone, ritonavir, thioridazine, tricyclic antidepressants, and venlafaxine and other CYP2D6 substrates. Chlorpromazine may increase the effects/toxicity of anticholinergics, antihypertensives, lithium (rare neurotoxicity), trazodone, or valproic acid. Concurrent use with TCA may produce increased toxicity or altered therapeutic response. Chloroquine and propranolol may increase chlorpromazine concentrations. Hypotension may occur when chlorpromazine is combined with epinephrine. May increase the risk of arrhythmia when combined with antiarrhythmics, cisapride, pimozide, or other drugs which prolong QT interval. Metoclopramide may increase risk of extrapyramidal symptoms (EPS). Acetylcholinesterase inhibitors (central) may increase the risk of antipsychotic-related EPS.

Decreased Effect: Chlorpromazine may decrease the levels/effects of CYP2D6 prodrug substrates; example prodrug substrates include codeine, hydrocodone, oxycodone, and tramadol. Phenothiazines inhibit the ability of bromocriptine to lower serum prolactin concentrations. Benztropine (and other anticholinergics) may inhibit the therapeutic response to chlorpromazine and excess anticholinergic effects may occur. Antihypertensive effects of guanethidine and guanadrel may be inhibited by chlorpromazine. Chlorpromazine may inhibit the antiparkinsonian effect of levodopa. Chlorpromazine and possibly other low potency antipsychotics may reverse the pressor effects of epinephrine.

Ethanol/Nutrition/Herb Interactions

Ethanol: Avoid ethanol (may increase CNS depression).

Herb/Nutraceutical: Avoid St John's wort (may decrease chlorpromazine levels, increase photosensitization, or enhance sedative effect). Avoid dong quai (may enhance photosensitization). Avoid kava kava, gotu kola, valerian (may increase CNS depression).

Storage/Stability Injection: Protect from light. A slightly yellowed solution does not indicate potency loss, but a markedly discolored solution should be discarded. Diluted injection (1 mg/mL) with NS and stored in 5 mL vials remains stable for 30 days.

Reconstitution Dilute injection (1 mg/mL) with NS for I.V. administration.

Compatibility Stable in dextran 6% in dextrose, dextran 6% in NS, D₅LR, D₅¼NS, D₅½NS, D₅NS, D₅W, D₁₀W, LR, ½NS, NS.

Y-site administration: Compatible: Amsacrine, cisatracurium, cisplatin, cladribine, cyclophosphamide, cytarabine, docetaxel, doxorubicin, doxorubicin liposome, famotidine, filgrastim, fluconazole, gatifloxacin,

CHLORPROMAZINE

gemcitabine, granisetron, heparin, hydrocortisone sodium succinate, ondansetron, potassium chloride, propofol, teniposide, thiotepa, vinorelbine, vitamin B complex with C. **Incompatible:** Allopurinol, amifostine, amphotericin B cholesteryl sulfate complex, aztreonam, cefepime, etoposide phosphate, fludarabine, furosemide, linezolid, melphalan, methotrexate, paclitaxel, piperacillin/tazobactam, sargramostim. **Variable (consult detailed reference):** Remifentanil, TPN.

Compatibility in syringe: Compatible: Atropine, benztropine, butorphanol, diphenhydramine, doxapram, droperidol, fentanyl, glycopyrrolate, hydromorphone, hydroxyzine, meperidine, metoclopramide, midazolam, morphine, pentazocine, perphenazine, prochlorperazine edisylate, promazine, promethazine, scopolamine. **Incompatible:** Cimetidine, dimenhydrinate, heparin, pentobarbital, thiopental. **Variable (consult detailed reference):** Ranitidine.

Compatibility when admixed: Compatible: Ascorbic acid injection, ethacrynate, netilmicin, theophylline, vitamin B complex with C. **Incompatible:** Aminophylline, amphotericin B, ampicillin, chloramphenicol, chlorothiazide, floxacillin, furosemide, methohexital, penicillin G potassium, penicillin G sodium, phenobarbital. **Variable (consult detailed reference):** Pentobarbital.

Mechanism of Action Chlorpromazine is an aliphatic phenothiazine antipsychotic which blocks postsynaptic mesolimbic dopaminergic receptors in the brain; exhibits a strong alpha-adrenergic blocking effect and depresses the release of hypothalamic and hypophyseal hormones; believed to depress the reticular activating system, thus affecting basal metabolism, body temperature, wakefulness, vasomotor tone, and emesis

Pharmacodynamics/Kinetics
Onset of action: I.M.: 15 minutes; Oral: 30-60 minutes
Absorption: Rapid
Distribution: V_d: 20 L/kg; crosses the placenta; enters breast milk
Protein binding: 92% to 97%
Metabolism: Extensively hepatic to active and inactive metabolites
Bioavailability: 20%
Half-life, biphasic: Initial: 2 hours; Terminal: 30 hours
Excretion: Urine (<1% as unchanged drug) within 24 hours

Dosage
Children ≥6 months:
Schizophrenia/psychoses:
Oral: 0.5-1 mg/kg/dose every 4-6 hours; older children may require 200 mg/day or higher
I.M., I.V.: 0.5-1 mg/kg/dose every 6-8 hours
<5 years (22.7 kg): Maximum: 40 mg/day
5-12 years (22.7-45.5 kg): Maximum: 75 mg/day
Nausea and vomiting:
Oral: 0.5-1 mg/kg/dose every 4-6 hours as needed
I.M., I.V.: 0.5-1 mg/kg/dose every 6-8 hours
<5 years (22.7 kg): Maximum: 40 mg/day
5-12 years (22.7-45.5 kg): Maximum: 75 mg/day
Adults:
Schizophrenia/psychoses:
Oral: Range: 30-2000 mg/day in 1-4 divided doses, initiate at lower doses and titrate as needed; usual dose: 400-600 mg/day; some patients may require 1-2 g/day
I.M., I.V.: Initial: 25 mg, may repeat (25-50 mg) in 1-4 hours, gradually increase to a maximum of 400 mg/dose every 4-6 hours until patient is controlled; usual dose: 300-800 mg/day
(Continued)

ChlorproMAZINE *(Continued)*

Intractable hiccups: Oral, I.M.: 25-50 mg 3-4 times/day

Nausea and vomiting:

Oral: 10-25 mg every 4-6 hours

I.M., I.V.: 25-50 mg every 4-6 hours

Elderly: Behavioral symptoms associated with dementia (unlabeled use): Initial: 10-25 mg 1-2 times/day; increase at 4- to 7-day intervals by 10-25 mg/day. Increase dose intervals (bid, tid, etc) as necessary to control behavior response or side effects; maximum daily dose: 800 mg; gradual increases (titration) may prevent some side effects or decrease their severity.

Dosing comments in renal impairment: Hemodialysis: Not dialyzable (0% to 5%)

Dosing adjustment/comments in hepatic impairment: Avoid use in severe hepatic dysfunction

Administration Note: Avoid skin contact with oral solution or injection solution; may cause contact dermatitis.

I.V.: Direct or intermittent infusion: Infuse 1 mg or portion thereof over 1 minute.

Monitoring Parameters Vital signs; lipid profile, fasting blood glucose/Hgb A_{1c}; BMI; mental status; abnormal involuntary movement scale (AIMS); extrapyramidal symptoms (EPS)

Test Interactions False-positives for phenylketonuria, amylase, uroporphyrins, urobilinogen. May cause false-positive pregnancy test.

Patient Information Do not stop taking unless informed by your prescriber. Do not take antacid within 1 hour of taking drug. Avoid alcohol. Avoid excess sun exposure (use sun block). May cause drowsiness; rise slowly from recumbent position. Use of supportive stockings may help prevent orthostatic hypotension.

Special Geriatric Considerations Many elderly patients receive antipsychotic medications for inappropriate nonpsychotic behavior. Before initiating antipsychotic medication, the clinician should investigate any possible reversible cause; any stress or stress from any disease can cause acute "confusion" or worsening of baseline nonpsychotic behavior. Most commonly acute changes in behavior are due to increases in drug dose or addition of new drug to regimen; fluid electrolyte loss; infections; and changes in environment.

Any changes in disease status in any organ system can result in behavior changes.

In the treatment of agitated, demented, elderly patients, authors of meta-analysis of controlled trials of the response to the traditional antipsychotics (phenothiazines, butyrophenones) in controlling agitation have concluded that the use of neuroleptics results in a response rate of 18%. Clearly neuroleptic therapy for behavior control should be limited with frequent attempts to withdraw the agent given for behavior control.

Emetic Potential Very low (<10%)

Vesicant No

Dosage Forms Excipient information presented when available (limited, particularly for generics); consult specific product labeling.

Injection, solution, as hydrochloride: 25 mg/mL (1 mL, 2 mL)

Tablet, as hydrochloride: 10 mg, 25 mg, 50 mg, 100 mg, 200 mg

References

American Academy of Pediatrics Committee on Drugs, "Reappraisal of Lytic Cocktail/Demerol®, Phenergan®, and Thorazine® (DPT) for the Sedation of Children," *Pediatrics*, 1995, 95(4):598-602.

"American Academy of Pediatrics Committee on Drugs. The Transfer of Drugs and Other Chemicals Into Human Milk," *Pediatrics*, 2001, 108(3):776-89.

Fernandes CM, "Parenteral Chlorpromazine and a Meningitis Headache," *J Emerg Med*, 1995, 13(4):577-9.

Gez E, Ben-Yosef R, Catane R, et al, "Chlorpromazine and Dexamethasone Versus High-Dose Metoclopramide and Dexamethasone in Patients Receiving Cancer Chemotherapy, Particularly Cis-Platinum: A Prospective Randomized Crossover Study," *Oncology*, 1989, 46(3):150-4.

Gez E, Brufman G, Kaufman B, et al, "Methylprednisolone and Chlorpromazine in Patients Receiving Cancer Chemotherapy: A Prospective Nonrandomized Study," *J Chemother*, 1989, 1(2):140-3.

Hutcheon AW, Palmer JB, Soukop M, et al, "A Randomized Multicentre Single Blind Comparison of a Cannabinoid Antiemetic (Levonantradol) With Chlorpromazine in Patients Receiving Their First Cytotoxic Chemotherapy," *Eur J Cancer Clin Oncol*, 1983, 19(8):1087-90.

Knight ME and Roberts RJ, "Phenothiazine and Butyrophenone Intoxication in Children," *Pediatr Clin North Am*, 1986, 33(2):299-309.

Lipka LJ, Lathers CM, and Roberts J, "Does Chlorpromazine Produce Cardiac Arrhythmia Via the Central Nervous System," *J Clin Pharmacol*, 1988, 28(11):968-83.

Mitchell AC and Brown KW, "Chlorpromazine-Induced Retinopathy," *Br J Psychiatry*, 1995, 166(6):822-3.

Oshika T, "Ocular Adverse Effects of Neuropsychiatric Agents. Incidence and Management," *Drug Saf*, 1995, 12(4):256-63.

Peabody CA, Warner MD, Whiteford HA, et al, "Neuroleptics and the Elderly," *J Am Geriatr Soc*, 1987, 35(3):233-8.

Relling MV, Mulhern RK, Fairclough D, et al, "Chlorpromazine With and Without Lorazepam as Antiemetic Therapy in Children Receiving Uniform Chemotherapy," *J Pediatr*, 1993, 123(5):811-6.

Risse SC and Barnes R, "Pharmacologic Treatment of Agitation Associated With Dementia," *J Am Geriatr Soc*, 1986, 34(5):368-76.

Rosenberg MR and Green M, "Neuroleptic Malignant Syndrome: Review of Response to Therapy," *Arch Intern Med*, 1989, 149(9):1927-31.

Saab GA, Shamseddine A, and Habbal Z, "Prolonged Chlorpromazine Infusion as Antiemetic in Patients on Daily Cisplating Infusion. A Pilot Study," *Am J Clin Oncol*, 1988, 11(4):470-3.

Saltz BL, Woerner MG, Kane JM, et al, "Prospective Study of Tardive Dyskinesia Incidence in the Elderly," *JAMA*, 1991, 266(17):2402-6.

Seifert RD, "Therapeutic Drug Monitoring: Psychotropic Drugs," *J Pharm Pract*, 1984, 6:403-16.

♦ **Chlorpromazine Hydrochloride** *see* ChlorproMAZINE *on page 208*

♦ **Ciloxan®** *see* Ciprofloxacin *on page 213*

♦ **Cipro®** *see* Ciprofloxacin *on page 213*

♦ **Cipro® XL (Can)** *see* Ciprofloxacin *on page 213*

Ciprofloxacin (sip roe FLOKS a sin)

Medication Safety Issues

Sound-alike/look-alike issues:

Ciprofloxacin may be confused with cephalexin

Ciloxan® may be confused with cinoxacin, Cytoxan®

Cipro® may be confused with Ceftin®

U.S. Brand Names Ciloxan®; Cipro®; Cipro® XR; Proquin® XR

Index Terms Ciprofloxacin Hydrochloride

Generic Available Yes: Excludes infusion, suspension, ointment

Canadian Brand Names Apo-Ciproflox®; Ciloxan®; Cipro®; Cipro® XL; CO Ciprofloxacin; Gen-Ciprofloxacin; Novo-Ciprofloxacin; PMS-Ciprofloxacin; RAN™-Ciprofloxacin; ratio-Ciprofloxacin; Rhoxal-ciprofloxacin; Sandoz-Ciprofloxacin; Taro-Ciprofloxacin
(Continued)

Ciprofloxacin *(Continued)*

Pharmacologic Category Antibiotic, Ophthalmic; Antibiotic, Quinolone

Use

Children: Complicated urinary tract infections and pyelonephritis due to *E. coli*. **Note:** Although effective, ciprofloxacin is not the drug of first choice in children.

Children and Adults: To reduce incidence or progression of disease following exposure to aerolized *Bacillus anthracis*. Ophthalmologically, for superficial ocular infections (corneal ulcers, conjunctivitis) due to susceptible strains

Adults: Treatment of the following infections when caused by susceptible bacteria: Urinary tract infections; acute uncomplicated cystitis in females; chronic bacterial prostatitis; lower respiratory tract infections (including acute exacerbations of chronic bronchitis); acute sinusitis; skin and skin structure infections; bone and joint infections; complicated intra-abdominal infections (in combination with metronidazole); infectious diarrhea; typhoid fever due to *Salmonella typhi* (eradication of chronic typhoid carrier state has not been proven); uncomplicated cervical and urethra gonorrhea (due to *N. gonorrhoeae*); nosocomial pneumonia; empirical therapy for febrile neutropenic patients (in combination with piperacillin)

Note: As of April 2007, the CDC no longer recommends the use of fluoroquinolones for the treatment of gonococcal disease.

Unlabeled/Investigational Use Acute pulmonary exacerbations in cystic fibrosis (children); cutaneous/gastrointestinal/oropharyngeal anthrax (treatment, children and adults); disseminated gonococcal infection (adults); chancroid (adults); prophylaxis to *Neisseria meningitidis* following close contact with an infected person; empirical therapy (oral) for febrile neutropenia in low-risk cancer patients; infectious diarrhea (children)

Pregnancy Risk Factor C

Lactation Enters breast milk/not recommended (AAP rates "compatible")

Labeled Contraindications Hypersensitivity to ciprofloxacin, any component of the formulation, or other quinolones; concurrent administration of tizanidine

Warnings/Precautions CNS stimulation may occur (tremor, restlessness, confusion, and very rarely hallucinations or seizures). Use with caution in patients with known or suspected CNS disorder. Potential for seizures, although very rare, may be increased with concomitant NSAID therapy. Use with caution in individuals at risk of seizures. Fluoroquinolones may prolong QT_c interval; avoid use in patients with a history of QT_c prolongation, uncorrected hypokalemia, hypomagnesemia, or concurrent administration of other medications known to prolong the QT interval (including Class Ia and Class III antiarrhythmics, cisapride, erythromycin, antipsychotics, and tricyclic antidepressants). Prolonged use may result in fungal or bacterial superinfection, including *C. difficile*-associated diarrhea (CDAD) and pseudomembranous colitis; CDAD has been observed >2 months postantibiotic treatment. Rarely crystalluria has occurred; urine alkalinity may increase the risk. Ensure adequate hydration during therapy. Tendon inflammation and/or rupture have been reported with ciprofloxacin and other quinolone antibiotics. Risk may be increased with concurrent corticosteroids, particularly in the elderly. Discontinue at first sign of tendon inflammation (commonly Achilles, shoulder, or hand tendons) or pain. Adverse effects, including those related to joints and/or surrounding tissues, are increased in pediatric patients and therefore, ciprofloxacin should not be considered as drug of choice in children (exception is anthrax treatment). Rare cases of peripheral neuropathy may occur.

Fluoroquinolones have been associated with the development of serious, and sometimes fatal, hypoglycemia, most often in elderly diabetics but also in patients without diabetes. This occurred most frequently with gatifloxacin (no longer available systemically), but may occur at a lower frequency with other quinolones.

Severe hypersensitivity reactions, including anaphylaxis, have occurred with quinolone therapy. Reactions may present as typical allergic symptoms after a single dose, or may manifest as severe idiosyncratic dermatologic, vascular, pulmonary, renal, hepatic, and/or hematologic events, usually after multiple doses. Prompt discontinuation of drug should occur if skin rash or other symptoms arise. Quinolones may exacerbate myasthenia gravis, use with caution (rare, potentially life-threatening weakness of respiratory muscles may occur). Use caution in renal impairment. Avoid excessive sunlight; may cause moderate-to-severe phototoxicity reactions.

Ciprofloxacin is a potent inhibitor of CYP1A2. Coadministration of drugs which depend on this pathway may lead to substantial increases in serum concentrations and adverse effects.

Adverse Reactions

1% to 10%:
Central nervous system: Neurologic events (children 2%, includes dizziness, insomnia, nervousness, somnolence); fever (children 2%); headache (I.V. administration); restlessness (I.V. administration)
Dermatologic: Rash (children 2%, adults 1%)
Gastrointestinal: Nausea (children/adults 3%); diarrhea (children 5%, adults 2%); vomiting (children 5%, adults 1%); abdominal pain (children 3%, adults <1%); dyspepsia (children 3%)
Hepatic: ALT/AST increased (adults 1%)
Local: Injection site reactions (I.V. administration)
Respiratory: Rhinitis (children 3%)
<1%: Abnormal gait, acute renal failure, agitation, allergic reactions, anaphylaxis, anemia, angina pectoris, angioedema, anorexia, arthralgia, ataxia, atrial flutter, breast pain, bronchospasm, candidiasis, cardiopulmonary arrest, cerebral thrombosis, chills, cholestatic jaundice, confusion, chromatopsia, crystalluria (particularly in alkaline urine), cylindruria, depersonalization, depression, dizziness, drowsiness, dyspnea, edema, eosinophilia, erythema nodosum, fever (adults), gastrointestinal bleeding, hallucinations, headache (oral), hematuria, hyperpigmentation, hyper-/hypotension, insomnia, interstitial nephritis, intestinal perforation, irritability, joint pain, laryngeal edema, lightheadedness, lymphadenopathy, malaise, manic reaction, migraine, MI, nephritis, nightmares, palpitation, paranoia, paresthesia, peripheral neuropathy, petechia, photosensitivity, pulmonary edema, seizure, syncope, tachycardia, thrombophlebitis, tinnitus, tremor, urethral bleeding, vaginitis, ventricular ectopy, visual disturbance, weakness
Postmarketing and/or case reports: Agranulocytosis, albuminuria, anaphylactic shock, anosmia, bone marrow depression (life-threatening), candiduria, constipation, delirium, dyspepsia (adults), dysphagia, erythema multiforme, exfoliative dermatitis, fixed eruption, flatulence, hemolytic anemia, hepatic failure (some fatal), hepatic necrosis, hyperesthesia, hyperglycemia, hypertonia, jaundice, methemoglobinemia, moniliasis, myalgia, myasthenia gravis, myoclonus, nystagmus, orthostatic hypotension, pancreatitis, pancytopenia (life-threatening or fatal), pneumonitis, prolongation of PT/INR, pseudomembranous colitis, psychosis, renal calculi, serum cholesterol increased, serum glucose increased, serum sickness-like reactions, serum triglycerides increased, Stevens-Johnson
(Continued)

Ciprofloxacin *(Continued)*

syndrome, taste loss, tendon rupture, tendonitis, toxic epidermal necrolysis (Lyell's syndrome), torsade de pointes, twitching, vaginal candidiasis, vasculitis

Overdosage/Toxicology Symptoms of overdose include acute renal failure and seizures. Treatment is supportive and should include adequate hydration and renal function monitoring. Magnesium- or calcium-containing antacids may be given to decrease absorption of oral ciprofloxacin. Only a small amount of ciprofloxacin (<10%) is removed from the body after hemodialysis or peritoneal dialysis.

Drug Interactions

Cytochrome P450 Effect: Inhibits CYP1A2 (strong), 3A4 (weak)

Increased Effect/Toxicity: Ciprofloxacin may increase serum levels of tizanidine; concurrent administration is contraindicated. Ciprofloxacin may increase the effects/toxicity of caffeine, CYP1A2 substrates (eg, aminophylline, fluvoxamine, mexiletine, mirtazapine, ropinirole, tizanidine, and trifluoperazine), glyburide, methotrexate, ropivacaine, theophylline, and warfarin. Headache has been observed with concomitant pentoxifylline therapy. Concomitant use with corticosteroids may increase the risk of tendon rupture. Concomitant use with foscarnet or NSAIDs may increase the risk of seizures. Probenecid may increase ciprofloxacin levels. Ciprofloxacin may enhance the QT-prolonging effects of known QT_c-prolonging agents; information based on rare case reports.

Decreased Effect: Concurrent administration of metal cations, including most antacids, oral electrolyte supplements, quinapril, sucralfate, some didanosine formulations (pediatric powder for oral suspension), other highly-buffered oral drugs, and sevelamer may decrease quinolone absorption; separate doses. Ciprofloxacin may decrease phenytoin levels. Antibiotics may decrease the therapeutic effect of live, attenuated Ty21a (typhoid) vaccine; delay vaccination for >24 hours after administration of antibacterial agents.

Ethanol/Nutrition/Herb Interactions

Food: Food decreases rate, but not extent, of absorption. Ciprofloxacin serum levels may be decreased if taken with dairy products or calcium-fortified juices. Ciprofloxacin may increase serum caffeine levels if taken with caffeine.

Enteral feedings may decrease plasma concentrations of ciprofloxacin probably by >30% inhibition of absorption. Ciprofloxacin should not be administered with enteral feedings. The feeding would need to be discontinued for 1-2 hours prior to and after ciprofloxacin administration. Nasogastric administration produces a greater loss of ciprofloxacin bioavailability than does nasoduodenal administration.

Herb/Nutraceutical: Avoid dong quai, St John's wort (may also cause photosensitization).

Storage/Stability

Injection:

Premixed infusion: Store between 5°C to 25°C (41°F to 77°F); avoid freezing. Protect from light.

Vial: Store between 5°C to 30°C (41°F to 86°F); avoid freezing. Protect from light. Diluted solutions of 0.5-2 mg/mL are stable for up to 14 days refrigerated or at room temperature.

Ophthalmic solution/ointment: Store at 36°F to 77°F (2°C to 25°C). Protect from light.

Microcapsules for oral suspension: Prior to reconstitution, store below 25°C (77°F). Protect from freezing. Following reconstitution, store below 30°C (86°F) for up to 14 days. Protect from freezing.

Tablet:

Immediate release: Store below 30°C (86°F).

Extended release: Store at room temperature of 15°C to 30°C (59°F to 86°F).

Reconstitution Injection, vial: May be diluted with NS, D_5W, SWFI, $D_{10}W$, $D_5{}^1/_4NS$, $D_5{}^1/_2NS$, LR.

Compatibility Stable in $D_5{}^1/_4NS$, $D_5{}^1/_2NS$, D_5W, $D_{10}W$, LR, NS; **variable stability (consult detailed reference)** in peritoneal dialysis solution.

Y-site administration: Compatible: Amifostine, amino acids (dextrose), aztreonam, calcium gluconate, ceftazidime, cisatracurium, clarithromycin, digoxin, diltiazem, diphenhydramine, dobutamine, docetaxel, dopamine, doxorubicin liposome, etoposide phosphate, gemcitabine, gentamicin, granisetron, hydroxyzine, lidocaine, linezolid, lorazepam, metoclopramide, midazolam, midodrine, piperacillin, potassium acetate, potassium chloride, potassium phosphates, promethazine, ranitidine, remifentanil, Ringer's injection (lactated), sodium chloride, tacrolimus, teniposide, thiotepa, tobramycin, verapamil. **Incompatible:** Aminophylline, ampicillin/sulbactam, cefepime, dexamethasone sodium phosphate, furosemide, heparin, hydrocortisone sodium succinate, methylprednisolone sodium succinate, phenytoin, propofol, sodium phosphates, warfarin. **Variable (consult detailed reference):** Magnesium sulfate, sodium bicarbonate, teicoplanin, TPN.

Compatibility when admixed: Compatible: Amikacin, aztreonam, ceftazidime, cyclosporine, gentamicin, metronidazole, netilmicin, piperacillin, potassium chloride, ranitidine, tobramycin, vitamin B complex. **Incompatible:** Aminophylline, clindamycin, floxacillin, heparin.

Mechanism of Action Inhibits DNA-gyrase in susceptible organisms; inhibits relaxation of supercoiled DNA and promotes breakage of double-stranded DNA

Pharmacodynamics/Kinetics

Absorption: Oral: Immediate release tablet: Rapid (~50% to 85%)

Distribution: V_d: 2.1-2.7 L/kg; tissue concentrations often exceed serum concentrations especially in kidneys, gallbladder, liver, lungs, gynecological tissue, and prostatic tissue; CSF concentrations: 10% of serum concentrations (noninflamed meninges), 14% to 37% (inflamed meninges); crosses placenta; enters breast milk

Protein binding: 20% to 40%

Metabolism: Partially hepatic; forms 4 metabolites (limited activity)

Half-life elimination: Children: 2.5 hours; Adults: Normal renal function: 3-5 hours

Time to peak: Oral:

Immediate release tablet: 0.5-2 hours

Extended release tablet: Cipro® XR: 1-2.5 hours, Proquin® XR: 3.5-8.7 hours

Excretion: Urine (30% to 50% as unchanged drug); feces (15% to 43%)

Dosage Note: Extended release tablets and immediate release formulations are not interchangeable. Unless otherwise specified, oral dosing reflects the use of immediate release formulations.

Usual dosage ranges:

Children (see Warnings/Precautions):

Oral: 20-30 mg/kg/day in 2 divided doses; maximum dose: 1.5 g/day

I.V.: 20-30 mg/kg/day divided every 12 hours; maximum dose: 800 mg/day

(Continued)

Ciprofloxacin *(Continued)*

Adults:
  Oral: 250-750 mg every 12 hours
  I.V.: 200-400 mg every 12 hours

Indication-specific dosing:

Children:

Anthrax:

Inhalational (postexposure prophylaxis):
  Oral: 15 mg/kg/dose every 12 hours for 60 days; maximum: 500 mg/dose
  I.V.: 10 mg/kg/dose every 12 hours for 60 days; do **not** exceed 400 mg/dose (800 mg/day)

Cutaneous (treatment, CDC guidelines): Oral: 10-15 mg/kg every 12 hours for 60 days (maximum: 1 g/day); amoxicillin 80 mg/kg/day divided every 8 hours is an option for completion of treatment after clinical improvement. **Note:** In the presence of systemic involvement, extensive edema, lesions on head/neck, refer to I.V. dosing for treatment of inhalational/gastrointestinal/oropharyngeal anthrax.

Inhalational/gastrointestinal/oropharyngeal (treatment, CDC guidelines): I.V.: Initial: 10-15 mg/kg every 12 hours for 60 days (maximum: 500 mg/dose); switch to oral therapy when clinically appropriate; refer to adult dosing for notes on combined therapy and duration

Bacterial conjunctivitis: See adult dosing

Corneal ulcer: See adult dosing

Cystic fibrosis (unlabeled use):
  Oral: 40 mg/kg/day divided every 12 hours administered following 1 week of I.V. therapy has been reported in a clinical trial; total duration of therapy: 10-21 days
  I.V.: 30 mg/kg/day divided every 8 hours for 1 week, followed by oral therapy, has been reported in a clinical trial

Urinary tract infection (complicated) or pyelonephritis:
  Oral: 20-30 mg/kg/day in 2 divided doses (every 12 hours) for 10-21 days; maximum: 1.5 g/day
  I.V.: 6-10 mg/kg every 8 hours for 10-21 days (maximum: 400 mg/dose)

Adults:

Anthrax:

Inhalational (postexposure prophylaxis):
  Oral: 500 mg every 12 hours for 60 days
  I.V.: 400 mg every 12 hours for 60 days

Cutaneous (treatment, CDC guidelines): Oral: Immediate release formulation: 500 mg every 12 hours for 60 days. **Note:** In the presence of systemic involvement, extensive edema, lesions on head/neck, refer to I.V. dosing for treatment of inhalational/gastrointestinal/oropharyngeal anthrax

Inhalational/gastrointestinal/oropharyngeal (treatment, CDC guidelines): I.V.: 400 mg every 12 hours. **Note:** Initial treatment should include two or more agents predicted to be effective (per CDC recommendations). Continue combined therapy for 60 days.

Bacterial conjunctivitis:
  Ophthalmic solution: Instill 1-2 drops in eye(s) every 2 hours while awake for 2 days and 1-2 drops every 4 hours while awake for the next 5 days

Ophthalmic ointment: Apply a ½" ribbon into the conjunctival sac 3 times/day for the first 2 days, followed by a ½" ribbon applied twice daily for the next 5 days

Bone/joint infections:

Oral: 500-750 mg twice daily for 4-6 weeks

I.V.: Mild to moderate: 400 mg every 12 hours for 4-6 weeks; Severe/complicated: 400 mg every 8 hours for 4-6 weeks

Chancroid (CDC guidelines): Oral: 500 mg twice daily for 3 days

Corneal ulcer: Ophthalmic solution: Instill 2 drops into affected eye every 15 minutes for the first 6 hours, then 2 drops into the affected eye every 30 minutes for the remainder of the first day. On day 2, instill 2 drops into the affected eye hourly. On days 3-14, instill 2 drops into affected eye every 4 hours. Treatment may continue after day 14 if re-epithelialization has not occurred.

Endocarditis due to HACEK organisms (AHA guidelines, unlabeled use): Note: Not first-line option; use only if intolerant of beta-lactam therapy:

Oral: 500 mg every 12 hours for 4 weeks

I.V.: 400 mg every 12 hours for 4 weeks

Febrile neutropenia*: I.V.: 400 mg every 8 hours for 7-14 days

Gonococcal infections:

Urethral/cervical gonococcal infections: Oral: 250-500 mg as a single dose (CDC recommends concomitant doxycycline or azithromycin due to possible coinfection with *Chlamydia*; **Note:** As of April 2007, the CDC no longer recommends the use of fluoroquinolones for the treatment of uncomplicated gonococcal disease.

Disseminated gonococcal infection (CDC guidelines): Oral: 500 mg twice daily to complete 7 days of therapy (initial treatment with ceftriaxone 1 g I.M./I.V. daily for 24-48 hours after improvement begins); **Note:** As of April 2007, the CDC no longer recommends the use of fluoroquinolones for the treatment of more serious gonococcal disease, unless no other options exist and susceptibility can be confirmed via culture.

Infectious diarrhea: Oral:

Salmonella: 500 mg twice daily for 5-7 days

Shigella: 500 mg twice daily for 3 days

Traveler's diarrhea: Mild: 750 mg for one dose; Severe: 500 mg twice daily for 3 days

Vibrio cholerae: 1 g for one dose

Intra-abdominal*:

Oral: 500 mg every 12 hours for 7-14 days

I.V.: 400 mg every 12 hours for 7-14 days

Lower respiratory tract, skin/skin structure infections:

Oral: 500-750 mg twice daily for 7-14 days

I.V.: Mild to moderate: 400 mg every 12 hours for 7-14 days; Severe/complicated: 400 mg every 8 hours for 7-14 days

Nosocomial pneumonia: I.V.: 400 mg every 8 hours for 10-14 days

Prostatitis (chronic, bacterial): Oral: 500 mg every 12 hours for 28 days

Sinusitis (acute): Oral: 500 mg every 12 hours for 10 days

Typhoid fever: Oral: 500 mg every 12 hours for 10 days

Urinary tract infection:

Acute uncomplicated, cystitis:

Oral:

Immediate release formulation: 250 mg every 12 hours for 3 days

(Continued)

Ciprofloxacin *(Continued)*

Extended release formulation (Cipro® XR, Proquin® XR): 500 mg every 24 hours for 3 days

I.V.: 200 mg every 12 hours for 7-14 days

Complicated (including pyelonephritis):

Oral:

Immediate release formulation: 500 mg every 12 hours for 7-14 days

Extended release formulation (Cipro® XR): 1000 mg every 24 hours for 7-14 days

I.V.: 400 mg every 12 hours for 7-14 days

*Combination therapy generally recommended.

Elderly: No adjustment needed in patients with normal renal function

Dosing adjustment in renal impairment: Adults:

Cl_{cr} 30-50 mL/minute: Oral: 250-500 mg every 12 hours

Cl_{cr} <30 mL/minute: Acute uncomplicated pyelonephritis or complicated UTI: Oral: Extended release formulation: 500 mg every 24 hours

Cl_{cr} 5-29 mL/minute:

Oral: 250-500 mg every 18 hours

I.V.: 200-400 mg every 18-24 hours

Dialysis: Only small amounts of ciprofloxacin are removed by hemo- or peritoneal dialysis (<10%); usual dose: Oral: 250-500 mg every 24 hours following dialysis

Continuous renal replacement therapy (CRRT): I.V.:

CVVH: 200 mg every 12 hours

CVVHD or CVVHDF: 200-400 mg every 12 hours

Administration

Oral: May administer with food to minimize GI upset; avoid antacid use; maintain proper hydration and urine output. Administer immediate release ciprofloxacin and Cipro® XR at least 2 hours before or 6 hours after, and Proquin® XR at least 4 hours before or 6 hours after antacids or other products containing calcium, iron, or zinc (including dairy products or calcium-fortified juices). Separate oral administration from drugs which may impair absorption (see Drug Interactions).

Oral suspension: Should not be administered through feeding tubes (suspension is oil-based and adheres to the feeding tube). Patients should avoid chewing on the microcapsules.

Nasogastric/orogastric tube: Crush immediate-release tablet and mix with water. Flush feeding tube before and after administration. Hold tube feedings at least 1 hour before and 2 hours after administration.

Tablet, extended release: Do not crush, split, or chew. May be administered with meals containing dairy products (calcium content <800 mg), but not with dairy products alone. Proquin® XR should be administered with a main meal of the day; evening meal is preferred.

Parenteral: Administer by slow I.V. infusion over 60 minutes to reduce the risk of venous irritation (burning, pain, erythema, and swelling); final concentration for administration should not exceed 2 mg/mL.

Monitoring Parameters Patients receiving concurrent ciprofloxacin, theophylline, or cyclosporine should have serum levels monitored; CBC, renal and hepatic function during prolonged therapy

Test Interactions Some quinolones may produce a false-positive urine screening result for opiates using commercially-available immunoassay kits. This has been demonstrated most consistently for levofloxacin and ofloxacin, but other quinolones have shown cross-reactivity in certain assay kits.

Confirmation of positive opiate screens by more specific methods should be considered.

Dietary Considerations

Food: Drug may cause GI upset; take without regard to meals (manufacturer prefers that immediate release tablet is taken 2 hours after meals). Extended release tablet may be taken with meals that contain dairy products (calcium content <800 mg), but not with dairy products alone.

Dairy products, calcium-fortified juices, oral multivitamins, and mineral supplements: Absorption of ciprofloxacin is decreased by divalent and trivalent cations. The manufacturer states that the usual dietary intake of calcium (including meals which include dairy products) has not been shown to interfere with ciprofloxacin absorption. Immediate release ciprofloxacin and Cipro® XR may be taken 2 hours before or 6 hours after, and Proquin® XR may be taken 4 hours before or 6 hours after, any of these products.

Caffeine: Patients consuming regular large quantities of caffeinated beverages may need to restrict caffeine intake if excessive cardiac or CNS stimulation occurs.

Patient Information Take as directed, preferably on an empty stomach, 2 hours after meals. Extended release tablet may be taken with meals containing dairy products, but not with dairy products alone; do not crush, split, or chew extended release tablet. Swallow oral suspension. Do not chew microcapsules. Take entire prescription even if feeling better. Maintain adequate hydration (2-3 L/day of fluids unless instructed to restrict fluid intake) to avoid concentrated urine and crystal formation. You may experience nausea, vomiting, or anorexia (small frequent meals, frequent mouth care, sucking lozenges, or chewing gum may help). You may experience increased sensitivity to sunlight; use sunblock, wear protective clothing and dark glasses, and avoid direct exposure to sunlight. Report immediately any signs of skin rash, joint or back pain, or difficulty breathing. Report unusual fever or chills; vaginal itching or foul-smelling vaginal discharge; easy bruising or bleeding. Report immediately any pain, inflammation, or rupture of tendon.

Special Geriatric Considerations Ciprofloxacin should not be used as first-line therapy unless the culture and sensitivity findings show resistance to usual therapy. The interactions with caffeine and theophylline can result in serious toxicity in the elderly. Adjust dose for renal function.

Additional Information Although the systemic use of ciprofloxacin is only FDA approved in children for the treatment of complicated UTI and postexposure treatment of inhalation anthrax, use of the fluoroquinolones in pediatric patients is increasing. Current recommendations by the American Academy of Pediatrics note that the systemic use of these agents in children should be restricted to infections caused by multidrug resistant pathogens with no safe or effective alternative, and when parenteral therapy is not feasible or other oral agents are not available.

Emetic Potential Very low (<10%)

Vesicant No

Dosage Forms Excipient information presented when available (limited, particularly for generics); consult specific product labeling.

Infusion [premixed in D_5W]:

Cipro®: 200 mg (100 mL); 400 mg (200 mL) [latex free]

Injection, solution: 10 mg/mL (20 mL, 40 mL)

Cipro®: 10 mg/mL (20 mL, 40 mL)

Microcapsules for suspension, oral:

Cipro®: 250 mg/5 mL (100 mL); 500 mg/5 mL (100 mL) [strawberry flavor]

(Continued)

Ciprofloxacin *(Continued)*

Ointment, ophthalmic, as hydrochloride:
   Ciloxan®: 3.33 mg/g [0.3% base] (3.5 g)
Solution, ophthalmic, as hydrochloride: 3.5 mg/mL (2.5 mL, 5mL, 10 mL) [0.3% base]
   Ciloxin®: 3.5 mg/mL (2.5 mL, 5mL, 10 mL) [0.3% base; contains benzalkonium chloride]
Tablet: 250 mg, 500 mg, 750 mg
   Cipro®: 250 mg, 500 mg, 750 mg
Tablet, extended release: 500 mg, 1000 mg
   Cipro® XR: 500 mg [equivalent to ciprofloxacin hydrochloride 287.5 mg and ciprofloxacin base 212.6 mg]; 1000 mg [equivalent to ciprofloxacin hydrochloride 574.9 mg and ciprofloxacin base 425.2 mg]
   Proquin® XR: 500 mg
Tablet, extended release [dose pack]:
   Proquin® XR: 500 mg (3s)

References

Abramowicz M, "Antimicrobial Prophylaxis in Surgery," *Medical Letter on Drugs and Therapeutics, Handbook of Antimicrobial Therapy*, 16th ed, New York, NY: Medical Letter, 2002.

American Academy of Pediatrics Committee on Drugs, "The Transfer of Drugs and Other Chemicals Into Human Milk," *Pediatrics*, 2001, 108(3):776-89.

American Thoracic Society and Infectious Diseases Society of America, "Guidelines for the Management of Adults With Hospital-Acquired, Ventilator-Associated, and Healthcare-Associated Pneumonia," *Am J Respir Crit Care Med*, 2005, 171(4):388-416.

Baddour LM, Wilson WR, Bayer AS, et al, "Infective Endocarditis. Diagnosis, Antimicrobial Therapy, and Management of Complications. A Statement for Healthcare Professionals from the Committee on Rheumatic Fever, Endocarditis, and Kawasaki Disease, Council on Cardiovascular Disease in the Young, and the Councils on Clinical Cardiology, Stroke, and Cardiovascular Surgery and Anesthesia, American Heart Association," *Circulation*, 2005, 111(23):e394-434.

Bayer A, Gajewska A, Stephens M, et al, "Pharmacokinetics of Ciprofloxacin in the Elderly," *Respiration*, 1987, 51(4):292-5.

Centers for Disease Control and Prevention, "Update to CDC's Sexually Transmitted Diseases Treatment Guidelines, 2006: Fluoroquinolones No Longer Recommended for Treatment of Gonococcal Infections," *MMWR Recomm Rep*, 2007, 56(14):332-6.

Centers for Disease Control and Prevention, "Prevention and Control of Meningococcal Disease. Recommendations of the Advisory Committee on Immunization Practices (ACIP)," *MMWR Recomm Rep*, 2000, 49(RR-7):1-10. Available at: http://www.cdc.gov/mmwr/preview/mmwrhtml/rr4907a1.htm. Accessed May 5, 2004.

Centers for Disease Control and Prevention, "Update: Investigation of Bioterrorism-Related Anthrax and Interim Guidelines for Exposure Management and Antimicrobial Therapy, October 2001," *MMWR*, October 26, 2001, 50(42):909-19. Available at: http://www.cdc.gov/mmwr/preview/mmwrhtml/mm5042a1.htm. Accessed October 26, 2001.

Chung AM, Reed MD, and Blumer JL, "Antibiotics and Breast-Feeding: A Critical Review of the Literature," *Paediatr Drugs*, 2002, 4(12):817-37.

Cohen H and Francisco DH, "Twelve Gram Overdose of Ciprofloxacin With Mild Symptomatology," *Ann Pharmacother*, 1994, 28(6):805-6.

Committee on Infectious Diseases, "The Use of Systemic Fluoroquinolones," *Pediatrics*, 2006, 118(3):1287-92.

Davies SP, Azadian BS, Kox WJ, et al, "Pharmacokinetics of Ciprofloxacin and Vancomycin in Patients With Acute Renal Failure Treated by Continuous Haemodialysis," *Nephrol Dial Transplant*, 1992, 7(8):848-54.

Food and Drug Administration (FDA), "CIPRO (Ciprofloxacin) Use by Pregnant and Lactating Women." Available at http://www.fda.gov/cder/drug/infopage/cipro/cipropreg.htm. Last accessed August 9, 2004.

Friedrich LV and Dougherty R, "Fatal Hypoglycemia Associated With Levofloxacin," *Pharmacotherapy*, 2004, 24(12):1807-12.

Frothingham R, "Glucose Homeostasis Abnormalities Associated With Use of Gatifloxacin," *Clin Infect Dis*, 2005, 41(9):1269-76.

Gamboa F, Rivera JM, Gomez Mateos JM, et al, "Ciprofloxacin-Induced Henoch-Schönlein Purpura," *Ann Pharmacother*, 1995, 29(1):84.

Gavin JR 3rd, Kubin R, Choudhri S, et al, "Moxifloxacin and Glucose Homeostasis: A Pooled-Analysis of the Evidence From Clinical and Postmarketing Studies," *Drug Saf*, 2004, 27(9):671-86.

Giamarellou H, Kolokythas E, Petrikkos G, et al, "Pharmacokinetics of Three Newer Quinolones in Pregnant and Lactating Women," *Am J Med*, 1989, 87(Suppl 5A):49-51.

Graumlich JF, Habis S, Avelino RR, et al, "Hypoglycemia in Inpatients After Gatifloxacin or Levofloxacin Therapy: Nested Case-Control Study," *Pharmacotherapy*, 2005, 25(10):1296-302.

Guay DRP, Awni WM, Peterson PK, et al, "Single and Multiple Dose Pharmacokinetics of Oral Ciprofloxacin in Elderly Patients," *Int J Clin Pharmacol Ther Toxicol*, 1988, 26(6):279-84.

Guharoy SR, "Serum Sickness Secondary to Ciprofloxacin Use," *Vet Hum Toxicol*, 1994, 36(6):540-1.

Hughes WT, Armstrong D, Bodey GP, et al, "2002 Guidelines for the Use of Antimicrobial Agents in Neutropenic Patients With Cancer," *Clin Infect Dis*, 2002, 15;34(6):730-51.

Kapila K, Chysky V, Hullman R, et al, "Worldwide Clinical Experience on Safety of Ciprofloxacin in Children on Compassionate Use Basis," *Proceedings of Third International Symposium on New Quinolones*, Vancouver, Canada, 1990, 9.

Khaliq Y and Zhanel GG, "Fluoroquinolone-Associated Tendinopathy: A Critical Review of the Literature," *Clin Infect Dis*, 2003, 36(11):1404-10.

Lawrence KR, Adra M, and Keir C, "Hypoglycemia-Induced Anoxic Brain Injury Possibly Associated With Levofloxacin," *J Infect*, 2006, 52(6):e177-80.

Loebstein R, Addis A, Ho E, et al, "Pregnancy Outcome Following Gestational Exposure to Fluoroquinolones: A Multicenter, Prospective Controlled Study," *Antimicrob Agents Chemother*, 1998, 42(6):1336-9.

Lomaestro BM and Bailie GR, "Quinolone-Cation Interactions: A Review," *DICP*, 1991, 25(11):1249-58.

Mackay AD and Mehta A, "Autoimmune Haemolytic Anemia Associated With Ciprofloxacin," *Clin Lab Haematol*, 1995, 17(1):98-8.

Malone RS, Fish DN, Abraham E, et al, "Pharmacokinetics of Levofloxacin and Ciprofloxacin During Continuous Renal Replacement Therapy in Critically Ill Patients," *Antimicrob Agents Chemother*, 2001, 45(10):2949-54.

Mohr JF, McKinnon PS, Peymann PJ, et al, "A Retrospective, Comparative Evaluation of Dysglycemias in Hospitalized Patients Receiving Gatifloxacin, Levofloxacin, Ciprofloxacin, or Ceftriaxone," *Pharmacotherapy*, 2005, 25(10):1303-9.

Mulhall JP and Bergmann LS, "Ciprofloxacin-Induced Acute Psychosis," *Urology*, 1995, 46(1):102-3.

Mullen CA, "Ciprofloxacin in Treatment of Fever and Neutropenia in Pediatric Cancer Patients,"*Pediatr Infect Dis J*, 2003, 22(12):1138-42.

Nilsson-Ehle I and Ljungberg B, "Quinolone Disposition in the Elderly: Practical Implications," *Drugs Aging*, 1991, 1(4):279-88.

Park-Wyllie LY, Juurlink DN, Kopp A, et al, "Outpatient Gatifloxacin Therapy and Dysglycemia in Older Adults," *N Engl J Med*, 2006, 354(13):1352-61.

Paul J and Brown NM, "Tinnitus and Ciprofloxacin," *BMJ*, 1995, 311(6999):232.

Rams TE and Slots J, "Antibiotics in Periodontal Therapy: An Update," *Compendium*, 1992, 13(12):1130, 1132, 1134.

Rfidah EI, Findlay CA, and Beattie TJ, "Reversible Encephalopathy After Intravenous Ciprofloxacin Therapy," *Pediatr Nephrol*, 1995, 9(2):250-1.

Rodriguez WJ, and Wiedermann BL, "The Role of Newer Oral Cephalosporins, Fluoroquinolones, and Macrolides in the Treatment of Pediatric Infections," *Adv Pediatr Infect Dis*, 1994, 9:125-59.

Rubio TT, Miles MV, Lettieri JT, et al, "Pharmacokinetic Disposition of Sequential Intravenous/ Oral Ciprofloxacin in Pediatric Cystic Fibrosis Patients With Acute Pulmonary Exacerbation," *Pediatr Infect Dis J*, 1997, 16:112-7

Schaad UB, abdus Salam M, Aujard Y, et al, "Use of Fluoroquinolones in Pediatrics: Consensus Report of an International Society of Chemotherapy Commission," *Pediatr Infect Dis J*, 1995, 14(1):1-9.

Sudip RG, "Serum Sickness Secondary to Ciprofloxacin Use," *Vet Hum Toxicol*, 36(6):540-1, 1994.

Szarfman A, Chen M, and Blum MD, "More on Fluoroquinolone Antibiotics and Tendon Rupture," *N Engl J Med*, 1995, 332(3):193.

Trotman RL, Williamson JC, Shoemaker DM, et al, "Antibiotic Dosing in Critically Ill Adult Patients Receiving Continuous Renal Replacement Therapy," *Clin Infect Dis*, 2005, 41(8):1159-66.

Villenueve JP, Davies C, and Cote J, "Suspected Ciprofloxacin-Induced Hepatotoxicity," *Ann Pharmacother*, 1995, 29(3):257-9.

Walker RC and Wright AJ, "The Fluoroquinolones," *Mayo Clin Proc*, 1991, 66(12):1249-59.

Wang S and Rizvi AA, "Levofloxacin-Induced Hypoglycemia in a Nondiabetic Patient," *Am J Med Sci*, 2006, 331(6):334-5.

Workowski KA and Berman SM, "Centers for Disease Control and Prevention: Sexually Transmitted Diseases Treatment Guidelines," *MMWR*, 2006, 55(RR-11):1-94.

(Continued)

Ciprofloxacin (Continued)

Yew WW, Chau CH, Wong PC, et al, "Ciprofloxacin-Induced Renal Dysfunction in Patients With Mycobacterial Lung Infections," *Tuber Lung Dis*, 1995, 76(2):173-5.

Zacher JL and Givone DM, "False-Positive Urine Opiate Screening Associated With Fluoroquinolone Use," *Ann Pharmacother*, 2004, 38:1525-28.

Zimbabwe, Bangladesh, South Africa (Zimbasa) Dysentery Study Group, "Multicenter, Randomized, Double Blind Clinical Trial of Short Course Versus Standard Course Oral Ciprofloxacin for *Shigella dysenteriae* Type 1 Dysentery in Children," *Pediatr Infect Dis J*, 2002, 21(12):1136-41.

♦ **Ciprofloxacin Hydrochloride** *see* Ciprofloxacin *on page 213*

♦ **Cipro® XR** *see* Ciprofloxacin *on page 213*

Cisplatin (SIS pla tin)

Medication Safety Issues

Sound-alike/look-alike issues:

Cisplatin may be confused with carboplatin

High alert medication: The Institute for Safe Medication Practices (ISMP) includes this medication among its list of drugs which have a heightened risk of causing significant patient harm when used in error.

Doses >100 mg/m^2 once every 3-4 weeks are rarely used and should be verified with the prescriber.

Related Information

Fertility and Cancer Therapy *on page 1298*

Hematopoietic Stem Cell Transplantation *on page 1366*

Management of Drug Extravasations *on page 1301*

Safe Handling of Hazardous Drugs *on page 1382*

Index Terms CDDP

Generic Available Yes

Pharmacologic Category Antineoplastic Agent, Alkylating Agent; Antineoplastic Agent, Platinum Analog

Use Treatment of bladder, testicular, and ovarian cancer

Unlabeled/Investigational Use Treatment of head and neck, breast, gastric, lung, esophageal, cervical, prostate and small cell lung cancer; Hodgkin's and non-Hodgkin's lymphoma; neuroblastoma; sarcomas, myeloma, melanoma, mesothelioma, and osteosarcoma

Pregnancy Risk Factor D

Lactation Enters breast milk/contraindicated

Labeled Contraindications Hypersensitivity to cisplatin, other platinum-containing compounds, or any component of the formulation (anaphylactic-like reactions have been reported); pre-existing renal insufficiency; myelosuppression; hearing impairment; pregnancy

Warnings/Precautions Hazardous agent - use appropriate precautions for handling and disposal. **[U.S. Boxed Warning]: Doses >100 mg/m^2 once every 3-4 weeks are rarely used and should be verified with the prescriber.** Patients should receive adequate hydration, with or without diuretics, prior to and for 24 hours after cisplatin administration. Reduce dosage in renal impairment. **[U.S. Boxed Warning]: Cumulative renal toxicity may be severe.** Elderly patients may be more susceptible to nephrotoxicity and peripheral neuropathy; select dose cautiously and monitor closely. **[U.S. Boxed Warnings]: Dose-related toxicities include myelosuppression, nausea, and vomiting. Ototoxicity, especially pronounced in children, is manifested by tinnitus or loss of high frequency hearing and occasionally, deafness.** Severe and possibly irreversible neuropathies may occur with higher than recommended doses or more frequent regimen.

Serum electrolytes, particularly magnesium and potassium, should be monitored and replaced as needed during and after cisplatin therapy. When administered as sequential infusions, taxane derivatives (docetaxel, paclitaxel) should be administered before platinum derivatives (carboplatin, cisplatin). **[U.S. Boxed Warnings]: Anaphylactic-like reactions have been reported; may be managed with epinephrine, corticosteroids, and/or antihistamines. Should be administered under the supervision of an experienced cancer chemotherapy physician.**

Adverse Reactions

>10%:

Central nervous system: Neurotoxicity: Peripheral neuropathy is dose- and duration-dependent.

Dermatologic: Mild alopecia

Gastrointestinal: Nausea and vomiting (76% to 100%)

Hematologic: Myelosuppression (25% to 30%; mild with moderate doses, mild to moderate with high-dose therapy)

WBC: Mild

Platelets: Mild

Onset: 10 days

Nadir: 14-23 days

Recovery: 21-39 days

Hepatic: Liver enzymes increased

Renal: Nephrotoxicity (acute renal failure and chronic renal insufficiency)

Otic: Ototoxicity (10% to 30%; manifested as high frequency hearing loss; ototoxicity is especially pronounced in children)

1% to 10%:

Gastrointestinal: Diarrhea

Local: Tissue irritation

<1%: Anaphylactic reaction, arrhythmias, blurred vision, bradycardia, hemolytic uremic syndrome, mild alopecia, mouth sores, optic neuritis, orthostatic hypotension, papilledema, phlebitis, SIADH, thrombophlebitis

Overdosage/Toxicology Symptoms of overdose include severe myelosuppression, intractable nausea and vomiting, kidney and liver failure, deafness, ocular toxicity, and neuritis. Overdose may be fatal. There is no known antidote. Hemodialysis appears to have little effect. Treatment is symptom-directed and supportive.

Drug Interactions

Increased Effect/Toxicity: Cisplatin and ethacrynic acid have resulted in severe ototoxicity in animals. Delayed bleomycin elimination with decreased glomerular filtration rate. When administered as sequential infusions, observational studies indicate a potential for increased toxicity when platinum derivatives (carboplatin, cisplatin) are administered before taxane derivatives (docetaxel, paclitaxel).

Decreased Effect: Sodium thiosulfate and amifostine theoretically inactivate drug systemically; have been used clinically to reduce systemic toxicity with administration of cisplatin.

Ethanol/Nutrition/Herb Interactions Herb/Nutraceutical: Avoid black cohosh, dong quai in estrogen-dependent tumors.

Storage/Stability Store intact vials at room temperature 15°C to 25°C (59°F to 77°F) and protect from light. Do not refrigerate solution as a precipitate may form. Further dilution **stability is dependent on the chloride ion concentration** and should be mixed in solutions of NS (at least 0.3% NaCl). After initial entry into the vial, solution is stable for 28 days protected from light or for at least 7 days under fluorescent room light at room temperature. (Continued)

Cisplatin *(Continued)*

Further dilutions in NS, $D_5/0.45\%$ NaCl or D_5/NS to a concentration of 0.05-2 mg/mL are stable for 72 hours at 4°C to 25°C. The infusion solution should have a final sodium chloride concentration ≥0.2%.

Reconstitution The infusion solution should have a final sodium chloride concentration ≥0.2%.

Compatibility Stable in $D_5^{1}/_4NS$, $D_5^{1}/_2NS$, D_5NS, $^{1}/_4NS$, $^{1}/_3NS$, $^{1}/_2NS$, NS; **incompatible** with sodium bicarbonate; **variable stability (consult detailed reference)** in D_5W.

Y-site administration: Compatible: Allopurinol, aztreonam, bleomycin, chlorpromazine, cimetidine, cladribine, cyclophosphamide, dexamethasone sodium phosphate, diphenhydramine, doxorubicin, doxorubicin liposome, droperidol, etoposide phosphate, famotidine, filgrastim, fludarabine, fluorouracil, furosemide, ganciclovir, gatifloxacin, gemcitabine, granisetron, heparin, hydromorphone, leucovorin, linezolid, lorazepam, melphalan, methotrexate, methylprednisolone sodium succinate, metoclopramide, mitomycin, morphine, ondansetron, paclitaxel, prochlorperazine edisylate, promethazine, propofol, ranitidine, sargramostim, teniposide, topotecan, vinblastine, vincristine, vinorelbine. **Incompatible:** Amifostine, amphotericin B cholesteryl sulfate complex, cefepime, piperacillin/tazobactam, thiotepa.

Compatibility in syringe: Compatible: Bleomycin, cyclophosphamide, doxapram, doxorubicin, droperidol, fluorouracil, furosemide, heparin, leucovorin, methotrexate, metoclopramide, mitomycin, vinblastine, vincristine.

Compatibility when admixed: Compatible: Carboplatin, cyclophosphamide with etoposide, etoposide, etoposide with floxuridine, floxuridine, floxuridine with leucovorin, hydroxyzine, ifosfamide, ifosfamide with etoposide, leucovorin, magnesium sulfate, mannitol, ondansetron. **Incompatible:** Fluorouracil, mesna, thiotepa. **Variable (consult detailed reference):** Etoposide with mannitol and potassium chloride, paclitaxel.

Mechanism of Action Inhibits DNA synthesis by the formation of DNA cross-links; denatures the double helix; covalently binds to DNA bases and disrupts DNA function; may also bind to proteins; the *cis*-isomer is 14 times more cytotoxic than the *trans*-isomer; both forms cross-link DNA but cis-platinum is less easily recognized by cell enzymes and, therefore, not repaired. Cisplatin can also bind two adjacent guanines on the same strand of DNA producing intrastrand cross-linking and breakage.

Pharmacodynamics/Kinetics

Distribution: I.V.: Rapidly into tissue; high concentrations in kidneys, liver, ovaries, uterus, and lungs

Protein binding: >90%

Metabolism: Nonenzymatic; inactivated (in both cell and bloodstream) by sulfhydryl groups; covalently binds to glutathione and thiosulfate

Half-life elimination: Initial: 20-30 minutes; Beta: 60 minutes; Terminal: ~24 hours; Secondary half-life: 44-73 hours

Excretion: Urine (>90%); feces (10%)

Dosage Refer to individual protocols. **VERIFY ANY CISPLATIN DOSE EXCEEDING 100 mg/m² PER COURSE.**

Children (unlabeled uses):

Intermittent dosing schedule: 37-75 mg/m² once every 2-3 weeks or 50-100 mg/m² over 4-6 hours, once every 21-28 days

Daily dosing schedule: 15-20 mg/m²/day for 5 days every 3-4 weeks

Osteogenic sarcoma or neuroblastoma: 60-100 mg/m² on day 1 every 3-4 weeks

Recurrent brain tumors: 60 mg/m^2 once daily for 2 consecutive days every 3-4 weeks

Bone marrow/blood cell transfusion: Continuous Infusion: High dose: 55 mg/m^2/day for 72 hours; total dose = 165 mg/m^2

Adults:

Advanced bladder cancer: 50-70 mg/m^2 every 3-4 weeks

Head and neck cancer (unlabeled use): 100-120 mg/m^2 every 3-4 weeks

Malignant pleural mesothelioma in combination with pemetrexed: 75 mg/m^2 on day 1 of each 21-day cycle; see Pemetrexed monograph for additional details

Metastatic ovarian cancer: 75-100 mg/m^2 every 3-4 weeks

Intraperitoneal: Cisplatin has been administered intraperitoneal with systemic sodium thiosulfate for ovarian cancer; doses up to 90-270 mg/m^2 have been administered and retained for 4 hours before draining

Testicular cancer: 10-20 mg/m^2/day for 5 days repeated every 3-4 weeks

Dosing adjustment in renal impairment: Note: The manufacturer(s) recommend that repeat courses of cisplatin should not be given until serum creatinine is <1.5 mg/dL and/or BUN is <25 mg/dL. The FDA-approved labeling does not contain renal dosing adjustment guidelines. The following guidelines have been used by some clinicians:

Aronoff, 2007:

Cl$_{cr}$ 10-50 mL/minute: Administer 75% of dose

Cl$_{cr}$ <10 mL/minute: Administer 50% of dose

Hemodialysis: Partially cleared by hemodialysis

Administer 50% of dose posthemodialysis

Continuous ambulatory peritoneal dialysis (CAPD): Administer 50% of dose

Continuous renal replacement therapy (CRRT): Administer 75% of dose

Kintzel, 1995:

Cl$_{cr}$ 46-60 mL/minute: Administer 75% of dose

Cl$_{cr}$ 31-45 mL/minute: Administer 50% of dose

Cl$_{cr}$ <30 mL/minute: Consider use of alternative drug

Combination Regimens

Adenocarcinoma, unknown primary: EP (Adenocarcinoma) *on page 1203*

Bladder cancer:

CAP *on page 1158*

CISCA *on page 1175*

Cisplatin-Docetaxel *on page 1176*

CMV *on page 1179*

Gemcitabine-Cisplatin (Bladder Cancer) *on page 1226*

M-VAC (Bladder Cancer) *on page 1255*

Brain tumors:

8 in 1 (Brain Tumors) *on page 1141*

CDDP/VP-16 *on page 1165*

COPE *on page 1182*

Breast Cancer:

Docetaxel-Trastuzumab-Cisplatin *on page 1193*

M-VAC (Breast Cancer) *on page 1258*

Cervical cancer:

BIP *on page 1152*

Cisplatin-Fluorouracil *on page 1176*

Cisplatin-Vinorelbine *on page 1177*

M-VAC (Cervical Cancer) *on page 1259*

(Continued)

Cisplatin *(Continued)*

Administration Pretreatment hydration with 1-2 L of fluid is recommended prior to cisplatin administration; adequate hydration and urinary output (>100 mL/hour) should be maintained for 24 hours after administration.

I.V.: Rate of administration has varied from a 15- to 120-minute infusion, 1 mg/minute infusion, 6- to 8-hour infusion, 24-hour infusion, or per protocol; maximum rate of infusion of 1 mg/minute in patients with CHF.

Monitoring Parameters Renal function (serum creatinine, BUN, Cl_{cr}); electrolytes (particularly magnesium, calcium, potassium) before and within 48 hours after cisplatin therapy; audiography (baseline and prior to each subsequent dose), neurologic exam (with high dose); liver function tests periodically, CBC with differential and platelet count; urine output, urinalysis

Dietary Considerations Sodium content: 9 mg/mL (equivalent to 0.9% sodium chloride solution)

Patient Information This drug is usually given I.V. and numerous adverse side effects can occur. Maintaining adequate hydration is extremely important to help avoid kidney damage (2-3 L/day of fluids unless instructed to restrict fluid intake). Nausea and vomiting can be severe and can be delayed for up to 48 hours after infusion and last for 1 week; consult prescriber immediately for appropriate antiemetic medication. May cause hair loss (reversible). You will be susceptible to infection; avoid crowds or infectious situations (do not have any vaccinations without consulting prescriber). Report all unusual symptoms promptly to prescriber. Contraceptive measures are recommended during therapy.

Emetic Potential High (>90%)

Vesicant No

(Continued)

Cisplatin *(Continued)*

High Dose Considerations

High Dose: Continuous I.V.: 55 mg/m^2/24 hours for 72 hours; total dose: 165 mg/m^2; generally combined with other high-dose chemotherapy

Unique Toxicities:

Central nervous system: Autonomic neuropathy, ototoxicity

Gastrointestinal: Highly emetogenic

Hematologic: Myelosuppression

Endocrine & metabolic: Hypokalemia, hypomagnesemia

Neuromuscular & skeletal: Peripheral neuropathy

Ocular: Optic neuropathy, retinal vascular occlusion and myelopathy (concurrent administration of high-dose carmustine)

Renal: Acute renal failure, serum creatinine increased, azotemia

Miscellaneous: Transient pain at tumor, transient autoimmune disorders

Dosage Forms Excipient information presented when available (limited, particularly for generics); consult specific product labeling.

Injection, solution [preservative free]: 1 mg/mL (50 mL, 100 mL, 200 mL)

References

Aronoff GR, Bennett WM, Berns JS, et al, *Drug Prescribing in Renal Failure: Dosing Guidelines for Adults and Children*, 5th ed. Philadelphia, PA: American College of Physicians; 2007, p 97, 170.

Bowman A, et al, 'Effect of Adding Glutathione to Cisplatin in the Treatment of Stage I-IV Ovarian Cancer," *Br J Cancer*, 1995, 71(Suppl XXIV):14

Costello MA, Dominick C, and Clerico A, "A Pilot Study of 5-Day Continuous Infusion of High-Dose Cisplatin and Pulsed Etoposide in Childhood Solid Tumors," *Am J Pediatr Hematol Oncol*, 1988, 10:103-8.

el Weshi A, Thieblemont C, Cottin V, et al, "Cisplatin-Induced Hyponatremia and Renal Sodium Wasting," *Acta Oncol*, 1995, 34(2):264-5.

Farris FF, Dedrick RL, and King FG, "Cisplatin Pharmacokinetics: Applications of a Physiological Model," *Toxicol Lett*, 1988, 43(1-3):117-37.

Go RS and Adjei AA, "Review of the Comparative Pharmacology and Clinical Activity of Cisplatin and Carboplatin," *J Clin Oncol*, 1999, 17(1):409-22.

Haupt R, Perin G, Dallorso S, et al, "Very High-Dose Cis-Platinum (450 mg/sq m) in an Infant With Rhabdomyosarcoma," *Anticancer Res*, 1989, 9(2):427-8.

Hebert ME, Blivin JL, Kessler J, et al, "Anaphylactoid Reactions With Intraperitoneal Cisplatin," *Ann Pharmacother*, 1995, 29(3):260-3.

Higa GM, Wise TC, and Crowell EB, "Severe, Disabling Neurologic Toxicity Following Cisplatin Retreatment," *Ann Pharmacother*, 1995, 29(2):134-7.

Howell SB, Pfeifle CL, Wung WE, et al, "Intraperitoneal Cisplatin With Systemic Thiosulfate Protection," *Ann Intern Med*, 1982, 97(6):845-51.

Kintzel PE and Dorr RT, "Anticancer Drug Renal Toxicity and Elimination: Dosing Guidelines for Altered Renal Function," *Cancer Treat Rev*, 1995, 21(1):33-64.

Loehrer PJ and Einhorn LH, "Drugs Five Years Later. Cisplatin," *Ann Intern Med*, 1984, 100(5):704-13.

Long DF and Repta AJ, "Cisplatin: Chemistry, Distribution and Biotransformation," *Biopharm Drug Dispos*, 1981, 2(1):1-16.

Prestayko AW, D'Aoust JC, Isell BF, et al, "Cisplatin (cis-diamminedichloroplatinum II)," *Cancer Treat Rev*, 1979, 6(1):17-39.

Reece PA, Stafford I, Abbott RL, et al, "Two- Hour 24-Hour Infusion of Cisplatin: Pharmacokinetic Considerations," *J Clin Oncol*, 1989, 7(2):270-5.

Reed E, "Cisplatin," *Cancer Chemother Biol Response Modif*, 1999, 18:144-51.

Rothmann SA and Weick JK, "Cisplatin Toxicity for Erythroid Precursors," *N Engl J Med*, 1981, 304(6):360.

Schilsky RL and Anderson T, "Hypomagnesemia and Renal Magnesium Wasting in Patients Receiving Cisplatin," *Ann Intern Med*, 1979, 90(6):929-31.

Schuchter LM, Hensley ML, Meropol NJ, et al, "2002 Update of Recommendations for the Use of Chemotherapy and Radiotherapy Protectants: Clinical Practice Guidelines of the American Society of Clinical Oncology," *J Clin Oncol*, 2002, 20(12):2895-903.

Shlebak AA, Clark PI, and Green JA, "Hypersensitivity and Cross-Reactivity to Cisplatin and Analogues," *Cancer Chemother Pharmacol*, 1995, 35(4):349-51.

Siddik ZH, "Cisplatin: Mode of Cytotoxic Action and Molecular Basis of Resistance," *Oncogene*, 2003, 22(47):7265-79.

Sleijfer DT, Meijer S, and Mulder NH, "Cisplatin: A Review of Clinical Applications and Renal Toxicity," *Pharm Weekbl Sci*, 1985, 7(6):237-44.

♦ **Citrovorum Factor** *see* Leucovorin Calcium *on page 668*

♦ **CL-118,532** *see* Triptorelin *on page 1077*

♦ **CL-184116** *see* Porfimer *on page 908*

Cladribine (KLA dri been)
Medication Safety Issues
Sound-alike/look-alike issues:
Cladribine may be confused with clofarabine
Leustatin® may be confused with lovastatin

High alert medication: The Institute for Safe Medication Practices (ISMP) includes this medication among its list of drugs which have a heightened risk of causing significant patient harm when used in error.
Related Information
Safe Handling of Hazardous Drugs *on page 1382*
U.S. Brand Names Leustatin®
Index Terms 2-CdA; 2-Chlorodeoxyadenosine; NSC-105014
Generic Available Yes
Canadian Brand Names Leustatin®
Pharmacologic Category Antineoplastic Agent, Antimetabolite; Antineoplastic Agent, Antimetabolite (Purine Antagonist)
Use Treatment of hairy cell leukemia
Unlabeled/Investigational Use Treatment of chronic lymphocytic leukemia (CLL), chronic myelogenous leukemia (CML), non-Hodgkin's lymphomas, progressive multiple sclerosis
Pregnancy Risk Factor D
Lactation Excretion in breast milk unknown/not recommended
Labeled Contraindications Hypersensitivity to cladribine or any component of the formulation
Warnings/Precautions Hazardous agent - use appropriate precautions for handling and disposal. **[U.S. Boxed Warnings]: Dose-dependent, reversible myelosuppression will occur; use with caution in patients with pre-existing hematologic or immunologic abnormalities. Neurologic toxicity has been reported, usually with higher doses, but may occur at normal doses. Acute renal toxicity has been reported with high doses; use caution when administering with other nephrotoxic agents.** Use caution with renal and hepatic impairment. Fever may occur, with or without neutropenia. Use caution in patients with high tumor burden; tumor lysis syndrome may occur. **[U.S. Boxed Warning]: Should be administered under the supervision of an experienced cancer chemotherapy physician.** Safety and efficacy in children have not been established.
Adverse Reactions
>10%:
Central nervous system: Fever (69%; ≥104°F: 11%), fatigue (11% to 45%), headache (7% to 22%)
Dermatologic: Rash (10% to 27%)
Gastrointestinal: Nausea (28%), appetite decreased (17%), vomiting (13%)
Hematologic: Myelosuppression, common, dose limiting (nadir: 5-10 days, recovery: 4-8 weeks); neutropenia (70%); anemia (37%); thrombocytopenia (12%)
Local: Injection site reactions (9% to 19%)
Respiratory: Abnormal breath sounds (11%)
(Continued)

Cladribine *(Continued)*

Miscellaneous: Infection (28%)

1% to 10%:

Cardiovascular: Edema (6%), tachycardia (6%), thrombosis (2%)

Central nervous system: Dizziness (9%), chills (9%), insomnia (7%), malaise (5% to 7%), pain (6%)

Dermatologic: Purpura (10%), petechiae (8%), pruritus (6%), erythema (6%)

Gastrointestinal: Diarrhea (10%), constipation (9%), abdominal pain (6%)

Local: Phlebitis (2%)

Neuromuscular & skeletal: Weakness (9%), myalgia (7%), arthralgia (5%)

Respiratory: Cough (7% to 10%), abnormal chest sounds (9%), dyspnea (7%), epistaxis (5%)

Miscellaneous: Diaphoresis (9%)

<1%, postmarketing and/or case reports: Aplastic anemia, bilirubin increased, hemolytic anemia, hypereosinophilia, myelodysplastic syndrome, neurologic toxicity, opportunistic infections, pancytopenia, paraparesis, pneumonia, polyneuropathy (with high doses), pulmonary interstitial infiltrates, quadriplegia (reported at high doses); renal dysfunction (with high doses), Stevens-Johnson syndrome, toxic epidermal necrolysis, transaminases increased, tumor lysis syndrome, urticaria

Overdosage/Toxicology High doses are associated with irreversible neurologic toxicity, nephrotoxicity, and severe bone marrow suppression. Treatment is symptom-directed and supportive.

Ethanol/Nutrition/Herb Interactions Ethanol: Avoid ethanol (due to GI irritation).

Storage/Stability Store intact vials under refrigeration 2°C to 8°C (36°F to 46°F). Protect from light. Dilutions in 500 mL NS are stable for 72 hours. Stable in PVC containers for 24 hours at room temperature of 15°C to 30°C (59°F to 86°F) and 7 days in Pharmacia Deltec® cassettes.

Reconstitution Dilute in 500 mL; dilute to a total volume of 100 mL for 7-day infusion. Solutions for 7-day infusion should be prepared in bacteriostatic NS; the manufacturer recommends filtering with a 0.22 micron filter when preparing 7-day infusions.

Compatibility Stable in NS; **incompatible** with D_5W.

Y-site administration: **Compatible:** Aminophylline, bumetanide, buprenorphine, butorphanol, calcium gluconate, carboplatin, chlorpromazine, cimetidine, cisplatin, cyclophosphamide, cytarabine, dexamethasone sodium phosphate, diphenhydramine, dobutamine, dopamine, doxorubicin, droperidol, enalaprilat, etoposide, famotidine, furosemide, granisetron, haloperidol, heparin, hydrocortisone sodium phosphate, hydrocortisone sodium succinate, hydromorphone, hydroxyzine, idarubicin, leucovorin, lorazepam, mannitol, meperidine, mesna, methylprednisolone sodium succinate, metoclopramide, mitoxantrone, morphine, nalbuphine, ondansetron, paclitaxel, potassium chloride, prochlorperazine edisylate, promethazine, ranitidine, sodium bicarbonate, teniposide, vincristine.

Mechanism of Action A purine nucleoside analogue; prodrug which is activated via phosphorylation by deoxycytidine kinase to a 5'-triphosphate derivative. This active form incorporates into DNA to result in the breakage of DNA strand and shutdown of DNA synthesis. This also results in a depletion of nicotinamide adenine dinucleotide and adenosine triphosphate (ATP). Cladribine is cell-cycle nonspecific.

Pharmacodynamics/Kinetics

Absorption: Oral: 55%; SubQ: 100%; Rectal: 20%

Distribution: V_d: 4.52 ± 2.82 L/kg

Protein binding: 20%

Metabolism: Hepatic; 5'-triphosphate moiety-active

Half-life elimination: Biphasic: Alpha: 25 minutes; Beta: 6.7 hours; Terminal, mean: Normal renal function: 5.4 hours

Excretion: Urine (18% to 44%)

Clearance: Estimated systemic: 640 mL/hour/kg

Dosage I.V.: Refer to individual protocols.

Children (unlabeled use): Acute leukemias: 6.2-7.5 mg/m^2/day continuous infusion for days 1-5; maximum tolerated dose was 8.9 mg/m^2/day.

Adults:

Hairy cell leukemia: Continuous infusion:

0.09 mg/kg/day days 1-7; may be repeated every 28-35 days **or**

3.4 mg/m^2/day SubQ days 1-7 (unlabeled dose)

Chronic lymphocytic leukemia (unlabeled use): Continuous infusion:

0.1 mg/kg/day days 1-7 **or**

0.028-0.14 mg/kg/day as a 2-hour infusion days 1-5

Chronic myelogenous leukemia (unlabeled use): 15 mg/m^2/day as a 1-hour infusion days 1-5; if no response, increase dose to 20 mg/m^2/day in the second course.

Dosing adjustment in renal impairment: The FDA-approved labeling recommends that caution should be used in patients with renal impairment; however, no specific dosage adjustment guidelines are available due to lack of data. The following guidelines have been used by some clinicians (Aronoff, 2007):

Children:

Cl_{cr} 10-50 mL/minute: Administer 50% of dose

Cl_{cr} <10 mL/minute: Administer 30% of dose

Hemodialysis: Administer 30% of dose

Continuous renal replacement therapy (CRRT): Administer 50% of dose

Adults:

Cl_{cr} 10-50 mL/minute: Administer 75% of dose

Cl_{cr} <10 mL/minute: Administer 50% of dose

Continuous ambulatory peritoneal dialysis (CAPD): Administer 50% of dose

Dosing adjustment in hepatic impairment: The FDA-approved labeling recommends that caution should be used in patients with hepatic impairment; however, no specific dosage adjustment guidelines are available due to lack of data.

Administration I.V.: Administer as a 1- to 2-hour infusion or by continuous infusion

Monitoring Parameters CBC with differential, renal and hepatic function; monitor for fever

Periodic assessment of peripheral blood counts, particularly during the first 4-8 weeks post-treatment, is recommended to detect the development of anemia, neutropenia, and thrombocytopenia and for early detection of any potential sequelae (eg, infection or bleeding)

Emetic Potential Very low (<10%)

Vesicant No

Dosage Forms Excipient information presented when available (limited, particularly for generics); consult specific product labeling.

Injection, solution [preservative free]: 1 mg/mL (10 mL)

References

Aronoff GR, Bennett WM, Berns JS, et al, *Drug Prescribing in Renal Failure: Dosing Guidelines for Adults and Children*, 5th ed. Philadelphia, PA: American College of Physicians; 2007, p 98, 170.

(Continued)

Cladribine *(Continued)*

Baltz JK and Montello MJ, "Cladribine for the Treatment of Hematologic Malignancies," *Clin Pharm*, 1993, 12(11):805-13.

Beutler E, "Cladribine (2-Chlorodeoxyadenosine)," *Lancet*, 1992, 340(8825):952-6.

Kearns CM, Biakley RL, Santane VM, et al, "Pharmacokinetics of Cladribine (2-Chlorodioxyadenosine) in Children With Acute Leukemia," *Cancer Res*, 1994, 54:1235-39.

Larson RA, Mick R, Spielberger RT, et al, "Dose Escalation Trial of Cladribine Using 5 Daily I.V. Infusions in Patients With Advanced Hematologic Malignancies," *J Clin Oncol*, 1996, 14(1):188-95.

Liliemark J, "The Clinical Pharmacokinetics of Cladribine," *Clin Pharmacokinet*, 1997, 32(2):120-31.

Piro LD, "2-Chlorodeoxyadenosine Treatment of Lymphoid Malignancies," *Blood*, 1992, 79(4):843-5.

Robak T, "Cladribine in the Treatment of Chronic Lymphocytic Leukemia," *Leuk Lymphoma*, 2001, 40(5-6):551-64.

Saven A and Piro LD, "2-Chlorodeoxyadenosine: A Potent Antimetabolite With Major Activity in the Treatment of Indolent Lymphoproliferative Disorders," *Hematol Cell Ther*, 1996, 38(Suppl 2):93-101.

Stine KC, Saylors RL, Williams LL, et al, "2-Chlorodeoxyadenosine (2-CDA) for the Treatment of Refractory or Recurrent Langerhans Cell Histiocytosis (LCH) in Pediatric Patients," *Med Pediatr Oncol*, 1997, 29:288-92.

Tallman MS and Hakimian D, "Current Results and Prospective Trials of Cladribine in Chronic Lymphocytic Leukemia," *Semin Hematol*, 1996, 33(Suppl 1):23-7.

Tortorella C, Rovaris M, and Filippi M, "Cladribine. Ortho Biotech Inc," *Curr Opin Investig Drugs*, 2001, 2(12):1751-6.

♦ **Clasteon®** **(Can)** see Clodronate on page 234

Clodronate *(KLOE droh nate)*

Index Terms Clodronate Disodium

Canadian Brand Names Bonefos®; Clasteon®

Pharmacologic Category Bisphosphonate Derivative

Use Management of hypercalcemia of malignancy

Restrictions Not available in U.S.

Pregnancy Risk Factor Not assigned; similar agents rated X

Lactation Excretion in breast milk unknown/contraindicated

Labeled Contraindications Hypersensitivity to clodronate, bisphosphonates, or any component of the formulation; severe GI inflammation; renal impairment (serum creatinine >5 mg/dL, SI 440 µmol/L); pregnancy or breast-feeding

Warnings/Precautions Use caution in patients with renal impairment. May cause irritation to upper gastrointestinal mucosa. Esophagitis, esophageal ulcers, esophageal erosions, and esophageal stricture (rare) have been reported with bisphosphonates (oral). Use with caution in patients with dysphagia, esophageal disease, gastritis, duodenitis, or ulcers (may worsen underlying condition).

Bisphosphonate therapy has been associated with osteonecrosis, primarily of the jaw; this has been observed mostly in cancer patients, but also in patients with postmenopausal osteoporosis and other diagnoses. Dental exams and preventative dentistry should be performed prior to placing patients with risk factors on chronic bisphosphonate therapy. Invasive dental procedures should be avoided during treatment.

Infrequently, severe (and occasionally debilitating) bone, joint, and/or muscle pain have been reported during bisphosphonate treatment. The onset of pain ranged from a single day to several months. Symptoms usually resolve upon discontinuation. Some patients experienced recurrence when rechallenged with same drug or another bisphosphonate; avoid use in patients with a history of these symptoms in association with bisphosphonate therapy.

For I.V. preparation: Dilute prior to use; adequate hydration should be ensured prior to infusion; avoid infiltration/extravasation. May cause venous irritation, hypocalcemia, or transient hypophosphatemia. Do not administer as bolus injection.

Adverse Reactions

1% to 10%:

Endocrine & metabolic: Hypocalcemia (2%)

Gastrointestinal: Incidence highest with oral administration: Vomiting (4%), nausea (3%), diarrhea (2%), anorexia (1%)

Renal: Serum creatinine increased (1%), BUN increased

<1%: Bronchospasm, hypersensitivity reactions (angioedema, pruritus, rash, urticaria), oliguria, proteinuria, transaminases increased

Postmarketing and/or case reports: Osteonecrosis

Overdosage/Toxicology Symptoms of overdose include hypocalcemia, ECG changes, seizures, bleeding, paresthesia, carpopedal spasm, and fever. Treat with I.V. calcium gluconate, and general supportive care; fever and hypotension can be treated with corticosteroids.

Drug Interactions

Increased Effect/Toxicity: Aminoglycosides may lower serum calcium levels with prolonged administration; concomitant use may have an additive hypocalcemic effect. NSAIDs may enhance the gastrointestinal adverse/toxic effects (increased incidence of GI ulcers) of bisphosphonate derivatives. Bisphosphonate derivatives may enhance the hypocalcemic effect of phosphate supplements.

Decreased Effect: The following agents may decrease the absorption of oral bisphosphonate derivatives: Antacids (aluminum, calcium, magnesium), oral calcium salts, oral iron salts, and oral magnesium salts.

Ethanol/Nutrition/Herb Interactions Food: All food and beverages may interfere with absorption. Coadministration with dairy products may decrease absorption. Beverages (especially orange juice and coffee), food, and medications (eg, antacids, calcium, iron, and multivalent cations) may reduce the absorption of bisphosphonates as much as 60%.

Storage/Stability Store capsules and undiluted ampuls at room temperature (15°C to 30°C). Diluted injection solution should be infused within 12 hours of preparation.

Reconstitution Injection must be diluted (in 500 mL of NS or D_5W).

Compatibility Stable in D_5W or 0.9% NS.

Mechanism of Action A bisphosphonate which inhibits bone resorption via actions on osteoclasts or on osteoclast precursors.

Pharmacodynamics/Kinetics

Onset of effect: 24-48 hours

Peak effect: 5-7 days

Duration: 2-3 weeks

Distribution: V_d: 20 L

Bioavailability: Oral: 1% to 3%

Half-life (terminal): 13 hours (serum); prolonged in bone tissue

Elimination: Urine (as unchanged drug)

Dosage

I.V.:

Multiple infusions: 300 mg/day; should not be prolonged beyond 10 days.

Single infusion: 1500 mg as a single dose

Oral: Recommended daily maintenance dose following I.V. therapy: Range: 1600 mg (4 capsules) to 2400 mg (6 capsules) given in single or 2 divided doses; maximum recommended daily dose: 3200 mg (8 capsules). Should (Continued)

Clodronate *(Continued)*

be taken at least 1 hour before or after food, because food may decrease the amount of clodronate absorbed by the body.

Dosage adjustment in renal impairment:

S_{cr} >5 mg/dL: Use is contraindicated

S_{cr} ≥2.5-5 mg/dL: Dosage reduction is recommended; no specific guidelines available

Administration

Capsules: Administer with copious fluids (not milk).

Injection: Do not administer as bolus injection; infuse over 2-6 hours.

Monitoring Parameters Serum electrolytes, monitor for hypocalcemia for at least 2 weeks after therapy; serum calcium, phosphate, magnesium, potassium, serum creatinine, CBC with differential, hepatic function

Test Interactions Bisphosphonates may interfere with diagnostic imaging agents such as technetium-99m-diphosphonate in bone scans.

Patient Information Take as directed, with a full glass of water first thing in the morning and at least 30 minutes before the first food or beverage of the day. Wait at least 30 minutes after taking clodronate before taking any supplement. Avoid NSAIDs, aspirin or aspirin-containing medications. You may experience GI upset (eg, flatulence, bloating, nausea, acid regurgitation); small, frequent meals may help. Report acute headache or gastric pain, unresolved GI upset, or acid stomach.

Additional Information Not available in U.S.

Dosage Forms Excipient information presented when available (limited, particularly for generics); consult specific product labeling. [CAN] = Canadian brand name

Injection:

Bonefos® [CAN]: 30 mg/mL (10 mL); 60 mg/mL (5 mL) [not available in the U.S.]

Capsule:

Bonefos® [CAN]: 400 mg [not available in the U.S.]

References
American Dental Association Council on Scientific Affairs, "Dental Management of Patients Receiving Oral Bisphosphonate Therapy," *JADA*, 2006, 137(8):1144-50. Available at http://www.ada.org/prof/resources/pubs/jada/reports/report bisphosphonate.pdf

Durie BG, Katz M, and Crowley J, "Osteonecrosis of the Jaw and Bisphosphonates," *N Engl J Med*, 2005, 353(1):99-102.

Maerevoet M, Martin C, and Duck L, "Osteonecrosis of the Jaw and Bisphosphonates," *N Engl J Med*, 2005, 353(1):99-102.

McMahon RE, Bouquot JE, Glueck CJ, et al, "Osteonecrosis: A Multifactorial Etiology," *J Oral Maxillofac Surg*, 2004, 62(7):904-5.

Ruggiero S, Gralow J, Marx RE, et al, "Practical Guidelines for the Prevention, Diagnosis, and Treatment of Osteonecrosis of the Jaw in Patients With Cancer," *J Clin Oncol*, 2006, 2(1):7-14.

Tarassoff P and Csermak K, "Avascular Necrosis of the Jaws: Risk Factors in Metastatic Cancer Patients," *J Oral Maxillofac Surg*, 2003, 61(10):1238-9.

♦ **Clodronate Disodium** *see* Clodronate *on page 234*

Clofarabine *(klo FARE a been)*

Medication Safety Issues

High alert medication: The Institute for Safe Medication Practices (ISMP) includes this medication among its list of drugs which have a heightened risk of causing significant patient harm when used in error.

Related Information

Safe Handling of Hazardous Drugs *on page 1382*

U.S. Brand Names Clolar™

Index Terms Clofarex; NSC606869

Generic Available No

Pharmacologic Category Antineoplastic Agent, Antimetabolite (Purine Antagonist)

Use Treatment of relapsed or refractory acute lymphoblastic leukemia

Unlabeled/Investigational Use Adults: Relapsed and refractory acute myeloid leukemia (AML), chronic myeloid leukemia (CML) in blast phase, acute lymphocytic leukemia (ALL), myelodysplastic syndrome

Pregnancy Risk Factor D

Lactation Excretion in breast milk unknown/not recommended

Labeled Contraindications Hypersensitivity to clofarabine or any component of the formulation

Warnings/Precautions Hazardous agent - use appropriate precautions for handling and disposal. Tumor lysis syndrome and cytokine release may develop into systemic inflammatory response syndrome (SIRS)/capillary leak syndrome, and organ dysfunction; discontinuation of clofarabine should be considered with the presentation of SIRS or capillary leak syndrome (see Tumor Lysis Syndrome) *on page 1340*. Safety and efficacy have not been established with renal or hepatic dysfunction; use with caution. Safety and efficacy in pediatric patients <1 year of age or adults >21 years have not been established.

Adverse Reactions

>10%:

Cardiovascular: Pericardial effusion (35%), tachycardia (34%), hypotension (29%), left ventricular systolic dysfunction (27%), edema (20%), flushing (18%), hypertension (11%)

Central nervous system: Headache (46%), pyrexia (41%), fatigue (36%), anxiety (22%), pain (19%), dizziness (16%), depression (11%), irritability (11%), lethargy (1%)

Dermatologic: Pruritus (47%), dermatitis (41%), petechiae (29%), erythema (18%), palmar-plantar erythrodysesthesia syndrome (13%), oral candidiasis (13%), cellulitis (11%)

Gastrointestinal: Vomiting (83%), nausea (75%), diarrhea (53%), abdominal pain (36%), anorexia (30%), constipation (21%), mucosal inflammation (18%), gingival bleeding (15%), sore throat (14%), appetite decreased (11%)

Genitourinary: Hematuria (17%)

Hematologic: Febrile neutropenia (57%)

Hepatic: ALT increased (44%), AST increased (38%), bilirubin increased (15%), hepatomegaly (15%), jaundice (15%)

Neuromuscular & skeletal: Rigors (38%), pain in limb (29%), myalgia (14%), back pain (13%), arthralgia (11%)

Respiratory: Epistaxis (31%), cough (19%), respiratory distress (14%), dyspnea (13%)

Miscellaneous: Infection (85%), injection site pain (14%), staphylococcal infection (13%), herpes simplex (11%)

1% to 10%:

Central nervous system: Somnolence (10%)

Gastrointestinal: Weight gain (10%)

Genitourinary: Creatinine increased (6%)

Neuromuscular & skeletal: Tremor (10%)

Respiratory: Pleural effusion (10%), pneumonia (10%), systemic inflammatory response syndrome (SIRS)/capillary leak syndrome

Miscellaneous: Transfusion reaction (10%), bacteremia (10%)

(Continued)

Clofarabine *(Continued)*

Overdosage/Toxicology No known overdoses have been reported; treatment should be symptom-directed and supportive.

Drug Interactions

Increased Effect/Toxicity: None known

Decreased Effect: None known

Storage/Stability Store undiluted and diluted solutions at room temperature of 15°C to 30°C (59°F to 86°F). Solutions diluted in 100-500 mL of D_5W or NS are stable for 24 hours at room temperature.

Reconstitution Clofarabine should be diluted with 100-500 mL NS or D_5W; manufacturer recommends the product be filtered through a 0.2 micrometer filter before dilution.

Compatibility Stable in D_5W or NS.

Mechanism of Action Clofarabine, a purine (deoxyadenosine) nucleoside analog, is metabolized to clofarabine 5'-triphosphate. Clofarabine 5'-triphosphate decreases cell replication and repair as well as causing cell death. To decrease cell replication and repair, clofarabine 5'-triphosphate competes with deoxyadenosine triphosphate for the enzymes ribonucleotide reductase and DNA polymerase. Cell replication is decreased when clofarabine 5'-triphosphate inhibits ribonucleotide reductase from reacting with deoxyadenosine triphosphate to produce deoxynucleotide triphosphate which is needed for DNA synthesis. Cell replication is also decreased when clofarabine 5'-triphosphate competes with DNA polymerase for incorporation into the DNA chain; when done during the repair process, cell repair is affected. To cause cell death, clofarabine 5'-triphosphate alters the mitochondrial membrane by releasing proteins, an inducing factor and cytochrome C.

Pharmacodynamics/Kinetics

Distribution: V_d: 172 L/m^2

Protein binding: 47%

Metabolism: Intracellulary by deoxycytidine kinase and mono- and diphosphokinases to active metabolite clofarabine 5'-triphosphate

Half-life elimination: ~5.2 hours

Excretion: Urine (49% to 60% unchanged)

Dosage I.V.: Children and Adults 1-21 years: ALL: 52 mg/m^2/day days 1 through 5; repeat every 2-6 weeks

Dosage adjustment in renal/hepatic impairment: Safety not established; use with caution

Administration I.V. infusion: Over 2 hours. Continuous I.V. fluids are encouraged to decrease adverse events and tumor lysis effects. Hypotension may be a sign of capillary leak syndrome or systemic inflammatory response syndrome (SIRS). Discontinue if the patient becomes hypotensive during administration. Retreatment should only be considered if the hypotension is not related to capillary leak syndrome or SIRS.

Monitoring Parameters Blood pressure, cardiac function, and respiratory status during infusion; periodic CBC with platelet count (increase frequency in patients who develop cytopenias); liver and kidney function during 5 days of clofarabine administration; signs and symptoms of tumor lysis syndrome and cytokine release syndrome (tachypnea, tachycardia, hypotension, pulmonary edema); hydration status

Additional Information The use of prophylactic steroids (hydrocortisone 100 mg/m^2 on days 1-3) may be of benefit in preventing signs of SIRS or capillary leak syndrome; allopurinol may be used if hyperuricemia is anticipated. Dosage should be based on BSA, calculated based upon height and weight prior to each cycle.

Emetic Potential High (60% to 90%)

Vesicant No

Dosage Forms Excipient information presented when available (limited, particularly for generics); consult specific product labeling.

Injection, solution [preservative free]: 1 mg/mL (20 mL)

References

"Clofarabine," *Drugs R D*, 2004, 5(4):213-7.

Faderl S, Gandhi V, Giles F, et al, "Clofarabine Plus Cytarabine (ara-C) Is an Active Induction Regimen for Newly Diagnosed Patients (pts) Age ≥50 With Acute Myeloid Leukemia (AML) and High-Risk Myelodysplastic Syndrome (MDS)" (abstract 6609). Presented at the ASCO Annual Meeting; June 5-8, 2004; New Orleans, LA, USA.

Kantarjian H, Gandhi V, Cortes J, et al, "Phase 2 Clinical and Pharmacologic Study of Clofarabine in Patients With Refractory or Relapsed Acute Leukemia," *Blood*, 2003, 102(7):2379-86.

Sternberg A, "Clofarabine. Bioenvision/ILEX," *Curr Opin Investig Drugs*, 2003, 4(12):1479-87.

♦ **Clofarex** *see* Clofarabine *on page 236*

♦ **Clolar**™ *see* Clofarabine *on page 236*

♦ **Clotrimaderm (Can)** *see* Clotrimazole *on page 239*

Clotrimazole (kloe TRIM a zole)

Medication Safety Issues

Sound-alike/look-alike issues:

Clotrimazole may be confused with co-trimoxazole

Lotrimin® may be confused with Lotrisone®, Otrivin®

Mycelex® may be confused with Myoflex®

International issues:

Cloderm®: Brand name for clocortolone in the United States

Canesten® [multiple international markets] may be confused with Cenestin® which is a brand name for estrogens (conjugated a/synthetic) in the U.S.

Canesten® [multiple international markets]: Brand name for fluconazole in Great Britain

Mycelex® may be confused with Mucolex® which is a brand name for carbocysteine in Ireland, Portugal, and Thailand; a brand name for guaifenesin in Hong Kong

U.S. Brand Names Cruex® Cream [OTC]; Gyne-Lotrimin® 3 [OTC]; Gyne-Lotrimin® 7 [OTC]; Lotrimin® AF Athlete's Foot Cream [OTC]; Lotrimin® AF for Her [OTC]; Lotrimin® AF Jock Itch Cream [OTC]; Mycelex®

Generic Available Yes: Cream, solution, troche

Canadian Brand Names Canesten® Topical; Canesten® Vaginal; Clotrimaderm; Trivagizole-3®

Pharmacologic Category Antifungal Agent, Oral Nonabsorbed; Antifungal Agent, Topical; Antifungal Agent, Vaginal

Use Treatment of susceptible fungal infections, including oropharyngeal candidiasis, dermatophytoses, superficial mycoses, and cutaneous candidiasis, as well as vulvovaginal candidiasis; limited data suggest that clotrimazole troches may be effective for prophylaxis against oropharyngeal candidiasis in neutropenic patients

Pregnancy Risk Factor B (topical); C (troches)

Lactation Excretion in breast milk unknown

Labeled Contraindications Hypersensitivity to clotrimazole or any component of the formulation

(Continued)

Clotrimazole *(Continued)*

Warnings/Precautions Clotrimazole should not be used for treatment of ocular or systemic fungal infection. Use with caution with hepatic impairment. Safety and effectiveness of clotrimazole lozenges (troches) in children <3 years of age have not been established. When using topical formulation, avoid contact with eyes.

Adverse Reactions

Oral:

>10%: Hepatic: Abnormal liver function tests

1% to 10%:

Gastrointestinal: Nausea and vomiting may occur in patients on clotrimazole troches

Local: Mild burning, irritation, stinging to skin or vaginal area

Vaginal:

1% to 10%: Genitourinary: Vulvar/vaginal burning

<1% (Limited to important or life-threatening): Vulvar itching, soreness, edema, or discharge; polyuria; burning or itching of penis of sexual partner

Drug Interactions

Cytochrome P450 Effect: Inhibits CYP1A2 (weak), 2A6 (weak), 2B6 (weak), 2C8 (weak), 2C9 (weak), 2C19 (weak), 2D6 (weak), 2E1 (weak), 3A4 (moderate)

Increased Effect/Toxicity: Clotrimazole may increase the levels/effects of selected benzodiazepines, calcium channel blockers, cisapride, cyclosporine, ergot derivatives, selected HMG-CoA reductase inhibitors, mesoridazine, mirtazapine, nateglinide, nefazodone, pimozide, quinidine, sildenafil (and other PDE-5 inhibitors), tacrolimus, thioridazine, venlafaxine, and other CYP3A4 substrates.

Mechanism of Action Binds to phospholipids in the fungal cell membrane altering cell wall permeability resulting in loss of essential intracellular elements

Pharmacodynamics/Kinetics

Absorption: Topical: Negligible through intact skin

Time to peak, serum:

Oral topical (troche): Salivary levels occur within 3 hours following 30 minutes of dissolution time

Vaginal cream: High vaginal levels: 8-24 hours

Vaginal tablet: High vaginal levels: 1-2 days

Excretion: Feces (as metabolites)

Dosage

Children >3 years and Adults:

Oral:

Prophylaxis: 10 mg troche dissolved 3 times/day for the duration of chemotherapy or until steroids are reduced to maintenance levels

Treatment: 10 mg troche dissolved slowly 5 times/day for 14 consecutive days

Topical (cream, solution): Apply twice daily; if no improvement occurs after 4 weeks of therapy, re-evaluate diagnosis

Children >12 years and Adults:

Vaginal:

Cream:

1%: Insert 1 applicatorful vaginal cream daily (preferably at bedtime) for 7 consecutive days

2%: Insert 1 applicatorful vaginal cream daily (preferably at bedtime) for 3 consecutive days

Tablet: Insert 100 mg/day for 7 days or 500 mg single dose

Topical (cream, solution): Apply to affected area twice daily (morning and evening) for 7 consecutive days

Administration

Oral (troche): Allow to dissolve slowly over 15-30 minutes.

Topical: Avoid contact with eyes. For external use only. Apply sparingly. Protect hands with latex gloves. Do not use occlusive dressings.

Monitoring Parameters Periodic liver function tests during oral therapy with clotrimazole troche

Patient Information Oral: Do not swallow oral medication whole; allow to dissolve slowly in mouth. You may experience nausea or vomiting (small frequent meals, frequent mouth care, chewing gum, or sucking lozenges may help). Report signs of opportunistic infection (eg, white plaques in mouth, fever, chills, perianal itching or vaginal discharge, fatigue, unhealed wounds or sores).

Topical: Wash hands before applying or wear gloves. Apply thin film to affected area. May apply porous dressing. Report persistent burning, swelling, itching, worsening of condition, or lack of response to therapy.

Vaginal: Wash hands before using. Insert full applicator into vagina gently and expel cream, or insert tablet into vagina, at bedtime. Wash applicator with soap and water following use. Remain lying down for 30 minutes following administration. Avoid intercourse during therapy (sexual partner may experience penile burning or itching). Report adverse reactions (eg, vulvar itching, frequent urination), worsening of condition, or lack of response to therapy. Contact prescriber if symptoms do not improve within 3 days or you do not feel well within 7 days. Do not use tampons until therapy is complete. Contact prescriber immediately if you experience abdominal pain, fever, or foul-smelling discharge.

Special Geriatric Considerations Localized fungal infections frequently follow broad-spectrum antimicrobial therapy. Specifically, oral and vaginal infections due to *Candida*.

Emetic Potential Very low (<10%)

Dosage Forms Excipient information presented when available (limited, particularly for generics); consult specific product labeling. [DSC] = Discontinued product

Cream, topical: 1% (15 g, 30 g, 45 g)

Cruex®: 1% (15 g) [contains benzyl alcohol]

Lotrimin® AF Athlete's Foot: 1% (12 g) [contains benzyl alcohol]

Lotrimin® AF Jock Itch: 1% (12 g) [contains benzyl alcohol]

Lotrimin® AF for Her: 1% (24 g) [contains benzyl alcohol]

Cream, topical/vaginal: 1% (45 g)

Gyne-Lotrimin® 7: 1% (45 g) [contains benzyl alcohol; packaged with refillable applicator]

Cream, vaginal: 2% (21 g)

Gyne-Lotrimin® 3: 2% (21 g) [contains benzyl alcohol; packaged with 3 disposable applicators]

Solution, topical: 1% (10 mL, 30 mL)

Tablet, vaginal:

Gyne-Lotrimin® 3: 200 mg (3s) [DSC]

Troche, oral: 10 mg

Mycelex®: 10 mg

References

Duhm B, Medenwald H, Puetter J, et al, "The Pharmacokinetics of Clotrimazole 14C," *Postgrad Med J*, 1974, 50(Suppl 1):13-6.

Hughes D and Kriedman T, "Treatment of Vulvovaginal Candidiasis With a 500 mg Vaginal Tablet of Clotrimazole," *Clin Ther*, 1984, 6(5):662-8.

- ◆ **CMA-676** *see* Gemtuzumab Ozogamicin *on page 508*
- ◆ **CMV-IGIV** *see* Cytomegalovirus Immune Globulin (Intravenous-Human) *on page 278*
- ◆ **Coagulation Factor VIIa** *see* Factor VIIa (Recombinant) *on page 416*
- ◆ **CO Bicalutamide (Can)** *see* Bicalutamide *on page 141*
- ◆ **CO Ciprofloxacin (Can)** *see* Ciprofloxacin *on page 213*

Codeine (KOE deen)

Medication Safety Issues

Sound-alike/look-alike issues:

Codeine may be confused with Cardene®, Cophene®, Cordran®, iodine, Lodine®

Index Terms Codeine Phosphate; Codeine Sulfate; Methylmorphine

Generic Available Yes

Canadian Brand Names Codeine Contin®

Pharmacologic Category Analgesic, Opioid; Antitussive

Use Treatment of mild-to-moderate pain; antitussive in lower doses; dextromethorphan has equivalent antitussive activity but has much lower toxicity in accidental overdose

Restrictions C-II

Pregnancy Risk Factor C/D (prolonged use or high doses at term)

Lactation Enters breast milk/use caution (AAP rates "compatible")

Labeled Contraindications Hypersensitivity to codeine or any component of the formulation; pregnancy (prolonged use or high doses at term)

Warnings/Precautions Use with caution in patients with hypersensitivity reactions to other phenanthrene-derivative opioid agonists (morphine, hydrocodone, hydromorphone, levorphanol, oxycodone, oxymorphone); respiratory diseases including asthma, emphysema, COPD, adrenal insufficiency; biliary tract impairment, CNS depression/coma, head trauma, morbid obesity, prostatic hyperplasia, urinary stricture, thyroid dysfunction, or severe liver or renal insufficiency; some preparations contain sulfites which may cause allergic reactions; tolerance or drug dependence may result from extended use. May obscure diagnosis or clinical course of patients with acute abdominal conditions. May cause CNS depression, which may impair physical or mental abilities; patients must be cautioned about performing tasks which require mental alertness (eg, operating machinery or driving). May cause hypotension; use with caution in patients with hypovolemia, cardiovascular disease (including acute MI), or drugs which may exaggerate hypotensive effects (including phenothiazines or general anesthetics). Use caution in patients with two or more copies of the variant CYP2D6*2 allele; may have extensive conversion to morphine and thus increased opioid-mediated effects.

Not recommended for use for cough control in patients with a productive cough; not recommended as an antitussive for children <2 years of age; the elderly and debilitated patients may be particularly susceptible to adverse effects of narcotics.

Not approved for I.V. administration (although this route has been used clinically). If given intravenously, must be given slowly and the patient should be lying down. Rapid intravenous administration of narcotics may increase the incidence of serious adverse effects, in part due to limited opportunity to assess response prior to administration of the full dose. Access to respiratory support should be immediately available.

Concurrent use of agonist/antagonist analgesics may precipitate withdrawal symptoms and/or reduced analgesic efficacy in patients following prolonged therapy with mu opioid agonists. Abrupt discontinuation following prolonged use may also lead to withdrawal symptoms.

Adverse Reactions

Frequency not defined: AST/ALT increased

>10%:

Central nervous system: Drowsiness

Gastrointestinal: Constipation

1% to 10%:

Cardiovascular: Tachycardia or bradycardia, hypotension

Central nervous system: Dizziness, lightheadedness, false feeling of well being, malaise, headache, restlessness, paradoxical CNS stimulation, confusion

Dermatologic: Rash, urticaria

Gastrointestinal: Xerostomia, anorexia, nausea, vomiting

Genitourinary: Urination decreased, ureteral spasm

Hepatic: LFTs increased

Local: Burning at injection site

Neuromuscular & skeletal: Weakness

Ocular: Blurred vision

Respiratory: Dyspnea

Miscellaneous: Histamine release

<1%: Convulsions, hallucinations, mental depression, nightmares, insomnia, paralytic ileus, biliary spasm, stomach cramps, muscle rigidity, trembling

Overdosage/Toxicology Symptoms of overdose include CNS and respiratory depression, GI cramping, and constipation. Naloxone, 2 mg I.V. with repeat administration as necessary up to a total of 10 mg, can also be used to reverse toxic effects of the opiate.

Drug Interactions

Cytochrome P450 Effect: Substrate of CYP2D6 (major), 3A4 (minor); **Inhibits** CYP2D6 (weak)

Increased Effect/Toxicity: May cause severely increased toxicity of codeine when taken with CNS depressants, phenothiazines, tricyclic antidepressants, other opioid analgesics, guanabenz, MAO inhibitors, and neuromuscular blockers.

Decreased Effect: CYP2D6 inhibitors may decrease the effects of codeine. Example inhibitors include chlorpromazine, delavirdine, fluoxetine, miconazole, paroxetine, pergolide, quinidine, quinine, ritonavir, and ropinirole. Decreased effect with cigarette smoking.

Ethanol/Nutrition/Herb Interactions

Ethanol: Avoid or limit ethanol (may increase CNS depression).

Herb/Nutraceutical: St John's wort may decrease codeine levels. Avoid valerian, St John's wort, kava kava, gotu kola (may increase CNS depression).

Storage/Stability Store injection between 15°C to 30°C; avoid freezing. Do not use if injection is discolored or contains a precipitate. Protect injection from light.

Compatibility Compatibility in syringe: **Compatible:** Glycopyrrolate, hydroxyzine.

Mechanism of Action Binds to opiate receptors in the CNS, causing inhibition of ascending pain pathways, altering the perception of and response to pain; causes cough supression by direct central action in the medulla; produces generalized CNS depression

Pharmacodynamics/Kinetics

Onset of action: Oral: 0.5-1 hour; I.M.: 10-30 minutes

Peak effect: Oral: 1-1.5 hours; I.M.: 0.5-1 hour

Duration: 4-6 hours

(Continued)

Codeine *(Continued)*

Absorption: Oral: Adequate

Distribution: Crosses placenta; enters breast milk

Protein binding: 7%

Metabolism: Hepatic to morphine (active)

Half-life elimination: 2.5-3.5 hours

Excretion: Urine (3% to 16% as unchanged drug, norcodeine, and free and conjugated morphine)

Dosage Note: These are guidelines and do not represent the maximum doses that may be required in all patients. Doses should be titrated to pain relief/prevention. Doses >1.5 mg/kg body weight are not recommended.

Analgesic:

Children: Oral, I.M., SubQ: 0.5-1 mg/kg/dose every 4-6 hours as needed; maximum: 60 mg/dose

Adults:

Oral: 30 mg every 4-6 hours as needed; patients with prior opiate exposure may require higher initial doses. Usual range: 15-120 mg every 4-6 hours as needed

Oral, controlled release formulation (Codeine Contin®, not available in U.S.): 50-300 mg every 12 hours. **Note:** A patient's codeine requirement should be established using prompt release formulations; conversion to long acting products may be considered when chronic, continuous treatment is required. Higher dosages should be reserved for use only in opioid-tolerant patients.

I.M., SubQ: 30 mg every 4-6 hours as needed; patients with prior opiate exposure may require higher initial doses. Usual range: 15-120 mg every 4-6 hours as needed; more frequent dosing may be needed

Antitussive: Oral (for nonproductive cough):

Children: 1-1.5 mg/kg/day in divided doses every 4-6 hours as needed: Alternative dose according to age:

2-6 years: 2.5-5 mg every 4-6 hours as needed; maximum: 30 mg/day

6-12 years: 5-10 mg every 4-6 hours as needed; maximum: 60 mg/day

Adults: 10-20 mg/dose every 4-6 hours as needed; maximum: 120 mg/day

Dosing adjustment in renal impairment:

Cl_{cr} 10-50 mL/minute: Administer 75% of dose

Cl_{cr} <10 mL/minute: Administer 50% of dose

Dosing adjustment in hepatic impairment: Probably necessary in hepatic insufficiency

Administration Not approved for I.V. administration (although this route has been used clinically). If given intravenously, must be given slowly and the patient should be lying down. Rapid intravenous administration of narcotics may increase the incidence of serious adverse effects, in part due to limited opportunity to assess response prior to administration of the full dose. Access to respiratory support should be immediately available.

Monitoring Parameters Pain relief, respiratory and mental status, blood pressure, heart rate

Test Interactions Some quinolones may produce a false-positive urine screening result for opiates using commercially-available immunoassay kits. This has been demonstrated most consistently for levofloxacin and ofloxacin, but other quinolones have shown cross-reactivity in certain assay kits. Confirmation of positive opiate screens by more specific methods should be considered.

Patient Information Avoid alcohol; may cause drowsiness, impaired judgment, or coordination; may cause physical and psychological dependence with prolonged use

Special Geriatric Considerations The elderly may be particularly susceptible to CNS depression and confusion as well as the constipating effects of narcotics.

Vesicant No

Dosage Forms Excipient information presented when available (limited, particularly for generics); consult specific product labeling. [CAN] = Canadian brand name

Injection, as phosphate: 15 mg/mL (2 mL); 30 mg/mL (2 mL) [contains sodium metabisulfite]

Powder, for prescription compounding: 10 g, 25 g

Tablet, as phosphate: 30 mg, 60 mg

Tablet, as sulfate: 15 mg, 30 mg, 60 mg

Tablet, controlled release (Codeine Contin®) [CAN]: 50 mg, 100 mg, 150 mg, 200 mg [not available in U.S.]

References

Cardan E, "Fatal Case of Codeine Poisoning," *Lancet*, 1981, 1(8233):1313.

de Groot AC and Conemans J, "Allergic Urticarial Rash From Oral Codeine," *Contact Dermatitis*, 1986, 14(4):209-14.

Desjardins PJ, Cooper SA, Gallegos TL, et al, "The Relative Analgesic Efficacy of Propiram Fumarate, Codeine, Aspirin, and Placebo in Postimpaction Dental Pain," *J Clin Pharmacol*, 1984, 24(1):35-42.

"Drugs for Pain," *Med Lett Drugs Ther*, 2000, 42(1085):73-8.

Ferrell BA, "Pain Management in Elderly People," *J Am Geriatr Soc*, 1991, 39(1):64-73.

Forbes JA, Keller CK, Smith JW, et al, "Analgesic Effect of Naproxen Sodium, Codeine, a Naproxen-Codeine Combination and Aspirin on the Postoperative Pain of Oral Surgery," *Pharmacotherapy*, 1986, 6(5):211-8.

Ivey HH and Kattwinkel J, "Danger of Actifed-C," *Pediatrics*, 1976, 57(1):164-5.

Jacobi J, Fraser GL, Coursin DB, et al, "Clinical Practice Guidelines for the Sustained Use of Sedatives and Analgesics in the Critically Ill Adult," *Crit Care Med*, 2002, 30(1):119-41. Available at: http://www.sccm.org/pdf/sedatives.pdf. Accessed August 2, 2003.

Kaiko RF, Wallenstein SL, Rogers AG, et al, "Narcotics in the Elderly," *Med Clin North Am*, 1982, 66(5):1079-89.

Khan K and Chang J, "Neonatal Abstinence Syndrome Due to Codeine," *Arch Dis Child Fetal Neonatal Ed*, 1997; 76(1): F59-60.

Koren G, Cairns J, Chitayat D, et al, "Pharmacogenetics of Morphine Poisoning in a Breastfed Neonate of a Codeine-Prescribed Mother," *Lancet*, 2006, 368(9536):704.

Mokhlesi B, Leikin JB, Murray P, et al, "Adult Toxicology in Critical Care: Part II: Specific Poisonings," *Chest*, 2003, 123(3):897-922.

"Principles of Analgesic Use in the Treatment of Acute Pain and Chronic Cancer Pain," 5th ed, Glenview, IL: American Pain Society, 2003.

Reynolds EW, Riel-Romero RM, and Bada HS, "Neonatal Abstinence Syndrome and Cerebral Infarction Following Maternal Codeine Use During Pregnancy," *Clin Pediatr*, 2007, 46(7):639-45.

Spigset O and Hagg S, "Analgesics and Breast-Feeding: Safety Considerations," *Paediatr Drugs*, 2000, 2(3):223-38.

U.S. Food and Drug Administration, Center for Drug Evaluation and Research, "Public Health Advisory: Use of Codeine by Some Breastfeeding Mothers May Lead to Life-Threatening Side Effects in Nursing Babies." available at http://www.fda.gov/cder/drug/advisory/codeine.htm

Wilkins D, Rollins DE, Seaman J, et al, "Quantitative Determination of Codeine and Its Major Metabolites in Human Hair by Gas Chromatography With Positive Ion Chemical Ionization Mass Spectrometry: A Clinical Application," *J Anal Toxicol*, 1995, 19(5):269-74.

Zacher JL and Givone DM, "False-Positive Urine Opiate Screening Associated With Fluoroquinolone Use," *Ann Pharmacother*, 2004, 38:1525-28.

- ♦ **Correctol® Tablets [OTC]** see Bisacodyl on page 144
- ♦ **Cortaid® Intensive Therapy [OTC]** see Hydrocortisone on page 545
- ♦ **Cortaid® Maximum Strength [OTC]** see Hydrocortisone on page 545
- ♦ **Cortaid® Sensitive Skin [OTC]** see Hydrocortisone on page 545
- ♦ **Cortamed® (Can)** see Hydrocortisone on page 545
- ♦ **Cortef®** see Hydrocortisone on page 545
- ♦ **Cortenema® (Can)** see Hydrocortisone on page 545
- ♦ **Corticool® [OTC]** see Hydrocortisone on page 545
- ♦ **Cortifoam®** see Hydrocortisone on page 545
- ♦ **Cortisol** see Hydrocortisone on page 545
- ♦ **Cortizone®-10 Maximum Strength [OTC]** see Hydrocortisone on page 545
- ♦ **Cortizone®-10 Plus Maximum Strength [OTC]** see Hydrocortisone on page 545
- ♦ **Cortizone®-10 Quick Shot [OTC]** see Hydrocortisone on page 545
- ♦ **Cosmegen®** see Dactinomycin on page 287
- ♦ **Co-Trimoxazole** see Sulfamethoxazole and Trimethoprim on page 982
- ♦ **Co-Vidarabine** see Pentostatin on page 891
- ♦ **CP358774** see Erlotinib on page 396
- ♦ **CPM** see Cyclophosphamide on page 246
- ♦ **CPT-11** see Irinotecan on page 626
- ♦ **CPZ** see ChlorproMAZINE on page 208
- ♦ **Cruex® Cream [OTC]** see Clotrimazole on page 239
- ♦ **CsA** see CycloSPORINE on page 254
- ♦ **CTX** see Cyclophosphamide on page 246
- ♦ **CyA** see CycloSPORINE on page 254

Cyclophosphamide (sye kloe FOS fa mide)

Medication Safety Issues

Sound-alike/look-alike issues:

Cyclophosphamide may be confused with cycloSPORINE, ifosfamide

Cytoxan® may be confused with cefoxitin, Centoxin®, Ciloxan®, cytarabine, CytoGam®, Cytosar®, Cytosar-U®, Cytotec®

High alert medication: The Institute for Safe Medication Practices (ISMP) includes this medication among its list of drugs which have a heightened risk of causing significant patient harm when used in error.

Related Information

Fertility and Cancer Therapy on page 1298
Hematopoietic Stem Cell Transplantation on page 1366
Management of Drug Extravasations on page 1301
Safe Handling of Hazardous Drugs on page 1382

U.S. Brand Names Cytoxan®

Index Terms CPM; CTX; CYT; Neosar; NSC-26271

Generic Available Yes: Tablet

Canadian Brand Names Cytoxan®; Procytox®

Pharmacologic Category Antineoplastic Agent, Alkylating Agent

Use

Oncologic: Treatment of Hodgkin's and non-Hodgkin's lymphoma, Burkitt's lymphoma, chronic lymphocytic leukemia (CLL), chronic myelocytic leukemia (CML), acute myelocytic leukemia (AML), acute lymphocytic leukemia (ALL), mycosis fungoides, multiple myeloma, neuroblastoma, retinoblastoma, rhabdomyosarcoma, Ewing's sarcoma; breast, testicular, endometrial, ovarian, and lung cancers, and in conditioning regimens for bone marrow transplantation

Nononcologic: Prophylaxis of rejection for kidney, heart, liver, and bone marrow transplants, severe rheumatoid disorders, nephrotic syndrome, Wegener's granulomatosis, idiopathic pulmonary hemosideroses, myasthenia gravis, multiple sclerosis, systemic lupus erythematosus, lupus nephritis, autoimmune hemolytic anemia, idiopathic thrombocytic purpura (ITP), macroglobulinemia, and antibody-induced pure red cell aplasia

Pregnancy Risk Factor D

Lactation Enters breast milk/contraindicated

Labeled Contraindications Hypersensitivity to cyclophosphamide or any component of the formulation; pregnancy

Warnings/Precautions Hazardous agent - use appropriate precautions for handling and disposal. Dosage adjustment may be needed for renal or hepatic failure. Hemorrhagic cystitis may occur; increased hydration and frequent voiding is recommended. Immunosuppression may occur; monitor for infections. May cause cardiotoxicity (CHF, usually with higher doses); may potentiate the cardiotoxicity of anthracyclines. May impair fertility; interferes with oogenesis and spermatogenesis. Secondary malignancies (usually delayed) have been reported

Adverse Reactions

>10%:

Dermatologic: Alopecia (40% to 60%) but hair will usually regrow although it may be a different color and/or texture. Hair loss usually begins 3-6 weeks after the start of therapy.

Endocrine & metabolic: Fertility: May cause sterility; interferes with oogenesis and spermatogenesis; may be irreversible in some patients; gonadal suppression (amenorrhea)

Gastrointestinal: Nausea and vomiting (usually beginning 6-10 hours after administration); anorexia, diarrhea, mucositis, and stomatitis are also seen

Genitourinary: Severe, potentially fatal, acute hemorrhagic cystitis or urinary fibrosis (7% to 40%)

Hematologic: Thrombocytopenia and anemia are less common than leukopenia

Onset: 7 days

Nadir: 10-14 days

Recovery: 21 days

1% to 10%:

Cardiovascular: Facial flushing

Central nervous system: Headache

Dermatologic: Skin rash

Renal: SIADH may occur, usually with doses >50 mg/kg (or 1 g/m^2); renal tubular necrosis, which usually resolves with discontinuation of the drug, is also reported

Respiratory: Nasal congestion occurs when I.V. doses are administered too rapidly; patients experience runny eyes, rhinorrhea, sinus congestion, and sneezing during or immediately after the infusion.

<1%, postmarketing, and/or case reports: High-dose therapy may cause cardiac dysfunction manifested as CHF; cardiac necrosis or hemorrhagic myocarditis has occurred, but may be fatal. Interstitial pneumonitis and pulmonary fibrosis are occasionally seen with high doses. Cyclophosphamide may also potentiate the cardiac toxicity of anthracyclines. Other adverse reactions include anaphylactic reactions, darkening of skin/fingernails, dizziness, hemorrhagic colitis, hemorrhagic ureteritis, hepatotoxicity,

(Continued)

Cyclophosphamide *(Continued)*

hyperuricemia, hypokalemia, jaundice, malaise, neutrophilic eccrine hidradenitis, radiation recall, renal tubular necrosis, secondary malignancy (eg, bladder carcinoma), SAIDH, Stevens-Johnson syndrome, toxic epidermal necrolysis, weakness.

Overdosage/Toxicology Symptoms of overdose include myelosuppression, alopecia, nausea, and vomiting. Treatment is symptom-directed and supportive.

Drug Interactions

Cytochrome P450 Effect: Substrate of CYP2A6 (minor), 2B6 (major), 2C9 (minor), 2C19 (minor), 3A4 (major); **Inhibits** CYP3A4 (weak); **Induces** CYP2B6 (weak), 2C8 (weak), 2C9 (weak)

Increased Effect/Toxicity: Allopurinol may cause an increase in bone marrow depression and may result in significant elevations of cyclophosphamide cytotoxic metabolites. CYP2B6 inducers may increase the levels/effects of acrolein (the active metabolite of cyclophosphamide); example inducers include carbamazepine, nevirapine, phenobarbital, phenytoin, and rifampin. CYP3A4 inducers may increase the levels/effects of acrolein (the active metabolite of cyclophosphamide); example inducers include aminoglutethimide, carbamazepine, nafcillin, nevirapine, phenobarbital, phenytoin, and rifamycins. Etanercept may enhance the adverse effects of cyclophosphamide. Cyclophosphamide reduces serum pseudocholinesterase concentrations and may prolong the neuromuscular blocking activity of succinylcholine and mivacurium.

Decreased Effect: Cyclophosphamide may decrease the absorption of digoxin tablets. CYP2B6 inhibitors may decrease the levels/effects of acrolein (the active metabolite of cyclophosphamide); example inhibitors include desipramine, paroxetine, and sertraline. CYP3A4 inhibitors may decrease the levels/effects of acrolein (the active metabolite of cyclophosphamide); example inhibitors include azole antifungals, ciprofloxacin, clarithromycin, diclofenac, doxycycline, erythromycin, imatinib, isoniazid, nefazodone, nicardipine, propofol, protease inhibitors, quinidine, and verapamil.

Ethanol/Nutrition/Herb Interactions Herb/Nutraceutical: Avoid black cohosh, dong quai in estrogen-dependent tumors.

Storage/Stability Store intact vials of powder at room temperature of 15°C to 30°C (59°F to 86°F). Reconstituted solutions are stable for 24 hours at room temperature and 6 days under refrigeration 2°C to 8°C (36°F to 46°F). Further dilutions in D_5W or NS are stable for 24 hours at room temperature (25°C) and 6 days at refrigeration.

Reconstitution Reconstitute vials with SWI, NS, or D_5W to a concentration of 20 mg/mL.

Compatibility Stable in D_5LR, D_5NS, D_5W, LR, ½NS, NS.

Y-site administration: Compatible: Allopurinol, amifostine, amikacin, ampicillin, azlocillin, aztreonam, bleomycin, cefamandole, cefazolin, cefepime, cefoperazone, cefotaxime, cefoxitin, cefuroxime, chloramphenicol, chlorpromazine, cimetidine, cisplatin, cladribine, clindamycin, co-trimoxazole, dexamethasone sodium phosphate, diphenhydramine, doxorubicin, doxorubicin liposome, doxycycline, droperidol, erythromycin lactobionate, etoposide phosphate, famotidine, filgrastim, fludarabine, fluorouracil, furosemide, ganciclovir, gatifloxacin, gemcitabine, gentamicin, granisetron, heparin, hydromorphone, idarubicin, kanamycin, leucovorin, linezolid, lorazepam, melphalan, methotrexate, methylprednisolone sodium succinate, metoclopramide, metronidazole, minocycline, mitomycin, morphine, nafcillin, ondansetron, oxacillin, paclitaxel, penicillin G potassium, pipera-cillin, piperacillin/tazobactam, prochlorperazine edisylate, promethazine, propofol, ranitidine, sargramostim, sodium bicarbonate, teniposide, thio-tepa, ticarcillin, ticarcillin/clavulanate, tobramycin, topotecan, vancomycin, vinblastine, vincristine, vinorelbine. **Incompatible:** Amphotericin B choles-teryl sulfate complex.

Compatibility in syringe: Compatible: Bleomycin, cisplatin, doxapram, doxorubicin, droperidol, fluorouracil, furosemide, heparin, leucovorin, methotrexate, metoclopramide, mitomycin, vinblastine, vincristine.

Compatibility when admixed: Compatible: Cisplatin with etoposide, dacarbazine, fluorouracil, hydroxyzine, mesna, methotrexate, metho-trexate with fluorouracil, mitoxantrone, ondansetron.

Mechanism of Action Cyclophosphamide is an alkylating agent that prevents cell division by cross-linking DNA strands and decreasing DNA synthesis. It is a cell cycle phase nonspecific agent. Cyclophosphamide also possesses potent immunosuppressive activity. Cyclophosphamide is a prodrug that must be metabolized to active metabolites in the liver.

Pharmacodynamics/Kinetics

Absorption: Oral: Well absorbed

Distribution: V_d: 0.48-0.71 L/kg; crosses placenta; crosses into CSF (not in high enough concentrations to treat meningeal leukemia)

Protein binding: 10% to 60%

Metabolism: Hepatic to active metabolites acrolein, 4-aldophosphamide, 4-hydroperoxycyclophosphamide, and nor-nitrogen mustard

Bioavailability: >75%

Half-life elimination: 3-12 hours

Time to peak, serum: Oral: ~1 hour

Excretion: Urine (<30% as unchanged drug, 85% to 90% as metabolites)

Dosage Refer to individual protocols

Children:

SLE: I.V.: 500-750 mg/m^2 every month; maximum dose: 1 g/m^2

JRA/vasculitis: I.V.: 10 mg/kg every 2 weeks

Children and Adults:

Oral: 50-100 mg/m^2/day as continuous therapy or 400-1000 mg/m^2 in divided doses over 4-5 days as intermittent therapy

I.V.:

Single doses: 400-1800 mg/m^2 (30-50 mg/kg) per treatment course (1-5 days) which can be repeated at 2-4 week intervals

Continuous daily doses: 60-120 mg/m^2 (1-2.5 mg/kg) per day

Autologous BMT: IVPB: 50 mg/kg/dose x 4 days or 60 mg/kg/dose for 2 days; total dose is usually divided over 2-4 days

Nephrotic syndrome: Oral: 2-3 mg/kg/day every day for up to 12 weeks when corticosteroids are unsuccessful

Dosing adjustment in renal impairment: The FDA-approved labeling states there is insufficient evidence to recommend dosage adjustment and therefore, does not contain renal dosing adjustment guidelines. The following guidelines have been used by some clinicians (Aronoff, 2007):

Children and Adults:

Cl$_{cr}$ <10 mL/minute: Administer 75% of normal dose

Hemodialysis effects: Moderately dialyzable (20% to 50%)

Administer 50% of dose posthemodialysis

Continuous ambulatory peritoneal dialysis (CAPD): Administer 75% of normal dose

Continuous renal replacement therapy (CRRT): Administer 100% of normal dose

(Continued)

Cyclophosphamide *(Continued)*

Dosing adjustment in hepatic impairment: The pharmacokinetics of cyclophosphamide are not significantly altered in the presence of hepatic insufficiency. The FDA-approved labeling does not contain hepatic dosing adjustment guidelines. The following guidelines have been used by some clinicians (Floyd, 2006):

Serum bilirubin 3.1-5 mg/dL or ALT/AST >3 times ULN: Administer 75% of dose

Serum bilirubin >5 mg/mL: Avoid use

Combination Regimens

Bladder cancer:
CAP *on page 1158*
CISCA *on page 1175*

Brain tumor:
8 in 1 (Brain Tumors) *on page 1141*
COPE *on page 1182*

Breast cancer:
AC *on page 1143*
AC/Paclitaxel (Sequential) *on page 1143*
AC-Paclitaxel-Trastuzumab *on page 1144*
CAF *on page 1157*
CEF *on page 1166*
CFP *on page 1170*
CMF *on page 1177*
CMF-IV *on page 1177*
CMFP *on page 1178*
CMFVP (Cooper Regimen, VPCMF) *on page 1178*
CNF *on page 1179*
Docetaxel-Cyclophosphamide *on page 1191*
Docetaxel-Trastuzumab-FEC *on page 1193*
Dox-CMF (Sequential) *on page 1195*
FAC *on page 1210*
FEC *on page 1214*
TAC *on page 1279*

Gestational trophoblastic tumor:
CHAMOCA (Modified Bagshawe Regimen) *on page 1170*
CHAMOMA (Bagshawe Regimen) *on page 1172*
EMA/CO *on page 1199*

Leukemia, acute lymphocytic:
Hyper-CVAD + Imatinib *on page 1229*
Hyper-CVAD (Leukemia, Acute Lymphocytic) *on page 1231*
Larson Regimen *on page 1242*
VAD/CVAD *on page 1287*

Leukemia, chronic lymphocytic:
CVP (Leukemia) *on page 1184*
Fludarabine-Cyclophosphamide (FC) *on page 1216*
Fludarabine-Cyclophosphamide-Rituximab *on page 1217*
PCR *on page 1267*
Pentostatin-Cyclophosphamide *on page 1270*

Lung cancer (small cell): CAVE *on page 1163*

Lymphoma, Hodgkin's disease:
BEACOPP *on page 1148*
COMP *on page 1182*

Lymphoma, non-Hodgkin's:
CEPP(B) *on page 1167*

(Continued)

Cyclophosphamide *(Continued)*

VAC Alternating With IE (Ewing's Sarcoma) *on page 1285*
Wilms' tumor: ACAV (J) *on page 1143*

Administration Administer I.P., intrapleurally, IVPB, or continuous I.V. infusion; may also be administered slow IVP in doses ≤1 g.

I.V. infusions may be administered over 1-24 hours

Doses >500 mg to approximately 2 g may be administered over 20-30 minutes

To minimize bladder toxicity, increase normal fluid intake during and for 1-2 days after cyclophosphamide dose. Most adult patients will require a fluid intake of at least 2 L/day. High-dose regimens should be accompanied by vigorous hydration with or without mesna therapy.

Oral: Tablets are not scored and should not be cut or crushed. To minimize the risk of bladder irritation, do not administer tablets at bedtime.

Monitoring Parameters CBC with differential and platelet count, BUN, UA, serum electrolytes, serum creatinine

Dietary Considerations Tablets should be administered during or after meals.

Patient Information Tablets may be taken during or after meals to reduce GI effects. Maintain adequate fluid balance (2-3 L/day of fluids unless instructed to restrict fluid intake). Void frequently and report any difficulty or pain with urination. May cause hair loss (reversible after treatment), sterility, or amenorrhea (sometimes reversible). If you are diabetic, you will need to monitor serum glucose closely to avoid hypoglycemia. You may be more susceptible to infection; avoid crowds and unnecessary exposure to infection. Report unusual bleeding or bruising; persistent fever or sore throat; blood in urine, stool (black stool), or vomitus; delayed healing of any wounds; skin rash; yellowing of skin or eyes; or changes in color of urine or stool. Contraceptive measures are recommended during therapy.

Special Geriatric Considerations Toxicity to immunosuppressives is increased in the elderly. Start with lowest recommended adult doses. Signs of infection, such as fever and WBC rise, may not occur. Lethargy and confusion may be more prominent signs of infection; adjust dose for renal function.

Additional Information In patients with CYP2B6 G516T variant allele, cyclophosphamide metabolism is markedly increased; metabolism is not influenced by CYP2C9 and CYP2C19 isotypes.

Emetic Potential

Very high (>90%): >1500 mg/m^2

High (60% to 90%): >750 mg/m^2, ≤1500 mg/m^2

Moderate (30% to 60%): ≤750 mg/m^2

Oral: Moderate (30% to 60%)

Vesicant No

High Dose Considerations

Comments: Approaches to reduction of hemorrhagic cystitis include infusion of 0.9% NaCl 3 L/m^2/24 hours, infusion of 0.9% NaCl 3 L/m^2/24 hours with continuous 0.9% NaCl bladder irrigation 300-1000 mL/hour, and infusion of 0.9% NaCl 1.5-3 L/m^2/24 hours with intravenous mesna. Hydration should begin at least 4 hours before cyclophosphamide and continue at least 24 hours after completion of cyclophosphamide. The dose of daily mesna used should equal the daily dose of cyclophosphamide. Mesna can be administered as a continuous 24-hour intravenous infusion or be given in divided doses every 4 hours. Mesna should begin at the start of treatment, and continue at least 24 hours following the last dose of cyclophosphamide.

Enhanced bioactivation of cyclophosphamide may increase the risk of cardiotoxicity. A 30-minute infusion of thiotepa administered 1 hour before a 60-minute infusion of cyclophosphamide reduced bioactivation of cyclophosphamide to 4-hydroxycyclophosphamide in 20 patients. This effect did not occur with administration of thiotepa 1 hour following infusion of cyclophosphamide. Intravascular red blood cell hemolysis requiring transfusion support occurred during continuous flow plasmapheresis performed 12 hours following infusion of cyclophosphamide 60 mg/kg.

High Dose:
I.V.:
60 mg/kg/day for 2 days (total dose: 120 mg/kg)
50 mg/kg/day for 4 days (total dose: 200 mg/kg)
1.8 g/m^2/day for 4 days (total dose: 7.2 g/m^2)
1875 mg/m^2/24 hours for 72 hours (total dose: 5625 mg/m^2)
Continuous I.V.: 1.5 g/m^2/24 hours for 96 hours (total dose: 6 g/m^2)
Duration of infusion is 1-24 hours; generally combined with other high-dose chemotherapeutic drugs, lymphocyte immune globulin, or total body irradiation (TBI).

Unique Toxicities:
Cardiovascular: Heart failure, cardiac necrosis, pericardial tamponade, heart block
Endocrine & metabolic: Hyponatremia, acquired pseudocholinesterase deficiency, transient diabetes insipidus
Hematologic: Methemoglobinemia
Neuromuscular & skeletal: Rhabdomyolysis
Respiratory: Pleural effusion, interstitial pneumonitis

Dosage Forms Excipient information presented when available (limited, particularly for generics); consult specific product labeling.

Injection, powder for reconstitution:
Cytoxan®: 500 mg, 1 g, 2 g [contains mannitol 75 mg per cyclophosphamide 100 mg]
Tablet: 25 mg, 50 mg
Cytoxan®: 25 mg, 50 mg

Extemporaneous Preparations A 2 mg/mL oral elixir was stable for 14 days when refrigerated when made as follows: Reconstitute a 200 mg vial with aromatic elixir, withdraw the solution, and add sufficient aromatic elixir to make a final volume of 100 mL (store in amber glass container).

Brook D, Davis RE, and Bequette RJ, "Chemical Stability of Cyclophosphamide in Aromatic Elixir U.S.P.," *Am J Health Syst Pharm*, 1973, 30:618-20.

References

Aronoff GR, Bennett WM, Berns JS, et al, *Drug Prescribing in Renal Failure: Dosing Guidelines for Adults and Children*, 5th ed. Philadelphia, PA: American College of Physicians; 2007, p 97, 170.

Ahmed AR and Hombal SM, "Cyclophosphamide (Cytoxan®). A Review on Relevant Pharmacology and Clinical Uses," *J Am Acad Dermatol*, 1984, 11(6):1115-26.

Brade W, Seeber S, and Herdrich K, "Comparative Activity of Ifosfamide and Cyclophosphamide," *Cancer Chemother Pharmacol*, 1986, 18(Suppl 2):1-9.

Colvin OM, "An Overview of Cyclophosphamide Development and Clinical Applications," *Curr Pharm Des*, 1999, 5(8):555-60.

deJonge ME, Huitema AD, vanDam SM, et al, "Significant Induction of Cyclophosphamide and Thiotepa Metabolism by Phenytoin," *Cancer Chemother Pharmacol*, 2005, 55(5):507-10.

Eder JP, Elias A, Shea TC, et al, "A Phase I-II Study of Cyclophosphamide, Thiotepa, and Carboplatin With Autologous Bone Marrow Transplantation in Solid Tumor Patients," *J Clin Oncol*, 1990, 8(7):1239-45.

Fleming RA, "An Overview of Cyclophosphamide and Ifosfamide Pharmacology," *Pharmacotherapy*, 1997, 17(5 Pt 2):146S-154S.

Floyd J, Mirza I, Sachs B, et al, "Hepatotoxicity of Chemotherapy," *Semin Oncol*, 2006, 33(1):50-67.

(Continued)

Cyclophosphamide *(Continued)*

Fraiser LH, Kanekal S, and Kehrer JP, "Cyclophosphamide Toxicity. Characterizing and Avoiding the Problem," *Drugs*, 1991, 42(5):781-95.

Giralt SA, LeMaistre CF, Vriesendorp HM, et al, "Etoposide, Cyclophosphamide, Total-Body Irradiation and Allogeneic Bone Marrow Transplantation for Hematologic Malignancies," *J Clin Oncol*, 1994, 12(9):1923-30.

Langford CA, "Complications of Cyclophosphamide Therapy," *Eur Arch Otorhinolaryngol*, 1997, 254(2):65-72.

Xie H, Griskevicius L, Stahle L, et al, "Pharmacogenetics of Cyclophosphamide in Patients With Hematologic Malignancies," *Eur J Pharm Sci*, 2006, 27(1):54-61.

♦ **Cyclosporin A** *see* CycloSPORINE *on page 254*

CycloSPORINE *(SYE kloe spor een)*

Medication Safety Issues
Sound-alike/look-alike issues:
CycloSPORINE may be confused with cyclophosphamide, Cyklokapron®, cycloSERINE
CycloSPORINE modified (Neoral®, Gengraf®) may be confused with cyclo-SPORINE non-modified (Sandimmne®)
Gengraf® may be confused with Prograf®
Neoral® may be confused with Neurontin®, Nizoral®
Sandimmune® may be confused with Sandostatin®

Related Information
Hematopoietic Stem Cell Transplantation *on page 1366*
Safe Handling of Hazardous Drugs *on page 1382*

U.S. Brand Names Gengraf®; Neoral®; Restasis®; Sandimmune®

Index Terms CsA; CyA; Cyclosporin A

Generic Available Yes

Canadian Brand Names Neoral®; Rhoxal-cyclosporine; Sandimmune® I.V.; Sandoz-Cyclosporine

Pharmacologic Category Immunosuppressant Agent

Use Prophylaxis of organ rejection in kidney, liver, and heart transplants, has been used with azathioprine and/or corticosteroids; severe, active rheumatoid arthritis (RA) not responsive to methotrexate alone; severe, recalcitrant plaque psoriasis in nonimmunocompromised adults unresponsive to or unable to tolerate other systemic therapy

Ophthalmic emulsion (Restasis®): Increase tear production when suppressed tear production is presumed to be due to keratoconjunctivitis sicca-associated ocular inflammation (in patients not already using topical anti-inflammatory drugs or punctal plugs)

Unlabeled/Investigational Use Short-term, high-dose cyclosporine as a modulator of multidrug resistance in cancer treatment; allogenic bone marrow transplants for prevention and treatment of graft-versus-host disease; also used in some cases of severe autoimmune disease (eg, SLE, myasthenia gravis, inflammatory bowel disease) that are resistant to corticosteroids and other therapy; focal segmental glomerulosclerosis

Pregnancy Risk Factor C

Lactation Enters breast milk/not recommended

Labeled Contraindications Hypersensitivity to cyclosporine or any component of the formulation. Rheumatoid arthritis and psoriasis: Abnormal renal function, uncontrolled hypertension, malignancies. Concomitant treatment with PUVA or UVB therapy, methotrexate, other immunosuppressive agents, coal tar, or radiation therapy are also contraindications for use in patients with psoriasis. Ophthalmic emulsion is contraindicated in patients with active ocular infections.

Warnings/Precautions [U.S. Boxed Warning]: Renal impairment, including structural kidney damage has occurred (when used at high doses); monitor renal function closely. Use caution with other potentially nephrotoxic drugs (eg, acyclovir, aminoglycoside antibiotics, amphotericin B, ciprofloxacin). **[U.S. Boxed Warning]: Increased risk of lymphomas and other malignancies, particularly those of the skin;** risk is related to intensity/duration of therapy and the use of >1 immunosuppressive agent; all patients should avoid excessive sun/UV light exposure. **[U.S. Boxed Warning]: Increased risk of infection; fatal infections have been reported. [U.S. Boxed Warning]: May cause hypertension.** Use caution when changing dosage forms. **[U.S. Boxed Warning]: Cyclosporine (modified) has increased bioavailability as compared to cyclosporine (non-modified) and cannot be used interchangeably without close monitoring.** Monitor cyclosporine concentrations closely following the addition, modification, or deletion of other medications; live, attenuated vaccines may be less effective; use should be avoided. Increased hepatic enzymes and bilirubin have occurred (when used at high doses); improvement usually seen with dosage reduction.

Transplant patients: To be used initially with corticosteroids. May cause significant hyperkalemia and hyperuricemia, seizures (particularly if used with high dose corticosteroids), and encephalopathy. Make dose adjustments based on cyclosporine blood concentrations. **[U.S. Boxed Warning]: Adjustment of dose should only be made under the direct supervision of an experienced physician.** Anaphylaxis has been reported with I.V. use; reserve for patients who cannot take oral form. **[U.S. Boxed Warning]: Risk of skin cancer may be increased in transplant patients.**

Psoriasis: Patients should avoid excessive sun exposure; safety and efficacy in children <18 years of age have not been established. **[U.S. Boxed Warning]: Risk of skin cancer may be increased with a history of PUVA and possibly methotrexate or other immunosuppressants, UVB, coal tar, or radiation.**

Rheumatoid arthritis: Safety and efficacy for use in juvenile rheumatoid arthritis have not been established. If receiving other immunosuppressive agents, radiation or UV therapy, concurrent use of cyclosporine is not recommended.

Ophthalmic emulsion: Safety and efficacy have not been established in patients <16 years of age.

Products may contain corn oil, castor oil, ethanol, or propylene glycol; injection also contains Cremophor® EL (polyoxyethylated castor oil), which has been associated with rare anaphylactic reactions.

Adverse Reactions Adverse reactions reported with systemic use, including rheumatoid arthritis, psoriasis, and transplantation (kidney, liver, and heart). Percentages noted include the highest frequency regardless of indication/dosage. Frequencies may vary for specific conditions or formulation.

>10%:
  Cardiovascular: Hypertension (8% to 53%), edema (5% to 14%)
  Central nervous system: Headache (2% to 25%)
  Dermatologic: Hirsutism (21% to 45%), hypertrichosis (5% to 19%)
  Endocrine & metabolic: Triglycerides increased (15%), female reproductive disorder (9% to 11%)
  Gastrointestinal: Nausea (23%), diarrhea (3% to 13%), gum hyperplasia (2% to 16%), abdominal discomfort (<1% to 15%), dyspepsia (2% to 12%)
(Continued)

CycloSPORINE *(Continued)*

Neuromuscular & skeletal: Tremor (7% to 55%), paresthesia (1% to 11%), leg cramps/muscle contractions (2% to 12%)

Renal: Renal dysfunction/nephropathy (10% to 38%), creatinine increased (16% to ≥50%)

Respiratory: Upper respiratory infection (1% to 14%)

Miscellaneous: Infection (3% to 25%)

Kidney, liver, and heart transplant only (≤2% unless otherwise noted):

Cardiovascular: Flushes (<1% to 4%), MI

Central nervous system: Convulsions (1% to 5%), anxiety, confusion, fever, lethargy

Dermatologic: Acne (1% to 6%), brittle fingernails, hair breaking, pruritus

Endocrine & metabolic: Gynecomastia (<1% to 4%), hyperglycemia

Gastrointestinal: Nausea (2% to 10%), vomiting (2% to 10%), diarrhea (3% to 8%), abdominal discomfort (<1% to 7%), cramps (0% to 4%), anorexia, constipation, gastritis, mouth sores, pancreatitis, swallowing difficulty, upper GI bleed, weight loss

Hematologic: Leukopenia (<1% to 6%), anemia, thrombocytopenia

Hepatic: Hepatotoxicity (<1% to 7%)

Neuromuscular & skeletal: Paresthesia (1% to 3%), joint pain, muscle pain, tingling, weakness

Ocular: Conjunctivitis, visual disturbance

Otic: Hearing loss, tinnitus

Renal: Hematuria

Respiratory: Sinusitis (<1% to 7%)

Miscellaneous: Lymphoma (<1% to 6%), allergic reactions, hiccups, night sweats

Rheumatoid arthritis only (1% to <3% unless otherwise noted):

Cardiovascular: Hypertension (8%), edema (5%), chest pain (4%), arrhythmia (2%), abnormal heart sounds, cardiac failure, MI, peripheral ischemia

Central nervous system: Dizziness (8%), pain (6%), insomnia (4%), depression (3%), migraine (2%), anxiety, hypoesthesia, emotional lability, impaired concentration, malaise, nervousness, paranoia, somnolence, vertigo

Dermatologic: Purpura (3%), abnormal pigmentation, angioedema, cellulitis, dermatitis, dry skin, eczema, folliculitis, nail disorder, pruritus, skin disorder, urticaria

Endocrine & metabolic: Menstrual disorder (3%), breast fibroadenosis, breast pain, diabetes mellitus, goiter, hot flashes, hyperkalemia, hyperuricemia, hypoglycemia, libido increased/decreased

Gastrointestinal: Vomiting (9%), flatulence (5%), gingivitis (4%), gum hyperplasia (2%), constipation, dry mouth, dysphagia, enanthema, eructation, esophagitis, gastric ulcer, gastritis, gastroenteritis, gingival bleeding, glossitis, peptic ulcer, salivary gland enlargement, taste perversion, tongue disorder, tooth disorder, weight loss/gain

Genitourinary: Leukorrhea (1%), abnormal urine, micturition urgency, nocturia, polyuria, pyelonephritis, urinary incontinence, uterine hemorrhage

Hematologic: Anemia, leukopenia

Hepatic: Bilirubinemia

Neuromuscular & skeletal: Paresthesia (8%), tremor (8%), leg cramps/muscle contractions (2%), arthralgia, bone fracture, joint dislocation, myalgia, neuropathy, stiffness, synovial cyst, tendon disorder, weakness

Ocular: Abnormal vision, cataract, conjunctivitis, eye pain

Otic: Tinnitus, deafness, vestibular disorder

Renal: BUN increased, hematuria, renal abscess

Respiratory: Cough (5%), dyspnea (5%), sinusitis (4%), abnormal chest sounds, bronchospasm, epistaxis

Miscellaneous: Infection (9%), abscess, allergy, bacterial infection, carcinoma, fungal infection, herpes simplex, herpes zoster, lymphadenopathy, moniliasis, diaphoresis increased, tonsillitis, viral infection

Psoriasis only (1% to <3% unless otherwise noted):

Cardiovascular: Chest pain, flushes

Central nervous system: Psychiatric events (4% to 5%), pain (3% to 4%), dizziness, fever, insomnia, nervousness, vertigo

Dermatologic: Hypertrichosis (5% to 7%), acne, dry skin, folliculitis, keratosis, pruritus, rash, skin malignancies

Endocrine & metabolic: Hot flashes

Gastrointestinal: Nausea (5% to 6%), diarrhea (5% to 6%), gum hyperplasia (4% to 6%), abdominal discomfort (3% to 6%), dyspepsia (2% to 3%), abdominal distention, appetite increased, constipation, gingival bleeding

Genitourinary: Micturition increased

Hematologic: Bleeding disorder, clotting disorder, platelet disorder, red blood cell disorder

Hepatic: Hyperbilirubinemia

Neuromuscular & skeletal: Paresthesia (5% to 7%), arthralgia (1% to 6%)

Ocular: Abnormal vision

Respiratory: Bronchospasm (5%), cough (5%), dyspnea (5%), rhinitis (5%), respiratory infection

Miscellaneous: Flu-like syndrome (8% to 10%)

Postmarketing and/or case reports (any indication): Anaphylaxis/anaphylactoid reaction (possibly associated with Cremophor® EL vehicle in injection formulation), benign intracranial hypertension, cholesterol increased, death (due to renal deterioration), encephalopathy, gout, hyperbilirubinemia, hyperkalemia, hypomagnesemia (mild), impaired consciousness, neurotoxicity, papilloedema, pulmonary edema (noncardiogenic), uric acid increased

Ophthalmic emulsion (Restasis®):

>10%: Ocular: Burning (17%)

1% to 10%: Ocular: Hyperemia (conjunctival 5%), eye pain, pruritus, stinging

Overdosage/Toxicology Symptoms of overdose include hepatotoxicity, nephrotoxicity, nausea, vomiting, tremor. CNS secondary to direct action of the drug may not be reflected in serum concentrations, may be more predictable by renal magnesium loss. Forced emesis may be beneficial if done within 2 hours of ingestion of oral cyclosporine. Treatment is symptom-directed and supportive. Cyclosporine is not dialyzable.

Drug Interactions

Cytochrome P450 Effect: Substrate of CYP3A4 (major); **Inhibits** CYP2C9 (weak), 3A4 (moderate)

Increased Effect/Toxicity: The levels/effects of cyclosporine may be increased by acetazolamide, allopurinol, amiodarone, androgens, antimalarials, azithromycin, azole antifungals, bromocriptine, clarithromycin, colchicine, dichlorphenamide, doxycycline, erythromycin, estrogens, ezetimibe, H₂-blockers, imatinib, imipenem, isoniazid, methazolamide, methotrexate, metoclopramide, nefazodone, nicardipine, norfloxacin, progestins, propofol, protease inhibitors, quinidine, quinupristin/dalfopristin, telithromycin, verapamil, and other CYP3A4 inhibitors. Cyclosporine may increase the levels/effects of selected benzodiazepines, calcium channel blockers, cisapride, ergot alkaloids, selected HMG-CoA reductase inhibitors, mirtazapine, nateglinide, nefazodone, pimozide, (Continued)

CycloSPORINE *(Continued)*

sildenafil (and other PDE-5 inhibitors), tacrolimus, venlafaxine, and other CYP3A4 substrates.

Drugs that enhance nephrotoxicity of cyclosporine include ACE inhibitors, aminoglycosides, amphotericin B, acyclovir, cimetidine, ciprofloxacin, keto-conazole, lovastatin, melphalan, NSAIDs, ranitidine, trimethoprim and sulfamethoxazole, and vancomycin. Cyclosporine increases toxicity of digoxin, methotrexate, minoxidil, nifedipine. Cyclosporine may increase the levels/effects of sirolimus, concurrent therapy with may increase the risk of HUS/TTP/TMA. Cyclosporine may increase the serum concentrations of antineoplastics (doxorubicin, etoposide, and etoposide phosphate), bosentan, caspofungin, diclofenac, ezetimibe, pimecrolimus, repaglinide, and sitaxsentan [CAN]. Cyclosporine may decrease the clearance of colchicine. Systemic corticosteroids may increase the serum concentration of cyclosporine (reported with methylprednisolone). Cyclosporine may increase the serum concentration of systemic corticosteroids. Convulsions have been reported with high-dose methylprednisolone.

Decreased Effect: Antacids, bosentan, griseofulvin, isoniazid octreotide, probucol, and ticlopidine may decrease cyclosporine concentrations. The levels/effects of cyclosporine may be decreased by aminoglutethimide, carbamazepine, nafcillin, nevirapine, oxcarbamazepine, phenobarbital, phenytoin, rifamycins, and other CYP3A4 inducers. Orlistat may decrease absorption of cyclosporine; avoid concomitant use. Vaccination may be less effective; avoid use of live vaccines during therapy. Sulfasalazine and sulfinpyrazone may decrease cyclosporine levels.

Ethanol/Nutrition/Herb Interactions

Food: Grapefruit juice increases absorption; unsupervised use should be avoided.

Herb/Nutraceutical: Avoid St John's wort; as an enzyme inducer, it may increase the metabolism of and decrease plasma levels of cyclosporine; organ rejection and graft loss have been reported. Avoid cat's claw, echinacea (have immunostimulant properties).

Storage/Stability

Capsule: Store at controlled room temperature.

Injection: Store at controlled room temperature; do not refrigerate. Ampuls should be protected from light. Stability of injection of parenteral admixture at room temperature (25°C) is 6 hours in PVC; 24 hours in Excel®, PAB® containers, or glass.

Ophthalmic emulsion: Store at 15°C to 25°C (59°F to 77°F). Vials are single-use; discard immediately following administration.

Oral solution: Store at controlled room temperature; do not refrigerate. Use within 2 months after opening; should be mixed in glass containers.

Reconstitution Sandimmune® injection: Injection should be further diluted [1 mL (50 mg)] of concentrate in 20-100 mL of D_5W or NS] for administration by intravenous infusion.

Compatibility Stable in D_5W, fat emulsion 10%, fat emulsion 20%, NS.

Y-site administration: Compatible: Alatrofloxacin, gatifloxacin, linezolid, propofol, sargramostim. **Incompatible:** Amphotericin B cholesteryl sulfate complex.

Compatibility when admixed: Compatible: Ciprofloxacin. **Incompatible:** Magnesium sulfate.

Mechanism of Action Inhibition of production and release of interleukin II and inhibits interleukin II-induced activation of resting T-lymphocytes.

Pharmacodynamics/Kinetics

Absorption:

Ophthalmic emulsion: Serum concentrations not detectable.

Oral:

Cyclosporine (non-modified): Erratic and incomplete; dependent on presence of food, bile acids, and GI motility; larger oral doses are needed in pediatrics due to shorter bowel length and limited intestinal absorption

Cyclosporine (modified): Erratic and incomplete; increased absorption, up to 30% when compared to cyclosporine (non-modified); less dependent on food, bile acids, or GI motility when compared to cyclosporine (non-modified)

Distribution: Widely in tissues and body fluids including the liver, pancreas, and lungs; crosses placenta; enters breast milk

V_{dss}: 4-6 L/kg in renal, liver, and marrow transplant recipients (slightly lower values in cardiac transplant patients; children <10 years have higher values)

Protein binding: 90% to 98% to lipoproteins

Metabolism: Extensively hepatic via CYP3A4; forms at least 25 metabolites; extensive first-pass effect following oral administration

Bioavailability: Oral:

Cyclosporine (non-modified): Dependent on patient population and transplant type (<10% in adult liver transplant patients and as high as 89% in renal transplant patients; bioavailability of Sandimmune® capsules and oral solution are equivalent; bioavailability of oral solution is ~30% of the I.V. solution

Children: 28% (range: 17% to 42%); gut dysfunction common in BMT patients and oral bioavailability is further reduced

Cyclosporine (modified): Bioavailability of Neoral® capsules and oral solution are equivalent:

Children: 43% (range: 30% to 68%)

Adults: 23% greater than with cyclosporine (non-modified) in renal transplant patients; 50% greater in liver transplant patients

Half-life elimination: Oral: May be prolonged in patients with hepatic impairment and shorter in pediatric patients due to the higher metabolism rate

Cyclosporine (non-modified): Biphasic: Alpha: 1.4 hours; Terminal: 19 hours (range: 10-27 hours)

Cyclosporine (modified): Biphasic: Terminal: 8.4 hours (range: 5-18 hours)

Time to peak, serum: Oral:

Cyclosporine (non-modified): 2-6 hours; some patients have a second peak at 5-6 hours

Cyclosporine (modified): Renal transplant: 1.5-2 hours

Excretion: Primarily feces; urine (6%, 0.1% as unchanged drug and metabolites)

Dosage Neoral®/Genraf® and Sandimmune® are not bioequivalent and cannot be used interchangeably.

Children: Transplant: Refer to adult dosing; children may require, and are able to tolerate, larger doses than adults.

Adults:

Newly-transplanted patients: Adjunct therapy with corticosteroids is recommended. Initial dose should be given 4-12 hours prior to transplant or may be given postoperatively; adjust initial dose to achieve desired plasma concentration

Oral: Dose is dependent upon type of transplant and formulation:

Cyclosporine (modified):

Renal: 9 ± 3 mg/kg/day, divided twice daily

(Continued)

CycloSPORINE *(Continued)*

Liver: 8 ± 4 mg/kg/day, divided twice daily

Heart: 7 ± 3 mg/kg/day, divided twice daily

Cyclosporine (non-modified): Initial dose: 15 mg/kg/day as a single dose (range 14-18 mg/kg); lower doses of 10-14 mg/kg/day have been used for renal transplants. Continue initial dose daily for 1-2 weeks; taper by 5% per week to a maintenance dose of 5-10 mg/kg/day; some renal transplant patients may be dosed as low as 3 mg/kg/day

Note: When using the non-modified formulation, cyclosporine levels may increase in liver transplant patients when the T-tube is closed; dose may need decreased

I.V.: Cyclosporine (non-modified): Manufacturer's labeling: Initial dose: 5-6 mg/kg/day as a single dose ($\frac{1}{3}$ the oral dose), infused over 2-6 hours; use should be limited to patients unable to take capsules or oral solution; patients should be switched to an oral dosage form as soon as possible

Note: Many transplant centers administer cyclosporine as "divided dose" infusions (in 2-3 doses/day) or as a continuous (24-hour) infusion; dosages range from 3-7.5 mg/kg/day. Specific institutional protocols should be consulted.

Conversion to cyclosporine (modified) from cyclosporine (non-modified): Start with daily dose previously used and adjust to obtain preconversion cyclosporine trough concentration. Plasma concentrations should be monitored every 4-7 days and dose adjusted as necessary, until desired trough level is obtained. When transferring patients with previously poor absorption of cyclosporine (non-modified), monitor trough levels at least twice weekly (especially if initial dose exceeds 10 mg/kg/day); high plasma levels are likely to occur.

Rheumatoid arthritis: Oral: Cyclosporine (modified): Initial dose: 2.5 mg/kg/day, divided twice daily; salicylates, NSAIDs, and oral glucocorticoids may be continued (refer to Drug Interactions); dose may be increased by 0.5-0.75 mg/kg/day if insufficient response is seen after 8 weeks of treatment; additional dosage increases may be made again at 12 weeks (maximum dose: 4 mg/kg/day). Discontinue if no benefit is seen by 16 weeks of therapy.

Note: Increase the frequency of blood pressure monitoring after each alteration in dosage of cyclosporine. Cyclosporine dosage should be decreased by 25% to 50% in patients with no history of hypertension who develop sustained hypertension during therapy and, if hypertension persists, treatment with cyclosporine should be discontinued.

Psoriasis: Oral: Cyclosporine (modified): Initial dose: 2.5 mg/kg/day, divided twice daily; dose may be increased by 0.5 mg/kg/day if insufficient response is seen after 4 weeks of treatment. Additional dosage increases may be made every 2 weeks if needed (maximum dose: 4 mg/kg/day). Discontinue if no benefit is seen by 6 weeks of therapy. Once patients are adequately controlled, the dose should be decreased to the lowest effective dose. Doses lower than 2.5 mg/kg/day may be effective. Treatment longer than 1 year is not recommended.

Note: Increase the frequency of blood pressure monitoring after each alteration in dosage of cyclosporine. Cyclosporine dosage should be decreased by 25% to 50% in patients with no history of hypertension who develop sustained hypertension during therapy and, if hypertension persists, treatment with cyclosporine should be discontinued.

Focal segmental glomerulosclerosis (unlabeled use): Initial: 3 mg/kg/day divided every 12 hours

Autoimmune diseases (unlabeled use): 1-3 mg/kg/day

Keratoconjunctivitis sicca: Ophthalmic (Restasis®): Children ≥16 years and Adults: Instill 1 drop in each eye every 12 hours

Dosage adjustment in renal impairment: For severe psoriasis:

Serum creatinine levels ≥25% above pretreatment levels: Take another sample within 2 weeks; if the level remains ≥25% above pretreatment levels, decrease dosage of cyclosporine (modified) by 25% to 50%. If two dosage adjustments do not reverse the increase in serum creatinine levels, treatment should be discontinued.

Serum creatinine levels ≥50% above pretreatment levels: Decrease cyclosporine dosage by 25% to 50%. If two dosage adjustments do not reverse the increase in serum creatinine levels, treatment should be discontinued.

Hemodialysis: Supplemental dose is not necessary.

Peritoneal dialysis: Supplemental dose is not necessary.

Dosage adjustment in hepatic impairment: Probably necessary; monitor levels closely

Administration

Oral solution: Do not administer liquid from plastic or styrofoam cup. May dilute Neoral® oral solution with orange juice or apple juice. May dilute Sandimmune® oral solution with milk, chocolate milk, or orange juice. Avoid changing diluents frequently. Mix thoroughly and drink at once. Use syringe provided to measure dose. Mix in a glass container and rinse container with more diluent to ensure total dose is taken. Do not rinse syringe before or after use (may cause dose variation).

I.V.: The manufacturer recommends that following dilution, intravenous admixture be administered over 2-6 hours. However, many transplant centers administer as divided doses (2-3 doses/day) or as a 24-hour continuous infusion. Discard solution after 24 hours. Anaphylaxis has been reported with I.V. use; reserve for patients who cannot take oral form. Patients should be under continuous observation for at least the first 30 minutes of the infusion, and should be monitored frequently thereafter. Maintain patent airway; other supportive measures and agents for treating anaphylaxis should be present when I.V. drug is given.

Ophthalmic emulsion: Prior to use, invert vial several times to obtain a uniform emulsion. Remove contact lenses prior to instillation of drops; may be reinserted 15 minutes after administration. May be used with artificial tears; allow 15 minute interval between products.

Monitoring Parameters Monitor blood pressure and serum creatinine after any cyclosporine dosage changes or addition, modification, or deletion of other medications. Monitor plasma concentrations periodically.

Transplant patients: Cyclosporine trough levels, serum electrolytes, renal function, hepatic function, blood pressure, lipid profile

Psoriasis therapy: Baseline blood pressure, serum creatinine (2 levels each), BUN, CBC, serum magnesium, potassium, uric acid, lipid profile. Biweekly monitoring of blood pressure, complete blood count, and levels of BUN, uric acid, potassium, lipids, and magnesium during the first 3 months of treatment for psoriasis. Monthly monitoring is recommended after this initial period. Also evaluate any atypical skin lesions prior to therapy. Increase the frequency of blood pressure monitoring after each alteration in dosage of cyclosporine. Cyclosporine dosage should be decreased by 25% to 50% in patients with no history of hypertension who develop sustained hypertension during therapy and, if hypertension persists, treatment with cyclosporine should be discontinued.

Rheumatoid arthritis: Baseline blood pressure, and serum creatinine (2 levels each); serum creatinine every 2 weeks for first 3 months, then

(Continued)

CycloSPORINE *(Continued)*

monthly if patient is stable. Increase the frequency of blood pressure monitoring after each alteration in dosage of cyclosporine. Cyclosporine dosage should be decreased by 25% to 50% in patients with no history of hypertension who develop sustained hypertension during therapy and, if hypertension persists, treatment with cyclosporine should be discontinued.

Test Interactions Specific whole blood, HPLC assay for cyclosporine may be falsely elevated if sample is drawn from the same line through which dose was administered (even if flush has been administered and/or dose was given hours before).

Dietary Considerations Administer this medication consistently with relation to time of day and meals. Avoid grapefruit juice.

Patient Information Use glass container for liquid solution (do not use plastic or styrofoam cup). Diluting oral solution improves flavor. May dilute Neoral® oral solution with orange juice or apple juice. May dilute Sandimmune® oral solution with milk, chocolate milk, or orange juice. Avoid changing what you mix with your cyclosporine. Mix thoroughly and drink at once. Use syringe provided to measure dose. Mix in a glass container and rinse container with more juice/milk to ensure total dose is taken. Do not rinse syringe before or after use (may cause dose variation). Take dose at the same time each day. You will be susceptible to infection; avoid crowds and exposure to any infectious diseases. Do not have any vaccinations without consulting prescriber. Practice good oral hygiene to reduce gum inflammation; see dentist regularly during treatment. Report severe headache; unusual hair growth or deepening of voice; mouth sores or swollen gums; persistent nausea, vomiting, or abdominal pain; muscle pain or cramping; unusual swelling of extremities, weight gain, or change in urination; or chest pain or rapid heartbeat. Increases in blood pressure or damage to the kidney are possible. Your prescriber will need to monitor closely. Do not change one brand of cyclosporine for another; any changes must be done by your prescriber. If you are taking this medication for psoriasis, your risk of cancer may be increased when taking additional medications.

Ophthalmic emulsion: Prior to use, invert vial several times to obtain a uniform emulsion. Remove contact lenses prior to instillation of drops; may be reinserted 15 minutes after administration. May be used with artificial tears; allow 15 minute interval between products.

Special Geriatric Considerations Cyclosporine has not been specifically studied in the elderly. Cyclosporine is being used in combination therapy for the treatment of severe rheumatoid arthritis.

Additional Information Cyclosporine (modified): Refers to the capsule dosage formulation of cyclosporine in an aqueous dispersion (previously referred to as "microemulsion"). Cyclosporine (modified) has increased bioavailability as compared to cyclosporine (non-modified) and cannot be used interchangeably without close monitoring.

Emetic Potential Very low (<10%)

Vesicant No

Dosage Forms Excipient information presented when available (limited, particularly for generics); consult specific product labeling.

Capsule, soft gel, modified: 25 mg, 100 mg [contains castor oil, ethanol]
Gengraf®: 25 mg, 100 mg [contains ethanol, castor oil, propylene glycol]
Neoral®: 25 mg, 100 mg [contains dehydrated ethanol, corn oil, castor oil, propylene glycol]
Capsule, soft gel, non-modified (Sandimmune®): 25 mg, 100 mg [contains dehydrated ethanol, corn oil]

Emulsion, ophthalmic [preservative free, single-use vial] (Restasis®): 0.05% (0.4 mL) [contains glycerin, castor oil, polysorbate 80, carbomer 1342; 32 vials/box]

Injection, solution, non-modified (Sandimmune®): 50 mg/mL (5 mL) [contains Cremophor® EL (polyoxyethylated castor oil), ethanol]

Solution, oral, modified:

Gengraf®: 100 mg/mL (50 mL) [contains castor oil, propylene glycol]

Neoral®: 100 mg/mL (50 mL) [contains dehydrated ethanol, corn oil, castor oil, propylene glycol]

Solution, oral, non-modified (Sandimmune®): 100 mg/mL (50 mL) [contains olive oil, ethanol]

References

"American Academy of Pediatrics Committee on Drugs. The Transfer of Drugs and Other Chemicals Into Human Milk," *Pediatrics*, 2001, 108(3):776-89.

Andrews DJ and Cramb R, "Cyclosporin: Revisions in Monitoring Guidelines and Review of Current Analytical Methods," *Ann Clin Biochem*, 2002, 39(Pt 5):424-35.

Bachmann K, Jauregui L, Chandra R, et al, "Influence of a 3-Day Regimen of Azithromycin on the Disposition Kinetics of Cyclosporine A in Stable Renal Transplant Patients," *Pharmacol Res*, 2003, 47(6):549-54.

Bachmann K, Sullivan TJ, Reese JH, et al, "The Influence of Dirithromycin on the Pharmacokinetics of Cyclosporine in Healthy Subjects and in Renal Transplant Patients," *Am J Ther*, 1995, 2(7):490-8.

Back DJ and Tjia JF, "Comparative Effects of the Antimycotic Drugs Ketoconazole, Fluconazole, Itraconazole and Terbinafine on the Metabolism of Cyclosporin by Human Liver Microsomes," *Br J Clin Pharmacol*, 1991, 32(5):624-6.

Benfield MR, Tejani A, Harmon WE, et al, "A Randomized Multicenter Trial of OKT3 mAbs Induction Compared With Intravenous Cyclosporine in Pediatric Renal Transplantation," *Pediatr Transplant*, 2005, 9(3):282-92.

Boni R and Dummer R, "Abscessed Inflammation as a Serious Complication of Low Dose Cyclosporin A in Atopic Dermatitis," *Eur J Dermatol*, 1995, 5:268-9.

Bulengo-Ransby SM, Sahn EE, Metcalf JS, et al, "Bowenoid Change in Association With Graft-Versus-Host Disease: A Cyclosporine Toxicity?" *J Am Acad Dermatol*, 1994, 31(6):1052-4.

Burckart GJ, Canafax DM, and Yee GC, "Cyclosporine Monitoring," *Drug Intell Clin Pharm*, 1986, 20(9):649-52.

Caforio AL, Gambino A, Tona F, "Sulfinpyrazone Reduces Cyclosporine Levels: A New Drug Interaction in Heart Transplant Recipients," *J Heart Lung Transplant*, 2000, 19(12):1205-8.

Calonge VM, Glotz D, Bouscary D, et al, "Hemophagocytic Histiocytosis (HH) in Renal Transplant Recipients Under Ciclosporin Therapy: Report of the First Two Cases," *Clin Transpl*, 1995, 9(2):88-91.

Cooney GF, Mochon M, Kaiser B, et al, "Effects of Carbamazepine on Cyclosporine Metabolism in Pediatric Renal Transplant Recipients," *Pharmacotherapy*, 1995, 15(3):353-6.

Davies MG and Bowers PW, "Alopecia Areata Arising in Patients Receiving Cyclosporin Immunosuppression," *Br J Dermatol*, 1995, 132(5):835-6.

Ducharme MP, Warbasse LH, and Edwards DJ, "Disposition of Intravenous and Oral Cyclosporine After Administration With Grapefruit Juice," *Clin Pharmacol Ther*, 1995, 57(5):485-91.

Dunn CJ, Wagstaff AJ, Perry CM, et al, "Cyclosporin: An Updated Review of the Pharmacokinetic Properties, Clinical Efficacy and Tolerability of a Microemulsion-Based Formulation (Neoral)1 in Organ Transplantation," *Drugs*, 2001, 61(13):1957-2016.

Finielz P, Mondon JM, Chuet C, et al, "Drug Interactions Between Midecamycin and Cyclosporin," *Nephron*, 1995, 70(1):136.

Higgins EM, Hughes JR, Snowden S, et al, "Cyclosporin-Induced Periungual Granulation Tissue," *Br J Dermatol*, 1995, 132(5):829-30.

Hollander AA, van Rooij J, Lentjes GW, et al, "The Effect of Grapefruit Juice on Cyclosporine and Prednisone Metabolism in Transplant Patients," *Clin Pharmacol Ther*, 1995, 57(3):318-24.

Holt DW, Mueller EA, Kovarik JM, et al, "Sandimmune® Neoral® Pharmacokinetics: Impact of the New Oral Formulation," *Transplant Proc*, 1995, 27(1):1434-7.

Honcharik N and Anthone S, "Activated Charcoal in Acute Cyclosporine Overdose," *Lancet*, 1985, 1(8436):1051.

Horton RC and Bonser RS, "Interaction Between Cyclosporin and Fluoxetine," *BMJ*, 1995, 311(7002):422.

Hughes RL, "Cyclosporine-Related Central Nervous System Toxicity in Cardiac Transplantation," *N Engl J Med*, 1990, 323(6):420-1.

(Continued)

CycloSPORINE (Continued)

Jensen P, Lehne G, Fauchald P, et al, "Effect of Oral Terbinafine Treatment on Cyclosporin Pharmacokinetics in Organ Transplant Recipients With Dermatophyte Nail Infection," *Acta Derm Venereol*, 1996, 76(4):280-1.

Kabeer MH, Filo RS, Milgrom ML, et al, "Central Pontine Myelinolysis Following Orthotopic Liver Transplant: Association With Cyclosporine Toxicity," *Postgrad Med J*, 1995, 71(834):239-41.

Kahan BD, "Cyclosporine," *N Engl J Med*, 1989, 321(25):1725-38.

Kaufman DB, Kaplan B, Kanwar YS, et al, "The Successful Use of Tacrolimus (FK506) in a Pancreas/Kidney Transplant Recipient With Recurrent Cyclosporine-Associated Hemolytic Uremic Syndrome," *Transplantation*, 1995, 59(12):1737-9.

Kino KJ and Wittkowsky AK, "Influence of Bile Acid Replacement on Cyclosporine Absorption in a Patient With Jejunoileal Bypass," *Pharmacotherapy*, 1995, 15(3):350-2.

Lichtenstein GR, Abreu MT, Cohen R, et al, "American Gastroenterological Association Institute Technical Review on Corticosteroids, Immunomodulators, and Infliximab in Inflammatory Bowel Disease," *Gastroenterology*, 2006, 30(3):940-87.

Lin CY and Lee SF, "Comparison of Pharmacokinetics Between CsA Capsules and Sandimmune® Neoral® in Pediatric Patients," *Transplant Proc*, 1994, 26(5):2973-4.

Ljutic D and Rumboldt Z, "Possible Interaction Between Azithromycin and Cyclosporin: A Case Report," *Nephron*, 1995, 70(1):130.

Long CC, Hill SA, Thomas RC, et al, "Effect of Terbinafine on the Pharmacokinetics of Cyclosporin in Humans,: *J Invest Dermatol*, 1994, 102(5):740-3.

McIntyre HD, Menzies B, Rigby R, et al, "Long-Term Bone Loss After Renal Transplantation: Comparison of Immunosuppressive Regimens," *Clin Transplant*, 1995, 9(1):20-4.

Memon M, de Magalhace-Silverman M, Bloom EJ, et al, "Reversible Cyclosporine-Induced Cortical Blindness in Allogeneic Bone Marrow Transplant Recipients," *Bone Marrow Transplant*, 1995, 15(2):283-6.

Morales JM, Muñoz MA, Fernandez Zatarain G, et al, "Reversible Acute Renal Failure Caused by the Combined Use of Foscarnet and Cyclosporin in Organ Transplanted Patients," *Nephrol Dial Transplant*, 1995, 10(6):882-3.

Niese D, "A Double-Blind Randomized Study of Sandimmune® Neoral® vs Sandimmune® in New Renal Transplant Recipients: Results After 12 Months," *Transplant Proc*, 1995, 27(2):1849-56.

Page RL 2nd, Ruscin JM, Fish D, et al, "Possible Interaction Between Intravenous Azithromycin and Oral Cyclosporine," *Pharmacotherapy*, 2001, 21(11):1436-43.

Passfall J, Schuller I, and Keller F, "Pharmacokinetics of Cyclosporin During Administration of Danazol," *Nephrol Dial Transplant*, 1994, 9(12):1807-8.

Pollard S, Nashan B, Johnston A, et al, "A Pharmacokinetic and Clinical Review of the Potential Clinical Impact of Using Different Formulations of Cyclosporin A. Berlin, Germany, November 19, 2001," *Clin Ther*, 2003, 25(6): 1654-69.

Ratanatharathorn V, Nash RA, Przepiorka D, et al, "Phase III Study Comparing Methotrexate and Tacrolimus (Prograf, FK506) With Methotrexate and Cyclosporine for Graft-Versus-Host Disease Prophylaxis After HLA-Identical Sibling Bone Marrow Transplantation," *Blood*, 1998, 92(7):2303-14.

Scalzini A, Barni C, Stellini R, et al, "Fatal Invasive Aspergillosis During Cyclosporine and Steroids Treatment for Crohn's Disease," *Dig Dis Sci*, 1995, 40(3):528.

Sharma RK, Kumar P, Rai P, et al, "Cyclosporine Neurotoxicity in a Renal-Transplant Recipient," *Nephron*, 1995, 70(2):269.

Taesch S, Niese D, and Mueller EA, "Sandimmune® Neoral®, A New Oral Formulation of Cyclosporine With Improved Pharmacokinetic Characteristics: Safety and Tolerability in Renal Transplant Patients," *Transplant Proc*, 1994, 26(6):3147-9.

Tugwell P, Pincus T, Yocum D, et al, "Combination Therapy With Cyclosporine and Methotrexate in Severe Rheumatoid Arthritis," *N Engl J Med*, 1995, 333(3):137-41.

Wahlstrom E, Zamora JU, and Teichman S, "Improvement in Cyclosporin-Associated Gingival Hyperplasia With Azithromycin Therapy," *N Engl J Med*, 1995, 332(11):753-4.

Wallemacq PE and Lesne ML, "Accidental Massive I.V. Administration of Cyclosporine in Man," *Drug Intell Clin Pharm*, 1985, 19(1):29-30.

Wandstrat TL, Schroeder TJ, and Myre SA, "Cyclosporine Pharmacokinetics in Pediatric Transplant Recipients," *Ther Drug Monit*, 1989, 11(5):493-6.

Wells G and Tugwell P, "Cyclosporin A in Rheumatoid Arthritis: Overview of Efficacy," *Br J Rheumatol*, 1993, 32(Suppl 1):51-6.

Yee GC and McGuire TR, "Pharmacokinetic Drug Interactions With Cyclosporine," *Clin Pharmacokinet*, 1990, 19(4):319-32 and 19(5):400-15.

Yee GC, "Recent Advances in Cyclosporine Pharmacokinetics," *Pharmacotherapy*, 1991, 11(5):130S-134S.

♦ **Cyklokapron**® *see* Tranexamic Acid *on page 1064*

Cyproheptadine (si proe HEP ta deen)

Medication Safety Issues

Sound-alike/look-alike issues:

Cyproheptadine may be confused with cyclobenzaprine

Periactin may be confused with Perative®, Percodan®, Persantine®

Index Terms Cyproheptadine Hydrochloride; Periactin

Generic Available Yes

Pharmacologic Category Antihistamine

Use Perennial and seasonal allergic rhinitis and other allergic symptoms including urticaria

Unlabeled/Investigational Use Appetite stimulation, blepharospasm, cluster headaches, migraine headaches, Nelson's syndrome, pruritus, schizophrenia, spinal cord damage associated spasticity, and tardive dyskinesia

Pregnancy Risk Factor B

Lactation Excretion in breast milk unknown/contraindicated

Labeled Contraindications Hypersensitivity to cyproheptadine or any component of the formulation; narrow-angle glaucoma; bladder neck obstruction; symptomatic prostatic hyperplasia; acute asthmatic attack; stenosing peptic ulcer; GI tract obstruction; concurrent use of MAO inhibitors; avoid use in premature and term newborns due to potential association with SIDS

Warnings/Precautions May cause CNS depression, which may impair physical or mental abilities; patients must be cautioned about performing tasks which require mental alertness (eg, operating machinery or driving). Effects may be potentiated when used with other sedative drugs or ethanol. Use with caution in patients with cardiovascular disease; increased intraocular pressure; respiratory disease; or thyroid dysfunction. Use with caution in the elderly; may be more sensitive to adverse effects. In case reports, cyproheptadine has promoted weight gain in anorexic adults, though it has not been specifically studied in the elderly. All cases of weight loss or decreased appetite should be adequately assessed. Antihistamines may cause excitation in young children. Safety and efficacy have not been established in children <2 years of age.

Adverse Reactions

>10%:

Central nervous system: Slight-to-moderate drowsiness

Respiratory: Thickening of bronchial secretions

1% to 10%:

Central nervous system: Dizziness, fatigue, headache, nervousness

Gastrointestinal: Abdominal pain, appetitie stimulation, diarrhea, nausea, xerostomia

Neuromuscular & skeletal: Arthralgia

Respiratory: Pharyngitis

<1%: Allergic reaction, angioedema, bronchospasm, CNS stimulation, depression, edema, epistaxis, hemolytic anemia, hepatitis, leukopenia, myalgia, palpitation, paresthesia, photosensitivity, rash, sedation, seizure, tachycardia, thrombocytopenia

Overdosage/Toxicology Symptoms of overdose include CNS depression or stimulation, dry mouth, flushed skin, fixed and dilated pupils, and apnea. There is no specific treatment for antihistamine overdose. Clinical toxicity is due to blockade of cholinergic receptors. For anticholinergic overdose with severe life-threatening symptoms, physostigmine 1-2 mg I.V. slowly, may be given to reverse these effects.

(Continued)

Cyproheptadine *(Continued)*

Drug Interactions
Increased Effect/Toxicity: Cyproheptadine may potentiate the effect of CNS depressants. MAO inhibitors may cause hallucinations when taken with cyproheptadine.

Ethanol/Nutrition/Herb Interactions Ethanol: Avoid ethanol (may increase CNS sedation).

Mechanism of Action A potent antihistamine and serotonin antagonist, competes with histamine for H_1-receptor sites on effector cells in the gastrointestinal tract, blood vessels, and respiratory tract

Pharmacodynamics/Kinetics
Absorption: Completely

Metabolism: Almost completely hepatic

Excretion: Urine (>50% primarily as metabolites); feces (~25%)

Dosage Oral:
Children:

Allergic conditions: 0.25 mg/kg/day or 8 mg/m^2/day in 2-3 divided doses **or**
2-6 years: 2 mg every 8-12 hours (not to exceed 12 mg/day)
7-14 years: 4 mg every 8-12 hours (not to exceed 16 mg/day)
Migraine headaches: 4 mg 2-3 times/day

Children ≥12 years and Adults: Spasticity associated with spinal cord damage: 4 mg at bedtime; increase by a 4 mg dose every 3-4 days; average daily dose: 16 mg in divided doses; not to exceed 36 mg/day

Children >13 years and Adults: Appetite stimulation (anorexia nervosa): 2 mg 4 times/day; may be increased gradually over a 3-week period to 8 mg 4 times/day

Adults:

Allergic conditions: 4-20 mg/day divided every 8 hours (not to exceed 0.5 mg/kg/day)
Cluster headaches: 4 mg 4 times/day
Migraine headaches: 4-8 mg 3 times/day

Dosage adjustment in hepatic impairment: Reduce dosage in patients with significant hepatic dysfunction

Test Interactions Diagnostic antigen skin test results may be suppressed; false positive serum TCA screen

Patient Information May stimulate appetite. Avoid alcohol and other CNS depressants. May cause drowsiness. May impair judgment and coordination.

Special Geriatric Considerations In case reports, cyproheptadine has promoted weight gain in anorexic adults, though it has not been specifically studied in the elderly. All cases of weight loss or decreased appetite should be adequately assessed. Cyproheptadine may cause less sedation than diphenhydramine or hydroxyzine and, therefore, may be useful for pruritus in elderly; however, elderly may not tolerate anticholinergic effects.

Additional Information May stimulate appetite. In case reports, cyproheptadine has promoted weight gain in anorexic adults.

Emetic Potential Very low (<10%)

Dosage Forms Excipient information presented when available (limited, particularly for generics); consult specific product labeling.

Syrup, as hydrochloride: 2 mg/5 mL (473 mL) [contains alcohol 5%; mint flavor]

Tablet, as hydrochloride: 4 mg

References
Carlton MC, Kunkel DB, and Curry SC, "Ergotism Treated With Cyproheptadine," *Clin Toxicol*, 1995, 33(5):552.

Craven JL and Rodin GM, "Cyproheptadine Dependence Associated With an Atypical Somato-
form Disorder," *Can J Psychiatry,* 1987, 32(2):143-5.

Herzog DB and Copeland PM, "Eating Disorders," *N Engl J Med,* 1985, 313(5):295-303.

Lappin RI and Auchincloss EL, "Treatment of the Serotonin Syndrome With Cyproheptadine," *N
Engl J Med,* 1994, 331(15):1021-2.

Wians FH, Norton JT, and Wirebaugh, "False-Positive Serum Tricyclic Antidepressant Screen
With Cyproheptadine," *Clin Chem,* 1993, 39(6):1355-6.

♦ **Cyproheptadine Hydrochloride** *see* Cyproheptadine *on page 265*

Cyproterone (sye PROE ter one)

Index Terms Cyproterone Acetate

Generic Available Yes

Canadian Brand Names Androcur®; Androcur® Depot; Apo-Cyproterone®;
Gen-Cyproterone; Novo-Cyproterone

Pharmacologic Category Antiandrogen

Use Palliative treatment of advanced prostate carcinoma

Restrictions Not available in U.S.

Pregnancy Risk Factor Not indicated for use in women

Labeled Contraindications Hypersensitivity to cyproterone or any component of the formulation; active liver disease or hepatic dysfunction; renal
impairment

Warnings/Precautions Cyproterone has been associated with hepatic
toxicity (jaundice, hepatitis, hepatic failure); typically this toxicity develops
after several months of therapy. Monitor hepatic function and consider
discontinuation of therapy in patients with evidence of hepatic injury.

Use caution in patients with a history of depression. Cyproterone has been
associated with an increased incidence of depression, particularly early in
the course of therapy (initial 6-8 weeks). Use with caution in patients with
diabetes or impaired glucose tolerance, may cause alterations in glucose
metabolism. Use with caution in conditions that may be aggravated by fluid
retention, or cardiovascular disease. May increase the risk of thromboembolism and/or alter lipid profiles.

Adverse Reactions Frequency not defined.

Cardiovascular: Heart failure, hemorrhage, hypotension, MI, stroke, shock,
stroke, syncope, tachycardia, thrombosis (DVT, pulmonary embolism,
retinal vein thrombosis)

Central nervous system: Depression, dizziness, encephalopathy, fatigue,
headache, lassitude

Dermatologic: Dry skin (sebum reduction), eczema, erythema, exfoliative
dermatitis, hirsutism, nodosum, patchy loss of body hair, photosensitivity,
pruritus, rash, scleroderma, skin discoloration, urticaria

Endocrine & metabolic: Adrenal suppression (dose related), benign nodular
breast hyperplasia, diabetes mellitus, galactorrhea, gynecomastia, hot
flashes, hypercalcemia, hyperglycemia, impotence, inhibition of spermatogenesis, libido increased, negative nitrogen balance, weight gain/loss

Gastrointestinal: Anorexia, constipation, diarrhea, dyspepsia, glossitis,
nausea, pancreatitis, vomiting

Genitourinary: Bladder carcinoma, hematuria, urinary frequency

Hematologic: Anemia, fibrinogen increased, hemolytic anemia, leukopenia,
leukocytosis, PT decreased, thrombocytopenia

Hepatic: Ascites, cholestatic jaundice, cirrhosis, hepatic dysfunction (dose
related), hepatic carcinoma, hepatic coma, hepatic failure, hepatic
necrosis, hepatitis, hepatoma, hepatomegaly, transaminases increased

Local: Injection site reaction

Neuromuscular and skeletal: Myasthenia, osteoporosis, weakness

(Continued)

Cyproterone (Continued)

Ocular: Abnormal accommodation, abnormal vision, blindness, optic neuritis, optic atrophy, retinal disorder

Renal: Renal failure, serum creatinine increased

Respiratory: Asthma, bronchospasm, cough, dyspnea, pulmonary embolism, pulmonary fibrosis

Miscellaneous: Allergic reaction

Overdosage/Toxicology Toxicity is unlikely following single exposures of excessive doses. Any treatment following emesis and charcoal administration should be supportive and symptomatic.

Ethanol/Nutrition/Herb Interactions

Ethanol: May reduce the effect of cyproterone (not established in the treatment of prostatic carcinoma); avoid concurrent use.

Storage/Stability Store at controlled room temperature of 25°C (77°F).

Mechanism of Action Cyproterone is a steroidal compound with antiandrogenic, antigonadotropic, and progestin-like activity.

Pharmacodynamics/Kinetics

Absorption: Oral: Rapid and complete

Metabolism: Hepatic, some metabolites have activity

Half-life elimination: Oral: 38 hours; Depot injection: 4 days

Time to peak, plasma: Oral: 3-4 hours; Depot injection: 3 days

Excretion: Urine (35%, as metabolites); feces (60%)

Dosage Adults: Males: Prostatic carcinoma (palliative treatment):

Oral: 200-300 mg/day in 2-3 divided doses; following orchiectomy, reduce dose to 100-200 mg/day; should be taken with meals

I.M. (depot): 300 mg (3 mL) once weekly; reduce dose in orchiectomized patients to 300 mg every 2 weeks

Dosage adjustment in renal impairment: Use is contraindicated

Dosage adjustment in hepatic impairment: Use is contraindicated with hepatic impairment or active liver disease

Administration Administer at the same time each day. Take with meals.

Monitoring Parameters Liver function tests should be performed at baseline and periodically thereafter, or whenever signs or symptoms suggestive of hepatotoxicity are noted. Adrenal function should be monitored periodically.

Patient Information Immediately report pain or muscle soreness; warmth, swelling, pain, or redness in calves; shortness of breath; sudden loss of vision; unresolved leg/foot swelling; acute abdominal cramping; CNS changes (blurred vision, confusion, acute anxiety, or unresolved depression); or significant weight gain (>5 lb/week). Notify prescriber of changes in contact lens tolerance.

Dosage Forms Excipient information presented when available (limited, particularly for generics); consult specific product labeling.

Injection, solution, as acetate (Androcur® Depot): 100 mg/mL (3 mL) [contains benzyl benzoate and castor oil]

Tablet, as acetate (Androcur®): 50 mg

References

Barradell LB and Faulds D, "Cyproterone. A Review of its Pharmacology and Therapeutic Efficacy in Prostate Cancer," *Drugs Aging*, 1994, 5(1):59-80.

Goldenberg SL and Bruchovsky N, "Use of Cyproterone Acetate in Prostate Cancer," *Urol Clin North Am*, 1991, 18(1):111-22.

Neumann F and Kalmus J, "Cyproterone Acetate in the Treatment of Sexual Disorders: Pharmacological Base and Clinical Experience," *Exp Clin Endocrinol*, 1991, 98(2):71-80.

Neumann F, "Pharmacology and Potential Use of Cyproterone Acetate," *Horm Metab Res*, 1977, 9(1):1-13.

Neumann F, "The Antiandrogen Cyproterone Acetate: Discovery, Chemistry, Basic Pharmacology, Clinical Use and Tool in Basic Research," *Exp Clin Endocrinol*, 1994, 102(1):1-32.

Schroder FH, "Cyproterone Acetate--Mechanism of Action and Clinical Effectiveness in Prostate Cancer Treatment," *Cancer*, 1993, 72(12 Suppl):3810-5.

♦ **Cyproterone Acetate** *see Cyproterone on page 267*
♦ **CYT** *see Cyclophosphamide on page 246*
♦ **Cytadren®** *see Aminoglutethimide on page 65*

Cytarabine (sye TARE a been)
Medication Safety Issues
Sound-alike/look-alike issues:
Cytarabine may be confused with Cytadren®, Cytosar®, Cytoxan®, vidarabine
Cytarabine (conventional) may be confused with cytarabine liposomal
Cytosar-U® may be confused with cytarabine, Cytovene®, Cytoxan®, Neosar®

High alert medication: The Institute for Safe Medication Practices (ISMP) includes this medication among its list of drugs which have a heightened risk of causing significant patient harm when used in error.
Related Information
Fertility and Cancer Therapy *on page 1298*
Hematopoietic Stem Cell Transplantation *on page 1366*
Safe Handling of Hazardous Drugs *on page 1382*
Index Terms Arabinosylcytosine; Ara-C; Cytarabine (Conventional); Cytarabine Hydrochloride; Cytosar-U; Cytosine Arabinosine Hydrochloride; NSC-63878
Generic Available Yes
Canadian Brand Names Cytosar®
Pharmacologic Category Antineoplastic Agent, Antimetabolite; Antineoplastic Agent, Antimetabolite (Pyrimidine Analog)
Use Treatment of acute myeloid leukemia (AML), acute lymphocytic leukemia (ALL), chronic myelocytic leukemia (CML; blast phase), and lymphomas; prophylaxis and treatment of meningeal leukemia
Pregnancy Risk Factor D
Lactation Excretion in breast milk unknown/not recommended
Labeled Contraindications Hypersensitivity to cytarabine or any component of the formulation
Warnings/Precautions Hazardous agent - use appropriate precautions for handling and disposal. **[U.S. Boxed Warning]: Potent myelosuppressive agent;** use with caution in patients with prior bone marrow suppression; monitor for signs of febrile neutropenia.

High-dose regimens are associated with CNS, gastrointestinal, ocular (prophylaxis with ophthalmic corticosteroid drops is recommended), pulmonary toxicities and cardiomyopathy. Neurotoxicity associated with high dose treatment may present as acute cerebellar toxicity, or may be severe with seizure and/or coma; may be delayed, occurring up to 3 to 8 days after treatment has begun. Risk factors for neurotoxicity include cumulative cytarabine dose, prior CNS disease and renal impairment. Tumor lysis syndrome and subsequent hyperuricemia may occur with high dose cytarabine; monitor, consider allopurinol and hydrate accordingly. There have been case reports of fatal cardiomyopathy when high dose cytarabine was used in combination with cyclophosphamide as a preparation regimen for transplantation.

Use with caution in patients with impaired renal and hepatic function; may be at higher risk for CNS toxicities; dosage adjustments may be necessary. Cytarabine syndrome is characterized by fever, myalgia, bone pain, chest (Continued)

Cytarabine *(Continued)*

pain, maculopapular rash, conjunctivitis, and malaise, and may occur 6-12 hours following administration; may be managed with corticosteroids. There have been reports of acute pancreatitis in patients receiving continuous infusion and in patients previously treated with L-asparaginase. **[U.S. Boxed Warning]: Should be administered under the supervision of an experienced cancer chemotherapy physician.** Some products may contain benzyl alcohol; do not use products containing benzyl alcohol or products reconstituted with bacteriostatic diluent intrathecally or for high-dose cytarabine regimens.

Adverse Reactions Note: Frequency not defined.

Frequent:

Central nervous system: Fever

Dermatologic: Rash

Gastrointestinal: Anal inflammation, anal ulceration, anorexia, diarrhea, mucositis, nausea, vomiting

Hematologic: Myelosuppression, neutropenia (onset: 1-7 days; nadir [biphasic]: 7-9 days and at 15-24 days; recovery [biphasic]: 9-12 and at 24-34 days), thrombocytopenia (onset: 5 days; nadir: 12-15 days; recovery 15-25 days), anemia, bleeding, leukopenia, megaloblastosis, reticulocytes decreased

Hepatic: Hepatic dysfunction, transaminases increased (acute)

Local: Thrombophlebitis

Less frequent:

Cardiovascular: Chest pain, pericarditis

Central nervous system: Dizziness, headache, neural toxicity, neuritis

Dermatologic: Alopecia, pruritus, skin freckling, skin ulceration, urticaria

Gastrointestinal: Abdominal pain, bowel necrosis, esophageal ulceration, esophagitis, pancreatitis, sore throat

Genitourinary: Urinary retention

Hepatic: Jaundice

Local: Injection site cellulitis

Ocular: Conjunctivitis

Renal: Renal dysfunction

Respiratory: Dyspnea

Miscellaneous: Allergic edema, anaphylaxis, sepsis

Infrequent and/or case reports: Amylase increased, aseptic meningitis, cardiopulmonary arrest (acute), cerebral dysfunction, cytarabine syndrome (bone pain, chest pain, conjunctivitis, fever, maculopapular rash, malaise, myalgia); exanthematous pustulosis, hyperuricemia, injection site inflammation (SubQ injection), injection site pain (SubQ injection), interstitial pneumonitis, lipase increased, paralysis (intrathecal and I.V. combination therapy), rhabdomyolysis, veno-occlusive liver disease

Adverse events associated with high-dose cytarabine (CNS, gastrointestinal, ocular and pulmonary toxicities are more common with high-dose regimens):

Cardiovascular: Cardiomegaly, cardiomyopathy (in combination with cyclophosphamide)

Central nervous system: Coma, neurotoxicity (dose-related, cerebellar toxicity may occur in patients receiving high-dose cytarabine [>36-48 g/m^2/cycle]; incidence may up to 55% in patients with renal impairment), personality change, somnolence

Dermatologic: Alopecia (complete), desquamation, rash (severe)

Gastrointestinal: Gastrointestinal ulcer, peritonitis, pneumatosis cystoides intestinalis

Hepatic: Hyperbilirubinemia, liver abscess, liver damage, necrotizing colitis

Neuromuscular & skeletal: Peripheral neuropathy (motor and sensory)

Ocular: Corneal toxicity, hemorrhagic conjunctivitis

Respiratory: Pulmonary edema, syndrome of sudden respiratory distress

Miscellaneous: Sepsis

Adverse events associated with intrathecal cytarabine administration:

Central nervous system: Accessory nerve paralysis, fever, necrotizing leukoencephalopathy (with concurrent cranial irradiation, I.T. methotrexate, and I.T. hydrocortisone), neurotoxicity, paraplegia

Gastrointestinal: Dysphagia, nausea, vomiting

Ocular: Blindness (with concurrent systemic chemotherapy and cranial irradiation), diplopia

Respiratory: Cough, hoarseness

Miscellaneous: Aphonia

Overdosage/Toxicology Doses of 4.5 g/m^2 every 12 hours for 12 doses (total of 54 g/m^2) have resulted in irreversible CNS toxicity and death. Symptoms of overdose include myelosuppression, megaloblastosis, nausea, vomiting, respiratory distress, and pulmonary edema. A syndrome of sudden respiratory distress progressing to pulmonary edema and cardiomegaly has been reported following high doses. Treatment is symptom-directed and supportive.

Drug Interactions

Decreased Effect: Cytarabine may decrease the effect of flucytosine; cytarabine may decrease digoxin absorption.

Storage/Stability

Powder for reconstitution: Store intact vials of powder at room temperature 15°C to 30°C (59°F to 86°F). Reconstituted solutions are stable for up to 8 days at room temperature, although the manufacturer recommends use within 48 hours.

Solution: Prior to dilution, store at room temperature, 15°C to 30°C (59°F to 86°F); protect from light. Do not refrigerate solution; precipitate may form.

Reconstitution Reconstitute powder with bacteriostatic water for injection, bacteriostatic 0.9% NaCl.

For I.T. use: Reconstitute with preservative free diluent.

For I.V. infusion: Dilute in 250-1000 mL 0.9% NaCl or D$_5$W.

Note: Solutions containing bacteriostatic agents should not be used for the preparation of either high doses or intrathecal doses of cytarabine; may be used for I.M., SubQ, and low-dose (100-200 mg/m^2) I.V. solution.

Compatibility Stable in D$_5$LR, D$_5$¼NS, D$_5$NS, D$_{10}$NS, D$_5$W, LR, NS.

Y-site administration: Compatible: Amifostine, amsacrine, aztreonam, cefepime, chlorpromazine, cimetidine, cladribine, dexamethasone sodium phosphate, diphenhydramine, doxorubicin liposome, droperidol, etoposide phosphate, famotidine, filgrastim, fludarabine, furosemide, gatifloxacin, gemcitabine, gentamicin, granisetron, heparin, hydrocortisone sodium succinate, hydromorphone, idarubicin, linezolid, lorazepam, melphalan, methotrexate, methylprednisolone sodium succinate, metoclopramide, morphine, ondansetron, paclitaxel, piperacillin/tazobactam, prochlorperazine edisylate, promethazine, propofol, ranitidine, sargramostim, sodium bicarbonate, teniposide, thiotepa, vinorelbine. **Incompatible:** Allopurinol, amphotericin B cholesteryl sulfate complex, ganciclovir.

Compatibility in syringe: Compatible: Metoclopramide.

Compatibility when admixed: Compatible: Corticotropin, dacarbazine, daunorubicin with etoposide, etoposide, hydroxyzine, lincomycin, methotrexate, mitoxantrone, ondansetron, potassium chloride, sodium bicarbonate, vincristine. **Incompatible:** Fluorouracil, heparin, insulin (regular), (Continued)

Cytarabine *(Continued)*

nafcillin, oxacillin, penicillin G sodium. **Variable (consult detailed reference):** Gentamicin, hydrocortisone sodium succinate, methylprednisolone sodium succinate.

Mechanism of Action Inhibits DNA synthesis. Cytosine gains entry into cells by a carrier process, and then must be converted to its active compound, aracytidine triphosphate. Cytosine is a pyrimidine analog and is incorporated into DNA; however, the primary action is inhibition of DNA polymerase resulting in decreased DNA synthesis and repair. The degree of cytotoxicity correlates linearly with incorporation into DNA; therefore, incorporation into the DNA is responsible for drug activity and toxicity. Cytarabine is specific for the S phase of the cell cycle (blocks progression from the G_1 to the S phase).

Pharmacodynamics/Kinetics

Distribution: V_d: Total body water; widely and rapidly since it enters the cells readily; crosses blood-brain barrier with CSF levels of 40% to 50% of plasma level

Metabolism: Primarily hepatic; metabolized by deoxycytidine kinase and other nucleotide kinases to aracytidine triphosphate (active); about 86% to 96% of dose is metabolized to inactive uracil arabinoside (ARA-U); intrathecal administration results in little conversion to ARA-U due to the low levels of deaminase in the cerebral spinal fluid

Half-life elimination: I.V.: Initial: 7-20 minutes; Terminal: 1-3 hours

Time to peak, plasma: I.M., SubQ: 20-60 minutes

Excretion: Urine (~80%; 90% as metabolite ARA-U) within 24 hours

Dosage Refer to individual protocols. Children and Adults:

Remission induction:

I.V.: 75-200 mg/m²/day for 5-10 days; a second course, beginning 2-4 weeks after the initial therapy, may be required in some patients.

or 100 mg/m² for 7 days

or 100 mg/m²/dose every 12 hours for 7 days

I.T.: Usual dose 30 mg/m² every 4 days; range: 5-75 mg/m² every 2-7 days until CNS findings normalize; or age-based dosing (frequency of administration usually defined by protocol):

<1 year of age: 15-20 mg per dose

1-2 years of age: 16-30 mg per dose

2-3 years of age: 20-50 mg per dose

>3 years of age: 24-75 mg per dose

Remission maintenance:

I.V.: 70-200 mg/m²/day for 2-5 days at monthly intervals

I.M., SubQ: 1-1.5 mg/kg single dose for maintenance at 1- to 4-week intervals

High-dose therapies (unlabeled use):

Doses as high as 1-3 g/m² have been used for refractory or secondary leukemias or refractory non-Hodgkin's lymphoma.

Doses of 1-3 g/m² every 12 hours for up to 12 doses have been used for leukemia

Bone marrow transplant (unlabeled use): 1.5 g/m² continuous infusion over 48 hours

Dosage adjustment in renal impairment: The FDA-approved labeling does not contain renal dosing adjustment guidelines; the following guidelines have been used by some clinicians:

Aronoff, 2007 (Cytarabine 100-200 mg/m²): Children and Adults: No adjustment necessary

Kintzel, 1995 (High-dose cytarabine 1-3 g/m²):

Cl_{cr} 46-60 mL/minute: Administer 60% of dose

Cl$_{cr}$ 31-45 mL/minute: Administer 50% of dose

Cl$_{cr}$ <30 mL/minute: Consider use of alternative drug

Smith, 1997 (High-dose cytarabine ≥2 g/m^2/dose):

Serum creatinine 1.5-1.9 mg/dL or increase (from baseline) of 0.5-1.2 mg/dL: Reduce dose to 1 g/m^2/dose

Serum creatinine ≥2 mg/dL or increase (from baseline) of >1.2 mg/dL: Reduce dose to 0.1 g/m^2/day as a continuous infusion

Dosage adjustment in hepatic impairment: Dose may need to be adjusted in patients with liver failure since cytarabine is partially detoxified in the liver. The FDA-approved labeling does not contain hepatic dosing adjustment guidelines; the following guideline has been used by some clinicians:

Floyd, 2006: AST/ALT (any elevation): Administer 50% of dose; may increase subsequent doses in the absence of toxicities

Koren, 1992 (dose level not specified): Bilirubin >2 mg/dL: Administer 50% of dose; may increase subsequent doses in the absence of toxicities

Combination Regimens

Brain tumors: 8 in 1 (Brain Tumors) *on page 1141*

Leukemia, acute lymphocytic:

FIS-HAM *on page 1214*

Hyper-CVAD + Imatinib *on page 1229*

Hyper-CVAD (Leukemia, Acute Lymphocytic) *on page 1231*

Linker Protocol *on page 1243*

PVA (POG 8602) *on page 1273*

Leukemia, acute myeloid:

5 + 2 *on page 1140*

7 + 3 (Daunorubicin) *on page 1140*

7 + 3 (Idarubicin) *on page 1140*

7 + 3 (Mitoxantrone) *on page 1140*

7 + 3 + 7 *on page 1141*

CA *on page 1156*

DA *on page 1187*

DAT *on page 1189*

DAV *on page 1189*

EMA 86 *on page 1199*

FIS-HAM *on page 1214*

FLAG *on page 1215*

FLAG-IDA *on page 1215*

Idarubicin, Cytarabine, Etoposide (ICE Protocol) *on page 1239*

Idarubicin, Cytarabine, Etoposide (IDA-Based BF12) *on page 1239*

TAD *on page 1279*

V-TAD *on page 1293*

Lymphoma, Hodgkin's disease: mini-BEAM *on page 1248*

Lymphoma, non-Hodgkin's:

CODOX-M *on page 1180*

COMLA *on page 1181*

DHAP *on page 1190*

ESHAP *on page 1206*

Hyper-CVAD (Lymphoma, non-Hodgkin's) *on page 1236*

IVAC *on page 1242*

Pro-MACE-CytaBOM *on page 1273*

Lymphoma, non-Hodgkin's (Burkitt's): CODOX-M/IVAC *on page 1180*

Lymphoma, non-Hodgkin's (Mantle cell): Hyper-CVAD + Rituximab *on page 1237*

Neuroblastoma: N4SE Protocol *on page 1260*

Retinoblastoma: 8 in 1 (Retinoblastoma) *on page 1142*

(Continued)

Cytarabine *(Continued)*

Administration May be administered I.M., I.T., or SubQ at a concentration not to exceed 100 mg/mL. When administered via I.V. infusion, infuse over 1-3 hours or as a continuous infusion. GI effects may be more pronounced with divided I.V. bolus doses than with continuous infusion.

Monitoring Parameters Liver function tests, CBC with differential and platelet count, serum creatinine, BUN, serum uric acid

Patient Information This drug can only be given by injection. You will be more susceptible to infection; avoid crowds and exposure to infection. Do not have any vaccinations without consulting prescriber. Small frequent meals, frequent mouth care, sucking lozenges, or chewing gum may reduce incidence of nausea or vomiting or loss of appetite. If these measures are ineffective, consult prescriber for antiemetic medication. Report immediately any signs of CNS changes or change in gait, easy bruising or bleeding, yellowing of eyes or skin, change in color of urine or blackened stool, respiratory difficulty, or palpitations. Contraceptive measures are recommended during therapy.

Additional Information I.V. doses ≥ 1.5 g/m^2 may produce conjunctivitis which can be ameliorated with prophylactic use of corticosteroid (0.1% dexamethasone) eye drops. Dexamethasone eye drops should be administered at 1-2 drops every 6 hours during and for 2-7 days after cytarabine is done.

Emetic Potential

Low dose (<200 mg/m^2): Low (10% to 30%)

High dose (>1 g/m^2): Moderate-to-high (30% to 90%)

Vesicant No

High Dose Considerations

Comments: Risk of cerebellar toxicity increases with creatinine clearance <60 mL/minute, age older than 50 years, pre-existing CNS lesion, and alkaline phosphatase levels exceeding 3 times the upper limit of normal. Conjunctivitis is prevented and treated with saline or corticosteroid eye drops. As prophylaxis, eye drops should be started 6-12 hours before initiation of cytarabine and continued 24 hours following the last dose.

High Dose: I.V.: 2-3 g/m^2/dose every 12-24 hours for 4-12 doses; duration of infusion is 1-3 hours; maximum single-agent dose: 36 g/m^2; generally combined with other high-dose chemotherapeutic drugs or total body irradiation (TBI).

Unique Toxicities:

Central nervous system: Cerebellar toxicity which includes nystagmus, dysarthria, disdiadochokinesis, slurred speech; cerebral toxicity which includes somnolence, confusion

Dermatologic: Rash, desquamation may occur

Gastrointestinal: Severe nausea and vomiting, mucositis, diarrhea, ageusia

Ocular: Photophobia, excessive tearing, blurred vision, local discomfort, chemical conjunctivitis, optic neuropathy, visual loss

Respiratory: Noncardiogenic pulmonary edema (onset 22-27 days following completion of therapy)

Miscellaneous: Anosmia

Dosage Forms Excipient information presented when available (limited, particularly for generics); consult specific product labeling.

Injection, powder for reconstitution: 100 mg, 500 mg, 1 g, 2 g

Injection, solution: 20 mg/mL (5 mL, 25 mL, 50 mL); 100 mg/mL (20 mL)

References

Capizzi RL, "Curative Chemotherapy for Acute Myeloid Leukemia: The Development of High-Dose Ara-C From the Laboratory to Bedside," *Invest New Drugs*, 1996, 14(3):249-56.

Capizzi RL, White JC, Powell BL, et al, "Effect of Dose on the Pharmacokinetic and Pharmaco-dynamic Effects of Cytarabine," *Semin Hematol*, 1991, 28(3 Suppl 4):54-69.

Hamada A, Kawaguchi T, and Nakano M, "Clinical Pharmacokinetics of Cytarabine Formulations," *Clin Pharmacokinet*, 2002, 41(10):705-18.

Hiddemann W, "Cytosine Arabinoside in the Treatment of Acute Myeloid Leukemia: The Role and Place of High-Dose Regimens," *Ann Hematol*, 1991, 62(4):119-28.

Stasi R, Venditti A, Del Poeta G, et al, "High-Dose Chemotherapy in Adult Acute Myeloid Leukemia: Rationale and Results," *Leuk Res*, 1996, 20(7):535-49.

Stentoft J, "The Toxicity of Cytarabine," *Drug Saf*, 1990, 5(1):7-27.

♦ **Cytarabine (Conventional)** *see* Cytarabine *on page 269*

♦ **Cytarabine Hydrochloride** *see* Cytarabine *on page 269*

Cytarabine (Liposomal) (sye TARE a been lip po SOE mal)

Medication Safety Issues

Sound-alike/look-alike issues:

Cytarabine may be confused with Cytadren®, Cytosar®, Cytoxan®, vidarabine

Cytarabine liposomal may be confused with conventional cytarabine

DepoCyt® may be confused with Depoject®

High alert medication: The Institute for Safe Medication Practices (ISMP) includes this medication among its list of drugs which have a heightened risk of causing significant patient harm when used in error.

Related Information

Safe Handling of Hazardous Drugs *on page 1382*

U.S. Brand Names DepoCyt®

Generic Available No

Canadian Brand Names DepoCyt®

Pharmacologic Category Antineoplastic Agent, Antimetabolite (Pyrimidine Antagonist)

Use Treatment of lymphomatous meningitis

Pregnancy Risk Factor D

Lactation Excretion in breast milk unknown/not recommended

Labeled Contraindications Hypersensitivity to cytarabine or any component of the formulation; active meningeal infection

Warnings/Precautions Hazardous agent - use appropriate precautions for handling and disposal. **[U.S. Boxed Warning]: Chemical arachnoiditis (nausea, vomiting, headache, fever) occurs commonly; may be fatal if untreated. The incidence and severity of chemical arachnoiditis is reduced by coadministration with dexamethasone.** Hydrocephalus has been reported and may be precipitated by chemical arachnoiditis. May cause neurotoxicity (including myelopathy), which may lead to permanent neurologic deficit. Blockage to CSF flow may increase the risk of neurotoxicity. Peripheral neurotoxicity has also been reported. Monitor for neurotoxicity; reduce subsequent doses; discontinue with persistent neurotoxicity. The risk of adverse events, including neurotoxicity, is increased with concurrent radiation therapy or systemic chemotherapy. Infectious meningitis may be associated with intrathecal administration. **[U.S. Boxed Warning]: Should be administered under the supervision of an experienced cancer chemotherapy physician.** For intrathecal use only. Safety and efficacy in pediatric patients have not been established.

Adverse Reactions

>10%:

Cardiovascular: Peripheral edema (11%)

Central nervous system: Chemical arachnoiditis (without dexamethasone premedication: 100%; with dexamethasone premedication: 33% to 42%; grade 4: 19% to 30%; onset: ≤5 days); headache (56%), confusion

(Continued)

Cytarabine (Liposomal) *(Continued)*

(33%), fever (32%), fatigue (25%), seizure (20% to 22%), dizziness (18%), lethargy (16%), insomnia (14%), memory impairment (14%), pain (14%)

Endocrine & metabolic: Dehydration (13%)

Gastrointestinal: Nausea (46%), vomiting (44%), constipation (25%), diarrhea (12%), appetite decreased (11%)

Genitourinary: Urinary tract infection (14%)

Hematologic: Anemia (12%), thrombocytopenia (3% to 11%)

Neuromuscular & skeletal: Weakness (40%), back pain (24%), abnormal gait (23%), limb pain (15%), neck pain (14%), arthralgia (11%), neck stiffness (11%)

Ocular: Blurred vision (11%)

1% to 10%:

Cardiovascular: Tachycardia (9%), hypotension (8%), hypertension (6%), syncope (3%), edema (2%)

Central nervous system: Agitation (10%), hypoesthesia (10%), depression (8%), anxiety (7%), sensory neuropathy (3%)

Dermatologic: Pruritus (2%)

Endocrine & metabolic: Hypokalemia (7%), hyponatremia (7%), hyperglycemia (6%)

Gastrointestinal: Abdominal pain (9%), dysphagia (8%), anorexia (5%), hemorrhoids (3%), mucosal inflammation (3%)

Genitourinary: Incontinence (7%), urinary retention (5%)

Hematologic: Neutropenia (10%), contusion (2%)

Neuromuscular & skeletal: Muscle weakness (10%), tremor (9%), peripheral neuropathy (4%), abnormal reflexes (3%)

Otic: Hypoacusis (6%)

Respiratory: Dyspnea (10%), cough (7%), pneumonia (6%)

Miscellaneous: Diaphoresis (2%)

<1%, postmarketing, and/or case reports: Anaphylaxis, bladder control impaired, blindness, bowel control impaired, cauda equine syndrome, cranial nerve palsies, CSF protein increased, CSF WBC increased, deafness, encephalopathy, hemiplegia, hydrocephalus, infectious meningitis, intracranial pressure increased, myelopathy, neurologic deficit, numbness, papilledema, somnolence, visual disturbance

Overdosage/Toxicology No overdosage with liposomal cytarabine has been reported. See Cytarabine *on page 269* for toxicology related to systemic administration. Overdose would likely result in severe chemical arachnoiditis, including encephalopathy; coadministration of dexamethasone should be continued. Exchange of CSF with isotonic saline may be considered; treatment is otherwise symptom-directed and supportive.

Drug Interactions

Increased Effect/Toxicity: No formal studies of interactions with other medications have been conducted. The limited systemic exposure minimizes the potential for interaction between cytarabine liposomal and other medications.

Decreased Effect: No formal studies of interactions with other medications have been conducted. The limited systemic exposure minimizes the potential for interaction between cytarabine liposomal and other medications.

Storage/Stability Store under refrigeration at 2°C to 8°C (36°F to 46°F). Protect from freezing and avoid aggressive agitation. Solutions should be used within 4 hours of withdrawal from the vial.

Reconstitution

Allow vial to warm to room temperature prior to withdrawal from vial. Particles may settle in diluent over time, and may be resuspended by gentle agitation or inversion of the vial. Further reconstitution or dilution is not required.

Mechanism of Action Cytarabine liposomal is a sustained-release formulation of the active ingredient cytarabine, an antimetabolite which acts through inhibition of DNA synthesis and is cell cycle-specific for the S phase of cell division. Cytarabine is converted intracellularly to its active metabolite cytarabine-5'-triphosphate (ara-CTP). Ara-CTP also appears to be incorporated into DNA and RNA; however, the primary action is inhibition of DNA polymerase, resulting in decreased DNA synthesis and repair. The liposomal formulation allows for gradual release, resulting in prolonged exposure.

Pharmacodynamics/Kinetics

Absorption: Systemic exposure following intrathecal administration is negligible since transfer rate from CSF to plasma is slow

Half-life elimination, CSF: 6-82 hours

Time to peak, CSF: Intrathecal: <1 hour

Dosage Note: Patients should be started on dexamethasone 4 mg twice daily (oral or I.V.) for 5 days, beginning on the day of cytarabine liposomal injection.

Intrathecal: Adults:

Induction: 50 mg every 14 days for a total of 2 doses (weeks 1 and 3)

Consolidation: 50 mg every 14 days for 3 doses (weeks 5, 7, and 9), followed by an additional dose at week 13

Maintenance: 50 mg every 28 days for 4 doses (weeks 17, 21, 25, and 29)

Dosage reduction for toxicity: If drug-related neurotoxicity develops, reduce dose to 25 mg. If toxicity persists, discontinue treatment.

Administration For intrathecal use only. Dose should be removed from vial immediately before administration (must be administered within 4 hours of removal). An in-line filter should **not** be used. Administer directly into the CSF via an intraventricular reservoir or by direct injection into the lumbar sac. Injection should be made slowly (over 1-5 minutes). Patients should lie flat for 1 hour after lumbar puncture.

Monitoring Parameters Monitor closely for signs of an immediate reaction; neurotoxicity

Test Interactions Since cytarabine liposomes are similar in appearance to WBCs, care must be taken in interpreting CSF examinations in patients receiving cytarabine liposomal.

Patient Information Report fever, sore throat, bleeding, or bruising. Contraceptive measures are recommended during therapy.

Emetic Potential Moderate (30% to 60%)

Vesicant No

Dosage Forms Excipient information presented when available (limited, particularly for generics); consult specific product labeling.

Injection, suspension [preservative free]:

Depocyt®: 10 mg/mL (5 mL)

References

Cole BF, Glantz MJ, Jaeckle KA, et al, "Quality-of-Life-Adjusted Survival Comparison of Sustained-Release Cytosine Arabinoside Versus Intrathecal Methotrexate for Treatment of Solid Tumor Neoplastic Meningitis," *Cancer*, 2003, 97(12):3053-60.

Glantz MJ, LaFollette S, Jaeckle KA, et al, "Randomized Trial of a Slow-Release Versus a Standard Formulation of Cytarabine for the Intrathecal Treatment of Lymphomatous Meningitis," *J Clin Oncol*, 1999, 17(10):3110-6.

(Continued)

Cytarabine (Liposomal) *(Continued)*

Jabbour E, O'Brien S, Kantarjian H, et al, "Neurologic Complications Associated With Intrathecal Liposomal Cytarabine in Combination With High-Dose Methotrexate and Cytarabine to Patients With Acute Lymphocytic Leukemia," *Blood*, 2007, 109(8):3214-8.

♦ **CytoGam®** *see* Cytomegalovirus Immune Globulin (Intravenous-Human) *on page 278*

Cytomegalovirus Immune Globulin (Intravenous-Human)

(sye toe meg a low VYE rus i MYUN GLOB yoo lin in tra VEE nus HYU man)

Medication Safety Issues

Sound-alike/look-alike issues:

CytoGam® may be confused with Cytoxan®, Gamimune® N

U.S. Brand Names CytoGam®

Index Terms CMV-IGIV

Generic Available No

Canadian Brand Names CytoGam®

Pharmacologic Category Immune Globulin

Use Prophylaxis of cytomegalovirus (CMV) disease associated with kidney, lung, liver, pancreas, and heart transplants; concomitant use with ganciclovir should be considered in organ transplants (other than kidney) from CMV seropositive donors to CMV seronegative recipients

Unlabeled/Investigational Use Adjunct therapy in the treatment of CMV disease in immunocompromised patients

Pregnancy Risk Factor C

Lactation Excretion in breast milk unknown

Labeled Contraindications Hypersensitivity to CMV-IGIV, other immunoglobulins, or any component of the formulation; immunoglobulin A deficiency

Warnings/Precautions Hypersensitivity and anaphylactic reactions can occur; immediate treatment (including epinephrine 1:1000) should be available. Aseptic meningitis syndrome (AMS) has been reported with intravenous immune globulin administration (rare); may occur with high doses (≥ 2 g/kg). Intravenous immune globulin has been associated with antiglobulin hemolysis; monitor for signs of hemolytic anemia. Monitor for transfusion-related acute lung injury (TRALI); noncardiogenic pulmonary edema has been reported with intravenous immune globulin use. Acute renal dysfunction (increased serum creatinine, oliguria, acute renal failure) can rarely occur; usually within 7 days of use (more likely with products stabilized with sucrose). Use with caution in the elderly, patients with renal disease, diabetes mellitus, volume depletion, sepsis, paraproteinemia, and nephrotoxic medications due to risk of renal dysfunction. In patients at risk of renal dysfunction, the rate of infusion and concentration of solution should be minimized. discontinue if renal function deteriorates. Patients should not be volume depleted prior to therapy. Thrombotic events have been reported with administration of intravenous immune globulin; use with caution in patients with cardiovascular risk factors. Use with caution in patients >65 years of age. Product is stabilized with albumin. Product of human plasma; may potentially contain infectious agents which could transmit disease. Screening of donors, as well as testing and/or inactivation or removal of certain viruses, reduces the risk. Infections thought to be transmitted by this product should be reported to the manufacturer. Product is stabilized with sucrose.

Adverse Reactions
<6%:
  Cardiovascular: Flushing
  Central nervous system: Chills, fever
  Gastrointestinal: Nausea, vomiting
  Neuromuscular & skeletal: Arthralgia, back pain, muscle cramps
  Respiratory: Wheezing
<1%: Blood pressure decreased
Postmarketing and/or case reports: Acute renal failure, acute tubular necrosis, anaphylactic shock, angioneurotic edema, anuria, aseptic meningitis syndrome (AMS), BUN increased, oliguria, osmotic nephrosis, proximal tubular nephropathy, serum creatinine increased

Overdosage/Toxicology Symptoms related to volume overload would be expected to occur with overdose; treatment is symptom-directed and supportive.

Drug Interactions
Decreased Effect: Decreased effect of live vaccines may be seen if given within 3 months of IGIV administration. Defer vaccination or revaccinate.

Storage/Stability Store between 2°C and 8°C (35.6°F and 46.4°F). Use reconstituted product within 6 hours.

Reconstitution Do not admix with other medications; do not use if turbid. Do not shake vials. Dilution is not recommended.

Compatibility Infusion with other products is not recommended. If unavoidable, may be piggybacked into an I.V. line of sodium chloride, 2.5% dextrose in water, 5% dextrose in water, 10% dextrose in water, or 20% dextrose in water. Do not dilute more than 1:2. Do not admix with other medications.

Mechanism of Action CMV-IGIV is a preparation of immunoglobulin G derived from pooled healthy blood donors with a high titer of CMV antibodies; administration provides a passive source of antibodies against cytomegalovirus

Dosage I.V.: Adults:
Kidney transplant:
  Initial dose (within 72 hours of transplant): 150 mg/kg/dose
  2-, 4-, 6-, and 8 weeks after transplant: 100 mg/kg/dose
  12 and 16 weeks after transplant: 50 mg/kg/dose
Liver, lung, pancreas, or heart transplant:
  Initial dose (within 72 hours of transplant): 150 mg/kg/dose
  2-, 4-, 6-, and 8 weeks after transplant: 150 mg/kg/dose
  12 and 16 weeks after transplant: 100 mg/kg/dose
Severe CMV pneumonia (unlabeled): Various regimens have been used, including 400 mg/kg CMV-IGIV in combination with ganciclovir on days 1, 2, 7, or 8, followed by 200 mg/kg CMV-IGIV on days 14 and 21
Elderly: Use with caution in patients >65 years of age, may be at increased risk of renal insufficiency

Dosage adjustment in renal impairment: Use with caution; specific dosing adjustments are not available. Infusion rate should be the minimum practical; do not exceed 180 mg/kg/hour

Administration Administer through an I.V. line containing an in-line filter (pore size 15 micron) using an infusion pump. Do not mix with other infusions; do not use if turbid. Begin infusion within 6 hours of entering vial, complete infusion within 12 hours.

Infuse at 15 mg/kg/hour. If no adverse reactions occur within 30 minutes, may increase rate to 30 mg/kg/hour. If no adverse reactions occur within the second 30 minutes, may increase rate to 60 mg/kg/hour; maximum rate of (Continued)

Cytomegalovirus Immune Globulin
(Intravenous-Human) *(Continued)*

infusion: 75 mL/hour. When infusing subsequent doses, may decrease titration interval from 30 minutes to 15 minutes. If patient develops nausea, back pain, or flushing during infusion, slow the rate or temporarily stop the infusion. Discontinue if blood pressure drops or in case of anaphylactic reaction.

Monitoring Parameters Vital signs (throughout infusion), flushing, chills, muscle cramps, back pain, fever, nausea, vomiting, wheezing, decreased blood pressure, or anaphylaxis; renal function and urine output

Dietary Considerations
CytoGam® solution for injection 50 mg (± 10 mg/mL) contains sodium 20-30 mEq/L

Emetic Potential Very low (<10%)

Vesicant No

Dosage Forms Excipient information presented when available (limited, particularly for generics); consult specific product labeling.

Injection, solution [preservative free]:
CytoGam®: 50 mg ± 10 mg/mL (50 mL) [contains sodium 20-30 mEq/L, human albumin, and sucrose]

References
Levinson ML and Jacobson PA, "Treatment and Prophylaxis of Cytomegalovirus Disease," *Pharmacotherapy*, 1992, 12(4):300-18.

Reed EC, Bowden RA, Dandliker PS, et al, "Efficacy of Cytomegalovirus Immunoglobulin in Marrow Transplant Recipients With Cytomegalovirus Pneumonia," *J Infect Dis*, 1987, 156:641-5.

Reed EC, Bowden RA, Dandliker PS, et al, "Treatment of Cytomegalovirus Pneumonia With Ganciclovir and Intravenous Cytomegalovirus Immunoglobulin in Patients With Bone Marrow Transplants," *Ann Intern Med*, 1988, 109:783-8.

"Renal Insufficiency and Failure Associated With Immune Globulin Intravenous Therapy - United States, 1985-1998." *MMWR*, 1999, 48(24):518-21.

Snydman DR, "Cytomegalovirus Immunoglobulins in the Prevention and Treatment of Cytomegalovirus Disease," *Rev Infect Dis*, 1990, 12(Suppl 7):839-48.

♦ **Cytosar® (Can)** *see* Cytarabine *on page 269*
♦ **Cytosar-U** *see* Cytarabine *on page 269*
♦ **Cytosine Arabinoside Hydrochloride** *see* Cytarabine *on page 269*
♦ **Cytovene®** *see* Ganciclovir *on page 492*
♦ **Cytoxan®** *see* Cyclophosphamide *on page 246*
♦ **DAB₃₈₉IL-2** *see* Denileukin Diftitox *on page 323*

Dacarbazine *(da KAR ba zeen)*
Medication Safety Issues
Sound-alike/look-alike issues:
Dacarbazine may be confused with Dicarbosil®, procarbazine

High alert medication: The Institute for Safe Medication Practices (ISMP) includes this medication among its list of drugs which have a heightened risk of causing significant patient harm when used in error.

Related Information
Management of Drug Extravasations *on page 1301*
Safe Handling of Hazardous Drugs *on page 1382*

U.S. Brand Names DTIC-Dome®

Index Terms DIC; Dimethyl Triazeno Imidazole Carboxamide; DTIC; Imidazole Carboxamide; Imidazole Carboxamide Dimethyltriazene; WR-139007

Generic Available Yes

Canadian Brand Names DTIC®

Pharmacologic Category Antineoplastic Agent, Alkylating Agent (Triazene)

Use Treatment of malignant melanoma, Hodgkin's disease, soft-tissue sarcomas, fibrosarcomas, rhabdomyosarcoma, islet cell carcinoma, medullary carcinoma of the thyroid, and neuroblastoma

Pregnancy Risk Factor C

Lactation Excretion in breast milk unknown/not recommended

Labeled Contraindications Hypersensitivity to dacarbazine or any component of the formulation

Warnings/Precautions Hazardous agent - use appropriate precautions for handling and disposal. **[U.S. Boxed Warnings]: Bone marrow suppression is a common toxicity; monitor closely. Hepatotoxicity with hepatocellular necrosis and hepatic vein thrombosis has been reported,** usually with combination chemotherapy, but may occur with dacarbazine alone. The half-life is increased in patients with renal and/or hepatic impairment; use caution, monitor for toxicity and consider dosage reduction. Anaphylaxis may occur. Extravasation may result in tissue damage and pain. **[U.S. Boxed Warnings]: May be carcinogenic and/or teratogenic. Should be administered under the supervision of an experienced cancer chemotherapy physician.**

Adverse Reactions
>10%:
  Gastrointestinal: Nausea and vomiting (>90%), can be severe and dose limiting; nausea and vomiting decrease on successive days when dacarbazine is given daily for 5 days; diarrhea
  Hematologic: Myelosuppression, leukopenia, thrombocytopenia - dose limiting
    Onset: 5-7 days
    Nadir: 7-10 days
    Recovery: 21-28 days
  Local: Pain on infusion, may be minimized by administration through a central line, or by administration as a short infusion (eg, 1-2 hours as opposed to bolus injection)
1% to 10%:
  Dermatologic: Alopecia, rash, photosensitivity
  Gastrointestinal: Anorexia, metallic taste
  Miscellaneous: Flu-like syndrome (fever, myalgia, malaise)
<1%: Anaphylactic reactions, diarrhea (following high-dose bolus injection), eosinophilia, headache, hepatic necrosis, hepatic vein occlusion, liver enzymes increased (transient), paresthesia

Overdosage/Toxicology Symptoms of overdose include myelosuppression and diarrhea. There are no known antidotes and treatment is symptomatic and supportive.

Drug Interactions
  Cytochrome P450 Effect: Substrate (major) of CYP1A2, 2E1
  Increased Effect/Toxicity: CYP1A2 inhibitors may increase the levels/effects of dacarbazine; example inhibitors include ciprofloxacin, fluvoxamine, ketoconazole, norfloxacin, ofloxacin, and rofecoxib. CYP2E1 inhibitors may increase the levels/effects of dacarbazine; example inhibitors include disulfiram, isoniazid, and miconazole.
  Decreased Effect: CYP1A2 inducers may decrease the levels/effects of dacarbazine; example inducers include aminoglutethimide, carbamazepine, phenobarbital, and rifampin. Patients may experience impaired
(Continued)

Dacarbazine *(Continued)*

immune response to vaccines; possible infection after administration of live vaccines in patients receiving immunosuppressants.

Ethanol/Nutrition/Herb Interactions

Ethanol: Avoid ethanol (due to GI irritation).

Herb/Nutraceutical: Avoid dong quai, St John's wort (may also cause photo-sensitization).

Storage/Stability Store intact vials under refrigeration (2°C to 8°C) and protect from light. Vials are stable for 4 weeks at room temperature. Reconstituted solution is stable for 24 hours at room temperature (20°C) and 96 hours under refrigeration (4°C). Solutions for infusion (in D_5W or NS) are stable for 24 hours at room temperature and protected from light. Decomposed drug turns pink.

Reconstitution The manufacturer recommends reconstituting 100 mg and 200 mg vials with 9.9 mL and 19.7 mL SWFI, respectively, to a concentration of 10 mg/mL; some institutions use different standard dilutions (eg, 20 mg/mL).

Standard I.V. dilution: Dilute in 250-1000 mL D_5W or NS.

Compatibility Stable in NS, sterile water for injection; **variable stability (consult detailed reference)** in D_5W.

Y-site administration: Compatible: Amifostine, aztreonam, etoposide phosphate, filgrastim, fludarabine, granisetron, melphalan, ondansetron, paclitaxel, sargramostim, teniposide, thiotepa, vinorelbine. **Incompatible:** Allopurinol, cefepime, piperacillin/tazobactam. **Variable (consult detailed reference):** Heparin.

Compatibility when admixed: Compatible: Bleomycin, carmustine, cyclophosphamide, cytarabine, dactinomycin, doxorubicin, fluorouracil, hydrocortisone sodium phosphate, lidocaine, mercaptopurine, methotrexate, ondansetron, vinblastine. **Incompatible:** Hydrocortisone sodium succinate. **Variable (consult detailed reference):** Ondansetron with doxorubicin.

Mechanism of Action Alkylating agent which appears to form methylcarbonium ions that attack nucleophilic groups in DNA; cross-links strands of DNA resulting in the inhibition of DNA, RNA, and protein synthesis, the exact mechanism of action is still unclear.

Pharmacodynamics/Kinetics

Onset of action: I.V.: 18-24 days

Distribution: V_d: 0.6 L/kg, exceeding total body water; suggesting binding to some tissue (probably liver)

Protein binding: 5%

Metabolism: Extensively hepatic; hepatobiliary excretion is probably of some importance; metabolites may also have an antineoplastic effect

Half-life elimination: Biphasic: Initial: 20-40 minutes; Terminal: 5 hours

Excretion: Urine (~30% to 50% as unchanged drug)

Dosage Refer to individual protocols. Some dosage regimens include:

Intra-arterial: 50-400 mg/m² for 5-10 days

I.V.:

Hodgkin's disease, ABVD: 375 mg/m² days 1 and 15 every 4 weeks **or** 100 mg/m²/day for 5 days

Metastatic melanoma (alone or in combination with other agents): 150-250 mg/m² days 1-5 every 3-4 weeks

Metastatic melanoma: 850 mg/m² every 3 weeks

High dose: Bone marrow/blood cell transplantation: I.V.: 1-3 g/m²; maximum dose as a single agent: 3.38 g/m²; generally combined with other high-dose chemotherapeutic drugs

Dosage adjustment in renal impairment: The FDA-approved labeling does not contain dosage adjustment guidelines. The following guidelines have been used by some clinicians (Kintzel, 1995):

Cl_{cr} 46-60 mL/minute: Administer 80% of dose

Cl_{cr} 31-45 mL/minute: Administer 75% of dose

Cl_{cr} <30 mL/minute: Administer 70% of dose

Dosage adjustment in hepatic impairment: The FDA-approved labeling does not contain adjustment guidelines. May cause hepatotoxicity; monitor closely for signs of toxicity.

Combination Regimens

Brain tumors: 8 in 1 (Brain Tumors) *on page 1141*

Lymphoma, Hodgkin's:

    ABVD *on page 1142*

    MOPP/ABVD *on page 1249*

Melanoma:

    BOLD *on page 1153*

    BOLD (Melanoma) *on page 1154*

    BOLD + Interferon *on page 1153*

    CCDT (Melonoma) *on page 1165*

    CVD *on page 1184*

    Dacarbazine-Carboplatin-Aldesleukin-Interferon *on page 1187*

    Dartmouth Regimen *on page 1187*

    IL-2 + IFN *on page 1240*

Neuroblastoma: CCDDT (Neuroblastoma) *on page 1164*

Sarcoma: CYVADIC *on page 1187*

Soft tissue sarcoma:

    AD *on page 1145*

    MAID *on page 1246*

Administration Infuse over 30-60 minutes; rapid infusion may cause severe venous irritation.

Extravasation management: Local pain, burning sensation, and irritation at the injection site may be relieved by local application of hot packs. If extravasation occurs, apply cold packs. Protect exposed tissue from light following extravasation.

Monitoring Parameters CBC with differential, liver function

Patient Information Limit oral intake for 4-6 hours before therapy. Do not use alcohol, aspirin-containing products, and/or OTC medications without consulting prescriber. It is important to maintain adequate nutrition and hydration (2-3 L/day of fluids unless instructed to restrict fluid intake) during therapy; frequent small meals may help. You may experience nausea or vomiting (frequent small meals, frequent mouth care, sucking lozenges, or chewing gum may help). If this is ineffective, consult prescriber for antiemetic medication. You may experience loss of hair (reversible); you will be more susceptible to infection (avoid crowds and exposure to infection as much as possible); you will be more sensitive to sunlight; use sunblock, wear protective clothing and dark glasses, or avoid direct exposure to sunlight. Flu-like symptoms (eg, malaise, fever, myalgia) may occur 1 week after infusion and persist for 1-3 weeks; consult prescriber for severe symptoms. Report fever, chills, unusual bruising or bleeding, signs of infection, excessive fatigue, yellowing of eyes or skin, or change in color of urine or stool. Contraceptive measures are recommended during therapy.

Emetic Potential High (>90%)

Vesicant No; irritant

(Continued)

Dacarbazine *(Continued)*

High Dose Considerations

Comments: Doses of 6591 mg/m^2 have been administered, although hypotension is considered the nonhematologic dose-limiting side effect for doses >3380 mg/m^2. Infusion-related hypotension may be secondary to calcium chelation by citric acid in formulation.

High Dose: I.V.: 1-3 g/m^2; maximum dose as a single agent: 3.38 g/m^2; generally combined with other high-dose chemotherapeutic drugs.

Unique Toxicities:

Cardiovascular: Hypotension (infusion-related)

Gastrointestinal: Severe nausea and vomiting

Dosage Forms Excipient information presented when available (limited, particularly for generics); consult specific product labeling.

Injection, powder for reconstitution: 100 mg, 200 mg, 500 mg

DTIC-Dome®: 200 mg

References

Berg SL, Grisell DL, DeLaney TF, et al, "Principles of Treatment of Pediatric Solid Tumors," *Pediatr Clin North Am*, 1991, 38(2):249-67.

Bonfante V, Santoro A, Viviani S, et al, "ABVD in the Treatment of Hodgkin's Disease," *Semin Oncol*, 1992, 19(2 Suppl 5):38-44.

Buesa JM and Urrechaga E, "Clinical Pharmacokinetics of High-Dose DTIC," *Cancer Chemother Pharmacol*, 1991, 28(6):475-9.

Eggermont AM and Kirkwood JM, "Re-Evaluating the Role of Dacarbazine in Metastatic Melanoma: What Have We Learned in 30 years?" *Eur J Cancer*, 2004, 40(12):1825-36.

Finklestein JZ, Albo V, Ertel I, et al, "5-(3,3-Dimethyl-l-triazeno) imidazole-4-carboxamide (NSC-45388) in the Treatment of Solid Tumors in Children," *Cancer Chemother Rep*, 1975, 59(2 Pt 1):351-7.

Keohan ML and Taub RN, "Chemotherapy for Advanced Sarcoma: Therapeutic Decisions and Modalities," *Semin Oncol*, 1997, 24(5):572-9.

Mutz ID and Urban CE, "Dimethyl-triazeno-imidazole-carboxamide (DTIC) in Combination Chemotherapy for Childhood Neuroblastoma," *Wien Klin Wochenschr*, 1978, 90(24):867-70.

Rusthoven JJ, Quirt IC, Iscoe NA, et al, "Randomized, Double-Blind, Placebo-Controlled Trial Comparing the Response Rates of Carmustine, Dacarbazine, and Cisplatin With and Without Tamoxifen in Patients With Metastatic Melanoma. National Cancer Institute of Canada Clinical Trials Group" *J Clin Oncol*, 1996, 14(7):2083-90.

Yuen AR and Horning SJ, "Hodgkin's Disease: Management of First Relapse," *Oncology*, 1996, 10(2):233-40, 245.

Daclizumab *(dac KLYE zue mab)*

Related Information

Investigational Drug Service *on page 1379*

U.S. Brand Names Zenapax®

Generic Available No

Canadian Brand Names Zenapax®

Pharmacologic Category Immunosuppressant Agent

Use Part of an immunosuppressive regimen (including cyclosporine and corticosteroids) for the prophylaxis of acute organ rejection in patients receiving renal transplant

Unlabeled/Investigational Use Graft-versus-host disease; prevention of organ rejection after heart transplant

Pregnancy Risk Factor C

Lactation Excretion in breast milk unknown/use caution

Labeled Contraindications Hypersensitivity to daclizumab or any component of the formulation

Warnings/Precautions Patients on immunosuppressive therapy are at increased risk for infectious complications and secondary malignancies. Long-term effects of daclizumab on immune function are unknown. Severe hypersensitivity reactions have been rarely reported; anaphylaxis has been observed on initial exposure and following re-exposure; medications for the management of severe allergic reaction should be available for immediate use. Anti-idiotype antibodies have been measured in patients who have received daclizumab (adults 14%; children 34%); detection of antibodies may be influenced by multiple factors and may therefore be misleading.

In cardiac transplant patients, the combined use of daclizumab, cyclosporine, mycophenolate mofetil, and corticosteroids has been associated with an increased mortality. Higher mortality may be associated with the use of antilymphocyte globulin and a higher incidence of severe infections. **[U.S. Boxed Warning]: Should be administered under the supervision of a physician experienced in immunosuppressive therapy.**

Adverse Reactions Although reported adverse events are frequent, when daclizumab is compared with placebo the incidence of adverse effects is similar between the two groups. Many of the adverse effects reported during clinical trial use of daclizumab may be related to the patient population, transplant procedure, and concurrent transplant medications. Diarrhea, fever, postoperative pain, pruritus, respiratory tract infection, urinary tract infection, and vomiting occurred more often in children than adults.

≥5%:
  Cardiovascular: Chest pain, edema, hyper-/hypotension, tachycardia, thrombosis
  Central nervous system: Dizziness, fatigue, fever, headache, insomnia, pain, post-traumatic pain, tremor
  Dermatologic: Acne, cellulitis, wound healing impaired
  Gastrointestinal: Abdominal distention, abdominal pain, constipation, diarrhea, dyspepsia, epigastric pain, nausea, pyrosis, vomiting
  Genitourinary: Dysuria
  Hematologic: Bleeding
  Neuromuscular & skeletal: Back pain, musculoskeletal pain
  Renal: Oliguria, renal tubular necrosis
  Respiratory: Cough, dyspnea, pulmonary edema
  Miscellaneous: Lymphocele, wound infection
≥2% to <5%:
  Central nervous system: Anxiety, depression, shivering
  Dermatologic: Hirsutism, pruritus, rash
  Endocrine & metabolic: Dehydration, diabetes mellitus, fluid overload
  Gastrointestinal: Flatulence, gastritis, hemorrhoids
  Genitourinary: Urinary retention, urinary tract bleeding
  Local: Application site reaction
  Neuromuscular & skeletal: Arthralgia, leg cramps, myalgia, weakness
  Ocular: Vision blurred
  Renal: Hydronephrosis, renal damage, renal insufficiency
  Respiratory: Atelectasis, congestion, hypoxia, pharyngitis, pleural effusion, rales, rhinitis
  Miscellaneous: Night sweats, prickly sensation, diaphoresis
<1%, postmarketing, and/or case reports: Severe hypersensitivity reactions (rare): Anaphylaxis, bronchospasm, cardiac arrest, cytokine release syndrome, hypotension, laryngeal edema, pulmonary edema, pruritus, urticaria

Overdosage/Toxicology Overdose has not been reported.
Drug Interactions
  Increased Effect/Toxicity: The combined use of daclizumab, cyclosporine, mycophenolate mofetil, and corticosteroids has been associated with an increased mortality in a population of cardiac transplant recipients, (Continued)

Daclizumab *(Continued)*

particularly in patients who received antilymphocyte globulin and in patients with severe infections.

Storage/Stability Refrigerate vials at 2°C to 8°C (36°F to 46°F). Do not shake or freeze; protect undiluted solution against direct sunlight. Diluted solution is stable for 24 hours at 4°C or for 4 hours at room temperature.

Reconstitution Dose should be further diluted in 50 mL 0.9% sodium chloride solution. When mixing, gently invert bag to avoid foaming; do not shake. Do not use if solution is discolored.

Compatibility Do not mix with other medications or infuse other medications through same I.V. line.

Mechanism of Action Daclizumab is a chimeric (90% human, 10% murine) monoclonal IgG antibody produced by recombinant DNA technology. Daclizumab inhibits immune reactions by binding and blocking the alpha-chain of the interleukin-2 receptor (CD25) located on the surface of activated lymphocytes.

Pharmacodynamics/Kinetics

Distribution: V_d:

Adults: Central compartment: 0.031 L/kg; Peripheral compartment: 0.043 L/kg

Children: Central compartment: 0.067 L/kg; Peripheral compartment: 0.047 L/kg

Half-life elimination (estimated): Adults: Terminal: 20 days; Children: 13 days

Dosage Daclizumab is used adjunctively with other immunosuppressants (eg, cyclosporine, corticosteroids, mycophenolate mofetil, and azathioprine): I.V.:

Children: Use same weight-based dose as adults

Adults:

Immunoprophylaxis against acute renal allograft rejection: 1 mg/kg infused over 15 minutes within 24 hours before transplantation (day 0), then every 14 days for 4 additional doses

Treatment of graft-versus-host disease (unlabeled use, limited data): 0.5-1.5 mg/kg, repeat same dosage for transient response. Repeat doses have been administered 11-48 days following the initial dose.

Prevention of organ rejection after heart transplant (unlabeled use): 1 mg/kg up to a maximum of 100 mg; administer within 12 hours after heart transplant and on days 8, 22, 36, and 50 post-transplant

Dosage adjustment in renal impairment: No adjustment needed.

Dosage adjustment in hepatic impairment: No data available for patients with severe impairment.

Administration For I.V. administration following dilution. Daclizumab solution should be administered within 4 hours of preparation if stored at room temperature; infuse over a 15-minute period via a peripheral or central vein.

Patient Information This medication can only be given by I.V. infusion by a healthcare professional. May cause side effects similar to those caused by surgery as well as other medications that you may be taking.

Emetic Potential Very low (<10%)

Vesicant No

Dosage Forms Excipient information presented when available (limited, particularly for generics); consult specific product labeling.

Injection, solution [preservative free]: 5 mg/mL (5 mL)

References

Carswell CI, Plosker GL, and Wagstaff AJ, "Daclizumab: A Review of its Use in the Management of Organ Transplantation," *BioDrugs*, 2001, 15(11):745-73.

Hershberger RE, Starling RC, Eisen HJ, et al, "Daclizumab to Prevent Rejection After Cardiac Transplantation," *N Engl J Med*, 2005, 352(26):2705-13.

Vincenti F, Kirkman R, Light S, et al, "Interleukin-2-Receptor Blockade With Daclizumab to Prevent Acute Rejection in Renal Transplantation. Daclizumab Triple Therapy Study Group," *N Engl J Med*, 1998, 338(3):161-5.

Wiseman LR and Faulds D, "Daclizumab: A Review of Its Use in the Prevention of Acute Rejection in Renal Transplant Recipients," *Drugs*, 1999, 58(6):1029-42.

♦ **Dacodyl™ [OTC]** *see* Bisacodyl *on page 144*

♦ **Dacogen™** *see* Decitabine *on page 313*

♦ **DACT** *see* Dactinomycin *on page 287*

Dactinomycin (dak ti noe MYE sin)

Medication Safety Issues

Sound-alike/look-alike issues:

Dactinomycin may be confused with daptomycin, DAUNOrubicin

Actinomycin may be confused with Achromycin

High alert medication: The Institute for Safe Medication Practices (ISMP) includes this medication among its list of drugs which have a heightened risk of causing significant patient harm when used in error.

Related Information

Management of Drug Extravasations *on page 1301*

Safe Handling of Hazardous Drugs *on page 1382*

U.S. Brand Names Cosmegen®

Index Terms ACT; Act-D; Actinomycin; Actinomycin Cl; Actinomycin D; DACT; NSC-3053

Generic Available No

Canadian Brand Names Cosmegen®

Pharmacologic Category Antineoplastic Agent, Antibiotic

Use Treatment of testicular tumors, melanoma, gestational trophoblastic neoplasm, Wilms' tumor, neuroblastoma, retinoblastoma, rhabdomyosarcoma, uterine sarcomas, Ewing's sarcoma, Kaposi's sarcoma, sarcoma botryoides, and soft tissue sarcoma

Pregnancy Risk Factor D

Lactation Excretion in breast milk unknown/contraindicated

Labeled Contraindications Hypersensitivity to dactinomycin or any component of the formulation; patients with concurrent or recent chickenpox or herpes zoster; avoid in infants <6 months of age

Warnings/Precautions [U.S. Boxed Warnings]: Hazardous agent - use appropriate precautions for handling and disposal. Dactinomycin is extremely irritating to tissues and must be administered I.V.; if extravasation occurs during I.V. use, severe damage to soft tissues will occur. Avoid inhalation of vapors or contact with skin, mucous membrane, or eyes; avoid exposure during pregnancy. Dosage is usually expressed in **MICRO**grams, **NOT** milligrams, and must be calculated on the basis of body surface area (BSA) in obese or edematous adult patients. Dactinomycin potentiates the effects of radiation therapy; use with caution in patients who have received radiation therapy; reduce dosages in patients who are receiving dactinomycin and radiation therapy simultaneously; combination with radiation therapy may result in increased GI toxicity and myelosuppression. Avoid dactinomycin use within 2 months of radiation treatment for right-sided Wilms' tumor, may increase the risk of hepatotoxicity. Toxic effects may be delayed in onset (2-4 days following a course of treatment) and may require 1-2 weeks to reach maximum severity. Avoid administration of live vaccines. Use caution in hepatobiliary dysfunction; may cause veno-occlusive liver disease, increased risk in children <4 years of age. Long-term observation of cancer survivors is recommended due to the potential for secondary primary tumors following treatment with radiation and (Continued)

Dactinomycin *(Continued)*

antineoplastic agents. **[U.S. Boxed Warning]: Should be administered under the supervision of an experienced cancer chemotherapy physician.**

Adverse Reactions Frequency not defined.

Central nervous system: Fatigue, fever, lethargy, malaise

Dermatologic: Acne, alopecia (reversible), cheilitis; increased pigmentation, sloughing, or erythema of previously irradiated skin; skin eruptions

Endocrine & metabolic: Growth retardation, hypocalcemia

Gastrointestinal: Abdominal pain, anorexia, diarrhea, dysphagia, esophagitis, GI ulceration, mucositis, nausea, pharyngitis, proctitis, stomatitis, vomiting

Hematologic: Agranulocytosis, anemia, aplastic anemia, leukopenia, pancytopenia, reticulocytopenia, thrombocytopenia, myelosuppression (onset: 7 days, nadir: 14-21 days, recovery: 21-28 days)

Hepatic: Ascites, hepatic failure, hepatitis, hepatomegaly, hepatotoxicity, liver function test abnormality, veno-occlusive disease

Local: Erythema, edema, epidermolysis, pain, tissue necrosis, and ulceration (following extravasation)

Neuromuscular & skeletal: Myalgia

Renal: Renal function abnormality

Respiratory: Pneumonitis

Miscellaneous: Anaphylactoid reaction, infection

Overdosage/Toxicology Symptoms of overdose include nausea, vomiting, diarrhea, depression, GI ulceration, mucositis, severe myelosuppression, skin disorders (eg, exanthema, desquamation, epidermolysis), stomatitis, veno-occlusive disease, acute renal failure and fatality. Treatment is symptom-directed and supportive. Toxic effects may not be apparent until 2-4 days after a treatment course (peak after 1-2 weeks).

Drug Interactions

Increased Effect/Toxicity: Administration of live vaccines during treatment with dactinomycin should be avoided.

Storage/Stability Store at controlled room temperature of 15°C to 30°C (59°F to 86°F). Protect from light and humidity. Solutions in 50 mL D_5W or NS are stable for 24 hours at room temperature.

Reconstitution Dilute with 1.1 mL of preservative-free SWI to yield a final concentration of 500 mcg/mL. Do not use preservative diluent as precipitation may occur. Cellulose ester membrane filters should not be used during preparation.

Compatibility Stable in D_5W, NS, SWFI.

Y-site administration: Compatible: Allopurinol, amifostine, aztreonam, cefepime, etoposide phosphate, fludarabine, gemcitabine, granisetron, melphalan, ondansetron, sargramostim, teniposide, thiotepa, vinorelbine. **Incompatible:** Filgrastim.

Compatibility when admixed: Compatible: Dacarbazine.

Mechanism of Action Binds to the guanine portion of DNA intercalating between guanine and cytosine base pairs inhibiting DNA and RNA synthesis and protein synthesis

Pharmacodynamics/Kinetics

Distribution: High concentrations found in bone marrow and tumor cells, submaxillary gland, liver, and kidney; crosses placenta; poor CSF penetration

Metabolism: Hepatic, minimal

Half-life elimination: ~36 hours

Time to peak, serum: I.V.: 2-5 minutes

Excretion: Bile (50%); feces (14%); urine (~10% as unchanged drug)

Dosage Refer to individual protocols:

Note: Medication orders for dactinomycin are commonly written in MICROgrams (eg, 150 mcg) although many regimens list the dose in MILLIgrams (eg, mg/kg or mg/m²). One-time doses for >1000 mcg, or multiple-day doses for >500 mcg/day are not common. The dose intensity per 2-week cycle for adults and children should not exceed 15 mcg/kg/day for 5 days or 400-600 mcg/m²/day for 5 days. Some practitioners recommend calculation of the dosage for obese or edematous adult patients on the basis of body surface area in an effort to relate dosage to lean body mass.

Children >6 months: I.V.: Usual dose: 15 mcg/kg/day **or** 400-600 mcg/m²/day for 5 days every 3-6 weeks

Wilms' tumor, rhabdomyosarcoma, Ewing's sarcoma: 15 mcg/kg/day for 5 days (in various combination regimens and schedules)

Adults: I.V.:

Usual doses:

2.5 mg/m² in divided doses over 1 week, repeated every 2 weeks **or** 0.75-2 mg/m² every 1-4 weeks **or** 400-600 mcg/m²/day for 5 days, repeated every 3-6 weeks

Testicular cancer: 1000 mcg/m² on day 1 (as part of a combination chemotherapy regimen)

Gestational trophoblastic neoplasm: 12 mcg/kg/day for 5 days **or** 500 mcg days 1 and 2 (as part of a combination chemotherapy regimen)

Wilms' tumor, Ewing's sarcoma: 15 mcg/kg/day for 5 days (in various combination regimens and schedules)

Elderly: Elderly patients are at increased risk of myelosuppression; dosing should begin at the low end of the dosing range.

Dosage adjustment in renal impairment: No adjustment required

Combination Regimens

Gestational trophoblastic tumor:

CHAMOCA (Modified Bagshawe Regimen) *on page 1170*
CHAMOMA (Bagshawe Regimen) *on page 1172*
EMA/CO *on page 1199*
EP/EMA *on page 1203*

Osteosarcoma: POG-8651 *on page 1272*
Retinoblastoma: VAC (Retinoblastoma) *on page 1286*
Rhabdomyosarcoma:

VAC Pulse *on page 1286*
VAC (Rhabdomyosarcoma) *on page 1286*

Sarcoma: VAC Alternating With IE (Ewing's Sarcoma) *on page 1285*
Wilms' tumor:

AAV (DD) *on page 1142*
ACAV (J) *on page 1143*
AV (EE) *on page 1147*
AV (K) *on page 1148*
AV (L) *on page 1148*
AV (Wilms' Tumor) *on page 1148*
AVD *on page 1147*
EE *on page 1198*
EE-4A *on page 1198*

Administration Do not administer I.M. or SubQ. Administer by slow I.V. push or infuse over 10-15 minutes. Avoid extravasation. Do not filter with cellulose ester membrane filters.

Monitoring Parameters CBC with differential and platelet count, liver function tests, and renal function tests

(Continued)

Dactinomycin *(Continued)*

Test Interactions May interfere with bioassays of antibacterial drug levels

Patient Information Limit oral intake for 4-6 hours before therapy. It is important to maintain adequate nutrition and hydration (2-3 L/day of fluids unless instructed to restrict fluid intake) during therapy; frequent small meals may help. You may experience nausea or vomiting (frequent small meals, frequent mouth care, sucking lozenges, or chewing gum may help). If this is ineffective, consult prescriber for antiemetic medication. You may experience loss of hair (reversible); you will be more susceptible to infection (avoid crowds and exposure to infection as much as possible); you will be more sensitive to sunlight; use sunblock, wear protective clothing and dark glasses, or avoid direct exposure to sunlight. Flu-like symptoms (eg, malaise, fever, myalgia) may occur 1 week after infusion and persist for 1-3 weeks; consult prescriber for severe symptoms. Report fever, chills, unusual bruising or bleeding, signs of infection, excessive fatigue, yellowing of eyes or skin, or change in color of urine or stool. Contraceptive measures are recommended during therapy.

Emetic Potential High (60% to 90%)

Vesicant Yes; see Management of Drug Extravasations *on page 1301.*

Dosage Forms Excipient information presented when available (limited, particularly for generics); consult specific product labeling.

Injection, powder for reconstitution:

Cosmegen®: 0.5 mg [contains mannitol 20 mg]

References

Berkowitz RS and Goldstein DP, "Gestational Trophoblastic Disease," *Cancer*, 1995, 76(10 Suppl):2079-85.

Blatt J, Trigg ME, Pizzo PA, et al, "Tolerance to Single-Dose Dactinomycin in Combination Chemotherapy for Solid Tumors," *Cancer Treat Rep*, 1981, 65(1-2):145-7.

Carli M, Pastore G, Perilongo G, et al, "Tumor Response and Toxicity After Single High-Dose Versus Standard Five-Day Divided Dose Dactinomycin in Childhood Rhabdomyosarcoma," *J Clin Oncol*, 1988, 6(4):654-8.

Czauderna P, Katski K, Kowalczyk J, et al, "Venoocclusive Liver Disease (VOD) as a Complication of Wilms' Tumour Management in the Series of Consecutive 206 Patients," *Eur J Pediatr Surg*, 2000, 10(5):300-3.

D'Antiga L, Baker A, Pritchard J. et al, "Veno-Occlusive Disease With Multi-Organ Involvement Following Actinomycin-D," *Eur J Cancer*, 2001, 37(9):1141-8.

Horowitz ME, "Ewing's Sarcoma: Current Status of Diagnosis and Treatment," *Oncology*, 1989, 3(3):101-6.

Mehta MP, Bastin KT, and Wiersma SR, "Treatment of Wilms' Tumor. Current Recommendations," *Drugs*, 1991, 42(5):766-80.

Sulis ML, Bessmertny O, Granowetter L, et al, "Veno-Occlusive Disease in Pediatric Patients Receiving Actinomycin D and Vincristine Only for the Treatment of Rhabdomyosarcoma, *J Pediatr Hematol Oncol*, 2004, 26(12):843-6.

♦ **DAD** *see* Mitoxantrone *on page 773*

Dalteparin *(dal TE pa rin)*

Medication Safety Issues

High alert medication: The Institute for Safe Medication Practices (ISMP) includes this medication among its list of drugs which have a heightened risk of causing significant patient harm when used in error.

U.S. Brand Names Fragmin®

Index Terms Dalteparin Sodium; NSC-714371

Generic Available No

Canadian Brand Names Fragmin®

Pharmacologic Category Low Molecular Weight Heparin

Use Prevention of deep vein thrombosis which may lead to pulmonary embolism, in patients requiring abdominal surgery who are at risk for thromboembolism complications (eg, patients >40 years of age, obesity, patients with malignancy, history of deep vein thrombosis or pulmonary embolism, and surgical procedures requiring general anesthesia and lasting >30 minutes); prevention of DVT in patients undergoing hip-replacement surgery; patients immobile during an acute illness; acute treatment of unstable angina or non-Q-wave myocardial infarction; prevention of ischemic complications in patients on concurrent aspirin therapy; in patients with cancer, extended treatment (6 months) of acute symptomatic venous thromboembolism (DVT and/or PE) to reduce the recurrence of venous thromboembolism

Unlabeled/Investigational Use Active treatment of deep vein thrombosis (noncancer patients)

Pregnancy Risk Factor B

Lactation Enters breast milk/use caution

Labeled Contraindications Hypersensitivity to dalteparin or any component of the formulation; thrombocytopenia associated with a positive *in vitro* test for antiplatelet antibodies in the presence of dalteparin; hypersensitivity to heparin or pork products; patients with active major bleeding; patients with unstable angina, non-Q-wave MI, or acute venous thromboembolism undergoing regional anesthesia; not for I.M. or I.V. use

Warnings/Precautions [U.S. Boxed Warning]: Patients with recent or anticipated neuraxial anesthesia (epidural or spinal anesthesia) are at risk of spinal or epidural hematoma and subsequent paralysis. Consider risk versus benefit prior to neuraxial anesthesia. Risk is increased by concomitant agents which may alter hemostasis, as well as traumatic or repeated epidural or spinal puncture. Patient should be observed closely for bleeding if dalteparin is administered during or immediately following diagnostic lumbar puncture, epidural anesthesia, or spinal anesthesia.

Not to be used interchangeably (unit for unit) with heparin or any other low molecular weight heparins. Use caution in patients with known hypersensitivity to methylparaben or propylparaben, renal failure, or a history of heparin-induced thrombocytopenia. Monitor platelet count closely. Rare thrombocytopenia may occur. Consider discontinuation of dalteparin in any patient developing significant thrombocytopenia related to initiation of dalteparin. Rare cases of thrombocytopenia with thrombosis have occurred. Use caution in patients with congenital or drug-induced thrombocytopenia or platelet defects. Cancer patients with thrombocytopenia may require dose adjustments for treatment of acute venous thromboembolism. Monitor patient closely for signs or symptoms of bleeding. Certain patients are at increased risk of bleeding. Risk factors include bacterial endocarditis; congenital or acquired bleeding disorders; active ulcerative or angiodysplastic GI diseases; severe uncontrolled hypertension; hemorrhagic stroke; or use shortly after brain, spinal, or ophthalmology surgery; in patient treated concomitantly with platelet inhibitors; recent GI bleeding; thrombocytopenia or platelet defects; severe liver disease; hypertensive or diabetic retinopathy; or in patients undergoing invasive procedures.

Rare cases of thrombocytopenia with thrombosis have occurred. Multidose vials contain benzyl alcohol and should not be used in pregnant women. In neonates, large amounts of benzyl alcohol (>100 mg/kg/day) have been associated with fatal toxicity (gasping syndrome). Heparin can cause hyperkalemia by affecting aldosterone. Similar reactions could occur with LMWHs. Monitor for hyperkalemia. Safety and efficacy in pediatric patients have not been established.

Adverse Reactions

Note: As with all anticoagulants, bleeding is the major adverse effect of dalteparin. Hemorrhage may occur at virtually any site. Risk is dependent on multiple variables.

(Continued)

Dalteparin *(Continued)*

>10%:

Hematologic: Bleeding (3% to 14%)

1% to 10%:

Hematologic: Wound hematoma (up to 3%)

Hepatic: AST >3 times upper limit of normal (5% to 9%), ALT >3 times upper limit of normal (4% to 10%)

Local: Pain at injection site (up to 12%), injection site hematoma (up to 7%)

<1% (Limited to important or life-threatening): Thrombocytopenia (including heparin-induced thrombocytopenia), allergic reaction (fever, pruritus, rash, injections site reaction, bullous eruption), alopecia, anaphylactoid reaction, operative site bleeding, gastrointestinal bleeding, hemoptysis, skin necrosis, subdural hematoma, thrombosis (associated with heparin-induced thrombocytopenia). Spinal or epidural hematomas can occur following neuraxial anesthesia or spinal puncture, resulting in paralysis.

Overdosage/Toxicology

Symptoms of overdose include hemorrhage. Protamine sulfate has been used to reverse effects (protamine 1 mg neutralizes dalteparin 100 int. units). Monitor aPTT 2-4 hours after first infusion; consider readministration of protamine (50% of original dose). **Note:** Anti-Xa activity is never completely neutralized (maximum of 60% to 75%). Avoid overdose of protamine. Treatment is otherwise symptom-directed and supportive.

Drug Interactions

Increased Effect/Toxicity: Anticoagulants, antiplatelet agents, dasatinib, NSAIDs, salicylates, and treprostinil may enhance the anticoagulant effect of dalteparin. Dalteparin, particularly at therapeutic doses, may enhance the bleeding complications of drotrecogin alfa.

Ethanol/Nutrition/Herb Interactions Herb/Nutraceutical: Alfalfa, anise, bilberry, bladderwrack, bromelain, cat's claw, celery, chamomile, coleus, cordyceps, dong quai, evening primrose oil, fenugreek, feverfew, garlic, ginger, ginkgo biloba, Ginseng (american), Ginseng (panax), Ginseng (siberian), grapeseed, green tea, guggul, horse chestnut seed, horseradish, licorice, prickly ash, red clover, reishi, SAMe (s-adenosylmethionine), sweet clover, turmeric, white willow (all have additional antiplatelet/anticoagulant activity)

Storage/Stability Store at temperatures of 20°C to 25°C (68°F to 77°F). Multidose vials may be stored for up to 2 weeks at room temperature after entering.

Mechanism of Action Low molecular weight heparin analog with a molecular weight of 4000-6000 daltons; the commercial product contains 3% to 15% heparin with a molecular weight <3000 daltons, 65% to 78% with a molecular weight of 3000-8000 daltons and 14% to 26% with a molecular weight >8000 daltons; while dalteparin has been shown to inhibit both factor Xa and factor IIa (thrombin), the antithrombotic effect of dalteparin is characterized by a higher ratio of antifactor Xa to antifactor IIa activity (ratio = 4)

Pharmacodynamics/Kinetics

Onset of action: 1-2 hours

Duration: >12 hours

Distribution: V_d: 40-60 mL/kg

Bioavailability: SubQ: 81% to 93%

Half-life elimination (route dependent): 2-5 hours

Time to peak, serum: 4 hours

Dosage Adults: SubQ:

Abdominal surgery:

Low-to-moderate DVT risk: 2500 int. units 1-2 hours prior to surgery, then once daily for 5-10 days postoperatively

High DVT risk: 5000 int. units the evening prior to surgery and then once daily for 5-10 days postoperatively. Alternatively in patients with malignancy: 2500 int. units 1-2 hours prior to surgery, 2500 int. units 12 hours later, then 5000 int. units once daily for 5-10 days postoperatively.

Patients undergoing total hip surgery: **Note:** Three treatment options are currently available. Dose is given for 5-10 days, although up to 14 days of treatment have been tolerated in clinical trials:

Postoperative start:

Initial: 2500 int. units 4-8 hours* after surgery

Maintenance: 5000 int. units once daily; start at least 6 hours after postsurgical dose

Preoperative (starting day of surgery):

Initial: 2500 int. units within 2 hours before surgery

Adjustment: 2500 int. units 4-8 hours* after surgery

Maintenance: 5000 int. units once daily; start at least 6 hours after postsurgical dose

Preoperative (starting evening prior to surgery):

Initial: 5000 int. units 10-14 hours before surgery

Adjustment: 5000 int. units 4-8 hours* after surgery

Maintenance: 5000 int. units once daily, allowing 24 hours between doses.

*Dose may be delayed if hemostasis is not yet achieved.

Unstable angina or non-Q-wave myocardial infarction: 120 int. units/kg body weight (maximum dose: 10,000 int. units) every 12 hours for 5-8 days with concurrent aspirin therapy. Discontinue dalteparin once patient is clinically stable.

Venous thromboembolism: Cancer patients:

Initial (month 1): 200 int. units/kg (maximum dose: 18,000 int. units) once daily for 30 days

Maintenance (months 2-6): ~150 int. units/kg (maximum dose: 18,000 int. units) once daily. If platelet count between 50,000-100,000/mm^3, reduce dose by 2,500 int. units until platelet count recovers to ≥100,000/mm^3. If platelet count <50,000/mm^3, discontinue dalteparin until platelet count recover to >50,000/mm^3.

Immobility during acute illness: 5000 int. units once daily

Dosing adjustment in renal impairment: Half-life is increased in patients with chronic renal failure, use with caution, accumulation can be expected; specific dosage adjustments have not been recommended. In cancer patients, receiving treatment for venous thromboembolism, if Cl$_{cr}$ <30 mL/ minute, manufacturer recommends monitoring anti-Xa levels to determine appropriate dose.

Dosing adjustment in hepatic impairment: Use with caution in patients with hepatic insufficiency; specific dosage adjustments have not been recommended

Administration For deep SubQ injection only. May be injected in a U-shape to the area surrounding the navel, the upper outer side of the thigh, or the upper outer quadrangle of the buttock. Apply pressure to injection site; do not massage. Use thumb and forefinger to lift a fold of skin when injecting dalteparin to the navel area or thigh. Insert needle at a 45- to 90-degree angle. The entire length of needle should be inserted. Do not expel air bubble from fixed-dose syringe prior to injection. Air bubble (and extra solution, if applicable) may be expelled from graduated syringes.

(Continued)

Dalteparin *(Continued)*

Administration once daily beginning prior to surgery and continuing 5-10 days after surgery prevents deep vein thrombosis in patients at risk for thromboembolic complications. For unstable angina or non-Q-wave myocardial infarction, dalteparin is administered every 12 hours until the patient is stable (5-8 days).

Monitoring Parameters Periodic CBC including platelet count; stool occult blood tests; monitoring of PT and PTT is not necessary. Once patient has received 3-4 doses, anti-Xa levels, drawn 4-6 hours after dalteparin administration, may be used to monitor effect in patients with severe renal dysfunction or if abnormal coagulation parameters or bleeding should occur.

Special Geriatric Considerations No specific recommendations are necessary for the elderly.

Additional Information Multidose vial contains 14 mg/mL benzyl alcohol.

Dosage Forms Excipient information presented when available (limited, particularly for generics); consult specific product labeling.

Injection, solution:

Fragmin®: Antifactor Xa 10,000 int. units per 1 mL (9.5 mL) [contains benzyl alcohol]; antifactor Xa 25,000 units per 1 mL (3.8 mL) [contains benzyl alcohol]

Injection, solution [preservative free]:

Fragmin®: Antifactor Xa 2500 int. units per 0.2 mL (0.2 mL); antifactor Xa 5000 int. units per 0.2 mL (0.2 mL); antifactor Xa 7500 int. units per 0.3 mL (0.3 mL); antifactor Xa 10,000 int. units per 1 mL (1 mL); antifactor Xa 12,500 int. units per 0.5 mL (0.5 mL); antifactor Xa 15,000 int. units per 0.6 mL (0.6 mL); antifactor Xa 18,000 int. units per 0.72 mL (0.72 mL)

References

Braunwald E, Antman EM, Beasley JW, et al, "ACC/AHA 2002 Guideline Update for the Management of Patients With Unstable Angina and Non-ST-Segment Elevation Myocardial Infarction - Summary Article: A Report of the American College of Cardiology/American Heart Association Task Force on Practice Guidelines (Committee on the Management of Patients With Unstable Angina)," *J Am Coll Cardiol*, 2002, 40(7):1366-74. Available at: http://www.acc.org/clinical/guidelines/unstable/incorporated/index.htm. Accessed May 20, 2003.

Frostfeldt G, Ahlberg G, Gustafsson G, et al, "Low Molecular Weight Heparin (Dalteparin) as Adjunctive Treatment of Thrombolysis in Acute Myocardial Infarction - A Pilot Study: Biochemical Markers in Acute Coronary Syndromes (BIOMACS II), *J Am Coll Cardiol*, 1999, 33(3):627-33.

"Invasive Compared With Noninvasive Treatment in Unstable Coronary-Artery Disease: FRISC II Prospective Randomised Multicentre Study. Fragmin® and Fast Revascularisation During Instability in Coronary Artery Disease Investigators," *Lancet*, 1999, 354(9180):708-15.

Klein W, Buchwald A, Hillis SE, et al, "Comparison of Low Molecular-Weight Heparin With Unfractionated Heparin Acutely and With Placebo for 6 Weeks in the Management of Unstable Coronary Artery Disease. Fragmin® in Unstable Coronary Artery Disease Study," *Circulation*, 1997, 96(1):61-8.

Kontny F, Dale, J Abildgaard U, et al, "Randomized Trial of Low Molecular Weight Heparin (Dalteparin) in Prevention of Left Ventricular Thrombus Formation and Arterial Embolism After Acute Anterior Myocardial Infarction: The Fragmin® in Acute Myocardial Infarction (FRAMI) Study," *J Am Coll Cardiol*, 1997, 30(4):962-9.

Lee AY, Levine MN, Baker RI, et al, "Low-Molecular-Weight Heparin Versus a Coumarin for the Prevention of Recurrent Venous Thromboembolism in Patients with Cancer," *N Engl J Med*, 2003, 349(2):146-53.

Lee AY, Rickels FR, Julian JA, et al, "Randomized Comparison of Low Molecular Weight Heparin and Coumarin Derivatives on the Survival of Patients With Cancer and Venous Thromboembolism," *J Clin Oncol*, 2005, 23(10):2123-9.

Long-Term Low-Molecular-Mass Heparin in Unstable Coronary-Artery Disease: FRISC II Prospective Randomised Multicentre Study. Fragmin® and Fast Revascularisation During Instability in Coronary Artery Disease Investigators," *Lancet*, 1999, 354(9180):701-7.

"Low-Molecular-Weight Heparin During Instability in Coronary Artery Disease, Fragmin® During Instability in Coronary Artery Disease (FRISC) Study Group," *Lancet*, 1996, 347(9001):561-8.

Nagge J, Crowther M, and Hirsh J, "Is Impaired Renal Function a Contraindication to the Use of Low-Molecular Weight Heparin?" *Arch Intern Med*, 2002, 162(22):2605-9.

Wallentin L, "ASSENT 3 PLUS," [Paper presented at] American Heart Association 75th Scientific Sessions, November 17-20, 2002; Chicago, Ill.

Wong GC, Giugliano RP, and Antman EM, "Use of Low-Molecular-Weight Heparins in the Management of Acute Coronary Artery Syndromes and Percutaneous Coronary Intervention," *JAMA*, 2003, 289(3):331-42.

Zed PJ, Tisdale JE, and Borzak S, "Low-Molecular-Weight Heparins in the Management of Acute Coronary Syndromes," *Arch Intern Med*, 1999, 159(16):1849-57.

♦ **Dalteparin Sodium** *see* Dalteparin *on page 290*

Darbepoetin Alfa (dar be POE e tin AL fa)

Medication Safety Issues
Sound-alike/look-alike issues:
Darbepoetin alfa may be confused with epoetin alfa

U.S. Brand Names Aranesp®

Index Terms Erythropoiesis-Stimulating Agent (ESA); Erythropoiesis-Stimulating Protein; NSC-729969

Generic Available No

Canadian Brand Names Aranesp®

Pharmacologic Category Colony Stimulating Factor; Growth Factor; Recombinant Human Erythropoietin

Use Treatment of anemia (elevate/maintain red blood cell level and decrease the need for transfusions) associated with chronic renal failure (CRF), including patients on dialysis (ESRD) and patients not on dialysis, and concurrent chemotherapy for nonmyeloid malignancies

Pregnancy Risk Factor C

Lactation Excretion in breast milk unknown/use caution

Labeled Contraindications Hypersensitivity to darbepoetin or any component of the formulation; uncontrolled hypertension

Warnings/Precautions [U.S. Boxed Warning]: ESAs increased the risk of cardiovascular events, thromboembolic events, mortality, and/or tumor progression in clinical studies; a rapid rise in hemoglobin and/or maintaining higher hemoglobin levels may contribute to these risks. **[U.S. Boxed Warning]: A shortened overall survival and/or time-to-tumor progression has been reported in studies with advanced breast, head and neck, lymphoid, and non small cell lung cancer patients receiving ESAs to a target hemoglobin of ≥12 g/dL; risk has not been excluded when ESAs are dosed to achieve a target hemoglobin of <12 g/dL.** Malignant cell lines and tumors may have surface receptors for erythropoietin; it is not known if darbepoetin stimulates these receptors. **To decrease these risks, and risk of cardio and thrombovascular events, use ESAs in cancer patients only for the treatment of anemia related to concurrent chemotherapy and use the lowest dose needed to avoid red blood cell transfusions. Discontinue ESA following completion of the chemotherapy course. [U.S. Boxed Warning]: An increased risk of death and serious cardiovascular events was reported in chronic renal failure patients administered ESAs to target higher versus lower hemoglobin levels (13.5 vs 11.3 g/dL; 14 vs 10 g/dL) in two clinical studies; dosing should be individualized to achieve and maintain hemoglobin levels within 10-12 g/dL range.** Chronic renal failure patients who exhibit an inadequate hemoglobin response to ESA therapy may be at a higher risk for cardiovascular and mortality compared to other patients. ESA therapy may reduce dialysis efficacy (due to increase in red blood cells and decrease in plasma volume); adjustments in dialysis parameters may be needed. An increased risk of DVT has been observed in patients treated with epoetin
(Continued)

Darbepoetin Alfa *(Continued)*

undergoing surgical orthopedic procedures. Darbepoetin is **not** approved for reduction in red blood cell transfusions in patients scheduled for surgical procedures. During therapy in any patient, hemoglobin levels should not exceed 12 g/dL and should not rise >1 g/dL per 2-week time period.

Use with caution in patients with hypertension or with a history of seizures; hypertensive encephalopathy and seizures have been reported. If hypertension is difficult to control, reduce or hold darbepoetin alfa. **Not** recommended for acute correction of severe anemia or as a substitute for transfusion. Consider discontinuing in patients who receive a renal transplant.

Prior to treatment, correct or exclude deficiencies of iron, vitamin B_{12}, and/or folate, as well as other factors which may impair erythropoiesis (aluminum toxicity, inflammatory conditions, infections). Prior to and during therapy, iron stores must be evaluated. Supplemental iron is recommended if serum ferritin <100 mcg/mL or serum transferrin saturation <20%. Poor response should prompt evaluation of these potential factors, as well as possible malignant processes, occult blood loss, hemolysis, and/or bone marrow fibrosis. Pure red cell aplasia (PRCA) with associated neutralizing antibodies to erythropoietin has been reported, predominantly in patients with CRF. Patients with loss of response to darbepoetin alfa should be evaluated. Discontinue treatment in patients with PRCA secondary to neutralizing antibodies to erythropoietin.

Due to the delayed onset of erythropoiesis, darbepoetin is of no value in the acute treatment of anemia. Safety and efficacy in patients with underlying hematologic diseases have not been established, including porphyria, thalassemia, hemolytic anemia, and sickle cell disease. Potentially serious allergic reactions have been reported. Some products may contain albumin and the packaging of some formulations may contain latex. Do not shake solution; vigorous shaking may denature darbepoetin alfa, rendering it biologically inactive. Safety and efficacy in children with cancer have not been established; children >1 year of age with CRF have been converted from epoetin alfa to darbepoetin.

Adverse Reactions

>10%:

Cardiovascular: Hypertension (4% to 23%), hypotension (22%), edema (21%), peripheral edema (11%)

Central nervous system: Fatigue (9% to 33%), fever (4% to 19%), headache (12% to 16%), dizziness (8% to 14%)

Gastrointestinal: Diarrhea (16% to 22%), constipation (5% to 18%), vomiting (2% to 15%), nausea (14%), abdominal pain (12%)

Neuromuscular & skeletal: Myalgia (8% to 21%), arthralgia (11% to 13%)

Respiratory: Upper respiratory infection (14%), dyspnea (2% to 12%)

Miscellaneous: Infection (27%)

1% to 10%:

Cardiovascular: Arrhythmia (10%), angina/chest pain (6% to 8%), fluid overload (6%), CHF (6%), thrombosis (6%), MI (2%)

Central nervous system: Seizure (≤1%), stroke (1%), TIA (1%)

Dermatologic: Pruritus (8%), rash (7%)

Endocrine & metabolic: Dehydration (3% to 5%)

Local: Vascular access thrombosis (8%), injection site pain (7%), vascular access hemorrhage (6%), vascular access infection (6%)

Neuromuscular & skeletal: Limb pain (10%), back pain (8%), weakness (5%)

Respiratory: Cough (10%), bronchitis (6%), pneumonia (3%), pulmonary embolism (1%)

Miscellaneous: Death (7% to 10 %; similar to placebo), flu-like syndrome (6%)

Postmarketing and/or case reports: CHF, deep vein thrombosis, GI hemorrhage, hypertensive encephalopathy, pure red cell aplasia, sepsis, severe anemia (with or without other cytopenias), thromboembolism, thrombophlebitis, thrombosis, tumor progression (cancer patients)

Overdosage/Toxicology The maximum amount of darbepoetin which may be safely administered has not been determined. However, cardiovascular and neurologic adverse events have been correlated to excessive and/or rapid rise in hemoglobin. Phlebotomy may be performed for polycythemia, if clinically indicated.

Ethanol/Nutrition/Herb Interactions Ethanol: Should be avoided due to adverse effects on erythropoiesis.

Storage/Stability Store at 2°C to 8°C (36°F to 46°F). Do not freeze or shake. Protect from light.

Compatibility Do not dilute or administer with other solutions.

Mechanism of Action Induces erythropoiesis by stimulating the division and differentiation of committed erythroid progenitor cells; induces the release of reticulocytes from the bone marrow into the bloodstream, where they mature to erythrocytes. There is a dose response relationship with this effect. This results in an increase in reticulocyte counts followed by a rise in hematocrit and hemoglobin levels. When administered SubQ or I.V., darbepoetin's half-life is ~3 times that of epoetin alfa concentrations.

Pharmacodynamics/Kinetics

Onset of action: Increased hemoglobin levels not generally observed until 2-6 weeks after initiating treatment

Absorption: SubQ: Slow

Distribution: V_d: 0.06 L/kg

Bioavailability: CRF: SubQ: Adults: ~37% (range: 30% to 50%); Children: 54% (range: 32% to 70%)

Half-life elimination:
CRF: Terminal: Adult: I.V.: 21 hours, SubQ: 49 hours (range: 27-89 hours)
Cancer: Adult: SubQ: 74 hours (range: 24-144 hours); Children: 49 hours
Note: Darbepoetin half-life is approximately threefold longer than epoetin alfa following I.V. administration

Time to peak: SubQ:
CRF: Adults: 34 hours (range: 24-72 hours); Children: 36 hours (range: 10-58 hours)
Cancer: Adults: 71-90 hours; Children: 71 hours (range: 21-143 hours)

Dosage Note: Hemoglobin levels should not exceed 12 g/dL and should not rise >1 g/dL per 2-week time period during therapy in any patient.

Anemia associated with CRF: Individualize dosing to achieve and maintain hemoglobin levels between 10-12 g/dL. Hemoglobin levels should not exceed 12 g/dL.
Children ≥1 year: Conversion from epoetin alfa: I.V., SubQ: Weekly epoetin alfa doses of 1500 to ≥90,000 units per week may be converted to doses ranging from 6.25-200 mcg darbepoetin alfa per week (see pediatric column in conversion table below).
Children 11-18 years: Initial treatment (unlabeled use): I.V., SubQ: Initial dose: 0.45 mcg/kg once weekly; titrate to response
Adults: I.V., SubQ: Initial: 0.45 mcg/kg once weekly; titrate to response; some patients may respond to doses given once every 2 weeks

(Continued)

Darbepoetin Alfa *(Continued)*

Dosage adjustment:

Decrease dose by ~25%: If hemoglobin approaches 12 g/dL **or** hemoglobin increases >1 g/dL in any 2"week period. If hemoglobin continues to increase, temporarily discontinue therapy until hemoglobin begins to decrease, then resume therapy with a ~25% reduction from previous dose.

Increase dose by ~25%: If hemoglobin does not increase by 1 g/dL after 4 weeks of therapy (with adequate iron stores). Do not increase dose more frequently than at 4-week intervals.

Inadequate or lack of response: If patient does not attain target hemoglobin range of 10-12 g/dL after appropriate dose titrations over 12 weeks:

Do not continue to increase dose and use the minimum effective dose that will maintain a hemoglobin level sufficient to avoid red blood cell transfusions **and** evaluate patient for other causes of anemia.

Monitor hemoglobin closely thereafter, and if responsiveness improves, may resume making dosage adjustments as recommended above. If responsiveness does not improve and recurrent red blood cell transfusions continue to be needed, discontinue therapy.

Maintenance dose: Individualize to target hemoglobin range of 10-12 g/dL; limit additional dosage increase to every 4 weeks or longer. Patients generally require lower maintenance doses than initial doses to maintain target range.

Anemia associated with chemotherapy: Titrate dosage to use the minimum effective dose that will maintain a hemoglobin level sufficient to avoid red blood cell transfusions. Target hemoglobin levels should not exceed 12 g/dL.

Children (unlabeled use): 2.25 mcg/kg once weekly

Adults: Initial: 2.25 mcg/kg once weekly

or

500 mcg once every 3 weeks

Conversion From Epoetin Alfa to Darbepoetin Alfa

Previous Dosage of Epoetin Alfa (units/week)	Children Darbepoetin Alfa Dosage (mcg/week)	Adults Darbepoetin Alfa Dosage (mcg/week)	Adults Darbepoetin Alfa Dosage (mcg/every 2 weeks)
<1500	Not established	6.25	12.5
1500-2499	6.25	6.25	12.5
2500-4999	10	12.5	25
5000-10,999	20	25	50
11,000-17,999	40	40	80
18,000-33,999	60	60	120
34,000-89,999	100	100	200
≥90,000	200	200	400

Note: In patients receiving epoetin alfa 2-3 times per week, darbepoetin alfa is administered once weekly. In patients receiving epoetin alfa once weekly, darbepoetin alfa is administered once every 2 weeks.

Dosage adjustment:

Increase dose: If hemoglobin does not increase by 1 g/dL after 6 weeks of therapy (for patients receiving weekly therapy), the dose should be increased up to 4.5 mcg/kg once weekly.

Decrease dose by 40%: If hemoglobin increases >1g/dL in any 2-week period **or** hemoglobin reaches a level sufficient to avoid red blood cell transfusion.

Withhold dose: If hemoglobin exceeds 12 g/dL. Resume treatment with a dose 40% below the previous dose when hemoglobin approaches a level where transfusions may be required.

Conversion from epoetin alfa to darbepoetin alfa: See table on previous page.

Dosage adjustment in renal impairment: Dosage requirements for patients with chronic renal failure who do not require dialysis may be lower than in dialysis patients. Monitor patients closely during the time period in which a dialysis regimen is initiated, dosage requirement may increase. The National Kidney Foundation Clinical Practice Guidelines for Anemia in Chronic Kidney Disease: 2007 Update of Hemoglobin Target (September, 2007) recommend hemoglobin levels in the range of 11-12 g/dL for dialysis and nondialysis patients receiving ESAs; hemoglobin levels should not be maintained >13 g/dL.

Administration May be administered by SubQ or I.V. injection. The I.V. route is recommended in hemodialysis patients. Do not shake; vigorous shaking may denature darbepoetin alfa, rendering it biologically inactive. Do not dilute or administer in conjunction with other drug solutions. Discard any unused portion of the vial; do not pool unused portions.

Monitoring Parameters Hemoglobin (at least once per week until maintenance dose established and after dosage changes; monitor at regular intervals at least once per month once hemoglobin is stabilized); iron stores (transferrin saturation and ferritin) prior to and during therapy; serum chemistry (CRF patients); blood pressure

Dietary Considerations Supplemental iron intake may be required in patients with low iron stores.

Patient Information You will require frequent blood tests to determine appropriate dosage. Do not take other medications, vitamin or iron supplements, or make significant changes in your diet without consulting prescriber. Report signs or symptoms of edema (eg, swollen extremities, difficulty breathing, rapid weight gain), onset of severe headache, acute back pain, chest pain, or muscular tremors or seizure activity. Be careful to check blood pressure regularly.

Additional Information Oncology Comment: The American Society of Hematology (ASH) and American Society of Clinical Oncology (ASCO) 2007 updates to the clinical practice guidelines for the use of erythropoiesis-stimulating agents (ESAs) indicate that ESAs are most appropriate when used according to the dosage parameters within the Food and Drug Administration (FDA) approved labeling for epoetin and darbepoetin (Rizzo, 2007). While the previous guidelines addressed only the use of epoetin, the 2007 guidelines also address the use of darbepoetin, which is assessed as being equivalent to epoetin with respect to safety and efficacy. When used as an option for the treatment of chemotherapy-associated anemia (to increase hemoglobin and decrease red blood cell transfusions), therapy with ESAs should begin as the hemoglobin level approaches or falls below 10 g/dL. The ASH/ASCO guidelines recommend following the FDA approved dosing (and dosing adjustment) guidelines and target hemoglobin ranges as alternate dosing and schedules have not demonstrated consistent differences in effectiveness with regard to hemoglobin response. In patients who (Continued)

299

Darbepoetin Alfa (Continued)

do not have a response within 6-8 weeks (hemoglobin rise <1-2 g/dL or no reduction in transfusions) ESA therapy should be discontinued.

The guidelines note that patients with an increased risk of thromboembolism (generally includes previous history of thrombosis, surgery, and/or prolonged periods of immobilization) and patients receiving concomitant medications that may increase thromboembolic risk, should begin ESA therapy only after careful consideration. With the exception of low-risk myelodysplasia-associated anemia (which has evidence supporting the use of ESAs without concurrent chemotherapy), the guidelines do not support the use of ESAs in the absence of concurrent chemotherapy.

Emetic Potential Low (10% to 30%)

Vesicant No

Dosage Forms Excipient information presented when available (limited, particularly for generics); consult specific product labeling.

Injection, solution [preservative free]:

Aranesp®: 25 mcg/0.42 mL (0.42 mL); 40 mcg/ 0.4 mL (0.4 mL); 60 mcg/ 0.3 mL (0.3 mL); 100 mcg/0.5 mL (0.5 mL); 150 mcg/0.3 mL (0.3 mL); 200 mcg/0.4 mL (0.4 mL); 300 mcg/0.6 mL (0.6 mL); 500 mcg/mL (1 mL) [contains polysorbate 80; prefilled syringe; needle cover contains latex]

Aranesp®: 25 mcg/mL (1 mL); 40 mcg/mL (1 mL); 60 mcg/mL (1 mL); 100 mcg/mL (1 mL); 150 mcg/0.75 mL (0.75 mL); 200 mcg/mL (1 mL); 300 mcg/mL (1 mL) [contains polysorbate 80; single-dose vial]

References

Andre JL, Deschenes G, Boudaillies B, et al, "Darbepoetin, Effective Treatment of Anaemia in Paediatric Patients With Chronic Renal Failure," *Pediatr Nephrol*, 2007, 22(5):708-14.

Besarab A, Bolton WK, Browne JK, et al, "The Effects of Normal as Compared With Low Hematocrit Values in Patients With Cardiac Disease Who Are Receiving Hemodialysis and Epoetin," *N Engl J Med*, 1998, 339(9):584-90.

Blumer J, Berg S, Adamson PC, et al, "Pharmacokinetic Evaluation of Darbepoetin Alfa for the Treatment of Pediatric Patients With Chemotherapy-Induced Anemia," *Pediatr Blood Cancer*, 2007, 49(5):687-93.

Canon JL, Vansteenkiste J, Bodoky G, et al, "Randomized, Double-Blind, Active-Controlled Trial of Every-3-Week Darbepoetin Alfa for the Treatment of Chemotherapy-Induced Anemia," *J Natl Cancer Inst*, 2006, 98(4):273-84.

Corwin HL, Gettinger A, Pearl RG, et al, "Efficacy of Recombinant Human Erythropoietin in Critically Ill Patients: A Randomized Controlled Trial," *JAMA*, 2002, 288(22):2827-35.

Drueke TB, Locatelli F, Clyne N, et al, "Normalization of Hemoglobin Level in Patients With Chronic Kidney Disease and Anemia," *N Engl J Med*, 2006, 355(20): 2071-84.

Egrie JC and Browne KJ, "Development and Characterization of Novel Erythropoiesis Stimulation Protein (NESP)," *Br J Cancer*, 2001, 84(Suppl 1):3-10.

Hebert PC, Wells G, Blajchman MA, et al, "A Multicenter, Randomized, Controlled Clinical Trial of Transfusion Requirements in Critical Care. Transfusion Requirements in Critical Care Investigators, Canadian Critical Care Trials Group," *N Engl J Med*, 1999, 340(6):409-17.

Hesketh PJ, Arena F, Patel D, et al, "A Randomized Controlled Trial of Darbepoetin Alfa Administered as a Fixed or Weight-Based Dose Using a Front-Loading Schedule in Patients With Anemia Who Have Nonmyeloid Malignancies," *Cancer*, 2004, 100(4):859-68.

Jadoul M, Vanrenterghem Y, Foret M, et al, "Darbepoetin Alfa Administered Once Monthly Maintains Haemoglobin Levels in Stable Dialysis Patients," *Nephrol Dial Transplant*, 2004, 19(4):898-903.

Lerner G, Kale AS, Warady BA, et al, "Pharmacokinetics of Darbepoetin Alfa in Pediatric Patients With Chronic Kidney Disease," *Pediatr Nephrol*, 2002, 17(11):933-7.

National Kidney Foundation, "KDOQI Clinical Practice Guidelines and Clinical Practice Recommentaions for Anemia in Chronic Kidney Disease," *Am J Kidney Dis*, 2007, 50(3):529-30. Available at http://www.kidney.org/professionals/kdoqi/pdf/KDOQI_finalPDF.pdf or http://www.kidney.org/professionals/KDOQI.

NCCN (National Comprehensive Cancer Network), "Practice Guidelines in Oncology: Cancer- and Treatment-Related Anemia Version 1.2007." Available at http://www.nccn.org/professionals/physician_gls/PDF/anemia.pdf

Phronmmintikul A, Haas SJ, Elsik M, et al, "Mortality and Target Haemoglobin Concentrations in Anaemic Patients with Chronic Kidney Disease Treated With Erythropoietin: A Meta-Analysis," *Lancet*, 2007, 369(9559):381-88.

Rizzo JD, Somerfield MR, Hagerty LK, et al, "American Society of Hematology/American Society of Clinical Oncology 2007 Clinical Practice Guideline Update on the Use of Epoetin and Darbepoetin," *Blood*, 2007, Oct 22 [Epub ahead of print]

Singh AJ, Szczech L, Tang KI, et al, "Correction of Anemia with Epoetin Alfa in Chronic Kidney Disease," *N Engl J Med*, 2006, 355(20):2085-98.

Thames W, Yao B, Scheifele A, et al, "Drug Use Evaluation (DUE) of Darbepoetin Alfa in Anemic Patients Undergoing Chemotherapy Supports a Fixed Dose of 200 mcg Q2W Given Every 2 Weeks (Q2W)," *Asco Annual Meeting*, 2003.

Toto RD, Pichette V, Brenner R, et al, "Darbepoetin Alfa Effectively Treats Anemia in Patients With Chronic Kidney Disease With de novo Every-Other-Week Administration," *Am J Nephrol*, 2004, 24(4):453-60.

Vadhan-Raj S, Mirtsching B, Charu V, et al, "Assessment of Hematologic Effects and Fatigue in Cancer Patients With Chemotherapy-Induced Anemia Given Darbepoetin Alfa Every Two Weeks," *J Support Oncol*, 2003, 1(2):131-8.

Warady BA, Arar MY, Lerner G, et al, "Darbepoetin Alfa for the Treatment of Anemia in Pediatric Patients With Chronic Kidney Disease," *Pediatr Nephrol*, 2006, 21(8):1144-52.

Dasatinib (da SA ti nib)

Medication Safety Issues
High alert medication: The Institute for Safe Medication Practices (ISMP) includes this medication among its list of classes of drugs which have a heightened risk of causing significant patient harm when used in error.

Related Information
Safe Handling of Hazardous Drugs *on page 1382*

U.S. Brand Names Sprycel®

Index Terms BMS-354825; NSC-732517

Generic Available No

Canadian Brand Names Sprycel®

Pharmacologic Category Antineoplastic Agent, Tyrosine Kinase Inhibitor

Use Treatment of chronic myelogenous leukemia (CML) in chronic, accelerated or blast (myeloid or lymphoid) phase resistant or intolerant to prior therapy (including imatinib); treatment of Philadelphia chromosome-positive (Ph+) acute lymphoblastic leukemia (ALL) resistant or intolerant to prior therapy

Pregnancy Risk Factor D

Lactation Excretion in breast milk unknown/not recommended

Labeled Contraindications There are no contraindications listed in the manufacturer's labeling.

Warnings/Precautions Hazardous agent - use appropriate precautions for handling and disposal. Severe dose-related bone marrow suppression (thrombocytopenia, neutropenia, anemia) is associated with treatment; dosage adjustment or temporary interruption may be required for severe myelosuppression; the incidence of myelosuppression is higher in patients with advanced CML and Ph+ ALL. Severe hemorrhages (including CNS, GI) may occur due to thrombocytopenia. Use caution with patients taking anticoagulants or medications interfering with platelet function; not studied in clinical trials. Use with caution in patients receiving concurrent therapy which alters CYP3A4 activity; avoid concomitant use or consider dasatinib dosage adjustments. Fluid retention, including pleural and pericardial effusions, severe ascites, severe pulmonary edema, and generalized edema were reported. Use caution in patients where fluid accumulation may be poorly tolerated, such as in cardiovascular disease (CHF or hypertension) and pulmonary disease. Elderly may be more likely to experience fluid retention.

May prolong QT interval; use caution in patients at risk for QT prolongation, including patients with pre-existing QT interval prolongation; patients taking (Continued)

Dasatinib *(Continued)*

antiarrhythmic medications or other medications that lead to QT prolongation or potassium-wasting diuretics; patients with cumulative high-dose anthracycline therapy, and conditions which cause hypokalemia or hypomagnesemia. Correct hypokalemia and hypomagnesemia prior to initiation of therapy. Use caution with hepatic impairment due to extensive hepatic metabolism; patients with ALT or AST >2.5 times the upper limit of normal (ULN) or total bilirubin >2 times the ULN were excluded from clinical trials. Safety and efficacy in children <18 years of age have not been established.

Adverse Reactions

≥10%:

Cardiovascular: Fluid retention (37%; grades 3/4: 8%), superficial edema (20%)

Central nervous system: Headache (24%), fatigue (21%), fever (13%)

Dermatologic: Rash (22%; includes erythema, erythema multiforme, erythematous rash, exfoliative rash, follicular rash, heat rash, maculopapular rash, milia, papular rash, pruritic rash, pustular rash, skin exfoliation, skin irritation, systemic lupus erythematosus rash, urticaria vesiculosa, vesicular rash)

Endocrine & metabolic: Hypophosphatemia (grades 3/4: 6% to 20%), hypocalcemia (grades 3/4: 1% to 16%)

Gastrointestinal: Diarrhea (31%; grades 3/4: 3%), nausea (22%), vomiting (13%)

Hematologic: Neutropenia (grades 3/4: 34% to 80%), thrombocytopenia (grades 3/4: 22% to 81%), anemia (grades 3/4: 10% to 75%), hemorrhage (21%; grades 3/4: 6%)

Neuromuscular & skeletal: Musculoskeletal pain (14%)

Respiratory: Pleural effusion (22%; grades 3/4: 5%), dyspnea (20%; grades 3/4: 4%)

1% to <10%:

Cardiovascular: Generalized edema (3%), pericardial effusion (3%; grades 3/4: 1%), CHF/cardiac dysfunction (2%; grades 3/4: 1%; includes cardiac failure, cardiopmyopathy, CHF, diastolic dysfunction, ejection fraction decreased, left ventricular dysfunction, ventricular failure); arrhythmia, chest pain, flushing, hypertension, palpitation

Central nervous system: CNS bleeding (1%), chills, depression, dizziness, insomnia, pain, somnolence

Dermatologic: Acne, alopecia, dermatitis, dry skin, eczema, hyperhydrosis, pruritus, urticaria

Gastrointestinal: Abdominal pain (10%), gastrointestinal bleeding (7%; grades 3/4: 4%), abdominal distention, colitis, constipation, dysgeusia, dyspepsia, enterocolitis, gastritis, mucositis/stomatitis, oral soft tissue disorder, weight loss/gain

Hematologic: Contusion, neutropenic fever, pancytopenia

Hepatic: ALT increased (grades 3/4: ≤7%), AST increased (grades 3/4: ≤5%), bilirubin increased (grades 3/4: ≤5%)

Neuromuscular & skeletal: Arthralgia, muscle inflammation, muscle weakness, myalgia, neuropathy, peripheral neuropathy, weakness

Ocular: Visual disorder, xerophthalmia

Renal: Serum creatinine increased (grades 3/4: ≤3%)

Respiratory: Pulmonary edema (2%; grades 3/4: 1%), pulmonary hypertension (1%), cough, lung infiltration, pneumonia, pneumonitis, upper respiratory tract infection/inflammation

Miscellaneous: Infection (bacterial, fungal, viral), herpes virus infection

<1%, postmarketing, and/or case reports (limited to important or life-threatening): Acute coronary syndrome, acute febrile neutrophilic dermatosis, acute respiratory distress syndrome, affect lability, amnesia, anal fissure, angina, ascites, asthma, bronchospasm, bullous conditions, cardiomegaly, cerebrovascular accident, cholecystitis, cholestasis, coagulopathy, confusion, conjunctivitis, creatine phosphokinase increased, dysphagia, erythema nodosum, esophagitis, gynecomastia, hand-foot syndrome, hepatitis, hypersensitivity, hyperuricemia, hypoalbuminemia, hypotension, ileus, libido decreased, livedo reticularis, menstrual irregularities, MI, musculoskeletal stiffness, myocarditis, neutropenic colitis, pancreatitis, panniculitis, pericarditis, periorbital edema, photosensitivity, platelet aggregation abnormal, polyuria, proteinuria, pure red cell aplasia, QT_c prolongation, renal failure, reversible posterior leukoencephalopathy syndrome, rhabdomyolysis, seizure, sepsis, skin ulcer, syncope, tendonitis, thrombophlebitis, TIA, tinnitus, tremor, troponin increased, tumor lysis syndrome, upper gastrointestinal ulcer, ventricular arrhythmia, ventricular tachycardia, vertigo

Overdosage/Toxicology Accidental overdose (280 mg daily for 1 week) resulted in severe myelosuppression and bleeding. Closely monitor hematologic parameters. Treatment is symptom-directed and supportive.

Drug Interactions

Cytochrome P450 Effect: Substrate of CYP3A4 (major); **Inhibits** CYP3A4 (weak)

Increased Effect/Toxicity:

The levels/effects of dasatinib may be increased by azole antifungals, clarithromycin, diclofenac, doxycycline, erythromycin, imatinib, isoniazid, nefazodone, nicardipine, propofol, protease inhibitors, quinidine, telithromycin, verapamil, and other CYP3A4 inhibitors. Concurrent use of dasatinib with other drugs which may prolong QT_c interval (ciprofloxacin, thioridazine) may increase the risk of potentially-fatal arrhythmias. Anticoagulants and antiplatelet agents may increase the risk of bleeding.

Decreased Effect: The levels/effects of dasatinib may be decreased by aminoglutethimide, carbamazepine, nafcillin, nevirapine, phenobarbital, phenytoin, rifamycins, and other CYP3A4 inducers. Antacids, H_2 blockers and proton pump inhibitors may decrease the absorption of dasatinib.

Ethanol/Nutrition/Herb Interactions Herb/Nutraceutical: Avoid St John's wort (may increase metabolism and decrease dasatinib plasma concentration).

Storage/Stability Store at 15°C to 30°C (59°F to 86°F).

Mechanism of Action BCR-ABL tyrosine kinase inhibitor; targets most imatinib-resistant BCR-ABL mutations (except the T315I and F317V mutants) by distinctly binding to ABL-kinase. Kinase inhibition halts proliferation of leukemia cells. Also inhibits SRC family (including SRC, LKC, YES, FYN); c-KIT, EPHA2 and platelet derived growth factor receptor (PDGFRβ)

Pharmacodynamics/Kinetics

Distribution: 2505 L

Protein binding: Dasatinib: 96%; metabolite (active): 93%

Metabolism: Hepatic (extensive); metabolized by CYP3A4 (primarily), flavin-containing mono-oxygenase-3 (FOM-3) and uridine diphosphate-glucuronosyltransferase (UGT) to an active metabolite and other inactive metabolites (the active metabolite plays only a minor role in the pharmacology of dasatinib)

Half-life elimination: Terminal: 3-5 hours

Time to peak, plasma: 0.5-6 hours

(Continued)

Dasatinib *(Continued)*

Excretion: Feces (85%, 19% as unchanged drug); urine (4%, 0.1% as unchanged drug)

Dosage Oral: Adults:

CML:

Chronic phase: 100 mg once daily. In clinical studies, a dose escalation to 140 mg once daily was allowed in patients not achieving cytogenetic response at recommended initial dosage.

Accelerated or blast phase: 70 mg twice daily. In clinical studies, a dose escalation to 100 mg twice daily was allowed in patients not achieving cytogenetic response at recommended initial dosage.

Ph+ ALL: 70 mg twice daily. In clinical studies, a dose escalation to 100 mg twice daily was allowed in patients not achieving cytogenetic response at recommended initial dosage.

Dosage adjustment for concomitant CYP3A4 inhibitors/inducers: Dose reductions are likely to be needed when dasatinib is administered concomitantly with a strong CYP3A4 inhibitor (an alternate medication for CYP3A4 enzyme inhibitors should be investigated first). In the event that dasatinib must be administered concomitantly with a potent enzyme inhibitor, consider reducing dasatinib to 20 mg daily with careful monitoring. If reduced dose is not tolerated, the strong CYP3A4 inhibitor must be discontinued or dasatinib therapy temporarily held until concomitant inhibitor use has ceased. When a strong CYP3A4 inhibitor is discontinued, allow a washout period (~1 week) prior to adjusting dasatinib dose upward. Likewise, concomitant administration with CYP3A4 inducers may require increased dasatinib doses, with careful monitoring; (alternatives to the enzyme inducing agent should be utilized first.) See Drug Interactions for examples of CYP3A4 inhibitors and inducers.

Dosage adjustment for toxicity: Dose increases or reductions should be made in 20 mg increments (per dose) or as follows:

Hematologic toxicity:

Chronic phase CML: For ANC <0.5 x 10^9/L or platelets <50 x 10^9/L, withhold treatment until ANC ≥1 x 10^9/L and platelets ≥50 x 10^9/L; then resume treatment at the original starting dose if recovery occurs in ≤7 days. If platelets <25 x 10^9/L or recurrence of ANC <0.5 x 10^9/L for >7 days, withhold treatment until ANC ≥1 x 10^9/L and platelets ≥50 x 10^9/L; then resume treatment at 80 mg once daily (2nd episode) or discontinue (3rd episode)

Accelerated or blast phase CML and Ph+ ALL: For ANC <0.5 x 10^9/L or platelets <10 x 10^9/L, if cytopenia unrelated to leukemia, withhold treatment until ANC ≥1 x 10^9/L and platelets ≥20 x 10^9/L; then resume treatment at the original starting dose. If cytopenia recurs, withhold treatment until ANC ≥1 x 10^9/L and platelets ≥20 x 10^9/L; then resume treatment at 50 mg twice daily (2nd episode) or 40 mg twice daily (3rd episode). For cytopenias related to leukemia (confirm with marrow aspirate or biopsy), consider dose escalation to 100 mg twice daily with careful monitoring.

Nonhematologic toxicity: Withhold treatment until toxicity improvement or resolution; if appropriate, resume treatment at a reduced dose based on the event severity.

Administration Administer once daily (morning or evening) or twice daily (morning and evening). May be taken without regard to food. Do not break, crush, or chew tablets.

Monitoring Parameters CBC with differential (weekly for 2 months, then monthly); bone marrow biopsy; liver function tests, electrolytes including calcium, phosphorus, magnesium; monitor for fluid retention; ECG monitoring if at risk for QT_c prolongation

Dietary Considerations May be taken without regard to food. Avoid grapefruit juice.

Special Geriatric Considerations Limited data available demonstrate no difference in safety or efficacy observed between elderly and younger adults. Elderly may be more sensitive to pharmacologic effects.

Additional Information In clinical trials, dasatinib was continued until disease progression or until the patient no longer tolerated treatment. Patients who did not achieve hematologic or cytogenetic response at 70 mg twice daily were allowed to escalate the dose to 90 mg twice daily (chronic phase CML) or 100 mg twice daily (advanced phase CML and Ph+ ALL)

Emetic Potential Low (10% to 30%)

Dosage Forms Excipient information presented when available (limited, particularly for generics); consult specific product labeling.
Tablet:
Sprycel®: 20 mg, 50 mg, 70 mg

References

Assouline S, Laneuville P and Gambacorti-Passerini C, "Panniculitis During Dasatinib Therapy for Imatinib-Resistant Chronic Myelogenous Leukemia," N Engl J Med, 2006, 354(24):2623-4.

Bradeen HA, Eide CA, O'Hare T, et al , "Comparison of Imatinib, Dasatinib (BMS-354825), and Nilotinib (AMN107) in an N-Ethyl-N-Nitrosourea (ENU)-Based Mutagenesis Screen: High Efficacy of Drug Combinations," Blood, 2006, 108(7):2332-8.

Copland M, Hamilton A, Elrick LJ, et al, "Dasatinib (BMS-354825) Targets an Earlier Progenitor Population Than Imatinib in Primary CML But Does Not Eliminate the Quiescent Fraction," Blood, 2006, 107(11):4532-9.

Cortes J, Rousselot P, Kim DW, et al, "Dasatinib Induces Complete Hematologic and Cytogenetic Responses in Patients With Imatinib-Resistant or Intolerant Chronic Myeloid Leukemia in Blast Crisis," Blood, 2007, 109(8):3207-13.

Guilhot F, Apperley J, Kim DW, et al, "Dasatinib Induces Significant Hematologic and Cytogenetic Responses in Patients with Imatinib-Resistant or Intolerant Chronic Myeloid Leukemia in Accelerated Phase," Blood, 2007, 109(10):4143-50.

Hochhaus A, Kantarjian HM, Baccarani M, et al, "Dasatinib Induces Notable Hematologic and Cytogenetic Responses in Chronic-Phase Chronic Myeloid Leukemia After Failure of Imatinib Therapy," Blood, 2007, 109(6):2303-09.

Ottmann O, Dombret H, Martinelli G, et al, "Dasatinib Induces Rapid Hematologic and Cytogenetic Responses in Adult Patients with Philadelphia Chromosome-Positive Acute Lymphoblastic Leukemia with Intolerance to Imatinib: Interim Results of a Phase 2 Study," Blood, 2007, 110(7):2309-15.

Talpaz M, Shah NP, Kantarjian H, et al, "Dasatinib in Imatinib-Resistant Philadelphia Chromosome-Positive Leukemias," N Engl J Med, 2006, 354(24):2531-41.

♦ **Daunomycin** see DAUNOrubicin Hydrochloride on page 308

DAUNOrubicin Citrate (Liposomal)
(daw noe ROO bi sin SI trate lip po SOE mal)

Medication Safety Issues
Sound-alike/look-alike issues:
DAUNOrubicin liposomal may be confused with dactinomycin, DOXOrubicin, DOXOrubicin liposomal, epirubicin, idarubicin
DAUNOrubicin liposomal may be confused with DOXOrubicin liposomal
Liposomal formulation (DaunoXome®) may be confused with the conventional formulation (Cerubidine®, Rubex®)

High alert medication: The Institute for Safe Medication Practices (ISMP) includes this medication among its list of classes of drugs which have a heightened risk of causing significant patient harm when used in error.

Related Information
Management of Drug Extravasations on page 1301
(Continued)

DAUNOrubicin Citrate (Liposomal) *(Continued)*

Safe Handling of Hazardous Drugs *on page 1382*

U.S. Brand Names DaunoXome®

Index Terms DAUNOrubicin Liposomal; Liposomal DAUNOrubicin; NSC-697732

Generic Available No

Pharmacologic Category Antineoplastic Agent, Anthracycline

Use First-line treatment of advanced HIV-associated Kaposi's sarcoma (KS)

Pregnancy Risk Factor D

Lactation Excretion in breast milk unknown/not recommended

Labeled Contraindications Hypersensitivity to daunorubicin citrate (liposomal), daunorubicin, or any component of the formulation

Warnings/Precautions Hazardous agent - use appropriate precautions for handling and disposal. **[U.S. Boxed Warning]: Monitor cardiac function regularly; especially in patients with previous therapy with high cumulative doses of anthracyclines, cyclophosphamide, or thoracic radiation, or who have pre-existing cardiac disease.** Although the risk increases with cumulative dose, irreversible cardiotoxicity may occur with anthracycline treatment at any dose level. Patients with pre-existing heart disease, hypertension, concurrent administration of other antineoplastic agents, prior or concurrent chest irradiation, and advanced age are at increased risk. Evaluate left ventricular ejection fraction (LVEF) prior to treatment and periodically during treatment.

[U.S. Boxed Warning]: May cause bone marrow suppression, particularly neutropenia; monitor closely for infections. **[U.S. Boxed Warning]: Use caution with hepatic impairment;** dosage reduction is recommended. Use caution with renal impairment; may require dose adjustment. **[U.S. Boxed Warning]: The lipid component is associated with infusion-related reactions (back pain, flushing, chest tightness) usually within the first 5 minutes of infusion;** monitor, interrupt infusion, and resume at reduced infusion rate. Safety and efficacy in children and the elderly have not been established. **[U.S. Boxed Warning]: Should be administered under the supervision of an experienced cancer chemotherapy physician.**

Adverse Reactions

>10%:

Cardiovascular: Edema (11%)

Central nervous system: Fatigue (49%), fever (47%), headache (25%), neutropenic fever (17%)

Gastrointestinal: Nausea (54%), diarrhea (38%), abdominal pain (23%), anorexia (23%), vomiting (23%)

Hematologic: Myelosuppression (onset: 7 days; nadir: 14 days; recovery 21 days), neutropenia (up to 55%; grade 4: 15%), anemia (up to 55%; grade 4: 2%), thrombocytopenia (up to 12%; grade 4: 1%)

Neuromuscular & skeletal: Rigors (19%), back pain (16%), neuropathy (13%)

Respiratory: Cough (28%), dyspnea (26%), rhinitis (12%)

Miscellaneous: Opportunistic infections (40%), allergic reactions (24%), diaphoresis (14%), infusion-related reactions (14%; includes back pain, flushing, chest tightness)

1% to 10%:

Cardiovascular: Chest pain (10%), hypertension (≤5%), palpitation (≤5%), syncope (≤5%), tachycardia (≤5%), LVEF decreased (3%), CHF/cardiomyopathy

Central nervous system: Depression (10%), malaise (10%), dizziness (8%), insomnia (6%), abnormal thinking (≤5%), amnesia (≤5%), anxiety (≤5%), ataxia (≤5%), confusion (≤5%), emotional lability (≤5%), hallucination (≤5%), meningitis (≤5%), seizure (≤5%), somnolence (≤5%)

Dermatologic: Alopecia (8%), pruritus (7%), dry skin (≤5%), folliculitis (≤5%), seborrhea (≤5%)

Endocrine & metabolic: Dehydration (≤5%), hot flashes (≤5%)

Gastrointestinal: Stomatitis (10%), constipation (7%), tenesmus (5%), appetite increased (≤5%), dental caries (≤5%), dysphagia (≤5%), gastrointestinal hemorrhage (≤5%), gastritis (≤5%), gingival bleeding (≤5%), hemorrhoids (≤5%), melena (≤5%), splenomegaly (≤5%), taste perversion (≤5%), xerostomia (≤5%)

Genitourinary: Dysuria (≤5%), nocturia (≤5%), polyuria (≤5%)

Hepatic: Hepatomegaly (≤5%)

Local: Injection site inflammation (≤5%)

Neuromuscular & skeletal: Arthralgia (7%), myalgia (7%), gait abnormal (≤5%), hyperkinesia (≤5%), hypertonia (≤5%), tremor (≤5%)

Ocular: Abnormal vision (5%) conjunctivitis (≤5%), eye pain (≤5%)

Otic: Deafness (≤5%), earache (≤5%), tinnitus (≤5%)

Respiratory: Sinusitis (8%), hemoptysis (≤5%), pulmonary infiltrate (≤5%), sputum increased (≤5%)

Miscellaneous: Flu-like syndrome (5%), hiccups (≤5%), lymphadenopathy (≤5%), thirst (≤5%)

Postmarketing and/or case reports: Angina, atrial fibrillation, cardiac arrest, MI, pericardial effusion, pericardial tamponade, pulmonary hypertension, supraventricular tachycardia, ventricular extrasystoles

Overdosage/Toxicology Symptoms of acute overdose are increased severity of the observed dose-limiting toxicities of therapeutic doses, myelosuppression (especially granulocytopenia), fatigue, nausea, and vomiting. Treatment is symptom-directed and supportive.

Drug Interactions

Increased Effect/Toxicity: Bevacizumab and trastuzumab may increase the cardiotoxic effects of anthracyclines. Daunorubicin citrate liposomal may increase the risk of vaccinal infection.

Decreased Effect: Daunorubicin citrate liposomal may decrease the effect of vaccines.

Storage/Stability Store intact vials of solution under refrigeration at 2°C to 8°C (36°F to 46°F); do not freeze. Protect from light. Diluted daunorubicin liposomal for infusion may be refrigerated at 2°C to 8°C (36°F to 46°F) for a maximum of 6 hours. Do not use with in-line filters.

Reconstitution Only fluid which may be mixed with DaunoXome® is D₅W. Dilute to a 1:1 solution (1 mg daunorubicin liposomal/mL D₅W). Must **not** be mixed with saline, bacteriostatic agents (such as benzyl alcohol), or any other solution.

Compatibility Stable in D₅W. **Incompatible** with normal saline, sodium bicarbonate and fluorouracil, heparin, dexamethasone.

Mechanism of Action Liposomes have been shown to penetrate solid tumors more effectively, possibly because of their small size and longer circulation time. Once in tissues, daunorubicin is released. Daunorubicin inhibits DNA and RNA synthesis by intercalation between DNA base pairs and by steric obstruction; and intercalates at points of local uncoiling of the double helix. Although the exact mechanism is unclear, it appears that direct binding to DNA (intercalation) and inhibition of DNA repair (topoisomerase II inhibition) result in blockade of DNA and RNA synthesis and fragmentation of DNA.

(Continued)

DAUNOrubicin Citrate (Liposomal) *(Continued)*

Pharmacodynamics/Kinetics

Distribution: V_d: 5-8 L

Metabolism: Similar to daunorubicin, but metabolite plasma levels are low

Half-life elimination: Distribution: 4.4 hours; Terminal: 3-5 hours

Excretion: Primarily feces; some urine

Clearance, plasma: 17.3 mL/minute

Dosage Refer to individual protocols. I.V.:

Adults: HIV-associated KS: 40 mg/m^2 every 2 weeks

Elderly: Use with caution.

Dosage adjustment for toxicity: Withhold treatment for ANC <750/mm^3

Elderly: Use with caution.

Dosing adjustment in renal impairment: Serum creatinine >3 mg/dL: Administer 50% of normal dose

Dosing adjustment in hepatic impairment:

Bilirubin 1.2-3 mg/dL: Administer 75% of normal dose

Bilirubin >3 mg/dL: Administer 50% of normal dose

Combination Regimens

Leukemia, acute lymphocytic: Hyper-CVAD (Leukemia, Acute Lymphocytic) *on page 1231*

Administration Infuse over 1 hour; do not mix with other drugs. Avoid extravasation.

Monitoring Parameters CBC with differential and platelets (prior to each dose), liver function tests, renal function tests; evaluate cardiac function (baseline left ventricular ejection fraction [LVEF] prior to treatment initiation; repeat LVEF at total cumulative doses of 320 mg/m^2, and every 160 mg/m^2 thereafter; patients with pre-existing cardiac disease, history of prior chest irradiation, or history of prior anthracycline treatment should have baseline LVEF and every 160 mg/m^2 thereafter); signs and symptoms of infection or disease progression; monitor closely for infusion reactions

Emetic Potential Moderate (30% to 60%)

Vesicant No; may be an irritant

Dosage Forms Excipient information presented when available (limited, particularly for generics); consult specific product labeling.

Injection, solution [preservative free]:

DaunoXome®: 2 mg/mL (25 mL) [contains sucrose 2125 mg/25 mL]

References

Eckardt JR, Campbell E, Burris HA, et al, "A Phase II Trial of DaunoXome®, Liposome-Encapsulated Daunorubicin, in Patients With Metastatic Adenocarcinoma of the Colon," *Am J Clin Oncol*, 1994, 17(6):498-501.

Gill PS, Espina BM, Muggia F, et al, "Phase I/II Clinical and Pharmacokinetic Evaluation of Liposomal Daunorubicin," *J Clin Oncol*, 1995, 13(4):996-1003.

Gill PS, Wernz J, Scadden DT, et al, "Randomized Phase III Trial of Liposomal Daunorubicin Versus Doxorubicin, Bleomycin, and Vincristine in AIDS-Related Kaposi's Sarcoma," *J Clin Oncol*, 1996, 14(8):2353-64.

Guaglianone P, Chan K, Dela Flor-Weiss E, et al, "Phase I and Pharmacologic Study of Liposomal Daunorubicin (DaunoXome®)," *Invest New Drugs*, 1994, 12(2):103-10.

Schurmann D, Dormann A, Grunewald T, et al, "Successful Treatment of AIDS-Related Pulmonary Kaposi's Sarcoma With Liposomal Daunorubicin," *Eur Respir J*, 1994, 7(4):824-5.

DAUNOrubicin Hydrochloride

(daw noe ROO bi sin hye droe KLOR ide)

Medication Safety Issues

Sound-alike/look-alike issues:

DAUNOrubicin may be confused with dactinomycin, DOXOrubicin, DOXOrubicin liposomal, epirubicin, idarubicin

Conventional formulation (Cerubidine®, DAUNOrubicin hydrochloride) may be confused with the liposomal formulation (DaunoXome®)

High alert medication: The Institute for Safe Medication Practices (ISMP) includes this medication among its list of classes of drugs which have a heightened risk of causing significant patient harm when used in error.

Related Information

Management of Drug Extravasations *on page 1301*
Safe Handling of Hazardous Drugs *on page 1382*

U.S. Brand Names Cerubidine®

Index Terms Daunomycin; NSC-82151; Rubidomycin Hydrochloride

Generic Available Yes

Canadian Brand Names Cerubidine®

Pharmacologic Category Antineoplastic Agent, Anthracycline

Use Treatment of acute lymphocytic (ALL) and nonlymphocytic (ANLL) leukemias

Pregnancy Risk Factor D

Lactation Excretion in breast milk unknown/not recommended

Labeled Contraindications Hypersensitivity to daunorubicin or any component of the formulation

Warnings/Precautions Hazardous agent - use appropriate precautions for handling and disposal. Use with caution in patients who have received radiation therapy; reduce dosage in patients who are receiving radiation therapy simultaneously. **[U.S. Boxed Warnings]: Use caution with renal impairment or in the presence of hepatic dysfunction; dosage reduction is recommended. Potent vesicant; if extravasation occurs, severe local tissue damage leading to ulceration and necrosis, and pain may occur. For I.V. administration only. Severe bone marrow suppression may occur.**

[U.S. Boxed Warning]: May cause cumulative, dose-related myocardial toxicity (concurrent or delayed). Total cumulative dose should take into account previous or concomitant treatment with cardiotoxic agents or irradiation of chest. The incidence of irreversible myocardial toxicity increases as the total cumulative (lifetime) dosages approach:

550 mg/m^2 in adults
400 mg/m^2 in adults receiving chest radiation
300 mg/m^2 in children >2 years of age
10 mg/kg in children <2 years of age

Although the risk increases with cumulative dose, irreversible cardiotoxicity may occur at any dose level. Patients with pre-existing heart disease, hypertension, concurrent administration of other antineoplastic agents, prior or concurrent chest irradiation, advanced age; and infants and children are at increased risk. Monitor left ventricular (LV) function (baseline and periodic) with ECHO or MUGA scan; monitor ECG.

Secondary leukemias may occur when used with combination chemotherapy or radiation therapy. **[U.S. Boxed Warning]: Should be administered under the supervision of an experienced cancer chemotherapy physician].**

Adverse Reactions

>10%:

Cardiovascular: Transient ECG abnormalities (supraventricular tachycardia, S-T wave changes, atrial or ventricular extrasystoles); generally asymptomatic and self-limiting. CHF, dose related, may be delayed for 7-8 years after treatment.

Dermatologic: Alopecia (reversible), radiation recall

(Continued)

DAUNOrubicin Hydrochloride *(Continued)*

Gastrointestinal: Mild nausea or vomiting, stomatitis

Genitourinary: Discoloration of urine (red)

Hematologic: Myelosuppression (onset: 7 days; nadir: 10-14 days; recovery: 21-28 days), primarily leukopenia; thrombocytopenia and anemia

1% to 10%:

Dermatologic: Skin "flare" at injection site; discoloration of saliva, sweat, or tears

Endocrine & metabolic: Hyperuricemia

Gastrointestinal: Abdominal pain, GI ulceration, diarrhea

<1%: Anaphylactoid reaction, bilirubin increased, hepatitis, infertility; local (cellulitis, pain, thrombophlebitis at injection site); MI, myocarditis, nail banding, onycholysis, pericarditis, pigmentation of nailbeds, secondary leukemia, skin rash, sterility, systemic hypersensitivity (including urticaria, pruritus, angioedema, dysphagia, dyspnea); transaminases increased

Overdosage/Toxicology Symptoms of overdose include myelosuppression, nausea, vomiting, and stomatitis. There are no known antidotes. Treatment is symptom-directed and supportive.

Drug Interactions

Increased Effect/Toxicity: Bevacizumab and trastuzumab may enhance the cardiotoxic effect of anthracycline antineoplastics. Docetaxel and paclitaxel may enhance the adverse/toxic effect of anthracycline antineoplastic agents; may increase the serum concentration of anthracycline antineoplastic agents and may also increase the formation of toxic anthracycline metabolites in heart tissue.

Decreased Effect: Digoxin may diminish the cardiotoxic effect of anthracycline antineoplastics. Daunorubicin may decrease the absorption of cardiac glycosides (may only affect digoxin tablets).

Ethanol/Nutrition/Herb Interactions Ethanol: Avoid ethanol (due to GI irritation).

Storage/Stability Store intact vials of powder for injection at room temperature of 15°C to 30°C (59°F to 86°F); intact vials of solution for injection should be refrigerated at 2°C to 8°C (36°F to 46°F). Protect from light. Reconstituted solution is stable for 4 days at 15°C to 25°C. Further dilution in D_5W, LR, or NS is stable at room temperature (25°C) for up to 4 weeks if protected from light.

Reconstitution Dilute vials of powder for injection with 4 mL SWFI for a final concentration of 5 mg/mL. May further dilute in 100 mL D_5W or NS.

Compatibility Stable in D_5W, LR, NS, sterile water for injection. **Incompatible** with heparin, sodium bicarbonate, fluorouracil, and dexamethasone.

Y-site administration: **Compatible:** Amifostine, etoposide phosphate, filgrastim, gemcitabine, granisetron, melphalan, methotrexate, ondansetron, sodium bicarbonate, teniposide, thiotepa, vinorelbine. **Incompatible:** Allopurinol, aztreonam, cefepime, fludarabine, piperacillin/tazobactam.

Compatibility when admixed: **Compatible:** Cytarabine with etoposide, hydrocortisone sodium succinate. **Incompatible:** Dexamethasone sodium phosphate, heparin.

Mechanism of Action Inhibition of DNA and RNA synthesis by intercalation between DNA base pairs and by steric obstruction. Daunomycin intercalates at points of local uncoiling of the double helix. Although the exact mechanism is unclear, it appears that direct binding to DNA (intercalation) and inhibition of DNA repair (topoisomerase II inhibition) result in blockade of DNA and RNA synthesis and fragmentation of DNA.

Pharmacodynamics/Kinetics

Distribution: Many body tissues, particularly the liver, kidneys, lung, spleen, and heart; not into CNS; crosses placenta; V_d: 40 L/kg

Metabolism: Primarily hepatic to daunorubicinol (active), then to inactive aglycones, conjugated sulfates, and glucuronides

Half-life elimination: Distribution: 2 minutes; Elimination: 14-20 hours; Terminal: 18.5 hours; Daunorubicinol plasma half-life: 24-48 hours

Excretion: Feces (40%); urine (~25% as unchanged drug and metabolites)

Dosage I.V. (refer to individual protocols):

Children: **Note:** Cumulative dose should not exceed 300 mg/m² in children >2 years or 10 mg/kg in children <2 years of age; maximum cumulative doses for younger children are unknown.

Children <2 years or BSA <0.5 m²: ALL combination therapy: 1 mg/kg/dose per protocol, with frequency dependent on regimen employed

Children ≥2 years and BSA ≥0.5 m²:

ALL combination therapy: Remission induction: 25 mg/m² on day 1 every week for up to 4-6 cycles

AML combination therapy: Induction: I.V. continuous infusion: 30-60 mg/m²/day on days 1-3 of cycle

Adults: **Note:** Cumulative dose should not exceed 550 mg/m² in adults without risk factors for cardiotoxicity and should not exceed 400 mg/m² in adults receiving chest irradiation.

Range: 30-60 mg/m²/day for 3 days, repeat dose in 3-4 weeks

ALL combination therapy: 45 mg/m²/day for 3 days

AML combination therapy:

Adults <60 years: Induction: 45 mg/m²/day for 3 days of the first course of induction therapy; subsequent courses: 45 mg/m²/day for 2 days

Adults ≥60 years: Induction: 30 mg/m²/day for 3 days of the first course of induction therapy; subsequent courses: 30 mg/m²/day for 2 days

Dosing adjustment in renal impairment:

The FDA-approved labeling recommends the following adjustment: S_{cr} >3 mg/dL: Administer 50% of normal dose

The following guidelines have been used by some clinicians (Aronoff, 2007):

Children:

Cl_{cr} <30 mL/minute: Administer 50% of dose

Hemodialysis/continuous ambulatory peritoneal dialysis (CAPD): Administer 50% of dose

Adults: No adjustment recommended

Dosing adjustment in hepatic impairment:

The FDA-approved labeling recommends the following adjustments:

Serum bilirubin 1.2-3 mg/dL: Administer 75% of dose

Serum bilirubin >3 mg/dL: Administer 50% of dose

The following guidelines have been used by some clinicians (Floyd, 2006):

Serum bilirubin 1.2-3 mg/dL: Administer 75% of dose

Serum bilirubin 3.1-5 mg/dL: Administer 50% of dose

Serum bilirubin >5 mg/dL: Avoid use

Combination Regimens

Leukemia, acute lymphocytic:

DVP *on page 1196*
Larson Regimen *on page 1242*
Linker Protocol *on page 1243*
PVDA *on page 1276*

Leukemia, acute myeloid:

5 + 2 *on page 1140*

(Continued)

DAUNOrubicin Hydrochloride *(Continued)*

7 + 3 (Daunorubicin) *on page 1140*
7 + 3 + 7 *on page 1141*
DA *on page 1187*
DAT *on page 1189*
DAV *on page 1189*
TAD *on page 1279*
V-TAD *on page 1293*

Administration Not for I.M. or SubQ administration. Administer as slow I.V. push over 1-5 minutes into the tubing of a rapidly infusing I.V. solution of D_5W or NS or dilute in 100 mL of D_5W or NS and infuse over 15-30 minutes.

Monitoring Parameters CBC with differential and platelet count, liver function test, ECG, left ventricular ejection function (echocardiography [ECHO] or multigated radionuclide angiography [MUGA] scan), renal function test

Patient Information This medication can only be administered I.V. During therapy, do not use alcohol, aspirin-containing products, and/or OTC medications without consulting prescriber. It is important to maintain adequate nutrition and hydration (2-3 L/day of fluids unless instructed to restrict fluid intake) during therapy; frequent small meals may help. You may experience nausea or vomiting (frequent small meals, frequent mouth care, sucking lozenges, or chewing gum may help). You may experience loss of hair (reversible); you will be more susceptible to infection (avoid crowds and exposure to infection as much as possible). Urine may turn red (normal). Yogurt or buttermilk may help reduce diarrhea (if unresolved, contact prescriber). Report fever, chills, unusual bruising or bleeding, signs of infection, abdominal pain or blood in stools, excessive fatigue, yellowing of eyes or skin, swelling of extremities, difficulty breathing, or unresolved diarrhea. Contraceptive measures are recommended during therapy.

Emetic Potential Moderate (30% to 60%)

Vesicant Yes; see Management of Drug Extravasations *on page 1301*.

Dosage Forms Excipient information presented when available (limited, particularly for generics); consult specific product labeling.

Injection, powder for reconstitution: 20 mg, 50 mg

Cerubidine®: 20 mg [contains mannitol 100 mg]

Injection, solution: 5 mg/mL (4 mL, 10 mL)

References

Aubel-Sadron G and Londos-Gagliardi D, "Daunorubicin and Doxorubicin, Anthracycline Antibiotics, a Physicochemical and Biological Review," *Biochimie*, 1984, 66(5):333-52.

Bassan R, Lerede T, Rambaldi A, et al, "Role of Anthracyclines in the Treatment of Adult Acute Lymphoblastic Leukemia," *Acta Haematol*, 1996, 95(3-4):188-92.

Crom WR, Glynn-Barnhart AM, Rodman JH, et al, "Pharmacokinetics of Anticancer Drugs in Children," *Clin Pharmacokinet*, 1987, 12(3):168-213.

Cuttner J, Mick R, Budman DR, et al, "Phase III Trial of Brief Intensive Treatment of Adult Acute Lymphocytic Leukemia Comparing Daunorubicin and Mitoxantrone: A CALGB Study," *Leukemia*, 1991, 5(5):425-31.

Davis HL and Davis TE, "Daunorubicin and Adriamycin in Cancer Treatment: An Analysis of Their Roles and Limitations," *Cancer Treat Rep*, 1979, 63(5):809-15.

Maral RJ and Jouanne M, "Toxicology of Daunorubicin in Animals and Man," *Cancer Treat Rep*, 1981, 65 Suppl 4:9-18.

Masaoka T, Ogawa M, Yamada K, et al, "A Phase II Comparative Study of Idarubicin Plus Cytarabine Versus Daunorubicin Plus Cytarabine in Adult Acute Myeloid Leukemia," *Semin Hematol*, 1996, 33(4 Suppl 3):12-7.

Riggs CE Jr., "Clinical Pharmacology of Daunorubicin in Patients With Acute Leukemia," *Semin Oncol*, 1984, 11(4 Suppl 3):2-11.

Speth PA, Minderman H, and Haanen C, "Idarubicin v Daunorubicin: Preclinical and Clinical Pharmacokinetic Studies," *Semin Oncol*, 1989, 16(1 Suppl 2):2-9.

Weick JK, Kopecky KJ, Appelbaum FR, et al, "A Randomized Investigation of High-Dose Versus Standard-Dose Cytosine Arabinoside With Daunorubicin in Patients With Previously

Untreated Acute Myeloid Leukemia: A Southwest Oncology Group Study," *Blood*, 1996, 88(8):2841-51.

Weiss RB and Bruno S, "Daunorubicin Treatment of Adult Solid Tumors," *Cancer Treat Rep*, 1981, 65 Suppl 4:25-8.

♦ **DAUNOrubicin Liposomal** *see* DAUNOrubicin Citrate (Liposomal) *on page 305*

♦ **DaunoXome®** *see* DAUNOrubicin Citrate (Liposomal) *on page 305*

♦ **DAVA** *see* Vindesine *on page 1105*

♦ **dCF** *see* Pentostatin *on page 891*

♦ **DDAVP®** *see* Desmopressin *on page 326*

♦ **Deacetyl Vinblastine Carboxamide** *see* Vindesine *on page 1105*

♦ **1-Deamino-8-D-Arginine Vasopressin** *see* Desmopressin *on page 326*

Decitabine (de SYE ta been)

Medication Safety Issues

High alert medication: The Institute for Safe Medication Practices (ISMP) includes this medication among its list of classes of drugs which have a heightened risk of causing significant patient harm when used in error.

Related Information

Safe Handling of Hazardous Drugs *on page 1382*

U.S. Brand Names Dacogen™

Index Terms 5-Aza-2'-deoxycytidine; 5-AzaC; NSC-127716

Generic Available No

Pharmacologic Category Antineoplastic Agent, DNA Methylation Inhibitor

Use Treatment of myelodysplastic syndrome (MDS)

Unlabeled/Investigational Use Treatment of acute myelogenous leukemia (AML), chronic myelogenous leukemia (CML), sickle cell anemia

Pregnancy Risk Factor D

Lactation Excretion in breast milk unknown/not recommended

Labeled Contraindications Hypersensitivity to decitabine or any component of the formulation

Warnings/Precautions Hazardous agent - use appropriate precautions for handling and disposal. The dose-limiting toxicity is bone marrow suppression; worsening neutropenia is common in first two treatment cycles and may not correlate with progression of underlying MDS; may require growth factor support. Not studied in hepatic and renal disease; use caution. Safety and efficacy in children have not been established.

Adverse Reactions

>10%:

Cardiovascular: Peripheral edema (25%), pallor (23%), edema (18%), cardiac murmur (16%)

Central nervous system: Pyrexia (6% to 53%), headache (28%), insomnia (28%), dizziness (18%), pain (13%), confusion (12%), lethargy (12%), anxiety (11%), hypoesthesia (11%)

Dermatologic: Petechiae (39%), bruising (22%), rash (19%), erythema (14%), cellulitis (12%), lesions (11%), pruritus (11%)

Endocrine & metabolic: Hyperglycemia (33%), hypoalbuminemia (7% to 24%), hypomagnesemia (24%), hypokalemia (22%), hyperkalemia (13%), hyponatremia (13%)

Gastrointestinal: Nausea (42%), constipation (35%), diarrhea (34%), vomiting (25%), anorexia (16%), appetite decreased (16%), abdominal pain (5% to 14%), oral mucosal petechiae (13%), stomatitis (12%), dyspepsia (12%)

(Continued)

Decitabine *(Continued)*

Hematologic: Neutropenia (90%; recovery 28-50 days), thrombocytopenia (89%), anemia (82%), febrile neutropenia (29%), leukopenia (28%), lymphadenopathy (12%)

Hepatic: Hyperbilirubinemia (14%), alkaline phosphatase increased (11%)

Local: Tenderness (11%)

Neuromuscular & skeletal: Rigors (22%), arthralgia (20%), limb pain (19%), back pain (17%)

Respiratory: Cough (40%), pneumonia (22%), pharyngitis (16%), lung crackles (14%)

5% to 10%:

Cardiovascular: Chest discomfort (7%), facial swelling (6%), hypotension (6%)

Central nervous system: Malaise (5%)

Dermatologic: Alopecia (8%), urticaria (6%)

Endocrine & metabolic: Hyperuricemia (10%), LDH increased (8%), bicarbonate increased (6%), dehydration (6%), hypochloremia (6%), bicarbonate decreased (5%), hypoproteinemia (5%)

Gastrointestinal: Gingival bleeding (8%), hemorrhoids (8%), loose stools (7%), tongue ulceration (7%), dysphagia (6%), oral candidiasis (6%), lip ulceration (5%), abdominal distension (5%), gastroesophageal reflux (5%), glossodynia (5%)

Genitourinary: Urinary tract infection (7%), dysuria (6%), polyuria (5%)

Hematologic: Hematoma (5%), thrombocythemia (5%), bacteremia (5%)

Hepatic: Ascites (10%), AST increased (10%), hypobilirubinemia (5%)

Local: Catheter infection (8%), catheter site erythema (5%), catheter site pain (5%), injection site swelling (5%)

Neuromuscular & skeletal: Falling (8%), chest wall pain (7%), musculoskeletal discomfort (6%), crepitation (5%), myalgia (5%)

Ocular: Blurred vision (6%)

Respiratory: Breath sounds diminished (10%), hypoxia (10%), rales (8%), pulmonary edema (6%), postnasal drip (5%), sinusitis (5%)

Miscellaneous: Candidal infection (10%), staphylococcal infection (7%), transfusion reaction (7%)

<5%, postmarketing, and/or case reports: Anaphylactic reaction, atrial fibrillation, bronchopulmonary aspergillosis, cardiomyopathy, cardiorespiratory failure, catheter site hemorrhage, chest pain, CHF, cholecystitis, dyspnea, fungal infection, gastrointestinal hemorrhage, gingival pain, hemoptysis, hypersensitivity, intracranial hemorrhage, mental status change, MI, mucosal inflammation, mycobacterium avium complex infection, peridiverticular abscess, pseudomonal lung infection, pulmonary embolism, pulmonary infiltrates, pulmonary mass, renal failure, respiratory arrest, respiratory tract infection, sepsis, splenomegaly, supraventricular tachycardia, urethral hemorrhage, weakness

Overdosage/Toxicology Higher doses are associated with increased and prolonged myelosuppression. Treatment is symptom-directed and supportive.

Storage/Stability Store vials at 15°C to 30°C (59°F to 86°F). Solutions diluted for infusion may be stored for up to 7 hours under refrigeration at 2°C to 8°C (36°F to 46°F) if prepared with cold infusion fluids.

Reconstitution Vials should be reconstituted with 10 mL SWFI to a concentration of 5 mg/mL. Further dilute with 50-250 mL NS, D_5W, or lactated Ringer's to a final concentration of 0.1-1 mg/mL. Solutions not administered within 15 minutes of preparation should be prepared with cold (2°C to 8°C [36°F to 46°F]) infusion solutions.

Compatibility Stable in NS, D$_5$W, and lactated Ringer's.

Mechanism of Action After phosphorylation, decitabine is incorporated into DNA and inhibits DNA methyltransferase causing hypomethylation and subsequent cell death.

Pharmacodynamics/Kinetics

Protein binding: <1%

Half-life elimination: ~30 minutes

Dosage Adults:

MDS: I.V.: 15 mg/m^2 over 3 hours every 8 hours (45 mg/m^2/day) for 3 days (135 mg/m^2/cycle) every 6 weeks (treatment is recommended for at least 4 cycles and may continue until the patient no longer continues to benefit) **or** Low-dose schedule (unlabeled): 20 mg/m^2 over 1 hour daily for 5 days every 28 days

AML (investigational use): I.V.:

5-15 mg/m^2 over 1 hour daily, 5 days/week for 2 weeks (5 days on, 2 days off, 5 days on; 10 doses total) every 6 weeks

or

15 mg/m^2 over 1 hour daily for 10 days every 6 weeks

CML (investigational use): I.V.:

20 mg/m^2 over 1 hour daily for 5 days every 28 days

or

10-15 mg/m^2 over 1 hour daily, 5 days/week for 2 weeks (5 days on, 2 days off, 5 days on; 10 doses total) every 6 weeks

or

50-75 mg/m^2 over 6 hours every 12 hours for 5 days every 4-8 weeks

Sickle cell anemia (investigational use): I.V., SubQ: 0.15-0.3 mg/kg/day over 2 minutes 5 days/week for 2 weeks (5 days on, 2 days off, 5 days on; 10 doses total) every 6 weeks

Dosage adjustment for toxicity:

For delayed hematologic recovery (ANC ≥1000/mm^3 and platelets ≥50,000/mm^3):

Greater than 6 weeks but less than 8 weeks: Delay dose for up to 2 weeks and temporarily reduce dose to 11 mg/m^2 every 8 hours (33 mg/m^2/day) for 3 days

Greater than 8 weeks but less than 10 weeks: Assess for disease progression; if no disease progression, delay dose for up to 2 weeks and reduce dose to 11 mg/m^2 every 8 hours (33 mg/m^2/day) for 3 days; maintain or increase dose with subsequent cycles if clinically indicated

Temporarily hold treatment until resolution for any of the following nonhematologic toxicities:

Serum creatinine ≥2 mg/dL

ALT, bilirubin ≥2 times ULN

Active or uncontrolled infection

Combination Regimens

Leukemia, chronic myelogenous: Decitabine (Low Dose) *on page 1189*

Myelodysplastic syndrome: Decitabine (Low Dose) *on page 1189*

Administration Infuse over 1-6 hours. Premedication with antiemetics is recommended.

Monitoring Parameters CBC and platelets with each cycle, more frequently if needed; liver enzymes; serum creatinine

Emetic Potential Moderate (30% to 60%)

Dosage Forms Excipient information presented when available (limited, particularly for generics); consult specific product labeling.

Injection, powder for reconstitution:

Dacogen™: 50 mg

(Continued)

Decitabine *(Continued)*

References

DeSimone J, Koshy M, Dorn L, et al, "Maintenance of Elevated Fetal Hemoglobin Levels by Decitabine During Dose Interval Treatment of Sickle Cell Anemia," *Blood*, 2002, 99(11):3905-8.

Issa JP, Garcia-Manero G, and Giles FJ, "Phase 1 Study of Low-Dose Prolonged Exposure Schedules of the Hypomethylating Agent 5-Aza-2'Deoxycytidine (Decitabine) in Hematopoietic Malignancies," *Blood*, 2004, 103(5):1635-40.

Issa JP, Gharibyan V, Cortes J, et al, "Phase II Study of Low-Dose Decitabine in Patients With Chronic Myelogenous Leukemia Resistant to Imatinib Mesylate," *J Clin Oncol*, 2005, 23(17):3948-56.

Kantarjian H, Issa JP, Rosenfeld CS, et al, "Decitabine Improves Patient Outcomes in Myelodysplastic Syndromes," *Cancer*, 2006, 106(8):1794-803.

Kantarjian HM, O'Brien S, Cortes J, et al, "Results of Decitabine (5-Aza-2'Deoxycytidine) Therapy in 130 Patients With Chronic Myelogenous Leukemia," *Cancer*, 2003, 98(3):522-8.

Kantarjian H, Oki Y, Garcia-Manero G, et al, "Results of a Randomized Study of 3 Schedules of Low-Dose Decitabine in Higher-Risk Myelodysplastic Syndrome and Chronic Myelomonocytic Leukemia," *Blood*, 2007, 109(1):52-7.

Momparler RL, "Pharmacology of 5-Aza-2'-Deoxycytidine (Decitabine)," *Semin Hematol*, 2005, 42(3 Suppl 2):S9-16.

Deferasirox *(de FER a sir ox)*

Medication Safety Issues

Sound-alike/look-alike issues:

Deferasirox may be confused with deferoxamine

U.S. Brand Names Exjade®

Index Terms ICL670

Generic Available No

Canadian Brand Names Exjade®

Pharmacologic Category Antidote; Chelating Agent

Use Treatment of chronic iron overload due to blood transfusions

Pregnancy Risk Factor B

Lactation Excretion in breast milk unknown/use caution

Labeled Contraindications Hypersensitivity to deferasirox or any component of the formulation

Warnings/Precautions Cases of acute renal failure (some fatal) and dose-related elevations in serum creatinine have been reported. Monitor serum creatinine in patients at risk for renal complications (eg, pre-existing renal conditions, elderly, comorbid conditions, and/or with concurrent medications that may affect renal function); consider dose reduction, interruption, or discontinuation for serum creatinine elevations. Patients with baseline serum creatinine above the upper limit of normal (ULN) were excluded from clinical trials. May cause proteinuria; closely monitor. Hepatitis, elevated transaminases and hepatic dysfunction have been reported; monitor LFTs and consider dose modifications. Use caution with hepatic impairment. May cause skin rash (dose-related); mild-to-moderate rashes may resolve without treatment interruption; for severe rash, interrupt and consider restarting at a lower dose with dose escalation and oral steroids. Hypersensitivity reactions, including severe reactions (anaphylaxis and angioedema) have been reported, usually within the first month of treatment. Auditory or ocular disturbances have been reported; monitor and consider dose reduction or treatment interruption. Cytopenias (including agranulocytosis, neutropenia, and thrombocytopenia) have been reported, predominately in patients with preexisting hematologic disorders; monitor closely; interrupt treatment for unexplained cytopenias. Do not combine with other iron chelation therapies; safety of combinations has not been established. Safety and efficacy in children <2 years of age have not been established.

Adverse Reactions

>10%:

Central nervous system: Fever (19%), headache (16%)

Gastrointestinal: Abdominal pain (8% to 14%), diarrhea (12%), nausea (11%)

Renal: Serum creatinine increased (11% to 38%), proteinuria (19%)

Respiratory: Cough (14%), nasopharyngitis (13%), pharyngolaryngeal pain (11%)

Miscellaneous: Influenza (11%)

1% to 10%:

Central nervous system: Fatigue (6%)

Dermatologic: Rash (8% to 11%), urticaria (4%)

Gastrointestinal: Vomiting (10%)

Hepatic: ALT increased (6% to 8%), transaminitis (4%)

Neuromuscular & skeletal: Arthralgia (7%), back pain (6%)

Otic: Ear infection (5%)

Respiratory: Respiratory tract infection (10%), bronchitis (9%), pharyngitis (8%), acute tonsillitis (6%), rhinitis (6%)

<1%, postmarketing, and/or case reports: Acute renal failure, agranulocytosis, anaphylaxis, angioedema, anxiety, cataract, cholelithiasis, cytopenias, dizziness, drug fever, edema, gastritis, glucosuria, hearing loss (including high frequency), Henoch-Schönlein purpura, hepatic dysfunction, hepatic transaminases increased, hepatitis, hyperactivity, hypersensitivity reaction, insomnia, intraocular pressure increased, lens opacities, leukocytoclastic vasculitis, maculopathy, neutropenia, pigment disorder, purpura, retinal disorder, sleep disorder, thrombocytopenia, urticaria, visual disturbance

Overdosage/Toxicology Overdose of 2-3 times the prescribed doses for several weeks resulted in hepatitis, which resolved upon treatment interruption. Single doses of up to 80 mg/kg have been tolerated with incidences of nausea and diarrhea. In case of overdose, induce vomiting and gastric lavage. Treatment is otherwise symptom-directed and supportive.

Drug Interactions

Decreased Effect: Aluminum-containing antacids may decrease absorption of deferasirox.

Storage/Stability Store at room temperature between 15°C and 30°C (59°F and 86°F). Protect from moisture.

Mechanism of Action Selectively binds iron, forming a complex which is excreted primarily through the feces.

Pharmacodynamics/Kinetics

Distribution: Adults: 11.7-17.1 L

Protein binding: ~99% to serum albumin

Metabolism: Hepatic via glucuronidation by UGT1A1 and UGT1A3; minor oxidation by CYP450; undergoes enterohepatic recirculation

Bioavailability: 70%

Half-life elimination: 8-16 hours

Time to peak, plasma: 1-4 hours

Excretion: Feces (84%), urine (6% to 8%)

Dosage Oral: Children ≥2 years and Adults:

Initial: 20 mg/kg daily (calculate dose to nearest whole tablet)

Maintenance: Adjust dose every 3-6 months based on serum ferritin levels; increase by 5-10 mg/kg/day (calculate dose to nearest whole tablet); titrate. Maximum dose: 30 mg/kg/day; consider interrupting therapy for serum ferritin <500 mcg/L. **Note:** Consider dose reduction or interruption for hearing loss or visual disturbances.

(Continued)

Deferasirox *(Continued)*

Dosage adjustment in renal impairment: Interrupt treatment for progressive increase in serum creatinine above the age-appropriate ULN; once serum creatinine recovers to within the normal range, reinitiate treatment at a reduced dose; gradually escalate the dose if the clinical benefit outweighs potential risk.

Children: For increase in serum creatinine above the age-appropriate ULN for 2 consecutive levels, reduce daily dose by 10 mg/kg

Adults: For increase in serum creatinine >33% above the average pretreatment level at 2 consecutive levels (and cannot be attributed to other causes), reduce daily dose by 10 mg/kg

Dosage adjustment in hepatic impairment: Consider dose adjustment or discontinuation for severe elevations in liver function tests.

Administration Do not chew or swallow whole tablets. Take at same time each day on an empty stomach, 30 minutes before food. Disperse tablets in water, orange juice, or apple juice (use 3.5 ounces for total doses <1 g; 7 ounces for doses ≥1 g); stir to form suspension and drink entire contents. Rinse remaining residue with more fluid; drink. Do not take simultaneously with aluminum-containing antacids.

Monitoring Parameters

CBC with differential, serum creatinine (twice prior to initiation, then monthly thereafter; monitor weekly in patients with renal risk factors or with changes in therapy; per Canadian labeling: 2 times prior to initiation, then weekly for the first month and monthly thereafter), urine protein (monthly), liver function tests (monthly), and serum ferritin (monthly); baseline and annual auditory and ophthalmic function

Dietary Considerations Bioavailability increased variably when taken with food; take on empty stomach 30 minutes before a meal.

Patient Information Take once daily on an empty stomach at least 30 minutes before food. Disperse tablets in water, orange juice, or apple juice to form suspension and drink. Rinse residue in container with more fluid and drink. Do not chew or swallow tablet whole. Do not take simultaneously with aluminum-containing antacids. Report any hearing loss or visual changes to prescriber. May cause dizziness; use caution when driving or operating machinery. Do not take iron supplements, including multivitamins which contain iron.

Special Geriatric Considerations Studies to date have not included sufficient numbers of subjects ≥65 years of age. Use caution in patients with liver dysfunction or low serum albumin. Monitor renal function. In general, this drug should be used with caution and close monitoring in elderly due to the greater incidence of decreased hepatic, renal, cardiac function, as well as concomitant disease and drug therapy.

Additional Information Deferasirox has a low affinity for binding with zinc and copper, may cause variable decreases in the serum concentration of these trace minerals.

Oncology Comment: The National Comprehensive Cancer Network (NCCN) guidelines for myelodysplastic syndromes (MDS) recommend iron chelation therapy in relatively low-risk MDS patients to reverse adverse effects (on cardiac, hepatic and endocrine function) from chronic iron overload due to multiple transfusions. Treatment is generally recommended in MDS patients who have received 20-30 units of RBC transfusions and for those with serum ferritin levels >2500 mcg/L. Although clinical trials in MDS are ongoing, deferasirox may be useful in the management of iron overload of these patients.

Emetic Potential Low (10% to 30%)

Dosage Forms Excipient information presented when available (limited, particularly for generics); consult specific product labeling.

Tablet, for oral suspension:

Exjade®: 125 mg, 250 mg, 500 mg

References

Cappellini MD, Cohen A, Piga A, et al, "A Phase 3 Study of Deferasirox (ICL670), a Once-Daily Oral Iron Chelator, in Patients With Beta-Thalassemia," *Blood*, 2006, 107(9):3455-62.

Galanello R, Piga A, Alberti D, et al, "Safety, Tolerability, and Pharmacokinetics of ICL670, a New Orally Active Iron-Chelating Agent in Patients With Transfusion-Dependent Iron Overload Due to Beta-Thalassemia," *J Clin Pharmacol*, 2003, 43(6):565-72.

NCCN (National Comprehensive Cancer Network), "Practice Guidelines in Oncology: Myelodysplastic Syndromes Version 1.2007," available at http://www.nccn.org/professionals/physician_gls/PDF/mds.pdf

Nisbet-Brown E, Oliveri NF, Giardina PJ, et al, "Effectiveness and Safety of ICL670 in Iron-Loaded Patients With Thalassaemia: A Randomised, Double-Blind, Placebo-Controlled, Dose-Escalation Trial," *Lancet*, 2003, 361(9369):1597-602.

Rund D and Rachmilewitz E, "Beta-Thalassemia," *N Engl J Med*, 2005, 353(11):1135-46.

Deferoxamine (de fer OKS a meen)

Medication Safety Issues

Sound-alike/look-alike issues:

Deferoxamine may be confused with cefuroxime, deferasirox

Desferal® may be confused with desflurane, Dexferrum®, Disophrol®

International issues:

Desferal® may be confused with Deseril® which is a brand name for methysergide in multiple international markets

U.S. Brand Names Desferal®

Index Terms Deferoxamine Mesylate; Desferrioxamine; NSC-644468

Generic Available Yes

Canadian Brand Names Desferal®; PMS-Deferoxamine

Pharmacologic Category Antidote; Chelating Agent

Use Acute iron intoxication or when clinical signs of significant iron toxicity exist; chronic iron overload secondary to multiple transfusions

Unlabeled/Investigational Use Removal of corneal rust rings following surgical removal of foreign bodies; diagnosis or treatment of aluminum induced toxicity associated with chronic kidney disease (CKD)

Pregnancy Risk Factor C

Lactation Excretion in breast milk unknown/use caution

Labeled Contraindications Hypersensitivity to deferoxamine or any component of the formulation; patients with severe renal disease or anuria, primary hemochromatosis

Warnings/Precautions Patients with iron overload are at increased susceptibility to infection with *Yersinia enterocolitica* and *Yersinia pseudotuberculosis;* treatment with deferoxamine may enhance this risk; if infection develops, discontinue deferoxamine until resolved. Rare and serious cases of mucormycosis have been reported with use; withhold treatment with signs and symptoms of mucormycosis. Combination treatment with ascorbic acid may impair cardiac function (rare). If combination treatment is warranted, therapy may need adjusted; monitor cardiac function. Do not administer deferoxamine in combination with ascorbic acid in patients with pre-existing cardiac failure.

High doses may exacerbate neurological symptoms, including seizure in patients with aluminum-related encephalopathy. Deferoxamine treatment in patients with aluminum toxicity may cause hypocalcemia and aggravate hyperparathyroidism. Deferoxamine is associated with dialysis dementia (Continued)

Deferoxamine *(Continued)*

onset. Ocular and auditory disturbances have been reported following prolonged administration at high doses, or in patients with low ferritin levels; elderly patients are at increased risk for ocular and auditory disorders. Has been associated with adult respiratory distress syndrome (ARDS) following excessively high-dose treatment of acute intoxication or thalassemia; has also been reported in children. Flushing, hypotension, urticaria and shock are associated with rapid infusions. Patients should be informed that urine may have a reddish color. High deferoxamine doses and low ferritin levels are also associated with growth retardation. Safety and efficacy have not been established in children <3 years of age.

Adverse Reactions Frequency not defined.

Cardiovascular: Flushing, hypotension, tachycardia, shock, edema

Central nervous system: Fever, dizziness, neuropathy, seizure, exacerbation of aluminum-related encephalopathy (dialysis), headache

Dermatologic: Angioedema, rash, urticaria

Endocrine & metabolic: Growth retardation (children), hypocalcemia

Gastrointestinal: Abdominal discomfort, abdominal pain, diarrhea, nausea, vomiting

Genitourinary: Dysuria

Hematologic: Thrombocytopenia, leukopenia

Local: Injection site: Burning, crust, edema, erythema, eschar, induration, infiltration, irritation, pain, pruritus, swelling, vesicles, wheal formation

Neuromuscular & skeletal: Arthralgia, leg cramps, metaphyseal dysplasia (dose related), myalgia, paresthesia

Ocular: Acuity decreased, blurred vision, dichromatopsia, maculopathy, night vision impaired, peripheral vision impaired, visual loss, scotoma, visual field defects, optic neuritis, cataracts, retinal pigmentary abnormalities, night blindness

Otic: Hearing loss, tinnitus

Renal: Renal impairment, urine discoloration (vin-rose color)

Respiratory: Acute/adult respiratory distress syndrome, asthma

Miscellaneous: Anaphylaxis, hypersensitivity reaction, infections (*Yersinia*, mucormycosis)

Overdosage/Toxicology Symptoms of overdose include aphasia, agitation, CNS depression, coma, bradycardia, acute renal failure, headache, hypotension, nausea, pallor, transient vision loss, and tachycardia. Treatment is symptom-directed and supportive. Deferoxamine is dialyzable.

Drug Interactions

Increased Effect/Toxicity: May cause loss of consciousness or coma when administered with prochlorperazine. Vitamin C (>500 mg/day) may increase the adverse/toxic effects of deferoxamine; may cause left ventricular dysfunction; avoid concomitant use.

Storage/Stability Prior to reconstitution, do not store above 25°C (77°F). Following reconstitution, may be stored at room temperature for 7 days; protect from light. Do not refrigerate reconstituted solution.

Reconstitution

I.M.: Reconstitute with sterile water for injection (500 mg vial with 2 mL to a final concentration of 210 mg/mL; 2000 mg vial with 8 mL to a final concentration of 213 mg/mL)

I.V.: Reconstitute with sterile water for injection to a final solution of 100 mg/mL

SubQ: Reconstitute with sterile water for injection (500 mg vial with 5 mL; 2000 mg vial with 20 mL) to a final concentration of 95 mg/mL

Compatibility Stable in D_5W, LR, NS, sterile water for injection.

Mechanism of Action Complexes with trivalent ions (ferric ions) to form ferrioxamine, which are removed by the kidneys

Pharmacodynamics/Kinetics

Absorption: I.M.: Erratic

Metabolism: Plasma enzymes; binds with iron to form ferrioxamine

Half-life elimination: Parent drug: 6.1 hours; Ferrioxamine: 5.8 hours

Excretion: Primarily urine (as unchanged drug and ferrioxamine); feces (via bile)

Dosage

Acute iron toxicity: **Note:** I.V. route is used when severe toxicity is evidenced by systemic symptoms (coma, shock, metabolic acidosis, or severe gastrointestinal bleeding) or potentially severe intoxications (serum iron level >500 mcg/dL). When severe symptoms are not present, the I.M. route may be preferred (per manufacturer); however, the use of deferoxamine in situations where the serum iron concentration is <500 mcg/dL or when severe toxicity is not evident is a subject of some clinical debate.

Children ≥3 years:

I.M.: 90 mg/kg/dose every 8 hours (maximum: 6 g/24 hours)

I.V.: 15 mg/kg/hour (maximum: 6 g/24 hours)

Adults: I.M., I.V.: Initial: 1000 mg, may be followed by 500 mg every 4 hours for up to 2 doses; subsequent doses of 500 mg have been administered every 4-12 hours

Maximum recommended dose: 6 g/day (per manufacturer, however, higher doses have been administered)

Chronic iron overload:

Children ≥3 years:

I.V.: 15 mg/kg/hour (maximum: 12 g/24 hours)

SubQ: 20-40 mg/kg/day over 8-12 hours (maximum: 1000-2000 mg/day)

Adults:

I.M., I.V.: 500-1000 mg/day I.M.; in addition, 2000 mg should be given I.V. with each unit of blood transfused (administer separately from blood); maximum: 1 g/day in absence of transfusions; 6 g/day if patient received transfusions

SubQ: 1-2 g every day or 20-40 mg/kg/day over 8-24 hours

Diagnosis of aluminum induced toxicity with CKD (unlabeled use): Children and Adults: I.V.: Test dose: 5 mg/kg during the last hour of dialysis if serum aluminum levels are 60-200 mcg/L and there are clinical signs/symptoms of toxicity. Do not use if aluminum serum levels are >200 mcg/L

Treatment of aluminum toxicity with CKD (unlabeled use): Children and Adults: I.V.: 5-10 mg/kg 4-6 hours before dialysis. Administer every 7-10 days with 3-4 dialysis procedures between doses. Do not use if aluminum serum levels are >200 mcg/L.

Dosing adjustment in renal impairment: Cl_{cr} <10 mL/minute: Administer 50% of dose

Administration

I.V.: Urticaria, hypotension, and shock have occurred following rapid I.V. administration; limiting infusion rate to 15mg/kg/hour may help avoid infusion-related adverse effects.

Acute iron toxicity: The manufacturer states that the I.M. route is preferred; however, the I.V. route is generally preferred in patients with severe toxicity (ie, patients in shock). For the first 1000 mg, infuse at 15 mg/kg/hour (although rates up to 40-50 mg/kg/hour have been given in patients with massive iron intoxication). Subsequent doses may be given over 4-12 hours at a rate not to exceed 125 mg/hour.

(Continued)

Deferoxamine *(Continued)*

Diagnosis or treatment of aluminum induced toxicity with CKD: Administer dose over 1 hour

SubQ: When administered for chronic iron overload, daily dose should be given over 8-24 hours using portable pump.

Monitoring Parameters Serum iron; ophthalmologic exam (fundoscopy, slit-lamp exam) and audiometry with chronic therapy; growth and body weight in children (every 3 months)

Dialysis patients: Serum aluminum (yearly; every 3 months in patients on aluminum-containing medications)

Aluminum-induced bone disease: Serum aluminum 2 days following test dose; test is considered positive if serum aluminum increases ≥50 mcg/L

Test Interactions TIBC may be falsely elevated with high serum iron concentrations or deferoxamine therapy. Imaging results may be distorted due to rapid urinary excretion of deferoxamine-bound gallium-67; discontinue deferoxamine 48 hours prior to scintigraphy.

Dietary Considerations Vitamin C supplements may need to be limited. The manufacturer recommends a maximum of 200 mg/day in adults (given in divided doses) and avoiding use in patients with heart failure.

Patient Information May turn urine pink; blood and urine tests are necessary to follow therapy

Dosage Forms Excipient information presented when available (limited, particularly for generics); consult specific product labeling.

Injection, powder for reconstitution, as mesylate: 500 mg, 2 g

Desferal®: 500 mg, 2 g

References

Allain P, Mauras Y, Chaleil D, et al, "Pharmacokinetics and Renal Elimination of Desferrioxamine and Ferrioxamine in Healthy Subjects and Patients With Haemochromatosis," *Br J Clin Pharmacol*, 1987, 24(2):207-12.

Bentur Y, McGuigan M, and Koren G, "Deferoxamine (Desferrioxamine): New Toxicities for an Old Drug," *Drug Saf*, 1991, 6(1):37-46.

Cheney K, Gumbiner C, Benson B, et al, "Survival After a Severe Iron Poisoning Treated With Intermittent Infusions of Deferoxamine," *J Toxicol Clin Toxicol*, 1995, 33(1):61-6.

Cohen AR, Mizanin J, and Schwartz E, "Rapid Removal of Excessive Iron With Daily, High-Dose Intravenous Chelation Therapy," *J Pediatr*, 1989, 115(1):151-5.

Douglas D and Smilkstein M, "Deferoxamine-Iron Induced Pulmonary Injury and N-Acetylcysteine," *Clin Toxicol*, 1995, 33(5):495.

Fouad AA, Eldin NAS, and Eweda MH, "Protective Effects of Desferrioxamine on Cadmium Induced Testicular Toxicity in Rats," *Clin Toxicol*, 1995, 33(5):539-40.

Freedman MH, Olivieri N, Benson L, et al, "Clinical Studies on Iron Chelation in Patients With Thalassemia Major," *Haematologica*, 1990, 75(Suppl 5):74-83.

Giardina PJ, Grady RW, Ehlers KH, et al, "Current Therapy of Cooley's Anemia: A Decade of Experience With Subcutaneous Desferrioxamine," *Ann N Y Acad Sci*, 1990, 612:275-85.

Gomez HF, McClafferty H, Flory D, et al, "Prevention of GI Iron Absorption by an Orally Administered Deferoxamine/Charcoal Mixture," *Clin Toxicol*, 1995, 33(5):556.

Hershko C, Konijn AM, and Link G, "Iron Chelators for Thalassaemia," *Br J Haematol*, 1998, 101(3):399-406.

Jackson TW, Ling LJ, and Washington V, "The Effect of Oral Deferoxamine on Iron Absorption in Humans," *J Toxicol Clin Toxicol*, 1995, 33(4):325-9.

Kirking MH, "Treatment of Chronic Iron Overload," *Clin Pharm*, 1991, 10(10):775-83.

Krishnan K, Trobe JD, and Adams PT, "Myasthenia Gravis Following Iron Chelation Therapy With Intravenous Desferrioxamine," *Eur J Haematol*, 1995, 55(2):138-9.

Metwalley HE and Melies AE, "Protective Effects of Desferrioxamine on Cadmium Induced Liver and Kidney Toxicity in Rats," *Clin Toxicol*, 1995, 33(5):541.

Mills KC and Curry SC, "Acute Iron Poisoning," *Emerg Med Clin North Am*, 1994, 12(2):397-413.

National Kidney Foundation, K/DOQI Clinical Practice Guidelines for Bone Metabolism and Disease in Chronic Kidney Failure," *Am J Kidney Dis*, 2003, 42(4 Supple3):1-201.

Pippard MJ, "Iron Metabolism and Iron Chelation in the Thalassemia Disorders," *Haematologica*, 1990, 75(Suppl 5):66-71.

Shannon M, "Desferrioxamine in Acute Iron Poisoning," *Lancet*, 1992, 339(8809):1601.

Stiles ML, Allen LV, and Prince SJ, "Stability of Deferoxamine Mesylate, Floxuridine, Fluorouracil, Hydromorphone Hydrochloride, Lorazepam, and Midazolam Hydrochloride in Polypropylene Infusion-Pump Syringes," *Am J Health Syst Pharm*, 1996, 53(13):1583-8.

Voest EE, Vreugdenhil G, and Marx JJ, "Iron-Chelating Agents in Noniron Overload Conditions," *Ann Intern Med*, 1994, 120(6):490-9.

Winship KA, "Toxicity of Aluminum: A Historical Review, Part 2," *Adverse Drug React Toxicol Rev*, 1993, 12(3):177-211.

Yatscoff RW, Wayne EA, and Tenenbein M, "An Objective Criterion for the Cessation of Deferoxamine Therapy in the Acutely Iron Poisoned Patient," *J Toxicol Clin Toxicol*, 1991, 29(1):1-10.

♦ **Deferoxamine Mesylate** *see Deferoxamine on page 319*

♦ **Dehydrobenzperidol** *see Droperidol on page 369*

♦ **Delta-9-tetrahydro-cannabinol** *see Dronabinol on page 367*

♦ **Delta-9-Tetrahydrocannabinol and Cannabinol** *see Tetrahydrocannabinol and Cannabidiol on page 1022*

♦ **Delta-9 THC** *see Dronabinol on page 367*

♦ **Deltacortisone** *see PredniSONE on page 919*

♦ **Deltadehydrocortisone** *see PredniSONE on page 919*

♦ **Deltahydrocortisone** *see PrednisoLONE on page 914*

♦ **Demerol®** *see Meperidine on page 715*

♦ **4-Demethoxydaunorubicin** *see Idarubicin on page 575*

Denileukin Diftitox (de ni LOO kin DIF ti toks)

Medication Safety Issues

High alert medication: The Institute for Safe Medication Practices (ISMP) includes this medication among its list of drugs which have a heightened risk of causing significant patient harm when used in error.

Related Information

Safe Handling of Hazardous Drugs *on page 1382*

U.S. Brand Names ONTAK®

Index Terms DAB$_{389}$IL-2; NSC-714744

Generic Available No

Pharmacologic Category Antineoplastic Agent, Miscellaneous

Use Treatment of persistent or recurrent cutaneous T-cell lymphoma whose malignant cells express the CD25 component of the IL-2 receptor

Pregnancy Risk Factor C

Lactation Excretion in breast milk unknown/contraindicated

Labeled Contraindications Hypersensitivity to denileukin diftitox, diphtheria toxin, interleukin-2, or any component of the formulation

Warnings/Precautions Hazardous agent - use appropriate precautions for handling and disposal. Acute hypersensitivity reactions, including anaphylaxis, may occur; most events (eg, hypotension, back pain, dyspnea, vasodilation, rash, chest pain, tachycardia, dysphagia, syncope) occur during or within 24 hours of infusion; with ~50% occurring on the day 1, regardless of treatment cycle. Denileukin diftitox has been associated with a potentially-severe, delayed-onset vascular leak syndrome, which may be severe. The onset of symptoms (hypotension, edema, hypoalbuminemia) of vascular leak syndrome usually occurred within the first 2 weeks of infusion and may persist or worsen after cessation of denileukin diftitox. Use caution in patients with pre-existing cardiovascular disease. Pre-existing low serum albumin levels (<3 g/dL) may predict or predispose to vascular leak syndrome. Immunogenicity may develop; patients with antibodies have a two- to threefold increase in clearance. The presence of antibodies does not correlate with risk for hypersensitivity/infusion related reactions. Denileukin diftitox may impair immune function. Loss of visual acuity with loss of color vision (with or without retinal pigment mottling) has been reported. Use with (Continued)

Denileukin Diftitox *(Continued)*

caution in patients >65 years of age; adverse events (anemia, anorexia, confusion, hypotension, rash, nausea/vomiting) occur more frequently. Safety and efficacy in children have not been established. **[U.S. Boxed Warning]: Should be administered under the supervision of an experienced cancer chemotherapy physician.**

Adverse Reactions

>10%:

Cardiovascular: Edema (47%; grade 3 and 4, 15%), hypotension (36%), chest pain (24%), vasodilation (22%), tachycardia (12%)

Central nervous system: Fever/chills (81%; grade 3 and 4, 22%), headache (26%), pain (48%; grade 3 and 4, 13%), dizziness (22%), nervousness (11%)

Dermatologic: Rash (34%; grade 3 and 4, 13%), pruritus (20%)

Endocrine & metabolic: Hypoalbuminemia (83%; grade 3 and 4, 14%), hypocalcemia (17%), weight loss (14%)

Gastrointestinal: Nausea/vomiting (64%; grade 3 and 4, 14%), anorexia (36%), diarrhea (29%)

Hematologic: Lymphocyte count decreased (34%), anemia (18%)

Hepatic: Transaminases increased (61%; grade 3 and 4, 15%)

Neuromuscular & skeletal: Weakness (66%; grade 3 and 4, 22%), myalgia (17%), paresthesia (13%)

Respiratory: Dyspnea (29%; grade 3 and 4, 14%), cough increased (26%), pharyngitis (17%), rhinitis (13%)

Miscellaneous: Flu-like syndrome (91%; beginning several hours to days following infusion), hypersensitivity (69%; reactions are variable, but may include hypotension, back pain, dyspnea, vasodilation, rash, chest pain, tachycardia, dysphagia, syncope, or anaphylaxis), infection (48%; grade 3 and 4, 24%), vascular leak syndrome (27%; characterized by hypotension, edema, or hypoalbuminemia; the syndrome usually developed within the first 2 weeks of infusion; 6% of patients who developed this syndrome required hospitalization; the symptoms may persist or even worsen despite cessation of denileukin diftitox)

1% to 10%:

Cardiovascular: Thrombotic events (7%), hypertension (6%), arrhythmia (6%), MI (1%)

Central nervous system: Insomnia (9%), confusion (8%)

Endocrine & metabolic: Dehydration (9%), hypokalemia (6%), hyperthyroidism (<5%), hypothyroidism (<5%)

Gastrointestinal: Constipation (9%), dyspepsia (7%), dysphagia (6%), oral ulcer (<5%), pancreatitis (<5%)

Hematologic: Thrombocytopenia (8%), leukopenia (6%)

Local: Injection site reaction (8%), anaphylaxis (1%)

Neuromuscular & skeletal: Arthralgia (8%)

Renal: Hematuria (10%), albuminuria (10%), pyuria (10%), creatinine increased (7%), acute renal insufficiency (<5%)

Respiratory: Lung disorder (8%)

Miscellaneous: Anaphylaxis (1%), diaphoresis decreased (10%)

Postmarketing and/or case reports: Toxic epidermal necrolysis, visual loss

Overdosage/Toxicology Although there is no human experience in overdose, dose-limiting toxicities include nausea, vomiting, fever, chills and persistent weakness. Treatment is supportive and symptom-directed. Fluid balance, as well as hepatic and renal function, should be closely monitored.

Storage/Stability Store frozen at or below -10°C (14°F); cannot be refrozen. Solutions ≥15 mcg/mL in NS should be used within 6 hours. Do **not** use glass syringes or containers.

Reconstitution Must be brought to room temperature (25°C or 77°F) before preparing the dose. Do **not** heat vials. Thaw in refrigerator for not more than 24 hours or at room temperature for 1-2 hours. Avoid vigorous agitation. Solution may be mixed by gentle swirling. Dilute with NS to a concentration of ≥15 mcg/mL; the concentration must be ≥15 mcg/mL during all steps of preparation. Add drug to the empty sterile I.V. bag first, then add NS.

Mechanism of Action Denileukin diftitox is a fusion protein (a combination of amino acid sequences from diphtheria toxin and interleukin-2) which selectively delivers the cytotoxic activity of diphtheria toxin to targeted cells. It interacts with the high-affinity IL-2 receptor on the surface of malignant cells to inhibit intracellular protein synthesis, rapidly leading to cell death.

Pharmacodynamics/Kinetics
Distribution: V_d: 0.06-0.08 L/kg
Metabolism: Hepatic via proteolytic degradation (animal studies)
Half-life elimination: Distribution: 2-5 minutes; Terminal: 70-80 minutes

Dosage Adults: I.V.: 9 or 18 mcg/kg/day days 1 through 5 every 21 days

Administration For I.V. use only. Infuse over at least 15 minutes. Should not be given as a rapid I.V. bolus. Discontinue or reduce infusion rate for infusion related reactions. There is no clinical experience with prolonged infusions (>80 minutes). Do not administer through an in-line filter. Consider premedication with antipyretics, antihistamines, and antiemetics.

Monitoring Parameters Baseline CD25 expression (on malignant cells); CBC, blood chemistry panel, renal and hepatic function tests as well as a serum albumin level; these tests should be done prior to initiation of therapy and repeated at weekly intervals during therapy. During the infusion, the patient should be monitored for symptoms of an acute hypersensitivity reaction. After infusion, the patient should be monitored for the development of a delayed vascular leak syndrome (usually in the first 2 weeks), including careful monitoring of weight, blood pressure, and serum albumin.

Additional Information Formulation includes polysorbate 20.

Emetic Potential High (60% to 90%)

Vesicant No

Dosage Forms Excipient information presented when available (limited, particularly for generics); consult specific product labeling.
Injection, solution [frozen]:
ONTAK®: 150 mcg/mL (2 mL) [contains EDTA]

References
Duvic M, "Bexarotene and DAB(389)IL-2 (denileukin diftitox, ONTAK) in Treatment of Cutaneous T-cell Lymphomas: Algorithms," *Clin Lymphoma*, 2000, 1(Suppl 1):51-5.

Figgitt DP, Lamb HM, and Goa KL "Denileukin Diftitox," *Am J Clin Dermatol*, 2000, 1(1):67-72.

Foss FM, "DAB(389)IL-2 (denileukin diftitox, ONTAK): A New Fusion Protein Technology," *Clin Lymphoma*, 2000, 1(Suppl 1):27-31.

Kuzel TM, "DAB(389)IL-2 (denileukin diftitox, ONTAK): Review of Clinical Trials to Date," *Clin Lymphoma*, 2000, 1(Suppl 1):33-6.

LeMaistre CF, "DAB(389)IL-2 (denileukin diftitox, ONTAK): Other Potential Applications," *Clin Lymphoma*, 2000, 1(Suppl 1):37-40.

Nichols J, Foss F, Kuzel TM, et al, "Interleukin-2 Fusion Protein: An Investigational Therapy for Interleukin-2 Receptor Expressing Malignancies," *Eur J Cancer*, 1997, 33(Suppl 1):34-6.

Olsen E, Duvic M, Frankel A, et al, "Pivotal Phase III Trial of Two Dose Levels of Denileukin Diftitox for the Treatment of Cutaneous T-Cell Lymphoma," *J Clin Oncol*, 2001, 19(2):376-88.

Polder K, Wang C, Duvic M, et al, "Toxic Epidermal Necrolysis Associated With Denileukin Diftitox (DAB389IL-2) Administration in a Patient With Follicular Large Cell Lymphoma," *Leuk Lymphoma*, 2005, 46(12):1807-11.

♦ **Deoxycoformycin** see Pentostatin on page 891
♦ **DepoCyt®** see Cytarabine (Liposomal) on page 275

+ **DepoDur™** *see* Morphine Sulfate *on page 779*
+ **Depo-Medrol®** *see* MethylPREDNISolone *on page 745*
+ **Depo-Prevera® (Can)** *see* MedroxyPROGESTERone *on page 703*
+ **Depo-Provera®** *see* MedroxyPROGESTERone *on page 703*
+ **Depo-Provera® Contraceptive** *see* MedroxyPROGESTERone *on page 703*
+ **depo-subQ provera 104™** *see* MedroxyPROGESTERone *on page 703*
+ **Dermarest Dricort® [OTC]** *see* Hydrocortisone *on page 545*
+ **Dermtex® HC [OTC]** *see* Hydrocortisone *on page 545*
+ **Desacetyl Vinblastine Amide Sulfate** *see* Vindesine *on page 1105*
+ **Desferal®** *see* Deferoxamine *on page 319*
+ **Desferrioxamine** *see* Deferoxamine *on page 319*

Desmopressin (des moe PRES in)

U.S. Brand Names DDAVP®; Stimate™

Index Terms 1-Deamino-8-D-Arginine Vasopressin; Desmopressin Acetate

Generic Available Yes

Canadian Brand Names Apo-Desmopressin®; DDAVP®; Minirin®; Nove-Desmopressin®; Octostim®

Pharmacologic Category Antihemophilic Agent; Hemostatic Agent; Vasopressin Analog, Synthetic

Use

Injection: Treatment of diabetes insipidus; control of bleeding in hemophilia A, and mild-to-moderate classic von Willebrand disease (type I)

Tablet, nasal solution: Treatment of diabetes insipidus; primary nocturnal enuresis

Pregnancy Risk Factor B

Lactation Excretion in breast milk unknown/use caution

Labeled Contraindications Hypersensitivity to desmopressin or any component of the formulation; moderate to severe renal impairment (Cl_{cr}<50 mL/minute)

Warnings/Precautions Fluid intake should be adjusted downward in the elderly and very young patients to decrease the possibility of water intoxication and hyponatremia. Avoid overhydration especially when drug is used for its hemostatic effect. Use may rarely lead to extreme decreases in plasma osmolality, resulting in seizures and coma. Use caution with cystic fibrosis or other conditions associated with fluid and electrolyte imbalance due to potential hyponatremia. Use caution with coronary artery insufficiency or hypertensive cardiovascular disease; may increase or decrease blood pressure leading to changes in heart rate. Consider switching from nasal to intravenous solution if changes in the nasal mucosa (scarring, edema) occur leading to unreliable absorption. Use caution in patients predisposed to thrombus formation; thrombotic events (acute cerebrovascular thrombosis, acute myocardial infarction) have occurred (rare). Injection is not for use in hemophilia B, severe classic von Willebrand disease (type IIB), or in patients with factor VIII antibodies. In general, the injection is also not recommended for use in patients with ≤5% factor VIII activity level, although it may be considered in selected patients with activity levels between 2% and 5%. Some patients may demonstrate a change in response after long-term therapy (>6 months) characterized as decreased response or a shorter duration of response.

Adverse Reactions Frequency not defined (may be dose or route related).

Cardiovascular: Acute cerebrovascular thrombosis, acute MI, blood pressure increased/decreased, chest pain, edema, facial flushing, palpitation

Central nervous system: Agitation, chills, coma, dizziness, headache, insomnia, somnolence

Dermatologic: Rash

Endocrine & metabolic: Hyponatremia, water intoxication

Gastrointestinal: Abdominal cramps, dyspepsia, nausea, sore throat, vomiting

Genitourinary: Balanitis, vulval pain

Local: Injection: Burning pain, erythema, and swelling at the injection site

Ocular: Conjunctivitis, eye edema, lacrimation disorder

Respiratory: Cough, epistaxis, nasal congestion, rhinitis

Miscellaneous: Allergic reactions (rare), anaphylaxis (rare)

Overdosage/Toxicology Symptoms of overdose include drowsiness, headache, confusion, anuria, and water intoxication. In case of overdose, decrease or discontinue desmopressin.

Drug Interactions

Increased Effect/Toxicity: Chlorpropamide, fludrocortisone may increase ADH response.

Decreased Effect: Demeclocycline and lithium may decrease ADH response.

Ethanol/Nutrition/Herb Interactions Ethanol: Avoid ethanol (may decrease antidiuretic effect).

Storage/Stability

DDAVP®:

Tablet, nasal spray: Store at controlled room temperature of 20°C to 25°C (68°F to 77°F). Keep nasal spray in upright position.

Rhinal tube: Store refrigerated at 2°C to 8°C (36°F to 46°F). May store at room temperature for up to 3 weeks.

Injection: Store refrigerated at 2°C to 8°C (36°F to 46°F).

Stimate™: Store refrigerated at 2°C to 8°C (36°F to 46°F). May store at room temperature for up to 3 weeks.

Reconstitution DDAVP®: Dilute solution for injection in 10-50 mL NS for I.V. infusion (10 mL for children ≤10 kg; 50 mL for adults and children >10 kg).

Compatibility Stable in NS.

Mechanism of Action Enhances reabsorption of water in the kidneys by increasing cellular permeability of the collecting ducts; possibly causes smooth muscle constriction with resultant vasoconstriction; raises plasma levels of von Willebrand factor and factor VIII

Pharmacodynamics/Kinetics

Intranasal administration:

Onset of increased factor VIII activity: 30 minutes (dose related)

Peak effect 1.5 hours

Bioavailability: 3.2%

I.V. infusion:

Onset of increased factor VIII activity: 30 minutes (dose related)

Peak effect: 1.5-2 hours

Half-life elimination: Terminal: 3 hours (up to 9 hours in renal dysfunction)

Excretion: Urine

Oral tablet:

Onset of action: ADH: ~1 hour

Peak effect: 4-7 hours

Bioavailability: 5% compared to intranasal; 0.16% compared to I.V.

Half-life elimination: 1.5-2.5 hours

(Continued)

Desmopressin *(Continued)*

Dosage

Children:

Diabetes insipidus:

Intranasal (using 100 mcg/mL nasal solution): 3 months to 12 years: Initial: 5 mcg/day (0.05 mL/day) divided 1-2 times/day; range: 5-30 mcg/day (0.05-0.3 mL/day) divided 1-2 times/day; adjust morning and evening doses separately for an adequate diurnal rhythm of water turnover; doses <10 mcg should be administered using the rhinal tube system

Oral: ≥4 years: Initial: 0.05 mg twice daily; total daily dose should be increased or decreased as needed to obtain adequate antidiuresis (range: 0.1-1.2 mg divided 2-3 times/day)

Hemophilia A and von Willebrand disease (type I):

I.V.: >3 months: 0.3 mcg/kg by slow infusion; may repeat dose if needed; begin 30 minutes before procedure

Intranasal: ≥11 months: Refer to adult dosing.

Nocturnal enuresis:

Intranasal (using 100 mcg/mL nasal solution): ≥6 years: Initial: 20 mcg (0.2 mL) at bedtime; range: 10-40 mcg; it is recommended that ¹/₂ of the dose be given in each nostril. **Note:** The nasal spray pump can only deliver doses of 10 mcg (0.1 mL) or multiples of 10 mcg (0.1 mL); if doses other than this are needed, the rhinal tube delivery system is preferred. For 10 mcg dose, administer in one nostril.

Oral: 0.2 mg at bedtime; dose may be titrated up to 0.6 mg to achieve desired response. Patients previously on intranasal therapy can begin oral tablets 24 hours after the last intranasal dose.

Children ≥12 years and Adults:

Diabetes insipidus:

I.V., SubQ: 2-4 mcg/day (0.5-1 mL) in 2 divided doses or ¹/₁₀ of the maintenance intranasal dose

Intranasal (using 100 mcg/mL nasal solution): 10-40 mcg/day (0.1-0.4 mL) divided 1-3 times/day; adjust morning and evening doses separately for an adequate diurnal rhythm of water turnover. **Note:** The nasal spray pump can only deliver doses of 10 mcg (0.1 mL) or multiples of 10 mcg (0.1 mL); if doses other than this are needed, the rhinal tube delivery system is preferred.

Oral: Initial: 0.05 mg twice daily; total daily dose should be increased or decreased as needed to obtain adequate antidiuresis (range: 0.1-1.2 mg divided 2-3 times/day)

Hemophilia A and mild to moderate von Willebrand disease (Type I):

I.V.: 0.3 mcg/kg by slow infusion, begin 30 minutes before procedure

Intranasal: Using high concentration spray (1.5 mg/mL): <50 kg: 150 mcg (1 spray); >50 kg: 300 mcg (1 spray each nostril); repeat use is determined by the patient's clinical condition and laboratory work; if using preoperatively, administer 2 hours before surgery

Dosage adjustment in renal impairment: Cl_{cr} <50 mL/minute: Use is contraindicated

Administration

I.V.: Infuse over 15-30 minutes

Intranasal:

DDAVP®: Nasal pump spray: Delivers 0.1 mL (10 mcg); for other doses which are not multiples, use rhinal tube. DDAVP® Nasal spray delivers fifty 10 mcg doses. For 10 mcg dose, administer in one nostril. Any solution remaining after 50 doses should be discarded. Pump must be primed prior to first use.

DDAVP® Rhinal tube: Insert top of dropper into tube (arrow marked end) in downward position. Squeeze dropper until solution reaches desired calibration mark. Disconnect dropper. Grasp the tube ³/₄ inch from the end and insert tube into nostril until the fingertips reach the nostril. Place opposite end of tube into the mouth (holding breath). Tilt head back and blow with a strong, short puff into the nostril (for very young patients, an adult should blow solution into the child's nose). Reseal dropper after use.

Monitoring Parameters Blood pressure and pulse should be monitored during I.V. infusion.

Diabetes insipidus: Fluid intake, urine volume, specific gravity, plasma and urine osmolality, serum electrolytes

Hemophilia A: Factor VIII coagulant activity, factor VIII ristocetin cofactor activity, and factor VIII antigen levels, aPTT

von Willebrand disease: Factor VIII coagulant activity, factor VIII ristocetin cofactor activity, and factor VIII von Willebrand antigen levels, bleeding time

Nocturnal enuresis: Serum electrolytes if used for >7 days

Patient Information Avoid overhydration. Report headache, shortness of breath, heartburn, nausea, abdominal cramps, or vulval pain.

Special Geriatric Considerations Elderly patients should be cautioned not to increase their fluid intake beyond that sufficient to satisfy their thirst in order to avoid water intoxication and hyponatremia. Under experimental conditions, elderly have been shown to have a decreased responsiveness to vasopressin with respect to its effects on water homeostasis.

Additional Information 10 mcg of desmopressin acetate is equivalent to 40 int. units

Emetic Potential Very low (<10%)

Vesicant No

Dosage Forms Excipient information presented when available (limited, particularly for generics); consult specific product labeling.

Injection, solution, as acetate (DDAVP®): 4 mcg/mL (1 mL, 10 mL)

Solution, intranasal, as acetate (DDAVP®): 100 mcg/mL (2.5 mL) [with rhinal tube]

Solution, intranasal, as acetate [spray]: 100 mcg/mL (5 mL) [delivers 10 mcg/spray]

DDAVP®: 100 mcg/mL (5 mL) [delivers 10 mcg/spray]

Stimate™: 1.5 mg/mL (2.5 mL) [delivers 150 mcg/spray]

Tablet, as acetate (DDAVP®): 0.1 mg, 0.2 mg

References

Asplund R and Aberg H, "Desmopressin in Elderly Subjects With Increased Nocturnal Diuresis: A Two-Month Treatment Study," *Scand J Urol Nephrol*, 1993, 27(1):77-82.

Brewster UC and Hayslett JP, "Diabetes Insipidus in the Third Trimester of Pregnancy," *Obstet Gynecol*, 2005, 105(5 Pt 2):1173-6.

Byrnes JJ, Larcada A, and Moake JL, "Thrombosis Following Desmopressin for Uremic Bleeding," *Am J Hematol*, 1988, 28(1):63-5.

Cattaneo M, "Review of Clinical Experience of Desmopressin in Patients With Congenital and Acquired Bleeding Disorder," *Eur J Anesthesiol Suppl*, 1997, 14:10-4.

Chistolini A, Dragoni F, Ferrari A, et al, "Intranasal DDAVP®: Biological and Clinical Evaluation in Mild Factor VIII Deficiency," *Haemostasis*, 1991, 21(5):273-7.

Couch P and Stumpf JL, "Management of Uremic Bleeding," *Clin Pharm*, 1990, 9(9):673-81.

Das P, Carcao M, and Hitzler J, "Use of Recombinant Factor VIIa Prior to Lumbar Puncture in Pediatric Patients With Acute Leukemia," *Pediatr Blood Cancer*, 2006, 47(2):206-9.

Dave SP, Greenstein AJ, Sachar DB, et al, "Bleeding Diathesis in Amyloidosis With Renal Insufficiency Associated With Crohn's Disease: Response to Desmopressin," *Am J Gastroenterol*, 2002, 97(1):187-9.

(Continued)

Desmopressin *(Continued)*

Lusher JM, "Response to 1-Deamino-8-D-Arginine Vasopressin in von Willebrand Disease," *Haemostasis*, 1994, 24(5):276-84.

Mannucci PM and Cattaneo M, "Desmopressin: A Nontransfusional Treatment of Hemophilia and von Willebrand Disease," *Haemostasis*, 1992, 22(5)276-80.

Rembratt A, Graugaard-Jensen C, Senderovitz T, et al, "Pharmacokinetics and Pharmacodynamics of Desmopressin Administered Orally Versus Intravenously at Daytime Versus Night-Time in Healthy Men Aged 55-70 Years," *Eur J Clin Pharmacol*, 2004, 60(6):397-402.

Rembratt A, Riis A, and Norgaard JP, "Desmopressin Treatment in Nocturia; An Analysis of Risk Factors for Hyponatremia," *Neurourol Urodyn*, 2005, 25(2):105-9.

Richardson DW and Robinson AG, "Desmopressin," *Ann Intern Med*, 1985, 103(2):228-39.

Stenberg A and Läckgren G, "Desmopressin Tablets in the Treatment of Severe Nocturnal Enuresis in Adolescents," *Pediatrics*, 1994, 94(6 Pt 1):841-46.

♦ **Desmopressin Acetate** *see Desmopressin on page 326*

Dexamethasone *(deks a METH a sone)*

Medication Safety Issues
Sound-alike/look-alike issues:

Dexamethasone may be confused with desoximetasone

Decadron® may be confused with Percodan®

Maxidex® may be confused with Maxzide®

Related Information
Management of Nausea and Vomiting *on page 1319*

U.S. Brand Names Dexamethasone Intensol™; DexPak® TaperPak®; Maxidex®

Index Terms Dexamethasone Sodium Phosphate

Generic Available Yes: Excludes ophthalmic suspension

Canadian Brand Names Apo-Dexamethasone®; Dexasone®; Diodex®; Maxidex®; PMS-Dexamethasone

Pharmacologic Category Anti-inflammatory Agent; Anti-inflammatory Agent, Ophthalmic; Antiemetic; Corticosteroid, Ophthalmic; Corticosteroid, Otic; Corticosteroid, Systemic

Use

Systemic: Primarily as an anti-inflammatory or immunosuppressant agent in the treatment of a variety of diseases including those of allergic, dermatologic, endocrine, hematologic, inflammatory, neoplastic, nervous system, renal, respiratory, rheumatic, and autoimmune origin; may be used in management of cerebral edema, septic shock, chronic swelling, as a diagnostic agent, diagnosis of Cushing's syndrome, antiemetic

Ophthalmic: Treatment of palpebral and bulbar conjunctivitis; corneal injury from chemical, radiation, thermal burns, or foreign body penetration

Otic: Treatment of inflammation of external auditory meatus; treatment of edema associated with infective otitis externa

Unlabeled/Investigational Use Dexamethasone suppression test: General indicator consistent with depression and/or suicide

Pregnancy Risk Factor C

Lactation Enters breast milk/use caution

Labeled Contraindications Hypersensitivity to dexamethasone or any component of the formulation; systemic fungal infections, cerebral malaria; ophthalmic use in viral (active ocular herpes simplex), fungal, or tuberculosis diseases of the eye

Warnings/Precautions Use with caution in patients with thyroid disease, hepatic impairment, renal impairment, cardiovascular disease, diabetes, glaucoma, cataracts, myasthenia gravis, patients at risk for osteoporosis, patients at risk for seizures, or GI diseases (diverticulitis, peptic ulcer, ulcerative colitis) due to perforation risk. Use caution following acute MI (corticosteroids have been associated with myocardial rupture). Because of the risk of adverse effects, systemic corticosteroids should be used cautiously in the elderly in the smallest possible effective dose for the shortest duration. May affect growth velocity; growth should be routinely monitored in pediatric patients. Withdraw therapy with gradual tapering of dose.

May cause hypercorticism or suppression of hypothalamic-pituitary-adrenal (HPA) axis, particularly in younger children or in patients receiving high doses for prolonged periods. HPA axis suppression may lead to adrenal crisis. Withdrawal and discontinuation of a corticosteroid should be done slowly and carefully. Particular care is required when patients are transferred from systemic corticosteroids to inhaled products due to possible adrenal insufficiency or withdrawal from steroids, including an increase in allergic symptoms. Patients receiving >20 mg per day of prednisone (or equivalent) may be most susceptible. Fatalities have occurred due to adrenal insufficiency in asthmatic patients during and after transfer from systemic corticosteroids to aerosol steroids; aerosol steroids do not provide the systemic steroid needed to treat patients having trauma, surgery, or infections. Dexamethasone does not provide adequate mineralocorticoid activity in adrenal insufficiency (may be employed as a single dose while cortisol assays are performed). The lowest possible dose should be used during treatment; discontinuation and/or dose reductions should be gradual.

Acute myopathy has been reported with high dose corticosteroids, usually in patients with neuromuscular transmission disorders; may involve ocular and/or respiratory muscles; monitor creatine kinase; recovery may be delayed. Corticosteroid use may cause psychiatric disturbances, including depression, euphoria, insomnia, mood swings, and personality changes. Pre-existing psychiatric conditions may be exacerbated by corticosteroid use. Prolonged use of corticosteroids may also increase the incidence of secondary infection, mask acute infection (including fungal infections), prolong or exacerbate viral infections, or limit response to vaccines. Exposure to chickenpox should be avoided; corticosteroids should not be used to treat ocular herpes simplex. Corticosteroids should not be used for cerebral malaria. Close observation is required in patients with latent tuberculosis and/or TB reactivity; restrict use in active TB (only in conjunction with antituberculosis treatment). Prolonged treatment with corticosteroids has been associated with the development of Kaposi's sarcoma (case reports); if noted, discontinuation of therapy should be considered.

Adverse Reactions Frequency not defined.

Cardiovascular: Arrhythmia, bradycardia, cardiac arrest, cardiomyopathy, CHF, circulatory collapse, edema, hypertension, myocardial rupture (post-MI), syncope, thromboembolism, vasculitis

Central nervous system: Depression, emotional instability, euphoria, headache, intracranial pressure increased, insomnia, malaise, mood swings, neuritis, personality changes, pseudotumor cerebri (usually following discontinuation), psychic disorders, seizure, vertigo

Dermatologic: Acne, allergic dermatitis, alopecia, angioedema, bruising, dry skin, erythema, fragile skin, hirsutism, hyper-/hypopigmentation, hypertrichosis, perianal pruritus (following I.V. injection), petechiae, rash, skin atrophy, skin test reaction impaired, striae, urticaria, wound healing impaired

Endocrine & metabolic: Adrenal suppression, carbohydrate tolerance decreased, Cushing's syndrome, diabetes mellitus, glucose intolerance decreased, growth suppression (children), hyperglycemia, hypokalemic
(Continued)

Dexamethasone *(Continued)*

alkalosis, menstrual irregularities, negative nitrogen balance, pituitary-adrenal axis suppression, protein catabolism, sodium retention

Gastrointestinal: Abdominal distention, appetite increased, gastrointestinal hemorrhage, gastrointestinal perforation, nausea, pancreatitis, peptic ulcer, ulcerative esophagitis, weight gain

Genitourinary: Altered (increased or decreased) spermatogenesis

Hepatic: Hepatomegaly, transaminases increased

Local: Postinjection flare (intra-articular use), thrombophlebitis

Neuromuscular & skeletal: Arthropathy, aseptic necrosis (femoral and humoral heads), fractures, muscle mass loss, myopathy (particularly in conjunction with neuromuscular disease or neuromuscular-blocking agents), neuropathy, osteoporosis, parasthesia, tendon rupture, vertebral compression fractures, weakness

Ocular: Cataracts, exophthalmos, glaucoma, intraocular pressure increased

Renal: Glucosuria

Respiratory: Pulmonary edema

Miscellaneous: Abnormal fat deposition, anaphylactoid reaction, anaphylaxis, avascular necrosis, diaphoresis, hiccups, hypersensitivity, impaired wound healing, infections, Kaposi's sarcoma, moon face, secondary malignancy

Overdosage/Toxicology When consumed in high doses over prolonged periods, systemic hypercorticism and adrenal suppression may occur. In these cases, discontinuation of the corticosteroid should be done judiciously.

Drug Interactions

Cytochrome P450 Effect: Substrate of CYP3A4 (major); **Induces** CYP2A6 (weak), 2B6 (weak), 2C8 (weak), 2C9 (weak), 3A4 (strong)

Increased Effect/Toxicity: Aprepitant, azole antifungals, calcium channel blockers (nondihydropyridine), cyclosporine, estrogens, and macrolides may increase the serum levels of corticosteroids. Corticosteroids may increase the hypokalemic effects of amphotericin B or potassium-wasting diuretics (loop or thiazide); monitor.

Concurrent use of nonsteroidal anti-inflammatory drugs (NSAIDs) and salicylates with corticosteroids may lead to an increased incidence of gastrointestinal adverse effects. Concurrent use with anticholinergic agents may lead to severe weakness in patients with myasthenia gravis. Concurrent use of fluoroquinolone antibiotics may increase the risk of tendon rupture, particularly in elderly patients (overall incidence rare). Concurrent use of neuromuscular-blocking agents with corticosteroids may increase the risk of myopathy. The concurrent use of thalidomide with corticosteroids may increase the risk of selected adverse effects (toxic epidermal necrolysis and DVT). Concurrent use with cyclosporine may increase cyclosporine levels. Concurrent use of ophthalmic NSAIDs may enhance the toxic effects of ophthalmic dexamethasone. The use of live vaccines is contraindicated in immunosuppressed patients (may increase the risk of vaccinal infection). In patients receiving high doses of systemic corticosteroids for ≥14 days, wait at least 1 month between discontinuing steroid therapy and administering immunization.

Decreased Effect: Antacids and bile acid sequestrants may reduce the absorption of corticosteroids; separate administration by 2 hours. Aminoglutethimide, barbiturates, and CYP3A4 inducers may reduce the serum levels/effects of dexamethasone and dexamethasone may decrease the levels/effects of other CYP3A4 substrates. Serum concentrations of isoniazid may be decreased by corticosteroids. Corticosteroids may lead to a reduction in warfarin effect. Corticosteroids may suppress the response to vaccinations.

Ethanol/Nutrition/Herb Interactions

Ethanol: Avoid ethanol (may enhance gastric mucosal irritation).

Food: Dexamethasone interferes with calcium absorption. Limit caffeine.

Herb/Nutraceutical: Avoid cat's claw, echinacea (have immunostimulant properties).

Storage/Stability

Injection solution: Store at room temperature; protect from light and freezing.

Stability of injection of parenteral admixture at room temperature (25°C): 24 hours.

Stability of injection of parenteral admixture at refrigeration temperature (4°C): 2 days; protect from light and freezing.

Reconstitution Injection should be diluted in 50-100 mL NS or D_5W.

Compatibility Stable in D_5W, NS.

Y-site administration: Compatible: Acyclovir, allopurinol, amifostine, amikacin, amphotericin B cholesteryl sulfate complex, amsacrine, aztreonam, cefepime, cefpirome, cisatracurium, cisplatin, cladribine, cyclophosphamide, cytarabine, docetaxel, doxorubicin, doxorubicin liposome, etoposide phosphate, famotidine, filgrastim, fluconazole, fludarabine, foscarnet, gatifloxacin, gemcitabine, granisetron, heparin, heparin with hydrocortisone sodium succinate, levofloxacin, linezolid, lorazepam, melphalan, meperidine, meropenem, morphine, ondansetron, paclitaxel, piperacillin/tazobactam, potassium chloride, propofol, remifentanil, sargramostim, sodium bicarbonate, sufentanil, tacrolimus, teniposide, theophylline, thiotepa, vinorelbine, vitamin B complex with C, zidovudine. **Incompatible:** Ciprofloxacin, idarubicin, midazolam, topotecan. **Variable (consult detailed reference):** Methotrexate.

Compatibility in syringe: Compatible: Granisetron, metoclopramide, palonosetron, ranitidine, sufentanil. **Incompatible:** Doxapram, glycopyrrolate. **Variable (consult detailed reference):** Diphenhydramine, hydromorphone, ondansetron.

Compatibility when admixed: Compatible: Aminophylline, bleomycin, cimetidine, floxacillin, furosemide, granisetron, lidocaine, meropenem, mitomycin, nafcillin, netilmicin, ondansetron, palonosetron, prochlorperazine edisylate, ranitidine, verapamil. **Incompatible:** Daunorubicin, diphenhydramine with lorazepam and metoclopramide, metaraminol, vancomycin. **Variable (consult detailed reference):** Amikacin.

Mechanism of Action Decreases inflammation by suppression of neutrophil migration, decreased production of inflammatory mediators, and reversal of increased capillary permeability; suppresses normal immune response. Dexamethasone's mechanism of antiemetic activity is unknown.

Pharmacodynamics/Kinetics

Onset of action: Acetate: Prompt

Duration of metabolic effect: 72 hours; acetate is a long-acting repository preparation

Metabolism: Hepatic

Half-life elimination: Normal renal function: 1.8-3.5 hours; Biological half-life: 36-54 hours

Time to peak, serum: Oral: 1-2 hours; I.M.: ~8 hours

Excretion: Urine and feces

Dosage Refer to individual protocols.

(Continued)

Dexamethasone *(Continued)*

Children:

Antiemetic (prior to chemotherapy): I.V.: 10 mg/m^2 (initial dose) followed by 5 mg/m^2 every 6 hours as needed **or** 5-20 mg given 15-30 minutes before treatment

Anti-inflammatory immunosuppressant: Oral, I.M., I.V.: 0.08-0.3 mg/kg/day **or** 2.5-10 mg/m^2/day in divided doses every 6-12 hours

Extubation or airway edema: Oral, I.M., I.V.: 0.5-2 mg/kg/day in divided doses every 6 hours beginning 24 hours prior to extubation and continuing for 4-6 doses afterwards

Cerebral edema: I.V.: Loading dose: 1-2 mg/kg/dose as a single dose; maintenance: 1-1.5 mg/kg/day (maximum: 16 mg/day) in divided doses every 4-6 hours, taper off over 1-6 weeks

Bacterial meningitis in infants and children >2 months: I.V.: 0.6 mg/kg/day in 4 divided doses every 6 hours for the first 4 days of antibiotic treatment; start dexamethasone at the time of the first dose of antibiotic

Physiologic replacement: Oral, I.M., I.V.: 0.03-0.15 mg/kg/day **or** 0.6-0.75 mg/m^2/day in divided doses every 6-12 hours

Adults:

Antiemetic:

Prophylaxis: Oral, I.V.: 10-20 mg 15-30 minutes before treatment on each treatment day

Continuous infusion regimen: Oral or I.V.: 10 mg every 12 hours on each treatment day

Mildly emetogenic therapy: Oral, I.M., I.V.: 4 mg every 4-6 hours

Delayed nausea/vomiting: Oral: 4-10 mg 1-2 times/day for 2-4 days **or**

8 mg every 12 hours for 2 days; then

4 mg every 12 hours for 2 days **or**

20 mg 1 hour before chemotherapy; then

10 mg 12 hours after chemotherapy; then

8 mg every 12 hours for 4 doses; then

4 mg every 12 hours for 4 doses

Anti-inflammatory:

Oral, I.M., I.V. (injections should be given as sodium phosphate): 0.75-9 mg/day in divided doses every 6-12 hours

Intra-articular, intralesional, or soft tissue (as sodium phosphate): 0.4-6 mg/day

Ophthalmic:

Solution: Instill 1-2 drops into conjunctival sac every hour during the day and every other hour during the night; gradually reduce dose to every 3-4 hours, then to 3-4 times/day

Suspension: Instill 1-2 drops into conjunctival sac up to 4-6 times per day; may use hourly in severe disease; taper prior to discontinuation

Otic: Instill 3-4 drops 2-3 times a day; reduce dose gradually prior to discontinuation

Multiple myeloma: Oral, I.V.: 40 mg/day, days 1 to 4, 9 to 12, and 17 to 20, repeated every 4 weeks (alone or as part of a regimen)

Cerebral edema: I.V. 10 mg stat, 4 mg I.M./I.V. every 6 hours until response is maximized, then switch to oral regimen, then taper off if appropriate; dosage may be reduced after 24 days and gradually discontinued over 5-7 days

Extubation or airway edema: Oral, I.M., I.V. (injections should be given as sodium phosphate): 0.5-2 mg/kg/day in divided doses every 6 hours beginning 24 hours prior to extubation and continuing for 4-6 doses afterwards

Dexamethasone suppression test (depression/suicide indicator) (unlabeled use): Oral: 1 mg at 11 PM, draw blood at 8 AM the following day for plasma cortisol determination

Cushing's syndrome, diagnostic: Oral: 1 mg at 11 PM, draw blood at 8 AM; greater accuracy for Cushing's syndrome may be achieved by the following:

Dexamethasone 0.5 mg by mouth every 6 hours for 48 hours (with 24-hour urine collection for 17-hydroxycorticosteroid excretion)

Differentiation of Cushing's syndrome due to ACTH excess from Cushing's due to other causes: Oral: Dexamethasone 2 mg every 6 hours for 48 hours (with 24-hour urine collection for 17-hydroxycorticosteroid excretion)

Multiple sclerosis (acute exacerbation): 30 mg/day for 1 week, followed by 4-12 mg/day for 1 month

Physiological replacement: Oral, I.M., I.V. (should be given as sodium phosphate): 0.03-0.15 mg/kg/day **or** 0.6-0.75 mg/m^2/day in divided doses every 6-12 hours

Treatment of shock:

Addisonian crisis/shock (ie, adrenal insufficiency/responsive to steroid therapy): I.V. (given as sodium phosphate): 4-10 mg as a single dose, which may be repeated if necessary

Unresponsive shock (ie, unresponsive to steroid therapy): I.V. (given as sodium phosphate): 1-6 mg/kg as a single I.V. dose or up to 40 mg initially followed by repeat doses every 2-6 hours while shock persists

Hemodialysis: Supplemental dose is not necessary

Peritoneal dialysis: Supplemental dose is not necessary

Combination Regimens

Leukemia, acute lymphocytic:

Hyper-CVAD + Imatinib *on page 1229*

Hyper-CVAD (Leukemia, Acute Lymphocytic) *on page 1231*

TVTG *on page 1285*

VAD/CVAD *on page 1287*

Leukemia, acute myeloid: TVTG *on page 1285*

Lymphoma, non-Hodgkin's:

DHAP *on page 1190*

Hyper-CVAD (Lymphoma, non-Hodgkin's) *on page 1236*

m-BACOD *on page 1246*

Lymphoma, non-Hodgkin's (Mantle cell): Hyper-CVAD + Rituximab *on page 1237*

Multiple myeloma:

DTPACE *on page 1196*

Doxorubicin (Liposomal)-Vincristine-Dexamethasone *on page 1195*

Hyper-CVAD (Multiple Myeloma) *on page 1237*

Lenalidomide-Dexamethasone *on page 1243*

Lenalidomide-Dexamethasone (Low Dose) *on page 1243*

Thalidomide-Dexamethasone *on page 1280*

VAD *on page 1287*

Prostate cancer: Cyclophosphamide + Vincristine + Dexamethasone *on page 1186*

Administration

Oral: Administer with meals to decrease GI upset.

I.V.: Administer as a 5-10 minute bolus; rapid injection is associated with a high incidence of perineal discomfort.

Ophthalmic: Remove soft contact lenses prior to using solutions containing benzalkonium chloride. Do not touch tip of container to eye.

(Continued)

Dexamethasone *(Continued)*

Otic: Use ophthalmic solution for otic administration. Instill directly into aural canal or may pack canal with gauze saturated with solution. Keep wick moist and remove after 12-24 hours.

Monitoring Parameters Hemoglobin, occult blood loss, serum potassium, and glucose; intraocular pressure (with use >6 weeks)

Dietary Considerations May be taken with meals to decrease GI upset. May need diet with increased potassium, pyridoxine, vitamin C, vitamin D, folate, calcium, and phosphorus.

Patient Information Notify prescriber of any signs of infection or injuries during therapy. Inform physician or dentist before surgery if you are taking a corticosteroid. May cause GI upset; take with food. Do not overuse; use only as prescribed and for no longer than the period prescribed. Notify prescriber if condition being treated persists or worsens.

Ophthalmic: For ophthalmic use only. Wash hands before using. Tilt head back and look upward. Put drops of suspension or solution inside lower eyelid. Close eye and roll eyeball in all directions. Do not blink for $1/2$ minute. Apply gentle pressure to inner corner of eye for 30 seconds. Do not use any other eye preparation for at least 10 minutes. Do not let tip of applicator touch eye; do not contaminate tip of applicator (may cause eye infection, eye damage, or vision loss). Do not share medication with anyone else. Wear sunglasses when in sunlight; you may be more sensitive to bright light. Inform prescriber if condition worsens or fails to improve or if you experience eye pain, disturbances of vision, or other adverse eye response.

Topical: Use only as prescribed, and for no longer than the period prescribed. A thin film of cream or ointment is effective; do not overuse. Rub in lightly; avoid contact with eyes. Do not use tight-fitting diapers or plastic pants on children being treated in the diaper area.

Special Geriatric Considerations Because of the risk of adverse effects, systemic corticosteroids should be used cautiously in the elderly in the smallest possible dose, and for the shortest possible time.

Additional Information Effects of inhaled/intranasal steroids on growth have been observed in the absence of laboratory evidence of HPA axis suppression, suggesting that growth velocity is a more sensitive indicator of systemic corticosteroid exposure in pediatric patients than some commonly used tests of HPA axis function. The long-term effects of this reduction in growth velocity associated with orally-inhaled and intranasal corticosteroids, including the impact on final adult height, are unknown. The potential for "catch up" growth following discontinuation of treatment with inhaled corticosteroids has not been adequately studied.

Withdrawal/tapering of therapy: Corticosteroid tapering following short-term use is limited primarily by the need to control the underlying disease state; tapering may be accomplished over a period of days. Following longer-term use, tapering over weeks to months may be necessary to avoid signs and symptoms of adrenal insufficiency and to allow recovery of the HPA axis. Testing of HPA axis responsiveness may be of value in selected patients. Subtle deficits in HPA response may persist for months after discontinuation of therapy, and may require supplemental dosing during periods of acute illness or surgical stress.

Emetic Potential Very low (<10%); may cause nausea/indigestion if taken orally on an empty stomach

Vesicant No

Dosage Forms Excipient information presented when available (limited, particularly for generics); consult specific product labeling. [DSC] = Discontinued product

Elixir, as base: 0.5 mg/5 mL (240 mL)

Injection, solution, as sodium phosphate: 4 mg/mL (1 mL, 5 mL, 30 mL); 10 mg/mL (10 mL)

Injection, solution, as sodium phosphate [preservative free]: 10 mg/mL (1 mL)

Solution, ophthalmic, as sodium phosphate: 0.1% (5 mL)

Solution, oral: 0.5 mg/5 mL (500 mL)

Solution, oral concentrate:

Dexamethasone Intensol™: 1 mg/mL (30 mL) [contains alcohol 30%]

Suspension, ophthalmic:

Maxidex®: 0.1% (5 mL; 15 mL [DSC]) [contains benzalkonium chloride]

Tablet [scored]: 0.5 mg, 0.75 mg, 1 mg, 1.5 mg, 2 mg, 4 mg, 6 mg

DexPak® TaperPak®: 1.5 mg [51 tablets on taper dose card]

References

American Academy of Pediatrics Committee on Infectious Diseases, "Dexamethasone Therapy for Bacterial Meningitis in Infants and Children," *Pediatrics*, 1990, 86(1):130-3.

Bahal N and Nahata MC, "The Role of Corticosteroids in Infants and Children With Bacterial Meningitis," *DICP*, 1991, 25(5):542-5.

Brophy TR, McCafferty J, Tyrer JH, et al, "Bioavailability of Oral Dexamethasone During High Dose Steroid Therapy in Neurological Patients," *Eur J Clin Pharmacol*, 1983, 24(1):103-8.

Coryell WH, "Clinical Assessment of Suicide Risk in Depressive Disorder," *CNS Spectr*, 2006, 11(6):455-61.

Couser RJ, Ferrara TB, Falde B, et al, "Effectiveness of Dexamethasone in Preventing Extubation Failure in Preterm Infants at Increased Risk for Airway Edema," *J Pediatr*, 1992, 121(4):591-6.

de los Reyes RA, Ausman JI, and Diaz FG, "Agents for Cerebral Edema," *Clin Neurosurg*, 1981, 28:98-107.

"Dexamethasone, Granisetron, or Both for the Prevention of Nausea and Vomiting During Chemotherapy for Cancer. The Italian Group for Antiemetic Research," *N Engl J Med*, 1995, 332(1):1-5.

Duggan DE, Matalia N, Ditzler, CA, et al, "Bioavailability of Oral Dexamethasone," *Clin Pharmacol Ther*, 1975, 18(2):205-9.

Durand M, Sardesai S, and McEvoy C, "Effects of Early Dexamethasone Therapy on Pulmonary Mechanics and Chronic Lung Disease in Very Low Birth Weight Infants: A Randomized, Controlled Trial," *Pediatrics*, 1995, 95(4):584-90.

Goedert JJ, Vitale F, Lauria C, et al, "Risk Factors for Classical Kaposi's Sarcoma," *J Natl Cancer Inst*, 2002, 94(22):1712-8.

Kyle RA and Rajkumar SV, "Multiple Myeloma," *N Engl J Med*, 2004, 351(18): 1860-73.

Kris MG, Baltzer L, Pisters KM, et al, "Enhancing the Effectiveness of the Specific Serotonin Antagonists. Combination Antiemetic Therapy With Dexamethasone," *Cancer*, 1993, 72(11 Suppl):3436-42.

Latreille J, Stewart D, Laberge F, et al, "Dexamethasone Improves the Efficacy of Granisetron in the First 24 h Following High-Dose Cisplatin Chemotherapy," *Support Care Cancer*, 1995, 3(5):307-12.

Mann JJ, Currier D, Stanley B, et al, "Can Biological Tests Assist Prediction of Suicide in Mood Disorders?" *Int J Neuropsychopharmacol*, 2006, 9(4):465-74.

McDonnell M and Evans N, "Upper and Lower Gastrointestinal Complications With Dexamethasone Despite H2 Antagonists," *J Paediatr Child Health*, 1995, 31(2):152-4.

Ng PC, "The Effectiveness and Side Effects of Dexamethasone in Preterm Infants With Bronchopulmonary Dysplasia," *Arch Dis Child*, 1993, 68(3 Spec No):330-6.

Peterson C, Hursti TJ, Borjeson S, et al, "Single High-Dose Dexamethasone Improves the Effect of Ondansetron on Acute Chemotherapy-Induced Nausea and Vomiting But Impairs the Control of Delayed Symptoms," *Support Care Cancer*, 1996, 4(6):440-6.

Randin D, Vollenweider P, Tappy L, et al, "Suppression of Alcohol-Induced Hypertension by Dexamethasone," *N Engl J Med*, 1995, 332(26):1733-7.

Ruvinsky ED, Douvas SG, Roberts WE, et al, "Maternal Administration of Dexamethasone in Severe Pregnancy-Induced Hypertension," *Am J Obstet Gynecol*, 1984, 149(7):722-6.

Trissel LA and Zhang Y, "Compatibility and Stability of Aloxi (Palonosetron Hydrochloride) Admixed With Dexamethasone Sodium Phosphate," *Intl J Pharm Compounding*, 2004, 8(5):398-403.

(Continued)

Dexamethasone *(Continued)*

Wald ER, Kaplan SL, and Mason, EO Jr, "Dexamethasone Therapy for Children With Bacterial Meningitis," *Pediatrics*, 1995, 95(1):21-8.

Yerevanian BI, Feusner JD, Koek RJ, et al, "The Dexamethasone Suppression Test as a Predictor of Suicidal Behavior in Unipolar Depression," *J Affect Disord*, 2004, 83(2-3):103-8.

- ◆ **Dexamethasone Intensol™** *see* Dexamethasone *on page 330*
- ◆ **Dexamethasone Sodium Phosphate** *see* Dexamethasone *on page 330*
- ◆ **Dexasone® (Can)** *see* Dexamethasone *on page 330*
- ◆ **Dexferrum®** *see* Iron Dextran Complex *on page 633*
- ◆ **Dexiron™ (Can)** *see* Iron Dextran Complex *on page 633*
- ◆ **DexPak® TaperPak®** *see* Dexamethasone *on page 330*

Dexrazoxane (deks ray ZOKS ane)

Medication Safety Issues

Sound-alike/look-alike issues:

Zinecard® may be confused with Gemzar®

Related Information

Management of Drug Extravasations *on page 1301*

Safe Handling of Hazardous Drugs *on page 1382*

U.S. Brand Names Totect™; Zinecard®

Index Terms ICRF-187; NSC-169780

Generic Available Yes

Canadian Brand Names Zinecard®

Pharmacologic Category Antidote; Cardioprotectant

Use

Zinecard®: Reduction of the incidence and severity of cardiomyopathy associated with doxorubicin administration in women with metastatic breast cancer who have received a cumulative doxorubicin dose of 300 mg/m² and who would benefit from continuing therapy with doxorubicin. (It is not recommended for use with initial doxorubicin therapy.)

Totect™: Treatment of anthracycline-induced extravasation.

Pregnancy Risk Factor C (Zinecard®) / D (Totect™)

Lactation Excretion in breast milk unknown/not recommended

Labeled Contraindications Hypersensitivity to dexrazoxane or any component of the formulation; use with chemotherapy regimens that do not contain an anthracycline

Warnings/Precautions Hazardous agent - use appropriate precautions for handling and disposal. Dexrazoxane may cause mild myelosuppression activity; myelosuppression may be additive with concurrently administered chemotherapeutic agents. Does not eliminate the potential for anthracycline-induced cardiac toxicity; carefully monitor cardiac function. May interfere with the antitumor effect of chemotherapy when given concurrently with fluorouracil, doxorubicin and cyclophosphamide (FAC). When used for the prevention of cardiomyopathy, doxorubicin should be administered 30 minutes after the beginning of the dexrazoxane infusion. Dosage adjustment required for moderate or severe renal insufficiency. Due to dosage adjustments for doxorubicin in hepatic impairment, a proportional dose reduction in dexrazoxane is recommended to maintain the dosage ratio of 10:1. Do not use DMSO in patients receiving dexrazoxane for anthracycline-induced extravasation; may diminish dexrazoxane efficacy. For I.V. administration; **not** for local infiltration into extravasation site. Safety and efficacy in children have not been established.

Adverse Reactions Adverse reactions listed are those which were greater in the dexrazoxane arm in a trial comparison of dexrazoxane plus fluorouracil, doxorubicin, and cyclophosphamide (FAC) to FAC alone for the prevention of cardiomyopathy. Most adverse reactions are thought to be attributed to chemotherapy, except for increased myelosuppression, pain at injection site, and phlebitis.

Central nervous system: Fatigue/malaise, fever

Dermatologic: Alopecia, streaking/erythema

Endocrine & metabolic: Serum amylase increased, serum calcium decreased, serum triglycerides increased

Hematologic: Anemia, granulocytopenia, hemorrhage, leukopenia, myelosuppression, thrombocytopenia

Hepatic: AST/ALT increased, bilirubin increased

Local: Injection site pain (12% to 16%), phlebitis (6% to 8%), extravasation,

Neuromuscular & skeletal: Neurotoxicity

Miscellaneous: Infection, sepsis

Overdosage/Toxicology Management includes supportive care until resolution of myelosuppression and related conditions is complete. Retention of a significant dose fraction of unchanged drug in the plasma pool, minimal tissue partitioning or binding, and availability of >90% of systemic drug levels in the unbound form suggest that dexrazoxane could be removed using conventional peritoneal or hemodialysis.

Storage/Stability Store intact vials at controlled room temperature of 15°C to 30°C (59°F to 86°F). Protect from light. According to the manufacturers, infusion solutions diluted in 1000 mL NS (Totect™) are stable for 4 hours when stored at temperatures <25°C (<77°F); solutions diluted in D₅W or NS (Zinecard®) are stable for 6 hours at room temperature of 15°C to 30°C (59°F to 86°F) or under refrigeration at 2°C to 8°C (36°F to 46°F). When studied as a 24-hour continuous infusion for the prevention of cardiomyopathy, solutions diluted to a final concentration of 0.1 or 0.5 mg/mL in D₅W were found to retain ≥90% of their initial concentration when stored at room temperature (ambient light conditions) for ≤24 hours (Tetef, 2007).

Reconstitution Must be reconstituted with 0.167 Molar (M/6) sodium lactate injection to a concentration of 10 mg dexrazoxane/mL sodium lactate. Reconstituted dexrazoxane solution may be diluted with either 0.9% sodium chloride injection or 5% dextrose injection to a final concentration of 1.3-5 mg/mL in intravenous infusion bags for prevention of cardiomyopathy. For anthracycline-induced extravasation, add the reconstituted solution to 1000 mL NS.

Compatibility Stable in NS, D₅W.

Mechanism of Action Derivative of EDTA; potent intracellular chelating agent. The mechanism of cardioprotectant activity is not fully understood. Appears to be converted intracellularly to a ring-opened chelating agent that interferes with iron-mediated oxygen free radical generation thought to be responsible, in part, for anthracycline-induced cardiomyopathy. In the management of anthracycline-induced extravasation, dexrazoxane may act by reversibly inhibiting topoisomerase II, protecting tissue from anthracycline cytotoxicity, thereby decreasing tissue damage.

Pharmacodynamics/Kinetics

Distribution: V_d: 22 L/m²

Protein binding: None

Half-life elimination: 2-2.5 hours

Excretion: Urine (42%)

Clearance, renal: 3.35 L/hour/m²; Plasma: 6.25-7.88 L/hour/m²

(Continued)

Dexrazoxane *(Continued)*

Dosage Adults: I.V.:

Prevention of doxorubicin cardiomyopathy: A 10:1 ratio of dexrazoxane:doxorubicin (500 mg/m^2 dexrazoxane: 50 mg/m^2 doxorubicin)

Treatment of anthracycline extravasation: 1000 mg/m^2 on days 1 and 2 (maximum dose: 2000 mg), followed by 500 mg/m^2 on day 3 (maximum dose 1000 mg); begin treatment as soon as possible, within 6 hours of extravasation

Dosage adjustment in renal impairment: Moderate-to-severe (Cl$_{cr}$<40 mL/minute):

Prevention of cardiomyopathy: Reduce dose by 50%, using a 5:1 ratio (250 mg/m^2 dexrazoxane: 50 mg/m^2 doxorubicin)

Anthracycline-induced extravasation: Reduce dose by 50%

Dosage adjustment in hepatic impairment: Since doxorubicin dosage is reduced in hyperbilirubinemia, a proportional reduction in dexrazoxane dosage is recommended (maintain ratio of 10:1).

Administration

Prevention of doxorubicin cardiomyopathy: Administer by slow I.V. push or rapid (5-15 minutes) I.V. infusion. Administer doxorubicin within 30 minutes after beginning the infusion with dexrazoxane.

Treatment of anthracycline extravasation: Administer over 1-2 hours; begin infusion as soon as possible, within 6 hours of extravasation. Infuse in a large vein in an area remote from the extravasation. If extravasation is also being managed with cooling, withhold cooling beginning 15 minutes before dexrazoxane infusion; continue withholding cooling until 15 minutes after infusion is completed. Day 2 and 3 doses should be administered at approximately the same time (±3 hours) as the dose on day 1. For I.V. administration; **not** for local infiltration into extravasation

Monitoring Parameters Since dexrazoxane will always be used with cytotoxic drugs, and since it may add to the myelosuppressive effects of cytotoxic drugs, frequent complete blood counts are recommended; liver function; serum creatinine; cardiac function (repeat monitoring at 400 mg/m^2, 500 mg/m^2 and with every 50 mg/m^2 of doxorubicin thereafter); monitor site of extravasation

Additional Information Oncology Comment: Guidelines from the American Society of Clinical Oncology (ASCO) for the use of chemotherapy and radiotherapy protectants (Schuchter, 2002) recommend the use of dexrazoxane as a cardioprotectant in patients with metastatic breast cancer who may benefit from further doxorubicin-based chemotherapy after a cumulative doxorubicin dose of 300 mg/m^2 has been reached. Dexrazoxane may also be considered in adults with malignancies other than breast cancer, who have received >300 mg/m^2 of doxorubicin-based therapy. Cardiac monitoring should continue during dexrazoxane therapy; doxorubicin/dexrazoxane should be discontinued in patients who develop a decline in LVEF or clinical CHF.

Emetic Potential Low (high incidence of mild nausea)

Vesicant No

Dosage . Forms Excipient information presented when available (limited, particularly for generics); consult specific product labeling.

Injection, powder for reconstitution: 250 mg, 500 mg

Totect™: 500 mg [provided with 0.167 Molar sodium lactate injection, USP]

Zinecard®: 250 mg, 500 mg [provided with 0.167 Molar sodium lactate injection, USP]

References

Hellmann K, "Overview and Historical Development of Dexrazoxane," *Semin Oncol*, 1998, 25(4 Suppl 10):48-54.

Hochster HS, "Clinical Pharmacology of Dexrazoxane," *Semin Oncol*, 1998, 25(4 Suppl 10):37-42.

Kwok JC and Richardson DR, "The Cardioprotective Effect of the Iron Chelator Dexrazoxane (ICRF-187) on Anthracycline-Mediated Cardiotoxicity," *Redox Rep*, 2000, 5(6):317-24.

Langer SW, Sehested M, and Jensen PB, "Treatment of Anthracycline Extravasation With Dexrazoxane," *Clin Cancer Res*, 2000, 6(9):3680-6.

Langer SW, Thougaard AV, Sehested M, et al, "Treatment of Anthracycline Extravasation in Mice With Dexrazoxane With or Without DMSO and Hydrocortisone," *Cancer Chemother Pharmacol*, 2006, 57(1):125-8.

Lopez M and Vici P, "European Trials With Dexrazoxane in Amelioration of Doxorubicin and Epirubicin-Induced Cardiotoxicity," *Semin Oncol*, 1998, 25(4 Suppl 10):55-60.

Mouridsen HT, Langer SW, Buter J, et al, "Treatment of Anthracycline Extravasation With Savene (Dexrazoxane): Results From Two Prospective Clinical Multicentre Studies," *Ann Oncol*, 2007, 18(3):546-50.

Schuchter LM, Hensley ML, Meropol NJ, et al, "2002 Update of Recommendations for the Use of Chemotherapy and Radiotherapy Protectants: Clinical Practice Guidelines of the American Society of Clinical Oncology," *J Clin Oncol*, 2002, 20(12):2895-903.

Sehested M, et al, "Dexrazoxane for Protection Against Cardiotoxic Effects of Anthracyclines," *J Clin Oncol*, 1996, 14:2884.

Tetef ML, Synold TW, Chow W, et al, "Phase I Trial of 96-Hour Continuous Infusion of Dexrazoxane I Patients With Advanced Malignancies," *Clin Cancer Res*, 2001, 7(6):1569-76.

Wiseman LR and Spencer CM, "Dexrazoxane. A Review of Its Use as a Cardioprotective Agent in Patients Receiving Anthracycline-Based Chemotherapy," *Drugs*, 1998. 56(3):385-403.

Docetaxel (doe se TAKS el)

Medication Safety Issues
Sound-alike/look-alike issues:
 Taxotere® may be confused with Taxol®

High alert medication: The Institute for Safe Medication Practices (ISMP) includes this medication among its list of drugs which have a heightened risk of causing significant patient harm when used in error.

Related Information
Management of Drug Extravasations *on page 1301*
Safe Handling of Hazardous Drugs *on page 1382*

U.S. Brand Names Taxotere®

Index Terms NSC-628503; RP-6976

Generic Available No

Canadian Brand Names Taxotere®

Pharmacologic Category Antineoplastic Agent, Antimicrotubular; Antineoplastic Agent, Natural Source (Plant) Derivative; Antineoplastic Agent, Taxane Derivative

Use Treatment of breast cancer; locally-advanced or metastatic nonsmall cell lung cancer (NSCLC); hormone refractory, metastatic prostate cancer; advanced gastric adenocarcinoma; locally-advanced squamous cell head and neck cancer

Unlabeled/Investigational Use Treatment of bladder cancer, ovarian cancer, small cell lung cancer, and soft tissue sarcoma

Pregnancy Risk Factor D

Lactation Excretion in breast milk unknown/not recommended

Labeled Contraindications Hypersensitivity to docetaxel or any component of the formulation; prior hypersensitivity to medications containing polysorbate 80; pre-existing bone marrow suppression (neutrophils <1500 cells/mm^3)

Warnings/Precautions Hazardous agent - use appropriate precautions for handling and disposal. **[U.S. Boxed Warnings]: Use caution in hepatic disease; avoid use in patients with bilirubin exceeding upper limit of normal (ULN) or AST and/or ALT >1.5 times ULN in conjunction with alkaline phosphatase >2.5 times ULN; patients with abnormal liver function are at increased risk of treatment-related adverse events. Severe hypersensitivity reactions characterized by rash/erythema, hypotension, bronchospasms, or anaphylaxis may occur; minor reactions including flushing or localized skin reactions may also occur. Fluid retention syndrome characterized by pleural effusions, ascites, edema, and weight gain (2-15 kg) has also been reported.** The incidence and severity of the syndrome increase sharply at cumulative doses ≥400 mg/m^2. Patients should be premedicated with a corticosteroid to prevent hypersensitivity reactions and fluid retention; severity is reduced with dexamethasone premedication starting one day prior to docetaxel administration.

[U.S. Boxed Warning]: Patients with abnormal liver function, those receiving higher doses, and patients with nonsmall cell lung cancer and a history of prior treatment with platinum derivatives who receive docetaxel doses higher than 100 mg/m2 are at higher risk for treatment-related mortality.

Neutropenia is the dose-limiting toxicity; however, this rarely results in treatment delays and prophylactic colony stimulating factors have not been routinely used. Patients with increased liver function tests experienced more episodes of neutropenia with a greater number of severe infections. **[U.S.**

Boxed Warning]: Patients with an absolute neutrophil count <1500 cells/mm³ should not receive docetaxel. When administered as sequential infusions, taxane derivatives (docetaxel, paclitaxel) should be administered before platinum derivatives (carboplatin, cisplatin) to limit myelosuppression and to enhance efficacy.

Cutaneous reactions including erythema and desquamation have been reported; may require dose reduction. Dosage adjustment is recommended with severe neurosensory symptoms (paresthesia, dysesthesia, pain). Safety and efficacy in children have not been established.

Adverse Reactions Percentages reported for docetaxel monotherapy; frequency may vary depending on diagnosis, dose, liver function, prior treatment, and premedication. The incidence of adverse events was usually higher in patients with elevated liver function tests.

>10%:
  Cardiovascular: Fluid retention (13% to 60%; dose dependent)
  Central nervous system: Neurosensory events (20% to 58%; including neuropathy), fever (31% to 35%), neuromotor events (16%)
  Dermatologic: Alopecia (56% to 76%), cutaneous events (20% to 48%), nail disorder (11% to 41%)
  Gastrointestinal: Stomatitis (19% to 53%; severe 1% to 8%), diarrhea (23% to 43%; severe: 5% to 6%), nausea (34% to 42%), vomiting (22% to 23%)
  Hematologic: Neutropenia (84% to 99%; grade 4: 75% to 86%; onset: 4-7 days, nadir: 5-9 days, recovery: 21 days; dose dependent), leukopenia (84% to 99%; grade 4: 32% to 44%), anemia (65% to 94%; dose dependent; grades 3/4: 8% to 9%), thrombocytopenia (8% to 14%; grade 4: 1%; dose dependent), febrile neutropenia (6% to 12%; dose dependent)
  Hepatic: Transaminases increased (4% to 19%)
  Neuromuscular and skeletal: Weakness (53% to 66%; severe 13% to 18%), myalgia (3% to 23%)
  Respiratory: Pulmonary events (41%)
  Miscellaneous: Infection (1% to 34%; dose dependent), hypersensitivity (1% to 21%; with premedication 15%)
1% to 10%:
  Cardiovascular: Left ventricular ejection fraction decreased (prostate cancer: 10%; metastatic breast cancer: 8%), hypotension (3%)
  Dermatologic: Rash/erythema (2%)
  Gastrointestinal: Taste perversion (6%)
  Hepatic: Bilirubin increased (9%), alkaline phosphatase increased (4% to 7%)
  Local: Infusion-site reactions (4%, including hyperpigmentation, inflammation, redness, dryness, phlebitis, extravasation, swelling of the vein)
  Neuromuscular and skeletal: Arthralgia (3% to 9%)
  Ocular: Epiphora associated with canalicular stenosis (≤77% with weekly administration; ≤1% with every-3-week administration)
<1%, postmarketing and/or case reports (limited to important or life-threatening): Acute myeloid leukemia (AML), acute respiratory distress syndrome (ARDS), anaphylactic shock, angina, ascites, atrial fibrillation, atrial flutter, bleeding episodes, bronchospasm, cardiac tamponade, chest pain, chest tightness, colitis, conjunctivitis, constipation, cutaneous lupus erythematosus, deep vein thrombosis, dehydration, disseminated intravascular coagulation (DIC), drug fever, duodenal ulcer, dyspnea, dysrhythmia, ECG abnormalities, erythema multiforme, esophagitis, gastrointestinal hemorrhage, gastrointestinal obstruction, gastrointestinal perforation, hand
(Continued)

Docetaxel *(Continued)*

and foot syndrome, hearing loss, heart failure, hepatitis, hypertension, ileus, interstitial pneumonia, ischemic colitis, lacrimal duct obstruction, loss of consciousness (transient), MI, multiorgan failure, myelodysplastic syndrome, neutropenic enterocolitis, ototoxicity, pleural effusion, pruritus, pulmonary edema, pulmonary embolism, pulmonary fibrosis, radiation pneumonitis, radiation recall, renal insufficiency, seizure, sepsis, sinus tachycardia, Stevens-Johnson syndrome, syncope, toxic epidermal necrolysis, tachycardia, thrombophlebitis, unstable angina, visual disturbances (transient)

Overdosage/Toxicology Symptoms of overdose may include bone marrow suppression, severe neutropenia, peripheral neural toxicity, paresthesia, weakness, cutaneous reactions and mucositis. Growth factor support should be administered immediately; treatment is otherwise symptom-directed and supportive.

Drug Interactions

Cytochrome P450 Effect: Substrate of CYP3A4 (major); **Inhibits** CYP3A4 (weak)

Increased Effect/Toxicity: CYP3A4 inhibitors may increase the levels/effects of docetaxel; example inhibitors include azole antifungals, clarithromycin, diclofenac, doxycycline, erythromycin, imatinib, isoniazid, nefazodone, nicardipine, propofol, protease inhibitors, quinidine, telithromycin, and verapamil. When administered as sequential infusions, observational studies indicate a potential for increased toxicity when platinum derivatives (carboplatin, cisplatin) are administered before taxane derivatives (docetaxel, paclitaxel). Taxane derivatives may enhance the adverse/toxic effect of anthracyclines.

Decreased Effect: CYP3A4 inducers may decrease the levels/effects of docetaxel; example inducers include aminoglutethimide, carbamazepine, nafcillin, nevirapine, phenobarbital, phenytoin, and rifamycins.

Ethanol/Nutrition/Herb Interactions

Ethanol: Avoid ethanol (due to GI irritation).

Herb/Nutraceutical: Avoid St John's wort (may decrease docetaxel levels).

Storage/Stability Intact vials should be stored at 2°C to 25°C (36°F to 77°F) and protected from light. Freezing does not adversely affect the product. If refrigerated, vials should be stored at room temperature for approximately 5 minutes before using. Diluted solutions in the vial are stable for 8 hours at room temperature or under refrigeration. Solutions diluted for infusion in D_5W or NS are stable for up to 4 weeks at room temperature of 15°C to 25°C (59°F to 77°F) in polyolefin containers; however, the manufacturer recommends use within 4 hours.

Reconstitution Vials should be diluted with 13% (w/w) ethanol/water (provided with the drug) to a final concentration of 10 mg/mL. The solution should be further diluted in 250-1000 mL of NS or D_5W to a final concentration of 0.3-0.9 mg/mL (although the manufacturer recommends a final concentration of 0.3-0.74) and dispensed in a non-DEHP container (eg, glass, polypropylene, polyolefin).

Compatibility Stable in D_5W, NS.

Y-site administration: Compatible: Acyclovir, amifostine, amikacin, aminophylline, ampicillin, ampicillin/sulbactam, aztreonam, bumetanide, buprenorphine, butorphanol, calcium gluconate, cefazolin, cefepime, cefoperazone, cefotaxime, cefotetan, cefoxitin, ceftazidime, ceftizoxime, ceftriaxone, cefuroxime, chlorpromazine, cimetidine, ciprofloxacin, clindamycin, co-trimoxazole, dexamethasone sodium phosphate, diphenhydramine, dobutamine, dopamine, doxycycline, droperidol, enalaprilat, famotidine, fluconazole, furosemide, ganciclovir, gemcitabine, gentamicin, granisetron, haloperidol, heparin, hydrocortisone sodium phosphate, hydrocortisone sodium succinate, hydromorphone, hydroxyzine, imipenem/cilastatin, leucovorin, lorazepam, magnesium sulfate, mannitol, meperidine, meropenem, mesna, metoclopramide, metronidazole, minocycline, morphine, netilmicin, ofloxacin, ondansetron, piperacillin, piperacillin/tazobactam, potassium chloride, prochlorperazine edisylate, promethazine, ranitidine, Ringer's injection (lactated), sodium bicarbonate, ticarcillin, ticarcillin/clavulanate, tobramycin, vancomycin, zidovudine. **Incompatible:** Amphotericin B, doxorubicin liposome, methylprednisolone sodium succinate, nalbuphine.

Mechanism of Action Docetaxel promotes the assembly of microtubules from tubulin dimers, and inhibits the depolymerization of tubulin which stabilizes microtubules in the cell. This results in inhibition of DNA, RNA, and protein synthesis. Most activity occurs during the M phase of the cell cycle.

Pharmacodynamics/Kinetics Exhibits linear pharmacokinetics at the recommended dosage range

Distribution: Extensive extravascular distribution and/or tissue binding; V_d: 80-90 L/m^2, V_{dss}: 113 L (mean steady state)

Protein binding: ~94% to 97%, primarily to alpha$_1$-acid glycoprotein, albumin, and lipoproteins

Metabolism: Hepatic; oxidation via CYP3A4 to metabolites

Half-life elimination: Terminal: 11 hours

Excretion: Feces (75%, <8% as unchanged drug); urine (6%); ~80% within 48 hours

Clearance: Total body: Mean: 21 L/hour/m^2

Dosage Adults: I.V. infusion: Refer to individual protocols: **Note:** Premedicate with corticosteroids, beginning the day before docetaxel administration, (administer for 1-5 days) to reduce the severity of hypersensitivity reactions and pulmonary/peripheral edema

Breast cancer:
Locally-advanced or metastatic: 60-100 mg/m^2 every 3 weeks; patients initially started at 60 mg/m^2 who do not develop toxicity may tolerate higher doses

Operable, node-positive (adjuvant treatment): 75 mg/m^2 every 3 weeks for 6 courses (in combination with doxorubicin and cyclophosphamide)

Nonsmall cell lung cancer: 75 mg/m^2 every 3 weeks (as monotherapy or in combination with cisplatin)

Prostate cancer: 75 mg/m^2 every 3 weeks (in combination with prednisone)

Gastric adenocarcinoma: 75 mg/m^2 every 3 weeks (in combination with cisplatin and fluorouracil)

Head and neck cancer: 75 mg/m^2 every 3 weeks (in combination with cisplatin and fluorouracil) for 3 or 4 cycles, followed by radiation therapy

Dosing adjustment for toxicity:
Note: Toxicity includes febrile neutropenia, neutrophils ≤500/mm^3 for >1 week, severe or cumulative cutaneous reactions; in nonsmall cell lung cancer, this may also include platelets <25,000/mm^3 and other grade 3/4 nonhematologic toxicities.

Breast cancer: Patients dosed initially at 100 mg/m^2; reduce dose to 75 mg/m^2; **Note:** If the patient continues to experience this adverse reactions, the dosage should be reduced to 55 mg/m^2 or therapy should be discontinued; discontinue for peripheral neuropathy ≥ grade 3

Breast cancer, adjuvant treatment: TAC regimen should be administered when neutrophils are ≥1500 cells/mm^3. Patients experiencing febrile neutropenia should receive G-CSF in all subsequent cycles. Patients

(Continued)

345

Docetaxel *(Continued)*

with persistent febrile neutropenia (while on G-CSF) or patients experiencing severe/cumulative cutaneous reactions or moderate neurosensory effects (signs/symptoms) should receive a reduced dose (60 mg/m^2) of docetaxel. Patients who experience grade 3 or 4 stomatitis should also receive a reduced dose (60 mg/m^2) of docetaxel. Discontinue therapy with persistent toxicities after dosage reduction.

Nonsmall cell lung cancer:

Monotherapy: Patients dosed initially at 75 mg/m^2 should have dose held until toxicity is resolved, then resume at 55 mg/m^2; discontinue for peripheral neuropathy $\geq$ grade 3.

Combination therapy (with cisplatin): Patients dosed initially at 75 mg/m^2 should have the docetaxel dosage reduced to 65 mg/m^2 in subsequent cycles; if further adjustment is required, dosage may be reduced to 50 mg/m^2

Prostate cancer: Reduce dose to 60 mg/m^2; discontinue therapy if toxicities persist at lower dose.

Gastric cancer, head and neck cancer: **Note:** Cisplatin may require dose reductions/therapy delays for peripheral neuropathy, ototoxicity, and/or nephrotoxicity. Patients experiencing febrile neutropenia, documented infection with neutropenia or neutropenia >7 days should receive G-CSF in all subsequent cycles. For neutropenic complications despite G-CSF use, further reduce dose to 60 mg/m^2. Neutropenic complications in subsequent cycles should be further dose reduced to 45 mg/m^2. Patients who experience grade 4 thrombocytopenia should receive a dose reduction from 75 mg/m^2 to 60 mg/m^2. Discontinue therapy for persistent toxicities.

Gastrointestinal toxicity for docetaxel in combination with cisplatin and fluorouracil for treatment of gastric cancer or head and neck cancer:

Diarrhea, grade 3:

First episode: Reduce fluorouracil dose by 20%

Second episode: Reduce docetaxel dose by 20%

Diarrhea, grade 4:

First episode: Reduce fluorouracil and docetaxel doses by 20%

Second episode: Discontinue treatment

Stomatitis, grade 3:

First episode: Reduce fluorouracil dose by 20%

Second episode: Discontinue fluorouracil for all subsequent cycles

Third episode: Reduce docetaxel dose by 20%

Stomatitis, grade 4:

First episode: Discontinue fluorouracil for all subsequent cycles

Second episode: Reduce docetaxel dose by 20%

Dosing adjustment in renal impairment: Docetaxel has minimal renal excretion; dosage adjustments for renal dysfunction may not be needed.

Dosing adjustment in hepatic impairment:

The FDA-approved labeling recommends the following adjustments:

Total bilirubin greater than the ULN, or AST/ALT >1.5 times ULN concomitant with alkaline phosphatase >2.5 times ULN: Docetaxel **generally should not be administered**.

Hepatic impairment dosing adjustment specific for gastric adenocarcinoma:

AST/ALT >2.5 to ≤5 times ULN and alkaline phosphatase ≤2.5 times ULN: Administer 80% of dose

AST/ALT >1.5 to ≤5 times ULN and alkaline phosphatase >2.5 to ≤5 times ULN: Administer 80% of dose

AST/ALT >5 times ULN and /or alkaline phosphatase >5 times ULN: Discontinue docetaxel

The following guidelines have been used by some clinicians (Floyd, 2006):

AST/ALT 1.6-6 times ULN: Administer 75% of dose

AST/ALT >6 times ULN: Use clinical judgment

Combination Regimens

Bladder cancer:

Cisplatin-Docetaxel on page 1176

Gemcitabine-Docetaxel (Bladder Cancer) on page 1227

Breast cancer:

AT on page 1146

Capecitabine + Docetaxel (Breast Cancer) on page 1158

Docetaxel-Cyclophosphamide (TC) on page 1191

Docetaxel-Trastuzumab on page 1192

Docetaxel-Trastuzumab-Carboplatin on page 1192

Docetaxel-Trastuzumab-Cisplatin on page 1193

Docetaxel-Trastuzumab-FEC on page 1193

Docetaxel (Weekly)-Trastuzumab on page 1194

TAC on page 1279

TEX (Capecitabine + Docetaxel + Epirubicin) on page 1280

Gastric cancer:

Capecitabine + Docetaxel (Gastric Cancer) on page 1159

Docetaxel-Cisplatin-Fluorouracil (Gastric Cancer) on page 1190

Head and neck cancer: Docetaxel-Cisplatin-Fluorouracil (Head and Neck Cancer) on page 1191

Lung cancer (nonsmall cell):

Capecitabine + Docetaxel (Nonsmall Cell Lung Cancer) on page 1159

Docetaxel-Cisplatin on page 1190

Prostate cancer:

Docetaxel-Prednisone on page 1192

Docetaxel-Thalidomide on page 1192

Docetaxel (Weekly) on page 1194

Estramustine + Docetaxel on page 1206

Estramustine + Docetaxel + Calcitriol on page 1207

Estramustine + Docetaxel + Carboplatin on page 1208

Estramustine + Docetaxel + Hydrocortisone on page 1208

Estramustine + Docetaxel + Prednisone on page 1208

Osteosarcoma: Gemcitabine-Docetaxel (Sarcoma) on page 1227

Soft tissue sarcoma: Gemcitabine-Docetaxel (Sarcoma) on page 1227

Administration Administer I.V. infusion over 1-hour through nonsorbing polyethylene lined (non-DEHP) tubing; in-line filter is not necessary. **Note:** Premedication with corticosteroids for 1-5 days, beginning the day before docetaxel administration, is recommended to prevent hypersensitivity reactions and pulmonary/peripheral edema (see Additional Information).

Monitoring Parameters CBC with differential, liver function tests, bilirubin, alkaline phosphatase, renal function; monitor for hypersensitivity reactions, fluid retention, epiphora, and canalicular stenosis

Patient Information This medication can only be administered intravenously. You may experience nausea or vomiting (frequent small meals, frequent mouth care, sucking lozenges, or chewing gum may help); you may experience loss of hair (reversible); you will be more susceptible to infection (avoid crowds and exposure to infection as much as possible). Yogurt or buttermilk may help reduce diarrhea (if unresolved, contact prescriber for medication relief). Report swelling of extremities, difficulty breathing, unusual weight gain, abdominal distention, fever, chills, unusual bruising or bleeding, (Continued)

Docetaxel *(Continued)*

signs of infection, excessive fatigue, or unresolved diarrhea. Contraceptive measures are recommended during therapy.

Additional Information Premedication with oral corticosteroids is recommended to decrease the incidence and severity of fluid retention and severity of hypersensitivity reactions. Dexamethasone 8-10 mg orally twice daily for 3-5 days, starting the day before docetaxel administration, is usually recommended. When prednisone is part of the antineoplastic regimen (eg, prostate cancer), the prednisone is sometimes withheld on the days dexamethasone is administered.

Emetic Potential Moderate (30% to 60%)

Vesicant No; may be an irritant

Dosage Forms Excipient information presented when available (limited, particularly for generics); consult specific product labeling.

Injection, solution [concentrate]:

Taxotere®: 20 mg/0.5 mL (0.5 mL, 2 mL) [contains Polysorbate 80®; diluent contains ethanol 13%]

References

Ajani JA, Fodor MD, Tjulandin SA, et al, "Phase II Multi-Institutional Randomized Trial of Docetaxel Plus Cisplatin With or Without Fluorouracil in Patients With Untreated, Advanced Gastric, or Gastroesophageal Adenocarcinoma," *J Clin Oncol*, 2005, 23(24):5660-7.

Bruno R and Sanderink GJ, "Pharmacokinetics and Metabolism of Taxotere® (Docetaxel)," *Cancer Surv*, 1993, 17:305-13.

Cortes JE and Pazdur R, "Docetaxel," *J Clin Oncol*, 1995, 13(10):2643-55.

De Santis M, Lucchese A, De Carolis S, et al, "Metastatic Breast Cancer in Pregnancy: First Case of Chemotherapy With Docetaxel," *Eur J Cancer Care (Engl)*, 2000, 9(4):235-7.

Floyd J, Mirza I, Sachs B, et al, "Hepatotoxicity of Chemotherapy," *Semin Oncol*, 2006, 33(1):50-67.

Fulton B and Spencer CM, "Docetaxel. A Review of Its Pharmacodynamic and Pharmacokinetic Properties and Therapeutic Efficacy in the Management of Metastatic Breast Cancer," *Drugs*, 1996, 51(6):1075-92.

Posner MR, Glisson B, Frenette G, et al, "Multicenter Phase I-II Trial of Docetaxel, Cisplatin, and Fluorouracil Induction Chemotherapy for Patients With Locally Advanced Squamous Cell Cancer of the Head and Neck," *J Clin Oncol*, 2001, 19(4):1096-104.

Posner MR, Hershock DM, Blajman CR, et al, "Cisplatin and Fluorouracil Alone or With Docetaxel in Head and Neck Cancer," *N Engl J Med*, 2007, 357(17):1705-15.

Ravdin PM, "The International Experience With Docetaxel in the Treatment of Breast Cancer," *Oncology*, 1997, 11(3 Suppl 2):38-42.

Schrijvers D, Van Herpen C, Kerger J, et al, "Docetaxel, Cisplatin and 5-Fluorouracil in Patients With Locally Advanced Unresectable Head and Neck Cancer: A Phase I-II Feasibility Study," *Ann Oncol*, 2004, 15(4):638-45.

Thiesen J and Kramer I, "Physico-Chemical Stability of Docetaxel Premix Solution and Docetaxel Infusion Solutions in PVC Bags and Polyolefine Containers," *Pharm World Sci*, 1999, 21(3):137-41.

Trudeau ME, "Docetaxel: A Review of Its Pharmacology and Clinical Activity," *Can J Oncol*, 1996, 6(1):443-57.

Vermorken JB, Remenar E, van Herpen C, et al, "Cisplatin, Fluorouracil, and Docetaxel in Unresectable Head and Neck Cancer," *N Engl J Med*, 2007, 357(17):1695-704.

Dolasetron *(dol A se tron)*

Medication Safety Issues

Sound-alike/look-alike issues:

Anzemet® may be confused with Aldomet® and Avandamet™

Dolasetron may be confused with granisetron, ondansetron, palonosetron

Related Information

Management of Nausea and Vomiting *on page 1319*

U.S. Brand Names Anzemet®

Index Terms Dolasetron Mesylate; MDL 73,147EF

Generic Available No

Canadian Brand Names Anzemet®

Pharmacologic Category Antiemetic; Selective 5-HT₃ Receptor Antagonist

Use Prevention of nausea and vomiting associated with emetogenic cancer chemotherapy; prevention of postoperative nausea and vomiting; treatment of postoperative nausea and vomiting (injectable form only).

Note: In Canada, the use of dolasetron is contraindicated for all uses in children <18 years of age or in the treatment of postoperative nausea and vomiting in adults. These are not labeled contraindications in the U.S.

Pregnancy Risk Factor B

Lactation Excretion in breast milk unknown/use caution

Labeled Contraindications Hypersensitivity to dolasetron or any component of the formulation

Note: In Canada, the use of dolasetron is contraindicated for all uses in children <18 years of age or in the treatment of postoperative nausea and vomiting in adults. These are not labeled contraindications in the U.S.

Warnings/Precautions Dose-related cardiac conduction abnormalities, including PR, QT_c, JT prolongation and QRS widening may occur; interval prolongation usually lasts 6-8 hours, however, may last ≥24 hours and rarely lead to heart block or arrhythmia. Dolasetron should be administered with caution in patients with congenital QT syndrome or other risk factors for QT prolongation (eg, medications known to prolong QT interval, electrolyte abnormalities, and cumulative high dose anthracycline therapy). Use with caution in children and adolescents who have or may develop QT_c prolongation; rare cases of supraventricular and ventricular arrhythmias, cardiac arrest, and MI have been reported in this population. Use with caution in patients allergic to other 5-HT₃ receptor antagonists; cross-reactivity has been reported. **For chemotherapy, should be used on a scheduled basis, not on an "as needed" (PRN) basis,** since data support the use of this drug only in the prevention of nausea and vomiting (due to antineoplastic therapy) and not in the rescue of nausea and vomiting. Not intended for treatment of nausea and vomiting or for chronic continuous therapy. Safety and efficacy in children <2 years of age have not been established.

Adverse Reactions Adverse events may vary according to indication
>10%:
  Central nervous system: Headache (7% to 24%)
  Gastrointestinal: Diarrhea (2% to 12%)
1% to 10%:
  Cardiovascular: Bradycardia (4% to 5%), hypotension (5%), hypertension (2% to 3%), tachycardia (2% to 3%)
  Central nervous system: Dizziness (1% to 6%), fatigue (3% to 6%), fever (4% to 5%), pain (≤3%), chills/shivering (1% to 2%), sedation (2%)
  Dermatologic: Pruritus (3% to 4%)
  Gastrointestinal: Dyspepsia (2% to 3%), abdominal pain (≤3%)
  Hepatic: Abnormal hepatic function (4%)
  Neuromuscular & skeletal: Pain (3%)
  Renal: Oliguria (1% to 3%)
<1% (Limited to important or life-threatening): Abnormal vision, abnormal dreaming, acute renal failure, alkaline phosphatase increased, ALT increased, anaphylactic reaction, anemia, anorexia, anxiety, arrhythmia (supraventricular and ventricular), AST increased, ataxia, AV block, bronchospasm, cardiac arrest, cardiac conduction abnormalities, chest pain, confusion, constipation, diaphoresis, dyspnea, dysuria, edema, epistaxis, facial edema, flushing, GGT increased, heart block, hematuria, hyperbilirubinemia, ischemia (peripheral), local injection site reaction, MI, myocardial
(Continued)

Dolasetron *(Continued)*

ischemia, orthostatic hypotension, palpitation, pancreatitis, paresthesia, peripheral edema, photophobia, polyuria; prolonged PR, QRS, JT, and QT_c intervals; prothrombin time increased, PTT increased, purpura/hematoma, rash, sleep disorder, syncope, taste perversion, thrombocytopenia, thrombophlebitis/phlebitis, tinnitus, tremor, twitching, urticaria, vertigo

Overdosage/Toxicology Prolongation of QT, AV block, severe hypotension, and dizziness have been reported. Treatment is symptom-directed and supportive; continuous ECG monitoring (telemetry) is recommended.

Drug Interactions

Cytochrome P450 Effect: Substrate (minor) of CYP2C9, 3A4; **Inhibits** CYP2D6 (weak)

Increased Effect/Toxicity: Due to reports of profound hypotension during concomitant therapy with ondansetron, the manufacturer of apomorphine contraindicates its use with all 5-HT$_3$ antagonists. Concurrent use of dolasetron with other drugs which may prolong QT_c interval may increase the risk of potentially-fatal arrhythmias; includes type Ia and type III antiarrhythmic agents, selected quinolones (ciprofloxacin, moxifloxacin), cisapride, thioridazine, and other agents

Storage/Stability Store intact vials and tablets at room temperature. Protect from light. A 20 mg/mL solution in syringes is stable for 8 months at room temperature. Solutions diluted for infusion are stable at room temperature for 24 hours or under refrigeration for 48 hours.

Reconstitution Dilute in 50-100 mL of a compatible solution (ie, 0.9% NS, D_5W, $D_5^1/_2NS$, D_5LR, LR, and 10% mannitol injection).

Compatibility Stable in 0.9% NS, D_5W, $D_5^1/_2NS$, D_5LR, LR, and 10% mannitol injection.

Mechanism of Action Selective serotonin receptor (5-HT$_3$) antagonist, blocking serotonin both peripherally (primary site of action) and centrally at the chemoreceptor trigger zone

Pharmacodynamics/Kinetics

Absorption: Rapid and complete

Distribution: Hydrodolasetron: 5.8 L/kg

Protein binding: Hydrodolasetron: 69% to 77% (50% bound to alpha$_1$-acid glycoprotein)

Metabolism: Hepatic; reduction by carbonyl reductase to hydrodolasetron (active metabolite); further metabolized by CYP2D6, CYP3A, and flavin monooxygenase

Bioavailability: 75%

Half-life elimination: Dolasetron: 10 minutes; hydrodolasetron: Adults: 6-8 hours; Children: 4-6 hours

Time to peak, plasma: Hydrodolasetron: I.V.: 0.6 hours; Oral: 1 hour

Excretion: Urine ~67% (53% to 61% as active metabolite hydrodolasetron); feces ~33%

Dosage Note: In Canada, the use of dolasetron is contraindicated in children <18 years of age or in the treatment of postoperative nausea and vomiting in adults. These are not labeled contraindications in the U.S.

Prevention of chemotherapy-associated nausea and vomiting (including initial and repeat courses):

Children 2-16 years:

Oral: 1.8 mg/kg within 1 hour before chemotherapy; maximum: 100 mg/dose

I.V.: 1.8 mg/kg ~30 minutes before chemotherapy; maximum: 100 mg/dose

Adults:

Oral:100 mg single dose 1 hour prior to chemotherapy

I.V.: 1.8 mg/kg or 100 mg 30 minutes prior to chemotherapy

Prevention of postoperative nausea and vomiting:

Children 2-16 years:

Oral: 1.2 mg/kg within 2 hours before surgery; maximum: 100 mg/dose

I.V.: 0.35 mg/kg (maximum: 12.5 mg) ~15 minutes before stopping anesthesia

Adults:

Oral: 100 mg within 2 hours before surgery

I.V.: 12.5 mg ~15 minutes before stopping anesthesia

Treatment of postoperative nausea and vomiting: I.V. (only):

Children: 0.35 mg/kg (maximum: 12.5 mg) as soon as needed

Adults: 12.5 mg as soon as needed

Dosing adjustment for elderly, renal/hepatic impairment: No dosage adjustment is recommended

Administration I.V. injection may be given either undiluted IVP over 30 seconds or diluted in 50 mL of compatible fluid and infused over 15 minutes. Line should be flushed, prior to and after, dolasetron administration. Dolasetron injection may be diluted in apple or apple-grape juice and taken orally; this dilution is stable for 2 hours at room temperature.

Monitoring Parameters Liver function tests, blood pressure and pulse, and ECG in patients with cardiovascular disease

Special Geriatric Considerations In controlled trials, no difference in overall safety and efficacy were observed between elderly and younger adults. Pharmacokinetics are similar in younger adults and elderly. No dosage adjustment necessary.

Additional Information Efficacy of dolasetron, for chemotherapy treatment, is enhanced with concomitant administration of dexamethasone 20 mg (increases complete response by 10% to 20%). Oral administration of the intravenous solution is equivalent to tablets. A single I.V. dose of dolasetron mesylate (1.8 or 2.4 mg/kg) has comparable safety and efficacy to a single 32 mg I.V. dose of ondansetron in patients receiving cisplatin chemotherapy.

Vesicant No

Dosage Forms Excipient information presented when available (limited, particularly for generics); consult specific product labeling.

Injection, solution, as mesylate:

Anzemet®: 20 mg/mL (0.625 mL) [single-use Carpuject® or vial; contains mannitol 38.2 mg/mL]; 20 mg/mL (5 mL) [single-use vial; contains mannitol 38.2 mg/mL]; 20 mg/mL (25 mL) [multidose vial; contains mannitol 29 mg/mL]

Tablet, as mesylate:

Anzemet®: 50 mg, 100 mg

Extemporaneous Preparations Dolasetron injection may be diluted in apple or apple-grape juice and taken orally; this dilution is stable for 2 hours at room temperature.

References

Dimmitt DC, Cramer MB, Keung A, et al, "Pharmacokinetics of Dolasetron With Coadministration of Cimetidine or Rifampin in Healthy Subjects," *Cancer Chemother Pharmacol*, 1999, 43(2):126-32.

Fauser AA, Russ W, and Bischoff M, "Oral Dolasetron Mesilate (MDL 73, 147EF) for the Control of Emesis During Fractionated Total-Body Irradiation and High-Dose Cyclophosphamide in Patients Undergoing Allogeneic Bone Marrow Transplantation," *Support Care Cancer*, 1997, 5(3):219-22.

Kovac AI, Scuderi PE, et al, "Treatment of Postoperative Nausea and Vomiting With Single Intravenous Doses of Dolasetron Mesylate: A Multicenter Trial," *Anesth Analg*, 1997, 85(3):546-52.

(Continued)

Dolasetron *(Continued)*

Kris MG, Hesketh PJ, Somerfield MR, et al, "American Society of Clinical Oncology Guideline for Antiemetics in Oncology: Update 2006," *J Clin Oncol*, 2006, 24(18):2932-47.

Kris MG, Pendergrass KB, Navari RM, et al, "Prevention of Acute Emesis in Cancer Patients Following High-Dose Cisplatin With the Combination of Oral Dolasetron and Dexamethasone," *J Clin Oncol*, 1997, 15(5):2135-8.

Sanwald P, David M, and Dow J, "Characterization of the Cytochrome P450 Enzymes Involved in the *in vitro* Metabolism of Dolasetron. Comparison With Other Indole-Containing 5-HT3 Antagonists," *Drug Metab Dispos*, 1996, 24(5):602-9.

Steiner ME, Lensmeyer G, and Vermeulen LC, "Stability and Sterility of Dolasetron Mesylate in Syringes Stored at Room Temperature," *Am J Health Syst Pharm*, 2005, 62(9):896-9.

- ◆ **Dolasetron Mesylate** *see* Dolasetron *on page 348*
- ◆ **Dolophine®** *see* Methadone *on page 726*
- ◆ **Dom-Benzydamine (Can)** *see* Benzydamine *on page 132*
- ◆ **Dom-Fluconazole (Can)** *see* Fluconazole *on page 449*
- ◆ **Dom-Furosemide (Can)** *see* Furosemide *on page 483*
- ◆ **Doxidan® [OTC]** *see* Bisacodyl *on page 144*
- ◆ **Doxil®** *see* DOXOrubicin (Liposomal) *on page 359*

DOXOrubicin *(doks oh ROO bi sin)*

Medication Safety Issues

Sound-alike/look-alike issues:

DOXOrubicin may be confused with dactinomycin, DAUNOrubicin, DAUNOrubicin liposomal, doxacurium, doxapram, doxazosin, DOXOrubicin liposomal, epirubicin, idarubicin

Adriamycin PFS® may be confused with achromycin, Aredia®, Idamycin®

Conventional formulation (Adriamycin PFS®, Adriamycin RDF®) may be confused with the liposomal formulation (Doxil®)

Use caution when selecting product for preparation and dispensing; indications, dosages and adverse event profiles differ between conventional DOXOrubicin hydrochloride solution and DOXOrubicin liposomal. Both formulations are the same concentration. As a result, serious errors have occurred.

High alert medication: The Institute for Safe Medication Practices (ISMP) includes this medication among its list of classes of drugs which have a heightened risk of causing significant patient harm when used in error.

ADR is an error-prone abbreviation

International issues:

Doxil® may be confused with Doxal® which is a brand name for doxepin in Finland, a brand name for doxycycline in Austria, and a brand name for pyridoxine/thiamine combination in Brazil

Rubex®: Brand name for ascorbic acid in Ireland

Related Information

Fertility and Cancer Therapy *on page 1298*
Hematopoietic Stem Cell Transplantation *on page 1366*
Management of Drug Extravasations *on page 1301*
Safe Handling of Hazardous Drugs *on page 1382*

U.S. Brand Names Adriamycin®; Rubex® [DSC]

Index Terms ADR (error-prone abbreviation); Adria; Doxorubicin Hydrochloride; Hydroxydaunomycin Hydrochloride; Hydroxyldaunorubicin Hydrochloride; NSC-123127

Generic Available Yes

Canadian Brand Names Adriamycin®

Pharmacologic Category Antineoplastic Agent, Anthracycline

Use Treatment of leukemias, lymphomas, multiple myeloma, osseous and nonosseous sarcomas, mesotheliomas, germ cell tumors of the ovary or testis, and carcinomas of the head and neck, thyroid, lung, breast, stomach, pancreas, liver, ovary, bladder, prostate, uterus, neuroblastoma, and Wilms' tumor.

Pregnancy Risk Factor D

Lactation Enters breast milk/not recommended

Labeled Contraindications Hypersensitivity to doxorubicin, any component of the formulation, or to other anthracyclines or anthracenediones; recent MI, severe myocardial insufficiency, severe arrhythmia; previous therapy with high cumulative doses of doxorubicin, daunorubicin, idarubicin, or other anthracycline and anthracenediones; baseline neutrophil count <1500/mm³; severe hepatic impairment

Warnings/Precautions Hazardous agent - use appropriate precautions for handling and disposal. **[U.S. Boxed Warning]: May cause cumulative, dose-related, myocardial toxicity (early or delayed).** Cardiotoxicity is dose-limiting. Total cumulative dose should take into account previous or concomitant treatment with cardiotoxic agents or irradiation of chest. The incidence of irreversible myocardial toxicity increases as the total cumulative (lifetime) dosages approach 450-500 mg/m². Although the risk increases with cumulative dose, irreversible cardiotoxicity may occur at any dose level. Patients with pre-existing heart disease, hypertension, concurrent administration of other antineoplastic agents, prior or concurrent chest irradiation, advanced age; and infants and children are at increased risk. Alternative administration schedules (weekly or continuous infusions) have are associated with less cardiotoxicity Baseline and periodic monitoring of ECG and LVEF (with either ECHO or MUGA scan) is recommended. **[U.S. Boxed Warnings]: Reduce dose in patients with impaired hepatic function; dose-limiting severe myelosuppression (primarily leukopenia and neutropenia) may occur. Secondary acute myelogenous leukemia and myelodysplastic syndrome have been reported following treatment.** May cause tumor lysis syndrome and hyperuricemia (in patients with rapidly growing tumors).

Children are at increased risk for developing delayed cardiotoxicity; follow-up cardiac function monitoring is recommended. Doxorubicin may contribute to prepubertal growth failure in children; may also contribute to gonadal impairment (usually temporary). Radiation recall pneumonitis has been reported in children receiving concomitant dactinomycin and doxorubicin. **[U.S. Boxed Warnings]: For I.V. administration only. Potent vesicant; if extravasation occurs, severe local tissue damage leading to ulceration, necrosis, and pain may occur. Should be administered under the supervision of an experienced cancer chemotherapy physician.**

Adverse Reactions Frequency not defined.

Cardiovascular:

Acute cardiotoxicity: Atrioventricular block, bradycardia, bundle branch block, ECG abnormalities, extrasystoles (atrial or ventricular), sinus tachycardia, ST-T wave changes, supraventricular tachycardia, tachyarrhythmia, ventricular tachycardia

Delayed cardiotoxicity: LVEF decreased, CHF (manifestations include ascites, cardiomegaly, dyspnea, edema, gallop rhythm, hepatomegaly, oliguria, pleural effusion, pulmonary edema, tachycardia); myocarditis, pericarditis

Central nervous system: Malaise

(Continued)

DOXOrubicin *(Continued)*

Dermatologic: Alopecia, itching, photosensitivity, radiation recall, rash; discoloration of saliva, sweat, or tears

Endocrine & metabolic: Amenorrhea, dehydration, infertility (may be temporary), hyperuricemia

Gastrointestinal: Abdominal pain, anorexia, colon necrosis, diarrhea, GI ulceration, mucositis, nausea, vomiting

Genitourinary: Discoloration of urine

Hematologic: Leukopenia/neutropenia (75%; nadir: 10-14 days; recovery: by day 21); thrombocytopenia and anemia

Local: Skin "flare" at injection site, urticaria

Neuromuscular & skeletal: Weakness

Postmarketing and/or case reports: Anaphylaxis, azoospermia, bilirubin increased, chills, coma (when in combination with cisplatin or vincristine), conjunctivitis, fever, gonadal impairment (children), growth failure (prepubertal), hepatitis, hyperpigmentation (nail, skin & oral mucosa), infection, keratitis, lacrimation, myelodysplastic syndrome, neutropenic fever, oligospermia, onycholysis, peripheral neurotoxicity (with intra-arterial doxorubicin), phlebosclerosis, radiation recall pneumonitis (children), secondary acute myelogenous leukemia, seizure (when in combination with cisplatin or vincristine), sepsis, shock, systemic hypersensitivity (including urticaria, pruritus, angioedema, dysphagia, and dyspnea), transaminases increased, urticaria

Overdosage/Toxicology Symptoms of overdose include myelosuppression, nausea, vomiting, and myocardial toxicity. Treatment of acute overdose consists of treatment of the severely myelosuppressed patient with hospitalization, antibiotics, growth factors (G-CSF), platelet and granulocyte transfusions, and symptomatic treatment of mucositis.

Drug Interactions

Cytochrome P450 Effect: Substrate (major) of CYP2D6, 3A4; **Inhibits** CYP2B6 (moderate), 2D6 (weak), 3A4 (weak)

Increased Effect/Toxicity: Bevacizumab, trastuzumab, and cyclophosphamide may enhance the cardiotoxic effect of anthracycline antineoplastics. Docetaxel and paclitaxel may enhance the adverse/toxic effect of anthracycline antineoplastic agents; may increase the serum concentration of anthracycline antineoplastic agents and may also increase the formation of toxic anthracycline metabolites in heart tissue. Cyclosporine and sorafenib may increase the levels/effects of doxorubicin. CYP2D6 inhibitors may increase the levels/effects of doxorubicin; example inhibitors include chlorpromazine, delavirdine, fluoxetine, miconazole, paroxetine, pergolide, quinidine, quinine, ritonavir, and ropinirole. CYP3A4 inhibitors may increase the levels/effects of doxorubicin; example inhibitors include azole antifungals, clarithromycin, diclofenac, doxycycline, erythromycin, imatinib, isoniazid, nefazodone, nicardipine, propofol, protease inhibitors, quinidine, telithromycin, and verapamil.

Doxorubicin may increase the levels/effects of CYP2B6 substrates; example substrates include bupropion, promethazine, propofol, selegiline, and sertraline. Doxorubicin may enhance the adverse/toxic hematologic effects of zidovudine.

Decreased Effect: Digoxin may diminish the cardiotoxic effect of anthracycline antineoplastics. Doxorubicin may decrease the absorption (may only affect digoxin tablets) and serum concentration of cardiac glycosides. CYP3A4 inducers may decrease the levels/effects of doxorubicin; example inducers include aminoglutethimide, carbamazepine, nafcillin, nevirapine, phenobarbital, phenytoin, and rifamycins. Doxorubicin may diminish the therapeutic effect of stavudine and zidovudine.

Ethanol/Nutrition/Herb Interactions Herb/Nutraceutical: Avoid St John's wort (may decrease doxorubicin levels). Avoid black cohosh, dong quai in estrogen-dependent tumors.

Storage/Stability Store intact vials of solution under refrigeration at 2°C to 8°C and protected from light. Store intact vials of lyophilized powder at room temperature (15°C to 30°C). Reconstituted vials are stable for 7 days at room temperature (25°C) and 15 days under refrigeration (5°C) when protected from light. Infusions are stable for 48 hours at room temperature (25°C) when protected from light. Solutions diluted in 50-1000 mL D_5W or NS are stable for 48 hours at room temperature (25°C) when protected from light.

Reconstitution Reconstitute lyophilized powder with NS to a final concentration of 2 mg/mL (may further dilute in 50-1000 mL D_5W or NS for infusion). Unstable in solutions with a pH <3 or >7.

Compatibility Stable in D_5W, LR, NS.

Y-site administration: Compatible: Amifostine, aztreonam, bleomycin, chlorpromazine, cimetidine, cisplatin, cladribine, cyclophosphamide, dexamethasone sodium phosphate, diphenhydramine, droperidol, etoposide phosphate, famotidine, filgrastim, fludarabine, fluorouracil, gatifloxacin, gemcitabine, granisetron, hydromorphone, leucovorin, linezolid, lorazepam, melphalan, methotrexate, methylprednisolone sodium succinate, metoclopramide, mitomycin, morphine, ondansetron, paclitaxel, prochlorperazine edisylate, promethazine, ranitidine, sargramostim, sodium bicarbonate, teniposide, thiotepa, topotecan, vinblastine, vincristine, vinorelbine. **Incompatible:** Allopurinol, amphotericin B cholesteryl sulfate complex, cefepime, ganciclovir, piperacillin/tazobactam, propofol. **Variable (consult detailed reference):** Furosemide, heparin.

Compatibility in syringe: Compatible: Bleomycin, cisplatin, cyclophosphamide, droperidol, leucovorin, methotrexate, metoclopramide, mitomycin, vinblastine, vincristine. **Incompatible:** Furosemide, heparin. **Variable (consult detailed reference):** Fluorouracil.

Compatibility when admixed: Compatible: Dacarbazine, ondansetron, ondansetron with vincristine, paclitaxel, vinblastine. **Incompatible:** Aminophylline, diazepam, fluorouracil. **Variable (consult detailed reference):** Dacarbazine with ondansetron, etoposide with vincristine.

Mechanism of Action Inhibition of DNA and RNA synthesis by intercalation between DNA base pairs by inhibition of topoisomerase II and by steric obstruction. Doxorubicin intercalates at points of local uncoiling of the double helix. Although the exact mechanism is unclear, it appears that direct binding to DNA (intercalation) and inhibition of DNA repair (topoisomerase II inhibition) result in blockade of DNA and RNA synthesis and fragmentation of DNA. Doxorubicin is also a powerful iron chelator; the iron-doxorubicin complex can bind DNA and cell membranes and produce free radicals that immediately cleave the DNA and cell membranes.

Pharmacodynamics/Kinetics

Absorption: Oral: Poor (<50%)

Distribution: V_d: 809-1214 L/m²; to many body tissues, particularly liver, spleen, kidney, lung, heart; does not distribute into the CNS; crosses placenta

Protein binding, plasma: 70% to 76%

Metabolism: Primarily hepatic to doxorubicinol (active), then to inactive aglycones, conjugated sulfates, and glucuronides

(Continued)

DOXOrubicin *(Continued)*

Half-life elimination:

Distribution: 5-10 minutes

Elimination: Doxorubicin: 1-3 hours; Metabolites: 3-3.5 hours

Terminal: 17-48 hours

Male: 54 hours; Female: 35 hours

Excretion: Feces (~40% to 50% as unchanged drug); urine (~5% to 12% as unchanged drug and metabolites)

Clearance: Male: 113 L/hour; Female: 44 L/hour

Dosage I.V.: Refer to individual protocols. **Note:** Lower dosage should be considered for patients with inadequate marrow reserve (due to old age, prior treatment or neoplastic marrow infiltration)

Children:

35-75 mg/m²/dose every 21 days **or**

20-30 mg/m²/dose once weekly **or**

60-90 mg/m²/dose given as a continuous infusion over 96 hours every 3-4 weeks

Adults: Usual or typical dose: 60-75 mg/m²/dose every 21 days **or**

60 mg/m²/dose every 2 weeks (dose dense) **or**

40-60 mg/m²/dose every 3-4 weeks **or**

20-30 mg/m²/day for 2-3 days every 4 weeks **or**

20 mg/m²/dose once weekly

Dosing adjustment in toxicity: The following delays and/or dose reductions have been used:

Neutropenic fever/infection: Consider reducing to 75% of dose in subsequent cycles

ANC <1000/mm³: Delay treatment until ANC recovers to ≥1000/mm³

Platelets <100,000/mm³: Delay treatment until platelets recover to ≥100,000/mm³

Dosing adjustment in renal impairment:

Adjustments are not required.

Hemodialysis: Supplemental dose is not necessary.

Dosing adjustment in hepatic impairment:

The FDA-approved labeling recommends the following adjustments:

Serum bilirubin 1.2-3 mg/dL: Administer 50% of dose

Serum bilirubin 3.1-5 mg/dL: Administer 25% of dose

Severe hepatic impairment: Use is contraindicated

The following guidelines have been used by some clinicians: Floyd, 2006:

ALT/AST 2-3 times ULN: Administer 75% of dose

ALT/AST >3 times ULN or serum bilirubin 1.2-3 mg/dL: Administer 50% of dose

Serum bilirubin 3.1-5 mg/dL: Administer 25% of dose

Serum bilirubin >5 mg/dL: Do not administer

Combination Regimens

Bladder cancer:

CAP *on page 1158*

CISCA *on page 1175*

M-VAC (Bladder Cancer) *on page 1255*

Breast cancer:

AC *on page 1143*

AC/Paclitaxel (Sequential) *on page 1143*

AC-Paclitaxel-Trastuzumab *on page 1144*

AT *on page 1146*

CAF *on page 1157*

(Continued)

DOXOrubicin *(Continued)*

VCAP *on page 1289*

Neuroblastoma:
CAV-P/VP *on page 1163*
CCDDT (Neuroblastoma) *on page 1164*
CE-CAdO *on page 1166*
HIPE-IVAD *on page 1229*
N4SE Protocol *on page 1260*
N6 Protocol *on page 1260*
OPEC-D *on page 1262*
PE-CAdO *on page 1270*
Regimen A1 *on page 1277*
Regimen A2 *on page 1277*

Osteosarcoma:
MTX-CDDPAdr *on page 1254*
POG-8651 *on page 1272*

Ovarian cancer: PAC (CAP) *on page 1262*

Pancreatic cancer: FAM *on page 1211*

Prostate cancer:
Cyclophosphamide + Doxorubicin *on page 1185*
Doxorubicin + Ketoconazole *on page 1195*
Doxorubicin + Ketoconazole/Estramustine + Vinblastine *on page 1195*

Retinoblastoma: CCCDE (Retinoblastoma) *on page 1164*

Sarcoma:
CYVADIC *on page 1187*
VAC Alternating With IE (Ewing's Sarcoma) *on page 1285*

Soft tissue sarcoma:
AD *on page 1145*
AI *on page 1145*
MAID *on page 1246*

Wilms' tumor:
AAV (DD) *on page 1142*
ACAV (J) *on page 1143*
AVD *on page 1147*

Administration Administer I.V. push over at least 3-5 minutes, IVPB over 15-60 minutes, or continuous infusion.

Monitoring Parameters CBC with differential and platelet count; liver function tests (bilirubin, ALT/AST, alkaline phosphatase); serum uric acid, calcium, potassium, phosphate and creatinine; cardiac function (baseline, periodic, and followup): ECG, left ventricular ejection fraction (echocardiography [ECHO] or multigated radionuclide angiography [MUGA])

Patient Information This medication can only be administered intravenously. During therapy, do not use aspirin-containing products, and/or OTC medications without consulting prescriber. It is important to maintain adequate nutrition during therapy; frequent small meals may help. You may experience nausea or vomiting (frequent small meals, frequent mouth care, sucking lozenges, or chewing gum may help). You may experience loss of hair (reversible); you will be more susceptible to infection (avoid crowds and exposure to infection as much as possible). Urine may turn darker yellow. Yogurt or buttermilk may help reduce diarrhea (if unresolved, contact prescriber for medication relief). Frequent mouth care and use of a soft toothbrush or cotton swabs may reduce mouth sores. Report fever, chills, unusual bruising or bleeding, signs of infection, abdominal pain or blood in stools, excessive fatigue, yellowing of eyes or skin, swelling of extremities, difficulty breathing, or unresolved diarrhea. Contraceptive measures are recommended during therapy.

Emetic Potential Moderate (30% to 60%)

Vesicant Yes; see Management of Drug Extravasations *on page 1301.*

Dosage Forms Excipient information presented when available (limited, particularly for generics); consult specific product labeling.

Injection, powder for reconstitution, as hydrochloride: 10 mg, 50 mg
  Adriamycin®: 10 mg, 20 mg, 50 mg, [contains lactose]
  Rubex®: 50 mg, 100 mg [contains lactose] [DSC]
Injection, solution, as hydrochloride: 2 mg/mL (5 mL, 10 mL, 25 mL, 100 mL)
  Adriamycin®: 2 mg/mL (5 mL, 10 mL, 25 mL, 100 mL)

References

Berg SL, Grisell DL, DeLaney TF, et al, "Principles of Treatment of Pediatric Solid Tumors," *Pediatr Clin North Am*, 1991, 38(2):249-67.

Brown JR and Iman SH, "Recent Studies on Doxorubicin and Its Analogues," *Prog Med Chem*, 1984, 21:169-236.

Cummings J and Smyth JF, "Pharmacology of Adriamycin: The Message to the Clinician," *Eur J Cancer Clin Oncol*, 1988, 24(4):579-82.

Curran CF, "Acute Doxorubicin Overdoses," *Ann Intern Med*, 1991, 115(11):913-4.

Curran CF and Luce JK, "Accidental Acute Exposure to Doxorubicin," *Cancer Nurs*, 1989, 12(6):329-31.

Davis HL and Davis TE, "Daunorubicin and Adriamycin in Cancer Treatment: An Analysis of Their Roles and Limitations," *Cancer Treat Rep*, 1979, 63(5):809-15.

Floyd J, Mirza I, Sachs B, et al, "Hepatotoxicity of Chemotherapy," *Semin Oncol*, 2006, 33(1):50-67.

Floyd JD, Nguyen DT, Lobins RL, et al, "Cardiotoxicity of Cancer Therapy," *J Clin Oncol*, 2005, 23(30):7685-96.

Gordon KB, Tajuddin A, Guitart J, et al, "Hand-Foot Syndrome Associated With Liposome-Encapsulated Doxorubicin Therapy," *Cancer*, 1995, 75(8):2169-73.

Ishii E, Hara T, Ohkubo K, et al, "Treatment of Childhood Acute Lymphoblastic Leukemia With Intermediate Dose Cytosine Arabinoside and Adriamycin," *Med Pediatr Oncol*, 1986, 14(2):73-7.

King PD and Perry MC, "Hepatotoxicity of Chemotherapy," *Oncologist*, 2001, 6(2):162-76.

Lauvin R, Miglianico L, and Hellegouarc'h R, "Skin Cancer Occurring 10 Years After the Extravasation of Doxorubicin," *N Engl J Med*, 1995, 332(11):754.

Legha SS, Benjamin RS, Mackay B, et al, "Reduction of Doxorubicin Cardiotoxicity by Prolonged Continuous Intravenous Infusion," *Ann Intern Med*, 1982, 96(2):133-9.

Namer M, "Anthracyclines in the Adjuvant Treatment of Breast Cancer," *Drugs*, 1993, 45(Suppl 2):4-9.

NCCN (National Comprehensive Cancer Network), "Practice Guidelines in Oncology: Breast Cancer Version 2.2007." Available at http://www.nccn.org/professionals/physician_gls/PDF/breast.pdf

Seifert CF, Nesser ME, and Thompson DF, "Dexrazoxane in the Prevention of Doxorubicin-Induced Cardiotoxicity," *Ann Pharmacother*, 1994, 28(9):1063-72.

Speth PA, van Hoesel QG, and Haanen C, "Clinical Pharmacokinetics of Doxorubicin," *Clin Pharmacokinet*, 1988, 15(1):15-31.

Speyer JL, Green MD, Kramer E, et al, "Protective Effect of the Bispiperazinedione ICRF-187 Against Doxorubicin-Induced Cardiac Toxicity in Women With Advanced Breast Cancer," *N Engl J Med*, 1988, 319(12):745-52.

Zimmerman S, Adkins D, Graham M, et al, "Irreversible, Severe, Congestive Cardiomyopathy Occurring in Association With Interferon Alpha Therapy," *Cancer Biother*, 1994, 9(4):291-9.

♦ **Doxorubicin Hydrochloride** *see* DOXOrubicin *on page 352*

♦ **DOXOrubicin Hydrochloride (Liposomal)** *see* DOXOrubicin (Liposomal) *on page 359*

DOXOrubicin (Liposomal) (doks oh ROO bi sin lip pah SOW mal)

Medication Safety Issues

Sound-alike/look-alike issues:
  DOXOrubicin liposomal may be confused with dactinomycin, DAUNOrubicin, DAUNOrubicin liposomal, doxacurium, doxapram, doxazosin, DOXOrubicin, epirubicin, idarubicin
  DOXOrubicin liposomal may be confused with DAUNOrubicin liposomal

(Continued)

DOXOrubicin (Liposomal) *(Continued)*

Doxil® may be confused with Doxy®, Paxil®

Liposomal formulation (Doxil®) may be confused with the conventional formulation (Adriamycin PFS®, Adriamycin RDF®)

High alert medication: The Institute for Safe Medication Practices (ISMP) includes this medication among its list of classes of drugs which have a heightened risk of causing significant patient harm when used in error.

Use caution when selecting product for preparation and dispensing; indications, dosages and adverse event profiles differ between conventional DOXOrubicin hydrochloride solution and DOXOrubicin liposomal. Both formulations are the same concentration. As a result, serious errors have occurred. Liposomal formulation of doxorubicin should NOT be substituted for doxorubicin hydrochloride on a mg-per-mg basis.

Related Information
Management of Drug Extravasations *on page 1301*
Safe Handling of Hazardous Drugs *on page 1382*

U.S. Brand Names Doxil®

Index Terms DOXOrubicin Hydrochloride (Liposomal); Liposomal DOXOrubicin; NSC-712227; Pegylated Liposomal DOXOrubicin

Generic Available No

Canadian Brand Names Caelyx®

Pharmacologic Category Antineoplastic Agent, Anthracycline

Use Treatment of ovarian cancer, multiple myeloma, and AIDS-related Kaposi's sarcoma

Unlabeled/Investigational Use
Treatment of metastatic breast cancer

Pregnancy Risk Factor D

Lactation Excretion in breast milk unknown/contraindicated

Labeled Contraindications Hypersensitivity to doxorubicin, other anthracyclines, or any component of the formulation; breast-feeding

Warnings/Precautions Hazardous agent - use appropriate precautions for handling and disposal.

[U.S. Boxed Warning]: Doxorubicin may cause cumulative, dose-related myocardial toxicity (concurrent or delayed). Doxorubicin liposomal should be used cautiously in patients with high cumulative doses of anthracyclines. Total cumulative dose should take into account previous or concomitant treatment with cardiotoxic agents or irradiation of chest. The incidence of irreversible myocardial toxicity increases as the total cumulative (lifetime) dosages approach 450-550 mg/m². Although the risk increases with cumulative dose, irreversible cardiotoxicity may occur with anthracycline treatment at any dose level. Patients with pre-existing heart disease, hypertension, concurrent administration of other antineoplastic agents, prior or concurrent chest irradiation, and advanced age are at increased risk. Evaluate left ventricular ejection fraction (LVEF) prior to treatment and periodically during treatment. The onset of symptoms of anthracycline-induced CHF and/or cardiomyopathy may be delayed. **[U.S. Boxed Warning]: Acute infusion reactions may occur, some may be serious/life-threatening;** fatal allergic/anaphylactoid-like infusion reactions have been reported. May include flushing, dyspnea, facial swelling, chills, back pain, hypotension and/or tightness of chest/throat. Medication for the treatment of reactions should be readily available. Infuse doxorubicin liposomal at 1 mg/minute initially to minimize risk of infusion reaction. **[U.S. Boxed Warning]: Use with caution in patients with hepatic impairment;** dosage reduction is recommended.

DOXORUBICIN (LIPOSOMAL)

[U.S. Boxed Warning]: Severe myelosuppression may occur. Hand-foot syndrome (palmar-plantar erythrodysesthesia) has been reported in up to 51% of patients with ovarian cancer, 19% of patients with multiple myeloma, and ~3% in patients with Kaposi's sarcoma. May occur early in treatment, but is usually seen after 2-3 treatment cycles. Dosage modification may be required. In severe cases, treatment discontinuation may be required. **[U.S. Boxed Warning]: Liposomal formulations of doxorubicin should NOT be substituted for conventional doxorubicin hydrochloride on a mg-per-mg basis.**

Doxorubicin may potentiate the toxicity of cyclophosphamide (hemorrhagic cystitis) and mercaptopurine (hepatotoxicity). Radiation recall reaction has been reported with doxorubicin liposomal treatment after radiation therapy. Radiation-induced toxicity (to the myocardium, mucosa, skin, and liver) may be increased by doxorubicin. Safety and efficacy in children have not been established.

Adverse Reactions

>10%:

Cardiovascular: Peripheral edema (≤11%)

Central nervous system: Fever (8% to 21%), headache (≤11%), pain (≤21%)

Dermatologic: Alopecia (9% to 19%); palmar-plantar erythrodysesthesia/hand-foot syndrome (≤51% in ovarian cancer, 3% in Kaposi's sarcoma), rash (≤29% in ovarian cancer, ≤5% in Kaposi's sarcoma)

Gastrointestinal: Stomatitis (5% to 41%), vomiting (8% to 33%), nausea (17% to 46%), mucositis (≤14%), constipation (≤30%), anorexia (≤20%), diarrhea (5% to 21%), dyspepsia (≤12%), intestinal obstruction (≤11%)

Hematologic: Myelosuppression (onset: 7 days; nadir: 10-14 days; recovery: 21-28 days), neutropenia (12% to 62%; grade 4: 4%), leukopenia (36%), thrombocytopenia (13% to 65%), anemia (6% to 74%; grade 4: <1%)

Neuromuscular & skeletal: Weakness (7% to 40%), back pain (≤12%)

Respiratory: Pharyngitis (≤16%), dyspnea (≤15%)

Miscellaneous: Infection (≤11%)

1% to 10%:

Cardiovascular: Cardiac arrest, chest pain, edema, hypotension, pallor, tachycardia, vasodilation

Central nervous system: Agitation, anxiety, chills, confusion, depression, dizziness, emotional lability, insomnia, somnolence, vertigo

Dermatologic: Acne, bruising, dry skin (6%), dermatitis (exfoliative and fungal), furunculosis, maculopapular rash, pruritus, skin discoloration, vesiculobullous rash

Endocrine & metabolic: Dehydration, hyperbilirubinemia, hypercalcemia, hyperglycemia, hypokalemia, hyponatremia

Gastrointestinal: Abdomen enlarged, anorexia, ascites, cachexia, dyspepsia, dysphagia, esophagitis, flatulence, gingivitis, glossitis, ileus, mouth ulceration, oral moniliasis, rectal bleeding, taste perversion, weight loss, xerostomia

Genitourinary: Cystitis, dysuria, leukorrhea, pelvic pain, polyuria, urinary incontinence, urinary tract infection, urinary urgency, vaginal bleeding, vaginal moniliasis

Hematologic: Hemolysis, prothrombin time increased

Hepatic: ALT increased

Local: Thrombophlebitis

(Continued)

361

DOXOrubicin (Liposomal) *(Continued)*

Neuromuscular & skeletal: Arthralgia, hypertonia, myalgia, neuralgia, neuritis (peripheral), neuropathy, paresthesia (≤10%), pathological fracture

Ocular: Conjunctivitis, dry eyes, retinitis

Otic: Ear pain

Renal: Albuminuria, hematuria

Respiratory: Apnea, cough (≤10%), epistaxis, pleural effusion, pneumonia, rhinitis, sinusitis

Miscellaneous: Allergic reaction; infusion-related reactions (7%; includes bronchospasm, chest tightness, chills, dyspnea, facial edema, flushing, headache, herpes simplex/zoster, hypotension, pruritus); moniliasis, diaphoresis

<1%, postmarketing, and/or case reports (limited to important or life-threatening): Abscess, acute brain syndrome, abnormal vision, acute myeloid leukemia (secondary), alkaline phosphatase increased, anaphylactic or anaphylactoid reaction, asthma, balanitis, blindness, bone pain, bronchitis, BUN increased, bundle branch block, cardiomegaly, cardiomyopathy, cellulitis, CHF, colitis, creatinine increased, cryptococcosis, diabetes mellitus, erythema multiforme, erythema nodosum, eosinophilia, fecal impaction, flu-like syndrome, gastritis, glucosuria, hemiplegia, hemorrhage, hepatic failure, hepatitis, hepatosplenomegaly, hyperkalemia, hypernatremia, hyperuricemia, hyperventilation, hypoglycemia, hypolipidemia, hypomagnesemia, hypophosphatemia, hypoproteinemia, hypothermia, injection site hemorrhage, injection site pain, jaundice, ketosis, lactic dehydrogenase increased, kidney failure, lymphadenopathy, lymphangitis, migraine, myositis, optic neuritis, palpitation, pancreatitis, pericardial effusion, petechia, pneumothorax, pulmonary embolism, radiation injury, sclerosing cholangitis, seizure, sepsis, skin necrosis, skin ulcer, syncope, tenesmus, thromboplastin decreased, thrombosis, tinnitus, urticaria, visual field defect, ventricular arrhythmia

Overdosage/Toxicology Symptoms of overdose include increases in mucositis, leukopenia, and thrombocytopenia. For acute overdose, treatment of the severely myelosuppressed patient consists of hospitalization, antibiotics, hematopoietic growth factors, platelet and granulocyte transfusion, and symptomatic treatment of mucositis. Treatment is otherwise symptom-directed and supportive.

Drug Interactions

Cytochrome P450 Effect: Substrate (major) of CYP2D6, 3A4; **Inhibits** CYP2B6 (moderate), 2D6 (weak), 3A4 (weak)

Increased Effect/Toxicity: Bevacizumab and trastuzumab may enhance the cardiotoxic effect of anthracycline antineoplastics. Cyclosporine may increase the levels/effects of doxorubicin; may increase neurotoxicity and/or enhance hematologic toxicity. CYP2D6 inhibitors may increase the levels/effects of doxorubicin (example inhibitors include chlorpromazine, delavirdine, fluoxetine, miconazole, paroxetine, pergolide, quinidine, quinine, ritonavir, and ropinirole). CYP3A4 inhibitors may increase the levels/effects of doxorubicin (example inhibitors include azole antifungals, clarithromycin, diclofenac, doxycycline, erythromycin, imatinib, isoniazid, nefazodone, nicardipine, propofol, protease inhibitors, quinidine, telithromycin, and verapamil). Sorafenib may increase the levels/effects of doxorubicin. Paclitaxel may reduce doxorubicin clearance and increase toxicity, including cardiotoxicity of doxorubicin.

Doxorubicin may enhance the adverse effects of zidovudine. Doxorubicin may increase the levels/effects of CYP2B6 substrates (example substrates include bupropion, efavirenz, promethazine, selegiline, and sertraline).

Decreased Effect: Doxorubicin liposomal may decrease the absorption of cardiac glycosides (may only affect digoxin tablets). CYP3A4 inducers may decrease the levels/effects of doxorubicin (example inducers include aminoglutethimide, carbamazepine, nafcillin, nevirapine, phenobarbital, phenytoin, and rifamycins). Doxorubicin may diminish the therapeutic effect of stavudine and zidovudine.

Ethanol/Nutrition/Herb Interactions

Ethanol: Avoid ethanol (due to GI irritation).

Herb/Nutraceutical: St John's wort may decrease doxorubicin levels.

Storage/Stability Store intact vials of solution under refrigeration at 2°C to 8°C (36°F to 46°F); avoid freezing. Prolonged freezing may adversely affect liposomal drug products, however, short-term freezing (<1 month) does not appear to have a deleterious effect. Diluted doxorubicin hydrochloride liposome injection may be refrigerated at 2°C to 8°C (36°F to 46°F); administer within 24 hours. **Do not infuse with in-line filters.**

Reconstitution Doses of doxorubicin liposomal ≤90 mg must be diluted in 250 mL of D_5W prior to administration. Doses >90 mg should be diluted in 500 mL D_5W.

Compatibility Stable in D_5W.

Y-site administration: Compatible: Acyclovir, allopurinol, aminophylline, ampicillin, aztreonam, bleomycin, butorphanol, calcium gluconate, carboplatin, cefazolin, cefepime, cefoxitin, ceftizoxime, ceftriaxone, chlorpromazine, cimetidine, ciprofloxacin, cisplatin, clindamycin, co-trimoxazole, cyclophosphamide, cytarabine, dexamethasone sodium phosphate, diphenhydramine, dobutamine, dopamine, droperidol, enalaprilat, etoposide, famotidine, fluconazole, ganciclovir, gentamicin, granisetron, haloperidol, hydrocortisone sodium succinate, hydromorphone, ifosfamide, leucovorin, lorazepam, magnesium sulfate, mesna, methotrexate, methylprednisolone sodium succinate, metronidazole, netilmicin, ondansetron, piperacillin, potassium chloride, prochlorperazine edisylate, ranitidine, ticarcillin, ticarcillin/clavulanate, tobramycin, vancomycin, vinblastine, vincristine, vinorelbine, zidovudine. Incompatible: Amphotericin B, amphotericin B cholesteryl sulfate complex, buprenorphine, cefoperazone, ceftazidime, docetaxel, fluorouracil, furosemide, heparin, hydroxyzine, mannitol, meperidine, metoclopramide, mitoxantrone, morphine, ofloxacin, paclitaxel, piperacillin/tazobactam, promethazine, sodium bicarbonate.

Mechanism of Action Doxorubicin inhibits DNA and RNA synthesis by intercalating between DNA base pairs causing steric obstruction and inhibits topoisomerase-II at the point of DNA cleavage. Doxorubicin is also a powerful iron chelator. The iron-doxorubicin complex can bind DNA and cell membranes, producing free hydroxyl (OH) radicals that cleave DNA and cell membranes. Active throughout entire cell cycle. Doxorubicin liposomal is a pegylated formulation which protects the liposomes, and thereby increases blood circulation time.

Pharmacodynamics/Kinetics

Distribution: V_{dss}: 2.7-2.8 L/m^2

Protein binding, plasma: Unknown; nonliposomal (conventional) doxorubicin: 70%

Half-life elimination: Terminal: Distribution: 4.7-5.2 hours, Elimination: 44-55 hours

Metabolism: Hepatic and in plasma to doxorubicinol and the sulfate and glucuronide conjugates of 4-demethyl,7-deoxyaglycones

Excretion: Urine (5% as doxorubicin or doxorubicinol)

(Continued)

DOXOrubicin (Liposomal) *(Continued)*

Recommended Dose Modification Guidelines

Toxicity Grade	Dose Adjustment
HAND FOOT SYNDROME (HFS)	
1 (Mild erythema, swelling, or desquamation not interfering with daily activities)	Redose unless patient has experienced previous Grade 3 or 4 toxicity. If so, delay up to 2 weeks and decrease dose by 25%; return to original dosing interval.
2 (Erythema, desquamation, or swelling interfering with, but not precluding, normal physical activities; small blisters or ulcerations <2 cm in diameter)	Delay dosing up to 2 weeks or until resolved to Grade 0-1. If after 2 weeks there is no resolution, liposomal doxorubicin should be discontinued. Otherwise, if no prior Grade 3-4 HFS, continue treatment at previous dose and dosage interval. If a prior Grade 3-4 HFS has occurred, continue prior dosage interval, but decrease dose by 25%.
3 (Blistering, ulceration, or swelling interfering with walking or normal daily activities; cannot wear regular clothing)	Delay dosing up to 2 weeks or until resolved to Grade 0-1. Decrease dose by 25% and return to original dosing interval; if after 2 weeks there is no resolution, liposomal doxorubicin should be discontinued.
4 (Diffuse or local process causing infectious complications, or a bedridden state or hospitalization)	Delay dosing up to 2 weeks or until resolved to Grade 0-1. Decrease dose by 25% and return to original dosing interval. If after 2 weeks there is no resolution, liposomal doxorubicin should be discontinued.
STOMATITIS	
1 (Painless ulcers, erythema, or mild soreness)	Redose unless patient has experienced previous Grade 3 or 4 toxicity. If so, delay up to 2 weeks and decrease by 25%. Return to original dosing interval.
2 (Painful erythema, edema, or ulcers, but can eat)	Delay dosing up to 2 weeks or until resolved to Grade 0-1. If after 2 weeks there is no resolution, liposomal doxorubicin should be discontinued. Otherwise, if not prior Grade 3-4 stomatitis, continue treatment at previous dose and dosage interval. If prior Grade 3-4 toxicity, continue treatment with previous dosage interval, but decrease dose by 25%.
3 (Painful erythema, edema, or ulcers, but cannot eat)	Delay dosing up to 2 weeks or until resolved to Grade 0-1. Decrease dose by 25% and return to original dosing interval. If after 2 weeks there is no resolution, liposomal doxorubicin should be discontinued.
4 (Requires parenteral or enteral support)	Delay dosing up to 2 weeks or until resolved to Grade 0-1. Decrease dose by 25% and return to original dosing interval. If after 2 weeks there is no resolution, liposomal doxorubicin should be discontinued.

Dosage Refer to individual protocols. **Liposomal formulations of doxorubicin should NOT be substituted for conventional doxorubicin hydrochloride on a mg-per-mg basis.**

AIDS-related Kaposi's sarcoma: I.V.: 20 mg/m^2/dose once every 3 weeks

Breast cancer (unlabeled use): I.V.: 50 mg/m^2/dose every 4 weeks

Multiple myeloma: I.V.: 30 mg/m^2/dose every 3 weeks (in combination with bortezomib) **or**

Unlabeled dosing: I.V.: 40 mg/m^2/dose every 4 weeks (in combination with vincristine and dexamethasone)

Ovarian cancer: I.V.: 50 mg/m^2/dose every 4 weeks

Dosing adjustment for toxicity in treatment with bortezomib (for multiple myeloma) (see Bortezomib monograph for bortezomib dosage reduction with toxicity guidelines):

Fever ≥38°C and ANC <1000/mm^3: If prior to doxorubicin liposomal treatment (day 4), do not administer; if after doxorubicin liposomal administered, reduce dose by 25% in next cycle.

ANC<500/mm^3, platelets <25,000/mm^3, hemoglobin <8 g/dL: If prior to doxorubicin liposomal treatment (day 4); do not administer; if after doxorubicin liposomal administered, reduce dose by 25% in next cycle if bortezomib dose reduction occurred for hematologic toxicity.

Grade 3 or 4 nonhematologic toxicity: Delay dose until resolved to grade <2; reduce dose by 25% for all subsequent doses.

Neuropathic pain or peripheral neuropathy: No dose reductions needed for doxorubicin liposomal, refer to Bortezomib monograph for bortezomib dosing adjustment.

See table "Recommended Dose Modification Guidelines" on previous page.

Dosing adjustment in hepatic impairment:

ALT/AST 2-3 times ULN: Administer 75% of dose

ALT/AST >3 times ULN **or** bilirubin 1.2-3 mg/dL (20-51 μmol/L): Administer 50% of dose

Bilirubin 3.1-5 mg/dL (51-85 μmol/L): Administer 25% of dose

Bilirubin >5 mg/dL (85 μmol/L): Do not administer

See table: "Hematological Toxicity"

Hematological Toxicity

Grade	ANC	Platelets	Modification
1	1500-1900	75,000-150,000	Resume treatment with no dose reduction.
2	1000-<1500	50,000-<75,000	Wait until ANC ≥1500 and platelets ≥75,000; redose with no dose reduction.
3	500-999	25,000-<50,000	Wait until ANC ≥1500 and platelets ≥75,000; redose with no dose reduction.
4	<500	<25,000	Wait until ANC ≥1500 and platelets ≥75,000; redose at 25% dose reduction or continue full dose with cytokine support.

Combination Regimens

Multiple myeloma:

Bortezomib-Doxorubicin (Liposomal) *on page 1155*

Doxorubicin (Liposomal)-Vincristine-Dexamethasone *on page 1195*

(Continued)

DOXOrubicin (Liposomal) *(Continued)*

Administration Administer IVPB over 60 minutes; manufacturer recommends administering at initial rate of 1 mg/minute to minimize risk of infusion reactions until the absence of a reaction has been established, then increase the infusion rate for completion over 1 hour. **Do not administer I.M. or SubQ. Do not infuse with in-line filters.** Avoid extravasation (irritant), monitor site; extravasation may occur without stinging or burning. Flush with 5-10 mL of D_5W solution before and after drug administration, incompatible with heparin flushes. Monitor for local erythematous streaking along vein and/or facial flushing (may indicate rapid infusion rate).

Monitoring Parameters CBC with differential and platelet count, liver function tests (ALT/AST, bilirubin, alkaline phosphatase); monitor for infusion reactions

Cardiac function should be carefully monitored; echocardiography, left ventricular ejection fraction (LVEF), MUGA scan may be used during therapy. Endomyocardial biopsy is the most definitive test for anthracycline myocardial injury.

Patient Information This medication can only be administered by infusion. During therapy, do not use alcohol, aspirin-containing products, and/or OTC medications without consulting prescriber. It is important to maintain adequate nutrition and hydration (2-3 L/day of fluids unless instructed to restrict fluid intake) during therapy; frequent small meals may help. You may experience nausea or vomiting (frequent small meals, frequent mouth care, sucking lozenges, or chewing gum may help). You may experience loss of hair (reversible); you will be more susceptible to infection (avoid crowds and exposure to infection as much as possible). Urine may turn red-brown (normal). Yogurt or buttermilk may help reduce diarrhea (if unresolved, contact prescriber for medication relief). Frequent mouth care and use of a soft toothbrush or cotton swabs may reduce mouth sores. Report fever, chills, unusual bruising or bleeding, signs of infection, abdominal pain or blood in stools, excessive fatigue, yellowing of eyes or skin, darkening in color of urine or pale colored stools, swelling of extremities, difficulty breathing, or unresolved diarrhea. Contraceptive measures are recommended during therapy

Additional Information Oncology Comment: Pegylated liposomal doxorubicin is listed within National Comprehensive Cancer Network (NCCN) guidelines for the treatment of the following malignancies: Breast cancer (as a preferred single-agent therapy for recurrent or metastatic breast cancer), ovarian cancer (an acceptable second-line agent for recurrent ovarian cancer), and multiple myeloma, (as primary induction therapy for both transplant candidates and nontransplant candidates [in combination with vincristine and dexamethasone]).

Emetic Potential Low (10% to 30%)

Vesicant No; may be an irritant

Dosage Forms Excipient information presented when available (limited, particularly for generics); consult specific product labeling.

Injection, solution, as hydrochloride: 2 mg/mL (10 mL, 25 mL)

References

Biehn SE, Moore DT, Voorhees PM, et al, "Extended Follow-Up of Outcome Measures in Multiple Myeloma Patients Treated on a Phase I Study With Bortezomib and Pegylated Liposomal Doxorubicin," *Ann Hematol*, 2007, 86(3):211-6.

Forbes C, Wilby J, Richardson G, et al, "A Systematic Review and Economic Evaluation of Pegylated Liposomal Doxorubicin Hydrochloride for Ovarian Cancer," *Health Technol Assess*, 2002, 6(23):1-119.

Gabizon A, Shmeeda H, and Barenholz Y, "Pharmacokinetics of Pegylated Liposomal Doxorubicin: Review of Animal and Human Studies," *Clin Pharmacokinet*, 2003, 42(5):419-36.

Gordon AN, Fleagle JT, Guthrie D, et al, "Recurrent Epithelial Ovarian Carcinoma: A Randomized Phase III Study of Pegylated Liposomal Doxorubicin Versus Topotecan," *J Clin Oncol*, 2001, 19(14):3312-22.

King PD and Perry MC, "Hepatotoxicity of Chemotherapy," *Oncologist*, 2001, 6(2):162-76.

NCCN (National Comprehensive Cancer Network), "Practice Guidelines in Oncology: Breast Cancer Version 2.2007." Available at http://www.nccn.org/professionals/physician_gls/PDF/breast.pdf

NCCN (National Comprehensive Cancer Network), "Practice Guidelines in Oncology: Multiple Myeloma Version 3.2007." Available at http://www.nccn.org/professionals/physician_gls/PDF/myeloma.pdf

NCCN (National Comprehensive Cancer Network), "Practice Guidelines in Oncology: Ovarian-Cancer Version 1.2007." Available at http://www.nccn.org/professionals/physician_gls/PDF/ovarian.pdf

Northfelt DW, Dezebe BJ, Thommes JA, et al, "Pegylated-Liposomal Doxorubicin Versus Doxorubicin, Bleomycin, and Vincristine in the Treatment of AIDS-Related Kaposi's Sarcoma: Results of a Randomized Phase III Clinical Trial," *J Clin Oncol*, 1998, 16(7):2445-51.

O'Brien ME, Wigler N, Inbar M, et al, "Reduced Cardiotoxicity and Comparable Efficacy in a Phase III Trial of Pegylated Liposomal Doxorubicin HCl (CAELYX™/Doxil®) Versus Conventional Doxorubicin for First-Line Treatment of Metastatic Breast Cancer," *Ann Oncol*, 2004, 15(3):440-9.

Orditura M, Quaglia F, Morgillo F, et al, "Pegylated Liposomal Doxorubicin: Pharmacologic and Clinical Evidence of Potent Antitumor Activity With Reduced Anthracycline-induced Cardiotoxicity (Review)," *Oncol Rep*, 2004, 12(3):549-56.

Orlowski RZ, Voorhees PM, Garcia RA, et al, "Phase I Trial of the Proteasome Inhibitor Bortezomib and Pegylated Liposomal Doxorubicin in Patients With Advanced Hematologic Malignancies," *Blood*, 2005, 105(8):3058-65.

O'Shaughnessy JA, "Pegylated Liposomal Doxorubicin in the Treatment of Breast Cancer," *Clin Breast Cancer*, 2003, 4(5):318-28.

Rifkin RM, Gregory SA, Mohrbacher A, et al, "Pegylated Liposomal Doxorubicin, Vincristine, and Dexamethasone Provide Significant Reduction in Toxicity Compared With Doxorubicin, Vincristine, and Dexamethasone in Patients With Newly Diagnosed Multiple Myeloma," *Cancer*, 2006, 106(4):848-58.

Sharpe M, Easthope SE, Keating GM, et al, "Polyethylene Glycol-Liposomal Doxorubicin: A Review of Its Use in the Management of Solid and Haematological Malignancies and AIDS-Related Kaposi's Sarcoma," *Drugs*, 2002, 62(14):2089-126.

Stebbing J and Gaya A, "Pegylated Liposomal Doxorubicin (Caelyx) in Recurrent Ovarian Cancer," *Cancer Treat Rev*, 2002, 28(2):121-5.

Theodoulou M and Hudis C, "Cardiac Profiles of Liposomal Anthracyclines: Greater Cardiac Safety Versus Conventional Doxorubicin?" *Cancer*, 2004, 100(10):2052-63.

Vorbiof DA, Rapoport BL, Chasen C, et al, "First Line Therapy With Paclitaxel (Taxol) and Pegylated Liposomal Doxorubicin (Caelyx) in Patients With Metastatic Breast Cancer: A Multicentre Phase II Study," *Breast*, 2004, 13(3):219-26.

Waterhouse DN, Tardi PG, Mayer LD, "A Comparison of Liposomal Formulations of Doxorubicin With Drug Administered in Free Form: Changing Toxicity Profiles," *Drug Saf*, 2001, 24(12):903-20.

Dronabinol (droe NAB i nol)

Medication Safety Issues
Sound-alike/look-alike issues:
Dronabinol may be confused with droperidol

Related Information
Management of Nausea and Vomiting *on page 1319*

U.S. Brand Names Marinol®

Index Terms Delta-9-tetrahydro-cannabinol; Delta-9 THC; Tetrahydrocannabinol; THC

Generic Available No

Canadian Brand Names Marinol®

Pharmacologic Category Antiemetic; Appetite Stimulant

Use Chemotherapy-associated nausea and vomiting refractory to other antiemetic(s); AIDS-related anorexia

Unlabeled/Investigational Use Cancer-related anorexia

Restrictions C-III

Pregnancy Risk Factor C
(Continued)

Dronabinol *(Continued)*

Lactation Enters breast milk/contraindicated

Labeled Contraindications Hypersensitivity to dronabinol, cannabinoids, sesame oil, or any component of the formulation, or marijuana; should be avoided in patients with a history of schizophrenia

Warnings/Precautions Use with caution in patients with hepatic disease or seizure disorders. Reduce dosage in patients with severe hepatic impairment. May cause additive CNS effects with sedatives, hypnotics or other psychoactive agents; patients must be cautioned about performing tasks which require mental alertness (eg, operating machinery or driving).

May have potential for abuse; drug is psychoactive substance in marijuana; use caution in patients with a history of substance abuse or potential. May cause withdrawal symptoms upon abrupt discontinuation. Use with caution in patients with mania, depression, or schizophrenia; careful psychiatric monitoring is recommended. Use caution in elderly; they are more sensitive to adverse effects. Safety and efficacy have not been established in children.

Adverse Reactions Frequency not always specified.

>1%:

Cardiovascular: Palpitations, tachycardia, vasodilation/facial flushing

Central nervous system: Euphoria (8% to 24%, dose related), abnormal thinking (3% to 10%), dizziness (3% to 10%), paranoia (3% to 10%), somnolence (3% to 10%), amnesia, anxiety, ataxia, confusion, depersonalization, hallucination

Gastrointestinal: Abdominal pain (3% to 10%), nausea (3% to 10%), vomiting (3% to 10%)

Neuromuscular & skeletal: Weakness

<1%, postmarketing, and/or case reports: Conjunctivitis, depression, diarrhea, fatigue, fecal incontinence, flushing, hypotension, myalgia, nightmares, seizure, speech difficulties, tinnitus, vision difficulties

Overdosage/Toxicology Symptoms of overdose may include tachycardia, hyper- or hypotension, behavioral disturbances, lethargy, panic reactions, seizures or motor incoordination. Benzodiazepines may be helpful for agitative behavior; Trendelenburg position and hydration may be helpful for hypotensive effects. For other manifestations, treatment should be symptom-directed and supportive.

Drug Interactions

Increased Effect/Toxicity: Sedative effects may be additive with CNS depressants (includes barbiturates, opioid analgesics, and other sedative agents). Use in combination with phenothiazines (prochlorperazine) may result in additive or synergistic effects (as antiemetics), but sedation must be monitored.

Ethanol/Nutrition/Herb Interactions

Ethanol: Avoid ethanol (may increase CNS depression).

Food: Administration with high-lipid meals may increase absorption.

Herb/Nutraceutical: St John's wort may decrease dronabinol levels.

Storage/Stability Store under refrigeration (or in a cool environment) between 8°C and 15°C (46°F and 59°F). Protect from freezing.

Mechanism of Action Unknown, may inhibit endorphins in the brain's emetic center, suppress prostaglandin synthesis, and/or inhibit medullary activity through an unspecified cortical action. Some pharmacologic effects appear to involve sympathomimetic activity; tachyphylaxis to some effect (eg, tachycardia) may occur, but appetite-stimulating effects do not appear to wane over time. Antiemetic activity may be due to effect on cannabinoid receptors (CB1) within the central nervous system.

Pharmacodynamics/Kinetics

Onset of action: Within 1 hour

Peak effect: 2-4 hours

Duration: 24 hours (appetite stimulation)

Absorption: Oral: 90% to 95%; 10% to 20% of dose gets into systemic circulation

Distribution: V_d: 10 L/kg; dronabinol is highly lipophilic and distributes to adipose tissue

Protein binding: 97% to 99%

Metabolism: Hepatic to at least 50 metabolites, some of which are active; 11-hydroxy-delta-9-tetrahydrocannabinol (11-OH-THC) is the major metabolite; extensive first-pass effect

Half-life elimination: Dronabinol: 25-36 hours (terminal); Dronabinol metabolites: 44-59 hours

Time to peak, serum: 0.5-4 hours

Excretion: Feces (50% as unconjugated metabolites, 5% as unchanged drug); urine (10% to 15% as acid metabolites and conjugates)

Dosage Refer to individual protocols. Oral:

Antiemetic: Children and Adults: 5 mg/m² 1-3 hours before chemotherapy, then 5 mg/m²/dose every 2-4 hours after chemotherapy for a total of 4-6 doses/day; increase doses in increments of 2.5 mg/m² to a maximum of 15 mg/m²/dose.

Appetite stimulant: Adults: Initial: 2.5 mg twice daily (before lunch and dinner); titrate up to a maximum of 20 mg/day.

Monitoring Parameters CNS effects, heart rate, blood pressure, behavioral profile

Test Interactions Decreased FSH, LH, growth hormone, and testosterone

Dietary Considerations Capsules contain sesame oil.

Patient Information Avoid activities such as driving which require motor coordination. Avoid alcohol and other CNS depressants. May impair coordination and judgment.

Special Geriatric Considerations Elderly patients may be more sensitive to the CNS effects and postural hypotensive effects of dronabinol. Titrate the dose slowly and monitor for adverse effects.

Emetic Potential Very low (<10%)

Dosage Forms Excipient information presented when available (limited, particularly for generics); consult specific product labeling.

Capsule, gelatin:

Marinol®: 2.5 mg, 5 mg, 10 mg [contains sesame oil]

References

Anderson PO and Muire GG, "Delta-9-Tetrahydrocannabinol as an Antiemetic," *Am J Hosp Pharm*, 1981, 38:639-46.

Cat LK and Coleman RL, "Treatment for HIV Wasting Syndrome," *Ann Pharmacother*, 1994, 28(5):595-7.

Plasse TF, Gorter RW, Krasnow SH, et al, "Recent Clinical Experience with Dronabinol," *Pharmacol Biochem Behav*, 1991, 40(3):695-700.

Struwe M, Kaempfer SH, Geiger CJ, et al, "Effect of Dronabinol on Nutritional Status in HIV Infection," *Ann Pharmacother*, 1993, 27(7-8):827-31.

Voth EA and Schwartz RH, "Medicinal Applications of Delta-9-Tetrahydrocannabinol and Marijuana," *Ann Intern Med*, 1979, 126(10):791-8.

Droperidol (droe PER i dole)

Medication Safety Issues

Sound-alike/look-alike issues:

Droperidol may be confused with dronabinol

Inapsine® may be confused with Nebcin®

(Continued)

Droperidol *(Continued)*

Related Information
Management of Nausea and Vomiting *on page 1319*

U.S. Brand Names Inapsine®

Index Terms Dehydrobenzperidol

Generic Available Yes

Canadian Brand Names Droperidol Injection, USP

Pharmacologic Category Antiemetic; Antipsychotic Agent, Typical

Use Antiemetic in surgical and diagnostic procedures; preoperative medication in patients when other treatments are ineffective or inappropriate

Pregnancy Risk Factor C

Lactation Excretion in breast milk unknown

Labeled Contraindications Hypersensitivity to droperidol or any component of the formulation; known or suspected QT prolongation, including congenital long QT syndrome (prolonged QT_c is defined as >440 msec in males or >450 msec in females)

Warnings/Precautions May alter cardiac conduction. **[U.S. Boxed Warning]: Cases of QT prolongation and torsade de pointes, including some fatal cases, have been reported.** Use extreme caution in patients with bradycardia (<50 bpm), cardiac disease, concurrent MAO inhibitor therapy, Class I and Class III antiarrhythmics or other drugs known to prolong QT interval, and electrolyte disturbances (hypokalemia or hypomagnesemia), including concomitant drugs which may alter electrolytes (diuretics).

Use with caution in patients with seizures or severe liver disease. May be sedating, use with caution in disorders where CNS depression is a feature. Caution in patients with hemodynamic instability, predisposition to seizures, subcortical brain damage, pheochromocytoma, or renal disease. Esophageal dysmotility and aspiration have been associated with antipsychotic use. Caution in breast cancer or other prolactin-dependent tumors. May cause orthostatic hypotension - use with caution in patients at risk of this effect. Significant hypotension may occur; injection contains benzyl alcohol; injection also contains sulfites which may cause allergic reaction.

Relative to other neuroleptics, droperidol has a low potency of cholinergic blockade. Use with caution in patients with decreased gastrointestinal motility, urinary retention, BPH, xerostomia, or visual problems. May worsen myasthenia gravis.

May cause extrapyramidal symptoms, including tardive dyskinesia. May be associated with neuroleptic malignant syndrome (NMS) or pigmentary retinopathy. May mask toxicity of other drugs or conditions (eg, intestinal obstruction, Reye's syndrome, brain tumor) due to antiemetic effects. Use with caution in the elderly; reduce initial dose. Safety in children <2 years of age has not been established.

Adverse Reactions
>10%:
Cardiovascular: QT_c prolongation (dose dependent)
Central nervous system: Restlessness, anxiety, extrapyramidal symptoms, dystonic reactions, pseudoparkinsonian signs and symptoms, tardive dyskinesia, seizure, altered central temperature regulation, sedation, drowsiness
Endocrine & metabolic: Swelling of breasts
Gastrointestinal: Weight gain, constipation

1% to 10%:
  Cardiovascular: Hypotension (especially orthostatic), tachycardia, abnormal T waves with prolonged ventricular repolarization, hypertension

  Central nervous system: Hallucinations, persistent tardive dyskinesia, akathisia

  Gastrointestinal: Nausea, vomiting

  Genitourinary: Dysuria

<1%: Adynamic ileus, agranulocytosis, alopecia, amenorrhea, arrhythmia, blurred vision, cholestatic jaundice, contact dermatitis, galactorrhea, gynecomastia, heat stroke, hyperpigmentation, laryngospasm, leukopenia (usually with large doses for prolonged periods), neuroleptic malignant syndrome (NMS), obstructive jaundice, overflow incontinence, photosensitivity (rare), priapism, pruritus, rash, respiratory depression, retinal pigmentation, sexual dysfunction, tardive dystonia, torsade de pointes, urinary retention, ventricular tachycardia, visual acuity decreased (may be irreversible), xerostomia

Overdosage/Toxicology Symptoms of overdose include hypotension, tachycardia, hallucinations, and extrapyramidal symptoms. Following initiation of essential overdose management, toxic symptom treatment and supportive treatment should be initiated. Prolonged QT interval, seizures, and arrhythmias have been reported.

Drug Interactions

Increased Effect/Toxicity: Droperidol in combination with certain forms of conduction anesthesia may produce peripheral vasodilitation and hypotension. Droperidol and CNS depressants will likely have additive CNS effects. Droperidol and cyclobenzaprine may have an additive effect on prolonging the QT interval. Use caution with other agents known to prolong QT interval (Class I or Class III antiarrhythmics, some quinolone antibiotics, cisapride, some phenothiazines, pimozide, tricyclic antidepressants). Potassium- or magnesium-depleting agents (diuretics, aminoglycosides, amphotericin B, cyclosporine) may increase risk of arrhythmias. Metoclopramide may increase risk of extrapyramidal symptoms (EPS). Acetylcholinesterase inhibitors (central) may increase the risk of antipsychotic-related EPS.

Storage/Stability Droperidol ampuls/vials should be stored at room temperature and protected from light. Solutions diluted in NS or D_5W are stable at room temperature for up to 7 days.

Compatibility Stable in D_5W, LR, NS.

Y-site administration: Compatible: Alatrofloxacin, amifostine, aztreonam, bleomycin, cisatracurium, cisplatin, cladribine, cyclophosphamide, cytarabine, docetaxel, doxorubicin, doxorubicin liposome, etoposide phosphate, famotidine, filgrastim, fluconazole, fludarabine, gatifloxacin, gemcitabine, granisetron, hydrocortisone sodium succinate, idarubicin, linezolid, melphalan, meperidine, metoclopramide, mitomycin, ondansetron, paclitaxel, potassium chloride, propofol, remifentanil, sargramostim, teniposide, thiotepa, vinblastine, vincristine, vinorelbine, vitamin B complex with C. **Incompatible:** Allopurinol, amphotericin B cholesteryl sulfate complex, cefepime, fluorouracil, foscarnet, furosemide, leucovorin, nafcillin, piperacillin/tazobactam. **Variable (consult detailed reference):** Heparin, methotrexate.

Compatibility in syringe: Compatible: Atropine, bleomycin, butorphanol, chlorpromazine, cimetidine, cisplatin, cyclophosphamide, dimenhydrinate, diphenhydramine, doxorubicin, fentanyl, glycopyrrolate, hydroxyzine, meperidine, metoclopramide, midazolam, mitomycin, morphine, nalbuphine, pentazocine, perphenazine, prochlorperazine edisylate, promazine, (Continued)

Droperidol *(Continued)*

promethazine, scopolamine, vinblastine, vincristine. **Incompatible:** Fluorouracil, furosemide, heparin, leucovorin, methotrexate, ondansetron, pentobarbital.

Mechanism of Action Droperidol is a butyrophenone antipsychotic; antiemetic effect is a result of blockade of dopamine stimulation of the chemoreceptor trigger zone. Other effects include alpha-adrenergic blockade, peripheral vascular dilation, and reduction of the pressor effect of epinephrine resulting in hypotension and decreased peripheral vascular resistance; may also reduce pulmonary artery pressure

Pharmacodynamics/Kinetics

Onset of action: Peak effect: Parenteral: ~30 minutes

Duration: Parenteral: 2-4 hours, may extend to 12 hours

Absorption: I.M.: Rapid

Distribution: Crosses blood-brain barrier and placenta

V_d: Children: ~0.25-0.9 L/kg; Adults: ~2 L/kg

Protein binding: Extensive

Metabolism: Hepatic, to *p*-fluorophenylacetic acid, benzimidazolone, *p*-hydroxypiperidine

Half-life elimination: Adults: 2.3 hours

Excretion: Urine (75%, <1% as unchanged drug); feces (22%, 11% to 50% as unchanged drug)

Dosage Titrate carefully to desired effect

Children 2-12 years: Nausea and vomiting: I.M., I.V.: 0.05-0.06 mg/kg (maximum initial dose: 0.1 mg/kg); additional doses may be repeated to achieve effect; administer additional doses with caution.

Adults: Prevention of postoperative nausea and vomiting (PONV): I.M., I.V.: Initial: 0.625-2.5 mg; additional doses of 1.25 mg may be administered to achieve desired effect; administer additional doses with caution. Consensus guidelines recommend 0.625-1.25 mg I.V. administered after surgery (Gan, 2003).

Administration Administer I.M. or I.V.; according to the manufacturer, I.V. push administration should be slow (generally regarded as 2-5 minutes); however, many clinicians administer I.V. doses rapidly (over 30-60 seconds) in an effort to reduce the incidence of EPS. The effect, if any, of rapid administration on QT prolongation is unclear. For I.V. infusion, dilute in 50-100 mL NS or D_5W; ECG monitoring for 2-3 hours after administration is recommended regardless of rate of infusion.

Monitoring Parameters To identify QT prolongation, a 12-lead ECG prior to use is recommended; continued ECG monitoring for 2-3 hours following administration is recommended. Vital signs; lipid profile, fasting blood glucose/Hgb A_{1c}, serum magnesium and potassium; BMI; mental status, abnormal involuntary movement scale (AIMS); observe for dystonias, extrapyramidal side effects, and temperature changes

Special Geriatric Considerations Many elderly patients receive antipsychotic medications for inappropriate nonpsychotic behavior although the use of droperidol is seldom used for this indication. Since elderly frequently have cardiac disease which may result in QT prolongation, evaluation should be made prior to considering use of this agent.

Additional Information Does not possess analgesic effects; has little or no amnesic properties.

Emetic Potential Very low (<10%)

Vesicant No

Dosage Forms Excipient information presented when available (limited, particularly for generics); consult specific product labeling.

Injection, solution: 2.5 mg/mL (1 mL, 2 mL)

References

Cersosimo RJ, Bromer R, Hoffer S, et al, "The Antiemetic Activity of Droperidol Administered by Intramuscular Injection During Cisplatin Chemotherapy: A Pilot Study," *Drug Intell Clin Pharm*, 1985, 19(2):118-21.

Foster PN, Stickle BR, Dale M, et al, "Akathisia After Low-Dose Droperidol," *Br J Anaesth*, 1995, 74:477P.

Gan TJ, Meyer T, Apfel CC, et al, "Consensus Guidelines for Managing Postoperative Nausea and Vomiting," *Anesth Analg*, 2003, 97(1):62-71.

Ghoneim MM and Korttila K, "Pharmacokinetics of Intravenous Anaesthetics: Implications for Clinical Use," *Clin Pharmacokinet*, 1977, 2(5):344-72.

Grunberg SM and Hesketh PJ, "Control of Chemotherapy-Induced Emesis," *N Engl J Med*, 1993, 329(24):1790-6.

Jackson CW, Sheehan AH, and Reddan JG, "Evidence-Based Review of the Black-Box Warning for Droperidol", *AJHP*, 2007, 64(11):1174-86.

Kao LW, Kirk MA, Evers SJ, et al, "Droperidol, QT Prolongation, and Sudden Death: What Is the Evidence," *Ann Emerg Med*, 2003, 41(4):546-58.

Leslie JB and Gan TJ, "Meta-Analysis of the Safety of 5-HT3 Antagonists With Dexamethasone or Droperidol for Prevention of PONV," *Ann Pharacother*, 2006, 40(5):856-72.

Nuttall G, Eckerman K, Jacob K, et al, " Does Low-dose Droperidol Administration Increase the Risk of Drug-induced QT Prolongation and Torsade de Pointes in the General Surgical Population?" *Anesthesiology*, 2007, 107(4):531-6.

Peabody CA, Warner MD, Whiteford HA, et al, "Neuroleptics and the Elderly," *J Am Geriatr Soc*, 1987, 35(3):233-8.

Risse SC and Barnes R, "Pharmacologic Treatment of Agitation Associated With Dementia," *J Am Geriatr Soc*, 1986, 34(5):368-76.

Rosen C, Ratliff AF, Wolfe RW, et al, "The Efficacy of Droperidol in the Prehospital Setting," *Acad Emerg Med*, 1995, 2:446.

Saltz BL, Woerner MG, Kane JM, et al, "Prospective Study of Tardive Dyskinesia Incidence in the Elderly," *JAMA*, 1991, 266(17):2402-6.

Seifert RD, "Therapeutic Drug Monitoring: Psychotropic Drugs," *J Pharm Pract*, 1984, 6:403-16.

Sridhar KS and Donnelly E, "Combination Antiemetics for Cisplatin Chemotherapy," *Cancer*, 1988, 61(8):1508-17.

Tortorice PV and O'Connell MB, "Management of Chemotherapy-Induced Nausea and Vomiting," *Pharmacotherapy*, 1990, 10(2):129-45.

Wilhelm SM, Dehoorne-Smith ML, and Kale-Pradhan PB, "Prevention of Postoperative Nausea and Vomiting," *Ann Pharmacother*, 2007, 41(1):68-78.

Wilson J, Weltz M, Solimando D, et al, "Continuous Infusion Droperidol: Antiemetic Therapy for Cis-Platinum (DDP) Toxicity," *Proc Am Soc Clin Oncol*, 1981, C-351.

Yaster M, Sola JE, Pegoli W Jr, et al, "The Night After Surgery: Postoperative Management of the Pediatric Outpatient - Surgical and Anesthetic Aspects," *Pediatr Clin North Am*, 1994, 41(1):199-220.

Eculizumab (e kue LIZ oo mab)

U.S. Brand Names Soliris™

Generic Available No

Pharmacologic Category Monoclonal Antibody; Monoclonal Antibody, Complement Inhibitor

Use Treatment of paroxysmal nocturnal hemoglobinuria (PNH) to reduce hemolysis

Restrictions Patients and providers must enroll with Soliris™ OneSource™ (1-888-765-4747) prior to treatment initiation.

An FDA-approved medication guide is available at http://www.fda.gov/cder/Offices/ODS/medication_guides.htm; distribute to each patient to whom this medication is dispensed.

Pregnancy Risk Factor C

Lactation Excretion in breast milk unknown/use caution

Labeled Contraindications Hypersensitivity to eculizumab or any component of the formulation; unresolved serious *Neisseria meningitidis* infection; use in patients who have not received *Neisseria meningitidis* vaccination at least 2 weeks prior to first treatment

Warnings/Precautions [U.S. Boxed Warning]: The risk for meningococcal *(Neisseria meningitides)* infections (septicemia and/or meningitis) is increased with PNH and may be further increased in patients receiving eculizumab; vaccinate with meningococcal vaccine at least 2 weeks prior to initiation of treatment; revaccinate according to current guidelines. Quadravalent, conjugated meningococcal vaccines are recommended. Meningococcal infections developed in some patients despite vaccination. Monitor for early signs of meningococcal infections; evaluate and treat promptly. Consider withholding eculizumab during the treatment of serious meningococcal infections. In addition to meningitis, the risk of other infections, especially with encapsulated bacteria (eg, *Streptococcus pneumoniae, H. influenzae*) is increased with eculizumab treatment. Use caution in patients with concurrent systemic infection. Patients should be brought up to date with all immunizations before initiating therapy.

Infusion reactions, including anaphylaxis or hypersensitivity, may occur; interrupt infusion for severe reaction. Continue monitoring for 1 hour after completion of infusion. Patients with PNH who discontinue treatment may be at increased risk for serious hemolysis; monitor closely for at least 8 weeks after treatment discontinuation. In clinical trials, anticoagulant therapy was continued in patients who were receiving these agents prior to initiation of eculizumab. The effect of anticoagulant therapy withdrawal is unknown. Safety and efficacy have not been established in children.

Adverse Reactions

>10%:

Central nervous system: Headache (2% to 44%), fatigue (12%)

Gastrointestinal: Nausea (16%)

Neuromuscular & skeletal: Back pain (19%)

Respiratory: Nasopharyngitis (23%), cough (12%)

1% to 10%:

Central nervous system: Fever (2%)

Gastrointestinal: Constipation (7%)

Hematologic: Anemia (2%)

Neuromuscular & skeletal: Limb pain (7%), myalgia (7%)

Respiratory: Respiratory tract infection (7%), sinusitis (7%)

Miscellaneous: Herpes infections (7%), flu-like syndrome (5%), viral infection (2%), meningococcal infection (1%)

<1%, postmarketing, and/or case reports: Chills, dizziness, infusion reaction, vomiting

Overdosage/Toxicology Treatment is symptom-directed and supportive.

Storage/Stability Prior to dilution, store vials at 2°C to 8°C (36°F to 46°F). Protect from light; do not freeze; do not shake. Following dilution, store at room temperature or refrigerate; protect from light; use within 24 hours.

Reconstitution Dilute with an equal volume of D_5W, sodium chloride 0.9% sodium chloride 0.45%, or Ringer's injection to a final concentration of 5 mg/mL. (eg, 600 mg in a total volume of 120 mL or 900 mg in a total volume of 180 mL). Gently invert bag to mix.

Compatibility Compatible with D_5W, sodium chloride 0.9%, sodium chloride 0.45%, Ringer's injection

Mechanism of Action Eculizumab is a humanized monoclonal IgG antibody that binds to complement protein C5, preventing cleavage into C5a and C5b. Blocking the formation of C5b inhibits the subsequent formation of terminal complex C5b-9 or membrane attack complex (MAC). Terminal complement-mediated intravascular hemolysis is a key clinical feature of paroxysmal nocturnal hemoglobinuria. Blocking the formation of MAC results in stabilization of hemoglobin and a reduction in the need for RBC transfusions.

Pharmacodynamics/Kinetics

Onset of action: PNH: Reduced hemolysis: ≤1 week

Distribution: 7.7 L

Half-life elimination: ~11 days (range: ~8-15 days)

Dosage Note: Patients must receive meningococcal vaccine at least 2 weeks prior to treatment initiation; revaccinate according to current guidelines.

I.V.: Adults: PNH: 600 mg once weekly (±2 days) for 4 weeks, followed by 900 mg 1 week (±2 days) later; then maintenance: 900 mg every 2 weeks (±2 days) thereafter

Treatment should be administered at the recommended time interval, however, the administration day may be varied by ±2 days if serum LDH levels suggest increased hemolysis before the end of the dosing interval.

Dosage adjustment in renal impairment: Not studied in renal dysfunction

Dosage adjustment in hepatic impairment: Not studied in hepatic dysfunction

Administration I.V.: Allow to warm to room temperature prior to administration. Infuse over 35 minutes. Decrease infusion rate or discontinue for infusion reactions; do not exceed a maximum 2-hour duration of infusion. Monitor for at least 1 hour following completion of infusion.

Monitoring Parameters Signs and symptoms of infusion reaction (during infusion and for 1 hour after infusion complete); CBC with differential, lactic dehydrogenase (LDH), AST, urinalysis

After discontinuation: Signs and symptoms of intravascular hemolysis, serum LDH (monitor for at least 8 weeks after discontinuation)

Emetic Potential Very low (<10%)

Dosage Forms Excipient information presented when available (limited, particularly for generics); consult specific product labeling.

Injection, solution [preservative free]:

Soliris™: 10 mg/ml (30 mL) [contains polysorbate 80]

References

Centers for Disease Control and Prevention, "Prevention and Control of Meningococcal Disease Recommendations of the Advisory Committee on Immunization Practices (ACIP)," *MMWR Recomm Rep*, 2005, 54(RR-7):1-21. Available at http://www.cdc.gov/mmwr/pdf/rr/rr5407.pdf (last accessed March 19, 2007).

Hill A, Hillmen P, Richards SJ, et al, "Sustained Response and Long-Term Safety of Eculizumab in Paroxysmal Nocturnal Hemoglobinuria," *Blood*, 2005, 106(7):2559-65.

(Continued)

Eculizumab *(Continued)*

Hillmen P, Hall C, Marsh JC, et al, "Effect of Eculizumab on Hemolysis and Transfusion Requirements in Patients With Paroxysmal Nocturnal Hemoglobinuria," *N Engl J Med*, 2004, 350(6):552-9.

Hillmen P, Young NS, Schubert J, et al, "The Complement Inhibitor Eculizumab in Paroxysmal Nocturnal Hemoglobinuria," *N Engl J Med*, 2006, 355(12):1233-43.

Enoxaparin (ee noks a PA rin)

Medication Safety Issues

Sound-alike/look-alike issues:

Lovenox® may be confused with Lotronex®, Protonix®

High alert medication: The Institute for Safe Medication Practices (ISMP) includes this medication among its list of drugs which have a heightened risk of causing significant patient harm when used in error.

International issues:

Lovenox® may be confused with Lotanax® which is a brand name for terfenadine in the Czech Republic

U.S. Brand Names Lovenox®

Index Terms Enoxaparin Sodium

Generic Available No

Canadian Brand Names Enoxaparin Injection; Lovenox®; Lovenox® HP

Pharmacologic Category Low Molecular Weight Heparin

Use

Acute coronary syndromes: Unstable angina (UA), non-ST-segment elevation (NSTEMI), and ST-segment elevation myocardial infarction (STEMI)

DVT prophylaxis: Following hip or knee replacement surgery, abdominal surgery, or in medical patients with severely-restricted mobility during acute illness in patients at risk of thromboembolic complications

DVT treatment (acute): Inpatient treatment (patients with and without pulmonary embolism) and outpatient treatment (patients without pulmonary embolism)

Note: High-risk patients include those with one or more of the following risk factors: >40 years of age, obesity, general anesthesia lasting >30 minutes, malignancy, history of deep vein thrombosis or pulmonary embolism

Unlabeled/Investigational Use Prophylaxis and treatment of thromboembolism in children

Pregnancy Risk Factor B

Lactation Excretion in breast milk unknown/use caution

Labeled Contraindications Hypersensitivity to enoxaparin, heparin, or any component of the formulation; thrombocytopenia associated with a positive *in vitro* test for antiplatelet antibodies in the presence of enoxaparin; hypersensitivity to pork products; active major bleeding; not for I.M. use

Warnings/Precautions

[U.S. Boxed Warning]: Patients with recent or anticipated neuraxial anesthesia (epidural or spinal anesthesia) are at risk of spinal or epidural hematoma and subsequent paralysis. Consider risk versus benefit prior to neuraxial anesthesia; risk is increased by concomitant agents which may alter hemostasis, as well as traumatic or repeated epidural or spinal puncture. Patient should be observed closely for bleeding if enoxaparin is administered during or immediately following diagnostic lumbar puncture, epidural anesthesia, or spinal anesthesia.

Do not administer intramuscularly. Not recommended for thromboprophylaxis in patients with prosthetic heart valves (especially pregnant women). Not to be used interchangeably (unit for unit) with heparin or any other low molecular weight heparins. Use caution in patients with history of heparin-induced thrombocytopenia. Monitor patient closely for signs or symptoms of bleeding. Certain patients are at increased risk of bleeding. Risk factors include bacterial endocarditis; congenital or acquired bleeding disorders; active ulcerative or angiodysplastic GI diseases; severe uncontrolled hypertension; hemorrhagic stroke; use shortly after brain, spinal, or ophthalmology surgery; patients treated concomitantly with platelet inhibitors; recent GI bleeding; thrombocytopenia or platelet defects; severe liver disease; hypertensive or diabetic retinopathy; or in patients undergoing invasive procedures. Monitor platelet count closely. Rare cases of thrombocytopenia have occurred. Manufacturer recommends discontinuation of therapy if platelets are <100,000/mm³. Rare cases of thrombocytopenia with thrombosis have occurred. Use caution in patients with congenital or drug-induced thrombocytopenia or platelet defects. Risk of bleeding may be increased in women <45 kg and in men <57 kg. Use caution in patients with renal failure; dosage adjustment needed if Cl_{cr} <30 mL/minute. Safety and efficacy in pediatric patients have not been established. Use with caution in the elderly (delayed elimination may occur); dosage alteration/adjustment may be required (eg, omission of I.V. bolus in acute STEMI in patients ≥75 years of age). Heparin can cause hyperkalemia by affecting aldosterone. Similar reactions could occur with LMWHs. Monitor for hyperkalemia. Multiple-dose vials contain benzyl alcohol (use caution in pregnant women). In neonates, large amounts of benzyl alcohol (>100 mg/kg/day) have been associated with fatal toxicity (gasping syndrome).

Adverse Reactions As with all anticoagulants, bleeding is the major adverse effect of enoxaparin. Hemorrhage may occur at virtually any site. Risk is dependent on multiple variables. At the recommended doses, single injections of enoxaparin do not significantly influence platelet aggregation or affect global clotting time (ie, PT or aPTT).

1% to 10%:

Central nervous system: Fever (5% to 8%), confusion, pain

Dermatologic: Erythema, bruising

Gastrointestinal: Nausea (3%), diarrhea

Hematologic: Hemorrhage (major, <1% to 4%; includes cases of intracranial, retroperitoneal, or intraocular hemorrhage; incidence varies with indication/population), thrombocytopenia (moderate 1%; severe 0.1% - see note below), hypochromic anemia (2%)

Hepatic: ALT/AST increased

(Continued)

377

Enoxaparin *(Continued)*

Local: Injection site hematoma (9%), local reactions (irritation, pain, ecchymosis, erythema)

<1% and/or postmarketing case reports (limited to important or life-threatening): Allergic reaction, anaphylactoid reaction, eczematous plaques, hematoma (see note on "Spinal or epidural hematomas" below), hyperlipidemia, hypertriglyceridemia, intracranial hemorrhage (up to 0.8%), erythematous pruritic patches, pruritus, purpura, retroperitoneal bleeding, skin necrosis, thrombocytosis, urticaria, vasculitis (cutaneous hypersensitive), vesicobullous rash

Notes:

Spinal or epidural hematomas: Can occur following neuraxial anesthesia or spinal puncture, resulting in paralysis. Risk is increased in patients with indwelling epidural catheters or concomitant use of other drugs affecting hemostasis. Prosthetic valve thrombosis, including fatal cases, has been reported in pregnant women receiving enoxaparin as thromboprophylaxis.

Thrombocytopenia with thrombosis: Cases of heparin-induced thrombocytopenia (some complicated by organ infarction, limb ischemia, or death) have been reported.

Overdosage/Toxicology Symptoms of overdose include hemorrhage. Protamine sulfate has been used to reverse effects (protamine 1 mg neutralizes enoxaparin 1 mg). Monitor aPTT 2-4 hours after first infusion; consider readministration of protamine (50% of original dose). **Note:** Anti-Xa activity is never completely neutralized (maximum of 60% to 75%). Avoid overdose of protamine.

Drug Interactions

Increased Effect/Toxicity: Risk of bleeding with enoxaparin may be increased with thrombolytic agents, oral anticoagulants (warfarin), drugs which affect platelet function (eg, aspirin, NSAIDs, dipyridamole, ticlopidine, clopidogrel, and IIb/IIIa antagonists). Although the risk of bleeding may be increased during concurrent therapy with warfarin, enoxaparin is commonly continued during the initiation of warfarin therapy to assure anticoagulation and to protect against possible transient hypercoagulability. Some cephalosporins and penicillins may block platelet aggregation, theoretically increasing the risk of bleeding.

Ethanol/Nutrition/Herb Interactions Herb/Nutraceutical: Avoid cat's claw, dong quai, evening primrose, feverfew, garlic, ginger, ginkgo, red clover, horse chestnut, green tea, ginseng (all have additional antiplatelet activity).

Storage/Stability Store at 15°C to 25°C (59°F to 77°F); do not freeze.

Compatibility Stable in NS; do not mix with other injections or infusions.

Mechanism of Action Standard heparin consists of components with molecular weights ranging from 4000-30,000 daltons with a mean of 16,000 daltons. Heparin acts as an anticoagulant by enhancing the inhibition rate of clotting proteases by antithrombin III impairing normal hemostasis and inhibition of factor Xa. Low molecular weight heparins have a small effect on the activated partial thromboplastin time and strongly inhibit factor Xa. Enoxaparin is derived from porcine heparin that undergoes benzylation followed by alkaline depolymerization. The average molecular weight of enoxaparin is 4500 daltons which is distributed as (≤20%) 2000 daltons (≥68%) 2000-8000 daltons, and (≤15%) >8000 daltons. Enoxaparin has a higher ratio of antifactor Xa to antifactor IIa activity than unfractionated heparin.

Pharmacodynamics/Kinetics

Onset of action: Peak effect: SubQ: Antifactor Xa and antithrombin (antifactor IIa): 3-5 hours

Duration: 40 mg dose: Antifactor Xa activity: ~12 hours

Metabolism: Hepatic, to lower molecular weight fragments (little activity)

Protein binding: Does not bind to heparin binding proteins

Half-life elimination, plasma: 2-4 times longer than standard heparin, independent of dose; based on anti-Xa activity: 4.5-7 hours

Excretion: Urine (40% of dose; 10% as active fragments)

Dosage SubQ:

Infants and Children (unlabeled use):

Infants <2 months: Initial:

Prophylaxis: 0.75 mg/kg every 12 hours

Treatment: 1.5 mg/kg every 12 hours

Infants >2 months and Children ≤18 years: Initial:

Prophylaxis: 0.5 mg/kg every 12 hours

Treatment: 1 mg/kg every 12 hours

Maintenance: See **Dosage Titration** table:

Enoxaparin Pediatric Dosage Titration

Antifactor Xa	Dose Titration	Time to Repeat Antifactor Xa Level
<0.35 units/mL	Increase dose by 25%	4 h after next dose
0.35-0.49 units/mL	Increase dose by 10%	4 h after next dose
0.5-1 unit/mL	Keep same dosage	Next day, then 1 wk later, then monthly (4 h after dose)
1.1-1.5 units/mL	Decrease dose by 20%	Before next dose
1.6-2 units/mL	Hold dose for 3 h and decrease dose by 30%	Before next dose, then 4 h after next dose
>2 units/mL	Hold all doses until antifactor Xa is 0.5 units/mL, then decrease dose by 40%	Before next dose and every 12 h until antifactor Xa <0.5 units/mL

Modified from Monagle P, Michelson AD, Bovill E, et al, "Antithrombotic Therapy in Children," *Chest*, 2001, 119:344S-70S.

Adults:

DVT prophylaxis:

Hip replacement surgery:

Twice-daily dosing: 30 mg twice daily, with initial dose within 12-24 hours after surgery, and every 12 hours until risk of DVT has diminished or the patient is adequately anticoagulated on warfarin.

Once-daily dosing: 40 mg once daily, with initial dose within 9-15 hours before surgery, and daily until risk of DVT has diminished or the patient is adequately anticoagulated on warfarin.

Knee replacement surgery: 30 mg twice daily, with initial dose within 12-24 hours after surgery, and every 12 hours until risk of DVT has diminished (usually 7-10 days).

Abdominal surgery: 40 mg once daily, with initial dose given 2 hours prior to surgery; continue until risk of DVT has diminished (usual 7-10 days).

Medical patients with severely-restricted mobility during acute illness: 40 mg once daily; continue until risk of DVT has diminished

DVT treatment (acute): **Note:** Start warfarin within 72 hours and continue enoxaparin until INR is between 2.0 and 3.0 (usually 7 days).

Inpatient treatment (with or without pulmonary embolism): 1 mg/kg/dose every 12 hours or 1.5 mg/kg once daily.

Outpatient treatment (without pulmonary embolism): 1 mg/kg/dose every 12 hours.

(Continued)

Enoxaparin *(Continued)*

ST-segment elevation myocardial infarction (STEMI):

Patients <75 years of age: Initial: 30 mg I.V. single bolus plus 1 mg/kg (maximum 100 mg for the first 2 doses only) SubQ every 12 hours. The first SubQ dose should be administered with the I.V. bolus. Maintenance: After first 2 doses, administer 1 mg/kg SubQ every 12 hours.

Patients ≥75 years of age: Initial: SubQ: 0.75 mg/kg every 12 hours (**Note:** No I.V. bolus is administered in this population); a maximum dose of 75 mg is recommended for the first 2 doses. Maintenance: After first 2 doses, administer 0.75 mg/kg SubQ every 12 hours

Additional notes on STEMI treatment: Therapy was continued for 8 days or until hospital discharge; optimal duration not defined. Unless contraindicated, all patients received aspirin (75-325 mg daily) in clinical trials. In patients with STEMI receiving thrombolytics, initiate enoxaparin dosing between 15 minutes before and 30 minutes after fibrinolytic therapy. In patients undergoing PCI, if balloon inflation occurs <8 hours after the last SubQ enoxaparin dose, no additional dosing is needed. If balloon inflation occurs ≥8 hours after last SubQ enoxaparin dose, a single I.V. dose of 0.3 mg/kg should be administered.

Unstable angina or non-ST-segment myocardial infarction (NSTEMI): 1 mg/kg every 12 hours in conjunction with oral aspirin therapy (100-325 mg once daily); continue until clinical stabilization (a minimum of at least 2 days)

Elderly: Refer to adult dosing. Increased incidence of bleeding with doses of 1.5 mg/kg/day or 1 mg/kg every 12 hours; injection-associated bleeding and serious adverse reactions are also increased in the elderly. Careful attention should be paid to elderly patients, particularly those <45 kg. **Note:** Dosage alteration/adjustment may be required.

Dosing adjustment in renal impairment: SubQ:

Cl_{cr} ≥30 mL/minute: No specific adjustment recommended (per manufacturer); monitor closely for bleeding

Cl_{cr} <30 mL/minute:

DVT prophylaxis in abdominal surgery, hip replacement, knee replacement, or in medical patients during acute illness: 30 mg once daily

DVT treatment (inpatient or outpatient treatment in conjunction with warfarin): 1 mg/kg once daily

STEMI: Initial: I.V.: 30 mg as a single dose in patients <75 years of age; omit I.V. bolus in patients ≥75 years of age. The first dose of the SubQ maintenance regimen is administered at the same time as the I.V. bolus. Maintenance: SubQ: 1 mg/kg every 24 hours in all patients

Unstable angina, NSTEMI: SubQ: 1 mg/kg once daily

Dialysis: Enoxaparin has not been FDA approved for use in dialysis patients. It's elimination is primarily via the renal route. Serious bleeding complications have been reported with use in patients who are dialysis dependent or have severe renal failure. LMWH administration at fixed doses without monitoring has greater unpredictable anticoagulant effects in patients with chronic kidney disease. If used, dosages should be reduced and anti-Xa activity frequently monitored, as accumulation may occur with repeated doses. Many clinicians would not use enoxaparin in this population especially without timely anti-Xa activity assay results.

Hemodialysis: Supplemental dose is not necessary.

Peritoneal dialysis: Significant drug removal is unlikely based on physiochemical characteristics.

Administration Should be administered by deep SubQ injection to the left or right anterolateral and left or right posterolateral abdominal wall. A single dose may be administered I.V. as part of treatment for ST-segment elevation myocardial infarction (STEMI) to patients <75 years of age; no I.V. bolus is given to patients ≥75 years of age. To avoid loss of drug from the 30 mg and 40 mg syringes, do not expel the air bubble from the syringe prior to injection. In order to minimize bruising, do not rub injection site. An automatic injector (Lovenox EasyInjector™) is available with the 30 mg and 40 mg syringes to aid the patient with self-injections. **Note:** Enoxaparin is available in 100 mg/mL and 150 mg/mL concentrations.

Monitoring Parameters Platelets, occult blood, and anti-Xa activity, if available; the monitoring of PT and/or aPTT is not necessary

Special Geriatric Considerations No specific dosage adjustment recommendations for most indications, however, total clearance is lower and elimination is delayed in patients with renal failure. Adjustment may be necessary if renal impairment is present. In the treatment of STEMI, a lower dosage (0.75 mg/kg every 12 hours) and omission of the I.V. bolus, are recommended in patients ≥75 years of age.

Over 2800 patients, ≥65 years of age, have received enoxaparin sodium in pivotal clinical trials. The efficacy of enoxaparin injection in elderly (≥65 years) was similar to that seen in younger patients (<65 years). The incidence of bleeding complications was similar between elderly and younger patients when 30 mg every 12 hours or 40 mg once daily doses of enoxaparin injection was administered at doses of 1.5 mg/kg/day or 1 mg/kg every 12 hours. The risk of enoxaparin injection associated bleeding increased with age. Serious adverse events increased with age for patients receiving enoxaparin injections. Other clinical experience (including postmarketing surveillance and literature reports) has not revealed additional differences in the safety of enoxaparin injection between elderly and younger patients. Careful attention to dosing intervals and concomitant medications (especially antiplatelet medications) is advised. Monitoring of elderly patients with low body weight (<45 kg) and those predisposed to decreased renal function should be considered.

Dosage Forms Excipient information presented when available (limited, particularly for generics); consult specific product labeling.

Injection, solution, as sodium [graduated prefilled syringe; preservative free]:
Lovenox®: 60 mg/0.6 mL (0.6 mL); 80 mg/0.8 mL (0.8 mL); 100 mg/mL (1 mL); 120 mg/0.8 mL (0.8 mL); 150 mg/mL (1 mL)

Injection, solution, as sodium [multidose vial]:
Lovenox®: 100 mg/mL (3 mL) [contains benzyl alcohol]

Injection, solution, as sodium [prefilled syringe; preservative free]:
Lovenox®: 30 mg/0.3 mL (0.3 mL); 40 mg/0.4 mL (0.4 mL)

References

Antman EM, Anbe SC, Alpert JS, et al, "ACC/AHA Guidelines for the Management of Patients With ST-Elevation Myocardial Infarction - Executive Summary: A Report of the American College of Cardiology/American Heart Association Task Force on Practice Guidelines (Writing Committee to Revise the 1999 Guidelines for the Management of Patients With Acute Myocardial Infarction)," *Circulation*, 2004, 110(5):588-636. Available at: http://www.circulationaha.org/cgi/content/full/110/5/588. Last accessed October 26, 2004.

Antman EM, Cohen M, Radley D, et al, "Assessment of the Treatment Effect of Enoxaparin for Unstable Angina/Non-Q-Wave Myocardial Infarction. TIMI 11B-ESSENCE Meta-analysis," *Circulation*, 1999, 100(15):1602-8.

Antman EM, McCabe CH, Gurfinkel EP, et al, "Enoxaparin Prevents Death and Cardiac Ischemic Events in Unstable Angina/Non-Q-Wave Myocardial Infarction. Results of the Thrombolysis in Myocardial Infarction (TIMI) 11B Trial," *Circulation*, 1999, 100(15):1593-601.

Antman EM, Morrow DA, McCabe CH, et al, "Enoxaparin Versus Unfractionated Heparin With Fibrinolysis for ST-Elevation Myocardial Infarction," *N Engl J Med*, 2006, 354(14):1477-88.

(Continued)

Enoxaparin *(Continued)*

Braunwald E, Antman EM, Beasley JW, et al, "ACC/AHA 2002 Guideline Update for the Management of Patients With Unstable Angina and Non-ST-Segment Elevation Myocardial Infarction - Summary Article: A Report of the American College of Cardiology/American Heart Association Task Force on Practice Guidelines (Committee on the Management of Patients With Unstable Angina)," *J Am Coll Cardiol*, 2002, 40(7):1366-74. Available at: http://www.acc.org/clinical/guidelines/unstable/incorporated/index.htm. Accessed May 20, 2003.

Cohen M, Bigonzi F, Le Louer V, et al, "One Year Follow-Up of the ESSENCE Trial (Enoxaparin Versus Heparin in Unstable Angina and Non-Q Wave Myocardial Infarction)," *J Am Coll Cardiol*, 1998, 31:79A.

Cohen M, Demers C, Gurfinkel EP, et al, "A Comparison of Low-Molecular-Weight Heparin With Unfractionated Heparin for Unstable Coronary Artery Disease. Efficacy and Safety of Subcutaneous Enoxaparin in Non-Q-Wave Coronary Events Study Group," *N Engl J Med*, 1997, 337(7):447-52.

Farooq V, Hegarty J, Chandrasekar T, et al, "Serious Adverse Incidents With the Usage of Low Molecular Weight Heparins in Patients With Chronic Kidney Disease," *Am J Kidney Dis*, 2004, 43(3):531-7.

Ferguson JJ, Califf RM, Antman EM, et al, "Enoxaparin vs. Unfractionated Heparin in High-Risk Patients With Non-ST-segment Elevation Acute Coronary Syndromes Managed With an Intended Early Invasive Strategy: Primary Results of the SYNERGY Randomized Trial," *JAMA*, 2004, 292(1):45-54.

Fox KA, "Low Molecular Weight Heparin (Enoxaparin) in the Management of Unstable Angina: The ESSENCE Study. Efficacy and Safety of Subcutaneous Enoxaparin in Non-Q wave Coronary Events," *Heart*, 1999, 82(Suppl 1):112-4.

Gerlach AT, Pickworth KK, Seth SK, et al, "Enoxaparin and Bleeding Complications: A Review in Patients With and Without Renal Insufficiency," *Pharmacotherapy*, 2000, 20(7):771-5.

Hirsh J, Dalen J, and Guyatt G, et al, "The Sixth (2000) ACCP Guidelines for Antithrombotic Therapy for Prevention and Treatment of Thrombosis. American College of Chest Physicians," *Chest*, 2001, 119(1 Suppl):346-7.

Monagle P, Michelson AD, Bovill E, et al, "Antithrombotic Therapy in Children," *Chest*, 2001, 119:344S-70S.

Montalescot G, Philippe F, Ankri A, et al, "Early Increase of von Willebrand Factor Predicts Adverse Outcome in Unstable Coronary Artery Disease: Beneficial Effects of Enoxaparin. French Investigators of the ESSENCE Trial," *Circulation*, 1998, 98(4):294-9.

Nagge J, Crowther M, and Hirsh J, "Is Impaired Renal Function a Contraindication to the Use of Low-Molecular Weight Heparin?" *Arch Intern Med*, 2002, 162(22):2605-9.

Polkinghorne KR, McMahon LP, and Becker GJ, "Pharmacokinetic Studies of Dalteparin (Fragmin), Enoxaparin (Clexane), and Danaparoid Sodium (Orgaran) in Stable Chronic Hemodialysis Patients," *Am J Kidney Dis*, 2002, 40(5):990-5.

Reach L, Debure A, de Groc F, et al, "Anticoagulation With Enoxaparin 0.5 mg/kg in 630 Dialysis Sessions," *Haemostasis*, 1994, 24(Suppl 1):280 [Abstract 281]

Simonneau G, Charbonnier B, Decousus H, et al, "Subcutaneous Low-Molecular-Weight Heparin Compared With Continuous Intravenous Unfractionated Heparin in the Treatment of Proximal Deep Vein Thrombosis," *Arch Intern Med*, 1993, 153(13):1541-6.

Von Visger J and Magee C, "Low Molecular Weight Heparins in Renal Failure," *J Nephrol*, 2003, 16(6):914-6.

Wallentin L, Goldstein P, Armstrong PW, et al, "Efficacy amd Safety of Tenecteplase in Combination With the Low-Molecular-Weight Heparin Enoxaparin or Unfractionated Heparin in the Prehospital Setting: The Assessment of the Safety and Efficacy of a New Thrombolytic Regimen (ASSENT)-3 PLUS Randomized Trial in Acute Myocardial Infarction," *Circulation*, 2003, 108(2): 135-42.

Wong GC, Giugliano RP, and Antman EM, "Use of Low-Molecular-Weight Heparins in the Management of Acute Coronary Artery Syndromes and Percutaneous Coronary Intervention," *JAMA*, 2003, 289:331-42.

Zed PJ, Tisdale JE, and Borzak S, "Low-Molecular-Weight Heparins in the Management of Acute Coronary Syndromes," *Arch Intern Med*, 1999, 159(16):1849-57.

- **Enoxaparin Injection (Can)** see Enoxaparin *on page 376*
- **Enoxaparin Sodium** see Enoxaparin *on page 376*
- **Entertainer's Secret®** [OTC] see Saliva Substitute *on page 960*
- **Epidermal Thymocyte Activating Factor** see Aldesleukin *on page 29*
- **Epipodophyllotoxin** see Etoposide *on page 402*

Epirubicin (ep i ROO bi sin)

Medication Safety Issues

Sound-alike/look-alike issues:

Epirubicin may be confused with DOXOrubicin, DAUNOrubicin, idarubicin

Ellence® may be confused with Elase®

High alert medication: The Institute for Safe Medication Practices (ISMP) includes this medication among its list of drugs which have a heightened risk of causing significant patient harm when used in error.

Related Information

Management of Drug Extravasations *on page 1301*

Safe Handling of Hazardous Drugs *on page 1382*

U.S. Brand Names Ellence®

Index Terms Epirubicin Hydrochloride; NSC-256942; Pidorubicin; Pidorubicin Hydrochloride

Generic Available Yes

Canadian Brand Names Ellence®; Pharmorubicin®

Pharmacologic Category Antineoplastic Agent, Anthracycline

Use Adjuvant therapy for primary breast cancer

Pregnancy Risk Factor D

Lactation Excretion in breast milk unknown/contraindicated

Labeled Contraindications Hypersensitivity to epirubicin or any component of the formulation, other anthracyclines, or anthracenediones; previous anthracycline treatment up to maximum cumulative dose; severe myocardial insufficiency, severe arrhythmias; recent myocardial infarction; severe hepatic dysfunction; baseline neutrophil count 1500 cells/mm^3; pregnancy

Warnings/Precautions Hazardous agent - use appropriate precautions for handling and disposal.

[U.S. Boxed Warning]: Potential cardiotoxicity, particularly in patients who have received prior anthracyclines, prior or concomitant radiotherapy to the mediastinal/pericardial area, or who have pre-existing cardiac disease, may occur. Acute toxicity (primarily arrhythmias) and delayed toxicity (CHF) have been described. Delayed toxicity usually develops late in the course of therapy or within 2-3 months after completion, however, events with an onset of several months to years after termination of treatment have been described. The risk of delayed cardiotoxicity increases more steeply with cumulative doses >900 mg/m^2, and this dose should be exceeded only with extreme caution. (The risk of CHF is ~0.9% at a cumulative dose of 550 mg/m^2, ~1.6% at a cumulative dose of 700 mg/m^2, and ~3.3% at a cumulative dose of 900 mg/m^2.) Toxicity may be additive with other anthracyclines or anthracenediones, and may be increased in pediatric patients. Regular monitoring of LVEF and discontinuation at the first sign of impairment is recommended especially in patients with cardiac risk factors or impaired cardiac function.

[U.S. Boxed Warning]: May cause severe myelosuppression; neutropenia is the dose-limiting toxicity; severe thrombocytopenia or anemia may occur. Thrombophlebitis and thromboembolic phenomena (including pulmonary embolism) have occurred.

[U.S. Boxed Warning]: Reduce dosage and use with caution in mild-to-moderate hepatic impairment or in severe renal dysfunction (serum creatinine >5 mg/dL). May cause tumor lysis syndrome. Radiation recall has been reported; epirubicin may have radiosensitizing activity. **[U.S. Boxed Warnings]: Treatment with anthracyclines may increase the risk of secondary leukemias. For I.V. administration only, severe local**

(Continued)

Epirubicin *(Continued)*

tissue damage and necrosis will result if extravasation occurs. Women ≥70 years of age should be especially monitored for toxicity; women of childbearing age should be advised to avoid becoming pregnant. **[U.S. Boxed Warning]: Should be administered under the supervision of an experienced cancer chemotherapy physician.** Safety and efficacy in children have not been established.

Adverse Reactions Percentages reported as part of combination chemotherapy regimens.

>10%:

Central nervous system: Lethargy (1% to 46%)

Dermatologic: Alopecia (69% to 96%)

Endocrine & metabolic: Amenorrhea (69% to 72%), hot flashes (5% to 39%)

Gastrointestinal: Nausea/vomiting (83% to 92%), mucositis (9% to 59%), diarrhea (7% to 25%)

Hematologic: Leukopenia (50% to 80%; grades 3/4: 2% to 59%), neutropenia (54% to 80%; grades 3/4: 11% to 67%; nadir: 10-14 days; recovery: 21 days), anemia (13% to 72%; grades 3/4: 6%), thrombocytopenia (5% to 49%; grades 3/4: 5%)

Local: Injection site reactions (3% to 20%)

Ocular: Conjunctivitis (1% to 15%)

Miscellaneous: Infection (15% to 21%)

1% to 10%:

Cardiovascular: CHF (0.4% to 1.5%), decreased LVEF (asymptomatic) (1% to 2%); recommended maximum cumulative dose: 900 mg/m^2

Central nervous system: Fever (1% to 5%)

Dermatologic: Rash (1% to 9%), skin changes (1% to 5%)

Gastrointestinal: Anorexia (2% to 3%)

Hematologic: Neutropenic fever (grades 3/4: 6%)

<1%, postmarketing, case reports, and/or frequency not defined: Acute lymphoid leukemia; acute myelogenous leukemia (0.3% at 3 years, 0.5% at 5 years, 0.6% at 8 years); anaphylaxis, atrioventricular block, bradycardia, bundle-branch block, cardiomyopathy, ECG abnormalities, hypersensitivity, myelodysplastic syndrome, photosensitivity, premature menopause, premature ventricular contractions, pulmonary embolism, radiation recall, sinus tachycardia, skin and nail hyperpigmentation, ST-T wave changes (nonspecific), tachyarrhythmias, thromboembolism, thrombophlebitis, transaminases increased, urticaria, ventricular tachycardia

Overdosage/Toxicology Symptoms of overdose are generally extensions of known cytotoxic effects, including myelosuppression, mucositis, gastrointestinal bleeding, lactic acidosis, multiple organ failure, and death. Treatment is symptom-directed and supportive; consider growth factor support and antimicrobial coverage. Patients should be followed long-term for delayed-onset CHF.

Drug Interactions

Increased Effect/Toxicity: Cimetidine may increase the levels/effects of epirubicin. Bevacizumab and trastuzumab may enhance the cardiotoxic effects of epirubicin.

Ethanol/Nutrition/Herb Interactions

Ethanol: Avoid ethanol (due to GI irritation).

Herb/Nutraceutical: Avoid black cohosh, dong quai in estrogen-dependent tumors.

Storage/Stability Store intact vials of solution under refrigeration at 2°C to 8°C (36°F to 46°F). Store intact vials of lyophilized powder at room temperature 15°C to 30°C (59°F to 86°F). Protect from light. Reconstituted solutions and solutions for infusion are stable for 24 hours when stored at 2°C to 8°C (36°F to 46°F).

Reconstitution Reconstitute lyophilized powder with SWFI to a final concentration of 2 mg/mL. May administer undiluted for IVP or dilute in 50-250 mL NS or D_5W for infusion.

Compatibility Stable in D_5W, LR, NS; **incompatible** with heparin, fluorouracil, or any solution of alkaline pH.

    Compatibility in syringe: Compatible: Ifosfamide. **Incompatible:** Fluorouracil, heparin, ifosfamide with mesna, any solution of alkaline pH.

Mechanism of Action Epirubicin is an anthracycline antibiotic; known to inhibit DNA and RNA synthesis by steric obstruction after intercalating between DNA base pairs; active throughout entire cell cycle. Intercalation triggers DNA cleavage by topoisomerase II, resulting in cytocidal activity. Also inhibits DNA helicase, and generates cytotoxic free radicals.

Pharmacodynamics/Kinetics

Distribution: V_{ss}: 21-27 L/kg

Protein binding: 77% to albumin

Metabolism: Extensively via hepatic and extrahepatic (including RBCs) routes

Half-life elimination: Triphasic; Mean terminal: 33 hours

Excretion: Feces (34% to 35%); urine (20% to 27%)

Dosage Adults: I.V.: 100-120 mg/m² once every 3-4 weeks **or** 50-60 mg/m² days 1 and 8 every 3-4 weeks

Breast cancer:

    CEF-120: 60 mg/m² on days 1 and 8 every 28 days for 6 cycles

    FEC-100: 100 mg/m² on day 1 every 21 days for 6 cycles

    Note: Note: Patients receiving 120 mg/m²/cycle as part of combination therapy should also receive prophylactic therapy with sulfamethoxazole/trimethoprim or a fluoroquinolone.

Dosage modifications:

    Delay day 1 dose until platelets are ≥100,000/mm³, ANC ≥1500/mm³, and nonhematologic toxicities have recovered to ≤grade 1

    Reduce day 1 dose in subsequent cycles to 75% of previous day 1 dose if patient experiences nadir platelet counts <50,000/mm³, ANC <250/mm³, neutropenic fever, or grade 3/4 nonhematologic toxicity during the previous cycle

    For divided doses (day 1 and day 8), reduce day 8 dose to 75% of day 1 dose if platelet counts are 75,000-100,000/mm³ and ANC is 1000-1499/mm³; omit day 8 dose if platelets are <75,000/mm³, ANC <1000/mm³, or grade 3/4 nonhematologic toxicity

Dosage adjustment in bone marrow dysfunction: Heavily-treated patients, patients with pre-existing bone marrow depression or neoplastic bone marrow infiltration: Lower starting doses (75-90 mg/mm²) should be considered.

Elderly: Plasma clearance of epirubicin in elderly female patients was noted to be reduced by 35%. Although no initial dosage reduction is specifically recommended, particular care should be exercised in monitoring toxicity and adjusting subsequent dosage in elderly patients (particularly females >70 years of age).

(Continued)

Epirubicin *(Continued)*

Dosage adjustment in renal impairment: The FDA-approved labeling recommends that in patients with severe renal impairment (serum creatinine >5 mg/dL), lower doses should be considered. Aronoff (2007) recommends no dosage adjustment needed for Cl_{cr} <50 mL/minute.

Dosage adjustment in hepatic impairment: The FDA-approved labeling recommends the following guidelines (based on clinical trial information):

Bilirubin 1.2-3 mg/dL or AST 2-4 times the upper limit of normal: Administer 50% of recommended starting dose

Bilirubin >3 mg/dL or AST >4 times the upper limit of normal: Administer 25% of recommended starting dose

Severe hepatic impairment: Use is contraindicated

Combination Regimens

Breast cancer:

CEF *on page 1166*

Docetaxel-Trastuzumab-FEC *on page 1193*

FEC *on page 1214*

Tamoxifen-Epirubicin *on page 1280*

TEX (Capecitabine + Docetaxel + Epirubicin) *on page 1280*

Gastric cancer: ECF *on page 1197*

Rhabdomyosarcoma: CEV *on page 1168*

Administration I.V.: Infuse over 15-20 minutes or slow I.V. push (for lower doses [due to dose modification or organ dysfunction]) over 3-10 minutes

Monitoring Parameters Monitor injection site during infusion for possible extravasation or local reactions; CBC with differential and platelet count, liver function tests, renal function, ECG, and left ventricular ejection fraction. Monitor during therapy for potential cardiotoxicity with ECHO or with MUGA scans (patients with higher cumulative doses).

Patient Information Report any stinging or change in sensation during the infusion. This medication can only be administered I.V. During therapy, do not use alcohol, aspirin-containing products, and OTC medications without consulting prescriber. It is important to maintain adequate nutrition and hydration (2-3 L/day of fluids unless instructed to restrict fluid intake) during therapy; frequent small meals may help. You may experience nausea or vomiting (frequent small meals, frequent mouth care, sucking lozenges, or chewing gum may help). You may experience loss of hair (reversible); you will be more susceptible to infection (avoid crowds and exposure to infection as much as possible). Yogurt or buttermilk may help reduce diarrhea (if unresolved, contact prescriber for medication relief). Frequent mouth care and use of a soft toothbrush or cotton swabs may reduce mouth sores. May discolor urine (red/pink). Report fever, chills, unusual bruising or bleeding, signs of infection, abdominal pain or blood in stools, excessive fatigue, yellowing of eyes or skin, swelling of extremities, difficulty breathing, or unresolved diarrhea. Barrier contraceptive measures are recommended for both males and females while receiving this drug and for at least one month following administration. Risks of treatment include irreversible heart damage, treatment-related leukemia, and premature menopause in women.

Emetic Potential High (60% to 90%)

Vesicant Yes

Dosage Forms Excipient information presented when available (limited, particularly for generics); consult specific product labeling.

Injection, powder for reconstitution, as hydrochloride, [preservative free]: 50 mg, 200 mg [contains lactose]

Injection, solution, as hydrochloride [preservative free]: 2 mg/mL (25 mL, 100 mL)

Ellence®: 2 mg/mL (25 mL, 100 mL)

References

Aronoff GR, Bennett WM, Berns JS, et al, *Drug Prescribing in Renal Failure: Dosing Guidelines for Adults and Children,* 5th ed. Philadelphia, PA: American College of Physicians; 2007, p 99.

Coukell AJ and Faulds D, "Epirubicin. An Updated Review of Its Pharmacodynamic and Pharmacokinetic Properties and Therapeutic Efficacy in the Management of Breast Cancer," *Drugs,* 1997, 53(3):453-82.

Gluck S, "The Expanding Role of Epirubicin in the Treatment of Breast Cancer," *Cancer Control,* 2002, 9(2 Suppl):16-27.

Murray LS, Jodrell DI, Morrison JG, et al, "The Effect of Cimetidine on the Pharmacokinetics of Epirubicin in Patients With Advanced Breast Cancer: Preliminary Evidence of a Potentially Common Drug Interaction," *Clin Oncol (R Coll Radiol),* 1998, 10(1):35-8.

Onrust SV, Wiseman LR, and Goa KL, "Epirubicin: A Review of Its Intravesical Use in Superficial Bladder Cancer," *Drugs Aging,* 1999, 15(4):307-33.

Trudeau M and Pagani O, "Epirubicin in Combination With the Taxanes," *Semin Oncol,* 2001, 28(4 Suppl 12):41-50.

♦ **Epirubicin Hydrochloride** *see* Epirubicin *on page 383*

♦ **EPO** *see* Epoetin Alfa *on page 387*

Epoetin Alfa (e POE e tin AL fa)

Medication Safety Issues

Sound-alike/look-alike issues:

Epoetin alfa may be confused with darbepoetin alfa

International issues:

Epopen® [Spain] may be confused with EpiPen® which is a brand name for epinephrine in the U.S.

U.S. Brand Names Epogen®; Procrit®

Index Terms EPO; Erythropoiesis-Stimulating Agent (ESA); Erythropoietin; NSC-724223; rHuEPO-α

Generic Available No

Canadian Brand Names Eprex®

Pharmacologic Category Colony Stimulating Factor

Use Treatment of anemia (elevate/maintain red blood cell level and decrease the need for transfusions) associated with HIV (zidovudine) therapy, chronic renal failure (including patients on dialysis and not on dialysis), antineoplastic therapy (for nonmyeloid malignancies) due to concurrent chemotherapy; reduction of allogeneic blood transfusion for elective, noncardiac, nonvascular surgery

Unlabeled/Investigational Use Anemia associated with rheumatic disease; anemia associated with heart failure; anemia of prematurity

Pregnancy Risk Factor C

Lactation Excretion in breast milk unknown/use caution

Labeled Contraindications Hypersensitivity to albumin (human) or mammalian cell-derived products; uncontrolled hypertension

Warnings/Precautions [U.S. Boxed Warning]: ESAs increased the risk of cardiovascular events, thromboembolic events, mortality, and/or tumor progression in clinical studies; a rapid rise in hemoglobin or maintaining higher hemoglobin levels may contribute to these risks. **[U.S. Boxed Warning]: A shortened overall survival and/or time-to-tumor progression has been reported in studies with advanced breast, head and neck, lymphoid, and non small cell lung cancer patients receiving ESAs to a target hemoglobin of ≥12 g/dL; risk has not been excluded when ESAs are dosed to achieve a target hemoglobin of <12 g/dL.** Malignant cell lines and tumors may have surface receptors for erythropoietin; it is not known if epoetin stimulates these receptors. **To decrease these risks, and risk of cardio and thrombovascular events, use ESAs in cancer patients only for the treatment of anemia related to concurrent** (Continued)

Epoetin Alfa *(Continued)*

chemotherapy and use the lowest dose needed to avoid red blood cell transfusions. Discontinue ESA following completion of the chemotherapy course. [U.S. Boxed Warning]: An increased risk of death and serious cardiovascular events was reported in chronic renal failure patients administered ESAs to target higher versus lower hemoglobin levels (13.5 vs. 11.3 g/dL; 14 vs. 10 g/dL) in two clinical studies; dosing should be individualized to achieve and maintain hemoglobin levels within 10-12 g/dL range. Chronic renal failure patients who exhibit an inadequate hemoglobin response to ESA therapy may be at a higher risk for cardiovascular and mortality compared to other patients. ESA therapy may reduce dialysis efficacy (due to increase in red blood cells and decrease in plasma volume); adjustments in dialysis parameters may be needed. [U.S. Boxed Warning]: Epoetin alfa increased the rate of DVT in perisurgery patients not receiving anticoagulant prophylaxis; consider DVT prophylaxis. Increased mortality was also observed in patients undergoing coronary artery bypass surgery who received epoetin alfa; these deaths were associated with thrombotic events. Epoetin is not approved for reduction of red blood cell transfusion in patients undergoing cardiac or vascular surgery. During therapy in any patient, hemoglobin levels should not exceed 12 g/dL and should not rise >1 g/dL per 2-week time period.

Use with caution in patients with hypertension or with a history of seizures; hypertensive encephalopathy and seizures have been reported. If hypertension is difficult to control, reduce or hold epoetin alfa. Not recommended for acute correction of severe anemia or as a substitute for transfusion.

Prior to treatment, correct or exclude deficiencies of iron, vitamin B_{12}, and/or folate, as well as other factors which may impair erythropoiesis (aluminum toxicity, inflammatory conditions, infections). Prior to and during therapy, iron stores must be evaluated. Supplemental iron is recommended if serum ferritin <100 mcg/mL or serum transferrin saturation <20%. Poor response should prompt evaluation of these potential factors, as well as possible malignant processes, occult blood loss, hemolysis, and/or bone marrow fibrosis. Pure red cell aplasia (PRCA) with associated neutralizing antibodies to erythropoietin has been reported, predominantly in patients with CRF. Patients with loss of response to epoetin alfa should be evaluated. Discontinue treatment in patients with PRCA secondary to neutralizing antibodies to epoetin.

Due to the delayed onset of erythropoiesis, epoetin is of no value in the acute treatment of anemia. Safety and efficacy in patients with underlying hematologic diseases have not been established, including porphyria, thalassemia, hemolytic anemia, and sickle cell disease. Potentially serious allergic reactions have been reported. Use caution with porphyria, exacerbation of porphyria has been reported (rarely) in patients with chronic renal failure. Some products may contain albumin. Multidose vials contain benzyl alcohol; do not use in premature infants. Safety and efficacy in children <1 month of age have not been established.

Adverse Reactions

>10%:

Cardiovascular: Hypertension (5% to 24%), thrombotic/vascular events (coronary artery bypass graft surgery: 23%), edema (6% to 17%), deep vein thrombosis (3% to 11%)

Central nervous system: Fever (29% to 51%), dizziness (<7% to 21%), insomnia (13% to 21%), headache (10% to 19%)

Dermatologic: Pruritus (14% to 22%), skin pain (4% to 18%), rash (≤16%)

Gastrointestinal: Nausea (11% to 58%), constipation (42% to 53%), vomiting (8% to 29%), diarrhea (9% to 21%), dyspepsia (7% to 11%)

Genitourinary: Urinary tract infection (3% to 12%)

Local: Injection site reaction (<10% to 29%)

Neuromuscular & skeletal: Arthralgia (11%), paresthesia (11%)

Respiratory: Cough (18%), congestion (15%), dyspnea (13% to 14%), upper respiratory infection (11%)

1% to 10%:

Central nervous system: Seizure (1% to 3%)

Local: Clotted vascular access (7%)

<1%, postmarketing, and/or case reports: Allergic reaction, anemia (severe; with or without other cytopenias), CVA, flu-like syndrome, hyperkalemia, hypersensitivity reactions, hypertensive encephalopathy, microvascular thrombosis, MI, myalgia, neutralizing antibodies, pulmonary embolism, pure red cell aplasia, renal vein thrombosis, retinal artery thrombosis, tachycardia, temporal vein thrombosis, thrombophlebitis, thrombosis, TIA, urticaria

Overdosage/Toxicology Symptoms of overdose include erythrocytosis and polycythemia. A rapid or excessive rise in hemoglobin may be associated with an increased risk for cardiovascular and/or thrombotic events. Phlebotomy may be indicated for polycythemia; treatment is otherwise symptom-directed and supportive.

Storage/Stability Vials should be stored at 2°C to 8°C (36°F to 46°F); **do not freeze or shake.**

Single-dose 1 mL vial contains no preservative: Use one dose per vial. Do not re-enter vial; discard unused portions.

Single-dose vials (except 40,000 units/mL vial) are stable for 2 weeks at room temperature. Single-dose 40,000 units/mL vial is stable for 1 week at room temperature.

Multidose 1 mL or 2 mL vial contains preservative. Store at 2°C to 8°C after initial entry and between doses. Discard 21 days after initial entry.

Multidose vials (with preservative) are stable for 1 week at room temperature.

Prefilled syringes containing the 20,000 units/mL formulation with preservative are stable for 6 weeks refrigerated (2°C to 8°C).

Dilutions of 1:10 in $D_{10}W$ with human albumin 0.05% or 0.1% are stable for 24 hours.

Reconstitution Prior to SubQ administration, preservative free solutions may be mixed with bacteriostatic NS containing benzyl alcohol 0.9% in a 1:1 ratio.

Compatibility Stable in $D_{10}W$ with albumin 0.05%, $D_{10}W$ with albumin 0.1%; **incompatible** with $D_{10}W$ with albumin 0.01%, $D_{10}W$, NS; **variable stability (consult detailed reference)** in TPN.

Mechanism of Action Induces erythropoiesis by stimulating the division and differentiation of committed erythroid progenitor cells; induces the release of reticulocytes from the bone marrow into the bloodstream, where they mature to erythrocytes. There is a dose response relationship with this effect. This results in an increase in reticulocyte counts followed by a rise in hematocrit and hemoglobin levels.

Pharmacodynamics/Kinetics

Onset of action: Several days

Peak effect: 2-3 weeks

Distribution: V_d: 9 L; rapid in the plasma compartment; concentrated in liver, kidneys, and bone marrow

Metabolism: Some degradation does occur

(Continued)

Epoetin Alfa *(Continued)*

Bioavailability: SubQ: ~21% to 31%; intraperitoneal epoetin: 3% (a few patients)

Half-life elimination: Cancer: SubQ: 16-67 hours; Chronic renal failure: I.V.: 4-13 hours

Time to peak, serum: Chronic renal failure: SubQ: 5-24 hours

Excretion: Feces (majority); urine (small amounts, 10% unchanged in normal volunteers)

Dosage Note: Hemoglobin levels should not exceed 12 g/dL and should not rise >1 g/dL per 2-week time period during therapy in any patient.

Chronic renal failure patients: Individualize dosing to achieve and maintain hemoglobin levels between 10-12 g/dL. Hemoglobin levels should not exceed 12 g/dL.

Children: SubQ, I.V.: Initial dose: 50 units/kg 3 times/week

Adults: SubQ, I.V.: Initial dose: 50-100 units/kg 3 times/week

Dosage adjustment in Children and Adults: SubQ, I.V.:

Decrease dose by 25%: If hemoglobin approaches 12 g/dL **or** hemoglobin increases >1 g/dL in any 2-week period. If hemoglobin continues to increase, temporarily discontinue therapy until hemoglobin begins to decrease, then resume therapy with a ~25% reduction from previous dose.

Increase dose by 25%: If hemoglobin <10 g/dL and does not increase by 1 g/dL after 4 weeks of therapy (with adequate iron stores) **or** hemoglobin decreases below 10 g/dL. Do not increase dose more frequently than at 4-week intervals.

Inadequate or lack of response: If patient does not attain target hemoglobin range of 10-12 g/dL after appropriate dose titrations over 12 weeks:

Do not continue to increase dose and use the minimum effective dose that will maintain a hemoglobin level sufficient to avoid red blood cell transfusions **and** evaluate patient for other causes of anemia.

Monitor hemoglobin closely thereafter, and if responsiveness improves, may resume making dosage adjustments as recommended above. If responsiveness does not improve and recurrent red blood cell transfusions continue to be needed, discontinue therapy.

Maintenance dose: Individualize to target hemoglobin range of 10-12 g/dL; limit additional dosage increases to every 4 weeks (or longer)

Dialysis patients: Median dose:

Children: 167 units/kg/week (hemodialysis) **or** 76 units/kg/week (peritoneal dialysis)

Adults: 75 units/kg 3 times/week

Nondialysis patients:

Children: Dosing range: 50-250 units/kg 1-3 times/week

Adults: Median range: 75-150 units/kg/week

Zidovudine-treated, HIV-infected patients (patients with erythropoietin levels >500 mU/mL are **unlikely** to respond): Titrate dosage to use the minimum effective dose that will maintain a hemoglobin level sufficient to avoid red blood cell transfusions. Hemoglobin levels should not exceed 12 g/dL.

Children: SubQ, I.V.: Limited data available; reported dosing range: 50-400 units/kg 2-3 times/week

Adults (with serum erythropoietin levels ≤500 and zidovudine doses ≤4200 mg/week): SubQ, I.V.: 100 units/kg 3 times/week for 8 weeks

Dosage adjustment:

Increase dose by 50-100 units/kg 3 times/week: If response is not satisfactory in terms of reducing transfusion requirements **or** increasing hemoglobin after 8 weeks of therapy. Evaluate response every 4-8 weeks thereafter, and adjust the dose accordingly by 50-100 units/kg increments 3 times/week. If patients has not responded satisfactorily to a 300 units/kg/dose 3 times/week, a response to higher doses is unlikely.

Withhold dose: If hemoglobin exceeds 12 g/dL. Resume treatment with a 25% dose reduction when hemoglobin approaches a level where transfusions may be required.

Cancer patient on chemotherapy: Treatment of patients with erythropoietin levels >200 mU/mL is **not recommended.** Titrate dosage to use the minimum effective dose that will maintain a hemoglobin level sufficient to avoid red blood cell transfusions. Hemoglobin levels should not exceed 12 g/dL.

Children: I.V.: 600 units/kg once weekly (maximum: 40,000 units)

Dosage adjustment:

Increase dose: If response is not satisfactory after a sufficient period of evaluation (no increase in hemoglobin by ≥1 g/dL after 4 weeks of once-weekly therapy), the dose may be increased every 4 weeks (or longer) to 900 units/kg/week; maximum 60,000 units. If patient does not respond, a response to higher doses is unlikely.

Withhold dose: If hemoglobin exceeds 12 g/dL. Resume treatment with a 25% dose reduction when hemoglobin approaches a level where transfusions may be required.

Reduce dose by 25%: If hemoglobin increases >1 g/dL in any 2-week period **or** hemoglobin reaches a level sufficient to avoid red blood cell transfusion.

Adults: SubQ: Initial dose: 150 units/kg 3 times/week or 40,000 units once weekly; commonly used doses range from 10,000 units 3 times/week to 40,000-60,000 units once weekly.

Dosage adjustment:

Increase dose: If response is not satisfactory after a sufficient period of evaluation (no reduction in transfusion requirements or increase in hemoglobin after 8 weeks of 3 times/week therapy) **or** (no increase in hemoglobin by ≥1 g/dL after 4 weeks of once-weekly therapy), the dose may be increased every 4 weeks (or longer) to 300 units/kg 3 times/week, **or** when dosed weekly, increased all at once to 60,000 units weekly. If patient does not respond, a response to higher doses is unlikely.

Withhold dose: If hemoglobin exceeds 12 g/dL. Resume treatment with a 25% dose reduction when hemoglobin approaches a level where transfusions may be required.

Reduce dose by 25%: If hemoglobin increases >1 g/dL in any 2-week period **or** hemoglobin reaches a level sufficient to avoid red blood cell transfusion.

Surgery patients: Prior to initiating treatment, obtain a hemoglobin to establish that it is >10 g/dL or ≤13 g/dL: Adults: SubQ: Initial dose: 300 units/kg/day for 10 days before surgery, on the day of surgery, and for 4 days after surgery

Alternative dose: 600 units/kg in once weekly doses (21, 14, and 7 days before surgery) plus a fourth dose on the day of surgery

Anemia of critical illness (unlabeled use): Adults: SubQ: 40,000 units once weekly

(Continued)

Epoetin Alfa *(Continued)*

Anemia of prematurity (unlabeled use): Infants: I.V., SubQ: Dosing range: 500-1250 units/kg/week; commonly used dose: 250 units/kg 3 times/week; supplement with oral iron therapy 3-8 mg/kg/day

Dosage adjustment in renal impairment: The National Kidney Foundation Clinical Practice Guideline for Anemia in Chronic Kidney Disease: 2007 Update of Hemoglobin Target (September, 2007) recommend hemoglobin levels in the range of 11-12 g/dL for dialysis and nondialysis patients receiving ESAs; hemoglobin levels should not be >13 g/dL.

Hemodialysis: Supplemental dose is not necessary.

Peritoneal dialysis: Supplemental dose is not necessary.

Administration SubQ, I.M. (I.V. not recommended unless on hemodialysis; I.V. administration may require up to 40% more drug as SubQ/I.M. administration to achieve the same therapeutic result)

Patients with CRF on dialysis: I.V. route preferred; may be administered I.V. bolus into the venous line after dialysis.

Patients with CRF not on dialysis: May be administered I.V. or SubQ

Monitoring Parameters Blood pressure; hemoglobin, CBC with differential and platelets, transferrin saturation and ferritin, serum chemistry (CRF patients)

Suggested tests to be monitored and their frequency: See table.

Test	Initial Phase Frequency	Maintenance Phase Frequency
Hemoglobin	2 x/week	2-4 x/month
Blood pressure	3 x/week	3 x/week
Serum ferritin	Monthly	Quarterly
Transferrin saturation	Monthly	Quarterly
Serum chemistries including CBC with differential, creatinine, blood urea nitrogen, potassium, phosphorous	Regularly per routine	Regularly per routine

Hemoglobin should be determined twice weekly until stabilization within the target range (30% to 36%), and twice weekly for at least 2-6 weeks after a dose increase. It may take 6-8 weeks to begin to see an effect and may take 16 weeks to see full therapeutic effect.

Patient Information You will require blood tests to determine appropriate dosage. Do not take other medications, vitamin or iron supplements, or make significant changes in your diet without consulting prescriber. Report signs or symptoms of edema (eg, swollen extremities, difficulty breathing, rapid weight gain), onset of severe headache, acute back pain, chest pain, muscular tremors, or seizure activity.

Special Geriatric Considerations There is limited information about the use of epoetin alfa in the elderly. Endogenous erythropoietin secretion has been reported to be decreased in elderly with normocytic or iron deficiency anemias or those with a serum hemoglobin concentration <12 g/dL; one study did not find such a relationship in the elderly with chronic anemia. A blunted erythropoietin response to anemia has been reported in patients with cancer, rheumatoid arthritis, and AIDS.

Additional Information Due to the delayed onset of erythropoiesis (7-10 days to increase reticulocyte count; 2-6 weeks to increase hemoglobin), erythropoietin is of no value in the acute treatment of anemia.

Factors Limiting Response to Epoetin Alfa

Factor	Mechanism
Iron deficiency	Limits hemoglobin synthesis
Blood loss/hemolysis	Counteracts epoetin alfa-stimulated erythropoiesis
Infection/inflammation	Inhibits iron transfer from storage to bone marrow
	Suppresses erythropoiesis through activated macrophages
Aluminum overload	Inhibits iron incorporation into heme protein
Bone marrow replacement Hyperparathyroidism Metastatic, neoplastic	Limits bone marrow volume
Folic acid/vitamin B_{12} deficiency	Limits hemoglobin synthesis
Patient compliance	Self-administered epoetin alfa or iron therapy

Professional Services:
Amgen (Epogen®): 1-800-772-6436
Ortho Biotech (Procrit®): 1-800-325-7504
Reimbursement Assistance:
Amgen: 1-800-272-9376
Ortho Biotech: 1-800-553-3851

Oncology Comment: The American Society of Hematology (ASH) and American Society of Clinical Oncology (ASCO) 2007 updates to the clinical practice guidelines for the use of erythropoiesis-stimulating agents (ESAs) indicate that ESAs are most appropriate when used according to the dosage parameters within the Food and Drug Administration (FDA) approved labeling for epoetin and darbepoetin (Rizzo, 2007). While the previous guidelines addressed only the use of epoetin, the 2007 guidelines also address the use of darbepoetin, which is assessed as being equivalent to epoetin with respect to safety and efficacy. When used as an option for the treatment of chemotherapy-associated anemia (to increase hemoglobin and decrease red blood cell transfusions), therapy with ESAs should begin as the hemoglobin level approaches or falls below 10 g/dL. The ASH/ASCO guidelines recommend following the FDA approved dosing (and dosing adjustment) guidelines and target hemoglobin ranges as alternate dosing and schedules have not demonstrated consistent differences in effectiveness with regard to hemoglobin response. In patients who do not have a response within 6-8 weeks (hemoglobin rise <1-2 g/dL or no reduction in transfusions) ESA therapy should be discontinued.

The guidelines note that patients with an increased risk of thromboembolism (generally includes previous history of thrombosis, surgery, and/or prolonged periods of immobilization) and patients receiving concomitant medications that may increase thromboembolic risk, should begin ESA therapy only after careful consideration. With the exception of low-risk myelodysplasia-associated anemia (which has evidence supporting the use of ESAs without concurrent chemotherapy), the guidelines do not support the use of ESAs in the absence of concurrent chemotherapy.

Emetic Potential Very low (<10%)

Vesicant No

Dosage Forms Excipient information presented when available (limited, particularly for generics); consult specific product labeling.
(Continued)

Epoetin Alfa *(Continued)*

Injection, solution [preservative free]:

Epogen®, Procrit®: 2000 units/mL (1 mL); 3000 units/mL (1 mL); 4000 units/mL (1 mL); 10,000 units/mL (1 mL); 40,000 units/mL (1 mL) [contains human albumin]

Injection, solution [with preservative]:

Epogen®, Procrit®: 10,000 units/mL (2 mL); 20,000 units/mL (1 mL) [contains human albumin and benzyl alcohol]

References

Bennett CL, Cournoyer D, Carson KR, et al, "Long-Term Outcome of Individuals With Pure Red Cell Aplasia and Antierythropoietin Antibodies in Patients Treated With Recombinant Epoetin: A Follow-up Report From the Research on Adverse Drug Events and Reports (RADAR) Project,"*Blood*, 2005, 106(10):3343-7.

Blanche S, Caniglia M, Fischer A, et al, "Zidovudine Therapy in Children With Acquired Immunodeficiency Syndrome," *Am J Med*, 1988, 85(2A):203-7.

Brown KR, Carter W Jr, and Lombardi GE, "Recombinant Erythropoietin Overdose," *Am J Emerg Med*, 1993, 11(6):619-21.

Brown MS and Keith JF 3rd, "Comparison Between Two and Five Doses a Week of Recombinant Human Erythropoietin for Anemia of Prematurity: A Randomized Trial," *Pediatrics*, 1999, 104(2 Pt 1):210-5.

Carpenter MA, Kendall RG, O'Brien AE, et al, "Reduced Erythropoietin Response to Anaemia in Elderly Patients With Normocytic Anaemia," *Eur J Haematol*, 1992, 49(3):119-21.

Corwin HL, Gettinger A, Pearl RG, et al, "Efficacy of Recombinant Human Erythropoietin in Critically Ill Patients: A Randomized Controlled Trial," *JAMA*, 2002, 288(22):2827-35.

Cournoyer D, Toffelmire EB, Wells GA, et al, "Anti-Erythropoietin Antibody-Mediated Pure Red Cell Aplasia After Treatment With Recombinant Erythropoietin Products: Recommendations for Minimization of Risk," *J Am Soc Nephrol*, 2004, 15(10):2728-34.

Dellinger RP, Carlet JM, Masur H, et al, "Surviving Sepsis Campaign Guidelines for Management of Severe Sepsis and Septic Shock," *Crit Care Med*, 2004, 32(3):858-73.

Donato H, Vain N, Rendo P, et al, "Effect of Early Versus Late Administration of Human Recombinant Erythropoietin on Transfusion Requirements in Premature Infants: Results of a Randomized, Placebo-Controlled, Multicenter Trial," *Pediatrics*, 2000, 105(5):1066-72.

Drueke TB, Locatelli F, Clyne N, et al, "Normalization of Hemoglobin Level in Patients With Chronic Kidney Disease and Anemia," *N Engl J Med*, 2006, 355(20): 2071-84.

Erslev AJ, "Erythropoietin," *N Engl J Med*, 1991, 324(19):1339-44.

Feusner J and Hastings C, "Recombinant Human Erythropoietin in Pediatric Oncology: A Review," *Med Pediatr Oncol*, 2002, 39(4):463-8.

Gareau R, Gagnon MG, Thellend C, et al, "Transferrin Soluble Receptor: A Possible Probe for Detection of Erythropoietin Abuse by Athletes," *Horm Metab Res*, 1994, 26(6):311-2.

Goodnough LT, Price TH, Parvin CA, "The Indigenous Erythropoietin Response and the Erythropoietic Response to Blood Loss Anemia: The Effects of Age and Gender," *J Lab Clin Med*, 1995, 126(1):57-64.

Halperin DS, Wacker P, Lacourt G, et al, "Effects of Recombinant Human Erythropoietin in Infants With the Anemia of Prematurity: A Pilot Study," *J Pediatr*, 1990, 116(5):779-86.

Hebert PC, Wells G, Blajchman MA, et al, "A Multicenter, Randomized, Controlled Clinical Trial of Transfusion Requirements in Critical Care. Transfusion Requirements in Critical Care Investigators, Canadian Critical Care Trials Group," *N Engl J Med*, 1999, 340(6):409-17.

Henry DH, "Recombinant Human Erythropoietin Treatment of Anemic Cancer Patients," *Cancer Pract*, 1996, 4(4):180-4.

Henry DH and Spivak JL, "Clinical Use of Erythropoietin," *Curr Opin Hematol*, 1995, 2(2):118-24.

Henry DH and Thatcher N, "Patient Selection and Predicting Response to Recombinant Human Erythropoietin in Anemic Cancer Patients," *Semin Hematol*, 1996, 33(1 Suppl 1):2-5.

Hunt SA, Abraham WT, Chin MH , et al, "ACC/AHA 2005 Guideline Update for the Diagnosis and Management of Chronic Heart Failure in the Adult: A Report of the American College of Cardiology/American Heart Association Task Force on Practice Guidelines (Writing Committee to Update the 2001 Guidelines for the Evaluation and Management of Heart Failure)," available at http://www.acc.org/qualityandscience/clinical/guidelines/failure/update/index.pdf.

Joosten E, Van Hove L, Lesaffre E, et al, "Serum Erythropoietin Levels in Elderly Inpatients With Anemia of Chronic Disorders and Iron Deficiency Anemia," *J Am Geriatr Soc*, 1993, 41(12):1301-4.

Juul SE and Christensen RD, "Absorption of Enteral Recombinant Human Erythropoietin By Neonates," *Ann Pharmacother*, 2003, 37(6):782-6.

Kario K, Matsuo T, and Nakao K, "Serum Erythropoietin Levels in the Elderly," *Gerontology*, 1991, 37(6):345-8.

Kharagjitsingh AV, Korevaar JC, Vandenbroucke JP, et al, "Incidence of Recombinant Erythropoietin (EPO) Hyporesponse, EPO-Associated Antibodies, and Pure Red Cell Aplasia in Dialysis Patients," *Kidney Int*, 2005, 68(3):1215-22.

MacDougall IC, "Adverse Reactions Profile: Erythropoietin in Chronic Renal Failure," *Prescribers J*, 1992, 32:40-4.

Maier RF, Obladen M, Muller-Hansen I, et al, "Early Treatment With Erythropoietin Beta Ameliorates Anemia and Reduces Transfusion Requirements in Infants With Birth Weights Below 1000 g," *J Pediatr*, 2002, 141(1):8-15.

Means RT Jr, "Erythropoietin in the Treatment of Anemia in Chronic Infectious, Inflammatory, and Malignant Diseases," *Curr Opin Hematol*, 1995, 2(3):210-3.

Nafziger J, Pailla K, Luciani L, et al, "Decreased Erythropoietin Responsiveness to Iron Deficiency Anemia in the Elderly," *Am J Hematol*, 1993, 43(3):172-6.

National Kidney Foundation, "KDOQI Clinical Practice Guidelines and Clinical Practice Recommentaions for Anemia in Chronic Kidney Disease," *Am J Kidney Dis*, 2007, 50(3):529-30. Available at http://www.kidney.org/professionals/kdoqi/pdf/KDOQI_finalPDF.pdf or http://www.kidney.org/professionals/KDOQI.

Naughton CA, Duppong LM, Forbes KD, et al, "Stability of Multidose, Preserved Formulation Epoetin Alfa in Syringes for Three and Six Weeks," *Am J Health Syst Pharm*, 2003, 60(5):464-8.

NCCN (National Comprehensive Cancer Network), "Practice Guidelines in Oncology: Cancer- and Treatment-Related Anemia Version 1.2007." Available at http://www.nccn.org/professionals/physician_gls/PDF/anemia.pdf

Ohls RK and Christensen, RD, "Stability of Human Recombinant Epoetin Alfa in Commonly Used Neonatal Intravenous Solutions," *Ann Pharmacother*, 1996, 30(5):466-468.

Ohls RK, Ehrenkranz RA, Wright LL, et al, "Effects of Early Erythropoietin Therapy on the Transfusion Requirements of Preterm Infants Below 1250 Grams Birth Weight: A Multicenter, Randomized, Controlled Trial," *Pediatrics*, 2001, 108(4):934-42.

Ohls RK, Veerman MW, and Christensen RD, "Pharmacokinetics and Effectiveness of Recombinant Erythropoietin Administered to Preterm Infants by Continuous Infusion in Total Parenteral Nutrition Solution," *J Pediatr*, 1996, 128(4):518-23.

Patton J, Kuzur M, Liggett W, et al, "Epoetin Alfa 60,000 U Once Weekly Followed by 120,000 U Every 3 Weeks Increases and Maintains Hemoglobin Levels in Anemic Cancer Patients Undergoing Chemotherapy," *Oncologist*, 2004, 9(1):90-6.

Phronmmintikul A, Haas SJ, Elsik M, et al, "Mortality and Target Haemoglobin Concentrations in Anaemic Patients with Chronic Kidney Disease Treated With Erythropoietin: A Meta-Analysis, *Lancet*, 2007, 369(9559):381-88.

Powers JS, Krantz SB, Collins JC, et al, "Erythropoietin Response to Anemia as a Function of Age," *J Am Geriatr Soc*, 1991, 39(1):30-2.

Rhondeau SM, Christensen RD, Ross MP, et al, "Responsiveness to Recombinant Human Erythropoietin of Marrow Erythroid Progenitors From Infants With the Anemia of Prematurity," *J Pediatr*, 1988, 112(6):935-40.

Rizzo JD, Lichten AE, Woolf SH, et al, "Use of Epoetin in Patients With Cancer: Evidence-Based Clinical Practice Guidelines of the American Society of Clinical Oncology and the American Society of Hematology," *Blood*, 2002, 100(7):2303-20.

Rizzo JD, Somerfield MR, Hagerty LK, et al, "American Society of Hematology/American Society of Clinical Oncology 2007 Clinical Practice Guideline Update on the Use of Epoetin and Darbepoetin," *Blood*, 2007, Oct 22 [Epub ahead of print]

Rubins J, "Metastatic Renal Cell Carcinoma: Response to Treatment With Human Recombinant Erythropoietin," *Ann Intern Med*, 1995, 122(9):676-7.

Schwenk MH and Halstenson CE, "Recombinant Human Erythropoietin," *DICP*, 1989, 23(7-8):528-36.

Shannon KM, Keith JF 3rd, Mentzer WC, et al, "Recombinant Human Erythropoietin Stimulates Erythropoiesis and Reduces Erythrocyte Transfusions in Very Low Birth Weight Preterm Infants," *Pediatrics*, 1995, 95(1):1-8.

Sinai-Trieman L, Salusky IB, and Fine RN, "Use of Subcutaneous Recombinant Human Erythropoietin in Children Undergoing Continuous Cycling Peritoneal Dialysis," *J Pediatr*, 1989, 114(4 Pt 1):550-4.

Singh AJ, Szczech L, Tang KI, et al, "Correction of Anemia With Epoetin Alfa in Chronic Kidney Disease," *N Engl J Med*, 2006, 355(20):2085-98.

Steinberg H, "Erythropoietin and Visual Hallucinations," *N Engl J Med*, 1991, 325(4):285.

Weinthal JA, "The Role of Cytokines Following Bone Marrow Transplantation: Indications and Controversies," *Bone Marrow Transplant*, 1996, 18(Suppl 3):10-4.

♦ **Epogen®** *see Epoetin Alfa on page 387*

♦ **Eprex® (Can)** *see Epoetin Alfa on page 387*

♦ **Epsilon Aminocaproic Acid** *see Aminocaproic Acid on page 62*

♦ **EPT** *see Teniposide on page 1018*

♦ **Eptacog Alfa (Activated)** *see* Factor VIIa (Recombinant) *on page 416*

♦ **Erbitux®** *see* Cetuximab *on page 201*

Erlotinib (er LOE tye nib)

Medication Safety Issues
Sound-alike/look-alike issues:
Erlotinib may be confused with gefitinib

High alert medication: The Institute for Safe Medication Practices (ISMP) includes this medication among its list of drugs which have a heightened risk of causing significant patient harm when used in error.

Related Information
Safe Handling of Hazardous Drugs *on page 1382*

U.S. Brand Names Tarceva®

Index Terms CP358774; Erlotinib Hydrochloride; NSC-718781; OSI-774; R 14-15

Generic Available No

Canadian Brand Names Tarceva®

Pharmacologic Category Antineoplastic Agent, Tyrosine Kinase Inhibitor; Epidermal Growth Factor Receptor (EGFR) Inhibitor

Use Treatment of refractory advanced or metastatic nonsmall cell lung cancer (NSCLC); pancreatic cancer (first-line therapy in combination with gemcitabine)

Pregnancy Risk Factor D

Lactation Excretion in breast milk unknown/not recommended

Labeled Contraindications Hypersensitivity to erlotinib or any component of the formulation; pregnancy

Warnings/Precautions Hazardous agent - use appropriate precautions for handling and disposal. Rare, sometimes fatal, pulmonary toxicity (interstitial pneumonia, interstitial lung disease, obliterative bronchiolitis, pulmonary fibrosis) has occurred; interrupt therapy for unexplained pulmonary symptoms (dyspnea, cough, and fever). Liver enzyme elevations have been reported; use caution in patients with hepatic impairment; dosage reductions may be needed. Acute renal failure and renal insufficiency (with/without hypokalemia) have been reported; use with caution in patients with or at risk for renal impairment. Use caution with cardiovascular disease; MI, CVA, and microangiopathic hemolytic anemia with thrombocytopenia have been noted in patients receiving concomitant erlotinib and gemcitabine. Elevated INR and bleeding events have been reported; use caution with concomitant anticoagulant therapy. Erlotinib levels may be lower in patients who smoke; for best effects, patients should be advised to stop smoking. Use with caution in patients taking strong CYP3A4 inhibitors and moderate or strong CYP3A4 inducers (see Drug Interactions). Consider alternative agents that avoid or lessen the potential for CYP-mediated interactions. Safety and efficacy in pediatric patients have not been established.

Adverse Reactions Percentages as reported with monotherapy; frequency of adverse event with combination chemotherapy (gemcitabine) noted where applicable

>10%:
Cardiovascular: Edema (37% combination)
Central nervous system: Fatigue (14% to 55%; 73% combination), pyrexia (36% combination), anxiety (21%), headache (17%), depression (16%; 19% combination), dizziness (15% combination), insomnia (12%; 15% combination)

Dermatologic: Acneiform rash (50% to 88%; grade 3/4: 9%), pruritus (13% to 55%), dry skin (12% to 35%), erythema (18%), alopecia (14% combination)

Gastrointestinal: Diarrhea (30% to 56%; grade 3/4: 6%), anorexia (23% to 52%), nausea (11% to 33%; 60% combination), vomiting (23%; 42% combination), mucositis (17% to 18%), glossodynia (18%), stomatitis (17%; 22% combination), xerostomia (17%), pain (14%), flatulence (13% combination); constipation (12%; 31% combination), dyspepsia (12%; 17% combination), dysphagia (12%), weight loss (12%; 39% combination), abnormal taste (11%), abdominal pain (11%; 46% combination)

Hepatic: ALT increased (grade 2: 4%; combination grade 2: 31%, grade 3: 13%, grade 4: <1%), AST increased (combination grade 2: 24%, grade 3: 10%, grade 4 <1%), hyperbilirubinemia (20%; combination grade 2: 17%, grade 3: 10%, grade 4: <1%)

Neuromuscular & skeletal: Bone pain (25% combination), myalgia (21% combination), arthralgia (14%), neuropathy (13% combination), rigors (12% combination), paresthesia (11%)

Ocular: Conjunctivitis (12%), keratoconjunctivitis sicca (12%)

Respiratory: Dyspnea (21% to 41%), cough (16% to 33%)

Miscellaneous: Infection (24%; 39% combination)

1% to 10%:

Cardiovascular (reported with combination chemotherapy): Deep venous thrombosis (4%), arrhythmia, cerebrovascular accidents (including cerebral hemorrhage), MI, myocardial ischemia, syncope

Gastrointestinal (reported with combination chemotherapy): Ileus, pancreatitis

Hematologic (reported with combination chemotherapy): Hemolytic anemia, microangiopathic hemolytic anemia with thrombocytopenia

Ocular: Keratitis (6%; <1% combination)

Renal (reported with combination chemotherapy): Renal insufficiency

Respiratory: Pneumonitis (6%)

<1%, postmarketing, and/or case reports: Acute renal failure, bronchiolitis, corneal ulcerations, epistaxis, gastritis, gastroduodenal ulcers, gastrointestinal bleeding, gastrointestinal hemorrhage, hematemesis, hematochezia, interstitial lung disease, melena, peptic ulcer bleeding, pulmonary fibrosis, pulmonary infiltrates, rash (acneiform; sparing prior radiation field)

Overdosage/Toxicology Single doses of up to 1000 mg in healthy patients and 1600 mg in cancer patients have been tolerated. Repeated doses of 200 mg twice daily in healthy subjects were poorly tolerated after a few days. Specific overdose-related toxicities include diarrhea, rash, and liver transaminase elevation. Overdose management should include withdrawal of erlotinib, and symptom-directed and supportive treatment.

Drug Interactions

Cytochrome P450 Effect: Substrate of CYP1A2 (minor), 3A4 (major)

Increased Effect/Toxicity: Azole antifungals (eg, fluconazole, itraconazole, ketoconazole, voriconazole) and CYP3A4 inhibitors may increase erlotinib levels/effects; example inhibitors include azole antifungals, clarithromycin, diclofenac, doxycycline, erythromycin, imatinib, isoniazid, nefazodone, nicardipine, propofol, protease inhibitors, quinidine, telithromycin, and verapamil. Concomitant therapy with warfarin and erlotinib may increase the risk of bleeding or INR elevations; monitor.

Decreased Effect: Rifamycins and CYP3A4 inducers may decrease erlotinib levels/effects; example inducers include aminoglutethimide, carbamazepine, nafcillin, nevirapine, phenobarbital, and phenytoin. Erlotinib may decrease the absorption of digoxin tablets.

(Continued)

Erlotinib *(Continued)*

Ethanol/Nutrition/Herb Interactions

Food: Erlotinib bioavailability is increased with food. Avoid grapefruit or grapefruit juice (may decrease the metabolism and increase erlotinib levels).

Herb/Nutraceutical: Avoid St John's wort (may increase metabolism and decrease erlotinib concentrations).

Storage/Stability Store at room temperature between 15°C and 30°C (59°F and 86°F).

Mechanism of Action The mechanism of erlotinib's antitumor action is not fully characterized. The drug is known to inhibit overall epidermal growth factor receptor (HER1/EGFR)- tyrosine kinase. Active competitive inhibition of adenosine triphosphate inhibits downstream signal transduction of ligand dependent HER1/EGFR activation.

Pharmacodynamics/Kinetics

Absorption: Oral: 60% on an empty stomach; ~100% on a full stomach

Distribution: 94-232 L

Protein binding: 92% to 95%, albumin and α_1-acid glycoprotein

Metabolism: Hepatic, CYP3A4 (major), CYP1A1 (minor), CYP1A2 (minor), and CYP1C (minor)

Bioavailability: 100% when given with food; 60% without food

Half-life elimination: 24-36 hours

Time to peak, plasma: 1-7 hours

Excretion: Primarily as metabolites: Feces (83%; 1% as unchanged drug); urine (8%)

Dosage Oral: Adults: **Note:** Dose adjustments are likely to be needed when erlotinib is administered concomitantly with strong CYP3A4 inducers or inhibitors.

NSCLC: 150 mg/day

Pancreatic cancer: 100 mg/day in combination with gemcitabine

Dosage adjustment for concomitant CYP3A4 inhibitors/inducers:

CYP3A4 inhibitors: Dose reductions are more likely to be needed when erlotinib is administered concomitantly with strong CYP3A4 inhibitors. Dose reduction (if required) should be done in decrements of 50 mg. See Drug Interactions for examples of CYP3A4 inhibitors.

CYP3A4 inducers: Concomitant administration with CYP3A4 inducers may require increased doses; doses >150 mg/day should be considered with rifampin. See Drug Interactions for examples of CYP3A4 inducers.

Dosage adjustment for toxicity: Patients experiencing poorly-tolerated diarrhea or a severe skin reaction may benefit from dose reductions or a brief therapy interruption. Dose reductions should be made in 50 mg decrements. Patients experiencing acute onset (or worsening) of pulmonary symptoms should have therapy interrupted and be evaluated for drug-induced interstitial lung disease. Discontinue permanently with development of interstitial lung disease.

Dosage adjustment in renal impairment: No adjustment required.

Dosage adjustment in hepatic impairment: Dose reduction or interruption should be considered if liver function changes are severe.

Combination Regimens

Pancreatic cancer: Gemcitabine-Erlotinib *on page 1227*

Administration The manufacturer recommends administration on an empty stomach (at least 1 hour before or 2 hours after the ingestion of food) even though this reduces drug absorption by approximately 40%. Administration after a meal results in nearly 100% absorption.

Monitoring Parameters Periodic liver function tests (asymptomatic increases in liver enzymes have occurred); periodic renal function tests and serum electrolytes (in patients at risk for dehydration); hydration status

Dietary Considerations Take this medicine an empty stomach, 1 hour before or 2 hours after a meal.

Special Geriatric Considerations In clinical trials, there was no significant difference between older and younger adults in survival benefit, safety, or pharmacokinetics. No dosage adjustment necessary in elderly patients.

Additional Information Oncology Comment:The National Comprehensive Cancer Network (NCCN) guidelines for NSCLC recommend erlotinib as single agent treatment after failure of first- or second-line treatment of NSCLC in patients with a performance status of 0-2. Erlotinib may be considered for patients with a performance status of 3.

According to the NCCN pancreatic adenocarcinoma guidelines, gemcitabine combination therapy (including gemcitabine + erlotinib) is a first-line option in the treatment of locally-advanced, unresectable, or metastatic pancreatic cancer.

Emetic Potential Low (10% to 30%)

Dosage Forms Excipient information presented when available (limited, particularly for generics); consult specific product labeling.

Tablet:

Tarceva®: 25 mg, 100 mg, 150 mg

References

Blank SV, Chang R, and Muggia F, "Epidermal Growth Factor Receptor Inhibitors for the Treatment of Epithelial Ovarian Cancer," *Oncology*, 2005, 19(4):553-9.

Bonomi P, "Erlotinib: A New Therapeutic Approach for Non-Small Cell Lung Cancer," *Expert Opin Investig Drugs*, 2003, 12(8):1395-1401.

Bulgaru AM, Mani S, Goel S, et al, "Erlotinib (Tarceva): A Promising Drug Targeting Epidermal Growth Factor Receptor Tyrosine Kinase," *Expert Rev Anticancer Ther*, 2001, 3(3):269-79.

Ciardiello F and Tortora G, "A Novel Approach in the Treatment of Cancer: Targeting the Epidermal Growth Factor Receptor," *Clin Cancer Res*, 2001, 7:2958-70.

Herbst RS, "Erlotinib (Tarceva): An Update on the Clinical Trial Program," *Semin Oncol*, 2003, 30(3 Suppl 7):34-46.

Hidalgo M, "Erlotinib: Preclinical Investigations," *Oncology (Williston Park)*, 2003, 17(11 Suppl 12):11-6.

Hidalgo M and Bloedow D, "Pharmacokinetics and Pharmacodynamics: Maximizing the Clinical Potential of Erlotinib (Tarceva)," *Semin Oncol*, 2003, 30(3 Suppl 7):25-33.

Kim TE and Murren JR, "Erlotinib OSI/Roche/Genentech," *Curr Opin Investig Drugs*, 2002, 3(9):1385-95.

Messersmith WA, Laheru DA, Senzer NN, et al, "Phase I Trial of Irinotecan, Infusional 5-Fluorouracil, and Leucovorin (FOLFIRI) With Erlotinib (OSI-774)," *Clin Cancer Res*, 2004, 10:6522-7.

Pérez-Soler R, Chachoua A, Hammond LA, et al, "Determinants of Tumor Response and Survival With Erlotinib in Patients With Non-Small-Cell Lung Cancer," *J Clin Oncol*, 2004, 22(16):3238-47.

Potti A and George DJ, "Tyrosine Kinase Inhibitors in Renal Cell Carcinoma," *Clinical Cancer Research*, 2004, 10(18 Pt 2):6371-6.

Soulieres D, Senzer NN, Vokes EE, et al, "A Multicenter Phase II, Study of Erlotinib, An Oral Epidermal Growth Factor Receptor Tyrosine Kinase Inhibitor, in Patients With Recurrent or Metastatic Squamous Cell Carcinoma of the Head and Neck," *J Clin Oncol*, 2004, 22(1):77-85.

Tan AR, Yang X, Hewitt SM, et al, "Evaluation of Biologic End Points and Pharmacokinetics in Patients With Metastatic Breast Cancer After Treatment With Erlotinib, an Epidermal Growth Factor Receptor Tyrosine Kinase Inhibitor," *J Clin Oncol*, 2004, 22(15):3080-90.

Willett CG, Czito BG, Bendell JC, et al, "Locally Advanced Pancreatic Cancer," *J Clin Oncol*, 2005, 23(20):4538-44.

♦ **Erlotinib Hydrochloride** *see* Erlotinib *on page 396*

♦ *Erwinia* **Asparaginase** *see* Asparaginase *on page 111*

♦ **Erythropoiesis-Stimulating Agent (ESA)** *see* Darbepoetin Alfa *on page 295*

♦ **Erythropoiesis-Stimulating Agent (ESA)** *see* Epoetin Alfa *on page 387*

♦ **Erythropoiesis-Stimulating Protein** *see* Darbepoetin Alfa *on page 295*

♦ **Erythropoietin** *see* Epoetin Alfa *on page 387*

Estramustine (es tra MUS teen)
Medication Safety Issues
Sound-alike/look-alike issues:

Emcyt® may be confused with Eryc®

Estramustine may be confused with exemestane.

High alert medication: The Institute for Safe Medication Practices (ISMP) includes this medication among its list of drugs which have a heightened risk of causing significant patient harm when used in error.

Related Information
Safe Handling of Hazardous Drugs *on page 1382*

U.S. Brand Names Emcyt®

Index Terms Estramustine Phosphate; Estramustine Phosphate Sodium; NSC-89199

Generic Available No

Canadian Brand Names Emcyt®

Pharmacologic Category Antineoplastic Agent, Alkylating Agent; Antineoplastic Agent, Hormone; Antineoplastic Agent, Hormone (Estrogen/Nitrogen Mustard)

Use Palliative treatment of prostatic carcinoma (progressive or metastatic)

Lactation Excretion in breast milk unknown/contraindicated

Labeled Contraindications Hypersensitivity to estramustine, estradiol, nitrogen mustard, or any component of the formulation; active thrombophlebitis or thromboembolic disorders (except where tumor mass is the cause of thromboembolic disorder and the benefit may outweigh the risk)

Warnings/Precautions Hazardous agent - use appropriate precautions for handling and disposal. Glucose tolerance may be decreased; use with caution in patients with diabetes. Elevated blood pressure may occur; exacerbation of peripheral edema or congestive heart disease may occur. Use with caution in patients with impaired liver function, renal insufficiency, metabolic bone diseases, seizure disorder, or migraines. Estrogen treatment for prostate cancer is associated with an increased risk of thrombosis and MI; use caution with history of cardiovascular disease (eg, thrombophlebitis, thrombosis, or thromboembolic disease) and cerebrovascular or coronary artery disease. Patients with prostate cancer and osteoblastic metastases should have their calcium monitored regularly. Estrogen use may cause gynecomastia and/or impotence.

Adverse Reactions
>10%:

Cardiovascular: Edema (20%)

Endocrine & metabolic: Gynecomastia (75%), breast tenderness (71%), libido decreased

Gastrointestinal: Nausea (16%), diarrhea (13%), gastrointestinal upset (12%)

Hepatic: LDH increased (2% to 33%), AST increased (2% to 33%)

Respiratory: Dyspnea (12%)

1% to 10%:

Cardiovascular: CHF (3%), MI (3%), cerebrovascular accident (2%), chest pain (1%), flushing (1%)

Central nervous system: Lethargy (4%), insomnia (3%), emotional lability (2%), anxiety (1%), headache (1%)

Dermatologic: Bruising (3%), pruritus (2%), dry skin (1%), hair thinning (1%), rash (1%), skin peeling (1%)

Gastrointestinal: Anorexia (4%), flatulence (2%), burning throat (1%), gastrointestinal bleeding (1%), thirst (1%), vomiting (1%)

Hematologic: Leukopenia (4%), thrombocytopenia (1%)

Hepatic: Bilirubin increased (1% to 2%)

Local: Thrombophlebitis (3%)

Neuromuscular & skeletal: Leg cramps (9%)

Ocular: Tearing (1%)

Respiratory: Pulmonary embolism (2%), upper respiratory discharge (1%), hoarseness (1%)

<1%, postmarketing, and/or case reports: Allergic reactions, angioedema, cerebrovascular ischemia, coronary ischemia, glucose tolerance decreased, hypercalcemia, impotence, venous thrombosis

Overdosage/Toxicology Symptoms of overdose include nausea, vomiting, and myelosuppression. There are no known antidotes; treatment is symptom-directed and supportive. Monitor CBC and liver function tests for at least 6 weeks following overdose.

Drug Interactions

Decreased Effect: Antacids containing calcium and calcium salts may decrease the absorption of estramustine.

Ethanol/Nutrition/Herb Interactions Food: Estramustine serum levels may be decreased if taken with milk and other dairy products, calcium supplements, and vitamins containing calcium.

Storage/Stability Refrigerate at 2°C to 8°C (36°F to 46°F). Capsules may be stored outside of refrigerator for up to 24-48 hours without affecting potency.

Mechanism of Action Combines the effects of estradiol and nitrogen mustard. It appears to bind to microtubule proteins, preventing normal tubulin function. The antitumor effect may be due solely to an estrogenic effect. Estramustine causes a marked decrease in plasma testosterone and an increase in estrogen levels.

Pharmacodynamics/Kinetics

Absorption: Oral: 75%

Metabolism:

GI tract: Initial dephosphorylation

Hepatic: Oxidation and hydrolysis; metabolites include estramustine, estrone analog, estrone, and estradiol

Half-life elimination: Terminal: 20-24 hours

Time to peak, serum: 2-3 hours

Excretion: Feces (2.9% to 4.8% as unchanged drug)

Dosage Refer to individual protocols.

Oral: Adults: Males: 14 mg/kg/day (range: 10-16 mg/kg/day) in 3 or 4 divided doses

Combination Regimens

Prostate cancer:

Cyclophosphamide + Estramustine *on page 1186*

Doxorubicin + Ketoconazole/Estramustine + Vinblastine *on page 1195*

Estramustine + Docetaxel *on page 1206*

Estramustine + Docetaxel + Calcitriol *on page 1207*

Estramustine + Docetaxel + Carboplatin *on page 1208*

Estramustine + Docetaxel + Hydrocortisone *on page 1208*

Estramustine + Docetaxel + Prednisone *on page 1208*

Estramustine + Etoposide *on page 1209*

Estramustine + Vinorelbine *on page 1209*

EV *on page 1210*

(Continued)

Estramustine *(Continued)*

Paclitaxel + Estramustine + Carboplatin *on page 1265*
Paclitaxel + Estramustine + Etoposide *on page 1265*
PE *on page 1269*

Administration Administer on an empty stomach, at least 1 hour before or 2 hours after eating.

Monitoring Parameters Serum calcium, liver function tests; blood pressure

Dietary Considerations Should be taken at least 1 hour before or 2 hours after eating. Milk products and calcium-rich foods or supplements may impair the oral absorption of estramustine phosphate sodium.

Patient Information It may take several weeks to manifest effects of this medication. Store capsules in refrigerator. Do not take with milk or milk products. Preferable to take on empty stomach (1 hour before or 2 hours after meals). Small frequent meals and frequent mouth care may reduce incidence of nausea or vomiting. You may experience flatulence, diarrhea, decreased libido (reversible), breast tenderness or enlargement. Report sudden acute pain or cramping in legs or calves, chest pain, shortness of breath, weakness or numbness of arms or legs, difficulty breathing, or edema (increased weight, swelling of legs or feet); contraceptive measures are recommended during therapy.

Emetic Potential Moderate (10% to 60%)

Dosage Forms Excipient information presented when available (limited, particularly for generics); consult specific product labeling.

Capsule, as phosphate sodium:
Emcyt®: 140 mg

References

Benson R and Hartley-Asp B, "Mechanisms of Action and Clinical Uses of Estramustine," *Cancer Invest*, 1990, 8(3-4):375-80.
Bergenheim AT and Henriksson R, "Pharmacokinetics and Pharmacodynamics of Estramustine Phosphate," *Clin Pharmacokinet*, 1998, 34(2):163-72.
Gunnarsson PO and Forshell GP, "Clinical Pharmacokinetics of Estramustine Phosphate," *Urology*, 1984, 23(6 Suppl):22-7.
Hudes GR, "Estramustine-Based Chemotherapy," *Semin Urol Oncol*, 1997, 15(1):13-9.
Kreis W, "Estramustine Revisited," *Cancer Treat Res*, 1995, 78:163-84.
Perry CM and McTavish D, "Estramustine Phosphate Sodium. A Review of Its Pharmacodynamic and Pharmacokinetic Properties, and Therapeutic Efficacy in Prostate Cancer," *Drugs Aging*, 1995, 7(1):49-74.

♦ **Estramustine Phosphate** *see* Estramustine *on page 400*

♦ **Estramustine Phosphate Sodium** *see* Estramustine *on page 400*

♦ **Ethiofos** *see* Amifostine *on page 53*

♦ **ETH-Oxydose**™ *see* Oxycodone *on page 849*

♦ **Ethoxynaphthamido Penicillin Sodium** *see* Nafcillin *on page 800*

♦ **Ethyol®** *see* Amifostine *on page 53*

♦ **Etopophos®** *see* Etoposide Phosphate *on page 409*

Etoposide *(e toe POE side)*

Medication Safety Issues

Sound-alike/look-alike issues:
Etoposide may be confused with teniposide
VePesid® may be confused with Versed

High alert medication: The Institute for Safe Medication Practices (ISMP) includes this medication among its list of drugs which have a heightened risk of causing significant patient harm when used in error.

Related Information

Hematopoietic Stem Cell Transplantation *on page 1366*

Safe Handling of Hazardous Drugs *on page 1382*

U.S. Brand Names Toposar®; VePesid®

Index Terms Epipodophyllotoxin; VP-16; VP-16-213

Generic Available Yes

Canadian Brand Names VePesid®

Pharmacologic Category Antineoplastic Agent, Podophyllotoxin Derivative

Use Treatment of refractory testicular tumors; treatment of small cell lung cancer

Unlabeled/Investigational Use Treatment of lymphomas, acute nonlymphocytic leukemia (ANLL); lung, bladder, and prostate carcinoma; hepatoma, rhabdomyosarcoma, uterine carcinoma, neuroblastoma, mycosis fungoides, Kaposi's sarcoma, histiocytosis, gestational trophoblastic disease, Ewing's sarcoma, Wilms' tumor, brain tumors

Pregnancy Risk Factor D

Lactation Enters breast milk/contraindicated

Labeled Contraindications Hypersensitivity to etoposide or any component of the formulation; pregnancy

Warnings/Precautions Hazardous agent - use appropriate precautions for handling and disposal. **[U.S. Boxed Warning]: Severe myelosuppression with resulting infection or bleeding may occur.** Treatment should be withheld for platelets <50,000/mm^3 or absolute neutrophil count (ANC) <500/mm^3. May cause anaphylactic reaction manifested by chills, fever, tachycardia, bronchospasm, dyspnea, and hypotension. In children, the use of concentrations higher than recommended were associated with higher rates of anaphylactic-like reactions. Infusion should be interrupted and medications for the treatment of anaphylaxis should be available for immediate use. Must be diluted; do not give I.V. push, infuse over at least 30-60 minutes; hypotension is associated with rapid infusion. Dosage should be adjusted in patients with hepatic or renal impairment. **[U.S. Boxed Warning]: Should be administered under the supervision of an experienced cancer chemotherapy physician.** Injectable formula contains polysorbate 80; do not use in premature infants. May contain benzyl alcohol; do not use in newborn infants.

Adverse Reactions

>10%:

Dermatologic: Alopecia (8% to 66%)

Endocrine & metabolic: Ovarian failure (38%), amenorrhea

Gastrointestinal: Nausea/vomiting (31% to 43%), anorexia (10% to 13%), diarrhea (1% to 13%), mucositis/esophagitis (with high doses)

Hematologic: Leukopenia (60% to 91%; grade 4: 3% to 17%; onset: 5-7 days; nadir: 7-14 days; recovery: 21-28 days), thrombocytopenia (22% to 41%; grades 3/4: 1% to 20%; nadir 9-16 days), anemia (up to 33%)

1% to 10%:

Cardiovascular: Hypotension (1% to 2%; due to rapid infusion)

Gastrointestinal: Stomatitis (1% to 6%), abdominal pain (up to 2%)

Hepatic: Hepatic toxicity (up to 3%)

Neuromuscular & skeletal: Peripheral neuropathy (1% to 2%)

Miscellaneous: Anaphylactic-like reaction (I.V. infusion: 1% to 2%; including chills, fever, tachycardia, bronchospasm, dyspnea)

<1%: Anovulatory cycles, back pain; blindness (transient, cortical); CHF, constipation, cough, cyanosis, diaphoresis, dysphagia, erythema; extravasation (induration, necrosis, swelling); facial swelling, fatigue, fever, headache, hepatic toxicity, hepatitis, hyperpigmentation, hypersensitivity, hypersensitivity-associated apnea, hypomenorrhea, interstitial pneumonitis, laryngospasm, maculopapular rash, malaise, metabolic acidosis, MI, (Continued)

Etoposide *(Continued)*

optic neuritis, perivasculitis, pruritus, pulmonary fibrosis, radiation-recall dermatitis, rash, seizure, somnolence, Stevens-Johnson syndrome, tachycardia, taste perversion, thrombophlebitis, tongue swelling, toxic epidermal necrolysis, urticaria, weakness

Overdosage/Toxicology Symptoms of overdose include bone marrow suppression, leukopenia, thrombocytopenia, nausea, and vomiting. Treatment is symptom-directed and supportive.

Drug Interactions

Cytochrome P450 Effect: Substrate of CYP1A2 (minor), 2E1 (minor), 3A4 (major); **Inhibits** CYP2C9 (weak), 3A4 (weak)

Increased Effect/Toxicity: Cyclosporine may increase the levels of etoposide; consider reducing the dose of etoposide by 50%. Etoposide may increase the effects/toxicity of warfarin. CYP3A4 inhibitors may increase the levels/effects of etoposide; example inhibitors include azole antifungals, clarithromycin, diclofenac, doxycycline, erythromycin, imatinib, isoniazid, nefazodone, nicardipine, propofol, protease inhibitors, quinidine, telithromycin, and verapamil.

Decreased Effect: Barbiturates and phenytoin may decrease the levels/effects of etoposide; monitor. CYP3A4 inducers may decrease the levels/effects of etoposide; example inducers include aminoglutethimide, carbamazepine, nafcillin, nevirapine, phenobarbital, phenytoin, and rifamycins.

Ethanol/Nutrition/Herb Interactions

Ethanol: Avoid ethanol (may increase GI irritation).

Herb/Nutraceutical: Avoid concurrent St John's wort; may decrease etoposide levels.

Storage/Stability Store intact vials of injection at 15°C to 30°C (59°F to 86°F). Protect from light. Store oral capsules at 2°C to 8°C (36°F to 46°F). Solutions for infusion, at room temperature, in D_5W or NS in polyvinyl chloride, the concentration is stable as follows:

0.2 mg/mL: 96 hours

0.4 mg/mL: 24 hours

Etoposide injection contains polysorbate 80 which may cause leaching of diethylhexyl phthalate (DEHP), a plasticizer contained in polyvinyl chloride (PVC) bags and tubing. Higher concentrations and longer storage time after preparation in PVC bags may increase DEHP leaching. Preparation in glass or polyolefin containers will minimize patient exposure to DEHP.

Etoposide injection diluted for oral use to 10 mg/mL in NS may be stored for 22 days in plastic oral syringes at room temperature. Mix with orange juice, apple juice, or lemonade to a concentration of ≤0.4 mg/mL, and use within a 3-hour period.

Reconstitution Etoposide should be diluted to a concentration of 0.2-0.4 mg/mL in D_5W or NS for administration. Diluted solutions have concentration-dependent stability: More concentrated solutions have shorter stability times. Precipitation may occur with concentrations >0.4 mg/mL.

Compatibility Variable stability (consult detailed reference) in D_5W, LR, NS.

Y-site administration: Compatible: Allopurinol, amifostine, aztreonam, cladribine, doxorubicin liposome, fludarabine, gemcitabine, granisetron, melphalan, ondansetron, paclitaxel, piperacillin/tazobactam, sargramostim, sodium bicarbonate, teniposide, thiotepa, topotecan, vinorelbine. **Incompatible:** Cefepime, filgrastim, idarubicin.

Compatibility when admixed: Compatible: Carboplatin, cisplatin, cisplatin with cyclophosphamide, cisplatin with floxuridine, cytarabine, cytarabine with daunorubicin, floxuridine, fluorouracil, hydroxyzine, ifosfamide, ifosfamide with carboplatin, ifosfamide with cisplatin, ondansetron. **Variable (consult detailed reference):** Cisplatin with mannitol and potassium chloride, doxorubicin with vincristine.

Mechanism of Action Etoposide has been shown to delay transit of cells through the S phase and arrest cells in late S or early G_2 phase. The drug may inhibit mitochondrial transport at the NADH dehydrogenase level or inhibit uptake of nucleosides into HeLa cells. It is a topoisomerase II inhibitor and appears to cause DNA strand breaks. Etoposide does not inhibit microtubular assembly.

Pharmacodynamics/Kinetics

Absorption: Oral: 25% to 75%; significant inter- and intrapatient variation

Distribution: Average V_d: 7-17 L/m²; poor penetration across the blood-brain barrier; CSF concentrations <10% of plasma concentrations

Protein binding: 94% to 97%

Metabolism: Hepatic to hydroxy acid and cislactone metabolites

Bioavailability: Oral: ~50% (range 25% to 75%)

Half-life elimination: Terminal: 4-11 hours; Children: Normal renal/hepatic function: 6-8 hours

Time to peak, serum: Oral: 1-1.5 hours

Excretion:

Children: Urine (≤55% as unchanged drug)

Adults: Urine (42% to 67%; 8% to 35% as unchanged drug) within 24 hours; feces (up to 44%)

Dosage Refer to individual protocols:

Children (unlabeled uses): I.V.: 60-120 mg/m²/day for 3-5 days every 3-6 weeks

AML:

Remission induction: 150 mg/m²/day for 2-3 days for 2-3 cycles

Intensification or consolidation: 250 mg/m²/day for 3 days, courses 2-5

Brain tumor: 150 mg/m²/day on days 2 and 3 of treatment course

Neuroblastoma: 100 mg/m²/day over 1 hour on days 1-5 of cycle; repeat cycle every 4 weeks

BMT conditioning regimen used in patients with rhabdomyosarcoma or neuroblastoma: I.V. continuous infusion: 160 mg/m²/day for 4 days

Conditioning regimen for allogenic BMT: 60 mg/kg/dose as a single dose

Adults:

Small cell lung cancer (in combination with other approved chemotherapeutic drugs):

Oral: Due to poor bioavailability, oral doses should be twice the I.V. dose, rounded to the nearest 50 mg given once daily

I.V.: 35 mg/m²/day for 4 days or 50 mg/m²/day for 5 days every 3-4 weeks

IVPB: 60-100 mg/m²/day for 3 days (with cisplatin)

CIV: 500 mg/m² over 24 hours every 3 weeks

Testicular cancer (in combination with other approved chemotherapeutic drugs):

IVPB: 50-100 mg/m²/day for 5 days repeated every 3-4 weeks

I.V.: 100 mg/m² every other day for 3 doses repeated every 3-4 weeks

BMT/relapsed leukemia (unlabeled uses): I.V.: 2.4-3.5 g/m² or 25-70 mg/kg administered over 4-36 hours

Dosing adjustment in renal impairment:

The FDA-approved labeling recommends the following adjustments:

Cl_{cr} 15-50 mL/minute: Administer 75% of dose

Cl_{cr} <15 mL minute: Data not available; consider further dose reductions

(Continued)

Etoposide *(Continued)*

The following guidelines have been used by some clinicians:

Aronoff, 2007:

Cl_{cr} 10-50 mL/minute: Children and Adults: Administer 75% of dose

Cl_{cr} <10 mL minute: Children and Adults: Administer 50% of dose

Hemodialysis:

Children: Administer 50% of dose

Adults: Supplemental dose is not necessary

Continuous ambulatory peritoneal dialysis (CAPD):

Children: Administer 50% of dose

Adults: Supplemental dose is not necessary

Continuous renal replacement therapy (CRRT): Children and Adults: Administer 75% of dose

Kintzel, 1995:

Cl_{cr} 46-60 mL/minute: Administer 85% of dose

Cl_{cr} 31-45 mL/minute: Administer 80% of dose

Cl_{cr} <30 mL/minute: Administer 75% of dose

Dosing adjustment in hepatic impairment: The FDA-approved labeling does not contain dosing adjustment guidelines. The following adjustments have been used by some clinicians:

Donelli, 1998: Liver dysfunction may reduce the metabolism and increase the toxicity of etoposide. Normal doses of I.V. etoposide should be given to patients with liver dysfunction (dose reductions may result in subtherapeutic concentrations); however, use caution with concomitant liver dysfunction (severe) and renal dysfunction as the decreased metabolic clearance cannot be compensated by increased renal clearance.

Floyd, 2006: Bilirubin 1.5-3 mg/dL or AST >3 times ULN: Administer 50% of dose

King, 2001: Bilirubin 1.5-3 mg/dL or ALT or AST >180 units/L: Administer 50% of dose

Koren, 1992: Bilirubin 1.5-3 mg/dL or AST >180 units/L: Administer 50% of dose

Perry, 1982:

Bilirubin 1.5-3 mg/dL or AST 60-180 units/L: Administer 50% of dose

Bilirubin >3 mg/dL or AST >180 units/L: Avoid use

Combination Regimens

Adenocarcinoma, unknown primary:

EP (Adenocarcinoma) *on page 1203*

Paclitaxel-Carboplatin-Etoposide *on page 1264*

PCE *on page 1266*

Brain tumors:

CDDP/VP-16 *on page 1165*

COPE *on page 1182*

Breast cancer: ICE-T *on page 1238*

Gastric cancer:

EAP *on page 1197*

EFP *on page 1198*

ELF *on page 1199*

Gestational trophoblastic tumor:

EMA/CO *on page 1199*

EP/EMA *on page 1203*

Leukemia, acute lymphocytic: Hyper-CVAD (Leukemia, Acute Lymphocytic) *on page 1231*

Leukemia, acute myeloid:

7 + 3 + 7 *on page 1141*

DAV *on page 1189*
EMA 86 *on page 1199*
Idarubicin, Cytarabine, Etoposide (ICE Protocol) *on page 1239*
Idarubicin, Cytarabine, Etoposide (IDA-Based BF12) *on page 1239*
MV *on page 1255*
V-TAD *on page 1293*
Lung cancer (small cell):
  CAVE *on page 1163*
  EC (Small Cell Lung Cancer) *on page 1198*
  EP (Small Cell Lung Cancer) *on page 1205*
  VIP (Small Cell Lung Cancer) *on page 1291*
  VP (Small Cell Lung Cancer) *on page 1293*
Lung cancer (nonsmall cell):
  EC (Nonsmall Cell Lung Cancer) *on page 1197*
  EP (Nonsmall Cell Lung Cancer) *on page 1204*
  EP/PE *on page 1204*
Lymphoma, Hodgkin's:
  BEACOPP *on page 1148*
  EVA *on page 1210*
  mini-BEAM *on page 1248*
  Stanford V *on page 1278*
Lymphoma, non-Hodgkin's:
  CEPP(B) *on page 1167*
  EPOCH *on page 1204*
  ESHAP *on page 1206*
  ICE (Lymphoma, non-Hodgkin's) *on page 1238*
  IMVP-16 *on page 1240*
  IVAC *on page 1242*
  MINE *on page 1247*
  MINE-ESHAP *on page 1247*
  Pro-MACE-CytaBOM *on page 1273*
  RICE *on page 1277*
Lymphoma, non-Hodgkin's (Burkitt's): CODOX-M/IVAC *on page 1180*
Multiple myeloma: DTPACE *on page 1196*
Neuroblastoma:
  CAV-P/VP *on page 1163*
  CDDP/VP-16 *on page 1165*
  CE (Neuroblastoma) *on page 1166*
  CE-CAdO *on page 1166*
  HIPE-IVAD *on page 1229*
  N6 Protocol *on page 1260*
  Regimen A2 *on page 1277*
Osteosarcoma: ICE (Sarcoma) *on page 1238*
Ovarian cancer:
  BEP (Ovarian Cancer) *on page 1149*
  BEP (Ovarian Cancer, Testicular Cancer) *on page 1149*
Prostate cancer:
  Cyclophosphamide + Etoposide *on page 1186*
  Estramustine + Etoposide *on page 1209*
  Paclitaxel + Estramustine + Etoposide *on page 1265*
Retinoblastoma:
  CCCDE (Retinoblastoma) *on page 1164*
  CE (Retinoblastoma) *on page 1167*
Sarcoma: VAC Alternating With IE (Ewing's Sarcoma) *on page 1285*
Soft tissue sarcoma
  ICE (Sarcoma) *on page 1238*
(Continued)

Etoposide *(Continued)*

ICE-T *on page 1238*
IE *on page 1239*
Testicular cancer:
BEP (Ovarian Cancer, Testicular Cancer) *on page 1149*
BEP (Testicular Cancer) *on page 1149*
EP (Testicular Cancer) *on page 1205*
VIP (Etoposide) (Testicular Cancer) *on page 1290*

Administration

Oral: Doses ≤400 mg/day as a single once daily dose; doses >400 mg should be given in 2-4 divided doses. If necessary, the injection may be used for oral administration.

I.V.: As a bolus or 24-hour continuous infusion; bolus infusions are usually administered over at least 45-60 minutes. Infusion of doses in ≤30 minutes greatly increases the risk of hypotension. Etoposide injection contains polysorbate 80 which may cause leaching of diethylhexyl phthalate (DEHP), a plasticizer contained in polyvinyl chloride (PVC) tubing. Administration through non-PVC (low sorbing) tubing will minimize patient exposure to DEHP. Concentrations >0.4 mg/mL are very unstable and may precipitate within a few minutes. For large doses, where dilution to ≤0.4 mg/mL is not feasible, consideration should be given to slow infusion of the undiluted drug through a running normal saline, dextrose or saline/dextrose infusion; or use of etoposide phosphate. Etoposide solutions of 0.1-0.4 mg/mL may be filtered through a 0.22 micron filter without damage to the filter or significant loss of drug.

Monitoring Parameters CBC with differential, platelet count, and hemoglobin, vital signs (blood pressure), bilirubin, and renal function tests

Patient Information During therapy, do not use alcohol, aspirin-containing products, and/or OTC medications without consulting prescriber. It is important to maintain adequate nutrition and hydration (2-3 L/day of fluids unless instructed to restrict fluid intake) during therapy; frequent small meals may help. You may experience mild nausea or vomiting (frequent small meals, frequent mouth care, sucking lozenges, or chewing gum may help). You may experience loss of hair (reversible); you will be more susceptible to infection (avoid crowds and exposure to infection as much as possible). Yogurt or buttermilk may help reduce diarrhea. Frequent mouth care and use of a soft toothbrush or cotton swabs may help prevent mouth sores. This drug may cause sterility or birth defects. Report extreme fatigue, pain or numbness in extremities, severe GI upset or diarrhea, bleeding or bruising, fever, chills, sore throat, vaginal discharge, difficulty breathing, yellowing of eyes or skin, and any changes in color of urine or stool. Contraceptive measures are recommended during therapy. The drug may be excreted in breast milk, therefore, an alternative form of feeding your baby should be used.

Emetic Potential Mild (10% to 30%)

Vesicant No; irritant

High Dose Considerations

Comments: The etoposide formulation contains ethanol 30.3% (v/v). Etoposide 2.4 mg/m^2 delivers ethanol 45 g/m^2 I.V. Adverse effects may be increased with administration of etoposide to patients with decreased creatinine clearance. Etoposide 400-1600 mg/m^2 has been drawn into plastic syringes undiluted (20 mg/mL) for administration over 3-4 hours. Etoposide 800 mg/m^2 was pharmacokinetically equivalent to etoposide phosphate 910 mg/m^2 in patients with refractory hematologic malignancies.

High Dose: I.V.: 750-2400 mg/m²; 10-60 mg/kg; duration of infusion is 1-4 hours to 24 hours; generally combined with other high-dose chemotherapeutic drugs or total body irradiation (TBI).

Unique Toxicities:

Cardiovascular: Hypotension (infusion-related)

Central nervous system: Confusion, somnolence, seizure activity increased

Dermatologic: Skin lesions resembling Stevens-Johnson syndrome, alopecia

Endocrine & metabolic: Metabolic acidosis, parotitis

Gastrointestinal: Severe nausea and vomiting, mucositis

Hepatic: Hepatitis

Neuromuscular & skeletal: Peripheral neuropathy, motor deficits exacerbated

Miscellaneous: Secondary malignancy, ethanol intoxication (infusion-related)

Dosage Forms Excipient information presented when available (limited, particularly for generics); consult specific product labeling.

Capsule, softgel:

VePesid®: 50 mg

Injection, solution: 20 mg/mL (5 mL, 25 mL, 50 mL)

Toposar®: 20 mg/mL (5 mL, 25 mL, 50 mL) [contains alcohol 33% and polysorbate 80]

References

Aronoff GR, Bennett WM, Berns JS, et al, *Drug Prescribing in Renal Failure: Dosing Guidelines for Adults and Children*, 5th ed. Philadelphia, PA: American College of Physicians; 2007, p 99, 171.

Clark PL and Slevin ML, "The Clinical Pharmacology of Etoposide and Teniposide," *Clin Pharmacokinet*, 1987, 12(4):223-52.

de Lemos ML, Hamata L, and Vu T, "Leaching of Diethylhexyl Phthalate from Polyvinyl Chloride Materials into Etoposide Intravenous Solutions," *J Oncol Pharm Pract*, 2005, 11(4):155-7.

Demoré B, Vigneron J, Perrin A, et al, "Leaching of Diethylhexyl Phthalate from Polyvinyl Chloride Bags into Intravenous Etoposide Solution," *J Clin Pharm Ther*, 2002, 27(2):139-42.

Donelli MG, Zucchetti M, Munzone E, et al, "Pharmacokinetics of Anticancer Agents in Patients With Impaired Liver Function," *Eur J Cancer*, 1998, 34(1):33-46.

Floyd J, Mirza I, Sachs B, et al, "Hepatotoxicity of Chemotherapy," *Semin Oncol*, 2006, 33(1):50-67.

Hainsworth JD and Greco FA, "Etoposide: Twenty Years Later," *Ann Oncol*, 1995, 6(4):325-41.

Joel SP, Shah R, and Slevin ML, "Etoposide Dosage and Pharmacodynamics," *Cancer Chemother Pharmacol*, 1994, 34(Suppl):69-75.

King PD and Perry MC, "Hepatotoxicity of Chemotherapy," *Oncologist*, 2001, 6(2):162-76.

Kintzel PE and Dorr RT, "Anticancer Drug Renal Toxicity and Elimination: Dosing Guidelines for Altered Renal Function," *Cancer Treat Rev*, 1995, 21(1):33-64.

Koren G, Beatty K, Seto A, et al, "The Effects of Impaired Liver Function on the Elimination of Antineoplastic Agents," *Ann Pharmacother*, 1992, 26(3):363-71.

McLeod HL and Relling MV, "Stability of Etoposide Solution for Oral Use," *Am J Hosp Pharm*, 1992, 49(11):2784-5.

Meresse P, Dechaux E, Monneret C, et al, "Etoposide: Discovery and Medicinal Chemistry," *Curr Med Chem*, 2004, 11(18):2443-66.

Perry MC, "Hepatotoxicity of Chemotherapeutic Agents," *Semin Oncol*, 1982, 9(1):65-73.

Toffoli G, Corona G, Basso B, et al "Pharmacokinetic Optimisation of Treatment with Oral Etoposide," *Clin Pharmacokinet*, 2004, 43(7):441-66.

Trissel L, *Handbook of Injectable Drugs*, 13th ed, Bethesda, MD: American Society of Health-System Pharmacists; 2005, p 590-6.

Etoposide Phosphate (e toe POE side FOS fate)

Medication Safety Issues

Sound-alike/look-alike issues:

Etoposide may be confused with teniposide

Etoposide phosphate is a prodrug of etoposide and is rapidly converted in the plasma to etoposide. To avoid confusion or dosing errors, **dosage**

(Continued)

Etoposide Phosphate *(Continued)*

should be expressed as the desired etoposide dose, not as the etoposide phosphate dose (eg, etoposide phosphate equivalent to _____ mg etoposide).

High alert medication: The Institute for Safe Medication Practices (ISMP) includes this medication among its list of drugs which have a heightened risk of causing significant patient harm when used in error.

Related Information

Safe Handling of Hazardous Drugs *on page 1382*

U.S. Brand Names Etopophos®

Generic Available No

Pharmacologic Category Antineoplastic Agent, Podophyllotoxin Derivative

Use Treatment of refractory testicular tumors; treatment of small cell lung cancer

Pregnancy Risk Factor D

Lactation Enters breast milk/contraindicated

Labeled Contraindications Hypersensitivity to etoposide, etoposide phosphate, or any component of the formulation; pregnancy

Warnings/Precautions Hazardous agent - use appropriate precautions for handling and disposal. **[U.S. Boxed Warning]: Severe myelosuppression with resulting infection or bleeding may occur.** Treatment should be withheld for platelets <50,000/mm³ or absolute neutrophil count (ANC) <500/mm³. May cause anaphylactic reaction manifested by chills, fever, tachycardia, bronchospasm, dyspnea, and hypotension (higher concentrations were associated with higher rates of reactions in children). Infusion should be interrupted and medications for the treatment of anaphylaxis should be available for immediate use. Dosage should be adjusted in patients with hepatic or renal impairment. Use with caution in patients with low serum albumin; may increase risk for toxicities. Doses of etoposide phosphate >175 mg/m² have not been evaluated. Use caution in elderly patients (may be more likely to develop severe myelosuppression and/or GI effects. **[U.S. Boxed Warning]: Should be administered under the supervision of an experienced cancer chemotherapy physician.** Safety and efficacy in children have not been established.

Adverse Reactions Note: Also see adverse reactions for **etoposide**. Since etoposide phosphate is converted to etoposide, adverse reactions experienced with etoposide would also be expected with etoposide phosphate.

>10%:

    Central nervous system: Chills/fever (24%)

    Dermatologic: Alopecia (33% to 44%)

    Gastrointestinal: Nausea/vomiting (37%), anorexia (16%), mucositis (11%)

    Hematologic: Leukopenia (91%; grade 4: 17%), neutropenia (88%; grade 4: 37%), anemia (72%; grades 3/4: 19%), thrombocytopenia (23%; grade 4: 9%)

    Neuromuscular and skeletal: Weakness/malaise (39%)

1% to 10%:

    Cardiovascular: Hypotension (5%), hypertension (3%), facial flushing (2%)

    Central nervous system: Dizziness (5%)

    Dermatologic: Skin rash (3%)

    Gastrointestinal: Constipation (8%), abdominal pain (7%), diarrhea (6%), taste perversion (6%)

    Local: Extravasation/phlebitis (5%)

    Miscellaneous: Anaphylactic-type reactions (3%; including chills, diaphoresis, fever, rigor, tachycardia, bronchospasm, dyspnea, pruritus)

<1%, postmarketing, and/or case reports: Acute leukemia (with/without preleukemia phase), anaphylactic-like reactions, back pain, blindness (transient, cortical), cough, cyanosis, diaphoresis, dysphagia, erythema, facial swelling, hepatic toxicity, hyperpigmentation, hypersensitivity-associated apnea, infection, interstitial pneumonitis, laryngospasm, maculopapular rash, neutropenic fever, optic neuritis, perivasculitis, pruritus, pulmonary fibrosis, radiation recall dermatitis, seizure, Stevens-Johnson syndrome, taste perversion, tongue swelling, toxic epidermal necrolysis, urticaria

Overdosage/Toxicology Symptoms of overdose include bone marrow suppression, leukopenia, thrombocytopenia, nausea, and vomiting. Treatment is symptom-directed and supportive.

Drug Interactions

Cytochrome P450 Effect: Substrate of CYP1A2 (minor), 2E1 (minor), 3A4 (major); **Inhibits** CYP2C9 (weak), 3A4 (weak)

Increased Effect/Toxicity: Cyclosporine may increase the levels/effects of etoposide phosphate, via CYP isoenzymes and may decrease the p-glycoprotein-mediated elimination of etoposide phosphate. CYP3A4 inhibitors may increase the levels/effects of etoposide; example inhibitors include azole antifungals, clarithromycin, diclofenac, doxycycline, erythromycin, imatinib, isoniazid, nefazodone, nicardipine, propofol, protease inhibitors, quinidine, telithromycin, and verapamil.

Decreased Effect: Barbiturates and phenytoin may decrease the levels/effects of etoposide; monitor. CYP3A4 inducers may decrease the levels/effects of etoposide; example inducers include aminoglutethimide, carbamazepine, nafcillin, nevirapine, phenobarbital, phenytoin, and rifamycins.

Ethanol/Nutrition/Herb Interactions

Ethanol: Avoid ethanol (may increase GI irritation).

Herb/Nutraceutical: Avoid St John's wort (may decrease etoposide levels).

Storage/Stability Store intact vials of injection under refrigeration 2°C to 8°C (36°F to 46°F). Protect from light. Reconstituted etoposide phosphate is stable refrigerated at 2°C to 8°C (36°F to 47°F) for 7 days. Undiluted solutions are stable for 24 hours at room temperature of 20°C to 25°C (68°F to 77°F) when reconstituted with SWI, D₅W or NS; and stable for 48 hours at room temperature when reconstituted with bacteriostatic SWI or NS. Further diluted solutions are stable at room temperature 20°C to 25°C (68°F to 77°F) or under refrigeration 2°C to 8°C (36°F to 47°F) for up to 24 hours.

Reconstitution Reconstitute with 5 mL or 10 mL SWI, D₅W, NS, bacteriostatic SWI, or bacteriostatic NS to a concentration of 20 mg/mL or 10 mg/mL etoposide equivalent. These solutions may be administered without further dilution or may be diluted in 50-500 mL of D₅W or NS to a concentration as low as 0.1 mg/mL.

Compatibility Stable in D₅W, NS, sterile water for injection.

Y-site administration: Compatible: Acyclovir, amikacin, aminophylline, ampicillin, ampicillin/sulbactam, aztreonam, bleomycin, bumetanide, buprenorphine, butorphanol, calcium gluconate, carboplatin, carmustine, cefazolin, cefoperazone, cefotaxime, cefotetan, cefoxitin, ceftazidime, ceftizoxime, ceftriaxone, cefuroxime, cimetidine, ciprofloxacin, cisplatin, clindamycin, co-trimoxazole, cyclophosphamide, cytarabine, dacarbazine, dactinomycin, daunorubicin, dexamethasone sodium phosphate, diphenhydramine, dobutamine, dopamine, doxorubicin, doxycycline, droperidol, enalaprilat, famotidine, floxuridine, fluconazole, fludarabine, fluorouracil, furosemide, ganciclovir, gatifloxacin, gemcitabine, gentamicin, granisetron, haloperidol, heparin, hydrocortisone sodium phosphate, hydrocortisone

(Continued)

411

Etoposide Phosphate *(Continued)*

sodium succinate, hydromorphone, hydroxyzine, idarubicin, ifosfamide, leucovorin, linezolid, lorazepam, magnesium sulfate, mannitol, meperidine, mesna, methotrexate, metoclopramide, metronidazole, minocycline, mito-xantrone, morphine, nalbuphine, netilmicin, ofloxacin, ondansetron, paclitaxel, piperacillin, piperacillin/tazobactam, plicamycin, potassium chloride, promethazine, ranitidine, sodium bicarbonate, streptozocin, tenipo-side, thiotepa, ticarcillin, ticarcillin/clavulanate, tobramycin, vancomycin, vinblastine, vincristine, zidovudine. **Incompatible:** Amphotericin B, cefepime, chlorpromazine, imipenem/cilastatin, methylprednisolone sodium succinate, mitomycin, prochlorperazine edisylate.

Mechanism of Action Etoposide phosphate is converted *in vivo* to the active moiety, etoposide, by dephosphorylation. Etoposide inhibits mitotic activity; inhibits cells from entering prophase; inhibits DNA synthesis. Initially thought to be mitotic inhibitors similar to podophyllotoxin, but actually have no effect on microtubule assembly. However, later shown to induce DNA strand breakage and inhibition of topoisomerase II (an enzyme which breaks and repairs DNA); etoposide acts in late S or early G2 phases.

Pharmacodynamics/Kinetics

Distribution: Average V_d: 7-17 L/m²; poor penetration across blood-brain barrier; concentrations in CSF being <10% that of plasma

Protein binding: 94% to 97%

Metabolism:

Etoposide phosphate: Rapidly and completely converted to etoposide in plasma

Etoposide: Hepatic, via CYP3A4, to hydroxy acid and cislactone metabolites

Half-life elimination: Terminal: 4-11 hours; Children: Normal renal/hepatic function: 6-8 hours

Excretion: Urine (56%; 45% as etoposide); feces (44% as etoposide and metabolites)

Children: I.V.: Urine (≤55% as etoposide)

Dosage Refer to individual protocols. Adults: Note: Etoposide phosphate is a prodrug of etoposide, doses should be expressed as the desired **ETOPO-SIDE** dose; **not** as the etoposide phosphate dose. (eg, etoposide phosphate equivalent to ____ mg etoposide).

Small cell lung cancer (in combination with other approved chemotherapeutic drugs): I.V.: Etoposide 35 mg/m²/day for 4 days to 50 mg/m²/day for 5 days. Courses are repeated at 3- to 4-week intervals after adequate recovery from any toxicity.

Testicular cancer (in combination with other approved chemotherapeutic agents): I.V.: Etoposide 50-100 mg/m²/day on days 1-5 to 100 mg/m²/day on days 1, 3, and 5. Courses are repeated at 3- to 4-week intervals after adequate recovery from any toxicity.

Dosage adjustment in renal impairment:

Manufacturer recommended guidelines:

Cl_{cr} 15-50 mL/minute: Administer 75% of normal dose

Cl_{cr} <15 mL minute: Data are available; consider further dose reductions

Aronoff, 1999:

Cl_{cr} 10-50 mL/minute: Administer 75% of normal dose

Cl_{cr} <10 mL/minute: Administer 50% of normal dose

Hemodialysis: Supplemental dose is not necessary

Peritoneal dialysis: Supplemental dose is not necessary

CAPD effects: Unknown

CAVH effects: Dose for Cl_{cr} 10-50 mL/minute (Aronoff, 1999)

Dosage adjustment in hepatic impairment:
Bilirubin 1.5-3 mg/dL or AST 60-180 units: Reduce dose by 50%
Bilirubin 3-5 mg/dL or AST >180 units: Reduce by 75%
Bilirubin >5 mg/dL: Do not administer

Administration Infuse over 5-210 minutes.

Monitoring Parameters CBC with differential, platelet count, bilirubin, renal function

Patient Information This drug can only be administered by infusion. During therapy, do not use alcohol, aspirin-containing products, and/or OTC medications without consulting prescriber. It is important to maintain adequate nutrition and hydration (2-3 L/day of fluids unless instructed to restrict fluid intake) during therapy; frequent small meals may help. You may experience mild nausea or vomiting (frequent small meals, frequent mouth care, sucking lozenges, or chewing gum may help). You may experience loss of hair (reversible); you will be more susceptible to infection (avoid crowds and exposure to infection as much as possible). Yogurt or buttermilk may help reduce diarrhea. Frequent mouth care and use of a soft toothbrush or cotton swabs may help prevent mouth sores. This drug may cause sterility or birth defects. Report extreme fatigue, pain or numbness in extremities, severe GI upset or diarrhea, bleeding or bruising, fever, chills, sore throat, vaginal discharge, difficulty breathing, yellowing of eyes or skin, and any changes in color of urine or stool. Contraceptive measures should be used during therapy. The drug may cause permanent sterility and may cause birth defects. The drug may be excreted in breast milk, therefore, an alternative form of feeding your baby should be used.

Special Geriatric Considerations Elderly patients may be more susceptible to severe myelosuppression. Other adverse effects including GI toxicity, infectious complications, weakness, and alopecia may occur more frequently in elderly.

Additional Information Etoposide phosphate 113.5 mg is equivalent to etoposide 100 mg. Dosages should always be expressed, and calculated, as the desired **etoposide** dose.

Emetic Potential Mild (10% to 30%)

Vesicant No

High Dose Considerations

Comments: In contrast to etoposide, metabolic acidosis is not a frequent adverse effect of high-dose etoposide phosphate. Etoposide 800 mg/m^2 was pharmacokinetically equivalent to etoposide phosphate 910 mg/m^2 in patients with refractory hematologic malignancies.

High Dose: I.V.: 0.5-2 g/m^2 divided into 2 daily doses; maximum single-dose agent: 3.2 g/m^2; generally combined with other high-dose chemotherapeutic drugs.

Unique Toxicities: Gastrointestinal: Nausea, vomiting, mucositis

Dosage Forms Excipient information presented when available (limited, particularly for generics); consult specific product labeling.
Injection, powder for reconstitution:
Etopophos®: 100 mg

References

Aronoff GR, Berns JS, Brier ME, et al, "Drug Prescribing in Renal Failure: Dosing Guidelines for Adults," 4th ed. Philadelphia, PA: American College of Physicians; 1999, p 73.

Budman DR, "Early Studies of Etoposide Phosphate, a Water-Soluble Prodrug," *Semin Oncol*, 1996, 23(6 Suppl 13):8-14.

Dorr RT, Briggs A, Kintzel P, et al, "Comparative Pharmacokinetic Study of High-Dose Etoposide and Etoposide Phosphate in Patients With Lymphoid Malignancy Receiving Autologous Stem Cell Transplantation," *Bone Marrow Transplant*, 2003, 31(8):643-9.

Greco FA and Hainsworth JD, "Clinical Studies With Etoposide Phosphate," *Semin Oncol*, 1996, 23(6 Suppl 13):45-50.

(Continued)

Etoposide Phosphate *(Continued)*

Mummaneni V, Kaul S, Igwemezie LN, et al, "Bioequivalence Assessment of Etoposide Phosphate and Etoposide Using Pharmacodynamic and Traditional Pharmacokinetic Parameters," *J Pharmacokinet Biopharm*, 1996, 24(4):313-25.

Schacter LP, Igwemezie LN, Seyedsadr M, et al, "Clinical and Pharmacokinetic Overview of Parenteral Etoposide Phosphate," *Cancer Chemother Pharmacol*, 1994, 34(Suppl):58-63.

Witterland AH, Koks CH, and Beijnen JH, "Etoposide Phosphate, the Water Soluble Prodrug of Etoposide," *Pharm World Sci*, 1996, 18(5):163-70.

♦ **Euflex® (Can)** *see* Flutamide *on page 470*

♦ **Eulexin®** *see* Flutamide *on page 470*

♦ **Evista®** *see* Raloxifene *on page 940*

Exemestane *(ex e MES tane)*

Medication Safety Issues

Sound-alike/look-alike issues:

Exemestane may be confused with estramustine.

Related Information

Safe Handling of Hazardous Drugs *on page 1382*

U.S. Brand Names Aromasin®

Generic Available No

Canadian Brand Names Aromasin®

Pharmacologic Category Antineoplastic Agent, Aromatase Inactivator

Use Treatment of advanced breast cancer in postmenopausal women whose disease has progressed following tamoxifen therapy; adjuvant treatment of postmenopausal estrogen receptor-positive early breast cancer following 2-3 years of tamoxifen (for a total of 5 years of adjuvant therapy)

Pregnancy Risk Factor D

Lactation Excretion in breast milk unknown/use caution

Labeled Contraindications Hypersensitivity to exemestane or any component of the formulation; pregnancy

Warnings/Precautions Hazardous agent - use appropriate precautions for handling and disposal. Not indicated for premenopausal women; not to be given with estrogen-containing agents.

Adverse Reactions

>10%:

Cardiovascular: Hypertension (5% to 15%)

Central nervous system: Fatigue (8% to 22%), insomnia (11% to 14%), pain (13%), headache (7% to 13%), depression (6% to 13%)

Dermatological: Hyperhidrosis (4% to 18%), alopecia (15%)

Endocrine & metabolic: Hot flashes (13% to 21%)

Gastrointestinal: Nausea (9% to 18%), abdominal pain (6% to 11%)

Hepatic: Alkaline phosphatase increased (14% to 15%)

Neuromuscular & skeletal: Arthralgia (15% to 29%)

1% to 10%:

Cardiovascular: Edema (6% to 7%); cardiac ischemic events (2%: MI, angina, myocardial ischemia); chest pain

Central nervous system: Dizziness (8% to 10%), anxiety (4% to 10%), fever (5%), confusion, hypoesthesia

Dermatologic: Dermatitis (8%), itching, rash

Endocrine & metabolic: Weight gain (8%)

Gastrointestinal: Diarrhea (4% to 10%), vomiting (7%), anorexia (6%), constipation (5%), appetite increased (3%), dyspepsia

Genitourinary: Urinary tract infection

Hepatic: Bilirubin increased (5% to 7%)

Neuromuscular & skeletal: Back pain (9%), limb pain (9%), osteoarthritis (6%), weakness (6%), osteoporosis (5%), pathological fracture (4%), paresthesia (3%), carpal tunnel syndrome (2%), cramps (2%)

Ocular: Visual disturbances (5%)

Renal: Creatinine increased (6%)

Respiratory: Dyspnea (10%), cough (6%), bronchitis, pharyngitis, rhinitis, sinusitis, upper respiratory infection

Miscellaneous: Influenza-like symptoms (6%), diaphoresis (6%), lymphedema, infection

<1%: Cardiac failure, endometrial hyperplasia, GGT increased, neuropathy, osteochondrosis, thromboembolism, transaminases increased, trigger finger, uterine polyps

A dose-dependent decrease in sex hormone-binding globulin has been observed with daily doses of 25 mg or more. Serum luteinizing hormone and follicle-stimulating hormone levels have increased with this medicine.

Overdosage/Toxicology In case of overdose, treatment should be symptom-directed and supportive.

Drug Interactions

Cytochrome P450 Effect: Substrate of CYP3A4 (major)

Decreased Effect: CYP3A4 inducers may decrease the levels/effects of exemestane; example inducers include aminoglutethimide, carbamazepine, efavirenz, fosphenytoin, nafcillin, nevirapine, oxcarbazepine, pentobarbital, phenobarbital, phenytoin, primidone, rifabutin, rifampin, and rifapentine; adjustment required with potent inducers.

Ethanol/Nutrition/Herb Interactions

Food: Plasma levels increased by 40% when exemestane was taken with a fatty meal.

Herb/Nutraceutical: St John's wort may decrease exemestane levels. Avoid black cohosh, dong quai in estrogen-dependent tumors.

Storage/Stability Store at 25°C (77°F)

Mechanism of Action Exemestane is an irreversible, steroidal aromatase inactivator. It prevents conversion of androgens to estrogens by tying up the enzyme aromatase. In breast cancers where growth is estrogen-dependent, this medicine will lower circulating estrogens.

Pharmacodynamics/Kinetics

Absorption: Rapid and moderate (~42%) following oral administration; absorption increases ~40% following high-fat meal

Distribution: Extensive

Protein binding: 90%, primarily to albumin and α_1-acid glycoprotein

Metabolism: Extensively hepatic; oxidation (CYP3A4) of methylene group, reduction of 17-keto group with formation of many secondary metabolites; metabolites are inactive

Half-life elimination: 24 hours

Time to peak: Women with breast cancer: 1.2 hours

Excretion: Urine (<1% as unchanged drug, 39% to 45% as metabolites); feces (36% to 48%)

Dosage Adults: Oral: 25 mg once daily

Dosage adjustment with CYP3A4 inducers: 50 mg once daily when used with potent inducers (eg, rifampin, phenytoin)

Dosing adjustment in renal/hepatic impairment: Safety of chronic doses has not been studied

Administration Administer after a meal.

Dietary Considerations Take after a meal; patients on aromatase inhibitor therapy should receive vitamin D and calcium supplements.

(Continued)

Exemestane *(Continued)*

Patient Information Take after a meal; use caution if you have uncontrolled high blood pressure. Avoid driving or doing other tasks or hobbies that require alertness until you know how this medicine affects you. Take at approximately the same time every day.

Special Geriatric Considerations In pharmacokinetic trials, no significant changes were seen in women <68 years of age.

Emetic Potential Low (10% to 30%)

Dosage Forms Excipient information presented when available (limited, particularly for generics); consult specific product labeling.

Tablet: 25 mg

References

Boeddinghaus IM and Dowsett M, "Comparative Clinical Pharmacology and Pharmacokinetic Interactions of Aromatase Inhibitors," *J Steroid Biochem Mol Biol*, 2001, 79(1-5):85-91.

Buzdar AU, Robertson JF, Eiermann W, et al, "An Overview of the Pharmacology and Pharmacokinetics of the Newer Generation Aromatase Inhibitors Anastrozole, Letrozole, and Exemestane," *Cancer*, 2002, 95(9):2006-16.

Lonning PE, "Pharmacological Profiles of Exemestane and Fromestane, Steroidal Aromatase Inhibitors Used for Treatment of Postmenopausal Breast Cancer," *Breast Cancer Res Treat*, 1998, 49(Suppl 1):45-52.

Morandi P, Rouzier R, Altundag K, et al, "The Role of Aromatase Inhibitors in the Adjuvant Treatment of Breast Carcinoma: The M. D. Anderson Cancer Center Evidence-Based Approach," *Cancer*, 2004, 101(7):1482-9.

Njar VC and Brodie AM, "Comprehensive Pharmacology and Clinical Efficacy of Aromatase Inhibitors," *Drugs*, 1999, 58(2):233-55.

Scott LJ and Wiseman LR, "Exemestane," *Drugs*, 1999, 58(4):675-80.

Winer EP, Hudis C, Burstein HJ, et al, "American Society of Clinical Oncology Technology Assessment on the Use of Aromatase Inhibitors as Adjuvant Therapy for Postmenopausal Women With Hormone Receptor-Positive Breast Cancer: Status Report 2004," *J Clin Oncol*, 2005, 23(3):619-29.

♦ **Exjade®** *see* Deferasirox *on page 316*

♦ **ex-lax® Ultra [OTC]** *see* Bisacodyl *on page 144*

♦ **Extina®** *see* Ketoconazole *on page 649*

♦ **309F** *see* Suramin *on page 991*

♦ **Factive®** *see* Gemifloxacin *on page 504*

Factor VIIa (Recombinant)

(FAK ter SEV en aye ree KOM be nant)

Medication Safety Issues

Sound-alike/look-alike issues:

NovoSeven® may be confused with Novacet®

U.S. Brand Names NovoSeven®

Index Terms Coagulation Factor VIIa; Eptacog Alfa (Activated); rFVIIa

Generic Available No

Canadian Brand Names Niastase®

Pharmacologic Category Antihemophilic Agent; Blood Product Derivative

Use Treatment of bleeding episodes and prevention of bleeding in surgical interventions in patients with hemophilia A or B with inhibitors to factor VIII or factor IX and in patients with congenital factor VII deficiency

Unlabeled/Investigational Use Reduction of hematoma growth in patients with acute intracerebral hemorrhage, warfarin-related intracerebral hemorrhage

Pregnancy Risk Factor C

Lactation Excretion in breast milk unknown/compatible

Labeled Contraindications Hypersensitivity to factor VII or any component of the formulation; hypersensitivity to mouse, hamster, or bovine proteins

Warnings/Precautions Patients should be monitored for signs and symptoms of activation of the coagulation system or thrombosis. Thrombotic events may be increased in patients with disseminated intravascular coagulation (DIC), advanced atherosclerotic disease, sepsis, crush injury, or concomitant treatment with prothrombin complex concentrates. Decreased dosage or discontinuation is warranted in confirmed DIC. Efficacy with prolonged infusions and data evaluating this agent's long-term adverse effects are limited.

Adverse Reactions

1% to 10%:

Cardiovascular: Hypertension

Central nervous system: Fever

Hematologic: Hemorrhage, plasma fibrinogen decreased

Neuromuscular & skeletal: Hemarthrosis

<1%: Abnormal renal function, allergic reactions, arthrosis, bradycardia, coagulation disorder, disseminated intravascular coagulation (DIC), edema, fibrinolysis increased, gastrointestinal bleeding, headache, hypotension, injection site reactions, intracranial hemorrhage, localized phlebitis, pain, pneumonia, prothrombin decreased, pruritus, purpura, rash, splenic hematoma, therapeutic response decreased, thrombosis, vomiting

Postmarketing and/or case reports: Anaphylactic reaction, arterial thrombosis, cerebral infarction and/or ischemia, consumptive coagulopathy, deep vein thrombosis, hypersensitivity, MI, myocardial ischemia, pulmonary embolism, thrombophlebitis

Overdosage/Toxicology Experience with overdose in humans is limited; an increased risk of thrombotic events may occur in overdosage. Treatment is symptomatic and supportive.

Storage/Stability Store under refrigeration (2°C to 8°C/36°F to 46°F). Protect from light. Reconstituted solutions may be stored at room temperature or under refrigeration, but must be infused within 3 hours of reconstitution. Do not freeze reconstituted solutions. Do not store reconstituted solutions in syringes.

Reconstitution Prior to reconstitution, bring vials to room temperature. Reconstitute each vial to a final concentration of 0.6 mg/mL as follows:

1.2 mg vial: 2.2 mL sterile water

2.4 mg vial: 4.3 mL sterile water

4.8 mg vial: 8.5 mL sterile water

Add diluent along wall of vial; do not inject directly into powder. Gently swirl until dissolved.

Mechanism of Action Recombinant factor VIIa, a vitamin K-dependent glycoprotein, promotes hemostasis by activating the extrinsic pathway of the coagulation cascade. It replaces deficient activated coagulation factor VII, which complexes with tissue factor and may activate coagulation factor X to Xa and factor IX to IXa. When complexed with other factors, coagulation factor Xa converts prothrombin to thrombin, a key step in the formation of a fibrin-platelet hemostatic plug.

Pharmacodynamics/Kinetics

Distribution: V_d: 103 mL/kg (78-139)

Half-life elimination: 2.3 hours (1.7-2.7)

Excretion: Clearance: 33 mL/kg/hour (27-49)

Dosage Children and Adults: I.V. administration only: Hemophilia A or B with inhibitors:

(Continued)

FACTOR IX

Factor VIIa (Recombinant) *(Continued)*

Bleeding episodes: 90 mcg/kg every 2 hours until hemostasis is achieved or until the treatment is judged ineffective. The dose and interval may be adjusted based upon the severity of bleeding and the degree of hemostasis achieved. For patients experiencing severe bleeds, dosing should be continued at 3- to 6-hour intervals after hemostasis has been achieved and the duration of dosing should be minimized.

Surgical interventions: 90 mcg/kg immediately before surgery; repeat at 2-hour intervals for the duration of surgery. Continue every 2 hours for 48 hours, then every 2-6 hours until healed for minor surgery; continue every 2 hours for 5 days, then every 4 hours until healed for major surgery.

Congenital factor VII deficiency: Bleeding episodes and surgical interventions: 15-30 mcg/kg every 4-6 hours until hemostasis. Doses as low as 10 mcg/kg have been effective.

Administration I.V. administration only; bolus over 2-5 minutes. Administer within 3 hours after reconstitution.

Monitoring Parameters Monitor for evidence of hemostasis; although the prothrombin time, aPTT, and factor VII clotting activity have no correlation with achieving hemostasis, these parameters may be useful as adjunct tests to evaluate efficacy and guide dose or interval adjustments

Dietary Considerations Contains sodium 0.44 mEq/mg rFVIIa

Dosage Forms Excipient information presented when available (limited, particularly for generics); consult specific product labeling.

Injection, powder for reconstitution [preservative free]: 1.2 mg, 2.4 mg, 4.8 mg [latex free; contains sodium 0.44 mEq/mg rFVIIa, polysorbate 80]

References

Broderick J, Connolly S, Feldmann E, et al, "Guidelines for the Management of Spontaneous Intracerebral Hemorrhage in Adults: 2007 Update: A Guideline From the American Heart Association/American Stroke Association Stroke Council, High Blood Pressure Research Council, and the Quality of Care and Outcomes in Research Interdisciplinary Working Group," *Stroke*, 2007, 38(6):2001-23. Available at http://stroke.ahajournals.org/cgi/content/short/STROKEAHA.107.183689.

Mayer SA, Brun NC, Begtrup K, et al, "Recombinant Activated Factor VII for Acute Intracerebral Hemorrhage," *N Engl J Med*, 2005, 352(8):777-85.

Mohr AM, Holcomb JB, Dutton RP, et al, "Recombinant Activated Factor VIIa and Hemostasis in Critical Care: A Focus on Trauma," *Crit Care*, 2005, 9 (Suppl 5):37-42.

♦ **Factor VIII (Human)** *see* Antihemophilic Factor (Human) *on page 92*
♦ **Factor VIII (Recombinant)** *see* Antihemophilic Factor (Recombinant) *on page 95*

Factor IX *(FAK ter nyne)*

U.S. Brand Names AlphaNine® SD; BeneFix®; Mononine®
Generic Available No
Canadian Brand Names BeneFix®; Immunine® VH; Mononine®
Pharmacologic Category Antihemophilic Agent; Blood Product Derivative
Use Control bleeding in patients with factor IX deficiency (hemophilia B or Christmas disease)
Pregnancy Risk Factor C
Labeled Contraindications Hypersensitivity to mouse protein (Mononine®), hamster protein (BeneFix®), or any component of the formulation
Warnings/Precautions Use with caution in patients with liver dysfunction; some products prepared from pooled human plasma - the risk of viral transmission is not totally eradicated; monitor patients who receive repeated doses twice daily with PTT and level of factor being replaced (eg, IX). Observe closely for signs or symptoms of intravascular coagulation or thrombosis. Caution should be exercised when administering to patients with liver disease, postoperatively, neonates, or patients at risk of thromboembolic phenomena or disseminated intravascular coagulation because of the potential risk of thromboembolic complications.

AlphaNine® SD, Mononine® contain **nondetectable levels of factors II, VII, and X** (<0.0025 units per factor IX unit using standard coagulation assays) and are, therefore, **NOT INDICATED** for replacement therapy of any of these clotting factors.

BeneFix®, Mononine® are **NOT INDICATED** in the treatment or reversal of coumarin-induced anticoagulation or in a hemorrhagic state caused by hepatitis-induced lack of production of liver dependent coagulation factors.

Adverse Reactions Frequency not defined.

Cardiovascular: Angioedema, cyanosis, flushing, hypotension, tightness in chest, tightness in neck, thrombosis (following high dosages because of presence of activated clotting factors)

Central nervous system: Fever, headache, chills, somnolence, dizziness, drowsiness, lightheadedness

Dermatologic: Urticaria, rash

Gastrointestinal: Nausea, vomiting, abnormal taste

Hematologic: Disseminated intravascular coagulation (DIC)

Local: Injection site discomfort

Neuromuscular & skeletal: Tingling

Respiratory: Dyspnea, laryngeal edema, allergic rhinitis

Miscellaneous: Transient fever (following rapid administration), anaphylaxis, burning sensation in jaw/skull

Overdosage/Toxicology Symptoms of overdose include disseminated intravascular coagulation (DIC).

Drug Interactions

Increased Effect/Toxicity: Do not coadminister with aminocaproic acid; may increase risk for thrombosis.

Storage/Stability When stored at refrigerator temperature, 2°C to 8°C (36°F to 46°F), coagulation factor IX is stable for the period indicated by the expiration date on its label. Avoid freezing which may damage container for the diluent.

AlphaNine® SD: May also be stored at ≤30°C (≤86°F) for up to 3 months.

BeneFix®: May also be stored at ≤25°C (≤77°F) for up to 6 months.

Mononine®: May also be stored at ≤30°C (≤86°F) for up to 1 month.

Stability of parenteral admixture at room temperature (25°C): 3 hours.

Reconstitution Mononine®: When reconstituted to ~100 int. units/mL, infusion rate should be up to 225 units/minute (2 mL/minute).

Mechanism of Action Replaces deficient clotting factor IX; concentrate of factor IX; hemophilia B, or Christmas disease, is an X-linked inherited disorder of blood coagulation characterized by insufficient or abnormal synthesis of the clotting protein factor IX. Factor IX is a vitamin K-dependent coagulation factor which is synthesized in the liver. Factor IX is activated by factor XIa in the intrinsic coagulation pathway. Activated factor IX (IXa), in combination with factor VII:C activates factor X to Xa, resulting ultimately in the conversion of prothrombin to thrombin and the formation of a fibrin clot. The infusion of exogenous factor IX to replace the deficiency present in hemophilia B temporarily restores hemostasis.

Pharmacodynamics/Kinetics Half-life elimination: IX component: 23-31 hours

Dosage Dosage is expressed in units of factor IX activity and must be individualized. I.V. only:

Formula for units required to raise blood level %:

AlphaNine® SD, Mononine®: Children and Adults:

Number of factor IX units required = body weight (in kg) x desired factor IX level increase (% normal) x 1 unit/kg

(Continued)

Factor IX *(Continued)*

For example, for a 100% level a patient who has an actual level of 20%:
Number of factor IX units needed = 70 kg x 80% x 1 unit/kg = 5600 units

BeneFix®:

Children <15 years:

Number of factor IX units required = body weight (in kg) x desired factor IX level increase (% normal) x 1.4 units/kg

Adults:

Number of factor IX units required = body weight (in kg) x desired factor IX level increase (% normal) x 1.2 units/kg

Guidelines: As a general rule, the level of factor IX required for treatment of different conditions is listed below:

Minor spontaneous hemorrhage, prophylaxis:

Desired levels of factor IX for hemostasis: 15% to 25%

Initial loading dose to achieve desired level: 20-30 units/kg

Frequency of dosing: Every 12-24 hours if necessary

Duration of treatment: 1-2 days

Moderate hemorrhage:

Desired levels of factor IX for hemostasis: 25% to 50%

Initial loading dose to achieve desired level: 25-50 units/kg

Frequency of dosing: Every 12-24 hours

Duration of treatment: 2-7 days

Major hemorrhage:

Desired levels of factor IX for hemostasis: >50%

Initial loading dose to achieve desired level: 30-50 units/kg

Frequency of dosing: Every 12-24 hours, depending on half-life and measured factor IX levels (after 3-5 days, maintain at least 20% activity)

Duration of treatment: 7-10 days, depending upon nature of insult

Surgery:

Desired levels of factor IX for hemostasis: 50% to 100%

Initial loading dose to achieve desired level: 50-100 units/kg

Frequency of dosing: Every 12-24 hours, depending on half-life and measured factor IX levels

Duration of treatment: 7-10 days, depending upon nature of insult

Administration Solution should be infused at room temperature

I.V. administration only: Should be infused **slowly**: The rate of administration should be determined by the response and comfort of the patient.

Mononine®: Intravenous dosage administration rates of up to 225 units/ minute (~2 mL/minute) have been regularly tolerated without incident. **Infuse at a rate not exceeding 2 mL/minute.**

Monitoring Parameters Levels of factors IX, PTT

Patient Information Early signs of hypersensitivity reactions, including hives, generalized urticaria, tightness of the chest, wheezing, hypotension, and anaphylaxis, indicate discontinuation of use of the concentrate and prescriber should be contacted if these symptoms occur.

Dosage Forms Excipient information presented when available (limited, particularly for generics); consult specific product labeling.

Injection, powder for reconstitution (**Note:** Exact potency labeled on each vial):

AlphaNine® SD [human derived; solvent detergent treated; virus filtered; contains nondetectable levels of factors II, VII, X; supplied with diluent]

BeneFix® [recombinant formulation; supplied with diluent]

Mononine® [human derived; monoclonal antibody purified; contains nondetectable levels of factors II, VII, X; supplied with diluent]

Factor IX Complex (Human)
(FAK ter nyne KOM pleks HYU man)

U.S. Brand Names Bebulin® VH; Profilnine® SD; Proplex® T [DSC]

Index Terms Prothrombin Complex Concentrate

Generic Available No

Pharmacologic Category Antihemophilic Agent; Blood Product Derivative

Use

Control bleeding in patients with factor IX deficiency (hemophilia B or Christmas disease) **Note:** Factor IX concentrate containing **only** factor IX is also available and preferable for this indication.

Prevention/control of bleeding in hemophilia A patients with inhibitors to factor VIII.

Prevention/control of bleeding in patients with factor VII deficiency.

Emergency correction of the coagulopathy of warfarin excess in critical situations.

Pregnancy Risk Factor C

Labeled Contraindications Liver disease with signs of intravascular coagulation or fibrinolysis; not for use in factor VII deficiencies, patients undergoing elective surgery

Warnings/Precautions Use with caution in patients with liver dysfunction. Prepared from pooled human plasma - the risk of viral transmission is not totally eradicated. Thromboembolic complications rarely occur; more likely to occur during postoperative period or in patients with risk factors. Treatment should stop if respiratory distress or any changes in blood pressure or pulse rate occur.

Adverse Reactions

1% to 10%:

Central nervous system: Fever, headache, chills

Neuromuscular & skeletal: Tingling

Miscellaneous: Following rapid administration: Transient fever

<1%: Disseminated intravascular coagulation (DIC), flushing, nausea, somnolence, thrombosis (following high dosages because of presence of activated clotting factors), tightness in chest, tightness in neck, urticaria, vomiting

Overdosage/Toxicology Symptoms of overdose include disseminated intravascular coagulation (DIC).

Drug Interactions

Increased Effect/Toxicity: Do not coadminister with aminocaproic acid; may increase risk for thrombosis.

Storage/Stability When stored at refrigerator temperature, 2°C to 8°C (36°F to 46°F), coagulation factor IX is stable for the period indicated by the expiration date on its label. Avoid freezing which may damage container for the diluent. Once diluted, should be used promptly; stable for up to 3 hours.

Reconstitution

Refer to instructions for individual products. Diluent and factor IX complex should come to room temperature before combining. Diluent vial should be inverted over concentrate vial. After diluent is pulled, disconnect. The provided filter needle should be used to withdraw concentrate. Remove needle and attach to infusion set or replace needle for infusion.

Mechanism of Action Replaces deficient clotting factor including factor X; hemophilia B, or Christmas disease, is an X-linked recessively inherited disorder of blood coagulation characterized by insufficient or abnormal synthesis of the clotting protein factor IX. Factor IX is a vitamin K-dependent coagulation factor which is synthesized in the liver. Factor IX is activated by factor XIa in the intrinsic coagulation pathway. Activated factor IX (IXa), in (Continued)

Factor IX Complex (Human) *(Continued)*

combination with factor VII:C, activates factor X to Xa, resulting ultimately in the conversion of prothrombin to thrombin and the formation of a fibrin clot. The infusion of exogenous factor IX to replace the deficiency present in hemophilia B temporarily restores hemostasis.

Pharmacodynamics/Kinetics

Half-life elimination:

VII component: Initial: 4-6 hours; Terminal: 22.5 hours

IX component: 24 hours

Dosage Children and Adults: Dosage is expressed in units of factor IX activity and must be individualized. I.V. only:

Formula for units required to raise blood level %:

Total blood volume (mL blood/kg) = 70 mL/kg (adults), 80 mL/kg (children)

Plasma volume = total blood volume (mL) x [1 - Hct (in decimals)]

For example, for a 70 kg adult with a Hct = 40%: Plasma volume = [70 kg x 70 mL/kg] x [1 - 0.4] = 2940 mL

To calculate number of units needed to increase level to desired range (highly individualized and dependent on patient's condition): Number of units = desired level increase [desired level - actual level] x plasma volume (in mL)

For example, for a 100% level in the above patient who has an actual level of 20%: Number of units needed = [1 (for a 100% level) - 0.2] x 2940 mL = 2352 units

As a general rule, the level of factor IX required for treatment of different conditions is listed below:

Minor Spontaneous Hemorrhage, Prophylaxis:

Desired levels of factor IX for hemostasis: 15% to 25%

Initial loading dose to achieve desired level: <20-30 units/kg

Frequency of dosing: Once; repeated in 24 hours if necessary

Duration of treatment: Once; repeated if necessary

Major Trauma or Surgery:

Desired levels of factor IX for hemostasis: 25% to 50%

Initial loading dose to achieve desired level: <75 units/kg

Frequency of dosing: Every 18-30 hours, depending on half-life and measured factor IX levels

Duration of treatment: Up to 10 days, depending upon nature of insult

Factor VIII inhibitor patients: 75 units/kg/dose; may be given every 6-12 hours

Anticoagulant overdosage: I.V.: 15 units/kg

Administration I.V. administration only; should be infused **slowly**. Rate should not exceed 2 mL/minute for Bebulin® VH, 3 mL/minute for Proplex® T, or 10 mL/minute for Profilnine® SD.

Monitoring Parameters Levels of factors being replaced (eg, VII or IX), PT, PTT

Patient Information Early signs of hypersensitivity reactions, including hives, generalized urticaria, tightness of the chest, wheezing, hypotension, and anaphylaxis, indicate discontinuation of use of the concentrate. Prescriber should be contacted if these symptoms occur.

Dosage Forms Excipient information presented when available (limited, particularly for generics); consult specific product labeling. [DSC] = Discontinued product

Injection, powder for reconstitution (**Note:** Exact potency labeled on each vial):

Bebulin® VH [single-dose vial; vapor heated; supplied with sterile water for injection]

Profilnine® SD [single-dose vial; solvent detergent treated]

Proplex® T [single-dose vial; heat treated; supplied with sterile water for injection] [DSC]

References

Broderick J, Connolly S, Feldmann E, et al, "Guidelines for the Management of Spontaneous Intracerebral Hemorrhage in Adults: 2007 Update: A Guideline From the American Heart Association/American Stroke Association Stroke Council, High Blood Pressure Research Council, and the Quality of Care and Outcomes in Research Interdisciplinary Working Group," *Stroke*, 2007, 38(6):2001-23. Available at http://stroke.ahajournals.org/cgi/content/short/STROKEAHA.107.183689.

Lusher JM, "Thrombogenicity Associated With Factor IX Complex Concentrates," *Semin Hematol*, 1991, 28(3 Suppl 6):3-5.

Famciclovir (fam SYE kloe veer)

U.S. Brand Names Famvir®

Generic Available Yes

Canadian Brand Names Apo-Famciclovir; Famvir®; PMS-Famciclovir

Pharmacologic Category Antiviral Agent

Use Treatment of acute herpes zoster (shingles); treatment and suppression of recurrent episodes of genital herpes in immunocompetent patients; treatment of herpes labialis (cold sores) in immunocompetent patients; treatment of recurrent mucocutaneous/genital herpes simplex in HIV-infected patients

Pregnancy Risk Factor B

Lactation Excretion in breast milk unknown/use caution

Labeled Contraindications Hypersensitivity to famciclovir, penciclovir, or any component of the formulation

Warnings/Precautions Has not been studied in immunocompromised patients or patients with ophthalmic, disseminated zoster, or with initial episode of genital herpes. Dosage adjustment is required in patients with renal insufficiency. Tablets contain lactose; do not use with galactose intolerance, severe lactase deficiency, or glucose-galactose malabsorption syndromes. Safety and efficacy have not been established in children <18 years of age

Adverse Reactions

Note: Frequencies vary with dose and duration. Single-dose treatment (herpes labialis) was associated only with headache (10%), diarrhea (2%), fatigue (1%), and dysmenorrhea (1%).

>10%:

Central nervous system: Headache (17% to 39%)

Gastrointestinal: Nausea (7% to 13%)

1% to 10%:

Central nervous system: Fatigue (4% to 6%), migraine (1% to 3%)

Dermatologic: Pruritus (1% to 4%), rash (<1% to 3%)

Endocrine and metabolic: Dysmenorrhea (up to 8%)

Gastrointestinal: Diarrhea (5% to 9%), flatulence (2% to 5%), vomiting (1% to 5%), abdominal pain (1% to 8%)

Hematologic: Neutropenia (3%), leukopenia (1%)

Hepatic: Transaminases increased (2% to 3%), bilirubin increased (2%)

Neuromuscular & skeletal: Paresthesia (1% to 3%)

Postmarketing and/or case reports: Confusion, delirium, disorientation, dizziness, erythema multiforme, hallucinations, jaundice, somnolence, thrombocytopenia, urticaria

(Continued)

Famciclovir *(Continued)*

Overdosage/Toxicology Supportive and symptomatic care is recommended. Hemodialysis may enhance elimination of penciclovir.

Ethanol/Nutrition/Herb Interactions Food: Rate of absorption and/or conversion to penciclovir and peak concentration are reduced with food, but bioavailability is not affected.

Storage/Stability Store at controlled room temperature.

Mechanism of Action Famciclovir undergoes rapid biotransformation to the active compound, penciclovir, which is phosphorylated by viral thymidine kinase in HSV-1, HSV-2, and VZV-infected cells to a monophosphate form; this is then converted to penciclovir triphosphate and competes with deoxyguanosine triphosphate to inhibit HSV-2 polymerase (eg, herpes viral DNA synthesis/replication is selectively inhibited)

Pharmacodynamics/Kinetics

Absorption: Food decreases maximum peak concentration and delays time to peak; AUC remains the same

Distribution: V_{dss}: 0.91-1.25 L/kg

Protein binding: ≤20%

Metabolism: Rapidly deacetylated and oxidized to penciclovir; not via CYP

Bioavailability: 69% to 85%

Half-life elimination: Penciclovir: 2-3 hours (10, 20, and 7 hours in HSV-1, HSV-2, and VZV-infected cells, respectively); prolonged with renal impairment

Time to peak: 0.9 hours; C_{max} and T_{max} are decreased and prolonged with noncompensated hepatic impairment

Excretion: Urine (73% primarily as penciclovir); feces (27%)

Dosage Adults: Oral:

Acute herpes zoster: 500 mg every 8 hours for 7 days (**Note:** Initiate therapy within 72 hours of rash onset.)

Recurrent genital herpes simplex in immunocompetent patients:

Initial: 1000 mg twice daily for 1 day (**Note:** Initiate therapy within 6 hours of symptoms/lesions.)

Suppressive therapy: 250 mg twice daily for up to 1 year

Recurrent herpes labialis (cold sores): 1500 mg as a single dose; initiate therapy at first sign or symptom such as tingling, burning, or itching (initiated within 1 hour in clinical studies)

Recurrent mucocutaneous/genital herpes simplex in HIV patients: 500 mg twice daily for 7 days

Dosing interval in renal impairment:

Herpes zoster:

Cl_{cr} 40-59 mL/minute: Administer 500 mg every 12 hours

Cl_{cr} 20-39 mL/minute: Administer 500 mg every 24 hours

Cl_{cr} <20 mL/minute: Administer 250 mg every 24 hours

Hemodialysis: Administer 250 mg after each dialysis session.

Recurrent genital herpes: Treatment (single day regimen):

Cl_{cr} 40-59 mL/minute: Administer 500 mg every 12 hours for 1 day

Cl_{cr} 20-39 mL/minute: Administer 500 mg as a single dose

Cl_{cr} <20 mL/minute: Administer 250 mg as a single dose

Hemodialysis: Administer 250 mg as a single dose after dialysis session.

Recurrent genital herpes: Suppression:

Cl_{cr} 20-39 mL/minute: Administer 125 mg every 12 hours

Cl_{cr} <20 mL/minute: Administer 125 mg every 24 hours

Hemodialysis: Administer 125 mg after each dialysis session.

Recurrent herpes labialis: Treatment (single dose regimen):

Cl_{cr} 40-59 mL/minute: Administer 750 mg as a single dose

Cl_{cr} 20-39 mL/minute: Administer 500 mg as a single dose

Cl_{cr} <20 mL/minute: Administer 250 mg as a single dose

Hemodialysis: Administer 250 mg as a single dose after dialysis session.

Recurrent orolabial or genital herpes in HIV-infected patients:

Cl_{cr} 20-39 mL/minute: Administer 500 mg every 12 hours

Cl_{cr} <20 mL/minute: Administer 250 mg every 24 hours

Hemodialysis: Administer 250 mg after each dialysis session.

Monitoring Parameters Periodic CBC during long-term therapy

Dietary Considerations May be taken with food or on an empty stomach.

Patient Information Initiate therapy as soon as herpes zoster is diagnosed. May take medication with food or on an empty stomach.

Special Geriatric Considerations For herpes zoster (shingles) infections, famciclovir should be started within 72 hours of the appearance of the rash to be effective. Famciclovir has been shown to accelerate healing, reduce the duration of viral shedding, and resolve posthepatic neuralgia faster than placebo. Comparison trials to acyclovir or valacyclovir are not available. Adjust dose for estimated renal function.

Additional Information Most effective for herpes zoster if therapy is initiated within 48 hours of initial lesion. Resistance may occur by alteration of thymidine kinase, resulting in loss of or reduced penciclovir phosphorylation (cross-resistance occurs between acyclovir and famciclovir). When treatment for herpes labialis is initiated within 1 hour of symptom onset, healing time is reduced by ~2 days.

Dosage Forms Excipient information presented when available (limited, particularly for generics); consult specific product labeling.

Tablet: 125 mg, 250 mg, 500 mg

Famvir®: 125 mg, 250 mg, 500 mg

References

Alrabiah FA and Sacks SL, "New Antiherpesvirus Agents. Their Targets and Therapeutic Potential," *Drugs*, 1996, 52(1):17-32.

Boike SC, Pue MA, and Freed MI, "Pharmacokinetics of Famciclovir in Subjects With Varying Degrees of Renal Impairment," *Clin Pharmacol Ther*, 1994, 55(4):418-26.

Boyd MR, Safrin S, and Kern ER, "Penciclovir: A Review of Its Spectrum of Activity, Selectivity, and Cross Resistance Pattern," *Antivir Chem Chemother*, 1993, 4:3-11.

Daniels S and Schentag JJ, "Drug Interaction Studies and Safety of Famciclovir in Healthy Volunteers: A Review," *Antivir Chem Chemother*, 1993, 4:57-64.

De Clercq E, "Antivirals for the Treatment of Herpesvirus Infections," *J Antimicrob Chemother*, 1993, 32(Suppl A):121-32.

Gill KS and Wood MJ, "The Clinical Pharmacokinetics of Famciclovir," *Clin Pharmacokinet*, 1996, 31(1):1-8.

Goffin E, Horsmans Y, Pirson Y, et al, "Acute Necrotico-Hemorrhagic Pancreatitis After Famciclovir Prescription," *Transplantation*, 1995, 59(8):1218-9.

Hodge RA, "Famciclovir and Penciclovir: The Mode of Action of Famciclovir Including Its Conversion to Penciclovir," *Antivir Chem Chemother*, 1993, 4:67-84.

Luber AD and Flaherty JF Jr, "Famciclovir for Treatment of Herpesvirus Infections," *Ann Pharmacother*, 1996, 30(9):978-85.

Perry CM and Wagstaff AJ, "Famciclovir. A Review of Its Pharmacological Properties and Therapeutic Efficacy in Herpesvirus Infections," *Drugs*, 1995, 50(2):396-415.

Pue MA and Benet LZ, "Pharmacokinetics of Famciclovir in Man," *Antivir Chem Chemother*, 1993, 4(Suppl 1):47-55.

Sacks SL, "Genital Herpes Simplex Virus and Its Treatment Focus on Famciclovir," *Semin Dermatol*, 1996, 15(2 Suppl 1):32-6.

Spruance SL, Bodsworth N, Resnick H, et al, "Single-Dose, Patient-Initiated Famciclovir: A Randomized, Double-Blind, Placebo-Controlled Trial for Episodic Treatment of Herpes Labialis," *J Am Acad Dermatol*, 2006, 55(1):47-53.

Tyring SK, Barbarash RA, Nahlik JE, et al, "Famciclovir for the Treatment of Acute Herpes Zoster: Effects on Acute Disease and Postherpetic Neuralgia," *Ann Intern Med*, 1995, 123(2):89-96.

Tyring SK, "Efficacy of Famciclovir in the Treatment of Herpes Zoster," *Semin Dermatol*, 1996, 15(2 Suppl 1):27-31.

♦ **Famvir**® *see Famciclovir on page 423*

- **Fareston®** *see* Toremifene *on page 1053*
- **Faslodex®** *see* Fulvestrant *on page 482*
- **Fasturtec® (Can)** *see* Rasburicase *on page 945*
- **5-FC** *see* Flucytosine *on page 454*
- **FC1157a** *see* Toremifene *on page 1053*
- **Femara®** *see* Letrozole *on page 665*
- **Fematrol [OTC]** *see* Bisacodyl *on page 144*
- **Femilax™ [OTC]** *see* Bisacodyl *on page 144*

Fentanyl (FEN ta nil)

Medication Safety Issues

Sound-alike/look-alike issues:
Fentanyl may be confused with alfentanil, sufentanil

Dosing of transdermal fentanyl patches may be confusing. Transdermal fentanyl patches should always be prescribed in mcg/hour, not size.

Fentora™ and Actiq® are not interchangeable; do not substitute doses on a mcg-per-mcg basis.

High alert medication: The Institute for Safe Medication Practices (ISMP) includes this medication among its list of drugs which have a heightened risk of causing significant patient harm when used in error.

New patch dosage form of Duragesic®-12 actually delivers 12.5 mcg/hour of fentanyl. Use caution, as orders may be written as "Duragesic 12.5" which can be erroneously interpreted as a 125 mcg dose.

Iontophoretic transdermal system (Ionsys™) may contain conducting metal (eg, aluminum); remove patch prior to MRI. Transdermal patch (eg, Duragesic®) does not contain any metal-based compounds; however, the printed ink used to indicate strength on the outer surface of the patch does contain titanium dioxide, but the amount is minimal.

U.S. Brand Names Actiq®; Duragesic®; Fentora™; Ionsys™; Sublimaze®

Index Terms Fentanyl Citrate; Fentanyl Hydrochloride; OTFC (Oral Transmucosal Fentanyl Citrate)

Generic Available Yes: Excludes buccal tablet and iontophoretic transdermal system

Canadian Brand Names Actiq®; Duragesic®; Fentanyl Citrate Injection, USP

Pharmacologic Category Analgesic, Opioid; General Anesthetic

Use

Injection: Sedation, relief of pain, preoperative medication, adjunct to general or regional anesthesia

Iontophoretic transdermal system (Ionsys™): Short-term in-hospital management of acute postoperative pain

Transdermal patch (eg, Duragesic®): Management of moderate-to-severe chronic pain

Transmucosal lozenge (eg, Actiq®), buccal tablet (Fentora™): Management of breakthrough cancer pain

Restrictions C-II

An FDA-approved medication guide for buccal tablet (Fentora™) and transmucosal lozenge (eg, Actiq®) must be distributed when dispensing an outpatient prescription (new or refill) where this medication is to be used without direct supervision of a healthcare provider. Medication guides are available at http://www.fda.gov/cder/Offices/ODS/medication_guides.htm.

Pregnancy Risk Factor C/D (prolonged use or high doses at term)

Lactation Enters breast milk/not recommended (AAP rates "compatible")

Labeled Contraindications Hypersensitivity to fentanyl or any component of the formulation; increased intracranial pressure; severe respiratory disease or depression including acute asthma (unless patient is mechanically ventilated); paralytic ileus; severe liver or renal insufficiency; pregnancy (prolonged use or high doses near term)

Iontophoretic transdermal system (Ionsys™): Hypersensitivity to fentanyl, cetylpyridinium chloride (eg, Cepacol®) or any component of Ionsys™ system

Transmucosal buccal tablets (Fentora™), lozenges (eg, Actiq®), and/or transdermal patches (eg, Duragesic®) are recommended for use only in patients who are opioid-tolerant. Patients are considered opioid-tolerant if they are taking at least 60 mg morphine/day, 30 mg oral oxycodone/day, 8 mg oral hydromorphone/day, 25 mcg transdermal fentanyl/hour, or an equivalent dose of another opioid for ≥1 week. Transmucosal buccal tablets (Fentora™), lozenges (eg, Actiq®), and transdermal patches (eg, Duragesic®) are not for use in acute pain, mild pain, intermittent pain, or postoperative pain management.

Warnings/Precautions An opioid-containing analgesic regimen should be tailored to each patient's needs and based upon the type of pain being treated (acute versus chronic), the route of administration, degree of tolerance for opioids (naive versus chronic user), age, weight, and medical condition. The optimal analgesic dose varies widely among patients. Doses should be titrated to pain relief/prevention. When using with other CNS depressants, reduce dose of one or both agents. Fentanyl shares the toxic potentials of opiate agonists, and precautions of opiate agonist therapy should be observed; use with caution in patients with bradycardia; rapid I.V. infusion may result in skeletal muscle and chest wall rigidity leading to respiratory distress and/or apnea, bronchoconstriction, laryngospasm; inject slowly over 3-5 minutes. Tolerance or drug dependence may result from extended use. Use caution in patients with a history of drug dependence or abuse. The elderly may be particularly susceptible to the CNS depressant and constipating effects of narcotics. Use extreme caution in patients with COPD or other chronic respiratory conditions. Use caution with head injuries, morbid obesity, or hepatic dysfunction. **[U.S. Boxed Warning]: Use with strong or moderate CYP3A4 inhibitors may result in increased effects and potential respiratory depression.** Concurrent use of agonist/antagonist analgesics may precipitate withdrawal symptoms and/or reduced analgesic efficacy in patients following prolonged therapy with mu opioid agonists. Abrupt discontinuation following prolonged use may also lead to withdrawal symptoms. Opioid-nontolerant patients should not receive some formulations/strengths of fentanyl, including buccal tablets (Fentora™), lozenges (Actiq®), or transdermal patches.

Transmucosal: Lozenge (eg, Actiq®), buccal tablet (Fentora™): **[U.S. Boxed Warning]: Do not substitute Fentora™ on a mcg-per-mcg basis when converting from transmucosal lozenge to buccal tablet. Buccal tablet has higher bioavailability. [U.S. Boxed Warning]: Should be used only for the care of opioid-tolerant cancer patients.** Not approved for use in management of acute or postoperative pain. **[U.S. Boxed Warning]: Buccal tablet and lozenge contain an amount of medication that can be fatal to children.** Keep all units out of the reach of children and discard any open units properly. Safety and efficacy have not been established in children <16 years of age for the lozenge and <18 years of age for the buccal tablet.

Transdermal patches (eg, Duragesic®): **[U.S. Boxed Warning]: Serious or life-threatening hypoventilation may occur, even in opioid-tolerant** (Continued)

Fentanyl *(Continued)*

patients. Serum fentanyl concentrations may increase approximately one-third for patients with a body temperature of 40°C secondary to a temperature-dependent increase in fentanyl release from the patch and increased skin permeability. Avoid exposure of application site to direct external heat sources. Patients who experience adverse reactions should be monitored for at least 24 hours after removal of the patch. Transdermal patch does not contain any metal-based compounds; the printed ink used to indicate strength on the outer surface of the patch does contain titanium dioxide but the amount is minimal; adverse events have not been reported while wearing during an MRI. **[U.S. Boxed Warning]: Safety and efficacy of transdermal patch have been limited to children ≥2 years of age who are opioid tolerant.**

Iontophoretic transdermal system (Ionsys™): **[U.S. Boxed Warning]: Should only be used for the treatment of hospitalized patients. To avoid overdose, the patient should be the only one to activate the system. Unintended exposure to fentanyl hydrogel could lead to absorption of fatal dose; hydrogel should not come in contact with fingers or mouth.** Should be used only in patients who are able to understand and follow instructions to operate the system. The error detection circuit uses a series of audible signals to alert the patient when a dose is not being delivered; use caution in patients who have high frequency hearing impairment. Remove prior to MRI procedure, cardioversion, or defibrillation. May interfere with radiographic image or CAT scan. Patients on chronic opioids or with a history of opioid abuse may require higher analgesic doses than Ionsys™ is able to provide. Prior to patient's hospital discharge, the system must be removed and disposed of in accordance with State and Federal regulations for a C-II substance. **[U.S. Boxed Warning]: Even if all 80 doses are used, a significant amount of fentanyl remains in the iontophoretic transdermal system and requires proper removal and disposal to avoid misuse, abuse, or diversion.** Safety and efficacy of iontophoretic transdermal system have not been established in children <18 years of age.

Adverse Reactions

>10%:
Cardiovascular: Hypotension, bradycardia
Central nervous system: CNS depression, confusion, drowsiness, sedation
Gastrointestinal: Nausea, vomiting, constipation, xerostomia
Local: Application-site reaction (iontophoretic system 14%)
Neuromuscular & skeletal: Chest wall rigidity (high dose I.V.), weakness
Ocular: Miosis
Respiratory: Respiratory depression
Miscellaneous: Diaphoresis

1% to 10%:
Cardiovascular: Cardiac arrhythmia, edema, orthostatic hypotension, hypertension, syncope, tachycardia
Central nervous system: Abnormal dreams, abnormal thinking, agitation, amnesia, anxiety, dizziness, euphoria, fatigue, fever, hallucinations, headache, insomnia, nervousness, paranoid reaction
Dermatologic: Erythema, papules, pruritus (iontophoretic system 6%), rash
Gastrointestinal: Abdominal pain, anorexia, biliary tract spasm, diarrhea, dyspepsia, flatulence, ileus
Genitourinary: Urinary retention (iontophoretic transdermal system 3%)
Hematologic: Anemia
Local: Application site reactions (buccal tablet)

Neuromuscular & skeletal: Abnormal coordination, abnormal gait, back pain, paresthesia, rigors, tremor

Respiratory: Apnea, bronchitis, dyspnea, hemoptysis, hypoxia, pharyngitis, rhinitis, sinusitis, upper respiratory infection

Miscellaneous: Hiccups, flu-like syndrome, speech disorder

<1%: Abdominal distention, ADH release, amblyopia, aphasia, bladder pain, bradycardia, bronchospasm, circulatory depression, CNS excitation or delirium, cold/clammy skin, convulsions, depersonalization, dysesthesia, exfoliative dermatitis, hostility, hyperpigmentation (application site of iontophoretic system), hyper-/hypotonia, laryngospasm, oliguria, paradoxical dizziness, physical and psychological dependence with prolonged use, polyuria, pustules, stertorous breathing, stupor, urinary tract spasm, urticaria, vertigo

Postmarketing and/or case reports: Anorgasmia, blurred vision, dental caries (Actiq®), ejaculatory difficulty, gum line erosion (Actiq®), libido decreased, tachycardia, tooth loss (Actiq®), weight loss

Overdosage/Toxicology Symptoms of overdose include CNS depression, respiratory depression, and miosis; muscle and chest wall rigidity (may require nondepolarizing skeletal muscle relaxant). Treatment is symptom-directed and supportive. If overdose from transdermal patch (eg, Duragesic®), remove system from patient's skin. Naloxone, 2 mg I.V. with repeat administration as necessary up to a total of 10 mg, can also be used to reverse toxic effects of the opiate. Use of an opioid antagonist can precipitate withdrawal in opioid-tolerant patients. Patients who experience adverse reactions during use of transdermal patch (eg, Duragesic®) should be monitored for at least 24 hours after removal of the patch.

Drug Interactions

Cytochrome P450 Effect: Substrate of CYP3A4 (major); **Inhibits** CYP3A4 (weak)

Increased Effect/Toxicity: Increased sedation with CNS depressants. Potential for serotonin syndrome if combined with other serotonergic drugs. Fentanyl may enhance the serotonergic effects of SSRIs and sibutramine. CYP3A4 inhibitors may increase the levels/effects of fentanyl; potentially fatal respiratory depression may occur when a potent inhibitor is used in a patient receiving chronic fentanyl (eg, transdermal patch); example inhibitors include azole antifungals, clarithromycin, diclofenac, doxycycline, erythromycin, imatinib, isoniazid, nefazodone, nicardipine, propofol, protease inhibitors, quinidine, telithromycin, and verapamil. Antipsychotic agents (phenothiazines) may increase hypotension. Protease inhibitors may increase effects of fentanyl.

Decreased Effect: Ammonium chloride may decrease the duration of opioid's analgesia. CYP3A4 inducers (including carbamazepine, phenytoin, phenobarbital, rifampin) may decrease serum levels of fentanyl by increasing metabolism. Pegvisomant effect may be decreased.

Ethanol/Nutrition/Herb Interactions

Ethanol: Avoid ethanol (may increase CNS depression).

Food: Glucose may cause hyperglycemia.

Herb/Nutraceutical: St John's wort may decrease fentanyl levels. Avoid valerian, St John's wort, kava kava, gotu kola (may increase CNS depression).

Storage/Stability

Injection formulation: Store at controlled room temperature of 15°C to 25°C (59°F to 86°F). Protect from light.

Iontophoretic transdermal system: Store at 15°C to 30°C (59°F to 86°F).

Transdermal patch: Do not store above 25°C (77°F).

(Continued)

Fentanyl *(Continued)*

Transmucosal (buccal tablets, lozenges): Store at controlled room temperature of 15°C to 30°C (59°F to 86°F). Protect from freezing and moisture.

Compatibility Stable in D_5W, NS.

Y-site administration: Compatible: Alatrofloxacin, amphotericin B cholesteryl sulfate complex, atracurium, cisatracurium, diltiazem, dobutamine, dopamine, enalaprilat, epinephrine, esmolol, etomidate, furosemide, gatifloxacin, heparin, hydrocortisone sodium succinate, hydromorphone, labetalol, levofloxacin, linezolid, lorazepam, midazolam, milrinone, morphine, nafcillin, nicardipine, nitroglycerin, norepinephrine, pancuronium, potassium chloride, propofol, ranitidine, remifentanil, sargramostim, thiopental, vecuronium, vitamin B complex with C.

Compatibility in syringe: Compatible: Atracurium, atropine, bupivacaine with ketamine, butorphanol, chlorpromazine, cimetidine, clonidine with lidocaine, dimenhydrinate, diphenhydramine, droperidol, heparin, hydromorphone, hydroxyzine, meperidine, metoclopramide, midazolam, morphine, ondansetron, pentazocine, perphenazine, prochlorperazine edisylate, promazine, promethazine, ranitidine, scopolamine. **Incompatible:** Pentobarbital.

Compatibility when admixed: Compatible: Bupivacaine. **Incompatible:** Fluorouracil, methohexital, pentobarbital, thiopental.

Mechanism of Action Binds with stereospecific receptors at many sites within the CNS, increases pain threshold, alters pain reception, inhibits ascending pain pathways

Pharmacodynamics/Kinetics

Onset of action: Analgesic: I.M.: 7-15 minutes; I.V.: Almost immediate; Transmucosal: 5-15 minutes

Peak effect: Transmucosal: Analgesic: 15-30 minutes

Duration: I.M.: 1-2 hours; I.V.: 0.5-1 hour; Transmucosal: Related to blood level; respiratory depressant effect may last longer than analgesic effect

Absorption:

Transmucosal, buccal tablet: Rapid, ~50% from the buccal mucosa; remaining 50% swallowed with saliva and slowly absorbed from GI tract.

Transmucosal, lozenge: Rapid, ~25% from the buccal mucosa; 75% swallowed with saliva and slowly absorbed from GI tract

Iontophoretic transdermal system (Ionsys™): Fentanyl levels continue to rise for 5 minutes after the completion of each 10-minute dose

Distribution: Highly lipophilic, redistributes into muscle and fat

Protein binding: 80% to 85%

Metabolism: Hepatic, primarily via CYP3A4

Bioavailability: Total (transmucosal and GI absorption): Buccal: 65% (range: 45% to 85%); Lozenge: 47% (range: 37% to 57%)

Half-life elimination:

I.V.: 2-4 hours

Iontophoretic transdermal system (Ionsys™): 11 hours

Transdermal patch: 17 hours (half-life is influenced by absorption rate)

Transmucosal: Lozenge: 7 hours; Buccal tablet: 100-200 mcg: 3-4 hours, 400-800 mcg: 11-12 hours

Time to peak: Buccal tablet: 46 minutes; Lozenge: ~91 minutes; Transdermal patch: 24-72 hours

Excretion: Urine (primarily as metabolites, <7% to 10% as unchanged drug)

Dosage Note: These are guidelines and do not represent the maximum doses that may be required in all patients. Doses should be titrated to pain relief/prevention. Monitor vital signs routinely. Single I.M. doses have a duration of 1-2 hours, single I.V. doses last 0.5-1 hour.

Sedation for minor procedures/analgesia:
Children 1-12 years:
  Sedation for minor procedures/analgesia: I.M., I.V.: 1-2 mcg/kg/dose; may repeat at 30- to 60-minute intervals. **Note:** Children 18-36 months of age may require 2-3 mcg/kg/dose
  Continuous sedation/analgesia: Initial I.V. bolus: 1-2 mcg/kg; then 1-3 mcg/kg/hour to a maximum dose of 5 mcg/kg/hour
Children >12 years and Adults: I.V.: 25-50 mcg; may repeat every 3-5 minutes to desired effect or adverse event; maximum dose of 500 mcg/4 hours; higher doses are used for major procedures

Surgery: Adults:
  Premedication: I.M., slow I.V.: 25-100 mcg/dose 30-60 minutes prior to surgery
  Adjunct to regional anesthesia: Slow I.V.: 25-100 mcg/dose over 1-2 minutes. **Note:** An I.V. should be in place with regional anesthesia so the I.M. route is rarely used but still maintained as an option in the package labeling.
  Adjunct to general anesthesia: Slow I.V.:
    Low dose: 0.5-2 mcg/kg/dose depending on the indication. For example, 0.5 mcg/kg will provide analgesia or reduce the amount of propofol needed for laryngeal mask airway insertion with minimal respiratory depression. However, to blunt the hemodynamic response to intubation 2 mcg/kg is often necessary.
    Moderate dose: Initial: 2-15 mcg/kg/dose; Maintenance (bolus or infusion): 1-2 mcg/kg/hour. Discontinuing fentanyl infusion 30-60 minutes prior to the end of surgery will usually allow adequate ventilation upon emergence from anesthesia. For "fast-tracking" and early extubation following major surgery, total fentanyl doses are limited to 10-15 mcg/kg.
    High dose: **Note:** High-dose (20-50 mcg/kg/dose) fentanyl is rarely used, but is still maintained in the package labeling.

Acute pain management: Adults:
  Severe: I.M, I.V.: 50-100 mcg/dose every 1-2 hours as needed; patients with prior opiate exposure may tolerate higher initial doses
  Patient-controlled analgesia (PCA): I.V.: Usual concentration: 10 mcg/mL
    Demand dose: Usual: 10 mcg; range: 10-50 mcg
    Lockout interval: 5-8 minutes
  Mechanically-ventilated patients (based on 70 kg patient): Slow I.V.: 0.35-1.5 mcg/kg every 30-60 minutes as needed; infusion: 0.7-10 mcg/kg/hour
  Iontophoretic transdermal system: 40 mcg per activation on-demand (maximum: 6 doses/hour). **Note:** Patient's pain should be controlled prior to initiating system. Instruct patient how to operate system. Only the patient should initiate system. Each system operates for 24 hours or until 80 doses have been administered, whichever comes first.

Breakthrough cancer pain: For patients who are tolerant to and currently receiving opioid therapy for persistent cancer pain; dosing should be individually titrated to provide adequate analgesia with minimal side effects. Dose titration should be done if patient requires more than 1 dose/breakthrough pain episode for several consecutive episodes. Patients experiencing >4 breakthrough pain episodes/day should have the dose of their long-term opioid re-evaluated.
  Children ≥16 years and Adults: Lozenge: Initial dose: 200 mcg; the second dose may be started 15 minutes after completion of the first dose. Consumption should be limited to ≤4 units/day.

(Continued)

Fentanyl *(Continued)*

Adults: Buccal tablet (Fentora™): Initial dose: 100 mcg; a second 100 mcg dose, if needed, may be started 30 minutes after the start of the first dose. **Note:** For patients previously using the transmucosal lozenge (Actiq®), the initial dose should be selected using the conversions listed below (maximum: 2 doses per breakthrough pain episode every 4 hours).

Dose titration, if required, should be done using multiples of the 100 mcg tablets. Patient can take two 100 mcg tablets (one on each side of mouth). If that dose is not successful, can use four 100 mcg tablets (two on each side of mouth). If titration requires >400 mcg/dose, then use 200 mcg tablets.

Conversion from lozenge to buccal tablet (Fentora™):

Lozenge dose 200-400 mcg, then buccal tablet 100 mcg

Lozenge dose 600-800 mcg, then buccal tablet 200 mcg

Lozenge dose 1200-1600 mcg, then buccal tablet 400 mcg

Note: Four 100 mcg buccal tablets deliver approximately 12% and 13% higher values of C_{max} and AUC, respectively, compared to one 400 mcg buccal tablet. To prevent confusion, patient should only have one strength available at a time. Using more than four buccal tablets at a time has not been studied.

Elderly >65 years: Transmucosal lozenge (eg, Actiq®): Dose should be reduced to 2.5-5 mcg/kg.

Chronic pain management: Children ≥2 years and Adults (opioid-tolerant patients): Transdermal patch (eg, Duragesic®):

Initial: To convert patients from oral or parenteral opioids to transdermal patch, a 24-hour analgesic requirement should be calculated (based on prior opiate use). Using the tables, the appropriate initial dose can be determined. The initial fentanyl dosage may be approximated from the 24-hour morphine dosage and titrated to minimize adverse effects and provide analgesia. With the initial application, the absorption of transdermal fentanyl requires several hours to reach plateau; therefore transdermal fentanyl is inappropriate for management of acute pain. Change patch every 72 hours.

Conversion from continuous infusion of fentanyl: In patients who have adequate pain relief with a fentanyl infusion, fentanyl may be converted to transdermal dosing at a rate equivalent to the intravenous rate. A two-step taper of the infusion to be completed over 12 hours has been recommended (Kornick, 2001) after the patch is applied. The infusion is decreased to 50% of the original rate six hours after the application of the first patch, and subsequently discontinued twelve hours after application.

Titration: Short-acting agents may be required until analgesic efficacy is established and/or as supplements for "breakthrough" pain. The amount of supplemental doses should be closely monitored. Appropriate dosage increases may be based on daily supplemental dosage using the ratio of 45 mg/24 hours of oral morphine to a 12.5 mcg/hour increase in fentanyl dosage.

Frequency of adjustment: The dosage should not be titrated more frequently than every 3 days after the initial dose or every 6 days thereafter. Patients should wear a consistent fentanyl dosage through two applications (6 days) before dosage increase based on supplemental opiate dosages can be estimated.

Recommended Initial Duragesic® Dose
Based Upon Daily Oral Morphine Dose[1]

Oral 24-Hour Morphine (mg/d)	Duragesic® Dose (mcg/h)
60-134[2]	25
135-224	50
225-314	75
315-404	100
405-494	125
495-584	150
585-674	175
675-764	200
765-854	225
855-944	250
945-1034	275
1035-1124	300

[1]The table should NOT be used to convert from transdermal fentanyl (eg, Duragesic®) to other opioid analgesics. Rather, following removal of the patch, titrate the dose of the new opioid until adequate analgesia is achieved.

[2]Pediatric patients initiating therapy on a 25 mcg/hour Duragesic® system should be opioid-tolerant and receiving at least 60 mg oral morphine equivalents per day.

Dosing Conversion Guidelines[1,2]

Current Analgesic	Daily Dosage (mg/day)			
Morphine (I.M./I.V.)	10-22	23-37	38-52	53-67
Oxycodone (oral)	30-67	67.5-112	112.5-157	157.5-202
Oxycodone (I.M./I.V.)	15-33	33.1-56	56.1-78	78.1-101
Codeine (oral)	150-447	448-747	748-1047	1048-1347
Hydromorphone (oral)	8-17	17.1-28	28.1-39	39.1-51
Hydromorphone (I.V.)	1.5-3.4	3.5-5.6	5.7-7.9	8-10
Meperidine (I.M.)	75-165	166-278	279-390	391-503
Methadone (oral)	20-44	45-74	75-104	105-134
Methadone (I.M.)	10-22	23-37	38-52	53-67
Fentanyl transdermal recommended dose (mcg/h)	25 mcg/h	50 mcg/h	75 mcg/h	100 mcg/h

[1]The table should NOT be used to convert from transdermal fentanyl (eg, Duragesic®) to other opioid analgesics. Rather, following removal of the patch, titrate the dose of the new opioid until adequate analgesia is achieved.

[2]Duragesic® product insert, Janssen Pharmaceutica, Feb 2005.

(Continued)

Opioid Analgesics Initial Oral Dosing
Commonly Used for Severe Pain

Drug	Equianalgesic Dose (mg)		Initial Oral Dose	
	Oral[1]	Parenteral[2]	Children (mg/kg)	Adults (mg)
Buprenorphine	—	0.4	—	—
Butorphanol	—	2	—	—
Hydromorphone	7.5	1.5	0.06	4-8
Levorphanol	4 (acute) 1 (chronic)	2 (acute) 1 (chronic)	0.04	2-4
Meperidine	300	75	Not Recommended	
Methadone	10	5	0.2	5-10
Morphine	30	10	0.3	15-30
Nalbuphine	—	10	—	—
Pentazocine	50	30	—	—
Oxycodone	20	—	0.3	10-20
Oxymorphone	—	1	—	—

From "Principles of Analgesic Use in the Treatment of Acute Pain and Cancer Pain," *Am Pain Soc*, Fifth Ed.

[1]Elderly: Starting dose should be lower for this population group

[2]Standard parenteral doses for acute pain in adults; can be used to doses for I.V. infusions and repeated small I.V. boluses. Single I.V. boluses, use half the I.M. dose. Children >6 months: I.V. dose = parenteral equianalgesic dose x weight (kg)/100

Frequency of application: The majority of patients may be controlled on every 72-hour administration; however, a small number of patients require every 48-hour administration.

Dose conversion guidelines for transdermal fentanyl [1] (see tables on previous page and above).

Dosing adjustment in hepatic impairment: Actiq®: Although fentanyl kinetics may be altered in hepatic disease, Actiq® can be used successfully in the management of breakthrough cancer pain. Doses should be titrated to reach clinical effect with careful monitoring of patients with severe hepatic disease.

Administration

I.V.: Muscular rigidity may occur with rapid I.V. administration.

Transdermal patch (eg, Duragesic®): Apply to nonirritated and nonirradiated skin, such as chest, back, flank, or upper arm. Do not shave skin; hair at application site should be clipped. Prior to application, clean site with clear water and allow to dry completely. Do not use damaged or cut patches; a rapid release of fentanyl and increased systemic absorption may occur. Firmly press in place and hold for 30 seconds. Change patch every 72 hours. Do **not** use soap, alcohol, or other solvents to remove transdermal gel if it accidentally touches skin; use copious amounts of water. Avoid exposing application site to external heat sources (eg, heating pad, electric blanket, heat lamp, hot tub).

Iontophoretic transdermal system: System should be tested and applied by healthcare professional. The sticker on the back of the pouch is intended for use by the registered nurse. The sticker should be removed and applied to the Ionsys™ system with a date and time of application so that subsequent healthcare providers will know when the system expires (24 hours after application). Apply to intact, nonirritated, nonirradiated skin on chest or upper outer arm. Do not apply to scarred, burned, or tattooed areas. Any excessive hair at application site should be clipped; do not shave. Remove clear, plastic release liner before placement on skin. Avoid pulling on red tab. To administer a dose, the patient must press the button twice firmly within 3 seconds. An audible tone (beep) indicates the start of the delivery of the dose; red light remains on throughout the 10-minute dosing period. Each system operates for 24 hours or until 80 doses have been used (whichever comes first). Rotate skin site if another system is required after the first one is finished. Do not touch sticky side of system or the gels. If the hydrogel (where fentanyl is housed) becomes separated from the delivery system during removal, use gloves or tweezers to remove the hydrogel from skin. Do not use soap, alcohol, or other solvents to remove the hydrogel as they can increase absorption of fentanyl. Once a system has been removed, the same system can not be reapplied. Contains metal; remove prior to MRi procedure, cardioversion, or defibrillation.

Lozenge: Foil overwrap should be removed just prior to administration. Place the unit in mouth and allow it to dissolve. Do not chew. Lozenge may be moved from one side of the mouth to the other. The unit should be consumed over a period of 15 minutes. Handle should be removed after it is consumed or if patient has achieved an adequate response and/or shows signs of respiratory depression.

Buccal tablet: Patient should not open blister until ready to administer. The blister backing should be peeled back to expose the tablet; tablet should not be pushed out through the blister. Immediately use tablet once removed from blister. Place entire tablet in the buccal cavity (above a rear molar, between the upper cheek and gum). Tablet should not be broken, sucked, chewed, or swallowed. Should dissolve in about 14-25 minutes when left between the cheek and the gum. If remnants remain they may be swallowed with water.

Monitoring Parameters Respiratory and cardiovascular status, blood pressure, heart rate; signs of misuse, abuse, or addiction

Transdermal patch: Monitor for 24 hours after application of first dose

Dietary Considerations Transmucosal lozenge contains 2 g sugar per unit.

Patient Information Actiq® preparations contain an amount of medication that can be fatal to children. Keep all units out of the reach of children and discard any open units properly. Actiq® Welcome Kits are available which contain educational materials, safe storage and disposal instructions.

Special Geriatric Considerations The elderly may be particularly susceptible to the CNS depressant and constipating effects of narcotics; therefore, use with caution. For Ionsys™, age does not significantly affect the extent of drug absorption. Before using Ionsys™ in elderly patients, assess cognitive function and ability to operate the dosage system. The effect of age on the pharmacokinetics of Fentora™ (oral transmucosal buccal tablets) has not been studied.

Additional Information Fentanyl is 50-100 times as potent as morphine; morphine 10 mg I.M. is equivalent to fentanyl 0.1-0.2 mg I.M.; fentanyl has less hypotensive effects than morphine due to lack of histamine release. However, fentanyl may cause rigidity with high doses. If the patient has required high-dose analgesia or has used for a prolonged period (~7 days), taper dose to prevent withdrawal; monitor for signs and symptoms of withdrawal.

(Continued)

Fentanyl *(Continued)*

Iontophoretic transdermal system: Pharmacist should test before dispensing for patient. Without opening pouch, pharmacist should locate button side, find button and firmly press and release button twice within 3 seconds. Listen for a single audible tone (beep) confirming that the system is functional. The pharmacist should sign the front of the pouch after performing the functionality test.

Four minutes after the functional test, the system will beep for 15 seconds indicating that it is not in contact with skin. Open by cutting on dotted line of pouch, remove and discard plastic liner covering adhesive. Do not pull on red tab while removing. Press system firmly in place with sticky side down, on skin for at least 15 seconds. Make sure all sides of outer edge stick to skin. May tape sides down if they loosen; don't tape over button or red light. To determine the number of doses delivered, the red light will flash between doses in one second pulses to indicate the approximate number of doses that have been administered up to the present time. Each flash indicates up to 5 doses have been administered: One flash 1-5 doses; two flashes 6-10 doses; three flashes 11-15 doses; four flashes 16-20 doses, continuing up to 16 flashes (76-80 doses).

To dispose of system, wear gloves and pull the red tab to separate the bottom from the top. Fold the bottom in half with the sticky side facing in and flush down the toilet (needs to be witnessed by second healthcare provider). Dispose of top section according to hospital procedures for batteries.

Transmucosal (oral lozenge): Disposal of lozenge units: After consumption of a complete unit, the handle may be disposed of in a trash container that is out of the reach of children. For a partially-consumed unit, or a unit that still has any drug matrix remaining on the handle, the handle should be placed under hot running tap water until the drug matrix has dissolved. Special child-resistant containers are available to temporarily store partially consumed units that cannot be disposed of immediately.

Transdermal patch (Duragesic®): Upon removal of the patch, ~17 hours are required before serum concentrations fall to 50% of their original values. Opioid withdrawal symptoms are possible. Gradual downward titration (potentially by the sequential use of lower-dose patches) is recommended. Keep transdermal patch (both used and unused) out of the reach of children. Do **not** use soap, alcohol, or other solvents to remove transdermal gel if it accidentally touches skin as they may increase transdermal absorption, use copious amounts of water. Avoid exposure of direct external heat sources (eg, heating pads, electric blankets, heat lamps, saunas, hot tubs, heated water beds) to application site.

Vesicant No

Dosage Forms Excipient information presented when available (limited, particularly for generics); consult specific product labeling.

Note: Strengths expressed as base.

Infusion, as citrate [premixed in NS]: 0.05 mg (10 mL); 1 mg (100 mL); 1.25 mg (250 mL); 2 mg (100 mL); 2.5 mg (250 mL)

Injection, solution, as citrate [preservative free]: 0.05 mg/mL (2 mL, 5 mL, 10 mL, 20 mL, 30 mL, 50 mL)

Sublimaze®: 0.05 mg/mL (2 mL, 5 mL, 10 mL, 20 mL)

Lozenge, oral, as citrate [transmucosal]: 200 mcg, 400 mcg, 600 mcg, 800 mcg, 1200 mcg, 1600 mcg

Actiq®: 200 mcg, 400 mcg, 600 mcg, 800 mcg, 1200 mcg, 1600 mcg [mounted on a plastic radiopaque handle; contains sugar 2 g/unit; raspberry flavor]

Tablet, for buccal application, as citrate:

Fentora™: 100 mcg, 200 mcg, 300 mcg, 400 mcg, 600 mcg, 800 mcg

Transdermal system, topical, as base: 12 (5s) [delivers 12.5 mcg/hour; 3.13 cm^2]; 12 (5s) [delivers 12.5 mcg/hour; 5 cm^2]; 25 (5s) [delivers 25 mcg/hour; 10 cm^2]; 25 (5s) [delivers 25 mcg/hour; 6.25 cm^2]; 50 (5s) [delivers 50 mcg/hour; 12.5 cm^2]; 50 (5s) [delivers 50 mcg/hour; 20 cm^2]; 75 (5s) [delivers 75 mcg/hour; 18.75 cm^2]; 75 (5s) [delivers 75 mcg/hour; 30 cm^2]; 100 (5s) [delivers 100 mcg/hour; 25 cm^2]; 100 (5s) [delivers 100 mcg/hour; 40 cm^2]

Duragesic®: 12 [delivers 12.5 mcg/hour; 5 cm^2; contains alcohol 0.1 mL/10 cm^2] (5s); 25 [delivers 25 mcg/hour; 10 cm^2; contains alcohol 0.1 mL/10 cm^2] (5s); 50 [delivers 50 mcg/hour; 20 cm^2; contains alcohol 0.1 mL/10 cm^2] (5s); 75 [delivers 75 mcg/hour; 30 cm^2; contains alcohol 0.1 mL/10 cm^2] (5s); 100 [delivers 100 mcg/hour; 40 cm^2; contains alcohol 0.1 mL/10 cm^2] (5s)

Transdermal iontophoretic system, topical, as hydrochloride:

Ionsys™: Fentanyl 40 mcg/dose [80 doses/patch; contains 3-volt lithium battery]

References

Anwar M, Garrettson L, Huddleston K, et al, "Withdrawal Seizures in a Neonate Following Prolonged Fentanyl Use," Clin Toxicol, 1995, 33(5):493.

Baraka A, "Fentanyl-Induced Laryngospasm Following Tracheal Extubation in a Child," Anaesthesia, 1995, 50(4):375.

Bedforth NM and Lockey DJ, "Raynaud's Syndrome Following Intravenous Induction of Anaesthesia," Anaesthesia, 1995, 50(3):248-9.

Bennett MR and Adams AP, "Postoperative Respiratory Complications of Opiates," Clin Anaesthesiol, 1983, 1:41-56.

Billmire DA, Neale HW, and Gregory RO, "Use of I.V. Fentanyl in the Outpatient Treatment of Pediatric Facial Trauma," J Trauma, 1985, 25(11):1079-80.

Chaturvedi AK, Rao NG, and Baird JR, "A Death Due to Self-Administered Fentanyl," J Anal Toxicol, 1990, 14(6):385-7.

"Drugs for Pain," Med Lett Drugs Ther, 2000, 42(1085):73-8.

Fine PG, "Fentanyl in the Treatment of Cancer Pain," Semin Oncol, 1997, 24(5 Suppl 16):16-20-7.

Furuya H and Okumura F, "Hemolysis After Administration of High Dose Fentanyl," Anesth Analg, 1986, 65(2):207-8.

Jacobi J, Fraser GL, Coursin DB, et al, "Clinical Practice Guidelines for the Sustained Use of Sedatives and Analgesics in the Critically Ill Adult," Crit Care Med, 2002, 30(1):119-41. Available at: http://www.sccm.org/pdf/sedatives.pdf. Accessed August 2, 2003.

Jeal W and Benfield P, "Transdermal Fentanyl. A Review of Its Pharmacological Properties and Therapeutic Efficacy in Pain Control," Drugs, 1997, 53(1):109-38.

Katz R, Kelly HW, and Hsi A, "Prospective Study on the Occurrence of Withdrawal in Critically Ill Children Who Receive Fentanyl by Continuous Infusion," Crit Care Med, 1994, 22(5):763-7.

Kornick CA, Santiago-Palma J, Khojainova N, et al, "A Safe and Effective Method for Converting Cancer Patients from Intravenous to Transdermal Fentanyl," Cancer, 2001, 92(12):3056-61.

Leuschen MP, Willett LD, Hoie EB, et al, "Plasma Fentanyl Levels in Infants Undergoing Extracorporeal Membrane Oxygenation," J Thorac Cardiovasc Surg, 1993, 105(5):885-91.

Maurer PM and Bartkowski RR, "Drug Interactions of Clinical Significance With Opiad Analgesics," Drug Saf, 1993, 8(1):30-48.

Mokhlesi B, Leikin JB, Murray P, et al, "Adult Toxicology in Critical Care: Part II: Specific Poisonings," Chest, 2003, 123(3):897-922.

Poklis A, "Fentanyl: A Review for Clinical and Analytical Toxicologists," J Toxicol Clin Toxicol, 1995, 33(5):439-47.

"Principles of Analgesic Use in the Treatment of Acute Pain and Chronic Cancer Pain," 5th ed, Glenview, IL: American Pain Society, 2003.

Roth B, Schlunder C, Houben F, et al, "Analgesia and Sedation in Neonatal Intensive Care Using Fentanyl by Continuous Infusion," Dev Pharmacol Ther, 1991, 17(3-4):121-7.

Schechter NL, Weisman SJ, Rosenblum M, et al, "The Use of Oral Transmucosal Fentanyl Citrate for Painful Procedures in Children," Pediatrics, 1995, 95(3):335-9.

Scholz J, Steinfath M, and Schulz M, "Clinical Pharmacokinetics of Alfentanil, Fentanyl, and Sufentanil. An Update," Clin Pharmacokinet, 1996, 31(4):275-92.

Spigset O and Hagg S, "Analgesics and Breast-feeding: Safety Considerations," Paediatr Drugs, 2000, 2(3):223-38.

(Continued)

Fentanyl *(Continued)*

Stoukides CA and Stegman M, "Diffuse Rash Associated With Transdermal Fentanyl," *Clin Pharm*, 1992, 11(3):222.

Zeltzer LK, Altman A, Cohen D, et al, "Report of the Subcommittee on the Management of Pain Associated With Procedures in Children With Cancer," *Pediatrics*, 1990, 86(5 Pt 2):826-31.

♦ **Fentanyl Citrate** *see Fentanyl on page 426*

♦ **Fentanyl Citrate Injection, USP (Can)** *see Fentanyl on page 426*

♦ **Fentanyl Hydrochloride** *see Fentanyl on page 426*

♦ **Fentora™** *see Fentanyl on page 426*

Ferric Gluconate *(FER ik GLOO koe nate)*

Medication Safety Issues
  Sound-alike/look-alike issues:
    Ferrlecit® may be confused with Ferralet®

U.S. Brand Names Ferrlecit®

Index Terms Sodium Ferric Gluconate

Generic Available No

Canadian Brand Names Ferrlecit®

Pharmacologic Category Iron Salt

Use Repletion of total body iron content in patients with iron-deficiency anemia who are undergoing hemodialysis in conjunction with erythropoietin therapy

Pregnancy Risk Factor B

Lactation Excretion in breast milk unknown/use caution

Labeled Contraindications Hypersensitivity to ferric gluconate or any component of the formulation; use in any anemia not caused by iron deficiency; iron overload

Warnings/Precautions Potentially serious hypersensitivity reactions may occur. Fatal immediate hypersensitivity reactions have occurred with other iron carbohydrate complexes. Avoid rapid administration. Flushing and transient hypotension may occur. May augment hemodialysis-induced hypotension. Use with caution in elderly patients. Use only in patients with documented iron deficiency; caution with hemoglobinopathies or other refractory anemias as iron overload may occur. Safety and efficacy in children <6 years of age have not been established. Contains benzyl alcohol; do not use in neonates.

Adverse Reactions
  Cardiovascular: Angina, bradycardia, chest pain, edema, hyper-/hypotension, hypervolemia, MI, pulmonary edema, syncope, tachycardia, thrombosis, vasodilation

  Central nervous system: Agitation, chills, dizziness, fatigue, fever, headache, insomnia, malaise, pain, somnolence

  Dermatologic: Pruritus, rash

  Endocrine & metabolic: Hyper-/hypokalemia, hypoglycemia

  Gastrointestinal: Abdominal pain, anorexia, diarrhea, dyspepsia, epigastric pain, eructation, flatulence, melena, nausea, vomiting

  Genitourinary: Urinary tract infection

  Hematologic: Abnormal erythrocytes, leukocytosis, lymphadenopathy

  Local: Injection site reactions, injection site pain

  Neuromuscular & skeletal: Arthralgia, back pain, cramps, groin pain, leg cramps, myalgia, paresthesia, rigors, weakness

  Ocular: Blurred vision, conjunctivitis

  Respiratory: Cough, dyspnea, pneumonia, rhinitis, upper respiratory infection

Miscellaneous: Carcinoma, diaphoresis increased, flu-like syndrome, hypersensitivity reactions, infection, sepsis

Postmarketing and/or case reports: Dry mouth, dysgeusia, hemorrhage, hypertonia, hypoesthesia, loss of consciousness, nervousness, pallor, phlebitis, seizure, shock, skin discoloration

Overdosage/Toxicology Serum iron levels >300 mcg/dL may indicate iron poisoning. Initially, symptoms include abdominal pain, diarrhea, and/or vomiting and may progress to pallor, cyanosis, lassitude, drowsiness, acidosis and cardiovascular collapse. Treatment is generally symptom-directed and supportive. Refer to more detailed reference on poisonings for details.

Drug Interactions

Decreased Effect: Ferric gluconate injection may decrease the absorption of oral iron.

Storage/Stability Store at 20°C to 25°C (68°F to 77°F). Do not freeze.

Reconstitution For I.V. infusion, dilute 10 mL ferric gluconate in 0.9% sodium chloride (children: 25 mL NS, adults: 100 mL NS); use immediately after dilution.

Compatibility Stable with 0.9% sodium chloride; do not mix with parenteral nutrition solutions or other medications.

Mechanism of Action Supplies a source to elemental iron necessary to the function of hemoglobin, myoglobin and specific enzyme systems; allows transport of oxygen via hemoglobin

Pharmacodynamics/Kinetics Half-life elimination: Bound: 1 hour

Dosage I.V.: Repletion of iron in hemodialysis patients:

Children ≥6 years: 1.5 mg/kg of elemental iron (maximum: 125 mg/dose) diluted in NS 25 mL, administered over 60 minutes at 8 sequential dialysis sessions

Adults: 125 mg elemental iron per 10 mL (either by I.V. infusion or slow I.V. injection). Most patients will require a cumulative dose of 1 g elemental iron over approximately 8 sequential dialysis treatments to achieve a favorable response.

Note: A test dose of 2 mL diluted in NS 50 mL administered over 60 minutes was previously recommended (not in current manufacturer labeling). Doses >125 mg are associated with increased adverse events.

Administration I.V.: Adults: May be diluted prior to administration; avoid rapid administration. Solutions diluted for infusion should be infused over 1 hour. If administered undiluted, infuse slowly at a rate of up to 12.5 mg/minute.

Monitoring Parameters Hemoglobin and hematocrit, serum ferritin, iron saturation; vital signs

NKF K/DOQI guidelines recommend that iron status should be monitored monthly during initiation through the percent transferrin saturation (TSAT) and serum ferritin.

Test Interactions Serum or transferrin bound iron levels may be falsely elevated if assessed within 24 hours of ferric gluconate administration. Serum ferritin levels may be falsely elevated for 5 days after ferric gluconate administration.

Special Geriatric Considerations Studies in the elderly have not been done, nor were there sufficient numbers of the elderly in premarketing studies to identify any differences in the elderly using this drug. Monitor dose closely so as to avoid iron overload.

Dosage Forms Excipient information presented when available (limited, particularly for generics); consult specific product labeling.

(Continued)

Ferric Gluconate *(Continued)*

Injection, solution:

Ferrlecit®: Elemental iron 12.5 mg/mL (5 mL) [contains benzyl alcohol and sucrose 20%]

References

National Kidney Foundation, "KDOQI Clinical Practice Guidelines and Clinical Practice Recommentaions for Anemia in Chronic Kidney Disease," Available at www.kidney.org/professionals/KDOQI/guidelines_anemia/cpr32.htm. Last accessed November 20, 2006.

♦ **Ferrlecit®** *see Ferric Gluconate on page 438*

Filgrastim *(fil GRA stim)*

Medication Safety Issues

Sound-alike/look-alike issues:

Neupogen® may be confused with Epogen®, Neumega®, Neupro®, Nutramigen®

Related Information

Hematopoietic Stem Cell Transplantation *on page 1366*

U.S. Brand Names Neupogen®

Index Terms G-CSF; Granulocyte Colony Stimulating Factor; NSC-614629

Generic Available No

Canadian Brand Names Neupogen®

Pharmacologic Category Colony Stimulating Factor

Use Stimulation of granulocyte production in chemotherapy-induced neutropenia (nonmyeloid malignancies, acute myeloid leukemia, and bone marrow transplantation); severe chronic neutropenia (SCN); patients undergoing peripheral blood progenitor cell (PBPC) collection

Unlabeled/Investigational Use Treatment of anemia in myelodysplastic syndrome; treatment of drug-induced (nonchemotherapy) agranulocytosis in the elderly

Pregnancy Risk Factor C

Lactation Excretion in breast milk unknown/use caution

Labeled Contraindications Hypersensitivity to filgrastim, *E. coli*-derived proteins, or any component of the formulation

Warnings/Precautions Do not use filgrastim in the period 24 hours before to 24 hours after administration of cytotoxic chemotherapy because of the potential sensitivity of rapidly dividing myeloid cells to cytotoxic chemotherapy. May potentially act as a growth factor for any tumor type, particularly myeloid malignancies; precaution should be exercised in the usage of filgrastim in any malignancy with myeloid characteristics. Safety and efficacy have not been established with patients receiving radiation therapy, or with chemotherapy associated with delayed myelosuppression (eg, nitrosoureas, mitomycin C).

Allergic-type reactions (rash, urticaria, wheezing, dyspnea, tachycardia and/or hypotension) have occurred with first or later doses. Reactions tended to occur more frequently with intravenous administration and within 30 minutes of administration. Rare cases of splenic rupture or acute respiratory distress syndrome have been reported in association with filgrastim; patients must be instructed to report left upper quadrant pain or shoulder tip pain or respiratory distress. Reports of alveolar hemorrhage, manifested as pulmonary infiltrates and hemoptysis, have occurred in healthy donors undergoing PBPC collection (not indicated for use in healthy donors); hemoptysis resolved upon discontinuation. Cutaneous vasculitis has been reported, generally occurring in SCN patients on long-term therapy; dose reductions may improve symptoms to allow for continued therapy. Use caution in patients with sickle cell diseases; sickle cell crises have been reported following filgrastim therapy. Cytogenetic abnormalities, transformation to AML and MDS have been observed in patients treated with filgrastim for congenital neutropenia; a longer duration of treatment and poorer ANC response appear to increase the risk. The packaging of some forms may contain latex.

Adverse Reactions

>10%:

Central nervous system: Fever (12%)

Dermatologic: Petechiae (17%), rash (12%)

Gastrointestinal: Splenomegaly (severe chronic neutropenia: 30%; rare in other patients)

Hepatic: Alkaline phosphatase increased (21%)

Neuromuscular & skeletal: Bone pain (22% to 33%), commonly in the lower back, posterior iliac crest, and sternum

Respiratory: Epistaxis (9% to 15%)

1% to 10%:

Cardiovascular: Hyper-/hypotension (4%), S-T segment depression (3%), myocardial infarction/arrhythmias (3%)

Central nervous system: Headache (7%)

Gastrointestinal: Nausea (10%), vomiting (7%), peritonitis (2%)

Hematologic: Leukocytosis (2%)

Miscellaneous: Transfusion reaction (10%)

<1%, postmarketing, and/or case reports: Acute respiratory distress syndrome, allergic reactions, alopecia, alveolar hemorrhage, arthralgia, capillary leak syndrome, cerebral hemorrhage, cutaneous vasculitis, dyspnea, edema (facial), erythema nodosum, hematuria, hemoptysis, hepatomegaly, hypersensitivity reaction, injection site reaction, osteoporosis, pericarditis, proteinuria, psoriasis exacerbation, pulmonary infiltrates, renal insufficiency, sickle cell crisis, splenic rupture, Sweet's syndrome (acute febrile dermatosis), tachycardia, thrombocytopenia (in PBPC mobilization), thrombophlebitis, transient supraventricular arrhythmia, urticaria, wheezing

Overdosage/Toxicology No clinical adverse effects have been seen with high doses producing ANC >10,000/mm^3. Filgrastim discontinuation should result in a 50% decrease in circulating neutrophils within 1-2 days and a return to pretreatment levels in 1-7 days.

Storage/Stability Intact vials and prefilled syringes should be stored under refrigeration at 2°C to 8°C (36°F to 46°F) and protected from direct sunlight. Filgrastim should be protected from freezing and temperatures >30°C to avoid aggregation. If inadvertently frozen, thaw in a refrigerator and use within 24 hours; do not use if frozen >24 hours or frozen more than once. Do not shake.

Filgrastim vials and prefilled syringes are stable for 24 hours at 9°C to 30°C (47°F to 86°F).

Undiluted filgrastim is stable for 24 hours at 15°C to 30°C (59°F to 86°F) and for up to 14 days at 2°C to 8°C (36°F to 46°F) (data on file, Amgen Medical Information) in BD tuberculin syringes; however, sterility has only been assessed and maintained for up to 7 days when prepared under strict aseptic conditions (Singh, 1994; Jacobson, 1996). The manufacturer recommends using syringes within 24 hours due to the potential for bacterial contamination.

Filgrastim diluted with D$_5$W or D$_5$W with albumin for I.V. infusion (5-15 mcg/mL) is stable for 7 days at 2°C to 8°C (36°F to 46°F), however, should be used within 24 hours due to the possibility for bacterial contamination.

(Continued)

Filgrastim *(Continued)*

Reconstitution Do not dilute with saline at any time; product may precipitate. Filgrastim may be diluted with D_5W or with D_5W with albumin to a concentration of 5-15 mcg/mL for I.V. infusion administration (minimum concentration: 5 mcg/mL). Dilution to <5 mcg/mL is not recommended. Concentrations 5-15 mcg/mL require addition of albumin (final concentration of 2 mg/mL) to prevent adsorption to plastics.

Compatibility Stable in D_5W; **incompatible** with NS.

Y-site administration: Compatible: Acyclovir, allopurinol, amikacin, aminophylline, ampicillin, ampicillin/sulbactam, aztreonam, bleomycin, bumetanide, buprenorphine, butorphanol, calcium gluconate, carboplatin, carmustine, cefazolin, cefotetan, ceftazidime, chlorpromazine, cimetidine, cisplatin, co-trimoxazole, cyclophosphamide, cytarabine, dacarbazine, daunorubicin, dexamethasone sodium phosphate, diphenhydramine, doxorubicin, doxycycline, droperidol, enalaprilat, famotidine, floxuridine, fluconazole, fludarabine, ganciclovir, granisetron, haloperidol, hydrocortisone sodium phosphate, hydrocortisone sodium succinate, hydromorphone, hydroxyzine, idarubicin, ifosfamide, leucovorin, lorazepam, mechlorethamine, melphalan, meperidine, mesna, methotrexate, metoclopramide, minocycline, mitoxantrone, morphine, nalbuphine, netilmicin, ondansetron, plicamycin, potassium chloride, promethazine, ranitidine, sodium bicarbonate, streptozocin, ticarcillin, ticarcillin/clavulanate, tobramycin, vancomycin, vinblastine, vincristine, vinorelbine, zidovudine. **Incompatible:** Amphotericin B, cefepime, cefoperazone, cefotaxime, cefoxitin, ceftizoxime, ceftriaxone, cefuroxime, clindamycin, dactinomycin, etoposide, fluorouracil, furosemide, heparin, mannitol, methylprednisolone sodium succinate, metronidazole, mitomycin, piperacillin, prochlorperazine edisylate, thiotepa. **Variable (consult detailed reference):** Gentamicin, imipenem/cilastatin.

Mechanism of Action Stimulates the production, maturation, and activation of neutrophils; filgrastim activates neutrophils to increase both their migration and cytotoxicity.

Pharmacodynamics/Kinetics

Onset of action: ~24 hours; plateaus in 3-5 days

Duration: ANC decreases by 50% within 2 days after discontinuing filgrastim; white counts return to the normal range in 4-7 days; peak plasma levels can be maintained for up to 12 hours

Absorption: SubQ: 100%

Distribution: V_d: 150 mL/kg; no evidence of drug accumulation over a 11- to 20-day period

Metabolism: Systemically degraded

Half-life elimination: 1.8-3.5 hours

Time to peak, serum: SubQ: 2-8 hours

Dosage Refer to individual protocols.

Dosing, even in morbidly obese patients, should be based on actual body weight. Rounding doses to the nearest vial size often enhances patient convenience and reduces costs without compromising clinical response.

Children and Adults:

Chemotherapy-induced neutropenia: SubQ, I.V.: 5 mcg/kg/day; doses may be increased by 5 mcg/kg according to the duration and severity of the neutropenia; continue for up to 14 days or until the ANC reaches 10,000/mm^3

Bone marrow transplantation: SubQ, I.V.: 10 mcg/kg/day; adjust the dose according to the duration and severity of neutropenia; recommended steps based on neutrophil response:

When ANC >1000/mm³ for 3 consecutive days: Reduce filgrastim dose to 5 mcg/kg/day

If ANC remains >1000/mm³ for 3 more consecutive days: Discontinue filgrastim

If ANC decreases to <1000/mm³: Resume at 5 mcg/kg/day

If ANC decreases <1000/mm³ during the 5 mcg/kg/day dose, increase filgrastim to 10 mcg/kg/day and follow the above steps

Peripheral blood progenitor cell (PBPC) collection: SubQ: 10 mcg/kg daily in donors, usually for 6-7 days. Begin at least 4 days before the first leukopheresis and continue until the last leukopheresis; consider dose adjustment for WBC >100,000/mm³

Severe chronic neutropenia: SubQ:

Congenital: 6 mcg/kg twice daily; adjust the dose based on ANC and clinical response

Idiopathic/cyclic: 5 mcg/kg/day; adjust the dose based on ANC and clinical response

Anemia in myelodysplastic syndrome (unlabeled use - in combination with epoetin): SubQ: 0.3-3 mcg/kg daily **or** 30-150 mcg daily **or** 1-2 mcg/kg 2-3 times weekly

Elderly: Refer to adult dosing.

Drug-induced agranulocytosis (nonchemotherapy) in the elderly (unlabeled use): SubQ: 300 mcg daily until ANC >1500/mm³

Combination Regimens

Breast cancer: AC/Paclitaxel (Sequential) *on page 1143*

Head and neck cancer: FU HURT *on page 1223*

Leukemia, acute myeloid:

FLAG *on page 1215*

FLAG-IDA *on page 1215*

Lymphoma, non-Hodgkin's:

ICE (Lymphoma, non-Hodgkin's) *on page 1238*

RICE *on page 1277*

Lymphoma, non-Hodgkin's (Burkitt's): CODOX-M/IVAC *on page 1180*

Prostate cancer: Cyclophosphamide + Doxorubicin *on page 1185*

Soft tissue sarcoma: AI *on page 1145*

Administration May be administered undiluted by SubQ injection. May also be administered by I.V. bolus over 15-30 minutes in D₅W, or by continuous SubQ or I.V. infusion. Do not administer earlier than 24 hours after or in the 24 hours prior to cytotoxic chemotherapy.

Monitoring Parameters CBC with differential prior to treatment and twice weekly during filgrastim treatment for chemotherapy-induced neutropenia (3 times a week following marrow transplantation). For severe chronic neutropenia, monitor CBC with differential twice weekly during the first month of therapy and for 2 weeks following dose adjustments; monthly thereafter. In PBPC mobilization, monitor platelets.

Test Interactions May interfere with bone imaging studies; increased hematopoietic activity of the bone marrow may appear as transient positive bone imaging changes

Dietary Considerations Solution for injection contains sodium 0.035 mg/mL and sorbitol.

Patient Information Follow directions for proper storage and administration of SubQ medication. Never reuse syringes or needles. You may experience bone pain (request analgesic); nausea or vomiting (small frequent meals (Continued)

Filgrastim *(Continued)*

may help); hair loss (reversible); or sore mouth (frequent mouth care with a soft toothbrush or cotton swab may help). Report unusual fever or chills; unhealed sores; severe bone pain; pain, redness, or swelling at injection site; unusual swelling of extremities or difficulty breathing; or chest pain and palpitations.

Special Geriatric Considerations No specific data available for the elderly.

Additional Information

Reimbursement Hotline: 1-800-272-9376

Professional Services [Amgen]: 1-800-77-AMGEN

Emetic Potential Low (10% to 30%)

Vesicant No

High Dose Considerations

High Dose: 5-10 mcg/kg/day

Dosage Forms Excipient information presented when available (limited, particularly for generics); consult specific product labeling.

Injection, solution [preservative free]:

Neupogen®: 300 mcg/mL (1 mL, 1.6 mL) [vial; contains sodium 0.035 mg/mL and sorbitol]

Injection, solution [preservative free]:

Neupogen®: 600 mcg/mL (0.5 mL, 0.8 mL) [prefilled Singleject® syringe; contains sodium 0.035 mg/mL and sorbitol; needle cover contains latex]

References

Andres E, Kurtz JE, Martin-Hunyadi C, et al, "Nonchemotherapy Drug-Induced Agranulocytosis in Elderly Patients: The Effects of Granulocyte Colony-Stimulating Factor," *Am J Med,* 2002, 112(6):460-4.

Jacobson PA, West NJ, Spadoni V, et al, "Sterility of Filgrastim (G-CSF) in Syringes," *Ann Pharmacother,* 1996, 30(11):1238-42.

Jädersten M, Montgomery SM, Dybedal I, et al, "Long-Term Outcome of Treatment of Anemia in MDS with Erythropoietin and G-CSF," *Blood,* 2005, 106(3):803-11.

Kuwabara T, Kobayashi S, and Sugiyama Y, "Pharmacokinetics and Pharmacodynamics of a Recombinant Human Granulocyte Colony-Stimulating Factor," *Drug Metab Rev,* 1996, 28(4):625-58.

NCCN (National Comprehensive Cancer Network), "Practice Guidelines in Oncology: Myelodysplastic Syndromes Version 3.2006" (available at http://www.nccn.org/professionals/physician_gls/PDF/mds.pdf)

Nemunaitis J, "A Comparative Review of Colony-Stimulating Factors," *Drugs,* 1997, 54(5):709-29.

Rosenberg PS, Alter BP, Bolyard AA, et al, "The Incidence of Leukemia and Mortality From Sepsis in Patients With Severe Congenital Neutropenia Receiving Long-Term G-CSF Therapy," *Blood,* 2006, 107(12): 4628-35.

Singh RF, Corelli RL, and Guglielmo BJ, "Sterility of Unit Dose Syringes of Filgrastim and Sargramostim," *Am J Hosp Pharm,* 1994, 51(15):2811-2.

Smith TJ, Khatcheressian J, Lyman GH, et al, "2006 Update of Recommendations for the Use of White Blood Cell Growth Factors: An Evidence-Based Clinical Practice Guideline," *J Clin Oncol,* 2006, 24(19):3187-205.

Finasteride *(fi NAS teer ide)*

Medication Safety Issues

Sound-alike/look-alike issues:

Proscar® may be confused with ProSom®, Prozac®, Psorcon®

High alert medication: The Institute for Safe Medication Practices (ISMP) includes this medication among its list of drugs which have a heightened risk of causing significant patient harm when used in error.

Related Information

Safe Handling of Hazardous Drugs *on page 1382*

U.S. Brand Names Propecia®; Proscar®

Generic Available Yes

Canadian Brand Names Propecia®; Proscar®

Pharmacologic Category 5 Alpha-Reductase Inhibitor

Use

Propecia®: Treatment of male pattern hair loss in **men only**. Safety and efficacy were demonstrated in men between 18-41 years of age.

Proscar®: Treatment of symptomatic benign prostatic hyperplasia (BPH); can be used in combination with an alpha-blocker, doxazosin

Unlabeled/Investigational Use Adjuvant monotherapy after radical prostatectomy in the treatment of prostatic cancer; female hirsutism

Pregnancy Risk Factor X

Lactation Excretion in breast milk unknown/contraindicated

Labeled Contraindications Hypersensitivity to finasteride or any component of the formulation; pregnancy; not for use in children

Warnings/Precautions Hazardous agent - use appropriate precautions for handling and disposal. Other urological diseases including cancer should be ruled out before initiating. A minimum of 6 months of treatment may be necessary to determine whether an individual will respond to finasteride. Reduces prostate specific antigen (PSA) by 50%; in patients treated for ≥6 months the PSA should be doubled when comparing to normal ranges in untreated patients. Use with caution in those patients with hepatic dysfunction. Carefully monitor patients with a large residual urinary volume or severely diminished urinary flow for obstructive uropathy. These patients may not be candidates for finasteride therapy. Safety and efficacy have not been established in children.

Adverse Reactions Note: "Combination therapy" refers to finasteride and doxazosin.

>10%:

Endocrine & metabolic: Impotence (19%; combination therapy 23%), libido decreased (10%; combination therapy 12%)

Genitourinary: Neuromuscular & skeletal: Weakness (5%; combination therapy 17%)

1% to 10%:

Cardiovascular: Postural hypotension (9%; combination therapy 18%), edema (1%, combination therapy 3%)

Central nervous system: Dizziness (7%; combination therapy 23%), somnolence (2%; combination therapy 3%)

Genitourinary: Ejaculation disturbances (7%; combination therapy 14%), decreased volume of ejaculate

Endocrine & metabolic: Gynecomastia (2%)

Respiratory: Dyspnea (1%; combination therapy 2%), rhinitis (1%; combination therapy 2%)

<1%, postmarketing and/or case reports: Hypersensitivity (pruritus, rash, urticaria, swelling of face/lips); breast tenderness, breast enlargement, breast cancer (males), prostate cancer (high grade), testicular pain

Drug Interactions

Cytochrome P450 Effect: Substrate of CYP3A4 (minor)

Ethanol/Nutrition/Herb Interactions

Herb/Nutraceutical: St John's wort may decrease finasteride levels. Avoid saw palmetto (concurrent use has not been adequately studied).

Storage/Stability Store below 30°C (86°F). Protect from light.

Mechanism of Action Finasteride is a competitive inhibitor of both tissue and hepatic 5-alpha reductase. This results in inhibition of the conversion of testosterone to dihydrotestosterone and markedly suppresses serum dihydrotestosterone levels

(Continued)

Finasteride *(Continued)*

Pharmacodynamics/Kinetics

Onset of action: 3-6 months of ongoing therapy

Duration:

After a single oral dose as small as 0.5 mg: 65% depression of plasma dihydrotestosterone levels persists 5-7 days

After 6 months of treatment with 5 mg/day: Circulating dihydrotestosterone levels are reduced to castrate levels without significant effects on circulating testosterone; levels return to normal within 14 days of discontinuation of treatment

Distribution: V_{dss}: 76 L

Protein binding: 90%

Metabolism: Hepatic via CYP3A4; two active metabolites (<20% activity of finasteride)

Bioavailability: Mean: 63%

Half-life elimination, serum: Elderly: 8 hours; Adults: 6 hours (3-16)

Time to peak, serum: 2-6 hours

Excretion: Feces (57%) and urine (39%) as metabolites

Dosage Oral: Adults:

Male:

Benign prostatic hyperplasia (Proscar®): 5 mg/day as a single dose; clinical responses occur within 12 weeks to 6 months of initiation of therapy; long-term administration is recommended for maximal response

Male pattern baldness (Propecia®): 1 mg daily

Female hirsutism (unlabeled use): 5 mg/day

Dosing adjustment in renal impairment: No dosage adjustment is necessary

Dosing adjustment in hepatic impairment: Use with caution in patients with liver function abnormalities because finasteride is metabolized extensively in the liver

Administration Administration with food may delay the rate and reduce the extent of oral absorption. Women of childbearing age should not touch or handle broken tablets.

Monitoring Parameters Objective and subjective signs of relief of benign prostatic hyperplasia, including improvement in urinary flow, reduction in symptoms of urgency, and relief of difficulty in micturition

Special Geriatric Considerations Clearance of finasteride is decreased in the elderly, but no dosage reductions are necessary.

Emetic Potential Very low (<10%)

Dosage Forms Excipient information presented when available (limited, particularly for generics); consult specific product labeling.

Tablet: 5 mg

Propecia®: 1 mg

Proscar®: 5 mg

References

Lepor H, Williford WO, Barry MJ, et al, "The Efficacy of Terazosin, Finasteride, or Both in Benign Prostatic Hyperplasia," *N Engl J Med*, 1996, 335(8):533-9.

McConnell JD, Roehrborn CG, Bautista OM, et al, "The Long-Term Effect of Doxazosin, Finasteride, and Combination Therapy on the Clinical Progression of Benign Prostatic Hyperplasia. Medical Therapy of Prostatic Symptoms (MTOPS) Research Group," *N Engl J Med*, 2003, 349(25):2387-98.

Pole M and Koren G, "Finasteride. Does It Affect Spermatogenesis and Pregnancy," *Can Fam Physician*, 2001, 47:2469-70.

Thompson IM, Goodman PJ, Tangen CM, et al, "The Influence of Finasteride on the Development of Prostate Cancer," *N Engl J Med*, 2003, Jul 349(3):215-24.

♦ **FK506** *see* Tacrolimus *on page 993*

- **Flagyl**® *see* Metronidazole *on page 755*
- **Flagyl ER**® *see* Metronidazole *on page 755*
- **Flebogamma**® *see* Immune Globulin (Intravenous) *on page 597*
- **Fleet**® **Bisacodyl [OTC]** *see* Bisacodyl *on page 144*
- **Fleet**® **Stimulant Laxative [OTC]** *see* Bisacodyl *on page 144*
- **Florazole**® **ER (Can)** *see* Metronidazole *on page 755*
- **Floxin**® *see* Ofloxacin *on page 825*
- **Floxin Otic Singles** *see* Ofloxacin *on page 825*

Floxuridine (floks YOOR i deen)

Medication Safety Issues

Sound-alike/look-alike issues:

Floxuridine may be confused with Fludara®, fludarabine

FUDR® may be confused with Fludara®

High alert medication: The Institute for Safe Medication Practices (ISMP) includes this medication among its list of drugs which have a heightened risk of causing significant patient harm when used in error.

Related Information

Management of Drug Extravasations *on page 1301*

Safe Handling of Hazardous Drugs *on page 1382*

U.S. Brand Names FUDR®

Index Terms Fluorodeoxyuridine; FUDR; 5-FUDR; NSC-27640

Generic Available Yes

Canadian Brand Names FUDR®

Pharmacologic Category Antineoplastic Agent, Antimetabolite (Pyrimidine Analog)

Use Management of hepatic metastases of colorectal and gastric cancers

Pregnancy Risk Factor D

Lactation Excretion in breast milk unknown/contraindicated

Labeled Contraindications Hypersensitivity to floxuridine, fluorouracil, or any component of the formulation; pregnancy

Warnings/Precautions Hazardous agent - use appropriate precautions for handling and disposal. Use caution with impaired kidney or liver function. Discontinue if intractable vomiting, diarrhea, precipitous fall in leukocyte or platelet counts, myocardial ischemia, hemorrhage, gastrointestinal ulcer, or stomatitis occur. Use with caution in patients with poor nutritional status; depressed (leukocyte count <5000/mm³ or platelet count <100,000/mm³) bone marrow function; potentially serious infections. Use with caution in patients who have had high-dose pelvic radiation or previous use of alkylating agents. **[U.S. Boxed Warnings]: Should be administered under the supervision of an experienced cancer chemotherapy physician. Patients should be hospitalized for initiation of the first course of therapy due to the risk for severe toxic reactions.**

Adverse Reactions

>10%:

Gastrointestinal: Stomatitis, diarrhea; may be dose-limiting

Hematologic: Myelosuppression, may be dose-limiting; leukopenia, thrombocytopenia, anemia

Onset: 4-7 days

Nadir: 5-9 days

Recovery: 21 days

1% to 10%:

Dermatologic: Alopecia, photosensitivity, hyperpigmentation of the skin, localized erythema, dermatitis

(Continued)

Floxuridine *(Continued)*

Gastrointestinal: Anorexia

Hepatic: Biliary sclerosis, cholecystitis, jaundice

<1%: Nausea, vomiting, intrahepatic abscess

Drug Interactions

Increased Effect/Toxicity: Any form of therapy which adds to the stress of the patient, interferes with nutrition, or depresses bone marrow function will increase the toxicity of floxuridine.

Decreased Effect: Patients may experience impaired immune response to vaccines; possible infection after administration of live vaccines in patients receiving immunosuppressants.

Ethanol/Nutrition/Herb Interactions Ethanol: Avoid ethanol (due to GI irritation).

Storage/Stability Store intact vials at room temperature of 15°C to 30°C (59°F to 86°F). Reconstituted vials are stable for up to 2 weeks under refrigeration at 2°C to 8°C (36°C to 46°C). Further dilution in 500-1000 mL D_5W or NS is stable for 2 weeks at room temperature. Solutions in 0.9% sodium chloride are stable in some ambulatory infusion pumps for up to 21 days.

Reconstitution Reconstitute with 5 mL SWI for a final concentration of 100 mg/mL. Further dilute in 500-1000 mL D_5W or NS for I.V. infusion.

Compatibility Stable in D_5W, NS, sterile water for injection.

Y-site administration: Compatible: Amifostine, aztreonam, etoposide phosphate, filgrastim, fludarabine, gemcitabine, granisetron, melphalan, ondansetron, paclitaxel, piperacillin/tazobactam, sargramostim, teniposide, thiotepa, vinorelbine. **Incompatible:** Allopurinol, cefepime.

Compatibility when admixed: Compatible: Carboplatin, cisplatin, cisplatin with etoposide, cisplatin with leucovorin, etoposide, fluorouracil, leucovorin.

Mechanism of Action Mechanism of action and pharmacokinetics are very similar to fluorouracil; floxuridine is the deoxyribonucleotide of fluorouracil. Floxuridine is a fluorinated pyrimidine antagonist which inhibits DNA and RNA synthesis and methylation of deoxyuridylic acid to thymidylic acid.

Pharmacodynamics/Kinetics

Metabolism: Hepatic; Active metabolites: Floxuridine monophosphate (FUDR-MP) and fluorouracil; Inactive metabolites: Urea, CO_2, α-fluoro-β-alanine, α-fluoro-β-guanidopropionic acid, α-fluoro-β-ureidopropionic acid, and dihydrofluorouracil

Excretion: Urine: Fluorouracil, urea, α-fluoro-β-alanine, α-fluoro-β-guanidopropionic acid, α-fluoro-β-ureidopropionic acid, and dihydrofluorouracil; exhaled gases (CO_2)

Dosage Refer to individual protocols.

Intra-arterial:

0.1-0.6 mg/kg/day

4-20 mg/day

I.V.: (unlabeled use)

0.15 mg/kg/day for 7-14 days

0.5-1 mg/kg/day for 6-15 days

30 mg/kg/day for 5 days, then 15 mg/kg/day every other day, up to 11 days

Dosage adjustment in renal impairment: The FDA-approved labeling does not contain dosing adjustment guidelines; use with extreme caution.

Dosage adjustment in hepatic impairment: The FDA-approved labeling does not contain dosing adjustment guidelines; use with extreme caution. The following guidelines have been used by some clinicians (Floyd, 2006):

Serum bilirubin 1.2 times ULN or alkaline phosphatase 1.2 times ULN: Administer 80% of dose

Serum bilirubin 1.5 times ULN; ALT/AST 3 times baseline or alkaline phosphatase 1.5 times ULN: Administer 50% of dose

Serum bilirubin 2 times ULN; ALT/AST >3 times baseline or alkaline phosphatase 2 times ULN: No recommendation is available

Administration Continuous intra-arterial or I.V. infusion (unlabeled use)

Emetic Potential Very low (<10%)

Vesicant No

Dosage Forms Excipient information presented when available (limited, particularly for generics); consult specific product labeling.

Injection, powder for reconstitution: 500 mg

References

Davidson BS, Izzo F, Chase JL, et al, "Alternating Floxuridine and 5-Fluorouracil Hepatic Arterial Chemotherapy for Colorectal Liver Metastases Minimizes Biliary Toxicity," *Am J Surg*, 1996, 172(3):244-7.

DeConti RC, Kaplan SR, Papac RJ, et al, "Continuous Infusions of 5-Fluoro-2-Deoxyuridine in the Treatment of Solid Tumors," *Cancer*, 1973, 31(4):894-8.

de Takats PG, Kerr DJ, Poole CJ, et al, "Hepatic Arterial Chemotherapy for Metastatic Colorectal Carcinoma," *Br J Cancer*, 1994, 69(2):372-8.

Floyd J, Mirza I, Sachs B, et al, "Hepatotoxicity of Chemotherapy," *Semin Oncol*, 2006, 33(1):50-67.

Hrushesky WJ, von Roemeling R, Lanning RM, et al, "Circadian-Shaped Infusions of Floxuridine for Progressive Metastatic Renal Cell Carcinoma," *J Clin Oncol*, 1990, 8(9):1504-13.

Kemeny N, Seiter K, Conti JA, et al, Hepatic Arterial Floxuridine and Leucovorin for Unresectable Liver Metastases From Colorectal Carcinoma. New Dose Schedules and Survival Update," *Cancer*, 1994, 73(4):1134-42.

Fluconazole (floo KOE na zole)

Medication Safety Issues

Sound-alike/look-alike issues:

Fluconazole may be confused with flecainide

Diflucan® may be confused with diclofenac, Diprivan®, disulfiram

International issues:

Canesten® [Great Britain]: Brand name for clotrimazole in multiple international markets

U.S. Brand Names Diflucan®

Generic Available Yes

Canadian Brand Names Apo-Fluconazole®; Diflucan®; Dom-Fluconazole; Fluconazole Injection; Fluconazole Omega; Gen-Fluconazole; GMD-Fluconazole; Novo-Fluconazole; PHL-Fluconazole; PMS-Fluconazole; Riva-Fluconazole; Taro-Fluconazole

Pharmacologic Category Antifungal Agent, Oral; Antifungal Agent, Parenteral

Use Treatment of candidiasis (vaginal, oropharyngeal, esophageal, urinary tract infections, peritonitis, pneumonia, and systemic infections); cryptococcal meningitis; antifungal prophylaxis in allogeneic bone marrow transplant recipients

Pregnancy Risk Factor C

Lactation Enters breast/not recommended (AAP rates "compatible")

Labeled Contraindications Hypersensitivity to fluconazole, other azoles, or any component of the formulation; concomitant administration with cisapride

(Continued)

Fluconazole *(Continued)*

Warnings/Precautions Should be used with caution in patients with renal and hepatic dysfunction or previous hepatotoxicity from other azole derivatives. Patients who develop abnormal liver function tests during fluconazole therapy should be monitored closely and discontinued if symptoms consistent with liver disease develop. Rare exfoliative skin disorders have been observed; monitor closely if rash develops. the manufacturer reports rare cases of QT_c prolongation and TdP associated with fluconazole use and advises caution in patients with concomitant medications or conditions which are arrhythmogenic. However, given the limited number of cases and the presence of multiple confounding variables, the likelihood that fluconazole causes conduction abnormalities appears remote.

Adverse Reactions Frequency not always defined.

Cardiovascular: Angioedema, pallor, QT prolongation (rare, case reports), torsade de pointes (rare, case reports)

Central nervous system: Headache (2% to 13%), seizure, dizziness

Dermatologic: Rash (2%), alopecia, toxic epidermal necrolysis, Stevens-Johnson syndrome

Endocrine & metabolic: Hypercholesterolemia, hypertriglyceridemia, hypokalemia

Gastrointestinal: Nausea (4% to 7%), vomiting (2%), abdominal pain (2% to 6%), diarrhea (2% to 3%), taste perversion, dyspepsia

Hematologic: Agranulocytosis, leukopenia, neutropenia, thrombocytopenia

Hepatic: Hepatic failure (rare), hepatitis, cholestasis, jaundice, increased ALT/AST, increased alkaline phosphatase

Respiratory: Dyspnea

Miscellaneous: Anaphylactic reactions (rare)

Overdosage/Toxicology Symptoms of overdose include decreased lacrimation, salivation, respiration and motility, urinary incontinence, and cyanosis. Treatment includes supportive measures. A 3-hour hemodialysis will remove 50%.

Drug Interactions

Cytochrome P450 Effect: Inhibits CYP1A2 (weak), 2C9 (strong), 2C19 (strong), 3A4 (moderate)

Increased Effect/Toxicity: Concurrent use of fluconazole with cisapride is contraindicated due to the potential for malignant arrhythmias. Fluconazole may increase the levels/effects of amiodarone, selected benzodiazepines, bosentan, calcium channel blockers, citalopram, cyclosporine, dapsone, diazepam, fluoxetine, glimepiride, glipizide, losartan, methsuximide, mirtazapine, montelukast, nateglinide, nefazodone, paclitaxel, phenytoin, propranolol, sertraline, sildenafil (and other PDE-5 inhibitors), tacrolimus, venlafaxine, warfarin, zafirlukast, and other substrates of CYP2C9, 2C19, and 3A4.

Decreased Effect: Rifampin decreases concentrations of fluconazole.

Storage/Stability

Powder for oral suspension: Store dry powder at ≤30°C (86°F). Following reconstitution, store at 5°C to 30°C (41°F to 86°F). Discard unused portion after 2 weeks. Do not freeze.

Injection: Store injection in glass at 5°C to 30°C (41°F to 86°F). Store injection in Viaflex® at 5°C to 25°C (41°F to 77°F). Do not freeze. Do not unwrap unit until ready for use.

Compatibility Stable in D_5W, LR, NS.

Y-site administration: Compatible: Acyclovir, aldesleukin, allopurinol, amifostine, amikacin, aminophylline, ampicillin/sulbactam, aztreonam, benztropine, cefazolin, cefepime, cefotetan, cefoxitin, cefpirome, chlorpromazine, cimetidine, cisatracurium, dexamethasone sodium phosphate, diltiazem, diphenhydramine, dobutamine, docetaxel, dopamine, doxorubicin liposome, droperidol, etoposide phosphate, famotidine, filgrastim, fludarabine, foscarnet, ganciclovir, gatifloxacin, gemcitabine, gentamicin, granisetron, heparin, hydrocortisone sodium phosphate, immune globulin intravenous, leucovorin, linezolid, lorazepam, melphalan, meperidine, meropenem, metoclopramide, metronidazole, midazolam, morphine, nafcillin, nitroglycerin, ondansetron, oxacillin, paclitaxel, pancuronium, penicillin G potassium, phenytoin, piperacillin/tazobactam, prochlorperazine edisylate, promethazine, propofol, ranitidine, remifentanil, sargramostim, tacrolimus, teniposide, theophylline, thiotepa, ticarcillin/clavulanate, tobramycin, vancomycin, vecuronium, vinorelbine, zidovudine. **Incompatible:** Amphotericin B, amphotericin B cholesteryl sulfate complex, ampicillin, calcium gluconate, cefotaxime, ceftazidime, ceftriaxone, cefuroxime, chloramphenicol, clindamycin, co-trimoxazole, diazepam, digoxin, erythromycin lactobionate, furosemide, haloperidol, hydroxyzine, imipenem/cilastatin, pentamidine, piperacillin, ticarcillin.

Compatibility when admixed: Compatible: Acyclovir, amikacin, amphotericin B, cefazolin, ceftazidime, clindamycin, gentamicin, heparin, meropenem, metronidazole, morphine, piperacillin, potassium chloride, ranitidine with ondansetron, theophylline. **Incompatible:** Co-trimoxazole.

Mechanism of Action Interferes with cytochrome P450 activity, decreasing ergosterol synthesis (principal sterol in fungal cell membrane) and inhibiting cell membrane formation

Pharmacodynamics/Kinetics

Distribution: Widely throughout body with good penetration into CSF, eye, peritoneal fluid, sputum, skin, and urine

Relative diffusion blood into CSF: Adequate with or without inflammation (exceeds usual MICs)

CSF:blood level ratio: Normal meninges: 70% to 80%; Inflamed meninges: >70% to 80%

Protein binding, plasma: 11% to 12%

Bioavailability: Oral: >90%

Half-life elimination: Normal renal function: ~30 hours

Time to peak, serum: Oral: 1-2 hours

Excretion: Urine (80% as unchanged drug)

Dosage The daily dose of fluconazole is the same for oral and I.V. administration

Usual dosage ranges:

Neonates: First 2 weeks of life, especially premature neonates: Same dose as older children every 72 hours

Children: Loading dose: 6-12 mg/kg; maintenance: 3-12 mg/kg/day; duration and dosage depends on severity of infection

Adults: 200-800 mg/day; duration and dosage depends on severity of infection

Indication-specific dosing:

Children:

Candidiasis:

Oropharyngeal: Loading dose: 6 mg/kg; maintenance: 3 mg/kg/day for 2 weeks

Esophageal: Loading dose: 6 mg/kg; maintenance: 3-12 mg/kg/day for 21 days and at least 2 weeks following resolution of symptoms

Systemic infection: 6 mg/kg every 12 hours for 28 days

(Continued)

Fluconazole *(Continued)*

Meningitis, cryptococcal: Loading dose: 12 mg/kg; maintenance: 6-12 mg/kg/day for 10-12 weeks following negative CSF culture; relapse suppression (HIV-positive): 6 mg/kg/day

Adults:

Candidiasis:

Candidemia (neutropenic and non-neutropenic): 400-800 mg/day for 14 days after last positive blood culture and resolution of signs/ symptoms

Chronic, disseminated: 400-800 mg/day for 3-6 months

Oropharyngeal (long-term suppression): 200 mg/day; chronic therapy is recommended in immunocompromised patients with history of oropharyngeal candidiasis (OPC)

Osteomyelitis: 400-800 mg/day for 6-12 months

Esophageal: 200 mg on day 1, then 100-200 mg/day for 2-3 weeks after clinical improvement

Prophylaxis in bone marrow transplant: 400 mg/day; begin 3 days before onset of neutropenia and continue for 7 days after neutrophils >1000 cells/mm^3

Urinary: 200 mg/day for 1-2 weeks

Vaginal: 150 mg as a single dose

Coccidiomycosis (unlabeled use, IDSA guideline): 400 mg/day; doses of 800-1000 mg/day have been used for meningeal disease; usual duration of therapy ranges from 3-6 months for primary uncomplicated infections and up to 1 year for pulmonary (chronic and diffuse) infection

Endocarditis, prosthetic valve, early (unlabeled use, IDSA guideline): 400-800 mg/day for 6 weeks after valve replacement; long-term suppression in absence of valve replacement: 200-400 mg/day

Endophthalmitis: 400-800 mg/day for 6-12 weeks after surgical intervention.

Meningitis, cryptococcal: Amphotericin 0.7-1 mg/kg +/- 5-FC for 2 weeks then fluconazole 400 mg/day for at least 10 weeks (consider life-long in HIV-positive); maintenance (HIV-positive): 200-400 mg/day life-long

Pneumonia, cryptococcal (mild-to-moderate) (unlabeled use, IDSA guideline): 200-400 mg/day for 6-12 months (consider life-long in HIV-positive patients)

Dosing adjustment/interval in renal impairment:

No adjustment for vaginal candidiasis single-dose therapy

For multiple dosing, administer usual load then adjust daily doses as follows:

Cl$_{cr}$ ≤50 mL/minute (no dialysis): Administer 50% of recommended dose or administer every 48 hours.

Hemodialysis: 50% is removed by hemodialysis; administer 100% of daily dose (according to indication) after each dialysis treatment.

Continuous renal replacement therapy (CRRT): Drug clearance is highly dependent on the method of renal replacement, filter type, and flow rate. Appropriate dosing requires close monitoring of pharmacologic response, signs of adverse reactions due to drug accumulation, as well as drug levels in relation to target trough (if appropriate). The following are general recommendations only (based on dialysate flow/ultrafiltration rates of 1 L/hour) and should not supersede clinical judgment:

CVVH: 200-400 mg every 24 hours

CVVHD/CVVHDF: 400-800 mg every 24 hours

Note: Higher daily doses of 400 mg (CVVH) and 800 mg (CVVHD/CVVHDF) should be considered when treating resistant organisms and/or when employing combined ultrafiltration and dialysis flow rates of ≥2 L/hour for CVVHD/CVVHDF (Trotman, 2005).

Administration

I.V.: Infuse over approximately 1-2 hours; do not exceed 200 mg/hour
Oral: May be administered with or without food

Monitoring Parameters Periodic liver function tests (AST, ALT, alkaline phosphatase) and renal function tests, potassium

Dietary Considerations Take with or without regard to food.

Patient Information May take with food; take entire course of medication; report if side effects develop

Special Geriatric Considerations Has not been specifically studied in the elderly.

Emetic Potential Very low (<10%)

Vesicant No

Dosage Forms Excipient information presented when available (limited, particularly for generics); consult specific product labeling.

Infusion [premixed in sodium chloride or dextrose]: 200 mg (100 mL); 400 mg (200 mL)

Diflucan® [premixed in sodium chloride or dextrose]: 200 mg (100 mL); 400 mg (200 mL)

Powder for oral suspension: 10 mg/mL (35 mL); 40 mg/mL (35 mL)

Diflucan®: 10 mg/mL (35 mL); 40 mg/mL (35 mL) [contains sodium benzoate; orange flavor]

Tablet: 50 mg, 100 mg, 150 mg, 200 mg

Diflucan®: 50 mg, 100 mg, 150 mg, 200 mg

References

Aleck KA and Bartley DL, "Multiple Malformation Syndrome Following Fluconazole Use in Pregnancy: Report of an Additional Patient," *Am J Med Genet*, 1997, 72(3):253-6.

"American Academy of Pediatrics Committee on Drugs. The Transfer of Drugs and Other Chemicals Into Human Milk," *Pediatrics*, 2001, 108(3):776-89.

Amichai B and Grunwald MH, "Adverse Drug Reactions of the New Oral Antifungal Agents - Terbinafine, Fluconazole, and Itraconazole," *Int J Dermatol*, 1998, 37(6):410-5.

Berl T, Wilner KD, Gardner M, et al, "Pharmacokinetics of Fluconazole in Renal Failure," *J Am Soc Nephrol*, 1995, 6(2):242-7.

Como JA and Dismukes WE, "Oral Azole Drugs as Systemic Antifungal Therapy," *N Engl J Med*, 1993, 330(4):263-72.

Edwards JE Jr, Bodey GP, Bowden RA, et al, "International Conference for the Development of a Consensus on the Management and Prevention of Severe Candidal Infections," *Clin Infect Dis*, 1997, 25(1):43-59.

Eggimann P, Francioli P, Bille J, et al, "Fluconazole Prophylaxis Prevents Intra-Abdominal Candidiasis in High-Risk Surgical Patients," *Crit Care Med*, 1999, 27(6):1066-72.

Force RW, "Fluconazole Concentrations in Breast Milk," *Pediatr Infect Dis J*, 1995, 14(3):235-6.

Goa KL and Barradell LB, "Fluconazole. An Update of Its Pharmacodynamic and Pharmacokinetic Properties and Therapeutic Use in Major Superficial and Systemic Mycoses in Immuno-compromised Patients," *Drugs*, 1995, 50(4):658-90.

Goodman JL, Winston DJ, Greenfield RA, et al, "A Controlled Trial of Fluconazole to Prevent Fungal Infections in Patients Undergoing Bone Marrow Transplantation," *N Engl J Med*, 1992, 326(13):845-51.

Grant SM and Clissold SP, "Fluconazole: A Review of Its Pharmacodynamic and Pharmacokinetic Properties and Therapeutic Potential in Superficial and Systemic Mycoses," *Drugs*, 1990, 39(6):877-916.

Kauffman CA and Carver PL, "Antifungal Agents in the 1990s. Current Status and Future Developments," *Drugs*, 1997, 53(4):539-49.

Kowalsky SF and Dixon DM, "Fluconazole: A New Antifungal Agent," *Clin Pharm*, 1991, 10(3):179-94.

Lee JW, Seibel NL, Amantea M, et al, "Safety and Pharmacokinetics of Fluconazole in Children With Neoplastic Diseases," *J Pediatr*, 1992, 120(6):987-93.

Lyman CA and Walsh TJ, "Systemically Administered Antifungal Agents. A Review of Their Clinical Pharmacology and Therapeutic Applications," *Drugs*, 1992, 44(1):9-35.

(Continued)

Fluconazole *(Continued)*

Mastroiacovo P, Mazzone T, Botto LD, et al, "Prospective Assessment of Pregnancy Outcomes After First-Trimester Exposure to Fluconazole," *Am J Obstet Gynecol*, 1996, 175(6):1645-50.

Mercurio MG and Elewski BE, "Thrombocytopenia Caused by Fluconazole Therapy," *J Am Acad Dermatol*, 1995, 32(3):525-6.

Moncino MD and Gutman LT, "Severe Systemic Cryptococcal Disease in a Child: Review of Prognostic Indicators Predicting Treatment Failure and an Approach to Maintenance Therapy With Oral Fluconazole," *Pediatr Infect Dis J*, 1990, 9(5):363-8.

Pappas PG, Rex JH, Sobel JD, et al, "Guidelines for Treatment of Candidiasis. Infectious Diseases Society of America," *Clin Infect Dis*, 2004, 38(2):161-89.

Pelz RK, Hendrix CW, Swoboda SM, et al, "Double-Blind Placebo-Controlled Trial of Fluconazole to Prevent Candidal Infections in Critically Ill Surgical Patients," *Ann Surg*, 2001, 233(4):542-8.

Perry CM, Whittington R, and McTavish D, "Fluconazole. An Update of Its Antimicrobial Activity, Pharmacokinetic Properties, and Therapeutic Use in Vaginal Candidiasis," *Drugs*, 1995, 49(6):984-1006.

Pham CP, de Feiter PW, van der Kuy PH, "Long QTc Interval and Torsade de Pointes Caused by Fluconazole," *Ann Pharmacother*, 2006, 40(7):1456-61.

Rex JH, Bennett JE, Sugar AM, "A Randomized Trial Comparing Fluconazole With Amphotericin B for the Treatment of Candidemia in Patients Without Neutropenia. Candidemia Study Group and the National Institute," *N Engl J Med*, 1994, 331(20):1325-30.

Rex JH, Walsh TJ, Sobel JD, et al, "Practice Guidelines for the Treatment of Candidiasis, Infectious Diseases Society of America," *Clin Infect Dis*, 2000, 30(4):662-78.

Saag MS, Graybill RJ, Larsen RA, et al, "Practice Guidelines for the Management of Cryptococcal Disease. Infectious Diseases Society of America," *Clin Infect Dis*, 2000, 30(4):710-8.

Sanchez JM and Moya G, "Fluconazole Teratogenicity," *Prenat Diagn*, 1998, 18(8):862-3.

Sorensen HT, Nielsen GL, Olesen C, et al, "Risk of Malformations and Other Outcomes in Children Exposed to Fluconazole in utero," *Br J Clin Pharmacol*, 1999, 48(2):234-8.

Terrell CL, "Antifungal Agents. Part II. The Azoles," *Mayo Clin Proc*, 1999, 74(1):78-100.

Trepanier EF and Amsden GW, "Current Issues in Onchomycosis," *Ann Pharmacother*, 1998, 32(2):204-14.

Trotman RL, Williamson JC, Shoemaker DM, et al, "Antibiotic Dosing in Critically Ill Adult Patients Receiving Continuous Renal Replacement Therapy," *Clin Infect Dis*, 2005, 41(8):1159-66.

Valtonen M, Tiula E, and Neuvonen PJ, "Effect of Continuous Veno-Venous Haemofiltration and Haemodiafiltration on the Elimination of Fluconazole in Patients With Acute Renal Failure," *J Antimicrob Chemother*, 1997, 40(5):695-700.

Viscoli C, Castagnola E, Fioredda F, et al, "Fluconazole in the Treatment of Candidiasis in Immunocompromised Children," *Antimicrob Agents Chemother*, 1991, 35(2):365-7.

Wassmann S, Nickenig G, and Bohm M, "Long QT Syndrome and Torsade de Pointes in a Patient Receiving Fluconazole," *Ann Inter Med*, 1999, 131(10):797.

♦ **Fluconazole Injection (Can)** *see* Fluconazole *on page 449*

♦ **Fluconazole Omega (Can)** *see* Fluconazole *on page 449*

Flucytosine *(floo SYE toe seen)*

Medication Safety Issues

Sound-alike/look-alike issues:

Flucytosine may be confused with fluorouracil

Ancobon® may be confused with Oncovin®

High alert medication: The Institute for Safe Medication Practices (ISMP) includes this medication among its list of drugs which have a heightened risk of causing significant patient harm when used in error.

U.S. Brand Names Ancobon®

Index Terms 5-FC; 5-Fluorocytosine; 5-Flurocytosine

Generic Available No

Canadian Brand Names Ancobon®

Pharmacologic Category Antifungal Agent, Oral

Use Adjunctive treatment of systemic fungal infections (eg, septicemia, endocarditis, UTI, meningitis, or pulmonary) caused by susceptible strains of *Candida* or *Cryptococcus*

Pregnancy Risk Factor C

Lactation Excretion in breast milk unknown/not recommended

Labeled Contraindications Hypersensitivity to flucytosine or any component of the formulation

Warnings/Precautions [U.S. Boxed Warning]: Use with extreme caution in patients with renal dysfunction; dosage adjustment required. Avoid use as monotherapy; resistance rapidly develops. Use with caution in patients with bone marrow depression; patients with hematologic disease or who have been treated with radiation or drugs that suppress the bone marrow may be at greatest risk. Bone marrow toxicity can be irreversible. **[U.S. Boxed Warning]: Closely monitor hematologic, renal, and hepatic status.** Hepatotoxicity and bone marrow toxicity appear to be dose related; monitor levels closely and adjust dose accordingly. Safety and efficacy in children have not been established.

Adverse Reactions Frequency not defined.

Cardiovascular: Cardiac arrest, myocardial toxicity, ventricular dysfunction, chest pain

Central nervous system: Ataxia, confusion, dizziness, drowsiness, fatigue, hallucinations, headache, parkinsonism, psychosis, pyrexia, sedation, seizure, vertigo

Dermatologic: Rash, photosensitivity, pruritus, toxic epidermal necrolysis, urticaria

Endocrine & metabolic: Hypoglycemia, hypokalemia

Gastrointestinal: Abdominal pain, diarrhea, dry mouth, duodenal ulcer, hemorrhage, loss of appetite, nausea, ulcerative colitis, vomiting

Hematologic: Agranulocytosis, anemia, aplastic anemia, eosinophilia, leukopenia, pancytopenia, thrombocytopenia

Hepatic: Acute hepatic injury, bilirubin increased, hepatic dysfunction, jaundice, liver enzymes increased

Neuromuscular & skeletal: Paresthesia, peripheral neuropathy, weakness

Otic: Hearing loss

Renal: Azotemia, BUN increased, crystalluria, renal failure, serum creatinine increased

Respiratory: Dyspnea, respiratory arrest

Miscellaneous: Allergic reaction

Overdosage/Toxicology Symptoms of overdose include nausea, vomiting, diarrhea, hepatitis, and bone marrow suppression. Monitor hematologic, renal, and hepatic parameters frequently. Treatment is symptom-directed and supportive. Removed by hemodialysis.

Drug Interactions

Decreased Effect: Cytarabine may decrease levels/effects of flucytosine.

Ethanol/Nutrition/Herb Interactions Food: Food decreases the rate, but not the extent of absorption.

Storage/Stability Store at room temperature of 15°C to 30°C (59°F to 86°F). Protect from light.

Mechanism of Action Penetrates fungal cells and is converted to fluorouracil which competes with uracil interfering with fungal RNA and protein synthesis

Pharmacodynamics/Kinetics

Absorption: 76% to 89%

Distribution: Into CSF, aqueous humor, joints, peritoneal fluid, and bronchial secretions; V_d: 0.6 L/kg

Protein binding: 3% to 4%

Metabolism: Minimally hepatic; deaminated, possibly via gut bacteria, to 5-fluorouracil

(Continued)

Flucytosine *(Continued)*

Half-life elimination:
Normal renal function: 2-5 hours
Anuria: 85 hours (range: 30-250)
End stage renal disease: 75-200 hours
Time to peak, serum: ~1-2 hours
Excretion: Urine (>90% as unchanged drug)

Dosage

Usual dosage ranges: Children (unlabeled use) and Adults: Oral: 50-150 mg/kg/day in divided doses every 6 hours

Indication-specific dosing:
Children (unlabeled use) and Adults: Oral:
Endocarditis: 25-37.5 mg/kg every 6 hours (with amphotericin B) for at least 6 weeks after valve replacement
Meningoencephalitis, cryptococcal: Induction: 25 mg/kg/dose (with amphotericin B) every 6 hours for 2 weeks; if clinical improvement, may discontinue both amphotericin and flucytosine and follow with an extended course of fluconazole (400 mg/day); alternatively, may continue flucytosine for 6-10 weeks (with amphotericin B) without conversion to fluconazole treatment

Dosing interval in renal impairment: Use lower initial dose:
Cl_{cr} 20-40 mL/minute: Administer 37.5 mg/kg every 12 hours
Cl_{cr} 10-20 mL/minute: Administer 37.5 mg/kg every 24 hours
Cl_{cr} <10 mL/minute: Administer 37.5 mg/kg every 24-48 hours, but monitor drug concentrations frequently
Hemodialysis: Dialyzable (50% to 100%); administer dose posthemodialysis
Peritoneal dialysis: Adults: Administer 0.5-1 g every 24 hours
Continuous arteriovenous or venovenous hemodiafiltration effects: Change dosing frequency to every 12-24 hours (monitor serum concentrations and adjust)

Administration Administer around-the-clock to promote less variation in peak and trough serum levels. To avoid nausea and vomiting, administer a few capsules at a time over 15 minutes until full dose is taken.

Monitoring Parameters

Pretreatment: Electrolytes (especially potassium), CBC with differential, BUN, renal function, blood culture
During treatment: CBC with differential, and LFTs (eg, alkaline phosphatase, AST/ALT) frequently, serum flucytosine concentration, renal function

Test Interactions Flucytosine causes markedly false elevations in serum creatinine values when the Ektachem® analyzer is used. The Jaffé reaction is recommended for determining serum creatinine.

Patient Information Take capsules a few at a time with food over a 15-minute period to avoid nausea

Special Geriatric Considerations Adjust for renal function.

Emetic Potential Very low (<10%)

Dosage Forms Excipient information presented when available (limited, particularly for generics); consult specific product labeling.
Capsule: 250 mg, 500 mg

Extemporaneous Preparations Flucytosine oral liquid has been prepared by using the contents of ten 500 mg capsules triturated in a mortar and pestle with a small amount of distilled water; the mixture was transferred to a 500 mL volumetric flask; the mortar was rinsed several times with a small amount of distilled water and the fluid added to the flask; sufficient distilled water was added to make a total volume of 500 mL of a 10 mg/mL liquid; oral liquid was stable for 70 days when stored in glass or plastic prescription bottles at 4°C or for up to 14 days at room temperature.

Wintermeyer SM and Nahata MC, "Stability of Flucytosine in an Extemporaneously Compounded Oral Liquid," *Am J Health Syst Pharm*, 1996, 53:407-9.

References
Aronoff GR, Berns JS, Brier ME, et al, "Drug Prescribing in Renal Failure: Dosing Guidelines for Adults," 4th ed. Philadelphia, PA: American College of Physicians; 1999.

Lau AH and Kronfol NO, "Elimination of Flucytosine by Continuous Hemofiltration," *Am J Nephrol*, 1995, 15(4):327-31.

Lyman CA and Walsh TJ, "Systemically Administered Antifungal Agents. A Review of Their Clinical Pharmacology and Therapeutic Applications," *Drugs*, 1992, 44(1):9-35.

Mofenson LM, Oleske J, Serchuck L, et al, "Treating Opportunistic Infections Among HIV-Exposed and Infected Children: Recommendations from CDC, the National Institutes of Health, and the Infectious Diseases Society of America," *MMWR Recomm Rep*, 2004, 53(RR-14):1-92. Available at http://www.cdc.gov/MMWR/preview/MMWRhtml/rr5314a1.htm

Patel R, "Antifungal Agents. Part I. Amphotericin B Preparations and Flucytosine," *Mayo Clin Proc*, 1998, 73(12):1205-25.

Saag MS, Graybill RJ, Larsen RA, et al, "Practice Guidelines for the Management of Cryptococcal Disease. Infectious Diseases Society of America," *Clin Infect Dis*, 2000, 30(4):710-8.

Vermes A, Guchelaar H, and Dankert J, "Flucytosine: A Review of its Pharmacology, Clinical Indications, Pharmacokinetics, Toxicity and Drug Interactions," *J Antimicrob Chemother*, 2000, 46(2):171-9.

♦ **Fludara**® *see Fludarabine on page 457*

Fludarabine (floo DARE a been)

Medication Safety Issues
Sound-alike/look-alike issues:

Fludarabine may be confused with floxuridine, Flumadine®

Fludara® may be confused with FUDR®

High alert medication: The Institute for Safe Medication Practices (ISMP) includes this medication among its list of drugs which have a heightened risk of causing significant patient harm when used in error.

Related Information
Hematopoietic Stem Cell Transplantation *on page 1366*

Safe Handling of Hazardous Drugs *on page 1382*

U.S. Brand Names Fludara®

Index Terms Fludarabine Phosphate; NSC-312887

Generic Available Yes

Canadian Brand Names Beneflur®; Fludara®

Pharmacologic Category Antineoplastic Agent, Antimetabolite (Purine Antagonist)

Use
I.V.: Treatment of chronic lymphocytic leukemia (CLL) (including refractory CLL); non-Hodgkin's lymphoma in adults

Oral (formulation not available in U.S.): Approved in Canada for treatment of CLL

Unlabeled/Investigational Use Treatment of non-Hodgkin's lymphoma and acute leukemias in pediatric patients; reduced-intensity conditioning regimens prior to allogeneic hematopoietic stem cell transplantation (generally administered in combination with busulfan and antithymocyte globulin or lymphocyte immune globulin, or in combination with melphalan and alemtuzumab)

Pregnancy Risk Factor D

Lactation Excretion in breast milk unknown/contraindicated

(Continued)

Fludarabine *(Continued)*

Labeled Contraindications Hypersensitivity of fludarabine or any component of the formulation; decompensated hemolytic anemia; breast-feeding, pregnancy

Warnings/Precautions Hazardous agent - use appropriate precautions for handling and disposal. Use with caution with renal insufficiency, patients with a fever, documented infection, or pre-existing hematological disorders (particularly granulocytopenia) or in patients with pre-existing central nervous system disorder (epilepsy), spasticity, or peripheral neuropathy. **[U.S. Boxed Warnings]: Higher doses are associated with severe neurologic toxicity (blindness, coma, death); similar toxicity was reported rarely at recommended doses. Life-threatening (and sometimes fatal) autoimmune hemolytic anemia has occurred; monitor closely for hemolysis. Severe bone marrow suppression may occur;** severe myelosuppression (trilineage bone marrow hypoplasia/aplasia) has been reported (rare); the duration of significant cytopenias in these cases may be prolonged (up to 1 year). May cause tumor lysis syndrome; risk is increased in patients with large tumor burden prior to treatment. Patients receiving blood products should only receive irradiated blood products due to the potential for transfusion related GVHD. **[U.S. Boxed Warnings]: Do not use in combination with pentostatin; may lead to severe, even fatal pulmonary toxicity. Should be administered under the supervision of an experienced cancer chemotherapy physician.**

Adverse Reactions

>10%:

Cardiovascular: Edema (8% to 19%)

Central nervous system: Fever (60% to 69%), fatigue (10% to 38%), pain (20% to 22%), chills (11% to 19%)

Dermatologic: Rash (15%)

Gastrointestinal: Nausea/vomiting (mild: 31% to 36%), anorexia (7% to 34%), diarrhea (13% to 15%), gastrointestinal bleeding (3% to 13%)

Genitourinary: Urinary tract infection (2% to 15%)

Hematologic: Myelosuppression (nadir: 10-14 days; recovery: 5-7 weeks; dose-limiting toxicity), anemia (60%), neutropenia (grade 4: 59%; nadir: ~13 days), thrombocytopenia (50% to 55%; nadir: ~16 days)

Neuromuscular & skeletal: Weakness (9% to 65%), myalgia (4% to 16%), paresthesia (4% to 12%)

Ocular: Visual disturbance (3% to 15%)

Respiratory: Cough (10% to 44%), pneumonia (16% to 22%), dyspnea (9% to 22%), upper respiratory infection (2% to 16%)

Miscellaneous: Infection (33% to 44%), diaphoresis (1% to 13%)

1% to 10%:

Cardiovascular: Angina (≤6%), CHF (≤3%), arrhythmia (≤3%), cerebrovascular accident (≤3%), MI (≤3%), supraventricular tachycardia (≤3%), deep vein thrombosis (1% to 3%), phlebitis (1% to 3%), aneurysm (≤1%), transient ischemic attack (≤1%)

Central nervous system: Malaise (6% to 8%), headache (≤3%), sleep disorder (1% to 3%), cerebellar syndrome (≤1%), depression (≤1%), mentation impaired (≤1%)

Dermatologic: Alopecia (≤3%), pruritus (1% to 3%), seborrhea (≤1%)

Endocrine & metabolic: Hyperglycemia (1% to 6%), dehydration (≤1%)

Gastrointestinal: Stomatitis (≤9%), esophagitis (≤3%), constipation (1% to 3%), mucositis (≤2%), dysphagia (≤3%)

Genitourinary: Dysuria (3% to 4%), hesitancy (≤3%)

Hematologic: Hemorrhage (≤1%)

Hepatic: Cholelithiasis (≤3%), liver function tests abnormal (1% to 3%), liver failure (≤1%)

Neuromuscular & skeletal: Osteoporosis (≤2%), arthralgia (≤1%)

Otic: Hearing loss (2% to 6%)

Renal: Hematuria (2% to 3%), renal failure (≤1%), renal function test abnormal (≤1%), proteinuria (≤1%)

Respiratory: Pharyngitis (≤9%), allergic pneumonitis (≤6%), hemoptysis (1% to 6%), sinusitis (≤5%), bronchitis (≤1%), epistaxis (≤1%), hypoxia (≤1%)

Miscellaneous: Anaphylaxis (≤1%), tumor lysis syndrome (1%)

<1%, postmarketing, and/or case reports: Agitation, ARDS, autoimmune hemolytic anemia, blurred vision, bone marrow fibrosis, coma, confusion, diplopia, eosinophilia, hemorrhagic cystitis, interstitial pneumonitis, metabolic acidosis, opportunistic infection, pancytopenia, pericardial effusion, peripheral neuropathy, photophobia (primarily with high doses), pulmonary fibrosis, pulmonary hemorrhage, pulmonary infiltrate, respiratory failure, trilineage bone marrow aplasia, trilineage bone marrow hypoplasia, urate crystalluria, wrist drop

Also observed: Neurologic syndrome characterized by cortical blindness, coma, and paralysis [36% at doses >96 mg/m^2 for 5-7 days; <0.2% at doses <125 mg/m^2/cycle (onset of neurologic symptoms may be delayed for 3-4 weeks)]

Overdosage/Toxicology High doses of fludarabine are associated with bone marrow depression including severe neutropenia and thrombocytopenia; irreversible central nervous system toxicity with delayed blindness, coma, and death has occurred. Discontinue drug; treatment is symptom-directed and supportive.

Drug Interactions

Increased Effect/Toxicity: Combined use with pentostatin may lead to severe, even fatal, pulmonary toxicity.

Ethanol/Nutrition/Herb Interactions Ethanol: Avoid ethanol (due to GI irritation).

Storage/Stability

I.V.: Store intact vials under refrigeration at 2°C to 8°C (36°F to 46°F). Reconstituted vials are stable for 16 days at room temperature of 15°C to 30°C (59°F to 86°F) or refrigerated. Solutions diluted in saline or dextrose are stable for 48 hours at room temperature or under refrigeration.

Tablet (formulation not available in U.S.): Store between 15°C to 30°C (59°F to 86°F); should be kept within packaging until use.

Reconstitution Reconstitute vials with SWI, NS, or D$_5$W to a concentration of 10-25 mg/mL. Standard I.V. dilution: 50-100 mL D$_5$W or NS.

Compatibility Stable in D$_5$W, NS, sterile water for injection.

Y-site administration: Compatible: Allopurinol, amifostine, amikacin, aminophylline, ampicillin, ampicillin/sulbactam, amsacrine, aztreonam, bleomycin, butorphanol, carboplatin, carmustine, cefazolin, cefepime, cefoperazone, cefotaxime, cefotetan, ceftazidime, ceftizoxime, ceftriaxone, cefuroxime, cimetidine, cisplatin, clindamycin, co-trimoxazole, cyclophosphamide, cytarabine, dacarbazine, dactinomycin, dexamethasone sodium phosphate, diphenhydramine, doxorubicin, doxycycline, droperidol, etoposide, etoposide phosphate, famotidine, filgrastim, floxuridine, fluconazole, fluorouracil, furosemide, gemcitabine, gentamicin, granisetron, haloperidol, heparin, hydrocortisone sodium phosphate, hydrocortisone sodium succinate, hydromorphone, ifosfamide, imipenem/cilastatin, lorazepam, magnesium sulfate, mannitol, mechlorethamine, melphalan, meperidine, mesna, methotrexate, methylprednisolone sodium succinate, metoclopramide, (Continued)

Fludarabine *(Continued)*

minocycline, mitoxantrone, morphine, multivitamins, nalbuphine, netilmicin, ondansetron, pentostatin, piperacillin, piperacillin/tazobactam, potassium chloride, promethazine, ranitidine, sodium bicarbonate, teniposide, thiotepa, ticarcillin, ticarcillin/clavulanate, tobramycin, vancomycin, vinblastine, vincristine, vinorelbine, zidovudine. **Incompatible:** Acyclovir, amphotericin B, chlorpromazine, daunorubicin, ganciclovir, hydroxyzine, prochlorperazine edisylate.

Mechanism of Action Fludarabine inhibits DNA synthesis by inhibition of DNA polymerase, ribonucleotide reductase and DNA primase.

Pharmacodynamics/Kinetics

Distribution: V_d: 38-96 L/m^2; widely with extensive tissue binding

Metabolism: I.V.: Fludarabine phosphate is rapidly dephosphorylated to 2-fluoro-vidarabine, which subsequently enters tumor cells and is phosphorylated by deoxycytidine kinase to the active triphosphate derivative; rapidly dephosphorylated in the serum

Bioavailability: 75%

Half-life elimination: 2-fluoro-vidarabine: 9 hours

Excretion: Urine (60%, 23% as 2-fluoro-vidarabine) within 24 hours

Dosage

I.V.:

Children (unlabeled use):

Acute leukemia: 10 mg/m^2 bolus over 15 minutes followed by continuous infusion of 30.5 mg/m^2/day for 5 days **or**

10.5 mg/m^2 bolus over 15 minutes followed by 30.5 mg/m^2/day for 48 hours

Solid tumors: 9 mg/m^2 bolus followed by 27 mg/m^2/day continuous infusion for 5 days

Adults:

Chronic lymphocytic leukemia: 25 mg/m^2/day for 5 days every 28 days

Non-hodgkin's lymphoma: Loading dose: 20 mg/m^2 followed by 30 mg/m^2/day for 48 hours

Reduced-intensity conditioning regimens prior to allogeneic hematopoietic stem cell transplantation (unlabeled use): 120-150 mg/m^2 administered in divided doses over 4-5 days

Oral: Adults: **Note:** Formulation available in Canada; not available in U.S.:

CLL: 40 mg/m^2 once daily for 5 days every 28 days

Dosing in renal impairment:

The FDA-approved labeling contains the following adjustment recommendations:

Cl_{cr} 30-70 mL/minute: Administer 80% of dose

Cl_{cr} <30 mL/minute: Avoid use

The Canadian labeling contains the following adjustment recommendations:

Cl_{cr} 30-70 mL/minute: Administer 50% of dose

Cl_{cr} <30 mL/minute: Not recommended

The following guidelines have been used by some clinicians:

Aronoff, 2007:

Children:

Cl_{cr} 30-50 mL/minute: Administer 80% of dose

Cl_{cr} <30 mL/minute: Not recommended

Hemodialysis: Administer 25% of dose

Continuous ambulatory peritoneal dialysis (CAPD): Not recommended

Continuous renal replacement therapy (CRRT): Administer 80% of dose

Adults:

Cl_{cr} 10-50 mL/minute: Administer 75% of dose

Cl_{cr} <10 mL/minute: Administer 50% of dose

Hemodialysis: Administer after dialysis

Continuous ambulatory peritoneal dialysis (CAPD): Administer 50% of dose

Continuous renal replacement therapy (CRRT): Administer 75% of dose

Kintzel, 1995:

Cl_{cr} 46-60 mL/minute: Administer 80% of dose

Cl_{cr} 31-45 mL/minute: Administer 75% of dose

Cl_{cr} <30 mL/minute: Administer 65% of dose

Combination Regimens

Leukemia, acute lymphocytic: FIS-HAM *on page 1214*

Leukemia, acute myeloid:

FIS-HAM *on page 1214*

FLAG *on page 1215*

FLAG-IDA *on page 1215*

Leukemia, chronic lymphocytic:

Fludarabine-Cyclophosphamide (FC) *on page 1216*

Fludarabine-Cyclophosphamide-Rituximab *on page 1217*

Fludarabine-Rituximab *on page 1217*

Administration

I.V.: Usually administered as a 15- to 30-minute infusion; continuous infusions are occasionally used

Oral: Tablet (formulation not available in U.S.) may be administered with or without food; should be swallowed whole; do not chew, break, or crush.

Monitoring Parameters CBC with differential, platelet count, AST, ALT, creatinine, serum albumin, uric acid

Emetic Potential Very low (<10%)

Vesicant No

Dosage Forms Excipient information presented when available (limited, particularly for generics); consult specific product labeling. [CAN] = Canadian brand name

Injection, powder for reconstitution, as phosphate: 50 mg

Tablet, as phosphate [CAN]: 10 mg [not available in U.S.]

References

Adkins JC, Peters DH, and Markham A, "Fludarabine. An Update of Its Pharmacology and Use in the Treatment of Haematological Malignancies," *Drugs*, 1997, 53(6):1005-37.

Avramis VI, Champagne J, Sato J, et al, "Pharmacology of Fludarabine Phosphate After a Phase I/II Trial by a Loading Bolus and Continuous Infusion in Pediatric Patients," *Cancer Res*, 1990, 50(22):7226-31.

Bacigalupo A, "Second EBMT Workshop on Reduced Intensity Allogeneic Hemopoietic Stem Cell Transplants (RI-HSCT)," *Bone Marrow Transplant*, 2002, 29(3):191-5.

Gandhi V and Plunkett W, "Cellular and Clinical Pharmacology of Fludarabine," *Clin Pharmacokinet*, 2002, 41(2):93-103.

Giralt S, Aleman A, Anagnostopoulos A, et al, "Fludarabine/Melphalan Conditioning for Allogeneic Transplantation in Patients With Multiple Myeloma," *Bone Marrow Transplant*, 2002, 30(6):367-73.

Hood MA and Finley RS, "Fludarabine: A Review," *DICP*, 1991, 25(5):518-24.

Johnson SA, "Clinical Pharmacokinetics of Nucleoside Analogues: Focus on Haematological Malignancies," *Clin Pharmacokinet*, 2000, 39(1):5-26.

Keating MJ, O'Brien S, McLaughlin P, et al, "Clinical Experience With Fludarabine in Hemato-Oncology," *Hematol Cell Ther*, 1996, 38(Suppl 2):83-91.

Plosker GL and Figgitt DP, "Oral fludarabine," *Drugs*, 2003, 63(21):2317-23.

Plunkett W, Gandhi V, Huang P, et al, "Fludarabine: Pharmacokinetics, Mechanisms of Action, and Rationales for Combination Therapies," *Semin Oncol*, 1993, 20(5 Suppl 7):2-12.

(Continued)

Fludarabine *(Continued)*

Rodriguez G, "Fludarabine Phosphate. A New Anticancer Drug With Significant Activity in Patients With Chronic Lymphocytic Leukemia and in Patients With Lymphoma," *Invest New Drugs*, 1994, 12(2):75-92.

Ross SR, McTavish D, and Faulds D, "Fludarabine. A Review of Its Pharmacological Properties and Therapeutic Potential in Malignancy," *Drugs*, 1993, 45(5):737-59.

Schetelig J, Bornhauser M, Kiehl M, et al, "Reduced-Intensity Conditioning With Busulfan and Fludarabine With or Without Antithymocyte Globulin in HLA-Identical Sibling Transplantation - A Retrospective Analysis," *Bone Marrow Transplant*, 2004, 33(5):483-90.

Van Besien K, Devine S, Wickrema A, et al, "Regimen-Related Toxicity After Fludarabine-Melphalan Conditioning: A Prospective Study of 31 Patients With Hematologic Malignancies," *Bone Marrow Transplant*, 2003, 32(5):471-6.

Von Hoff DD, "Phase I Clinical Trials With Fludarabine Phosphate," *Semin Oncol*, 1990, 17(5 Suppl 8):33-8.

Wright SJ, Robertson LE, O'Brien S, et al, "The Role of Fludarabine in Hematological Malignancies," *Blood Rev*, 1994, 8(3):125-34.

♦ **Fludarabine Phosphate** *see* Fludarabine *on page 457*

♦ **5-Fluorocytosine** *see* Flucytosine *on page 454*

♦ **Fluorodeoxyuridine** *see* Floxuridine *on page 447*

♦ **Fluoroplex®** *see* Fluorouracil *on page 462*

Fluorouracil *(flure oh YOOR a sil)*

Medication Safety Issues

Sound-alike/look-alike issues:

Fluorouracil may be confused with flucytosine

Efudex® may be confused with Efidac (Efidac 24®), Eurax®

High alert medication: The Institute for Safe Medication Practices (ISMP) includes this medication among its list of drugs which have a heightened risk of causing significant patient harm when used in error.

International issues:

Carac™ may be confused with Carace® which is a brand name for lisinopril in Ireland and Great Britain

Related Information

Fertility and Cancer Therapy *on page 1298*

Management of Drug Extravasations *on page 1301*

Safe Handling of Hazardous Drugs *on page 1382*

U.S. Brand Names Adrucil®; Carac™; Efudex®; Fluoroplex®

Index Terms 5-Fluorouracil; FU; 5-FU

Generic Available Yes: Injection, topical solution

Canadian Brand Names Efudex®

Pharmacologic Category Antineoplastic Agent, Antimetabolite (Pyrimidine Analog)

Use Treatment of carcinomas of the breast, colon, head and neck, pancreas, rectum, or stomach; topically for the management of actinic or solar keratoses and superficial basal cell carcinomas

Pregnancy Risk Factor D (injection); X (topical)

Lactation Excretion in breast milk unknown/not recommended

Labeled Contraindications Hypersensitivity to fluorouracil or any component of the formulation; dihydropyrimidine dehydrogenase (DPD) enzyme deficiency; pregnancy

Warnings/Precautions Hazardous agent - use appropriate precautions for handling and disposal. Use with caution in patients with impaired kidney or liver function. The drug should be discontinued if intractable vomiting or diarrhea, precipitous falls in leukocyte or platelet counts, stomatitis, hemorrhage, or myocardial ischemia occurs. Use with caution in patients who have had high-dose pelvic radiation or previous use of alkylating agents.

Palmar-plantar erythrodysesthesia (hand-foot) syndrome has been associated with use. Safety and efficacy have not been established in pediatric patients.

Administration to patients with a genetic deficiency of dihydropyrimidine dehydrogenase (DPD) has been associated with increased toxicity following administration (diarrhea, neutropenia, and neurotoxicity). Systemic toxicity normally associated with parenteral administration has also been associated with topical use, particularly in patients with DPD. Discontinue if symptoms of DPD occur. **[U.S. Boxed Warning]: Should be administered under the supervision of an experienced cancer chemotherapy physician.**

Avoid topical application to mucous membranes due to potential for local inflammation and ulceration. The use of occlusive dressings with topical preparations may increase the severity of inflammation in nearby skin areas. Avoid exposure to ultraviolet rays during and immediately following therapy.

Adverse Reactions Toxicity depends on route and duration of treatment

I.V.:

Cardiovascular: Angina, myocardial ischemia, nail changes

Central nervous system: Acute cerebellar syndrome, confusion, disorientation, euphoria, headache, nystagmus

Dermatologic: Alopecia, dermatitis, dry skin, fissuring, palmar-plantar erythrodysesthesia syndrome, pruritic maculopapular rash, photosensitivity, vein pigmentations

Gastrointestinal: Anorexia, bleeding, diarrhea, esophagopharyngitis, nausea, sloughing, stomatitis, ulceration, vomiting

Hematologic: Agranulocytosis, anemia, leukopenia, pancytopenia, thrombocytopenia

Myelosuppression:

Onset: 7-10 days

Nadir: 9-14 days

Recovery: 21-28 days

Local: Thrombophlebitis

Ocular: Lacrimation, lacrimal duct stenosis, photophobia, visual changes

Respiratory: Epistaxis

Miscellaneous: Anaphylaxis, generalized allergic reactions, nail loss

Topical: Note: Systemic toxicity normally associated with parenteral administration (including neutropenia, neurotoxicity, and gastrointestinal toxicity) has been associated with topical use particularly in patients with a genetic deficiency of dihydropyrimidine dehydrogenase (DPD).

Central nervous system: Headache, insomnia, irritability

Dermatologic: Alopecia, photosensitivity, pruritus, rash, scarring, telangiectasia

Gastrointestinal: Medicinal taste, stomatitis

Hematologic: Leukocytosis, thrombocytopenia

Local: Application site reactions: Allergic contact dermatitis, burning, crusting, dryness, edema, erosion, erythema, hyperpigmentation, irritation, pain, soreness, ulceration

Ocular: Eye irritation (burning, watering, sensitivity, stinging, itching)

Miscellaneous: Birth defects, herpes simplex, miscarriage

Overdosage/Toxicology Symptoms of overdose include myelosuppression, nausea, vomiting, diarrhea, and alopecia. No specific antidote exists. Monitor hematologically for at least 4 weeks. Treatment is supportive.
(Continued)

Fluorouracil *(Continued)*

Drug Interactions
Increased Effect/Toxicity: Fluorouracil may increase effects of warfarin.

Ethanol/Nutrition/Herb Interactions
Ethanol: Avoid ethanol (due to GI irritation).

Herb/Nutraceutical: Avoid black cohosh, dong quai in estrogen-dependent tumors.

Storage/Stability
Injection: Store intact vials at room temperature and protect from light; slight discoloration does not usually denote decomposition. If exposed to cold, a precipitate may form; **gentle** heating to 60°C will dissolve the precipitate without impairing the potency. Solutions in 50-1000 mL NS or D$_5$W, or undiluted solutions in syringes are stable for 72 hours at room temperature.

Topical: Store at controlled room temperature of 15°C to 30°C (59°F to 86°F).

Reconstitution Dilute in 50-1000 mL NS, D$_5$W, or bacteriostatic NS for infusion.

Compatibility Stable in D$_5$LR, D$_5$W, NS, bacteriostatic NS; **incompatible** with concentrations >25 mg/mL of fluorouracil and >2 mg/mL of leucovorin (precipitation occurs).

Y-site administration: Compatible: Allopurinol, amifostine, aztreonam, bleomycin, cefepime, cisplatin, cyclophosphamide, doxorubicin, doxorubicin liposome, etoposide phosphate, fludarabine, furosemide, gatifloxacin, gemcitabine, granisetron, heparin, hydrocortisone sodium succinate, leucovorin, linezolid, mannitol, melphalan, methotrexate, metoclopramide, mitomycin, paclitaxel, piperacillin/tazobactam, potassium chloride, propofol, sargramostim, teniposide, thiotepa, vinblastine, vincristine, vitamin B complex with C. **Incompatible:** Amphotericin B cholesteryl sulfate complex, droperidol, filgrastim, ondansetron, topotecan, vinorelbine.

Compatibility in syringe: Compatible: Bleomycin, cisplatin, cyclophosphamide, furosemide, heparin, leucovorin, methotrexate, metoclopramide, mitomycin, vinblastine, vincristine. **Incompatible:** Droperidol, epirubicin. **Variable (consult detailed reference):** Doxorubicin.

Compatibility when admixed: Compatible: Bleomycin, cyclophosphamide, cyclophosphamide with methotrexate, etoposide, floxuridine, hydromorphone, ifosfamide, methotrexate, mitoxantrone, vincristine. **Incompatible:** Carboplatin, cisplatin, cytarabine, diazepam, doxorubicin, fentanyl, leucovorin, metoclopramide, morphine.

Mechanism of Action A pyrimidine antimetabolite that interferes with DNA synthesis by blocking the methylation of deoxyuridylic acid; fluorouracil inhibits thymidylate synthetase (TS), or is incorporated into RNA. The reduced folate cofactor is required for tight binding to occur between the 5-FdUMP and TS.

Pharmacodynamics/Kinetics
Duration: ~3 weeks

Distribution: V$_d$: ~22% of total body water; penetrates extracellular fluid, CSF, and third space fluids (eg, pleural effusions and ascitic fluid)

Metabolism: Hepatic (90%); via a dehydrogenase enzyme; FU must be metabolized to be active

Bioavailability: <75%, erratic and undependable

Half-life elimination: Biphasic: Initial: 6-20 minutes; two metabolites, FdUMP and FUTP, have prolonged half-lives depending on the type of tissue

Excretion: Lung (large amounts as CO_2); urine (5% as unchanged drug) in 6 hours

Dosage Adults:

Refer to individual protocols:

I.V. bolus: 500-600 mg/m² every 3-4 weeks **or** 425 mg/m² on days 1-5 every 4 weeks

Continuous I.V. infusion: 1000 mg/m²/day for 4-5 days every 3-4 weeks **or** 2300-2600 mg/m² on day 1 every week **or**

300-400 mg/m²/day **or**

225 mg/m²/day for 5-8 weeks (with radiation therapy)

Actinic keratoses: Topical:

Carac™: Apply thin film to lesions once daily for up to 4 weeks, as tolerated

Efudex®: Apply to lesions twice daily for 2-4 weeks; complete healing may not be evident for 1-2 months following treatment

Fluoroplex®: Apply to lesions twice daily for 2-6 weeks

Superficial basal cell carcinoma: Topical: Efudex® 5%: Apply to affected lesions twice daily for 3-6 weeks; treatment may be continued for up to 10-12 weeks

Dosage adjustment for renal impairment: The FDA-approved labeling does not contain specific dosing adjustment guidelines; however, it is stated that extreme caution should be used in patients with renal impairment.

Hemodialysis: Administer dose following hemodialysis.

Aronoff (2007): Recommends that dosage adjustment is not needed in adult patients with Cl_{cr} <50 mL/minute and patients receiving hemodialysis should be administered 50% of dose.

Dosage adjustment for hepatic impairment: The FDA-approved labeling does not contain specific dosing adjustment guidelines; however, it is stated that extreme caution should be used in patients with hepatic impairment. The following guidelines have been used by some clinicians:

Floyd, 2006: Bilirubin >5 mg/dL: Avoid use.

Koren, 1992: Hepatic impairment (degree not specified): Administer <50% of dose, then increase if toxicity does not occur.

Combination Regimens

Breast cancer:
CAF *on page 1157*

CEF *on page 1166*

CFP *on page 1170*

CMF *on page 1177*

CMF-IV *on page 1177*

CMFP *on page 1178*

CMFVP (Cooper Regimen, VPCMF) *on page 1178*

CNF *on page 1179*

Docetaxel-Trastuzumab-FEC *on page 1193*

Dox-CMF (Sequential) *on page 1195*

FAC *on page 1210*

FEC *on page 1214*

MF *on page 1247*

NFL *on page 1261*

Cervical cancer: Cisplatin-Fluorouracil *on page 1176*
Colorectal cancer:
Bevacizumab-Fluorouracil-Leucovorin *on page 1151*

Bevacizumab-Irinotecan-Fluorouracil-Leucovorin *on page 1151*

Bevacizumab-Oxaliplatin-Fluorouracil-Leucovorin *on page 1152*

FLOX (Nordic FLOX) *on page 1216*
(Continued)

Fluorouracil *(Continued)*

Administration

I.V.: I.V. bolus as a slow push or short (5-15 minutes) bolus infusion, or as a continuous infusion. Doses >1000 mg/m^2 are usually administered as a 24-hour infusion. Toxicity may be reduced by giving the drug as a constant infusion. Bolus doses may be administered by slow IVP or IVPB.

Note: I.V. formulation may be given orally mixed in water, grape juice, or carbonated beverage. It is generally best to drink undiluted solution, then rinse the mouth. CocaCola® has been recommended as the "best chaser" for oral fluorouracil.

Topical: Apply 10 minutes after washing, rinsing, and drying the affected area. Apply using fingertip (wash hands immediately after application) or nonmetal applicator. Do not cover area with an occlusive dressing. Wash hands immediately after topical application of the 5% cream. Topical preparations are for external use only; not for ophthalmic, oral, or intravaginal use.

Monitoring Parameters CBC with differential and platelet count, renal function tests, liver function tests

Dietary Considerations Increase dietary intake of thiamine.

Patient Information Avoid alcohol and all OTC drugs unless approved by your prescriber. Maintain adequate hydration (2-3 L/day of fluids unless instructed to restrict fluid intake) and nutrition (small frequent meals may help). You may experience sensitivity to sunlight (use sunblock, wear protective clothing, or avoid direct sunlight); susceptibility to infection (avoid crowds or infected persons or persons with contagious diseases); nausea, vomiting, diarrhea, or loss of appetite (frequent small meals may help - request medication); weakness, lethargy, dizziness, decreased vision (use caution when driving or engaging in tasks requiring alertness until response to drug is known); or headache (request medication). Report signs and symptoms of infection (eg, fever, chills, sore throat, burning urination, vaginal itching or discharge, fatigue, mouth sores); bleeding (eg, black or tarry stools, easy bruising, unusual bleeding); vision changes; unremitting nausea, vomiting, or abdominal pain; CNS changes; respiratory difficulty; chest pain or palpitations; severe skin reactions to topical application; or any other adverse reactions. Contraceptive measures are recommended during therapy. The drug may be excreted in breast milk, therefore, an alternative form of feeding your baby should be used.

Topical: Use as directed; do not overuse. Wash hands thoroughly before and after applying medication. Avoid contact with eyes and mouth. Avoid occlusive dressings; use a porous dressing. May cause local reaction (pain, burning, or swelling); if severe, contact prescriber.

Emetic Potential Very low (<10%)

Vesicant No

Dosage Forms Excipient information presented when available (limited, particularly for generics); consult specific product labeling.

Cream, topical:
Carac™: 0.5% (30 g)
Efudex®: 5% (25 g, 40 g)
Fluoroplex®: 1% (30 g) [contains benzyl alcohol]
Injection, solution: 50 mg/mL (10 mL, 20 mL, 50 mL, 100 mL)
Adrucil®: 50 mg/mL (10 mL, 50 mL, 100 mL)
Solution, topical (Efudex®): 2% (10 mL); 5% (10 mL)

References

Aronoff GR, Bennett WM, Berns JS, et al, *Drug Prescribing in Renal Failure: Dosing Guidelines for Adults and Children*, 5th ed. Philadelphia, PA: American College of Physicians; 2007, p 100.

Balis FM, Holcenberg JS, and Bleyer WA, "Clinical Pharmacokinetics of Commonly Used Anti-cancer Drugs," *Clin Pharmacokinet*, 1983, 8(3):202-32.

Curran CF and Luce JK, "Fluorouracil and Palmar-Plantar Erythrodysesthesia," *Ann Intern Med*, 1989, 111(10):858.

Diasio RB and Harris BE, "Clinical Pharmacology of 5-Fluorouracil," *Clin Pharmacokinet*, 1989, 16(4):215-37.

Diasio RB and Johnson MR, "The Role of Pharmacogenetics and Pharmacogenomics in Cancer Chemotherapy With 5-Fluorouracil," *Pharmacology*, 2000, 61(3):199-203.

Floyd J, Mirza I, Sachs B, et al, "Hepatotoxicity of Chemotherapy," *Semin Oncol*, 2006, 33(1):50-67.

Grem JL, "5-Fluorouracil: Forty-Plus and Still Ticking. A Review of its Preclinical and Clinical Development," *Invest New Drugs*, 2000, 18(4):299-313.

Grem JL, "Systemic Treatment Options in Advanced Colorectal Cancer: Perspectives on Combination 5-Fluorouracil Plus Leucovorin," *Semin Oncol*, 1997, 24(5 Suppl 18):13-8, 18.

Iyer L and Ratain MJ, "5-Fluorouracil Pharmacokinetics: Causes for Variability and Strategies for Modulation in Cancer Chemotherapy," *Cancer Invest*, 1999, 17(7):494-506.

Kleiman NS, Lehane DE, Geyer CE Jr, et al, "Prinzmetal's Angina During 5-Fluorouracil Chemotherapy," *Am J Med*, 1987, 82(3):566-8.

Koren G, Beatty K, Seto A, et al, "The Effects of Impaired Liver Function on the Elimination of Antineoplastic Agents," *Ann Pharmacother*, 1992, 26(3):363-71.

Kuhn JG, "Fluorouracil and the New Oral Fluorinated Pyrimidines," *Ann Pharmacother*, 2001, 35(2):217-27.

Macdonald JS, "Toxicity of 5-Fluorouracil," *Oncology*, 1999, 13(7 Suppl 3):33-4.

Machover D, "A Comprehensive Review of 5-Fluorouracil and Leucovorin in Patients With Metastatic Colorectal Carcinoma," *Cancer*, 1997, 80(7):1179-87.

Mainwaring P and Grygiel JJ, "Interaction of 5-Fluorouracil With Folates," *Aust N Z J Med*, 1995, 25(1):60.

(Continued)

Fluorouracil *(Continued)*

Milano G and Chamorey AL, "Clinical Pharmacokinetics of 5-Fluorouracil With Consideration of Chronopharmacokinetics," *Chronobiol Int*, 2002, 19(1):177-89.

Parker WB and Cheng YC, "Metabolism and Mechanism of Action of 5-Fluorouracil," *Pharmacol Ther*, 1990, 48(3):381-95.

Pottage A, Holt S, Ludgate S, et al, "Fluorouracil Cardiotoxicity," *Br Med J*, 1978, 1(6112):547.

Schalhorn A and Kuhl M, "Clinical Pharmacokinetics of Fluorouracil and Folinic Acid," *Semin Oncol*, 1992, 19(2 Suppl 3):82-92.

Schilsky RL, "Biochemical and Clinical Pharmacology of 5-Fluorouracil," *Oncology*, 1998, 12(10 Suppl 7):13-8.

Trissel LA, Martinez JF, and Xu QA, "Incompatibility of Fluorouracil With Leucovorin Calcium or Levoleucovorin Calcium," *Am J Health Syst Pharm*, 1995, 52(7):710-5.

♦ **5-Fluorouracil** *see* Fluorouracil *on page 462*

Fluoxymesterone *(floo oks i MES te rone)*

Medication Safety Issues
Sound-alike/look-alike issues:
Halotestin® may be confused with Haldol®, haloperidol, halothane

Related Information
Safe Handling of Hazardous Drugs *on page 1382*

U.S. Brand Names Halotestin®

Generic Available Yes

Pharmacologic Category Androgen

Use Replacement of endogenous testicular hormone; in females, palliative treatment of breast cancer

Unlabeled/Investigational Use Stimulation of erythropoiesis, angioneurotic edema

Restrictions C-III

Pregnancy Risk Factor X

Lactation Excretion in breast milk unknown/contraindicated

Labeled Contraindications Hypersensitivity to fluoxymesterone or any component of the formulation; serious cardiac disease; liver or kidney disease; pregnancy

Warnings/Precautions Prolonged use and/or high doses may cause peliosis hepatis or liver cell tumors which may not be apparent until liver failure or intra-abdominal hemorrhage develops. Discontinue in case of cholestatic hepatitis with jaundice or abnormal liver function tests. Use with caution in patients with breast cancer; may cause hypercalcemia by stimulating osteolysis. Use with caution in patients with diabetes mellitus; monitor carefully. Use with caution in patients with conditions influenced by edema (eg, cardiovascular disease, migraine, seizure disorder, renal impairment); may cause fluid retention. Discontinue with evidence of mild virilization in women. Use with caution in hepatic impairment. Use with caution in elderly. May accelerate bone maturation without producing compensatory gain in linear growth in children. In prepubertal children, perform radiographic examination of the hand and wrist every 6 months to determine the rate of bone maturation and to assess the effect of treatment on the epiphyseal centers. Product may contain tartrazine.

Adverse Reactions
>10%:
Male: Priapism
Female: Menstrual problems (amenorrhea), virilism, breast soreness
Cardiovascular: Edema
Dermatologic: Acne

1% to 10%:

Male: Prostatic carcinoma, hirsutism (increase in pubic hair growth), impotence, testicular atrophy

Cardiovascular: Edema

Gastrointestinal: GI irritation, nausea, vomiting

Genitourinary: Prostatic hyperplasia

Hepatic: Hepatic dysfunction

<1%:

Male: Gynecomastia

Female: Amenorrhea

Hypercalcemia, leukopenia, polycythemia, hepatic necrosis, cholestatic hepatitis, hypersensitivity reactions

Overdosage/Toxicology Symptoms of overdose include water retention. Abnormal liver function tests have been observed.

Drug Interactions

Increased Effect/Toxicity: Fluoxymesterone may suppress clotting factors II, V, VII, and X; therefore, bleeding may occur in patients on anticoagulant therapy May elevate cyclosporine serum levels. May enhance hypoglycemic effect of insulin therapy; may decrease blood glucose concentrations and insulin requirements in patients with diabetes. Lithium may potentiate EPS and other CNS effect. May potentiate the effects of narcotics including respiratory depression

Decreased Effect: May decrease barbiturate levels and fluphenazine effectiveness.

Storage/Stability Protect from light.

Mechanism of Action Synthetic androgenic anabolic hormone responsible for the normal growth and development of male sex hormones and development of male sex organs and maintenance of secondary sex characteristics; synthetic testosterone derivative with significant androgen activity; stimulates RNA polymerase activity resulting in an increase in protein production; increases bone development; halogenated derivative of testosterone with up to 5 times the activity of methyltestosterone

Pharmacodynamics/Kinetics

Absorption: Rapid

Protein binding: 98%

Metabolism: Hepatic; enterohepatic recirculation

Half-life elimination: 10-100 minutes

Excretion: Urine (90%)

Dosage Adults: Oral:

Male:

Hypogonadism: 5-20 mg/day

Delayed puberty: 2.5-20 mg/day for 4-6 months

Female: Inoperable breast carcinoma: 10-40 mg/day in divided doses for 1-3 months

Combination Regimens

Breast cancer: VATH on page 1287

Monitoring Parameters In prepubertal children, perform radiographic examination of the hand and wrist every 6 months

Test Interactions Decreased levels of thyroxine-binding globulin; decreased total T_4 serum levels; increased resin uptake of T_3 and T_4

Patient Information Take as directed; do not discontinue without consulting prescriber. Diabetics should monitor serum glucose closely and notify prescriber of changes; this medication can alter hypoglycemic requirements. You may experience acne, growth of body hair, loss of libido, impotence, or menstrual irregularity (usually reversible); nausea or vomiting (small frequent (Continued)

Fluoxymesterone *(Continued)*

meals, frequent mouth care, sucking lozenges, or chewing gum may help). Report changes in menstrual pattern; deepening of voice or unusual growth of body hair; fluid retention (swelling of ankles, feet, or hands, difficulty breathing, or sudden weight gain); change in color of urine or stool; yellowing of eyes or skin; unusual bruising or bleeding; or other adverse reactions.

Emetic Potential Very low (<10%)

Dosage Forms Excipient information presented when available (limited, particularly for generics); consult specific product labeling. [DSC] = Discontinued product

Tablet: 10 mg

Halotestin®: 2 mg, 5 mg, 10 mg [contains tartrazine; 10 mg tablet DSC]

♦ **5-Flurocytosine** *see Flucytosine on page 454*

Flutamide *(FLOO ta mide)*

Medication Safety Issues

Sound-alike/look-alike issues:

Flutamide may be confused with Flumadine®, thalidomide

Eulexin® may be confused with Edecrin®, Eurax®

Related Information

Safe Handling of Hazardous Drugs *on page 1382*

U.S. Brand Names Eulexin®

Index Terms Niftolid; NSC-147834; 4'-Nitro-3'-Trifluoromethylisobutyranilide; SCH 13521

Generic Available Yes

Canadian Brand Names Apo-Flutamide®; Euflex®; Eulexin®; Novo-Flutamide

Pharmacologic Category Antineoplastic Agent, Antiandrogen

Use Treatment of metastatic prostatic carcinoma in combination therapy with LHRH agonist analogues

Unlabeled/Investigational Use Female hirsutism

Pregnancy Risk Factor D

Lactation Excretion in breast milk unknown/not recommended

Labeled Contraindications Hypersensitivity to flutamide or any component of the formulation; severe hepatic impairment; pregnancy

Warnings/Precautions Hazardous agent - use appropriate precautions for handling and disposal. Product labeling states flutamide is not for use in women, particularly for nonlife-threatening conditions. Patients with glucose-6 phosphate dehydrogenase deficiency or hemoglobin M disease or smokers are at risk of toxicities associated with aniline exposure, including methemoglobinemia, hemolytic anemia, and cholestatic jaundice. Monitor methemoglobin levels. **[U.S. Boxed Warning]: Hospitalization and, rarely, death due to liver failure have been reported in patients taking flutamide.** Severe and potentially fatal hepatic injury may occur (50% of cases within first 3 months of therapy). Serum transaminases should be monitored at baseline and monthly for the first four months of therapy, and periodically thereafter. These should also be repeated at the first sign and symptom of liver dysfunction. Use of flutamide is not recommended in patients with baseline elevation of transaminase levels (>2 times the upper limit of normal). Flutamide should be discontinued immediately at any time if the patient develops jaundice or elevation in serum transaminase levels (>2 times upper limit of normal).

Adverse Reactions

>10%:

Endocrine & metabolic: Breast tenderness, galactorrhea (9% to 42%), gynecomastia, hot flashes, impotence, libido decreased, tumor flare

Gastrointestinal: Nausea, vomiting (11% to 12%)

Hepatic: AST and LDH levels increased, transient, mild

1% to 10%:

Cardiovascular: Edema, hypertension (1%)

Central nervous system: Anxiety, confusion, depression, dizziness, drowsiness, headache, insomnia, nervousness

Dermatologic: Pruritus, ecchymosis, photosensitivity

Gastrointestinal: Anorexia, appetite increased, constipation, diarrhea, indigestion, upset stomach (4% to 6%)

Hematologic: Anemia (6%), leukopenia (3%), thrombocytopenia (1%)

Neuromuscular & skeletal: Weakness (1%)

Miscellaneous: Herpes zoster

<1%: Discoloration of urine (yellow), hepatic failure, hepatitis, hypersensitivity pneumonitis, jaundice, malignant breast neoplasm (male), MI, pulmonary embolism, sulfhemoglobinemia, thrombophlebitis

Overdosage/Toxicology Symptoms of overdose include hypoactivity, ataxia, anorexia, vomiting, slow respiration, and lacrimation. Induce vomiting. Management is supportive. Dialysis is of no benefit.

Drug Interactions

Cytochrome P450 Effect: Substrate (major) of CYP1A2, 3A4; **Inhibits** CYP1A2 (weak)

Increased Effect/Toxicity: CYP1A2 inhibitors may increase the levels/effects of flutamide; example inhibitors include ciprofloxacin, fluvoxamine, ketoconazole, lomefloxacin, ofloxacin, and rofecoxib. CYP3A4 inhibitors may increase the levels/effects of flutamide; example inhibitors include azole antifungals, clarithromycin, diclofenac, doxycycline, erythromycin, imatinib, isoniazid, nefazodone, nicardipine, propofol, protease inhibitors, quinidine, telithromycin, and verapamil. Warfarin effects may be increased.

Decreased Effect: CYP1A2 inducers may decrease the levels/effects of flutamide; example inducers include aminoglutethimide, carbamazepine, phenobarbital, and rifampin. CYP3A4 inducers may decrease the levels/effects of flutamide; example inducers include aminoglutethimide, carbamazepine, nafcillin, nevirapine, phenobarbital, phenytoin, and rifamycins.

Ethanol/Nutrition/Herb Interactions

Food: No effect on bioavailability of flutamide.

Herb/Nutraceutical: St John's wort may decrease flutamide levels.

Storage/Stability Store at room temperature.

Mechanism of Action Nonsteroidal antiandrogen that inhibits androgen uptake or inhibits binding of androgen in target tissues

Pharmacodynamics/Kinetics

Absorption: Oral: Rapid and complete

Protein binding: Parent drug: 94% to 96%; 2-hydroxyflutamide: 92% to 94%

Metabolism: Extensively hepatic to more than 10 metabolites, primarily 2-hydroxyflutamide (active)

Half-life elimination: 5-6 hours (2-hydroxyflutamide)

Excretion: Primarily urine (as metabolites)

Dosage Oral: Adults:

Prostatic carcinoma: 250 mg 3 times/day; alternatively, once-daily doses of 0.5-1.5 g have been used (unlabeled dosing)

Female hirsutism (unlabeled use): 250 mg daily

(Continued)

Flutamide *(Continued)*

Combination Regimens

Prostate cancer:

FL *on page 1215*

FZ *on page 1224*

Administration Usually administered orally in 3 divided doses. Contents of capsule may be opened and mixed with applesauce, pudding, or other soft foods. Mixing with a beverage is not recommended.

Monitoring Parameters Serum transaminase levels should be measured prior to starting treatment and should be repeated monthly for the first 4 months of therapy, and periodically thereafter. LFTs should be checked at the first sign or symptom of liver dysfunction (eg, nausea, vomiting, abdominal pain, fatigue, anorexia, flu-like symptoms, hyperbilirubinuria, jaundice, or right upper quadrant tenderness). Other parameters include tumor reduction, testosterone/estrogen, and phosphatase serum levels.

Patient Information Take as directed; do not discontinue without consulting prescriber. You may experience decreased libido, impotence, swelling of breasts, or decreased appetite (small frequent meals may help). Report chest pain or palpitation; acute abdominal pain; pain, tingling, or numbness of extremities; swelling of extremities or unusual weight gain; difficulty breathing; or other persistent adverse effects.

Special Geriatric Considerations A study has shown that the addition of flutamide to leuprolide therapy in patients with advanced prostatic cancer increased median actuarial survival time to 34.9 months versus 27.9 months with leuprolide alone. No specific dose alterations are necessary in the elderly.

Emetic Potential Low (10% to 30%)

Dosage Forms Excipient information presented when available (limited, particularly for generics); consult specific product labeling.

Capsule: 125 mg

References

Airhart RA, Barnett TF, Sullivan JW, "Flutamide Therapy for Carcinoma of the Prostate," *South Med J*, 1978, 71(7):798-801.

Azziz R, "The Evaluation and Management of Hirsutism," *Obstet Gynecol*, 2003, 101(5 Pt 1):995-1007.

Brogden RN and Chrisp P, "Flutamide. A Review of Its Pharmacodynamic and Pharmacokinetic Properties, and Therapeutic Use in Advanced Prostatic Cancer," *Drugs Aging*, 1991, 1(2):104-15.

Brogden RN and Clissold SP, "Flutamide. A Preliminary Review of Its Pharmacodynamic and Pharmacokinetic Properties, and Therapeutic Efficacy in Advanced Prostate Cancer," *Drugs*, 1989, 38(2):185-203.

Delaere KP and Van Thillo EL, "Flutamide Monotherapy as Primary Treatment in Advanced Prostatic Carcinoma," *Semin Oncol*, 1991, 18(5 Suppl 6):13-8.

Goldspiel BR and Kohler DR, "Flutamide: An Antiandrogen for Advanced Prostate Cancer," *DICP Ann Pharmacother*, 1990, 24(6):616-23.

Hunter MH and Carek PJ, "Evaluation and Treatment of Women With Hirsutism," *Am Fam Physician*, 2003, 67(12):2565-72.

Kassem NY, Nero RO, and Munroe JS, "Effect of Flutamide, An Antiandrogen, on Stage D Cancer of the Prostate," *Clin Pharmacol Ther*, 1981, 29:256.

Labrie F, "Mechanism of Action and Pure Antiandrogenic Properties of Flutamide," *Cancer*, 1993, 72(12 Suppl):3816-27.

Luo S, Martel C, Chen C, "Daily Dosing With Flutamide or Casodex Exerts Maximal Antiandrogenic Activity," *Urology*, 1997, 50(6):913-9.

Moghetti P, Tosi F, Tosti A, et al, "Comparison of Spironolactone, Flutamide, and Finasteride Efficacy in the Treatment of Hirsutism: A Randomized, Double Blind, Placebo-Controlled Trial," *J Clin Endocrinol Metab*, 2000, 85(1):89-94.

Thrasher JB, Deeths J, and Bennett C, "Comparative Study of the Clinical Efficacy of Two Dosing Regimens of Flutamide," *Mol Urol*, 2000, 4(3):259-63.

♦ **Folinic Acid (error prone synonym)** *see* Leucovorin Calcium *on page 668*

Fondaparinux (fon da PARE i nuks)

Medication Safety Issues

High alert medication: The Institute for Safe Medication Practices (ISMP) includes this medication among its list of drugs which have a heightened risk of causing significant patient harm when used in error.

U.S. Brand Names Arixtra®

Index Terms Fondaparinux Sodium

Generic Available No

Canadian Brand Names Arixtra®

Pharmacologic Category Factor Xa Inhibitor

Use Prophylaxis of deep vein thrombosis (DVT) in patients undergoing surgery for hip replacement, knee replacement, hip fracture (including extended prophylaxis following hip fracture surgery), or abdominal surgery (in patients at risk for thromboembolic complications); treatment of acute pulmonary embolism (PE); treatment of acute DVT without PE

Note: Additional Canadian approvals (not approved in U.S.): Unstable angina or non-ST segment elevation myocardial infarction (UA/NSTEMI) for the prevention of death and subsequent MI; ST segment elevation MI (STEMI) for the prevention of death and myocardial reinfarction

Unlabeled/Investigational Use Prophylaxis of DVT in patients with a history of heparin-induced thrombocytopenia (HIT)

Pregnancy Risk Factor B

Lactation Excretion in breast milk unknown/use caution

Labeled Contraindications Hypersensitivity to fondaparinux or any component of the formulation; severe renal impairment (Cl_{cr} <30 mL/minute); body weight <50 kg (prophylaxis); active major bleeding; bacterial endocarditis; thrombocytopenia associated with a positive *in vitro* test for antiplatelet antibody in the presence of fondaparinux

Warnings/Precautions [U.S. Boxed Warning]: Patients with recent or anticipated neuraxial anesthesia (epidural or spinal anesthesia) are at risk of spinal or epidural hematoma and subsequent paralysis. Not to be used interchangeably (unit-for-unit) with heparin, low molecular weight heparins (LMWHs), or heparinoids. Use caution in patients with moderate renal dysfunction (Cl_{cr} 30-50 mL/minute). Discontinue if severe dysfunction or labile function develops.

Use caution in congenital or acquired bleeding disorders; active ulcerative or angiodysplastic gastrointestinal disease; hemorrhagic stroke; shortly after brain, spinal, or ophthalmologic surgery; or in patients taking platelet inhibitors. Risk of major bleeding may be increased if initial dose is administered earlier then recommended (initiation recommended at 6-8 hours following surgery). Discontinue agents that may enhance the risk of hemorrhage if possible. Use caution in patients <50 kg who are being treated for DVT/PE; fondaparinux clearance may be decreased. Use with caution in the elderly. Safety and efficacy in pediatric patients have not been established.

Canadian labeling warnings/precautions: The administration of fondaparinux is not recommended prior to and during primary percutaneous coronary intervention (PCI) for reperfusion in STEMI patients, due to an increased risk for guiding catheter thrombosis. UA/NSTEMI and STEMI patients undergoing any PCI should not receive fondaparinux as a sole anticoagulant agent. Use of an antithrombin regimen (eg, unfractionated heparin) is recommended as adjunctive therapy to PCI. Following sheath removal, fondaparinux therapy should not resume for at least 2 hours in UA/NSTEMI patients and 3 hours in STEMI patients. Use caution in
(Continued)

Fondaparinux *(Continued)*

UA/NSTEMI/STEMI patients <50 kg. Avoid administration 24 hours before and 48 hours after coronary artery bypass graft (CABG) surgery.

Adverse Reactions As with all anticoagulants, bleeding is the major adverse effect. Hemorrhage may occur at any site. Risk appears increased by a number of factors including renal dysfunction, age (>75 years), and weight (<50 kg).

>10%:

Central nervous system: Fever (4% to 14%)

Gastrointestinal: Nausea (11%)

Hematologic: Anemia (20%)

1% to 10%:

Cardiovascular: Edema (9%), hypotension (4%), thrombosis PCI catheter (without heparin 1%)

Central nervous system: Insomnia (5%), dizziness (4%), headache (2% to 5%), confusion (3%), pain (2%)

Dermatologic: Rash (8%), purpura (4%), bullous eruption (3%)

Endocrine & metabolic: Hypokalemia (1% to 4%)

Gastrointestinal: Constipation (5% to 9%), nausea (3%), vomiting (6%), diarrhea (3%), dyspepsia (2%)

Genitourinary: Urinary tract infection (4%), urinary retention (3%)

Hematologic: Moderate thrombocytopenia (50,000-100,000/mm^3: 3%), major bleeding (1% to 3%), minor bleeding (2% to 4%), hematoma (3%); risk of major bleeding increased as high as 5% in patients receiving initial dose <6 hours following surgery

Hepatic: AST increased (2%), ALT increased (3%)

Local: Injection site reaction (bleeding, rash, pruritus)

Miscellaneous: Wound drainage increased (5%)

<1%: Heparin-induced thrombocytopenia (1 case report), hepatic enzymes increased, severe thrombocytopenia (<50,000/mm^3)

Overdosage/Toxicology Treatment is symptom-directed and supportive. Hemodialysis may increase clearance by 20%.

Drug Interactions

Increased Effect/Toxicity: Anticoagulants, antiplatelet agents, drotrecogin alfa, NSAIDs, salicylates, and thrombolytic agents may enhance the anticoagulant effect and/or increase the risk of bleeding.

Ethanol/Nutrition/Herb Interactions Herb/Nutraceutical: Avoid alfalfa, anise, bilberry, bladderwrack, bromelain, cat's claw, celery, coleus, cordyceps, dong quai, evening primrose oil, fenugreek, feverfew, garlic, ginger, ginkgo biloba, ginseng (American/Panax/Siberian), grapeseed, green tea, guggul, horse chestnut seed, horseradish, licorice, prickly ash, red clover, reishi, sweet clover, turmeric, white willow (all possess anticoagulant or antiplatelet activity and as such, may enhance the anticoagulant effects of fondaparinux).

Storage/Stability Store at 15°C to 30°C (59°F to 86°F).

Canadian labeling: For I.V. administration: Manufacturer recommends immediate use once diluted in NS, but is stable for up to 24 hours at 15°C to 30°C (59°F to 86°F).

Reconstitution Canadian labeling: For I.V. administration: May mix with 25 mL or 50 mL NS

Compatibility

Do not mix with other injections or infusions.

Canadian labeling: Stable in NS

Mechanism of Action Fondaparinux is a synthetic pentasaccharide that causes an antithrombin III-mediated selective inhibition of factor Xa. Neutralization of factor Xa interrupts the blood coagulation cascade and inhibits thrombin formation and thrombus development.

Pharmacodynamics/Kinetics

Absorption: SubQ: Rapid and complete

Distribution: V_d: 7-11 L; mainly in blood

Protein binding: ≥94% to antithrombin III

Bioavailability: SubQ: 100%

Half-life elimination: 17-21 hours; prolonged with worsening renal impairment

Time to peak: SubQ: 2-3 hours

Excretion: Urine (as unchanged drug); decreased clearance in patients <50 kg

Dosage SubQ: Adults:

DVT prophylaxis: Adults ≥50 kg: 2.5 mg once daily. **Note:** Initiate dose after hemostasis has been established, 6-8 hours postoperatively.

DVT prophylaxis with history of HIT (unlabeled use): 2.5 mg once daily

Usual duration: 5-9 days (up to 10 days following abdominal surgery or up to 11 days following hip replacement or knee replacement)

Extended prophylaxis is recommended following hip fracture surgery (has been tolerated for up to 32 days).

Acute DVT/PE treatment: **Note:** Concomitant treatment with warfarin sodium should be initiated as soon as possible, usually within 72 hours:

<50 kg: 5 mg once daily

50-100 kg: 7.5 mg once daily

>100 kg: 10 mg once daily

Usual duration: 5-9 days (has been administered up to 26 days)

Canadian labeling only: Adults:

UA/NSTEMI: SubQ: 2.5 mg once daily; initiate as soon as possible after diagnosis; treat for up to 8 days or until hospital discharge.

STEMI: I.V.: 2.5 mg once; subsequent doses: SubQ: 2.5 mg once daily; treat for up to 8 days or until hospital discharge

Dosage adjustment in renal impairment:

Cl_{cr} 30-50 mL/minute: Use caution

Cl_{cr} <30 mL/minute: Contraindicated

Administration Do not administer I.M.; for SubQ administration only. Do not mix with other injections or infusions. Do not expel air bubble from syringe before injection. Administer according to recommended regimen; early initiation (before 6 hours after surgery) has been associated with increased bleeding.

Canadian labeling only: STEMI patients: I.V. push or mixed in 25-50 mL of NS and infused over 1-2 minutes. Flush tubing with NS after infusion to ensure complete administration of fondaparinux. Infusion bag should not be mixed with other agents.

Monitoring Parameters Periodic monitoring of CBC, serum creatinine, occult blood testing of stools recommended. Antifactor Xa activity of fondaparinux can be measured by the assay if fondaparinux is used as the calibrator. PT and aPTT are insensitive measures of fondaparinux activity.

Test Interactions International standards of heparin or LMWH are not the appropriate calibrators for antifactor Xa activity of fondaparinux.

Patient Information This drug can only be administered by injection. You may have a tendency to bleed easily while taking this drug; brush teeth with soft brush, floss with waxed floss, use electric razor, avoid scissors or sharp knives, and potentially harmful activities. Report unusual bleeding or bruising (Continued)

Fondaparinux *(Continued)*

(bleeding gums, nosebleed, blood in urine, dark stool); any falls or accidents; new joint pain or swelling; or dizziness, severe headache, shortness of breath, weakness, fainting, or passing out.

Special Geriatric Considerations Patients studied for DVT prophylaxis following elective knee or hip fracture surgery averaged 67.5 and 77 years of age, respectively. Use with caution in patients with estimated or actual creatinine clearance between 30-50 mL/minute. Contraindicated in patients with Cl_{cr} <30 mL/minute.

Dosage Forms Excipient information presented when available (limited, particularly for generics); consult specific product labeling.

Injection, solution, as sodium [preservative free]: 2.5 mg/0.5 mL (0.5 mL); 5 mg/0.4 mL (0.4 mL); 7.5 mg/0.6 mL (0.6 mL); 10 mg/0.8 mL (0.8 mL) [prefilled syringe]

References

Bauer KA, Eriksson BI, Lassen MR, et al, "Fondaparinux Compared With Enoxaparin for the Prevention of Venous Thromboembolism After Elective Major Knee Surgery," *N Engl J Med*, 2001, 345:1305-10.

Bauer KA, "Fondaparinux Sodium: A Selective Inhibitor of Factor Xa," *Am J Health Syst Pharm*, 2001, 58(Suppl 2):14-7.

Buller HR, Davidson BL, Decousus H, et al, "Fondaparinux or Enoxaparin for the Initial Treatment of Symptomatic Deep Venous Thrombosis: A Randomized Trial," *Ann Intern Med*, 2004, 140(11):867-73.

Buller HR, Davidson BL, Decousus H, et al, "Subcutaneous Fondaparinux Versus Intravenous Unfractionated Heparin in the Initial Treatment of Pulmonary Embolism," *N Engl J Med*, 2003, 349(18):1695-702.

Dempfle CE, "Minor Transplacental Passage of Fondaparinux in vivo," *N Engl J Med*, 2004, 350(18):1914-5.

Eriksson BI, Bauer KA, Lassen MR, et al, "Fondaparinux Compared With Enoxaparin for the Prevention of Venous Thromboembolism After Hip-Fracture Surgery," *N Engl J Med*, 2001, 345:1298-304.

Hassell K, "The Management of Patients With Heparin-Induced Thrombocytopenia Who Require Anticoagulation Therapy," *Chest*, 2005, 127(2 Suppl):1-8.

Warkentin TE, Maurer BT, and Aster RH, "Heparin-Induced Thrombocytopenia Associated With Fondaparinux," *N Engl J Med*, 2007, 356(25):2653-55.

Yusuf S, Mehta SR, Chrolavicius S, et al, "Comparison of Fondaparinux and Enoxaparin in Acute Coronary Syndromes — The Fifth Organization to Assess Strategies in Acute Ischemic Syndromes Investigators," *N Engl J Med*, 2006, 354(14):1464-76.

Foscarnet *(fos KAR net)*

U.S. Brand Names Foscavir®

Index Terms PFA; Phosphonoformate; Phosphonoformic Acid

Generic Available Yes

Canadian Brand Names Foscavir®

Pharmacologic Category Antiviral Agent

Use

Treatment of mucotaneous herpesvirus infections suspected to be caused by acyclovir-resistant (HSV, VZV) or ganciclovir-resistant (CMV) strains; this occurs almost exclusively in immunocompromised persons (eg, with advanced AIDS) who have received prolonged treatment for a herpesvirus infection

Treatment of CMV retinitis in persons with AIDS

Unlabeled/Investigational Use Other CMV infections (eg, colitis, esophagitis, neurological disease)

Pregnancy Risk Factor C

Lactation Excretion in breast milk unknown/contraindicated

Labeled Contraindications Hypersensitivity to foscarnet or any component of the formulation; Cl_{cr} <0.4 mL/minute/kg during therapy

Warnings/Precautions Hazardous agent - use appropriate precautions for handling and disposal. **[U.S. Boxed Warning]: Indicated only for immunocompromised patients with CMV retinitis and mucocutaneous acyclovir-resistant HSV infection. [U.S. Boxed Warning]: Renal impairment occurs to some degree in the majority of patients treated with foscarnet;** renal impairment may occur at any time and is usually reversible within 1 week following dose adjustment or discontinuation of therapy, however, several patients have died with renal failure within 4 weeks of stopping foscarnet; therefore, renal function should be closely monitored. To reduce the risk of nephrotoxicity and the potential to administer a relative overdose, always calculate the Cl_{cr} even if serum creatinine is within the normal range. Adequate hydration may reduce the risk of nephrotoxicity; the manufacturer makes specific recommendations regarding this (see Administration).

Imbalance of serum electrolytes or minerals occurs in at least 15% of patients (hypocalcemia, low ionized calcium, hyper/hypophosphatemia, hypomagnesemia, or hypokalemia). Patients with low ionized calcium may experience perioral tingling, numbness, paresthesias, tetany, and seizures. Correct electrolytes before initiating therapy. Use caution when administering other medications that cause electrolyte imbalances. Patients who experience signs or symptoms of an electrolyte imbalance should be assessed immediately. **[U.S. Boxed Warning]: Seizures related to plasma electrolyte/mineral imbalance may occur;** incidence has been reported in up to 10% of AIDS patients. Risk factors for seizures include impaired baseline renal function, low total serum calcium, and underlying CNS conditions. May cause anemia and granulocytopenia. Safety and efficacy in children have not been established.

Adverse Reactions

>10%:

Central nervous system: Fever (65%), headache (26%)

Endocrine & metabolic: Hypokalemia (16% to 48%), hypocalcemia (15% to 30%), hypomagnesemia (15% to 30%), hypophosphatemia (8% to 26%)

Gastrointestinal: Nausea (47%), diarrhea (30%), vomiting (26%)

Hematologic: Anemia (33%), granulocytopenia (17%)

Renal: Abnormal renal function/decreased creatinine clearance (27%)

1% to 10%:

Cardiovascular: Chest pain (1% to 5%), edema (1% to 5%), facial edema (1% to 5%), flushing (1% to 5%), hyper-/hypotension (1% to 5%), palpitation (1% to 5%), sinus tachycardia, first degree AV block, nonspecific ST-T segment changes

Central nervous system: Seizure (10%), fatigue (>5%), malaise (>5%), dizziness (>5%), hypoesthesia (>5%), depression (>5%), confusion (>5%), anxiety (≥5%), aphasia (1% to 5%), ataxia (1% to 5%), dementia (1% to 5%), meningitis (1% to 5%), stupor (1% to 5%), insomnia (1% to 5%), somnolence (1% to 5%), nervousness (1% to 5%), amnesia (1% to 5%), agitation (1% to 5%), aggressiveness (1% to 5%), hallucination (1% to 5%)

(Continued)

Foscarnet *(Continued)*

Dermatologic: Rash (>5%), pruritus (1% to 5%), skin ulceration (1% to 5%), seborrhea (1% to 5%), erythematous rash, maculopapular rash, skin discoloration

Endocrine & metabolic: Hyperphosphatemia (6%), acidosis (1% to 5%), hyponatremia (1% to 5%)

Gastrointestinal: Anorexia (>5%), abdominal pain (>5%), constipation (1% to 5%), dysphasia (1% to 5%), dyspepsia (1% to 5%), flatulence (1% to 5%), melena (1% to 5%), pancreatitis (1% to 5%), rectal hemorrhage (1% to 5%), taste perversion (1% to 5%), ulcerative stomatitis (1% to 5%), weight loss (1% to 5%), xerostomia (1% to 5%)

Genitourinary: Urinary retention (1% to 5%), dysuria (1% to 5%), nocturia (1% to 5%)

Hematologic: Leukopenia (≥5%), thrombocytopenia (1% to 5%), thrombosis (1% to 5%), lymphadenopathy (1% to 5%)

Local: Injection site pain

Neuromuscular & skeletal: Paresthesia (>5%), involuntary muscle contractions (>5%), rigors (>5%), neuropathy (peripheral; >5%), weakness (>5%), arthralgia (1% to 5%), back pain (1% to 5%), leg cramps (1% to 5%), myalgia (1% to 5%), tremor (1% to 5%)

Ocular: Vision abnormalities (>5%), conjunctivitis (1% to 5%), eye pain (1% to 5%)

Renal: Acute renal failure (1% to 5%), albuminuria (1% to 5%), BUN increased (1% to 5%), polyuria (1% to 5%), urinary tract infection (1% to 5%)

Respiratory: Cough (>5%), dyspnea (≥5%), bronchospasm (1% to 5%), hemoptysis (1% to 5%), pharyngitis (1% to 5%), pneumonia (1% to 5%), pneumothorax (1% to 5%), rhinitis (1% to 5%), sinusitis (1% to 5%), stridor (1% to 5%)

Miscellaneous: Sepsis (>5%), diaphoresis (increased), flu-like syndrome (1% to 5%), infection (1% to 5%), thirst (1% to 5%)

<1%: Amylase increased, cardiac arrest, coma, creatinine phosphokinase increased, dehydration, hematuria, hypoproteinemia, neutropenia, pancytopenia, syndrome of inappropriate antidiuretic hormone (SIADH)

Postmarketing and/or case reports: Diabetes insipidus (usually nephrogenic), erythema multiforme, muscle weakness, myopathy, myositis, QT_c prolongation, renal calculus, rhabdomyolysis, Stevens-Johnson syndrome, toxic epidermal necrolysis, ventricular arrhythmia, vesiculobullous eruptions

Overdosage/Toxicology Overdoses, up to 20 times the recommended dose, have been observed. Symptoms of overdose include seizures, renal dysfunction, perioral or limb paresthesia, and electrolyte disturbances including hypocalcemia and hypophosphatemia. Treatment is symptom-directed and supportive. Hydration and monitoring for electrolyte abnormalities are necessary. Hemodialysis may be helpful for foscarnet removal.

Drug Interactions

Increased Effect/Toxicity: Concurrent use with ciprofloxacin (or other fluoroquinolone) increases seizure potential. Ciprofloxacin may enhance the neuroexcitatory effect of foscarnet. Foscarnet may enhance the neurotoxic (peripheral) effect of zalcitabine. Nephrotoxic drugs (amphotericin B, I.V. pentamidine, aminoglycosides, etc) should be avoided, if possible, to minimize additive renal risk with foscarnet. Concurrent use of pentamidine also increases the potential for hypocalcemia. Protease inhibitors (ritonavir, saquinavir) have been associated with an increased risk of renal impairment during concurrent use of foscarnet. QT_c-prolonging agents may enhance the adverse/toxic effect of foscarnet. Foscarnet may enhance the QT_c-prolonging effect of thioridazine.

Storage/Stability Foscarnet injection is a clear, colorless solution. It should be stored at room temperature and protected from temperatures >40°C and from freezing. Diluted solution is stable for 24 hours at room temperature or under refrigeration.

Reconstitution Foscarnet should be diluted in D_5W or NS. For peripheral line administration, foscarnet **must** be diluted to ≤12 mg/mL with D_5W or NS. For central line administration, foscarnet may be administered undiluted.

Compatibility Stable in D_5W; **incompatible** with dextrose 30%, LR, TPN, and I.V. solutions containing calcium, magnesium, vancomycin.

  Y-site administration: Compatible: Aldesleukin, amikacin, aminophylline, ampicillin, aztreonam, cefazolin, cefoperazone, cefoxitin, ceftazidime, ceftizoxime, ceftriaxone, cefuroxime, chloramphenicol, cimetidine, clindamycin, dexamethasone sodium phosphate, dopamine, erythromycin lactobionate, fluconazole, flucytosine, furosemide, gentamicin, heparin, hydrocortisone sodium succinate, hydromorphone, hydroxyzine, imipenem/cilastatin, metoclopramide, metronidazole, morphine, nafcillin, oxacillin, penicillin G potassium, phenytoin, piperacillin, ranitidine, ticarcillin/clavulanate, tobramycin. **Incompatible:** Acyclovir, amphotericin B, diazepam, digoxin, diphenhydramine, dobutamine, droperidol, ganciclovir, haloperidol, leucovorin, midazolam, pentamidine, prochlorperazine edisylate, promethazine. **Variable (consult detailed reference):** Co-trimoxazole, lorazepam, vancomycin.

  Compatibility when admixed: Compatible: Potassium chloride.

Mechanism of Action Pyrophosphate analogue which acts as a noncompetitive inhibitor of many viral RNA and DNA polymerases as well as HIV reverse transcriptase. Similar to ganciclovir, foscarnet is a virostatic agent. Foscarnet does not require activation by thymidine kinase.

Pharmacodynamics/Kinetics

Distribution: Up to 28% of cumulative I.V. dose may be deposited in bone

Metabolism: Biotransformation does not occur

Half-life elimination: ~3 hours

Excretion: Urine (≤28% as unchanged drug)

**Induction Dosing of Foscarnet in Patients
With Abnormal Renal Function**

Cl_{cr} (mL/min/kg)	HSV Equivalent to 40 mg/kg q12h	HSV Equivalent to 40 mg/kg q8h	CMV Equivalent to 60 mg/kg q8h	CMV Equivalent to 90 mg/kg q12h
<0.4	Not recommended	Not recommended	Not recommended	Not recommended
≥0.4-0.5	20 mg/kg every 24 hours	35 mg/kg every 24 hours	50 mg/kg every 24 hours	50 mg/kg every 24 hours
>0.5-0.6	25 mg/kg every 24 hours	40 mg/kg every 24 hours	60 mg/kg every 24 hours	60 mg/kg every 24 hours
>0.6-0.8	35 mg/kg every 24 hours	25 mg/kg every 12 hours	40 mg/kg every 12 hours	80 mg/kg every 24 hours
>0.8-1.0	20 mg/kg every 12 hours	35 mg/kg every 12 hours	50 mg/kg every 12 hours	50 mg/kg every 12 hours
>1.0-1.4	30 mg/kg every 12 hours	30 mg/kg every 8 hours	45 mg/kg every 8 hours	70 mg/kg every 12 hours
>1.4	40 mg/kg every 12 hours	40 mg/kg every 8 hours	60 mg/kg every 8 hours	90 mg/kg every 12 hours

(Continued)

Foscarnet *(Continued)*

Dosage

CMV retinitis: I.V.:

Induction treatment: 60 mg/kg/dose every 8 hours **or** 90 mg/kg every 12 hours for 14-21 days

Maintenance therapy: 90-120 mg/kg/day as a single infusion

Herpes simplex infections (acyclovir-resistant): Induction: I.V.: 40 mg/kg/dose every 8-12 hours for 14-21 days

Dosage adjustment in renal impairment:

Induction and maintenance dosing schedules based on creatinine clearance (mL/minute/kg): See tables on previous page and below.

Maintenance Dosing of Foscarnet in Patients With Abnormal Renal Function

Cl_cr (mL/min/kg)	CMV Equivalent to 90 mg/kg q24h	CMV Equivalent to 120 mg/kg q24h
<0.4	Not recommended	Not recommended
≥0.4-0.5	50 mg/kg every 48 hours	65 mg/kg every 48 hours
>0.5-0.6	60 mg/kg every 48 hours	80 mg/kg every 48 hours
>0.6-0.8	80 mg/kg every 48 hours	105 mg/kg every 48 hours
>0.8-1.0	50 mg/kg every 24 hours	65 mg/kg every 24 hours
>1.0-1.4	70 mg/kg every 24 hours	90 mg/kg every 24 hours
>1.4	90 mg/kg every 24 hours	120 mg/kg every 24 hours

Hemodialysis:

Foscarnet is highly removed by hemodialysis (30% in 4 hours HD)

Doses of 50 mg/kg/dose posthemodialysis have been found to produce similar serum concentrations as doses of 90 mg/kg twice daily in patients with normal renal function

Doses of 60-90 mg/kg/dose loading dose (posthemodialysis) followed by 45 mg/kg/dose posthemodialysis (3 times/week) with the monitoring of weekly plasma concentrations to maintain peak plasma concentrations in the range of 400-800 µMolar have been recommended by some clinicians

Continuous arteriovenous or venovenous hemodiafiltration effects: Dose as for Cl_cr 10-50 mL/minute

Administration Foscarnet is administered by intravenous infusion, using an infusion pump, at a rate not exceeding 1 mg/kg/minute. Undiluted (24 mg/mL) solution can be administered without further dilution when using a central venous catheter for infusion. For peripheral vein administration, the solution **must** be diluted to a final concentration **not to exceed** 12 mg/mL. The manufacturer recommends 750-1000 mL of NS or D_5W be administered prior to first infusion. With subsequent infusions of 90-120 mg/kg, this volume would be repeated. If the dose were 40-60 mg/kg, then the volume could be reduced to 500 mL. After the first dose, the hydration fluid should be administered concurrently with foscarnet.

Monitoring Parameters 24-hour creatinine clearance at baseline and periodically thereafter. During induction therapy: Obtain complete blood counts, and electrolytes (including serum creatinine, calcium, magnesium, potassium and phosphorus) twice weekly and then one weekly during maintenance therapy. More frequent monitoring may be required in some patients. Check hydration status before and after infusion.

Patient Information Close monitoring is important and any symptoms of electrolyte abnormalities should be reported immediately. Maintain adequate fluid intake and hydration. Regular ophthalmic examinations are necessary. Report any numbness in the extremities, paresthesias, or perioral tingling.

Special Geriatric Considerations Information on the use of foscarnet is lacking in the elderly. Dose adjustments and proper monitoring must be performed because of the decreased renal function common in older patients.

Additional Information CMV retinitis maintenance treatment may be discontinued if immune reconstitution occurs as a result of ART.

Emetic Potential Moderate (30% to 60%)

Vesicant No

Dosage Forms Excipient information presented when available (limited, particularly for generics); consult specific product labeling.

Injection, solution: 24 mg/mL (250 mL, 500 mL)

Foscavir®: 24 mg/mL (500 mL)

References

Benson CA, Kaplan JE, Masur H, et al, "Treating Opportunistic Infections Among HIV-Exposed and Infected Children: Recommendations from CDC, the National Institutes of Health and the HIV Medicine Association/IDSA," available at http://aidsinfo.nih.gov/ContentFiles/TreatmentofOI_AA.pdf; last accessed July 11, 2006.

Butler KM, DeSmet MD, Husson RN, et al, "Treatment of Aggressive Cytomegalovirus Retinitis With Ganciclovir in Combination With Foscarnet in a Child Infected With Human Immunodeficiency Virus," J Pediatr, 1992, 120(3):483-6.

Calligaro KD, Stern J, and DeLaurentis DA, "Foscarnet: A Possible Cause of Ulnar Artery Thrombosis in a Patient With AIDS," J Vasc Surg, 1994, 20(6):1007-8.

Chilukuri S and Rosen T, "Management of Acycovir-Resistant Herpes Simplex Virus," Dermatol Clin, 2003, 21(2):311-20.

Chrisp P and Clissold SP, "Foscarnet. A Review of Its Antiviral Activity, Pharmacokinetic Properties and Therapeutic Use in Immunocompromised Patients With Cytomegalovirus Retinitis," Drugs, 1991, 41(1):104-29.

Deray G, Martinez F, Katlama C, et al, "Foscarnet Nephrotoxicity: Mechanism, Incidence and Prevention," Am J Nephrol, 1989, 9:316-21.

"Drugs for Non-HIV Viral Infections," Med Lett Drugs Ther, 1994, 36(919):27.

Jacobson MA, "Review of the Toxicities of Foscarnet," J Acquir Immune Defic Syndr, 1992, 5(Suppl 1):11-7.

Jayaweera DT, "Minimizing the Dosage-Limiting Toxicities of Foscarnet Induction Therapy," Drug Saf, 1997, 16(4):258-66.

Keating MR, "Antiviral Agents," Mayo Clin Proc, 1992, 67(2):160-78.

Morales JM, Munoz MA, Fernandez Zatarain G, et al, "Reversible Acute Renal Failure Caused by the Combined Use of Foscarnet and Cyclosporin in Organ Transplanted Patients," Nephrol Dial Transplant, 1995, 10(6):882-3.

Polis MA, "Foscarnet and Ganciclovir in the Treatment of Cytomegalovirus Retinitis," J Acquir Immune Defic Syndr, 1992, 5(Suppl 1):3-10.

Whitley RJ, Jacobson MA, Friedberg DN, et al, "Guidelines for the Treatment of Cytomegalovirus Diseases in Patients With AIDS in the Era of Potent Antiretroviral Therapy: Recommendations of an International Panel. International AIDS Society-USA," Arch Intern Med, 1998, 158(9):957-69.

Fulvestrant (fool VES trant)

U.S. Brand Names Faslodex®

Index Terms ICI-182,780; Zeneca 182,780; ZM-182,780

Generic Available No

Pharmacologic Category Antineoplastic Agent, Estrogen Receptor Antagonist

Use Treatment of hormone receptor positive metastatic breast cancer in postmenopausal women with disease progression following antiestrogen therapy

Unlabeled/Investigational Use Endometriosis; uterine bleeding

Pregnancy Risk Factor D

Lactation Excretion in breast milk unknown/contraindicated

Labeled Contraindications Hypersensitivity to fulvestrant or any component of the formulation; contraindications to I.M. injections (bleeding diatheses, thrombocytopenia, or therapeutic anticoagulation); pregnancy

Warnings/Precautions Hazardous agent - use appropriate precautions for handling and disposal. Use caution in hepatic impairment. Safety and efficacy have not been established in children.

Adverse Reactions

>10%:
  Cardiovascular: Vasodilation (18%)
  Central nervous system: Pain (19%), headache (15%)
  Endocrine & metabolic: Hot flushes (19% to 24%)
  Gastrointestinal: Nausea (26%), vomiting (13%), constipation (13%), diarrhea (12%), abdominal pain (12%)
  Local: Injection site reaction (11%)
  Neuromuscular & skeletal: Weakness (23%), bone pain (16%), back pain (14%)
  Respiratory: Pharyngitis (16%), dyspnea (15%)

1% to 10%:
  Cardiovascular: Edema (9%), chest pain (7%)
  Central nervous system: Dizziness (7%), insomnia (7%), paresthesia (6%), fever (6%), depression (6%), anxiety (5%)
  Dermatologic: Rash (7%)
  Gastrointestinal: Anorexia (9%), weight gain (1% to 2%)
  Genitourinary: Pelvic pain (10%), urinary tract infection (6%), vaginitis (2% to 3%)
  Hematologic: Anemia (5%)
  Neuromuscular and skeletal: Arthritis (3%)
  Respiratory: Cough (10%)
  Miscellaneous: Diaphoresis increased (5%)

<1%: Angioedema, hypersensitivity reactions, leukopenia, myalgia, thrombosis, urticaria, vaginal bleeding, vertigo

Overdosage/Toxicology No specific experience in overdose. Treatment is supportive.

Drug Interactions

Cytochrome P450 Effect: Substrate of CYP3A4 (minor)

Storage/Stability Store under refrigeration at 2°C to 8°C (36°F to 46°F).

Mechanism of Action Steroidal compound which competitively binds to estrogen receptors on tumors and other tissue targets, producing a nuclear complex that decreases DNA synthesis and inhibits estrogen effects. Fulvestrant has no estrogen-receptor agonist activity. Causes down-regulation of estrogen receptors and inhibits tumor growth.

Pharmacodynamics/Kinetics

Duration: I.M.: Plasma levels maintained for at least 1 month

Distribution: V_d: 3-5 L/kg

Protein binding: 99%

Metabolism: Hepatic via multiple pathways (CYP3A4 substrate, relative contribution to metabolism unknown)

Bioavailability: Oral: Poor

Half-life elimination: ~40 days

Time to peak, plasma: I.M.: 7-9 days

Excretion: Feces (>90%); urine (<1%)

Dosage I.M.: Adults (postmenopausal women): 250 mg at 1-month intervals

Dosage adjustment in renal impairment: No adjustment required.

Dosage adjustment in hepatic impairment: Use in moderate-to-severe hepatic impairment has not been evaluated; use caution.

Administration I.M. injection into a relatively large muscle (ie, buttock); do not administer I.V., SubQ, or intra-arterially. May be administered as a single 5 mL injection or two concurrent 2.5 mL injections.

Dosage Forms Excipient information presented when available (limited, particularly for generics); consult specific product labeling.

Injection, solution: 50 mg/mL (2.5 mL, 5 mL) [prefilled syringe; contains alcohol, benzyl alcohol, benzyl stearate, castor oil]

References
Bundred N and Howell A, "Fulvestrant (Faslodex): Current Status in the Therapy of Breast Cancer," *Expert Rev Anticancer Ther*, 2002, 2(2):151-60.

Curran M and Wiseman L, "Fulvestrant," *Drugs*, 2001, 61(6):807-13.

Wardley AM, "Fulvestrant: A Review of Its Development, Preclinical and Clinical Data," *Int J Clin Pract*, 2002, 56(4):305-9.

♦ **Fungizone® (Can)** *see* Amphotericin B (Conventional) *on page 71*

Furosemide (fyoor OH se mide)

Medication Safety Issues
Sound-alike/look-alike issues:

Furosemide may be confused with torsemide

Lasix® may be confused with Esidrix®, Lanoxin®, Lidex®, Lomotil®, Luvox®, Luxiq®

International issues:

Urex® [Australia] may be confused with Eurax® which is a brand name for crotamiton in the U.S.

Urex® [Australia]: Brand name for methenamine in the U.S.

U.S. Brand Names Lasix®

Index Terms Frusemide

Generic Available Yes

Canadian Brand Names Apo-Furosemide®; Dom-Furosemide; Furosemide Injection, USP; Furosemide Special; Lasix®; Lasix® Special; Novo-Semide; Nu-Furosemide; PMS-Furosemide

Pharmacologic Category Diuretic, Loop

Use Management of edema associated with congestive heart failure and hepatic or renal disease; alone or in combination with antihypertensives in treatment of hypertension

Pregnancy Risk Factor C

Lactation Enters breast milk/use caution

Labeled Contraindications Hypersensitivity to furosemide, any component, or sulfonylureas; anuria; patients with hepatic coma or in states of severe electrolyte depletion until the condition improves or is corrected

Warnings/Precautions Loop diuretics are potent diuretics; excess amounts can lead to profound diuresis with fluid and electrolyte loss; close medical
(Continued)

Furosemide *(Continued)*

supervision and dose evaluation are required. Watch for and correct electrolyte disturbances; adjust dose to avoid dehydration. In cirrhosis, avoid electrolyte and acid/base imbalances that might lead to hepatic encephalopathy. Coadministration of antihypertensives may increase the risk of hypotension.

Monitor fluid status and renal function in an attempt to prevent oliguria, azotemia, and reversible increases in BUN and creatinine; close medical supervision of aggressive diuresis is required. Rapid I.V. administration, renal impairment, excessive doses, and concurrent use of other ototoxins is associated with ototoxicity. Asymptomatic hyperuricemia has been reported with use.

Chemical similarities are present among sulfonamides, sulfonylureas, carbonic anhydrase inhibitors, thiazides, and loop diuretics (except ethacrynic acid). Use in patients with sulfonylurea allergy is specifically contraindicated in product labeling, however, a risk of cross-reaction exists in patients with allergy to any of these compounds; avoid use when previous reaction has been severe. Discontinue if signs of hypersensitivity are noted.

Adverse Reactions Frequency not defined.

Cardiovascular: Acute hypotension, chronic aortitis, necrotizing angiitis, orthostatic hypotension, thrombophlebitis, sudden death from cardiac arrest (with I.V. or I.M. administration)

Central nervous system: Blurred vision, dizziness, fever, headache, lightheadedness, restlessness, vertigo, xanthopsia

Dermatologic: Cutaneous vasculitis, erythema multiforme, exfoliative dermatitis, photosensitivity, pruritus, purpura, rash, urticaria

Endocrine & metabolic: Gout, hyperglycemia, hyperuricemia, hypocalcemia, hypochloremia, hypokalemia, hypomagnesemia, hyponatremia, metabolic alkalosis

Gastrointestinal: Anorexia, constipation, cramping, diarrhea, intrahepatic cholestatic jaundice, ischemia hepatitis, nausea, oral and gastric irritation, pancreatitis, vomiting

Genitourinary: Urinary bladder spasm, urinary frequency

Hematological: Agranulocytosis (rare), anemia, aplastic anemia (rare), hemolytic anemia, leukopenia, purpura, thrombocytopenia

Neuromuscular & skeletal: Muscle spasm, paresthesia, weakness

Otic: Hearing impairment (reversible or permanent with rapid I.V. or I.M. administration), reversible deafness (with rapid I.V. or I.M. administration), tinnitus

Renal: Allergic interstitial nephritis, fall in glomerular filtration rate and renal blood flow (due to overdiuresis), glycosuria, transient rise in BUN, vasculitis

Miscellaneous: Anaphylaxis (rare), exacerbate or activate systemic lupus erythematosus

Overdosage/Toxicology Symptoms of overdose include electrolyte depletion, volume depletion, hypotension, dehydration, and circulatory collapse. Treatment is supportive.

Drug Interactions

Increased Effect/Toxicity: Furosemide-induced hypokalemia may predispose to digoxin toxicity and may increase the risk of arrhythmia with drugs which may prolong QT interval, including type Ia and type III antiarrhythmic agents, cisapride, and some quinolones (sparfloxacin, gatifloxacin, and moxifloxacin). The risk of toxicity from lithium and salicylates (high dose) may be increased by loop diuretics. Hypotensive effects and/or adverse renal effects of ACE inhibitors and NSAIDs are potentiated by furosemide-induced hypovolemia. The effects of peripheral adrenergic-blocking drugs or ganglionic blockers may be increased by furosemide.

Furosemide may increase the risk of ototoxicity with other ototoxic agents (aminoglycosides, cis-platinum), especially in patients with renal dysfunction. Synergistic diuretic effects occur with thiazide-type diuretics. Diuretics tend to be synergistic with other antihypertensive agents, and hypotension may occur.

Decreased Effect: Indomethacin, aspirin, phenobarbital, phenytoin, and NSAIDs may reduce natriuretic and hypotensive effects of furosemide. Colestipol, cholestyramine, and sucralfate may reduce the effect of furosemide; separate administration by 2 hours. Furosemide may antagonize the effect of skeletal muscle relaxants (tubocurarine). Glucose tolerance may be decreased by furosemide, requiring an adjustment in the dose of hypoglycemic agents. Metformin may decrease furosemide concentrations.

Ethanol/Nutrition/Herb Interactions

Food: Furosemide serum levels may be decreased if taken with food.

Herb/Nutraceutical: Avoid dong quai if using for hypertension (has estrogenic activity). Avoid ephedra, yohimbe, and ginseng (may worsen hypertension). Limit intake of natural licorice. Avoid garlic (may have increased antihypertensive effect).

Storage/Stability Furosemide injection should be stored at controlled room temperature and protected from light. Exposure to light may cause discoloration. Do not use furosemide solutions if they have a yellow color. Refrigeration may result in precipitation or crystallization, however, resolubilization at room temperature or warming may be performed without affecting the drugs stability. I.V. infusion solution mixed in NS or D_5W solution is stable for 24 hours at room temperature.

Reconstitution I.V. infusion solution may also be diluted for infusion 1-2 mg/mL (maximum: 10 mg/mL) over 10-15 minutes (following infusion rate parameters).

Compatibility Stable in D_5LR, D_5NS, D_5W, $D_{10}W$, $D_{20}W$, mannitol 20%, LR, NS.

Y-site administration: Compatible: Allopurinol, amifostine, amikacin, amphotericin B cholesteryl sulfate complex, aztreonam, bleomycin, cefepime, cisplatin, cladribine, cyclophosphamide, cytarabine, docetaxel, doxorubicin liposome, epinephrine, etoposide phosphate, fentanyl, fludarabine, fluorouracil, foscarnet, granisetron, heparin, hydrocortisone sodium succinate, hydromorphone, indomethacin, kanamycin, leucovorin, linezolid, lorazepam, melphalan, meropenem, methotrexate, mitomycin, nitroglycerin, norepinephrine, paclitaxel, piperacillin/tazobactam, potassium chloride, propofol, ranitidine, remifentanil, sargramostim, tacrolimus, teniposide, thiotepa, tobramycin, tolazoline, vitamin B complex with C. **Incompatible:** Alatrofloxacin, amsacrine, chlorpromazine, ciprofloxacin, clarithromycin, diltiazem, droperidol, esmolol, filgrastim, fluconazole, gatifloxacin, gemcitabine, gentamicin, hydralazine, idarubicin, levofloxacin, metoclopramide, midazolam, milrinone, netilmicin, nicardipine, ondansetron, quinidine gluconate, thiopental, vecuronium, vinblastine, vincristine, vinorelbine. **Variable (consult detailed reference):** Cisatracurium, dobutamine, dopamine, doxorubicin, famotidine, labetalol, meperidine, morphine.

Compatibility in syringe: Compatible: Bleomycin, cisplatin, cyclophosphamide, fluorouracil, heparin, leucovorin, methotrexate, mitomycin. **Incompatible:** Doxapram, doxorubicin, droperidol, metoclopramide, milrinone, vinblastine, vincristine.

(Continued)

Furosemide *(Continued)*

Compatibility when admixed: Compatible: Amikacin, aminophylline, ampicillin, atropine, bumetanide, calcium gluconate, cefamandole, cefoperazone, cefuroxime, cimetidine, dexamethasone sodium phosphate, diamorphine, digoxin, epinephrine, heparin, isosorbide, kanamycin, lidocaine, meropenem, morphine, nitroglycerin, penicillin G, potassium chloride, ranitidine, scopolamine, sodium bicarbonate, sulfadimidine, theophylline, tobramycin. **Incompatible:** Buprenorphine, chlorpromazine, diazepam, dobutamine, erythromycin lactobionate, isoproterenol, meperidine, metoclopramide, netilmicin, prochlorperazine edisylate, promethazine. **Variable (consult detailed reference):** Amiodarone, gentamicin, hydrocortisone sodium succinate, verapamil.

Mechanism of Action Inhibits reabsorption of sodium and chloride in the ascending loop of Henle and distal renal tubule, interfering with the chloride-binding cotransport system, thus causing increased excretion of water, sodium, chloride, magnesium, and calcium

Pharmacodynamics/Kinetics

Onset of action: Diuresis: Oral: 30-60 minutes; I.M.: 30 minutes; I.V.: ~5 minutes

Peak effect: Oral: 1-2 hours

Duration: Oral: 6-8 hours; I.V.: 2 hours

Absorption: Oral: 60% to 67%

Protein binding: >98%

Metabolism: Minimally hepatic

Half-life elimination: Normal renal function: 0.5-1.1 hours; End-stage renal disease: 9 hours

Excretion: Urine (Oral: 50%, I.V.: 80%) within 24 hours; feces (as unchanged drug); nonrenal clearance prolonged in renal impairment

Dosage

Infants and Children:

Oral: 0.5-2 mg/kg/dose increased in increments of 1 mg/kg/dose with each succeeding dose until a satisfactory effect is achieved to a maximum of 6 mg/kg/dose no more frequently than 6 hours.

I.M., I.V.: 1 mg/kg/dose, increasing by each succeeding dose at 1 mg/kg/dose at intervals of 6-12 hours until a satisfactory response up to 6 mg/kg/dose.

Adults:

Oral: 20-80 mg/dose initially increased in increments of 20-40 mg/dose at intervals of 6-8 hours; usual maintenance dose interval is twice daily or every day; may be titrated up to 600 mg/day with severe edematous states.

Hypertension (JNC 7): 20-80 mg/day in 2 divided doses

I.M., I.V.: 20-40 mg/dose, may be repeated in 1-2 hours as needed and increased by 20 mg/dose until the desired effect has been obtained. Usual dosing interval: 6-12 hours; for acute pulmonary edema, the usual dose is 40 mg I.V. over 1-2 minutes. If not adequate, may increase dose to 80 mg. **Note:** ACC/AHA 2005 guidelines for chronic congestive heart failure recommend a maximum single dose of 160-200 mg.

Continuous I.V. infusion: Initial I.V. bolus dose 20-40 mg, followed by continuous I.V. infusion doses of 10-40 mg/hour. If urine output is <1 mL/kg/hour, double as necessary to a maximum of 80-160 mg/hour. The risk associated with higher infusion rates (80-160 mg/hour) must be weighed against alternative strategies. **Note:** ACC/AHA 2005 guidelines for chronic congestive heart failure recommend 40 mg I.V. load, then 10-40 mg/hour infusion.

Refractory heart failure: Oral, I.V.: Doses up to 8 g/day have been used.
Elderly: Oral, I.M., I.V.: Initial: 20 mg/day; increase slowly to desired response.

Dosing adjustment/comments in renal impairment: Acute renal failure: High doses (up to 1-3 g/day - oral/I.V.) have been used to initiate desired response; avoid use in oliguric states.

Dialysis: Not removed by hemo- or peritoneal dialysis; supplemental dose is not necessary.

Dosing adjustment/comments in hepatic disease: Diminished natriuretic effect with increased sensitivity to hypokalemia and volume depletion in cirrhosis; monitor effects, particularly with high doses.

Administration

I.V.: I.V. injections should be given slowly. In adults, undiluted direct I.V. injections may be administered at a rate of 40 mg over 1-2 minutes; maximum rate of administration for IVPB or continuous infusion: 4 mg/minute. In children, a maximum rate of 0.5 mg/kg/minute has been recommended.

Oral: May be taken with or without food.

Monitoring Parameters Monitor weight and I & O daily; blood pressure, orthostasis, serum electrolytes, renal function; in high doses, monitor hearing

Dietary Considerations May cause a potassium loss; potassium supplement or dietary changes may be required. Administer on an empty stomach. May be administered with food or milk if GI distress occurs. Do not mix with acidic solutions.

Patient Information May be taken with food or milk. Take last dose of day early in the evening to prevent nocturia. Rise slowly from a lying or sitting position to minimize dizziness, lightheadedness, or fainting. Also use extra care when exercising, standing for long periods of time, and during hot weather.

Special Geriatric Considerations Loop diuretics are potent diuretics; excess amounts can lead to profound diuresis with fluid and electrolyte loss; close medical supervision and dose evaluation is required, particularly in the elderly. Severe loss of sodium and/or increase in BUN can cause confusion. For any change in mental status in patients on furosemide, monitor electrolytes and renal function.

Emetic Potential Very low (<10%)

Vesicant No

Dosage Forms Excipient information presented when available (limited, particularly for generics); consult specific product labeling.

Injection, solution: 10 mg/mL (2 mL, 4 mL, 8 mL, 10 mL)

Solution, oral: 10 mg/mL (60 mL, 120 mL) [orange flavor]; 40 mg/5 mL (5 mL, 500 mL) [pineapple-peach flavor]

Tablet (Lasix®): 20 mg, 40 mg, 80 mg

References

Brown CB, Ogg CS, and Cameron JS, "High-Dose Frusemide in Acute Renal Failure: A Controlled Trial," *Clin Nephrol*, 1981, 15(2):90-6.

Chaudhry AY, Bing RF, Castleden CM, et al, "The Effect of Aging on the Response to Frusemide in Normal Subjects," *Eur J Clin Pharmacol*, 1984, 27(3):303-6.

Chobanian AV, Bakris GL, Black HR, et al, "The Seventh Report of the Joint National Committee on Prevention, Detection, Evaluation, and Treatment of High Blood Pressure: The JNC 7 Report," *JAMA*, 2003, 289(19):2560-71.

Gerlag PG and van Meijel JJ, "High-Dose Furosemide in the Treatment of Refractory Congestive Heart Failure," *Arch Intern Med*, 1988, 148(2):286-91.

Howard PA and Dunn MI, "Aggressive Diuresis for Severe Heart Failure in the Elderly," *Chest*, 2001, 119(3):807-10.

Hunt SA, Abraham WT, Chin MH , et al, "ACC/AHA 2005 Guideline Update for the Diagnosis and Management of Chronic Heart Failure in the Adult: A Report of the American College of

(Continued)

Furosemide *(Continued)*

Cardiology/American Heart Association Task Force on Practice Guidelines (Writing Committee to Update the 2001 Guidelines for the Evaluation and Management of Heart Failure)," available at http://www.acc.org/qualityandscience/clinical/guidelines/failure/update/index.pdf.

Kuchar DL and O'Rourke MF, "High Dose Furosemide in Refractory Cardiac Failure," *Eur Heart J*, 1985, 6(11):954-8.

National High Blood Pressure Education Program Working Group on High Blood Pressure in Children and Adolescents, "The Fourth Report on the Diagnosis, Evaluation, and Treatment of High Blood Pressure in Children and Adolescents," *Pediatrics*, 2004, 114(2 Suppl):555-76.

Rudy DW, Voelker JR, Greene PK, et al, "Loop Diuretics for Chronic Renal Insufficiency: A Continuous Infusion Is More Efficacious Than Bolus Therapy," *Ann Intern Med*, 1991, 115(5):360-6.

Schuller D, Lynch JP, and Fine D, "Protocol-Guided Diuretic Management: Comparison of Furosemide by Continuous Infusion and Intermittent Bolus," *Crit Care Med*, 1997, 25(12):1969-75.

♦ **Furosemide Injection, USP (Can)** *see* Furosemide *on page 483*

♦ **Furosemide Special (Can)** *see* Furosemide *on page 483*

Fusidic Acid *(fyoo SI dik AS id)*

Index Terms Sodium Fusidate

Generic Available No

Canadian Brand Names Fucidin®; Fucithalmic®

Pharmacologic Category Antibiotic, Miscellaneous

Use

Systemic: Treatment of skin and soft tissue infections, or osteomyelitis, caused by susceptible organisms, including *Staphylococcus aureus* (penicillinase-producing or nonpenicillinase strains); may be used in the treatment of pneumonia, septicemia, endocarditis, burns, and cystic fibrosis caused by susceptible organisms when other antibiotics have failed

Topical: Treatment of primary and secondary skin infections caused by susceptible organisms

Ophthalmic: Treatment of superficial infections of the eye and conjunctiva caused by susceptible organisms

Restrictions Not available in U.S.

Lactation Enters breast milk/use caution

Labeled Contraindications Hypersensitivity to fusidic acid or any component of the formulation

Warnings/Precautions Use with extreme caution in hepatic impairment; monitor liver function regularly during treatment. Intravenous formulation contains phosphate/citrate buffer; excessive amounts may lead to hypocalcemia. Use with extreme caution in patients with pre-existing hypocalcemia. Should not be administered I.M. or SubQ; local tissue injury may occur.

Adverse Reactions

Cardiovascular: Edema (leg), thrombophlebitis, venospasm

Central nervous system: Dizziness, headache, psychic disturbance

Dermatologic: Pruritus, rash

Gastrointestinal: Anorexia, dyspepsia, diarrhea, epigastric distress, nausea, vomiting

Hepatic: Jaundice

Local: Injection site reaction (redness, irritation)

Ocular: Blurred vision

Ophthalmic suspension: Ocular: Transient stinging, tearing, eyelid edema, temporary blurred vision

Overdosage/Toxicology Limited experience in overdose. Symptoms may include gastrointestinal distress, diarrhea, jaundice, and hepatic injury. Large amounts of intravenous solution may lead to hypophosphatemia (due to phosphate/citrate buffer). Not significantly removed by dialysis.

Drug Interactions

Increased Effect/Toxicity: Concurrent administration of rifampin (or other drugs with extensive biliary secretion) may increase the risk of jaundice.

Decreased Effect:

Fusidic acid may decrease penicillin effectiveness.

Storage/Stability

Cream: Store below 25°C.

Injection, powder for reconstitution: Store below 25°C.

Ointment: Store below 30°C.

Ophthalmic suspension: Store at 2°C to 25°C. Discard multidose vials 1 month after opening.

Reconstitution Injection, powder for reconstitution: Reconstitute 500 mg vial of powder for injection by adding 10 mL of supplied diluent containing phosphate/citrate buffer. Reconstituted solution may be further diluted with NS or D_5W; should be used within 24 hours. Add to NS or D_5W to produce a final concentration of 1-2 mg/mL. For patients weighing <50 kg, reconstituted drug should be diluted at least 10-fold in a compatible solution. Discard solution if opalescence is observed.

Compatibility Stable in NS, D_5W, or LR.

Incompatible with whole blood or amino acid solutions.

Compatibility when admixed: Incompatible with calcium solutions, carbenicillin, gentamicin, kanamycin.

Mechanism of Action Inhibits protein synthesis by blocking aminoacyl-sRNA transfer to protein in susceptible bacteria.

Pharmacodynamics/Kinetics

Protein binding: 97%

Metabolism: Hepatic, to multiple metabolites

Half-life elimination: 5-6 hours

Time to peak, serum: Oral: 2-4 hours

Excretion: Feces (~100%, via bile)

Dosage

I.V.:

Children ≤12 years: 20 mg/kg/day in 3 divided doses

Children >12 years and Adults: 500 mg sodium fusidate 3 times/day

Ophthalmic: Children ≥2 years and Adults: Instill 1 drop in each eye every 12 hours for 7 days

Topical: Children and Adults: Apply to affected area 3-4 times/day until favorable results are achieved. If a gauze dressing is used, frequency of application may be reduced to 1-2 times/day.

Oral: Adults: 500 mg sodium fusidate 3 times/day. (**Note:** Oral dosage may be increased to 1000 mg 3 times/day in fulminating infections.)

Dosage adjustment in renal impairment: No dosage adjustment required

Dosage adjustment in hepatic impairment: Oral, I.V.: Use with extreme caution in patients with hepatic impairment; monitor liver function periodically during therapy

Administration I.V.: Should not be administered I.M. or SubQ. Intravenous administration should be via a large bore vein with good blood flow. Administer over 2 hours or more. Do not administer with whole blood or amino acid solutions.

Monitoring Parameters Monitor liver function tests, including bilirubin periodically during systemic therapy

Dietary Considerations May take tablets with food to minimize gastrointestinal upset.

(Continued)

Fusidic Acid *(Continued)*

Dosage Forms Excipient information presented when available (limited, particularly for generics); consult specific product labeling. [CAN] = Canadian brand name

Cream, as fusidic acid:
Fucidin®: 2% (15 g, 30 g)

Injection, powder for reconstitution, as sodium fusidate:
Fucidin®: 500 mg [packaged with 10 mL diluent/buffer solution]

Ointment, topical, as sodium fusidate:
Fucidin®: 2% (15 g, 30 g) [contains lanolin]

Suspension, ophthalmic, as fusidic acid:
Fucithalmic®: 10 mg/g [1%] (0.2 g) [unit-dose, without preservative]; (3 g, 5 g) [multidose, contains benzalkonium chloride]

Tablet, as sodium fusidate:
Fucidin®: 250 mg

Gallium Nitrate *(GAL ee um NYE trate)*

Related Information
Safe Handling of Hazardous Drugs *on page 1382*

U.S. Brand Names Ganite™

Index Terms NSC-15200

Generic Available No

Pharmacologic Category Calcium-Lowering Agent

Use Treatment of symptomatic cancer-related hypercalcemia

Pregnancy Risk Factor C

Lactation Excretion in breast milk unknown/not recommended

Labeled Contraindications Hypersensitivity to gallium nitrate or any component of the formulation; severe renal dysfunction (serum creatinine >2.5 mg/dL)

Warnings/Precautions Hazardous agent - use appropriate precautions for handling and disposal. BUN and serum creatinine elevations have been observed with gallium nitrate use; monitor closely; discontinue with serum creatinine >2.5 mg/dL. **[U.S. Boxed Warning]: Concurrent administration with other nephrotoxic drugs (eg, aminoglycosides, amphotericin B) may increase the risk for renal insufficiency; discontinue gallium nitrate during treatment with nephrotoxic drugs.** Establish and maintain adequate hydration with normal saline. Urinary output of ≥2 liters/day should be established prior to treatment initiation. Use with caution in patients where aggressive hydration may be poorly tolerated, such as in cardiovascular disease (CHF or hypertension) and pulmonary disease. Therapy may result in mild-to-moderate hypocalcemia. Safety and efficacy in pediatric patients have not been established.

Adverse Reactions Not all frequencies defined.

Cardiovascular: Edema (lower extremity), hypotension, tachycardia

Central nervous system: Coma, confusion, dreams, encephalopathy, fever, hallucinations, hypothermia, lethargy

Dermatologic: Rash

Endocrine & metabolic: Hypophosphatemia (up to 79%), serum bicarbonate decreased (40% to 50%), hypocalcemia (38%), respiratory alkalosis (mild)

Hematologic: Anemia, leukopenia

Gastrointestinal: Constipation, diarrhea, nausea, vomiting

Neuromuscular & skeletal: Paresthesia, positive Cvostek's sign

Ocular: Optic neuritis

Otic: Auditory acuity decreased (<1%), hearing decreased, tinnitus (<1%)

Renal: BUN increased (13%), creatinine increased (13%), acute renal failure

Respiratory: Dyspnea, pleural effusion, pulmonary infiltrates, rales, rhonchi

Overdosage/Toxicology Symptoms of overdose include nausea, vomiting, and increased risk of nephrotoxicity. Continue I.V. hydration; monitor serum calcium, renal function and urine output. Treatment is otherwise symptom-directed and supportive.

Drug Interactions

Increased Effect/Toxicity: Concurrent use of low-dose gallium nitrate with cyclophosphamide has been associated with dyspnea, stomatitis, asthenia, and rarely interstitial pneumonitis. Concurrent use nephrotoxic drugs (eg, aminoglycosides, amphotericin B) with gallium nitrate may increase nephrotoxic effects.

Storage/Stability Store unopened vials (25 mg/mL) at room temperature of 20°C to 25°C (68°F to 77°F); not light sensitive. Solutions in 0.9% NaCl or D_5W are stable for 48 hours at room temperature or for 7 days under refrigeration at 2°C to 8°C (36°F to 46°F).

Reconstitution Dilute in 1000 mL NS (preferred) or D_5W for infusion.

Compatibility Stable in NS, D_5W.

Mechanism of Action Inhibits bone resorption by inhibiting osteoclast function. Gallium nitrate appears to be effective in parathyroid hormone-related protein (PTHrP) and non-PTHrP-associated hypercalcemia.

Pharmacodynamics/Kinetics

Onset of calcium lowering: Seen within 24-48 hours of beginning therapy, with normocalcemia achieved within 4-7 days of beginning therapy

Duration: Normocalcemia: 7-10 days

Bioavailability: Oral: 5%

Distribution: Tissue concentrations were determined postmortem in one patient and concentrations were higher in liver and kidney than in lung, skin, muscle, heart, and cervix tumor; in dogs, tissue gallium concentrations were higher in renal cortex, bone, bone marrow, small intestine, and liver than in skeletal muscle and brain

Half-life elimination: Alpha: 1.25 hours; Beta: ~24 hours

Elimination half-life varies with method of administration (72-115 hours with prolonged intravenous infusion versus 24 hours with bolus administration); long elimination half-life may be related to slow release from tissue such as bone

Excretion: Primarily renal with no prior metabolism in the liver or kidney

Dosage Note: Initiate I.V. hydration prior to treatment; maintain throughout treatment.

I.V.: Adults: 200 mg/m²/day for 5 days; duration may be shortened during a course if normocalcemia is achieved. If hypercalcemia is mild and with very few symptoms, 100 mg/m²/day may be used.

Dosage adjustment in renal impairment:

Serum creatinine >2.5 mg/dL: Contraindicated

Serum creatinine 2 to ≤2.5 mg/dL: No guidelines exist; frequent monitoring is recommended

Administration The manufacturer recommends continuous I.V. infusion over 24 hours.

Monitoring Parameters Renal function (BUN, serum creatinine); serum calcium (baseline, then daily); serum phosphorus (baseline, then twice weekly); fluid intake, urine output

Additional Information

In addition to the hypocalcemic effect, gallium nitrate has also been studied for its antitumor effects. Gallium nitrate was studied at higher doses infused over 30 minutes every 2 weeks in bladder cancer and lymphoma (Einhorn, 2003; Straus, 2003). Rapid infusion rates and higher doses are associated (Continued)

Gallium Nitrate *(Continued)*

with an increased risk of toxicity, including nephrotoxicity and gastrointestinal toxicity.

Emetic Potential Low (10% to 30%)

Vesicant No

Dosage Forms Excipient information presented when available (limited, particularly for generics); consult specific product labeling.

Injection, solution [preservative free]:

Ganite™: 25 mg/mL (20 mL)

References
Chitambar CR, "Gallium Nitrate Revisited," *Semin Oncol*, 2003, 30(2 Suppl 5):1-4.

Cvitkovic F, Armand JP, Tubiana-Hulin M, et al, "Randomized, Double-Blind, Phase II Trial of Gallium Nitrate Compared With Pamidronate for Acute Control of Cancer-Related Hypercalcemia," *Cancer J*, 2006, 12(1):47-53.

Einhorn L, "Gallium Nitrate in the Treatment of Bladder Cancer," *Sem Oncol*, 2003, 30(2 Suppl 5): 34-41.

Hortobagyi GN, "Novel Approaches to the Management of Bone Metastases," *Semin Oncol*, 2003, 30(5 Suppl 16):161-6.

Leyland-Jones B, "Pharmacokinetics and Therapeutic Index of Gallium Nitrate," *Semin Oncol*, 1991, 18(4 Suppl 5):16-20.

Leyland-Jones B, "Treatment of Cancer-Related Hypercalcemia: The Role of Gallium Nitrate," *Semin Oncol*, 2003, 30(2 Suppl 5):13-9.

Straus DJ, "Gallium Nitrate in the Treatment of Lymphoma", *Sem Oncol*, 2003, 30(2 Suppl 5):25-33.

♦ **Gamimune® N (Can)** *see* Immune Globulin (Intravenous) *on page 597*

♦ **Gammagard Liquid** *see* Immune Globulin (Intravenous) *on page 597*

♦ **Gammagard S/D** *see* Immune Globulin (Intravenous) *on page 597*

♦ **Gammaphos** *see* Amifostine *on page 53*

♦ **Gammar®-P I.V.** *see* Immune Globulin (Intravenous) *on page 597*

♦ **Gamunex®** *see* Immune Globulin (Intravenous) *on page 597*

Ganciclovir *(gan SYE kloe veer)*

Medication Safety Issues
Sound-alike/look-alike issues:

Cytovene® may be confused with Cytosar®, Cytosar-U®

Related Information
Safe Handling of Hazardous Drugs *on page 1382*

U.S. Brand Names Cytovene®; Vitrasert®

Index Terms DHPG Sodium; GCV Sodium; Nordeoxyguanosine

Generic Available Yes: Capsule

Canadian Brand Names Cytovene®; Vitrasert®

Pharmacologic Category Antiviral Agent

Use
Parenteral: Treatment of CMV retinitis in immunocompromised individuals, including patients with acquired immunodeficiency syndrome; prophylaxis of CMV infection in transplant patients

Oral: Alternative to the I.V. formulation for maintenance treatment of CMV retinitis in immunocompromised patients, including patients with AIDS, in whom retinitis is stable following appropriate induction therapy and for whom the risk of more rapid progression is balanced by the benefit associated with avoiding daily I.V. infusions.

Implant: Treatment of CMV retinitis

Unlabeled/Investigational Use May be given in combination with foscarnet in patients who relapse after monotherapy with either drug

Pregnancy Risk Factor C

Lactation Excretion in breast milk unknown/contraindicated

Labeled Contraindications Hypersensitivity to ganciclovir, acyclovir, or any component of the formulation; absolute neutrophil count <500/mm³; platelet count <25,000/mm³

Warnings/Precautions Hazardous agent - use appropriate precautions for handling and disposal. **[U.S. Boxed Warning]: Granulocytopenia (neutropenia), anemia, and thrombocytopenia may occur.** Dosage adjustment or interruption of ganciclovir therapy may be necessary in patients with neutropenia and/or thrombocytopenia and patients with impaired renal function. Use with extreme caution in children since long-term safety has not been determined and **[U.S. Boxed Warning]: Animal studies have demonstrated carcinogenic and teratogenic effects, and inhibition of spermatogenesis;** contraceptive precautions for female and male patients need to be followed during and for at least 90 days after therapy with the drug. Take care to administer only into veins with good blood flow. **[U.S. Boxed Warning]: Indicated only for treatment of CMV retinitis in the immunocompromised and CMV prevention in transplant patients at risk.**

Adverse Reactions

>10%:

Central nervous system: Fever (38% to 48%)

Dermatologic: Rash (15% oral, 10% I.V.)

Gastrointestinal: Abdominal pain (17% to 19%), diarrhea (40%), nausea (25%), anorexia (15%), vomiting (13%)

Hematologic: Anemia (20% to 25%), leukopenia (30% to 40%)

1% to 10%:

Central nervous system: Confusion, neuropathy (8% to 9%), headache (4%)

Dermatologic: Pruritus (5%)

Hematologic: Thrombocytopenia (6%), neutropenia with ANC <500/mm³ (5% oral, 14% I.V.)

Neuromuscular & skeletal: Paresthesia (6% to 10%), weakness (6%)

Ocular: Retinal detachment (8% oral, 11% I.V.; relationship to ganciclovir not established)

Miscellaneous: Sepsis (4% oral, 15% I.V.)

<1% (Limited to important or life-threatening): Alopecia, arrhythmia, ataxia, bronchospasm, coma, dyspnea, encephalopathy, exfoliative dermatitis, extrapyramidal symptoms, nervousness, pancytopenia, psychosis, seizure, alopecia, urticaria, eosinophilia, hemorrhage, Stevens-Johnson syndrome, torsade de pointes, renal failure, SIADH, visual loss

Overdosage/Toxicology Symptoms of overdose include neutropenia, vomiting, hypersalivation, bloody diarrhea, cytopenia, and testicular atrophy. Treatment is supportive. Hemodialysis removes 50% of the drug. Hydration may be of some benefit.

Drug Interactions

Increased Effect/Toxicity: Immunosuppressive agents may increase hematologic toxicity of ganciclovir. Imipenem/cilastatin may increase seizure potential. Oral ganciclovir increases blood levels of zidovudine, although zidovudine decreases steady-state levels of ganciclovir. Since both drugs have the potential to cause neutropenia and anemia, some patients may not tolerate concomitant therapy with these drugs at full dosage. Didanosine levels are increased with concurrent ganciclovir. Other nephrotoxic drugs (eg, amphotericin and cyclosporine) may have additive nephrotoxicity with ganciclovir.

Decreased Effect: A decrease in blood levels of ganciclovir AUC may occur when used with didanosine.

(Continued)

Ganciclovir *(Continued)*

Storage/Stability Intact vials should be stored at room temperature and protected from temperatures >40°C. Reconstituted solution is stable for 12 hours at room temperature, however, conflicting data indicates that reconstituted solution is stable for 60 days under refrigeration (4°C). Stability of parenteral admixture at room temperature (25°C) and at refrigeration temperature (4°C) is 5 days.

Reconstitution Reconstitute powder with unpreserved sterile water not bacteriostatic water because parabens may cause precipitation. Dilute in 250-1000 mL D_5W or NS to a concentration ≤10 mg/mL for infusion.

Compatibility Stable in D_5W, LR, NS; **incompatible** with paraben preserved bacteriostatic water for injection (may cause precipitation).

Y-site administration: Compatible: Allopurinol, amphotericin B cholesteryl sulfate complex, cisplatin, cyclophosphamide, docetaxel, doxorubicin liposome, enalaprilat, etoposide phosphate, filgrastim, fluconazole, gatifloxacin, granisetron, linezolid, melphalan, methotrexate, paclitaxel, propofol, remifentanil, tacrolimus, teniposide, thiotepa. **Incompatible:** Aldesleukin, amifostine, amsacrine, aztreonam, cefepime, cytarabine, doxorubicin, fludarabine, foscarnet, gemcitabine, ondansetron, piperacillin/tazobactam, sargramostim, vinorelbine. **Variable (consult detailed reference):** Cisatracurium.

Mechanism of Action Ganciclovir is phosphorylated to a substrate which competitively inhibits the binding of deoxyguanosine triphosphate to DNA polymerase resulting in inhibition of viral DNA synthesis

Pharmacodynamics/Kinetics

Distribution: V_d: 15.26 L/1.73 m²; widely to all tissues including CSF and ocular tissue

Protein binding: 1% to 2%

Bioavailability: Oral: Fasting: 5%; Following food: 6% to 9%; Following fatty meal: 28% to 31%

Half-life elimination: 1.7-5.8 hours; prolonged with renal impairment; End-stage renal disease: 5-28 hours

Excretion: Urine (80% to 99% as unchanged drug)

Dosage

CMV retinitis: Slow I.V. infusion (dosing is based on total body weight):

Children >3 months and Adults:

Induction therapy: 5 mg/kg/dose every 12 hours for 14-21 days followed by maintenance therapy

Maintenance therapy: 5 mg/kg/day as a single daily dose for 7 days/week or 6 mg/kg/day for 5 days/week

CMV retinitis: Oral: 1000 mg 3 times/day with food **or** 500 mg 6 times/day with food

Prevention of CMV disease in patients with advanced HIV infection and normal renal function: Oral: 1000 mg 3 times/day with food

Prevention of CMV disease in transplant patients: Same initial and maintenance dose as CMV retinitis except duration of initial course is 7-14 days, duration of maintenance therapy is dependent on clinical condition and degree of immunosuppression

Intravitreal implant: One implant for 5- to 8-month period; following depletion of ganciclovir, as evidenced by progression of retinitis, implant may be removed and replaced

Elderly: Refer to adult dosing; in general, dose selection should be cautious, reflecting greater frequency of organ impairment

Dosing adjustment in renal impairment:
I.V. (Induction):
Cl_{cr} 50-69 mL/minute: Administer 2.5 mg/kg/dose every 12 hours
Cl_{cr} 25-49 mL/minute: Administer 2.5 mg/kg/dose every 24 hours
Cl_{cr} 10-24 mL/minute: Administer 1.25 mg/kg/dose every 24 hours
Cl_{cr} <10 mL/minute: Administer 1.25 mg/kg/dose 3 times/week following hemodialysis
I.V. (Maintenance):
Cl_{cr} 50-69 mL/minute: Administer 2.5 mg/kg/dose every 24 hours
Cl_{cr} 25-49 mL/minute: Administer 1.25 mg/kg/dose every 24 hours
Cl_{cr} 10-24 mL/minute: Administer 0.625 mg/kg/dose every 24 hours
Cl_{cr} <10 mL/minute: Administer 0.625 mg/kg/dose 3 times/week following hemodialysis
Oral:
Cl_{cr} 50-69 mL/minute: Administer 1500 mg/day or 500 mg 3 times/day
Cl_{cr} 25-49 mL/minute: Administer 1000 mg/day or 500 mg twice daily
Cl_{cr} 10-24 mL/minute: Administer 500 mg/day
Cl_{cr} <10 mL/minute: Administer 500 mg 3 times/week following hemodialysis
Hemodialysis effects: Dialyzable (50%) following hemodialysis; administer dose postdialysis. During peritoneal dialysis, dose as for Cl_{cr} <10 mL/minute. During continuous arteriovenous or venovenous hemofiltration, administer 2.5 mg/kg/dose every 24 hours.

Administration Oral: Should be administered with food.
I.V.: Should not be administered by I.M., SubQ, or rapid IVP; administer by slow I.V. infusion over at least 1 hour

Monitoring Parameters CBC with differential and platelet count, serum creatinine, ophthalmologic exams

Dietary Considerations Sodium content of 500 mg vial: 46 mg

Patient Information Regular ophthalmologic examinations should be done; close monitoring of blood counts should be done while on therapy and dosage adjustments may need to be made; take with food to increase absorption

Special Geriatric Considerations Adjust dose based upon renal function.
Vesicant No

Dosage Forms Excipient information presented when available (limited, particularly for generics); consult specific product labeling.
Capsule: 250 mg, 500 mg
Implant, intravitreal:
Vitrasert®: 4.5 mg [released gradually over 5-8 months]
Injection, powder for reconstitution, as sodium:
Cytovene®: 500 mg

References
Alraiabiah FA and Sacks SL, "New Antiherpesvirus Agents. Their Targets and Therapeutic Potential," *Drugs*, 1996, 52(1):17-32.
"Drugs for Non-HIV Viral Infections," *Med Lett Drugs Ther*, 1994, 36(919):27.
Fletcher C, Sawchuk R, Chinnock B, et al, "Human Pharmacokinetics of the Antiviral Drug DHPG," *Clin Pharmacol Ther*, 1986, 40(3):281-6.
Gando S, Kameue T, Nanzaki S, et al, "Pharmacokinetics and Clearance of Ganciclovir During Continuous Hemodiafiltration," *Crit Care Med*, 1998, 26(1):184-7.
Goodrich JM, Bowden RA, Fisher L, et al, "Ganciclovir Prophylaxis to Prevent Cytomegalovirus Disease After Allogeneic Marrow Transplant," *Ann Intern Med*, 1993, 118(3):173-8.
Gudnason T, Belani KK, and Balfour HH Jr, "Ganciclovir Treatment of Cytomegalovirus Disease in Immunocompromised Children," *Pediatr Infect Dis J*, 1989, 8(7):436-40.
Keating MR, "Antiviral Agents," *Mayo Clin Proc*, 1992, 67(2):160-78.
Lake KD, Fletcher CV, Love KR, et al, "Ganciclovir Pharmacokinetics During Renal Impairment," *Antimicrob Agents Chemother*, 1988, 32(12):1899-900.
(Continued)

Ganciclovir *(Continued)*

Matthews T and Boehme R, "Antiviral Activity and Mechanism of Action of Ganciclovir," *Rev Infect Dis*, 1988, 10(Suppl 3):490-4.

Merigan TC, Renlund DG, Keay S, et al, "A Controlled Trial of Ganciclovir to Prevent Cytomegalovirus Disease After Heart Transplantation," *N Engl J Med*, 1992, 326(18):1182-6.

Morris DJ, "Adverse Effects and Drug Interactions of Clinical Importance With Antiviral Drugs," *Drug Saf*, 1994, 10(4):281-91.

Paul S and Dummer S, "Topics in Clinical Pharmacology, Ganciclovir," *Am J Med Sci*, 1992, 304(4):272-7.

Sommadossi JP, Bevan R, Ling T, et al, "Clinical Pharmacokinetics of Ganciclovir in Patients With Normal and Impaired Renal Function," *Rev Infect Dis*, 1988, 10(Suppl 3):507-14.

Whitley RJ, Jacobson MA, Friedberg DN, et al, "Guidelines for the Treatment of Cytomegalovirus Diseases in Patients With AIDS in the Era of Potent Antiretroviral Therapy: Recommendations of an International Panel. International AIDS Society-USA," *Arch Intern Med*, 1998, 158(9):957-69.

♦ **Ganite™** *see* Gallium Nitrate *on page 490*

♦ **Garamycin® (Can)** *see* Gentamicin *on page 512*

♦ **Gardasil®** *see* Papillomavirus (Types 6, 11, 16, 18) Recombinant Vaccine *on page 878*

♦ **G-CSF** *see* Filgrastim *on page 440*

♦ **GCV Sodium** *see* Ganciclovir *on page 492*

Gefitinib *(ge FI tye nib)*

Medication Safety Issues

Sound-alike/look-alike issues:

Gefitinib may be confused with erlotinib

High alert medication: The Institute for Safe Medication Practices (ISMP) includes this medication among its list of drugs which have a heightened risk of causing significant patient harm when used in error.

U.S. Brand Names IRESSA®

Index Terms NSC-715055; ZD1839

Generic Available No

Pharmacologic Category Antineoplastic Agent, Tyrosine Kinase Inhibitor

Use

U.S. labeling: Treatment of locally advanced or metastatic nonsmall cell lung cancer after failure of platinum-based and docetaxel therapies. Treatment is limited to patients who are benefiting or have benefited from treatment with gefitinib.

Note: Due to the lack of improved survival data from clinical trials of gefitinib, and in response to positive survival data with another EGFR inhibitor, physicians are advised to use other treatment options in advanced nonsmall cell lung cancer patients following one or two prior chemotherapy regimens when they are refractory/intolerant to their most recent regimen.

Canada labeling: Approved indication is limited to NSCLC patients with epidermal growth factor receptor (EGFR) expression status positive or unknown.

Restrictions As of September 15, 2005, distribution will be limited to patients enrolled in the Iressa Access Program. Under this program, access to gefitinib will be limited to the following groups:

Patients who are currently receiving and benefitting from gefitinib (IRESSA®)

Patients who have previously received and benefited from gefitinib (IRESSA®)

Previously-enrolled patients or new patients in non-Investigational New Drug (IND) clinical trials involving gefitinib (IRESSA®) if these protocols were approved by an IRB prior to June 17, 2005

New patients may also receive Iressa if the manufacturer (AstraZeneca) decides to make it available under IND, and the patients meet the criteria for enrollment under the IND

Additional information on the IRESSA® Access Program, including enrollment forms, may be obtained by calling AstraZeneca at 1-800-601-8933 or via the web at www.Iressa-access.com

Pregnancy Risk Factor D

Lactation Excretion in breast milk unknown/not recommended

Labeled Contraindications Hypersensitivity to gefitinib or any component of the formulation; pregnancy

Warnings/Precautions Hazardous agent - use appropriate precautions for handling and disposal. Rare, sometimes fatal, pulmonary toxicity (eg, alveolitis, interstitial pneumonia, pneumonitis) has occurred. Therapy should be interrupted in patients with acute onset or worsening pulmonary symptoms; discontinue gefitinib if interstitial pneumonitis is confirmed. Use caution in hepatic or severe renal impairment. May cause hepatic injury and elevation of transaminases; discontinue if elevations/changes are severe. Interruption of therapy may be required in patients with poorly tolerated diarrhea or adverse skin reactions. Eye pain should be promptly evaluated and therapy may be interrupted based on appropriate medical evaluation; may be reinitiated following resolution of symptoms and eye changes. Safety and efficacy in pediatric patients have not been established.

Adverse Reactions

>10%:

Dermatologic: Rash (43% to 54%), acne (25% to 33%), dry skin (13% to 26%)

Gastrointestinal: Diarrhea (48% to 76%), nausea (13% to 18%), vomiting (9% to 12%)

1% to 10%:

Cardiovascular: Peripheral edema (2%)

Dermatologic: Pruritus (8% to 9%)

Gastrointestinal: Anorexia (7% to 10%), weight loss (3% to 5%), mouth ulceration (1%)

Neuromuscular & skeletal: Weakness (4% to 6%)

Ocular: Amblyopia (2%), conjunctivitis (1%)

Respiratory: Dyspnea (2%), interstitial lung disease (1% to 2%)

<1%: Aberrant eyelash growth, angioedema, corneal erosion and membrane sloughing, epistaxis, erythema multiforme, eye pain, hematuria, hemorrhage, ocular hemorrhaging, ocular ischemia, pancreatitis, toxic epidermal necrolysis, urticaria

Postmarketing and/or case reports: CNS hemorrhage and death were reported in clinical trials of pediatric patients with primary CNS tumors

Overdosage/Toxicology No specific overdose-related toxicities reported; Overdose management should be symptom-based and supportive.

Drug Interactions

Cytochrome P450 Effect: Substrate of CYP3A4 (major); **Inhibits** CYP2C19 (weak), 2D6 (weak)

Increased Effect/Toxicity: Gefitinib may increase the effects of warfarin. CYP3A4 inhibitors may increase the levels/effects of gefitinib; example inhibitors include azole antifungals, clarithromycin, diclofenac, doxycycline, erythromycin, imatinib, isoniazid, nefazodone, nicardipine, propofol, protease inhibitors, quinidine, telithromycin, and verapamil.

(Continued)

Gefitinib *(Continued)*

Decreased Effect: Gefitinib effects may be decreased by H_2-receptor blockers and sodium bicarbonate. CYP3A4 inducers may decrease the levels/effects of gefitinib; example inducers include aminoglutethimide, carbamazepine, nafcillin, nevirapine, phenobarbital, phenytoin, and rifamycins.

Ethanol/Nutrition/Herb Interactions Food: Grapefruit juice may increase serum gefitinib concentrations; St John's wort may decrease serum gefitinib concentrations.

Storage/Stability Store tablets at controlled room temperature of 20°C to 25°C (68°F to 77°F).

Mechanism of Action The mechanism of antineoplastic action is not fully understood. Gefitinib inhibits tyrosine kinases (TK) associated with transmembrane cell surface receptors found on both normal and cancer cells. One such receptor is epidermal growth factor receptor. TK activity appears to be vitally important to cell proliferation and survival.

Pharmacodynamics/Kinetics

Absorption: Oral: slow

Distribution: I.V.: 1400 L

Protein binding: 90%, albumin and alpha$_1$-acid glycoprotein

Metabolism: Hepatic, primarily via CYP3A4; forms metabolites

Bioavailability: 60%

Half-life elimination: I.V.: 48 hours

Time to peak, plasma: Oral: 3-7 hours

Excretion: Feces (86%); urine (<4%)

Dosage Note: In response to the lack of improved survival data from the ISEL trial, AstraZeneca has temporarily suspended promotion of this drug.

Oral: Adults: 250 mg/day; consider 500 mg/day in patients receiving effective CYP3A4 inducers (eg, rifampin, phenytoin)

Dosage adjustment in renal/hepatic impairment: No adjustment necessary

Dosage adjustment for toxicity: Consider interruption of therapy in any patient with evidence of pulmonary decompensation or severe hepatic injury; discontinuation may be required if toxicity is confirmed. Poorly tolerated diarrhea or adverse skin reactions may be managed by a brief interruption of therapy (up to 14 days), followed by reinitiation of therapy at 250 mg/day. Eye pain should be promptly evaluated and therapy may be interrupted based on appropriate medical evaluation; may be reinitiated following resolution of symptoms and eye changes.

Administration May administer with or without food.

For patients unable to swallow tablets or for administration via NG tube: Tablets may be dispersed in noncarbonated drinking water. Drop whole tablet (do not crush) into $^1/_2$ glass of water; stir until tablet is dispersed (~10 minutes). Drink immediately. Rinse with $^1/_2$ glass of water and drink.

Monitoring Parameters Periodic liver function tests (asymptomatic increases in liver enzymes have occurred)

Dietary Considerations Food does not affect gefitinib absorption.

Patient Information Contact prescriber if any of the following symptoms occur: Severe, persistent diarrhea; nausea or vomiting; breathing difficulties (shortness of breath, painful breathing, cough); eye irritation. Avoid becoming pregnant while on this medication.

Dosage Forms Excipient information presented when available (limited, particularly for generics); consult specific product labeling.

Tablet: 250 mg

References

Cohen EE, Rosen F, Stadler WM, et al, "Phase II Trial of ZD1839 in Recurrent or Metastatic Squamous Cell Carcinoma of the Head and Neck," *J Clin Oncol*, 2003, 21(10):1980-7.

Culy CR and Faulds D, "Gefitinib," *Drugs*, 2002, 62(15):2237-48.

Fukuoka M, Yano S, Giaccone G, et al, "Multi-Institutional Randomized Phase II Trial of Gefitinib for Previously Treated Patients With Advanced Non-Small-Cell Lung Cancer," *J Clin Oncol*, 2003, 21(12):2237-46.

Gemcitabine (jem SITE a been)

Medication Safety Issues

Sound-alike/look-alike issues:

Gemzar® may be confused with Zinecard®

High alert medication: The Institute for Safe Medication Practices (ISMP) includes this medication among its list of drugs which have a heightened risk of causing significant patient harm when used in error.

Related Information

Management of Drug Extravasations *on page 1301*

Safe Handling of Hazardous Drugs *on page 1382*

U.S. Brand Names Gemzar®

Index Terms Gemcitabine Hydrochloride; NSC-613327

Generic Available No

Canadian Brand Names Gemzar®

Pharmacologic Category Antineoplastic Agent, Antimetabolite (Pyrimidine Analog)

Use Treatment of metastatic breast cancer; locally-advanced or metastatic nonsmall cell lung cancer (NSCLC) or pancreatic cancer; advanced, relapsed ovarian cancer

Unlabeled/Investigational Use Treatment of bladder cancer, acute leukemia

Pregnancy Risk Factor D

Lactation Excretion in breast milk unknown/not recommended

Labeled Contraindications Hypersensitivity to gemcitabine or any component of the formulation; pregnancy

Warnings/Precautions Hazardous agent - use appropriate precautions for handling and disposal. Prolongation of the infusion time >60 minutes and more frequent than weekly dosing have been shown to increase toxicity. Gemcitabine can suppress bone marrow function (leukopenia, thrombocytopenia and anemia); myelosuppression is usually the dose-limiting toxicity. Gemcitabine may cause fever in the absence of clinical infection. Pulmonary toxicity has occurred; discontinue if severe.

Hemolytic uremic syndrome has been reported; monitor for evidence of microangiopathic hemolysis (elevation of bilirubin or LDH, reticulocytosis, severe thrombocytopenia, and/or renal failure); use with caution in patients with pre-existing renal impairment. Serious hepatotoxicity has been reported. Use caution with hepatic impairment (history of cirrhosis, hepatitis, or alcoholism) or in patients with hepatic metastases; may lead to exacerbation of hepatic impairment. Use caution with concurrent radiation therapy; radiation toxicity has been reported with concurrent and nonconcurrent administration; may have radiosensitizing activity when gemcitabine and radiation therapy are given ≤7 days apart; optimum regimen for combination therapy has not been determined for all tumor types. Use caution in the elderly; clearance is affected by age. Efficacy in children has not been established

Adverse Reactions

>10%:

Cardiovascular: Peripheral edema (20%), edema (13%)

(Continued)

Gemcitabine *(Continued)*

Central nervous system: Pain (10% to 48%), fever (30% to 41%), somnolence (5% to 11%)

Dermatologic: Rash (24% to 30%), alopecia (15% to 18%), pruritus (13%)

Gastrointestinal: Nausea/vomiting (64% to 71%; grades 3/4: 1% to 13%), constipation (10% to 31%), diarrhea (19% to 30%), stomatitis (10% to 14%)

Hematologic: Anemia (65% to 73%; grade 4: 1% to 3%), leukopenia (62% to 71%; grade 4: ≤1%), neutropenia (61% to 63%; grade 4: 6% to 7%), thrombocytopenia (24% to 47%; grade 4: ≤1%), hemorrhage (4% to 17%; grades 3/4: <1% to 2%); myelosuppression is the dose-limiting toxicity

Hepatic: Transaminases increased (67% to 78%; grades 3/4: 1% to 12%), alkaline phosphatase increased (55% to 77%; grades 3/4: 2% to 16%), bilirubin increased (13% to 26%; grades 3/4: <1% to 6%)

Renal: Proteinuria (10% to 45%; grades 3/4: <1%), hematuria (13% to 35%; grades 3/4: <1%), BUN increased (8% to 16%; grades 3/4: 0%)

Respiratory: Dyspnea (6% to 23%)

Miscellaneous: Flu-like syndrome (19%), infection (8% to 16%; grades 3/4: <1% to 2%)

1% to 10%:

Local: Injection site reactions (4%)

Neuromuscular & skeletal: Paresthesia (2% to 10%)

Renal: Creatinine increased (2% to 8%)

Respiratory: Bronchospasm (<2%)

<1%, postmarketing, and/or case reports (reported with single-agent use or with combination therapy, all reported rarely): Adult respiratory distress syndrome, anaphylactoid reaction, anorexia, arrhythmias, bullous skin eruptions, cellulitis, cerebrovascular accident, CHF, chills, cough, desquamation, diaphoresis, gangrene, GGT increased, headache, hemolytic uremic syndrome (HUS), hepatotoxic reaction (rare), hypertension, insomnia, interstitial pneumonitis, liver failure, malaise, MI, peripheral vasculitis, petechiae, pulmonary edema, pulmonary fibrosis, radiation recall, renal failure, respiratory failure, rhinitis, sepsis, supraventricular arrhythmia, weakness

Overdosage/Toxicology Symptoms of overdose include myelosuppression, paresthesia, and severe rash. The principle toxicities were seen when a single dose as high as 5700 mg/m^2 was administered by I.V. infusion over 30 minutes every 2 weeks. Monitor blood counts. Treatment is symptom-directed and supportive.

Drug Interactions

Increased Effect/Toxicity: Gemcitabine may increase the levels/effects of fluorouracil. Gemcitabine may enhance the adverse pulmonary effects of bleomycin.

Ethanol/Nutrition/Herb Interactions Ethanol: Avoid ethanol (due to GI irritation).

Storage/Stability Store intact vials at room temperature of 20°C to 25°C (68°F to 77°F). Reconstituted vials are stable for up to 35 days and infusion solutions diluted in 0.9% sodium chloride are stable up to 7 days at 23°C when protected from light ; however, the manufacturer recommends use within 24 hours for both reconstituted vials and infusion solutions. Do not refrigerate.

Reconstitution Reconstitute the 200 mg vial with preservative free 0.9% NaCl 5 mL or the 1000 mg vial with preservative free 0.9% NaCl 25 mL.

Resulting solution is 38 mg/mL. Dilute with 50-500 mL 0.9% sodium chloride injection or D_5W to concentrations as low as 0.1 mg/mL.

Compatibility Stable in D_5W, NS.

Y-site administration: Compatible: Amifostine, amikacin, aminophylline, ampicillin, ampicillin/sulbactam, aztreonam, bleomycin, bumetanide, buprenorphine, butorphanol, calcium gluconate, carboplatin, carmustine, cefazolin, cefotetan, cefoxitin, ceftazidime, ceftizoxime, ceftriaxone, cefuroxime, chlorpromazine, cimetidine, ciprofloxacin, cisplatin, clindamycin, co-trimoxazole, cyclophosphamide, cytarabine, dactinomycin, daunorubicin, dexamethasone sodium phosphate, dexrazoxane, diphenhydramine, dobutamine, docetaxel, dopamine, doxorubicin, doxycycline, droperidol, enalaprilat, etoposide, etoposide phosphate, famotidine, floxuridine, fluconazole, fludarabine, fluorouracil, gatifloxacin, gentamicin, granisetron, haloperidol, heparin, hydrocortisone sodium phosphate, hydrocortisone sodium succinate, hydromorphone, hydroxyzine, idarubicin, ifosfamide, leucovorin, linezolid, lorazepam, mannitol, meperidine, mesna, metoclopramide, metronidazole, minocycline, mitoxantrone, morphine, nalbuphine, netilmicin, ofloxacin, ondansetron, paclitaxel, plicamycin, potassium chloride, promethazine, ranitidine, sodium bicarbonate, streptozocin, teniposide, thiotepa, ticarcillin, ticarcillin/clavulanate, tobramycin, topotecan, vancomycin, vinblastine, vincristine, vinorelbine, zidovudine. **Incompatible:** Acyclovir, amphotericin B, cefoperazone, cefotaxime, furosemide, ganciclovir, imipenem/cilastatin, irinotecan, methotrexate, methylprednisolone sodium succinate, mitomycin, piperacillin, piperacillin/tazobactam, prochlorperazine edisylate.

Mechanism of Action A pyrimidine antimetabolite that inhibits DNA synthesis by inhibition of DNA polymerase and ribonucleotide reductase, specific for the S-phase of the cycle. Gemcitabine is phosphorylated intracellularly by deoxycytidine kinase to gemcitabine monophosphate, which is further phosphorylated to active metabolites gemcitabine diphosphate and gemcitabine triphosphate. Gemcitabine diphosphate inhibits DNA synthesis by inhibiting ribonucleotide reductase; gemcitabine triphosphate incorporates into DNA and inhibits DNA polymerase.

Pharmacodynamics/Kinetics

Distribution: Infusions <70 minutes: 50 L/m^2; Long infusion times: 370 L/m^2

Protein binding: Low

Metabolism: Metabolized intracellularly by nucleoside kinases to the active diphosphate (dFdCDP) and triphosphate (dFdCTP) nucleoside metabolites

Half-life elimination:

Gemcitabine: Infusion time ≤1 hour: 42-94 minutes; infusion time 3-4 hours: 4-10.5 hours

Metabolite (gemcitabine triphosphate), terminal phase: 1.7-19.4 hours

Time to peak, plasma: 30 minutes after completion of infusion

Excretion: Urine (92% to 98%; primarily as inactive uracil metabolite); feces (<1%)

Dosage Refer to individual protocols. **Note**: Prolongation of the infusion time >60 minutes and administration more frequently than once weekly have been shown to increase toxicity. I.V.:

Pancreatic cancer: Initial: 1000 mg/m^2 weekly for up to 7 weeks followed by 1 week rest; then weekly for 3 weeks out of every 4 weeks.

Dose adjustment: Patients who complete an entire cycle of therapy may have the dose in subsequent cycles increased by 25% as long as the absolute granulocyte count (AGC) nadir is >1500 x 10^6/L, platelet nadir is >100,000 x 10^6/L, and nonhematologic toxicity is less than WHO Grade 1. If the increased dose is tolerated (with the same parameters) the dose in subsequent cycles may again be increased by 20%.

(Continued)

Gemcitabine *(Continued)*

Nonsmall cell lung cancer:

1000 mg/m^2 days 1, 8, and 15; repeat cycle every 28 days

or

1250 mg/m^2 days 1 and 8; repeat cycle every 21 days

Breast cancer: 1250 mg/m^2 days 1 and 8; repeat cycle every 21 days

Ovarian cancer: 1000 mg/m^2 days 1 and 8; repeat cycle every 21 days

Bladder cancer (unlabeled use):

I.V.: 1000 mg/m^2 once weekly for 3 weeks; repeat cycle every 4 weeks

Intravesicular instillation: 2000 mg (in 100 mL NS; retain for 1 hour) twice weekly for 3 weeks; repeat cycle every 4 weeks (for at least 2 cycles)

Dosing adjustment for toxicity:

Pancreatic cancer: Hematologic toxicity:

AGC ≥1000 x 10^6/L and platelet count ≥100,000 x 10^6/L: Administer 100% of full dose

AGC 500-999 x 10^6/L or platelet count 50,000-90,000 x 10^6/L: Administer 75% of full dose

AGC <500 x 10^6/L or platelet count <50,000 x 10^6/L: Hold dose

Nonsmall cell lung cancer:

Hematologic toxicity: Refer to guidelines for pancreatic cancer. Cisplatin dosage may also need adjusted.

Severe (grades 3 or 4) nonhematologic toxicity (except alopecia, nausea and vomiting): Hold or decrease dose by 50%.

Breast cancer:

Hematologic toxicity: Adjustments based on granulocyte and platelet counts on day 8:

AGC ≥1200 x 10^6/L and platelet count >75,000 x 10^6/L: Administer 100% of full dose

AGC 1000-1199 x 10^6/L or platelet count 50,000-75,000 x 10^6/L: Administer 75% of full dose

AGC 700-999 x 10^6/L and platelet count ≥50,000 x 10^6/L: Administer 50% of full dose

AGC <700 x 10^6/L or platelet count <50,000 x 10^6/L: Hold dose

Severe (grades 3 or 4) nonhematologic toxicity (except alopecia, nausea, and vomiting): Hold or decrease dose by 50%. Paclitaxel dose may also need adjusted.

Ovarian cancer:

Hematologic toxicity: Adjustments based on granulocyte and platelet counts on day 8:

AGC ≥1500 x 10^6/L and platelet count ≥100,000 x 10^6/L: Administer 100% of full dose

AGC 1000-1499 x 10^6/L and/or platelet count 75,000-99,999 x 10^6/L: Administer 50% of full dose

AGC <1000 x 10^6/L and/or platelet count <75,000 x 10^6/L: Hold dose

Severe (grades 3 or 4) nonhematologic toxicity (except nausea and vomiting): Hold or decrease dose by 50%. Carboplatin dose may also need adjusted.

Dose adjustment for subsequent cycles:

AGC < 500 x 10^6/L for >5 days, AGC <100 x 10^6/L for >3 days, febrile neutropenia, platelet count <25,000 x 10^6/L, cycle delay >1 week due to toxicity: Reduce gemcitabine to 800 mg/m2 on days 1 and 8.

For recurrence of any of the above toxicities after initial dose reduction: Administer gemcitabine 800 mg/m^2 on day 1 only for the subsequent cycle

Dosing adjustment in renal impairment: The FDA-approved labeling does not contain dosing adjustment guidelines; use caution. Gemcitabine has not been studied in patients with significant renal dysfunction.

Dosing adjustment in hepatic impairment: The FDA-approved labeling does not contain dosing adjustment guidelines; use caution. Gemcitabine has not been studied in patients with significant hepatic dysfunction. The following guidelines have been used by some clinicians (Floyd, 2006): Serum bilirubin >1.6 mg/dL: Use starting dose of 800 mg/m^2

Combination Regimens

Biliary adenocarcinoma:
Gemcitabine-Capecitabine *on page 1225*
GEMOX *on page 1229*
Bladder cancer:
Gemcitabine-Carboplatin (Bladder Cancer) *on page 1225*
Gemcitabine-Cisplatin (Bladder Cancer) *on page 1226*
Gemcitabine-Docetaxel (Bladder Cancer) *on page 1227*
Paclitaxel-Carboplatin-Gemcitabine *on page 1264*
Paclitaxel-Gemcitabine *on page 1265*
Leukemia, acute lymphocytic: TVTG *on page 1285*
Leukemia, acute myeloid: TVTG *on page 1285*
Lung cancer (nonsmall cell):
GC *on page 1225*
Gemcitabine-Carboplatin (Nonsmall Cell Lung Cancer) *on page 1226*
Gemcitabine-Cisplatin (Lung Cancer) *on page 1226*
Gemcitabine-Vinorelbine *on page 1228*
Vinorelbine-Gemcitabine *on page 1289*
Osteosarcoma: Gemcitabine-Docetaxel (Sarcoma) *on page 1227*
Ovarian cancer:
Gemcitabine-Carboplatin (Ovarian Cancer) *on page 1226*
Gemcitabine-Paclitaxel *on page 1228*
Pancreatic cancer:
Gemcitabine-Capecitabine *on page 1225*
Gemcitabine-Erlotinib *on page 1227*
Gemcitabine-Irinotecan *on page 1228*
Soft tissue sarcoma: Gemcitabine-Docetaxel (Sarcoma) *on page 1227*

Administration Infuse over 30 minutes. **Note**: Prolongation of the infusion time >60 minutes has been shown to increase toxicity. Gemcitabine is being investigated in clinical trials for fixed dose rate (FDR) infusion administration at doses from 1000 mg/m^2 to 2200 mg/m^2 at a rate of 10 mg/m^2/minute. Prolonged infusion times increase the accumulation of the active metabolite, gemcitabine triphosphate. Patients who receive gemcitabine FDR experience more grade 3/4 hematologic toxicity.

Monitoring Parameters CBC with differential and platelet count (prior to each dose); hepatic and renal function (prior to initiation of therapy and periodically, thereafter); monitor electrolytes, including potassium, magnesium, and calcium (when in combination therapy with cisplatin)

Special Geriatric Considerations Clearance is affected by age. There is no evidence; however, that unusual dose adjustment is necessary in patients older than 65 years of age. In general, adverse reaction rates were similar to patients older and younger than 65 years. Grade 3/4 thrombocytopenia was more common in the elderly. Older women were more likely to experience grade 3/4 neutropenia and thrombocytopenia.

Emetic Potential Low (10% to 30%)

Vesicant No

(Continued)

Gemcitabine *(Continued)*

Dosage Forms Excipient information presented when available (limited, particularly for generics); consult specific product labeling.

Injection, powder for reconstitution:

Gemzar®: 200 mg, 1 g

References

Aapro MS, Martin C, and Hatty S, "Gemcitabine - A Safety Review," *Anticancer Drugs*, 1998, 9(3):191-201.

Bredenfeld H, Franklin J, Nogova L, et al, "Severe Pulmonary Toxicity in Patients With Advanced-Stage Hodgkin's Disease Treated With a Modified Bleomycin, Doxorubicin, Cyclo-phosphamide, Vincristine, Procarbazine, Prednisone, and Gemcitabine (BEACOPP) Regimen is Probably Related to the Combination of Gemcitabine and Bleomycin: A Report of the German Hodgkin's Lymphoma Study Group," *J Clin Oncol*, 2004, 22(12):2424-9.

Correale P, Cerretani D, Marsili S, et al, "Gemcitabine Increases Systemic 5-Fluorouracil Exposure in Advanced Cancer Patients," *Eur J Cancer*, 2003, 39(11):1547-51.

Dalbagni G, Russo P, Bochner B, et al, "Phase II Trial of Intravesical Gemcitabine in Bacille Calmette-Guerin-Refractory Transitional Cell Carcinoma of the Bladder," *J Clin Oncol*, 2006, 24(18):2729-34.

Floyd J, Mirza I, Sachs B, et al, "Hepatotoxicity of Chemotherapy," *Semin Oncol*, 2006, 33(1):50-67.

Guchelaar HJ, Richel DJ, and van Knapen A, "Clinical, Toxicological and Pharmacological Aspects of Gemcitabine," *Cancer Treat Rev*, 1996, 22(1):15-31.

Noble S and Goa KL, "Gemcitabine. A Review of its Pharmacology and Clinical Potential in Nonsmall Cell Lung Cancer and Pancreatic Cancer," *Drugs*, 1997, 54(3):447-72.

Pfisterer J, Vergote I, Du Bois A, et al, "Combination Therapy with Gemcitabine and Carboplatin in Recurrent Ovarian Cancer," *Int J Gynecol Cancer*, 2005, 15(4 Suppl 1):36-41.

Plunkett W, Huang P, Xu YZ, et al, "Gemcitabine: Metabolism, Mechanisms of Action, and Self-Potentiation," *Semin Oncol*, 1995, 22(4 Suppl 11):3-10.

Storniolo AM, Allerheiligen SR, and Pearce HL, "Preclinical, Pharmacologic, and Phase I Studies of Gemcitabine," *Semin Oncol* 1997, 24(2 Suppl 7):7-12.

Tempero M, Plunkett W, Ruiz Van Haperen V, "Randomized Phase II Comparison of Dose-Intense Gemcitabine: Thirty-Minute Infusion and Fixed Dose Rate Infusion in Patients With Pancreatic Adenocarcinoma," *J Clin Oncol*, 2003, 21(18):3402-8.

Xu Q, Zhang Y, and Trissel LA, "Physical and Chemical Stability of Gemcitabine Hydrochloride Solutions," *J Am Pharm Assoc*, 1999, 39(4):509-13.

♦ **Gemcitabine Hydrochloride** *see* Gemcitabine *on page 499*

Gemifloxacin *(je mi FLOKS a sin)*

U.S. Brand Names Factive®

Index Terms DW286; Gemifloxacin Mesylate; LA 20304a; SB-265805

Generic Available No

Canadian Brand Names Factive®

Pharmacologic Category Antibiotic, Quinolone

Use Treatment of acute exacerbation of chronic bronchitis; treatment of community-acquired pneumonia (CAP), including pneumonia caused by multidrug-resistant strains of *S. pneumoniae* (MDRSP)

Unlabeled/Investigational Use Acute sinusitis

Pregnancy Risk Factor C

Lactation Excretion in breast milk unknown/not recommended

Labeled Contraindications Hypersensitivity to gemifloxacin, other fluoro-quinolones, or any component of the formulation

Warnings/Precautions Fluoroquinolones may prolong QT_c interval; avoid use of gemifloxacin in patients with a history of QT_c prolongation, uncor-rected hypokalemia, hypomagnesemia, or concurrent administration of other medications known to prolong the QT interval (including Class Ia and Class III antiarrhythmics, cisapride, erythromycin, antipsychotics, and tricyclic anti-depressants). Use with caution in patients with significant bradycardia or acute myocardial ischemia. Use with caution in individuals at risk of seizures (CNS disorders or concurrent therapy with medications which may lower seizure threshold). Potential for seizures, although very rare, may be increased with concomitant NSAID therapy. Discontinue in patients who experience significant CNS adverse effects (dizziness, hallucinations, suicidal ideation or actions). Use caution in renal dysfunction; dosage adjustment required for $Cl_{cr} \leq 40$ mL/minute.

Fluoroquinolones have been associated with the development of serious, and sometimes fatal, hypoglycemia, most often in elderly diabetics, but also in patients without diabetes. This occurred most frequently with gatifloxacin (no longer available systemically) but may occur at a lower frequency with other quinolones.

Severe hypersensitivity reactions, including anaphylaxis, have occurred with quinolone therapy. Reactions may present as typical allergic symptoms after a single dose, or may manifest as severe idiosyncratic dermatologic, vascular, pulmonary, renal, hepatic, and/or hematologic events, usually after multiple doses. May cause maculopapular rash, usually 8-10 days after treatment initiation; risk factors may include age <40 years, female gender (including postmenopausal women on HRT), and treatment duration >7 days. Prompt discontinuation of drug should occur if skin rash or other symptoms arise. Avoid excessive sunlight; may rarely cause moderate-to-severe phototoxicity reactions similar to ciprofloxacin. Prolonged use may result in fungal or bacterial superinfection, including *C. difficile*-associated diarrhea (CDAD) and pseudomembranous colitis; CDAD has been observed >2 months postantibiotic treatment. Tendon inflammation and/or rupture has been reported with other quinolone antibiotics; risk may increase with concurrent corticosteroids, particularly in the elderly. Discontinue at first sign of tendon inflammation or pain. Peripheral neuropathy has been linked to the use of quinolones; these cases were rare. Safety and effectiveness in pediatric patients (<18 years of age) have not been established.

Adverse Reactions

1% to 10%:
Central nervous system: Headache (1%), dizziness (1%)
Dermatologic: Rash (3%)
Endocrine & metabolic: Hyperkalemia (1%)
Gastrointestinal: Diarrhea (4%), nausea (3%), abdominal pain (1%), vomiting (1%)
Hematologic: Thrombocythemia (1%), neutropenia/neutrophilia (1%)
Hepatic: Transaminases increased (1% to 2%), GGT increased (1%)
Neuromuscular & skeletal: CPK increased (1%)
<1%: Alkaline phosphatase increased, anemia, anorexia, arthralgia, asthenia, back pain, bilirubin increased, BUN increased, constipation, cramps (leg), dermatitis, dry mouth, dyspepsia, dyspnea, eczema, eosinophilia, fatigue, flatulence, flushing, fungal infection, gastritis, gastroenteritis, genital moniliasis, granulocytopenia, hematocrit increased, hemoglobin increased, hot flashes, hyperglycemia, hyper-/hypocalcemia, hypoalbuminemia, hyponatremia, insomnia, leukopenia, moniliasis, myalgia, nervousness, pharyngitis, photosensitivity, pneumonia, pruritus, pseudomembranous colitis, QT_c prolongation, serum creatinine increased, somnolence, taste perversion, thrombocytopenia, tremor, urticaria, vaginitis, vertigo, vision abnormal
Postmarketing and/or case reports: Anaphylaxis, colitis (antibiotic associated), edema (peripheral), erythema multiforme, facial edema, GGT increased, hemorrhage, renal failure, retinal hemorrhage, SVT, TIA
Important adverse effects reported with other agents in this drug class include (not reported for gemifloxacin): Agranulocytosis, allergic reactions, (Continued)

Gemifloxacin *(Continued)*

aplastic anemia, CNS stimulation, hemolytic anemia, hepatic necrosis/failure, hepatitis, hypersensitivity, jaundice, pain, pancytopenia, peripheral neuropathy, pneumonitis (eosinophilic), seizure, sensorimotor-axonal neuropathy (paresthesia, hypoesthesias, dysesthesias, weakness), serum sickness, severe dermatologic reactions (toxic epidermal necrolysis, Stevens-Johnson syndrome), tendon rupture, thrombotic thrombocytopenia purpura, torsade de pointes, vasculitis

Overdosage/Toxicology Based on animal data, acute toxicity may manifest as ataxia, lethargy, tremor and/or seizures. Treatment is symptom-directed and supportive; 20% to 30% removed by hemodialysis.

Drug Interactions

Increased Effect/Toxicity: Gemifloxacin may increase the effects/toxicity of glyburide and warfarin. Concomitant use with corticosteroids may increase the risk of tendon rupture. Concomitant use with other QT_c-prolonging agents (eg, Class Ia and Class III antiarrhythmics, erythromycin, cisapride, antipsychotics, and cyclic antidepressants) may result in arrhythmias, such as torsade de pointes. Probenecid may increase gemifloxacin levels. Concomitant use with NSAIDs may rarely increase risk of seizure.

Decreased Effect: Concurrent administration of metal cations, including most antacids, oral electrolyte supplements, quinapril, sucralfate, some didanosine formulations (pediatric powder for oral suspension), and other highly-buffered oral drugs, may decrease quinolone levels; separate doses. Gemifloxacin may diminish the therapeutic effect of the live, attenuated Ty21a strain of typhoid vaccine.

Ethanol/Nutrition/Herb Interactions Herb/Nutraceutical: Avoid dong quai, St John's wort (may also cause photosensitization).

Storage/Stability Store at 15°C to 30°C (59°F to 86°F). Protect from light.

Mechanism of Action Gemifloxacin is a DNA gyrase inhibitor and also inhibits topoisomerase IV. DNA gyrase (topoisomerase IV) is an essential bacterial enzyme that maintains the superhelical structure of DNA. DNA gyrase is required for DNA replication and transcription, DNA repair, recombination, and transposition; bactericidal

Pharmacodynamics/Kinetics

Absorption: Well absorbed from the GI tract

Distribution: V_{dss}: 4.2 L/kg

Bioavailability: 71%

Metabolism: Hepatic (minor); forms metabolites (CYP isoenzymes are not involved)

Time to peak, plasma: 0.5-2 hours

Protein binding: 60% to 70%

Half-life elimination: 7 hours (range 4-12 hours)

Excretion: Feces (61%); urine (36%)

Dosage

Usual dosage range:

Adults: Oral: 320 mg once daily

Indication-specific dosing:

Adults: Oral:

Acute exacerbations of chronic bronchitis: 320 mg once daily for 5 days

Community-acquired pneumonia (mild to moderate): 320 mg once daily for 5 or 7 days (decision to use 5- or 7-day regimen should be guided by initial sputum culture; 7 days are recommended for MDRSP, *Klebsiella*, or *M. catarrhalis* infection)

Sinusitis (unlabeled use): 320 mg once daily for 10 days
Elderly: Refer to adult dosing.

Dosage adjustment in renal impairment: Cl_{cr} ≤40 mL/minute (or patients on hemodialysis/CAPD): 160 mg once daily (administer dose following hemodialysis)

Dosage adjustment in hepatic impairment: No adjustment required.

Administration May be administered with or without food, milk, or calcium supplements. Gemifloxacin should be taken 3 hours before or 2 hours after supplements (including multivitamins) containing iron, zinc, or magnesium.

Monitoring Parameters WBC, signs/symptoms of infection, renal function

Dietary Considerations May take tablets with or without food, milk, or calcium supplements. Gemifloxacin should be taken 3 hours before or 2 hours after supplements (including multivitamins) containing iron, zinc, or magnesium.

Special Geriatric Considerations The risk of torsade de pointes and tendon inflammation and/or rupture associated with the concomitant use of corticosteroids and quinolones is increased in the elderly population.

Dosage Forms Excipient information presented when available (limited, particularly for generics); consult specific product labeling.
Tablet:
Factive®: 320 mg

References

Calvo A, Gimenez MJ, Alou L, et al, "*Ex Vivo* Serum Activity (Killing Rates) After Gemifloxacin 320 mg Versus Trovafloxacin 200 mg Single Doses Against Ciprofloxacin-Susceptible and -Resistant *Streptococcus pneumoniae*," *Int J Antimicrob Agents*, 2002, 20(2):144-6.

Friedrich LV and Dougherty R, "Fatal Hypoglycemia Associated With Levofloxacin," *Pharmacotherapy*, 2004, 24(12):1807-12.

Frothingham R, "Glucose Homeostasis Abnormalities Associated With Use of Gatifloxacin," *Clin Infect Dis*, 2005, 41(9):1269-76.

Gavin JR 3rd, Kubin R, Choudhri S, et al, "Moxifloxacin and Glucose Homeostasis: A Pooled-Analysis of the Evidence From Clinical and Postmarketing Studies," *Drug Saf*, 2004, 27(9):671-86.

Graumlich JF, Habis S, Avelino RR, et al, "Hypoglycemia in Inpatients After Gatifloxacin or Levofloxacin Therapy: Nested Case-Control Study," *Pharmacotherapy*, 2005, 25(10):1296-302.

Khaliq Y and Zhanel GG, "Fluoroquinolone-Associated Tendinopathy: A Critical Review of the Literature," *Clin Infect Dis*, 2003, 36(11):1404-10.

Kutlin A, Roblin PM, and Hammerschlag MR, "Effect of Gemifloxacin on Viability of *Chlamydia pneumoniae* (*Chlamydophila pneumoniae*) in an *In Vitro* Continuous Infection Model," *J Antimicrob Chemother*, 2002, 49(5):763-7.

Lawrence KR, Adra M, and Keir C, "Hypoglycemia-Induced Anoxic Brain Injury Possibly Associated With Levofloxacin," *J Infect*, 2006, 52(6):e177-80.

Lode H, File TM Jr, Mandell L, et al, "Oral Gemifloxacin Versus Sequential Therapy With Intravenous Ceftriaxone/Oral Cefuroxime With or Without a Macrolide in the Treatment of Patients Hospitalized With Community-Acquired Pneumonia: A Randomized, Open-Label, Multicenter Study of Clinical Efficacy and Tolerability. 185 Gemifloxacin Study Group," *Clin Ther*, 2002, 24(11):1915-36.

Malone RS, Fish DN, Abraham E, et al, "Pharmacokinetics of Levofloxacin and Ciprofloxacin During Continuous Renal Replacement Therapy in Critically Ill Patients," *Antimicrob Agents Chemother*, 2001, 45(10):2949-54.

Mandell LA, Wunderink RG, Anzueto A, et al, "Infectious Diseases Society of America/American Thoracic Society Consensus Guidelines on the Management of Community-Acquired Pneumonia in Adults," *Clin Infect Dis*, 2007, 44 (Suppl 2):27-72.

Mohr JF, McKinnon PS, Peymann PJ, et al, "A Retrospective, Comparative Evaluation of Dysglycemias in Hospitalized Patients Receiving Gatifloxacin, Levofloxacin, Ciprofloxacin, or Ceftriaxone," *Pharmacotherapy*, 2005, 25(10):1303-9.

Park-Wyllie LY, Juurlink DN, Kopp A, et al, "Outpatient Gatifloxacin Therapy and Dysglycemia in Older Adults," *N Engl J Med*, 2006, 354(13):1352-61.

Trotman RL, Williamson JC, Shoemaker DM, et al, "Antibiotic Dosing in Critically Ill Adult Patients Receiving Continuous Renal Replacement Therapy," *Clin Infect Dis*, 2005, 41(8):1159-66.

(Continued)

Gemifloxacin *(Continued)*

Wang S and Rizvi AA, "Levofloxacin-Induced Hypoglycemia in a Nondiabetic Patient," *Am J Med Sci*, 2006, 331(6):334-5.

Wilson R, Langan C, Ball P, et al, "Oral Gemifloxacin Once Daily for 5 Days Compared With Sequential Therapy With I.V. Ceftriaxone/Oral Cefuroxime (Maximum of 10 Days) in the Treatment of Hospitalized Patients With Acute Exacerbations of Chronic Bronchitis. Gemifloxacin 207 Clinical Study Group," *Respir Med*, 2003, 97(3):242-9.

♦ **Gemifloxacin Mesylate** *see* Gemifloxacin *on page 504*

Gemtuzumab Ozogamicin *(gem TOO zoo mab oh zog a MY sin)*

Medication Safety Issues

High alert medication: The Institute for Safe Medication Practices (ISMP) includes this medication among its list of drugs which have a heightened risk of causing significant patient harm when used in error.

Related Information

Management of Drug Extravasations *on page 1301*
Safe Handling of Hazardous Drugs *on page 1382*

U.S. Brand Names Mylotarg®

Index Terms CMA-676; NSC-720568

Generic Available No

Canadian Brand Names Mylotarg®

Pharmacologic Category Antineoplastic Agent, Monoclonal Antibody

Use Treatment of relapsed CD33 positive acute myeloid leukemia (AML) in patients ≥60 years of age who are not candidates for cytotoxic chemotherapy

Unlabeled/Investigational Use Salvage therapy for acute promyelocytic leukemia (APL), relapsed/ refractory CD33 positive acute myeloid leukemia in children and adults <60 years

Pregnancy Risk Factor D

Lactation Excretion in breast milk unknown/not recommended

Labeled Contraindications Hypersensitivity to gemtuzumab ozogamicin, calicheamicin derivatives, or any component of the formulation; patients with anti-CD33 antibody; pregnancy

Warnings/Precautions Hazardous agent - use appropriate precautions for handling and disposal.

[U.S. Boxed Warning]: Gemtuzumab has been associated with severe hepatic veno-occlusive disease (VOD) or hepatotoxicity. Symptoms of VOD include right upper quadrant pain, rapid weight gain, ascites, hepatomegaly, and bilirubin/transaminase elevations. Risk may be increased by combination chemotherapy, underlying hepatic disease, or hematopoietic stem cell transplant.

[U.S. Boxed Warning]: Infusion-related reactions may be severe (including anaphylaxis, pulmonary edema, or ARDS). Infusion-related events are common, generally reported to occur with the first dose after the end of the 2-hour intravenous infusion. These symptoms usually resolved after 2-4 hours with a supportive therapy of acetaminophen, diphenhydramine, and intravenous fluids. Other severe and potentially fatal infusion related pulmonary events (including dyspnea and hypoxia) have been reported infrequently. Symptomatic intrinsic lung disease or high peripheral blast counts may increase the risk of severe reactions. Fewer infusion-related events were observed after the second dose. Postinfusion reactions (may include fever, chills, hypotension, or dyspnea) may occur during the first 24 hours after administration. Consider discontinuation in patients who develop severe infusion-related reactions. In addition to infusion related pulmonary events, gemtuzumab therapy is also associated with pulmonary infiltrates, pleural effusion, noncardiogenic pulmonary edema, and pulmonary insufficiency.

[U.S. Boxed Warning]: Severe myelosuppression occurs in all patients at recommended dosages. Use caution in patients with renal impairment and hepatic impairment. Tumor lysis syndrome may occur as a consequence of leukemia treatment, adequate hydration and prophylactic allopurinol must be instituted prior to use. Other methods to lower WBC <30,000 cells/mm^3 may be considered (hydroxyurea or leukapheresis) to minimize the risk of tumor lysis syndrome, and/or severe infusion reactions. **[U.S. Boxed Warnings]: Should be administered under the supervision of an experienced cancer chemotherapy physician. Safety and efficacy have not been established in combination with other chemotherapy agents,** in pediatric patients, patients with poor performance status, or in patients with organ dysfunction.

Adverse Reactions Percentages established in adults ≥60 years of age. **Note:** A postinfusion symptom complex (fever, chills, less commonly hypertension, and/or dyspnea) may occur within 24 hours of administration; the incidence of infusion-related events decreases with repeat administration.

>10%:
Cardiovascular: Peripheral edema (19%), hypotension (18%), hypertension (17%), tachycardia (11%)
Central nervous system: Fever (78%), chills (64%), headache (27%), pain (18%), insomnia (11%)
Dermatologic: Petechiae (19%), rash (18%), bruising (11%)
Endocrine & metabolic: Hypokalemia (24%), hyperglycemia (11%)
Gastrointestinal: Nausea (63%), vomiting (53%), diarrhea (30%), anorexia (27%), abdominal pain (26%), constipation (23%), stomatitis/mucositis (22%)
Hematologic: Neutropenia (grades 3/4: 98%; median recovery 40.5 days), lymphopenia (grades 3/4: 93%), thrombocytopenia (49%; grades 3/4: 48%; median recovery 39 days), hemoglobin decreased (grades 3/4: 50%), leukopenia (grades 3/4: 43%), anemia (22%, grades 3/4: 12%)
Hepatic: Abnormal liver function tests (20%; grade 3/4: 7%), LDH increased (18%), hyperbilirubinemia (11%)
Local: Local reaction (17%)
Neuromuscular & skeletal: Weakness (36%), back pain (12%)
Respiratory: Dyspnea (26%), epistaxis (24%; grade 3/4: 3%), cough (18%), pneumonia (13%)
Miscellaneous: Sepsis (25%), neutropenic fever (19%), cutaneous herpes simplex (18%),
1% to 10%:
Central nervous system: Anxiety (10%), depression (10%), dizziness (10%), cerebral hemorrhage (2%), intracranial hemorrhage (1%)
Dermatologic: Pruritus (4%)
Endocrine & metabolic: Hypocalcemia (10%), hypophosphatemia (6%) hypomagnesemia (3%)
Gastrointestinal: Dyspepsia (8%), gingival hemorrhage (5%)
Genitourinary: Vaginal hemorrhage (5%), vaginal bleeding 2%, hematuria (grade 3/4: 1%)
Hematologic: Hemorrhage (9%), disseminated intravascular coagulation (DIC) (1%)
Hepatic: Alkaline phosphatase increased (10%), PT/PTT increased, veno-occlusive disease (5% to 10%; up to 20% in relapsed patients; higher frequency in patients with prior history of subsequent hematopoietic stem cell transplant)
(Continued)

Gemtuzumab Ozogamicin *(Continued)*

Neuromuscular & skeletal: Arthralgia (10%), myalgia (3%)

Respiratory: Pharyngitis (10%), rhinitis (7%), hypoxia (5%)

Miscellaneous: Infection (10%)

<1% (Limited to important or life-threatening symptoms): Hepatic failure, jaundice, hepatosplenomegaly

Postmarketing and/or case reports: Acute respiratory distress syndrome, anaphylaxis, gastrointestinal hemorrhage, hypersensitivity reactions, noncardiogenic pulmonary edema, pulmonary hemorrhage, renal impairment, renal failure, renal failure secondary to tumor lysis syndrome

Overdosage/Toxicology Symptoms are unknown. Closely monitor vital signs and blood counts. Treatment is symptom-directed and supportive. Gemtuzumab ozogamicin is not dialyzable.

Drug Interactions

Increased Effect/Toxicity: Monoclonal antibodies may increase the risk for allergic reactions to gemtuzumab due to the presence of HACA antibodies

Ethanol/Nutrition/Herb Interactions Ethanol: Avoid ethanol (due to GI irritation).

Storage/Stability Light sensitive; protect from light. The infusion container should be placed in a UV protectant bag immediately after preparation. Store vials under refrigeration 2°C to 8°C (36°F to 46°F). Reconstituted solutions may be stored for up to 2 hours at room temperature or under refrigeration. Following dilution, solutions are stable for up to 16 hours at room temperature. Administration requires 2 hours; therefore, the maximum elapsed time from initial reconstitution to completion of infusion should be 20 hours.

Reconstitution Prepare in a darkened room with the lights in the biologic safety cabinet turned **off**. Allow to warm to room temperature prior to reconstitution. Reconstitute vial with sterile water for injection. Final concentration of 1 mg/mL. Dilute in 100 mL of 0.9% sodium chloride injection.

Compatibility No information; infuse via separate line.

Mechanism of Action Antibody to CD33 antigen. Binding results in internalization of the antibody-antigen complex. Following internalization, the calicheamicin derivative is released inside the myeloid cell. The calicheamicin derivative binds to DNA resulting in double strand breaks and cell death. Pluripotent stem cells and nonhematopoietic cells are not affected.

Pharmacodynamics/Kinetics

Distribution: V_{ss}: Adults: Initial dose: 21 L; Repeat dose: 10 L

Half-life elimination: Total calicheamicin: Initial: 41-45 hours, Repeat dose: 60-64 hours; Unconjugated: 100-143 hours (no change noted in repeat dosing)

Time to peak, plasma: Immediate; higher concentrations observed after repeat dose

Dosage I.V.:

Children: **Note:** Patients should receive diphenhydramine (1 mg/kg) 1 hour prior to infusion and acetaminophen 15 mg/kg 1 hour prior to infusion and every 4 hours for 2 additional doses.

AML (unlabeled use): 4-9 mg/m² infused over 2 hours every 2 weeks for a total of 1-3 doses per treatment course. Patients received the second and third doses and/or dose escalation if no dose-limiting toxicities were observed. (**Note:** Higher incidences of liver toxicities were observed in children at the 9 mg/m² dose level.)

or

Children <3 years: 0.2 mg/kg infused over 2 hours every 2 weeks for a
total of 2 doses

Children ≥3 years: 6 mg/m^2 infused over 2 hours every 2 weeks for a
total of 2 doses

Adults: **Note:** Patients should receive diphenhydramine 50 mg orally and
acetaminophen 650-1000 mg orally 1 hour prior to administration of each
dose. Acetaminophen dosage should be repeated as needed every 4
hours for 2 additional doses. Pretreatment with methylprednisolone may
ameliorate infusion-related symptoms.

AML:

≥60 years: 9 mg/m^2 infused over 2 hours. A full treatment course is a total
of 2 doses administered with 14 days between doses. Full hematologic
recovery is not necessary for administration of the second dose. There
has been only limited experience with repeat courses of gemtuzumab
ozogamicin.

<60 years (unlabeled use): 9 mg/m^2 infused over 2 hours. A full treatment
course is a total of 2 doses administered with 14 days between doses.

APL (unlabeled use): 6 mg/m^2 infused over 2 hours. A full treatment course
is a total of 2 doses administered with 15 days between doses.

Dosage adjustment in renal impairment: No recommendation (not
studied)

Dosage adjustment in hepatic impairment: No recommendation (not
studied)

Administration Do not administer as I.V. push or bolus. Administer via I.V.
infusion, over at least 2 hours. Use of a low protein-binding (0.2-1.2 micron)
in-line filter is recommended. Protect from light during infusion. Premedication with acetaminophen and diphenhydramine should be administered prior
to each infusion.

Monitoring Parameters Monitor vital signs during the infusion and for 4
hours following the infusion. Monitor for signs/symptoms of postinfusion
reaction. Monitor electrolytes, LFTs, CBC with differential, and platelet
counts frequently. Monitor for signs and symptoms of hepatitis reaction
(weight gain, right upper quadrant abdominal pain, hepatomegaly, ascites).

Test Interactions None known

Patient Information This medication can only be administered as an I.V.
infusion. During therapy do not use ethanol, aspirin-containing products,
antiplatelet medications (ticlopidine, clopidogrel, or dipyridamole), OTC
medications, or supplements/herbal products without consulting prescriber. It
is important to maintain adequate nutrition and hydration. You may experience nausea and vomiting (small frequent meals, frequent mouth care,
sucking lozenges or chewing gum may help). Frequent mouth care and use
of a soft toothbrush or cotton swabs may reduce mouth sores. You will be
susceptible to infection (avoid crowds and exposure to infection). Report
fever, chills, unusual bruising or bleeding, signs of infection, dizziness, lightheadedness, difficulty breathing, or yellowing of the eyes or skin to
prescriber. Keep all appointments and get required blood work done.

Emetic Potential High (60% to 90%)

Vesicant No

Dosage Forms Excipient information presented when available (limited,
particularly for generics); consult specific product labeling.

Injection, powder for reconstitution:

Mylotarg®: 5 mg

References

Arceci RJ, Sande J, Lange B, et al, "Safety and Efficacy of Gemtuzumab Ozogamicin in
Pediatric Patients With Advanced CD33+ Acute Myeloid Leukemia," *Blood*, 2005,
106(4):1183-8.

(Continued)

Gemtuzumab Ozogamicin *(Continued)*

Buckwalter M, Dowell JA, Korth-Bradley J, et al, "Pharmacokinetics of Gemtuzumab Ozogamicin as a Single-Agent Treatment of Pediatric Patients With Refractory or Relapsed Acute Myeloid Leukemia," *J Clin Pharmacol*, 2004, 44(8):873-80.

Dowell JA, Korth-Bradley J, Liu H, et al, "Pharmacokinetics of Gemtuzumab Ozogamicin, an Antibody-Targeted Chemotherapy Agent for the Treatment of Patients With Acute Myeloid Leukemia in First Relapse," *J Clin Pharmacol*, 2001, (11):1206-14.

Giles F, Estey E, and O'Brien S, "Gemtuzumab Ozogamicin in the Treatment of Acute Myeloid Leukemia," *Cancer*, 2003, 98(10):2095-104.

Giles FJ, "Gemtuzumab Ozogamicin: Promise and Challenge in Patients With Acute Myeloid Leukemia," *Expert Rev Anticancer Ther*, 2002, 2(6):630-40.

Larson RA, "Current Use and Future Development of Gemtuzumab Ozogamicin," *Semin Hematol*, 2001, 38(3 Suppl 6):24-31.

Larson RA, Sievers EL, Stadtmauer EA, et al, "Final Report of the Efficacy and Safety of Gemtuzumab Ozogamicin (Mylotarg) in Patients With CD33-Positive Acute Myeloid Leukemia in First Recurrence," *Cancer*, 2005, 104(7):1442-52.

Lo-Coco F, Cimino G, Breccia M, et al, "Gemtuzumab Ozogamicin (Mylotarg) as a Single Agent for Molecularly Relapsed Acute Promyelocytic Leukemia," *Blood*, 2004, 104(7):1995-9.

McGavin JK and Spencer CM, "Gemtuzumab Ozogamicin," *Drugs*, 2001, 61(9):1317-22.

Stadtmauer EA, "Gemtuzumab Ozogamicin in the Treatment of Acute Myeloid Leukemia," *Curr Oncol Rep*, 2002, 4(5):375-80.

Zwaan CM, Reinhardt D, Corbacioglu S, et al, "Gemtuzumab Ozogamicin: First Clinical Experiences in Children With Relapsed/Refractory Acute Myeloid Leukemia Treated on Compassionate-Use Basis," *Blood*, 2003, 101(10):3868-71.

- **Gemzar®** *see* Gemcitabine *on page 499*
- **Gen-Acyclovir (Can)** *see* Acyclovir *on page 22*
- **Gen-Anagrelide (Can)** *see* Anagrelide *on page 87*
- **Gen-Ciprofloxacin (Can)** *see* Ciprofloxacin *on page 213*
- **Gen-Cyproterone (Can)** *see* Cyproterone *on page 267*
- **Gen-Fluconazole (Can)** *see* Fluconazole *on page 449*
- **Gengraf®** *see* CycloSPORINE *on page 254*
- **Gen-Hydroxyurea (Can)** *see* Hydroxyurea *on page 559*
- **Gen-Medroxy (Can)** *see* MedroxyPROGESTERone *on page 703*
- **Genoptic® [DSC]** *see* Gentamicin *on page 512*
- **Gentak®** *see* Gentamicin *on page 512*

Gentamicin *(jen ta MYE sin)*

Medication Safety Issues
Sound-alike/look-alike issues:
Gentamicin may be confused with kanamycin
Garamycin® may be confused with kanamycin, Terramycin®

U.S. Brand Names Genoptic® [DSC]; Gentak®

Index Terms Gentamicin Sulfate

Generic Available Yes

Canadian Brand Names Alcomicin®; Diogent®; Garamycin®; Gentamicin Injection, USP; SAB-Gentamicin

Pharmacologic Category Antibiotic, Aminoglycoside; Antibiotic, Ophthalmic; Antibiotic, Topical

Use Treatment of susceptible bacterial infections, normally gram-negative organisms including *Pseudomonas*, *Proteus*, *Serratia*, and gram-positive *Staphylococcus*; treatment of bone infections, respiratory tract infections, skin and soft tissue infections, as well as abdominal and urinary tract infections, endocarditis, and septicemia; used topically to treat superficial infections of the skin or ophthalmic infections caused by susceptible bacteria; prevention of infective endocarditis prior to dental or surgical procedures

Pregnancy Risk Factor C (ophthalmic, topical); C/D (injection; varies per manufacturer)

Lactation Enters breast milk (small amounts)/use caution (AAP rates "compatible")

Labeled Contraindications Hypersensitivity to gentamicin or other aminoglycosides

Warnings/Precautions [U.S. Boxed Warning]: Aminoglycosides may cause neurotoxicity and/or nephrotoxicity; usual risk factors include pre-existing renal impairment, concomitant neuro-/nephrotoxic medications, advanced age and dehydration. Ototoxicity may be directly proportional to the amount of drug given and the duration of treatment; tinnitus or vertigo are indications of vestibular injury and impending hearing loss; renal damage is usually reversible. May cause neuromuscular blockade and respiratory paralysis; especially when given soon after anesthesia or muscle relaxants.

Not intended for long-term therapy due to toxic hazards associated with extended administration; use caution in pre-existing renal insufficiency, vestibular or cochlear impairment, myasthenia gravis, hypocalcemia, conditions which depress neuromuscular transmission. Dosage modification required in patients with impaired renal function. Prolonged use may result in fungal or bacterial superinfection, including *C. difficile*-associated diarrhea (CDAD) and pseudomembranous colitis; CDAD has been observed <2 months postantibiotic treatment.

Adverse Reactions

>10%:

Central nervous system: Neurotoxicity (vertigo, ataxia)

Neuromuscular & skeletal: Gait instability

Otic: Ototoxicity (auditory), ototoxicity (vestibular)

Renal: Nephrotoxicity, decreased creatinine clearance

1% to 10%:

Cardiovascular: Edema

Dermatologic: Skin itching, reddening of skin, rash

<1%: Drowsiness, headache, pseudomotor cerebri, photosensitivity, allergic reaction, erythema, anorexia, nausea, vomiting, weight loss, increased salivation, enterocolitis, granulocytopenia, agranulocytosis, thrombocytopenia, elevated LFTs, burning, stinging, tremor, muscle cramps, weakness, dyspnea

Overdosage/Toxicology Symptoms of overdose include ototoxicity, nephrotoxicity, and neuromuscular toxicity. Serum level monitoring is recommended. The treatment of choice, following a single acute overdose, appears to be maintenance of urine output of at least 3 mL/kg/hour during the acute treatment phase. Dialysis is of questionable value in enhancing aminoglycoside elimination.

Drug Interactions

Increased Effect/Toxicity: Penicillins, cephalosporins, amphotericin B, loop diuretics may increase nephrotoxic potential. Aminoglycosides may potentiate the effects of neuromuscular blocking agents.

Storage/Stability Gentamicin is a colorless to slightly yellow solution which should be stored between 2°C to 30°C, but refrigeration is not recommended. I.V. infusion solutions mixed in NS or D_5W solution are stable for 24 hours at room temperature and refrigeration. Premixed bag: Manufacturer expiration date; remove from overwrap stability: 30 days.

Compatibility Stable in dextran 40, D_5W, $D_{10}W$, mannitol 20%, LR, NS; **incompatible** with fat emulsion 10%; **variable stability (consult detailed reference)** in peritoneal dialysis solution.

Y-site administration: Compatible: Acyclovir, alatrofloxacin, amifostine, amiodarone, amsacrine, atracurium, aztreonam, cefpirome, ciprofloxacin, cisatracurium, clarithromycin, cyclophosphamide, cytarabine, diltiazem, (Continued)

Gentamicin *(Continued)*

docetaxel, doxorubicin liposome, enalaprilat, esmolol, etoposide phosphate, famotidine, fluconazole, fludarabine, foscarnet, gatifloxacin, gemcitabine, granisetron, hydromorphone, IL-2, insulin (regular), labetalol, levofloxacin, linezolid, lorazepam, magnesium sulfate, melphalan, meperidine, meropenem, midazolam, morphine, multivitamins, ondansetron, paclitaxel, pancuronium, perphenazine, remifentanil, sargramostim, tacrolimus, teniposide, theophylline, thiotepa, tolazoline, vecuronium, vinorelbine, vitamin B complex with C, zidovudine. **Incompatible:** Allopurinol, amphotericin B cholesteryl sulfate complex, cefamandole, furosemide, heparin, hetastarch, idarubicin, indomethacin, iodipamide meglumine, phenytoin, propofol, warfarin. **Variable (consult detailed reference):** Filgrastim.

Compatibility in syringe: Compatible: Clindamycin, diatrizoate meglumine 52% and diatrizoate sodium 8%, diatrizoate sodium 60%, iohexol, iopamidol, iothalamate meglumine 60%, penicillin G sodium. **Incompatible:** Ampicillin, cefamandole, heparin. **Variable (consult detailed reference):** Ioxaglate meglumine 39.3% and ioxaglate sodium 19.6%.

Compatibility when admixed: Compatible: Atracurium, aztreonam, bleomycin, cefoxitin, cimetidine, chloroprocaine, ciprofloxacin, fluconazole, hexylcaine, lidocaine, lidocaine with epinephrine, mepivacaine, meropenem, metronidazole, metronidazole with sodium bicarbonate, ofloxacin, penicillin G sodium, piperocaine, procaine, ranitidine, verapamil. **Incompatible:** Amphotericin B, ampicillin, cefamandole, cefazolin with clindamycin, cefepime, heparin, nafcillin, ticarcillin. **Variable (consult detailed reference):** Cefotaxime, cefotetan, cefuroxime, clindamycin, cytarabine, dopamine, floxacillin, furosemide.

Mechanism of Action Interferes with bacterial protein synthesis by binding to 30S and 50S ribosomal subunits resulting in a defective bacterial cell membrane

Pharmacodynamics/Kinetics

Absorption:

Intramuscular: Rapid and complete

Oral: None

Distribution: Primarily into extracellular fluid (highly hydrophilic); high concentration in the renal cortex; minimal penetration to ocular tissues via I.V. route

V_d: Increased by edema, ascites, fluid overload; decreased with dehydration

Neonates: 0.4-0.6 L/kg

Children: 0.3-0.35 L/kg

Adults: 0.2-0.3 L/kg

Relative diffusion from blood into CSF: Minimal even with inflammation

CSF:blood level ratio: Normal meninges: Nil; Inflamed meninges: 10% to 30%

Protein binding: <30%

Half-life elimination:

Infants: <1 week: 3-11.5 hours; 1 week to 6 months: 3-3.5 hours

Adults: 1.5-3 hours; End-stage renal disease: 36-70 hours

Time to peak, serum: I.M.: 30-90 minutes; I.V.: 30 minutes after 30-minute infusion

Excretion: Urine (as unchanged drug)

Clearance: Directly related to renal function

Dosage Note: Dosage Individualization is **critical** because of the low therapeutic index.

Use of ideal body weight (IBW) for determining the mg/kg/dose appears to be more accurate than dosing on the basis of total body weight (TBW). In morbid obesity, dosage requirement may best be estimated using a dosing weight of IBW + 0.4 (TBW - IBW).

Initial and periodic plasma drug levels (eg, peak and trough with conventional dosing) should be determined, particularly in critically-ill patients with serious infections or in disease states known to significantly alter aminoglycoside pharmacokinetics (eg, cystic fibrosis, burns, or major surgery).

Usual dosage ranges:

Infants and Children <5 years: I.M., I.V.: 2.5 mg/kg/dose every 8 hours*

Children ≥5 years: I.M., I.V.: 2-2.5 mg/kg/dose every 8 hours*

*Note: Higher individual doses and/or more frequent intervals (eg, every 6 hours) may be required in selected clinical situations (cystic fibrosis) or serum levels document the need

Children and Adults:

Intrathecal: 4-8 mg/day

Ophthalmic:

Ointment: Instill 1/2" (1.25 cm) 2-3 times/day to every 3-4 hours

Solution: Instill 1-2 drops every 2-4 hours, up to 2 drops every hour for severe infections

Topical: Apply 3-4 times/day to affected area

Adults: I.M., I.V.:

Conventional: 1-2.5 mg/kg/dose every 8-12 hours; to ensure adequate peak concentrations early in therapy, higher initial dosage may be considered in selected patients when extracellular water is increased (edema, septic shock, postsurgical, or trauma)

Once daily: 4-7 mg/kg/dose once daily; some clinicians recommend this approach for all patients with normal renal function; this dose is at least as efficacious with similar, if not less, toxicity than conventional dosing

Indication-specific dosing:

Neonates: I.V.:

Meningitis:

0-7 days of age: <2000 g: 2.5 mg/kg every 18-24 hours; >2000 g: 2.5 mg/kg every 12 hours

8-28 days of age: <2000 g: 2.5 mg/kg every 8-12 hours; >2000 g: 2.5 mg/kg every 8 hours

Children and Adults: I.M., I.V.:

Brucellosis: 240 mg (I.M.) daily or 5 mg/kg (I.V.) daily for 7 days; either regimen recommended in combination with doxycycline

Cholangitis: 4-6 mg/kg once daily with ampicillin

Diverticulitis (complicated): 1.5-2 mg/kg every 8 hours (with ampicillin and metronidazole)

Endocarditis:

Prophylaxis for dental, oral, upper respiratory procedures: 1.5 mg/kg with ampicillin (50 mg/kg) 30 minutes prior to procedure. **Note:** American Heart Association (AHA) guidelines now recommend prophylaxis only in patients undergoing invasive procedures and in whom underlying cardiac conditions may predispose to a higher risk of adverse outcomes should infection occur. As of April 2007, routine prophylaxis for GI/GU procedures is no longer recommended by the AHA.

Treatment: 3 mg/kg/day in 1-3 divided doses

(Continued)

Gentamicin *(Continued)*

Meningitis:

(Enterococcus sp or *Pseudomonas aeruginosa):* Loading dose 2 mg/kg, then 1.7 mg/kg/dose every 8 hours (administered with another bacteriocidal drug)

Listeria: 5-7 mg/kg/day (with penicillin) for 1 week

Pelvic inflammatory disease: Loading dose: 2 mg/kg, then 1.5 mg/kg every 8 hours

Alternate therapy: 4.5 mg/kg once daily

Plague (*Yersinia pestis*): Treatment: 5 mg/kg/day, followed by postexposure prophylaxis with doxycycline

Pneumonia, hospital- or ventilator-associated: 7 mg/kg/day (with antipseudomonal beta-lactam or carbapenem)

Synergy (for gram-positive infections): 3 mg/kg/day in 1-3 divided doses (with ampicillin)

Tularemia: 5 mg/kg/day divided every 8 hours for 1-2 weeks

Urinary tract infection: 1.5 mg/kg/dose every 8 hours

Dosing interval in renal impairment:

Conventional dosing:

Cl_{cr} ≥60 mL/minute: Administer every 8 hours

Cl_{cr} 40-60 mL/minute: Administer every 12 hours

Cl_{cr} 20-40 mL/minute: Administer every 24 hours

Cl_{cr} <20 mL/minute: Loading dose, then monitor levels

High-dose therapy: Interval may be extended (eg, every 48 hours) in patients with moderate renal impairment (Cl_{cr} 30-59 mL/minute) and/or adjusted based on serum level determinations.

Hemodialysis: Dialyzable; removal by hemodialysis: 30% removal of aminoglycosides occurs during 4 hours of HD; administer dose after dialysis and follow levels

Removal by continuous ambulatory peritoneal dialysis (CAPD):

Administration via CAPD fluid:

Gram-negative infection: 4-8 mg/L (4-8 mcg/mL) of CAPD fluid

Gram-positive infection (eg, synergy): 3-4 mg/L (3-4 mcg/mL) of CAPD fluid

Administration via I.V., I.M. route during CAPD: Dose as for Cl_{cr} <10 mL/minute and follow levels

Removal via continuous arteriovenous or venovenous hemofiltration: Dose as for Cl_{cr} 10-40 mL/minute and follow levels

Dosing adjustment/comments in hepatic disease: Monitor plasma concentrations

Administration

I.M.: Administer by deep I.M. route if possible. Slower absorption and lower peak concentrations, probably due to poor circulation in the atrophic muscle, may occur following I.M. injection; in paralyzed patients, suggest I.V. route.

Ophthalmic: Administer any other ophthalmics 10 minutes before or after gentamicin preparations.

Some penicillins (eg, carbenicillin, ticarcillin and piperacillin) have been shown to inactivate aminoglycosides *in vitro.* This has been observed to a greater extent with tobramycin and gentamicin, while amikacin has shown greater stability against inactivation. Concurrent use of these agents may pose a risk of reduced antibacterial efficacy *in vivo,* particularly in the setting of profound renal impairment. However, definitive clinical evidence is lacking. If combination penicillin/aminoglycoside therapy is desired in a patient with renal dysfunction, separation of doses (if feasible), and routine monitoring of aminoglycoside levels, CBC, and clinical response should be considered.

Monitoring Parameters Urinalysis, urine output, BUN, serum creatinine; hearing should be tested before, during, and after treatment; particularly in those at risk for ototoxicity or who will be receiving prolonged therapy (>2 weeks)

Some penicillin derivatives may accelerate the degradation of aminoglyco-sides *in vitro*. This may be clinically-significant for certain penicillin (ticar-cillin, piperacillin, carbenicillin) and aminoglycoside (gentamicin, tobramycin) combination therapy in patients with significant renal impairment. Close monitoring of aminoglycoside levels is warranted.

Test Interactions

Some penicillin derivatives may accelerate the degradation of aminoglyco-sides *in vitro*, leading to a potential underestimation of aminoglycoside serum concentration.

Dietary Considerations Calcium, magnesium, potassium: Renal wasting may cause hypocalcemia, hypomagnesemia, and/or hypokalemia.

Patient Information Report any dizziness or sensations of ringing or fullness in ears; do not touch ophthalmics to eye; use no other eye drops within 5-10 minutes of instilling ophthalmic

Special Geriatric Considerations The aminoglycosides are important therapeutic interventions for infections due to susceptible organisms and as empiric therapy in seriously ill patients. Their use is not without risk of toxicity, however, these risks can be minimized if initial dosing is adjusted for estimated renal function and appropriate monitoring performed. High dose, once daily aminoglycosides have been advocated as an alternative to traditional dosing regimens. Once daily or extended interval dosing is as effective and may be safer than traditional dosing. The interval must be adjusted for renal function.

Emetic Potential Very low (<10%)

Vesicant No

Dosage Forms Excipient information presented when available (limited, particularly for generics); consult specific product labeling. [DSC] = Discontinued product

Cream, topical, as sulfate: 0.1% (15 g, 30 g)

Infusion, as sulfate [premixed in NS]: 40 mg (50 mL); 60 mg (50 mL, 100 mL); 70 mg (50 mL); 80 mg (50 mL, 100 mL); 90 mg (100 mL); 100 mg (50 mL, 100 mL); 120 mg (100 mL)

Injection, solution, as sulfate [ADD-Vantage® vial]: 10 mg/mL (6 mL, 8 mL, 10 mL)

Injection, solution, as sulfate: 40 mg/mL (2 mL, 20 mL) [may contain sodium metabisulfite]

Injection, solution, pediatric, as sulfate: 10 mg/mL (2 mL) [may contain sodium metabisulfite]

Injection, solution, pediatric, as sulfate [preservative free]: 10 mg/mL (2 mL)

Ointment, ophthalmic, as sulfate (Gentak®): 0.3% [3 mg/g] (3.5 g)

Ointment, topical, as sulfate: 0.1% (15 g, 30 g)

Solution, ophthalmic, as sulfate: 0.3% (5 mL, 15 mL) [contains benzalkonium chloride]

Genoptic®: 0.3% (1 mL) [contains benzalkonium chloride] [DSC]

Gentak®: 0.3% (5 mL; 15 mL [DSC]) [contains benzalkonium chloride]

References

Abramowicz M, "Antimicrobial Prophylaxis in Surgery," *Medical Letter on Drugs and Therapeutics, Handbook of Antimicrobial Therapy*, 16th ed, New York, NY: Medical Letter, 2002.

Ahkee S, Smith R, and Ritter GW, "Once-Daily Aminoglycoside Dosing in Lower Respiratory Tract Infections," *Pharm Therapeut*, 1995, 20:226-34.

(Continued)

Gentamicin (Continued)

"American Academy of Pediatrics Committee on Drugs. The Transfer of Drugs and Other Chemicals Into Human Milk," Pediatrics, 2001, 108(3):776-89.

American Thoracic Society and Infectious Diseases Society of America, "Guidelines for the Management of Adults With Hospital-Acquired, Ventilator-Associated, and Health-care-Associated Pneumonia," Am J Respir Crit Care Med, 2005, 171(4):388-416.

Baddour LM, Wilson WR, Bayer AS, et al, "Infective Endocarditis. Diagnosis, Antimicrobial Therapy, and Management of Complications. A Statement for Healthcare Professionals from the Committee on Rheumatic Fever, Endocarditis, and Kawasaki Disease, Council on Cardio-vascular Disease in the Young, and the Councils on Clinical Cardiology, Stroke, and Cardio-vascular Surgery and Anesthesia, American Heart Association," Circulation, 2005, 111(23):e394-434.

Begg EJ and Barclay ML, "Aminoglycosides - 50 Years On," Br J Clin Pharmacol, 1995, 39(6):597-603.

Bhatt-Mehta V, Johnson CE and Schumacher RE, "Gentamicin Pharmacokinetics in Term Neonates Receiving Extracorporeal Membrane Oxygenation," Pharmacotherapy, 1992, 12(1):28-32.

Brummett RE, Bendrick T, and Himes D, "Comparative Ototoxicity of Bumetanide and Furosemide When Used in Combination With Kanamycin," J Clin Pharmacol, 1981, 21(11-12 Pt 2):628-36.

Chow MS, Quintiliani, and Nightingale CH, "In Vivo Inactivation of Tobramycin by Ticarcillin. A Case Report," JAMA, 1982, 247(5):658-9.

Council on Dental Therapeutics, American Heart Association, "Preventing Bacterial Endocarditis," J Am Dent Assoc, 1991, 122(2):87-92.

Cunha BA, "Aminoglycosides: Current Role in Antimicrobial Therapy," Pharmacotherapy, 1988, 8(6):334-50.

Dajani AS, Bisno AL, Chung KJ, et al, "Prevention of Bacterial Endocarditis, Recommendations by the American Heart Association," JAMA, 1990, 264(22):2919-22.

Daly JS, Dodge RA, Glew RH, et al, "Effect of Time and Temperature on Inactivation of Aminoglycosides by Ampicillin at Neonatal Dosages," J Perinatol, 1997, 17(1):42-5.

Dowell JA, Korth-Bradley J, Milisci M, et al, "Evaluating Possible Pharmacokinetic Interactions Between Tobramycin, Piperacillin, and a Combination of Piperacillin and Tazobactam in Patients With Various Degrees of Renal Impairment," J Clin Pharmacol, 2001, 41:979-86.

Edson RS and Terrell CL, "The Aminoglycosides," Mayo Clin Proc, 1999, 74(5):519-28.

Farchione LA, "Inactivation of Aminoglycosides by Penicillins," J Antimicrob Chemother, 1982, 8(Suppl A):27-36.

Fuchs PC, Stickel S, Anderson PH, et al, "In Vitro Inactivation of Aminoglycosides by Sulbactam, Other Beta-Lactams, and Sulbactam-Beta-Lactam Combinations," Antimicrob Agents Chemother, 1991, 35(1):182-4.

Fuquay D, Koup J, and Smith AL, "Management of Neonatal Gentamicin Overdosage," J Pediatr, 1981, 99(3):473-6.

Gilbert DN, Moellering RC, Eliopoulos GM, et al, eds, The Sanford Guide To Antimicrobial Therapy, 2006, 36th ed, Hyde Park, VT: Antimicrobial Therapy, Inc, 2006, 6-7.

Gilbert DN, "Once-Daily Aminoglycoside Therapy," Antimicrob Agents Chemother, 1991, 35(3):399-405.

Halstenson CE, Wong MO, Herman CS, et al, "Effect of Concomitant Administration of Pipera-cillin on the Dispositions on Isepamicin and Gentamicin in Patients With End-Stage Renal Disease," Antimicrob Agents Chemother, 1992, 36(9):1832-36.

Hitt CM, Patel KB, Nicolau DP, et al, "Influence of Piperacillin-Tazobactam on Pharmacokinetics of Gentamicin Given Once Daily," Am J Health Syst Pharm, 1997, 54(23):2704-8.

Hustinx WN and Hoepelman IM, "Aminoglycoside Dosage Regimens. Is Once a Day Enough?" Clin Pharmacokinet, 1993, 25(6):427-32.

Iseman MD, "Treatment of Multidrug-Resistant Tuberculosis," N Engl J Med, 1993, 329(11):784-91.

Kaka JS, Lyman C, and Kilarski DJ, "Tobramycin-Furosemide Interaction," Drug Intell Clin Pharm, 1984, 18(3):235-8.

Konishi H, Goto M, Nakamoto Y, et al, "Tobramycin Inactivation by Carbenicillin, Ticarcillin, and Piperacillin," Antimicrob Agents Chemother, 1983, 23(5):653-57.

Lau A, Lee M, Flascha S, et al, "Effect of Piperacillin on Tobramycin Pharmacokinetics in Patients with Normal Renal Function," Antimicrob Agents Chemother, 1983, 24(4):533-37.

Lawson DH, Tilstone WJ, Gray JM, et al, "Effect of Furosemide on the Pharmacokinetics of Gentamicin in Patients," J Clin Pharmacol, 1982, 22(5-6):254-8.

Lortholary O, Tod M, Cohen Y, et al, "Aminoglycosides," Med Clin North Am, 1995, 79(4):761-87.

Lucena MI, Andrade RJ, Cabello MR, et al, "Aminoglycoside-Associated Nephrotoxicity in Extra-hepatic Obstructive Jaundice," J Hepatol, 1995, 22(2):189-96.

Mann HJ, Fuhs DW, Awang R, et al, "Altered Aminoglycoside Pharmacokinetics in Critically Ill Patients With Sepsis," *Clin Pharm*, 1987, 6(2):148-53.

Matz GJ, "Aminoglycoside Ototoxicity," *Am J Otolaryngol*, 1986, 7(2):117-9.

Matzke GR, Jameson JJ, and Halstenson CE, "Gentamicin Disposition in Young and Elderly Patients With Various Degrees of Renal Function," *J Clin Pharmacol*, 1987, 27(3):216-20.

McCormack JP and Jewesson PJ, "A Critical Re-Evaluation of the "Therapeutic Range" of Aminoglycosides," *Clin Infect Dis*, 1992, 14(1):320-39.

Nicolau DP, Freeman CD, Belliveau PP, et al, "Experience With a Once-Daily Aminoglycoside Program Administered to 2184 Adult Patients," *Antimicrob Agents Chemother*, 1995, 39(3):650-5.

O'Brien RK and Sparling TG, "Gentamicin and Fludarabine Ototoxicity," *Ann Pharmacother*, 1995, 29(2):200-1.

Oparaoji EC, Siram S, Shoheiber O, et al, "Appropriateness of a 4 mg/kg Gentamicin or Tobramycin Loading Dose in Post-Operative Septic Shock Patients," *J Clin Pharm Ther*, 1998, 23(3):185-90.

Preston SL and Briceland LL, "Single Daily Dosing of Aminoglycosides," *Pharmacotherapy*, 1995, 15(3):297-316.

Reimche LD, Rooney, ME, Hindmarsh KW, et al, "An Evaluation of Gentamicin Dosing According to Renal Function in Neonates With Suspected Sepsis," *Am J Perinatol*, 1987, 4(3):262-5.

Russoe ME and Atkins-Thor E, "Gentamicin and Ticarcillin in Subjects With End-Stage Renal Disease. Comparison of Two Assay Methods and Evaluation of Inactivation Rate," *Clin Nephrol*, 1981, 15(4):175-80.

Schentag JJ, Simons GW, Schultz RW, et al, "Complexation Versus Hemodialysis to Reduce Elevated Aminoglycoside Serum Concentrations," *Pharmacotherapy*, 1984, 4(6):374-80.

Shevchuk YM and Taylor DM, "Aminoglycoside Volume of Distribution in Pediatric Patients," *DICP*, 1990, 24(3):273-6.

Smith CR and Lietman PS, "Effect of Furosemide on Aminoglycoside-Induced Nephrotoxicity and Auditory Toxicity in Humans," Antimicrob Agents Chemother, 1983, 23(1):133-7.

Terrell CL, "Antifungal Agents. Part II. The Azoles," *Mayo Clin Proc*, 1999, 74(1):78-100.

Thompson MIB, Russo ME, Saxon BJ, et al, "Gentamicin Inactivation by Piperacillin or Carbenicillin in Patients With End-Stage Renal Disease," *Antimicrob Agents Chemother*, 1982, 21(2):268-73.

Townsend PL, Fink MP, Stein KL, et al, "Aminoglycoside Pharmacokinetics: Dosage Requirements and Nephrotoxicity in Trauma Patients," *Crit Care Med*, 1989, 17(2):154-7.

Tunkel AR, Hartman BJ, Kaplan SL, et al, "Practice Guidelines for the Management of Bacterial Meningitis," *Clin Infect Dis*, 2004, 39(9):1267-84.

Viollier AF, Standiford HC, Drusano GL, et al, "Comparative Pharmacokinetics and Serum Bactericidal Activity of Mezlocillin, Ticarcillin and Piperacillin, With and Without Gentamicin," *J Antimicrob Chemother*, 1985, 15(5):597-606.

Walterspiel JN, Feldman S, Van R, et al, "Comparative Inactivation of Isepamicin, Amikacin, and Gentamicin by Nine Beta-Lactams and Two Beta-Lactamase Inhibitors, Cilastatin and Heparin," *Antimicrob Agents Chemother*, 1991, 35(9):1875-8.

Watling SM and Dasta JF, "Aminoglycoside Dosing Considerations in Intensive Care Unit Patients," *Ann Pharmacother*, 1993, 27(3):351-7.

Wilson W, Taubert KA, Gewitz M, et al, "Prevention of Infective Endocarditis. Guidelines From the American Heart Association. A Guideline From the American Heart Association Rheumatic Fever, Endocarditis, and Kawasaki Disease Committee, Council on Cardiovascular Disease in the Young, and the Council on Clinical Cardiology, Council on Cardiovascular Surgery and Anesthesia, and the Quality of Care and Outcomes Research Interdisciplinary Working Group," *Circulation*, 2007, 115. Available at http://circ.ahajournals.org/cgi/reprint/CIRCULATIONAHA.106.183095v1; last accessed July 26, 2007.

Wynn RL, "Gentamicin for Prophylaxis of Bacterial Endocarditis: A Review for the Dentist," *Oral Surg Oral Med Oral Pathol*, 1975, 60(2):159-65.

Zaske DE, Irvine P, Strand LM, et al, "Wide Interpatient Variations in Gentamicin Dose Requirements for Geriatric Patients," *JAMA*, 1982, 248(23):3122-6.

◆ **Gentamicin Injection, USP (Can)** *see* Gentamicin *on page 512*

◆ **Gentamicin Sulfate** *see* Gentamicin *on page 512*

◆ **Gen-Tamoxifen (Can)** *see* Tamoxifen *on page 1002*

◆ **Gentlax® (Can)** *see* Bisacodyl *on page 144*

◆ **Gleevec®** *see* Imatinib *on page 583*

◆ **Gliadel®** *see* Carmustine *on page 178*

◆ **Gliadel Wafer® (Can)** *see* Carmustine *on page 178*

◆ **Glivec** *see* Imatinib *on page 583*

◆ **GM-CSF** *see* Sargramostim *on page 962*

♦ **GMD-Fluconazole (Can)** *see* Fluconazole *on page 449*

♦ **GnRH Agonist** *see* Histrelin *on page 540*

Goserelin (GOE se rel in)

Related Information

Safe Handling of Hazardous Drugs *on page 1382*

U.S. Brand Names Zoladex®

Index Terms D-Ser(Bu^t)^6,Azgly^{10}-LHRH; Goserelin Acetate; ICI-118630; NSC-606864

Generic Available No

Canadian Brand Names Zoladex®; Zoladex® LA

Pharmacologic Category Gonadotropin Releasing Hormone Agonist

Use Palliative treatment of advanced breast cancer and carcinoma of the prostate; treatment of endometriosis, including pain relief and reduction of endometriotic lesions; endometrial thinning agent as part of treatment for dysfunctional uterine bleeding

Pregnancy Risk Factor X (endometriosis, endometrial thinning); D (advanced breast cancer)

Lactation Enters breast milk/contraindicated

Labeled Contraindications Hypersensitivity to goserelin or any component of the formulation; pregnancy (or potential to become pregnant); breast-feeding

Warnings/Precautions Hazardous agent - use appropriate precautions for handling and disposal. Transient worsening of signs and symptoms (tumor flare) may develop during the first few weeks of treatment. Urinary tract obstruction or spinal cord compression have been reported when used for prostate cancer; closely observe patients for weakness, paresthesias, and urinary tract obstruction in first few weeks of therapy. Decreased bone density has been reported in women and may be irreversible; use caution if other risk factors are present; evaluate and institute preventative treatment if necessary. Rare cases of pituitary apoplexy (frequently secondary to pituitary adenoma) have been observed with leuprolide administration (onset from 1 hour to usually <2 weeks); may present as sudden headache, vomiting, visual or mental status changes, and infrequently cardiovascular collapse; immediate medical attention required. Safety and efficacy have not been established in pediatric patients.

Adverse Reactions Percentages reported in males with prostatic carcinoma and females with endometriosis using the 1-month implant:

>10%:

Central nervous system: Headache (female 75%, male 1% to 5%), emotional lability (female 60%), depression (female 54%, male 1% to 5%), pain (female 17%, male 8%), insomnia (female 11%, male 5%)

Endocrine & metabolic: Hot flashes (female 96%, male 62%), sexual dysfunction (21%), erections decreased (18%), libido decreased (female 61%), breast enlargement (female 18%)

Genitourinary: Lower urinary symptoms (male 13%), vaginitis (75%), dyspareunia (female 14%)

Miscellaneous: Diaphoresis (female 45%, male 6%); infection (female 13%)

1% to 10%:

Cardiovascular: CHF (male 5%), arrhythmia, cerebrovascular accident, hypertension, MI, peripheral vascular disorder, chest pain, palpitation, tachycardia, edema

Central nervous system: Lethargy (male 8%), dizziness (female 6%, male 5%), abnormal thinking, anxiety, chills, fever, malaise, migraine, somnolence

Dermatologic: Rash (female >1%, male 6%), alopecia, bruising, dry skin, skin discoloration

Endocrine & metabolic: Breast pain (female 7%), breast swelling/tenderness (male 1% to 5%), dysmenorrhea, gout, hyperglycemia

Gastrointestinal: Anorexia (female >1%, male 5%), nausea (male 5%), constipation, diarrhea, flatulence, dyspepsia, ulcer, vomiting, weight increased, xerostomia

Genitourinary: Renal insufficiency, urinary frequency, urinary obstruction, urinary tract infection, vaginal hemorrhage

Hematologic: Anemia, hemorrhage

Neuromuscular & skeletal: Arthralgia, bone mineral density decreased (female; ~4% decrease in 6 months), joint disorder, paresthesia

Ocular: Amblyopia, dry eyes

Respiratory: Upper respiratory tract infection (male 7%), COPD (male 5%), pharyngitis (female 5%), bronchitis, cough, epistaxis, rhinitis, sinusitis

Miscellaneous: Allergic reaction

Postmarketing and/or case reports: Pituitary apoplexy

Overdosage/Toxicology Symptomatic management

Storage/Stability Zoladex® should be stored at room temperature not to exceed 25°C (77°F). Protect from light. Should be dispensed in a lightproof bag.

Mechanism of Action Goserelin is a synthetic analog of luteinizing-hormone-releasing hormone (LHRH). Following an initial increase in luteinizing hormone (LH) and follicle stimulating hormone (FSH), chronic administration of goserelin results in a sustained suppression of pituitary gonadotropins. Serum testosterone falls to levels comparable to surgical castration. The exact mechanism of this effect is unknown, but may be related to changes in the control of LH or down-regulation of LH receptors.

Pharmacodynamics/Kinetics Note: Data reported using the 1-month implant.

Absorption: SubQ: Rapid and can be detected in serum in 10 minutes

Distribution: V_d: Male: 44.1 L; Female: 20.3 L

Time to peak, serum: SubQ: Male: 12-15 days, Female: 8-22 days

Half-life elimination: SubQ: Male: ~4 hours, Female: ~2 hours; Renal impairment: Male: 12 hours

Excretion: Urine (90%)

Dosage SubQ: Adults:

Prostate cancer:

Monthly implant: 3.6 mg injected into upper abdomen every 28 days

3-month implant: 10.8 mg injected into the upper abdominal wall every 12 weeks

Breast cancer, endometriosis, endometrial thinning: Monthly implant: 3.6 mg injected into upper abdomen every 28 days

Note: For breast cancer, treatment may continue indefinitely; for endometriosis, it is recommended that duration of treatment not exceed 6 months. Only 1-2 doses are recommended for endometrial thinning.

Dosing adjustment in renal/hepatic impairment: No adjustment is necessary

Combination Regimens

Prostate cancer:

Bicalutamide + LHRH-A *on page 1152*

FZ *on page 1224*

(Continued)

Goserelin *(Continued)*

Administration Subcutaneous implant: Insert the hypodermic needle into the subcutaneous fat. Do not try to aspirate with the goserelin syringe. If the needle is in a large vessel, blood will immediately appear in the syringe chamber. Change the direction of the needle so it parallels the abdominal wall. Push the needle in until the barrel hub touches the patient's skin. Fully depress the plunger to discharge. Withdraw needle and bandage the site. Confirm discharge by ensuring tip of the plunger is visible within the tip of the needle.

Test Interactions Serum alkaline phosphatase, serum acid phosphatase, serum testosterone, serum LH and FSH, serum estradiol

Patient Information This drug must be implanted under the skin of your abdomen every 28 days; it is important to maintain appointment schedule. You may experience systemic hot flashes (cool clothes and temperatures may help), headache (analgesic may help), constipation (increased bulk and water in diet or stool softener may help), sexual dysfunction (decreased libido, decreased erection). Symptoms may worsen temporarily during first weeks of therapy. Report unusual nausea or vomiting, any chest pain, respiratory difficulty, unresolved dizziness, or constipation. Females must use reliable contraception during therapy.

Special Geriatric Considerations No dosage adjustments are needed in the elderly. Monitoring for bone density changes, serum lipid and serum calcium changes is recommended.

Emetic Potential Low (10% to 30%)

Vesicant No

Dosage Forms Excipient information presented when available (limited, particularly for generics); consult specific product labeling.

Implant, subcutaneous:

Zoladex®:

3.6 mg [1-month implant packaged with 16-gauge hypodermic needle]

10.8 mg [3-month implant packaged with 14-gauge hypodermic needle]

References

Ahmann FR, Citrin DL, deHaan HA, et al, "Zoladex: A Sustained-Release, Monthly Luteinizing Hormone-Releasing Hormone Analog for the Treatment of Advanced Prostate Cancer," *J Clin Oncol*, 1987, 5(6):912-7.

Brogden RN and Faulds D, "Goserelin. A Review of Its Pharmacodynamic and Pharmacokinetic Properties and Therapeutic Efficacy in Prostate Cancer," *Drugs Aging*, 1995, 6(4);324-43.

Goldspiel BR and Kohler DR, "Goserelin Acetate Implant: A Depot Luteinizing Hormone-Releasing Hormone Analog for Advanced Prostate Cancer," *DICP*, 1991, 25(7-8):796-804.

♦ **Goserelin Acetate** *see* Goserelin *on page 520*

♦ **GR38032R** *see* Ondansetron *on page 837*

Granisetron *(gra NI se tron)*

Medication Safety Issues

Sound-alike/look-alike issues:

Granisetron may be confused with dolasetron, ondansetron, palonosetron

Related Information

Management of Nausea and Vomiting *on page 1319*

U.S. Brand Names Kytril®

Index Terms BRL 43694

Generic Available No

Canadian Brand Names Kytril®

Pharmacologic Category Antiemetic; Selective 5-HT$_3$ Receptor Antagonist

Use Prophylaxis of nausea and vomiting associated with emetogenic chemotherapy and radiation therapy, (including total body irradiation and fractionated abdominal radiation); prophylaxis and treatment of postoperative nausea and vomiting (PONV)

Generally **not** recommended for treatment of existing chemotherapy-induced emesis (CIE) or for prophylaxis of nausea from agents with a low emetogenic potential.

Pregnancy Risk Factor B

Lactation Excretion in breast milk unknown/use caution

Labeled Contraindications Previous hypersensitivity to granisetron, other 5-HT$_3$ receptor antagonists, or any component of the formulation

Warnings/Precautions For chemotherapy-related emesis, **granisetron should be used on a scheduled basis, not on an "as needed" (PRN) basis**, since data support the use of this drug in the prevention of nausea and vomiting and not in the rescue of nausea and vomiting. Granisetron should be used only in the first 24-48 hours of receiving chemotherapy or radiation. Data do not support any increased efficacy of granisetron in delayed nausea and vomiting.

Use with caution in patients allergic to other 5-HT$_3$ receptor antagonists; cross-reactivity has been reported. Routine prophylaxis for PONV is not recommended in patients where there is little expectation of nausea and vomiting postoperatively. In patients where nausea and vomiting must be avoided postoperatively, administer to all patients even when expected incidence of nausea and vomiting is low. Use caution following abdominal surgery or in chemotherapy-induced nausea and vomiting; may mask progressive ileus or gastric distention. Safety and efficacy in children <2 years of age have not been established. Injection contains benzyl alcohol (1 mg/mL) and should not be used in neonates.

Adverse Reactions
>10%:
Central nervous system: Headache (9% to 21%)
Gastrointestinal: Constipation (3% to 18%)
Neuromuscular & skeletal: Weakness (5% to 18%)
1% to 10%:
Cardiovascular: Hypertension (1% to 2%)
Central nervous system: Pain (10%), fever (3% to 9%), dizziness (4% to 5%), insomnia (<2% to 5%), somnolence (1% to 4%), anxiety (2%), agitation (<2%), CNS stimulation (<2%)
Dermatologic: Rash (1%)
Gastrointestinal: Diarrhea (3% to 9%), abdominal pain (4% to 6%), dyspepsia (3% to 6%), taste perversion (2%)
Hepatic: Liver enzymes increased (5% to 6%)
Renal: Oliguria (2%)
Respiratory: Cough (2%)
Miscellaneous: Infection (3%)
<1%: Agitation, allergic reactions; anaphylaxis (including hypotension, dyspnea, urticaria); angina, arrhythmias, atrial fibrillation, extrapyramidal syndrome, hot flashes, hypotension, hypersensitivity, syncope

Overdosage/Toxicology Overdoses of up to 38.5 mg have been reported without symptoms or with only slight headache. In the event of an overdose, treatment should be symptomatic and supportive.

Drug Interactions
Cytochrome P450 Effect: Substrate of CYP3A4 (minor)
Increased Effect/Toxicity: Granisetron may enhance the hypotensive effect of apomorphine.
(Continued)

Granisetron *(Continued)*

Ethanol/Nutrition/Herb Interactions Herb/Nutraceutical: St John's wort may decrease granisetron levels.

Storage/Stability

I.V.: Store at 15°C to 30°C (59°F to 86°F). Protect from light. Do not freeze vials. Stable when mixed in NS or D₅W for 7 days under refrigeration and for 3 days at room temperature.

Oral: Store tablet or oral solution at 15°C to 30°C (59°F to 86°F). Protect from light.

Compatibility Stable in $D_5^1/_2NS$, D_5NS, D_5W, NS, bacteriostatic water.

Y-site administration: Compatible: Acyclovir, allopurinol, amifostine, amikacin, aminophylline, amphotericin B cholesteryl sulfate complex, ampicillin, ampicillin/sulbactam, amsacrine, aztreonam, bleomycin, bumetanide, buprenorphine, butorphanol, calcium gluconate, carboplatin, carmustine, cefazolin, cefepime, cefoperazone, cefotaxime, cefotetan, cefoxitin, ceftazidime, ceftizoxime, ceftriaxone, cefuroxime, chlorpromazine, cimetidine, ciprofloxacin, cisplatin, cladribine, clindamycin, co-trimoxazole, cyclophosphamide, cytarabine, dacarbazine, dactinomycin, daunorubicin, dexamethasone sodium phosphate, diphenhydramine, dobutamine, docetaxel, dopamine, doxorubicin, doxorubicin liposome, doxycycline, droperidol, enalaprilat, etoposide, etoposide phosphate, famotidine, filgrastim, floxuridine, fluconazole, fludarabine, fluorouracil, furosemide, ganciclovir, gatifloxacin, gemcitabine, gentamicin, haloperidol, heparin, hydrocortisone sodium phosphate, hydrocortisone sodium succinate, hydromorphone, hydroxyzine, idarubicin, ifosfamide, imipenem/cilastatin, leucovorin, levoleucovorin, linezolid, lorazepam, magnesium sulfate, mechlorethamine, melphalan, meperidine, mesna, methotrexate, methylprednisolone sodium succinate, metoclopramide, metronidazole, minocycline, mitomycin, mitoxantrone, morphine, nalbuphine, netilmicin, ofloxacin, paclitaxel, piperacillin, piperacillin/tazobactam, plicamycin, potassium chloride, prochlorperazine edisylate, promethazine, propofol, ranitidine, sargramostim, sodium bicarbonate, streptozocin, teniposide, thiotepa, ticarcillin, ticarcillin/clavulanate, tobramycin, topotecan, vancomycin, vinblastine, vincristine, vinorelbine, zidovudine. Incompatible: Amphotericin B.

Compatibility in syringe: Compatible: Dexamethasone sodium phosphate, methylprednisolone sodium succinate.

Compatibility when admixed: Compatible: Dexamethasone sodium phosphate, methylprednisolone sodium succinate.

Mechanism of Action Selective 5-HT₃-receptor antagonist, blocking serotonin, both peripherally on vagal nerve terminals and centrally in the chemoreceptor trigger zone

Pharmacodynamics/Kinetics

Duration: Generally up to 24 hours

Absorption: Tablets and oral solution are bioequivalent

Distribution: V_d: 2-4 L/kg; widely throughout body

Protein binding: 65%

Metabolism: Hepatic via N-demethylation, oxidation, and conjugation; some metabolites may have 5-HT₃ antagonist activity

Half-life elimination: Terminal: 5-9 hours

Excretion: Urine (12% as unchanged drug, 48% to 49% as metabolites); feces (34% to 38% as metabolites)

Dosage

Oral: Adults:

Prophylaxis of chemotherapy-related emesis: 2 mg once daily up to 1 hour before chemotherapy or 1 mg twice daily; the first 1 mg dose should be given up to 1 hour before chemotherapy.

Prophylaxis of radiation therapy-associated emesis: 2 mg once daily given 1 hour before radiation therapy.

I.V.:

Children ≥2 years and Adults: Prophylaxis of chemotherapy-related emesis:

Within U.S.: 10 mcg/kg/dose (maximum: 1 mg/dose) given 30 minutes prior to chemotherapy; for some drugs (eg, carboplatin, cyclophosphamide) with a later onset of emetic action, 10 mcg/kg every 12 hours may be necessary

Outside U.S.: 40 mcg/kg/dose (or 3 mg/dose); maximum: 9 mg/24 hours

Breakthrough: Granisetron has not been shown to be effective in terminating nausea or vomiting once it occurs and should not be used for this purpose.

Adults: PONV:

Prevention: 1 mg given undiluted over 30 seconds; administer before induction of anesthesia or immediately before reversal of anesthesia

Treatment: 1 mg given undiluted over 30 seconds

Dosing interval in renal impairment: No dosage adjustment required.

Dosing interval in hepatic impairment: Kinetic studies in patients with hepatic impairment showed that total clearance was approximately halved, however, standard doses were very well tolerated, and dose adjustments are not necessary.

Administration

Oral: Doses should be given up to 1 hour prior to initiation of chemotherapy/radiation

I.V.: Administer I.V. push over 30 seconds or as a 5-10 minute-infusion

Prevention of PONV: Administer before induction of anesthesia or immediately before reversal of anesthesia.

Treatment of PONV: Administer undiluted over 30 seconds.

Special Geriatric Considerations Clinical trials with patients older than 65 years of age are limited; however, the data indicates that safety and efficacy are similar to that observed in younger adults. No adjustment in dose necessary for elderly.

Vesicant No

Dosage Forms Excipient information presented when available (limited, particularly for generics); consult specific product labeling.

Injection, solution: 1 mg/mL (1 mL, 4 mL) [contains benzyl alcohol]

Injection, solution [preservative free]: 0.1 mg/mL (1 mL)

Solution, oral: 2 mg/10 mL (30 mL) [contains sodium benzoate; orange flavor]

Tablet: 1 mg

References

Andrews PL, "The Pharmacologic Profile of Granisetron (Kytril®)," *Semin Oncol*, 1994, 21(3 Suppl 5):3-9.

Blower P, "A Pharmacologic Profile of Oral Granisetron (Kytril® Tablets)," *Semin Oncol*, 1995, 22(4 Suppl 10):3-5.

Kris MG, Hesketh PJ, Somerfield MR, et al, "American Society of Clinical Oncology Guideline for Antiemetics in Oncology: Update 2006," *J Clin Oncol*, 2006, 24(18):2932-47.

Morrow GR, Hickok JT, and Rosenthal SN, "Progress in Reducing Nausea and Emesis. Comparisons of Ondansetron (Zofran®), Granisetron (Kytril®), and Tropisetron (Navoban®)," *Cancer*, 1995, 76(3):343-57.

(Continued)

Granisetron *(Continued)*

Palmer R, "Efficacy and Safety of Granisetron (Kytril®) in Two Special Populations: Children and Adults With Impaired Hepatic Function," *Semin Oncol*, 1994, 21(3 Suppl 5):22-5.

Plosker GL and Goa KL, "Granisetron: A Review of Its Pharmacological Properties and Therapeutic Use as an Antiemetic," *Drugs*, 1991, 42(5):805-24.

Yarker YE and McTavish D, "Granisetron. An Update of Its Therapeutic Use in Nausea and Vomiting Induced by Antineoplastic Therapy," *Drugs*, 1994, 48(5):761-93.

♦ **Granulocyte Colony Stimulating Factor** *see* Filgrastim *on page 440*

♦ **Granulocyte-Macrophage Colony Stimulating Factor** *see* Sargramostim *on page 962*

♦ **GW506U78** *see* Nelarabine *on page 804*

♦ **GW-1000-02** *see* Tetrahydrocannabinol and Cannabidiol *on page 1022*

♦ **GW572016** *see* Lapatinib *on page 656*

♦ **Gyne-Lotrimin® 3 [OTC]** *see* Clotrimazole *on page 239*

♦ **Gyne-Lotrimin® 7 [OTC]** *see* Clotrimazole *on page 239*

♦ **Haldol®** *see* Haloperidol *on page 526*

♦ **Haldol® Decanoate** *see* Haloperidol *on page 526*

Haloperidol *(ha loe PER i dole)*

Medication Safety Issues
Sound-alike/look-alike issues:

Haloperidol may be confused Halotestin®

Haldol® may be confused with Halcion®, Halenol®, Halog®, Halotestin®, Stadol®

Related Information
Management of Nausea and Vomiting *on page 1319*

U.S. Brand Names Haldol®; Haldol® Decanoate

Index Terms Haloperidol Decanoate; Haloperidol Lactate

Generic Available Yes

Canadian Brand Names Apo-Haloperidol®; Apo-Haloperidol LA®; Haloperidol Injection, USP; Haloperidol-LA; Haloperidol-LA Omega; Haloperidol Long Acting; Novo-Peridol; Peridol; PMS-Haloperidol LA

Pharmacologic Category Antipsychotic Agent, Typical

Use Management of schizophrenia; control of tics and vocal utterances of Tourette's disorder in children and adults; severe behavioral problems in children

Unlabeled/Investigational Use Treatment of psychosis; may be used for the emergency sedation of severely-agitated or delirious patients; adjunctive treatment of ethanol dependence; antiemetic

Pregnancy Risk Factor C

Lactation Enters breast milk/not recommended (AAP rates "of concern")

Labeled Contraindications Hypersensitivity to haloperidol or any component of the formulation; Parkinson's disease; severe CNS depression; bone marrow suppression; severe cardiac or hepatic disease; coma

Warnings/Precautions Hypotension may occur, particularly with parenteral administration. Although the short-acting form (lactate) is used clinically, the I.V. use of the injection is not an FDA-approved route of administration; the decanoate form should never be administered intravenously.

May alter cardiac conduction and prolong QT interval; life-threatening arrhythmias have occurred with therapeutic doses of antipsychotics but risk may be increased with doses exceeding recommendations and/or intravenous administration (unlabeled route). Use caution or avoid use in patients with electrolyte abnormalities (eg, hypokalemia, hypomagnesemia), hypothyroidism, familial long QT syndrome, concomitant medications which may augment QT prolongation, or any underlying cardiac abnormality which may also potentiate risk. Monitor ECG closely for dose-related QT effects. Adverse effects of decanoate may be prolonged. Avoid in thyrotoxicosis. May be sedating, use with caution in disorders where CNS depression is a feature. Caution in patients with hemodynamic instability, predisposition to seizures, subcortical brain damage, renal or respiratory disease. Esophageal dysmotility and aspiration have been associated with antipsychotic use - use with caution in patients at risk of pneumonia (eg, Alzheimer's disease). Caution in breast cancer or other prolactin-dependent tumors (may elevate prolactin levels). May alter temperature regulation or mask toxicity of other drugs due to antiemetic effects. May cause orthostatic hypotension; use with caution in patients at risk of this effect or those who would tolerate transient hypotensive episodes (cerebrovascular disease, cardiovascular disease, or other medications which may predispose). Some tablets contain tartrazine.

May cause anticholinergic effects (confusion, agitation, constipation, xerostomia, blurred vision, urinary retention). Therefore, they should be used with caution in patients with decreased gastrointestinal motility, urinary retention, BPH, xerostomia, or visual problems. Conditions which also may be exacerbated by cholinergic blockade include narrow-angle glaucoma (screening is recommended) and worsening of myasthenia gravis. Relative to other neuroleptics, haloperidol has a low potency of cholinergic blockade.

May cause extrapyramidal symptoms, including pseudoparkinsonism, acute dystonic reactions, akathisia, and tardive dyskinesia (risk of these reactions is high relative to other neuroleptics). May be associated with neuroleptic malignant syndrome (NMS) or pigmentary retinopathy.

Adverse Reactions Frequency not defined.

Cardiovascular: Abnormal T waves with prolonged ventricular repolarization, arrhythmia, hyper-/hypotension, QT prolongation, sudden death, tachycardia, torsade de pointes

Central nervous system: Agitation, akathisia, altered central temperature regulation, anxiety, confusion, depression, drowsiness, dystonic reactions, euphoria, extrapyramidal reactions, headache, insomnia, lethargy, neuroleptic malignant syndrome (NMS), pseudoparkinsonian signs and symptoms, restlessness, seizure, tardive dyskinesia, tardive dystonia, vertigo

Dermatologic: Alopecia, contact dermatitis, hyperpigmentation, photosensitivity (rare), pruritus, rash

Endocrine & metabolic: Amenorrhea, breast engorgement, galactorrhea, gynecomastia, hyper-/hypoglycemia, hyponatremia, lactation, mastalgia, menstrual irregularities, sexual dysfunction

Gastrointestinal: Anorexia, constipation, diarrhea, dyspepsia, hypersalivation, nausea, vomiting, xerostomia

Genitourinary: Priapism, urinary retention

Hematologic: Cholestatic jaundice, obstructive jaundice

Ocular: Blurred vision

Respiratory: Bronchospasm, laryngospasm

Miscellaneous: Diaphoresis, heat stroke

Overdosage/Toxicology Symptoms of overdose include deep sleep, dystonia, agitation, dysrhythmias, and extrapyramidal symptoms. Treatment is supportive and symptomatic.

Drug Interactions

Cytochrome P450 Effect: **Substrate** of CYP1A2 (minor), 2D6 (major), 3A4 (major); **Inhibits** CYP2D6 (moderate), 3A4 (moderate)

Increased Effect/Toxicity: Haloperidol concentrations/effects may be increased by chloroquine, propranolol, and sulfadoxine-pyridoxine. The (Continued)

Haloperidol *(Continued)*

levels/effects of haloperidol may be increased by azole antifungals, chlorpromazine, clarithromycin, delavirdine, diclofenac, doxycycline, erythromycin, fluoxetine, imatinib, isoniazid, miconazole, nefazodone, nicardipine, paroxetine, pergolide, propofol, protease inhibitors, quinidine, quinine, ritonavir, ropinirole, telithromycin, verapamil, and other CYP2D6 or 3A4 inhibitors.

Haloperidol may increase the levels/effects of amphetamines, selected beta-blockers, selected benzodiazepines, calcium channel blockers, cisapride, cyclosporine, dextromethorphan, ergot alkaloids, fluoxetine, selected HMG-CoA reductase inhibitors, lidocaine, mesoridazine, mirtazapine, nateglinide, nefazodone, paroxetine, risperidone, ritonavir, sildenafil (and other PDE-5 inhibitors), tacrolimus, thioridazine, tricyclic antidepressants, venlafaxine, and other substrates of CYP2D6 or 3A4.

Haloperidol may increase the effects of antihypertensives, CNS depressants (ethanol, opioid analgesics, sedative-hypnotics), lithium, trazodone, and TCAs. Haloperidol in combination with indomethacin may result in drowsiness, tiredness, and confusion. Metoclopramide may increase risk of extrapyramidal symptoms (EPS). QT-prolonging agents may further increase haloperidol's QT prolongation potential. Acetylcholinesterase inhibitors (central) may increase the risk of antipsychotic-related EPS.

Decreased Effect: Haloperidol may inhibit the ability of bromocriptine to lower serum prolactin concentrations. Benztropine (and other anticholinergics) may inhibit the therapeutic response to haloperidol and excess anticholinergic effects may occur. Barbiturates, carbamazepine, and cigarette smoking may enhance the hepatic metabolism of haloperidol. Haloperidol may inhibit the antiparkinsonian effect of levodopa; avoid this combination. The levels/effects of haloperidol may be decreased by aminoglutethimide, carbamazepine, nafcillin, nevirapine, phenobarbital, phenytoin, rifamycins, and other CYP3A4 inducers. Haloperidol may decrease the levels/effects of CYP2D6 prodrug substrates (eg, codeine, hydrocodone, oxycodone, tramadol).

Ethanol/Nutrition/Herb Interactions

Ethanol: Avoid ethanol (may increase CNS depression).

Herb/Nutraceutical: Avoid valerian, St John's wort, kava kava, gotu kola (may increase CNS depression).

Storage/Stability Protect oral dosage forms from light. Haloperidol lactate injection should be stored at controlled room temperature; do not freeze or expose to temperatures >40°C. Protect from light; exposure to light may cause discoloration and the development of a grayish-red precipitate over several weeks. Stability of standardized solutions is 38 days at room temperature (24°C).

Reconstitution Haloperidol lactate may be administered IVPB or I.V. infusion in D_5W solutions. NS solutions should not be used due to reports of decreased stability and incompatibility.

Standardized dose: 0.5-100 mg/50-100 mL D_5W.

Compatibility Stable in D_5W; **variable stability (consult detailed reference)** in $D_5^{1}/_4NS$, LR, $^{1}/_2NS$, NS.

Y-site administration: Compatible: Amifostine, amsacrine, aztreonam, cimetidine, cisatracurium, cladribine, dobutamine, docetaxel, dopamine, doxorubicin liposome, etoposide phosphate, famotidine, filgrastim, fludarabine, gatifloxacin, gemcitabine, granisetron, lidocaine, linezolid, lorazepam, melphalan, midazolam, nitroglycerin, norepinephrine ondansetron, paclitaxel, phenylephrine, propofol, remifentanil, sufentanil, tacrolimus, teniposide, theophylline, thiotepa, vinorelbine. **Incompatible:** Allopurinol, amphotericin B cholesteryl sulfate complex, cefepime, fluconazole, foscarnet, heparin, piperacillin/tazobactam, sargramostim. **Variable (consult detailed reference):** Sodium nitroprusside.

Compatibility in syringe: Compatible: Hydromorphone, sufentanil. **Incompatible:** Diphenhydramine, heparin, hydroxyzine, ketorolac. **Variable (consult detailed reference):** Benztropine, cyclizine, diamorphine, morphine.

Mechanism of Action Haloperidol is a butyrophenone antipsychotic which blocks postsynaptic mesolimbic dopaminergic D_1 and D_2 receptors in the brain; depresses the release of hypothalamic and hypophyseal hormones; believed to depress the reticular activating system thus affecting basal metabolism, body temperature, wakefulness, vasomotor tone, and emesis

Pharmacodynamics/Kinetics

Onset of action: Sedation: I.M., I.V.: 30-60 minutes

Duration: Decanoate: 2-4 weeks

Distribution: V_d: 8-18 L/kg; crosses placenta; enters breast milk

Protein binding: 90%

Metabolism: Hepatic to inactive compounds

Bioavailability: Oral: 60%

Half-life elimination: 18 hours; Decanoate: ~1 day

Time to peak, serum: Oral: 2-6 hours; I.M.: 20 minutes; Decanoate: 7 days

Excretion: Urine (33% to 40% as metabolites) within 5 days; feces (15%)

Clearance: 550 ± 133 mL/minute

Dosage

Children: 3-12 years (15-40 kg): Oral:

Initial: 0.05 mg/kg/day or 0.25-0.5 mg/day given in 2-3 divided doses; increase by 0.25-0.5 mg every 5-7 days; maximum: 0.15 mg/kg/day

Usual maintenance:

Agitation or hyperkinesia: 0.01-0.03 mg/kg/day once daily

Nonpsychotic disorders: 0.05-0.075 mg/kg/day in 2-3 divided doses

Psychotic disorders: 0.05-0.15 mg/kg/day in 2-3 divided doses

Children 6-12 years: Sedation/psychotic disorders: I.M. (as lactate): 1-3 mg/ dose every 4-8 hours to a maximum of 0.15 mg/kg/day; change over to oral therapy as soon as able

Adults:

Psychosis:

Oral: 0.5-5 mg 2-3 times/day; usual maximum: 30 mg/day

I.M. (as lactate): 2-5 mg every 4-8 hours as needed

I.M. (as decanoate): Initial: 10-20 times the daily oral dose administered at 4-week intervals

Maintenance dose: 10-15 times initial oral dose; used to stabilize psychiatric symptoms

Delirium in the intensive care unit (unlabeled use, unlabeled route):

I.V.: 2-10 mg; may repeat bolus doses every 20-30 minutes until calm achieved then administer 25% of the maximum dose every 6 hours; monitor ECG and QT_c interval

Intermittent I.V.: 0.03-0.15 mg/kg every 30 minutes to 6 hours

Oral: Agitation: 5-10 mg

Continuous intravenous infusion (100 mg/100 mL D_5W): Rates of 3-25 mg/hour have been used

Rapid tranquilization of severely-agitated patient (unlabeled use): Administer every 30-60 minutes:

Oral: 5-10 mg

I.M. (as lactate): 5 mg

Average total dose (oral or I.M.) for tranquilization: 10-20 mg

(Continued)

Haloperidol *(Continued)*

Elderly: Nonpsychotic patient, dementia behavior (unlabeled use): Initial: Oral: 0.25-0.5 mg 1-2 times/day; increase dose at 4- to 7-day intervals by 0.25-0.5 mg/day; increase dosing intervals (twice daily, 3 times/day, etc) as necessary to control response or side effects

Hemodialysis/peritoneal dialysis: Supplemental dose is not necessary

Administration The decanoate injectable formulation should be administered I.M. only, **do not administer decanoate I.V.** Dilute the oral concentrate with water or juice before administration. Avoid skin contact with oral suspension or solution; may cause contact dermatitis.

Monitoring Parameters Vital signs; lipid profile, fasting blood glucose/Hgb A_{1c}; BMI; mental status, abnormal involuntary movement scale (AIMS), extrapyramidal symptoms (EPS); ECG (with off-label intravenous administration)

Patient Information May cause drowsiness, restlessness; avoid alcohol and other CNS depressants; rise slowly from recumbent position; use of supportive stockings may help prevent orthostatic hypotension; do not alter dosage or discontinue without consulting prescriber; oral concentrate must be diluted in 2-4 oz of liquid (water, fruit juice, carbonated drinks, milk, or pudding)

Special Geriatric Considerations Many elderly patients receive antipsychotic medications for inappropriate nonpsychotic behavior. Before initiating antipsychotic medication, the clinician should investigate any possible reversible cause; any stress or stress from any disease can cause acute "confusion" or worsening of baseline nonpsychotic behavior. Most commonly acute changes in behavior are due to increases in drug dose or addition of new drug to regimen; fluid electrolyte loss; infections; and changes in environment.

Any changes in disease status in any organ system can result in behavior changes.

In the treatment of agitated, demented, elderly patients, authors of meta-analysis of controlled trials of the response to the traditional antipsychotics (phenothiazines, butyrophenones) in controlling agitation have concluded that the use of neuroleptics results in a response rate of 18%. Clearly neuroleptic therapy for behavior control should be limited with frequent attempts to withdraw the agent given for behavior control.

Clinical studies of haloperidol did not include sufficient numbers of subjects ≥65 years of age to determine whether they respond differently from younger subjects. Other reported clinical experience has not consistently identified differences between the elderly and younger patients. However, the prevalence of tardive dyskinesia appears to be highest among the elderly, especially elderly women. Also, the pharmacokinetics of haloperidol in geriatric patients generally warrants the use of lower doses.

Emetic Potential Very low (<10%)

Vesicant No

Dosage Forms Excipient information presented when available (limited, particularly for generics); consult specific product labeling. [DSC] = Discontinued product

Note: Strength expressed as base.

Injection, oil, as decanoate: 50 mg/mL (1 mL, 5 mL); 100 mg/mL (1 mL, 5 mL)

Haldol® Decanoate: 50 mg/mL (1 mL; 5 mL [DSC]); 100 mg/mL (1 mL; 5 mL [DSC]) [contains benzyl alcohol, sesame oil]

Injection, solution, as lactate: 5 mg/mL (1 mL, 10 mL)

Haldol®: 5 mg/mL (1 mL)
Solution, oral concentrate, as lactate: 2 mg/mL (15 mL, 120 mL)
Tablet: 0.5 mg, 1 mg, 2 mg, 5 mg, 10 mg, 20 mg

References

"American Academy of Pediatrics Committee on Drugs. The Transfer of Drugs and Other Chemicals Into Human Milk," *Pediatrics*, 2001, 108(3):776-89.

Aunsholt NA, "Prolonged QT Interval and Hypokalemia Caused by Haloperidol," *Acta Psychiatr Scand*, 1989, 79(4):411-2.

Barton MD, Libonati M, and Cohen PJ, "The Use of Haloperidol for Treatment of Postoperative Nausea and Vomiting - A Double-Blind Placebo-Controlled Trial," *Anesthesiology*, 1975, 42(4):508-12.

Bauer M, "Concurrent Agranulocytosis and Acute Hepatitis Resulting From Combination of Classic Neuroleptics and Subsequent Successful Clozapine Treatment," *Pharmacopsychiatry*, 1995, 28(1):29-31.

Cole RM, Robinson F, Harvey L, et al, "Successful Control of Intractable Nausea and Vomiting Requiring Combined Ondansetron and Haloperidol in a Patient With Advanced Cancer," *J Pain Symptom Manage*, 1994, 9(1):48-50.

Di Salvo TG and O'Gara PT, "Torsade de Pointes Caused by High-Dose Intravenous Haloperidol in Cardiac Patients," *Clin Cardiol*, 1995, 18(5):285-90.

Doenecke AL and Heuermann RC, "Treatment of Haloperidol Abuse With Diphenhydramine," *Am J Psychiatry*, 1980, 137(4):487-8.

Fisher H, "A New Approach to Emergency Department Therapy of Migraine Headache With Intravenous Haloperidol: A Case Series," *J Emerg Med*, 1995, 13(1):119-22.

Harada H, Igarashi M, Sugae S, et al, "A Schizophrenic Patient Who Developed Extreme Hypothermia After an Increase in the Dose of Haloperidol: A Case Report," *Jpn J Psychiatry Neurol*, 1994, 48(3):595-8.

Jacobi J, Fraser GL, Coursin DB, et al, "Clinical Practice Guidelines for the Sustained Use of Sedatives and Analgesics in the Critically Ill Adult," *Crit Care Med*, 2002, 30(1):119-41. Available at: http://www.sccm.org/pdf/sedatives.pdf. Accessed August 2, 2003.

Kubota T, Ishikura T, and Jibiki I, "Alopecia Areata Associated With Haloperidol," *Jpn J Psychiatry Neurol*, 1994, 48(3):579-81.

Mahutte CK, Nakasato SK, and Light RW, "Haloperidol and Sudden Death Due to Pulmonary Edema," *Arch Intern Med*, 1982, 142(10):1951-2.

Medlin R, Ransom M, and Kline J, "Ethanol Potentiates Electromechanical Depression Induced by Haloperidol," *Clin Toxicol*, 1995, 33(5):499.

Neidhart JA, Gagen MM, Wilson HE, et al, "Comparative Trial of the Antiemetic Effects of THC and Haloperidol," *J Clin Pharmacol*, 1981, 21(8-9 Suppl):38-42.

Peabody CA, Warner MD, Whiteford HA, et al, "Neuroleptics and the Elderly," *J Am Geriatr Soc*, 1987, 35(3):233-8.

Plotkin DA, Plotkin D, and Okun R, "Haloperidol in the Treatment of Nausea and Vomiting Due to Cytotoxic Drug Administration," *Curr Ther Res Clin Exp*,1973, 15(9):599-602.

Riker RR, Fraser GL, and Cox PM, "Continuous Infusion of Haloperidol Controls Agitation in Critically Ill Patients," *Crit Care Med*, 1994, 22(3):433-40.

Risse SC and Barnes R, "Pharmacologic Treatment of Agitation Associated With Dementia," *J Am Geriatr Soc*, 1986, 34(5):368-76.

Saltz BL, Woerner MG, Kane JM, et al, "Prospective Study of Tardive Dyskinesia Incidence in the Elderly," *JAMA*, 1991, 266(17):2402-6.

Schwartz M, Weller B, Erdreich M, et al, "Rabbit Syndrome and Tardive Dyskinesia: Two Complications of Chronic Neuroleptic Treatment," *J Clin Psychiatry*, 1995, 56(5):212.

Seifert RD, "Therapeutic Drug Monitoring: Psychotropic Drugs," *J Pharm Pract*, 1984, 6:403-16.

Serrano AC, "Haloperidol - Its Use in Children," *J Clin Psychiatry*, 1981, 42(4):154-6.

Sharma ND, Rosman HS, Padhi ID, et al, "Torsades de Pointes Associated With Intravenous Haloperidol in Critically Ill Patients," *Am J Cardiol*, 1998, 81(2):238-40.

Silvey L, Carpenter JT Jr, Wheeler RH, et al, "A Randomized Comparison of Haloperidol Plus Dexamethasone Versus Prochlorperazine Plus Dexamethasone in Preventing Nausea and Vomiting in Patients Receiving Chemotherapy for Breast Cancer," *J Clin Oncol*, 1988, 6(9):1397-400.

Spencer EK, Kafantaris V, Padron-Gayol MV, et al, "Haloperidol in Schizophrenic Children: Early Findings From a Study in Progress," *Psychopharmacol Bull*, 1992, 28(2):183-6.

Wilt JL, Minnema AM, Johnson RF, et al, "Torsade de Pointes Associated With the Use of Intravenous Haloperidol," *Ann Intern Med*, 1993, 119(3):391-4.

♦ **Haloperidol Decanoate** *see Haloperidol on page 526*
♦ **Haloperidol Injection, USP (Can)** *see Haloperidol on page 526*
♦ **Haloperidol-LA (Can)** *see Haloperidol on page 526*
♦ **Haloperidol Lactate** *see Haloperidol on page 526*

♦ **Haloperidol-LA Omega (Can)** *see Haloperidol on page 526*
♦ **Haloperidol Long Acting (Can)** *see Haloperidol on page 526*
♦ **Halotestin**® *see Fluoxymesterone on page 468*
♦ **Helixate**® **FS** *see Antihemophilic Factor (Recombinant) on page 95*
♦ **Hemofil M** *see Antihemophilic Factor (Human) on page 92*
♦ **Hemorrhoidal HC** *see Hydrocortisone on page 545*
♦ **Hemril**®**-30** *see Hydrocortisone on page 545*
♦ **Hepalean**® **(Can)** *see Heparin on page 532*
♦ **Hepalean**® **Leo (Can)** *see Heparin on page 532*
♦ **Hepalean**®**-LOK (Can)** *see Heparin on page 532*

Heparin (HEP a rin)
Medication Safety Issues
Sound-alike/look-alike issues:
Heparin may be confused with Hespan®

High alert medication: The Institute for Safe Medication Practices (ISMP) includes this medication among its list of drugs which have a heightened risk of causing significant patient harm when used in error.

Heparin sodium injection 10,000 units/mL and Hep-Lock U/P 10 units/mL have been confused with each other. Fatal medication errors have occurred between the two whose labels are both blue. **Never rely on color as a sole indicator to differentiate product identity.**

Heparin lock flush solution is intended only to maintain patency of I.V. devices and is **not** to be used for anticoagulant therapy.

Note: The 100 unit/mL concentration should not be used in neonates or infants <10 kg. The 10 unit/mL concentration may cause systemic anticoagulation in infants <1 kg who receive frequent flushes.

U.S. Brand Names HepFlush®-10; Hep-Lock®; Hep-Lock U/P
Index Terms Heparin Calcium; Heparin Lock Flush; Heparin Sodium
Generic Available Yes
Canadian Brand Names Hepalean®; Hepalean® Leo; Hepalean®-LOK
Pharmacologic Category Anticoagulant
Use Prophylaxis and treatment of thromboembolic disorders
Note: Heparin lock flush solution is intended only to maintain patency of I.V. devices and is **not** to be used for anticoagulant therapy.
Unlabeled/Investigational Use Acute MI - combination regimen of heparin (unlabeled dose), tenecteplase (half dose), and abciximab (full dose)
Pregnancy Risk Factor C
Lactation Does not enter breast milk/compatible
Labeled Contraindications Hypersensitivity to heparin or any component of the formulation; severe thrombocytopenia; uncontrolled active bleeding except when due to DIC; suspected intracranial hemorrhage; not for I.M. use; not for use when appropriate monitoring parameters cannot be obtained
Warnings/Precautions Hemorrhage is the most common complication. Risk factors for bleeding include bacterial endocarditis; congenital or acquired bleeding disorders; active ulcerative or angiodysplastic GI diseases; severe uncontrolled hypertension; hemorrhagic stroke; or use shortly after brain, spinal, or ophthalmology surgery; patient treated concomitantly with platelet inhibitors; conditions associated with increased bleeding tendencies (hemophilia, vascular purpura); recent GI bleeding; thrombocytopenia or platelet defects; severe liver disease; hypertensive or diabetic retinopathy; or in patients undergoing invasive procedures. A higher incidence of bleeding has

been reported in women >60 years of age. Discontinue heparin if hemorrhage occurs; severe hemorrhage or overdosage may require protamine.

May cause thrombocytopenia; monitor platelet count closely. Patients who develop thrombocytopenia on heparin may be at risk of developing a new thrombus (heparin-induced thrombocytopenia and thrombosis [HITT]). Discontinue therapy and consider alternatives if platelets are <100,000/mm^3 and/or thrombosis develops. HIT or HITT can occur up to several weeks after discontinuation of heparin. Hypersensitivity reactions can occur. Osteoporosis can occur following long-term use (>6 months). Monitor for hyperkalemia. Patients >60 years of age may require lower doses of heparin.

Some preparations contain benzyl alcohol as a preservative. In neonates, large amounts of benzyl alcohol (>100 mg/kg/day) have been associated with fatal toxicity (gasping syndrome). The use of preservative-free heparin is, therefore, recommended in neonates. Some preparations contain sulfite which may cause allergic reactions.

Heparin resistance may occur in patients with fever, thrombosis, thrombophlebitis, infections with thrombosing tendencies, MI, cancer, and in postsurgical patients.

Adverse Reactions
Cardiovascular: Chest pain, hemorrhagic shock, thrombosis, vasospasm (possibly related to thrombosis)

Central nervous system: Fever, headache, chills

Dermatologic: Unexplained bruising, urticaria, alopecia, dysesthesia pedis, purpura, eczema, cutaneous necrosis (following deep SubQ injection), erythematous plaques (case reports)

Endocrine & metabolic: Hyperkalemia (supression of aldosterone), rebound hyperlipidemia on discontinuation

Gastrointestinal: Nausea, vomiting, constipation, hematemesis

Genitourinary: Frequent or persistent erection

Hematologic: Hemorrhage, blood in urine, bleeding from gums, epistaxis, adrenal hemorrhage, ovarian hemorrhage, retroperitoneal hemorrhage, thrombocytopenia (see note)

Hepatic: Elevated liver enzymes (AST/ALT)

Local: Irritation, ulceration, cutaneous necrosis have been rarely reported with deep SubQ injections, I.M. injection (not recommended) is associated with a high incidence of these effects

Neuromuscular & skeletal: Peripheral neuropathy, osteoporosis (chronic therapy effect)

Ocular: Conjunctivitis (allergic reaction)

Respiratory: Hemoptysis, pulmonary hemorrhage, asthma, rhinitis, bronchospasm (case reports)

Miscellaneous: Allergic reactions, anaphylactoid reactions

Note: Thrombocytopenia has been reported to occur at an incidence between 0% and 30%. It is often of no clinical significance. However, immunologically mediated heparin-induced thrombocytopenia has been estimated to occur in 1% to 2% of patients, and is marked by a progressive fall in platelet counts and, in some cases, thromboembolic complications (skin necrosis, pulmonary embolism, gangrene of the extremities, stroke or MI). For recommendations regarding platelet monitoring during heparin therapy, consult "Seventh ACCP Consensus Conference on Antithrombotic and Thrombolytic Therapy."

Overdosage/Toxicology The primary symptom of overdose is bleeding. Antidote is protamine; dose 1 mg neutralizes 1 mg (100 units) of heparin. (Continued)

Heparin *(Continued)*

Discontinue all heparin if evidence of progressive immune thrombocytopenia occurs.

Drug Interactions

Increased Effect/Toxicity: The risk of hemorrhage associated with heparin may be increased by oral anticoagulants (warfarin), thrombolytics, dextran, and drugs which affect platelet function (eg, aspirin, NSAIDs, dipyridamole, ticlopidine, clopidogrel, IIb/IIIa antagonists). However, heparin is often used in conjunction with thrombolytic therapy or during the initiation of warfarin therapy to assure anticoagulation and to protect against possible transient hypercoagulability. Cephalosporins which contain the MTT side chain and parenteral penicillins (may inhibit platelet aggregation) may increase the risk of hemorrhage. Other drugs reported to increase heparin's anticoagulant effect include antihistamines, tetracycline, quinine, nicotine, and cardiac glycosides (digoxin).

Decreased Effect: Nitroglycerin (I.V.) may decrease heparin's anticoagulant effect. This interaction has not been validated in some studies, and may only occur at high nitroglycerin dosages.

Ethanol/Nutrition/Herb Interactions

Food: When taking for >6 months, may interfere with calcium absorption.

Herb/Nutraceutical: Avoid cat's claw, dong quai, evening primrose, feverfew, red clover, horse chestnut, garlic, green tea, ginseng, ginkgo (all have additional antiplatelet activity).

Storage/Stability Heparin solutions are colorless to slightly yellow. Minor color variations do not affect therapeutic efficacy. Heparin should be stored at controlled room temperature. Protect from freezing and temperatures >40°C.

Stability at room temperature and refrigeration:

Prepared bag: 24 hours.

Premixed bag: After seal is broken 4 days.

Out of overwrap stability: 30 days.

Reconstitution

Standard diluent: 25,000 units/500 mL D_5W (premixed).

Minimum volume: 250 mL D_5W.

Compatibility Stable in dextran 6% in dextrose, dextran 6% in NS, D_5LR, $D_5^1/_4NS$, $D_5^1/_2NS$, $D_{25}W$, fat emulsion 10%, $^1/_2NS$, NS; **variable stability (consult detailed reference)** in D_5NS, D_5W, $D_{10}W$, LR, peritoneal dialysis solutions, TPN.

Y-site administration: Compatible: Acyclovir, aldesleukin, allopurinol, amifostine, aminophylline, ampicillin, ampicillin/sulbactam, atracurium, atropine, aztreonam, betamethasone sodium phosphate, bleomycin, calcium gluconate, cefazolin, cefotetan, ceftazidime, ceftriaxone, chlordiazepoxide, chlorpromazine, cimetidine, cisplatin, cladribine, clindamycin, cyanocobalamin, cyclophosphamide, cytarabine, dexamethasone sodium phosphate, digoxin, diphenhydramine, docetaxel, dopamine, doxorubicin liposome, edrophonium, enalaprilat, epinephrine, erythromycin lactobionate, esmolol, estrogens (conjugated), ethacrynate, etoposide, famotidine, fentanyl, fluconazole, fludarabine, fluorouracil, foscarnet, furosemide, gemcitabine, granisetron, hydralazine, hydrocortisone sodium succinate, hydromorphone, insulin (regular), isoproterenol, kanamycin, leucovorin, lidocaine, linezolid, lorazepam, magnesium sulfate, melphalan, menadiol sodium diphosphate, meperidine, meropenem, methotrexate, methoxamine, methyldopate, methylergonovine, metoclopramide, metronidazole, midazolam, milrinone, minocycline, mitomycin, morphine, nafcillin, neostigmine, nitroglycerin, norepinephrine, ondansetron, oxacillin, oxytocin, paclitaxel, pancuronium, penicillin G potassium, pentazocine, phytonadione, piperacillin, piperacillin/tazobactam, potassium chloride, procainamide, prochlorperazine edisylate, propofol, propranolol, pyridostigmine, ranitidine, remifentanil, sargramostim, scopolamine, sodium bicarbonate, sodium nitroprusside, streptokinase, succinylcholine, tacrolimus, theophylline, thiopental, thiotepa, ticarcillin, ticarcillin/clavulanate potassium, tirofiban, trimethobenzamide, trimethaphan camsylate, vecuronium, vinblastine, vincristine, warfarin, zidovudine. **Incompatible:** Alatrofloxacin, alteplase, amiodarone, amphotericin B cholesteryl sulfate complex, amsacrine, ciprofloxacin, clarithromycin, diazepam, doxycycline, ergotamine, filgrastim, gatifloxacin, gentamicin, haloperidol, idarubicin, isosorbide dinitrate, levofloxacin, methotrimeprazine, nicardipine, phenytoin, tobramycin, triflupromazine, vancomycin. **Variable (consult detailed reference):** Cisatracurium, dacarbazine, diltiazem, dobutamine, doxorubicin, droperidol, droperidol and fentanyl, labetalol, methylprednisolone sodium succinate, promethazine, quinidine gluconate, TPN, vinorelbine.

Compatibility in syringe: Compatible: Aminophylline, amphotericin B, ampicillin, atropine, azlocillin, bleomycin, cefamandole, cefazolin, cefoperazone, cefotaxime, cefoxitin, chloramphenicol, cimetidine, cisplatin, clindamycin, cyclophosphamide, diatrizoate meglumine 52%, diatrizoate sodium 8%, diatrizoate sodium 60%, diazoxide, digoxin, dimenhydrinate, dobutamine, dopamine, epinephrine, fentanyl, fluorouracil, furosemide, iohexol, iopamidol, iothalamate meglumine 60%, ioxaglate meglumine 39.3%, ioxaglate sodium 19.6%, leucovorin, lidocaine, lincomycin, methotrexate, metoclopramide, mitomycin, nafcillin, naloxone, neostigmine, nitroglycerin, norepinephrine, pancuronium, penicillin G, phenobarbital, piperacillin, sodium nitroprusside, succinylcholine, trimethoprim/sulfamethoxazole, verapamil, vincristine. **Incompatible:** Amikacin, amiodarone, chlorpromazine, diazepam, doxorubicin, droperidol, droperidol and fentanyl, erythromycin, erythromycin lactobionate, gentamicin, haloperidol, kanamycin, meperidine, methotrimeprazine, pentazocine, promethazine, streptomycin, tobramycin, triflupromazine, vancomycin, warfarin. **Variable (consult detailed reference):** Morphine, vinblastine.

Compatibility when admixed: Compatible: Aminophylline, amphotericin B, amphotericin B with hydrocortisone sodium succinate, ascorbic acid injection, bleomycin, calcium gluconate, cefepime, chloramphenicol, clindamycin, colistimethate, dimenhydrinate, dopamine, enalaprilat, esmolol, floxacillin, fluconazole, flumazenil, furosemide, isoproterenol, lidocaine, lincomycin, magnesium sulfate, meropenem, methyldopate, methylprednisolone sodium succinate, metronidazole with sodium bicarbonate, nafcillin, norepinephrine, octreotide, penicillin G, potassium chloride, promazine, ranitidine, sodium bicarbonate, teicoplanin, verapamil, vitamin B complex, vitamin B complex with C. **Incompatible:** Alteplase, amikacin, atracurium, ciprofloxacin, cytarabine, daunorubicin, erythromycin lactobionate, gentamicin, hyaluronidase, kanamycin, levorphanol, meperidine, morphine, polymyxin B sulfate, promethazine, streptomycin. **Variable (consult detailed reference):** Dobutamine, hydrocortisone sodium succinate, mitomycin, penicillin G potassium, penicillin G sodium, vancomycin.

Mechanism of Action Potentiates the action of antithrombin III and thereby inactivates thrombin (as well as activated coagulation factors IX, X, XI, XII, and plasmin) and prevents the conversion of fibrinogen to fibrin; heparin also stimulates release of lipoprotein lipase (lipoprotein lipase hydrolyzes triglycerides to glycerol and free fatty acids)

(Continued)

Heparin *(Continued)*

Pharmacodynamics/Kinetics

Onset of action: Anticoagulation: I.V.: Immediate; SubQ: ~20-30 minutes

Absorption: Oral, rectal, I.M.: Erratic at best from all these routes of administration; SubQ absorption is also erratic, but considered acceptable for prophylactic use

Distribution: Does not cross placenta; does not enter breast milk

Metabolism: Hepatic; may be partially metabolized in the reticuloendothelial system

Half-life elimination: Mean: 1.5 hours; Range: 1-2 hours; affected by obesity, renal function, hepatic function, malignancy, presence of pulmonary embolism, and infections

Excretion: Urine (small amounts as unchanged drug)

Dosage

Children:

Intermittent I.V.: Initial: 50-100 units/kg, then 50-100 units/kg every 4 hours

I.V. infusion: Initial: 50 units/kg, then 15-25 units/kg/hour; increase dose by 2-4 units/kg/hour every 6-8 hours as required

Adults:

Prophylaxis (low-dose heparin): SubQ: 5000 units every 8-12 hours

Intermittent I.V.: Initial: 10,000 units, then 50-70 units/kg (5000-10,000 units) every 4-6 hours

I.V. infusion (weight-based dosing per institutional nomogram recommended):

Acute coronary syndromes: MI: Fibrinolytic therapy:

Full-dose alteplase, reteplase, or tenecteplase with dosing as follows: Concurrent bolus of 60 units/kg (maximum: 4000 units), then 12 units/kg/hour (maximum: 1000 units) as continuous infusion. Check aPTT every 4-6 hours; adjust to target of 1.5-2 times the upper limit of control (50-70 seconds in clinical trials); usual range 10-30 units/kg/hour. Duration of heparin therapy depends on concurrent therapy and the specific patient risks for systemic or venous thromboembolism.

Combination regimen (unlabeled): Half-dose tenecteplase (15-25 mg based on weight) and abciximab 0.25 mg/kg bolus then 0.125 mcg/kg/minute (maximum 10 mcg/minute) for 12 hours with heparin dosing as follows: Concurrent bolus of 40 units/kg (maximum 3000 units), then 7 units/kg/hour (maximum: 800 units/hour) as continuous infusion. Adjust to a aPTT target of 50-70 seconds.

Streptokinase: Heparin use optional depending on concurrent therapy and specific patient risks for systemic or venous thromboembolism (anterior MI, CHF, previous embolus, atrial fibrillation, LV thrombus): If heparin is administered, start when aPTT <2 times the upper limit of control; do not use a bolus, but initiate infusion adjusted to a target aPTT of 1.5-2 times the upper limit of control (50-70 seconds in clinical trials). If heparin is not administered by infusion, 7500-12,500 units SubQ every 12 hours (when aPTT <2 times the upper limit of control) is recommended.

Percutaneous coronary intervention: Heparin bolus and infusion may be administered to an activated clotting time (ACT) of 300-350 seconds if no concurrent GPIIb/IIIa receptor antagonist is administered or 200-250 seconds if a GPIIb/IIIa receptor antagonist is administered.

Treatment of unstable angina (high-risk and some intermediate-risk patients): Initial bolus of 60-70 units/kg (maximum: 5000 units), followed by an initial infusion of 12-15 units/kg/hour (maximum: 1000 units/hour). The American College of Chest Physicians consensus conference has recommended dosage adjustments to correspond to a therapeutic range equivalent to heparin levels of 0.3-0.7 units/mL by antifactor Xa determinations.

Treatment of venous thromboembolism:

DVT/PE: I.V. push: 80 units/kg followed by continuous infusion of 18 units/kg/hour

DVT: SubQ: 17,500 units every 12 hours

Line flushing: When using daily flushes of heparin to maintain patency of single and double lumen central catheters, 10 units/mL is commonly used for younger infants (eg, <10 kg) while 100 units/mL is used for older infants, children, and adults. Capped PVC catheters and peripheral heparin locks require flushing more frequently (eg, every 6-8 hours). Volume of heparin flush is usually similar to volume of catheter (or slightly greater). Additional flushes should be given when stagnant blood is observed in catheter, after catheter is used for drug or blood administration, and after blood withdrawal from catheter.

Addition of heparin (0.5-3 unit/mL) to peripheral and central parenteral nutrition has not been shown to decrease catheter-related thrombosis. The final concentration of heparin used for TPN solutions may need to be decreased to 0.5 units/mL in small infants receiving larger amounts of volume in order to avoid approaching therapeutic amounts. Arterial lines are heparinized with a final concentration of 1 unit/mL.

Dosing adjustments in the elderly: Patients >60 years of age may have higher serum levels and clinical response (longer aPTTs) as compared to younger patients receiving similar dosages; lower dosages may be required

Administration SubQ: Inject in subcutaneous tissue only (not muscle tissue). Injection sites should be rotated (usually left and right portions of the abdomen, above iliac crest).

Do not administer I.M. due to pain, irritation, and hematoma formation; central venous catheters must be flushed with heparin solution when newly inserted, daily (at the time of tubing change), after blood withdrawal or transfusion, and after an intermittent infusion through an injectable cap. A volume of at least 10 mL of blood should be removed and discarded from a heparinized line before blood samples are sent for coagulation testing.

Monitoring Parameters Platelet counts, hemoglobin, hematocrit, signs of bleeding; aPTT or ACT depending upon indication

For intermittent I.V. injections, aPTT is measured 3.5-4 hours after I.V. injection

Note: Continuous I.V. infusion is preferred over I.V. intermittent injections. For full-dose heparin (ie, nonlow-dose), the dose should be titrated according to aPTT results. For anticoagulation, an aPTT 1.5-2.5 times normal is usually desired. Because of variation among hospitals in the control aPTT values, nomograms should be established at each institution, designed to achieve aPTT values in the target range (eg, for a control aPTT of 30 seconds, the target range [1.5-2.5 times control] would be 45-75 seconds). Measurements should be made prior to heparin therapy, 6 hours after initiation, and 6 hours after any dosage change, and should be used to adjust the heparin infusion until the aPTT exhibits a therapeutic level. When two consecutive aPTT values are therapeutic, the measurements may be made every 24 hours, and if necessary, dose adjustment carried out. In (Continued)

Heparin *(Continued)*

addition, a significant change in the patient's clinical condition (eg, recurrent ischemia, bleeding, hypotension) should prompt an immediate aPTT determination, followed by dose adjustment if necessary. Increase or decrease infusion by 2-4 units/kg/hour dependent upon aPTT.

Heparin infusion dose adjustment:
aPTT >3x control: Decrease infusion rate 50%
aPTT 2-3x control: Decrease infusion rate 25%
aPTT 1.5-2x control: No change
aPTT <1.5x control: Increase rate of infusion 25%; max 2500 units/hour

Test Interactions Increased thyroxine (S) (competitive protein binding methods); increased PT

Aprotinin significantly increases aPTT and celite Activated Clotting Time (ACT) which may not reflect the actual degree of anticoagulation by heparin. Kaolin-based ACTs are not affected by aprotinin to the same degree as celite ACTs. While institutional protocols may vary, a minimal celite ACT of 750 seconds or kaolin-ACT of 480 seconds is recommended in the presence of aprotinin. Consult the manufacturer's information on specific ACT test interpretation in the presence of aprotinin.

Special Geriatric Considerations In the clinical setting, age has not been shown to be a reliable predictor of a patient's anticoagulant response to heparin. However, it is common for the elderly to have a "standard" response for the first 24-48 hours after a loading dose (5000 units) and a maintenance infusion of 800-1000 units/hour. After this period, they then have an exaggerated response (ie, elevated PTT), requiring a lower infusion rate. Hence, monitor closely during this period of therapy. Elderly women are more likely to have bleeding complications and osteoporosis may be a problem when used >3 months or total daily dose exceeds 30,000 units.

Additional Information Heparin lock flush solution is intended only to maintain patency of I.V. devices and is **not** to be used for anticoagulant therapy.

Dosage Forms Excipient information presented when available (limited, particularly for generics); consult specific product labeling.

Infusion, as sodium [premixed in NaCl 0.45%; porcine intestinal mucosa source]: 12,500 units (250 mL); 25,000 units (250 mL, 500 mL)

Infusion, as sodium [preservative free; premixed in D₅W; porcine intestinal mucosa source]: 10,000 units (100 mL) [contains sodium metabisulfite]; 12,500 units (250 mL) [contains sodium metabisulfite]; 20,000 units (500 mL) [contains sodium metabisulfite]; 25,000 units (250 mL, 500 mL) [contains sodium metabisulfite]

Infusion, as sodium [preservative free; premixed in NaCl 0.9%; porcine intestinal mucosa source]: 1000 units (500 mL); 2000 units (1000 mL)

Injection, solution, as sodium [lock flush preparation; porcine intestinal mucosa source; multidose vial]: 10 units/mL (1 mL, 10 mL, 30 mL) [contains parabens]; 100 units/mL (1 mL, 5 mL) [contains parabens]

Injection, solution, as sodium [lock flush preparation; porcine intestinal mucosa source; multidose vial]: 10 units/mL (10 mL, 30 mL); 100 units/mL (10 mL, 30 mL)

Hep-Lock®: 10 units/mL (1 mL, 2 mL, 10 mL, 30 mL); 100 units/mL (1 mL, 2 mL, 10 mL, 30 mL) [contains benzyl alcohol]

Injection, solution, as sodium [lock flush preparation; porcine intestinal mucosa source; prefilled syringe]: 10 units/mL (1 mL, 2 mL, 3 mL, 5 mL); 100 units/mL (1 mL, 2 mL, 3 mL, 5 mL) [contains benzyl alcohol]

Injection, solution, as sodium [preservative free; lock flush preparation; porcine intestinal mucosa source; prefilled syringe]: 100 units/mL (5 mL)

Injection, solution, as sodium [preservative free; lock flush preparation; porcine intestinal mucosa source; vial]:

HepFlush®-10: 10 units/mL (10 mL)

Hep-Lock U/P: 10 units/mL (1 mL); 100 units/mL (1 mL)

Injection, solution, as sodium [porcine intestinal mucosa source; multidose vial]: 1000 units/mL (1 mL, 10 mL, 30 mL) [contains benzyl alcohol]; 1000 units/mL (1 mL, 10 mL, 30 mL) [contains methylparabens]; 5000 units/mL (1 mL, 10 mL) [contains benzyl alcohol]; 5000 units/mL (1 mL) [contains methylparabens]; 10,000 units/mL (1 mL, 4 mL) [contains benzyl alcohol]; 10,000 units/mL (1 mL, 5 mL) [contains methylparabens]; 20,000 units/mL (1 mL) [contains methylparabens]

Injection, solution, as sodium [porcine intestinal mucosa source; prefilled syringe]: 5000 units/mL (1 mL) [contains benzyl alcohol]

Injection, solution, as sodium [preservative free; porcine intestinal mucosa source; prefilled syringe]: 10,000 units/mL (0.5 mL)

Injection, solution, as sodium [preservative free; porcine intestinal mucosa source; vial]: 1000 units/mL (2 mL); 2000 units/mL (5 mL); 2500 units/mL (10 mL)

References

Anderson JL, Adams CD, Antman EM, et al, "ACC/AHA 2007 Guidelines for the Management of Patients With Unstable Angina/Non-ST-Elevation Myocardial Infarction: A Report of the American College of Cardiology/American Heart Association Task Force on Practice Guidelines (Writing Committee to Revise the 2002 Guidelines for the Management of Patients With Unstable Angina/Non-ST-Elevation Myocardial Infarction) Developed in Collaboration With the American College of Emergency Physicians, the Society for Cardiovascular Angiography and Interventions, and the Society of Thoracic Surgeons endorsed by the American Association of Cardiovascular and Pulmonary Rehabilitation and the Society for Academic Emergency Medicine" *J Am Coll Cardiol*, 2007, 50(7):e1-e157.

Antman EM, Anbe DT, Armstrong PW, et al, "ACC/AHA Guidelines for the Management of Patients With ST-Elevation Myocardial Infarction: A Report of the American College of Cardiology/American Heart Association Task Force on Practice Guidelines (Committee to Revise the 1999 Guidelines for the Management of Patients with Acute Myocardial Infarction)," *Circulation*, 2004, 110(9):e82-292.

Broderick J, Connolly S, Feldmann E, et al, "Guidelines for the Management of Spontaneous Intracerebral Hemorrhage in Adults: 2007 Update: A Guideline From the American Heart Association/American Stroke Association Stroke Council, High Blood Pressure Research Council, and the Quality of Care and Outcomes in Research Interdisciplinary Working Group," *Stroke*, 2007, 38(6):2001-23. Available at http://stroke.ahajournals.org/cgi/content/short/STROKEAHA.107.183689.

Dager WE and White RH, "Pharmacotherapy of Heparin-Induced Thrombocytopenia," *Expert Opin Pharmacother*, 2003, 4(6):919-40.

Greinacher A, Janssens U, Berg G, et al, "Lepirudin (Recombinant Hirudin) for Parenteral Anticoagulation in Patients With Heparin-Induced Thrombocytopenia. Heparin-Associated Thrombocytopenia Study (HAT) Investigators," *Circulation*, 1999, 100(6):587-93.

Greinacher A, Volpel H, Janssens U, et al, "Recombinant Hirudin (Lepirudin) Provides Safe and Effective Anticoagulation in Patients With Heparin-Induced Thrombocytopenia: A Prospective Study," *Circulation*, 1999, 99(1):73-80.

Klerk CP, Smorenburg SM, and Buller HR, "Thrombosis Prophylaxis in Patient Populations With a Central Venous Catheter: A Systematic Review," *Arch Intern Med*, 2003, 163(16):1913-21.

Raschke RA, Reilly BM, Guidry JR, et al, "The Weight-Based Heparin Dosing Nomogram Compared With a "Standard Care" Nomogram: A Randomized Controlled Trial," *Ann Intern Med*, 1993, 119(9):874-81.

Savi P, Chong BH, Greinacher A, et al, "Effect of Fondaparinux on Platelet Activation in the Presence of Heparin-Dependent Antibodies: A Blinded Comparative Multicenter Study With Unfractionated Heparin," *Blood*, 2005, 105(1):139-44.

"Seventh ACCP Consensus Conference on Antithrombotic and Thrombolytic Therapy," *Chest*, 2004, 126(3 Suppl):172-608.

Sinnaeve PR, Alexander JH, Bogaerts K, et al, "Efficacy of Tenecteplase in Combination With Enoxaparin, Abciximab, or Unfractionated Heparin: One-Year Follow-Up Results of the Assessment of the Safety of a New Thrombolytic-3 (ASSENT-3) Randomized Trial in Acute Myocardial Infarction," *Am Heart J*, 2004, 147(6):993-8.

Verma AK, Levine M, Shalansky SJ, et al, "Frequency of Heparin-Induced Thrombocytopenia in Critical Care Patients," *Pharmacotherapy*, 2003, 23(6):745-53.

(Continued)

Heparin *(Continued)*

Warkentin TE and Greinacher A, "Heparin-Induced Thrombocytopenia: Recognition, Treatment, and Prevention: The Seventh ACCP Conference on Antithrombotic and Thrombolytic Therapy," *Chest*, 2004, 126(3 Suppl):311-37.

Warkentin TE and Kelton JG, "Temporal Aspects of Heparin-Induced Thrombocytopenia," *N Engl J Med*, 2001, 344(17):1286-92.

Warkentin TE, "Heparin-Induced Thrombocytopenia: A Clinicopathologic Syndrome," *Thromb Haemost*, 1999, 82(2):439-47.

Warkentin TE, Levine MN, Hirsch J, et al, "Heparin-Induced Thrombocytopenia in Patients Treated With Low-Molecular Weight Heparin or Unfractionated Heparin," *N Engl J Med*, 1995, 332(20):1330-5.

Histrelin *(his TREL in)*

U.S. Brand Names Supprelin® LA; Vantas™

Index Terms GnRH Agonist; Histrelin Acetate; LH-RH Agonist

Generic Available No

Canadian Brand Names Vantas™

Pharmacologic Category Gonadotropin Releasing Hormone Agonist

Use Palliative treatment of advanced prostate cancer; treatment of children with central precocious puberty (CPP)

Pregnancy Risk Factor X

Lactation Excretion in breast milk unknown/contraindicated

Labeled Contraindications Hypersensitivity to histrelin acetate, GnRH, GnRH-agonist analogs, or any component of the formulation; pregnancy

Warnings/Precautions

CPP: Transient increases in estradiol serum levels (female) or testosterone levels (female and male) may occur during the first week of use. Worsening symptoms may occur, however, manifestations of puberty should decrease within 4 weeks. Safety and efficacy have not been established in children <2 years of age

Prostate cancer: Transient increases in testosterone serum levels occur during the first week of use (initial flare). Worsening symptoms such as bone pain, hematuria, neuropathy, ureteral or bladder outlet obstruction, and spinal cord compression have been reported. Spinal cord compression and ureteral obstruction may contribute to paralysis; close attention should be given during the first few weeks of therapy to both patients having metastatic vertebral lesions and/or urinary tract obstructions, and to any patients reporting weakness, paresthesias or poor urine output. Safety and efficacy have not been established in patients with hepatic dysfunction.

Adverse Reactions

CPP:

>10%: Local: Insertion site reaction (51%; includes bruising, discomfort, itching, pain, protrusion of implant area, soreness, swelling, tingling)

>2% to 10%:
  Endocrine & metabolic: Metrorrhagia (4%)
  Local: Keloid scar (6%), scar (6%), suture-related complication (6%), pain at the application site (4%), post procedural pain (4%)
≤2%: Amblyopia, breast tenderness, cold feeling, disease progression, dysmenorrhea, epistaxis, erythema, flu-like syndrome, gynecomastia, headache, infection at the implant site, menorrhagia, migraine, mood swings, pituitary adenoma, pruritus, weight increase

Prostate cancer:
>10%:
  Endocrine & metabolic: Hot flashes (66%)
  Local: Implant site reaction (6% to 14%; includes bruising, erythema, pain, soreness, swelling, tenderness)
2% to 10%:
  Central nervous system: Fatigue (10%), headache (3%), insomnia (3%)
  Endocrine & metabolic: Gynecomastia (4%), sexual dysfunction (4%), libido decreased (2%)
  Gastrointestinal: Constipation (4%), weight gain (2%)
  Genitourinary: Expected pharmacological consequence of testosterone suppression: Testicular atrophy (5%)
  Renal: Renal impairment (5%)
<2%: Abdominal discomfort, alopecia, anemia, appetite increased, arthralgia, AST increased, back pain, bone density decreased, bone pain, breast pain, breast tenderness, cold feeling, contusion, craving food, creatinine increased, depression, diaphoresis, dizziness, dyspnea (exertional), dysuria, fluid retention, flushing, genital pruritus, hematoma, hematuria, hypercalcemia, hypercholesterolemia, hyperglycemia, irritability, LDH increased, lethargy, limb pain, liver disorder, malaise, muscle twitching, myalgia, nausea, neck pain, night sweats, palpitation, peripheral edema, prostatic acid phosphatase increased, pruritus, renal calculi, renal failure, stent occlusion, testosterone increased, tremor, urinary frequency, urinary retention, ventricular asystoles, weakness, weight loss

Drug Interactions
  Decreased Effect: Histrelin may decrease the absorption of digoxin tablets.

Storage/Stability Supprelin® LA, Vantas™: Upon delivery, separate contents of implant carton. Store implant under refrigeration at 2°C to 8°C (36°F to 46°F), wrapped in the amber pouch for protection from light. Do not freeze. The implantation kit does not require refrigeration.

Mechanism of Action Potent inhibitor of gonadotropin secretion; continuous administration results in, after an initiation phase, the suppression of luteinizing hormone (LH), follicle-stimulating hormone (FSH), and a subsequent decrease in testosterone (females and males) and estrogen (premenopausal females). Additionally, in patients with CPP, linear growth velocity is slowed (improves chance of attaining predicted adult height).

Pharmacodynamics/Kinetics
  Onset: Prostate cancer: Chemical castration: 2-4 weeks; CPP: progression of sexual development stops and growth is decreased in ~1 month
  Duration: 1 year
  Distribution: Adults: V_d: ~58 L
  Protein binding: Adults: 70% ± 9%
  Metabolism: Hepatic via C-terminal dealkylation and hydrolysis
  Bioavailability: Adults: 92%
  Half-life elimination: Adults: Terminal: ~4 hours
  Time to peak, serum: Adults: 12 hours
  (Continued)

Histrelin *(Continued)*

Dosage SubQ:

Children ≥2 years: CPP (Supprelin® LA): 50 mg implant surgically inserted every 12 months. Discontinue at the appropriate time for the onset of puberty.

Adults: Prostate cancer (Vantas™): 50 mg implant surgically inserted every 12 months

Elderly: See adult dosing

Dosage adjustment in renal impairment: Cl_{cr}: 15-60 mL/minute: Adjustment not needed

Administration SubQ: Surgical implantation into the inner portion of the upper arm requires the use of the implantation device provided. Use the patient's nondominant arm for placement. Removal must occur after 12 months; a replacement implant may be required. Palpate area of incision to locate implant for removal. If not readily palpated, ultrasound, CT or MRI may be used to locate implant; plain films are not recommended because the implant is not radiopaque.

Monitoring Parameters

CPP: LH, FSH, estradiol or testosterone (after 1 month then every 6 months); height, bone age (every 6-12 months); tanner staging

Prostate cancer: LH and FSH levels, serum testosterone levels, prostate specific antigen (PSA), bone mineral density; weakness, paresthesias, and urinary tract obstruction (especially during first few weeks of therapy)

Test Interactions Results of diagnostic test of pituitary gonadotropic and gonadal functions may be affected during and after therapy

Patient Information May experience disease flare (increased bone pain) and urinary retention during early treatment (usually resolves). Until response to drug is known use caution when driving or engaging in tasks that require alertness; dizziness, headache, lethargy or faintness may occur. Wait at least 24 hours before allowing moisture or water to touch the arm and 7 days before participating in strenuous exertion or heavy lifting. Wear lighter clothing or seek a cooler environment if hot flashes or flushing occur. May develop swelling or tenderness of the breast or a decrease in libido. Notify prescriber if any of the following occur: rapid heartbeat, palpitations, chest pain, inability to void or changes in urinary pattern; continual nausea or vomiting, numbness of extremities, or pain or swelling at implantation site.

Dosage Forms Excipient information presented when available (limited, particularly for generics); consult specific product labeling.

Implant, subcutaneous:

Supprelin® LA: 50 mg (1) [releases ~65 mcg/day over 12 months; packaged with implantation kit]

Vantas™: 50 mg (1) [releases 50-60 mcg/day over 12 months; packaged with implantation kit]

References

Dineen MK, Tierney DS, Kuzma P, et al, "An Evaluation of the Pharmacokinetics and Pharmacodynamics of the Histrelin Implant for the Palliative Treatment of Prostate Cancer," *J Clin Pharmacol*, 2005, 45(11):1245-9.

Schlegel PN, Histrelin Study Group, "Efficacy and Safety of Histrelin Subdermal Implant in Patients With Advanced Prostate Cancer," *J Urol*, 2006, 175(4):1353-8.

♦ **Histrelin Acetate** *see* Histrelin *on page 540*

♦ **HMM** *see* Altretamine *on page 50*

♦ **HMR 3647** *see* Telithromycin *on page 1007*

♦ **HN₂** *see* Mechlorethamine *on page 700*

♦ **Horse Antihuman Thymocyte Gamma Globulin** *see* Antithymocyte Globulin (Equine) *on page 100*

+ **HPV Vaccine** *see* Papillomavirus (Types 6, 11, 16, 18) Recombinant Vaccine *on page 878*

+ **Humanized IgG1 Anti-CD52 Monoclonal Antibody** *see* Alemtuzumab *on page 34*

+ **Human Papillomavirus Vaccine** *see* Papillomavirus (Types 6, 11, 16, 18) Recombinant Vaccine *on page 878*

+ **HXM** *see* Altretamine *on page 50*

Hyaluronidase (hye al yoor ON i dase)
Medication Safety Issues
Sound-alike/look-alike issues:
Wydase may be confused with Lidex®, Wyamine®

U.S. Brand Names Amphadase™; Hydase™; Hylenex™; Vitrase®

Generic Available No

Pharmacologic Category Enzyme

Use Increase the dispersion and absorption of other drugs; increase rate of absorption of parenteral fluids given by hypodermoclysis; adjunct in subcutaneous urography for improving resorption of radiopaque agents

Unlabeled/Investigational Use Management of drug extravasations

Pregnancy Risk Factor C

Lactation Excretion in breast milk unknown/use caution

Labeled Contraindications Hypersensitivity to hyaluronidase or any component of the formulation

Warnings/Precautions Do not inject in or around infected or inflamed areas; may spread localized infection. Should not be used for extravasation management of dopamine or alpha agonists or to reduce swelling of bites or stings. Do not administer intravenously. Do not apply directly to the cornea. Discontinue if sensitization occurs.

Adverse Reactions
Frequency not defined:
Cardiovascular: Edema
Local: Injection site reactions
<1%: Allergic reactions, anaphylactic-like reactions (retrobulbar block or I.V. injections), angioedema, urticaria

Overdosage/Toxicology Symptoms of overdose include local edema, urticaria, erythema, chills, nausea, vomiting, dizziness, tachycardia, and hypotension. Treatment is symptom-directed and supportive.

Drug Interactions
Increased Effect/Toxicity: Absorption and toxicity of local anesthetics may be increased.

Storage/Stability
Amphadase™, Hydase™, Hylenex™: Store in refrigerator at 2°C to 8°C (35°F to 46°F); do not freeze.

Vitrase®: Store unopened vial in refrigerator at 2°C to 8°C (35°F to 46°F). After reconstitution, store at 20°C to 25°C (68°F to 77°F) and use within 6 hours.

Reconstitution Vitrase®: Add 6.2 mL of NaCl to vial (1000 units/mL). Further dilute with NaCl before administration.

For 50 units/mL, draw up 0.05 mL of hyaluronidase reconstituted solution (1000 units/mL) and add 0.95 mL of NaCl.

For 75 units/mL, draw up 0.075 mL of hyaluronidase reconstituted solution and add 0.925 mL of NaCl.

For 150 units/mL, draw up 0.15 mL of hyaluronidase reconstituted solution and add 0.85 mL of NaCl.

(Continued)

Hyaluronidase *(Continued)*

For 300 units/mL, draw up 0.3 mL of hyaluronidase reconstituted solution and add 0.7 mL of NaCl.

Compatibility Stable in dextran 6% in dextrose, dextran 6% in NS, D$_5$LR, D$_5$1/4NS, D$_5$1/2NS, D$_5$NS, D$_5$W, D$_{10}$W, LR, 1/2NS, NS.

Compatibility in syringe: Compatible: Diatrizoate meglumine 34.3%, diatrizoate sodium 35%, iothalamate meglumine 60%, iothalamate sodium 80%, pentobarbital, thiopental. **Incompatible:** Hydromorphone. **Variable (consult detailed reference):** Diatrizoate meglumine 52%, diatrizoate sodium 8%, diatrizoate sodium 75%, iodipamide meglumine 52%.

Compatibility when admixed: Compatible: Amikacin, sodium bicarbonate. **Incompatible:** Benzodiazepines, epinephrine, furosemide, heparin, phenytoin.

Mechanism of Action Modifies the permeability of connective tissue through hydrolysis of hyaluronic acid, one of the chief components of tissue cement which offers resistance to diffusion of liquids through tissues; hyaluronidase increases both the distribution and absorption of locally injected substances.

Pharmacodynamics/Kinetics

Onset of action: SubQ: Immediate

Duration: 24-48 hours

Dosage Note: A preliminary skin test for hypersensitivity can be performed. ACTH, antihistamines, corticosteroids, estrogens, and salicylates, when used in large doses, may cause tissues to be partly resistant to hyaluronidase. May require larger doses of hyaluronidase for the same effect.

Skin test: Intradermal: 0.02 mL (3 units) of a 150 units/mL solution. Positive reaction consists of a wheal with pseudopods appearing within 5 minutes and persisting for 20-30 minutes with localized itching.

Hypodermoclysis: SubQ: 15 units is added to each 100 mL of I.V. fluid to be administered; 150 units facilitates absorption of >1000 mL of solution

Premature Infants and Neonates: Volume of a single clysis should not exceed 25 mL/kg and the rate of administration should not exceed 2 mL/minute

Children <3 years: Volume of a single clysis should not exceed 200 mL

Children ≥3 years and Adults: Rate and volume of a single clysis should not exceed those used for infusion of I.V. fluids

Urography: Children and Adults: SubQ: 75 units over each scapula followed by injection of contrast medium at the same site; patient should be in the prone position.

Extravasation (unlabeled use): Adults: SubQ: Inject 1 mL of a 150 unit/mL solution (as 5-10 injections of 0.1-0.2 mL) into affected area; doses of 15-250 units have been reported. **Note:** Do not use for extravasation of pressor agents (eg, dopamine, norepinephrine).

Elderly: See adult dosing. Adjust dose carefully to individual patient.

Administration Do **not** administer I.V.

Special Geriatric Considerations The most common use of hyaluronidase in the elderly is in hypodermoclysis. Hypodermoclysis is very useful in dehydrated patients in whom oral intake is minimal and I.V. access is a problem.

Additional Information

Amphadase™ pH: 6.8

Hydase™: pH: 6.9, osmolality: 275-305 mOsm

Hylenex™: pH: 7.4, osmolality: 290-350 mOsm

Vitrase® pH: ~6.7

Dosage Forms Excipient information presented when available (limited, particularly for generics); consult specific product labeling.

Injection, powder for reconstitution:
   Vitrase®: 6200 units [ovine derived; contains lactose]
Injection, solution:
   Amphadase™: 150 units/mL (1 mL) [bovine derived; contains edetate diso-
   dium 1 mg, thimerosal ≤0.1 mg]
Injection, solution [preservative free]:
   Hydase™: 150 units/mL (1 mL) [bovine derived; contains edetate disodium
   1 mg]
   Hylenex™: 150 units/mL (1 mL, 2 mL) [recombinant; contains human
   albumin and edetate disodium]
   Vitrase®: 200 units/mL (2 mL) [ovine derived; contains lactose]

References

Albanell J and Baselga J, "Systemic Therapy Emergencies," *Semin Oncol*, 2000, 27(3):347-61.
Berger EY, "Nutrition by Hypodermoclysis," *J Am Geriatr Soc*, 1984, 32(3):199-203.
Bertelli G, "Prevention and Management of Extravasation of Cytotoxic Drugs," *Drug Saf*, 1995, 12(4):245-55.
Bertelli G, Dini D, Forno GB, et al, "Hyaluronidase as an Antidote to Extravasation of Vinca Alkaloids: Clinical Results," *J Cancer Res Clin Oncol*, 1994, 120(8):505-6.
Cochran ST, Bomyea K, and Kahn M, "Treatment of Iodinated Contrast Material Extravasation With Hyaluronidase," *Acad Radiol*, 2002, 9(Suppl 2):544-6.
Dorr RT, "Vinca Alkaloid Ulceration: Experimental Mouse Model and Effects of Local Antidotes," *Proc Am Soc Clin Oncol*, 1982, 1:428.
Elam EA, Dorr RT, Lagel KE, et al, "Cutaneous Ulceration Due to Contrast Extravasation. Experimental Assessment of Injury and Potential Antidotes," *Invest Radiol*, 1991, 26(1):13-6.
Kumar MM and Sprung J, "The Use of Hyaluronidase to Treat Mannitol Extravasation," *Anesth Analg*, 2003, 97(4):1199-200.
Lipschitz S, Campbell AJ, Roberts MS, et al, "Subcutaneous Fluid Administration in Elderly Subjects: Validation of an Underused Technique," *J Am Geriatr Soc*, 1991, 39(1):6-9.
Raszka WV Jr, Kueser TK, Smith FR, et al, "The Use of Hyaluronidase in the Treatment of Intravenous Extravasation Injuries," *J Perinatol*, 19909, 10(2):146-9.
Sokol DK, Dahlmann A, and Dunn DW, "Hyaluronidase Treatment for Intravenous Phenytoin Extravasation," *J Child Neurol*, 1998, 13(5):246-7.
Zenk KE, "Hyaluronidase: An Antidote for Intravenous Extravasations," *CSHP Voice*, 1981, 66-8.
Zenk KE, "Management of Intravenous Extravasations," *Infusion*, 1981, 5:77-9.
Zenk KE, "Treating I.V. Extravasations With Hyaluronidase," *ASHP Signal*, 1986, 10:25,29.
Zenk KE, Dungy CI, and Greene GR, "Nafcillin Extravasation Injury: Use of Hyaluronidase as an Antidote," *Am J Dis Child*, 1981, 135(12):1113-4.

- **Hycamptamine** *see* Topotecan *on page 1048*
- **Hycamtin®** *see* Topotecan *on page 1048*
- **Hycort™ (Can)** *see* Hydrocortisone *on page 545*
- **Hydase™** *see* Hyaluronidase *on page 543*
- **Hydeltra T.B.A.® (Can)** *see* PrednisoLONE *on page 914*
- **Hyderm (Can)** *see* Hydrocortisone *on page 545*
- **Hydrea®** *see* Hydroxyurea *on page 559*

Hydrocortisone (hye droe KOR ti sone)

Medication Safety Issues

Sound-alike/look-alike issues:
   Hydrocortisone may be confused with hydrocodone, hydroxychloroquine, hydrochlorothiazide
   Anusol® may be confused with Anusol-HC®, Aplisol®, Aquasol®
   Anusol-HC® may be confused with Anusol®
   Cortef® may be confused with Lortab®
   Cortizone® may be confused with cortisone
   HCT (occasional abbreviation for hydrocortisone) is an error-prone abbre-
   viation (mistaken as hydrochlorothiazide)
   Hytone® may be confused with Vytone®
   Proctocort® may be confused with ProctoCream®
(Continued)

Hydrocortisone *(Continued)*

ProctoCream® may be confused with Proctocort®

International issues:

Hytone® may be confused with Hysone® [Australia]

Nutracort® may be confused with Nitrocor® which is a brand name of nitroglycerin in Chile and Italy

U.S. Brand Names Anucort-HC®; Anusol-HC®; Anusol® HC-1 [OTC]; Aquanil™ HC [OTC]; Beta-HC®; Caldecort® [OTC]; Cetacort® [DSC]; Colocort®; Cortaid® Intensive Therapy [OTC]; Cortaid® Maximum Strength [OTC]; Cortaid® Sensitive Skin [OTC]; Cortef®; Corticool® [OTC]; Cortifoam®; Cortizone®-10 Maximum Strength [OTC]; Cortizone®-10 Plus Maximum Strength [OTC]; Cortizone®-10 Quick Shot [OTC]; Dermarest Dricort® [OTC]; Dermtex® HC [OTC]; EarSol® HC; Encort™; Hemril®-30; HydroZone Plus [OTC]; Hytone®; IvySoothe® [OTC]; Locoid®; Locoid Lipocream®; Nupercainal® Hydrocortisone Cream [OTC]; Nutracort®; Pandel®; Post Peel Healing Balm [OTC]; Preparation H® Hydrocortisone [OTC]; Proctocort®; ProctoCream® HC; Procto-Kit™; Procto-Pak™; Proctosert; Proctosol-HC®; Proctozone-HC™; Sarnol®-HC [OTC]; Solu-Cortef®; Summer's Eve® Special-Care™ Medicated Anti-Itch Cream [OTC] [DSC]; Texacort®; Tucks® Anti-Itch [OTC]; Westcort®

Index Terms A-hydroCort; Compound F; Cortisol; Hemorrhoidal HC; Hydrocortisone Acetate; Hydrocortisone Butyrate; Hydrocortisone Probutate; Hydrocortisone Sodium Succinate; Hydrocortisone Valerate

Generic Available Yes: Excludes acetate foam, butyrate cream and ointment, gel as base, otic drops as base, probutate cream, sodium succinate injection

Canadian Brand Names Aquacort®; Cortamed®; Cortef®; Cortenema®; Cortifoam™; Emo-Cort®; Hycort™; Hyderm; HydroVal®; Locoid®; Prevex® HC; Sarna® HC; Solu-Cortef®; Westcort®

Pharmacologic Category Corticosteroid, Rectal; Corticosteroid, Systemic; Corticosteroid, Topical

Use Management of adrenocortical insufficiency; relief of inflammation of corticosteroid-responsive dermatoses (low and medium potency topical corticosteroid); adjunctive treatment of ulcerative colitis

Pregnancy Risk Factor C

Lactation Excretion in breast milk unknown/use caution

Labeled Contraindications Hypersensitivity to hydrocortisone or any component of the formulation; serious infections, except septic shock or tuberculous meningitis; viral, fungal, or tubercular skin lesions

Warnings/Precautions Use with caution in patients with thyroid disease, hepatic impairment, renal impairment, cardiovascular disease, diabetes, glaucoma, cataracts, myasthenia gravis, patients at risk for osteoporosis, patients at risk for seizures, or GI diseases (diverticulitis, peptic ulcer, ulcerative colitis) due to perforation risk. Use caution following acute MI (corticosteroids have been associated with myocardial rupture). Because of the risk of adverse effects, systemic corticosteroids should be used cautiously in the elderly in the smallest possible effective dose for the shortest duration. May affect growth velocity; growth should be routinely monitored in pediatric patients. Withdraw therapy with gradual tapering of dose.

May cause hypercorticism or suppression of hypothalamic-pituitary-adrenal (HPA) axis, particularly in younger children or in patients receiving high doses for prolonged periods. HPA axis suppression may lead to adrenal crisis. Withdrawal and discontinuation of a corticosteroid should be done slowly and carefully. Particular care is required when patients are transferred from systemic corticosteroids to inhaled products due to possible adrenal insufficiency or withdrawal from steroids, including an increase in allergic symptoms. Patients receiving >20 mg per day of prednisone (or equivalent) may be most susceptible. Fatalities have occurred due to adrenal insufficiency in asthmatic patients during and after transfer from systemic corticosteroids to aerosol steroids; aerosol steroids do not provide the systemic steroid needed to treat patients having trauma, surgery, or infections. Avoid use of topical preparations with occlusive dressings or on weeping or exudative lesions.

Acute myopathy has been reported with high dose corticosteroids, usually in patients with neuromuscular transmission disorders; may involve ocular and/or respiratory muscles; monitor creatine kinase; recovery may be delayed. Corticosteroid use may cause psychiatric disturbances, including depression, euphoria, insomnia, mood swings, and personality changes. Pre-existing psychiatric conditions may be exacerbated by corticosteroid use. Prolonged use of corticosteroids may also increase the incidence of secondary infection, mask acute infection (including fungal infections), prolong or exacerbate viral infections, or limit response to vaccines. Exposure to chickenpox should be avoided; corticosteroids should not be used to treat ocular herpes simplex. Corticosteroids should not be used for cerebral malaria. Close observation is required in patients with latent tuberculosis and/or TB reactivity; restrict use in active TB (only in conjunction with anti-tuberculosis treatment). Prolonged treatment with corticosteroids has been associated with the development of Kaposi's sarcoma (case reports); if noted, discontinuation of therapy should be considered.

Adverse Reactions
Systemic:
>10%:
  Central nervous system: Insomnia, nervousness
  Gastrointestinal: Increased appetite, indigestion
1% to 10%:
  Dermatologic: Hirsutism
  Endocrine & metabolic: Diabetes mellitus
  Neuromuscular & skeletal: Arthralgia
  Ocular: Cataracts
  Respiratory: Epistaxis
<1%: Hypertension, edema, euphoria, headache, delirium, hallucinations, seizure, mood swings, acne, dermatitis, skin atrophy, bruising, hyperpigmentation, hypokalemia, hyperglycemia, Cushing's syndrome, sodium and water retention, bone growth suppression, amenorrhea, peptic ulcer, abdominal distention, ulcerative esophagitis, pancreatitis, muscle wasting, hypersensitivity reactions, immunosuppression

Topical:
>10%: Dermatologic: Eczema (12.5%)
1% to 10%: Dermatologic: Pruritus (6%), stinging (2%), dry skin (2%)
<1%: Allergic contact dermatitis, burning, dermal atrophy, folliculitis, HPA axis suppression, hypopigmentation; metabolic effects (hyperglycemia, hypokalemia); striae

Overdosage/Toxicology When consumed in high doses for prolonged periods, systemic hypercorticism and adrenal suppression may occur. In those cases, discontinuation of the corticosteroid should be done judiciously.

Drug Interactions
Cytochrome P450 Effect: Substrate of CYP3A4 (minor); **Induces** CYP3A4 (weak)
(Continued)

Hydrocortisone *(Continued)*

Increased Effect/Toxicity: Aprepitant, azole antifungals, calcium channel blockers (nondihydropyridine), cyclosporine, estrogens, and macrolides may increase the serum levels of corticosteroids. Corticosteroids may increase the hypokalemic effects of amphotericin B or potassium-wasting diuretics (loop or thiazide); monitor.

Concurrent use of nonsteroidal anti-inflammatory drugs (NSAIDs) and salicylates with corticosteroids may lead to an increased incidence of gastrointestinal adverse effects. Concurrent use with anticholinergic agents may lead to severe weakness in patients with myasthenia gravis. Concurrent use of fluoroquinolone antibiotics may increase the risk of tendon rupture, particularly in elderly patients (overall incidence rare). Concurrent use of neuromuscular-blocking agents with corticosteroids may increase the risk of myopathy. Concurrent use with cyclosporine may increase cyclosporine levels. The use of live vaccines is contraindicated in immunosuppressed patients (may increase the risk of vaccinal infection). In patients receiving high doses of systemic corticosteroids for ≥14 days, wait at least 1 month between discontinuing steroid therapy and administering immunization.

Decreased Effect: Antacids and bile acid sequestrants may reduce the absorption of corticosteroids; separate administration by 2 hours. Aminoglutethimide, barbiturates and rifamycin derivatives may reduce the serum levels/effects of hydrocortisone (systemic). Serum concentrations of isoniazid may be decreased by corticosteroids. Corticosteroids may lead to a reduction in warfarin effect. Corticosteroids may suppress the response to vaccinations.

Ethanol/Nutrition/Herb Interactions

Ethanol: Avoid ethanol (may enhance gastric mucosal irritation).

Food: Hydrocortisone interferes with calcium absorption.

Herb/Nutraceutical: St John's wort may decrease hydrocortisone levels. Avoid cat's claw, echinacea (have immunostimulant properties).

Storage/Stability Store at controlled room temperature 20°C to 25°C (59°F to 86°F). Hydrocortisone sodium phosphate and hydrocortisone sodium succinate are clear, light yellow solutions which are heat labile.

Sodium succinate: After initial reconstitution, hydrocortisone sodium succinate solutions are stable for 3 days at room temperature or under refrigeration when protected from light. Stability of parenteral admixture (Solu-Cortef®) at room temperature (25°C) and at refrigeration temperature (4°C) is concentration-dependent:

Stability of concentration 1 mg/mL: 24 hours.

Stability of concentration 2 mg/mL to 60 mg/mL: At least 4 hours.

Reconstitution

Sodium succinate: Reconstitute 100 mg vials with bacteriostatic water (not >2 mL). Act-O-Vial (self-contained powder for injection plus diluent) may be reconstituted by pressing the activator to force diluent into the powder compartment. Following gentle agitation, solution may be withdrawn via syringe through a needle inserted into the center of the stopper. May be administered (I.V. or I.M.) without further dilution.

Solutions for I.V. infusion: Reconstituted solutions may be added to an appropriate volume of compatible solution for infusion. Concentration should generally not exceed 1 mg/mL. However, in cases where administration of a small volume of fluid is desirable, 100-3000 mg may be added to 50 mL of D_5W or NS (stability limited to 4 hours).

Compatibility

Hydrocortisone sodium phosphate: Stable in D_5W, NS, fat emulsion 10%.

Y-site administration: Compatible: Allopurinol, amifostine, aztreonam, cefepime, cladribine, clarithromycin, docetaxel, etoposide, famotidine, filgrastim, fluconazole, fludarabine, gemcitabine, granisetron, melphalan, ondansetron, paclitaxel, piperacillin/tazobactam, teniposide, thiotepa, vinorelbine. **Incompatible:** Sargramostim.

Compatibility in syringe: Compatible: Metoclopramide. **Incompatible:** Doxapram.

Compatibility when admixed: Compatible: Amikacin, amphotericin B, amphotericin B with heparin, bleomycin, dacarbazine, metaraminol, sodium bicarbonate, verapamil. **Variable (consult detailed reference):** Mitoxantrone.

Hydrocortisone sodium succinate: Stable in dextran 6% in dextrose, dextran 6% in NS, D_5LR, $D_5\frac{1}{4}NS$, $D_5\frac{1}{2}NS$, D_5NS, D_5W, $D_{10}W$, $D_{20}W$, LR, $\frac{1}{2}NS$, NS, fat emulsion 10%.

Y-site administration: Compatible: Acyclovir, allopurinol, amifostine, aminophylline, amphotericin B cholesteryl sulfate complex, ampicillin, amsacrine, atracurium, atropine, aztreonam, betamethasone sodium phosphate, calcium gluconate, cefepime, chlordiazepoxide, chlorpromazine, cisatracurium, cladribine, cyanocobalamin, cytarabine, dexamethasone sodium phosphate, digoxin, diphenhydramine, docetaxel, dopamine, doxorubicin liposome, droperidol, droperidol and fentanyl, edrophonium, enalaprilat, epinephrine, esmolol, estrogens (conjugated), ethacrynate sodium, etoposide, famotidine, fentanyl, filgrastim, fludarabine, fluorouracil, foscarnet, furosemide, gatifloxacin, gemcitabine, granisetron, heparin, hydralazine, inamrinone, insulin (regular), isoproterenol, kanamycin, lidocaine, linezolid, lorazepam, magnesium sulfate, melphalan, menadiol sodium diphosphate, meperidine, methoxamine, methylergonovine, minocycline, morphine, neostigmine, norepinephrine, ondansetron, oxacillin, oxytocin, paclitaxel, pancuronium, penicillin G potassium, pentazocine, phytonadione, piperacillin/tazobactam, procainamide, prochlorperazine edisylate, propofol, propranolol, pyridostigmine, remifentanil, scopolamine, sodium bicarbonate, succinylcholine, tacrolimus, teniposide, theophylline, thiotepa, trimethaphan camsylate, trimethobenzamide, vecuronium, vinorelbine. **Incompatible:** Ciprofloxacin, diazepam, ergotamine, idarubicin, midazolam, phenytoin, sargramostim. **Variable (consult detailed reference):** Diltiazem, methylprednisolone sodium succinate, promethazine.

Compatibility in syringe: Compatible: Diatrizoate meglumine 52%, diatrizoate sodium 8%, diatrizoate sodium 60%, iohexol, iopamidol, iothalamate meglumine 60%, ioxaglate meglumine 39.3%, ioxaglate sodium 19.6%, metoclopramide, thiopental. **Incompatible:** Doxapram.

Compatibility when admixed: Compatible: Amikacin, aminophylline, amphotericin B, calcium chloride, calcium gluconate, chloramphenicol, clindamycin, corticotropin, daunorubicin, diphenhydramine, dopamine, erythromycin lactobionate, floxacillin, lidocaine, magnesium sulfate, mephentermine, metronidazole, metronidazole with sodium bicarbonate, mitomycin, mitoxantrone, norepinephrine, penicillin G potassium, penicillin G sodium, piperacillin, polymyxin B sulfate, potassium chloride, procaine, sodium bicarbonate, theophylline, thiopental, vancomycin, verapamil, vitamin B complex with C. **Incompatible:** Aminophylline with cephalothin, bleomycin, colistimethate, ephedrine, hydralazine, nafcillin, pentobarbital, phenobarbital, prochlorperazine edisylate, promethazine. **Variable (consult detailed reference):** Amobarbital, ampicillin, cytarabine, dimenhydrinate, furosemide, heparin, kanamycin, metaraminol.

(Continued)

Hydrocortisone *(Continued)*

Mechanism of Action Decreases inflammation by suppression of migration of polymorphonuclear leukocytes and reversal of increased capillary permeability

Pharmacodynamics/Kinetics

Onset of action:

Hydrocortisone acetate: Slow

Hydrocortisone sodium succinate (water soluble): Rapid

Duration: Hydrocortisone acetate: Long

Absorption: Rapid by all routes, except rectally

Metabolism: Hepatic

Half-life elimination: Biologic: 8-12 hours

Excretion: Urine (primarily as 17-hydroxysteroids and 17-ketosteroids)

Dosage Dose should be based on severity of disease and patient response

Acute adrenal insufficiency: I.M., I.V.:

Infants and young Children: Succinate: 1-2 mg/kg/dose bolus, then 25-150 mg/day in divided doses every 6-8 hours

Older Children: Succinate: 1-2 mg/kg bolus then 150-250 mg/day in divided doses every 6-8 hours

Adults: Succinate: 100 mg I.V. bolus, then 300 mg/day in divided doses every 8 hours or as a continuous infusion for 48 hours; once patient is stable change to oral, 50 mg every 8 hours for 6 doses, then taper to 30-50 mg/day in divided doses

Chronic adrenal corticoid insufficiency: Adults: Oral: 20-30 mg/day

Anti-inflammatory or immunosuppressive:

Infants and Children:

Oral: 2.5-10 mg/kg/day **or** 75-300 mg/m^2/day every 6-8 hours

I.M., I.V.: Succinate: 1-5 mg/kg/day **or** 30-150 mg/m^2/day divided every 12-24 hours

Adolescents and Adults: Oral, I.M., I.V.: Succinate: 15-240 mg every 12 hours

Congenital adrenal hyperplasia: Oral: Initial: 10-20 mg/m^2/day in 3 divided doses; a variety of dosing schedules have been used. **Note:** Inconsistencies have occurred with liquid formulations; tablets may provide more reliable levels. Doses must be individualized by monitoring growth, bone age, and hormonal levels. Mineralocorticoid and sodium supplementation may be required based upon electrolyte regulation and plasma renin activity.

Physiologic replacement: Children:

Oral: 0.5-0.75 mg/kg/day **or** 20-25 mg/m^2/day every 8 hours

I.M.: Succinate: 0.25-0.35 mg/kg/day **or** 12-15 mg/m^2/day once daily

Shock: I.M., I.V.: Succinate:

Children: Initial: 50 mg/kg, then repeated in 4 hours and/or every 24 hours as needed

Adolescents and Adults: 500 mg to 2 g every 2-6 hours

Status asthmaticus: Children and Adults: I.V.: Succinate: 1-2 mg/kg/dose every 6 hours for 24 hours, then maintenance of 0.5-1 mg/kg every 6 hours

Adults:

Rheumatic diseases:

Intralesional, intra-articular, soft tissue injection: Acetate:

Large joints: 25 mg (up to 37.5 mg)

Small joints: 10-25 mg

Tendon sheaths: 5-12.5 mg

Soft tissue infiltration: 25-50 mg (up to 75 mg)

Bursae: 25-37.5 mg

    Ganglia: 12.5-25 mg
    Stress dosing (surgery) in patients known to be adrenally-suppressed or
        on chronic systemic steroids: I.V.:
        Minor stress (ie, inguinal herniorrhaphy): 25 mg/day for 1 day
        Moderate stress (ie, joint replacement, cholecystectomy): 50-75 mg/day
            (25 mg every 8-12 hours) for 1-2 days
        Major stress (pancreatoduodenectomy, esophagogastrectomy, cardiac
            surgery): 100-150 mg/day (50 mg every 8-12 hours) for 2-3 days
    Dermatosis: Children >2 years and Adults: Topical: Apply to affected area
        2-4 times/day (Buteprate: Apply once or twice daily). Therapy should be
        discontinued when control is achieved; if no improvement is seen, reas-
        sessment of diagnosis may be necessary.
    Ulcerative colitis: Adults: Rectal: 10-100 mg 1-2 times/day for 2-3 weeks
Combination Regimens
    Prostate cancer:
        Estramustine + Docetaxel + Hydrocortisone *on page 1208*
        Mitoxantrone + Hydrocortisone *on page 1248*
Administration
    Oral: Administer with food or milk to decrease GI upset
    Parenteral: Hydrocortisone sodium succinate may be administered by I.M. or
        I.V. routes
        I.V. bolus: Dilute to 50 mg/mL and administer over 30 seconds to several
            minutes (depending on the dose)
        I.V. intermittent infusion: Dilute to 1 mg/mL and administer over 20-30
            minutes
    Topical: Apply a thin film to clean, dry skin and rub in gently
Monitoring Parameters Blood pressure, weight, serum glucose, and elec-
    trolytes
Dietary Considerations Systemic use of corticosteroids may require a diet
    with increased potassium, vitamins A, B_6, C, D, folate, calcium, zinc, phos-
    phorus, and decreased sodium. Sodium content of 1 g (sodium succinate
    injection): 47.5 mg (2.07 mEq)
Patient Information Notify surgeon or dentist before surgical repair; oral
    formulation may cause GI upset, take with food; report if any sign of infection
    occurs; avoid abrupt withdrawal when on long-term therapy. Before applying,
    gently wash area to reduce risk of infection; apply a thin film to cleansed area
    and rub in gently and thoroughly until medication vanishes; avoid exposure
    to sunlight, severe sunburn may occur.
Special Geriatric Considerations Because of the risk of adverse effects,
    systemic corticosteroids should be used cautiously in the elderly, in the
    smallest possible dose, and for the shortest possible time.
Additional Information Hydrocortisone base topical cream, lotion, and oint-
    ments in concentrations of 0.25%, 0.5%, and 1% may be OTC or prescrip-
    tion depending on the product labeling.
Dosage Forms Excipient information presented when available (limited,
    particularly for generics); consult specific product labeling. [DSC] = Discon-
    tinued product
    Aerosol, rectal, as acetate (Cortifoam®): 10% (15 g) [90 mg/applicator]
    Cream, rectal, as acetate (Nupercainal® Hydrocortisone Cream): 1% (30 g)
        [strength expressed as base]
    Cream, rectal, as base:
        Cortizone®-10: 1% (30 g) [contains aloe]
        Preparation H® Hydrocortisone: 1% (27 g)
    Cream, topical, as acetate: 0.5% (9 g, 30 g, 60 g) [available with aloe]; 1%
        (30 g, 454 g) [available with aloe]
(Continued)

Hydrocortisone *(Continued)*

Cream, topical, as base: 0.5% (30 g); 1% (1.5 g, 30 g, 114 g, 454 g); 2.5% (20 g, 30 g, 454 g)

Anusol-HC®: 2.5% (30 g) [contains benzyl alcohol]

Caldecort®: 1% (30 g) [contains aloe vera gel]

Cortaid® Intensive Therapy: 1% (60 g)

Cortaid® Maximum Strength: 1% (15 g, 30 g, 40 g, 60 g) [contains aloe vera gel and benzyl alcohol]

Cortaid® Sensitive Skin: 0.5% (15 g) [contains aloe vera gel]

Cortizone®-10 Maximum Strength: 1% (15 g, 30 g, 60 g) [contains aloe]

Cortizone®-10 Plus Maximum Strength: 1% (30 g, 60 g) [contains vitamins A, D, E and aloe]

Dermarest® Dricort®: 1% (15 g, 30 g)

HydroZone Plus, Proctocort®, Procto-Pak™: 1% (30 g)

Hytone®: 2.5% (30 g, 60 g)

IvySoothe®: 1% (30 g) [contains aloe]

Post Peel Healing Balm: 1% (23 g)

ProctoCream® HC: 2.5% (30 g) [contains benzyl alcohol]

Procto-Kit™: 1% (30 g) [packaged with applicator tips and finger cots]; 2.5% (30 g) [packaged with applicator tips and finger cots]

Proctosol-HC®, Proctozone-HC™: 2.5% (30 g)

Summer's Eve® SpecialCare™ Medicated Anti-Itch Cream: 1% (30 g) [DSC]

Cream, topical, as butyrate (Locoid®, Locoid Lipocream®): 0.1% (15 g, 45 g)

Cream, topical, as probutate (Pandel®): 0.1% (15 g, 45 g, 80 g)

Cream, topical, as valerate (Westcort®): 0.2% (15 g, 45 g, 60 g)

Gel, topical, as base (Corticool®): 1% (45 g)

Injection, powder for reconstitution, as sodium succinate:

A-Hydrocort®: 100 mg

Solu-Cortef®: 100 mg, 250 mg, 500 mg, 1 g [diluent contains benzyl alcohol; strength expressed as base]

Lotion, topical, as base: 1% (120 mL); 2.5% (60 mL)

Aquanil™ HC: 1% (120 mL)

Beta-HC®, Cetacort® [DSC], Sarnol®-HC: 1% (60 mL)

HydroZone Plus: 1% (120 mL)

Hytone®: 2.5% (60 mL)

Nutracort®: 1% (60 mL, 120 mL); 2.5% (60 mL, 120 mL)

Ointment, topical, as acetate: 1% (30 g) [strength expressed as base; available with aloe]

Anusol® HC-1: 1% (21 g) [strength expressed as base]

Cortaid® Maximum Strength: 1% (15 g, 30 g) [strength expressed as base]

Ointment, topical, as base: 0.5% (30 g); 1% (30 g, 454 g); 2.5% (20 g, 30 g, 454 g)

Cortizone®-10 Maximum Strength: 1% (30 g, 60 g)

Hytone®: 2.5% (30 g) [DSC]

Ointment, topical, as butyrate (Locoid®): 0.1% (15 g, 45 g)

Ointment, topical, as valerate (Westcort®): 0.2% (15 g, 45 g, 60 g)

Solution, otic, as base (EarSol® HC): 1% (30 mL) [contains alcohol 44%, benzyl benzoate, yerba santa]

Solution, topical, as base (Texacort®): 2.5% (30 mL) [contains alcohol]

Solution, topical, as butyrate (Locoid®): 0.1% (20 mL, 60 mL) [contains alcohol 50%]

Solution, topical spray, as base:

Cortaid® Intensive Therapy: 1% (60 mL) [contains alcohol]

Cortizone®-10 Quick Shot: 1% (44 mL) [contains benzyl alcohol]

Dermtex® HC: 1% (52 mL) [contains menthol 1%]

Suppository, rectal, as acetate: 25 mg (12s, 24s, 100s)

Anucort-HC®, Tucks® Anti-Itch: 25 mg (12s, 24s, 100s) [strength expressed as base; Anucort-HC® renamed Tucks® Anti-Itch]

Anusol-HC®, Proctosol-HC®: 25 mg (12s, 24s)

Encort™, Proctocort®: 30 mg (12s)

Hemril®-30, Proctosert: 30 mg (12s, 24s)

Suspension, rectal, as base: 100 mg/60 mL (7s)

Colocort®: 100 mg/60 mL (1s, 7s)

Tablet, as base: 20 mg

Cortef®: 5 mg, 10 mg, 20 mg

References

Abraham E and Evans T, "Corticosteroids and Septic Shock [editorial]," *JAMA*, 2002, 288(7):886-7.

Annane D, Sebille V, Charpentier C, et al, "Effect of Treatment With Low Doses of Hydrocortisone and Fludrocortisone on Mortality in Patients With Septic Shock," *JAMA*, 2002, 288(7):862-71.

Cooper MS and Stewart PM, "Corticosteroid Insufficiency in Acutely Ill Patients," *N Engl J Med*, 2003, 348(8):727-34.

Coursin DB and Wood KE, "Corticosteroid Supplementation for Adrenal Insufficiency," *JAMA*, 2002, 287(2):236-40.

de Jonghe B, Sharshar T, Lefaucheur JP, et al, "Paresis Acquired in the Intensive Care Unit. A Prospective Multicenter Study," *JAMA*, 2002, 288(22):2859-67.

Dellinger RP, Carlet JM, Masur H, et al, "Surviving Sepsis Campaign Guidelines for Management of Severe Sepsis and Septic Shock," *Crit Care Med*, 2004, 32(3):858-73.

Gamsu HR, Mullinger BM, Donnai P, et al, "Antenatal Administration of Betamethasone to Prevent Respiratory Distress Syndrome in Preterm Infants: Report of a UK Multicentre Trial," *Br J Obstet Gynaecol*, 1989, 96(4):401-10.

Goedert JJ, Vitale F, Lauria C, et al, "Risk Factors for Classical Kaposi's Sarcoma," *J Natl Cancer Inst*, 2002, 94(22):1712-8.

Hotchkiss RS and Karl IE, "The Pathophysiology and Treatment of Sepsis," *N Engl J Med*, 2003, 348(2):138-50.

Liggins GC and Howie RN, "A Controlled Trial of Antepartum Glucocorticoid Treatment of Respiratory Distress Syndrome in Premature Infants," *Pediatrics*, 1972, 50:515-25.

Salem M, Tainsh RE Jr, Bromberg J, et al, "Perioperative Glucocorticoid Coverage. A Reassessment 42 Years After Emergence of a Problem," *Ann Surg*, 1994, 219(4):416-25.

"Technical Report: Congenital Adrenal Hyperplasia," American Academy of Pediatrics, Section on Endocrinology and Committee on Genetics, *Pediatrics*, 2000, 106(6):1511-8.

♦ **Hydrocortisone Acetate** *see* Hydrocortisone *on page 545*

♦ **Hydrocortisone Butyrate** *see* Hydrocortisone *on page 545*

♦ **Hydrocortisone Probutate** *see* Hydrocortisone *on page 545*

♦ **Hydrocortisone Sodium Succinate** *see* Hydrocortisone *on page 545*

♦ **Hydrocortisone Valerate** *see* Hydrocortisone *on page 545*

♦ **Hydromorph Contin® (Can)** *see* Hydromorphone *on page 553*

♦ **Hydromorph-IR® (Can)** *see* Hydromorphone *on page 553*

Hydromorphone (hye droe MOR fone)

Medication Safety Issues

Sound-alike/look-alike issues:

Dilaudid® may be confused with Demerol®, Dilantin®

Hydromorphone may be confused with morphine; significant overdoses have occurred when hydromorphone products have been inadvertently administered instead of morphine sulfate. Commercially available prefilled syringes of both products looks similar and are often stored in close proximity to each other. **Note:** Hydromorphone 1 mg oral is approximately equal to morphine 4 mg oral; hydromorphone 1 mg I.V. is approximately equal to morphine 5 mg I.V.

(Continued)

Hydromorphone *(Continued)*

Dilaudid®, Dilaudid-HP®: Extreme caution should be taken to avoid confusing the highly-concentrated (Dilaudid-HP®) injection with the less-concentrated (Dilaudid®) injectable product.

Significant differences exist between oral and I.V. dosing. Use caution when converting from one route of administration to another.

U.S. Brand Names Dilaudid®; Dilaudid-HP®

Index Terms Dihydromorphinone; Hydromorphone Hydrochloride

Generic Available Yes: Excludes capsule, liquid, powder for injection

Canadian Brand Names Dilaudid®; Dilaudid-HP®; Dilaudid-HP-Plus®; Dilaudid® Sterile Powder; Dilaudid-XP®; Hydromorph Contin®; Hydromorph-IR®; Hydromorphone HP; Hydromorphone HP® 10; Hydromorphone HP® 20; Hydromorphone HP® 50; Hydromorphone HP® Forte; Hydromorphone Hydrochloride Injection, USP; PMS-Hydromorphone

Pharmacologic Category Analgesic, Opioid

Use Management of moderate-to-severe pain

Unlabeled/Investigational Use Antitussive

Restrictions C-II

Pregnancy Risk Factor C/D (prolonged use or high doses at term)

Lactation Excretion in breast milk unknown/not recommended

Labeled Contraindications Hypersensitivity to hydromorphone, any component of the formulation; acute or severe asthma, severe respiratory depression (in absence of resuscitative equipment or ventilatory support); severe CNS depression; pregnancy (prolonged use or high doses at term); obstetrical analgesia

Warnings/Precautions Use with caution in patients with hypersensitivity reactions to other phenanthrene derivative opioid agonists (codeine, hydrocodone, levorphanol, oxycodone, oxymorphone). Hydromorphone shares toxic potential of opiate agonists, including CNS depression and respiratory depression. Precautions associated with opiate agonist therapy should be observed. May cause CNS depression, which may impair physical or mental abilities; patients must be cautioned about performing tasks which require mental alertness (eg, operating machinery or driving). Myoclonus and seizures have been reported with high doses. Critical respiratory depression may occur, even at therapeutic dosages, particularly in elderly or debilitated patients or in patients with pre-existing respiratory compromise (hypoxia and/or hypercapnia). Use caution in COPD or other obstructive pulmonary disease. Use with caution in patients with hypersensitivity to other phenanthrene opiates, kyphoscoliosis, biliary tract disease, acute pancreatitis, morbid obesity, adrenocortical insufficiency, hypothyroidism, acute alcoholism, toxic psychoses, prostatic hyperplasia and/or urinary stricture, or severe liver or renal failure. Use extreme caution in patients with head injury, intracranial lesions, or elevated intracranial pressure; exaggerated elevation of ICP may occur (in addition, hydromorphone may complicate neurologic evaluation due to pupillary dilation and CNS depressant effects). Use with caution in patients with depleted blood volume or drugs which may exaggerate hypotensive effects (including phenothiazines or general anesthetics). May obscure diagnosis or clinical course of patients with acute abdominal conditions.

[U.S. Boxed Warning]: Hydromorphone has a high potential for abuse. Those at risk for opioid abuse include patients with a history of substance abuse or mental illness. Tolerance or drug dependence may result from extended use; however, concerns for abuse should not prevent effective management of pain. In general, abrupt discontinuation of therapy in dependent patients should be avoided.

An opioid-containing analgesic regimen should be tailored to each patient's needs and based upon the type of pain being treated (acute versus chronic), the route of administration, degree of tolerance for opioids (naive versus chronic user), age, weight, and medical condition. The optimal analgesic dose varies widely among patients. Doses should be titrated to pain relief/ prevention. I.M. use may result in variable absorption and a lag time to peak effect.

Dosage form specific warnings:

[U.S. Boxed Warning]: Dilaudid-HP®: Extreme caution should be taken to avoid confusing the highly-concentrated (Dilaudid-HP®) injection with the less-concentrated (Dilaudid®) injectable product. Dilaudid-HP® should only be used in patients who are opioid-tolerant.

Controlled release: Capsules should only be used when continuous analgesia is required over an extended period of time. Controlled release products are not to be used on an "as needed" (PRN) basis.

Some dosage forms contain trace amounts of sodium metabisulfite which may cause allergic reactions in susceptible individuals.

Adverse Reactions Frequency not defined.

Cardiovascular: Bradycardia, flushing of face, hyper-/hypotension, palpitation, peripheral vasodilation, syncope, tachycardia

Central nervous system: Agitation, chills, CNS depression, dizziness, drowsiness, dysphoria, euphoria, fatigue, hallucinations, headache, increased intracranial pressure, insomnia, lightheadedness, mental depression, nervousness, restlessness, sedation, seizure

Dermatologic: Pruritus, rash, urticaria

Endocrine & metabolic: Antidiuretic hormone release

Gastrointestinal: Anorexia, biliary tract spasm, constipation, diarrhea, nausea, paralytic ileus, stomach cramps, taste perversion, vomiting, xerostomia

Genitourinary: Ureteral spasm, urinary retention, urinary tract spasm, urination decreased

Hepatic: AST/ALT increased, LFTs increased

Local: Pain at injection site (I.M.), wheal/flare over vein (I.V.)

Neuromuscular & skeletal: Myoclonus, paresthesia, trembling, tremor, weakness

Ocular: Blurred vision, diplopia, miosis, nystagmus

Respiratory: Apnea, bronchospasm, dyspnea, laryngospasm, respiratory depression

Miscellaneous: Diaphoresis, histamine release, physical and psychological dependence

Overdosage/Toxicology Symptoms of overdose include CNS depression, bradycardia, hypotension, respiratory depression, miosis, apnea, pulmonary edema, and convulsions. Along with supportive measures, naloxone, 2 mg I.V. with repeat administration as necessary up to a total of 10 mg, can also be used to reverse toxic effects of the opiate. Longer observation times may be required with overdose of longer duration products. Activated charcoal or gut decontamination may be used with oral overdose.

Drug Interactions

Increased Effect/Toxicity: Effects may be additive with CNS depressants; hypotensive effects may be increased with phenothiazines or general anesthetics; serotonergic effects may be additive with SSRIs
(Continued)

Hydromorphone *(Continued)*

Decreased Effect: Hydromorphone may diminish the effects of pegvisomant. Ammonium chloride may decrease the levels/effects of hydromorphone.

Ethanol/Nutrition/Herb Interactions

Ethanol: Avoid ethanol (may increase CNS depression).

Herb/Nutraceutical: Avoid valerian, St John's wort, kava kava, gotu kola (may increase CNS depression).

Storage/Stability Store injection and oral dosage forms at 15°C to 30°C (59°F to 86°F). Protect tablets from light. A slightly yellowish discoloration has not been associated with a loss of potency.

Compatibility Stable in D_5LR, D_5W, $D_5^1/_2NS$, D_5NS, LR, $^1/_2NS$, NS.

Y-site administration: Compatible: Acyclovir, allopurinol, amifostine, amikacin, amsacrine, aztreonam, cefamandole, cefepime, cefoperazone, cefotaxime, cefoxitin, ceftazidime, ceftizoxime, cefuroxime, chloramphenicol, cisatracurium, cisplatin, cladribine, clindamycin, cyclophosphamide, cytarabine, diltiazem, dobutamine, docetaxel, dopamine, doxorubicin, doxorubicin liposome, doxycycline, epinephrine, erythromycin lactobionate, etoposide, famotidine, fentanyl, filgrastim, fludarabine, foscarnet, furosemide, gatifloxacin, gemcitabine, gentamicin, granisetron, heparin, kanamycin, labetalol, linezolid, lorazepam, magnesium sulfate, melphalan, methotrexate, metronidazole, midazolam, milrinone, morphine, nafcillin, nicardipine, nitroglycerin, norepinephrine, ondansetron, oxacillin, paclitaxel, penicillin G potassium, piperacillin, piperacillin/tazobactam, propofol, ranitidine, remifentanil, tacrolimus, teniposide, thiotepa, ticarcillin, tobramycin, trimethoprim/sulfamethoxazole, vancomycin, vecuronium, vinorelbine. **Incompatible:** Amphotericin B cholesteryl sulfate complex, diazepam, minocycline, phenobarbital, phenytoin, sargramostim, tetracycline, thiopental. **Variable (consult detailed reference):** Ampicillin, cefazolin.

Compatibility in syringe: Compatible: Albuterol, atropine, bupivacaine, ceftazidime, chlorpromazine, cimetidine, dimenhydrinate, diphenhydramine, fentanyl, glycopyrrolate, haloperidol, hydroxyzine, lorazepam, midazolam, pentazocine, pentobarbital, prochlorperazine mesylate, promethazine, ranitidine, scopolamine, thiethylperazine, trimethobenzamide. **Incompatible:** Ampicillin, diazepam, hyaluronidase, phenobarbital, phenytoin. **Variable (consult detailed reference):** Cefazolin, dexamethasone sodium phosphate, ketorolac, prochlorperazine edisylate.

Compatibility when admixed: Compatible: Bupivacaine, fluorouracil, midazolam, ondansetron, promethazine, verapamil. **Incompatible:** Sodium bicarbonate, thiopental. **Variable (consult detailed reference):** Tetracaine.

Mechanism of Action Binds to opiate receptors in the CNS, causing inhibition of ascending pain pathways, altering the perception of and response to pain; causes cough supression by direct central action in the medulla; produces generalized CNS depression

Pharmacodynamics/Kinetics

Onset of action: Analgesic: Immediate release formulations:

Oral: 15-30 minutes

Peak effect: Oral: 30-60 minutes

Duration: Immediate release formulations: 4-5 hours

Absorption: I.M.: Variable and delayed

Distribution: V_d: 4 L/kg

Protein binding: ~8% to 19%

Metabolism: Hepatic via glucuronidation; to inactive metabolites

Bioavailability: 62%

Half-life elimination: Immediate release formulations: 1-3 hours

Excretion: Urine (primarily as glucuronide conjugates)

Dosage

Acute pain (moderate to severe): **Note:** These are guidelines and do not represent the maximum doses that may be required in all patients. Doses should be titrated to pain relief/prevention.

Children ≥6 months and <50 kg:

Oral: 0.03-0.08 mg/kg/dose every 3-4 hours as needed

I.V.: 0.015 mg/kg/dose every 3-6 hours as needed

Children >50 kg and Adults:

Oral: Initial: Opiate-naive: 2-4 mg every 3-6 hours as needed; elderly/debilitated patients may require lower doses; patients with prior opiate exposure may require higher initial doses; usual dosage range: 2-8 mg every 3-4 hours as needed

I.V.: Initial: Opiate-naive: 0.2-0.6 mg every 2-3 hours as needed; patients with prior opiate exposure may tolerate higher initial doses

Note: More frequent dosing may be needed.

Mechanically-ventilated patients (based on 70 kg patient): 0.7-2 mg every 1-2 hours as needed; infusion (based on 70 kg patient): 0.5-1 mg/hour

Patient-controlled analgesia (PCA): (Opiate-naive: Consider lower end of dosing range)

Usual concentration: 0.2 mg/mL

Demand dose: Usual: 0.1-0.2 mg; range: 0.05-0.5 mg

Lockout interval: 5-15 minutes

4-hour limit: 4-6 mg

Epidural:

Bolus dose: 1-1.5 mg

Infusion concentration: 0.05-0.075 mg/mL

Infusion rate: 0.04-0.4 mg/hour

Demand dose: 0.15 mg

Lockout interval: 30 minutes

I.M., SubQ: **Note:** I.M. use may result in variable absorption and a lag time to peak effect.

Initial: Opiate-naive: 0.8-1 mg every 4-6 hours as needed; patients with prior opiate exposure may require higher initial doses; usual dosage range: 1-2 mg every 3-6 hours as needed

Rectal: 3 mg every 4-8 hours as needed

Chronic pain: Adults: Oral: **Note:** Patients taking opioids chronically may become tolerant and require doses higher than the usual dosage range to maintain the desired effect. Tolerance can be managed by appropriate dose titration. There is no optimal or maximal dose for hydromorphone in chronic pain. The appropriate dose is one that relieves pain throughout its dosing interval without causing unmanageable side effects.

Controlled release formulation (Hydromorph Contin®, not available in U.S.): 3-30 mg every 12 hours. **Note:** A patient's hydromorphone requirement should be established using prompt release formulations; conversion to long acting products may be considered when chronic, continuous treatment is required. Higher dosages should be reserved for use only in opioid-tolerant patients.

Antitussive (unlabeled use): Oral:

Children 6-12 years: 0.5 mg every 3-4 hours as needed

Children >12 years and Adults: 1 mg every 3-4 hours as needed

Dosing adjustment in hepatic impairment: Should be considered

(Continued)

Hydromorphone *(Continued)*

Administration

Parenteral: May be given SubQ or I.M.; vial stopper contains latex

I.V.: For IVP, must be given slowly over 2-3 minutes (rapid IVP has been associated with an increase in side effects, especially respiratory depression and hypotension)

Oral: Hydromorph Contin®: Capsule should be swallowed whole; do not crush or chew; contents may be sprinkled on soft food and swallowed

Monitoring Parameters Pain relief, respiratory and mental status, blood pressure

Test Interactions Some quinolones may produce a false-positive urine screening result for opiates using commercially-available immunoassay kits. This has been demonstrated most consistently for levofloxacin and ofloxacin, but other quinolones have shown cross-reactivity in certain assay kits. Confirmation of positive opiate screens by more specific methods should be considered.

Patient Information May cause drowsiness and may impair ability to drive or operate heavy machinery. Avoid alcohol and other CNS depressants. Do not exceed recommended dose or take for more than 10 days without prescriber's advice. Take with food or milk to minimize GI distress

Special Geriatric Considerations Elderly may be particularly susceptible to the CNS depressant and constipating effects of narcotics.

Additional Information Equianalgesic doses: Morphine 10 mg I.M. = hydromorphone 1.5 mg I.M.

Vesicant No

Dosage Forms Excipient information presented when available (limited, particularly for generics); consult specific product labeling. [CAN] = Canadian brand name

Capsule, controlled release:

Hydromorph Contin® [CAN]: 3 mg, 6 mg, 12 mg, 18 mg, 24 mg, 30 mg [not available in U.S.]

Injection, powder for reconstitution, as hydrochloride:

Dilaudid-HP®: 250 mg [may contain trace amounts of sodium bisulfite]

Injection, solution, as hydrochloride: 1 mg/mL (1 mL); 2 mg/mL (1 mL, 20 mL); 4 mg/mL (1 mL); 10 mg/mL (1 mL, 5 mL, 10 mL, 50 mL)

Dilaudid®: 1 mg/mL (1 mL); 2 mg/mL (1 mL, 20 mL) [20 mL size contains edetate sodium; vial stopper contains latex]; 4 mg/mL (1 mL)

Dilaudid-HP®: 10 mg/mL (1 mL, 5 mL, 50 mL) [50 mL packaging contains latex]

Liquid, oral, as hydrochloride:

Dilaudid®: 1 mg/mL (480 mL) [may contain trace amounts of sodium bisulfite]

Suppository, rectal, as hydrochloride: 3 mg

Dilaudid®: 3 mg (6s)

Tablet, as hydrochloride: 2 mg, 4 mg, 8 mg

Dilaudid®: 2 mg, 4 mg, 8 mg (8 mg tablets may contain trace amounts of sodium bisulfite)

References

Agency for Health Care Policy and Research, "Acute Pain Management in Infants, Children and Adolescents: Operative and Medical Procedures," *Am Fam Physician*, 1992, 46(2):469-79.

"Clinical Practice Guidelines for the Sustained Use of Sedatives and Analgesics in the Critically Ill Adult. Task Force of the American College of Critical Care Medicine (ACCM) of the Society of Critical Care Medicine (SCCM), American Society of Health-System Pharmacists (ASHP), American College of Chest Physicians," *Am J Health Syst Pharm*, 2002, 59(2):150-78.

"Drugs for Pain," *Med Lett Drugs Ther*, 2000, 42(1085):73-8.

Ferrell BA, "Pain Management in Elderly People," *J Am Geriatr Soc*, 1991, 39(1):64-73.

Honigberg IL, and Stewart JT, "Radioimmunoassay of Hydromorphone and Hydrocodone in Human Plasma," *J Pharm Sci*, 1980, 69(10):1171-3.

Inturrisi CE, "Narcotic Drugs," *Med Clin North Am*, 1982, 66(5):1061-71.

Jacobi J, Fraser GL, Coursin DB, et al, "Clinical Practice Guidelines for the Sustained Use of Sedatives and Analgesics in the Critically Ill Adult," *Crit Care Med*, 2002, 30(1):119-41. Available at: http://www.sccm.org/pdf/sedatives.pdf. Accessed August 2, 2003.

Kaiko RF, Wallenstein SL, Rogers AG, et al, "Narcotics in the Elderly," *Med Clin North Am*, 1982, 66(5):1079-89.

Levy MH, "Pharmacologic Treatment of Cancer Pain," *N Engl J Med*, 1996, 335(15):1124-32.

Mokhlesi B, Leikin JB, Murray P, et al, "Adult Toxicology in Critical Care: Part II: Specific Poisonings," *Chest*, 2003, 123(3):897-922.

Nasraway SA, "Use of Sedative Medications in the Intensive Care Unit," *Sem Resp Crit Care Med*, 2001, 22(2):165-74.

"Principles of Analgesic Use in the Treatment of Acute Pain and Cancer Pain," 5th ed, Glenview, IL: American Pain Society, 2003.

Zacher JL and Givone DM, "False-Positive Urine Opiate Screening Associated With Fluoroquinolone Use," *Ann Pharmacother*, 2004, 38:1525-28.

♦ **Hydromorphone HP (Can)** *see* Hydromorphone *on page 553*

♦ **Hydromorphone HP® 10 (Can)** *see* Hydromorphone *on page 553*

♦ **Hydromorphone HP® 20 (Can)** *see* Hydromorphone *on page 553*

♦ **Hydromorphone HP® 50 (Can)** *see* Hydromorphone *on page 553*

♦ **Hydromorphone HP® Forte (Can)** *see* Hydromorphone *on page 553*

♦ **Hydromorphone Hydrochloride** *see* Hydromorphone *on page 553*

♦ **Hydromorphone Hydrochloride Injection, USP (Can)** *see* Hydromorphone *on page 553*

♦ **HydroVal® (Can)** *see* Hydrocortisone *on page 545*

♦ **Hydroxycarbamide** *see* Hydroxyurea *on page 559*

♦ **Hydroxydaunomycin Hydrochloride** *see* DOXOrubicin *on page 352*

♦ **Hydroxyldaunorubicin Hydrochloride** *see* DOXOrubicin *on page 352*

Hydroxyurea (hye droks ee yoor EE a)

Medication Safety Issues
Sound-alike/look-alike issues:
Hydroxyurea may be confused with hydrOXYzine

High alert medication: The Institute for Safe Medication Practices (ISMP) includes this medication among its list of drugs which have a heightened risk of causing significant patient harm when used in error.

International issues:
Hydrea® may be confused with Hydra® which is a brand name for isoniazid in Japan

Related Information
Safe Handling of Hazardous Drugs *on page 1382*

U.S. Brand Names Droxia®; Hydrea®; Mylocel™

Index Terms Hydroxycarbamide

Generic Available Yes: Capsule

Canadian Brand Names Apo-Hydroxyurea®; Gen-Hydroxyurea; Hydrea®

Pharmacologic Category Antineoplastic Agent, Antimetabolite

Use Treatment of melanoma, refractory chronic myelocytic leukemia (CML), relapsed and refractory metastatic ovarian cancer; radiosensitizing agent in the treatment of squamous cell head and neck cancer (excluding lip cancer); adjunct in the management of sickle cell patients who have had at least three painful crises in the previous 12 months (to reduce frequency of these crises and the need for blood transfusions)

Unlabeled/Investigational Use Treatment of HIV; treatment of psoriasis, treatment of hematologic conditions such as essential thrombocythemia, polycythemia vera, hypereosinophilia, and hyperleukocytosis due to acute (Continued)

Hydroxyurea *(Continued)*

leukemia; treatment of uterine, cervix and nonsmall cell lung cancers; radiosensitizing agent in the treatment of primary brain tumors; has shown activity against renal cell cancer and prostate cancer

Pregnancy Risk Factor D

Lactation Enters breast milk/contraindicated

Labeled Contraindications Hypersensitivity to hydroxyurea or any component of the formulation; severe anemia; severe bone marrow suppression; WBC <2500/mm³ or platelet count <100,000/mm³ (neutrophils <2000/mm³, platelets <80,000/mm³, and hemoglobin <4.5 g/dL for sickle cell anemia); pregnancy

Warnings/Precautions Hazardous agent - use appropriate precautions for handling and disposal. Patients with a history of prior cytotoxic chemotherapy and radiation therapy are more likely to experience bone marrow depression. Patients with a history of radiation therapy are also at risk for exacerbation of post irradiation erythema. Megaloblastic erythropoiesis may be seen early in hydroxyurea treatment; plasma iron clearance may be delayed and the rate of utilization of iron by erythrocytes may be delayed. HIV-infected patients treated with hydroxyurea and antiretroviral agents (including didanosine) are at higher risk for potentially fatal pancreatitis, hepatotoxicity, hepatic failure, and severe peripheral neuropathy. **[U.S. Boxed Warning]: Hydroxyurea is mutagenic and clastogenic. Treatment of myeloproliferative disorders (polycythemia vera and thrombocythemia) with long-term hydroxyurea is associated with secondary leukemia**; it is unknown if this is drug-related or disease-related. Cutaneous vasculitic toxicities (vasculitic ulceration and gangrene) have been reported with hydroxyurea treatment, most often in patients with a history of or receiving concurrent interferon therapy; discontinue hydroxyurea and consider alternate cytoreductive therapy if cutaneous vasculitic toxicity develops. Use caution with renal dysfunction; may require dose reductions. **[U.S. Boxed Warning]: Should be administered under the supervision of a physician experienced in cancer chemotherapy or in the treatment of sickle cell anemia.**

Adverse Reactions Frequency not defined.

Cardiovascular: Edema

Central nervous system: Chills, disorientation, dizziness, drowsiness (dose-related), fever, hallucinations, headache, malaise, seizure

Dermatologic: Alopecia (rare), cutaneous vasculitic toxicities, dermatomyositis-like skin changes, dry skin, facial erythema, gangrene, hyperpigmentation, maculopapular rash, nail atrophy, nail pigmentation, peripheral erythema, scaling, skin atrophy, skin cancer, skin ulcer, vasculitis ulcerations, violet papules

Endocrine & metabolic: Hyperuricemia

Gastrointestinal: Anorexia, constipation, diarrhea, gastrointestinal irritation and mucositis, (potentiated with radiation therapy), nausea, pancreatitis, stomatitis, vomiting

Genitourinary: Dysuria (rare)

Hematologic: Myelosuppression (primarily leukopenia; onset: 24-48 hours; nadir: 10 days; recovery: 7 days after stopping drug; reversal of WBC count occurs rapidly but the platelet count may take 7-10 days to recover); thrombocytopenia and anemia, megaloblastic erythropoiesis, macrocytosis, hemolysis, serum iron decreased, persistent cytopenias, secondary leukemias (long-term use)

Hepatic: Hepatic enzymes increased, hepatotoxicity

Neuromuscular & skeletal: Peripheral neuropathy, weakness

Renal: BUN increased, creatinine increased

Respiratory: Acute diffuse pulmonary infiltrates (rare), dyspnea, pulmonary fibrosis (rare)

Overdosage/Toxicology Symptoms of overdose include myelosuppression, facial swelling, hallucinations, disorientation, soreness, violet erythema, edema on palms and soles, scaling on hands and feet, severe generalized hyperpigmentation of the skin, and stomatitis. Treatment is symptom-directed and supportive.

Drug Interactions

Increased Effect/Toxicity: Hydroxyurea may increase the toxicity of didanosine.

Storage/Stability Store at room temperature between 15°C and 30°C (59°F and 86°F).

Mechanism of Action Thought to interfere (unsubstantiated hypothesis) with synthesis of DNA, during the S phase of cell division, without interfering with RNA synthesis; inhibits ribonucleoside diphosphate reductase, preventing conversion of ribonucleotides to deoxyribonucleotides; cell-cycle specific for the S phase and may hold other cells in the G_1 phase of the cell cycle. In sickle cell anemia, hydroxyurea increases red blood cell (RBC) hemoglobin F levels, RBC water content, deformability of sickled cells, and alters adhesion of RBCs to endothelium.

Pharmacodynamics/Kinetics

Absorption: Readily ($\geq$80%)

Distribution: Readily crosses blood-brain barrier; distributes into intestine, brain, lung, kidney tissues, effusions and ascites

Metabolism: 60% via hepatic and GI tract

Half-life elimination: 3-4 hours

Time to peak: 1-4 hours

Excretion: Urine (80%, 50% as unchanged drug, 30% as urea); exhaled gases (as CO_2)

Dosage Oral (refer to individual protocols): All doses should be based on ideal or actual body weight, whichever is less:

Children (unlabeled use):

No FDA-approved dosage regimens have been established; dosages of 1500-3000 mg/m^2 as a single dose in combination with other agents every 4-6 weeks have been used in the treatment of pediatric astrocytoma, medulloblastoma, and primitive neuroectodermal tumors

CML: Initial: 10-20 mg/kg/day once daily; adjust dose according to hematologic response

Adults: Dose should always be titrated to patient response and WBC counts; usual oral doses range from 10-30 mg/kg/day or 500-3000 mg/day; if WBC count falls to <2500 cells/mm^3, or the platelet count to <100,000/mm^3, therapy should be stopped for at least 3 days and resumed when values rise toward normal

Solid tumors:

Intermittent therapy: 80 mg/kg as a single dose every third day

Continuous therapy: 20-30 mg/kg/day given as a single dose/day

Concomitant therapy with irradiation: 80 mg/kg as a single dose every third day starting at least 7 days before initiation of irradiation

Resistant chronic myelocytic leukemia: Continuous therapy: 20-30 mg/kg once daily

HIV (unlabeled use; in combination with antiretroviral agents): 1000-1500 mg daily in a single dose or divided doses

Psoriasis (unlabeled use): 1000-1500 mg/day in a single dose or divided doses

(Continued)

Hydroxyurea *(Continued)*

Sickle cell anemia (moderate/severe disease): Initial: 15 mg/kg/day, increased by 5 mg/kg every 12 weeks if blood counts are in an acceptable range until the maximum tolerated dose of 35 mg/kg/day is achieved or the dose that does not produce toxic effects

Acceptable range:

Neutrophils ≥2500 cells/mm^3

Platelets ≥95,000/mm^3

Hemoglobin >5.3 g/dL, and

Reticulocytes ≥95,000/mm^3 if the hemoglobin concentration is <9 g/dL

Toxic range:

Neutrophils <2000 cells/mm^3

Platelets <80,000/mm^3

Hemoglobin <4.5 g/dL

Reticulocytes <80,000/mm^3 if the hemoglobin concentration is <9 g/dL

Monitor for toxicity every 2 weeks; if toxicity occurs, stop treatment until the bone marrow recovers; restart at 2.5 mg/kg/day less than the dose at which toxicity occurs; if no toxicity occurs over the next 12 weeks, then the subsequent dose should be increased by 2.5 mg/kg/day; reduced dosage of hydroxyurea alternating with erythropoietin may decrease myelotoxicity and increase levels of fetal hemoglobin in patients who have not been helped by hydroxyurea alone

Dosing adjustment in renal impairment:

The FDA-approved labeling recommends the following adjustment:

Sickle cell anemia: Cl$_{cr}$ <60 mL/minute or ESRD: Reduce initial dose to 7.5 mg/kg; titrate to response/avoidance of toxicity (refer to usual dosing).

Other indications: It is recommended to reduce the initial dose; however, no specific guidelines are available.

The following guidelines have been used by some clinicians:

Aronoff, 2007: Adults:

Cl$_{cr}$ 10-50 mL/minute: Administer 50% of dose

Cl$_{cr}$ <10 mL/minute: Administer 20% of dose

Hemodialysis: Administer dose after dialysis on dialysis days; supplemental dose is not necessary. Hydroxyurea is a low molecular weight compound with high aqueous solubility that may be freely dialyzable, however, clinical studies confirming this hypothesis have not been performed.

Continuous renal replacement therapy (CRRT): Administer 50% of dose

Kintzel, 1995:

Cl$_{cr}$ 46-60 mL/minute: Administer 85% of dose

Cl$_{cr}$ 31-45 mL/minute: Administer 80% of dose

Cl$_{cr}$ <30 mL/minute: Administer 75% of dose

Dosing adjustment in hepatic impairment: Specific guidelines are not available for dosage adjustment in hepatic impairment. The FDA-approved labeling recommends closely monitoring for bone marrow toxicity in patients with hepatic impairment.

Combination Regimens

Brain tumors: 8 in 1 (Brain Tumors) *on page 1141*

Gestational trophoblastic tumor:

CHAMOCA (Modified Bagshawe Regimen) *on page 1170*

CHAMOMA (Bagshawe Regimen) *on page 1172*

Head and neck cancer: FU HURT *on page 1223*

Neuroblastoma: N4SE Protocol *on page 1260*

Retinoblastoma: 8 in 1 (Retinoblastoma) *on page 1142*

Administration Capsules may be opened and emptied into water (will not dissolve completely); observe proper handling procedures

Monitoring Parameters CBC with differential and platelets, renal function and liver function tests, serum uric acid

Sickle cell disease: Monitor for toxicity every 2 weeks. If toxicity occurs, stop treatment until the bone marrow recovers; restart at 2.5 mg/kg/day less than the dose at which toxicity occurs. If no toxicity occurs over the next 12 weeks, then the subsequent dose should be increased by 2.5 mg/kg/day. Reduced dosage of hydroxyurea alternating with erythropoietin may decrease myelotoxicity and increase levels of fetal hemoglobin in patients who have not been helped by hydroxyurea alone.

Acceptable range: Neutrophils ≥2500 cells/mm^3, platelets ≥95,000/mm^3, hemoglobin >5.3 g/dL, and reticulocytes ≥95,000/mm^3 if the hemoglobin concentration is <9 g/dL

Toxic range: Neutrophils <2000 cells/mm^3, platelets <80,000/mm^3, hemoglobin <4.5 g/dL, and reticulocytes <80,000/mm^3 if the hemoglobin concentration is <9 g/dL

Dietary Considerations In sickle cell patients, supplemental administration of folic acid is recommended; hydroxyurea may mask development of folic acid deficiency.

Patient Information Take capsules exactly on schedule directed by prescriber (dosage and timing will be specific to purpose of therapy). Contents of capsule may be emptied into a glass of water and taken immediately. You will require frequent monitoring and blood tests while taking this medication to assess effectiveness and monitor adverse reactions. You will be susceptible to infection; avoid crowds, infected persons, and persons with contagious diseases. You may experience nausea, vomiting, or loss of appetite (small frequent meals, frequent mouth care, sucking lozenges, or chewing gum may help); constipation (increased exercise, fluid, or dietary fiber may help); diarrhea (buttermilk, boiled milk, or yogurt may help); mouth sores (frequent mouth care will help). Report persistent vomiting, diarrhea, constipation, stomach pain, or mouth sores; skin rash, redness, irritation, or sores; painful or difficult urination; increased confusion, depression, hallucinations, lethargy, or seizures; persistent fever or chills, unusual fatigue, white plaques in mouth, vaginal discharge, or unhealed sores; unusual lassitude, weakness, or muscle tremors; easy bruising/bleeding; or blood in vomitus, stool, or urine. People not taking hydroxyurea should not be exposed to it; if powder from capsule is spilled, wipe up with damp, disposable towel immediately, and discard the towel in a closed container, such as a plastic bag; wash hands thoroughly. Contraceptive measures are recommended during therapy.

Special Geriatric Considerations Elderly may be more sensitive to the effects of this drug and may require a lower dosage regimen; advance dose slowly and adjust dose for renal function with careful monitoring.

Additional Information Although I.V. use is reported, no parenteral product is commercially available in the U.S.

If WBC decreases to <2500/mm^3 or platelet count to <100,000/mm^3 (neutrophils <2000/mm^3 and platelets <80,000/mm^3 for patients with sickle cell anemia), interrupt therapy until values rise significantly toward normal. Treat anemia with whole blood replacement; do not interrupt therapy (for sickle cell anemia patients, withhold treatment for hemoglobin <4.5 g/dL until recovery to >5.3 g/dL). Adequate trial period to determine the antineoplastic effectiveness is 6 weeks. Almost all patients receiving hydroxyurea in clinical trials needed to have their medication stopped for a time to allow their low blood count to return to acceptable levels.

(Continued)

Hydroxyurea *(Continued)*

Emetic Potential Low (10% to 30%)

Dosage Forms Excipient information presented when available (limited, particularly for generics); consult specific product labeling.

Capsule: 500 mg

Droxia®: 200 mg, 300 mg, 400 mg

Hydrea®: 500 mg

Tablet:

Mylocel™: 1000 mg

References

Aronoff GR, Bennett WM, Berns JS, et al, *Drug Prescribing in Renal Failure: Dosing Guidelines for Adults and Children*, 5th ed. Philadelphia, PA: American College of Physicians; 2007, p 100.

Garcia F, Plana M, Arnedo M, et al, "A Cytostatic Drug Improves Control of HIV-1 Replication During Structured Treatment Interruptions: A Randomized Study," *AIDS*, 2003, 17(1):43-51.

Gwilt PR and Tracewell WG, "Pharmacokinetics and Pharmacodynamics of Hydroxyurea," *Clin Pharmacokinet*, 1998, 34(5):347-58.

Howard LW and Kennedy LD, "Hydroxyurea in the Treatment of Sickle-Cell Anemia," *Ann Pharmacother*, 1997, 31(11):1393-6.

Kintzel PE and Dorr RT, "Anticancer Drug Renal Toxicity and Elimination: Dosing Guidelines for Altered Renal Function," *Cancer Treat Rev*, 1995, 21(1):33-64.

Kumar B, Saraswat A, and Kaur I, "Rediscovering Hydroxyurea: Its Role in Recalcitrant Psoriasis," *Int J Dermatol*, 2001, 40(8):530-4.

Lafeuillade A, Hittinger G, Chadapaud S, et al, "The HYDILE Trial: Efficacy and Tolerance of a Quadruple Combination of Reverse Transcriptase Inhibitors Versus the Same Regimen Plus Hydroxyurea or Hydroxyurea and Interleukin-2 in HIV-infected Patients Failing Protease Inhibitor-based Combinations," *HIV Clin Trials*, 2002, 3(4):263-71.

Longhurst HJ, and Pinching AJ, "Pancreatitis Associated With Hydroxyurea in Combination With Didanosine," *Br Med J*, 2001, 322(7278):81.

Lossos IS and Matzner Y, "Hydroxyurea-Induced Fever: Case Report and Review of the Literature," *Ann Pharmacother*, 1995, 29(2):132-3.

Maier-Redelsperger M, de Montalembert M, Flahault A, et al, "Fetal Hemoglobin and F-Cell Responses to Long-Term Hydroxyurea Treatment in Young Sickle Cell Patients. The French Study Group on Sickle Cell Disease," *Blood*, 1998, 91(12):4472-9.

Montaner JS, Zala C, Conway B, et al, "A Pilot Study of Hydroxyurea Among Patients With Advanced Human Immunodeficiency Virus (HIV) Disease Receiving Chronic Didanosine Therapy: Canadian HIV Trials Network Protocol 080," *J Infect Dis*, 1997, 175(4):801-6.

Navarra P and Preziosi P, "Hydroxyurea: New Insights on an Old Drug," *Crit Rev Oncol Hematol*, 1999, 29(3):249-55.

Stevens MR, "Hydroxyurea: An Overview," *J Biol Regul Homeost Agents*, 1999, 13(3):172-5.

Yarboro JW, "Mechanism of Action of Hydroxyurea," *Semin Oncol*, 1992, 19(3 Suppl 9):1-10.

HydrOXYzine *(hye DROKS i zeen)*

Medication Safety Issues

Sound-alike/look-alike issues:

HydrOXYzine may be confused with hydrALAZINE, hydroxyurea

Atarax® may be confused with amoxicillin, Ativan®

Vistaril® may be confused with Restoril®, Versed, Zestril®

International issues:

Vistaril® may be confused with Vastarel® which is a brand name for trimetazidine in multiple international markets

Related Information

Management of Nausea and Vomiting *on page 1319*

U.S. Brand Names Vistaril®

Index Terms Hydroxyzine Hydrochloride; Hydroxyzine Pamoate

Generic Available Yes

Canadian Brand Names Apo-Hydroxyzine®; Atarax®; Hydroxyzine Hydrochloride Injection, USP; Novo-Hydroxyzin; PMS-Hydroxyzine; Vistaril®

Pharmacologic Category Antiemetic; Antihistamine

Use Treatment of anxiety; preoperative sedative; antipruritic

Unlabeled/Investigational Use Antiemetic; ethanol withdrawal symptoms

Pregnancy Risk Factor C

Lactation Excretion in breast milk unknown/not recommended

Labeled Contraindications Hypersensitivity to hydroxyzine or any component of the formulation; early pregnancy; SubQ, intra-arterial, or I.V. administration of injection

Warnings/Precautions Causes sedation, caution must be used in performing tasks which require alertness (eg, operating machinery or driving). Sedative effects of CNS depressants or ethanol are potentiated. SubQ, I.V., and intra-arterial administration are contraindicated since tissue damage, intravascular hemolysis, thrombosis, and digital gangrene can occur. Use with caution with narrow-angle glaucoma, prostatic hyperplasia, bladder neck obstruction, asthma, or COPD. Not recommended for use as a sedative or anxiolytic in the elderly.

Adverse Reactions Frequency not defined.

Central nervous system: Dizziness, drowsiness, fatigue, hallucination, headache, nervousness, seizure

Dermatologic: Pruritus, rash, urticaria

Gastrointestinal: Xerostomia

Neuromuscular & skeletal: Involuntary movements, paresthesia, tremor

Ocular: Blurred vision

Respiratory: Thickening of bronchial secretions

Miscellaneous: Allergic reaction

Overdosage/Toxicology Symptoms of overdose include seizures, sedation, and hypotension. There is no specific treatment for antihistamine overdose. Clinical toxicity is due to blockade of cholinergic receptors. For anticholinergic overdose with severe life-threatening symptoms, physostigmine 1-2 mg I.V. slowly, may be given to reverse these effects.

Drug Interactions

Cytochrome P450 Effect: Inhibits CYP2D6 (weak)

Increased Effect/Toxicity: CNS depressants, anticholinergics, and pramlintide used in combination with hydroxyzine may result in additive effects.

Decreased Effect:

Acetylcholinesterase Inhibitors (Central) may diminish the anticholinergic of hydroxyzine. If the anticholinergic effect is a side effect of the agent, as is the case with hydroxyzine, the result may be beneficial.

Ethanol/Nutrition/Herb Interactions

Ethanol: Avoid ethanol (may increase CNS depression).

Herb/Nutraceutical: Avoid valerian, St John's wort, kava kava, gotu kola (may increase CNS depression).

Storage/Stability Injection: Store at 15°C to 30°C. Protect from light.

Compatibility Compatibility in syringe: Compatible: Atropine, atropine with meperidine, butorphanol, chlorpromazine, cimetidine, codeine, diphenhydramine, doxapram, droperidol, fentanyl, fluphenazine, glycopyrrolate, hydromorphone, lidocaine, meperidine, methotrimeprazine, metoclopramide, midazolam, morphine, nalbuphine, oxymorphone, pentazocine, perphenazine, procaine, prochlorperazine edisylate, promazine, promethazine, scopolamine, sufentanil. **Incompatible:** Dimenhydrinate, haloperidol, ketorolac, pentobarbital, ranitidine.

Mechanism of Action Competes with histamine for H_1-receptor sites on effector cells in the gastrointestinal tract, blood vessels, and respiratory tract. Possesses skeletal muscle relaxing, bronchodilator, antihistamine, antiemetic, and analgesic properties.

Pharmacodynamics/Kinetics

Onset of action: Oral: 15-30 minutes

(Continued)

HydrOXYzine *(Continued)*

Duration: 4-6 hours

Absorption: Oral: Rapid

Metabolism: Forms metabolites

Half-life elimination: 3-7 hours

Time to peak: ~2 hours

Excretion: Urine

Dosage

Children:

Preoperative sedation:

Oral: 0.6 mg/kg/dose

I.M.: 0.5-1 mg/kg/dose

Pruritus, anxiety: Oral:

<6 years: 50 mg daily in divided doses

≥6 years: 50-100 mg daily in divided doses

Adults:

Antiemetic (unlabeled use): I.M.: 25-100 mg/dose every 4-6 hours as needed

Anxiety: Oral, I.M.: 50-100 mg 4 times/day

Preoperative sedation:

Oral: 50-100 mg

I.M.: 25-100 mg

Pruritus: Oral, I.M.: 25 mg 3-4 times/day

Dosing interval in hepatic impairment: Change dosing interval to every 24 hours in patients with primary biliary cirrhosis

Administration Do not administer SubQ or intra-arterially. Administer I.M. deep in large muscle. With I.V. administration, extravasation can result in sterile abscess and marked tissue induration.

Monitoring Parameters Relief of symptoms, mental status, blood pressure

Patient Information Will cause drowsiness, avoid alcohol and other CNS depressants, avoid driving and other hazardous tasks until the CNS effects are known

Special Geriatric Considerations Anticholinergic effects are not well tolerated in the elderly and frequently result in bowel, bladder, and mental status changes (ie, constipation, confusion, and urinary retention). Hydroxyzine may be useful as a short-term antipruritic, but it is not recommended for use as a sedative or anxiolytic in the elderly.

Emetic Potential Very low (<10%)

Dosage Forms Excipient information presented when available (limited, particularly for generics); consult specific product labeling. [DSC] = Discontinued product

Capsule, as pamoate: 25 mg, 50 mg, 100 mg

Vistaril®: 25 mg, 50 mg

Injection, solution, as hydrochloride: 25 mg/mL (1 mL); 50 mg/mL (1 mL, 2 mL, 10 mL)

Suspension, oral, as pamoate:

Vistaril®: 25 mg/5 mL (120 mL, 480 mL) [lemon flavor] [DSC]

Syrup, as hydrochloride: 10 mg/5 mL (120 mL, 480 mL)

Tablet, as hydrochloride: 10 mg, 25 mg, 50 mg

References

Baumgartner T, "Administration of Hydroxyzine Injection," *Am J Hosp Pharm*, 1979, 36(12):1660.

Serreau R, Komiha M, Blanc F, et al, "Neonatal Seizures Associated With Maternal Hydroxyzine Hydrochloride in Late Pregnancy," *Reprod Toxicol*, 2005, 20(4):573-4.

Simons FE, Simons KJ, and Frith EM, "The Pharmacokinetics and Antihistaminic of the H₁ Receptor Antagonist Hydroxyzine," *J Allergy Clin Immunol*, 1984, 73(1 Pt 1):69-75.

Simons FE, Watson WT, Chen XY, et al, "The Pharmacokinetics and Pharmacodynamics of Hydroxyzine in Patients With Primary Biliary Cirrhosis," *J Clin Pharmacol*, 1989, 29(9):809-15.

Simons KJ, Watson WT, Chen XY, et al, "Pharmacokinetic and Pharmacodynamic Studies of the H₁-Receptor Antagonist Hydroxyzine in the Elderly," *Clin Pharmacol Ther*, 1989, 45(1):9-14.

♦ **Hydroxyzine Hydrochloride** *see* HydrOXYzine *on page 564*

♦ **Hydroxyzine Hydrochloride Injection, USP (Can)** *see* HydrOXYzine *on page 564*

♦ **Hydroxyzine Pamoate** *see* HydrOXYzine *on page 564*

♦ **HydroZone Plus [OTC]** *see* Hydrocortisone *on page 545*

♦ **Hylenex™** *see* Hyaluronidase *on page 543*

♦ **HyperRHO™ S/D Full Dose** *see* Rhₒ(D) Immune Globulin *on page 948*

♦ **HyperRHO™ S/D Mini Dose** *see* Rhₒ(D) Immune Globulin *on page 948*

♦ **Hytone®** *see* Hydrocortisone *on page 545*

Ibandronate (eye BAN droh nate)

Related Information

Safe Handling of Hazardous Drugs *on page 1382*

U.S. Brand Names Boniva®

Index Terms Ibandronate Sodium; Ibandronic Acid; NSC-722623

Generic Available No

Canadian Brand Names Bondronat®

Pharmacologic Category Bisphosphonate Derivative

Use Treatment and prevention of osteoporosis in postmenopausal females

Unlabeled/Investigational Use Hypercalcemia of malignancy; corticosteroid-induced osteoporosis; Paget's disease; reduce bone pain and skeletal complications from metastatic bone disease

Pregnancy Risk Factor C

Lactation Excretion in breast milk unknown/use caution

Labeled Contraindications Hypersensitivity to ibandronate, other bisphosphonates, or any component of the formulation; hypocalcemia; oral tablets are also contraindicated in patients unable to stand or sit upright for at least 60 minutes

Warnings/Precautions Hypocalcemia must be corrected before therapy initiation. Ensure adequate calcium and vitamin D intake. Bisphosphonate therapy has been associated with osteonecrosis, primarily of the jaw; this has been observed mostly in cancer patients, but also in patients with postmenopausal osteoporosis and other diagnoses. Dental exams and preventative dentistry should be performed prior to placing patients with risk factors on chronic bisphosphonate therapy. Invasive dental procedures should be avoided during treatment.

Infrequently, severe (and occasionally debilitating) bone, joint, and/or muscle pain have been reported during bisphosphonate treatment. The onset of pain ranged from a single day to several months. Symptoms usually resolve upon discontinuation. Some patients experienced recurrence when rechallenged with same drug or another bisphosphonate; avoid use in patients with a history of these symptoms in association with bisphosphonate therapy.

Oral bisphosphonates may cause dysphagia, esophagitis, esophageal or gastric ulcer; risk may increase in patients unable to comply with dosing instructions. Intravenous bisphosphonates may cause transient decreases in serum calcium and have also been associated with renal toxicity.
(Continued)

Ibandronate *(Continued)*

Use not recommended with severe renal impairment (Cl$_{cr}$ <30 mL/minute or serum creatinine >2.3 mg/dL). Safety and efficacy have not been established in patients <18 years of age.

Adverse Reactions Percentages vary based on frequency of administration (daily vs monthly). Unless specified, percentages are reported with oral use.

>10%:

Gastrointestinal: Dyspepsia (6% to 12%)

Neuromuscular & skeletal: Back pain (4% to 14%)

1% to 10%:

Central nervous system: Headache (3% to 7%), dizziness (1% to 4%), insomnia (1% to 2%)

Dermatologic: Rash (1% to 2%)

Endocrine & metabolic: Hypercholesterolemia (5%)

Gastrointestinal: Abdominal pain (5% to 8%), diarrhea (4% to 7%), nausea (5%), tooth disorder (4%), vomiting (3%), constipation (3% to 4%)

Genitourinary: Urinary tract infection (2% to 6%)

Hepatic: Alkaline phosphatase decreased (frequency not defined)

Local: Injection site reaction (<2%)

Neuromuscular & skeletal: Pain in extremity (8%), myalgia (1% to 6%), joint disorder (4%), weakness (4%), muscle cramp (2%)

Respiratory: Bronchitis (3% to 10%), pneumonia (6%), pharyngitis/nasopharyngitis (3% to 4%), upper respiratory infection (2%)

Miscellaneous: Acute phase reaction (I.V. 10%; oral 4%), allergic reaction (3%), flu-like syndrome (1% to 3%)

Postmarketing and/or case reports: Incapacitating bone, joint or muscle pain, ocular inflammation, scleritis, uveitis

Overdosage/Toxicology Dyspepsia, esophagitis, gastritis, ulcer, hypocalcemia, hypophosphatemia, hypomagnesemia, or upset stomach may be seen with overdose. Milk or antacids may be used to bind ibandronate. Patient should remain fully upright, and vomiting should not be induced to avoid esophageal irritation. Following overdose with I.V. formulation, dialysis may be of benefit if administered within 2 hours of overdose.

Drug Interactions

Increased Effect/Toxicity: Aminoglycosides may lower serum calcium levels with prolonged administration; concomitant use may have an additive hypocalcemic effect. Nonsteroidal anti-inflammatory drugs may enhance the gastrointestinal adverse/toxic effects (increased incidence of GI ulcers) of bisphosphonate derivatives. Bisphosphonate derivatives may enhance the hypocalcemic effect of phosphate supplements.

Decreased Effect: The following agents may decrease the absorption of oral bisphosphonate derivatives: Antacids (aluminum, calcium, magnesium), oral calcium salts, oral iron salts, and oral magnesium salts

Ethanol/Nutrition/Herb Interactions

Ethanol: Avoid ethanol (may increase risk of osteoporosis).

Food: May reduce absorption; mean oral bioavailability is decreased up to 90% when given with food.

Storage/Stability Store at controlled room temperature of 15°C to 30°C (59°F to 86°F).

Mechanism of Action A bisphosphonate which inhibits bone resorption via actions on osteoclasts or on osteoclast precursors; decreases the rate of bone resorption, leading to an indirect increase in bone mineral density.

Pharmacodynamics/Kinetics

Distribution: Terminal V$_d$: 90 L; 40% to 50% of circulating ibandronate binds to bone

Protein binding: 85% to 99%

Bioavailability: Oral: Reduced by 90% following standard breakfast

Half-life elimination:

Oral: 150 mg dose: Terminal: 37-157 hours

I.V.: Terminal: ~5-25 hours

Time to peak, plasma: Oral: 0.5-2 hours

Excretion: Urine (50% to 60% of absorbed dose, excreted as unchanged drug); feces (unabsorbed drug)

Dosage

Oral:

Treatment of postmenopausal osteoporosis: 2.5 mg/day or 150 mg once a month

Prevention of postmenopausal osteoporosis: 2.5 mg/day; 150 mg once a month may be considered

Metastatic bone disease (unlabeled use): 50 mg once daily

I.V.:

Treatment of postmenopausal osteoporosis: 3 mg every 3 months

Hypercalcemia of malignancy (unlabeled use): 2-4 mg over 2 hours

Metastatic bone disease (unlabeled use): 6 mg over 1 hour every 3-4 weeks

Dosage adjustment in renal impairment:

Mild or moderate impairment: Dosing adjustment not needed

Severe impairment (Cl_{cr} <30 mL/minute): Use not recommended

Dose adjustment in renal impairment for oncologic uses (unlabeled):

Severe impairment (Cl_{cr} <30 mL/minute):

Oral: 50 mg once weekly

I.V.: 2 mg over 1 hour every 3-4 weeks

Dosage adjustment in hepatic impairment: Dosing adjustment not needed

Administration

Oral: Should be administered 60 minutes before the first food or drink of the day (other than water). Ibandronate should be taken in an upright position with a full glass (6-8 oz) of plain water and the patient should avoid lying down for 60 minutes to minimize the possibility of GI side effects. Mineral water with a high calcium content should be avoided. The tablet should be swallowed whole; do not chew or suck.

Once-monthly dosing: The 150 mg tablet should be taken on the same date each month. In case of a missed dose, do not take two 150 mg tablets within the same week. If the next scheduled dose is 1-7 days away, wait until the next scheduled dose to take the tablet. If the next scheduled dose is >7 days away, take the dose the morning it is remembered, and then resume taking the once-monthly dose on the originally scheduled day.

I.V.: Administer as a 15-30 second bolus. Do not mix with calcium-containing solutions or other drugs. For osteoporosis, do not administer more frequently than every 3 months. Infuse over 1 hour for metastatic bone disease and over 2 hours for hypercalcemia of malignancy.

Monitoring Parameters Bone mineral density; serum creatinine prior to each I.V. dose

Test Interactions Bisphosphonates may interfere with diagnostic imaging agents such as technetium-99m-diphosphonate in bone scans.

Dietary Considerations Supplemental calcium or vitamin D may be required if dietary intake is not adequate. Tablet should be taken with a full

(Continued)

Ibandronate *(Continued)*

glass (6-8 oz) of plain water, at least 60 minutes prior to any food, beverages, or medications. Mineral water with a high calcium content should be avoided.

Special Geriatric Considerations Studies with elderly found no difference between younger adults and the elderly. No special dosage changes are necessary.

Dosage Forms Excipient information presented when available (limited, particularly for generics); consult specific product labeling.

Injection, solution: 1 mg/mL (3 mL) [prefilled syringe]

Tablet: 2.5 mg [once-daily formulation]; 150 mg [once-monthly formulation]

References

Author Unknown, "Safety Update: Bone-Building Drugs: Risks Explained," *Consum Rep Health*, 2006, 18(5):3.

Barrett J, Worth E, Bauss F, et al, "Ibandronate: A Clinical Pharmacological and Pharmacokinetic Update," *J Clin Pharmacol*, 2004, 44(9):951-65.

Marx RE, Sawatari Y, Fortin M, et al, "Bisphosphonate-Induced Exposed Bone (Osteonecrosis/Osteopetrosis) of the Jaws: Risk Factors, Recognition, Prevention, and Treatment," *J Oral Maxillofac Surg*, 2005, 63(11):1567-75.

McCormack PL and Plosker GL, "Ibandronic Acid: A Review of its Use in the Treatment of Bone Metastases of Breast Cancer," *Drugs*, 2006, 66(5):711-28.

Tripathy D, Body JJ, and Bergstrom B, "Review of Ibandronate in the Treatment of Metastatic Bone Disease: Experience From Phase III Trials," *Clin Ther*, 2004, 26(12):1947-59.

Von Moos R, "Bisphosphonate Treatment Recommendations for Oncologists," *Oncologist*, 2005, 10 (Suppl 1):19-24.

♦ **Ibandronate Sodium** see Ibandronate *on page 567*

♦ **Ibandronic Acid** see Ibandronate *on page 567*

Ibritumomab *(ib ri TYOO mo mab)*

Medication Safety Issues

High alert medication: The Institute for Safe Medication Practices (ISMP) includes this medication among its list of drugs which have a heightened risk of causing significant patient harm when used in error.

Dosage maximum: Do not exceed the Y-90 Ibritumomab maximum allowable dose of 32 mCi, regardless of the patient's body weight.

Related Information

Safe Handling of Hazardous Drugs *on page 1382*

U.S. Brand Names Zevalin®

Index Terms Ibritumomab Tiuxetan; IDEC-Y2B8; In-111 Ibritumomab; In-111 Zevalin; Y-90 Ibritumomab; Y-90 Zevalin

Generic Available No

Canadian Brand Names Zevalin®

Pharmacologic Category Antineoplastic Agent, Monoclonal Antibody; Radiopharmaceutical

Use Treatment of relapsed or refractory low-grade, follicular, or transformed B-cell non-Hodgkin's lymphoma

Pregnancy Risk Factor D

Lactation Excretion in breast milk unknown/contraindicated

Labeled Contraindications Known type I hypersensitivity or anaphylactic reactions to ibritumomab, indium chloride, yttrium chloride, or any component of the formulation; murine proteins, rituximab; ≥25% lymphoma marrow involvement; prior myeloablative therapies; platelet count <100,000 cells/mm^3; neutrophil count <1500 cells/mm^3; hypocellular bone marrow (≤15% cellularity of marked reduction in bone marrow precursors); history of failed stem cell collection; pregnancy; breast-feeding. Y-90 ibritumomab should not be administered to patients with altered In-111 ibritumomab biodistribution.

Warnings/Precautions Hazardous agent - use appropriate precautions for handling and disposal. **[U.S. Boxed Warning]: Severe cutaneous and mucocutaneous skin reactions have been reported (with fatalities) in postmarketing experience.** These include erythema multiforme, Stevens-Johnson syndrome, toxic epidermal necrolysis, bullous dermatitis, and exfoliative dermatitis. Onset may occur within days to 3-4 months following infusion. Patients experiencing severe cutaneous or mucocutaneous skin reactions should not receive any further component of the ibritumomab tiuxetan regimen.

To be used as part of the Zevalin® therapeutic regimen (in combination with rituximab). **[U.S. Boxed Warnings]: Do not exceed the Y-90 Ibritumomab maximum allowable dose of 32 mCi; do not administer to patients with altered biodistribution. Use should be reserved to physicians and other professionals qualified and experienced in the safe handling of radiopharmaceuticals, and in monitoring and emergency treatment of infusion reactions.** The contents of the kit are not radioactive until radiolabeling occurs. During and after radiolabeling, adequate shielding should be used with this product, in accordance with institutional radiation safety practices.

[U.S. Boxed Warning]: Severe, potentially-fatal infusion reactions (angioedema, bronchospasm, hypotension, hypoxia) have been reported, typically with the first rituximab infusion (during infusion or within 30-120 minutes of infusion). Patients should be screened for human antimouse antibodies (HAMA); may be at increased risk of allergic or serious hypersensitivity reactions. Medications for the treatment of hypersensitivity reactions should be available for immediate use.

[U.S. Boxed Warning]: Prolonged and severe cytopenias are common. Do not administer with ≥25% lymphoma marrow involvement and/or impaired bone marrow reserve. Hemorrhage may occur due to thrombocytopenia; use caution with patients taking anticoagulants or medications interfering with platelet function. Closely monitor patients for up to 3 months after administration.

Secondary malignancies (acute myelogenous leukemia and myelodysplastic syndrome) have been reported following use. Product contains albumin, which confers a theoretical risk of transmission of viral disease or Creutzfeldt-Jakob disease. Safety and efficacy of repeated courses of the therapeutic regimen have not been established. Safety and efficacy have not been established in pediatric patients.

Adverse Reactions Severe, potentially life-threatening allergic reactions have occurred in association with infusions. Also refer to Rituximab monograph.

>10%:
 Central nervous system: Chills (24%), fever (17%), pain (13%), headache (12%)
 Gastrointestinal: Nausea (31%), abdominal pain (16%), vomiting (12%)
 Hematologic: Thrombocytopenia (95%; grades 3/4: 63%; nadir: 53 days), neutropenia (77%; grades 3/4: 60%; nadir: 62 days), anemia (61%; grades 3/4: 17%; nadir: 68 days), myelosuppression (nadir: 7-9 weeks; duration: 22-35 days)
 Neuromuscular & skeletal: Weakness (43%)
 Respiratory: Dyspnea (14%)
 Miscellaneous: Infection (29%)
1% to 10%:
 Cardiovascular: Peripheral edema (8%), hypotension (6%), flushing (6%), angioedema (5%)
(Continued)

Ibritumomab *(Continued)*

Central nervous system: Dizziness (10%), insomnia (5%), anxiety (4%)

Dermatologic: Pruritus (9%), rash (8%), bruising (7%), angioedema (5%; severe: <1%), urticaria (4%), petechia (3%)

Gastrointestinal: Diarrhea (9%), anorexia (8%), abdominal distension (5%), constipation (5%), dyspepsia (4%), melena (2%; life threatening in 1%), gastrointestinal hemorrhage (1%)

Hematologic: Pancytopenia (2%), secondary malignancies (2% to 6%; includes acute myelogenous leukemia and myelodysplastic syndrome)

Neuromuscular & skeletal: Back pain (8%), arthralgia (7%), myalgia (7%)

Respiratory: Cough (10%), throat irritation (10%), rhinitis (6%), bronchospasm (5%), epistaxis (3%), apnea (1%)

Miscellaneous: Diaphoresis (4%), allergic reaction (2%; life-threatening in 1%)

<1%: Anaphylactic reactions, arthritis, cerebral hemorrhage, cytogenetic abnormalities, encephalopathy, hematemesis, hemorrhage, hypersensitivity, infusion reaction, lung edema, meningioma (benign), pulmonary edema, pulmonary embolism, stroke (hemorrhagic), subdural hematoma, tachycardia, vaginal hemorrhage

Postmarketing and/or case reports: Cutaneous and mucocutaneous reactions (eg, erythema multiforme, Stevens-Johnson Syndrome, toxic epidermal necrolysis, bullous dermatitis and exfoliative dermatitis)

Overdosage/Toxicology Symptoms include severe hematological toxicity. Treatment is symptom-directed and supportive. In early clinical experience with high dosages, some patients required autologous stem cell transplantation.

Drug Interactions

Increased Effect/Toxicity: Due to the high incidence of thrombocytopenia associated with ibritumomab, the use of agents which decrease platelet function may be associated with a higher risk of bleeding (includes aspirin, NSAIDs, glycoprotein IIb/IIIa antagonists, clopidogrel and ticlopidine). In addition, the risk of bleeding may be increased with anticoagulant agents, including heparin, low molecular weight heparins, thrombolytics, and warfarin. The safety of live viral vaccines has not been established.

Decreased Effect: Response to vaccination may be impaired.

Ethanol/Nutrition/Herb Interactions Herb/Nutraceutical: Avoid cat's claw, dong quai, evening primrose, feverfew, garlic, ginger, ginkgo, red clover, horse chestnut, green tea, ginseng (all have antiplatelet activity).

Storage/Stability Store at 2°C to 8°C (36°F to 46°F); do not freeze. Kit is not radioactive.

Reconstitution To prepare radiolabeled injection, follow preparation guidelines provided by manufacturer.

Mechanism of Action Ibritumomab is a monoclonal antibody directed against the CD20 antigen found on B lymphocytes (normal and malignant). Ibritumomab binding induces apoptosis in B lymphocytes *in vitro*. It is combined with the chelator tiuxetan, which acts as a specific chelation site for either Indium-111 (In-111) or Yttrium-90 (Y-90). The monoclonal antibody acts as a delivery system to direct the radioactive isotope to the targeted cells, however, binding has been observed in lymphoid cells throughout the body and in lymphoid nodules in organs such as the large and small intestines. Indium-111 is a gamma-emitter used to assess biodistribution of ibritumomab, while Y-90 emits beta particles. Beta-emission induces cellular damage through the formation of free radicals (in both target cells and surrounding cells).

Pharmacodynamics/Kinetics

Duration: Beta cell recovery begins in ~12 weeks; generally in normal range within 9 months

Distribution: To lymphoid cells throughout the body and in lymphoid nodules in organs such as the large and small intestines, spleen, testes, and liver

Metabolism: Has not been characterized; the product of yttrium-90 radioactive decay is zirconium-90 (nonradioactive); Indium-111 decays to cadmium-111 (nonradioactive)

Half-life elimination: Y-90 ibritumomab: 30 hours; Indium-111 decays with a physical half-life of 67 hours; Yttrium-90 decays with a physical half-life of 64 hours

Excretion: A median of 7.2% of the radiolabeled activity was excreted in urine over 7 days

Dosage I.V.: Adults: Ibritumomab is administered **only** as part of the Zevalin™ therapeutic regimen (a combined treatment regimen with rituximab). The regimen consists of two steps:

Step 1:

Rituximab infusion: 250 mg/m^2 at an initial rate of 50 mg/hour. If hypersensitivity or infusion-related events do not occur, increase infusion in increments of 50 mg/hour every 30 minutes, to a maximum of 400 mg/hour. Infusions should be temporarily slowed or interrupted if hypersensitivity or infusion-related events occur. The infusion may be resumed at one-half the previous rate upon improvement of symptoms.

In-111 ibritumomab infusion: Within 4 hours of the completion of rituximab infusion, inject 5 mCi (1.6 mg total antibody dose) over 10 minutes.

Biodistribution of In-111 ibritumomab should be assessed by imaging at 48-72 hours postinjection. Optional additional imaging may be performed to resolve ambiguities. If biodistribution is not acceptable, the patient should not proceed to Step 2.

Step 2 (initiated 7-9 days following Step 1):

Rituximab infusion: 250 mg/m^2 at an initial rate of 100 mg/hour (50 mg/hour if infusion-related events occurred with the first infusion). If hypersensitivity or infusion-related events do not occur, increase infusion in increments of 100 mg/hour every 30 minutes, to a maximum of 400 mg/hour, as tolerated.

Y-90 ibritumomab infusion: Within 4 hours of the completion of rituximab infusion:

Platelet count >150,000 cells/mm^3: Inject 0.4 mCi/kg (14.8 MBq/kg actual body weight) over 10 minutes; maximum dose: 32 mCi (1184 MBq)

Platelet count between 100,000-149,000 cells/mm^3: Inject 0.3 mCi/kg (11.1 MBq/kg actual body weight) over 10 minutes; maximum dose: 32 mCi (1184 MBq)

Platelet count <100,000 cells/mm^3: Do **not** administer

Maximum dose: The prescribed, measured, and administered dose of Y-90 ibritumomab must not exceed 32 mCi (1184 MBq), regardless of the patient's body weight

Administration

Rituximab: Administer the first infusion of rituximab at an initial rate of 50 mg/hour. If hypersensitivity or infusion-related events do not occur, escalate the infusion rate in 50 mg/hour increments every 30 minutes, to a maximum of 400 mg/hour. If hypersensitivity or an infusion-related event develops, temporarily slow or interrupt the infusion (discontinue if reaction is severe). The infusion can continue at one-half the previous rate upon improvement of patient symptoms. Subsequent rituximab infusion can be (Continued)

Ibritumomab *(Continued)*

administered at an initial rate of 100 mg/hour and increased in 100 mg/hour increments at 30-minute intervals, to a maximum of 400 mg/hour as tolerated.

In-111 and Y-90 ibritumomab: Inject slowly, over 10 minutes through a 0.22 micron low protein binding in-line filter. After injection, flush line with at least 10 mL normal saline. Y-90 ibritumomab: establish free-flowing I.V. line prior to administration; avoid extravasation.

Monitoring Parameters Human antimurine antibody (HAMA) prior to treatment (if positive, may have an allergic or hypersensitivity reaction when treated with this or other murine or chimeric monoclonal antibodies).

Patients must be monitored for infusion-related allergic reactions (typically within 30-120 minutes of administration). Obtain complete blood counts (with differential) and platelet counts at regular intervals during rituximab therapy (at least weekly and more frequently in patients who develop cytopenia). Platelet count must be obtained prior to step 2. Monitor for up to 3 months after use.

Biodistribution of In-111 ibritumomab should be assessed by imaging at 48-72 hours post injection. Optional additional imaging may be performed to resolve ambiguities. If biodistribution is not acceptable, the patient should not proceed to Step 2.

Patient Information

Inform prescriber of all prescriptions, OTC medications, or herbal products you are taking, and any allergies you have. Do not take any new medication during therapy unless approved by prescriber. This medication is used in combination with another medication called rituximab and can only be administered by infusion. You may experience a reaction during the infusion of this medication including high fever, chills, or respiratory difficulty. You will be closely monitored and comfort measures provided. Maintain adequate hydration (2-3 L/day of fluids) during entire course of therapy unless instructed to restrict fluid intake. You will be susceptible to infection and people may wear masks and gloves while caring for you to protect you (avoid crowds and exposure to infection and do not have any vaccinations without consulting prescriber). Report skin reactions, swelling of extremities, unusual weight gain, respiratory difficulty, chest pain or tightness; symptoms of respiratory infection, wheezing or bronchospasms, or respiratory difficulty; unresolved GI effects; sore or irritated throat; fatigue, chills, fever, or other unusual effects related to this medication.

Additional Information Ibritumomab tiuxetan is produced in Chinese hamster ovary cell cultures. Kit is not radioactive. Radiolabeling of ibritumomab with Yttrium-90 and Indium-111 (not included in kit) must be performed by appropriate personnel in a specialized facility.

Dosage Forms Excipient information presented when available (limited, particularly for generics); consult specific product labeling.

Each kit contains 4 vials for preparation of either In-111 or Y-90 conjugate (as indicated on container label)

Injection, solution:

Zevalin®: 1.6 mg/mL (2 mL) [supplied with sodium acetate solution, formulation buffer vial (includes albumin 750 mg), and an empty reaction vial]

References

Borghaei H and Schilder RJ, "Safety and Efficacy of Radioimmunotherapy with Yttrium 90 Ibritumomab Tiuxetan (Zevalin)," *Semin Nucl Med*, 2004, 34(1 Suppl 1):4-9.

Krasner C and Joyce RM, "Zevalin: 90yttrium Labeled Anti-CD20 (Ibritumomab Tiuxetan), A New Treatment for Non-Hodgkin's Lymphoma," *Curr Pharm Biotechnol*, 2001, 2(4):341-9.

Smith BE, "Ibritumomab Tiuxetan: The Cancer Smart Bomb," *J Am Pharm Assoc (Wash DC)*, 2003, 43(3):437-8.

Witzig TE, "Yttrium-90-Ibritumomab Tiuxetan Radioimmunotherapy: A New Treatment Approach for B-Cell Non-Hodgkin's Lymphoma," *Drugs Today (Barc)*, 2004, 40(2):111-9.

- **Ibritumomab Tiuxetan** *see Ibritumomab on page 570*
- **ICI-182,780** *see Fulvestrant on page 482*
- **ICI-46474** *see Tamoxifen on page 1002*
- **ICI-118630** *see Goserelin on page 520*
- **ICI-176334** *see Bicalutamide on page 141*
- **ICI-D1033** *see Anastrozole on page 89*
- **ICI-D1694** *see Raltitrexed on page 943*
- **ICL670** *see Deferasirox on page 316*
- **ICRF-187** *see Dexrazoxane on page 338*
- **Idamycin® (Can)** *see Idarubicin on page 575*
- **Idamycin PFS®** *see Idarubicin on page 575*

Idarubicin (eye da ROO bi sin)

Medication Safety Issues
Sound-alike/look-alike issues:

Idarubicin may be confused with DOXOrubicin, DAUNOrubicin, epirubicin

Idamycin PFS® may be confused with Adriamycin

High alert medication: The Institute for Safe Medication Practices (ISMP) includes this medication among its list of drugs which have a heightened risk of causing significant patient harm when used in error.

Related Information
Management of Drug Extravasations *on page 1301*

Safe Handling of Hazardous Drugs *on page 1382*

U.S. Brand Names Idamycin PFS®

Index Terms 4-Demethoxydaunorubicin; 4-DMDR; Idarubicin Hydrochloride; IDR; IMI 30; NSC-256439; SC 33428

Generic Available Yes

Canadian Brand Names Idamycin®

Pharmacologic Category Antineoplastic Agent, Anthracycline; Antineoplastic Agent, Antibiotic

Use Treatment of acute leukemias (AML, ANLL, ALL), accelerated phase or blast crisis of chronic myelogenous leukemia (CML), breast cancer

Unlabeled/Investigational Use Autologous hematopoietic stem cell transplantation

Pregnancy Risk Factor D

Lactation Excretion in breast milk unknown

Labeled Contraindications Hypersensitivity to idarubicin, other anthracyclines, or any component of the formulation; bilirubin >5 mg/dL; pregnancy

Warnings/Precautions Hazardous agent - use appropriate precautions for handling and disposal. **[U.S. Boxed Warning]: May cause myocardial toxicity (CHF, arrhythmias or cardiomyopathies) and is more common in patients who have previously received anthracyclines or have pre-existing cardiac disease.** The risk of myocardial toxicity is also increased in patients with concomitant or prior mediastinal/pericardial irradiation, patients with anemia, bone marrow depression, infections, leukemic pericarditis or myocarditis. Monitor cardiac function during treatment.

[U.S. Boxed Warnings]: May cause severe myelosuppression; use caution in patients with pre-existing myelosuppression from prior treatment or radiation. Use caution with renal or hepatic impairment; (Continued)

Idarubicin *(Continued)*

may required dosage reductions. For I.V. administration only; may cause severe local tissue damage and necrosis if extravasation occurs. Rapid lysis of leukemic cells may lead to hyperuricemia. Systemic infections should be managed prior to initiation of treatment. **[U.S. Boxed Warning]: Should be administered under the supervision of an experienced cancer chemotherapy physician. Safety and efficacy in children have not been established.**

Adverse Reactions

>10%:

Cardiovascular: Transient ECG abnormalities (supraventricular tachycardia, S-T wave changes, atrial or ventricular extrasystoles); generally asymptomatic and self-limiting. CHF, dose related. The relative cardiotoxicity of idarubicin compared to doxorubicin is unclear. Some investigators report no increase in cardiac toxicity at cumulative oral idarubicin doses up to 540 mg/m^2; other reports suggest a maximum cumulative intravenous dose of 150 mg/m^2.

Central nervous system: Headache

Dermatologic: Alopecia (25% to 30%), radiation recall, skin rash (11%), urticaria

Gastrointestinal: Nausea, vomiting (30% to 60%); diarrhea (9% to 22%); stomatitis (11%); GI hemorrhage (30%)

Genitourinary: Discoloration of urine (darker yellow)

Hematologic: Myelosuppression, primarily leukopenia; thrombocytopenia and anemia. Effects are generally less severe with oral dosing.

Nadir: 10-15 days

Recovery: 21-28 days

Hepatic: Bilirubin and transaminases increased (44%)

1% to 10%:

Central nervous system: Seizure

Neuromuscular & skeletal: Peripheral neuropathy

<1%: Hyperuricemia

Overdosage/Toxicology Symptoms of overdose include severe myelosuppression and increased GI toxicity. Treatment is supportive. It is unlikely that therapeutic efficacy or toxicity would be altered by conventional peritoneal or hemodialysis.

Drug Interactions

Decreased Effect: Patients may experience impaired immune response to vaccines; possible infection after administration of live vaccines in patients receiving immunosuppressants.

Storage/Stability Store intact vials of solution under refrigeration (2°C to 8°C/36°F to 46°F). Protect from light. Solutions diluted in D$_5$W or NS for infusion are stable for 4 weeks at room temperature, protected from light. Syringe and IVPB solutions are stable for 72 hours at room temperature and 7 days under refrigeration.

Compatibility Stable in D$_5$NS, D$_5$W, LR, NS, sterile water for injection, **incompatible** with bacteriostatic water.

Y-site administration: Compatible: Amifostine, amikacin, aztreonam, cimetidine, cladribine, cyclophosphamide, cytarabine, diphenhydramine, droperidol, erythromycin lactobionate, etoposide phosphate, filgrastim, gemcitabine, granisetron, imipenem/cilastatin, magnesium sulfate, mannitol, melphalan, metoclopramide, potassium chloride, ranitidine, sargramostim, thiotepa, vinorelbine. **Incompatible:** Acyclovir, allopurinol, ampicillin/sulbactam, cefazolin, cefepime, ceftazidime, clindamycin, dexamethasone sodium phosphate, etoposide, fluorouracil, furosemide, gentamicin, heparin, hydrocortisone sodium succinate, lorazepam, meperidine, methotrexate, piperacillin/tazobactam, sodium bicarbonate, teniposide, vancomycin, vincristine.

Compatibility when admixed: Incompatible: Heparin.

Mechanism of Action Similar to doxorubicin and daunorubicin; inhibition of DNA and RNA synthesis by intercalation between DNA base pairs

Pharmacodynamics/Kinetics

Absorption: Oral: Variable (4% to 77%; mean: ~30%)

Distribution: V_d: 64 L/kg (some reports indicate 2250 L); extensive tissue binding; CSF

Protein binding: 94% to 97%

Metabolism: Hepatic to idarubicinol (pharmacologically active)

Half-life elimination: Oral: 14-35 hours; I.V.: 12-27 hours

Time to peak, serum: 1-5 hours

Excretion:

Oral: Urine (~5% of dose; 0.5% to 0.7% as unchanged drug, 4% as idarubicinol); hepatic (8%)

I.V.: Urine (13% as idarubicinol, 3% as unchanged drug); hepatic (17%)

Dosage Refer to individual protocols. I.V.:

Children:

Leukemia: 10-12 mg/m²/day for 3 days every 3 weeks

Solid tumors: 5 mg/m²/day for 3 days every 3 weeks

Adults:

Leukemia induction: 12 mg/m²/day for 3 days

Leukemia consolidation: 10-12 mg/m²/day for 2 days

Stem cell transplantation (unlabeled use): 20 mg/m²/24 hours continuous I.V. infusion **or** 21 mg/m²/24 hours continuous infusion for 48 hours (both with high-dose oral busulfan)

Dosing adjustment in renal impairment: The FDA-approved labeling does not contain specific dosing adjustment guidelines; however, it does reccomend that dosage reductions be made. Patients with S_{cr}: ≥2 mg/dL did not receive treatment in many clinical trials. The following guidelines have been used by some clinicians (Aronoff, 2007):

Children:

Cl_{cr} <50 mL/minute: Administer 75% of dose

Hemodialysis: Administer 75% of dose

Continuous ambulatory peritoneal dialysis (CAPD): Administer 75% of dose

Continuous renal replacement therapy (CRRT): Administer 75% of dose

Adults:

Cl_{cr} 10-50 mL/minute: Administer 75% of dose

Cl_{cr} <10 mL/minute: Administer 50% of dose

Hemodialysis/CAPD: Supplemental dose not needed

Dosing adjustment/comments in hepatic impairment:

Bilirubin 2.6-5 mg/dL: Administer 50% of dose

Bilirubin >5 mg/dL: Avoid use

Combination Regimens

Leukemia, acute myeloid:

7 + 3 (Idarubicin) *on page 1140*

FLAG-IDA *on page 1215*

Idarubicin, Cytarabine, Etoposide (ICE Protocol) *on page 1239*

Idarubicin, Cytarabine, Etoposide (IDA-Based BF12) *on page 1239*

Leukemia, acute promyelocytic: Tretinoin-Idarubicin *on page 1283*

(Continued)

Idarubicin *(Continued)*

Administration Do not administer I.M. or SubQ; administer as slow push over 3-5 minutes, preferably into the side of a freely-running saline or dextrose infusion **or** as intermittent infusion over 10-15 minutes into a free-flowing I.V. solution of NS or D_5W; also occasionally administered as a bladder lavage.

Extravasation management: Topical cooling may be achieved using ice packs or cooling pad with circulating ice water. Cooling of site for 24 hours as tolerated by the patient. Elevate and rest extremity 24-48 hours, then resume normal activity as tolerated. Application of cold inhibits vesicant's cytotoxicity. **Application of heat can be harmful and is contraindicated.** If pain, erythema, and/or swelling persist beyond 48 hours, refer patient immediately to plastic surgeon for consultation and possible debridement.

Monitoring Parameters CBC with differential, platelet count, cardiac function, serum electrolytes, creatinine, uric acid, ALT, AST, bilirubin, signs of extravasation

Patient Information This drug can only be administered I.V. Maintain adequate nutrition and hydration (2-3 L/day of fluids unless instructed to restrict fluid intake). May cause hair loss (will grow back); nausea or vomiting (consult prescriber for antiemetic medication); you will be susceptible to infection (avoid crowds and exposure to infection); or urine may turn darker (normal). Report immediately any pain, burning, or stinging at infusion site; difficulty breathing; or swelling of extremities. Contraceptive measures are recommended during therapy.

Special Geriatric Considerations During induction therapy, patients >60 years of age experience CHF, arrhythmias, MI, and decline in LVEF more frequently than younger populations.

Emetic Potential Moderate (30% to 60%)

Vesicant Yes; see Management of Drug Extravasations *on page 1301.*

Dosage Forms Excipient information presented when available (limited, particularly for generics); consult specific product labeling.

Injection, solution, as hydrochloride [preservative free] (Idamycin PFS®): 1 mg/mL (5 mL, 10 mL, 20 mL)

References

Arlin ZA, "Idarubicin in Acute Leukemia: An Effective New Therapy for the Future," *Semin Oncol*, 1989, 16(1 Suppl 2):35-6.

Berman E, "A Review of Idarubicin in Acute Leukemia," *Oncology*, 1993, 7(10):91-8, 104.

Blijlevens NM, Donnelly JP, and de Pauw BE, "Prospective Evaluation of Gut Mucosal Barrier Injury Following Various Myeloablative Regimens for Haematopoietic Stem Cell Transplant," *Bone Marrow Transplant*, 2005, 35:707-11.

Borchmann P, Hubel K, Schnell R, et al, "Idarubicin: A Brief Overview on Pharmacology and Clinical Use," *Int J Clin Pharmacol Ther*, 1997, 35(2):80-3.

Buckley MM and Lamb HM, "Oral Idarubicin. A Review of its Pharmacological Properties and Clinical Efficacy in the Treatment of Haematological Malignancies and Advanced Breast Cancer," *Drugs Aging*, 1997, 11(1):61-86.

Ferrara F, Palmieri S, Annunziata M, et al, "Continuous Infusion Idarubicin and Oral Busulfan as Conditioning for Patients With Acute Myeloid Leukemia Aged Over 60 Years Undergoing Autologous Stem Cell Transplantation," *Bone Marrow Transplant*, 2004, 34(7):73-576.

Fields SM and Koeller JM, "Idarubicin: A Second Generation Anthracycline," *DICP*, 1991, 25(5):505-17.

Goebel M, "Oral Idarubicin--An Anthracycline Derivative With Unique Properties," *Ann Hematol*, 1993, 66(1):33-43.

Hollingshead LM and Faulds D, "Idarubicin: A Review of Its Pharmacodynamic and Pharmacokinetic Properties, and Therapeutic Potential in the Chemotherapy of Cancer," *Drugs*, 1991, 42(4):690-719.

Mengarelli A, Iori AP, Guglielmi C, et al, "Idarubicin Intensified BUCY2 Regimen in Allogeneic Unmanipulated Transplant for High-Risk Hematological Malignancies," *Leukemia*, 2000, 14(12):2052-8.

Robert J, "Clinical Pharmacokinetics of Edarubicin," *Clin Pharmacokinet*, 1993, 24(4):275-88.

- ♦ **Idarubicin Hydrochloride** *see Idarubicin on page 575*
- ♦ **IDEC-C2B8** *see Rituximab on page 953*
- ♦ **IDEC-Y2B8** *see Ibritumomab on page 570*
- ♦ **IDR** *see Idarubicin on page 575*
- ♦ **Ifex®** *see Ifosfamide on page 579*
- ♦ **IFLrA** *see Interferon Alfa-2a on page 611*

Ifosfamide (eye FOSS fa mide)

Medication Safety Issues

Sound-alike/look-alike issues:

Ifosfamide may be confused with cyclophosphamide

High alert medication: The Institute for Safe Medication Practices (ISMP) includes this medication among its list of drugs which have a heightened risk of causing significant patient harm when used in error.

Related Information

Hematopoietic Stem Cell Transplantation *on page 1366*
Management of Drug Extravasations *on page 1301*
Safe Handling of Hazardous Drugs *on page 1382*

U.S. Brand Names Ifex®

Index Terms Isophosphamide; NSC-109724; Z4942

Generic Available Yes

Canadian Brand Names Ifex®

Pharmacologic Category Antineoplastic Agent, Alkylating Agent; Antineoplastic Agent, Alkylating Agent (Nitrogen Mustard)

Use Treatment of testicular cancer

Unlabeled/Investigational Use Treatment of bladder, breast, cervical, ovarian, pancreatic and lung cancers; Hodgkin's and non-Hodgkin's lymphoma; acute lymphocytic leukemia; Ewing's sarcoma, osteosarcoma, and soft tissue sarcomas

Pregnancy Risk Factor D

Lactation Enters breast milk/not recommended

Labeled Contraindications Hypersensitivity to ifosfamide or any component of the formulation; patients with severely depressed bone marrow function

Warnings/Precautions Hazardous agent - use appropriate precautions for handling and disposal. **[U.S. Boxed Warning: Urotoxic side effects, primarily hemorrhagic cystitis, may occur (dose-limiting toxicity).** Hydration (at least 2 L/day) and/or mesna administration will protect against hemorrhagic cystitis. **[U.S. Boxed Warning: Severe bone marrow suppression may occur (dose-limiting toxicity);** use is contraindicated in patients with severely depressed bone marrow function. **[U.S. Boxed Warning]: May cause CNS toxicity, including confusion and coma;** usually reversible upon discontinuation of treatment. Encephalopathy, ranging from mild somnolence to hallucinations and/or coma may occur; risk factors may include hypoalbuminemia, renal dysfunction and prior history of ifosfamide-induced encephalopathy. Use with caution in patients with impaired renal function or those with compromised bone marrow reserve. May interfere with wound healing. **[U.S. Boxed Warning]: Should be administered under the supervision of an experienced cancer chemotherapy physician.** Safety and efficacy in children have not been established.
(Continued)

Ifosfamide *(Continued)*

Adverse Reactions

>10%:

Central nervous system: CNS toxicity or encephalopathy (10% to 30%; includes somnolence, agitation, confusion, delirium, hallucinations, depressive psychosis, incontinence, palsy, diplopia, aphasia, or coma)

Dermatologic: Alopecia (83%)

Endocrine & metabolic: Metabolic acidosis (31%)

Gastrointestinal: Nausea/vomiting (58%), may be more common with higher doses or bolus infusion

Hematologic: Myelosuppression (onset: 7-14 days; nadir: 21-28 days; recovery: 21-28 days), leukopenia (50% to ≤100%; grade 4: ≤50%), thrombocytopenia (20%; grades 3/4: 8%)

Renal: Hematuria (6% to 92%; grade 2 [gross hematuria]: 8% to 12%)

1% to 10%:

Central nervous system: Fever

Hepatic: Bilirubin increased (3%), liver dysfunction (3%), transaminases increased (3%)

Local: Phlebitis (2%)

Renal: Renal impairment (6%)

Miscellaneous: Infection (8%)

<1%, postmarketing, and/or case reports: Acidosis, acute renal failure, acute tubular necrosis, allergic reaction, anemia, anorexia, BUN increased, cardiotoxicity, chronic renal failure, coagulopathy, constipation, creatinine increased, dermatitis, diarrhea, Fanconi syndrome, fatigue, hyper-/hypotension, hyperpigmentation, malaise, nail banding/ridging, nonconvulsive status epilepticus, polyneuropathy, proteinuria, pulmonary fibrosis, renal rickets, renal tubular acidosis, salivation, SIADH, sterility, stomatitis

Overdosage/Toxicology Symptoms of overdose include myelosuppression, nausea, vomiting, diarrhea, and alopecia; direct extensions of the drug's pharmacologic effect. Treatment is symptom-directed and supportive. Limited case reports indicate that methylene blue may be useful in the treatment or prophylaxis of ifosfamide-induced encephalopathy.

Drug Interactions

Cytochrome P450 Effect: Substrate of CYP2A6 (major), 2B6 (minor), 2C8 (minor), 2C9 (minor), 2C19 (major), 3A4 (major); **Inhibits** CYP3A4 (weak); **Induces** CYP2C8 (weak), 2C9 (weak)

Increased Effect/Toxicity: Ifosfamide may enhance the anticoagulant effect of coumarin derivatives. CYP2A6 inhibitors may increase the levels/effects of ifosfamide; example inhibitors include isoniazid, methoxsalen, and miconazole. CYP2C19 inhibitors may increase the levels/effects of ifosfamide; example inhibitors include delavirdine, fluconazole, fluvoxamine, gemfibrozil, isoniazid, omeprazole, and ticlopidine. CYP3A4 inhibitors may increase the levels/effects of ifosfamide; example inhibitors include azole antifungals, clarithromycin, diclofenac, doxycycline, erythromycin, imatinib, isoniazid, nefazodone, nicardipine, propofol, protease inhibitors, quinidine, telithromycin, and verapamil.

Decreased Effect: CYP2A6 inducers may decrease the levels/effects of ifosfamide; example inducers include amobarbital, pentobarbital, phenobarbital, rifampin, and secobarbital. CYP2C19 inducers may decrease the levels/effects of ifosfamide; example inducers include carbamazepine, phenobarbital, phenytoin, rifampin, rifapentine, and secobarbital. CYP3A4 inducers may decrease the levels/effects of ifosfamide; example inducers include aminoglutethimide, carbamazepine, nafcillin, nevirapine, phenobarbital, phenytoin, and rifamycins

Ethanol/Nutrition/Herb Interactions Herb/Nutraceutical: St John's wort may decrease ifosfamide levels.

Storage/Stability Store intact vials of powder for injection at room temperature of 20°C to 25°C (68°F to 77°F). Store intact vials of solution under refrigeration at 2°C to 8°C (36°F to 46°F). Reconstituted solutions may be stored under refrigeration for up to 21 days. Solutions diluted for administration are stable for 7 days at room temperature and for 6 weeks under refrigeration.

Reconstitution Dilute powder with SWFI or bacteriostatic SWFI to a concentration of 50 mg/mL. Further dilution in 50-1000 mL D_5W or NS (to a final concentration of 0.6-20 mg/mL) is recommended for I.V. infusion.

Compatibility Stable in D_5LR, D_5NS, D_5W, LR, ½NS, NS.

    Y-site administration: Compatible: Allopurinol, amifostine, amphotericin B cholesteryl sulfate complex, aztreonam, doxorubicin liposome, etoposide phosphate, filgrastim, fludarabine, gatifloxacin, gemcitabine, granisetron, linezolid, melphalan, ondansetron, paclitaxel, piperacillin/tazobactam, propofol, sargramostim, sodium bicarbonate, teniposide, thiotepa, topotecan, vinorelbine. **Incompatible:** Cefepime, methotrexate.

    Compatibility in syringe: Compatible: Epirubicin, mesna. **Incompatible:** Mesna with epirubicin.

    Compatibility when admixed: Compatible: Carboplatin, carboplatin with etoposide, cisplatin, cisplatin with etoposide, epirubicin, etoposide, fluorouracil, mesna. **Incompatible:** Mesna with epirubicin.

Mechanism of Action Causes cross-linking of strands of DNA by binding with nucleic acids and other intracellular structures; inhibits protein synthesis and DNA synthesis

Pharmacodynamics/Kinetics Pharmacokinetics are dose dependent

    Distribution: V_d: 5.7-49 L; does penetrate CNS, but not in therapeutic levels

    Protein binding: Negligible

    Metabolism: Hepatic to active metabolites isofosforamide mustard, 4-hydroxy-ifosfamide, acrolein, and inactive dichloroethylated and carboxy metabolites; acrolein is the agent implicated in development of hemorrhagic cystitis

    Half-life elimination:

    High dose (3800-5000 mg/m²): ~15 hours

    Lower dose (1600-2400 mg/m²): ~7 hours

    Excretion:

    High dose (5000 mg/m²): Urine (70% to 86%; 61% as unchanged drug)

    Lower dose (1600-2400 mg/m²): Urine (12% to 18% as unchanged drug)

Dosage Refer to individual protocols. To prevent bladder toxicity, ifosfamide should be given with the urinary protector mesna and hydration of at least 2 L of oral or I.V. fluid per day.

    Children (unlabeled use): I.V.

    1200-1800 mg/m²/day for 3-5 days every 21-28 days **or**

    5 g/m² once every 21-28 days **or**

    3 g/m²/day for 2 days every 21-28 days

    Adults: I.V.:

    Testicular cancer: 1200 mg/m²/day for 5 days every 3 weeks

    Dose ranges used in other cancers (unlabeled uses):

        4000-5000 mg/m²/day for 1 day every 14-28 days **or**

        1000-3000 mg/m²/day for 2-5 days every 21-28 days

(Continued)

Ifosfamide *(Continued)*

Dosing adjustment in renal impairment: The FDA-approved labeling does not contain dosage adjustment guidelines (has not been studied). The following guidelines have been used by some clinicians:

Aronoff, 2007:

Cl_{cr} <10 mL/minute: Children and Adults: Administer 75% of dose

Hemodialysis:

Children: 1 g/m^2 followed by hemodialysis 6-8 hours later

Adults: No supplemental dose needed

Kintzel, 1995:

Cl_{cr} 46-60 mL/minute: Administer 80% of dose

Cl_{cr} 31-45 mL/minute: Administer 75% of dose

Cl_{cr} <30 mL/minute: Administer 70% of dose

Dosing adjustment in hepatic impairment: The FDA-approved labeling does not contain dosage adjustment guidelines (has not been studied). The following guidelines have been used by some clinicians (Floyd, 2006):

Bilirubin >3 mg/dL: Administer 25% of dose

Combination Regimens

Breast cancer: ICE-T *on page 1238*

Cervical cancer: BIP *on page 1152*

Esophageal cancer: TIP *on page 1281*

Head and neck cancer: TIP *on page 1281*

Hepatoblastoma: IPA *on page 1241*

Lung cancer (small cell): VIP (Small Cell Lung Cancer) *on page 1291*

Lymphoma, non-Hodgkin's:

ICE (Lymphoma, non-Hodgkin's) *on page 1238*

IMVP-16 *on page 1240*

IVAC *on page 1242*

MINE *on page 1247*

MINE-ESHAP *on page 1247*

RICE *on page 1277*

Lymphoma, non-Hodgkin's (Burkitt's): CODOX-M/IVAC *on page 1180*

Neuroblastoma:

CI (Neuroblastoma) *on page 1174*

HIPE-IVAD *on page 1229*

Osteosarcoma: ICE (Sarcoma) *on page 1238*

Sarcoma: VAC Alternating With IE (Ewing's Sarcoma) *on page 1285*

Soft tissue sarcoma:

AI *on page 1145*

ICE (Sarcoma) *on page 1238*

ICE-T *on page 1238*

IE *on page 1239*

MAID *on page 1246*

Testicular cancer:

Paclitaxel-Ifosfamide-Cisplatin *on page 1265*

VIP (Etoposide) (Testicular Cancer) *on page 1290*

VIP (Vinblastine) (Testicular Cancer) *on page 1291*

Administration Administer I.V. over 30 minutes to several hours or continuous I.V. over 5 days

Monitoring Parameters CBC with differential, hemoglobin, and platelet count, urine output, urinalysis (prior to each dose), liver function, and renal function tests

Patient Information This drug can only be administered I.V. Report immediately any pain, stinging, or burning at infusion site. It is vital to maintain adequate hydration (2-3 L/day of fluids unless instructed to restrict fluid intake) for 3 days prior to infusion and each day of therapy. May cause hair loss (will grow back); nausea or vomiting (consult prescriber for antiemetic medication); and you will be susceptible to infection (avoid crowds and exposure to infection). Report immediately pain or irritation on urination, severe diarrhea, CNS changes (eg, hallucinations, confusion, somnolence), signs of opportunistic infection (eg, fever, chills, easy bruising or unusual bleeding), difficulty breathing, swelling of extremities, or any other adverse effects. Contraceptive measures are recommended during therapy.

Emetic Potential Moderate (30% to 60%)

Vesicant No

High Dose Considerations

High Dose: I.V.: 7.5-16 g/m^2 in divided doses over several days; generally combined with other high-dose chemotherapy

Dosage Forms Excipient information presented when available (limited, particularly for generics); consult specific product labeling.

Injection, powder for reconstitution: 1 g

Ifex®: 1 g, 3 g

Injection, solution: 50 mg/mL (20 mL, 60 mL)

References

Brade WP, Herdrich K, Kachel-Fischer U, et al, "Dosing and Side-Effects of Ifosfamide Plus Mesna," *J Cancer Res Clin Oncol*, 1991, 117(Suppl 4):164-86.

Furlanut M and Franceschi L, "Pharmacology of Ifosfamide," *Oncology*, 2003, 65 Suppl 2:2-6.

Kerbusch T, de Kraker J, Keizer HJ, et al, "Clinical Pharmacokinetics and Pharmacodynamics of Ifosfamide and its Metabolites," *Clin Pharmacokinet*, 2001, 40(1):41-62.

Klastersky J, "Side Effects of Ifosfamide," *Oncology*, 2003, 65 Suppl 2:7-10.

Lotz JP, Bouleuc C, Andre T, et al, "Tandem High-Dose Chemotherapy With Ifosfamide, Carboplatin, and Teniposide With Autologous Bone Marrow Transplantation for the Treatment of Poor Prognosis Common Epithelial Ovarian Carcinoma," *Cancer*, 1996, 77(12):2550-9.

Patterson WP and Reams GP, "Renal and Electrolyte Abnormalities Due to Chemotherapy," *The Chemotherapy Sourcebook*, 3rd ed, Perry MC, ed, Philadelphia, PA: Lippincott, Williams, and Wilkins, 2001, 494-504.

Sarosy G, "Ifosfamide - Pharmacologic Overview," *Semin Oncol*, 1989, 16(1 Suppl 3):2-8.

Wagner T, "Ifosfamide Clinical Pharmacokinetics," *Clin Pharmacokinet*, 1994, 26(6):439-56.

Wilson WH, Jain V, Bryant G, et al, "Phase I and II Study of High-Dose Ifosfamide, Carboplatin, and Etoposide With Autologous Bone Marrow Rescue in Lymphomas and Solid Tumors," *J Clin Oncol*, 1992, 10(11):1712-22.

♦ **IGIV** see Immune Globulin (Intravenous) on page 597

♦ **IL-2** see Aldesleukin on page 29

♦ **IL-11** see Oprelvekin on page 842

Imatinib (eye MAT eh nib)

Medication Safety Issues

High alert medication: The Institute for Safe Medication Practices (ISMP) includes this medication among its list of drugs which have a heightened risk of causing significant patient harm when used in error.

Related Information

Safe Handling of Hazardous Drugs on page 1382

U.S. Brand Names Gleevec®

Index Terms CGP-57148B; Glivec; Imatinib Mesylate; NSC-716051; STI571

Generic Available No

Canadian Brand Names Gleevec®

Pharmacologic Category Antineoplastic Agent, Tyrosine Kinase Inhibitor

Use Treatment of:

Gastrointestinal stromal tumors (GIST) kit-positive (CD117) unresectable and/or (metastatic) malignant

Philadelphia chromosome-positive (Ph+) chronic myeloid leukemia (CML) in chronic phase (newly-diagnosed)

(Continued)

Imatinib *(Continued)*

Ph+ CML in blast crisis, accelerated phase, or chronic phase after failure of interferon therapy

Ph+ acute lymphoblastic leukemia (ALL) (relapsed or refractory)

Ph+ ALL induction therapy (newly diagnosed) [**not** an approved indication in the U.S.]

Note: The following indications are **not** approved in Canada:

Aggressive systemic mastocytosis (ASM) without D816V c-Kit mutation (or c-Kit mutation status unknown)

Dermatofibrosarcoma protuberans (DFSP) (unresectable, recurrent and metastatic)

Hypereosinophilic syndrome (HES) and/or chronic eosinophilic leukemia (CEL)

Myelodysplastic/myeloproliferative disease (MDS/MPD) associated with platelet-derived growth factor receptor (PDGFR) gene rearrangements

Ph+ CML in chronic phase in pediatric patients recurring following stem cell transplant or who are resistant to interferon-alpha therapy

Pregnancy Risk Factor D

Lactation Excretion in breast milk unknown/not recommended

Labeled Contraindications Hypersensitivity to imatinib or any component of the formulation

Warnings/Precautions Hazardous agent - use appropriate precautions for handling and disposal. Often associated with fluid retention, weight gain, and edema (probability increases with higher doses and age >65 years); occasionally leading to significant complications, including pleural effusion, pericardial effusion, pulmonary edema, and ascites. Use caution in patients where fluid accumulation may be poorly tolerated, such as in cardiovascular disease (CHF or hypertension) and pulmonary disease. Severe CHF and left ventricular dysfunction (LVD) have been reported rarely; carefully monitor patients with pre-existing cardiac disease or risk factors for heart failure. Cardiogenic shock and/or LVD have been reported in patients with hypereosinophilic syndrome and cardiac involvement (reversible with systemic steroids, circulatory support and temporary cessation of imatinib). Patients with an abnormal echocardiogram or abnormal serum troponin level may benefit from prophylactic systemic steroids with the initiation of imatinib.

Severe dermatologic reactions (including erythema multiforme and Stevens-Johnson syndrome) have been reported; reintroduction has been attempted following resolution. Successful resumption at a lower dose (with corticosteroids and/or antihistamine) has been described; however, some patients may experience recurrent reactions.

Use with caution in renal impairment, hematologic impairment, or hepatic disease. May cause GI irritation, severe hemorrhage (grades 3 and 4), hepatotoxicity, or hematologic toxicity (anemia, neutropenia, and thrombocytopenia); median duration of neutropenia is 2-3 weeks; median duration of thrombocytopenia is 3-4 weeks. Hepatotoxic reactions may be severe and interruption of therapy or dose reductions may be necessary. Has been associated with development of opportunistic infections. Use with caution in patients receiving concurrent therapy with drugs which alter cytochrome P450 activity or require metabolism by these isoenzymes. Safety and efficacy in patients <2 years of age have not been established.

Adverse Reactions

>10%:

Cardiovascular: Edema/fluid retention (33% to 81%; grades 3/4: 3% to 12%; includes aggravated edema, anasarca, pericardial effusion, peripheral edema, pulmonary edema and superficial edema); facial edema (DFSP: 17%), chest pain (CML: 7% to 11%)

Central nervous system: Fatigue (29% to 53%), fever (16% to 41%), headache (27% to 39%), dizziness (11% to 19%), insomnia (10% to 19%), depression (≤15%), anxiety (7% to 12%)

Dermatologic: Rash (25% to 53%; grades 3/4: 3% to 5%), pruritus (8% to 14%)

Endocrine & metabolic: Hypokalemia (CML: 6% to 13%)

Gastrointestinal: Nausea (42% to 74%), diarrhea (25% to 70%), vomiting (23% to 58%), abdominal pain (30% to 40%), flatulence (≤34%), weight gain (5% to 32%), dyspepsia (12% to 27%), anorexia (≤17%), constipation (9% to 16%), taste disturbance (GIST: 3% to 15%), loose stools (GIST: 10% to 12%)

Hematologic: Hemorrhage (26% to 53%; grades 3/4: 2% to 19%), neutropenia (grade 3: 7% to 27%; grade 4: 3% to 48%), thrombocytopenia (grade 3: 1% to 31%; grade 4: <1% to 33%), anemia (grade 3: 3% to 42%; grade 4: 1% to 11%)

Hepatic: Ascites/pleural effusion (GIST: 12% to 15%), hepatotoxicity (6% to 12%; grades 3/4: 3% to 8%)

Neuromuscular & skeletal: Muscle cramps (28% to 62%), musculoskeletal pain (adults 30% to 49%; children 21%), arthralgia (≤40%), joint pain (11% to 31%), myalgia (9% to 27%), back pain (GIST: 23% to 26%), weakness (≤21%), rigors (CML: 10% to 12%), bone pain (≤11%)

Ocular: Periorbital edema (DFSP: 33%; MPD: 29%), lacrimation increased (DFSP: 25%; GIST: 16% to 18%)

Respiratory: Nasopharyngitis (10% to 31%), cough (14% to 27%), dyspnea (≤21%), upper respiratory tract infection (3% to 21%), pharyngolaryngeal pain (7% to 18%), rhinitis (DFSP: 17%), pharyngitis (CML: 10% to 15%), pneumonia (CML: 4% to 13%), sinusitis (4% to 11%)

Miscellaneous: Night sweats (CML: 13% to 17%), influenza (1% to 14%)

1% to 10%:

Central nervous system: CNS/cerebral hemorrhage (≤9%)

Dermatologic: Alopecia, dry skin

Endocrine & metabolic: Albumin decreased (grade 3: ≤4%)

Gastrointestinal: Gastrointestinal hemorrhage (2% to 8%), abdominal distension, gastroesophageal reflux, mouth ulceration

Hepatic: Alkaline phosphatase increased (grade 3: ≤6%; grade 4: <1%), ALT increased (grade 3: 2% to 7%; grade 4: <1%), AST increased (grade 3: 2% to 4%; grade 4: ≤3%), bilirubin increased (grade 3: 1% to 4%; grade 4: ≤3%)

Neuromuscular & skeletal: Joint swelling, paresthesia

Ocular: Blurred vision, conjunctivitis

Renal: Serum creatinine increased (grade 3: ≤3%; DFSP: grade 4: 8%)

Miscellaneous: Tumor hemorrhage (GIST: 1% to 4%)

<1%, postmarketing, and/or case reports (limited to important or life-threatening): Acute febrile neutropenic dermatosis (Sweet's syndrome), angioedema, aplastic anemia, avascular necrosis, breast enlargement, bullous eruption, cardiac failure, cardiac tamponade, cardiogenic shock, cerebral edema, CHF (severe), colitis, confusion, conjunctival hemorrhage, CPK increased, dehydration, diverticulitis, embolism, (Continued)

Imatinib *(Continued)*

erythema multiforme, exanthematous pustulosis (acute generalized), exfoliative dermatitis, flushing, gastric ulcer, gastritis, gastroenteritis, gastrointestinal obstruction, gastrointestinal perforation, glaucoma, gout, hematuria, hepatic failure, hepatitis, herpes simplex, herpes zoster, hip osteonecrosis, hyperkalemia, hyper-/hypotension, hyponatremia, hypophosphatemia, ileus, intracranial pressure increased, interstitial pneumonitis, LDH increased, leukopenia, left ventricular dysfunction, lymphopenia, macular edema, memory impairment, menorrhagia, migraine, pancreatitis, pancytopenia, papilledema, pericarditis, peripheral neuropathy, photosensitivity, pulmonary fibrosis, purpura, renal failure, respiratory tract (lower) infection, retinal hemorrhage, sciatica, seizure, sepsis, sexual dysfunction, skin pigment changes, somnolence, Stevens-Johnson syndrome, syncope, tachycardia, thrombosis, tinnitus, tumor necrosis, vertigo, vesicular rash, vitreous hemorrhage

Overdosage/Toxicology Experience with overdose (>800 mg/day) is limited. Patients taking doses of 1200-1600 mg per day experienced ascites, elevated transaminases, elevated bilirubin, and muscle cramps; treatment was interrupted until reversal of abnormalities, then resumed at the normal doses without recurrence of symptoms. Hematologic adverse effects are more common at dosages >750 mg/day. Treatment is symptom-directed and supportive

Drug Interactions

Cytochrome P450 Effect: Substrate of CYP1A2 (minor), 2D6 (minor), 2C9 (minor), 2C19 (minor), 3A4 (major), **Inhibits** CYP2C9 (weak), 2D6 (moderate), 3A4 (strong)

Increased Effect/Toxicity: Imatinib may increase the levels/effects of amphetamines, selected beta-blockers, dextromethorphan, fluoxetine, lidocaine, maraviroc, mirtazapine, nefazodone, paroxetine, risperidone, ritonavir, thioridazine, tricyclic antidepressants, venlafaxine and other CYP2D6 substrates. Imatinib may increase the risk of myopathy/rhabdomyolysis with HMG-CoA reductase inhibitors (except pravastatin/fluvastatin). Imatinib may increase the toxicity of pimecrolimus (in patients with widespread and/or erythrodermic disease). Imatinib may increase the levels/effects of benzodiazepines, calcium channel blockers, clarithromycin, cyclosporine, erythromycin, estrogens, mirtazapine, nateglinide, nefazodone, nevirapine, protease inhibitors, tacrolimus, venlafaxine and other CYP3A4 substrates. (Selected benzodiazepines [midazolam and triazolam], cisapride, ergot alkaloids, selected HMG-CoA reductase inhibitors [lovastatin and simvastatin], and pimozide are generally contraindicated with strong CYP3A4 inhibitors.)

The levels/effects of imatinib may be increased by azole antifungals, clarithromycin, diclofenac, doxycycline, erythromycin, isoniazid, nefazodone, nicardipine, propofol, protease inhibitors, quinidine, telithromycin, verapamil, and other CYP3A4 inhibitors. Lansoprazole may enhance the dermatologic adverse effects of Imatinib.

Decreased Effect: The levels/effects of imatinib may be decreased by aminoglutethimide, carbamazepine, nafcillin, nevirapine, phenobarbital, phenytoin, rifamycins, and other CYP3A4 inducers. Dosage of imatinib should be increased by at least 50% (with careful monitoring) when used concurrently with a strong inducer.

Imatinib may decrease the levels/effects of codeine, hydrocodone, oxycodone, tramadol, and other CYP2D6 prodrug substrates. Imatinib may decrease the absorption of digoxin (tablet formulation).

Ethanol/Nutrition/Herb Interactions
Ethanol: Avoid ethanol.

Food: Food may reduce gastrointestinal irritation.

Herb/Nutraceutical: Avoid St John's wort (may increase metabolism and decrease imatinib plasma concentration).

Storage/Stability Store at 15°C to 30°C (59°F to 86°F). Protect from moisture.

Mechanism of Action Inhibits Bcr-Abl tyrosine kinase, the constitutive abnormal gene product of the Philadelphia chromosome in chronic myeloid leukemia (CML). Inhibition of this enzyme blocks proliferation and induces apoptosis in Bcr-Abl positive cell lines as well as in fresh leukemic cells in Philadelphia chromosome positive CML. Also inhibits tyrosine kinase for platelet-derived growth factor (PDGF), stem cell factor (SCF), c-Kit, and cellular events mediated by PDGF and SCF.

Pharmacodynamics/Kinetics
Absorption: Rapid

Protein binding: 95% to albumin and alpha$_1$-acid glycoprotein

Metabolism: Hepatic via CYP3A4 (minor metabolism via CYP1A2, CYP2D6, CYP2C9, CYP2C19); primary metabolite (active): N-demethylated piperazine derivative (CGP74588); severe hepatic impairment (bilirubin >3-10 times ULN) increases AUC by 45% to 55% for imatinib and its active metabolite, respectively

Bioavailability: 98%

Half-life elimination: Adults: Parent drug: ~18 hours; N-desmethyl metabolite: ~40 hours; Children: Parent drug: ~15 hours

Time to peak: 2-4 hours

Excretion: Feces (68% primarily as metabolites, 20% as unchanged drug); urine (13% primarily as metabolites, 5% as unchanged drug)

Clearance: Highly variable; Mean: 8-14 L/hour (for 50 kg and 100 kg male, respectively)

Dosage Oral: **Note:** For concurrent use with a strong CYP3A4 enzyme-inducing agent (eg, rifampin, phenytoin), imatinib dosage should be increased by at least 50%.

Children ≥2 years: **Note:** May be administered once daily or in 2 divided doses.

Ph+ CML (chronic phase, recurrent or resistant): 260 mg/m^2/day

Ph+ CML (chronic phase, newly diagnosed): 340 mg/m^2/day; maximum: 600 mg /day

Adults:

Ph+ CML:

Chronic phase: 400 mg once daily; may be increased to 600 mg daily

Canadian labeling: Includes range up to 800 mg/day (400 mg twice daily)

Accelerated phase or blast crisis: 600 mg once daily; may be increased to 800 mg daily (400 mg twice daily)

Ph+ ALL (induction, newly diagnosed): *Canadian labeling* (not an approved use in the U.S.): 600 mg once daily

Ph+ ALL (relapsed or refractory): 600 mg once daily

GIST: 400-600 mg/day

Canadian labeling: Includes range up to 800 mg/ day (400 mg twice daily)

ASM with eosinophilia: Initiate at 100 mg once daily; titrate up to a maximum of 400 mg once daily (if tolerated) for insufficient response to lower dose

ASM without D816V c-Kit mutation or c-Kit mutation status unknown: 400 mg once daily

(Continued)

Imatinib *(Continued)*

DFSP: 400 mg twice daily

HES/CEL: 400 mg once daily

HES/CEL with FIP1L1-PDGFRα fusion kinase: Initiate at 100 mg once daily; titrate up to a maximum of 400 mg once daily (if tolerated) if insufficient response to lower dose

MDS/MPD: 400 mg once daily

Dosage adjustment with concomitant strong CYP3A4 inducers: Avoid concomitant use if possible; if concomitant use can not be avoided, increase imatinib dose by at least 50% with careful monitoring.

Dosage adjustment for hepatic impairment: Treatment initiation:

Mild-to-moderate impairment: No adjustment necessary

Canadian labeling: Minimum effective dose: 400 mg once daily

Severe impairment: Reduce dose by 25%; usual initial dose: 300 mg/day (depending on indication)

Canadian labeling: 200 mg dose once daily with titration to 300 mg once daily in the absence of severe toxicity

Dosage adjustment for hepatotoxicity or other nonhematologic adverse reactions: If elevations of bilirubin >3 times upper limit of normal (ULN) or transaminases (ALT/AST) >5 times ULN occur, withhold until bilirubin <1.5 times ULN or transaminases <2.5 times ULN. Resume treatment at a reduced dose:

Children ≥2 years:

If initial dose 260 mg/m^2/day, reduce dose to 200 mg/m^2/day

If initial dose 340 mg/m^2/day, reduce dose to 260 mg/m^2/day

Adults:

If initial dose 400 mg, reduce dose to 300 mg

If initial dose 600 mg, reduce dose to 400 mg

If initial dose 800 mg, reduce dose to 600 mg

Dosage adjustment for hematologic adverse reactions:

Chronic phase CML (initial dose 400 mg/day in adults or 260-340 mg/m^2/day in children), ASM, MDS/MPD, and HES/CEL (initial dose 400 mg/day), or GIST (initial dose 400 mg or 600 mg): If ANC <1 x 10^9/L and/or platelets <50 x 10^9/L: Withhold until ANC ≥1.5 x 10^9/L and platelets ≥75 x 10^9/L; resume treatment at previous dose. For recurrent neutropenia or thrombocytopenia, withhold until recovery, and reinstitute treatment at a reduced dose:

Children ≥2 years:

If initial dose 260 mg/m^2/day, reduce dose to 200 mg/m^2/day

If initial dose 340 mg/m^2/day, reduce dose to 260 mg/m^2/day

Adults:

If initial dose 400 mg, reduce dose to 300 mg

If initial dose 600 mg, reduce dose to 400 mg

CML (accelerated phase or blast crisis) and PH+ ALL: Adults (initial dose 600 mg): If ANC <0.5 x 10^9/L and/or platelets <10 x 10^9/L, establish whether cytopenia is related to leukemia (bone marrow aspirate or biopsy). If unrelated to leukemia, reduce dose to 400 mg. If cytopenia persists for an additional 2 weeks, further reduce dose to 300 mg. If cytopenia persists for 4 weeks and is still unrelated to leukemia, withhold treatment until ANC ≥1 x 10^9/L and platelets ≥20 x 10^9/L, then resume treatment at 300 mg.

ASM associated with eosinophilia and HES/CEL with FIP1L1-PDGFRα fusion kinase (starting dose 100 mg/day): If ANC <1 x 10^9/L and/or platelets <50 x 10^9/L: Withhold until ANC ≥1.5 x 10^9/L and platelets ≥75 x 10^9/L; resume treatment at previous dose.

DFSP (initial dose 800 mg/day): If ANC <1 x 10^9/L and/or platelets <50 x 10^9/L , withhold until ANC ≥1.5 x 10^9/L and platelets ≥75 x 10^9/L; resume treatment at reduced dose of 600 mg/day. If depression in neutrophils or platelets recurs, withhold until recovery, and reinstitute treatment with a further dose reduction to 400 mg/day.

Combination Regimens

Leukemia, acute lymphocytic: Hyper-CVAD + Imatinib *on page 1229*

Administration Should be administered with food and a large glass of water. Tablets may be dispersed in water or apple juice (using ~50 mL for 100 mg tablet, ~200 mL for 400 mg tablet); stir until dissolved and use immediately. For daily dosing ≥800 mg, the 400 mg tablets should be used in order to reduce iron exposure.

Monitoring Parameters CBC (weekly for first month, biweekly for second month, then periodically thereafter), liver function tests (at baseline and monthly or as clinically indicated), renal function, calcium and phosphorus levels, thyroid function tests; fatigue, weight, and edema/fluid status; consider echocardiogram and serum troponin levels in patients with HES/CEL, and in patients with MDS/MPD or ASM with high eosinophil levels

Monitor for CHF in patients with at risk for cardiac failure or patients with pre-existing cardiac disease. In Canada, a baseline evaluation of left ventricular ejection fraction is recommended prior to initiation of imatinib therapy in all patients with known underlying heart disease or in elderly patients.

Dietary Considerations Should be taken with food and a large glass of water to decrease gastrointestinal irritation.

Patient Information Take exactly as directed; do not alter or discontinue dose without consulting prescriber. Take with food and a large glass of water. For patients unable to swallow tablets, tablet may be dispersed in water or apple juice (using ~50 mL for 100 mg tablet, ~200 mL for 400 mg tablet); stir until dissolved and use immediately. Avoid alcohol, chronic use of acetaminophen or aspirin, OTC or prescription medications, or herbal products unless approved by prescriber. Maintain adequate hydration (2-3 L/day) unless instructed to restrict fluids. You will be required to have regularly scheduled laboratory tests while on this medication. You will be more susceptible to infection (avoid crowds or contagious persons, and do not receive any vaccination unless approved by prescriber). You may experience headache or fatigue (use caution when driving or engaged in tasks requiring alertness until response to drug in known); loss of appetite, nausea, vomiting, or mouth sores (small frequent meals, frequent mouth care, chewing gum, or sucking lozenges may help); constipation (increased dietary fiber and fluids, exercise may help); or diarrhea (buttermilk, boiled milk, or yogurt may reduce diarrhea). Report chest pain, palpitations, or swelling of extremities; cough, difficulty breathing, or wheezing; weight gain greater than 5 lb; skin rash; muscle or bone pain, tremors, or cramping; persistent fatigue or weakness; easy bruising or unusual bleeding (eg, tarry stools, blood in vomitus, stool, urine, or mouth); persistent gastrointestinal problems or pain; or other adverse effects.

Special Geriatric Considerations Incidence of edema and edema-related adverse effects is increased in elderly patients.

Additional Information Median time to hematologic response was one month; only short-term studies have been completed. Follow-up is insufficient to estimate duration of cytogenic response. Patients with HES/CEL, MDS/MPD or ASM with an abnormal echocardiogram or abnormal serum (Continued)

Imatinib *(Continued)*

troponin level may benefit from prophylactic systemic steroids (1-2 mg/kg for 1-2 weeks) with the initiation of imatinib.

Emetic Potential Moderate (30% to 60%)

Dosage Forms Excipient information presented when available (limited, particularly for generics); consult specific product labeling.

Tablet:

Gleevec®: 100 mg; 400 mg

References

Atallah E, Durand JB, Kantarjian H, et al, "Congestive Heart Failure is a Rare Event in Patients Receiving Imatinib Therapy," *Blood*, 2007, 110(4):1233-7.

Ault P, Kantarjian H, O'Brien S, et al, "Pregnancy Among Patients with Chronic Myeloid Leukemia Treated with Imatinib," *J Clin Oncol*, 2006, 24(7):1204-8.

Berman E, Nicolaides M, Maki RG, et al, "Altered Bone and Mineral Metabolism in Patients Receiving Imatinib Mesylate," *N Engl J Med*, 2006, 354(19):2006-13.

Brunstein CG and McGlave PB, "The Biology and Treatment of Chronic Myelogenous Leukemia," *Oncology*, 2001, 15:23-31.

de Groot JW, Zonnenberg BA, Plukker JT, et al, "Imatinib Induces Hypothyroidism in Patients Receiving Levothyroxine," *Clin Pharmacol Ther*, 2005, 78(4):433-8.

Dewar AL, Farrugia AN, Condina MR, et al, "Imatinib as a Potential Antiresorptive Therapy for Bone Disease," *Blood*, 2006, 107(11):4334-7.

Droogendijk HJ, Kluin-Nelemans HJ, van Doormaal JJ, et al, "Imatinib Mesylate in the Treatment of Systemic Mastocytosis: A Phase II Trial," *Cancer*, 2006, 107(2):345-51

Druker BJ, Sawyers CL, Kantarjian H, et al, "Activity of a Specific Inhibitor of the BCR-ABL Tyrosine Kinase in the Blast Crisis of Chronic Myeloid Leukemia and Acute Lymphoblastic Leukemia With the Philadelphia Chromosome," *N Engl J Med*, 2001, 344(14):1038-42.

Druker BJ, Talpaz M, Resta DJ, et al, "Efficacy and Safety of a Specific Inhibitor of the BCR-ABL Tyrosine Kinase in Chronic Myeloid Leukemia," *N Engl J Med*, 2001, 344(14):1031-7.

Gotlib J, Cools J, Malone JM 3rd, et al, "The FIP1L1-PDGFRalpha Fusion Tyrosine Kinase in Hypereosinophilic Syndrome and Chronic Eosinophilic Leukemia: Implications for Diagnosis, Classification, and Management," *Blood*, 2004, 103(8):2879-91.

Hehlmann R, Hochhaus A, Berger U, et al, "Current Trends in the Management of Chronic Myelogenous Leukemia," *Ann Hematol*, 2000, 79:345-54.

Joensuu H, Roberts PJ, Sarlomo-Rikala M, et al, "Effect of the Tyrosine Kinase Inhibitor STI571 in a Patient With a Metastatic Gastrointestinal Stromal Tumor," *N Engl J Med*, 2001, 344(14):1052-6.

Kantarjian H, Sawyers C, Hochhaus A, et al, "Hematologic and Cytogenetic Responses to Imatinib Mesylate in Chronic Myelogenous Leukemia," *N Engl J Med*, 2002, 346:645-52.

Kerkela R, Grazette L, Yacobi R, et al, "Cardiotoxicity of the Cancer Therapeutic Agent Imatinib Mesylate," *Nat Med*, 2006, 12(8):908-16.

McArthur GA, Demetri GD, van Oosterom A, et al, "Molecular and Clinical Analysis of Locally Advanced Dermatofibrosarcoma Protuberans Treated with Imatinib: Imatinib Target Exploration Consortium Study B2225," *J Clin Oncol*, 2005, 23(4):866-73.

Ottmann OG, Wassmann B, Pfeifer H, et al, "Imatinib Compared With Chemotherapy as Front-Line Treatment of Elderly Patients With Philadelphia Chromosome-Positive Acute Lymphoblastic Leukemia (Ph+ALL)," *Cancer*, 2007, 109(10):2068-76.

Yanada M, Takeuchi J, Sugiura I, et al, "High Complete Remission Rate and Promising Outcome by Combination of Imatinib and Chemotherapy for Newly Diagnosed BCR-ABL-Positive Acute Lymphoblastic Leukemia: A Phase II Study by the Japan Adult Leukemia Study Group," *J Clin Oncol*, 2006, 24(3):460-6.

♦ **Imatinib Mesylate** *see* Imatinib *on page 583*

♦ **IMC-C225** *see* Cetuximab *on page 201*

♦ **IMI 30** *see* Idarubicin *on page 575*

♦ **IMid-3** *see* Lenalidomide *on page 659*

♦ **Imidazole Carboxamide** *see* Dacarbazine *on page 280*

♦ **Imidazole Carboxamide Dimethyltriazene** *see* Dacarbazine *on page 280*

♦ **Imipemide** *see* Imipenem and Cilastatin *on page 591*

Imipenem and Cilastatin (i mi PEN em & sye la STAT in)

Medication Safety Issues

Sound-alike/look-alike issues:

Primaxin® may be confused with Premarin®, Primacor®

U.S. Brand Names Primaxin®

Index Terms Imipemide

Generic Available No

Canadian Brand Names Primaxin®; Primaxin® I.V.

Pharmacologic Category Antibiotic, Carbapenem

Use Treatment of lower respiratory tract, urinary tract, intra-abdominal, gynecologic, bone and joint, skin and skin structure, and polymicrobic infections as well as bacterial septicemia and endocarditis. Antibacterial activity includes resistant gram-negative bacilli (*Pseudomonas aeruginosa* and *Enterobacter* sp), gram-positive bacteria (methicillin-sensitive *Staphylococcus aureus* and *Streptococcus* sp) and anaerobes.

Unlabeled/Investigational Use Hepatic abscess; neutropenic fever; melioidosis

Pregnancy Risk Factor C

Lactation Enters breast milk/use caution

Labeled Contraindications Hypersensitivity to imipenem/cilastatin or any component of the formulation

I.M. formulation (due to lidocaine diluent) additional contraindications: Hypersensitivity to amide-type anesthetics; severe shock or heart block

Warnings/Precautions Dosage adjustment required in patients with impaired renal function; elderly patients often require lower doses (adjust carefully to renal function). Prolonged use may result in fungal or bacterial superinfection, including *C. difficile*-associated diarrhea (CDAD) and pseudomembranous colitis; CDAD has been observed <2 months postantibiotic treatment. Has been associated with CNS adverse effects, including confusional states and seizures (myoclonic); use with caution in patients with a history of seizures or hypersensitivity to beta-lactams (including penicillins and cephalosporins); patients with impaired renal function are at increased risk of seizures if not properly dose adjusted. Not recommended in pediatric CNS infections due to seizure potential. Serious hypersensitivity reactions, including anaphylaxis, have been reported (some without a history of previous allergic reactions to beta-lactams). Doses for I.M. administration are mixed with lidocaine; consult information on lidocaine for associated warnings/precautions. Two different imipenem/cilastatin products are available; due to differences in formulation, the I.V. and I.M. preparations **cannot** be interchanged. Safety and efficacy of I.M. administration in children <12 years of age have not been established.

Adverse Reactions Adverse reactions reported with use for both I.V. and I.M. formulations in adults, except where noted.

1% to 10%:

Cardiovascular: Tachycardia (infants 2%; adults <1%)

Central nervous system: Seizure (infants 6%; adults <1%)

Dermatologic: Rash (≤1%, children 2%)

Gastrointestinal: Nausea (1% to 2%), diarrhea (children 3% to 4%; adults 1% to 2%), vomiting (≤2%)

Genitourinary: Oliguria/anuria (infants 2%; adults <1%)

Local: Phlebitis/thrombophlebitis (3%), pain at I.M. injection site (1.2%)

<1%, postmarketing and/or case reports: Abdominal pain, abnormal urinalysis, acute renal failure, alkaline phosphatase increased, anaphylaxis, anemia, angioneurotic edema, asthenia, bilirubin increased, bone marrow depression, BUN/creatinine increased, candidiasis, confusion, cyanosis, (Continued)

Imipenem and Cilastatin *(Continued)*

dizziness, drug fever, dyspnea, encephalopathy, eosinophilia, erythema multiforme, fever, flushing, gastroenteritis, glossitis, hallucinations, headache, hearing loss, hematocrit decreased, hemoglobin decreased, hemolytic anemia, hemorrhagic colitis, hepatitis (including fulminant onset), hepatic failure, hyperchloremia, hyperhidrosis, hyperkalemia, hypersensitivity, hyperventilation, hyponatremia, hypotension, injection site erythema, jaundice, lactate dehydrogenase increased, leukocytosis, leukopenia, myoclonus, neutropenia (including agranulocytosis), palpitation, pancytopenia, paresthesia, pharyngeal pain, polyarthralgia, polyuria, positive Coombs' test, prothrombin time increased, pruritus, pruritus vulvae, pseudomembranous colitis, psychic disturbances, rash, resistant *P. aeruginosa*, salivation increased, somnolence, staining of teeth, Stevens-Johnson syndrome, taste perversion, thoracic spine pain, thrombocythemia, thrombocytopenia, tinnitus, tongue/tooth discoloration, tongue papillar hypertrophy, toxic epidermal necrolysis, transaminases increased, tremor, urine discoloration, urticaria, vertigo

Overdosage/Toxicology Symptoms of overdose include neuromuscular hypersensitivity and seizures. Hemodialysis may be helpful to aid in removal of the drug from blood; otherwise, treatment is supportive or symptom-directed.

Drug Interactions

Increased Effect/Toxicity: Ganciclovir may increase the risk of seizures; concomitant use not recommended. Uricosuric agents (eg, probenecid) may increase the levels/effects of imipenem; monitor. Concurrent cyclosporine may increase the neurotoxic effects of imipenem and cyclosporine levels may also be increased; monitor.

Decreased Effect: Imipenem may decrease valproic acid concentrations to subtherapeutic levels; monitor. Antibiotics may decrease therapeutic effects of Ty21a typhoid vaccine.

Storage/Stability Imipenem/cilastatin powder for injection should be stored at <25°C (77°F).

I.M.: The I.M. suspension should be used within 1 hour of reconstitution.

I.V.: Reconstituted I.V. solutions are stable for 4 hours at room temperature and 24 hours when refrigerated. Do not freeze.

Reconstitution

I.M.: Prepare 500 mg vial with 2 mL 1% lidocaine (do not use lidocaine with epinephrine). The I.V. formulation does not form a stable suspension in lidocaine and cannot be used to prepare an I.M. dose.

I.V.: Prior to use, dilute dose into 100-250 mL of an appropriate solution. Imipenem is inactivated at acidic or alkaline pH. Final concentration should not exceed 5 mg/mL. The I.M. formulation is not buffered and cannot be used to prepare I.V. solutions.

Compatibility I.V. formulation:

Variable stability (consult detailed reference) in D_5W, D_5LR, $D_5^{1}/_4NS$, $D_5^{1}/_2NS$, D_5NS, $D_{10}W$, mannitol 2.5%, mannitol 5%, mannitol 10%, NS, TPN.

Y-site administration: Compatible: Acyclovir, amifostine, aztreonam, cefepime, cisatracurium, diltiazem, docetaxel, famotidine, fludarabine, foscarnet, gatifloxacin, granisetron, idarubicin, insulin (regular), linezolid, melphalan, methotrexate, ondansetron, propofol, remifentanil, tacrolimus, teniposide, thiotepa, vinorelbine, zidovudine. **Incompatible:** Allopurinol, amphotericin B cholesteryl sulfate complex, etoposide phosphate, fluconazole, gemcitabine, lorazepam, meperidine, midazolam, sargramostim, sodium bicarbonate. **Variable (consult detailed reference):** Filgrastim, TPN.

Mechanism of Action Inhibits bacterial cell wall synthesis by binding to one or more of the penicillin binding proteins (PBPs); which in turn inhibits the final transpeptidation step of peptidoglycan synthesis in bacterial cell walls, thus inhibiting cell wall biosynthesis. Bacteria eventually lyse due to ongoing activity of cell wall autolytic enzymes (autolysins and murein hydrolases) while cell wall assembly is arrested. Cilastatin prevents renal metabolism of imipenem by competitive inhibition of dehydropeptidase along the brush border of the renal tubules.

Pharmacodynamics/Kinetics

Absorption: I.M.: Imipenem: 60% to 75%; cilastatin: 95% to 100%

Distribution: Rapidly and widely to most tissues and fluids including sputum, pleural fluid, peritoneal fluid, interstitial fluid, bile, aqueous humor, and bone; highest concentrations in pleural fluid, interstitial fluid, and peritoneal fluid; low concentrations in CSF

Protein binding: Imipenem: 20%; cilastatin: 40%

Metabolism: Imipenem is metabolized in the kidney by dehydropeptidase I; cilastatin prevents imipenem metabolism by this enzyme; cilastatin is partially metabolized renally

Half-life elimination: I.V.: Both drugs: 60 minutes; prolonged with renal impairment; I.M.: Imipenem: 2-3 hours

Time to peak: I.M.: 3.5 hours

Excretion: Both drugs: Urine (~70% as unchanged drug)

Dosage

Usual dosage ranges: Note: Dosage based on **imipenem** content:

Neonates ≤3 months and weight ≥1500 g: Non-CNS infections: I.V.:

<1 week: 25 mg/kg every 12 hours

1-4 weeks: 25 mg/kg every 8 hours

4 weeks to 3 months: 25 mg/kg every 6 hours

Children >3 months: Non-CNS infections: I.V.: 15-25 mg/kg every 6 hours; maximum dosage: Susceptible infections: 2 g/day; moderately-susceptible organisms: 4 g/day

Adults:

I.M.: 500-750 mg every 12 hours; maximum: 1500 mg/day

I.V.: Weight ≥70 kg: 250-1000 mg every 6-8 hours; maximum: 4 g/day. **Note:** For adults weighing <70 kg, refer to Dosing Adjustment in Renal Impairment:

Indication-specific dosing: Note: Doses based on imipenem content. I.M. administration is not intended for severe or life-threatening infections (eg, septicemia, endocarditis, shock), UTI, bone/joint or polymicrobic infections:

Children: I.V.:

Burkholderia mallei (melioidosis) (unlabeled use): 20 mg/kg every 8 hours for 10 days

Cystic fibrosis: Doses up to 90 mg/kg/day have been used

Adults:

Burkholderia mallei (melioidosis) (unlabeled use): I.V.: 20 mg/kg (up to 1 g) every 6-8 hours for 10 days

Intra-abdominal infections:

I.V.: Mild infection: 250-500 mg every 6 hours; severe: 500 mg every 6 hours

I.M.: Mild-to-moderate infection: 750 mg every 12 hours

Liver abscess (unlabeled use): I.V.: 500 mg every 6 hours for 2-3 weeks, then appropriate oral therapy for a total of 4-6 weeks

Lower respiratory tract, skin/skin structure, gynecologic infections:

I.M.: Mild/moderate: 500-750 mg every 12 hours

(Continued)

Imipenem and Cilastatin *(Continued)*

Mild infection: Note: Rarely a suitable option in mild infections; normally reserved for moderate-severe cases:
I.M.: 500 mg every 12 hours

Imipenem and Cilastatin Dosage in Renal Impairment

Reduced I.V. Dosage Regimen Based on Creatinine Clearance (mL/minute/1.73 m^2) and/or Body Weight <70 kg					
	Body Weight (kg)				
	≥70	**60**	**50**	**40**	**30**
Total daily dose for normal renal function: 1 g/day					
Cl$_{cr}$ ≥71	250 mg q6h	250 mg q8h	125 mg q6h	125 mg q6h	125 mg q8h
Cl$_{cr}$ 41-70	250 mg q8h	125 mg q6h	125 mg q6h	125 mg q8h	125 mg q8h
Cl$_{cr}$ 21-40	250 mg q12h	250 mg q12h	125 mg q8h	125 mg q12h	125 mg q12h
Cl$_{cr}$ 6-20	250 mg q12h	125 mg q12h	125 mg q12h	125 mg q12h	125 mg q12h
Total daily dose for normal renal function: 1.5 g/day					
Cl$_{cr}$ ≥71	500 mg q8h	250 mg q6h	250 mg q6h	250 mg q8h	125 mg q6h
Cl$_{cr}$ 41-70	250 mg q6h	250 mg q8h	250 mg q8h	125 mg q6h	125 mg q8h
Cl$_{cr}$ 21-40	250 mg q8h	250 mg q8h	250 mg q12h	125 mg q8h	125 mg q8h
Cl$_{cr}$ 6-20	250 mg q12h	250 mg q12h	250 mg q12h	125 mg q12h	125 mg q12h
Total daily dose for normal renal function: 2 g/day					
Cl$_{cr}$ ≥71	500 mg q6h	500 mg q8h	250 mg q6h	250 mg q6h	250 mg q8h
Cl$_{cr}$ 41-70	500 mg q8h	250 mg q6h	250 mg q6h	250 mg q8h	125 mg q6h
Cl$_{cr}$ 21-40	250 mg q6h	250 mg q8h	250 mg q8h	250 mg q12h	125 mg q8h
Cl$_{cr}$ 6-20	250 mg q12h	250 mg q12h	250 mg q12h	250 mg q12h	125 mg q12h
Total daily dose for normal renal function: 3 g/day					
Cl$_{cr}$ ≥71	1000 mg q8h	750 mg q8h	500 mg q6h	500 mg q8h	250 mg q6h
Cl$_{cr}$ 41-70	500 mg q6h	500 mg q8h	500 mg q8h	250 mg q6h	250 mg q8h
Cl$_{cr}$ 21-40	500 mg q8h	500 mg q8h	250 mg q6h	250 mg q8h	250 mg q8h
Cl$_{cr}$ 6-20	500 mg q12h	500 mg q12h	250 mg q12h	250 mg q12h	250 mg q12h
Total daily dose for normal renal function: 4 g/day					
Cl$_{cr}$ ≥71	1000 mg q6h	1000 mg q8h	750 mg q8h	500 mg q6h	500 mg q8h
Cl$_{cr}$ 41-70	750 mg q8h	750 mg q8h	500 mg q6h	500 mg q8h	250 mg q6h
Cl$_{cr}$ 21-40	500 mg q6h	500 mg q8h	500 mg q8h	250 mg q6h	250 mg q8h
Cl$_{cr}$ 6-20	500 mg q12h	500 mg q12h	500 mg q12h	250 mg q12h	250 mg q12h

I.V.:
Fully-susceptible organisms: 250 mg every 6 hours
Moderately-susceptible organisms: 500 mg every 6 hours

Moderate infection:
I.M.: 750 mg every 12 hours
I.V.:
Fully-susceptible organisms: 500 mg every 6-8 hours
Moderately-susceptible organisms: 500 mg every 6 hours or 1 g every 8 hours

Neutropenic fever (unlabeled use): I.V.: 500 mg every 6 hours

***Pseudomonas* infections:** I.V.: 500 mg every 6 hours; **Note:** Higher doses may be required based on organism sensitivity.

Severe infection: I.V.:
Fully-susceptible organisms: 500 mg every 6 hours
Moderately-susceptible organisms: 1 g every 6-8 hours
Maximum daily dose should not exceed 50 mg/kg or 4 g/day, whichever is lower

Urinary tract infection: I.V.:
Uncomplicated: 250 mg every 6 hours
Complicated: 500 mg every 6 hours

Dosage adjustment in renal impairment: I.V.: **Note:** Adjustments have not been established for I.M. dosing:

Patients with a Cl_{cr} ≤5 mL/minute/1.73 m^2 should not receive imipenem/cilastatin unless hemodialysis is instituted within 48 hours.

Patients weighing <30 kg with impaired renal function should not receive imipenem/cilastatin.

Hemodialysis: Use the dosing recommendation for patients with a Cl_{cr} 6-20 mL/minute; administer dose after dialysis session and every 12 hours thereafter

Peritoneal dialysis: Dose as for Cl_{cr} 6-20 mL/minute

Continuous renal replacement therapy (CRRT): Drug clearance is highly dependent on the method of renal replacement, filter type, and flow rate. Appropriate dosing requires close monitoring of pharmacologic response, signs of adverse reactions due to drug accumulation, as well as drug levels in relation to target trough (if appropriate). The following are general recommendations only (based on dialysate flow/ultrafiltration rates of 1 L/hour) and should not supersede clinical judgment:

CVVH: 250 mg every 6 hours or 500 mg every 8 hours

CVVHD/CVVHDF: 250 mg every 6 hours or 500 mg every 6-8 hours

Note: Data suggest that 500 mg every 12 hours may provide sufficient T>MIC to cover organisms with MIC values ≤2 mg/L; however, a higher dose of 500 mg every 6 hours is recommended for resistant organisms (particularly *Pseudomonas*) with MIC ≥4 mg/L (Fish, 2005).

Dosage adjustment in hepatic impairment: Hepatic dysfunction may further impair cilastatin clearance; consider decreasing the dosing frequency.

See table on previous page.

Administration

I.M.: **Note:** I.M. administration is not intended for severe or life-threatening infections (eg, septicemia, endocarditis, shock). Administer by deep injection into a large muscle (gluteal or lateral thigh). **Only the I.M. formulation can be used for I.M. administration.**

I.V.: Do not administer I.V. push. Infuse doses ≤500 mg over 20-30 minutes; infuse doses ≥750 mg over 40-60 minutes. **Only the I.V. formulation can be used for I.V. administration.**

(Continued)

Imipenem and Cilastatin *(Continued)*

Monitoring Parameters Periodic renal, hepatic, and hematologic function tests; monitor for signs of anaphylaxis during first dose

Test Interactions Interferes with urinary glucose determination using Clinitest®

Dietary Considerations Sodium content of 500 mg injection:
- I.M.: 32 mg (1.4 mEq)
- I.V.: 37.5 mg (1.6 mEq)

Special Geriatric Considerations Imipenem/cilastatin's role is limited to the treatment of infections caused by susceptible multiresistant organism(s) and in patients whose bacterial infection(s) have failed to respond to other appropriate antimicrobials; many of the seizures attributed to imipenem/ cilastatin were in elderly patients; dose must be adjusted for creatinine clearance and body weight.

Emetic Potential Very low (<10%)

Vesicant No

Dosage Forms Excipient information presented when available (limited, particularly for generics); consult specific product labeling.

Injection, powder for reconstitution [I.M.]:
Primaxin®: Imipenem 500 mg and cilastatin 500 mg [contains sodium 32 mg (1.4 mEq)]

Injection, powder for reconstitution [I.V.]:
Primaxin®: Imipenem 250 mg and cilastatin 250 mg [contains sodium 18.8 mg (0.8 mEq)]; imipenem 500 mg and cilastatin 500 mg [contains sodium 37.5 mg (1.6 mEq)]

References

Ahonkhai VI, Cyhan GM, Wilson SE, et al, "Imipenem-Cilastatin in Pediatric Patients: An Overview of Safety and Efficacy in Studies Conducted in the United States," *Pediatr Infect Dis J*, 1989, 8(11):740-4.

American Thoracic Society and Infectious Diseases Society of America, "Guidelines for the Management of Adults With Hospital-Acquired, Ventilator-Associated, and Healthcare-Associated Pneumonia," *Am J Respir Crit Care Med*, 2005, 171(4):388-416.

Asensi AV, Rodriguez-Guardado A, Carton Sanchez JA, et al, "Pyogenic Hepatic Abscess. Review of 59 Cases and Experience With imipenem," *Rev Clin Esp*, 1997, 197(7):494-9.

Balfour JA, Bryson HM, and Brogden RN, "Imipenem/Cilastatin: An Update of Its Antibacterial Activity, Pharmacokinetics, and Therapeutic Efficacy in the Treatment of Serious Infections," *Drugs*, 1996, 51(1):99-136.

Bomback T, Sesin GP, and Mucciardi N, "Possible Imipenem/Cilastatin-Induced Aplastic Anemia," *Pharm Therapeut*, 1995, 20(5):293-302.

Chung AM, Reed MD, and Blumer JL, "Antibiotics and Breast-Feeding: A Critical Review of the Literature," *Paediatr Drugs*, 2002, 4(12):817-37.

Finch RG, Craddock C, Kelly J, et al, "Pharmacokinetic Studies of Imipenem/Cilastatin in Elderly Patients," *J Antimicrob Chemother*, 1986, 18(Suppl E):103-7.

Fish DN, Teitelbaum I, and Abraham E, "Pharmacokinetics and Pharmacodynamics of Imipenem During Continuous Renal Replacement Therapy in Critically Ill Patients," *Antimicrob Agents Chemother*, 2005, 49(6):2421-8.

Hughes WT, Armstrong D, Bodey GP, et al, "2002 Guidelines for the Use of Antimicrobial Agents in Neutropenic Patients With Cancer," *Clin Infect Dis*, 2002, 34(6):730-51.

Leo RJ and Ballow CH, "Seizure Activity Associated With Imipenem Use: Clinical Case Reports and Review of the Literature," *DICP*, 1991, 25(4):351-4.

Lin JC, Siu LK, Fung CP, et al, "Nosocomial Liver Abscess Caused by Extended-Spectrum Beta-Lactamase-Producing *Klebsiella pneumoniae*," *J Clin Microbiol*, 2007, 45(1):266-9.

Norrby SR, "Carbapenems," *Med Clin North Am*, 1995, 79(4):745-59.

O'Donovan CA, White ML, Cheung A, et al, "Seizure Incidence With Imipenem Use at VA Hospital," *Hosp Formul*, 1995, 30:172-5.

Overturf GD, "Use of Imipenem-Cilastatin in Pediatrics," *Pediatr Infect Dis J*, 1989, 8(11):792-4.

Somani P, Freimer EH, Gross ML, et al, "Pharmacokinetics of Imipenem-Cilastatin in Patients With Renal Insufficiency Undergoing Continuous Ambulatory Peritoneal Dialysis," *Antimicrob Agents Chemother*, 1988, 32(4):530-4.

Tegeder I, Bremer F, Oelkers R, et al, "Pharmacokinetics of Imipenem-Cilastatin in Critically Ill Patients Undergoing continuous Veno-Venous Hemofiltration," *Antimicrob Agents Chemother*, 1997, 41(12):2640-5.

Trotman RL, Williamson JC, Shoemaker DM, et al, "Antibiotic Dosing in Critically Ill Adult Patients Receiving Continuous Renal Replacement Therapy," *Clin Infect Dis*, 2005, 41(8):1159-66.

Toon S, Hopkins KJ, Garstang FM, et al, "Pharmacokinetics of Imipenem and Cilastatin After Their Simultaneous Administration to the Elderly," *Br J Clin Pharmacol*, 1987, 23(2):143-9.

Wong VK, Wright HT Jr, Ross LA, et al, "Imipenem/Cilastatin Treatment of Bacterial Meningitis in Children," *Pediatr Infect Dis J*, 1991, 10(2):122-5.

Yoshikawa TT, "Antimicrobial Therapy for the Elderly Patient," *J Am Geriatr Soc*, 1990, 38(12):1353-72.

♦ **ImmuCyst® (Can)** see BCG Vaccine on page 128

Immune Globulin (Intravenous)
(i MYUN GLOB yoo lin, IN tra VEE nus)

Medication Safety Issues
Sound-alike/look-alike issues:
Gamimune® N may be confused with CytoGam®

U.S. Brand Names Carimune® NF; Flebogamma®; Gammagard Liquid; Gammagard S/D; Gammar®-P I.V.; Gamunex®; Octagam®; Panglobulin® NF; Polygam® S/D

Index Terms IGIV; IVIG

Generic Available No

Canadian Brand Names Gamimune® N; Gammagard Liquid; Gammagard S/D; Gamunex®

Pharmacologic Category Immune Globulin

Use
Treatment of primary immunodeficiency syndromes (congenital agammaglobulinemia, severe combined immunodeficiency syndromes [SCIDS], common variable immunodeficiency, X-linked immunodeficiency, Wiskott-Aldrich syndrome) (Carimune® NF, Flebogamma®, Gammagard Liquid, Gammagard S/D, Gammar®-P I.V., Gamunex®, Octagam®, Panglobulin® NF, Polygam® S/D)

Treatment of immune (idiopathic) thrombocytopenic purpura (ITP) (Carimune® NF, Gammagard S/D, Gamunex®, Panglobulin® NF, Polygam® S/D)

Prevention of coronary artery aneurysms associated with Kawasaki disease (in combination with aspirin) (Gammagard S/D, Polygam® S/D)

Prevention of bacterial infection in B-cell chronic lymphocytic leukemia (CLL) (Gammagard S/D, Polygam® S/D)

Unlabeled/Investigational Use Prevention of serious bacterial infections among HIV-infected children with hypogammaglobulinemia (IgG <400 mg/dL) (CDC guidelines); hematopoietic stem cell transplantation (HSCT), to prevent bacterial infections among allogeneic recipients with severe hypogammaglobulinemia (IgG <400 mg/dL) at <100 days post transplant (CDC guidelines); fetal-neonatal alloimmune thrombocytopenia; pregnancy-associated ITP; prevention of gastroenteritis in children; multiple sclerosis (relapsing, remitting when other therapies cannot be used); hemolytic disease of the newborn; HIV-associated thrombocytopenia; acquired hypogammaglobulinemia secondary to malignancy; chronic inflammatory demyelinating polyneuropathy; myasthenia gravis; refractory dermatomyositis/polymyositis

Pregnancy Risk Factor C

Lactation Excretion in breast milk unknown

Labeled Contraindications Hypersensitivity to immune globulin or any component of the formulation; selective IgA deficiency
(Continued)

Immune Globulin (Intravenous) *(Continued)*

Warnings/Precautions [U.S. Boxed Warning]: Acute renal dysfunction (increased serum creatinine, oliguria, acute renal failure, osmotic nephrosis) can rarely occur; usually within 7 days of use (more likely with products stabilized with sucrose). Use with caution in the elderly, patients with renal disease, diabetes mellitus, volume depletion, sepsis, paraproteinemia, and nephrotoxic medications due to risk of renal dysfunction. In patients at risk of renal dysfunction, the rate of infusion and concentration of solution should be minimized. discontinue if renal function deteriorates. Hypersensitivity and anaphylactic reactions can occur; immediate treatment (including epinephrine 1:1000) should be available; product of human plasma; may potentially contain infectious agents which could transmit disease. Screening of donors, as well as testing and/or inactivation or removal of certain viruses, reduces the risk. Infections thought to be transmitted by this product should be reported to the manufacturer. Aseptic meningitis may occur with high doses (≥2 g/kg); syndrome usually appears within several hours to 2 days following treatment; usually resolves within several days after IVIG is discontinued.

Intravenous immune globulin has been associated with antiglobulin hemolysis; monitor for signs of hemolytic anemia. Patients should be adequately hydrated prior to therapy. Use caution in patients with a history of thrombotic events or cardiovascular disease; there is clinical evidence of a possible association between thrombotic events and administration of intravenous immune globulin. For intravenous administration only. Patients should be monitored for adverse events during and after the infusion. Stop administration with signs of infusion reaction (fever, chills, nausea, vomiting, and rarely shock). Risk may be increased with initial treatment, when switching brands of immune globulin, and with treatment interruptions of >8 weeks. Monitor for transfusion-related acute lung injury (TRALI); noncardiogenic pulmonary edema has been reported with intravenous immune globulin use. Response to live vaccinations may be impaired. Some products may contain maltose, which may result in falsely-elevated blood glucose readings. Product may contain sucrose. Some products may contain sorbitol; do not use in patients with fructose intolerance. Packaging of some products may contain natural latex/natural rubber.

Adverse Reactions Frequency not defined.

Cardiovascular: Chest tightness, edema, flushing of the face, hyper-/hypotension, palpitation, tachycardia

Central nervous system: Anxiety, chills, dizziness, drowsiness, fatigue, fever, headache, irritability, lethargy, lightheadedness, malaise, migraine, pain

Dermatologic: Pruritus, rash, urticaria

Gastrointestinal: Abdominal cramps, diarrhea, nausea, sore throat, vomiting

Hematologic: Autoimmune hemolytic anemia, hematocrit decreased, mild hemolysis

Hepatic: Liver function test increased

Local: Pain or irritation at the infusion site

Neuromuscular & skeletal: Arthralgia, back or hip pain, leg cramps, muscle cramps, myalgia, neck pain, weakness

Renal: Acute renal failure, acute tubular necrosis, anuria, BUN increased, creatinine increased, oliguria, proximal tubular nephropathy, osmotic nephrosis

Respiratory: Asthma aggravated, bronchitis, cough, dyspnea, nasal congestion, pharyngeal pain, rhinorrhea, sinus headache, sinusitis, upper respiratory infection, wheezing

Miscellaneous: Anaphylaxis, diaphoresis, hypersensitivity reactions, infusion reaction

Postmarketing and/or case reports: Abdominal pain, apnea, ARDS, aseptic meningitis syndrome, bronchospasm, bullous dermatitis, cardiac arrest, coma, Coombs' test positive, cyanosis, epidermolysis, erythema multiforme, hepatic dysfunction, hypoxemia, leukopenia, loss of consciousness, pancytopenia, papular rash, pulmonary edema, rigors, seizure, Stevens-Johnson syndrome, thromboembolism, transfusion-related acute lung injury (TRALI), tremor, vascular collapse

Drug Interactions

Decreased Effect: Decreased effect of live virus vaccines (eg, measles, mumps, rubella). Recommended separation of administration interval varies by product; refer to individual product labeling or current practice guidelines.

Storage/Stability Stability is dependent upon the manufacturer and brand. Do not freeze.

Carimune® NF, Panglobulin® NF: Prior to reconstitution, store at or below 30°C (86°F). Following reconstitution, store under refrigeration. Begin infusion within 24 hours.

Flebogamma®: Store at 2°C to 25°C (36°F to 77°F).

Gammagard Liquid: Prior to use, store at 2°C to 8°C (36°F to 46°F) for up to 36 months. May store at room temperature of 25°C (77°F) within the first 24 months of manufacturing. Storage time at room temperature varies with length of time previously refrigerated; refer to product labeling for details.

Gammagard S/D, Polygam® S/D: Store at ≤25°C (≤77°F).

Gammar®-P I.V.: Store at ≤25°C (≤77°F).

Gamunex®: May be stored for up to 36 months at 2°C to 8°C (36°F to 46°F); may be stored at ≤25°C (≤77°F) for up to 6 months.

Octagam®: Store at 2°C to 25°C (36°F to 77°F).

Reconstitution Dilution is dependent upon the manufacturer and brand. Gently swirl; do not shake; avoid foaming. Discard unused portion:

Carimune® NF, Panglobulin® NF: Reconstitute with NS, D_5W, or SWFI.

Flebogamma®: Dilution is not recommended.

Gammagard Liquid: May dilute in D_5W only.

Gammagard S/D, Gammar®-P I.V., Polygam® S/D: Reconstitute with SWFI.

Gamunex®:Dilute in D_5W only.

Compatibility Stable in D_5W, $D_{15}W$, $D_51/4NS$; **variable stability (consult detailed reference)** in TPN.

Y-site administration: Compatible: Fluconazole, sargramostim.

Mechanism of Action Replacement therapy for primary and secondary immunodeficiencies; interference with F_c receptors on the cells of the reticuloendothelial system for autoimmune cytopenias and ITP; possible role of contained antiviral-type antibodies

Pharmacodynamics/Kinetics

Onset of action: I.V.: Provides immediate antibody levels

Duration: Immune effect: 3-4 weeks (variable)

Distribution: V_d: 0.09-0.13 L/kg

Intravascular portion (primarily): Healthy subjects: 41% to 57%; Patients with congenital humoral immunodeficiencies: ~70%

Half-life elimination: IgG (variable among patients): Healthy subjects: 14-24 days; Patients with congenital humoral immunodeficiencies: 26-40 days; hypermetabolism associated with fever and infection have coincided with a shortened half-life

(Continued)

Immune Globulin (Intravenous) *(Continued)*

Dosage Approved doses and regimens may vary between brands; check manufacturer guidelines. **Note:** Some clinicians dose IVIG on ideal body weight or an adjusted ideal body weight in morbidly-obese patients.

Children: I.V.: Pediatric HIV, prevention of infection (CDC guidelines): 400 mg/kg every 2-4 weeks

Children and Adults: I.V.:

Primary immunodeficiency disorders: **Note:** Adjust dose/frequency based desired IgG levels and clinical response:

General dosing range: 200-800 mg/kg per month

Carimune® NF, Panglobulin® NF: 200 mg/kg every 4 weeks. May increase dose to 300 mg/kg every 4 weeks or may increase frequency based on patient response.

Flebogamma®, Gammagard Liquid, Gammagard S/D, Gamunex®, Octagam®, Polygam® S/D: 300-600 mg/kg every 3-4 weeks; adjusted based on dosage and interval in conjunction with monitored serum IgG concentrations

Gamma®-P I.V.:

Children and Adolescents: Initial dose: 200 mg/kg every 3-4 weeks

Adults: 200-400 mg/kg every 3-4 weeks

B-cell chronic lymphocytic leukemia (CLL) (Gammagard S/D, Polygam® S/D): 400 mg/kg/dose every 3-4 weeks

Immune (idiopathic) thrombocytopenic purpura (ITP):

Carimune® NF, Panglobulin® NF:

Acute: 400 mg/kg/day for 2-5 days

Chronic: 400 mg/kg as needed to maintain platelet count ≥30,000/mm^3 or to control significant bleeding; may increase dose if needed (range: 800-1000 mg/kg)

Gammagard S/D, Polygam® S/D: 1000 mg/kg; adjust additional doses based on patient response or platelet count. Up to 3 separate doses may be administered on alternate days if required.

Gamunex®: 1000 mg/kg/day for 1-2 days, **or** 400 mg/kg/day for 5 days

Kawasaki disease: Initiate IVIG therapy within 10 days of disease onset:

Must be used in combination with aspirin: 80-100 mg/kg/day in 4 divided doses for 14 days; when fever subsides, dose aspirin at 3-5 mg/kg once daily for ≥6-8 weeks

AHA guidelines: 2000 mg/kg as a single dose

Gammagard S/D, Polygam® S/D: 1000 mg/kg as a single dose administered over 10 hours, **or** 400 mg/kg/day for 4 days. Begin within 7 days of onset of fever.

Hematopoietic stem cell transplantation with hypogammaglobulinemia (CDC guidelines):

Children: 400 mg/kg per month; increase dose or frequency to maintain IgG levels >400 mg/dL

Adolescents and Adults: 500 mg/kg/week

Unlabeled uses:

Acquired hypogammaglobulinemia secondary to malignancy (unlabeled use): Adults: 400 mg/kg/dose every 3 weeks; reevaluate every 4-6 months

Chronic inflammatory demyelinating polyneuropathy (unlabeled use): Adults: Various regimens have been used, including:

400 mg/kg/day for 5 doses once each month

or

1000 mg/kg/day for 2 days once each month

Guillain-Barré syndrome (unlabeled use): Children and Adults: Various regimens have been used, including:

400 mg/kg/day for 5 days

or

2000 mg/kg in divided doses administered over 2 days

HIV-associated thrombocytopenia (unlabeled use): Adults: 1000 mg/kg/day for 2 days

Multiple sclerosis (relapsing-remitting, when other therapies cannot be used) (unlabeled use): Adults: 1000 mg/kg per month, with or without an induction of 400 mg/kg/day for 5 days

Myasthenia gravis (severe exacerbation) (unlabeled use): Adults: Total dose of 2000 mg/kg over 2-5 days

Refractory dermatomyositis (unlabeled use): Adults: 2000 mg/kg per month administered over 2-5 days

Refractory polymyositis (unlabeled use): Adults: 2000 mg/kg per course administered over 2-5 days

Dosing adjustment/comments in renal impairment: Cl_{cr} <10 mL/minute: Avoid use; in patients at risk of renal dysfunction, consider infusion at a rate less than maximum.

Administration I.V. infusion over 2-24 hours; for initial treatment, a lower concentration and/or a slower rate of infusion should be used. Administer in separate infusion line from other medications; if using primary line, flush with saline prior administration. Refrigerated product should be warmed to room temperature prior to infusion. Some products require filtration; refer to individual product labeling. Antecubital veins should be used, especially with concentrations ≥10% to prevent injection site discomfort. Decrease dose, rate and/or concentration of infusion in patients who may be at risk of renal failure. Decreasing the rate or stopping the infusion may help relieve some adverse effects (flushing, changes in pulse rate, changes in blood pressure). Epinephrine should be available during administration.

Monitoring Parameters Renal function, urine output, hemoglobin and hematocrit, platelets (in patients with ITP); infusion-related adverse reactions, anaphylaxis, signs and symptoms of hemolysis; blood viscosity (in patients at risk for hyperviscosity)

Test Interactions Octagam® contains maltose. Falsely-elevated blood glucose levels may occur when glucose monitoring devices and test strips utilizing the glucose dehydrogenase pyrroloquinolinequinone (GDH-PQQ) based methods are used. Glucose monitoring devices and test strips which utilize the glucose-specific method are recommended.

Dietary Considerations Octagam® contains sodium 30 mmol/L

Emetic Potential Low

Vesicant No

Dosage Forms Excipient information presented when available (limited, particularly for generics); consult specific product labeling.

Injection, powder for reconstitution [preservative free]:

Gammar®-P I.V.: 5 g, 10 g [stabilized with human albumin and sucrose]

Injection, powder for reconstitution [preservative free, nanofiltered]:

Carimune® NF: 3 g, 6 g, 12 g [contains sucrose]

Panglobulin® NF: 6 g, 12 g [contains sucrose]

Injection, powder for reconstitution [preservative free, solvent detergent-treated]:

Gammagard S/D: 2.5 g, 5 g, 10 g [stabilized with human albumin, glycine, glucose, and polyethylene glycol; packaging may contain natural latex/natural rubber]

(Continued)

Immune Globulin (Intravenous) *(Continued)*

Polygam® S/D: 5 g, 10 g [stabilized with human albumin, glycine, glucose, and polyethylene glycol]

Injection, solution [preservative free; solvent detergent-treated]:

Gammagard Liquid: 10% (10 mL, 25 mL, 50 mL, 100 mL, 200 mL) [latex free, sucrose free; stabilized with glycine]

Octagam®: 5% (20 mL, 50 mL, 100 mL, 200 mL) [sucrose free; contains sodium 30 mmol/L and maltose]

Injection, solution [preservative free]

Flebogamma®: 5% (10 mL, 50 mL, 100 mL, 200 mL) [contains polyethylene glycol and sorbitol]

Gamunex®: 10% (10 mL, 25 mL, 50 mL, 100 mL, 200 mL) [caprylate/ chromatography purified]

References

American Academy of Pediatrics Subcommittee on Hyperbilirubinemia, "Management of Hyperbilirubinemia in the Newborn Infant 35 or More Weeks of Gestation," *Pediatrics*, 2004, 114(1):297-316.

Anderson D, Ali K, Blanchette V, et al, "Guidelines on the Use of Intravenous Immune Globulin for Hematologic Conditions," *Transfus Med Rev*, 2007, 21(2 Suppl 1):9-56.

ASHP Commission on Therapeutics, "ASHP Therapeutic Guidelines for Intravenous Immune Globulin," *Am J Hosp Pharm*, 1992, 49(3):652-4.

Blanchette VS, Luke B, Andrew M, et al, "A Prospective Randomized Trial of High-Dose Intravenous Immune Globulin G Therapy, Oral Prednisone Therapy, and No Therapy in Childhood Acute Immune Thrombocytopenic Purpura," *J Pediatr*, 1993, 123(6):989-95.

British Committee for Standards in Haematology General Haematology Task Force, "Guidelines for the Investigation and Management of Idiopathic Thrombocytopenic Purpura in Adults, Children and in Pregnancy," *Br J Haematol*, 2003, 120(4):574-96.

Centers for Disease Control and Prevention, "Guidelines for Preventing Opportunistic Infections Among HIV-Infected Persons - 2002 Recommendations of the U.S. Public Health Service and the Infectious Diseases Society of America," *MMWR Recomm Rep*, 2002, 51(RR-8):1-52.

Centers for Disease Control and Prevention, "Guidelines for Preventing Opportunistic Infections Among Hematopoietic Stem Cell Transplant Recipients: Recommendations of CDC, the Infectious Disease Society of America, and the American Society of Blood and Marrow Transplantation," *MMWR Recomm Rep*, 2000, 49(RR-10):1-125.

Dalakas MC, "Intravenous Immunoglobulin In Autoimmune Neuromuscular Diseases," *JAMA*, 2004, 291(19):2367-75.

Dalakas MC and Hohlfeld R, "Polymyositis and Dermatomyositis," *Lancet*, 2003, 362(9388):971-82.

Dalakas MC, Illa I, Dambrosia JM, et al, "A Controlled Trial of High-Dose Intravenous Immune Globulin Infusions as Treatment for Dermatomyositis," *N Engl J Med*, 1993, 329(27):1993-2000.

Dattani SJ and Connelly JF, "Oral Immunoglobulins for Gastroenteritis," *Ann Pharmacother*, 1996, 30(11):1323-4.

Eijkhout HW, van Der Meer JW, Kallenberg CG, et al, "The Effect of Two Different Dosages of Intravenous Immunoglobulin on the Incidenceof Recurrent Infections In Patients With Primary Hypogammaglobulinemia. A Randomized, Double-Blind, Multicenter Crossover Trial," *Ann Intern Med*, 2001, 135(3):165-74.

Feasby T, Banwell B, Benstead T, et al, "Guidelines on the Use of Intravenous Immune Globulin for Neurologic Conditions," *Transfus Med Rev*, 2007, 21(2 Suppl 1):57-107.

Gottstein R and Cooke RW, "Systematic Review of Intravenous Immunoglobulin in Haemolytic Disease of the Newborn," *Arch Dis Child Fetal Neonatal Ed*, 2003, 88(1):F6-10.

Grillo JA, Gorson, KC, Ropper AH, et al, "Rapid Infusion of Intravenous Immune Globulin in Patients With Neuromuscular Disorders," *Neurology*, 2001, 57:1699-1701.

Gurcan HM and Ahmed AR, "Efficacy of Various Intravenous Immunoglobulin Therapy Protocols in Autoimmune and Chronic Inflammatory Disorders," *Ann Pharmacother*, 2007, 41(5):812-23.

Hilgartner MW and Bussel J, "Use of Intravenous Gamma Globulin for the Treatment of Autoimmune Neutropenia of Childhood and Autoimmune Hemolytic Anemia," *Am J Med*, 1987, 83(4A):25-9.

Hughes RA, Bouche P, Cornblath DR, et al, "European Federation of Neurological Societies/ Peripheral Nerve Society Guideline on Management of Chronic Inflammatory Demyelinating Polyradiculoneuropathy: Report of a Joint Task Force of the European Federation of Neurological Societies and the Peripheral Nerve Society," *Eur J Neurol*, 2006, 13(4):326-32.

Hughes RA, Wijdicks EF, Barohn R, et al, "Practice Parameter: Immunotherapy for Guillain-Barré Syndrome: Report of the Quality Standards Subcommittee of the American Academy of Neurology," *Neurology*, 2003, 61(6):736-40.

Kuwabara S, "Guillain-Barré Syndrome: Epidemiology, Pathophysiology and Management," *Drugs*, 2004, 64(6):597-610.

Morrell A, "Pharmacokinetics of Intravenous Immunoglobulin Preparations," *Intravenous Immunoglobulins in Clinical Practice*, Lee ML and Strand V eds, New York, NY: Marcel Dekker, Inc, 1997, 1-18.

NIH Consensus Conference, "Intravenous Immunoglobulin, Prevention and Treatment of Disease," *JAMA*, 1990, 264(24):3189-93.

Newburger JW, Takahashi M, Gerber MA, et al, "Diagnosis, Treatment, and Long-Term Management of Kawasaki Disease: A Statement for Health Professionals From the Committee on Rheumatic Fever, Endocarditis, and Kawasaki Disease, Council on Cardiovascular Disease in the Young, American Heart Association," *Pediatrics*, 2004, 114(6):1708-33.

Skvaril F and Gardi A, "Differences Among Available Immunoglobulin Preparations for Intravenous Use," *Pediatr Infect Dis J*, 1988, 7:543-48.

"University Hospital Consortium Expert Panel for Off-Label Use of Polyvalent Intravenously Administered Immunoglobulin Preparations Consensus Statement," *JAMA*, 1995, 273(23):1865-70.

van Schaik IN, Winer JB, de Haan R, et al, "Intravenous Immunoglobulin for Chronic Inflammatory Demyelinating Polyradiculoneuropathy: A Systematic Review," *Lancet Neurol*, 2002, 1(8):491-8.

Immune Globulin (Subcutaneous)
(i MYUN GLOB yoo lin sub kyoo TAY nee us)

U.S. Brand Names Vivaglobin®

Index Terms Immune Globulin Subcutaneous (Human); SCIG

Generic Available No

Pharmacologic Category Immune Globulin

Use Treatment of primary immune deficiency (PID)

Pregnancy Risk Factor C

Lactation Excretion in breast milk unknown/use caution

Labeled Contraindications Hypersensitivity to immune globulin or any component of the formulation; history of anaphylactic or severe systemic reaction to immune globulin preparations; selective IgA deficiency with known antibody against IgA

Warnings/Precautions For subcutaneous administration only; not for I.V. use. Hypersensitivity reactions and anaphylactic reactions can occur; use caution with initial treatment, when switching brands of immune globulin, and with treatment interruptions of >8 weeks. Patients should be monitored for adverse events during and after the first infusion. Stop infusion with signs of infusion reaction (fever, chills, nausea, vomiting, and rarely shock); medications for the treatment of hypersensitivity reactions should be available for immediate use. Use caution with IgA deficiency; sensitization to IgA may cause anaphylactic reaction. Product of human plasma; may potentially contain infectious agents which could transmit disease. Screening of donors, as well as testing and/or inactivation or removal of certain viruses, reduces the risk. Infections thought to be transmitted by this product should be reported to the manufacturer. Safety and effectiveness for children <2 years of age have not been established.

Adverse Reactions Adverse reactions can be expected to be similar to those experienced with other immune globulin products; percentages are reported as adverse events per patient; injection site reactions decreased with subsequent infusions

>10%:

Central nervous system: Headache (32% to 48%), fever (3% to 25%)

Dermatologic: Rash (6% to 17%)

Gastrointestinal: Gastrointestinal disorder (5% to 37%), nausea (11% to 18%), sore throat (17%)

(Continued)

Immune Globulin (Subcutaneous) *(Continued)*

Local: Injection site reactions (swelling, redness, itching; 92%)
Miscellaneous: Allergic reaction (11%)
1% to 10%:
Cardiovascular: Tachycardia (3%)
Central nervous system: Pain (10%)
Dermatologic: Skin disorder (3%)
Gastrointestinal: Diarrhea (10%)
Genitourinary: Urine abnormality (3%)
Neuromuscular & skeletal: Weakness (5%)
Respiratory: Cough (10%)
<1%: Abdominal pain, dyspnea, nervousness

Overdosage/Toxicology Treatment should be symptom-directed and supportive.

Drug Interactions
   Decreased Effect: Immune globulin may decrease the efficacy of immune response to live vaccines.

Storage/Stability Store at 2°C to 8°C (36°F to 46°F); do not freeze. Do not shake. Store in original box until ready to use. Allow vial(s) to reach room temperature prior to use. The appearance of immune globulin (subcutaneous) may vary from colorless to light brown; do not use if cloudy or contains precipitate.

Compatibility Do not mix with other products.

Mechanism of Action Immune globulin replacement therapy of IgG antibodies against bacteria and viral agents.

Pharmacodynamics/Kinetics
Bioavailability: 73% (compared to I.V.)
Time to peak, plasma: 2.5 days

Dosage Note: Consider premedicating with acetaminophen and diphenhydramine.
   SubQ infusion: Children ≥2 years and Adults: 100-200 mg/kg weekly (maximum rate: 20 mL/hour; doses >15 mL should be divided between sites); adjust the dose over time to achieve desired clinical response or target IgG levels
   Conversion from I.V. to SubQ: Multiply previous I.V. dose by 1.37, then divide into a weekly regimen by dividing by the previous I.V. dosing interval (eg, if the dosing interval was every 3 weeks, divide by 3); adjust the dose over time to achieve desired clinical response or target IgG levels. SubQ infusion administration should begin 1 week after the last I.V. dose.

Administration Subcutaneous: Initial dose should be administered in a healthcare setting capable of providing monitoring and treatment in the event of hypersensitivity. Using aseptic technique, follow the infusion device manufacturer's instructions for filling the reservoir and preparing the pump. Remove air from administration set and needle by priming. Inject via infusion pump into the abdomen, thigh, upper arm, and/or lateral hip. The maximum rate is 20 mL/hour and maximum volume per injection site is 15 mL (doses >15 mL should be divided and infused into several sites). Select the number of required infusion sites; multiple concurrent injection sites may be achieved with the use of Y-site connection tubing; injection sites must be at least 2 inches apart. After the sites are clean and dry, insert subcutaneous needle and prime administration set. Attach sterile needle to administration set, gently pull back on the syringe to assure a blood vessel has not been inadvertently accessed. Repeat for each injection site; infuse following instructions for the infusion device. Rotate the site(s) weekly. Treatment may be transitioned to the home/home care setting in the absence of adverse reactions.

Monitoring Parameters Infusion-related adverse reactions, anaphylaxis, IgG levels, clinical response

Test Interactions Passively-transferred antibodies may yield false-positive serologic testing results; may yield false-positive direct and indirect Coombs' test

Patient Information Do not have live virus vaccinations within 3 months of receiving this medication. This medication can only be administered by infusion under the skin. Report immediately any difficulty breathing; chills; fever; rapid heart beat; skin rash; pain; or redness, swelling, or pain at injection site. You may experience headache or mild headache (consult prescriber for appropriate analgesic). Report any acute or persistent adverse effects.

Special Geriatric Considerations No clinical data specific to elderly at this time. Use caution and monitor closely.

Additional Information Serum IgG levels may be drawn at any time. Subcutaneous weekly treatments provide more constant levels rather than the more pronounced peak and trough patterns observed with I.V. monthly immune globulin treatments.

Dosage Forms Excipient information presented when available (limited, particularly for generics); consult specific product labeling.

Injection, solution [preservative free]: IgG 160 mg/mL (3 mL, 10 mL, 20 mL)

References

Chapel HM, Spickett GP, Ericson D, et al, "The Comparison of the Efficacy and Safety of Intravenous Versus Subcutaneous Immunoglobulin Replacement Therapy," *J Clin Immunol*, 2000, 20(2):94-100.

Gardulf A, Hammerstrom L, and Smith CI, "Home Treatment of Hypogammaglobulinaemia With Subcutaneous Gammaglobulin by Rapid Infusion," *Lancet*, 1991, 338(8760):162-6.

Stiehm ER, Casillas AM, Finkelstein JZ, et al, "Slow Subcutaneous Human Intravenous Immunoglobulin in the Treatment of Antibody Immunodeficiency: Use of an Old Method With a New Product," *J Allergy Clin Immunol*, 1998, 101(6):848-9.

♦ **Immune Globulin Subcutaneous (Human)** *see* Immune Globulin (Subcutaneous) *on page 603*

♦ **Immunine® VH (Can)** *see* Factor IX *on page 418*

♦ **In-111 Ibritumomab** *see* Ibritumomab *on page 570*

♦ **In-111 Zevalin** *see* Ibritumomab *on page 570*

♦ **Inapsine®** *see* Droperidol *on page 369*

♦ **INF-alpha 2** *see* Interferon Alfa-2b *on page 617*

♦ **INFeD®** *see* Iron Dextran Complex *on page 633*

♦ **Inflamase® Mild (Can)** *see* PrednisoLONE *on page 914*

Infliximab (in FLIKS e mab)

Medication Safety Issues

Sound-alike/look-alike issues:

Remicade® may be confused with Renacidin®, Rituxan®

Infliximab may be confused with rituximab

U.S. Brand Names Remicade®

Index Terms Infliximab, Recombinant; NSC-728729

Generic Available No

Canadian Brand Names Remicade®

Pharmacologic Category Antirheumatic, Disease Modifying; Gastrointestinal Agent, Miscellaneous; Monoclonal Antibody; Tumor Necrosis Factor (TNF) Blocking Agent

Use Treatment of rheumatoid arthritis (moderate-to-severe, with methotrexate); treatment of Crohn's disease (moderate-to-severe with inadequate
(Continued)

Infliximab *(Continued)*

response to conventional therapy) for induction and maintenance of remission, and/or to reduce the number of draining enterocutaneous and rectovaginal fistulas, and to maintain fistula closure; treatment of psoriatic arthritis; treatment of plaque psoriasis (chronic severe); treatment of ankylosing spondylitis; treatment of and maintenance of healing of ulcerative colitis (moderately- to severely-active with inadequate response to conventional therapy)

Note: In Canada, infliximab is not approved for use in children.

Unlabeled/Investigational Use Acute graft-versus-host disease (GVHD)

Restrictions An FDA-approved medication guide is available at www.fda.gov/cder/Offices/ODS/labeling.htm; distribute to each patient to whom this medication is dispensed.

Pregnancy Risk Factor B

Lactation Excretion in breast milk unknown/not recommended

Labeled Contraindications Hypersensitivity to infliximab, murine proteins or any component of the formulation; doses >5 mg/kg in patients with moderate or severe congestive heart failure (NYHA Class III/IV)

Warnings/Precautions [U.S. Boxed Warning]: Opportunistic infections and/or reactivation of latent infections have been associated with infliximab therapy. Tuberculosis (may be disseminated or extrapulmonary) has been reactivated in patients previously exposed to TB while on infliximab. Most cases have been reported within the first 3-6 months of treatment. Other opportunistic infections (eg, invasive fungal infections, listeriosis, *Pneumocystis*) have occurred during therapy. Patients should be evaluated for latent tuberculosis infection with a tuberculin skin test prior to infliximab therapy. Treatment of latent tuberculosis should be initiated before infliximab is used. The risk/benefit ratio should be weighed in patients who have resided in regions where histoplasmosis is endemic.

Serious infections (including sepsis, pneumonia, and fatal infections) have been reported in patients receiving TNF-blocking agents. Many of the serious infections in patients treated with infliximab have occurred in patients on concomitant immunosuppressive therapy. Serious infections were reported when used in combination with anakinra or etanercept. Caution should be exercised when considering the use of infliximab in patients with a chronic infection or history of recurrent infection. Infliximab should not be given to patients with a clinically important, active infection. Patients who develop a new infection while undergoing treatment with infliximab should be monitored closely. If a patient develops a serious infection or sepsis, infliximab should be discontinued. Patients should be brought up to date with all immunizations before initiating therapy. Live vaccines should not be given concurrently; there is no data available concerning secondary transmission of live vaccines in patients receiving therapy. Rare reactivation of hepatitis B virus (HBV) has occurred in chronic virus carriers; use with caution; evaluate prior to initiation and during treatment.

[U.S. Boxed Warning]: Hepatosplenic T-cell lymphoma has been reported (rarely) in adolescent and young adults with Crohn's disease treated with infliximab and azathioprine or 6-mercaptopurine. The impact of infliximab on the development and course of malignancies is not fully defined, but may be dose dependent. As compared to the general population, an increased risk of lymphoma has been noted in clinical trials; however, rheumatoid arthritis alone has been previously associated with an increased rate of lymphoma. Use caution in patients with a history of COPD, higher rates of malignancy were reported in COPD patients treated with infliximab. Psoriasis patients with a history of phototherapy had a higher incidence of nonmelanoma skin cancers.

Severe hepatic reactions have been reported during treatment; discontinue with jaundice or marked increase in liver enzymes (≥5 times ULN). Use caution with heart failure; if a decision is made to use with heart failure, monitor closely and discontinue if exacerbated or new symptoms occur. Use caution with history of hematologic abnormalities; hematologic toxicities (eg, leukopenia, neutropenia, thrombocytopenia, pancytopenia) have been reported; discontinue if significant abnormalities occur. Autoimmune antibodies and a lupus-like syndrome have been reported. If antibodies to double-stranded DNA are confirmed in a patient with lupus-like symptoms, infliximab should be discontinued. Rare cases of optic neuritis and demyelinating disease have been reported; use with caution in patients with pre-existing or recent onset CNS demyelinating disorders, or seizures; discontinue if significant CNS adverse reactions develop.

Acute infusion reactions may occur. Hypersensitivity reaction may occur within 2 hours of infusion. Medication and equipment for management should be available for immediate use. Interruptions and/or reinstitution at a slower rate may be required (consult protocols). Pretreatment may be considered, and may be warranted in all patients with prior infusion reactions. Serum sickness-like reactions have occurred; may be associated with a decreased response to treatment. Safety and efficacy for use in juvenile rheumatoid arthritis, pediatric plaque psoriasis, or pediatric ulcerative colitis have not been established.

Adverse Reactions Although profile is similar, frequency of adverse effects may vary with disease state. Except where noted, percentages reported in adults with rheumatoid arthritis:

>10%:
   Central nervous system: Headache (18%)
   Gastrointestinal: Nausea (21%), diarrhea (12%), abdominal pain (12%, Crohn's 26%)
   Hepatic: ALT increased (risk increased with concomitant methotrexate)
   Local: Infusion reactions (20%; severe: <1%)
   Respiratory: Upper respiratory tract infection (32%), sinusitis (14%), cough (12%), pharyngitis (12%)
   Miscellaneous: Development of antinuclear antibodies (~50%), infection (36%), development of antibodies to double-stranded DNA (17%); Crohn's patients with fistulizing disease: Development of new abscess (15%)

5% to 10%:
   Cardiovascular: Hypertension (7%)
   Central nervous system: Fatigue (9%), pain (8%), fever (7%)
   Dermatologic: Rash (1% to 10%), pruritus (7%)
   Gastrointestinal: Dyspepsia (10%)
   Genitourinary: Urinary tract infection (8%)
   Neuromuscular & skeletal: Arthralgia (1% to 8%), back pain (8%)
   Respiratory: Bronchitis (10%), rhinitis (8%), dyspnea (6%)
   Miscellaneous: Moniliasis (5%)

<5%: Abscess, adult respiratory distress syndrome, allergic reaction, anemia, arrhythmia, basal cell carcinoma, biliary pain, bradycardia, brain infarction, breast cancer, cardiac arrest, cellulitis, cholecystitis, cholelithiasis, circulatory failure, confusion, constipation, dehydration, delayed hypersensitivity (plaque psoriasis), diaphoresis increased, dizziness, edema, gastrointestinal hemorrhage, heart failure, hemolytic anemia, hepatitis, hypersensitivity reactions, hypotension, ileus, intervertebral disk
(Continued)

Infliximab *(Continued)*

herniation, intestinal obstruction, intestinal perforation, intestinal stenosis, leukopenia, lupus-like syndrome, lymphadenopathy, lymphoma, malignancies, meningitis, menstrual irregularity, MI, myalgia, neuritis, pancreatitis, pancytopenia, peripheral neuropathy, peritonitis, pleural effusion, pleurisy, proctalgia, pulmonary edema, pulmonary embolism, renal calculus, renal failure, respiratory insufficiency, seizure, sepsis, serum sickness, suicide attempt, syncope, tachycardia, tendon disorder, thrombocytopenia, thrombophlebitis (deep), ulceration

The following adverse events were reported in children with Crohn's disease and were found more frequently in children than adults:

>10%:
Hepatic: Liver enzymes increased (18%; ≥5 times ULN: 1%)
Hematologic: Anemia (11%)
Miscellaneous: Infections (56%; more common with every 8-week versus every 12-week infusions)

1% to 10%:
Central nervous system: Flushing (9%)
Gastrointestinal: Blood in stool (10%)
Hematologic: Leukopenia (9%), neutropenia (7%)
Neuromuscular & skeletal: Bone fracture (7%)
Respiratory: Respiratory tract allergic reaction (6%)
Miscellaneous: Viral infection (8%), bacterial infection (6%), antibodies to infliximab (3%)

Postmarketing and/or case reports (adults or children): Anaphylactic reactions, angina, angioedema, autoimmune hepatitis, bronchospasm, cholestasis, demyelinating disorders (eg, multiple sclerosis, optic neuritis); drug-induced lupus-like syndrome, erythema multiforme, Guillain-Barré syndrome, heart failure (worsening), hepatitis B reactivation, hepatosplenic T-cell lymphoma (HSTCL), Hodgkin's disease, idiopathic thrombocytopenia purpura, interstitial fibrosis, interstitial pneumonitis, jaundice, laryngeal/pharyngeal edema, latent tuberculosis reactivation, liver failure, liver function tests increased, metallic taste, neuropathy, neutropenia, opportunistic infection, pericardial effusion, pneumonia, Stevens-Johnson syndrome, thrombotic thrombocytopenia purpura, toxic epidermal necrolysis, transverse myelitis, tuberculosis, urticaria, vasculitis (systemic and cutaneous)

Overdosage/Toxicology Doses of up to 20 mg/kg have been given without toxic effects. In case of overdose, treatment is symptom-directed and supportive.

Drug Interactions

Increased Effect/Toxicity: Specific drug interaction studies have not been conducted. Anti-TNF agents may be associated with increased risk of serious infection when used in combination with anakinra. Abciximab may increase potential for hypersensitivity reaction to infliximab, and may increase risk of thrombocytopenia and/or reduced therapeutic efficacy of infliximab. Infliximab may enhance the adverse/toxic effects of abatacept and live vaccines.

Decreased Effect: Infliximab may decrease the effect of vaccines (dead organisms).

Ethanol/Nutrition/Herb Interactions Herb/Nutraceutical: Echinacea may diminish the therapeutic effect of infliximab.

Storage/Stability Store vials at 2°C to 8°C (36°F to 46°F); do not freeze.

Reconstitution Reconstitute vials with 10 mL sterile water for injection. Swirl vial gently to dissolve powder; do not shake. Allow solution to stand for 5 minutes. Total dose of reconstituted product should be further diluted to 250 mL of 0.9% sodium chloride injection to a final concentration of 0.4-4 mg/mL. Infusion of dose should begin within 3 hours of preparation.

Compatibility Do not infuse with other agents.

Mechanism of Action Infliximab is a chimeric monoclonal antibody that binds to human tumor necrosis factor alpha (TNFα), thereby interfering with endogenous TNFα activity. Biological activities of TNFα include the induction of proinflammatory cytokines (interleukins), enhancement of leukocyte migration, activation of neutrophils and eosinophils, and the induction of acute phase reactants and tissue degrading enzymes. Animal models have shown TNFα expression causes polyarthritis, and infliximab can prevent disease as well as allow diseased joints to heal.

Pharmacodynamics/Kinetics

Onset of action: Crohn's disease: ~2 weeks

Distribution: V_d: 3-6 L

Half-life elimination: 7-12 days

Dosage I.V.: **Note:** Premedication with antihistamines (anti-H_1 and/or anti-H_2), acetaminophen and/or corticosteroids may be considered to prevent and/or manage infusion-related reactions:

Children ≥6 years: Crohn's disease: 5 mg/kg at 0, 2, and 6 weeks, followed by a maintenance dose of 5 mg/kg every 8 weeks

Adults:

Crohn's disease: Induction regimen: 5 mg/kg at 0, 2, and 6 weeks, followed by 5 mg/kg every 8 weeks thereafter; dose may be increased to 10 mg/kg in patients who respond but then lose their response. If no response by week 14, consider discontinuing therapy.

Psoriatic arthritis (with or without methotrexate): 5 mg/kg at 0, 2, and 6 weeks, then every 8 weeks

Rheumatoid arthritis (in combination with methotrexate therapy): 3 mg/kg at 0, 2, and 6 weeks, then every 8 weeks thereafter; doses have ranged from 3-10 mg/kg intravenous infusion repeated at 4- to 8-week intervals

Ankylosing spondylitis: 5 mg/kg at 0, 2, and 6 weeks, followed by 5 mg/kg every 6 weeks thereafter

Plaque psoriasis: 5 mg/kg at 0, 2, and 6 weeks, then every 8 weeks thereafter

Ulcerative colitis: 5 mg/kg at 0, 2, and 6 weeks, followed by 5 mg/kg every 8 weeks thereafter

Acute GVHD (unlabeled use): 10 mg/kg weekly for up to 8 weeks (median 4 weeks of treatment)

Dosage adjustment with CHF: Weigh risk versus benefits for individual patient:

NYHA Class III or IV: ≤5 mg/kg

Dosage adjustment in renal impairment: No specific adjustment is recommended

Dosage adjustment in hepatic impairment: No specific adjustment is recommended

Administration Infuse over at least 2 hours; do not infuse with other agents; use in-line low protein binding filter (≤1.2 micron). Temporarily discontinue or decrease infusion rate with infusion-related reactions. Antihistamines (anti-H_1 and/or anti-H_2), acetaminophen and/or corticosteroids may be used to manage reactions. Infusion may be reinitiated at a lower rate upon resolution of mild-to-moderate symptoms.

(Continued)

Infliximab *(Continued)*

Guidelines for the treatment and prophylaxis of infusion reactions: (Note: Limited to dosages used in Crohn's; prospective information on other indications/dosing such as in GVHD are not available).

Treatment of infusion reactions: Medications for the treatment of hypersensitivity reactions should be available for immediate use. A protocol for the treatment of acute infusion reactions, as well a prophylactic therapy for repeat infusions, has been published (Cheifetz, 2003). Decreasing the rate of infusion to 10 mL/hour (mild-to-moderate reactions) or a 20-minute interruption of the infusion (moderate-to-severe reactions) is recommended. Monitor vital signs every 10 minutes until normal. Administration of appropriate symptomatic treatment (acetaminophen and diphenhydramine, as well as hydrocortisone and epinephrine for severe reactions) should be instituted (consult institutional policies, if available). Following initial treatment, the infusion may be reinstituted at 10 mL/hour; then increased at 15-minute intervals, as tolerated (first to 20 mL/hour, then 40 mL/hour, then 80 mL/hour to completion).

Prophylaxis of infusion reactions: Premedication with acetaminophen and diphenhydramine 90 minutes prior to infusion may be considered in all patients with prior infusion reactions, and in patients with severe reactions corticosteroid administration is recommended (Cheifetz, 2003). Steroid dosing may be oral (prednisone 50 mg orally for 3 doses over a 24-hour period prior to infusion) or intravenous (a single dose of hydrocortisone 100 mg or methylprednisolone 20-240 mg administered 20 minutes prior to the infusion) (Cheifetz, 2003). On initiation of the infusion, a test dose (infusion at 10 mL/hour for 15 minutes) may be considered. If tolerated, for patients with mild reactions, the infusion may be completed over 3 hours. For patients with prior moderate-to-severe reactions, the infusion may be increased at 15-minute intervals, as tolerated, to completion (first to 20 mL/ hour, then 40 mL/hour, then 100 mL/hour, and finally 125 mL/hour to completion). A maximum rate of 100 mL/hour is recommended in patients who experienced prior severe reactions. In patients with cutaneous flushing, aspirin may be considered (Becker, 2004).

Monitoring Parameters During infusion, if reaction is noted, monitor vital signs every 10 minutes until normal. Follow-up monitoring includes monitoring for improvement of symptoms; signs of infection; LFTs (discontinue if >5 times ULN); place and read PPD before initiation. Psoriasis patients with history of phototherapy should be monitored for nonmelanoma skin cancer.

Dosage Forms Excipient information presented when available (limited, particularly for generics); consult specific product labeling.

Injection, powder for reconstitution [preservative free]:

Remicade®: 100 mg [contains sucrose 500 mg and polysorbate 80]

References

Antoni CE, Kavanaugh A, Kirkham B, et al, "Sustained Benefits of Infliximab Therapy for Dermatologic and Articular Manifestations of Psoriatic Arthritis: Results from the Infliximab Multinational Psoriatic Arthritis Controlled Trial (IMPACT)," *Arthritis Rheum*, 2005, 52(4):1227-36.

Becker M, Rose CD, and McIlvain-Simpson G, "Niacin-Like Reaction to Infliximab Infusion in Systemic Juvenile Rheumatoid Arthritis," *J Rheumatol*, 2004, 31(12):2529-30.

Bongartz T, Sutton AJ, Sweeting MJ, et al, "Anti-TNF Antibody Therapy In Rheumatoid Arthritis and the Risk of Serious Infections and Malignancies: Systematic Review and Meta-Analysis of Rare Harmful Effects in Randomized Controlled Trials," *JAMA*, 2006, 295(19):2275-85.

Carpenter PA and Sanders JE, "Steroid-Refractory Graft-vs-Host Disease: Past, Present and Future," *Pediatr Transplant*, 2003, 7(Suppl 3):19-31.

Centers for Disease Control, "Testing and Treatment of Latent Tuberculosis Infection," *MMWR Recomm Rep*, 2000, 49(RR-6).

Cheifetz A, Smedley M, Martin S, et al, "The Incidence and Management of Infusion Reactions to Infliximab: A Large Center Experience," *Am J Gastroenterol*, 2003, 98(6):1315-24.

Chung ES, Packer M, Lo KH, et al, "Randomized, Double-Blind, Placebo-Controlled, Pilot Trial of Infliximab, a Chimeric Monoclonal Antibody to Tumor Necrosis Factor-Alpha, in Patients with Moderate-to-Severe Heart Failure: Results of the Anti-TNF Therapy Against Congestive Heart Failure (ATTACH) Trial," *Circulation*, 2003, 107(25):3133-40.

Couriel D, Saliba R, Hicks K, et al, "Tumor Necrosis Factor-Alpha Blockade for the Treatment of Acute GVHD," *Blood*, 2004, 104(3):649-54.

"Diagnostic Standards and Classification of Tuberculosis in Adults and Children. Official Statement of the American Thoracic Society and the Centers for Disease Control and Prevention," *Am J Respir Crit Care Med*, 2000, 161:1376-95.

Klotz U, Teml A, and Schwab M, "Clinical Pharmacokinetics and Use of Infliximab," *Clin Pharmacokinet*, 2007, 45(8):645-60.

Thayu M, Markowitz JE, Mamula P, et al, "Hepatosplenic T-Cell Lymphoma in an Adolescent Patient After Immunomodulator and Biologic Therapy for Crohn Disease," *J Pediatr Gastroenterol Nutr*, 2005, 40(2):220-2.

♦ **Infliximab, Recombinant** *see* Infliximab *on page 605*

♦ **Infufer® (Can)** *see* Iron Dextran Complex *on page 633*

♦ **Infumorph®** *see* Morphine Sulfate *on page 779*

♦ **α-2-interferon** *see* Interferon Alfa-2b *on page 617*

Interferon Alfa-2a (in ter FEER on AL fa too aye)

Medication Safety Issues

Sound-alike/look-alike issues:

Interferon alfa-2a may be confused with interferon alfa-2b, interferon alfa-n3, pegylated interferon alfa-2b

Roferon-A® may be confused with Rocephin®

International issues:

Interferon alfa-2a may be confused with interferon alpha multi-subtype which is available in international markets

Related Information

Safe Handling of Hazardous Drugs *on page 1382*

U.S. Brand Names Roferon®-A

Index Terms IFLrA; Interferon Alpha-2a; NSC-367982; rIFN-A

Generic Available No

Canadian Brand Names Roferon®-A

Pharmacologic Category Interferon

Use

Patients >18 years of age: Treatment of hairy cell leukemia, chronic hepatitis C

Children and Adults: Treatment of Philadelphia chromosome-positive (Ph+) chronic myelogenous leukemia (CML) in chronic phase, within 1 year of diagnosis (limited experience in children)

Unlabeled/Investigational Use Adjuvant therapy for malignant melanoma; treatment of AIDS-related Kaposi's sarcoma, carcinoid tumors; bladder, cervical, and ovarian cancers; hemangioma; chronic hepatitis D; low-grade non-Hodgkin's lymphoma; multiple myeloma; renal cell carcinoma; basal and squamous cell skin cancer; cutaneous T-cell lymphoma

Restrictions An FDA-approved medication guide must be distributed when dispensing an outpatient prescription (new or refill) where this medication is to be used without direct supervision of a healthcare provider. Medication guides are available at http://www.fda.gov/cder/Offices/ODS/medication_guides.htm.

Pregnancy Risk Factor C

Lactation Enters breast milk/not recommended (AAP rates "compatible") (Continued)

Interferon Alfa-2a *(Continued)*

Labeled Contraindications Hypersensitivity to interferon alfa or any component of the formulation; autoimmune hepatitis; hepatic decompensation (Child-Pugh class B or C)

Warnings/Precautions Hazardous agent - use appropriate precautions for handling and disposal.

[U.S. Boxed Warning]: May cause or aggravate fatal or life-threatening autoimmune disorders, neuropsychiatric symptoms (including depression and/or suicidal thoughts/behaviors), ischemic and/or infectious disorders; discontinue treatment for persistent severe or worsening symptoms.

Neuropsychiatric disorders: May cause severe psychiatric adverse events (eg, depression, psychosis, mania, suicidal behavior/ideation) in patients with and without previous psychiatric symptoms; use with extreme caution in patients with a history of depression. Careful neuropsychiatric monitoring is required during therapy. Patients developing severe depression may require discontinuation of treatment. Although dose reduction or discontinuation may resolve symptoms, depression may persist; suicides have been reported after therapy has been discontinued. Use with caution in patients with seizure disorders, brain metastases, or compromised CNS function. Higher doses in the elderly or in malignancies other than hairy cell leukemia may result in severe obtundation.

Hepatic disease: Transient liver abnormalities may occur when treating chronic hepatitis C with interferon alfa-2a; increased ascites, hepatic failure, and death may occur with poorly-compensated liver disease.

Bone marrow suppression: Causes bone marrow suppression, including potentially severe cytopenias, and very rarely, aplastic anemia. Use caution in patients with pre-existing myelosuppression and/or with concomitant medications which cause myelosuppression.

Cardiovascular disease: Use caution and monitor closely in patients with history of cardiovascular disease; acute toxicities may exacerbate pre-existing cardiac conditions. MI has been observed (rarely) in patients receiving interferon alfa-2a; cardiomyopathy has been reported (rarely) in patients receiving interferon alfa.

Gastrointestinal disorders: Pancreatitis (occasionally fatal) has been observed; hypertriglyceridemia increases the risk for pancreatitis; consider discontinuing treatment in patients with pancreatitis. Hypertriglyceridemia has been reported; consider discontinuing with persistent elevations, particularly if combined with symptoms of pancreatitis. Gastrointestinal hemorrhage, ulcerative and hemorrhagic/ischemic colitis have been observed with interferon alfa treatment; may be severe and/or life-threatening; discontinue if symptoms (eg, abdominal pain, bloody diarrhea, and/or fever) develop.

Pulmonary disease: Dyspnea, pulmonary infiltrates, pneumonia, bronchiolitis obliterans, interstitial pneumonia, and sarcoidosis, resulting in potential fatal respiratory failure may occur with interferon alfa treatment. Discontinue with unexplained pulmonary infiltrates or evidence of impaired pulmonary function. Use caution in patients with a history of pulmonary disease.

Endocrine disorders: Thyroid disorders (hyper- or hypothyroidism) have been reported; use caution in patients with pre-existing thyroid disease. Hyperglycemia has been reported; use caution in patients with diabetes mellitus, may require adjustments in medications.

Autoimmune disorders: Avoid use in patients with history of autoimmune disorders. Development or exacerbation of autoimmune disorders (thrombocytopenic purpura, vasculitis, Raynaud's disease, rheumatoid arthritis, interstitial nephritis, thyroiditis, lupus erythematosus, and rhabdomyolysis) has been associated with interferon alfa. Monitor closely and consider discontinuing if autoimmune disease develops.

Ophthalmic disorders: Decreased/loss of vision, retinopathy (including macular edema), retinal artery or vein thrombosis, retinal hemorrhages, cotton wool spots, optic neuritis and papilledema have occurred in patients receiving interferon alfa. Use caution in patients with pre-existing ophthalmic disorders; monitor closely and discontinue with new or worsening ophthalmic symptoms.

Infections: Commonly associated with flu-like symptoms, including fever; rule out other causes/infection with persistent or high fever. Serious and severe infections (bacterial, viral and fungal) have been reported in with treatment; evaluate and treat promptly; consider discontinuing interferon.

Renal disorders: Renal toxicities, some requiring dialysis, have been reported with interferon alfa (alone or in combination with interleukin-2). Use caution in patients with renal impairment (Cl_{cr} <50 mL/minute); monitor closely for signs/symptoms of toxicity.

Acute hypersensitivity reactions have been reported. **Due to differences in dosage, patients should not change brands of interferons without the concurrence of their healthcare provider.** Injection solution contains benzyl alcohol; do not use in neonates or infants. Safety and efficacy have not been established in children <18 years for uses other than Ph+ CML or in organ transplant recipients.

Adverse Reactions Note: A flu-like syndrome (fever, chills, tachycardia, malaise, myalgia, arthralgia, headache) occurs within 1-2 hours of administration; may last up to 24 hours and may be dose-limiting.

>10%:

Cardiovascular: Chest pain (<4% to 11%), edema (1% to 11%), hypertension (11%)

Central nervous system: Fever (28% to 92%), fatigue (58% to 88%), headache (44% to 64%), chills (23% to 64%), depression (16% to 28%), pain (24%), dizziness (11% to 21%), mental status decreased (10% to 16%), irritability (15%), insomnia (14%), sleep disturbances (10% to 11%)

Dermatologic: Rash (8% to 44%), alopecia (17% to 19%), pruritus (7% to 13%), dry skin (7% to 17%)

Endocrine & metabolic: Hypocalcemia (28%), hypophosphatemia (22%)

Gastrointestinal: Anorexia (14% to 48%), nausea (33% to 39%), vomiting (33% to 39%), diarrhea (20% to 37%), weight loss (33%), throat irritation (21%), abdominal pain (12%)

Hematologic (often due to underlying disease): Myelosuppression (onset: 7-10 days; nadir 14 days [may be delayed 20-40 days in hairy cell leukemia], recovery: 21 days), neutropenia (≤68%; dose dependant); thrombocytopenia (5% to 62%), leukopenia (2% to 45%), anemia (≤31%)

Hepatic: Alkaline phosphatase increased (≤50%), transaminases increased (≤50%)

Local: Injection site reaction (29%)

Neuromuscular & skeletal: Weakness (6% to 88%) myalgia (51% to 71%), arthralgia (47% to 51%), bone pain (25% to 47%), joint pain (25%), back pain (16%), numbness (12%), paresthesia (7% to 12%)

Respiratory: Cough (1% to 19%), rhinorrhea/rhinitis (3% to 12%), dyspnea (1% to 12%), pneumonia (11%), sinusitis (11%)

(Continued)

Interferon Alfa-2a *(Continued)*

Miscellaneous: Flu-like syndrome (16% to 33%), diaphoresis (1% to 22%)

1% to 10%:

Cardiovascular: Dysrhythmia (7%), hypotension (<5%), syncope (<5%), murmur (<5%), thrombophlebitis (<5%), palpitations (<3%), vasculitis (<3%), arrhythmia (1%)

Central nervous system: Confusion (<4% to 7%), anxiety (5% to 6%), lethargy (1% to 6%), nervousness (<5%), vertigo (<5%), concentration impaired (4%), memory loss (<4%), seizure (<4%), behavior disturbances (3%), malaise (1%)

Dermatologic: Bruising (<4%), skin lesions (1% to 3%)

Endocrine & metabolic: Hyperphosphatemia (9%), diabetes (<5%), hyper-/hypothyroidism (<5%), hypertriglyceridemia (<4%), libido changes (<4%), sexual dysfunction (1% to 3%), menstrual irregularity (2%)

Gastrointestinal: Colitis (<5%), gastrointestinal hemorrhage (<5%), pancreatitis (<5%), flatulence (3%), taste change (3% to <4%), stomatitis (1% to <5%), constipation (<3%), digestion impaired (2%), gingival bleeding (≤2%)

Genitourinary: Impotence (<4%), urinary tract infection (1% to 3%)

Hematologic: Coagulopathy (<4%), hemolytic anemia (<3%), hematoma (1%)

Hepatic: Liver pain (3%)

Neuromuscular & skeletal: Involuntary movements (7%), arthritis (≤5%), polyarthritis (5%), gait disturbance (<5%), leg cramps (3%), muscle cramps (1% to 3%)

Ocular: Visual disturbance (6%), conjunctivitis (4%), eye pain (1% to 3%)

Otic: Hearing alteration (<4%)

Renal: Proteinuria (≤10%)

Respiratory: Oropharynx dryness/inflammation (6%), pneumonitis (<5%), epistaxis (≤4%), bronchospasm (<4%), chest congestion (<3%)

Miscellaneous: Herpes virus reactivation (1% to 3%), lupus erythematosus syndrome (<3%)

<1%, postmarketing, and/or case reports (limited to important or life-threatening): Anaphylactic reaction, anaphylaxis, angioedema, aplastic anemia, ascites, autoimmune reaction with worsening of liver disease, bronchiolitis obliterans, BUN/creatinine increased, cardiomyopathy, coma, CHF, cutaneous eruptions, cyanosis, dysphasia, EEG abnormalities, encephalopathy, hallucinations, hearing loss, hemolytic anemia (Coombs' positive), hemorrhagic colitis, hepatic failure, hepatitis, hyperglycemia, hyperlipidemia, hypersensitivity, hyponatremia (SIADH), inflammation (injection site), macular edema, mania, idiopathic thrombocytopenia purpura, interstitial nephritis, interstitial pneumonitis, ischemic colitis, ischemic retinopathy, LDH increased, MI, myositis, nephrotic syndrome, obtundation, optic neuritis, petechiae, pneumonia, pneumonitis, presenile dementia, proteinuria, psoriasis, psychomotor retardation, psychotic episodes, pulmonary edema, pulmonary infiltrates, Raynaud's phenomenon, renal failure (acute), retinopathy, rhabdomyolysis, sarcoidosis, seizure, serum creatinine increased, somnolence, stroke, suicidal behavior/ideation, syncope, tachypnea, transient ischemic attacks, ulcerative colitis, uric acid increased, urticaria (injection site), vasculitis, visual acuity decreased

Overdosage/Toxicology Symptoms of overdose include CNS depression, obtundation, flu-like symptoms, and myelosuppression. Treatment is symptom-directed and supportive.

Drug Interactions
  Cytochrome P450 Effect: Inhibits CYP1A2 (weak)
  Increased Effect/Toxicity: Concurrent therapy with ribavirin may increase the risk of hemolytic anemia. Interferon alfa may increase the levels/effects of theophylline derivatives. Interferons may decrease the metabolism of zidovudine; the neutropenic effects of zidovudine and interferon may be synergistic.

Storage/Stability Refrigerate (2°C to 8°C/36°F to 46°F); do not freeze. Protect from light. Do not shake.

Compatibility Stable in LR, NS; **incompatible** with D₅W.

Mechanism of Action Following activation, multiple effects can be detected including induction of gene transcription. Inhibits cellular growth, alters the state of cellular differentiation, interferes with oncogene expression, alters cell surface antigen expression, increases phagocytic activity of macrophages, and augments cytotoxicity of lymphocytes for target cells

Pharmacodynamics/Kinetics
  Distribution: V$_d$: 0.223-0.748 L/kg
  Metabolism: Primarily renal; filtered through glomeruli and undergoes rapid proteolytic degradation during tubular reabsorption
  Bioavailability: I.M.: 83%; SubQ: 90%
  Half-life elimination: I.V.: 3.7-8.5 hours (mean ~5 hours)
  Time to peak, serum: I.M., SubQ: ~4-7 hours

Dosage Refer to individual protocols
  Children (limited data):
    Ph+ chronic myelogenous leukemia (CML): I.M.: 2.5-5 million units/m²/day;
      Note: In juveniles, higher dosages (30 million units/m²/day) have been associated with severe adverse events, including death
  Adults:
    Hairy cell leukemia: SubQ: 3 million units/day for 16-24 weeks, then 3 million units 3 times/week for up to 6-24 months
    Ph+ chronic myelogenous leukemia (CML): SubQ: 9 million units/day, continue treatment until disease progression **or** 3 million units/day for 3 days, followed by 6 million units/day for 3 days, followed by 9 million units daily until disease progression
    AIDS-related Kaposi's sarcoma (unlabeled use): SubQ, I.M.: 36 million units/day for 10-12 weeks, then 36 million units 3 times/week; to minimize adverse reactions, can use escalating dose (3-, 9-, then 18 million units each day for 3 days, then 36 million units daily thereafter).
    Chronic hepatitis C: SubQ: 3 million units 3 times/week for 12 months **or** 6 million units 3 times/week for 12 weeks followed by 3 million units 3 times/week for 36 weeks

Dosage adjustment in renal impairment: Not removed by hemodialysis

Combination Regimens
  Leukemia, acute lymphocytic: Hyper-CVAD (Leukemia, Acute Lymphocytic) *on page 1231*
  Melanoma: Dacarbazine-Carboplatin-Aldesleukin-Interferon *on page 1187*
  Renal cell cancer:
    Bevacizumab-Interferon Alfa-2a *on page 1151*
    Interleukin 2-Interferon Alfa-2 *on page 1240*
    Interleukin 2-Interferon Alfa-2-Fluorouracil *on page 1241*

Administration
  SubQ: For SubQ administration, rotate SubQ injection site.
  I.M.: May also be administered I.M. (unlabeled route).
  (Continued)

Interferon Alfa-2a *(Continued)*

Monitoring Parameters CBC with differential and platelets, liver function, electrolytes, triglycerides. Baseline chest x-ray and ECG. Baseline ophthalmologic exam should be performed in all patients, with periodic reassessment in patients with impairment. Patients with thyroid dysfunction should be monitored by TSH levels at baseline and every 3 months during therapy.

Chronic hepatitis C: Monitor ALT (at baseline, after 2 weeks, and monthly thereafter) and HCV-RNA (particularly in first 3 months of therapy)

CML/hairy cell leukemia: Hematologic monitoring should be performed monthly

Patient Information Use as directed; do not change dosage or schedule of administration without consulting prescriber. Maintain adequate hydration (2-3 L/day of fluids unless instructed to restrict fluid intake). You may experience flu-like syndrome (acetaminophen may help); this syndrome subsides after several weeks of continuous dosing, but usually recurs during each cycle of intermittent therapy. You may also experience nausea, vomiting, dry mouth, or metallic taste (frequent small meals, frequent mouth care, sucking lozenges, or chewing gum may help); drowsiness, dizziness, agitation, abnormal thinking (use caution when driving or engaging in tasks requiring alertness until response to drug is known). Inform prescriber **immediately** if you feel depressed or have any thoughts of suicide. Report unusual bruising or bleeding; persistent abdominal disturbances; unusual fatigue; muscle pain or tremors; chest pain or palpitation; swelling of extremities or unusual weight gain; difficulty breathing; pain, swelling, or redness at injection site; or other unusual symptoms.

Special Geriatric Considerations No specific data is available for the elderly; however, pay close attention to Warnings/Precautions since the elderly often have reduced Cl_{cr} (<50 mL/minute), diabetes, and hyper-/hypo-thyroidism.

Emetic Potential Moderate (30% to 60%); usually mild to moderate, aggressive therapy with serotonin antagonists is usually not necessary

Vesicant No

Dosage Forms Excipient information presented when available (limited, particularly for generics); consult specific product labeling.

Injection, solution:

Roferon®-A: 3 million units/0.5 mL (0.5 mL) [contains benzyl alcohol and polysorbate 80]; 6 million units/0.5 mL (0.5 mL) [contains benzyl alcohol and polysorbate 80]; 9 million units/0.5 mL (0.5 mL) [contains benzyl alcohol and polysorbate 80]

References

ACOG Practice Bulletin No. 86: "Viral Hepatitis in Pregnancy," *Obstet Gynecol*, 2007, 110(4):941-56.

"American Academy of Pediatrics Committee on Drugs. The Transfer of Drugs and Other Chemicals Into Human Milk," *Pediatrics*, 2001, 108(3):776-89.

Centers for Disease Control and Prevention, "Sexually Transmitted Diseases Treatment Guidelines, 2006," *MMWR*, 2006, 55(RR-11):1-94.

Gresser I, "Biologic Effects of Interferons," *J Invest Dermatol*, 1990, 95(6 Suppl):66-71.

Haria M and Benfield P, "Interferon-Alpha-2a. A Review of Its Pharmacological Properties and Therapeutic Use in the Management of Viral Hepatitis," *Drugs*, 1995, 50(5):873-96.

Lebon P, Girard S, Thepot F, et al, "The Presence of Alpha-Interferon in Human Amniotic Fluid," *J Gen Virol*, 1982, 59(Pt 2):393-6.

"Perinatal HIV Guidelines Working Group. Public Health Service Task Force Recommendations for Use of Antiretroviral Drugs in Pregnant HIV-Infected Women for Maternal Health and Interventions to Reduce Perinatal HIV Transmission in the United States," November 2, 2007, 1-96. Available at http://aidsinfo.nih.gov/ContentFiles/PerinatalGL.pdf.

Waysbort A, Giroux M, Mansat V, et al, "Experimental Study of Transplacental Passage of Alpha Interferon by Two Assay Techniques," *Antimicrob Agents Chemother*, 1993, 37(6):1232-7.

White CW, Sondheimer HM, Crouch EC, et al, "Treatment of Pulmonary Hemangiomatosis With Recombinant Interferon Alfa-2a," *N Engl J Med*, 1989, 320(18):1197-200.

Williams CD and Linch DC, "Interferon Alfa-2a," *Br J Hosp Med*, 1997, 57(9):436-9.

Wills RJ, "Clinical Pharmacokinetics of Interferons," *Clin Pharmacokinet*, 1990, 19(5):390-9.

Interferon Alfa-2b (in ter FEER on AL fa too bee)

Medication Safety Issues

Sound-alike/look-alike issues:

Interferon alfa-2b may be confused with interferon alfa-2a, interferon alfa-n3, pegylated interferon alfa-2b

Intron® A may be confused with PEG-Intron®

International issues:

Interferon alfa-2b may be confused with interferon alpha multi-subtype which is available in international markets

Related Information

Safe Handling of Hazardous Drugs *on page 1382*

U.S. Brand Names Intron® A

Index Terms α-2-interferon; INF-alpha 2; Interferon Alpha-2b; NSC-377523; rLFN-α2

Generic Available No

Canadian Brand Names Intron® A

Pharmacologic Category Interferon

Use

Patients ≥1 year of age: Chronic hepatitis B

Patients ≥3 years of age: Chronic hepatitis C (in combination with ribavirin)

Patients ≥18 years of age: Condyloma acuminata, chronic hepatitis B, chronic hepatitis C, hairy cell leukemia, malignant melanoma, AIDS-related Kaposi's sarcoma, follicular non-Hodgkin's lymphoma

Unlabeled/Investigational Use AIDS-related thrombocytopenia, cutaneous ulcerations of Behçet's disease, carcinoid syndrome, cervical cancer, cutaneous T-Cell lymphoma, lymphomatoid granulomatosis, genital herpes, hepatitis D, chronic myelogenous leukemia (CML), non-Hodgkin's lymphomas (other than follicular lymphoma, see approved use), polycythemia vera, medullary thyroid carcinoma, multiple myeloma, renal cell carcinoma, basal and squamous cell skin cancers, essential thrombocytopenia, thrombocytopenic purpura, West Nile virus

Restrictions An FDA-approved medication guide is available at http://www.fda.gov/cder/Offices/ODS/labeling.htm; distribute to each patient to whom this medication is dispensed.

Pregnancy Risk Factor C / X in combination with ribavirin

Lactation Enters breast milk/not recommended (AAP rates "compatible")

Labeled Contraindications Hypersensitivity to interferon alfa or any component of the formulation; decompensated liver disease; autoimmune hepatitis

Warnings/Precautions Hazardous agent - use appropriate precautions for handling and disposal.

[U.S. Boxed Warning]: May cause or aggravate fatal or life-threatening autoimmune disorders, neuropsychiatric symptoms (including depression and/or suicidal thoughts/behaviors), ischemic, and/or infectious disorders; discontinue treatment for persistent severe or worsening symptoms.

Neuropsychiatric disorders: May cause severe psychiatric adverse events (eg, depression, psychosis, mania, suicidal behavior/ideation) in patients with and without previous psychiatric symptoms, avoid use in patients with pre-existing psychiatric condition, severe psychiatric disorder or history of

(Continued)

Interferon Alfa-2b *(Continued)*

severe depression; careful neuropsychiatric monitoring is required during and for 6 months after therapy. Suicidal ideation or attempts may occur more frequently in pediatric patients when compared to adults. Discontinue in patients developing severe depression or psychiatric disorders. Higher doses in elderly patients, or diseases other than hairy cell leukemia, may result in increased CNS toxicity.

Hepatic disease: May cause hepatotoxicity; monitor closely if abnormal liver function tests develop. A transient increase in ALT ($\geq$2 times baseline) may occur in patients treated with interferon alfa-2b for chronic hepatitis B. Therapy generally may continue; monitor. Worsening and potentially fatal liver disease, including jaundice, hepatic encephalopathy, and hepatic failure have been reported in patients receiving interferon alfa for chronic hepatitis B and C with decompensated liver disease, autoimmune hepatitis, history of autoimmune disease, and immunosuppressed transplant recipients; avoid use in these patients. Chronic hepatitis B or C patients with a history of autoimmune disease or who are immunosuppressed transplant recipients should not receive interferon alfa 2-b. Discontinue treatment in any patient developing signs or symptoms of liver failure.

Bone marrow suppression: Causes bone marrow suppression, including potentially severe cytopenias, and very rarely, aplastic anemia. Hemolytic anemia (hemoglobin <10 g/dL) was observed when combined with ribavirin; anemia occurred within 1-2 weeks of initiation of therapy. Use caution in patients with pre-existing myelosuppression and in patients with concomitant medications which cause myelosuppression.

Autoimmune disorders: Avoid use in patients with history of autoimmune disorders; development of autoimmune disorders (thrombocytopenia, vasculitis, Raynaud's disease, rheumatoid arthritis, lupus erythematosus and rhabdomyolysis) has been associated with use. Monitor closely; consider discontinuing. Worsening of psoriasis and sarcoidosis (and the development of new sarcoidosis) have been reported; use caution.

Cardiovascular disease/coagulation disorders: Use caution and monitor closely in patients with cardiovascular disease (ischemic or thromboembolic), arrhythmias, hypertension, and in patients with a history of MI or prior therapy with cardiotoxic drugs. Patients with pre-existing cardiac disease and/or advanced cancer should have baseline and periodic ECGs. May cause hypotension (during administration or delayed), arrhythmia, tachycardia, cardiomyopathy (~2% in AIDS-related Kaposi's Sarcoma patients) and/or MI. Use caution in patients with coagulopathy.

Endocrine disorders: Thyroid disorders (possibly reversible) have been reported; use caution in patients with pre-existing thyroid disease. Discontinue use in patients who cannot maintain normal ranges with thyroid medication. Diabetes mellitus has been reported; discontinue if cannot effectively manage with medication. Use caution in patients with a history of diabetes mellitus, particularly if prone to DKA. Hypertriglyceridemia has been reported; discontinue if severe, and/or combined with symptoms of pancreatitis.

Pulmonary disease: Pulmonary infiltrates, pneumonitis and pneumonia have been reported with interferon alfa therapy; occurs more frequently in patients being treated for chronic hepatitis C. Patients with fever, cough, dyspnea or other respiratory symptoms should be evaluated with a chest x-ray; monitor closely and consider discontinuing treatment with evidence of impaired pulmonary function. Use with caution in patients with a history of pulmonary disease.

Ophthalmic disorders: Decreased/loss of vision, macular edema, optic neuritis, retinal hemorrhages, cotton wool spots, papilledema, and retinal artery or vein thrombosis have occurred (or been aggravated) in patients receiving alpha interferons. Use caution in patients with pre-existing eye disorders; monitor closely; discontinue with new or worsening ophthalmic disorders.

Commonly associated with fever and flu-like symptoms; rule out other causes/infection with persistent fever; use with caution in patients with debilitating conditions. Acute hypersensitivity reactions have been reported. Do not treat patients with visceral AIDS-related Kaposi's sarcoma associated with rapidly-progressing or life-threatening disease. Some formulations contain albumin, which may carry a remote risk of viral transmission. Due to differences in dosage, patients should not change brands of interferons without the concurrence of their healthcare provider. Safety and efficacy in children <1 year of age have not been established.

Adverse Reactions Note: In a majority of patients, a flu-like syndrome (fever, chills, tachycardia, malaise, myalgia, headache), occurs within 1-2 hours of administration; may last up to 24 hours and may be dose-limiting.

>10%:
  Cardiovascular: Chest pain (≤28%)
  Central nervous system: Fatigue (8% to 96%), fever (34% to 94%), headache (21% to 62%), chills (≤54%), depression (3% to 40%; grades 3/4: 2%), somnolence (≤33%), dizziness (≤24%), irritability (≤22%), pain (≤18%), amnesia (≤14%), concentration impaired (≤14%), malaise (≤14%), confusion (≤12%), insomnia (≤12%)
  Dermatologic: Alopecia (≤38%), rash (≤25%), pruritus (≤11%)
  Endocrine & metabolic: Amenorrhea (≤12%)
  Gastrointestinal: Anorexia (1% to 69%), nausea, (17% to 66%), diarrhea (2% to 45%), vomiting (2% to 32%), xerostomia (≤28%), taste alteration (≤24%), abdominal pain (1% to 23%), constipation (≤14%), gingivitis (≤14%), weight loss (<1% to 13%)
  Hematologic: Neutropenia (≤92%; grade 4: 1% to 4%), leukopenia (≤68%), anemia (≤32%), thrombocytopenia (≤15%)
  Hepatic: AST increased (≤63%; grades 3/4: 14%), ALT increased (≤15%), pain (upper right quadrant: up to 15%); alkaline phosphatase increased (≤13%)
  Local: Injection site reaction (≤20%)
  Neuromuscular & skeletal: Myalgia (28% to 75%), weakness (≤63%), rigors (≤42%), paresthesia (1% to 21%), skeletal pain (≤21%), arthralgia (≤19%), back pain (≤19%)
  Renal: BUN increased (≤12%)
  Respiratory: Dyspnea (≤34%), cough (≤31%), pharyngitis (≤31%), sinusitis (≤21%)
  Miscellaneous: Flu-like syndrome (≤79%), diaphoresis (1% to 21%), moniliasis (≤17%)
5% to 10%:
  Cardiovascular: Edema (≤10%), hypertension (≤9%)
  Central nervous system: Hypoesthesia (≤10%), anxiety (≤9%), vertigo (≤8%), agitation (≤7%)
  Dermatologic: Dry skin (≤10%), dermatitis (≤8%), purpura (≤5%)
  Endocrine & metabolic: Libido decreased (≤5%)
  Gastrointestinal: Loose stools (≤10%), dyspepsia (≤8%)
  Genitourinary: Urinary tract infection (≤5%)
(Continued)

Interferon Alfa-2b *(Continued)*

Renal: Polyuria (≤10%), serum creatinine increased (≤6%)

Respiratory: Bronchitis (≤10%), nasal congestion (≤10%), epistaxis (≤7%)

Miscellaneous: Infection (≤7%), herpes virus infections (≤5%)

<5%, postmarketing, and/or case reports (limited to important or life-threatening):

Cardiovascular: Angina, arrhythmia, arteritis, atrial fibrillation, bradycardia, cardiac failure, cardiomegaly, cardiomyopathy, coronary artery disorder, ejection fraction decreased, extrasystoles, flushing, heart valve disorder, hypotension, MI, palpitation, peripheral ischemia, polyarteritis, Raynaud's disease, syncope, tachycardia, thrombosis, vasculitis

Central nervous system: Nervousness (≤3%), aggression, alcohol intolerance, aphasia, ataxia, Bell's palsy, coma, extrapyramidal disorder, hallucination, hypothermia, mania, migraine, neurosis, paranoia, psychosis, stroke, suicidal attempt/ideation, seizure

Dermatologic: Angioedema, cellulitis, dermatitis lichenoides, eczema, epidermal necrolysis, erythema, erythema multiforme, erythematous rash, folliculitis, hirsutism, lipoma, maculopapular rash, photosensitivity, psoriasis, psoriasis exacerbation, sebaceous cyst, Stevens-Johnson syndrome, toxic epidermal necrolysis, urticaria

Endocrine & metabolic: Dehydration, diabetes mellitus, goiter, hot flashes, hypercalcemia, hyperglycemia, hyper-/hypothyroidism, hypertriglyceridemia, mastitis, menorrhagia, sexual dysfunction

Gastrointestinal: Colitis, dysphasia, esophagitis, gastritis, gastrointestinal hemorrhage, mucositis, pancreatitis, rectal bleeding/hemorrhage, stomatitis, ulcerative stomatitis

Genitourinary: Cystitis, dysuria, incontinence, impotence, leukorrhea, nocturia, pelvic pain, uterine bleeding

Hematologic: Aplastic anemia (rarely), granulocytopenia, hemolytic anemia, hypochromic anemia, lymphopenia, lymphadenitis, lymphadenopathy, lymphocytosis, pure red cell aplasia, thrombocytopenia purpura

Hepatic: Ascites, biliary pain, bilirubinemia, hepatic encephalopathy, hepatic failure, hepatitis, hepatotoxicity, jaundice, lactate dehydrogenase increased (up to 1%), liver function test abnormal

Local: Injection site necrosis

Neuromuscular & skeletal: Arthritis, carpal tunnel syndrome, hyporeflexia, leg cramps, muscle atrophy, myositis, neuralgia, neuropathy, rhabdomyolysis, rheumatoid arthritis, spondylitis, tendonitis, tremor

Ocular: Blurred vision, conjunctivitis, cotton wool spots, macular edema, nystagmus, optic neuritis, papilledema, photophobia, retinal artery thrombosis, retinal vein thrombosis

Otic: Hearing impairment, hearing loss

Renal: Albuminuria, hematuria, nephrotic syndrome, proteinuria, renal failure, renal insufficiency

Respiratory: Asthma, bronchoconstriction, bronchospasm, cyanosis, hemoptysis, hypoventilation, pleural effusion, pneumonitis, pneumothorax, pulmonary embolism, pulmonary fibrosis, respiratory insufficiency, upper respiratory tract infection, wheezing

Miscellaneous: Abscess, acute hypersensitivity reaction, allergic reactions, anaphylaxis, fungal infection, lupus erythematosus, sarcoidosis, sarcoidosis exacerbation, sepsis

Overdosage/Toxicology Symptoms of overdose include CNS depression, obtundation, flu-like symptoms, hepatic enzyme abnormalities, renal failure, and myelosuppression. Treatment is symptom-directed and supportive.

Hemodialysis and peritoneal dialysis are not effective in the treatment of overdose.

Drug Interactions

Cytochrome P450 Effect: Inhibits CYP1A2 (weak)

Increased Effect/Toxicity: Interferons may increase serum levels and neutropenic effects of zidovudine. Concurrent therapy with ribavirin may increase the risk of hemolytic anemia. Interferon alfa may increase the levels/effects of theophylline.

Storage/Stability Store powder and solution for injection (vials and pens) under refrigeration at 2°C to 8°C (36°F to 46°F). Do not freeze.

Powder for injection: Following reconstitution, should be used immediately, but may be stored under refrigeration for up to 24 hours.

Prefilled pens: After first use, discard unused portion after 4 weeks.

Reconstitution The manufacturer recommends reconstituting vial with the diluent provided (SWFI). To prepare solution for infusion, further dilute appropriate dose in NS 100 mL. Final concentration should be ≥10 million units/100 mL.

Compatibility Stable in LR, NS; **incompatible** with D_5W.

Mechanism of Action Following activation, multiple effects can be detected including induction of gene transcription. Inhibits cellular growth, alters the state of cellular differentiation, interferes with oncogene expression, alters cell surface antigen expression, increases phagocytic activity of macrophages, and augments cytotoxicity of lymphocytes for target cells

Pharmacodynamics/Kinetics

Distribution: V_d: 31 L; but has been noted to be much greater (370-720 L) in leukemia patients receiving continuous infusion IFN; IFN does not penetrate the CSF

Metabolism: Primarily renal

Bioavailability: I.M.: 83%; SubQ: 90%

Half-life elimination: I.V.: 2 hours; I.M., SubQ: 2-3 hours

Time to peak, serum: I.M., SubQ: ~3-12 hours

Dosage Refer to individual protocols. **Note:** Withhold treatment for ANC <500/mm^3 or platelets <25,000/mm^3. Consider premedication with acetaminophen prior to administration to reduce the incidence of some adverse reactions. Not all dosage forms and strengths are appropriate for all indications; refer to product labeling for details.

Children 1-17 years: Chronic hepatitis B: SubQ: 3 million units/m^2 3 times/week for 1 week; then 6 million units/m^2 3 times/week; maximum: 10 million units 3 times/week; total duration of therapy 16-24 weeks

Children ≥3 years: Chronic hepatitis C: In combination with ribavirin (refer to Interferon Alfa-2b/Ribavirin combination pack monograph)

Adults:

Hairy cell leukemia: I.M., SubQ: 2 million units/m^2 3 times/week for up to 6 months (may continue treatment with continued treatment response)

Lymphoma (follicular): SubQ: 5 million units 3 times/week for up to 18 months

Malignant melanoma: Induction: 20 million units/m^2 I.V. for 5 consecutive days per week for 4 weeks, followed by maintenance dosing of 10 million units/m^2 SubQ 3 times/week for 48 weeks

AIDS-related Kaposi's sarcoma: I.M., SubQ: 30 million units/m^2 3 times/week

Chronic hepatitis B: I.M., SubQ: 5 million units/day or 10 million units 3 times/week for 16 weeks

Chronic hepatitis C: I.M., SubQ: 3 million units 3 times/week for 16 weeks. In patients with normalization of ALT at 16 weeks, continue treatment for

(Continued)

Interferon Alfa-2b *(Continued)*

18-24 months; consider discontinuation if normalization does not occur at 16 weeks. **Note:** May be used in combination therapy with ribavirin in previously untreated patients or in patients who relapse following alpha interferon therapy.

Condyloma acuminata: Intralesionally: 1 million units/lesion (maximum: 5 lesions/treatment) 3 times/week (on alternate days) for 3 weeks; may administer a second course at 12-16 weeks

Dosage adjustment in renal impairment: Combination therapy with ribavirin (hepatitis C) should not be used in patients with reduced renal function (Cl_{cr} <50 mL/minute).

Not removed by peritoneal or hemodialysis

Dosage adjustment for toxicity: Manufacturer-recommended adjustments, listed according to indication:

Lymphoma (follicular):

Neutrophils >1000/mm^3 to <1500/mm^3: Reduce dose by 50%; may re-escalate to starting dose when neutrophils return to >1500/mm^3

Severe toxicity (neutrophils <1000/mm^3 or platelets <50,000/mm^3): Temporarily withhold

AST >5 times ULN or serum creatinine >2 mg/dL: Permanently discontinue

Hairy cell leukemia, chronic hepatitis C: Severe toxicity: Reduce dose by 50% or temporarily withhold and resume with 50% dose reduction; permanently discontinue if persistent or recurrent severe toxicity is noted

Chronic hepatitis B:

WBC <1500/mm^3, granulocytes <750/mm^3, or platelet count <50,000/mm^3, or other laboratory abnormality or severe adverse reaction: Reduce dose by 50%; may re-escalate to starting dose upon resolution of hematologic toxicity. Discontinue for persistent intolerance.

WBC <1000/mm^3, granulocytes <500/mm^3, or platelet count <25,000/mm^3: Permanently discontinue

Kaposi sarcoma: Severe toxicity: Reduce dose by 50% or temporarily withhold; may resume at reduced dose with toxicity resolution; permanently discontinue for persistent/recurrent toxicities

Malignant melanoma:

Severe toxicity (neutrophils >250/mm^3 to <500/mm^3 or AST/ALT >5-10 times ULN): Temporarily withhold; resume with a 50% dose reduction when adverse reaction abates

Neutrophils <250/mm^3, AST/ALT >10 times ULN, or severe/persistent adverse reactions: Permanently discontinue

Combination Regimens

Head and neck cancer: PFL + IFN *on page 1271*

Leukemia, acute lymphocytic: Hyper-CVAD (Leukemia, Acute Lymphocytic) *on page 1231*

Melanoma:

BOLD + Interferon *on page 1153*

IL-2 + IFN *on page 1240*

Renal cell cancer:

Interleukin 2-Interferon Alfa-2 *on page 1240*

Interleukin 2-Interferon Alfa-2-Fluorouracil *on page 1241*

Administration

I.M.: Administer in evening (if possible)

I.V.: Infuse over ~20 minutes

SubQ: Suggested for those who are at risk for bleeding or are thrombocytopenic. Rotate SubQ injection site. Administer in evening (if possible). Patient should be well hydrated. Reconstitute with recommended amount of SWFI and agitate gently; do not shake. **Note:** Different vial strengths require different amounts of diluent. Not every dosage form is appropriate for every indication; refer to manufacturer's labeling.

Monitoring Parameters Baseline chest x-ray, ECG; CBC with differential and platelets (baseline and routinely during treatment), liver function tests, serum creatinine, electrolytes, triglycerides, thyroid function tests (baseline and periodically during treatment); weight; ophthalmic exam (baseline and periodic, or with new ocular symptoms); patients with pre-existing cardiac abnormalities or in advanced stages of cancer should have ECGs taken before and during treatment

Patient Information Without the advice of prescriber, do not change brands of interferon as changes in dosage may result; do not operate heavy machinery while on therapy since changes in mental status may occur; report any persistent or severe sore throat, fever, fatigue, unusual bleeding, or bruising. You may experience flu-like syndrome (acetaminophen may help); this syndrome subsides after several weeks of continuous dosing, but usually recurs during each cycle of intermittent therapy.

Emetic Potential Moderate (10% to 30%); usually mild to moderate, aggressive therapy with serotonin antagonists is usually not necessary

Vesicant No

Dosage Forms Excipient information presented when available (limited, particularly for generics); consult specific product labeling.

Injection, powder for reconstitution [preservative free]:

Intron® A: 10 million units; 18 million units; 50 million units [contains human albumin]

Injection, solution [multidose prefilled pen]:

Intron® A:

Delivers 3 million units/0.2 mL (1.5 mL) [delivers 6 doses; 18 million units; contains polysorbate 80; edetate disodium]

Delivers 5 million units/0.2 mL (1.5 mL) [delivers 6 doses; 30 million units; contains polysorbate 80; edetate disodium]

Delivers 10 million units/0.2 mL (1.5 mL) [delivers 6 doses; 60 million units; contains polysorbate 80; edetate disodium]

Injection, solution [multidose vial]:

Intron® A: 6 million units/mL (3 mL); 10 million units/mL (2.5 mL) [contains polysorbate 80; edetate disodium]

Injection, solution [single-dose vial]:

Intron® A: 10 million units/ mL (1 mL) [contains polysorbate 80; edetate disodium]

See also Interferon Alfa-2b and Ribavirin Combination Pack monograph.

References

ACOG Practice Bulletin No. 86: "Viral Hepatitis in Pregnancy," *Obstet Gynecol*, 2007, 110(4):941-56.

"American Academy of Pediatrics Committee on Drugs. The Transfer of Drugs and Other Chemicals Into Human Milk," *Pediatrics*, 2001, 108(3):776-89.

Balkwill FR and Smyth JF, "Interferons in Cancer Therapy: A Reappraisal," *Lancet*, 1987, 2(8554):317-9.

Centers for Disease Control and Prevention, "Sexually Transmitted Diseases Treatment Guidelines, 2006," *MMWR*, 2006, 55(RR-11):1-94.

Gresser I, "Biologic Effects of Interferons," *J Invest Dermatol*, 1990, 95(6 Suppl):66-71.

Houglum JE, "Interferon: Mechanisms of Action and Clinical Value," *Clin Pharm*, 1983, 2(1):20-8.

Lebon P, Girard S, Thepot F, et al, "The Presence of Alpha-Interferon in Human Amniotic Fluid," *J Gen Virol*, 1982, 59(Pt 2):393-6.

Legha SS, "The Role of Interferon Alfa in the Treatment of Metastatic Melanoma," *Semin Oncol*, 1997, 24(1 Suppl 4):24-31.

(Continued)

Interferon Alfa-2b *(Continued)*

Musselman DL, Lawson DH, Gumnick JF, et al, "Paroxetine for the Prevention of Depression Induced by High-Dose Interferon Alfa," *N Engl J Med*, 2001, 344(13):961-6.

"Perinatal HIV Guidelines Working Group. Public Health Service Task Force Recommendations for Use of Antiretroviral Drugs in Pregnant HIV-Infected Women for Maternal Health and Interventions to Reduce Perinatal HIV Transmission in the United States," November 2, 2007, 1-96. Available at http://aidsinfo.nih.gov/ContentFiles/PerinatalGL.pdf.

Tilg H, "New Insights Into the Mechanisms of Interferon Alfa: An Immunoregulatory and Anti-Inflammatory Cytokine," *Gastroenterology*, 1997, 112(3):1017-21.

Vial T and Descotes J, "Clinical Toxicity of the Interferons," *Drug Saf*, 1994, 10(2):115-50.

Waysbort A, Giroux M, Mansat V, et al, "Experimental Study of Transplacental Passage of Alpha Interferon by Two Assay Techniques," *Antimicrob Agents Chemother*, 1993, 37(6):1232-7.

Wills RJ, "Clinical Pharmacokinetics of Interferons," *Clin Pharmacokinet*, 1990, 19(5):390-9.

◆ **Interferon Alpha-2a** *see* Interferon Alfa-2a *on page 611*
◆ **Interferon Alpha-2b** *see* Interferon Alfa-2b *on page 617*

Interferon Gamma-1b (in ter FEER on GAM ah won bee)

Related Information
  Safe Handling of Hazardous Drugs *on page 1382*

U.S. Brand Names Actimmune®

Generic Available No

Canadian Brand Names Actimmune®

Pharmacologic Category Interferon

Use Reduce frequency and severity of serious infections associated with chronic granulomatous disease; delay time to disease progression in patients with severe, malignant osteopetrosis

Pregnancy Risk Factor C

Lactation Excretion in breast milk unknown/not recommended

Labeled Contraindications Hypersensitivity to interferon gamma, *E. coli* derived proteins, or any component of the formulation

Warnings/Precautions Hypersensitivity reactions have been reported (rarely). Transient cutaneous rashes may occur. Dose-related bone marrow toxicity has been reported; use caution in patients with myelosuppression. May cause hepatotoxicity and the incidence may be increased in children <1 year of age. Doses >10 times the weekly recommended dose (used in studies for unlabeled indications) have been associated with a different pattern/frequency of adverse effects. Flu-like symptoms which may exacerbate pre-existing cardiovascular disorders (including ischemia, CHF, or arrhythmias) and the development of neurologic disorders have been noted at the higher doses. Caution should also be used in patients with seizure disorders or compromised CNS function.

Adverse Reactions Based on 50 mcg/m^2 dose administered 3 times weekly for chronic granulomatous disease
  >10%:
    Central nervous system: Fever (52%), headache (33%), chills (14%), fatigue (14%)
    Dermatologic: Rash (17%)
    Gastrointestinal: Diarrhea (14%), vomiting (13%)
    Local: Injection site erythema or tenderness (14%)
  1% to 10%:
    Central nervous system: Depression (3%)
    Gastrointestinal: Nausea (10%), abdominal pain (8%)
    Neuromuscular & skeletal: Myalgia (6%), arthralgia (2%), back pain (2%)
  Postmarketing and/or case reports: Alkaline phosphatase elevated, atopic dermatitis, granulomatous colitis, hepatomegaly, hypersensitivity reactions, hypokalemia, neutropenia, Stevens-Johnson syndrome

Additional adverse reactions noted at doses >100 mcg/m^2 administered 3 times weekly: ALT increased, AST increased, autoantibodies increased, bronchospasm, chest discomfort, confusion, dermatomyositis exacerbation, disorientation, DVT, gait disturbance, GI bleeding, hallucinations, heart block, heart failure, hepatic insufficiency, hyperglycemia, hypertriglyceridemia, hyponatremia, hypotension, interstitial pneumonitis, lupus-like syndrome, MI, neutropenia, pancreatitis (may be fatal), Parkinsonian symptoms, PE, proteinuria, renal insufficiency (reversible), seizure, syncope, tachyarrhythmia, tachypnea, thrombocytopenia, TIA

Overdosage/Toxicology Decreased mental status, dizziness, gait disturbances, hepatic enzyme elevation, neutropenia, thrombocytopenia, and triglyceride elevation have been reported at higher doses and generally respond to a dose reduction or discontinuation of therapy. Treatment is otherwise symptom-directed and supportive.

Drug Interactions

   Cytochrome P450 Effect: Inhibits CYP1A2 (weak), 2E1 (weak)

   Increased Effect/Toxicity: Interferons may decrease the metabolism of theophylline derivatives.

Storage/Stability Store in refrigerator at 2°C to 8°C (36°F to 46°F); do not freeze. Do not shake. Discard if left unrefrigerated for >12 hours.

Mechanism of Action Interferon gamma participates in immunoregulation by enhancing the oxidative metabolism of macrophages; it also enhances antibody dependent cellular cytotoxicity, activates natural killer cells and has a role in the expression of Fc receptors and histocompatibility antigens. The exact mechanism of action for the treatment of chronic granulomatous disease or osteopetrosis has not been defined.

Pharmacodynamics/Kinetics

   Absorption: I.M., SubQ: >89%

   Half-life elimination: I.V.: 38 minutes; I.M.: ~3 hours, SubQ: ~6 hours

   Time to peak, plasma: I.M.: 4 hours (1.5 ng/mL); SubQ: 7 hours (0.6 ng/mL)

Dosage If severe reactions occur, reduce dose by 50% or therapy should be interrupted until adverse reaction abates.

   Children: Severe, malignant osteopetrosis: SubQ:

      BSA ≤0.5 m^2: 1.5 mcg/kg/dose 3 times/week

      BSA >0.5 m^2: 50 mcg/m^2 (1 million int. units/m^2) 3 times/week

   Children and Adults: Chronic granulomatous disease: SubQ:

      BSA ≤0.5 m^2: 1.5 mcg/kg/dose 3 times/week

      BSA >0.5 m^2: 50 mcg/m^2 (1 million int. units/m^2) 3 times/week

   Note: Previously expressed as 1.5 million units/m^2; 50 mcg is equivalent to 1 million int. units/m^2.

Administration Administer by SubQ injection into the right and left deltoid or anterior thigh.

Monitoring Parameters CBC with differential, platelets, LFTs (monthly in children <1 year), electrolytes, BUN, creatinine, and urinalysis prior to therapy and at 3-month intervals

Patient Information Use as directed; do not change the dosage or schedule of administration without consulting prescriber. Maintain adequate hydration (2-3 L/day of fluids unless instructed to restrict fluid intake). You may experience flu-like syndrome (acetaminophen may help or can administer dose at bedtime); nausea, vomiting, or loss of appetite (frequent small meals, frequent mouth care, sucking lozenges, or chewing gum may help); drowsiness, dizziness, agitation, or abnormal thinking (use caution when driving or engaging in tasks requiring alertness until response to drug is known). Report unusual bruising or bleeding; persistent abdominal disturbances; (Continued)

Interferon Gamma-1b *(Continued)*

unusual fatigue; muscle pain or tremors; chest pain or palpitations; swelling of extremities; visual disturbances; pain, swelling, or redness at injection site; or other unusual symptoms.

Emetic Potential Very low (<10%)

Vesicant No

Dosage Forms Excipient information presented when available (limited, particularly for generics); consult specific product labeling.

Injection, solution [preservative free]:

Actimmune®: 100 mcg [2 million int. units] (0.5 mL)

References

Key LL, Rodriguiz RM, Willi SM, et al, "Long-Term Treatment of Osteopetrosis With Recombinant Human Interferon Gamma," *N Engl J Med* 1995, 332(24):1594-9.

Marciano BE, Wesley R, DeCarlo E, et al, "Long-Term Interferon-Gamma Therapy for Patients With Chronic Granulomatous Disease," *Clin Infect Dis*, 2004, 39(5):692-9.

Raghu G, Brown KK, Bradford WZ, et al, "A Placebo-Controlled Trial of Interferon Gamma-1b in Patients With Idiopathic Pulmonary Fibrosis," *N Engl J Med*, 2004 Jan 8;350(2):125-33.

- ◆ **Interleukin-2** *see* Aldesleukin *on page 29*
- ◆ **Interleukin-11** *see* Oprelvekin *on page 842*
- ◆ **Intron® A** *see* Interferon Alfa-2b *on page 617*
- ◆ **Iodine I 131 Tositumomab and Tositumomab** *see* Tositumomab and Iodine I 131 Tositumomab *on page 1056*
- ◆ **Ionsys™** *see* Fentanyl *on page 426*
- ◆ **Iquix®** *see* Levofloxacin *on page 678*
- ◆ **IRESSA®** *see* Gefitinib *on page 496*

Irinotecan *(eye rye no TEE kan)*

Medication Safety Issues

High alert medication: The Institute for Safe Medication Practices (ISMP) includes this medication among its list of classes of drugs which have a heightened risk of causing significant patient harm when used in error.

Related Information

Management of Drug Extravasations *on page 1301*
Management of Nausea and Vomiting *on page 1319*
Safe Handling of Hazardous Drugs *on page 1382*

U.S. Brand Names Camptosar®

Index Terms Camptothecin-11; CPT-11; NSC-616348

Generic Available No

Canadian Brand Names Camptosar®; Irinotecan Hydrochloride Trihydrate

Pharmacologic Category Antineoplastic Agent, Camptothecin; Antineoplastic Agent, Natural Source (Plant) Derivative

Use Treatment of metastatic carcinoma of the colon or rectum

Unlabeled/Investigational Use Lung cancer (small cell and nonsmall cell), cervical cancer, gastric cancer, pancreatic cancer, leukemia, lymphoma, breast cancer, brain tumors

Pregnancy Risk Factor D

Lactation Excretion in breast milk unknown/not recommended

Labeled Contraindications Hypersensitivity to irinotecan or any component of the formulation; concurrent use of ketoconazole, St John's wort

Warnings/Precautions Hazardous agent - use appropriate precautions for handling and disposal. Severe hypersensitivity reactions have occurred.

Patients with diarrhea should be carefully monitored and treated promptly. **[U.S. Boxed Warning]: Severe diarrhea may be dose-limiting and potentially fatal; two severe (life-threatening) forms of diarrhea may occur.**

Early diarrhea occurs during or within 24 hours of receiving irinotecan and is characterized by cholinergic symptoms (eg, increased salivation, diaphoresis, abdominal cramping); it is usually responsive to atropine. Late diarrhea occurs more than 24 hours after treatment which may lead to dehydration, electrolyte imbalance, or sepsis; it should be promptly treated with loperamide. Colitis, complicated by ulceration, bleeding, ileus, and infection has been reported.

[U.S. Boxed Warning]: May cause severe myelosuppression. Deaths due to sepsis following severe myelosuppression have been reported. Therapy should be temporarily discontinued if neutropenic fever occurs or if the absolute neutrophil count is <1000/mm^3. The dose of irinotecan should be reduced if there is a clinically significant decrease in the total WBC (<200/mm^3), neutrophil count (<1500/mm^3), hemoglobin (<8 g/dL), or platelet count (<100,000/mm^3). Routine administration of a colony-stimulating factor is generally not necessary, but may be considered for patients experiencing significant neutropenia.

Patients with even modest elevations in total serum bilirubin levels (1-2 mg/dL) have a significantly greater likelihood of experiencing first-course grade 3 or 4 neutropenia than those with bilirubin levels that were <1 mg/dL. Patients with abnormal glucuronidation of bilirubin, such as those with Gilbert's syndrome, may also be at greater risk of myelosuppression when receiving therapy with irinotecan. Use caution when treating patients with known hepatic dysfunction or hyperbilirubinemia. Dosage adjustments should be considered.

Patients homozygous for the UGT1A1*28 allele are at increased risk of neutropenia; initial one-level dose reduction should be considered for both single-agent and combination regimens. Heterozygous carriers of the UGT1A1*28 allele may also be at increased risk; however, most patients have tolerated normal starting doses.

Renal impairment and acute renal failure have been reported, possibly due to dehydration secondary to diarrhea. Patients with bowel obstruction should not be treated with irinotecan until resolution of obstruction. Use caution in patients who previously received pelvic/abdominal radiation, elderly patients with comorbid conditions, or baseline performance status of 2; close monitoring and dosage adjustments are recommended. Contains sorbitol; do not use in patients with hereditary fructose intolerance. **[U.S. Boxed Warning]: Should be administered under the supervision of an experienced cancer chemotherapy physician.** Except as part of a clinical trial, use in combination with fluorouracil and leucovorin "Mayo Clinic" regimen is not recommended. Increased toxicity has also been noted in patients with a baseline performance status of 2 in other combination regimens containing irinotecan, leucovorin, and fluorouracil.

Adverse Reactions Frequency of adverse reactions reported for single-agent use of irinotecan only.
>10%:
Cardiovascular: Vasodilation (9% to 11%)
Central nervous system: Cholinergic toxicity (47% - includes rhinitis, increased salivation, miosis, lacrimation, diaphoresis, flushing and intestinal hyperperistalsis); fever (44% to 45%), pain (23% to 24%), dizziness (15% to 21%), insomnia (19%), headache (17%), chills (14%)
Dermatologic: Alopecia (46% to 72%), rash (13% to 14%)
Endocrine & metabolic: Dehydration (15%)
Gastrointestinal: Diarrhea, late (83% to 88%; grade 3/4: 6% to 31%), diarrhea, early (43% to 51%; grade 3/4: 6% to 22%), nausea (70% to (Continued)

Irinotecan *(Continued)*

86%), abdominal pain (57% to 68%), vomiting (62% to 67%), cramps (57%), anorexia (44% to 55%), constipation (30% to 32%), mucositis (30%), weight loss (30%), flatulence (12%), stomatitis (12%)

Hematologic: Anemia (60% to 97%; grades 3/4: 5% to 22%), leukopenia (63% to 96%, grades 3/4: 14% to 28%), thrombocytopenia (96%, grades 3/4: 1% to 4%), neutropenia (30% to 96%; grades 3/4: 14% to 31%)

Hepatic: Bilirubin increased (84%), alkaline phosphatase increased (13%)

Neuromuscular & skeletal: Weakness (69% to 76%), back pain (14%)

Respiratory: Dyspnea (22%), cough (17% to 20%), rhinitis (16%)

Miscellaneous: Diaphoresis (16%), infection (14%)

1% to 10%:

Cardiovascular: Edema (10%), hypotension (6%), thromboembolic events (5%)

Central nervous system: Somnolence (9%), confusion (3%)

Gastrointestinal: Abdominal fullness (10%), dyspepsia (10%)

Hematologic: Neutropenic fever (grades 3/4: 2% to 6%), hemorrhage (grades 3/4: 1% to 5%), neutropenic infection (grades 3/4: 1% to 2%)

Hepatic: AST increased (10%), ascites and/or jaundice (grades 3/4: 9%)

Respiratory: Pneumonia (4%)

<1%, postmarketing, and/or case reports: ALT increased, amylase increased, anaphylactoid reaction, anaphylaxis, angina, arterial thrombosis, bleeding, bradycardia, cardiac arrest, cerebral infarct, cerebrovascular accident, circulatory failure, colitis, deep thrombophlebitis, dysrhythmia, embolus, gastrointestinal bleeding, gastrointestinal obstruction, hepatomegaly, hiccups, hyperglycemia, hypersensitivity, hyponatremia, ileus, interstitial lung disease, intestinal perforation, ischemic colitis, lipase increased, lymphocytopenia, megacolon, MI, muscle cramps, myocardial ischemia, pancreatitis, paresthesia, peripheral vascular disorder, pulmonary embolus; pulmonary toxicity (dyspnea, fever, reticulonodular infiltrates on chest x-ray); renal failure (acute), renal impairment, syncope, thrombophlebitis, thrombosis, typhlitis, ulceration, ulcerative colitis, vertigo

Note: In limited pediatric experience, dehydration (often associated with severe hypokalemia and hyponatremia) was among the most significant grade 3/4 adverse events, with a frequency up to 29%. In addition, grade 3/4 infection was reported in 24%.

Overdosage/Toxicology Symptoms of overdose include bone marrow suppression, including leukopenia, severe neutropenia and thrombocytopenia; nausea, vomiting and severe diarrhea. Treatment is symptom-directed and supportive, including prevention/treatment of dehydration due to diarrhea.

Drug Interactions

Cytochrome P450 Effect: Substrate (major) of CYP2B6, 3A4

Increased Effect/Toxicity: CYP2B6 inhibitors may increase the levels/effects of irinotecan; example inhibitors include desipramine, paroxetine, and sertraline. CYP3A4 inhibitors may increase the levels/effects of irinotecan; example inhibitors include azole antifungals, clarithromycin, diclofenac, doxycycline, erythromycin, imatinib, isoniazid, nefazodone, nicardipine, propofol, protease inhibitors, quinidine, telithromycin, and verapamil. Atazanavir may increase the levels/effects of irinotecan (SN-38) by CYP3A4 and UGT1A1 inhibition. Bevacizumab may increase the adverse effects of irinotecan (eg, diarrhea, neutropenia). Ketoconazole increases the levels/effects of irinotecan and active metabolite; discontinue ketoconazole 1 week prior to irinotecan therapy; **concurrent use is contraindicated.**

Decreased Effect: CYP2B6 inducers may decrease the levels/effects of irinotecan; example inducers include carbamazepine, nevirapine, phenobarbital, phenytoin, and rifampin. CYP3A4 inducers may decrease the levels/effects of irinotecan; example inducers include aminoglutethimide, carbamazepine, nafcillin, nevirapine, phenobarbital, phenytoin, and rifamycins. St John's wort decreases therapeutic effect of irinotecan; discontinue ≥2 weeks prior to irinotecan therapy; **concurrent use is contraindicated.**

Ethanol/Nutrition/Herb Interactions Herb/Nutraceutical: Avoid St John's wort (decreases the efficacy of irinotecan).

Storage/Stability Store intact vials of injection at room temperature of 15°C to 30°C (59°F to 86°F). Protect from light. Solutions diluted in NS may precipitate if refrigerated. Solutions diluted in D_5W are stable for 24 hours at room temperature or 48 hours under refrigeration at 2°C to 8°C. Do not freeze.

Reconstitution Dilute in 250-500 mL D_5W or NS to a final concentration of 0.12-2.8 mg/mL. Due to the relatively acidic pH, irinotecan appears to be more stable in D_5W than NS.

Compatibility Stable in D_5W, NS.

Y-site administration: Compatible: Leucovorin; **Incompatible:** Gemcitabine.

Compatibility when admixed: Incompatible: Methylprednisolone sodium succinate.

Mechanism of Action Irinotecan and its active metabolite (SN-38) bind reversibly to topoisomerase I-DNA complex preventing religation of the cleaved DNA strand. This results in the accumulation of cleavable complexes and double-strand DNA breaks. As mammalian cells cannot efficiently repair these breaks, cell death consistent with S-phase cell cycle specificity occurs, leading to termination of cellular replication.

Pharmacodynamics/Kinetics

Distribution: V_d: 33-150 L/m^2

Protein binding, plasma: Predominantly albumin; Parent drug: 30% to 68%, SN-38 (active metabolite): ~95%

Metabolism: Primarily hepatic to SN-38 (active metabolite) by carboxylesterase enzymes; SN-38 undergoes conjugation by UDP- glucuronosyl transferase 1A1 (UGT1A1) to form a glucuronide metabolite. Conversion of irinotecan to SN-38 is decreased and glucuronidation of SN-38 is increased patients who smoke cigarettes, resulting in lower levels of the metabolite and overall decreased systemic exposure. SN-38 is increased by UGT1A1*28 polymorphism (10% of North Americans are homozygous for UGT1A1*28 allele). The lactones of both irinotecan and SN-38 undergo hydrolysis to inactive hydroxy acid forms.

Half-life elimination: SN-38: Mean terminal: 10-20 hours

Time to peak: SN-38: Following 90-minute infusion: ~1 hour

Excretion: Within 24 hours: Urine: Irinotecan (11% to 20%), metabolites (SN-38 <1%, SN-38 glucuronide, 3%)

Dosage I.V. (Refer to individual protocols): **Note:** A reduction in the starting dose by one dose level should be considered for patients ≥65 years of age, prior pelvic/abdominal radiotherapy, performance status of 2, homozygosity for UGT1A1*28 allele, or increased bilirubin (dosing for patients with a bilirubin >2 mg/dL cannot be recommended based on lack of data per manufacturer).

(Continued)

Irinotecan *(Continued)*

Single-agent therapy:

125 mg/m^2 over 90 minutes on days 1, 8, 15, and 22 of a 6-week treatment cycle

Adjusted dose level -1: 100 mg/m^2

Adjusted dose level -2: 75 mg/m^2

Once-every-3-week regimen: 350 mg/m^2 over 90 minutes, once every 3 weeks

Adjusted dose level -1: 300 mg/m^2

Adjusted dose level -2: 250 mg/m^2

Depending on the patient's ability to tolerate therapy, doses should be adjusted in increments of 25-50 mg/m^2. Irinotecan doses may range from 50-150 mg/m^2 for the weekly regimen. Patients may be dosed as low as 200 mg/m^2 (in 50 mg/m^2 decrements) for the once-every-3-week regimen.

Combination therapy with fluorouracil and leucovorin: Six-week (42-day) cycle:

Regimen 1: 125 mg/m^2 over 90 minutes on days 1, 8, 15, and 22; to be given in combination with bolus leucovorin and fluorouracil (leucovorin administered immediately following irinotecan; fluorouracil immediately following leucovorin)

Adjusted dose level -1: 100 mg/m^2

Adjusted dose level -2: 75 mg/m^2

Regimen 2: 180 mg/m^2 over 90 minutes on days 1, 15, and 29; to be given in combination with infusional leucovorin and bolus/infusion fluorouracil (leucovorin administered immediately following irinotecan; fluorouracil immediately following leucovorin)

Adjusted dose level -1: 150 mg/m^2

Adjusted dose level -2: 120 mg/m^2

Note: For all regimens: It is recommended that new courses begin only after the granulocyte count recovers to ≥1500/mm^3, the platelet count recovers to ≥100,000/mm^3, and treatment-related diarrhea has fully resolved. Treatment should be delayed 1-2 weeks to allow for recovery from treatment-related toxicities. If the patient has not recovered after a 2-week delay, consideration should be given to discontinuing irinotecan.

Dosing adjustment in renal impairment: Effects have not been evaluated; not recommended for use in patients on dialysis

Dosing adjustment in hepatic impairment: The manufacturer recommends that no change in dosage or administration be made for patients with liver metastases and normal hepatic function.

Consideration may be given to starting irinotecan at a lower dose (eg, 100 mg/m^2) if bilirubin is 1-2 mg/dL; for total serum bilirubin elevations >2 mg/dL, specific recommendations are not available in the FDA labeling. The following guidelines have been used by some clinicians:

Bilirubin 1.5-3 mg/dL: Administer 75% of dose (Floyd, 2006).

Dosage adjustment for toxicities: It is recommended that new courses begin only after the granulocyte count recovers to ≥1500/mm^3, the platelet counts recovers to ≥100,000/mm^3, and treatment-related diarrhea has fully resolved. Depending on the patient's ability to tolerate therapy, doses should be adjusted in increments of 25-50 mg/m^2. Treatment should be delayed 1-2 weeks to allow for recovery from treatment-related toxicities. If the patient has not recovered after a 2-week delay, consideration should be given to discontinuing irinotecan. See tables on following pages.

Combination Regimens

Brain tumors: Bevacizumab-Irinotecan (Glioblastoma) *on page 1151*

Colorectal cancer:

Bevacizumab-Irinotecan-Fluorouracil-Leucovorin *on page 1151*

Cetuximab-Irinotecan *on page 1167*

Fluorouracil-Leucovorin-Irinotecan (Saltz Regimen) *on page 1220*

FOIL *on page 1221*

FU-LV-CPT-11 *on page 1223*

Esophageal cancer: Irinotecan-Cisplatin *on page 1241*

Pancreatic cancer: Gemcitabine-Irinotecan *on page 1228*

Administration Administer by I.V. infusion, usually over 90 minutes.

Monitoring Parameters CBC with differential, platelet count, and hemoglobin with each dose; bilirubin, electrolytes (with severe diarrhea); bowel movements and hydration status; monitor infusion site for signs of inflammation and avoid extravasation

Dietary Considerations Contains sorbitol; do not use in patients with hereditary fructose intolerance.

Single-Agent Schedule: Recommended Dosage Modifications[1]

Toxicity NCI Grade[2] (Value)	During a Cycle of Therapy	At Start of Subsequent Cycles of Therapy (After Adequate Recovery), Compared to Starting Dose in Previous Cycle[1]	
	Weekly	Weekly	Once Every 3 Weeks
No toxicity	Maintain dose level	↑ 25 mg/m² up to a maximum dose of 150 mg/m²	Maintain dose level
Neutropenia			
1 (1500-1999/mm³)	Maintain dose level	Maintain dose level	Maintain dose level
2 (1000-1499/mm³)	↓ 25 mg/m²	Maintain dose level	Maintain dose level
3 (500-999/mm³)	Omit dose until resolved to ≤ grade 2, then ↓ 25 mg/m²	↓ 25 mg/m²	↓ 50 mg/m²
4 (<500/mm³)	Omit dose until resolved to ≤ grade 2, then ↓ 50 mg/m²	↓ 50 mg/m²	↓ 50 mg/m²
Neutropenic Fever (grade 4 neutropenia and ≥ grade 2 fever)	Omit dose until resolved, then ↓ 50 mg/m²	↓ 50 mg/m²	↓ 50 mg/m²
Other Hematologic Toxicities	Dose modifications for leukopenia, thrombocytopenia, and anemia during a course of therapy and at the start of subsequent courses of therapy are also based on NCI toxicity criteria and are the same as recommended for neutropenia above.		
Diarrhea			
1 (2-3 stools/day > pretreatment)	Maintain dose level	Maintain dose level	Maintain dose level
2 (4-6 stools/day > pretreatment)	↓ 25 mg/m²	Maintain dose level	Maintain dose level
3 (7-9 stools/day > pretreatment)	Omit dose until resolved to ≤ grade 2, then ↓ 25 mg/m²	↓ 25 mg/m²	↓ 50 mg/m²
4 (≥10 stools/day > pretreatment)	Omit dose until resolved to ≤ grade 2, then ↓ 50 mg/m²	↓ 50 mg/m²	↓ 50 mg/m²
Other Nonhematologic Toxicities[3]			
1	Maintain dose level	Maintain dose level	Maintain dose level
2	↓ 25 mg/m²	↓ 25 mg/m²	↓ 50 mg/m²
3	Omit dose until resolved to ≤ grade 2, then ↓ 25 mg/m²	↓ 25 mg/m²	↓ 50 mg/m²
4	Omit dose until resolved to ≤ grade 2, then ↓ 50 mg/m²	↓ 50 mg/m²	↓ 50 mg/m²

[1]All dose modifications should be based on the worst preceding toxicity.

[2]National Cancer Institute Common Toxicity Criteria (version 1.0).

[3]Excludes alopecia, anorexia, asthenia.

(Continued)

Irinotecan *(Continued)*

Combination Schedules: Recommended Dosage Modifications[1]

Toxicity NCI[2] Grade (Value)	During a Cycle of Therapy	At the Start of Subsequent Cycles of Therapy (After Adequate Recovery), Compared to the Starting Dose in the Previous Cycle[1]
No toxicity	Maintain dose level	Maintain dose level
Neutropenia		
1 (1500-1999/mm³)	Maintain dose level	Maintain dose level
2 (1000-1499/mm³)	↓ 1 dose level	Maintain dose level
3 (500-999/mm³)	Omit dose until resolved to ≤ grade 2, then ↓ 1 dose level	↓ 1 dose level
4 (<500/mm³)	Omit dose until resolved to ≤ grade 2, then ↓ 2 dose levels	↓ 2 dose levels
Neutropenic Fever (grade 4 neutropenia and ≥ grade 2 fever)	Omit dose until resolved, then ↓ 2 dose levels	
Other Hematologic Toxicities	Dose modifications for leukopenia or thrombocytopenia during a course of therapy and at the start of subsequent courses of therapy are also based on NCI toxicity criteria and are the same as recommended for neutropenia above.	
Diarrhea		
1 (2-3 stools/day > pretreatment)	Delay dose until resolved to baseline, then give same dose	Maintain dose level
2 (4-6 stools/day > pretreatment)	Omit dose until resolved to baseline, then ↓ 1 dose level	Maintain dose level
3 (7-9 stools/day > pretreatment)	Omit dose until resolved to baseline, then ↓ by 1 dose level	↓ 1 dose level
4 (≥10 stools/day > pretreatment)	Omit dose until resolved to baseline, then ↓ 2 dose levels	↓ 2 dose levels
Other Nonhematologic Toxicities[3]		
1	Maintain dose level	Maintain dose level
2	Omit dose until resolved to ≤ grade 1, then ↓ 1 dose level	Maintain dose level
3	Omit dose until resolved to ≤ grade 2, then ↓ 1 dose level	↓ 1 dose level
4	Omit dose until resolved to ≤ grade 2, then ↓ 2 dose levels	↓ 2 dose levels
Mucositis and/or stomatitis	Decrease only 5-FU, not irinotecan	Decrease only 5-FU, not irinotecan

[1]All dose modifications should be based on the worst preceding toxicity.

[2]National Cancer Institute Common Toxicity Criteria (version 1.0).

[3]Excludes alopecia, anorexia, asthenia.

Patient Information Patients and patients' caregivers should be informed of the expected toxic effects of irinotecan, particularly of its gastrointestinal manifestations, such as nausea, vomiting, and diarrhea. Each patient should be instructed to have loperamide readily available and to begin treatment for late diarrhea (occurring >24 hours after administration of irinotecan) at the first episode of poorly formed or loose stools or the earliest onset of bowel movements more frequent than normally expected for the patient. Refer to Warnings/Precautions. The patient should also be instructed to notify the prescriber if diarrhea occurs. Premedication with loperamide is not recommended. The use of drugs with laxative properties should be avoided because of the potential for exacerbation of diarrhea. Patients should be advised to contact their prescriber to discuss any laxative use. Patients should consult their prescriber if vomiting occurs, fever or evidence of infection develops, or if symptoms of dehydration, such as fainting, lightheadedness, or dizziness, are noted following therapy.

Additional Information Patients who are homozygous for the UGT1A1*28 allele are at increased risk for neutropenia; a decreased dose is recommended. Clinical research of patients who are heterozygous for UGT1A1*28 have been variable for increased neutropenic risk and such patients have tolerated normal starting doses. An FDA-approved test (Invader® Molecular Assay) is available for clinical determination of UGT phenotype.

The recommended regimen to manage late diarrhea is loperamide 4 mg orally at onset of late diarrhea, followed by 2 mg every 2 hours (or 4 mg every 4 hours at night) until 12 hours have passed without a bowel movement. If diarrhea recurs, then repeat administration. Loperamide should not be used for more than 48 consecutive hours.

Emetic Potential High (60% to 90%, usually mild)

Vesicant No

Dosage Forms Excipient information presented when available (limited, particularly for generics); consult specific product labeling.

Injection, solution, as hydrochloride:

Camptosar®: 20 mg/mL (2 mL, 5 mL) [contains sorbitol 45 mg/mL]

References

Floyd J, Mirza I, Sachs B, et al, "Hepatotoxicity of Chemotherapy," *Semin Oncol*, 2006, 33(1):50-67.

Marsh S and McLeod HL, "Pharmacogenetics of Irinotecan Toxicity," *Pharmacogenomics*, 2004, 5(7):835-43.

Mathijssen RH, Loos WJ, Verweij J, et al, "Pharmacology of Topoisomerase I Inhibitors Irinotecan (CPT-11) and Topotecan," *Curr Cancer Drug Targets*, 2002, 2(2):103-23.

Mathijssen RH, van Alphen RJ, Verweij J, et al, "Clinical Pharmacokinetics and Metabolism of Irinotecan (CPT-11)," *Clin Cancer Res*, 2001, 7(8):2182-94.

Tofffoli G, Cecchin E, Corona G, et al "Pharmacogenetics of Irinotecan," *Curr Med Chem Anti-Canc Agents*, 2003, 3(3):225-37.

Tofffoli G, Cecchin E, Corona G, et al, "The Role of UGT1A1*28 Polymorphism in the Pharmacodynamics and Pharmacokinetics of Irinotecan in Patients With Metastatic Colorectal Cancer," *J Clin Oncol*, 2006, 24(19):3061-8.

Walker SE, Law S, and Puodziunas A, "Simulation of Y-Site Compatibility of Irinotecan and Leucovorin at Room Temperature in 5% Dextrose in Water in 3 Different Containers," *Can J Hosp Pharm*, 2005, 58(4): 212-22.

van der Bol JM, Mathijssen RH, Loos WJ, et al, "Cigarette Smoking and Irinotecan Treatment: Pharmacokinetic Interaction and Effects on Neutropenia," *J Clin Oncol*, 2007, 25(19):2719-26.

♦ **Irinotecan Hydrochloride Trihydrate (Can)** *see* Irinotecan *on page 626*

Iron Dextran Complex (EYE ern DEKS tran KOM pleks)

Medication Safety Issues

Sound-alike/look-alike issues:

Dexferrum® may be confused with Desferal®

U.S. Brand Names Dexferrum®; INFeD®

Generic Available No

Canadian Brand Names Dexiron™; Infufer®

Pharmacologic Category Iron Salt

Use Treatment of microcytic hypochromic anemia resulting from iron deficiency in patients in whom oral administration is infeasible or ineffective

Pregnancy Risk Factor C

Lactation Enters breast milk/contraindicated

(Continued)

Iron Dextran Complex *(Continued)*

Labeled Contraindications Hypersensitivity to iron dextran or any component of the formulation; all anemias that are not involved with iron deficiency; hemochromatosis; hemolytic anemia

Warnings/Precautions Use with caution in patients with history of asthma, hepatic impairment, or rheumatoid arthritis. Not recommended in children <4 months of age. **[U.S. Boxed Warning]: Deaths associated with parenteral administration following anaphylactic-type reactions have been reported.** Use only in patients where the iron deficient state is not amenable to oral iron therapy. A test dose of 0.5 mL I.V. or I.M. should be given to observe for adverse reactions. I.V. administration of iron dextran is often preferred.

Adverse Reactions

>10%:
  Cardiovascular: Flushing
  Central nervous system: Dizziness, fever, headache, pain
  Gastrointestinal: Nausea, vomiting, metallic taste
  Local: Staining of skin at the site of I.M. injection
  Miscellaneous: Diaphoresis

1% to 10%:
  Cardiovascular: Hypotension (1% to 2%)
  Dermatologic: Urticaria (1% to 2%), phlebitis (1% to 2%)
  Gastrointestinal: Diarrhea
  Genitourinary: Discoloration of urine

<1%: Cardiovascular collapse, leukocytosis, chills, arthralgia, respiratory difficulty, lymphadenopathy, anaphylaxis, shock

Note: Diaphoresis, urticaria, arthralgia, fever, chills, dizziness, headache, and nausea may be delayed 24-48 hours after I.V. administration or 3-4 days after I.M. administration.

Anaphylactoid reactions: Respiratory difficulties and cardiovascular collapse have been reported and occur most frequently within the first several minutes of administration.

Overdosage/Toxicology Symptoms of overdose include erosion of GI mucosa, pulmonary edema, hyperthermia, convulsions, tachycardia, hepatic and renal impairment, coma, hematemesis, lethargy, tachycardia, and acidosis. Serum iron level >300 mcg/mL requires treatment of overdose due to severe toxicity. If severe iron overdose (when the serum iron concentration exceeds the total iron-binding capacity) occurs, it may be treated with deferoxamine. Deferoxamine may be administered I.V. (80 mg/kg over 24 hours) or I.M. (40-90 mg/kg every 8 hours).

Drug Interactions

Decreased Effect: Decreased effect with chloramphenicol.

Ethanol/Nutrition/Herb Interactions Food: Iron bioavailability may be decreased if taken with dairy products.

Storage/Stability Store at room temperature. Stability of parenteral admixture is 3 months refrigerated.

Reconstitution Solutions for infusion should be diluted in 250-1000 mL NS.

Compatibility Stable in D_5W, NS; **variable stability (consult detailed reference)** in TPN.

  Compatibility when admixed: Compatible: Cyanocobalamin, netilmicin.

Mechanism of Action The released iron, from the plasma, eventually replenishes the depleted iron stores in the bone marrow where it is incorporated into hemoglobin

Pharmacodynamics/Kinetics

Absorption:

I.M.: 50% to 90% is promptly absorbed, balance is slowly absorbed over month

I.V.: Uptake of iron by the reticuloendothelial system appears to be constant at about 10-20 mg/hour

Excretion: Urine and feces via reticuloendothelial system

Dosage I.M. (Z-track method should be used for I.M. injection), I.V.:

A 0.5 mL test dose (0.25 mL in infants) should be given prior to starting iron dextran therapy; total dose should be divided into a daily schedule for I.M., total dose may be given as a single continuous infusion

Iron-deficiency anemia:

Children 5-15 kg: Should not normally be given in the first 4 months of life:

Dose (mL) = 0.0442 (desired hemoglobin - observed hemoglobin) x W + (0.26 x W)

Desired hemoglobin: Usually 12 g/dL

W = Total body weight in kg

Children >15 kg and Adults:

Dose (mL) = 0.0442 (desired hemoglobin - observed hemoglobin) x LBW + (0.26 x LBW)

Desired hemoglobin: Usually 14.8 g/dL

LBW = Lean body weight in kg

Iron replacement therapy for blood loss: Replacement iron (mg) = blood loss (mL) x hematocrit

Maximum daily dosage:

Manufacturer's labeling: **Note:** Replacement of larger estimated iron deficits may be achieved by serial administration of smaller incremental dosages. Daily dosages should be limited to:

Children:

5-15 kg: 50 mg iron (1 mL)

15-50 kg: 100 mg iron (2 mL)

Adults >50 kg: 100 mg iron (2 mL)

Total dose infusion (unlabeled): The entire dose (estimated iron deficit) may be diluted and administered as a one-time I.V. infusion.

Administration Note: Test dose: A test dose should be given on the first day of therapy; patient should be observed for 1 hour for hypersensitivity reaction, then the remaining dose (dose minus test dose) should be given. Epinephrine should be available.

I.M.: Use Z-track technique (displacement of the skin laterally prior to injection); injection should be deep into the upper outer quadrant of buttock; subsequent injections should be given into alternate buttock

I.V.: Test dose should be given gradually over at least 5 minutes. Subsequent dose(s) may be administered by I.V. bolus at rate of ≤50 mg/minute or diluted in 250-1000 mL NS and infused over 1-6 hours (initial 25 mL should be given slowly and patient should be observed for allergic reactions); avoid dilutions with dextrose (increased incidence of local pain and phlebitis)

Monitoring Parameters Hemoglobin, hematocrit, reticulocyte count, serum ferritin, serum iron, TIBC

Test Interactions May cause falsely elevated values of serum bilirubin and falsely decreased values of serum calcium

Special Geriatric Considerations Anemia in the elderly is most often caused by "anemia of chronic disease", a result of aging effect in bone marrow, or associated with inflammation rather than blood loss. Iron stores are usually normal or increased, with a serum ferritin >50 ng/mL and a (Continued)

Iron Dextran Complex *(Continued)*

decreased total iron binding capacity. Hence, the anemia is not secondary to iron deficiency but the inability of the reticuloendothelial system to use available iron stores. I.V. administration of iron dextran is often preferred over I.M. in the elderly secondary to a decreased muscle mass and the need for daily injections.

Dosage Forms Excipient information presented when available (limited, particularly for generics); consult specific product labeling.

Note: Strength expressed as elemental iron

Injection, solution:

Dexferrum®: 50 mg/mL (1 mL, 2 mL)

INFeD®: 50 mg/mL (2 mL)

References

Auerbach M, Witt D, and Toler W, "Clinical Use of the Total Dose Intravenous Infusion of Iron Dextran," *J Lab Clin Med*, 1988, 111(5):566-70.

Benito RP and Guerrero TC, "Response to a Single Intravenous Dose Versus Multiple Intramuscular Administration of Iron Dextran Complex: A Comparative Study," *Curr Ther Res Clin Exp*, 1973, 15(7):373-82.

Burns DL, Mascioli EA, and Bistrian BR, "Parenteral Iron Dextran Therapy: A Review," *Nutrition*, 1995, 11(2):163-8.

Kumpf VJ and Holland EG, "Parenteral Iron Dextran Therapy," *DICP*, 1990, 24(2):162-6.

Lipschitz DA, "The Anemia of Chronic Disease," *J Am Geriatr Soc*, 1990, 38(11):1258-64.

Iron Sucrose *(EYE ern SOO krose)*

U.S. Brand Names Venofer®

Generic Available No

Canadian Brand Names Venofer®

Pharmacologic Category Iron Salt

Use Treatment of iron-deficiency anemia in chronic renal failure, including nondialysis-dependent patients (with or without erythropoietin therapy) and dialysis-dependent patients receiving erythropoietin therapy

Pregnancy Risk Factor B

Lactation Excretion in breast milk unknown/use caution

Labeled Contraindications Hypersensitivity to iron sucrose or any component of the formulation; evidence of iron overload; anemia not caused by iron deficiency

Warnings/Precautions Rare anaphylactic and anaphylactoid reactions, including serious or life-threatening reactions, have been reported. Facilities (equipment and personnel) for cardiopulmonary resuscitation should be available during initial administration until response/tolerance has been established. Hypotension has been reported frequently in hemodialysis dependent patients. The incidence of hypotension in nondialysis patients is substantially lower. Hypotension may be related to total dose or rate of administration (avoid rapid I.V. injection), follow recommended guidelines. Withhold iron in the presence of tissue iron overload; periodic monitoring of hemoglobin, hematocrit, serum ferritin, and transferrin saturation is recommended. Safety and efficacy in children have not been established.

Adverse Reactions

>10%:

Cardiovascular: Hypotension (1% to 7%; 39% in hemodialysis patients; may be related to total dose or rate of administration), peripheral edema (2% to 13%)

Central nervous system: Headache (3% to 13%)

Gastrointestinal: Nausea (1% to 15%)

Neuromuscular & skeletal: Muscle cramps (1% to 3%; 29% in hemodialysis patients)

1% to 10%:

Cardiovascular: Hypertension (6% to 8%), edema (1% to 7%), chest pain (1% to 6%), murmur (<1% to 3%), CHF

Central nervous system: Dizziness (1% to 10%), fatigue (2% to 5%), fever (1% to 3%), anxiety

Dermatologic: Pruritus (1% to 7%), rash (<1% to 2%)

Endocrine & metabolic: Gout (2% to 7%), hypoglycemia (<1% to 4%), hyperglycemia (3% to 4%), fluid overload (1% to 3%)

Gastrointestinal: Diarrhea (1% to 10%), vomiting (5% to 9%), taste perversion (1% to 9%), peritoneal infection (8%), constipation (1% to 7%), abdominal pain (1% to 4%), positive fecal occult blood (1% to 3%)

Genitourinary: Urinary tract infection (≤1%)

Local: Injection site reaction (2% to 4%), catheter site infection (4%)

Neuromuscular & skeletal: Muscle pain (1% to 7%), extremity pain (3% to 6%), arthralgia (1% to 4%), weakness (1% to 3%), back pain (1% to 3%)

Ocular: Conjunctivitis (<1% to 3%)

Otic: Ear pain (1% to 7%)

Respiratory: Dyspnea (1% to 10%), pharyngitis (<1% to 7%), cough (1% to 7%), sinusitis (1% to 4%), rhinitis (1% to 3%), upper respiratory infection (1% to 3%), nasal congestion (1%)

Miscellaneous: Graft complication (1% to 10%), hypersensitivity, sepsis <1%, postmarketing, and/or case reports: Anaphylactoid reactions, anaphylactic shock, bronchospasm (with dyspnea), collapse, facial rash, loss of consciousness, hypoesthesia, necrotizing enterocolitis (reported in premature infants, no causal relationship established), seizure, urticaria

Overdosage/Toxicology Symptoms associated with overdose or rapid infusion include hypotension, headache, vomiting, nausea, dizziness, joint aches, paresthesia, abdominal and muscle pain, edema, and cardiovascular collapse. Reducing rate of infusion can alleviate some symptoms. Most symptoms can be treated with I.V. fluids, hydrocortisone, and/or antihistamines.

For severe iron overdose (serum iron concentration exceeds TIBC), deferoxamine may be administered intravenously.

Drug Interactions

Increased Effect/Toxicity: Iron sucrose injection may reduce the absorption of oral iron preparations.

Storage/Stability Store vials at room temperature of 15°C to 30°C (59°F to 86°F); do not freeze. Following dilution, solutions are stable for 48 hours at room temperature or under refrigeration.

Reconstitution May be administered via the dialysis line as an undiluted solution or by diluting 100 mg (5 mL) in 100 mL normal saline. Doses ≥200 mg should be diluted in a maximum of 250 mL normal saline.

Compatibility Do not mix with other medications.

Mechanism of Action Iron sucrose is dissociated by the reticuloendothelial system into iron and sucrose. The released iron increases serum iron concentrations and is incorporated into hemoglobin.

Pharmacodynamics/Kinetics

Distribution: V_{dss}: Healthy adults: 7.9 L

Metabolism: Dissociated into iron and sucrose by the reticuloendothelial system

Half-life elimination: Healthy adults: 6 hours

Excretion: Healthy adults: Urine (5%) within 24 hours

Dosage Doses expressed in mg of **elemental** iron. **Note:** Test dose: Product labeling does not indicate need for a test dose in product-naive patients. (Continued)

Iron Sucrose *(Continued)*

I.V.: Adults: Iron-deficiency anemia in chronic renal disease:

Hemodialysis-dependent patient: 100 mg (5 mL of iron sucrose injection) administered 1-3 times/week during dialysis; administer no more than 3 times/week to a cumulative total dose of 1000 mg (10 doses); may continue to administer at lowest dose necessary to maintain target hemoglobin, hematocrit, and iron storage parameters

Peritoneal dialysis-dependent patient: Slow intravenous infusion at the following schedule: Two infusions of 300 mg each over $1^1/_2$ hours 14 days apart followed by a single 400 mg infusion over $2^1/_2$ hours 14 days later (total cumulative dose of 1000 mg in 3 divided doses)

Nondialysis-dependent patient: 200 mg slow injection (over 2-5 minutes) on 5 different occasions within a 14-day period. Total cumulative dose: 1000 mg in 14-day period. **Note:** Dosage has also been administered as two infusions of 500 mg in a maximum of 250 mL 0.9% NaCl infused over 3.5-4 hours on day 1 and day 14 (limited experience)

Elderly: Insufficient data to identify differences between elderly and other adults; use caution

Administration Not for rapid (bolus) I.V. injection; can be administered through dialysis line. Do not mix with other medications or parenteral nutrient solutions.

Slow I.V. injection: 1 mL (20 mg iron) of undiluted solution per minute (100 mg over 2-5 minutes)

Infusion: Dilute 1 vial (100 mg/5 mL) in maximum of 100 mL 0.9% NaCl; infuse over at least 15 minutes; 300 mg/250 mL should be infused over at least $1^1/_2$ hours; 400 mg/250 mL should be infused over at least $2^1/_2$ hours; 500 mg/250 mL should be infused over at least $3^1/_2$ hours.

Monitoring Parameters Hematocrit, hemoglobin, serum ferritin, transferrin, percent transferrin saturation, TIBC; takes about 4 weeks of treatment to see increased serum iron and ferritin, and decreased TIBC. Serum iron concentrations should be drawn 48 hours after last dose.

Dosage Forms Excipient information presented when available (limited, particularly for generics); consult specific product labeling.

Injection, solution [preservative free]: 20 mg of elemental iron/mL (5 mL)

References

al-Momen AK, al-Meshari A, al-Nuaim L, et al "Intravenous Iron Sucrose Complex in the Treatment of Iron Deficiency Anemia During Pregnancy," *Eur J Obstet Gynecol Reprod Biol*, 1996, 69(2):121-4.

Aronoff GR, Bennett WM, Blumenthal S, et al, "Iron Sucrose in Hemodialysis Patients: Safety of Replacement and Maintenance Regimens," *Kidney Int*, 2004, 66(3):1193-8.

Goodnough LT, "The Use of Erythropoietin to Increase Red Cell Mass," *Can J Anaesth*, 2003, 50(6 Suppl):10-8.

Goodnough LT, Skikne B, and Brugnara C, "Erythropoietin, Iron, and Erythropoiesis," *Blood*, 2000, 96(3):823-33.

"K/DOQI Guidelines for Anemia of Chronic Kidney Disease: NKF K/DOQI Guidelines 2000. Kidney Disease Outcome Quality Initiative." Available at http://www.kidney.org/professionals/kdoqi/guidelines_updates/doqiupan_iii.html. Last accessed November 7, 2005.

♦ **Isonipecaine Hydrochloride** *see* Meperidine *on page 715*

♦ **Isophosphamide** *see* Ifosfamide *on page 579*

♦ **Isopto® Carpine** *see* Pilocarpine *on page 899*

Itraconazole *(i tra KOE na zole)*

Medication Safety Issues

Sound-alike/look-alike issues:

Sporanox® may be confused with Suprax®

U.S. Brand Names Sporanox®
Generic Available Yes: Capsule
Canadian Brand Names Sporanox®
Pharmacologic Category Antifungal Agent, Oral
Use Treatment of susceptible fungal infections in immunocompromised and immunocompetent patients including blastomycosis and histoplasmosis; indicated for aspergillosis, and onychomycosis of the toenail; treatment of onychomycosis of the fingernail without concomitant toenail infection via a pulse-type dosing regimen; has activity against *Aspergillus*, *Candida*, *Coccidioides*, *Cryptococcus*, *Sporothrix*, tinea unguium

Oral: Useful in superficial mycoses including dermatophytoses (eg, tinea capitis), pityriasis versicolor, sebopsoriasis, vaginal and chronic mucocutaneous candidiases; systemic mycoses including candidiasis, meningeal and disseminated cryptococcal infections, paracoccidioidomycosis, coccidioidomycoses; miscellaneous mycoses such as sporotrichosis, chromomycosis, leishmaniasis, fungal keratitis, alternariosis, zygomycosis
Oral solution: Treatment of oral and esophageal candidiasis
Intravenous solution: Indicated in the treatment of blastomycosis, histoplasmosis (nonmeningeal), and aspergillosis (in patients intolerant or refractory to amphotericin B therapy); empiric therapy of febrile neutropenic fever

Pregnancy Risk Factor C
Lactation Enters breast milk/not recommended
Labeled Contraindications Hypersensitivity to itraconazole, any component of the formulation, or to other azoles; concurrent administration with cisapride, dofetilide, ergot derivatives, levomethadyl, lovastatin, midazolam, pimozide, quinidine, simvastatin, or triazolam; treatment of onychomycosis in patients with evidence of left ventricular dysfunction, CHF, or a history of CHF

Warnings/Precautions Discontinue if signs or symptoms of CHF or neuropathy occur during treatment. **[U.S. Boxed Warning]: Rare cases of serious cardiovascular adverse events (including death), ventricular tachycardia, and torsade de pointes have been observed due to increased cisapride, pimozide, quinidine, dofetilide or levomethadyl concentrations induced by itraconazole; concurrent use contraindicated. Use with caution in patients with left ventricular dysfunction or a history of CHF; not recommended for treatment of onychomycosis in these patients.** Not recommended for use in patients with active liver disease, elevated liver enzymes, or prior hepatotoxic reactions to other drugs. Itraconazole has been associated with rare cases of serious hepatotoxicity (including fatal cases and cases within the first week of treatment); treatment should be discontinued in patients who develop clinical symptoms of liver dysfunction or abnormal liver function tests during itraconazole therapy except in cases where expected benefit exceeds risk. Large differences in itraconazole pharmacokinetic parameters have been observed in cystic fibrosis patients receiving the solution; if a patient with cystic fibrosis does not respond to therapy, alternate therapies should be considered. Due to differences in bioavailability, oral capsules and oral solution **cannot be used interchangeably.** Intravenous formulation should be used with caution in renal impairment; consider conversion to oral therapy if renal dysfunction/toxicity is noted. Initiation of treatment with oral solution is not recommended in patients at immediate risk for systemic candidiasis (eg, patients with severe neutropenia).

Adverse Reactions Listed incidences are for higher doses appropriate for systemic fungal infection.

>10%: Gastrointestinal: Nausea (11%)
(Continued)

Itraconazole *(Continued)*

1% to 10%:

Cardiovascular: Edema (4%), hypertension (3%)

Central nervous system: Headache (4%), fatigue (2% to 3%), malaise (1%), fever (3%), dizziness (2%)

Dermatologic: Rash (9%), pruritus (3%)

Endocrine & metabolic: Decreased libido (1%), hypertriglyceridemia, hypokalemia (2%)

Gastrointestinal: Abdominal pain (2%), anorexia (1%), vomiting (5%), diarrhea (3%)

Hepatic: Abnormal LFTs (3%), hepatitis

Renal: Albuminuria (1%)

<1%: Adrenal suppression, constipation, gastritis, gynecomastia, impotence, somnolence, tinnitus

Postmarketing and/or case reports: Allergic reactions (urticaria, angioedema); alopecia, anaphylactoid reactions, anaphylaxis, arrhythmia, CHF, hepatic failure, menstrual disorders, neutropenia, peripheral neuropathy, photosensitivity, pulmonary edema, Stevens-Johnson syndrome

Overdosage/Toxicology Overdoses are well tolerated. Treatment is supportive. Dialysis is not effective.

Drug Interactions

Cytochrome P450 Effect: Substrate of CYP3A4 (major); **Inhibits** CYP3A4 (strong)

Increased Effect/Toxicity: Itraconazole is a strong inhibitor of CYP3A4, and is contraindicated with cisapride, dofetilide, ergot derivatives, lovastatin, midazolam, pimozide, quinidine, simvastatin, and triazolam. Itraconazole may also increase the levels of alfentanil, benzodiazepines (alprazolam, diazepam, and others), buspirone, busulfan, calcium channel blockers (felodipine, nifedipine, verapamil), carbamazepine, corticosteroids, cyclosporine, digoxin, docetaxel, eletriptan, HMG-CoA reductase inhibitors (except fluvastatin, pravastatin), indinavir, oral hypoglycemics (sulfonylureas), phenytoin, rifabutin, ritonavir, saquinavir, sirolimus, tacrolimus, vincristine, vinblastine, warfarin, and zolpidem. Other medications metabolized by CYP3A4 should be used with caution. Serum concentrations of itraconazole may be increased by strong CYP3A4 inhibitors. Serum concentrations of PDE-5 inhibitors (sildenafil, tadalafil, and vardenafil) are increased by itraconazole; specific dosage reductions/limitations are recommended.

Decreased Effect: Absorption of itraconazole requires gastric acidity; therefore, antacids, H_2 antagonists (cimetidine, famotidine, nizatidine, and ranitidine), proton pump inhibitors (omeprazole, lansoprazole, rabeprazole), and sucralfate may significantly reduce bioavailability resulting in treatment failures and should not be administered concomitantly. Antacids may decrease serum concentration of itraconazole; administer antacids 1 hour before or 2 hours after itraconazole capsules. Serum levels of itraconazole may be decreased by didanosine, isoniazid, and nevirapine. The levels/effects of itraconazole may be reduced by aminoglutethimide, carbamazepine, nafcillin, phenobarbital, phenytoin, rifamycins, and other CYP3A4 inducers. Oral contraceptive efficacy may be reduced (limited data).

Ethanol/Nutrition/Herb Interactions

Food:

Capsules: Enhanced by food and possibly by gastric acidity. Cola drinks have been shown to increase the absorption of the capsules in patients with achlorhydria or those taking H_2-receptor antagonists or other gastric acid suppressors. Avoid grapefruit juice.

Solution: Decreased by food, time to peak concentration prolonged by food.

Herb/Nutraceutical: St John's wort may decrease itraconazole levels.

Storage/Stability

Capsule: Store at room temperature, 15°C to 25°C (59°F to 77°F). Protect from light and moisture.

Oral solution: Store at ≤25°C (77°F); do not freeze.

Solution for injection: Store at ≤25°C (77°F); do not freeze. Protect from light. Stable for 48 hours at room temperature or under refrigeration.

Reconstitution Dilute solution for injection with 0.9% sodium chloride. A precise mixing ratio is required to maintain stability (3.33:1) and avoid precipitate formation. Add 25 mL (1 ampul) to 50 mL 0.9% sodium chloride. Mix and withdraw 15 mL of solution before infusing.

Compatibility Stable in NS.

Mechanism of Action Interferes with cytochrome P450 activity, decreasing ergosterol synthesis (principal sterol in fungal cell membrane) and inhibiting cell membrane formation

Pharmacodynamics/Kinetics

Absorption: Requires gastric acidity; capsule better absorbed with food, solution better absorbed on empty stomach

Distribution: V_d (average): 796 ± 185 L or 10 L/kg; highly lipophilic and tissue concentrations are higher than plasma concentrations. The highest concentrations are: adipose, omentum, endometrium, cervical and vaginal mucus, and skin/nails. Aqueous fluids (eg, CSF and urine) contain negligible amounts.

Protein binding, plasma: 99.9%; metabolite hydroxy-itraconazole: 99.5%

Metabolism: Extensively hepatic via CYP3A4 into >30 metabolites including hydroxy-itraconazole (major metabolite); appears to have *in vitro* antifungal activity. Main metabolic pathway is oxidation; may undergo saturation metabolism with multiple dosing

Bioavailability: Variable, ~55% (oral solution) in 1 small study; **Note:** Oral solution has a higher degree of bioavailability (149% ± 68%) relative to oral capsules; should not be interchanged

Half-life elimination: Oral: After single 200 mg dose: 21 ± 5 hours; 64 hours at steady-state; I.V.: steady-state: 35 hours; steady-state concentrations are achieved in 13 days with multiple administration of itraconazole 100-400 mg/day.

Excretion: Feces (~3% to 18%); urine (~0.03% as parent drug, 40% as metabolites)

Dosage

Usual dosage ranges:

Children: Efficacy and safety have not been established; a small number of patients 3-16 years of age have been treated with 100 mg/day for systemic fungal infections with no serious adverse effects reported. A dose of 5 mg/kg once daily was used in a pharmacokinetic study using the oral solution in patients 6 months to 12 years; duration of study was 2 weeks.

Adults: Oral, I.V.: 100-400 mg/day; doses >200 mg/day are given in 2 divided doses; length of therapy varies from 1 day to >6 months depending on the condition and mycological response

(Continued)

Itraconazole *(Continued)*

Indication-specific dosing:

Adults:

Aspergillosis:
Oral: 200-400 mg/day

I.V.: 200 mg twice daily for 4 doses, followed by 200 mg daily

Blastomycosis/histoplasmosis:
Oral: 200 mg once daily, if no obvious improvement or there is evidence of progressive fungal disease, increase the dose in 100 mg increments to a maximum of 400 mg/day; doses >200 mg/day are given in 2 divided doses; length of therapy varies from 1 day to >6 months depending on the condition and mycological response

I.V.: 200 mg twice daily for 4 doses, followed by 200 mg/day

Brain abscess: Cerebral phaeohyphomycosis (dematiaceous): Oral:
200 mg twice daily for at least 6 months with amphotericin

Candidiasis:
Oropharyngeal: Oral solution: 200 mg once daily for 1-2 weeks; in patients unresponsive or refractory to fluconazole: 100 mg twice daily (clinical response expected in 1-2 weeks)

Esophageal: Oral solution: 100-200 mg once daily for a minimum of 3 weeks; continue dosing for 2 weeks after resolution of symptoms

Coccidioides: Oral: 200 mg twice daily

Infections, life-threatening:
Oral: 200 mg 3 times/day (600 mg/day) should be given for the first 3 days of therapy

I.V.: 200 mg twice daily for 4 doses, followed by 200 mg/day

Meningitis:
Coccidioides: Oral: 400-800 mg/day

Cryptococcal: HIV positive (unlabeled use): Induction: Oral: 400 mg/day for 10-12 weeks; maintenance: 200 mg twice daily lifelong

Onychomycosis: Oral: 200 mg once daily for 12 consecutive weeks

Pneumonia:
Coccidioides: Mild to moderate: Oral, I.V.: 200 mg twice daily

Cryptococcal: Mild to moderate (unlabeled use): 200-400 mg/day for 6-12 months (lifelong for HIV positive)

Protothecal infection: 200 mg once daily for 2 months

Sporotrichosis: Oral:
Lymphocutaneous: 100-200 mg/day for 3-6 months

Osteoarticular and pulmonary: 200 mg twice daily for 1-2 years (may use amphotericin B initially for stabilization)

Dosing adjustment in renal impairment: Not necessary; itraconazole injection is not recommended in patients with Cl_{cr} <30 mL/minute; hydroxy-propyl-β-cyclodextrin (the excipient) is eliminated primarily by the kidneys.

Hemodialysis: Not dialyzable

Dosing adjustment in hepatic impairment: May be necessary, but specific guidelines are not available. Risk-to-benefit evaluation should be undertaken in patients who develop liver function abnormalities during treatment.

Administration

Oral: Doses >200 mg/day are given in 2 divided doses; do not administer with antacids. Capsule absorption is best if taken with food, therefore, it is best to administer itraconazole after meals; solution should be taken on an empty stomach. When treating oropharyngeal and esophageal candidiasis, solution should be swished vigorously in mouth, then swallowed.

I.V.: Infuse 60 mL of the dilute solution (3.33 mg/mL = 200 mg itraconazole, pH ~4.8) over 60 minutes; flush with 15-20 mL of 0.9% sodium chloride over 30 seconds to 15 minutes

Monitoring Parameters Liver function in patients with pre-existing hepatic dysfunction, and in all patients being treated for longer than 1 month

Dietary Considerations

Capsule: Administer with food.

Solution: Take without food, if possible.

Patient Information Take capsule with food; take solution on an empty stomach; stop therapy and report any signs and symptoms that may suggest liver dysfunction immediately so that the appropriate laboratory testing can be done; signs and symptoms may include unusual fatigue, anorexia, nausea and/or vomiting, jaundice, dark urine, or pale stool

Special Geriatric Considerations No specific data for the elderly.

Additional Information Due to potential toxicity, the manufacturer recommends confirmation of diagnosis testing of nail specimens prior to treatment of onychomycosis.

Dosage Forms Excipient information presented when available (limited, particularly for generics); consult specific product labeling. [DSC] = Discontinued product

Capsule: 100 mg

Sporanox®: 100 mg

Injection, solution:

Sporanox®: 10 mg/mL (25 mL) [packaged in a kit containing sodium chloride 0.9% (50 mL); filtered infusion set (1)] [DSC]

Solution, oral:

Sporanox®: 100 mg/10 mL (150 mL) [cherry flavor]

References

"1997 USPHS/IDSA Guidelines for the Prevention of Opportunistic Infections in Persons Infected With Human Immunodeficiency Virus. USPHS/IDSA Prevention of Opportunistic Infections Working Group," *MMWR Recomm Rep*, 1997, 46(RR-12):1-46.

Ahmad SR, Singer SJ, and Leissa BG, "Congestive Heart Failure Associated With Itraconazole," *Lancet*, 2001, 357(9270):1766-7.

Amichai B and Grunwald MH, "Adverse Drug Reactions of the New Oral Antifungal Agents - Terbinafine, Fluconazole, and Itraconazole," *Int J Dermatol*, 1998, 37(6):410-5.

Cleary JD, Taylor JW, and Chapman SW, "Itraconazole in Antifungal Therapy," *Ann Pharmacother*, 1992, 26(4):502-9.

Cowie F, Meller ST, Cushing P, et al, "Chemoprophylaxis for Pulmonary Aspergillosis During Intensive Chemotherapy," *Arch Dis Child*, 1994, 70(2):136-8.

De Backer M, De Vroey C, Lesaffre E, et al, "Twelve Weeks of Continuous Oral Therapy for Toenail Onychomycosis Caused by Dermatophytes: A Double-Blind Comparative Trial of Terbinafine 250 mg/day Versus Itraconazole 200 mg/day," *J Am Acad Dermatol*, 1998, 38(5 Pt 3):S57-63.

Grant SM and Clissold SP, "Itraconazole. A Review of Its Pharmacodynamic and Pharmacokinetic Properties, and Therapeutic Use in Superficial and Systemic Mycoses," *Drugs*, 1989, 37(3):310-44.

Haria M, Bryson HM, and Goa KL, "Itraconazole: A Reappraisal of Its Pharmacological Properties and Therapeutic Use in the Management of Superficial Fungal Infections," *Drugs*, 1996, 51(4):585-620.

Heymann WR and Manders SM, "Itraconazole-Induced Acute Generalized Exanthemic Pustulosis," *J Am Acad Dermatol*, 1995, 33(1):130-1.

Jennings TS and Hardin TC, "Treatment of Aspergillosis With Itraconazole," *Ann Pharmacother*, 1993, 27(10):1206-11.

Kauffman CA and Carver PL, "Antifungal Agents in the 1990s. Current Status and Future Developments," *Drugs*, 1997, 53(4):539-49.

Kintzel PE, Rollins CJ, Yee WJ, et al, "Low Itraconazole Serum Concentrations Following Administration of Itraconazole Suspension to Critically Ill Allogenic Bone Marrow Transplant Recipients," *Ann Pharmacother*, 1995, 29(2):140-3.

Lyman CA and Walsh TJ, "Systemically Administered Antifungal Agents. A Review of Their Clinical Pharmacology and Therapeutic Applications," *Drugs*, 1992, 44(1):9-35.

(Continued)

Itraconazole *(Continued)*

Mouy R, Veber F, Blanche S, et al, "Long-Term Itraconazole Prophylaxis Against *Aspergillus* Infections in Thirty-Two Patients With Chronic Granulomatous Disease," *J Pediatr*, 1994, 125(6 Pt 1):998-1003.

Neuvonen PJ and Suhonen R, "Itraconazole Interacts With Felodipine," *J Am Acad Dermatol*, 1995, 33(1):134-5.

Terrell CL, "Antifungal Agents. Part II. The Azoles," *Mayo Clin Proc*, 1999, 74(1):78-100.

Tobon AM, Franco L, Espinal D, et al, "Disseminated Histoplasmosis in Children: The Role of Itraconazole Therapy," *Pediatr Infect Dis J*, 1996; 15:1002-8.

Trepanier EF and Amsden GW, "Current Issues in Onchomycosis," *Ann Pharmacother*, 1998, 32(2):204-14.

Tucker RM, Haq Y, Denning DW, et al, "Adverse Effects Associated With Itraconazole in 189 Patients on Chronic Therapy," *J Antimicrob Chemother*, 1990, 26(4):561-6.

Varhe A, Olkkola KT, and Neuvonen PJ, "Oral Triazolam is Potentially Hazardous to Patients Receiving Systemic Antimycotics Ketoconazole or Itraconazole," *Clin Pharmacol Ther*, 1994, 56(6 Pt 1):601-7.

Wheat J, Hafner R, Korzun AH, et al, "Itraconazole Treatment of Disseminated Histoplasmosis in Patients With the Acquired Immunodeficiency Syndrome," *Am J Med*, 1995, 98(4):336-42.

♦ **IVIG** *see* Immune Globulin (Intravenous) *on page 597*

♦ **IvySoothe® [OTC]** *see* Hydrocortisone *on page 545*

Ixabepilone *(ix ab EP i lone)*

Medication Safety Issues

High alert medication: The Institute for Safe Medication Practices (ISMP) includes this medication among its list of the classes of drugs which have a heightened risk of causing significant patient harm when used in error.

Related Information

Common Toxicity Criteria *on page 1353*
Management of Nausea and Vomiting *on page 1319*
Safe Handling of Hazardous Drugs *on page 1382*

U.S. Brand Names Ixempra™

Index Terms BMS-247550; NSC-710428

Generic Available No

Pharmacologic Category Antineoplastic Agent, Antimicrotubular; Antineoplastic Agent, Epothilone B Analog

Use Treatment of metastatic or locally-advanced breast cancer (refractory or resistant)

Pregnancy Risk Factor D

Lactation Excretion in breast milk unknown/not recommended

Labeled Contraindications History of severe hypersensitivity to Cremophor® EL or its derivatives (eg, polyoxyethylated castor oil); neutrophil count <1500/mm^3 or platelet count <100,000mm^3; combination therapy with ixabepilone and capecitabine in patients with AST or ALT >2.5 times ULN or bilirubin >1 times ULN

Warnings/Precautions Hazardous agent – use appropriate precautions for handling and disposal. **[U.S. Boxed Warning]: Combination therapy with capecitabine is contraindicated in patients with AST or ALT >2.5 times ULN or bilirubin >1 times ULN;** the risk of toxicity and neutropenia-related death is increased. Use (as monotherapy) is not recommended if AST or ALT >10 times ULN or bilirubin >3 times ULN; use caution in patients with AST or ALT >5 times ULN. Toxicities and serious adverse reactions are increased (in mono- and combination therapy) with hepatic dysfunction; dosage reductions are necessary. Diluent contains Cremophor® EL, which is associated with hypersensitivity reactions; use is contraindicated in patients with a history of severe hypersensitivity to Cremophor® EL. Medications for the treatment of reaction should be available for immediate use; reactions may also be managed with a reduction of infusion rate. Premedicate with an

H_1- and H_2-antagonist 1 hour prior to infusion; patients who experience hypersensitivity (eg, bronchospasm, dyspnea, flushing, rash) should also be premedicated with a corticosteroid for all subsequent cycles if treatment is continued.

Dose-dependent myelosuppression, particularly neutropenia, may occur with mono- or combination therapy. Neutropenic fever and infection have been reported with use. The risk for neutropenia is increased with hepatic dysfunction, especially when used in combination with capecitabine. Severe neutropenia and/or thrombocytopenia may require dosage adjustment and/or treatment delay. Peripheral (sensory and motor) neuropathy occurs commonly; may require dose reductions, treatment delays or discontinuation. Usually occurs during the first 3 cycles. Use with caution in patients with pre-existing neuropathy. Patients with diabetes may have an increased risk for severe peripheral neuropathy. Use with caution in patients with cardiovascular disease; the incidence of MI, ventricular dysfunction, and supraventricular arrhythmias is higher when ixabepilone is used in combination with capecitabine (as compared to capecitabine alone). Consider discontinuing ixabepilone in patients who develop cardiac ischemia or impaired cardiac function.

Due to the ethanol content in the diluent, may cause cognitive impairment; patients must be cautioned about performing tasks which require mental alertness (eg, operating machinery or driving). Toxicities or serious adverse events with combination therapy may be increased in the elderly. Safety and efficacy have not been established in children.

Adverse Reactions

Percentages reported with monotherapy:

>10%:

Central nervous system: Headache (11%)

Dermatologic: Alopecia (48%)

Gastrointestinal: Nausea (42%), vomiting (29%), mucositis/stomatitis (29%), diarrhea (22%), anorexia (19%), constipation (16%), abdominal pain (13%)

Hematologic: Leukopenia (36%; grade 4: 13%), neutropenia (31%; grade 4: 23%)

Neuromuscular & skeletal: Peripheral neuropathy (~75%; grades 3/4: 14%; median onset: cycle 4), sensory neuropathy (62%; grades 3/4: 14%), weakness (56%), myalgia/arthralgia (49%), musculoskeletal pain (20%)

1% to 10%:

Cardiovascular: Edema (9%), hot flush (6%), chest pain (5%)

Central nervous system: Fever (8%), pain (8%), dizziness (7%), insomnia (5%)

Dermatologic: Nail disorder (9%), rash (9%), palmar-plantar erythrodysesthesia/hand-and-foot syndrome (8%), pruritus (6%), skin exfoliation (2%), hyperpigmentation (2%)

Endocrine & metabolic: Dehydration (2%)

Gastrointestinal: Gastroesophageal reflux disease (6%), taste perversion (6%), weight loss (6%)

Hematologic: Anemia (6%; grade 4: 2%), neutropenic fever (3%; grade 3: 3%), thrombocytopenia (5%; grade 4: 2%)

Neuromuscular & skeletal: Motor neuropathy (10%; grade 3: 1%)

Ocular: Lacrimation increased (4%)

Respiratory: Dyspnea (9%), upper respiratory tract infection (6%), cough (2%)

Miscellaneous: Hypersensitivity (5%; grade 3: 1%), infection (5%)

(Continued)

Ixabepilone *(Continued)*

Mono- and combination therapy: <1%, postmarketing, and/or case reports (limited to important or life-threatening): Alkaline phosphatase increased, angina, atrial flutter, autonomic neuropathy, cardiomyopathy, cerebral hemorrhage, coagulopathy, colitis, embolism, dysphagia, enterocolitis, erythema multiforme, gastrointestinal hemorrhage, gastroparesis, GGT increased, hemorrhage, hepatic failure (acute), hypokalemia, hyponatremia, hypotension, hypovolemia, hypovolemic shock, hypoxia, ileus, interstitial pneumonia, jaundice, left ventricular dysfunction, metabolic acidosis, MI, nephrolithiasis, neutropenic infection, orthostatic hypotension, pneumonia, pneumonitis, pulmonary edema (acute), renal failure, respiratory failure, sepsis, septic shock, supraventricular arrhythmia, syncope, thrombosis, transaminases increased, trismus, urinary tract infection, vasculitis

Overdosage/Toxicology Myalgia and fatigue were reported following overdose of 100 mg/m^2. Treatment is symptom-directed and supportive.

Drug Interactions

Cytochrome P450 Effect: Substrate of CYP3A4 (major)

Increased Effect/Toxicity: CYP3A4 inhibitors may increase the levels/effects of ixabepilone (example inhibitors include azole antifungals, clarithromycin, diclofenac, doxycycline, erythromycin, imatinib, isoniazid, nefazodone, nicardipine, propofol, protease inhibitors, quinidine, telithromycin, and verapamil).

Decreased Effect: CYP3A4 inducers may decrease the levels/effects of ixabepilone (example inducers include aminoglutethimide, carbamazepine, nafcillin, nevirapine, phenobarbital, phenytoin, and rifamycins).

Ethanol/Nutrition/Herb Interactions Herb/Nutraceutical: Avoid St John's wort (may decrease ixabepilone levels).

Storage/Stability Store intact vials under refrigeration at 2°C to 8°C (36°F to 46°F); protect from light. Reconstituted solution (in the vial) is stable for 1 hour at room temperature; infusion solution diluted in lactated Ringer's is stable for 6 hours at room temperature.

Reconstitution Allow to reach room temperature for ~30 minutes prior to reconstitution. Diluent vial may contain a white precipitate which should dissolve upon reaching room temperature. **Reconstitute only with the provided diluent.** Dilute the 15 mg vial with 8 mL and the 45 mg vial with 23.5 mL (using provided diluent) to a concentration of 2 mg/mL (contains overfill). Gently swirl and invert vial until dissolved completely. Prior to administration, further dilute in lactated Ringer's (~250 mL) using a non-DEHP container (eg, glass, polypropylene or polyolefin), to a final concentration of 0.2-0.6 mg/mL.

Compatibility Stable in lactated Ringer's injection.

Mechanism of Action Epothilone B analog; binds to the beta-tubulin subunit of the microtubule, stabilizing microtubular function, thus arresting the cell cycle at the G2/M phase) and inducing apoptosis

Pharmacodynamics/Kinetics

Distribution: >1000 L/m^2

Protein binding: 67% to 77%

Metabolism: Extensively hepatic, via CYP3A4; >30 metabolites (inactive) formed

Half-life elimination: ~52 hours

Time to peak, plasma: At the end of infusion (3 hours)

Excretion: Feces (65%; 2% as unchanged drug); urine (21%; 6% as unchanged drug)

Dosage Note: Premedicate with an oral H_1-antagonist (eg, diphenhydramine 50 mg) and an oral H_2-antagonist (eg, ranitidine 150-300 mg) 1 hour prior to infusion. Patients with a history of hypersensitivity should also be premedicated with corticosteroids (orally 1 hour before or I.V. 30 minutes before infusion). Body surface area (BSA) is capped at a maximum of 2.2 m^2.
I.V.: Adults: 40 mg/m^2 every 3 weeks (maximum dose: 88 mg)

Dosage adjustment with concurrent strong CYP3A4 inhibitor: If concurrent use can not be avoided, reduce ixabepilone dose to 20 mg/m^2. When a strong CYP3A4 inhibitor is discontinued, allow ~1 week to elapse prior to adjusting ixabepilone dose upward. (See Drug Interactions for examples of CYP3A4 inhibitors.)

Ixabepilone dosage adjustments for toxicity for monotherapy or combination therapy:
Hematologic:
Neutrophils <500/mm^3 for ≥7 days: Reduce dose by 20%
Neutropenic fever: Reduce dose by 20%
Platelets <25,000/mm^3 (or <50,000/mm^3 with bleeding): Reduce dose by 20%

Nonhematologic:
Neuropathy:
Grade 2 (moderate) for ≥7 days: Reduce dose by 20%
Grade 3 (severe) for <7days: Reduce dose by 20%
Grade 3 (severe or disabling) for ≥7 days: Discontinue treatment
Grade 3 toxicity (severe; other than neuropathy): Reduce dose by 20%
Grade 3 arthralgia/myalgia or fatigue (transient): Continue at current dose
Grade 3 hand-foot syndrome: Continue at current dose
Grade 4 toxicity (disabling): Discontinue treatment

Note: Adjust dosage at the start of a cycle are based on toxicities (hematologic and nonhematologic) from the previous cycle; delay new cycles until neutrophils have recovered to >1500/mm^3, platelets have recovered to >100,000/mm^3 and nonhematologic toxicities have resolved to at least grade 1. If toxicities persist despite initial dose reduction, reduce dose an additional 20%.

Capecitabine dosage adjustments for toxicity in combination therapy with ixabepilone:
Hematologic:
Neutrophils <500/mm^3 for ≥7 days or neutropenic fever: Hold for concurrent diarrhea or stomatitis until neutrophils recover to >1000/mm3, then continue at same dose
Platelets <25,000/mm^3 (or <50,000/mm^3 with bleeding): Hold for concurrent diarrhea or stomatitis until platelets recover to >50,000/mm^3, then continue at same dose

Nonhematologic: Refer to Capecitabine monograph.

Dosage adjustment in renal impairment: Pharmacokinetics (monotherapy) are not affected in patients with mild-to-moderate renal insufficiency (Cl_{cr} >30 mL/minute); monotherapy has not been studied in patients with serum creatinine >1.5 times ULN. Combination therapy with capecitabine has not been studied in patients with Cl_{cr} <50 mL/minute.

Dosage adjustment in hepatic impairment:
Ixabepilone monotherapy (initial cycle; adjust doses for subsequent cycles based on toxicity):
AST and ALT ≤2.5 times ULN and bilirubin ≤1 times ULN: No adjustment necessary

(Continued)

Ixabepilone *(Continued)*

AST or ALT ≤10 times ULN and bilirubin ≤1.5 times ULN: Reduce dose to 32 mg/m^2

AST and ALT ≤10 times ULN and bilirubin >1.5 - ≤3 times ULN: Reduce dose to 20-30 mg/m^2

AST or ALT >10 times ULN or bilirubin >3 times ULN: Use is not recommended

Combination therapy of ixabepilone with capecitabine:

AST and ALT ≤2.5 times ULN and bilirubin ≤1 times ULN: No adjustment necessary

AST or ALT >2.5 times ULN or bilirubin >1 times ULN: Use is contraindicated

Combination Regimens

Breast cancer: Ixabepilone-Capecitabine *on page 1242*

Administration Infuse over 3 hours. Use non-DEHP administration set (eg, polyethylene); filter with a 0.2-1.2 micron inline filter.

Monitoring Parameters CBC with differential; hepatic function (ALT, AST, bilirubin); monitor for hypersensitivity

Dietary Considerations Avoid grapefruit juice.

Emetic Potential Low (10% to 30%)

Dosage Forms Excipient information presented when available (limited, particularly for generics); consult specific product labeling.

Injection, powder for reconstitution:

Ixempra™: 15 mg, 45 mg [packaged with diluent; diluent contains alcohol and purified polyoxyethylated castor oil (Cremophor® EL)]

References

Dendurali N, Low JA, Lee JJ, et al, "Phase II Trial of Ixabepilone, an Epothilone B Analog, in Patients With Metastatic Breast Cancer Previously Untreated With Taxanes," *J Clin Oncol*, 2007, 25(23):3421-7.

Lee JJ, Low JA, Croarkin E, et al, "Changes in Neurologic Function Tests May Predict Neurotoxicity Caused by Ixabepilone," *J Clin Oncol*, 2006, 24(13):2084-91.

Low JA, Wedam SB, Lee JJ, et al, "Phase II Clinical Trial of Ixabepilone (BMS-247550), an Epothilone B Analog, in Metastatic and Locally Advanced Breast Cancer," *J Clin Oncol*, 2005, 23(12):2726-34.

Mani S, McDid H, Hamilton A, et al, "Phase I and Clinical Pharmacokinetic Study of BMS-247550, a Novel Derivative of Epothilone B,in Solid Tumors," *Clin Cancer Res*, 2004, 10(4):1289-98.

Perez EA, Lerzo G, Pivot X, et al, "Efficacy and Safety of Ixabepilone (BMS-247550), in a Phase II Study of Patients With Advanced Breast Cancer Resistant to an Anthracycline, a Taxane and Capecitabine," *J Clin Oncol*, 2007, 25(23):3407-14.

Roche H, Yelle L, Cognetti F, et al, "Phase II Clinical Trial of Ixabepilone (BMS-247550), an Epothilone B Analog, as First Line Therapy in Patients With Metastatic Breast Cancer Previously Treated With Anthracycline Chemotherapy," *J Clin Oncol*, 2007, 25(23):3415-20.

Takimoto CH, Liu PY, Lenz H, et al, "A Phase I Pharmacokinetic (PK) Study of the Epothilone B Analogue, Ixabepilone (BMS-247550) in Patients (pts) With Advanced Malignancies and Varying Degrees of Hepatic Impairment: A SWOG Early Therapeutics Committee and NCI Organ Dysfunction Working Group Trial," *J Clin Oncol*, 2006, 24(18S):2004 [abstract from 2006 ASCO Annual Meeting Proceedings]

Thomas E, Tabernero J, Fornier M, et al, "Phase II Clinical Trial of Ixabepilone (BMS-247550), an Epothilone B Analog, in Patients With Taxane-Resistant Metastatic Breast Cancer," *J Clin Oncol*, 2007, 25(23):3399-406.

♦ **Ixempra**™ *see* Ixabepilone *on page 644*

♦ **Kadian**® *see* Morphine Sulfate *on page 779*

♦ **Keoxifene Hydrochloride** *see* Raloxifene *on page 940*

♦ **Kepivance**™ *see* Palifermin *on page 868*

♦ **Ketek**® *see* Telithromycin *on page 1007*

Ketoconazole (kee toe KOE na zole)

Medication Safety Issues

Sound-alike/look-alike issues:

Nizoral® may be confused with Nasarel®, Neoral®, Nitrol®

U.S. Brand Names Extina®; Kuric™; Nizoral®; Nizoral® A-D [OTC]; Xolegel™

Generic Available Yes: Cream, shampoo, tablet

Canadian Brand Names Apo-Ketoconazole®; Ketoderm®; Novo-Ketoconazole; Xolegel™

Pharmacologic Category Antifungal Agent, Oral; Antifungal Agent, Topical

Use

Systemic: Treatment of susceptible fungal infections, including candidiasis, oral thrush, blastomycosis, histoplasmosis, paracoccidioidomycosis, coccidioidomycosis, chromomycosis, candiduria, chronic mucocutaneous candidiasis, as well as certain recalcitrant cutaneous dermatophytoses

Topical:

Cream: Treatment of tinea corporis, tinea cruris, tinea versicolor, cutaneous candidiasis, seborrheic dermatitis

Foam, gel: Treatment of seborrheic dermatitis

Shampoo: Treatment of dandruff, seborrheic dermatitis, tinea versicolor

Unlabeled/Investigational Use Tablet: Treatment of prostate cancer (androgen synthesis inhibitor)

Pregnancy Risk Factor C

Lactation Enters breast milk/not recommended

Labeled Contraindications Hypersensitivity to ketoconazole or any component of the formulation; CNS fungal infections (due to poor CNS penetration); coadministration with ergot derivatives or cisapride is contraindicated due to risk of potentially fatal cardiac arrhythmias

Warnings/Precautions [U.S. Boxed Warning]: Ketoconazole has been associated with hepatotoxicity, including some fatalities; use with caution in patients with impaired hepatic function and perform periodic liver function tests. **[U.S. Boxed Warning]: Concomitant use with cisapride is contraindicated due to the occurrence of ventricular arrhythmias.** High doses of ketoconazole may depress adrenocortical function.

Topical: Formulations may contain sulfites. Avoid exposure of gel to open flames during or immediately after application. Foam formulation contains alcohol and propane/butane; do not expose to open flame or smoking during or immediately after application; do not puncture or incinerate container.

Adverse Reactions

Oral:

1% to 10%:

Dermatologic: Pruritus (2%)

Gastrointestinal: Nausea/vomiting (3% to 10%), abdominal pain (1%)

<1%: Bulging fontanelles, chills, depression, diarrhea, dizziness, fever, gynecomastia, headache, hemolytic anemia, hepatotoxicity, impotence, leukopenia, photophobia, somnolence, thrombocytopenia

Topical cream/gel: Allergic reaction, contact dermatitis (possibly related to sulfites or propylene glycol), facial swelling, headache, impetigo, local burning, ocular irritation, paresthesia, pruritus, severe irritation, stinging (~5%)

Topical foam: Application site burning (10%), application site reaction (6%), contact sensitization, dryness, erythema, pruritus, rash

Shampoo: Abnormal hair texture, hair loss increase, irritation (<1%), itching, mild dryness of skin, oiliness/dryness of hair, scalp pustules

(Continued)

Ketoconazole *(Continued)*

Overdosage/Toxicology Oral: Symptoms of overdose include dizziness, headache, nausea, vomiting, diarrhea. Overdoses are well tolerated. Treatment includes supportive measures and gastric decontamination.

Drug Interactions

Cytochrome P450 Effect: Substrate of CYP3A4 (major); **Inhibits** CYP1A2 (strong), 2A6 (moderate), 2B6 (weak), 2C8 (weak), 2C9 (strong), 2C19 (moderate), 2D6 (moderate), 3A4 (strong)

Increased Effect/Toxicity: Due to inhibition of hepatic CYP3A4, ketoconazole use is contraindicated with cisapride, lovastatin, midazolam, simvastatin, and triazolam due to large substantial increases in the toxicity of these agents. Ketoconazole may increase the serum levels/effects of amphetamines, benzodiazepines, beta-blockers, bosentan, buspirone, busulfan, calcium channel blockers, citalopram, dapsone, dexmedetomidine, dextromethorphan, diazepam, digoxin, docetaxel, fluoxetine, fluvoxamine, glimepiride, glipizide, ifosfamide, inhalational anesthetics, lidocaine, losartan, mesoridazine, methsuximide, mexiletine, mirtazapine, montelukast, nateglinide, nefazodone, paclitaxel, paroxetine, phenytoin, propranolol, risperidone, ritonavir, ropinirole, sertraline, sirolimus, tacrolimus, theophylline, thioridazine, tricyclic antidepressants, trifluoperazine, venlafaxine, vincristine, vinblastine, warfarin, zafirlukast, zolpidem, and other substrates of CYP1A2, 2A6, 2C9, 2C19, 2D6, or 3A4. Selected benzodiazepines (midazolam and triazolam), cisapride, ergot alkaloids, selected HMG-CoA reductase inhibitors (lovastatin and simvastatin), and pimozide are generally contraindicated with strong CYP3A4 inhibitors. Mesoridazine and thioridazine are generally contraindicated with strong CYP2D6 inhibitors. When used with strong CYP3A4 inhibitors, dosage adjustment/limits are recommended for sildenafil and other PDE-5 inhibitors; consult individual monographs.

Decreased Effect: Oral: Absorption requires gastric acidity; therefore, antacids, H_2 antagonists (cimetidine, famotidine, nizatidine, and ranitidine), proton pump inhibitors (omeprazole, lansoprazole, rabeprazole), and sucralfate may significantly reduce bioavailability resulting in treatment failures and should not be administered concomitantly. Decreased serum levels with didanosine and isoniazid. The levels/effects of ketoconazole may be decreased by aminoglutethimide, carbamazepine, nafcillin, nevirapine, phenobarbital, phenytoin, rifamycins, or other CYP3A4 inducers. **Should not be administered concomitantly with rifampin.** Oral contraceptive efficacy may be reduced (limited data). Ketoconazole may decrease the levels/effects of CYP2D6 prodrug substrates (eg, codeine, hydrocodone, oxycodone, tramadol).

Ethanol/Nutrition/Herb Interactions

Food: Ketoconazole peak serum levels may be prolonged if taken with food.

Herb/Nutraceutical: St John's wort may decrease ketoconazole levels.

Storage/Stability

Cream: Store at <25°C (<77°F).

Foam: Store at 20°C to 25°C (68°F to 77°F). Do not refrigerate. Do not store in direct sunlight. Contents are flammable.

Gel: Store at 15°C to 30°C (59°F to 86°F).

Shampoo: Store between 2°C to 30°C (35°F to 86°F); protect from freezing. Protect from light.

Tablet: Store at 15°C to 25°C (59°F to 77°F).

Mechanism of Action Alters the permeability of the cell wall by blocking fungal cytochrome P450; inhibits biosynthesis of triglycerides and phospholipids by fungi; inhibits several fungal enzymes that results in a build-up of toxic concentrations of hydrogen peroxide; also inhibits androgen synthesis

Pharmacodynamics/Kinetics

Absorption: Oral: Rapid (~75%); Shampoo: None; Gel: Minimal

Distribution: Well into inflamed joint fluid, saliva, bile, urine, breast milk, sebum, cerumen, feces, tendons, skin and soft tissue, and testes; crosses blood-brain barrier poorly; only negligible amounts reach CSF

Protein binding: 93% to 96%

Metabolism: Partially hepatic via CYP3A4 to inactive compounds

Bioavailability: Decreases as gastric pH increases

Half-life elimination: Biphasic: Initial: 2 hours; Terminal: 8 hours

Time to peak, serum: 1-2 hours

Excretion: Feces (57%); urine (13%)

Dosage

Oral:

Fungal infections:

Children ≥2 years: 3.3-6.6 mg/kg/day as a single dose for 1-2 weeks for candidiasis, for at least 4 weeks in recalcitrant dermatophyte infections, and for up to 6 months for other systemic mycoses

Adults: 200-400 mg/day as a single daily dose for durations as stated above

Prostate cancer (unlabeled use): Adults: 400 mg 3 times/day

Shampoo: Seborrheic dermatitis, tinea versicolor: Children ≥12 years and Adults: Apply twice weekly for 4 weeks with at least 3 days between each shampoo

Topical:

Tinea infections: Adults: Cream: Rub gently into the affected area once daily. Duration of treatment: Tinea corporis, cruris: 2 weeks; tinea pedis: 6 weeks

Seborrheic dermatitis: Children ≥12 years and Adults:

Cream: Rub gently into the affected area twice daily for 4 weeks or until clinical response is noted

Foam: Apply to affected area twice daily for 4 weeks

Gel: Rub gently into the affected area once daily for 2 weeks

Dosing adjustment in hepatic impairment: Dose reductions should be considered in patients with severe liver disease

Hemodialysis: Not dialyzable (0% to 5%)

Combination Regimens

Prostate cancer:

Doxorubicin + Ketoconazole *on page 1195*

Doxorubicin + Ketoconazole/Estramustine + Vinblastine *on page 1195*

Administration

Oral: Administer oral tablets 2 hours prior to antacids to prevent decreased absorption due to the high pH of gastric contents.

Cream, foam, gel, and shampoo are for external use only. Avoid exposure to flame or smoking immediately following application of gel or foam; do not apply directly to hands.

Monitoring Parameters Liver function tests

Dietary Considerations Tablet: May be taken with food or milk to decrease GI adverse effects.

Patient Information Cream is for topical application to the skin only. Avoid contact with the eye. Avoid taking antacids at the same time as ketoconazole. May take with food. May cause drowsiness, impaired judgment or (Continued)

Ketoconazole *(Continued)*

coordination. Report unusual fatigue, anorexia, vomiting, dark urine, or pale stools.

Special Geriatric Considerations No specific recommendations.

Dosage Forms Excipient information presented when available (limited, particularly for generics); consult specific product labeling. [DSC] = Discontinued product

Aerosol, topical [foam]:
  Extina®: 2% (50 g, 100 g)
Cream, topical: 2% (15 g, 30 g, 60 g)
  Kuric™: 2%: (25 g [DSC]; 75 g)
Gel, topical:
  Xolegel™: 2% (15 g) [contains dehydrated alcohol 34%]
Shampoo, topical: 1% (120 mL), 2% (120 mL)
  Nizoral®: 2% (120 mL)
  Nizoral® A-D: 1% (120 mL, 210 mL)
Tablet: 200 mg
  Nizoral®: 200 mg

Extemporaneous Preparations A 20 mg/mL suspension may be made by pulverizing twelve 200 mg ketoconazole tablets to a fine powder; add 40 mL Ora-Plus® in small portions with thorough mixing; incorporate Ora-Sweet® to make a final volume of 120 mL and mix thoroughly; refrigerate (no stability information is available)

Allen LV, "Ketoconazole Oral Suspension," *US Pharm*, 1993, 18(2):98-9, 101.

References

Como JA and Dismukes WE, "Oral Azole Drugs as Systemic Antifungal Therapy," *N Engl J Med*, 1994, 330(4):263-72.

Ginsburg AM, McCracken GH Jr, and Olsen K, "Pharmacology of Ketoconazole Suspension in Infants and Children," *Antimicrob Agents Chemother*, 1983, 23(5):787-9.

Gorman SE, Dela Cruz F, and Paloucek F, "Ketoconazole and Zidovudine Overdose," *Am J Emerg Med*, 1995, 13(1):115-6.

Greenblatt DJ, von Moltke LL, Harmatz JS, et al, "Interaction of Triazolam and Ketoconazole," *Lancet*, 1995, 345(8943):191.

Herrod HG, "Chronic Mucocutaneous Candidiasis in Childhood and Complications of non-*Candida* Infection: A Report of the Pediatric Immunodeficiency Collaborative Study Group," *J Pediatr*, 1990, 116(3):377-82.

Hwang WL, Gau JP, Young JH, et al, "Ketoconazole and High-Dose Methylprednisolone Predisposing to Cyclosporine-Induced Seizures: A Report of Three Cases," *Acta Haematol*, 1992, 88(2-3):139-41.

Janssen PA and Symoens JE, "Hepatic Reactions During Ketoconazole Treatment," *Am J Med*, 1983, 74(1B):80-5.

Lyman CA and Walsh TJ, "Systemically Administered Antifungal Agents. A Review of Their Clinical Pharmacology and Therapeutic Applications," *Drugs*, 1992, 44(1):9-35.

Small EJ, Halabi S, Dawson NA, et al, "Antiandrogen Withdrawal Alone or in Combination With Ketoconazole in Androgen-Independent Prostate Cancer Patients: A Phase III Trial (CALGB 9583)," *J Clin Oncol*, 2004, 22(6):1025-33.

Terrell CL, "Antifungal Agents. Part II. The Azoles," *Mayo Clin Proc*, 1999, 74(1):78-100.

Trachtenberg J and Pont A, "Ketoconazole Therapy for Advanced Prostate Cancer," *Lancet*, 1984, (8400):433-5.

Varhe A, Olkkola KT, and Neuvonen PJ, "Oral Triazolam Is Potentially Hazardous to Patients Receiving Systemic Antimycotics Ketoconazole or Itraconazole," *Clin Pharmacol Ther*, 1994, 56(6 Pt 1):601-7.

Wynn RL, "Erythromycin and Ketoconazole (Nizoral®) Associated With Terfenadine (Seldane®)-Induced Ventricular Arrhythmias," *Gen Dent*, 1993, 41(1):27-9.

♦ **Ketoderm® (Can)** *see* Ketoconazole *on page 649*

♦ **Kidrolase® (Can)** *see* Asparaginase *on page 111*

♦ **Kogenate® (Can)** *see* Antihemophilic Factor (Recombinant) *on page 95*

♦ **Kogenate® FS** *see* Antihemophilic Factor (Recombinant) *on page 95*

- **Konakion (Can)** *see* Phytonadione *on page 895*
- **Koāte®-DVI** *see* Antihemophilic Factor (Human) *on page 92*
- **Kuric™** *see* Ketoconazole *on page 649*
- **Kytril®** *see* Granisetron *on page 522*
- **L 754030** *see* Aprepitant *on page 104*
- **LA 20304a** *see* Gemifloxacin *on page 504*
- **Ladakamycin** *see* Azacitidine *on page 117*
- **L-AmB** *see* Amphotericin B (Liposomal) *on page 80*

Lanreotide (lan REE oh tide)

Medication Safety Issues

Sound-alike/look-alike issues:

Somatuline® may be confused with somatropin, sumatriptan

International issues:

Somatuline® may be confused with Soma® which is a brand name for carisoprodol in the U.S.

U.S. Brand Names Somatuline® Depot

Index Terms Lanreotide Acetate

Canadian Brand Names Somatuline® Autogel®

Pharmacologic Category Somatostatin Analog

Use Long-term treatment of acromegaly in patients who are not candidates for or are unresponsive to surgery and/or radiotherapy

Note: Also approved in Canada for relief of symptoms of acromegaly

Pregnancy Risk Factor C

Lactation

Excretion into breast milk unknown/not recommended

Labeled Contraindications

There are no contraindications listed in the manufacturer's labeling.

Note: Canadian labeling contraindications: Hypersensitivity to lanreotide, somatostatin (or related peptides), or any component of the formulation; complicated, untreated lithiasis of the bile ducts

Warnings/Precautions Inhibition of insulin and glucagon secretion may affect glucose regulation, leading to hyper-/hypoglycemia, especially in patients with diabetes. Monitor serum glucose levels with the initiation of therapy and with dosage changes; dose adjustments in antidiabetic medications may be necessary. May reduce gall bladder motility, leading to cholelithiasis (may be dose- or duration-related); monitor. **Note:** In Canada, ultrasonography is recommended when initiating therapy and periodically thereafter. Slight decreases in thyroid function have been observed during therapy; may require monitoring of thyroid function tests.

Bradycardia, sinus bradycardia and hypertension have been observed with therapy; use with caution in patients with preexisting cardiac disease. Patients without preexisting cardiac disease may experience a decrease in heart rate though not to the level of bradycardia. Concurrent use with cyclosporine may lead to decreased levels of cyclosporine; monitor cyclosporine levels during therapy. Use with caution in patients with renal and hepatic impairment; lower doses are recommended at therapy initiation in patients with moderate-to-severe impairment. The packaging (needle cover) may contain latex. Safety and efficacy have not been established in children. **Note:** In Canada, safety and efficacy have not been established in children <16 years of age.

(Continued)

Lanreotide *(Continued)*

Adverse Reactions

>10%:

Cardiovascular: Bradycardia (5% to 18%)

Gastrointestinal: Diarrhea (26% to 65%; dose related), abdominal pain (7% to 19%; dose related), flatulence (≤14%; dose related), nausea (11%), weight loss (5% to 11%)

Hematologic: Anemia (3% to 14%)

Hepatic: Cholelithiasis/gall bladder sludge (2% to 20%)

Local: Injection site reaction (6% to 22%; induration: 5%; pain: 4%; mass: 2%)

1% to 10%:

Cardiovascular: Hypertension (5%), sinus bradycardia (3%)

Central nervous system: Headache (7%)

Endocrine & metabolic: Hyper-/hypoglycemia/diabetes (7%)

Gastrointestinal: Constipation (8%), vomiting (7%), loose stools (6%)

Neuromuscular & skeletal: Arthralgia (7%)

<1%, postmarketing, and/or case reports: Allergic skin reaction, aortic valve regurgitation, dysautonomia, injection site pruritus, mitral valve regurgitation, steatorrhea

Overdosage/Toxicology A single case of overdose has been reported with a patient receiving lanreotide 30 mg daily for 2 months. No acute signs or symptoms of overdose were reported. The patient experienced an MI 1 week after the last injection. Treatment of a suspected overdose is symptom-directed and supportive.

Drug Interactions

Increased Effect/Toxicity: Lanreotide may increase the effects of bromocriptine, codeine, insulin, and antidiabetic agents.

Decreased Effect: Lanreotide may decrease the levels/effects of cyclosporine.

Ethanol/Nutrition/Herb Interactions Herb/Nutraceutical: Avoid hypoglycemic herbs, including alfalfa, aloe, bilberry, bitter melon, burdock, celery, damiana, fenugreek, garcinia, garlic, ginger, ginseng, gymnema, marshmallow, and stinging nettle (may enhance the hypoglycemic effect of lanreotide).

Storage/Stability Store under refrigeration 2°C to 8°C (36°F to 46°F). Protect from light. Allow to reach room temperature by removing sealed pouch from refrigerator 30 minutes prior to administration; keep in sealed pouch until just prior to administration.

Mechanism of Action Synthetic octapeptide analogue of somatostatin which is a peptide inhibitor of multiple endocrine, neuroendocrine, and exocrine mechanisms. Displays a greater affinity for somatostatin type 2 (SSTR2) and type 5 (SSTR5) receptors found in pituitary gland, pancreas, and growth hormone (GH) secreting neoplasms of pituitary gland and a lesser affinity for somatostatin receptors 1, 3, and 4. Reduces GH secretion and also reduces the levels of insulin-like growth factor 1.

Pharmacodynamics/Kinetics

Distribution: V_{ss}: ~0.2 L/kg

Protein binding: 79% to 83%

Metabolism: Extensively within GI tract after biliary excretion

Bioavailability: 69% to 83%

Half-life, elimination: 23-36 days

Time to peak, plasma: Mean: 7-12 hours

Excretion: Urine (<1% to 5% as unchanged drug); feces (<0.5% as unchanged drug)

Dosage SubQ: **Note: Differences in U.S. and Canadian labeled dosing:**

U.S. labeling: Adults: Acromegaly: 90 mg once every 4 weeks for 3 months; after initial 90 days of therapy, adjust dose based on clinical response of patient, growth hormone (GH) levels, and/or insulin-like growth factor 1 (IGF-1) levels as follows:

GH ≤1 ng/mL, IGF-1 normal, symptoms stable:60 mg once every 4 weeks

GH >1-2.5 ng/mL, IGF-1 normal, symptoms stable: 90 mg once every 4 weeks

GH >2.5 ng/mL, IGF-1 elevated and/or uncontrolled symptoms: 120 mg once every 4 weeks

Canadian labeling: Children ≥16 years and Adults: Acromegaly: 90 mg once every 4 weeks for 3 months; after initial 90 days of therapy, adjust dose based on clinical response of patient, growth hormone (GH) levels, and/or insulin-like growth factor 1 (IGF-1) levels as follows:

GH = 1 ng/mL, IGF-1 normal, symptoms stable: 60 mg once every 4 weeks

GH >1-2.5 ng/mL, IGF-1 normal, symptoms stable: 90 mg once every 4 weeks

GH >2.5 ng/mL, IGF-1 elevated and/or uncontrolled symptoms: 120 mg once every 4 weeks

Dosing adjustment in renal impairment:

U.S. labeling: Moderate-to-severe impairment: Recommended starting dose: 60 mg

Canadian labeling: No adjustment is necessary

Dosing adjustment in hepatic impairment:

U.S. labeling: Moderate-to-severe impairment: Recommended starting dose: 60 mg

Canadian labeling: No adjustment is necessary

Administration Administer by deep subcutaneous injection into superior outer quadrant of buttocks. Do not fold skin. Alternate injection sites.

Monitoring Parameters Serum GH, IGF-1, glucose levels, thyroid function (where clinically indicated); heart rate, gall bladder ultrasonography (prior to initiation and periodically during therapy)

Dosage Forms Excipient information presented when available (limited, particularly for generics); consult specific product labeling. [CAN] = Canadian brand name

Injection, solution, as acetate [preservative free; prefilled syringe]:

Somatuline® Autogel® [CAN]: 60 mg/ 0.3 mL (0.3 mL); 90 mg/ 0.3 mL (0.3 mL); 120 mg/0.5 mL (0.5 mL) [packaged with needle; needle cover contains latex]

Somatuline® Depot®: 60 mg/0.3 mL (0.3 mL); 90 mg/0.3 mL (0.3 mL); 120 mg/0.5 mL (0.5 mL) [packaged with needle; needle cover contains latex]

References

Caron P, Beckers A, Cullen DR, et al, "Efficacy of the New Long-Acting Formulation of Lanreotide (Lanreotide Autogel) in the Management of Acromegaly," *J Clin Endocrinol Metab*, 2002, 87(1):99-104.

Rasmussen E, Eriksson B, Oberg K, et al, "Selective Effects of Somatostatin Analogs on Human Drug-Metabolizing Enzymes," *Clin Pharmacol Ther*, 1998, 64(2):150-9.

Reubi JC, Waser B, Schaer JC, et al, "Somatostatin Receptor sst1-sst5 Expression in Normal and Neoplastic Human Tissues Using Receptor Autoradiography With Subtype-Selective Ligands," *Eur J Nucl Med*, 2001, 28(7):836-46.

♦ **Lanreotide Acetate** *see* Lanreotide *on page 653*

♦ **Lanvis® (Can)** *see* Thioguanine *on page 1030*

Lapatinib (la PA ti nib)

Medication Safety Issues
Sound-alike/look-alike issues:
Lapatinib may be confused with dasatinib, erlotinib, imatinib

High alert medication: The Institute for Safe Medication Practices (ISMP) includes this medication among its list of drugs which have a heightened risk of causing significant patient harm when used in error.

Related Information
Common Toxicity Criteria *on page 1353*
Management of Nausea and Vomiting *on page 1319*

U.S. Brand Names Tykerb®

Index Terms GW572016; Lapatinib Ditosylate; NSC-727989

Generic Available No

Pharmacologic Category Antineoplastic Agent, Tyrosine Kinase Inhibitor; Epidermal Growth Factor Receptor (EGFR) Inhibitor

Use Treatment (in combination with capecitabine) of HER2/neu overexpressing advanced or metastatic breast cancer, in patients who have received prior therapy (with an anthracycline, a taxane, and trastuzumab)

Unlabeled/Investigational Use Treatment of head and neck cancers

Restrictions Lapatinib is available **only** at specialty pharmacies through a restricted-access program, Tykerb® CARES. Information is available at www.tykerbcares.com or 1-866-489-5372.

Pregnancy Risk Factor D

Lactation Excretion in breast milk unknown/not recommended

Labeled Contraindications Hypersensitivity to lapatinib or any component of the formulation

Warnings/Precautions Hazardous agent - use appropriate precautions for handling and disposal.

Decreases in left ventricular ejection fraction (LVEF) have been reported; baseline and periodic LVEF evaluations are recommended; interrupt therapy or decrease dose with with decreased LVEF ≥ grade 2 or LVEF < LLN. QT_c prolongation has been observed; use caution in patients with a history of QT_c prolongation or with medications known to prolong the QT interval; a baseline and periodic 12-lead ECG should be considered; correct electrolyte (potassium, calcium and magnesium) abnormalities prior to and during treatment. Use caution in patients with a history of or predisposed (prior treatment with anthracyclines, chest wall irradiation) to left ventricular dysfunction. Interstitial lung disease (ILD) and pneumonitis have been reported (with lapatinib monotherapy and with combination chemotherapy); discontinue therapy for grade 3 (or higher) pulmonary symptoms indicative of ILD or pneumonitis (eg, dyspnea, dry cough).

Avoid concurrent use with strong CYP3A4 inhibitors or inducers; if concurrent use is necessary, consider lapatinib dosage adjustments. Use caution in patients with hepatic dysfunction. Dose reductions should be considered in patients with severe (Child-Pugh class C) hepatic impairment. May cause diarrhea (may be severe); manage with antidiarrheal agents; severe diarrhea may require hydration, electrolytes, and or interruption of therapy. Safety and efficacy have not been established in children.

Adverse Reactions Percentages reported for combination chemotherapy.
>10%:
Central nervous system: Fatigue (10% to 18%)
Dermatologic: Palmar-plantar erythrodysesthesia (hand-and-foot syndrome) (53%; grade 3: 12%), rash (28%)

Gastrointestinal: Diarrhea (65%; grade 3: 13%; grade 4: 1%), nausea (44%), vomiting (26%), abdominal pain (15%), mucosal inflammation (15%), stomatitis (14%), dyspepsia (11%)

Hematologic: Anemia (56%; grade 3: <1%), neutropenia (22%; grade 3: 3%; grade 4: <1%), thrombocytopenia (18%; grade 3: <1%)

Hepatic:AST increased (49%; grade 3: 2%; grade 4: <1%), total bilirubin increased (45%; grade 3: 4%), ALT increased (37%; grade 3: 2%)

Neuromuscular and skeletal: Limb pain (12%), back pain (11%)

Respiratory: Dyspnea (12%)

1% to 10%:

Cardiovascular: LVEF decreased (grade 2: 2%; grade 3: <1%)

Central nervous system: Insomnia (10%)

Dermatologic: Dry skin (10%)

<1%, postmarketing, and/or case reports: Interstitial lung disease, pneumonitis, Prinzmetal's angina, QT$_c$ prolongation

Overdosage/Toxicology The maximum dose administered in clinical trials was 1800 mg once daily. Severe diarrhea and vomiting were reported following exposure to 3000 mg daily for 10 days. This was managed with I.V. hydration. Treatment is otherwise symptom-directed and supportive. Dialysis is unlikely to be of benefit in lapatinib elimination.

Drug Interactions

Cytochrome P450 Effect: Substrate of CYP2C8 (minor), 3A4 (major), P-glycoprotein; **Inhibits** CYP2C8, 3A4

Increased Effect/Toxicity: CYP3A4 inhibitors may increase the levels/effects of lapatinib; example inhibitors include azole antifungals, clarithromycin, diclofenac, doxycycline, erythromycin, imatinib, isoniazid, nefazodone, nicardipine, propofol, protease inhibitors, quinidine, telithromycin, and verapamil. Concurrent use of lapatinib with other drugs which may prolong QT$_c$ interval may increase the risk of potentially-fatal arrhythmias; includes type Ia and type III antiarrhythmic agents, selected quinolones (eg, ciprofloxacin, moxifloxacin), cisapride, dolasetron, thioridazine, and other agents.

Lapatinib may increase levels/effects of CYP2C8 substrates; example substrates include amiodarone, paclitaxel, pioglitazone, repaglinide and rosiglitazone. Lapatinib may increase the levels/effects of CYP3A4 substrates; example substrates include benzodiazepines, calcium channel blockers, cyclosporine, mirtazapine, nateglinide, nefazodone, sildenafil (and other PDE-5 inhibitors), tacrolimus, and venlafaxine. Selected benzodiazepines (midazolam, triazolam), cisapride, ergot alkaloids, selected HMG-CoA reductase inhibitors (lovastatin and simvastatin), and pimozide are generally contraindicated with strong CYP3A4 inhibitors. Lapatinib may increase the levels/effects of pimecrolimus, especially in patients with widespread and/or erythrodermic disease; these patients are likely to experience increased absorption of pimecrolimus.

Decreased Effect: CYP3A4 inducers may decrease the levels/effects of lapatinib; example inducers include aminoglutethimide, carbamazepine, dexamethasone, nafcillin, nevirapine, phenobarbital, phenytoin, and rifamycins.

Ethanol/Nutrition/Herb Interactions

Food: Systemic exposure of lapatinib is increased when administered with food (AUC three- to fourfold higher). Avoid grapefruit juice (may increase the levels/effects of lapatinib).

Herb/Nutraceutical: Avoid St John's wort (may increase metabolism and decrease lapatinib concentrations).

(Continued)

Lapatinib (Continued)

Storage/Stability Store at room temperature between 15°C and 30°C (59°F and 86°F).

Mechanism of Action Tyrosine kinase (dual kinase) inhibitor; inhibitor of EGFR (ErbB1) and HER2 (ErbB2) by reversibly binding to tyrosine kinase, blocking phosphorylation and activation of downstream second messengers (Erk1/2 and Akt), regulating cellular proliferation and survival in ErbB- and ErbB2-expressing tumors.

Pharmacodynamics/Kinetics

Absorption: Incomplete and variable

Protein binding: >99% to albumin and alpha$_1$-acid glycoprotein

Metabolism: Hepatic; extensive via CYP3A4 and 3A5, and to a lesser extent via CYP2C19 and 2C8 to oxidized metabolites

Half-life elimination: ~24 hours

Time to peak, plasma: 3-6 hours

Excretion: Feces (27% as unchanged drug; range 3% to 67%); urine (<2%)

Dosage Refer to individual protocols. **Note:** Dose reductions are likely to be needed when lapatinib is administered concomitantly with a strong CYP3A4 inhibitor (an alternate medication for CYP3A4 enzyme inhibitors should be investigated first).

Oral: Adults: 1250 mg once daily

Dosage adjustment for concomitant CYP3A4 inhibitors/inducers:

CYP3A4 inhibitors: Dose reductions are likely to be needed when lapatinib is administered concomitantly with a strong CYP3A4 inhibitor (an alternate medication for CYP3A4 enzyme inhibitors should be investigated first); in the event that lapatinib must be administered concomitantly with a potent enzyme inhibitor, consider reducing lapatinib to 500 mg once daily with careful monitoring. (When a strong CYP3A4 inhibitor is discontinued; allow ~1 week to elapse prior to adjusting the lapatinib dose upward.) See Drug Interactions for examples of CYP3A4 inhibitors.

CYP3A4 inducers: Concomitant administration with CYP3A4 inducers may require increased lapatinib doses (alternatives to the enzyme-inducing agent should be utilized first); consider titrating gradually up to 4500 mg/day, with careful monitoring. (If the strong CYP3A4 enzyme inducer is discontinued, reduce the lapatinib dose to the indicated dose.) See Drug Interactions for examples of CYP3A4 inducers.

Dosage adjustment for toxicity:

Cardiac toxicity: Discontinue treatment for decreased LVEF ≥ grade 2 or LVEF < LLN; may be restarted after 2 weeks at 1000 mg once daily if LVEF recovers to normal and patient is asymptomatic

Other toxicities: Withhold for any toxicity (other than cardiac) ≥ grade 2 until toxicity resolves to ≤ grade 1; reduce dosage to 1000 mg once daily for persistent toxicity

Dosage adjustment in renal impairment: Not studied in renal dysfunction, however, due to the minimal renal elimination (<2%), dosage adjustments for renal dysfunction may not be necessary.

Dosage adjustment in hepatic impairment: Severe hepatic impairment (Child-Pugh class C): Consider a dose reduction to 750 mg once daily.

Combination Regimens

Breast cancer: Capecitabine + Lapatinib *on page 1160*

Administration Administer once daily, on an empty stomach, 1 hour before or 1 hour after a meal. Take at the same time each day; dividing doses is not recommended.

Monitoring Parameters LVEF (baseline and periodic), CBC with differential, liver function tests, electrolytes including calcium, potassium, magnesium; monitor for fluid retention; ECG monitoring if at risk for QT_c prolongation; symptoms of ILD

Dietary Considerations Take on an empty stomach, 1 hour before or 1 hour after a meal. (**Note:** For combination with capecitabine treatment, capecitabine should be taken with food, or within 30 minutes after a meal.)

Special Geriatric Considerations No differences in safety or effectiveness were observed between elderly and younger patients.

Additional Information Oncology Comment: The National Comprehensive Cancer Network (NCCN) has added lapatinib to the breast cancer guidelines as an option for the treatment of HER2-positive breast cancer that is hormone receptor-negative, symptomatic visceral disease, or hormone refractory in patients who have previously received anthracycline, taxane and trastuzumab treatment. In a randomized phase III study (Geyer, 2006) of lapatinib plus capecitabine versus capecitabine alone in HER2-positive advanced breast cancer, the addition of lapatinib was associated with a 51% reduction in the risk of disease progression in heavily pretreated patients. Lapatinib shows activity in HER2-positive metastatic breast cancer that has progressed after trastuzumab treatment.

Emetic Potential Low (10% to 30%)

Dosage Forms Excipient information presented when available (limited, particularly for generics); consult specific product labeling.
Tablet:
Tykerb®: 250 mg

References
Burris HA 3rd, Hurwitz HI, Dees EC, et al, "Phase I Safety, Pharmacokinetics, and Clinical Activity Study of Lapatinib (GW572016), a Reversible Dual Inhibitor of Epidermal Growth Factor Receptor Tyrosine Kinases, in Heavily Pretreated Patients with Metastatic Carcinomas," *J Clin Oncol*, 2005, 23(23):5305-13.

Geyer CE, Forster J, Lindquist D, et al "Lapatinib Plus Capecitabine for HER2-Positive Advanced Breast Cancer," *N Engl J Med*, 2006, 355(26):2733-43.

NCCN (National Comprehensive Cancer Network), "Practice Guidelines in Oncology: Breast Cancer Version 2.2007." Accessible at http://www.nccn.org/professionals/physician_gls/PDF/breast.pdf

Nelson MH and Dolder CR, "Lapatinib: A Novel Dual Tyrosine Kinase Inhibitor with Activity in Solid Tumors," *Ann Pharmacother*, 2006, 40(2):261-9.

Spector NL, Xia W, Burris H 3rd, et al, "Study of the Biologic Effects of Lapatinib, a Reversible Inhibitor of ErbB1 and ErbB2 Tyrosine Kinases, on Tumor Growth and Survival Pathways in Patients with Advanced Malignancies," *J Clin Oncol*, 2005, 23(11):2502-12.

♦ **Lapatinib Ditosylate** *see* Lapatinib *on page 656*
♦ **Largactil® (Can)** *see* ChlorproMAZINE *on page 208*
♦ **Lasix®** *see* Furosemide *on page 483*
♦ **Lasix® Special (Can)** *see* Furosemide *on page 483*
♦ **L-asparaginase** *see* Asparaginase *on page 111*
♦ **LDP-341** *see* Bortezomib *on page 150*

Lenalidomide (le na LID oh mide)

Medication Safety Issues
High alert medication: The Institute for Safe Medication Practices (ISMP) includes this medication among its list of drugs which have a heightened risk of causing significant patient harm when used in error.

Related Information
Safe Handling of Hazardous Drugs *on page 1382*

U.S. Brand Names Revlimid®

Index Terms CC-5013; IMid-3; NSC-703813

Generic Available No

(Continued)

Lenalidomide *(Continued)*

Pharmacologic Category Angiogenesis Inhibitor; Antineoplastic Agent; Immunosuppressant Agent; Tumor Necrosis Factor (TNF) Blocking Agent

Use Treatment of myelodysplastic syndrome (MDS) in patients with deletion 5q (del 5q) cytogenetic abnormality; treatment of multiple myeloma

Unlabeled/Investigational Use Treatment of metastatic malignant melanoma; treatment of myelofibrosis

Restrictions Lenalidomide is approved for marketing only under a Food and Drug Administration (FDA) approved, restricted distribution program called RevAssist^SM (www.REVLIMID.com or 1-888-423-5436). Physicians, pharmacies, and patients must be registered; a maximum 28-day supply may be dispensed; a new prescription is required each time it is filled; pregnancy testing is required for females of childbearing potential.

An FDA-approved medication guide must be distributed when dispensing an outpatient prescription (new or refill) where this medication is to be used without direct supervision of a healthcare provider. Medication guides are available at http://www.fda.gov/cder/Offices/ODS/medication_guides.htm.

Pregnancy Risk Factor X

Lactation Excretion in breast milk unknown/not recommended

Labeled Contraindications Hypersensitivity to lenalidomide or any component of the formulation; pregnancy or women capable of becoming pregnant; patients unable to comply with the RevAssist^SM program

Warnings/Precautions Hazardous agent - use appropriate precautions for handling and disposal. **[U.S. Boxed Warning]: Hematologic toxicity (neutropenia and thrombocytopenia) occurs in a majority of patients (grade 3/4: 80%)** and may require dose reductions and/or delays; the use of blood product support and/or growth factors may be needed. **[U.S. Boxed Warning]: Lenalidomide has been associated with a significant increase in risk for thrombosis and embolism in multiple myeloma patients treated with combination therapy. Deep vein thrombosis (DVT) and pulmonary embolism (PE) have occurred;** monitor for signs and symptoms of thromboembolism (shortness of breath, chest pain, or arm or leg swelling) and seek prompt medical attention with development of these symptoms. Use caution in renal impairment; may experience an increased rate of toxicities.

[U.S. Boxed Warning]: Lenalidomide is an analogue of thalidomide (a human teratogen) and could potentially cause birth defects in humans. Distribution of lenalidomide is restricted; physicians, pharmacists, and patients must be registered with the RevAssist^SM program. Safety and effectiveness in children <18 years of age have not been established.

Adverse Reactions

>10%:

Cardiovascular: Peripheral edema (8% to 21%)

Central nervous system: Fatigue (31% to 38%), pyrexia (21% to 23%), dizziness (20% to 21%), headache (20%)

Dermatologic: Pruritus (42%), rash (16% to 36%), dry skin (14%)

Endocrine & metabolic: Hyperglycemia (15%), hypokalemia (11%)

Gastrointestinal: Diarrhea (29% to 49%), constipation (24% to 39%), nausea (22% to 24%), weight loss (18%), dyspepsia (14%), anorexia (10% to 14%), taste perversion (6% to 13%), abdominal pain (8% to 12%)

Genitourinary: Urinary tract infection (11%)

Hematologic: Thrombocytopenia (17% to 62%; grades 3/4: 10% to 50%), neutropenia (28% to 59%; grades 3/4: 21% to 53%), anemia (12% to

24%; grades 3/4: 6% to 9%); myelosuppression is dose-dependent and reversible with treatment interruption and/or dose reduction

Neuromuscular & skeletal: Muscle cramp (18% to 30%), arthralgia (10% to 22%), back pain (15% to 21%), tremor (20%), weakness (15%), paresthesia (12%), limb pain (11%)

Ocular: Blurred vision (15%)

Respiratory: Nasopharyngitis (23%), cough (20%), dyspnea (7% to 20%), pharyngitis (16%), epistaxis (15%), upper respiratory infection (14% to 15%), pneumonia (11% to 12%)

1% to 10%:

Cardiovascular: Edema (10%), deep vein thrombosis (≤8%; grades 3/4: 7%), hypertension (6%), chest pain (5%), palpitation (5%), atrial fibrillation (grades 3/4: 3%), syncope (grade 3: 2%)

Central nervous system: Insomnia (10%), hypoesthesia (7%), pain (7%), depression (5%)

Dermatologic: Bruising (5% to 8%), cellulitis (5%), erythema (5%)

Endocrine & metabolic: Hypothyroidism (7%), hypomagnesemia (6%), hypocalcemia (grades 3/4: 4%)

Gastrointestinal: Vomiting (10%), xerostomia (7%), loose stools (6%)

Genitourinary: Dysuria (7%)

Hematologic: Leukopenia (8%; grade 3: 4%), febrile neutropenia (5%), lymphopenia (grade 3: 2%)

Hepatic: ALT increased (8%)

Neuromuscular & skeletal: Myalgia (9%), rigors (6%), neuropathy (peripheral 5%)

Respiratory: Sinusitis (8%), rhinitis (7%), bronchitis (6%), pulmonary embolism (≤3%; grades 3/4: 3%)

Miscellaneous: Night sweats (8%), diaphoresis increased (7%)

<1% or frequency not defined: Acute febrile neutrophilic dermatosis, acute leukemia, acute myeloid leukemia (AML), adrenal insufficiency, angina, aortic disorder, aphasia, arthritis, azotemia, bacteremia, Basedow's disease, biliary obstruction, blindness, bone marrow depression, bradycardia, brain edema, c-reactive protein decreased, cardiac arrest, cardiac failure, cardiogenic shock, cardiomyopathy, cardiopulmonary arrest, cellulitis, cerebellar infarction, cerebral infarction, cerebrovascular accident, CHF, cholecystitis, chondrocalcinosis, chronic obstructive airway disease, circulatory collapse, coagulopathy, colonic polyp, confusion, consciousness decreased, dehydration, delirium, delusion, diabetes mellitus, diabetic ketoacidosis, diverticulitis, dysarthria, dysphagia, encephalitis, falls, fractures, gait abnormal, gastritis, gastroenteritis, gastroesophageal reflux disease, gastrointestinal hemorrhage, gout, hematuria, hemoglobin decreased, hemolysis, hemolytic anemia, hemorrhage, hepatitis, herpesvirus infection, hyperbilirubinemia, hypernatremia, hypersensitivity, hypoglycemia, hypotension, hypoxia, infection, influenza, inguinal hernia, INR increased, interstitial lung disease, intestinal perforation, intracranial hemorrhage, intracranial venous sinus thrombosis, irritable bowel syndrome, ischemia, ischemic colitis, kidney infection, leukoencephalopathy, liver failure, liver function tests abnormal, lung cancer, lung infiltration, lymphoma, melena, MI, migraine, myocardial ischemia, myopathy, neutropenic sepsis, orthostatic hypotension, otitis media, pancreatitis, pancytopenia, pelvic pain, performance status decreased, peripheral ischemia, perirectal abscess, phlebitis, post procedural hemorrhage, pseudomembranous colitis, pulmonary edema, rectal hemorrhage, refractory anemia, renal calculus, renal failure, renal mass, renal tubular necrosis, respiratory failure, septic shock, sepsis, serum creatinine increased, skin desquamation, small bowel obstruction, somnolence, (Continued)

Lenalidomide *(Continued)*

spinal cord compression, splenic infarction, subarachnoid hemorrhage, sudden death, supraventricular arrhythmia, tachyarrhythmia, thrombophlebitis, thrombosis, transient ischemic attack, troponin I increased, urinary retention, urosepsis, urticaria, ventricular dysfunction, vertigo, wheezing

Overdosage/Toxicology Treatment is symptomatic and supportive.

Drug Interactions

Increased Effect/Toxicity: Abatacept and anakinra may increase the risk of serious infection when used in combination with lenalidomide. Lenalidomide may increase the risk of infections associated with vaccines (live organism).

Decreased Effect: Lenalidomide may decrease the effect of vaccines (dead organisms).

Ethanol/Nutrition/Herb Interactions Herb/Nutraceutical: Avoid echinacea (has immunostimulant properties; consider therapy modifications).

Storage/Stability Store at controlled room temperature between 15°C and 30°C (59°F and 86°F).

Mechanism of Action Immunomodulatory and antiangiogenic characteristics via multiple mechanisms. Selectively inhibits secretion of proinflammatory cytokines (potent inhibitor of tumor necrosis factor-alpha secretion); enhances cell-mediated immunity by stimulating proliferation of anti-CD3 stimulated T cells (resulting in increased IL-2 and interferon gamma secretion); inhibits trophic signals to angiogenic factors in cells. Inhibits the growth of myeloma cells by inducing cell cycle arrest and cell death.

Pharmacodynamics/Kinetics

Absorption: Rapid

Protein binding: ~30%

Half-life elimination: ~3 hours

Time, to peak, plasma: Healthy volunteers: 0.6-1.5 hours; Myeloma patients: 0.5-4 hours

Excretion: Urine (~67% as unchanged drug)

Dosage Oral:

Adults:

Myelodysplastic syndrome (MDS): 10 mg once daily

Multiple myeloma: 25 mg once daily for 21 days of a 28-day treatment cycle (in combination with dexamethasone)

Metastatic malignant melanoma (unlabeled/investigational use): 10-25 mg once daily

Myelofibrosis (unlabeled/investigational use): 5-10 mg once daily

Elderly: Refer to adult dosing; due to the potential for decreased renal function in the elderly, select dose carefully and closely monitor renal function

Dosage adjustment in renal impairment: Select dose carefully and closely monitor renal function. The FDA-approved labeling does not contain renal dosing adjustment guidelines. Lenalidomide AUC is increased 56% in multiple myeloma patients with mild renal impairment. Consider dose reductions in patients with renal dysfunction. Lenalidomide use with renal dysfunction has been studied in a limited number of patients with the following initial dosage recommendations (Chen, 2007):

MDS:

Cl_{cr} 30-49 mL/minute: 5 mg once daily

Cl_{cr} <30 mL/minute (nondialysis dependent): 5 mg every 48 hours

Cl_{cr} <30 mL/minute (dialysis dependent): 5 mg 3 times/week (administer following dialysis)

Multiple myeloma:

Cl$_{cr}$ 30-49 mL/minute: 10 mg once daily (may increase to 15 mg once daily for inadequate treatment response after 2 cycles)

Cl$_{cr}$ <30 mL/minute (nondialysis dependent): 15 mg every 48 hours

Cl$_{cr}$ <30 mL/minute (dialysis dependent): 15 mg 3 times/week (administer following dialysis)

Dosage adjustment for toxicity:

Adjustment for thrombocytopenia in MDS:

Thrombocytopenia developing within 4 weeks of beginning treatment at 10 mg/day:

Baseline platelets ≥100,000/mcL:

If platelets <50,000/mcL: Hold treatment

When platelets return to ≥50,000/mcL: Resume treatment at 5 mg/day

Baseline platelets <100,000/mcL:

If platelets fall to 50% of baseline: Hold treatment

If baseline ≥60,000/mcL and platelet level returns to ≥50,000/mcL: Resume at 5 mg/day

If baseline <60,000/mcL and platelet level returns to ≥30,000/mcL: Resume at 5 mg/day

Thrombocytopenia developing after 4 weeks of beginning treatment at 10 mg/day:

Platelets <30,000/mcL **or** <50,000/mcL with platelet transfusions: Hold treatment

Platelets ≥30,000/mcL (without hemostatic failure): Resume at 5 mg/day

Thrombocytopenia developing with treatment at 5 mg/day:

Platelets <30,000/mcL **or** <50,000/mcL with platelet transfusions: Hold treatment

Platelets ≥30,000/mcL (without hemostatic failure): Resume at 5 mg every other day day

Adjustment for neutropenia in MDS:

Neutropenia developing within 4 weeks of beginning treatment at 10 mg/day:

For baseline absolute neutrophil count (ANC) ≥1000/mcL:

ANC <750/mcL: Hold treatment

When ANC returns to ≥1000/mcL: Resume at 5 mg/day

For baseline absolute neutrophil count (ANC) <1000/mcL:

ANC <500/mcL: Hold treatment

When ANC returns to ≥500/mcL: Resume at 5 mg/day

Neutropenia developing after 4 weeks of beginning treatment at 10 mg/day:

ANC <500/mcL for ≥7 days or associated with fever: Hold treatment

When ≥500/mcL: Resume at 5 mg/day

Neutropenia developing with treatment at 5 mg/day:

ANC <500/mcL for ≥7 days or associated with fever: Hold treatment

When ≥500/mcL: Resume at 5 mg every other day

Adjustment for thrombocytopenia in multiple myeloma:

Platelets <30,000/mcL: Hold treatment, check CBC weekly

When platelets ≥30,000/mcL: Resume at 15 mg daily

Additional occurrence of platelets <30,000/mcL: Hold treatment

When platelets ≥30,000/mcL: Resume treatment at 5 mg below previous dose; do not dose below 5 mg daily

Adjustment for neutropenia in multiple myeloma:

ANC <1000/mcL: Hold treatment, add G-CSF, check CBC weekly

(Continued)

Lenalidomide *(Continued)*

When ≥1000/mcL (with neutropenia as only toxicity): Resume at 25 mg/day

When ≥1000/mcL (with additional toxicities): Resume at 15 mg/day

Additional occurrence of ANC <1000/mcL: Hold treatment

When ≥1000/mcL: Resume treatment at 5 mg below previous dose; do not dose below 5 mg daily.

Adjustment for other toxicities in multiple myeloma: For additional treatment-related grade 3/4 toxicities, hold treatment and restart at next dose level when toxicity has resolved to ≤ grade 2.

Combination Regimens

Multiple myeloma:

Lenalidomide-Dexamethasone *on page 1243*

Lenalidomide-Dexamethasone (Low Dose) *on page 1243*

Administration Administer with water. Swallow capsule whole; do not break, open, or chew.

Monitoring Parameters CBC with differential (MDS: weekly for first 8 weeks; MM: every 2 weeks for the first 3 months), then monthly thereafter; serum creatinine, liver function tests, thyroid function tests; monitor for signs and symptoms of thromboembolism

Women of childbearing potential: Pregnancy test 10-14 days **and** 24 hours prior to initiating therapy, then every 2-4 weeks through 4 weeks after therapy discontinued

Patient Information You will be given oral and written instructions about the necessity of using two methods of contraception and the necessity of keeping return visits for pregnancy testing. Do not donate blood while taking this medicine. Male patients should not donate sperm. May cause low white blood cells and platelets, blood clots in the veins or lungs, diarrhea or constipation, itching or rash, or fatigue (use caution when operating heavy machinery). Report any of the above if persistent or severe. Report chest pain or shortness of breath, or swelling of extremities; skin rash; excessive tiredness; or any other symptom of adverse reactions.

Special Geriatric Considerations The manufacturer reports that the frequency of serious adverse effects was higher in patients >65 years of age compared to younger patients (54% vs 33%). More older patients withdrew from the clinical studies because of side effects. There was no significant difference in efficacy in older versus younger patients.

Additional Information Pregnancy tests are required prior to beginning therapy, throughout treatment and during therapy interruptions for all women of childbearing age. The pregnancy test must be verified by the prescriber and the pharmacist prior to dispensing. Effective contraception with at least two reliable forms of contraception (IUD, hormonal contraception, tubal ligation or partner's vasectomy plus latex condom, diaphragm, or cervical cap) should be used for 4 weeks prior to beginning therapy, during therapy, and for 4 weeks following discontinuance of therapy. Women who have undergone a hysterectomy or have been postmenopausal for at least 24 consecutive months are the only exception. Do not prescribe, administer, or dispense to women of childbearing age or males who may have intercourse with women of childbearing age unless both female and male are capable of complying with contraceptive measures. Even males who have undergone vasectomy must acknowledge these risks in writing, and must use a latex condom during any sexual contact with women of childbearing age. Oral and written warnings concerning contraception and the hazards of thalidomide must be conveyed to females and males and they must acknowledge their understanding in writing. Parents or guardians must consent and sign acknowledgment for patients 12-18 years of age following therapy. A maximum 28-day supply should be dispensed.

Emetic Potential Low (10% to 30%)

Dosage Forms Excipient information presented when available (limited, particularly for generics); consult specific product labeling.

Capsule:

Revlimid®: 5 mg, 10 mg, 15 mg, 25 mg

References

Barlogie B, Shaughnessy J, Tricot G, et al, "Treatment of Multiple Myeloma," *Blood*, 2004, 103(1):20-32.

Bartlett JB, Michael A, Clarke IA, et al, "Phase I Study to Determine the Safety, Tolerability and Immunostimulatory Activity of Thalidomide Analogue CC-5013 in Patients With Metastatic Malignant Melanoma and Other Advanced Cancers," *Br J Cancer*, 2004, 90(5):955-61.

Chen N, Lau H, Kong L, et al, "Pharmacokinetics of Lenalidomide in Subjects With Various Degrees of Renal Function," *J Clin Oncol*, 2007, 25(18S):2520 [abstract from ASCO Annual Meeting Proceedings, Part I]

Dimopoulos MA, Anagnostopoulos A, and Weber D, "Treatment of Plasma Cell Dyscrasias With Thalidomide and Its Derivatives," *J Clin Oncol*, 2003, 21(23):4444-54.

Fadern S and Kantarjian HM, "Novel Therapies for Myelodysplastic Syndromes," *Cancer*, 2004, 101(2): 226-41.

Giagounidis AA, Germing U, Strupp C, et al, "Prognosis of Patients with del(5q) MDS and Complex Karyotype and the Possible Role of Lenalidomide in this Patient Subgroup," *Ann Hematol*, 2005, 84(9):569-71.

Kyle RA and Rajkumar SV, "Multiple Myeloma," *N Engl J Med*, 2004, 351(18):1860-73.

List A, Dewald G, Bennett J, et al, "Lenalidomide in Myelodysplastic Syndrome With Chromosome 5q Deletion," *N Engl J Med*, 2006, 355(14):1456-65.

List A, Kurtin S, Roe DJ, et al, "Efficacy of Lenalidomide in Myelodysplastic Syndromes," *N Engl J Med*, 2005, 352(6):549-57.

Rajkumar SV, Hayman SR, Lacy MQ, et al, "Combination Therapy With Lenalidomide Plus Dexamethasone (Rev/Dex) for Newly Diagnosed Myeloma," *Blood*, 2005, 106(13):4050-3.

Richardson PG, Schlossman RL, Weller E, et al, "Immunomodulatory Drug CC-5013 Overcomes Drug Resistance and Is Well Tolerated in Patients With Relapsed Multiple Myeloma," *Blood*, 2002, 100(9):3063-7.

Tefferi A, Cortes J, Verstovsek S, et al, "Lenalidomide Therapy in Myelofibrosis With Myeloid Metaplasia," *Blood*, 2006, 108(4):1158-64.

Teo SK, "Properties of Thalidomide and Its Analogues: Implications for Anticancer Therapy," *AAPSJ*, 2005, 7(1):e14-9.

Letrozole (LET roe zole)

Medication Safety Issues

Sound-alike/look-alike issues:

Femara® may be confused with femhrt®

Related Information

Safe Handling of Hazardous Drugs *on page 1382*

U.S. Brand Names Femara®

Index Terms CGS-20267; NSC-719345

Generic Available No

Canadian Brand Names Femara®

Pharmacologic Category Antineoplastic Agent, Aromatase Inhibitor

Use Adjuvant treatment of postmenopausal hormone receptor positive early breast cancer; treatment of postmenopausal hormone receptor positive or hormone receptor unknown, locally-advanced, or metastatic breast cancer

Pregnancy Risk Factor D

Lactation Excretion in breast milk unknown/use caution

Labeled Contraindications Hypersensitivity to letrozole or any component of the formulation; women of premenopausal endocrine status; pregnancy

Warnings/Precautions Hazardous agent - use appropriate precautions for handling and disposal. Use caution with hepatic impairment; dose adjustment may be required. Increases in transaminases ≥5 times the upper limit (Continued)

Letrozole *(Continued)*

of normal and in bilirubin ≥1.5 times the upper limit of normal were most often, but not always, associated with metastatic liver disease. May cause dizziness, fatigue, and somnolence; patients should be cautioned before performing tasks which require mental alertness (eg, operating machinery or driving). May increase total serum cholesterol. May cause decreases in bone mineral density. Safety and efficacy have not been established in children.

Adverse Reactions

>10%:
  Cardiovascular: Edema (7% to 18%)
  Central nervous system: Headache (4% to 20%), dizziness (2% to 14%), fatigue (6% to 13%)
  Endocrine & metabolic: Hot flashes (5% to 50%), hypercholesterolemia (3% to 16%)
  Gastrointestinal: Nausea (9% to 17%), constipation (2% to 11%), weight gain (2% to 11%)
  Neuromuscular & skeletal: Weakness (4% to 34%), bone pain (22%), arthralgia (8% to 22%), arthritis (7% to 21%), back pain (5% to 18%)
  Respiratory: Dyspnea (6% to 18%), cough (5% to 13%)
  Miscellaneous: Diaphoresis (<5% to 24%), night sweats (14%)

2% to 10%:
  Cardiovascular: Chest pain (3% to 8%), hypertension (5% to 8%), peripheral edema (5%)
  Central nervous system: Insomnia (6% to 7%), pain (5%), somnolence (2% to 3%), depression (<5%), anxiety (<5%), vertigo (<5%)
  Dermatologic: Rash (4% to 5%), alopecia (<5%), pruritus (1% to 2%)
  Endocrine & metabolic: Breast pain (7%), hypercalcemia (<5%)
  Gastrointestinal: Diarrhea (5% to 8%), vomiting (3% to 7%), weight loss (7%), abdominal pain (5% to 6%), anorexia (3% to 5%), dyspepsia (3% to 4%)
  Genitourinary: Urinary tract infection (6%), vaginal bleeding (5%), vaginal dryness (5%), vaginal hemorrhage (5%), vaginal irritation (4%)
  Hepatic: Transaminases increased (<1% to 3%)
  Neuromuscular & skeletal: Limb pain (10%), myalgia (6% to 7%), bone fractures (<5% to 6%), bone mineral density decreased/osteoporosis (2% to 7%)
  Renal: Renal disorder (5%)
  Respiratory: Pleural effusion (<5%)
  Miscellaneous: Infection (7%), flu (6%), viral infection (5% to 6%)

<2%, postmarketing, and/or case reports: Angina, appetite increase, arterial thrombosis, bilirubin increased, blurred vision, cardiac ischemia, cardiac failure, cataract, coronary artery disease, dry skin, dysesthesia, endometrial cancer, endometrial proliferation disorder, eye irritation, fever, hemiparesis, hemorrhagic stroke, hypoesthesia, irritability, leukopenia, lymphopenia, MI, memory impairment, nervousness, palpitations, paresthesia, portal vein thrombosis, pulmonary embolism, secondary malignancy, stomatitis, tachycardia, taste disturbance, thirst, thrombocytopenia, thrombophlebitis, thromboembolic event, thrombotic stroke, transient ischemic attack, urinary frequency increased, urticaria, vaginal discharge, venous thrombosis, xerostomia

Overdosage/Toxicology Firm recommendations for treatment are not possible; emesis could be induced if the patient is alert. In general, treatment is symptom-directed and supportive. Frequent monitoring of vital signs is appropriate.

Drug Interactions

Cytochrome P450 Effect: Substrate (minor) of CYP2A6, 3A4; **Inhibits** CYP2A6 (strong), 2C19 (weak)

Increased Effect/Toxicity: Letrozole may increase the levels/effects of CYP2A6 substrates; example substrates include dexmedetomidine and ifosfamide.

Decreased Effect: Tamoxifen may decrease serum concentrations of letrozole.

Storage/Stability Store at 15°C to 30°C (59°F to 86°F).

Mechanism of Action Nonsteroidal competitive inhibitor of the aromatase enzyme system which binds to the heme group of aromatase, a cytochrome P450 enzyme which catalyzes conversion of androgens to estrogens (specifically, androstenedione to estrone and testosterone to estradiol). This leads to inhibition of the enzyme and a significant reduction in plasma estrogen levels. Does not affect synthesis of adrenal or thyroid hormones, aldosterone, or androgens.

Pharmacodynamics/Kinetics

Absorption: Rapid and well absorbed; not affected by food

Distribution: V_d: ~1.9 L/kg

Protein binding, plasma: Weak

Metabolism: Hepatic via CYP3A4 and 2A6 to an inactive carbinol metabolite

Half-life elimination: Terminal: ~2 days

Time to steady state, plasma: 2-6 weeks

Excretion: Urine (90%; 6% as unchanged drug, 75% as glucuronide carbinol metabolite, 9% as unidentified metabolites)

Dosage Oral (refer to individual protocols): Adults: Female: Breast cancer: 2.5 mg once daily

Elderly: No dosage adjustments required

Dosage adjustment in renal impairment: No dosage adjustment is required in patients with renal impairment if Cl_{cr} ≥10 mL/minute

Dosage adjustment in hepatic impairment:

Mild-to-moderate impairment (Child-Pugh class A and B): No adjustment recommended

Severe impairment (Child-Pugh class C): 2.5 mg every other day

Monitoring Parameters Monitor periodically during therapy: Complete blood counts, thyroid function tests; serum electrolytes, cholesterol, transaminases, and creatinine; blood pressure; bone density

Dietary Considerations May be taken without regard to meals. Calcium and vitamin D supplementation are recommended.

Patient Information May experience nausea, vomiting, hot flashes, or loss of appetite; musculoskeletal pain or headache; sleepiness, fatigue, or dizziness (use caution when driving, climbing stairs, or engaging in tasks that require alertness until response to drug is known); constipation; diarrhea; or loss of hair. Report chest pain, pressure, palpitations, or swollen extremities; weakness, severe headache, numbness, or loss of strength in any part of the body, difficulty speaking; vaginal bleeding; unusual signs of bleeding or bruising; difficulty breathing; severe nausea, or muscle pain; or skin rash. For use in postmenopausal women only.

Special Geriatric Considerations No dosage adjustment recommended.

Emetic Potential Low (10% to 30%)

Dosage Forms Excipient information presented when available (limited, particularly for generics); consult specific product labeling.

Tablet: 2.5 mg

Femara®: 2.5 mg

(Continued)

Letrozole *(Continued)*

References

Boeddinghaus IM and Dowsett M, "Comparative Clinical Pharmacology and Pharmacokinetic Interactions of Aromatase Inhibitors," *J Steroid Biochem Mol Biol*, 2001, 79(1-5):85-91.

Buzdar AU, Robertson JF, Eiermann W, et al, "An Overview of the Pharmacology and Pharmacokinetics of the Newer Generation Aromatase Inhibitors Anastrozole, Letrozole, and Exemestane," *Cancer*, 2002, 95(9):2006-16.

Coates AS, Keshaviah A, Thurlimann B, et al, "Five Years of Letrozole Compared With Tamoxifen as Initial Adjuvant Therapy for Postmenopausal Women With Endocrine-Responsive Early Breast Cancer: Update of Study BIG 1-98," *J Clin Oncol*, 2007, 25(5):486-92.

Haynes BP, Dowsett M, Miller WR, et al, "The Pharmacology of Letrozole," *J Steroid Biochem Mol Biol*, 2003, 87(1):35-45.

Simpson D, Curran MP, and Perry CM, "Letrozole: A Review of Its Use in Postmenopausal Women With Breast Cancer," *Drugs*, 2004, 64(11):1213-30.

Smith IE and Dowsett M, "Aromatase Inhibitors in Breast Cancer," *N Engl J Med*, 2003, 348(24):2431-42.

Thurlimann B, Keshaviah A, Coates AS, et al, "A Comparison of Letrozole and Tamoxifen in Postmenopausal Women with Early Breast Cancer," *N Engl J Med*, 2005, 353(26):2747-57.

Winer EP, Hudis C, Burstein HJ, et al, "American Society of Clinical Oncology Technology Assessment on the Use of Aromatase Inhibitors as Adjuvant Therapy for Postmenopausal Women With Hormone Receptor-Positive Breast Cancer: Status Report 2004," *J Clin Oncol*, 2005, 23(3):619-29.

Leucovorin Calcium *(loo koe VOR in KAL see um)*

Medication Safety Issues

Sound-alike/look-alike issues:

Leucovorin may be confused with Leukeran®, Leukine®

Folinic acid may be confused with folic acid

Folinic acid is an error prone synonym and should not be used

Index Terms
Calcium Leucovorin; Citrovorum Factor; Folinic Acid (error prone synonym); 5-Formyl Tetrahydrofolate

Generic Available
Yes

Pharmacologic Category
Antidote; Vitamin, Water Soluble

Use
Antidote for folic acid antagonists (methotrexate, trimethoprim, pyrimethamine) and rescue therapy following high-dose methotrexate; in combination with fluorouracil in the treatment of colon cancer; treatment of megaloblastic anemias when folate is deficient as in infancy, sprue, pregnancy, and nutritional deficiency when oral folate therapy is not possible

Unlabeled/Investigational Use
I.T. administration following I.T. methotrexate overdose

Pregnancy Risk Factor
C

Lactation
Excretion in breast milk unknown/use caution

Labeled Contraindications
Pernicious anemia or vitamin B_{12}-deficient megaloblastic anemias

Warnings/Precautions
When used for the treatment of accidental folic acid antagonist overdose, administer as soon as possible. When used for methotrexate rescue therapy, methotrexate serum concentrations should be monitored to determine dose and duration of leucovorin therapy. Dose may need increased or administration prolonged in situations where methotrexate excretion may be delayed (eg, ascites, pleural effusion, renal insufficiency, inadequate hydration). Combination of leucovorin and sulfamethoxazole-trimethoprim for the acute treatment of PCP in patients with HIV infection has been reported to cause increased rates of treatment failure. Leucovorin may increase the toxicity of 5-fluorouracil; dose of 5-fluorouracil may need decreased.

Powder for injection: When doses >10 mg/m^2 are required, reconstitute using sterile water for injection, not a solution containing benzyl alcohol.

Injection: Due to calcium content, do not administer I.V. solutions at a rate >160 mg/ minute. Not intended for intrathecal use.

Adverse Reactions Frequency not defined. Toxicities (especially gastrointestinal toxicity) of fluorouracil is higher when used in combination with leucovorin.

Dermatologic: Rash, pruritus, erythema, urticaria

Hematologic: Thrombocytosis

Respiratory: Wheezing

Miscellaneous: Allergic reactions, anaphylactoid reactions

Drug Interactions

Decreased Effect: May decrease efficacy of trimethoprim/sulfamethoxazole against *Pneumocystis carinii* pneumonia; may diminish therapeutic effect of Raltitrexed [CAN; not available in U.S.].

Storage/Stability

Powder for injection: Store at room temperature of 25°C (77°F). Protect from light. Solutions reconstituted with bacteriostatic water for injection U.S.P., must be used within 7 days. Solutions reconstituted with SWFI must be used immediately. Parenteral admixture is stable for 24 hours stored at room temperature (25°C) and for 4 days when stored under refrigeration (4°C).

Solution for injection: Prior to dilution, store vials under refrigeration at 2°C to 8°C (36°F to 46°F). Protect from light.

Tablet: Store at room temperature of 15°C to 30°C (59°F to 86°F).

Reconstitution Powder for injection: Reconstitute with SWFI or BWFI; dilute in 100-1000 mL NS, D_5W for infusion. When doses >10 mg/m^2 are required, reconstitute using sterile water for injection, not a solution containing benzyl alcohol.

Compatibility Stable in $D_{10}NS$, D_5W, $D_{10}W$, LR, sterile water for injection, bacteriostatic water, bacteriostatic NS; **variable stability (consult detailed reference)** in NS.

Y-site administration: Compatible: Amifostine, aztreonam, bleomycin, cefepime, cisplatin, cladribine, cyclophosphamide, docetaxel, doxorubicin, doxorubicin liposome, etoposide phosphate, filgrastim, fluconazole, fluorouracil, furosemide, gatifloxacin, gemcitabine, granisetron, heparin, irinotecan, linezolid, methotrexate, metoclopramide, mitomycin, piperacillin/tazobactam, tacrolimus, teniposide, thiotepa, vinblastine, vincristine. Incompatible: Amphotericin B cholesteryl sulfate complex, droperidol, foscarnet, sodium bicarbonate.

Compatibility in syringe: Compatible: Bleomycin, cisplatin, cyclophosphamide, doxorubicin, fluorouracil, furosemide, heparin, methotrexate, metoclopramide, mitomycin, vinblastine, vincristine. Incompatible: Droperidol.

Compatibility when admixed: Compatible: Cisplatin, cisplatin with floxuridine, floxuridine. Incompatible: Concentrations >2 mg/mL of leucovorin and >25 mg/mL of fluorouracil.

Mechanism of Action A reduced form of folic acid, leucovorin supplies the necessary cofactor blocked by methotrexate, enters the cells via the same active transport system as methotrexate. Stabilizes the binding of 5-dUMP and thymidylate synthetase, enhancing the activity of fluorouracil.

Pharmacodynamics/Kinetics

Absorption: Oral, I.M.: Well absorbed

Metabolism: Intestinal mucosa and hepatically to 5-methyl-tetrahydrofolate (5MTHF; active)

Bioavailability: Saturable at oral doses >25 mg; 25 mg (97%), 50 mg (75%), 100 mg (37%)

Half-life elimination: ~4-8 hours

(Continued)

Leucovorin Calcium *(Continued)*

Time to peak: Oral: ~2 hours; I.V.: Total folates: 10 minutes; 5MTHF: ~1 hour

Excretion: Urine (primarily); feces

Dosage

Children and Adults:

Treatment of folic acid antagonist overdosage: Oral: 5-15 mg/day

Folate-deficient megaloblastic anemia: I.M.: ≤1 mg/day

High-dose methotrexate-rescue dose: Initial: Oral, I.M., I.V.: 15 mg (~10 mg/m²); start 24 hours after beginning methotrexate infusion; continue every 6 hours for 10 doses, until methotrexate level is <0.05 micromole/L. Adjust dose as follows:

Normal methotrexate elimination: Oral, I.M., I.V.: 15 mg every 6 hours

Delayed early methotrexate elimination: I.V.: 150 mg every 3 hours until methotrexate level is <1 micromole/L, then 15 mg every 3 hours until methotrexate level is <0.05 micromole/L

Adults:

Colorectal cancer (also refer to Combination Regimens):

I.V.: 200 mg/m² over at least 3 minutes (used in combination with fluorouracil 370 mg/m²)

or

I.V.: 20 mg/m² (used in combination with fluorouracil 425 mg/m²)

Pemetrexed toxicity (unlabeled dose): I.V.: 100 mg/m² once, followed by 50 mg/m² every 6 hours for 8 days was used in clinical trial for CTC grade 4 leukopenia ≥3 days; CTC grade 4 neutropenia ≥3 days; immediately for CTC grade 4 thrombocytopenia, bleeding associated with grade 3 thrombocytopenia, or grade 3 or 4 mucositis

Combination Regimens

Bladder cancer: M-VAC (Bladder Cancer) *on page 1255*

Breast cancer:

MF *on page 1247*

M-VAC (Breast Cancer) *on page 1258*

NFL *on page 1261*

Colorectal cancer:

Bevacizumab-Fluorouracil-Leucovorin *on page 1151*

Bevacizumab-Irinotecan-Fluorouracil-Leucovorin *on page 1151*

Bevacizumab-Oxaliplatin-Fluorouracil-Leucovorin *on page 1152*

FLOX (Nordic FLOX) *on page 1216*

Fluorouracil-Leucovorin *on page 1218*

Fluorouracil-Leucovorin-Irinotecan (Saltz Regimen) *on page 1220*

FOIL *on page 1221*

FOLFOX 1 *on page 1221*

FOLFOX 2 *on page 1221*

FOLFOX 3 *on page 1222*

FOLFOX 4 *on page 1222*

FOLFOX 6 *on page 1222*

FOLFOX 7 *on page 1222*

FU-LV-CPT-11 *on page 1223*

PFL (Colorectal Cancer) *on page 1270*

Gastric cancer:

ELF *on page 1199*

FAMTX *on page 1213*

Gestational trophoblastic tumor:

CHAMOCA (Modified Bagshawe Regimen) *on page 1170*

CHAMOMA (Bagshawe Regimen) *on page 1172*

EMA/CO *on page 1199*

Administration Due to calcium content, do not administer I.V. solutions at a rate >160 mg/ minute.

Refer to individual protocols. Should be administered I.M., I.V. push, or I.V. infusion (15 minutes to 2 hours). Leucovorin should not be administered concurrently with methotrexate. It is commonly initiated 24 hours after the start of methotrexate. Toxicity to normal tissues may be irreversible if leucovorin is not initiated by ~40 hours after the start of methotrexate.

As a rescue after folate antagonists: Administer by I.V. bolus, I.M., or orally. Do not administer orally in the presence of nausea or vomiting. Doses >25 mg should be administered parenterally.

In combination with fluorouracil: Fluorouracil activity, the fluorouracil is usually given after, or at the midpoint, of the leucovorin infusion. Leucovorin is usually administered by I.V. bolus injection or short (10-120 minutes) I.V. infusion. Other administration schedules have been used; refer to individual protocols.

Monitoring Parameters

High-dose methotrexate therapy: Plasma methotrexate concentration; leucovorin is continued until the plasma methotrexate level <0.05 micromole/L. With 4- to 6-hour high-dose methotrexate infusions, plasma drug values in excess of 50 and 1 micromole/L at 24 and 48 hours after starting the infusion, respectively, are often predictive of delayed methotrexate clearance.

Fluorouracil therapy: CBC with differential and platelets, liver function tests, electrolytes

Dietary Considerations Solutions for injection contain calcium 0.004 mEq per leucovorin 1 mg

Patient Information Contact prescriber immediately if you have an allergic reaction after taking leucovorin calcium (trouble breathing, wheezing, fainting, skin rash, or hives). Inform prescriber if you are pregnant or are trying to get pregnant before taking leucovorin calcium. Leucovorin calcium can be taken with or without food. Take as directed, at evenly spaced intervals around-the-clock. Maintain hydration (2-3 L of water/day while taking for rescue therapy). For folic acid deficiency, eat foods high in folic *(Continued)*

Leucovorin Calcium *(Continued)*

acid (eg, meat proteins, bran, dried beans, asparagus, green leafy vegetables).

Emetic Potential Low

Vesicant No

Dosage Forms Excipient information presented when available (limited, particularly for generics); consult specific product labeling. **Note:** Strength expressed as base

Injection, powder for reconstitution: 50 mg, 100 mg, 200 mg, 350 mg

Injection, solution: 10 mg/mL (50 mL)

Tablet: 5 mg, 10 mg, 15 mg, 25 mg

References

Bleyer WA, "New Vistas for Leucovorin in Cancer Chemotherapy," *Cancer*, 1989, 63(6 Suppl):995-1007.

Grogan L, Sotos GA, and Allegra CJ, "Leucovorin Modulation of Fluorouracil," *Oncology (Huntingt)*, 1993, 7(8):63-72.

Hansen RM, "Systemic Therapy in Metastatic Colorectal Cancer," *Arch Intern Med*, 1990, 150(11):2265-9.

Jacobsen D and McMartin KE, "Methanol and Ethylene Glycol Poisonings. Mechanism of Toxicity, Clinical Course, Diagnosis and Treatment," *Med Toxicol*, 1986, 1(5):309-34.

Jolivet J, "Role of Leucovorin Dosing and Administration Schedule," *Eur J Cancer*, 1995, 31A(7-8):1311-5.

Machover D, "A Comprehensive Review of 5-Fluorouracil and Leucovorin in Patients With Metastatic Colorectal Carcinoma," *Cancer*, 1997, 80(7):1179-87.

McGuire BW, Sia LL, Leese PT, et al, "Pharmacokinetics of Leucovorin Calcium After Intravenous, Intramuscular, and Oral Administration," *Clin Pharm*, 1988, 7(1):52-8.

Rustum SE, Law S, and Puodziunas A, "Modulation of Fluoropyrimidines by Leucovorin: Rationale and Status," *J Surg Oncol Suppl*, 1991, 2:116-23.

Stover P and Schirch V, "The Metabolic Role of Leucovorin," *Trends Biochem Sci*, 1993, 18(3):102-6.

Trissel LA, Martinez JF, and Xu QA, "Incompatibility of Fluorouracil With Leucovorin Calcium or Levoleucovorin Calcium," *Am J Health Syst Pharm*, 1995, 52(7):710-5.

Walker SE, Law S, and Puodziunas A, "Simulation of Y-Site Compatibility of Irinotecan and Leucovorin at Room Temperature in 5% Dextrose in Water in 3 Different Containers," *Can J Hosp Pharm*, 2005, 58(4): 212-22.

♦ **Leukeran**® *see* Chlorambucil *on page 205*

♦ **Leukine**® *see* Sargramostim *on page 962*

Leuprolide *(loo PROE lide)*

Medication Safety Issues

Sound-alike/look-alike issues:

Lupron® may be confused with Nuprin®

Lupron Depot®-3 Month may be confused with Lupron Depot-Ped®

Related Information

Safe Handling of Hazardous Drugs *on page 1382*

U.S. Brand Names Eligard®; Lupron®; Lupron Depot®; Lupron Depot-Ped®; Viadur®

Index Terms Abbott-43818; Leuprolide Acetate; Leuprorelin Acetate; NSC-377526; TAP-144

Generic Available Yes: Injection (solution)

Canadian Brand Names Eligard®; Lupron®; Lupron® Depot®; Viadur®

Pharmacologic Category Antineoplastic Agent, Gonadotropin-Releasing Hormone Agonist; Gonadotropin Releasing Hormone Agonist

Use Palliative treatment of advanced prostate carcinoma; management of endometriosis; treatment of anemia caused by uterine leiomyomata (fibroids); central precocious puberty

Unlabeled/Investigational Use Treatment of breast, ovarian, and endometrial cancer; infertility; prostatic hyperplasia

Pregnancy Risk Factor X

Lactation Excretion in breast milk unknown/contraindicated

Labeled Contraindications Hypersensitivity to leuprolide, GnRH, GnRH-agonist analogs, or any component of the formulation; spinal cord compression (orchiectomy suggested); undiagnosed abnormal vaginal bleeding; pregnancy; breast-feeding

Warnings/Precautions Hazardous agent - use appropriate precautions for handling and disposal. Transient increases in testosterone serum levels occur at the start of treatment. Tumor flare, bone pain, neuropathy, urinary tract obstruction, and spinal cord compression have been reported when used for prostate cancer; closely observe patients for weakness, paresthesias, hematuria, and urinary tract obstruction in first few weeks of therapy. Observe patients with metastatic vertebral lesions or urinary obstruction closely. Exacerbation of endometriosis or uterine leiomyomata may occur initially. Decreased bone density has been reported when used for ≥6 months. Use caution in patients with a history of psychiatric illness; alteration in mood, memory impairment, and depression have been associated with use. Rare cases of pituitary apoplexy (frequently secondary to pituitary adenoma) have been observed with leuprolide administration (onset from 1 hour to usually <2 weeks); may present as sudden headache, vomiting, visual or mental status changes, and infrequently cardiovascular collapse; immediate medical attention required. Females treated for precocious puberty may experience menses or spotting during the first 2 months of treatment; notify healthcare provider if bleeding continues after the second month.

Adverse Reactions

Children:

2% to 10%:

Central nervous system: Pain (2%)

Dermatologic: Acne (2%), rash (2% including erythema multiforme), seborrhea (2%)

Genitourinary: Vaginitis (2%), vaginal bleeding (2%), vaginal discharge (2%)

Local: Injection site reaction (5%)

<2%: Alopecia, body odor, cervix disorder, dysphagia, emotional lability, epistaxis, fever, gingivitis, gynecomastia, headache, nausea, nervousness, peripheral edema, personality disorder, sexual maturity accelerated, skin striae, somnolence, syncope, urinary incontinence, vasodilation, vomiting, weight gain

Adults: Note: For prostate cancer treatment, an initial rise in serum testosterone concentrations may cause "tumor flare" or worsening of symptoms, including bone pain, neuropathy, hematuria, or ureteral or bladder outlet obstruction during the first 2 weeks. Similarly, an initial increase in estradiol levels, with a temporary worsening of symptoms, may occur in women treated with leuprolide.

Delayed release formulations:

10%:

Cardiovascular: Edema (≤14%)

Central nervous system: Headache (≤65%), pain (<2% to 33%), depression (≤31%), insomnia (≤31%), fatigue (≤17%), dizziness/vertigo (≤16%)

Dermatologic: Skin reaction (≤12%)

Endocrine & metabolic: Hot flashes (47% to 98%), testicular atrophy (≤20%), hyperlipidemia (≤12%), libido decreased (≤11%)

Gastrointestinal: Nausea/vomiting (≤25%), weight gain/loss (≤13%)

Genitourinary: Vaginitis (11% to 28%), urinary disorder (13% to 15%)

(Continued)

LEUPROLIDE

Leuprolide *(Continued)*

Local: Implant site bruising (35%), injection site reaction (≤16%)
Neuromuscular & skeletal: Joint disorder (≤12%), weakness (≤12%)
Miscellaneous: Flu-like syndrome (≤12%)
1% to 10% (limited to important or life-threatening):
Cardiovascular: Angina (<5%), arrhythmia (<5%), atrial fibrillation (<5%), bradycardia (<5%), CHF (<5%), deep thrombophlebitis (<5%), hyper-/hypotension (<5%), palpitation (<5%), syncope (<5%), tachycardia (<5%)
Central nervous system: Nervousness (≤8%), anxiety (≤6%), confusion (<5%), delusions (<5%), dementia (<5%), fever (<5%), seizure (<5%)
Dermatologic: Acne (≤10%), alopecia (<5%), bruising (≤5%), cellulitis (<5%), pruritus (≤3%), hirsutism (<2%), rash (<2%)
Endocrine & metabolic: Dehydration (≤8%), gynecomastia (≤7%), breast tenderness/pain (≤6%), bicarbonate decreased (≥5%), hyper-/hypocholesterolemia (≥5%), hyperglycemia (≥5%), hyperphosphatemia (≥5%), hyperuricemia (≥5%), hypoalbuminemia (≥5%), hypoproteinemia (≥5%), lactation (<5%), testicular pain (≤4%), menstrual disorder (≤2%)
Gastrointestinal: Dysphagia (<5%), gastrointestinal hemorrhage (<5%), intestinal obstruction (<5%), ulcer (<5%), gastroenteritis/colitis (≤3%), diarrhea (≤2%), constipation (≤2%)
Genitourinary: Prostatic acid phosphatase increased/decreased (≥5%), urine specific gravity increased/decreased (≥5%), impotence (≤5%), balanitis (<5%), incontinence (<5%), penile/testis disorder (<5%), urinary tract infection (<5%), nocturia (≤4%), urinary frequency (4%), dysuria (<2%), urinary retention (<2%), urinary urgency (<2%)
Hematologic: Eosinophilia (≥5%), leukopenia (≥5%), platelets increased (≥5%), anemia
Hepatic: Liver function tests abnormal (≥5%), partial thromboplastin time increased (≥5%), prothrombin time increased (≥5%), hepatomegaly (<5%)
Local: Implant site reaction (persistent or delayed: 9% to 10%), implant site burning (6%)
Neuromuscular & skeletal: Myalgia (≤8%), paresthesia (≤8%), neuropathy (<5%), paralysis (<5%), pathologic fracture (<5%), bone pain (<2%)
Renal: BUN increased (≥5%), creatinine increased (≥5%)
Respiratory: Emphysema (<5%), epistaxis (<5%), hemoptysis (<5%), pleural effusion (<5%), pulmonary edema (<5%), dyspnea (≤2%)
Miscellaneous: Diaphoresis (≤5%), allergic reaction (<5%), infection (5%), lymphadenopathy (<5%)
Immediate release formulation:
>10%:
Cardiovascular: ECG changes/ischemia (19%), peripheral edema (12%)
Central nervous system: Pain (13%)
Endocrine & metabolic: Hot flashes (55%)
1% to 10% (limited to important or life-threatening):
Cardiovascular: Hypertension (8%), murmur (3%), thrombosis/phlebitis (2%), CHF (1%), angina, arrhythmia, MI, syncope
Central nervous system: Headache (7%), insomnia (7%), dizziness/lightheadedness (5%), anxiety, depression, fatigue, fever, nervousness
Dermatologic: Dermatitis (5%), alopecia, bruising, itching, lesions, pigmentation
Endocrine & metabolic: Gynecomastia/breast tenderness/pain (7%), testicular size decreased (7%), diabetes, hypercalcemia, hypoglycemia, libido decreased, thyroid enlarged

674

Gastrointestinal: Constipation (7%), anorexia (6%), nausea/vomiting (5%), diarrhea, dysphagia, gastrointestinal bleeding, peptic ulcer, rectal polyps

Genitourinary: Urinary frequency/urgency (6%), impotence (4%), urinary tract infection (3%), bladder spasm, dysuria, incontinence, testicular pain, urinary obstruction

Hematologic: Anemia (5%)

Local: Injection site reaction

Neuromuscular & skeletal: Weakness (10%), bone pain (5%), peripheral neuropathy

Ocular: Blurred vision

Renal: Hematuria (6%), BUN increased, creatinine increased

Respiratory: Dyspnea (2%), cough, pneumonia, pulmonary embolus, pulmonary fibrosis

Miscellaneous: Infection, inflammation

Children and Adults: *All formulations:* Postmarketing and/or case reports (limited to important or life-threatening): Anaphylactic/anaphylactoid reactions, asthmatic reactions, bone density decreased; fibromyalgia-like symptoms (arthralgia/myalgia, headaches, GI distress); hemoptysis, hepatic dysfunction, hypokalemia, hypoproteinemia, implant extrusion, implant migration, injection site induration/abscess, MI, pelvic fibrosis, penile swelling, photosensitivity; pituitary apoplexy (cardiovascular collapse, mental status altered, ophthalmoplegia, sudden headache, visual changes, vomiting); prostate pain, pulmonary embolism, pulmonary infiltrate, spinal fracture/paralysis, stroke, tenosynovitis-like symptoms, thrombocytopenia, transient ischemia attack, uric acid increased, urticaria, WBC increased

Overdosage/Toxicology Treatment is symptom-directed and supportive.

Storage/Stability

Lupron®: Store unopened vials of injection in refrigerator, vial in use can be kept at room temperature of ≤30°C (86°F) for several months with minimal loss of potency. Protect from light and store vial in carton until use. Do not freeze.

Eligard®: Store at 2°C to 8°C (36°F to 46°F). Allow to reach room temperature prior to using; once mixed, must be administered within 30 minutes.

Lupron Depot® may be stored at room temperature of 15°C to 30°C (59°F to 86°F). Upon reconstitution, the suspension does not contain a preservative and should be used immediately.

Viadur® may be stored at room temperature of 15°C to 30°C (59°F and 86°F).

Reconstitution

Eligard®: Packaged in two syringes; one contains the Atrigel® polymer system and the second contains leuprolide acetate powder; follow package instructions for mixing

Lupron Depot®: Reconstitute only with diluent provided

Mechanism of Action Leuprolide, is an agonist of luteinizing hormone-releasing hormone (LHRH). Acting as a potent inhibitor of gonadotropin secretion; continuous daily administration results in suppression of ovarian and testicular steroidogenesis due to decreased levels of LH and FSH with subsequent decrease in testosterone (male) and estrogen (female) levels. Leuprolide may also have a direct inhibitory effect on the testes, and act by a different mechanism not directly related to reduction in serum testosterone.

Pharmacodynamics/Kinetics

Onset of action: Following transient increase, testosterone suppression occurs in ~2-4 weeks of continued therapy

(Continued)

Leuprolide *(Continued)*

Distribution: Males: V_d: 27 L

Protein binding: 43% to 49%

Metabolism: Major metabolite, pentapeptide (M-1)

Bioavailability: Oral: None; SubQ: 94%

Half-life elimination: I.V.: 3 hours

Excretion: Urine (<5% as parent and major metabolite)

Dosage

Children: Precocious puberty (consider discontinuing by age 11 for females and by age 12 for males):

SubQ (Lupron®): Initial: 50 mcg/kg/day (per manufacturer, doses of 20-45 mcg/kg/day have also been reported); titrate dose upward by 10 mcg/kg/day if down-regulation is not achieved

I.M. (Lupron Depot-Ped®): 0.3 mg/kg/dose given every 28 days (minimum dose: 7.5 mg)

≤25 kg: 7.5 mg

>25-37.5 kg: 11.25 mg

>37.5 kg: 15 mg

Titrate dose upward in increments of 3.75 mg every 4 weeks if down-regulation is not achieved.

Adults:

Advanced prostatic carcinoma:

SubQ:

Eligard®: 7.5 mg monthly **or** 22.5 mg every 3 months **or** 30 mg every 4 months **or** 45 mg every 6 months

Lupron®: 1 mg/day

Viadur®: 65 mg implanted subcutaneously every 12 months

I.M.:

Lupron Depot®: 7.5 mg/dose given monthly (every 28-33 days) **or**

Lupron Depot®-3: 22.5 mg every 3 months **or**

Lupron Depot®-4: 30 mg every 4 months

Breast cancer, premenopausal ovarian ablation (unlabeled use): I.M.:

Lupron Depot®: 3.75 mg every 28 days **or**

Lupron Depot®-3: 11.25 mg every 3 months

Endometriosis: I.M.: Initial therapy may be with leuprolide alone or in combination with norethindrone; if retreatment for an additional 6 months is necessary, norethindrone should be used. Retreatment is not recommended for longer than one additional 6-month course.

Lupron Depot®: 3.75 mg/month for up to 6 months **or**

Lupron Depot®-3: 11.25 mg every 3 months for up to 2 doses (6 months total duration of treatment)

Uterine leiomyomata (fibroids): I.M. (in combination with iron):

Lupron Depot®: 3.75 mg/month for up to 3 months **or**

Lupron Depot®-3: 11.25 mg as a single injection

Combination Regimens

Prostate cancer:

Bicalutamide + LHRH-A *on page 1152*

FL *on page 1215*

Administration

I.M.: Lupron Depot®: Vary injection site periodically

SubQ:

Eligard®: Vary injection site; choose site with adequate subcutaneous tissue (eg, abdomen, upper buttocks)

Lupron®: Vary injection site; if an alternate syringe from the syringe provided is required, insulin syringes should be used

Other: Viadur® implant: Requires surgical implantation (subcutaneous) and removal at 12-month intervals

Monitoring Parameters Bone mineral density

Precocious puberty: GnRH testing (blood LH and FSH levels), measurement of bone age every 6-12 months, testosterone in males and estradiol in females; Tanner staging

Prostatic cancer: LH and FSH levels, serum testosterone (2-4 weeks after initiation of therapy), PSA; weakness, paresthesias, and urinary tract obstruction in first few weeks of therapy

Test Interactions Interferes with pituitary gonadotropic and gonadal function tests during and up to 3 months after monthly administration of leuprolide therapy. Viadur®: Efficacy and stability of product not affected by MRI or radiographic exposure, although device will be visualized during these diagnostic procedures.

Patient Information Do not discontinue medication without prescriber's advice. May cause depression; report changes in mood or memory immediately. For self administration, patient must be taught aseptic technique and SubQ injection technique; rotate SubQ injection sites frequently. Disease flare can briefly occur with initiation of therapy.

Special Geriatric Considerations Leuprolide has the advantage of not increasing risk of atherosclerotic vascular disease, causing swelling of breasts, fluid retention, and thromboembolism as compared to estrogen therapy.

Additional Information

Eligard® Atrigel®: A nongelatin-based, biodegradable, polymer matrix

Viadur®: Leuprolide acetate implant containing 72 mg of leuprolide acetate, equivalent to 65 mg leuprolide free base. One Viadur® implant delivers 120 mcg of leuprolide/day over 12 months.

Guidelines from the American Society of Clinical Oncology (ASCO) for hormonal management of advanced prostate cancer which is androgen-sensitive (Loblaw, 2007) recommend either orchiectomy or luteinizing hormone-releasing hormone (LHRH) agonists as initial treatment for androgen deprivation.

Emetic Potential Very low (<10%)

Vesicant No

Dosage Forms Excipient information presented when available (limited, particularly for generics); consult specific product labeling.

Implant, subcutaneous:

Viadur®: 65 mg [released over 12 months; packaged with administration kit]

Injection, solution, as acetate: 5 mg/mL (2.8 mL)

Lupron®: 5 mg/mL (2.8 mL) [contains benzyl alcohol; packaged with syringes and alcohol swabs]

Injection, powder for reconstitution, as acetate [depot formulation]:

Eligard®:

7.5 mg [released over 1 month]

22.5 mg [released over 3 months]

30 mg [released over 4 months]

45 mg [released over 6 months]

Lupron Depot®: 3.75 mg, 7.5 mg [released over 1 month; contains polysorbate 80]

Lupron Depot®-3 Month: 11.25 mg, 22.5 mg [released over 3 months; contains polysorbate 80]

Lupron Depot®-4 Month: 30 mg [released over 4 months; contains polysorbate 80]

(Continued)

Leuprolide *(Continued)*

Lupron Depot-Ped®: 7.5 mg, 11.25 mg, 15 mg [released over 1 month; contains polysorbate 80]

References

Adjei AL and Hsu L, "Leuprolide and Other LH-RH Analogues," *Pharm Biotechnol*, 1993, 5:159-99.

Chrisp P and Sorkin EM, "Leuprorelin. A Review of Its Pharmacology and Therapeutic Use in Prostatic Disorders," *Drugs Aging*, 1991, 1(6):487-509.

Crawford ED, Eisenberger MA, McLeod DG, et al, "A Controlled Trial of Leuprolide With and Without Flutamide in Prostatic Carcinoma," *N Engl J Med*, 1989, 321(7):419-24.

Drago JR, Rohner T, Santen R, et al, "Leuprolide: A Review of its Effects in Animals and Man," *Br J Clin Pract Suppl*, 1985, 37:4-7, 16-9.

Kappy MS, Stuart T, and Perelman A, "Efficacy of Leuprolide Therapy in Children With Central Precocious Puberty," *Am J Dis Child*, 1988, 142(10):1061-4.

Kavanagh JJ, Roberts W, Townsend P, et al, "Leuprolide Acetate in the Treatment of Refractory or Persistent Epithelial Ovarian Cancer," *J Clin Oncol*, 1989, 7(1):115-8.

Lee PA and Page JG, "Effects of Leuprolide in the Treatment of Central Precocious Puberty," *J Pediatr*, 1989, 114(2):321-4.

Plosker GL and Brogden RN, "Leuprorelin. A Review of Its Pharmacology and Therapeutic Use in Prostate Cancer, Endometriosis and Other Sex Hormone-Related Disorders," *Drugs*, 1994, 48(6):930-67.

- ♦ **Leuprolide Acetate** *see* Leuprolide *on page 672*
- ♦ **Leuprorelin Acetate** *see* Leuprolide *on page 672*
- ♦ **Leurocristine Sulfate** *see* VinCRIStine *on page 1099*
- ♦ **Leustatin®** *see* Cladribine *on page 231*
- ♦ **Levaquin®** *see* Levofloxacin *on page 678*
- ♦ **Levo-Dromoran®** *see* Levorphanol *on page 685*

Levofloxacin *(lee voe FLOKS a sin)*

U.S. Brand Names Iquix®; Levaquin®; Quixin™

Generic Available No

Canadian Brand Names Levaquin®; Novo-Levofloxacin

Pharmacologic Category Antibiotic, Quinolone

Use

Systemic: Treatment of mild, moderate, or severe infections caused by susceptible organisms. Includes the treatment of community-acquired pneumonia, including multidrug resistant strains of *S. pneumoniae* (MDRSP); nosocomial pneumonia; chronic bronchitis (acute bacterial exacerbation); acute bacterial sinusitis; urinary tract infection (uncomplicated or complicated); acute pyelonephritis; skin or skin structure infections (uncomplicated or complicated); reduce incidence or disease progression of inhalational anthrax (postexposure)

Ophthalmic: Treatment of bacterial conjunctivitis caused by susceptible organisms (Quixin™ 0.5% ophthalmic solution); treatment of corneal ulcer caused by susceptible organisms (Iquix® 1.5% ophthalmic solution)

Unlabeled/Investigational Use Diverticulitis, enterocolitis (*Shigella* spp.), epididymitis (nongonococcal), gonococcal infections, Legionnaires' disease, peritonitis, PID

Note: As of April 2007, the CDC no longer recommends the use of fluoroquinolones for the treatment of gonococcal disease.

Pregnancy Risk Factor C

Lactation Excretion in breast milk unknown/not recommended

Labeled Contraindications Hypersensitivity to levofloxacin, any component of the formulation, or other quinolones

Warnings/Precautions Systemic: Not recommended in children <18 years of age; CNS stimulation may occur (tremor, restlessness, confusion, and very rarely hallucinations or seizures). Potential for seizures, although very rare, may be increased with concomitant NSAID therapy. Use with caution in individuals at risk of seizures, with known or suspected CNS disorders or renal dysfunction; use caution to avoid possible photosensitivity reactions during and for several days following fluoroquinolone therapy

Rare cases of torsade de pointes have been reported in patients receiving levofloxacin. Risk may be minimized by avoiding use in patients with known prolongation of QT interval, bradycardia, hypokalemia, hypomagnesemia, cardiomyopathy, or in those receiving concurrent therapy with Class Ia or Class III antiarrhythmics.

Severe hypersensitivity reactions, including anaphylaxis, have occurred with quinolone therapy. Reactions may present as typical allergic symptoms after a single dose, or may manifest as severe idiosyncratic dermatologic, vascular, pulmonary, renal, hepatic, and/or hematologic events, usually after multiple doses. Prompt discontinuation of drug should occur if skin rash or other symptoms arise. Prolonged use may result in fungal or bacterial super-infection, including *C. difficile*-associated diarrhea (CDAD) and pseudomembranous colitis; CDAD has been observed >2 months postantibiotic treatment. Tendon inflammation and/or rupture have been reported with quinolone antibiotics. Risk may be increased with concurrent corticosteroids, particularly in the elderly. Discontinue at first sign of tendon inflammation or pain. Peripheral neuropathies have been linked to levofloxacin use; discontinue if numbness, tingling, or weakness develops. Quinolones may exacerbate myasthenia gravis.

Fluoroquinolones have been associated with the development of serious, and sometimes fatal, hypoglycemia, most often in elderly diabetics, but also in patients without diabetes. This occurred most frequently with gatifloxacin (no longer available systemically) but may occur at a lower frequency with other quinolones.

Ophthalmic solution: For topical use only. Do not inject subconjunctivally or introduce into anterior chamber of the eye. Contact lenses should not be worn during treatment for bacterial conjunctivitis. Safety and efficacy in children <1 year of age (Quixin™) or <6 years of age (Iquix®) have not been established. **Note:** Indications for ophthalmic solutions are product concentration-specific and should not be used interchangeably.

Adverse Reactions

1% to 10%:
  Cardiovascular: Chest pain (1%), edema (1%)
  Central nervous system: Headache (6%), insomnia (4%), dizziness (3%), fatigue (1%), pain (1%)
  Dermatologic: Rash (2%), pruritus (1%)
  Gastrointestinal: Nausea (7%), diarrhea (5%), constipation (3%), abdominal pain (2%), dyspepsia (2%), vomiting (2%)
  Genitourinary: Vaginitis (1%)
  Local: Injection site reaction (1%)
  Ocular (with ophthalmic solution use): Decreased vision (transient), foreign body sensation, transient ocular burning, ocular pain or discomfort, photophobia
  Respiratory: Pharyngitis (4%), dyspnea (1%)
<1%, postmarketing, and/or case reports (limited to important or life-threatening):
  Systemic: Acute renal failure, agitation, agranulocytosis; allergic reaction (including anaphylaxis, angioedema, pneumonitis rash, pneumonitis, and serum sickness); anaphylactoid reaction, arrhythmia (including atrial/ventricular tachycardia/fibrillation and torsade de pointes), aplastic
(Continued)

Levofloxacin *(Continued)*

anemia, arthralgia, ascites, bradycardia, bronchospasm, carcinoma, cardiac failure, cholecystitis, cholelithiasis, confusion, depression, EEG abnormalities, encephalopathy, eosinophilia, erythema multiforme, GI hemorrhage, granulocytopenia, hallucination, heart block, hemolytic anemia, hemoptysis, hepatic failure (some fatal), hepatitis, hyper-/hypoglycemia, hyperkalemia, hyperkinesias, hyper-/hypotension, infection, INR increased, intestinal obstruction, intracranial hypertension, involuntary muscle contractions, jaundice, leukocytosis, leukopenia, leukorrhea, lymphadenopathy, MI, migraine, multiple organ failure, nephritis (interstitial), palpitation, pancreatitis, pancytopenia, paralysis, paresthesia, peripheral neuropathy, photosensitivity (<0.1%), pleural effusion, pneumonitis, postural hypotension, prothrombin time increased/decreased, pseudomembraneous colitis, psychosis, pulmonary edema, pulmonary embolism, purpura, QT_c prolongation, respiratory depression, rhabdomyolysis, seizure, skin disorder, somnolence, speech disorder, Stevens-Johnson syndrome, stupor, syncope, tendon rupture, tongue edema, transaminases increased, thrombocythemia, thrombocytopenia, tremor, urticaria, WBC abnormality

Ophthalmic solution: Allergic reaction, lid edema, ocular dryness, ocular itching

Overdosage/Toxicology

Symptoms of overdose include acute renal failure, seizures

Treatment should include GI decontamination and supportive care; not removed by peritoneal or hemodialysis

Drug Interactions

Increased Effect/Toxicity: Levofloxacin may increase the effects/toxicity of glyburide and warfarin (and other coumarin-type anticoagulants). Concomitant use with corticosteroids may increase the risk of tendon rupture. Concomitant use with other QT_c-prolonging agents (eg, Class Ia and Class III antiarrhythmics, erythromycin, cisapride, antipsychotics [thioridazine is contraindicated], and cyclic antidepressants) may result in arrhythmias, such as torsade de pointes. Probenecid may increase levofloxacin levels. Concomitant use with NSAIDs may rarely increase risk of seizure.

Decreased Effect: Concurrent administration of metal cations, including most antacids, oral electrolyte supplements, quinapril, sevelamer, sucralfate, some didanosine formulations (pediatric powder for oral suspension), and other highly-buffered oral drugs, may decrease quinolone levels; separate doses. Antibiotics may decrease the therapeutic effect of live, attenuated Ty21a vaccine; delay vaccination for >24 hours after administration of antibacterial agents.

Storage/Stability

Solution for injection:

Vial: Store at room temperature. Protect from light. Diluted solution is stable for 72 hours when stored at room temperature; stable for 14 days when stored under refrigeration. When frozen, stable for 6 months; do not refreeze. Do not thaw in microwave or by bath immersion.

Premixed: Store at ≤25°C (77°F); do not freeze. Brief exposure to 40°C (104°F) does not affect product. Protect from light.

Tablet, oral solution: Store at 25°C (77°F); excursions permitted to 15°C to 25°C (59°F to 77°F).

Ophthalmic solution: Store at 15°C to 25°C (59°F to 77°F).

Reconstitution Solution for injection: Single-use vials must be further diluted in compatible solution to a final concentration of 5 mg/mL prior to infusion.

Compatibility Stable in D₅LR, D₅NS, D₅¹/₂NS with 0.15% KCl, D₅W, NS, Plasma-Lyte® 56/5% dextrose, sodium lactate (M/6); **incompatible** with mannitol 20%, sodium bicarbonate 5%.

Y-site administration: Compatible: Amikacin, aminophylline, ampicillin, caffeine citrate, cefotaxime, cimetidine, clindamycin, dexamethasone sodium phosphate, dobutamine, dopamine, epinephrine, fentanyl, gentamicin, isoproterenol, lidocaine, linezolid, lorazepam, metoclopramide, morphine, oxacillin, pancuronium, penicillin G sodium, phenobarbital, phenylephrine, sodium bicarbonate, vancomycin. **Incompatible:** Acyclovir, alprostadil, furosemide, heparin, indomethacin, nitroglycerin, sodium nitroprusside. **Variable (consult detailed reference):** Insulin (regular).

Mechanism of Action As the S (-) enantiomer of the fluoroquinolone, ofloxacin, levofloxacin, inhibits DNA-gyrase in susceptible organisms thereby inhibits relaxation of supercoiled DNA and promotes breakage of DNA strands. DNA gyrase (topoisomerase II), is an essential bacterial enzyme that maintains the superhelical structure of DNA and is required for DNA replication and transcription, DNA repair, recombination, and transposition.

Pharmacodynamics/Kinetics

Absorption: Rapid and complete

Distribution: V_d: 1.25 L/kg; CSF concentrations ~15% of serum levels; high concentrations are achieved in prostate, lung, and gynecological tissues, sinus, saliva

Protein binding: 50%

Metabolism: Minimally hepatic

Bioavailability: 99%

Half-life elimination: 6-8 hours

Time to peak, serum: 1-2 hours

Excretion: Primarily urine (as unchanged drug)

Dosage Note: Sequential therapy (intravenous to oral) may be instituted based on prescriber's discretion.

Usual dosage range:

Children ≥1 year: Ophthalmic: 1-2 drops every 2-6 hours

Adults:

Ophthalmic: 1-2 drops every 2-6 hours

Oral, I.V.: 250-500 mg every 24 hours; severe or complicated infections: 750 mg every 24 hours

Indication-specific dosing:

Children ≥1 year and Adults: Ophthalmic:

Conjunctivitis (0.5% ophthalmic solution):

Treatment day 1 and day 2: Instill 1-2 drops into affected eye(s) every 2 hours while awake, up to 8 times/day

Treatment day 3 through day 7: Instill 1-2 drops into affected eye(s) every 4 hours while awake, up to 4 times/day

Children ≥6 years and Adults: Ophthalmic:

Corneal ulceration (1.5% ophthalmic solution): Treatment day 1 through day 3: Instill 1-2 drops into affected eye(s) every 30 minutes to 2 hours while awake and 4-6 hours after retiring.

Adults: Oral, I.V.:

Anthrax (inhalational): 500 mg every 24 hours for 60 days, beginning as soon as possible after exposure

Chronic bronchitis (acute bacterial exacerbation): 500 mg every 24 hours for at least 7 days

Diverticulitis, peritonitis (unlabeled use): 750 mg every 24 hours for 7-10 days; use adjunctive metronidazole therapy

Dysenteric enterocolitis, _Shigella_ spp. (unlabeled use): 500 mg every 24 hours for 3-5 days

(Continued)

Levofloxacin *(Continued)*

Epididymitis, nongonococcal (unlabeled use): 500 mg once daily for 10 days

Gonococcal infection (unlabeled use):

Cervicitis, urethritis: 250 mg for one dose with azithromycin or doxycycline; **Note:** As of April 2007, the CDC no longer recommends the use of fluoroquinolones for the treatment of uncomplicated gonococcal disease.

Disseminated infection: 250 mg I.V. once daily; 24 hours after symptoms improve may change to 500 mg orally every 24 hours to complete total therapy of 7 days; **Note:** As of April 2007, the CDC no longer recommends the use of fluoroquinolones for the treatment of more serious gonococcal disease, unless no other options exist and susceptibility can be confirmed via culture.

Pelvic inflammatory disease (unlabeled use): 500 mg once daily for 14 days with or without adjunctive metronidazole; **Note:** The CDC recommends use only if standard cephalosporin therapy is not feasible and community prevalence of quinolone-resistant gonococcal organisms is low. Culture sensitivity must be confirmed.

Pneumonia:

Community-acquired: 500 mg every 24 hours for 7-14 days or 750 mg every 24 hours for 5 days (efficacy of 5-day regimen for MDRSP not established)

Nosocomial: 750 mg every 24 hours for 7-14 days

Prostatitis (chronic bacterial): 500 mg every 24 hours for 28 days

Sinusitis (acute bacterial): 500 mg every 24 hours for 10-14 days or 750 mg every 24 hours for 5 days

Skin and skin structure infections:

Uncomplicated: 500 mg every 24 hours for 7-10 days

Complicated: 750 mg every 24 hours for 7-14 days

Traveler's diarrhea (unlabeled use): 500 mg for one dose

Urinary tract infections:

Uncomplicated: 250 mg once daily for 3 days

Complicated, including pyelonephritis: 250 mg once daily for 10 days **or** 750 mg once daily for 5 days

Dosing adjustment in renal impairment:

Normal renal function dosing of 750 mg/day:

Cl_{cr} 20-49 mL/minute: Administer 750 mg every 48 hours

Cl_{cr} 10-19 mL/minute: Administer 750 mg initial dose, followed by 500 mg every 48 hours

Hemodialysis/CAPD: Administer 750 mg initial dose, followed by 500 mg every 48 hours

Normal renal function dosing of 500 mg/day:

Cl_{cr} 20-49 mL/minute: Administer 500 mg initial dose, followed by 250 mg every 24 hours

Cl_{cr} 10-19 mL/minute: Administer 500 mg initial dose, followed by 250 mg every 48 hours

Hemodialysis/CAPD: Administer 500 mg initial dose, followed by 250 mg every 48 hours

Normal renal function dosing of 250 mg/day:

Cl_{cr} 20-49 mL/minute: No dosage adjustment required

Cl_{cr} 10-19 mL/minute: Administer 250 mg every 48 hours (except in uncomplicated UTI, where no dosage adjustment is required)

Hemodialysis/CAPD: No information available

CRRT: **Note:** Clearance dependent on filter type, flow rates, and other variables.

CVVH/CVVHD/CVVHDF: Alternative recommendations exist:

500 mg every 48 hours **or**

250 mg every 24 hours (**Note:** This regimen has been shown to be equivalent to 500 mg/day in normal renal function. Appropriateness of this regimen for target dosing equal to 750 mg/day is not known.)

Administration

Oral: Tablets may be administered without regard to meals. Oral solution should be administered 1 hour before or 2 hours after meals.

I.V.: Infuse 250-500 mg I.V. solution over 60 minutes; infuse 750 mg I.V. solution over 90 minutes. Too rapid of infusion can lead to hypotension. Avoid administration through an intravenous line with a solution containing multivalent cations (eg, magnesium, calcium).

Monitoring Parameters Evaluation of organ system functions (renal, hepatic, ophthalmologic, and hematopoietic) is recommended periodically during therapy; the possibility of crystalluria should be assessed; WBC and signs of infection

Test Interactions Some quinolones may produce a false-positive urine screening result for opiates using commercially-available immunoassay kits. This has been demonstrated most consistently for levofloxacin and ofloxacin, but other quinolones have shown cross-reactivity in certain assay kits. Confirmation of positive opiate screens by more specific methods should be considered.

Dietary Considerations Tablets may be taken without regard to meals. Oral solution should be administered on an empty stomach (1 hour before or 2 hours after a meal).

Patient Information

Oral: Take per recommended schedule, preferably on an empty stomach (1 hour before or 2 hours after meals). Maintain adequate hydration (2-3 L/day of fluids unless instructed to restrict fluid intake). Take entire course of medication. Do not take with antacids; separate by 2 hours. You may experience dizziness, lightheadedness, or confusion; use caution when driving or engaging in tasks that require alertness until response to drug is known. Small frequent meals and frequent mouth care may reduce nausea or vomiting. You may experience photosensitivity; use sunscreen, wear protective clothing and eyewear, and avoid direct sunlight. Report palpitations or chest pain, persistent diarrhea, GI disturbances or abdominal pain, muscle tremor or pain, yellowing of eyes or skin, easy bruising or bleeding, unusual fatigue, fever, chills, signs of infection, or worsening of condition. Report immediately any rash, itching, unusual CNS changes, or any facial swelling. Report immediately any pain, inflammation, or rupture of tendon.

Ophthalmic: Wash hands before instilling solution. Sit or lie down to instill. Open eye, look at ceiling, and instill prescribed amount of solution. Close eye and roll eye in all directions, and apply gentle pressure to inner corner of eye. Do not let tip of applicator touch eye or contaminate tip of applicator. Temporary stinging or blurred vision may occur. Report persistent pain, burning, vision disturbances, swelling, itching, or worsening of condition. Discontinue medication and contact prescriber immediately if you develop a rash or allergic reaction. Do not wear contact lenses.

Special Geriatric Considerations The risk of torsade de pointes and tendon inflammation and/or rupture associated with the concomitant use of corticosteroids and quinolones is increased in the elderly population. Adjust dose for renal function.

(Continued)

Levofloxacin *(Continued)*

Dosage Forms Excipient information presented when available (limited, particularly for generics); consult specific product labeling.

Infusion [premixed in D_5W] (Levaquin®): 250 mg (50 mL); 500 mg (100 mL); 750 mg (150 mL)

Injection, solution [preservative free] (Levaquin®): 25 mg/mL (20 mL, 30 mL)

Solution, ophthalmic:

Iquix®: 1.5% (5 mL)

Quixin™: 0.5% (5 mL) [contains benzalkonium chloride]

Solution, oral (Levaquin®): 25 mg/mL (480 mL) [contains benzyl alcohol]

Tablet (Levaquin®): 250 mg, 500 mg, 750 mg

Levaquin® Leva-Pak: 750 mg (5s)

References

American Thoracic Society and Infectious Diseases Society of America, "Guidelines for the Management of Adults With Hospital-Acquired, Ventilator-Associated, and Health-care-Associated Pneumonia," *Am J Respir Crit Care Med*, 2005, 171(4):388-416.

Centers for Disease Control and Prevention, "Update to CDC's Sexually Transmitted Diseases Treatment Guidelines, 2006: Fluoroquinolones No Longer Recommended for Treatment of Gonococcal Infections," *MMWR Recomm Rep*, 2007, 56(14):332-6.

Centers for Disease Control and Prevention, "Sexually Transmitted Diseases Treatment Guidelines, 2006," *MMWR*, 2006, 55(RR-11): 1-94.

Ernst ME, Ernst EJ, and Klepser ME, "Levofloxacin and Trovafloxacin: The Next Generation of Fluoroquinolones?" *Am J Health Syst Pharm*, 1997, 54(22):2569-84.

Friedrich LV and Dougherty R, "Fatal Hypoglycemia Associated With Levofloxacin," *Pharmacotherapy*, 2004, 24(12):1807-12.

Frothingham R, "Glucose Homeostasis Abnormalities Associated With Use of Gatifloxacin," *Clin Infect Dis*, 2005, 41(9):1269-76.

Gavin JR 3rd, Kubin R, Choudhri S, et al, "Moxifloxacin and Glucose Homeostasis: A Pooled-Analysis of the Evidence From Clinical and Postmarketing Studies," *Drug Saf*, 2004, 27(9):671-86.

Graumlich JF, Habis S, Avelino RR, et al, "Hypoglycemia in Inpatients After Gatifloxacin or Levofloxacin Therapy: Nested Case-Control Study," *Pharmacotherapy*, 2005, 25(10):1296-302.

Hoogkamp-Korstanje JA, "*In vitro* Activities of Ciprofloxacin, Levofloxacin, Lomefloxacin, Ofloxacin, Pefloxacin, Sparfloxacin, and Trovafloxacin Against Gram-Positive and Gram-Negative Pathogens From Respiratory Tract Infections," *J Antimicrob Chemother*, 1997, 40(3):427-31.

Khaliq Y and Zhanel GG, "Fluoroquinolone-Associated Tendinopathy: A Critical Review of the Literature," *Clin Infect Dis*, 2003, 36(11):1404-10.

Lawrence KR, Adra M, and Keir C, "Hypoglycemia-Induced Anoxic Brain Injury Possibly Associated With Levofloxacin," *J Infect*, 2006, 52(6):e177-80.

Malone RS, Fish DN, Abraham E, et al, "Pharmacokinetics of Levofloxacin and Ciprofloxacin During Continuous Renal Replacement Therapy in Critically Ill Patients," *Antimicrob Agents Chemother*, 2001, 45(10):2949-54.

Martin SJ, Meyer JM, Chuck SK, et al, "Levofloxacin and Sparfloxacin: New Quinolone Antibiotics," *Ann Pharmacother*, 1998, 32(3):320-36.

Mohr JF, McKinnon PS, Peymann PJ, et al, "A Retrospective, Comparative Evaluation of Dysglycemias in Hospitalized Patients Receiving Gatifloxacin, Levofloxacin, Ciprofloxacin, or Ceftriaxone," *Pharmacotherapy*, 2005, 25(10):1303-9.

Nicolle LN, Bradley S, Colgan R et al, "Infectious Disease Society of America Guidelines for the Diagnosis and Treatment of Asymptomatic Bacteriuria in Adults," *Clinical Infectious Diseases*, 2005, 40:643-54.

North DS, Fish DN, and Redington JJ, "Levofloxacin, A Second-Generation Fluoroquinolone," *Pharmacotherapy*, 1998, 18(5):915-35.

Park-Wyllie LY, Juurlink DN, Kopp A, et al, "Outpatient Gatifloxacin Therapy and Dysglycemia in Older Adults," *N Engl J Med*, 2006, 354(13):1352-61.

Pfaller MA and Jones RN, "Comparative Antistreptococcal Activity of Two Newer Fluoroquinolones, Levofloxacin and Sparfloxacin," *Diagn Microbiol Infect Dis*, 1997, 29(3):199-201.

"Sparfloxacin and Levofloxacin," *Med Lett Drugs Ther*, 1997, 39(999):41-3.

Trotman RL, Williamson JC, Shoemaker DM, et al, "Antibiotic Dosing in Critically Ill Adult Patients Receiving Continuous Renal Replacement Therapy," *Clin Infect Dis*, 2005, 41(8):1159-66.

Wang S and Rizvi AA, "Levofloxacin-Induced Hypoglycemia in a Nondiabetic Patient," *Am J Med Sci*, 2006, 331(6):334-5.

Zacher JL and Givone DM, "False-Positive Urine Opiate Screening Associated With Fluoroquinolone Use," *Ann Pharmacother*, 2004, 38:1525-28.

Levorphanol (lee VOR fa nole)

U.S. Brand Names Levo-Dromoran®

Index Terms Levorphanol Tartrate; Levorphan Tartrate

Generic Available Yes: Tablet

Pharmacologic Category Analgesic, Opioid

Use Relief of moderate to severe pain; also used parenterally for preoperative sedation and an adjunct to nitrous oxide/oxygen anesthesia

Restrictions C-II

Pregnancy Risk Factor B/D (prolonged use or high doses at term)

Lactation Excretion in breast milk unknown/not recommended

Labeled Contraindications Hypersensitivity to levorphanol or any component of the formulation; pregnancy (prolonged use or high doses at term)

Warnings/Precautions An opioid-containing analgesic regimen should be tailored to each patient's needs and based upon the type of pain being treated (acute versus chronic), the route of administration, degree of tolerance for opioids (naive versus chronic user), age, weight, and medical condition. The optimal analgesic dose varies widely among patients. Doses should be titrated to pain relief/prevention.

May cause CNS depression, which may impair physical or mental abilities; patients must be cautioned about performing tasks which require mental alertness (eg, operating machinery or driving). Effects may be potentiated when used with other sedative drugs or ethanol. Use with caution in patients with hypersensitivity reactions to other phenanthrene derivative opioid agonists (morphine, hydrocodone, hydromorphone, oxycodone, oxymorphone); respiratory diseases including asthma, emphysema, COPD, hypothyroidism, head trauma, morbid obesity, adrenal insufficiency, prostatic hyperplasia/urinary stricture, or severe liver or renal insufficiency. Use with caution in patients with biliary tract dysfunction; acute pancreatitis may cause constriction of sphincter of Oddi. Some preparations contain sulfites which may cause allergic reactions. May be habit-forming. May cause hypotension; use with caution in patients with depleted blood volume or drugs which may exaggerate hypotensive effects (including phenothiazines or general anesthetics). May obscure diagnosis or clinical course of patients with acute abdominal conditions. Concurrent use of agonist/antagonist analgesics may precipitate withdrawal symptoms and/or reduced analgesic efficacy in patients following prolonged therapy with mu opioid agonists. Abrupt discontinuation following prolonged use may also lead to withdrawal symptoms. Elderly and debilitated patients may be particularly susceptible to the adverse effects of narcotics. Safety and efficacy have not been established in children.

Adverse Reactions Frequency not defined.

Cardiovascular: Palpitation, hypotension, bradycardia, peripheral vasodilation, cardiac arrest, shock, tachycardia

Central nervous system: CNS depression, fatigue, drowsiness, dizziness, nervousness, headache, restlessness, anorexia, malaise, confusion, coma, convulsion, insomnia, amnesia, mental depression, hallucinations, paradoxical CNS stimulation, intracranial pressure (increased)

Dermatologic: Pruritus, urticaria, rash

Endocrine & metabolic: Antidiuretic hormone release

Gastrointestinal: Nausea, vomiting, dyspepsia, stomach cramps, xerostomia, constipation, abdominal pain, dry mouth, biliary tract spasm, paralytic ileus

Genitourinary: Decreased urination, urinary tract spasm, urinary retention

(Continued)

Levorphanol *(Continued)*

Local: Pain at injection site

Neuromuscular & skeletal: Weakness

Ocular: Miosis, diplopia

Respiratory: Respiratory depression, apnea, hypoventilation, cyanosis

Miscellaneous: Histamine release, physical and psychological dependence

Overdosage/Toxicology Symptoms of overdose include CNS depression, respiratory depression, miosis, apnea, pulmonary edema, and convulsions. Naloxone, 2 mg I.V. with repeat administration as necessary up to a total dose of 10 mg, can be used to reverse opiate effects.

Drug Interactions

Increased Effect/Toxicity: CNS depression is enhanced with coadministration of other CNS depressants.

Ethanol/Nutrition/Herb Interactions

Ethanol: Avoid or limit ethanol (may increase CNS depression). Watch for sedation.

Herb/Nutraceutical: Avoid valerian, St John's wort, kava kava, gotu kola (may increase CNS depression).

Storage/Stability Store at room temperature; do not freeze.

Compatibility

Y-site administration: Compatible: Propofol.

Compatibility in syringe: Compatible: Glycopyrrolate.

Compatibility when admixed: Incompatible: Aminophylline, ammonium chloride, amobarbital, chlorothiazide, heparin, pentobarbital, phenobarbital, phenytoin, sodium bicarbonate, thiopental.

Mechanism of Action Levorphanol tartrate is a synthetic opioid agonist that is classified as a morphinan derivative. Opioids interact with stereospecific opioid receptors in various parts of the central nervous system and other tissues. Analgesic potency parallels the affinity for these binding sites. These drugs do not alter the threshold or responsiveness to pain, but the perception of pain.

Pharmacodynamics/Kinetics

Onset of action: Oral: 10-60 minutes

Duration: 4-8 hours

Metabolism: Hepatic

Half-life elimination: 11-16 hours

Excretion: Urine (as inactive metabolite)

Dosage Adults: **Note:** These are guidelines and do not represent the maximum doses that may be required in all patients. Doses should be titrated to pain relief/prevention.

Acute pain (moderate to severe):

Oral: Initial: Opiate-naive: 2 mg every 6-8 hours as needed; patients with prior opiate exposure may require higher initial doses; usual dosage range: 2-4 mg every 6-8 hours as needed

I.M., SubQ: Initial: Opiate-naive: 1 mg every 6-8 hours as needed; patients with prior opiate exposure may require higher initial doses; usual dosage range: 1-2 mg every 6-8 hours as needed

Slow I.V.: Initial: Opiate-naive: Up to 1 mg/dose every 3-6 hours as needed; patients with prior opiate exposure may require higher initial doses

Chronic pain: Patients taking opioids chronically may become tolerant and require doses higher than the usual dosage range to maintain the desired effect. Tolerance can be managed by appropriate dose titration. **There is no optimal or maximal dose for levorphanol in chronic pain. The**

appropriate dose is one that relieves pain throughout its dosing interval without causing unmanageable side effects.

Premedication: I.M., SubQ: 1-2 mg/dose 60-90 minutes prior to surgery; older or debilitated patients usually require less drug

Dosing adjustment in hepatic disease: Reduction is necessary in patients with liver disease

Administration I.V.: Inject 3 mg over 4-5 minutes

Monitoring Parameters Pain relief, respiratory and mental status, blood pressure

Patient Information Avoid alcohol, may cause drowsiness, impaired judgment or coordination; may cause physical and psychological dependence with prolonged use

Special Geriatric Considerations The elderly may be particularly susceptible to the CNS depressant and constipating effects of narcotics.

Vesicant No

Dosage Forms Excipient information presented when available (limited, particularly for generics); consult specific product labeling.

Injection, solution, as tartrate: 2 mg/mL (1 mL, 10 mL)

Tablet, as tartrate: 2 mg

References

"Drugs for Pain," *Med Lett Drugs Ther*, 2000, 42(1085):73-8.

Mokhlesi B, Leikin JB, Murray P, et al, "Adult Toxicology in Critical Care: Part II: Specific Poisonings," *Chest*, 2003, 123(3):897-922.

"Principles of Analgesic Use in the Treatment of Acute Pain and Chronic Cancer Pain," 5th ed, Glenview, IL: American Pain Society, 2003.

Sinclair JG and Lo GF, "The Blockade of Serotonin Uptake and the Meperidine-Monoamine Oxidase Inhibitor Interaction," *Proc West Pharmacol Soc*, 1977, 20:373-4.

♦ **Levorphanol Tartrate** *see* Levorphanol *on page 685*

♦ **Levorphan Tartrate** *see* Levorphanol *on page 685*

♦ **LH-RH Agonist** *see* Histrelin *on page 540*

Lidocaine and Prilocaine (LYE doe kane & PRIL oh kane)

U.S. Brand Names EMLA®; Oraquix®

Index Terms Prilocaine and Lidocaine

Generic Available Yes: Cream

Canadian Brand Names EMLA®

Pharmacologic Category Local Anesthetic

Use Topical anesthetic for use on normal intact skin to provide local analgesia for minor procedures such as I.V. cannulation or venipuncture; has also been used for painful procedures such as lumbar puncture and skin graft harvesting; for superficial minor surgery of genital mucous membranes and as an adjunct for local infiltration anesthesia in genital mucous membranes.

Pregnancy Risk Factor B

Lactation Enters breast milk/compatible

Labeled Contraindications Hypersensitivity to amide-type anesthetic agents (eg, lidocaine, prilocaine, dibucaine, mepivacaine, bupivacaine, etidocaine); hypersensitivity to any component of the formulation selected; application on mucous membranes or broken or inflamed skin; infants <1 month of age if gestational age is <37 weeks; infants <12 months of age receiving therapy with methemoglobin-inducing agents; children with congenital or idiopathic methemoglobinemia, or in children who are receiving medications associated with drug-induced methemoglobinemia (eg, acetaminophen [overdosage], benzocaine, chloroquine, dapsone, nitrofurantoin, nitroglycerin, nitroprusside, phenazopyridine, phenelzine, phenobarbital, phenytoin, quinine, sulfonamides)

(Continued)

Lidocaine and Prilocaine *(Continued)*

Warnings/Precautions Use with caution in patients with severe hepatic impairment. Use with caution in the debilitated or acutely ill patients and the elderly. Use with caution in patients receiving class I and III antiarrhythmic drugs, since systemic absorption occurs and synergistic toxicity is possible. Although the incidence of systemic adverse reactions with EMLA® is very low, caution should be exercised, particularly when applying over large areas and leaving on for longer than 2 hours. Avoid use on open wounds or near the eyes.

Adverse Reactions Frequency not defined.

Cardiovascular: Hypotension, angioedema

Central nervous system: Shock

Dermatologic: Hyperpigmentation, erythema, itching, rash, burning, urticaria

Genitourinary: Blistering of foreskin (rare)

Local: Burning, stinging, edema

Respiratory: Bronchospasm

Miscellaneous: Alteration in temperature sensation, hypersensitivity reactions

Drug Interactions

Cytochrome P450 Effect: Lidocaine: **Substrate** of CYP1A2 (minor), 2A6 (minor), 2B6 (minor), 2C9 (minor), 2D6 (major), 3A4 (major); **Inhibits** CYP1A2 (strong), 2D6 (strong), 3A4 (moderate)

Increased Effect/Toxicity: The effects of class I antiarrhythmic drugs (eg, mexiletine) are additive and potentially synergistic. The cardiac effects of class III antiarrhythmic drugs (eg, amiodarone, sotalol, dofetilide) may be additive; consider ECG monitoring. Prilocaine may enhance the effect of other drugs known to induce methemoglobinemia.

Storage/Stability Store at room temperature.

Mechanism of Action Local anesthetic action occurs by stabilization of neuronal membranes and inhibiting the ionic fluxes required for the initiation and conduction of impulses

Pharmacodynamics/Kinetics

EMLA®:

Onset of action: 1 hour

Peak effect: 2-3 hours

Duration: 1-2 hours after removal

Absorption: Related to duration of application and area where applied

3-hour application: 3.6% lidocaine and 6.1% prilocaine

24-hour application: 16.2% lidocaine and 33.5% prilocaine

See individual agents.

Dosage Although the incidence of systemic adverse effects with EMLA® is very low, caution should be exercised, particularly when applying over large areas and leaving on for >2 hours

Children (intact skin): EMLA® should **not** be used in neonates with a gestation age <37 weeks nor in infants <12 months of age who are receiving treatment with methemoglobin-inducing agents

Dosing is based on child's age and weight:

Age 0-3 months or <5 kg: Apply a maximum of 1 g over no more than 10 cm^2 of skin; leave on for no longer than 1 hour

Age 3 months to 12 months and >5 kg: Apply no more than a maximum 2 g total over no more than 20 cm^2 of skin; leave on for no longer than 4 hours

Age 1-6 years and >10 kg: Apply no more than a maximum of 10 g total over no more than 100 cm^2 of skin; leave on for no longer than 4 hours.

Age 7-12 years and >20 kg: Apply no more than a maximum 20 g total over no more than 200 cm² of skin; leave on for no longer than 4 hours.

Note: If a patient greater than 3 months old does not meet the minimum weight requirement, the maximum total dose should be restricted to the corresponding maximum based on patient weight.

Adults (intact skin):

EMLA® cream and EMLA® anesthetic disc: A thick layer of EMLA® cream is applied to intact skin and covered with an occlusive dressing, or alternatively, an EMLA® anesthetic disc is applied to intact skin

Minor dermal procedures (eg, I.V. cannulation or venipuncture): Apply 2.5 g of cream (1/2 of the 5 g tube) over 20-25 cm of skin surface area, or 1 anesthetic disc (1 g over 10 cm²) for at least 1 hour. **Note:** In clinical trials, 2 sites were usually prepared in case there was a technical problem with cannulation or venipuncture at the first site.

Major dermal procedures (eg, more painful dermatological procedures involving a larger skin area such as split thickness skin graft harvesting): Apply 2 g of cream per 10 cm² of skin and allow to remain in contact with the skin for at least 2 hours.

Adult male genital skin (eg, pretreatment prior to local anesthetic infiltration): Apply a thick layer of cream (1 g/10 cm²) to the skin surface for 15 minutes. Local anesthetic infiltration should be performed immediately after removal of EMLA® cream.

Note: Dermal analgesia can be expected to increase for up to 3 hours under occlusive dressing and persist for 1-2 hours after removal of the cream

Adult females: Genital mucous membranes: Minor procedures (eg, removal of condylomata acuminata, pretreatment for local anesthetic infiltration): Apply 5-10 g (thick layer) of cream for 5-10 minutes

Periodontal gel (Oraqix®): Adults: Apply on gingival margin around selected teeth using the blunt-tipped applicator included in package. Wait 30 seconds, then fill the periodontal pockets using the blunt-tipped applicator until gel becomes visible at the gingival margin. Wait another 30 seconds before starting treatment. Maximum recommended dose: One treatment session: 5 cartridges (8.5 g)

Administration For external use only. Avoid application to open wounds or near the eyes. In small infants and children, observe patient to prevent accidental ingestion of cream, disc, or dressing. Choose two application sites available for intravenous access. Apply a thick layer (2.5 g/site ~½ of a 5 g tube) of cream to each designated site of intact skin. Cover each site with the occlusive dressing (Tegaderm®). Mark the time on the dressing. **Allow at least 1 hour for optimum therapeutic effect.** Remove the dressing and wipe off excess EMLA® cream (gloves should be worn). **Smaller areas of treatment are recommended for debilitated patients.**

Patient Information Not for ophthalmic use; for external use only. EMLA® may block sensation in the treated skin.

Emetic Potential Very low (<10%)

Dosage Forms Excipient information presented when available (limited, particularly for generics); consult specific product labeling.

Cream, topical: Lidocaine 2.5% and prilocaine 2.5% (5 g, 30 g)

EMLA®: Lidocaine 2.5% and prilocaine 2.5% (5 g, 30 g) [each packaged with Tegaderm® dressings]

Disc, topical: Lidocaine 2.5% and prilocaine 2.5% per disc (2s, 10s) [each 1 g disc is 10 cm²]

Gel, periodontal: Lidocaine 2.5% and prilocaine 2.5% (1.7 g) [cartridge]

(Continued)

Lidocaine and Prilocaine *(Continued)*

References

Broadman LM, Soliman IE, Hannallah RS, et al, "Analgesic Efficacy of Eutectic Mixture of Local Anesthetics (EMLA®) vs Intradermal Infiltration Prior to Venous Cannulation in Children," *Am J Anaesthesiol*, 1987, 34:S56.

Halperin DL, Koren G, Attias D, et al, "Topical Skin Anesthesia for Venous Subcutaneous Drug Reservoir and Lumbar Puncture in Children," *Pediatrics*, 1989, 84(2):281-4.

Robieux I, Kumar R, Radhakrishnan S, et al, "Assessing Pain and Analgesia With a Lido-caine-Prilocaine Emulsion in Infants and Toddlers During Venipuncture," *J Pediatr*, 1991, 118(6):971-3.

Taddio A, Shennan AT, Stevens B, et al, "Safety of Lidocaine-Prilocaine Cream in the Treatment of Preterm Neonates," *J Pediatr*, 1995, 127(6):1002-5.

Vickers ER, Mazbani N, Gerzina TM, et al, "Pharmacokinetics of EMLA Cream 5% Application to Oral Mucosa," *Anesth Prog*, 1997, 44:32-7.

♦ **Lilly CT-3231** *see* Vindesine *on page 1105*

♦ **Liposomal DAUNOrubicin** *see* DAUNOrubicin Citrate (Liposomal) *on page 305*

♦ **Liposomal DOXOrubicin** *see* DOXOrubicin (Liposomal) *on page 359*

♦ **Locoid**® *see* Hydrocortisone *on page 545*

♦ **Locoid Lipocream**® *see* Hydrocortisone *on page 545*

♦ **L-OHP** *see* Oxaliplatin *on page 845*

Lomustine *(loe MUS teen)*

Medication Safety Issues

Sound-alike/look-alike issues:

Lomustine may be confused with carmustine

High alert medication: The Institute for Safe Medication Practices (ISMP) includes this medication among its list of drugs which have a heightened risk of causing significant patient harm when used in error.

Lomustine should only be administered as a single dose once every 6 weeks; serious errors have occurred when lomustine was inadvertently administered daily.

Related Information

Safe Handling of Hazardous Drugs *on page 1382*

U.S. Brand Names CeeNU®

Index Terms CCNU; NSC-79037

Generic Available No

Canadian Brand Names CeeNU®

Pharmacologic Category Antineoplastic Agent, Alkylating Agent

Use Treatment of brain tumors and Hodgkin's disease

Unlabeled/Investigational Use Non-Hodgkin's lymphoma, melanoma, renal carcinoma, lung cancer, colon cancer

Pregnancy Risk Factor D

Lactation Enters breast milk/contraindicated

Labeled Contraindications Hypersensitivity to lomustine, any component of the formulation, or other nitrosoureas; pregnancy

Warnings/Precautions Hazardous agent - use appropriate precautions for handling and disposal. **[U.S. Boxed Warnings]: Bone marrow suppression, notably thrombocytopenia and leukopenia, may lead to bleeding and overwhelming infections in an already compromised patient;** will last for at least 6 weeks after a dose. Do not administer courses more frequently than every 6 weeks because the toxicity is delayed. Use with caution in patients with depressed platelet, leukocyte or erythrocyte counts, renal (may require dosage adjustment) or hepatic impairment. Bone marrow toxicity is cumulative; dose adjustments should be based on nadir counts from prior dose. May cause delayed pulmonary toxicity (infiltrates and/or fibrosis); usually related to cumulative doses >1100 mg/m^2. Long-term use may be associated with the development of secondary malignancies. **[U.S. Boxed Warning]: Should be administered under the supervision of an experienced cancer chemotherapy physician.**

Adverse Reactions

>10%:

Gastrointestinal: Nausea and vomiting, usually within 3-6 hours after oral administration. Administration of the dose at bedtime, with an antiemetic, significantly reduces both the incidence and severity of nausea.

Hematologic: Myelosuppression, common, dose-limiting, may be cumulative and irreversible; leukopenia (65%; nadir: 5-6 weeks; recovery 6-8 weeks); thrombocytopenia (nadir: 4 weeks; recovery 5-6 weeks)

Frequency not defined: Acute leukemia, alkaline phosphatase increased, alopecia, anemia, ataxia, azotemia (progressive), bilirubin increased, blindness, bone marrow dysplasia, disorientation, dysarthria, kidney size decreased, lethargy, optic atrophy, pulmonary fibrosis, pulmonary infiltrates, renal failure, stomatitis, transaminases increased, visual disturbances

Overdosage/Toxicology Symptoms of overdose include nausea, vomiting, and leukopenia. There are no known antidotes. Treatment is symptom-directed and supportive.

Drug Interactions

Cytochrome P450 Effect: Substrate of CYP2D6 (major); **Inhibits** CYP2D6 (weak), 3A4 (weak)

Increased Effect/Toxicity: CYP2D6 inhibitors may increase the levels/effects of lomustine; example inhibitors include chlorpromazine, delavirdine, fluoxetine, miconazole, paroxetine, pergolide, quinidine, quinine, ritonavir, and ropinirole.

Ethanol/Nutrition/Herb Interactions Ethanol: Avoid ethanol (due to GI irritation).

Storage/Stability Store at 15°C to 30°C (59°F to 86°F).

Mechanism of Action Inhibits DNA and RNA synthesis via carbamylation of DNA polymerase, alkylation of DNA, and alteration of RNA, proteins, and enzymes

Pharmacodynamics/Kinetics

Duration: Marrow recovery: ~5-8 weeks

Absorption: Complete

Distribution: Crosses blood-brain barrier to a greater degree than BCNU; CNS concentrations are ≥50% of plasma concentrations

Metabolism: Rapidly hepatic via hydroxylation producing at least two active metabolites; enterohepatically recycled

Half-life elimination: Parent drug: 16-72 hours; Active metabolite: 16-48 hours

Time to peak, serum: Active metabolite: ~3 hours

Excretion: Urine (~50%); feces (<5%); expired air (<10%)

Dosage Oral (refer to individual protocols):

Children: 75-150 mg/m^2 as a single dose once every 6 weeks; subsequent doses are readjusted after initial treatment according to platelet and leukocyte counts

Adults: 100-130 mg/m^2 as a single dose once every 6 weeks; readjust after initial treatment according to platelet and leukocyte counts

With compromised marrow function: Initial dose: 100 mg/m^2 as a single dose once every 6 weeks

(Continued)

Lomustine *(Continued)*

Repeat courses should only be administered after adequate recovery: Leukocytes >4000/mm^3 and platelet counts >100,000/mm^3

Subsequent dosing adjustment based on nadir:

Leukocytes 2000-2999/mm^3, platelets 25,000-74,999/mm^3: Administer 70% of prior dose

Leukocytes <2000/mm^3, platelets <25,000/mm^3: Administer 50% of prior dose

Dosage adjustment in renal impairment: The FDA-approved labeling does not contain renal dosing adjustment guidelines. The following guidelines have been used by some clinicians:

Aronoff, 2007: Adults:

Cl$_{cr}$ 10-50 mL/minute: Administer 75% of dose

Cl$_{cr}$ <10 mL/minute: Administer 25% to 50% of dose

Hemodialysis: Supplemental dose is not necessary

Continuous ambulatory peritoneal dialysis (CAPD): Administer 25% to 50% of dose

Kintzel, 1995:

Cl$_{cr}$ 46-60 mL/minute: Administer 75% of normal dose

Cl$_{cr}$ 31-45 mL/minute: Administer 70% of normal dose

Cl$_{cr}$ ≤30 mL/minute: Avoid use

Dosage adjustment in hepatic impairment: The FDA-approved labeling does not contain hepatic adjustment guidelines; lomustine is hepatically metabolized and caution should be used in patients with hepatic dysfunction.

Combination Regimens

Brain tumors:

8 in 1 (Brain Tumors) *on page 1141*

PCV *on page 1268*

POC *on page 1271*

Gastric cancer: FAMe *on page 1213*

Lymphoma, Hodgkin's disease: CAD/MOPP/ABV *on page 1157*

Melanoma:

BOLD *on page 1153*

BOLD + Interferon *on page 1153*

BOLD (Melanoma) *on page 1154*

Retinoblastoma: 8 in 1 (Retinoblastoma) *on page 1142*

Administration Take with fluids on an empty stomach; no food or drink for 2 hours after administration.

Monitoring Parameters CBC with differential and platelet count (for at least 6 weeks after dose), hepatic and renal function tests (periodic), pulmonary function tests (baseline and periodic)

Test Interactions Liver function tests

Dietary Considerations Should be taken with fluids on an empty stomach; no food or drink for 2 hours after administration to decrease nausea.

Patient Information Take with fluids on an empty stomach; do not eat or drink for 2 hours following administration. Do not use alcohol, aspirin, or aspirin-containing medications and/or OTC medications without consulting prescriber. Maintain adequate fluid balance (2-3 L/day of fluids unless instructed to restrict fluid intake). May cause hair loss (reversible); easy bleeding or bruising (use soft toothbrush or cotton swabs and frequent mouth care, use electric razor, avoid sharp knives or scissors); increased susceptibility to infection (avoid crowds or exposure to infection - do not have any vaccinations unless approved by prescriber). Report unusual bleeding or bruising or persistent fever or sore throat; blood in urine, stool, or vomitus;

delayed healing of any wounds; skin rash; yellowing of skin or eyes; changes in color of urine of stool. Contraceptive measures are recommended during therapy.

Emetic Potential High (60% to 90%)

Dosage Forms Excipient information presented when available (limited, particularly for generics); consult specific product labeling.

Capsule:

CeeNU®: 10 mg, 40 mg, 100 mg

Capsule [dose pack]:

CeeNU®: 10 mg (2s); 40 mg (2s); 100 mg (2s)

References

Aronoff GR, Bennett WM, Berns JS, et al, *Drug Prescribing in Renal Failure: Dosing Guidelines for Adults and Children*, 5th ed. Philadelphia, PA: American College of Physicians; 2007, p 101.

Berg SL, Grisell DL, DeLaney TF, et al, "Principles of Treatment of Pediatric Solid Tumors," *Pediatr Clin North Am*, 1991, 38(2):249-67.

Bono VH, "Review of Mechanism of Action Studies of the Nitrosoureas," *Cancer Treat Rep*, 1976, 60(6):699-702.

Kintzel PE and Dorr RT, "Anticancer Drug Renal Toxicity and Elimination: Dosing Guidelines for Altered Renal Function," *Cancer Treat Rev*, 1995, 21(1):33-64.

Lee FY, Workman P, Roberts JT, et al, "Clinical Pharmacokinetics or Oral CCNU (Lomustine)," *Cancer Chemother Pharmacol*, 1985, 14(2):125-31.

Oliverio VT, "Pharmacology of the Nitrosoureas: An Overview," *Cancer Treat Rep*, 1976, 60(6):703-7.

Pendergrass TW, Milstein JM, Geyer JR, et al, "Eight Drugs in One Day Chemotherapy for Brain Tumors: Experience in 107 Children and Rationale for Preradiation Chemotherapy," *J Clin Oncol*, 1987, 5(8):1221-31.

Wasserman TH, Slavik M, and Carter SK, "Clinical Comparison of the Nitrosoureas," *Cancer*, 1975, 36(4):1258-68.

Weiss RB and Issell BF, "The Nitrosoureas: Carmustine (BCNU) and Lomustine (CCNU)," *Cancer Treat Rev*, 1982, 9(4):313-30.

Lorazepam (lor A ze pam)

Medication Safety Issues

Sound-alike/look-alike issues:

Lorazepam may be confused with alprazolam, clonazepam, diazepam, temazepam

Ativan® may be confused with Atarax®, Atgam®, Avitene®

Injection dosage form contains propylene glycol. Monitor for toxicity when administering continuous lorazepam infusions.

Related Information

Management of Nausea and Vomiting *on page 1319*

U.S. Brand Names Ativan®; Lorazepam Intensol®

Generic Available Yes

Canadian Brand Names Apo-Lorazepam®; Ativan®; Lorazepam Injection, USP; Novo-Lorazepam; Nu-Loraz; PHL-Lorazepam; PMS-Lorazepam; Riva-Lorazepam

Pharmacologic Category Benzodiazepine

Use

Oral: Management of anxiety disorders or short-term (≤4 months) relief of the symptoms of anxiety or anxiety associated with depressive symptoms

I.V.: Status epilepticus, preanesthesia for desired amnesia

Unlabeled/Investigational Use Ethanol detoxification; insomnia; psychogenic catatonia; partial complex seizures; agitation (I.V.); antiemetic adjunct

Restrictions C-IV

Pregnancy Risk Factor D

Lactation Enters breast milk/not recommended (AAP rates "of concern")

(Continued)

Lorazepam *(Continued)*

Labeled Contraindications Hypersensitivity to lorazepam or any component of the formulation (cross-sensitivity with other benzodiazepines may exist); acute narrow-angle glaucoma; sleep apnea (parenteral); intra-arterial injection of parenteral formulation; severe respiratory insufficiency (except during mechanical ventilation)

Warnings/Precautions Use with caution in elderly or debilitated patients, patients with hepatic disease (including alcoholics) or renal impairment. Use with caution in patients with respiratory disease (COPD or sleep apnea) or limited pulmonary reserve, or impaired gag reflex. Initial doses in elderly or debilitated patients should be at the lower end of the dosing range. May worsen hepatic encephalopathy.

Causes CNS depression (dose-related) resulting in sedation, dizziness, confusion, or ataxia which may impair physical and mental capabilities. Patients must be cautioned about performing tasks which require mental alertness (eg, operating machinery or driving). Use with caution in patients receiving other CNS depressants or psychoactive agents. Effects with other sedative drugs or ethanol may be potentiated. Benzodiazepines have been associated with falls and traumatic injury and should be used with extreme caution in patients who are at risk of these events (especially the elderly).

Lorazepam may cause anterograde amnesia. Paradoxical reactions, including hyperactive or aggressive behavior have been reported with benzodiazepines, particularly in adolescent/pediatric or psychiatric patients. Does not have analgesic, antidepressant, or antipsychotic properties.

Use caution in patients with depression, particularly if suicidal risk may be present. Pre-existing depression may worsen or emerge during therapy. Not recommended for use in primary depressive or psychotic disorders. Use with caution in patients with a history of drug dependence, alcoholism, or significant personality disorders. Benzodiazepines have been associated with dependence and acute withdrawal symptoms on discontinuation or reduction in dose. Acute withdrawal, including seizures, may be precipitated after administration of flumazenil to patients receiving long-term benzodiazepine therapy.

As a hypnotic agent, should be used only after evaluation of potential causes of sleep disturbance. Failure of sleep disturbance to resolve after 7-10 days may indicate psychiatric or medical illness. A worsening of insomnia or the emergence of new abnormalities of thought or behavior may represent unrecognized psychiatric or medical illness and requires immediate and careful evaluation.

The parenteral formulation of lorazepam contains polyethylene glycol and propylene glycol which have resulted in toxicity during high dose and/or longer term infusions. Also contains benzyl alcohol; avoid in neonates.

Safety and efficacy have not been established in children <12 years of age.

Adverse Reactions

>10%:
  Central nervous system: Sedation
  Respiratory: Respiratory depression
1% to 10%:
  Cardiovascular: Hypotension
  Central nervous system: Confusion, dizziness, akathisia, ataxia, headache, depression, disorientation, amnesia
  Dermatologic: Dermatitis, rash
  Gastrointestinal: Weight gain/loss, nausea, changes in appetite

Neuromuscular & skeletal: Weakness

Ocular: Visual disturbances

Respiratory: Nasal congestion, hyperventilation, apnea

<1% or frequency not defined: Asthenia, blood dyscrasias, disinhibition, euphoria, fatigue, increased salivation, menstrual irregularities, physical and psychological dependence (with prolonged use), reflex slowing, polyethylene glycol or propylene glycol poisoning (prolonged I.V. infusion), suicidal ideation, seizure, vertigo

Overdosage/Toxicology Symptoms of overdose include confusion, coma, hypoactive reflexes, dyspnea, labored breathing. **Note:** Prolonged infusions have been associated with toxicity from propylene glycol and/or polyethylene glycol. Treatment for benzodiazepine overdose is supportive. Flumazenil has been shown to selectively block the binding of benzodiazepines to CNS receptors, resulting in a reversal of benzodiazepine-induced CNS depression but not respiratory depression

Drug Interactions

Increased Effect/Toxicity: CNS depressants may increase the CNS effects of lorazepam. Probenecid and/or valproic acid derivatives may increase the levels/effects or lorazepam; adjust lorazepam dose (decrease by 50%).There are rare reports of significant respiratory depression, stupor, and/or hypotension with concomitant use of loxapine and lorazepam. Use caution if concomitant administration of loxapine and CNS drugs is required. Benzodiazepines may enhance the toxic effects of clozapine sedation, hypersalivation, hypotension, ataxia, delirium and respiratory distress reported).

Decreased Effect: Theophylline and other CNS stimulants may antagonize the sedative effects of lorazepam.

Ethanol/Nutrition/Herb Interactions

Ethanol: Avoid or limit ethanol (may increase CNS depression).

Herb/Nutraceutical: Avoid valerian, St John's wort, kava kava, gotu kola (may increase CNS depression).

Storage/Stability

I.V.: Intact vials should be refrigerated. Protect from light. Do not use discolored or precipitate-containing solutions. May be stored at room temperature for up to 60 days. Parenteral admixture is stable at room temperature (25°C) for 24 hours.

Tablet: Store at room temperature.

Reconstitution

Injection: Dilute with equal volume of compatible diluent (D_5W, NS, SWI).

Infusion: Use 2 mg/mL injectable vial to prepare; there may be deceased stability when using 4 mg/mL vial. Dilute ≤1 mg/mL and mix in glass bottle. Precipitation may develop. Can also be administered undiluted via infusion.

Compatibility Variable stability (consult detailed reference) in D_5W, LR, NS.

Y-site administration: Compatible: Acyclovir, alatrofloxacin, albumin, allopurinol, amifostine, amikacin, amphotericin B cholesteryl sulfate complex, amsacrine, atracurium, bumetanide, cefepime, cefotaxime, ciprofloxacin, cisatracurium, cisplatin, cladribine, clonidine, co-trimoxazole, cyclophosphamide, cytarabine, dexamethasone sodium phosphate, diltiazem, dobutamine, docetaxel, dopamine, doxorubicin, doxorubicin liposome, epinephrine, erythromycin lactobionate, etomidate, etoposide phosphate, famotidine, fentanyl, filgrastim, fluconazole, fludarabine, fosphenytoin, (Continued)

Lorazepam *(Continued)*

furosemide, gatifloxacin, gemcitabine, gentamicin, granisetron, haloperidol, heparin, hydrocortisone sodium succinate, hydromorphone, ketanserin, labetalol, levofloxacin, linezolid, melphalan, methotrexate, metronidazole, midazolam, milrinone, morphine, nicardipine, nitroglycerin, norepinephrine, paclitaxel, pancuronium, piperacillin, piperacillin/tazobactam, potassium chloride, propofol, ranitidine, remifentanil, tacrolimus, teniposide, thiotepa, vancomycin, vecuronium, vinorelbine, zidovudine. **Incompatible:** Aldesleukin, aztreonam, floxacillin, idarubicin, imipenem/cilastatin, omeprazole, ondansetron, sargramostim, sufentanil. **Variable (consult detailed reference):** Foscarnet, thiopental, TPN.

Compatibility in syringe: Compatible: Cimetidine, hydromorphone. **Incompatible:** Sufentanil. **Variable (consult detailed reference):** Ranitidine.

Compatibility when admixed: Incompatible: Buprenorphine, dexamethasone sodium phosphate with diphenhydramine and metoclopramide.

Mechanism of Action Binds to stereospecific benzodiazepine receptors on the postsynaptic GABA neuron at several sites within the central nervous system, including the limbic system, reticular formation. Enhancement of the inhibitory effect of GABA on neuronal excitability results by increased neuronal membrane permeability to chloride ions. This shift in chloride ions results in hyperpolarization (a less excitable state) and stabilization.

Pharmacodynamics/Kinetics

Onset of action:
  Hypnosis: I.M.: 20-30 minutes
  Sedation: I.V.: 5-20 minutes
  Anticonvulsant: I.V.: 5 minutes, oral: 30-60 minutes
Duration: 6-8 hours
Absorption: Oral, I.M.: Prompt
Distribution:
  V_d: Neonates: 0.76 L/kg, Adults: 1.3 L/kg; crosses placenta; enters breast milk
Protein binding: 85%; free fraction may be significantly higher in elderly
Metabolism: Hepatic to inactive compounds
Bioavailability: Oral: 90%
Half-life elimination: Neonates: 40.2 hours; Older children: 10.5 hours; Adults: 12.9 hours; Elderly: 15.9 hours; End-stage renal disease: 32-70 hours
Time to peak: Oral: 2 hours
Excretion: Urine; feces (minimal)

Dosage

Antiemetic (unlabeled use):
  Children 2-15 years: I.V.: 0.05 mg/kg (up to 2 mg/dose) prior to chemotherapy
  Adults: Oral, I.V. (**Note:** May be administered sublingually; not a labeled route): 0.5-2 mg every 4-6 hours as needed
Anxiety and sedation (unlabeled in children except for oral use in children >12 years):
  Infants and Children: Oral, I.M., I.V.: Usual: 0.05 mg/kg/dose (range: 0.02-0.09 mg/kg) every 4-8 hours
    I.V.: May use smaller doses (eg, 0.01-0.03 mg/kg) and repeat every 20 minutes, as needed to titrate to effect
  Adults: Oral: 1-10 mg/day in 2-3 divided doses; usual dose: 2-6 mg/day in divided doses
  Elderly: 0.5-4 mg/day; initial dose not to exceed 2 mg

Insomnia: Adults: Oral: 2-4 mg at bedtime

Preoperative: Adults:

I.M.: 0.05 mg/kg administered 2 hours before surgery (maximum: 4 mg/dose)

I.V.: 0.044 mg/kg 15-20 minutes before surgery (usual maximum: 2 mg/dose)

Preprocedural anxiety (dental use): Adults: Oral: 1-2 mg 1 hour before procedure

Operative amnesia: Adults: I.V.: Up to 0.05 mg/kg (maximum: 4 mg/dose)

Sedation (preprocedure): Infants and Children (unlabeled):

Oral, I.M., I.V.: Usual: 0.05 mg/kg (range: 0.02-0.09 mg/kg)

I.V.: May use smaller doses (eg, 0.01-0.03 mg/kg) and repeat every 20 minutes, as needed to titrate to effect

Status epilepticus: I.V.:

Infants and Children (unlabeled): 0.1 mg/kg slow I.V. over 2-5 minutes; do not exceed 4 mg/single dose; may repeat second dose of 0.05 mg/kg slow I.V. in 10-15 minutes if needed

Adolescents: 0.07 mg/kg slow I.V. over 2-5 minutes; maximum: 4 mg/dose; may repeat in 10-15 minutes

Adults: 4 mg/dose slow I.V. over 2-5 minutes; may repeat in 10-15 minutes; usual maximum dose: 8 mg

Rapid tranquilization of agitated patient (administer every 30-60 minutes): Adults:

Oral: 1-2 mg

I.M.: 0.5-1 mg

Average total dose for tranquilization: Oral, I.M.: 4-8 mg

Agitation in the ICU patient (unlabeled): Adults:

I.V.: 0.02-0.06 mg/kg every 2-6 hours

I.V. infusion: 0.01-0.1 mg/kg/hour

Concurrent use of probenecid or valproic acid: Reduce lorazepam dose by 50%

Dosage adjustment in renal impairment: I.V.: Risk of propylene glycol toxicity. Monitor closely if using for prolonged periods of time or at high doses.

Dosage adjustment in hepatic impairment: Use cautiously.

Administration May be administered by I.M., I.V., or orally

I.M.: Should be administered deep into the muscle mass

I.V.: Do not exceed 2 mg/minute or 0.05 mg/kg over 2-5 minutes; dilute I.V. dose with equal volume of compatible diluent (D_5W, NS, SWI). Avoid intra-arterial administration. Monitor I.V. site for extravasation.

Monitoring Parameters Respiratory and cardiovascular status, blood pressure, heart rate, symptoms of anxiety

Patient Information Advise patient of potential for physical and psychological dependence with chronic use; advise patient of possible retrograde amnesia after I.V. or I.M. use; will cause drowsiness, impairment of judgment or coordination

Special Geriatric Considerations Because lorazepam is relatively short-acting with an inactive metabolite, it is a preferred agent to use in elderly patients when a benzodiazepine is indicated.

Additional Information Oral doses >0.09 mg/kg produced increased ataxia without increased sedative benefit vs lower doses; preferred anxiolytic when I.M. route needed. Abrupt discontinuation after sustained use (generally >10 days) may cause withdrawal symptoms.

Emetic Potential Very low (<10%)

Vesicant No

(Continued)

Lorazepam *(Continued)*

Dosage Forms Excipient information presented when available (limited, particularly for generics); consult specific product labeling.

Injection, solution: 2 mg/mL (1 mL, 10 mL); 4 mg/mL (1 mL, 10 mL)
    Ativan®: 2 mg/mL (1 mL, 10 mL); 4 mg/mL (1 mL, 10 mL) [contains benzyl alcohol, polyethylene glycol, and propylene glycol]

Solution, oral concentrate:
    Lorazepam Intensol®: 2 mg/mL (30 mL) [alcohol free, dye free]

Tablet: 0.5 mg, 1 mg, 2 mg
    Ativan®: 0.5 mg, 1 mg, 2 mg

References

Abernethy DR, Greenblatt DJ, Ameer B, et al, "Probenecid Impairment of Acetaminophen and Lorazepam Clearance: Direct Inhibition of Ether Glucuronide Formation," *J Pharmacol Exp Ther*, 1985, 234(2):345-9.

Alldredge BK, Gelb AM, Isaacs SM, et al, "A Comparison of Lorazepam, Diazepam, and Placebo for the Treatment of Out-of-Hospital Status Epilepticus," *N Engl J Med*, 2001, 345(9):631-7.

Ameer B and Greenblatt DJ, "Lorazepam: A Review of Its Clinical Pharmacological Properties and Therapeutic Uses," *Drugs*, 1981, 21(3):162-200.

"American Academy of Pediatrics Committee on Drugs. The Transfer of Drugs and Other Chemicals Into Human Milk," *Pediatrics*, 2001, 108(3):776-89.

Anderson GD, Gidal BE, Kantor ED, et al, "Lorazepam-Valproate Interaction: Studies in Normal Subjects and Isolated Perfused Rat Liver," *Epilepsia*, 1994, 35(1):221-5.

Arroliga AC, Shehab N, McCarthy K, et al, "Relationship of Continuous Infusion Lorazepam to Serum Propylene Glycol Concentration in Critically Ill Adults," *Crit Care Med*, 2004, 32(8):1709-14.

Barnes BJ, Gerst C, Smith JR, et al, "Osmol Gap as a Surrogate Marker for Serum Propylene Glycol Concentrations in Patients Receiving Lorazepam for Sedation," *Pharmacotherapy*, 2006, 26(1):23-33.

Bishop JF, Olver IN, Wolf MM, et al, "Lorazepam: A Randomized, Double-Blind, Crossover Study of a New Antiemetic in Patients Receiving Cytotoxic Chemotherapy and Prochlorpera-zine," *J Clin Oncol*, 1984, 2(5):691-5.

Bleck TB, Seizures, Stroke, and Other Neurologic Emergencies. In: Zimmerman JL, Roberts PR, eds. *Multidisciplinary Critical Care Review*, Des Plains, IL: Society of Critical Care Medicine; 2003:325-34.

Buzdar AU, Esparza L, Natale R, et al, "Lorazepam-Enhancement of the Antiemetic Efficacy of Dexamethasone and Promethazine. A Placebo-Controlled Study," *Am J Clin Oncol*, 1994, 17(5):417-21.

Clark RF, Sage TA, Tunget C, et al, "Delayed Onset Lorazepam Poisoning Successfully Reversed by Flumazenil in a Child: Case Report and Review of the Literature," *Pediatr Emerg Care*, 1995, 11(1):32-4.

Crawford TO, Mitchell WG, and Snodgrass SR, "Lorazepam in Childhood Status Epilepticus and Serial Seizures: Effectiveness and Tachyphylaxis," *Neurology*, 1987, 37(2):190-5.

Deshmukh A, Wittert W, Schnitzler E, et al, "Lorazepam in the Treatment of Refractory Neonatal Seizures: A Pilot Study," *Am J Dis Child*, 1986, 140(10):1042-4.

Divoll M and Greenblatt DJ, "Effect of Age and Sex on Lorazepam Protein Binding," *J Pharm Pharmacol*, 1982, 34(2):122-3.

Fraser AD and Bryan W, "Evaluation of the Abbott TDx® Serum Benzodiazepine Immunoassay for the Analysis of Lorazepam, Adinazolam, and N-Desmethyladinazolam," *J Anal Toxicol*, 1995, 19(5):281-4.

Greenblatt DJ, Allen MD, Locniskar A, et al, "Lorazepam Kinetics in the Elderly," *Clin Pharmacol Ther*, 1979, 26(1):103-13.

Guterman B, Sebastian P, and Sodha N, "Recovery From Alpha Coma After Lorazepam Over-dose," *Clin Electroencephalogr*, 1981, 12(4):205-8.

Hayman M, Seidl EC, Ali M, et al, "Acute Tubular Necrosis Associated With Propylene Glycol From Concomitant Administration of Intravenous Lorazepam and Trimetho-prim-sulfamethoxazole," *Pharmacotherapy*, 2003, 23(9):1190-4.

Henry DW, Burwinkle JW, and Klutman NE, "Determination of Sedative and Amnestic Doses of Lorazepam in Children," *Clin Pharm*, 1991, 10(8):625-9.

Jacobi J, Fraser GL, Coursin DB, et al, "Clinical Practice Guidelines for the Sustained Use of Sedatives and Analgesics in the Critically Ill Adult," *Crit Care Med*, 2002, 30(1):119-41. Available at: http://www.sccm.org/pdf/sedatives.pdf. Accessed August 2, 2003.

Lapierre YD and Labelle A, "Manic-Like Reaction Induced by Lorazepam Withdrawal," *Can J Psychiatry*, 1987, 32(8):697-8.

Laszlo J, Clark RA, Hanson DC, et al, "Lorazepam in Cancer Patients Treated With Cisplatin: A Drug Having Antiemetic, Amnesic, and Anxiolytic Effects," *J Clin Oncol*, 1985, 3(6):864-9.

Lee SA, Lee JK, Heo K, "Coma Probably Induced by Lorazepam-Valproate Interaction," *Seizure*, 2002, 11(2):124-5.

Lee DS, Wong HA, and Knoppert DC, "Myoclonus Associated With Lorazepam Therapy in Very-Low-Birth-Weight Infants," *Biol Neonate*, 1994, 66(6):311-5.

Lheureux P and Askenasi R, "Specific Treatment of Benzodiazepine Overdose," *Hum Toxicol*, 1988, 7(2):165-70.

Malik IA, Khan WA, Qazilbash M, et al, "Clinical Efficacy of Lorazepam in Prophylaxis of Anticipatory, Acute, and Delayed Nausea and Vomiting Induced by High Doses of Cisplatin. A Prospective Randomized Trial," *Am J Clin Oncol*, 1995, 18(2):170-5.

Manno EM, "New Management Strategies in the Treatment of Status Epilepticus," *Mayo Clin Proc*, 2003, 78(4):508-18.

Marshall JD, Farrar HC, and Kearns GL, "Diarrhea Associated With Enteral Benzodiazepine Solutions," *J Pediatr*, 1995, 126(4):657-9.

McDermott CA, Kowalczyk AL, Schnitzler ER, et al, "Pharmacokinetics of Lorazepam in Critically Ill Neonates With Seizures," *J Pediatr*, 1992, 120(3):479-83.

Mokhlesi B, Leikin JB, Murray P, et al, "Adult Toxicology in Critical Care: Part II: Specific Poisonings," *Chest*, 2003, 123(3):897-922.

Samara EE, Granneman RG, Witt GF, et al, "Effect of Valproate on the Pharmacokinetics and Pharmacodynamics of Lorazepam," *J Clin Pharmacol*, 1997, 37(5):442-50.

Stanford GK and Pine RH, "Postburn Delirium Associated With Use of Intravenous Lorazepam," *J Burn Care Rehabil*, 1988, 9(2):160-1.

"Treatment of Convulsive Status Epilepticus. Recommendations of the Epilepsy Foundation of America's Working Group on Status Epilepticus," *JAMA*, 1993, 270(7):854-9.

Treiman DM, Meyers PD, Walton NY, et al, "A Comparison of Four Treatments for Generalized Convulsive Status Epilepticus. Veterans Affairs Status Epilepticus Cooperative Study Group," *N Engl J Med*, 1998, 339(12):792-8.

Uchaipichat V, Mackenzie PI, Guo XH, et al, "Human UDP-Glucuronosyltransferases: Isoform Selectivity and Kinetics of 4-Methylumbelliferone and 1-Naphthol Glucuronidation, Effects of Organic Solvents, and Inhibition by Diclofenac and Probenecid," *Drug Metab Dispos*, 2004, 32(4):413-23.

Vlachos P, Kentarchou P, Poulosa L, et al, "Lorazepam Poisoning," *Toxicol Lett*, 1978, 2:109-10.

von Moltke LL, Manis M, Harmatz JS, et al, "Inhibition of Acetaminophen and Lorazepam Glucuronidation In Vitro by Probenecid," *Biopharm Drug Dispos*, 1993, 14(2):119-30.

Wiley JF and Wiley C, "Benzodiazepine Ingestions in Children," *Clin Toxicol*, 1995, 33(5):520.

Yaucher NE, Fish JT, Smith HW, et al, "Propylene Glycol-Associated Renal Toxicity From Lorazepam Infusion," *Pharmacotherapy*, 2003, 23(9):1094-9.

- **Lorazepam Injection, USP (Can)** see Lorazepam on page 693
- **Lorazepam Intensol®** see Lorazepam on page 693
- **Lotrimin® AF Athlete's Foot Cream [OTC]** see Clotrimazole on page 239
- **Lotrimin® AF for Her [OTC]** see Clotrimazole on page 239
- **Lotrimin® AF Jock Itch Cream [OTC]** see Clotrimazole on page 239
- **Lovenox®** see Enoxaparin on page 376
- **Lovenox® HP (Can)** see Enoxaparin on page 376
- **L-PAM** see Melphalan on page 710
- **L-Sarcolysin** see Melphalan on page 710
- **Lupron®** see Leuprolide on page 672
- **Lupron Depot®** see Leuprolide on page 672
- **Lupron® Depot® (Can)** see Leuprolide on page 672
- **Lupron Depot-Ped®** see Leuprolide on page 672
- **LY170053** see Olanzapine on page 831
- **LY231514** see Pemetrexed on page 884
- **Lymphocyte Immune Globulin** see Antithymocyte Globulin (Equine) on page 100
- **Lymphocyte Mitogenic Factor** see Aldesleukin on page 29
- **Lysodren®** see Mitotane on page 771
- **MabCampath® (Can)** see Alemtuzumab on page 34
- **m-AMSA** see Amsacrine on page 85
- **Marinol®** see Dronabinol on page 367

♦ **Matulane**® *see* Procarbazine *on page 926*
♦ **Maxidex**® *see* Dexamethasone *on page 330*
♦ **Maxipime**® *see* Cefepime *on page 186*
♦ **MDL 73,147EF** *see* Dolasetron *on page 348*

Mechlorethamine (me klor ETH a meen)

Medication Safety Issues
High alert medication: The Institute for Safe Medication Practices (ISMP) includes this medication among its list of drugs which have a heightened risk of causing significant patient harm when used in error.

Related Information
Management of Drug Extravasations *on page 1301*

U.S. Brand Names Mustargen®

Index Terms Chlorethazine; Chlorethazine Mustard; HN$_2$; Mechlorethamine Hydrochloride; Mustine; Nitrogen Mustard; NSC-762

Generic Available No

Canadian Brand Names Mustargen®

Pharmacologic Category Antineoplastic Agent, Alkylating Agent (Nitrogen Mustard)

Use Hodgkin's disease; non-Hodgkin's lymphoma; intracavitary injection for treatment of metastatic tumors; pleural and other malignant effusions; topical treatment of mycosis fungoides

Pregnancy Risk Factor D

Lactation Excretion in breast milk unknown/not recommended

Labeled Contraindications Hypersensitivity to mechlorethamine or any component of the formulation; pre-existing profound myelosuppression or infection

Warnings/Precautions [U.S. Boxed Warnings]: Hazardous agent - use appropriate precautions for handling and disposal. Avoid contact with skin or eyes; avoid exposure during pregnancy. Mechlorethamine is a potent vesicant; if extravasation occurs, severe tissue damage (leading to ulceration and necrosis) and pain may occur. Sodium thiosulfate should be available for treatment of extravasation. May cause lymphopenia, granulocytopenia, thrombocytopenia and anemia. Hyperuricemia may occur, especially with lymphomas; ensure adequate hydration. **[U.S. Boxed Warning]: Should be administered under the supervision of an experienced cancer chemotherapy physician.**

Adverse Reactions
>10%:
  Dermatologic: Alopecia; hyperpigmentation of veins; contact and allergic dermatitis (50% with topical use)
  Endocrine & metabolic: Chromosomal abnormalities, delayed menses, oligomenorrhea, amenorrhea, impaired spermatogenesis
  Gastrointestinal: Nausea and vomiting (almost 100%), onset may be within minutes of drug administration
  Genitourinary: Azoospermia
  Hematologic: Myelosuppression, leukopenia, and thrombocytopenia
    Onset: 4-7 days
    Nadir: 14 days
    Recovery: 21 days
1% to 10%:
  Central nervous system: Fever
  Gastrointestinal: Diarrhea, anorexia, metallic taste
  Otic: Tinnitus

<1%: Vertigo, rash, hemolytic anemia, hepatotoxicity, weakness, peripheral neuropathy

Overdosage/Toxicology Suppression of all formed elements of blood, uric acid crystals, nausea, vomiting, and diarrhea. Sodium thiosulfate is the specific antidote for nitrogen mustard extravasations. Treatment of systemic overdose is supportive.

Drug Interactions

Decreased Effect: Patients may experience impaired immune response to vaccines; possible infection after administration of live vaccines in patients receiving immunosuppressants.

Ethanol/Nutrition/Herb Interactions Ethanol: Avoid ethanol (due to GI irritation).

Storage/Stability Store intact vials at room temperature. Solution is stable for only 15-60 minutes after dilution

Reconstitution Must be prepared immediately before use. Dilute powder with 10 mL SWI to a final concentration of 1 mg/mL. May be diluted in up to 100 mL NS for intracavitary or topical administration.

Compatibility Stable in sterile water for injection; **incompatible** with D_5W; **variable stability (consult detailed reference)** in NS.

Y-site administration: Compatible: Amifostine, aztreonam, filgrastim, fludarabine, granisetron, melphalan, ondansetron, sargramostim, teniposide, vinorelbine. **Incompatible:** Allopurinol, cefepime.

Compatibility when admixed: Incompatible: Methohexital.

Mechanism of Action Bifunctional alkylating agent that inhibits DNA and RNA synthesis via formation of carbonium ions; cross-links strands of DNA, causing miscoding, breakage, and failure of replication; produces interstrand and intrastrand cross-links in DNA resulting in miscoding, breakage, and failure of replication. Although not cell phase-specific *per se*, mechlorethamine effect is most pronounced in the S phase, and cell proliferation is arrested in the G_2 phase.

Pharmacodynamics/Kinetics

Duration: Unchanged drug is undetectable in blood within a few minutes

Absorption: Intracavitary administration: Incomplete secondary to rapid deactivation by body fluids

Metabolism: Rapid hydrolysis and demethylation, possibly in plasma

Half-life elimination: <1 minute

Excretion: Urine (50% as metabolites, <0.01% as unchanged drug)

Dosage Refer to individual protocols.

Children and Adults: I.V.: 6 mg/m² on days 1 and 8 of a 28-day cycle (MOPP regimen)

Adults:

I.V.: 0.4 mg/kg **or** 12-16 mg/m² for one dose **or** divided into 0.1 mg/kg/day for 4 days, repeated at 4- to 6-week intervals

Intracavitary: 0.2-0.4 mg/kg (10-20 mg) as a single dose; may be repeated if fluid continues to accumulate.

Intrapericardially: 0.2-0.4 mg/kg as a single dose; may be repeated if fluid continues to accumulate.

Topical: 0.01% to 0.02% solution, lotion, or ointment

Hemodialysis: Not removed; supplemental dosing is not required.

Peritoneal dialysis: Not removed; supplemental dosing is not required.

Combination Regimens

Brain tumors:

MOP *on page 1249*
MOPP (Medulloblastoma) *on page 1253*

(Continued)

Mechlorethamine *(Continued)*

Lymphoma, Hodgkin's:
CAD/MOPP/ABV *on page 1157*
MOPP (Lymphoma, Hodgkin's Disease) *on page 1252*
MOPP/ABV Hybrid *on page 1251*
MOPP/ABVD *on page 1249*
MVPP *on page 1259*
Stanford V *on page 1278*

Administration I.V. as a slow push through the side of a freely-flowing saline or dextrose solution. Due to the limited stability of the drug, and the increased risk of phlebitis and venous irritation and blistering with increased contact time, infusions of the drug are not recommended.

Mechlorethamine may cause extravasation. Use within 1 hour of preparation. Avoid extravasation since mechlorethamine is a potent vesicant.

Monitoring Parameters CBC with differential, hemoglobin, and platelet count

Patient Information This medication can only be given by infusion, usually in cycles of therapy. You will need frequent laboratory and medical monitoring during treatment. Do not use alcohol, aspirin or aspirin-containing medications, and/or OTC medications without consulting prescriber. Maintain adequate fluid balance (2-3 L/day of fluids unless instructed to restrict fluid intake) and adequate nutrition (small frequent meals, frequent mouth care, sucking lozenges, or chewing gum may reduce anorexia and nausea). May cause discoloration (brown color) of veins used for infusion; hair loss (reversible); easy bleeding or bruising (use soft toothbrush or cotton swabs and frequent mouth care, use electric razor, avoid sharp knives or scissors); increased susceptibility to infection (avoid crowds or exposure to infection - do not have any vaccinations unless approved by prescriber). This drug may cause menstrual irregularities, permanent sterility, and birth defects. Report changes in auditory or visual acuity; unusual bleeding or bruising or persistent fever or sore throat; blood in urine, stool, or vomitus; delayed healing of any wounds; skin rash; yellowing of skin or eyes; changes in color of urine or stool; acute or unresolved nausea or vomiting; diarrhea; or loss of appetite. The drug may be excreted in breast milk, therefore, an alternative form of feeding your baby should be used. Contraceptive measures are recommended during therapy.

Emetic Potential Very high (>90%)

Vesicant Yes; see Management of Drug Extravasations *on page 1301*.

High Dose Considerations

High Dose: I.V.: 0.3-2 mg/kg

Dosage Forms Excipient information presented when available (limited, particularly for generics); consult specific product labeling.

Injection, powder for reconstitution, as hydrochloride: 10 mg

References

Bonadonna G, Valagussa P, and Santoro A, "Alternating Non-Cross-Resistant Combination Chemotherapy or MOPP in Stage IV Hodgkin's Disease. A Report of 8-Year Results," *Ann Intern Med*, 1986, 104(6):739-46.

DeVita VT, Serpick A, and Carbone PP, "Combination Chemotherapy in the Treatment of Advanced Hodgkin's Disease," *Ann Intern Med*, 1970, 73:881-95.

Dorr RT, Soble M, and Alberts DS, "Efficacy of Sodium Thiosulfate as a Local Antidote to Mechlorethamine Skin Toxicity in the Mouse," *Cancer Chemother Pharmacol*, 1988, 22(4):299-302.

Loutsidis A, Bellenis I, Argiriou M, et al, "Tetracycline Compared With Mechlorethamine in the Treatment of Malignant Pleural Effusions. A Randomized Trial," *Respir Med*, 1994, 88(7):523-6.

Price NM, Hoppe RT, and Deneau DG, "Ointment Based Mechlorethamine Treatment for Mycosis Fungoides," *Cancer*, 1983, 52:2214-9.

Taylor JR, Halprin KM, Levine V, et al, "Mechlorethamine Hydrochloride Solutions and Oint-
ments," *Arch Dermatol*, 1980, 116:783-5.

Vonderheid EC, "Topical Mechlorethamine Chemotherapy: Considerations on its Use in Mycosis
Fungoides," *Int J Dermatol*, 1984, 23(3):180-6.

♦ **Mechlorethamine Hydrochloride** *see* Mechlorethamine *on page 700*

♦ **Medrol**® *see* MethylPREDNISolone *on page 745*

MedroxyPROGESTERone (me DROKS ee proe JES te rone)

Medication Safety Issues

Sound-alike/look-alike issues:

MedroxyPROGESTERone may be confused with hydroxyprogesterone,
methylPREDNISolone, methylTESTOSTERone

Provera® may be confused with Covera®, Parlodel®, Premarin®

The injection dosage form is available in different formulations. Carefully
review prescriptions to assure the correct formulation and route of administration.

U.S. Brand Names Depo-Provera®; Depo-Provera® Contraceptive;
depo-subQ provera 104™; Provera®

Index Terms Acetoxymethylprogesterone; Medroxyprogesterone Acetate;
Methylacetoxyprogesterone; MPA

Generic Available Yes

Canadian Brand Names Alti-MPA; Apo-Medroxy®; Depo-Prevera®;
Depo-Provera®; Gen-Medroxy; Novo-Medrone; Provera®; Provera-Pak

Pharmacologic Category Contraceptive; Progestin

Use Endometrial carcinoma or renal carcinoma; secondary amenorrhea or
abnormal uterine bleeding due to hormonal imbalance; reduction of endometrial hyperplasia in nonhysterectomized postmenopausal women receiving
conjugated estrogens; prevention of pregnancy; management of endometri-
osis-associated pain

Pregnancy Risk Factor X

Lactation Enters breast milk/compatible

Labeled Contraindications Hypersensitivity to medroxyprogesterone or
any component of the formulation; history of or current thrombophlebitis or
venous thromboembolic disorders (including DVT, PE); cerebral vascular
disease; severe hepatic dysfunction or disease; carcinoma of the breast or
genital organs; undiagnosed vaginal bleeding; missed abortion, diagnostic
test for pregnancy; pregnancy

**Warnings/Precautions [U.S. Boxed Warning]: Prolonged use of
medroxyprogesterone contraceptive injection may result in a loss of
bone mineral density (BMD).** Loss is related to the duration of use, and
may not be completely reversible on discontinuation of the drug. The impact
on peak bone mass in adolescents should be considered in treatment decisions. **[U.S. Boxed Warning]: Long-term use (ie, >2 years) should be
limited to situations where other birth control methods are inadequate.**
Consider other methods of birth control in women with (or at risk for) osteoporosis.

Use caution with cardiovascular disease or dysfunction. MPA used in combination with estrogen may increase the risks of hypertension, myocardial
infarction (MI), stroke, pulmonary emboli (PE), and deep vein thrombosis;
incidence of these effects was shown to be significantly increased in postmenopausal women using conjugated equine estrogens (CEE) in combination with MPA. MPA in combination with estrogens should not be used to
prevent coronary heart disease. Use with caution in patients with diabetes
mellitus; may cause glucose intolerance.
(Continued)

MedroxyPROGESTERone *(Continued)*

The risk of dementia may be increased in postmenopausal women; increased incidence was observed in women ≥65 years of age taking MPA in combination with CEE. An increased risk of invasive breast cancer was observed in postmenopausal women using MPA in combination with CEE. An increase in abnormal mammograms has also been reported with estrogen and progestin therapy.

Discontinue pending examination in cases of sudden partial or complete vision loss, sudden onset of proptosis, diplopia, or migraine; discontinue permanently if papilledema or retinal vascular lesions are observed on examination. Use with caution in patients with diseases that may be exacerbated by fluid retention (including asthma, epilepsy, migraine, diabetes, or renal dysfunction). Use caution with history of depression. Whenever possible, progestins in combination with estrogens should be discontinued at least 4-6 weeks prior to surgeries associated with an increased risk of thromboembolism or during periods of prolonged immobilization. Progestins used in combination with estrogen should be used for shortest duration possible consistent with treatment goals. Conduct periodic risk:benefit assessments. Not for use prior to menarche.

Adverse Reactions Adverse effects as reported with any dosage form; percent ranges presented are noted with the MPA contraceptive injection:

>5%:
Central nervous system: Dizziness, headache, nervousness
Endocrine & metabolic: Libido decreased, menstrual irregularities (includes bleeding, amenorrhea, or both)
Gastrointestinal: Abdominal pain/discomfort, weight changes (average 3-5 pounds after 1 year, 8 pounds after 2 years)
Neuromuscular & skeletal: Weakness

1% to 5%:
Cardiovascular: Edema
Central nervous system: Depression, fatigue, insomnia, irritability, pain
Dermatologic: Acne, alopecia, rash
Endocrine & metabolic: Anorgasmia, breast pain, hot flashes
Gastrointestinal: Bloating, nausea
Genitourinary: Cervical smear abnormal, leukorrhea, menometrorrhagia, menorrhagia, pelvic pain, urinary tract infection, vaginitis, vaginal infection, vaginal hemorrhage
Local: Injection site atrophy, injection site reaction, injection site pain
Neuromuscular & skeletal: Arthralgia, backache, leg cramp
Respiratory: Respiratory tract infections

<1%: Allergic reaction, anemia, angioedema, appetite changes, asthma, axillary swelling, blood dyscrasia, body odor, breast cancer, breast changes, cervical cancer, chest pain, chills, chloasma, convulsions, deep vein thrombosis, diaphoresis, drowsiness, dry skin, dysmenorrhea, dyspareunia, dyspnea, facial palsy, fever, galactorrhea, genitourinary infections, glucose tolerance decreased, hirsutism, hoarseness, jaundice, lack of return to fertility, lactation decreased, libido increased, melasma, nipple bleeding, osteoporosis, paralysis, paresthesia, pruritus, pulmonary embolus, rectal bleeding, scleroderma, sensation of pregnancy, somnolence, syncope, tachycardia, thirst, thrombophlebitis, uterine hyperplasia, vaginal cysts, varicose veins; residual lump, sterile abscess, or skin discoloration at the injection site

Postmarketing and/or case reports: Anaphylaxis, anaphylactoid reactions, bone mineral density decreased, osteoporotic fractures

Overdosage/Toxicology Toxicity is unlikely following single exposure of excessive doses. Supportive treatment is adequate in most cases.

Drug Interactions

Cytochrome P450 Effect: Substrate of CYP3A4 (major); **Induces** CYP3A4 (weak)

Decreased Effect: Acitretin, and griseofulvin may diminish the therapeutic effect of progestin contraceptives (contraceptive failure is possible). CYP3A4 inducers may decrease the levels/effects of medroxyprogesterone; example inducers include aminoglutethimide, carbamazepine, nafcillin, nevirapine, phenobarbital, phenytoin, and rifamycins. Progestins may diminish the anticoagulant effect of coumarin derivatives; and in contrast, enhanced anticoagulant effects have also been noted with some products.

Ethanol/Nutrition/Herb Interactions

Ethanol: Avoid ethanol (may increase risk of osteoporosis).

Food: Bioavailability of the oral tablet is increased when taken with food; half-life is unchanged.

Herb/Nutraceutical: St John's wort may diminish the therapeutic effect of progestin contraceptives (contraceptive failure is possible).

Storage/Stability Store at controlled room temperature.

Mechanism of Action Inhibits secretion of pituitary gonadotropins, which prevents follicular maturation and ovulation; causes endometrial thinning

Pharmacodynamics/Kinetics

Absorption: Oral: Well absorbed; I.M.: Slow

Protein binding: 86% to 90% primarily to albumin; does not bind to sex hormone-binding globulin

Metabolism: Extensively hepatic via hydroxylation and conjugation; forms metabolites

Time to peak: Oral: 2-4 hours

Half-life elimination: Oral: 12-17 hours; I.M. (Depo-Provera® Contraceptive): 50 days; SubQ: ~40 days

Excretion: Urine

Dosage

Adolescents and Adults:

Amenorrhea: Oral: 5-10 mg/day for 5-10 days

Abnormal uterine bleeding: Oral: 5-10 mg for 5-10 days starting on day 16 or 21 of cycle

Contraception:

Depo-Provera® Contraceptive: I.M.: 150 mg every 3 months

depo-subQ provera 104™: SubQ: 104 mg every 3 months (every 12-14 weeks)

Endometriosis: depo-subQ provera 104™: SubQ: 104 mg every 3 months (every 12-14 weeks)

Adults:

Endometrial or renal carcinoma (Depo-Provera®): I.M.: 400-1000 mg/week

Accompanying cyclic estrogen therapy, postmenopausal: Oral: 5-10 mg for 12-14 consecutive days each month, starting on day 1 or day 16 of the cycle; lower doses may be used if given with estrogen continuously throughout the cycle

Dosing adjustment in hepatic impairment: Use is contraindicated with severe impairment. Consider lower dose or less frequent administration with mild-to-moderate impairment. Use of the contraceptive injection has not been studied in patients with hepatic impairment; consideration should be given to not readminister if jaundice develops

(Continued)

MedroxyPROGESTERone *(Continued)*

Administration

I.M.: Depo-Provera® Contraceptive: Administer first dose during the first 5 days of menstrual period, or within the first 5 days postpartum if not breast-feeding, or at the sixth week postpartum if breast feeding exclusively. Shake vigorously prior to administration. Administer by deep I.M. injection in the gluteal or deltoid muscle.

SubQ: depo-subQ provera 104™: Administer first dose during the first 5 days of menstrual period, or at the sixth week postpartum if breast-feeding. Shake vigorously prior to administration. Administer by SubQ injection in the upper thigh or abdomen; avoid boney areas and the umbilicus. Administer over 5-7 seconds. Do not rub the injection area. When switching from combined hormonal contraceptives (estrogen plus progestin), the first injection should be within 7 days after the last active pill, or removal of patch or ring. If switching from the I.M. to SubQ formulation, the next dose should be given within the prescribed dosing period for the I.M. injection.

Monitoring Parameters Before starting therapy, a physical exam with reference to the breasts and pelvis are recommended, including a Papanicolaou smear. Exam may be deferred if appropriate prior to administration of MPA contraceptive injection; pregnancy should be ruled out prior to use. Monitor patient closely for loss of vision; sudden onset of proptosis, diplopia, or migraine; signs and symptoms of thromboembolic disorders; signs or symptoms of depression; glucose in patients with diabetes; or blood pressure.

Test Interactions

The following tests may be decreased: Steroid levels (plasma and urinary), gonadotropin levels, SHBG concentration, T_3 uptake

The following tests may be increased: Protein-bound iodine, butanol extractable protein-bound iodine, Factors II, VII, VIII, IX, X

Pathologist should be advised of estrogen/progesterone therapy when specimens are submitted.

Dietary Considerations Ensure adequate calcium and vitamin D intake when used for the prevention of pregnancy

Patient Information Follow dosage schedule and do not take more than prescribed. You may experience sensitivity to sunlight (use sunblock, wear protective clothing and eyewear, and avoid extensive exposure to direct sunlight); dizziness, anxiety, depression (use caution when driving or engaging in tasks that require alertness until response to drug is known); changes in appetite (maintain adequate hydration and diet - 2-3 L/day of fluids unless instructed to restrict fluid intake); decreased libido or increased body hair (reversible when drug is discontinued); hot flashes (cool clothes and environment may help). May cause discoloration of stool (green). Report swelling of face, lips, or mouth; absent or altered menses; abdominal pain; vaginal itching, irritation, or discharge; heat, warmth, redness, or swelling of extremities; or sudden change in vision.

Injection for contraception: This product does not protect against HIV or other sexually-transmitted diseases.

Emetic Potential Very low (<10%)

Vesicant No

Dosage Forms Excipient information presented when available (limited, particularly for generics); consult specific product labeling.

Injection, suspension, as acetate: 150 mg/mL (1 mL)

Depo-Provera®: 400 mg/mL (2.5 mL)

Depo-Provera® Contraceptive: 150 mg/mL (1 mL) [prefilled syringe or vial]

depo-subQ provera 104™: 104 mg/0.65 mL (0.65 mL) [prefilled syringe]

Tablet, as acetate: 2.5 mg, 5 mg, 10 mg
Provera®: 2.5 mg, 5 mg, 10 mg

♦ **Medroxyprogesterone Acetate** *see* MedroxyPROGESTERone *on page 703*

♦ **Megace®** *see* Megestrol *on page 707*

♦ **Megace® ES** *see* Megestrol *on page 707*

♦ **Megace® OS (Can)** *see* Megestrol *on page 707*

Megestrol (me JES trole)

Medication Safety Issues

Sound-alike/look-alike issues:
Megace® may be confused with Reglan®

U.S. Brand Names Megace®; Megace® ES

Index Terms 5071-1DL(6); Megestrol Acetate; NSC-71423

Generic Available Yes

Canadian Brand Names Apo-Megestrol®; Megace®; Megace® OS; Nu-Megestrol

Pharmacologic Category Antineoplastic Agent, Hormone; Appetite Stimulant; Progestin

Use Palliative treatment of breast and endometrial carcinoma; treatment of anorexia, cachexia, or unexplained significant weight loss in patients with AIDS

Pregnancy Risk Factor X

Lactation Enters breast milk/contraindicated

Labeled Contraindications Hypersensitivity to megestrol or any component of the formulation; pregnancy

Warnings/Precautions Hazardous agent - use appropriate precautions for handling and disposal. May suppress hypothalamic-pituitary-adrenal (HPA) axis during chronic administration; consider the possibility of adrenal suppression in any patient receiving or being withdrawn from chronic therapy when signs/symptoms suggestive of hypoadrenalism are noted (during stress or in unstressed state). Laboratory evaluation and replacement/stress doses of rapid-acting glucocorticoid should be considered. New-onset diabetes and exacerbation of pre-existing diabetes have been reported with long-term use. Use with caution in patients with a history of thromboembolic disease. Vaginal bleeding or discharge may occur in elderly females. Megace® ES suspension is not equivalent to other formulations on a mg per mg basis; Megace® ES suspension 625 mg/5 mL is equivalent to megestrol acetate suspension 800 mg/20 mL. Safety and efficacy in children have not been established.

Adverse Reactions

Frequency not always defined.

Cardiovascular: Hypertension (≤8%), cardiomyopathy (1% to 3%), chest pain (1% to 3%), edema (1% to 3%), palpitation (1% to 3%), peripheral edema (1% to 3%), heart failure

Central nervous system: Headache (≤10%), insomnia (≤6%), fever (1% to 6%), pain (≤6%, similar to placebo), abnormal thinking (1% to 3%), confusion (1% to 3%), seizure (1% to 3%), depression (1% to 3%), hypoesthesia (1% to 3%), mood changes, malaise, lethargy

Dermatologic: Rash (2% to 12%), alopecia (1% to 3%), pruritus (1% to 3%), vesiculobullous rash (1% to 3%)

Endocrine & metabolic: Breakthrough bleeding and amenorrhea, spotting, changes in menstrual flow, changes in cervical erosion and secretions, (Continued)

Megestrol *(Continued)*

increased breast tenderness, changes in vaginal bleeding pattern, hyperglycemia (≤6%), gynecomastia (1% to 3%), diabetes, HPA axis suppression, adrenal insufficiency, Cushing's syndrome, hypercalcemia, hot flashes

Gastrointestinal: Weight gain (not attributed to edema or fluid retention), diarrhea (6% to 15%, similar to placebo), flatulence (≤10%), vomiting (≤6%), nausea (≤5%), dyspepsia (≤4%), abdominal pain (1% to 3%), constipation (1% to 3%), salivation increased (1% to 3%), xerostomia (1% to 3%)

Genitourinary: Impotence (4% to 14%), decreased libido (≤5%), urinary incontinence (1% to 3%), urinary tract infection (1% to 3%), urinary frequency (≤2%)

Hematologic: Anemia (≤5%), leukopenia (1% to 3%)

Hepatic: Hepatomegaly (1% to 3%), LDH increased (1% to 3%), cholestatic jaundice, hepatotoxicity

Neuromuscular & skeletal: Carpal tunnel syndrome, weakness (2% to 8%), neuropathy (1% to 3%), paresthesia (1% to 3%)

Ocular: Amblyopia (1% to 3%)

Renal: Albuminuria (1% to 3%)

Respiratory: Dyspnea (1% to 3%), cough (1% to 3%), pharyngitis (1% to 3%), pneumonia (≤2%), hyperpnea

Miscellaneous: Diaphoresis (1% to 3%), herpes infection (1% to 3%), infection (1% to 3%), tumor flare

Postmarketing and/or case reports: Glucose intolerance, pulmonary embolism, thromboembolic phenomena, thrombophlebitis

Overdosage/Toxicology Toxicity is unlikely following single exposure of excessive doses. Although not tested for dialyzability, dialysis would not likely be effective in treating an overdose.

Drug Interactions

Increased Effect/Toxicity: Megestrol may enhance the hepatotoxic effect of cyclosporine; megestrol may increase the serum concentration of cyclosporine.

Decreased Effect: Aminoglutethimide may decrease the levels/effects of megestrol.

Ethanol/Nutrition/Herb Interactions Herb/Nutraceutical: Avoid herbs with progestogenic properties (eg, bloodroot, chasteberry, damiana, oregano, and yucca); may enhance the adverse/toxic effect of megestrol.

Storage/Stability Store at 15°C to 30°C (59°F to 86°F).

Mechanism of Action A synthetic progestin with antiestrogenic properties which disrupt the estrogen receptor cycle. Megestrol interferes with the normal estrogen cycle and results in a lower LH titer. May also have a direct effect on the endometrium. Megestrol is an antineoplastic progestin thought to act through an antileutenizing effect mediated via the pituitary. May stimulate appetite by antagonizing the metabolic effects of catabolic cytokines.

Pharmacodynamics/Kinetics

Absorption: Well absorbed orally

Metabolism: Hepatic (to free steroids and glucuronide conjugates)

Half-life elimination: 13-105 hours

Time to peak, serum: 1-3 hours

Excretion: Urine (57% to 78%; 5% to 8% as metabolites); feces (8% to 30%)

Dosage Adults: Oral: **Note:** Megace® ES suspension is not equivalent to other formulations on a mg-per-mg basis:

Tablet: Female (refer to individual protocols):

Breast carcinoma: 40 mg 4 times/day

Endometrial carcinoma: 40-320 mg/day in divided doses; use for 2 months to determine efficacy; maximum doses used have been up to 800 mg/day

Suspension: Male/Female: HIV-related cachexia:

Megace®: Initial dose: 800 mg/day; daily doses of 400 and 800 mg/day were found to be clinically effective

Megace® ES: 625 mg/day

Dosing adjustment in renal impairment: No data available; however, the urinary excretion of megestrol acetate administered in doses of 4-90 mg ranged from 56% to 78% within 10 days

Administration Megestrol acetate (Megace®) oral suspension is compatible with water, orange juice, apple juice, or Sustacal H.C. for immediate consumption.

Monitoring Parameters Observe for signs of thromboembolic phenomena; blood pressure, weight; serum glucose

Test Interactions Altered thyroid and liver function tests

Patient Information Follow dosage schedule and do not take more than prescribed. You may experience sensitivity to sunlight (use sunblock, wear protective clothing, and avoid extended exposure to direct sunlight); dizziness, anxiety, depression (use caution when driving or engaging in tasks that require alertness until response to drug is known); change in appetite (maintain adequate hydration and diet - 2-3 L/day of fluids unless instructed to restrict fluid intake); decreased libido or increased body hair (reversible when drug is discontinued); hot flashes (cool clothes and environment may help). Report swelling of face, lips, or mouth; absence or altered menses; abdominal pain; vaginal itching, irritation, or discharge; heat, warmth, redness, or swelling of extremities; or sudden onset change in vision.

Special Geriatric Considerations Elderly females may have vaginal bleeding or discharge and need to be forewarned of this side effect and inconvenience. No specific changes in dose are required for the elderly. Megestrol has been used in the treatment of the failure to thrive syndrome in cachectic elderly in addition to proper nutrition. Data does not support the use of megestrol for weight gain. The increase in weight tends to be mostly fat instead of lean body mass. Also, this agent is associated with DVTs.

Emetic Potential Very low (<10%)

Dosage Forms Excipient information presented when available (limited, particularly for generics); consult specific product labeling.

Suspension, oral, as acetate: 40 mg/mL (10 mL, 20 mL, 240 mL, 480 mL)

Megace®: 40 mg/mL (240 mL) [contains alcohol 0.06% and sodium benzoate; lemon-lime flavor]

Megace® ES: 125 mg/mL (150 mL) [contains alcohol 0.06% and sodium benzoate; lemon-lime flavor]

Tablet, as acetate: 20 mg, 40 mg

References

Canetta R, Florentine S, Hunter H, et al, "Megestrol Acetate," *Cancer Treat Rev*, 1983, 10(3);141-57.

Chang AY, "Megestrol Acetate as a Biomodulator," *Semin Oncol*, 1998, 25(2 Suppl 6):58-61.

Farrar DJ, "Megestrol Acetate: Promises and Pitfalls," *AIDS Patient Care STDS*, 1999, 13(3):149-52.

Fietkau R, Riepl M, Kettner H, et al, "Supportive Use of Megestrol Acetate in Patients With Head and Neck Cancer During Radio(Chemo)Therapy," *Eur J Cancer*, 1997, 33(1):75-9.

Lentz SS, Brady MF, Major FJ, et al, "High-Dose Megestrol Acetate in Advanced or Recurrent Endometrial Carcinoma: A Gynecologic Oncology Group Study," *J Clin Oncol*, 1996, 14(2):357-61.

Schacter L, Rozenzweig M, Canett R, et al, "Megestrol Acetate: Clinical Experience," *Cancer Treat Rev*, 1989, 16(1):49-63.

Strang P, "The Effect of Megestrol Acetate on Anorexia, Weight Loss and Cachexia in Cancer and AIDS Patients," *Anticancer Res*, 1997, 17(1B):657-62.

♦ **Megestrol Acetate** see Megestrol on page 707

Melphalan (MEL fa lan)

Medication Safety Issues

Sound-alike/look-alike issues:

Melphalan may be confused with Mephyton®, Myleran®

Alkeran® may be confused with Alferon®, Leukeran®

High alert medication: The Institute for Safe Medication Practices (ISMP) includes this medication among its list of drugs which have a heightened risk of causing significant patient harm when used in error.

Related Information

Hematopoietic Stem Cell Transplantation on page 1366

Safe Handling of Hazardous Drugs on page 1382

U.S. Brand Names Alkeran®

Index Terms L-PAM; L-Sarcolysin; NSC-8806; Phenylalanine Mustard

Generic Available No

Canadian Brand Names Alkeran®

Pharmacologic Category Antineoplastic Agent, Alkylating Agent

Use Palliative treatment of multiple myeloma and nonresectable epithelial ovarian carcinoma

Unlabeled/Investigational Use Treatment of neuroblastoma, rhabdomyosarcoma, breast cancer; part of an induction regimen for marrow and stem cell transplantation

Pregnancy Risk Factor D

Lactation Excretion in breast milk unknown/not recommended

Labeled Contraindications Hypersensitivity to melphalan or any component of the formulation; severe bone marrow suppression; patients whose disease was resistant to prior melphalan therapy; pregnancy

Warnings/Precautions Hazardous agent - use appropriate precautions for handling and disposal. **[U.S. Boxed Warning]: Is potentially mutagenic, leukemogenic,** and carcinogenic. Suppresses ovarian function and produces amenorrhea; may also cause testicular suppression. **[U.S. Boxed Warning]: Bone marrow suppression is common.** Use with caution in patients with prior bone marrow suppression, impaired renal function (consider dose reduction), or who have received prior chemotherapy or irradiation. Toxicity to immunosuppressives is increased in elderly; start with lowest recommended adult doses. Signs of infection, such as fever and WBC rise, may not occur. Lethargy and confusion may be more prominent signs of infection. **[U.S. Boxed Warning]: Hypersensitivity has been reported with I.V. administration** and oral melphalan; may occur after multiple treatment cycles. **[U.S. Boxed Warning]: Should be administered under the supervision of an experienced cancer chemotherapy physician.** Safety and efficacy in children have not been established.

Adverse Reactions

>10%:

Gastrointestinal: Vomiting (oral low-dose: <10%; I.V.: 30% to 90%)

Hematologic: Myelosuppression, leukopenia (onset 7 days; nadir 14-35 days; recovery 28-56 days), thrombocytopenia (onset 7 days; nadir 14-35 days; recovery 28-56 days)

Miscellaneous: Secondary malignancy (<2% to 20%; cumulative dose and duration dependent)

1% to 10%: Miscellaneous: Hypersensitivity (I.V.: 2%)

Infrequent, frequency undefined, postmarketing, and/or case reports: Agranulocytosis, allergic reactions, alopecia, amenorrhea, anaphylaxis, anemia, bladder irritation, bone marrow failure (irreversible), diarrhea, hemolytic anemia, hemorrhagic cystitis, hemorrhagic necrotic enterocolitis, hepatic veno-occlusive disease (I.V. melphalan), hepatitis, interstitial pneumonitis, jaundice, nausea, ovarian suppression, pruritus, pulmonary fibrosis, radiation myelopathy, rash, secondary carcinoma, secondary leukemia, secondary myeloproliferative syndrome, SIADH, skin hypersensitivity, skin necrosis, skin ulceration (injection site), skin vesiculation, sterility, stomatitis, testicular suppression, transaminases increased, vasculitis

Overdosage/Toxicology Symptoms of overdose include hypocalcemia, hyponatremia, pulmonary fibrosis, severe nausea and vomiting, diarrhea, GI hemorrhage, mucositis, stomatitis, and bone marrow suppression (including pancytopenia). Deaths have been reported with I.V. overdoses. Monitor hematologic parameters closely for 3-6 weeks; consider growth factor support, transfusions, and antibiotics. Treatment is otherwise symptom-directed and supportive. Not removed by hemodialysis.

Drug Interactions

Increased Effect/Toxicity: Risk of nephrotoxicity of cyclosporine is increased by melphalan. Concomitant use of I.V. melphalan may cause serious GI toxicity. Cisplatin may increase the levels/effects of melphalan (I.V.). Melphalan may increase risk of vaccinal infection.

Decreased Effect: Melphalan may decrease the levels/effects of digoxin.

Ethanol/Nutrition/Herb Interactions

Ethanol: Avoid ethanol (due to GI irritation).

Food: Food interferes with oral absorption.

Storage/Stability

Tablet: Store in refrigerator at 2°C to 8°C (36°F to 46°F). Protect from light.

Injection: Store at room temperature (15°C to 30°C). Protect from light. Reconstituted solution is chemically and physically stable for at least 90 minutes when stored at 25°C (77°F). Diluted solution is physically and chemically stable for at least 60 minutes at 25°C (77°F).

Reconstitution Injection must be prepared fresh. **The time between reconstitution/dilution and administration of parenteral melphalan must be kept to a minimum (manufacturer recommends <60 minutes) because reconstituted and diluted solutions are unstable.** Dissolve powder initially with 10 mL of diluent to a concentration of 5 mg/mL. Shake vigorously to dissolve. Immediately dilute dose in 250-500 mL NS to a concentration of 0.1-0.45 mg/mL.

Compatibility Incompatible with D_5W, LR; **variable stability (consult detailed reference)** in NS.

Y-site administration: Compatible: Acyclovir, amikacin, aminophylline, ampicillin, aztreonam, bleomycin, bumetanide, buprenorphine, butorphanol, calcium gluconate, carboplatin, carmustine, cefazolin, cefepime, cefoperazone, cefotaxime, cefotetan, ceftazidime, ceftizoxime, ceftriaxone, cefuroxime, cimetidine, cisplatin, clindamycin, co-trimoxazole, cyclophosphamide, cytarabine, dacarbazine, dactinomycin, daunorubicin, dexamethasone sodium phosphate, diphenhydramine, doxorubicin, doxycycline, droperidol, enalaprilat, etoposide, famotidine, floxuridine, fluconazole, fludarabine, fluorouracil, furosemide, ganciclovir, gentamicin, granisetron, haloperidol, heparin, hydrocortisone sodium phosphate, hydrocortisone sodium succinate, hydromorphone, hydroxyzine, idarubicin, ifosfamide, imipenem/cilastatin, lorazepam, mannitol, mechlorethamine, meperidine, mesna, methotrexate, methylprednisolone sodium succinate, metoclopramide, metronidazole, minocycline, mitomycin, mitoxantrone, morphine, nalbuphine, netilmicin, ondansetron, pentostatin, piperacillin, plicamycin, potassium chloride, prochlorperazine edisylate, promethazine, ranitidine, sodium bicarbonate, streptozocin, teniposide, thiotepa, ticarcillin, ticarcillin/

(Continued)

Melphalan *(Continued)*

clavulanate, tobramycin, vancomycin, vinblastine, vincristine, vinorelbine, zidovudine. **Incompatible:** Amphotericin B, chlorpromazine.

Mechanism of Action Alkylating agent which is a derivative of mechlorethamine that inhibits DNA and RNA synthesis via formation of carbonium ions; cross-links strands of DNA; acts on both resting and rapidly dividing tumor cells.

Pharmacodynamics/Kinetics

Absorption: Oral: Variable and incomplete

Distribution: V_d: 0.5-0.6 L/kg throughout total body water

Protein binding: 60% to 90%; primarily to albumin, 20% to α_1-acid glycoprotein

Metabolism: Hepatic; chemical hydrolysis to monohydroxymelphalan and dihydroxymelphalan

Bioavailability: Unpredictable; 61% ± 26%, decreasing with repeated doses

Half-life elimination: Terminal: I.V.: 1.5 hours; oral: 1-1.25 hours

Time to peak, serum: ~1-2 hours

Excretion: Oral: Feces (20% to 50%); urine (10% to 30% as unchanged drug)

Dosage Refer to individual protocols.

Oral: Dose should always be adjusted to patient response and weekly blood counts:

Children (unlabeled use): 4-20 mg/m^2/day for 1-21 days

Adults:

Multiple myeloma (multiple regimens have been employed): **Note:** Response is gradual; may require repeated courses to realize benefit:

6 mg daily for 2-3 weeks initially, followed by up to 4 weeks rest, then a maintenance dose of 2 mg daily as hematologic recovery begins **or**

10 mg daily for 7-10 days; institute 2 mg daily maintenance dose after WBC >4000 cells/mcL and platelets >100,000 cells/mcL (~4-8 weeks); titrate maintenance dose to hematologic response **or**

0.15 mg/kg/day for 7 days, with a 2-6 week rest, followed by a maintenance dose of ≤0.05 mg/kg/day as hematologic recovery begins **or**

0.25 mg/kg/day for 4 days (or 0.2 mg/kg/day for 5 days); repeat at 4- to 6-week intervals as ANC and platelet counts return to normal

Ovarian carcinoma: 0.2 mg/kg/day for 5 days, repeat every 4-5 weeks.

I.V.:

Children (unlabeled use):

Pediatric rhabdomyosarcoma: 10-35 mg/m^2/dose every 21-28 days

High-dose melphalan with bone marrow transplantation for neuroblastoma: I.V.: 100-220 mg/m^2 as a single dose or divided into 2-5 daily doses. Infuse over 20-60 minutes.

Adults: Multiple myeloma: 16 mg/m^2 administered at 2-week intervals for 4 doses, then administer at 4-week intervals after adequate hematologic recovery.

Dosing adjustment in renal impairment: The FDA-approved labeling contains the following adjustment recommendations based on route of administration:

Oral: Moderate-to-severe renal impairment: Consider a reduced dose initially

I.V.: BUN >30 mg/dL: Reduce dose by up to 50%

The following guidelines have been used by some clinicians:

Aronoff, 2007 (route of administration not specified): Adults:

Cl_{cr} 10-50 mL/minute: Administer 75% of dose

Cl_{cr} <10 mL/minute: Administer 50% of dose

Hemodialysis: Administer dose after hemodialysis

Continuous ambulatory peritoneal dialysis (CAPD): Administer 50% of dose

Continuous renal replacement therapy (CRRT): Administer 75% of dose

Kintzel, 1995:

Oral: Adjust dose in the presence of hematologic toxicity

I.V.:

Cl_{cr} 46-60 mL/minute: Administer 85% of normal dose

Cl_{cr} 31-45 mL/minute: Administer 75% of normal dose

Cl_{cr} <30 mL/minute: Administer 70% of normal dose

Dosing adjustment in hepatic impairment: Melphalan is hepatically metabolized; however, dosage adjustment does not appear to be necessary (King, 2001).

Combination Regimens

Gestational trophoblastic tumor:

CHAMOCA (Modified Bagshawe Regimen) *on page 1170*

CHAMOMA (Bagshawe Regimen) *on page 1172*

Lymphoma, Hodgkin's disease:

CAD/MOPP/ABV *on page 1157*

mini-BEAM *on page 1248*

Multiple myeloma:

Bortezomib-Melphalan-Prednisone *on page 1156*

Bortezomib-Melphalan-Prednisone-Thalidomide *on page 1156*

M-2 *on page 1245*

Melphalan-Prednisone-Thalidomide *on page 1246*

MP (Multiple Myeloma) *on page 1254*

VBMCP *on page 1288*

Administration

Oral: Administer on an empty stomach (1 hour prior to or 2 hours after meals)

Parenteral: Due to limited stability, complete administration of I.V. dose should occur within 60 minutes of reconstitution

I.V. infusion: Infuse over 15-20 minutes

I.V. bolus:

Central line: I.V. bolus doses of 17-200 mg/m² (reconstituted and not diluted) have been infused over 2-20 minutes

Peripheral line: I.V. bolus doses of 2-23 mg/m² (reconstituted and not diluted) have been infused over 1-4 minutes

Monitoring Parameters CBC with differential and platelet count, serum electrolytes, serum uric acid

Test Interactions False-positive Coombs' test [direct]

Dietary Considerations Should be taken on an empty stomach (1 hour prior to or 2 hours after meals).

Patient Information

Do not take alcohol, aspirin or aspirin-containing medications, and/or OTC medications without consulting prescriber. Inform prescriber of all prescription medication you are taking. Maintain adequate fluid balance (2-3 L/day of fluids unless instructed to restrict fluid intake). May cause hair loss (reversible); easy bleeding or bruising (use a soft toothbrush or cotton swabs and frequent mouth care, use electric razor, avoid sharp knives or scissors); increased susceptibility to infection (avoid crowds or exposure to infection - do (Continued)

Melphalan *(Continued)*

not have any vaccinations unless approved by prescriber). Report unusual bleeding or bruising or persistent fever or sore throat; blood in urine, stool, or vomitus; delayed healing of any wounds; skin rash; yellowing of skin or eyes; changes in color of urine or black stool; pain or burning on urination; respiratory difficulty; or other severe adverse reactions. Contraceptive measures should be used during therapy. The drug may be excreted in breast milk, therefore, an alternative form of feeding your baby should be used.

I.V.: Report promptly any pain, irritation, or redness at infusion site.

Oral: Preferable to take on an empty stomach, 1 hour prior to or 2 hours after meals.

Special Geriatric Considerations Toxicity to immunosuppressives is increased in the elderly. Start with lowest recommended adult doses. Signs of infection, such as fever and WBC rise, may not occur. Lethargy and confusion may be more prominent signs of infection.

Emetic Potential
Oral: Very low (<10%)
I.V. (>50 mg/m^2): High (60% to 90%)

Vesicant No

High Dose Considerations
    Comments: Saline-based hydration (100-125 mg/m^2/hour) preceding (2-4 hours), during, and following (6-12 hours) administration reduces risk of drug precipitation in renal tubules. Hydrolysis causes loss of 1% melphalan injection per 10 minutes. Infusion of admixture must be completed within 100 minutes of preparation to deliver ordered dose. Reconstitute dose to 5 mg/mL in diluent provided by manufacturer. Dose may be infused via central or peripheral venous access without further dilution to minimize volume of infusion.

    High Dose: I.V.: 100-240 mg/m^2 administered as a single dose or divided into 2-4 daily doses. Maximum dose as a single agent: 200-400 mg/m^2. Maximum dose with total body irradiation (TBI): 110-140 mg/m^2; other high-dose chemotherapeutic drugs: 100-180 mg/m^2. Generally infused over 20-60 minutes.

    Unique Toxicities:
        Cardiovascular: Atrial fibrillation, left ventricular heart failure
        Dermatologic: Alopecia
        Gastrointestinal: Mucositis (severity increases with Cl$_{cr}$ ≤40 mL/minute; pretreatment with amifostine or glutamine may decrease mucositis), nausea and vomiting (moderate), diarrhea
        Hematologic: Myelosuppression, secondary leukemia
        Renal: Increased serum creatinine and azotemia possible without adequate hydration
        Rare side effects: Abnormal LFTs, atrial fibrillation, interstitial pneumonitis, secondary leukemia, SIADH, vasculitis

Dosage Forms Excipient information presented when available (limited, particularly for generics); consult specific product labeling.
    Injection, powder for reconstitution: 50 mg [diluent contains ethanol and propylene glycol]
    Tablet: 2 mg

References
Alberts DS, Chang SY, Chen HS, et al, "Oral Melphalan Kinetics," *Clin Pharmacol Ther*, 1979, 26(6):737-45.

Aronoff GR, Bennett WM, Berns JS, et al, *Drug Prescribing in Renal Failure: Dosing Guidelines for Adults and Children*, 5th ed. Philadelphia, PA: American College of Physicians; 2007, p 100.

Berg SL, Grisell DL, DeLaney TF, et al, "Principles of Treatment of Pediatric Solid Tumors," *Pediatr Clin North Am*, 1991, 38(2):249-67.

Coates TD, "Survival From Melphalan Overdose," *Lancet*, 1984, 2(8410):1048.

Hutchins LF and Lipschitz DA, "Cancer, Clinical Pharmacology, and Aging," *Clin Geriatr Med*, 1987, 3(3):483-503.

Kaplan HG, "Use of Cancer Chemotherapy in the Elderly," *Drug Treatment in the Elderly*, Vestal RE, ed, Boston, MA: ADIS Health Science Press, 1984, 338-49.

Kellie SJ and Kingston JE, "Ovarian Failure After High-Dose Melphalan in Adolescents," *Lancet*, 1987, 1(8547):1425.

King PD and Perry MC, "Hepatotoxicity of Chemotherapy," *Oncologist*, 2001, 6(2):162-76.

Kintzel PE and Dorr RT, "Anticancer Drug Renal Toxicity and Elimination: Dosing Guidelines for Altered Renal Function," *Cancer Treat Rev*, 1995, 21(1):33-64.

Kyle RA and Rajkumar SV, "Multiple Myeloma," *N Engl J Med*, 2004, 351(18):1860-73.

NCCN (National Comprehensive Cancer Network) "Practice Guidelines in Oncology: Antiemesis Version 2.2006." Available at http://www.nccn.org/professionals/physician_gls/PDF/antiemesis.pdf

Pole JG, Casper J, Elfenbein G, et al, "High-Dose Chemoradiotherapy Supported by Marrow Infusions for Advanced Neuroblastoma: A Pediatric Oncology Group Study," *J Clin Oncol*, 1991, 9(1):152-8.

Schroeder H, Pinkerton CR, Powles RL, et al, "High-Dose Melphalan and Total Body Irradiation With Autologous Marrow Rescue in Childhood Acute Lymphoblastic Leukemia After Relapse," *Bone Marrow Transplant*, 1991, 7(1):11-15.

Seddon BM, Cassoni AM, Galloway MJ, et al, "Fatal Radiation Myelopathy After High-Dose Busulfan and Melphalan Chemotherapy and Radiotherapy for Ewing's Sarcoma: A Review of the Literature and Implications for Practice," Clin Oncol, 2005, 17(5):385-90.

Meperidine (me PER i deen)

Medication Safety Issues

Avoid the use of meperidine for pain control, especially in elderly and renally-compromised patients (Institute for Safe Medication Practices [ISMP], 2007)

Sound-alike/look-alike issues:

Meperidine may be confused with meprobamate

Demerol® may be confused with Demulen®, Desyrel®, dicumarol, Dilaudid®, Dymelor®, Pamelor®

U.S. Brand Names Demerol®; Meperitab®

Index Terms Isonipecaine Hydrochloride; Meperidine Hydrochloride; Pethidine Hydrochloride

Generic Available Yes

Canadian Brand Names Demerol®

Pharmacologic Category Analgesic, Opioid

Use Management of moderate-to-severe pain; adjunct to anesthesia and preoperative sedation

Unlabeled/Investigational Use

Reduce postoperative shivering; reduce rigors from amphotericin

Restrictions C-II

Pregnancy Risk Factor C/D (prolonged use or high doses at term)

Lactation Enters breast milk/contraindicated (AAP rates "compatible")

Labeled Contraindications Hypersensitivity to meperidine or any component of the formulation; use with or within 14 days of MAO inhibitors; pregnancy (prolonged use or high doses near term)

Warnings/Precautions Meperidine is not recommended for the management of pain; its use in this setting should be avoided (American Pain Society [APS], 2003; ISMP, 2007). Oral meperidine is not recommended for acute pain management. Normeperidine (an active metabolite and CNS stimulant) may accumulate and precipitate anxiety, tremors, or seizures; risk increases (Continued)

Meperidine *(Continued)*

with renal dysfunction and cumulative dose. Effects may be potentiated when used with other sedative drugs or ethanol.

May cause CNS depression, which may impair physical or mental abilities; patients must be cautioned about performing tasks which require mental alertness (eg, operating machinery or driving). Use only with extreme caution (if at all) in patients with head injury or increased intracranial pressure (ICP); potential to elevate ICP may be greatly exaggerated in these patients. Use caution with pulmonary, hepatic, or renal disorders, supraventricular tachycardias, acute abdominal conditions, hypothyroidism, toxic psychosis, kyphoscoliosis, morbid obesity, Addison's disease, BPH, or urethral stricture. Use with caution in patients with biliary tract dysfunction; acute pancreatitis may cause constriction of sphincter of Oddi. May cause hypotension; use with caution in patients with depleted blood volume or drugs which may exaggerate hypotensive effects (including phenothiazines or general anesthetics).

An opioid-containing analgesic regimen should be tailored to each patient's needs and based upon the type of pain being treated (acute versus chronic), the route of administration, degree of tolerance for opioids (naive versus chronic user), age, weight, and medical condition. The optimal analgesic dose varies widely among patients. Doses should be titrated to pain relief/prevention.

Some preparations contain sulfites which may cause allergic reaction. Tolerance or drug dependence may result from extended use. Healthcare provider should be alert to problems of abuse, misuse, and diversion. Concurrent use of agonist/antagonist analgesics may precipitate withdrawal symptoms and/or reduced analgesic efficacy in patients following prolonged therapy with mu opioid agonists. Abrupt discontinuation following prolonged use may also lead to withdrawal symptoms. Avoid use in the elderly.

Adverse Reactions Frequency not defined.

Cardiovascular: Hypotension

Central nervous system: Fatigue, drowsiness, dizziness, nervousness, headache, restlessness, malaise, confusion, mental depression, hallucinations, paradoxical CNS stimulation, increased intracranial pressure, seizure (associated with metabolite accumulation), serotonin syndrome

Dermatologic: Rash, urticaria

Gastrointestinal: Nausea, vomiting, constipation, anorexia, stomach cramps, xerostomia, biliary spasm, paralytic ileus, sphincter of Oddi spasm

Genitourinary: Ureteral spasms, decreased urination

Local: Pain at injection site

Neuromuscular & skeletal: Weakness

Respiratory: Dyspnea

Miscellaneous: Histamine release, physical and psychological dependence

Overdosage/Toxicology Symptoms of overdose include CNS depression, respiratory depression, mydriasis, bradycardia, pulmonary edema, chronic tremor, CNS excitability, and seizures. Treatment is symptomatic. Naloxone, 2 mg I.V. with repeat administration as necessary up to a total dose of 10 mg, can be used to reverse opiate effects. Naloxone should not be used to treat meperidine-induced seizures. Naloxone does not reverse the adverse effects of normeperidine, and may even exacerbate the hyperexcitability.

Drug Interactions

Cytochrome P450 Effect: Substrate (minor) of CYP2B6, 2C19, 3A4

Increased Effect/Toxicity: MAO inhibitors may enhance the serotonergic effect of meperidine, which may cause serotonin syndrome; concurrent use with or within 14 days of an MAO inhibitor is contraindicated. CNS depressants may potentiate the sedative effects of meperidine or increase respiratory depression. Phenothiazines may potentiate the sedative effects of meperidine and may increase the incidence of hypotension. Serotonin agonists, serotonin reuptake inhibitors, sibutramine, and tricyclic antidepressants may potentiate the effects of meperidine. In addition, concurrent therapy with these drugs potentially may increase the risk of serotonin syndrome. A number of drugs may increase meperidine metabolite concentrations (including acyclovir, cimetidine, and ritonavir).

Decreased Effect: Barbiturates may decrease the analgesic efficacy and increase the sedative effects of meperidine. Phenytoin may decrease the analgesic effects of meperidine.

Ethanol/Nutrition/Herb Interactions

Ethanol: Avoid or limit ethanol (may increase CNS depression). Watch for sedation.

Herb/Nutraceutical: Avoid valerian, St John's wort, kava kava, gotu kola (may increase CNS depression).

Storage/Stability Meperidine injection should be stored at room temperature; do not freeze. Protect from light. Protect oral dosage forms from light.

Compatibility Stable in dextran 6% in dextrose, dextran 6% in NS, D_5LR, $D_5^1/_4NS$, $D_5^1/_2NS$, D_5NS, D_5W, $D_{10}W$, LR, $^1/_2NS$, NS.

Y-site administration: Compatible: Amifostine, amikacin, ampicillin, ampicillin/sulbactam, atenolol, aztreonam, bumetanide, cefamandole, cefazolin, cefotaxime, cefotetan, cefoxitin, ceftazidime, ceftizoxime, ceftriaxone, cefuroxime, chloramphenicol, cisatracurium, cladribine, clindamycin, co-trimoxazole, dexamethasone sodium phosphate, diltiazem, diphenhydramine, dobutamine, docetaxel, dopamine, doxycycline, droperidol, erythromycin lactobionate, etoposide phosphate, famotidine, filgrastim, fluconazole, fludarabine, gatifloxacin, gemcitabine, gentamicin, granisetron, heparin, hydrocortisone sodium succinate, insulin (regular), kanamycin, labetalol, lidocaine, linezolid, magnesium sulfate, melphalan, methyldopa, methylprednisolone sodium succinate, metoclopramide, metoprolol, metronidazole, ondansetron, oxacillin, oxytocin, paclitaxel, penicillin G potassium, piperacillin, piperacillin/tazobactam, potassium chloride, propofol, propranolol, ranitidine, remifentanil, sargramostim, teniposide, thiotepa, ticarcillin, ticarcillin/clavulanate, tobramycin, vancomycin, verapamil, vinorelbine. **Incompatible:** Allopurinol, amphotericin B cholesteryl sulfate complex, cefepime, cefoperazone, doxorubicin liposome, idarubicin, imipenem/cilastatin, minocycline. **Variable (consult detailed reference):** Acyclovir, furosemide, nafcillin.

Compatibility in syringe: Compatible: Atropine, atropine with hydroxyzine, atropine with promethazine, butorphanol, chlorpromazine, cimetidine, dimenhydrinate, diphenhydramine, droperidol, fentanyl, glycopyrrolate, hydroxyzine, ketamine, metoclopramide, midazolam, ondansetron, pentazocine, pentazocine with perphenazine, perphenazine, prochlorperazine edisylate, promazine, promethazine, ranitidine, scopolamine. **Incompatible:** Heparin, morphine, pentobarbital.

Compatibility when admixed: Compatible: Cefazolin, dobutamine, metoclopramide, ondansetron, scopolamine, succinylcholine, triflupromazine, verapamil. **Incompatible:** Aminophylline, amobarbital, floxacillin, furosemide, heparin, morphine, phenobarbital, phenytoin, thiopental. **Variable (consult detailed reference):** Sodium bicarbonate.

Mechanism of Action Binds to opiate receptors in the CNS, causing inhibition of ascending pain pathways, altering the perception of and response to pain; produces generalized CNS depression
(Continued)

Meperidine *(Continued)*

Pharmacodynamics/Kinetics

Onset of action: Analgesic: Oral, SubQ: 10-15 minutes; I.V.: ~5 minutes

Peak effect: SubQ.: ~1 hour; Oral: 2 hours

Duration: Oral, SubQ: 2-4 hours

Absorption: I.M.: Erratic and highly variable

Distribution: Crosses placenta; enters breast milk

Protein binding: 65% to 75%

Metabolism: Hepatic; hydrolyzed to meperidinic acid (inactive) or undergoes N-demethylation to normeperidine (active; has $1/2$ the analgesic effect and 2-3 times the CNS effects of meperidine)

Bioavailability: ~50% to 60%; increased with liver disease

Half-life elimination:

Parent drug: Terminal phase: Adults: 2.5-4 hours, Liver disease: 7-11 hours

Normeperidine (active metabolite): 15-30 hours; can accumulate with high doses (>600 mg/day) or with decreased renal function

Excretion: Urine (as metabolites)

Dosage Note: The American Pain Society (2003) and ISMP (2007) do not recommend meperidine's use as an analgesic.

Children: Pain: Oral, I.M., I.V., SubQ: 1-1.5 mg/kg/dose every 3-4 hours as needed; 1-2 mg/kg as a single dose preoperative medication may be used; maximum 100 mg/dose (**Note:** Oral route is not recommended for acute pain.)

Adults: Pain:

Oral: Initial: Opiate-naive: 50 mg every 3-4 hours as needed; usual dosage range: 50-150 mg every 2-4 hours as needed (manufacturers recommendation; oral route is not recommended for acute pain)

I.M., SubQ: Initial: Opiate-naive: 50-75 mg every 3-4 hours as needed; patients with prior opiate exposure may require higher initial doses

Preoperatively: 50-100 mg given 30-90 minutes before the beginning of anesthesia

Note: If use in acute pain (in patients without renal or CNS disease) cannot be avoided, treatment should be limited to ≤48 hours and doses should not exceed 600 mg/24 hours.

Elderly:

Oral: 50 mg every 4 hours

I.M.: 25 mg every 4 hours

Dosing adjustment in renal impairment: Avoid use in renal impairment

Dosing adjustment/comments in hepatic disease: Increased narcotic effect in cirrhosis; reduction in dose more important for oral than I.V. route

Administration Meperidine may be administered I.M., SubQ, or I.V.; I.V. push should be administered slowly, use of a 10 mg/mL concentration has been recommended. For continuous I.V. infusions, a more dilute solution (eg, 1 mg/mL) should be used.

Oral: Administer syrup diluted in $1/2$ glass of water; undiluted syrup may exert topical anesthetic effect on mucous membranes

Monitoring Parameters Pain relief, respiratory and mental status, blood pressure; observe patient for excessive sedation, CNS depression, seizures, respiratory depression

Test Interactions Increased amylase (S), increased BSP retention, increased CPK (I.M. injections)

Patient Information Avoid alcohol; may cause drowsiness

Special Geriatric Considerations Meperidine is not recommended as a drug of first choice for the treatment of chronic pain in the elderly due to the accumulation of its metabolite, normeperidine, which leads to serious CNS side effects (eg, tremor, seizures). For acute pain, its use should be limited to 1-2 doses.

Vesicant No

Dosage Forms Excipient information presented when available (limited, particularly for generics); consult specific product labeling. [DSC] = Discontinued product

Injection, solution, as hydrochloride [ampul]: 25 mg/0.5 mL (0.5 mL); 25 mg/mL (1 mL); 50 mg/mL (1 mL, 1.5 mL, 2 mL); 75 mg/mL (1 mL); 100 mg/mL (1 mL)

Injection, solution, as hydrochloride [prefilled syringe]: 25 mg/mL (1 mL); 50 mg/mL (1 mL); 75 mg/mL (1 mL); 100 mg/mL (1 mL)

Injection, solution, as hydrochloride [for PCA pump]: 10 mg/mL (30 mL, 50 mL, 60 mL)

Injection, solution, as hydrochloride [vial]: 25 mg/mL (1 mL); 50 mg/mL (1 mL, 30 mL); 75 mg/mL (1 mL); 100 mg/mL (1 mL, 20 mL) [may contain sodium metabisulfite]

Solution, oral, as hydrochloride: 50 mg/5 mL (500 mL)

Syrup, as hydrochloride:
Demerol®: 50 mg/5 mL (480 mL) [contains benzoic acid; banana flavor] [DSC]

Tablet, as hydrochloride: 50 mg, 100 mg
Demerol®, Meperitab®: 50 mg, 100 mg

References
"American Academy of Pediatrics Committee on Drugs. The Transfer of Drugs and Other Chemicals Into Human Milk," *Pediatrics*, 2001, 108(3):776-89.

American Academy of Pediatrics Committee on Drugs, "Reappraisal of Lytic Cocktail/Demerol®, Phenergan®, and Thorazine® (DPT) for the Sedation of Children," *Pediatrics*, 1995, 95(4):598-602.

Armstrong PJ and Bersten A, "Normeperidine Toxicity," *Anesth Analg*, 1986, 65(5):536-8.

Buchanan JF and Brown CR, "Designer Drugs: A Problem in Clinical Toxicology," *Med Toxicol Adverse Drug Exp*, 1988, 3(1):1-17.

Clark RF, Wei EM, and Anderson PO, "Meperidine: Therapeutic Use and Toxicity," *J Emerg Med*, 1995,13(6):797-802.

Cole TB, Sprinkle RH, Smith SJ, et al, "Intravenous Narcotic Therapy for Children With Severe Sickle Cell Pain Crisis," *Am J Dis Child*, 1986, 140(12):1255-9.

Ferrell BA, "Pain Management in Elderly People," *J Am Geriatr Soc*, 1991, 39(1):64-73.

Golembiewski J, "Safety Concerns With Meperidine," *J Perianesth Nurs*, 2002, 17(2):123-5.

Institute for Safe Medication Practice, "High Alert Medication Feature: Reducing Patient Harm From Opiates," *ISMP Medication Safety Alert*, February 22, 2007. Available online at http://www.ismp.org/Newsletters/acutecare/articles/20070222.asp.

Jacobi J, Fraser GL, Coursin DB, et al, "Clinical Practice Guidelines for the Sustained Use of Sedatives and Analgesics in the Critically Ill Adult," *Crit Care Med*, 2002, 30(1):119-41. Available at: http://www.sccm.org/pdf/sedatives.pdf. Accessed August 2, 2003.

Kyff JV and Rice TL, "Meperidine-Associated Seizures in a Child," *Clin Pharm*, 1990, 9(5):337-8.

Latta KS, Ginsberg B, and Barkin RL, "Meperidine: A Critical Review," *Am J Ther*, 2002, 9(1):53-68.

Miller RR and Jick H, "Clinical Effects of Meperidine in Hospitalized Medical Patients," *J Clin Pharmacol*, 1978, 18(4):180-9.

Mokhlesi B, Leikin JB, Murray P, et al, "Adult Toxicology in Critical Care: Part II: Specific Poisonings," *Chest*, 2003, 123(3):897-922.

Olkkola KT, Hamunen K, and Maunuksela EL, "Clinical Pharmacokinetics and Pharmacodynamics of Opioid Analgesics in Infants and Children," *Clin Pharmacokinet*, 1995, 28(5):385-404.

Pokela ML, Olkkola KT, Koivisto ME, et al, "Pharmacokinetics and Pharmacodynamics of Intravenous Meperidine in Neonates and Infants," *Clin Pharmacol Ther*, 1992, 52(4):342-9.

"Principles of Analgesic Use in the Treatment of Acute Pain and Chronic Cancer Pain," 5th ed, Glenview, IL: American Pain Society, 2003.

Stone PA, Macintyre PE, and Jarvis DA, "Norpethidine Toxicity and Patient Controlled Analgesia," *Br J Anaesth*, 1993, 71(5):738-40.

♦ **Meperidine Hydrochloride** *see* Meperidine *on page 715*

♦ **Meperitab®** *see* Meperidine *on page 715*

♦ **Mephyton®** *see* Phytonadione *on page 895*

Mercaptopurine (mer kap toe PYOOR een)

Medication Safety Issues

Sound-alike/look-alike issues:
Purinethol® may be confused with propylthiouracil

High alert medication: The Institute for Safe Medication Practices (ISMP) includes this medication among its list of drugs which have a heightened risk of causing significant patient harm when used in error.

To avoid potentially serious dosage errors, the terms "6-mercaptopurine" or "6-MP" should be avoided; use of these terms has been associated with sixfold overdosages.

Azathioprine is metabolized to mercaptopurine; concurrent use of these commercially-available products has resulted in profound myelosuppression.

Related Information

Investigational Drug Service *on page 1379*
Safe Handling of Hazardous Drugs *on page 1382*

U.S. Brand Names Purinethol®

Index Terms 6-Mercaptopurine (error-prone abbreviation); 6-MP (error-prone abbreviation); NSC-755

Generic Available Yes

Canadian Brand Names Purinethol®

Pharmacologic Category Antineoplastic Agent, Antimetabolite; Immunosuppressant Agent

Use Treatment (maintenance and induction) of acute lymphoblastic leukemia (ALL)

Unlabeled/Investigational Use Steroid-sparing agent for corticosteroid-dependent Crohn's disease (CD) and ulcerative colitis (UC); maintenance of remission in CD; fistulizing Crohn's disease

Pregnancy Risk Factor D

Lactation Enters breast milk/contraindicated

Labeled Contraindications Hypersensitivity to mercaptopurine or any component of the formulation; patients whose disease showed prior resistance to mercaptopurine or thioguanine; severe liver disease, severe bone marrow suppression; pregnancy

Warnings/Precautions Hazardous agent - use appropriate precautions for handling and disposal. Use with caution in patients with prior bone marrow suppression. Common signs of infection, such as fever and leukocytosis may not occur; lethargy and confusion may be more prominent signs of infection. Use caution with other hepatotoxic drugs or in dosages >2.5 mg/kg/day; hepatotoxicity may occur. Patients with genetic deficiency of thiopurine methyltransferase (TPMT) or concurrent therapy with drugs which may inhibit TPMT (eg, olsalazine) or xanthine oxidase (eg, allopurinol) may be sensitive to myelosuppressive effects. Azathioprine is metabolized to mercaptopurine; concomitant use may result in profound myelosuppression and should be avoided. Immune response to vaccines may be diminished.

To avoid potentially serious dosage errors, the terms "6-mercaptopurine" or "6-MP" should be avoided; use of these terms has been associated with sixfold overdosages.

Adverse Reactions

>10%:

Hematologic: Myelosuppression; leukopenia, thrombocytopenia, anemia
Onset: 7-10 days
Nadir: 14-16 days
Recovery: 21-28 days

Hepatic: Intrahepatic cholestasis and focal centralobular necrosis (40%), characterized by hyperbilirubinemia, increased alkaline phosphatase and AST, jaundice, ascites, encephalopathy; more common at doses >2.5 mg/kg/day. Usually occurs within 2 months of therapy but may occur within 1 week, or be delayed up to 8 years.

1% to 10%:

Central nervous system: Drug fever
Dermatologic: Hyperpigmentation, rash
Endocrine & metabolic: Hyperuricemia
Gastrointestinal: Nausea, vomiting, diarrhea, stomatitis, anorexia, stomach pain, mucositis
Renal: Renal toxicity

<1%: Alopecia, dry and scaling rash, glossitis, oligospermia, tarry stools, eosinophilia

Overdosage/Toxicology Symptoms of overdose include nausea and vomiting (immediate); bone marrow suppression, hepatic necrosis, and gastroenteritis (delayed). Treatment is supportive. Efforts to minimize absorption (charcoal, gastric lavage) may be ineffective unless instituted within 60 minutes of ingestion.

Drug Interactions

Increased Effect/Toxicity: Allopurinol can cause increased levels of mercaptopurine by inhibition of xanthine oxidase. Decrease dose of mercaptopurine by 75% when both drugs are used concomitantly. May potentiate effect of bone marrow suppression (reduce mercaptopurine to 25% of dose). Synergistic liver toxicity between doxorubicin and mercaptopurine has been reported. Any agent which could potentially alter the metabolic function of the liver could produce higher drug levels and greater toxicities from either mercaptopurine or thioguanine (6-TG). Aminosalicylates (eg, olsalazine, mesalamine, sulfasalazine) may inhibit TPMT, increasing toxicity/myelosuppression of mercaptopurine. Azathioprine is metabolized to mercaptopurine; concomitant use may result in profound myelosuppression and should be avoided

Decreased Effect: Mercaptopurine inhibits the anticoagulation effect of warfarin by an unknown mechanism.

Storage/Stability Store at room temperature of 15°C to 25°C (59°F to 77°F). Protect from moisture.

Mechanism of Action Purine antagonist which inhibits DNA and RNA synthesis; acts as false metabolite and is incorporated into DNA and RNA, eventually inhibiting their synthesis; specific for the S phase of the cell cycle

Pharmacodynamics/Kinetics

Absorption: Variable and incomplete (16% to 50%)

Distribution: V_d = total body water; CNS penetration is poor

Protein binding: 19%

Metabolism: Hepatic and in GI mucosa; hepatically via xanthine oxidase and methylation via TPMT to sulfate conjugates, 6-thiouric acid, and other inactive compounds; first-pass effect

Half-life elimination (age dependent): Children: 21 minutes; Adults: 47 minutes

Time to peak, serum: ~2 hours

(Continued)

Mercaptopurine *(Continued)*

Excretion: Urine (46% as mercaptopurine and metabolites)

Dosage Oral (refer to individual protocols):

Children: ALL:

Induction: 2.5-5 mg/kg/day **or** 70-100 mg/m^2/day given once daily

Maintenance: 1.5-2.5 mg/kg/day **or** 50-75 mg/m^2/day given once daily

Adults:

ALL:

Induction: 2.5-5 mg/kg/day (100-200 mg)

Maintenance: 1.5-2.5 mg/kg/day **or** 80-100 mg/m^2/day given once daily

Reduction of steroid use in CD or UC, maintenance of remission in CD or fistulizing disease (unlabeled uses): Initial: 50 mg daily; may increase by 25 mg/day every 1-2 weeks as tolerated to target dose of 1-1.5 mg/kg/day

Dosage adjustment with concurrent allopurinol: Reduce mercaptopurine dosage to $^1/_4$ to $^1/_3$ the usual dose.

Dosage adjustment in TPMT-deficiency: Not established; substantial reductions are generally required only in homozygous deficiency.

Elderly: Due to renal decline with age, start with lower recommended doses for adults

Note: In ALL, administration in the evening (vs morning administration) may lower the risk of relapse.

Dosing adjustment in renal impairment: The FDA-approved labeling recommends starting with reduced doses in patients with renal impairment to avoid accumulation; however, specific guidelines are not available. The following guidelines have been used by some clinicians (Aronoff, 2007):

Children:

Cl$_{cr}$ <50 mL/minute: Administer every 48 hours

Hemodialysis: Administer every 48 hours

Continuous ambulatory peritoneal dialysis (CAPD): Administer every 48 hours

Continuous renal replacement therapy (CRRT): Administer every 48 hours

Dosing adjustment in hepatic impairment: The FDA-approved labeling recommends considering a reduced dose in patients with hepatic impairment; however, specific guidelines are not available.

Combination Regimens

Leukemia, acute lymphocytic:

Hyper-CVAD (Leukemia, Acute Lymphocytic) *on page 1231*

MTX/6-MP/VP (Maintenance) *on page 1254*

POMP *on page 1273*

PVA (POG 8602) *on page 1273*

Leukemia, acute promyelocytic: Tretinoin-Idarubicin *on page 1283*

Administration Preferably on an empty stomach (1 hour before or 2 hours after meals)

Monitoring Parameters CBC with differential and platelet count, liver function tests, uric acid, urinalysis; TPMT genotyping may identify individuals at risk for toxicity

For use as immunomodulatory therapy in CD or UC, monitor CBC with differential weekly for 1 month, then biweekly for 1 month, followed by monitoring every 1-2 months throughout the course of therapy. LFTs should be assessed every 3 months.

Dietary Considerations Should not be administered with meals.

Patient Information Take daily dose at the same time each day. Preferable to take an on empty stomach (1 hour before or 2 hours after meals). Maintain adequate hydration (2-3 L/day of fluids unless instructed to restrict fluid intake). You may experience nausea and vomiting, diarrhea, or loss of appetite (frequent small meals may help/request medication) or weakness or lethargy (use caution when driving or engaging in tasks that require alertness until response to drug is known). Use good oral care to reduce incidence of mouth sores. You may be more susceptible to infection (avoid crowds or exposure to infection). May cause headache (request medication). Report signs of opportunistic infection (eg, fever, chills, sore throat, burning urination, fatigue); bleeding (eg, tarry stools, easy bruising); unresolved mouth sores, nausea, or vomiting; swelling of extremities, difficulty breathing, or unusual weight gain. The drug may be excreted in breast milk, therefore, an alternative form of feeding your baby should be used. Contraceptive measures are recommended during therapy.

Special Geriatric Considerations Toxicity to immunosuppressives is increased in the elderly. Start with lowest recommended adult doses. Signs of infection, such as fever and WBC rise, may not occur. Lethargy and confusion may be more prominent signs of infection.

Emetic Potential Very low (<10%)

Vesicant No

Dosage Forms Excipient information presented when available (limited, particularly for generics); consult specific product labeling.
Tablet [scored]: 50 mg

Extemporaneous Preparations A 50 mg/mL oral suspension can be prepared by crushing thirty 50 mg tablets in a mortar, and then mixing in a small amount of vehicle (a 1:1 combination of methylcellulose 1% and syrup) to create a uniform paste. Add a sufficient quantity of vehicle to make 30 mL of suspension. Label "shake well." Room temperature stability is 14 days.

Dressman JB and Poust RI, "Stability of Allopurinol and of Five Antineoplastics in Suspension," *Am J Hosp Pharm*, 1983, 40:616-8.

Nahata MC, Morosco RS, and Hipple TF, 4th ed, *Pediatric Drug Formulations*, Cincinnati, OH: Harvey Whitney Books Co, 2000.

References

Bostrom B and Erdmann G, "Cellular Pharmacology of 6-Mercaptopurine in Acute Lymphoblastic Leukemia," *Am J Pediatr Hematol Oncol*, 1993, 15(1):80-6.

Elgemeie GH, "Thioguanine, Mercaptopurine: Their Analogs and Nucleosides as Antimetabolites," *Curr Pharm Des*, 2003, 9(31):2627-42.

Grindey GB, "Clinical Pharmacology of the 6-Thiopurines," *Cancer Treat Rev*, 1979, 6(Suppl):19-25.

Hutchins LF and Lipschitz DA, "Cancer, Clinical Pharmacology, and Aging," *Clin Geriatr Med*, 1987, 3(3):483-503.

Kaplan HG, "Use of Cancer Chemotherapy in the Elderly," *Drug Treatment in the Elderly*, Vestal RE, ed, Boston, MA: ADIS Health Science Press, 1984, 338-49.

Lennard L, "The Clinical Pharmacology of 6-Mercaptopurine," *Eur J Clin Pharmacol*, 1992, 43(4):329-39.

Mosesso P and Palitti F, "The Genetic Toxicology of 6-Mercaptopurine," *Mutat Res*, 1993, 296(3):279-94.

Pinkel D, "Intravenous Mercaptopurine: Life Begins at 40," *J Clin Oncol*, 1993, 11(9):1826-31.

Van Scoik KG, Johnson CA, and Porter WR, "The Pharmacology and Metabolism of the Thiopurine Drugs 6-Mercaptopurine and Azathioprine," *Drug Metab Rev*, 1985, 16(1-2):157-74.

Zimm S, Ettinger LJ, Holcenberg JS, et al, "Phase I and Clinical Pharmacological Study of Mercaptopurine Administered as a Prolonged Intravenous Infusion," *Cancer Res*, 1988, 45(4):1869-73.

♦ **6-Mercaptopurine (error-prone abbreviation)** *see* Mercaptopurine *on* page 720

♦ **M-Eslon® (Can)** *see* Morphine Sulfate *on* page 779

Mesna (MES na)

Related Information
Safe Handling of Hazardous Drugs *on page 1382*

U.S. Brand Names Mesnex®

Index Terms Sodium 2-Mercaptoethane Sulfonate

Generic Available Yes

Canadian Brand Names Mesnex®; Uromitexan

Pharmacologic Category Antidote

Use Orphan drug: Prevention of hemorrhagic cystitis induced by ifosfamide

Unlabeled/Investigational Use Prevention of hemorrhagic cystitis induced by cyclophosphamide

Pregnancy Risk Factor B

Lactation Excretion in breast milk unknown/not recommended

Labeled Contraindications Hypersensitivity to mesna or other thiol compounds, or any component of the formulation

Warnings/Precautions Examine morning urine specimen for hematuria prior to ifosfamide or cyclophosphamide treatment; if hematuria (>50 RBC/HPF) develops, reduce the ifosfamide/cyclophosphamide dose or discontinue the drug; will not prevent or alleviate other toxicities associated with ifosfamide or cyclophosphamide and will not prevent hemorrhagic cystitis in all patients. Allergic reactions have been reported; patients with autoimmune disorders may be at increased risk. Symptoms ranged from mild hypersensitivity to systemic anaphylactic reactions. I.V. formulation contains benzyl alcohol; do not use in neonates or infants.

Adverse Reactions Reported as part of a chemotherapy regimen.
>10%: Gastrointestinal: Bad taste in mouth with oral administration (100%), vomiting (secondary to the bad taste after oral administration, or with high I.V. doses)
<1%: Anaphylaxis, hypersensitivity, hypertonia, injection site reaction, limb pain, myalgia, platelet count decreased, tachycardia, tachypnea

Drug Interactions
Decreased Effect: Warfarin: Questionable alterations in coagulation control.

Storage/Stability Store intact vials and tablets at controlled room temperature of 20°C to 25°C (68°F to 77°F). Opened multidose vials may be stored and used for use to 8 days after opening. Infusion solutions diluted in D_5W or lactated Ringer's are stable for at least 48 hours at room temperature. Solutions in NS are stable for at least 24 hours at room temperature. Solutions in plastic syringes are stable for 9 days under refrigeration, or at room or body temperature. Solutions of mesna and ifosfamide in lactated Ringer's are stable for 7 days in a PVC ambulatory infusion pump reservoir. Mesna injection is stable for at least 7 days when diluted 1:2 or 1:5 with grape- and orange-flavored syrups or 11:1 to 1:100 in carbonated beverages for oral administration.

Reconstitution Dilute in 50-1000 mL NS, D_5W, or lactated Ringer's.

Compatibility Stable in $D_5^1/_4NS$, $D_5^1/_3NS$, $D_5^1/_2NS$, D_5W, LR, NS.
Y-site administration: Compatible: Allopurinol, amifostine, aztreonam, cefepime, cladribine, docetaxel, doxorubicin liposome, etoposide phosphate, filgrastim, fludarabine, gatifloxacin, gemcitabine, granisetron, linezolid, melphalan, methotrexate, ondansetron, paclitaxel, piperacillin/tazobactam, sargramostim, sodium bicarbonate, teniposide, thiotepa, vinorelbine. **Incompatible:** Amphotericin B cholesteryl sulfate complex.
Compatibility in syringe: Compatible: Ifosfamide. **Incompatible:** Ifosfamide with epirubicin.

Compatibility when admixed: Compatible: Cyclophosphamide, hydroxyzine, ifosfamide. **Incompatible:** Carboplatin, cisplatin, ifosfamide with epirubicin.

Mechanism of Action In blood, mesna is oxidized to dimesna which in turn is reduced in the kidney back to mesna, supplying a free thiol group which binds to and inactivates acrolein, the urotoxic metabolite of ifosfamide and cyclophosphamide

Pharmacodynamics/Kinetics

Distribution: No tissue penetration

Protein binding: 69% to 75%

Metabolism: Rapidly oxidized intravascularly to mesna disulfide; mesna disulfide is reduced in renal tubules back to mesna following glomerular filtration.

Bioavailability: Oral: 45% to 79%

Half-life elimination: Parent drug: 24 minutes; Mesna disulfide: 72 minutes

Time to peak, plasma: 2-3 hours

Excretion: Urine; as unchanged drug (18% to 26%) and metabolites

Dosage Children and Adults (refer to individual protocols):

I.V.: Recommended dose is 60% of the ifosfamide dose given in 3 divided doses (0, 4, and 8 hours after the start of ifosfamide)

Alternative I.V. regimens include 80% of the ifosfamide dose given in 4 divided doses (0, 3, 6, and 9 hours after the start of ifosfamide) and continuous infusions

Oral, I.V.: Recommended dose is 100% of the ifosfamide dose, given as 20% of the ifosfamide dose I.V. at hour 0, followed by 40% of the ifosfamide dose given orally 2 and 6 hours after start of ifosfamide

Combination Regimens

Breast cancer: ICE-T *on page 1238*

Cervical cancer: BIP *on page 1152*

Esophageal cancer: TIP *on page 1281*

Head and neck cancer: TIP *on page 1281*

Leukemia, acute lymphocytic:

Hyper-CVAD + Imatinib *on page 1229*

Hyper-CVAD (Leukemia, Acute Lymphocytic) *on page 1231*

Lung cancer (small cell): VIP (Small Cell Lung Cancer) *on page 1291*

Lymphoma, non-Hodgkin's:

ICE (Lymphoma, non-Hodgkin's) *on page 1238*

IMVP-16 *on page 1240*

IVAC *on page 1242*

MINE *on page 1247*

MINE-ESHAP *on page 1247*

RICE *on page 1277*

Lymphoma, non-Hodgkin's (Burkitt's): CODOX-M/IVAC *on page 1180*

Lymphoma, non-Hodgkin's (Mantle cell): Hyper-CVAD + Rituximab *on page 1237*

Multiple myeloma: Hyper-CVAD (Multiple Myeloma) *on page 1237*

Neuroblastoma:

CI (Neuroblastoma) *on page 1174*

HIPE-IVAD *on page 1229*

Osteosarcoma: ICE (Sarcoma) *on page 1238*

Soft tissue sarcoma:

AI *on page 1145*

ICE (Sarcoma) *on page 1238*

ICE-T *on page 1238*

IE *on page 1239*

MAID *on page 1246*

(Continued)

Mesna *(Continued)*

Testicular cancer:

Paclitaxel-Ifosfamide-Cisplatin *on page 1265*
VIP (Etoposide) (Testicular Cancer) *on page 1290*
VIP (Vinblastine) (Testicular Cancer) *on page 1291*

Administration

Oral: Administer orally in tablet formulation or parenteral solution diluted in water, milk, juice, or carbonated beverages; patients who vomit within 2 hours of taking oral mesna should repeat the dose or receive I.V. mesna

I.V.: Administer by short (15-30 minutes) infusion or continuous (24 hour) infusion

Monitoring Parameters Urinalysis

Test Interactions False-positive urinary ketones with Multistix® or Labstix®

Additional Information A parenteral formulation without benzyl alcohol can be requested directly from the manufacturer.

Emetic Potential Low (10% to 30%); when administered orally, the unpleasant taste may result in vomiting

Vesicant No

Dosage Forms Excipient information presented when available (limited, particularly for generics); consult specific product labeling.

Injection, solution: 100 mg/mL (10 mL) [contains benzyl alcohol]
Tablet: 400 mg

References

Ben Yehuda A, Heyman A and Steiner Salz D, "False Positive Reaction for Urinary Ketones With Mesna," *Drug Intell Clin Pharm*, 1987, 21(6):547-8.

Brock N and Pohl J, "The Development of Mesna for Regional Detoxification," *Cancer Treat Rev*, 1983, 10(Suppl A):33-43.

"Cancer Chemotherapy," *Med Lett Drugs Ther*, 1989, 31(793):49-56.

Goren MP, "Oral Administration of Mesna With Ifosfamide," *Semin Oncol*, 1996, 23(3 Suppl 6):91-6.

Goren MP, "Oral Mesna: A Review," *Semin Oncol*, 1992, 19(6 Suppl 12):65-71.

Pohl J, "Toxicology, Pharmacology, and Interactions of Sodium 2-Mercaptoethane Sulfonate (Mesna)," *Curr Chemotherapy*, 1981, 2:1387-9.

Schoenike SE and Dana WJ, "Ifosfamide and Mesna," *Clin Pharm*, 1990, 9(3):179-91.

Shaw IC and Graham MI, "Mesna - A Short Review," *Cancer Treat Rev*, 1987, 14(2):67-86.

Siu LL and Moore MJ, "Use of Mesna to Prevent Ifosfamide-Induced Urotoxicity," *Support Care Cancer*, 1998, 6(2):144-54.

♦ **Mesnex®** *see* Mesna *on page 724*
♦ **Metacortandralone** *see* PrednisoLONE *on page 914*
♦ **Metadol™ (Can)** *see* Methadone *on page 726*
♦ **Metastron®** *see* Strontium-89 *on page 981*

Methadone *(METH a done)*

Medication Safety Issues

Sound-alike/look-alike issues:

Methadone may be confused with Mephyton®, methylphenidate, Metadate®, and Metadate® ER

U.S. Brand Names Dolophine®; Methadone Diskets®; Methadone Intensol™; Methadose®

Index Terms Methadone Hydrochloride

Generic Available Yes

Canadian Brand Names Metadol™

Pharmacologic Category Analgesic, Opioid

Use Management of moderate-to-severe pain; detoxification and maintenance treatment of opioid addiction (if used for detoxification and maintenance treatment of narcotic addiction, it must be part of an FDA-approved program)

Restrictions C-II

When used for treatment of opioid addiction: May only be dispensed in accordance to guidelines established by the Substance Abuse and Mental Health Services Administration's (SAMHSA) Center for Substance Abuse Treatment (CSAT). Regulations regarding methadone use may vary by state and/or country. Obtain advice from appropriate regulatory agencies and/or consult with pain management/palliative care specialists.

Note: Regulatory Exceptions to the General Requirement to Provide Opioid Agonist Treatment (per manufacturer's labeling):
1. During inpatient care, when the patient was admitted for any condition other than concurrent opioid addiction, to facilitate the treatment of the primary admitting diagnosis.
2. During an emergency period of no longer than 3 days while definitive care for the addiction is being sought in an appropriately licensed facility.

Pregnancy Risk Factor C/D (prolonged use or high doses at term)

Lactation Enters breast milk/not recommended (AAP rates "compatible")

Labeled Contraindications Hypersensitivity to methadone or any component of the formulation; respiratory depression (in the absence of resuscitative equipment or in an unmonitored setting); acute bronchial asthma or hypercarbia; paralytic ileus; concurrent use of selegiline

Warnings/Precautions An opioid-containing analgesic regimen should be tailored to each patient's needs and based upon the type of pain being treated (acute versus chronic), the route of administration, degree of tolerance for opioids (naive versus chronic user), age, weight, and medical condition. The optimal analgesic dose varies widely among patients. Doses should be titrated to pain relief/prevention. Patients maintained on stable doses of methadone may need higher and/or more frequent doses in case of acute pain (eg, postoperative pain, physical trauma). Methadone is ineffective for the relief of anxiety.

[U.S. Boxed Warning]: May prolong the QT interval; use caution in patients at risk for QT prolongation, with medications known to prolong the QT interval, or history of conduction abnormalities. QT interval prolongation and torsade de pointes may be associated with doses >200 mg/day, but have also been observed with lower doses. Correct potassium and magnesium abnormalities prior to initiation. May cause severe hypotension; use caution with severe volume depletion or other conditions which may compromise maintenance of normal blood pressure. Use caution with cardiovascular disease or patients predisposed to dysrhythmias.

[U.S. Boxed Warning]: May cause respiratory depression. Use caution in patients with respiratory disease or pre-existing respiratory conditions (eg, severe obesity, asthma, COPD, sleep apnea, CNS depression). Because the respiratory effects last longer than the analgesic effects, slow titration is required. Use extreme caution during treatment initiation, dose titration and conversion from other opioid agonists. Incomplete cross tolerance may occur; patients tolerant to other mu opioid agonists may not be tolerant to methadone. Abrupt cessation may precipitate withdrawal symptoms.

May cause CNS depression, which may impair physical or mental abilities. Patients must be cautioned about performing tasks which require mental alertness (eg, operating machinery or driving). Effects with other sedative drugs or ethanol may be potentiated. Use with caution in patients with depression or suicidal tendencies, or in patients with a history of drug abuse. Tolerance or psychological and physical dependence may occur with prolonged use.
(Continued)

Methadone *(Continued)*

Use with caution in patients with head injury or increased intracranial pressure. May obscure diagnosis or clinical course of patients with acute abdominal conditions. Elderly may be more susceptible to adverse effects (eg, CNS, respiratory, gastrointestinal). Decrease initial dose and use caution in the elderly or debilitated; with hyper/hypothyroidism, morbid obesity, adrenal insufficiency, prostatic hyperplasia, or urethral stricture; or with severe renal or hepatic failure. Use with caution in patients with biliary tract dysfunction; acute pancreatitis may cause constriction of sphincter of Oddi. Safety and efficacy have not been established in children. **[U.S. Boxed Warning]: For oral administration only;** excipients to deter use by injection are contained in tablets.

[U.S. Boxed Warning]: When used for treatment of narcotic addiction: May only be dispensed by opioid treatment programs certified by the Substance Abuse and Mental Health Services Administration (SAMHSA) and certified by the designated state authority. Exceptions include inpatient treatment of other conditions and emergency period (not >3 days) while definitive substance abuse treatment is being sought.

Adverse Reactions Frequency not defined. During prolonged administration, adverse effects may decrease over several weeks; however, constipation and sweating may persist.

Cardiovascular: Bradycardia, peripheral vasodilation, cardiac arrest, syncope, faintness, shock, hypotension, edema, arrhythmia, bigeminal rhythms, extrasystoles, tachycardia, torsade de pointes, ventricular fibrillation, ventricular tachycardia, ECG changes, QT interval prolonged, T-wave inversion, cardiomyopathy, flushing, heart failure, palpitation, phlebitis, orthostatic hypotension

Central nervous system: Euphoria, dysphoria, hallucination, headache, insomnia, agitation, disorientation, drowsiness, dizziness, lightheadedness, sedation, confusion, seizure

Dermatologic: Pruritus, urticaria, rash, hemorrhagic urticaria

Endocrine & metabolic: Libido decreased, hypokalemia, hypomagnesemia, antidiuretic effect, amenorrhea

Gastrointestinal: Nausea, vomiting, constipation, anorexia, stomach cramps, xerostomia, biliary tract spasm, abdominal pain, glossitis, weight gain

Genitourinary: Urinary retention or hesitancy, impotence

Hematologic: Thrombocytopenia (reversible, reported in patients with chronic hepatitis)

Neuromuscular & skeletal: Weakness

Local: I.M./SubQ injection: Pain, erythema, swelling; I.V. injection: pruritus, urticaria, rash, hemorrhagic urticaria (rare)

Ocular: Miosis, visual disturbances

Respiratory: Respiratory depression, respiratory arrest, pulmonary edema

Miscellaneous: Physical and psychological dependence, death, diaphoresis

Overdosage/Toxicology Symptoms include respiratory depression, CNS depression, miosis, hypothermia, circulatory collapse, and convulsions. Treatment includes naloxone 2 mg I.V. (0.01 mg/kg for children), with repeat administration as necessary, up to a total of 10 mg, or as a continuous infusion. Nalmefene may also be used to reverse signs of intoxication. Patient should be monitored for depressant effects of methadone for 36-48 hours and other supportive measures should be employed as needed. Forced diuresis, peritoneal dialysis, hemodialysis, or charcoal hemoperfusion have not been established as beneficial for increasing methadone or metabolite elimination.

Drug Interactions

Cytochrome P450 Effect: Substrate of CYP2C9 (minor), 2C19 (minor), 2D6 (minor), 3A4 (major); **Inhibits** CYP2D6 (moderate), 3A4 (weak)

Increased Effect/Toxicity: CYP3A4 inhibitors may increase the levels/ effects of methadone (eg, azole antifungals, clarithromycin, diclofenac, doxycycline, erythromycin, imatinib, isoniazid, nefazodone, nicardipine, propofol, protease inhibitors, quinidine, telithromycin, verapamil). Methadone may increase the levels/effects of CYP2D6 substrates (eg, amphetamines, selected beta-blockers, dextromethorphan, fluoxetine, lidocaine, mirtazapine, nefazodone, paroxetine, risperidone, ritonavir, thioridazine, tricyclic antidepressants, venlafaxine). Methadone may increase bioavailability and toxic effects of zidovudine. CNS depressants (including but not limited to opioid analgesics, general anesthetics, sedatives, hypnotics, ethanol) may cause respiratory depression, hypotension, profound sedation, or coma. Levels of desipramine may be increased by methadone. Effects/toxicity of QT$_c$ interval-prolonging agents may be increased; use with caution (including but may not be limited to amitriptyline, astemizole, bepridil, disopyramide, erythromycin, haloperidol, imipramine, quinidine, pimozide, procainamide, sotalol, thioridazine). Ritonavir may increase levels/effects of methadone shortly after initiation. SSRIs may increase the levels/effects of methadone; the serotonergic effects of SSRIs or selegiline may be increased by methadone.

Decreased Effect: Agonist/antagonist analgesics (buprenorphine, butorphanol, nalbuphine, pentazocine) may decrease analgesic effect of methadone and precipitate withdrawal symptoms; use is not recommended. Efavirenz and nevirapine may decrease levels of methadone (opioid withdrawal syndrome has been reported). Methadone may decrease bioavailability of didanosine and stavudine. Ritonavir (and combinations) may decrease levels of methadone during prolonged therapy; withdrawal symptoms have inconsistently been observed, monitor. CYP3A4 inducers may decrease the levels/effects of methadone (eg, aminoglutethimide, carbamazepine, nafcillin, nevirapine, phenobarbital, phenytoin, rifamycins). Monitor for methadone withdrawal. Larger doses of methadone may be required. Methadone may decrease the levels/effects of CYP2D6 prodrug substrates (eg, codeine, hydrocodone, oxycodone, tramadol). Methadone may decrease the effects of pegvisomant.

Ethanol/Nutrition/Herb Interactions

Ethanol: Avoid ethanol (may increase CNS effects). Watch for sedation.

Herb/Nutraceutical: Avoid St John's wort (may decrease methadone levels; may increase CNS depression). Avoid valerian, kava kava, gotu kola (may increase CNS depression). Methadone is metabolized by CYP3A4 in the intestines; avoid concurrent use of grapefruit juice.

Storage/Stability

Injection: Store at controlled room temperature of 15°C to 30°C (59°F to 86°F). Protect from light.

Oral concentrate, oral solution, tablet: Store at controlled room temperature of 15°C to 30°C (59°F to 86°F).

Compatibility Stable in NS.

Mechanism of Action Binds to opiate receptors in the CNS, causing inhibition of ascending pain pathways, altering the perception of and response to pain; produces generalized CNS depression

Pharmacodynamics/Kinetics

Onset of action: Oral: Analgesic: 0.5-1 hour; Parenteral: 10-20 minutes
Peak effect: Parenteral: 1-2 hours; Oral: continuous dosing: 3-5 days
(Continued)

Methadone *(Continued)*

Duration of analgesia: Oral: 4-8 hours, increases to 22-48 hours with repeated doses

Distribution: V_{dss}: 1-8 L/kg

Protein binding: 85% to 90%

Metabolism: Hepatic; N-demethylation primarily via CYP3A4, CYP2B6, and CYP2C19 to inactive metabolites

Bioavailability: Oral: 36% to 100%

Half-life elimination: 8-59 hours; may be prolonged with alkaline pH, decreased during pregnancy

Time to peak, plasma: 1-7.5 hours

Excretion: Urine (<10% as unchanged drug); increased with urine pH <6

Dosage Note: These are guidelines and do not represent the maximum doses that may be required in all patients. Methadone accumulates with repeated doses and dosage may need reduction after 3-5 days to prevent CNS depressant effects. Some patients may benefit from every 8-12 hour dosing interval for chronic pain management. Doses should be titrated to appropriate effects.

Children (unlabeled use):

Pain (analgesia):

Oral: Initial: 0.1-0.2 mg/kg 4-8 hours initially for 2-3 doses, then every 6-12 hours as needed. Dosing interval may range from 4-12 hours during initial therapy; decrease in dose or frequency may be required (~days 2-5) due to accumulation with repeated doses (maximum dose: 5-10 mg)

I.V.: 0.1 mg/kg every 4-8 hours initially for 2-3 doses, then every 6-12 hours as needed. Dosing interval may range from 4-12 hours during initial therapy; decrease in dose or frequency may be required (~ days 2-5) due to accumulation with repeated doses (maximum dose: 5-8 mg)

Iatrogenic narcotic dependency: Oral: General guidelines: Initial: 0.05-0.1 mg/kg/dose every 6 hours; increase by 0.05 mg/kg/dose until withdrawal symptoms are controlled; after 24-48 hours, the dosing interval can be lengthened to every 12-24 hours; to taper dose, wean by 0.05 mg/kg/day; if withdrawal symptoms recur, taper at a slower rate

Adults:

Acute pain (moderate-to-severe):

Oral: Opioid-naive: Initial: 2.5-10 mg every 8-12 hours; more frequent administration may be required during initiation to maintain adequate analgesia. Dosage interval may range from 4-12 hours, since duration of analgesia is relatively short during the first days of therapy, but increases substantially with continued administration.

Chronic pain (opioid-tolerant): **Conversion from oral morphine to oral methadone:**

Daily oral morphine dose <100 mg: Estimated daily oral methadone dose: 20% to 30% of total daily morphine dose

Daily oral morphine dose 100-300 mg: Estimated daily oral methadone dose: 10% to 20% of total daily morphine dose

Daily oral morphine dose 300-600 mg: Estimated daily oral methadone dose: 8% to 12% of total daily morphine dose

Daily oral morphine dose 600-1000 mg: Estimated daily oral methadone dose: 5% to 10% of total daily morphine dose.

Daily oral morphine dose >1000 mg: Estimated daily oral methadone dose: <5% of total daily morphine dose.

Note: The total daily methadone dose should then be divided to reflect the intended dosing schedule.

I.V.: Manufacturers labeling: Initial: 2.5-10 mg every 8-12 hours in opioid-naive patients; titrate slowly to effect; may also be administered by SubQ or I.M. injection

Conversion from oral methadone to parenteral methadone dose: Initial dose: Parenteral:Oral ratio: 1:2 (eg, 5 mg parenteral methadone equals 10 mg oral methadone)

Detoxification: Oral:

Initial: A single dose of 20-30 mg is generally sufficient to suppress symptoms. Should not exceed 30 mg; lower doses should be considered in patients with low tolerance at initiation (eg, absence of opioids ≥5 days); an additional 5-10 mg of methadone may be provided if withdrawal symptoms have not been suppressed or if symptoms reappear after 2-4 hours; total daily dose on the first day should not exceed 40 mg, unless the program physician documents in the patient's record that 40 mg did not control opiate abstinence symptoms.

Maintenance: Titrate to a dosage which attenuates craving, blocks euphoric effects of other opiates, and tolerance to sedative effect of methadone. Usual range: 80-120 mg/day (titration should occur cautiously)

Withdrawal: Dose reductions should be <10% of the maintenance dose, every 10-14 days

Detoxification (short-term): Oral:

Initial: Titrate to ~40 mg/day in divided doses to achieve stabilization, may continue 40 mg dose for 2-3 days

Maintenance: Titrate to a dosage which prevents/attenuates euphoric effects of self-administered opioids, reduces drug craving, and withdrawal symptoms are prevented for 24 hours.

Withdrawal: Requires individualization. Decrease daily or every other day, keeping withdrawal symptoms tolerable; hospitalized patients may tolerate a 20% reduction/day; ambulatory patients may require a slower reduction

Dosage adjustment during pregnancy: Methadone dose may need to be increased, or the dosing interval decreased; see Pregnancy Implications - use should be reserved for cases where the benefits clearly outweigh the risks

Dosage adjustment in renal impairment: Cl_{cr} <10 mL/minute: Administer 50% to 75% of normal dose

Dosage adjustment in hepatic impairment: Avoid in severe liver disease

Administration Oral dose for detoxification and maintenance may be administered in fruit juice or water. Dispersible tablet should not be chewed or swallowed; add to liquid and allow to dissolve before administering. May rinse if residual remains.

Monitoring Parameters Pain relief, respiratory and mental status, blood pressure

Test Interactions Some quinolones may produce a false-positive urine screening result for opiates using commercially-available immunoassay kits. This has been demonstrated most consistently for levofloxacin and ofloxacin, but other quinolones have shown cross-reactivity in certain assay kits. Confirmation of positive opiate screens by more specific methods should be considered.

(Continued)

Methadone *(Continued)*

Patient Information May cause drowsiness, avoid alcohol and other CNS depressants

Special Geriatric Considerations Because of it's long half-life and risk of accumulation, methadone is difficult to titrate and is not considered a drug of first choice. It should be prescribed only by physicians who are experienced in using it. Elderly may be particularly susceptible to the CNS depressant and constipating effects of narcotics.

Vesicant No

Dosage Forms Excipient information presented when available (limited, particularly for generics); consult specific product labeling.

Injection, solution, as hydrochloride: 10 mg/mL (20 mL)

Solution, oral, as hydrochloride: 5 mg/5 mL (500 mL); 10 mg/5 mL (500 mL) [contains alcohol 8%; citrus flavor]

Solution, oral, as hydrochloride [concentrate]: 10 mg/mL (946 mL)

Methadone Intensol™: 10 mg/mL (30 mL)

Methadose®: 10 mg/mL (1000 mL) [cherry flavor]

Methadose®: 10 mg/mL (1000 mL) [dye free, sugar free, unflavored]

Tablet, as hydrochloride: 5 mg, 10 mg

Dolophine®: 5 mg, 10 mg

Methadose®: 5 mg, 10 mg [DSC]

Tablet, dispersible, as hydrochloride: 40 mg

Methadose®: 40 mg

Methadone Diskets®: 40 mg [orange-pineapple flavor]

References

Anand KJ and Arnold JH, "Opioid Tolerance and Dependence in Infants and Children," *Crit Care Med*, 1994, 22(2):334-42.

Berde C, Ablin A, Glazer J, et al, "American Academy of Pediatrics Report of the Subcommittee on Disease-Related Pain in Childhood Cancer," *Pediatrics*, 1990, 86(5 Pt 2):818-25.

Berde CB and Sethna NF, "Analgesics for the Treatment of Pain in Children," *N Engl J Med*, 2002, 347(14):1094-103.

Department of Health and Human Services: Substance Abuse and Mental Health Services Administration, "Opioid Drugs in Maintenance and Detoxification of Opiate Addiction; Final Rule," *Fed Regist*, 2001, 66(11): 4075-102.

"Drugs for Pain," *Med Lett Drugs Ther*, 2000, 42(1085):73-8.

Ferrell BA, "Pain Management in Elderly People," *J Am Geriatr Soc*, 1991, 39(1):64-73.

Gayle MO, Ryan CA, and Nazarali S, "Unusual Cause of Methadone Poisoning," *Acta Paediatr Scand*, 1991, 80(4):486-7.

Gazelle G and Fine PG, "Methadone for the Treatment of Pain #75," *J Palliat Med*, 2003, 6(4):620-1.

Geller RJ and Garrettson LK, "Delayed Onset of Toxicity After Methadone Ingestion Due to Therapeutic Error," *Vet Hum Toxicol*, 1994, 36:367.

Lauriault G, LeBelle MJ, Lodge BA, et al, "Stability of Methadone in Four Vehicles for Oral Administration," *Am J Hosp Pharm*, 1991, 48(6):1252-6.

Mokhlesi B, Leikin JB, Murray P, et al, "Adult Toxicology in Critical Care: Part II: Specific Poisonings," *Chest*, 2003, 123(3):897-922.

Molyneux E, Ahern R, and Baldwin B, "Accidental Ingestion of Methadone," *BMJ*, 1991, 303(6807):922-3.

Olkkola KT, Hamunen K, and Maunuksela EL, "Clinical Pharmacokinetics and Pharmacodynamics of Opioid Analgesics in Infants and Children," *Clin Pharmacokinet*, 1995, 28(5):385-404.

"Principles of Analgesic Use in the Treatment of Acute Pain and Chronic Cancer Pain," 5th ed, Glenview, IL: American Pain Society, 2003.

Wasserman S and Yahr MD, "Choreic Movements Induced by the Use of Methadone," *Arch Neurol*, 1980, 37(11):727-8.

Wu CH and Henry JA, "Deaths of Heroin Addicts Starting on Methadone Maintenance," *Lancet*, 1990, 335(8686):424.

Wunsch MJ, Stanard V, and Schnoll SH, "Treatment of Pain in Pregnancy," *Clin J Pain*, 2003, 19(3):148-55.

Zacher JL and Givone DM, "False-Positive Urine Opiate Screening Associated With Fluoroquinolone Use," *Ann Pharmacother*, 2004, 38:1525-28.

♦ **Methadone Diskets**® *see* Methadone *on page 726*
♦ **Methadone Hydrochloride** *see* Methadone *on page 726*
♦ **Methadone Intensol**™ *see* Methadone *on page 726*
♦ **Methadose**® *see* Methadone *on page 726*

Methotrexate (meth oh TREKS ate)

Medication Safety Issues

Sound-alike/look-alike issues:

Methotrexate may be confused with metolazone, mitoxantrone

MTX is an error-prone abbreviation (mistaken as mitoxantrone)

High alert medication: The Institute for Safe Medication Practices (ISMP) includes this medication among its list of drugs which have a heightened risk of causing significant patient harm when used in error.

Errors have occurred (resulting in death) when methotrexate was administered as "daily" dose instead of the recommended "weekly" dose.

International issues:

Trexall™ may be confused with Truxal® which is a brand name for chlorprothixene in Belgium

Trexall™ may be confused with Trexol® which is a brand name for tramadol in Mexico

Related Information

Fertility and Cancer Therapy *on page 1298*
Hematopoietic Stem Cell Transplantation *on page 1366*
Safe Handling of Hazardous Drugs *on page 1382*

U.S. Brand Names Rheumatrex® Dose Pack®; Trexall™

Index Terms Amethopterin; Methotrexate Sodium; MTX (error-prone abbreviation); NSC-740

Generic Available Yes

Canadian Brand Names Apo-Methotrexate®; ratio-Methotrexate

Pharmacologic Category Antineoplastic Agent, Antimetabolite (Antifolate); Antirheumatic, Disease Modifying

Use Treatment of trophoblastic neoplasms; leukemias; psoriasis; rheumatoid arthritis (RA), including polyarticular-course juvenile rheumatoid arthritis (JRA); breast, head and neck, and lung carcinomas; osteosarcoma; soft-tissue sarcomas; carcinoma of gastrointestinal tract, esophagus, testes; lymphomas

Unlabeled/Investigational Use Treatment and maintenance of remission in Crohn's disease; ectopic pregnancy

Pregnancy Risk Factor X (psoriasis, rheumatoid arthritis)

Lactation Enters breast milk/contraindicated

Labeled Contraindications Hypersensitivity to methotrexate or any component of the formulation; severe renal or hepatic impairment; pre-existing profound bone marrow suppression in patients with psoriasis or rheumatoid arthritis, alcoholic liver disease, AIDS, pre-existing blood dyscrasias; pregnancy (in patients with psoriasis or rheumatoid arthritis); breast-feeding

Warnings/Precautions Hazardous agent - use appropriate precautions for handling and disposal.

[U.S. Boxed Warning]: Methotrexate has been associated with acute (elevated transaminases) and potentially fatal chronic (fibrosis, cirrhosis) hepatotoxicity. Risk is related to cumulative dose and prolonged exposure. Monitor closely (with liver function tests, including serum albumin) for liver toxicities. Liver enzyme elevations may be noted, but may not be
(Continued)

Methotrexate *(Continued)*

predictive of hepatic disease in long term treatment for psoriasis (but generally is predictive in rheumatoid arthritis [RA] treatment). With long-term use, liver biopsy may show histologic changes, fibrosis or cirrhosis; periodic liver biopsy is recommended with long-term use for psoriasis and for persistent abnormal liver function tests with RA; discontinue methotrexate with moderate-to-severe change in liver biopsy. Ethanol abuse, obesity, advanced age, and diabetes may increase the risk of hepatotoxic reactions. Use caution with preexisting liver impairment; may require dosage reduction. Use caution when used with other hepatotoxic agents (azathioprine, retinoids, sulfasalazine). **[U.S. Boxed Warning]: Methotrexate elimination is reduced in patients with ascites;** may require dose reduction or discontinuation. Monitor closely for toxicity.

[U.S. Boxed Warning]: May cause renal damage leading to acute renal failure, especially with high-dose methotrexate; monitor renal function and methotrexate levels closely, maintain adequate hydration and urinary alkalinization. Use caution in osteosarcoma patients treated with high-dose methotrexate in combination with nephrotoxic chemotherapy (eg, cisplatin). **[U.S. Boxed Warning]: Methotrexate elimination is reduced in patients with renal impairment;** may require dose reduction or discontinuation; monitor closely for toxicity. **[U.S. Boxed Warning]: Tumor lysis syndrome may occur in patients with high tumor burden;** use appropriate prevention and treatment.

[U.S. Boxed Warning]: May cause potentially life-threatening pneumonitis (may occur at any time during therapy and at any dosage); monitor closely for pulmonary symptoms, particularly dry, nonproductive cough. Other potential symptoms include fever, dyspnea, hypoxemia, or pulmonary infiltrate. **[U.S. Boxed Warning]: Methotrexate elimination is reduced in patients with pleural effusions;** may require dose reduction or discontinuation. Monitor closely for toxicity.

[U.S. Boxed Warning]: Bone marrow suppression may occur, resulting in anemia, aplastic anemia, pancytopenia, leukopenia, neutropenia, and/or thrombocytopenia. Use caution in patients with pre-existing bone marrow suppression. Discontinue therapy in RA or psoriasis if a significant decrease in hematologic components is noted. **[U.S. Boxed Warning]: Use of low dose methotrexate has been associated with the development of malignant lymphomas;** may regress upon discontinuation of therapy; treat lymphoma appropriately if regression is not induced by cessation of methotrexate.

[U.S. Boxed Warning]: Diarrhea and ulcerative stomatitis may require interruption of therapy; death from hemorrhagic enteritis or intestinal perforation has been reported. Use with caution in patients with peptic ulcer disease, ulcerative colitis.

May cause neurotoxicity including seizures (usually in pediatric ALL patients), leukoencephalopathy (usually with concurrent cranial irradiation) and stroke-like encephalopathy (usually with high-dose regimens). Chemical arachnoiditis (headache, back pain, nuchal rigidity, fever), myelopathy and chronic leukoencephalopathy may result from intrathecal administration.

[U.S. Boxed Warning]: Any dose level or route of administration may cause severe and potentially fatal dermatologic reactions, including toxic epidermal necrolysis, Stevens-Johnson syndrome, exfoliative dermatitis, skin necrosis, and erythema multiforme. Radiation dermatitis and sunburn may be precipitated by methotrexate administration. Psoriatic lesions may be worsened by concomitant exposure to ultraviolet radiation.

[U.S. Boxed Warning]: Concomitant administration with NSAIDs may cause severe bone marrow suppression, aplastic anemia, and GI toxicity. Do not administer NSAIDs prior to or during high dose methotrexate therapy; may increase and prolong serum methotrexate levels. Doses used for psoriasis may still lead to unexpected toxicities; use caution when administering NSAIDs or salicylates with lower doses of methotrexate for RA. Methotrexate may increase the levels and effects of mercaptopurine; may require dosage adjustments. Vitamins containing folate may decrease response to systemic methotrexate; folate deficiency may increase methotrexate toxicity. **[U.S. Boxed Warning]: Concomitant methotrexate administration with radiotherapy may increase the risk of soft tissue necrosis and osteonecrosis.**

[U.S. Boxed Warnings]: Should be administered under the supervision of a physician experienced in the use of antimetabolite therapy; serious and fatal toxicities have occurred at all dose levels. Immune suppression may lead to potentially fatal opportunistic infections. For rheumatoid arthritis and psoriasis, immunosuppressive therapy should only be used when disease is active and less toxic, traditional therapy is ineffective. Methotrexate formulations and/or diluents containing preservatives should not be used for intrathecal or high-dose therapy. May cause fetal death or congenital abnormalities; do not use for psoriasis or RA treatment in pregnant women. May cause impairment of fertility, oligospermia, and menstrual dysfunction. Toxicity from methotrexate or any immunosuppressive is increased in the elderly. Methotrexate injection may contain benzyl alcohol and should not be used in neonates.

Adverse Reactions Note: Adverse reactions vary by route and dosage. Hematologic and/or gastrointestinal toxicities may be common at dosages used in chemotherapy; these reactions are much less frequent when used at typical dosages for rheumatic diseases.

>10%:
Central nervous system (with I.T. administration or very high-dose therapy):
    Arachnoiditis: Acute reaction manifested as severe headache, nuchal rigidity, vomiting, and fever; may be alleviated by reducing the dose
    Subacute toxicity: 10% of patients treated with 12-15 mg/m^2 of I.T. methotrexate may develop this in the second or third week of therapy; consists of motor paralysis of extremities, cranial nerve palsy, seizure, or coma. This has also been seen in pediatric cases receiving very high-dose I.V. methotrexate.
    Demyelinating encephalopathy: Seen months or years after receiving methotrexate; usually in association with cranial irradiation or other systemic chemotherapy
Dermatologic: Reddening of skin
Endocrine & metabolic: Hyperuricemia, defective oogenesis or spermatogenesis
Gastrointestinal: Ulcerative stomatitis, glossitis, gingivitis, nausea, vomiting, diarrhea, anorexia, intestinal perforation, mucositis (dose dependent; appears in 3-7 days after therapy, resolving within 2 weeks)
Hematologic: Leukopenia, thrombocytopenia
Renal: Renal failure, azotemia, nephropathy
Respiratory: Pharyngitis
(Continued)

Methotrexate *(Continued)*

1% to 10%:

Cardiovascular: Vasculitis

Central nervous system: Dizziness, malaise, encephalopathy, seizure, fever, chills

Dermatologic: Alopecia, rash, photosensitivity, depigmentation or hyper-pigmentation of skin

Endocrine & metabolic: Diabetes

Genitourinary: Cystitis

Hematologic: Hemorrhage

Myelosuppressive: This is the primary dose-limiting factor (along with mucositis) of methotrexate; occurs about 5-7 days after methotrexate therapy, and should resolve within 2 weeks

WBC: Mild

Platelets: Moderate

Onset: 7 days

Nadir: 10 days

Recovery: 21 days

Hepatic: Cirrhosis and portal fibrosis have been associated with chronic methotrexate therapy; acute elevation of liver enzymes are common after high-dose methotrexate, and usually resolve within 10 days.

Neuromuscular & skeletal: Arthralgia

Ocular: Blurred vision

Renal: Renal dysfunction: Manifested by an abrupt rise in serum creatinine and BUN and a fall in urine output; more common with high-dose metho-trexate, and may be due to precipitation of the drug.

Respiratory: Pneumonitis: Associated with fever, cough, and interstitial pulmonary infiltrates; treatment is to withhold methotrexate during the acute reaction; interstitial pneumonitis has been reported to occur with an incidence of 1% in patients with RA (dose 7.5-15 mg/week)

<1% (Limited to important or life-threatening): Acute neurologic syndrome (at high dosages - symptoms include confusion, hemiparesis, transient blind-ness, and coma); anaphylaxis, alveolitis, cognitive dysfunction (has been reported at low dosage), decreased resistance to infection, erythema multi-forme, hepatic failure, leukoencephalopathy (especially following cranio-spinal irradiation or repeated high-dose therapy), lymphoproliferative disorders, osteonecrosis and soft tissue necrosis (with radiotherapy), peri-carditis, plaque erosions (psoriasis), seizure (more frequent in pediatric patients with ALL), Stevens-Johnson syndrome, thromboembolism

Overdosage/Toxicology Symptoms of overdose include nausea, vomiting, alopecia, melena, and renal failure. Administer leucovorin (see Dosage).

Hydration and alkalinization may be used to prevent precipitation of metho-trexate or methotrexate metabolites in the renal tubules. Severe bone marrow toxicity can result from overdose. Generally, neither peritoneal nor hemodialysis have been shown to increase elimination. However, effective clearance of methotrexate has been reported with acute, intermittent hemodialysis using a high-flux dialyzer.

Drug Interactions

Increased Effect/Toxicity: Concurrent therapy with NSAIDs has resulted in severe bone marrow suppression, aplastic anemia, and GI toxicity. NSAIDs should not be used during moderate or high-dose methotrexate due to increased and prolonged methotrexate levels (may increase toxicity); NSAID use during treatment of rheumatoid arthritis has not been fully explored, but continuation of prior regimen has been allowed in some circumstances, with cautious monitoring. Salicylates may increase methotrexate levels, however salicylate doses used for prophylaxis of cardiovascular events are not likely to be of concern.

Penicillins, probenecid, sulfonamides, tetracyclines may increase methotrexate concentrations due to a reduction in renal tubular secretion; primarily a concern with high doses of methotrexate. Hepatotoxic agents (acitretin, azathioprine, retinoids, sulfasalazine) may increase the risk of hepatotoxic reactions with methotrexate.

Concomitant administration of cyclosporine with methotrexate may increase levels and toxicity of each. Methotrexate may increase mercaptopurine or theophylline levels. Methotrexate, when administered prior to cytarabine, may enhance the efficacy and toxicity of cytarabine; some combination treatment regimens (eg, hyper-CVAD) have been designed to take advantage of this interaction.

Concurrent use of live virus vaccines may result in infections.

Decreased Effect: Cholestyramine may decrease levels of methotrexate. Corticosteroids may decrease uptake of methotrexate into leukemia cells. Administration of these drugs should be separated by 12 hours. Dexamethasone has been reported to not affect methotrexate influx into cells.

Ethanol/Nutrition/Herb Interactions

Ethanol: Avoid ethanol (may be associated with increased liver injury).

Food: Methotrexate peak serum levels may be decreased if taken with food. Milk-rich foods may decrease methotrexate absorption. Folate may decrease drug response.

Herb/Nutraceutical: Avoid echinacea (has immunostimulant properties).

Storage/Stability Store tablets and intact vials at room temperature (15°C to 25°C). Protect from light. Solution diluted in D_5W or NS is stable for 24 hours at room temperature (21°C to 25°C). Reconstituted solutions with a preservative may be stored under refrigeration for up to 3 months, and up to 4 weeks at room temperature. Intrathecal dilutions are stable at room temperature for 7 days, but it is generally recommended that they be used within 4-8 hours.

Reconstitution Dilute powder with D_5W or NS to a concentration ≤25 mg/mL (20 mg and 50 mg vials) and 50 mg/mL (1 g vial). Intrathecal solutions may be reconstituted to 2.5-5 mg/mL with NS, D_5W, lactated Ringer's, or Elliott's B solution. **Use preservative free preparations for intrathecal or high-dose administration.**

Compatibility Stable in D_5NS, D_5W, NS.

Y-site administration: Compatible: Allopurinol, amifostine, amphotericin B cholesteryl sulfate complex, asparaginase, aztreonam, bleomycin, cefepime, ceftriaxone, cimetidine, cisplatin, cyclophosphamide, cytarabine, daunorubicin, dexchlorpheniramine, diphenhydramine, doxorubicin, doxorubicin liposome, etoposide, etoposide phosphate, famotidine, filgrastim, fludarabine, fluorouracil, furosemide, ganciclovir, gatifloxacin, granisetron, heparin, hydromorphone, imipenem/cilastatin, leucovorin, linezolid, lorazepam, melphalan, mesna, methylprednisolone sodium succinate, metoclopramide, mitomycin, morphine, ondansetron, oxacillin, paclitaxel, piperacillin/tazobactam, prochlorperazine edisylate, ranitidine, sargramostim, teniposide, thiotepa, vinblastine, vincristine, vindesine, vinorelbine. **Incompatible:** Chlorpromazine, gemcitabine, idarubicin, ifosfamide, midazolam, nalbuphine, promethazine, propofol. **Variable (consult detailed reference):** Dexamethasone sodium phosphate, droperidol, vancomycin.

(Continued)

Methotrexate *(Continued)*

Compatibility in syringe: Compatible: Bleomycin, cisplatin, cyclophospha-mide, doxapram, doxorubicin, fluorouracil, furosemide, heparin, leucovorin, mitomycin, vinblastine, vincristine. **Incompatible:** Droperidol. **Variable (consult detailed reference):** Metoclopramide.

Compatibility when admixed: Compatible: Cyclophosphamide, cyclo-phosphamide with fluorouracil, cytarabine, dacarbazine, fluorouracil, hydrocortisone, hydroxyzine, mercaptopurine, ondansetron, sodium bicar-bonate, vincristine. **Incompatible:** Bleomycin.

Mechanism of Action Methotrexate is a folate antimetabolite that inhibits DNA synthesis. Methotrexate irreversibly binds to dihydrofolate reductase, inhibiting the formation of reduced folates, and thymidylate synthetase, resulting in inhibition of purine and thymidylic acid synthesis. Methotrexate is cell cycle specific for the S phase of the cycle.

The MOA in the treatment of rheumatoid arthritis is unknown, but may affect immune function. In psoriasis, methotrexate is thought to target rapidly prolif-erating epithelial cells in the skin.

In Crohn's disease, it may have immune modulator and anti-inflammatory activity.

Pharmacodynamics/Kinetics

Onset of action: Antirheumatic: 3-6 weeks; additional improvement may continue longer than 12 weeks

Absorption: Oral: Rapid; well absorbed at low doses (<30 mg/m^2), incom-plete after large doses; I.M.: Complete

Distribution: Penetrates slowly into 3rd space fluids (eg, pleural effusions, ascites), exits slowly from these compartments (slower than from plasma); crosses placenta; small amounts enter breast milk; sustained concentra-tions retained in kidney and liver

Protein binding: 50%

Metabolism: $<10\%$; degraded by intestinal flora to DAMPA by carboxypepti-dase; hepatic aldehyde oxidase converts methotrexate to 7-OH metho-trexate; polyglutamates are produced intracellularly and are just as potent as methotrexate; their production is dose- and duration-dependent and they are slowly eliminated by the cell once formed

Half-life elimination: Low dose: 3-10 hours; High dose: 8-12 hours

Time to peak, serum: Oral: 1-2 hours; I.M.: 30-60 minutes

Excretion: Urine (44% to 100%); feces (small amounts)

Dosage Refer to individual protocols.

Note: Doses between 100-500 mg/m^2 **may require** leucovorin rescue. Doses >500 mg/m^2 **require** leucovorin rescue: Oral, I.M., I.V.: Leucovorin 10-15 mg/m^2 every 6 hours for 8 or 10 doses, starting 24 hours after the start of methotrexate infusion. Continue until the methotrexate level is ≤0.1 micromolar (10^{-7}M). Some clinicians continue leucovorin until the metho-trexate level is <0.05 micromolar (5×10^{-8}M) or 0.01 micromolar (10^{-8}M).

If the 48-hour methotrexate level is >1 micromolar (10^{-7}M) or the 72-hour methotrexate level is >0.2 micromolar (2×10^{-7}M): I.V., I.M, Oral: Leuco-vorin 100 mg/m^2 every 6 hours until the methotrexate level is ≤0.1 micro-molar (10^{-7}M). Some clinicians continue leucovorin until the methotrexate level is <0.05 micromolar (5×10^{-8}M) or 0.01 micromolar (10^{-8}M).

Children:

Dermatomyositis: Oral: 15-20 mg/m^2/week as a single dose once weekly **or** 0.3-1 mg/kg/dose once weekly

Juvenile rheumatoid arthritis: Oral, I.M.: 10 mg/m^2 once weekly, then 5-15 mg/m^2/week as a single dose **or** as 3 divided doses given 12 hours apart

Antineoplastic dosage range:

Oral, I.M.: 7.5-30 mg/m^2/week **or** every 2 weeks

I.V.: 10-18,000 mg/m^2 bolus dosing **or** continuous infusion over 6-42 hours

Pediatric solid tumors (high-dose): I.V.:

<12 years: 12-25 g/m^2

≥12 years: 8 g/m^2

Acute lymphocytic leukemia (intermediate-dose): I.V.: Loading: 100 mg/m^2 bolus dose, followed by 900 mg/m^2/day infusion over 23-41 hours.

Meningeal leukemia: I.T.: 10-15 mg/m^2 (maximum dose: 15 mg) **or** an age-based dosing regimen; one possible system is:

≤3 months: 3 mg/dose

4-11 months: 6 mg/dose

1 year: 8 mg/dose

2 years: 10 mg/dose

≥3 years: 12 mg/dose

Adults: I.V.: Range is wide from 30-40 mg/m^2/week to 100-12,000 mg/m^2 with leucovorin rescue

Trophoblastic neoplasms:

Oral, I.M.: 15-30 mg/day for 5 days; repeat in 7 days for 3-5 courses

I.V.: 11 mg/m^2 days 1 through 5 every 3 weeks

Head and neck cancer: Oral, I.M., I.V.: 25-50 mg/m^2 once weekly

Mycosis fungoides (cutaneous T-cell lymphoma): Oral, I.M.: Initial (early stages):

5-50 mg once weekly **or**

15-37.5 mg twice weekly

Bladder cancer: I.V.:

30 mg/m^2 day 1 and 8 every 3 weeks **or**

30 mg/m^2 day 1, 15, and 22 every 4 weeks

Breast cancer: I.V.: 30-60 mg/m^2 days 1 and 8 every 3-4 weeks

Gastric cancer: I.V.: 1500 mg/m^2 every 4 weeks

Lymphoma, non-Hodgkin's: I.V.:

30 mg/m^2 days 3 and 10 every 3 weeks **or**

120 mg/m^2 day 8 and 15 every 3-4 weeks **or**

200 mg/m^2 day 8 and 15 every 3 weeks **or**

400 mg/m^2 every 4 weeks for 3 cycles **or**

1 g/m^2 every 3 weeks **or**

1.5 g/m^2 every 4 weeks

Sarcoma: I.V.: 8-12 g/m^2 weekly for 2-4 weeks

Rheumatoid arthritis: Oral: 7.5 mg once weekly **or** 2.5 mg every 12 hours for 3 doses/week, not to exceed 20 mg/week

Psoriasis:

Oral: 2.5-5 mg/dose every 12 hours for 3 doses given weekly **or**

Oral, I.M.: 10-25 mg/dose given once weekly

Ectopic pregnancy (unlabeled use): I.M.: 50 mg/m^2 as a single dose

Active Crohn's disease (unlabeled use): Induction of remission: I.M., SubQ: 15-25 mg once weekly; remission maintenance: 15 mg once weekly

Note: Oral dosing has been reported as effective but oral absorption is highly variable. If patient relapses after a switch to oral, may consider returning to injectable.

Elderly: Rheumatoid arthritis/psoriasis: Oral: Initial: 5-7.5 mg/week, not to exceed 20 mg/week

(Continued)

739

Methotrexate *(Continued)*

Dosing adjustment in renal impairment: The FDA-approved labeling does not contain dosage adjustment guidelines. The following guidelines have been used by some clinicians:

Cl$_{cr}$ 61-80 mL/minute: Administer 75% of dose

Cl$_{cr}$ 51-60 mL/minute: Administer 70% of dose

Cl$_{cr}$ 10-50 mL/minute: Administer 30% to 50% of dose

Cl$_{cr}$ <10 mL/minute: Avoid use

Hemodialysis: Not dialyzable (0% to 5%); supplemental dose is not necessary

Peritoneal dialysis effects: Supplemental dose is not necessary

CAVH effects: Unknown

Aronoff, 2007:

Children:

Cl$_{cr}$ 10-50 mL/minute: Administer 50% of dose

Cl$_{cr}$ <10 mL/minute: Administer 30% of dose

Hemodialysis: Administer 30% of dose

Continuous ambulatory peritoneal dialysis (CAPD): Administer 30% of dose

Continuous renal replacement therapy (CRRT): Administer 50% of dose

Adults:

Cl$_{cr}$ 10-50 mL/minute: Administer 50% of dose

Cl$_{cr}$ <10 mL/minute: Avoid use

Hemodialysis: Administer 50% of dose

Continuous renal replacement therapy (CRRT): Administer 50% of dose

Kintzel, 1995:

Cl$_{cr}$ 46-60 mL/minute: Administer 65% of normal dose

Cl$_{cr}$ 31-45 mL/minute: Administer 50% of normal dose

Cl$_{cr}$ <30 mL/minute: Avoid use

Dosage adjustment in hepatic impairment: The FDA-approved labeling does not contain dosage adjustment guidelines. The following guidelines have been used by some clinicians (Floyd, 2006):

Bilirubin 3.1-5 mg/dL **or** ALT/AST >3 times ULN: Administer 75% of dose

Bilirubin >5 mg/dL: Avoid use

Combination Regimens

Bladder cancer:

CMV *on page 1179*

M-VAC (Bladder Cancer) *on page 1255*

Breast cancer:

CMF *on page 1177*

CMF-IV *on page 1177*

CMFP *on page 1178*

CMFVP (Cooper Regimen, VPCMF) *on page 1178*

Dox-CMF (Sequential) *on page 1195*

MF *on page 1247*

M-VAC (Breast Cancer) *on page 1258*

Cervical Cancer: M-VAC (Cervical Cancer) *on page 1259*

Endometrial cancer: M-VAC (Endometrial Cancer) *on page 1259*

Gastric cancer: FAMTX *on page 1213*

Gestational trophoblastic tumor:

CHAMOCA (Modified Bagshawe Regimen) *on page 1170*

CHAMOMA (Bagshawe Regimen) *on page 1172*

Administration Methotrexate may be administered I.M., I.V., or I.T.; I.V. administration may be as slow push, short bolus infusion, or 24- to 42-hour continuous infusion

Specific dosing schemes vary, but high dose should be followed by leucovorin calcium to prevent toxicity; refer to Leucovorin monograph *on page 668*

Monitoring Parameters For prolonged use (especially rheumatoid arthritis, psoriasis) a baseline liver biopsy, repeated at each 1-1.5 g cumulative dose interval, should be performed; WBC and platelet counts every 4 weeks; CBC and creatinine, LFTs every 3-4 months; chest x-ray

Dietary Considerations
Sodium content of 100 mg injection: 20 mg (0.86 mEq)
Sodium content of 100 mg (low sodium) injection: 15 mg (0.65 mEq)

Patient Information Avoid alcohol to prevent serious side effects. Avoid intake of extra dietary folic acid, maintain adequate hydration (2-3 L/day of fluids unless instructed to restrict fluid intake) and adequate nutrition (frequent small meals may help). You may experience nausea and vomiting (small frequent meals may help or request antiemetic from prescriber); drowsiness, tingling, numbness, or blurred vision (avoid driving or engaging in tasks that require alertness until response to drug is known); mouth sores (frequent oral care is necessary); loss of hair; skin rash; photosensitivity (use sunscreen, wear protective clothing and eyewear, and avoid direct sunlight). *(Continued)*

Methotrexate *(Continued)*

Report black or tarry stools, fever, chills, unusual bleeding or bruising, shortness of breath or difficulty breathing, yellowing of skin or eyes, dark or bloody urine, or acute joint pain or other side effects you may experience. The drug may cause permanent sterility and may cause birth defects; contraceptive measures are recommended during therapy. Pregnancy should be avoided for a minimum of 3 months after completion of therapy in male patients, and at least one ovulatory cycle in female patients. The drug is excreted in breast milk, therefore, an alternative form of feeding your baby should be used.

Special Geriatric Considerations Toxicity to methotrexate or any immunosuppressive is increased in the elderly. Must monitor carefully. For rheumatoid arthritis and psoriasis, immunosuppressive therapy should only be used when disease is active and less toxic, traditional therapy is ineffective. Recommended doses should be reduced when initiating therapy in the elderly due to possible decreased metabolism, reduced renal function, and presence of interacting diseases and drugs. Adjust dose as needed for renal function (Cl_{cr}).

Additional Information Latex-free products: 50 mg/2 mL, 100 mg/4 mL, and 250 mg/10 mL vials with and without preservatives by Immunex

Emetic Potential

Low (10% to 30%): <250 mg/m^2

Moderate (30% to 90%): ≥250 mg/m^2

Vesicant No

Dosage Forms Excipient information presented when available (limited, particularly for generics); consult specific product labeling.

Injection, powder for reconstitution [preservative free]: 20 mg, 1 g

Injection, solution: 25 mg/mL (2 mL, 10 mL) [contains benzyl alcohol]

Injection, solution [preservative free]: 25 mg/mL (2 mL, 4 mL, 8 mL, 10 mL, 40 mL)

Tablet: 2.5 mg

Trexall™: 5 mg, 7.5 mg, 10 mg, 15 mg

Tablet, as sodium [dose pack] (Rheumatrex® Dose Pack): 2.5 mg (4 cards with 2, 3, 4, 5, or 6 tablets each)

References

Aronoff GR, Bennett WM, Berns JS, et al, *Drug Prescribing in Renal Failure: Dosing Guidelines for Adults and Children*, 5th ed. Philadelphia, PA: American College of Physicians; 2007, p 101.

Egan LJ, Sandborn WJ, Tremaine WJ, et al, "A Randomized Dose-Response and Pharmacokinetic Study of Methotrexate for Refractory Inflammatory Crohn's Disease and Ulcerative Colitis," *Aliment Pharmacol Ther*, 1999, 13(12):1597-604.

Evans WE, Pratt CB, Taylor RH, et al, "Pharmacokinetic Monitoring of High-Dose Methotrexate: Early Recognition of High-Risk Patients," *Cancer Chemother Pharmacol*, 1979, 3:161-6.

Feagan BG, Fedorak RN, Irvine EJ, et al, "A Comparison of Methotrexate With Placebo for the Maintenance of Remission in Crohn's Disease. North American Crohn's Study Group Investigators." *N Engl J Med*, 2000, 342(22):1627-32.

Floyd J, Mirza I, Sachs B, et al, "Hepatotoxicity of Chemotherapy," *Semin Oncol*, 2006, 33(1):50-67.

Furst DE, "Methotrexate: New Mechanisms and Old Toxicities," *Agents Actions Suppl*, 1993, 44:131-7.

Grem JL, King SA, Wittes RE, et al, "The Role of Methotrexate in Osteosarcoma," *J Natl Cancer Inst*, 1988, 80(9):626-55.

Jolivet J, Cowan KH, Curt GA, et al, "The Pharmacology and Clinical Use of Methotrexate," *N Engl J Med*, 1983, 309(18):1094-104.

Kintzel PE and Dorr RT, "Anticancer Drug Renal Toxicity and Elimination: Dosing Guidelines for Altered Renal Function," *Cancer Treat Rev*, 1995, 21(1):33-64.

Seeber BE and Barnhart KT, "Suspected Ectopic Pregnancy," *Obstet Gynecol*, 2006, 107(2 Pt 1):399-413.

Treon SP and Chabner BA, "Concepts in Use of High-Dose Methotrexate Therapy," *Clin Chem*, 1996, 42(8 Pt 2):1322-9.

- **Methotrexate Sodium** *see* Methotrexate *on page 733*
- **Methylacetoxyprogesterone** *see* MedroxyPROGESTERone *on page 703*

Methylene Blue (METH i leen bloo)

Medication Safety Issues Due to potential toxicity (hemolytic anemia), do not use methylene blue to color enteral feedings to detect aspiration.

U.S. Brand Names Urolene Blue®

Generic Available Yes: Injection

Pharmacologic Category Antidote

Use Antidote for cyanide poisoning and drug-induced methemoglobinemia, indicator dye

Unlabeled/Investigational Use Treatment/prevention of ifosfamide-induced encephalopathy; topically, in conjunction with polychromatic light to photoinactivate viruses such as herpes simplex; alone or in combination with vitamin C for the management of chronic urolithiasis

Pregnancy Risk Factor C

Labeled Contraindications Hypersensitivity to methylene blue or any component of the formulation; intraspinal injection; renal insufficiency

Warnings/Precautions Do not inject SubQ or intrathecally; use with caution in young patients and in patients with G6PD deficiency; continued use can cause profound anemia. At high doses or in patients with G6PD-deficiency and infants, methylene blue may catalyze the oxidation of ferrous iron in hemoglobin to ferric iron causing paradoxical methemoglobinemia; monitor methemoglobin concentrations regularly during administration.

Adverse Reactions Frequency not defined.

Cardiovascular: Hypertension, precordial pain

Central nervous system: Dizziness, mental confusion, headache, fever

Dermatologic: Staining of skin

Gastrointestinal: Fecal discoloration (blue-green), nausea, vomiting, abdominal pain

Genitourinary: Discoloration of urine (blue-green), bladder irritation

Hematologic: Anemia

Miscellaneous: Diaphoresis

Overdosage/Toxicology

Symptoms of overdose include nausea, vomiting, precordial pain, hypertension, methemoglobinemia, cyanosis; overdosage has resulted in methemoglobinemia and cyanosis

Treatment is symptom-directed and supportive

Mechanism of Action Weak germicide in low concentrations, hastens the conversion of methemoglobin to hemoglobin; has opposite effect at high concentrations by converting ferrous ion of reduced hemoglobin to ferric ion to form methemoglobin; in cyanide toxicity, it combines with cyanide to form cyanmethemoglobin preventing the interference of cyanide with the cytochrome system

Pharmacodynamics/Kinetics

Onset of action: Reduction of methemoglobin: I.V.: 30-60 minutes

Absorption: Oral: 53% to 97%

Excretion: Urine and feces

Dosage

Children: NADPH-methemoglobin reductase deficiency: Oral: 1-1.5 mg/kg/day (maximum: 300 mg/day) given with 5-8 mg/kg/day of ascorbic acid

Children and Adults: Methemoglobinemia: I.V.: 1-2 mg/kg or 25-50 mg/m² over several minutes; may be repeated in 1 hour if necessary
(Continued)

Methylene Blue *(Continued)*

Adults:

Genitourinary antiseptic: Oral: 65-130 mg 3 times/day with a full glass of water (maximum: 390 mg/day)

Ifosfamide-induced encephalopathy (unlabeled use): Oral, I.V.:

Prevention: 50 mg every 6-8 hours

Treatment: 50 mg as a single dose or every 4-8 hours until symptoms resolve

Administration

I.V.: Administer undiluted by direct I.V. injection over several minutes. For the treatment of ifosfamide-induced encephalopathy, methylene blue may be administered either undiluted as a slow I.V. push over at least 5 minutes or diluted in 50 mL NS or D_5W and infused over at least 5 minutes. Consider concomitant dextrose administration, especially in patients who are hypoglycemic, to ensure efficacy of methylene blue.

Oral: Administer after meals with a full glass of water. When given for the treatment of ifosfamide-induced encephalopathy, may be mixed with fruit juice to mask unpleasant taste.

Monitoring Parameters Arterial blood gases; cardiac monitoring (patients with pre-existing pulmonary and/or cardiac disease); CBC; methemoglobin levels (co-oximetry yields a direct and accurate measure of methemoglobin levels); pulse oximeter (will not provide accurate measurement of oxygenation when methemoglobin levels are >35%); renal function; signs and symptoms of methemoglobinemia such as pallor, cyanosis, nausea, muscle weakness, dizziness, confusion, agitation, dyspnea and tachycardia; transcutaneous O_2 saturation

Patient Information May discolor urine and feces blue-green; take oral formulation after meals with a glass of water; skin stains may be removed using a hypochlorite solution

Additional Information Skin stains may be removed using a hypochlorite solution.

Dosage Forms Excipient information presented when available (limited, particularly for generics); consult specific product labeling.

Injection, solution: 10 mg/mL (1 mL, 10 mL)

Tablet:

Urolene Blue®: 65 mg

References

Burnakis TG, "Inadvertent Substitution of Methylene Blue for Indigo Carmine to Detect Premature Rupture of Membranes," *Hosp Pharm*, 1995, 30(4):336-8.

David KA and Picus J, "Evaluating Risk Factors for the Development of Ifosfamide Encephalopathy," *Am J Clin Oncol*, 2005, 28(3):277-80.

Dawson AH and Whyte IM, "Management of Dapsone Poisoning Complicated by Methaemoglobinaemia," *Med Toxicol Adverse Drug Exp*, 1989, 4(5):387-92.

DiSanto AR and Wagner JG, "Pharmacokinetics of Highly Ionized Drugs II: Methylene Blue - Absorption, Metabolism, and Excretion in Man and Dog After Oral Administration," *J Pharm Sci*, 1972, 61(7):1086-90.

Harvey JW and Keitt AS, "Studies of the Efficacy and Potential Hazards of Methylene Blue Therapy in Aniline-Induced Methaemoglobinaemia," *Br J Haematol*, 1983, 54(1):29-41.

Jahns BE, Rynn KO, and Paloucek FP, "Interference of Methylene Blue (MthB) in the Determination of Whole Blood Methemoglobin (MtHgb) Concentrations," *Vet Hum Toxicol*, 1994, 36:342.

Mokhlesi B, Leikin JB, Murray P, et al, "Adult Toxicology in Critical Care: Part II: Specific Poisonings," *Chest*, 2003, 123(3):897-922.

Patel PN, "Methylene Blue for Management of Ifosfamide-Induced Encephalopathy," *Ann Pharmacother*, 2006, 40(2):299-303.

Pelgrims J, DeVos F, Van den Brande J, et al, "Methylene Blue in the Treatment and Prevention of Ifosfamide-Induced Encephalopathy: Report of 12 Cases and a Review of the Literature," *Br J Cancer*, 2000, 82(2) 291-4.

Preiser JC, Lejeune P, Roman A, et al, "Methylene Blue Administration in Septic Shock: A Clinical Trial," *Crit Care Med*, 1995, 23(2):259-64.

Turner AR, Duong CD, and Good DJ, "Methylene Blue for the Treatment and Prophylaxis of Ifosfamide-Induced Encephalopathy," *Clin Oncol (R Coll Radiol)*, 2003, 15(7):435-9.

Wright RO, Lewander WJ, and Woolf AD, "Methemoglobinemia: Etiology, Pharmacology, and Clinical Management," *Ann Emerg Med*, 1999, 34(5):646-56.

Zulian GB, Tullen E, and Maton B, "Methylene Blue for Ifosfamide-Associated Encephalopathy," *N Engl J Med*, 1995, 332(18):1239-40.

♦ **Methylmorphine** *see Codeine on page 242*

♦ **Methylphytyl Napthoquinone** *see Phytonadione on page 895*

MethylPREDNISolone (meth il pred NIS oh lone)

Medication Safety Issues

Sound-alike/look-alike issues:

MethylPREDNISolone may be confused with medroxyPROGESTERone, predniSONE

Depo-Medrol® may be confused with Solu-Medrol®

Medrol® may be confused with Mebaral®

Solu-Medrol® may be confused with Depo-Medrol®

International issues:

Medor® may be confused with Medral® which is a brand name for omeprazole in Mexico

Related Information

Hematopoietic Stem Cell Transplantation *on page 1366*

U.S. Brand Names Depo-Medrol®; Medrol®; Solu-Medrol®

Index Terms 6-α-Methylprednisolone; A-Methapred; Methylprednisolone Acetate; Methylprednisolone Sodium Succinate

Generic Available Yes

Canadian Brand Names Depo-Medrol®; Medrol®; Methylprednisolone Acetate; Solu-Medrol®

Pharmacologic Category Corticosteroid, Systemic

Use Primarily as an anti-inflammatory or immunosuppressant agent in the treatment of a variety of diseases including those of hematologic, allergic, inflammatory, neoplastic, and autoimmune origin. Prevention and treatment of graft-versus-host disease following allogeneic bone marrow transplantation.

Pregnancy Risk Factor C

Lactation Excretion in breast milk unknown

Labeled Contraindications Hypersensitivity to methylprednisolone or any component of the formulation; viral, fungal, or tubercular skin lesions; administration of live virus vaccines; serious infections, except septic shock or tuberculous meningitis. Methylprednisolone formulations containing benzyl alcohol preservative are contraindicated in infants.

Warnings/Precautions Use with caution in patients with thyroid disease, hepatic impairment, renal impairment, cardiovascular disease, diabetes, glaucoma, cataracts, myasthenia gravis, patients at risk for osteoporosis, patients at risk for seizures, or GI diseases (diverticulitis, peptic ulcer, ulcerative colitis) due to perforation risk. Use caution following acute MI (corticosteroids have been associated with myocardial rupture). Because of the risk of adverse effects, systemic corticosteroids should be used cautiously in the elderly in the smallest possible effective dose for the shortest duration. May affect growth velocity; growth should be routinely monitored in pediatric patients. Withdraw therapy with gradual tapering of dose.

May cause hypercorticism or suppression of hypothalamic-pituitary-adrenal (HPA) axis, particularly in younger children or in patients receiving high (Continued)

MethylPREDNISolone *(Continued)*

doses for prolonged periods. HPA axis suppression may lead to adrenal crisis. Withdrawal and discontinuation of a corticosteroid should be done slowly and carefully. Particular care is required when patients are transferred from systemic corticosteroids to inhaled products due to possible adrenal insufficiency or withdrawal from steroids, including an increase in allergic symptoms. Patients receiving >20 mg per day of prednisone (or equivalent) may be most susceptible. Fatalities have occurred due to adrenal insufficiency in asthmatic patients during and after transfer from systemic corticosteroids to aerosol steroids; aerosol steroids do not provide the systemic steroid needed to treat patients having trauma, surgery, or infections.

Acute myopathy has been reported with high dose corticosteroids, usually in patients with neuromuscular transmission disorders; may involve ocular and/or respiratory muscles; monitor creatine kinase; recovery may be delayed. Corticosteroid use may cause psychiatric disturbances, including depression, euphoria, insomnia, mood swings, and personality changes. Pre-existing psychiatric conditions may be exacerbated by corticosteroid use. Prolonged use of corticosteroids may also increase the incidence of secondary infection, mask acute infection (including fungal infections), prolong or exacerbate viral infections, or limit response to vaccines. Exposure to chickenpox should be avoided; corticosteroids should not be used to treat ocular herpes simplex. Corticosteroids should not be used for cerebral malaria. Close observation is required in patients with latent tuberculosis and/or TB reactivity; restrict use in active TB (only in conjunction with anti-tuberculosis treatment). Prolonged treatment with corticosteroids has been associated with the development of Kaposi's sarcoma (case reports); if noted, discontinuation of therapy should be considered.

Adverse Reactions Frequency not defined.

Cardiovascular: Edema, hypertension, arrhythmia

Central nervous system: Insomnia, nervousness, vertigo, seizure, psychoses, pseudotumor cerebri, headache, mood swings, delirium, hallucinations, euphoria

Dermatologic: Hirsutism, acne, skin atrophy, bruising, hyperpigmentation

Endocrine & metabolic: Diabetes mellitus, adrenal suppression, hyperlipidemia, Cushing's syndrome, pituitary-adrenal axis suppression, growth suppression, glucose intolerance, hypokalemia, alkalosis, amenorrhea, sodium and water retention, hyperglycemia

Gastrointestinal: Increased appetite, indigestion, peptic ulcer, nausea, vomiting, abdominal distention, ulcerative esophagitis, pancreatitis

Hematologic: Transient leukocytosis

Neuromuscular & skeletal: Arthralgia, muscle weakness, osteoporosis, fractures

Ocular: Cataracts, glaucoma

Miscellaneous: Infections, hypersensitivity reactions, avascular necrosis, secondary malignancy, intractable hiccups

Overdosage/Toxicology When consumed in high doses for prolonged periods, systemic hypercorticism and adrenal suppression may occur. In these cases, discontinuation should be done judiciously. Arrhythmias and cardiovascular collapse are possible with rapid intravenous infusion of high-dose methylprednisolone. May mask signs and symptoms of infection.

Drug Interactions

Cytochrome P450 Effect: Substrate of CYP3A4 (major); **Inhibits** CYP2C8 (weak), 3A4 (weak)

Increased Effect/Toxicity: Aprepitant, azole antifungals, calcium channel blockers (nondihydropyridine), cyclosporine, estrogens, and macrolides may increase the serum levels of corticosteroids. Corticosteroids may increase the hypokalemic effects of amphotericin B or potassium-wasting diuretics (loop or thiazide); monitor.

Concurrent use of nonsteroidal anti-inflammatory drugs (NSAIDs) and salicylates with corticosteroids may lead to an increased incidence of gastrointestinal adverse effects. Concurrent use with anticholinergic agents may lead to severe weakness in patients with myasthenia gravis. Concurrent use of fluoroquinolone antibiotics may increase the risk of tendon rupture, particularly in elderly patients (overall incidence rare). Concurrent use of neuromuscular-blocking agents with corticosteroids may increase the risk of myopathy. Concurrent use with cyclosporine may increase cyclosporine levels. The use of live vaccines is contraindicated in immunosuppressed patients (may increase the risk of vaccinal infection). In patients receiving high doses of systemic corticosteroids for ≥14 days, wait at least 1 month between discontinuing steroid therapy and administering immunization.

Decreased Effect: Aminoglutethimide, barbiturates and rifamycin derivatives may reduce the serum levels/effects of methylprednisolone. Serum concentrations of isoniazid may be decreased by corticosteroids. Corticosteroids may lead to a reduction in warfarin effect. Corticosteroids may suppress the response to vaccinations.

Ethanol/Nutrition/Herb Interactions

Ethanol: Avoid ethanol (may increase gastric mucosal irritation).

Food: Methylprednisolone interferes with calcium absorption. Limit caffeine.

Herb/Nutraceutical: St John's wort may decrease methylprednisolone levels. Avoid cat's claw, echinacea (have immunostimulant properties).

Storage/Stability Intact vials of methylprednisolone sodium succinate should be stored at controlled room temperature. Reconstituted solutions of methylprednisolone sodium succinate should be stored at room temperature (15°C to 30°C) and used within 48 hours. Stability of parenteral admixture at room temperature (25°C) and at refrigeration temperature (4°C) is 48 hours.

Reconstitution

Standard diluent (Solu-Medrol®): 40 mg/50 mL D₅W; 125 mg/50 mL D₅W.

Minimum volume (Solu-Medrol®): 50 mL D₅W.

Compatibility Incompatible with D₅¹/₂NS; **variable stability (consult detailed reference)** in D₅NS, D₅W, LR, NS.

Y-site administration: Compatible: Acyclovir, amifostine, amphotericin B cholesteryl sulfate complex, aztreonam, cefepime, cisplatin, cladribine, cyclophosphamide, cytarabine, dopamine, doxorubicin, doxorubicin liposome, enalaprilat, famotidine, fludarabine, gatifloxacin, granisetron, heparin, inamrinone, linezolid, melphalan, meperidine, methotrexate, metronidazole, midazolam, morphine, piperacillin/tazobactam, remifentanil, sodium bicarbonate, tacrolimus, teniposide, theophylline, thiotepa, topotecan. **Incompatible:** Allopurinol, amsacrine, ciprofloxacin, docetaxel, etoposide phosphate, filgrastim, gemcitabine, ondansetron, paclitaxel, propofol, sargramostim, vinorelbine. **Variable (consult detailed reference):** Cisatracurium, diltiazem, heparin with hydrocortisone sodium succinate, potassium chloride, vitamin B complex with C.

Compatibility in syringe: Compatible: Diatrizoate meglumine 52% and diatrizoate sodium 8%, diatrizoate sodium 60%, granisetron, iohexol, iopamidol, iothalamate meglumine 60%, ioxaglate meglumine 39.3% and ioxaglate sodium 19.6%, metoclopramide. **Incompatible:** Doxapram.

Compatibility when admixed: Compatible: Chloramphenicol, cimetidine, clindamycin, dopamine, granisetron, heparin, norepinephrine, penicillin G potassium, ranitidine, theophylline, verapamil. **Incompatible:** Calcium

(Continued)

MethylPREDNISolone *(Continued)*

gluconate, glycopyrrolate, insulin (regular), metaraminol, nafcillin, penicillin G sodium. **Variable (consult detailed reference):** Aminophylline, amphotericin B, cytarabine.

Mechanism of Action In a tissue-specific manner, corticosteroids regulate gene expression subsequent to binding specific intracellular receptors and translocation into the nucleus. Corticosteroids exert a wide array of physiologic effects including modulation of carbohydrate, protein, and lipid metabolism and maintenance of fluid and electrolyte homeostasis. Moreover cardiovascular, immunologic, musculoskeletal, endocrine, and neurologic physiology are influenced by corticosteroids. Decreases inflammation by suppression of migration of polymorphonuclear leukocytes and reversal of increased capillary permeability.

Pharmacodynamics/Kinetics

Onset of action: Peak effect (route dependent): Oral: 1-2 hours; I.M.: 4-8 days; Intra-articular: 1 week; methylprednisolone sodium succinate is highly soluble and has a rapid effect by I.M. and I.V. routes

Duration (route dependent): Oral: 30-36 hours; I.M.: 1-4 weeks; Intra-articular: 1-5 weeks; methylprednisolone acetate has a low solubility and has a sustained I.M. effect

Distribution: V_d: 0.7-1.5 L/kg

Half-life elimination: 3-3.5 hours; reduced in obese

Excretion: Clearance: Reduced in obese

Dosage Dosing should be based on the lesser of ideal body weight or actual body weight

Only sodium succinate may be given I.V.; methylprednisolone sodium succinate is highly soluble and has a rapid effect by I.M. and I.V. routes. Methylprednisolone acetate has a low solubility and has a sustained I.M. effect.

Children:

Anti-inflammatory or immunosuppressive: Oral, I.M., I.V. (sodium succinate): 0.5-1.7 mg/kg/day **or** 5-25 mg/m²/day in divided doses every 6-12 hours; "Pulse" therapy: 15-30 mg/kg/dose over ≥30 minutes given once daily for 3 days

Status asthmaticus: I.V. (sodium succinate): Loading dose: 2 mg/kg/dose, then 0.5-1 mg/kg/dose every 6 hours for up to 5 days

Acute spinal cord injury: I.V. (sodium succinate): 30 mg/kg over 15 minutes, followed in 45 minutes by a continuous infusion of 5.4 mg/kg/hour for 23 hours

Lupus nephritis: I.V. (sodium succinate): 30 mg/kg over ≥30 minutes every other day for 6 doses

Adults: **Only sodium succinate may be given I.V.;** methylprednisolone sodium succinate is highly soluble and has a rapid effect by I.M. and I.V. routes. Methylprednisolone acetate has a low solubility and has a sustained I.M. effect.

Acute spinal cord injury: I.V. (sodium succinate): 30 mg/kg over 15 minutes, followed in 45 minutes by a continuous infusion of 5.4 mg/kg/hour for 23 hours

Anti-inflammatory or immunosuppressive:

Oral: 2-60 mg/day in 1-4 divided doses to start, followed by gradual reduction in dosage to the lowest possible level consistent with maintaining an adequate clinical response.

I.M. (sodium succinate): 10-80 mg/day once daily

I.M. (acetate): 10-80 mg every 1-2 weeks

I.V. (sodium succinate): 10-40 mg over a period of several minutes and repeated I.V. or I.M. at intervals depending on clinical response; when high dosages are needed, give 30 mg/kg over a period ≥30 minutes and may be repeated every 4-6 hours for 48 hours.

Status asthmaticus: I.V. (sodium succinate): Loading dose: 2 mg/kg/dose, then 0.5-1 mg/kg/dose every 6 hours for up to 5 days

Lupus nephritis: High-dose "pulse" therapy: I.V. (sodium succinate): 1 g/ day for 3 days

Aplastic anemia: I.V. (sodium succinate): 1 mg/kg/day or 40 mg/day (whichever dose is higher), for 4 days. After 4 days, change to oral and continue until day 10 or until symptoms of serum sickness resolve, then rapidly reduce over approximately 2 weeks.

Pneumocystis pneumonia in AIDs patients: I.V.: 40-60 mg every 6 hours for 7-10 days

Intra-articular (acetate): Administer every 1-5 weeks.

Large joints: 20-80 mg

Small joints: 4-10 mg

Intralesional (acetate): 20-60 mg every 1-5 weeks

Combination Regimens

Brain tumors: 8 in 1 (Brain Tumors) *on page 1141*

Leukemia, acute lymphocytic: Hyper-CVAD (Leukemia, Acute Lymphocytic) *on page 1231*

Lymphoma, non-Hodgkin's: ESHAP *on page 1206*

Retinoblastoma: 8 in 1 (Retinoblastoma) *on page 1142*

Administration

Oral: Administer after meals or with food or milk

Parenteral: Methylprednisolone sodium succinate may be administered I.M. or I.V.; I.V. administration may be IVP over one to several minutes or IVPB or continuous I.V. infusion. **Acetate salt should not be given I.V.**

I.V.: Succinate:

Low dose: ≤1.8 mg/kg or ≤125 mg/dose: I.V. push over 3-15 minutes

Moderate dose: ≥2 mg/kg or 250 mg/dose: I.V. over 15-30 minutes

High dose: 15 mg/kg or ≥500 mg/dose: I.V. over ≥30 minutes

Doses >15 mg/kg or ≥1 g: Administer over 1 hour

Do **not** administer high-dose I.V. push; hypotension, cardiac arrhythmia, and sudden death have been reported in patients given high-dose methylprednisolone I.V. push over <20 minutes; intermittent infusion over 15-60 minutes; maximum concentration: I.V. push 125 mg/mL

Monitoring Parameters Blood pressure, blood glucose, electrolytes

Test Interactions Interferes with skin tests

Dietary Considerations Should be taken after meals or with food or milk; need diet rich in pyridoxine, vitamin C, vitamin D, folate, calcium, phosphorus, and protein.

Sodium content of 1 g sodium succinate injection: 2.01 mEq; 53 mg of sodium succinate salt is equivalent to 40 mg of methylprednisolone base

Methylprednisolone acetate: Depo-Medrol®

Methylprednisolone sodium succinate: Solu-Medrol®

Patient Information Do not discontinue or decrease the drug without contacting your prescriber; carry an identification card or bracelet advising that you are on steroids; may take with meals to decrease GI upset

Special Geriatric Considerations Because of the risk of adverse effects, systemic corticosteroids should be used cautiously in the elderly, in the smallest possible dose, and for the shortest possible time.

(Continued)

MethylPREDNISolone *(Continued)*

Additional Information Sodium content of 1 g sodium succinate injection: 2.01 mEq; 53 mg of sodium succinate salt is equivalent to 40 mg of methylprednisolone base

Methylprednisolone acetate: Depo-Medrol®

Methylprednisolone sodium succinate: Solu-Medrol®

Emetic Potential Very low (<10%)

Vesicant No

Dosage Forms Excipient information presented when available (limited, particularly for generics); consult specific product labeling.

Injection, powder for reconstitution, as sodium succinate: 40 mg, 125 mg, 500 mg, 1 g [strength expressed as base]

Solu-Medrol®: 40 mg, 125 mg, 500 mg, 1 g, 2 g [packaged with diluent; diluent contains benzyl alcohol; strength expressed as base]

Solu-Medrol®: 500 mg, 1 g

Injection, suspension, as acetate: 40 mg/mL (5 mL, 10 mL); 80 mg/mL (5 mL)

Depo-Medrol®: 20 mg/mL (5 mL); 40 mg/mL (5 mL); 80 mg/mL (5 mL) [contains benzyl alcohol; strength expressed as base]

Injection, suspension, as acetate: 40 mg/mL (1 mL); 80 mg/mL (1 mL) [single-dose vial]

Depo-Medrol®: 40 mg/mL (1 mL, 10 mL); 80 mg/mL (1 mL) [single-dose vial]

Tablet: 4 mg

Medrol®: 2 mg, 4 mg, 8 mg, 16 mg, 32 mg

Tablet, dose-pack: 4 mg (21s)

Medrol® Dosepak™: 4 mg (21s)

References

Abraham E and Evans T, "Corticosteroids and Septic Shock [editorial]," *JAMA*, 2002, 288(7):886-7.

Annane D, Sebille V, Charpentier C, et al, "Effect of Treatment With Low Doses of Hydrocortisone and Fludrocortisone on Mortality in Patients With Septic Shock," *JAMA*, 2002, 288(7):862-71.

Bracken MB, Shepard MJ, Collins WF, et al, "A Randomized, Controlled Trial of Methylprednisolone or Naloxone in the Treatment of Acute Spinal-Cord Injury. Results of the Second National Acute Spinal Cord Injury Study," *N Engl J Med*, 1990, 322(20):1405-11.

Cooper MS and Stewart PM, "Corticosteroid Insufficiency in Acutely Ill Patients," *N Engl J Med*, 2003, 348(8):727-34.

Coursin DB and Wood KE, "Corticosteroid Supplementation for Adrenal Insufficiency," *JAMA*, 2002, 287(2):236-40.

de Jonghe B, Sharshar T, Lefaucheur JP, et al, "Paresis Acquired in the Intensive Care Unit. A Prospective Multicenter Study," *JAMA*, 2002, 288(22):2859-67.

Gamsu HR, Mullinger BM, Donnai P, et al, "Antenatal Administration of Betamethasone to Prevent Respiratory Distress Syndrome in Preterm Infants: Report of a UK Multicentre Trial," *Br J Obstet Gynaecol*, 1989, 96(4):401-10.

Goedert JJ, Vitale F, Lauria C, et al, "Risk Factors for Classical Kaposi's Sarcoma," *J Natl Cancer Inst*, 2002, 94(22):1712-8.

Hotchkiss RS and Karl IE, "The Pathophysiology and Treatment of Sepsis," *N Engl J Med*, 2003, 348(2):138-50.

Liggins GC and Howie RN, "A Controlled Trial of Antepartum Glucocorticoid Treatment of Respiratory Distress Syndrome in Premature Infants," *Pediatrics*, 1972, 50:515-25.

Salem M, Tainsh RE Jr, Bromberg J, et al, "Perioperative Glucocorticoid Coverage. A Reassessment 42 Years After Emergence of a Problem," *Ann Surg*, 1994, 219(4):416-25.

Steinberg KP, Hudson LD, Goodman RB, et al, "Efficacy and Safety of Corticosteroids for Persistent Acute Respiratory Distress Syndrome. National Heart, Lung and Blood Institute Acute Respiratory Distress Syndrome (ARDS) Clinical Trials Network," *N Engl J Med*, 2006, 354(16):1671-84.

Tornatore KM, Logue G, Venuto RC, et al, "Pharmacokinetics of Methylprednisolone in Elderly and Young Healthy Males," *J Am Geriatr Soc*, 1994, 42(10):1118-22.

♦ **6-α-Methylprednisolone** *see* MethylPREDNISolone *on page 745*

♦ **Methylprednisolone Acetate** *see* MethylPREDNISolone *on page 745*
♦ **Methylprednisolone Sodium Succinate** *see* MethylPREDNISolone *on page 745*

Metoclopramide (met oh KLOE pra mide)

Medication Safety Issues

Sound-alike/look-alike issues:
   Metoclopramide may be confused with metolazone
   Reglan® may be confused with Megace®, Regonol®, Renagel®

Related Information

Management of Nausea and Vomiting *on page 1319*

U.S. Brand Names Reglan®

Generic Available Yes

Canadian Brand Names Apo-Metoclop®; Metoclopramide Hydrochloride Injection; Nu-Metoclopramide

Pharmacologic Category Antiemetic; Gastrointestinal Agent, Prokinetic

Use

Oral: Symptomatic treatment of diabetic gastric stasis; gastroesophageal reflux

I.V., I.M.: Symptomatic treatment of diabetic gastric stasis; postpyloric placement of enteral feeding tubes; prevention and/or treatment of nausea and vomiting associated with chemotherapy, or postsurgery; to stimulate gastric emptying and intestinal transit of barium during radiological examination

Pregnancy Risk Factor B

Lactation Enters breast milk/use caution

Labeled Contraindications Hypersensitivity to metoclopramide or any component of the formulation; GI obstruction, perforation or hemorrhage; pheochromocytoma; history of seizures

Warnings/Precautions Use caution with a history of mental illness; has been associated with extrapyramidal symptoms (EPS) and depression. The frequency of EPS is higher in pediatric patients and adults <30 years of age; risk is increased at higher dosages. Extrapyramidal reactions typically occur within the initial 24-48 hours of treatment. Use caution with concurrent use of other drugs associated with EPS. Use caution in the elderly and with Parkinson's disease; may have increased risk of tardive dyskinesia. Neuroleptic malignant syndrome (NMS) has been reported (rarely) with metoclopramide. Use lowest recommended doses initially; may cause transient increase in serum aldosterone; use caution in patients who are at risk of fluid overload (CHF, cirrhosis). Use caution in patients with hypertension or following surgical anastomosis/closure. Patients with NADH-cytochrome b5 reductase deficiency are at increased risk of methemoglobinemia and/or sulfhemoglobinemia. Abrupt discontinuation may (rarely) result in withdrawal symptoms (dizziness, headache, nervousness). Use caution and adjust dose in renal impairment.

Adverse Reactions Frequency not always defined.

Cardiovascular: AV block, bradycardia, CHF, fluid retention, flushing (following high I.V. doses), hyper-/hypotension, supraventricular tachycardia

Central nervous system: Drowsiness (~10% to 70%; dose related), fatigue (~10%), restlessness (~10%), acute dystonic reactions (<1% to 25%; dose and age related), akathisia, confusion, depression, dizziness, hallucinations (rare), headache, insomnia, neuroleptic malignant syndrome (rare), Parkinsonian-like symptoms, suicidal ideation, seizure, tardive dyskinesia

Dermatologic: Angioneurotic edema (rare), rash, urticaria

(Continued)

Metoclopramide *(Continued)*

Endocrine & metabolic: Amenorrhea, galactorrhea, gynecomastia, impotence

Gastrointestinal: Diarrhea, nausea

Genitourinary: Incontinence, urinary frequency

Hematologic: Agranulocytosis, leukopenia, neutropenia, porphyria

Hepatic: Hepatotoxicity (rare)

Ocular: Visual disturbance

Respiratory: Bronchospasm, laryngeal edema (rare)

Miscellaneous: Allergic reactions, methemoglobinemia, sulfhemoglobinemia

Overdosage/Toxicology Symptoms of overdose include drowsiness, ataxia, extrapyramidal symptoms, seizures, methemoglobinemia (in infants). Disorientation, muscle hypertonia, irritability, and agitation are common. Metoclopramide often causes extrapyramidal symptoms (eg, dystonic reactions) requiring management with diphenhydramine 1-2 mg/kg (adults) up to a maximum of 50-100 mg I.M. or I.V. slow push followed by a maintenance dose (25-50 mg orally every 4-6 hours) for 48-72 hours. When these reactions are unresponsive to diphenhydramine, benztropine mesylate I.V. 1-2 mg (adults) may be effective. These agents are generally effective within 2-5 minutes. Methylene blue is not recommended in patients with G6PD deficiency who experience methemoglobinemia due to metoclopramide.

Drug Interactions

Cytochrome P450 Effect: Substrate (minor) of CYP1A2, 2D6; **Inhibits** CYP2D6 (weak)

Increased Effect/Toxicity: Opiate analgesics may increase CNS depression. Metoclopramide may increase extrapyramidal symptoms (EPS) or risk when used concurrently with antipsychotic agents. Metoclopramide may increase cyclosporine levels.

Decreased Effect: Anticholinergic agents antagonize metoclopramide's actions.

Ethanol/Nutrition/Herb Interactions Ethanol: Avoid ethanol (may increase CNS depression).

Storage/Stability

Injection: Store intact vial at controlled room temperature; injection is photosensitive and should be protected from light during storage; parenteral admixtures in D₅W or NS are stable for at least 24 hours and do not require light protection if used within 24 hours.

Tablet: Store at controlled room temperature.

Compatibility Stable in D₅¹/₂NS, D₅W, mannitol 20%, LR, NS; **variable stability (consult detailed reference)** in TPN.

Y-site administration: Compatible: Acyclovir, aldesleukin, amifostine, aztreonam, bleomycin, ciprofloxacin, cisatracurium, cisplatin, cladribine, clarithromycin, cyclophosphamide, cytarabine, diltiazem, docetaxel, doxorubicin, droperidol, etoposide phosphate, famotidine, filgrastim, fluconazole, fludarabine, fluorouracil, foscarnet, gatifloxacin, gemcitabine, granisetron, heparin, idarubicin, leucovorin, levofloxacin, linezolid, melphalan, meperidine, meropenem, methotrexate, mitomycin, morphine, ondansetron, paclitaxel, piperacillin/tazobactam, remifentanil, sargramostim, sufentanil, tacrolimus, teniposide, thiotepa, topotecan, vinblastine, vincristine, vinorelbine, zidovudine. **Incompatible:** Allopurinol, amphotericin B cholesteryl sulfate complex, amsacrine, cefepime, doxorubicin liposome, furosemide, propofol. **Variable (consult detailed reference):** TPN.

Compatibility in syringe: Compatible: Aminophylline, ascorbic acid injection, atropine, benztropine, bleomycin, butorphanol, chlorpromazine, cisplatin, cyclophosphamide, cytarabine, dexamethasone sodium phosphate, diamorphine, dimenhydrinate, diphenhydramine, doxorubicin, droperidol, fentanyl, fluorouracil, heparin, hydrocortisone sodium phosphate, hydrocortisone sodium succinate, hydroxyzine, insulin (regular), leucovorin, lidocaine, magnesium sulfate, meperidine, methotrimeprazine, methylprednisolone sodium succinate, midazolam, mitomycin, morphine, ondansetron, pentazocine, perphenazine, prochlorperazine edisylate, promazine, promethazine, ranitidine, scopolamine, sufentanil, vinblastine, vincristine, vitamin B complex with C. **Incompatible:** Ampicillin, calcium gluconate, chloramphenicol, furosemide, penicillin G potassium, sodium bicarbonate. **Variable (consult detailed reference):** Methotrexate.

Compatibility when admixed: Compatible: Cimetidine, clindamycin, diamorphine, meperidine, meropenem, morphine, multivitamins, potassium acetate, potassium chloride, potassium phosphate, verapamil. **Incompatible:** Dexamethasone sodium phosphate with lorazepam and diphenhydramine, erythromycin lactobionate, floxacillin, fluorouracil, furosemide.

Mechanism of Action Blocks dopamine receptors and (when given in higher doses) also blocks serotonin receptors in chemoreceptor trigger zone of the CNS; enhances the response to acetylcholine of tissue in upper GI tract causing enhanced motility and accelerated gastric emptying without stimulating gastric, biliary, or pancreatic secretions; increases lower esophageal sphincter tone

Pharmacodynamics/Kinetics
Onset of action: Oral: 0.5-1 hour; I.V.: 1-3 minutes; I.M.: 10-15 minutes
Duration: Therapeutic: 1-2 hours, regardless of route
Distribution: V_d: 2-4 L/kg
Protein binding: 30%
Bioavailability: Oral: 65% to 95%
Half-life elimination: Normal renal function: 4-6 hours (may be dose dependent)
Time to peak, serum: Oral: 1-2 hours
Excretion: Urine ($\sim$85%)

Dosage
Children:
Gastroesophageal reflux (unlabeled use): Oral: 0.1-0.2 mg/kg/dose 4 times/day
Antiemetic (chemotherapy-induced emesis) (unlabeled): I.V.: 1-2 mg/kg 30 minutes before chemotherapy and every 2-4 hours
Postpyloric feeding tube placement: I.V.:
<6 years: 0.1 mg/kg
6-14 years: 2.5-5 mg
>14 years: Refer to adult dosing.
Adults:
Gastroesophageal reflux: Oral: 10-15 mg/dose up to 4 times/day 30 minutes before meals or food and at bedtime; single doses of 20 mg are occasionally needed for provoking situations. Treatment >12 weeks has not been evaluated.
Diabetic gastric stasis:
Oral: 10 mg 30 minutes before each meal and at bedtime
I.M., I.V. (for severe symptoms): 10 mg over 1-2 minutes; 10 days of I.V. therapy may be necessary for best response
Chemotherapy-induced emesis:
I.V.: 1-2 mg/kg 30 minutes before chemotherapy and repeated every 2 hours for 2 doses, then every 3 hours for 3 doses (manufacturer labeling)
(Continued)

Metoclopramide *(Continued)*

Alternate dosing (with or without diphenhydramine):
   Moderate emetic risk chemotherapy: 0.5 mg/kg every 6 hours on days 2-4
   Low and minimal risk chemotherapy: 1-2 mg/kg every 3-4 hours
   Breakthrough treatment: 1-2 mg/kg every 3-4 hours
Oral (unlabeled use; with or without diphenhydramine):
   Moderate emetic risk chemotherapy: 0.5 mg/kg every 6 hours or 20 mg 4 times/day on days 2-4
   Low and minimal risk chemotherapy: 20-40 mg every 4-6 hours
   Breakthrough treatment: 20-40 mg every 4-6 hours
Postoperative nausea and vomiting: I.M., I.V.: 10-20 mg near end of surgery
Postpyloric feeding tube placement, radiological exam: I.V.: 10 mg
Elderly:
   Gastroesophageal reflux: Oral: 5 mg 4 times/day (30 minutes before meals or food and at bedtime); increase dose to 10 mg 4 times/day if no response at lower dose
   Gastrointestinal hypomotility:
      Oral: Initial: 5 mg 30 minutes before meals and at bedtime; increase if necessary to 10 mg doses
      I.V.: Initiate at 5 mg over 1-2 minutes; increase to 10 mg if necessary
   Postoperative nausea and vomiting: I.M., I.V.: 5 mg near end of surgery; may repeat dose if necessary

Dosing adjustment in renal impairment: Cl_{cr} <40 mL/minute: Administer at 50% of normal dose
Hemodialysis: Not dialyzable (0% to 5%); supplemental dose is not necessary

Administration Injection solution may be given I.M., direct I.V. push, short infusion (15-30 minutes), or continuous infusion; lower doses (≤10 mg) of metoclopramide can be given I.V. push undiluted over 1-2 minutes; higher doses to be given IVPB over at least 15 minutes; continuous SubQ infusion and rectal administration have been reported. **Note:** Rapid I.V. administration may be associated with a transient (but intense) feeling of anxiety and restlessness, followed by drowsiness.

Monitoring Parameters Dystonic reactions; signs of hypoglycemia in patients using insulin and those being treated for gastroparesis; agitation, and onfusion

Test Interactions Increased aminotransferase [ALT/AST] (S), increased amylase (S)

Patient Information May impair mental alertness or physical coordination; avoid alcohol, barbiturates or other CNS depressants; take 30 minutes before meals; report if involuntary movements occur

Special Geriatric Considerations Elderly are more likely to develop tardive dyskinesia syndrome (especially elderly females) reactions than younger adults. Use lowest recommended doses initially. Must consider renal function (estimate creatinine clearance). It is recommended to do involuntary movement assessments on elderly using this medication at high doses and for long-term therapy.

Emetic Potential Very low (<10%)

Vesicant No

Dosage Forms Excipient information presented when available (limited, particularly for generics); consult specific product labeling.
Injection, solution (Reglan®): 5 mg/mL (2 mL, 10 mL, 30 mL)
Syrup: 5 mg/5 mL (10 mL, 480 mL)

Tablet (Reglan®): 5 mg, 10 mg

References

"American Academy of Pediatrics Committee on Drugs. The Transfer of Drugs and Other Chemicals Into Human Milk," *Pediatrics*, 2001, 108(3):776-89.

Bruera E, Seifert L, Watanabe S, et al, "Chronic Nausea in Advanced Cancer Patients: A Retrospective Assessment of a Metoclopramide-Based Antiemetic Regimen," *J Pain Symptom Manage*, 1996, 11(3):147-53.

Desmond PV and Watson KJ, "Metoclopramide - A Review," *Med J Aust*, 1986, 144(7):366-9.

DiPalma JR, "Metoclopramide: A Dopamine Receptor Antagonist," *Am Fam Physician*, 1990, 41(3):919-24.

Gan TJ, Meyer T, Apfel CC, et al, "Consensus Guidelines for Managing Postoperative Nausea and Vomiting," *Anesth Analg*, 2003, 97(1):62-71.

Harrington RA, Hamilton CW, Brogden RN, et al, "Metoclopramide. An Updated Review of Its Pharmacological Properties and Clinical Use," *Drugs*, 1983, 25(5):451-94.

Hart J, "Pediatric Gastroesophageal Reflux," *Am Fam Physician*, 1996, 54(8):2463-72.

Karadsheh NS, Shaker Q, and Ratroat B, "Metoclopramide-Induced Methemoglobinemia in a Patient With Co-Existing Deficiency of Glucose-6-Phosphate Dehydrogenase and NADH-Cytochrome b5 Reductase: Failure of Methylene Blue Treatment," *Haematologica*, 2001, 86(6):659-60.

Mary AM and Bhupalam L, "Metoclopramide-induced Methemoglobinemia in an Adult," *J KY Med Assoc*, 2000, 98(6):245-7.

McGovern EM, Grevel J, and Bryson SM, "Pharmacokinetics of High-Dose Metoclopramide in Cancer Patients," *Clin Pharmacokinet*, 1986, 11(6):415-24.

"National Comprehensive Cancer Network Practice Guidelines in Oncology," (version 1.2005); available at: http://www.nccn.org/professionals/physician_gls/PDF/antiemesis.pdf

Parrish RH and Bonzo SM, "Use of Metoclopramide Suppositories," *Clin Pharm*, 1983, 2:395-6.

Patterson JF, "Neuroleptic Malignant Syndrome Associated With Metoclopramide," *South Med J*, 1988, 81(5):674-5.

Schulze-Delrieu K, "Drug Therapy. Metoclopramide," *N Engl J Med*, 1981, 305(1):28-33.

Van Veldhuizen PJ and Wyatt A, "Metoclopramide-induced Sulfhemoglobinemia," *Am J Gastroenterol*, 1995, 90(6):1010-1.

♦ **Metoclopramide Hydrochloride Injection (Can)** *see* Metoclopramide *on page 751*

♦ **MetroCream®** *see* Metronidazole *on page 755*

♦ **MetroGel®** *see* Metronidazole *on page 755*

♦ **Metrogel® (Can)** *see* Metronidazole *on page 755*

♦ **MetroGel-Vaginal®** *see* Metronidazole *on page 755*

♦ **MetroLotion®** *see* Metronidazole *on page 755*

Metronidazole (met roe NYE da zole)

Medication Safety Issues

Sound-alike/look-alike issues:

Metronidazole may be confused with metformin.

U.S. Brand Names Flagyl®; Flagyl ER®; MetroCream®; MetroGel®; MetroGel-Vaginal®; MetroLotion®; Noritate®; Vandazole™

Index Terms Metronidazole Hydrochloride

Generic Available Yes: Capsule, cream, gel, infusion, lotion, tablet

Canadian Brand Names Apo-Metronidazole®; Flagyl®; Florazole® ER; MetroCream®; Metrogel®; Nidagel™; Noritate®; Trikacide

Pharmacologic Category Amebicide; Antibiotic, Miscellaneous; Antibiotic, Topical; Antiprotozoal; Nitroimidazole

Use Treatment of susceptible anaerobic bacterial and protozoal infections in the following conditions: Amebiasis, symptomatic and asymptomatic trichomoniasis; skin and skin structure infections; CNS infections; intra-abdominal infections (as part of combination regimen); systemic anaerobic infections; treatment of antibiotic-associated pseudomembranous colitis (AAPC), bacterial vaginosis; as part of a multidrug regimen for *H. pylori* eradication to reduce the risk of duodenal ulcer recurrence

Topical: Treatment of inflammatory lesions and erythema of rosacea

Unlabeled/Investigational Use Crohn's disease

(Continued)

Metronidazole *(Continued)*

Pregnancy Risk Factor B (may be contraindicated in 1st trimester)

Lactation Enters breast milk/not recommended (AAP rates "of concern")

Labeled Contraindications Hypersensitivity to metronidazole, nitroimidazole derivatives, or any component of the formulation; pregnancy (1st trimester - found to be carcinogenic in rats)

Warnings/Precautions Use with caution in patients with liver impairment due to potential accumulation, blood dyscrasias; history of seizures, CHF, or other sodium retaining states; reduce dosage in patients with severe liver impairment, CNS disease, and consider dosage reduction in longer-term therapy with severe renal failure (Cl_{cr} <10 mL/minute); if *H. pylori* is not eradicated in patients being treated with metronidazole in a regimen, it should be assumed that metronidazole-resistance has occurred and it should not again be used; seizures and neuropathies have been reported especially with increased doses and chronic treatment; if this occurs, discontinue therapy. **[U.S. Boxed Warning]: Possibly carcinogenic based on animal data.** Prolonged use may result in fungal or bacterial superinfection, including *C. difficile*-associated diarrhea (CDAD) and pseudomembranous colitis. CDAD has been observed <2 months postantibiotic treatment.

Adverse Reactions

Systemic: Frequency not defined:

Cardiovascular: Flattening of the T-wave, flushing

Central nervous system: Ataxia, confusion, coordination impaired, dizziness, fever, headache, insomnia, irritability, seizure, vertigo

Dermatologic: Erythematous rash, urticaria

Endocrine & metabolic: Disulfiram-like reaction, dysmenorrhea, libido decreased

Gastrointestinal: Nausea (~12%), anorexia, abdominal cramping, constipation, diarrhea, furry tongue, glossitis, proctitis, stomatitis, unusual/metallic taste, vomiting, xerostomia

Genitourinary: Cystitis, darkened urine (rare), dysuria, incontinence, polyuria, vaginitis

Hematologic: Neutropenia (reversible), thrombocytopenia (reversible, rare)

Neuromuscular & skeletal: Peripheral neuropathy, weakness

Respiratory: Nasal congestion, rhinitis, sinusitis, pharyngitis

Miscellaneous: Flu-like syndrome, moniliasis

Topical: Frequency not defined:

Central nervous system: Headache

Dermatologic: Burning, contact dermatitis, dryness, erythema, irritation, pruritus, rash

Gastrointestinal: Unusual/metallic taste, nausea, constipation

Local: Local allergic reaction

Neuromuscular & skeletal: Tingling/numbness of extremities

Ocular: Eye irritation

Vaginal:

>10%: Genitourinary: Vaginal discharge (12%)

1% to 10%:

Central nervous system: Headache (5%), dizziness (2%)

Gastrointestinal: Gastrointestinal discomfort (7%), nausea and/or vomiting (4%), unusual/metallic taste (2%), diarrhea (1%)

Genitourinary: Vaginitis (10%), vulva/vaginal irritation (9%), pelvic discomfort (3%)

Hematologic: WBC increased (2%)

<1%: Abdominal bloating, abdominal gas, darkened urine, depression, fatigue, itching, rash, thirst, xerostomia

Overdosage/Toxicology Symptoms of overdose include nausea, vomiting, ataxia, seizures, and peripheral neuropathy. Treatment is symptomatic and supportive.

Drug Interactions

Cytochrome P450 Effect: Inhibits CYP2C9 (weak), 3A4 (moderate)

Increased Effect/Toxicity: Ethanol may cause a disulfiram-like reaction. Warfarin and metronidazole may increase bleeding times (PT) which may result in bleeding. Cimetidine may increase metronidazole levels. Metronidazole may inhibit metabolism of cisapride, causing potential arrhythmias; avoid concurrent use. Metronidazole may increase lithium levels/toxicity. Metronidazole may increase the levels/effects of selected benzodiazepines, calcium channel blockers, cyclosporine, ergot derivatives, selected HMG-CoA reductase inhibitors, mirtazapine, nateglinide, nefazodone, sildenafil (and other PDE-5 inhibitors), tacrolimus, venlafaxine, and other CYP3A4 substrates.

Decreased Effect: Phenytoin, phenobarbital (potentially other enzyme inducers) may decrease metronidazole half-life and effects.

Ethanol/Nutrition/Herb Interactions

Ethanol: The manufacturer recommends to avoid all ethanol or any ethanol-containing drugs (may cause disulfiram-like reaction characterized by flushing, headache, nausea, vomiting, sweating or tachycardia).

Food: Peak antibiotic serum concentration lowered and delayed, but total drug absorbed not affected.

Storage/Stability Metronidazole injection should be stored at 15°C to 30°C and protected from light. Product may be refrigerated but crystals may form. Crystals redissolve on warming to room temperature. Prolonged exposure to light will cause a darkening of the product. However, short-term exposure to normal room light does not adversely affect metronidazole stability. Direct sunlight should be avoided. Stability of parenteral admixture at room temperature (25°C): Out of overwrap stability: 30 days.

Reconstitution Standard diluent: 500 mg/100 mL NS.

Compatibility Stable in D_5W, NS.

Y-site administration: Compatible: Acyclovir, allopurinol, amiodarone, amifostine, cefepime, cisatracurium, clarithromycin, cyclophosphamide, diltiazem, docetaxel, dopamine, doxorubicin liposome, enalaprilat, esmolol, etoposide phosphate, fluconazole, foscarnet, gatifloxacin, gemcitabine, granisetron, heparin, hydromorphone, labetalol, linezolid, lorazepam, magnesium sulfate, melphalan, meperidine, methylprednisolone sodium succinate, midazolam, morphine, perphenazine, piperacillin/tazobactam, remifentanil, sargramostim, tacrolimus, teniposide, theophylline, thiotepa, vinorelbine. **Incompatible:** Amphotericin B cholesteryl sulfate complex, aztreonam, filgrastim, meropenem, warfarin.

Compatibility when admixed: Compatible: Amikacin, aminophylline, ampicillin, cefazolin, cefotaxime, cefoxitin, ceftazidime, ceftizoxime, ceftriaxone, cefuroxime, chloramphenicol, ciprofloxacin, clindamycin, disopyramide, floxacillin, fluconazole, gentamicin, heparin, hydrocortisone sodium succinate, multivitamins, netilmicin, penicillin G potassium, tobramycin. **Incompatible:** Aztreonam, dopamine, meropenem. **Variable (consult detailed reference):** Cefamandole, cefepime.

Mechanism of Action After diffusing into the organism, interacts with DNA to cause a loss of helical DNA structure and strand breakage resulting in inhibition of protein synthesis and cell death in susceptible organisms

(Continued)

Metronidazole *(Continued)*

Pharmacodynamics/Kinetics

Absorption: Oral: Well absorbed; Topical: Concentrations achieved systemically after application of 1 g topically are 10 times less than those obtained after a 250 mg oral dose

Distribution: To saliva, bile, seminal fluid, breast milk, bone, liver, and liver abscesses, lung and vaginal secretions; crosses placenta and blood-brain barrier

CSF:blood level ratio: Normal meninges: 16% to 43%; Inflamed meninges: 100%

Protein binding: <20%

Metabolism: Hepatic (30% to 60%)

Half-life elimination: Neonates: 25-75 hours; Others: 6-8 hours, prolonged with hepatic impairment; End-stage renal disease: 21 hours

Time to peak, serum: Oral: Immediate release: 1-2 hours

Excretion: Urine (20% to 40% as unchanged drug); feces (6% to 15%)

Dosage

Infants and Children:

Amebiasis: Oral: 35-50 mg/kg/day in divided doses every 8 hours for 10 days

Trichomoniasis: Oral: 15-30 mg/kg/day in divided doses every 8 hours for 7 days

Anaerobic infections:

Oral: 15-35 mg/kg/day in divided doses every 8 hours

I.V.: 30 mg/kg/day in divided doses every 6 hours

Clostridium difficile (antibiotic-associated colitis): Oral: 20 mg/kg/day divided every 6 hours

Maximum dose: 2 g/day

Adults:

Anaerobic infections (diverticulitis, intra-abdominal, peritonitis, cholangitis, or abscess): Oral, I.V.: 500 mg every 6-8 hours, not to exceed 4 g/day

Acne rosacea: Topical:

0.75%: Apply and rub a thin film twice daily, morning and evening, to entire affected areas after washing. Significant therapeutic results should be noticed within 3 weeks. Clinical studies have demonstrated continuing improvement through 9 weeks of therapy.

1%: Apply thin film to affected area once daily

Amebiasis: Oral: 500-750 mg every 8 hours for 5-10 days

Antibiotic-associated pseudomembranous colitis: Oral: 250-500 mg 3-4 times/day for 10-14 days

Note: Due to the emergence of a new strain of *C. difficile*, some clinicians recommend converting to oral vancomycin therapy if the patient does not show a clear clinical response after 2 days of metronidazole therapy.

Giardiasis: 500 mg twice daily for 5-7 days

Helicobacter pylori eradication: Oral: 250-500 mg with meals and at bedtime for 14 days; requires combination therapy with at least one other antibiotic and an acid-suppressing agent (proton pump inhibitor or H_2 blocker)

Bacterial vaginosis or vaginitis due to *Gardnerella, Mobiluncus*:

Oral: 500 mg twice daily (regular release) or 750 mg once daily (extended release tablet) for 7 days

Vaginal: 1 applicatorful (~37.5 mg metronidazole) intravaginally once or twice daily for 5 days; apply once in morning and evening if using twice daily, if daily, use at bedtime

Trichomoniasis: Oral: 250 mg every 8 hours for 7 days **or** 375 mg twice daily for 7 days **or** 2 g as a single dose

Elderly: Use lower end of dosing recommendations for adults, do not administer as a single dose

Dosing adjustment in renal impairment: Cl_{cr} <10 mL/minute, but not on dialysis: Recommendations vary: To reduce possible accumulation in patients receiving multiple doses, consider reduction to 50% of dose or every 12 hours; **Note:** Dosage reduction is unnecessary in short courses of therapy. Clinical recommendations and practice vary. Some references do not recommend reduction at any level of renal impairment (Lamp, 1999).

Hemodialysis: Extensively removed by hemodialysis and peritoneal dialysis (50% to 100%); dosage reduction not recommended; administer full dose posthemodialysis

Peritoneal dialysis: Dose as for Cl_{cr} <10 mL/minute

Continuous arteriovenous or venovenous hemofiltration: Administer usual dose

Dosing adjustment/comments in hepatic disease: Unchanged in mild liver disease; reduce dosage in severe liver disease

Administration

Oral: May be taken with food to minimize stomach upset. Extended release tablets should be taken on an empty stomach (1 hour before or 2 hours after meals).

Topical: No disulfiram-like reactions have been reported after **topical** application, although metronidazole can be detected in the blood. Apply to clean, dry skin. Cosmetics may be used after application (wait at least 5 minutes after using lotion).

Test Interactions May interfere with AST, ALT, triglycerides, glucose, and LDH testing

Dietary Considerations Take on an empty stomach. Drug may cause GI upset; if GI upset occurs, take with food. Extended release tablets should be taken on an empty stomach (1 hour before or 2 hours after meals). Sodium content of 500 mg (I.V.): 322 mg (14 mEq). The manufacturer recommends that ethanol be avoided during treatment and for 3 days after therapy is complete.

Patient Information Urine may be discolored to a dark or reddish-brown; do not take alcohol for at least 24 hours after the last dose; avoid beverage alcohol or any topical products containing alcohol during therapy; may cause metallic taste; may be taken with food to minimize stomach upset; report numbness or tingling in extremities; avoid contact of the topical product with the eyes; cleanse areas to be treated well before application

Special Geriatric Considerations Adjust dose based on renal function.

Emetic Potential Low (10% to 30%)

Vesicant No

Dosage Forms Excipient information presented when available (limited, particularly for generics); consult specific product labeling.

Capsule: 375 mg
  Flagyl®: 375 mg
Cream, topical: 0.75% (45 g)
  MetroCream®: 0.75% (45 g) [contains benzyl alcohol]
  Noritate®: 1% (60 g)
Gel, topical: 0.75% (45 g)
  MetroGel®: 1% (46 g, 60 g) [60 g tube also packaged in a kit with Cetaphil® skin cleanser]
Gel, vaginal: 0.75% (70 g)
(Continued)

Metronidazole (Continued)

MetroGel-Vaginal®, Vandazole™: 0.75% (70 g)

Infusion [premixed iso-osmotic sodium chloride solution]: 500 mg (100 mL)

Lotion, topical: 0.75% (60 mL)

MetroLotion®: 0.75% (60 mL) [contains benzyl alcohol]

Tablet: 250 mg, 500 mg

Flagyl®: 250 mg, 500 mg

Tablet, extended release:

Flagyl® ER: 750 mg

Extemporaneous Preparations A 20 mg/mL oral suspension can be prepared by crushing ten 250 mg tablets in a mortar, and then adding 10 mL purified water USP to create a uniform paste. Add a small quantity of syrup, then transfer to a graduate and add a sufficient quantity of syrup to make 125 mL. Label "shake well" and "refrigerate." Refrigerated stability is 10 days.

Irwin DB, Dupuis LL, Prober CG, et al, "The Acceptability, Stability, and Relative Bioavailability of an Extemporaneous Metronidazole Suspension," *Can J Hosp Pharm*, 1987, 40:42-6.

Nahata MC, Morosco RS, and Hipple TF, 4th ed, *Pediatric Drug Formulations*, Cincinnati, OH: Harvey Whitney Books Co, 2000.

References

Abramowicz M, "Antimicrobial Prophylaxis in Surgery," *Medical Letter on Drugs and Therapeutics, Handbook of Antimicrobial Therapy*, 16th ed, New York, NY: Medical Letter, 2002.

Ahmed A, Loes DJ, and Bressler EL, "Reversible Magnetic Resonance Imaging Findings in Metronidazole-Induced Encephalopathy," *Neurology*, 1995, 45(3 Pt 1):588-9.

"American Academy of Pediatrics Committee on Drugs. The Transfer of Drugs and Other Chemicals Into Human Milk," *Pediatrics*, 2001, 108(3):776-89.

Bartlett JG and Perl TM, "The New *Clostridium difficile*- What Does it Mean?" *N Engl J Med*, 2005, 353(23):2503-5.

Belliveau PP, Nightingale CH, and Quintiliani R, "Stability of Cefotaxime Sodium and Metronidazole in 0.9% Sodium Chloride Injection or in Ready-to-Use Metronidazole Bags," *Am J Health Syst Pharm*, 1995, 52(14):1561-3.

Bradley WG, Karlsson IJ, and Russo ICG, "Metronidazole Neuropathy," *Br Med J*, 1977, 2:610-1.

Brodgen RN, Heel RC, Speight TM, et al, "Metronidazole in Anaerobic Infections: A Review of Its Activity, Pharmacokinetics and Therapeutic Use," *Drugs*, 1978, 16(5):387-417.

Canto JM and Carcia-Cruz D, "Midline Facial Defect as a Teratogenic Effect of Metronidazole," *Birth Defects*, 1982, 18:85-8.

Cassey JG, Clark DA, Merrick P, et al, "Pharmacokinetics of Metronidazole in Patients Undergoing Peritoneal Dialysis," *Antimicrob Agents Chemother*, 1983, 24:950-1.

Committee on Adolescence, American Academy of Pediatrics, "Sexual Assault and the Adolescent," *Pediatrics*, 1994, 94(5):761-5.

Coronado BE, Opal SM, and Yoburn DC, "Antibiotic-Induced D-Lactic Acidosis," *Ann Intern Med*, 1995, 122(11):839-42.

Eisenberg L, Suchow R, Coles RS, et al, "The Effects of Metronidazole Administration on Clinical and Microbiologic Parameters of Periodontal Disease," *Clin Prev Dent*, 1991, 13(1):28-34.

Falagas ME and Gorbach SL, "Clindamycin and Metronidazole," *Med Clin North Am*, 1995, 79(4):845-67.

Fekety R and Shah AB, "Diagnosis and Treatment of *Clostridium difficile* Colitis," *JAMA*, 1993, 269(1):71-5.

Freeman CD, Klutman NE, and Lamp KC, "Metronidazole. A Therapeutic Review and Update," *Drugs*, 1997, 54(5):679-708.

Hager WD and Rapp RP, "Metronidazole," *Obstet Gynecol Clin North Am*, 1992, 19(3):497-510.

Hampson JP, "The Use of Metronidazole in the Treatment of Malodorous Wounds," *J Wound Care*, 1996, 5(9):421-5.

Israel DM and Hassall E, "Treatment and Long-Term Follow-up of *Helicobacter pylori*-Associated Duodenal Ulcer Disease in Children," *J Pediatr*, 1993, 123(1):53-8.

Jenkins WM, MacFarlane TW, Gilmour WH, et al, "Systemic Metronidazole in the Treatment of Periodontitis," *J Clin Periodontol*, 1989, 16(7):433-50.

Kelly CP, Pothoulakis C, and LaMont JT, "*Clostridium difficile* Colitis," *N Engl J Med*, 1994, 330(4):257-62.

Lam S and Bank S, "Hepatotoxicity Caused by Metronidazole Overdose," *Ann Intern Med*, 1995, 122(10):803.

Lamp KC, Freeman CD, Klutman NE, et al, "Pharmacokinetics and Pharmacodynamics of the Nitroimidazole Antimicrobials," *Clin Pharmacokinet*, 1999, 36(5):353-73.

Lau AH, Chang CW, and Sabatini S, "Hemodialysis Clearance of Metronidazole and its Metabolites," *Antimicrob Agents Chemother*, 1986, 29(2):235-8.

Loesche WJ, Giordano JR, Hujoel P, et al, "Metronidazole in Periodontitis: Reduced Need for Surgery," *J Clin Periodontol*, 1992, 19(2):103-12.

Loesche WJ, Schmidt E, Smith BA, et al, "Effects of Metronidazole on Periodontal Treatment Needs," *J Periodontol*, 1991, 62(4):247-57.

Lorber B, "Update in Infectious Diseases," *Ann Intern Med*, 2006, 145:356-7.

Ludwig E, Csiba A, Magyar T, et al, "Age-Associated Pharmacokinetic Changes of Metronidazole," *Int J Clin Pharmacol Ther Toxicol*, 1983, 21(2):87-91.

Oldenburg B and Speck WT, "Metronidazole," *Pediatr Clin North Am*, 1983, 30(1):71-5.

Patterson BD, "Possible Interaction Between Metronidazole and Carbamazepine," *Ann Pharmacother*, 1994, 28(11):1303-4.

Ralph ED, "Clinical Pharmacokinetics of Metronidazole," *Clin Pharmacokinet*, 1983, 8:43-62.

Smilack JD, Wilson WR, and Cockerill FR 3d, "Tetracyclines, Chloramphenicol, Erythromycin, Clindamycin, and Metronidazole," *Mayo Clin Proc*, 1991, 66(12):1270-80.

Smogyi A, Kong C, Sabto J, et al, "Disposition and Removal of Metronidazole in Patients Undergoing Haemodialysis," *Eur J Clin Pharmacol*, 1983, 25:683-7.

Soder PO, Frithiof L, Wikner S, et al, "The Effect of Systemic Metronidazole After Nonsurgical Treatment in Moderate and Advanced Periodontitis in Young Adults," *J Periodontol*, 1990, 61(5):281-8.

"Treatment of *Clostridium difficile* Diarrhea," *Med Lett Drugs Ther*, 1989, 31(803):94-5.

♦ **Metronidazole Hydrochloride** *see* Metronidazole *on page 755*

♦ **M-FA-142** *see* Amonafide *on page 67*

♦ **Miacalcin®** *see* Calcitonin *on page 160*

♦ **Miacalcin® NS (Can)** *see* Calcitonin *on page 160*

Micafungin (mi ka FUN gin)

U.S. Brand Names Mycamine®

Index Terms Micafungin Sodium

Generic Available No

Canadian Brand Names Mycamine®

Pharmacologic Category Antifungal Agent, Parenteral; Echinocandin

Use Esophageal candidiasis; *Candida* prophylaxis in patients undergoing hematopoietic stem cell transplant

Unlabeled/Investigational Use Treatment of infections due to *Aspergillus* spp; prophylaxis of HIV-related esophageal candidiasis

Pregnancy Risk Factor C

Lactation Excretion in breast milk unknown/use caution

Labeled Contraindications Hypersensitivity to micafungin or any component of the formulation

Warnings/Precautions Anaphylactic reactions, including shock, have been reported. New onset or worsening hepatic failure has been reported; use caution in pre-existing mild-moderate hepatic impairment; safety in severe liver failure has not been evaluated. Hemolytic anemia and hemoglobinuria have been reported. Increased BUN, serum creatinine, renal dysfunction, and/or acute renal failure has been reported; use with caution in patients with pre-existing renal impairment and monitor closely. Safety and efficacy in pediatric patients have not been established.

Adverse Reactions

1% to 10%:

Cardiovascular: Phlebitis (2%), hypertension (1%), flushing (1%)

Central nervous system: Headache (2%), pyrexia (2%), dizziness (1%), somnolence (1%)

Dermatologic: Rash (2%), pruritus (1%), febrile neutropenia (1%)

Endocrine & metabolic: Hypokalemia (1%), hypocalcemia (1%), hypomagnesemia (1%), hypophosphatemia (1%)

(Continued)

Micafungin *(Continued)*

Gastrointestinal: Nausea (3%), diarrhea (2%), vomiting (2%), abdominal pain (1%), appetite decreased (1%), dysgeusia (1%), dyspepsia (1%)

Hematologic: Leukopenia (2%), neutropenia (1%), thrombocytopenia (1%), anemia (1%), lymphopenia (1%), eosinophilia (1%)

Hepatic: Transaminase increased (≤3%), serum alkaline phosphatase increased (2%), hyperbilirubinemia (1%)

Local: Infusion site reactions (1%)

Neuromuscular & skeletal: Rigors (1%), lactate dehydrogenase increased (1%)

Renal: Serum creatinine increased (1%), serum urea increased (1%)

<1%, postmarketing and/or case reports, or frequency not defined: Acidosis, anorexia, anuria, apnea, arrhythmia, arthralgia, cardiac arrest, coagulopathy, constipation, cyanosis, deep vein thrombosis, delirium, dyspnea, hypoxia, encephalopathy, erythema multiforme, facial edema, hemoglobinuria, hemolysis, hemolytic anemia, hepatic failure, hepatocellular damage, hepatomegaly, hiccups, hyponatremia, hypotension, infection, injection site necrosis, intracranial hemorrhage, jaundice, MI, mycosal inflammation, oliguria, pancytopenia, pneumonia, pulmonary embolism, renal failure, renal tubular necrosis, seizure, sepsis, shock, skin necrosis, tachycardia, thrombotic thrombocytopenia purpura, thrombophlebitis, urticaria, vasodilatation

Overdosage/Toxicology Treatment is symptom-directed and supportive. Not removed by dialysis.

Drug Interactions

Cytochrome P450 Effect: Substrate of CYP3A4 (minor); **Inhibits** CYP3A4 (weak)

Increased Effect/Toxicity: No clinically-significant interactions have been identified.

Decreased Effect: Antifungal agents may dimmish the activity of *Saccharomyces boulardii*

Storage/Stability Store at 15°C to 30°C (59°F to 86°F). Reconstituted and diluted solutions are stable for 24 hours at room temperature. Protect from light.

Reconstitution Aseptically add 5 mL of NS (preservative-free) to each 50 or 100 mg vial. Swirl to dissolve; do not shake. Further dilute 50-150 mg in 100 mL NS. Protect from light. Alternatively, D_5W may be used for reconstitution and dilution.

Compatibility Do not mix or coinfuse with other intravenous solutions.

Mechanism of Action Concentration-dependent inhibition of 1,3-beta-D-glucan synthase resulting in reduced formation of 1,3-beta-D-glucan, an essential polysaccharide comprising 30% to 60% of *Candida* cell walls (absent in mammalian cells); decreased glucan content leads to osmotic instability and cellular lysis

Pharmacodynamics/Kinetics

Distribution: 0.28-0.5 L/kg

Protein binding: >99%; primarily to albumin

Metabolism: Hepatic; forms M-1 (catechol) and M-2 (methoxy) metabolites (activity unknown)

Half-life elimination: 11-21 hours

Excretion: Primarily feces (71%); urine (<15%)

Dosage I.V.: Adults:

Esophageal candidiasis: 150 mg daily; mean duration of therapy (from clinical trials) was 15 days (range: 10-30 days)

Prophylaxis of *Candida* infection in hematopoietic stem cell transplantation: 50 mg daily

Dosing adjustment in renal impairment: No adjustment required

Dosing adjustment in hepatic impairment: No dosage adjustment required for moderate hepatic impairment (Child-Pugh score 7-9). Patients with severe hepatic dysfunction have not been studied.

Administration For intravenous use only; infuse over 1 hour. Flush line with NS prior to administration.

Monitoring Parameters Liver function tests

Patient Information Inform prescriber of all prescriptions, OTC medications, or herbal products you are taking, and any allergies you have. This medication can only be administered by infusion. Report immediately any pain, burning, or swelling at infusion site, or any signs of allergic reaction (eg, respiratory difficulty or swallowing, back pain, chest tightness, rash, hives, or swelling of lips or mouth). Report nausea, vomiting, abdominal pain, or diarrhea.

Dosage Forms Excipient information presented when available (limited, particularly for generics); consult specific product labeling.

Injection, powder for reconstitution, as sodium [preservative-free]:

Mycamine®: 50 mg, 100 mg [contains lactose]

References

Carver PL, "Micafungin," *Ann Pharmacother*, 2004, 38(10):1707-21.

de Wet N, Llanos-Cuentas A, Suleiman J, et al, "A Randomized, Double-Blind, Parallel-Group, Dose-Response Study of Micafungin Compared With Fluconazole for the Treatment of Esophageal Candidiasis in HIV-Positive Patients," *Clin Infect Dis*, 2004, 39(6):842-9.

Kohno S, Masaoka T, Yamaguchi H, et al, "A Multicenter, Open-Label Clinical Study of Micafungin (FK463) in the Treatment of Deep-Seated Mycosis in Japan," *Scand J Infect Dis*, 36(5):372-9.

Pettengell K, Mynhardt J, Kluyts T, et al, "Successful Treatment of Oesophageal Candidiasis by Micafungin: A Novel Systemic Antifungal Agent," *Aliment Pharmacol Ther*, 2004, 20(4):475-81.

Yokote T, Akioka T, Oka S, et al, "Successful Treatment With Micafungin of Invasive Pulmonary Aspergillosis in Acute Myeloid Leukemia, With Renal Failure Due to Amphotericin B Therapy," *Ann Hematol*, 2004, 83(1):64-6.

♦ **Micafungin Sodium** *see* Micafungin *on page 761*

♦ **MICRhoGAM®** *see* Rh₀(D) Immune Globulin *on page 948*

♦ **Mifeprex®** *see* Mifepristone *on page 763*

Mifepristone (mi FE pris tone)

Medication Safety Issues

Sound-alike/look-alike issues:

Mifeprex® may be confused with Mirapex®

Related Information

Investigational Drug Service *on page 1379*

U.S. Brand Names Mifeprex®

Index Terms RU-486; RU-38486

Generic Available No

Pharmacologic Category Abortifacient; Antineoplastic Agent, Hormone Antagonist; Antiprogestin

Use Medical termination of intrauterine pregnancy, through day 49 of pregnancy. Patients may need treatment with misoprostol and possibly surgery to complete therapy

Unlabeled/Investigational Use Treatment of unresectable meningioma; has been studied in the treatment of breast cancer, ovarian cancer, and adrenal cortical carcinoma

(Continued)

Mifepristone *(Continued)*

Restrictions Investigators wishing to obtain the agent for use in oncology patients must apply for a patient-specific IND from the FDA. Mifepristone will be supplied only to licensed physicians who sign and return a "Prescriber's Agreement." Distribution of mifepristone will be subject to specific requirements imposed by the distributor. Mifepristone will **not** be available to the public through licensed pharmacies. An FDA-approved medication guide must be distributed when dispensing an outpatient prescription (new or refill) where this medication is to be used without direct supervision of a healthcare provider. Medication guides are available at http://www.fda.gov/cder/Offices/ODS/medication_guides.htm.

Not available in Canada

Pregnancy Risk Factor X

Lactation Excretion in breast milk unknown/contraindicated

Labeled Contraindications Hypersensitivity to mifepristone, misoprostol, other prostaglandins, or any component of the formulation; chronic adrenal failure; porphyrias; hemorrhagic disorder or concurrent anticoagulant therapy; pregnancy termination >49 days; intrauterine device (IUD) in place; ectopic pregnancy or undiagnosed adnexal mass; concurrent long-term corticosteroid therapy; inadequate or lack of access to emergency medical services; inability to understand effects and/or comply with treatment

Warnings/Precautions [U.S. Boxed Warning]: Patient must be instructed of the treatment procedure and expected effects. A signed agreement form must be kept in the patient's file. Physicians may obtain patient agreement forms, physician enrollment forms, and medical consultation directly from Danco Laboratories at 1-877-432-7596. Adverse effects (including blood transfusions, hospitalization, ongoing pregnancy, and other major complications) must be reported in writing to the medication distributor. To be administered only by physicians who can date pregnancy, diagnose ectopic pregnancies, provide access to surgical abortion (if needed), and can provide access to emergency care. Medication will be distributed directly to these physicians following signed agreement with the distributor. Must be administered under supervision by the qualified physician. Pregnancy is dated from day 1 of last menstrual period (presuming a 28-day cycle, ovulation occurring midcycle). Pregnancy duration can be determined using menstrual history and clinical examination. Ultrasound should be used if an ectopic pregnancy is suspected or if duration of pregnancy is uncertain. Ultrasonography may not identify all ectopic pregnancies, and healthcare providers should be alert for signs and symptoms which may be related to undiagnosed ectopic pregnancy in any patient who receives mifepristone

[U.S. Boxed Warning]: Patients should be counseled to seek medical attention in cases of excessive bleeding. Bleeding occurs and should be expected (average 9-16 days, may be ≥30 days). In some cases, bleeding may be prolonged and heavy, potentially leading to hypovolemic shock; the manufacturer cites soaking through two thick sanitary pads per hour for two consecutive hours as an example of excessive bleeding. Bleeding may require blood transfusion (rare), curettage, saline infusions, and/or vasoconstrictors. Use caution in patients with severe anemia. Confirmation of pregnancy termination by clinical exam or ultrasound must be made 14 days following treatment. Manufacturer recommends surgical termination of pregnancy when medical termination fails or is not complete. Prescriber should determine in advance whether they will provide such care themselves or through other providers. Preventative measures to prevent rhesus immunization must be taken prior to surgical abortion. Prescriber should also give the patient clear instructions on whom to call and what to do in the event of an emergency following administration of mifepristone.

[U.S. Boxed Warning]: Bacterial infections have been reported following use of this product. In rare cases, these infections may be serious and/or fatal, with septic shock as a potential complication. A causal relationship has not been established. Sustained fever, abdominal pain, or pelvic tenderness should prompt evaluation; however, healthcare professionals are warned that atypical presentations of serious infection without these symptoms have also been noted. Patients presenting with nausea, vomiting, diarrhea, or weakness, with or without abdominal pain or fever, should be evaluated for serious bacterial infection when symptoms occur >24 hours after taking misoprostol. Treatment with antibiotics, including coverage for anaerobic bacteria (eg, *Clostridium sordellii*) should be initiated.

[U.S. Boxed Warning]: Patients undergoing treatment with mifepristone should be instructed to bring their Medication Guide with them when an obtaining treatment from an emergency room or healthcare provider that did not prescribe the medication initially in order to identify that they are undergoing a medical abortion.

Safety and efficacy have not been established for use in women with chronic cardiovascular, hypertensive, hepatic, respiratory, or renal disease, insulin-dependent diabetes mellitus, severe anemia, or heavy smokers. Women >35 years of age and smokers (>10 cigarettes/day) were excluded from clinical trials. Safety and efficacy in pediatric patients have not been established.

Adverse Reactions Vaginal bleeding and uterine cramping are expected to occur when this medication is used to terminate a pregnancy; 90% of women using this medication for this purpose also report adverse reactions. Bleeding or spotting occurs in most women for a period of 9-16 days. Up to 8% of women will experience some degree of bleeding or spotting for 30 days or more. In some cases, bleeding may be prolonged and heavy, potentially leading to hypovolemic shock.

>10%:
 Central nervous system: Headache (2% to 31%), dizziness (1% to 12%)
 Gastrointestinal: Abdominal pain (cramping) (96%), nausea (43% to 61%), vomiting (18% to 26%), diarrhea (12% to 20%)
 Genitourinary: Uterine cramping (83%)
1% to 10%:
 Cardiovascular: Syncope (1%)
 Central nervous system: Fatigue (10%), fever (4%), insomnia (3%), anxiety (2%), fainting (2%)
 Gastrointestinal: Dyspepsia (3%)
 Genitourinary: Uterine hemorrhage (5%), vaginitis (3%), pelvic pain (2%), endometriosis/salpingitis/pelvic inflammatory disease (1%)
 Hematologic: Decreased hemoglobin >2 g/dL (6%), anemia (2%), leukorrhea (2%)
 Neuromuscular & skeletal: Back pain (9%), rigors (3%), leg pain (2%), weakness (2%)
 Respiratory: Sinusitis (2%)
 Miscellaneous: Viral infection (4%)
<1%: Significant ALT/AST, alkaline phosphatase, and GT changes have been reported rarely
Postmarketing and/or case reports: Adult respiratory distress syndrome (ADRS), allergic reaction including urticaria and hives, bacterial infection
(Continued)

Mifepristone *(Continued)*

(including an ectopic bacteria such as *Clostridium sordellii*), Crohn's disease (exacerbation), disseminated intravascular coagulopathy (DIC), dyspnea, hypotension, lightheadedness, loss of consciousness, MI, pancreatitis (acute), postabortal infection, QT prolongation, ruptured ectopic pregnancy, sepsis, septic shock, sickle cell crisis (exacerbation), tachycardia, toxic shock syndrome

In trials for unresectable meningioma, the most common adverse effects included fatigue, hot flashes, gynecomastia or breast tenderness, hair thinning, and rash. In premenopausal women, vaginal bleeding may be seen shortly after beginning therapy and cessation of menses is common. Thyroiditis and effects related to antiglucocorticoid activity have also been noted.

Overdosage/Toxicology In studies using 3 times the recommended dose for termination of pregnancy, no serious maternal adverse effects were reported. This medication is supplied in single-dose containers to be given under physician supervision, therefore, the risk of overdose should be low. In case of massive ingestion, treat symptomatically and monitor for signs of adrenal failure.

Drug Interactions

Cytochrome P450 Effect: Substrate of CYP3A4 (minor); **Inhibits** CYP2D6 (weak), 3A4 (weak)

Increased Effect/Toxicity: There are no reported interactions. It might be anticipated that the concurrent administration of mifepristone and a progestin would result in an attenuation of the effects of one or both agents.

Ethanol/Nutrition/Herb Interactions

Food: Do not take with grapefruit juice; grapefruit juice may inhibit mifepristone metabolism leading to increased levels.

Herb/Nutraceutical: Avoid St John's wort (may induce mifepristone metabolism, leading to decreased levels).

Storage/Stability Store at room temperature of 25°C (77°F).

Mechanism of Action Mifepristone, a synthetic steroid, competitively binds to the intracellular progesterone receptor, blocking the effects of progesterone. When used for the termination of pregnancy, this leads to contraction-inducing activity in the myometrium. In the absence of progesterone, mifepristone acts as a partial progesterone agonist. Mifepristone also has weak antiglucocorticoid and antiandrogenic properties; it blocks the feedback effect of cortisol on corticotropin secretion.

Pharmacodynamics/Kinetics

Absorption: Oral: rapid

Protein binding: 98% to albumin and α_1-acid glycoprotein

Metabolism: Hepatic via CYP3A4 to three metabolites (may possess some antiprogestin and antiglucocorticoid activity)

Bioavailability: Oral: 69%

Half-life elimination: Terminal: 18 hours following a slower phase where 50% eliminated between 12-72 hours

Time to peak: Oral: 90 minutes

Excretion: Feces (83%); urine (9%)

Dosage Oral:

Adults:

Termination of pregnancy: Treatment consists of three office visits by the patient; the patient must read medication guide and sign patient agreement prior to treatment:

Day 1: 600 mg (three 200 mg tablets) taken as a single dose under physician supervision

Day 3: Patient must return to the healthcare provider 2 days following administration of mifepristone; unless abortion has occurred (confirmed using ultrasound or clinical examination): 400 mcg (two 200 mcg tablets) of misoprostol; patient may need treatment for cramps or gastrointestinal symptoms at this time

Day 14: Patient must return to the healthcare provider ~14 days after administration of mifepristone; confirm complete termination of pregnancy by ultrasound or clinical exam. Surgical termination is recommended to manage treatment failures.

Meningioma (unlabeled use): Refer to individual protocols. The dose used in meningioma is usually 200 mg/day, continued based on toxicity and response.

Elderly: Safety and efficacy have not been established

Dosage adjustment in renal impairment: Safety and efficacy have not been established

Dosage adjustment in hepatic impairment: Safety and efficacy have not been established; use with caution due to CYP3A4 metabolism

Monitoring Parameters Clinical exam and/or ultrasound to confirm complete termination of pregnancy; hemoglobin, hematocrit, and red blood cell count in cases of heavy bleeding. Consider CBC in any patient who reports nausea, vomiting, or diarrhea and weakness with or without abdominal pain, and without fever or other signs of infection more than 24 hours after administration of misoprostol.

Test Interactions hCG levels will not be useful to confirm pregnancy termination until at least 10 days following mifepristone treatment

Patient Information This medication is used to terminate pregnancy. It is not to be used for pregnancies >49 days (7 weeks). Vaginal bleeding and cramping are expected to occur and may require medical treatment if severe. Most women report that this is heavier bleeding than experienced during a heavy menstrual period. Other side effects that may be expected include abdominal pain, nausea, vomiting, and diarrhea. *Report symptoms that last more than 24 hours after misoprostol to your healthcare provider.* Follow-up with prescriber at approximately 3 days and 14 days following initial treatment. Surgical termination of pregnancy may be required if medication fails. There is a risk of fetal malformation if treatment fails. Your prescriber will give you a phone number to call for problems, questions, or emergencies; you should not use this medication if you do not have access to emergency care. It is possible to become pregnant again following treatment with this medication but before your next period starts. Contraception should be started once the pregnancy's end has been proven and before resuming sexual intercourse. You will be given a medication guide to help you understand this medication and its effects. It is important to review this carefully. Ask any questions you may have. You will also be required to sign a form saying that you understand the effects of this treatment and are able to return to the prescriber for follow-up appointments. Do not breast feed while using this medication.

(Continued)

Mifepristone *(Continued)*

Additional Information Medication will be distributed directly to qualified physicians following signed agreement with the distributor, Danco Laboratories. It will not be available through pharmacies. Major adverse reactions (hospitalization, blood transfusion, ongoing pregnancy, etc) should be reported to Danco Laboratories.

Emetic Potential Mild

Vesicant No

Dosage Forms Excipient information presented when available (limited, particularly for generics); consult specific product labeling.

Tablet: 200 mg

References

ACOG, ACOG Practice Bulletin, Clinical Management Guidelines of Obstetrician-Gynecologists, Number 67, October 2005, "Medical Management of Abortion," *Obstet Gynecol*, 2005, 106(4):871-82.

Fischer M, Bhatnagar J, Guarner J, et al, "Fatal Toxic Shock Syndrome Associated With *Clostridium sordellii* After Medical Abortion," *N Engl J Med*, 2005, 353(22):2352-60.

Gary M and Harrison D, "Analysis of Severe Adverse Events Related to the Use of Mifepristone as an Abortifacient," *Ann Pharmacother*, 2005, 40(2):191-7.

Grumberg SM, Weiss MH, Spitz IM, et al, "Treatment of Unresectable Meningiomas With the Antiprogesterone Agent Mifepristone," *J Neurosurg*, 1991, 74(6):861-6.

Perrault D, Eisenhauer EA, Pritchard KI, et al, "Phase II Study of the Progesterone Antagonist Mifepristone in Patients With Untreated Metastatic Breast Carcinoma: A National Cancer Institute of Canada Clinical Trials Group Study," *J Clin Oncol*, 1996, 14(10):2709-12.

Rocereto TF, Saul HM, Aikins JA, et al, "Phase II Study of Mifepristone (RU486) in Refractory Ovarian Cancer," *Gynecol Oncol*, 2000, 77(3):429-32.

Spitz IM and Bardin CW, "Mifepristone (RU486) - A Modulator of Progestin and Glucocorticoid Action," *N Engl J Med*, 1993, 329(6):404-12.

♦ **Minirin® (Can)** *see* Desmopressin *on page 326*

Mitomycin *(mye toe MYE sin)*

Medication Safety Issues

Sound-alike/look-alike issues:

Mitomycin may be confused with mithramycin, mitotane, mitoxantrone

High alert medication: The Institute for Safe Medication Practices (ISMP) includes this medication among its list of drugs which have a heightened risk of causing significant patient harm when used in error.

Related Information

Management of Drug Extravasations *on page 1301*

Safe Handling of Hazardous Drugs *on page 1382*

U.S. Brand Names Mutamycin®

Index Terms Mitomycin-C; Mitomycin-X; MTC; NSC-26980

Generic Available Yes

Canadian Brand Names Mutamycin®

Pharmacologic Category Antineoplastic Agent, Antibiotic

Use Treatment of adenocarcinoma of stomach or pancreas, bladder cancer, breast cancer, or colorectal cancer

Unlabeled/Investigational Use Prevention of excess scarring in glaucoma filtration procedures in patients at high risk of bleb failure

Pregnancy Risk Factor D

Lactation Enters breast milk/contraindicated

Labeled Contraindications Hypersensitivity to mitomycin or any component of the formulation; thrombocytopenia; coagulation disorders, increased bleeding tendency; pregnancy

Warnings/Precautions Hazardous agent - use appropriate precautions for handling and disposal. **[U.S. Boxed Warning]: May cause bone marrow**

suppression (thrombocytopenia and leukopenia); monitor for infections. Use with caution in patients who have received radiation therapy or in the presence of hepatobiliary dysfunction; reduce dosage in patients who are receiving radiation therapy simultaneously. Monitor for renal toxicity; do not administer if serum creatinine is >1.7 mg/dL. **[U.S. Boxed Warning]: Hemolytic-uremic syndrome, potentially fatal, has been reported;** is correlated with total dose (single doses ≥60 mg or cumulative doses ≥50 mg/m^2) and total duration of therapy (>5-11 months). Bladder fibrosis/contraction has been reported with intravesical administration. **Mitomycin is a potent vesicant, may cause ulceration, necrosis, cellulitis, and tissue sloughing if infiltrated.** Shortness of breath and bronchospasm have been reported in patients receiving vinca alkaloids in combination with or after mitomycin; may be managed with bronchodilators, steroids and/or oxygen. Safety and efficacy in children have not been established. **[U.S. Boxed Warning]: Should be administered under the supervision of an experienced cancer chemotherapy physician.**

Adverse Reactions

>10%:
  Cardiovascular: CHF (3% to 15%) (doses >30 mg/m^2)
  Central nervous system: Fever (14%)
  Dermatologic: Alopecia, nail banding/discoloration
  Gastrointestinal: Nausea, vomiting and anorexia (14%)
  Hematologic: Anemia (19% to 24%); myelosuppression, common, dose-limiting, delayed
    Onset: 3 weeks
    Nadir: 4-6 weeks
    Recovery: 6-8 weeks
1% to 10%:
  Dermatologic: Rash
  Gastrointestinal: Stomatitis
  Neuromuscular: Paresthesia
  Renal: Creatinine increased (2%)
  Respiratory: Interstitial pneumonitis, infiltrates, dyspnea, cough (7%)
<1%: Malaise, pruritus, extravasation reactions, hemolytic uremic syndrome, renal failure, bladder fibrosis/contraction (intravesical administration)

Overdosage/Toxicology
Symptoms of overdose include bone marrow suppression, nausea, vomiting, and alopecia. Treatment is symptom-directed and supportive.

Drug Interactions
Increased Effect/Toxicity: *Vinca* alkaloids or doxorubicin may enhance cardiac toxicity when coadministered with mitomycin.

Ethanol/Nutrition/Herb Interactions Herb/Nutraceutical: Avoid black cohosh, dong quai in estrogen-dependent tumors.

Storage/Stability Store intact vials at controlled room temperature. Mitomycin solution is stable for 7 days at room temperature and 14 days when refrigerated if protected from light. Solution of 0.5 mg/mL in a syringe is stable for 7 days at room temperature and 14 days when refrigerated and protected from light.
Further dilution to 20-40 mcg/mL:
  In normal saline: Stable for 12 hours at room temperature.
  In sodium lactate: Stable for 24 hours at room temperature.

Reconstitution Dilute powder with SWFI or 0.9% sodium chloride to a concentration of 0.5-1 mg/mL.

Compatibility Stable in LR; **variable stability (consult detailed reference)** in D$_5$W, NS.

(Continued)

Mitomycin *(Continued)*

Y-site administration: Compatible: Amifostine, bleomycin, cisplatin, cyclophosphamide, doxorubicin, droperidol, fluorouracil, furosemide, granisetron, heparin, leucovorin, melphalan, methotrexate, metoclopramide, ondansetron, teniposide, thiotepa, vinblastine, vincristine. **Incompatible:** Aztreonam, cefepime, etoposide phosphate, filgrastim, gemcitabine, piperacillin/tazobactam, sargramostim, topotecan, vinorelbine.

Compatibility in syringe: Compatible: Bleomycin, cisplatin, cyclophosphamide, doxorubicin, droperidol, fluorouracil, furosemide, heparin, leucovorin, methotrexate, metoclopramide, vinblastine, vincristine.

Compatibility when admixed: Compatible: Dexamethasone sodium phosphate, hydrocortisone sodium succinate. **Incompatible:** Bleomycin. **Variable (consult detailed reference):** Heparin.

Mechanism of Action Acts like an alkylating agent and produces DNA cross-linking (primarily with guanine and cytosine pairs); cell-cycle nonspecific; inhibits DNA and RNA synthesis; degrades preformed DNA, causes nuclear lysis and formation of giant cells. While not phase-specific *per se*, mitomycin has its maximum effect against cells in late G and early S phases.

Pharmacodynamics/Kinetics

Distribution: V_d: 22 L/m^2; high drug concentrations found in kidney, tongue, muscle, heart, and lung tissue; probably not distributed into the CNS

Metabolism: Hepatic

Half-life elimination: 23-78 minutes; Terminal: 50 minutes

Excretion: Urine (<10% as unchanged drug), with elevated serum concentrations

Dosage Refer to individual protocols. Children (unlabeled use) and Adults:

Single agent therapy: I.V.: 20 mg/m^2 every 6-8 weeks

Combination therapy: I.V.: 10 mg/m^2 every 6-8 weeks

Bladder carcinoma: Intravesical instillation (unapproved route): 20-40 mg instilled into the bladder and retained for 3 hours up to 3 times/week for up to 20 procedures per course

Glaucoma surgery (unlabeled use): 0.2-0.5 mg (0.2-0.5 mg/mL solution)

Dosage adjustment in renal impairment: The FDA-approved labeling states to avoid use in patients with serum creatine >1.7 mg/dL, but offers no other dosage adjustment guidelines. The following guidelines have been used by some clinicians (Aronoff, 2007): Adults:

Cl_{cr} <10 mL/minute: Administer 75% of dose

Continuous ambulatory peritoneal dialysis (CAPD): Administer 75% of dose

Dosage adjustment in hepatic impairment: Although some mitomycin may be excreted in the bile, no specific guidelines regarding dosage adjustment in hepatic impairment are available.

Combination Regimens

Breast cancer:

Mitomycin-Vinblastine *on page 1248*

VM *on page 1292*

Gastric cancer: FAM *on page 1211*

Pancreatic cancer: FAM *on page 1211*

Administration

I.V.: Administer slow I.V. push or by slow (15-30 minute) infusion via a freely-running dextrose or saline infusion. Consider using a central venous catheter.

Intravesicular (unlabeled route): Instill into bladder for up to 3 hours (rotate patient every 15-30 minutes)

Glaucoma surgery (unlabeled route): Apply to pledget and place in contact with surgical wound for 2-5 minutes (doses and techniques may vary)

Monitoring Parameters Platelet count, CBC with differential, hemoglobin, prothrombin time, renal and pulmonary function tests

Patient Information Make note of scheduled return dates. You may experience, rash, skin lesions, loss of hair, or permanent sterility. Small frequent meals may help if you experience nausea, vomiting, or loss of appetite. Frequent mouth care will help reduce the incidence of mouth sores. Use caution when driving or engaging in tasks that require alertness because you may experience dizziness, drowsiness, syncope, or blurred vision. Report difficulty breathing, swelling of extremities, or sudden weight gain; burning, pain, or redness at infusion site; unusual bruising or bleeding; pain on urination; or other adverse effects. The drug may be excreted in breast milk, therefore, an alternative form of feeding your baby should be used. Contraceptive measures are recommended during therapy.

Emetic Potential Mild (10% to 30%)

Vesicant Yes; see Management of Drug Extravasations *on page 1301.*

Dosage Forms Excipient information presented when available (limited, particularly for generics); consult specific product labeling.

Injection, powder for reconstitution: 5 mg, 20 mg, 40 mg

References

Aronoff GR, Bennett WM, Berns JS, et al, *Drug Prescribing in Renal Failure: Dosing Guidelines for Adults and Children,* 5th ed. Philadelphia, PA: American College of Physicians; 2007, p 101.

Bradner WT, "Mitomycin C: A Clinical Update," *Cancer Treat Rev,* 2001, 27(1):35-50.

den Hartigh J, Verweij J, and Pinedo HM, "Mitomycin C," *Cancer Chemother Biol Response Modif,* 1987, 9:56-62.

Doll DC, Weiss RB and Issell BF, "Mitomycin: Ten Years After Approval for Marketing," *J Clin Oncol,* 1985, 3(2):276-86.

Gandolfi SA, Vecchi M and Braccio L, "Decrease of Intraocular Pressure After Subconjunctival Injection of Mitomycin in Human Glaucoma," *Arch Ophthalmol,* 1995, 113(5):582-5.

Gibson NW, Phillips RM, and Ross D, "Mitomycin C," *Cancer Chemother Biol Response Modif,* 1994, 15:51-7.

Hortobagyi GN, "Mitomycin: Its Evolving Role in the Treatment of Breast Cancer," *Oncology,* 1993, 50(Suppl 1):1-8.

Rodriguez JA, Ferrari C, and Hernandez GA, "Intraoperative Application of Topical Mitomycin C 0.05% for Pterygium Surgery," *Bol Asoc Med P R,* 2004, 96(2):100-2.

Verweij J, "Mitomycins," *Cancer Chemother Biol Response Modif,* 1996, 16:48-56.

Verweij J and Pinedo HM, "Mitomycin C: Mechanism of Action, Usefulness and Limitations," *Anticancer Drugs,* 1990, 1(1):5-13.

Wilkins M, Indar A, and Wormald R, "Intra-Operative Mitomycin C for Glaucoma Surgery," *Cochrane Database Syst Rev,* 2001, (1):CD002897.

♦ **Mitomycin-X** *see* Mitomycin *on page 768*

♦ **Mitomycin-C** *see* Mitomycin *on page 768*

Mitotane (MYE toe tane)

Medication Safety Issues

Sound-alike/look-alike issues:

Mitotane may be confused with mitomycin

High alert medication: The Institute for Safe Medication Practices (ISMP) includes this medication among its list of drugs which have a heightened risk of causing significant patient harm when used in error.

Related Information

Safe Handling of Hazardous Drugs *on page 1382*

U.S. Brand Names Lysodren®

Index Terms NSC-38721; o,p'-DDD

Generic Available No

(Continued)

Mitotane *(Continued)*

Canadian Brand Names Lysodren®

Pharmacologic Category Antineoplastic Agent, Miscellaneous

Use Treatment of adrenocortical carcinoma

Unlabeled/Investigational Use Treatment of Cushing's syndrome

Pregnancy Risk Factor C

Lactation Excretion in breast milk unknown/not recommended

Labeled Contraindications Hypersensitivity to mitotane or any component of the formulation

Warnings/Precautions Hazardous agent - use appropriate precautions for handling and disposal. Steroid replacement with glucocorticoid, and sometimes mineralocorticoid, is necessary. It has been recommended that replacement therapy be initiated at the start of therapy, rather than waiting for evidence of adrenal insufficiency. Because mitotane can increase the metabolism of hydrocortisone, higher than usual replacement doses of the latter may be required. Surgically remove tumor tissues from metastatic masses prior to initiation of treatment; rapid cytotoxic effect may cause tumor hemorrhage. Observe patients for neurotoxicity with long-term (>2 years) use. Use caution with hepatic impairment; metabolism may be decreased. **[U.S. Boxed Warnings]: Acute adrenal insufficiency may occur in the face of shock, trauma, or infection. Mitotane should be discontinued temporarily in this setting and appropriate steroid coverage should be administered. Should be administered under the supervision of an experienced cancer chemotherapy physician.** Safety and efficacy in children have not been established.

Adverse Reactions

>10%:

Central nervous system: CNS depression (32%), somnolence (25%), dizziness/vertigo (15%)

Dermatologic: Skin rash (15%)

Gastrointestinal: Anorexia (24%), nausea (39%), vomiting (37%), diarrhea (13%)

Neuromuscular & skeletal: Weakness (12%)

1% to 10%:

Central nervous system: Headache (5%), confusion (3%)

Neuromuscular & skeletal: Muscle tremor (3%)

<1% and/or frequency not defined: Albuminuria, blurred vision, diplopia, flushing, hematuria, hemorrhagic cystitis, hypertension, hyperpyrexia, lens opacity, myalgia, orthostatic hypotension, protein bound iodine decreased, toxic retinopathy

Overdosage/Toxicology Symptoms of overdose include diarrhea, vomiting, numbness of limbs, and weakness. Treatment is symptom-directed and supportive.

Drug Interactions

Decreased Effect: Potassium-sparing diuretics (spironolactone) may decrease the effect of mitotane. Mitotane may decrease the effects of warfarin.

Ethanol/Nutrition/Herb Interactions Ethanol: Avoid ethanol (may increase CNS depression).

Storage/Stability Store at room temperature.

Mechanism of Action Causes adrenal cortical atrophy; drug affects mitochondria in adrenal cortical cells and decreases production of cortisol; also alters the peripheral metabolism of steroids

Pharmacodynamics/Kinetics

Absorption: Oral: ~35% to 40%

Distribution: Stored mainly in fat tissue but is found in all body tissues

Metabolism: Hepatic and other tissues

Half-life elimination: 18-159 days

Time to peak, serum: 3-5 hours

Excretion: Urine (10% as metabolites) and feces (1% to 17% as metabolites)

Dosage Adrenocortical carcinoma: Oral:

Children (unlabeled use): 1-2 g/day in divided doses, increasing gradually to a maximum of 5-7 g/day

Adults: Start at 2-6 g/day in 3-4 divided doses, then increase incrementally to 9-10 g/day in 3-4 divided doses (maximum daily dose: 18 g)

Dosing adjustment in hepatic impairment: Dose may need to be decreased in patients with liver disease

Monitoring Parameters Adrenal function; neurologic assessments with chronic (>2 years) use

Patient Information Desired effects of this drug may not be seen for 2-3 months. Wear identification that alerts medical personnel that you are taking this drug in event of shock or trauma. Maintain adequate hydration (2-3 L/day of fluids unless instructed to restrict fluid intake) and nutrition. May cause dizziness and vertigo (avoid driving or performing tasks requiring alertness until response to drug is known); nausea, vomiting, or loss of appetite (small frequent meals, frequent mouth care, sucking lozenges, or chewing gum may help); orthostatic hypotension (use caution when rising from sitting or lying position or climbing stairs); muscle aches or pain (if severe, request medication from prescriber). Report severe vomiting or acute loss of appetite, muscular twitching, fever or infection, blood in urine or pain on urinating, or darkening of skin. Contraceptive measures are recommended during therapy.

Emetic Potential Moderate (30% to 60%)

Dosage Forms Excipient information presented when available (limited, particularly for generics); consult specific product labeling.

Tablet [scored]:

Lysodren®: 500 mg

References

Boscaro M, Barzon L, Fallo F, et al, "Cushing's Syndrome," *Lancet*, 2001, 357(9258):783-91.

De Leon DD, Lange BJ, Walterhouse D, et al, "Long-Term (15 years) Outcome in an Infant with Metastatic Adrenocortical Carcinoma," *J Clin Endocrinol Metab*, 2002, 87(10):4452-6.

Kasperlik-Zaluska AA, "Clinical Results of the Use of Mitotane for Adrenocortical Carcinoma," *Braz J Med Biol Res*, 2000, 33(10):1191-6.

Newell-Price J, Bertagna X, Grossman AB, et al, "Cushing's Syndrome," *Lancet*, 2006, 367(9522):1605-17.

Rodriguez-Galindo C, Figueiredo BC, Zambetti GP, et al, "Biology, Clinical Characteristics, and Management of Adrenocortical Tumors in Children," *Pediatr Blood Cancer*, 2005, 45(3):265-73.

Mitoxantrone (mye toe ZAN trone)

Medication Safety Issues

Sound-alike/look-alike issues:

Mitoxantrone may be confused with methotrexate, mitomycin

High alert medication: The Institute for Safe Medication Practices (ISMP) includes this medication among its list of drugs which have a heightened risk of causing significant patient harm when used in error.

Related Information

Hematopoietic Stem Cell Transplantation *on page 1366*

Management of Drug Extravasations *on page 1301*

Safe Handling of Hazardous Drugs *on page 1382*

(Continued)

Mitoxantrone *(Continued)*

U.S. Brand Names Novantrone®

Index Terms DAD; DHAD; DHAQ; Dihydroxyanthracenedione Dihydrochloride; Mitoxantrone Hydrochloride CL-232315; Mitozantrone; NSC-301739

Generic Available Yes

Canadian Brand Names Mitoxantrone Injection®; Novantrone®

Pharmacologic Category Antineoplastic Agent, Anthracenedione

Use Treatment of acute leukemias, lymphoma, breast cancer, pediatric sarcoma, secondary progressive or relapsing-remitting multiple sclerosis, prostate cancer

Pregnancy Risk Factor D

Lactation Enters breast milk/contraindicated

Labeled Contraindications Hypersensitivity to mitoxantrone or any component of the formulation; multiple sclerosis with left ventricular ejection fraction (LVEF) <50% or clinically significant decrease in LVEF

Warnings/Precautions Hazardous agent - use appropriate precautions for handling and disposal.

[U.S. Boxed Warning]: Do not use if baseline neutrophil count <1500 cells/mm³ (except for treatment of ANLL). Treatment may lead to severe myelosuppression; use with caution in patients with pre-existing myelosuppression.

[U.S. Boxed Warning]: May cause myocardial toxicity and potentially-fatal CHF; risk increases with cumulative dosing. Effects may be delayed. Predisposing factors for mitoxantrone-induced cardiotoxicity include prior anthracycline therapy, prior cardiovascular disease, concomitant use of cardiotoxic drugs, and mediastinal/pericardial irradiation. Not recommended for use when left ventricular ejection fraction (LVEF) <50%. Use in multiple sclerosis should be limited to a cumulative dose of ≤140 mg/m², and discontinued if a significant decrease in LVEF is observed.

[U.S. Boxed Warnings]: For I.V. administration only; may cause severe local tissue damage if extravasation occurs. Do not administer intrathecally; may cause serious and permanent neurologic damage. May cause urine, saliva, tears, and sweat to turn blue-green for 24 hours postinfusion. Whites of eyes may have blue-green tinge. **[U.S. Boxed Warning]: Has been associated with the development of secondary acute myelogenous leukemia and myelodysplasia.**

[U.S. Boxed Warning]: Should be administered under the supervision of an experienced cancer chemotherapy physician. Dosage should be reduced in patients with impaired hepatobiliary function; not for treatment of multiple sclerosis in patients with concurrent hepatic impairment. Not for treatment of primary progressive multiple sclerosis. Safety and efficacy in children have not been established.

Adverse Reactions Includes events reported with any indication; incidence varies based on treatment/dose

>10%:

Cardiovascular: Arrhythmia (3% to 18%), edema (10% to 31%), ECG changes (11%)

Central nervous system: Pain (8% to 41%), fatigue (up to 39%), fever (6% to 78%), headache (6% to 13%)

Dermatologic: Alopecia (20% to 61%), nail bed changes (11%)

Endocrine & metabolic: Amenorrhea (28% to 53%), menstrual disorder (26% to 61%), hyperglycemia (10% to 31%)

Gastrointestinal: Abdominal pain (9% to 15%), anorexia (22% to 25%), nausea (26% to 76%), constipation (10% to 16%), diarrhea (14% to 47%), GI bleeding (2% to 16%), mucositis (10% to 29%), stomatitis (8% to 29%), dyspepsia (5% to 14%), vomiting (6% to 11%), weight gain/loss (13% to 17%)

Genitourinary: Abnormal urine (6% to 11%), urinary tract infection (7% to 32%)

Hematologic: Neutropenia (79% to 100%), leukopenia (9% to 100%), lymphopenia (72% to 95%), anemia (5% to 75%), hemoglobin decreased (43%), thrombocytopenia (33% to 39%), petechiae/bruising (6% to 11%); myelosuppression (WBC: mild; platelets: mild; onset: 7-10 days; nadir: 14 days; recovery: 21 days)

Hepatic: Alkaline phosphatase increased (37%), transaminases increased (5% to 20%), GGT increased (3% to 15%)

Neuromuscular & skeletal: Weakness (24%)

Renal: BUN increased (22%), creatinine increased (13%), hematuria (11%)

Respiratory: Cough (5% to 13%), dyspnea (6% to 18%), upper respiratory tract infection (7% to 53%)

Miscellaneous: Fungal infection (9% to 15%), infection (4% to 18%), sepsis (ANLL 31% to 34%)

1% to 10%:

Cardiovascular: Ischemia (5%), LVEF decreased (≤5%), hypertension (4%), CHF (2% to 5%, risk is much lower with anthracyclines, some reports suggest cumulative doses >160 mg/mL cause CHF in ~10% of patients)

Central nervous system: Chills (5%), anxiety (5%), depression (5%), seizure (2% to 4%)

Dermatologic: Skin infection

Endocrine & metabolic: Hypocalcemia (10%), hypokalemia (7% to 10%), hyponatremia (9%), menorrhagia (7%)

Gastrointestinal: Aphthosis (10%)

Genitourinary: Impotence (7%), sterility (5%)

Hematologic: Granulocytopenia (6%), hemorrhage (6%)

Hepatic: Jaundice (3% to 7%)

Neuromuscular & skeletal: Back pain (8%), myalgia (5%), arthralgia (5%)

Ocular: Conjunctivitis (5%), blurred vision (3%)

Renal: Renal failure (8%), proteinuria (6%)

Respiratory: Rhinitis (10%), pneumonia (9%), sinusitis (6%)

Miscellaneous: Systemic infection, diaphoresis (9%), development of secondary leukemia (~1% to 2%)

<1% or frequency not defined: Acute leukemia, allergic reaction, anaphylactoid reactions, anaphylaxis, chest pain, extravasation and phlebitis at the infusion site, interstitial pneumonitis (has occurred during combination chemotherapy), irritant chemotherapy with blue skin discoloration, rash, tachycardia

Overdosage/Toxicology Symptoms of overdose include leukopenia, tachycardia, and marrow hypoplasia. No known antidote. Treatment is symptom-directed and supportive.

Drug Interactions

Cytochrome P450 Effect: Inhibits CYP3A4 (weak)

Decreased Effect: Patients may experience impaired immune response to vaccines; possible infection after administration of live vaccines in patients receiving immunosuppressants.

Ethanol/Nutrition/Herb Interactions Herb/Nutraceutical: Avoid black cohosh, dong quai in estrogen-dependent tumors.

(Continued)

Mitoxantrone *(Continued)*

Storage/Stability Store intact vials at 15°C to 25°C (59°F to 77°F); do not freeze. Opened vials may be stored at room temperature for 7 days or under refrigeration for up to 14 days. Solutions diluted for administration are stable for 7 days at room temperature or under refrigeration.

Reconstitution Dilute in at least 50 mL of NS or D_5W.

Compatibility Stable in D_5NS, D_5W, NS.

Y-site administration: Compatible: Allopurinol, amifostine, cladribine, etoposide phosphate, filgrastim, fludarabine, gatifloxacin, gemcitabine, granisetron, linezolid, melphalan, ondansetron, sargramostim, teniposide, thiotepa, vinorelbine. **Incompatible:** Amphotericin B cholesteryl sulfate complex, aztreonam, cefepime, doxorubicin liposome, paclitaxel, piperacillin/tazobactam, propofol.

Compatibility when admixed: Compatible: Cyclophosphamide, cytarabine, fluorouracil, hydrocortisone sodium succinate, potassium chloride. **Incompatible:** Heparin. **Variable (consult detailed reference):** Hydrocortisone sodium phosphate.

Mechanism of Action Analogue of the anthracyclines, mitoxantrone intercalates DNA; binds to nucleic acids and inhibits DNA and RNA synthesis by template disordering and steric obstruction; replication is decreased by binding to DNA topoisomerase II and seems to inhibit the incorporation of uridine into RNA and thymidine into DNA; active throughout entire cell cycle

Pharmacodynamics/Kinetics

Absorption: Oral: Poor

Distribution: V_d: 14 L/kg; distributes into pleural fluid, kidney, thyroid, liver, heart, and red blood cells

Protein binding: >95%, 76% to albumin

Metabolism: Hepatic; pathway not determined

Half-life elimination: Terminal: 23-215 hours; may be prolonged with hepatic impairment

Excretion: Urine (6% to 11%; 65% as unchanged drug); feces (25%; 65% as unchanged drug)

Dosage Refer to individual protocols. I.V. (dilute in D_5W or NS):

Acute leukemias:

Children ≤2 years (unlabeled use): 0.4 mg/kg/day once daily for 3-5 days

Children >2 years (unlabeled use): 8-12 mg/m^2/day once daily for 4-5 days

Adults:

Induction: 12 mg/m^2 once daily for 3 days; for incomplete response, may repeat at 12 mg/m^2 once daily for 2 days

Consolidation: 12 mg/m^2 once daily for 2 days, repeat in 4 weeks

Solid tumors:

Children (unlabeled use): 18-20 mg/m^2 every 3-4 weeks **or** 5-8 mg/m^2 every week

Adults: 12-14 mg/m^2 every 3-4 weeks **or** 2-4 mg/m^2/day for 5 days every 4 weeks

Hormone-refractory prostate cancer: Adults: 12-14 mg/m^2 every 3 weeks

Multiple sclerosis: Adults: 12 mg/m^2 every 3 months (maximum lifetime cumulative dose: 140 mg/m^2

Dosing adjustment in renal impairment: Safety and efficacy have not been established

Hemodialysis: Supplemental dose is not necessary

Peritoneal dialysis: Supplemental dose is not necessary

Elderly: Clearance is decreased in elderly patients; use with caution

Dosing adjustment in hepatic impairment: Official dosage adjustment recommendations have not been established. Clearance is reduced in hepatic dysfunction; patients with severe hepatic dysfunction (bilirubin >3.4 mg/dL) have an AUC of 3 times greater than patients with normal hepatic function. Consider dose adjustments. **Note:** MS patients with hepatic impairment should not receive mitoxantrone.

Combination Regimens

Breast cancer:

CNF *on page 1179*

NFL *on page 1261*

Leukemia, acute lymphocytic: FIS-HAM *on page 1214*

Leukemia, acute myeloid:

7 + 3 (Mitoxantrone) *on page 1140*

EMA 86 *on page 1199*

FIS-HAM *on page 1214*

MV *on page 1255*

Leukemia, acute promyelocytic: Tretinoin-Idarubicin *on page 1283*

Lymphoma, non-Hodgkin's:

CNOP *on page 1179*

MINE *on page 1247*

MINE-ESHAP *on page 1247*

Prostate cancer:

Mitoxantrone + Hydrocortisone *on page 1248*

MP (Prostate Cancer) *on page 1254*

Administration Administered as a short (5-30 minutes) I.V. infusion; continuous 24-hour infusions are occasionally used. Although not generally recommended, mitoxantrone has been given as a rapid bolus over 1-3 minutes. High doses for bone marrow transplant are usually given as 1- to 4-hour infusions.

Monitoring Parameters CBC, serum uric acid (for treatment of leukemia), liver function tests, signs and symptoms of CHF; evaluate LVEF prior to start of therapy and regularly during treatment, especially with the development of signs and symptoms of CHF. In addition, for the treatment of multiple sclerosis, obtain pregnancy test and monitor LVEF prior to all doses

Patient Information This drug can only be given I.V. Make note of scheduled return dates. Your urine may turn blue-green for 24 hours after infusion and the whites of your eyes may have a blue-green tinge; this is normal. Maintain adequate hydration (2-3 L/day of fluids unless instructed to restrict fluid intake) and nutrition. You may experience rash, skin lesions, or loss of hair. Small frequent meals may help if you experience nausea, vomiting, or loss of appetite. Frequent mouth care will help reduce the incidence of mouth sores. Use caution when driving or engaging in tasks that require alertness because you may experience dizziness, drowsiness, syncope, or blurred vision. Report chest pain or heart palpitations; difficulty breathing or constant cough; swelling of extremities or sudden weight gain; burning, pain, or redness at the I.V. infusion site; persistent fever or chills; unusual bruising or bleeding; twitching or tremors; or pain on urination. Contraceptive measures are recommended during therapy.

Emetic Potential Moderate (30% to 60%)

Vesicant No; may be an irritant

High Dose Considerations

Comments: Extensive pretreatment with anthracyclines increases risk of cardiac toxicity.

(Continued)

Mitoxantrone *(Continued)*

High Dose: I.V.: 24-48 mg/m^2 as a single dose; duration of infusion is 1-4 hours; total doses of 75-90 mg/m^2 have been used. Generally combined with other high-dose chemotherapeutic drugs.

Unique Toxicities:

Cardiovascular: Bradycardia (infusion-related), heart failure

Dermatologic: Alopecia

Gastrointestinal: Severe mucositis, skin discoloration

Dosage Forms Excipient information presented when available (limited, particularly for generics); consult specific product labeling. [DSC] = Discontinued product

Injection, solution: 2 mg/mL (10 mL, 12.5 mL, 15 mL)

Novantrone®: 2 mg/mL (10 mL; 12.5 mL [DSC]; 15 mL)

References

Birchall LA, Bailey NP, and Blackledge GR, "An Overview of Mitozantrone," *Br J Clin Pract*, 1991, 45(3):208-11.

Donelli MG, Zuchetti M, Munzone E, et al, "Pharmacokinetics of Anticancer Agents in Patients With Impaired Liver Function," *Eur J Cancer*, 1998, 34(1):33-46.

Dunn CJ and Goa KL, "Mitoxantrone: A Review of Its Pharmacological Properties and Use in Acute Nonlymphoblastic Leukaemia," *Drugs Aging*, 1996, 9(2):122-47.

Ehninger G, Schuler U, Proksch B, et al, "Pharmacokinetics and Metabolism of Mitoxantrone. A Review,"*Clin Pharmacokinet*, 1990, 18(5):365-80.

Faulds D, Balfour JA, Chrisp P, et al, "Mitoxantrone. A Review of Its Pharmacodynamic and Pharmacokinetic Properties, and Therapeutic Potential in the Chemotherapy of Cancer," *Drugs*, 1991, 41(3):400-49.

Jeffrey LP, Chairman, National Study Commission on Cytotoxic Exposure. Position Statement. "The Handling of Cytotoxic Agents by Women Who Are Pregnant, Attempting to Conceive, or Breast-Feeding," January 12, 1987.

Koeller J and Eble M, "Mitoxantrone: A Novel Anthracycline Derivative," *Clin Pharm*, 1988, 7(8):574-81.

LeMaistre CF and Herzig R, "Mitoxantrone: Potential for Use in Intensive Therapy," *Semin Oncol*, 1990, 17(1 Suppl 3):43-8.

Lenk H, Muller U, and Tanneberger S, "Mitoxantrone: Mechanism of Action, Antitumor Activity, Pharmacokinetics, Efficacy in the Treatment of Solid Tumors and Lymphomas, and Toxicity," *Anticancer Res*, 1987, 7(6):1257-64.

Nathanson L, "Mitoxantrone," *Cancer Treat Rev*, 1984, 11(4):289-93.

Poirier TI, "Mitoxantrone," *Drug Intell Clin Pharm*, 1986, 20(2):97-105.

Pratt CB, Vietti TJ, Etcubanas E, et al, "Novantrone® for Childhood Malignant Solid Tumors. A Pediatric Oncology Group Phase II Study," *Invest New Drugs*, 1986, 4(1):43-8.

Scott LJ and Figgitt DP, "Mitoxantrone: A Review of its Use in Multiple Sclerosis," *CNS Drugs*, 2004, 18(6):379-96.

Shenkenberg TD and Von Hoff DD, "Mitoxantrone: A New Anticancer Drug With Significant Clinical Activity," *Ann Intern Med*, 1986, 105(1):67-81.

Wiseman LR and Spencer CM, "Mitoxantrone. A Review of its Pharmacology and Clinical Efficacy in the Management of Hormone-Resistant Advanced Prostate Cancer," *Drugs Aging*, 1997, 10(6):473-85.

Morphine Sulfate (MOR feen SUL fate)

Medication Safety Issues

Sound-alike/look-alike issues:

Morphine may be confused with hydromorphone

Morphine sulfate may be confused with magnesium sulfate

MSO₄ is an error-prone abbreviation (mistaken as magnesium sulfate)

Avinza® may be confused with Evista®, Invanz®

Roxanol™ may be confused with OxyFast®, Roxicet™

Use care when prescribing and/or administering morphine solutions. These products are available in different concentrations. Always prescribe dosage in mg; **not** by volume (mL).

Use caution when selecting a morphine formulation for use in neurologic infusion pumps (eg, Medtronic delivery systems). The product should be appropriately labeled as "preservative-free" and suitable for intraspinal use via continuous infusion. In addition, the product should be formulated in a pH range that is compatible with the device operation specifications.

Significant differences exist between oral and I.V. dosing. Use caution when converting from one route of administration to another.

U.S. Brand Names Astramorph/PF™; Avinza®; DepoDur™; Duramorph®; Infumorph®; Kadian®; MS Contin®; Oramorph SR®; RMS® [DSC]; Roxanol™

Index Terms MSO₄ (error-prone abbreviation and should not be used)

Generic Available Yes: Excludes capsule, controlled release tablet, sustained release tablet, extended release liposomal suspension for injection

Canadian Brand Names Kadian®; M-Eslon®; Morphine HP®; Morphine LP® Epidural; M.O.S.® 10; M.O.S.® 20; M.O.S.® 30; M.O.S.-SR®; M.O.S.-Sulfate®; MS Contin®; MS-IR®; PMS-Morphine Sulfate SR; ratio-Morphine SR; Statex®; Zomorph®

Pharmacologic Category Analgesic, Opioid

Use Relief of moderate to severe acute and chronic pain; relief of pain of myocardial infarction; relief of dyspnea of acute left ventricular failure and pulmonary edema; preanesthetic medication

DepoDur™: Epidural (lumbar) single-dose management of surgical pain

Infumorph®: Used in microinfusion devices for intraspinal administration in treatment of intractable chronic pain

Restrictions C-II

Pregnancy Risk Factor C/D (prolonged use or high doses at term)

Lactation Enters breast milk/use caution (AAP rates "compatible")

Labeled Contraindications Hypersensitivity to morphine sulfate or any component of the formulation; increased intracranial pressure; severe respiratory depression; acute or severe asthma; known or suspected paralytic ileus; sustained release products are not recommended with gastrointestinal obstruction or in acute/postoperative pain; pregnancy (prolonged use or high doses at term)

Warnings/Precautions An opioid-containing analgesic regimen should be tailored to each patient's needs and based upon the type of pain being treated (acute versus chronic), the route of administration, degree of tolerance for opioids (naive versus chronic user), age, weight, and medical condition. The optimal analgesic dose varies widely among patients. Doses should be titrated to pain relief/prevention. When used as an epidural injection, monitor for delayed sedation.

May cause respiratory depression; use with caution in patients (particularly elderly or debilitated) with impaired respiratory function, morbid obesity, (Continued)

Morphine Sulfate *(Continued)*

adrenal insufficiency, prostatic hyperplasia, urinary stricture, renal impairment, or severe hepatic dysfunction and in patients with hypersensitivity reactions to other phenanthrene derivative opioid agonists (codeine, hydrocodone, hydromorphone, levorphanol, oxycodone, oxymorphone). Use with caution in patients with biliary tract dysfunction; acute pancreatitis may cause constriction of sphincter of Oddi. Some preparations contain sulfites which may cause allergic reactions; infants <3 months of age are more susceptible to respiratory depression, use with caution and generally in reduced doses in this age group. May cause CNS depression, which may impair physical or mental abilities; patients must be cautioned about performing tasks which require mental alertness (eg, operating machinery or driving). Effects may be potentiated when used with other sedative drugs or ethanol. May cause hypotension in patients with acute myocardial infarction, volume depletion, or concurrent drug therapy which may exaggerate vasodilation. Use with extreme caution in patients with head injury, intracranial lesions, or elevated intracranial pressure; exaggerated elevation of ICP may occur. May obscure diagnosis or clinical course of patients with acute abdominal conditions. Tolerance or drug dependence may result from extended use. Concurrent use of agonist/antagonist analgesics may precipitate withdrawal symptoms and/or reduced analgesic efficacy in patients following prolonged therapy with mu opioid agonists. Abrupt discontinuation following prolonged use may also lead to withdrawal symptoms. Elderly may be particularly susceptible to adverse effects of narcotics.

Extended or sustained-release formulations:

[U.S. Boxed Warning]: **Extended or sustained release dosage forms should not be crushed or chewed.** Controlled-, extended-, or sustained-release products are not intended for "as needed (PRN)" use. MS Contin® 100 or 200 mg tablets are for use only in opioid-tolerant patients requiring >400 mg/day.

[U.S. Boxed Warning]: Avinza®: **Do not administer with alcoholic beverages or ethanol-containing products, which may disrupt extended-release characteristic of product.**

Injections: Note: Products are designed for administration by specific routes (I.V., intrathecal, epidural). Use caution when prescribing, dispensing, or administering to use formulations only by intended route(s).

[U.S. Boxed Warning]: Duramorph®: **Due to the risk of severe and/or sustained cardiopulmonary depressant effects of Duramorph® must be administered in a fully equipped and staffed environment.** Naloxone injection should be immediately available. Patient should remain in this environment for at least 24 hours following the initial dose.

Infumorph® solutions are **for use in microinfusion devices only**; not for I.V., I.M., or SubQ administration.

Depo-Dur™: **For epidural administration only.** Intrathecal administration has resulted in prolonged respiratory depression. Freezing may adversely affect modified-release mechanism of drug; check freeze indicator within carton prior to administration.

Adverse Reactions Note: Individual patient differences are unpredictable, and percentage may differ in acute pain (surgical) treatment.

Frequency not defined: Flushing, CNS depression, sedation, antidiuretic hormone release, physical and psychological dependence, diaphoresis

>10%:

Cardiovascular: Palpitation, hypotension, bradycardia

Central nervous system: Drowsiness (48%, tolerance usually develops to drowsiness with regular dosing for 1-2 weeks); dizziness (20%), confusion, headache (following epidural or intrathecal use)

Dermatologic: Pruritus (may be secondary to histamine release)

Note: Pruritus may be dose-related, but not confined to the site of administration.

Gastrointestinal: Nausea (28%, tolerance usually develops to nausea and vomiting with chronic use); constipation (40%, tolerance develops very slowly if at all); xerostomia (78%)

Genitourinary: Urinary retention (16%; may be prolonged, up to 20 hours, following epidural or intrathecal use)

Local: Pain at injection site

Neuromuscular & skeletal: Weakness

Miscellaneous: Histamine release

1% to 10%:

Cardiovascular: Atrial fibrillation (<3%), chest pain (<3%), edema (<3%), syncope (<3%), tachycardia (<3%)

Central nervous system: Amnesia, anxiety, apathy, ataxia, chills, depression, euphoria, false feeling of well being, fever, headache, hypoesthesia, insomnia, lethargy, malaise, restlessness, seizure, vertigo

Endocrine & metabolic: Gynecomastia (<3%), hyponatremia (<3%)

Gastrointestinal: Anorexia, biliary colic, dyspepsia, dysphagia, GERD, GI irritation, paralytic ileus, vomiting (9%)

Genitourinary: Decreased urination

Hematologic: Anemia (<3%), leukopenia (<3%), thrombocytopenia (<3%)

Neuromuscular & skeletal: Arthralgia, back pain, bone pain, paresthesia, trembling

Ocular: Vision problems

Respiratory: Asthma, atelectasis, dyspnea, hiccups, hypoxia, noncardiogenic pulmonary edema, respiratory depression, rhinitis

Miscellaneous: Diaphoresis, flu-like syndrome, withdrawal syndrome

<1%: Amenorrhea, anaphylaxis, biliary tract spasm, hallucinations, intestinal obstruction, intracranial pressure increased, liver function tests increased, menstrual irregularities, mental depression, miosis, muscle rigidity, myoclonus, oliguria, paradoxical CNS stimulation, peripheral vasodilation, urinary tract spasm, transaminases increased

Overdosage/Toxicology Symptoms of overdose include respiratory depression, miosis, hypotension, bradycardia, apnea, and pulmonary edema. Treatment is symptomatic. Naloxone, 2 mg I.V. with repeat administration as necessary up to a total dose of 10 mg, can be used to reverse opiate effects.

Drug Interactions

Cytochrome P450 Effect: Substrate of CYP2D6 (minor)

Increased Effect/Toxicity: Antipsychotic agents may increase the hypotensive effects of morphine. Use of selective serotonin reuptake inhibitors (SSRIs) or meperidine may lead to additive serotonergic effects with concomitant morphine, possibly precipitating serotonin syndrome. CNS depressants and tricyclic antidepressants may potentiate the effects of morphine. Concurrent use of MAO inhibitors and meperidine has been associated with significant adverse effects; use caution with morphine. Some manufacturers recommend avoiding use within 14 days of MAO inhibitors.

Decreased Effect: The therapeutic efficacy of pegvisomant may be decreased by concomitant opiates, possibly requiring dosage adjustment
(Continued)

Morphine Sulfate *(Continued)*

of pegvisomant. Rifamycin derivatives may decrease levels or effects of morphine.

Ethanol/Nutrition/Herb Interactions

Ethanol: Avoid ethanol (may increase CNS depression).

Avinza®: Alcoholic beverages or ethanol-containing products may disrupt extended-release formulation resulting in rapid release of entire morphine dose.

Food: Administration of oral morphine solution with food may increase bioavailability (ie, a report of 34% increase in morphine AUC when morphine oral solution followed a high-fat meal). The bioavailability of Oramorph SR® or Kadian® does not appear to be affected by food.

Herb/Nutraceutical: Avoid valerian, St John's wort, kava kava, gotu kola (may increase CNS depression).

Storage/Stability

Capsule, sustained release (Kadian®): Store at controlled room temperature 15°C to 30°C (59°F to 86°F). Protect from light and moisture.

Suppositories: Store at controlled room temperature 25°C (77°F). Protect from light.

Injection: Store at controlled room temperature. Protect from light. Degradation depends on pH and presence of oxygen; relatively stable in pH ≤4; darkening of solutions indicate degradation.

DepoDur™: Store under refrigeration, 2°C to 8°C (36°F to 46°F); do not freeze. Check freeze indicator before administration; do not administer if bulb is pink or purple. May store at room temperature for up to 30 days in sealed, unopened vials. Gently invert to suspend particles prior to removal from vial. Once vial is opened, use within 4 hours.

Reconstitution Usual concentration for continuous I.V. infusion: 0.1-1 mg/mL in D_5W. DepoDur™ may be diluted in preservative-free NS to a volume of 5 mL.

Compatibility Stable in dextran 6% in dextrose, dextran 6% in NS, D_5LR, $D_5^1/_4NS$, $D_5^1/_2NS$, D_5NS, D_5W, $D_{10}W$, LR, $^1/_2NS$, NS; **variable stability (consult detailed reference)** in TPN.

Y-site administration: Compatible: Allopurinol, amifostine, amikacin, aminophylline, amiodarone, ampicillin, ampicillin/sulbactam, amsacrine, atenolol, atracurium, aztreonam, bumetanide, calcium chloride, cefamandole, cefazolin, cefoperazone, cefotaxime, cefotetan, cefoxitin, ceftazidime, ceftizoxime, ceftriaxone, cefuroxime, chloramphenicol, cisatracurium, cisplatin, cladribine, clindamycin, co-trimoxazole, cyclophosphamide, cytarabine, dexamethasone sodium phosphate, digoxin, diltiazem, dobutamine, docetaxel, dopamine, doxorubicin, doxycycline, enalaprilat, epinephrine, erythromycin lactobionate, esmolol, etomidate, etoposide phosphate, famotidine, fentanyl, filgrastim, fluconazole, fludarabine, foscarnet, gatifloxacin, gemcitabine, gentamicin, granisetron, heparin, hydrocortisone sodium succinate, hydromorphone, IL-2, insulin (regular), kanamycin, labetalol, levofloxacin, lidocaine, linezolid, lorazepam, magnesium sulfate, melphalan, meropenem, methotrexate, methyldopate, methylprednisolone sodium succinate, metoclopramide, metoprolol, metronidazole, midazolam, milrinone, nafcillin, nicardipine, nitroglycerin, norepinephrine, ondansetron, oxacillin, oxytocin, paclitaxel, pancuronium, penicillin G potassium, piperacillin, piperacillin/tazobactam, potassium chloride, propofol, propranolol, ranitidine, remifentanil, sodium bicarbonate, sodium nitroprusside, tacrolimus, teniposide, thiotepa, ticarcillin, ticarcillin/clavulanate, tobramycin, vancomycin, vecuronium, vinorelbine, vitamin B complex with C, warfarin, zidovudine. **Incompatible:**

Alatrofloxacin, amphotericin B cholesteryl sulfate complex, cefepime, doxorubicin liposome, minocycline, sargramostim. **Variable (consult detailed reference):** Acyclovir, furosemide, thiopental, TPN.

Compatibility in syringe: Compatible: Atropine, bupivacaine, bupivacaine with clonidine, butorphanol, cimetidine, dimenhydrinate, diphenhydramine, droperidol, fentanyl, glycopyrrolate, hydroxyzine, hyoscine, ketamine, ketamine with lidocaine, metoclopramide, midazolam, milrinone, ondansetron, pentazocine, perphenazine, promazine, ranitidine, Sthf067200albutamol, scopolamine. **Incompatible:** Meperidine, thiopental. **Variable (consult detailed reference):** Chlorpromazine, haloperidol, heparin, pentobarbital, prochlorperazine edisylate, promethazine.

Compatibility when admixed: Compatible: Alteplase, atracurium, baclofen, bupivacaine, dobutamine, fluconazole, furosemide, ketamine, meropenem, metoclopramide, ondansetron, succinylcholine, verapamil. **Incompatible:** Aminophylline, amobarbital, chlorothiazide, floxacillin, fluorouracil, heparin, meperidine, phenobarbital, phenytoin, sodium bicarbonate, thiopental.

DepoDur™: Do not mix with other medications.

Mechanism of Action Binds to opiate receptors in the CNS, causing inhibition of ascending pain pathways, altering the perception of and response to pain; produces generalized CNS depression

Pharmacodynamics/Kinetics

Onset of action: Oral (immediate release): ~30 minutes; I.V.: 5-10 minutes

Duration: Pain relief:

Immediate release formulations: 4 hours

Extended release epidural injection (DepoDur™): >48 hours

Absorption: Variable

Distribution: V_d: 3-4 L/kg; binds to opioid receptors in the CNS and periphery (eg, GI tract)

Protein binding: 30% to 35%

Metabolism: Hepatic via conjugation with glucuronic acid to morphine-3-glucuronide (inactive), morphine-6-glucuronide (active), and in lesser amounts, morphine-3-6-diglucuronide; other minor metabolites include normorphine (active) and the 3-ethereal sulfate

Bioavailability: Oral: 17% to 33% (first-pass effect limits oral bioavailability; oral:parenteral effectiveness reportedly varies from 1:6 in opioid naive patients to 1:3 with chronic use)

Half-life elimination: Adults: 2-4 hours (immediate release forms)

Time to peak, plasma: Kadian®: ~10 hours

Excretion: Urine (primarily as morphine-3-glucuronide, ~2% to 12% excreted unchanged); feces (~7% to 10%). It has been suggested that accumulation of morphine-6-glucuronide might cause toxicity with renal insufficiency. All of the metabolites (ie, morphine-3-glucuronide, morphine-6-glucuronide, and normorphine) have been suggested as possible causes of neurotoxicity (eg, myoclonus).

Dosage Note: These are guidelines and do not represent the doses that may be required in all patients. Doses should be titrated to pain relief/prevention.

Children >6 months and <50 kg: Acute pain (moderate-to-severe):

Oral (prompt release): 0.15-0.3 mg/kg every 3-4 hours as needed

I.M.: 0.1 mg/kg every 3-4 hours as needed

I.V.: 0.05-0.1 mg/kg every 3-4 hours as needed

I.V. infusion: Range: 10-30 mcg/kg/hour

Adolescents >12 years: Sedation/analgesia for procedures: I.V.: 3-4 mg and repeat in 5 minutes if necessary

(Continued)

Morphine Sulfate *(Continued)*

Adults:

Acute pain (moderate-to-severe):

Oral: Prompt release formulations: Opiate-naive: Initial: 10 mg every 3-4 hours as needed; patients with prior opiate exposure may require higher initial doses: usual dosage range: 10-30 mg every 3-4 hours as needed

I.M., SubQ: **Note:** Repeated SubQ administration causes local tissue irritation, pain, and induration.

Initial: Opiate-naive: 5-10 mg every 3-4 hours as needed; patients with prior opiate exposure may require higher initial doses; usual dosage range: 5-20 mg every 3-4 hours as needed

Rectal: 10-20 mg every 3-4 hours

I.V.: Initial: Opiate-naive: 2.5-5 mg every 3-4 hours; patients with prior opiate exposure may require higher initial doses. **Note:** Repeated doses (up to every 5 minutes if needed) in small increments (eg, 1-4 mg) may be preferred to larger and less frequent doses.

I.V., SubQ continuous infusion: 0.8-10 mg/hour; usual range: Up to 80 mg/hour

Mechanically-ventilated patients (based on 70 kg patient): 0.7-10 mg every 1-2 hours as needed; infusion: 5-35 mg/hour

Patient-controlled analgesia (PCA): (Opiate-naive: Consider lower end of dosing range):

Usual concentration: 1 mg/mL

Demand dose: Usual: 1 mg; range: 0.5-2.5 mg

Lockout interval: 5-10 minutes

Intrathecal (I.T.): **Note:** Administer with extreme caution and in reduced dosage to geriatric or debilitated patients.

Opioid-naive: 0.2-0.25 mg/dose (may provide adequate relief for 24 hours); repeat doses are **not** recommended.

Epidural: **Note:** Administer with extreme caution and in reduced dosage to geriatric or debilitated patients. Vigilant monitoring is particularly important in these patients.

Pain management:

Single-dose (Duramorph®): Initial: 3-5 mg

Infusion:

Bolus dose: 1-6 mg

Infusion rate: 0.1-0.2 mg/hour

Maximum dose: 10 mg/24 hours

Surgical anesthesia: Epidural: Single-dose (extended release, Depo-Dur™): Lumbar epidural only; not recommended in patients <18 years of age:

Cesarean section: 10 mg

Lower abdominal/pelvic surgery: 10-15 mg

Major orthopedic surgery of lower extremity: 15 mg

For Depo-Dur™: To minimize the pharmacokinetic interaction resulting in higher peak serum concentrations of morphine, administer the test dose of the local anesthetic at least 15 minutes prior to Depo-Dur™ administration. Use of Depo-Dur™ with epidural local anesthetics has not been studied. Other medications should not be administered into the epidural space for at least 48 hours after administration of DepoDur™.

Note: Some patients may benefit from a 20 mg dose, however, the incidence of adverse effects may be increased.

Chronic pain: Note: Patients taking opioids chronically may become tolerant and require doses higher than the usual dosage range to maintain the desired effect. Tolerance can be managed by appropriate dose titration. There is no optimal or maximal dose for morphine in chronic pain. The appropriate dose is one that relieves pain throughout its dosing interval without causing unmanageable side effects.

Oral: Controlled-, extended-, or sustained-release formulations: A patient's morphine requirement should be established using prompt-release formulations. Conversion to long-acting products may be considered when chronic, continuous treatment is required. Higher dosages should be reserved for use only in opioid-tolerant patients.

Capsules, extended release (Avinza™): Daily dose administered once daily (for best results, administer at same time each day)

Capsules, sustained release (Kadian®): Daily dose administered once daily or in 2 divided doses daily (every 12 hours)

Tablets, controlled release (MS Contin®), sustained release (Oramorph SR®), or extended release: Daily dose divided and administered every 8 or every 12 hours

Elderly or debilitated patients: Use with caution; may require dose reduction

Dosing adjustment in renal impairment:

Cl_{cr} 10-50 mL/minute: Administer at 75% of normal dose

Cl_{cr} <10 mL/minute: Administer at 50% of normal dose

Dosing adjustment/comments in hepatic disease: Unchanged in mild liver disease; substantial extrahepatic metabolism may occur; excessive sedation may occur in cirrhosis

Administration

Oral: Do not crush controlled release drug product, swallow whole. Kadian® and Avinza® can be opened and sprinkled on applesauce; do not crush or chew the beads. Contents of Kadian® capsules may be opened and sprinkled over 10 mL water and flushed through prewetted 16F gastrostomy tube; do not administer Kadian® through nasogastric tube. Administration of oral morphine solution with food may increase bioavailability (not observed with Oramorph SR®).

I.V.: When giving morphine I.V. push, it is best to first dilute in 4-5 mL of sterile water, and then to administer slowly (eg, 15 mg over 3-5 minutes)

Epidural: Use preservative-free solutions

Epidural, extended release liposomal suspension (DepoDur™): Intended for lumbar administration only. Thoracic administration has not been studied. May be administered undiluted or diluted up to 5 mL total volume in preservative-free NS. Do not use an in-line filter during administration. Not for I.V., I.M., or intrathecal administration.

Resedation may occur following epidural administration; this may be delayed ≥48 hours in patients receiving extended-release (DepoDur™) injections.

Administration of an epidural test dose (lidocaine 1.5% and epinephrine 1:200,000) may affect the release of morphine from the liposomal preparation. Delaying the dose for an interval of at least 15 minutes following the test dose minimizes this pharmacokinetic interaction. Except for a test dose, other epidural local anesthetics should not be used before or after this product.

Intrathecal: Use preservative-free solutions

Monitoring Parameters Pain relief, respiratory and mental status, blood pressure

Infumorph®: Patients should be observed in a fully-equipped and staffed environment for at least 24 hours following initiation, and as appropriate for the first several days after catheter implantation.

(Continued)

Morphine Sulfate *(Continued)*

DepoDur™: Patient should be monitored for at least 48 hours following administration.

Test Interactions Some quinolones may produce a false-positive urine screening result for opiates using commercially-available immunoassay kits. This has been demonstrated most consistently for levofloxacin and ofloxacin, but other quinolones have shown cross-reactivity in certain assay kits. Confirmation of positive opiate screens by more specific methods should be considered.

Dietary Considerations Morphine may cause GI upset; take with food if GI upset occurs. Be consistent when taking morphine with or without meals.

Patient Information Avoid alcohol, may cause drowsiness, impaired judgment or coordination; may cause physical and psychological dependence with prolonged use

Special Geriatric Considerations The elderly may be particularly susceptible to the CNS depressant and constipating effects of narcotics. For chronic administration of narcotic analgesics, morphine is preferable in the elderly due to its pharmacokinetics and side effect profile as compared to meperidine and methadone.

Emetic Potential High (60% to 90%)

Vesicant No

Dosage Forms Excipient information presented when available (limited, particularly for generics); consult specific product labeling. [DSC] = Discontinued product

Capsule, extended release:
  Avinza®: 30 mg, 60 mg, 90 mg, 120 mg

Capsule, sustained release:
  Kadian®: 20 mg, 30 mg, 50 mg, 60 mg, 80 mg, 100 mg, 200 mg

Infusion [premixed in D_5W]: 1 mg/mL (100 mL, 250 mL)

Injection, extended release liposomal suspension [lumbar epidural injection, preservative free]:
  DepoDur™: 10 mg/mL (1 mL, 1.5 mL, 2 mL)

Injection, solution: 2 mg/mL (1 mL); 4 mg/mL (1 mL); 5 mg/mL (1 mL); 8 mg/mL (1 mL); 10 mg/0.7 mL (0.7 mL); 10 mg/mL (1 mL, 10 mL); 15 mg/mL (1 mL, 20 mL); 25 mg/mL (4 mL, 10 mL, 20 mL, 40 mL, 50 mL, 100 mL, 250 mL); 50 mg/mL (20 mL, 40 mL) [some preparations contain sodium metabisulfite]

Injection, solution [epidural, intrathecal, or I.V. infusion; preservative free]:
  Astramorph/PF™: 0.5 mg/mL (2 mL, 10 mL); 1 mg/mL (2 mL, 10 mL)
  Duramorph®: 0.5 mg/mL (10 mL); 1 mg/mL (10 mL)

Injection, solution [epidural or intrathecal infusion via microinfusion device; preservative free]:
  Infumorph®: 10 mg/mL (20 mL); 25 mg/mL (20 mL)

Injection, solution [I.V. infusion via PCA pump]: 0.5 mg/mL (30 mL); 1 mg/mL (30 mL, 50 mL); 2 mg/mL (30 mL); 5 mg/mL (30 mL, 50 mL)

Injection, solution [preservative free]: 0.5 mg/mL (10 mL); 1 mg/mL (10 mL); 25 mg/mL (4 mL, 10 mL, 20 mL)

Solution, oral: 10 mg/5 mL (5 mL, 10 mL, 100 mL, 500 mL); 20 mg/5 mL (100 mL, 500 mL); 20 mg/mL (30 mL, 120 mL, 240 mL)
  Roxanol™: 20 mg/mL (30 mL, 120 mL); 100 mg/5 mL (240 mL) [with calibrated spoon]

Solution, oral [concentrate]: 5 mg/0.25 mL (0.25 mL); 10 mg/0.5 mL (0.5 mL); 20 mg/mL (1 mL)

Suppository, rectal: 5 mg (12s), 10 mg (12s), 20 mg (12s), 30 mg (12s)
  RMS®: 5 mg (12s), 10 mg (12s), 20 mg (12s), 30 mg (12s) [DSC]

Tablet: 10 mg, 15 mg, 30 mg
Tablet, controlled release:
 MS Contin®: 15 mg, 30 mg, 60 mg, 100 mg, 200 mg
Tablet, extended release: 15 mg, 30 mg, 60 mg, 100 mg, 200 mg
Tablet, sustained release:
 Oramorph SR®: 15 mg, 30 mg, 60 mg, 100 mg

References

"Acute Pain Management in Infants, Children, and Adolescents: Operative and Medical Procedures. Agency for Health Care Policy and Research," *Am Fam Physician*, 1992, 46(2):469-79.

"American Academy of Pediatrics Committee on Drugs. The Transfer of Drugs and Other Chemicals Into Human Milk," *Pediatrics*, 2001, 108(3):776-89.

Antman EM, Anbe SC, Alpert JS, et al, "ACC/AHA Guidelines for the Management of Patients With ST-Elevation Myocardial Infarction - Executive Summary: A Report of the American College of Cardiology/American Heart Association Task Force on Practice Guidelines (Writing Committee to Revise the 1999 Guidelines for the Management of Patients With Acute Myocardial Infarction)," *Circulation*, 2004, 110(5):588-636. Available at: http://www.circulationaha.org/cgi/content/full/110/5/588. Last accessed October 26, 2004.

Berde C, Ablin A, Glazer J, et al, "American Academy of Pediatrics Report of the Subcommittee on Disease-Related Pain in Childhood Cancer," *Pediatrics*, 1990, 86(5 Pt 2):818-25.

Braunwald E, Antman EM, Beasley JW, et al, "ACC/AHA 2002 Guideline Update for the Management of Patients With Unstable Angina and Non-ST-Segment Elevation Myocardial Infarction - Summary Article: A Report of the American College of Cardiology/American Heart Association Task Force on Practice Guidelines (Committee on the Management of Patients With Unstable Angina)," *J Am Coll Cardiol*, 2002, 40(7):1366-74. Available at: http://www.acc.org/clinical/guidelines/unstable/incorporated/index.htm. Accessed May 20, 2003.

Brunk SF and Delle M, "Morphine Metabolism in Man," *Clin Pharmacol Ther*, 1974, 16(1):51-7.

Capogna G, Celleno D, Zangrillo A, et al, "Addition of Clonidine to Epidural Morphine Enhances Postoperative Analgesia After Cesarean Delivery," *Reg Anesth*, 1995, 20(1):57-61.

Dampier CD, Setty BN, Logan J, et al, "Intravenous Morphine Pharmacokinetics in Pediatric Patients With Sickle Cell Disease," *J Pediatr*, 1995, 126(3):461-7.

"Drugs for Pain," *Med Lett Drugs Ther*, 2000, 42(1085):73-8.

Duthie DJ and Nimmo WS, "Adverse Effects of Opioid Analgesic Drugs," *Br J Anaesth*, 1987, 59(1):61-77.

Ferrell BA, "Pain Management in Elderly People," *J Am Geriatr Soc*, 1991, 39(1):64-73.

Gerber N and Apseloff G, "Death From a Morphine Infusion During a Sickle Cell Crisis," *J Pediatr*, 1993, 123(2):322-5.

Golianu B, Krane EJ, Galloway KS, et al, "Pediatric Acute Pain Management," *Pediatr Clin North Am*, 2000, 47(3):559-87.

Groudine SB, Cresanti-Daknis C, and Lumb PD, "Successful Treatment of a Massive Intrathecal Morphine Overdose," *Anesthesiology*, 1995, 82(1):292-5.

Henneberg SW, Hole P, Madsen de Haas I, et al, "Epidural Morphine for Postoperative Pain Relief in Children," *Acta Anaesthesiol Scand*, 1993, 37(7):664-7.

Henry J and Volans GJ, "ABC of Poisoning. Analgesics: Opioids," *Br Med J (Clin Res Ed)*, 1984, 289(6450):990-3.

Holdsworth MT, Adams VR, Chavez CM, et al, "Continuous Midazolam Infusion for the Management of Morphine-Induced Myoclonus," *Ann Pharmacother*, 1995, 29(1):25-9.

Inturrisi CE, "Narcotic Drugs," *Med Clin North Am*, 1982, 66(5):1061-71.

Jacobi J, Fraser GL, Coursin DB, et al, "Clinical Practice Guidelines for the Sustained Use of Sedatives and Analgesics in the Critically Ill Adult," *Crit Care Med*, 2002, 30(1):119-41. Available at: http://www.sccm.org/pdf/sedatives.pdf. Accessed August 2, 2003.

June HL, Stitzer ML, and Cone E, "Acute Physical Dependence: Time Course and Relation to Human Plasma Morphine Concentrations," *Clin Pharmacol Ther*, 1995, 57(3):270-80.

Kaiko RF, "Age and Morphine Analgesia in Cancer Patients With Postoperative Pain," *Clin Pharmacol Ther*, 1980, 28(6):823-6.

Kaiko RF, Wallenstein SL, Rogers AG, et al, "Narcotics in the Elderly," *Med Clin North Am*, 1982, 66(5):1079-89.

Meine TJ, Roe MT, Chen AY, et al, "Association of Intravenous Morphine Use and Outcomes in Acute Coronary Syndromes: Results From the CRUSADE Quality Improvement Initiative," *Am Heart J*, 2005, 149(6):1043-9.

McRorie TI, Lynn AM, Nespeca MK, et al, "The Maturation of Morphine Clearance and Metabolism," *Am J Dis Child*, 1992, 147(8):972-6.

Mignault GG, Latreille J, Viguie F, et al, "Control of Cancer-Related Pain With MS Contin: A Comparison Between 12-Hourly and 8-Hourly Administration," *J Pain Symptom Manage*, 1995, 10(6):416-22.

Mokhlesi B, Leikin JB, Murray P, et al, "Adult Toxicology in Critical Care: Part II: Specific Poisonings," *Chest*, 2003, 123(3):897-922.

(Continued)

Morphine Sulfate *(Continued)*

Olkkola KT, Hamunen K, and Maunuksela EL, "Clinical Pharmacokinetics and Pharmacodynamics of Opioid Analgesics in Infants and Children," *Clin Pharmacokinet,* 1995,
28(5):385-404.

"Principles of Analgesic Use in the Treatment of Acute Pain and Chronic Cancer Pain," 5th ed,
Glenview, IL: American Pain Society, 2003.

Rathmell JP, Viscomi CM, and Ashburn MA, "Management of Nonobstetric Pain During Pregnancy and Lactation," *Anesth Analg,* 1997, 85(5):1074-87.

Schug SA, Zech D, and Grond S, "Adverse Effects of Systemic Opioid Analgesics," *Drug Saf,*
1992, 7(3):200-13.

Spigset O and Hagg S, "Analgesics and Breast-feeding: Safety Considerations," *Paediatr Drugs,*
2000, 2(3):223-38.

Wunsch MJ, Stanard V, and Schnoll SH, "Treatment of Pain in Pregnancy," *Clin J Pain,* 2003,
19(3):148-55.

Zacher JL and Givone DM, "False-Positive Urine Opiate Screening Associated With Fluoroquinolone Use," *Ann Pharmacother,* 2004, 38:1525-28.

- ◆ M.O.S.® 10 (Can) *see* Morphine Sulfate *on page 779*
- ◆ M.O.S.® 20 (Can) *see* Morphine Sulfate *on page 779*
- ◆ M.O.S.® 30 (Can) *see* Morphine Sulfate *on page 779*
- ◆ M.O.S.-SR® (Can) *see* Morphine Sulfate *on page 779*
- ◆ M.O.S.-Sulfate® (Can) *see* Morphine Sulfate *on page 779*
- ◆ Mouthkote® [OTC] *see* Saliva Substitute *on page 960*
- ◆ MPA *see* MedroxyPROGESTERone *on page 703*
- ◆ MPA *see* Mycophenolate *on page 791*
- ◆ 6-MP (error-prone abbreviation) *see* Mercaptopurine *on page 720*
- ◆ MS Contin® *see* Morphine Sulfate *on page 779*
- ◆ MS-IR® (Can) *see* Morphine Sulfate *on page 779*
- ◆ MSO₄ (error-prone abbreviation and should not be used) *see* Morphine
Sulfate *on page 779*
- ◆ MTA *see* Pemetrexed *on page 884*
- ◆ MTC *see* Mitomycin *on page 768*
- ◆ MTX (error-prone abbreviation) *see* Methotrexate *on page 733*
- ◆ Multitargeted Antifolate *see* Pemetrexed *on page 884*

Muromonab-CD3 (myoo roe MOE nab see dee three)

Related Information
Safe Handling of Hazardous Drugs *on page 1382*

U.S. Brand Names Orthoclone OKT® 3

Index Terms Monoclonal Antibody; OKT3

Generic Available No

Canadian Brand Names Orthoclone OKT® 3

Pharmacologic Category Immunosuppressant Agent

Use Treatment of acute allograft rejection in renal transplant patients; treatment of acute hepatic, kidney, and pancreas rejection episodes resistant to
conventional treatment. Acute graft-versus-host disease following bone
marrow transplantation resistant to conventional treatment.

Pregnancy Risk Factor C

Lactation Excretion in breast milk unknown/contraindicated

Labeled Contraindications Hypersensitivity to OKT3 or any murine
product; patients in fluid overload or those with >3% weight gain within 1
week prior to start of OKT3; mouse antibody titers >1:1000

Warnings/Precautions It is imperative, especially prior to the first few
doses, that there be no clinical evidence of volume overload, uncontrolled
hypertension, or uncompensated heart failure, including a clear chest x-ray

and weight restriction of ≤3% above the patient's minimum weight during the week prior to injection.

Risk of development of lymphoproliferative disorders (particularly of the skin) is increased. May result in an increased susceptibility to infection; dosage of concomitant immunosuppressants should be reduced during OKT3 therapy; cyclosporine should be decreased to 50% usual maintenance dose and maintenance therapy resumed about 4 days before stopping OKT3.

Severe pulmonary edema has occurred in patients with fluid overload. Use with caution in patients with a history of seizure disorder.

[U.S. Boxed Warning]: First dose effect (flu-like symptoms, anaphylactic-type reaction) may occur within 30 minutes to 6 hours up to 24 hours after the first dose and may be minimized by using the recommended regimens. See Dosage.

Cardiopulmonary resuscitation may be needed. If the patient's temperature is >37.8°C, reduce before administering OKT3. **[U.S. Boxed Warning]: Should be administered under the supervision of a physician experienced in immunosuppressive therapy in a facility appropriate for monitoring and resuscitation.**

Adverse Reactions Note: Signs and symptoms of Cytokine Release Syndrome (characterized by pyrexia, chills, dyspnea, nausea, vomiting, chest pain, diarrhea, tremor, wheezing, headache, tachycardia, rigor, hypertension, pulmonary edema and/or other cardiorespiratory manifestations) occurs in a significant proportion of patients following the first couple of doses of muromonab-CD3. See Warnings/Precautions. Additionally, some patients have experienced immediate hypersensitivity reactions to muromonab-CD3 (characterized by cardiovascular collapse, cardiorespiratory arrest, loss of consciousness, hypotension/shock, tachycardia, tingling, angioedema (including laryngeal, pharyngeal, or facial edema), airway obstruction, bronchospasm, dyspnea, urticaria, and/or pruritus) upon initial exposure and re-exposure.

>10%:
  Cardiovascular: Tachycardia (26%), hypotension (25%), hypertension (19%), edema (12%)
  Central nervous system: Pyrexia (77%), chills (43%), headache (28%)
  Dermatologic: Rash (14%; erythematous 2%)
  Gastrointestinal: Diarrhea (37%), nausea (32%), vomiting (25%)
  Respiratory: Dyspnea (16%)
1% to 10%:
  Cardiovascular: Chest pain (9%), vasodilation (7%), arrhythmia (4%), bradycardia (4%), vascular occlusion (2%)
  Central nervous system: Fatigue (9%), confusion (6%), dizziness (6%), lethargy (6%), pain trunk (6%), malaise (5%), nervousness (5%), depression (3%), somnolence (2%), meningitis (1%), seizure (1%)
  Dermatologic: Pruritus (7%)
  Gastrointestinal: Gastrointestinal pain (7%), abdominal pain (6%), anorexia (4%)
  Hematologic: Leukopenia (7%), anemia (2%), thrombocytopenia (2%), leukocytosis (1%)
  Neuromuscular & skeletal: Weakness (10%), arthralgia (7%), myalgia (1%), tremor (14%)
  Ocular: Photophobia (1%)
  Otic: Tinnitus (1%)
  Renal: Renal dysfunction (3%)
(Continued)

Muromonab-CD3 *(Continued)*

Respiratory: Abnormal chest sound (10%), hyperventilation (7%), wheezing (6%), respiratory congestion (4%), pulmonary edema (2%), hypoxia (1%), pneumonia (1%)

Miscellaneous: Diaphoresis (7%), infections (various)

<1%: ALT/AST increased, angina, anuria, apnea, cardiac arrest, coagulation disorder, coma, conjunctivitis, encephalopathy, epilepsy, GI hemorrhage, hallucinations, hearing decreased, heart failure, hepatitis, hypotonia, lymphadenopathy, lymphopenia, MI, mood changes, neoplasms (various), oliguria, paranoia, pneumonitis, psychosis, shock, thrombosis

Drug Interactions

Increased Effect/Toxicity: Recommend decreasing dose of prednisone to 0.5 mg/kg, azathioprine to 0.5 mg/kg (approximate 50% decrease in dose), and discontinuing cyclosporine while patient is receiving OKT3.

Decreased Effect: Decreased effect with immunosuppressive drugs.

Storage/Stability Refrigerate; do not freeze. Do not shake. Stable in Becton Dickinson syringe for 16 hours at room temperature or refrigeration.

Mechanism of Action Reverses graft rejection by binding to T cells and interfering with their function by binding T-cell receptor-associated CD3 glycoprotein

Pharmacodynamics/Kinetics

Duration: 7 days after discontinuation

Time to peak: Steady-state: Trough: 3-14 days

Dosage I.V. (refer to individual protocols):

Children <30 kg: 2.5 mg/day once daily for 7-14 days

Children >30 kg: 5 mg/day once daily for 7-14 days

OR

Children <12 years: 0.1 mg/kg/day once daily for 10-14 days

Children ≥12 years and Adults: 5 mg/day once daily for 10-14 days

Hemodialysis: Molecular size of OKT3 is 150,000 daltons; not dialyzed by most standard dialyzers; however, may be dialyzed by high flux dialysis; OKT3 will be removed by plasmapheresis; administer following dialysis treatments

Peritoneal dialysis: Significant drug removal is unlikely based on physiochemical characteristics

Note: Suggested prevention/treatment of muromonab-CD3 first-dose effects (grouped by adverse reaction):

Severe pulmonary edema:
- Effective prevention or palliation: Clear chest x-ray within 24 hours preinjection; weight restriction to ≤3% gain over 7days preinjection
- Supportive treatment: Prompt intubation and oxygenation; 24 hours close observation

Fever, chills:
- Effective prevention or palliation: 15 mg/kg methylprednisolone sodium succinate 1 hour preinjection; fever reduction to <37.8°C (100°F) 1 hour preinjection; acetaminophen (1 g orally) and diphenhydramine(50 mg orally) 1 hour preinjection
- Supportive treatment: Cooling blanket; acetaminophen as needed

Respiratory effects:
- Effective prevention or palliation: 100 mg hydrocortisone sodium succinate 30 minutes postinjection
- Supportive treatment: Additional 100 mg hydrocortisone sodium succinate as needed for wheezing; if respiratory distress, give epinephrine 1:1000 (0.3 mL SubQ)

Administration Not for I.M. administration. Filter each dose through a low protein-binding 0.22 micron filter (Millex GV) before administration; administer I.V. push over <1 minute at a final concentration of 1 mg/mL

Children and Adults:

Methylprednisolone sodium succinate 15 mg/kg I.V. administered prior to first muromonab-CD3 administration and I.V. hydrocortisone sodium succinate 50-100 mg given 30 minutes after administration are strongly recommended to decrease the incidence of reactions to the first dose

Patient temperature should not exceed 37.8°C (100°F) at time of administration

Monitoring Parameters Chest x-ray, weight gain, CBC with differential, temperature, vital signs (blood pressure, temperature, pulse, respiration); immunologic monitoring of T cells, serum levels of OKT3

Dietary Considerations Injection solution contains sodium 43 mg/5 mL.

Patient Information Inform patient of expected first dose effects which are markedly reduced with subsequent treatments

Emetic Potential Moderate (30% to 60%)

Vesicant No

Dosage Forms Excipient information presented when available (limited, particularly for generics); consult specific product labeling.

Injection, solution: 1 mg/mL (5 mL) [contains sodium 43 mg/5 mL]

References

Ettenger RB, Marik JL, Rosenthal JT, et al, "OKT3 for Rejection Reversal in Pediatric Renal Transplantation," *Clin Transpl*, 1988, 2:180-4.

Hooks MA, Wade CS, and Millikan WJ Jr, "Muromonab CD-3: A Review of Its Pharmacology, Pharmacokinetics, and Clinical Use in Transplantation," *Pharmacotherapy*, 1991, 11(1):26-37.

Niaudet P, Murcia I, Jean G, et al, "A Comparative Trial of OKT3 and Antilymphocyte Serum in the Preventive Treatment of Rejection After Kidney Transplantation in Children," *Ann Pediatr (Paris)*, 1990, 37(2):83-5.

Ross SJ, "Immunologic Monitoring of OKT3 Therapy," *Transplantation Pharm Newslet*, 1995;2-5.

Todd PA and Brogden RN, "Muromonab CD3 A Review of Its Pharmacology and Therapeutic Potential," *Drugs*, 1989, 37(6):871-99.

♦ **Mustargen**® *see* Mechlorethamine *on page 700*

♦ **Mustine** *see* Mechlorethamine *on page 700*

♦ **Mutamycin**® *see* Mitomycin *on page 768*

♦ **Mycamine**® *see* Micafungin *on page 761*

♦ **Mycelex**® *see* Clotrimazole *on page 239*

Mycophenolate (mye koe FEN oh late)

Related Information

Hematopoietic Stem Cell Transplantation *on page 1366*
Safe Handling of Hazardous Drugs *on page 1382*

U.S. Brand Names CellCept®; Myfortic®

Index Terms MMF; MPA; Mycophenolate Mofetil; Mycophenolate Sodium; Mycophenolic Acid

Generic Available No

Canadian Brand Names CellCept®; Myfortic®

Pharmacologic Category Immunosuppressant Agent

Use Prophylaxis of organ rejection concomitantly with cyclosporine and corticosteroids in patients receiving allogeneic renal (CellCept®, Myfortic®), cardiac (CellCept®), or hepatic (CellCept®) transplants

Unlabeled/Investigational Use Treatment of rejection in liver transplant patients unable to tolerate tacrolimus or cyclosporine due to neurotoxicity; mild rejection in heart transplant patients; treatment of moderate-severe

(Continued)

Mycophenolate *(Continued)*

psoriasis; treatment of proliferative lupus nephritis; treatment of myasthenia gravis; prevention and treatment of graft-versus-host disease (GVHD)

Pregnancy Risk Factor D

Lactation Excretion in breast milk unknown/not recommended

Labeled Contraindications Hypersensitivity to mycophenolate mofetil, mycophenolic acid, mycophenolate sodium, or any component of the formulation; intravenous formulation is contraindicated in patients who are allergic to polysorbate 80

Warnings/Precautions Hazardous agent - use appropriate precautions for handling and disposal. **[U.S. Boxed Warning]: Risk for infection and development of lymphoma and skin malignancy is increased.** Patients should be monitored appropriately, instructed to limit exposure to sunlight/ UV light, and given supportive treatment should these conditions occur. Severe neutropenia may occur, requiring interruption of treatment (risk greater from day 31-180 post-transplant). Use caution with active peptic ulcer disease; may be associated with GI bleeding and/or perforation. Use caution in renal impairment as toxicity may be increased; may require dosage adjustment in severe impairment. Patients may be at increased risk of infection.

[U.S. Boxed Warning]: Mycophenolate is associated with an increased risk of congenital malformations and spontaneous abortions when used during pregnancy. Females of childbearing potential should have a negative pregnancy test within 1 week prior to beginning therapy. Two reliable forms of contraception should be used beginning 4 weeks prior to, during, and for 6 weeks after therapy. Because mycophenolate mofetil has demonstrated teratogenic effects in rats and rabbits, tablets should not be crushed, and capsules should not be opened or crushed. Avoid inhalation or direct contact with skin or mucous membranes of the powder contained in the capsules and the powder for oral suspension. Caution should be exercised in the handling and preparation of solutions of intravenous mycophenolate. Avoid skin contact with the intravenous solution and reconstituted suspension. If such contact occurs, wash thoroughly with soap and water, rinse eyes with plain water.

Theoretically, use should be avoided in patients with the rare hereditary deficiency of hypoxanthine-guanine phosphoribosyltransferase (such as Lesch-Nyhan or Kelley-Seegmiller syndrome). Intravenous solutions should be given over at least 2 hours; **never** administer intravenous solution by rapid or bolus injection. **[U.S. Boxed Warning]: Should be administered under the supervision of a physician experienced in immunosuppressive therapy.**

Note: CellCept® and Myfortic® dosage forms should not be used interchangeably due to differences in absorption. Some dosage forms may contain phenylalanine.

Adverse Reactions As reported in adults following oral dosing of CellCept® alone in renal, cardiac, and hepatic allograft rejection studies. In general, lower doses used in renal rejection patients had less adverse effects than higher doses. Rates of adverse effects were similar for each indication, except for those unique to the specific organ involved. The type of adverse effects observed in pediatric patients was similar to those seen in adults; abdominal pain, anemia, diarrhea, fever, hypertension, infection, pharyngitis, respiratory tract infection, sepsis, and vomiting were seen in higher proportion; lymphoproliferative disorder was the only type of malignancy observed.

Percentages of adverse reactions were similar in studies comparing CellCept® to Myfortic® in patients following renal transplant.

>20%:

Cardiovascular: Hypertension (28% to 77%), hypotension (up to 33%), peripheral edema (27% to 64%), edema (27% to 28%), tachycardia (20% to 22%)

Central nervous system: Pain (31% to 76%), headache (16% to 54%), insomnia (41% to 52%), fever (21% to 52%), dizziness (up to 29%), anxiety (28%)

Dermatologic: Rash (up to 22%)

Endocrine & metabolic: Hyperglycemia (44% to 47%), hypercholesterolemia (41%), hypokalemia (32% to 37%), hypocalcemia (up to 30%), hypomagnesemia (up to 39%), hyperkalemia (up to 22%)

Gastrointestinal: Abdominal pain (25% to 62%), nausea (20% to 54%), diarrhea (31% to 52%), constipation (18% to 41%), vomiting (33% to 34%), anorexia (up to 25%), dyspepsia (22%)

Genitourinary: Urinary tract infection (37%)

Hematologic: Leukopenia (23% to 46%), leukocytosis (22% to 40%), hypochromic anemia (26% to 43%), thrombocytopenia (24% to 36%)

Hepatic: Liver function tests abnormal (up to 25%), ascites (24%)

Neuromuscular & skeletal: Back pain (35% to 47%), weakness (35% to 43%), tremor (24% to 34%), paresthesia (21%)

Renal: BUN increased (up to 35%), creatinine increased (up to 39%)

Respiratory: Dyspnea (31% to 37%), respiratory tract infection (22% to 37%), cough (31%), lung disorder (22% to 30%)

Miscellaneous: Infection (18% to 27%), *Candida* (11% to 22%), herpes simplex (10% to 21%)

3% to <20%:

Cardiovascular: Angina, arrhythmia, arterial thrombosis, atrial fibrillation, atrial flutter, bradycardia, cardiac arrest, cardiac failure, CHF, extrasystole, facial edema, hypervolemia, pallor, palpitation, pericardial effusion, peripheral vascular disorder, postural hypotension, supraventricular extrasystoles, supraventricular tachycardia, syncope, thrombosis, vasodilation, vasospasm, venous pressure increased, ventricular extrasystole, ventricular tachycardia

Central nervous system: Agitation, chills with fever, confusion, convulsion, delirium, depression, emotional lability, hallucinations, hypoesthesia, malaise, nervousness, psychosis, somnolence, thinking abnormal, vertigo

Dermatologic: Acne, alopecia, bruising, cellulitis, hirsutism, petechia, pruritus, skin carcinoma, skin hypertrophy, skin ulcer, vesiculobullous rash

Endocrine & metabolic: Acidosis, Cushing's syndrome, dehydration, diabetes mellitus, gout, hypercalcemia, hyperlipemia, hyperphosphatemia, hyperuricemia, hypochloremia, hypoglycemia, hyponatremia, hypoproteinemia, hypothyroidism, parathyroid disorder, weight gain/loss

Gastrointestinal: Abdomen enlarged, dry mouth, dysphagia, esophagitis, flatulence, gastritis, gastroenteritis, gastrointestinal hemorrhage, gastrointestinal moniliasis, gingivitis, gum hyperplasia, ileus, melena, mouth ulceration, oral moniliasis, stomach disorder, stomatitis

Genitourinary: Impotence, nocturia, pelvic pain, prostatic disorder, scrotal edema, urinary frequency, urinary incontinence, urinary retention, urinary tract disorder

(Continued)

Mycophenolate *(Continued)*

Hematologic: Coagulation disorder, hemorrhage, neutropenia, pancytopenia, polycythemia, prothrombin time increased, thromboplastin increased

Hepatic: Alkaline phosphatase increased, alkalosis, bilirubinemia, cholangitis, cholestatic jaundice, GGT increased, hepatitis, jaundice, liver damage, transaminases increased

Local: Abscess

Neuromuscular & skeletal: Arthralgia, hypertonia, joint disorder, leg cramps, myalgia, myasthenia, neck pain, neuropathy, osteoporosis

Ocular: Amblyopia, cataract, conjunctivitis, eye hemorrhage, lacrimation disorder, vision abnormal

Otic: Deafness, ear disorder, ear pain, tinnitus

Renal: Albuminuria, creatinine increased, dysuria, hematuria, hydronephrosis, kidney failure, kidney tubular necrosis, oliguria

Respiratory: Apnea, asthma, atelectasis, bronchitis, epistaxis, hemoptysis, hiccup, hyperventilation, hypoxia, respiratory acidosis, lung edema, pharyngitis, pleural effusion, pneumonia, pneumothorax, pulmonary hypertension, respiratory moniliasis, rhinitis, sinusitis, sputum increased, voice alteration

Miscellaneous: *Candida* (mucocutaneous 15% to 18%), CMV viremia/syndrome (12% to 14%), CMV tissue invasive disease (6% to 11%), herpes zoster cutaneous disease (4% to 10%), cyst, diaphoresis, flu-like syndrome, fungal dermatitis, healing abnormal, hernia, ileus infection, lactic dehydrogenase increased, peritonitis, pyelonephritis, thirst

Postmarketing and/or case reports: Atypical mycobacterial infection, colitis, gastrointestinal perforation, gastrointestinal ulcers, infectious endocarditis, interstitial lung disorder, intestinal villous atrophy, meningitis, pancreatitis, pulmonary fibrosis (fatal), tuberculosis

Overdosage/Toxicology There are no reported overdoses with mycophenolate. At plasma concentrations >100 mcg/mL, small amounts of the inactive metabolite MPAG are removed by hemodialysis. Excretion of the active metabolite, MPA, may be increased by using bile acid sequestrants (cholestyramine).

Drug Interactions

Increased Effect/Toxicity: Acyclovir, valacyclovir, ganciclovir, and valganciclovir levels may increase due to competition for tubular secretion of these drugs. Probenecid may increase mycophenolate levels due to inhibition of tubular secretion. High doses of salicylates may increase free fraction of mycophenolic acid. Azathioprine's bone marrow suppression may be potentiated; do not administer together.

Decreased Effect: Antacids decrease serum levels (C_{max} and AUC); **do not administer together.** Cholestyramine resin decreases serum levels; **do not administer together.** Avoid use of live vaccines; vaccinations may be less effective. Influenza vaccine may be of value. During concurrent use of oral contraceptives, progesterone levels may be decreased, however, effect on estrogen component varies; an additional form of contraception should be used.

Ethanol/Nutrition/Herb Interactions

Food: Decreases C_{max} of MPA by 40% following CellCept® administration and 33% following Myfortic® use; the extent of absorption is not changed

Herb/Nutraceutical: Avoid cat's claw, echinacea (have immunostimulant properties)

Storage/Stability

Capsules: Store at room temperature of 15°C to 39°C (59°F to 86°F).

Tablets: Store at room temperature of 15°C to 39°C (59°F to 86°F). Protect from light.

Oral suspension: Store powder for oral suspension at room temperature of 15°C to 39°C (59°F to 86°F). Once reconstituted, the oral solution may be stored at room temperature or under refrigeration. Do not freeze. The mixed suspension is stable for 60 days.

Injection: Store intact vials at room temperature 15°C to 30°C (59°F to 86°F). Store solutions at 15°C to 30°C (59°F to 86°F). Begin infusion within 4 hours of reconstitution.

Reconstitution

Oral suspension: Should be constituted prior to dispensing to the patient and **not** mixed with any other medication. Add 47 mL of water to the bottle and shake well for ~1 minute. Add another 47 mL of water to the bottle and shake well for an additional minute. Final concentration is 200 mg/mL of mycophenolate mofetil.

I.V.: Reconstitute the contents of each vial with 14 mL of 5% dextrose injection; dilute the contents of a vial with 5% dextrose in water to a final concentration of 6 mg mycophenolate mofetil per mL. **Note:** Vial is vacuum-sealed; if a lack of vacuum is noted during preparation, the vial should not be used.

Compatibility Stable in D_5W.

Mechanism of Action MPA exhibits a cytostatic effect on T and B lymphocytes. It is an inhibitor of inosine monophosphate dehydrogenase (IMPDH) which inhibits de novo guanosine nucleotide synthesis. T and B lymphocytes are dependent on this pathway for proliferation.

Pharmacodynamics/Kinetics

Onset of action: Peak effect: Correlation of toxicity or efficacy is still being developed, however, one study indicated that 12-hour AUCs >40 mcg/mL/hour were correlated with efficacy and decreased episodes of rejection

T_{max}: Oral: MPA:
  CellCept®: 1-1.5 hours
  Myfortic®: 1.5-2.5 hours

Absorption: AUC values for MPA are lower in the early post-transplant period versus later (>3 months) post-transplant period. The extent of absorption in pediatrics is similar to that seen in adults, although there was wide variability reported.
  Oral: Myfortic®: 93%

Distribution:
  CellCept®: MPA: Oral: 4 L/kg; I.V.: 3.6 L/kg
  Myfortic®: MPA: Oral: 54 L (at steady state); 112 L (elimination phase)

Protein binding: MPA: 97%, MPAG 82%

Metabolism: Hepatic and via GI tract; CellCept® is completely hydrolyzed in the liver to mycophenolic acid (MPA; active metabolite); enterohepatic recirculation of MPA may occur; MPA is glucuronidated to MPAG (inactive metabolite)

Bioavailability: Oral: CellCept®: 94%; Myfortic®: 72%

Half-life elimination:
  CellCept®: MPA: Oral: 18 hours; I.V.: 17 hours
  Myfortic®: MPA: Oral: 8-16 hours; MPAG: 13-17 hours

Excretion:
  CellCept®: MPA: Urine (<1%), feces (6%); MPAG: Urine (87%)
  Myfortic®: MPA: Urine (3%), feces; MPAG: Urine (>60%)

Dosage

Children: Renal transplant: Oral:
  CellCept® suspension: 600 mg/m²/dose twice daily; maximum dose: 1 g twice daily

(Continued)

795

Mycophenolate *(Continued)*

Alternatively, may use solid dosage forms according to BSA as follows:
BSA 1.25-1.5 m^2: 750 mg capsule twice daily
BSA >1.5 m^2: 1 g capsule or tablet twice daily
Myfortic®: 400 mg/m^2/dose twice daily; maximum dose: 720 mg twice daily
BSA <1.19 m^2: Use of this formulation is not recommended
BSA 1.19-1.58 m^2: 540 mg twice daily (maximum: 1080 mg/day)
BSA >1.58 m^2: 720 mg twice daily (maximum: 1440 mg/day)
Adults: **Note:** May be used I.V. for up to 14 days; transition to oral therapy as
soon as tolerated.
Renal transplant:
CellCept®:
Oral: 1 g twice daily. Doses >2 g/day are not recommended.
I.V.: 1 g twice daily
Myfortic®: Oral: 720 mg twice daily (1440 mg/day)
Cardiac transplantation:
Oral (CellCept®): 1.5 g twice daily
I.V. (CellCept®): 1.5 g twice daily
Hepatic transplantation:
Oral (CellCept®): 1.5 g twice daily
I.V. (CellCept®): 1 g twice daily
Myasthenia gravis (unlabeled use): Oral (CellCept®): 1 g twice daily (range
1-3 g/day)

Dosing adjustment in renal impairment:
Renal transplant: GFR <25 mL/minute in patients outside the immediate
post-transplant period:
CellCept®: Doses of >1 g administered twice daily should be avoided;
patients should also be carefully observed; no dose adjustments are
needed in renal transplant patients experiencing delayed graft function
postoperatively
Myfortic®: Cl_{cr} <25 mL/minute: Monitor carefully
Cardiac or liver transplant: No data available; mycophenolate may be used
in cardiac or hepatic transplant patients with severe chronic renal impairment if the potential benefit outweighs the potential risk
Hemodialysis: Not removed; supplemental dose is not necessary
Peritoneal dialysis: Supplemental dose is not necessary
Dosage adjustment in hepatic impairment: No dosage adjustment is
recommended for renal patients with severe hepatic parenchymal disease;
however, it is not currently known whether dosage adjustments are necessary for hepatic disease with other etiologies
Elderly: Dosage is the same as younger patients, however, dosing should be
cautious due to possibility of increased hepatic, renal or cardiac dysfunction; elderly patients may be at an increased risk of certain infections,
gastrointestinal hemorrhage, and pulmonary edema, as compared to
younger patients
Dosing adjustment for toxicity (neutropenia): ANC <1.3 x 10^3/μL: Dosing
should be interrupted or the dose reduced, appropriate diagnostic tests
performed and patients managed appropriately
Administration
Oral dosage formulations (tablet, capsule, suspension) should be administered on an empty stomach to avoid variability in MPA absorption. The oral
solution may be administered via a nasogastric tube (minimum 8 French,
1.7 mm interior diameter); oral suspension should not be mixed with other
medications. Delayed release tablets should not be crushed, cut, or
chewed.

Intravenous solutions should be administered over at least 2 hours (either peripheral or central vein); do **not** administer intravenous solution by rapid or bolus injection.

Monitoring Parameters Complete blood count; signs and symptoms of infection; pregnancy test (prior to initiation in females of childbearing potential)

Dietary Considerations Oral dosage formulations should be taken on an empty stomach to avoid variability in MPA absorption. However, in stable renal transplant patients, may be administered with food if necessary. Oral suspension contains 0.56 mg phenylalanine/mL; use caution if administered to patients with phenylketonuria.

Patient Information Take as directed, preferably 1 hour before or 2 hours after meals. Do not take within 1 hour before or 2 hours after antacids or cholestyramine medications. Do not alter dose and do not discontinue without consulting prescriber. Maintain adequate hydration (2-3 L/day of fluids unless instructed to restrict fluid intake) during entire course of therapy. You will be susceptible to infection (avoid crowds and people with infections or contagious diseases). If you are diabetic, monitor glucose levels closely (may alter glucose levels). You may experience dizziness or trembling (use caution until response to medication is known); nausea or vomiting (frequent small meals, frequent mouth care may help); diarrhea (boiled milk, yogurt, or buttermilk may help); sores or white plaques in mouth (frequent rinsing of mouth and frequent mouth care may help); or muscle or back pain (mild analgesics may be recommended). Report chest pain; acute headache or dizziness; swelling of extremities; unusual weight gain; symptoms of respiratory infection, cough, or difficulty breathing; unresolved gastrointestinal effects; fatigue, chills, fever unhealed sores, white plaques in mouth; irritation in genital area or unusual discharge; unusual bruising or bleeding; or other unusual effects related to this medication. May be at increased risk for skin cancer; wear protective clothing and use sunscreen with high protective factor to help limit exposure to sunlight and UV light. Two reliable forms of contraception should be used prior to, during, and for 6 weeks after therapy.

Dosage Forms Excipient information presented when available (limited, particularly for generics); consult specific product labeling.

Capsule, as mofetil:
CellCept®: 250 mg

Injection, powder for reconstitution, as mofetil hydrochloride:
CellCept®: 500 mg [contains polysorbate 80]

Powder for oral suspension, as mofetil:
CellCept®: 200 mg/mL (225 mL) [provides 175 mL suspension following reconstitution; contains phenylalanine 0.56 mg/mL; mixed fruit flavor]

Tablet, as mofetil:
CellCept®: 500 mg [may contain ethyl alcohol]

Tablet, delayed release, as mycophenolic acid:
Myfortic®: 180 mg, 360 mg [formulated as a sodium salt]

References
Cahoon WD Jr and Kockler DR, "Mycophenolate Mofetil Treatment of Myasthenia Gravis," *Ann Pharmacother*, 2006, 40(2):295-8.

Chaudhry V, Cornblath DR, Griffin JW, et al, "Mycophenolate Mofetil: A Safe and Promising Immunosuppressant in Neuromuscular Diseases," *Neurology*, 2001, 56(1):94-6.

Ciafaloni E, Massey JM, Tucker-Lipscomb B, et al, "Mycophenolate Mofetil for Myasthenia Gravis: An Open-Label Pilot Study," *Neurology*, 200, 56(1):97-9.

Contreras G, Pardo V, Leclercq B, et al, "Sequential Therapies for Proliferative Lupus Nephritis," *N Engl J Med*, 2004, 350(10):971-80.

Ettenger R, Warshaw B, Menster M, et al, "Mycophenolate Mofetil in Pediatric Renal Transplantation: A Report of the Ped MMF Study Group." Abstract: 1996, Annual Meeting, ASTP.

Gabardi S, Tran JL, and Clarkson MR, "Enteric-Coated Mycophenolate Sodium," *Ann Pharmacother*, 2003, 37(11):1685-93.

(Continued)

Mycophenolate *(Continued)*

Lipsky JJ, "Mycophenolate Mofetil," *Lancet*, 1996, 348(9038):1357-9.

Meriggioli MN, Ciafaloni E, Al-Hayk KA, et al, "Mycophenolate Mofetil for Myasthenia Gravis: An Analysis of Efficacy, Safety, and Tolerability," *Neurology*, 2003, 61(10):1438-40.

Shaw LM, Sollinger HW, Halloran P, et al, "Mycophenolate Mofetil: A Report of the Consensus Panel," *Ther Drug Monit*, 1995, 17(6):690-9.

Sifontis NM, Coscia LA, Constantinescu S, et al, "Pregnancy Outcomes in Solid Organ Transplant Recipients With Exposure to Mycophenolate Mofetil Or Sirolimus," *Transplantation*, 2006 Dec 27;82(12):1698-702.

Sollinger HW, "Mycophenolate Mofetil for the Prevention of Acute Rejection in Primary Cadaveric Renal Allograft Recipients. U.S. Renal Transplant Mycophenolate Mofetil Study Group," *Transplantation*, 1995, 60:225-32.

Vogelsang GB, and Arai S, "Mycophenolate Mofetil for the Prevention and Treatment of Graft-Versus-Host Disease Following Stem Cell Transplantation: Preliminary Findings," *Bone Marrow Transplant*, 2001, 27(12):1255-62.

- ◆ **Mycophenolate Mofetil** *see* Mycophenolate *on page 791*
- ◆ **Mycophenolate Sodium** *see* Mycophenolate *on page 791*
- ◆ **Mycophenolic Acid** *see* Mycophenolate *on page 791*
- ◆ **Mycostatin**® *see* Nystatin *on page 817*
- ◆ **Myfortic**® *see* Mycophenolate *on page 791*
- ◆ **Myleran**® *see* Busulfan *on page 154*
- ◆ **Mylocel**™ *see* Hydroxyurea *on page 559*
- ◆ **Mylotarg**® *see* Gemtuzumab Ozogamicin *on page 508*

Nabilone *(NA bi lone)*

Related Information

Management of Nausea and Vomiting *on page 1319*

U.S. Brand Names Cesamet™

Generic Available No

Canadian Brand Names Cesamet™

Pharmacologic Category Antiemetic

Use Treatment of refractory nausea and vomiting associated with cancer chemotherapy

Restrictions C-II

Pregnancy Risk Factor C

Lactation Excretion in breast milk unknown/not recommended

Labeled Contraindications Hypersensitivity to nabilone, cannabinoids, tetrahydrocannabinol, or any component of the formulation

Warnings/Precautions May affect CNS function; use with caution in the elderly and those with pre-existing CNS depression. May cause additive CNS effects with sedatives, hypnotics, or other psychoactive agents; patients must be cautioned about performing tasks which require mental alertness (eg, operating machinery or driving). Use caution with current or previous history of mental illness; cannabinoid use may reveal symptoms of psychiatric disorders. Psychiatric adverse reactions may persist for up to 3 days after discontinuing treatment. Has potential for abuse and or dependence, use caution in patients with substance abuse history or potential. May cause tachycardia and orthostatic hypotension; use caution with cardiovascular disease. Safety and efficacy in children have not been established.

Adverse Reactions

>10%:

Central nervous system: Dizziness (59%), drowsiness (52% to 66%), vertigo (52% to 59%), euphoria (11% to 38%), ataxia (13% to 14%), depression (14%), concentration decreased (12%), sleep disturbance (11%)

Gastrointestinal: Xerostomia (22% to 36%)

Ocular: Visual disturbance (13%)

1% to 10%:

Cardiovascular: Hypotension (8%)

Central nervous system: Dysphoria (9%), headache (6% to 7%), sedation (3%), depersonalization (2%), disorientation (2%)

Gastrointestinal: Anorexia (8%), nausea (4%), appetite increased (2%)

Neuromuscular & skeletal: Weakness (8%)

<1%, postmarketing, or frequency not reported: Abdominal pain, abnormal dreams, akathisia, allergic reaction, amblyopia, anemia, anhydrosis, anxiety, apathy, aphthous ulcer, arrhythmia, back pain, cerebral vascular accident, chest pain, chills, constipation, cough, diaphoresis, diarrhea, dyspepsia, dyspnea, dystonia, emotional disorder, emotional lability, epistaxis, equilibrium dysfunction, eye irritation, fatigue, fever, flushing, gastritis, hallucinations, hot flashes, hyperactivity, hypertension, infection, insomnia, irritation, joint pain, leukopenia, lightheadedness, malaise, memory disturbance, mood swings, mouth irritation, muscle pain, nasal congestion, neck pain, nervousness, neurosis (phobic), numbness, orthostatic hypotension, pain, palpitation, panic disorder, paranoia, paresthesia, perception disturbance, pharyngitis, photophobia, photosensitivity, polyuria, pruritus, psychosis (toxic), pupil dilation, rash, seizure, sinus headache, speech disorder, stupor, syncope, tachycardia, taste perversion, thirst, thought disorder, tinnitus, tremor, urination decreased, urinary retention, vomiting, wheezing, withdrawal, xerophthalmia

Overdosage/Toxicology Symptoms of overdose include nausea, vomiting, disorientation, CNS/respiratory depression, dysphoria, and euphoria. Although hypertension and hypotension may occur, orthostatic hypotension and tachycardia are most commonly reported. Large overdoses may present with psychotic episodes, hallucinations, anxiety, respiratory depression, and/or coma. Consider overdose in the presence of disturbing psychiatric symptoms. Monitor vital signs, serum electrolytes, and blood gases. Activated charcoal may be used to decrease gastrointestinal absorption. Treatment is otherwise symptom-directed and supportive.

Drug Interactions

Increased Effect/Toxicity: CNS depressants and ethanol may increase sedation. Anticholinergic agents may increase tachycardia and drowsiness. Naltrexone may increase the levels/effects of cannabinoids. Sympathomimetic agents may increase hypertension and tachycardia. Opioids may increase the effects of cannabinoids.

Decreased Effect: Opioids may cause tolerance to cannabinoids.

Ethanol/Nutrition/Herb Interactions Ethanol: Avoid ethanol (may increase CNS depression).

Storage/Stability Store at room temperature between 15°C and 30°C (59°F and 86°F).

Mechanism of Action Not fully characterized; antiemetic activity may be due to effect on cannabinoid receptors (CB1) within the central nervous system.

Pharmacodynamics/Kinetics

Absorption: Rapid and complete

Distribution: ~12.5 L/kg

Metabolism: To several active metabolites by oxidation and stereospecific enzyme reduction; CYP450 enzymes may also be involved

Half-life elimination: Parent compound: 2 hours; Metabolites: 35 hours

Time to peak, serum: Within 2 hours

Excretion: Feces (~60%); renal (~24%)

(Continued)

Nabilone *(Continued)*

Dosage Refer to individual protocols. Oral:

Children >4 years (unlabeled use):
- <18 kg: 0.5 mg twice daily
- 18-30 kg: 1 mg twice daily
- >30 kg: 1 mg 3 times/day

Adults: 1-2 mg twice daily (maximum: 6 mg divided in 3 doses daily)

Dosage adjustment in renal impairment: No adjustment required.

Administration Initial dose should be given 1-3 hours before chemotherapy; may be given 2-3 times a day during the entire chemotherapy course and for up to 48 hours after the last dose of chemotherapy; a dose of 1-2 mg the night before chemotherapy may be useful.

Monitoring Parameters Blood pressure; heart rate; signs and symptoms of excessive use, abuse, or misuse

Patient Information May cause drowsiness, impaired judgment or coordination. Avoid alcohol and other CNS depressants. Can cause disorientation.

Emetic Potential Very low (<10%)

Dosage Forms Excipient information presented when available (limited, particularly for generics); consult specific product labeling.

Capsule:

Cesamet™: 1 mg

References

Dupuis LL and Nathan PC, "Options for the Prevention and Management of Acute Chemotherapy-Induced Nausea and Vomiting in Children," *Pediatr Drug*, 2003, 5(9):597-613.

Tramer MR, Carroll D, Campbell FA, et al, "Cannabinoids for Control of Chemotherapy Induced Nausea and Vomiting: Quantitative Systematic Review," *BMJ*, 2001, 323(7303):16-21.

Ward A and Holmes B, "Nabilone: A Preliminary Review of Its Pharmacological Properties and Therapeutic Use," *Drugs*, 1985, 30(2):127-44.

♦ **NAB-Paclitaxel** *see* Paclitaxel (Protein Bound) *on page 865*

Nafcillin *(naf SIL in)*

Index Terms Ethoxynaphthamido Penicillin Sodium; Nafcillin Sodium; Nallpen; Sodium Nafcillin

Generic Available Yes

Canadian Brand Names Nallpen®; Unipen®

Pharmacologic Category Antibiotic, Penicillin

Use Treatment of infections such as osteomyelitis, septicemia, endocarditis, and CNS infections caused by susceptible strains of staphylococci species

Pregnancy Risk Factor B

Lactation Enters breast milk/use caution

Labeled Contraindications Hypersensitivity to nafcillin, or any component of the formulation, or penicillins

Warnings/Precautions Serious and occasionally severe or fatal hypersensitivity (anaphylactoid) reactions have been reported in patients on penicillin therapy, especially with a history of beta-lactam hypersensitivity, history of sensitivity to multiple allergens, or previous IgE-mediated reactions (eg, anaphylaxis, angioedema, urticaria). Use with caution in asthmatic patients. Extravasation of I.V. infusions should be avoided. Modification of dosage is necessary in patients with both severe renal and hepatic impairment. Elimination rate will be slow in neonates. Prolonged use may result in fungal or bacterial superinfection, including *C. difficile*-associated diarrhea (CDAD) and pseudomembranous colitis; CDAD has been observed <2 months postantibiotic treatment.

Adverse Reactions Frequency not defined.

Central nervous system: Pain, fever

Dermatologic: Rash

Gastrointestinal: Nausea, diarrhea, pseudomembranous colitis

Hematologic: Agranulocytosis, bone marrow depression, neutropenia

Local: Pain, swelling, inflammation, phlebitis, skin sloughing, and thrombo-phlebitis at the injection site; oxacillin (less likely to cause phlebitis) is often preferred in pediatric patients

Renal: Interstitial nephritis (acute)

Miscellaneous: Hypersensitivity reactions

Overdosage/Toxicology Symptoms of penicillin overdose include neuro-muscular hypersensitivity (eg, agitation, hallucinations, asterixis, encepha-lopathy, confusion, and seizures). Electrolyte imbalance may occur if the preparation contains potassium or sodium salts, especially in renal failure. Treatment is supportive or symptom-directed.

Drug Interactions

Cytochrome P450 Effect: Induces CYP3A4 (strong)

Increased Effect/Toxicity: Probenecid may cause an increase in nafcillin levels. Penicillins may increase the exposure to methotrexate during concurrent therapy; monitor.

Decreased Effect: Nafcillin may decrease levels/effects of calcium channel blockers. If taken concomitantly with warfarin, nafcillin may inhibit the anticoagulant response to warfarin. This effect may persist for up to 30 days after nafcillin has been discontinued. Subtherapeutic cyclosporine levels may result when taken concomitantly with nafcillin. Although anec-dotal reports suggest oral contraceptive efficacy could be reduced by penicillins, this has been refuted by more rigorous scientific and clinical data. Nafcillin may decrease the levels/effects of benzodiazepines, calcium channel blockers, clarithromycin, cyclosporine, erythromycin, estrogens, mirtazapine, nateglinide, nefazodone, nevirapine, protease inhibitors, tacrolimus, venlafaxine, and other CYP3A4 substrates. Fusidic acid, tetra-cyclines may decrease the effects of penicillins. The effects of the typhoid vaccine may be decreased by nafcillin.

Storage/Stability Reconstituted parenteral solution is stable for 3 days at room temperature, 7 days when refrigerated, or 12 weeks when frozen. For I.V. infusion in NS or D_5W, solution is stable for 24 hours at room tempera-ture and 96 hours when refrigerated.

Compatibility Stable in dextran 40 10% in dextrose, D_5LR, $D_5\frac{1}{4}NS$, $D_5\frac{1}{2}NS$, D_5NS, D_5W, $D_{10}NS$, $D_{10}W$, LR, NS; **variable stability (consult detailed reference)** in peritoneal dialysis solution, TPN.

Y-site administration: Compatible: Acyclovir, atropine, cyclophosphamide, diazepam, enalaprilat, esmolol, famotidine, fentanyl, fluconazole, foscarnet, hydromorphone, magnesium sulfate, morphine, perphenazine, propofol, theophylline, zidovudine. **Incompatible:** Droperidol, fentanyl and droperidol, insulin (regular), labetalol, midazolam, nalbuphine, pentazo-cine, verapamil. **Variable (consult detailed reference):** Diltiazem, meper-idine, TPN, vancomycin.

Compatibility in syringe: Compatible: Cimetidine, heparin.

Compatibility when admixed: Compatible: Chloramphenicol, chlorothia-zide, dexamethasone sodium phosphate, diphenhydramine, ephedrine, heparin, hydroxyzine, lidocaine, potassium chloride, prochlorperazine edis-ylate, sodium bicarbonate, sodium lactate. **Incompatible:** Ascorbic acid injection, aztreonam, bleomycin, cytarabine, gentamicin, hydrocortisone sodium succinate, methylprednisolone sodium succinate, promazine. **Vari-able (consult detailed reference):** Aminophylline, verapamil, vitamin B complex with C.

(Continued)

Nafcillin *(Continued)*

Mechanism of Action Interferes with bacterial cell wall synthesis during active multiplication, causing cell wall death and resultant bactericidal activity against susceptible bacteria

Pharmacodynamics/Kinetics

Distribution: Widely distributed; CSF penetration is poor but enhanced by meningeal inflammation; crosses placenta

Protein binding: 70% to 90%

Metabolism: Primarily hepatic; undergoes enterohepatic recirculation

Half-life elimination:

Neonates: <3 weeks: 2.2-5.5 hours; 4-9 weeks: 1.2-2.3 hours

Children 3 months to 14 years: 0.75-1.9 hours

Adults: 30 minutes to 1.5 hours with normal renal and hepatic function

Time to peak, serum: I.M.: 30-60 minutes

Excretion: Primarily feces; urine (10% to 30% as unchanged drug)

Dosage

Usual dosage range:

Neonates: I.M., I.V.:

1200-2000 g, <7 days: 50 mg/kg/day divided every 12 hours

>2000 g, <7 days: 75 mg/kg/day divided every 8 hours

1200-2000 g, ≥7 days: 75 mg/kg/day divided every 8 hours

>2000 g, ≥7 days: 100-140 mg/kg/day divided every 6 hours

Children:

I.M.: 25 mg/kg twice daily

I.V.: 50-200 mg/kg/day in divided doses every 4-6 hours (maximum: 12 g/day)

Adults:

I.M.: 500 mg every 4-6 hours

I.V.: 500-2000 mg every 4-6 hours

Indication-specific dosing:

Children:

Mild-to-moderate infections: I.M., I.V.: 50-100 mg/kg/day in divided doses every 6 hours

Severe infections: I.M., I.V.: 100-200 mg/kg/day in divided doses every 4-6 hours (maximum dose: 12 g/day)

Staphylococcal endocarditis: I.V.:

Native valve: 200 mg/kg/day in divided doses every 4-6 hours for 6 weeks

Prosthetic valve: 200 mg/kg/day in divided doses every 4-6 hours for ≥6 weeks (use with rifampin and gentamicin)

Adults: I.V.:

Endocarditis: MSSA:

Native valve: 12 g/24 hours in 4-6 divided doses for 6 weeks

Prosthetic valve: 12 g/24 hours in 4-6 divided doses for ≥6 weeks (use with rifampin and gentamicin)

Joint:

Bursitis, septic: 2 g every 4 hours

Prosthetic: 2 g every 4-6 hours with rifampin for 6 weeks

***Staphylococcus aureus,* methicillin-susceptible infections, including brain abscess, empyema, erysipelas, mastitis, myositis, osteomyelitis, pneumonia, toxic shock, urinary tract (perinephric abscess):** 2 g every 4 hours

Dosing adjustment in renal impairment: Not necessary

Dosing adjustment in hepatic impairment: In patients with both hepatic and renal impairment, modification of dosage may be necessary; no data available.

Dialysis: Not dialyzable (0% to 5%) via hemodialysis; supplemental dosage not necessary with hemo- or peritoneal dialysis or continuous arteriovenous or venovenous hemofiltration

Administration

I.M.: Rotate injection sites

I.V.: Vesicant. Administer around-the-clock to promote less variation in peak and trough serum levels; infuse over 30-60 minutes

Extravasation management: Use cold packs. Hyaluronidase: Add 1 mL NS to 150 unit vial to make 150 units/mL of concentration; mix 0.1 mL of above with 0.9 mL NS in 1 mL syringe to make final concentration = 15 units/mL.

Monitoring Parameters Periodic CBC, urinalysis, BUN, serum creatinine, AST and ALT; observe for signs and symptoms of anaphylaxis during first dose

Test Interactions Positive Coombs' test (direct), false-positive urinary and serum proteins; may inactivate aminoglycosides *in vitro*

Dietary Considerations Sodium content of 1 g: 76.6 mg (3.33 mEq)

Special Geriatric Considerations Nafcillin has not been studied exclusively in the elderly, however, given its route of elimination, dosage adjustments based upon age and renal function is not necessary

Emetic Potential Very low (<10%)

Vesicant Yes; see Management of Drug Extravasations *on page 1301.*

Dosage Forms Excipient information presented when available (limited, particularly for generics); consult specific product labeling.

Infusion [premixed iso-osmotic dextrose solution]: 1 g (50 mL); 2 g (100 mL)

Injection, powder for reconstitution, as sodium: 1 g, 2 g, 10 g

References

Baddour LM, Wilson WR, Bayer AS, et al, "Infective Endocarditis. Diagnosis, Antimicrobial Therapy, and Management of Complications. A Statement for Healthcare Professionals from the Committee on Rheumatic Fever, Endocarditis, and Kawasaki Disease, Council on Cardiovascular Disease in the Young, and the Councils on Clinical Cardiology, Stroke, and Cardiovascular Surgery and Anesthesia, American Heart Association," *Circulation,* 2005, 111(23):e394-434.

Banner W Jr, Gooch WM 3d, Burckart G, et al, "Pharmacokinetics of Nafcillin in Infants With Low Birth Weights," *Antimicrob Agents Chemother,* 1980, 17(4):691-4.

Donowitz GR and Mandell GL, "Beta-Lactam Antibiotics," *N Engl J Med,* 1988, 318(7):419-26 and 318(8):490-500.

Wright AJ, "The Penicillins," *Mayo Clin Proc,* 1999, 74(3):290-307.

Zenk KE, Dungy CL, and Greene CR, "Nafcillin Extravasation Injury: Use of Hyaluronidase as an Antidote," *Am J Dis Child,* 1981, 135(12):1113-4.

- ♦ **Nafcillin Sodium** *see* Nafcillin *on page 800*
- ♦ **Nafidimide** *see* Amonafide *on page 67*
- ♦ **Nallpen** *see* Nafcillin *on page 800*
- ♦ **Nallpen® (Can)** *see* Nafcillin *on page 800*
- ♦ **Naphuride Sodium** *see* Suramin *on page 991*
- ♦ **Natulan® (Can)** *see* Procarbazine *on page 926*
- ♦ **Navelbine®** *see* Vinorelbine *on page 1107*
- ♦ **NC-722665** *see* Bicalutamide *on page 141*
- ♦ **NebuPent®** *see* Pentamidine *on page 887*

Nelarabine (nel AY re been)

Medication Safety Issues

High alert medication: The Institute for Safe Medication Practices (ISMP) includes this medication among its list of drugs which have a heightened risk of causing significant patient harm when used in error.

Related Information

Safe Handling of Hazardous Drugs *on page 1382*

U.S. Brand Names Arranon®

Index Terms 2-Amino-6-Methoxypurine Arabinoside; GW506U78; 506U78

Generic Available No

Canadian Brand Names Atriance™

Pharmacologic Category Antineoplastic Agent, Antimetabolite

Use Treatment of relapsed or refractory T-cell acute lymphoblastic leukemia (ALL) and T-cell lymphoblastic lymphoma

Unlabeled/Investigational Use CML (Philadelphia chromosome positive) T-Cell blast phase

Pregnancy Risk Factor D

Lactation Excretion in breast milk unknown/not recommended

Labeled Contraindications Hypersensitivity to nelarabine or any component of the formulation

Warnings/Precautions Hazardous agent - use appropriate precautions for handling and disposal. **[U.S. Boxed Warning]: Neurotoxicity is the dose-limiting toxicity;** observe closely for signs and symptoms of neurotoxicity (somnolence, confusion, convulsions, ataxia, paresthesia, hypoesthesia, coma, status epilepticus, craniospinal demyelination, or ascending neuropathy). Risk of neurotoxicity may increase in patients with concurrent or previous intrathecal chemotherapy or history of craniospinal irradiation. Appropriate measures must be taken to prevent hyperuricemia and tumor lysis syndrome; use extreme caution in patients with increased uric acid, gout, and history of uric acid stones; monitor, consider allopurinol and hydrate accordingly. Bone marrow suppression is common. Avoid administration of live vaccines. Use caution in patients with renal impairment; ara-G clearance may be reduced with renal dysfunction. Use caution with severe hepatic impairment; risk of adverse reactions may be higher with hepatic dysfunction.

[U.S. Boxed Warning]: Should be administered under the supervision of an experienced cancer chemotherapy physician.

Adverse Reactions Note: Pediatric adverse reactions fell within a range similar to adults except where noted.

>10%:

Cardiovascular: Peripheral edema (15%), edema (11%)

Central nervous system: Fatigue (50%), fever (23%), somnolence (7% to 23%; grades 2-4: 1% to 6%), dizziness (21%; grade 2: 8% adults), headache (15% to 17%; grades 2-4: 4% to 8%), hypoesthesia (6% to 17%; grades 2-4: children 5%, adults 12%), pain (11%)

Dermatologic: Petechiae (12%)

Endocrine & metabolic: Hypokalemia (11%)

Gastrointestinal: Nausea (41%), diarrhea (22%), vomiting (10% to 22%), constipation (21%)

Hematologic: Anemia (95% to 99%; grade 4: 10% to 14%), neutropenia (81% to 94%; grade 4: children 62%, adults 49%), thrombocytopenia (86% to 88%; grade 4: 22% to 32%), leukopenia (38%; grade 4: 7%), febrile neutropenia (12%; grade 4: 1%)

Hepatic: Transaminases increased (12%)

Neuromuscular & skeletal: Peripheral neuropathy (12% to 21%; grades 2-4: 11% to 14%), weakness (6% to 17%; grade 4: 1%), paresthesia (4% to 15%; grades 2-4: 3% to 4%), myalgia (13%)

Respiratory: Cough (25%), dyspnea (7% to 20%)

1% to 10%:

Cardiovascular: Hypotension (8%), tachycardia (8%), chest pain (5%)

Central nervous system: Ataxia (2% to 9%; grades 2-4: children 1%, adults 8%), confusion (8%), insomnia (7%), depressed level of consciousness (6%; grades 2-4: 2%), depression (6%), seizure (grade 3: 1% adults; grade 4: 6% children), motor dysfunction (4%; grades 2-4: 2%), amnesia (3%; grades 2-4: 1%), balance disorder (2%; grades 2-4: 1%), nerve paralysis (2%), sensory loss (1% to 2%), aphasia (1%), cerebral hemorrhage (1%), coma (1%), encephalopathy (1%), hemiparesis (1%), hydrocephalus (1%), lethargy (1%), leukoencephalopathy (1%), loss of consciousness (1%), mental impairment (1%), neuropathic pain (1%), nerve palsy (1%), nystagmus (1%), paralysis (1%), sciatica (1%), sensory disturbance (1%), speech disorder (1%), demyelination, ascending peripheral neuropathy

Endocrine & Metabolic: Hypocalcemia (8%), dehydration (7%), hyper-/hypoglycemia (6%), hypomagnesemia (6%)

Gastrointestinal: Abdominal pain (9%), anorexia (9%), stomatitis (8%), abdominal distension (6%), taste perversion (3%)

Hepatic: Albumin decreased (10%), bilirubin increased (10%), AST increased (6%)

Neuromuscular & skeletal: Arthralgia (9%), back pain (8%), muscle weakness (8%), rigors (8%), limb pain (7%), abnormal gait (6%), noncardiac chest pain (5%), tremor (4% to 5%; grades 2-4: 2% to 3%), dysarthria (1%), hyporeflexia (1%), hypertonia (1%), incoordination (1%)

Ocular: Blurred vision (4%)

Renal: Creatinine increased (6%)

Respiratory: Pleural effusion (10%), epistaxis (8%), pneumonia (8%), sinusitis (7%), wheezing (5%), sinus headache (1%)

Miscellaneous: Infection (5% to 9%)

Postmarketing and/or case reports: Tumor lysis syndrome

Overdosage/Toxicology Nelarabine was administered to two adult patients at doses up to 2900 mg/m^2 on days 1, 3, and 5 in clinical trials. Two patients developed grade 3 neuropathy at a dose of 2200 mg/m^2 given on days 1, 3, and 5. A single dose of 4800 mg/m^2 produced neurotoxicity and was fatal in animal studies. If an overdose occurs, it would be expected to cause severe and potentially fatal neurotoxicity and myelosuppression; treatment should be symptom-directed and supportive.

Drug Interactions

Increased Effect/Toxicity: Avoid administration of live vaccines in immunosuppressive therapy.

Decreased Effect: Pentostatin may decrease conversion of prodrug to active; concomitant use is not recommended.

Storage/Stability Store unopened vials at 15°C to 30°C (59°F to 86°F). Stable in plastic or glass containers for up to 8 hours at room temperature.

Reconstitution Reconstitution is not required; the appropriate dose should be added to empty plastic bag or glass container.

Compatibility Stable in sodium chloride 0.45%.

Mechanism of Action Nelarabine, a prodrug of ara-G, is demethylated by adenosine deaminase to ara-G and then converted to ara-GTP. Ara-GTP is incorporated into the DNA of the leukemic blasts, leading to inhibition of DNA (Continued)

Nelarabine (Continued)

synthesis and inducing apoptosis. Ara-GTP appears to accumulate at higher levels in T-cells, which correlates to clinical response.

Pharmacodynamics/Kinetics

Distribution: V_{ss}:

Nelarabine: Children: ~213 L/m^2; Adults: ~197 L/m^2

Ara-G: Children: ~50 L/m^2; Adults: ~33 L/m^2

Protein binding: Nelarabine and ara-G: <25%

Metabolism: Hepatic; demethylated by adenosine deaminase to form ara-G (active); also hydrolyzed to form methylguanine. Both ara-G and methylguanine metabolized to guanine. Guanine is deaminated into xanthine, which is further oxidized to form uric acid, which is then oxidized to form allantoin.

Half-life elimination: Nelarabine: 30 minutes; ara-G: 3 hours

Time to peak: Ara-G: 3-25 hours

Excretion: Urine (nelarabine 7%, ara-G 27%) within 24 hours of infusion on day 1

Dosage I.V.: T-cell ALL, T-cell lymphoblastic lymphoma:

Children: 650 mg/m^2/day on days 1 through 5; repeat every 21 days

Adults: 1500 mg/m^2/day on days 1, 3, and 5; repeat every 21 days

Dosage adjustment for toxicity:

Neurologic toxicity ≥ grade 2: Discontinue treatment.

Hematologic or other (non-neurologic) toxicity: Consider treatment delay.

Dosage adjustment in renal impairment:

Cl_{cr} ≥50 mL/minute: No adjustment recommended

Cl_{cr} <50 mL/minute: Safety has not been established

Cl_{cr} <30 mL/minute: Closely monitor

Dosage adjustment in hepatic impairment: Safety has not been established; closely monitor with severe impairment (bilirubin >3 mg/dL)

Administration Adequate I.V. hydration recommended to prevent tumor lysis syndrome; allopurinol may be used if hyperuricemia is anticipated.

Children: Infuse over 1 hour daily for 5 consecutive days

Adults: Infuse over 2 hours on days 1, 3, and 5

Monitoring Parameters Closely monitor for neurologic toxicity (severe somnolence, seizure, peripheral neuropathy, confusion, ataxia, paresthesia, hypoesthesia, coma, or craniospinal demyelination); signs and symptoms of tumor lysis syndrome; hydration status; CBC with platelet counts, liver and kidney function

Emetic Potential Low (10% to 30%)

Vesicant No

Dosage Forms Excipient information presented when available (limited, particularly for generics); consult specific product labeling. [CAN] = Canadian brand name

Injection, solution:

Arranon®: 5 mg/mL (50 mL)

Atriance™ [CAN]: 5 mg/ml (50 mL)

References

Aguayo A, Cortes JF, Kantarjian HM, et al, "Complete Hematologic and Cytogenetic Response to 2-Amino-9-Beta-D-Arabinosul-6-Methoxy-9H-Guanine in a Patient With Chronic Myelogenous Leukemia in T-Cell Blastic Phase: A Case Report and Review of the Literature," *Cancer*, 1999, 85(1):58-64.

Berg SL, Blaney SM, Devidas M, et al, "Phase II Study of Nelarabine (Compound 506U78) in Children and Young Adults With Refractory T-Cell Malignancies: A Report from the Children's Oncology Group," *J Clin Oncol*, 2005, 23(15):3376-82.

Gandhi V, Plunkett W, Weller S, et al, "Evaluation of the Combination of Nelarabine and Fludarabine in Leukemias: Clinical Response, Pharmacokinetics, and Pharmacodynamics in Leukemia Cells," *J Clin Oncol*, 2001, 19(8):2142-52.

Kisor DF, "Nelarabine: A Nucleoside Analog With Efficacy in T-Cell and Other Leukemias," *Ann Pharmacother*, 2005, 39(6):1056-63.

Kurtzberg J, Ernst TJ, Keating MJ, et al, "Phase I Study of 506U78 Administered on a Consecutive 5-Day Schedule in Children and Adults With Refractory Hematologic Malignancies," *J Clin Oncol*, 2005, 23(15):3396-403.

♦ **Neoral**® *see* CycloSPORINE *on page 254*
♦ **Neosar** *see* Cyclophosphamide *on page 246*
♦ **Neumega**® *see* Oprelvekin *on page 842*
♦ **Neupogen**® *see* Filgrastim *on page 440*
♦ **Nexavar**® *see* Sorafenib *on page 974*
♦ **Niastase**® **(Can)** *see* Factor VIIa (Recombinant) *on page 416*
♦ **Nidagel**™ **(Can)** *see* Metronidazole *on page 755*
♦ **Niftolid** *see* Flutamide *on page 470*
♦ **Nilandron**® *see* Nilutamide *on page 812*

Nilotinib (nye LOE ti nib)

Medication Safety Issues

Sound-alike/look-alike issues:
Nilotinib may be confused with nilutamide

High alert medication: The Institute for Safe Medication Practices (ISMP) includes this medication among its list of the classes of drugs which have a heightened risk of causing significant patient harm when used in error.

Related Information

Common Toxicity Criteria *on page 1353*
Management of Nausea and Vomiting *on page 1319*
Safe Handling of Hazardous Drugs *on page 1382*

U.S. Brand Names Tasigna®

Index Terms AMN107; Nilotinib Hydrochloride Monohydrate

Generic Available No

Pharmacologic Category Antineoplastic Agent, Tyrosine Kinase Inhibitor

Use Treatment of Philadelphia chromosome-positive chronic myelogenous leukemia (Ph+ CML) in chronic and accelerated phase (refractory or intolerant to prior therapy, including imatinib)

Unlabeled/Investigational Use Treatment of Ph+ acute lymphoblastic leukemia (ALL), systemic mastocytosis (with c-kit activation), hypereosinophilic syndrome

Pregnancy Risk Factor D

Lactation Excretion in breast milk unknown/not recommended

Labeled Contraindications Use in patients with hypokalemia, hypomagnesemia, or long QT syndrome

Warnings/Precautions Hazardous agent - use appropriate precautions for handling and disposal. **[U.S. Boxed Warning]: May prolong the QT interval; sudden deaths have been reported.** Sudden deaths appear to be related to dose-dependent ventricular repolarization abnormalities. Prolonged QT interval may result in torsade de pointes, which may cause syncope, seizure, and/or death. Use in patients with hypokalemia, hypomagnesemia, or long QT syndrome is contraindicated. Electrolyte abnormalities may occur during treatment, including hypophosphatemia, hyper-/hypokalemia, hypocalcemia, and hyponatremia. Correct electrolyte abnormalities prior to treatment initiation; monitor ECG. Concurrent use with other drugs which may prolong QT interval may increase the risk of potentially-fatal (Continued)

Nilotinib *(Continued)*

arrhythmias. Concurrent use with CYP3A4 inhibitors/inducers is not recommended; dosage adjustments are recommended if concurrent use cannot be avoided. Patients with uncontrolled or significant cardiovascular disease were excluded from studies.

[U.S. Boxed Warning]: Use with caution in patients with hepatic impairment; nilotinib metabolism is primarily hepatic; carefully monitor for QT prolongation. Nilotinib use in patients with ALT/AST >2.5 times ULN (>5 times ULN if disease-related) and/or bilirubin >1.5 times ULN has not been studied. May cause hepatotoxicity, including dose-limiting elevations in bilirubin, ALT/AST and alkaline phosphatase; monitor liver function.

Reversible myelosuppression, including grades 3 and 4 thrombocytopenia, neutropenia, and anemia may occur; may require dose reductions and/or treatment delay. **[U.S. Boxed Warning]: Administer on an empty stomach, at least 1 hour before and 2 hours after food.** Use with caution in patients with a history of pancreatitis, may cause dose-limiting elevations of serum lipase and amylase; monitor. Capsules contain lactose; do not use with galactose intolerance, severe lactase deficiency, or glucose-galactose malabsorption syndromes. Safety and efficacy have not been established in children.

Adverse Reactions Frequency not always defined.

10%:

Cardiovascular: Peripheral edema (11%)

Central nervous system: Headache (21% to 31%), fatigue (16% to 28%), fever (14% to 24%)

Dermatologic: Rash (28% to 33%), pruritus (20% to 29%)

Endocrine & metabolic: Hyperglycemia (grades 3/4: 4% to 11%)

Gastrointestinal: Nausea (18% to 31%), diarrhea (19% to 22%), constipation (18% to 21%), vomiting (10% to 21%), lipase increased (grades 3/4: 15% to 17%), abdominal pain (11% to 13%)

Hematologic: Neutropenia (grades 3/4: 28% to 37%; median duration: 15 days), thrombocytopenia (grade 3: 7% to 11%; grade 4: 17% to 30%; median duration: 22 days), anemia (grades 3/4: 8% to 23%)

Neuromuscular & skeletal: Arthralgia (16% to 18%), limb pain (13% to 16%), myalgia (14%), weakness (12% to 14%), muscle spasm (11% to 14%), bone pain (11% to 13%), back pain (10% to 12%)

Respiratory: Cough (13% to 17%), nasopharyngitis (11% to 16%), dyspnea (8% to 11%)

1% to 10%:

Cardiovascular: Flushing, hypertension, palpitation, QT interval prolonged

Central nervous system: Dizziness, dysphonia, insomnia, vertigo

Dermatologic: Alopecia, dry skin, eczema, erythema, hyperhidrosis, urticaria

Endocrine & metabolic: Hypophosphatemia (grades 3/4: 10%), hypokalemia (grades 3/4: 1% to 5%), hyperkalemia (grades 3/4: 3% to 4%), hypocalcemia (grades 3/4: 1% to 4%), hyponatremia (grades 3/4: 3%), albumin decreased (grades 3/4: 1%), hypomagnesemia

Gastrointestinal: Abdominal discomfort, amylase increased, anorexia, dyspepsia, flatulence, pancreatitis (≤1%)

Hematologic: Neutropenic fever, pancytopenia

Hepatic: Hyperbilirubinemia (grades 3/4: 9% to 10%), ALT increased (grades 3/4: 2% to 4%), alkaline phosphatase increased (grades 3/4: 1% to 3%), AST increased (grades 3/4: 1%), GGT increased

Neuromuscular & skeletal: Musculoskeletal pain, paresthesia

Respiratory: Dyspnea (exertional), pleural effusion (≤1%)

Miscellaneous: Night sweats

<1%, postmarketing, and/or case reports (limited to important or life-threatening): Angina, atrial fibrillation, blurred vision, bradycardia, brain edema, bruising, BUN increased, candidiasis, cardiac failure, cardiac flutter, cardiac murmur, cardiomegaly, chest pain, confusion, coronary artery disease, creatinine elevated, depression, diabetes mellitus, diplopia, dysuria, epistaxis, erectile dysfunction, erythema nodosum, exfoliative rash, extrasystoles, eye hemorrhage, facial edema, gastroenteritis, gastrointestinal hemorrhage, gastrointestinal ulcer perforation, gynecomastia, hematemesis, hematoma, hematuria, hemorrhagic shock, hepatitis, hepatomegaly, hepatotoxicity, herpes simplex, hypercalcemia, hyper-/hypothyroidism, hyperphosphatemia, hypertensive crisis, hypoglycemia, hypotension, influenza-like illness, interstitial lung disease, intracranial hemorrhage, jaundice, joint swelling, lactic dehydrogenase increased, leukocytosis, loss of consciousness, melena, MI, migraine, mouth ulceration, optic neuritis, papilledema, pericardial effusion, pericarditis, periorbital edema, peripheral neuropathy, petechiae, pneumonia, pulmonary edema, pulmonary hypertension, renal failure, retroperitoneal hemorrhage, sepsis, stomatitis, subileus, thrombocytosis, thrombosis, thyroiditis, troponin increased, ulcerative esophagitis, urinary tract infection, ventricular dysfunction, visual acuity decreased

Overdosage/Toxicology Treatment is symptom-directed and supportive.

Drug Interactions

Cytochrome P450 Effect: Substrate of CYP3A4 (major), P-glycoprotein (P-gp, ABCB1); **Induces** CYP2C8, 2C9, 2D6

Increased Effect/Toxicity: Nilotinib may increase levels/effects of CYP2C8 substrates; example substrates include amiodarone, paclitaxel, pioglitazone, repaglinide, and rosiglitazone. Nilotinib may increase levels/effects of CYP2C9 substrates; example substrates include bosentan, dapsone, fluoxetine, glimepiride, glipizide, losartan, montelukast, nateglinide, paclitaxel, phenytoin, warfarin, and zafirlukast. Nilotinib may increase the levels/effects of CYP2D6 substrates; example substrates include amphetamines, selected beta-blockers, dextromethorphan, fluoxetine, lidocaine, mirtazapine, nefazodone, paroxetine, risperidone, ritonavir, thioridazine, tricyclic antidepressants, and venlafaxine. Nilotinib may increase the levels/effects of CYP3A4 substrates; example substrates include benzodiazepines, calcium channel blockers, cyclosporine, midazolam, mirtazapine, nateglinide, nefazodone, sildenafil (and other PDE5 inhibitors), tacrolimus, and venlafaxine. Nilotinib may increase the levels/effects of P-glycoprotein substrates and UGT1A1 substrates. Nilotinib may increase the levels/effects of warfarin.

CYP3A4 inhibitors may increase the levels/effects of nilotinib; example inhibitors include azole antifungals, clarithromycin, diclofenac, doxycycline, erythromycin, imatinib, isoniazid, nefazodone, nicardipine, propofol, protease inhibitors, quinidine, telithromycin, and verapamil. Concurrent use with other drugs may prolong the QT_c interval (class Ia and class III antiarrhythmic agents, selected quinolones [moxifloxacin], cisapride, dolasetron, thioridazine, and other agents) may increase the risk of potentially-fatal arrhythmias. P-glycoprotein inhibitors may increase the levels/effects of nilotinib.

Decreased Effect: Nilotinib may decrease the levels/effects of CYP2B6 substrates; example substrates include bupropion, efavirenz, promethazine, selegiline, and sertraline. Nilotinib may decrease levels/effects of CYP2C8 substrates; example substrates include amiodarone, paclitaxel, (Continued)

Nilotinib *(Continued)*

pioglitazone, repaglinide, rosiglitazone. Nilotinib may decrease levels/ effects of CYP2C9 substrates; example substrates include bosentan, celecoxib, dapsone, fluoxetine, glimepiride, glipizide, losartan, montelukast, nateglinide, paclitaxel, phenytoin, sulfonamides, trimetho-prim, warfarin, zafirlukast. Nilotinib may decrease the levels/effects of active metabolites generated by CYP2D6; example prodrug substrates include codeine and tramadol. CYP3A4 inducers may decrease the levels/ effects of nilotinib; example inducers include aminoglutethimide, carbam-azepine, nafcillin, nevirapine, phenobarbital, phenytoin, and rifamycins.

Ethanol/Nutrition/Herb Interactions Herb/Nutraceutical: Avoid St John's wort (may decrease nilotinib levels).

Storage/Stability Store at 15°C to 30°C (59°F to 86°F).

Mechanism of Action Selective tyrosine kinase inhibitor that targets BCR-ABL kinase, c-KIT and platelet derived growth factor receptor (PDGFR); does not have activity against the SRC family. Inhibits BCR-ABL mediated proliferation of leukemic cell lines by binding to the ATP-binding site of BCR-ABL and inhibiting tyrosine kinase activity. Nilotinib has activity in imatinib-resistant BCR-ABL kinase mutations.

Pharmacodynamics/Kinetics

Protein binding: ~98%

Metabolism: Hepatic; oxidation and hydroxylation, via CYP3A4 to primarily inactive metabolites

Bioavailability: Increased 82% when administered 30 minutes after a high-fat meal

Half-life elimination: ~15-17 hours

Time to peak: 3 hours

Excretion: Feces (93%; 69% as parent drug)

Dosage Oral: Adults: 400 mg twice daily (continue treatment until disease progression or unacceptable toxicity)

Dosage adjustment for concomitant CYP3A4 inhibitors/inducers:

CYP3A4 inhibitors: The concomitant use of a strong CYP3A4 inhibitor with nilotinib is not recommended. If a strong CYP3A4 inhibitor is required, interruption of nilotinib treatment is recommended; if therapy cannot be interrupted and concurrent use can not be avoided, consider reducing the nilotinib dose by 50%, to 400 mg once daily, with careful monitoring, especially of the QT interval. When a strong CYP3A4 inhibitor is discon-tinued, allow a washout period prior to adjusting nilotinib dose upward. (See Drug Interactions for examples of CYP3A4 inhibitors.)

CYP3A4 inducers: The concomitant use of a strong CYP3A4 inducer with nilotinib is not recommended. If a strong CYP3A4 inducer is required, the nilotinib dose may need to be increased, with careful monitoring. When the strong CYP3A4 inducer is discontinued, reduce nilotinib to the indicated dose. (See Drug Interactions for examples of CYP3A4 inducers.)

Dosage adjustment in renal impairment: Not studied in patients with serum creatinine >1.5 times ULN, however, nilotinib and its metabolites have minimal renal excretion; dosage adjustments for renal dysfunction may not be needed.

Dosage adjustment in hepatic impairment: Not studied in patients with hepatic impairment; nilotinib metabolism is primarily hepatic, use caution.

For hepatotoxicity during treatment:

If bilirubin >3 times ULN (≥ grade 3): Withhold treatment, monitor bili-rubin, resume treatment at 400 mg once daily when bilirubin returns to ≤1.5 times ULN (≤ grade 1)

If ALT or AST >5 times ULN (≥ grade 3): Withhold treatment, monitor transaminases, resume treatment at 400 mg once daily when ALT or AST returns to ≤2.5 times ULN (≤ grade 1)

Dosage adjustment for hematologic toxicity:

ANC <1000/mm^3 and/or platelets <50,000/mm^3: Withhold treatment, monitor blood counts

If ANC >1000/mm^3 and platelets >50,000/mm^3 within 2 weeks: Continue at 400 mg twice daily

If ANC <1000/mm^3 and/or platelets <50,000/mm^3 for >2 weeks: Reduce dose to 400 mg once daily

Dosage adjustment for nonhematologic toxicity:

Amylase or lipase ≥2 times ULN (≥ grade 3): Withhold treatment, monitor serum amylase or lipase, resume treatment at 400 mg once daily when lipase or amylase returns to ≤1.5 times ULN (≤ grade 1)

Clinically-significant moderate or severe nonhematologic toxicity: Withhold treatment, upon resolution of toxicity, resume at 400 mg once daily; may escalate back to 400 mg twice daily if clinically appropriate.

Dosage adjustment for QT prolongation:

QT_c >480 msec: Withhold treatment, monitor and correct potassium and magnesium levels.

If within 2 weeks:

QT_cF returns to <450 msec and to within 20 msec of baseline within 2 weeks: Continue at 400 mg twice daily

QT_cF returns to 450-480 msec: Reduce dose to 400 mg once daily

If QT_cF >480 msec after dosage reduction to 400 mg once daily, discontinue therapy.

Administration Administer twice daily, ~12 hours apart. Swallow capsules whole with water. Administer on an empty stomach, at least 1 hour before or 2 hours after food.

Monitoring Parameters CBC with differential (every 2 weeks for first 2 months, then monthly); electrolytes (including potassium and magnesium; baseline and periodic); hepatic function (ALT/AST, bilirubin, alkaline phosphatase; baseline and periodic); serum lipase (baseline and periodic); bone marrow assessments; ECG (baseline, 7 days after treatment initiation or dosage adjustments, and periodically thereafter)

Dietary Considerations The bioavailability of nilotinib is increased with food. Take on an empty stomach, at least 1 hour before or 2 hours after food. Avoid grapefruit juice.

Additional Information If clinically indicated, may be administered in combination with hematopoietic growth factors (eg, erythropoietin, filgrastim) and with hydroxyurea or anagrelide.

Emetic Potential Low (10% to 30%)

Dosage Forms Excipient information presented when available (limited, particularly for generics); consult specific product labeling.

Capsule, as monohydrate hydrochloride:

Tasigna®: 200 mg

References

Kantarjian HM, Giles F, Gattermann N, et al, "Nilotinib (Formerly AMN107), a Highly Selective Bcr-Abl Tyrosine Kinase Inhibitor, is Effective in Patients With Philadelphia Chromosome-Positive Chronic Myelogenous Leukemia in Chronic Phase Following Imatinib Resistance and Intolerance," *Blood*, 2007 [epub ahead of print]

Kantarjian H, Giles F, Wunderle L, et al, "Nilotinib in Imatinib-Resistant CML and Philadelphia Chromosome-Positive ALL," *N Engl J Med*, 2006, 354(24):2542-51.

Verstovsek S, Akin C, Manshouri T, et al, "Effects of AMN107, a Novel Aminopyrimidine Tyrosine Kinase Inhibitor, on Human Mast Cells Bearing Wild-Type or Mutated Codon 816 c-kit," *Leuk Res*, 2006, 30(11):1365-70.

(Continued)

Nilotinib *(Continued)*

Verstovsek S, Giles FJ, Quintas-Cardama A, et al, "Activity of AMN107, a Novel Aminopyrimidine Tyrosine Kinase Inhibitor, Against Human FIP1L1-PDGFR-Alpha-Expressing Cells, *Leuk Res*, 2006, 30(12):1499-505.

Verstovsek S, Golemovic M, Kantarjian H, et al, "AMN107, a Novel Aminopyrimidine Inhibitor of p190 Bcr-Abl Activation and of *in vitro* Proliferation of Philadelphia-Positive Acute Lymphoblastic Leukemia Cells," *Cancer*, 2005, 104(6):1230-6.

Weisberg E, Manley P, Mestan J, et al, "AMN107 (Nilotinib): A Novel and Selective Inhibitor of BCR-ABL," *Br J Cancer*, 2006, 94(12):1765-9.

♦ **Nilotinib Hydrochloride Monohydrate** *see* Nilotinib *on page 807*

♦ **Nilstat (Can)** *see* Nystatin *on page 817*

Nilutamide *(ni LOO ta mide)*

Medication Safety Issues
Sound-alike/look-alike issues:
Nilutamide may be confused with nilotinib

Related Information
Safe Handling of Hazardous Drugs *on page 1382*

U.S. Brand Names Nilandron®

Index Terms NSC-684588; RU-23908

Generic Available No

Canadian Brand Names Anandron®

Pharmacologic Category Antiandrogen; Antineoplastic Agent, Antiandrogen

Use Treatment of metastatic prostate cancer

Pregnancy Risk Factor C

Lactation Not indicated for use in women

Labeled Contraindications Hypersensitivity to nilutamide or any component of the formulation; severe hepatic impairment; severe respiratory insufficiency

Warnings/Precautions Hazardous agent - use appropriate precautions for handling and disposal. **[U.S. Boxed Warning]: May cause interstitial pneumonitis;** the suggestive signs of pneumonitis most often occurred within the first 3 months of nilutamide treatment. Has been associated with severe hepatitis, which has resulted in fatality. In addition, foreign postmarketing surveillance has revealed isolated cases of aplastic anemia (a causal relationship with nilutamide could not be ascertained).

May alter time for visual adaptation to darkness, ranging from seconds to a few minutes. This effect sometimes does not abate as drug treatment is continued. Caution patients who experience this effect about driving at night or through tunnels. This effect can be alleviated by wearing tinted glasses.

Adverse Reactions
>10%:
Central nervous system: Headache, insomnia
Endocrine & metabolic: Hot flashes (30% to 67%), gynecomastia (10%)
Gastrointestinal: Nausea (mild - 10% to 32%), abdominal pain (10%), constipation, anorexia
Genitourinary: Testicular atrophy (16%), libido decreased
Hepatic: Transaminases increased (8% to 13%; transient)
Ocular: Impaired dark adaptation (13% to 57%), usually reversible with dose reduction, may require discontinuation of the drug in 1% to 2% of patients
Respiratory: Dyspnea (11%)
1% to 10%:
Cardiovascular: Chest pain, edema, heart failure, hypertension, syncope

Central nervous system: Dizziness, drowsiness, malaise, hypoesthesia, depression

Dermatologic: Pruritus, alopecia, dry skin, rash

Endocrine & metabolic: Disulfiram-like reaction (hot flashes, rash) (5%); Flu-like syndrome, fever

Gastrointestinal: Vomiting, diarrhea, dyspepsia, GI hemorrhage, melena, weight loss, xerostomia

Genitourinary: Hematuria, nocturia

Hematologic: Anemia

Hepatic: Hepatitis (1%)

Neuromuscular & skeletal: Arthritis, paresthesia

Ocular: Chromatopsia (9%), abnormal vision (6% to 7%), cataracts, photophobia

Respiratory: Interstitial pneumonitis (2% - typically exertional dyspnea, cough, chest pain, and fever; most often occurring within the first 3 months of treatment); rhinitis

Miscellaneous: Diaphoresis

<1%, postmarketing, and/or case reports: Aplastic anemia

Overdosage/Toxicology Symptoms of overdose may include nausea, vomiting, malaise, headache, dizziness, and elevated liver enzymes. Management is supportive. Dialysis is of no benefit.

Drug Interactions

Cytochrome P450 Effect: Substrate of CYP2C19 (major); **Inhibits** CYP2C19 (weak)

Increased Effect/Toxicity: CYP2C19 inhibitors may increase the levels/ effects of nilutamide; example inhibitors include delavirdine, fluconazole, fluvoxamine, gemfibrozil, isoniazid, omeprazole, and ticlopidine.

Decreased Effect: CYP2C19 inducers may decrease the levels/effects of nilutamide; example inducers include aminoglutethimide, carbamazepine, phenytoin, and rifampin.

Ethanol/Nutrition/Herb Interactions

Ethanol: Avoid ethanol. Up to 5% of patients may experience a systemic reaction (flushing, hypotension, malaise) when combined with nilutamide.

Herb/Nutraceutical: St John's wort may decrease nilutamide levels.

Storage/Stability Store at room temperature of 15°C to 30°C (59°F to 86°F). Protect from light.

Mechanism of Action Nonsteroidal antiandrogen that inhibits androgen uptake or inhibits binding of androgen in target tissues. It specifically blocks the action of androgens by interacting with cytosolic androgen receptor F sites in target tissue

Pharmacodynamics/Kinetics

Absorption: Rapid and complete

Protein binding: 72% to 85%

Metabolism: Hepatic, forms active metabolites

Half-life elimination: Terminal: 23-87 hours; Metabolites: 35-137 hours

Excretion: Urine (up to 78% at 120 hours; <1% as unchanged drug); feces (1% to 7%)

Dosage Refer to individual protocols.

Adults: Oral: 300 mg daily for 30 days starting the same day or day after surgical castration, then 150 mg/day

Monitoring Parameters Obtain a chest x-ray if a patient reports dyspnea; if there are findings suggestive of interstitial pneumonitis, discontinue treatment with nilutamide. Measure serum hepatic enzyme levels at baseline and at regular intervals (3 months); if transaminases increase over 2-3 times the upper limit of normal, discontinue treatment. Perform appropriate laboratory (Continued)

Nilutamide *(Continued)*

testing at the first symptom/sign of liver injury (eg, jaundice, dark urine, fatigue, abdominal pain or unexplained GI symptoms).

Dietary Considerations May be taken without regard to food.

Patient Information Take as prescribed; do not change dosing schedule or stop taking without consulting prescriber. May cause a severe reaction with alcohol. Use alcohol cautiously while taking this medication; if the reaction occurs, avoid alcohol. Periodic laboratory tests are necessary while taking this medication. You may experience dizziness, confusion, or blurred vision (avoid driving or engaging in tasks that require alertness until response to drug is known); loss of light accommodation (avoid night driving and use caution in poorly lighted or changing light situations); impotence; or loss of libido (discuss with prescriber). Report yellowing of skin or eyes; change in color of urine or stool; unusual bruising or bleeding; chest pain; difficulty or painful voiding. Report immediately any shortness of breath, difficulty breathing, or increased cough.

Special Geriatric Considerations Your eyes may be slow to adapt to darkness; be careful when driving at night; tinted glasses may help.

Emetic Potential Low (10% to 30)

Dosage Forms Excipient information presented when available (limited, particularly for generics); consult specific product labeling.
Tablet: 150 mg

References

Bertagna C, DeGery A, Hucher M, et al, "Efficacy of the Combination of Nilutamide Plus Orchidectomy in Patients With Metastatic Prostatic Cancer, A Meta-Analysis of Seven Randomized Double-Blind Trials (1056 Patients)," *Br J Urol*, 1994, 73(4):396-402.

Creaven PJ, Pendyala L, and Tremblay D, "Pharmacokinetics and Metabolism of Nilutamide," *Urology*, 1991, 37(2 Suppl):13-9.

Dijkman GA, Janknegt RA, De Reijke TM, et al, "Long-Term Efficacy and Safety of Nilutamide Plus Castration in Advanced Prostate Cancer, and the Significance of Early Prostate Specific Antigen Normalization. International Anandron Study Group," *J Urol*, 1997, 158(1):160-3.

Dole EJ and Holdsworth MT, "Nilutamide: An Antiandrogen for the Treatment of Prostate Cancer," *Ann Pharmacother*, 1997, 31(1):65-75.

Du Plessis DJ, "Castration Plus Nilutamide vs Castration Plus Placebo in Advanced Prostate Cancer. A Review, *Urology*, 1991, 37(2 Suppl):20-4.

Harris MG, Coleman SG, Faulds D, et al, "Nilutamide. A Review of Its Pharmacodynamic and Pharmacokinetic Properties, and Therapeutic Efficacy in Prostate Cancer," *Drugs Aging*, 1993, 3(1):9-25.

Pendyala L, Creaven PJ, Huben R, et al, "Pharmacokinetics of Anandron in Patients With Advanced Carcinoma of the Prostate," *Cancer Chemother Pharmacol*, 1988, 22(1):69-76.

♦ **Nipent**® *see* Pentostatin *on page 891*

♦ **Nitrogen Mustard** *see* Mechlorethamine *on page 700*

♦ **Nizoral**® *see* Ketoconazole *on page 649*

♦ **Nizoral**® **A-D [OTC]** *see* Ketoconazole *on page 649*

♦ **N-Methylhydrazine** *see* Procarbazine *on page 926*

♦ **Nolvadex**® **[DSC]** *see* Tamoxifen *on page 1002*

♦ **Nolvadex**® **(Can)** *see* Tamoxifen *on page 1002*

♦ **Nolvadex**®**-D (Can)** *see* Tamoxifen *on page 1002*

♦ **Nordeoxyguanosine** *see* Ganciclovir *on page 492*

♦ **Noritate**® *see* Metronidazole *on page 755*

♦ **Novantrone**® *see* Mitoxantrone *on page 773*

♦ **Nove-Desmopressin**® **(Can)** *see* Desmopressin *on page 326*

♦ **Novo-Benzydamine (Can)** *see* Benzydamine *on page 132*

♦ **Novo-Bicalutamide (Can)** *see* Bicalutamide *on page 141*

♦ **Novo-Chlorpromazine (Can)** *see* ChlorproMAZINE *on page 208*

♦ **Novo-Ciprofloxacin (Can)** *see* Ciprofloxacin *on page 213*

- **Novo-Cyproterone (Can)** *see* Cyproterone *on page 267*
- **Novo-Fluconazole (Can)** *see* Fluconazole *on page 449*
- **Novo-Flutamide (Can)** *see* Flutamide *on page 470*
- **Novo-Hydroxyzin (Can)** *see* HydrOXYzine *on page 564*
- **Novo-Ketoconazole (Can)** *see* Ketoconazole *on page 649*
- **Novo-Levofloxacin (Can)** *see* Levofloxacin *on page 678*
- **Novo-Lorazepam (Can)** *see* Lorazepam *on page 693*
- **Novo-Medrone (Can)** *see* MedroxyPROGESTERone *on page 703*
- **Novo-Ofloxacin (Can)** *see* Ofloxacin *on page 825*
- **Novo-Olanzapine (Can)** *see* Olanzapine *on page 831*
- **Novo-Ondansetron (Can)** *see* Ondansetron *on page 837*
- **Novo-Peridol (Can)** *see* Haloperidol *on page 526*
- **Novo-Prednisolone (Can)** *see* PrednisoLONE *on page 914*
- **Novo-Prednisone (Can)** *see* PredniSONE *on page 919*
- **Novo-Purol (Can)** *see* Allopurinol *on page 40*
- **Novo-Semide (Can)** *see* Furosemide *on page 483*
- **NovoSeven®** *see* Factor VIIa (Recombinant) *on page 416*
- **Novo-Tamoxifen (Can)** *see* Tamoxifen *on page 1002*
- **Novo-Trimel (Can)** *see* Sulfamethoxazole and Trimethoprim *on page 982*
- **Novo-Trimel D.S. (Can)** *see* Sulfamethoxazole and Trimethoprim *on page 982*
- **Noxafil®** *see* Posaconazole *on page 912*
- **NSC-740** *see* Methotrexate *on page 733*
- **NSC-750** *see* Busulfan *on page 154*
- **NSC-752** *see* Thioguanine *on page 1030*
- **NSC-755** *see* Mercaptopurine *on page 720*
- **NSC-762** *see* Mechlorethamine *on page 700*
- **NSC-3053** *see* Dactinomycin *on page 287*
- **NSC-3088** *see* Chlorambucil *on page 205*
- **NSC-8806** *see* Melphalan *on page 710*
- **NSC-13875** *see* Altretamine *on page 50*
- **NSC-15200** *see* Gallium Nitrate *on page 490*
- **NSC-26271** *see* Cyclophosphamide *on page 246*
- **NSC-26980** *see* Mitomycin *on page 768*
- **NSC-27640** *see* Floxuridine *on page 447*
- **NSC-34936** *see* Suramin *on page 991*
- **NSC-38721** *see* Mitotane *on page 771*
- **NSC-49842** *see* VinBLAStine *on page 1095*
- **NSC-63878** *see* Cytarabine *on page 269*
- **NSC-66847** *see* Thalidomide *on page 1025*
- **NSC-67574** *see* VinCRIStine *on page 1099*
- **NSC-71423** *see* Megestrol *on page 707*
- **NSC-77213** *see* Procarbazine *on page 926*
- **NSC-79037** *see* Lomustine *on page 690*
- **NSC-82151** *see* DAUNOrubicin Hydrochloride *on page 308*
- **NSC-85998** *see* Streptozocin *on page 979*
- **NSC-89199** *see* Estramustine *on page 400*
- **NSC-102816** *see* Azacitidine *on page 117*
- **NSC-105014** *see* Cladribine *on page 231*
- **NSC-106977 (*Erwinia*)** *see* Asparaginase *on page 111*

- **NSC-109229 (*E. coli*)** *see* Asparaginase *on page 111*
- **NSC-109724** *see* Ifosfamide *on page 579*
- **NSC-122758** *see* Tretinoin (Oral) *on page 1069*
- **NSC-123127** *see* DOXOrubicin *on page 352*
- **NSC-125066** *see* Bleomycin *on page 146*
- **NSC-125973** *see* Paclitaxel *on page 858*
- **NSC-127716** *see* Decitabine *on page 313*
- **NSC-147834** *see* Flutamide *on page 470*
- **NSC-169780** *see* Dexrazoxane *on page 338*
- **NSC-180973** *see* Tamoxifen *on page 1002*
- **NSC-218321** *see* Pentostatin *on page 891*
- **NSC-241240** *see* Carboplatin *on page 173*
- **NSC-245467** *see* Vindesine *on page 1105*
- **NSC-249992** *see* Amsacrine *on page 85*
- **NSC-256439** *see* Idarubicin *on page 575*
- **NSC-256942** *see* Epirubicin *on page 383*
- **NSC-266046** *see* Oxaliplatin *on page 845*
- **NSC-301739** *see* Mitoxantrone *on page 773*
- **NSC-308847** *see* Amonafide *on page 67*
- **NSC-312887** *see* Fludarabine *on page 457*
- **NSC-362856** *see* Temozolomide *on page 1010*
- **NSC-367982** *see* Interferon Alfa-2a *on page 611*
- **NSC-373364** *see* Aldesleukin *on page 29*
- **NSC-377523** *see* Interferon Alfa-2b *on page 617*
- **NSC-377526** *see* Leuprolide *on page 672*
- **NSC-409962** *see* Carmustine *on page 178*
- **NSC-603071** *see* Aminocamptothecin *on page 61*
- **NSC-606864** *see* Goserelin *on page 520*
- **NSC606869** *see* Clofarabine *on page 236*
- **NSC-609699** *see* Topotecan *on page 1048*
- **NSC-613327** *see* Gemcitabine *on page 499*
- **NSC-613795** *see* Sargramostim *on page 962*
- **NSC-614629** *see* Filgrastim *on page 440*
- **NSC-616348** *see* Irinotecan *on page 626*
- **NSC-628503** *see* Docetaxel *on page 342*
- **NSC-639186** *see* Raltitrexed *on page 943*
- **NSC-644468** *see* Deferoxamine *on page 319*
- **NSC-644954** *see* Pegaspargase *on page 880*
- **NSC-671663** *see* Octreotide *on page 819*
- **NSC-673089** *see* Paclitaxel *on page 858*
- **NSC-681239** *see* Bortezomib *on page 150*
- **NSC-683864** *see* Temsirolimus *on page 1014*
- **NSC-684588** *see* Nilutamide *on page 812*
- **NSC-687451** *see* Rituximab *on page 953*
- **NSC-688097** *see* Trastuzumab *on page 1066*
- **NSC-697732** *see* DAUNOrubicin Citrate (Liposomal) *on page 305*
- **NSC-698037** *see* Pemetrexed *on page 884*
- **NSC-701852** *see* Vorinostat *on page 1116*
- **NSC-703813** *see* Lenalidomide *on page 659*
- **NSC-704865** *see* Bevacizumab *on page 133*

Nystatin (nye STAT in)

Medication Safety Issues

Sound-alike/look-alike issues:

Nystatin may be confused with Nilstat®, Nitrostat®

(Continued)

Nystatin *(Continued)*

Nilstat may be confused with Nitrostat®, nystatin

Related Information

Oral Mucositis / Stomatitis *on page 1332*

U.S. Brand Names Bio-Statin®; Mycostatin®; Nyamyc™; Nystat-Rx®; Nystop®; Pedi-Dri®

Generic Available Yes: Cream, ointment, powder, suspension, tablet

Canadian Brand Names Candistatin®; Nilstat; Nyaderm; PMS-Nystatin

Pharmacologic Category Antifungal Agent, Oral Nonabsorbed; Antifungal Agent, Topical; Antifungal Agent, Vaginal

Use Treatment of susceptible cutaneous, mucocutaneous, and oral cavity fungal infections normally caused by the *Candida* species

Pregnancy Risk Factor B/C (oral)

Lactation Does not enter breast milk/compatible (not absorbed orally)

Labeled Contraindications Hypersensitivity to nystatin or any component of the formulation

Adverse Reactions

Frequency not defined: Dermatologic: Contact dermatitis, Stevens-Johnson syndrome

1% to 10%: Gastrointestinal: Nausea, vomiting, diarrhea, stomach pain

<1%: Hypersensitivity reactions

Overdosage/Toxicology Symptoms of overdose include nausea, vomiting, and diarrhea. Treatment is supportive.

Storage/Stability

Vaginal insert: Store in refrigerator. Protect from temperature extremes, moisture, and light.

Oral tablet, ointment, topical powder, and oral suspension: Store at controlled room temperature 15°C to 25°C (59°F to 77°F).

Mechanism of Action Binds to sterols in fungal cell membrane, changing the cell wall permeability allowing for leakage of cellular contents

Pharmacodynamics/Kinetics

Onset of action: Symptomatic relief from candidiasis: 24-72 hours

Absorption: Topical: None through mucous membranes or intact skin; Oral: Poorly absorbed

Excretion: Feces (as unchanged drug)

Dosage

Oral candidiasis:

Suspension (swish and swallow orally):

Premature infants: 100,000 units 4 times/day

Infants: 200,000 units 4 times/day or 100,000 units to each side of mouth 4 times/day

Children and Adults: 400,000-600,000 units 4 times/day

Powder for compounding: Children and Adults: $1/8$ teaspoon (500,000 units) to equal approximately $1/2$ cup of water; give 4 times/day

Mucocutaneous infections: Children and Adults: Topical: Apply 2-3 times/day to affected areas; very moist topical lesions are treated best with powder

Intestinal infections: Adults: Oral: 500,000-1,000,000 units every 8 hours

Vaginal infections: Adults: Vaginal tablets: Insert 1 tablet/day at bedtime for 2 weeks

Administration Suspension: Shake well before using. Should be swished about the mouth and retained in the mouth for as long as possible (several minutes) before swallowing.

Patient Information The oral suspension should be swished about the mouth and retained in the mouth for as long as possible (several minutes)

before swallowing. For neonates and infants, paint nystatin suspension into recesses of the mouth. Troches must be allowed to dissolve slowly and should not be chewed or swallowed whole. If topical irritation occurs, discontinue; for external use only; do not discontinue therapy even if symptoms are gone

Special Geriatric Considerations For oral infections, patients who wear dentures must have them removed and cleaned in order to eliminate source of reinfection.

Emetic Potential Low (10% to 30%)

Dosage Forms Excipient information presented when available (limited, particularly for generics); consult specific product labeling.

Capsule:

Bio-Statin®: 500,000 units, 1 million units

Cream: 100,000 units/g (15 g, 30 g)

Mycostatin®: 100,000 units/g (30 g)

Ointment, topical: 100,000 units/g (15 g, 30 g)

Powder, for prescription compounding: 50 million units (10 g); 150 million units (30 g); 500 million units (100 g); 2 billion units (400 g)

Nystat-Rx®: 50 million units (10 g); 150 million units (30 g); 500 million units (100 g); 1 billion units (190 g); 2 billion units (350 g)

Powder, topical:

Mycostatin®: 100,000 units/g (15 g) [contains talc]

Nyamyc™: 100,000 units/g (15 g, 30 g) [contains talc]

Nystop®: 100,000 units/g (15 g, 30 g, 60 g) [contains talc]

Pedi-Dri®: 100,000 units/g (56.7 g) [contains talc]

Suspension, oral: 100,000 units/mL (5 mL, 60 mL, 480 mL)

Tablet: 500,000 units

Tablet, vaginal: 100,000 units (15s) [packaged with applicator]

References

Dismukes WE, Wade JS, Lee JY, et al, "A Randomized, Double-Blind Trial of Nystatin Therapy for the Candidiasis Hypersensitivity Syndrome," *N Engl J Med*, 1990, 323(25):1717-23.

Epstein JB, Vickars L, Spinelli J, et al, "Efficacy of Chlorhexidine and Nystatin Rinses in Prevention of Oral Complications in Leukemia and Bone Marrow Transplantation," *Oral Surg Oral Med Oral Pathol*, 1992, 73(6):682-9.

Meunier-Carpentier F, "Symposium on Infectious Complications of Neoplastic Disease (Part II). Chemoprophylaxis of Fungal Infections," *Am J Med*, 1984, 76(4):652-6.

Poland JM, "Oral Thrush in the Oncologic Patient. Therapy Must Be Tailored," *Am J Hosp Care* 1987, 4(5):30-2.

Wasilewski C Jr, "Allergic Contact Dermatitis From Nystatin," *Arch Dermatol*, 1971, 104(4):437.

♦ **Nystat-Rx®** see Nystatin on page 817

♦ **Nystop®** see Nystatin on page 817

♦ **Oasis®** see Saliva Substitute on page 960

♦ **Octagam®** see Immune Globulin (Intravenous) on page 597

♦ **Octostim® (Can)** see Desmopressin on page 326

Octreotide (ok TREE oh tide)

Medication Safety Issues

Sound-alike/look-alike issues:

Sandostatin® may be confused with Sandimmune®

U.S. Brand Names Sandostatin®; Sandostatin LAR®

Index Terms NSC-671663; Octreotide Acetate

Generic Available Yes: Solution

Canadian Brand Names Octreotide Acetate Injection; Octreotide Acetate Omega; Sandostatin®; Sandostatin LAR®

(Continued)

Octreotide *(Continued)*

Pharmacologic Category Antidiarrheal; Somatostatin Analog

Use Control of symptoms in patients with metastatic carcinoid and vasoactive intestinal peptide-secreting tumors (VIPomas); acromegaly

Unlabeled/Investigational Use AIDS-associated secretory diarrhea (including *Cryptosporidiosis*); control of bleeding of esophageal varices; breast cancer; cryptosporidiosis; Cushing's syndrome (ectopic); insulinomas; small bowel fistulas; pancreatic tumors; gastrinoma; postgastrectomy dumping syndrome; chemotherapy-induced diarrhea; graft-versus-host disease (GVHD) induced diarrhea; Zollinger-Ellison syndrome; congenital hyperinsulinism; hypothalamic obesity; treatment of hypoglycemia secondary to sulfonylurea poisoning

Pregnancy Risk Factor B

Lactation Excretion in breast milk unknown/use caution

Labeled Contraindications Hypersensitivity to octreotide or any component of the formulation

Warnings/Precautions May impair gallbladder function; monitor patients for cholelithiasis. Use with caution in patients with renal impairment. Somatostatin analogs may affect glucose regulation. In type I diabetes, severe hypoglycemia may occur; in type II diabetes or patients without diabetes, hyperglycemia may occur. Insulin and other hypoglycemic medication requirements may change. Do not use depot formulation for the treatment of sulfonylurea-induced hypoglycemia. Bradycardia, conduction abnormalities, and arrhythmia have been observed in acromegalic patients; use caution with CHF or concomitant medications that alter heart rate or rhythm. Octreotide may enhance the adverse/toxic effects of other QT_c-prolonging agents. May alter absorption of dietary fats; monitor for pancreatitis. Chronic treatment has been associated with abnormal Schillings test; monitor vitamin B_{12} levels. Tumors which secrete growth hormone may increase in size; monitor. Suppresses secretion of TSH; monitor for hypothyroidism.

Adverse Reactions Adverse reactions vary by route of administration. Frequency of cardiac, endocrine, and gastrointestinal adverse reactions was generally higher in acromegalics.

>16%:

Cardiovascular: Sinus bradycardia (19% to 25%), chest pain (16% to 20%)

Central nervous system: Fatigue (1% to 20%), malaise (16% to 20%), dizziness (5% to 20%), headache (6% to 20%), fever (16% to 20%)

Endocrine & metabolic: Hyperglycemia (15% to 27%)

Gastrointestinal: Diarrhea (36% to 58%), abdominal discomfort (5% to 61%), flatulence (<10% to 38%), constipation (9% to 21%), nausea (5% to 61%), cholelithiasis (27%; length of therapy dependent), biliary duct dilatation (12%), biliary sludge (24%; length of therapy dependent), loose stools (5% to 61%), vomiting (4% to 21%)

Hematologic: Antibodies to octreotide (up to 25%; no efficacy change)

Local: Injection pain (2% to 50%; dose and formulation related)

Neuromuscular & skeletal: Backache (1% to 20%), arthropathy (16% to 20%)

Respiratory: Dyspnea (16% to 20%), upper respiratory infection (16% to 20%)

Miscellaneous: Flu symptoms (1% to 20%)

5% to 15%:

Cardiovascular: Conduction abnormalities (9% to 10%), arrhythmia (3% to 9%), hypertension, palpitation, peripheral edema

Central nervous system: Anxiety, confusion, depression, hypoesthesia, insomnia

Dermatologic: Pruritus, rash

Endocrine & metabolic: Hypothyroidism (2% to 12%), goiter (2% to 8%)

Gastrointestinal: Abdominal pain, anorexia, cramping, dehydration, discomfort, hemorrhoids, tenesmus (4% to 6%), dyspepsia (4% to 15%), steatorrhea (4% to 6%), feces discoloration (4% to 6%), weight loss

Genitourinary: UTI

Hematologic: Anemia

Hepatic: Hepatitis

Neuromuscular & skeletal: Arthralgia, leg cramps, myalgia, paresthesia, rigors, weakness

Otic: Earache, otitis media

Renal: Renal calculus

Respiratory: Coughing, pharyngitis, sinusitis, rhinitis

Miscellaneous: Allergy, diaphoresis

1% to 4%:

Cardiovascular: Angina, cardiac failure, cerebral vascular disorder, edema, flushing, hematoma, phlebitis, tachycardia

Central nervous system: Abnormal gait, amnesia, dysphonia, hallucinations, nervousness, neuralgia, neuropathy, somnolence, tremor, vertigo

Dermatologic: Acne, alopecia, bruising, cellulitis, urticaria

Endocrine & metabolic: Hypoglycemia (2% to 4%), hypokalemia, hypoproteinemia, gout, cachexia, menstrual irregularities, breast pain, impotence

Gastrointestinal: Colitis, diverticulitis, dysphagia, fat malabsorption, gastritis, gastroenteritis, gingivitis, glossitis, melena, rectal bleeding, stomatitis, taste perversion, xerostomia

Genitourinary: Incontinence

Hematologic: Epistaxis

Hepatic: Ascites, jaundice

Local: Injection hematoma

Neuromuscular & skeletal: Hyperkinesia, hypertonia, joint pain

Ocular: Blurred vision, visual disturbance

Otic: Tinnitus

Renal: Albuminuria, renal abscess

Respiratory: Bronchitis, pleural effusion, pneumonia, pulmonary embolism

Miscellaneous: Bacterial infection, cold symptoms, moniliasis

<1%: Abdomen enlarged, anaphylactic shock, anaphylactoid reaction, aneurysm, aphasia, appendicitis, arthritis, atrial fibrillation, basal cell carcinoma, Bell's palsy, breast carcinoma, burning eyes, cardiac arrest, CHF, CK increased, creatinine increased, deafness, diabetes insipidus, diabetes mellitus, facial edema, fatty liver, galactorrhea, gallbladder polyp, gallstones, GI hemorrhage, glaucoma, gynecomastia, hematuria, hemiparesis, hepatitis, hyperesthesia, hypertensive reaction, hypoadrenalism, intestinal obstruction, intracranial hemorrhage, iron deficiency, ischemia, joint effusion, lactation, leg cramps, LFTs increased, libido decreased, malignant hyperpyrexia, MI, migraine, muscle cramping, nephrolithiasis, orthostatic hypotension, pancreatitis, paranoia, paresis, peptic ulcer, petechiae, pituitary apoplexy, pneumothorax, pulmonary hypertension, pulmonary nodule, Raynaud's syndrome, renal insufficiency, retinal vein thrombosis, rhinorrhea, scotoma, seizure, status asthmaticus, suicide attempt, throat discomfort, thrombocytopenia, thrombophlebitis, thrombosis, vaginitis, visual field defect, wheal/erythema

Overdosage/Toxicology Symptoms of overdose include hypo- or hyperglycemia, blurred vision, dizziness, drowsiness, nausea, flushing, and loss of motor function. Well-tolerated bolus doses up to 1000 mcg have failed to produce adverse effects. Treatment is symptom-directed and supportive. (Continued)

Octreotide *(Continued)*

Drug Interactions

Increased Effect/Toxicity: Octreotide may increase the levels/effects of bromocriptine. Octreotide may enhance the adverse/toxic effects of other QT_c-prolonging agents, including thioridazine. Ciprofloxacin may enhance the QT_c-prolonging effects of octreotide.

Decreased Effect: Octreotide may decrease the levels/effects of cyclosporine and codeine.

Ethanol/Nutrition/Herb Interactions

Herb/Nutraceutical: Avoid hypoglycemic herbs, including alfalfa, aloe, bilberry, bitter melon, burdock, celery, damiana, fenugreek, garcinia, garlic, ginger, ginseng, gymnema, marshmallow, and stinging nettle (may enhance the hypoglycemic effect of octreotide).

Storage/Stability

Solution: Octreotide is a clear solution and should be stored under refrigeration. May be stored at room temperature for up to 14 days when protected from light. Stability of parenteral admixture is stable in NS for 96 hours at room temperature (25°C) and in D_5W for 24 hours.

Suspension: Prior to dilution, store under refrigeration and protect from light. May be at room temperature for 30-60 minutes prior to use. Use suspension immediately after preparation.

Compatibility Solution: Stable in D_5W, NS; **incompatible** with fat emulsion 10%; **variable stability** in TPN (The manufacturer states that octreotide solution is not compatible in TPN solutions due to the formation of a glycosyl octreotide conjugate which may have decreased activity; other sources give it limited compatibility.)

Y-site administration: Variable (consult detailed reference): TPN.
Compatibility when admixed: Compatible: Heparin.

Mechanism of Action Mimics natural somatostatin by inhibiting serotonin release, and the secretion of gastrin, VIP, insulin, glucagon, secretin, motilin, and pancreatic polypeptide. Decreases growth hormone and IGF-1 in acromegaly.

Pharmacodynamics/Kinetics

Duration: SubQ: 6-12 hours

Absorption: SubQ: Rapid

Distribution: V_d: 14 L (13-30 L in acromegaly)

Protein binding: 65%, mainly to lipoprotein (41% in acromegaly)

Metabolism: Extensively hepatic

Bioavailability: SubQ: 100%; I.M.: 60% to 63% of SubQ dose

Half-life elimination: 1.7-1.9 hours; up to 3.7 hours with cirrhosis

Time to peak, plasma: SubQ: 0.4 hours (0.7 hours acromegaly); I.M.: 1 hour

Excretion: Urine (32%)

Dosage

Infants and Children:

Secretory diarrhea (unlabeled use): I.V., SubQ: Doses of 1-10 mcg/kg every 12 hours have been used in children beginning at the low end of the range and increasing by 0.3 mcg/kg/dose at 3-day intervals. Suppression of growth hormone (animal data) is of concern when used as long-term therapy.

Congenital hyperinsulinism (unlabeled use): SubQ: Doses of 3-40 mcg/kg/day have been used

Adults: SubQ, I.V.: Initial: 50 mcg 2-3 times/day and titrate dose based on patient tolerance, response, and indication

Carcinoid: Initial 2 weeks: 100-600 mcg/day in 2-4 divided doses; usual range 50-1500 mcg/day

VIPomas: Initial 2 weeks: 200-300 mcg/day in 2-4 divided doses; usual range 150-750 mcg/day

Diarrhea (unlabeled use): Initial: I.V.: 50-100 mcg every 8 hours; increase by 100 mcg/dose at 48-hour intervals; maximum dose: 500 mcg every 8 hours

Esophageal varices bleeding (unlabeled use): I.V. bolus: 25-50 mcg followed by continuous I.V. infusion of 25-50 mcg/hour

Hypoglycemia in sulfonylurea poisoning (unlabeled use): SubQ (preferred route of administration): 50-100 mcg; repeat in 8-12 hours as needed based on clinical response (most patients will not require more than 2-3 doses)

Acromegaly: Initial: SubQ: 50 mcg 3 times/day; titrate to achieve growth hormone levels <5 ng/mL or IGF-I (somatomedin C) levels <1.9 units/mL in males and <2.2 units/mL in females; usual effective dose 100 mcg 3 times/day; range 300-1500 mcg/day

Note: Should be withdrawn yearly for a 4-week interval (8 weeks for depot injection) in patients who have received irradiation. Resume if levels increase and signs/symptoms recur.

Acromegaly, carcinoid tumors, and VIPomas (depot injection): Patients must be stabilized on subcutaneous octreotide for at least 2 weeks before switching to the long-acting depot: Upon switch: 20 mg I.M. intragluteally every 4 weeks for 2-3 months, then the dose may be modified based upon response. Patients receiving depot injection for carcinoid tumor or VIPoma should continue to receive their SubQ injections for the first 2 weeks at the same dose in order to maintain therapeutic levels.

Dosage adjustment for acromegaly: After 3 months of depot injections the dosage may be continued or modified as follows:

GH ≤2.5 ng/mL, IGF-1 is normal, symptoms controlled: Maintain octreotide LAR® at 20 mg I.M. every 4 weeks

GH >2.5 ng/mL, IGF-1 is elevated, and/or symptoms uncontrolled: Increase octreotide LAR® to 30 mg I.M. every 4 weeks

GH ≤1 ng/mL, IGF-1 is normal, symptoms controlled: Reduce octreotide LAR® to 10 mg I.M. every 4 weeks

Note: Patients not adequately controlled may increase dose to 40 mg every 4 weeks. Dosages >40 mg are not recommended.

Dosage adjustment for carcinoid tumors and VIPomas: After 2 months of depot injections the dosage may be continued or modified as follows:

Increase to 30 mg I.M. every 4 weeks if symptoms are inadequately controlled

Decrease to 10 mg I.M. every 4 weeks, for a trial period, if initially responsive to 20 mg dose

Dosage >30 mg is not recommended

Elderly: Elimination half-life is increased by 46% and clearance is decreased by 26%; dose adjustment may be required.

Dosage adjustment in renal impairment: Severe renal failure requiring dialysis: Clearance is reduced by ~50%; specific dosing guidelines not available

Administration

Regular injection formulation (do not use if solution contains particles or is discolored): Administer SubQ or I.V.; I.V. administration may be IVP, IVPB, or continuous I.V. infusion:

IVP should be administered undiluted over 3 minutes

IVPB should be administered over 15-30 minutes

(Continued)

Octreotide *(Continued)*

Continuous I.V. infusion rates have ranged from 25-50 mcg/hour for the treatment of esophageal variceal bleeding

Depot formulation: Administer I.M. intragluteal (avoid deltoid administration); alternate gluteal injection sites to avoid irritation. Do not administer Sandostatin LAR® intravenously or subcutaneously; must be administered immediately after mixing.

Monitoring Parameters

Acromegaly: Growth hormone, somatomedin C (IGF-1)

Carcinoid: 5-HIAA, plasma serotonin and plasma substance P

VIPomas: Vasoactive intestinal peptide

Chronic therapy: Thyroid function (baseline and periodic), vitamin B_{12} level, blood glucose, cardiac function (heart rate, EKG)

Dietary Considerations
Schedule injections between meals to decrease GI effects. May alter absorption of dietary fats.

Emetic Potential
Very low (<10%)

Vesicant
No

Dosage Forms
Excipient information presented when available (limited, particularly for generics); consult specific product labeling.

Injection, microspheres for suspension, as acetate [depot formulation]:
Sandostatin LAR®: 10 mg, 20 mg, 30 mg [with diluent and syringe]

Injection, solution, as acetate: 0.2 mg/mL (5 mL); 1 mg/mL (5 mL)
Sandostatin®: 0.2 mg/mL (5 mL); 1 mg/mL (5 mL)

Injection, solution, as acetate [preservative free]: 0.05 mg/mL (1 mL); 0.1 mg/mL (1 mL); 0.5 mg/mL (1 mL)
Sandostatin®: 0.05 mg/mL (1 mL); 0.1 mg/mL (1 mL); 0.5 mg/mL (1 mL)

References

Baillie-Johnson HR, "Octreotide in the Management of Treatment-Related Diarrhoea," *Anticancer Drugs*, 1996, 7(Suppl 1):11-5.

Barrons RW, "Octreotide in Hyperinsulinism," *Ann Pharmacother*, 1997, 31(2):239-41.

Behrman RE, Kliegman RM, and Jenson HB, *Nelson's Textbook of Pediatrics*, 17th ed, Philadelphia, PA: WB Saunders Co, 2004.

Braatvedt GD, "Octreotide for the Treatment of Sulphonylurea Induced Hypoglycaemia in Type 2 Diabetes," *N Z Med J*, 1997, 110(1044):189-90.

Bui L, Adler D, and Keller KH, "Prolonged Octreotide Infusion to Treat Glyburide-Induced Hypoglycemia," *J Toxicol Clin Toxicol*, 2000, 38(5):576.

Carr R and Zed PJ, "Octreotide for Sulfonylurea-Induced Hypoglycemia Following Overdose," *Ann Pharmacother*, 2002, 36(11):1727-32.

Corley DA, Cello JP, Adkisson W, et al, "Octreotide for Acute Esophageal Variceal Bleeding: A Meta-analysis," *Gastroenterology*, 2001, 120(4):946-54.

Couper RT, Berzen A, Berall G, et al, "Clinical Response to the Long-Acting Somatostatin Analogue SMS 201-995 in a Child With Congenital Microvillus Atrophy," *Gut*, 1989, 30(7):1020-4.

Erstad BL, "Octreotide for Acute Variceal Bleeding," *Ann Pharmacother*, 2001, 35(5):618-26.

Heikenen JB, Pohl JF, Werlin SL, et al, "Octreotide in Pediatric Patients," *J Pediatr Gastroenterol Nutr*, 2002, 35(5):600-9.

Hejna M, Schmidinger M, and Raderer M, "The Clinical Role of Somatostatin Analogues as Antineoplastic Agents: Much Ado About Nothing?" *Ann Oncol*, 2002, 13(5):653-68.

Jaros W, Biller J, Greer S, et al, "Successful Treatment of Idiopathic Secretory Diarrhea of Infancy With the Somatostatin Analogue SMS 201-995," *Gastroenterology*, 1988, 94(1):189-93.

Jenkins SA, "Somatostatin in Acute Bleeding Oesophageal Varices. Clinical Evidence," *Drugs*, 1992, 44(Suppl 2):36-55.

Katz MD and Erstad BL, "Octreotide, A New Somatostatin Analogue," *Clin Pharm*, 1989, 8(4):255-73.

Lustig RH, Hinds PS, Ringwald-Smith K, et al, "Octreotide Therapy of Pediatric Hypothalamic Obesity: A Double-Blind, Placebo-Controlled Trial," *J Clin Endocrinol Metab*, 2003, 88(6):2586-92.

McLaughlin SA, Crandall CS, and McKinney PE, "Octreotide: An Antidote for Sulfonylurea-Induced Hypoglycemia," *Ann Emerg Med*, 2000, 36(2):133-6.

Mordel A, Sivilotti ML, Old AC, et al, "Octreotide for Pediatric Sulfonylurea Poisoning," *J Toxicol Clin Toxicol*, 1998, 36(5):437.

Mulvihill SJ, "Perioperative Use of Octreotide in Gastrointestinal Surgery," *Digestion*, 1993, 54(Suppl 1):33-7.

Oberg K, "Established Clinical Use of Octreotide and Lanreotide in Oncology," *Chemotherapy*, 2001, 47(Suppl 2):40-53.

Pollak M, "The Potential Role of Somatostatin Analogues in Breast Cancer Treatment," *Yale J Biol Med*, 1997, 70(5-6):535-9.

Szilagyi A and Shrier I, "Systematic Review: The Use of Somatostatin or Octreotide in Refractory Diarrhoea," *Aliment Pharmacol Ther*, 2001, 15(12):1889-97.

Tassiopoulos AK, Baum G, and Halverson JD, "Small Bowel Fistulas," *Surg Clin North Am*, 1996, 76(5):1175-81

von Werder K, Muller OA, and Stalla GK, "Somatostatin Analogs in Ectopic Corticotropin Production," *Metabolism*, 1996, 45(8 Suppl 1):129-31.

- ◆ **Octreotide Acetate** *see* Octreotide *on page 819*
- ◆ **Octreotide Acetate Injection (Can)** *see* Octreotide *on page 819*
- ◆ **Octreotide Acetate Omega (Can)** *see* Octreotide *on page 819*
- ◆ **Ocuflox®** *see* Ofloxacin *on page 825*

Ofloxacin (oh FLOKS a sin)

Medication Safety Issues

Sound-alike/look-alike issues:

Floxin® may be confused with Flexeril®

Ocuflox® may be confused with Ocufen®

International issues:

Floxin® may be confused with Flogen® which is a brand name for naproxen in Mexico

Floxin® may be confused with Fluoxin® which is a brand name for fluoxetine in the Czech Republic and Romania

Floxin® may be confused with Flexin® which is a brand name for orphenadrine in Israel and indomethacin in Great Britain

U.S. Brand Names Floxin®; Ocuflox®

Index Terms Floxin Otic Singles

Generic Available Yes: Tablet, ophthalmic solution

Canadian Brand Names Apo-Oflox®; Apo-Ofloxacin®; Floxin®; Novo-Ofloxacin; Ocuflox®; PMS-Ofloxacin

Pharmacologic Category Antibiotic, Quinolone

Use Quinolone antibiotic for the treatment of acute exacerbations of chronic bronchitis, community-acquired pneumonia, skin and skin structure infections (uncomplicated), urethral and cervical gonorrhea (acute, uncomplicated), urethritis and cervicitis (nongonococcal), mixed infections of the urethra and cervix, pelvic inflammatory disease (acute), cystitis (uncomplicated), urinary tract infections (complicated), prostatitis

Note: As of April 2007, the CDC no longer recommends the use of fluoroquinolones for the treatment of gonococcal disease.

Ophthalmic: Treatment of superficial ocular infections involving the conjunctiva or cornea due to strains of susceptible organisms

Otic: Otitis externa, chronic suppurative otitis media, acute otitis media

Unlabeled/Investigational Use Epididymitis (nongonococcal), leprosy, Traveler's diarrhea

Pregnancy Risk Factor C

Lactation Enters breast milk/not recommended (AAP rates "compatible")

Labeled Contraindications Hypersensitivity to ofloxacin or other members of the quinolone group, such as nalidixic acid, oxolinic acid, cinoxacin, norfloxacin, and ciprofloxacin; hypersensitivity to any component of the formulation

(Continued)

Ofloxacin *(Continued)*

Warnings/Precautions Use with caution in patients with epilepsy or other CNS diseases which could predispose seizures; potential for seizures, although very rare, may be increased with concomitant NSAID therapy. Tremor, restlessness, confusion, and very rarely hallucinations or seizures may occur; use with caution in patients with known or suspected CNS disorder. Discontinue in patients who experience significant CNS adverse effects (eg, dizziness, hallucinations, suicidal ideations or actions). Use with caution in patients with renal or hepatic impairment. Has been associated with rare tendonitis or ruptured tendons (discontinue immediately with signs of inflammation or tendon pain). Risk may be increased with concurrent corticosteroids, particularly in the elderly. Discontinue at first sign of tendon inflammation or pain. Peripheral neuropathies have been linked to ofloxacin use; discontinue if numbness, tingling, or weakness develops.

Fluoroquinolones have been associated with the development of serious, and sometimes fatal, hypoglycemia, most often in elderly diabetics, but also in patients without diabetes. This occurred most frequently with gatifloxacin (no longer available systemically) but may occur at a lower frequency with other quinolones.

Rare cases of torsade de pointes have been reported in patients receiving ofloxacin and other quinolones. Risk may be minimized by avoiding use in patients with known prolongation of the QT interval, bradycardia, hypokalemia, hypomagnesemia, cardiomyopathy, or in those receiving concurrent therapy with Class Ia or Class III antiarrhythmics.

Severe hypersensitivity reactions, including anaphylaxis, have occurred with quinolone therapy. Reactions may present as typical allergic symptoms after a single dose, or may manifest as severe idiosyncratic dermatologic, vascular, pulmonary, renal, hepatic, and/or hematologic events, usually after multiple doses. Prompt discontinuation of drug should occur if skin rash or other symptoms arise. Prolonged use may result in fungal or bacterial superinfection, including *C. difficile*-associated diarrhea (CDAD) and pseudomembranous colitis; CDAD has been observed >2 months postantibiotic treatment. Quinolones may exacerbate myasthenia gravis. Avoid excessive sunlight; may cause moderate-to-severe phototoxicity reactions. Safety and efficacy have not been established in children.

Adverse Reactions
Systemic:
1% to 10%:
Cardiovascular: Chest pain (1% to 3%)
Central nervous system: Headache (1% to 9%), insomnia (3% to 7%), dizziness (1% to 5%), fatigue (1% to 3%), somnolence (1% to 3%), sleep disorders (1% to 3%), nervousness (1% to 3%), pyrexia (1% to 3%)
Dermatologic: Rash/pruritus (1% to 3%)
Gastrointestinal: Diarrhea (1% to 4%), vomiting (1% to 4%), GI distress (1% to 3%), abdominal cramps (1% to 3%), flatulence (1% to 3%), abnormal taste (1% to 3%), xerostomia (1% to 3%), appetite decreased (1% to 3%), nausea (3% to 10%), constipation (1% to 3%)
Genitourinary: Vaginitis (1% to 5%), external genital pruritus in women (1% to 3%)
Ocular: Visual disturbances (1% to 3%)
Respiratory: Pharyngitis (1% to 3%)
Miscellaneous: Trunk pain
<1%, postmarketing, and/or case reports (limited to important or life-threatening): Anaphylaxis reactions, anxiety, blurred vision, chills,

cognitive change, cough, depression, dream abnormality, ecchymosis, edema, erythema nodosum, euphoria, extremity pain, hallucinations, hearing acuity decreased, hepatic dysfunction, hepatic failure (some fatal), hepatitis, hyper-/hypoglycemia, hypertension, interstitial nephritis, light-headedness, malaise, myasthenia gravis exacerbation, palpitation, paresthesia, peripheral neuropathy, photophobia, photosensitivity, pneumonitis, psychotic reactions, rhabdomyolysis, seizure, Stevens-Johnson syndrome, syncope, tendonitis and tendon rupture, thirst, tinnitus, torsade de pointes, Tourette's syndrome, toxic epidermal necrolysis, vasculitis, vasodilation, vertigo, weakness, weight loss

Ophthalmic: Frequency not defined:
Central nervous system: Dizziness
Gastrointestinal: Nausea
Ocular: Blurred vision, burning, chemical conjunctivitis/keratitis, discomfort, dryness, edema, eye pain, foreign body sensation, itching, photophobia, redness, stinging, tearing

Otic:
>10%: Local: Application site reaction (<1% to 17%)
1% to 10%:
Central nervous system: Dizziness (≤1%), vertigo (≤1%)
Dermatologic: Pruritus (1% to 4%), rash (1%)
Gastrointestinal: Taste perversion (7%)
Neuromuscular & skeletal: Paresthesia (1%)
<1% (Limited to important or life-threatening): Diarrhea, fever, headache, hearing loss (transient), hypertension, nausea, otorrhagia, tinnitus, tremor, vomiting, xerostomia
Postmarketing and/case reports: Transient neuropsychiatric disturbances

Overdosage/Toxicology Symptoms of overdose include acute renal failure, seizures, nausea, and vomiting. Treatment includes GI decontamination, if possible, and supportive care. Not removed by peritoneal or hemodialysis.

Drug Interactions

Cytochrome P450 Effect: Inhibits CYP1A2 (strong)

Increased Effect/Toxicity: Ofloxacin may increase the effects/toxicity of CYP1A2 substrates (eg, aminophylline, fluvoxamine, mexiletine, mirtazapine, ropinirole, and trifluoperazine), glyburide, theophylline, and warfarin. Concomitant use with corticosteroids may increase the risk of tendon rupture. Concomitant use with other QT_c-prolonging agents (eg, Class Ia and Class III antiarrhythmics, erythromycin, cisapride, antipsychotics, and cyclic antidepressants) may result in arrhythmias, such as torsade de pointes. Probenecid may increase ofloxacin levels. Concomitant use with NSAIDs may rarely increase risk of seizure.

Decreased Effect: Concurrent administration of metal cations, including most antacids, oral electrolyte supplements, quinapril, sucralfate, some didanosine formulations (pediatric powder for oral suspension), and other highly-buffered oral drugs, may decrease quinolone levels; separate doses. Antibiotics may decrease the therapeutic effect of live, attenuated Ty21a (typhoid) vaccine; delay vaccination for >24 hours after administration of antibacterial agents.

Ethanol/Nutrition/Herb Interactions

Food: Ofloxacin average peak serum concentrations may be decreased by 20% if taken with food.
Herb/Nutraceutical: Avoid dong quai, St John's wort (may also cause photosensitization).

Storage/Stability

Ophthalmic and otic solution: Store between 15°C to 25°C (59°F to 77°F). (Continued)

Ofloxacin *(Continued)*

Otic Singles™: Store between 15°C to 30°C (59°F to 86°F). Store in pouch to protect from light.

Tablet: Store below 30°C (86°F).

Mechanism of Action Ofloxacin is a DNA gyrase inhibitor. DNA gyrase is an essential bacterial enzyme that maintains the superhelical structure of DNA. DNA gyrase is required for DNA replication and transcription, DNA repair, recombination, and transposition; bactericidal

Pharmacodynamics/Kinetics

Absorption: Well absorbed; food causes only minor alterations

Distribution: V_d: 2.4-3.5 L/kg

Protein binding: 20%

Bioavailability: Oral: 98%

Half-life elimination: Biphasic: 5-7.5 hours and 20-25 hours (accounts for <5%); prolonged with renal impairment

Excretion: Primarily urine (as unchanged drug)

Dosage

Usual dosage range:

Children ≥6 months: Otic: 5 drops daily

Children >1 year: Ophthalmic: 1-2 drops every 30 minutes to 4 hours initially, decreasing to every 4-6 hours

Children >12 years: Otic: 10 drops once or twice daily

Adults:

Ophthalmic: 1-2 drops every 30 minutes to 4 hours initially, decreasing to every 4-6 hours

Oral: 200-400 mg every 12 hours

Otic: 10 drops once or twice daily

Indication-specific dosing:

Children 6 months to 13 years: Otic:

Otitis externa: Instill 5 drops (or the contents of 1 single-dose container) into affected ear(s) once daily for 7 days

Children 1-12 years: Otic:

Acute otitis media with tympanostomy tubes: Instill 5 drops (or the contents of 1 single-dose container) into affected ear(s) twice daily for 10 days

Children >1 year and Adults: Ophthalmic:

Conjunctivitis: Instill 1-2 drops in affected eye(s) every 2-4 hours for the first 2 days, then use 4 times/day for an additional 5 days

Corneal ulcer: Instill 1-2 drops every 30 minutes while awake and every 4-6 hours after retiring for the first 2 days; beginning on day 3, instill 1-2 drops every hour while awake for 4-6 additional days; thereafter, 1-2 drops 4 times/day until clinical cure.

Children >12 years and Adults: Otic:

Otitis media, chronic suppurative with perforated tympanic membranes: Instill 10 drops (or the contents of 2 single-dose containers) into affected ear twice daily for 14 days

Children ≥13 years and Adults: Otic:

Otitis externa: Instill 10 drops (or the contents of 2 single-dose containers) into affected ear(s) once daily for 7 days

Adults: Oral:

Cervicitis/urethritis:

Nongonococcal: 300 mg every 12 hours for 7 days

Gonococcal (acute, uncomplicated): 400 mg as a single dose; **Note:** As of April 2007, the CDC no longer recommends the use of fluoroquinolones for the treatment of uncomplicated gonococcal disease.

Chronic bronchitis (acute exacerbation), community-acquired pneumonia, skin and skin structure infections (uncomplicated): 400 mg every 12 hours for 10 days

Epididymitis, nongonococcal (unlabeled use): 300 mg twice daily for 10 days

Leprosy (unlabeled use): 400 mg once daily

Pelvic inflammatory disease (acute): 400 mg every 12 hours for 10-14 days with or without metronidazole; **Note:** The CDC recommends use only if standard cephalosporin therapy is not feasible and community prevalence of quinolone-resistant gonococcal organisms is low. Culture sensitivity must be confirmed.

Prostatitis:
Acute: 400 mg for 1 dose, then 300 mg twice daily for 10 days
Chronic: 200 mg every 12 hours for 6 weeks

Traveler's diarrhea (unlabeled use): 300 mg twice daily for 3 days

UTI:
Uncomplicated: 200 mg every 12 hours for 3-7 days
Complicated: 200 mg every 12 hours for 10 days

Dosing adjustment/interval in renal impairment: Adults: Oral: After a normal initial dose, adjust as follows:

Cl_{cr} 20-50 mL/minute: Administer usual dose every 24 hours

Cl_{cr} <20 mL/minute: Administer half the usual dose every 24 hours

Continuous arteriovenous or venovenous hemodiafiltration effects: Administer 300 mg every 24 hours

Dosing adjustment in hepatic impairment: Severe impairment: Maximum dose: 400 mg/day

Administration

Ophthalmic: For ophthalmic use only; avoid touching tip of applicator to eye or other surfaces.

Oral: Do not take within 2 hours of food or any antacids which contain zinc, magnesium, or aluminum.

Otic: Prior to use, warm solution by holding container in hands for 1-2 minutes. Patient should lie down with affected ear upward and medication instilled. Pump tragus 4 times to ensure penetration of medication. Patient should remain in this position for 5 minutes.

Test Interactions Some quinolones may produce a false-positive urine screening result for opiates using commercially-available immunoassay kits. This has been demonstrated most consistently for levofloxacin and ofloxacin, but other quinolones have shown cross-reactivity in certain assay kits. Confirmation of positive opiate screens by more specific methods should be considered.

Patient Information Do not take with food. Do not take within 2 hours of any products including antacids which contain calcium, magnesium, or aluminum. Contact your prescriber immediately with signs of inflammation or tendon pain. Report any skin rash or other allergic reactions. Avoid excessive sunlight.

Special Geriatric Considerations Dosage must be carefully adjusted to renal function. The half-life of ofloxacin may be prolonged and serum concentrations are elevated in elderly patients even in the absence of overt renal impairment. The risk of torsade de pointes and tendon inflammation and/or rupture associated with the concomitant use of corticosteroids and quinolones is increased in the elderly population.

Emetic Potential Very low (<10%)

Vesicant No

(Continued)

Ofloxacin *(Continued)*

Dosage Forms Excipient information presented when available (limited, particularly for generics); consult specific product labeling. [DSC] = Discontinued product

Solution, ophthalmic (Ocuflox®): 0.3% (5 mL; 10 mL [DSC]) [contains benzalkonium chloride]

Solution, otic:

Floxin®: 0.3% (5 mL, 10 mL) [contains benzalkonium chloride]

Floxin® Otic Singles™: 0.3% (0.25 mL) [contains benzalkonium chloride; packaged as 2 single-dose containers per pouch, 10 pouches per carton, total net volume 5 mL]

Tablet (Floxin®): 200 mg, 300 mg, 400 mg

References

Abramowicz M, "Antimicrobial Prophylaxis in Surgery," *Medical Letter on Drugs and Therapeutics, Handbook of Antimicrobial Therapy*, 16th ed, New York, NY: Medical Letter, 2002.

American Academy of Pediatrics Committee on Drugs, "The Transfer of Drugs and Other Chemicals Into Human Milk," *Pediatrics*, 2001, 108(3):776-89.

Centers for Disease Control and Prevention, "Update to CDC's Sexually Transmitted Diseases Treatment Guidelines, 2006: Fluoroquinolones No Longer Recommended for Treatment of Gonococcal Infections," *MMWR Recomm Rep*, 2007, 56(14):332-6.

Centers for Disease Control and Prevention, "Sexually Transmitted Diseases Treatment Guidelines, 2006," *MMWR*, 2006, 55(RR-11): 1-94.

Friedrich LV and Dougherty R, "Fatal Hypoglycemia Associated With Levofloxacin," *Pharmacotherapy*, 2004, 24(12):1807-12.

Frothingham R, "Glucose Homeostasis Abnormalities Associated With Use of Gatifloxacin," *Clin Infect Dis*, 2005, 41(9):1269-76.

Gavin JR 3rd, Kubin R, Choudhri S, et al, "Moxifloxacin and Glucose Homeostasis: A Pooled-Analysis of Three Experience From Clinical and Postmarketing Studies," *Drug Saf*, 2004, 27(9):671-86.

Giamarellou H, Kolokythas E, Petrikkos G, et al, "Pharmacokinetics of Three Newer Quinolones in Pregnant and Lactating Women," *Am J Med*, 1989, 87(Suppl 5A):49-51.

Graumlich JF, Habis S, Avelino RR, et al, "Hypoglycemia in Inpatients After Gatifloxacin or Levofloxacin Therapy: Nested Case-Control Study," *Pharmacotherapy*, 2005, 25(10):1296-302.

Hoogkamp-Korstanje JA, "*In vitro* Activities of Ciprofloxacin, Levofloxacin, Lomefloxacin, Ofloxacin, Pefloxacin, Sparfloxacin, and Trovafloxacin Against Gram-Positive and Gram-Negative Pathogens From Respiratory Tract Infections," *J Antimicrob Chemother*, 1997, 40(3):427-31.

Hooper DC and Wolfson JS, "Fluoroquinolone Antimicrobial Agents," *N Engl J Med*, 1991, 324(6):384-94.

Jacobs MR, Felmingham D, Appelbaum PC, et al, "The Alexander Project 1998-2000: Susceptibility of Pathogens Isolated From Community-Acquired Respiratory Tract Infection to Commonly Used Antimicrobial Agents," *J Antimicrob Chemother*, 2003, 52(2):229-46.

Khaliq Y and Zhanel GG, "Fluoroquinolone-Associated Tendinopathy: A Critical Review of the Literature," *Clin Infect Dis*, 2003, 36(11):1404-10.

Kohler RB, Arkins N, and Tack KJ, "Accidental Overdose of Intravenous Ofloxacin With Benign Outcome," *Antimicrob Agents Chemother*, 1991, 35(6):1239-40.

Lawrence KR, Adra M, and Keir C, "Hypoglycemia-Induced Anoxic Brain Injury Possibly Associated With Levofloxacin," *J Infect*, 2006, 52(6):e177-80.

Loebstein R, Addis A, Ho E, et al, "Pregnancy Outcome Following Gestational Exposure to Fluoroquinolones: A Multicenter, Prospective Controlled Study," *Antimicrob Agents Chemother*, 1998, 42(6):1336-9.

Lomaestro BM and Bailie GR, "Quinolone-Cation Interactions: A Review," *DICP*, 1991, 25(11):1249-58.

Malone RS, Fish DN, Abraham E, et al, "Pharmacokinetics of Levofloxacin and Ciprofloxacin During Continuous Renal Replacement Therapy in Critically Ill Patients," *Antimicrob Agents Chemother*, 2001, 45(10):2949-54.

Mohr JF, McKinnon PS, Peymann PJ, et al, "A Retrospective, Comparative Evaluation of Dysglycemias in Hospitalized Patients Receiving Gatifloxacin, Levofloxacin, Ciprofloxacin, or Ceftriaxone," *Pharmacotherapy*, 2005, 25(10):1303-9.

Monk JP and Campoli-Richards DM, "Ofloxacin. A Review of Its Antibacterial Activity, Pharmacokinetic Properties, and Therapeutic Use," *Drugs*, 1987, 33(4):346-91.

Nilsson-Ehle I and Ljungberg B, "Quinolone Disposition in the Elderly: Practical Implications," *Drugs Aging*, 1991, 1(4):279-88.

Park-Wyllie LY, Juurlink DN, Kopp A, et al, "Outpatient Gatifloxacin Therapy and Dysglycemia in Older Adults," N Engl J Med, 2006, 354(13):1352-61.

Peled Y, Friedman S, Hod M, et al, "Ofloxacin During the Second Trimester of Pregnancy," DICP, 1991, 25(11):1181-2.

Stein GE, "The 4-Quinolone Antibiotics: Past, Present, and Future," Pharmacotherapy, 1988, 8(6):301-14.

Szarfman A, Chen M, and Blum MD, "More on Fluoroquinolone Antibiotics and Tendon Rupture," N Engl J Med, 1995, 332(3):193.

Thalhammer F, Kletzmayr J, El Menyawi I, et al, "Ofloxacin Clearance During Hemodialysis: A Comparison of Polysulfone and Cellulose Acetate Hemodialyzers," Am J Kidney Dis, 1998, 32(4):642-5.

Thomas RJ and Reagan DR, "Association of a Tourette-Like Syndrome With Ofloxacin," Ann Pharmacother, 1996, 30(2):138-41.

Trotman RL, Williamson JC, Shoemaker DM, et al, "Antibiotic Dosing in Critically Ill Adult Patients Receiving Continuous Renal Replacement Therapy," Clin Infect Dis, 2005, 41(8):1159-66.

Walker RC and Wright AJ, "The Fluoroquinolones," Mayo Clin Proc, 1991, 66(12):1249-59.

Wang S and Rizvi AA, "Levofloxacin-Induced Hypoglycemia in a Nondiabetic Patient," Am J Med Sci, 2006, 331(6):334-5.

Zacher JL and Givone DM, "False-Positive Urine Opiate Screening Associated With Fluoroquinolone Use," Ann Pharmacother, 2004, 38:1525-28.

♦ **OKT3** see Muromonab-CD3 on page 788

Olanzapine (oh LAN za peen)

Medication Safety Issues
Sound-alike/look-alike issues:
Olanzapine may be confused with olsalazine
Zyprexa® may be confused with Celexa™, Zyrtec®

U.S. Brand Names Zyprexa®; Zyprexa® Zydis®

Index Terms LY170053; Zyprexa Zydis

Generic Available No

Canadian Brand Names Novo-Olanzapine; Zyprexa®; Zyprexa® Zydis®

Pharmacologic Category Antipsychotic Agent, Atypical

Use Treatment of the manifestations of schizophrenia; treatment of acute or mixed mania episodes associated with Bipolar I Disorder (as monotherapy or in combination with lithium or valproate); maintenance treatment of bipolar disorder; acute agitation (patients with schizophrenia or bipolar mania)

Unlabeled/Investigational Use Treatment of psychosis/schizophrenia in children or adolescents; chronic pain; prevention of chemo-therapy-associated delayed nausea or vomiting; psychosis/agitation related to Alzheimer's dementia

Pregnancy Risk Factor C

Lactation Enters breast milk/not recommended

Labeled Contraindications Hypersensitivity to olanzapine or any component of the formulation

Warnings/Precautions [U.S. Boxed Warning]: Patients with dementia-related psychosis treated with atypical antipsychotics are at an increased risk of death compared to placebo. An increased incidence of cerebrovascular adverse events (including fatalities) has been reported in elderly patients with dementia-related psychosis. Risk may be increased by dehydration; use caution with concurrent diuretics. Olanzapine is not approved for this indication.

Moderate to highly sedating, use with caution in disorders where CNS depression is a feature; patients must be cautioned about performing tasks which require mental alertness (eg, operating machinery or driving). Use caution in patients with cardiac disease. Use with caution in Parkinson's disease, predisposition to seizures, or severe hepatic or renal disease. Life-threatening arrhythmias have occurred with therapeutic doses of some
(Continued)

Olanzapine *(Continued)*

neuroleptics. May induce orthostatic hypotension; use caution with history of cardiovascular disease. Esophageal dysmotility and aspiration have been associated with antipsychotic use; use with caution in patients at risk of aspiration pneumonia. Caution in breast cancer or other prolactin-dependent tumors (elevates prolactin levels). Significant weight gain (>7% of baseline weight) may occur; monitor waist circumference and BMI. Impaired core body temperature regulation may occur; caution with strenuous exercise, heat exposure, dehydration, and concomitant medication possessing anticholinergic effects.

May cause anticholinergic effects; use with caution in patients with decreased gastrointestinal motility, urinary retention, BPH, xerostomia, glaucoma, or myasthenia gravis. Relative to other neuroleptics, olanzapine has a moderate potency of cholinergic blockade.

May cause extrapyramidal symptoms, although risk of these reactions is lower relative to other neuroleptics). May be associated with neuroleptic malignant syndrome (NMS). May cause extreme and life-threatening hyperglycemia; use with caution in patients with diabetes or other disorders of glucose regulation; monitor. Olanzapine levels may be lower in patients who smoke, requiring dosage adjustment.

The possibility of a suicide attempt is inherent in psychotic illness or bipolar disorder; use caution in high-risk patients during initiation of therapy. Prescriptions should be written for the smallest quantity consistent with good patient care. Safety and efficacy in pediatric patients have not been established.

Intramuscular administration: Patients should remain recumbent if drowsy/dizzy until hypotension, bradycardia, and/or hypoventilation has been ruled out. Concurrent use of I.M./I.V. benzodiazepines is not recommended (fatalities have been reported, though causality not determined).

Adverse Reactions

>10%:

Central nervous system: Somnolence (6% to 39% dose dependent), extrapyramidal symptoms (15% to 32% dose dependent), insomnia (up to 12%), dizziness (4% to 18%)

Gastrointestinal: Dyspepsia (7% to 11%), constipation (9% to 11%), weight gain (5% to 6%, has been reported as high as 40%), xerostomia (9% to 22% dose dependent)

Neuromuscular & skeletal: Weakness (2% to 20% dose dependent)

Miscellaneous: Accidental injury (12%)

1% to 10%:

Cardiovascular: Postural hypotension (1% to 5%), tachycardia (up to 3%), peripheral edema (up to 3%), chest pain (up to 3%), hyper-/hypotension (up to 2%)

Central nervous system: Personality changes (8%), speech disorder (7%), fever (up to 6%), abnormal dreams, euphoria, amnesia, delusions, emotional lability, mania, schizophrenia

Dermatologic: Bruising (up to 5%)

Endocrine & metabolic: Cholesterol increased (4%), prolactin increased

Gastrointestinal: Nausea (up to 9% dose dependent), appetite increased (3% to 6%), vomiting (up to 4%), flatulence, salivation increased, thirst

Genitourinary: Incontinence (up to 2%), UTI (up to 2%), vaginitis

Hepatic: ALT increased (2%)

Local: Injection site pain (I.M. administration)

Neuromuscular & skeletal: Tremor (1% to 7% dose dependent), abnormal gait (6%), back pain (up to 5%), joint/extremity pain (up to 5%), akathisia (3% to 5% dose dependent), hypertonia (up to 3%), articulation impairment (up to 2%), falling (particularly in older patients), joint stiffness, paresthesia, twitching

Ocular: Amblyopia (up to 3%), conjunctivitis

Respiratory: Rhinitis (up to 7%), cough (up to 6%), pharyngitis (up to 4%), dyspnea

Miscellaneous: Dental pain, diaphoresis, flu-like syndrome

<1%, postmarketing, and/or case report (limited to important or life-threatening): Acidosis, akinesia, albuminuria, anaphylactoid reaction, anemia, angioedema, apnea, arteritis, asthma, ataxia, atelectasis, atrial fibrillation, AV block, cerebrovascular accident, coma, confusion, congestive heart failure, deafness, diabetes mellitus, diabetic acidosis, diabetic coma, dyskinesia, dysphagia, dysuria, encephalopathy, facial paralysis, glaucoma, gynecomastia, heart arrest, heart block, heart failure, hematuria, hemoptysis, hemorrhage (eye, rectal, subarachnoid, vaginal), hepatitis, hyper-/hypoglycemia, hyper-/hypokalemia, hyperlipemia, hyper-/hyponatremia, hyperuricemia, hyper-/hypoventilation, hypoesthesia, hypokinesia, hypoproteinemia, hypoxia, jaundice, ileus, ketosis, leukocytosis (eosinophilia), leukopenia, liver damage (cholestatic or mixed), liver fatty deposit, lung edema, lymphadenopathy, menstrual irregularities, migraine, myasthenia, myopathy, neuralgia, neuroleptic malignant syndrome, neuropathy, neutropenia, osteoporosis, pancreatitis, paralysis, priapism, pulmonary embolus, rhabdomyolysis, seizure, stridor, sudden death, suicide attempt, syncope, tardive dyskinesia, thrombocythemia, thrombocytopenia, tongue edema, venous thrombotic events, vomiting, withdrawal syndrome

Overdosage/Toxicology Signs and symptoms of overdose include CNS depression (ranging from drowsiness to coma), extrapyramidal movements, fasciculations, hypotension (possible, though not described), miosis, respiratory depression, rhinitis (10%), slurred speech, tachycardia, trismus, and possible NMS. Treatment is symptom-directed and supportive. Cardiac monitoring should be initiated, including continuous EEG monitoring. Activated charcoal (1 g) may reduce the C_{max} and AUC of olanzapine by ~60%.

Drug Interactions

Cytochrome P450 Effect: Substrate of CYP1A2 (major), 2D6 (minor); **Inhibits** CYP1A2 (weak), 2C9 (weak), 2C19 (weak), 2D6 (weak), 3A4 (weak)

Increased Effect/Toxicity: Olanzapine levels may be increased by CYP1A2 inhibitors such as cimetidine and fluvoxamine. Sedation from olanzapine is increased with ethanol or other CNS depressants. Concomitant use with pramlintide and other anticholinergic agents may result in increased anticholinergic adverse effects. Concomitant use with ciprofloxacin may increase the levels/effects of olanzapine. Use of acetylcholinesterase inhibitors (central) or lithium may increase the risk of antipsychotic-related EPS. Concurrent use of intramuscular olanzapine and parenteral benzodiazepines may increase the risk of cardiopulmonary toxicity.

Decreased Effect: Olanzapine levels may be decreased by CYP1A2 inducers such as rifampin, omeprazole, and carbamazepine (also cigarette smoking).

Ethanol/Nutrition/Herb Interactions

Ethanol: Avoid ethanol (may increase CNS depression).
(Continued)

Olanzapine *(Continued)*

Herb/Nutraceutical: Avoid dong quai, St John's wort (may also cause photo-sensitization). Avoid kava kava, gotu kola, valerian, St John's wort (may increase CNS depression).

Storage/Stability

Injection, powder for reconstitution: Store at room temperature 15°C to 30°C (59°F to 86°F); do not freeze. Protect from light.

Tablet and orally-disintegrating tablet: Store at room temperature of 15°C to 30°C (59°F to 86°F). Protect from light and moisture.

Reconstitution Injection, powder for reconstitution: Reconstitute 10 mg vial with 2.1 mL SWFI. Resulting solution is ~5 mg/mL. Use immediately (within 1 hour) following reconstitution. Discard any unused portion.

Mechanism of Action Olanzapine is a second generation thienobenzodiazepine antipsychotic which displays potent antagonist of serotonin 5-HT$_{2A}$ and 5-HT$_{2C}$, dopamine D$_{1-4}$, muscarinic M$_{1-5}$, histamine H$_1$- and alpha$_1$-adrenergic receptors. Olanzapine shows moderate antagonism of 5-HT$_3$ and muscarinic M$_{1-5}$ receptors, and weak binding to GABA-A, BZD, and beta-adrenergic receptors. Although the precise mechanism of action in schizophrenia and bipolar disorder is not known, the efficacy of olanzapine is thought to be mediated through combined antagonism of dopamine and serotonin type 2 receptor sites.

Pharmacodynamics/Kinetics

Absorption:

I.M.: Rapidly absorbed

Oral: Well absorbed; not affected by food; tablets and orally-disintegrating tablets are bioequivalent

Distribution: V$_d$: Extensive, 1000 L

Protein binding, plasma: 93% bound to albumin and alpha$_1$-glycoprotein

Metabolism: Highly metabolized via direct glucuronidation and cytochrome P450 mediated oxidation (CYP1A2, CYP2D6); 40% removed via first pass metabolism

Bioavailability: >57%

Half-life elimination: 21-54 hours; ~1.5 times greater in elderly

Time to peak, plasma: Maximum plasma concentrations after I.M. administration are 5 times higher than maximum plasma concentrations produced by an oral dose.

I.M.: 15-45 minutes

Oral: ~6 hours

Excretion: Urine (57%, 7% as unchanged drug); feces (30%)

Clearance: 40% increase in olanzapine clearance in smokers; 30% decrease in females

Dosage

Children: Schizophrenia/bipolar disorder (unlabeled use): Oral: Initial: 2.5 mg/day; titrate as necessary to 20 mg/day (0.12-0.29 mg/kg/day)

Adults:

Schizophrenia: Oral: Initial: 5-10 mg once daily (increase to 10 mg once daily within 5-7 days); thereafter, adjust by 5 mg/day at 1-week intervals, up to a recommended maximum of 20 mg/day. Maintenance: 10-20 mg once daily. **Note:** Doses of 30-50 mg/day have been used; however, doses >10 mg/day have not demonstrated better efficacy, and safety and efficacy of doses >20 mg/day have not been evaluated.

Bipolar I acute mixed or manic episodes: Oral:

Monotherapy: Initial: 10-15 mg once daily; increase by 5 mg/day at intervals of not less than 24 hours. Maintenance: 5-20 mg/day; recommended maximum dose: 20 mg/day.

Combination therapy (with lithium or valproate): Initial: 10 mg once daily; dosing range: 5-20 mg/day

Agitation (acute, associated with bipolar I mania or schizophrenia): I.M.: Initial dose: 5-10 mg (a lower dose of 2.5 mg may be considered when clinical factors warrant); additional doses (2.5-10 mg) may be considered; however, 2-4 hours should be allowed between doses to evaluate response (maximum total daily dose: 30 mg, per manufacturer's recommendation)

Prevention of chemotherapy-associated delayed nausea or vomiting (unlabeled use; in combination with a corticosteroid and serotonin [5HT$_3$] antagonist): Oral: 10 mg once daily for 3-5 days, beginning on day 1 of chemotherapy **or** 5 mg once daily for 2 days before chemotherapy, followed by 10 mg once daily (beginning on the day of chemotherapy) for 3-8 days

Elderly: Oral, I.M.: Consider lower starting dose of 2.5-5 mg/day for elderly or debilitated patients; may increase as clinically indicated and tolerated with close monitoring of orthostatic blood pressure

Psychosis/agitation related to Alzheimer's dementia (unlabeled use): Initial: 1.25-5 mg/day; if necessary, gradually increase as tolerated not to exceed 10 mg/day

Dosage adjustment in renal impairment: No adjustment required. Not removed by dialysis.

Dosage adjustment in hepatic impairment: Dosage adjustment may be necessary, however, there are no specific recommendations. Monitor closely.

Administration

Injection: For I.M. administration only; do not administer injection intravenously; inject slowly, deep into muscle. If dizziness and/or drowsiness are noted, patient should remain recumbent until examination indicates postural hypotension and/or bradycardia are not a problem. Concurrent use of I.M./I.V. benzodiazepines is not recommended (fatalities have been reported, though causality not determined).

Tablet: May be administered with or without food.

Orally-disintegrating: Remove from foil blister by peeling back (do not push tablet through the foil); place tablet in mouth immediately upon removal; tablet dissolves rapidly in saliva and may be swallowed with or without liquid. May be administered with or without food/meals.

Monitoring Parameters Vital signs; fasting lipid profile and fasting blood glucose/Hgb A$_{1c}$ (prior to treatment, at 3 months, then annually); periodic assessment of hepatic transaminases (in patients with hepatic disease); BMI, personal/family history of obesity, waist circumference; orthostatic blood pressure; mental status, abnormal involuntary movement scale (AIMS), extrapyramidal symptoms (EPS). Weight should be assessed prior to treatment, at 4 weeks, 8 weeks, 12 weeks, and then at quarterly intervals. Consider titrating to a different antipsychotic agent for a weight gain ≥5% of the initial weight.

Dietary Considerations Tablets may be taken with or without food. Zyprexa® Zydis®: 5 mg tablet contains phenylalanine 0.34 mg; 10 mg tablet contains phenylalanine 0.45 mg; 15 mg tablet contains phenylalanine 0.67 mg; 20 mg tablet contains phenylalanine 0.9 mg.

Special Geriatric Considerations Elderly patients have an increased risk of adverse response to side effects or adverse reactions to antipsychotics. A higher incidence of falls has been reported in elderly patients, particularly in debilitated patients. Olanzapine half-life that was 1.5 times that of younger (<65 years of age) adults; therefore, lower initial doses are recommended. Olanzapine is not indicated in dementia-related psychosis.

(Continued)

Olanzapine *(Continued)*

Studies with patients ≥65 years of age with schizophrenia showed no difference in tolerability compared to younger adults. Studies in the elderly with dementia-related psychosis suggested a different tolerability compared to younger patients with schizophrenia. In light of significant risks and adverse effects in the elderly population (compared with limited data demonstrating efficacy in the treatment of dementia-related psychosis, aggression, and agitation), an extensive risk:benefit analysis should be performed prior to use. Therefore, use with caution and at lower recommended doses.

Dosage Forms Excipient information presented when available (limited, particularly for generics); consult specific product labeling.

Injection, powder for reconstitution (Zyprexa® IntraMuscular): 10 mg [contains lactose 50 mg]

Tablet (Zyprexa®): 2.5 mg, 5 mg, 7.5 mg, 10 mg, 15 mg, 20 mg

Tablet, orally disintegrating (Zyprexa® Zydis®): 5 mg [contains phenylalanine 0.34 mg/tablet], 10 mg [contains phenylalanine 0.45 mg/tablet], 15 mg [contains phenylalanine 0.67 mg/tablet], 20 mg [contains phenylalanine 0.9 mg/tablet]

References

American Diabetes Association; American Psychiatric Association; American Association of Clinical Endocrinologists; North American Association for the Study of Obesity, "Consensus Development Conference on Antipsychotic Drugs and Obesity and Diabetes," *Diabetes Care*, 2004, 27(2):596-601.

Baldwin DS and Montgomery SA, "First Clinical Experience With Olanzapine (LY 170053): Results of an Open-Label Safety and Dose-Ranging Study in Patients With Schizophrenia," *Int Clin Psychopharmacol*, 1995, 10(4):239-44.

Carrillo JA, Herraiz AG, Ramos SI, et al, "Role of the Smoking-Induced Cytochrome P450 (CYP)1A2 and Polymorphic CYP2D6 in Steady-State Concentration of Olanzapine," *J Clin Psychopharmacol*, 23(2):119-27.

Davis JM, Chen N, and Glick ID, "A Meta-analysis of the Efficacy of Second-Generation Antipsychotics," *Arch Gen Psychiatry*, 2003, 60(6):553-64.

Duggal HS, Gates C, and Pathak PC, "Olanzapine-Induced Neutropenia: Mechanism and Treatment," *J Clin Psychopharmacol*, 2004, 24(2):234-5.

Farwell WR, Stump TE, Wang J, et al, "Weight Gain and New Onset Diabetes Associated With Olanzapine and Risperidone," *J Gen Intern Med*, 2004, 19(12):1200-5.

Goldberg RJ, "Managing Psychosis-Related Behavioral Problems in the Elderly," *Consult Pharm*, 1997, 12(Suppl C):4-10.

Gorski ED and Willis KC, "Report of Three Cases Studied With Olanzapine for Chronic Pain," *J Pain*, 2003, 4:166-8.

Khojainova N, Santiago-Palma J, Kornick C, et al, "Olanzapine in the Management of Cancer Pain," *J Pain Symptom Manage*, 2002, 23(4):346-50.

Kiser RS, Cohen HM, Freedenfeld RN, et al, "Olanzapine for the Treatment of Fibromyalgia Symptoms," *J Pain Symptom Manage*, 2001, 22(2):704-8.

Krishnamoorthy J and King BH, "Open-Label Olanzapine Treatment in Five Preadolescent Children," *J Child Adolesc Psychopharmacol*, 1998, 8(2):107-13.

Kumra S, Jacobsen LK, Lenane M et al, "Childhood-Onset Schizophrenia: An Open-Label Study of Olanzapine in Adolescents," *J Am Acad Child Adolesc Psychiatry*, 1998, 37(4):377-85.

Navari RM, Einhorn LH, Loehrer PJ, et al, "A Phase II Trial of Olanzapine, Dexamethasone, and Palonosetron for the Prevention of Chemotherapy-Induced Nausea and Vomiting: A Hoosier Oncology Group Study," *Support Care Cancer*, 2007, 15(11):1285-91.

Navari RM, Einhorn LH, Passik SD, et al, "A Phase II Trial of Olanzapine for the Prevention of Chemotherapy-Induced Nausea and Vomiting: A Hoosier Oncology Group Study," *Support Care Cancer*, 2005, 13(7):529-34.

Passick SD, Navari RM, Jung SH, et al, "A Phase I Trial of Olanzapine (Zyprexa) for the Prevention of Delayed Emesis in Cancer Patients: A Hoosier Oncology Group Study," *Cancer Invest*, 2004, 22(3):383-8.

Rabins PV, Blacker D, Rovner BW, et al, "Practice Guidelines for the Treatment of Patients With Alzheimer's Disease and Other Dementias," October, 2007. Available at http://www.psych.org/psych_pract/treatg/pg/prac_guide.cfm.

Rozen TD, "New Treatments in Cluster Headache," *Curr Neurol Neurosci Rep*, 2002, 2(2):114-21.

Schneider LS, Tariot PN, Dagerman KS, et al, "Effectiveness of Atypical Antipsychotic Drugs in Patients With Alzheimer's Disease," *N Engl J Med*, 2006, 355(15):1525-38.

Shaw P, Sporn A, Gogtay N et al, "Childhood-Onset Schizophrenia: A Double-Blind, Randomized Clozapine-Olanzapine Comparison," *Arch Gen Psychiatry*, 2006, 63(7):721-30.

Sorsaburu S, Hornbuckle K, Blake D, et al, "The First 21 Months of Safety Experience With Postmarketing Use of Olanzapine's Intramuscular Formulation," College of Psychiatric and Neurologic Pharmacists, April, 2006, Baltimore, MD.

Soutullo CA, Sorter MT, Foster KD, et al, "Olanzapine in the Treatment of Adolescent Acute Mania: A Report of Seven Cases," *J Affect Disord*, 1999, 53(3):279-83.

Thangadurai P, Jyothi KS, Gopalakrishman R, et al, "Reversible Neutropenia With Olanzapine Following Clozapine-Induced Neutropenia," *Am J Psychiatry*, 2006, 163(7):1298.

Thinn SS, Liew E, May AL, et al, "Reversible Delayed Onset Olanzapine-Associated Leukopenia and Neutropenia in a Clozapine-Naive Patient on Concomitant Depot Antipsychotic," *J Clin Psychopharmacol*, 2007, 27(4):394-5.

♦ **Oncaspar®** *see* Pegaspargase *on page 880*

♦ **Oncotice™ (Can)** *see* BCG Vaccine *on page 128*

♦ **Oncovin** *see* VinCRIStine *on page 1099*

Ondansetron (on DAN se tron)

Medication Safety Issues

Sound-alike/look-alike issues:

Ondansetron may be confused with dolasetron, granisetron, palonosetron

Zofran® may be confused with Zantac®, Zosyn®

Related Information

Management of Nausea and Vomiting *on page 1319*

U.S. Brand Names Zofran®; Zofran® ODT

Index Terms GR38032R; Ondansetron Hydrochloride

Generic Available Yes

Canadian Brand Names Apo-Ondansetron®; Novo-Ondansetron; Ondansetron-Omega; PHL-Ondansetron; PMS-Ondansetron; Ratio-Ondansetron; Sandoz-Ondansetron; Zofran®; Zofran® ODT

Pharmacologic Category Antiemetic; Selective 5-HT$_3$ Receptor Antagonist

Use Prevention of nausea and vomiting associated with moderately- to highly-emetogenic cancer chemotherapy; radiotherapy in patients receiving total body irradiation or fractions to the abdomen; prevention of postoperative nausea and vomiting (PONV); treatment of PONV if no prophylactic dose received

Unlabeled/Investigational Use Treatment of early-onset alcoholism; hyperemesis gravidarum

Pregnancy Risk Factor B

Lactation Excretion in breast milk unknown/use caution

Labeled Contraindications Hypersensitivity to ondansetron, other selective 5-HT$_3$ antagonists, or any component of the formulation

Warnings/Precautions **Ondansetron should be used on a scheduled basis, not on an "as needed" (PRN) basis,** since data support the use of this drug only in the prevention of nausea and vomiting (due to antineoplastic therapy) and not in the rescue of nausea and vomiting. Ondansetron should only be used in the first 24-48 hours of chemotherapy. Data do not support any increased efficacy of ondansetron in delayed nausea and vomiting. Does not stimulate gastric or intestinal peristalsis; may mask progressive ileus and/or gastric distension. Use with caution in patients allergic to other 5-HT$_3$ receptor antagonists; cross-reactivity has been reported. Transient ECG changes (including QT interval prolongation) have been reported (rarely) with I.V. use. Orally-disintegrating tablets contain phenylalanine. Safety and efficacy for children <1 month of age have not been established. (Continued)

Ondansetron *(Continued)*

Adverse Reactions Note: Percentages reported in adult patients.

>10%:

Central nervous system: Headache (9% to 27%), malaise/fatigue (9% to 13%)

Gastrointestinal: Constipation (6% to 11%)

1% to 10%:

Central nervous system: Drowsiness (8%), fever (2% to 8%), dizziness (4% to 7%), anxiety (6%), cold sensation (2%)

Dermatologic: Pruritus (2% to 5%), rash (1%)

Gastrointestinal: Diarrhea (2% to 7%)

Genitourinary: Gynecological disorder (7%), urinary retention (5%)

Hepatic: ALT/AST increased (1% to 5%)

Local: Injection site reaction (4%; pain, redness, burning)

Neuromuscular & skeletal: Paresthesia (2%)

Respiratory: Hypoxia (9%)

<1%: Anaphylaxis, angina, bronchospasm, ECG changes, extrapyramidal symptoms, grand mal seizure, hypokalemia, tachycardia, vascular occlusive events

Postmarketing and/or case reports: Anaphylactoid reactions, angioedema, arrhythmia, blindness (transient/following infusion; lasting ≤48 hours), blurred vision (transient/following infusion), bradycardia, cardiopulmonary arrest, dyspnea, dystonic reaction, electrocardiographic alterations (second degree heart block and ST-segment depression), flushing, hiccups, hypersensitivity reaction, hypotension, laryngeal edema, laryngospasm, oculogyric crisis, palpitation, premature ventricular contractions (PVC), QT interval increased, shock, stridor, supraventricular tachycardia, syncope, urticaria, ventricular arrhythmia

Overdosage/Toxicology Sudden transient blindness, severe constipation, hypotension, and vasovagal episode with transient secondary heart block have been reported in some cases of overdose. I.V. doses of up to 252 mg/day have been inadvertently given without adverse effects. There is no specific antidote. Treatment is symptom-directed and supportive.

Drug Interactions

Cytochrome P450 Effect: Substrate of CYP1A2 (minor), 2C9 (minor), 2D6 (minor), 2E1 (minor), 3A4 (major); **Inhibits** CYP1A2 (weak), 2C9 (weak), 2D6 (weak)

Increased Effect/Toxicity: Ondansetron may enhance the hypotensive effect of apomorphine; concurrent use is contraindicated.

Decreased Effect: CYP3A4 inducers may decrease the levels/effects of ondansetron; example inducers include aminoglutethimide, carbamazepine, nafcillin, nevirapine, phenobarbital, phenytoin, and rifamycins. The manufacturer does not recommend dosage adjustment in patients receiving CYP3A4 inducers.

Ethanol/Nutrition/Herb Interactions

Food: Food increases the extent of absorption. The C_{max} and T_{max} do not change much.

Herb/Nutraceutical: St John's wort may decrease ondansetron levels.

Storage/Stability

Oral solution: Store between 15°C and 30°C (59°F and 86°F). Protect from light.

Premixed bag: Store between 2°C and 30°C (36°F and 86°F). Protect from light.

Tablet: Store between 2°C and 30°C (36°F and 86°F).

Vial: Store between 2°C and 30°C (36°F and 86°F). Protect from light. Stable when mixed in D$_5$W or NS for 48 hours at room temperature.

Reconstitution Prior to I.V. infusion, dilute in 50 mL D$_5$W or NS.

Compatibility Stable in D$_5$¹/₂NS, D$_5$NS, D$_5$W, mannitol 10%, LR, NS, sodium chloride 3%; do not mix injection with alkaline solutions.

Y-site administration: Compatible: Alatrofloxacin, aldesleukin, amifostine, amikacin, aztreonam, bleomycin, carboplatin, carmustine, cefazolin, cefotaxime, cefoxitin, ceftazidime, ceftizoxime, cefuroxime, chlorpromazine, cimetidine, cisatracurium, cisplatin, cladribine, clindamycin, cyclophosphamide, cytarabine, dacarbazine, dactinomycin, daunorubicin, dexamethasone sodium phosphate, diphenhydramine, docetaxel, dopamine, doxorubicin, doxorubicin liposome, doxycycline, droperidol, etoposide, etoposide phosphate, famotidine, filgrastim, floxuridine, fluconazole, fludarabine, gatifloxacin, gemcitabine, gentamicin, haloperidol, heparin, hydrocortisone sodium phosphate, hydrocortisone sodium succinate, hydromorphone, hydroxyzine, ifosfamide, imipenem/cilastatin, linezolid, magnesium sulfate, mannitol, mechlorethamine, melphalan, meperidine, mesna, methotrexate, metoclopramide, mitomycin, mitoxantrone, morphine, paclitaxel, paclitaxel with ranitidine, pentostatin, piperacillin/tazobactam, potassium chloride, prochlorperazine edisylate, promethazine, ranitidine, remifentanil, sodium acetate, streptozocin, teniposide, thiotepa, ticarcillin, ticarcillin/clavulanate, topotecan, vancomycin, vinblastine, vincristine, vinorelbine, zidovudine. Incompatible: Acyclovir, allopurinol, aminophylline, amphotericin B, amphotericin B cholesteryl sulfate complex, ampicillin, ampicillin/sulbactam, amsacrine, cefepime, cefoperazone, furosemide, ganciclovir, lorazepam, methylprednisolone sodium succinate, piperacillin, sargramostim, sodium bicarbonate. Variable (consult detailed reference): Fluorouracil, meropenem.

Mechanism of Action Selective 5-HT$_3$-receptor antagonist, blocking serotonin, both peripherally on vagal nerve terminals and centrally in the chemoreceptor trigger zone

Pharmacodynamics/Kinetics

Onset of action: ~30 minutes

Distribution: V$_d$: Children: 1.7-3.7 L/kg; Adults: 2.2-2.5 L/kg

Protein binding, plasma: 70% to 76%

Metabolism: Extensively hepatic via hydroxylation, followed by glucuronide or sulfate conjugation; CYP1A2, CYP2D6, and CYP3A4 substrate; some demethylation occurs

Bioavailability: Oral: 56% to 71%; Rectal: 58% to 74%

Half-life elimination: Children <15 years: 2-7 hours; Adults: 3-6 hours

Mild-to-moderate hepatic impairment: Adults: 12 hours

Severe hepatic impairment (Child-Pugh C): Adults: 20 hours

Time to peak: Oral: ~2 hours

Excretion: Urine (44% to 60% as metabolites, 5% to 10% as unchanged drug); feces (~25%)

Dosage Note: Studies in adults have shown a single daily dose of 8-12 mg I.V. or 8-24 mg orally to be as effective as mg/kg dosing, and should be considered for **all** patients whose mg/kg dose exceeds 8-12 mg I.V.; oral solution and ODT formulations are bioequivalent to corresponding doses of tablet formulation

Children:

I.V.:

Prevention of chemotherapy-induced emesis: 6 months to 18 years: 0.15 mg/kg/dose administered 30 minutes prior to chemotherapy, 4 and 8 hours after the first dose **or** 0.45 mg/kg/day as a single dose

(Continued)

Ondansetron *(Continued)*

Prevention of postoperative nausea and vomiting: 1 month to 12 years:
≤40 kg: 0.1 mg/kg as a single dose
>40 kg: 4 mg as a single dose

Oral: Prevention of chemotherapy-induced emesis:
4-11 years: 4 mg 30 minutes before chemotherapy; repeat 4 and 8 hours after initial dose, then 4 mg every 8 hours for 1-2 days after chemotherapy completed
≥12 years: Refer to adult dosing.

Adults:
I.V.:
Prevention of chemotherapy-induced emesis:
0.15 mg/kg 3 times/day beginning 30 minutes prior to chemotherapy **or**
0.45 mg/kg once daily **or**
8-10 mg 1-2 times/day **or**
24 mg or 32 mg once daily

Treatment of hyperemesis gravidum (unlabeled use): 8 mg administered over 15 minutes every 12 hours **or** 1 mg/hour infused continuously for up to 24 hours

I.M., I.V.: Postoperative nausea and vomiting: 4 mg as a single dose approximately 30 minutes before the end of anesthesia, or as treatment if vomiting occurs after surgery
Note: Repeat doses given in response to inadequate control of nausea/vomiting from preoperative doses are generally ineffective.

Oral:
Chemotherapy-induced emesis:
Highly-emetogenic agents/single-day therapy: 24 mg given 30 minutes prior to the start of therapy
Moderately-emetogenic agents: 8 mg every 12 hours beginning 30 minutes before chemotherapy, continuously for 1-2 days after chemotherapy completed

Total body irradiation: 8 mg 1-2 hours before daily each fraction of radiotherapy
Single high-dose fraction radiotherapy to abdomen: 8 mg 1-2 hours before irradiation, then 8 mg every 8 hours after first dose for 1-2 days after completion of radiotherapy
Daily fractionated radiotherapy to abdomen: 8 mg 1-2 hours before irradiation, then 8 mg 8 hours after first dose for each day of radiotherapy
Postoperative nausea and vomiting: 16 mg given 1 hour prior to induction of anesthesia
Treatment of hyperemesis gravidum (unlabeled use): 8 mg every 12 hours

Elderly: No dosing adjustment required

Dosage adjustment in renal impairment: No dosing adjustment required
Dosage adjustment in hepatic impairment: Severe liver disease (Child-Pugh C): Maximum daily dose: 8 mg

Administration

Oral: Oral dosage forms should be administered 30 minutes prior to chemotherapy; 1-2 hours before radiotherapy; 1 hour prior to the induction of anesthesia.

Orally-disintegrating tablets: Do not remove from blister until needed. Peel backing off the blister, do not push tablet through. Using dry hands, place tablet on tongue and allow to dissolve. Swallow with saliva.

I.M.: Should be administered undiluted.

I.V.: Give first dose 30 minutes prior to beginning chemotherapy; the I.V. preparation has been successful when administered orally.

I.V. injection: Single doses for prevention of postoperative nausea and vomiting may be administered I.V. over 2-5 minutes as undiluted solution.

IVPB: Dilute in 50 mL D_5W or NS. Infuse over 15-30 minutes; 24-hour continuous infusions have been reported, but are rarely used.

Monitoring Parameters Closely monitor patients <4 months of age

Dietary Considerations Take without regard to meals.

Orally-disintegrating tablet contains <0.03 mg phenylalanine

Patient Information Orally-disintegrating tablets: Do not remove from blister until needed. Peel backing off the blister, do not push tablet through. Using dry hands, place tablet on tongue and allow to dissolve. Swallow with saliva. Contains <0.03 mg phenylalanine/tablet.

Special Geriatric Considerations Elderly have a slightly decreased hepatic clearance rate. This does not, however, require a dose adjustment.

Emetic Potential Very low (<10%)

Vesicant No

Dosage Forms Excipient information presented when available (limited, particularly for generics); consult specific product labeling.

Infusion [premixed in D_5W, preservative free]: 32 mg (50 mL)
Zofran®: 32 mg (50 mL)
Injection, solution: 2 mg/mL (2 mL, 20 mL)
Zofran®: 2 mg/mL (2 mL, 20 mL)
Solution, oral: 4 mg/5 mL (50 mL)
Zofran®: 4 mg/5 mL (50 mL) [contains sodium benzoate; strawberry flavor]
Tablet: 4 mg; 8 mg
Zofran®: 4 mg; 8 mg
Tablet, orally disintegrating: 4 mg; 8 mg
Zofran® ODT: 4 mg, 8 mg [each strength contains phenylalanine <0.03 mg/tablet; strawberry flavor]

Extemporaneous Preparations A 0.8 mg/mL syrup may be made by crushing ten 8 mg tablets; flaking of the tablet coating occurs. Mix thoroughly with 50 mL of the suspending vehicle, Ora-Plus® (Paddock), in 5 mL increments. Add sufficient volume of any of the following syrups: Cherry syrup USP, Syrpalta® (Humco), Ora-Sweet® (Paddock), or Ora-Sweet® Sugar-Free (Paddock) to make a final volume of 100 mL. Stability is 42 days refrigerated.

Trissel LA, "Trissel's Stability of Compounded Formulations," American Pharmaceutical Association, 1996.

Rectal suppositories: Calibrate a suppository mold for the base being used. Determine the displacement factor (DF) for ondansetron for the base being used (Fattibase® = 1.1; Polybase® = 0.6). Weigh the ondansetron tablet. Divide the tablet weight by the DF. Subtract the weight of base displaced from the calculated weight of base required for each suppository. Grind the ondansetron tablets to a fine powder in a mortar. Weigh out the appropriate weight of suppository base. Melt the base over a water bath (<55°C). Add the ondansetron powder to the suppository base and mix well. Pour the mixture into the suppository mold and cool. Stable for at least 30 days under refrigeration.

Allen LV, "Ondansetron Suppositories," *US Pharm*, 20(7):84-6.

References
American College of Obstetrics and Gynecology, ACOG (American College of Obstetrics and Gynecology) Practice Bulletin: "Nausea and Vomiting of Pregnancy," *Obstet Gynecol*, 2004, 103(4):803-14.

Chaffee BJ and Tankanow RM, "Ondansetron - the First of a New Class of Antiemetic Agents," *Clin Pharm*, 1991, 10(6):430-6.
(Continued)

Ondansetron *(Continued)*

Kris MG, Hesketh PJ, Somerfield MR, et al, "American Society of Clinical Oncology Guideline for Antiemetics in Oncology: Update 2006," *J Clin Oncol*, 2006, 24(18):2932-47.

Levichek Z, Atanackovic G, Oepkes D, et al, "Nausea and Vomiting of Pregnancy. Evidence-Based Treatment Algorithm," *Can Fam Physician*, 2002, 48:267-8, 277.

Roila F and Del Favero A, "Ondansetron Clinical Pharmacokinetics," *Clin Pharmacokinet*, 1995, 29(2):95-109.

Siu SS, Yip SK, Cheung CW, et al, "Treatment of Intractable Hyperemesis Gravidarum by Ondansetron," *Eur J Obstet Gynecol Reprod Biol*, 2002, 105(1):73-4.

Tramer MR, Moore RA, Reynolds DJ, et al, "A Quantitative Systematic Review of Ondansetron in Treatment of Established Postoperative Nausea and Vomiting," *BMJ*, 1997, 314(7087):1088-92.

Wilde MI and Markham A, "Ondansetron. A Review of Its Pharmacology and Preliminary Clinical Findings in Novel Application," *Drugs*, 1996, 52(5):773-94.

- **Ondansetron Hydrochloride** *see* Ondansetron *on page 837*
- **Ondansetron-Omega (Can)** *see* Ondansetron *on page 837*
- **ONTAK®** *see* Denileukin Diftitox *on page 323*
- **Onxol™** *see* Paclitaxel *on page 858*
- **Opana®** *see* Oxymorphone *on page 853*
- **Opana® ER** *see* Oxymorphone *on page 853*
- **Ophtho-Tate® (Can)** *see* PrednisoLONE *on page 914*

Oprelvekin *(oh PREL ve kin)*

Medication Safety Issues

Sound-alike/look-alike issues:

Oprelvekin may be confused with aldesleukin, Proleukin®

Neumega® may be confused with Neulasta®, Neupogen®

U.S. Brand Names Neumega®

Index Terms IL-11; Interleukin-11; NSC-722848; Recombinant Human Interleukin-11; Recombinant Interleukin-11; rhIL-11; rIL-11

Generic Available No

Pharmacologic Category Biological Response Modulator; Human Growth Factor

Use Prevention of severe thrombocytopenia; reduce the need for platelet transfusions following myelosuppressive chemotherapy

Pregnancy Risk Factor C

Lactation Excretion in breast milk unknown/not recommended

Labeled Contraindications Hypersensitivity to oprelvekin or any component of the formulation

Warnings/Precautions [U.S. Boxed Warning]: Allergic or hypersensitivity reactions, including anaphylaxis have been reported. May occur with the first or with subsequent doses. Permanently discontinue in any patient developing an allergic reaction. May cause serious fluid retention; use cautiously in patients with conditions where expansion of plasma volume should be avoided (eg, left ventricular dysfunction, CHF, hypertension). Closely monitor fluid and electrolytes in patient on chronic diuretic therapy; severe hypokalemia contributing to sudden death have been reported in these patients. Arrhythmia, pulmonary edema, and cardiac arrest have been reported; use in patients with a history of atrial arrhythmia only if the potential benefit exceeds possible risks. Patients experiencing arrhythmia may be at risk for stroke; use caution in patients with a history of transient ischemic attack or stroke. Ventricular arrhythmia has also been reported, occurring within 2-7 days of treatment initiation. Use caution in patients with conduction defects, respiratory disease; history of thromboembolic problems; pre-existing pericardial effusions or ascites. Use with caution in hepatic or renal dysfunction. Not indicated following myeloablative chemotherapy; increased toxicities were reported when used following myeloablative therapy. Efficacy has not been established with chemotherapy regimens >5 days duration or with regimens associated with delayed myelosuppression (eg, nitrosoureas, mitomycin C). Safety and efficacy have not been established with chronic administration. Papilledema, more frequently associated with use in children, has occurred; use caution in patients with pre-existing papilledema or with tumors involving the central nervous system. Papilledema is dose limiting. Patients experiencing oprelvekin-related papilledema may be at risk for visual acuity changes, including blurred vision or blindness. Although used in children in clinical trials, safety and efficacy have not been established in pediatric patients.

Adverse Reactions

>10%:

Cardiovascular: Tachycardia (children 84%; adults 20%), edema (59%), palpitation (14%), cardiomegaly (children 21%), vasodilation (19%), syncope (13%), atrial arrhythmia (12%)

Central nervous system: Headache (41%), dizziness (38%), fever (36%), insomnia (33%), fatigue (30%)

Dermatologic: Rash (25%)

Endocrine & metabolic: Fluid retention

Gastrointestinal: Nausea/vomiting (77%), diarrhea (43%), oral moniliasis (14%)

Hematologic: Anemia (dilutional); appears within 3 days of initiation of therapy, resolves in about 1 week after cessation of oprelvekin

Neuromuscular & skeletal: Weakness (severe 14%), arthralgia, periostitis (children 11%)

Ocular: Conjunctival injection/redness/swelling (children 57%; adults 19%), papilledema (children 16%; adults 1%)

Respiratory: Dyspnea (48%), rhinitis (42%), cough (29%), pharyngitis (25%)

1% to 10%:

Gastrointestinal: Weight gain (5%)

Respiratory: Pleural effusion (10%)

Postmarketing and/or case reports: Allergic reaction, amblyopia, anaphylaxis/anaphylactoid reactions, blindness, blurred vision, capillary leak syndrome, CHF, dehydration, exfoliative dermatitis, eye hemorrhage, facial edema, fibrinogen increased, fluid overload, hypoalbuminemia, hypocalcemia, hypotension, injection site reactions (dermatitis, pain, discoloration), optic neuropathy, paresthesia, pericardial effusion, pulmonary edema, renal failure, skin discoloration, stroke, ventricular arrhythmia

Overdosage/Toxicology Doses of oprelvekin >50 mcg/kg may be associated with an increased incidence of cardiovascular events. If an overdose is administered, discontinue oprelvekin and closely observe patient for signs of toxicity. Treatment is symptom-directed and supportive. Base reinstitution of therapy on individual patient factors (evidence of toxicity and continued need for therapy).

Drug Interactions

Increased Effect/Toxicity: Hypokalemia may increase the risk of adverse cardiovascular events with oprelvekin; monitor.

Storage/Stability Store vials under refrigeration between 2°C to 8°C (36°F to 46°F); do not freeze. Protect from light. Use reconstituted oprelvekin within 3 hours of reconstitution and store in the vial at either 2°C to 8°C (36°F to 46°F) or room temperature of ≤25°C (77°F). Do not freeze or shake reconstituted solution.

(Continued)

Oprelvekin *(Continued)*

Reconstitution Reconstitute to a final concentration of 5 mg/mL with SWFI; swirl gently, do not shake.

Mechanism of Action Oprelvekin is a growth factor which stimulates multiple stages of megakaryocytopoiesis and thrombopoiesis, resulting in proliferation of megakaryocyte progenitors and megakaryocyte maturation, or increased platelet production.

Pharmacodynamics/Kinetics

Bioavailability: >80%

Half-life elimination: Terminal: 5-9 hours

Time to peak, serum: 1-6 hours

Excretion: Urine (primarily as metabolites)

Dosage SubQ: Administer first dose ~6-24 hours after the end of chemotherapy. Discontinue at least 48 hours before beginning the next cycle of chemotherapy.

Children (unlabeled use): 75-100 mcg/kg once daily for 10-21 days (until postnadir platelet count ≥50,000 cells/µL).

Note: A safe and effective dose for use in children has not been established by the manufacturer.

Adults: 50 mcg/kg once daily for ~10-21 days (until postnadir platelet count ≥50,000 cells/µL)

Dosage adjustment in renal impairment: Cl_{cr} <30 mL/minute: 25 mcg/kg once daily

Administration Subcutaneously in the abdomen, thigh, hip, or upper arm.

Monitoring Parameters Monitor electrolytes and fluid balance during therapy; obtain a CBC at regular intervals during therapy; monitor platelet counts until adequate recovery has occurred

Test Interactions Decrease in hemoglobin concentration, serum concentration of albumin and other proteins (result of expansion of plasma volume)

Patient Information Report any swelling in the arms or legs (peripheral edema), shortness of breath (congestive failure, anemia), irregular heartbeat, or headaches.

Emetic Potential Moderate (30% to 60%)

Vesicant No

Dosage Forms Excipient information presented when available (limited, particularly for generics); consult specific product labeling.

Injection, powder for reconstitution:

Neumega®: 5 mg [packaged with diluent]

References

Du X and Williams DA, "Interleukin-11: Review of Molecular, Cell Biology, and Clinical Use," *Blood*, 1997, 89(11):3897-908.

Gordon MS, "Thrombopoietic Activity of Recombinant Human Interleukin 11 in Cancer Patients Receiving Chemotherapy," *Cancer Chemother Pharmacol*, 1996, 38 (Suppl):96-8.

Sitaraman SV and Gewirtz AT, "Oprelvekin. Genetics Institute," *Curr Opin Investig Drugs*, 2001, 2(10):1395-400.

Tepler I, Elias L, Smith JW 2d, et al, "A Randomized Placebo-Controlled Trial of Recombinant Human Interleukin-11 in Cancer Patients With Severe Thrombocytopenia Due to Chemotherapy," *Blood*, 1996, 87(9):3607-14.

Teramura M, Kobayashi S, Yoshinaga K, et al, "Effect of Interleukin 11 on Normal and Pathological Thrombopoiesis," *Cancer Chemother Pharmacol*, 1996, 38 (Suppl):99-102.

- **Oraquix**® *see Lidocaine and Prilocaine on page 687*
- **Orthoclone OKT**® **3** *see Muromonab-CD3 on page 788*
- **Orzel**® *see UFT on page 1079*
- **OSI-774** *see Erlotinib on page 396*
- **OTFC (Oral Transmucosal Fentanyl Citrate)** *see Fentanyl on page 426*

Oxaliplatin (ox AL i pla tin)

Medication Safety Issues

Sound-alike/look-alike issues:

Oxaliplatin may be confused with Aloxi®, carboplatin

High alert medication: The Institute for Safe Medication Practices (ISMP) includes this medication among its list of drugs which have a heightened risk of causing significant patient harm when used in error.

Related Information

Investigational Drug Service *on page 1379*
Management of Drug Extravasations *on page 1301*
Safe Handling of Hazardous Drugs *on page 1382*

U.S. Brand Names Eloxatin®

Index Terms Diaminocyclohexane Oxalatoplatinum; L-OHP; NSC-266046

Generic Available No

Pharmacologic Category Antineoplastic Agent, Alkylating Agent; Antineoplastic Agent, Platinum Analog

Use Treatment of stage III colon cancer and advanced colorectal cancer

Unlabeled/Investigational Use Head and neck cancer, nonsmall-cell lung cancer, non-Hodgkin's lymphoma, ovarian cancer

Pregnancy Risk Factor D

Lactation Excretion in breast milk unknown/not recommended

Labeled Contraindications Hypersensitivity to oxaliplatin, other platinum-containing compounds, or any component of the formulation

Warnings/Precautions Hazardous agent - use appropriate precautions for handling and disposal. **[U.S. Boxed Warning]: Anaphylactic-like reaction may occur within minutes of oxaliplatin administration; symptoms may be managed with epinephrine, corticosteroids, and antihistamines.** Two different types of neuropathy may occur: First, an acute (within first 2 days), reversible (resolves within 14 days), with primarily peripheral symptoms that are often exacerbated by cold (may include pharyngolaryngeal dysesthesia; avoid mucositis prophylaxis with ice chips during oxaliplatin infusion). Secondly, a more persistent (>14 days) presentation that often interferes with daily activities (eg, writing, buttoning, swallowing), these symptoms may improve upon discontinuing treatment. May cause pulmonary fibrosis or hepatotoxicity. The presence of hepatic vascular disorders (including veno-occlusive disease) should be considered, especially in individuals developing portal hypertension or who present with increased liver function tests. Use caution with renal dysfunction; increased toxicity may occur. When administered as sequential infusions, taxane derivatives (docetaxel, paclitaxel) should be administered before platinum derivatives (carboplatin, cisplatin, oxaliplatin) to limit myelosuppression and enhance efficacy. Elderly patients are more sensitive to some adverse events including diarrhea, dehydration, hypokalemia, leukopenia, fatigue and syncope. **[U.S. Boxed Warning]: Should be administered under the supervision of an experienced cancer chemotherapy physician.** Safety and efficacy in children have not been established.

Adverse Reactions Percentages reported with monotherapy.

(Continued)

Oxaliplatin *(Continued)*

>10%:

Central nervous system: Fatigue (61%), fever (25%), pain (14%), headache (13%), insomnia (11%)

Gastrointestinal: Nausea (64%), diarrhea (46%), vomiting (37%), abdominal pain (31%), constipation (31%), anorexia (20%), stomatitis (14%)

Hematologic: Anemia (64%), thrombocytopenia (30%), leukopenia (13%)

Hepatic: AST increased (54%; grades 3/4: 4%), ALT increased (36%; grades 3/4: 1%), total bilirubin increased (13%; grades 3/4: 5%)

Neuromuscular & skeletal: Peripheral neuropathy (may be dose limiting; 76%; acute 65%; grades 3/4: 5%; persistent 43%; grades 3/4: 3%), back pain (11%)

Respiratory: Dyspnea (13%), cough (11%)

1% to 10%:

Cardiovascular: Edema (10%), chest pain (5%), peripheral edema (5%), flushing (3%), thromboembolism (2%)

Central nervous system: Dizziness (7%)

Dermatologic: Rash (5%), alopecia (3%), hand-foot syndrome (1%)

Endocrine & metabolic: Dehydration (5%), hypokalemia (3%)

Gastrointestinal: Dyspepsia (7%), taste perversion (5%), flatulence (3%), mucositis (2%), gastroesophageal reflux (1%), dysphagia (acute 1% to 2%)

Genitourinary: Dysuria (1%)

Hematologic: Neutropenia (7%)

Local: Injection site reaction (9%; redness/swelling/pain)

Neuromuscular & skeletal: Rigors (9%), arthralgia (7%)

Ocular: Abnormal lacrimation (1%)

Renal: Serum creatinine increased (5% to 10%)

Respiratory: URI (7%), rhinitis (6%), epistaxis (2%), pharyngitis (2%), pharyngolaryngeal dysesthesia (grades 3/4: 1% to 2%)

Miscellaneous: Allergic reactions (3%); hypersensitivity (includes urticaria, pruritus, facial flushing, shortness of breath, bronchospasm, diaphoresis, hypotension, syncope: grades 3/4: 2% to 3%); hiccup (2%)

Postmarketing and/or case reports: Acute renal failure, alkaline phosphatase increased, anaphylactic shock, angioedema, colitis, cranial nerve palsies, deep tendon reflex loss, deafness, dysarthria, eosinophilic pneumonia, extravasation (including necrosis), fasciculations, hemolytic anemia (immuno-allergic), hemolytic uremia syndrome, hepatotoxicity, hypokalemia (due to severe diarrhea, vomiting), ileus, INR increased, interstitial lung diseases, interstitial nephropathy (acute), intestinal obstruction, Lhermittes' sign, metabolic acidosis, optic neuritis, pancreatitis, prothrombin time increased, pulmonary fibrosis, thrombocytopenia (immuno-allergic), veno-occlusive liver disease (sinusoidal obstruction syndrome and perisinusoidal fibrosis), visual acuity decreased, visual field disturbance

Overdosage/Toxicology Overdose symptoms are extensions of known side effects (eg, thrombocytopenia, myelosuppression, nausea, vomiting, neurotoxicity, respiratory symptoms). Monitor closely. Treatment is symptom-directed and supportive.

Drug Interactions

Increased Effect/Toxicity: Taxane derivatives may increase oxaliplatin toxicity if administered before the platin as a sequential infusion. Nephrotoxic agents may increase oxaliplatin toxicity.

Decreased Effect: Oxaliplatin may decrease plasma levels of digoxin.

Storage/Stability Store intact vials in original outer carton at room temperature of 15°C to 30°C (59°F to 86°F); do not freeze. According to the manufacturer, solutions diluted for infusion are stable up to 6 hours at room temperature of 20°C to 25°C (68°F to 77°F) or up to 24 hours under refrigeration at 2°C to 8°C (36°F to 46°F). Oxaliplatin solution diluted with D$_5$W to a final concentration of 0.7 mg/mL (polyolefin container) has been shown to retain >90% of it's original concentration for up to 30 days when stored at room temperature or refrigerated; artificial light did not affect the concentration (Andre, 2007). As this study did not examine sterility, refrigeration would be preferred to limit microbial growth.

Reconstitution Do not prepare using a chloride-containing solution (eg, NaCl). Dilution with D$_5$W (250 or 500 mL) is required prior to administration. Infusion solutions do not require protection from light.

Compatibility Incompatible with alkaline solutions (eg, fluorouracil) and chloride-containing solutions. Flush infusion line with D$_5$W prior to, and following, administration of concomitant medications via same I.V. line.

Y-site administration: Compatible: Allopurinol, aminophylline, bumetanide, buprenorphine, butorphanol, calcium gluconate, carboplatin, chlorpromazine, cimetidine, cyclophosphamide, dexamethasone, diphenhydramine, dobutamine, docetaxel, dolasetron, dopamine, doxorubicin, droperidol, enalaprilat, epirubicin, etoposide phosphate, famotidine, fentanyl, furosemide, gemcitabine, granisetron, haloperidol, heparin, hydrocortisone sodium succinate, hydromorphone, hydroxyzine, ifosfamide, irinotecan, leucovorin, lorazepam, magnesium sulfate, mannitol, meperidine, mesna, methotrexate, methylprednisolone sodium succinate, metoclopramide, mitoxantrone, morphine, nalbuphine, ondansetron, paclitaxel, potassium chloride, prochlorperazine, promethazine, ranitidine, sodium bicarbonate, theophylline, topotecan, verapamil, vincristine, vinorelbine. **Incompatible:** Diazepam.

Mechanism of Action Oxaliplatin, a platinum derivative, is an alkylating agent. Following intracellular hydrolysis, the platinum compound binds to DNA forming cross-links which inhibit DNA replication and transcription, resulting in cell death. Cytotoxicity is cell-cycle nonspecific.

Pharmacodynamics/Kinetics

Distribution: V$_d$: 440 L

Protein binding: >90% primarily albumin and gamma globulin (irreversible binding to platinum)

Metabolism: Nonenzymatic (rapid and extensive), forms active and inactive derivatives

Half-life elimination: Terminal: 391 hours; Distribution: Alpha phase: 0.4 hours, Beta phase: 16.8 hours

Excretion: Primarily urine (~54%); feces (~2%)

Dosage Refer to individual protocols.

Adults: Stage III colon cancer and colorectal cancer: I.V.:

85 mg/m^2 every 2 weeks **or**

Unlabeled doses:

20-25 mg/m^2 days 1-5 every 3 weeks **or**

100-130 mg/m^2 every 2-3 weeks

Elderly: No dosing adjustment recommended

Dosage adjustments for toxicity: Acute toxicities: Longer infusion times may mitigate acute toxicities.

(Continued)

Oxaliplatin *(Continued)*

Neurosensory events:

Persistent (>7 days) grade 2 neurosensory events: Consider oxaliplatin dose reduction if symptoms do not resolve:

Stage III colon cancer: Reduce dose to 75 mg/m^2

Advanced colorectal cancer: Reduce dose to 65 mg/m^2

Consider withholding oxaliplatin for grade 2 neuropathy lasting >7 days despite dose reduction.

Grade 3 neurosensory events: Consider discontinuing oxaliplatin

Other toxicities (grade 3/4 gastrointestinal toxicity, grade 4 neutropenia, or grade 3/4 thrombocytopenia): After recovery from toxicity, oxaliplatin dose reductions are recommended:

Stage III colon cancer: Reduce dose to 75 mg/m^2

Advanced colorectal cancer: Reduce dose to 65 mg/m^2

Dosage adjustment in renal impairment: The FDA-approved labeling does not contain renal dosing adjustment guidelines. Oxaliplatin is primarily eliminated renally; in patients with Cl_{cr} <30 mL/minute, the AUC is increased ~190%. Oxaliplatin use has been studied in 25 patients with renal dysfunction; treatment was well-tolerated in patients with mild-to-moderate impairment (Cl_{cr} 20-59 mL/minute), suggesting that dose reduction is not necessary in this patient population (Takimoto, 2003). Patients with severe renal impairment (Cl_{cr} <20 mL/minute) have not been adequately studied; consider omitting dose or changing chemotherapy regimen if Cl_{cr} <20 mL/minute.

Combination Regimens

Biliary adenocarcinoma: GEMOX *on page 1229*

Colorectal cancer:

Bevacizumab-Oxaliplatin-Fluorouracil-Leucovorin *on page 1152*

FLOX (Nordic FLOX) *on page 1216*

FOIL *on page 1221*

FOLFOX 1 *on page 1221*

FOLFOX 2 *on page 1221*

FOLFOX 3 *on page 1222*

FOLFOX 4 *on page 1222*

FOLFOX 6 *on page 1222*

FOLFOX 7 *on page 1222*

XelOx *on page 1293*

Lymphoma, non-Hodgkin's: DHAP *on page 1190*

Administration Administer as I.V. infusion over 2-6 hours. Flush infusion line with D_5W prior to administration of any concomitant medication. Patients should receive an antiemetic premedication regimen. Avoid mucositis prophylaxis with ice chips during oxaliplatin infusion.

Monitoring Parameters CBC with differential, serum creatinine, liver function tests (including ALT, AST and bilirubin); signs of neuropathy, hypersensitivity, and/or respiratory effects; delay dosage until recovery of neutrophils ≥1.5 x 10^9/L and platelets ≥75 x 10^9/L

Patient Information Maintain adequate nutrition (frequent small meals may help) and adequate hydration (2-3 L/day of fluids unless instructed to restrict fluid intake). Nausea and vomiting may be severe; request antiemetic. You will be susceptible to infection; avoid crowds or exposure to infection. Report sore throat, fever, chills; unusual fatigue or unusual bruising/bleeding; difficulty breathing; muscle cramps or twitching; or tingling/numbness in arms, fingers, legs, or toes (may be increased by cold temperature). Inform prescriber if you are pregnant. Do not get pregnant during or for 1 month following therapy. Male: Do not cause a female to become pregnant. Male/

female: Consult prescriber for instruction on appropriate barrier contraceptive measures. This drug may cause severe fetal defects. Do not breast-feed.

Additional Information Cold temperature may exacerbate acute neuropathy. Do not use ice for mucositis prophylaxis.

Emetic Potential High (60% to 90%)

Vesicant No; may be an irritant. Cool compress may be used for immediate management of extravasation, with consideration of potential for peripheral neuropathy exacerbated by cold. Warm compresses will avoid peripheral neuropathy, however, while possibly increasing drug removal through local vasodilation, may increase cellular uptake and injury.

Dosage Forms Excipient information presented when available (limited, particularly for generics); consult specific product labeling.

Injection, solution [preservative free]:

Eloxatin®: 5 mg/mL (10 mL, 20 mL, 40 mL)

References

Andre T, Boni C, Mounedji-Boudiaf L, et al, "Oxaliplatin, Fluorouracil, and Leucovorin as Adjuvant Treatment for Colon Cancer," *N Engl J Med*, 2004, 350(23):2343-51.

Cassidy J and Misset JL, "Oxaliplatin-Related Side Effects: Characteristics and Management," *Semin Oncol*, 2002, 29(5 Suppl 15):11-20.

Culy CR, Clemett D, and Wiseman LR, "Oxaliplatin. A Review of Its Pharmacological Properties and Clinical Efficacy in Metastatic Colorectal Cancer and Its Potential in Other Malignancies," *Drugs*, 2000, 60(4):895-924.

Graham MA, Lockwood GF, Greenslade D, et al, "Clinical Pharmacokinetics of Oxaliplatin: A Critical Review," *Clin Cancer Res*, 2000, 6(4):1205-18.

Levi F, Metzger G, Massari C, et al, "Oxaliplatin: Pharmacokinetics and Chronopharmacological Aspects," *Clin Pharmacokinet*, 2000, 38(1):1-21.

Mani S, Graham MA, Bregman DB, et al, "Oxaliplatin: A Review of Evolving Concepts," *Cancer Invest*, 2002, 20(2):246-63.

Misset JL, Bleiberg H, Sutherland W, et al, "Oxaliplatin Clinical Activity: A Review," *Crit Rev Oncol Hematol*, 2000, 35(2):75-93.

Raymond E, Faivre S, Woynarowski JM, et al, "Oxaliplatin: Mechanism of Action and Antineoplastic Activity," *Semin Oncol*, 1998, 25(2 Suppl 5):4-12.

Takimoto CH, Remick SC, Sharma S, et al, "Dose-Escalating and Pharmacological Study of Oxaliplatin in Adult Cancer Patients With Impaired Renal Function: A National Cancer Institute Organ Dysfunction Working Group Study," *J Clin Oncol*, 2003, 21(14):2664-72.

Trissel LA, Saenz CA, Ingram DS, et al, "Compatibility Screening of Oxaliplatix During Simulated Y-Site Administration With Other Drugs," *J Oncol Pharm Practice*, 2002, 8(1):33-7.

Wiseman LR, Adkins JC, Plosker GL, et al, "Oxaliplatin: A Review of Its Use in the Management of Metastatic Colorectal Cancer," *Drugs Aging*, 1999, 14(6):459-75.

Oxycodone (oks i KOE done)

Medication Safety Issues

Sound-alike/look-alike issues:

Oxycodone may be confused with OxyContin®, oxymorphone

OxyContin® may be confused with oxybutynin

OxyFast® may be confused with Roxanol™

U.S. Brand Names ETH-Oxydose™; OxyContin®; OxyFast®; OxyIR®; Roxicodone®

Index Terms Dihydrohydroxycodeinone; Oxycodone Hydrochloride

Generic Available Yes

Canadian Brand Names OxyContin®; Oxy.IR®; Supeudol®

Pharmacologic Category Analgesic, Opioid

Use Management of moderate-to-severe pain, normally used in combination with nonopioid analgesics

OxyContin® is indicated for around-the-clock management of moderate-to-severe pain when an analgesic is needed for an extended period of time.

Restrictions C-II

(Continued)

Oxycodone *(Continued)*

Pregnancy Risk Factor B/D (prolonged use or high doses at term)

Lactation Enters breast milk/use caution

Labeled Contraindications Hypersensitivity to oxycodone or any component of the formulation; significant respiratory depression; hypercarbia; acute or severe bronchial asthma; OxyContin® is also contraindicated in paralytic ileus (known or suspected); pregnancy (prolonged use or high doses at term)

Warnings/Precautions May cause CNS depression, which may impair physical or mental abilities; patients must be cautioned about performing tasks which require mental alertness (eg, operating machinery or driving). Effects may be potentiated when used with other sedative drugs or ethanol. Use with caution in patients with hypersensitivity reactions to other phenanthrene derivative opioid agonists (morphine, hydrocodone, hydromorphone, levorphanol, oxymorphone), respiratory diseases including asthma, emphysema, or COPD. Use with caution in pancreatitis or biliary tract disease, acute alcoholism (including delirium tremens), morbid obesity, adrenocortical insufficiency, history of seizure disorders, CNS depression/coma, kyphoscoliosis (or other skeletal disorder which may alter respiratory function), hypothyroidism (including myxedema), prostatic hyperplasia, urethral stricture, and toxic psychosis. May obscure diagnosis or clinical course of patients with acute abdominal conditions.

Use with caution in the elderly, debilitated, severe hepatic or renal function. Hemodynamic effects (hypotension, orthostasis) may be exaggerated in patients with hypovolemia, concurrent vasodilating drugs, or in patients with head injury. Respiratory depressant effects and capacity to elevate CSF pressure may be exaggerated in presence of head injury, other intracranial lesion, or pre-existing intracranial pressure.

Concurrent use of agonist/antagonist analgesics may precipitate withdrawal symptoms and/or reduced analgesic efficacy in patients following prolonged therapy with mu opioid agonists. Abrupt discontinuation following prolonged use may also lead to withdrawal symptoms.

[U.S. Boxed Warning]: Healthcare provider should be alert to problems of abuse, misuse, and diversion. Tolerance or drug dependence may result from extended use.

Controlled-release formulations:

[U.S. Boxed Warning]: OxyContin® is not intended for use as an "as needed" analgesic or for immediately-postoperative pain management (should be used postoperatively only if the patient has received it prior to surgery or if severe, persistent pain is anticipated). **[U.S. Boxed Warning]: Do NOT crush, break, or chew controlled-release tablets;** 60 mg, 80 mg, and 160 mg strengths are for use only in opioid-tolerant patients.

Adverse Reactions

>10%:

Central nervous system: Somnolence (23% to 24%), dizziness (13% to 16%)

Dermatologic: Pruritus (12% to 13%)

Gastrointestinal: Nausea (23% to 27%), constipation (23% to 26%), vomiting (12% to 14%)

1% to 10%:

Cardiovascular: Postural hypotension (1% to 5%)

Central nervous system: Headache (7% to 8%), abnormal dreams (1% to 5%), anxiety (1% to 5%), chills (1% to 5%), confusion (1% to 5%), euphoria (1% to 5%), fever (1% to 5%), insomnia (1% to 5%), nervousness (1% to 5%), thought abnormalities (1% to 5%)

Dermatologic: Rash (1% to 5%)

Gastrointestinal: Xerostomia (6% to 7%), abdominal pain (1% to 5%), anorexia (1% to 5%), diarrhea (1% to 5%), dyspepsia (1% to 5%), gastritis (1% to 5%)

Neuromuscular & skeletal: Weakness (6% to 7%), twitching (1% to 5%)

Respiratory: Dyspnea (1% to 5%), hiccups (1% to 5%)

Miscellaneous: Diaphoresis (5% to 6%)

<1% (Limited to important or life-threatening): Agitation, amenorrhea, amnesia, anaphylaxis, anaphylactoid reaction, appetite increased, chest pain, cough, dehydration, depression, dysphagia, dysuria, edema, emotional lability, eructation, exfoliative dermatitis, facial edema, hallucinations, hematuria, histamine release, hyperkinesia, hypoesthesia, hyponatremia, hypotonia, ileus, impotence, intracranial pressure increased, libido decreased, malaise, migraine, paradoxical CNS stimulation, paralytic ileus, paresthesia, pharyngitis, physical dependence, polyuria, psychological dependence, seizure, SIADH, speech disorder, ST segment depression, stomatitis, stupor, syncope, tablet in stool (OxyCodone®), taste perversion, thirst, tinnitus, tremor, urinary retention, urticaria, vasodilation, vertigo, vision change, voice alteration, withdrawal syndrome

Overdosage/Toxicology Symptoms of toxicity include CNS depression, respiratory depression, and miosis. Treatment is symptom-directed and supportive. Naloxone can reverse opioid-induced hypotension and respiratory depression. An initial I.V. dose of 0.2-0.4 mg can be administered. Lower initial doses should be considered in opioid-dependent patients or if suspected concurrent stimulant overdose. If no response in 2-3 minutes after initial dose, consider an additional 1-2 mg every 2-3 minutes up to a total dose of 10 mg. There is no role for dialysis or hemoperfusion.

Drug Interactions

Cytochrome P450 Effect: Substrate (minor) of CYP2D6, 3A

Increased Effect/Toxicity: Phenothiazine antipsychotic agents may enhance the hypotensive effect of analgesics (opioid). CNS depressants may enhance the adverse/toxic effect of analgesics (opioids).

Decreased Effect: Analgesics (opioid) may diminish the therapeutic effect of pegvisomant. Ammonium chloride may increase the excretion of analgesics (opioid). Analgesics (opioid) may enhance the serotonergic effect of SSRIs (may cause serotonin syndrome).

Ethanol/Nutrition/Herb Interactions

Ethanol: Avoid ethanol (may increase CNS depression).

Food: When taken with a high-fat meal, peak concentration is 25% greater following a single OxyContin® 160 mg tablet as compared to two 80 mg tablets.

Herb/Nutraceutical: Avoid valerian, St John's wort, kava kava, gotu kola (may increase CNS depression).

Storage/Stability Store at 15°C to 30°C (59°F to 86°F). Protect from light.

Mechanism of Action Binds to opiate receptors in the CNS, causing inhibition of ascending pain pathways, altering the perception of and response to pain; produces generalized CNS depression

Pharmacodynamics/Kinetics

Onset of action: Pain relief: 10-15 minutes

Peak effect: 0.5-1 hour

Duration: Immediate release: 3-6 hours; Controlled release: ≤12 hours

Distribution: V_d: 2.6 L/kg; distributed to skeletal muscle, liver, intestinal tract, lungs, spleen, brain, and breast milk

(Continued)

Oxycodone *(Continued)*

Protein binding: ~45%

Metabolism: Hepatically via CYP2D6 to various metabolites including noroxycodone (weak analgesic activity), oxymorphone (has analgesic activity; low concentrations in plasma) and their glucuronides

Bioavailability: Controlled release, immediate release: 60% to 87%

Half-life elimination: Immediate release: 2-3 hours; controlled release: ~5 hours

Excretion: Urine (~19% as parent; > 64% as metabolites)

Dosage Oral:

Children: Immediate release:

6-12 years: 1.25 mg every 6 hours as needed

>12 years: 2.5 mg every 6 hours as needed

Adults:

Immediate release: 5 mg every 6 hours as needed

Controlled release:

Opioid naive: 10 mg every 12 hours

Concurrent CNS depressants: Reduce usual dose by $1/3$ to $1/2$

Conversion from transdermal fentanyl: For each 25 mcg/hour transdermal dose, substitute 10 mg controlled release oxycodone every 12 hours; should be initiated 18 hours after the removal of the transdermal fentanyl patch

Currently on opioids: Use standard conversion chart to convert daily dose to oxycodone equivalent. Divide daily dose in 2 (for twice-daily dosing, usually every 12 hours) and round down to nearest dosage form.

Note: 60 mg, 80 mg, or 160 mg tablets are for use **only** in opioid-tolerant patients. Special safety considerations must be addressed when converting to OxyContin® doses ≥160 mg every 12 hours. Dietary caution must be taken when patients are initially titrated to 160 mg tablets. Using different strengths to obtain the same daily dose is equivalent (eg, four 40 mg tablets, two 80 mg tablets, one 160 mg tablet); all produce similar blood levels.

Multiplication factors for converting the daily dose of current oral opioid to the daily dose of oral oxycodone:

Current opioid mg/day dose x factor = Oxycodone mg/day dose

Codeine mg/day oral dose **x** 0.15 = Oxycodone mg/day dose

Hydrocodone mg/day oral dose **x** 0.9 = Oxycodone mg/day dose

Hydromorphone mg/day oral dose **x** 4 = Oxycodone mg/day dose

Levorphanol mg/day oral dose **x** 7.5 = Oxycodone mg/day dose

Meperidine mg/day oral dose **x** 0.1 = Oxycodone mg/day dose

Methadone mg/day oral dose **x** 1.5 = Oxycodone mg/day dose

Morphine mg/day oral dose **x** 0.5 = Oxycodone mg/day dose

Note: Divide the oxycodone mg/day dose into the appropriate dosing interval for the specific form being used.

Dosing adjustment in hepatic impairment: Reduce dosage in patients with severe liver disease

Administration Do not crush, break, or chew controlled-release tablets; 60 mg, 80 mg, and 160 mg tablets are for use **only** in opioid-tolerant patients. Do not administer OxyContin® 160 mg tablet with a high-fat meal. Controlled release tablets are not indicated for rectal administration; increased risk of adverse events due to better rectal absorption.

Monitoring Parameters Pain relief, respiratory and mental status, blood pressure

Test Interactions Some quinolones may produce a false-positive urine screening result for opiates using commercially-available immunoassay kits. This has been demonstrated most consistently for levofloxacin and ofloxacin, but other quinolones have shown cross-reactivity in certain assay kits. Confirmation of positive opiate screens by more specific methods should be considered.

Dietary Considerations Instruct patient to avoid high-fat meals when taking OxyContin® 160 mg tablets.

Patient Information Avoid alcohol. May cause drowsiness, impaired judgment or coordination. May be addicting if used for prolonged periods. Do not crush or chew the controlled-release product. The wax matrix from OxyContin® tablets may appear in stool.

Special Geriatric Considerations The elderly may be particularly susceptible to the CNS depressant and constipating effects of narcotics. Prophylactic use of a laxative should be considered. Serum levels at a given dose may also be increased relative to concentrations in younger patients.

Additional Information Prophylactic use of a laxative should be considered. OxyContin® 60 mg, 80 mg, and 160 mg tablets are for use in opioid-tolerant patients only.

Dosage Forms Excipient information presented when available (limited, particularly for generics); consult specific product labeling.
Capsule, as hydrochloride: 5 mg
  OxyIR®: 5 mg
Solution, oral, as hydrochloride: 5 mg/5 mL (500 mL)
  Roxicodone®: 5 mg/5 mL (5 mL, 500 mL) [contains alcohol]
Solution, oral, as hydrochloride [concentrate]: 20 mg/mL (30 mL)
  ETH-Oxydose™: 20 mg/mL (1 mL, 30 mL) [contains sodium benzoate; berry flavor]
  OxyFast®: 20 mg/mL (30 mL) [contains sodium benzoate and dry natural rubber]
  Roxicodone®: 20 mg/mL (30 mL) [contains sodium benzoate]
Tablet, as hydrochloride: 5 mg, 15 mg, 30 mg
  Roxicodone®: 5 mg, 15 mg, 30 mg
Tablet, controlled release, as hydrochloride:
  OxyContin®: 10 mg, 20 mg, 40 mg, 60 mg, 80 mg, 160 mg
Tablet, extended release, as hydrochloride: 10 mg, 20 mg, 40 mg, 80 mg

References
"Drugs for Pain," *Med Lett Drugs Ther*, 2000, 42(1085):73-8.
Kalso E and Vainio A, "Morphine and Oxycodone Hydrochloride in the Management of Cancer Pain," *Clin Pharmacol Ther*, 1990, 47(5):639-46.
Mokhlesi B, Leikin JB, Murray P, et al, "Adult Toxicology in Critical Care: Part II: Specific Poisonings," *Chest*, 2003, 123(3):897-922.
Turturro MA and O'Toole KS, "Oxycodone-Induced Pulmonary Edema," *Am J Emerg Med*, 1991, 9(2):201-3.
Zacher JL and Givone DM, "False-Positive Urine Opiate Screening Associated With Fluoroquinolone Use," *Ann Pharmacother*, 38:1525-28.

♦ **Oxycodone Hydrochloride** *see* Oxycodone *on page 849*
♦ **OxyContin®** *see* Oxycodone *on page 849*
♦ **OxyFast®** *see* Oxycodone *on page 849*
♦ **OxyIR®** *see* Oxycodone *on page 849*
♦ **Oxy.IR® (Can)** *see* Oxycodone *on page 849*

Oxymorphone (oks i MOR fone)
Medication Safety Issues
Sound-alike/look-alike issues:
Oxymorphone may be confused with oxycodone, oxymetholone
(Continued)

Oxymorphone *(Continued)*

U.S. Brand Names Numorphan® [DSC]; Opana®; Opana® ER

Index Terms Oxymorphone Hydrochloride

Generic Available No

Pharmacologic Category Analgesic, Opioid

Use

Parenteral: Management of moderate-to-severe pain and preoperatively as a sedative and/or supplement to anesthesia

Oral, regular release: Management of moderate-to-severe pain

Oral, extended release: Management of moderate-to-severe pain in patients requiring around-the-clock opioid treatment for an extended period of time

Restrictions C-II

Pregnancy Risk Factor C/D (prolonged use or high doses at term)

Lactation Excretion in breast milk unknown/use caution

Labeled Contraindications Hypersensitivity to oxymorphone, other morphine analogs (phenanthrene derivatives), or any component of the formulation; paralytic ileus (known or suspected); increased intracranial pressure; moderate-to-severe hepatic impairment; severe respiratory depression (unless in monitored setting with resuscitative equipment); acute/severe bronchial asthma; hypercarbia; pregnancy (prolonged use or high doses at term).

Note: Injection formulation is also contraindicated in the treatment of upper airway obstruction and pulmonary edema due to a chemical respiratory irritant.

Warnings/Precautions An opioid-containing analgesic regimen should be tailored to each patient's needs and based upon the type of pain being treated (acute versus chronic), the route of administration, degree of tolerance for opioids (naive versus chronic user), age, weight, and medical condition. The optimal analgesic dose varies widely among patients. Doses should be titrated to pain relief/prevention.

May cause CNS depression, which may impair physical or mental abilities; patients must be cautioned about performing tasks which require mental alertness (eg, operating machinery or driving). Effects may be potentiated when used with other sedative drugs or ethanol. Use with caution in patients with hypersensitivity reactions to other phenanthrene-derivative opioid agonists (codeine, hydrocodone, hydromorphone, levorphanol, oxycodone). May cause respiratory depression. Use extreme caution in patients with COPD or other chronic respiratory conditions characterized by hypoxia, hypercapnia, or diminished respiratory reserve (myxedema, cor pulmonale, kyphoscoliosis, obstructive sleep apnea, severe obesity). Use with caution in patients (particularly elderly or debilitated) with impaired respiratory function, adrenal disease, morbid obesity, thyroid dysfunction, prostatic hyperplasia, or renal impairment. Use caution in mild hepatic dysfunction; use is contraindicated in moderate-to-severe hepatic impairment. Use only with extreme caution (if at all) in patients with head injury or increased intracranial pressure (ICP); potential to elevate ICP and/or blunt papillary response may be greatly exaggerated in these patients. Use with caution in biliary tract disease or acute pancreatitis (may cause constriction of sphincter of Oddi). May obscure diagnosis or clinical course of patients with acute abdominal conditions.

Oxymorphone shares the toxic potential of opiate agonists and usual precautions of opiate agonist therapy should be observed; may cause hypotension in patients with acute myocardial infarction, volume depletion, or concurrent drug therapy which may exaggerate vasodilation. The elderly may be particularly susceptible to adverse effects of narcotics. Safety and efficacy have not been established in children <18 years of age.

[U.S. Boxed Warning]: Healthcare provider should be alert to problems of abuse, misuse, and diversion. Tolerance or drug dependence may result from extended use. Use caution in patients with a history of drug dependence or abuse. Abrupt discontinuation may precipitate withdrawal syndrome.

Extended release formulation:

[U.S. Boxed Warnings]: Opana® ER is an extended release oral formulation of oxymorphone and is not suitable for use as an "as needed" analgesic. Tablets should not be broken, chewed, dissolved, or crushed; tablets should be swallowed whole. Opana® ER is intended for use in long-term, continuous management of moderate to severe chronic pain. It is not indicated for use in the immediate postoperative period (12-24 hours). **[U.S. Boxed Warning]: The coingestion of ethanol or ethanol-containing medications with Opana® ER may result in accelerated release of drug from the dosage form, abruptly increasing plasma levels, which may have fatal consequences.**

Adverse Reactions Frequency not defined.

Cardiovascular: Bradycardia, cardiac shock, flushing, hypotension, orthostatic hypotension, palpitation, peripheral vasodilation, shock, tachycardia

Central nervous system: Agitation, amnesia, anorexia, anxiety, CNS depression, coma, confusion, convulsion, dizziness, drowsiness, dysphoria, euphoria, fatigue, fever, hallucinations, headache, insomnia, intracranial pressure increased, malaise, mental depression, mental impairment, nervousness, restlessness, paradoxical CNS stimulation

Dermatologic: Pruritus, urticaria, rash

Endocrine & metabolic: Antidiuretic hormone release, weight loss

Gastrointestinal: Abdominal pain, appetite depression, biliary tract spasm, constipation, dehydration, dry mouth, dyspepsia, flatulence, nausea, paralytic ileus, stomach cramps, vomiting, xerostomia

Genitourinary: Urination decreased, urinary retention, urinary tract spasm

Local: Pain/reaction at injection site

Neuromuscular & skeletal: Weakness

Ocular: Blurred vision, diplopia, miosis

Renal: Oliguria

Respiratory: Apnea, bronchospasm, cyanosis, dyspnea, hypoventilation, laryngeal edema, laryngeal spasm, respiratory depression

Miscellaneous: Diaphoresis, histamine release, physical and psychological dependence

Overdosage/Toxicology Symptoms of overdose include respiratory depression, miosis, hypotension, bradycardia, apnea, and pulmonary edema. Treatment of overdose includes maintaining patent airway and establishing an I.V. line. Naloxone, 2 mg I.V., with repeat administration as necessary up to a total of 10 mg, can also be used to reverse toxic effects of the opiate.

Drug Interactions

Increased Effect/Toxicity: Increased effect/toxicity with CNS depressants (phenothiazines, tricyclic antidepressants, anxiolytics, sedatives, hypnotics, alcohol, and anesthetics). Dextroamphetamine may increase the analgesic effects of opiate agonists. Concurrent use with SSRIs may enhance serotonergic activity and may increase the risk of serotonin syndrome.

(Continued)

Oxymorphone *(Continued)*

Ethanol/Nutrition/Herb Interactions

Ethanol: Avoid ethanol (may increase CNS depression). Ethanol ingestion with extended-release tablets is specifically contraindicated due to possible accelerated release and potentially fatal overdose.

Food: When taken orally with a high-fat meal, peak concentration is 38% to 50% greater. Both immediate-release and extended-release tablets should be taken 1 hour before or 2 hours after eating.

Herb/Nutraceutical: Avoid valerian, St John's wort, kava kava, gotu kola (may increase CNS depression).

Storage/Stability Injection solution, tablet: Store at 15°C to 30°C (59°F to 86°F).

Compatibility Compatibility in syringe: Compatible: Glycopyrrolate, hydroxyzine, ranitidine.

Mechanism of Action Oxymorphone hydrochloride (Numorphan®) is a potent narcotic analgesic with uses similar to those of morphine. The drug is a semisynthetic derivative of morphine (phenanthrene derivative) and is closely related to hydromorphone chemically (Dilaudid®).

Pharmacodynamics/Kinetics

Onset of action: Parenteral: 5-10 minutes

Duration: Analgesic: Parenteral: 3-6 hours

Distribution: V_d: I.V.: 1.94-4.22 L/kg

Protein binding: 10% to 12%

Metabolism: Hepatic via glucuronidation to active and inactive metabolites

Bioavailability: Oral: 10%

Half-life elimination: Oral: Immediate release: 7-9 hours; Extended release: 9-11 hours

Excretion: Urine (<1% as unchanged drug); feces

Dosage Adults: **Note:** Dosage must be individualized.

I.M., SubQ: Initial: 1-1.5 mg; may repeat every 4-6 hours as needed

Labor analgesia: I.M.: 0.5-1 mg

I.V.: Initial: 0.5 mg

Oral:

Immediate release:

Opioid-naive: 10-20 mg every 4-6 hours as needed. Initial dosages as low as 5 mg may be considered in selected patients and/or patients with renal impairment. Dosage adjustment should be based on level of analgesia, side effects, and pain intensity. Initiation of therapy with initial dose >20 mg is **not** recommended.

Currently on stable dose of parenteral oxymorphone: ~10 times the daily parenteral requirement. The calculated amount should be divided and given in 4-6 equal doses.

Currently on other opioids: Use standard conversion chart to convert daily dose to oxymorphone equivalent. Generally start with $^1/_2$ the calculated daily oxymorphone dosage and administered in divided doses every 4-6 hours.

Extended release (Opana® ER):

Opioid-naive: Initial: 5 mg every 12 hours. Supplemental doses of immediate-release oxymorphone may be used as "rescue" medication as dosage is titrated.

Note: Continued requirement for supplemental dosing may be used to titrate the dose of extended-release continuous therapy. Adjust therapy incrementally, by 5-10 mg every 12 hours at intervals of every 3-7 days. Ideally, basal dosage may be titrated to generally mild pain or no pain with the regular use of fewer than 2 supplemental doses per 24 hours.

Currently on stable dose of parenteral oxymorphone: Approximately 10 times the daily parenteral requirement. The calculated amount should be given in 2 divided doses (every 12 hours).

Currently on opioids: Use conversion chart (see Note below) to convert daily dose to oxymorphone equivalent. Generally start with $1/2$ the calculated daily oxymorphone dosage. Divide daily dose in 2 (for every 12-hour dosing) and round down to nearest dosage form. **Note:** Per manufacturer, the following approximate oral dosages are equivalent to oxymorphone 10 mg:

Hydrocodone 20 mg
Oxycodone 20 mg
Methadone 20 mg
Morphine 30 mg

Conversion of stable dose of immediate-release oxymorphone to extended-release oxymorphone: Administer $1/2$ of the daily dose of immediate-release oxymorphone (Opana®) as the extended-release formulation (Opana® ER) every 12 hours

Elderly: Initiate dosing at the lower end of the dosage range

Dosing adjustment in renal impairment: Cl_{cr} <50 mL/minute: Reduce initial dosage of oral formulations (bioavailability increased 57% to 65%). Begin therapy at lowest dose and titrate carefully.

Dosing adjustment in hepatic impairment: Generally, contraindicated for use in patients with moderate-to-severe liver disease. Initiate with lowest possible dose and titrate slowly in mild impairment.

Administration Administer immediate release and extended release tablets 1 hour before or 2 hours after eating. Opana® ER tablet should be swallowed; do not break, crush, or chew.

Monitoring Parameters Respiratory rate, heart rate, blood pressure, CNS activity

Test Interactions

Some quinolones may produce a false-positive urine screening result for opiates using commercially-available immunoassay kits. This has been demonstrated most consistently for levofloxacin and ofloxacin, but other quinolones have shown cross-reactivity in certain assay kits. Confirmation of positive opiate screens by more specific methods should be considered. May cause elevation in amylase (due to constriction of the sphincter of Oddi).

Dietary Considerations Immediate release and extended release tablets should be taken 1 hour before or 2 hours after eating.

Patient Information Avoid alcohol. May cause drowsiness, impaired judgment or coordination. May cause physical and psychological dependence with prolonged use.

Special Geriatric Considerations Elderly may be particularly susceptible to the CNS depressant and constipating effects of narcotics. Plasma levels of oxymorphone were about 40% higher in elderly patients as compared to younger patients.

Vesicant No

Dosage Forms Excipient information presented when available (limited, particularly for generics); consult specific product labeling. [DSC] = Discontinued product

Injection, solution, as hydrochloride:
Numorphan® [DSC], Opana®: 1 mg/mL (1 mL)
Tablet, as hydrochloride:
Opana®: 5 mg, 10 mg
(Continued)

Oxymorphone *(Continued)*

Tablet, extended release, as hydrochloride:
Opana®: ER: 5 mg, 10 mg, 20 mg, 40 mg

References

Adams MP and Ahdieh H, "Pharmacokinetics and Dose-Proportionality of Oxymorphone Extended Release and its Metabolites: Results of a Randomized Crossover Study," *Pharmacotherapy*, 2004, 24(4):468-76.

Adams MP and Ahdieh H, "Single- and Multiple-Dose Pharmacokinetic and Dose-Proportionality Study of Oxymorphone Immediate-Release Tablets," *Drugs R D*, 2005, 6(2):91-9.

"Drugs for Pain," *Med Lett Drugs Ther*, 2000, 42(1085):73-8.

Gabrail NY, Dvergsten C, and Ahdieh H, "Establishing the Dosage Equivalency of Oxymorphone Extended Release and Oxycodone Controlled Release in Patients With Cancer Pain: A Randomized Controlled Study," *Curr Med Res Opin*, 2004, 20(6):911-8.

Gimbel J and Ahdieh H, "The Efficacy and Safety of Oral Immediate-Release Oxymorphone for Postsurgical Pain," *Anesth Analg*, 2004, 99(5):1472-7.

Gimbel J, Walker D, Ma T, et al, "Efficacy and Safety of Oxymorphone Immediate Release for the Treatment of Mild to Moderate Pain After Ambulatory Orthopedic Surgery: Results of a Randomized, Double-Blind, Placebo-Controlled Trial," *Arch Phys Med Rehabil*, 2005, 86(12):2284-9

Matsumoto AK, Babul N, and Ahdieh H, "Oxymorphone Extended-Release Tablets Relieve Moderate to Severe Pain and Improve Physical Function in Osteoarthritis: Results of a Randomized, Double-Blind, Placebo- and Active-Controlled Phase III Trial," *Pain Med*, 2005, 6(5):357-66.

McIlwain H and Ahdieh H, "Safety, Tolerability, and Effectiveness of Oxymorphone Extended Release for Moderate to Severe Osteoarthritis Pain: A One-Year Study," *Am J Ther*, 2005, 12(2):106-12.

Mokhlesi B, Leikin JB, Murray P, et al, "Adult Toxicology in Critical Care: Part II: Specific Poisonings," *Chest*, 2003, 123(3):897-922.

"Principles of Analgesic Use in the Treatment of Acute Pain and Chronic Cancer Pain," 5th ed, Glenview, IL: American Pain Society, 2003.

Prommer E, "Oxymorphone: A Review," *Support Care Cancer*, 2006, 14(2):109-15.

Rathmell JP, Viscomi CM, and Ashburn MA, "Management of Nonobstetric Pain During Pregnancy and Lactation," *Anesth Analg*, 1997, 85(5):1074-87.

Sinatra RS and Harrison DM, "Oxymorphone in Patient-Controlled Analgesia," *Clin Pharm*, 1989, 8(8):541, 544.

Zacher JL and Givone DM, "False-Positive Urine Opiate Screening Associated With Fluoroquinolone Use," *Ann Pharmacother*, 2004, 38:1525-28.

♦ **Oxymorphone Hydrochloride** *see Oxymorphone on page 853*
♦ **Pacis™ (Can)** *see BCG Vaccine on page 128*

Paclitaxel *(pac li TAKS el)*

Medication Safety Issues

Sound-alike/look-alike issues:

Paclitaxel may be confused with paroxetine, Paxil®

Paclitaxel (conventional) may be confused with paclitaxel (protein-bound)

Taxol® may be confused with Abraxane®, Paxil®, Taxotere®

High alert medication: The Institute for Safe Medication Practices (ISMP) includes this medication among its list of drugs which have a heightened risk of causing significant patient harm when used in error.

Related Information

Hematopoietic Stem Cell Transplantation *on page 1366*
Management of Drug Extravasations *on page 1301*
Safe Handling of Hazardous Drugs *on page 1382*

U.S. Brand Names Onxol™; Taxol®

Index Terms NSC-125973; NSC-673089

Generic Available Yes

Canadian Brand Names Apo-Paclitaxel®; Taxol®

Pharmacologic Category Antineoplastic Agent, Antimicrotubular; Antineoplastic Agent, Natural Source (Plant) Derivative; Antineoplastic Agent, Taxane Derivative

Use Treatment of breast, nonsmall cell lung, and ovarian cancers; treatment of AIDS-related Kaposi's sarcoma (KS)

Unlabeled/Investigational Use Treatment of bladder, cervical, prostate, small cell lung, and head and neck cancers; treatment of (unknown primary) adenocarcinoma

Pregnancy Risk Factor D

Lactation Excretion in breast milk unknown/contraindicated

Labeled Contraindications Hypersensitivity to paclitaxel, Cremophor® EL (polyoxyethylated castor oil), or any component of the formulation

Warnings/Precautions Hazardous agent - use appropriate precautions for handling and disposal. **[U.S. Boxed Warning]: Severe hypersensitivity reactions have been reported;** premedication may minimize this effect. Stop infusion and do not rechallenge for severe hypersensitivity reactions (hypotension requiring treatment, dyspnea requiring bronchodilators, angioedema, urticaria). Minor hypersensitivity reactions (flushing, skin reactions, dyspnea, hypotension, or tachycardia) do not require interruption of treatment. **[U.S. Boxed Warning]: Bone marrow suppression is the dose-limiting toxicity; do not administer if baseline absolute neutrophil count (ANC) is <1500 cells/mm³ (<1000 cells/mm³ for patients with AIDS-related KS);** reduce future doses by 20% for severe neutropenia (<500 cells/mm³ for 7 days or more) and consider the use of supportive therapy, including growth factor treatment.

Use extreme caution with hepatic dysfunction (myelotoxicity may be worsened); dose reductions are recommended. Peripheral neuropathy may occur; patients with pre-existing neuropathies from chemotherapy or coexisting conditions (eg, diabetes mellitus) may be at a higher risk; reduce dose by 20% for severe neuropathy. Paclitaxel formulations contain dehydrated alcohol; may cause adverse CNS effects. Infusion-related hypotension, bradycardia, and/or hypertension may occur; frequent monitoring of vital signs is recommended, especially during the first hour of the infusion. Rare but severe conduction abnormalities have been reported; conduct cardiac monitoring during subsequent infusions for these patients. When administered as sequential infusions, taxane derivatives (docetaxel, paclitaxel) should be administered before platinum derivatives (carboplatin, cisplatin) to limit myelosuppression. Elderly patients have an increased risk of toxicity (neutropenia, neuropathy). **[U.S. Boxed Warning]: Should be administered under the supervision of an experienced cancer chemotherapy physician.** Safety and efficacy in children have not been established.

Adverse Reactions Percentages reported with single-agent therapy. **Note:** Myelosuppression is dose related, schedule related, and infusion-rate dependent (increased incidences with higher doses, more frequent doses, and longer infusion times) and, in general, rapidly reversible upon discontinuation.

>10%:

Cardiovascular: Flushing (28%), ECG abnormal (14% to 23%), edema (21%), hypotension (4% to 12%)

Dermatologic: Alopecia (87%), rash (12%)

Gastrointestinal: Nausea/vomiting (52%), diarrhea (38%), mucositis (17% to 35%; grades 3/4: up to 3%), stomatitis (15%; most common at doses >390 mg/m²), abdominal pain (with intraperitoneal paclitaxel)

Hematologic: Neutropenia (78% to 98%; grade 4: 14% to 75%; onset 8-10 days, median nadir 11 days, recovery 15-21 days), leukopenia (90%; grade 4: 17%), anemia (47% to 90%; grades 3/4: 2% to 16%), thrombocytopenia (4% to 20%; grades 3/4: 1% to 7%), bleeding (14%)

Hepatic: Alkaline phosphatase increased (22%), AST increased (19%)

(Continued)

Paclitaxel *(Continued)*

Local: Injection site reaction (erythema, tenderness, skin discoloration, swelling: 13%)

Neuromuscular & skeletal: Peripheral neuropathy (42% to 70%; grades 3/4: up to 7%), arthralgia/myalgia (60%), weakness (17%)

Renal: Creatinine increased (observed in KS patients only: 18% to 34%; severe: 5% to 7%)

Miscellaneous: Hypersensitivity reaction (31% to 45%; grades 3/4: up to 2%), infection (15% to 30%)

1% to 10%:

Cardiovascular: Bradycardia (3%), tachycardia (2%), hypertension (1%), rhythm abnormalities (1%), syncope (1%), venous thrombosis (1%)

Dermatologic: Nail changes (2%)

Hematologic: Febrile neutropenia (2%)

Hepatic: Bilirubin increased (7%)

Respiratory: Dyspnea (2%)

<1%, postmarketing, and/or case reports: Anaphylaxis, ataxia, atrial fibrillation, AV block, back pain, cardiac conduction abnormalities, cellulitis, CHF, chills, conjunctivitis, dehydration, enterocolitis, extravasation recall, hepatic encephalopathy, hepatic necrosis, induration, intestinal obstruction, intestinal perforation, interstitial pneumonia, ischemic colitis, lacrimation increased, maculopapular rash, malaise, MI, necrotic changes and ulceration following extravasation, neuroencephalopathy, neutropenic enterocolitis, ototoxicity (tinnitus and hearing loss), pancreatitis, paralytic ileus, phlebitis, pruritus, pulmonary embolism, pulmonary fibrosis, radiation recall, radiation pneumonitis, pruritus, renal insufficiency, seizure, skin exfoliation, skin fibrosis, skin necrosis, Stevens-Johnson syndrome, supraventricular tachycardia, toxic epidermal necrolysis, ventricular tachycardia (asymptomatic), visual disturbances (scintillating scotomata)

Overdosage/Toxicology Potential symptoms of overdose would include bone marrow suppression, peripheral neurotoxicity, and mucositis. Overdoses in children would be associated with acute ethanol toxicity. There is no known antidote; treatment is symptom-directed and supportive.

Drug Interactions

Cytochrome P450 Effect: Substrate (major) of CYP2C8, 3A4; **Induces** CYP3A4 (weak)

Increased Effect/Toxicity: CYP2C8 inhibitors may increase the levels/effects of paclitaxel; example inhibitors include gemfibrozil, ketoconazole, montelukast and ritonavir. CYP3A4 inhibitors may increase the levels/effects of paclitaxel; example inhibitors include azole antifungals, clarithromycin, diclofenac, doxycycline, erythromycin, imatinib, isoniazid, nefazodone, nicardipine, propofol, protease inhibitors, quinidine, telithromycin, and verapamil. Paclitaxel may increase anthracycline (doxorubicin, epirubicin) levels/toxicity. Concomitant therapy with taxane derivatives (docetaxel, paclitaxel) and platinum derivatives (carboplatin, cisplatin, oxaliplatin) may cause increased hematologic toxicity if the platinum agent is administered first (taxanes should be administered first).

Decreased Effect: CYP2C8 inducers may decrease the levels/effects of paclitaxel; example inducers include carbamazepine, phenobarbital, phenytoin, rifampin, rifapentine, and secobarbital. CYP3A4 inducers may decrease the levels/effects of paclitaxel; example inducers include aminoglutethimide, carbamazepine, nafcillin, nevirapine, phenobarbital, phenytoin, and rifamycins. Paclitaxel may decrease the absorption of digoxin (tablets).

Ethanol/Nutrition/Herb Interactions Herb/Nutraceutical: Avoid black cohosh, dong quai in estrogen-dependent tumors. Avoid valerian, St John's wort (may decrease paclitaxel levels), kava kava, gotu kola (may increase CNS depression).

Storage/Stability Store intact vials at room temperature of 20°C to 25°C (68°F to 77°F). Protect from light. Solutions in D_5W and NS are stable for up to 3 days at room temperature (25°C).

Paclitaxel should be dispensed in either glass or non-PVC containers (eg, Excel™/PAB™). Use **nonpolyvinyl** (non-PVC) tubing (eg, polyethylene) to minimize leaching. Formulated in a vehicle known as Cremophor® EL (poly-oxyethylated castor oil). Cremophor® EL has been found to leach the plasti-cizer DEHP from polyvinyl chloride infusion bags or administration sets. Contact of the undiluted concentrate with plasticized polyvinyl chloride (PVC) equipment or devices is not recommended.

Reconstitution Dilute in 250-1000 mL D_5W, D_5LR, D_5NS, or NS to a concen-tration of 0.3-1.2 mg/mL. Chemotherapy dispensing devices (eg, Chemo Dispensing Pin™) should not be used to withdraw paclitaxel from the vial.

Compatibility Stable in D_5W, D_5LR, D_5NS, NS.

Y-site administration: Compatible: Acyclovir, amikacin, aminophylline, ampicillin/sulbactam, bleomycin, butorphanol, calcium chloride, carbo-platin, cefepime, cefotetan, ceftazidime, ceftriaxone, cimetidine, cisplatin, cladribine, cyclophosphamide, cytarabine, dacarbazine, dexamethasone sodium phosphate, diphenhydramine, doxorubicin, droperidol, etoposide, etoposide phosphate, famotidine, floxuridine, fluconazole, fluorouracil, furosemide, ganciclovir, gatifloxacin, gemcitabine, gentamicin, granisetron, haloperidol, heparin, hydrocortisone sodium phosphate, hydrocortisone sodium succinate, hydromorphone, ifosfamide, linezolid, lorazepam, magnesium sulfate, mannitol, meperidine, mesna, methotrexate, metoclo-pramide, morphine, nalbuphine, ondansetron, ondansetron with ranitidine, pentostatin, potassium chloride, prochlorperazine edisylate, propofol, rani-tidine, sodium bicarbonate, thiotepa, topotecan, vancomycin, vinblastine, vincristine, zidovudine. **Incompatible:** Amphotericin B, amphotericin B cholesteryl sulfate complex, chlorpromazine, doxorubicin liposome, hydroxyzine, methylprednisolone sodium succinate, mitoxantrone.

Compatibility when admixed: Compatible: Carboplatin, doxorubicin. **Vari-able (consult detailed reference):** Cisplatin.

Mechanism of Action Paclitaxel promotes microtubule assembly by enhancing the action of tubulin dimers, stabilizing existing microtubules, and inhibiting their disassembly, interfering with the late G_2 mitotic phase, and inhibiting cell replication. In addition, the drug can distort mitotic spindles, resulting in the breakage of chromosomes. Paclitaxel may also suppress cell proliferation and modulate immune response.

Pharmacodynamics/Kinetics

Distribution:

V_d: Widely distributed into body fluids and tissues; affected by dose and duration of infusion

V_{dss}:

1- to 6-hour infusion: 67.1 L/m^2

24-hour infusion: 227-688 L/m^2

Protein binding: 89% to 98%

Metabolism: Hepatic via CYP2C8 and 3A4; forms metabolites (primarily 6α-hydroxypaclitaxel)

Half-life elimination:

1- to 6-hour infusion: Mean (beta): 6.4 hours

3-hour infusion: Mean (terminal): 13.1-20.2 hours

(Continued)

Paclitaxel *(Continued)*

24-hour infusion: Mean (terminal): 15.7-52.7 hours

Excretion: Feces (~70%, 5% as unchanged drug); urine (14%)

Clearance: Mean: Total body: After 1- and 6-hour infusions: 5.8-16.3 L/hour/m^2; After 24-hour infusions: 14.2-17.2 L/hour/m^2

Dosage Premedication with dexamethasone (20 mg orally or I.V. at 12 and 6 hours **or** 14 and 7 hours before the dose; reduce dexamethasone dose to 10 mg orally with advanced HIV disease), diphenhydramine (50 mg I.V. 30-60 minutes prior to the dose), and cimetidine, famotidine or ranitidine (I.V. 30-60 minutes prior to the dose) is recommended.

Adults: I.V.: Refer to individual protocols

Ovarian carcinoma: 135-175 mg/m^2 over 3 hours every 3 weeks **or**

135 mg/m^2 over 24 hours every 3 weeks **or**

50-80 mg/m^2 over 1-3 hours weekly **or**

1.4-4 mg/m^2/day continuous infusion for 14 days every 4 weeks

Metastatic breast cancer: 175-250 mg/m^2 over 3 hours every 3 weeks **or**

50-80 mg/m^2 weekly **or**

1.4-4 mg/m^2/day continuous infusion for 14 days every 4 weeks

Nonsmall cell lung carcinoma: 135 mg/m^2 over 24 hours every 3 weeks

AIDS-related Kaposi's sarcoma: 135 mg/m^2 over 3 hours every 3 weeks **or**

100 mg/m^2 over 3 hours every 2 weeks

Intraperitoneal (unlabeled route): Ovarian carcinoma: 60 mg/m^2 on day 8 of a 21-day treatment cycle for 6 cycles, in combination with I.V. paclitaxel and intraperitoneal cisplatin. **Note:** Administration of intraperitoneal paclitaxel should include the standard paclitaxel premedication regimen.

Dosage modification for toxicity (solid tumors, including ovary, breast, and lung carcinoma): Courses of paclitaxel should not be repeated until the neutrophil count is ≥1500 cells/mm^3 and the platelet count is ≥100,000 cells/mm^3; reduce dosage by 20% for patients experiencing severe peripheral neuropathy or severe neutropenia (neutrophil <500 cells/mm^3 for a week or longer)

Dosage modification for immunosuppression in advanced HIV disease: Paclitaxel should not be given to patients with HIV if the baseline or subsequent neutrophil count is <1000 cells/mm^3. Additional modifications include: Reduce dosage of dexamethasone in premedication to 10 mg orally; reduce dosage by 20% in patients experiencing severe peripheral neuropathy or severe neutropenia (neutrophil <500 cells/mm^3 for a week or longer); initiate concurrent hematopoietic growth factor (G-CSF) as clinically indicated

Dosage adjustment in renal impairment: There are no FDA-approved labeling guidelines for dosage adjustment in patients with renal impairment. Arnoff (2007) recommends no dosage adjustment necessary for adults with Cr$_{cl}$ <50 mL/minute.

Dosage adjustment in hepatic impairment: Note: The FDA-approved labeling recommendations are based upon the patient's first course of therapy where the usual dose would be 135 mg/m^2 dose over 24 hours or the 175 mg/m^2 dose over 3 hours in patients with normal hepatic function. Dosage in subsequent courses should be based upon individual tolerance. Adjustments for other regimens are not available.

24-hour infusion:

ALT/AST <2 times upper limit of normal (ULN) and bilirubin level ≤1.5 mg/dL: 135 mg/m^2

ALT/AST 2-<10 times ULN and bilirubin level ≤1.5 mg/dL: 100 mg/m^2

ALT/AST <10 times ULN and bilirubin level 1.6-7.5 mg/dL: 50 mg/m^2

ALT/AST ≥10 times ULN **or** bilirubin level >7.5 mg/dL: Avoid use
3-hour infusion:
ALT/AST <10 times ULN and bilirubin level ≤1.25 times ULN: 175 mg/m²
ALT/AST <10 times ULN and bilirubin level 1.26-2 times ULN: 135 mg/m²
ALT/AST <10 times ULN and bilirubin level 2.01-5 times ULN: 90 mg/m²
ALT/AST ≥10 times ULN **or** bilirubin level >5 times ULN: Avoid use

Combination Regimens
Adenocarcinoma, unknown primary:
Carbo-Tax (Adenocarcinoma) *on page 1161*
Paclitaxel-Carboplatin-Etoposide *on page 1264*
PCE *on page 1266*
Bladder cancer:
Paclitaxel-Carboplatin (Bladder Cancer) *on page 1264*
Paclitaxel-Carboplatin-Gemcitabine *on page 1264*
Paclitaxel-Gemcitabine *on page 1265*
Breast cancer:
AC/Paclitaxel (Sequential) *on page 1143*
AC-Paclitaxel-Trastuzumab *on page 1144*
ICE-T *on page 1238*
Paclitaxel-Bevacizumab *on page 1263*
Paclitaxel-Vinorelbine *on page 1266*
Trastuzumab-Paclitaxel *on page 1283*
Esophageal cancer:
TCF *on page 1280*
TIP *on page 1281*
Head and neck cancer:
FU HURT *on page 1223*
TIP *on page 1281*
Lung cancer (nonsmall cell):
Carbo-Tax (Nonsmall Cell Lung Cancer) *on page 1161*
CaT (Nonsmall Cell Lung Cancer) *on page 1162*
Paclitaxel-Carboplatin-Bevacizumab *on page 1263*
PC (Nonsmall Cell Lung Cancer) *on page 1267*
Ovarian cancer:
Carbo-Tax (Ovarian Cancer) *on page 1162*
CaT (Ovarian Cancer) *on page 1163*
CT *on page 1184*
Gemcitabine-Paclitaxel *on page 1228*
Prostate cancer:
Paclitaxel + Estramustine + Carboplatin *on page 1265*
Paclitaxel + Estramustine + Etoposide *on page 1265*
PE *on page 1269*
Soft tissue sarcoma: ICE-T *on page 1238*
Testicular cancer: Paclitaxel-Ifosfamide-Cisplatin *on page 1265*

Administration
I.V.: Infuse over 1-96 hours. When administered as sequential infusions, taxane derivatives should be administered before platinum derivatives (cisplatin, carboplatin) to limit myelosuppression and to enhance efficacy. Premedication with dexamethasone (20 mg orally or I.V. at 12 and 6 hours **or** 14 and 7 hours before the dose; reduce to 10 mg with advanced HIV disease), diphenhydramine (50 mg I.V. 30-60 minutes prior to the dose), and cimetidine 300 mg, famotidine 20 mg, or ranitidine 50 mg (I.V. 30-60 minutes prior to the dose) is recommended.
Administer I.V. infusion over 1-24 hours; infuse through a 0.22 micron in-line filter and nonsorbing administration set.
(Continued)

Paclitaxel *(Continued)*

Intraperitoneal: 1-2 hour infusion

Monitoring Parameters CBC with differential; monitor for hypersensitivity reactions, vital signs (frequently during the first hour of infusion), continuous cardiac monitoring (patients with conduction abnormalities)

Patient Information This medication can only be administered by I.V. infusion, usually on a cyclic basis. Maintain adequate hydration (2-3 L/day of fluids unless instructed to restrict fluid intake) and nutrition (small frequent meals will help). You will most likely lose your hair (will grow back after therapy); experience some nausea or vomiting (request antiemetic); feel weak or lethargic (use caution when driving or engaging in tasks that require alertness until response to drug is known). Use good oral care to reduce incidence of mouth sores. You will be more susceptible to infection; avoid crowds or exposure to infection. Report numbness or tingling in fingers or toes (use care to prevent injury); signs of infection (fever, chills, sore throat, burning urination, fatigue); unusual bleeding (tarry stools, easy bruising, or blood in stool, urine, or mouth); unresolved mouth sores; nausea or vomiting; or skin rash or itching. Contraceptive measures are recommended during therapy.

Special Geriatric Considerations Elderly patients may have a higher incidence of severe neuropathy, severe myelosuppression, or cardiovascular events as compared to younger patients.

Additional Information Sensory neuropathy is almost universal at doses >250 mg/m^2; motor neuropathy is uncommon at doses <250 mg/m^2. Myopathic effects are common with doses >200 mg/m^2, generally occur within 2-3 days of treatment, and resolve over 5-6 days. Intraperitoneal administration of paclitaxel is associated with a higher incidence of chemotherapy related toxicity.

Emetic Potential Low (10% to 30%)

Vesicant No; the drug is an irritant. See Management of Drug Extravasations *on page 1301.*

High Dose Considerations

Comments: Glutamine may decrease mucositis

High Dose: I.V.: 250-775 mg/m^2; generally combined with other high-dose chemotherapy; maximum dose as single agent: 825 mg/m^2

Dosage Forms Excipient information presented when available (limited, particularly for generics); consult specific product labeling.

Injection, solution: 6 mg/mL (5 mL, 16.7 mL, 25 mL, 50 mL) [contains alcohol and purified Cremophor® EL (polyoxyethylated castor oil)]

Onxol™: 6 mg/mL (5 mL, 25 mL, 50 mL) [contains alcohol and purified Cremophor® EL (polyoxyethylated castor oil)]

Taxol®: 6 mg/mL (5 mL, 16.7 mL, 50 mL) [contains alcohol and purified Cremophor® EL (polyoxyethylated castor oil)]

References

Armstrong DK, Bundy B, Wenzel L, et al, "Intraperitoneal Cisplatin and Paclitaxel in Ovarian Cancer," *N Engl J Med*, 2006, 354(1):34-43.

Aronoff GR, Bennett WM, Berns JS, et al, *Drug Prescribing in Renal Failure: Dosing Guidelines for Adults and Children*, 5th ed. Philadelphia, PA: American College of Physicians; 2007, p 101.

Baker AF and Dorr RT, "Drug Interactions With the Taxanes: Clinical Implications," *Cancer Treat Rev*, 2001, 27(4):221-33.

Hesketh PJ, Kris MG, Grunberg SM, et al, "Proposal for Classifying the Acute Emetogenicity of Cancer Chemotherapy," *J Clin Oncol*, 1997, 15(1):103-9.

Holmes FA, "Paclitaxel Combination Therapy in the Treatment of Metastatic Breast Cancer: A Review," *Semin Oncol*, 1996, 23(5 Suppl 11):46-56.

Longnecker SM, Donehower RC, Cates AE, et al, "High-Performance Liquid Chromatographic Assay for Taxol in Human Plasma and Urine and Pharmacokinetics in a Phase I Trial," *Cancer Treat Rep*, 1987, 71(1):53-9.

Mekhail TM and Markman M, "Paclitaxel in Cancer Therapy," *Expert Opin Pharmacother*, 2002, 3(6):755-66.

Rowinsky EK and Donehower RC, "Paclitaxel (Taxol)," *N Engl J Med*, 1995, 332(15):1004-14.

Rowinsky EK, "The Taxanes: Dosing and Scheduling Considerations," *Oncology*, 1997, 11(3 Suppl 2):7-19.

Seetalarom K, Kudelka AP, Verschraegen CF, et al, "Taxanes in Ovarian Cancer Treatment," *Curr Opin Obstet Gynecol*, 1997, 9(1):14-20.

Sonnichsen DS and Relling MV, "Clinical Pharmacokinetics of Paclitaxel," *Clin Pharmacokinet*, 1994, 27(4):256-69.

Spencer CM and Faulds D, "Paclitaxel. A Review of Its Pharmacodynamic and Pharmacokinetic Properties and Therapeutic Potential in the Treatment of Cancer," *Drugs*, 1994, 48(5):794-847.

Paclitaxel (Protein Bound) (pac li TAKS el PROE teen bownd)

Medication Safety Issues
Sound-alike/look-alike issues:

Paclitaxel (protein bound) may be confused with paclitaxel (conventional)
Abraxane® may be confused with Paxil®, Taxol®, Taxotere®

High alert medication: The Institute for Safe Medication Practices (ISMP) includes this medication among its list of drugs which have a heightened risk of causing significant patient harm when used in error.

Related Information
Safe Handling of Hazardous Drugs *on page 1382*

U.S. Brand Names Abraxane®

Index Terms ABI-007; Albumin-Bound Paclitaxel; NAB-Paclitaxel; NSC-736631; Protein-Bound Paclitaxel

Generic Available No

Pharmacologic Category Antineoplastic Agent, Antimicrotubular; Antineoplastic Agent, Natural Source (Plant) Derivative; Antineoplastic Agent, Taxane Derivative

Use Treatment of relapsed or refractory breast cancer

Pregnancy Risk Factor D

Lactation Excretion in breast milk unknown/not recommended

Labeled Contraindications Hypersensitivity to paclitaxel or any component of the formulation; baseline neutrophils <1500/mm³

Warnings/Precautions Hazardous agent - use appropriate precautions for handling and disposal.

[U.S. Boxed Warning]: Paclitaxel (protein-bound) is not interchangeable with other forms of paclitaxel, including Cremophor®-based or unbound paclitaxel.

[U.S. Boxed Warning]: Baseline neutrophils should be ≥1,500 cells/mm³ for administration; platelets should recover to >100,000/mm³ prior to the next treatment cycle. Dose-dependent bone marrow suppression (primarily neutropenia) is the dose-limiting toxicity. When administered as sequential infusions, taxane derivatives (docetaxel, paclitaxel) should be administered before platinum derivatives (carboplatin, cisplatin) to limit myelosuppression. Dose-related sensory neuropathy is common; severe sensory neuropathy may occur. Use caution in hepatic and renal dysfunction; not studied in these populations.

[U.S. Boxed Warning]: Should be administered under the supervision of an experienced cancer chemotherapy physician. Safety and efficacy in children have not been established.
(Continued)

Paclitaxel (Protein Bound) *(Continued)*

Adverse Reactions
>10%:

Cardiovascular: EKG abnormal (60%)

Dermatologic: Alopecia (90%)

Gastrointestinal: Nausea (30%; grades 3/4: 3%), diarrhea (27%; grades 3/4: <1%), vomiting (18%; grades 3/4: 4%)

Hematologic: Neutropenia (80%; grade 4: 9%), anemia (33%; grades 3/4: 1%)

Hepatic: AST increased (39%), alkaline phosphatase increased (36%), GGT increased (grades 3/4: 14%)

Neuromuscular & skeletal: Sensory neuropathy (71%; grades 3/4: 10%; dose dependent; may be cumulative), weakness (47%), myalgia/arthralgia (44%)

Ocular: Vision disturbance (13%; severe [keratitis, blurred vision]: 1%)

Respiratory: Dyspnea (12%)

Miscellaneous: Infection (24%; primarily included oral candidiasis, respiratory tract infection, and pneumonia)

1% to 10%:

Cardiovascular: Edema (10%), hypotension (5%), cardiovascular events (grades 3/4: 3%; included chest pain, cardiac arrest, supraventricular tachycardia, edema, thrombosis, pulmonary thromboembolism, pulmonary emboli, and hypertension)

Gastrointestinal: Mucositis (7%; grades 3/4: <1%)

Hematologic: Bleeding (2%), neutropenic fever (2%), thrombocytopenia (2%; grades 3/4: 1%)

Hepatic: Bilirubin increased (7%)

Neuromuscular and skeletal: Peripheral neuropathy (grade 3: 10%)

Renal: Creatinine increased (11%; severe 1%)

Respiratory: Cough (7%)

Miscellaneous: Hypersensitivity reaction (4%)

<1%: Bradycardia, cardiac ischemia, cerebrovascular attack, cranial nerve palsies, embolism, erythema, hand-foot syndrome (in patients previously exposed to capecitabine), injection site reaction, maculopapular rash, MI, motor neuropathy, nail discoloration, nail pigmentation changes, photosensitivity reaction, pneumothorax, pruritus, radiation recall, stroke, thrombosis, transient ischemic attack

Adverse reactions reported with paclitaxel, which may occur with paclitaxel (protein bound): Autonomic neuropathy, cellulitis, conjunctivitis, extravasation recall, fibrosis, hepatic necrosis, hepatic encephalopathy, induration, intestinal obstruction, intestinal perforation, interstitial pneumonia, ischemic colitis, lacrimation increased, lung fibrosis, necrosis, neutropenic enterocolitis (typhlitis), optic nerve damage (persistent), pancreatitis, paralytic ileus, phlebitis, radiation pneumonitis with concurrent radiation therapy, skin exfoliation, Stevens-Johnson syndrome, toxic epidermal necrolysis

Overdosage/Toxicology Overdose would likely result in severe bone marrow suppression, sensory neuropathy, and mucositis. Treatment is symptom-directed and supportive.

Drug Interactions

Cytochrome P450 Effect: Substrate (major) of CYP2C8, 2C9, 3A4; **Induces** CYP3A4 (weak)

Increased Effect/Toxicity: CYP2C8 Inhibitors may increase the levels/effects of paclitaxel; example inhibitors include gemfibrozil, ketoconazole, montelukast, and ritonavir. CYP3A4 inhibitors may increase the levels/

effects of paclitaxel; example inhibitors include azole antifungals, clarithromycin, diclofenac, doxycycline, erythromycin, imatinib, isoniazid, nefazodone, nicardipine, propofol, protease inhibitors, quinidine, telithromycin, and verapamil. Paclitaxel may increase anthracycline (doxorubicin, epirubicin) levels/toxicity. Concomitant therapy with taxane derivatives (docetaxel, paclitaxel) and platinum derivatives (carboplatin, cisplatin, oxaliplatin) may cause increased hematologic toxicity if the platinum agent is administered first (taxanes should be administered first).

Decreased Effect: CYP2C8 inducers may decrease the levels/effects of paclitaxel; example inducers include carbamazepine, phenobarbital, phenytoin, rifampin, rifapentine, and secobarbital. CYP3A4 inducers may decrease the levels/effects of paclitaxel; example inducers include aminoglutethimide, carbamazepine, nafcillin, nevirapine, phenobarbital, phenytoin, and rifamycins. Paclitaxel may decrease the absorption of digoxin (tablets).

Ethanol/Nutrition/Herb Interactions Herb/Nutraceutical: Avoid St John's wort (may decrease paclitaxel levels and may increase CNS depression). Avoid black cohosh, dong quai in estrogen-dependent tumors. Avoid valerian, kava kava, gotu kola (may increase CNS depression).

Storage/Stability Store intact vial at room temperature of 20°C to 25°C (68°F to 77°F) and protect from bright light. Reconstituted solution may be stored under refrigeration 2°C to 8°C (36°F to 46°F) for up to 8 hours. The solution for administration is stable for up to 8 hours at room temperature and ambient light.

Reconstitution Reconstitute vial with 20 mL NS to a concentration of 5 mg/mL. Place dose without further dilution into an empty sterile container. **Note:** Use of DEHP-free containers or administration sets is not necessary. **Do not use an in-line filter.**

Compatibility Stable in NS. Formulation contains albumin; do not mix with other drugs.

Mechanism of Action Paclitaxel promotes microtubule assembly by enhancing the action of tubulin dimers, stabilizing existing microtubules, and inhibiting their disassembly, interfering with the late G_2 mitotic phase, and inhibiting cell replication. In addition, the drug can distort mitotic spindles, resulting in the breakage of chromosomes. Paclitaxel may also suppress cell proliferation and modulate immune response.

Pharmacodynamics/Kinetics

Distribution: V_d: 632 L/m^2

Protein binding: 89% to 98%

Metabolism: Hepatic via CYP3A4 (to minor metabolites) and 2C8 (primarily to 6-alpha-hydroxypaclitaxel)

Half-life elimination: Terminal: 27 hours

Excretion: Urine (4% as unchanged drug, 1% as metabolites); feces (20%) Clearance 15 L/hour/m^2

Dosage I.V.: Adults: Breast cancer: 260 mg/m^2 every 3 weeks **or** alternate weekly schedule (unlabeled): 100-125 mg/m^2 on days 1, 8, and 15 of a 28-day cycle

Dosage adjustment for toxicity:

Severe neutropenia (<500 cells/mm^3) ≥1 week: Reduce dose to 220 mg/m^2 for subsequent courses

Recurrent severe neutropenia: Reduce dose to 180 mg/m^2

Severe sensory neuropathy: Reduce dose to 180 mg/m^2

Sensory neuropathy grade 3 or 4: Hold treatment until resolved to grade 1 or 2, then resume with reduced dose

(Continued)

Paclitaxel (Protein Bound) *(Continued)*

Dosage adjustment in renal impairment: Safety not established for serum creatinine >2 mg/dL; use with caution

Dosage adjustment in hepatic impairment: Effects of hepatic dysfunction (serum bilirubin >1.5 mg/dL) unknown; dosage adjustment recommendations are not available

Administration I.V.: Administer over 30 minutes; do not use an in-line filter

Monitoring Parameters CBC, BP (during infusion), baseline ECG, infusion site

Emetic Potential Very low (<10%)

Vesicant No

High Dose Considerations

Comments: Glutamine may decrease mucositis.

Dosage Forms Excipient information presented when available (limited, particularly for generics); consult specific product labeling.

Injection, powder for reconstitution:

Abraxane®: 100 mg [contains human albumin 900 mg]

References

Baker AF and Dorr RT, "Drug Interactions With the Taxanes: Clinical Implications," *Cancer Treat Rev*, 2001, 27(4):221-33.

Gradishar WJ, Tjulandin S, Davidson N, et al, "Phase III Trial of Nanoparticle Albumin-Bound Paclitaxel Compared With Polyethylated Castor Oil-Based Paclitaxel in Women With Breast Cancer," *J Clin Oncol*, 2005, 23(31):7794-803.

Ibrahim NK, Samuels B, Page R, et al, "Multicenter Phase II Trial of ABI-007, an Albumin-Bound Paclitaxel, in Women With Metastatic Breast Cancer," *J Clin Oncol*, 2005, 23(25):6019-26.

Nyman DW, Campbell KJ, Hersh E, et al, "Phase I and Pharmacokinetics Trial of ABI-007, a Novel Nanoparticle Formulation of Paclitaxel in Patients With Advanced Nonhematologic Malignancies," *J Clin Oncol*, 2005, 23(31):7785-93.

Palifermin *(pal ee FER min)*

Related Information

Oral Mucositis / Stomatitis *on page 1332*

U.S. Brand Names Kepivance™

Index Terms AMJ 9701; rHu-KGF

Generic Available No

Pharmacologic Category Keratinocyte Growth Factor

Use Decrease the incidence and severity of severe oral mucositis associated with hematologic malignancies in patients receiving myelotoxic therapy requiring hematopoietic stem cell support

Pregnancy Risk Factor C

Lactation Excretion in breast milk unknown/use caution

Labeled Contraindications Hypersensitivity to palifermin, *E. coli*-derived proteins, or any component of the formulation

Warnings/Precautions Safety and efficacy have not been established with nonhematologic malignancies; effect on the growth of nonhematopoietic human tumors is not known. Palifermin should be administered prior to and following, but not with, chemotherapy. If administered within 24 hours of chemotherapy, palifermin may increase the severity and duration of mucositis due to the increased sensitivity of rapidly-dividing epithelial cells. Safety and efficacy have not been established in children.

Adverse Reactions

>10%:

Cardiovascular: Edema (28%), hypertension (7% to 14%)

Central nervous system: Fever (39%), pain (16%), dysesthesia (12%)

Dermatologic: Rash (62%), pruritus (35%), erythema (32%)

Gastrointestinal: Mouth/tongue discoloration or thickness (17%), taste alteration (16%)

Miscellaneous: Serum amylase increased (grade 3/4, 38%); serum lipase increased (grade 3/4, 11%)

1% to 10%: Neuromuscular & skeletal: Arthralgia (10%)

Overdosage/Toxicology Specific information is not available. Doses higher than those recommended were associated with the reported adverse events, but in general were more severe.

Drug Interactions

Increased Effect/Toxicity: Drug interaction studies have not been conducted.

Storage/Stability Store intact vials under refrigeration at 2°C to 8°C (36°F to 46°F). Protect from light. Following reconstitution, vials are stable for up to 72 hours under refrigeration protected from light; do not freeze. Reconstituted solution should not be used if left at room temperature >2 hours.

Reconstitution To reconstitute, slowly add SWFI 1.2 mL to vial; final concentration will be 5 mg/mL. Do not shake or vigorously agitate.

Compatibility Incompatible: Heparin.

Mechanism of Action Palifermin is a recombinant keratinocyte growth factor (KGF) produced in *E. coli*. Endogenous KGF is produced by mesenchymal cells in response to epithelial tissue injury. KGF binds to the KGF receptor resulting in proliferation, differentiation and migration of epithelial cells in multiple tissues, including (but not limited to) the tongue, buccal mucosa, esophagus, and salivary gland.

Pharmacodynamics/Kinetics Half-life elimination: 4.5 hours (range: 3.3-5.7 hours)

Dosage I.V.: Adults: 60 mcg/kg/day for 3 consecutive days before and after myelotoxic therapy; total of 6 doses

Note: Administer first 3 doses prior to myelotoxic therapy, with the 3rd dose given 24-48 hours before therapy begins. The last 3 doses should be administered after myelotoxic therapy, with the first of these doses after but on the same day of hematopoietic stem cell infusion and at least 4 days after the most recent dose of palifermin.

Administration Administer by I.V. bolus. If heparin is used to maintain the patency of the I.V. line, flush line with saline prior to and after palifermin administration. Do not administer palifermin with or within 24 hours of chemotherapy. Allow solution to reach room temperature prior to administration; do not use if at room temperature >1 hour.

Dosage Forms Excipient information presented when available (limited, particularly for generics); consult specific product labeling.

Injection, powder for reconstitution [preservative free]: 6.25 mg [contains mannitol 50 mg, sucrose 25 mg]

References

Finch PW and Rubin JS, "Keratinocyte Growth Factor/Fibroblast Growth Factor 7, a Homeostatic Factor With Therapeutic Potential for Epithelial Protection and Repair," *Adv Cancer Res*, 2004;91:69-136.

Meropol NJ, Somer RA, Gutheil J, et al, "Randomized Phase I Trial of Recombinant Human Keratinocyte Growth Factor Plus Chemotherapy: Potential Role as Mucosal Protectant," *J Clin Oncol*, 2003, 21(8):1452-8.

Spielberger R, Stiff P, Bensinger W, et al, "Palifermin for Oral Mucositis After Intensive Therapy for Hematologic Cancers," *N Engl J Med*, 2004, 351(25):2590-8.

Palonosetron (pal oh NOE se tron)

Medication Safety Issues

Sound-alike/look-alike issues:

Aloxi® may be confused with Eloxatin®, oxaliplatin

Palonosetron may be confused with dolasetron, granisetron, ondansetron

(Continued)

Palonosetron *(Continued)*

U.S. Brand Names Aloxi®

Index Terms Palonosetron Hydrochloride; RS-25259; RS-25259-197

Generic Available No

Pharmacologic Category Antiemetic; Selective 5-HT$_3$ Receptor Antagonist

Use Prevention of chemotherapy-associated nausea and vomiting; indicated for prevention of acute (highly-emetogenic therapy) as well as acute and delayed (moderately-emetogenic therapy) nausea and vomiting

Pregnancy Risk Factor B

Lactation Excretion in breast milk unknown/not recommended

Labeled Contraindications Hypersensitivity to palonosetron or any component of the formulation

Warnings/Precautions Use caution in patients allergic to other 5-HT$_3$ receptor antagonists; cross-reactivity is possible. Use with caution in patients with congenital QT syndrome or other risk factors for QT prolongation (eg, medications known to prolong QT interval, electrolyte abnormalities, and cumulative high dose anthracycline therapy). Not intended for treatment of nausea and vomiting or for chronic continuous therapy. **For chemotherapy, should be used on a scheduled basis, not on an "as needed" (PRN) basis,** since data support the use of this drug only in the prevention of nausea and vomiting (due to antineoplastic therapy) and not in the rescue of nausea and vomiting. Safety and efficacy in children have not been established.

Adverse Reactions

1% to 10%:

Cardiovascular: Bradycardia (1%), hypotension (1%), tachycardia (nonsustained) (1%)

Central nervous system: Headache (5% to 9%), anxiety (1%), dizziness (1%)

Endocrine & metabolic: Hyperkalemia (1%)

Gastrointestinal: Constipation (2% to 5%), diarrhea (1%)

Neuromuscular & skeletal: Weakness (1%)

<1%, postmarketing, and/or case reports: Abdominal pain, allergic dermatitis, ALT increased, amblyopia, anorexia, appetite decreased, arthralgia, AST increased, bilirubin increased, dyspepsia, electrolyte fluctuations, euphoric mood, extrasystoles, eye irritation, fatigue, fever, flatulence, flu-like syndrome, glycosuria, hiccups, hot flash, hyperglycemia, hypersensitivity, hypersomnia, hypertension, injection site reactions (burning/discomfort/induration/pain), insomnia, metabolic acidosis, motion sickness, myocardial ischemia, paresthesia, QT prolongation, rash, sinus arrhythmia, sinus tachycardia, somnolence, supraventricular extrasystoles, tinnitus, urinary retention, vein discoloration, vein distention, xerostomia

Overdosage/Toxicology Dose-ranging studies in humans using doses up to 25 times the recommended dose of 0.25 mg revealed no increase in the incidence of adverse effects compared to lower dose groups. Due to the large volume of distribution, dialysis would not be effective in the event of an overdose. Treatment is symptom-directed and supportive.

Drug Interactions

Cytochrome P450 Effect: Substrate (minor) of CYP1A2, 2D6, 3A4

Increased Effect/Toxicity: Palonosetron may enhance the hypotensive effect of apomorphine; concurrent use is contraindicated.

Storage/Stability Store intact vials at room temperature of 15°C to 30°C (59°F to 86°F); do not freeze. Protect from light. Solutions of 5 mcg/mL and

30 mcg/mL in NS, D_5W, $D_5$1/2NS, and D_5LR injection are stable for 48 hours at room temperature and 14 days under refrigeration.

Compatibility Stable in D_5W, NS, $D_5$1/2NS, and D_5LR.

Y-site administration: Compatible: Cyclophosphamide, doxorubicin, epirubicin, fentanyl, hydromorphone, ifosfamide, meperidine, morphine, sufentanil

Compatibility in syringe: Compatible: Dexamethasone

Compatibility when admixed: Compatible: Dexamethasone

Mechanism of Action Selective 5-HT_3 receptor antagonist, blocking serotonin, both peripherally on vagal nerve terminals and centrally in the chemoreceptor trigger zone

Pharmacodynamics/Kinetics

Distribution: V_d: 8.3 ± 2.5 L/kg

Protein binding: ~62%

Metabolism: ~50% metabolized via CYP enzymes (and likely other pathways) to relatively inactive metabolites (N-oxide-palonosetron and 6-S-hydroxy-palonosetron); CYP1A2, 2D6, and 3A4 contribute to its metabolism

Half-life elimination: Terminal: ~40 hours

Excretion: Urine (80%, 40% as unchanged drug)

Dosage I.V.: Adults:

Chemotherapy-induced nausea and vomiting: 0.25 mg 30 minutes prior to the start of chemotherapy administration, day 1 of each cycle

Breakthrough: Palonosetron has not been shown to be effective in terminating nausea or vomiting once it occurs and should not be used for this purpose.

Elderly: No dosage adjustment necessary

Dosage adjustment in renal/hepatic impairment: No dosage adjustment necessary

Administration I.V.: Infuse over 30 seconds, 30 minutes prior to the start of chemotherapy; flush I.V. line with NS prior to and following administration.

Patient Information Inform prescriber of all prescriptions, OTC medications, or herbal products you are taking, and any allergies you have. Do not take anything new during treatment unless approved by prescriber. May cause drowsiness or dizziness (use caution when driving or engaging in tasks that require alertness until response to drug is known): or fatigue, diarrhea, constipation, or headache (request appropriate treatment from prescriber). Do not change position rapidly (rise slowly). Report persistent headache, excessive drowsiness, fever, numbness or tingling, or changes in elimination patterns (constipation or diarrhea); or chest pain or palpitations.

Dosage Forms Excipient information presented when available (limited, particularly for generics); consult specific product labeling.

Injection, solution:

Aloxi®: 0.05 mg/mL (5 mL) [contains disodium edetate and mannitol]

References

Aapro MS, Grunberg SM, Manikhas GM, et al, "A Phase III, Double-Blind, Randomized Trial of Palonosetron Compared With Ondansetron in Preventing Chemotherapy-Induced Nausea and Vomiting Following Highly Emetogenic Chemotherapy," *Ann Oncol*, 2006, 17(9):1441-9.

Eisenberg P, Figueroa-Vadillo J, Zamora R, et al, "Improved Prevention of Moderately Emetogenic Chemotherapy-Induced Nausea and Vomiting With Palonosetron, a Pharmacologically Novel 5-HT3 Receptor Antagonist: Results of a Phase III, Single-Dose Trial Versus Dolasetron," *Cancer*, 2003, 98(11):2473-82.

Eisenberg P, MacKintosh FR, Ritch P, et al, "Efficacy, Safety and Pharmacokinetics of Palonosetron in Patients Receiving Highly Emetogenic Cisplatin-Based Chemotherapy: A Dose-Ranging Clinical Study," *Ann Oncol*, 2004, 15(2):330-7.

Gralla R, Lichinister M, Van Der Vegt S, et al, "Palonosetron Improves Prevention of Chemotherapy-Induced Nausea and Vomiting Following Moderately Emetogenic Chemotherapy:

(Continued)

Palonosetron *(Continued)*

Results of a Double-Blind Randomized Phase III Trial Comparing Single Doses of Palonose-tron With Ondansetron," *Ann Oncol*, 2003, 14(10):1570-7.

Kris MG, Hesketh PJ, Somerfield MR, et al, "American Society of Clinical Oncology Guideline for Antiemetics in Oncology: Update 2006," *J Clin Oncol*, 2006, 24(18):2932-47.

NCCN (National Comprehensive Cancer Network) "Practice Guidelines in Oncology: Antiemesis Version 2.2006." Available at http://www.nccn.org/professionals/physician_gls/PDF/antiemesis.pdf. Last accessed August 15, 2006.

Trissel LA, Trusley C, Ben M, et al, "Physical and Chemical Stability of Palonosetron Hydrochlo-ride With Five Opiate Agonists During Simulated Y-Site Administration," *Am J Health-Syst Pharm*, 2007, 64 (11):1209-13.

Trissel LA and Xu QA, "Physical and Chemical Stability of Palonosetron HCl in 4 Infusion Solutions," *Ann Pharmacother*, 2004, 38(10):1608-11.

Trissel LA and Zhang Y. "Compatibility and Stability of Aloxi (Palonosetron Hydrochloride) Admixed With Dexamethasone Sodium Phosphate," *Intl J Pharm Compounding*, 2004, 8(5):398-403.

Trissel LA and Zhang Y, "Palonosetron HCl Compatibility and Stability with Doxorubicin HCl and Epirubicin HCl During Simulated Y-Site Administration," *Ann Pharmacother*, 2005, 39(2):280-3.

Xu QA, and Trissel LA, "Compatibility of Palonosetron With Cyclophosphamide and With Ifos-famide During Simulated Y-site Administration," *Am J Health Syst Pharm*, 2005, 62(19):1998-2000.

♦ **Palonosetron Hydrochloride** *see* Palonosetron *on page 869*

Pamidronate *(pa mi DROE nate)*

Medication Safety Issues

Sound-alike/look-alike issues:

Aredia® may be confused with Adriamycin, Meridia®

International issues:

Linoten® [Spain] may be confused with Lidopen® which is a brand name for lidocaine in the U.S.

Related Information

Safe Handling of Hazardous Drugs *on page 1382*

U.S. Brand Names Aredia®

Index Terms Pamidronate Disodium

Generic Available Yes

Canadian Brand Names Aredia®; Pamidronate Disodium®; Rhoxal-pamidronate

Pharmacologic Category Antidote; Bisphosphonate Derivative

Use Treatment of hypercalcemia associated with malignancy; treatment of osteolytic bone lesions associated with multiple myeloma or metastatic breast cancer; moderate to severe Paget's disease of bone

Unlabeled/Investigational Use Treatment of pediatric osteoporosis, treat-ment of osteogenesis imperfecta

Pregnancy Risk Factor D

Lactation Excretion in breast milk unknown/use caution

Labeled Contraindications Hypersensitivity to pamidronate, other bisphosphonates, or any component of the formulation; pregnancy

Warnings/Precautions Bisphosphonate therapy has been associated with osteonecrosis, primarily of the jaw; this has been observed mostly in cancer patients, but also in patients with postmenopausal osteoporosis and other diagnoses. Dental exams and preventative dentistry should be performed prior to placing patients with risk factors on chronic bisphosphonate therapy. Invasive dental procedures should be avoided during treatment.

Infrequently, severe (and occasionally debilitating) bone, joint, and/or muscle pain have been reported during bisphosphonate treatment. The onset of pain ranged from a single day to several months. Symptoms usually resolve upon discontinuation. Some patients experienced recurrence when rechallenged with same drug or another bisphosphonate; avoid use in patients with a history of these symptoms in association with bisphosphonate therapy.

May cause deterioration in renal function. Use caution in patients with renal impairment and avoid in severe renal impairment. Assess serum creatinine prior to each dose; withhold dose in patients with bone metastases who experience deterioration in renal function. Use has been associated with asymptomatic electrolyte abnormalities (including hypophosphatemia, hypokalemia, hypomagnesemia, and hypocalcemia). Rare cases of symptomatic hypocalcemia, including tetany have been reported. Leukopenia has been observed with oral pamidronate and monitoring of white blood cell counts is suggested. Patients with pre-existing anemia, leukopenia, or thrombocytopenia should be closely monitored during the first 2 weeks of treatment.

Vein irritation and thrombophlebitis may occur with infusions. Advise women of childbearing age against becoming pregnant. Safety and efficacy have not been established in children.

Adverse Reactions Percentage of adverse effect varies upon dose and duration of infusion.

>10%:

Central nervous system: Fatigue (12% to 40%), fever (18% to 39%), headache (24% to 27%), anxiety (8% to 18%), insomnia (1% to 25%), pain (13% to 15%)

Endocrine & metabolic: Hypophosphatemia (9% to 18%), hypokalemia (4% to 18%), hypomagnesemia (4% to 12%), hypocalcemia (1% to 12%)

Gastrointestinal: Nausea (4% to 64%), vomiting (4% to 46%), anorexia (1% to 31%), abdominal pain (1% to 24%), dyspepsia (4% to 23%)

Genitourinary: Urinary tract infection (15% to 20%)

Hematologic: Anemia (6% to 48%), leukopenia (4% to 21%)

Local: Infusion site reaction (4% to 18%)

Neuromuscular & skeletal: Weakness (16% to 26%), myalgia (1% to 26%), arthralgia (11% to 15%)

Renal: Serum creatinine increased (19%)

Respiratory: Dyspnea (22% to 35%), cough (25% to 26%), upper respiratory tract infection (3% to 20%), sinusitis (15% to 16%), pleural effusion (3% to 15%)

1% to 10%:

Cardiovascular: Atrial fibrillation (6%), hypertension (6%), syncope (6%), tachycardia (6%), atrial flutter (1%), cardiac failure (1%), edema (1%)

Central nervous system: Somnolence (1% to 6%), psychosis (4%)

Endocrine & metabolic: Hypothyroidism (6%)

Gastrointestinal: Constipation (4% to 6%), gastrointestinal hemorrhage (6%), diarrhea (1%), stomatitis (1%)

Hematologic: Neutropenia (1%), thrombocytopenia (1%)

Neuromuscular & skeletal: Back pain (5%), bone pain (5%)

Renal: Uremia (4%)

Respiratory: Rales (6%), rhinitis (6%)

Miscellaneous: Moniliasis (6%)

<1%: Episcleritis, iritis, scleritis, uveitis

Postmarketing and/or case reports: Allergic reaction, anaphylactic shock, angioedema, hypotension, interstitial pneumonitis, joint and/or muscle pain, malaise, osteonecrosis (primarily jaws), renal deterioration

Overdosage/Toxicology Symptoms of overdose include hypocalcemia, hypotension, ECG changes, seizures, bleeding, paresthesia, carpopedal spasm, and fever. Treat with I.V. calcium gluconate, and general supportive care; fever and hypotension can be treated with corticosteroids.

(Continued)

Pamidronate *(Continued)*

Drug Interactions

Increased Effect/Toxicity: Aminoglycosides may lower serum calcium levels with prolonged administration; concomitant use may have an additive hypocalcemic effect. NSAIDs may enhance the gastrointestinal adverse/toxic effects (increased incidence of GI ulcers) of bisphosphonate derivatives. Bisphosphonate derivatives may enhance the hypocalcemic effect of phosphate supplements.

Decreased Effect: The following agents may decrease the absorption of oral bisphosphonate derivatives: Antacids (aluminum, calcium, magnesium), oral calcium salts, oral iron salts, and oral magnesium salts.

Storage/Stability

Powder for reconstitution: Store below 30°C (86°F). The reconstituted solution is stable for 24 hours stored under refrigeration at 2°C to 8°C (36°F to 46°F).

Solution for injection: Store below 25°C (77°F).

Pamidronate solution for infusion is stable at room temperature for up to 24 hours.

Reconstitution Powder for injection: Reconstitute by adding 10 mL of SWFI to each vial of lyophilized pamidronate disodium powder, the resulting solution will be 30 mg/10 mL or 90 mg/10 mL.

Pamidronate may be further diluted in 250-1000 mL of 0.45% or 0.9% sodium chloride or 5% dextrose.

Compatibility Incompatible with calcium-containing infusion solutions such as Ringer's injection.

Mechanism of Action A bisphosphonate which inhibits bone resorption via actions on osteoclasts or on osteoclast precursors. Does not appear to produce any significant effects on renal tubular calcium handling and is poorly absorbed following oral administration (high oral doses have been reported effective); therefore, I.V. therapy is preferred.

Pharmacodynamics/Kinetics

Onset of action: 24-48 hours

Peak effect: Maximum: 5-7 days

Absorption: Poor; pharmacokinetic studies lacking

Metabolism: Not metabolized

Half-life elimination: 21-35 hours

Excretion: Biphasic; urine (~50% as unchanged drug) within 120 hours

Dosage Drug must be diluted properly before administration and infused intravenously slowly. Due to risk of nephrotoxicity, doses should not exceed 90 mg. I.V.: Adults:

Hypercalcemia of malignancy:

Moderate cancer-related hypercalcemia (corrected serum calcium: 12-13.5 mg/dL): 60-90 mg, as a single dose

Severe cancer-related hypercalcemia (corrected serum calcium: >13.5 mg/dL): 90 mg, as a single dose

A period of 7 days should elapse before the use of second course; repeat infusions every 2-3 weeks have been suggested, however, could be administered every 2-3 months according to the degree and of severity of hypercalcemia and/or the type of malignancy.

Osteolytic bone lesions with multiple myeloma: 90 mg monthly

Osteolytic bone lesions with metastatic breast cancer: 90 mg repeated every 3-4 weeks

Paget's disease: 30 mg daily for 3 consecutive days

Elderly: Begin at lower end of adult dosing range.

Dosing adjustment in renal impairment: Not recommended in severe renal impairment (patients with bone metastases); safety and efficacy have not been established in patients with serum creatinine >5 mg/dL; studies are limited in multiple myeloma patients with serum creatinine ≥3 mg/dL

Dosing adjustment in renal toxicity: In patients with bone metastases, treatment should be withheld in patients who experience deterioration in renal function (increase of serum creatinine ≥0.5 mg/dL in patients with normal baseline or ≥1.0 mg/dL in patients with abnormal baseline). Resumption of therapy may be considered when serum creatinine returns to within 10% of baseline.

Administration I.V. infusion over 2-24 hours.

Monitoring Parameters Serum calcium, electrolytes, phosphate, magnesium, CBC with differential; monitor for hypocalcemia for at least 2 weeks after therapy; monitor serum creatinine prior to each dose; dental exam and preventative dentistry for patients at risk for osteonecrosis; patients with pre-existing anemia, leukopenia or thrombocytopenia should be closely monitored during the first 2 weeks of treatment

Test Interactions Bisphosphonates may interfere with diagnostic imaging agents such as technetium-99m-diphosphonate in bone scans.

Patient Information This medication can only be administered I.V. Avoid foods high in calcium, or vitamins with minerals, during infusion or for 2-3 hours after completion. You may experience nausea or vomiting (small frequent meals and good mouth care may help); or recurrent bone pain (consult prescriber for analgesic). Report unusual muscle twitching or spasms, severe diarrhea/constipation, or acute bone pain.

Special Geriatric Considerations Has not been studied exclusively in the elderly. Monitor serum electrolytes periodically since the elderly are often receiving diuretics which can result in decreases in serum calcium, potassium, and magnesium.

Emetic Potential Low

Vesicant No

Dosage Forms Excipient information presented when available (limited, particularly for generics); consult specific product labeling.

Injection, powder for reconstitution, as disodium: 30 mg, 90 mg
Aredia®: 30 mg, 90 mg

Injection, solution: 3 mg/mL (10 mL); 6 mg/mL (10 mL); 9 mg/mL (10 mL)

References

American Dental Association Council on Scientific Affairs, "Dental Management of Patients Receiving Oral Bisphosphonate Therapy," *JADA*, 2006, 137(8):1144-50. Available at http://www.ada.org/prof/resources/pubs/jada/reports/report bisphosphonate.pdf

Body JJ, Pot M, Borkowski A, et al, "Dose/Response Study of Aminohydroxypropylidene Bisphosphonate in Tumor-Associated Hypercalcemia," *Am J Med*, 1987, 82(5):957-63.

De S, Meyer P, and Crisp AJ, "Pamidronate and Uveitis," *Br J Rheumatol*, 1995, 34(5):479.

Durie BG, Katz M, and Crowley J, "Osteonecrosis of the Jaw and Bisphosphonates," *N Engl J Med*, 2005, 353(1):99-102.

Fitton A and McTavish D, "Pamidronate: A Review of Its Pharmacological Properties and Therapeutic Efficacy in Resorptive Bone Disease," *Drugs*, 1991, 41(2):289-318.

French AE, Kaplan N, Lishner M, et al, "Taking Bisphosphonates During Pregnancy," *Can Fam Physician*, 2003, 49:1281-2.

Glorieux FH, Bishop NH, Plotkin H, et al, "Cyclic Administration of Pamidronate in Children With Severe Osteogenesis Imperfecta," *N Engl J Med*, 1998, 339(14):947-52.

Kellihan MJ and Mangino PD, "Pamidronate," *Ann Pharmacother*, 1992, 26(10):1262-9.

Lteif AN and Zimmerman D, "Bisphosphonates for Treatment of Childhood Hypercalcemia," *Pediatrics*, 1998, 102(4 Pt 1):990-3.

Maerevoet M, Martin C, and Duck L, "Osteonecrosis of the Jaw and Bisphosphonates," *N Engl J Med*, 2005, 353(1):99-102.

McMahon RE, Bouquot JE, Glueck CJ, et al, "Osteonecrosis: A Multifactorial Etiology," *J Oral Maxillofac Surg*, 2004, 62(7):904-5.

(Continued)

Pamidronate *(Continued)*

Ralston SH, Gallacher SJ, Patel U, et al, "Cancer-Associated Hypercalcemia: Morbidity and Mortality, Clinical Experience in 126 Treated Patients," *Ann Intern Med*, 1990, 112(7):499-504.

Rauch F and Glorieux FH, "Osteogenesis Imperfecta," *Lancet*, 2004, 363(9418):1377-85.

Ruggiero S, Gralow J, Marx RE, et al, "Practical Guidelines for the Prevention, Diagnosis, and Treatment of Osteonecrosis of the Jaw in Patients With Cancer," *J Clin Oncol*, 2006, 2(1):7-14.

Steelman J and Zeitler P, "Treatment of Symptomatic Pediatric Osteoporosis With Cyclic Single-Day Intravenous Pamidronate Infusions," *J Pediatr*, 2003, 142(4):417-23.

Tarassoff P and Csermak K, "Avascular Necrosis of the Jaws: Risk Factors in Metastatic Cancer Patients," *J Oral Maxillofac Surg*, 2003, 61(10):1238-9.

◆ **Pamidronate Disodium** *see* Pamidronate *on page 872*

◆ **Pamidronate Disodium® (Can)** *see* Pamidronate *on page 872*

◆ **Pandel®** *see* Hydrocortisone *on page 545*

◆ **Panglobulin® NF** *see* Immune Globulin (Intravenous) *on page 597*

Panitumumab *(pan i TOOM yoo mab)*

U.S. Brand Names Vectibix™

Index Terms ABX-EGF; NSC-742319; rHuMAb-EGFr

Generic Available No

Pharmacologic Category Antineoplastic Agent, Monoclonal Antibody; Epidermal Growth Factor Receptor (EGFR) Inhibitor

Use Monotherapy in treatment of refractory (EGFR positive) metastatic colorectal cancer

Pregnancy Risk Factor C

Lactation Excretion in breast milk unknown/not recommended

Labeled Contraindications There are no contraindications listed in manufacturer's labeling.

Warnings/Precautions [U.S. Boxed Warning]: Dermatologic toxicities have been reported in ~90% of patients; may include dermatitis acneiform, pruritus, erythema, rash, skin exfoliation, paronychia, dry skin and skin fissures. Severe skin toxicities may be complicated by infection, sepsis, or abscesses. The median time to development of skin (or ocular) toxicity was 2 weeks, with resolution ~7 weeks after discontinuation. Hold treatment and monitor with severe dermatologic toxicities; may require dose reduction. Patients should minimize sunlight exposure; may exacerbate skin reactions. Gastric mucosal, ocular and nail toxicities have also been reported.

[U.S. Boxed Warning]: Severe infusion reactions (anaphylactic reaction, bronchospasm, fever, chills, and hypotension) have been reported in ~1% of patients. Discontinue infusion for severe reactions; permanently discontinue in patients with persistent severe infusion reactions. Appropriate medical support for the management of infusion reactions should be readily available. Mild to moderate infusion reactions are managed by slowing the infusion rate.

Pulmonary fibrosis has been reported (rarely); permanently discontinue treatment if interstitial lung disease, pneumonitis or lung infiltrates develop. Use caution with lung disease; patients with underlying lung disease were excluded from clinical trials. May cause diarrhea; the incidence and severity of chemotherapy-induced diarrhea and other toxicities (rash, electrolyte abnormalities, stomatitis) is increased with combination chemotherapy; combined use with chemotherapy regimens is not recommended. In addition to increased toxicity, studies using panitumumab in combination with chemotherapy (with or without bevacizumab) resulted in decreased progression-free survival compared to regimens without panitumumab; therefore, not indicated for use in combination with chemotherapy. Electrolyte depletion may occur during treatment and after treatment is discontinued; monitor for hypomagnesemia and hypocalcemia. Safety and efficacy in children have not been established.

Adverse Reactions

>10%:

Cardiovascular: Peripheral edema (12%)

Central nervous system: Fatigue (28%)

Dermatologic: Skin toxicity (90%; grades 3/4: 16%), erythema (65%; grades 3/4: 5%), acneiform rash (57%; grades 3/4: 7%), pruritus (57%; grades 3/4: 2%), exfoliation (25%; grades 3/4: 2%), paronychia (25%), rash (22%; grades 3/4: 1%), fissures (20%; grades 3/4: 1%), acne (13%; grades 3/4: 1%)

Endocrine & metabolic: Hypomagnesemia (39%; grades 3/4: 4%)

Gastrointestinal: Abdominal pain (25%), nausea (23%), diarrhea (21%; grades 3/4: 2%), constipation (21%), vomiting (19%)

Respiratory: Cough (14%)

1% to 10%:

Dermatologic: Dry skin (10%), nail disorder (other than paronychia) (9%)

Gastrointestinal: Stomatitis (7%), mucositis (6%)

Ocular: Eyelash growth (6%), conjunctivitis (4%), ocular hyperemia (3%), lacrimation increased (2%), eye/eye lid irritation (1%)

Miscellaneous: Infusion reactions (3%; grades 3/4: 1%)

<1%, postmarketing, and/or case reports: Allergic reaction, anaphylactoid reaction, chills, dyspnea, fever, hypocalcemia, pulmonary fibrosis

Overdosage/Toxicology Treatment is symptom-directed and supportive.

Storage/Stability Store unopened vials under refrigeration at 2°C to 8°C (36°F to 46°F). Do not freeze; do not shake; protect from light. Preparations in infusion containers are stable for 24 hours under refrigeration at 2°C to 8°C (36°F to 46°F) or for 6 hours at room temperature.

Reconstitution Dilute in 100-150 mL of normal saline to a final concentration of ≤10 mg/mL. Do not shake, invert gently to mix.

Mechanism of Action Recombinant human IgG2 monoclonal antibody which binds specifically to the epidermal growth factor receptor (EGFR, HER1, c-ErbB-1) and competitively inhibits the binding of epidermal growth factor (EGF) and other ligands. Binding to the EGFR blocks phosphorylation and activation of intracellular tyrosine kinases, resulting in inhibition of cell survival, growth, proliferation and transformation.

Pharmacodynamics/Kinetics Half-life elimination: ~7.5 days (range: 4-11 days)

Dosage I.V.: Adults: Colorectal cancer: 6 mg/kg every 2 weeks

Dosing adjustment for toxicity:

Infusion reactions, mild-to-moderate (grade 1 or 2): Reduce the infusion rate by 50% for the duration of infusion

Infusion reactions, severe (grade 3 or 4): Immediately and permanently discontinue treatment

Skin toxicity (grade 3 or 4): Withhold treatment; if skin toxicity does not improve to ≤ grade 2 within 1 month, permanently discontinue. If skin toxicity improves to ≤ grade 2 within 1 month (with patient missing ≤2 doses), resume treatment at 50% of the original dose. Dose may be increased in increments of 25% of the original dose (up to 6 mg/kg) if skin toxicities do not recur. For recurrent skin toxicity, permanently discontinue.

Dosage adjustment in renal impairment: Has not been studied

Dosage adjustment in hepatic impairment: Has not been studied

(Continued)

Panitumumab *(Continued)*

Administration Doses ≤1000 mg - infuse over 1 hour; doses >1000 mg - infuse over 90 minutes; reduce infusion rate by 50% for mild-to-moderate infusion reactions; discontinue for severe infusion reactions. Administer through a low protein-binding 0.2 or 0.22 micrometer in-line filter. Flush with NS before and after infusion.

Monitoring Parameters EGF receptor expression testing should be completed prior to treatment. Monitor serum electrolytes, including magnesium and calcium (periodically during and for at least 8 weeks after therapy). Monitor vital signs and temperature before, during, and after infusion. Monitor for skin toxicity.

Patient Information Do not take any new medication during therapy unless approved by prescriber. This medication can only be administered by infusion and you will be closely monitored during each infusion.

Emetic Potential Low (10% to 30%)

Vesicant No

Dosage Forms Excipient information presented when available (limited, particularly for generics); consult specific product labeling.

Injection, solution [preservative free]:

Vectibix™: 20 mg/mL (5 mL, 10 mL, 20 mL)

References

Lynch DH and Yang XD, "Therapeutic Potential of ABX-EGF: A Fully Human Anti-Epidermal Growth Factor Receptor Monoclonal Antibody for Cancer Treatment," *Sem Oncol*, 2002, 29(1 Suppl 4):47-50.

Rowinsky EK, Schwartz GH, Gollob JA, et al, "Safety, Pharmacokinetics, and Activity of ABX-EGF, a Fully Human Anti-Epidermal Growth Factor Receptor Monoclonal Antibody in Patients with Metastatic Renal Cell Cancer," *J Clin Oncol*, 2004, 22(15):3003-15.

Segaert S and Van Cutsem E, "Clinical Signs, Pathophysiology and Management of Skin Toxicity During Therapy with Epidermal Growth Factor Receptor Inhibitors," *Ann Oncol*, 2005, 16(9): 1425-33.

♦ **Panretin**® *see Alitretinoin on page 39*

Papillomavirus (Types 6, 11, 16, 18) Recombinant Vaccine

(pap ih LO ma VYE rus typs six e LEV en SIX teen aye teen ree KOM be nant vak SEEN)

U.S. Brand Names Gardasil®

Index Terms HPV Vaccine; Human Papillomavirus Vaccine; Papillomavirus Vaccine, Recombinant; Quadrivalent Human Papillomavirus Vaccine

Generic Available No

Pharmacologic Category Vaccine

Use Females: Prevention of cervical cancer, genital warts, cervical adenocarcinoma *in situ*, and vulvar, vaginal, or cervical intraepithelial neoplasia caused by human papillomavirus (HPV) types 6, 11, 16, 18

Pregnancy Risk Factor B

Lactation Excretion in breast milk unknown/use caution

Labeled Contraindications Hypersensitivity to papillomavirus recombinant vaccine or any component of the formulation

Warnings/Precautions Immediate treatment for anaphylactoid reaction should be available during vaccine use. There is no evidence that individuals already infected with HPV will be protected; those already infected with 1 or more HPV types were protected from disease in the remaining HPV types. Not for the treatment of active disease; will not protect against diseases not caused by human papillomavirus (HPV) vaccine types 6, 11, 16, and 18.

May administer with mild concurrent febrile illness; consider deferring vaccination with serious illness. Immunocompromised patients may have a reduced response to vaccination. Administered I.M., therefore use caution in patients at risk for bleeding. The entire 3 dose regimen should be completed for maximum efficacy. Not recommended for use during pregnancy. Safety and efficacy in girls <9 years of age or women >26 years have not been established. Safety and efficacy have not been established in males.

Adverse Reactions All serious adverse reactions must be reported to the U.S. Department of Health and Human Services (DHHS) Vaccine Adverse Event Reporting System (VAERS) 1-800-822-7967.

>10%:
  Central nervous system: Fever (10% to 13%)
  Local: Injection site: Pain (84%), swelling (25%), erythema (25%)
1% to 10%:
  Central nervous system: Dizziness (4%), malaise (1%), insomnia (1%)
  Gastrointestinal: Nausea (7%), diarrhea (4%), vomiting (2%), toothache (2%)
  Local: Injection site pruritus (3%)
  Neuromuscular & skeletal: Arthralgia (1%)
  Respiratory: Cough (2%), nasal congestion (1%)
<1%, postmarketing, and/or case reports: Anaphylactic/anaphylactoid reaction, appendicitis, arthritis, asthma, bronchospasm, gastroenteritis, headache, hypersensitivity reaction, JRA, pelvic inflammatory disease, RA, syncope, urticaria

Drug Interactions
  Decreased Effect: Immunosuppressants may decrease the effect of vaccines.

Storage/Stability Store at 2°C to 8°C (36°F to 46°F); do not freeze. Protect from light.

Mechanism of Action Contains inactive human papillomavirus (HPV) proteins HPV 6 L1, HPV 11 L1, HPV 16 L1, and HPV 18 L1 which produce neutralizing antibodies to prevent cervical cancer, cervical adenocarcinoma, cervical, vaginal and vulvar neoplasia and genital warts caused by HPV.

Dosage I.M.: Females: Children ≥9 years and Adults ≤26 years: 0.5 mL followed by 0.5 mL at 2 and 6 months after initial dose
  CDC recommended immunization schedule: Administer first dose to females at age 11-12 years; begin series in females aged 13-26 years if not previously vaccinated. Minimum interval between first and second doses is 4 weeks; the minimum interval between second and third doses is 12 weeks.

Administration Shake suspension well before use. Inject I.M. into the deltoid region of the upper arm or higher anterolateral thigh area.

Monitoring Parameters Gynecologic screening exam, papillomavirus test; observe for syncope/fainting for ~15 minutes after administration of vaccine

Patient Information Vaccination consists of a 3-dose regimen; it is important to receive all 3 doses for maximum benefit. Vaccination is not a substitute for routine cervical cancer screening.

Additional Information Federal law requires that the date of administration, the vaccine manufacturer, lot number of vaccine, and the administering person's name, title and address be entered into the patient's permanent medical record. Ideally, administration of vaccine should occur prior to potential HPV exposure. Benefits of vaccine decrease once infected with ≥1 of the HPV vaccine types.

Dosage Forms Excipient information presented when available (limited, particularly for generics); consult specific product labeling.
(Continued)

Papillomavirus (Types 6, 11, 16, 18) Recombinant Vaccine *(Continued)*

Injection, suspension [preservative free]:

Gardasil®: HPV 6 L1 protein 20 mcg, HPV 11 L1 protein 40 mcg, HPV 16 L1 protein 40 mcg, and HPV 18 L1 protein 20 mcg per 0.5 mL (0.5 mL) [contains aluminum, polysorbate 80; manufactured using *S. cerevisiae* (bakers yeast)]

References

Centers for Disease Control and Prevention, "HPV Vaccine Questions and Answers" at http://www.cdc.gov/std/hpv/STDFact-HPV-vaccine.htm. Last accessed June 9, 2006.

Centers for Disease Control and Prevention, "Quadrivalent Human Papillomavirus Vaccine. Recommendations of the Advisory Committee on Immunization Practices (ACIP)," *MMWR Recomm Rep*, 2007, 56(RR-2):1-24.

FUTURE II Study Group, "Quadrivalent Vaccine Against Human Papillomavirus to Prevent High-Grade Cervical Lesions," *N Engl J Med*, 2007, 356(19):1915-27.

Garland SM, Hernandez-Avila M, Wheeler CM, et al, "Quadrivalent Vaccine Against Human Papillomavirus to Prevent Anogenital Diseases," *N Engl J Med*, 2007, 356(19):1928-43.

Koutsky LA, Ault KA, Wheeler CM, et al, "A Controlled Trial of a Human Papillomavirus Type 16 Vaccine," *N Engl J Med*, 2002, 347(21):1645-51.

Mao C, Koutsky LA, Ault KA, et al, "Efficacy of Human Papillomavirus-16 Vaccine to Prevent Cervical Intraepithelial Neoplasia: A Randomized Controlled Trial," *Obstet Gynecol*, 2006, 107(1):18-27.

National Advisory Committee on Immunization (NACI), "Statement on Human Papillomavirus Vaccine. An Advisory Committee Statement (ACS)," *Can Commun Dis Rep*, 2007, 33(ACS-2):1-31.

Saslow D, Castle PE, Cox JT, et al, "American Cancer Society Guideline for Human Papillomavirus (HPV) Vaccine Use to Prevent Cervical Cancer and Its Precursors," *CA Cancer J Clin*, 2007, 57(1):7-28.

Steinbrook R, "The Potential of Human Papillomavirus Vaccines," *N Engl J Med*, 2006, 354(11):1109-11.

♦ **Papillomavirus Vaccine, Recombinant** *see* Papillomavirus (Types 6, 11, 16, 18) Recombinant Vaccine *on page 878*

♦ **Paraplatin® [DSC]** *see* Carboplatin *on page 173*

♦ **Paraplatin-AQ (Can)** *see* Carboplatin *on page 173*

♦ **Pediapred®** *see* PrednisoLONE *on page 914*

♦ **Pedi-Dri®** *see* Nystatin *on page 817*

♦ **PEG-L-asparaginase** *see* Pegaspargase *on page 880*

Pegaspargase *(peg AS par jase)*

Medication Safety Issues

Sound-alike/look-alike issues:

Pegaspargase may be confused with asparaginase

High alert medication: The Institute for Safe Medication Practices (ISMP) includes this medication among its list of drugs which have a heightened risk of causing significant patient harm when used in error.

Related Information

Safe Handling of Hazardous Drugs *on page 1382*

U.S. Brand Names Oncaspar®

Index Terms NSC-644954; PEG-L-asparaginase

Generic Available No

Pharmacologic Category Antineoplastic Agent, Miscellaneous

Use Treatment of acute lymphocytic leukemia (ALL); treatment of ALL with previous hypersensitivity to native L-asparaginase

Pregnancy Risk Factor C

Lactation Excretion in breast milk unknown/not recommended

Labeled Contraindications Hypersensitivity to pegaspargase or any component of the formulation; history of serious thrombosis with previous

L-asparaginase treatment; pancreatitis or a history of pancreatitis; previous serious allergic reactions (urticaria, bronchospasm, laryngeal edema, hypotension) or other unacceptable adverse reactions to pegaspargase; previous hemorrhagic event with L-asparaginase

Warnings/Precautions Hazardous agent - use appropriate precautions for handling and disposal. Monitor for severe allergic reactions; may be used cautiously in patients who have had hypersensitivity reactions to *E. coli* asparaginase; however, up to 32% of patients who have an allergic reaction to *E. coli* asparaginase will also react to pegaspargase; immediate treatment for hypersensitivity reactions should be available during administration. Thrombotic events may occur; discontinue with serious thrombotic event. Discontinue if pancreatitis occurs during treatment. May cause (possibly irreversible) glucose intolerance. Coagulopathy has been reported; monitor coagulation parameters. Use cautiously in patients with an underlying coagulopathy or previous hematologic complications from asparaginase, hepatic dysfunction, concomitant hepatotoxic medications, hyperglycemia, or diabetes.

Adverse Reactions In general, pegaspargase toxicities tend to be less frequent and appear somewhat later than comparable toxicities of asparaginase. Intramuscular rather than intravenous injection may decrease the incidence of coagulopathy; GI, hepatic, and renal toxicity. Except for hypersensitivity reactions, adults tend to have a higher incidence than children.

>5%:

Cardiovascular: Edema

Central nervous system: Fever, malaise

Dermatologic: Rash (1% to >5%)

Gastrointestinal: Nausea, vomiting

Hematologic: Coagulopathy (7%; grades 3/4: 2%)

Hepatic: Transaminases increased (11%; grades 3/4: 3%), ALT increased

Miscellaneous: Allergic reactions (including bronchospasm, chills, dyspnea, edema, erythema, fever, rash, urticaria: 1% to 10%; 32% in patients with prior hypersensitivity to asparaginase products)

1% to 5%:

Cardiovascular: Hypotension, peripheral edema, tachycardia, thrombosis (4%)

Central nervous system: Chills, CNS thrombosis/hemorrhage (2%), headache, seizure

Dermatologic: Lip edema, urticaria

Endocrine & metabolic: Hyperglycemia (3% to 5%), hyperuricemia, hypoglycemia, hypoproteinemia

Gastrointestinal: Abdominal pain, anorexia, diarrhea, pancreatitis (1% to 2%; grades 3/4: 2%)

Hematologic: Anticoagulant effect decreased, disseminated intravascular coagulation (DIC), fibrinogen decreased, hemolytic anemia, leukopenia, pancytopenia, thrombocytopenia, thromboplastin increased, myelosuppression (mild to moderate; onset: 7 days; nadir: 14 days; recovery: 21 days)

Hepatic: Liver function tests abnormal (5%), hyperbilirubinemia, jaundice, AST increased

Local: Injection site hypersensitivity, pain or reaction

Neuromuscular & skeletal: Arthralgia, limb pain, myalgia, paresthesia

Respiratory: Dyspnea

Miscellaneous: Anaphylactic reactions, night sweats

<1%, postmarketing, and/or case reports: Abnormal renal function, alopecia, amylase increased, anemia, antithrombin III decreased, appetite
(Continued)

Pegaspargase *(Continued)*

increased, ascites, bone pain, bronchospasm, bruising, BUN increased, chest pain, coagulation disorder, coagulation time increased, colitis, coma, confusion, constipation, cough, creatinine increased, dizziness, DVT, emotional lability, endocarditis, epistaxis, erythema, excessive thirst, face edema, fatigue, fatty liver deposits, flatulence, gastrointestinal pain, glucose intolerance, hematuria, hemorrhagic cystitis, hepatomegaly, hyperammonemia, hypertension, hypoalbuminemia, hyponatremia, joint disorder, lesional edema, lipase increased, liver failure, metabolic acidosis, mucositis, petechial rash, polyuria, proteinuria, prothrombin time increased, pruritus, purpura, renal failure, sagittal sinus thrombosis, sepsis, septic shock, somnolence, subacute bacterial endocarditis, superficial venous thrombosis, thirst, upper respiratory infection, uric acid nephropathy, urinary frequency, weight loss

Overdosage/Toxicology Symptoms of overdose include nausea, diarrhea, rash, and increased liver enzymes. Treatment is symptom-directed and supportive.

Storage/Stability Refrigerate at 2°C to 8°C (36°F to 46°F); do not freeze. Do not use product if it is known to have been frozen. Do not use if stored at room temperature for >48 hours. Avoid excessive agitation; do not shake. Do not use if cloudy or if precipitate is present.

Reconstitution

Standard I.M. dilution: Do not exceed 2 mL volume per injection site.

Standard I.V. dilution: Dilute in 100 mL NS or D_5W; stable for 48 hours at room temperature.

Compatibility Stable in NS, D_5W.

Mechanism of Action Pegaspargase is a modified version of asparaginase. Leukemic cells, especially lymphoblasts, require exogenous asparagine; normal cells can synthesize asparagine. Asparaginase contains L-asparaginase amidohydrolase type EC-2 which inhibits protein synthesis by deaminating asparagine to aspartic acid and ammonia in the plasma and extracellular fluid and therefore deprives tumor cells of the amino acid for protein synthesis. Asparaginase is cycle-specific for the G_1 phase of the cell cycle.

Pharmacodynamics/Kinetics

Duration: Asparaginase was measurable for at least 20 days following initial treatment with pegaspargase

Distribution: V_d: 4-5 L/kg; 70% to 80% of plasma volume; does not penetrate the CSF

Metabolism: Systemically degraded

Half-life elimination: 5.8 days; unaffected by age, renal or hepatic function; half life decreased to 3.2 days in patients with previous hypersensitivity to native L-asparaginase

Excretion: Urine (trace amounts)

Dosage Usually administered as part of a combination chemotherapy regimen.

I.M. administration is **preferred** over I.V. administration due to lower incidence of hepatotoxicity, coagulopathy, gastrointestinal and renal disorders with I.M. administration.

Children: I.M., I.V.:

Body surface area <0.6 m²: 82.5 int. units/kg every 14 days

Body surface area ≥0.6 m²: 2500 int. units/m² every 14 days

Adults: I.M., I.V.: 2500 int. units/m² every 14 days

Hemodialysis: Significant drug removal is unlikely based on physiochemical characteristics

Peritoneal dialysis: Significant drug removal is unlikely based on physiochemical characteristics

Combination Regimens

Leukemia, acute lymphocytic: Hyper-CVAD (Leukemia, Acute Lymphocytic) on page 1231

Administration

I.M.: Must only be administered as a deep intramuscular injection into a large muscle; if I.M. injection volume is >2 mL, use multiple injection sites.

I.V.: May be administered as a 1 - to 2-hour I.V. infusion; **do not administer I.V. push**.

Monitoring Parameters Vital signs during administration, CBC with differential, platelets, amylase, liver enzymes, fibrinogen, PT, PTT, renal function tests, urine dipstick for glucose, blood glucose; monitor for onset of abdominal pain and mental status changes

Patient Information This drug can only be given I.M. or I.V. Inform prescriber if you are using any other medications that may increase risk of bleeding. Possibility of hypersensitivity reactions includes anaphylaxis. Maintain adequate hydration (2-3 L/day of fluids unless instructed to restrict fluid intake) and nutrition (small frequent meals may help if you experience nausea, vomiting, or loss of appetite). You may experience dizziness, drowsiness, syncope, or blurred vision (use caution when driving or engaging in tasks that require alertness until response to drug is known). You may experience increased sweating, decreased sexual drive, or cough. Report immediately chest pain or heart palpitations; difficulty breathing or constant cough; rash, hives, or swelling of lips or mouth; or abdominal pain. Report swelling of extremities or sudden weight gain; burning, pain, or redness at infusion site; persistent fever or chills; unusual bruising or bleeding; twitching or tremors; pain on urination; or persistent nausea or diarrhea.

Emetic Potential Very low (<10%)

Vesicant No

Dosage Forms Excipient information presented when available (limited, particularly for generics); consult specific product labeling.

Injection, solution [preservative free]:

Oncaspar®: 750 units/mL (5 mL)

References

Abshire TC, Pollock BH, Billett AL, et al, "Weekly Polyethylene Glycol Conjugated L-Asparaginase Compared With Biweekly Dosing Produces Superior Induction Remission Rates in Childhood Relapsed Acute Lymphoblastic Leukemia: A Pediatric Oncology Group Study," Blood, 2000, 96(5):1709-15.

Asselin BL, Whitin JC, Cappola DJ, et al, "Comparative Pharmacokinetic Studies of Three Asparaginase Preparations," J Clin Oncol, 1993, 11(9):1780-6.

Avramis VI, Sencer S, Periclou AP, et al, "A Randomized Comparison of Native Escherichia Coli Asparaginase and Polyethylene Glycol Conjugated Asparaginase for Treatment of Children With Newly Diagnosed Standard-Risk Acute Lymphoblastic Leukemia: A Children's Cancer Group Study," Blood, 2002, 99(6):1986-94.

Graham ML, "Pegaspargase: A Review of Clinical Studies," Adv Drug Deliv Rev, 2003, 55(10):1293-302.

Holle LM, "Pegaspargase: An Alternative?" Ann Pharmacother, 1997, 31(5):616-24.

Keating MJ, Holmes R, Lerner S, et al, "L-Asparaginase and PEG Asparaginase - Past, Present, and Future," Leuk Lymphoma, 1993, 10(Suppl):153-7.

Muss HB, Spell N, Scudiery D, et al, "A Phase II Trial of PEG-L-Asparaginase in the Treatment of Non-Hodgkin's Lymphoma," Invest New Drugs, 1990, 8(1):125-30.

Patel SS and Benfield P, "Pegaspargase (Polyethylene Glycol-L-Asparaginase)," Clin Immunother, 1996, 5:490-6.

♦ **Pegylated Liposomal DOXOrubicin** see DOXOrubicin (Liposomal) on page 359

Pemetrexed (pem e TREKS ed)

Medication Safety Issues

High alert medication: The Institute for Safe Medication Practices (ISMP) includes this medication among its list of drugs which have a heightened risk of causing significant patient harm when used in error.

Related Information

Safe Handling of Hazardous Drugs *on page 1382*

U.S. Brand Names Alimta®

Index Terms LY231514; MTA; Multitargeted Antifolate; NSC-698037; Pemetrexed Disodium

Generic Available No

Canadian Brand Names Alimta®

Pharmacologic Category Antineoplastic Agent, Antimetabolite; Antineoplastic Agent, Antimetabolite (Antifolate)

Use Treatment of malignant pleural mesothelioma; treatment of nonsmall cell lung cancer

Unlabeled/Investigational Use Bladder, breast, cervical, colorectal, esophageal, gastric, head and neck, ovarian, pancreatic, and renal cell cancers

Pregnancy Risk Factor D

Lactation Excretion in breast milk unknown/not recommended

Labeled Contraindications Hypersensitivity to pemetrexed or any component of the formulation

Warnings/Precautions Hazardous agent - use appropriate precautions for handling and disposal. May cause bone marrow suppression (anemia, neutropenia, thrombocytopenia and/or pancytopenia). Prophylactic folic acid and vitamin B_{12} supplements are necessary to reduce hematologic and gastrointestinal toxicity and should be started 1 week before the first dose of pemetrexed. Pretreatment with corticosteroids reduces the incidence and severity of cutaneous reactions. Effects of third space fluid on drug disposition is unknown; consider removal of effusions prior to treatment. Use caution with hepatic dysfunction not due to metastases; may require dose adjustment. Decreased renal function results in increased toxicity. Use caution in patients receiving concurrent nephrotoxins; may result in delayed pemetrexed clearance. The manufacturer does not recommend use for Cl_{cr} <45 mL/minute. Safety and efficacy in children have not been established.

Adverse Reactions Note: Percentages reported with single-agent therapy (in patients who received folate and B_{12} supplementation); dose limiting toxicities include myelosuppression (neutropenia, thrombocytopenia); fatigue and dermatitis.

>10%:
Cardiovascular: Chest pain (38%), edema (19%), hypertension (11%; grades 3/4 incidence higher in patients >65 years)

Central nervous system: Fatigue (87%; grade 3: 14%; grade 4: 2%), fever (26%), depression (11%)

Dermatologic: Rash/desquamation (17%), alopecia (11%)

Gastrointestinal: Anorexia (62%), nausea (39%), constipation (30%), vomiting (25%), diarrhea (21%), stomatitis (20%)

Hematologic: Anemia (33%; grade 4: 2%), leukopenia (13%), neutropenia (11%; grade 4: 2%; nadir: 8-10 days; recovery: 12-17 days)

Neuromuscular & skeletal: Neuropathy (29%), myalgia (13%)

Respiratory: Dyspnea (72%), pharyngitis (20%)

Miscellaneous: Infection (23%)

1% to 10%:
Cardiovascular: Thrombosis/embolism (4%), cardiac ischemia (3%)

Endocrine & metabolic: Dehydration (3%)

Gastrointestinal: Dysphagia/esophagitis/odynophagia (5%)
Hematologic: Thrombocytopenia (9%), febrile neutropenia (2% to 6%)
Hepatic: ALT increased (10%; grade 3: 2%; grade 4: 1%), AST increased (8%; grade 3: <1%; grade 4: 1%)
Neuromuscular & skeletal: Arthralgia (8%)
Renal: Creatinine clearance decreased (5%), serum creatinine increased (3%)
Miscellaneous: Allergic reaction/hypersensitivity (8%)
<1%, postmarketing, and/or case reports: Colitis, renal failure

Overdosage/Toxicology Toxicities include neutropenia, anemia, thrombocytopenia, mucositis, rash, infection, and diarrhea. Treatment is supportive and symptom-directed. Continuing leucovorin may help minimize additional hematologic toxicity. The intravenous leucovorin doses used in clinical trials were 100 mg/m² once, followed by 50 mg/m² every 6 hours for 8 days. It is unknown if pemetrexed is removed by hemodialysis.

Drug Interactions

Increased Effect/Toxicity: NSAIDs may increase the toxicity of pemetrexed.

Ethanol/Nutrition/Herb Interactions Lower ANC nadirs occur in patients with elevated baseline cystathionine or homocysteine concentrations. Levels of these substances can be reduced by folic acid and vitamin B_{12} supplementation.

Storage/Stability Store unopened vials at 15°C to 30°C (59°F to 86°F). Reconstituted and infusion solutions are stable for 24 hours when refrigerated at 2°C to 8°C (36°F to 46°F) or stored at room temperature of 15°C to 30°C (59°F to 86°F). Concentrations at 25 mg/mL are stable in polypropylene syringes for 2 days at room temperature (23°C).

Reconstitution Add 20 mL of 0.9% preservative free sodium chloride injection to make a 25 mg/mL solution. Gently swirl. Solution may be colorless to green-yellow. Further dilute in 50-200 mL of 0.9% sodium chloride for administration.

Compatibility Stable in NS; physically **incompatible** with calcium-containing products.

Y-site administration: Compatible: Acyclovir, amifostine, amikacin sulfate, aminophylline, ampicillin sodium, ampicillin sodium-sulbactam sodium, aztreonam, bumetanide, buprenorphine hydrochloride, butorphanol tartrate, carboplatin, ceftizoxime sodium, ceftriaxone sodium, cefuroxime sodium, cimetidine hydrochloride, cisplatin, clindamycin phosphate, co-trimoxazole, cyclophosphamide, cytarabine, dexamethasone sodium phosphate, dexrazoxane, diphenhydramine hydrochloride, docetaxel, dopamine hydrochloride, enalaprilat, famotidine, fluconazole, fluorouracil, ganciclovir sodium, granisetron hydrochloride, haloperidol lactate, heparin sodium, hydromorphone hydrochloride, hydroxyzine hydrochloride, ifosfamide, leucovorin calcium, lorazepam, mannitol, meperidine hydrochloride, mesna, methylprednisolone sodium succinate, metoclopramide hydrochloride, morphine sulfate, paclitaxel, potassium chloride, promethazine hydrochloride, ranitidine hydrochloride, sodium bicarbonate, ticarcillin disodium, ticarcillin disodium-clavulanate potassium, vancomycin hydrochloride, vinblastine sulfate, vincristine sulfate, zidovudine. **Incompatible:** Amphotericin B, calcium gluconate, cefazolin sodium, cefotaxime sodium, cefotetan disodium, cefoxitin sodium, ceftazidime, chlorpromazine hydrochloride, ciprofloxacin, dobutamine hydrochloride, doxorubicin hydrochloride, doxycycline hyclate, droperidol, gemcitabine hydrochloride, gentamicin sulfate, irinotecan hydrochloride, metronidazole, minocycline hydrochloride, mitoxantrone hydrochloride, nalbuphine hydrochloride, (Continued)

Pemetrexed *(Continued)*

ondansetron hydrochloride, prochlorperazine edisylate, tobramycin sulfate, topotecan hydrochloride.

Mechanism of Action Inhibits thymidylate synthase (TS), dihydrofolate reductase (DHFR), glycinamide ribonucleotide formyltransferase (GARFT), and aminoimidazole carboxamide ribonucleotide formyltransferase (AICARFT), the enzymes involved in folate metabolism and DNA synthesis, resulting in inhibition of purine and thymidine nucleotide and protein synthesis.

Pharmacodynamics/Kinetics

Duration: V_{dss}: 16.1 L

Protein binding: ~73% to 81%

Metabolism: Minimal

Half-life elimination: Normal renal function: 3.5 hours; Cl_{cr} 40-59 mL/minute: 5.3-5.8 hours

Excretion: Urine (70% to 90% as unchanged drug)

Dosage I.V.: Adults: Refer to individual protocols:

Nonsmall cell lung cancer: 500 mg/m^2 on day 1 of each 21-day cycle

Malignant pleural mesothelioma: 500 mg/m^2 on day 1 of each 21-day cycle (in combination with cisplatin)

Note: Start vitamin supplements 1 week before initial dose of pemetrexed. Folic acid 350-1000 mcg/day orally (continuing for 21 days after last dose of pemetrexed) and vitamin B_{12} 1000 mcg I.M. every 9 weeks. Dexamethasone 4 mg twice daily can be started the day before therapy, and continued the day of and the day after to minimize cutaneous reactions.

Dosage adjustments for toxicities:

Toxicity: Discontinue if patient develops grade 3 or 4 toxicity after two dose reductions (except grade 3 transaminase elevations) or immediately if grade 3 or 4 neurotoxicity develops

Hematologic toxicity: Upon recovery, reinitiate therapy

Nadir ANC <500/mm^3 and nadir platelets ≥50,000/mm^3: Reduce dose to 75% of previous dose of pemetrexed and cisplatin

Nadir platelets <50,000/mm^3 (regardless of nadir ANC): Reduce dose to 50% of previous dose of pemetrexed and cisplatin

Nonhematologic toxicity (excluding neurotoxicity or grade 3 transaminase elevations): Withhold treatment until recovery to baseline, upon recovery, reinitiate therapy

Grade 3 or 4 toxicity (excluding mucositis or grade 3 transaminase elevations): Reduce dose to 75% of previous dose of pemetrexed and cisplatin

Grade 3 or 4 diarrhea or any diarrhea requiring hospitalization: Reduce dose to 75% of previous dose of pemetrexed and cisplatin

Grade 3 or 4 mucositis: Reduce dose to 50% of previous dose of pemetrexed; continue cisplatin at 100% of previous dose

Neurotoxicity:

Common Toxicity Criteria (CTC) Grade 0-1: Continue at 100% of previous dose of pemetrexed and cisplatin.

CTC Grade 2: Continue at previous dose of pemetrexed; Reduce dose to 50% of previous dose of cisplatin.

Dosage adjustment in renal impairment:

Cl_{cr} ≥45 mL/minute: No dosage adjustment required.

Cl_{cr} <45 mL/minute: No dosage adjustment guidelines are available; manufacturer recommends not using the drug.

Dosage adjustment in hepatic impairment: Grade 4 transaminase elevation (>20 times ULN): Reduce dose to 75% of previous dose

Combination Regimens

Bladder cancer: Pemetrexed (Bladder Cancer) *on page 1270*

Malignant pleural mesothelioma: Cisplatin-Pemetrexed *on page 1176*

Administration I.V.: Infuse over 10 minutes.

Monitoring Parameters CBC with differential and platelets (before each dose); serum creatinine, total bilirubin, ALT, AST (day 1 of each, or every other, cycle)

Dietary Considerations Initiate folic acid supplementation 1 week before first dose of pemetrexed, continue for full course of therapy, and for 21 days after last dose. Institute vitamin B_{12} 1 week before the first dose; administer every 9 weeks thereafter.

Emetic Potential Moderate (30% to 60%)

Vesicant No

Dosage Forms Excipient information presented when available (limited, particularly for generics); consult specific product labeling.

Injection, powder for reconstitution:

Alimta®: 500 mg

References

Adjei AA, "Pemetrexed (Alimta): A Novel Multitargeted Antifolate Agent," *Expert Rev Anticancer Ther*, 2003, 3(2):145-56.

Goldman ID and Zhao R, "Molecular, Biochemical, and Cellular Pharmacology of Pemetrexed," *Semin Oncol*, 2002, 29(6 Suppl 18):3-17.

Hanna N, Shepherd FA, Fossella FV, et al, "Randomized Phase III Trial of Pemetrexed Versus Docetaxel in Patients With Non-Small-Cell Lung Cancer Previously Treated With Chemotherapy," *J Clin Oncol*, 2004, 22(9):1589-97.

Manegold C, "Pemetrexed (Alimta, MTA, Multitargeted Antifolate, LY231514) for Malignant Pleural Mesothelioma," *Semin Oncol*, 2003, 30(4 Suppl 10):32-6.

Mita AC, Sweeney CJ, Baker SD, et al, "Phase I and Pharmacokinetic Study of Pemetrexed Administered Every 3 Weeks to Advanced Cancer Patients With Normal and Impaired Renal Function," *J Clin Oncol*, 2006, 24(4):552-62.

Niyikiza C, Hanauske AR, Rusthoven JJ, et al, "Pemetrexed Safety and Dosing Strategy," *Semin Oncol*, 2002, 29(6 Suppl 18):24-9.

Ouellet D, Periclou AP, Johnson RD, et al, "Population Pharmacokinetics of Pemetrexed Disodium (ALIMTA) in Patients With Cancer," *Cancer Chemother Pharmacol*, 2000, 46(3):227-34.

Paz-Ares L, Bezares S, Tabernero JM, et al, "Review of a Promising New Agent - Pemetrexed Disodium," *Cancer*, 2003, 97(8 Suppl):2056-63.

Rusch VW, "Pemetrexed and Cisplatin for Malignant Pleural Mesothelioma: A New Standard of Care?" *J Clin Oncol*, 2003, 21(14):2629-30.

Sweeney CJ, Takimoto CH, Latz JE, et al, "Two Drug Interaction Studies Evaluating the Pharmacokinetics and Toxicity of Pemetrexed When Coadministered with Aspirin or Ibuprofen in Patients with Advanced Cancer," *Clin Cancer Res*, 2006, 12(2):536-42.

Trissel LA, Saenz CA, Ogundele AB, et al, "Physical Compatibility of Pemetrexed Disodium With Other Drugs During Simulated Y-Site Administration," *Am J Health Syst Pharm*, 2004, 61(21):2289-93.

Zhang Y and Trissel LA, "Physical and Chemical Stability of Pemetrexed Solutions in Plastic Syringes," *Ann Pharmacother*, 2005, 39(12):2026-8.

♦ **Pemetrexed Disodium** *see* Pemetrexed *on page 884*

♦ **Pentahydrate** *see* Sodium Thiosulfate *on page 972*

♦ **Pentam-300®** *see* Pentamidine *on page 887*

Pentamidine (pen TAM i deen)

Related Information

Safe Handling of Hazardous Drugs *on page 1382*

U.S. Brand Names NebuPent®; Pentam-300®

Index Terms Pentamidine Isethionate

Generic Available No

(Continued)

PENTAMIDINE

Pentamidine *(Continued)*

Canadian Brand Names Pentamidine Isetionate for Injection

Pharmacologic Category Antibiotic, Miscellaneous

Use Treatment and prevention of pneumonia caused by *Pneumocystis carinii* (PCP)

Unlabeled/Investigational Use Treatment of trypanosomiasis and visceral leishmaniasis

Pregnancy Risk Factor C

Lactation Excretion in breast milk unknown/contraindicated

Labeled Contraindications Hypersensitivity to pentamidine isethionate or any component of the formulation (inhalation and injection)

Warnings/Precautions Use with caution in patients with diabetes mellitus, renal or hepatic dysfunction, cardiovascular disease, pancreatitis, leukopenia, thrombocytopenia, asthma, or hypo-/hyperglycemia. Severe hypotension (some fatalities) has been observed, even after a single dose; more common with rapid I.V. administration. Prolonged use may result in fungal or bacterial superinfection, including *C. difficile*-associated diarrhea (CDAD) and pseudomembranous colitis; CDAD has been observed <2 months postantibiotic treatment.

Adverse Reactions Injection (I); Aerosol (A)

>10%:

Cardiovascular: Chest pain (A - 10% to 23%)

Central nervous system: Fatigue (A - 50% to 70%); dizziness (A - 31% to 47%)

Dermatologic: Rash (31% to 47%)

Endocrine & metabolic: Hyperkalemia

Gastrointestinal: Anorexia (A - 50% to 70%), nausea (A - 10% to 23%)

Local: Local reactions at injection site

Renal: Increased creatinine (I - 23%)

Respiratory: Wheezing (A - 10% to 23%), dyspnea (A - 50% to 70%), cough (A - 31% to 47%), pharyngitis (10% to 23%)

1% to 10%:

Cardiovascular: Hypotension (I - 4%)

Central nervous system: Confusion/hallucinations (1% to 2%), headache (A - 1% to 5%)

Dermatologic: Rash (I - 3.3%)

Endocrine & metabolic: Hypoglycemia <25 mg/dL (I - 2.4%)

Gastrointestinal: Nausea/anorexia (I - 6%), diarrhea (A - 1% to 5%), vomiting

Hematologic: Severe leukopenia (I - 2.8%), thrombocytopenia <20,000/mm^3 (I - 1.7%), anemia (A - 1% to 5%)

Hepatic: Increased LFTs (I - 8.7%)

<1%: Hypotension <60 mm Hg systolic (I - 0.9%), tachycardia, arrhythmia, dizziness (I), fever, fatigue (I), hyperglycemia or hypoglycemia, hypocalcemia, pancreatitis, megaloblastic anemia, granulocytopenia, leukopenia, renal insufficiency, extrapulmonary pneumocystosis, irritation of the airway, pneumothorax, Jarisch-Herxheimer-like reaction, mild renal or hepatic injury

Overdosage/Toxicology Symptoms of overdose include hypotension, hypoglycemia, and cardiac arrhythmias. Treatment is supportive.

Drug Interactions

Cytochrome P450 Effect: Substrate of CYP2C19 (major); **Inhibits** CYP2C8/9 (weak), 2C19 (weak), 2D6 (weak), 3A4 (weak)

Increased Effect/Toxicity: CYP2C19 inhibitors may increase the levels/effects of pentamidine; example inhibitors include delavirdine, fluconazole, fluvoxamine, gemfibrozil, isoniazid, omeprazole, and ticlopidine. Pentamidine may potentiate the effect of other drugs which prolong QT interval (cisapride, moxifloxacin, pimozide, and type Ia and type III antiarrhythmics).

Decreased Effect: CYP2C19 inducers may decrease the levels/effects of pentamidine; example inducers include aminoglutethimide, carbamazepine, phenytoin, and rifampin.

Ethanol/Nutrition/Herb Interactions Ethanol: Avoid ethanol (may increase CNS depression or aggravate hypoglycemia).

Storage/Stability Store intact vials at controlled room temperature and protect from light. Do not refrigerate due to the possibility of crystallization. Reconstituted solutions (60-100 mg/mL) are stable for 48 hours at room temperature and do not require light protection. Diluted solutions for injection (1-2.5 mg/mL) in D₅W are stable for at least 24 hours at room temperature. The manufacturer recommends D₅W, however stability in NS has also been documented; in addition, light protection is recommended by the manufacturer, but stability has been documented without protection from light.

Reconstitution Powder for inhalation should be reconstituted with SWFI. Powder for injection may be reconstituted with SWFI or D₅W. Precipitation may occur if products are reconstituted with NS.

Compatibility Solutions for injection (1-2.5 mg/mL) in D₅W are stable for at least 24 hours at room temperature. The manufacturer's labeling recommends D₅W, however stability in NS has also been documented.

Y-site administration: Compatible: Diltiazem, gatifloxacin, zidovudine.
Incompatible: Aldesleukin, cefazolin, cefoperazone, cefotaxime, cefoxitin, ceftazidime, ceftriaxone, fluconazole, foscarnet, linezolid.

Mechanism of Action Interferes with RNA/DNA, phospholipids and protein synthesis, through inhibition of oxidative phosphorylation and/or interference with incorporation of nucleotides and nucleic acids into RNA and DNA, in protozoa

Pharmacodynamics/Kinetics
Absorption: I.M.: Well absorbed; Inhalation: Limited systemic absorption
Half-life elimination: Terminal: 6.4-9.4 hours; may be prolonged with severe renal impairment
Excretion: Urine (33% to 66% as unchanged drug)

Dosage
Children:
Treatment of PCP pneumonia: I.M., I.V. (I.V. preferred): 4 mg/kg/day once daily for 10-14 days
Prevention of PCP pneumonia:
I.M., I.V.: 4 mg/kg monthly or every 2 weeks
Inhalation (aerosolized pentamidine in children ≥5 years): 300 mg/dose given every 3-4 weeks via Respirgard® II inhaler (8 mg/kg dose has also been used in children <5 years)
Treatment of trypanosomiasis (unlabeled use): I.V.: 4 mg/kg/day once daily for 10 days
Adults:
Treatment: I.M., I.V. (I.V. preferred): 4 mg/kg/day once daily for 14-21 days
Prevention: Inhalation: 300 mg every 4 weeks via Respirgard® II nebulizer
Dialysis: Not removed by hemo or peritoneal dialysis or continuous arteriovenous or venovenous hemofiltration; supplemental dosage is not necessary
Dosing adjustment in renal impairment: Adults: I.V.:
Cl_cr 10-50 mL/minute: Administer 4 mg/kg every 24-36 hours
(Continued)

Pentamidine *(Continued)*

Cl_{cr} <10 mL/minute: Administer 4 mg/kg every 48 hours

Administration

Inhalation: Deliver until nebulizer is gone (30-45 minutes)

I.V.: Infuse slowly over a period of at least 60 minutes or administer deep I.M.

Monitoring Parameters Liver function tests, renal function tests, blood glucose, serum potassium and calcium, ECG, blood pressure

Patient Information PCP pneumonia may still occur despite pentamidine use; report fever, shortness of breath, or coughing up blood; maintain adequate fluid intake

Special Geriatric Considerations Ten percent of acquired immunodeficiency syndrome (AIDS) cases are in the elderly and this figure is expected to increase. Pentamidine has not as yet been studied exclusively in this population. Adjust dose for renal function.

Additional Information Virtually undetectable amounts are transferred to healthcare personnel during aerosol administration.

Vesicant No

Dosage Forms Excipient information presented when available (limited, particularly for generics); consult specific product labeling.

Injection, powder for reconstitution, as isethionate [preservative free]:

Pentam-300®: 300 mg

Powder for nebulization, as isethionate [preservative free]:

NebuPent®: 300 mg

References

"1997 USPHS/IDSA Guidelines for the Prevention of Opportunistic Infections in Persons Infected With Human Immunodeficiency Virus," *MMWR Recomm Rep*, 1997, 46(RR-12):1-46.

Centers for Disease Control, "Guidelines for Prophylaxis Against *Pneumocystis carinii* Pneumonia for Children Infected With Human Immunodeficiency Virus," *JAMA*, 1991, 265(13):1637-40, 1643-4.

Comtois R, Pouliot J, Gervais S, et al, "High Pentamidine Levels Associated With Hypoglycemia and Azotemia in a Patient With *Pneumocystis carinii* Pneumonia," *Diagn Microbiol Infect Dis*, 1992, 15(6):523-6.

Conte JE Jr, "Pharmacokinetics of Intravenous Pentamidine in Patients With Normal Renal Function or Receiving Hemodialysis," *J Infect Dis*, 1991, 163(1):169-75.

Cortese LM, Gasser RA, Jr, Bjornson DC, et al, "Prolonged Recurrence of Pentamidine-Induced Torsade de Pointes," *Ann Pharmacother*, 1992, 26(11):1365-9.

Goa KL and Campoli-Richards DM, "Pentamidine Isethionate. A Review of Its Antiprotozoal Activity, Pharmacokinetic Properties and Therapeutic Use in *Pneumocystis carinii* Pneumonia," *Drugs*, 1987, 33(3):242-58.

Hand IL, Wiznia AA, Porricolo M, et al, "Aerosolized Pentamidine for Prophylaxis of *Pneumocystis carinii* Pneumonia in Infants With Human Immunodeficiency Virus Infection," *Pediatr Infect Dis J*, 1994, 13(2):100-4.

Hughes WT, "*Pneumocystis carinii* Pneumonia: New Approaches to Diagnosis, Treatment, and Prevention," *Pediatr Infect Dis J*, 1991, 10(5):391-9.

Ito S and Koren G, "Estimation of Fetal Risk From Aerosolized Pentamidine in Pregnant Healthcare Workers," *Chest*, 1994, 106(5):1460-2.

Masur H, "Prevention and Treatment of *Pneumocystis* Pneumonia," *N Engl J Med*, 1992, 327(26):1853-60.

Monk JP and Benfield P, "Inhaled Pentamidine. An Overview of Its Pharmacological Properties and a Review of Its Therapeutic Use in *Pneumocystis carinii* Pneumonia," *Drugs*, 1990, 39(5):741-56.

Pelucio MT, Rothenhaus T, Smith M, et al, "Fatal Pancreatitis as a Complication of Therapy for HIV Infection," *J Emerg Med*, 1995, 13(5):633-7.

Sattler FR, Cowan R, Nielsen DM, et al, " Trimethoprim-Sulfamethoxazole Compared With Pentamidine for Treatment of *Pneumocystis carinii* Pneumonia in the Acquired Immunodeficiency Syndrome," *Ann Intern Med*, 1988, 109(4):280-7.

Singh G, el-Gadi SM, and Sparks RA, "Pancreatitis Associated With Aerosolized Pentamidine," *Genitourin Med*, 1995, 71(2):130-1.

◆ **Pentamidine Isethionate** *see* Pentamidine *on page 887*

♦ **Pentamidine Isetionate for Injection (Can)** *see* Pentamidine *on page 887*

Pentostatin (pen toe STAT in)

Medication Safety Issues

Sound-alike/look-alike issues:

Pentostatin may be confused with pentamidine, pentosan

High alert medication: The Institute for Safe Medication Practices (ISMP) includes this medication among its list of classes of drugs which have a heightened risk of causing significant patient harm when used in error.

International issues:

Nipent® may be confused with Nipin® which is a brand name for nifedipine in Italy and Singapore

Related Information

Safe Handling of Hazardous Drugs *on page 1382*

U.S. Brand Names Nipent®

Index Terms Co-Vidarabine; dCF; Deoxycoformycin; NSC-218321; 2'-Deoxycoformycin

Generic Available Yes

Canadian Brand Names Nipent®

Pharmacologic Category Antineoplastic Agent, Antibiotic; Antineoplastic Agent, Antimetabolite (Purine Antagonist)

Use Treatment of hairy cell leukemia

Unlabeled/Investigational Use Treatment of cutaneous T-cell lymphoma, chronic lymphocytic leukemia (CLL), and acute and chronic graft-versus-host-disease (GVHD)

Pregnancy Risk Factor D

Lactation Excretion in breast milk unknown/not recommended

Labeled Contraindications Hypersensitivity to pentostatin or any component of the formulation

Warnings/Precautions Hazardous agent - use appropriate precautions for handling and disposal. **[U.S. Boxed Warnings]: Severe renal, liver, pulmonary and CNS toxicities have occurred with doses higher than recommended; do not exceed the recommended dose. Do not administer concurrently with fludarabine; concomitant use has resulted in serious or fatal pulmonary toxicity.** Bone marrow suppression may occur, primarily early in treatment; if neutropenia persists beyond early cycles, evaluate for disease status. In patients who present with infections prior to treatment, infections should be resolved, if possible, prior to initiation of treatment; treatment should be temporarily withheld for active infections during therapy. Use cautiously in patients with renal dysfunction (the half-life is prolonged); appropriate dosing guidelines in renal insufficiency have not been determined. May cause elevations (reversible) in liver function tests. Withhold treatment for CNS toxicity or severe rash. Fatal pulmonary edema and hypotension have been reported in patients treated with pentostatin in combination with carmustine, etoposide, or high-dose cyclophosphamide as part of a myeloablative regimen for bone marrow transplant. **[U.S. Boxed Warning]: Should be administered under the supervision of an experienced cancer chemotherapy physician.** Safety and efficacy in children have not been established.
(Continued)

Pentostatin *(Continued)*

Adverse Reactions

>10%:

Central nervous system: Fever (42% to 46%), fatigue (29% to 42%), pain (8% to 20%), chills (11% to 19%), headache (13% to 17%), CNS toxicity (1% to 11%)

Dermatologic: Rash (26% to 43%), pruritus (10% to 21%), skin disorder (4% to 17%)

Gastrointestinal: Nausea/vomiting (22% to 63%), diarrhea (15% to 17%), anorexia (13% to 16%), abdominal pain (4% to 16%), stomatitis (5% to 12%)

Hematologic: Myelosuppression (nadir: 7 days; recovery: 10-14 days), leukopenia (22% to 60%), anemia (8% to 35%), thrombocytopenia (6% to 32%)

Hepatic: Transaminases increased (2% to 19%)

Neuromuscular & skeletal: Myalgia (11% to 19%), weakness (10% to 12%)

Respiratory: Cough (17% to 20%), upper respiratory infection (13% to 16%), rhinitis (10% to 11%), dyspnea (8% to 11%)

Miscellaneous: Infection (7% to 36%), allergic reaction (2% to 11%)

1% to 10%:

Cardiovascular: Chest pain (3% to 10%), facial edema (3% to 10%), hypotension (3% to 10%), peripheral edema (3% to 10%), angina (<3%), arrhythmia (<3%), AV block (<3%), bradycardia (<3%), cardiac arrest (<3%), deep thrombophlebitis (<3%), heart failure (<3%), hypertension (<3%), pericardial effusion (<3%), sinus arrest (<3%), syncope (<3%), tachycardia (<3%), vasculitis (<3%), ventricular extrasystoles (<3%)

Central nervous system: Anxiety (3% to 10%), confusion (3% to 10%), depression (3% to 10%), dizziness (3% to 10%), insomnia (3% to 10%), nervousness (3% to 10%), somnolence (3% to 10%), abnormal dreams/thinking (<3%), amnesia (<3%), ataxia (<3%), emotional lability (<3%), encephalitis (<3%), hallucination (<3%), hostility (<3%), meningism (<3%), neuritis (<3%), neurosis (<3%), seizure (<3%), vertigo (<3%)

Dermatologic: Cellulitis (6%), furunculosis (4%), dry skin (3% to 10%), urticaria (3% to 10%), acne (<3%), alopecia (<3%), eczema (<3%), petechial rash (<3%), photosensitivity (<3%), abscess (2%)

Endocrine & metabolic: Amenorrhea (<3%), hypercalcemia (<3%), hyponatremia (<3%), gout (<3%), libido decreased/loss (<3%)

Gastrointestinal: Dyspepsia (3% to 10%) flatulence (3% to 10%), gingivitis (3% to 10%), constipation (<3%), dysphagia (<3%), glossitis (<3%), ileus (<3%), taste perversion (<3%), oral moniliasis (2%)

Genitourinary: Urinary tract infection (3%), impotence (<3%)

Hematologic: Agranulocytosis (3% to 10%), hemorrhage (3% to 10%), acute leukemia (<3%), aplastic anemia (<3%), hemolytic anemia (<3%)

Local: Phlebitis (<3%)

Neuromuscular & skeletal: Arthralgia (3% to 10%), paresthesia (3% to 10%), arthritis (<3%), dysarthria (<3%), hyperkinesia (<3%), neuralgia (<3%), neuropathy (<3%), paralysis (<3%), twitching (<3%), osteomyelitis (1%)

Ocular: Conjunctivitis (4%), amblyopia (<3%), eyes nonreactive (<3%), lacrimation disorder (<3%), photophobia (<3%), retinopathy (<3%), vision abnormal (<3%), watery eyes (<3%), xerophthalmia (<3%)

Otic: Deafness (<3%), earache (<3%), labyrinthitis (<3%), tinnitus (<3%)

Renal: Creatinine increased (3% to 10%), nephropathy (<3%), renal failure (<3%), renal insufficiency (<3%), renal function abnormal (<3%), renal stone (<3%)

Respiratory: Pharyngitis (8% to 10%), sinusitis (6%), pneumonia (5%), asthma (3% to 10%), bronchitis (3%), bronchospasm (<3%), laryngeal edema (<3%), pulmonary embolus (<3%)

Miscellaneous: Diaphoresis (8% to 10%), herpes zoster (8%), viral infection (≤8%), bacterial infection (5%), herpes simplex (4%), sepsis (3%), flu-like syndrome (<3%)

<1%, postmarketing, and/or case reports: Dysuria, fungal infection (skin), hematuria, lethargy, pulmonary edema, pulmonary toxicity (fatal; in combination with fludarabine), uveitis/vision loss

Overdosage/Toxicology Doses higher than recommended (20-50mg/m2 divided over 5 days) are associated with deaths due to severe renal, hepatic, pulmonary, and CNS toxicity. Treatment of overdose is symptom-directed and supportive

Drug Interactions

Increased Effect/Toxicity: Fludarabine may enhance the pulmonary adverse/toxic effect of pentostatin; concurrent is not recommended.

Decreased Effect: Pentostatin may diminish the antineoplastic effect of nelarabine; conversion of nelarabine, a prodrug, to ARA-G (active form) may be inhibited by pentostatin.

Storage/Stability Store intact vials under refrigeration at 2°C to 8°C (36°F to 46°F); reconstituted, or further dilutions, are stable at room temperature for 8 hours in D_5W or 48 hours in NS.

Reconstitution Reconstitute with 5 mL SWFI to a concentration of 2 mg/mL. The solution may be further diluted in 25-50 mL NS or D_5W for infusion.

Compatibility Stable in LR, NS; **variable stability (consult detailed reference)** in D_5W.

Y-site administration: Compatible: Fludarabine, melphalan, ondansetron, paclitaxel, sargramostim.

Mechanism of Action Pentostatin is a purine antimetabolite that inhibits adenosine deaminase, preventing the deamination of adenosine to inosine. Accumulation of deoxyadenosine (dAdo) and deoxyadenosine 5'-triphosphate (dATP) results in a reduction of purine metabolism and DNA synthesis and cell death.

Pharmacodynamics/Kinetics

Distribution: I.V.: V_d: 36.1 L (20.1 L/m²); rapidly to body tissues

Protein binding: ~4%

Half-life elimination: Distribution half-life: 11-85 minutes; Terminal: 3-7 hours; renal impairment (Cl_{cr} <50 mL/minute): 4-18 hours

Excretion: Urine (~50% to 96%) within 24 hours (30% to 90% as unchanged drug)

Dosage I.V.: Adults (refer to individual protocols):

Hairy cell leukemia: 4 mg/m² every 2 weeks

CLL (unlabeled use): 4 mg/m² weekly for 3 weeks, then every 2 weeks

Cutaneous T-cell lymphoma (unlabeled use): 3.75-5 mg/m² daily for 3 days every 3 weeks

Acute GVHD (unlabeled use): 1.5 mg/m² daily for 3 days; may repeat after 2 weeks if needed

Chronic GVHD (unlabeled use): 4 mg/m² every 2 weeks for 12 doses; then 4 mg/m² every 3-4 weeks (if still improving)

Dosage adjustment in renal impairment: The FDA-approved labeling does not contain renal dosage adjustment guidelines; use with caution in patients with Cl_{cr} <60 mL/minute. Two patients with Cl_{cr} 50-60 mL/minute

(Continued)

Pentostatin *(Continued)*

achieved responses when treated with 2 mg/m^2/dose. The following guidelines have been used by some clinicians:

Kintzel, 1995:

Cl$_{cr}$ 46-60 mL/minute: Administer 70% of dose

Cl$_{cr}$ 31-45 mL/minute: Administer 60% of dose

Cl$_{cr}$ <30 mL/minute: Consider use of alternative drug

Lathia, 2002:

Cl$_{cr}$ 40-59 mL/minute: Administer 3 mg/m^2/dose

Cl$_{cr}$ 20-39 mL/minute: Administer 2 mg/m^2/dose

Combination Regimens

Leukemia, chronic lymphocytic:

PCR *on page 1267*

Pentostatin-Cyclophosphamide *on page 1270*

Administration Administer I.V. 20- to 30-minute infusion or I.V. bolus over 5 minutes. Hydrate with 500-1000 mL fluid prior to infusion and 500 mL after infusion.

Monitoring Parameters CBC with differential, platelet count, liver function, serum uric acid, renal function (creatinine clearance), bone marrow evaluation

Emetic Potential Moderate (30% to 60%)

Vesicant No

Dosage Forms Excipient information presented when available (limited, particularly for generics); consult specific product labeling.

Injection, powder for reconstitution [preservative free]: 10 mg [contains mannitol 50 mg]

Nipent®: 10 mg [contains mannitol 50 mg]

References

al-Razzak LA, Benedetti AE, Waugh WN, et al, "Chemical Stability of Pentostatin (NSC-218321), a Cytotoxic and Immunosuppressant Agent," *Pharm Res*, 1990, 7(5):452-60.

Bolanos-Meade J, Jacobsohn DA, Margolis J, et al, "Pentostatin in Steroid-Refractory Acute Graft-Versus-Host Disease," *J Clin Oncol*, 2005, 23(12):2661-8.

Brogden RN and Sorkin EM, "Pentostatin. A Review of Its Pharmacodynamic and Pharmacokinetic Properties, and Therapeutic Potential in Lymphoproliferative Disorders," *Drugs*, 1993, 46(4):652-77.

Catovsky D, "Clinical Experience With 2'-Deoxycoformycin," *Hematol Cell Ther*, 1996, 38(Suppl 2):103-7.

Dillman RO, "A New Chemotherapeutic Agent: Deoxycoformycin (Pentostatin)," *Semin Hematol*, 1994, 31(1):16-27.

Dillman RO, Mick R and McIntyre OR, "Pentostatin in Chronic Lymphocytic Leukemia: A Phase II Trial of Cancer and Leukemia Group B," *J Clin Oncol*, 1989, 7(4):433-8.

Grever MR, Siaw MFE, Jacob WF, et al, "The Biochemical and Clinical Consequences of 2'-Deoxycoformycin in Refractory Lymphoproliferative Malignancy," *Blood*, 1981, 57(3):406-17.

Jacobsohn DA, Chen AR, Zahurak M, et al, "Phase II Study of Pentostatin in Patients With Corticosteroid-Refractory Chronic Graft-Versus-Host Disease," *J Clin Oncol*, 2007, 25(27):4255-61.

Kane BJ, Kuhn JG, and Roush MK, "Pentostatin: An Adenosine Deaminase Inhibitor For the Treatment of Hairy Cell Leukemia," *Ann Pharmacother*, 1992, 26(7-8):939-47.

Kintzel PE and Dorr RT, "Anticancer Drug Renal Toxicity and Elimination: Dosing Guidelines for Altered Renal Function," *Cancer Treat Rev*, 1995, 21(1):33-64.

Kurzrock R, Pilat S, and Duvic M, "Pentostatin Therapy of T-Cell Lymphomas With Cutaneous Manifestations," *J Clin Oncol*, 1999, 17(10):3117-21.

Lathia C, Fleming GF, Meyer M, et al, "Pentostatin Pharmacokinetics and Dosing Recommendations in Patients With Mild Renal Impairment," *Cancer Chemother Pharmacol*, 2002, 50(2):121-6.

Margolis J and Grever MR, "Pentostatin (Nipent): A Review of Potential Toxicity and its Management," *Semin Oncol*, 2000, 27(2 Suppl 5):9-14.

Tsimberidou AM, Giles F, Duvic M, et al, "Phase II Study of Pentostatin in Advanced T-Cell Lymphoid Malignancies: Update of an M.D. Anderson Cancer Center Series," *Cancer*, 2004, 100(2):342-9.

Phytonadione (fye toe na DYE one)

Medication Safety Issues
Sound-alike/look-alike issues:
Mephyton® may be confused with melphalan, methadone

U.S. Brand Names Mephyton®

Index Terms Methylphytyl Napthoquinone; Phylloquinone; Phytomenadione; Vitamin K₁

Generic Available Yes

Canadian Brand Names AquaMEPHYTON®; Konakion; Mephyton®

Pharmacologic Category Vitamin, Fat Soluble

Use Prevention and treatment of hypoprothrombinemia caused by coumarin derivative-induced or other drug-induced vitamin K deficiency, hypoprothrombinemia caused by malabsorption or inability to synthesize vitamin K; hemorrhagic disease of the newborn

Unlabeled/Investigational Use Treatment of hypoprothrombinemia caused by anticoagulant rodenticides

Pregnancy Risk Factor C

Lactation Enters breast milk/use caution (AAP rates "compatible")

Labeled Contraindications Hypersensitivity to phytonadione or any component of the formulation

Warnings/Precautions [U.S. Boxed Warning]: Severe reactions resembling hypersensitivity (eg, anaphylaxis) reactions have occurred rarely during or immediately after I.V. administration. Allergic reactions have also occurred with I.M. and SubQ injections; oral administration is the safest. In obstructive jaundice or with biliary fistulas concurrent administration of bile salts is necessary. Manufacturers recommend the SubQ route over other parenteral routes. SubQ is less predictable when compared to the oral route. The American College of Chest Physicians recommends the I.V. route in patients with serious or life-threatening bleeding secondary to warfarin. The I.V. route should be restricted to emergency situations where oral phytonadione cannot be used. Efficacy is delayed regardless of route of administration; patient management may require other treatments in the interim. Administer a dose that will quickly lower the INR into a safe range without causing resistance to warfarin. Use caution in newborns especially premature infants; hemolysis, jaundice and hyperbilirubinemia have been reported (Continued)

Phytonadione *(Continued)*

with larger than recommended doses. Some dosage forms contain benzyl alcohol. In liver disease, if initial doses do not reverse coagulopathy then higher doses are unlikely to have any effect. Ineffective in hereditary hypo-prothrombinemia. Use caution with renal dysfunction (including premature infants). Injectable products may contain aluminum.

Adverse Reactions Parenteral administration: Frequency not defined.

Cardiovascular: Cyanosis, flushing, hypotension

Central nervous system: Dizziness

Dermatologic: Scleroderma-like lesions

Endocrine & metabolic: Hyperbilirubinemia (newborn; greater than recommended doses)

Gastrointestinal: Abnormal taste

Local: Injection site reactions

Respiratory: Dyspnea

Miscellaneous: Anaphylactoid reactions, diaphoresis, hypersensitivity reactions

Drug Interactions

Decreased Effect: Phytonadione may diminish the anticoagulant effect of coumarin derivatives (monitor INR). Phytonadione (oral) may not be properly absorbed when administered concurrently with orlistat (separate doses by at least 2 hours).

Storage/Stability

Injection: Store at 15°C to 30°C (59°F to 86°F). **Note:** Store Hospira product at 20°C to 25°C (68°F to 77°F).

Oral: Store tablets at 15°C to 30°C (59°F to 86°F). Protect from light.

Reconstitution Dilute injection solution in preservative-free NS, D_5W, or D_5NS.

Mechanism of Action Promotes liver synthesis of clotting factors (II, VII, IX, X); however, the exact mechanism as to this stimulation is unknown. Menadiol is a water soluble form of vitamin K; phytonadione has a more rapid and prolonged effect than menadione; menadiol sodium diphosphate (K_4) is half as potent as menadione (K_3).

Pharmacodynamics/Kinetics

Onset of action: Increased coagulation factors: Oral: 6-10 hours; I.V.: 1-2 hours

Peak effect: INR values return to normal: Oral: 24-48 hours; I.V.: 12-14 hours

Absorption: Oral: From intestines in presence of bile; SubQ: Variable

Metabolism: Rapidly hepatic

Excretion: Urine and feces

Dosage Note: According to the manufacturer, SubQ is the preferred parenteral route; I.M. route should be avoided due to the risk of hematoma formation; I.V. route should be restricted for emergency use only. The American College of Chest Physicians recommends the I.V. route in patients with serious or life-threatening bleeding secondary to use of vitamin K antagonists.

Adequate intake:

Children:

1-3 years: 30 mcg/day

4-8 years: 55 mcg/day

9-13 years: 60 mcg/day

14-18 years: 75 mcg/day

Adults: Males: 120 mcg/day; Females: 90 mcg/day

Hemorrhagic disease of the newborn:

Prophylaxis: I.M.: 0.5-1 mg within 1 hour of birth

Treatment: I.M., SubQ: 1 mg/dose/day; higher doses may be necessary if mother has been receiving oral anticoagulants

Hypoprothrombinemia due to drugs (other than coumarin derivatives) or factors limiting absorption or synthesis: Adults: Oral, SubQ, I.M., I.V.: Initial: 2.5-25 mg (rarely up to 50 mg)

Vitamin K deficiency secondary to coumarin derivative: Adults: See table:

Management of Elevated INR

INR	Symptom	Action
Above therapeutic range to <5	No significant bleeding	Lower or hold the next dose and monitor frequently; when INR approaches desired range, may resume dosing with a lower dose if INR was significantly above therapeutic range.
≥5 and <9	No significant bleeding	Omit the next 1or 2 doses; monitor INR and resume with a lower dose when the INR approaches the desired range. Alternatively, if there are other risk factors for bleeding, omit the next dose and give vitamin K_1 orally ≤5 mg; resume with a lower dose when the INR approaches the desired range. If rapid reversal is required for surgery, then given vitamin K_1 orally 2-4 mg and hold warfarin. Expect a response within 24 hours; another 1-2 mg may be given orally if needed.
≥9	No significant bleeding	Hold warfarin, give vitamin K_1 orally 5-10 mg, expect the INR to be reduced within 24-48 hours; monitor INR and administer additional vitamin K if necessary. Resume warfarin at lower doses when INR is in the desired range.
Any INR elevation	Serious bleeding	Hold warfarin, give vitamin K_1 (10 mg by slow I.V. infusion), and supplement with fresh plasma transfusion or prothrombin complex concentrate; recombinant factor VIIa is an alternative to prothrombin complex concentrate. Vitamin K_1 injection can be repeated every 12 hours.
Any INR elevation	Life-threatening bleeding	Hold warfarin, give prothrombin complex concentrate, supplemented with vitamin K_1 (10 mg by slow I.V. infusion); repeat if necessary. Recombinant factor VIIa is an alternative to prothrombin complex concentrate.

Note: Use of high doses of vitamin K_1 (10-15 mg) may cause resistance to warfarin for up to a week. Heparin or low molecular weight heparin can be given until the patient becomes responsive to warfarin.

Reference: Ansell J, Hirsh J, Poller L et al, "The Pharmacology and Management of the Vitamin K Antagonists," *Chest*, 2004, 126 (3 Suppl):204-33.

(Continued)

Phytonadione *(Continued)*

Administration

I.V. administration: Infuse slowly; rate of infusion should not exceed 1 mg/minute (3 mg/m²/minute in children and infants). The injectable route should be used only if the oral route is not feasible or there is a greater urgency to reverse anticoagulation.

Oral: The parenteral preparation has been administered orally to neonates.

Monitoring Parameters PT, INR

Emetic Potential Very low (<10%)

Vesicant No

Dosage Forms Excipient information presented when available (limited, particularly for generics); consult specific product labeling.

Injection, aqueous colloidal: 2 mg/mL (0.5 mL); 10 mg/mL (1 mL)

Tablet: 100 mcg [OTC]

Mephyton®: 5 mg

Extemporaneous Preparations A 1 mg/mL oral suspension was stable for only 3 days when refrigerated when compounded as follows:

Triturate six 5 mg tablets in a mortar, reduce to a fine powder, then add 5 mL each of water and methylcellulose 1% while mixing; then transfer to a graduate and qs to 30 mL with sorbitol

Shake well before using and keep in refrigerator

Nahata MC and Hipple TF, *Pediatric Drug Formulations*, 3rd ed, Cincinnati, OH: Harvey Whitney Books Co, 1997.

References

Andersen P and Godal HC, "Predictable Reduction in Anticoagulant Activity of Warfarin by Small Amounts of Vitamin K," *Acta Med Scand*, 1975, 198:269-70.

Ansell J, Hirsh J, Poller L, et al, "The Pharmacology and Management of the Vitamin K Antagonists: The Seventh ACCP Conference on Antithrombotic and Thrombolytic Therapy," *Chest*, 2004, 126(3 Suppl):204-33.

Barash P, Kitahata LM, and Mandel S, "Acute Cardiovascular Collapse After Intravenous Phytonadione," *Anesth Analg*, 1976, 55(2):304-6.

Crowther MA, Douketis JD, Schnurr T, et al, "Oral Vitamin K Lowers the International Normalized Ratio More Rapidly Than Subcutaneous Vitamin K in the Treatment of Warfarin-Associated Coagulopathy. A Randomized, Controlled Trial," *Ann Intern Med*, 2002, 137(4):251-4.

"Dietary Reference Intakes for Vitamin A, Vitamin K, Arsenic, Boron, Chromium, Copper, Iodine, Iron, Manganese, Molybdenum, Nickel, Silicon, Vanadium, and Zinc," Food and Nutrition Board, Institute of Medicine. National Academy of Sciences, Washington, DC: National Academy Press, 2001, 162-84.

Fiore LD, Scola MA, Cantillon CE, et al, "Anaphylactoid Reactions to Vitamin K," *J Thromb Thrombolysis*, 2001, 11(2): 175-83.

Harrell CC and Kline SS, "Oral Vitamin K1: An Option to Reduce Warfarin's Activity," *Ann Pharmacother*, 1995, 29(12):1228-32.

Hopkins CS, "Adverse Reaction to a Cremophor-Containing Preparation of Intravenous Vitamin K," *Intensive Therapy Clin Monit*, 1988, 9:254-5.

Martinez-Abad M, Delgado F, Palop V, et al, "Vitamin K₁ and Anaphylactic Shock," *DICP*, 1991, 25(7-8):871-2.

Monagle P, Michelson AD, Bovill E, et al, "Antithrombotic Therapy in Children," *Chest*, 2001, 119(1 Suppl):344-70.

Shearer MJ, "Vitamin K," *Lancet*, 1995, 345(8944):229-34.

Watt BE, Proudfoot AT, Bradberry SM, et al, "Anticoagulant Rodenticides," *Toxicol Rev*, 2005, 24(4):259-69.

Weibert RT, Le DT, Kayser SR, et al, "Correction of Excessive Anticoagulation With Low-Dose Oral Vitamin K1," *Ann Intern Med*, 1997, 126(12):959-62.

- ◆ **Pidorubicin** *see* Epirubicin *on page 383*
- ◆ **Pidorubicin Hydrochloride** *see* Epirubicin *on page 383*

Pilocarpine (pye loe KAR peen)

Medication Safety Issues
Sound-alike/look-alike issues:
Isopto® Carpine may be confused with Isopto® Carbachol
Salagen® may be confused with Salacid®, selegiline

International issues:
Salagen® may be confused with Poagen® which is a brand name for grass pollen extract in Portugal

Related Information
Oral Mucositis / Stomatitis *on page 1332*

U.S. Brand Names Isopto® Carpine; Pilopine HS®; Salagen®

Index Terms Pilocarpine Hydrochloride

Generic Available Yes: Hydrochloride solution, tablet

Canadian Brand Names Diocarpine; Isopto® Carpine; Pilopine HS®; Salagen®

Pharmacologic Category Cholinergic Agonist; Ophthalmic Agent, Antiglaucoma; Ophthalmic Agent, Miotic

Use
Ophthalmic: Management of chronic simple glaucoma, chronic and acute angle-closure glaucoma

Oral: Symptomatic treatment of xerostomia caused by salivary gland hypofunction resulting from radiotherapy for cancer of the head and neck or Sjögren's syndrome

Unlabeled/Investigational Use Counter effects of cycloplegics

Pregnancy Risk Factor C

Lactation Excretion in breast milk unknown/not recommended

Labeled Contraindications Hypersensitivity to pilocarpine or any component of the formulation; acute inflammatory disease of the anterior chamber of the eye; in addition, tablets are also contraindicated in patients with uncontrolled asthma, angle-closure glaucoma, severe hepatic impairment

Warnings/Precautions Use caution with cardiovascular disease; patients may have difficulty compensating for transient changes in hemodynamics or rhythm induced by pilocarpine.

Ophthalmic products: May cause decreased visual acuity, especially at night or with reduced lighting.

Oral tablets: Use caution with controlled asthma, chronic bronchitis or COPD; may increase airway resistance, bronchial smooth muscle tone, and bronchial secretions. Use caution with cholelithiasis, biliary tract disease, nephrolithiasis; adjust dose with moderate hepatic impairment.

Adverse Reactions
Ophthalmic: Frequency not defined:
Cardiovascular: Hypertension, tachycardia
Gastrointestinal: Diarrhea, nausea, salivation, vomiting
Ocular: Burning, ciliary spasm, conjunctival vascular congestion, corneal granularity (gel 10%), lacrimation, lens opacity, myopia, retinal detachment, supraorbital or temporal headache, visual acuity decreased
Respiratory: Bronchial spasm, pulmonary edema
Miscellaneous: Diaphoresis

Oral (frequency varies by indication and dose):
>10%:
Cardiovascular: Flushing (8% to 13%)
Central nervous system: Chills (3% to 15%), dizziness (5% to 12%), headache (11%)

(Continued)

Pilocarpine *(Continued)*

Gastrointestinal: Nausea (6% to 15%)

Genitourinary: Urinary frequency (9% to 12%)

Neuromuscular & skeletal: Weakness (2% to 12%)

Respiratory: Rhinitis (5% to 14%)

Miscellaneous: Diaphoresis (29% to 68%)

1% to 10%:

Cardiovascular: Edema (<1% to 5%), facial edema, hypertension (3%), palpitation, tachycardia

Central nervous system: Pain (4%), fever, somnolence

Dermatologic: Pruritus, rash

Gastrointestinal: Diarrhea (4% to 7%), dyspepsia (7%), vomiting (3% to 4%), constipation, flatulence, glossitis, salivation increased, stomatitis, taste perversion

Genitourinary: Vaginitis, urinary incontinence

Neuromuscular & skeletal: Myalgias, tremor

Ocular: Lacrimation (6%), amblyopia (4%), abnormal vision, blurred vision, conjunctivitis

Otic: Tinnitus

Respiratory: Cough increased, dysphagia, epistaxis, sinusitis

Miscellaneous: Allergic reaction, voice alteration

<1%: Abnormal dreams, abnormal thinking, alopecia, angina pectoris, anorexia, anxiety, aphasia, appetite increased, arrhythmia, arthralgia, arthritis, bilirubinemia, body odor, bone disorder, bradycardia, breast pain, bronchitis, cataract, cholelithiasis, colitis, confusion, contact dermatitis, cyst, deafness, depression, dry eyes, dry mouth, dry skin, dyspnea, dysuria, ear pain, ECG abnormality, eczema, emotional lability, eructation, erythema nodosum, esophagitis, exfoliative dermatitis, eye hemorrhage, eye pain, gastritis, gastroenteritis, gastrointestinal disorder, gingivitis, glaucoma, hematuria, hepatitis, herpes simplex, hiccup, hyperkinesias, hypoesthesia, hypoglycemia, hypotension, hypothermia, insomnia, intracranial hemorrhage, laryngismus, laryngitis, leg cramps, leukopenia, liver function test abnormal, lymphadenopathy, mastitis, melena, menorrhagia, metrorrhagia, migraine, moniliasis, myasthenia, MI, neck pain, photosensitivity reaction, nervousness, ovarian disorder, pancreatitis, paresthesia, parotid gland enlargement, peripheral edema, platelet abnormality, pneumonia, pyuria, salivary gland enlargement, salpingitis, seborrhea, skin ulcer, speech disorder, sputum increased, stridor, syncope, taste loss, tendon disorder, tenosynovitis, thrombocythemia, thrombocytopenia, thrombosis, tongue disorder, twitching, urethral pain, urinary impairment, urinary urgency, vaginal hemorrhage, vaginal moniliasis, vesiculobullous rash, WBC abnormality, yawning

Overdosage/Toxicology Symptoms of overdose include bronchospasm, bradycardia, involuntary urination, vomiting, hypotension, and tremor. Atropine is the treatment of choice for intoxications manifesting with significant muscarinic symptoms. Atropine I.V. 2-4 mg every 3-60 minutes should be repeated to control symptoms and then continued as needed for 1-2 days following acute ingestion. Epinephrine 0.1-1 mg SubQ may be useful for reversing severe cardiovascular or pulmonary sequelae.

Drug Interactions

Cytochrome P450 Effect: Inhibits CYP2A6 (weak), 2E1 (weak), 3A4 (weak)

Increased Effect/Toxicity: Concurrent use with beta-blockers may cause conduction disturbances.

Decreased Effect: May decrease effects of anticholinergic drugs (atropine, ipratropium).

Ethanol/Nutrition/Herb Interactions Food: Avoid administering oral formulation with high-fat meal; fat decreases the rate of absorption, maximum concentration and increases the time it takes to reach maximum concentration.

Storage/Stability

Gel: Store at room temperature of 2°C to 27°C (36°F to 80°F); do not freeze. Avoid excessive heat.

Tablets: Store at controlled room temperature of 15°C to 30°C (59°F to 86°F).

Mechanism of Action Directly stimulates cholinergic receptors in the eye causing miosis (by contraction of the iris sphincter), loss of accommodation (by constriction of ciliary muscle), and lowering of intraocular pressure (with decreased resistance to aqueous humor outflow)

Pharmacodynamics/Kinetics

Onset of action:

Ophthalmic: Miosis: 10-30 minutes; Intraocular pressure reduction: 1 hour

Oral: 20 minutes

Duration:

Ophthalmic: Miosis: 4-8 hours; Intraocular pressure reduction: 4-12 hours

Oral: 3-5 hours

Half-life elimination: Oral: 0.76-1.35 hours; increased with hepatic impairment

Excretion: Urine

Dosage Adults:

Ophthalmic:

Glaucoma:

Solution: Instill 1-2 drops up to 6 times/day; adjust the concentration and frequency as required to control elevated intraocular pressure

Gel: Instill 0.5" ribbon into lower conjunctival sac once daily at bedtime

To counteract the mydriatic effects of sympathomimetic agents (unlabeled use): Solution: Instill 1 drop of a 1% solution in the affected eye

Oral: Xerostomia:

Following head and neck cancer: 5 mg 3 times/day, titration up to 10 mg 3 times/day may be considered for patients who have not responded adequately; do not exceed 2 tablets/dose

Sjögren's syndrome: 5 mg 4 times/day

Dosage adjustment in hepatic impairment: Oral: Patients with moderate impairment: 5 mg 2 times/day regardless of indication; adjust dose based on response and tolerability. Do not use with severe impairment (Child-Pugh score 10-15).

Administration

Oral: Avoid administering with high-fat meal. Fat decreases the rate of absorption, maximum concentration, and increases the time it takes to reach maximum concentration.

Ophthalmic: If both solution and gel are used, the solution should be applied first, then the gel at least 5 minutes later. Following administration of the solution, finger pressure should be applied on the lacrimal sac for 1-2 minutes.

Monitoring Parameters Intraocular pressure, funduscopic exam, visual field testing

Patient Information Ophthalmic: May sting on instillation; report sweating, urinary retention; usually causes difficulty in dark adaptation; advise patients to use caution while night driving or performing hazardous tasks in poor (Continued)

Pilocarpine *(Continued)*

illumination; after topical instillation, finger pressure should be applied to lacrimal sac to decrease drainage into the nose and throat and minimize possible systemic absorption

Special Geriatric Considerations Assure the patient or a caregiver can adequately administer ophthalmic medication dosage form.

Emetic Potential Very low (<10%)

Dosage Forms Excipient information presented when available (limited, particularly for generics); consult specific product labeling.

Gel, ophthalmic, as hydrochloride (Pilopine HS®): 4% (4 g) [contains benzalkonium chloride]

Solution, ophthalmic, as hydrochloride: 0.5% (15 mL); 1% (2 mL, 15 mL); 2% (2 mL, 15 mL); 3% (15 mL); 4% (2 mL, 15 mL); 6% (15 mL) [may contain benzalkonium chloride]

Isopto® Carpine: 1% (15 mL); 2% (15 mL); 4% (15 mL) [contains benzalkonium chloride]

Tablet, as hydrochloride: 5 mg, 7.5 mg

Salagen®: 5 mg, 7.5 mg

References

Hawthorne M and Sullivan K, "Pilocarpine for Radiation-Induced Xerostomia in Head and Neck Cancer," *Int J Palliat Nurs*, 2000, 6(5):228-32.

Jacobs CD and van der Pas M, "A Multicenter Maintenance Study of Oral Pilocarpine Tablets for Radiation-Induced Xerostomia," *Oncology*, 1996, 10(3 Suppl):16-20.

Johnson JT, Ferretti GA, Nethery WJ, et al, "Oral Pilocarpine for Postirradiation Xerostomia in Patients With Head and Neck Cancer," *N Engl J Med*, 1993, 329(6):390-5.

LeVeque FG, Montgomery M, Potter D, et al, "A Multicenter, Randomized, Double-Blind, Placebo-Controlled, Dose-Titration Study of Oral Pilocarpine for Treatment of Radiation-Induced Xerostomia in Head and Neck Cancer Patients," *J Clin Oncol*, 1993, 11(6):1124-31.

Rieke JW, Hafermann MD, Johnson JT, et al, "Oral Pilocarpine for Radiation-Induced Xerostomia: Integrated Efficacy and Safety Results From Two Prospective Randomized Clinical Trials," *Int J Radiat Oncol Biol Phys*, 1995, 31(3):661-9.

Schuller DE, Stevens P, Clausen KP, et al, "Treatment of Radiation Side Effects With Oral Pilocarpine," *J Surg Oncol*, 1989, 42(4):272-6.

Taylor SE, "Efficacy and Economic Evaluation of Pilocarpine in Treating Radiation-Induced Xerostomia," *Expert Opin Pharmacother*, 2003, 4(9):1489-97.

♦ **Pilocarpine Hydrochloride** *see* Pilocarpine *on page 899*

♦ **Pilopine HS®** *see* Pilocarpine *on page 899*

Piperacillin and Tazobactam Sodium

(pi PER a sil in & ta zoe BAK tam SOW dee um)

Medication Safety Issues

Sound-alike/look-alike issues:

Zosyn® may be confused with Zofran®, Zyvox®

U.S. Brand Names Zosyn®

Index Terms Piperacillin Sodium and Tazobactam Sodium; Tazobactam and Piperacillin

Generic Available No

Canadian Brand Names Tazocin®

Pharmacologic Category Antibiotic, Penicillin

Use Treatment of moderate-to-severe infections caused by susceptible organisms, including infections of the lower respiratory tract (community-acquired pneumonia, nosocomial pneumonia); urinary tract; uncomplicated and complicated skin and skin structures; gynecologic (endometritis, pelvic inflammatory disease); bone and joint infections; intra-abdominal infections (appendicitis with rupture/abscess, peritonitis); and septicemia. Tazobactam expands activity of piperacillin to include beta-lactamase producing strains of *S. aureus, H. influenzae, Bacteroides,* and other gram-negative bacteria.

Pregnancy Risk Factor B

Lactation Enters breast milk/use caution

Labeled Contraindications Hypersensitivity to penicillins, beta-lactamase inhibitors, or any component of the formulation

Warnings/Precautions Bleeding disorders have been observed, particularly in patients with renal impairment; discontinue if thrombocytopenia or bleeding occurs. Due to sodium load and to the adverse effects of high serum concentrations of penicillins, dosage modification is required in patients with impaired or underdeveloped renal function; use with caution in patients with seizures or in patients with history of beta-lactam allergy; associated with an increased incidence of rash and fever in cystic fibrosis patients. Prolonged use may result in fungal or bacterial superinfection, including *C. difficile*-associated diarrhea (CDAD) and pseudomembranous colitis; CDAD has been observed <2 months postantibiotic treatment. Safety and efficacy have not been established in children <2 months of age.

Adverse Reactions

>10%: Gastrointestinal: Diarrhea (7% to 11%)

>1% to 10%:

Cardiovascular: Hypertension (2%)

Central nervous system: Insomnia (7%), headache (8%), fever (2% to 5%), agitation (2%), pain (2%)

Dermatologic: Rash (4%), pruritus (3%)

Gastrointestinal: Constipation (1% to 8%), nausea (7%), vomiting (3% to 4%), dyspepsia (3%), stool changes (2%), abdominal pain (1% to 2%)

Hepatic: Transaminases increased

Local: Local reaction (3%), abscess (2%)

Respiratory: Pharyngitis (2%)

Miscellaneous: Moniliasis (2%), sepsis (2%), infection (2%)

≤1%, postmarketing, and/or case reports: Agranulocytosis, anaphylaxis/anaphylactoid reaction, anemia, anxiety, arrhythmia, arthralgia, atrial fibrillation, back pain, bradycardia, bronchospasm, candidiasis, cardiac arrest, cardiac failure, circulatory failure, chest pain, cholestatic jaundice, confusion, convulsions, coughing, depression, diaphoresis, dizziness, dyspnea, dysuria, edema, epistaxis, erythema multiforme, flatulence, flushing, gastritis, genital pruritus, hallucination, hematuria, hemolytic anemia, hemorrhage, hepatitis, hiccough, hypoglycemia, hypotension, ileus, incontinence, inflammation, injection site reaction, interstitial nephritis, leukorrhea, malaise, mesenteric embolism, myalgia, myocardial infarction, oliguria, pancytopenia, phlebitis, photophobia, pseudomembranous colitis, pulmonary edema, pulmonary embolism, purpura, renal failure, rhinitis, rigors, Stevens-Johnson syndrome, syncope, tachycardia (supraventricular and ventricular), taste perversion, thirst, thrombocytopenia, thrombocytosis, thrombophlebitis, tinnitus, toxic epidermal necrolysis, tremor, ulcerative stomatitis, urinary retention, vaginitis, ventricular fibrillation, vertigo

Overdosage/Toxicology Symptoms of penicillin overdose include neuromuscular hypersensitivity (eg, agitation, hallucinations, asterixis, encephalopathy, confusion, and seizures). Electrolyte imbalance may occur if the preparation contains potassium or sodium salts, especially in renal dysfunction. Hemodialysis may be helpful to aid in removal of the drug from blood; otherwise, treatment is supportive or symptom-directed.

(Continued)

Piperacillin and Tazobactam Sodium *(Continued)*

Drug Interactions

Increased Effect/Toxicity: Probenecid may increase penicillin levels. Neuromuscular blockers may increase duration of blockade. Penicillins may increase methotrexate exposure; clinical significance has not been established.

Decreased Effect: Fusidic acid and tetracyclines may decrease penicillin effectiveness. Aminoglycosides may cause physical inactivation of aminoglycosides in the presence of high concentrations of piperacillin and potential toxicity in patients with mild-moderate renal dysfunction. Although anecdotal reports suggest oral contraceptive efficacy could be reduced by penicillins, this has been refuted by more rigorous scientific and clinical data.

Storage/Stability

Vials: Store at controlled room temperature of 20°C to 25°C (68°F to 77°F). Use single-dose vials immediately after reconstitution (discard unused portions after 24 hours at room temperature and 48 hours if refrigerated). After reconstitution, vials or solution are stable in NS or D_5W for 24 hours at room temperature and 48 hours (vials) or 7 days (solution) when refrigerated.

Premixed solution: Store frozen at -20°C (-4°F). Thawed solution is stable for 24 hours at room temperature or 14 days under refrigeration; do not refreeze.

Reconstitution Reconstitute with 5 mL of diluent per 1 g of piperacillin and then further dilute.

Compatibility Stable in dextran 6% in NS, D_5W, NS, sterile water for injection; LR (EDTA-formulated product only); **variable stability (consult detailed reference)** in peritoneal dialysis solution.

Y-site administration: Compatible: Amikacin (EDTA formulated product only), aminophylline, aztreonam, bleomycin, bumetanide, buprenorphine, butorphanol, calcium gluconate, carboplatin, carmustine, cefepime, cimetidine, clindamycin, co-trimoxazole, cyclophosphamide, cytarabine, dexamethasone sodium phosphate, diphenhydramine, docetaxel, dopamine, enalaprilat, etoposide, etoposide phosphate, floxuridine, fluconazole, fludarabine, fluorouracil, furosemide, gentamicin (EDTA formulated product only), granisetron, heparin, hydrocortisone sodium phosphate, hydrocortisone sodium succinate, hydromorphone, ifosfamide, leucovorin, linezolid, lorazepam, magnesium sulfate, mannitol, meperidine, mesna, methotrexate, methylprednisolone sodium succinate, metoclopramide, metronidazole, morphine, ondansetron, plicamycin, potassium chloride, ranitidine, remifentanil, sargramostim, sodium bicarbonate, thiotepa, vinblastine, vincristine, zidovudine. **Incompatible:** Acyclovir, alatrofloxacin, amphotericin B, amphotericin B cholesteryl sulfate complex, chlorpromazine, cisplatin, dacarbazine, daunorubicin, dobutamine, doxorubicin, doxorubicin liposome, doxycycline, droperidol, famotidine, ganciclovir, gatifloxacin, gemcitabine, haloperidol, hydroxyzine, idarubicin, minocycline, mitomycin, mitoxantrone, nalbuphine, prochlorperazine edisylate, promethazine, streptozocin, tobramycin. **Variable (consult detailed reference):** Cisatracurium, vancomycin.

Compatibility when admixed: Compatible: Potassium chloride. **Incompatible:** Aminoglycosides.

Mechanism of Action Inhibits bacterial cell wall synthesis by binding to one or more of the penicillin binding proteins (PBPs); which in turn inhibits the final transpeptidation step of peptidoglycan synthesis in bacterial cell walls, thus inhibiting cell wall biosynthesis. Bacteria eventually lyse due to ongoing activity of cell wall autolytic enzymes (autolysins and murein hydrolases) while cell wall assembly is arrested. Tazobactam inhibits many beta-lactamases, including staphylococcal penicillinase and Richmond and Sykes types II, III, IV, and V, including extended spectrum enzymes; it has only limited activity against class I beta-lactamases other than class Ic types.

Pharmacodynamics/Kinetics Both AUC and peak concentrations are dose proportional; hepatic impairment does not affect kinetics

Distribution: Well into lungs, intestinal mucosa, skin, muscle, uterus, ovary, prostate, gallbladder, and bile; penetration into CSF is low in subject with noninflamed meninges

Protein binding: Piperacillin and tazobactam: ~30%

Metabolism:

Piperacillin: 6% to 9% to desethyl metabolite (weak activity)

Tazobactam: ~26% to inactive metabolite

Half-life elimination: Piperacillin and tazobactam: 0.7-1.2 hours

Time to peak, plasma: Immediately following infusion of 30 minutes

Excretion: Clearance of both piperacillin and tazobactam are directly proportional to renal function

Piperacillin: Urine (68% as unchanged drug); feces (10% to 20%)

Tazobactam: Urine (80% as inactive metabolite)

Dosage

Usual dosage range:

Children: I.V.:

2-8 months: 80 mg of piperacillin component/kg every 8 hours

≥9 months and ≤40 kg: 100 mg of piperacillin component/kg every 8 hours

Adults: I.V.: 3.375 g every 6 hours **or** 4.5 g every 6-8 hours; maximum: 18 g/day

Indication-specific dosing: I.V.:

Children: **Note:** Dosing based on piperacillin component:

Appendicitis, peritonitis:

2-8 months: 80 mg/kg every 8 hours

≥9 months and ≤40 kg: 100 mg/kg every 8 hours

>40 kg: refer to Adult dosing

Cystic fibrosis, pseudomonal infections (unlabeled use): 350-450 mg/kg/day in divided doses

Adults:

Diverticulitis, intra-abdominal abscess, peritonitis: I.V.: 3.375 g every 6 hours; **Note:** Some clinicians use 4.5 g every 8 hours for empiric coverage since the %time>MIC is similar between the regimens for most pathogens; however, this regimen is NOT recommended for nosocomial pneumonia or *Pseudomonas* coverage.

Pneumonia (nosocomial): I.V.: 4.5 g every 6 hours for 7-14 days (when used empirically, combination with an aminoglycoside or antipseudomonal fluoroquinolone is recommended; consider discontinuation of additional agent if *P. aeruginosa* is not isolated)

Severe infections: I.V.: 3.375 g every 6 hours for 7-10 days; **Note:** Some clinicians use 4.5 g every 8 hours for empiric coverage since the %time>MIC is similar between the regimens for most pathogens; however, this regimen is NOT recommended for nosocomial pneumonia or *Pseudomonas* coverage.

Dosing interval in renal impairment:

Cl_{cr} 20-40 mL/minute: Administer 2.25 g every 6 hours (3.375 g every 6 hours for nosocomial pneumonia)

(Continued)

Piperacillin and Tazobactam Sodium *(Continued)*

Cl_{cr} <20 mL/minute: Administer 2.25 g every 8 hours (2.25 g every 6 hours for nosocomial pneumonia)

Hemodialysis/CAPD: Administer 2.25 g every 12 hours (2.25 g every 8 hours for nosocomial pneumonia) with an additional dose of 0.75 g after each hemodialysis session

Continuous renal replacement therapy (CRRT): Drug clearance is highly dependent on the method of renal replacement, filter type, and flow rate. Appropriate dosing requires close monitoring of pharmacologic response, signs of adverse reactions due to drug accumulation, as well as drug levels in relation to target trough (if appropriate). The following are general recommendations only (based on dialysate flow/ultrafiltration rates of 1 L/hour) and should not supersede clinical judgment:

CVVH: 2.25 g every 6 hours

CVVHD/CVVHDF: 2.25-3.375 g every 6 hours

Note: Higher dose of 3.375 g should be considered when treating resistant pathogens (especially *Pseudomonas*); alternative recommendations suggest dosing of 4.5 g every 8 hours; regardless of regimen, there is some concern of tazobactam (TAZ) accumulation, given its lower clearance relative to piperacillin (PIP). Some clinicians advocate dosing with PIP to alternate with PIP/TAZ, particularly in CVVH-dependent patients, to lessen this concern.

Administration Administer by I.V. infusion over 30 minutes

Some penicillins (eg, carbenicillin, ticarcillin and piperacillin) have been shown to inactivate aminoglycosides *in vitro*. This has been observed to a greater extent with tobramycin and gentamicin, while amikacin has shown greater stability against inactivation. Concurrent use of these agents may pose a risk of reduced antibacterial efficacy *in vivo*, particularly in the setting of profound renal impairment. However, definitive clinical evidence is lacking. If combination penicillin/aminoglycoside therapy is desired in a patient with renal dysfunction, separation of doses (if feasible), and routine monitoring of aminoglycoside levels, CBC, and clinical response should be considered. **Note:** Reformulated Zosyn® containing EDTA has been shown to be compatible *in vitro* for Y-site infusion with amikacin and gentamicin, but not compatible with tobramycin.

Monitoring Parameters Creatinine, BUN, CBC with differential, PT, PTT; signs of bleeding; monitor for signs of anaphylaxis during first dose

Test Interactions Positive Coombs' [direct] test; false positive reaction for urine glucose using copper-reduction method (Clinitest®); may result in false positive results with the Platelia® *Aspergillus* enzyme immunoassay (EIA)

Some penicillin derivatives may accelerate the degradation of aminoglycosides *in vitro*, leading to a potential underestimation of aminoglycoside serum concentration. **Note:** Reformulated Zosyn® containing EDTA has been shown to be compatible *in vitro* for Y-site infusion with amikacin and gentamicin, but not compatible with tobramycin.

Dietary Considerations

Infusion, premixed: 2.25 g contains sodium 5.58 mEq (128 mg); 3.375 g contains sodium 8.38 mEq (192 mg); 4.5 g contains sodium 11.17 mEq (256 mg)

Injection, powder for reconstitution: 2.25 g contains sodium 5.58 mEq (128 mg); 3.375 g contains sodium 8.38 mEq (192 mg); 4.5 g contains sodium 11.17 mEq (256 mg); 40.5 g contains sodium 100.4 mEq (2304 mg, bulk pharmacy vial)

Special Geriatric Considerations Has not been studied exclusively in the elderly.

Emetic Potential Very low (<10%)

Vesicant No

Dosage Forms Excipient information presented when available (limited, particularly for generics); consult specific product labeling.

Note: 8:1 ratio of piperacillin sodium/tazobactam sodium

Infusion [premixed iso-osmotic solution, frozen]:

2.25 g: Piperacillin 2 g and tazobactam 0.25 g (50 mL) [contains sodium 5.58 mEq (128 mg) and EDTA]

3.375 g: Piperacillin 3 g and tazobactam 0.375 g (50 mL) [contains sodium 8.38 mEq (192 mg) and EDTA]

4.5 g: Piperacillin 4 g and tazobactam 0.5 g (50 mL) [contains sodium 11.17 mEq (256 mg) and EDTA]

Injection, powder for reconstitution:

2.25 g: Piperacillin 2 g and tazobactam 0.25 g [contains sodium 5.58 mEq (128 mg) and EDTA]

3.375 g: Piperacillin 3 g and tazobactam 0.375 g [contains sodium 8.38 mEq (192 mg) and EDTA]

4.5 g: Piperacillin 4 g and tazobactam 0.5 g [contains sodium 11.17 mEq (256 mg) and EDTA]

40.5 g: Piperacillin 36 g and tazobactam 4.5 g [contains sodium 100.4 mEq (2304 mg) and EDTA; bulk pharmacy vial]

References

American Thoracic Society and Infectious Diseases Society of America, "Guidelines for the Management of Adults With Hospital-Acquired, Ventilator-Associated, and Health-care-Associated Pneumonia," *Am J Respir Crit Care Med*, 2005, 171(4):388-416.

Bryson HM and Brogden RN, "Piperacillin/Tazobactam. A Review of its Antibacterial Activity, Pharmacokinetic Properties, and Therapeutic Potential," *Drugs*, 1994, 47(3):506-35.

Chow MS, Quintiliani, and Nightingale CH, "*In Vivo* Inactivation of Tobramycin by Ticarcillin. A Case Report," *JAMA*, 1982, 247(5):658-9.

Daly JS, Dodge RA, Glew RH, et al, "Effect of Time and Temperature on Inactivation of Aminoglycosides by Ampicillin at Neonatal Dosages," *J Perinatol*, 1997, 17(1):42-5.

Dowell JA, Korth-Bradley J, Milisci M, et al, "Evaluating Possible Pharmacokinetic Interactions Between Tobramycin, Piperacillin, and a Combination of Piperacillin and Tazobactam in Patients With Various Degrees of Renal Impairment," *J Clin Pharmacol*, 2001, 41:979-86.

Farchione LA, "Inactivation of Aminoglycosides by Penicillins," *J Antimicrob Chemother*, 1982, 8(Suppl A):27-36.

Fuchs PC, Stickel S, Anderson PH, et al, "*In Vitro* Inactivation of Aminoglycosides by Sulbactam, Other Beta-Lactams, and Sulbactam-Beta-Lactam Combinations," *Antimicrob Agents Chemother*, 1991, 35(1):182-4.

Halstenson CE, Wong MO, Herman CS, et al, "Effect of Concomitant Administration of Piperacillin on the Dispositions on Isepamicin and Gentamicin in Patients With End-Stage Renal Disease," *Antimicrob Agents Chemother*, 1992, 36(9):1832-36.

Hitt CM, Patel KB, Nicolau DP, et al, "Influence of Piperacillin-Tazobactam on Pharmacokinetics of Gentamicin Given Once Daily," *Am J Health Syst Pharm*, 1997, 54(23):2704-8.

Kim M-K, Capitano B, Mattoes HM, et al, "Pharmacokinetic and Pharmacodynamic Evaluation of Two Dosing Regimens for Piperacillin-Tazobactam," *Pharmacother*, 2002, 22(5):569-77.

Konishi H, Goto M, Nakamoto Y, et al, "Tobramycin Inactivation by Carbenicillin, Ticarcillin, and Piperacillin," *Antimicrob Agents Chemother*, 1983, 23(5):653-57.

Lambourne J, Kitchen J, Hughes C, et al, "Piperacillin/Tazobactam-Induced Paresthesiae," *Ann Pharmacother*, 2006, 40(5):977-9.

Lau A, Lee M, Flascha S, et al, "Effect of Piperacillin on Tobramycin Pharmacokinetics in Patients with Normal Renal Function," *Antimicrob Agents Chemother*, 1983, 24(4):533-37.

Nelson Textbook of Pediatrics, 17th ed, Behrman RE, Kliegman RM, and Jenson HB, eds, Philadelphia, PA: WB Saunders Co, 2004.

Perez-Vazquez A, Pastor JM, and Riancho JA, "Immune Thrombocytopenia Caused by Piperacillin/Tazobactam," *Clin Infect Dis*, 1998, 27(3):650-1.

Reed MD, "The Pathophysiology and Treatment of Cystic Fibrosis," *J Pediatr Pharm Pract*, 1997, 2:285"305.

Reichardt P, Handrick W, Linke A, et al, "Leukocytopenia, Thrombocytopenia and Fever Related to Piperacillin/Tazobactam Treatment — a Retrospective Analysis in 38 Children With Cystic Fibrosis," *Infection*, 1999, 27(6):355-6.

(Continued)

Piperacillin and Tazobactam Sodium *(Continued)*

Russoe ME and Atkins-Thor E, "Gentamicin and Ticarcillin in Subjects With End-Stage Renal Disease. Comparison of Two Assay Methods and Evaluation of Inactivation Rate," *Clin Nephrol*, 1981, 15(4):175-80.

Sanders WE Jr and Sanders CC, "Piperacillin/Tazobactam: A Critical Review of the Evolving Clinical Literature," *Clin Infect Dis*, 1996, 22(1):107-23.

Schoonover LL, Occhipinti DJ, Rodvold KA, et al, "Piperacillin/Tazobactam: A New Beta-Lactam/Beta-Lactamase Inhibitor Combination," *Ann Pharmacother*, 1995, 29(5):501-14.

Sorgel F and Kinzig M, "The Chemistry, Pharmacokinetics and Tissue Distribution of Piperacillin/ Tazobactam," *J Antimicrob Chemother*, 1993, 31(Suppl A):39-60.

Teddy Bear Book: Pediatric Injectable Drugs, 7th ed, Phelps SJ and Hak EB, eds, Bethesda, MD: American Society of Health-System Pharmacists, 2003.

Thompson MIB, Russo ME, Saxon BJ, et al, "Gentamicin Inactivation by Piperacillin or Carbenicillin in Patients With End-Stage Renal Disease," *Antimicrob Agents Chemother*, 1982, 21(2):268-73.

Trotman RL, Williamson JC, Shoemaker DM, et al, "Antibiotic Dosing in Critically Ill Adult Patients Receiving Continuous Renal Replacement Therapy," *Clin Infect Dis*, 2005, 41(8):1159-66.

Valtonen M, Tiula E, Takkunen O, et al, "Elimination of the Piperacillin/Tazobactam Combination During Continuous Venovenous Haemofiltration and Haemodiafiltration in Patients With Acute Renal Failure," *J Antimicrob Chemother*, 2001, 48(6):881-5.

van der Werf TS, Mulder PO, Zijlstra JG, et al, "Pharmacokinetics of Piperacillin and Tazobactam in Critically Ill Patients With Renal Failure, Treated With Continuous Veno-Venous Hemofiltration (CVVH)," *Intensive Care Med*, 1997, 23(8):873-7.

Viollier AF, Standiford HC, Drusano GL, et al, "Comparative Pharmacokinetics and Serum Bactericidal Activity of Mezlocillin, Ticarcillin and Piperacillin, With and Without Gentamicin," *J Antimicrob Chemother*, 1985, 15(5):597-606.

Walterspiel JN, Feldman S, Van R, et al, "Comparative Inactivation of Isepamicin, Amikacin, and Gentamicin by Nine Beta-Lactams and Two Beta-Lactamase Inhibitors, Cilastatin and Heparin," *Antimicrob Agents Chemother*, 1991, 35(9):1875-8.

♦ **Piperacillin Sodium and Tazobactam Sodium** *see* Piperacillin and Tazobactam Sodium *on page 902*

♦ **Plenaxis™ [DSC]** *see* Abarelix *on page 20*

♦ **PMS-Anagrelide (Can)** *see* Anagrelide *on page 87*

♦ **PMS-Benzydamine (Can)** *see* Benzydamine *on page 132*

♦ **PMS-Bicalutamide (Can)** *see* Bicalutamide *on page 141*

♦ **PMS-Ciprofloxacin (Can)** *see* Ciprofloxacin *on page 213*

♦ **PMS-Deferoxamine (Can)** *see* Deferoxamine *on page 319*

♦ **PMS-Dexamethasone (Can)** *see* Dexamethasone *on page 330*

♦ **PMS-Famciclovir (Can)** *see* Famciclovir *on page 423*

♦ **PMS-Fluconazole (Can)** *see* Fluconazole *on page 449*

♦ **PMS-Furosemide (Can)** *see* Furosemide *on page 483*

♦ **PMS-Haloperidol LA (Can)** *see* Haloperidol *on page 526*

♦ **PMS-Hydromorphone (Can)** *see* Hydromorphone *on page 553*

♦ **PMS-Hydroxyzine (Can)** *see* HydrOXYzine *on page 564*

♦ **PMS-Lorazepam (Can)** *see* Lorazepam *on page 693*

♦ **PMS-Morphine Sulfate SR (Can)** *see* Morphine Sulfate *on page 779*

♦ **PMS-Nystatin (Can)** *see* Nystatin *on page 817*

♦ **PMS-Ofloxacin (Can)** *see* Ofloxacin *on page 825*

♦ **PMS-Ondansetron (Can)** *see* Ondansetron *on page 837*

♦ **PMS-Tobramycin (Can)** *see* Tobramycin *on page 1041*

♦ **Polygam® S/D** *see* Immune Globulin (Intravenous) *on page 597*

Porfimer *(POR fi mer)*

Related Information

Safe Handling of Hazardous Drugs *on page 1382*

U.S. Brand Names Photofrin®

Index Terms CL-184116; Dihematoporphrin Ether; Porfimer Sodium

Generic Available No

Canadian Brand Names Photofrin®

Pharmacologic Category Antineoplastic Agent, Miscellaneous

Use Adjunct to laser light therapy for obstructing esophageal cancer, obstructing endobronchial nonsmall cell lung cancer (NSCLC), ablation of high-grade dysplasia in Barrett's esophagus

Unlabeled/Investigational Use Transitional cell carcinoma *in situ* of the urinary bladder; gastric and rectal cancers

Pregnancy Risk Factor C

Lactation Excretion in breast milk unknown/contraindicated

Labeled Contraindications Hypersensitivity to porfimer, porphyrins, or any component of the formulation; porphyria; photodynamic therapy is contraindicated in tracheoesophageal or bronchoesophageal fistula; tumors eroding into a major blood vessel; severe acute respiratory distress when caused by endobronchial lesion; esophageal ulcers >1 cm

Warnings/Precautions Hazardous agent - use appropriate precautions for handling and disposal. When treating endobronchial tumors, use caution if treatment-induced inflammation may obstruct airway. Assess patient for possibility of tumor erosion into a pulmonary blood vessel; fatal massive pulmonary hemoptysis (FMH) may occur. Risk factors for FMH include large, centrally located tumors, cavitating tumors, or extensive tumor extrinsic to the bronchus. Generally not suited for treatment of patients with esophageal or gastric varices; if used in esophageal varices, extreme caution is warranted and light exposure to the varices should be avoided. In patients with Barrett's esophagus, rigorous surveillance (endoscopic biopsy every 3 months until 4 consecutive negative results for high-grade dysplasia followed by further follow-up per physician judgement). Esophageal strictures are common adverse events associated with photodynamic therapy of Barrett's esophagus; esophageal dilation may be required.

Photosensitivity reactions are common is patients are exposed to direct sunlight or bright indoor light (eg fluorescent lights, unshaded light bulbs, examination/operating lights). Photosensitivity may last 30-90 days. Ocular discomfort has been reported; for at least 30 days, when outdoors, patients should wear dark sunglasses which have an average white light transmittance of <4%. Patients should be educated to test for residual photosensitivity before resuming exposure to sunlight. Conventional sunscreens are NOT protective. Allow 2-4 weeks to elapse after phototherapy prior to initiating radiation therapy; 4 weeks should elapse after radiation therapy prior to initiating phototherapy. Safety and efficacy in children have not been established.

Adverse Reactions

>10%:

    Cardiovascular: Chest pain (7% to 35%), edema (3% to 18%)

    Central nervous system: Fever (5% to 31%), pain (1% to 22%), insomnia (4% to 14%)

    Dermatologic: Photosensitivity reaction (4% to 37%, minor reactions may occur in up to 100%; severe: 10%)

    Endocrine & metabolic: Dehydration (7% to 11%)

    Gastrointestinal: Esophageal stricture (6% in esophageal cancer patients; up to 39% in Barrett's esophagus patients), nausea (24% to 39%), vomiting (17% to 34%), constipation (5% to 24%), dysphagia (10% to 24%), abdominal pain (12% to 20%)

(Continued)

Porfimer *(Continued)*

Genitourinary: Urinary tract irritation including frequency, urgency, nocturia, painful urination, or bladder spasm (~100% of bladder cancer patients)

Hematologic: Anemia (32% in esophageal cancer patients)

Neuromuscular & skeletal: Back pain (3% to 11%)

Respiratory: Pleural effusion (32% in esophageal cancer patients; 11% in Barrett's esophagus patients), dyspnea (6% to 20%), pneumonia (6% to 18%), hemoptysis (7% to 16%), cough (6% to 15%), pharyngitis (11%)

Miscellaneous: Mild-moderate allergic-type reactions (34% of lung cancer patients)

5% to 10%:

Cardiovascular: Atrial fibrillation (10%), hyper-/hypotension (3% to 7%), cardiac failure (7% in esophageal cancer), tachycardia (6%), chest pain (substernal; 5%)

Central nervous system: Confusion (7% to 8%), headache (6%), anxiety (3% to 7%), depression (3% to 5%)

Dermatologic: Rash (7%), pruritus (4%)

Gastrointestinal: Diarrhea (5% to 10%), weight loss (6% to 9%), esophageal edema (8%), esophageal tumor bleeding (8%), anorexia (4% to 8%), dyspepsia (1% to 6%), eructation (5%), esophagitis (5%), hematemesis (5%), melena (5%), odynophagia (5%)

Genitourinary: Urinary tract infection (7%)

Neuromuscular & skeletal: Weakness (6%), arthralgia (3% to 5%)

Respiratory: Respiratory insufficiency (6% to 10%), bronchitis (4% to 10%), tracheoesophageal fistula (6%), sinusitis (4%)

Miscellaneous: Moniliasis (9%), surgical complication (5% in esophageal cancer patients)

<5% (Limited to important or life-threatening): Abnormal vision, bronchospasm, bradycardia, cataracts, diplopia, esophageal perforation, eye pain, fluid imbalance, gastric ulcer, hair growth increased, ileus, jaundice, lung abscess, myocardial infarction, peritonitis, photophobia, pulmonary edema, pulmonary embolism, pulmonary hemorrhage, pulmonary thrombosis, respiratory failure, sepsis, sick sinus syndrome, skin discoloration, skin fragility, skin nodules, skin wrinkles, stridor, supraventricular tachycardia

Overdosage/Toxicology Laser treatment should not be given if an overdose of porfimer is administered. In the event of overdose, patients should protect their eyes and skin from direct sunlight or bright indoor lights for 30 days. Patients should be tested for residual photosensitivity. Porfimer is not dialyzable.

Drug Interactions

Increased Effect/Toxicity: Concomitant administration of other photosensitizing agents (eg, tetracyclines, sulfonamides, phenothiazines, sulfonylureas, thiazide diuretics, griseofulvin) could increase the photosensitivity reaction.

Decreased Effect: Compounds that quench active oxygen species or scavenge radicals (eg, dimethyl sulfoxide, beta-carotene, ethanol, mannitol) would be expected to decrease photodynamic therapy (PDT) activity. Allopurinol, calcium channel blockers, and some prostaglandin synthesis inhibitors could interfere with porfimer. Drugs that decrease clotting, vasoconstriction, or platelet aggregation could decrease the efficacy of PDT. Glucocorticoid hormones may decrease the efficacy of the treatment.

Storage/Stability Store intact vials at controlled room temperature of 20°C to 25°C (68°F to 77°F). Reconstituted solutions are stable for 24 hours under refrigeration and protected from light.

Reconstitution Reconstitute each vial of porfimer with 31.8 mL of either D_5W or NS injection resulting in a final concentration of 2.5 mg/mL. Shake well until dissolved. Protect the reconstituted product from bright light and use immediately.

Compatibility Do not mix porfimer with other drugs in the same solution.

Mechanism of Action Porfimer's cytotoxic activity is dependent on light and oxygen. Following administration, the drug is selectively retained in neoplastic tissues. Exposure of the drug to laser light at wavelengths >630 nm results in the production of oxygen free-radicals. Release of thromboxane A_2, leading to vascular occlusion and ischemic necrosis, may also occur.

Pharmacodynamics/Kinetics

Distribution: V_{dss}: 0.49 L/kg

Protein binding, plasma: 90%

Half-life elimination: Mean: 21.5 days (range: 11-28 days)

Time to peak, serum: ~2 hours

Excretion: Feces; Clearance: Plasma: Total: 0.051 mL/minute/kg

Dosage I.V. (refer to individual protocols):

Children: Safety and efficacy have not been established

Adults: 2 mg/kg, followed by exposure to the appropriate laser light; repeat courses must be separated by at least 30 days (esophageal or endobronchial cancer) or 90 days (Barrett's esophagus) for a maximum of 3 courses

Administration Administer slow I.V. injection over 3-5 minutes.

Patient Information This medication can only be administered I.V. and will be followed by laser light therapy. Avoid any exposure to sunlight or bright indoor light for 30 days following therapy (cover skin with protective clothing and wear dark sunglasses with light transmittance <4% when outdoors - severe blistering, burning, and skin/eye damage can result). After 30 days, test a small area of skin (not face) for remaining sensitivity. Retest sensitivity if traveling to a different geographic area with greater sunshine. Exposure to indoor normal light is beneficial since it will help dissipate photosensitivity gradually. Maintain adequate hydration (2-3 L/day of fluids unless instructed to restrict fluid intake); maintain good oral hygiene (use a soft toothbrush or cotton applicators several times a day and rinse mouth frequently). Small frequent meals, frequent mouth care, sucking lozenges, or chewing gum may reduce nausea or vomiting. Report rapid heart rate, chest pain or palpitations, difficulty breathing or air hunger, persistent fever or chills, foul-smelling urine or burning on urination, swelling of extremities, increased anxiety, confusion, or hallucination.

Emetic Potential Low (10% to 30%)

Vesicant No

Dosage Forms Excipient information presented when available (limited, particularly for generics); consult specific product labeling.

Injection, powder for reconstitution, as sodium:

Photofrin®: 75 mg

References

Evensen JF, "The Use of Porphyrins and Nonionizing Radiation for Treatment of Cancer," *Acta Oncol*, 1995, 34(8):1103-10.

Levy JG, "Photosensitizers in Photodynamic Therapy," *Semin Oncol*, 1994, 21(6 Suppl 15):4-10.

Rosenthal DI and Glatstein E, "Clinical Applications of Photodynamic Therapy," *Ann Med*, 1994, 26(6):405-9.

Van Hillegersberg R, Kort WJ, and Wilson JH, "Current Status of Photodynamic Therapy in Oncology," *Drugs*, 1994, 48(4):510-27.

♦ **Porfimer Sodium** *see* Porfimer *on page 908*

Posaconazole (poe sa KON a zole)
Medication Safety Issues
Sound-alike/look-alike issues:

Noxafil® may be confused with minoxidil

International issues:

Noxafil® may be confused with Noxidil® which is a brand name for minoxidil in Thailand

U.S. Brand Names Noxafil®

Index Terms SCH 56592

Generic Available No

Canadian Brand Names Spriafil®

Pharmacologic Category Antifungal Agent, Oral

Use Prophylaxis of invasive *Aspergillus* and *Candida* infections in severely-immunocompromised patients [eg, hematopoietic stem cell transplant (HSCT) recipients with graft-versus-host disease (GVHD) or those with prolonged neutropenia secondary to chemotherapy for hematologic malignancies]; treatment of oropharyngeal candidiasis (including patients refractory to itraconazole and/or fluconazole)

Unlabeled/Investigational Use Salvage therapy of refractory invasive fungal infections

Pregnancy Risk Factor C

Lactation Excretion in breast milk unknown/use caution

Labeled Contraindications Hypersensitivity to posaconazole or any component of the formulation; coadministration of cisapride, pimozide, quinidine, or ergot alkaloids

Warnings/Precautions Use caution in hepatic impairment; hepatic dysfunction has occurred, ranging from mild/moderate increases of ALT/AST, alkaline phosphatase, and/or clinical hepatitis to severe reactions (cholestasis, hepatic failure including death). Use caution in patients with an increased risk of arrhythmia (concurrent QT_c-prolonging drugs, hypokalemia). Correct electrolyte abnormalities (eg, potassium, magnesium, and calcium) before initiating therapy.

Use caution in hypersensitivity with other azole antifungal agents; cross-reaction may occur, but has not been established. Alternative antifungal therapy should be considered in any patient unable to eat or tolerate an oral liquid nutritional supplement. Use caution in severe renal impairment; monitor for breakthrough fungal infections. Safety and efficacy have not been established in children <13 years of age.

Adverse Reactions Note: A higher frequency of adverse reactions was observed in studies with refractory oropharyngeal candidiasis patients and percentages are included below.

>10%: Gastrointestinal: Diarrhea (3% to 11%)

1% to 10%:

Cardiovascular: QT_c prolongation (up to 4%), hypertension (1%)

Central nervous system: Headache (1% to 8%), dizziness (1% to 3%), fatigue (1% to 3%), insomnia (1% to 3%), fever (up to 3%), somnolence (1%)

Dermatologic: Rash (1% to 4%), pruritus (1% to 2%)

Endocrine & metabolic: Hypokalemia (3%)

Gastrointestinal: Nausea (5% to 8%), vomiting (4% to 7%), abdominal pain (1% to 5%), flatulence (1% to 5%), anorexia (1% to 3%), mucositis (2%), dyspepsia (1% to 2%), xerostoma (1% to 2%), taste perversion (1%), constipation (up to 1%)

Hematologic: Neutropenia (2% to 8%), anemia (up to 3%), thrombocytopenia (up to 2%)

Hepatic: Bilirubin increased (2% to 3%), ALT increased (2% to 3%), AST increased (2% to 3%), GGT increased (2% to 3%), alkaline phosphatase increased (2%), hepatocellular damage (1%)

Neuromuscular & skeletal: Weakness (1% to 3%), myalgia (up to 2%), tremor (1%)

Ocular: Blurred vision (1%)

Renal: Serum creatinine increased (2%)

<1%, postmarketing, and/or case reports: Adrenal insufficiency, allergic/ hypersensitivity reactions, cholestasis, hemolytic uremic syndrome, hepatic failure, hepatitis, pulmonary embolus, thrombotic thrombocytopenic purpura, torsade de pointes

Overdosage/Toxicology Experience with overdosage is limited; treatment is symptom-directed and supportive. Posaconazole is not removed by hemodialysis.

Drug Interactions

Cytochrome P450 Effect: Inhibits CYP3A4 (moderate)

Increased Effect/Toxicity: Posaconazole may increase the levels/effects of calcium channel blockers (eg, felodipine, nifedipine, verapamil), cyclosporine, CYP3A4 substrates, ergot alkaloids, HMG-CoA reductase inhibitors, midazolam, phenytoin, rifabutin, sirolimus, tacrolimus and vinca alkaloids. Use with QT_c-prolonging agents may increase risk of malignant arrhythmias

Decreased Effect: Cimetidine, phenytoin, and rifabutin may decrease the effects/levels of posaconazole.

Ethanol/Nutrition/Herb Interactions Food: Bioavailability increased ~3-4 times when posaconazole administered with a meal or an oral liquid nutritional supplement.

Storage/Stability Store at 15°C to 30°C (59°F to 86°F);do not freeze.

Mechanism of Action Interferes with fungal cytochrome P450 activity, decreasing ergosterol synthesis (principal sterol in fungal cell membrane) and inhibiting fungal cell membrane formation.

Pharmacodynamics/Kinetics

Absorption: Food and/or liquid nutritional supplements increase absorption; fasting states do not provide sufficient absorption to ensure adequate plasma concentrations

Distribution: V_d: 465-1774 L

Protein binding: ≥97%; predominantly bound to albumin

Metabolism: Not significantly metabolized; ~15% to 17% undergoes non-CYP-mediated metabolism, primarily via hepatic glucuronidation into metabolites

Half-life elimination: 35 hours (range: 20-66 hours)

Time to peak, plasma: 3-5 hours

Excretion: Feces 71% to 77% (~66% as unchanged drug); urine 13% to 14% (<0.2% as unchanged drug)

Dosage Oral: Children ≥13 years and Adults:

Prophylaxis of invasive *Aspergillus* and *Candida* species: 200 mg 3 times/ day

Treatment of oropharyngeal candidiasis: Initial: 100 mg twice daily for 1 day; maintenance: 100 mg once daily for 13 days

Treatment of refractory oropharyngeal candidiasis: 400 mg twice daily

(Continued)

Posaconazole *(Continued)*

Treatment of refractory invasive fungal infections (unlabeled use): 800 mg/ day in divided doses

Dosage adjustment in renal impairment: No adjustment necessary; use caution in severe renal impairment and monitor for breakthrough fungal infections. Variability in posaconazole exposure observed with Cl_{cr}<20 mL/ minute.

Dosage adjustment in hepatic impairment: No adjustment necessary; use with caution

Administration Must be administered with a full meal or an oral liquid nutritional supplement.

Monitoring Parameters Hepatic function (eg, AST/ALT, alkaline phosphatase and bilirubin) prior to initiation and during treatment; renal function; electrolyte disturbances (eg, calcium, magnesium, potassium)

Dietary Considerations Give with meals. If alternative antifungal therapy can not be given to patients without food intake or severe diarrhea/vomiting, close monitoring for breakthrough fungal infections must be performed. Adequate posaconazole absorption from GI tract and subsequent plasma concentrations are dependent on food for efficacy. Lower average plasma concentrations have been associated with an increased risk of treatment failure.

Special Geriatric Considerations Dosage adjustment not necessary.

Dosage Forms Excipient information presented when available (limited, particularly for generics); consult specific product labeling.

Suspension, oral:

Noxafil®: 40 mg/mL (123 mL) [contains sodium benzoate; delivers 105 mL of suspension; cherry flavor; packaged with calibrated dosing spoon]

References

Herbrecht R, "Posaconazole: A Potent, Extended-Spectrum Triazole Anti-Fungal for the Treatment of Serious Fungal Infections," *Int J Clin Pract*, 2004, 58(6): 612-24.

Keating G, "Posaconazole," *Drugs*, 2005, 65(11):1553-67.

Krieter P, Flannery B, Musick T, et al, "Disposition of Posaconazole Following Single-Dose Oral Administration in Healthy Subjects," *Antimicrob Agents Chemother*, 2004, 48(9):3543-51.

Raad II, Graybill JR, Bustamante AB, "Safety of Long-Term Oral Posaconazole Use in the Treatment of Refractory Invasive Fungal Infections," *Clin Infect Dis*, 2006, 42(12):1726-34.

- ◆ **Post Peel Healing Balm [OTC]** *see* Hydrocortisone *on page 545*
- ◆ **PPI-149** *see* Abarelix *on page 20*
- ◆ **Pred Forte®** *see* PrednisoLONE *on page 914*
- ◆ **Pred Mild®** *see* PrednisoLONE *on page 914*

PrednisoLONE *(pred NISS oh lone)*

Medication Safety Issues

Sound-alike/look-alike issues:

PrednisoLONE may be confused with predniSONE

Pediapred® may be confused with Pediazole®

U.S. Brand Names Econopred® Plus; Orapred®; Orapred ODT™; Pediapred®; Pred Forte®; Pred Mild®; Prelone®

Index Terms Deltahydrocortisone; Metacortandralone; Prednisolone Acetate; Prednisolone Acetate, Ophthalmic; Prednisolone Sodium Phosphate; Prednisolone Sodium Phosphate, Ophthalmic

Generic Available Yes

Canadian Brand Names Diopred®; Hydeltra T.B.A.®; Inflamase® Mild; Novo-Prednisolone; Ophtho-Tate®; Pediapred®; Pred Forte®; Pred Mild®; Sab-Prenase

Pharmacologic Category Corticosteroid, Ophthalmic; Corticosteroid, Systemic

Use Treatment of palpebral and bulbar conjunctivitis; corneal injury from chemical, radiation, thermal burns, or foreign body penetration; endocrine disorders, rheumatic disorders, collagen diseases, dermatologic diseases, allergic states, ophthalmic diseases, respiratory diseases, hematologic disorders, neoplastic diseases, edematous states, and gastrointestinal diseases; resolution of acute exacerbations of multiple sclerosis; management of fulminating or disseminated tuberculosis and trichinosis; acute or chronic solid organ rejection

Pregnancy Risk Factor C

Lactation Enters breast milk/use caution (AAP rates "compatible")

Labeled Contraindications Hypersensitivity to prednisolone or any component of the formulation; acute superficial herpes simplex keratitis; live or attenuated virus vaccines (with immunosuppressive doses of corticosteroids); systemic fungal infections; varicella

Warnings/Precautions May cause hypercorticism or suppression of hypothalamic-pituitary-adrenal (HPA) axis, particularly in younger children or in patients receiving high doses for prolonged periods. HPA axis suppression may lead to adrenal crisis. Withdrawal and discontinuation of a corticosteroid should be done slowly and carefully. Particular care is required when patients are transferred from systemic corticosteroids to inhaled products due to possible adrenal insufficiency or withdrawal from steroids, including an increase in allergic symptoms. Patients receiving >20 mg per day of prednisone (or equivalent) may be most susceptible. Fatalities have occurred due to adrenal insufficiency in asthmatic patients during and after transfer from systemic corticosteroids to aerosol steroids; aerosol steroids do **not** provide the systemic steroid needed to treat patients having trauma, surgery, or infections.

Acute myopathy has been reported with high dose corticosteroids, usually in patients with neuromuscular transmission disorders; may involve ocular and/or respiratory muscles; monitor creatine kinase; recovery may be delayed. Corticosteroid use may cause psychiatric disturbances, including depression, euphoria, insomnia, mood swings, and personality changes. Pre-existing psychiatric conditions may be exacerbated by corticosteroid use. Prolonged use of corticosteroids may also increase the incidence of secondary infection, mask acute infection (including fungal infections), prolong or exacerbate viral infections, or limit response to vaccines. Exposure to chickenpox should be avoided; corticosteroids should not be used to treat ocular herpes simplex. Corticosteroids should not be used for cerebral malaria. Close observation is required in patients with latent tuberculosis and/or TB reactivity; restrict use in active TB (only in conjunction with anti-tuberculosis treatment). Prolonged use of corticosteroids may result in glaucoma; damage to the optic nerve (not indicated for treatment of optic neuritis), defects in visual acuity and fields of vision, and posterior subcapsular cataract formation may occur. Use following cataract surgery may delay healing or increase the incidence of bleb formation. Prolonged treatment with corticosteroids has been associated with the development of Kaposi's sarcoma (case reports); if noted, discontinuation of therapy should be considered.

Use with caution in patients with thyroid disease, hepatic impairment, renal impairment, cardiovascular disease, diabetes, glaucoma, cataracts, myasthenia gravis, patients at risk for osteoporosis, patients at risk for seizures, or GI diseases (diverticulitis, peptic ulcer, ulcerative colitis) due to perforation risk. Use caution following acute MI (corticosteroids have been associated (Continued)

PrednisoLONE *(Continued)*

with myocardial rupture). Because of the risk of adverse effects, systemic corticosteroids should be used cautiously in the elderly in the smallest possible effective dose for the shortest duration. Do not use occlusive dressings on weeping or exudative lesions and general caution with occlusive dressings should be observed; adverse effects may be increased. Discontinue if skin irritation or contact dermatitis should occur; do not use in patients with decreased skin circulation. Withdraw therapy with gradual tapering of dose. May affect growth velocity; growth should be routinely monitored in pediatric patients.

Adverse Reactions Frequency not defined.

Ophthalmic formulation:

Endocrine & metabolic: Hypercorticoidism (rare)

Ocular: Conjunctival hyperemia, conjunctivitis, corneal ulcers, delayed wound healing, glaucoma, intraocular pressure increased, keratitis, loss of accommodation, optic nerve damage, mydriasis, posterior subcapsular cataract formation, ptosis, secondary ocular infection

Oral formulation:

Cardiovascular: Cardiomyopathy, CHF, edema, facial edema, hypertension

Central nervous system: Convulsions, headache, insomnia, malaise, nervousness, pseudotumor cerebri, psychic disorders, vertigo

Dermatologic: Bruising, facial erythema, hirsutism, petechiae, skin test reaction suppression, thin fragile skin, urticaria

Endocrine & metabolic: Carbohydrate tolerance decreased, Cushing's syndrome, diabetes mellitus, growth suppression, hyperglycemia, hypernatremia, hypokalemia, hypokalemic alkalosis, menstrual irregularities, negative nitrogen balance, pituitary adrenal axis suppression

Gastrointestinal: Abdominal distention, increased appetite, indigestion, nausea, pancreatitis, peptic ulcer, ulcerative esophagitis, weight gain

Hepatic: LFTs increased (usually reversible)

Neuromuscular & skeletal: Arthralgia, aseptic necrosis (humeral/femoral heads), fractures, muscle mass decreased, muscle weakness, osteoporosis, steroid myopathy, tendon rupture, weakness

Ocular: Cataracts, exophthalmus, eyelid edema, glaucoma, intraocular pressure increased, irritation

Respiratory: Epistaxis

Miscellaneous: Diaphoresis increased, impaired wound healing

Overdosage/Toxicology When consumed in high doses for prolonged periods, systemic hypercorticism and adrenal suppression may occur, in those cases discontinuation of the corticosteroid should be done judiciously. Treatment should be symptom-directed and supportive.

Drug Interactions

Cytochrome P450 Effect: Substrate of CYP3A4 (minor); **Inhibits** CYP3A4 (weak)

Increased Effect/Toxicity: Aprepitant, azole antifungals, calcium channel blockers (nondihydropyridine), cyclosporine, estrogens, and macrolides may increase the serum levels of corticosteroids. Corticosteroids may increase the hypokalemic effects of amphotericin B or potassium-wasting diuretics (loop or thiazide); monitor.

Concurrent use of nonsteroidal anti-inflammatory drugs (NSAIDs) and salicylates with corticosteroids may lead to an increased incidence of gastrointestinal adverse effects. Concurrent use with anticholinergic agents may lead to severe weakness in patients with myasthenia gravis. Concurrent use of fluoroquinolone antibiotics may increase the risk of tendon rupture, particularly in elderly patients (overall incidence rare). Concurrent use of neuromuscular-blocking agents with corticosteroids may increase the risk of myopathy. Concurrent use with cyclosporine may increase cyclosporine levels. Concurrent use of ophthalmic NSAIDs may enhance the toxic effects of ophthalmic prednisolone. The use of live vaccines is contraindicated in immunosuppressed patients (may increase the risk of vaccinal infection). In patients receiving high doses of systemic corticosteroids for ≥14 days, wait at least 1 month between discontinuing steroid therapy and administering immunization.

Decreased Effect: Antacids and bile acid sequestrants may reduce the absorption of corticosteroids; separate administration by 2 hours. Aminoglutethimide, barbiturates and rifamycin derivatives may reduce the serum levels/effects of prednisolone (systemic). Serum concentrations of isoniazid may be decreased by corticosteroids. Corticosteroids may lead to a reduction in warfarin effect. Corticosteroids may suppress the response to vaccinations.

Ethanol/Nutrition/Herb Interactions

Ethanol: Avoid ethanol (may increase gastric mucosal irritation).

Food: Prednisolone interferes with calcium absorption. Limit caffeine.

Herb/Nutraceutical: St John's wort may decrease prednisolone levels. Avoid cat's claw, echinacea (have immunostimulant properties).

Storage/Stability Store Orapred ODT™ at 20°C to 25°C (68°F to 77°F) in blister pack. Protect from moisture.

Mechanism of Action Decreases inflammation by suppression of migration of polymorphonuclear leukocytes and reversal of increased capillary permeability; suppresses the immune system by reducing activity and volume of the lymphatic system

Pharmacodynamics/Kinetics

Duration: 18-36 hours

Protein binding (concentration dependent): 65% to 91%; decreased in elderly

Metabolism: Primarily hepatic, but also metabolized in most tissues, to inactive compounds

Half-life elimination: 3.6 hours; End-stage renal disease: 3-5 hours

Excretion: Primarily urine (as glucuronides, sulfates, and unconjugated metabolites)

Dosage Dose depends upon condition being treated and response of patient; dosage for infants and children should be based on severity of the disease and response of the patient rather than on strict adherence to dosage indicated by age, weight, or body surface area. Consider alternate day therapy for long-term therapy. Discontinuation of long-term therapy requires gradual withdrawal by tapering the dose. Patients undergoing unusual stress while receiving corticosteroids, should receive increased doses prior to, during, and after the stressful situation.

Children: Oral:

Acute asthma: 1-2 mg/kg/day in divided doses 1-2 times/day for 3-5 days

Anti-inflammatory or immunosuppressive dose: 0.1-2 mg/kg/day in divided doses 1-4 times/day

Nephrotic syndrome:

Initial (first 3 episodes): 2 mg/kg/day **or** 60 mg/m^2/day (maximum: 80 mg/day) in divided doses 3-4 times/day until urine is protein free for 3 consecutive days (maximum: 28 days); followed by 1-1.5 mg/kg/dose **or** 40 mg/m^2/dose given every other day for 4 weeks

Maintenance (long-term maintenance dose for frequent relapses): 0.5-1 mg/kg/dose given every other day for 3-6 months

(Continued)

PrednisoLONE *(Continued)*

Adults: Oral:
Usual range: 5-60 mg/day
Multiple sclerosis: 200 mg/day for 1 week followed by 80 mg every other
day for 1 month
Rheumatoid arthritis: Initial: 5-7.5 mg/day; adjust dose as necessary

Ophthalmic suspension/solution: Conjunctivitis, corneal injury: Children and
Adults: Instill 1-2 drops into conjunctival sac every hour during day, every 2
hours at night until favorable response is obtained, then use 1 drop every 4
hours.

Elderly: Use lowest effective dose

Dosing adjustment in hyperthyroidism: Prednisolone dose may need to
be increased to achieve adequate therapeutic effects

Hemodialysis: Slightly dialyzable (5% to 20%); administer dose posthemodialysis

Peritoneal dialysis: Supplemental dose is not necessary

Combination Regimens

Lymphoma, Hodgkin's:
LOPP *on page 1244*
MOPP (Lymphoma, Hodgkin's Disease) *on page 1252*

Administration Administer oral formulation with food or milk to decrease GI
effects.
Orapred ODT™: Do not break or use partial tablet. Remove tablet from
blister pack just prior to use. May swallow whole or allow to dissolve on
tongue.

Monitoring Parameters Blood pressure; blood glucose, electrolytes; intraocular pressure (use >6 weeks); bone mineral density

Test Interactions Response to skin tests

Dietary Considerations Should be taken after meals or with food or milk to
decrease GI effects; increase dietary intake of pyridoxine, vitamin C, vitamin
D, folate, calcium, and phosphorus.

Patient Information Notify surgeon or dentist before surgical repair; may
cause GI upset, take orally with food; notify prescriber if any sign of infection
occurs; avoid abrupt withdrawal when on long-term therapy

Special Geriatric Considerations Useful in patients with inability to activate prednisone (liver disease). Because of the risk of adverse effects,
systemic corticosteroids should be used cautiously in the elderly, in the
smallest possible dose, and for the shortest possible time. For long-term use,
monitor bone mineral density and institute fracture prevention strategies.

Dosage Forms Excipient information presented when available (limited,
particularly for generics); consult specific product labeling.
Solution, ophthalmic, as sodium phosphate: 1% (5 mL, 10 mL, 15 mL)
[contains benzalkonium chloride]
Solution, oral, as base: Prednisolone 15 mg/5 mL (240 mL, 480 mL)
Solution, oral, as sodium phosphate: Prednisolone base 5 mg/5 mL (120 mL,
240 mL); prednisolone base 15 mg/5 mL (240 mL)
Orapred®: 20 mg/5 mL (20 mL, 240 mL) [equivalent to prednisolone base
15 mg/5 mL; dye free; contains alcohol 2%, sodium benzoate; grape
flavor]
Pediapred®: 6.7 mg/5 mL (120 mL) [equivalent to prednisolone base 5 mg/
5 mL; dye free; raspberry flavor]
Suspension, ophthalmic, as acetate: 1% (5 mL, 10 mL, 15 mL)
Econopred® Plus: 1% (5 mL, 10 mL) [contains benzalkonium chloride]

Pred Forte®: 1% (1 mL, 5 mL, 10 mL, 15 mL) [contains benzalkonium chloride and sodium bisulfite]

Pred Mild®: 0.12% (5 mL, 10 mL) [contains benzalkonium chloride and sodium bisulfite]

Syrup, as base: 5 mg/5 mL (120 mL); 15 mg/5 mL (5 mL, 240 mL, 480 mL)

Prelone®: 15 mg/5 mL (240 mL, 480 mL) [contains alcohol 5%, benzoic acid; cherry flavor]

Tablet, as base: 5 mg

Tablet, orally disintegrating, as sodium phosphate [strength expressed as base]:

Orapred ODT™: 10 mg, 15 mg, 30 mg [grape flavor]

References

Abraham E and Evans T, "Corticosteroids and Septic Shock [editorial]," *JAMA*, 2002, 288(7):886-7.

Annane D, Sebille V, Charpentier C, et al, "Effect of Treatment With Low Doses of Hydrocortisone and Fludrocortisone on Mortality in Patients With Septic Shock," *JAMA*, 2002, 288(7):862-71.

Cooper MS and Stewart PM, "Corticosteroid Insufficiency in Acutely Ill Patients," *N Engl J Med*, 2003, 348(8):727-34.

Coursin DB and Wood KE, "Corticosteroid Supplementation for Adrenal Insufficiency," *JAMA*, 2002, 287(2):236-40.

Frey BM and Frey FJ, "Clinical Pharmacokinetics of Prednisone and Prednisolone," *Clin Pharmacokinet*, 1990, 19(2):126-46.

Frey FJ, "Kinetics and Dynamics of Prednisolone," *Endocr Rev*, 1987, 8(4):453-73.

Gambertoglio JG, Amend WJ Jr and Benet LZ, "Pharmacokinetics and Bioavailability of Prednisone and Prednisolone in Healthy Volunteers and Patients: A Review," *J Pharmacokinet Biopharm*, 1980, 8(1):1-52.

Gamsu HR, Mullinger BM, Donnai P, et al, "Antenatal Administration of Betamethasone to Prevent Respiratory Distress Syndrome in Preterm Infants: Report of a UK Multicentre Trial," *Br J Obstet Gynaecol*, 1989, 96(4):401-10.

Goedert JJ, Vitale F, Lauria C, et al, "Risk Factors for Classical Kaposi's Sarcoma," *J Natl Cancer Inst*, 2002, 94(22):1712-8.

Hotchkiss RS and Karl IE, "The Pathophysiology and Treatment of Sepsis," *N Engl J Med*, 2003, 348(2):138-50.

Liggins GC and Howie RN, "A Controlled Trial of Antepartum Glucocorticoid Treatment of Respiratory Distress Syndrome in Premature Infants," *Pediatrics*, 1972, 50:515-25.

Report of a Workshop by the British Association for Paediatric Nephrology and Research Unit, Royal College of Physicians, "Consensus Statement on Management and Audit Potential for Steroid Responsive Nephrotic Syndrome," *Arch Dis Child*, 1994, 70(2):151-7.

Salem M, Tainsh RE Jr, Bromberg J, et al, "Perioperative Glucocorticoid Coverage. A Reassessment 42 Years After Emergence of a Problem," *Ann Surg*, 1994, 219(4):416-25.

♦ **Prednisolone Acetate** *see* PrednisoLONE *on page 914*

♦ **Prednisolone Acetate, Ophthalmic** *see* PrednisoLONE *on page 914*

♦ **Prednisolone Sodium Phosphate** *see* PrednisoLONE *on page 914*

♦ **Prednisolone Sodium Phosphate, Ophthalmic** *see* PrednisoLONE *on page 914*

PredniSONE (PRED ni sone)

Medication Safety Issues

Sound-alike/look-alike issues:

PredniSONE may be confused with methylPREDNISolone, Pramosone®, prazosin, prednisoLONE, Prilosec®, primidone, promethazine

U.S. Brand Names PredniSONE Intensol™; Sterapred®; Sterapred® DS

Index Terms Deltacortisone; Deltadehydrocortisone

Generic Available Yes

Canadian Brand Names Apo-Prednisone®; Novo-Prednisone; Winpred™

Pharmacologic Category Corticosteroid, Systemic

Use Treatment of a variety of diseases including adrenocortical insufficiency, hypercalcemia, rheumatic, and collagen disorders; dermatologic, ocular, respiratory, gastrointestinal, and neoplastic diseases; organ transplantation (Continued)

PredniSONE *(Continued)*

and a variety of diseases including those of hematologic, allergic, inflammatory, and autoimmune in origin; not available in injectable form, prednisolone must be used

Unlabeled/Investigational Use Investigational: Prevention of postherpetic neuralgia and relief of acute pain in the early stages

Pregnancy Risk Factor B

Lactation Enters breast milk/compatible

Labeled Contraindications Hypersensitivity to prednisone or any component of the formulation; serious infections, except tuberculous meningitis; systemic fungal infections; varicella

Warnings/Precautions May cause hypercorticism or suppression of hypothalamic-pituitary-adrenal (HPA) axis, particularly in younger children or in patients receiving high doses for prolonged periods. HPA axis suppression may lead to adrenal crisis. Withdrawal and discontinuation of a corticosteroid should be done slowly and carefully. Particular care is required when patients are transferred from systemic corticosteroids to inhaled products due to possible adrenal insufficiency or withdrawal from steroids, including an increase in allergic symptoms. Patients receiving >20 mg per day of prednisone (or equivalent) may be most susceptible. Fatalities have occurred due to adrenal insufficiency in asthmatic patients during and after transfer from systemic corticosteroids to aerosol steroids; aerosol steroids do **not** provide the systemic steroid needed to treat patients having trauma, surgery, or infections.

Acute myopathy has been reported with high dose corticosteroids, usually in patients with neuromuscular transmission disorders; may involve ocular and/or respiratory muscles; monitor creatine kinase; recovery may be delayed. Corticosteroid use may cause psychiatric disturbances, including depression, euphoria, insomnia, mood swings, and personality changes. Pre-existing psychiatric conditions may be exacerbated by corticosteroid use. Prolonged use of corticosteroids may also increase the incidence of secondary infection, mask acute infection (including fungal infections), prolong or exacerbate viral infections, or limit response to vaccines. Exposure to chickenpox should be avoided; corticosteroids should not be used to treat ocular herpes simplex. Corticosteroids should not be used for cerebral malaria. Close observation is required in patients with latent tuberculosis and/or TB reactivity; restrict use in active TB (only in conjunction with anti-tuberculosis treatment). Prolonged treatment with corticosteroids has been associated with the development of Kaposi's sarcoma (case reports); if noted, discontinuation of therapy should be considered.

Use with caution in patients with thyroid disease, hepatic impairment, renal impairment, cardiovascular disease, diabetes, glaucoma, cataracts, myasthenia gravis, patients at risk for osteoporosis, patients at risk for seizures, or GI diseases (diverticulitis, peptic ulcer, ulcerative colitis) due to perforation risk. Use caution following acute MI (corticosteroids have been associated with myocardial rupture). Because of the risk of adverse effects, systemic corticosteroids should be used cautiously in the elderly in the smallest possible effective dose for the shortest duration. Withdraw therapy with gradual tapering of dose. May affect growth velocity; growth should be routinely monitored in pediatric patients.

Adverse Reactions

>10%:

Central nervous system: Insomnia, nervousness

Gastrointestinal: Increased appetite, indigestion

1% to 10%:
  Dermatologic: Hirsutism
  Endocrine & metabolic: Diabetes mellitus, glucose intolerance, hypergly-
    cemia
  Neuromuscular & skeletal: Arthralgia
  Ocular: Cataracts, glaucoma
  Respiratory: Epistaxis
<1%: Edema, hypertension, vertigo, seizure, psychoses, pseudotumor
  cerebri, headache, mood swings, delirium, hallucinations, euphoria, acne,
  skin atrophy, bruising, hyperpigmentation, Cushing's syndrome, pituitary-adrenal axis suppression, growth suppression, glucose intolerance,
  hypokalemia, alkalosis, amenorrhea, sodium and water retention, hyperglycemia, peptic ulcer, nausea, vomiting, abdominal distention, ulcerative
  esophagitis, pancreatitis, muscle weakness, osteoporosis, fractures,
  muscle wasting, hypersensitivity reactions

Overdosage/Toxicology When consumed in high doses for prolonged
periods, systemic hypercorticism and adrenal suppression may occur. In
those cases, discontinuation of the corticosteroid should be done judiciously.

Drug Interactions

Cytochrome P450 Effect: Substrate of CYP3A4 (minor); **Induces**
CYP2C19 (weak), 3A4 (weak)

Increased Effect/Toxicity: Aprepitant, azole antifungals, calcium channel
blockers (nondihydropyridine), cyclosporine, estrogens, and macrolides
may increase the serum levels of corticosteroids. Corticosteroids may
increase the hypokalemic effects of amphotericin B or potassium-wasting
diuretics (loop or thiazide); monitor.

Concurrent use of nonsteroidal anti-inflammatory drugs (NSAIDs) and
salicylates with corticosteroids may lead to an increased incidence of
gastrointestinal adverse effects. Concurrent use with anticholinergic
agents may lead to severe weakness in patients with myasthenia gravis.
Concurrent use of fluoroquinolone antibiotics may increase the risk of
tendon rupture, particularly in elderly patients (overall incidence rare).
Concurrent use of neuromuscular-blocking agents with corticosteroids may
increase the risk of myopathy. Concurrent use with cyclosporine may
increase cyclosporine levels. The use of live vaccines is contraindicated in
immunosuppressed patients (may increase the risk of vaccinal infection).
In patients receiving high doses of systemic corticosteroids for ≥14 days,
wait at least 1 month between discontinuing steroid therapy and administering immunization.

Decreased Effect: Antacids and bile acid sequestrants may reduce the
absorption of corticosteroids; separate administration by 2 hours. Aminoglutethimide, barbiturates and rifamycin derivatives may reduce the serum
levels/effects of betamethasone (systemic). Serum concentrations of isoniazid may be decreased by corticosteroids. Corticosteroids may lead to a
reduction in warfarin effect. Corticosteroids may suppress the response to
vaccinations.

Ethanol/Nutrition/Herb Interactions

Ethanol: Avoid ethanol (may increase gastric mucosal irritation)
Food: Prednisone interferes with calcium absorption, Limit caffeine.
Herb/Nutraceutical: St John's wort may decrease prednisone levels. Avoid
cat's claw, echinacea (have immunostimulant properties).

Mechanism of Action Decreases inflammation by suppression of migration
of polymorphonuclear leukocytes and reversal of increased capillary permeability; suppresses the immune system by reducing activity and volume of
the lymphatic system; suppresses adrenal function at high doses. Antitumor
(Continued)

PredniSONE *(Continued)*

effects may be related to inhibition of glucose transport, phosphorylation, or induction of cell death in immature lymphocytes. Antiemetic effects are thought to occur due to blockade of cerebral innervation of the emetic center via inhibition of prostaglandin synthesis.

Pharmacodynamics/Kinetics

Protein binding (concentration dependent): 65% to 91%

Metabolism: Hepatically converted from prednisone (inactive) to prednisolone (active); may be impaired with hepatic dysfunction

Half-life elimination: Normal renal function: 2.5-3.5 hours

See Prednisolone monograph for complete information.

Dosage Oral: Dose depends upon condition being treated and response of patient; dosage for infants and children should be based on severity of the disease and response of the patient rather than on strict adherence to dosage indicated by age, weight, or body surface area. Consider alternate day therapy for long-term therapy. Discontinuation of long-term therapy requires gradual withdrawal by tapering the dose.

Children:

Anti-inflammatory or immunosuppressive dose: 0.05-2 mg/kg/day divided 1-4 times/day

Acute asthma: 1-2 mg/kg/day in divided doses 1-2 times/day for 3-5 days

Alternatively (for 3- to 5-day "burst"):

<1 year: 10 mg every 12 hours

1-4 years: 20 mg every 12 hours

5-13 years: 30 mg every 12 hours

>13 years: 40 mg every 12 hours

Asthma long-term therapy (alternative dosing by age):

<1 year: 10 mg every other day

1-4 years: 20 mg every other day

5-13 years: 30 mg every other day

>13 years: 40 mg every other day

Nephrotic syndrome:

Initial (first 3 episodes): 2 mg/kg/day **or** 60 mg/m^2/day (maximum: 80 mg/day) in divided doses 3-4 times/day until urine is protein free for 3 consecutive days (maximum: 28 days); followed by 1-1.5 mg/kg/dose **or** 40 mg/m^2/dose given every other day for 4 weeks

Maintenance dose (long-term maintenance dose for frequent relapses): 0.5-1 mg/kg/dose given every other day for 3-6 months

Children and Adults: Physiologic replacement: 4-5 mg/m^2/day

Children ≥5 years and Adults: Asthma:

Moderate persistent: Inhaled corticosteroid (medium dose) or inhaled corticosteroid (low-medium dose) with a long-acting bronchodilator

Severe persistent: Inhaled corticosteroid (high dose) and corticosteroid tablets or syrup long term: 2 mg/kg/day, generally not to exceed 60 mg/day

Adults:

Immunosuppression/chemotherapy adjunct: Range: 5-60 mg/day in divided doses 1-4 times/day

Allergic reaction (contact dermatitis):

Day 1: 30 mg divided as 10 mg before breakfast, 5 mg at lunch, 5 mg at dinner, 10 mg at bedtime

Day 2: 5 mg at breakfast, 5 mg at lunch, 5 mg at dinner, 10 mg at bedtime

Day 3: 5 mg 4 times/day (with meals and at bedtime)

Day 4: 5 mg 3 times/day (breakfast, lunch, bedtime)

Day 5: 5 mg 2 times/day (breakfast, bedtime)

Day 6: 5 mg before breakfast

Pneumocystis carinii pneumonia (PCP):

40 mg twice daily for 5 days **followed by**

40 mg once daily for 5 days **followed by**

20 mg once daily for 11 days or until antimicrobial regimen is completed

Thyrotoxicosis: Oral: 60 mg/day

Chemotherapy (refer to individual protocols): Oral: Range: 20 mg/day to 100 mg/m^2/day

Rheumatoid arthritis: Oral: Use lowest possible daily dose (often ≤7.5 mg/day)

Idiopathic thrombocytopenia purpura (ITP): Oral: 60 mg daily for 4-6 weeks, gradually tapered over several weeks

Systemic lupus erythematosus (SLE): Oral:

Acute: 1-2 mg/kg/day in 2-3 divided doses

Maintenance: Reduce to lowest possible dose, usually <1 mg/kg/day as single dose (morning)

Elderly: Use the lowest effective dose

Dosing adjustment in hepatic impairment: Prednisone is inactive and must be metabolized by the liver to prednisolone. This conversion may be impaired in patients with liver disease, however, prednisolone levels are observed to be higher in patients with severe liver failure than in normal patients. Therefore, compensation for the inadequate conversion of prednisone to prednisolone occurs.

Dosing adjustment in hyperthyroidism: Prednisone dose may need to be increased to achieve adequate therapeutic effects

Hemodialysis: Supplemental dose is not necessary

Peritoneal dialysis: Supplemental dose is not necessary

Combination Regimens Note: In the U.S. prednisone is the preferred corticosteroid. However, in the British literature prednisolone is often used. The oral doses of these two agents are equivalent (ie, 1 mg prednisone = 1 mg prednisolone). Also, early clinical trials gave prednisone only with the first and fourth cycles. Some clinicians give prednisone with every cycle.

Brain tumors:

MOPP (Medulloblastoma) *on page 1253*

POC *on page 1271*

Breast cancer:

CFP *on page 1170*

CMFP *on page 1178*

CMFVP (Cooper Regimen, VPCMF) *on page 1178*

Leukemia, acute lymphocytic:

DVP *on page 1196*

Hyper-CVAD + Imatinib *on page 1229*

Hyper-CVAD (Leukemia, Acute Lymphocytic) *on page 1231*

Larson Regimen *on page 1242*

Linker Protocol *on page 1243*

MTX/6-MP/VP (Maintenance) *on page 1254*

POMP *on page 1273*

PVA (POG 8602) *on page 1273*

PVDA *on page 1276*

Leukemia, chronic lymphocytic:

CHL + PRED *on page 1173*

CP (Leukemia) *on page 1183*

CVP (Leukemia) *on page 1184*

Lymphoma, Hodgkin's:

BEACOPP *on page 1148*

(Continued)

PredniSONE *(Continued)*

CAD/MOPP/ABV *on page 1157*
ChIVPP *on page 1173*
COMP *on page 1182*
LOPP *on page 1244*
MOPP (Lymphoma, Hodgkin's Disease) *on page 1252*
MOPP/ABV Hybrid *on page 1251*
MOPP/ABVD *on page 1249*
MVPP *on page 1259*
OPA *on page 1261*
OPPA *on page 1262*
Stanford V *on page 1278*
Lymphoma, non-Hodgkin's:
CEPP(B) *on page 1167*
CHOP *on page 1173*
CNOP *on page 1179*
COMP *on page 1182*
COP-BLAM *on page 1182*
COPP *on page 1183*
CVP (Lymphoma, non-Hodgkin's) *on page 1185*
EPOCH *on page 1204*
MACOP-B *on page 1245*
Pro-MACE-CytaBOM *on page 1273*
R-CVP *on page 1276*
Rituximab-CHOP *on page 1278*
Multiple myeloma:
Bortezomib-Melphalan-Prednisone *on page 1156*
Bortezomib-Melphalan-Prednisone-Thalidomide *on page 1156*
M-2 *on page 1245*
Melphalan-Prednisone-Thalidomide *on page 1246*
MP (Multiple Myeloma) *on page 1254*
VBAP *on page 1287*
VBMCP *on page 1288*
VCAP *on page 1289*
Prostate cancer:
Docetaxel-Prednisone *on page 1192*
Estramustine + Docetaxel + Prednisone *on page 1208*
MP (Prostate Cancer) *on page 1254*

Administration Administer with meals to decrease gastrointestinal upset

Monitoring Parameters Blood pressure, blood glucose, electrolytes

Test Interactions Response to skin tests

Dietary Considerations Should be taken after meals or with food or milk; increase dietary intake of pyridoxine, vitamin C, vitamin D, folate, calcium, and phosphorus.

Patient Information Notify surgeon or dentist before surgical repair; may cause GI upset, take with food; notify prescriber if any sign of infection occurs; avoid abrupt withdrawal when on long-term therapy; do not discontinue or decrease drug without contacting prescriber, carry an identification card or bracelet advising that you are on steroids

Special Geriatric Considerations Because of the risk of adverse effects, systemic corticosteroids should be used cautiously in the elderly, in the smallest possible dose, and for the shortest possible time.

Additional Information Tapering of corticosteroids after a short course of therapy (<7-10 days) is generally not required unless the disease/inflammatory process is slow to respond. Tapering after prolonged exposure is dependent upon the individual patient, duration of corticosteroid treatments, and size of steroid dose. Recovery of the HPA axis may require several months. Subtle but important HPA axis suppression may be present for as long as several months after a course of as few as 10-14 days duration. Testing of HPA axis (cosyntropin) may be required, and signs/symptoms of adrenal insufficiency should be monitored in patients with a history of use.

Emetic Potential Very low (<10%)

Vesicant No

Dosage Forms Excipient information presented when available (limited, particularly for generics); consult specific product labeling.

Solution, oral: 1 mg/mL (5 mL, 120 mL, 500 mL) [contains alcohol 5%, sodium benzoate; peppermint vanilla flavor]

Solution, oral [concentrate]:

PredniSONE Intensol™: 5 mg/mL (30 mL) [contains alcohol 30%]

Tablet: 1 mg, 2.5 mg, 5 mg, 10 mg, 20 mg, 50 mg

Sterapred®: 5 mg [supplied as 21 tablet 6-day unit-dose package or 48 tablet 12-day unit-dose package]

Sterapred® DS: 10 mg [supplied as 21 tablet 6-day unit-dose package or 48 tablet 12-day unit-dose package]

References

Boot AM, Nauta J, Hokken-Koelega AC, et al, "Renal Transplantation and Osteoporosis," *Arch Dis Child*, 1995, 72(6):502-6.

Bowman H and Lennard TW, "Immunosuppressive Drugs," *Br J Hosp Med*, 1992, 48(9):570-3.

Frey BM and Frey FJ, "Clinical Pharmacokinetics of Prednisone and Prednisolone," *Clin Pharmacokinet*, 1990, 19(2):126-46.

Gambertoglio JG, Amend WJ Jr, and Benet LZ, "Pharmacokinetics and Bioavailability of Prednisone and Prednisolone in Healthy Volunteers and Patients: A Review," *J Pharmacokinet Biopharm*, 1980 , 8(1):1-52.

Grotz WH, Mundinger FA, Gugel B, et al, "Bone Mineral Density After Kidney Transplantation: A Cross-Sectional Study in 190-Graft Recipients Up to 20 Years After Transplantation," *Transplantation*, 1995, 59(7):982-6.

Gutin PH, "Corticosteroid Therapy in Patients With Brain Tumors," *Natl Cancer Inst Monogr*, 1977, 46:151-6.

Jusko WJ and Rose JQ, "Monitoring Prednisone and Prednisolone," *Ther Drug Monit*, 1980, 2(2):169-76.

Kimberly RP, "Glucocorticoids," *Curr Opin Rheumatol*, 1994, 6(3):273-80.

Lowenthal RM and Jestrimski KW, "Corticosteroid Drugs: Their Role in Oncological Practice," *Med J Aust*, 1986, 144(2):81-5.

Murphy CM, Coonce SL, and Simon PA, "Treatment of Asthma in Children," *Clin Pharm*, 1991, 10(9):685-703.

Report of a Workshop by the British Association for Paediatric Nephrology and Research Unit, Royal College of Physicians, "Consensus Statement on Management and Audit Potential for Steroid Responsive Nephrotic Syndrome," *Arch Dis Child*, 1994, 70(2):151-7.

Verbeek PR and Geerts WH, "Nontapering Versus Tapering Prednisone in Acute Exacerbations of Asthma: A Pilot Trial," *J Emerg Med*, 1995, 13(5):715-9.

Wolkowitz OM, "Long-Lasting Behavioral Changes Following Prednisone Withdrawal," *JAMA*, 1989, 261(12):1731-2.

Procarbazine (proe KAR ba zeen)

Medication Safety Issues

Sound-alike/look-alike issues:

Procarbazine may be confused with dacarbazine

Matulane® may be confused with Modane®

High alert medication: The Institute for Safe Medication Practices (ISMP) includes this medication among its list of drugs which have a heightened risk of causing significant patient harm when used in error.

Related Information

Fertility and Cancer Therapy *on page 1298*

Management of Nausea and Vomiting *on page 1319*

Safe Handling of Hazardous Drugs *on page 1382*

U.S. Brand Names Matulane®

Index Terms Benzmethyzin; N-Methylhydrazine; NSC-77213; Procarbazine Hydrochloride

Generic Available No

Canadian Brand Names Matulane®; Natulan®

Pharmacologic Category Antineoplastic Agent, Alkylating Agent

Use Treatment of Hodgkin's disease

Unlabeled/Investigational Use Treatment of non-Hodgkin's lymphoma, brain tumors, melanoma, lung cancer, multiple myeloma

Pregnancy Risk Factor D

Lactation Excretion in breast milk unknown/not recommended

Labeled Contraindications Hypersensitivity to procarbazine or any component of the formulation; pre-existing bone marrow aplasia; ethanol ingestion; pregnancy

Warnings/Precautions Hazardous agent - use appropriate precautions for handling and disposal. Use with caution in patients with pre-existing renal or hepatic impairment. Procarbazine possesses MAO inhibitor activity and has potential for severe drug and food interactions; follow MAOI diet. Avoid ethanol consumption, may cause disulfiram-like reaction. May cause hemolysis and/or presence of Heinz inclusion bodies in erythrocytes. Bone marrow depression may occur 2-8 weeks after treatment initiation. Allow ≥1 month interval between radiation therapy or myelosuppressive chemotherapy and initiation of treatment. Withhold treatment for CNS toxicity, leukopenia (WBC <4000/mm³), thrombocytopenia (platelets <100,000/mm³), hypersensitivity, stomatitis, diarrhea or hemorrhage. Procarbazine is a carcinogen which may cause acute leukemia. May cause infertility. **[U.S. Boxed Warning]: Should be administered under the supervision of an experienced cancer chemotherapy physician.**

Adverse Reactions Most frequencies not defined.

Cardiovascular: Edema, flushing, hypotension, syncope, tachycardia

Central nervous system: Apprehension, ataxia, chills, coma, confusion, depression, dizziness, drowsiness, fatigue, fever, hallucination, headache, insomnia, lethargy, nervousness, nightmares, pain, seizure, slurred speech

Dermatologic: Alopecia, dermatitis, hyperpigmentation, petechiae, pruritus, purpura, rash, urticaria

Endocrine & metabolic: Gynecomastia (in prepubertal and early pubertal males)

Hematologic: Eosinophilia; hemolysis (in patients with G6PD deficiency); hemolytic anemia; myelosuppression (leukopenia, anemia, thrombocytopenia); pancytopenia

Gastrointestinal: Abdominal pain, anorexia, constipation, diarrhea, dysphagia, hematemesis, melena; nausea and vomiting ([60% to 90%], increasing the dose in a stepwise fashion over several days may minimize); stomatitis, xerostomia

Genitourinary: Azoospermia (reported with combination chemotherapy), hematuria, nocturia, polyuria, reproductive dysfunction (>10%)

Hepatic: Hepatic dysfunction, jaundice

Neuromuscular & skeletal: Arthralgia, falling, foot drop, myalgia, neuropathy, paresthesia, reflex diminished, tremor, unsteadiness, weakness

Ocular: Diplopia, inability to focus, nystagmus, papilledema, photophobia, retinal hemorrhage

Otic: Hearing loss

Respiratory: Cough, epistaxis, hemoptysis, hoarseness, pleural effusion, pneumonitis, pulmonary toxicity (<1%)

Miscellaneous: Allergic reaction, diaphoresis, herpes, infection, secondary malignancies (2% to 15%; reported with combination therapy)

Overdosage/Toxicology Symptoms of overdose include hypotension, paresthesia, bone marrow suppression, hallucinations, nausea, vomiting, diarrhea, enteritis, tremors, seizures, and coma. In addition to I.V. hydration, treatment is symptom-directed and supportive. Emesis and/or gastric lavage may be useful. Adverse effects such as marrow toxicity may begin as late as 2 weeks after exposure. Monitor CBC and liver function tests for at least 2 weeks.

Drug Interactions

Increased Effect/Toxicity: Procarbazine may enhance the vasopressor effect of direct-acting alpha-/beta-agonists. Procarbazine may enhance the hypertensive effect of indirect-acting alpha-/beta-agonists, alpha$_1$-agonists, alpha$_2$-agonists (ophthalmic), amphetamines, dexmethylphenidate, and methylphenidate. Procarbazine may enhance the serotonergic effect of serotonin/norepinephrine reuptake inhibitors, cyclobenzaprine, dextromethorphan, meperidine, selective serotonin reuptake inhibitors, serotonin modulators, and tricyclic antidepressants. Procarbazine may enhance the neurotoxic (central) effect of atomoxetine, bupropion, lithium and mirtazapine. Procarbazine may enhance the adverse/toxic effect of disulfiram and rauwolfia alkaloids. Procarbazine may increase the levels/effects of serotonin 5-HT$_{1D}$ receptor agonists. Altretamine may enhance the orthostatic effect of procarbazine. Buspirone may enhance the adverse/toxic effect of procarbazine. COMT Inhibitors may enhance the cardiovascular adverse/toxic effects of procarbazine. Levodopa may enhance the hypertensive effect of procarbazine. Sibutramine may enhance the serotonergic effect of procarbazine. Tramadol may enhance the neurotoxic effects of procarbazine.

Decreased Effect: Procarbazine may decrease the absorption of digoxin tablets. Procarbazine may diminish the antihypertensive effect of false neurotransmitters.

Ethanol/Nutrition/Herb Interactions

Ethanol: May enhance the adverse/toxic effects of procarbazine; concurrent use not recommended.

Food: Concurrent ingestion of foods rich in tyramine may cause sudden and severe high blood pressure (hypertensive crisis). Avoid tyramine-containing foods with MAOIs. Food's freshness is also an important concern; improperly stored or spoiled food can create an environment where tyramine concentrations may increase.

Herb/Nutraceuticals: Avoid supplements containing caffeine, tyrosine, tryptophan or phenylalanine. Ingestion of large quantities may increase the risk of severe side effects (eg, hypertensive reactions, serotonin syndrome).

(Continued)

Procarbazine *(Continued)*

Storage/Stability Protect from light.

Mechanism of Action Mechanism of action is not clear, methylating of nucleic acids; inhibits DNA, RNA, and protein synthesis; may damage DNA directly and suppresses mitosis; metabolic activation required by host

Pharmacodynamics/Kinetics

Absorption: Rapid and complete

Distribution: Crosses blood-brain barrier; equilibrates between plasma and CSF

Metabolism: Hepatic and renal

Half-life elimination: 1 hour

Time to peak, plasma: 1 hour

Excretion: Urine and respiratory tract (<5% as unchanged drug, 70% as metabolites)

Dosage Refer to individual protocols. Manufacturer states that the dose is based on patient's ideal weight if the patient is obese or has abnormal fluid retention. Other studies suggest that ideal body weight may not be necessary. Oral (may be given as a single daily dose or in 2-3 divided doses):

Children:

BMT aplastic anemia conditioning regimen: 12.5 mg/kg/day every other day for 4 doses

Hodgkin's disease: MOPP/IC-MOPP regimens: 100 mg/m^2/day for 14 days and repeated every 4 weeks

Neuroblastoma and medulloblastoma: Doses as high as 100-200 mg/m^2/day once daily have been used

Adults: Initial: 2-4 mg/kg/day in single or divided doses for 7 days then increase dose to 4-6 mg/kg/day until response is obtained or leukocyte count decreased <4000/mm^3 or the platelet count decreased <100,000/mm^3; maintenance: 1-2 mg/kg/day

Dosing in renal impairment: The FDA-approved labeling does not contain dosing adjustment guidelines; use with caution; may result in increased toxicity.

Dosing in hepatic impairment: The FDA-approved labeling does not contain dosing adjustment guidelines; use with caution; may result in increased toxicity. The following guidelines have been used by some clinicians:

Floyd, 2006:

ALT/AST 1.6-6 times ULN: Administer 75% of dose

ALT/AST >6 times ULN: Use clinical judgment

Serum bilirubin >5 mg/dL or ALT/AST >3 times ULN: Avoid use

King, 2001: Serum bilirubin >5 mg/dL or ALT/AST >180 units/L: Avoid use

Combination Regimens

Brain tumors:

8 in 1 (Brain tumors) *on page 1141*

MOP *on page 1249*

MOPP (Medulloblastoma) *on page 1253*

PCV *on page 1268*

Lymphoma, Hodgkin's:

BEACOPP *on page 1148*

CAD/MOPP/ABV *on page 1157*

ChlVPP *on page 1173*

LOPP *on page 1244*

MOPP (Lymphoma, Hodgkin's Disease) *on page 1252*

MOPP/ABV Hybrid *on page 1251*

MOPP/ABVD *on page 1249*

Administration May be given as a single daily dose or in 2-3 divided doses.

Monitoring Parameters CBC with differential, platelet and reticulocyte count, urinalysis, liver function test, renal function test.

Dietary Considerations Avoid tyramine-containing foods/beverages. Some examples include aged or matured cheese, air-dried or cured meats (including sausages and salamis), fava or broad bean pods, tap/draft beers, Marmite concentrate, sauerkraut, soy sauce and other soybean condiments.

Patient Information Take as directed. Maintain adequate hydration (2-3 L/ day of fluids unless instructed to restrict fluid intake). Avoid aspirin and aspirin-containing substances; use alcohol cautiously, may cause acute disulfiram-like reaction - flushing, headache, acute vomiting, chest and/or abdominal pain; avoid tyramine-containing foods. Avoid tobacco. You may experience mental depression, nervousness, insomnia, nightmares, dizziness, confusion, or lethargy (use caution when driving or engaging in tasks that require alertness until response to drug is known); photosensitivity (use sunscreen, wear protective clothing and eyewear, and avoid direct sunlight). You may experience rash or hair loss (reversible), loss of libido, increased sensitivity to infection (avoid crowds and infected persons). Report persistent fever, chills, sore throat; unusual bleeding; blood in urine, stool (black stool), or vomitus; unresolved depression; mania; hallucinations; nightmares; disorientation; seizures; chest pain or palpitations; or difficulty breathing.

Emetic Potential Moderately high (60% to 90%)

Dosage Forms Excipient information presented when available (limited, particularly for generics); consult specific product labeling.

Capsule, as hydrochloride:
Matulane®: 50 mg

References

Floyd J, Mirza I, Sachs B, et al, "Hepatotoxicity of Chemotherapy," *Semin Oncol*, 2006, 33(1):50-67.

King PD and Perry MC, "Hepatotoxicity of Chemotherapy," *Oncologist*, 2001, 6(2):162-76.

Longo DL, Young RC, Wesley M, et al, "Twenty Years of MOPP Therapy for Hodgkin's Disease," *J Clin Oncol*, 1986, 4(9):1295-306.

Rodriguez LA, Prados M, Silver P, et al, "Re-evaluation of Procarbazine for the Treatment of Recurrent Malignant Central Nervous System Tumors," *Cancer*, 1989, 64(12):2420-3.

Shulman KI and Walker SE, "A Reevaluation of Dietary Restrictions for Irreversible Monoamine Oxidase Inhibitors," *Psychiatr Ann*, 2001, 31(6):378-84.

Shulman KI and Walker SE, "Refining the MAOI Diet: Tyramine Content of Pizzas and Soy Products," *J Clin Psychiatry*, 1999, 60(3):191-3.

Spivack SD, "Procarbazine," *Ann Intern Med*, 1974, 81:795-800.

Toth B, "A Review of the Antineoplastic Action of Certain Hydrazines and Hydrazine-Containing Natural Products," *In Vivo*, 1996, 10(1):65-96.

Walker SE, Shulman KI, Tailor SA, et al, "Tyramine Content of Previously Restricted Foods in Monoamine Oxidase Inhibitor Diets," *J Clin Psychopharmacol*, 1996, 16(5):383-8.

♦ **Procarbazine Hydrochloride** *see* Procarbazine *on page 926*

Prochlorperazine (proe klor PER a zeen)
Medication Safety Issues

Sound-alike/look-alike issues:

Prochlorperazine may be confused with chlorproMAZINE
Compazine® may be confused with Copaxone®, Coumadin®

(Continued)

Prochlorperazine *(Continued)*

CPZ (occasional abbreviation for Compazine®) is an error-prone abbreviation (mistaken as chlorpromazine)

U.S. Brand Names Compro™

Index Terms Chlormeprazine; Compazine; Prochlorperazine Edisylate; Prochlorperazine Maleate

Generic Available Yes: Injection, tablet, suppository

Canadian Brand Names Apo-Prochlorperazine®; Compazine®; Nu-Prochlor; Stemetil®

Pharmacologic Category Antiemetic; Antipsychotic Agent, Typical, Phenothiazine

Use Management of nausea and vomiting; psychotic disorders including schizophrenia; anxiety

Unlabeled/Investigational Use Behavioral syndromes in dementia

Lactation Excretion in breast milk unknown/use caution

Labeled Contraindications Hypersensitivity to prochlorperazine or any component of the formulation (cross-reactivity between phenothiazines may occur); severe CNS depression; coma; pediatric surgery; Reye's syndrome; should not be used in children <2 years of age or <9 kg

Warnings/Precautions May be sedating; use with caution in disorders where CNS depression is a feature. May obscure intestinal obstruction or brain tumor. May impair physical or mental abilities; patients must be cautioned about performing tasks which require mental alertness (eg, operating machinery or driving). Effects with other sedative drugs or ethanol may be potentiated. Use with caution in Parkinson's disease; hemodynamic instability; bone marrow suppression; predisposition to seizures; subcortical brain damage; and in severe cardiac, hepatic, renal or respiratory disease. Caution in breast cancer or other prolactin-dependent tumors (may elevate prolactin levels). May alter temperature regulation or mask toxicity of other drugs. Use caution with exposure to heat. May alter cardiac conduction - life threatening arrhythmias have occurred with therapeutic doses of phenothiazines. May cause orthostatic hypotension; use with caution in patients at risk of hypotension or where transient hypotensive episodes would be poorly tolerated (cardiovascular disease or cerebrovascular disease). Hypotension may occur following administration, particularly when parenteral form is used or in high dosages. Antipsychotic use has been associated with esophageal dysmotility and aspiration; use with caution in patients at risk of pneumonia (ie, Alzheimer's disease). May be associated with pigmentary retinopathy.

Phenothiazines may cause anticholinergic effects (eg, constipation, xerostomia, blurred vision, urinary retention); therefore, they should be used with caution in patients with decreased gastrointestinal motility, urinary retention, BPH, xerostomia, or visual problems. Conditions which also may be exacerbated by cholinergic blockade include narrow-angle glaucoma (screening is recommended) and worsening of myasthenia gravis. May cause extrapyramidal symptoms, including pseudoparkinsonism, acute dystonic reactions, akathisia, and tardive dyskinesia (TD). Use caution in the elderly; incidence of TD may be increased. Children with acute illness or dehydration are more susceptible to neuromuscular reactions (eg, dystonias); use cautiously. May be associated with neuroleptic malignant syndrome (NMS).

Adverse Reactions Reported with prochlorperazine or other phenothiazines. Frequency not defined

Cardiovascular: Cardiac arrest, hypotension, peripheral edema, Q-wave distortions, T-wave distortions

Central nervous system: Agitation, catatonia, cerebral edema, cough reflex suppressed, dizziness, drowsiness, fever (mild - I.M.), headache, hyperactivity, hyperpyrexia, impairment of temperature regulation, insomnia, neuroleptic malignant syndrome (NMS), paradoxical excitement, restlessness, seizure

Dermatologic: Angioedema, contact dermatitis, discoloration of skin (blue-gray), epithelial keratopathy, erythema, eczema, exfoliative dermatitis (injectable), itching, photosensitivity, rash, skin pigmentation, urticaria

Endocrine & metabolic: Amenorrhea, breast enlargement, galactorrhea, gynecomastia, glucosuria, hyperglycemia, hypoglycemia, lactation, libido (changes in), menstrual irregularity, SIADH

Gastrointestinal: Appetite increased, atonic colon, constipation, ileus, nausea, weight gain, xerostomia

Genitourinary: Ejaculating dysfunction, ejaculatory disturbances, impotence, incontinence, polyuria, priapism, urinary retention, urination difficulty

Hematologic: Agranulocytosis, aplastic anemia, eosinophilia, hemolytic anemia, leukopenia, pancytopenia, thrombocytopenic purpura

Hepatic: Biliary stasis, cholestatic jaundice, hepatotoxicity

Neuromuscular & skeletal: Dystonias (torticollis, opisthotonos, carpopedal spasm, trismus, oculogyric crisis, protusion of tongue); extrapyramidal symptoms (pseudoparkinsonism, akathisia, dystonias, tardive dyskinesia); SLE-like syndrome, tremor

Ocular: blurred vision, cornea and lens changes, lenticular/corneal deposits, miosis, mydriasis, pigmentary retinopathy

Respiratory: Asthma, laryngeal edema, nasal congestion

Miscellaneous: Allergic reactions, diaphoresis

Overdosage/Toxicology Symptoms of overdose include deep sleep, coma, extrapyramidal symptoms, abnormal involuntary muscle movements, seizures, and hypotension. Treatment is symptom-directed and supportive. Do not induce emesis because of risk of aspiration if acute dystonic reaction occurred. Extrapyramidal symptoms may be treated with an anticholinergic such as diphenhydramine or benztropine. Treat hypotension with norepinephrine or phenylephrine. Phenothiazines are not dialyzable.

Drug Interactions

Increased Effect/Toxicity: Prochlorperazine plus lithium may rarely produce neurotoxicity. Prochlorperazing may produce additive CNS depressant effects with other CNS depressants. Acetylcholinesterase inhibitors may increase the risk of EPS. Alpha-/beta-agonists, antihistamines, QT_c-prolonging agents may enhance the arrhythmogenic effects of phenothiazines. Concurrent use may enhance the hypotensive effects of narcotics and beta-blockers. SSRIs may increase risk of hypotension. Antimalarials and beta-blockers may increase serum levels of prochlorperazine. Pramlintide may increase anticholinergic effects of prochlorperazine.

Decreased Effect: The antihypertensive effects of methyldopa and guanadrel may be inhibited by prochlorperazine. Prochlorperazine may inhibit the antiparkinsonian effect of levodopa. Prochlorperazine may reverse the pressor effects of epinephrine. Antacids and attapulgite may decreased absorption of phenothiazines. Anticholinertics may decrease the therapeutic response to phenothiazines.

Ethanol/Nutrition/Herb Interactions

Ethanol: Avoid ethanol (may increase CNS depression).

Food: Limit caffeine.

Herb/Nutraceutical: Avoid dong quai, St John's wort (may also cause photosensitization). Avoid kava kava, gotu kola, valerian, St John's wort (may increase CNS depression).

(Continued)

Prochlorperazine *(Continued)*

Storage/Stability

Injection: Store at <30°C (<86°F); do not freeze. Protect from light. Clear or slightly yellow solutions may be used.

I.V. infusion: Injection may be diluted in 50-100 mL NS or D_5W.

Suppository, tablet: Store at 15°C to 30°C (59°F to 86°F). Protect from light.

Compatibility Stable in dextran 6% in dextrose, dextran 6% in NS, D_5W, $D_{10}W$, D_5LR, $D_5\frac{1}{4}NS$, $D_5\frac{1}{2}NS$, D_5NS, LR, $\frac{1}{2}NS$, NS.

Y-site administration: Compatible: Amsacrine, calcium gluconate, cisatracurium, cisplatin, cladribine, clarithromycin, cyclophosphamide, cytarabine, docetaxel, doxorubicin, doxorubicin liposome, fluconazole, gatifloxacin, granisetron, heparin, hydrocortisone sodium succinate, linezolid, melphalan, methotrexate, ondansetron, paclitaxel, potassium chloride, propofol, remifentanil, sargramostim, sufentanil, teniposide, thiotepa, topotecan, vinorelbine, vitamin B complex with C. **Incompatible:** Aldesleukin, allopurinol, amifostine, amphotericin B cholesteryl sulfate complex, aztreonam, cefepime, etoposide phosphate, fludarabine, foscarnet, filgrastim, gemcitabine, piperacillin/tazobactam.

Compatibility in syringe: Compatible: Atropine, butorphanol, chlorpromazine, cimetidine, diamorphine, diphenhydramine, droperidol, fentanyl, glycopyrrolate, hydroxyzine, meperidine, metoclopramide, nalbuphine, pentazocine, perphenazine, promazine, promethazine, ranitidine, scopolamine, sufentanil. **Incompatible:** Dimenhydrinate, ketorolac, midazolam, morphine tartrate, pentobarbital, thiopental. **Variable (consult detailed reference):** Hydromorphone, morphine sulfate.

Compatibility when admixed: Compatible: Amikacin, ascorbic acid injection, cephalothin, dexamethasone sodium phosphate, dimenhydrinate, erythromycin lactobionate, ethacrynate, lidocaine, nafcillin, sodium bicarbonate, vitamin B complex with C. **Incompatible:** Aminophylline, amphotericin B, ampicillin, chloramphenicol, chlorothiazide, floxacillin, furosemide, heparin, hydrocortisone sodium succinate, methohexital, penicillin G sodium, phenobarbital, phenytoin, thiopental. **Variable (consult detailed reference):** Calcium gluconate, penicillin G potassium.

Mechanism of Action Prochlorperazine is a piperazine phenothiazine antipsychotic which blocks postsynaptic mesolimbic dopaminergic D_1 and D_2 receptors in the brain, including the chemoreceptor trigger zone; exhibits a strong alpha-adrenergic and anticholinergic blocking effect and depresses the release of hypothalamic and hypophyseal hormones; believed to depress the reticular activating system, thus affecting basal metabolism, body temperature, wakefulness, vasomotor tone and emesis

Pharmacodynamics/Kinetics

Onset of action: Oral: 30-40 minutes; I.M.: 10-20 minutes; Rectal: ~60 minutes

Peak antiemetic effect: I.V.: 30-60 minutes

Duration: Rectal: 12 hours; Oral: 3-4 hours; I.M., I.V.: Adults: 4-6 hours; I.M.: Children: 12 hours

Distribution: V_d: 1400-1548 L; crosses placenta; enters breast milk

Metabolism: Primarily hepatic; N-desmethyl prochlorperazine (major active metabolite)

Bioavailability: Oral: 12.5%

Half-life elimination: Oral: 3-5 hours; I.V.: ~7 hours

Dosage

Antiemetic: Children (therapy >1 day usually not required): **Note:** Not recommended for use in children <9 kg or <2 years:

Oral, rectal: >9 kg: 0.4 mg/kg/24 hours in 3-4 divided doses; **or**

9-13 kg: 2.5 mg every 12-24 hours as needed; maximum: 7.5 mg/day
13.1-17 kg: 2.5 mg every 8-12 hours as needed; maximum: 10 mg/day
17.1-37 kg: 2.5 mg every 8 hours or 5 mg every 12 hours as needed; maximum: 15 mg/day

I.M.: 0.13 mg/kg/dose; change to oral as soon as possible

Antiemetic: Adults:
   Oral (tablet): 5-10 mg 3-4 times/day; usual maximum: 40 mg/day; larger doses may rarely be required
   I.M. (deep): 5-10 mg every 3-4 hours; usual maximum: 40 mg/day
   I.V.: 2.5-10 mg; maximum 10 mg/dose or 40 mg/day; may repeat dose every 3-4 hours as needed
   Rectal: 25 mg twice daily

Surgical nausea/vomiting: Adults: **Note:** Should not exceed 40 mg/day
   I.M.: 5-10 mg 1-2 hours before induction or to control symptoms during or after surgery; may repeat once if necessary
   I.V. (administer slow IVP <5 mg/minute): 5-10 mg 15-30 minutes before induction or to control symptoms during or after surgery; may repeat once if necessary
   Rectal (unlabeled use): 25 mg

Antipsychotic:
   Children 2-12 years (not recommended in children <9 kg or <2 years):
      Oral, rectal: 2.5 mg 2-3 times/day; do not give more than 10 mg the first day; increase dosage as needed to maximum daily dose of 20 mg for 2-5 years and 25 mg for 6-12 years
      I.M.: 0.13 mg/kg/dose; change to oral as soon as possible
   Adults:
      Oral: 5-10 mg 3-4 times/day; titrate dose slowly every 2-3 days; doses up to 150 mg/day may be required in some patients for treatment of severe disturbances
      I.M.: Initial: 10-20 mg; if necessary repeat initial dose every 1-4 hours to gain control; more than 3-4 doses are rarely needed. If parenteral administration is still required; give 10-20 mg every 4-6 hours; change to oral as soon as possible.

Nonpsychotic anxiety: Oral (tablet): Adults: Usual dose: 15-20 mg/day in divided doses; do not give doses >20 mg/day or for longer than 12 weeks

Elderly: Behavioral symptoms associated with dementia (unlabeled use): Initial: 2.5-5 mg 1-2 times/day; increase dose at 4- to 7-day intervals by 2.5-5 mg/day; increase dosing intervals (twice daily, 3 times/day, etc) as necessary to control response or side effects; maximum daily dose should probably not exceed 75 mg in elderly; gradual increases (titration) may prevent some side effects or decrease their severity

Administration May be administered orally, I.M., or I.V.
   I.M.: Inject by deep IM into outer quadrant of buttocks.
   I.V.: Doses should be given as a short (~30 minute) infusion to avoid orthostatic hypotension; administer at ≤5 mg/minute

Monitoring Parameters Vital signs; lipid profile, fasting blood glucose/Hgb A_{1c}; BMI; mental status, abnormal involuntary movement scale (AIMS); periodic ophthalmic exams (if chronically used); extrapyramidal symptoms (EPS)

Test Interactions False-positives for phenylketonuria, pregnancy, urinary amylase, uroporphyrins, urobilinogen

Dietary Considerations Increase dietary intake of riboflavin; should be administered with food or water. Rectal suppositories may contain coconut and palm oil.

Patient Information May cause drowsiness, impair judgment and coordination; may cause photosensitivity; avoid excessive sunlight; report involuntary movements or feelings of restlessness
(Continued)

Prochlorperazine *(Continued)*

Special Geriatric Considerations Due to side effect profile (dystonias, EPS) this is not a preferred drug in the elderly for antiemetic therapy.

Many elderly patients receive antipsychotic medications for inappropriate nonpsychotic behavior. Before initiating antipsychotic medication, the clinician should investigate any possible reversible cause; any stress or stress from any disease can cause acute "confusion" or worsening of baseline nonpsychotic behavior. Most commonly acute changes in behavior are due to increases in drug dose or addition of new drug to regimen, fluid electrolyte loss, infections, and changes in environment.

Any changes in disease status in any organ system can result in behavior changes.

In the treatment of agitated, demented, older adult patients, authors of meta-analysis of controlled trials of the response to the traditional antipsychotics (phenothiazines, butyrophenones) in controlling agitation have concluded that the use of neuroleptics results in a response rate of 18%. Clearly neuroleptic therapy for behavior control should be limited with frequent attempts to withdraw the agent given for behavior control.

Additional Information Not recommended as an antipsychotic due to inferior efficacy compared to other phenothiazines.

Emetic Potential Very low (<10%)

Vesicant No

Dosage Forms Excipient information presented when available (limited, particularly for generics); consult specific product labeling.

Injection, solution, as edisylate: 5 mg/mL (2 mL, 10 mL) [contains benzyl alcohol]

Suppository, rectal: 25 mg (12s) [may contain coconut and palm oil]

Compro™: 25 mg (12s) [contains coconut and palm oils]

Tablet, as maleate: 5 mg, 10 mg [strength expressed as base]

References

Ernst AA, Weiss SJ, Park S, et al, "Prochlorperazine Versus Promethazine for Uncomplicated Nausea and Vomiting in the Emergency Department: A Randomized, Double-Blind Clinical Trial," *Ann Emerg Med*, 2000, 36 (2):89-94.

Gan TJ, Meyer T, Apfel CC, et al, "Consensus Guidelines for Managing Postoperative Nausea and Vomiting," *Anesth Analg*, 2003, 97(1):62-71.

Goldstein D, Levi JA, Woods RL, et al, "Double-Blind Randomized Cross-Over Trial of Dexamethasone and Prochlorperazine as Antiemetics for Cancer Chemotherapy," *Oncology*, 1989, 46(2):105-8.

Golembiewski J, Chernin E, and Chopra T, "Prevention and Treatment of Postoperative Nausea and Vomiting," *Am J Health-Syst Pharm*, 2005, 62:1247-60.

Hesketh PJ, Gandara DR, Hesketh AM, et al, "Improved Control of High-Dose-Cisplatin-Induced Acute Emesis With the Addition of Prochlorperazine to Granisetron/Dexamethasone," *Cancer J Sci Am*, 1997, 3(3):180-3.

Lapierre J, Amin M, and Hattangadi S, "Prochlorperazine - A Review of the Literature Since 1956," *Can Psychiatr Assoc J*, 1969, 14(3):267-74.

Olver IN, Webster LK, Bishop JF, et al, "A Dose Finding Study of Prochlorperazine as an Antiemetic for Cancer Chemotherapy," *Eur J Cancer Clin Oncol*, 1989, 25(10):1457-61.

Owens NH, Schauer AR, Nightingale CH, et al, "Antiemetic Efficacy of Prochlorperazine, Haloperidol, Droperidol in Cisplatin-Induced Emesis," *Clin Pharm*, 1984, 3(2):167-70.

Peabody CA, Warner MD, Whiteford HA, et al, "Neuroleptics and the Elderly," *J Am Geriatr Soc*, 1987, 35(3):233-8.

♦ **Prochlorperazine Edisylate** *see* Prochlorperazine *on page 929*

♦ **Prochlorperazine Maleate** *see* Prochlorperazine *on page 929*

♦ **Procrit®** *see* Epoetin Alfa *on page 387*

♦ **Proctocort®** *see* Hydrocortisone *on page 545*

♦ **ProctoCream® HC** *see* Hydrocortisone *on page 545*

Promethazine (proe METH a zeen)

Medication Safety Issues

Sound-alike/look-alike issues:

Promethazine may be confused with chlorproMAZINE, predniSONE, promazine

Phenergan® may be confused with Phenaphen®, Phrenilin®, Theragran®

High alert medication: The Institute for Safe Medication Practices (ISMP) includes this medication among its list of drugs which have a heightened risk of causing significant patient harm when used in error.

Administration issues:

To prevent or minimize tissue damage during I.V. administration, the Institute for Safe Medication Practices (ISMP) has the following recommendations:

Limit concentration available to the 25 mg/mL product

Consider limiting initial doses to 6.25-12.5 mg

Further dilute the 25 mg/mL strength into 10-20 mL NS

Administer through a large bore vein (not hand or wrist)

Administer via running I.V. line at port furthest from patient's vein

Consider administering over 10-15 minutes

Instruct patients to report immediately signs of pain or burning

Related Information

Management of Drug Extravasations *on page 1301*
Management of Nausea and Vomiting *on page 1319*

U.S. Brand Names Phenadoz™; Phenergan®; Promethegan™

Index Terms Promethazine Hydrochloride

Generic Available Yes

Canadian Brand Names Phenergan®

Pharmacologic Category Antiemetic; Antihistamine; Phenothiazine Derivative; Sedative

Use Symptomatic treatment of various allergic conditions; antiemetic; motion sickness; sedative; postoperative pain (adjunctive therapy); anesthetic (adjunctive therapy); anaphylactic reactions (adjunctive therapy)

Pregnancy Risk Factor C

Lactation Excretion in breast milk unknown/use caution

Labeled Contraindications Hypersensitivity to promethazine or any component of the formulation (cross-reactivity between phenothiazines may occur); coma; treatment of lower respiratory tract symptoms, including asthma; children <2 years of age

Warnings/Precautions [U.S. Boxed Warning]: Respiratory fatalities have been reported in children <2 years of age. In children ≥2 years, use the lowest possible dose; other drugs with respiratory depressant effects should be avoided. Not for SubQ or intra-arterial administration. (Continued)

Promethazine *(Continued)*

Injection may contain sodium metabisulfite (may cause allergic reaction). I.M. is the preferred route of parenteral administration. I.V. use has been associated with severe tissue damage; discontinue immediately if burning or pain occurs with administration. May be sedating; use with caution in disorders where CNS depression is a feature. May impair physical or mental abilities; patients must be cautioned about performing tasks which require mental alertness (eg, operating machinery or driving). Use with caution in Parkinson's disease; hemodynamic instability; bone marrow suppression; subcortical brain damage; and in severe cardiac, hepatic, renal, or respiratory disease. Avoid use in Reye's syndrome. May lower seizure threshold; use caution in persons with seizure disorders or in persons using narcotics or local anesthetics which may also affect seizure threshold. May alter temperature regulation or mask toxicity of other drugs due to antiemetic effects. May alter cardiac conduction (life-threatening arrhythmias have occurred with therapeutic doses of phenothiazines). May cause orthostatic hypotension; use with caution in patients at risk of hypotension or where transient hypotensive episodes would be poorly tolerated (cardiovascular disease or cerebrovascular disease).

Phenothiazines may cause anticholinergic effects (constipation, xerostomia, blurred vision, urinary retention); therefore, they should be used with caution in patients with decreased gastrointestinal motility, urinary retention, BPH, xerostomia, or visual problems. Conditions which also may be exacerbated by cholinergic blockade include narrow-angle glaucoma (screening is recommended) and worsening of myasthenia gravis. May cause extrapyramidal symptoms, including pseudoparkinsonism, acute dystonic reactions, akathisia, and tardive dyskinesia. May be associated with neuroleptic malignant syndrome (NMS).

Adverse Reactions Frequency not defined.

Cardiovascular: Bradycardia, hypertension, postural hypotension, tachycardia, nonspecific QT changes

Central nervous system: Akathisia, catatonic states, confusion, delirium, disorientation, dizziness, drowsiness, dystonias, euphoria, excitation, extrapyramidal symptoms, fatigue, hallucinations, hysteria, insomnia, lassitude, pseudoparkinsonism, tardive dyskinesia, nervousness, neuroleptic malignant syndrome, nightmares, sedation, seizure, somnolence

Dermatologic: Angioneurotic edema, photosensitivity, dermatitis, skin pigmentation (slate gray), urticaria

Endocrine & metabolic: Lactation, breast engorgement, amenorrhea, gynecomastia, hyper-/hypoglycemia

Gastrointestinal: Xerostomia, constipation, nausea, vomiting

Genitourinary: Urinary retention, ejaculatory disorder, impotence

Hematologic: Agranulocytosis, eosinophilia, leukopenia, hemolytic anemia, aplastic anemia, thrombocytopenia, thrombocytopenic purpura

Hepatic: Jaundice

Local: Venous thrombosis; injection site reactions (burning, erythema, pain, edema)

Neuromuscular & skeletal: Incoordination, tremor

Ocular: Blurred vision, corneal and lenticular changes, diplopia, epithelial keratopathy, pigmentary retinopathy

Otic: Tinnitus

Respiratory: Apnea, asthma, nasal congestion, respiratory depression

Overdosage/Toxicology Symptoms of overdose include CNS depression, respiratory depression, possible CNS stimulation, dry mouth, fixed and dilated pupils, and hypotension. Treatment is symptom-directed and supportive. Epinephrine should not be used. Hemodialysis: Not dialyzable (0% to 5%)

Drug Interactions

Cytochrome P450 Effect: Substrate (major) of CYP2B6, 2D6; **Inhibits** CYP2D6 (weak)

Increased Effect/Toxicity: CYP2B6 inhibitors may increase the levels/effects of promethazine; example inhibitors include desipramine, paroxetine, and sertraline. CYP2D6 inhibitors may increase the levels/effects of promethazine; example inhibitors include chlorpromazine, delavirdine, fluoxetine, miconazole, paroxetine, pergolide, quinidine, quinine, ritonavir, and ropinirole. Pramlintide may enhance the gastrointestinal anticholinergic effects of promethazine.

Decreased Effect: Acetylcholinesterase inhibitors (centrally-acting) may diminish the effects of promethazine. CYP2B6 inducers may decrease the levels/effects of promethazine; example inducers include carbamazepine, nevirapine, phenobarbital, phenytoin, and rifampin. Benztropine (and other anticholinergics) may inhibit the therapeutic response to promethazine. Promethazine may diminish the effect of centrally-acting acetylcholinesterase inhibitors.

Ethanol/Nutrition/Herb Interactions

Ethanol: Avoid ethanol (may increase CNS depression).

Herb/Nutraceutical: Avoid valerian, St John's wort, kava kava, gotu kola (may increase CNS depression).

Storage/Stability

Injection: Prior to dilution, store at room temperature. Protect from light. Solutions in NS or D_5W are stable for 24 hours at room temperature.

Suppositories: Store refrigerated at 2°C to 8°C (36°F to 46°F).

Tablets: Store at room temperature. Protect from light.

Compatibility Stable in dextran 6% in dextrose, dextran 6% in NS, D_5W, $D_{10}W$, D_5LR, $D_5\frac{1}{4}NS$, $D_5\frac{1}{2}NS$, D_5NS, LR, $\frac{1}{2}NS$, NS.

Y-site administration: Compatible: Amifostine, amsacrine, aztreonam, ciprofloxacin, cisatracurium, cisplatin, cladribine, cyclophosphamide, cytarabine, docetaxel, doxorubicin, etoposide phosphate, filgrastim, fluconazole, fludarabine, gatifloxacin, gemcitabine, granisetron, linezolid, melphalan, ondansetron, remifentanil, sargramostim, teniposide, thiotepa, vinorelbine. **Incompatible:** Aldesleukin, allopurinol, amphotericin B cholesteryl sulfate complex, cefazolin, cefepime, cefoperazone, cefotetan, doxorubicin liposome, foscarnet, methotrexate, piperacillin/tazobactam. **Variable (consult detailed reference):** Cefazolin, ceftizoxime, heparin, hydrocortisone sodium succinate, potassium chloride, vitamin B complex with C.

Compatibility in syringe: Compatible: Atropine, atropine with meperidine, butorphanol, chlorpromazine, cimetidine, dihydroergotamine, diphenhydramine, droperidol, fentanyl, glycopyrrolate, hydromorphone, hydroxyzine, meperidine, metoclopramide, midazolam, pentazocine, perphenazine, prochlorperazine edisylate, promazine, ranitidine, scopolamine. **Incompatible:** Cefotetan, chloroquine, diatrizoate sodium 75%, diatrizoate meglumine 52% with diatrizoate sodium 8%, diatrizoate meglumine 34.3% with diatrizoate sodium 35%, dimenhydrinate, heparin, iodipamide meglumine 52%, iothalamate meglumine 60%, iothalamate sodium 80%, ketorolac, pentobarbital, thiopental. **Variable (consult detailed reference):** Morphine, nalbuphine.

Compatibility when admixed: Compatible: Amikacin, ascorbic acid injection, buprenorphine, butorphanol, chloroquine, hydromorphone, netilmicin, vitamin B complex with C. **Incompatible:** Aminophylline, chloramphenicol, (Continued)

Promethazine *(Continued)*

chlorothiazide, dimenhydrinate, floxacillin, furosemide, heparin, hydrocortisone sodium succinate, methohexital, penicillin G sodium, pentobarbital, phenobarbital, phenytoin, thiopental. **Variable (consult detailed reference):** Penicillin G potassium.

Mechanism of Action Blocks postsynaptic mesolimbic dopaminergic receptors in the brain; exhibits a strong alpha-adrenergic blocking effect and depresses the release of hypothalamic and hypophyseal hormones; competes with histamine for the H_1-receptor; reduces stimuli to the brainstem reticular system

Pharmacodynamics/Kinetics

Onset of action: I.M.: ~20 minutes; I.V.: 3-5 minutes
 Peak effect: C_{max}: 9.04 ng/mL (suppository); 19.3 ng/mL (syrup)
Duration: 2-6 hours
Absorption:
 I.M.: Bioavailability may be greater than with oral or rectal administration
 Oral: Rapid and complete; large first pass effect limits systemic bioavailability
Distribution: V_d: 171 L
Protein binding: 93%
Metabolism: Hepatic; primarily oxidation; forms metabolites
Half-life elimination: 9-16 hours
Time to maximum serum concentration: 4.4 hours (syrup); 6.7-8.6 hours (suppositories)
Excretion: Primarily urine and feces (as inactive metabolites)

Dosage

Children ≥2 years:
 Allergic conditions: Oral, rectal: 0.1 mg/kg/dose (maximum: 12.5 mg) every 6 hours during the day and 0.5 mg/kg/dose (maximum: 25 mg) at bedtime as needed
 Antiemetic: Oral, I.M., I.V., rectal: 0.25-1 mg/kg 4-6 times/day as needed (maximum: 25 mg/dose)
 Motion sickness: Oral, rectal: 0.5 mg/kg/dose 30 minutes to 1 hour before departure, then every 12 hours as needed (maximum dose: 25 mg twice daily)
 Sedation: Oral, I.M., I.V., rectal: 0.5-1 mg/kg/dose every 6 hours as needed (maximum: 50 mg/dose)

Adults:
 Allergic conditions (including allergic reactions to blood or plasma):
  Oral, rectal: 25 mg at bedtime **or** 12.5 mg before meals and at bedtime (range: 6.25-12.5 mg 3 times/day)
  I.M., I.V.: 25 mg, may repeat in 2 hours when necessary; switch to oral route as soon as feasible
 Antiemetic: Oral, I.M., I.V., rectal: 12.5-25 mg every 4-6 hours as needed
 Motion sickness: Oral, rectal: 25 mg 30-60 minutes before departure, then every 12 hours as needed
 Sedation: Oral, I.M., I.V., rectal: 12.5-50 mg/dose

Administration Formulations available for oral, rectal, I.M./I.V.; not for SubQ or intra-arterial administration. Administer I.M. into deep muscle (preferred route of administration). I.V. administration is **not** the preferred route; severe tissue damage may occur. Solution for injection should be administered in a maximum concentration of 25 mg/mL (more dilute solutions are recommended). Administer via running I.V. line at port furthest from patient's vein, or through a large bore vein (not hand or wrist). Consider administering over

10-15 minutes (maximum: 25 mg/minute). Discontinue immediately if burning or pain occurs with administration.

Monitoring Parameters Relief of symptoms, mental status

Test Interactions Alters the flare response in intradermal allergen tests; hCG-based pregnancy tests may result in false-negatives or false-positives; increased serum glucose may be seen with glucose tolerance tests.

Dietary Considerations Increase dietary intake of riboflavin.

Patient Information May cause drowsiness, impair judgment and coordination; may cause photosensitivity; avoid excessive sunlight; report involuntary movements or feelings of restlessness

Special Geriatric Considerations Because promethazine is a phenothiazine (and can, therefore, cause side effects such as extrapyramidal symptoms), it is not considered an antihistamine of choice in the elderly.

Emetic Potential Very low (<10%)

Vesicant No; may be an irritant

Dosage Forms Excipient information presented when available (limited, particularly for generics); consult specific product labeling. [DSC] = Discontinued product

Injection, solution, as hydrochloride: 25 mg/mL (1 mL); 50 mg/mL (1 mL)
Phenergan®: 25 mg/mL (1 mL); 50 mg/mL (1 mL) [contains sodium metabisulfite]

Suppository, rectal, as hydrochloride: 12.5 mg, 25 mg, 50 mg
Phenadoz™: 12.5 mg, 25 mg
Phenergan®: 25 mg, 50 mg [DSC]
Promethegan™: 12.5 mg, 25 mg, 50 mg

Syrup, as hydrochloride: 6.25 mg/5 mL (120 mL, 480 mL) [contains alcohol]

Tablet, as hydrochloride: 12.5 mg, 25 mg, 50 mg
Phenergan®: 25 mg [DSC]

References

Blanc VF, Ruest P, Milot J, et al, "Antiemetic Prophylaxis With Promethazine or Droperidol in Paediatric Outpatient Strabismus Surgery," Can J Anaesth, 1991, 38(1):54-60.

Grunberg SM and Hesketh PJ, "Control of Chemotherapy-Induced Emesis," N Engl J Med, 1993, 329(24):1790-6.

http://www.ismp.org/Newsletters/acutecare/articles/20060810.asp

McGee JL and Alexander MR, "Phenothiazine Analgesia - Fact or Fantasy?" Am J Hosp Pharm, 1979, 36(5):633-40.

Starke PR, Weaver J, and Chowdhury BA, "Boxed Warning Added to Promethazine Labeling for Pediatric Use," N Engl J Med, 2005, 352(25):2653.

Strenkoski-Nix LC, Ermer J, DeCleene S, et al, "Pharmacokinetics of Promethazine Hydrochloride After Administration of Rectal Suppositories and Oral Syrup to Healthy Subjects," Am J Health Syst Pharm, 2000, 57(16):1499-505.

Tavorath R and Hesketh PJ, "Drug Treatment of Chemotherapy-Induced Delayed Emesis," Drugs, 1996, 52(5):639-48.

Tortorice PV and O'Connell MB, "Management of Chemotherapy-Induced Nausea and Vomiting," Pharmacotherapy, 1990, 10(2):129-45.

◆ **Promethazine Hydrochloride** see Promethazine on page 935
◆ **Promethegan™** see Promethazine on page 935
◆ **Propecia®** see Finasteride on page 444
◆ **Proplex® T [DSC]** see Factor IX Complex (Human) on page 421
◆ **Proquin® XR** see Ciprofloxacin on page 213
◆ **Proscar®** see Finasteride on page 444
◆ **Protein-Bound Paclitaxel** see Paclitaxel (Protein Bound) on page 865
◆ **Prothrombin Complex Concentrate** see Factor IX Complex (Human) on page 421
◆ **Protopic®** see Tacrolimus on page 993
◆ **Provera®** see MedroxyPROGESTERone on page 703
◆ **Provera-Pak (Can)** see MedroxyPROGESTERone on page 703

- **PS-341** *see* Bortezomib *on page 150*
- **Purinethol**® *see* Mercaptopurine *on page 720*
- **Quadrivalent Human Papillomavirus Vaccine** *see* Papillomavirus (Types 6, 11, 16, 18) Recombinant Vaccine *on page 878*
- **Quixin**™ *see* Levofloxacin *on page 678*
- **R 14-15** *see* Erlotinib *on page 396*
- **R-3827** *see* Abarelix *on page 20*
- **rAHF** *see* Antihemophilic Factor (Recombinant) *on page 95*
- **Ralivia**™ **ER (Can)** *see* Tramadol *on page 1059*

Raloxifene (ral OKS i feen)

Medication Safety Issues
Sound-alike/look-alike issues:
   Evista® may be confused with Avinza™

Related Information
Safe Handling of Hazardous Drugs *on page 1382*

U.S. Brand Names Evista®

Index Terms Keoxifene Hydrochloride; NSC-706725; Raloxifene Hydrochloride

Generic Available No

Canadian Brand Names Evista®

Pharmacologic Category Selective Estrogen Receptor Modulator (SERM)

Use Prevention and treatment of osteoporosis in postmenopausal women; risk reduction for invasive breast cancer in postmenopausal women with osteoporosis and in postmenopausal women with high risk for invasive breast cancer

Pregnancy Risk Factor X

Lactation Excretion in breast milk unknown/contraindicated

Labeled Contraindications History of or current venous thromboembolic disorders (including DVT, PE, and retinal vein thrombosis); pregnancy; breast-feeding

Warnings/Precautions Hazardous agent - use appropriate precautions for handling and disposal. **[U.S. Boxed Warning]: May increase the risk for DVT or PE;** use with caution in patients at high risk for venous thromboembolism; the risk for DVT and PE are higher in the first 4 months of treatment. Discontinue at least 72 hours prior to and during prolonged immobilization (postoperative recovery or prolonged bedrest). Use is contraindicated with a history of or current venous thromboembolic disorders. **[U.S. Boxed Warning]: The risk of death due to stroke may be increased in women with coronary heart disease or in women at risk for coronary events;** use with caution in patients with cardiovascular disease. Not be used for the prevention of cardiovascular disease. Use caution with moderate-to-severe renal dysfunction, hepatic impairment, unexplained uterine bleeding, and in women with a history of elevated triglycerides in response to treatment with oral estrogens (or estrogen/progestin). Safety with concomitant estrogen therapy has not been established. Safety and efficacy in premenopausal women or men have not been established. Not indicated for treatment of invasive breast cancer, to reduce the risk of recurrence of invasive breast cancer or to reduce the risk of noninvasive breast cancer. The efficacy (for breast cancer risk reduction) in women with inherited BRCA1 and BRCA1 mutations has not been established.

Adverse Reactions Note: Raloxifene has been associated with increased risk of thromboembolism (DVT, PE) and superficial thrombophlebitis; risk is similar to reported risk of HRT

>10%:
  Cardiovascular: Peripheral edema (3% to 14%)
  Endocrine & metabolic: Hot flashes (8% to 29%)
  Neuromuscular & skeletal: Arthralgia (11% to 16%), leg cramps/muscle spasm (6% to 12%)
  Miscellaneous: Flu syndrome (14% to 15%), infection (11% to 15%)
1% to 10%:
  Cardiovascular: Chest pain (3% to 4%), syncope (2%), varicose vein (2%), venous thromboembolism (1% to 2%)
  Central nervous system: Headache (9%), depression (6%), insomnia (6%), vertigo (4%), fever (3% to 4%), migraine (2%), hypoesthesia (≤2%)
  Dermatologic: Rash (6%)
  Endocrine & metabolic: Breast pain (4%)
  Gastrointestinal: Nausea (8% to 9%), weight gain (9%), abdominal pain (7%), diarrhea (7%), dyspepsia (6%), vomiting (3% to 5%), flatulence (2% to 3%), cholelithiasis (≤3%), gastroenteritis (≤3%)
  Genitourinary: Vaginal bleeding (6%), cystitis (3% to 5%), urinary tract infection (4%), vaginitis (4%), leukorrhea (3%), urinary tract disorder (3%), uterine disorder (3%), vaginal hemorrhage (3%), endometrial disorder (≤3%)
  Neuromuscular & skeletal: Myalgia (8%), arthritis (4%), tendon disorder (4%), neuralgia (≤2%)
  Ocular: Conjunctivitis (2%)
  Respiratory: Bronchitis (10%), rhinitis (10%), sinusitis (8% to 10%), cough (6% to 9%), pharyngitis (5% to 8%), pneumonia (3%), laryngitis (≤2%)
  Miscellaneous: Diaphoresis (3%)
<1%, postmarketing, and/or case reports: Apolipoprotein A1 increased, apolipoprotein B decreased, death related to VTE, fibrinogen decreased, hypertriglyceridemia (in women with a history of increased triglycerides in response to oral estrogens), intermittent claudication, LDL cholesterol decreased, lipoprotein decreased, muscle spasm, retinal vein occlusion, stroke related to VTE, superficial thrombophlebitis, total serum cholesterol decreased

Overdosage/Toxicology In an 8-week study of postmenopausal women, a dose of raloxifene 600 mg/day was safely tolerated. Leg cramps and dizziness have been reported in women taking doses ≥180 mg. Ataxia, diarrhea, dizziness, flushing, rash, tremor, and increased alkaline phosphatase have been reported following overdose (180 mg) in children. There is no specific antidote for raloxifene. Treatment is symptom-directed and supportive.

Drug Interactions
  Decreased Effect: Cholestyramine decreases raloxifene absorption (separate doses by at least 2 hours); raloxifene may decrease levothyroxine absorption

Ethanol/Nutrition/Herb Interactions Ethanol: Avoid ethanol (may increase risk of osteoporosis).

Storage/Stability Store between 15°C to 30°C (59°F to 86°F).

Mechanism of Action A selective estrogen receptor modulator (SERM), meaning that it affects some of the same receptors that estrogen does, but not all, and in some instances, it antagonizes or blocks estrogen; it acts like estrogen to prevent bone loss and has the potential to block some estrogen effects in the breast and uterine tissues. Raloxifene decreases bone resorption, increasing bone mineral density and decreasing fracture incidence.

Pharmacodynamics/Kinetics
  Onset of action: 8 weeks
  Absorption: Rapid; ~60%
  (Continued)

Raloxifene *(Continued)*

Distribution: 2348 L/kg

Protein binding: >95% to albumin and α-glycoprotein; does not bind to sex-hormone-binding globulin

Metabolism: Hepatic, extensive first-pass effect; metabolized to glucuronide conjugates

Bioavailability: ~2%

Half-life elimination: 28-33 hours

Excretion: Primarily feces; urine (<0.2% as unchanged drug; <6% as glucuronide conjugates)

Dosage Adults: Female: Oral:

Osteoporosis: 60 mg/day

Invasive breast cancer risk reduction: 60 mg/day

Dosage adjustment in hepatic impairment: Child-Pugh class A: Plasma concentrations were higher and correlated with total bilirubin. Safety and efficacy in hepatic insufficiency have not been established.

Administration May be administered any time of the day without regard to meals.

Monitoring Parameters Bone mineral density (BMD), CBC, lipid profile; adequate diagnostic measures, including endometrial sampling, if indicated, should be performed to rule out malignancy in all cases of undiagnosed abnormal vaginal bleeding

Dietary Considerations Supplemental calcium or vitamin D may be required if dietary intake is not adequate.

Special Geriatric Considerations No need to cycle with progesterone.

Additional Information The decrease in estrogen-related adverse effects with the selective estrogen-receptor modulators in general and raloxifene in particular should improve compliance and decrease the incidence of cardiovascular events and fractures while not increasing breast cancer.

Dosage Forms Excipient information presented when available (limited, particularly for generics); consult specific product labeling.

Tablet, as hydrochloride:

Evista®: 60 mg

References

Barrett-Connor E, Mosca L, Collins P, et al, "Raloxifene Use for The Heart (RUTH) Trial Investigators. Effects of Raloxifene on Cardiovascular Events and Breast Cancer in Postmenopausal Women," *N Engl J Med*, 2006, 355(2):125-37.

Chlebowski RT, Col N, Winer EP, et al, "American Society of Clinical Oncology Technology Assessment of Pharmacologic Interventions for Breast Cancer Risk Reduction Including Tamoxifen, Raloxifene, and Aromatase Inhibition," *J Clin Oncol*, 2002, 20(15):3328-43.

Cummings SR, Eckert S, Krueger KA, et al, "The Effect of Raloxifene on Risk of Breast Cancer in Postmenopausal Women: Results from the MORE Randomized Trial," *JAMA*, 1999, 281(23) 2189-97.

Delmas PD, Bjarnason NH, Mitlak BH, et al, "Effects of Raloxifene on Bone Mineral Density, Serum Cholesterol Concentrations, and Uterine Endometrium in Postmenopausal Women," *N Engl J Med*, 1997, 337(23):1641-7.

Draper MW, Flowers DE, Huster WJ, et al, "A Controlled Trial of Raloxifene (LY139481) HCl: Impact on Bone Turnover and Serum Lipid Profile in Healthy Postmenopausal Women," *J Bone Miner Res*, 1996, 11(6):835-42.

Heaney RP and Draper MW, "Raloxifene and Estrogen: Comparative Bone-Remodeling Kinetics," *J Clin Endocrinol Metab*, 1997, 2(10):3425-9.

Land SR, Wickerham DL, Costantino JP, et al, "Patient-Reported Symptoms and Quality of Life During Treatment With Tamoxifen or Raloxifene for Breast Cancer Prevention: The NSABP Study of Tamoxifen and Raloxifene (STAR) P-2 Trial," *JAMA*, 2006, 295(23):2742-51.

Martino S, Cauley JA, Barrett-Connor E, et al, "Continuing Outcomes Relevant to Evista: Breast Cancer Incident in Postmenopausal Women in a Randomized Trial of Raloxifene," *J Natl Cancer Inst*, 2004, 96(23):1751-61.

NCCN (National Comprehensive Cancer Network), "Practice Guidelines in Oncology: Breast Cancer Risk Reduction Version 1.2007," available at http://www.nccn.org/professionals/physician_gls/PDF/breast_risk.pdf.

Siris ES, Harrris ST, Eastell R, et al, "Skeletal Effects of Raloxifene After 8 Years: Results From the Continuing Outcomes Relevant to Evista (CORE) Study," *J Bone Miner Res*, 2005, 20(9):1514-24.

Vogel VG, Costantino JP, Wickerham DL, "Effects of Tamoxifen vs Raloxifene on the Risk of Developing Invasive Breast Cancer and Other Disease Outcomes: The NSABP Study of Tamoxifen and Raloxifene (STAR) P-2 Trial," *JAMA*, 2006, 295(23):2727-41.

♦ **Raloxifene Hydrochloride** *see* Raloxifene *on page 940*

Raltitrexed (ral ti TREX ed)

Related Information
Investigational Drug Service *on page 1379*
Safe Handling of Hazardous Drugs *on page 1382*

Index Terms ICI-D1694; NSC-639186; Raltitrexed Disodium; ZD1694
Generic Available No
Canadian Brand Names Tomudex®
Pharmacologic Category Antineoplastic Agent, Antimetabolite
Use Treatment of advanced colorectal neoplasms
Unlabeled/Investigational Use Undergoing clinical trials for a variety of neoplasms, including breast, colorectal nonsmall cell lung, ovarian and pancreatic cancers
Restrictions Not available in U.S./Investigational
Pregnancy Risk Factor X
Lactation Excretion in breast milk unknown/contraindicated
Labeled Contraindications Hypersensitivity to raltitrexed or any component of the formulation; uncontrolled diarrhea; severe renal or hepatic impairment; pregnancy or breast-feeding
Warnings/Precautions Hazardous agent - use appropriate precautions for handling and disposal. Use caution in patients heavily pretreated with chemotherapy or radiation, especially if myelosuppression, stomatitis, renal toxicity persist. Therapy interruption is required in patients with hepatotoxicity. Use caution in elderly, mild-to-moderate hepatic or renal dysfunction, or a history of gastrointestinal problems (particularly diarrhea). Folinic acid, folic acid, or folate-containing medications (eg, multivitamins) may interfere with raltitrexed; do not administer immediately prior to or concurrently with raltitrexed. May cause malaise/weakness (caution patients concerning operation of machinery/driving). Safety and efficacy in pediatric patients have not been established.

Adverse Reactions
>10%:

Central nervous system: Fever (2% to 23%), may be delayed until several days after administration

Dermatologic: Rashes (14%), usually pruritic papular lesions on head and thorax

Gastrointestinal: Nausea (58%; grade 3 or 4 in 12%), mucositis/stomatitis (12% to 48%; grade 3 or 4 in 2%), diarrhea (38%; grade 3 or 4 in 11%), vomiting (37%), anorexia (27%), abdominal pain (18%), constipation (13% to 15%; grade 3 or 4 in 2%)

Hematologic: Myelosuppression; leukopenia occurs in about 21% of patients (grade 3 or 4 in 12%), nadirs occur in ~8 days, but may be delayed to day 21, with recovery in ~10 days; thrombocytopenia (5% to 6%; grade 3 or 4 in 4%), anemia (15% to 18%; grade 3 or 4 in 7%)

Hepatic: Transaminases increased (14% to 18%; grade 3 or 4 in 10%)

Neuromuscular & skeletal: Weakness (46% to 48%; grade 3 or 4 in 9%)

(Continued)

Raltitrexed *(Continued)*

1% to 10%:

Cardiovascular: Arrhythmias (3%), edema (9% to 10%), CHF (2%)

Central nervous system: Malaise, headache, pain, chills, insomnia, depression, paresthesia

Dermatologic: Alopecia, cellulitis, exfoliative eruptions

Endocrine & metabolic: Dehydration, hypokalemia

Gastrointestinal: Dyspepsia, flatulence, xerostomia, weight loss, taste perversion

Genitourinary: Urinary tract infection

Hepatic: Alkaline phosphatase increased, bilirubin increased

Neuromuscular & skeletal: Arthralgia, myalgia, hypotonia

Ocular: Conjunctivitis

Renal: Serum creatinine increased

Respiratory: Cough (increased), dyspnea, pharyngitis

Miscellaneous: Flu-like syndrome (6% to 8%), diaphoresis, infection, sepsis

<1%: Hypersensitivity/allergic reaction (including stridor and wheezing following the first dose), desquamation

Overdosage/Toxicology Symptoms may include severe hematologic and gastrointestinal toxicity. Treatment is symptom-directed and supportive. Anecdotal reports suggest potential benefit of folinic acid (25 mg/m^2 every 6 hours) if administered early.

Drug Interactions

Decreased Effect: Folic acid, folinic acid, and multivitamins with folic acid may decrease the effectiveness of raltitrexed.

Ethanol/Nutrition/Herb Interactions Herb/Nutraceutical: Avoid folic acid and multivitamins with folic acid close to and during administration.

Storage/Stability Intact vials should be refrigerated at 2°C to 25°C. Protect from light. Solutions reconstituted with saline or dextrose to a concentrate of 0.5 mg/mL are stable for up to 24 hours under refrigeration at 2°C to 8°C.

Reconstitution Reconstitute 2 mg vial with 4 mL SWFI; add to 50-250 mL NS or D_5W.

Compatibility Stable in D_5W, NS. Do not mix with other medications.

Mechanism of Action Raltitrexed is a folate analogue that inhibits thymidylate synthase, blocking purine synthesis. This results in an overall inhibition of DNA synthesis.

Pharmacodynamics/Kinetics

Distribution: V_{ss}: 548 L

Protein binding: 93%

Metabolism: Undergoes extensive intracellular metabolism to active polyglutamate forms; appears to be little or no systemic metabolism of the drug

Half-life elimination: Triphasic; Beta: 2 hours; Terminal: Up to 198 hours

Excretion: Urine (50% as unchanged drug); feces (15%)

Dosage Refer to individual protocols.

I.V.: 3 mg/m^2 every 3 weeks

Dosage adjustment in renal impairment:

Cl_{cr} 55-65 mL/minute: Administer 75% of dose every 4 weeks

Cl_{cr} 25-54 mL/minute: Administer % of dose equivalent to Cl_{cr} every 4 weeks (ie, 25% of dose for Cl_{cr} of 25 mL/minute)

Cl_{cr} <25 mL/minute: Do not administer

Dosage adjustment for hepatic impairment: No adjustment required for mild-moderate hepatic insufficiency. Patients who develop hepatic toxicity should have treatment held until returns to grade 2.

Dosage adjustment for toxicity:
Grade 4 gastrointestinal toxicity or grade 3 gastrointestinal toxicity in combination with grade 4 hematologic toxicity: Discontinue therapy
Grade 3 hematologic toxicity or grade 2 gastrointestinal toxicity: Reduce dose by 25%
Grade 4 hematologic toxicity or grade 3 gastrointestinal toxicity: Reduce dose by 50%

Administration Infuse over 15 minutes.

Monitoring Parameters CBC with differential, hepatic function tests, serum lipids, serum creatinine

Dietary Considerations Avoid folic acid, folinic acid, and multivitamins with folic acid close to and during administration.

Patient Information This medication can only be given intravenously. Avoid folic acid and multivitamins with folate. Inform prescriber if you are pregnant. Do not get pregnant during or for 6 months following therapy. Male: Do not cause a female to become pregnant. Male/female: Consult prescriber for instruction on appropriate contraceptive measures. This drug may cause severe fetal defects. Do not breast-feed.

Additional Information Not available in U.S.

Emetic Potential Mild to moderate (30% to 60%)

Vesicant No

Dosage Forms Excipient information presented when available (limited, particularly for generics); consult specific product labeling.
Injection, powder for reconstitution, as disodium: 2 mg

References
Clarke SJ, Beale PJ, and Rivory LP, "Clinical and Preclinical Pharmacokinetics of Raltitrexed," *Clin Pharmacokinet*, 2000, 39(6):429-43.
Taylor SC, "Raltitrexed for Advanced Colorectal Cancer. The Story So Far," *Cancer Pract*, 2000, 8(1):51-4.
Van Cutsem E, Cunningham D, Maroun J, et al, "Raltitrexed: Current Clinical Status and Future Directions," *Ann Oncol*, 2002, 13(4):513-22.

- **Raltitrexed Disodium** *see* Raltitrexed *on page 943*
- **RAN™-Ciprofloxacin (Can)** *see* Ciprofloxacin *on page 213*
- **Rapamune®** *see* Sirolimus *on page 966*

Rasburicase (ras BYOOR i kayse)

U.S. Brand Names Elitek™

Index Terms NSC-721631; Recombinant Urate Oxidase

Generic Available No

Canadian Brand Names Fasturtec®

Pharmacologic Category Enzyme; Enzyme, Urate-Oxidase (Recombinant)

Use Initial management of uric acid levels in pediatric patients with leukemia, lymphoma, and solid tumor malignancies receiving anticancer therapy expected to result in tumor lysis and elevation of plasma uric acid

Unlabeled/Investigational Use Prevention and treatment of malignancy-associated hyperuricemia in adults

Pregnancy Risk Factor C

Lactation Excretion in breast milk unknown/not recommended

Labeled Contraindications Hypersensitivity, hemolytic or methemoglobinemia reactions to rasburicase or any component of the formulation; glucose-6-phosphatase dehydrogenase (G6PD) deficiency

Warnings/Precautions [U.S. Boxed Warning]: Hypersensitivity reactions (including anaphylaxis), methemoglobinemia, and severe hemolysis have been reported; reactions may occur at any time during treatment (Continued)

Rasburicase *(Continued)*

(including the initial dose); discontinue **immediately and permanently** in patients developing any of these reactions. Hemolysis may be associated with G6PD deficiency; patients at higher risk for G6PD deficiency should be screened prior to therapy. **[U.S. Boxed Warning]: Enzymatic degradation of uric acid in blood samples will occur if left at room temperature;** specific guidelines for the collection of plasma uric acid samples must be followed. Rasburicase is immunogenic and can elicit an antibody response; administration of more than one course is not recommended.

Adverse Reactions As reported in patients receiving rasburicase with anti-tumor therapy versus active-control:

>10%:

Central nervous system: Fever (5% to 46%), headache (26%)

Dermatologic: Rash (13%)

Gastrointestinal: Vomiting (50%), nausea (27%), abdominal pain (20%), constipation (20%), diarrhea (≤1% to 20%), mucositis (2% to 15%)

1% to 10%:

Hematologic: Neutropenia with fever (4%), neutropenia (2%)

Respiratory: Respiratory distress (3%)

Miscellaneous: Sepsis (3%)

<1%: Acute renal failure, anaphylaxis, arrhythmia, cardiac arrest, cardiac failure, cellulitis, cerebrovascular disorder, chest pain, convulsions, cyanosis, dehydration, hemolysis, hemorrhage, hot flashes, ileus, infection, intestinal obstruction, methemoglobinemia, MI, pancytopenia, paresthesia, pneumonia, pulmonary edema, pulmonary hypertension, retinal hemorrhage, rigors, thrombosis, thrombophlebitis

Overdosage/Toxicology No cases of overdose have been reported; low or undetectable serum levels of uric acid would be expected. Treatment should be symptom-directed and supportive.

Storage/Stability Prior to reconstitution, store with diluent at 2°C to 8°C (36°F to 46°F); do not freeze. Protect from light. Reconstituted and final solution may be stored up to 24 hours at 2°C to 8°C (36°F to 46°F). Discard unused product.

Reconstitution Reconstitute each vial with 1 mL of the provided diluent. Mix by gently swirling; do **not** shake or vortex. Discard if discolored or containing particulate matter. Total dose should be further diluted in NS to a final volume of 50 mL.

Mechanism of Action Rasburicase is a recombinant urate-oxidase enzyme, which converts uric acid to allantoin (an inactive and soluble metabolite of uric acid); it does not inhibit the formation of uric acid.

Pharmacodynamics/Kinetics

Distribution: Pediatric patients: 110-127 mL/kg

Half-life elimination: Pediatric patients: 18 hours

Dosage I.V.:

Children: Management of uric acid levels: 0.15 mg/kg or 0.2 mg/kg once daily for 5 days (manufacturer-recommended duration); begin chemotherapy 4-24 hours after the first dose

Limited data suggest that a single prechemotherapy dose (versus multiple-day administration) may be sufficiently efficacious. Monitoring electrolytes, hydration status, and uric acid concentrations are necessary to identify the need for additional doses. Other clinical manifestations of tumor lysis syndrome (eg, hyperphosphatemia, hypocalcemia, and hyperkalemia) may occur.

Adults (unlabeled use): Management of malignancy-associated hyperuricemia: 0.2 mg/kg/day for 3-7 days, beginning the day before or day of chemotherapy **or** 0.15-0.2 mg/kg as a single dose, repeated if needed based on uric acid levels **or** 3-6 mg as a single dose, repeated (1.5-6 mg) if needed based on uric acid levels

Administration I.V. infusion over 30 minutes; do **not** administer as a bolus infusion. Do **not** filter during infusion. If not possible to administer through a separate line, I.V. line should be flushed with at least 15 mL saline prior to and following rasburicase infusion.

Monitoring Parameters Plasma uric acid levels, CBC

Test Interactions Specific handling procedures must be followed to prevent the degradation of uric acid in plasma samples. Blood must be collected in prechilled tubes containing heparin anticoagulant. Samples must then be **immediately** immersed in an ice water bath. Prepare samples by centrifugation in a precooled centrifuge (4°C). Samples must be kept in ice water bath and analyzed within 4 hours of collection.

Patient Information This medication can only be given by injection. Notify prescriber immediately for chest pain, difficulty breathing, or itching. May cause headache, nausea, vomiting, constipation, or fever.

Additional Information

Specific handling procedures must be followed to prevent the degradation of uric acid in plasma samples. Blood must be collected in prechilled tubes containing heparin anticoagulant. Samples must then be **immediately** immersed in an ice water bath. Prepare samples by centrifugation in a precooled centrifuge (4°C). Samples must be kept in ice water bath and analyzed within 4 hours of collection.

Dosage Forms Excipient information presented when available (limited, particularly for generics); consult specific product labeling.

Injection, powder for reconstitution:

Elitek™: 1.5 mg [packaged with three 1 mL ampuls of diluent]; 7.5 mg [packaged with 5 mL of diluent]

References

Lee AC, Li CH, So KT, et al, "Treatment of Impending Tumor Lysis With Single-Dose Rasburicase," *Ann Pharmacother*, 2003, 37(11):1614-7.

Pui CH, "Rasburicase: A Potent Uricolytic Agent," *Expert Opin Pharmacother*, 2002, 3(4):433-42.

- **rATG** *see* Antithymocyte Globulin (Rabbit) *on page 102*
- **ratio-Acyclovir (Can)** *see* Acyclovir *on page 22*
- **ratio-Benzydamine (Can)** *see* Benzydamine *on page 132*
- **ratio-Bicalutamide (Can)** *see* Bicalutamide *on page 141*
- **ratio-Ciprofloxacin (Can)** *see* Ciprofloxacin *on page 213*
- **ratio-Methotrexate (Can)** *see* Methotrexate *on page 733*
- **ratio-Morphine SR (Can)** *see* Morphine Sulfate *on page 779*
- **Ratio-Ondansetron (Can)** *see* Ondansetron *on page 837*
- **Reclast®** *see* Zoledronic Acid *on page 1122*
- **Recombinant Human Interleukin-11** *see* Oprelvekin *on page 842*
- **Recombinant Interleukin-11** *see* Oprelvekin *on page 842*
- **Recombinant Urate Oxidase** *see* Rasburicase *on page 945*
- **Recombinate** *see* Antihemophilic Factor (Recombinant) *on page 95*
- **ReFacto®** *see* Antihemophilic Factor (Recombinant) *on page 95*
- **Reglan®** *see* Metoclopramide *on page 751*
- **Remicade®** *see* Infliximab *on page 605*
- **Restasis®** *see* CycloSPORINE *on page 254*
- **Revlimid®** *see* Lenalidomide *on page 659*
- **rFVIIa** *see* Factor VIIa (Recombinant) *on page 416*

- ◆ **rGM-CSF** see Sargramostim on page 962
- ◆ **Rheumatrex® Dose Pack®** see Methotrexate on page 733
- ◆ **RhIG** see Rh$_o$(D) Immune Globulin on page 948
- ◆ **rhIL-11** see Oprelvekin on page 842
- ◆ **Rho(D) Immune Globulin (Human)** see Rh$_o$(D) Immune Globulin on page 948

Rh$_o$(D) Immune Globulin (ar aych oh (dee) i MYUN GLOB yoo lin)

U.S. Brand Names HyperRHO™ S/D Full Dose; HyperRHO™ S/D Mini Dose; MICRhoGAM®; RhoGAM®; Rhophylac®; WinRho® SDF

Index Terms RhIG; Rho(D) Immune Globulin (Human); RhoIGIV; RhoIVIM

Generic Available No

Canadian Brand Names WinRho® SDF

Pharmacologic Category Immune Globulin

Use

Suppression of Rh isoimmunization: Use in the following situations when an Rh$_o$(D)-negative individual is exposed to Rh$_o$(D)-positive blood: During delivery of an Rh$_o$(D)-positive infant; abortion; amniocentesis; chorionic villus sampling; ruptured tubal pregnancy; abdominal trauma; hydatidiform mole; transplacental hemorrhage. Used when the mother is Rh$_o$(D) negative, the father of the child is either Rh$_o$(D) positive or Rh$_o$(D) unknown, the baby is either Rh$_o$(D) positive or Rh$_o$(D) unknown.

Transfusion: Suppression of Rh isoimmunization in Rh$_o$(D)-negative individuals transfused with Rh$_o$(D) antigen-positive RBCs or blood components containing Rh$_o$(D) antigen-positive RBCs

Treatment of idiopathic thrombocytopenic purpura (ITP): Used in the following nonsplenectomized Rh$_o$(D) positive individuals: Children with acute or chronic ITP, adults with chronic ITP, children and adults with ITP secondary to HIV infection

Pregnancy Risk Factor C

Lactation Does not enter breast milk

Labeled Contraindications Hypersensitivity to immune globulins or any component of the formulation; prior sensitization to Rh$_o$(D)

Warnings/Precautions Rare but serious signs and symptoms (eg, back pain, shaking, chills, fever, discolored urine; onset within 4 hours of infusion) of intravascular hemolysis (IVH) have been reported in postmarketing experience in patients treated for ITP. Clinically-compromising anemia, acute renal insufficiency and disseminated intravascular coagulation (DIC) have also been reported. ITP patients should be advised of the signs and symptoms of IVH and instructed to report them immediately.

Product of human plasma; may potentially contain infectious agents which could transmit disease. Screening of donors, as well as testing and/or inactivation or removal of certain viruses, reduces the risk. Infections thought to be transmitted by this product should be reported to the manufacturer. Not for replacement therapy in immune globulin deficiency syndromes. Use caution with IgA deficiency, may contain trace amounts of IgA; patients who are IgA deficient may have the potential for developing IgA antibodies, anaphylactic reactions may occur. Administer I.M. injections with caution in patients with thrombocytopenia or coagulation disorders. Some products may contain maltose, which may result in falsely-elevated blood glucose readings. Use caution with renal dysfunction; may require an infusion rate reduction or discontinuation. Safety and efficacy have not been established for Rhophylac® in patients with anemia.

ITP: Do not administer I.M. or SubQ for the treatment of ITP; administer dose I.V. only. Safety and efficacy not established in Rh₀(D) negative, non-ITP thrombocytopenia, or splenectomized patients. When using WinRho® SDF, decrease dose with hemoglobin <10 g/dL; use with extreme caution if hemoglobin <8 g/dL. Safety and efficacy have not been established for Rhophylac® in patients with anemia.

Rh₀(D) suppression: For use in the mother; do not administer to the neonate.

Adverse Reactions Frequency not defined.

Cardiovascular: Hyper-/hypotension, pallor, tachycardia, vasodilation

Central nervous system: Chills, dizziness, fever, headache, malaise, somnolence

Dermatologic: Pruritus, rash

Gastrointestinal: Abdominal pain, diarrhea, nausea, vomiting

Hematologic: Haptoglobin decreased, hemoglobin decreased (patients with ITP), intravascular hemolysis (patients with ITP)

Hepatic: Bilirubin increased, LDH increased

Local: Injection site reaction: Discomfort, induration, mild pain, redness, swelling

Neuromuscular & skeletal: Arthralgia, back pain, hyperkinesia, myalgia, weakness

Renal: Acute renal insufficiency

Miscellaneous: Anaphylaxis, diaphoresis, infusion-related reactions, positive anti-C antibody test (transient), shivering

Postmarketing and/or case reports: Anemia (clinically-compromising), DIC, dyspnea, erythema, hemoglobinuria (transient in patients with ITP), injection site irritation, vertigo

Overdosage/Toxicology No symptoms are likely, however, high doses have been associated with a mild, transient hemolytic anemia. Treatment should be symptom-directed and supportive.

Drug Interactions

Decreased Effect: Rh₀(D) immune globulin may interfere with the response of live vaccines; vaccines should not be administered within 3 months after Rh₀(D)

Storage/Stability Store at 2°C to 8°C (35°F to 46°F); do not freeze.

Rhophylac®: Protect from light.

Mechanism of Action

Rh suppression: Prevents isoimmunization by suppressing the immune response and antibody formation by Rh₀(D) negative individuals to Rh₀(D) positive red blood cells.

ITP: Not completely characterized; Rh₀(D) immune globulin is thought to form anti-D-coated red blood cell complexes which bind to macrophage Fc receptors within the spleen; blocking or saturating the spleens ability to clear antibody-coated cells, including platelets. In this manner, platelets are spared from destruction.

Pharmacodynamics/Kinetics

Onset of platelet increase: ITP: Platelets should rise within 1-2 days

Peak effect: In 7-14 days

Duration: Suppression of Rh isoimmunization: ~12 weeks; Treatment of ITP: 30 days (variable)

Distribution: V_d: I.M.: 8.59 L

Bioavailability: I.M.: Rhophylac®: 69%

Half-life elimination: 12-30 days

Time to peak, plasma: I.M.: 5-10 days; I.V. (WinRho® SDF): ≤2 hours

(Continued)

Rhₒ(D) Immune Globulin *(Continued)*

Dosage

ITP: Children and Adults:

Rhophylac®: I.V.: 50 mcg/kg

WinRho® SDF: I.V.:

Initial: 50 mcg/kg as a single injection, or can be given as a divided dose on separate days. If hemoglobin is <10 g/dL: Dose should be reduced to 25-40 mcg/kg.

Subsequent dosing: 25-60 mcg/kg can be used if required to elevate platelet count

Maintenance dosing if patient **did respond** to initial dosing: 25-60 mcg/kg based on platelet and hemoglobin levels

Maintenance dosing if patient **did not respond** to initial dosing:

Hemoglobin 8-10 g/dL: Redose between 25-40 mcg/kg

Hemoglobin >10 g/dL: Redose between 50-60 mcg/kg

Hemoglobin <8 g/dL: Use with caution

Rhₒ(D) suppression: Adults: **Note:** One "full dose" (300 mcg) provides enough antibody to prevent Rh sensitization if the volume of RBC entering the circulation is ≤15 mL. When >15 mL is suspected, a fetal red cell count should be performed to determine the appropriate dose.

Pregnancy:

Antepartum prophylaxis: In general, dose is given at 28 weeks. If given early in pregnancy, administer every 12 weeks to ensure adequate levels of passively acquired anti-Rh

HyperRHO™ S/D Full Dose, RhoGAM®: I.M.: 300 mcg

Rhophylac®, WinRho® SDF: I.M., I.V.: 300 mcg

Postpartum prophylaxis: In general, dose is administered as soon as possible after delivery, preferably within 72 hours. Can be given up to 28 days following delivery

HyperRHO™ S/D Full Dose, RhoGAM®: I.M.: 300 mcg

Rhophylac®: I.M., I.V.: 300 mcg

WinRho® SDF: I.M., I.V.: 120 mcg

Threatened abortion, any time during pregnancy (with continuation of pregnancy):

HyperRHO™ S/D Full Dose, RhoGAM®: I.M.: 300 mcg; administer as soon as possible

Rhophylac®, WinRho® SDF: I.M., I.V.: 300 mcg; administer as soon as possible

Abortion, miscarriage, termination of ectopic pregnancy:

RhoGAM®: I.M.: ≥13 weeks gestation: 300 mcg.

HyperRHO™ S/D Mini Dose, MICRhoGAM®: <13 weeks gestation: I.M.: 50 mcg

Rhophylac®: I.M., I.V.: 300 mcg

WinRho® SDF: I.M., I.V.: After 34 weeks gestation: 120 mcg; administer immediately or within 72 hours

Amniocentesis, chorionic villus sampling:

HyperRHO™ S/D Full Dose, RhoGAM®: I.M.: At 15-18 weeks gestation or during the 3rd trimester: 300 mcg. If dose is given between 13-18 weeks, repeat at 26-28 weeks and within 72 hours of delivery.

Rhophylac®: I.M., I.V.: 300 mcg

WinRho® SDF: I.M., I.V.: Before 34 weeks gestation: 300 mcg; administer immediately, repeat dose every 12 weeks during pregnancy; After 34 weeks gestation: 120 mcg, administered immediately or within 72 hours

Excessive fetomaternal hemorrhage (>15 mL): Rhophylac®: I.M., I.V.: 300 mcg within 72 hours plus 20 mcg/mL fetal RBCs in excess of 15 mL if excess transplacental bleeding is quantified **or** 300 mcg/dose if bleeding cannot be quantified

Abdominal trauma, manipulation:

HyperRHO™ S/D Full Dose, RhoGAM®: I.M.: 2nd or 3rd trimester: 300 mcg. If dose is given between 13-18 weeks, repeat at 26-28 weeks and within 72 hours of delivery

Rhophylac®: I.M., I.V.: 300 mcg within 72 hours

WinRho® SDF: I.M./I.V.: After 34 weeks gestation: 120 mcg; administer immediately or within 72 hours

Transfusion:

Children and Adults: WinRho® SDF: Administer within 72 hours after exposure of incompatible blood transfusions or massive fetal hemorrhage.

I.V.: Calculate dose as follows; administer 600 mcg every 8 hours until the total dose is administered:

Exposure to Rh₀(D) positive whole blood: 9 mcg/mL blood

Exposure to Rh₀(D) positive red blood cells: 18 mcg/mL cells

I.M.: Calculate dose as follows; administer 1200 mcg every 12 hours until the total dose is administered:

Exposure to Rh₀(D) positive whole blood: 12 mcg/mL blood

Exposure to Rh₀(D) positive red blood cells: 24 mcg/mL cells

Adults:

HyperRHO™ S/D Full Dose, RhoGAM®: I.M.: Multiply the volume of Rh positive whole blood administered by the hematocrit of the donor unit to equal the volume of RBCs transfused. The volume of RBCs is then divided by 15 mL, providing the number of 300 mcg doses (vials/syringes) to administer. If the dose calculated results in a fraction, round up to the next higher whole 300 mcg dose (vial/syringe).

Rhophylac®: I.M., I.V.: 20 mcg/2 mL transfused blood or 20 mcg/mL erythrocyte concentrate

Dosage adjustment in renal impairment: I.V. infusion: Use caution; may require infusion rate reduction or discontinuation.

Administration The total volume can be administered in divided doses at different sites at one time or may be divided and given at intervals, provided the total dosage is given within 72 hours of the fetomaternal hemorrhage or transfusion.

I.M.: Administer into the deltoid muscle of the upper arm or anterolateral aspect of the upper thigh; avoid gluteal region due to risk of sciatic nerve injury. If large doses (>5 mL) are needed, administration in divided doses at different sites is recommended. **Note:** Do not administer I.M. Rho(D) immune globulin for ITP.

I.V.:

WinRho® SDF: Infuse over at least 3-5 minutes; do not administer with other medications

Rhophylac®: ITP: Infuse at 2 mL per 15-60 seconds

Note: If preparing dose using liquid formulation, withdraw the entire contents of the vial to ensure accurate calculation of the dosage requirement.

Monitoring Parameters Signs and symptoms of intravascular hemolysis (IVH), anemia, and renal insufficiency; observe patient for side effects for at least 20 minutes following administration; patients with suspected IVH should have CBC, haptoglobin, plasma hemoglobin, urine dipstick, BUN, serum creatinine, liver function tests, DIC-specific tests (D-dimer, fibrin degradation products [FDP] or fibrin split products [FSP]) for differential (Continued)

Rhₒ(D) Immune Globulin (Continued)

diagnosis. Clinical response may be determined by monitoring platelets, red blood cell (RBC) counts, hemoglobin, and reticulocyte levels.

Test Interactions Some infants born to women given Rhₒ(D) antepartum have a weakly positive Coombs' test at birth. Fetal-maternal hemorrhage may cause false blood-typing result in the mother; when there is any doubt to the patients' Rh type, Rhₒ(D) immune globulin should be administered. WinRho® SDF liquid contains maltose; may result in falsely elevated blood glucose levels with dehydrogenase pyrroloquinolinequinone or glucose-dye-oxidoreductase testing methods. WinRho® SDF contains trace amounts of anti-A, B, C and E; may alter Coombs' tests following administration.

Patient Information This medication is only given by injection. It may be given as a one-time dose, or may need repeated. You may experience pain at the injection site. Notify prescriber if you experience chills, headache, dizziness, fever or rash. In ITP, report any back pain, shaking, chills, fever, weight gain/edema, shortness of breath, or discolored urine immediately.

Additional Information A "full dose" of Rhₒ(D) immune globulin has previously been referred to as a 300 mcg dose. It is not the actual anti-D content. Although dosing has traditionally been expressed in mcg, potency is listed in int. units (1 mcg = 5 int. units). ITP patients requiring transfusions should be transfused with Rho-negative blood cells to avoid exacerbating hemolysis; platelet products may contain red blood cells; caution should be exercised if platelets are from Rhₒ-positive donors.

Dosage Forms Excipient information presented when available (limited, particularly for generics); consult specific product labeling.

Injection, solution [preservative free]:

HyperRHO™ S/D Full Dose, RhoGAM®: 300 mcg [for I.M. use only]

HyperRHO™ S/D Mini Dose, MICRhoGAM®: 50 mcg [for I.M. use only]

Rhophylac®: 300 mcg/2 mL (2 mL) [1500 int. units; for I.M. or I.V. use; contains human albumin]

WinRho® SDF:

120 mcg/~0.5 mL (~0.5 mL) [600 int. units; contains maltose and polysorbate 80; for I.M. or I.V. use]

300 mcg/~1.3 mL (~1.3 mL) [1500 int. units; contains maltose and polysorbate 80; for I.M. or I.V. use]

500 mcg/~2.2 mL (~2.2 mL) [2500 int. units; contains maltose and polysorbate 80; for I.M. or I.V. use]

1000 mcg/~4.4 mL (~4.4 mL) [5000 int. units; contains maltose and polysorbate 80; for I.M. or I.V. use]

3000 mcg/~13 mL (~13 mL) [15,000 int. units; contains maltose and polysorbate 80; for I.M. or I.V. use]

References

Gaines AR, "Acute Onset Hemoglobinemia and/or Hemoglobinuria and Sequelae Following Rho(D) Immune Globulin Intravascular Administration in Immune Thrombocytopenic Purpura Patients," *Blood*, 2000, 95(8):2523-9.

Gaines AR, "Disseminated Intravascular Coagulation Associated with Acute Hemoglobinemia or Hemoglobinuria Following Rho(D) Immune Globulin Intravascular Administration for Immune Thrombocytopenic Purpura," *Blood*, 2005, 106(5):1532-37.

George JN, Woolf SH, Raskob GE, et al, "Clinical Guideline: Diagnosis and Treatment of Idiopathic Thrombocytopenic Purpura: Recommendations of the American Society of Hematology," *Ann Intern Med*, 1997, 126(4):319-26.

Hartwell EA, "Use of Rh Immune Globulin: ASCP Practice Parameter. American Society of Clinical Pathologists," *Am J Clin Pathol*, 1998, 110(3):281-92.

"Rhₒ(D) Immune Globulin I.V. for Prevention of Rh Isoimmunization and for Treatment of ITP," *Med Lett Drugs Ther*, 1996, 38(966):6-8.

Simpson KN, Coughlin CM, Eron J, et al, "Idiopathic Thrombocytopenia Purpura: Treatment Patterns and an Analysis of Cost Associated With Intravenous Immunoglobulin and Anti-D Therapy," *Semin Hematol*, 1998, 35(1 Suppl 1):58-64.

Scaradavou A, Bussel J. "Clinical Experience With Anti-D in the Treatment of Idiopathic Thrombocytopenic Purpura." *Semin Hematol*, 1998, 35(1 Suppl 1):52-7.

Ware RE and Zimmerman SA, "Anti-D: Mechanisms of Action," *Semin Hematol*, 1998, 35(1 Suppl 1):14-22.

- **RhoGAM**® *see* Rh$_o$(D) Immune Globulin *on page 948*
- **RhoIGIV** *see* Rh$_o$(D) Immune Globulin *on page 948*
- **RhoIVIM** *see* Rh$_o$(D) Immune Globulin *on page 948*
- **Rhophylac**® *see* Rh$_o$(D) Immune Globulin *on page 948*
- **Rhoxal-anagrelide (Can)** *see* Anagrelide *on page 87*
- **Rhoxal-ciprofloxacin (Can)** *see* Ciprofloxacin *on page 213*
- **Rhoxal-cyclosporine (Can)** *see* CycloSPORINE *on page 254*
- **Rhoxal-pamidronate (Can)** *see* Pamidronate *on page 872*
- **rHuEPO-**α *see* Epoetin Alfa *on page 387*
- **rHu-KGF** *see* Palifermin *on page 868*
- **rHuMAb-EGFr** *see* Panitumumab *on page 876*
- **rhuMAb-VEGF** *see* Bevacizumab *on page 133*
- **rIFN-A** *see* Interferon Alfa-2a *on page 611*
- **rIL-11** *see* Oprelvekin *on page 842*
- **Rituxan**® *see* Rituximab *on page 953*

Rituximab (ri TUK si mab)

Medication Safety Issues

Sound-alike/look-alike issues:

Rituxan® may be confused with Remicade®

Rituximab may be confused with infliximab

High alert medication: The Institute for Safe Medication Practices (ISMP) includes this medication among its list of classes of drugs which have a heightened risk of causing significant patient harm when used in error.

The rituximab dose for rheumatoid arthritis is a flat dose (1000 mg) and is not based on body surface area (BSA).

Related Information

Safe Handling of Hazardous Drugs *on page 1382*

U.S. Brand Names Rituxan®

Index Terms Anti-CD20 Monoclonal Antibody; C2B8 Monoclonal Antibody; IDEC-C2B8; NSC-687451

Generic Available No

Canadian Brand Names Rituxan®

Pharmacologic Category Antineoplastic Agent, Monoclonal Antibody; Monoclonal Antibody

Use Treatment of low-grade or follicular CD20-positive, B-cell non-Hodgkin's lymphoma (NHL); treatment of diffuse large B-cell CD20-positive NHL; treatment of rheumatoid arthritis (RA) in combination with methotrexate

Unlabeled/Investigational Use Treatment of autoimmune hemolytic anemia (AIHA) in children; chronic immune thrombocytopenic purpura (ITP); chronic lymphocytic leukemia (CLL); small lymphocytic lymphoma (SLL); pemphigus vulgaris, Waldenström's macroglobulinemia (WM); treatment of systemic autoimmune diseases (other than rheumatoid arthritis); treatment of refractory chronic graft-versus-host disease (GVHD)

Restrictions An FDA-approved medication guide is available; distribute to each patient to whom this medication is dispensed.

Pregnancy Risk Factor C

(Continued)

Rituximab *(Continued)*

Lactation Excretion in breast milk unknown/not recommended

Labeled Contraindications There are no contraindications listed in the manufacturer's labeling.

Warnings/Precautions [U.S. Boxed Warning]: Severe and occasionally fatal infusion-related reactions have been reported during the first 30-120 minutes of the first infusion. Reactions include hypotension, angioedema, bronchospasm, hypoxia, and in more severe cases pulmonary infiltrates, acute respiratory distress syndrome, myocardial infarction, ventricular fibrillation, and/or cardiogenic shock. Risk factors associated with fatal outcomes include chronic lymphocytic leukemia, female gender, mantle cell lymphoma, or pulmonary infiltrates. Discontinue infusion for severe reactions; treatment is symptomatic. Medications for the treatment of hypersensitivity reactions (eg, epinephrine, antihistamines, corticosteroids) should be available for immediate use. Discontinue infusion for serious or life-threatening cardiac arrhythmias; subsequent doses should include cardiac monitoring during and after the infusion. Mild-to-moderate infusion-related reactions (eg, chills, fever, rigors) occur frequently and are typically managed through slowing or interrupting the infusion. Infusion may be resumed at a 50% infusion rate reduction upon resolution of symptoms. Due to the potential for hypotension, consider withholding antihypertensives 12 hours prior to treatment.

[U.S. Boxed Warning]: Progressive multifocal leukoencephalopathy (PML) due to JC virus has been reported with rituximab use. Cases were reported in patients with hematologic malignancies receiving rituximab either with combination chemotherapy, or with hematopoietic stem cell transplant. Cases were also reported in patients receiving rituximab for autoimmune disease (not an approved use) and may have received prior or concurrent immunosuppressant therapy. Onset may be delayed. Evaluate any neurological change promptly. Other serious and potentially fatal viral infections, either new or reactivated, associated with rituximab use include cytomegalovirus, herpes simplex virus, parvovirus B19, varicella zoster virus, West Nile virus, and hepatitis C. Viral infections may be delayed; occurring up to 1 year after discontinuation of rituximab. Reactivation of hepatitis B has been reported in association with rituximab (rare); consider screening in high-risk patients.

[U.S. Boxed Warning]: Tumor lysis syndrome leading to acute renal failure requiring dialysis may occur 12-24 hours following the first dose. Consider prophylaxis (allopurinol, hydration) in patients at high risk (high numbers of circulating malignant cells $\geq 25,000/mm^3$ or high tumor burden). May cause renal toxicity; consider discontinuation with increasing serum creatinine or oliguria. **[U.S. Boxed Warning]: Severe and sometimes fatal mucocutaneous reactions (lichenoid dermatitis, paraneoplastic pemphigus, Stevens-Johnson syndrome, toxic epidermal necrolysis and vesiculobullous dermatitis) have been reported,** occurring from 1-13 weeks following exposure. Patients experiencing severe mucocutaneous skin reactions should not receive further rituximab infusions and should seek prompt medical evaluation. Use caution with pre-existing cardiac or pulmonary disease, or prior cardiopulmonary events. Rheumatoid arthritis patients are at increased risk for cardiovascular events; monitor closely during and after each infusion. Elderly patients are at higher risk for cardiac (supraventricular arrhythmia) and pulmonary adverse events (pneumonia, pneumonitis). Bowel obstruction and perforation have been reported with an average onset of symptoms of ~6 days; complaints of abdominal pain should be evaluated, especially if early in the treatment course. Live vaccines should not be given concurrently with rituximab; there is no data available concerning secondary transmission of live vaccines with or following rituximab treatment. RA patients should be brought up to date with nonlive immunizations (following current guidelines) before initiating therapy; evaluate risks of therapy delay versus benefit (of nonlive vaccines) for NHL patients. Safety and efficacy of rituximab in combination with biologic agents or disease-modifying antirheumatic drugs (DMARD) other than methotrexate have not been established. Safety and efficacy of retreatment for RA have not been established. Safety and efficacy in children have not been established.

Adverse Reactions Note: Patients treated with rituximab for rheumatoid arthritis (RA) may experience fewer adverse reactions.

>10%:

Central nervous system: Fever (5% to 53%), chills (3% to 33%), headache (19%), pain (12%)

Dermatologic: Rash (15%; grades 3/4: 1%), pruritus (5% to 14%), angioedema (11%)

Gastrointestinal: Nausea (8% to 23%), abdominal pain (2% to 14%)

Hematologic: Lymphopenia (48%; grade 3/4: 40%; median duration 14 days), leukopenia (14%; grade 3/4: 4%), neutropenia (14%; grade 3/4: 6%; median duration 13 days), thrombocytopenia (12%; grade 3/4: 2%)

Neuromuscular & skeletal: Weakness (2% to 26%)

Respiratory: Cough (13%), rhinitis (3% to 12%)

Miscellaneous: Infection (31%; grade 3/4: 2%; bacterial: 19%; viral 10%; fungal: 1%), night sweats (15%)

Mild-to-moderate infusion-related reactions: Chills, fever, rigors, dizziness, hypertension, myalgia, nausea, pruritus, rash, and vomiting (lymphoma: first dose 77%; fourth dose 30%; eighth dose 14%); infusion-related reactions reported are lower in RA

1% to 10%:

Cardiovascular: Hypotension (10%), peripheral edema (8%), hypertension (6% to 8%), flushing (5%), edema (<5%)

Central nervous system: Dizziness (10%), anxiety (2% to 5%), agitation (<5%), depression (<5%), hypoesthesia (<5%), insomnia (<5%), malaise (<5%), nervousness (<5%), neuritis (<5%), somnolence (<5%), vertigo (<5%), migraine (RA: 2%)

Dermatologic: Urticaria (2% to 8%)

Endocrine & metabolic: Hyperglycemia (9%), hypoglycemia (<5%), hypercholesterolemia (2%)

Gastrointestinal: Diarrhea (10%), vomiting (10%), dyspepsia (3% to 5%), anorexia (<5%), weight loss (<5%)

Hematologic: Anemia (8%; grade 3/4: 3%)

Local: Pain at the injection site (<5%)

Neuromuscular & skeletal: Back pain (10%), myalgia (10%), arthralgia (6% to 10%), paresthesia (2% to 5%), arthritis (<5%), hyperkinesia (<5%), hypertonia (<5%), neuropathy (<5%)

Ocular: Conjunctivitis (<5%), lacrimation disorder (<5%)

Respiratory: Throat irritation (2% to 9%), bronchospasm (8%), dyspnea (7%), upper respiratory tract infection (RA: 7%), sinusitis (6%)

Miscellaneous: LDH increased (7%)

Postmarketing and/or case reports: Acute renal failure (associated with tumor lysis syndrome), anaphylactoid reaction/anaphylaxis, angina, aplastic anemia, ARDS, arrhythmia, bowel obstruction, bronchiolitis obliterans, cardiac failure, cardiogenic shock, disease progression (Kaposi's sarcoma), fatal infusion-related reactions, gastrointestinal perforation, (Continued)

Rituximab *(Continued)*

hemolytic anemia, hepatic failure, hepatitis, hepatitis B reactivation, hyper-viscosity syndrome (in Waldenström's macroglobulinemia), hypoxia, interstitial pneumonitis, lichenoid dermatitis, lupus-like syndrome, marrow hypoplasia, MI, neutropenia (late-onset occurring >40 days after last dose), optic neuritis, pancytopenia, paraneoplastic pemphigus (uncommon), pleuritis, pneumonia, pneumonitis, polyarticular arthritis, pure red cell aplasia, renal toxicity, serum sickness, Stevens-Johnson syndrome, supraventricular arrhythmia, systemic vasculitis, toxic epidermal necrolysis, urticaria, uveitis, vasculitis with rash, ventricular fibrillation, ventricular tachycardia, vesiculobullous dermatitis, viral reactivation (includes JC virus [PML], cytomegalovirus, herpes simplex virus, parvovirus B19, varicella zoster virus, West Nile virus, and hepatitis C)

Overdosage/Toxicology There has been no experience with overdosage in human clinical trials. Treatment is symptom-directed and supportive.

Drug Interactions

Increased Effect/Toxicity: Monoclonal antibodies may increase the risk for allergic reactions to rituximab due to the presence of HACA antibody. Antihypertensive medications may exacerbate hypotension.

Decreased Effect: Currently recommended not to administer live vaccines during rituximab treatment.

Ethanol/Nutrition/Herb Interactions Herb/Nutraceutical: Avoid hypoglycemic herbs, including alfalfa, bilberry, bitter melon, burdock, celery, damiana, fenugreek, garcinia, garlic, ginger, ginseng, gymnema, marshmallow, and stinging nettle (may enhance the hypoglycemic effect of rituximab). Monitor.

Storage/Stability Store vials at refrigeration at 2°C to 8°C (36°F to 46°F); do not freeze. Do not shake. Protect vials from direct sunlight. Solutions for infusion are stable at 2°C to 8°C (36°F to 46°F) for 24 hours and at room temperature for an additional 24 hours.

Reconstitution Withdraw necessary amount of rituximab and dilute to a final concentration of 1-4 mg/mL with 0.9% sodium chloride or 5% dextrose in water. Gently invert the bag to mix the solution. Do not shake.

Mechanism of Action Rituximab is a monoclonal antibody directed against the CD20 antigen on B-lymphocytes. CD20 regulates cell cycle initiation; and, possibly, functions as a calcium channel. Rituximab binds to the antigen on the cell surface, activating complement-dependent cytotoxicity; and to human Fc receptors, mediating cell killing through an antibody-dependent cellular toxicity. B-cells are believed to play a role in the development and progression of rheumatoid arthritis. Signs and symptoms of RA are reduced by targeting B-cells.

Pharmacodynamics/Kinetics

Duration: Detectable in serum 3-6 months after completion of treatment; B-cell recovery begins ~6 months following completion of treatment; median B-cell levels return to normal by 12 months following completion of treatment

Absorption: I.V.: Immediate and results in a rapid and sustained depletion of circulating and tissue-based B cells

Distribution: 4.3 L (following two 1000 mg doses for rheumatoid arthritis)

Half-life elimination:

Cancer: Proportional to dose; wide ranges reflect variable tumor burden and changes in CD20 positive B-cell populations with repeated doses:

>100 mg/m^2: 4.4 days (range 1.6-10.5 days)

375 mg/m^2:

Following first dose: Mean half-life: 3.2 days (range 1.3-6.4 days)

Following fourth dose: Mean half-life: 8.6 days (range 3.5-17 days)
RA: Mean terminal half-life: 19 days

Excretion: Uncertain; may undergo phagocytosis and catabolism in the reticuloendothelial system (RES)

Dosage Note: Pretreatment with acetaminophen and diphenhydramine is recommended.

Children: AIHA, chronic ITP (unlabeled uses): I.V.: 375 mg/m² once weekly for 2-4 doses

Adults: I.V. infusion (refer to individual protocols):

NHL (relapsed/refractory, low-grade or follicular CD20-positive, B-cell): 375 mg/m² once weekly for 4 or 8 doses

Retreatment following disease progression: 375 mg/m² once weekly for 4 doses

NHL (diffuse large B-cell): 375 mg/m² given on day 1 of each chemotherapy cycle for up to 8 doses

NHL (follicular, CD20-positive, B-cell, previously untreated): 375 mg/m² given on day 1 of each chemotherapy cycle for up to 8 doses

NHL (low-grade, CD20-positive, B-cell, previously untreated): 375 mg/m² once weekly for 4 doses every 6 months for up to 4 cycles (initiate after 6-8 cycles of chemotherapy are completed)

Rheumatoid arthritis: 1000 mg on days 1 and 15 in combination with methotrexate

Note: Premedication with a corticosteroid (eg, methylprednisolone 100 mg I.V.) prior to each rituximab dose is recommended. In clinical trials, patients received oral corticosteroids on a tapering schedule from baseline through day 16.

CLL/SLL (unlabeled use): 100 mg day 1, then 375 mg/m² 3 times/week for 11 doses

Refractory pemphigus vulgaris (unlabeled use): 375 mg/m² once weekly of weeks 1, 2, and 3 of a 4-week cycle, repeat for 1 additional cycle, then 1 dose per month for 4 months (total of 10 doses in 6 months)

Refractory chronic GVHD, Waldenström's macroglobulinemia (unlabeled uses): 375 mg/m² once weekly for 4 weeks

Combination therapy with ibritumomab: 250 mg/m² I.V. day 1; repeat in 7-9 days with ibritumomab (also see Ibritumomab monograph):

Combination Regimens

Leukemia, chronic lymphocytic:
Fludarabine-Cyclophosphamide-Rituximab *on page 1217*
Fludarabine-Rituximab *on page 1217*
PCR *on page 1267*

Lymphoma, non-Hodgkin's:
R-CVP *on page 1276*
RICE *on page 1277*
Rituximab-CHOP *on page 1278*

Lymphoma, non-Hodgkin's (Mantle cell): Hyper-CVAD + Rituximab *on page 1237*

Administration Do **not** administer I.V. push or bolus.

Initial infusion: Start rate of 50 mg/hour; if there is no reaction, increase the rate 50 mg/hour every 30 minutes, to a maximum of 400 mg/hour.

Subsequent infusions: If patient did not tolerate initial infusion follow initial infusion guidelines. If patient tolerated initial infusion, start at 100 mg/hour; if there is no reaction, increase the rate 100 mg/hour every 30 minutes, to a maximum of 400 mg/hour.

Note: If a reaction occurs, slow or stop the infusion. If the reaction abates, restart infusion at 50% of the previous rate.

(Continued)

Rituximab *(Continued)*

In patients with NHL who are receiving a corticosteroid as part of their combination chemotherapy regimen and after tolerance has been established at the recommended infusion rate in cycle 1, a rapid infusion rate has been used beginning with cycle 2. The daily corticosteroid, acetaminophen, and diphenhydramine are administered prior to treatment, then the rituximab dose is administered over 90 minutes, with 20% of the dose administered in the first 30 minutes and the remaining 80% is given over 60 minutes (Sehn, 2007).

Monitoring Parameters CBC with differential and platelets, peripheral CD20+ cells; HAMA/HACA titers (high levels may increase the risk of allergic reactions); renal function, fluid balance; vital signs; cardiac monitoring during and after infusion in rheumatoid arthritis patients and in patients with pre-existing cardiac disease or if arrhythmias develop during or after subsequent infusions

Screening for hepatitis B in high-risk persons may be considered prior to initiation of rituximab therapy. In addition, carriers and patients with evidence of recovery from prior hepatitis B infection should be monitored closely for clinical and laboratory signs of HBV infection during therapy and for up to a year following completion of treatment.

Complaints of abdominal pain, especially early in the course of treatment, should prompt a thorough diagnostic evaluation and appropriate treatment. Signs or symptoms of progressive multifocal leukoencephalopathy (focal neurologic deficits, which may present as hemiparesis, visual field deficits, cognitive impairment, aphasia, ataxia, and/or cranial nerve deficits).

Emetic Potential Low (10% to 30%)

Vesicant No

Dosage Forms Excipient information presented when available (limited, particularly for generics); consult specific product labeling.

Injection, solution [preservative free]:

Rituxan®: 10 mg/mL (10 mL, 50 mL) [contains polysorbate 80]

References

Ahmed AR, Spigelman Z, Cavacini LA, et al, "Treatment of Pemphigus Vulgaris With Rituximab and Intravenous Immune Globulin," *N Engl J Med*, 2006, 355(17):1772-9.

Avivi I, Robinson S, and Goldstone A, "Clinical Use of Rituximab in Haematological Malignancies," *Br J Cancer*, 2003, 89(8):1389-94.

Boye J, Elter T, and Engert A, "An Overview of the Current Clinical Use of the Anti-CD20 Monoclonal Antibody Rituximab," *Ann Oncol*, 2003, 14(4):520-35.

Byrd JC, Murphy T, Howard RS, et al, "Rituximab Using a Thrice Weekly Dosing Schedule in B-Cell Chronic Lymphocytic Leukemia and Small Lymphocytic Lymphoma Demonstrates Clinical Activity and Acceptable Toxicity," *J Clin Oncol*, 2001, 19(8):2153-64.

Coiffier B, "State-of-the-Art Therapeutics: Diffuse Large B-Cell Lymphoma," *J Clin Oncol*, 2005, 23(26): 6387-93.

Coiffier B, Haioun C, Ketterer N, et al, "Rituximab (Anti-CD20 Monoclonal Antibody) for the Treatment of Patients With Relapsing or Refractory Aggressive Lymphoma: A Multicenter Phase II Study," *Blood*, 1998, 92(6):1927-32.

Coiffier B, Lepage E, Briere J, "CHOP Chemotherapy Plus Rituximab Compared With CHOP Alone in Elderly Patients With Diffuse Large-B-Cell Lymphoma," *N Engl J Med*, 2002, 346(4):235-42.

Cutler C, Miklos D, Kim HT, et al, "Rituximab for Steroid-Refractory Chronic Graft-Versus-Host Disease," *Blood*, 2006, 108(2):756-62.

Dimopoulos MA, Kyle RA, Anagnostopoulos A, et al, "Diagnosis and Management of Waldenstrom's Macroglobulinemia," *J Clin Oncol*, 2005, 23(7):1564-77.

Edwards JC, Szczepanski L, Szechinski J, et al, "Efficacy of B-Cell-Targeted Therapy With Rituximab in Patients With Rheumatoid Arthritis," *N Engl J Med*, 2004, 350(25):2572-81.

Garcia-Suarez J, de Miguel D, Krsnik I, et al, "Changes in the Natural History of Progressive Multifocal Leukoencephalopathy in HIV-Negative Lymphoproliferative Disorders: Impact of Novel Therapies," *Am J Hematol*, 2005, 80(4):271-81.

Goldberg SL, Pecora AL, Alter RS, et al, "Unusual Viral Infections (Progressive Multifocal Leukoencephalopathy and Cytomegalovirus Disease) After High-Dose Chemotherapy With Autologous Blood Stem Cell Rescue and Peritransplantation Rituximab," *Blood*, 2002, 99(4):1486-8.

Gottenberg JE, Guillevin L, Lambotte O, et al, "Tolerance and Short Term Efficacy of Rituximab in 43 Patients With Systemic Autoimmune Diseases," *Ann Rheum Dis*, 2005, 64(6):913-20.

Grillo-Lopez AJ, "Rituximab (Rituxan/MabThera): The First Decade (1993-2003)," *Expert Rev Anticancer Ther*, 2003, 3(6):767-79.

Higashida J, Wun T, Schmidt S, et al, "Safety and Efficacy of Rituximab in Patients With Rheumatoid Arthritis Refractory to Disease Modifying Antirheumatic Drugs and Anti-Tumor Necrosis Factor-Alpha Treatment," *J Rheumatol*, 2005, 32(11):2109-15.

Johnson P and Glennie M, "The Mechanisms of Action of Rituximab in the Elimination of Tumor Cells," *Semin Oncol*, 2003, 30(1 Suppl 2):3-8.

Keating MJ, O'Brien S, Albitar M, et al, "Early Results of a Chemoimmunotherapy Regimen of Fludarabine, Cyclophosphamide, and Rituximab as Initial Therapy for Chronic Lymphocytic Leukemia," *J Clin Oncol*, 2005, 23(18):4079-88.

Maloney DG, Smith B, and Rose A, "Rituximab: Mechanism of Action and Resistance," *Semin Oncol*, 2002, 29(1 Suppl 2):2-9.

Marcus R, Imrie K, Belch A, et al, "CVP Chemotherapy Plus Rituximab Compared With CVP as First-Line Treatment for Advanced Follicular Lymphoma," *Blood*, 2005, 105(4):1417-23.

McLaughlin P, Grillo-Lopez AJ, Link BK, et al, "Rituximab Chimeric Anti-CD20 Monoclonal Antibody Therapy for Relapsed Indolent Lymphoma: Half of Patients Respond to a Four-Dose Treatment Program," *J Clin Oncol*, 1998, 16(8):2825-33.

Moore J, Ma D, Will R, et al, "A phase II Study of Rituximab in Rheumatoid Arthritis Patients With Recurrent Disease Following Haematopoietic Stem Cell Transplantation," *Bone Marrow Transplant*, 2004, 34(3):241-7

Ng CM, Bruno R, Combs D, et al, "Population Pharmacokinetics of Rituximab (Anti-CD20 Monoclonal Antibody) in Rheumatoid Arthritis Patients During a Phase II Clinical Trial," *J Clin Pharmacol*, 2005, 45(7):792-801

Panayi GS, "B Cell-Directed Therapy in Rheumatoid Arthritis - Clinical Experience," *J Rheumatol Suppl*, 2005, 73:19-24.

Sehn LH, Donaldson J, Filewich A, et al, "Rapid Infusion Rituximab in Combination With Corticosteroid-Containing Chemotherapy or as Maintenance Therapy is Well Tolerated and Can Safely be Delivered in the Community Setting," *Blood*, 2007, 109(4):4171-3.

Wang J, Wiley JM, Luddy R, et al, "Chronic Immune Thrombocytopenic Purpura in Children: Assessment of Rituximab Treatment," *J Pediatr*, 2005, 146(2):217-21.

Zecca M, Nobili B, Ramenghi U, et al, "Rituximab in the Treatment of Refractory Autoimmune Hemolytic Anemia in Children," *Blood*, 2003, 101(10): 3857-61.

♦ **Salagen**® see Pilocarpine on page 899

♦ **Salivart**® [OTC] see Saliva Substitute on page 960

Saliva Substitute (sa LYE va SUB stee tute)

U.S. Brand Names Aquoral™; Caphosol®; Entertainer's Secret® [OTC]; Moi-Stir® [OTC]; Mouthkote® [OTC]; Numoisyn™; Oasis®; Oral Balance® [OTC]; Salivart® [OTC]; Saliva Substitute™ [OTC]; SalivaSure™ [OTC]

Index Terms Artificial Saliva

Generic Available No

Pharmacologic Category Gastrointestinal Agent, Miscellaneous

Use Relief of dry mouth and throat in xerostomia or hyposalivation; adjunct to standard oral care in relief of symptoms associated with chemotherapy or radiation therapy-induced mucositis

Storage/Stability

Caphosol®: Store at room temperature; do not refrigerate.

Numoisyn™ liquid: Store at room temperature; do not refrigerate. Use within 3 months after opening.

Numoisyn™ lozenges: Store at room temperature.

Reconstitution Caphosol®: Mix contents of 1 blue (A) and 1 clear (B) ampul in clean container; use immediately after mixing.

Mechanism of Action Protein or electrolyte mixtures which restore/replace saliva, lubricate, moisten, and provide a coating on oral mucosa

Dosage Adults: Use as needed or product-specific dosing:

Caphosol®:

Mucositis symptoms: Swish and spit 4-10 doses per day (begin at onset of chemo-or radiation therapy)

Xerostomia: Swish and spit 2-10 doses per day

Numoisyn™ liquid: Use 2 mL as needed

Numoisyn™ lozenges: Dissolve 1 slowly; maximum 16 lozenges/day

Oasis® mouthwash: Rinse mouth with ~30 mL twice daily or as needed; do not swallow

Oasis® spray: 1-2 sprays as needed; maximum 60 sprays/day

Oral Balance®: Use after meals, at bedtime and as needed

Administration Oral:

Caphosol®: Mix contents of 1 blue (A) and 1 clear (B) ampul in clean container, swish thoroughly with ½ of mixture (15 mL) for 1 minute and spit; repeat. Avoid eating or drinking for at least 15 minutes after use.

Numoisyn™ liquid: Rinse in mouth before swallowing.

Numoisyn™ lozenges: Dissolve slowly in mouth.

Oasis® mouthwash: Rinse for 30 seconds.

Oasis® spray: Spray into mouth holding bottle upright; do not rinse.

Dietary Considerations Caphosol®: Contains sodium 75 mg/30 mL dose

Special Geriatric Considerations Saliva production has not been shown to change with aging, however, many drugs used by elderly can cause dry mouth. These patients may benefit from a saliva substitute.

Dosage Forms Excipient information presented when available (limited, particularly for generics); consult specific product labeling. [DSC] = Discontinued product

Liquid:

Numoisyn™: Water, sorbitol, linseed extract, *Chondrus crispus*, methylparaben, sodium benzoate, potassium sorbate, dipotassium phosphate, propylparaben (300 mL)

Oral Balance®: Water, starch, sunflower oil, propylene glycol, xylitol, glycerine, purified milk extract (45 mL) [sugar-free]

Lozenge:
Numoisyn™: Sorbitol 0.3 g/lozenge, polyethylene glycol, malic acid, sodium citrate, calcium phosphate dibasic, hydrogenated cottonseed oil, citric acid, magnesium stearate, silicon dioxide (100s)
SalivaSure™: Xylitol, citric acid, apple acid, sodium citrate dihydrate, sodium carboxymethylcellulose, dibasic calcium phosphate, silica colloidal, magnesium stearate, stearic acid (90s)

Solution, oral:
Caphosol®: Dibasic sodium phosphate 0.032%, monobasic sodium phosphate 0.009%, calcium chloride 0.052%, sodium chloride 0.569%, purified water (30 mL) [packaged in two 15 mL ampuls when mixed together provide one 30 mL dose]
Entertainer's Secret®: Sodium carboxymethylcellulose, aloe vera gel, glycerin (60 mL) [honey-apple flavor]
Saliva Substitute®: Sorbitol, sodium carboxymethylcellulose, methylparaben (120 mL) [alcohol free, dye free, sugar free]

Solution, oral [rinse]:
Oasis®: Water, glycerin, sorbitol, poloxamer 338, PEG-60, hydrogenated castor oil, copvodine, sodium benzoate, carboxymethycellulose (473 mL) [alcohol free, mild mint flavor]

Solution, oral [spray]:
Aquoral™: Oxidized glycerol triesters and silicon dioxide (40 mL) [contains aspartame; delivers 400 sprays, citrus flavor]
Moi-Stir®: Water, sorbitol, sodium carboxymethylcellulose, methylparaben, propylparaben, potassium chloride, dibasic sodium phosphate, calcium chloride, magnesium chloride, sodium chloride (120 mL)
Mouthkote®: Water, xylitol, sorbitol, yerba santa, citric acid, ascorbic acid, sodium saccharin, sodium benzoate (5 mL, 60 mL, 240 mL) [alcohol free, sugar free; lemon-lime flavor]
Oasis®: Glycerin, cetylpyridinium, copovidone (30 mL) [alcohol free, delivers ~150 sprays, mild mint flavor]
Salivart®: Water, sodium carboxymethylcellulose, sorbitol, sodium chloride, potassium chloride, calcium chloride, magnesium chloride, potassium phosphate (74 mL) [alcohol free]

References

Narhi TO, Meurman JH, and Ainamo A, "Xerostomia and Hyposalivation: Causes, Consequences and Treatment in the Elderly," Drugs Aging, 1999, 15(2):103-16.
Papas AS, Clark RE, Martuscelli G, et al, "A Prospective, Randomized Trial for the Prevention of Mucositis in Patients Undergoing Hematopoietic Stem Cell Transplantation," Bone Marrow Transplant, 2003, 31(8): 705-12.
Scully C and Epstein JB, " Oral Health Care for the Cancer Patient," Oral Oncology, 1996, 32(5): 281-92.
Sweeney MP and Bagg J, "The Mouth and Palliative Care," Am J Palliat Care, 2000, 17(2):118-24.

Sargramostim (sar GRAM oh stim)

Medication Safety Issues
Sound-alike/look-alike issues:
Leukine® may be confused with Leukeran®, leucovorin

Related Information
Hematopoietic Stem Cell Transplantation *on page 1366*

U.S. Brand Names Leukine®

Index Terms GM-CSF; Granulocyte-Macrophage Colony Stimulating Factor; NSC-613795; rGM-CSF

Generic Available No

Canadian Brand Names Leukine®

Pharmacologic Category Colony Stimulating Factor

Use
Acute myelogenous leukemia (AML) following induction chemotherapy in older adults (≥55 years of age) to shorten time to neutrophil recovery and to reduce the incidence of severe and life-threatening infections and infections resulting in death

Bone marrow transplant (allogeneic or autologous) failure or engraftment delay

Myeloid reconstitution after allogeneic bone marrow transplantation

Myeloid reconstitution after autologous bone marrow transplantation: Non-Hodgkin's lymphoma (NHL), acute lymphoblastic leukemia (ALL), Hodgkin's lymphoma

Peripheral stem cell transplantation: Mobilization and myeloid reconstitution following peripheral stem cell transplantation

Pregnancy Risk Factor C

Lactation Excretion in breast milk unknown/use caution

Labeled Contraindications Hypersensitivity to sargramostim, yeast-derived products, or any component of the formulation; concurrent (24 hours preceding/following) myelosuppressive chemotherapy or radiation therapy; patients with excessive (≥10%) leukemic myeloid blasts in bone marrow or peripheral blood

Warnings/Precautions Simultaneous administration, or administration 24 hours preceding/following cytotoxic chemotherapy or radiotherapy is not recommended. Use with caution in patients with pre-existing cardiac problems or CHF; supraventricular arrhythmias have been reported in patients with history of arrhythmias. Edema, capillary leak syndrome, pleural and/or pericardial effusion have been reported; use with caution in patients with pre-existing fluid retention; may worsen. Use with caution in patients with hepatic or renal impairment; monitor hepatic and/or renal function in patients with history of hepatic or renal dysfunction. Dyspnea may occur; monitor respiratory symptoms during and following infusion; use with caution in patients with hypoxia or pulmonary infiltrates.

With rapid increase in blood counts (ANC >20,000/mm^3 or platelets >500,000/mm^3); decrease dose by 50% or discontinue drug (counts will fall to normal within 3-7 days after discontinuing drug). May potentially act as a growth factor for any tumor type, particularly myeloid malignancies; caution should be exercised when using in any malignancy with myeloid characteristics; tumors of nonhematopoietic origin may have surface receptors for sargramostim.

There is a "first-dose effect" (refer to Adverse Reactions for details) which is seen (rarely) with the first dose of a cycle and does not usually occur with subsequent doses within that cycle. Anaphylaxis or other serious allergic reactions have been reported; discontinue immediately if occur. Solution contains benzyl alcohol; do not use in premature infants or neonates.

Adverse Reactions

>10%:

Cardiovascular: Hypertension (34%), pericardial effusion (4% to 25%), edema (13% to 25%), chest pain (15%), peripheral edema (11%), tachycardia (11%)

Central nervous system: Fever (81%), malaise (57%), headache (26%), chills (25%), anxiety (11%), insomnia (11%)

Dermatologic: Rash (44%), pruritus (23%)

Endocrine & metabolic: Hyperglycemia (25%), hypercholesterolemia (17%)

Gastrointestinal: Diarrhea (52% to 89%), nausea (58% to 70%), vomiting (46% to 70%), abdominal pain (38%), weight loss (37%), hematemesis (13%), dysphagia (11%), gastrointestinal hemorrhage (11%)

Genitourinary: Urinary tract disorder (14%)

Hepatic: Hyperbilirubinemia (30%)

Neuromuscular & skeletal: Weakness (66%), bone pain (21%), arthralgia (11% to 21%) myalgia (18%)

Ocular: Eye hemorrhage (11%)

Renal: BUN increased (23%), serum creatinine increased (15%)

Respiratory: Pharyngitis (23%), epistaxis (17%), dyspnea (15%)

1% to 10%: Respiratory: Pleural effusion (1%)

<1%, postmarketing, and/or case reports: Allergic reaction, anaphylaxis, anorexia, arrhythmia, capillary leak syndrome, constipation, eosinophilia, fever, first-dose effect (syndrome with respiratory distress, hypoxia, flushing, hypotension, syncope, and/or tachycardia occurring with the first dose of a treatment cycle); injection site reaction, lethargy, leukocytosis, malaise, pain, pericarditis, rigors, sore throat, supraventricular arrhythmia (transient), thrombocytosis, thrombophlebitis, thrombosis

Overdosage/Toxicology
Symptoms of overdose include dyspnea, malaise, nausea, fever, sinus tachycardia, headache, and chills. Discontinue drug and wait for levels to fall. Treatment is symptom-directed and supportive. Monitor CBC, respiratory symptoms, fluid status, and for pulmonary edema. Toxicity of GM-CSF is dose dependent. Severe reactions such as capillary leak syndrome are seen at higher doses (>15 mcg/kg/day).

Storage/Stability
Store at 2°C to 8°C (36°F to 46°F); do not freeze. Do not shake.

Solution for injection: May be stored for up to 20 days at 2°C to 8°C (36°F to 46°F) once the vial has been entered. Discard remaining solution after 20 days.

Powder for injection: Preparations made with SWFI should be administered as soon as possible, and discarded within 6 hours of reconstitution. Preparations made with bacteriostatic water may be stored for up to 20 days at 2°C to 8°C (36°F to 46°F).

I.V. infusion administration: Preparations diluted with NS are stable for 48 hours at room temperature and refrigeration.

Reconstitution
Powder for injection: May be reconstituted with preservative free SWFI or bacteriostatic water for injection (with benzyl alcohol 0.9%). Gently swirl to reconstitute; do not shake.

Sargramostim may also be further diluted in 25-50 mL NS to a concentration ≥10 mcg/mL for I.V. infusion administration.

If the final concentration of sargramostim is <10 mcg/mL, 1 mg of human albumin/1 mL of NS (eg, 1 mL of 5% human albumin/50 mL of NS) should be added.

(Continued)

Sargramostim (Continued)

Compatibility Stable in NS, sterile water for injection, bacteriostatic water; **incompatible** with dextrose-containing solutions.

Y-site administration: Compatible: Amikacin, aminophylline, aztreonam, bleomycin, butorphanol, calcium gluconate, carboplatin, carmustine, cefazolin, cefepime, cefotaxime, cefotetan, ceftizoxime, ceftriaxone, cefuroxime, cimetidine, cisplatin, clindamycin, co-trimoxazole, cyclophosphamide, cyclosporine, cytarabine, dacarbazine, dactinomycin, dexamethasone sodium phosphate, diphenhydramine, dopamine, doxorubicin, doxycycline, droperidol, etoposide, famotidine, fentanyl, floxuridine, fluconazole, fluorouracil, furosemide, gentamicin, granisetron, heparin, idarubicin, ifosfamide, immune globulin, magnesium sulfate, mannitol, mechlorethamine, meperidine, mesna, methotrexate, metoclopramide, metronidazole, minocycline, mitoxantrone, netilmicin, pentostatin, piperacillin/tazobactam, potassium chloride, prochlorperazine edisylate, promethazine, ranitidine, teniposide, ticarcillin, ticarcillin/clavulanate, vinblastine, vincristine, zidovudine. **Incompatible:** Acyclovir, ampicillin, ampicillin/sulbactam, cefoperazone, chlorpromazine, ganciclovir, haloperidol, hydrocortisone sodium phosphate, hydrocortisone sodium succinate, hydromorphone, hydroxyzine, imipenem/cilastatin, lorazepam, methylprednisolone sodium succinate, mitomycin, morphine, nalbuphine, ondansetron, piperacillin, sodium bicarbonate, tobramycin. **Variable (consult detailed reference):** Amphotericin B, amsacrine, ceftazidime, vancomycin.

Mechanism of Action Stimulates proliferation, differentiation and functional activity of neutrophils, eosinophils, monocytes, and macrophages, as indicated.

Pharmacodynamics/Kinetics

Onset of action: Increase in WBC: 7-14 days

Duration: WBCs return to baseline within 1 week of discontinuing drug

Half-life elimination: I.V.: 60 minutes; SubQ: 2.7 hours

Time to peak, serum: SubQ: 1-2 hours

Dosage

Children (unlabeled use) and Adults: I.V. infusion over ≥2 hours or SubQ: **Rounding the dose to the nearest vial size enhances patient convenience and reduces costs without clinical detriment**

Myeloid reconstitution after peripheral stem cell, allogeneic or autologous bone marrow transplant: I.V.: 250 mcg/m²/day (over 2 hours), begin 2-4 hours after the marrow infusion and ≥24 hours after chemotherapy or radiotherapy, when the post marrow infusion ANC is <500 cells/mm³, and continue until ANC >1500 cells/mm³ for 3 consecutive days

If a severe adverse reaction occurs, reduce or temporarily discontinue the dose until the reaction abates

If blast cells appear or progression of the underlying disease occurs, disrupt treatment

Interrupt or reduce the dose by half if ANC is >20,000 cells/mm³

Neutrophil recovery following chemotherapy in AML: I.V.: 250 mcg/m²/day (over 4 hours) starting approximately day 11 or 4 days following the completion of induction chemotherapy, if day 10 bone marrow is hypoblastic with <5% blasts

If a second cycle of chemotherapy is necessary, administer ~4 days after the completion of chemotherapy if the bone marrow is hypoblastic with <5% blasts

Continue sargramostim until ANC is >1500 cells/mm³ for 3 consecutive days or a maximum of 42 days

Discontinue sargramostim immediately if leukemic regrowth occurs

If a severe adverse reaction occurs, reduce the dose by 50% or temporarily discontinue the dose until the reaction abates

Mobilization of peripheral blood progenitor cells: I.V., SubQ: 250 mcg/m^2/day I.V. over 24 hours or SubQ once daily

Continue the same dose through the period of PBPC collection

The optimal schedule for PBPC collection has not been established (usually begun by day 5 and performed daily until protocol specified targets are achieved)

If WBC >50,000 cells/mm^3, reduce the dose by 50%

If adequate numbers of progenitor cells are not collected, consider other mobilization therapy

Postperipheral blood progenitor cell transplantation: I.V., SubQ: 250 mcg/m^2/day I.V. over 24 hours or SubQ once daily beginning immediately following infusion of progenitor cells and continuing until ANC is >1500 cells/mm^3 for 3 consecutive days is attained

BMT failure or engraftment delay: I.V.: 250 mcg/m^2/day over 2 hours for 14 days

May be repeated after 7 days off therapy if engraftment has not occurred

If engraftment still has not occurred, a third course of 500 mcg/m^2/day for 14 days may be tried after another 7 days off therapy; if there is still no improvement, it is unlikely that further dose escalation will be beneficial

If a severe adverse reaction occurs, reduce or temporarily discontinue the dose until the reaction abates

If blast cells appear or disease progression occurs, discontinue treatment

Combination Regimens

Lymphoma, non-Hodgkin's:

CODOX-M *on page 1180*

IVAC *on page 1242*

Administration Can premedicate with analgesics and antipyretics; control bone pain with non-narcotic analgesics. Sargramostim is administered as a subcutaneous injection or intravenous infusion; intravenous infusion should be over 2-24 hours; continuous infusions may be more effective than short infusion or bolus injection. An in-line membrane filter should not be used for intravenous administration. When administering GM-CSF subcutaneously, rotate injection sites.

Monitoring Parameters Vital signs, weight, CBC with differential, platelets, renal/liver function tests, especially with previous dysfunction, pulmonary function

Test Interactions May interfere with bone imaging studies; increased hematopoietic activity of the bone marrow may appear as transient positive bone imaging changes

Patient Information You may experience bone pain (request analgesic), nausea and vomiting (small frequent meals may help), hair loss (reversible). Report fever, chills, unhealed sores, severe bone pain, difficulty breathing, swelling or pain at infusion site. Avoid crowds or exposure to infected persons; you will be susceptible to infection.

Additional Information Reimbursement Hotline (Leukine®): 1-800-321-4669

Emetic Potential Very low (<10%)

Vesicant No

Dosage Forms Excipient information presented when available (limited, particularly for generics); consult specific product labeling.

Injection, powder for reconstitution:

Leukine®: 250 mcg [contains mannitol 40 mg/mL and sucrose 10 mg/mL]

(Continued)

Sargramostim *(Continued)*

Injection, solution:

Leukine®: 500 mcg/mL (1 mL) [contains benzyl alcohol, disodium edetate, mannitol 40 mg/mL, and sucrose 10 mg/mL]

References

Lieschke GJ and Burgess AW, "Granulocyte Colony-Stimulating Factor and Granulo-cyte-Macrophage Colony-Stimulating Factor," (1) *N Engl J Med*, 1992, 327(1):28-35.

Lieschke GJ and Burgess AW, "Granulocyte Colony-Stimulating Factor and Granulo-cyte-Macrophage Colony-Stimulating Factor," (2) *N Engl J Med*, 1992, 327(2):99-106.

Mayer D and Bednarczyk EM, "Interaction of Colony-Stimulating Factors and Fluorodeox-yglucose F[18] Positron Emission Tomography," *Ann Pharmacother*, 2002, 36(11):1796-9.

Smith TJ, Khatcheressian J, Lyman GH, et al, "2006 Update of Recommendations for the Use of White Blood Cell Growth Factors: An Evidence-Based Clinical Practice Guideline," *J Clin Oncol*, 2006, 24(19):3187-205.

Stute N, Furman WL, Schell M, et al, "Pharmacokinetics of Recombinant Human Granulocyte - Macrophage Colony - Stimulating Factor in Children After Intravenous and Subcutaneous Administration," *J Pharm Sci*, 1995, 84(7):824-8.

◆ **Sarna® HC (Can)** *see* Hydrocortisone *on page 545*

◆ **Sarnol®-HC [OTC]** *see* Hydrocortisone *on page 545*

◆ **Sativex® (Can)** *see* Tetrahydrocannabinol and Cannabidiol *on page 1022*

◆ **SB-265805** *see* Gemifloxacin *on page 504*

◆ **SC 33428** *see* Idarubicin *on page 575*

◆ **SCH 13521** *see* Flutamide *on page 470*

◆ **SCH 56592** *see* Posaconazole *on page 912*

◆ **SCIG** *see* Immune Globulin (Subcutaneous) *on page 603*

◆ **Septra®** *see* Sulfamethoxazole and Trimethoprim *on page 982*

◆ **Septra® DS** *see* Sulfamethoxazole and Trimethoprim *on page 982*

◆ **Septra® Injection (Can)** *see* Sulfamethoxazole and Trimethoprim *on page 982*

◆ **Simulect®** *see* Basiliximab *on page 126*

Sirolimus *(sir OH li mus)*

Medication Safety Issues

Sound-alike/look-alike issues:

Sirolimus may be confused with tacrolimus, temsirolimus

U.S. Brand Names Rapamune®

Generic Available No

Canadian Brand Names Rapamune®

Pharmacologic Category Immunosuppressant Agent; mTOR Kinase Inhibitor

Use Prophylaxis of organ rejection in patients receiving renal transplants, in combination with corticosteroids and cyclosporine (cyclosporine may be withdrawn in low-to-moderate immunological risk patients after 2-4 months, in conjunction with an increase in sirolimus dosage)

Unlabeled/Investigational Use Investigational: Immunosuppression in peripheral stem cell/bone marrow transplantation

Pregnancy Risk Factor C

Lactation Excretion in breast milk unknown/not recommended

Labeled Contraindications Hypersensitivity to sirolimus or any component of the formulation

Warnings/Precautions [U.S. Boxed Warning]: Immunosuppressive agents, including sirolimus, increase the risk of infection and may be associated with the development of lymphoma. Immune suppression may also increase the risk of opportunistic infections and sepsis. Prophylactic treatment for *Pneumocystis jirovec* pneumonia (PCP) should be administered for 1 year post-transplant; prophylaxis for cytomegalovirus (CMV) should be taken for 3 months in patients at risk for CMV.

In renal transplant patients, *de novo* use without cyclosporine has been associated with higher rates of acute rejection. May increase serum lipids (cholesterol and triglycerides). Use with caution in patients with hyperlipidemia. May increase serum creatinine and decrease GFR. Use caution in patients with renal impairment, or when used concurrently with medications which may alter renal function. May delay recovery of renal function in patients with delayed allograft function. Monitor renal function closely when combined with cyclosporine; consider dosage adjustment or discontinue in patients with increasing serum creatinine. Increased urinary protein excretion has been observed when converting renal transplant patients from calcineurin inhibitors to sirolimus during maintenance therapy. A higher level of proteinuria prior to sirolimus conversion correlates with a higher degree of proteinuria after conversion. In some patients, proteinuria may reach nephrotic levels.

Use caution with hepatic impairment; reduced dosage is recommended. Has been associated with an increased risk of lymphocele. Cases of interstitial lung disease (eg, pneumonitis, bronchiolitis obliterans organizing pneumonia, pulmonary fibrosis) have been observed; risk may be increased with higher trough levels. Avoid concurrent use of strong CYP3A4 inhibitors or strong inducers of either CYP3A4 or P-glycoprotein. Concurrent use with a calcineurin inhibitor (cyclosporine, tacrolimus) may increase the risk of calcineurin inhibitor-induced hemolytic uremic syndrome/thrombotic thrombocytopenic purpura/thrombotic microangiopathy (HUS/TTP/TMA). Hypersensitivity reactions, including anaphylactic/anaphylactoid reactions, angioedema, exfoliative dermatitis, and hypersensitivity vasculitis have been reported. Concurrent use with other drugs known to cause angioedema (eg, ACE inhibitors) may increase risk. May increase sensitivity to UV light; use appropriate sun protection.

Sirolimus is not recommended for use in liver transplant patients; studies indicate an association with an increase risk of hepatic artery thrombosis, graft failure, and increased mortality in these patients. Cases of bronchial anastomotic dehiscence have been reported in lung transplant patients when sirolimus was used as part of an immunosuppressive regimen; most of these reactions were fatal. Use in patients with lung transplants is not recommended. Safety and efficacy of cyclosporine withdrawal in high-risk patients has not been established and is not currently recommended. Safety and efficacy in children <13 years of age, or in adolescent patients <18 years of age considered at high immunological risk, have not been established.

Adverse Reactions Incidence of many adverse effects is dose related.
>20%:
    Cardiovascular: Peripheral edema (54% to 64%), hypertension (39% to 49%), edema (16% to 24%), chest pain (16% to 24%)
    Central nervous system: Fever (23% to 34%), headache (23% to 34%), pain (24% to 33%), insomnia (13% to 22%)
    Dermatologic: Acne (20% to 31%), rash (10% to 20%)
    Endocrine & metabolic: Hyperlipidemia (38% to 57%), hypercholesterolemia (38% to 46%), hypophosphatemia (15% to 23%), hypokalemia (11% to 21%)
    Gastrointestinal: Diarrhea (25% to 42%), constipation (28% to 38%), abdominal pain (28% to 36%), nausea (25% to 36%), vomiting (19% to 25%), dyspepsia (17% to 25%), weight gain (8% to 21%)
    Genitourinary: Urinary tract infection (20% to 33%)
    Hematologic: Anemia (23% to 37%), thrombocytopenia (13% to 30%)
(Continued)

Sirolimus *(Continued)*

Neuromuscular & skeletal: Weakness (22% to 40%), arthralgia (25% to 31%), tremor (21% to 31%), back pain (16% to 26%)

Renal: Serum creatinine increased (35% to 40%)

Respiratory: Dyspnea (22% to 30%), upper respiratory infection (20% to 26%), pharyngitis (16% to 21%)

3% to 20%:

Cardiovascular: Atrial fibrillation, CHF, facial edema, hypervolemia, hypotension, palpitation, peripheral vascular disorder, postural hypotension, syncope, tachycardia, thrombosis, vasodilation, venous thromboembolism

Central nervous system: Chills, malaise, anxiety, confusion, depression, dizziness, emotional lability, hypoesthesia, hypotonia, neuropathy, somnolence

Dermatologic: Dermatitis (fungal), hirsutism, pruritus, skin hypertrophy, dermal ulcer, ecchymosis, cellulitis, skin carcinoma (up to 3%)

Endocrine & metabolic: Cushing's syndrome, diabetes mellitus, glycosuria, acidosis, dehydration, hypercalcemia, hyperglycemia, hyperphosphatemia, hypocalcemia, hypoglycemia, hypomagnesemia, hyponatremia, hyperkalemia (12% to 17%)

Gastrointestinal: Enlarged abdomen, anorexia, dysphagia, eructation, esophagitis, flatulence, gastritis, gastroenteritis, gingivitis, gingival hyperplasia, ileus, mouth ulceration, oral moniliasis, stomatitis, weight loss

Genitourinary: Pelvic pain, scrotal edema, testis disorder, impotence

Hematologic: Leukocytosis, polycythemia, TTP, hemolytic-uremic syndrome, hemorrhage, leukopenia (9% to 15%)

Hepatic: Abnormal liver function tests, alkaline phosphatase increased, ascites, LDH increased, transaminases increased

Local: Thrombophlebitis

Neuromuscular & skeletal: Arthrosis, bone necrosis, CPK increased, leg cramps, myalgia, osteoporosis, tetany, hypertonia, paresthesia

Ocular: Abnormal vision, cataract, conjunctivitis

Otic: Ear pain, deafness, otitis media, tinnitus

Renal: Albuminuria, bladder pain, BUN increased, dysuria, hematuria, hydronephrosis, kidney pain, tubular necrosis, nocturia, oliguria, pyelonephritis, pyuria, nephropathy (toxic), urinary frequency, urinary incontinence, urinary retention

Respiratory: Asthma, atelectasis, bronchitis, cough, epistaxis, hypoxia, lung edema, pleural effusion, pneumonia, rhinitis, sinusitis

Miscellaneous: Abscess, diaphoresis, flu-like syndrome, herpesvirus infection, hernia, infection (including opportunistic), lymphadenopathy, lymphocele, lymphoproliferative disease, lymphoma (1% to 3%), peritonitis, sepsis

Postmarketing and/or case reports: Abnormal wound healing, anaphylactoid reaction, anaphylaxis, anastomotic disruption, angioedema, exfoliative dermatitis, fascial dehiscence, hepatic necrosis, hepatotoxicity, hypersensitivity vasculitis; interstitial lung disease (dose "related; includes pneumonitis, pulmonary fibrosis, and bronchiolitis obliterans organizing pneumonia [BOOP]) with no identified infectious etiology, joint disorders, lymphedema, nephrotic syndrome, neutropenia, pancreatitis, pancytopenia, *Pneumocystis* pneumonia, proteinuria, pulmonary hemorrhage. In liver transplant patients (not an approved use), an increase in hepatic artery thrombosis and graft failure were noted in clinical trials. In lung transplant patients (not an approved use), bronchial anastomotic dehiscence has been reported. Calcineurin inhibitor-induced hemolytic uremic syndrome/thrombotic thrombocytopenic purpura/thrombotic microangiopathy (HUS/TTP/TMA) have been reported (with concurrent cyclosporine or tacrolimus).

Overdosage/Toxicology Experience with overdosage has been limited. Dose-limiting toxicities include immune suppression. Reported symptoms of overdose include atrial fibrillation. Treatment is symptom-directed and supportive; dialysis is not likely to facilitate removal.

Drug Interactions

Cytochrome P450 Effect: Substrate of CYP3A4 (major); **Inhibits** CYP3A4 (weak)

Increased Effect/Toxicity: Cyclosporine may increase sirolimus concentrations during concurrent therapy, and cyclosporine levels may be increased; sirolimus should be taken 4 hours after cyclosporine oral solution (modified) and/or cyclosporine capsules (modified). CYP3A4 inhibitors may increase the levels/effects of sirolimus; example inhibitors include azole antifungals (fluconazole, itraconazole, ketoconazole, voriconazole), clarithromycin, diclofenac, diltiazem, doxycycline, erythromycin, imatinib, isoniazid, nefazodone, nicardipine, propofol, protease inhibitors, quinidine, telithromycin, and verapamil; avoid concurrent use. Concurrent use of ACE inhibitors may increase the risk of angioedema. Concurrent live organism vaccines may increase the adverse/toxic effect of the vaccine; vaccinial infections are possible (avoid concurrent use). Concurrent therapy with calcineurin inhibitors (cyclosporine, tacrolimus) may increase the risk of HUS/TTP/TMA.

Decreased Effect: CYP3A4 inducers may decrease the levels/effects of sirolimus; example inducers include aminoglutethimide, carbamazepine, nafcillin, nevirapine, phenobarbital, phenytoin, and rifamycins. Vaccination (dead organisms) may be less effective with concurrent sirolimus (monitor).

Ethanol/Nutrition/Herb Interactions

Food: Do not administer with grapefruit juice; may decrease clearance of sirolimus. Ingestion with high-fat meals decreases peak concentrations but increases AUC by 23% to 35%. Sirolimus should be taken consistently either with or without food to minimize variability.

Herb/Nutraceutical: St John's wort may decrease sirolimus levels; avoid concurrent use. Avoid cat's claw, echinacea (have immunostimulant properties; consider therapy modifications). Herbs with hypoglycemic properties may increase the risk of sirolimus-induced hypoglycemia; includes alfalfa, aloe, bilberry, bitter melon, burdock, celery, damiana, fenugreek, garcinia, garlic, ginger, ginseng (American), gymnema, marshmallow, stinging nettle.

Storage/Stability

Oral solution: Store under refrigeration, 2°C to 8°C (36°F to 46°F). Protect from light. A slight haze may develop in refrigerated solutions, but the quality of the product is not affected. After opening, solution should be used in 1 month. If necessary, may be stored at temperatures up to 25°C (77°F) for ≤15 days after opening. Product may be stored in amber syringe for a maximum of 24 hours (at room temperature or refrigerated). Solution should be used immediately following dilution.

Tablet: Store at room temperature of 20°C to 25°C (68°F to 77°F). Protect from light.

Mechanism of Action Sirolimus inhibits T-lymphocyte activation and proliferation in response to antigenic and cytokine stimulation and inhibits antibody production. Its mechanism differs from other immunosuppressants. Sirolimus binds to FKBP-12, an intracellular protein, to form an immunosuppressive complex which inhibits the regulatory kinase, mTOR (mammalian (Continued)

Sirolimus *(Continued)*

target of rapamycin). This inhibition suppresses cytokine mediated T-cell proliferation, halting progression from the G1 to the S phase of the cell cycle. It inhibits acute rejection of allografts and prolongs graft survival.

Pharmacodynamics/Kinetics

Absorption: Rapid

Distribution: 12 L/kg (range: 4-20 L/kg)

Protein binding: 92%, primarily to albumin

Metabolism: Extensively hepatic via CYP3A4; to 7 major metabolites

Bioavailability: Oral solution: 14%; Oral tablet: 18%

Half-life elimination: Mean: 62 hours (range: 46-78 hours); extended in hepatic impairment (Child-Pugh class A or B) to 113 hours

Time to peak: 1-2 hours

Excretion: Feces (91% due to P-glycoprotein-mediated efflux into gut lumen); urine (2%)

Dosage Oral:

Combination therapy with cyclosporine: Doses should be taken 4 hours after cyclosporine, and should be taken consistently either with or without food.

Low- to moderate-risk renal transplant patients: Children ≥13 years and Adults: Dosing by body weight:

<40 kg: Loading dose: 3 mg/m^2 on day 1, followed by maintenance dosing of 1 mg/m^2 once daily

≥40 kg: Loading dose: 6 mg on day 1; maintenance: 2 mg once daily

High-risk renal transplant patients: Adults: Loading dose: Up to 15 mg on day 1; maintenance: 5 mg/day; obtain trough concentration between days 5-7. Continue concurrent cyclosporine/sirolimus therapy for 1 year following transplantation. Further adjustment of the regimen must be based on clinical status.

Dosage adjustment: Sirolimus dosages should be adjusted to maintain trough concentrations within desired range based on risk and concomitant therapy. Maximum daily dose: 40 mg. Dosage should be adjusted at intervals of 7-14 days to account for the long half-life of sirolimus. In general, dose proportionality may be assumed. New sirolimus dose **equals** current dose **multiplied by** (target concentration/current concentration). **Note:** If large dose increase is required, consider loading dose calculated as:

Loading dose **equals** (new maintenance dose **minus** current maintenance dose) **multiplied by** 3

Doses >40 mg (with inclusion of loading dose) may be administered over 2 days. Serum concentrations should not be used as the sole basis for dosage adjustment (monitor clinical signs/symptoms, tissue biopsy, and laboratory parameters).

Maintenance therapy after withdrawal of cyclosporine: Cyclosporine withdrawal is not recommended in high immunological risk patients. Following 2-4 months of combined therapy, withdrawal of cyclosporine may be considered in low-to-moderate risk patients. Cyclosporine should be discontinued over 4-8 weeks, and a necessary increase in the dosage of sirolimus (up to fourfold) should be anticipated due to removal of metabolic inhibition by cyclosporine and to maintain adequate immunosuppressive effects. Dose-adjusted trough target concentrations are typically 16-24 ng/mL for the first year post-transplant and 12-20 ng/mL thereafter (measured by chromatographic methodology).

Dosage adjustment in renal impairment: No dosage adjustment is necessary in renal impairment. However, adjustment of regimen (including discontinuation of therapy) should be considered when used concurrently with cyclosporine and elevated or increasing serum creatinine is noted.

Dosage adjustment in hepatic impairment: Reduce maintenance dose by approximately 33% in hepatic impairment. Loading dose is unchanged.

Administration The solution should be mixed with at least 2 ounces of water or orange juice. No other liquids should be used for dilution. Patient should drink diluted solution immediately. The cup should then be refilled with an additional 4 ounces of water or orange juice, stirred vigorously, and the patient should drink the contents at once. Sirolimus should be taken 4 hours after cyclosporine oral solution (modified) or cyclosporine capsules (modified)

Monitoring Parameters Monitor sirolimus levels in pediatric patients, patients ≥13 years of age weighing <40 kg, patients with hepatic impairment, or on concurrent potent inhibitors or inducers of CYP3A4, and/or if cyclosporine dosing is markedly reduced or discontinued. Also monitor serum cholesterol and triglycerides, blood pressure, serum creatinine, and urinary protein. Serum drug concentrations should be determined 3-4 days after loading doses; however, these concentrations should not be used as the sole basis for dosage adjustment, especially during withdrawal of cyclosporine (monitor clinical signs/symptoms, tissue biopsy, and laboratory parameters). **Note:** Specific ranges will vary with assay methodology (chromatographic or immunoassay) and are not interchangeable.

Dietary Considerations Take consistently, with or without food, to minimize variability of absorption.

Patient Information Do not get pregnant while taking this medication. Use reliable contraception while on this medication and for 3 months after discontinuation. May be taken with or without food but take medication consistently with respect to meals (always take with food or always take on an empty stomach). Wear protective clothing and use sunscreen to limit exposure to sunlight and UV light; decreases risk of skin cancer.

Additional Information Sirolimus tablets and oral solution are not bioequivalent, due to differences in absorption. Clinical equivalence was seen using 2 mg tablet and 2 mg solution. It is not known if higher doses are also clinically equivalent.

High-risk renal transplant patients are defined (per the manufacturer's labeling) as African-American transplant recipients and/or repeat renal transplant recipients who lost a previous allograft based on an immunologic process and/or patients with high PRA (panel-reactive antibodies; peak PRA level >80%). Individual transplant centers may have differences in their definitions. For example, some centers would consider a PRA >50% to be at higher risk of rejection.

Dosage Forms Excipient information presented when available (limited, particularly for generics); consult specific product labeling.

Solution, oral:

Rapamune®: 1 mg/mL (60 mL) [contains ethanol 1.5% to 2.5%; packaged with oral syringes and a carrying case]

Tablet:

Rapamune®: 1 mg, 2 mg

References

Antin J, Kim H, Cutler C, et al, "Sirolimus, Tacrolimus, and Low-Dose Methotrexate for Graft-Versus-Host Disease Prophylaxis in Mismatched Related Donor or Unrelated Donor Transplantation," *Blood*, 2003, 102(5):1601-5.

Cutler C, Kim H, Hochberg E, et al, "Sirolimus and Tacrolimus Without Methotrexate as Graft-Versus-Host Disease Prophylaxis After Matched Related Donor Peripheral Blood Stem Cell Transplantation," *Biol Blood Marrow Transplant*, 2004, 10(5):328-36.

(Continued)

Sirolimus *(Continued)*

Ettinger RB and Grimm EM, "Safety and Efficacy of TOR Inhibitors in Pediatric Renal Transplant Recipients," *Am J Kidney Dis*, 2001, 38(4 Suppl 2):22-8.

Kahan BD, "Efficacy of Sirolimus Compared With Azathioprine for Reduction of Acute Renal Allograft Rejection: A Randomised Multicentre Study. The Rapamune US Study Group," *Lancet*, 2000, 356(9225):194-202.

McDonald AS, "A Worldwide, Phase III, Randomized, Controlled, Safety and Efficacy Study of a Sirolimus/Cyclosporine Regimen for Prevention of Acute Rejection in Recipients of Primary Mismatched Renal Allografts. RAPAMUNE Global Study Group," *Transplantation*, 2001, 71(2):271-80.

Sifontis NM, Coscia LA, Constantinescu S, et al, "Pregnancy Outcomes in Solid Organ Transplant Recipients With Exposure to Mycophenolate Mofetil or Sirolimus," *Transplantation*, 2006, 82(12):1698-1702.

Stenton SB, Partovi N, and Ensom MH, "Sirolimus: The Evidence for Clinical Pharmacokinetic Monitoring," *Clin Pharmacokinet*, 2005, 44(8):769-86.

- **SKF 104864** *see* Topotecan *on page 1048*
- **SKF 104864-A** *see* Topotecan *on page 1048*
- **SMZ-TMP** *see* Sulfamethoxazole and Trimethoprim *on page 982*
- **Sodium 2-Mercaptoethane Sulfonate** *see* Mesna *on page 724*
- **Sodium Ferric Gluconate** *see* Ferric Gluconate *on page 438*
- **Sodium Fusidate** *see* Fusidic Acid *on page 488*
- **Sodium Hyposulfate** *see* Sodium Thiosulfate *on page 972*
- **Sodium Nafcillin** *see* Nafcillin *on page 800*

Sodium Thiosulfate *(SOW dee um thye oh SUL fate)*

Related Information
  Management of Drug Extravasations *on page 1301*

U.S. Brand Names Versiclear™

Index Terms Disodium Thiosulfate Pentahydrate; Pentahydrate; Sodium Hyposulfate; Sodium Thiosulphate; Thiosulfuric Acid Disodium Salt

Generic Available Yes: Injection

Pharmacologic Category Antidote

Use
  Parenteral: Used alone or with sodium nitrite or amyl nitrite in cyanide poisoning; reduce the risk of nephrotoxicity associated with cisplatin therapy

  Topical: Treatment of tinea versicolor

Unlabeled/Investigational Use Management of I.V. extravasation

Pregnancy Risk Factor C

Labeled Contraindications Hypersensitivity to sodium thiosulfate or any component of the formulation

Warnings/Precautions Discontinue topical use if irritation or sensitivity occurs. Rapid I.V. infusion has caused transient hypotension and ECG changes in dogs. May increase risk of thiocyanate intoxication. Use caution with renal impairment.

Collection of pretreatment blood cyanide concentrations does not preclude administration and should not delay administration in the emergency management of highly suspected or confirmed cyanide toxicity. Patients receiving treatment for acute cyanide toxicity must be monitored for return of symptoms for 24-48 hours.

Adverse Reactions
  1% to 10%:
    Cardiovascular: Hypotension
    Central nervous system: Coma, CNS depression secondary to thiocyanate intoxication, psychosis, confusion

Dermatologic: Contact dermatitis, local irritation

Neuromuscular & skeletal: Weakness

Otic: Tinnitus

<1%: Gastrointestinal: Diarrhea (following large oral doses)

Mechanism of Action

Cyanide toxicity: Increases the rate of detoxification of cyanide by the enzyme rhodanese by providing an extra sulfur

Cisplatin toxicity: Complexes with cisplatin to form a compound that is nontoxic to either normal or cancerous cells

Pharmacodynamics/Kinetics

Absorption: Oral: Poor

Distribution: Extracellular fluid

Half-life elimination: 0.65 hour

Excretion: Urine (28.5% as unchanged drug)

Dosage

Cyanide and nitroprusside antidote: I.V.:

Children <25 kg: 50 mg/kg after receiving 4.5-10 mg/kg sodium nitrite; a half dose of each may be repeated if necessary

Children >25 kg and Adults: 12.5 g after 300 mg of sodium nitrite; a half dose of each may be repeated if necessary

Cyanide poisoning: I.V.: Dose should be based on determination as with nitrite, at rate of 2.5-5 mL/minute to maximum of 50 mL.

Variation of sodium nitrite and sodium thiosulfate dose, based on hemoglobin concentration: See table.

Variation of Sodium Nitrite and Sodium Thiosulfate Dose With Hemoglobin Concentration[1]

Hemoglobin (g/dL)	Initial Dose Sodium Nitrite (mg/kg)	Initial Dose Sodium Nitrite 3% (mL/kg)	Initial Dose Sodium Thiosulfate 25% (mL/kg)
7	5.8	0.19	0.95
8	6.6	0.22	1.10
9	7.5	0.25	1.25
10	8.3	0.27	1.35
11	9.1	0.30	1.50
12	10.0	0.33	1.65
13	10.8	0.36	1.80
14	11.6	0.39	1.95

[1]Adapted from Berlin DM Jr, "The Treatment of Cyanide Poisoning in Children," *Pediatrics*, 1970, 46:793.

Cisplatin rescue should be given before or during cisplatin administration: I.V. infusion (in sterile water): 12 g/m² over 6 hours or 9 g/m² I.V. push followed by 1.2 g/m² continuous infusion for 6 hours

Tinea versicolor: Children and Adults: Topical: 20% to 25% solution: Apply a thin layer to affected areas twice daily

Drug extravasation (unlabeled use): Children and Adults: SubQ:

2% solution: Infiltrate SubQ into the affected area

1/6 M (~4%) solution: 5-10 mL infused through I.V. line and SubQ into the affected area

Administration

I.V.: Inject slowly, over at least 10 minutes; rapid administration may cause hypotension.

Topical: Do not apply to or near eyes.

(Continued)

Sodium Thiosulfate *(Continued)*

Monitoring Parameters Monitor for signs of thiocyanate toxicity

Patient Information Avoid topical application near the eyes, mouth, or other mucous membranes; notify prescriber if condition worsens or burning or irritation occurs; shake well before using

Emetic Potential Very low (<10%)

Vesicant No

Dosage Forms Excipient information presented when available (limited, particularly for generics); consult specific product labeling.

Injection, solution [preservative free]: 100 mg/mL (10 mL); 250 mg/mL (50 mL)

Lotion: Sodium thiosulfate 25% and salicylic acid 1% (120 mL) [contains isopropyl alcohol 10%]

References

Bertelli G, "Prevention and Management of Extravasation of Cytotoxic Drugs," *Drug Saf*, 1995, 12(4):245-55.

Fuks JZ, Wadler S, and Wiernik PH, "Phase I and II Agents in Cancer Therapy: Two Cisplatin Analogues and High-Dose Cisplatin in Hypertonic Saline or With Thiosulfate Protection," *J Clin Pharmacol*, 1987, 27(5):357-65.

Gandara DR, Wiebe VJ, Perez EA, et al, "Cisplatin Rescue Therapy: Experience With Sodium Thiosulfate, WR2721, and Diethyldithiocarbamate," *Crit Rev Oncol Hematol*, 1990, 10(4):353-65.

Geller RJ, Barthold C, Saiers JA, et al, "Pediatric Cyanide Poisoning: Causes, Manifestations, Management, and Unmet Needs," *Pediatrics*, 2006, 118(5):2146-58.

Gracia R and Shepherd G, "Cyanide Poisoning and Its Treatment," *Pharmacotherapy*, 2004, 24(10):1358-65.

Hall AH and Rumack BH, "Hydroxocobalamin/Sodium Thiosulfate as a Cyanide Antidote," *J Emerg Med*, 1987, 5(2):115-21.

Howell SB, Pfeifle CL, Wung WE, et al, "Intraperitoneal Cisplatin With Systemic Thiosulfate Protection," *Ann Intern Med*, 1982, 97(6):845-51.

Mokhlesi B, Leikin JB, Murray P, et al, "Adult Toxicology in Critical Care: Part II: Specific Poisonings," *Chest*, 2003, 123(3):897-922.

Naughton M, "Acute Cyanide Poisoning," *Anaesth Intensive Care*, 1974, 2(4):351-6.

Pfeifle CE, Howell SB, Felthouse RD, et al, "High-Dose Cisplatin With Sodium Thiosulfate," *J Clin Oncol*, 1985, 3(2):237-44.

Skinner R, "Strategies to Prevent Nephrotoxicity of Anticancer Drugs," *Curr Opin Oncol*, 1995, 7(4):310-5.

Tognella S, "Pharmacological Interventions to Reduce Platinum-Induced Toxicity," *Cancer Treat Rev*, 1990, 17(2-3):139-42.

Willhite CC, "Inhalation Toxicology of Acute Exposure to Aliphatic Nitriles," *Clin Toxicol*, 1981, 18(8):991-1003.

♦ **Sodium Thiosulphate** *see* Sodium Thiosulfate *on page 972*

♦ **Soliris™** *see* Eculizumab *on page 374*

♦ **Soltamox™** *see* Tamoxifen *on page 1002*

♦ **Solu-Cortef®** *see* Hydrocortisone *on page 545*

♦ **Solu-Medrol®** *see* MethylPREDNISolone *on page 745*

♦ **Somatuline® Autogel® (Can)** *see* Lanreotide *on page 653*

♦ **Somatuline® Depot** *see* Lanreotide *on page 653*

Sorafenib *(sor AF e nib)*

Medication Safety Issues

High alert medication: The Institute for Safe Medication Practices (ISMP) includes this medication among its list of classes of drugs which have a heightened risk of causing significant patient harm when used in error.

Related Information

Safe Handling of Hazardous Drugs *on page 1382*

U.S. Brand Names Nexavar®

Index Terms BAY 43-9006; NSC-724772; Sorafenib Tosylate

Generic Available No

Pharmacologic Category Antineoplastic Agent, Tyrosine Kinase Inhibitor; Vascular Endothelial Growth Factor (VEGF) Inhibitor

Use Treatment of advanced renal cell cancer (RCC), unresectable hepatocellular cancer (HCC)

Unlabeled/Investigational Use Treatment of nonsmall cell lung cancer, ovarian cancer, pancreatic cancer, and melanoma

Pregnancy Risk Factor D

Lactation Excretion in breast milk unknown/not recommended

Labeled Contraindications Hypersensitivity to sorafenib or any component of the formulation

Warnings/Precautions Hazardous agent - use appropriate precautions for handling and disposal. May cause hypertension, especially in the first 6 weeks of treatment; monitor; use caution in patients with underlying or poorly-controlled hypertension. May cause cardiac ischemia or infarction; consider discontinuing (temporarily or permanently) in patients who develop these; use in patients with unstable coronary artery disease or recent myocardial infarction has not been studied. Use with caution in patients with cardiovascular disease. Serious bleeding events may occur; monitor PT/INR in patients on warfarin therapy. May complicate wound healing; temporarily withhold treatment for patients undergoing major surgical procedures. Gastrointestinal perforation has been reported (rare); monitor patients for signs/symptoms (abdominal pain, constipation, or vomiting); discontinue treatment if gastrointestinal perforation occurs. Use caution when administering sorafenib with compounds that are metabolized predominantly via UGT1A1 (eg, irinotecan). Hand-foot skin reaction and rash are the most common adverse events; usually managed with topical treatment, treatment delays, and/or dose reductions. Sorafenib levels may be lower in HCC patients with mild-to-moderate hepatic impairment (Child-Pugh classes A and B); has not been studied in patients with severe hepatic impairment or in patients on dialysis. Safety and efficacy have not been established in children.

Adverse Reactions

>10%:

Cardiovascular: Hypertension (9% to 17%; grade 3: 3% to 4%; grade 4: <1%; onset: ~3 weeks)

Central nervous system: Fatigue (37% to 46%), sensory neuropathy (≤13%), pain

Dermatologic: Rash/desquamation (19% to 40%; grade 3: ≤1%), hand-foot syndrome (21% to 30%; grade 3: 6% to 8%), alopecia (14% to 27%), pruritus (14% to 19%), dry skin (10% to 11%), erythema

Endocrine & metabolic: Hypoalbuminemia (≤59%), hypophosphatemia (35% to 45%; grade 3: 11% to 13%; grade 4: <1%)

Gastrointestinal: Diarrhea (43% to 55%; grade 3: 2% to 10%; grade 4: <1%), lipase increased (40% to 41% [usually transient]), amylase increased (30% to 34% [usually transient]), abdominal pain (11% to 31%), weight loss (10% to 30%), anorexia (16% to 29%), nausea (23% to 24%), vomiting (15% to 16%), constipation (14% to 15%)

Hematologic: Lymphopenia (23% to 47%; grades 3/4: 13%), thrombocytopenia (12% to 46%; grades 3/4: 1% to 4%), INR elevated (≤42%), neutropenia (≤18%; grades 3/4: ≤5%), hemorrhage (2% to 15%; grade 3: 2%), leukopenia

Hepatic: Liver dysfunction (≤11%)

(Continued)

Sorafenib *(Continued)*

Neuromuscular & skeletal: Muscle pain, weakness

Respiratory: Dyspnea (≤14%), cough (≤13%)

1% to 10%:

Cardiovascular: Cardiac ischemia/infarction (≤3%), flushing

Central nervous system: Headache (10%), depression, fever

Dermatologic: Acne, exfoliative dermatitis

Gastrointestinal: Appetite decreased, dyspepsia, dysphagia, glossodynia, mucositis, stomatitis, xerostomia

Genitourinary: Erectile dysfunction

Hepatic: Transaminases increased (transient)

Neuromuscular & skeletal: Joint pain (10%), arthralgia, myalgia

Respiratory: Hoarseness

Miscellaneous: Influenza-like symptoms

<1%, postmarketing, and/or case reports: Acute renal failure, alkaline phosphatase increased, arrhythmia, bilirubin increased, bone pain, cardiac failure, cerebral hemorrhage, CHF, dehydration, eczema, erythema multiforme, folliculitis, gastritis, gastrointestinal hemorrhage, gastrointestinal perforation, gastrointestinal reflux, gynecomastia, hypersensitivity (skin reaction, urticaria), hypertensive crisis, hyponatremia, hypothyroidism, infection, jaundice, MI, mouth pain, myocardial ischemia, pancreatitis, respiratory hemorrhage, reversible posterior leukoencephalopathy syndrome (RPLS), rhinorrhea, skin cancer (squamous cell/keratoacanthomas), thromboembolism, tinnitus, transient ischemic attack, tumor pain

Overdosage/Toxicology In clinical trials, doses of 800 mg twice daily produced diarrhea and dermatologic reactions. In the event of an overdose, treatment is symptom-directed and supportive.

Drug Interactions

Cytochrome P450 Effect: Substrate of CYP3A4 (minor); **Inhibits** CYP2B6 (weak) and 2C8 (weak)

Increased Effect/Toxicity: Sorafenib may increase the levels/effects of doxorubicin.

Decreased Effect: Sorafenib may decrease the absorption of digoxin tablets. CYP3A4 inducers may decrease the levels/effects of sorafenib; example inducers include aminoglutethimide, carbamazepine, nafcillin, nevirapine, phenobarbital, phenytoin, and rifamycins.

Ethanol/Nutrition/Herb Interactions

Food: Bioavailability is decreased 29% with a high-fat meal (bioavailability is similar to fasting state when administered with a moderate-fat meal).

Herb/Nutraceutical: Avoid St John's wort (may decrease the levels/effects of sorafenib).

Storage/Stability Store at room temperature between 15°C and 30°C (59°F and 86°F). Protect from moisture.

Mechanism of Action Multikinase inhibitor; inhibits tumor growth and angiogenesis by inhibiting intracellular Raf kinases (CRAF, BRAF, and mutant BRAF), and cell surface kinase receptors (VEGFR-2, VEGFR-3, PDGFR-beta, cKIT, and FLT-3)

Pharmacodynamics/Kinetics

Protein binding: 99.5%

Metabolism: Hepatic, via CYP3A4 (primarily oxidated to the pyridine N-oxide; active, minor) and UGT1A9 (glucuronidation)

Bioavailability: 38% to 49%

Half-life elimination: 25-48 hours

Time to peak, plasma: ~3 hours

Excretion: Feces (77%, 51% as unchanged drug); urine (19%, as metabolites)

Dosage Oral: Adults:

Advanced renal cell carcinoma: 400 mg twice daily

Hepatocellular cancer: 400 mg twice daily

Nonsmall cell lung cancer (unlabeled use): 400 mg twice daily

Pancreatic cancer (unlabeled use): 400 mg twice daily in combination with gemcitabine

Dosage adjustment for concomitant CYP3A4 inducers: Avoid the concomitant use of a strong CYP3A4 inducer with sorafenib. If a strong CYP3A4 inducer is required, the sorafenib dose may need to be increased, with careful monitoring. When the strong CYP3A4 inducer is discontinued, reduce sorafenib to the indicated dose. (See Drug Interactions for examples of CYP3A4 inducers.)

Dosage adjustment in renal impairment: No adjustment is required for mild, moderate, or severe renal impairment (not dependant on dialysis); has not been studied in dialysis patients.

Dosage adjustment in hepatic impairment: No adjustment required for mild (Child-Pugh class A) to moderate (Child-Pugh class B) hepatic impairment; not studied in severe hepatic impairment (Child-Pugh class C)

Dosage adjustment for toxicity: Temporary interruption and/or dosage reduction may be necessary for management of adverse drug reactions. The dose may be reduced to 400 mg once daily and then further reduced to 400 mg every other day.

Dose modification for skin toxicity:

Grade 1 (numbness, dysesthesia, paresthesia, tingling, painless swelling, erythema or discomfort of the hands or feet which do not disrupt normal activities): Continue sorafenib and consider symptomatic treatment with topical therapy.

Grade 2 (painful erythema and swelling of the hands or feet and/or discomfort affecting normal activities):

1st occurrence: Continue sorafenib and consider symptomatic treatment with topical therapy. **Note:** If no improvement within 7 days, see dosing for 2nd or 3rd occurrence.

2nd or 3rd occurrence: Hold treatment until resolves to grade 0-1; resume treatment with dose reduced by one dose level (400 mg daily or 400 mg every other day)

4th occurrence: Discontinue treatment

Grade 3 (moist desquamation, ulceration, blistering, or severe pain of the hands or feet or severe discomfort that prevents working or performing daily activities):

1st or 2nd occurrence: Hold treatment until resolves to grade 0-1; resume treatment with dose reduced by one dose level (400 mg daily or 400 mg every other day)

3rd occurrence: Discontinue treatment

Administration Administer on an empty stomach (1 hour before or 2 hours after eating).

Monitoring Parameters CBC with differential, electrolytes, phosphorus; blood pressure (baseline, weekly for the first 6 weeks, then periodic)

Dietary Considerations Take without food (1 hour before or 2 hours after eating).

Patient Information Take exactly as directed; 1 hour before or 2 hours after food. Maintain adequate nutrition and fluid intake. May cause hand or foot skin reaction or rash; notify prescriber. May cause hypertension, especially during the first 6 weeks of treatment; monitor blood pressure. May increase (Continued)

Sorafenib *(Continued)*

the risk of bleeding; report any bleeding episodes to prescriber. May cause cardiac ischemia or infarction; report chest pain to prescriber immediately. May cause fatigue (adequate rest periods may help), rash or dry skin (use nonirritating skin lotion that does not contain alcohol or other irritants), nausea or anorexia (small frequent meals, good mouth care, or sucking lozenges may help), or diarrhea (boiled milk, yogurt).

Special Geriatric Considerations No difference in efficacy or safety was observed between older and younger patients, but only 4% of patients studied were >75 years of age.

Emetic Potential Low (10% to 30%)

Dosage Forms Excipient information presented when available (limited, particularly for generics); consult specific product labeling.

Tablet, as tosylate: 200 mg

Nexavar®: 200 mg

References

Abou-Alfa GK, Schwarts L, Ricci S, et al, "Phase II Study of Sorafenib in Patients With Advanced Hepatocellular Carcinoma," *J Clin Oncol*, 2006, 24(26):4293-300.

Ahmad T and Eisen T, "Kinase Inhibition With BAY 43-9006 in Renal Cell Carcinoma," *Clin Cancer Res*, 2004, 10(18 Suppl 2):6388-92.

Clark JW, Eder JP, Ryan D, et al, "Safety and Pharmacokinetics of the Dual Action Raf Kinase and Vascular Endothelial Growth Factor Receptor Inhibitor, BAY 43-9006, in Patients With Advanced, Refractory Solid Tumors," *Clin Cancer Res*, 2005, 11(15):5472-80.

Escudier B, Eisen T, Stadler WM, et al, "Sorafenib in Advanced Clear-Cell Renal-Cell Carcinoma," *N Engl J Med*, 2007, 356(2):125-34.

Herbst RS, Onn A, and Sandler A, "Angiogenesis and Lung Cancer: Prognostic and Therapeutic Implications," *J Clin Oncol*, 2005, 23(14):3243-56.

Llovet J Ricci S, Mazzaferro V, et al, "Sorafenib Improves Survival in Advanced Hepatocellular Carcinoma (HCC): Results of a Phase III Randomized Placebo-Controlled Trial (SHARP Trial)," *J Clin Oncol*, 2007, 25(18S):LBA1 [abstract from 2007 ASCO Annual Meeting Proceedings, Part I]

Miller AA, Murry DJ, Owzar K, et al, "Pharmacokinetic (PK) and Phase I Study of Sorafenib (S) for Solid Tumors and Hematologic Malignancies in Patients With Hepatic or Renal Dysfunction," *J Clin Oncol*, 2007, 25(18S):3538 [abstract from 2007 ASCO Annual Meeting Proceedings, Part I]

Mross K, Steinbild S, Baas F, et al, "Drug-Drug Interaction Pharmacokinetic Study With the Raf Kinase Inhibitor (RKI) BAY 43-9006 Administered in Combination With Irinotecan (CPT-11) in Patients With Solid Tumors," *Int J Clin Pharmacol Ther*, 2003, 41(12):618-9.

Ratain, MJ, Eisen T, Stadler WM, et al, "Phase II Placebo-Controlled Randomized Discontinuation Trial of Sorafenib in Patients With Metastatic Renal Cell Carcinoma," *J Clin Oncol*, 2006, 24(16):2505-12.

Richly H, Kupsch P, Passage K, et al, "A Phase I Clinical and Pharmacokinetic Study of the Raf Kinase Inhibitor (RKI) BAY 43-9006 Administered in Combination With Doxorubicin in Patients With Solid Tumors," *Int J Clin Pharmacol Ther*, 2003, 41(12):620-1.

Rini BI and Small EJ, "Biology and Clinical Development of Vascular Endothelial Growth Factor-Targeted Therapy in Renal Cell Carcinoma," *J Clin Oncol*, 2005, 23(5):1028-43.

Siu LL, Awada A, Takimoto CH, et al, "Phase I Trial of Sorafenib and Gemcitabine in Advanced Solid Tumors with an Expanded Cohort in Advanced Pancreatic Cancer," *Clin Cancer Res*, 2006, 12(1):144-51.

Strumberg D, Richly H, Hilger RA, et al, "Phase I Clinical and Pharmacokinetic Study of the Novel Raf Kinase and Vascular Endothelial Growth Factor Receptor Inhibitor BAY 43-9006 in Patients With Advanced Refractory Solid Tumors," *J Clin Oncol*, 2005, 23(5):965-72.

Veronese ML, Mosenkis A, Flaherty KT, et al , "Mechanisms of Hypertension Associated With BAY 43-9006," *J Clin Oncol*, 2006, 24(9):1363-9.

+ **Sterapred® DS** *see* PredniSONE *on page 919*
+ **STI571** *see* Imatinib *on page 583*
+ **Stimate™** *see* Desmopressin *on page 326*

Streptozocin (strep toe ZOE sin)

Medication Safety Issues

Sound-alike/look-alike issues:

Streptozocin may be confused with streptomycin

High alert medication: The Institute for Safe Medication Practices (ISMP) includes this medication among its list of drugs which have a heightened risk of causing significant patient harm when used in error.

Related Information

Management of Drug Extravasations *on page 1301*
Management of Nausea and Vomiting *on page 1319*
Safe Handling of Hazardous Drugs *on page 1382*

U.S. Brand Names Zanosar®

Index Terms NSC-85998

Generic Available No

Canadian Brand Names Zanosar®

Pharmacologic Category Antineoplastic Agent, Alkylating Agent

Use Treatment of metastatic islet cell carcinoma of the pancreas, carcinoid tumor and syndrome, Hodgkin's disease, palliative treatment of colorectal cancer

Pregnancy Risk Factor D

Lactation Enters breast milk/contraindicated

Labeled Contraindications Pregnancy

Warnings/Precautions Hazardous agent - use appropriate precautions for handling and disposal. **[U.S. Boxed Warnings]: Renal toxicity is dose-related and cumulative and may be severe or fatal; other major toxicities include liver dysfunction, diarrhea, nausea, and vomiting. Should be administered under the supervision of an experienced cancer chemotherapy physician.** There may be an acute release of insulin during treatment. Keep syringe of $D_{50}W$ at bedside during administration. Local tissue irritation may occur; extravasation may cause local tissue lesions and necrosis.

Adverse Reactions

>10%:

Gastrointestinal: Nausea and vomiting (100%)

Hepatic: Increased LFTs

Miscellaneous: Hypoalbuminemia

Renal: BUN increased, Cl_{cr} decreased, hypophosphatemia, nephrotoxicity (25% to 75%), proteinuria, renal dysfunction (65%), renal tubular acidosis

1% to 10%:

Endocrine & metabolic: Hypoglycemia (6%)

Gastrointestinal: Diarrhea (10%)

Local: Pain at injection site

<1%: Confusion, lethargy, depression, leukopenia, thrombocytopenia, liver dysfunction, secondary malignancy

Myelosuppressive:

WBC: Mild

Platelets: Mild

Onset: 7 days

Nadir: 14 days

(Continued)

Streptozocin *(Continued)*

Recovery: 21 days

Overdosage/Toxicology Symptoms of overdose include bone marrow suppression, nausea, and vomiting. Treatment of bone marrow suppression is supportive.

Drug Interactions

Increased Effect/Toxicity: Doxorubicin toxicity may be increased with concurrent use of streptozocin. Manufacturer recommends doxorubicin dosage adjustment be considered.

Decreased Effect: Phenytoin results in negation of streptozocin cytotoxicity.

Storage/Stability Store intact vials under refrigeration. Vials are stable for 1 year at room temperature. Solution reconstituted with SWFI or NS is stable for 48 hours at room temperature and 96 hours under refrigeration. Further dilution in D_5W or NS is stable for 48 hours at room temperature and 96 hours under refrigeration when protected from light.

Reconstitution Dilute powder with 9.5 mL SWFI or NS to a concentration of 100 mg/mL.

Compatibility Stable in D_5W, NS.

Y-site administration: Compatible: Amifostine, etoposide phosphate, filgrastim, gemcitabine, granisetron, melphalan, ondansetron, teniposide, thiotepa, vinorelbine. **Incompatible:** Allopurinol, aztreonam, cefepime, piperacillin/tazobactam.

Mechanism of Action Interferes with the normal function of DNA by alkylation and cross-linking the strands of DNA, and by possible protein modification

Pharmacodynamics/Kinetics

Duration: Disappears from serum in 4 hours

Distribution: Concentrates in liver, intestine, pancreas, and kidney

Metabolism: Rapidly hepatic

Half-life elimination: 35-40 minutes

Excretion: Urine (60% to 70% as metabolites); exhaled gases (5%); feces (1%)

Dosage I.V. (refer to individual protocols):

Children and Adults:

Single-agent therapy: 1-1.5 g/m^2 weekly for 6 weeks followed by a 4-week rest period

Combination therapy: 0.5-1 g/m^2 for 5 consecutive days followed by a 4- to 6-week rest period

Dosing adjustment in renal impairment: The FDA-approved labeling does not contain dosing adjustments; however, it is recommended to use clinical judgment weighing benefit vs risk of renal toxicity in patients with pre-existing renal impairment. The following dosing adjustments have been used by some clinicians (Aronoff, 2007): Adults:

Cl_{cr} 10-50 mL/minute: Administer 75% of dose

Cl_{cr} <10 mL/minute: Administer 50% of dose

Dosing adjustment in hepatic impairment: There are no specific guidelines on dosage adjustment in patients with hepatic impairment. Streptozocin is rapidly hepatically metabolized; dose should be decreased in patients with severe liver disease.

Administration Administer as short (30-60 minutes) or 6-hour infusion; may be given by rapid I.V. push

Monitoring Parameters Monitor renal function closely

Emetic Potential Very high (>90%)

Vesicant Yes; see Management of Drug Extravasations *on page 1301*.

Dosage Forms Excipient information presented when available (limited, particularly for generics); consult specific product labeling.

Injection, powder for reconstitution: 1 g

References
Aronoff GR, Bennett WM, Berns JS, et al, *Drug Prescribing in Renal Failure: Dosing Guidelines for Adults and Children*, 5th ed. Philadelphia, PA: American College of Physicians; 2007, p 101.

Bolzan AD and Bianchi MS, "Genotoxicity of Streptozotocin," *Mutat Res*, 2002, 512(2-3):121-34.

♦ **Strontium-89 Chloride** *see* Strontium-89 *on page 981*

Strontium-89 (STRON shee um atey nine)

U.S. Brand Names Metastron®

Index Terms Strontium-89 Chloride

Generic Available No

Canadian Brand Names Metastron®

Pharmacologic Category Radiopharmaceutical

Use Relief of bone pain in patients with skeletal metastases

Pregnancy Risk Factor D

Labeled Contraindications Hypersensitivity to any strontium-containing compounds or any other component of the formulation; pregnancy; breast-feeding

Warnings/Precautions Use caution in patients with bone marrow compromise; incontinent patients may require urinary catheterization. Body fluids may remain radioactive up to one week after injection. Not indicated for use in patients with cancer not involving bone and should be used with caution in patients whose platelet counts fall <60,000/mm^3 or whose white blood cell counts fall <2400/mm^3. A small number of patients have experienced a transient increase in bone pain at 36-72 hours postdose; this reaction is generally mild and self-limiting. Use with caution in patients with renal impairment; renally eliminated. It should be handled cautiously, in a similar manner to other radioactive drugs. Appropriate safety measures to minimize radiation to personnel should be instituted. Safety and efficacy have not been established in children.

Adverse Reactions Most severe reactions of marrow toxicity can be managed by conventional means

Frequency not defined:

Cardiovascular: Flushing (most common after rapid injection)

Central nervous system: Fever and chills (rare)

Hematologic: Thrombocytopenia, leukopenia

Neuromuscular & skeletal: Increase in bone pain may occur (10% to 20% of patients)

Storage/Stability Store vial and its contents inside its transportation container at room temperature.

Dosage Adults: I.V.: 148 megabecquerel (4 millicurie) administered by slow I.V. injection over 1-2 minutes or 1.5-2.2 megabecquerel (40-60 microcurie)/kg; repeated doses are generally not recommended at intervals <90 days; measure the patient dose by a suitable radioactivity calibration system immediately prior to administration

Monitoring Parameters Routine blood tests

Patient Information Eat and drink normally, there is no need to avoid alcohol or caffeine unless already advised to do so; may be advised to take analgesics until Metastron® begins to become effective; the effect lasts for several months, if pain returns before that, notify medical personnel

(Continued)

Strontium-89 *(Continued)*

Additional Information During the first week after injection, strontium-89 will be present in the blood and urine, therefore, the following common sense precautions should be instituted:
1. Where a normal toilet is available, use in preference to a urinal, flush the toilet twice
2. Wipe away any spilled urine with a tissue and flush it away
3. Have patient wash hands after using the toilet
4. Immediately wash any linen or clothes that become stained with blood or urine
5. Wash away any spilled blood if a cut occurs

Emetic Potential Low (<10%)

Vesicant No

Dosage Forms Excipient information presented when available (limited, particularly for generics); consult specific product labeling.

Injection, solution, as chloride [preservative free]: 10.9-22.6 mg/mL [148 megabecquerel, 4 millicurie] (10 mL)

References
Brandi ML, "New Treatment Strategies: Ipriflavone Strontium, Vitamin D Metabolites and Analogs," *Am J Med*, 1993, 95(Suppl 5A):5A-69S-5A-74S.

Lincoln TA, "Importance of Initial Management of Persons Internally Contaminated With Radio-nuclides," *Am Ind Hyg Assoc J*, 1976, 37(1):16-21.

Robinson RG, Preston DF, Schiefelbein M, et al, "Strontium 89 Therapy for the Palliation of Pain Due to Osseous Metastases," *JAMA*, 1995, 274(5):420-4.

♦ **SU11248** *see Sunitinib on page 988*

♦ **Suberoylanilide Hydroxamic Acid** *see Vorinostat on page 1116*

♦ **Sublimaze**® *see Fentanyl on page 426*

Sulfamethoxazole and Trimethoprim
(sul fa meth OKS a zole & trye METH oh prim)

Medication Safety Issues

Sound-alike/look-alike issues:

Bactrim™ may be confused with bacitracin, Bactine®

Co-trimoxazole may be confused with clotrimazole

Septra® may be confused with Ceptaz®, Sectral®, Septa®

U.S. Brand Names Bactrim™; Bactrim™ DS; Septra®; Septra® DS

Index Terms Co-Trimoxazole; SMZ-TMP; Sulfatrim; TMP-SMZ; Trimethoprim and Sulfamethoxazole

Generic Available Yes

Canadian Brand Names Apo-Sulfatrim®; Apo-Sulfatrim® DS; Apo-Sulfatrim® Pediatric; Novo-Trimel; Novo-Trimel D.S.; Nu-Cotrimox; Septra® Injection

Pharmacologic Category Antibiotic, Miscellaneous; Antibiotic, Sulfonamide Derivative

Use

Oral treatment of urinary tract infections due to *E. coli*, *Klebsiella* and *Enterobacter* sp, *M. morganii*, *P. mirabilis* and *P. vulgaris*; acute otitis media in children; acute exacerbations of chronic bronchitis in adults due to susceptible strains of *H. influenzae* or *S. pneumoniae*; treatment and prophylaxis of *Pneumocystis jiroveci* pneumonitis (PCP); traveler's diarrhea due to enterotoxigenic *E. coli*; treatment of enteritis caused by *Shigella flexneri* or *Shigella sonnei*

I.V. treatment of severe or complicated infections when oral therapy is not feasible, for documented PCP, empiric treatment of PCP in immune compromised patients; treatment of documented or suspected shigellosis, typhoid fever, *Nocardia asteroides* infection, or other infections caused by susceptible bacteria

Unlabeled/Investigational Use Cholera and *Salmonella*-type infections and nocardiosis; chronic prostatitis; as prophylaxis in neutropenic patients with *P. jiroveci* infections, in leukemics, and in patients following renal transplantation, to decrease incidence of PCP; treatment of *Cyclospora* infection, typhoid fever, *Nocardia asteroides* infection

Pregnancy Risk Factor C/D (at term - expert analysis)

Lactation Enters breast milk/contraindicated (AAP rates "compatible with restrictions")

Labeled Contraindications Hypersensitivity to any sulfa drug, trimethoprim, or any component of the formulation; porphyria; megaloblastic anemia due to folate deficiency; infants <2 months of age; marked hepatic damage; severe renal disease; pregnancy (at term)

Warnings/Precautions Use with caution in patients with G6PD deficiency, impaired renal or hepatic function. Adjust dosage in patients with renal impairment. Injection vehicle contains benzyl alcohol and sodium metabisulfite. Fatalities associated with severe reactions including Stevens-Johnson syndrome, toxic epidermal necrolysis, hepatic necrosis, agranulocytosis, aplastic anemia, and other blood dyscrasias. Discontinue use at first sign of rash. Elderly patients and patients with HIV appear at greater risk for more severe adverse reactions. May cause hypoglycemia (particularly in malnourished, renal, or hepatic impairment). Use caution in patients with porphyria or thyroid dysfunction. May cause hyperkalemia. Slow acetylators may be more prone to adverse reactions.

Chemical similarities are present among sulfonamides, sulfonylureas, carbonic anhydrase inhibitors, thiazides, and loop diuretics (except ethacrynic acid). Use in patients with sulfonamide allergy is specifically contraindicated in product labeling, however, a risk of cross-reaction exists in patients with allergy to any of these compounds; avoid use when previous reaction has been severe. Prolonged use may result in fungal or bacterial superinfection, including *C. difficile*-associated diarrhea (CDAD) and pseudomembranous colitis; CDAD has been observed <2 months postantibiotic treatment.

Adverse Reactions The most common adverse reactions include gastrointestinal upset (nausea, vomiting, anorexia) and dermatologic reactions (rash or urticaria). Rare, life-threatening reactions have been associated with co-trimoxazole, including severe dermatologic reactions and hepatotoxic reactions. Most other reactions listed are rare, however, frequency cannot be accurately estimated.

Cardiovascular: Allergic myocarditis

Central nervous system: Confusion, depression, hallucinations, seizure, aseptic meningitis, peripheral neuritis, fever, ataxia, kernicterus in neonates

Dermatologic: Rashes, pruritus, urticaria, photosensitivity; rare reactions include erythema multiforme, Stevens-Johnson syndrome, toxic epidermal necrolysis, exfoliative dermatitis, and Henoch-Schönlein purpura

Endocrine & metabolic: Hyperkalemia (generally at high dosages), hypoglycemia

Gastrointestinal: Nausea, vomiting, anorexia, stomatitis, diarrhea, pseudomembranous colitis, pancreatitis

Hematologic: Thrombocytopenia, megaloblastic anemia, granulocytopenia, eosinophilia, pancytopenia, aplastic anemia, methemoglobinemia, hemolysis (with G6PD deficiency), agranulocytosis

(Continued)

Sulfamethoxazole and Trimethoprim *(Continued)*

Hepatic: Hepatotoxicity (including hepatitis, cholestasis, and hepatic necrosis), hyperbilirubinemia, transaminases increased

Neuromuscular & skeletal: Arthralgia, myalgia, rhabdomyolysis

Renal: Interstitial nephritis, crystalluria, renal failure, nephrotoxicity (in association with cyclosporine), diuresis

Respiratory: Cough, dyspnea, pulmonary infiltrates

Miscellaneous: Serum sickness, angioedema, periarteritis nodosa (rare), systemic lupus erythematosus (rare)

Overdosage/Toxicology Symptoms of overdose include nausea, vomiting, GI distress, hematuria, and crystalluria. Bone marrow suppression may occur. Treatment is supportive. Adequate fluid intake is essential. Peritoneal dialysis is not effective and hemodialysis is only moderately effective in removing co-trimoxazole. Leucovorin 5-15 mg/day may accelerate hematologic recovery.

Drug Interactions

Cytochrome P450 Effect:

Sulfamethoxazole: **Substrate** of CYP2C9 (major), 3A4 (minor); **Inhibits** CYP2C9 (moderate)

Trimethoprim: **Substrate** (major) of CYP2C9, 3A4; **Inhibits** CYP2C8 (moderate), 2C9 (moderate)

Increased Effect/Toxicity: Sulfamethoxazole/trimethoprim may increase toxicity of methotrexate. Sulfamethoxazole/trimethoprim may increase the serum levels of procainamide. Concurrent therapy with pyrimethamine (in doses >25 mg/week) may increase the risk of megaloblastic anemia. Sulfamethoxazole/trimethoprim may increase the levels/effects of amiodarone, fluoxetine, glimepiride, glipizide, nateglinide, phenytoin, pioglitazone, rosiglitazone, sertraline, warfarin, and other CYP2C8 and 2C9 substrates.

ACE Inhibitors, angiotensin receptor antagonists, or potassium-sparing diuretics may increase the risk of hyperkalemia. Concurrent use with cyclosporine may result in an increased risk of nephrotoxicity when used with sulfamethoxazole/trimethoprim. Trimethoprim may increase the serum concentration of dapsone.

Decreased Effect: The levels/effects of sulfamethoxazole may be decreased by carbamazepine, phenobarbital, phenytoin, rifampin, rifapentine, secobarbital, and other CYP2C9 inducers. Although occasionally recommended to limit or reverse hematologic toxicity of high-dose sulfamethoxazole/trimethoprim, concurrent use has been associated with a decreased effectiveness in treating *Pneumocystis carinii*.

Ethanol/Nutrition/Herb Interactions Herb/Nutraceutical: Avoid dong quai, St John's wort (may also cause photosensitization).

Storage/Stability

Injection: Store at room temperature; do not refrigerate. Less soluble in more alkaline pH. Protect from light. Solution must be diluted prior to administration. Following dilution, store at room temperature; do not refrigerate. Manufacturer recommended dilutions and stability of parenteral admixture at room temperature (25°C):

5 mL/125 mL D_5W; stable for 6 hours.

5 mL/100 mL D_5W; stable for 4 hours.

5 mL/75 mL D_5W; stable for 2 hours.

Studies have also confirmed limited stability in NS; detailed references should be consulted.

Suspension, tablet: Store at room temperature. Protect from light.

Compatibility Stable in D$_5$^{1}/$_2$NS, LR, ^{1}/$_2$NS; **variable stability (consult detailed reference)** in D$_5$W, NS.

Y-site administration: Compatible: Acyclovir, aldesleukin, allopurinol, amifostine, amphotericin B cholesteryl sulfate complex, atracurium, aztreonam, cefepime, cyclophosphamide, diltiazem, docetaxel, doxorubicin liposome, enalaprilat, esmolol, etoposide phosphate, filgrastim, fludarabine, gatifloxacin, gemcitabine, granisetron, hydromorphone, labetalol, linezolid, lorazepam, magnesium sulfate, melphalan, meperidine, morphine, pancuronium, perphenazine, piperacillin/tazobactam, remifentanil, sargramostim, tacrolimus, teniposide, thiotepa, vecuronium, zidovudine. **Incompatible:** Fluconazole, midazolam, vinorelbine. **Variable (consult detailed reference):** Cisatracurium, foscarnet.

Compatibility in syringe: Compatible: Heparin.

Compatibility when admixed: Incompatible: Fluconazole, verapamil.

Mechanism of Action Sulfamethoxazole interferes with bacterial folic acid synthesis and growth via inhibition of dihydrofolic acid formation from para-aminobenzoic acid; trimethoprim inhibits dihydrofolic acid reduction to tetrahydrofolate resulting in sequential inhibition of enzymes of the folic acid pathway

Pharmacodynamics/Kinetics

Absorption: Oral: Almost completely, 90% to 100%

Protein binding: SMX: 68%, TMP: 45%

Metabolism: SMX: N-acetylated and glucuronidated; TMP: Metabolized to oxide and hydroxylated metabolites

Half-life elimination: SMX: 9 hours, TMP: 6-17 hours; both are prolonged in renal failure

Time to peak, serum: Within 1-4 hours

Excretion: Both are excreted in urine as metabolites and unchanged drug

Effects of aging on the pharmacokinetics of both agents has been variable; increase in half-life and decreases in clearance have been associated with reduced creatinine clearance

Dosage Dosage recommendations are based on the trimethoprim component. Double-strength tablets are equivalent to sulfamethoxazole 800 mg and trimethoprim 160 mg.

Children >2 months:

General dosing guidelines:

Mild-to-moderate infections: Oral: 8-12 mg TMP/kg/day in divided doses every 12 hours

Serious infection:

Oral: 20 mg TMP/kg/day in divided doses every 6 hours

I.V.: 8-12 mg TMP/kg/day in divided doses every 6 hours

Acute otitis media: Oral: 8 mg TMP/kg/day in divided doses every 12 hours for 10 days

Urinary tract infection:

Treatment:

Oral: 6-12 mg TMP/kg/day in divided doses every 12 hours

I.V.: 8-10 mg TMP/kg/day in divided doses every 6, 8, or 12 hours for up to 4 days with serious infections

Prophylaxis: Oral: 2 mg TMP/kg/dose daily or 5 mg TMP/kg/dose twice weekly

Pneumocystis:

Treatment: Oral, I.V.: 15-20 mg TMP/kg/day in divided doses every 6-8 hours

Prophylaxis: Oral, 150 mg TMP/m^2/day in divided doses every 12 hours for 3 days/week; dose should not exceed trimethoprim 320 mg and sulfamethoxazole 1600 mg daily

(Continued)

Sulfamethoxazole and Trimethoprim *(Continued)*

Alternative prophylaxis dosing schedules include:

150 mg TMP/m^2/day as a single daily dose 3 times/week on consecutive days

or

150 mg TMP/m^2/day in divided doses every 12 hours administered 7 days/week

or

150 mg TMP/m^2/day in divided doses every 12 hours administered 3 times/week on alternate days

Shigellosis:

Oral: 8 mg TMP/kg/day in divided doses every 12 hours for 5 days

I.V.: 8-10 mg TMP/kg/day in divided doses every 6, 8, or 12 hours for up to 5 days

Cyclospora (unlabeled use): Oral, I.V.: 5 mg TMP/kg twice daily for 7-10 days

Adults:

Urinary tract infection:

Oral: One double-strength tablet every 12 hours

Duration of therapy: Uncomplicated: 3-5 days; Complicated: 7-10 days

Pyelonephritis: 14 days

Prostatitis: Acute: 2 weeks; Chronic: 2-3 months

I.V.: 8-10 mg TMP/kg/day in divided doses every 6, 8, or 12 hours for up to 14 days with severe infections

Chronic bronchitis: Oral: One double-strength tablet every 12 hours for 10-14 days

Meningitis (bacterial): I.V.: 10-20 mg TMP/kg/day in divided doses every 6-12 hours

Shigellosis:

Oral: One double strength tablet every 12 hours for 5 days

I.V.: 8-10 mg TMP/kg/day in divided doses every 6, 8, or 12 hours for up to 5 days

Travelers' diarrhea: Oral: One double strength tablet every 12 hours for 5 days

Sepsis: I.V.: 20 TMP/kg/day divided every 6 hours

Pneumocystis jiroveci:

Prophylaxis: Oral: 1 double strength tablet daily or 3 times/week

Treatment: Oral, I.V.: 15-20 mg TMP/kg/day in 3-4 divided doses

Cyclospora (unlabeled use): Oral, I.V.: 160 mg TMP twice daily for 7-10 days

Nocardia (unlabeled use): Oral, I.V.:

Cutaneous infections: 5 mg TMP/kg/day in 2 divided doses

Severe infections (pulmonary/cerebral): 10-15 mg TMP/kg/day in 2-3 divided doses. Treatment duration is controversial; an average of 7 months has been reported.

Note: Therapy for severe infection may be initiated I.V. and converted to oral therapy (frequently converted to approximate dosages of oral solid dosage forms: 2 DS tablets every 8-12 hours). Although not widely available, sulfonamide levels should be considered in patients with questionable absorption, at risk for dose-related toxicity, or those with poor therapeutic response.

Dosing adjustment in renal impairment: Oral, I.V.:

Cl$_{cr}$ 15-30 mL/minute: Administer 50% of recommended dose

Cl$_{cr}$ <15 mL/minute: Use is not recommended

Administration

I.V.: Infuse over 60-90 minutes, must dilute well before giving; may be given less diluted in a central line; not for I.M. injection

Oral: May be taken with or without food. Administer with at least 8 ounces of water.

Test Interactions Increased creatinine (Jaffé alkaline picrate reaction); increased serum methotrexate by dihydrofolate reductase method

Dietary Considerations Should be taken with 8 oz of water.

Patient Information Take oral medication with 8 oz of water; report any skin rashes immediately; finish all medication, do not skip doses

Special Geriatric Considerations Elderly patients appear at greater risk for more severe adverse reactions.

Vesicant No

Dosage Forms Excipient information presented when available (limited, particularly for generics); consult specific product labeling. **Note:** The 5:1 ratio (SMX:TMP) remains constant in all dosage forms.

Injection, solution: Sulfamethoxazole 80 mg and trimethoprim 16 mg per mL (5 mL, 10 mL, 30 mL)

Suspension, oral: Sulfamethoxazole 200 mg and trimethoprim 40 mg per 5 mL (480 mL)

Tablet: Sulfamethoxazole 400 mg and trimethoprim 80 mg

Bactrim™: Sulfamethoxazole 400 mg and trimethoprim 80 mg

Septra®: Sulfamethoxazole 400 mg and trimethoprim 80 mg

Tablet, double strength: Sulfamethoxazole 800 mg and trimethoprim 160 mg

Bactrim™ DS: Sulfamethoxazole 800 mg and trimethoprim 160 mg

Septra® DS: Sulfamethoxazole 800 mg and trimethoprim 160 mg

References

"1997 USPHS/IDSA Guidelines for the Prevention of Opportunistic Infections in Persons Infected With Human Immunodeficiency Virus. USPHS/IDSA Prevention of Opportunistic Working Group," *MMWR Recomm Rep*, 1997, 46(RR-12):1-46.

"American Academy of Pediatrics Committee on Drugs. The Transfer of Drugs and Other Chemicals Into Human Milk," *Pediatrics*, 2001, 108(3):776-89.

Bissuel F, Cotte L, Crapanne JB, et al, "Trimethoprim-Sulphamethoxazole Rechallenge in 20 Previously Allergic HIV-Infected Patients After Homeopathic," *AIDS*, 1995, 9(4):407-8.

Choo V, "UK Revises Indications for Co-Trimoxazole," *Lancet*, 1995, 346:175.

Cockerill FR and Edson RS, "Trimethoprim-Sulfamethoxazole," *Mayo Clin Proc*, 1991, 66(12):1260-9.

Cook DE and Ponte CD, "Suspected Trimethoprim/Sulfamethoxazole-Induced Hypoprothrombinemia," *J Fam Pract*, 1994, 39(6):589-91.

Dawkins B, Albury D, and Olsen TE, "Trimethoprim/Sulfamethoxazole-Induced Thrombocytopenia - A Case Report Supported by the Laboratory Diagnosis," *Aust N Z J Med*, 1995, 25:83.

Domingo P, Ferrer S, Cruz J, et al, "Trimethoprim-Sulfamethoxazole-Induced Renal Tubular Acidosis in a Patient With AIDS," *Clin Infect Dis*, 1995, 20(5):143, 45-7.

Fischl MA, Dickinson GM, and La Voie L, "Safety and Efficacy of Sulfamethoxazole and Trimethoprim Chemoprophylaxis for *Pneumocystis carinii* Pneumonia in AIDS," *JAMA*, 1988, 259(8):1185-9.

Gilbert DN, Moellering RC, Eliopoulos GM, et al, eds, *The Sanford Guide To Antimicrobial Therapy*, 2006, 36th ed, Hyde Park, VT: Antimicrobial Therapy, Inc, 2006, 6-7.

Hennessy S, Strom BL, Berlin JA, et al, "Predicting Cutaneous Hypersensitivity Reactions to Co-Trimoxazole in HIV-Infected Individuals Receiving Primary *Pneumocystis carinii* Pneumonia Prophylaxis," *J Gen Intern Med*, 1995, 10(7):380-6.

Hughes W, Leoung G, Kramer F, et al, "Comparison of Atovaquone (566C80) With Trimethoprim-Sulfamethoxazole to Treat *Pneumocystis carinii* Pneumonia in Patients With AIDS," *N Engl J Med*, 1993, 328(21):1521-7.

Hughes WT, "*Pneumocystis carinii* Pneumonia: New Approaches to Diagnosis, Treatment, and Prevention," *Pediatr Infect Dis J*, 1991, 10(5):391-9.

Jick H and Derby LE, "A Large Population-Based Follow-Up Study of Trimethoprim-Sulfamethoxazole, Trimethoprim, and Cephalexin for Uncommon Serious Drug Toxicity," *Pharmacotherapy*, 1995, 15(4):428-32.

Jick H and Derby LE, "Is Co-Trimoxazole Safe?" *Lancet*, 1995, 345(8957):1118-9.

Lerner PI, "Nocardiosis," *Clinical Infectious Disease*, 1996, 22(6):891-903.

(Continued)

Sulfamethoxazole and Trimethoprim *(Continued)*

Lundstrom TS and Sobel JD, "Vancomycin, Trimethoprim-Sulfamethoxazole, and Rifampin," *Infect Dis Clin North Am*, 1995, 9(3):747-67.

Masur H, "Prevention and Treatment of *Pneumocystis* Pneumonia," *N Engl J Med*, 1992, 327(26):1853-60.

Naber K, Vergin H, and Weigand W, "Pharmacokinetics of Co-trimoxazole and Co-tetroxazine in Geriatric Patients," *Infection*, 1981, 9(5):239-43.

Noto H, Kaneko Y, Takano T, et al, "Severe Hyponatremia and Hyperkalemia Induced by Trimethoprim-Sulfamethoxazole in Patients With *Pneumocystis carinii* Pneumonia," *Intern Med*, 1995, 34(2):96-9.

"Practice Parameter: The Diagnosis, Treatment, and Evaluation of the Initial Urinary Tract Infection in Febrile Infants and Young Children. American Academy of Pediatrics, Committee on Quality Improvement, Subcommittee on Urinary Tract Infection," *Pediatrics*, 1999, 103(4 Pt 1: 843-52.

Sattler FR, Cowan R, Nielsen DM, et al, "Trimethoprim-Sulfamethoxazole Compared With Pentamidine for Treatment of *Pneumocystis carinii* Pneumonia in the Acquired Immunodeficiency Syndrome," *Ann Intern Med*, 1988, 109(4):280-7.

Singh N, Gayowski T, Yu VL, et al, "Trimethoprim-Sulfamethoxazole for the Prevention of Spontaneous Bacterial Peritonitis in Cirrhosis: A Randomized Trial," *Ann Intern Med*, 1995, 122(8):595-8.

Torre D, Casari S, Speranza F, et al, "Randomized Trial of Trimethoprim-Sulfamethoxazole Versus Pyrimethamine-Sulfadiazine for Therapy of Toxoplasmic Encephalitis in Patients With AIDS. Italian Collaborative Study Group," *Antimicrob Agents Chemother*, 1998, 42(6):1346-9.

Tunkel AR, Hartman BJ, Kaplan SL, et al, "Practice Guidelines for the Management of Bacterial Meningitis," *Clin Infect Dis*, 2004, 39(9):1267-84.

Varoquaux O, Lajoie D, Gobert C, et al, "Pharmacokinetics of the Trimethoprim-Sulfamethoxazole Combination in the Elderly," *Br J Clin Pharmacol*, 1985, 20(6):575-81.

- ◆ **Sulfatrim** *see* Sulfamethoxazole and Trimethoprim *on page 982*
- ◆ **Summer's Eve® SpecialCare™ Medicated Anti-Itch Cream [OTC] [DSC]** *see* Hydrocortisone *on page 545*
- ◆ **Sun-Benz® (Can)** *see* Benzydamine *on page 132*

Sunitinib (su NIT e nib)

Medication Safety Issues

High alert medication: The Institute for Safe Medication Practices (ISMP) includes this medication among its list of drugs which have a heightened risk of causing significant patient harm when used in error.

Related Information

Safe Handling of Hazardous Drugs *on page 1382*

U.S. Brand Names Sutent®

Index Terms NSC736511; SU11248; Sunitinib Maleate

Generic Available No

Pharmacologic Category Antineoplastic Agent, Tyrosine Kinase Inhibitor; Vascular Endothelial Growth Factor (VEGF) Inhibitor

Use Treatment of gastrointestinal stromal tumor (GIST) following failure of or intolerance to imatinib; treatment of advanced renal cell cancer (RCC)

Pregnancy Risk Factor D

Lactation Excretion in breast milk unknown/not recommended

Labeled Contraindications Hypersensitivity to sunitinib or any other component of the formulation; pregnancy

Warnings/Precautions May cause a decrease in left ventricular ejection fraction (LVEF), including grade 3 reductions; monitor with baseline and periodic LVEF evaluations. Interrupt therapy or decrease dose with LVEF <50% or >20% reduction from baseline. Discontinue with clinical signs and symptoms of congestive heart failure (CHF). QT_c prolongation and torsade de pointes have been observed; a baseline and periodic ECG should be obtained; correct electrolyte abnormalities prior to treatment and monitor and correct potassium, calcium and magnesium levels during therapy; use caution in patients with a history of QT_c prolongation or with medications known to prolong the QTc$_c$ interval. Use caution with cardiac dysfunction; patients with MI, bypass grafts, CHF, vascular diseases (including CVA and TIA), and PE were excluded from clinical trials. May cause hypertension; monitor and control with antihypertensives if needed; interrupt therapy until hypertension is controlled for severe hypertension. Use caution and closely monitor in patients with underlying or poorly-controlled hypertension. Use with caution in patients concurrently taking strong CYP3A4 inhibitors or inducers; dosage adjustments of sunitinib may be required.

Hemorrhagic events have been reported including epistaxis, rectal, gingival, upper GI, genital, wound bleeding, and tumor-related and pulmonary hemorrhage. Serious and fatal gastrointestinal complications have occurred. Hypothyroidism may occur; risk for hypothyroidism appears to increase with duration of therapy; monitor thyroid function if symptomatic. Adrenal function abnormalities have been reported; monitor for adrenal insufficiency for patients with trauma, severe infection, or undergoing surgery. May cause skin and/or hair depigmentation or discoloration. Safety and effectiveness in children have not been established.

Adverse Reactions

>10%:

Cardiovascular: Hypertension (15% to 30%; grades 3/4: 4% to 10%), LVEF decreased (11% to 21%; grades 3/4: 1%), peripheral edema (11%)

Central nervous system: Fatigue (42% to 58%), fever (17% to 18%), headache (13% to 18%), chills (11%), insomnia (11%)

Dermatologic: Hyperpigmentation (19% to 33%), skin discoloration (19% to 30%), rash (14% to 27%), hand-foot syndrome (12% to 21%), dry skin (17% to 18%), hair color changes (7% to 16%)

Endocrine & metabolic: Hyperuricemia (15% to 41%), hypophosphatemia (9% to 36%), hypocalcemia (35%), hypoglycemia (19%), hypoalbuminemia (18%), hyperglycemia (15%), hyponatremia (6% to 14%), hypokalemia (12%), hyperkalemia (6% to 11%), hypernatremia (10% to 11%)

Gastrointestinal: Diarrhea (40% to 58%), lipase increased (25% to 52%), nausea (31% to 49%), taste perversion (21% to 44%), mucositis/stomatitis (29% to 43%), anorexia (31% to 38%), constipation (16% to 34%), abdominal pain (22% to 33%), dyspepsia (28%), vomiting (24% to 28%), amylase increased (5% to 17%), weight loss (12%), xerostomia (12%), GERD/reflux (11%)

Hematologic: Leukopenia (up to 78%; grades 3/4: 5%), neutropenia (53% to 72%; grades 3/4: 10% to 12%), anemia (26% to 72%; grades 3/4: 3% to 7%), thrombocytopenia (38% to 65%; grades 3/4: 5% to 8%), lymphopenia (38% to 59%; grades 3/4: up to 59%), hemorrhage/bleeding (18% to 30%)

Hepatic: AST increased (39% to 52%), ALT increased (39% to 46%), alkaline phosphatase increased (24% to 42%), hyperbilirubinemia (10% to 19%)

Neuromuscular & skeletal: Creatine kinase increased (41%), weakness (21% to 22%), back pain (11% to 19%), arthralgia (12% to 18%), limb pain (14% to 17%), myalgia (14%)

Renal: Creatinine increased (12% to 66%)

Respiratory: Dyspnea (10% to 28%), cough (8% to 17%)

1% to 10%:

Cardiovascular: Venous thrombotic events (2% to 3%), DVT (1% to 3%), myocardial ischemia (1%)

Central nervous system: Depression (8%), dizziness (7%)

Dermatologic: Skin blistering (7%), alopecia (5%)

Endocrine & metabolic: Dehydration (8%), hypothyroidism (3% to 7%)

(Continued)

Sunitinib *(Continued)*

Gastrointestinal: Flatulence (10%), glossodynia (10%), oral pain (6% to 10%), appetite disturbance (9%), pancreatitis (1%)

Neuromuscular & skeletal: Peripheral neuropathy (10%)

Ocular: Periorbital edema (7%), lacrimation increased (6%)

Respiratory: Pulmonary embolism (1%)

<1%, postmarketing, and/or case reports: Adrenal dysfunction, CHF, febrile neutropenia, gastrointestinal perforation, hepatic failure, MI, pulmonary hemorrhage, QT_c prolongation (dose dependent), reversible posterior leukoencephalopathy syndrome (RPLS), seizure, torsade de pointes

Overdosage/Toxicology There is no antidote for sunitinib overdose; emesis or gastric lavage may eliminate unabsorbed drug. Treatment is symptom-directed and supportive.

Drug Interactions

Cytochrome P450 Effect: Substrate of CYP3A4 (major)

Increased Effect/Toxicity: CYP3A4 inhibitors may increase the levels/effects of sunitinib (example inhibitors include azole antifungals, clarithromycin, diclofenac, doxycycline, erythromycin, imatinib, isoniazid, nefazodone, nicardipine, propofol, protease inhibitors, quinidine, telithromycin, and verapamil). Ketoconazole may increase the effects of sunitinib. Concurrent use of sunitinib with other drugs which may prolong QT_c interval may increase the risk of potentially-fatal arrhythmias; includes type Ia and type III antiarrhythmic agents, selected quinolones (eg, moxifloxacin), cisapride, dolasetron, thioridazine, and other agents.

Decreased Effect: CYP3A4 inducers may decrease the levels/effects of sunitinib (example inducers include aminoglutethimide, carbamazepine, dexamethasone, nafcillin, nevirapine, phenobarbital, and phenytoin. Rifamycins may decrease the effects of sunitinib.

Ethanol/Nutrition/Herb Interactions

Food: Grapefruit juice may increase the levels/effects of sunitinib. Food has no effect on the bioavailability of sunitinib.

Herb/Nutraceutical: Avoid St John's wort (may increase metabolism and decrease sunitinib concentrations).

Storage/Stability Store at room temperature between 15°C and 30°C (59°F and 86°F).

Mechanism of Action Exhibits antitumor and antiangiogenic properties by inhibiting multiple receptor tyrosine kinases, including platelet-derived growth factors (PDGFRα and PDGFRβ), vascular endothelial growth factors (VEGFR1, VEGFR2, and VEGFR3), FMS-like tyrosine kinase-3 (FLT3), colony-stimulating factor type 1 (CSF-1R), and glial cell-line-derived neurotrophic factor receptor (RET).

Pharmacodynamics/Kinetics

Distribution: V_d/F: 2230 L

Protein binding: Sunitinib: 95%; SU12662: 90%

Metabolism: Hepatic; primarily metabolized by CYP3A4 to the N-desethyl metabolite SU12662 (active)

Half-life elimination: Sunitinib: 40-60 hours; SU12662: 80-110 hours

Time to peak, plasma: 6-12 hours

Excretion: Feces (61%); urine (16%)

Dosage Oral: Adults: Gastrointestinal stromal tumor, renal cell cancer: 50 mg once daily for 4 weeks of a 6-week treatment cycle (4 weeks on, 2 weeks off). **Note:** Dose increase or reduction should be done in increments of 12.5 mg; individualize based on safety and tolerability.

Dosage adjustment with concurrent CYP3A4 inhibitor: Dose reductions are more likely to be needed when sunitinib is administered concomitantly with strong CYP3A4 inhibitors; dose reductions to a minimum of 37.5 mg/day should be considered with ketoconazole or other strong CYP3A4 inhibitor. (See Drug Interactions for examples of CYP3A4 inhibitors.)

Dosage adjustment with concurrent CYP3A4 inducer: May require increased doses; dosage increases to a maximum of 87.5 mg/day should be considered with rifampin or other strong CYP3A4 inducer. (See Drug Interactions for examples of CYP3A4 inducers).

Dosage adjustment in renal impairment: Not studied in patients with serum creatinine >2 x ULN; pharmacokinetics were unaltered in patients with $Cl_{cr} \geq 42$.

Dosage adjustment in hepatic impairment: No adjustment is necessary with mild-to-moderate (Child-Pugh Class A or B) hepatic impairment; not studied in patients with severe (Child-Pugh Class C) hepatic impairment. Studies excluded patients with ALT/AST >2.5 x ULN, or if due to liver metastases, ALT/AST >5 x ULN.

Administration May be taken with or without food.

Monitoring Parameters LVEF, baseline (and periodic with cardiac risk factors), ECG (12-lead; baseline and periodic), blood pressure, adrenal function, CBC with differential and platelets (prior to each treatment cycle), serum chemistries including magnesium, phosphate, and potassium (prior to each treatment cycle), thyroid function (baseline; then if symptomatic)

Dietary Considerations May be taken with or without food. Avoid grapefruit juice.

Special Geriatric Considerations Of the 450 patients studied, 115 (25.6%) were ≥65 years of age. No overall differences in safety or effectiveness were noted between younger adults and geriatric patients. Note, however, warning of left ventricular changes in ejection fraction as many elderly have systolic failure.

Emetic Potential Moderate (30% to 60%)

Dosage Forms Excipient information presented when available (limited, particularly for generics); consult specific product labeling.

Capsule:

Sutent®: 12.5 mg, 25 mg, 50 mg

References

Desai J, Yassa L, Marqusee E, et al, "Hypothyroidism After Sunitinib Treatment for Patients With Gastrointestinal Stromal Tumors," *Ann Intern Med*, 2006, 145(9):660-4.

Faivre S, Delbaldo C, and Vera K, "Safety, Pharmacokinetic, and Antitumor Activity of SU11248, a Novel Oral Multitarget Tyrosine Kinase Inhibitor, in Patients With Cancer," *J Clin Oncol*, 2006, 24(1):25-35.

Motzer RJ, Hutson TE, Tomczak P, et al, "Sunitinib Versus Interferon Alfa in Metastatic Renal-Cell Cancer," *N Engl J Med*, 2007, 356(2):115-24.

Moltzer RJ, Michaelson MD, and Redman BG, "Activity of SU11248, a Multitargeted Inhibitor of Vascular Endothelial Growth Factor Receptor, in Patients With Metastatic Renal Cell Cancer," *J Clin Oncol*, 2006, 24(1):16-24.

O'Farrell AM, Foran JM, Fiedler W, et al, "An Innovative Phase I Clinical Study Demonstrates Inhibition of FLT3 Phosphorylation by SU11248 in Acute Myeloid Leukemia Patients," *Clin Cancer Res*, 2003, 9(15):5465-76.

Rini BI, Tamaskar I, Shaheen P, et al, "Hypothyroidism in Patients With Metastatic Renal Cell Carcinoma Treated With Sunitinib," *J Natl Cancer Inst*, 2007, 99(1):81-3.

♦ **Sunitinib Maleate** *see* Sunitinib *on page 988*

♦ **Supeudol® (Can)** *see* Oxycodone *on page 849*

♦ **Supprelin® LA** *see* Histrelin *on page 540*

Suramin (SUR a min)

Related Information

Investigational Drug Service *on page 1379*
Safe Handling of Hazardous Drugs *on page 1382*
(Continued)

Suramin *(Continued)*

Index Terms Antrypol; Bayer 205; 309F; Forneau-309; Naphuride Sodium; NSC-34936; Suramin Sodium

Generic Available No

Pharmacologic Category Antineoplastic Agent

Unlabeled/Investigational Use Investigational: Treatment of prostate cancer; chemosensitizing agent in treatment of various solid tumors

Labeled Contraindications Hypersensitivity to suramin or any component of the formulation

Warnings/Precautions Hazardous agent - use appropriate precautions for handling and disposal. Use cautiously in patients with significant hepatic dysfunction, malnourishment, or with decreased serum albumin levels.

Adverse Reactions

>10%:

Central nervous system: Fever (78%), headache; palmar and plantar hyperesthesia occur at levels >350 mcg/mL

Dermatologic: Rash (48%)

Endocrine & metabolic: Adrenal insufficiency (23%), patients usually require adrenocorticoid therapy; transaminases increased (transient 14%)

Gastrointestinal: Nausea (20%), vomiting (35%), metallic taste

Hematologic: Leukopenia, agranulocytosis, thrombocytopenia (12% to 26%), usually not dose-limiting

Hepatic: Transient increases in bilirubin levels (14%)

Neuromuscular & skeletal: Paresthesia, peripheral neuropathies (33%), may be dose-limiting; areflexia and paralysis may occur at levels >375 mcg/mL

Ocular: Keratopathy (11%), possibly related to dose and/or rate of infusion

Renal: Mild, nondose-limiting, proteinuria (33%); decrease in creatinine clearance

1% to 10%:

Gastrointestinal: Stomatitis (5%)

Neuromuscular & skeletal: Myalgia (3%)

<1%: Abdominal pain, atrial fibrillation, diarrhea; coagulopathy (dose-limiting, inhibits factors V, VIII, IX, X, XI, and XII)

Immediate hypersensitivity reactions, including nausea, vomiting, shock, and loss of consciousness (0.1% to 0.3%); a 100-200 mg (10-20 mg in children) test dose prior to the first treatment cycle is occasionally given

Storage/Stability Solutions of 10 mg/mL in saline or dextrose solutions are stable for up to 2 weeks at room temperature of 15°C to 30°C (59°F to 86°F).

Mechanism of Action Suramin inhibits a number of growth factors and enzymes essential to cell proliferation including platelet-derived growth factor (PDGF), fibroblast growth factor, DNA polymerase, glycerol phosphate oxidase, reverse transcriptase, and various lysosomal enzymes. Suramin may also have some angiogenic inhibitory activity.

Pharmacodynamics/Kinetics

Absorption: Not absorbed orally

Distribution: V_d: 31-46 L; does not penetrate the CNS

Protein binding: >99%

Half-life elimination: Triphasic, terminal half-life: 50 days

Excretion: Urine (as unchanged drug); bile (small amounts)

Dosage Refer to individual protocols. I.V.: Adults:

Prostate cancer: 350 mg/m²/day continuous I.V. infusion for 7 days, then titrated to a plasma level of 250-300 mcg/mL for 7 days, repeated after an 8-week interval.

Titrate to a plasma level of 300 mcg/mL for 14 days, repeat after an 8-week interval.

Chemosensitizing agent: Doses are not yet established; anticipated to be significantly lower than cancer treatment doses.

Dosage adjustment in renal impairment: Dosage reductions have been suggested for "severe" renal dysfunction; however, specific guidelines have not been published.

Dosage adjustment in hepatic impairment: Dosage reductions of 50% to 75% have been suggested for "severe" hepatic dysfunction; however, specific guidelines have not been published.

Administration I.V.: Usually administered as a carefully titrated continuous infusion

Emetic Potential Moderate (30% to 60%)

Vesicant No; may be an irritant

Dosage Forms Excipient information presented when available (limited, particularly for generics); consult specific product labeling.

Injection, powder for reconstitution: 600 mg

References

Eisenberger MA and Reyno LM, "Suramin," *Cancer Treat Rev*, 1994, 20(3):259-73.
Larsen AK, "Suramin: An Anticancer Drug With Unique Biological Effects," *Cancer Chemother Pharmacol*, 1993, 32(2):96-8.
Stein CA, "Suramin: A Novel Antineoplastic Agent With Multiple Potential Mechanisms of Action," *Cancer Res*, 1993, 53(10 Suppl):2239-48.
Voogd TE, Vansterkenburg EL, Wilting J, et al, "Recent Research on the Biological Activity of Suramin," *Pharmacol Rev*, 1993, 45(2):177-203.

♦ **Suramin Sodium** *see* Suramin *on page 991*

♦ **Sutent**® *see* Sunitinib *on page 988*

♦ **Tabloid**® *see* Thioguanine *on page 1030*

Tacrolimus (ta KROE li mus)

Medication Safety Issues
Sound-alike/look-alike issues:
Prograf® may be confused with Gengraf®
Temsirolimus may be confused with sirolimus, tacrolimus

Related Information
Hematopoietic Stem Cell Transplantation *on page 1366*
Safe Handling of Hazardous Drugs *on page 1382*

U.S. Brand Names Prograf®; Protopic®

Index Terms FK506

Generic Available No

Canadian Brand Names Prograf®; Protopic®

Pharmacologic Category Immunosuppressant Agent; Topical Skin Product

Use
Oral/injection: Potent immunosuppressive drug used in heart, kidney, or liver transplant recipients

Topical: Moderate-to-severe atopic dermatitis in patients not responsive to conventional therapy or when conventional therapy is not appropriate

Unlabeled/Investigational Use Potent immunosuppressive drug used in lung, small bowel transplant recipients; immunosuppressive drug for peripheral stem cell/bone marrow transplantation

Restrictions An FDA-approved medication guide must be distributed when dispensing the outpatient prescription (new or refill) for tacrolimus ointment where this medication is to be used without direct supervision of a healthcare (Continued)

Tacrolimus *(Continued)*

provider. Medication guides are available at http://www.fda.gov/cder/Offices/ODS/medication_guides.htm.

Pregnancy Risk Factor C

Lactation Enters breast milk/contraindicated

Labeled Contraindications Hypersensitivity to tacrolimus or any component of the formulation

Warnings/Precautions

Oral/injection: Insulin-dependent post-transplant diabetes mellitus (PTDM) has been reported (1% to 20%); risk increases in African-American and Hispanic kidney transplant patients. **[U.S. Boxed Warning]: Increased susceptibility to infection and the possible development of lymphoma may occur after administration of tacrolimus.** Nephrotoxicity and neurotoxicity have been reported, especially with higher doses; to avoid excess nephrotoxicity do not administer simultaneously with cyclosporine; monitoring of serum concentrations (trough for oral therapy) is essential to prevent organ rejection and reduce drug-related toxicity; tonic clonic seizures may have been triggered by tacrolimus. A period of 24 hours should elapse between discontinuation of cyclosporine and the initiation of tacrolimus. Use caution in renal or hepatic dysfunction, dosing adjustments may be required. Delay initiation if postoperative oliguria occurs. Use may be associated with the development of hypertension (common). Myocardial hypertrophy has been reported (rare). Each mL of injection contains polyoxyl 60 hydrogenated castor oil (HCO-60) (200 mg) and dehydrated alcohol USP 80% v/v. Anaphylaxis has been reported with the injection, use should be reserved for those patients not able to take oral medications.

Topical: [U.S. Boxed Warning]: Topical calcineurin inhibitors have been associated with rare cases of malignancy. Avoid use on malignant or premalignant skin conditions (eg cutaneous T-cell lymphoma). Topical calcineurin agents are considered second-line therapies in the treatment of atopic dermatitis/eczema, and should be limited to use in patients who have failed treatment with other therapies. **[U.S. Boxed Warning]: They should be used for short-term and intermittent treatment using the minimum amount necessary for the control of symptoms should be used.** Application should be limited to involved areas. Safety of intermittent use for >1 year has not been established.

Should not be used in immunocompromised patients. Do not apply to areas of active viral infection; infections at the treatment site should be cleared prior to therapy. Patients with atopic dermatitis are predisposed to skin infections, and tacrolimus therapy has been associated with risk of developing eczema herpeticum, varicella zoster, and herpes simplex. May be associated with development of lymphadenopathy; possible infectious causes should be investigated. Discontinue use in patients with unknown cause of lymphadenopathy or acute infectious mononucleosis. Not recommended for use in patients with skin disease which may increase systemic absorption (eg, Netherton's syndrome). Avoid artificial or natural sunlight exposure, even when Protopic® is not on the skin. Safety not established in patients with generalized erythroderma. **[U.S. Boxed Warning]: The use of Protopic® in children <2 years of age is not recommended,** particularly since the effect on immune system development is unknown.

Adverse Reactions
Oral, I.V.:
≥15%:

Cardiovascular: Chest pain, hypertension, pericardial effusion (heart transplant)

Central nervous system: Dizziness, headache, insomnia, tremor (headache and tremor are associated with high whole blood concentrations and may respond to decreased dosage)

Dermatologic: Pruritus, rash

Endocrine & metabolic: Diabetes mellitus, hyperglycemia, hyper-/hypokalemia, hyperlipemia, hypomagnesemia, hypophosphatemia

Gastrointestinal: Abdominal pain, constipation, diarrhea, dyspepsia, nausea, vomiting

Genitourinary: Urinary tract infection

Hematologic: Anemia, leukocytosis, leukopenia, thrombocytopenia

Hepatic: Ascites

Neuromuscular & skeletal: Arthralgia, back pain, paresthesia, tremor, weakness

Renal: Abnormal kidney function, BUN increased, creatinine increased, oliguria, urinary tract infection

Respiratory: Atelectasis, bronchitis, dyspnea, increased cough, pleural effusion

Miscellaneous: CMV infection, infection

<15%:

Cardiovascular: Abnormal ECG (QRS or ST segment abnormal), angina pectoris, cardiopulmonary failure, deep thrombophlebitis, heart rate decreased, hemorrhage, hemorrhagic stroke, hypervolemia, hypotension, generalized edema, peripheral vascular disorder, phlebitis, postural hypotension, tachycardia, thrombosis, vasodilation

Central nervous system: Abnormal dreams, abnormal thinking, agitation, amnesia, anxiety, chills, confusion, depression, dizziness, elevated mood, emotional lability, encephalopathy, hallucinations, nervousness, paralysis, psychosis, quadriparesis, seizure, somnolence

Dermatologic: Acne, alopecia, cellulitis, exfoliative dermatitis, fungal dermatitis, hirsutism, increased diaphoresis, photosensitivity reaction, skin discoloration, skin disorder, skin ulcer

Endocrine & metabolic: Acidosis, alkalosis, Cushing's syndrome, decreased bicarbonate, decreased serum iron, diabetes mellitus, hypercalcemia, hypercholesterolemia, hyperphosphatemia, hypoproteinemia, increased alkaline phosphatase

Gastrointestinal: Anorexia, appetite increased, cramps, duodenitis, dysphagia, enlarged abdomen, esophagitis (including ulcerative), flatulence, gastritis, gastroesophagitis, GI perforation/hemorrhage, ileus, oral moniliasis, pancreatic pseudocyst, rectal disorder, stomatitis, weight gain

Genitourinary: Bladder spasm, cystitis, dysuria, nocturia, oliguria, urge incontinence, urinary frequency, urinary incontinence, urinary retention, vaginitis

Hematologic: Bruising, coagulation disorder, decreased prothrombin, hypochromic anemia, polycythemia

Hepatic: Abnormal liver function tests, ALT/AST increased, bilirubinemia, cholangitis, cholestatic jaundice, GGT increased, hepatitis (including granulomatous), jaundice, liver damage, increase LDH

Neuromuscular & skeletal: Hypertonia, incoordination, joint disorder, leg cramps, myalgia, myasthenia, myoclonus, nerve compression, neuropathy, osteoporosis

Ocular: Abnormal vision, amblyopia

(Continued)

Tacrolimus *(Continued)*

Otic: Ear pain, otitis media, tinnitus

Renal: Albuminuria, renal tubular necrosis, toxic nephropathy

Respiratory: Asthma, lung disorder, pharyngitis, pneumonia, pneumo-thorax, pulmonary edema, respiratory disorder, rhinitis, sinusitis, voice alteration

Miscellaneous: Abscess, abnormal healing, allergic reaction, crying, flu-like syndrome, generalized spasm, hernia, herpes simplex, perito-nitis, sepsis, writing impaired

Topical (as reported in children and adults, unless otherwise noted):

>10%:

Central nervous system: Headache (5% to 20%), fever (1% to 21%)

Dermatologic: Skin burning (43% to 58%; tends to improve as lesions resolve), pruritus (41% to 46%), erythema (12% to 28%)

Respiratory: Increased cough (18% children)

Miscellaneous: Flu-like syndrome (23% to 28%), allergic reaction (4% to 12%)

1% to 10%:

Cardiovascular: Peripheral edema (3% to 4% adults)

Central nervous system: Hyperesthesia (3% to 7% adults), pain (1% to 2%)

Dermatologic: Skin tingling (2% to 8%), acne (4% to 7% adults), localized flushing (following ethanol consumption 3% to 7% adults), folliculitis (2% to 6%), urticaria (1% to 6%), rash (2% to 5%), pustular rash (2% to 4%), vesiculobullous rash (4% children), contact dermatitis (3% to 4%), cyst (1% to 3% adults), eczema herpeticum (1% to 2%), fungal dermatitis (1% to 2% adults), sunburn (1% to 2% adults), dry skin (1% children)

Endocrine & metabolic: Dysmenorrhea (4% women)

Gastrointestinal: Diarrhea (3% to 5%), dyspepsia (1% to 4% adults), abdominal pain (3% children), vomiting (1% adults), gastroenteritis (adults 2%), nausea (1% children)

Neuromuscular & skeletal: Myalgia (2% to 3% adults), weakness (2% to 3% adults), back pain (2% adults)

Ocular: Conjunctivitis (2% adults)

Otic: Otitis media (12% children)

Respiratory: Rhinitis (6% children), sinusitis (2% to 4% adults), bronchitis (2% adults), pneumonia (1% adults)

Miscellaneous: Varicella/herpes zoster (1% to 5%), lymphadenopathy (3% children)

Oral, I.V., topical: Postmarketing and/or case reports (limited to important or life-threatening): Acute renal failure, alopecia, anaphylaxis, anaphylactoid reaction, angioedema, ARDS, arrhythmia, atrial fibrillation, atrial flutter, bile duct stenosis, blindness, cardiac arrest, cerebral infarction, cerebrovas-cular accident, deafness, delirium, depression, DIC, hemiparesis, hemo-lytic-uremic syndrome, hemorrhagic cystitis, hepatic necrosis, hepatotoxicity, hyperglycemia, leukoencephalopathy, lymphoproliferative disorder (related to EBV), myocardial hypertrophy (associated with ventric-ular dysfunction; reversible upon discontinuation), MI, neutropenia, pancreatitis (hemorrhagic and necrotizing), pancytopenia, paresthesia, photosensitivity reaction (topical), quadriplegia, QT_c prolongation, respira-tory failure, seizure, skin discoloration (topical), Stevens-Johnson syndrome, syncope, toxic epidermal necrolysis, thrombocytopenic purpura, torsade de pointes, TTP, veno-occlusive hepatic disease, venous thrombosis, ventricular fibrillation

Note: Calcineurin inhibitor-induced hemolytic uremic syndrome/thrombotic thrombocytopenic purpura/thrombotic microangiopathy (HUS/TTP/TMA) have been reported (with concurrent sirolimus).

Overdosage/Toxicology Symptoms are extensions of immunosuppressive activity and adverse effects. Symptomatic and supportive treatment is required. Hemodialysis is not effective.

Drug Interactions

Cytochrome P450 Effect: Substrate of CYP3A4 (major); **Inhibits** CYP3A4 (weak)

Increased Effect/Toxicity: Amphotericin B and other nephrotoxic antibiotics have the potential to increase tacrolimus-associated nephrotoxicity. Cisapride and metoclopramide may increase tacrolimus levels. Synergistic immunosuppression results from concurrent use of cyclosporine. Voriconazole may increase tacrolimus serum concentrations; decrease tacrolimus dosage by 66% when initiating voriconazole. CYP3A4 inhibitors may increase the levels/effects of tacrolimus; example inhibitors include azole antifungals, clarithromycin, diclofenac, doxycycline, erythromycin, imatinib, isoniazid, nefazodone, nicardipine, propofol, protease inhibitors, quinidine, telithromycin, and verapamil. Macrolides may increase tacrolimus concentration (limited documentation). Calcium channel blockers (dihydropyridine) may increase tacrolimus serum concentrations (monitor). Concurrent therapy with sirolimus may increase the risk of HUS/TTP/TMA.

Decreased Effect: Antacids impair tacrolimus absorption (separate administration by at least 2 hours). St John's wort may reduce tacrolimus serum concentrations (avoid concurrent use). CYP3A4 inducers may decrease the levels/effects of tacrolimus; example inducers include aminoglutethimide, carbamazepine, nafcillin, nevirapine, phenobarbital, phenytoin, and rifamycins. Caspofungin and sirolimus may decrease the serum concentrations of tacrolimus.

Ethanol/Nutrition/Herb Interactions

Ethanol: Localized flushing (redness, warm sensation) may occur at application site of topical tacrolimus following ethanol consumption.

Food: Decreases rate and extent of absorption. High-fat meals have most pronounced effect (35% decrease in AUC, 77% decrease in C_{max}). Grapefruit juice, CYP3A4 inhibitor, may increase serum level and/or toxicity of tacrolimus; avoid concurrent use.

Herb/Nutraceutical: St John's wort: May reduce tacrolimus serum concentrations (avoid concurrent use).

Storage/Stability

Injection: Prior to dilution, store at 5°C to 25°C (41°F to 77°F). Following dilution, stable for 24 hours in D_5W or NS in glass or polyolefin containers.

Capsules and ointment: Store at room temperature of 15°C to 30°C (59°F to 86°F).

Reconstitution Dilute with 5% dextrose injection or 0.9% sodium chloride injection to a final concentration between 0.004 mg/mL and 0.02 mg/mL.

Compatibility Variable stability (consult detailed reference) in D_5W, NS (only in glass or polyolefin containers).

Y-site administration: Compatible: Acyclovir, aminophylline, amphotericin B, ampicillin, ampicillin/sulbactam, benztropine, calcium gluconate, cefazolin, cefotetan, ceftazidime, ceftriaxone, cefuroxime, chloramphenicol, cimetidine, ciprofloxacin, clindamycin, co-trimoxazole, dexamethasone sodium phosphate, digoxin, diphenhydramine, dobutamine, dopamine, doxycycline, erythromycin lactobionate, esmolol, fluconazole, furosemide, (Continued)

Tacrolimus *(Continued)*

ganciclovir, gentamicin, haloperidol, heparin, hydrocortisone sodium succinate, hydromorphone, imipenem/cilastatin, insulin (regular), isoproterenol, leucovorin, lorazepam, methylprednisolone sodium succinate, metoclopramide, metronidazole, morphine, multivitamins, nitroglycerin, oxacillin, penicillin G potassium, perphenazine, phenytoin, piperacillin, potassium chloride, propranolol, ranitidine, sodium bicarbonate, sodium nitroprusside, sodium tetradecyl sulfate, tobramycin, vancomycin.

Compatibility when admixed: Compatible: Cimetidine.

Mechanism of Action Suppresses cellular immunity (inhibits T-lymphocyte activation), possibly by binding to an intracellular protein, FKBP-12

Pharmacodynamics/Kinetics

Absorption: Better in resected patients with a closed stoma; unlike cyclosporine, clamping of the T-tube in liver transplant patients does not alter trough concentrations or AUC

Oral: Incomplete and variable; food within 15 minutes of administration decreases absorption (27%)

Topical: Serum concentrations range from undetectable to 20 ng/mL (<5 ng/mL in majority of adult patients studied)

Protein binding: 99%

Metabolism: Extensively hepatic via CYP3A4 to eight possible metabolites (major metabolite, 31-demethyl tacrolimus, shows same activity as tacrolimus *in vitro*)

Bioavailability: Oral: Adults: 7% to 28%, Children: 10% to 52%; Topical: <0.5%; Absolute: Unknown

Half-life elimination: Variable, 21-61 hours in healthy volunteers

Time to peak: 0.5-4 hours

Excretion: Feces (~92%); feces/urine (<1% as unchanged drug)

Dosage

Oral:

Children: **Notes:** Patients without pre-existing renal or hepatic dysfunction have required (and tolerated) higher doses than adults to achieve similar blood concentrations. It is recommended that therapy be initiated at high end of the recommended adult I.V. and oral dosing ranges; dosage adjustments may be required. If switching from I.V. to oral, the oral dose should be started 8-12 hours after stopping the infusion. Adjunctive therapy with corticosteroids is recommended early post-transplant.

Liver transplant: Initial dose: 0.15-0.20 mg/kg/day in 2 divided doses, given every 12 hours; begin oral dose no sooner than 6 hours post-transplant

Adults: **Notes:** If switching from I.V. to oral, the oral dose should be started 8-12 hours after stopping the infusion. Adjunctive therapy with corticosteroids is recommended early post-transplant.

Heart transplant: Initial dose: 0.075 mg/kg/day in 2 divided doses, given every 12 hours; begin oral dose no sooner than 6 hours post-transplant

Kidney transplant: Initial dose: 0.2 mg/kg/day in 2 divided doses, given every 12 hours; initial dose may be given within 24 hours of transplant, but should be delayed until renal function has recovered; African-American patients may require larger doses to maintain trough concentration

Liver transplant: Initial dose: 0.1-0.15 mg/kg/day in 2 divided doses, given every 12 hours; begin oral dose no sooner than 6 hours post-transplant

I.V.: Children and Adults: **Note:** I.V. route should only be used in patients not able to take oral medications and continued only until oral medication can be tolerated; anaphylaxis has been reported. Begin no sooner than 6 hours post-transplant; adjunctive therapy with corticosteroids is recommended.

Heart transplant: Initial dose: 0.01 mg/kg/day as a continuous infusion

Kidney, liver transplant: Initial dose: 0.03-0.05 mg/kg/day as a continuous infusion

Prevention of graft-vs-host disease: 0.03 mg/kg/day as continuous infusion

Topical: Children ≥2 years and Adults: Atopic dermatitis (moderate to severe): Apply minimum amount of 0.03% or 0.1% ointment to affected area twice daily; rub in gently and completely. Discontinue use when symptoms have cleared. If no improvement within 6 weeks, patients should be re-examined to confirm diagnosis.

Dosing adjustment in renal impairment: Evidence suggests that lower doses should be used; patients should receive doses at the lowest value of the recommended I.V. and oral dosing ranges; further reductions in dose below these ranges may be required.

Tacrolimus therapy should usually be delayed up to 48 hours or longer in patients with postoperative oliguria.

Hemodialysis: Not removed by hemodialysis; supplemental dose is not necessary.

Peritoneal dialysis: Significant drug removal is unlikely based on physiochemical characteristics.

Dosing adjustment in hepatic impairment: Use of tacrolimus in liver transplant recipients experiencing post-transplant hepatic impairment may be associated with increased risk of developing renal insufficiency related to high whole blood levels of tacrolimus. The presence of moderate-to-severe hepatic dysfunction (serum bilirubin >2 mg/dL; Child-Pugh score ≥10) appears to affect the metabolism of tacrolimus. The half-life of the drug was prolonged and the clearance reduced after I.V. administration. The bioavailability of tacrolimus was also increased after oral administration. The higher plasma concentrations as determined by ELISA, in patients with severe hepatic dysfunction are probably due to the accumulation of metabolites of lower activity. These patients should be monitored closely and dosage adjustments should be considered. Some evidence indicates that lower doses could be used in these patients.

Administration

I.V.: Administer by I.V. continuous infusion only. Do not use PVC tubing when administering dilute solutions. Usually intended to be administered as a continuous infusion over 24 hours.

Oral: If dosed once daily (not common), administer in the morning. If dosed twice daily, doses should be 12 hours apart. If the morning and evening doses differ, the larger dose (differences are never >0.5-1 mg) should be given in the morning. If dosed 3 times/day, separate doses by 8 hours.

Topical: Do not use with occlusive dressings. Burning at the application site is most common in first few days; improves as atopic dermatitis improves. Limit application to involved areas. Continue as long as signs and symptoms persist; discontinue if resolution occurs; re-evaluate if symptoms persist >6 weeks.

Monitoring Parameters Renal function, hepatic function, serum electrolytes (especially potassium), glucose and blood pressure, measure 3 times/week for first few weeks, then gradually decrease frequency as patient stabilizes. Whole blood concentrations should be used for monitoring (trough for oral therapy). Signs/symptoms of anaphylactic reactions during infusion should also be monitored. Patients should be monitored during the first 30 minutes of the infusion, and frequently thereafter.

(Continued)

Tacrolimus *(Continued)*

Dietary Considerations Capsule: Take on an empty stomach; be consistent with timing and composition of meals if GI intolerance occurs (per manufacturer).

Patient Information You will be susceptible to infection (avoid crowds and people with infections or contagious diseases). May lead to diabetes mellitus, notify prescriber if you develop increased urination, increased thirst, or increased hunger. If you are diabetic, monitor glucose levels closely (may alter glucose levels). You may experience nausea, vomiting, loss of appetite (frequent small meals, frequent mouth care may help); diarrhea (boiled milk, yogurt, or buttermilk may help); constipation (increased exercise or dietary fruit, fluid, or fiber may help, if not consult prescriber); muscle or back pain (mild analgesics may be recommended). Report chest pain; acute headache or dizziness; symptoms of respiratory infection, cough, or difficulty breathing; unresolved gastrointestinal effects; fatigue, chills, fever, unhealed sores, white plaques in mouth, irritation in genital area; unusual bruising or bleeding; pain or irritation on urination or change in urinary patterns; rash or skin irritation; or other unusual effects related to this medication.

Oral: Take as directed, preferably 30 minutes before or 30 minutes after meals. Do not take within 2 hours before or after antacids. Do not alter dose and do not discontinue without consulting prescriber. Maintain adequate hydration (2-3 L/day of fluids unless instructed to restrict fluid intake) during entire course of therapy.

Topical: For external use only. Avoid exposure to sunlight or tanning beds. Apply to clean, dry skin. Do not cover with occlusive dressings. Burning and itching are most common in the first few days of use and improve as atopic dermatitis improves. Wash hands after use, unless hands are an area of treatment. Caution with alcohol consumption; may cause localized flushing at application site.

Additional Information Additional dosing considerations:

Switch from I.V. to oral therapy: Threefold increase in dose

Pediatric patients: About 2 times higher dose compared to adults

Liver dysfunction: Decrease I.V. dose; decrease oral dose

Renal dysfunction: Does not affect kinetics; decrease dose to decrease levels if renal dysfunction is related to the drug

Vesicant No

Dosage Forms Excipient information presented when available (limited, particularly for generics); consult specific product labeling.

Capsule (Prograf®): 0.5 mg, 1 mg, 5 mg

Injection, solution (Prograf®): 5 mg/mL (1 mL) [contains dehydrated alcohol 80% and polyoxyl 60 hydrogenated castor oil]

Ointment, topical (Protopic®): 0.03% (30 g, 60 g, 100 g); 0.1% (30 g, 60 g, 100 g)

Extemporaneous Preparations Tacrolimus 0.5 mg/mL oral suspension: Mix the contents of six 5-mg tacrolimus capsules with equal amounts of Ora-Plus® and Simple Syrup, N.F., to make a final volume of 60 mL. The suspension is stable for 56 days at room temperature in glass or plastic amber prescription bottles.

Esquivel C, So S, McDiarmid S, Andrews W, and Colombani PM, "Suggested Guidelines for the Use of Tacrolimus in Pediatric Liver Transplant Patients," *Transplantation*, 1996, 61(5):847-8.

Foster JA, Jacobson PA, Johnson CE, et al, "Stability of Tacrolimus in an Extemporaneously Compounded Oral Liquid (Abstract of Meeting

Presentation)," *American Society of Health-System Pharmacists Annual Meeting*, 1996, 53:P-52(E).

Tacrolimus 1 mg/mL oral suspension: Mix the contents of six 5-mg capsules in approximately 5 mL of sterile water; add capsule contents to an empty amber bottle first, then add sterile water and agitate bottle until drug disperses and a slurry is formed. Add equal parts of Ora-Plus® (suspending agent) and Ora-Sweet® (sweetening agent) to a total volume of 30 mL. The suspension is stable for 4 months at room temperature in plastic amber prescription bottles.

Elefante A, Muindi J, West K, et al, "Long-Term Stability of a Patient-Convenient 1 mg/mL Suspension of Tacrolimus for Accurate Maintenance of Stable Therapeutic Levels," *Bone Marrow Transplant*, 2006, 37(8):781-4.

References

Asante-Korang A, Boyle GJ, Webber SA, et al, "Experience of FK506 Immune Suppression in Pediatric Heart Transplantation: A Study of Long-Term Adverse Effects," *J Heart Lung Transplant*, 1996, 15(4):415-22.

Atkison P, Joubert G, Barron A, et al, "Hypertrophic Cardiomyopathy Associated With Tacrolimus in Paediatric Transplant Patients," *Lancet*, 1995, 345(8954):894-6.

Bronster DJ, Yonover P, Stein J, et al, "Demyelinating Sensorimotor Polyneuropathy After Administration of FK506," *Transplantation*, 1995, 59(7):1066-8.

Cerra FB and Gruber SA, "Critical Care of the Transplant Patient," *Crit Care Clin*, 6:813-1034.

Ehst BD and Warshaw EM, "Alcohol-Induced Application Site Erythema After Topical Immunomodulator Use and Its Inhibition by Aspirin," *Arch Dermatol*, 2004, 140(8):1014-5.

Furlan V, Perello L, Jacquemin E, et al, "Interactions Between FK506 and Rifampicin or Erythromycin in Pediatric Liver Recipients," *Transplantation*, 1995, 59(8):1217-8.

Hodak SP, Moubarak JB, Rodriguez I, et al, "QT Prolongation and Near Fatal Cardiac Arrhythmia After Intravenous Tacrolimus Administration: A Case Report," *Transplantation*, 1998, 66(4):535-7.

Johnson MC, So S, March JW, et al, "QT Prolongation and Torsades de Pointes After Administration of FK506," *Transplantation*, 1992, 53(4):929-30.

Jusko WJ, Piekoszewski W, Klintmalm GB, et al, "Pharmacokinetics of Tacrolimus in Liver Transplant Patients," *Clin Pharmacol Ther*, 1995, 57(3):281-96.

Kaufman DB, Kaplan B, Kanwar YS, et al, "The Successful Use of Tacrolimus (FK506) in a Pancreas/Kidney Transplant Recipient With Recurrent Cyclosporine-Associated Hemolytic Uremic Syndrome," *Transplantation*, 1995, 59(12):1737-9.

Kelly PA, Burckart GJ, and Venkataramanan R, "Tacrolimus: A New Immunosuppressive Agent," *Am J Health Syst Pharm*, 1995, 52(14):1521-35.

Lubbe J and Milingou M, "Images in Clinical Medicine. Tacrolimus Ointment, Alcohol, and Facial Flushing," *N Engl J Med*, 2004, 351(26):2740.

MacDonald AS and Sketris IS, "Tacrolimus in Transplantation," *Am J Health Syst Pharm*, 1995, 52(14):1569-71.

McDiarmid SV, Colonna JO, Shaked A, et al, "Differences in Oral FK506 Dose Requirements Between Adults and Pediatric Liver Transplant Patients," *Transplantation*, 1993, 55(6):1328-32.

Menegaux F, Keeffe EB, Andrews BT, et al, "Neurological Complications of Liver Transplantation in Adult Versus Pediatric Patients," *Transplantation*, 1994, 58(4):447-50.

Minematsu T, Ohtani H, Sato H, et al, "Sustained QT Prolongation Induced by Tacrolimus in Guinea Pigs," *Life Sci*, 1999, 65(14):PL197-202.

Mrvos R, Hodgman M, Dean B, et al, "FK506 Overdose: A Report of Four Cases," *Clin Toxicol*, 1995, 33(5):487-8.

Natazuka T, Ogawa R, Kizaki T, et al, "Immunosuppressive Drugs and Hypertrophic Cardiomyopathy," *Lancet*, 1995, 345(8965):1644.

Podesser BK, Rinaldi M, Yona NA, et al, "Comparison of Low and High Initial Tacrolimus Dosing in Primary Heart Transplant Recipients: A Prospective European Multicenter Study," *Transplantation*, 2005, 79(1):65-71.

Przepiorka D, Suzuki J, Ippoliti C, et al, "Blood Tacrolimus Concentration Unchanged by Plasmapheresis," *Am J Hosp Pharm*, 1994, 51(13):1708.

Schachner LA, Lamerson C, Sheehan MP, et al, "U.S. Tacrolimus Ointment Study Group: Tacrolimus Ointment 0.03% is Safe and Effective for the Treatment of Mild to Moderate Atopic Dermatitis in Pediatric Patients: Results From a Randomized, Double-Blind, Vehicle-Controlled Study," *Pediatrics*, 2005, 116(3):e334-42.

Starzl TE, Fung J, Jordan M, et al, "Kidney Transplantation Under FK506," *JAMA*, 1990, 264(1):63-7.

(Continued)

Tacrolimus *(Continued)*

Winkel E, DiSesa VJ, and Costanzo MR, "Advances in Heart Transplantation," *Dis Mon*, 1999, 45(3):62-87.

Winkler M and Christians U, "A Risk-Benefit Assessment of Tacrolimus in Transplantation," *Drug Saf*, 1995, 12(5):348-57.

♦ **TAM** *see* Tamoxifen *on page 1002*

♦ **Tamofen®** **(Can)** *see* Tamoxifen *on page 1002*

Tamoxifen *(ta MOKS i fen)*

Medication Safety Issues
Sound-alike/look-alike issues:
Tamoxifen may be confused with pentoxifylline, Tambocor™

Related Information
Safe Handling of Hazardous Drugs *on page 1382*

U.S. Brand Names Nolvadex® [DSC]; Soltamox™

Index Terms ICI-46474; NSC-180973; TAM; Tamoxifen Citrate

Generic Available Yes: Tablet

Canadian Brand Names Apo-Tamox®; Gen-Tamoxifen; Nolvadex®; Nolvadex®-D; Novo-Tamoxifen; Tamofen®

Pharmacologic Category Antineoplastic Agent, Estrogen Receptor Antagonist; Selective Estrogen Receptor Modulator (SERM)

Use Palliative or adjunctive treatment of advanced breast cancer; reduce the incidence of breast cancer in women at high risk; reduce risk of invasive breast cancer in women with ductal carcinoma *in situ* (DCIS); metastatic female and male breast cancer

Unlabeled/Investigational Use Treatment of mastalgia, gynecomastia, pancreatic carcinoma, melanoma and desmoid tumors; induction of ovulation; treatment of precocious puberty in females, secondary to McCune-Albright syndrome

Restrictions An FDA-approved medication guide must be distributed when dispensing the outpatient prescription (new or refill) to females for breast cancer prevention or treatment of ductal carcinoma *in situ* where this medication is to be used without direct supervision of a healthcare provider. Medication guides are available at http://www.fda.gov/cder/Offices/ODS/medication_guides.htm.

Pregnancy Risk Factor D

Lactation Excretion in breast milk unknown/contraindicated

Labeled Contraindications Hypersensitivity to tamoxifen or any component of the formulation; concurrent warfarin therapy or history of deep vein thrombosis or pulmonary embolism (when tamoxifen is used for cancer risk reduction); pregnancy

Warnings/Precautions Hazardous agent - use appropriate precautions for handling and disposal. **[U.S. Boxed Warning]: Serious and life-threatening events (including stroke, pulmonary emboli, and uterine malignancy) have occurred at an incidence greater than placebo during use for cancer risk reduction;** these events are rare, but require consideration in risk:benefit evaluation. An increased incidence of thromboembolic events has been associated with use for breast cancer; risk may increase with chemotherapy addition; use caution in individuals with a history of thromboembolic events. Use with caution in patients with leukopenia, thrombocytopenia, or hyperlipidemias. Decreased visual acuity, retinopathy, corneal changes, and increased incidence of cataracts have been reported. Hypercalcemia has occurred in patients with bone metastasis. Significant bone loss of the lumbar spine and hip was associated with use in premenopausal women. Liver abnormalities such as cholestasis, fatty liver, hepatitis, and hepatic necrosis have occurred. Hepatocellular carcinomas have been reported in some studies; relationship to treatment is unclear. Endometrial hyperplasia, polyps, endometriosis, uterine fibroids, and ovarian cysts have occurred. Increased risk of uterine or endometrial cancer; monitor. Safety and efficacy in children <2 years of age, or for treatment durations >1 year in children 2-10 years, have not been established.

Adverse Reactions

>10%:

Cardiovascular: Flushing (33% to 41%), hypertension (11%), peripheral edema (11%)

Central nervous system: Pain (3% to 16%), mood changes (12% to 18%), depression (2% to 12%)

Dermatologic: Skin changes (6% to 19%), rash (13%)

Endocrine & metabolic: Hot flashes (3% to 80%), fluid retention (32%), altered menses (13% to 25%), amenorrhea (16%)

Gastrointestinal: Nausea (5% to 26%), weight loss (23%)

Genitourinary: Vaginal bleeding (2% to 23%), vaginal discharge (13% to 55%)

Neuromuscular & skeletal: Weakness (19%), arthritis (14%), arthralgia (11%)

Respiratory: Pharyngitis (14%)

1% to 10%:

Cardiovascular: Chest pain (5%), venous thrombotic events (5%), edema (4%), cardiovascular ischemia (3%), cerebrovascular ischemia (3%), angina (2%), deep venous thrombus (2%), MI (1%)

Central nervous system: Insomnia (9%), dizziness (8%), headache (8%), anxiety (6%), fatigue (4%)

Dermatologic: Alopecia (<1% to 5%)

Endocrine & metabolic: Oligomenorrhea (9%), breast pain (6%), menstrual disorder (6%), breast neoplasm (5%), hypercholesterolemia (4%)

Gastrointestinal: Abdominal pain (9%), weight gain (9%), throat irritation (oral solution 5%), constipation (4% to 8%), diarrhea (7%), dyspepsia (6%), abdominal cramps (1%), anorexia (1%)

Genitourinary: Urinary tract infection (10%), leukorrhea (9%), vaginal hemorrhage (6%), vaginitis (5%), ovarian cyst (3%)

Hematologic: Thrombocytopenia (<1% to 10%), anemia (5%)

Hepatic: AST increased (5%), serum bilirubin increased (2%)

Neuromuscular & skeletal: Bone pain (6% to 10%), osteoporosis (7%), fracture (7%), arthrosis (5%), myalgia (5%), paresthesia (5%), musculo-skeletal pain (3%)

Ocular: Cataract (7%)

Renal: Serum creatinine increased (up to 2%)

Respiratory: Cough (4% to 9%), dyspnea (8%), bronchitis (5%), sinusitis (5%)

Miscellaneous: Infection/sepsis (up to 9%), diaphoresis (6%), flu-like syndrome (6%), allergic reaction (3%)

<1%, infrequent, or frequency not defined: Cholestasis, corneal changes, endometriosis, endometrial cancer, endometrial hyperplasia, endometrial polyps, fatty liver, hepatic necrosis, hepatitis, hypercalcemia, hyperlipid-emia, lightheadedness, phlebitis, pruritus vulvae, pulmonary embolism, retinal vein thrombosis, retinopathy, second primary tumors, stroke, taste disturbances, tumor pain and local disease flare (including increase in lesion size and erythema) during treatment of metastatic breast cancer (generally resolves with continuation), uterine fibroids, vaginal dryness

Postmarketing and/or case reports: Angioedema, bullous pemphigoid, erythema multiforme, hypersensitivity reactions, hypertriglyceridemia, (Continued)

Tamoxifen *(Continued)*

impotence (males), interstitial pneumonitis, loss of libido (males), pancreatitis, Stevens-Johnson syndrome

Overdosage/Toxicology Overdose produced respiratory difficulties and seizure in animal studies. In humans, loading doses of 400 mg/m^2 followed by 150 mg/m^2 twice daily produced reversible neurotoxicity (tremor, hyper-reflexia, unsteady gait, and dizziness). Loading doses of >250 mg/m^2 followed by 80 mg/m^2 twice daily produced QT prolongation in some patients. In the case of an overdose, treatment is symptom-directed and supportive.

Drug Interactions

Cytochrome P450 Effect: Substrate of CYP2A6 (minor), 2B6 (minor), 2C9 (major), 2D6 (major), 2E1 (minor), 3A4 (major); **Inhibits** CYP2B6 (weak), 2C8 (moderate), 2C9 (weak), 3A4 (weak)

Increased Effect/Toxicity: Concomitant use of warfarin is contraindicated when used for risk reduction; results in significant enhancement of the anticoagulant effects of warfarin. Tamoxifen may increase the levels/effects of CYP2C8 substrates; example substrates include amiodarone, paclitaxel, pioglitazone, repaglinide, and rosiglitazone. CYP2C9 inhibitors may increase the levels/effects of tamoxifen; example inhibitors include delavirdine, fluconazole, gemfibrozil, ketoconazole, nicardipine, NSAIDs, sulfonamides, and tolbutamide. CYP2D6 inhibitors may increase the levels/effects of tamoxifen; example inhibitors include chlorpromazine, delavirdine, fluoxetine, miconazole, paroxetine, pergolide, quinidine, quinine, ritonavir, and ropinirole. CYP3A4 inhibitors may increase the levels/effects of tamoxifen; example inhibitors include azole antifungals, clarithromycin, diclofenac, doxycycline, erythromycin, imatinib, isoniazid, nefazodone, nicardipine, propofol, protease inhibitors, quinidine, telithromycin, and verapamil. Rifamycin derivatives may increase the metabolism (via CYP isoenzymes) of tamoxifen.

Decreased Effect: CYP2C9 inducers may decrease the levels/effects of tamoxifen; example inducers include carbamazepine, phenobarbital, phenytoin, rifampin, rifapentine, and secobarbital. CYP3A4 inducers may decrease the levels/effects of tamoxifen; example inducers include aminoglutethimide, carbamazepine, nafcillin, nevirapine, phenobarbital, phenytoin, and rifamycins. Tamoxifen may reduce the levels/effects of anastrozole (concurrent therapy is not recommended per manufacturer).

Ethanol/Nutrition/Herb Interactions Herb/Nutraceutical: Avoid black cohosh, dong quai in estrogen-dependent tumors. Avoid St John's wort (may decrease levels/effects of tamoxifen).

Storage/Stability

Solution: Store at room temperature at or below 25°C (77°F); do not refrigerate or freeze. Protect from light. Use within 3 months of opening.

Tablet: Store at room temperature of 20°C to 25°C (68°F to 77°F).

Mechanism of Action Competitively binds to estrogen receptors on tumors and other tissue targets, producing a nuclear complex that decreases DNA synthesis and inhibits estrogen effects; nonsteroidal agent with potent antiestrogenic properties which compete with estrogen for binding sites in breast and other tissues; cells accumulate in the G$_0$ and G$_1$ phases; therefore, tamoxifen is cytostatic rather than cytocidal.

Pharmacodynamics/Kinetics

Absorption: Well absorbed; tablet and oral solution are bioequivalent

Distribution: High concentrations found in uterus, endometrial and breast tissue

Protein binding: 99%

Metabolism: Hepatic (via CYP3A4) to major metabolites, N-desmethyl tamoxifen (major) and 4-hydroxytamoxifen (minor), and a tamoxifen derivative (minor); undergoes enterohepatic recirculation

Half-life elimination: Distribution: 7-14 hours; Elimination: 5-7 days; Metabolites: 14 days

Time to peak, serum: 5 hours

Excretion: Feces (26% to 51%); urine (9% to 13%)

Dosage Oral (refer to individual protocols):

Children: Female: Precocious puberty and McCune-Albright syndrome (unlabeled use): A dose of 20 mg/day has been reported in patients 2-10 years of age; safety and efficacy have not been established for treatment of longer than 1 year duration

Adults:

Breast cancer:

Metastatic (males and females) or adjuvant therapy (females): 20-40 mg/day; daily doses >20 mg should be given in 2 divided doses (morning and evening)

Prevention (high-risk females): 20 mg/day for 5 years

DCIS (females): 20 mg once daily for 5 years

Note: Higher dosages (up to 700 mg/day) have been investigated for use in modulation of multidrug resistance (MDR), but are not routinely used in clinical practice

Induction of ovulation (unlabeled use): 5-40 mg twice daily for 4 days

Combination Regimens

Breast cancer: Tamoxifen-Epirubicin *on page 1280*

Melanoma:

CCDT (Melanoma) *on page 1165*

Dartmouth Regimen *on page 1187*

Administration Administer once or twice daily. Doses >20 mg/day should be given in divided doses.

Monitoring Parameters CBC with platelets, serum calcium, LFTs; abnormal vaginal bleeding; annual gynecologic exams, mammogram

Test Interactions T_4 elevations (which may be explained by increases in thyroid-binding globulin) have been reported; not accompanied by clinical hyperthyroidism

Patient Information Take as directed, morning and night, and maintain adequate hydration (2-3 L/day of fluids unless instructed to restrict fluid intake). You may experience menstrual irregularities, vaginal bleeding, hot flashes, hair loss, loss of libido (these will subside when treatment is completed). Bone pain may indicate a good therapeutic response (consult prescriber for mild analgesics). For nausea/vomiting, small frequent meals, chewing gum, or sucking lozenges may help. You may experience photosensitivity (use sunscreen, wear protective clothing and eyewear, and avoid direct sunlight). Report unusual bleeding or bruising, severe weakness, sedation, mental changes, swelling or pain in calves, difficulty breathing, or any changes in vision.

Special Geriatric Considerations Studies have shown tamoxifen to be effective in the treatment of primary breast cancer in elderly women. Comparative studies with other antineoplastic agents in elderly women with breast cancer had more favorable survival rates with tamoxifen. Initiation of hormone therapy rather than chemotherapy is justified for elderly patients with metastatic breast cancer who are responsive. Reduction of mortality and recurrence was greater in those studies that used tamoxifen for ≥2 years than those that use it for <2 years.

(Continued)

Tamoxifen *(Continued)*

Additional Information Oral clonidine is being studied for the treatment of tamoxifen-induced "hot flashes." The tumor flare reaction may indicate a good therapeutic response, and is often considered a good prognostic factor.

Emetic Potential Low (10% to 30%)

Dosage Forms Excipient information presented when available (limited, particularly for generics); consult specific product labeling.

Solution, oral:

Soltamox™: 10 mg/5 mL (150 mL) [licorice flavor]

Tablet: 10 mg, 20 mg

Nolvadex®: 10 mg, 20 mg [DSC]

References

Benson JR and Pitsinis V, "Update on Clinical Role of Tamoxifen," *Curr Opin Obstet Gynecol*, 2003, 15(1):13-23.

Boostanfar R, Jain JK, Mishell DR Jr, et al, "A Prospective Randomized Trial Comparing Clomiphene Citrate With Tamoxifen Citrate for Ovulation Induction," *Fertil Steril*, 2001, 75(5):1024-6.

Clemons M, Danson S, and Howell A, "Tamoxifen ("Nolvadex"): A Review," *Cancer Treat Rev*, 2002, 28(4):165-80.

Cohen I, Altaras MM, Lew S, et al, "Ovarian Endometrioid Carcinoma and Endometriosis Developing in a Postmenopausal Breast Cancer Patient During Tamoxifen Therapy: A Case Report and Review of the Literature," *Gynecol Oncol*, 1994, 55(3 Pt 1):443-7.

Eugster EA, Rubin SD, Reiter EO, et al, "Tamoxifen Treatment for Precocious Puberty in McCune-Albright Syndrome: A Multicenter Trial," *J Pediatr*, 2003, 143(1):60-6.

Hochner-Celnikier D, Anteby E, and Yagel S, "Ovarian Cysts in Tamoxifen-Treated Premenopausal Women With Breast Cancer - A Management Dilemma," *Am J Obstet Gynecol*, 1995, 172(4 Pt 1):1323-4.

Jordan VC, "Tamoxifen: A Most Unlikely Pioneering Medicine," *Nat Rev Drug Discov*, 2003, 2(3):205-13.

Jordan VC, "Tamoxifen: Toxicities and Drug Resistance During Treatment and Prevention of Breast Cancer," *Annu Rev Pharmacol Toxicol*, 1995, 35:195-211.

Jubelirer SJ, "The Management of Menopausal Symptoms in Women With Breast Cancer," *W V Med J*, 1995, 91(2):54-6.

LiVolsi VA, Salhany KE, and Dowdy YG, "Endocervical Adenocarcinoma in Tamoxifen-Treated Patient," *Am J Obstet Gynecol*, 1995, 172(3):1065.

Pandya KJ, Raubertas RF, Flynn PJ, et al, "Oral Clonidine in Postmenopausal Patients With Breast Cancer Experiencing Tamoxifen-Induced Hot Flashes: A University of Rochester Cancer Center Community Clinical Oncology Program Study," *Ann Intern Med*, 2000, 132:788-93.

Rutqvist LE, Johansson H, Signomklao T, et al, "Adjuvant Tamoxifen Therapy for Early Stage Breast Cancer and Second Primary Malignancies. Stockholm Breast Cancer Study Group," *J Natl Cancer Inst*, 1995, 87(9):645-51.

Wickerham L, "Tamoxifen - An Update on Current Data and Where it Can Now Be Used," *Breast Cancer Res Treat*, 2002, 75(Suppl 1):S7-12.

Winer EP, Hudis C, Burstein HJ, et al, "American Society of Clinical Oncology Technology Assessment on the Use of Aromatase Inhibitors as Adjuvant Therapy for Postmenopausal Women With Hormone Receptor-Positive Breast Cancer: Status Report 2004," *J Clin Oncol*, 2005, 23(3):619-29.

♦ **Tamoxifen Citrate** *see Tamoxifen on page 1002*

♦ **Tantum® (Can)** *see Benzydamine on page 132*

♦ **TAP-144** *see Leuprolide on page 672*

♦ **Tarceva®** *see Erlotinib on page 396*

♦ **Targretin®** *see Bexarotene on page 138*

♦ **Taro-Ciprofloxacin (Can)** *see Ciprofloxacin on page 213*

♦ **Taro-Fluconazole (Can)** *see Fluconazole on page 449*

♦ **Tasigna®** *see Nilotinib on page 807*

♦ **Taxol®** *see Paclitaxel on page 858*

♦ **Taxotere®** *see Docetaxel on page 342*

♦ **Tazicef®** *see Ceftazidime on page 190*

Telithromycin (tel ith roe MYE sin)

U.S. Brand Names Ketek®

Index Terms HMR 3647

Generic Available No

Canadian Brand Names Ketek®

Pharmacologic Category Antibiotic, Ketolide

Use Treatment of community-acquired pneumonia (mild-to-moderate) caused by susceptible strains of *Streptococcus pneumoniae* (including multi-drug-resistant isolates), *Haemophilus influenzae*, *Chlamydophila pneumoniae*, *Moraxella catarrhalis*, and *Mycoplasma pneumoniae*

Restrictions

An FDA-approved Medication Guide is available and must be dispensed with every prescription. Copies may be found at: http://www.fda.gov/cder/foi/label/2007/021144s012medg.pdf

Pregnancy Risk Factor C

Lactation Excretion in breast milk unknown/use caution

Labeled Contraindications Hypersensitivity to telithromycin, macrolide antibiotics, or any component of the formulation; myasthenia gravis; history of hepatitis and/or jaundice associated with telithromycin or other macrolide antibiotic use; concurrent use of cisapride or pimozide

Warnings/Precautions Acute hepatic failure and severe liver injury, including hepatitis and hepatic necrosis (leading to some fatalities) have been reported, in some cases after only a few doses; if signs/symptoms of hepatitis or liver damage occur, discontinue therapy and initiate liver function tests. **[U.S. Boxed Warning]: Life-threatening (including fatal) respiratory failure has occurred in patients with myasthenia gravis;** use in these patients is contraindicated. May prolong QT_c interval, leading to a risk of ventricular arrhythmias; closely-related antibiotics have been associated with malignant ventricular arrhythmias and torsade de pointes. Avoid in patients with prolongation of QTc interval due to congenital causes, history of long QT syndrome, uncorrected electrolyte disturbances (hypokalemia or hypomagnesemia), significant bradycardia (<50 bpm), or concurrent therapy with QT_c-prolonging drugs (eg, class Ia and class III antiarrhythmics). Avoid use in patients with a prior history of confirmed cardiogenic syncope or ventricular arrhythmias while receiving macrolide antibiotics or other QT_c-prolonging drugs. May cause severe visual disturbances (eg, changes in accommodation ability, diplopia, blurred vision). May cause loss of consciousness (possibly vagal-related); caution patients that these events may interfere with ability to operate machinery or drive, and to use caution until effects are known. Use caution in renal impairment; severe impairment (Cl_{cr} <30 mL/minute) requires dosage adjustment. Pseudomembranous colitis has been reported. Safety and efficacy not established in pediatric patients <13 years of age per Canadian approved labeling and <18 years of age per U.S. approved labeling.

Adverse Reactions

>10%: Gastrointestinal: Diarrhea (10% to 11%)

2% to 10%:

Central nervous system: Headache (2% to 6%), dizziness (3% to 4%)

(Continued)

Telithromycin *(Continued)*

Gastrointestinal: Nausea (7% to 8%), vomiting (2% to 3%), loose stools (2%), dysgeusia (2%)

≥0.2% to <2%:

Central nervous system: Vertigo, fatigue, somnolence, insomnia

Dermatologic: Rash

Gastrointestinal: Abdominal distension, abdominal pain, anorexia, constipation, dyspepsia, flatulence, gastritis, gastroenteritis, GI upset, glossitis, stomatitis, watery stools, xerostomia

Genitourinary: Vaginal candidiasis, vaginitis

Hematologic: Platelets increased

Hepatic: Transaminases increased

Ocular: Blurred vision, accommodation delayed, diplopia

Miscellaneous: Candidiasis, diaphoresis increased

<0.2%: Alkaline phosphatase increased, anxiety, bilirubin increased, bradycardia, eczema, eosinophilia, erythema multiforme, flushing, hepatitis, hypotension, jaundice, paresthesia, pruritus, urticaria

Postmarketing and/or case reports: Acute respiratory failure, allergic reaction, anaphylaxis, angioedema, arrhythmia, edema (facial), hepatocellular injury (including necrosis), liver failure, loss of consciousness (may be vagal-related), muscle cramps, myasthenia gravis exacerbation (rare), pancreatitis, palpitation, pseudomembranous colitis, QT_c prolongation, syncope, torsade de pointes

Overdosage/Toxicology Treatment should be symptomatic and supportive. Gastric lavage recommended. ECG and electrolytes should be monitored. Effectiveness of dialysis unknown. Maintain adequate hydration.

Drug Interactions

Cytochrome P450 Effect: Substrate of CYP1A2 (minor), 3A4 (major); **Inhibits** CYP2D6 (weak), 3A4 (strong)

Increased Effect/Toxicity: Concurrent use of cisapride or pimozide is contraindicated. Concurrent use with antiarrhythmics (eg, class Ia and class III) or other drugs which prolong QT_c (eg, disopyramide, moxifloxacin, pimozide, thioridazine) may be additive; serious arrhythmias may occur. Neuromuscular-blocking agents may be potentiated by telithromycin.

Telithromycin may increase the levels/effects of alfentanil, selected benzodiazepines, buspirone, calcium channel blockers, cilostazol, clozapine, corticosteroids, cyclosporine, eletriptan, eplerenone, ergot alkaloids, selected HMG-CoA reductase inhibitors, mirtazapine, nateglinide, nefazodone, pimozide, repaglinide, quinidine, sildenafil (and other PDE-5 inhibitors), SSRIs, tacrolimus, venlafaxine, warfarin (monitor), and other CYP3A4 substrates. Selected benzodiazepines (midazolam, triazolam), and selected HMG-CoA reductase inhibitors (atorvastatin, lovastatin and simvastatin) are generally contraindicated with strong CYP3A4 inhibitors. When used with strong CYP3A4 inhibitors, dosage adjustment/limits are recommended for sildenafil and other PDE-5 inhibitors; refer to individual monographs.

The levels/effects of telithromycin may be increased by azole antifungals, clarithromycin, diclofenac, doxycycline, erythromycin, imatinib, isoniazid, nefazodone, nicardipine, propofol, protease inhibitors, quinidine, verapamil, and other CYP3A4 inhibitors.

Decreased Effect: The levels/effects of telithromycin may be decreased by aminoglutethimide, carbamazepine, nafcillin, nevirapine, phenobarbital, phenytoin, rifamycins, and other CYP3A4 inducers; avoid concurrent use.

Telithromycin may decrease the levels/effects of clopidogrel, or the live, attenuated Ty21a strain of typhoid vaccine.

Ethanol/Nutrition/Herb Interactions Herb/nutraceutical: St John's wort: May decrease the levels/effects of telithromycin.

Storage/Stability Store at 15°C to 30°C (59°F to 86°F).

Mechanism of Action Inhibits bacterial protein synthesis by binding to two sites on the 50S ribosomal subunit. Telithromycin has also been demonstrated to alter secretion of IL-1alpha and TNF-alpha; the clinical significance of this immunomodulatory effect has not been evaluated.

Pharmacodynamics/Kinetics

Absorption: Rapid

Distribution: 2.9 L/kg

Protein binding: 60% to 70%

Metabolism: Hepatic, via CYP3A4 (50%) and non-CYP-mediated pathways

Bioavailability: 57% (significant first-pass metabolism)

Half-life elimination: 10 hours

Time to peak, plasma: 1 hour

Excretion: Urine (13% unchanged drug, remainder as metabolites); feces (7%)

Dosage Oral:

Children ≥13 years and Adults: Tonsillitis/pharyngitis (unlabeled use; Canadian indication): 800 mg once daily for 5 days

Adults:

Community-acquired pneumonia: 800 mg once daily for 7-10 days

Dosage adjustment in renal impairment:

U.S. product labeling: Cl_{cr} <30 mL/minute, including dialysis: 600 mg once daily; when renal impairment is accompanied by hepatic impairment, reduce dosage to 400 mg once daily

Canadian product labeling: Cl_{cr} <30 mL/minute: Reduce dose to 400 mg once daily

Hemodialysis: Administer following dialysis

Dosage adjustment in hepatic impairment: No adjustment recommended, unless concurrent severe renal impairment is present

Administration May be administered with or without food.

Monitoring Parameters Liver function tests; signs/symptoms of liver failure (eg, jaundice, fatigue, malaise, anorexia, nausea, bilirubinemia, acholic stools, liver tenderness, hepatomegaly); visual acuity

Dietary Considerations May be taken with or without food.

Special Geriatric Considerations Bioavailability (57%) equivalent in persons ≥65 years compared to younger adults; although a 1.4- to 2-fold increase in AUC found in older adults. No dosage adjustment required.

Dosage Forms Excipient information presented when available (limited, particularly for generics); consult specific product labeling.

Tablet:

Ketek®: 300 mg [not available in Canada], 400 mg

Ketek Pak™ [blister pack]: 400 mg (10s) [packaged as 10 tablets/card; 2 tablets/blister]

References

Araujo FG, Slifer TL, and Remington JS, "Inhibition of Secretion of Interleukin-1alpha and Tumor Necrosis Factor Alpha by the Ketolide Antibiotic Telithromycin," *Antimicrob Agents Chemother*, 2002, 46(10):3327-30.

Bhargava V, Lenfant B, Perret C, et al, "Lack of Effect of Food on the Bioavailability of a New Ketolide Antibacterial, Telithromycin," *Scand J Infect Dis*, 2002, 34(11):823-6.

Cantalloube C, Bhargava V, Sultan E, et al, "Pharmacokinetics of the Ketolide Telithromycin After Single and Repeated Doses in Patients With Hepatic Impairment," *Int J Antimicrob Agents*, 2003, 22(2):112-21.

(Continued)

Telithromycin (Continued)

Canton R, Morosini M, Enright MC, et al, "Worldwide Incidence, Molecular Epidemiology and Mutations Implicated in Fluoroquinolone-Resistant *Streptococcus pneumoniae*: Data From the Global PROTEKT Surveillance Programme," *J Antimicrob Chemother*, 2003, 52(6):944-52.

Carbon C, "A Pooled Analysis of Telithromycin in the Treatment of Community-Acquired Respiratory Tract Infections in Adults," *Infection*, 2003, 31(5):308-17.

Clay KD, Hanson JS, Pope SD, et al, "Brief Communication: Severe Hepatotoxicity of Telithromycin: Three Case Reports and Literature Review," *Ann Int Med*, 2006, 144(6):451-20.

Demolis JL, Vacheron F, Cardus S, et al, "Effect of Single and Repeated Oral Doses of Telithromycin on Cardiac QT Interval in Healthy Subjects," *Clin Pharmacol Ther*, 2003, 73(3):242-52.

Perret C, Lenfant B, Weinling E, et al, "Pharmacokinetics and Absolute Oral Bioavailability of an 800-mg Oral Dose of Telithromycin in Healthy Young and Elderly Volunteers," *Chemotherapy*, 2002, 48(5):217-23.

Nieman RB, Sharma K, Edelberg H, et al, "Telithromycin and Myasthenia Gravis," *Clin Infect Dis*, 2003, 37(11):1579.

Quinn J, Ruoff GE, and Ziter PS, "Efficacy and Tolerability of 5-Day, Once-Daily Telithromycin Compared With 10-Day, Twice-Daily Clarithromycin for the Treatment of Group A Beta-Hemolytic Streptococcal Tonsillitis/Pharyngitis: A Multicenter, Randomized, Double-Blind, Parallel-Group Study," *Clin Ther*, 2003, 25(2):422-43.

Ubukata K, Iwata S, and Sunakawa K, "*In vitro* Activities of New Ketolide, Telithromycin, and Eight Other Macrolide Antibiotics Against *Streptococcus pneumoniae* Having mefA and ermB Genes That Mediate Macrolide Resistance," *J Infect Chemother*, 2003, 9(3):221-6.

Zervos MJ, Heyder AM, and Leroy B, "Oral Telithromycin 800 mg Once Daily for 5 Days Versus Cefuroxime Axetil 500 mg Twice Daily for 10 Days in Adults With Acute Exacerbations of Chronic Bronchitis," *J Int Med Res*, 2003, 31(3):157-69.

♦ **Temodal® (Can)** *see* Temozolomide *on page 1010*

♦ **Temodar®** *see* Temozolomide *on page 1010*

Temozolomide (te moe ZOE loe mide)

Medication Safety Issues

High alert medication: The Institute for Safe Medication Practices (ISMP) includes this medication among its list of drugs which have a heightened risk of causing significant patient harm when used in error.

Related Information

Safe Handling of Hazardous Drugs *on page 1382*

U.S. Brand Names Temodar®

Index Terms NSC-362856; TMZ

Generic Available No

Canadian Brand Names Temodal®; Temodar®

Pharmacologic Category Antineoplastic Agent, Alkylating Agent (Triazene)

Use Treatment of adult patients with refractory anaplastic astrocytoma; newly-diagnosed glioblastoma multiforme

Unlabeled/Investigational Use Metastatic melanoma

Pregnancy Risk Factor D

Lactation Excretion in breast milk unknown/not recommended

Labeled Contraindications Hypersensitivity to temozolomide or any component of the formulation; hypersensitivity to dacarbazine (since both drugs are metabolized to MTIC); pregnancy

Warnings/Precautions Hazardous agent - use appropriate precautions for handling and disposal. Pneumocystis *jiroveci* pneumonia (PCP) may occur; risk is increased in those receiving steroids or longer dosing regimens; PCP prophylaxis is required in patients receiving radiotherapy in combination with the 42-day temozolomide regimen. Myelosuppression may occur; an increased incidence has been reported in geriatric and female patients. Rare cases of myelodysplastic syndrome and secondary malignancies, including acute myeloid leukemia have been reported. Use caution in patients with severe hepatic or renal impairment.

Adverse Reactions Note: With CNS malignancies, it is difficult to distinguish between CNS adverse events caused by temozolomide versus the effects of progressive disease.

>10%:

Cardiovascular: Peripheral edema (11%)

Central nervous system: Fatigue (34% to 61%), headache (23% to 41%), seizure (6% to 23%), hemiparesis (18%), fever (13%), dizziness (5% to 12%), coordination abnormality (11%)

Dermatologic: Alopecia (55%), rash (8% to 13%)

Gastrointestinal: Nausea (49% to 53%; grades 3/4: 1% to 10%), vomiting (29% to 42%; grades 3/4: 2% to 6%), constipation (22% to 33%), anorexia (9% to 27%), diarrhea (10% to 16%)

Hematologic: Lymphopenia (grades 3/4: 55%), thrombocytopenia (grades 3/4: adults: 4% to 19%; children: 25%), neutropenia (grades 3/4: adults: 8% to 14%; children: 20%), leukopenia (grades 3/4: 11%)

Neuromuscular & skeletal: Weakness (7% to 13%)

Miscellaneous: Viral infection (11%)

1% to 10%:

Central nervous system: Amnesia (10%), insomnia (4% to 10%), somnolence (9%), ataxia (8%), paresis (8%), anxiety (7%), memory impairment (7%), depression (6%), confusion (5%)

Dermatologic: Pruritus (5% to 8%), dry skin (5%), radiation injury (2% maintenance phase after radiotherapy), erythema (1%)

Endocrine & metabolic: Hypercorticism (8%), breast pain (females 6%)

Gastrointestinal: Stomatitis (9%), abdominal pain (5% to 9%), dysphagia (7%), taste perversion (5%), weight gain (5%)

Genitourinary: Incontinence (8%), urinary tract infection (8%), urinary frequency (6%)

Hematologic: Anemia (grades 3/4: 4%)

Neuromuscular & skeletal: Paresthesia (9%), back pain (8%), abnormal gait (6%), arthralgia (6%), myalgia (5%)

Ocular: Blurred vision (5% to 8%), diplopia (5%), vision abnormality (visual deficit/vision changes 5%)

Respiratory: Pharyngitis (8%), upper respiratory tract infection (8%), cough (5% to 8%), sinusitis (6%), dyspnea (5%)

Miscellaneous: Allergic reaction (up to 3%)

Postmarketing and/or case reports: Anaphylaxis, aplastic anemia, erythema multiforme, myelodysplastic syndrome, opportunistic infection (eg, PCP), pancytopenia, secondary malignancies (including myeloid leukemia)

Overdosage/Toxicology An overdose of 2000 mg/day for 5 days resulted in pancytopenia, pyrexia, multiorgan failure and death. There are also case reports of overdoses involving extended durations of treatment (beyond 5 days) which have resulted in potentially severe and prolonged bone marrow suppression and infections and resulted in death. Monitor hematologic parameters closely. Treatment is symptom-directed and supportive

Ethanol/Nutrition/Herb Interactions Food: Food reduces rate and extent of absorption.

Storage/Stability Store at room temperature of 15°C to 30°C (59°F to 86°F).

Mechanism of Action Like dacarbazine, temozolomide is converted to the active alkylating metabolite MTIC [(methyl-triazene-1-yl)-imidazole-4-carboxamide]. Unlike dacarbazine, however, this conversion is spontaneous, nonenzymatic, and occurs under physiologic conditions in all tissues to which the drug distributes.

(Continued)

Temozolomide *(Continued)*

Pharmacodynamics/Kinetics

Absorption: Rapid and complete

Distribution: V_d: Parent drug: 0.4 L/kg; penetrates blood brain barrier; CSF levels are ~35% to 39% of plasma levels

Protein binding: 15%

Metabolism: Prodrug, hydrolyzed to the active form, MTIC; MTIC is eventually eliminated as CO_2 and 5-aminoimidazole-4-carboxamide (AIC), a natural constituent in urine

Bioavailability: 100%

Half-life elimination: Mean: Parent drug: 1.8 hours

Time to peak: Empty stomach: 1 hour

Excretion: Urine (~38%; parent drug 6%); feces 0.8%

Dosage Oral (refer to individual protocols): Adults:

Anaplastic astrocytoma (refractory): Initial dose: 150 mg/m²/day for 5 days; repeat every 28 days. Subsequent doses of 100-200 mg/m²/day for 5 days per treatment cycle; based upon hematologic tolerance.

ANC <1000/mm³ or platelets <50,000/mm³ on day 22 or day 29 (day 1 of next cycle): Postpone therapy until ANC >1500/mm³ and platelets >100,000/mm³; reduce dose by 50 mg/m²/day for subsequent cycle

ANC 1000-1500/mm³ or platelets 50,000-100,000/mm³ on day 22 or day 29 (day 1 of next cycle): Postpone therapy until ANC >1500/mm³ and platelets >100,000/mm³; maintain initial dose

ANC >1500/mm³ and platelets >100,000/mm³ on day 22 or day 29 (day 1 of next cycle): Increase dose to or maintain dose at 200 mg/m²/day for 5 days for subsequent cycle

Glioblastoma multiforme (high-grade glioma):

Concomitant phase: 75 mg/m²/day for 42 days with radiotherapy (60Gy administered in 30 fractions). **Note:** PCP prophylaxis is required during concomitant phase and should continue in patients who develop lymphocytopenia until recovery (common toxicity criteria [CTC] ≤1). Obtain weekly CBC.

ANC ≥1500/mm³, platelet count ≥100,000/mm³, and nonhematologic CTC ≤grade 1 (excludes alopecia, nausea/vomiting): Temodar® 75 mg/m²/day may be continued throughout the 42-day concomitant period up to 49 days

Dosage modification:

ANC ≥500/mm³ but <1500/mm³ **or** platelet count ≥10,000/mm³ but <100,000/mm³ **or** nonhematologic CTC grade 2 (excludes alopecia, nausea/vomiting): Interrupt therapy

ANC <500/mm³ **or** platelet count <10,000/mm³ **or** nonhematologic CTC grade 3/4 (excludes alopecia, nausea/vomiting): Discontinue therapy

Maintenance phase (consists of 6 treatment cycles): Begin 4 weeks after concomitant phase completion. **Note:** Each subsequent cycle is 28 days (consisting of 5 days of drug treatment followed by 23 days without treatment). Draw CBC within 48 hours of day 22; hold next cycle and do weekly CBC until ANC >1500/mm³ and platelet count >100,000/mm³; dosing modification should be based on lowest blood counts and worst nonhematologic toxicity during the previous cycle.

Cycle 1: 150 mg/m²/day for 5 days; repeat every 28 days

Dosage modification for next cycle:

ANC <1000/mm³, platelet count <50,000/mm³, or nonhematologic CTC grade 3 (excludes for alopecia, nausea/vomiting) during previous cycle: Decrease dose by 50 mg/m²/day for 5 days, unless dose has already been lowered to 100 mg/m²/day, then discontinue therapy.

If dose reduction <100 mg/m²/day is required or nonhematologic CTC grade 4 (excludes for alopecia, nausea/vomiting), or if the same grade 3 nonhematologic toxicity occurs after dose reduction: Discontinue therapy

Cycle 2: 200 mg/m²/day for 5 days every 28 days, unless prior toxicity, then refer to Dosage Modifications under "Cycle 1" and give adjusted dose for 5 days

Cycles 3-6: Continue with previous cycle's dose for 5 days every 28 days unless toxicity has occurred then, refer to Dosage Modifications under "Cycle 1" and give adjusted dose for 5 days

Metastatic melanoma (unlabeled use): 200 mg/m²/day for 5 days every 28 days (for up to 12 cycles). For subsequent cycles reduce dose to 75% of the original dose for grade 3/4 hematologic toxicity and reduce the dose to 50% of the original dose for grade 3/4 nonhematologic toxicity.

Elderly: Refer to adult dosing. **Note:** Patients ≥70 years of age had a higher incidence of grade 4 neutropenia and thrombocytopenia in the first cycle of therapy than patients <70 years of age.

Dosage adjustment in renal impairment: No guidelines exist. Caution should be used when administered to patients with severe renal impairment (Cl_{cr} <36 mL/minute). Temozolomide has not been studied in dialysis patients.

Dosage adjustment in hepatic impairment: Caution should be used when administering to patients with severe hepatic impairment.

Administration Capsules should not be opened or chewed but swallowed whole with a glass of water. May be administered on an empty stomach to reduce nausea and vomiting. Bedtime administration may be advised.

Monitoring Parameters CBC with differential and platelets (prior to each cycle; weekly during glioma concomitant phase treatment; at or within 48 hours of day 22 and weekly until ANC >1500/mm³ for glioma maintenance and astrocytoma treatment)

Dietary Considerations The incidence of nausea/vomiting is decreased when the drug is taken on an empty stomach.

Patient Information Swallow capsules whole with a glass of water. Take on an empty stomach at similar time each day. If you have nausea and vomiting, contact prescriber for medicine to decrease this. Male and female patients who take temozolomide should protect against pregnancy (use effective contraception). Do not breast-feed while on medicine.

Emetic Potential Moderate (30% to 60%)

Dosage Forms Excipient information presented when available (limited, particularly for generics); consult specific product labeling.

Capsule:

Temodar®: 5 mg, 20 mg, 100 mg, 140 mg, 180 mg, 250 mg

Extemporaneous Preparations Temozolomide 10 mg/mL oral suspension: In a glass mortar, mix the contents of ten 100-mg capsules and 500 mg of povidone K-30 powder; add 25 mg anhydrous citric acid dissolved in 1.5 mL purified water; mix to form a paste; add 50 mL Ora-Plus® (add a small amount at first, mix, add balance); mix; transfer to amber plastic bottle; add enough Ora-Sweet® or Ora-Sweet® SF to bring a total volume of 100 mL by rinsing the mortar with small amounts of Ora-Sweet®; repeat rinsing 3 more times. The suspension is stable for 7 days at room temperature or 60 days refrigerated in plastic amber prescription bottles. **Note:** Use appropriate handling precautions during preparation.

Trissel LA, Yanping Z, and Koontz SE. "Temozolomide Stability in Extemporaneously Compounded Oral Suspension," *Int J Pharm Compounding*, 2006, 10(5):396-9.

(Continued)

Temozolomide *(Continued)*

References

Agarwala SS, Kirkwood JM, Gore M, et al, " Temozolomide for the Treatment of Brain metastases Associated With Metastatic Melanoma: A Phase II Study," *J Clin Oncol*, 2004, 22(11):2101-7.

Agarwala SS and Kirkwood JM, "Temozolomide, A Novel Alkylating Agent With Activity in the Central Nervous System, May Improve the Treatment of Advanced Metastatic Melanoma," *Oncologist*, 2000, 5(2):144-51.

Gaya A, Rees J, Greenstein A, et al, "The Use of Temozolomide in Recurrent Malignant Gliomas," *Cancer Treat Rev*, 2002, 28(2):115-20.

Jalali R, Singh P, Menon H, et al, "Unexpected Case of Aplastic Anemia in a Patient With Glioblastoma Multiforme Treated With Temozolomide," *J Neurooncol*, 2007, 85(1):105-7.

Middleton MR, Grob JJ, Aaronson N, et al, "Randomized Phase III Study of Temozolomide Versus Dacarbazine in the Treatment of Patients With Advanced Metastatic Malignant Melanoma," *J Clin Oncol*, 2000, 18(1):158-66.

Newlands ES, Stevens MF, Wedge SR, et al, "Temozolomide: A Review of Its Discovery, Chemical Properties, Pre-Clinical Development and Clinical Trials," *Cancer Treat Rev*, 1997, 23(1):35-61.

Schwenka J and Ignoffo RJ, "Temozolomide. A New Option for High-Grade Astrocytomas," *Cancer Pract*, 2000, 8(6):311-3.

Stupp R, Dietrich PY, Ostermann Kraljevic S, et al, "Promising Survival for Patients With Newly Diagnosed Glioblastoma Multiforme Treated With Concomitant Radiation Plus Temozolomide Followed by Adjuvant Temozolomide," *J Clin Oncol*, 2002, 20(5):1375-82.

Stupp R, Gander M, Leyvraz S, et al, "Current and Future Developments in the Use of Temozolomide for the Treatment of Brain Tumours," *Lancet Oncol*, 2001, 2(9):552-60.

Stupp R, Mason WP, van den Bent MJ, et al, "Radiotherapy Plus Concomitant and Adjuvant Temozolomide for Glioblastoma," *N Engl J Med*, 2005, 352(10):987-96.

Villano JL, Collins CA, Manasanch EE, et al, "Aplastic Anaemia in Patient With Glioblastoma Multiforme Treated With Temozolomide," *Lancet Oncol*, 2006, 7(5):436-8.

Yung WK, Prados MD, Yaya-Tur R, et al, "Multicenter Phase II Trial of Temozolomide in Patients With Anaplastic Astrocytoma or Anaplastic Oligoastrocytoma at First Relapse," *J Clin Oncol*, 1999, 17(9):2762-71.

Temsirolimus *(tem sir OH li mus)*

Medication Safety Issues

Sound-alike/look-alike issues:

Temsirolimus may be confused with sirolimus, tacrolimus

High alert medication: The Institute for Safe Medication Practices (ISMP) includes this medication among its list of drugs which have a heightened risk of causing significant patient harm when used in error.

Temsirolimus, for the treatment of advanced renal cell cancer, is a flat dose (25 mg) and is not based on body surface area (BSA).

Related Information

Common Toxicity Criteria *on page 1353*
Management of Nausea and Vomiting *on page 1319*
Safe Handling of Hazardous Drugs *on page 1382*

U.S. Brand Names Torisel™

Index Terms CCI-779; NSC-683864

Generic Available No

Pharmacologic Category Antineoplastic Agent, mTOR Kinase Inhibitor

Use Treatment of advanced renal cell cancer (RCC)

Pregnancy Risk Factor D

Lactation Excretion in breast milk unknown/not recommended

Labeled Contraindications Hypersensitivity to temsirolimus, sirolimus, or any component of the formulation

Warnings/Precautions Hazardous agent - use appropriate precautions for handling and disposal.

Hypersensitivity reactions have been reported; symptoms include anaphylaxis, dyspnea, flushing, and/or chest pain; premedicate with an antihistamine prior to infusion. Use with caution in patients with hypersensitivity to polysorbate 80. Angioneurotic edema has been reported; concurrent use with other drugs known to cause angioedema (eg, ACE inhibitors) may increase risk.

Use with caution in patients taking strong CYP3A4 inhibitors and moderate or strong CYP3A4 inducers (see Drug Interactions); consider alternative agents that avoid or lessen the potential for CYP-mediated interactions. Patients should not be immunized with live, viral vaccines during or shortly after treatment and should avoid close contact with recently vaccinated (live vaccine) individuals. Patients who are receiving anticoagulant therapy or those with CNS tumors/metastases may be at increased risk for developing intracranial hemorrhage.

Increases in serum glucose are common; may alter insulin and/or oral hypoglycemic therapy requirements in patients with diabetes; monitor. Serum cholesterol and triglyceride elevations are also common; may require initiation or dose increases of antihyperlipidemic agents. Treatment may result in immunosuppression, may increase risk of opportunistic infections and/or sepsis. Interstitial lung disease (ILD), sometimes fatal, has been reported; symptoms include dyspnea, cough, hypoxia, and/or fever, although asymptomatic cases may present; promptly evaluate worsening respiratory symptoms. Cases of bowel perforation (fatal) have occurred; promptly evaluate any new or worsening abdominal pain or bloody stools. Temsirolimus may be associated with impaired wound healing; use caution in the perioperative period. Cases of acute renal failure with rapid progression have been reported, including cases unresponsive to dialysis.

Has not been studied in patients with hepatic impairment; use caution; temsirolimus is predominantly cleared by the liver. Safety and efficacy in children have not been established.

Adverse Reactions

>10%:

Cardiovascular: Edema (35%), peripheral edema (27%), chest pain (16%)

Central nervous system: Pain (28%), fever (24%), headache (15%), insomnia (12%)

Dermatologic: Rash (47%), pruritus (19%), nail disorder/thinning (14%), dry skin (11%)

Endocrine & metabolic: Hyperglycemia (26% to 89%; grades 3/4: 16%), hypercholesterolemia (24% to 87%; grades 3/4: 2%), hyperlipidemia (27% to 83%; grades 3/4: 44%), hypophosphatemia (49%; grades 3/4: 18%), hypokalemia (21%; grades 3/4: 5%)

Gastrointestinal: Mucositis (41%), nausea (37%), anorexia (32%), diarrhea (27%), abdominal pain (21%), constipation (20%), stomatitis (20%), taste disturbance (20%), vomiting (19%), weight loss (19%)

Genitourinary: Urinary tract infection (15%)

Hematologic: Anemia (45% to 94%; grades 3/4: 20%), lymphopenia (53%; grades 3/4: 16%), thrombocytopenia (14% to 40%; grades 3/4: 1%; dose-limiting toxicity), leukopenia (6% to 32%; grades 3/4: 1%), neutropenia (7% to 19%; grades 3/4: 3% to 5%)

Hepatic: Alkaline phosphatase increased (68%; grades 3/4: 3%), AST increased (8% to 38%; grades 3/4: 1% to 2%)

Neuromuscular & skeletal: Weakness (51%), back pain (20%), arthralgia (18%)

Renal: Creatinine increased (14% to 57%; grades 3/4: 3%)

(Continued)

Temsirolimus *(Continued)*

Respiratory: Dyspnea (28%), cough (26%), epistaxis (12%), pharyngitis (12%)

Miscellaneous: Infection (20% to 27%; includes abscess, bronchitis, cellulitis, herpes simplex, herpes zoster)

1% to 10%:

Cardiovascular: Hypertension (7%), venous thromboembolism (2%, includes DVT and PE), thrombophlebitis (1%)

Central nervous system: Chills (8%), depression (4%)

Dermatologic: Acne (10%), wound healing impaired (1%)

Gastrointestinal: Bowel perforation (fatal: 1%)

Hepatic: Hyperbilirubinemia (8%)

Neuromuscular & skeletal: Myalgia (8%)

Ocular: Conjunctivitis (7%)

Respiratory: Rhinitis (10%), pneumonia (8%), upper respiratory tract infection (7%), interstitial lung disease (2%)

Miscellaneous: Allergic/hypersensitivity reaction (9%)

<1%, postmarketing, and/or case reports: Angioneurotic edema, pneumonitis

Overdosage/Toxicology Treatment is symptom-directed and supportive. Doses as high as 220 mg/m^2 were administered in phase I and II trials with toxicities (dose-limiting) including manic-depressive syndrome, stomatitis, and weakness; in the same trials, dose-limiting thrombocytopenia occurred at 34-45 mg/m^2. The risk of serious adverse events (thrombosis, bowel perforation, interstitial lung disease, seizure and/or psychosis) increases with doses >25 mg/week.

Drug Interactions

Cytochrome P450 Effect: Substrate of CYP3A4 (major); **Inhibits** CYP3A4 (weak), 2D6 (weak)

Increased Effect/Toxicity: Azole antifungal agents (itraconazole, ketoconazole, voriconazole) may increase the levels/effects of the active metabolite of temsirolimus (sirolimus). CYP3A4 inhibitors may increase the levels/effects of the active metabolite of temsirolimus (sirolimus); example inhibitors include azole antifungals, clarithromycin, diclofenac, doxycycline, erythromycin, imatinib, isoniazid, nefazodone, nicardipine, propofol, protease inhibitors, quinidine, telithromycin, and verapamil. Macrolide antibiotics may increase the levels/effects of the active metabolite of temsirolimus (sirolimus).

Concurrent use of ACE inhibitors with temsirolimus may increase the risk of angioedema. Concurrent therapy with calcineurin inhibitors (cyclosporine, tacrolimus) may increase the risk of HUS/TTP/TMA. Concomitant use of sunitinib with temsirolimus may lead to dose-limiting toxicity. Concurrent vaccination (live organisms) with temsirolimus may increase the adverse/toxic effect of the live vaccine; vaccinial infections are possible.

Decreased Effect:

CYP3A4 inducers may decrease the levels/effects of the active metabolite of temsirolimus (sirolimus); example inducers include aminoglutethimide, carbamazepine, nafcillin, nevirapine, phenobarbital, phenytoin, and rifamycins. Rifampin may decrease the levels/effects of the active metabolite of temsirolimus (sirolimus). Vaccination (dead organisms) may be less effective during temsirolimus therapy.

Ethanol/Nutrition/Herb Interactions Herb/Nutraceutical: St John's wort may decrease sirolimus (the active metabolite of temsirolimus) levels; avoid concurrent use. Herbs with hypoglycemic properties may increase the risk of temsirolimus-induced hypoglycemia; includes alfalfa, aloe, bilberry, bitter melon, burdock, celery, damiana, fenugreek, garcinia, garlic, ginger, ginseng (American), gymnema, marshmallow, stinging nettle. Avoid grapefruit and grapefruit juice (may increase the levels/effects of sirolimus).

Storage/Stability Store intact vials under refrigeration at 2°C to 8°C (36°F to 46°F). Diluted solution in the vial (10 mg/mL) is stable for 24 hours at room temperature. Solutions diluted for infusion (in normal saline) must be infused within 6 hours of preparation. Protect from light during storage, preparation, and handling.

Reconstitution Vials should be diluted with 1.8 mL of provided diluent to a concentration of 10 mg/mL (vial contains overfill). Mix by inverting vial. After allowing air bubbles to subside, further dilute in 250 mL of NS in a non-DEHP/non-PVC container (glass, polyolefin or polypropylene). Avoid excessive shaking (may result in foaming).

Compatibility Compatible with normal saline; do not mix with other solutions or medications. Temsirolimus is degraded by acids and bases.

Mechanism of Action Temsirolimus and its active metabolite, sirolimus, are targeted inhibitors of mTOR (mammalian target of rapamycin) kinase activity. Temsirolimus (and sirolimus) bind to FKBP-12, an intracellular protein, to form a complex which inhibits mTOR signaling, halting the cell cycle at the G1 phase in tumor cells. In renal cell carcinoma, mTOR inhibition also exhibits anti-angiogenesis activity by reducing levels of HIF-1 and HIF-2 alpha (hypoxia inducible factors) and vascular endothelial growth factor (VEGF).

Pharmacodynamics/Kinetics

Distribution: V_{dss}: 172 L

Metabolism: Hepatic; via CYP3A4 to sirolimus (primary active metabolite) and 4 minor metabolites

Half-life elimination: Temsirolimus: ~17 hours; Sirolimus: ~55 hours

Time to peak, plasma: Temsirolimus: At end of infusion; Sirolimus: 0.5-2 hours after temsirolimus infusion

Excretion: Feces (78%); urine (<5%)

Dosage Note: For infusion reaction prophylaxis, premedicate with diphenhydramine 25-50 mg I.V. 30 minutes prior to infusion.

I.V.: Adults: RCC: 25 mg weekly

Dosage adjustment for concomitant CYP3A4 inhibitors/inducers:

CYP3A4 inhibitors: Dose reductions are likely to be needed when temsirolimus is administered concomitantly with a strong CYP3A4 inhibitor (an alternate medication for CYP3A4 enzyme inhibitors should be investigated first); in the event that temsirolimus must be administered concomitantly with a potent enzyme inhibitor, consider reducing temsirolimus to 12.5 mg/week with careful monitoring. (When a strong CYP3A4 inhibitor is discontinued; allow ~1 week to elapse prior to adjusting the temsirolimus upward to the dose used prior to initiation of the CYP3A4 inhibitor.) See Drug Interactions for examples of CYP3A4 inhibitors.

CYP3A4 inducers: Concomitant administration with CYP3A4 inducers may require increased temsirolimus doses (alternatives to the enzyme-inducing agent should be utilized first); consider adjusting temsirolimus dose to 50 mg/week, with careful monitoring. (If the strong CYP3A4 enzyme inducer is discontinued, reduce the temsirolimus to the dose used prior to initiation of the CYP3A4 inducer.) See Drug Interactions for examples of CYP3A4 inducers.

(Continued)

Temsirolimus *(Continued)*

Dosage adjustment for toxicity :

Hematologic toxicity: ANC <1000/mm^3 or platelets <75,000/mm^3: Withhold treatment until resolves and reinitiate treatment with a 5 mg/week dose reduction; minimum dose: 15 mg/week if adjustment for toxicity is needed.

Nonhematologic toxicity: Any toxicity ≥grade 3: Withhold treatment until resolves to ≤grade 2; reinitiate treatment with a 5 mg/week dose reduction; minimum dose: 15 mg/week if adjustment for toxicity is needed.

Dosage adjustment in renal impairment: Not studied in renal dysfunction, however, due to the minimal renal elimination (<5%), dosage adjustment for renal dysfunction is not recommended.

Dosage adjustment in hepatic impairment (DOH) The FDA-approved labeling does not contain hepatic dosing adjustment guidelines. Patients with AST >3 times ULN (>5 times ULN in the presence of liver metastases) and total bilirubin >1.5 times ULN were excluded from clinical trials.

Administration Infuse over 30-60 minute via an infusion pump (preferred). Use non-DEHP containing administration tubing. Administer through an inline polyethersulfone filter ≤5 micron. Premedicate with diphenhydramine 25-50 mg I.V. 30 minutes prior to infusion. Stop infusion for hypersensitivity reaction; monitor for 30-60 minutes; may reinitiate at a reduced infusion rate (over 60 minutes) with discretion, 30 minutes after administration of a histamine H$_1$ antagonist and/or a histamine H$_2$ antagonist.

Monitoring Parameters CBC with differential and platelets (weekly), serum chemistries including glucose (baseline and every other week), serum cholesterol and triglycerides (baseline and periodic), liver and renal function tests

Monitor for infusion reactions; infection; symptoms of ILD (or radiographic changes)

Emetic Potential Low (10% to 30%)

Vesicant No

Dosage Forms Excipient information presented when available (limited, particularly for generics); consult specific product labeling.

Injection, solution [concentrate]:

Torisel™: 25 mg/mL [contains dehydrated alcohol, propylene glycol; diluent contains dehydrated alcohol, polyethylene glycol, polysorbate 80]

References

Atkins MB, Hidalgo M, Stadler WM, et al, "Randomized Phase II Study of Multiple Dose Levels of CCI-779, a Novel Mammalian Target of Rapamycin Kinase Inhibitor, in Patients With Advanced Refractory Renal Cell Carcinoma," *J Clin Oncol*, 2004, 22(5): 909-18.

Hidalgo M, Buckner JC, Erlichman C, et al, "A Phase I and Pharmacokinetics Study of Temsirolimus (CCI-779) Administered Intravenously Daily for 5 Days Every 2 Weeks to Patients With Advanced Cancer," *Clin Cancer Res*, 2006, 12(19):5755-63.

Hudes G, Carducci M, Tomczak P, et al, "Temsirolimus, Interferon Alfa, or Both for Advanced Renal-Cell Carcinoma," *N Engl J Med*, 2007, 356(22):2271-81.

Raymond E, Alexandre J, Faivre S, et al, "Safety and Pharmacokinetics of Escalated Doses of Weekly Intravenous Infusion of CCI-779, a Novel mTOR Inhibitor, in Patients With Cancer," *J Clin Oncol*, 2004, 22(12): 2336-47.

Witzig TE, Geyer SM, Ghobrial I, et al, "Phase II Trial of Single-Agent Temsirolimus (CCI-779) for Relapsed Mantle Cell Lymphoma," *J Clin Oncol*, 2005, 23(23):5347-56.

Teniposide *(ten i POE side)*

Medication Safety Issues

Sound-alike/look-alike issues:

Teniposide may be confused with etoposide

High alert medication: The Institute for Safe Medication Practices (ISMP) includes this medication among its list of drugs which have a heightened risk of causing significant patient harm when used in error.

Related Information

Management of Drug Extravasations *on page 1301*
Safe Handling of Hazardous Drugs *on page 1382*

U.S. Brand Names Vumon®

Index Terms EPT; VM-26

Generic Available No

Canadian Brand Names Vumon®

Pharmacologic Category Antineoplastic Agent, Miscellaneous

Use Treatment of acute lymphocytic leukemia, small cell lung cancer

Pregnancy Risk Factor D

Lactation Not recommended

Labeled Contraindications Hypersensitivity to teniposide, Cremophor® EL (polyoxyethylated castor oil), or any component of the formulation; pregnancy

Warnings/Precautions Hazardous agent - use appropriate precautions for handling and disposal. **[U.S. Boxed Warning]: Severe myelosuppression may occur;** monitor for infection and bleeding. **[U.S. Boxed Warning]: Hypersensitivity reactions, including anaphylaxis-like reactions, have been reported;** monitor during infusion; immediate treatment for anaphylactic reaction should be available during administration. Teniposide injection contains benzyl alcohol and should be avoided in neonates. The injection contains about 43% alcohol. For I.V. use only; may cause local tissue necrosis or thrombophlebitis if extravasation occurs. **[U.S. Boxed Warning]: Should be administered under the supervision of an experienced cancer chemotherapy physician.**

Adverse Reactions

>10%:

  Gastrointestinal: Mucositis (75%); diarrhea, nausea, vomiting (20% to 30%); anorexia

  Hematologic: Myelosuppression, leukopenia, neutropenia (95%), thrombocytopenia (65% to 80%), anemia

    Onset: 5-7 days

    Nadir: 7-10 days

    Recovery: 21-28 days

1% to 10%:

  Cardiovascular: Hypotension (2%), associated with rapid (<30 minutes) infusions

  Dermatologic: Alopecia (9%), rash (3%)

  Miscellaneous: Anaphylactoid reactions (5%) (fever, rash, hyper-/hypotension, dyspnea, bronchospasm), usually seen with rapid (<30 minutes) infusions

<1%: Lethargy, peripheral neuropathies, somnolence

Overdosage/Toxicology Symptoms of overdose include bone marrow suppression, leukopenia, thrombocytopenia, nausea, and vomiting. Treatment is supportive.

Drug Interactions

Cytochrome P450 Effect: Substrate of CYP3A4 (major); **Inhibits** CYP2C9 (weak), 3A4 (weak)

Increased Effect/Toxicity: May increase toxicity of methotrexate. Sodium salicylate, sulfamethizole, and tolbutamide displace teniposide from protein-binding sites which could cause substantial increases in free drug levels, resulting in potentiation of toxicity. Concurrent use of vincristine (Continued)

Teniposide *(Continued)*

may increase the incidence of peripheral neuropathy. CYP3A4 inhibitors may increase the levels/effects of teniposide; example inhibitors include azole antifungals, clarithromycin, diclofenac, doxycycline, erythromycin, imatinib, isoniazid, nefazodone, nicardipine, propofol, protease inhibitors, quinidine, telithromycin, and verapamil.

Decreased Effect: CYP3A4 inducers may decrease the levels/effects of teniposide; example inducers include aminoglutethimide, carbamazepine, nafcillin, nevirapine, phenobarbital, phenytoin, and rifamycins.

Ethanol/Nutrition/Herb Interactions Herb/Nutraceutical: St John's wort may decrease teniposide levels.

Storage/Stability Store ampuls in refrigerator at 2°C to 8°C (36°F to 46°F). Reconstituted solutions are stable at room temperature for up to 24 hours after preparation.

Reconstitution Teniposide must be diluted with either D_5W or 0.9% sodium chloride solutions to a final concentration of 0.1, 0.2, 0.4, or 1 mg/mL. However, precipitation may occur at any concentration. **Solutions should be prepared in non-DEHP-containing containers such as glass or poly-olefin containers.** The use of polyvinyl chloride (PVC) containers is not recommended. Administer 1 mg/mL solutions within 4 hours of preparation to reduce the potential for precipitation.

Compatibility Stable in D_5W, LR, NS.

Y-site administration: Compatible: Acyclovir, allopurinol, amifostine, amikacin, aminophylline, amphotericin B, ampicillin, ampicillin/sulbactam, aztreonam, bleomycin, bumetanide, buprenorphine, butorphanol, calcium gluconate, carboplatin, carmustine, cefazolin, cefoperazone, cefotaxime, cefotetan, cefoxitin, ceftazidime, ceftizoxime, ceftriaxone, cefuroxime, chlorpromazine, cimetidine, ciprofloxacin, cisplatin, cladribine, clinda-mycin, co-trimoxazole, cyclophosphamide, cytarabine, dacarbazine, dacti-nomycin, daunorubicin, dexamethasone sodium phosphate, diphenhydramine, doxorubicin, doxycycline, droperidol, enalaprilat, etopo-side, etoposide phosphate, famotidine, floxuridine, fluconazole, fludarabine, fluorouracil, furosemide, ganciclovir, gemcitabine, gentamicin, granisetron, haloperidol, hydrocortisone sodium phosphate, hydrocorti-sone sodium succinate, hydromorphone, hydroxyzine, ifosfamide, imipenem/cilastatin, leucovorin, lorazepam, mannitol, mechlorethamine, melphalan, meperidine, mesna, methotrexate, methylprednisolone sodium succinate, metoclopramide, metronidazole, minocycline, mitomycin, mito-xantrone, morphine, nalbuphine, netilmicin, ondansetron, piperacillin, plicamycin, potassium chloride, prochlorperazine edisylate, promethazine, ranitidine, sargramostim, sodium bicarbonate, streptozocin, thiotepa, ticar-cillin, ticarcillin/clavulanate, tobramycin, vancomycin, vinblastine, vincris-tine, vinorelbine, zidovudine. **Incompatible:** Idarubicin, heparin.

Mechanism of Action Teniposide does not inhibit microtubular assembly; it has been shown to delay transit of cells through the S phase and arrest cells in late S or early G_2 phase. Teniposide is a topoisomerase II inhibitor, and appears to cause DNA strand breaks by inhibition of strand-passing and DNA ligase action.

Pharmacodynamics/Kinetics

Distribution: V_d: 0.28 L/kg; Adults: 8-44 L; Children: 3-11 L; mainly into liver, kidneys, small intestine, and adrenals; crosses blood-brain barrier to a limited extent

Protein binding: 99.4%

Metabolism: Extensively hepatic

Half-life elimination: 5 hours

Excretion: Urine (44%, 21% as unchanged drug); feces (≤10%)

Dosage I.V.:

Children: 130 mg/m²/week, increasing to 150 mg/m² after 3 weeks and up to 180 mg/m² after 6 weeks

Acute lymphoblastic leukemia (ALL): 165 mg/m² twice weekly for 8-9 doses **or** 250 mg/m² weekly for 4-8 weeks

Adults: 50-180 mg/m² once or twice weekly for 4-6 weeks or 20-60 mg/m²/ day for 5 days

Small cell lung cancer: 80-90 mg/m²/day for 5 days every 4-6 weeks

Dosage adjustment in renal/hepatic impairment: Data is insufficient, but dose adjustments may be necessary in patient with significant renal or hepatic impairment

Dosage adjustment in Down syndrome patients: Reduce initial dosing; administer the first course at half the usual dose. Patients with both Down syndrome and leukemia may be especially sensitive to myelosuppressive chemotherapy.

Combination Regimens

Leukemia, acute lymphocytic: Linker Protocol *on page 1243*

Neuroblastoma:

CCDDT (Neuroblastoma) *on page 1164*

CCT (Neuroblastoma) *on page 1165*

OPEC *on page 1261*

OPEC-D *on page 1262*

PE-CAdO *on page 1270*

Administration Must be administered slowly (over at least 30-60 minutes).

Emetic Potential Moderate (30% to 60%)

Vesicant No; may be an irritant

High Dose Considerations

High Dose: I.V.: 750-1000 mg/m²

Dosage Forms Excipient information presented when available (limited, particularly for generics); consult specific product labeling.

Injection, solution: 10 mg/mL (5 mL) [contains benzyl alcohol, dehydrated alcohol, and polyoxyethylated castor oil]

References

Clark PI and Slevin ML, "The Clinical Pharmacology of Etoposide and Teniposide," *Clin Pharmacokinet*, 1987, 12(4):223-52.

Muggia FM, "Teniposide: Overview of Its Therapeutic Potential in Adult Cancers," *Cancer Chemother Pharmacol*, 1994, 34(Suppl):127-33.

O'Dwyer PJ, Alonso MT, Leyland-Jones B, et al, "Teniposide: A Review of 12 Years of Experience," *Cancer Treat Rep*, 1984, 68(12):1455-66.

Rivera GK and Evans WE, "Clinical Trials of Teniposide (VM-26) in Childhood Acute Lymphocytic Leukemia," *Semin Oncol*, 1992, 19(2 Suppl 6):51-8.

Sonneveld P, "Teniposide in Lymphomas and Leukemias," *Semin Oncol*, 1992, 19(2 Suppl 6):59-64.

♦ **Teslac**® *see* Testolactone *on page 1021*

♦ **TESPA** *see* Thiotepa *on page 1033*

Testolactone (tes toe LAK tone)

Medication Safety Issues

Sound-alike/look-alike issues:

Testolactone may be confused with testosterone

U.S. Brand Names Teslac®

Generic Available No

Canadian Brand Names Teslac®

Pharmacologic Category Androgen

Use Palliative treatment of advanced or disseminated breast carcinoma

(Continued)

Testolactone *(Continued)*

Restrictions C-III

Pregnancy Risk Factor C

Lactation Excretion in breast milk unknown/not recommended

Labeled Contraindications Hypersensitivity to testolactone or any component of the formulation; treatment of breast cancer in men

Warnings/Precautions Use with caution in hepatic, renal, or cardiac disease; history of porphyria. For use in postmenopausal women or in premenopausal women without ovarian function only. Safety and efficacy in pediatric patients have not been established.

Adverse Reactions Frequency not defined.

Cardiovascular: Blood pressure increased, edema

Central nervous system: Malaise

Dermatologic: Alopecia (rare), maculopapular rash

Endocrine & metabolic: Hypercalcemia

Gastrointestinal: Anorexia, diarrhea, nausea, tongue edema

Neuromuscular & skeletal: Paresthesia, peripheral neuropathies

Miscellaneous: Nail growth disturbance (rare)

Drug Interactions

Increased Effect/Toxicity: Increased effects of oral anticoagulants.

Mechanism of Action Testolactone is a synthetic testosterone derivative without significant androgen activity. The drug inhibits steroid aromatase activity, thereby blocking the production of estradiol and estrone from androgen precursors such as testosterone and androstenedione. Unfortunately, the enzymatic block provided by testolactone is transient and is usually limited to a period of 3 months.

Pharmacodynamics/Kinetics

Absorption: Well absorbed

Metabolism: Hepatic (forms metabolites)

Excretion: Urine

Dosage Adults: Female: Oral: 250 mg 4 times/day for at least 3 months; desired response may take as long as 3 months

Monitoring Parameters Plasma calcium levels

Test Interactions Plasma estradiol concentrations by RIA

Patient Information Passive exercises should be maintained throughout therapy to keep patient mobile; report numbness of fingers, toes, or face

Emetic Potential Very low (<10%)

Dosage Forms Excipient information presented when available (limited, particularly for generics); consult specific product labeling.

Tablet: 50 mg

♦ **Tetrahydrocannabinol** *see Dronabinol on page 367*

Tetrahydrocannabinol and Cannabidiol

(TET ra hye droe can NAB e nol & can nab e DYE ol)

Index Terms Cannabidiol and Tetrahydrocannabinol; Delta-9-Tetrahydrocannabinol and Cannabinol; GW-1000-02; THC and CBD

Generic Available No

Canadian Brand Names Sativex®

Pharmacologic Category Analgesic, Miscellaneous

Use Adjunctive treatment of neuropathic pain in multiple sclerosis; adjunctive treatment of moderate-to-severe pain in advanced cancer

Restrictions Not available in U.S.; CDSA-II

Lactation Enters breast milk/contraindicated

Labeled Contraindications Hypersensitivity to cannabinoids or any component of the formulation; serious cardiovascular disease (including arrhythmias, severe heart failure, poorly controlled hypertension, and ischemic heart disease); history of psychotic disorders (including schizophrenia); women of childbearing potential who are not using a reliable form of contraception; males intending to start a family; children <18 years of age; pregnancy; breast-feeding

Warnings/Precautions [Canadian Boxed Warnings]: May cause physical and psychological dependence in long-term use; avoid use in patients with a history or risk of drug or alcohol dependency. Prescriptions should be written for the minimal amount needed between clinic visits. Use may be associated with changes in mood, cognitive performance, memory, impulsivity, and coordination, as well as an altered perception of reality, particularly with respect to an awareness/sensation of time. May impair physical or mental abilities; patients must be cautioned about performing tasks which require mental alertness (eg, operating machinery or driving). **[Canadian Boxed Warnings]: Use with caution in patients with a history of seizures. Concurrent use of ethanol or other CNS active drugs may be additive.** Dosage must be carefully titrated and monitored, with downward adjustment in patients with unacceptable adverse events. Drug discontinuation is recommended, and a period of close observation should be instituted, in patients experiencing a psychotic reaction.

[Canadian Boxed Warning]: May be associated with adverse cardiovascular effects, including tachycardia and alterations in blood pressure (including orthostatic changes).

Use with caution in severe hepatic and renal dysfunction. Use with caution in elderly patients. May be irritating to the buccal mucosa; avoid administration in an area of soreness or inflammation. Use in cancer patients associated with increased risk of urinary retention and infection. Formulation contains ethanol; use may be harmful in patients with alcoholism. Due to accumulation in body fat, cannabinoids may be detectable in the urine and serum for several weeks following drug discontinuation.

Adverse Reactions

>10%:

Central nervous system: Dizziness (up to 32%), somnolence (9% to 15%), fatigue (14%)

Gastrointestinal: Oral application site events (≤20%), nausea (12%)

1% to 10%:

Cardiovascular: Hypotension (2% to 5%), hypertension (2%), flushing (1%), syncope (1%),

Central nervous system: Headache (3%), confusion (1% to 7%), disorientation (5%), impaired balance (3% to 5%), vertigo (4% to 5%), attention disturbance (3% to 5%), memory impairment (1%), dissociation (3%), euphoria (3%), hallucination (up to 3%), insomnia (3%), panic attack (3%), anxiety (2%), lethargy (2%), malaise (2%), amnesia (2%), depression (1% to 2%), paranoia (1%)

Endocrine & metabolic: Thirst (1%)

Gastrointestinal: Xerostomia (8%), diarrhea (5% to 7%), oral discomfort/pain (up to 8%), vomiting (4% to 8%), constipation (4% to 5%), abnormal taste (4%), tooth discoloration (4%), dysgeusia (3% to 5%), oral candidiasis (3%), anorexia (2%), appetite increased (2%), abdominal pain (1%), appetite decreased (1%)

Genitourinary: Urinary retention (5%)

Hepatic: ALT/AST increased (2.6%)

(Continued)

Tetrahydrocannabinol and Cannabidiol *(Continued)*

Neuromuscular & skeletal: Weakness (5% to 6%), muscle spasticity (3%), dysarthria (2%), fall (2%), paresthesia (2%)

Ocular: Vision blurred (2%)

Renal: Hematuria (3%)

Respiratory: Pharyngitis (2%), cough (1%), respiratory tract infection (1%), throat irritation (1%)

Miscellaneous: Drunken feeling (5%), sensation of heaviness (1%)

<1% and/or frequency not defined: Auditory hallucination, delusions, suicidal ideation, tachycardia, urinary infection

Overdosage/Toxicology Symptoms of overdose may include bradycardia, tachycardia, hyper- or hypotension, behavioral disturbances, lethargy, panic reactions, seizures or motor incoordination. Oral benzodiazepines may be helpful for agitative behavior; Trendelenburg position and hydration may be helpful for hypotensive effects. For other manifestations, treatment is symptom-directed and supportive.

Drug Interactions

Cytochrome P450 Effect: Substrate (minor) of CYP2C9, 2C19, 2D6, 3A4; **Inhibits** (weak) CYP1A2, 2C19, 2D6, 3A4

Increased Effect/Toxicity: CNS depressants and alcohol may increase sedation. Anticholinergic agents may increase tachycardia and drowsiness. Naltrexone may increase the levels/effects of cannabinoids. Sympathomimetic agents may increase hypertension, tachycardia, and cardiotoxicity. Opioids may increase the effects of cannabinoids.

Decreased Effect: Opioids may cause tolerance to cannabinoids.

Ethanol/Nutrition/Herb Interactions

Ethanol: Avoid ethanol (may increase CNS depression).

Food: Administration with high-lipid meals may increase absorption.

Storage/Stability Prior to first use, store unopened at 2°C to 8°C (36°F to 46°F); do not freeze. After opening, may be stored at room temperature of 15°C to 25°C (59°F to 77°F) for up to 28 days. Avoid heat and direct sunlight.

Mechanism of Action Stimulates cannabinoid receptors CB1 and CB2 in the CNS and dorsal root ganglia as well as other sites in the body. Cannabinoid receptors in the pain pathways of the brain and spinal cord mediate cannabinoid-induced analgesia. Peripheral CB2 receptors modulate immune function through cytokine release.

Pharmacodynamics/Kinetics

Absorption: Rapidly absorbed from the buccal mucosa

Distribution: Widely distributed, particularly to fatty tissues

Protein binding: Extensive

Metabolism: Hepatic, via CYP isoenzymes (2C9, 2C19, 2D6 and 3A4) to THC metabolite 11-hydroxy-tetrahydrocannabinol (11-OH-THC, psycho-active) and CBD metabolite 7-hydroxy-cannabidiol.

Half-life elimination: Initial: 1-2 hours; terminal half-life may require 24-36 hours (or longer) due to redistribution from fatty tissue

Time to peak, plasma: 2-4 hours

Excretion: As metabolites, urine and feces

Dosage Buccal spray: Adults: Neuropathic pain (MS), cancer pain: Initial: One spray every 4 hours to a maximum of 4 sprays on first day

Titration and individualization: Dosage is self-titrated by the patient. In the treatment of MS, the mean daily dosage after titration in clinical trials was 5 sprays per day. The usual maximum dose is 12 sprays per day although some patients may require and tolerate a higher number of sprays per day. In the treatment of cancer pain, the mean daily dosage after titration was 8 sprays per day. Dosage should be adjusted as necessary, based on effect and tolerance. Sprays should be evenly distributed over the course of the day during initial titration. If adverse reactions, including intoxication-type symptoms, are noted the dosage should be suspended until resolution of the symptoms; a dosage reduction or extension of the interval between doses may be used to avoid a recurrence of symptoms. Retitration may be required in the event of adverse reactions and/or worsening of symptoms.

Elderly: Refer to adult dosing. Use with caution and monitor closely.

Dosage adjustment in renal impairment: Use with caution; has not been studied in patients with significant renal dysfunction.

Dosage adjustment in hepatic impairment: Use with caution; has not been studied in patients with significant hepatic dysfunction.

Administration Note: For buccal use only; spray should be directed below the tongue or on the inside of the cheeks (the site should be varied); avoid direction to the pharynx.

Shake vial before use and remove protective cap; replace protective cap following use. Do not apply spray to sore or inflamed mucosa.

Priming: Vial should be held in an upright position and primed prior to the initial use by depression of the actuator 2-3 times until a fine spray appears. Priming should not be required for subsequent uses. Do not spray near an open flame.

Normal use: Hold vial in upright position and spray into mouth; spray should be directed below the tongue or on the inside of the cheeks, avoiding direction to the pharynx. The site should be varied.

Monitoring Parameters Mental status, response to pain; mucosal integrity and inflammation

Dosage Forms Excipient information presented when available (limited, particularly for generics); consult specific product labeling. [CAN] = Canadian brand name

Solution, buccal [spray]:

Sativex® [CAN]: Delta-9 tetrahydrocannabinol 27 mg/mL and cannabidiol 25 mg/mL (5.5 mL) [delivers 100 microliters/spray; 51 metered sprays; contains ethanol 50%, peppermint oil, and propylene glycol] [not available in U.S.]

References
Berman JS, Symonds C, and Birch R, "Efficacy of Two Cannabis Based Medicinal Extracts for Relief of Central Neuropathic Pain From Brachial Plexus Avulsion: Results of a Randomised Controlled Trial," *Pain*, 2004, 112(3):299-306.

Djulus J, Moretti M, and Koren G, "Marijuana Use and Breastfeeding," *Can Fam Physician*, 2005, 51:349-50.

Kozer E and Koren G, "Effects of Prenatal Exposure to Marijuana," *Can Fam Physician*, 2001, 47:263-4.

Smith, PF, "GW-1000. GW Pharmaceuticals," *Curr Opin Investig Drugs*, 2004, 5(7):748-54.

Wade DT, Makela P, Robson P, et al, "Do Cannabis-Cased Medicinal Extracts Have General or Specific Effects on Symptoms in Multiple Sclerosis? A Double-Blind, Randomized, Placebo-Controlled Study on 160 Patients," *Mult Scler*, 2004, 10(4):434-41.

♦ **Texacort®** *see Hydrocortisone on page 545*

♦ **TG** *see Thioguanine on page 1030*

♦ **6-TG (error-prone abbreviation)** *see Thioguanine on page 1030*

Thalidomide (tha LI doe mide)

Medication Safety Issues

Sound-alike/look-alike issues:

Thalidomide may be confused with flutamide

High alert medication: The Institute for Safe Medication Practices (ISMP) includes this medication among its list of drugs which have a heightened risk of causing significant patient harm when used in error.

(Continued)

Thalidomide *(Continued)*

International issues:

Thalomid® may be confused with Thilomide® which is a brand name for Iodoxamide in Greece and Turkey

Related Information

Safe Handling of Hazardous Drugs *on page 1382*

U.S. Brand Names Thalomid®

Index Terms NSC-66847

Generic Available No

Canadian Brand Names Thalomid®

Pharmacologic Category Angiogenesis Inhibitor; Immunosuppressant Agent; Tumor Necrosis Factor (TNF) Blocking Agent

Use Treatment of multiple myeloma; treatment and maintenance of cutaneous manifestations of erythema nodosum leprosum (ENL)

Unlabeled/Investigational Use Treatment of Crohn's disease; graft-versus-host reactions after bone marrow transplantation; AIDS-related aphthous stomatitis; Behçet's syndrome; Waldenström's macroglobulinemia; Langerhans cell histiocytosis; may be effective in rheumatoid arthritis, discoid lupus erythematosus, and erythema multiforme

Restrictions Thalidomide is approved for marketing only under a special distribution program. This program, called the "System for Thalidomide Education and Prescribing Safety" (STEPS® 1-888-423-5436), has been approved by the FDA. Prescribers and pharmacists must be registered with the program. No more than a 4-week supply should be dispensed. Blister packs should be dispensed intact (do not repackage capsules). Prescriptions must be filled within 7 days. Subsequent prescriptions may be filled only if fewer than 7 days of therapy remain on the previous prescription. A new prescription is required for further dispensing (a telephone prescription may not be accepted.)

Pregnancy Risk Factor X

Lactation Excretion in breast milk unknown/not recommended

Labeled Contraindications Hypersensitivity to thalidomide or any component of the formulation; neuropathy (peripheral); patient unable to comply with STEPS® program (including males); women of childbearing potential unless alternative therapies are inappropriate and adequate precautions are taken to avoid pregnancy; pregnancy

Warnings/Precautions Hazardous agent - use appropriate precautions for handling and disposal. **[U.S. Boxed Warning]: Thalidomide is a known teratogen; effective contraception must be used for at least 4 weeks before initiating therapy, during therapy, and for 4 weeks following discontinuation of thalidomide for women of childbearing potential.** Use caution with drugs which may decrease the efficacy of hormonal contraceptives.

[U.S. Boxed Warning]: Thrombotic events have been reported, generally in patients with other risk factors for thrombosis (neoplastic disease, inflammatory disease, or concurrent therapy with combination chemotherapy. Use in combination with dexamethasone is associated with increased risk for deep vein thrombosis (DVT) and pulmonary embolism (PE), monitor for signs and symptoms of thromboembolism; patients at risk may benefit from prophylactic anticoagulation or aspirin.

May cause sedation; patients must be warned to use caution when performing tasks which require alertness. Use caution in patients with renal or hepatic impairment, neurological disorders, or constipation. Thalidomide has been associated with the development of peripheral neuropathy, which may be irreversible; use caution with other medications which may cause peripheral neuropathy. Consider immediate discontinuation (if clinically appropriate) in patients who develop neuropathy. May cause seizures; use caution in patients with a history of seizures, concurrent therapy with drugs which alter seizure threshold, or conditions which predispose to seizures. May cause neutropenia; discontinue therapy if absolute neutrophil count decreases to <750/mm^3. Use caution in patients with HIV infection; has been associated with increased viral loads. May cause orthostasis and/or brady-cardia; use with caution in patients with cardiovascular disease or in patients who would not tolerate transient hypotensive episodes. Hypersensitivity, Stevens-Johnson syndrome (SJS) and toxic epidermal necrolysis (TEN) have been reported; withhold therapy and evaluate with skin rashes; perma-nently discontinue if rash is exfoliative, purpuric, bullous or if SJS or TEN is suspected. Safety and efficacy have not been established in children <12 years of age.

Adverse Reactions

>10%:

Cardiovascular: Edema (57%), thrombosis/embolism (23%; grade 3: 13%, grade 4: 9%), hypotension (16%)

Central nervous system: Fatigue (79%; grade 3: 3%, grade 4: 1%), somno-lence (36% to 38%), dizziness (4% to 20%), sensory neuropathy (54%), confusion (28%), anxiety/agitation (9% to 26%), fever (19% to 23%), motor neuropathy (22%), headache (13% to 19%)

Dermatologic: Rash (21% to 31%), rash/desquamation (30%; grade 3: 4%), dry skin (21%), maculopapular rash (4% to 19%), acne (3% to 11%)

Endocrine & metabolic: Hypocalcemia (72%)

Gastrointestinal: Constipation (3% to 55%), anorexia (3% to 28%), nausea (4% to 24%), weight loss (23%), weight gain (22%), diarrhea (4% to 19%), oral moniliasis (4% to 11%)

Hematologic: Leukopenia (17% to 35%), neutropenia (31%), anemia (6% to 13%), lymphadenopathy (6% to 13%)

Hepatic: AST increased (3% to 25%), bilirubin increased (14%)

Neuromuscular & skeletal: Muscle weakness (40%), tremor (4% to 26%), weakness (6% to 22%), myalgia (17%), paresthesia (6% to 16%), arthralgia (13%)

Renal: Hematuria (11%)

Respiratory: Dyspnea (42%)

Miscellaneous: Diaphoresis (13%)

1% to 10%:

Cardiovascular: Facial edema (4%), peripheral edema (3% to 8%)

Central nervous system: Insomnia (9%), nervousness (3% to 9%), malaise (8%), vertigo (8%), pain (3% to 8%)

Dermatologic: Dermatitis (fungal 4% to 9%), pruritus (3% to 8%), nail disorder (3% to 4%)

Endocrine & metabolic: Hyperlipemia (6% to 9%)

Gastrointestinal: Xerostomia (8% to 9%), flatulence (8%), tooth pain (4%)

Genitourinary: Impotence (3% to 8%)

Hepatic: LFTs abnormal (9%)

Neuromuscular & skeletal: Neuropathy (8%), back pain (4% to 6%), neck pain (4%), neck rigidity (4%)

Renal: Albuminuria (3% to 8%)

Respiratory: Pharyngitis (4% to 8%), rhinitis (4%), sinusitis (4% to 8%)

Miscellaneous: Infection (6% to 8%)

(Continued)

Thalidomide *(Continued)*

Postmarketing and/or case reports (limited to important or life-threatening): Acute renal failure, alkaline phosphatase increased, ALT increased, amenorrhea, aphthous stomatitis, arrhythmia, atrial fibrillation, bile duct obstruction, bradycardia, BUN increased, carpal tunnel, CML, creatinine clearance decreased, creatinine increased, deafness, depression, diplopia, dysesthesia, ECG abnormalities, electrolyte imbalances, enuresis, eosinophilia, epistaxis, erythema multiforme, erythema nodosum, erythroleukemia, exfoliative dermatitis, febrile neutropenia, foot drop, galactorrhea, granulocytopenia, gynecomastia, hepatomegaly, Hodgkin's disease, hypercalcemia, hyper-/hypokalemia, hypersensitivity, hypertension, hyper-/hypothyroidism, hyperuricemia, hypomagnesemia, hyponatremia, hypoproteinemia, intestinal obstruction, intestinal perforation, interstitial pneumonitis, LDH increased, lethargy, leukocytosis, lymphedema, lymphopenia, mental status changes, metrorrhagia, migraine, myxedema, nystagmus, oliguria, orthostatic hypotension, pancytopenia, paresthesia, petechiae, peripheral neuritis, photosensitivity, pleural effusion, prothrombin time changes, psychosis, pulmonary embolus, pulmonary hypertension, purpura, Raynaud's syndrome, seizure, status epilepticus, Stevens-Johnson syndrome, stomach ulcer, stupor, suicide attempt, syncope, tachycardia, thrombocytopenia, toxic epidermal necrolysis, tumor lysis syndrome

Overdosage/Toxicology Doses of up to 14.4 g have been reported (in suicide attempts) without fatalities. Treatment is symptom-directed and supportive.

Drug Interactions

Increased Effect/Toxicity: Thalidomide may enhance the sedative activity of other drugs such as ethanol, barbiturates, reserpine, and chlorpromazine. Thalidomide may be associated with increased risk of serious infection when used in combination with abatacept or anakinra. Thalidomide may increase the risk of vaccinal infection with vaccine (live attenuated). Thalidomide may enhance the adverse/toxic effect(s) of zoledronic acid. Dexamethasone may enhance the dermatologic adverse effects of thalidomide.

Decreased Effect: Thalidomide may decrease the effect of vaccines (killed).

Ethanol/Nutrition/Herb Interactions

Ethanol: Avoid ethanol (may increase sedation).

Herb/Nutraceutical: Avoid cat's claw and echinacea (have immunostimulant properties; consider therapy modifications).

Storage/Stability Store at 15°C to 30°C (50°F to 86°F). Protect from light. Keep in original package.

Mechanism of Action Has immunomodulatory and antiangiogenic characteristics. Immunologic effects may vary based on conditions; may suppress excessive tumor necrosis factor-alpha production in patients with ENL, yet may increase plasma tumor necrosis factor-alpha levels in HIV-positive patients. In multiple myeloma, thalidomide is associated with an increase in natural killer cells and increased levels of interleukin-2 and interferon gamma. Other proposed mechanisms of action include suppression of angiogenesis, prevention of free-radical-mediated DNA damage, increased cell mediated cytotoxic effects, and altered expression of cellular.

Pharmacodynamics/Kinetics

Distribution: V_d: 120 L

Protein binding: 55% to 66%

Metabolism: Nonenzymatic hydrolysis in plasma; forms multiple metabolites

Half-life elimination: 5-7 hours

Time to peak, plasma: 3-6 hours

Excretion: Urine (<1% as unchanged drug)

Dosage Oral:

Multiple myeloma: 200 mg once daily (with dexamethasone 40 mg daily on days 1-4, 9-12, and 17-20 of a 28-day treatment cycle)

Cutaneous ENL:

Initial: 100-300 mg/day taken once daily at bedtime with water (at least 1 hour after evening meal)

Patients weighing <50 kg: Initiate at lower end of the dosing range

Severe cutaneous reaction or patients previously requiring high dose may be initiated at 400 mg/day; doses may be divided, but taken 1 hour after meals

Maintenance: Dosing should continue until active reaction subsides (usually at least 2 weeks), then tapered in 50 mg decrements every 2-4 weeks

Patients who flare during tapering or with a history or requiring prolonged maintenance should be maintained on the minimum dosage necessary to control the reaction. Efforts to taper should be repeated every 3-6 months, in increments of 50 mg every 2-4 weeks.

Behçet's syndrome (unlabeled use): 100-400 mg/day

Graft-vs-host reactions (unlabeled use): 100-1600 mg/day; usual initial dose: 200 mg 4 times/day for use up to 700 days

AIDS-related aphthous stomatitis (unlabeled use): 200 mg twice daily for 5 days, then 200 mg/day for up to 8 weeks

Discoid lupus erythematosus (unlabeled use): 100-400 mg/day; maintenance dose: 25-50 mg

Combination Regimens

Multiple myeloma:

Bortezomib-Melphalan-Prednisone-Thalidomide *on page 1156*

DTPACE *on page 1196*

Melphalan-Prednisone-Thalidomide *on page 1246*

Thalidomide-Dexamethasone *on page 1280*

Prostate cancer: Docetaxel-Thalidomide *on page 1192*

Administration Oral: Administer with water, preferably at bedtime once daily on an empty stomach, at least 1 hour after the evening meal. Doses >400 mg/day may be given in 2-3 divided doses. Avoid extensive handling of capsules; capsules should remain in blister pack until ingestion. If exposed to the powder content from broken capsules or body fluids from patients receiving thalidomide, the exposed area should be washed with soap and water.

Monitoring Parameters CBC with differential, platelets; signs of neuropathy monthly for the first 3 months, then periodically during treatment; consider monitoring of sensory nerve application potential amplitudes (at baseline and every 6 months) to detect asymptomatic neuropathy. In HIV-seropositive patients: viral load after 1 and 3 months, then every 3 months. Pregnancy testing (sensitivity of at least 50 mIU/mL) is required within 24 hours prior to initiation of therapy, weekly during the first 4 weeks, then every 4 weeks in women with regular menstrual cycles or every 2 weeks in women with irregular menstrual cycles.

Dietary Considerations Should be taken at least 1 hour after the evening meal.

Patient Information Thalidomide must be obtained via "STEPS® Program" (1-888-423-5436). Effective contraception must be used for at least 1 month prior to beginning therapy, during therapy, and continued for 1 month after (Continued)

Thalidomide *(Continued)*

thalidomide has been discontinued. Two reliable forms of contraception must be used. Males must use a latex condom during sexual contact with women of childbearing age. Thalidomide may cause drowsiness and/or orthostatic hypotension. Patients should not donate blood. Patients should report signs of tingling, numbness, or pain in hands or feet.

Emetic Potential Very low (<10%)

Dosage Forms Excipient information presented when available (limited, particularly for generics); consult specific product labeling.

Capsule:

Thalomid®: 50 mg, 100 mg, 200 mg

References

Antonioli E, Nozzoli C, Gianfaldoni G, et al, "Pulmonary Hypertension Related to Thalidomide Therapy in Refractory Multiple Myeloma," *Ann Oncol*, 2005, 16(11):1849-50.

Bessmertny O and Pham T, "Thalidomide Use in Pediatric Patients," *Ann Pharmacother*, 2002, 36(3):521-5.

Diggle GE, "Thalidomide: 40 years On," *Int J Clin Pract*, 2001, 55(9):627-31.

Eriksson T, Bjorkman S, and Hoglund P, "Clinical Pharmacology of Thalidomide," *Eur J Clin Pharmacol*, 2001, 57(5):365-76.

Franks ME, Macpherson GR, and Figg WD, "Thalidomide," *Lancet*, 2004, 363(9423):1802-11.

Hamuryudan V, Mat C, Saip S, et al, "Thalidomide in the Treatment of the Mucocutaneous Lesions of the Behçet Syndrome. A Randomized, Double-Blind, Placebo-Controlled Trial," *Ann Intern Med*, 1998, 128(6):443-50.

Jacobson JM, Greenspan JS, Spritzler J, et al, "Thalidomide for the Treatment of Oral Aphthous Ulcers in Patients With Human Immunodeficiency Virus Infection. National Institute of Allergy and Infectious Diseases AIDS Clinical Trials Group," *N Engl J Med*, 1997, 336(21):1487-93.

Kyle RA and Rajkumar SV, "Multiple Myeloma," *N Engl J Med*, 2004, 351(18): 1860-73.

Onozawa M, Hashino S, Sogabe S, et al, "Side Effects and Good Effects from New Chemotherapeutic Agents. Case 2. Thalidomide-Induced Interstitial Pneumonitis," *J Clin Oncol*, 2005, 23(10):2425-6.

Rajkumar SV, Blood E, Vesole D, et al, "Phase III Clinical Trial of Thalidomide Plus Dexamethasone Compared With Dexamethasone Alone in Newly Diagnosed Multiple Myeloma: A Clinical Trial Coordinated by the Eastern Cooperative Oncology Group," *J Clin Oncol*, 2006, 24(3):431-6.

Teo SK, Colburn WA, Tracewell WG, et al, "Clinical Pharmacokinetics of Thalidomide," *Clin Pharmacokinet*, 2004, 43(5):311-27.

Uhl K, Cox E, Rogan R, et al, "Thalidomide Use in the US: Experience With Pregnancy Testing in the S.T.E.P.S.® Programme," *Drug Saf*, 2006, 29(4):231-9.

♦ **Thalomid®** *see* Thalidomide *on page 1025*

♦ **THC** *see* Dronabinol *on page 367*

♦ **THC and CBD** *see* Tetrahydrocannabinol and Cannabidiol *on page 1022*

♦ **TheraCys®** *see* BCG Vaccine *on page 128*

Thioguanine *(thye oh GWAH neen)*

Medication Safety Issues

High alert medication: The Institute for Safe Medication Practices (ISMP) includes this medication among its list of drugs which have a heightened risk of causing significant patient harm when used in error.

6-thioguanine and 6-TG are error-prone abbreviations (associated with six-fold overdoses of thioguanine)

Related Information

Investigational Drug Service *on page 1379*

Management of Nausea and Vomiting *on page 1319*

Safe Handling of Hazardous Drugs *on page 1382*

U.S. Brand Names Tabloid®

Index Terms 2-Amino-6-Mercaptopurine; NSC-752; TG; 6-TG (error-prone abbreviation); 6-Thioguanine (error-prone abbreviation); Tioguanine

Generic Available No

Canadian Brand Names Lanvis®

Pharmacologic Category Antineoplastic Agent, Antimetabolite (Purine Antagonist)

Use Treatment of acute myelogenous (nonlymphocytic) leukemia; treatment of chronic myelogenous leukemia and granulocytic leukemia

Restrictions The I.V. formulation is not available in U.S.

Pregnancy Risk Factor D

Lactation Excretion in breast milk unknown

Labeled Contraindications Hypersensitivity to thioguanine or any component of the formulation; pregnancy

Warnings/Precautions Hazardous agent - use appropriate precautions for handling and disposal. Use with caution and reduce dose in patients with renal or hepatic impairment. Not recommended for long-term continuous therapy due to potential for hepatotoxicity (hepatic veno-occlusive disease). Discontinue in patients with evidence of hepatotoxicity. Caution with history of previous therapy resistance with either thioguanine or mercaptopurine (there is usually complete cross resistance between these two). Thioguanine is potentially carcinogenic and teratogenic. Patients with genetic deficiency of thiopurine methyltransferase (TPMT) or who are receiving drugs which inhibit this enzyme (mesalazine, olsalazine, sulfasalazine) may be highly sensitive to myelosuppressive effects.

Adverse Reactions

>10%: Hematologic: Myelosuppressive:
WBC: Moderate
Platelets: Moderate
Onset: 7-10 days
Nadir: 14 days
Recovery: 21 days

1% to 10%:
Dermatologic: Skin rash
Endocrine & metabolic: Hyperuricemia
Gastrointestinal: Mild nausea or vomiting, anorexia, stomatitis, diarrhea
Neuromuscular & skeletal: Unsteady gait

<1%: Ascites, esophageal varices, hepatic necrosis, hepatitis, jaundice, LFTs increased, neurotoxicity, photosensitivity, portal hypertension, splenomegaly, thrombocytopenia, veno-occlusive hepatic disease

Overdosage/Toxicology Symptoms of overdose include bone marrow suppression, nausea, vomiting, malaise, hypertension, and sweating. Treatment is supportive. Dialysis is not useful.

Drug Interactions

Increased Effect/Toxicity: Allopurinol can be used in full doses with thioguanine unlike mercaptopurine. Use with busulfan may cause hepatotoxicity and esophageal varices. Aminosalicylates (olsalazine, mesalamine, sulfasalazine) may inhibit TPMT, increasing toxicity/myelosuppression of thioguanine.

Ethanol/Nutrition/Herb Interactions Food: Enhanced absorption if administered between meals.

Storage/Stability Store tablet at room temperature.

Reconstitution

Compatibility

Mechanism of Action Purine analog that is incorporated into DNA and RNA resulting in the blockage of synthesis and metabolism of purine nucleotides

Pharmacodynamics/Kinetics

Absorption: 30% (highly variable)
Distribution: Crosses placenta
(Continued)

Thioguanine *(Continued)*

Metabolism: Hepatic; rapidly and extensively via TPMT to 2-amino-6-methylthioguanine (active) and inactive compounds

Half-life elimination: Terminal: 11 hours

Time to peak, serum: Within 8 hours

Excretion: Urine

Dosage Total daily dose can be given at one time.

Oral (refer to individual protocols):

Infants and Children <3 years: Combination drug therapy for acute nonlymphocytic leukemia: 3.3 mg/kg/day in divided doses twice daily for 4 days

Children and Adults: 2-3 mg/kg/day calculated to nearest 20 mg or 75-200 mg/m²/day in 1-2 divided doses for 5-7 days or until remission is attained

Dosing comments in renal or hepatic impairment: Reduce dose

Combination Regimens

Leukemia, acute myeloid:

DAT *on page 1189*

TAD *on page 1279*

V-TAD *on page 1293*

Monitoring Parameters CBC with differential and platelet count; liver function tests (weekly when beginning therapy then monthly, more frequently in patients with liver disease or concurrent hepatotoxic drugs); hemoglobin, hematocrit, serum uric acid; some laboratories offer testing for TPMT deficiency

Hepatotoxicity may present with signs of portal hypertension (splenomegaly, esophageal varices, thrombocytopenia) or veno-occlusive disease (fluid retention, ascites, hepatomegaly with tenderness, or hyperbilirubinemia)

Patient Information You may experience nausea and vomiting, diarrhea, or loss of appetite (frequent small meals may help/request medication) or weakness or lethargy (use caution when driving or engaging in tasks requiring alertness until response to drug is known). Use good oral care to reduce incidence of mouth sores. May cause headache (request medication). Report signs or symptoms of infection (eg, fever, chills, sore throat, burning urination, fatigue), bleeding (eg, tarry stools, easy bruising), vision changes, unresolved mouth sores, nausea or vomiting, CNS changes (hallucinations), or respiratory difficulty. Avoid crowds or exposure to infected persons; you will be susceptible to infection. The drug may cause permanent sterility and may cause birth defects. Contraceptive measures should be used during therapy. The drug may be excreted in breast milk, therefore, an alternative form of feeding your baby should be used.

Emetic Potential Very low (<10%)

Dosage Forms Excipient information presented when available (limited, particularly for generics); consult specific product labeling.

Tablet [scored]:

Tabloid®: 40 mg

Extemporaneous Preparations A 20 mg/mL oral suspension can be prepared by crushing fifteen 40 mg tablets in a mortar, and then adding 10 mL of methylcellulose 1% (in small amounts). Transfer to a graduate, then add a sufficient quantity of syrup to make 30 mL of suspension. Label "shake well." Room temperature stability is 60 days.

Dressman JB and Poust RI, "Stability of Allopurinol and Five Antineoplastics in Suspension," *Am J Hosp Pharm*, 1983, 40:616-8.

Nahata MC, Morosco RS, and Hipple TF, 4th ed, *Pediatric Drug Formulations*, Cincinnati, OH: Harvey Whitney Books Co, 2000.

References

Broxson EH, Dole M, Wong R, et al, "Portal Hypertension Develops in a Subset of Children With Standard Risk Acute Lymphoblastic Leukemia Treated With Oral 6-Thioguanine During Maintenance Therapy," *Pediatr Blood Cancer*, 2004 [Epub October 24, 2004, prior to print].

Elgemeie GH, "Thioguanine, Mercaptopurine: Their Analogs and Nucleosides as Antimetabolites," *Curr Pharm Des*, 2003, 9(31):2627-42.

Estlin EJ, "Continuing Therapy for Childhood Acute Lymphoblastic Leukaemia: Clinical and Cellular Pharmacology of Methotrexate, 6-Mercaptopurine and 6-Thioguanine," *Cancer Treat Rev*, 2001, 27(6):351-63.

♦ **6-Thioguanine (error-prone abbreviation)** see Thioguanine on page 1030

♦ **Thiophosphoramide** see Thiotepa on page 1033

♦ **Thiosulfuric Acid Disodium Salt** see Sodium Thiosulfate on page 972

Thiotepa (thye oh TEP a)

Medication Safety Issues

High alert medication: The Institute for Safe Medication Practices (ISMP) includes this medication among its list of drugs which have a heightened risk of causing significant patient harm when used in error.

Related Information

Hematopoietic Stem Cell Transplantation on page 1366
Safe Handling of Hazardous Drugs on page 1382

Index Terms TESPA; Thiophosphoramide; Triethylenethiophosphoramide; TSPA

Generic Available Yes

Pharmacologic Category Antineoplastic Agent, Alkylating Agent

Use Treatment of superficial tumors of the bladder; palliative treatment of adenocarcinoma of breast or ovary; lymphomas and sarcomas; controlling intracavitary effusions caused by metastatic tumors; I.T. use: CNS leukemia/lymphoma, CNS metastases

Pregnancy Risk Factor D

Lactation Enters breast milk/not recommended

Labeled Contraindications Hypersensitivity to thiotepa or any component of the formulation; pregnancy

Warnings/Precautions Hazardous agent - use appropriate precautions for handling and disposal. Myelosuppression is common. Potentially mutagenic, carcinogenic, and teratogenic. Reduce dosage and use extreme caution in patients with hepatic, renal, or bone marrow damage. Use should be limited to cases where benefit outweighs risk.

Adverse Reactions

>10%:

Hematopoietic: Dose-limiting toxicity which is dose related and cumulative; moderate to severe leukopenia and severe thrombocytopenia have occurred. Anemia and pancytopenia may become fatal, so careful hematologic monitoring is required; intravesical administration may cause bone marrow suppression as well.

Hematologic: Myelosuppression (WBC: moderate; platelets: severe; onset: 7-10 days, nadir: 14 days, recovery: 28 days)

Local: Injection site pain

1% to 10%:

Central nervous system: Dizziness, fatigue, fever, headache

Dermatologic: Alopecia, depigmentation (with topical treatment), hyperpigmentation (with high-dose therapy), pruritus, rash, urticaria

Endocrine & metabolic: Amenorrhea, hyperuricemia

Gastrointestinal: Anorexia, nausea and vomiting rarely occur

Emetic potential: Low (<10%)

(Continued)

Thiotepa *(Continued)*

Genitourinary: Dysuria, hemorrhagic cystitis (intravesicular administration: rare), urinary retention

Neuromuscular & skeletal: Weakness

Ocular: Conjunctivitis

Renal: Hematuria

Miscellaneous: Tightness of the throat, allergic reactions

<1%: Stomatitis, anaphylaxis; like other alkylating agents, this drug is carcinogenic

Overdosage/Toxicology Symptoms of overdose include nausea, vomiting, precipitation of uric acid in kidney tubules, bone marrow suppression, and bleeding. Treatment is symptom-directed and supportive. Thiotepa is dialyzable. Transfusions of whole blood or platelets have been proven beneficial.

Drug Interactions

Cytochrome P450 Effect: Inhibits CYP2B6 (strong)

Increased Effect/Toxicity: Phenytoin may increase the levels/effects of TEPA (active metabolite). Thiotepa may increase the levels/effects of CYP2B6 substrates; example substrates include bupropion, promethazine, propofol, selegiline, and sertraline.

Decreased Effect: Phenytoin may decrease the levels/effects of thiotepa.

Ethanol/Nutrition/Herb Interactions

Ethanol: Avoid ethanol (due to GI irritation).

Herb/Nutraceutical: Avoid black cohosh, dong quai in estrogen-dependent tumors.

Storage/Stability Store intact vials under refrigeration (2°C to 8°C). Protect from light. Reconstituted solutions (10 mg/mL) are stable for up to 28 days under refrigeration (4°C to 8°C) or 7 days at room temperature (25°C).

Solutions for infusion in D_5W (≥5 mg/mL) are stable for 14 days under refrigeration (4°C) or 3 days at room temperature (23°C).

Solutions for infusion in NS (1, 3, or 5 mg/mL) are stable for 48 hours under refrigeration (4°C to 8°C) or 24 hours at room temperature (25°C). Solutions in NS at a concentration ≤0.5 mg/mL are stable for <1 hour.

Reconstitution Reconstitute each vial to 10 mg/mL. Solutions for infusion should be diluted to a concentration ≥5 mg/mL in 5% dextrose or 1, 3, or 5 mg/mL in 0.9% sodium chloride injection. Solutions for intravesicular administration should be diluted in 30-60 mL SWFI or NS. Solutions for intrathecal administration should be diluted in 1-5 mL NS or Elliott's B solution. Filter through a 0.22 micron filter prior to administration.

Compatibility Variable stability (consult detailed reference) in D_5W, NS.

Y-site administration: Compatible: Acyclovir, allopurinol, amifostine, amikacin, aminophylline, amphotericin B, ampicillin, ampicillin/sulbactam, aztreonam, bleomycin, bumetanide, buprenorphine, butorphanol, calcium gluconate, carboplatin, carmustine, cefazolin, cefepime, cefoperazone, cefotaxime, cefotetan, cefoxitin, ceftazidime, ceftizoxime, ceftriaxone, cefuroxime, chlorpromazine, cimetidine, ciprofloxacin, clindamycin, co-trimoxazole, cyclophosphamide, cytarabine, dacarbazine, dactinomycin, daunorubicin, dexamethasone sodium phosphate, diphenhydramine, dobutamine, dopamine, doxorubicin, doxycycline, droperidol, enalaprilat, etoposide, etoposide phosphate, famotidine, floxuridine, fluconazole, fludarabine, fluorouracil, furosemide, ganciclovir, gemcitabine, gentamicin, granisetron, haloperidol, heparin, hydrocortisone sodium phosphate, hydrocortisone sodium succinate, hydromorphone, hydroxyzine, idarubicin, ifosfamide, imipenem/cilastatin, leucovorin, lorazepam,

magnesium sulfate, mannitol, melphalan, meperidine, mesna, methotrexate, methylprednisolone sodium succinate, metoclopramide, metronidazole, , mitomycin, mitoxantrone, morphine, nalbuphine, netilmicin,
ofloxacin, ondansetron, paclitaxel, piperacillin, piperacillin/tazobactam,
plicamycin, potassium chloride, prochlorperazine edisylate, promethazine,
ranitidine, sodium bicarbonate, streptozocin, teniposide, ticarcillin, ticar-
cillin/clavulanate, tobramycin, vancomycin, vinblastine, vincristine, zidovudine. **Incompatible:** Cisplatin, filgrastim, minocycline, vinorelbine.
Variable (consult detailed reference): TPN.

Compatibility when admixed: Compatible: Epinephrine, lidocaine. **Incompatible:** Cisplatin.

Mechanism of Action Alkylating agent that reacts with DNA phosphate
groups to produce cross-linking of DNA strands leading to inhibition of DNA,
RNA, and protein synthesis; mechanism of action has not been explored as
thoroughly as the other alkylating agents, it is presumed that the aziridine
rings open and react as nitrogen mustard; reactivity is enhanced at a lower
pH

Pharmacodynamics/Kinetics

Absorption: Intracavitary instillation: Unreliable (10% to 100%) through
bladder mucosa; I.M.: variable

Metabolism: Extensively hepatic; major metabolite (active): TEPA

Half-life elimination: Terminal (dose-dependent clearance): 109 minutes

Excretion: Urine (as metabolites and unchanged drug)

Dosage Refer to individual protocols.

Children: Sarcomas: I.V.: 25-65 mg/m² as a single dose every 21 days

Adults:

I.M., I.V., SubQ: 30-60 mg/m² once weekly

I.V.: 0.3-0.4 mg/kg by rapid I.V. administration every 1-4 weeks, **or** 0.2 mg/
kg or 6-8 mg/m²/day for 4-5 days every 2-4 weeks

High-dose therapy for bone marrow transplant: I.V.: 500 mg/m², up to 900
mg/m²

I.M.: 15-30 mg in various schedules have been given

Intracavitary: 0.6-0.8 mg/kg or 30-60 mg weekly

Intrapericardial: 15-30 mg

Intrathecal: 10-15 mg or 5-11.5 mg/m²

Dosing comments/adjustment in renal impairment: Use with extreme
caution, reduced dose may be warranted.

Combination Regimens

Breast cancer: VATH *on page 1287*

Leukemia, acute lymphocytic: TVTG *on page 1285*

Leukemia, acute myeloid: TVTG *on page 1285*

Administration

I.V.: Administer either as a short (10-60 minute) infusion or 1-2 minute push;
a 1 mg/mL solution is considered isotonic; not a vesicant

Intravesical lavage: Instill directly into the bladder and retain for at least 2
hours; patient should be repositioned every 15-30 minutes for maximal
exposure

Monitoring Parameters CBC with differential and platelet count (monitor for
at least 3 weeks after treatment); uric acid, urinalysis

Patient Information This drug can only be administered I.V. You will require
regular blood tests to assess response to therapy. Avoid alcohol and aspirin
or aspirin-containing medications unless approved by prescriber. Maintain
adequate hydration (2-3 L/day of fluids unless instructed to restrict fluid
intake) to prevent kidney damage. For nausea and vomiting, small frequent
meals, chewing gum, or sucking lozenges may help, antiemetics may be
(Continued)

Thiotepa *(Continued)*

prescribed. You may experience amenorrhea or changed sperm production, rash, hair loss, or loss of appetite (maintaining adequate nutrition is important). You may have increased sensitivity to infection (avoid crowds and infected persons). Report unusual bleeding or bruising, persistent fever or chills, sore throat, sores in mouth or vagina, blackened stool, or difficulty breathing. The drug may cause permanent sterility and may cause birth defects. The drug may be excreted in breast milk, therefore, an alternative form of feeding your baby should be used. Contraceptive measures are recommended during therapy.

Additional Information A 1 mg/mL solution is considered isotonic.

Emetic Potential Very low (<10%)

Vesicant No

High Dose Considerations

Comments: Administration of thiotepa over 30 minutes, 1 hour before infusion of cyclophosphamide over 60 minutes, reduced bioactivation of cyclophosphamide to 4-hydroxycyclophosphamide in 20 patients. This effect did not occur with administration of thiotepa 1 hour following infusion of cyclophosphamide.

High Dose: I.V.: 360-1125 mg/m^2 as a single dose or divided into 2 daily doses; generally combined with other high-dose chemotherapeutic drugs.

Unique Toxicities:

Central nervous system: Effect increased with doses >1000 mg/m^2: Confusion, inappropriate behavior, somnolence

Dermatologic: Hyperpigmentation (most common on occluded areas of skin)

Gastrointestinal: Mucositis, mild nausea and vomiting

Hepatic: Serum transaminitis, hyperbilirubinemia

Dosage Forms Excipient information presented when available (limited, particularly for generics); consult specific product labeling.

Injection, powder for reconstitution: 15 mg, 30 mg

References

Antman K, Eder JP, Elias A, et al, "High-Dose Thiotepa Alone and in Combination Regimens With Bone Marrow Support," *Semin Oncol*, 1990, 17(1 Suppl 3):33-8.

Badalament RA and Farah RN, "Treatment of Superficial Bladder Cancer With Intravesicle Chemotherapy," *Semin Surg Oncol*, 1997, 13(5):335-41.

deJonge ME, Huitema AD, vanDam SM, et al, "Significant Induction of Cyclophosphamide and Thiotepa Metabolism by Phenytoin," *Cancer Chemother Pharmacol*, 2005, 55(5):507-10.

Dimopoulos MA, Alexanian R, Przepiorka D, et al, "Thiotepa, Busulfan, and Cyclophosphamide: A New Preparative Regimen for Autologous Marrow or Blood Stem Cell Transplantation in High-Risk Multiple Myeloma," *Blood*, 1993, 82(8):2324-8.

Gutin PH, Weiss HD, Wiernik PH, et al, "Intrathecal N,N',N"-triethylenethiophosphoramide [thio-TEPA (NSC-6396)] in the Treatment of Malignant Meningeal Disease: Phase I-II Study," *Cancer*, 1976, 38(4):1471-5.

Hart RD, Perloff M, and Holland JF, "One-Day VATH (Vinblastine, Adriamycin, Thiotepa, and Halotestin) Therapy for Advanced Breast Cancer Refractory to Chemotherapy," *Cancer*, 1981, 48(7):1522-7.

Heideman R, Cole D, Balis F, et al, "Phase I and Pharmacokinetic Evaluation of Thiotepa in the Cerebrospinal Fluid and Plasma of Pediatric Patients: Evidence for Dose-Dependent Plasma Clearance of Thiotepa," *Cancer Res*, 1989, 49(3):736-41.

Herzig GP, "Phase I-II Studies of High-Dose Thiotepa and Autologous BMT in Patients With Refractory Malignancies," *Adv Cancer Chemotherapy*, 1987, 17-29 (proceedings of a symposium, Oct 1986)

Maanen MJ, Smeets CJ, and Beijnen JH, "Chemistry, Pharmacology and Pharmacokinetics of N,N',N", -Triethylenethiophosphoramide (ThioTEPA)," *Cancer Treat Rev*, 2000, 26(4):257-68.

Saarinen UM, Hovi L, and Makipern CA, "High Dose Thiotepa With Autologous Bone Marrow Rescue in Pediatric Solid Tumors," *Proc Am Soc Clin Oncol*, 1989, 8:303.

♦ **Thrombate III**® *see* Antithrombin III *on page 98*
♦ **Thymocyte Stimulating Factor** *see* Aldesleukin *on page 29*

♦ **Thymoglobulin**® *see* Antithymocyte Globulin (Rabbit) *on page 102*

Ticarcillin and Clavulanate Potassium
(tye kar SIL in & klav yoo LAN ate poe TASS ee um)

U.S. Brand Names Timentin®

Index Terms Ticarcillin and Clavulanic Acid

Generic Available No

Canadian Brand Names Timentin®

Pharmacologic Category Antibiotic, Penicillin

Use Treatment of lower respiratory tract, urinary tract, skin and skin structures, bone and joint, gynecologic (endometritis) and intra-abdominal (peritonitis) infections, and septicemia caused by susceptible organisms. Clavulanate expands activity of ticarcillin to include beta-lactamase producing strains of *S. aureus, H. influenzae, Bacteroides* species, and some other gram-negative bacilli

Pregnancy Risk Factor B

Lactation Enters breast milk (other penicillins are compatible with breast-feeding)/use caution

Labeled Contraindications Hypersensitivity to ticarcillin, clavulanate, any penicillin, or any component of the formulation

Warnings/Precautions Use with caution and modify dosage in patients with renal impairment; serious and occasionally severe or fatal hypersensitivity (anaphylactoid) reactions have been reported in patients on penicillin therapy (especially with a history of beta-lactam hypersensitivity and/or a history of sensitivity to multiple allergens); use with caution in patients with seizures and in patients with CHF due to high sodium load. Particularly in patients with renal impairment, bleeding disorders have been observed; discontinue if thrombocytopenia or bleeding occurs. Prolonged use may result in fungal or bacterial superinfection, including *C. difficile*-associated diarrhea (CDAD) and pseudomembranous colitis; CDAD has been observed <2 months postantibiotic treatment. Safety and efficacy have not been established in children <3 months of age.

Adverse Reactions Frequency not defined.

Central nervous system: Confusion, drowsiness, fever, headache, Jarisch-Herxheimer reaction, seizure

Dermatologic: Erythema multiforme, pruritus, rash, Stevens-Johnson syndrome, toxic epidermal necrolysis, urticaria

Endocrine & metabolic: Electrolyte imbalance

Gastrointestinal: *Clostridium difficile* colitis, diarrhea, nausea, vomiting

Hematologic: Bleeding, eosinophilia, hemolytic anemia, leukopenia, neutropenia, positive Coombs' reaction, prothrombin time prolonged, thrombocytopenia

Hepatic: Hepatotoxicity, jaundice

Local: Injection site reaction (pain, burning, induration); thrombophlebitis

Neuromuscular & skeletal: Myoclonus

Renal: BUN increased, interstitial nephritis (acute), serum creatinine increased

Miscellaneous: Anaphylaxis, hypersensitivity reactions

Overdosage/Toxicology Symptoms of overdose include neuromuscular hypersensitivity and seizures. Hemodialysis may be helpful to aid in removal of the drug from blood; otherwise, treatment is supportive or symptom-directed.
(Continued)

Ticarcillin and Clavulanate Potassium *(Continued)*

Drug Interactions

Increased Effect/Toxicity: Penicillins may increase the exposure to methotrexate during concurrent therapy; monitor. Uricosuric agents (eg, probenecid, sulfinpyrazone) may decrease the excretion of penicillins.

Decreased Effect: Fusidic acid and tetracyclines may decrease penicillin effectiveness. Antibiotics may decrease the therapeutic effect of typhoid vaccine (live, attenuated Ty21a strain). Penicillins may cause physical inactivation of aminoglycosides in the presence of high concentrations of ticarcillin and potential toxicity in patients with mild-moderate renal dysfunction.

Storage/Stability

Vials: Store intact vials at <24°C (<75°F). Reconstituted solution is stable for 6 hours at room temperature and 72 hours when refrigerated. I.V. infusion in NS or LR is stable for 24 hours at room temperature, 7 days when refrigerated, or 30 days when frozen. I.V. infusion in D_5W solution is stable for 24 hours at room temperature, 3 days when refrigerated, or 7 days when frozen. After freezing, thawed solution is stable for 8 hours at room temperature. Darkening of drug indicates loss of potency of clavulanate potassium.

Premixed solution: Store frozen at ≤-20°C (-4°F). Thawed solution is stable for 24 hours at room temperature or 7 days under refrigeration; do not refreeze.

Compatibility

Stable in D_5W, LR, NS, sterile water for injection.

Y-site administration: Compatible: Allopurinol, amifostine, aztreonam, cefepime, clarithromycin, cyclophosphamide, diltiazem, docetaxel, doxorubicin liposome, etoposide, famotidine, filgrastim, fluconazole, fludarabine, foscarnet, gatifloxacin, gemcitabine, granisetron, heparin, insulin (regular), melphalan, meperidine, morphine, ondansetron, perphenazine, propofol, remifentanil, sargramostim, teniposide, theophylline, thiotepa, vinorelbine. **Incompatible:** Alatrofloxacin, amphotericin B cholesteryl sulfate complex. **Variable (consult detailed reference):** Cisatracurium, topotecan, vancomycin.

Compatibility when admixed: Incompatible: Sodium bicarbonate, aminoglycosides.

Mechanism of Action

Inhibits bacterial cell wall synthesis by binding to one or more of the penicillin binding proteins (PBPs); which in turn inhibits the final transpeptidation step of peptidoglycan synthesis in bacterial cell walls, thus inhibiting cell wall biosynthesis. Bacteria eventually lyse due to ongoing activity of cell wall autolytic enzymes (autolysins and murein hydrolases) while cell wall assembly is arrested.

Pharmacodynamics/Kinetics

Ticarcillin: See Ticarcillin monograph.

Clavulanic acid:

Protein binding: 9% to 30%

Metabolism: Hepatic

Half-life elimination: 66-90 minutes

Excretion: Urine (45% as unchanged drug)

Clearance: Does not affect clearance of ticarcillin

Dosage Note: Timentin® (ticarcillin/clavulanate) is a combination product; each 3.1 g dosage form contains 3 g ticarcillin disodium and 0.1 g clavulanic acid.

Usual dosage range:

Children and Adults <60 kg: I.V.: 200-300 mg of ticarcillin component/kg/day in divided doses every 4-6 hours

Children ≥60 kg and Adults: I.V.: 3.1 g (ticarcillin 3 g plus clavulanic acid 0.1 g) every 4-6 hours (maximum: 24 g of ticarcillin component/day)
Indication-specific dosing:
Children: I.V.:
Bite wounds (animal): 200 mg of ticarcillin component/kg/day in divided doses
Neutropenic fever: 75 mg of ticarcillin component/kg every 6 hours (maximum 3.1 g/dose)
Pneumonia (nosocomial): 300 mg of ticarcillin component/kg/day in 4 divided doses (maximum: 18-24 g of ticarcillin component/day)
Children ≥60 kg and Adults: I.V.:
Amnionitis, cholangitis, diverticulitis, endometritis, epididymo-orchitis, mastoiditis, orbital cellulitis, peritonitis, pneumonia (aspiration): 3.1 g every 6 hours
Liver abscess, parafascial space infections, septic thrombophlebitis: 3.1 g every 4 hours
***Pseudomonas* infections:** 3.1 g every 4 hours
Urinary tract infections: 3.1 g every 6-8 hours

Dosing adjustment in renal impairment: Loading dose: I.V.: 3.1 g one dose, followed by maintenance dose based on creatinine clearance:
Cl_{cr} 30-60 mL/minute: Administer 2 g of ticarcillin component every 4 hours or 3.1 g every 8 hours
Cl_{cr} 10-30 mL/minute: Administer 2 g of ticarcillin component every 8 hours or 3.1 g every 12 hours
Cl_{cr} <10 mL/minute: Administer 2 g of ticarcillin component every 12 hours
Cl_{cr} <10 mL/minute with concomitant hepatic dysfunction: 2 g of ticarcillin component every 24 hours
Moderately dialyzable (20% to 50%)
Continuous ambulatory peritoneal dialysis: 3.1 g every 12 hours
Hemodialysis: 2 g of ticarcillin component every 12 hours; supplemented with 3.1 g after each dialysis
Continuous renal replacement therapy (CRRT): Drug clearance is highly dependent on the method of renal replacement, filter type, and flow rate. Appropriate dosing requires close monitoring of pharmacologic response, signs of adverse reactions due to drug accumulation, as well as drug levels in relation to target trough (if appropriate). The following are general recommendations only (based on dialysate flow/ultrafiltration rates of 1 L/hour) and should not supersede clinical judgment:
CVVH: 2 g every 6-8 hours
CVVHD/CVVHDF: 3.1 g every 6 hours
Note: Do not administer in intervals exceeding every 8 hours. Clavulanate component is hepatically eliminated; extending the dosing interval beyond 8 hours may result in loss of beta-lactamase inhibition.

Dosing adjustment in hepatic dysfunction: With concomitant renal dysfunction (Cl_{cr} <10 mL/minute): 2 g of ticarcillin component every 24 hours
Administration Infuse over 30 minutes.
Some penicillins (eg, carbenicillin, ticarcillin and piperacillin) have been shown to inactivate aminoglycosides *in vitro*. This has been observed to a greater extent with tobramycin and gentamicin, while amikacin has shown greater stability against inactivation. Concurrent use of these agents may pose a risk of reduced antibacterial efficacy *in vivo*, particularly in the setting of profound renal impairment. However, definitive clinical evidence is lacking. If combination penicillin/aminoglycoside therapy is desired in a patient with renal dysfunction, separation of doses (if feasible), and routine
(Continued)

Ticarcillin and Clavulanate Potassium *(Continued)*

monitoring of aminoglycoside levels, CBC, and clinical response should be considered.

Monitoring Parameters Observe for signs and symptoms of anaphylaxis during first dose.

Test Interactions Positive Coombs' test, false-positive urinary proteins

Some penicillin derivatives may accelerate the degradation of aminoglycosides *in vitro*, leading to a potential underestimation of aminoglycoside serum concentration.

Dietary Considerations Sodium content of 1 g: 4.51 mEq; potassium content of 1 g: 0.15 mEq

Special Geriatric Considerations When used as empiric therapy or for a documented pseudomonal pneumonia, it is best to combine with an aminoglycoside such as gentamicin or tobramycin. High sodium content may limit use in patients with congestive heart failure. Adjust dose for renal function.

Emetic Potential Very low (<10%)

Vesicant No

Dosage Forms Excipient information presented when available (limited, particularly for generics); consult specific product labeling.

Infusion [premixed, frozen]: Ticarcillin 3 g and clavulanic acid 0.1 g (100 mL) [contains sodium 4.51 mEq and potassium 0.15 mEq per g]

Injection, powder for reconstitution: Ticarcillin 3 g and clavulanic acid 0.1 g (3.1 g, 31 g) [contains sodium 4.51 mEq and potassium 0.15 mEq per g]

References

Begue P, Quiniou F, Quinet B, "Efficacy and Pharmacokinetics of Timentin® in Paediatric Infections," *J Antimicrob Chemother*, 1986, 17(Suppl C):81-91.

Chow MS, Quintiliani, and Nightingale CH, "*In Vivo* Inactivation of Tobramycin by Ticarcillin. A Case Report," *JAMA*, 1982, 247(5):658-9.

Daly JS, Dodge RA, Glew RH, et al, "Effect of Time and Temperature on Inactivation of Aminoglycosides by Ampicillin at Neonatal Dosages," *J Perinatol*, 1997, 17(1):42-5.

Donowitz GR and Mandell GL, "Beta-Lactam Antibiotics," *N Engl J Med*, 1988, 318(7):419-26 and 318(8):490-500.

Dowell JA, Korth-Bradley J, Milisci M, et al, "Evaluating Possible Pharmacokinetic Interactions Between Tobramycin, Piperacillin, and a Combination of Piperacillin and Tazobactam in Patients With Various Degrees of Renal Impairment," *J Clin Pharmacol*, 2001, 41:979-86.

Farchione LA, "Inactivation of Aminoglycosides by Penicillins," *J Antimicrob Chemother*, 1982, 8(Suppl A):27-36.

Fuchs PC, Stickel S, Anderson PH, et al, "*In Vitro* Inactivation of Aminoglycosides by Sulbactam, Other Beta-Lactams, and Sulbactam-Beta-Lactam Combinations," *Antimicrob Agents Chemother*, 1991, 35(1):182-4.

Halstenson CE, Wong MO, Herman CS, et al, "Effect of Concomitant Administration of Piperacillin on the Dispositions on Isepamicin and Gentamicin in Patients With End-Stage Renal Disease," *Antimicrob Agents Chemother*, 1992, 36(9):1832-36.

Hitt CM, Patel KB, Nicolau DP, et al, "Influence of Piperacillin-Tazobactam on Pharmacokinetics of Gentamicin Given Once Daily," *Am J Health Syst Pharm*, 1997, 54(23):2704-8.

Itokazu GS and Danziger LH, "Ampicillin-Sulbactam and Ticarcillin-Clavulanic Acid: A Comparison of Their *In Vitro* Activity and Review of Their Clinical Efficacy," *Pharmacotherapy*, 1991, 11(5):382-414.

Konishi H, Goto M, Nakamoto Y, et al, "Tobramycin Inactivation by Carbenicillin, Ticarcillin, and Piperacillin," *Antimicrob Agents Chemother*, 1983, 23(5):653-57.

Lau A, Lee M, Flascha S, et al, "Effect of Piperacillin on Tobramycin Pharmacokinetics in Patients With Normal Renal Function," *Antimicrob Agents Chemother*, 1983, 24(4):533-37.

Reed MD, Yamashita TS, and Blumer JL, "Pharmacokinetic-Based Ticarcillin/Clavulanic Acid Dose Recommendations for Infants and Children," *J Clin Pharmacol*, 1995, 35(7):658-65.

Russoe ME and Atkins-Thor E, "Gentamicin and Ticarcillin in Subjects With End-Stage Renal Disease. Comparison of Two Assay Methods and Evaluation of Inactivation Rate," *Clin Nephrol*, 1981, 15(4):175-80.

Stutman HR and Marks MI, "Review of Pediatric Antimicrobial Therapies," *Semin Pediatr Infect Dis*, 1991, 2:3-17.

Thompson MIB, Russo ME, Saxon BJ, et al, "Gentamicin Inactivation by Piperacillin or Carbenicillin in Patients With End-Stage Renal Disease," *Antimicrob Agents Chemother*, 1982, 21(2):268-73.

Trotman RL, Williamson JC, Shoemaker DM, et al, "Antibiotic Dosing in Critically Ill Adult Patients Receiving Continuous Renal Replacement Therapy," *Clin Infect Dis*, 2005, 41(8):1159-66.

Viollier AF, Standiford HC, Drusano GL, et al, "Comparative Pharmacokinetics and Serum Bactericidal Activity of Mezlocillin, Ticarcillin and Piperacillin, With and Without Gentamicin," *J Antimicrob Chemother*, 1985, 15(5):597-606.

Walterspiel JN, Feldman S, Van R, et al, "Comparative Inactivation of Isepamicin, Amikacin, and Gentamicin by Nine Beta-Lactams and Two Beta-Lactamase Inhibitors, Cilastatin and Heparin," *Antimicrob Agents Chemother*, 1991, 35(9):1875-8.

Wright AJ, "The Penicillins," *Mayo Clin Proc*, 1999, 74(3):290-307.

♦ **Ticarcillin and Clavulanic Acid** *see* Ticarcillin and Clavulanate Potassium *on page 1037*

♦ **TICE® BCG** *see* BCG Vaccine *on page 128*

♦ **Tigan®** *see* Trimethobenzamide *on page 1073*

♦ **Timentin®** *see* Ticarcillin and Clavulanate Potassium *on page 1037*

♦ **Tioguanine** *see* Thioguanine *on page 1030*

♦ **TMP** *see* Trimethoprim *on page 1075*

♦ **TMP-SMZ** *see* Sulfamethoxazole and Trimethoprim *on page 982*

♦ **TMZ** *see* Temozolomide *on page 1010*

♦ **TOBI®** *see* Tobramycin *on page 1041*

Tobramycin® (toe bra MYE sin)

Medication Safety Issues

Sound-alike/look-alike issues:

Tobramycin may be confused with Trobicin®

AKTob® may be confused with AK-Trol®

Nebcin® may be confused with Inapsine®, Naprosyn®, Nubain®

Tobrex® may be confused with TobraDex®

U.S. Brand Names AKTob®; TOBI®; Tobrex®

Index Terms Tobramycin Sulfate

Generic Available Yes: Excludes ophthalmic ointment, solution for nebulization

Canadian Brand Names PMS-Tobramycin; Sandoz-Tobramycin; TOBI®; Tobramycin Injection, USP; Tobrex®

Pharmacologic Category Antibiotic, Aminoglycoside; Antibiotic, Ophthalmic

Use Treatment of documented or suspected infections caused by susceptible gram-negative bacilli including *Pseudomonas aeruginosa*; topically used to treat superficial ophthalmic infections caused by susceptible bacteria. Tobramycin solution for inhalation is indicated for the management of cystic fibrosis patients (>6 years of age) with *Pseudomonas aeruginosa*.

Pregnancy Risk Factor D (injection, inhalation); B (ophthalmic)

Lactation Enters breast milk/not recommended

Labeled Contraindications Hypersensitivity to tobramycin, other aminoglycosides, or any component of the formulation; pregnancy (injection/inhalation)

Warnings/Precautions [U.S. Boxed Warning]: Aminoglycosides may cause neurotoxicity and/or nephrotoxicity; usual risk factors include pre-existing renal impairment, concomitant neuro-/nephrotoxic medications, advanced age and dehydration. Ototoxicity may be directly proportional to the amount of drug given and the duration of treatment; tinnitus or vertigo are indications of vestibular injury and impending hearing loss; renal damage is usually reversible. May cause neuromuscular blockade and respiratory paralysis; especially when given soon after anesthesia or muscle relaxants. Not intended for long-term therapy due to toxic hazards associated with extended administration; use caution in pre-existing renal insufficiency, (Continued)

Tobramycin *(Continued)*

vestibular or cochlear impairment, myasthenia gravis, hypocalcemia, conditions which depress neuromuscular transmission. Dosage modification required in patients with impaired renal function. Prolonged use may result in fungal or bacterial superinfection, including *C. difficile*-associated diarrhea (CDAD) and pseudomembranous colitis; CDAD has been observed <2 months postantibiotic treatment. Solution may contain sodium metabisulfate; use caution in patients with sulfite allergy.

Adverse Reactions

Injection: Frequency not defined:

Central nervous system: Confusion, disorientation, dizziness, fever, headache, lethargy, vertigo

Dermatologic: Exfoliative dermatitis, itching, rash, urticaria

Endocrine & metabolic: Serum calcium, magnesium, potassium, and/or sodium decreased

Gastrointestinal: Diarrhea, nausea, vomiting

Hematologic: Anemia, eosinophilia, granulocytopenia, leukocytosis, leukopenia, thrombocytopenia

Hepatic: ALT, AST, bilirubin, and/or LDH increased

Local: Pain at the injection site

Otic: Hearing loss, tinnitus, ototoxicity (auditory), ototoxicity (vestibular), roaring in the ears

Renal: BUN increased, cylindruria, serum creatinine increased, oliguria, proteinuria

Inhalation:

>10%:

Gastrointestinal: Sputum discoloration (21%)

Respiratory: Voice alteration (13%)

1% to 10%:

Central nervous system: Malaise (6%)

Otic: Tinnitus (3%)

Postmarketing and/or case reports: Hearing loss

Ophthalmic: <1%: Ocular: Conjunctival erythema, lid itching, lid swelling

Overdosage/Toxicology Symptoms of overdose include ototoxicity, nephrotoxicity, and neuromuscular toxicity. Treatment of choice following a single acute overdose appears to be maintenance of urine output of at least 3 mL/kg/hour during the acute treatment phase. Dialysis is of questionable value in enhancing aminoglycoside elimination. If required, hemodialysis is preferred over peritoneal dialysis in patients with normal renal function. Chelation with penicillins is investigational.

Drug Interactions

Increased Effect/Toxicity: Increased antimicrobial effect of tobramycin with extended spectrum penicillins (synergistic). Neuromuscular blockers may have an increased duration of action (neuromuscular blockade). Amphotericin B, cephalosporins, and loop diuretics may increase the risk of nephrotoxicity.

Storage/Stability

Injection: Stable at room temperature both as the clear, colorless solution and as the dry powder. Reconstituted solutions remain stable for 24 hours at room temperature and 96 hours when refrigerated.

Ophthalmic solution: Store at 8°C to 27°C (46°F to 80°F).

Solution, for inhalation (TOBI®): Store under refrigeration at 2°C to 8°C (36°F to 46°F). May be stored in foil pouch at room temperature of 25°C (77°F)

for up to 28 days. Avoid intense light. Solution may darken over time; however, do not use if cloudy or contains particles.

Reconstitution Dilute in 50-100 mL NS, D_5W for I.V. infusion.

Compatibility Stable in dextran 40 10% in dextrose, D_5NS, D_5W, $D_{10}W$, mannitol 20%, LR, NS; **variable stability (consult detailed reference)** in peritoneal dialysis solutions.

Y-site administration: Compatible: Acyclovir, alatrofloxacin, amifostine, amiodarone, amsacrine, aztreonam, ciprofloxacin, cisatracurium, cyclophosphamide, diltiazem, docetaxel, doxorubicin liposome, enalaprilat, esmolol, etoposide phosphate, filgrastim, fluconazole, fludarabine, foscarnet, furosemide, gatifloxacin, gemcitabine, granisetron, hydromorphone, IL-2, insulin (regular), labetalol, linezolid, magnesium sulfate, melphalan, meperidine, midazolam, morphine, perphenazine, remifentanil, tacrolimus, teniposide, theophylline, thiotepa, tolazoline, vinorelbine, zidovudine. **Incompatible:** Allopurinol, amphotericin B cholesteryl sulfate complex, cefoperazone, heparin, hetastarch, indomethacin, propofol, sargramostim.

Compatibility in syringe: Compatible: Doxapram. **Incompatible:** Cefamandole, clindamycin, heparin.

Compatibility when admixed: Compatible: Aztreonam, bleomycin, calcium gluconate, cefoxitin, ciprofloxacin, clindamycin, furosemide, metronidazole, metronidazole with sodium bicarbonate, ofloxacin, ranitidine, verapamil. **Incompatible:** Cefamandole, cefepime, cefotaxime, cefotetan, floxacillin, heparin.

Mechanism of Action Interferes with bacterial protein synthesis by binding to 30S and 50S ribosomal subunits resulting in a defective bacterial cell membrane

Pharmacodynamics/Kinetics

Absorption:

Oral: Poorly absorbed

I.M.: Rapid and complete

Inhalation: Peak serum concentrations are ~1 mcg/mL following a 300 mg dose

Distribution: V_d: 0.2-0.3 L/kg; Pediatrics: 0.2-0.7 L/kg; to extracellular fluid including serum, abscesses, ascitic, pericardial, pleural, synovial, lymphatic, and peritoneal fluids; poor penetration into CSF, eye, bone, prostate

Inhalation: Tobramycin remains concentrated primarily in the airways

Protein binding: <30%

Half-life elimination:

Neonates: ≤1200 g: 11 hours; >1200 g: 2-9 hours

Adults: 2-3 hours; directly dependent upon glomerular filtration rate

Adults with impaired renal function: 5-70 hours

Time to peak, serum: I.M.: 30-60 minutes; I.V.: ~30 minutes

Excretion: Normal renal function: Urine (~90% to 95%) within 24 hours

Dosage Note: Dosage individualization is **critical** because of the low therapeutic index.

Use of ideal body weight (IBW) for determining the mg/kg/dose appears to be more accurate than dosing on the basis of total body weight (TBW). In morbid obesity, dosage requirement may best be estimated using a dosing weight of IBW + 0.4 (TBW - IBW).

Initial and periodic plasma drug levels (eg, peak and trough with conventional dosing) should be determined, particularly in critically-ill patients with serious infections or in disease states known to significantly alter aminoglycoside pharmacokinetics (eg, cystic fibrosis, burns, or major surgery).

(Continued)

Tobramycin *(Continued)*

Usual dosage range:

Infants and Children <5 years: I.M., I.V.: 2.5 mg/kg/dose every 8 hours

Children ≥5 years: I.M., I.V.: 2-2.5 mg/kg/dose every 8 hours

Note: Higher individual doses and/or more frequent intervals (eg, every 6 hours) may be required in selected clinical situations (cystic fibrosis) or serum levels document the need.

Children and Adults:

Inhalation:

Children: 40-80 mg 2-3 times/day

Adults: 60-80 mg 3 times/day

High-dose regimen: Children ≥6 years and Adults: 300 mg every 12 hours (do not administer doses <6 hours apart); administer in repeated cycles of 28 days on drug followed by 28 days off drug

Intrathecal: 4-8 mg/day

Ophthalmic: Children ≥2 months and Adults:

Ointment: Instill ½" (1.25 cm) 2-3 times/day every 3-4 hours

Solution: Instill 1-2 drops every 2-4 hours, up to 2 drops every hour for severe infections

Topical: Apply 3-4 times/day to affected area

Adults: I.M., I.V.:

Conventional: 1-2.5 mg/kg/dose every 8-12 hours; to ensure adequate peak concentrations early in therapy, higher initial dosage may be considered in selected patients when extracellular water is increased (edema, septic shock, postsurgical, and/or trauma)

Once-daily: 4-7 mg/kg/dose once daily; some clinicians recommend this approach for all patients with normal renal function; this dose is at least as efficacious with similar, if not less, toxicity than conventional dosing.

Indication-specific dosing:

Neonates: I.M., I.V.:

Meningitis:

0-7 days: <2000 g: 2.5 mg/kg every 18-24 hours; >2000 g: 2.5 mg/kg every 12 hours

8-28 days: <2000 g: 2.5 mg/kg every 8-12 hours; >2000 g: 2.5 mg/kg every 8 hours

Children:

Cystic fibrosis:

I.M., I.V.: 2.5-3.3 mg/kg every 6-8 hours; **Note:** Some patients may require larger or more frequent doses if serum levels document the need (eg, cystic fibrosis or febrile granulocytopenic patients).

Inhalation:

Standard aerosolized tobramycin: 40-80 mg 2-3 times/day

High-dose regimen (TOBI®): Children ≥6 years: See adult dosing.

Adults: I.M., I.V.:

Brucellosis: 240 mg (I.M.) daily or 5 mg/kg (I.V.) daily for 7 days; either regimen recommended in combination with doxycycline

Cholangitis: 4-6 mg/kg once daily with ampicillin

Diverticulitis, complicated: 1.5-2 mg/kg every 8 hours (with ampicillin and metronidazole)

Infective endocarditis or synergy (for gram-positive infections): I.M., I.V.: 1 mg/kg every 8 hours (with ampicillin)

Meningitis *(Enterococcus* or *Pseudomonas aeruginosa):* I.V.: Loading dose: 2 mg/kg, then 1.7 mg/kg/dose every 8 hours (administered with another bacteriocidal drug)

Pelvic inflammatory disease: Loading dose: 2 mg/kg, then 1.5 mg/kg every 8 hours **or** 4.5 mg/kg once daily

Plague *(Yersinia pestis):* Treatment: 5 mg/kg/day, followed by postexposure prophylaxis with doxycycline

Pneumonia, hospital- or ventilator-associated: 7 mg/kg/day (with antipseudomonal beta-lactam or carbapenem)

Prophylaxis against endocarditis (dental, oral, upper respiratory procedures, GI/GU procedures): 1.5 mg/kg with ampicillin (50 mg/kg) 30 minutes prior to procedure. **Note:** AHA guidelines now recommend prophylaxis only in patients undergoing invasive procedures and in whom underlying cardiac conditions may predispose to a higher risk of adverse outcomes should infection occur. As of April 2007, routine prophylaxis no longer recommended by the AHA.

Tularemia: 5 mg/kg/day divided every 8 hours for 1-2 weeks

Urinary tract infection: 1.5 mg/kg/dose every 8 hours

Dosing interval in renal impairment: I.M., I.V.:

Conventional dosing:

Cl_{cr} ≥60 mL/minute: Administer every 8 hours

Cl_{cr} 40-60 mL/minute: Administer every 12 hours

Cl_{cr} 20-40 mL/minute: Administer every 24 hours

Cl_{cr} 10-20 mL/minute: Administer every 48 hours

Cl_{cr} <10 mL/minute: Administer every 72 hours

High-dose therapy: Interval may be extended (eg, every 48 hours) in patients with moderate renal impairment (Cl_{cr} 30-59 mL/minute) and/or adjusted based on serum level determinations.

Hemodialysis: Dialyzable; 30% removal of aminoglycosides occurs during 4 hours of HD - administer dose after dialysis and follow levels

Continuous arteriovenous or venovenous hemofiltration: Dose as for Cl_{cr} of 10-40 mL/minute and follow levels

Administration in CAPD fluid:

Gram-negative infection: 4-8 mg/L (4-8 mcg/mL) of CAPD fluid

Gram-positive infection (ie, synergy): 3-4 mg/L (3-4 mcg/mL) of CAPD fluid

Administration IVPB/I.M.: Dose as for Cl_{cr} <10 mL/minute and follow levels

Dosing adjustment/comments in hepatic disease: Monitor plasma concentrations

Administration

I.V.: Infuse over 30-60 minutes. Flush with saline before and after administration.

Inhalation (TOBI®): To be inhaled over ~15 minutes using a handheld nebulizer.

Ophthalmic: Contact lenses should not be worn during treatment of ophthalmic infections.

Ointment: Do not touch tip of tube to eye. Instill ointment into pocket between eyeball and lower lid; patient should look downward before closing eye.

Solution: Allow 5 minutes between application of "multiple-drop" therapy.

Suspension: Shake well before using; tilt head back, instill suspension in conjunctival sac and close eye(s). Do not touch dropper to eye. Apply light finger pressure on lacrimal sac for 1 minute following instillation.

Some penicillins (eg, carbenicillin, ticarcillin and piperacillin) have been shown to inactivate aminoglycosides *in vitro*. This has been observed to a greater extent with tobramycin and gentamicin, while amikacin has shown greater stability against inactivation. Concurrent use of these agents may pose a risk of reduced antibacterial efficacy *in vivo*, particularly in the (Continued)

Tobramycin *(Continued)*

setting of profound renal impairment. However, definitive clinical evidence is lacking. If combination penicillin/aminoglycoside therapy is desired in a patient with renal dysfunction, separation of doses (if feasible), and routine monitoring of aminoglycoside levels, CBC, and clinical response should be considered.

Monitoring Parameters Urinalysis, urine output, BUN, serum creatinine, peak and trough plasma tobramycin levels; be alert to ototoxicity; hearing should be tested before and during treatment

Some penicillin derivatives may accelerate the degradation of aminoglycosides *in vitro*. This may be clinically-significant for certain penicillin (ticarcillin, piperacillin, carbenicillin) and aminoglycoside (gentamicin, tobramycin) combination therapy in patients with significant renal impairment. Close monitoring of aminoglycoside levels is warranted.

Test Interactions Some penicillin derivatives may accelerate the degradation of aminoglycosides *in vitro*, leading to a potential underestimation of aminoglycoside serum concentration.

Dietary Considerations May require supplementation of calcium, magnesium, potassium.

Patient Information Report symptoms of superinfection; for eye drops - no other eye drops 5-10 minutes before or after tobramycin; report any dizziness or sensations of ringing or fullness in ears

Special Geriatric Considerations The aminoglycosides are an important therapeutic intervention for susceptible organisms and as empiric therapy in seriously ill patients. Their use is not without risk of toxicity; however, these risks can be minimized if initial dosing is adjusted for estimated renal function and appropriate monitoring is performed. High dose, once daily aminoglycosides have been advocated as an alternative to traditional dosing regimens. Once daily or extended interval dosing is as effective and may be safer than traditional dosing. Interval must be adjusted for renal function.

Additional Information Once-daily dosing: Higher peak serum drug concentration to MIC ratios, demonstrated aminoglycoside postantibiotic effect, decreased renal cortex drug uptake, and improved cost-time efficiency are supportive reasons for the use of once daily dosing regimens for aminoglycosides. Current research indicates these regimens to be as effective for nonlife-threatening infections, with no higher incidence of nephrotoxicity, than those requiring multiple daily doses. Doses are determined by calculating the entire day's dose via usual multiple dose calculation techniques and administering this quantity as a single dose. Doses are then adjusted to maintain mean serum concentrations above the MIC(s) of the causative organism(s). (Example: 2.5-5 mg/kg as a single dose; expected Cp_{max}: 10-20 mcg/mL and Cp_{min}: <1 mcg/mL). Further research is needed for universal recommendation in all patient populations and gram-negative disease; exceptions may include those with known high clearance (eg, children, patients with cystic fibrosis, or burns who may require shorter dosage intervals) and patients with renal function impairment for whom longer than conventional dosage intervals are usually required.

Emetic Potential Very low (<10%)

Vesicant No

Dosage Forms Excipient information presented when available (limited, particularly for generics); consult specific product labeling.

Infusion [premixed in NS]: 60 mg (50 mL); 80 mg (100 mL)

Injection, powder for reconstitution: 1.2 g

Injection, solution: 10 mg/mL (2 mL, 8 mL); 40 mg/mL (2 mL, 30 mL, 50 mL) [may contain sodium metabisulfite]

Ointment, ophthalmic (Tobrex®): 0.3% (3.5 g)

Solution for nebulization [preservative free] (TOBI®): 60 mg/mL (5 mL)

Solution, ophthalmic (AKTob®, Tobrex®): 0.3% (5 mL) [contains benzalkonium chloride]

References

American Thoracic Society and Infectious Diseases Society of America, "Guidelines for the Management of Adults With Hospital-Acquired, Ventilator-Associated, and Health-care-Associated Pneumonia," *Am J Respir Crit Care Med*, 2005, 171(4):388-416.

Bauer LA and Blouin RA, "Influence of Age on Tobramycin. Pharmacokinetics in Patients With Normal Renal Function," *Antimicrob Agents Chemother*, 1981, 20:587-9.

Begg EJ and Barclay ML, "Aminoglycosides - 50 Years On," *Br J Clin Pharmacol*, 1995, 39(6):597-603.

Chow MS, Quintiliani, and Nightingale CH, "*In Vivo* Inactivation of Tobramycin by Ticarcillin. A Case Report," *JAMA*, 1982, 247(5):658-9.

Cunha BA, "Aminoglycosides: Current Role in Antimicrobial Therapy," *Pharmacotherapy*, 1988, 8(6):334-50.

Daly JS, Dodge RA, Glew RH, et al, "Effect of Time and Temperature on Inactivation of Aminoglycosides by Ampicillin at Neonatal Dosages," *J Perinatol*, 1997, 17(1):42-5.

Dowell JA, Korth-Bradley J, Milisci M, et al, "Evaluating Possible Pharmacokinetic Interactions Between Tobramycin, Piperacillin, and a Combination of Piperacillin and Tazobactam in Patients With Various Degrees of Renal Impairment," *J Clin Pharmacol*, 2001, 41:979-86.

Edson RS and Terrell CL, "The Aminoglycosides," *Mayo Clin Proc*, 1991, 66(11):1158-64.

Farchione LA, "Inactivation of Aminoglycosides by Penicillins," *J Antimicrob Chemother*, 1982, 8(Suppl A):27-36.

Fuchs PC, Stickel S, Anderson PH, et al, "*In Vitro* Inactivation of Aminoglycosides by Sulbactam, Other Beta-Lactams, and Sulbactam-Beta-Lactam Combinations," *Antimicrob Agents Chemother*, 1991, 35(1):182-4.

Gilbert DN, "Once-Daily Aminoglycoside Therapy," *Antimicrob Agents Chemother*, 1991, 35(3):399-405.

Green TP, Mirkin BL, Peterson PK, et al, "Tobramycin Serum Level Monitoring in Young Patients With Normal Renal Function," *Clin Pharmacokinet*, 1984, 9(5):457-68.

Halstenson CE, Wong MO, Herman CS, et al, "Effect of Concomitant Administration of Piperacillin on the Dispositions of Isepamicin and Gentamicin in Patients With End-Stage Renal Disease," *Antimicrob Agents Chemother*, 1992, 36(9):1832-36.

Hitt CM, Patel KB, Nicolau DP, et al, "Influence of Piperacillin-Tazobactam on Pharmacokinetics of Gentamicin Given Once Daily," *Am J Health Syst Pharm*, 1997, 54(23):2704-8.

Hustinx WN and Hoepelman IM, "Aminoglycoside Dosage Regimens. Is Once a Day Enough?" *Clin Pharmacokinet*, 1993, 25(6):427-32.

Kahler DA, Schowengerdt KO, Fricker FJ, et al, "Toxic Serum Trough Concentrations After Administration of Nebulized Tobramycin," *Pharmacotherapy*, 2003, 23(4):543-5.

Konishi H, Goto M, Nakamoto Y, et al, "Tobramycin Inactivation by Carbenicillin, Ticarcillin, and Piperacillin," *Antimicrob Agents Chemother*, 1983, 23(5):653-57.

Lau A, Lee M, Flascha S, et al, "Effect of Piperacillin on Tobramycin Pharmacokinetics in Patients With Normal Renal Function," *Antimicrob Agents Chemother*, 1983, 24(4):533-37.

Lortholary O, Tod M, Cohen Y, et al, "Aminoglycosides," *Med Clin North Am*, 1995, 79(4):761-87.

Matzke GR, Jameson JJ, and Halstenson CE, "Gentamicin Disposition in Young and Elderly Patients With Various Degrees of Renal Function," *J Clin Pharmacol*, 1987, 27(3):216-20.

Mayer PR, Brown CH, Carter RA, et al, "Intramuscular Tobramycin Pharmacokinetics in Geriatric Patients," *Drug Intell Clin Pharm*, 1986, 20:611-5.

McCormack JP and Jewesson PJ, "A Critical Re-evaluation of the "Therapeutic Range" of Aminoglycosides," *Clin Infect Dis*, 1992, 14(1):320-39.

Nahata MC, Powell DA, Durrell DE, et al, "Effect of Gestational Age and Birth Weight on Tobramycin Kinetics in Newborn Infants," *J Antimicrob Chemother*, 1984, 14(1):59-65.

Nicolau DP, Freeman CD, Belliveau PP, et al, "Experience With a Once-Daily Aminoglycoside Program Administered to 2184 Adult Patients," *Antimicrob Agents Chemother*, 1995, 39(3):650-5.

Preston SL and Briceland LL, "Single Daily Dosing of Aminoglycosides," *Pharmacotherapy*, 1995, 15(3):297-316.

Ramsey BW, Burns J, Smith A, et al, "Safety and Efficacy of Tobramycin for Inhalation in Patients With Cystic Fibrosis: The Results of Two Phase III Placebo Controlled Clinical Trials," *Pediatr Pulmonol*, 1997, (Suppl 14):137-8, S10.3.

Ramsey BW, Dorkin HL, Eisenberg JD, et al, "Efficacy of Aerosolized Tobramycin in Patients With Cystic Fibrosis," *N Engl J Med*, 1993, 328(24):1740-6.

Russoe ME and Atkins-Thor E, "Gentamicin and Ticarcillin in Subjects With End-Stage Renal Disease. Comparison of Two Assay Methods and Evaluation of Inactivation Rate," *Clin Nephrol*, 1981, 15(4):175-80.

(Continued)

Tobramycin *(Continued)*

Shaw PK, Braun TL, Liebergen A, et al, "Aerosolized Tobramycin Pharmacokinetics in Cystic Fibrosis Patients," *J Pediatr Pharm Pract*, 1997, 2(1):23-6.

Smith PF, Ballow CH, Booker BM, et al, "Pharmacokinetics and Pharmacodynamics of Aztreonam and Tobramycin in Hospitalized Patients," *Clin Ther*, 2001, 23(8):1231-44.

Thompson MIB, Russo ME, Saxon BJ, et al, "Gentamicin Inactivation by Piperacillin or Carbenicillin in Patients With End-Stage Renal Disease," *Antimicrob Agents Chemother*, 1982, 21(2):268-73.

Tunkel AR, Hartman BJ, Kaplan SL, et al, "Practice Guidelines for the Management of Bacterial Meningitis," *Clin Infect Dis*, 2004, 39(9):1267-84.

Viollier AF, Standiford HC, Drusano GL, et al, "Comparative Pharmacokinetics and Serum Bactericidal Activity of Mezlocillin, Ticarcillin and Piperacillin, With and Without Gentamicin," *J Antimicrob Chemother*, 1985, 15(5):597-606.

Walterspiel JN, Feldman S, Van R, et al, "Comparative Inactivation of Isepamicin, Amikacin, and Gentamicin by Nine Beta-Lactams and Two Beta-Lactamase Inhibitors, Cilastatin and Heparin," *Antimicrob Agents Chemother*, 1991, 35(9):1875-8.

Wilson W, Taubert KA, Gewitz M, et al, "Prevention of Infective Endocarditis. Guidelines From the American Heart Association. A Guideline From the American Heart Association Rheumatic Fever, Endocarditis, and Kawasaki Disease Committee, Council on Cardiovascular Disease in the Young, and the Council on Clinical Cardiology, Council on Cardiovascular Surgery and Anesthesia, and the Quality of Care and Outcomes Research Interdisciplinary Working Group," *Circulation*, 2007, 115. Available at http://circ.ahajournals.org/cgi/reprint/CIRCULATIONAHA.106.183095v1; last accessed July 26, 2007.

Zaske DE, Irvine P, Strand LM, et al, "Wide Interpatient Variations in Gentamicin Dose Requirements for Geriatric Patients," *JAMA*, 1982, 248(23):3122-6.

♦ **Tobramycin Injection, USP (Can)** *see* Tobramycin *on page 1041*

♦ **Tobramycin Sulfate** *see* Tobramycin *on page 1041*

♦ **Tobrex®** *see* Tobramycin *on page 1041*

♦ **Tomudex® (Can)** *see* Raltitrexed *on page 943*

♦ **Toposar®** *see* Etoposide *on page 402*

Topotecan *(toe poe TEE kan)*

Medication Safety Issues

Sound-alike/look-alike issues:

Hycamtin® may be confused with Hycomine®, Mycamine®

High alert medication: The Institute for Safe Medication Practices (ISMP) includes this medication among its list of drugs which have a heightened risk of causing significant patient harm when used in error.

Related Information

Management of Drug Extravasations *on page 1301*
Management of Nausea and Vomiting *on page 1319*
Safe Handling of Hazardous Drugs *on page 1382*

U.S. Brand Names Hycamtin®

Index Terms Hycamptamine; NSC-609699; SKF 104864; SKF 104864-A; Topotecan Hydrochloride

Generic Available No

Canadian Brand Names Hycamtin®

Pharmacologic Category Antineoplastic Agent, Camptothecin; Antineoplastic Agent, Natural Source (Plant) Derivative

Use Treatment of nonsmall cell lung cancer, myelodysplastic syndrome, sarcoma (pediatrics), neuroblastoma (pediatrics), refractory solid tumors (pediatrics)

Unlabeled/Investigational Use Investigational: Treatment of nonsmall cell lung cancer, sarcoma (pediatrics)

Pregnancy Risk Factor D

Lactation Excretion in breast milk unknown/contraindicated

Labeled Contraindications Hypersensitivity to topotecan or any component of the formulation; severe bone marrow depression; pregnancy; breast-feeding

Warnings/Precautions Hazardous agent - use appropriate precautions for handling and disposal. The dose-limiting toxicity is bone marrow suppression (primarily neutropenia; may also cause thrombocytopenia and anemia); monitor bone marrow function. Neutropenia is not cumulative overtime. **[U.S. Boxed Warning]: Should only administer to patients with adequate bone marrow reserves, baseline neutrophils at least 1500 cells/mm³** and platelet counts at least 100,000/mm³. In a clinical study comparing I.V. to oral topotecan, G-CSF support was administered in a higher percentage of patients receiving oral topotecan. Topotecan-induced neutropenia may lead to neutropenic colitis; should be considered in patients presenting with neutropenia, fever and abdominal pain. Diarrhea has been reported with oral topotecan; may be severe; incidence may be higher in the elderly; educate patients on proper management. Use caution in renal impairment; may require dose adjustment. Safety and efficacy in children have not been established.

Adverse Reactions

>10%:

Central nervous system: Fatigue (11% to 29%), fever (5% to 28%), pain (23%), headache (18%)

Dermatologic: Alopecia (10% to 49%), rash (16%)

Gastrointestinal: Nausea (27% to 64%), vomiting (19% to 45%), diarrhea (14% to 32%; Oral: grade 3: 4%; grade 4: ≤1%; onset: 9 days), constipation (29%), abdominal pain (22%), anorexia (7% to 19%), stomatitis (18%)

Hematologic: Neutropenia (83% to 97%; grade 4: 32% to 80%; nadir 8-11 days; duration: 7 days; recovery <21 days), leukopenia (86% to 97%; grade 4: 15% to 32%), anemia (89% to 98%; grade 4: 7% to 10%), thrombocytopenia (69% to 81%; grade 4: 6% to 29%; duration: 3 days), neutropenic fever/sepsis (2% to 28%)

Neuromuscular & skeletal: Weakness (3% to 25%)

Respiratory: Dyspnea (22%), cough (15%)

1% to 10%:

Hepatic: Transient increases in liver enzymes (8%)

Neuromuscular & skeletal: Paresthesia (7%)

Miscellaneous: Sepsis (grades 3/4: 5%)

<1%, postmarketing, and/or case reports: Abdominal pain, allergic reactions, anaphylactoid reactions, angioedema, bleeding (severe, associated with thrombocytopenia), dermatitis (severe), injection site reactions (mild erythema, bruising), neutropenic colitis, pancytopenia, pruritus (severe)

Overdosage/Toxicology Anticipated effects of overdose include bone marrow suppression. Treatment is symptom-directed and supportive.

Drug Interactions

Increased Effect/Toxicity: BCRP (ABCG2) inhibitors (dipyridamole, gefitinib, imatinib, pantoprazole) may increase the levels/effects of oral topotecan. Filgrastim may cause prolonged and severe neutropenia and thrombocytopenia if administered concurrently with topotecan; initiate filgrastim at least 24 hours after topotecan. P-glycoprotein (ABCB1) inhibitors may increase the levels/effects of oral topotecan (example inhibitors include amiodarone, atorvastatin, clarithromycin, cyclosporine, erythromycin, itraconazole, ketoconazole, ritonavir, saquinavir and verapamil); avoid concurrent use. Platinum derivatives (carboplatin, cisplatin, oxaliplatin) may enhance the adverse/toxic effects of topotecan; monitor (Continued)

Topotecan *(Continued)*

for hematologic toxicity, especially if the platinum derivative is administered prior to topotecan.

Ethanol/Nutrition/Herb Interactions Ethanol: Avoid ethanol (due to GI irritation).

Storage/Stability

I.V.: Store intact vials of lyophilized powder for injection at room temperature of 20°C to 25°C (68°F to 77°F); protect from light. Reconstituted solution is stable for up to 28 days at room temperature of 20°C to 25°C (68°F to 77°F). When further diluted in 50-100 mL D_5W or NS, solution is stable for 24 hours at room temperature or up to 7 days under refrigeration.

Oral: Store at 15°C to 30°C (59°F to 86°F). Protect from light

Reconstitution Reconstitute vials with 4 mL SWFI. May be further diluted in 50-100 mL D_5W or NS for infusion.

Compatibility Stable in D_5W, NS.

Y-site administration: Compatible: Carboplatin, cimetidine, cisplatin, cyclophosphamide, doxorubicin, etoposide, gemcitabine, granisetron, ifosfamide, methylprednisolone sodium succinate, metoclopramide, ondansetron, paclitaxel, prochlorperazine edisylate, vincristine. **Incompatible:** Dexamethasone sodium phosphate, fluorouracil, mitomycin. **Variable (consult detailed reference):** Ticarcillin/clavulanate.

Mechanism of Action Binds to topoisomerase I and stabilizes the cleavable complex so that religation of the cleaved DNA strand cannot occur. This results in the accumulation of cleavable complexes and single-strand DNA breaks. Topotecan acts in S phase of the cell cycle.

Pharmacodynamics/Kinetics

Absorption: Oral: Rapid

Distribution: V_{dss} of the lactone is high (mean: 87.3 L/mm²; range: 25.6-186 L/mm²), suggesting wide distribution and/or tissue sequestering

Protein binding: ~35%

Metabolism: Undergoes a rapid, pH-dependent hydrolysis of the lactone ring to yield a relatively inactive hydroxy acid in plasma; metabolized in the liver to N-demethylated metabolite

Bioavailability: Oral: ~40%

Half-life elimination: I.V.: 2-3 hours; renal impairment: 5 hours; Oral: 3-6 hours

Time to peak, plasma: Oral 1-2 hours; delayed with high-fat meal (1.5-4 hours)

Excretion:

I.V.: Urine (51%; 3% as N-desmethyl topotecan); feces (18%; 2% as N-desmethyl topotecan)

Oral: Urine (20%; 2% as N-desmethyl topotecan); feces (33%; <2% as N-desmethyl topotecan)

Dosage Adults (refer to individual protocols): **Note:** Baseline neutrophil count should be >1500/mm³; retreatment neutrophil count should be >1000/mm³; baseline and retreatment platelet count should be >100,000/mm³; (also, for oral topotecan, retreatment hemoglobin should be ≥9 g/dL):

Small cell lung cancer:

IVPB: 1.5 mg/m²/day for 5 days; repeated every 21 days

Oral: 2.3 mg/m²/day for 5 days; repeated every 21 days (round dose to the nearest 0.25 mg); if patient vomits after dose is administered, do not give a replacement dose.

Metastatic ovarian cancer:

IVPB: 1.5 mg/m²/day for 5 days; repeated every 21 days

I.V. continuous infusion (unlabeled dose) 0.2-0.7 mg/m²/day for 7-21 days

Cervical cancer: IVPB: 0.75 mg/m²/day for 3 days (followed by cisplatin 50 mg/m² on day 1 only, [with hydration]); repeated every 21 days

Dosage adjustment for toxicity:

I.V.:

Ovarian and small cell lung cancer: Dosage adjustment for hematological effects: Severe neutropenia or platelet count <25,000/mm³: Reduce dose to 1.25 mg/m²/day for subsequent cycles (may consider G-CSF support [beginning on day 6] prior to instituting dose reduction for neutropenia)

Cervical cancer: Severe febrile neutropenia (ANC <1000/mm³ with temperature of 38°C) or platelet count <10,000/mm³: Reduce topotecan to 0.6 mg/m²/day for subsequent cycles (may consider C-CSF support [beginning on day 4] prior to instituting dose reduction for neutropenic fever. For neutropenic fever despite G-CSF use, reduce dose to 0.45 mg/m²/day for subsequent cycles). **Note:** Cisplatin may also require dose adjustment.

Oral:

Small cell lung cancer: Severe neutropenia (neutrophils <500/mm³ associated with fever or infection or lasting >7 days) or prolonged neutropenia (neutrophils ≥500/mm³ to ≤1000/mm³ lasting beyond day 21) or platelets <25,000/mm³ or grades 3/4 diarrhea: Reduce dose to 1.9 mg/m²/day for subsequent cycles (may consider same dosage reduction for grade 2 diarrhea if clinically indicated).

Dosing adjustment in renal impairment:

The FDA-approved labeling recommends the following dosage adjustment:

I.V.:

Cl_{cr} 20-39 mL/minute: Reduce to 0.75 mg/m²/dose

Cl_{cr} <20 mL/minute: Insufficient data available for dosing recommendation

Note: For topotecan in combination with cisplatin for cervical cancer, do not initiate treatment in patients with serum creatinine >1.5 mg/dL; consider discontinuing treatment in patients with serum creatinine >1.5 mg/dL in subsequent cycles.

Oral:

Cl_{cr} 30-49 mL/minute: Reduce dose to 1.8 mg/m²/day

Cl_{cr} <30 mL/minute: Insufficient data available for dosing recommendation

The following guidelines have been used by some clinicians:

Aronoff, 2007: *I.V.:*

Children:

Cl_{cr} 30-50 mL/minute: Administer 75% of dose

Cl_{cr} 10-29 mL/minute: Administer 50% of dose or reduce by 0.75 mg/m²/dose

Cl_{cr} <10 mL/minute: Administer 25% of dose

Hemodialysis: 0.75 mg/m²

Continuous renal replacement therapy (CRRT): Administer 50% of dose or reduce by 0.75 mg/m²/dose

Adults:

Cl_{cr} >50 mL/minute: Administer 75% of dose

Cl_{cr} 10-50 mL/minute: Administer 50% of dose

Cl_{cr} <10 mL/minute: Administer 25% of dose

Hemodialysis: Avoid use

Continuous ambulatory peritoneal dialysis (CAPD): Avoid use

Continuous renal replacement therapy (CRRT): 0.75 mg/m²

(Continued)

Topotecan *(Continued)*

Kintzel, 1995:

Cl_{cr} 46-60 mL/minute: Administer 80% of dose
Cl_{cr} 31-45 mL/minute: Administer 75% of dose
Cl_{cr} <30 mL/minute: Administer 70% of dose

Dosing adjustment in hepatic impairment: The FDA-approved labeling recommends the following:

I.V.: Bilirubin 1.5-10 mg/dL: No adjustment necessary
Oral: Bilirubin >1.5 mg/dL: No adjustment necessary

Combination Regimens

Cervical cancer: Topotecan-Cisplatin *on page 1282*
Leukemia, acute lymphocytic: TVTG *on page 1285*
Leukemia, acute myeloid: TVTG *on page 1285*
Lung cancer, nonsmall cell: Topotecan (Oral) *on page 1282*
Lung cancer, small cell:

Topotecan (Oral) *on page 1282*
Topotecan (Oral)-Cisplatin *on page 1282*
Topotecan (Weekly) *on page 1283*

Ovarian cancer:

Topotecan (Oral) *on page 1282*
Topotecan (Weekly) *on page 1283*

Administration

I.V.: Administer IVPB over 30 minutes or by 24-hour continuous infusion. For combination chemotherapy with cisplatin, administer pretreatment hydration.

Oral: Administer with or without food. Swallow whole; do not crush, chew, or divide capsule. If vomiting occurs after dose, do not take replacement dose.

Monitoring Parameters CBC with differential and platelet count, renal function tests, bilirubin

Test Interactions None known

Dietary Considerations May be taken with or without food.

Patient Information This medication can only be administered I.V. and frequent blood tests may be necessary to monitor effects of the drug. Report pain, swelling, or irritation at infusion site. Do not use alcohol, prescription, and/or OTC medications without consulting prescriber. Maintain adequate hydration (2-3 L/day of fluids unless instructed to restrict fluid intake); maintain good oral hygiene (use a soft toothbrush or cotton applicators several times a day and rinse mouth frequently). You may experience nausea, vomiting, or loss of appetite (frequent small meals, frequent mouth care, sucking lozenges, or chewing gum may help, or consult prescriber). Hair loss may occur (reversible). You will be susceptible to infection; avoid crowds and infected persons and do not receive any vaccinations unless approved by prescriber. Report persistent fever or chills, unhealed sores, oral or vaginal sores, foul-smelling urine, painful urination, easy bruising or bleeding, yellowing of eyes or skin, and change in color of urine or stool. The drug may cause permanent sterility and may cause birth defects. Contraceptive measures should be used during therapy. The drug may be excreted in breast milk, therefore, an alternative form of feeding your baby should be used.

Emetic Potential Low (10% to 30%)

Vesicant I.V.: No; inadvertent extravasation may result in mild erythema and bruising

Dosage Forms Excipient information presented when available (limited, particularly for generics); consult specific product labeling.
Capsule, as hydrochloride:
Hycamtin®: 0.25 mg, 1 mg
Injection, powder for reconstitution, as hydrochloride:
Hycamtin®: 4 mg [base]

References

Aronoff GR, Bennett WM, Berns JS, et al, *Drug Prescribing in Renal Failure: Dosing Guidelines for Adults and Children*, 5th ed. Philadelphia, PA: American College of Physicians; 2007, p 102, 174.

Arun B and Frenkel EP, "Topoisomerase I Inhibition With Topotecan: Pharmacologic and Clinical Issues," *Expert Opin Pharmacother*, 2001, 2(3):491-505.

Cersosimo RJ, "Topotecan: A New Topoisomerase I Inhibiting Antineoplastic Agent," *Ann Pharmacother*, 1998, 32(12):1334-43.

Craig SB, Bhatt UH, and Patel K, "Stability and Compatibility of Topotecan Hydrochloride for Injection With Common Infusion Solutions and Containers," *J Pharm Biomed Anal*, 1997, 16(2):199-205.

Dennis MJ, Beijnen JH, Grochow LB, et al, "An Overview of the Clinical Pharmacology of Topotecan," *Semin Oncol*, 1997, 24(1 Suppl 5):5-12, 5-18.

Eckardt JR, von Pawel J, Pujol JL, et al, "Phase III Study of Oral Compared With Intravenous Topotecan as Second-Line Therapy in Small-Cell Lung Cancer," *J Clin Oncol*, 2007, 25(15):2086-92.

Herben VM, ten Bokkel Huinink WW, and Beijnen JH, "Clinical Pharmacokinetics of Topotecan," *Clin Pharmacokinet*, 1996, 31(2):85-102.

Kintzel PE and Dorr RT, "Anticancer Drug Renal Toxicity and Elimination: Dosing Guidelines for Altered Renal Function," *Cancer Treat Rev*, 1995, 21(1):33-64.

Kollmannsberger C, Mross K, Jakob A, et al, "Topotecan - A Novel Topoisomerase I Inhibitor: Pharmacology and Clinical Experience," *Oncology*, 1999, 56(1):1-12.

Kruijtzer CMF, Beijnen JH, Rosing H, et al, "Increased Oral Bioavailability of Topotecan in Combination With the Breast Cancer Resistance Protein and P-Glycoprotein Inhibitor GF120918," *J Clin Oncol*, 2002, 20(13):2943-50.

Long HJ 3rd, Bundy BN, Grendys EC Jr, et al, "Randomized Phase III Trial of Cisplatin With or Without Topotecan in Carcinoma of the Uterine Cervix: a Gynecologic Oncology Group Study," *J Clin Oncol*, 2005, 23(21):4626-33.

Mathijssen RH, Loos WJ, Verweij J, et al, "Pharmacology of Topoisomerase I Inhibitors Irinotecan (CPT-11) and Topotecan," *Curr Cancer Drug Targets*, 2002, 2(2):103-23.

O'Brien ME, Ciuleanu TE, Tsekov H, et al, "Phase III Trial Comparing Supportive Care Alone With Supportive Care With Oral Topotecan in Patients With Relapsed Small-Cell Lung Cancer," *J Clin Oncol*, 2006, 24(34):5441-7.

O'Reilly S, Rowinsky EK, Slichenmyer W, et al, "Phase I and Pharmacologic Study of Topotecan in Patients With Impaired Hepatic Function," *J Natl Cancer Inst*, 1996, 88(12):817-24.

O'Reilly S, Rowinsky EK, Slichenmyer W, et al, "Phase I and Pharmacologic Study of Topotecan in Patients With Impaired Renal Function," *J Clin Oncol*, 1996, 14(12):3062-73.

Patel K, Craig SB, McBride MG, et al, "Microbial Inhibitory Properties and Stability of Topotecan Hydrochloride Injection," *Am J Health Syst Pharm*, 1998, 55(15):1584-7.

♦ **Topotecan Hydrochloride** see Topotecan *on page 1048*

Toremifene (tore EM i feen)

Related Information
Safe Handling of Hazardous Drugs *on page 1382*

U.S. Brand Names Fareston®

Index Terms FC1157a; Toremifene Citrate

Generic Available No

Canadian Brand Names Fareston®

Pharmacologic Category Antineoplastic Agent, Estrogen Receptor Antagonist; Selective Estrogen Receptor Modulator (SERM)

Use Treatment of advanced breast cancer; management of desmoid tumors and endometrial carcinoma

Pregnancy Risk Factor D

Lactation Excretion in breast milk unknown/contraindicated

Labeled Contraindications Hypersensitivity to toremifene or any component of the formulation; pregnancy

(Continued)

Toremifene *(Continued)*

Warnings/Precautions Hazardous agent - use appropriate precautions for handling and disposal. Hypercalcemia and tumor flare have been reported in some breast cancer patients with bone metastases during the first weeks of treatment. Tumor flare is a syndrome of diffuse musculoskeletal pain and erythema with increased size of tumor lesions that later regress. It is often accompanied by hypercalcemia. Tumor flare does not imply treatment failure or represent tumor progression. Institute appropriate measures if hypercalcemia occurs, and if severe, discontinue treatment. Drugs that decrease renal calcium excretion (eg, thiazide diuretics) may increase the risk of hypercalcemia in patients receiving toremifene. Leukopenia and thrombocytopenia have been reported rarely. Use cautiously in patients with anemia, hepatic failure, or thromboembolic disease.

Adverse Reactions

>10%:

Endocrine & metabolic: Vaginal discharge, hot flashes

Gastrointestinal: Nausea, vomiting

Miscellaneous: Diaphoresis

1% to 10%:

Cardiovascular: Thromboembolism: Toremifene has been associated with the occurrence of venous thrombosis and pulmonary embolism; arterial thrombosis has also been described in a few case reports; cardiac failure, MI, edema

Central nervous system: Dizziness

Endocrine & metabolic: Hypercalcemia may occur in patients with bone metastases; galactorrhea and vitamin deficiency, menstrual irregularities

Genitourinary: Vaginal bleeding or discharge, endometriosis, priapism, possible endometrial cancer

Ocular: Ophthalmologic effects (visual acuity changes, cataracts, or retinopathy), corneal opacities, dry eyes

Overdosage/Toxicology Theoretically, overdose may manifest as an increase of antiestrogenic effects such as hot flashes; estrogenic effects such as vaginal bleeding; or nervous system disorders such as vertigo, dizziness, ataxia, and nausea. No specific antidote exists and treatment is symptomatic.

Drug Interactions

Cytochrome P450 Effect: Substrate of CYP1A2 (minor), 3A4 (major)

Increased Effect/Toxicity: Concurrent therapy with warfarin results in significant enhancement of anticoagulant effects; has been speculated that a decrease in antitumor effect of tamoxifen may also occur due to alterations in the percentage of active tamoxifen metabolites.

Decreased Effect: CYP3A4 inducers may decrease the levels/effects of toremifene; example inducers include aminoglutethimide, carbamazepine, nafcillin, nevirapine, phenobarbital, phenytoin, and rifamycins.

Storage/Stability Store at 25°C (77°F); excursions permitted to 15°C to 30°C (59°F to 86°F). Protect from heat and light.

Mechanism of Action Nonsteroidal, triphenylethylene derivative. Competitively binds to estrogen receptors on tumors and other tissue targets, producing a nuclear complex that decreases DNA synthesis and inhibits estrogen effects. Nonsteroidal agent with potent antiestrogenic properties which compete with estrogen for binding sites in breast and other tissues; cells accumulate in the G_0 and G_1 phases; therefore, toremifene is cytostatic rather than cytocidal.

Pharmacodynamics/Kinetics

Absorption: Well absorbed

Distribution: V_d: 580 L

Protein binding, plasma: >99.5%, primarily to albumin

Metabolism: Extensively hepatic, principally by CYP3A4 to N-demethyltoremifene, which is also antiestrogenic but with weak *in vivo* antitumor potency

Half-life elimination: ~5 days

Time to peak, serum: ~3 hours

Excretion: Primarily feces; urine (10%) during a 1-week period

Dosage Refer to individual protocols.

Adults: Oral: 60 mg once daily, generally continued until disease progression is observed

Dosage adjustment in renal impairment: No dosage adjustment necessary

Dosage adjustment in hepatic impairment: Toremifene is extensively metabolized in the liver and dosage adjustments may be indicated in patients with liver disease; however, no specific guidelines have been developed

Administration Orally, usually as a single daily dose; occasionally in 2 or 3 divided doses

Monitoring Parameters Obtain periodic complete blood counts, calcium levels, and liver function tests. Closely monitor patients with bone metastases for hypercalcemia during the first few weeks of treatment. Leukopenia and thrombocytopenia have been reported rarely; monitor leukocyte and platelet counts during treatment.

Patient Information Take as directed, without regard to food. You may experience an initial "flare" of this disease (increased bone pain and hot flashes) which will subside with continued use. You may experience nausea, vomiting, or loss of appetite (frequent mouth care, frequent small meals, chewing gum, or sucking lozenges may help); dizziness (use caution when driving, climbing stairs, or engaging in tasks requiring alertness until response to drug is known); or loss of hair (reversible). Report vomiting that occurs immediately after taking medication; chest pain, palpitations or swollen extremities; vaginal bleeding, hot flashes, or excessive perspiration; chest pain, unusual coughing, or difficulty breathing; or any changes in vision or dry eyes.

Special Geriatric Considerations No specific information concerning elderly patients.

Additional Information Increase of bone pain usually indicates a good therapeutic response

Emetic Potential Moderate (30% to 40%)

Dosage Forms Excipient information presented when available (limited, particularly for generics); consult specific product labeling.

Tablet: 60 mg

References

Gams R, "Phase III Trials of Toremifene vs Tamoxifen," *Oncology*, 1997, 11(5 Suppl 4):23-8.

Hamm JT, "Phase I and II Studies of Toremifene," *Oncology*, 1997, 11(5 Suppl 4):19-22.

Holli K, "Evolving Role of Toremifene in the Adjuvant Setting," *Oncology*, 1997, 11(5 Suppl 4):48-51.

Kangas L, "Review of the Pharmacological Properties of Toremifene," *J Steroid Biochem*, 1990, 36(3):191-5.

Pyrhönen S, Valavaara R, Modig H, et al, "Comparison of Toremifene and Tamoxifen in Post-menopausal Patients With Advanced Breast Cancer: A Randomized Double-Blind, the "Nordic" Phase III Study," *Br J Cancer*, 1997, 76(2):270-7.

Taras TL, Wurz GT, Linares GR, et al, "Clinical Pharmacokinetics of Toremifene," *Clin Pharmacokinet*, 2000, 39(5):327-34.

Williams GM and Jeffrey AM, "Safety Assessment of Tamoxifen and Toremifene," *Oncology*, 1997, 11(5 Suppl 4):41-7.

- **Toremifene Citrate** *see* Toremifene *on page 1053*
- **Torisel™** *see* Temsirolimus *on page 1014*
- **Tositumomab I-131** *see* Tositumomab and Iodine I 131 Tositumomab *on page 1056*

Tositumomab and Iodine I 131 Tositumomab

(toe si TYOO mo mab & EYE oh dyne eye one THUR tee one toe si TYOO mo mab)

Medication Safety Issues

High alert medication: The Institute for Safe Medication Practices (ISMP) includes this medication among its list of drugs which have a heightened risk of causing significant patient harm when used in error.

Related Information

Safe Handling of Hazardous Drugs *on page 1382*

U.S. Brand Names Bexxar®

Index Terms Anti-CD20-Murine Monoclonal Antibody I-131; B1; B1 Antibody; 131 I Anti-B1 Antibody; 131 I-Anti-B1 Monoclonal Antibody; Iodine I 131 Tositumomab and Tositumomab; Tositumomab I-131

Generic Available No

Pharmacologic Category Antineoplastic Agent, Monoclonal Antibody; Radiopharmaceutical

Use Treatment of relapsed or refractory CD20 positive, low-grade, follicular, or transformed non-Hodgkin's lymphoma

Pregnancy Risk Factor X

Lactation Enters breast milk/contraindicated

Labeled Contraindications Hypersensitivity to murine proteins or any component of the formulation; pregnancy; breast-feeding

Warnings/Precautions Hazardous agent - use appropriate precautions for handling and disposal. **[U.S. Boxed Warning]: Hypersensitivity reactions (including anaphylaxis) have been reported.** Patients should be screened for human antimouse antibodies (HAMA); may be at increased risk of allergic or serious hypersensitivity reactions. Hematologic toxicity was reported to be the most common adverse effect with 27% patients requiring supportive care. **[U.S. Boxed Warning]: Severe or life-threatening cytopenias (NCI CTC grade 3 or 4) have been reported in a large number of patients; may be prolonged and severe.** Secondary malignancies have been reported following use.

[U.S. Boxed Warning]: Treatment involves radioactive isotopes; appropriate precautions in handling and administration must be followed. Patients must be instructed in measures to minimize exposure of others. **[U.S. Boxed Warning]: Women of childbearing potential should be advised of potential fetal risk;** effective contraceptive measures should be used for 12 months following treatment (males and females). Treatment may lead to hypothyroidism; patients should receive thyroid-blocking medications prior to the start of therapy. Patients should be premedicated to prevent infusion related reactions. For a single course of therapy only; multiple courses or use in combination with other chemotherapy or irradiation have not been studied.

Safety has not been established in patients with >25% lymphoma marrow involvement, platelet count <100,000 cells/mm³ or neutrophil count <1500 cells/mm³. Use caution with cardiovascular disease, renal, or hepatic impairment. Safety and efficacy have not been established with impaired renal function or in pediatric patients.

Adverse Reactions
>10%:

Central nervous system: Fever (37%), pain (19%), chills (18%), headache (16%)

Dermatologic: Rash (17%)

Endocrine & metabolic: Hypothyroidism (7% to 19%)

Gastrointestinal: Nausea (36%), abdominal pain (15%), vomiting (15%), anorexia (14%), diarrhea (12%)

Hematologic:

Neutropenia (grade 3 or 4, 63%); thrombocytopenia (grade 3 or 4, 53%)

Time to nadir: 4-7 weeks

Duration: 30 days (>90 days in 5% to 7% of patients)

Neuromuscular & skeletal: Weakness (46%), myalgia (13%)

Respiratory: Cough (21%), pharyngitis (12%), dyspnea (11%)

Miscellaneous: Infusion-related reactions (26%, occurred within 14 days of infusion, included bronchospasm, chills, dyspnea, fever, hypotension, nausea, rigors, diaphoresis), infection (21%), HAMA-positive seroconversion (11%; up to 21% at 1 year)

1% to 10%:

Cardiovascular: Hypotension (7% to 10%), peripheral edema (9%), chest pain (7%), vasodilation (5%)

Central nervous system: Dizziness (5%), somnolence (5%)

Dermatologic: Pruritus (10%)

Gastrointestinal: Constipation (6%), dyspepsia (6%), weight loss (6%)

Local: Injection site hypersensitivity

Neuromuscular & skeletal: Arthralgia (10%), back pain (8%), neck pain (6%)

Respiratory: Rhinitis (10%), pneumonia (6%), laryngismus

Miscellaneous: Diaphoresis (8%), hypersensitivity reaction (6%), secondary leukemia/myelodysplastic syndrome (3%; up to 6% at 5 years), anaphylactoid reaction, secondary malignancies, serum sickness

Overdosage/Toxicology Grade 4 hematologic toxicity lasting 18 days was reported in one patient accidentally receiving a total body dose of 88 cGy. Monitor for cytopenias and radiation-related toxicity.

Drug Interactions
Increased Effect/Toxicity: No formal drug interaction studies have been conducted.

Decreased Effect: No formal drug interaction studies have been conducted. The ability of patients receiving tositumomab to generate humoral response (primary or anamnestic) to vaccination is unknown; safety of live vaccines has not been established.

Storage/Stability
Tositumomab: Store under refrigeration at 2°C to 8°C (36°F to 46°F); do not freeze. Protect from strong light. Following dilution, tositumomab is stable for 24 hour when refrigerated or 8 hours at room temperature.

Iodine I 131 tositumomab: Store frozen at less than or equal to -20°C in the original lead pots. Allow 60 minutes for thawing at ambient temperature. Solutions for infusion are stable for up to 8 hours at 2°C to 8°C (36°F to 46°F) or room temperature.

Reconstitution
Tositumomab: Withdraw and discard 32 mL of saline from a 50 mL bag of NS. Add contents of both 225 mg vials of tositumomab (total 32 mL) to remaining NS to make a final volume of 50 mL. Gently mix by inverting bag; do not shake.

(Continued)

Tositumomab and Iodine I 131 Tositumomab
(Continued)

Iodine I 131 tositumomab: Calculate volume required for an iodine I 131 tositumomab activity of 5 mCi (specification sheet provided with product). If the amount of tositumomab contained in the iodine I 131 tositumomab solution contains <35 mg of tositumomab, use the 35 mg vial of tositumomab to prepare a final concentration of tositumomab 35 mg. Using NS, the final volume should equal 30 mL.

Mechanism of Action Tositumomab is a murine IgG2a lambda monoclonal antibody which binds to the CD20 antigen, expressed on B-lymphocytes and on >90% of B-cell non-Hodgkin's lymphomas. Iodine I 131 tositumomab is a radio-iodinated derivative of tositumomab covalently linked to iodine 131. The possible actions of the regimen include apoptosis, complement-dependent cytotoxicity, antibody-dependent cellular cytotoxicity, and cell death. Administration results in depletion of CD20 positive cells.

Pharmacodynamics/Kinetics

Distribution: Tositumomab: V_d increased with high tumor burden, splenomegaly, or bone marrow involvement

Half-life elimination: Tositumomab:

Elimination: 36-48 hours

Terminal half-life decreased with high tumor burden, splenomegaly, or bone marrow involvement

Clearance: Blood: 68.2 mg/hour

Excretion: Iodine-131: Urine (98%) and decay

Dosage I.V.: Adults: Dosing consists of four components administered in 2 steps. Thyroid protective agents (SSKI, Lugol's solution or potassium iodide), acetaminophen and diphenhydramine should be given prior to or with treatment. Refer to Additional Information.

Step 1: Dosimetric step (Day 0):

Tositumomab 450 mg in NS 50 mL administered over 60 minutes

Iodine I 131 tositumomab (containing I-131 5.0 mCi and tositumomab 35mg) in NS 30 mL administered over 20 minutes

Note: Whole body dosimetry and biodistribution should be determined on Day 0; days 2, 3, or 4; and day 6 or 7 prior to administration of Step 2. If biodistribution is not acceptable, do not administer the therapeutic step. On day 6 or 7, calculate the patient specific activity of iodine I 131 tositumomab to deliver 75 cGy TBD or 65 cGy TBD (in mCi).

Step 2: Therapeutic step (Day 7):

Tositumomab 450 mg in NS 50 mL administered over 60 minutes

Iodine I 131 tositumomab:

Platelets ≥150,000/mm^3: Iodine I 131 calculated to deliver 75 cGy total body irradiation and tositumomab 35 mg over 20 minutes

Platelets ≥100,000/mm^3 and <150,000/mm^3: Iodine I 131 calculated to deliver 65 cGy total body irradiation and tositumomab 35 mg over 20 minutes

Administration I.V.:

Tositumomab: Infuse over 60 minutes

Iodine I 131 tositumomab: Infuse over 20 minutes

Reduce the rate of tositumomab or iodine 131 tositumomab infusion by 50% for mild-to-moderate infusion-related toxicities; interrupt for severe toxicity. Once severe toxicity has resolved, infusion may be restarted at half the previous rate. Prior to infusion, patients should be premedicated and a thyroid-protective agent should be started.

Monitoring Parameters CBC with differential (prior to therapy and at least weekly for a minimum of 10 weeks); TSH (prior to therapy and yearly); serum creatinine (immediately prior to administration)

Following infusion of the iodine I 131 tositumomab dosimetric dose, the total body gamma camera counts and whole body images should be taken within 1 hour of the infusion and prior to urination, and 2-4 days after the infusion and following urination, and 6-7 days after the infusion and following urination.

Test Interactions May interfere with tests using murine antibody technology.

Patient Information This medication is given only by injection. Follow instructions to limit exposure of radioactivity to family and friends. Notify prescriber if pregnant or if pregnancy occurs within 12 months after completion of therapy; effective birth control should be used by male and female patients during treatment and for 12 months following therapy. Breast-feeding is not recommended; discontinue and change to formula feedings prior to therapy.

Additional Information Thyroid protective agent: One of the following agents should be used starting at least 24 hours prior to the dosimetric dose and continued for 2 weeks after the therapeutic dose. Therapy should not begin without using one of the following agents:

SSKI: 4 drops 3 times/day

Lugol's solution: 20 drops 3 times/day

Potassium iodide: 130 mg once daily

Dosage Forms Excipient information presented when available (limited, particularly for generics); consult specific product labeling.

Note: Not all components are shipped from the same facility. When ordering, ensure that all will arrive on the same day.

Kit [dosimetric package]: Tositumomab 225 mg/16.1 mL [2 vials], tositumomab 35 mg/2.5 mL [1 vial], and iodine I 131 tositumomab 0.1 mg/mL and 0.61mCi/mL (20 mL) [1 vial]

Kit [therapeutic package]: Tositumomab 225 mg/16.1 mL [2 vials], tositumomab 35 mg/2.5 mL [1 vial], and iodine I 131 tositumomab 1.1 mg/mL and 5.6 mCi/mL (20 mL) [1 or 2 vials]

References

Kaminski MS, Zelenetz AD, Press OW, et al, "Pivotal Study of Iodine I 131 Tositumomab for Chemotherapy-Refractory Low-Grade or Transformed Low-Grade B-Cell Non-Hodgkin's Lymphomas," *J Clin Oncol*, 2001, 19(19):3918-28.

Press OW, Eary JF, Appelbaum FR, et al, "Phase II Trial of 131I-B1 (Anti-CD20) Antibody Therapy With Autologous Stem Cell Transplantation for Relapsed B Cell Lymphomas," *Lancet*, 1995, 346(8971):336-40.

Press OW, Eary JF, Appelbaum FR, et al, "Radiolabeled-Antibody Therapy of B-Cell Lymphoma With Autologous Bone Marrow Support," *N Engl J Med*, 1993, 329(17):1219-24.

Zelenetz AD, "A Clinical and Scientific Overview of Tositumomab and Iodine I 131 Tositumomab," *Semin Oncol*, 2003, 30(2 Suppl 4):22-30.

♦ **Totect**™ *see* Dexrazoxane *on page 338*

♦ **tPA** *see* Alteplase *on page 45*

♦ **tRA** *see* Tretinoin (Oral) *on page 1069*

Tramadol (TRA ma dole)

Medication Safety Issues

Sound-alike/look-alike issues:

Tramadol may be confused with Toradol®, Trandate®, Voltaren®

Ultram® may be confused with Ultane®, Voltaren®

International issues:

Theradol® [Netherlands] may be confused with Foradil® which is a brand name for formoterol in the U.S.

(Continued)

Tramadol *(Continued)*

Theradol® [Netherlands] may be confused with Terazol® which is a brand name for terconazole in the U.S.

Theradol® [Netherlands] may be confused with Toradol® which is a brand name for ketorolac in the U.S.

U.S. Brand Names Ultram®; Ultram® ER

Index Terms Tramadol Hydrochloride

Generic Available Yes: Excludes extended release tablet

Canadian Brand Names Ralivia™ ER; Tridural™; Zytram® XL

Pharmacologic Category Analgesic, Nonopioid

Use Relief of moderate to moderately-severe pain

Pregnancy Risk Factor C

Lactation Enters breast milk/not recommended

Labeled Contraindications Hypersensitivity to tramadol, opioids, or any component of the formulation; opioid-dependent patients; acute intoxication with alcohol, hypnotics, centrally-acting analgesics, opioids, or psychotropic drugs

Note: Based on Canadian product labeling:

Tramadol is contraindicated during or within 14 days following MAO inhibitor therapy

Extended release formulations (Ralivia™ ER [CAN], Tridural™[CAN], and Zytram® XL [CAN]): Additional contraindications: Severe (Cl_{cr} <30 mL/minute) renal dysfunction, severe (Child-Pugh Class C) hepatic dysfunction

Warnings/Precautions Rare but serious anaphylactoid reactions (including fatalities) often following initial dosing have been reported. Pruritus, hives, bronchospasm, angioedema, toxic epidermal necrolysis (TEN) and Stevens-Johnson syndrome also have been reported with use. Previous anaphylactoid reactions to opioids may increase risks for similar reactions to tramadol. Caution patients to swallow tablets whole. Rapid release and absorption of tramadol from tablets that are broken, crushed, or chewed may lead to a potentially lethal overdose. May cause CNS depression, which may impair physical or mental abilities; patients must be cautioned about performing tasks which require mental alertness (eg, operating machinery or driving). May cause CNS depression and/or respiratory depression, particularly when combined with other CNS depressants. Use with caution and reduce dosage when administered to patients receiving other CNS depressants. An increased risk of seizures may occur in patients receiving serotonin reuptake inhibitors (SSRIs or anorectics), tricyclic antidepressants, other cyclic compounds (including cyclobenzaprine, promethazine), neuroleptics, or drugs which may lower seizure threshold. Should be used only with extreme caution in patients receiving MAO inhibitors (contraindicated in Canadian product labeling). Patients with a history of seizures, or with a risk of seizures (head trauma, metabolic disorders, CNS infection, or malignancy, or during ethanol/drug withdrawal) are also at increased risk.

Elderly (particularly >75 years of age), debilitated patients and patients with chronic respiratory disorders may be at greater risk of adverse events. Use with caution in patients with increased intracranial pressure or head injury. Avoid use in patients who are suicidal or addiction prone. Use caution in heavy alcohol users. Use caution in treatment of acute abdominal conditions; may mask pain. Use tramadol with caution and reduce dosage in patients with liver disease or renal dysfunction. Tolerance or drug dependence may result from extended use (withdrawal symptoms have been reported); abrupt discontinuation should be avoided. Tapering of dose at the time of discontinuation limits the risk of withdrawal symptoms. Safety and efficacy in pediatric patients have not been established.

Adverse Reactions

>10%:

Cardiovascular: Flushing (8% to 16%)

Central nervous system: Dizziness (16% to 33%), headache (12% to 32%), insomnia (7% to 11%), somnolence (7% to 25%)

Dermatologic: Pruritus (6% to 12%)

Gastrointestinal: Constipation (10% to 46%), nausea (15% to 40%), vomiting (5% to 17%), dyspepsia (1% to 13%)

Neuromuscular & skeletal: Weakness (4% to 12%)

1% to 10%:

Cardiovascular: Chest pain (1% to <5%), postural hypotension (2% to 5%), vasodilation (1% to <5%)

Central nervous system: Agitation, anxiety (1% to <5%), confusion (1% to <5%), coordination impaired (1% to <5%), depression (1% to <5%), euphoria (1% to <5%), hypoesthesia (1% to <5%), lethargy (1% to <5%), malaise, nervousness (1% to <5%), pain (1% to <5%), pyrexia (1% to <5%), restlessness (1% to <5%)

Dermatologic: Dermatitis (1% to <5%), rash (1% to <5%)

Endocrine & metabolic: Hot flashes (2% to 9%), menopausal symptoms (1% to <5%)

Gastrointestinal: Diarrhea (5% to 10%), xerostomia (5% to 10%), anorexia (1% to <6%), abdominal pain (1% to <5%), appetite decreased (1% to <5%), flatulence (1% to <5%), weight loss (1% to <5%)

Genitourinary: Urinary frequency (1% to <5%), urinary retention (1% to <5%), urinary tract infection (1% to <5%)

Neuromuscular & skeletal: Arthralgia (1% to <5%), back pain (1% to <5%), hypertonia (1% to <5%), rigors (1% to <5%), paresthesia (1% to <5%), tremor (1% to <5%), creatinine phosphokinase increased (1% to <5%)

Ocular: Blurred vision (1% to <5%), miosis (1% to <5%)

Respiratory: Bronchitis (1% to <5%), congestion (nasal/sinus) (1% to <5%), cough (1% to <5%), dyspnea (1% to <5%), nasopharyngitis (1% to <5%), rhinorrhea (1% to <5%), sinusitis (1% to <5%), sore throat (1% to <5%), upper respiratory infection (1% to <5%)

Miscellaneous: Diaphoresis (2% to 9%), flu-like syndrome (1% to < 5%)

<1%: Abnormal ECG, abnormal gait, allergic reaction, amnesia, anaphylactoid reactions, anaphylaxis, angioedema, appendicitis, bronchospasm, cataracts, cholecystitis, cholelithiasis, clamminess, cognitive dysfunction, concentration difficulty, creatinine increased, deafness, dysuria, edema, gastrointestinal bleeding, hallucination, hemoglobin decreased, hepatitis, hyperglycemia, hyper-/hypotension, joint stiffness, libido decreased, liver enzymes increased, liver failure, menstrual disorder, MI, migraine, muscle cramps, muscle spasms, myalgia, myocardial ischemia, night sweats, palpitation, pancreatitis, peripheral ischemia, proteinuria, pulmonary edema, pulmonary embolism, seizure, serotonin syndrome, speech disorder, Stevens-Johnson syndrome, stomatitis, suicidal tendency, syncope, taste perversion, tachycardia, tinnitus, toxic epidermal necrolysis, urticaria, vertigo, vesicles, yawning

A withdrawal syndrome may occur with abrupt discontinuation; includes anxiety, diarrhea, hallucinations (rare), nausea, pain, piloerection, rigors, sweating, and tremor. Uncommon discontinuation symptoms may include severe anxiety, panic attacks, or paresthesia.

Overdosage/Toxicology Symptoms of overdose include CNS and respiratory depression, lethargy, somnolence leading to stupor or coma, skeletal (Continued)

Tramadol *(Continued)*

muscle flaccidity, cold clammy skin, miosis, seizure, cardiac arrest, and death. Treatment is symptom-directed and supportive. Naloxone may reverse some overdose symptoms, but may increase the risk of seizures. Hemodialysis is not helpful in removal of tramadol.

Drug Interactions

Cytochrome P450 Effect: Substrate of CYP2D6 (major), 3A4 (minor)

Increased Effect/Toxicity: Tramadol may enhance the CNS depressant effect of ethanol and other CNS depressants. Cyclobenzaprine, MAO inhibitors, SSRIs, and tricyclic antidepressants may enhance the neuroexcitatory and/or seizure-potentiating effects of tramadol. Naloxone may increase the risk of seizures in tramadol overdose. Quinidine may increase tramadol serum concentrations. Naloxone may increase risk of seizures if administered in tramadol overdose. Serotonin modulators and sibutramine may enhance the serotonergic effects of tramadol.

Decreased Effect: Carbamazepine may decrease analgesic efficacy of tramadol (increased metabolism) and tramadol may increase the risk of seizures in patients on carbamazepine. CYP2D6 inhibitors may decrease the effects of tramadol; examples include chlorpromazine, delavirdine, fluoxetine, miconazole, paroxetine, pergolide, quinidine, quinine, ritonavir, and ropinirole. Quinidine may decrease M1 (active metabolite) serum concentrations.

Ethanol/Nutrition/Herb Interactions

Ethanol: Avoid ethanol (may increase CNS depression).

Food:

Immediate release: Does not affect the rate or extent of absorption.

Extended release: Reduced C_{max} and AUC and T_{max} occurred 3 hours earlier when taken with a high-fat meal.

Herb/Nutraceutical: Avoid valerian, St John's wort, kava kava, gotu kola (may increase CNS depression).

Storage/Stability Store at 15°C to 30°C (59°F to 86°F).

Mechanism of Action Tramadol and active metabolite (M1) binds to μ-opiate receptors in the CNS causing inhibition of ascending pain pathways, altering the perception of and response to pain; also inhibits the reuptake of norepinephrine and serotonin, which also modifies the ascending pain pathway

Pharmacodynamics/Kinetics

Onset of action: Immediate release: ~1 hour

Duration of action: 9 hours

Absorption: Immediate release formulation: Rapid and complete; Extended release formulation: Delayed

Distribution: V_d: 2.5-3 L/kg

Protein binding, plasma: 20%

Metabolism: Extensively hepatic via demethylation, glucuronidation, and sulfation; has pharmacologically active metabolite formed by CYP2D6 (M1; O-desmethyl tramadol)

Bioavailability: Immediate release: 75%; Extended release: 85% to 90% as compared to immediate release; Zytram® XL, Tridural™: 70%

Half-life elimination: Tramadol: ~6-8 hours; Active metabolite: 7-9 hours; prolonged in elderly, hepatic or renal impairment; Zytram® XL: ~16 hours; Ralivia™ ER, Tridural™: ~5-9 hours

Time to peak: Immediate release: ~2 hours; Extended release: ~12 hours, Tridural™: ~4 hours

Excretion: Urine (30% as unchanged drug; 60% as metabolites)

Dosage Moderate-to-severe chronic pain: Oral:

Adults:

Immediate release formulation: 50-100 mg every 4-6 hours (not to exceed 400 mg/day)

For patients not requiring rapid onset of effect, tolerability may be improved by starting dose at 25 mg/day and titrating dose by 25 mg every 3 days, until reaching 25 mg 4 times/day. The total daily dose may then be increased by 50 mg every 3 days as tolerated, to reach dose of 50 mg 4 times/day. After titration, 50-100 mg may be given every 4-6 hours as needed up to a maximum 400 mg/day.

Extended release formulations:

Ultram® ER: 100 mg once daily; titrate every 5 days (maximum: 300 mg/day)

Ralivia™ ER (Canadian labeling, not available in U.S.): 100 mg once daily; titrate every 5 days as needed based on clinical response and severity of pain (maximum: 300 mg/day)

Tridural™ (Canadian labeling, not available in U.S.): 100 mg once daily; titrate by 100 mg/day every 2 days as needed based on clinical response and severity of pain (maximum: 300 mg/day)

Zytram® XL (Canadian labeling, not available in U.S.): 150 mg once daily; if pain relief is not achieved may titrate by increasing dosage incrementally, with sufficient time to evaluate effect of increased dosage; generally not more often than every 7 days (maximum: 400 mg/day)

Elderly >75 years:

Immediate release: 50 mg every 6 hours (not to exceed 300 mg/day); see dosing adjustments for renal and hepatic impairment.

Extended release formulation: Use with great caution. See adult dosing.

Dosing adjustment in renal impairment:

Immediate release: Cl_{cr} <30 mL/minute: Administer 50-100 mg dose every 12 hours (maximum: 200 mg/day)

Extended release: Should not be used in patients with Cl_{cr} <30 mL/minute

Dosing adjustment in hepatic impairment:

Immediate release: Cirrhosis: Recommended dose: 50 mg every 12 hours

Extended release: Should not be used in patients with severe (Child-Pugh Class C) hepatic dysfunction

Administration Do not crush or chew extended release tablet.

Monitoring Parameters Pain relief, respiratory rate, blood pressure, and pulse; signs of tolerance or abuse

Dietary Considerations May be taken with or without food. Extended release formulation: Be consistent; always give with food or always give on an empty stomach.

Patient Information Avoid driving or operating machinery until the effect of drug wears off. Report cravings to your prescriber immediately.

Special Geriatric Considerations One study in the elderly found that tramadol 50 mg was similar in efficacy as acetaminophen 300 mg with codeine 30 mg. In Ultram® ER trials, elderly patients experienced more adverse effects than younger adults, particularly constipation, fatigue, weakness, postural hypotension, and dyspepsia. For this reason, the extended release formulation should probably be avoided in the elderly, or only used with great caution.

Dosage Forms Excipient information presented when available (limited, particularly for generics); consult specific product labeling. [CAN] = Canadian brand name

Tablet, as hydrochloride: 50 mg

Ultram®: 50 mg

(Continued)

Tramadol *(Continued)*

Tablet, extended release, as hydrochloride:
Ultram® ER: 100 mg, 200 mg, 300 mg
Ralivia™ ER [CAN]: 100 mg, 200 mg, 300 mg [not available in the U.S.]
Tridural™ [CAN]: 100 mg, 200 mg, 300 mg [not available in the U.S.]
Zytram® XL [CAN]: 150 mg, 200 mg, 300 mg, 400 mg [not available in the U.S.]

References

Collins M, Young I, Sweeney P, et al, "The Effect of Tramadol on Dento-Alveolar Surgical Pain," *Br J Oral Maxillofac Surg*, 1997, 35(1):54-8.

Dayer P, Collart L, and Desmeules J, "The Pharmacology of Tramadol," *Drugs*, 1994, 47(Suppl 1):3-7.

"Drugs for Pain," *Treat Guidel Med Lett*, 2004, 2(23):47-54.

Kahn LH, Alderfer RJ, and Graham DJ, "Seizures Reported With Tramadol," *JAMA*, 1997, 278(20):1661.

Lewis KS and Han NH, "Tramadol: A New Centrally Acting Analgesic," *Am J Health Syst Pharm*, 1997, 54(6):643-52.

Mehlisch DR, Minn F, and Brown P, "Tramadol Hydrochloride: Efficacy Compared to Codeine Sulfate, Acetaminophen With Dextropropoxyphene and Placebo in Dental Extraction Pain," *Clin Pharmacol Ther*, 1992.

Mokhlesi B, Leikin JB, Murray P, et al, "Adult Toxicology in Critical Care: Part II: Specific Poisonings," *Chest*, 2003, 123(3):897-922.

Olson NZ, Sunshine A, O'Neill, et al, *Tramadol Hydrochloride: Oral Efficacy in Postoperative Pain*, American Pain Society 9th Annual Scientific Meeting, St Louis, MO, October, 1990.

Rauck RL, Ruoff GE, and McGillen, "Comparison of Tramadol and Acetaminophen With Codeine for Long-Term Pain Management in Elderly Patients," *Curr Ther Res*, 1994, 556:1417-31.

Riedel F and von Stockhausen HB, "Severe Cerebral Depression After Intoxication With Tramadol in a 6-Month-Old Infant," *Eur J Clin Pharmacol*, 1984, 26(5):631-2.

Ruoff GE, "Slowing the Initial Titration Rate of Tramadol Improves Tolerability," *Pharmacotherapy*, 1999, 19(1):88-93.

Sunshine A, Olson NZ, Zighelboim I, et al, "Analgesic Oral Efficacy of Tramadol Hydrochloride in Postoperative Pain," *Clin Pharmacol Ther*, 1992; 51(6):740-6.

Sunshine A, "New Clinical Experience With Tramadol," *Drugs*, 1994, 47(Suppl 1):8-18.

Voorhees F, Leibold DG, Stumpf, et al, "Tramadol Hydrochloride: Efficacy Compared to Codeine Sulfate, Aspirin With Codeine Phosphate, and Placebo in Dental Extraction Pain," *Clin Pharmacol Ther*, 1992, 51:122.

Wynn RL, "Tramadol (Ultram) - A New Kind of Analgesic," *Gen Dent*, 1996, 44(3):216-8,220.

♦ **Tramadol Hydrochloride** *see* Tramadol *on page 1059*

Tranexamic Acid *(tran eks AM ik AS id)*

Medication Safety Issues

Sound-alike/look-alike issues:
Cyklokapron® may be confused with cycloSPORINE

U.S. Brand Names Cyklokapron®

Generic Available No

Canadian Brand Names Cyklokapron®; Tranexamic Acid Injection BP

Pharmacologic Category Antihemophilic Agent

Use Short-term use (2-8 days) in hemophilia patients during and following tooth extraction to reduce or prevent hemorrhage

Unlabeled/Investigational Use Has been used as an alternative to aminocaproic acid for subarachnoid hemorrhage

Pregnancy Risk Factor B

Lactation Enters breast milk/use caution

Labeled Contraindications Acquired defective color vision; active intravascular clotting; subarachnoid hemorrhage; concurrent factor IX complex or anti-inhibitor coagulant concentrates

Warnings/Precautions Dosage modification required in patients with renal impairment; ophthalmic exam before and during therapy required if patient is treated beyond several days; caution in patients with cardiovascular, renal, or cerebrovascular disease; caution in patients with a history of thromboembolic disease (may increase risk of thrombosis); when used for subarachnoid hemorrhage, ischemic complications may occur

Adverse Reactions

>10%: Gastrointestinal: Nausea, diarrhea, vomiting

1% to 10%:

Cardiovascular: Hypotension, thrombosis

Ocular: Blurred vision

<1%: Unusual menstrual discomfort

Postmarketing and/or case reports: Deep venous thrombosis (DVT), pulmonary embolus (PE), renal cortical necrosis, retinal artery obstruction, retinal vein obstruction, ureteral obstruction

Drug Interactions

Increased Effect/Toxicity: Chlorpromazine may increase cerebral vasospasm and ischemia. Coadministrations of Factor IX complex or anti-inhibitor coagulant concentrates may increase risk of thrombosis.

Compatibility Stable in dextrose, saline, electrolyte solutions; **incompatible** with solutions containing penicillin.

Mechanism of Action Forms a reversible complex that displaces plasminogen from fibrin resulting in inhibition of fibrinolysis; it also inhibits the proteolytic activity of plasmin

Pharmacodynamics/Kinetics

Half-life elimination: 2-10 hours

Excretion: Urine (>90% as unchanged drug)

Dosage Children and Adults: I.V.: 10 mg/kg immediately before surgery, then 25 mg/kg/dose orally 3-4 times/day for 2-8 days

Alternatively:

Oral: 25 mg/kg 3-4 times/day beginning 1 day prior to surgery

I.V.: 10 mg/kg 3-4 times/day in patients who are unable to take oral

Dosing adjustment/interval in renal impairment:

Cl_{cr} 50-80 mL/minute: Administer 50% of normal dose or 10 mg/kg twice daily I.V. or 15 mg/kg twice daily orally

Cl_{cr} 10-50 mL/minute: Administer 25% of normal dose or 10 mg/kg/day I.V. or 15 mg/kg/day orally

Cl_{cr} <10 mL/minute: Administer 10% of normal dose or 10 mg/kg/dose every 48 hours I.V. or 15 mg/kg/dose every 48 hours orally

Administration May be administered by direct I.V. injection at a maximum rate of 100 mg/minute; compatible with dextrose, saline, and electrolyte solutions; use plastic syringe only for I.V. push

Patient Information Report any signs of bleeding or myopathy, changes in vision; GI upset usually disappears when dose is reduced

Emetic Potential Low (10% to 30%)

Vesicant No

Dosage Forms Excipient information presented when available (limited, particularly for generics); consult specific product labeling.

Injection, solution: 100 mg/mL (10 mL)

Tablet: 500 mg [Not marketed in U.S.; available from manufacturer for select cases]

References

Astedt B, "Clinical Pharmacology of Tranexamic Acid," *Scand J Gastroenterol Suppl*, 1987, 137:22-5.

Nilsson IM, "Clinical Pharmacology of Aminocaproic and Tranexamic Acids," *J Clin Pathol Suppl* (Royal College of Pathologists), 1980, 14:41-7.

Royston D, "Blood-Sparing Drugs: Aprotinin, Tranexamic Acid, and Epsilon-Aminocaproic Acid," *Int Anesthesiol Clin*, 1995, 33(1):155-79.

(Continued)

Tranexamic Acid *(Continued)*

Seto AH and Dunlap DS, "Tranexamic Acid in Oncology," *Ann Pharmacother*, 1996, 30(7-8):868-70.

Wellington K and Wagstaff AJ, "Tranexamic Acid: A Review of Its Use in the Management of Menorrhagia," *Drugs*, 2003, 63(13):1417-33.

♦ **Tranexamic Acid Injection BP (Can)** *see* Tranexamic Acid *on page 1064*

♦ **trans-Retinoic Acid** *see* Tretinoin (Oral) *on page 1069*

Trastuzumab *(tras TU zoo mab)*

Medication Safety Issues

High alert medication: The Institute for Safe Medication Practices (ISMP) includes this medication among its list of drugs which have a heightened risk of causing significant patient harm when used in error.

Related Information

Safe Handling of Hazardous Drugs *on page 1382*

U.S. Brand Names Herceptin®

Index Terms NSC-688097

Generic Available No

Canadian Brand Names Herceptin®

Pharmacologic Category Antineoplastic Agent, Monoclonal Antibody; Monoclonal Antibody

Use Treatment of HER-2/*neu* overexpressing metastatic breast cancer; adjuvant treatment of HER-2/*neu* overexpressing node-positive breast cancer

Unlabeled/Investigational Use Treatment of ovarian, gastric, colorectal, endometrial, lung, bladder, prostate, and salivary gland tumors

Pregnancy Risk Factor B

Lactation Excretion in breast milk unknown/not recommended

Labeled Contraindications Hypersensitivity to trastuzumab, Chinese hamster ovary cell proteins, or any component of the formulation

Warnings/Precautions Hazardous agent - use appropriate precautions for handling and disposal. **[U.S. Boxed Warning]: Congestive heart failure associated with trastuzumab may be severe and has been associated with disabling cardiac failure, death, mural thrombus, and stroke.** Left ventricular function should be evaluated in all patients prior to and during treatment with trastuzumab. Discontinuation should be strongly considered in patients who develop a clinically significant decrease in ejection fraction during therapy. Combination therapy with anthracyclines increases the risk of cardiac dysfunction. Prior or concurrent use of antihypertensive medications may increase the risk of cardiac toxicity. Extreme caution should be used when treating patients with pre-existing cardiac disease or dysfunction, and in patients with previous exposure to anthracyclines or radiation therapy. Advanced age may also predispose to cardiac toxicity.

[U.S. Boxed Warning]: Serious adverse events, including hypersensitivity reaction (anaphylaxis), infusion reactions (including fatalities), and pulmonary events (including acute respiratory distress syndrome) have been associated with trastuzumab. Most of these events occur with the first infusion; pulmonary events may occur during or within 24 hours of administration; delayed reactions have occurred. Discontinuation of trastuzumab should be strongly considered in any patient who develops anaphylaxis, angioedema, or acute respiratory distress syndrome. Retreatment of patients who experienced severe hypersensitivity reactions has been attempted (with premedication). Some patients tolerated retreatment, while others experienced a second severe reaction. When used in combination with myelosuppressive chemotherapy, trastuzumab may increase the incidence of neutropenia (moderate-to-severe) and febrile neutropenia. May cause serious pulmonary toxicity (pneumonitis, pulmonary infiltrates, pleural effusion, noncardiogenic pulmonary edema, pulmonary insufficiency, acute respiratory distress syndrome, and/or pulmonary fibrosis); use caution in patients with pre-existing pulmonary disease or patients with extensive pulmonary tumor involvement. Safety and efficacy in children have not been established.

Adverse Reactions Note: Percentages reported with single-agent therapy.

>10%:

Central nervous system: Pain (47%), fever (36%), chills (32%), headache (26%), insomnia (14%), dizziness (13%)

Dermatologic: Rash (18%)

Gastrointestinal: Nausea (8% to 33%), diarrhea (25%), vomiting (8% to 23%), abdominal pain (22%), anorexia (14%)

Neuromuscular & skeletal: Weakness (42%), back pain (22%)

Respiratory: Cough (26%), dyspnea (22%), rhinitis (14%), pharyngitis (12%)

Miscellaneous: Infusion reaction (21% to 40%, chills and fever most common; severe: 1%), infection (20%)

1% to 10%:

Cardiovascular: Peripheral edema (10%), edema (8%), CHF (7%), tachycardia (5%)

Central nervous system: Depression (6%)

Dermatologic: Acne (2%)

Genitourinary: Urinary tract infection (5%)

Hematologic: Anemia (4%), leukopenia (3%)

Neuromuscular & skeletal: Paresthesia (9%), bone pain (7%), arthralgia (6%), peripheral neuritis (2%), neuropathy (1%)

Respiratory: Sinusitis (9%)

Miscellaneous: Flu syndrome (10%), accidental injury (6%), allergic reaction (3%), herpes simplex (2%)

<1%: Acute respiratory distress syndrome (ARDS), amblyopia, anaphylaxis, anaphylactoid reaction, angioedema, apnea, arrhythmia, ascites, asthma, ataxia, bone necrosis, bronchospasm, cardiac arrest, cardiomyopathy, cellulitis, coagulopathy, colitis, confusion, deafness, esophageal ulcer, gastroenteritis, glomerulonephritis (membraneous and fibrillary), glomerulosclerosis, hematemesis, hemorrhage, hemorrhagic cystitis, hepatic failure, hepatitis, herpes zoster, hydrocephalus, hydronephrosis, hypercalcemia, hypotension, hypothyroidism, hypoxia, ileus, intestinal obstruction, laryngitis, leukemia (acute), lymphangitis, mania, mural thrombosis, myopathy, nephritic syndrome, neutropenia, pancreatitis, pancytopenia, paroxysmal nocturnal dyspnea, pathological fracture, pericardial effusion, pleural effusion, pneumonitis, pneumothorax, pulmonary edema (noncardiogenic), pulmonary fibrosis, pulmonary infiltrate, pyelonephritis, radiation injury, renal failure, respiratory distress, respiratory failure, seizure, sepsis, severe infusion reaction, shock, skin ulcers, stroke, syncope, stomatitis, vascular thrombosis, volume overload

Overdosage/Toxicology There is no experience with overdose in human clinical trials. Treatment is symptom-directed and supportive.

Drug Interactions

Increased Effect/Toxicity: Paclitaxel may result in a decrease in clearance of trastuzumab, increasing serum concentrations. Combined use with anthracyclines may increase the incidence/severity of cardiac dysfunction. Monoclonal antibodies may increase the risk for allergic reactions to trastuzumab due to the presence of HACA antibodies. Trastuzumab may (Continued)

Trastuzumab *(Continued)*

increase the incidence of neutropenia and/or febrile neutropenia when used in combination with myelosuppressive chemotherapy.

Storage/Stability Store intact vials under refrigeration 2°C to 8°C (36°F to 46°F) prior to reconstitution. Stable for 28 days after reconstitution if refrigerated; do not freeze. If sterile water for injection without preservative is used for reconstitution, it must be used immediately. After dilution in 0.9% sodium chloride for injection in polyethylene bags, solution is stable for 24 hours at room temperature or refrigerated.

Reconstitution Reconstitute each vial with 20 mL of bacteriostatic sterile water for injection to a concentration of 21 mg/mL. Swirl gently; do not shake. Allow vial to rest for ~5 minutes. Avoid rapid expulsion from syringe. If patient has a known hypersensitivity to benzyl alcohol, it may be reconstituted with sterile water for injection. Further dilute in 250 mL NS prior to administration.

Compatibility Stable in NS; **incompatible** with D_5W.

Mechanism of Action Trastuzumab is a monoclonal antibody which binds to the extracellular domain of the human epidermal growth factor receptor 2 protein (HER-2); it mediates antibody-dependent cellular cytotoxicity against cells which overproduce HER-2

Pharmacodynamics/Kinetics

Distribution: V_d: 44 mL/kg

Half-life elimination: Mean: 5.8 days (range: 1-32 days)

Dosage Refer to individual protocols. Adults: I.V. infusion:

Metastatic breast cancer:

Initial loading dose: 4 mg/kg infused over 90 minutes

Maintenance dose: 2 mg/kg infused over 90 minutes (can be administered over 30 minutes if prior infusions are well tolerated) weekly until disease progression

Node-positive breast cancer:

Initial loading dose: 4 mg/kg infused over 90 minutes

Maintenance dose: 2 mg/kg infused over 90 minutes (can be administered over 30 minutes if prior infusions are well tolerated) weekly for 51 weeks (total of 52 weeks)

Every 3-week schedule (unlabeled schedule):

Initial loading dose: 8 mg/kg infused over 90 minutes

Maintenance dose: 6 mg/kg infused over 90 minutes every 3 weeks

Dosage adjustment for toxicity:

Cardiotoxicity: LVEF ≥16% decrease from baseline within normal limits or LVEF below normal limits and ≥10% decrease from baseline: Withhold treatment for 4 weeks and repeat LVEF every 4 weeks. May resume trastuzumab treatment if LVEF returns to normal limits within 4-8 weeks and remains at ≤15% decrease from baseline value. Discontinue permanently for persistent LVEF decline or for >3 incidents of treatment interruptions for cardiomyopathy.

Infusion-related events:

Mild-moderate infusion reactions: Decrease infusion rate

Dyspnea, hypotension: Interrupt infusion

Severe reactions: Consider permanent discontinuation

Dosing adjustment in renal impairment: Data suggest that the disposition of trastuzumab is not altered based on age or serum creatinine (up to 2 mg/dL); however, no formal interaction studies have been performed

Dosing adjustment in hepatic impairment: No data is currently available

Combination Regimens

Breast cancer:
AC-Paclitaxel-Trastuzumab *on page 1144*
Capecitabine-Trastuzumab *on page 1160*
Docetaxel-Trastuzumab *on page 1192*
Docetaxel-Trastuzumab-Carboplatin *on page 1192*
Docetaxel-Trastuzumab-Cisplatin *on page 1193*
Docetaxel-Trastuzumab-FEC *on page 1193*
Docetaxel (Weekly)-Trastuzumab *on page 1194*
Trastuzumab-Paclitaxel *on page 1283*
Vinorelbine-Trastuzumab *on page 1290*

Administration Administered by I.V. infusion; loading doses are infused over 90 minutes; maintenance doses may be infused over 30 minutes if tolerated. Do not administer with D_5W. Do not administer I.V. push or by rapid bolus. Treatment with acetaminophen, diphenhydramine, and/or meperidine is usually effective for managing infusion-related events.

Monitoring Parameters Signs and symptoms of cardiac dysfunction; monitor vital signs during infusion; LVEF (baseline & periodic)

Emetic Potential Moderate (30% to 60%)

Vesicant No

Dosage Forms Excipient information presented when available (limited, particularly for generics); consult specific product labeling.
Injection, powder for reconstitution:
Herceptin®: 440 mg [packaged with bacteriostatic water for injection; diluent contains benzyl alcohol]

References
Baselga J, Albanell J, Molina MA, et al, "Mechanism of Action of Trastuzumab and Scientific Update," *Semin Oncol*, 2001, 28(5 Suppl 16):4-11.
Baselga J, Carbonell X, Castaneda-Soto NJ, et al, "Phase II Study of Efficacy, Safety, and Pharmacokinetics of Trastuzumab Monotherapy Administered on a 3-Weekly Schedule," *J Clin Oncol*, 2005, 23(10):2162-71.
Floyd JD, Nguyen DT, Lobins RL, et al, "Cardiotoxicity of Cancer Therapy," *J Clin Oncol*, 2005, 23(30):7685-96.
Jones RL and Smith IE, "Efficacy and Safety of Trastuzumab," *Expert Opin Drug Saf*, 2004, 3(4):317-27.
Leyland-Jones B, Gelmon K, Ayoub JP, et al, "Pharmacokinetics, Safety, and Efficacy of Trastuzumab Administered Every Three Weeks in Combination With Paclitaxel," *J Clin Oncol*, 2003, 21(21):3965-71.
Romond EH, Perez EA, Bryant J, et al, "Trastuzumab Plus Adjuvant Chemotherapy for Operable HER2-Positive Breast Cancer," *N Engl J Med*, 2005, 353(16):1673-84.
Treish I, Schwartz R, and Lindley C, "Pharmacology and Therapeutic Use of Trastuzumab in Breast Cancer," *Am J Health Syst Pharm*, 2000, 57(22):2063-76.
Vogel CL and Franco SX, "Clinical Experience With Trastuzumab (Herceptin)," *Breast J*, 2003, 9(6):452-62.
Watson WJ, "Herceptin (Trastuzumab) Therapy During Pregnancy: Association With Reversible Anhydramnios," *Obstet Gynecol*, 2005, 105(3):642-3.

♦ **Trelstar™ (Can)** *see* Triptorelin *on page 1077*
♦ **Trelstar™ Depot** *see* Triptorelin *on page 1077*
♦ **Trelstar™ LA** *see* Triptorelin *on page 1077*

Tretinoin (Oral) (TRET i noyn, oral)

Medication Safety Issues

Sound-alike/look-alike issues:
Tretinoin may be confused with trientine

High alert medication: The Institute for Safe Medication Practices (ISMP) includes this medication among its list of drugs which have a heightened risk of causing significant patient harm when used in error.
(Continued)

Tretinoin (Oral) *(Continued)*

Related Information
Safe Handling of Hazardous Drugs *on page 1382*

U.S. Brand Names Vesanoid®

Index Terms All-*trans*-Retinoic Acid; ATRA; NSC-122758; Ro 5488; tRA; *trans*-Retinoic Acid

Generic Available No

Canadian Brand Names Vesanoid®

Pharmacologic Category Antineoplastic Agent, Miscellaneous

Use Induction of remission in patients with acute promyelocytic leukemia (APL), French American British (FAB) classification M3 (including the M3 variant)

Pregnancy Risk Factor D

Lactation Enters breast milk/not recommended

Labeled Contraindications Sensitivity to parabens, vitamin A, other retinoids, or any component of the formulation; pregnancy

Warnings/Precautions Hazardous agent - use appropriate precautions for handling and disposal. **[U.S. Boxed Warning]: Patients with acute promyelocytic leukemia (APL) are at high risk and can have severe adverse reactions to tretinoin.**

[U.S. Boxed Warning]: About 25% of patients with APL and treated with tretinoin, have experienced retinoic acid-APL (RA-APL) syndrome, characterized by fever, dyspnea, acute respiratory distress, weight gain, radiographic pulmonary infiltrates and pleural or pericardial effusions, edema, and hepatic, renal, and/or multiorgan failure. This syndrome has occasionally been accompanied by impaired myocardial contractility and episodic hypotension. It has been observed with or without concomitant leukocytosis. Endotracheal intubation and mechanical ventilation have been required in some cases due to progressive hypoxemia, and several patients have expired with multiorgan failure. The syndrome usually occurs during the first month of treatment, with some cases reported following the first dose.

[U.S. Boxed Warning]: High risk of teratogenicity; not to be used in women of childbearing potential unless the woman is capable of complying with effective contraceptive measures. Repeat pregnancy testing and contraception counseling monthly throughout the period of treatment.

Retinoids have been associated with pseudotumor cerebri (benign intracranial hypertension), especially in children. Concurrent use of other drugs associated with this effect (eg, tetracyclines) may increase risk. Up to 60% of patients experienced reversible hypercholesterolemia or hypertriglyceridemia. Monitor liver function during treatment. **[U.S. Boxed Warning]: Should be administered under the supervision of an experienced cancer chemotherapy physician.**

Adverse Reactions Virtually all patients experience some drug-related toxicity, especially headache, fever, weakness and fatigue. These adverse effects are seldom permanent or irreversible nor do they usually require therapy interruption.

>10%:

Cardiovascular: Peripheral edema (52%), chest discomfort (32%), edema (29%), arrhythmias (23%), flushing (23%), hypotension (14%), hypertension (11%)

Central nervous system: Headache (86%), fever (83%), malaise (66%), pain (37%), dizziness (20%), anxiety (17%), insomnia (14%), depression (14%), confusion (11%)

Dermatologic: Skin/mucous membrane dryness (77%), pruritus (20%), rash (54%), alopecia (14%)

Endocrine & metabolic: Hypercholesterolemia and/or hypertriglyceridemia (60%)

Gastrointestinal: Nausea/vomiting (57%), liver function tests increased (50% to 60%), GI hemorrhage (34%), abdominal pain (31%), mucositis (26%), diarrhea (23%), constipation (17%), dyspepsia (14%), abdominal distention (11%), weight gain (23%), weight loss (17%), xerostomia, anorexia (17%)

Hematologic: Hemorrhage (60%), leukocytosis (40%), disseminated intra-vascular coagulation (DIC) (26%)

Local: Phlebitis (11%), injection site reactions (17%)

Neuromuscular & skeletal: Bone pain (77%), myalgia (14%), paresthesia (17%)

Ocular: Visual disturbances (17%)

Otic: Earache/ear fullness (23%)

Renal: Renal insufficiency (11%)

Respiratory: Upper respiratory tract disorders (63%), dyspnea (60%), respiratory insufficiency (26%), pleural effusion (20%), pneumonia (14%), rales (14%), expiratory wheezing (14%), dry nose

Miscellaneous: Infections (58%), shivering (63%), retinoic acid-acute promyelocytic leukemia syndrome (25%), diaphoresis increased (20%)

1% to 10%:

Cardiovascular: Cerebral hemorrhage (9%), pallor (6%), cardiac failure (6%), cardiac arrest (3%), MI (3%), enlarged heart (3%), heart murmur (3%), ischemia, stroke (3%), myocarditis (3%), pericarditis (3%), pulmonary hypertension (3%), secondary cardiomyopathy (3%), Central nervous system: Intracranial hypertension (9%), agitation (9%), hallucination (6%), agnosia (3%), aphasia (3%), cerebellar edema (3%), cerebral hemorrhage (9%), seizure (3%), coma (3%), CNS depression (3%), dysarthria (3%), encephalopathy (3%), hypotaxia (3%), light reflex absent (3%), spinal cord disorder (3%), unconsciousness (3%), dementia (3%), forgetfulness (3%), somnolence (3%), slow speech (3%), hypothermia (3%)

Dermatologic: Cellulitis (8%), photosensitivity

Endocrine & metabolic: Acidosis (3%)

Gastrointestinal: Hepatosplenomegaly (9%), hepatitis (3%), ulcer (3%)

Genitourinary: Dysuria (9%), acute renal failure (3%), micturition frequency (3%), renal tubular necrosis (3%), enlarged prostate (3%)

Hepatic: Ascites (3%), hepatitis

Neuromuscular & skeletal: Tremor (3%), leg weakness (3%), hyporeflexia, dysarthria, facial paralysis, hemiplegia, flank pain, asterixis, abnormal gait (3%), bone inflammation (3%)

Ocular: Dry eyes, visual acuity change (6%), visual field deficit (3%)

Otic: Hearing loss

Renal: Acute renal failure, renal tubular necrosis

Respiratory: Lower respiratory tract disorders (9%), pulmonary infiltration (6%), bronchial asthma (3%), pulmonary/larynx edema

Miscellaneous: Face edema

<1%: Arterial thrombosis, basophilia, cataracts, conjunctivitis, corneal opacities, erythema nodosum, erythrocyte sedimentation rate increased, gum bleeding, hematocrit decreased, hemoglobin decreased, hypercalcemia, (Continued)

Tretinoin (Oral) *(Continued)*

hyperhistaminemia, hyperuricemia, inflammatory bowel syndrome, irreversible hearing loss, mood changes, myositis, optic neuritis, pancreatitis, pseudomotor cerebri, renal infarct, Sweet's syndrome, vasculitis, venous thrombosis

Overdosage/Toxicology Symptoms of overdose include transient headache, facial flushing, cheilosis, abdominal pain, dizziness, and ataxia. All signs or symptoms have been transient and have resolved without apparent residual effects.

Drug Interactions

Cytochrome P450 Effect: Substrate (minor) of CYP2A6 (minor), 2B6 (minor), 2C8 (major), 2C9 (minor); **Inhibits** CYP2C9 (weak); **Induces** CYP2E1 (weak)

Increased Effect/Toxicity: Ketoconazole increases the mean plasma AUC of tretinoin. Concurrent use with antifibrinolytic agents (eg, aminocaproic acid, aprotinin, tranexamic acid) may increase risk of thrombosis. Concurrent use with tetracyclines may increase risk of pseudotumor cerebri. CYP2C8 Inhibitors may increase the levels/effects of tretinoin; example inhibitors include atazanavir, gemfibrozil, and ritonavir.

Ethanol/Nutrition/Herb Interactions

Ethanol: Avoid ethanol (may increase CNS depression).

Food: Absorption of retinoids has been shown to be enhanced when taken with food.

Herb/Nutraceutical: St John's wort may decrease tretinoin levels. Avoid dong quai, St John's wort (may also cause photosensitization). Avoid additional vitamin A supplementation. May lead to vitamin A toxicity.

Storage/Stability Store capsule at 15°C to 30°C (59°F to 86°F). Protect from light.

Mechanism of Action Tretinoin appears to bind one or more nuclear receptors and inhibits clonal proliferation and/or granulocyte differentiation

Pharmacodynamics/Kinetics

Protein binding: >95%

Metabolism: Hepatic via CYP; primary metabolite: 4-oxo-all-*trans*-retinoic acid

Half-life elimination: Terminal: Parent drug: 0.5-2 hours

Time to peak, serum: 1-2 hours

Excretion: Urine (63%); feces (30%)

Dosage Oral: Children and Adults:

Remission induction: 45 mg/m^2/day in 2-3 divided doses for up to 30 days after complete remission (maximum duration of treatment: 90 days)

Remission maintenance: 45-200 mg/m^2/day in 2-3 divided doses for up to 12 months.

Combination Regimens

Leukemia, acute promyelocytic: Tretinoin-Idarubicin *on page 1283*

Administration Administer with meals; do not crush capsules

Monitoring Parameters Monitor the patient's hematologic profile, coagulation profile, liver function test results and triglyceride and cholesterol levels frequently

Dietary Considerations To enhance absorption, some clinicians recommend giving with a fatty meal. Capsule contains soybean oil.

Patient Information Take with food; do not crush, chew, or dissolve capsules. You will need frequent blood tests while taking this medication. Maintain adequate hydration (2-3 L/day of fluids unless instructed to restrict fluid intake), avoid alcohol and foods containing vitamin A, and foods with high fat content. You may experience lethargy, dizziness, visual changes, confusion, anxiety (avoid driving or engaging in tasks requiring alertness until response to drug is known). For nausea/vomiting, loss of appetite, or dry mouth, small frequent meals, chewing gum, or sucking lozenges may help. You may experience photosensitivity (use sunscreen, wear protective clothing and eyewear, and avoid direct sunlight). You may experience dry, itchy, skin, and dry or irritated eyes (avoid contact lenses). Report persistent vomiting or diarrhea, difficulty breathing, unusual bleeding or bruising, acute GI pain, bone pain, or vision changes immediately.

Emetic Potential Moderate (30% to 60%)

Dosage Forms Excipient information presented when available (limited, particularly for generics); consult specific product labeling.

Capsule: 10 mg [contains soybean oil and parabens]

References

Chen GQ, Shen ZX, Wu F, et al, "Pharmacokinetics and Efficacy of Low-Dose All-*trans* Retinoic Acid in the Treatment of Acute Promyelocytic Leukemia," *Leukemia*, 1996, 10(5):825-8.

Kurzrock R, Estey E, and Talpaz M, "All-*trans* Retinoic Acid: Tolerance and Biologic Effects in Myelodysplastic Syndrome," *J Clin Oncol*, 1993, 11(8):1489-95.

Lazzarino M, Regazzi MB, and Corso A, "Clinical Relevance of All-*trans* Retinoic Acid Pharmacokinetics and Its Modulation in Acute Promyelocytic Leukemia," *Leuk Lymphoma*, 1996, 23(5-6):539-43.

Muindi JR, Frankel SR, Huselton C, et al, "Clinical Pharmacology of Oral All-*trans* Retinoic Acid in Patients With Acute Promyelocytic Leukemia," *Cancer Res*, 1992, 52(8):2138-42.

Smith MA, Adamson PC, Balis FM, et al, "Phase I and Pharmacokinetic Evaluation of All-*trans*-Retinoic Acid in Pediatric Patients With Cancer," *J Clin Oncol*, 1992, 10(11):1666-73.

♦ **Trexall™** *see* Methotrexate *on page 733*

♦ **Tridural™ (Can)** *see* Tramadol *on page 1059*

♦ **Triethylenethiophosphoramide** *see* Thiotepa *on page 1033*

♦ **Trikacide (Can)** *see* Metronidazole *on page 755*

Trimethobenzamide (trye meth oh BEN za mide)

Medication Safety Issues

Sound-alike/look-alike issues:

Tigan® may be confused with Tiazac®, Ticar®

Related Information

Management of Nausea and Vomiting *on page 1319*

U.S. Brand Names Tigan®

Index Terms Trimethobenzamide Hydrochloride

Generic Available Yes: Injection

Canadian Brand Names Tigan®

Pharmacologic Category Anticholinergic Agent; Antiemetic

Use Treatment of nausea and vomiting

Pregnancy Risk Factor C

Lactation Excretion in breast milk unknown

Labeled Contraindications Hypersensitivity to trimethobenzamide, benzocaine (or similar local anesthetics), or any component of the formulation; injection contraindicated in children

Warnings/Precautions May mask emesis due to Reye's syndrome or mimic CNS effects of Reye's syndrome in patients with emesis of other etiologies. May cause drowsiness; patient should avoid tasks requiring alertness (eg, driving, operating machinery). May cause extrapyramidal symptoms (EPS) which may be confused with CNS symptoms of primary disease responsible for emesis. Risk of adverse effects (eg, EPS, seizure) may be increased in patients with acute febrile illness, dehydration, or electrolyte imbalance; use caution.

Adverse Reactions Frequency not defined.

(Continued)

Trimethobenzamide *(Continued)*

Cardiovascular: Hypotension

Central nervous system: Coma, depression, disorientation, dizziness, drowsiness, EPS, headache, opisthotonos, Parkinson-like syndrome, seizure

Gastrointestinal: Diarrhea

Hematologic: Blood dyscrasias

Hepatic: Jaundice

Neuromuscular & skeletal: Muscle cramps

Ocular: Blurred vision

Miscellaneous: Hypersensitivity reactions

Overdosage/Toxicology Symptoms of overdose include hypotension, seizures, CNS depression, cardiac arrhythmias, disorientation, and confusion. Treatment is symptom-directed and supportive.

Ethanol/Nutrition/Herb Interactions Ethanol: Concomitant use should be avoided (sedative effects may be additive).

Storage/Stability Store capsules and injection solution at room temperature.

Mechanism of Action Acts centrally to inhibit the medullary chemoreceptor trigger zone

Pharmacodynamics/Kinetics

Onset of action: Antiemetic: Oral: 10-40 minutes; I.M.: 15-35 minutes

Duration: 3-4 hours

Bioavailability: Oral: 60% to 100%

Half-life elimination: 7-9 hours

Time to peak: Oral: 45 minutes; I.M.: 30 minutes

Excretion: Urine (30% to 50%)

Dosage

Children >40 kg: Oral: 300 mg 3-4 times/day

Adults:

Oral: 300 mg 3-4 times/day

I.M.: 200 mg 3-4 times/day

Postoperative nausea and vomiting (PONV): I.M.: 200 mg, followed 1 hour later by a second 200 mg dose

Administration Administer I.M. only; not for I.V. administration. Inject deep into upper outer quadrant of gluteal muscle.

Patient Information May cause drowsiness, impair judgment and coordination; report any restlessness or involuntary movements

Special Geriatric Considerations No specific data for use in the elderly have been established; as with any drug which has EPS adverse effects and possibility of confusion, caution should be used when administering to elderly.

Emetic Potential Very low (<10%)

Vesicant No

Dosage Forms Excipient information presented when available (limited, particularly for generics); consult specific product labeling.

Capsule, as hydrochloride:

Tigan®: 300 mg

Injection, solution, as hydrochloride: 100 mg/mL (2 mL)

Tigan®: 100 mg/mL (2 mL [preservative free], 20 mL)

References

ACOG (American College of Obstetrics and Gynecology) Practice Bulletin: "Nausea and Vomiting of Pregnancy," *Obstet Gynecol*, 2004, 103(4):803-14.

Ginsburg CM and Clahsen J, "Evaluation of Trimethobenzamide Hydrochloride (Tigan®) Suppositories for Treatment of Nausea and Vomiting in Children," *J Pediatr*, 1980, 96(4):767-9.

Hurley JD and Eshelman FN, "Trimethobenzamide HCl in the Treatment of Nausea and Vomiting Associated With Antineoplastic Chemotherapy," *J Clin Pharmacol*, 1980, 20(5-6 Pt1):352-6.

Kaan SK and Eshelman FN, "The Antiemetic Effects of Trimethobenzamide During Chemotherapy: A Controlled Study," *Curr Ther Res*, 1979, 26:210-3.

♦ **Trimethobenzamide Hydrochloride** *see* Trimethobenzamide *on page 1073*

Trimethoprim (trye METH oh prim)

Medication Safety Issues
Sound-alike/look-alike issues:
Trimethoprim may be confused with trimethaphan
Proloprim® may be confused with Prolixin®, Protropin®

U.S. Brand Names Primsol®; Proloprim® [DSC]

Index Terms TMP

Generic Available Yes: Tablet

Canadian Brand Names Apo-Trimethoprim®

Pharmacologic Category Antibiotic, Miscellaneous

Use Treatment of urinary tract infections due to susceptible strains of *E. coli*, *P. mirabilis*, *K. pneumoniae*, *Enterobacter* sp and coagulase-negative *Staphylococcus* including *S. saprophyticus*; acute otitis media in children; acute exacerbations of chronic bronchitis in adults; in combination with other agents for treatment of toxoplasmosis, *Pneumocystis carinii*; treatment of superficial ocular infections involving the conjunctiva and cornea

Pregnancy Risk Factor C

Lactation Enters breast milk/use caution (AAP rates "compatible")

Labeled Contraindications Hypersensitivity to trimethoprim or any component of the formulation; megaloblastic anemia due to folate deficiency

Warnings/Precautions Use with caution in patients with impaired renal or hepatic function or with possible folate deficiency. Prolonged use may result in fungal or bacterial superinfection, including *C. difficile*-associated diarrhea (CDAD) and pseudomembranous colitis; CDAD has been observed <2 months postantibiotic treatment.

Adverse Reactions Frequency not defined.
Central nervous system: Aseptic meningitis (rare), fever
Dermatologic: Maculopapular rash (3% to 7% at 200 mg/day; incidence higher with larger daily doses), erythema multiforme (rare), exfoliative dermatitis (rare), pruritus (common), phototoxic skin eruptions, Stevens-Johnson syndrome (rare), toxic epidermal necrolysis (rare)
Endocrine & metabolic: Hyperkalemia, hyponatremia
Gastrointestinal: Epigastric distress, glossitis, nausea, vomiting
Hematologic: Leukopenia, megaloblastic anemia, methemoglobinemia, neutropenia, thrombocytopenia
Hepatic: Liver enzyme elevation, cholestatic jaundice (rare)
Renal: BUN and creatinine increased
Miscellaneous: Anaphylaxis, hypersensitivity reactions

Overdosage/Toxicology Symptoms of acute toxicity include nausea, vomiting, confusion, and dizziness. Chronic overdose results in bone marrow suppression. Treatment of acute overdose is supportive following GI decontamination. Use oral leucovorin 5-15 mg/day for treatment of chronic overdose. Hemodialysis is only moderately effective in eliminating drug.

Drug Interactions
Cytochrome P450 Effect: Substrate (major) of CYP2C9, 3A4; **Inhibits** CYP2C8 (moderate), 2C9 (moderate)

Increased Effect/Toxicity: Increased effect/toxicity/levels of phenytoin. Concurrent use with ACE inhibitors increases risk of hyperkalemia.
(Continued)

Trimethoprim *(Continued)*

Increased myelosuppression with methotrexate. May increase levels of digoxin. Concurrent use with dapsone may increase levels of dapsone and trimethoprim. Concurrent use with procainamide may increase levels of procainamide and trimethoprim. Trimethoprim may increase the levels/ effects of amiodarone, fluoxetine, glimepiride, glipizide, nateglinide, phenytoin, pioglitazone, rosiglitazone, sertraline, warfarin, and other CYP2C8 and 2C9 substrates.

Decreased Effect: The levels/effects of trimethoprim may be decreased by aminoglutethimide, carbamazepine, nafcillin, nevirapine, phenobarbital, phenytoin, rifampin, rifapentine, secobarbital, and other CYP2C9 or 3A4 inducers.

Storage/Stability Protect the 200 mg tablet from light.

Mechanism of Action Inhibits folic acid reduction to tetrahydrofolate, and thereby inhibits microbial growth

Pharmacodynamics/Kinetics

Absorption: Readily and extensive

Distribution: Widely into body tissues and fluids (middle ear, prostate, bile, aqueous humor, CSF); crosses placenta; enters breast milk

Protein binding: 42% to 46%

Metabolism: Partially hepatic

Half-life elimination: 8-14 hours; prolonged with renal impairment

Time to peak, serum: 1-4 hours

Excretion: Urine (60% to 80%) as unchanged drug

Dosage Oral:

Children: 4 mg/kg/day in divided doses every 12 hours

Adults: 100 mg every 12 hours or 200 mg every 24 hours for 10 days; longer treatment periods may be necessary for prostatitis (ie, 4-16 weeks); in the treatment of *Pneumocystis carinii* pneumonia; dose may be as high as 15-20 mg/kg/day in 3-4 divided doses

Dosing interval in renal impairment:

Cl_{cr} 15-30 mL/minute: Administer 100 mg every 18 hours or 50 mg every 12 hours

Cl_{cr} <15 mL/minute: Administer 100 mg every 24 hours or avoid use

Hemodialysis: Moderately dialyzable (20% to 50%)

Administration Administer with milk or food.

Dietary Considerations May cause folic acid deficiency, supplements may be needed. Should be taken with milk or food.

Patient Information Take with milk or food; report any skin rash, persistent or severe fatigue, fever, sore throat, or unusual bleeding or bruising; complete full course of therapy

Special Geriatric Considerations Trimethoprim is often used in combination with sulfamethoxazole; it can be used alone in patients who are allergic to sulfonamides; adjust dose for renal function (see Pharmacodynamics/Kinetics and Dosage).

Emetic Potential Very low (<10%)

Dosage Forms Excipient information presented when available (limited, particularly for generics); consult specific product labeling. [DSC] = Discontinued product

Solution, oral:

Primsol®: 50 mg (base)/5 mL (480 mL) [contains sodium benzoate; bubble gum flavor]

Tablet: 100 mg

Proloprim®: 100 mg [DSC]

References
"American Academy of Pediatrics Committee on Drugs. The Transfer of Drugs and Other Chemicals Into Human Milk," *Pediatrics*, 2001, 108(3):776-89.

Hoppu K, Koskimies O, and Vilska J, "Trimethoprim in the Treatment of Acute Urinary Tract Infections in Children," *Int J Clin Pharmacol Ther Toxicol*, 1988, 26(2):65-8.

Hoppu K, "Age Differences in Trimethoprim Pharmacokinetics: Need for Revised Dosing in Children?" *Clin Pharmacol Ther*, 1987, 41(3):336-43.

Varoquaux O, Lajoie D, Gobert C, et al, "Pharmacokinetics of the Trimethoprim-Sulfamethoxazole Combination in the Elderly," *Br J Clin Pharmacol*, 1985, 20:575-81.

♦ **Trimethoprim and Sulfamethoxazole** *see* Sulfamethoxazole and Trimethoprim *on page 982*

♦ **Triptoraline** *see* Triptorelin *on page 1077*

Triptorelin (trip toe REL in)

Related Information
Safe Handling of Hazardous Drugs *on page 1382*

U.S. Brand Names Trelstar™ Depot; Trelstar™ LA

Index Terms AY-25650; CL-118,532; D-Trp(6)-LHRH; Triptoraline; Triptorelin Pamoate; Tryptoreline

Generic Available No

Canadian Brand Names Trelstar™; Trelstar™ Depot; Trelstar™ LA

Pharmacologic Category Gonadotropin Releasing Hormone Agonist

Use Palliative treatment of advanced prostate cancer as an alternative to orchiectomy or estrogen administration

Unlabeled/Investigational Use Treatment of endometriosis, growth hormone deficiency, hyperandrogenism, *in vitro* fertilization, ovarian carcinoma, pancreatic carcinoma, precocious puberty, uterine leiomyomata

Pregnancy Risk Factor X

Lactation Excretion in breast milk unknown/contraindicated

Labeled Contraindications Hypersensitivity to triptorelin or any component of the formulation, other LHRH agonists or LHRH; pregnancy

Warnings/Precautions Hazardous agent - use appropriate precautions for handling and disposal. Transient increases in testosterone can lead to worsening symptoms (bone pain, hematuria, bladder outlet obstruction) of prostate cancer during the first few weeks of therapy. Cases of spinal cord compression have been reported with LHRH agonists. Closely observe patients with metastatic vertebral lesions or lower urinary tract obstruction. Hypersensitivity reactions including angioedema and anaphylaxis have rarely occurred. Rare cases of pituitary apoplexy (frequently secondary to pituitary adenoma) have been observed with leuprolide administration (onset from 1 hour to usually <2 weeks); may present as sudden headache, vomiting, visual or mental status changes, and infrequently cardiovascular collapse; immediate medical attention required. Safety and efficacy has not established in pediatric population.

Adverse Reactions As reported with Trelstar™ Depot and Trelstar™ LA; frequency of effect may vary by product:

>10%:
  Central nervous system: Headache (30% to 60%)
  Endocrine & metabolic: Hot flashes (95% to 100%), glucose increased
  Hematologic: Hemoglobin decreased, RBC count decreased
  Hepatic: Alkaline phosphatase increased, ALT increased, AST increased
  Neuromuscular & skeletal: Skeletal pain (12% to 13%)
  Renal: BUN increased

1% to 10%:
  Cardiovascular: Leg edema (6%), hypertension (4%), chest pain (2%), peripheral edema (1%)

(Continued)

Triptorelin *(Continued)*

Central nervous system: Dizziness (1% to 3%), pain (2% to 3%), emotional lability (1%), fatigue (2%), insomnia (2%)

Dermatologic: Rash (2%), pruritus (1%)

Endocrine & metabolic: Alkaline phosphatase increased (2%), breast pain (2%), gynecomastia (2%), libido decreased (2%), tumor flare (8%)

Gastrointestinal: Nausea (3%), anorexia (2%), constipation (2%), dyspepsia (2%), vomiting (2%), abdominal pain (1%), diarrhea (1%)

Genitourinary: Dysuria (5%), impotence (2% to 7%), urinary retention (1%), urinary tract infection (1%)

Hematologic: Anemia (1%)

Local: Injection site pain (4%)

Neuromuscular & skeletal: Leg pain (2% to 5%), back pain (3%), arthralgia (2%), leg cramps (2%), myalgia (1%), weakness (1%)

Ocular: Conjunctivitis (1%), eye pain (1%)

Respiratory: Cough (2%), dyspnea (1%), pharyngitis (1%)

Postmarketing and/or case reports: Anaphylaxis, angioedema, hypersensitivity reactions, pituitary apoplexy, spinal cord compression, renal dysfunction

Overdosage/Toxicology Accidental or intentional overdose unlikely. If it were to occur, supportive and symptomatic treatment would be indicated.

Drug Interactions

Increased Effect/Toxicity: Not studied. Hyperprolactinemic drugs (dopamine antagonists such as antipsychotics, and metoclopramide) are contraindicated.

Decreased Effect: Not studied. Hyperprolactinemic drugs (dopamine antagonists such as antipsychotics, and metoclopramide) are contraindicated.

Storage/Stability

Trelstar™ Depot: Store at 15°C to 30°C (59°F to 86°F).

Trelstar™ LA: Store at 20°C to 25°C (68°F to 77°F).

Reconstitution Reconstitute with 2 mL sterile water for injection. Shake well to obtain a uniform suspension.

Debioclip™: Follow manufacturer's instructions for mixing prior to use.

Mechanism of Action Causes suppression of ovarian and testicular steroidogenesis due to decreased levels of LH and FSH with subsequent decrease in testosterone (male) and estrogen (female) levels. After chronic and continuous administration, usually 2-4 weeks after initiation, a sustained decrease in LH and FSH secretion occurs.

Pharmacodynamics/Kinetics

Absorption: Oral: Not active

Distribution: V_d: 30-33 L

Protein binding: None

Metabolism: Unknown; unlikely to involve CYP; no known metabolites

Half-life elimination: 2.8 ± 1.2 hours

Moderate to severe renal impairment: 6.5-7.7 hours

Hepatic impairment: 7.6 hours

Time to peak: 1-3 hours

Excretion: Urine (42% as intact peptide); hepatic

Dosage I.M.: Adults: Prostate cancer:

Trelstar™ Depot: 3.75 mg once every 28 days

Trelstar™ LA: 11.25 mg once every 84 days

Dosage adjustment in renal/hepatic impairment: Although this drug is excreted renally, no guidelines for adjustments are available.

Administration Administer by I.M. injection into the buttock; alternate injection sites.

Monitoring Parameters Serum testosterone levels, prostate-specific antigen

Test Interactions Pituitary-gonadal function may be suppressed with chronic administration and for up to 8 weeks after triptorelin therapy has been discontinued.

Patient Information Use as directed. Do not miss monthly appointment for injection. You may experience disease flare (increased bone pain), blood in urine, and urinary retention during early treatment (usually resolves within 1 week). Hot flashes are common; you may feel flushed and hot (wearing layers of clothes or summer clothes and cool environment may help). If it becomes annoying and bothersome, let prescriber know. Report irregular or rapid heartbeat, unresolved nausea or vomiting, numbness of extremities, breast swelling or pain, difficulty breathing, or infection at injection sites.

Special Geriatric Considerations Since many elderly men may have hypertension, blood pressure needs be monitored closely for the first 4-8 weeks.

Dosage Forms Excipient information presented when available (limited, particularly for generics); consult specific product labeling.

Injection, powder for reconstitution, as pamoate [also available packaged with Debioclip™ (prefilled syringe containing sterile water)]:
Trelstar™ Depot: 3.75 mg
Trelstar™ LA: 11.25 mg

References

Anonymous, "Triptorelin Pamoate. Phase III Drug Profiles," 1993, 3:1-8.

Filicor M, "Gonadotrophin-Releasing Hormone Agonists. A Guide to Use and Selection," *Drugs*, 1994, 48(1):41-58.

Swanson LJ, Seely JH, and Garnick MB, "Gonadotropin-Releasing Hormone Analogs and Prostatic Cancer," *Crit Rev Oncol Hematol*, 1988, 8(1):1-26.

- ◆ **Triptorelin Pamoate** see Triptorelin on page 1077
- ◆ **Trisenox®** see Arsenic Trioxide on page 107
- ◆ **Trivagizole-3® (Can)** see Clotrimazole on page 239
- ◆ **Tryptoreline** see Triptorelin on page 1077
- ◆ **TSPA** see Thiotepa on page 1033
- ◆ **Tucks® Anti-Itch [OTC]** see Hydrocortisone on page 545
- ◆ **Tykerb®** see Lapatinib on page 656
- ◆ **506U78** see Nelarabine on page 804

UFT

Related Information
Investigational Drug Service on page 1379
Safe Handling of Hazardous Drugs on page 1382

U.S. Brand Names Orzel®

Index Terms Uracil and Ftorafur; Uracil and Tegafur; Uracil and Tetrahydrofuranyl-5-Fluorouracil

Generic Available No

Pharmacologic Category Antineoplastic Agent, Antimetabolite (Pyrimidine Antagonist)

Unlabeled/Investigational Use Investigational: Treatment of unresectable or metastatic colorectal cancer

Warnings/Precautions
Hazardous agent - use appropriate precautions for handling and disposal.

Adverse Reactions Frequency not defined.
Central nervous system: Fatigue, cerebellar toxicity (rare)
(Continued)

UFT *(Continued)*

Dermatologic: Rash, skin pigmentation, photosensitivity, hand-foot syndrome (rare)

Gastrointestinal: Nausea, vomiting, anorexia, diarrhea (may be dose limiting)

Hematologic: Neutropenia (may be dose limiting)

Neuromuscular & skeletal: Neurotoxicity (peripheral neuropathy)

Ocular: Lacrimation

Mechanism of Action Tegafur is a prodrug of fluorouracil. It is converted *in vivo* to fluorouracil through hepatic microsomal cytochrome P450, and also via thymidine phosphorylase and spontaneous anabolic conversion. Uracil is a competitive inhibitor of dihydropyrimidine dehydrogenase (DPD), the enzyme responsible for catabolism of approximately 85% of fluorouracil to fluoro-β alanine.

Pharmacodynamics/Kinetics

Plasma levels: Tegafur > uracil > fluorouracil

Time to C_{pmax}: Tegafur: 0.6-2.1 hours; uracil: 0.6-4.1 hours; fluorouracil: 0.7-2.0 hours; the relationship between UFT dose and fluorouracil C_{pmax} is not linear

Dosage Refer to individual protocols.

Oral: Adults: 300 mg/m^2/day (expressed as tegafur) in combination with oral leucovorin

Emetic Potential Moderate (30% to 60%)

Vesicant No

Dosage Forms Excipient information presented when available (limited, particularly for generics); consult specific product labeling.

Capsule: Tegafur 100 mg and uracil 224 mg

References

Ho DH, Covington WP, Pazdur R, et al, "Clinical Pharmacology of Combined Oral Uracil and Ftorafur," *Drug Metab Disp*, 1992, 20(6):936-40.

Kohne CH and Peters GJ, "UFT: Mechanism of Drug Action," *Oncology (Huntingt)*, 2000, 14(10 Suppl 9):13-8.

Sun W and Haller D, "UFT in the Treatment of Colorectal and Breast Cancer," *Oncology (Huntingt)*, 2001, 15(1 Suppl 2):49-56.

♦ **UK109496** *see* Voriconazole *on page 1111*

♦ **Ultram®** *see* Tramadol *on page 1059*

♦ **Ultram® ER** *see* Tramadol *on page 1059*

♦ **Unipen® (Can)** *see* Nafcillin *on page 800*

♦ **Uracil and Ftorafur** *see* UFT *on page 1079*

♦ **Uracil and Tegafur** *see* UFT *on page 1079*

♦ **Uracil and Tetrahydrofuranyl-5-Fluorouracil** *see* UFT *on page 1079*

♦ **Urolene Blue®** *see* Methylene Blue *on page 743*

♦ **Uromitexan (Can)** *see* Mesna *on page 724*

Valacyclovir *(val ay SYE kloe veer)*

Medication Safety Issues

Sound-alike/look-alike issues:

Valtrex® may be confused with Valcyte™

Valacyclovir may be confused with valganciclovir

U.S. Brand Names Valtrex®

Index Terms Valacyclovir Hydrochloride

Generic Available No

Canadian Brand Names Valtrex®

Pharmacologic Category Antiviral Agent, Oral

Use Treatment of herpes zoster (shingles) in immunocompetent patients; treatment of first-episode genital herpes; episodic treatment of recurrent genital herpes; suppression of recurrent genital herpes and reduction of heterosexual transmission of genital herpes in immunocompetent patients; suppression of genital herpes in HIV-infected individuals; treatment of herpes labialis (cold sores)

Pregnancy Risk Factor B

Lactation Enters breast milk/use caution

Labeled Contraindications Hypersensitivity to valacyclovir, acyclovir, or any component of the formulation

Warnings/Precautions Hazardous agent - use appropriate precautions for handling and disposal. Thrombotic thrombocytopenic purpura/hemolytic uremic syndrome has occurred in immunocompromised patients (at doses of 8 g/day); use caution and adjust the dose in elderly patients or those with renal insufficiency and in patients receiving concurrent nephrotoxic agents. For genital herpes, treatment should begin as soon as possible after the first signs and symptoms (within 72 hours of onset of first diagnosis or within 24 hours of onset of recurrent episodes). For herpes zoster, treatment should begin within 72 hours of onset of rash. For cold sores, treatment should begin at with earliest symptom (tingling, itching, burning). Safety and efficacy in prepubertal patients have not been established.

Adverse Reactions

>10%: Central nervous system: Headache (14% to 35%)

1% to 10%:

Central nervous system: Dizziness (2% to 4%), depression (0% to 7%)

Endocrine: Dysmenorrhea (≤1% to 8%)

Gastrointestinal: Abdominal pain (2% to 11%), nausea (6% to 15%), vomiting (<1% to 6%)

Hematologic: Leukopenia (≤1%), thrombocytopenia (≤1%)

Hepatic: AST increased (1% to 4%)

Neuromuscular & skeletal: Arthralgia (≤1 to 6%)

<1%: Anemia

Postmarketing and/or case reports: Acute hypersensitivity reactions (angioedema, anaphylaxis, dyspnea, pruritus, rash, urticaria), aggression, agitation, alopecia, aplastic anemia, ataxia, creatinine increased, coma, confusion, consciousness decreased, diarrhea, dysarthria, encephalopathy, facial edema, erythema multiforme, hallucinations (auditory and visual), hemolytic uremic syndrome (HUS), hepatitis, hypertension, leukocytoclastic vasculitis, mania, photosensitivity reaction, psychosis, rash, renal failure, seizure, tachycardia, thrombotic thrombocytopenic purpura/ hemolytic uremic syndrome, tremor, visual disturbances

Overdosage/Toxicology Precipitation in renal tubules may occur. Treatment is symptomatic and includes hemodialysis, especially if compromised renal function develops.

Drug Interactions

Increased Effect/Toxicity: Valacyclovir and acyclovir have increased CNS side effects with zidovudine and probenecid.

Decreased Effect: Cimetidine and/or probenecid has decreased the rate but not the extent of valacyclovir conversion to acyclovir leading to decreased effectiveness of valacyclovir.

Storage/Stability Store at 15°C to 25°C (59°F to 77°F).

Mechanism of Action Valacyclovir is rapidly and nearly completely converted to acyclovir by intestinal and hepatic metabolism. Acyclovir is (Continued)

Valacyclovir *(Continued)*

converted to acyclovir monophosphate by virus-specific thymidine kinase then further converted to acyclovir triphosphate by other cellular enzymes. Acyclovir triphosphate inhibits DNA synthesis and viral replication by competing with deoxyguanosine triphosphate for viral DNA polymerase and being incorporated into viral DNA.

Pharmacodynamics/Kinetics

Absorption: Rapid

Distribution: Acyclovir is widely distributed throughout the body including brain, kidney, lungs, liver, spleen, muscle, uterus, vagina, and CSF

Protein binding: 13.5% to 17.9%

Metabolism: Hepatic; valacyclovir is rapidly and nearly completely converted to acyclovir and L-valine by first-pass effect; acyclovir is hepatically metabolized to a very small extent by aldehyde oxidase and by alcohol and aldehyde dehydrogenase (inactive metabolites)

Bioavailability: ~55% once converted to acyclovir

Half-life elimination: Normal renal function: Adults: Acyclovir: 2.5-3.3 hours, Valacyclovir: ~30 minutes; End-stage renal disease: Acyclovir: 14-20 hours

Excretion: Urine, primarily as acyclovir (88%); **Note:** Following oral administration of radiolabeled valacyclovir, 46% of the label is eliminated in the feces (corresponding to nonabsorbed drug), while 47% of the radiolabel is eliminated in the urine.

Dosage Oral:

Adolescents and Adults: Herpes labialis (cold sores): 2 g twice daily for 1 day (separate doses by ~12 hours)

Adults:

Herpes zoster (shingles): 1 g 3 times/day for 7 days

Genital herpes:

Initial episode: 1 g twice daily for 10 days

Recurrent episode: 500 mg twice daily for 3 days

Reduction of transmission: 500 mg once daily (source partner)

Suppressive therapy:

Immunocompetent patients: 1000 mg once daily (500 mg once daily in patients with <9 recurrences per year)

HIV-infected patients (CD4 ≥100 cells/mm^3): 500 mg twice daily

Dosing interval in renal impairment:

Herpes zoster: Adults:

Cl_{cr} 30-49 mL/minute: 1 g every 12 hours

Cl_{cr} 10-29 mL/minute: 1 g every 24 hours

Cl_{cr} <10 mL/minute: 500 mg every 24 hours

Genital herpes: Adults:

Initial episode:

Cl_{cr} 10-29 mL/minute: 1 g every 24 hours

Cl_{cr} <10 mL/minute: 500 mg every 24 hours

Recurrent episode: Cl_{cr} <10-29 mL/minute: 500 mg every 24 hours

Suppressive therapy: Cl_{cr} <10-29 mL/minute:

For usual dose of 1 g every 24 hours, decrease dose to 500 mg every 24 hours

For usual dose of 500 mg every 24 hours, decrease dose to 500 mg every 48 hours

HIV-infected patients: 500 mg every 24 hours

Herpes labialis: Adolescents and Adults:

Cl_{cr} 30-49 mL/minute: 1 g every 12 hours for 2 doses

Cl_{cr} 10-29 mL/minute: 500 mg every 12 hours for 2 doses

Cl_{cr} <10 mL/minute: 500 mg as a single dose

Hemodialysis: Dialyzable (~33% removed during 4-hour session); administer dose postdialysis

Chronic ambulatory peritoneal dialysis/continuous arteriovenous hemofiltration dialysis: Pharmacokinetic parameters are similar to those in patients with ESRD; supplemental dose not needed following dialysis

Administration If GI upset occurs, administer with meals.

Monitoring Parameters Urinalysis, BUN, serum creatinine, liver enzymes, and CBC

Dietary Considerations May be taken with or without food.

Patient Information

Herpes zoster: Therapy is most effective when started within 48 hours of onset of zoster rash.

Recurrent genital herpes: Therapy should be initiated within 24 hours after the onset of signs or symptoms.

Special Geriatric Considerations More convenient dosing and increased bioavailability, without increasing side effects, make valacyclovir a favorable choice compared to acyclovir. Has been shown to accelerate resolution of postherpetic pain. Adjust dose for renal impairment.

Dosage Forms Excipient information presented when available (limited, particularly for generics); consult specific product labeling.

Caplet: 500 mg, 1000 mg

References

Acosta EP and Fletcher CV, "Valacyclovir," *Ann Pharmacother*, 1997, 31(2):185-91.

Alrabiah FA and Sacks SL, "New Antiherpesvirus Agents. Their Targets and Therapeutic Potential," *Drugs*, 1996, 52(1):17-32.

Beutner KR, Friedman DJ, Forszpaniak C, et al, "Valacyclovir Compared With Acyclovir for Improved Therapy for Herpes Zoster in Immunocompetent Adults," *Antimicrob Agents Chemother*, 1995, 39(7):1546-53.

Bodsworth NJ, Crooks RJ, Borelli S, et al, "Valacyclovir Versus Aciclovir in Patients Initiated Treatment of Recurrent Genital Herpes: A Randomized, Double-Blind Clinical Trial. International Valaciclovir HSV Study Group," *Genitourin Med*, 1997, 73(2):110-6.

Grant DM, Mauskopf JA, Bell L, et al, "Comparison of Valaciclovir and Acyclovir for the Treatment of Herpes Zoster in Immunocompetent Patients Over 50 Years of Age: A Cost-Consequence Model," *Pharmacotherapy*, 1997, 17(2):333-41.

Patel R, Bodsworth NJ, Woolley P, et al, "Valaciclovir for the Suppression of Recurrent Genital HSV Infection: A Placebo Controlled Study of Once Daily Therapy. International Valaciclovir HSV Study Group," *Genitourin Med*, 1997, 73(2):105-9.

Perry CM and Faulds D, "Valaciclovir. A Review of Its Antiviral Activity, Pharmacokinetic Properties and Therapeutic Efficacy in Herpesvirus Infections," *Drugs*, 1996, 52(5):754-72.

Reitano M, Tyring S, Lang W, et al, "Valaciclovir for the Suppression of Recurrent Genital Herpes Simplex Virus Infection: A Large-Scale Dose Range-Finding Study. International Valaciclovir HSV Study Group," *J Infect Dis*, 1998, 178(3):603-10.

Tyring SK, Douglas JM Jr, Corey L, et al, "A Randomized, Placebo-Controlled Comparison of Oral Valacyclovir and Acyclovir in Immunocompetent Patients With Recurrent Genital Herpes Infections. The Valaciclovir International Study Group," *Arch Dermatol*, 1998, 134(2):185-91.

"Valaciclovir," *Med Lett Drugs Ther*, 1996, 38(965):3-4.

Weller S, Blum MR, Doucette M, et al, "Pharmacokinetics of the Acyclovir Prodrug Valaciclovir After Escalating Single- and Multiple-Dose Administration to Normal Volunteers," *Clin Pharmacol Ther*, 1993, 54(6):595-605.

♦ **Valacyclovir Hydrochloride** *see Valacyclovir on page 1080*

♦ **Valcyte™** *see Valganciclovir on page 1083*

Valganciclovir (val gan SYE kloh veer)

Medication Safety Issues

Sound-alike/look-alike issues:

Valcyte™ may be confused with Valium®, Valtrex®

Valganciclovir may be confused with valacyclovir

Related Information

Safe Handling of Hazardous Drugs *on page 1382*

(Continued)

Valganciclovir *(Continued)*

U.S. Brand Names Valcyte™

Index Terms Valganciclovir Hydrochloride

Generic Available No

Canadian Brand Names Valcyte™

Pharmacologic Category Antiviral Agent

Use Treatment of cytomegalovirus (CMV) retinitis in patients with acquired immunodeficiency syndrome (AIDS); prevention of CMV disease in high-risk patients (donor CMV positive/recipient CMV negative) undergoing kidney, heart, or kidney/pancreas transplantation

Pregnancy Risk Factor C

Lactation Excretion in breast milk unknown/contraindicated

Labeled Contraindications Hypersensitivity to valganciclovir, ganciclovir, acyclovir, or any component of the formulation; absolute neutrophil count <500/mm^3; platelet count <25,000/mm^3; hemoglobin <8 g/dL

Warnings/Precautions [U.S. Boxed Warning]: May cause dose- or therapy-limiting granulocytopenia, anemia, and/or thrombocytopenia; use caution in patients with impaired renal function (dose adjustment required). **[U.S. Boxed Warning]: Ganciclovir may adversely affect spermatogenesis and fertility.** Not approved for use in children. Due to differences in bioavailability, valganciclovir tablets cannot be substituted for ganciclovir capsules on a one-to-one basis. Not indicated for use in liver transplant patients (higher incidence of tissue-invasive CMV relative to oral ganciclovir was observed in trials). Safety and efficacy not established in pediatric patients.

Adverse Reactions

>10%:

Central nervous system: Fever (31%), headache (9% to 22%), insomnia (16%)

Gastrointestinal: Diarrhea (16% to 41%), nausea (8% to 30%), vomiting (21%), abdominal pain (15%)

Hematologic: Granulocytopenia (11% to 27%), anemia (8% to 26%)

Ocular: Retinal detachment (15%)

1% to 10%:

Central nervous system: Peripheral neuropathy (9%), paresthesia (8%), seizure (<5%), psychosis, hallucinations (<5%), confusion (<5%), agitation (<5%)

Hematologic: Thrombocytopenia (8%), pancytopenia (<5%), bone marrow depression (<5%), aplastic anemia (<5%), bleeding (potentially life-threatening due to thrombocytopenia <5%)

Renal: Renal function decreased (<5%)

Miscellaneous: Local and systemic infection, including sepsis (<5%); allergic reaction (<5%)

<1%: Valganciclovir is expected to share the toxicities which may occur at a low incidence or due to idiosyncratic reactions which have been associated with ganciclovir

Overdosage/Toxicology Symptoms of overdose with ganciclovir include neutropenia, vomiting, hypersalivation, bloody diarrhea, cytopenia, and testicular atrophy. Treatment is supportive. Hemodialysis removes 50% of the drug. Hydration may be of some benefit.

Drug Interactions

Increased Effect/Toxicity: Reported for ganciclovir: Immunosuppressive agents may increase hematologic toxicity of ganciclovir. Imipenem/cilastatin may increase seizure potential. Oral ganciclovir increases blood levels of zidovudine, although zidovudine decreases steady-state levels of ganciclovir. Since both drugs have the potential to cause neutropenia and anemia, some patients may not tolerate concomitant therapy with these drugs at full dosage. Didanosine levels are increased with concurrent ganciclovir. Other nephrotoxic drugs (eg, amphotericin and cyclosporine) may have additive nephrotoxicity with ganciclovir.

Decreased Effect: Reported for ganciclovir: A decrease in blood levels of ganciclovir AUC may occur when used with didanosine.

Ethanol/Nutrition/Herb Interactions Food: Coadministration with a high-fat meal increased AUC by 30%.

Storage/Stability Store at 25°C (77°F); excursions permitted to 15°C to 30°C (59°F to 86°F).

Mechanism of Action Valganciclovir is rapidly converted to ganciclovir in the body. The bioavailability of ganciclovir from valganciclovir is increased 10-fold compared to oral ganciclovir. A dose of 900 mg achieved systemic exposure of ganciclovir comparable to that achieved with the recommended doses of intravenous ganciclovir of 5 mg/kg. Ganciclovir is phosphorylated to a substrate which competitively inhibits the binding of deoxyguanosine triphosphate to DNA polymerase resulting in inhibition of viral DNA synthesis.

Pharmacodynamics/Kinetics

Absorption: Well absorbed; high-fat meal increases AUC by 30%

Distribution: Ganciclovir: V_d: 15.26 L/1.73 m^2; widely to all tissue including CSF and ocular tissue

Protein binding: 1% to 2%

Metabolism: Converted to ganciclovir by intestinal mucosal cells and hepatocytes

Bioavailability: With food: 60%

Half-life elimination: Ganciclovir: 4.08 hours; prolonged with renal impairment; Severe renal impairment: Up to 68 hours

Excretion: Urine (primarily as ganciclovir)

Dosage Oral: Adults:

CMV retinitis:

Induction: 900 mg twice daily for 21 days (with food)

Maintenance: Following induction treatment, or for patients with inactive CMV retinitis who require maintenance therapy: Recommended dose: 900 mg once daily (with food)

Prevention of CMV disease following transplantation: 900 mg once daily (with food) beginning within 10 days of transplantation; continue therapy until 100 days post-transplantation

Dosage adjustment in renal impairment:

Induction dose:

Cl_{cr} 40-59 mL/minute: 450 mg twice daily

Cl_{cr} 25-39 mL/minute: 450 mg once daily

Cl_{cr} 10-24 mL/minute: 450 mg every 2 days

Maintenance dose:

Cl_{cr} 40-59 mL/minute: 450 mg once daily

Cl_{cr} 25-39 mL/minute: 450 mg every 2 days

Cl_{cr} 10-24 mL/minute: 450 mg twice weekly

Note: Valganciclovir is not recommended in patients receiving hemodialysis. For patients on hemodialysis (Cl_{cr} <10 mL/minute), it is recommended that ganciclovir be used (dose adjusted as specified for ganciclovir).

Administration Avoid direct contact with broken or crushed tablets. Consideration should be given to handling and disposal according to guidelines (Continued)

Valganciclovir *(Continued)*

issued for antineoplastic drugs. However, there is no consensus on the need for these precautions.

Monitoring Parameters Retinal exam (at least every 4-6 weeks), CBC, platelet counts, serum creatinine

Dietary Considerations Should be taken with meals.

Patient Information Valganciclovir is not a cure for CMV retinitis. For oral administration, take as directed (with food) and maintain adequate hydration (2-3 L/day of fluids unless instructed to restrict fluid intake). Swallow tablets whole; do not break or crush. Avoid handling broken or crushed tablets. Wash area thoroughly if contact occurs. Report fever, chills, unusual bleeding or bruising, infection, or unhealed sores or white plaques in mouth.

Dosage Forms Excipient information presented when available (limited, particularly for generics); consult specific product labeling.

Tablet, as hydrochloride: 450 mg [valganciclovir hydrochloride 496.3 mg equivalent to valganciclovir 450 mg]

References

Ljungman P, de La Camara R, Milpied N, et al, "Randomized Study of Valacyclovir as Prophylaxis Against Cytomegalovirus Reactivation in Recipients of Allogeneic Bone Marrow Transplants," *Blood*, 2002, 99(8):3050-6.

Pescovitz MD, Rabkin J, Merion RM, et al, "Valganciclovir Results in Improved Oral Absorption of Ganciclovir in Liver Transplant Recipients," *Antimicrob Agents Chemother*, 2000, 44(10):2811-5.

♦ **Valganciclovir Hydrochloride** *see* Valganciclovir *on page 1083*

Valrubicin *(val ROO bi sin)*

Medication Safety Issues

Sound-alike/look-alike issues:

Valstar® may be confused with valsartan

High alert medication: The Institute for Safe Medication Practices (ISMP) includes this medication among its list of drugs which have a heightened risk of causing significant patient harm when used in error.

Related Information

Management of Drug Extravasations *on page 1301*

Safe Handling of Hazardous Drugs *on page 1382*

U.S. Brand Names Valstar® [DSC]

Index Terms AD3L; *N*-trifluoroacetyladriamycin-14-valerate

Generic Available No

Canadian Brand Names Valstar®; Valtaxin®

Pharmacologic Category Antineoplastic Agent, Anthracycline

Use Intravesical therapy of BCG-refractory carcinoma *in situ* of the urinary bladder

Pregnancy Risk Factor C

Lactation Excretion in breast milk unknown/not recommended

Labeled Contraindications Hypersensitivity to anthracyclines, Cremophor® EL, or any component of the formulation; concurrent urinary tract infection or small bladder capacity (unable to tolerate a 75 mL instillation)

Warnings/Precautions Hazardous agent - use appropriate precautions for handling and disposal. Do not administer if mucosal integrity of bladder has been compromised or bladder perforation is present. Irritable bladder symptoms may occur during instillation and retention. Use caution in patients with severe irritable bladder symptoms. Valrubicin should be used cautiously (if at all) in patients having a history of hypersensitivity reactions to other medications prepared with Cremophor® EL.

Adverse Reactions

>10%: Genitourinary: Frequency (61%), dysuria (56%), urgency (57%), bladder spasm (31%), hematuria (29%), bladder pain (28%), urinary incontinence (22%), cystitis (15%), urinary tract infection (15%)

1% to 10%:

Cardiovascular: Chest pain (2%), vasodilation (2%), peripheral edema (1%)

Central nervous system: Headache (4%), malaise (4%), dizziness (3%), fever (2%)

Dermatologic: Rash (3%)

Endocrine & metabolic: Hyperglycemia (1%)

Gastrointestinal: Abdominal pain (5%), nausea (5%), diarrhea (3%), vomiting (2%), flatulence (1%)

Genitourinary: Nocturia (7%), burning symptoms (5%), urinary retention (4%), urethral pain (3%), pelvic pain (1%), hematuria (microscopic) (3%)

Hematologic: Anemia (2%)

Neuromuscular & skeletal: Weakness (4%), back pain (3%), myalgia (1%)

Respiratory: Pneumonia (1%)

<1%: Tenesmus, pruritus, taste disturbance, skin irritation, urine flow decreased, urethritis

Overdosage/Toxicology Inadvertent paravenous extravasation has not been associated with skin ulceration or necrosis. Myelosuppression is possible following inadvertent systemic administration, or following significant systemic absorption from intravesical instillation.

Drug Interactions

Increased Effect/Toxicity: No specific drug interactions studies have been performed. Systemic exposure to valrubicin is negligible, and interactions are unlikely.

Decreased Effect: No specific drug interactions studies have been performed. Systemic exposure to valrubicin is negligible, and interactions are unlikely.

Storage/Stability Store unopened vials under refrigeration at 2°C to 8°C (36°F to 48°F). Stable for 12 hours when diluted in 0.9% sodium chloride.

Reconstitution Allow vial to warm to room temperature without heating. Dilute 800 mg (20 mL) with 55 mL NS.

Mechanism of Action Blocks function of DNA topoisomerase II; inhibits DNA synthesis, causes extensive chromosomal damage, and arrests cell development; unlike other anthracyclines, does not appear to intercalate DNA

Pharmacodynamics/Kinetics

Absorption: Well absorbed into bladder tissue, negligible systemic absorption. Trauma to mucosa may increase absorption, and perforation greatly increases absorption with significant systemic myelotoxicity.

Metabolism: Negligible after intravesical instillation and 2-hour retention

Excretion: Urine when expelled from urinary bladder (98.6% as intact drug; 0.4% as N-trifluoroacetyladriamycin)

Dosage Adults: Intravesical: 800 mg once weekly for 6 weeks

Dosing adjustment in renal impairment: No specific adjustment recommended

Dosing adjustment in hepatic impairment: No specific adjustment recommended

Administration Intravesicular bladder lavage, usually in 75 mL of 0.9% sodium chloride injection. Retain in the bladder for 2 hours, then void. Due to the Cremophor® EL diluent, valrubicin should be administered through non-PVC tubing.

(Continued)

Valrubicin *(Continued)*

Monitoring Parameters Cystoscopy, biopsy, and urine cytology every 3 months for recurrence or progression

Patient Information This medication will be instilled into your bladder through a catheter to be retained for as long as possible. Your urine will be red tinged for the next 24 hours; report promptly if this continues for a longer period. You may experience altered urination patterns (frequency, dysuria, or incontinence), some bladder pain, pain on urination, or pelvic pain; report if these persist. Diabetics should monitor glucose levels closely (may cause hyperglycemia). It is important that you maintain adequate hydration (2-3 L/ day of fluids unless instructed to restrict fluid intake). You may experience some dizziness (use caution when driving or engaging in tasks requiring alertness until response to drug is known); or nausea, vomiting, or taste disturbance (small frequent meals, frequent mouth care, chewing gum, or sucking lozenges may help). Report chest pain or palpitations; persistent dizziness; swelling of extremities; persistent nausea, vomiting, diarrhea, or abdominal pain; muscle weakness, pain, or tremors; unusual cough or difficulty breathing; or other adverse effects related to this medication.

Dosage Forms Excipient information presented when available (limited, particularly for generics); consult specific product labeling. [DSC] = Discontinued product

Injection, solution [DSC]: 40 mg/mL (5 mL) [contains Cremophor® EL 50% (polyoxyethyleneglycol triricinoleate) and dehydrated alcohol 50%]

References

Greenberg RE, Bahnson RR, Wood D, et al, "Initial Report on Intravesical Administration of N-trifluoroacetyldoxorubicin-14-valerate (AD32) to Patients With Refractory Superficial Transitional Cell Carcinoma of the Urinary Bladder," *Urology,* 1997, 49(3):471-5.

Markman M, Homesley H, Norberts DA, et al, "Phase 1 Trial of Intraperitoneal AD-32 in Gynecologic Malignancies," *Gynecol Oncol,* 1996, 61(1):90-3.

Onrust SV and Lamb HM, "Valrubicin," *Drugs Aging,* 1999, 15(1):69-75.

♦ **Valstar® [DSC]** *see* Valrubicin *on page 1086*

♦ **Valstar® (Can)** *see* Valrubicin *on page 1086*

♦ **Valtaxin® (Can)** *see* Valrubicin *on page 1086*

♦ **Valtrex®** *see* Valacyclovir *on page 1080*

♦ **Vancocin®** *see* Vancomycin *on page 1088*

Vancomycin *(van koe MYE sin)*

Medication Safety Issues

Sound-alike/look-alike issues:

I.V. vancomycin may be confused with Invanz®

Vancomycin may be confused with vecuronium

U.S. Brand Names Vancocin®

Index Terms Vancomycin Hydrochloride

Generic Available Yes: Injection

Canadian Brand Names Vancocin®

Pharmacologic Category Antibiotic, Miscellaneous

Use Treatment of patients with infections caused by staphylococcal species and streptococcal species; used orally for staphylococcal enterocolitis or for antibiotic-associated pseudomembranous colitis produced by *C. difficile*

Unlabeled/Investigational Use Bacterial endophthalmitis

Pregnancy Risk Factor C

Lactation Enters breast milk/use caution

Labeled Contraindications Hypersensitivity to vancomycin or any component of the formulation; avoid in patients with previous severe hearing loss

Warnings/Precautions May cause nephrotoxicity; usual risk factors include pre-existing renal impairment, concomitant nephrotoxic medications, advanced age, and dehydration. Discontinue treatment if signs of nephrotoxicity occur; renal damage is usually reversible. May cause neurotoxicity; usual risk factors include pre-existing renal impairment, concomitant neuro-/nephrotoxic medications, advanced age, and dehydration. Ototoxicity is proportional to the amount of drug given and the duration of treatment. Tinnitus or vertigo may be indications of vestibular injury and impending bilateral irreversible damage. Discontinue treatment if signs of ototoxicity occur. Prolonged therapy (>1 week) or total doses exceeding 25 g may increase the risk of neutropenia; prompt reversal of neutropenia is expected after discontinuation of therapy. Prolonged use may result in fungal or bacterial superinfection, including *C. difficile*-associated diarrhea (CDAD) and pseudomembranous colitis; CDAD has been observed <2 months postantibiotic treatment. Use with caution in patients with renal impairment or those receiving other nephrotoxic or ototoxic drugs; dosage modification required in patients with impaired renal function (especially elderly). Rapid I.V. administration may result in hypotension, flushing, erythema, urticaria, and/or pruritus; rate of infusion should be ≥60 minutes.

Adverse Reactions
Oral:
>10%: Gastrointestinal: Bitter taste, nausea, vomiting
1% to 10%:
Central nervous system: Chills, drug fever
Hematologic: Eosinophilia
<1%: Interstitial nephritis, ototoxicity, renal failure, thrombocytopenia, vasculitis
Parenteral:
>10%:
Cardiovascular: Hypotension accompanied by flushing
Dermatologic: Erythematous rash on face and upper body (red neck or red man syndrome - infusion rate related)
1% to 10%:
Central nervous system: Chills, drug fever
Dermatologic: Rash
Hematologic: Eosinophilia, reversible neutropenia
<1%: Ototoxicity (especially with large doses), thrombocytopenia, renal failure (especially with renal dysfunction or pre-existing hearing loss), Stevens-Johnson syndrome, vasculitis

Overdosage/Toxicology Symptoms of overdose include ototoxicity and nephrotoxicity. There is no specific therapy for overdose with vancomycin. Care is symptomatic and supportive. Peritoneal filtration and hemofiltration (not dialysis) have been shown to reduce the serum concentration of vancomycin. High flux dialysis may remove up to 25% of the drug.

Drug Interactions
Increased Effect/Toxicity: Increased toxicity with other ototoxic or nephrotoxic drugs. Increased neuromuscular blockade with most neuromuscular blocking agents.

Storage/Stability Reconstituted 500 mg and 1 g vials are stable for at either room temperature or under refrigeration for 14 days. **Note:** Vials contain no bacteriostatic agent. Solutions diluted for administration in either D_5W or NS are stable under refrigeration for 14 days or at room temperature for 7 days.

Reconstitution Reconstitute vials with 20 mL of SWFI for each 1 g of vancomycin (10 mL/500 mg vial; 20 mL/1 g vial; 100 mL/5 g vial; 200 mL/10 g vial). The reconstituted solution must be further diluted with at least 100 mL of a
(Continued)

Vancomycin *(Continued)*

compatible diluent per 500 mg of vancomycin prior to parenteral administration.

Intrathecal: Vancomycin is available as a powder for injection and may be diluted to 1-5 mg/mL concentration in preservative free 0.9% sodium chloride for administration into the CSF.

Compatibility Stable in dextran 6% in NS, D_5LR, D_5NS, D_5W, $D_{10}W$, LR, NS; **variable stability (consult detailed reference)** in peritoneal dialysis solutions, TPN.

Y-site administration: Compatible: Acyclovir, alatrofloxacin, allopurinol, amifostine, amiodarone, amsacrine, atracurium, cefpirome, cisatracurium, clarithromycin, cyclophosphamide, diltiazem, docetaxel, doxorubicin liposome, enalaprilat, esmolol, etoposide phosphate, filgrastim, fluconazole, fludarabine, gemcitabine, granisetron, hydromorphone, insulin (regular), labetalol, levofloxacin, linezolid, lorazepam, magnesium sulfate, melphalan, meperidine, meropenem, midazolam, morphine, ondansetron, paclitaxel, pancuronium, perphenazine, propofol, remifentanil, sodium bicarbonate, tacrolimus, teniposide, theophylline, thiotepa, tolazoline, vecuronium, vinorelbine, zidovudine. **Incompatible:** Albumin, amphotericin B cholesteryl sulfate complex, cefepime, gatifloxacin, heparin, idarubicin, omeprazole. **Variable (consult detailed reference):** Ampicillin, ampicillin/sulbactam, aztreonam, cefazolin, cefotaxime, cefotetan, cefoxitin, ceftazidime, ceftizoxime, ceftriaxone, cefuroxime, foscarnet, methotrexate, nafcillin, piperacillin, piperacillin/tazobactam, sargramostim, ticarcillin, ticarcillin/clavulanate, TPN, warfarin.

Compatibility in syringe: Incompatible: Heparin.

Compatibility when admixed: Compatible: Amikacin, atracurium, calcium gluconate, cefepime, cimetidine, corticotropin, dimenhydrinate, famotidine, hydrocortisone sodium succinate, meropenem, ofloxacin, potassium chloride, ranitidine, verapamil, vitamin B complex with C. **Incompatible:** Amobarbital, chloramphenicol, chlorothiazide, dexamethasone sodium phosphate, penicillin G potassium, pentobarbital, phenobarbital, phenytoin. **Variable (consult detailed reference):** Aminophylline, aztreonam, heparin, sodium bicarbonate.

Mechanism of Action Inhibits bacterial cell wall synthesis by blocking glycopeptide polymerization through binding tightly to D-alanyl-D-alanine portion of cell wall precursor

Pharmacodynamics/Kinetics

Absorption: Oral: Poor; I.M.: Erratic; Intraperitoneal: ~38%

Distribution: Widely in body tissue and fluids. except for CSF

Relative diffusion from blood into CSF: Good only with inflammation (exceeds usual MICs)

CSF:blood level ratio: Normal meninges: Nil; Inflamed meninges: 20% to 30%

Protein binding: 10% to 50%

Half-life elimination: Biphasic: Terminal:

Newborns: 6-10 hours

Infants and Children 3 months to 4 years: 4 hours

Children >3 years: 2.2-3 hours

Adults: 5-11 hours; significantly prolonged with renal impairment

End-stage renal disease: 200-250 hours

Time to peak, serum: I.V.: 45-65 minutes

Excretion: I.V.: Urine (80% to 90% as unchanged drug); Oral: Primarily feces

Dosage

Usual dosage range:

Infants >1 month and Children: I.V.: 10-15 mg/kg every 6 hours

Adults:

I.V.: 2-3 g/day (20-45 mg/kg/day) in divided doses every 6-12 hours; maximum 3 g/day; **Note:** Dose requires adjustment in renal impairment

Oral: 500-1000 mg/day in divided doses every 6 hours

Indication-specific dosing:

Infants >1 month and Children:

Colitis (*C. difficile*): Oral: 40 mg/kg/day in divided doses added to fluids

Meningitis/CNS infection:

I.V.: 15 mg/kg every 6 hours

Intrathecal: 5-20 mg/day

Prophylaxis against infective endocarditis: I.V.:

Dental, oral, or upper respiratory tract surgery: 20 mg/kg 1 hour prior to the procedure. **Note:** American Heart Association (AHA) guidelines now recommend prophylaxis only in patients undergoing invasive procedures and in whom underlying cardiac conditions may predispose to a higher risk of adverse outcomes should infection occur.

GI/GU procedure: 20 mg/kg plus gentamicin 2 mg/kg 1 hour prior to surgery. **Note:** As of April 2007, routine prophylaxis no longer recommended by the AHA.

Susceptible gram-positive infections: I.V.: 10 mg/kg every 6 hours

Adults:

Catheter-related infections: Antibiotic lock technique: 2 mg/mL in SWFI/NS or D_5W; instill 3-5 mL into catheter port as a flush solution instead of heparin lock (**Note:** Do not mix with any other solutions.)

Colitis (*C. difficile*) (unlabeled use): Oral: 125-250 mg every 6 hours for 10 days

Endophthalmitis (unlabeled use): Intravitreal: Usual dose: 1 mg/0.1 mL NS instilled into vitreum; may repeat administration if necessary in 3-4 days, usually in combination with ceftazidime or an aminoglycoside **Note:** Some clinicians have recommended using a lower dose of 0.2 mg/0.1 mL, based on concerns for retinotoxicity.

Hospital-acquired pneumonia (HAP): I.V.: 15 mg/kg/dose every 12 hours (American Thoracic Society [ATS] 2005 guidelines)

Meningitis (*Pneumococcus* or *Staphylococcus*):

I.V.: 30-45 mg/kg/day in divided doses every 8-12 hours **or** 500-750 mg every 6 hours (with third-generation cephalosporin for PCN-resistant *Streptococcus pneumoniae*); maximum dose: 2-3 g/day

Intrathecal: Up to 20 mg/day

Prophylaxis against infective endocarditis: I.V.:

Dental, oral, or upper respiratory tract surgery: 1 g 1 hour before surgery. **Note:** AHA guidelines now recommend prophylaxis only in patients undergoing invasive procedures and in whom underlying cardiac conditions may predispose to a higher risk of adverse outcomes should infection occur

GI/GU procedure: 1 g plus 1.5 mg/kg gentamicin 1 hour prior to surgery. **Note:** As of April 2007, routine prophylaxis no longer recommended by the AHA.

Susceptible gram-positive infections: I.V.: 15-20 mg/kg/dose (usual: 750-1500 mg) every 12 hours

(Continued)

Vancomycin *(Continued)*

Dosing interval in renal impairment (vancomycin levels should be monitored in patients with any renal impairment):

Cl_{cr} >50 mL/minute: Start with 15-20 mg/kg/dose (usual: 750-1500 mg) every 12 hours

Cl_{cr} 20-49 mL/minute: Start with 15-20 mg/kg/dose (usual: 750-1500 mg) every 24 hours

Cl_{cr} <20 mL/minute: Will need longer intervals; determine by serum concentration monitoring

Dialysis: Variable, depending on method; poorly dialyzable by conventional hemodialysis (0% to 5%). Use of high-flux membranes and continuous renal replacement therapy (CRRT) increases vancomycin clearance, and generally requires replacement dosing.

Hemodialysis (HD): Following loading dose of 15-20 mg/kg, give 500 mg to 1 g after each dialysis session, depending on factors such as HD membrane type and flow rate; monitor levels closely.

Continuous ambulatory peritoneal dialysis (CAPD):

Administration via CAPD fluid: 15-30 mg/L (15-30 mcg/mL) of CAPD fluid

Systemic: 1 g loading dose, followed by 500 mg to 1 g every 48-72 hours with close monitoring of levels

Continuous renal replacement therapy (CRRT): Removal of vancomycin is highly dependent on the method of replacement, filter type, and flow rate. Appropriate dosing requires close monitoring of levels in relation to target trough. The following are general recommendations only (based on Trotman, et al, 2005), and require consideration of the aforementioned parameters.

CVVH: Following loading dose of 15-20 mg/kg, give 1 g every 48 hours

CVVHD or CVVHDF: Following loading dose of 15-20 mg/kg, give 1 g every 24 hours

Trotman RL, Williamson JC, Shoemaker DM, et al, "Antibiotic Dosing in Critically Ill Adult Patients Receiving Continuous Renal Replacement Therapy," *Clin Infect Dis*, 2005, 41:1159-66.

Administration Administer vancomycin by I.V. intermittent infusion over at least 60 minutes at a final concentration not to exceed 5 mg/mL. If a maculopapular rash appears on the face, neck, trunk, and/or upper extremities (red man syndrome), slow the infusion rate to over $1^1/_2$ to 2 hours and increase the dilution volume. Hypotension, shock, and cardiac arrest (rare) have also been reported with too rapid of infusion. Reactions are often treated with antihistamines and steroids.

Vancomycin is available as a powder for injection and may be diluted to 1-5 mg/mL concentration in preservative free 0.9% sodium chloride for administration into the CSF.

Extravasation treatment: Monitor I.V. site closely; extravasation will cause serious injury with possible necrosis and tissue sloughing. Rotate infusion site frequently.

Monitoring Parameters Periodic renal function tests, urinalysis, serum vancomycin concentrations, WBC, audiogram

Dietary Considerations May be taken with food.

Patient Information Report pain at infusion site, dizziness, fullness or ringing in ears with I.V. use; nausea or vomiting with oral use

Special Geriatric Considerations As a result of age-related changes in renal function and volume of distribution, accumulation and toxicity are a risk in the elderly. Careful monitoring and dosing adjustment is necessary.

Additional Information Because of its long half-life, vancomycin should be dosed on an every 12-hour basis. Monitoring of peak and trough serum levels is advisable. "Red man syndrome", characterized by skin rash and hypotension, is not an allergic reaction but rather is associated with too rapid infusion of the drug. To alleviate or prevent the reaction, infuse vancomycin at a rate of ≥30 minutes for each 500 mg of drug being administered (eg, 1 g over ≥60 minutes); 1.5 g over ≥90 minutes.

Vesicant No

Dosage Forms Excipient information presented when available (limited, particularly for generics); consult specific product labeling.

Capsule (Vancocin®): 125 mg, 250 mg

Infusion [premixed in iso-osmotic dextrose] (Vancocin®): 500 mg (100 mL); 1 g (200 mL)

Injection, powder for reconstitution: 500 mg, 1 g, 5 g, 10 g

References

Abramowicz M, "Antimicrobial Prophylaxis in Surgery," *Medical Letter on Drugs and Therapeutics, Handbook of Antimicrobial Therapy*, 16th ed, New York, NY: Medical Letter, 2002.

Ahkee S, Smith R, and Ritter GW, "Once-Daily Aminoglycoside Dosing in Lower Respiratory Tract Infections," *Pharm Therapeut*, 1995, 20:226-34.

American Academy of Pediatrics Committee on Infectious Diseases, "Treatment of Bacterial Meningitis," *Pediatrics*, 1988, 81(6):904-7.

American Thoracic Society and Infectious Diseases Society of America, "Guidelines for the Management of Adults With Hospital-Acquired, Ventilator-Associated, and Health-care-Associated Pneumonia," *Am J Respir Crit Care Med*, 2005, 171(4):388-416.

Baddour LM, Wilson WR, Bayer AS, et al, "Infective Endocarditis. Diagnosis, Antimicrobial Therapy, and Management of Complications. A Statement for Healthcare Professionals from the Committee on Rheumatic Fever, Endocarditis, and Kawasaki Disease, Council on Cardiovascular Disease in the Young, and the Councils on Clinical Cardiology, Stroke, and Cardiovascular Surgery and Anesthesia, American Heart Association," *Circulation*, 2005, 111(23):e394-434.

Burkhart KK, Metcalf S, Shurnas E, et al, "Exchange Transfusion and Multidose Activated Charcoal Following Vancomycin Overdose," *J Toxicol Clin Toxicol*, 1992, 30(2):285-94.

Cantù TG, Yamanaka-Yuen NA, and Lietman PS, "Serum Vancomycin Concentrations: Reappraisal of Their Clinical Value," *Clin Infect Dis*, 1994, 18(4):533-43.

Centers for Disease Control and Prevention, "Recommendations for Preventing the Spread of Vancomycin Resistance - Recommendations of the Hospital Infection Control Practice Advisory Committee (HICPAC)," *MMWR Recomm Rep*, 1995, 44(RR-12):1-9.

Chang D, Liem L, and Malogolowkin M, "A Prospective Study of Vancomycin Pharmacokinetics and Dosage Requirements in Pediatric Cancer Patients," *Pediatr Infect Dis J*, 1994, 13(11):969-74.

Chang D, "Influence of Malignancy on the Pharmacokinetics of Vancomycin in Infants and Children," *Pediatr Infect Dis J*, 1995, 14(8):667-73.

Cunha BA, "Vancomycin," *Med Clin North Am*, 1995, 79(4):817-31.

Cutler NR, Narang PK, Lesko LJ, et al, "Vancomycin Disposition: The Importance of Age," *Clin Pharmacol Ther*, 1984, 36(6):803-10.

DeVries E, van Rossum MAJ, Garritsen EJA, et al, "No Difference in Frequency of Adverse Reactions to Either Vancomycin or Teicoplanin in 70 Pediatric Bone Marrow Transplant Patients," *Bone Marrow Transplant*, 1995, 15(Suppl 2):124.

Duffull SB and Begg EJ, "Vancomycin Toxicity. What Is the Evidence for Dose Dependency?" *Adverse Drug React Toxicol Rev*, 1994, 13(2):103-14.

French GL, "Enterococci and Vancomycin Resistance," *Clin Infect Dis*, 1998, 27(Suppl 1):75-83.

Frimat L, Hestin D, Hanesse B, et al, "Acute Renal Failure Due to Vancomycin Alone," *Nephrol Dial Transplant*, 1995, 10(4):550-1.

Geissmann C, Beylot-Barry M, Doutre M-S, et al, "Drug-Induced Linear IgA Bullous Dermatosis," *J Am Acad Dermatol*, 1995, 32(2 Pt 1):296.

Gilbert DN, Moellering RC, Eliopoulos GM, et al, eds, *The Sanford Guide To Antimicrobial Therapy*, 36th ed, Hyde Park, VT: Antimicrobial Therapy, Inc, 2006, 6-7.

Hill LM, "Fetal Distress Secondary to Vancomycin-Induced Maternal Hypotension," *Am J Obstet Gynecol*, 1985, 153(1):74-5.

Joy MS, Matzke GR, Frye RF, et al, "Determinants of Vancomycin Clearance by Continuous Veno-Venous Hemofiltration and Continuous Veno-Venous Hemodialysis," *Am J Kidney Dis*, 1998, 31(6):1019-27.

Kelly CP, Pothoulakis C, and LaMont JT, "*Clostridium difficile* colitis," *N Engl J Med*, 1994, 330(4):257-62.

(Continued)

Vancomycin *(Continued)*

Leader WG, Chandler MH, and Castiglia M, "Pharmacokinetic Optimization of Vancomycin Therapy," *Clin Pharmacokinet*, 1995, 28(4):327-42.

Leonard MB, Koren G, Stevenson DK, et al, "Vancomycin Pharmacokinetics in Very Low Birth Weight Neonates," *Pediatr Infect Dis J*, 1989, 8(5):282-6.

Linden P, "Antibiotic Therapy in Critical Illness," *Multidisciplinary Critical Care Review*, Zimmerman JL and Roberts PR, eds, Des Plaines, IL: Society of Critical Care Medicine, 2003,192.

Luer MS and Hatton J, "Vancomycin Administration Into the Cerebrospinal Fluid: A Review," *Ann Pharmacother*, 1993, 27(7-8):912-21.

Lundstrom TS and Sobel JD, "Vancomycin, Trimethoprim-Sulfamethoxazole, and Rifampin," *Infect Dis Clin North Am*, 1995, 9(3):747-67.

Lyon GD and Bruce DL, "Diphenhydramine Reversal of Vancomycin-Induced Hypotension," *Anesth Analg*, 1988, 67(11):1109-10.

Matzke GR, Zhanel GG, and Guay DRP, "Clinical Pharmacokinetics of Vancomycin," *Clin Pharmacokinet*, 1986, 11(4):257-82.

Morris JG Jr, Shay DK, Hebden JN, et al, "Enterococci Resistant to Multiple Antimicrobial Agents, Including Vancomycin. Establishment of Endemicity in a University Medical Center," *Ann Intern Med*, 1995, 123(4):250-9.

Murray BE, "Vancomycin-Resistant Enterococcal Infections," *N Engl J Med*, 2000, 342(10):710-21.

Nielsen HE, Sorensen I, and Hansen HE, "Peritoneal Transport of Vancomycin During Peritoneal Dialysis," *Nephron*, 1979, 24(6):274-7.

Quagliarello VJ and Scheld WM, "Treatment of Bacterial Meningitis," *N Engl J Med*, 1997, 336(10):708-16.

"Results of the Endophthalmitis Vitrectomy Study. A Randomized Trial of Immediate Vitrectomy and of Intravenous Antibiotics for the Treatment of Postoperative Bacterial Endophthalmitis. Endophthalmitis Vitrectomy Study Group," *Arch Ophthalmol*, 1995, 113(12):1479-96.

Rodvold KA, Blum RA, Fischer JH, et al, "Vancomycin Pharmacokinetics in Patients With Various Degrees of Renal Function," *Antimicrob Agents Chemother*, 1988, 32(6):848-52.

Rodvold KA, Everett JA, Pryka RD, and Kraus DM, "Pharmacokinetics and Administration Regimens of Vancomycin in Neonates, Infants and Children," *Clin Pharmacokinet*, 1997, 33(1):32-51.

Roth DB and Flynn HW Jr, "Antibiotic Selection in the Treatment of Endophthalmitis: The Significance of Drug Combinations and Synergy," *Surv Ophthalmol*, 1997, 41(5):395-401.

Rybak MJ, Albrecht LM, Boike SC, et al, "Nephrotoxicity of Vancomycin, Alone and With an Aminoglycoside," *J Antimicrob Chemother*, 1990, 25(4):679-87.

Schenfeld LA and Pote HH Jr, "Diarrhea Associated With Parenteral Vancomycin Therapy," *Clin Infect Dis*, 1995, 20(6):1578-9.

Trotman RL, Williamson JC, Shoemaker DM, et al, "Antibiotic Dosing in Critically Ill Adult Patients Receiving Continuous Renal Replacement Therapy," *Clin Infect Dis*, 2005, 41:1159-66.

Tunkel AR, Hartman BJ, Kaplan SL, et al, "Practice Guidelines for the Management of Bacterial Meningitis," *Clin Infect Dis*, 2004, 39(9):1267-84.

Wilhelm MP, "Vancomycin," *Mayo Clin Proc*, 1991, 66(11):1165-70.

Wilson W, Taubert KA, Gewitz M, et al, "Prevention of Infective Endocarditis. Guidelines From the American Heart Association. A Guideline From the American Heart Association Rheumatic Fever, Endocarditis, and Kawasaki Disease Committee, Council on Cardiovascular Disease in the Young, and the Council on Clinical Cardiology, Council on Cardiovascular Surgery and Anesthesia, and the Quality of Care and Outcomes Research Interdisciplinary Working Group," *Circulation*, 2007, 115. Available at http://circ.ahajournals.org/cgi/reprint/CIRCULATIONAHA.106.183095v1; last accessed July 26, 2007.

- ◆ **Vancomycin Hydrochloride** *see* Vancomycin *on page 1088*
- ◆ **Vandazole™** *see* Metronidazole *on page 755*
- ◆ **Vantas™** *see* Histrelin *on page 540*
- ◆ **Vectibix™** *see* Panitumumab *on page 876*
- ◆ **Velcade®** *see* Bortezomib *on page 150*
- ◆ **Venofer®** *see* Iron Sucrose *on page 636*
- ◆ **VePesid®** *see* Etoposide *on page 402*
- ◆ **Veracolate [OTC]** *see* Bisacodyl *on page 144*
- ◆ **Versiclear™** *see* Sodium Thiosulfate *on page 972*
- ◆ **Vesanoid®** *see* Tretinoin (Oral) *on page 1069*
- ◆ **VFEND®** *see* Voriconazole *on page 1111*

♦ **Viadur**® *see* Leuprolide *on page 672*
♦ **Vidaza**® *see* Azacitidine *on page 117*

VinBLAStine (vin BLAS teen)

Medication Safety Issues

Sound-alike/look-alike issues:

VinBLAStine may be confused with vinCRIStine, vinorelbine

High alert medication: The Institute for Safe Medication Practices (ISMP) includes this medication among its list of drugs which have a heightened risk of causing significant patient harm when used in error.

Note: Must be dispensed in overwrap which bears the statement **"Do not remove covering until the moment of injection. Fatal if given intrathecally. For I.V. use only."** Syringes should be labeled: **"Fatal if given intrathecally. For I.V. use only."**

Related Information

Management of Drug Extravasations *on page 1301*
Management of Nausea and Vomiting *on page 1319*
Safe Handling of Hazardous Drugs *on page 1382*

Index Terms NSC-49842; Vinblastine Sulfate; VLB

Generic Available Yes

Pharmacologic Category Antineoplastic Agent, Natural Source (Plant) Derivative; Antineoplastic Agent, Vinca Alkaloid

Use Treatment of Hodgkin's and non-Hodgkin's lymphoma; testicular, lung, head and neck, breast, and renal carcinomas; Mycosis fungoides; Kaposi's sarcoma; histiocytosis; choriocarcinoma; and idiopathic thrombocytopenic purpura

Pregnancy Risk Factor D

Lactation Enters breast milk/not recommended

Labeled Contraindications For I.V. use only; **I.T. use may result in death**; hypersensitivity to vinblastine or any component of the formulation; pregnancy

Warnings/Precautions Hazardous agent - use appropriate precautions for handling and disposal. **[U.S. Boxed Warning]: Vinblastine is a moderate vesicant; avoid extravasation.** Dosage modification required in patients with impaired liver function and neurotoxicity. **[U.S. Boxed Warning]: For I.V. use only. Intrathecal administration results in death.** Use with caution in patients with cachexia or ulcerated skin. Monitor closely for shortness of breath or bronchospasm in patients receiving in combination with mitomycin C. **[U.S. Boxed Warning]: Should be administered under the supervision of an experienced cancer chemotherapy physician.**

Adverse Reactions

>10%:

Dermatologic: Alopecia

Endocrine & metabolic: SIADH

Gastrointestinal: Diarrhea (less common), stomatitis, anorexia, metallic taste

Hematologic: May cause severe bone marrow suppression and is the dose-limiting toxicity of vinblastine (unlike vincristine); severe granulocytopenia and thrombocytopenia may occur following the administration of vinblastine and nadir 5-10 days after treatment

Myelosuppression (primarily leukopenia, may be dose limiting)

Onset: 4-7 days
Nadir: 5-10 days
Recovery: 4-21 days

(Continued)

VinBLAStine *(Continued)*

1% to 10%:

Cardiovascular: Hypertension, Raynaud's phenomenon

Central nervous system: Depression, malaise, headache, seizure

Dermatologic: Rash, photosensitivity, dermatitis

Endocrine & metabolic: Hyperuricemia

Gastrointestinal: Constipation, abdominal pain, nausea (mild), vomiting (mild), paralytic ileus, stomatitis

Genitourinary: Urinary retention

Neuromuscular & skeletal: Jaw pain, myalgia, paresthesia

Respiratory: Bronchospasm

<1%: Vinblastine rarely produces neurotoxicity at clinical doses; however, neurotoxicity may be seen, especially at high doses; if it occurs, symptoms are similar to vincristine toxicity (ie, peripheral neuropathy, loss of deep tendon reflexes, headache, weakness, urinary retention, and GI symptoms, tachycardia, orthostatic hypotension, convulsions); hemorrhagic colitis

Overdosage/Toxicology Symptoms of overdose include bone marrow suppression, mental depression, paresthesia, loss of deep tendon reflexes, and neurotoxicity. There are no antidotes for vinblastine. Treatment is supportive and symptomatic, including fluid restriction or hypertonic saline (3% sodium chloride) for drug-induced secretion of inappropriate antidiuretic hormone (SIADH).

Drug Interactions

Cytochrome P450 Effect: Substrate of CYP2D6 (minor), 3A4 (major); **Inhibits** CYP2D6 (weak), 3A4 (weak)

Increased Effect/Toxicity: CYP3A4 inhibitors may increase the levels/effects of vinblastine; example inhibitors include azole antifungals, clarithromycin, diclofenac, doxycycline, erythromycin, imatinib, isoniazid, nefazodone, nicardipine, propofol, protease inhibitors, quinidine, telithromycin, and verapamil.

Previous or simultaneous use with mitomycin-C has resulted in acute shortness of breath and severe bronchospasm within minutes or several hours after vinca alkaloid injection and may occur up to 2 weeks after the dose of mitomycin. Mitomycin-C, in combination with administration of vinblastine, may cause acute shortness of breath and severe bronchospasm. Onset may be within minutes or several hours after vinblastine injection.

Decreased Effect: CYP3A4 inducers may decrease the levels/effects of vinblastine; example inducers include aminoglutethimide, carbamazepine, nafcillin, nevirapine, phenobarbital, phenytoin (may reduce vinblastine serum concentrations), and rifamycins.

Ethanol/Nutrition/Herb Interactions Herb/Nutraceutical: St John's wort may decrease vinblastine levels. Avoid black cohosh, dong quai in estrogen-dependent tumors.

Storage/Stability Store intact vials under refrigeration (2°C to 8°C). Protect from light. Solutions reconstituted in bacteriostatic water or bacteriostatic NS are stable for 21 days at room temperature or under refrigeration.

Note: Must be dispensed in overwrap which bears the statement "Do not remove covering until the moment of injection. Fatal if given intrathecally. For I.V. use only." Syringes should be labeled: "Fatal if given intrathecally. For I.V. use only."

Reconstitution Reconstitute to a concentration of 1 mg/mL with bacteriostatic water, bacteriostatic NS, SWFI, NS, or D_5W. For infusion, may be diluted with 50-1000 mL NS or D_5W.

Compatibility Stable in D_5W, LR, NS, bacteriostatic water.

Y-site administration: Compatible: Allopurinol, amifostine, amphotericin B cholesteryl sulfate complex, aztreonam, bleomycin, cisplatin, cyclophosphamide, doxorubicin, doxorubicin liposome, droperidol, etoposide phosphate, filgrastim, fludarabine, fluorouracil, gatifloxacin, gemcitabine, granisetron, heparin, leucovorin, melphalan, methotrexate, metoclopramide, mitomycin, ondansetron, paclitaxel, piperacillin/tazobactam, sargramostim, teniposide, thiotepa, vincristine, vinorelbine. **Incompatible:** Cefepime, furosemide.

Compatibility in syringe: Compatible: Bleomycin, cisplatin, cyclophosphamide, droperidol, fluorouracil, leucovorin, methotrexate, metoclopramide, mitomycin, vincristine. **Incompatible:** Furosemide. **Variable (consult detailed reference):** Doxorubicin, heparin.

Compatibility when admixed: Compatible: Bleomycin, dacarbazine. **Variable (consult detailed reference):** Doxorubicin.

Mechanism of Action Vinblastine binds to tubulin and inhibits microtubule formation, therefore, arresting the cell at metaphase by disrupting the formation of the mitotic spindle; it is specific for the M and S phases. Vinblastine may also interfere with nucleic acid and protein synthesis by blocking glutamic acid utilization.

Pharmacodynamics/Kinetics

Distribution: V_d: 27.3 L/kg; binds extensively to tissues; does not penetrate CNS or other fatty tissues; distributes to liver

Protein binding: 99%

Metabolism: Hepatic to active metabolite

Half-life elimination: Biphasic: Initial: 0.164 hours; Terminal: 25 hours

Excretion: Feces (95%); urine (<1% as unchanged drug)

Dosage Refer to individual protocols.

Children and Adults: I.V.: 4-20 mg/m^2 (0.1-0.5 mg/kg) every 7-10 days **or** 5-day continuous infusion of 1.5-2 mg/m^2/day **or** 0.1-0.5 mg/kg/week

Dosing adjustment in renal impairment: According to FDA-approved labeling, no adjustment is necessary in patients with renal impairment.

Dosing adjustment in hepatic impairment:

The FDA-approved labeling recommends the following guidelines: Serum bilirubin >3 mg/dL: Administer 50% of dose

The following guidelines have been used by some clinicians:

Serum bilirubin 1.5-3 mg/dL or AST 60-180 units: Administer 50% of dose

Serum bilirubin 3-5 mg/dL: Administer 25% of dose

Serum bilirubin >5 mg/dL or AST >180 units: Avoid use

Floyd, 2006: Serum bilirubin >3.1 or ALT/AST >3 times ULN: Avoid use

Combination Regimens

Bladder cancer:

CMV *on page 1179*

M-VAC (Bladder Cancer) *on page 1255*

Breast cancer:

Mitomycin-Vinblastine *on page 1248*

M-VAC (Breast Cancer) *on page 1258*

VATH *on page 1287*

VM *on page 1292*

Cervical cancer: M-VAC (Cervical Cancer) *on page 1259*

Endometrial cancer: M-VAC (Endometrial Cancer) *on page 1259*

Head and Neck cancer: M-VAC (Head and Neck Cancer) *on page 1259*

(Continued)

VinBLAStine *(Continued)*

Lymphoma, Hodgkin's:

ABVD *on page 1142*

CAD/MOPP/ABV *on page 1157*

ChlVPP *on page 1173*

EVA *on page 1210*

MOPP/ABV Hybrid *on page 1251*

MOPP/ABVD *on page 1249*

MVPP *on page 1259*

Stanford V *on page 1278*

Melanoma:

CVD *on page 1184*

IL-2 + IFN *on page 1240*

Prostate cancer:

Doxorubicin + Ketoconazole/Estramustine + Vinblastine *on page 1195*

EV *on page 1210*

Testicular cancer:

PVB *on page 1275*

VBP *on page 1288*

VIP (Vinblastine) (Testicular Cancer) *on page 1291*

Administration FATAL IF GIVEN INTRATHECALLY. For I.V. administration only, usually as a slow (2-3 minutes) push, or a bolus (5-15 minutes) infusion. It is occasionally given as a 24-hour continuous infusion.

Monitoring Parameters CBC with differential and platelet count, serum uric acid, hepatic function tests

Patient Information This medication can only be administered by infusion, usually on a cyclic basis. Maintain adequate hydration (2-3 L/day of fluids unless instructed to restrict fluid intake) and nutrition (small frequent meals will help). You will most likely lose your hair (reversible after therapy); experience nausea or vomiting (request antiemetic); experience photosensitivity (use sunscreen, wear protective clothing and eyewear, and avoid direct sunlight); or feel weak or lethargic (use caution when driving or engaging in tasks requiring alertness until response to drug is known). Use good oral care to reduce incidence of mouth sores. You will be more susceptible to infection; avoid crowds or exposure to infection. Report numbness or tingling in fingers or toes (use care to prevent injury); signs of infection (eg, fever, chills, sore throat, burning urination, fatigue); unusual bleeding (eg, tarry stools, easy bruising, blood in stool, urine, or mouth); unresolved mouth sores; skin rash or itching; or difficulty breathing. The drug may cause permanent sterility and may cause birth defects. Contraceptive measures are recommended during therapy. The drug may be excreted in breast milk, therefore, an alternative form of feeding your baby should be used.

Emetic Potential Very low (<10%)

Vesicant Yes; see Management of Drug Extravasations *on page 1301*.

Dosage Forms Excipient information presented when available (limited, particularly for generics); consult specific product labeling.

Injection, powder for reconstitution, as sulfate: 10 mg

Injection, solution, as sulfate: 1 mg/mL (10 mL) [contains benzyl alcohol]

References

Bonadonna G, Valagussa P, and Santoro A, "Alternating Non-Cross-Resistant Combination Chemotherapy or MOPP in Stage IV Hodgkin's Disease: A Report of 8-Year Results," *Ann Intern Med*, 1986, 104(6):739-46.

Chong CD, Logothetis CJ, Savaraj N, et al, "The Correlation of Vinblastine Pharmacokinetics to Toxicity in Testicular Cancer Patients," *J Clin Pharmacol*, 1998, 28(8):714-8.

Floyd J, Mirza I, Sachs B, et al, "Hepatotoxicity of Chemotherapy," *Semin Oncol*, 2006, 33(1):50-67.

Friedman M, Venkatesan TK, and Caldarelli DD, "Intralesional Vinblastine for Treating AIDS-Associated Kaposi's Sarcoma of the Oropharynx and Larynx," *Ann Otol Rhinol Laryngol*, 1996, 105(4):272-4.

Pronzato P, Queirolo P, Vidili MG, et al, "Continuous Venous Infusion of Vinblastine in Metastatic Breast Cancer," *Chemotherapy*, 1991, 37(2):146-9.

Williams SD, Birch R, Einhorn LH, et al, "Treatment of Disseminated Germ-Cell Tumors With Cisplatin, Bleomycin, and Either Vinblastine or Etoposide," *N Engl J Med*, 1987, 316(23):1435-40.

♦ **Vinblastine Sulfate** *see* VinBLAStine *on page 1095*

♦ **Vincasar PFS®** *see* VinCRIStine *on page 1099*

♦ **Vincasar® PFS® (Can)** *see* VinCRIStine *on page 1099*

VinCRIStine (vin KRIS teen)

Medication Safety Issues

Sound-alike/look-alike issues:

VinCRIStine may be confused with vinBLAStine

Oncovin® may be confused with Ancobon®

High alert medication: The Institute for Safe Medication Practices (ISMP) includes this medication among its list of drugs which have a heightened risk of causing significant patient harm when used in error.

To prevent fatal inadvertent intrathecal injection, it is recommended that all doses be dispensed in a small minibag. If dispensing vincristine in a syringe, vincristine must be packaged in the manufacturer-provided overwrap which bears the statement **"Do not remove covering until the moment of injection. For intravenous use only. Fatal if given intrathecally."**

Related Information

Management of Drug Extravasations *on page 1301*
Safe Handling of Hazardous Drugs *on page 1382*

U.S. Brand Names Vincasar PFS®

Index Terms Leurocristine Sulfate; NSC-67574; Oncovin; Vincristine Sulfate

Generic Available Yes

Canadian Brand Names Vincasar® PFS®

Pharmacologic Category Antineoplastic Agent, Natural Source (Plant) Derivative; Antineoplastic Agent, Vinca Alkaloid

Use Treatment of leukemias, Hodgkin's disease, non-Hodgkin's lymphomas, Wilms' tumor, neuroblastoma, rhabdomyosarcoma

Pregnancy Risk Factor D

Lactation Enters breast milk/not recommended

Labeled Contraindications Hypersensitivity to vincristine or any component of the formulation; **for I.V. use only, fatal if given intrathecally**; patients with demyelinating form of Charcot-Marie-Tooth syndrome; pregnancy

Warnings/Precautions Hazardous agent - use appropriate precautions for handling and disposal. **[U.S. Boxed Warning]: Vincristine is a vesicant; avoid extravasation. (Individuals administering should be experienced in vincristine administration.)**

Dosage modification required in patients with impaired hepatic function or who have pre-existing neuromuscular disease. Use with caution in the elderly. Avoid eye contamination. Observe closely for shortness of breath, bronchospasm, especially in patients treated with mitomycin C. Alterations in mental status such as depression, confusion, or insomnia; constipation, paralytic ileus, and urinary tract disturbances may occur. All patients should be on a prophylactic bowel management regimen.

(Continued)

VinCRIStine *(Continued)*

[U.S. Boxed Warning]: Intrathecal administration of vincristine has uniformly caused severe neurologic damage and/or death; vincristine should never be administered by this route. For I.V. use only. Neurologic effects of vincristine may be additive with those of other neurotoxic agents and spinal cord irradiation.

Adverse Reactions

>10%: Dermatologic: Alopecia (20% to 70%)

1% to 10%:

Cardiovascular: Orthostatic hypotension or hypertension, hyper-/hypotension

Central nervous system: CNS depression, confusion, cranial nerve paralysis, fever, headache, insomnia, motor difficulties, seizure

Intrathecal administration of vincristine has uniformly caused death; vincristine should never be administered by this route. Neurologic effects of vincristine may be additive with those of other neurotoxic agents and spinal cord irradiation.

Dermatologic: Rash

Endocrine & metabolic: Hyperuricemia

Gastrointestinal: Abdominal cramps, anorexia, bloating, constipation (and possible paralytic ileus secondary to neurologic toxicity), diarrhea, metallic taste, nausea (mild), oral ulceration, vomiting, weight loss

Genitourinary: Bladder atony (related to neurotoxicity), dysuria, polyuria, urinary retention

Hematologic: Leukopenia (mild), thrombocytopenia, myelosuppression (onset: 7 days; nadir: 10 days; recovery: 21 days)

Local: Phlebitis, tissue irritation and necrosis if infiltrated

Neuromuscular & skeletal: Cramping, jaw pain, leg pain, myalgia, numbness, weakness

Peripheral neuropathy: Frequently the dose-limiting toxicity of vincristine. Most frequent in patients >40 years of age; occurs usually after an average of 3 weekly doses, but may occur after just one dose. Manifested as loss of the deep tendon reflexes in the lower extremities, numbness, tingling, pain, paresthesia of the fingers and toes (stocking glove sensation), and "foot drop" or "wrist drop."

Ocular: Optic atrophy, photophobia

<1%: SIADH (rare), stomatitis

Overdosage/Toxicology

Symptoms of overdose include bone marrow suppression, mental depression, paresthesia, loss of deep tendon reflexes, alopecia, and nausea. Severe symptoms may occur with 3-4 mg/m^2.

There are no antidotes for vincristine. Treatment is supportive and symptomatic, including fluid restriction or hypertonic saline (3% sodium chloride) for drug-induced secretion of inappropriate antidiuretic hormone (SIADH). Case reports suggest that folinic acid may be helpful in treating vincristine overdose. It is suggested that 100 mg folinic acid be given I.V. every 3 hours for 24 hours, then every 6 hours for 48 hours. This is in addition to supportive care. The use of pyridoxine, leucovorin factor, cyanocobalamin, or thiamine has been used with little success for drug-induced peripheral neuropathy.

Drug Interactions

Cytochrome P450 Effect: Substrate of CYP3A4 (major); **Inhibits** CYP3A4 (weak)

Increased Effect/Toxicity: Vincristine should be given 12-24 hours before asparaginase to minimize toxicity (may decrease the hepatic clearance of vincristine). Acute pulmonary reactions may occur with mitomycin-C. Previous or simultaneous use with mitomycin-C has resulted in acute shortness of breath and severe bronchospasm within minutes or several hours after vinca alkaloid injection and may occur up to 2 weeks after the dose of mitomycin. Itraconazole may enhance the neurotoxicity of vincristine.

CYP3A4 inhibitors may increase the levels/effects of vincristine. Example inhibitors include azole antifungals, clarithromycin, diclofenac, doxycycline, erythromycin, imatinib, isoniazid, nefazodone, nicardipine, propofol, protease inhibitors, quinidine, telithromycin, and verapamil. Digoxin plasma levels and renal excretion may decrease with combination chemotherapy including vincristine. Nifedipine may increase the levels/effects of vincristine.

Decreased Effect: Digoxin levels may decrease with combination chemotherapy. CYP3A4 inducers may decrease the levels/effects of vincristine; example inducers include aminoglutethimide, carbamazepine, nafcillin, nevirapine, phenobarbital, phenytoin, and rifamycins.

Ethanol/Nutrition/Herb Interactions Herb/Nutraceutical: St John's wort may decrease vincristine levels.

Storage/Stability
Undiluted vials: Store under refrigeration. May be stable for up to 30 days at room temperature.
I.V. solution: Diluted in 20-50 mL NS or D_5W, stable for 7 days under refrigeration, or 2 days at room temperature. In ambulatory pumps, solution is stable for 7-10 days at room temperature.

Reconstitution Solutions for I.V. infusion may be mixed in NS or D_5W. **Note:** The World Health Organization (WHO) recommends dispensing vincristine in a minibag, rather than a syringe.

Compatibility Stable in D_5W, LR, NS.
Y-site administration: Compatible: Allopurinol, amifostine, amphotericin B cholesteryl sulfate complex, aztreonam, bleomycin, cisplatin, cladribine, cyclophosphamide, doxorubicin, doxorubicin liposome, droperidol, etoposide phosphate, filgrastim, fludarabine, fluorouracil, gatifloxacin, gemcitabine, granisetron, heparin, leucovorin, linezolid, melphalan, methotrexate, metoclopramide, mitomycin, ondansetron, paclitaxel, piperacillin/tazobactam, sargramostim, teniposide, thiotepa, topotecan, vinblastine, vinorelbine. **Incompatible:** Cefepime, furosemide, idarubicin, sodium bicarbonate.
Compatibility in syringe: Compatible: Bleomycin, cisplatin, cyclophosphamide, doxapram, doxorubicin, droperidol, fluorouracil, heparin, leucovorin, methotrexate, metoclopramide, mitomycin, vinblastine. **Incompatible:** Furosemide.
Compatibility when admixed: Compatible: Bleomycin, cytarabine, doxorubicin with ondansetron, fluorouracil, methotrexate. **Variable (consult detailed reference):** Doxorubicin with etoposide.

Mechanism of Action Binds to tubulin and inhibits microtubule formation, therefore, arresting the cell at metaphase by disrupting the formation of the mitotic spindle; it is specific for the M and S phases. Vincristine may also interfere with nucleic acid and protein synthesis by blocking glutamic acid utilization.

Pharmacodynamics/Kinetics
Absorption: Oral: Poor
Distribution: V_d: 163-165 L/m^2; poor penetration into CSF; rapidly removed from bloodstream and tightly bound to tissues; penetrates blood-brain barrier poorly
Protein binding: 75%
Metabolism: Extensively hepatic
(Continued)

VinCRIStine *(Continued)*

Half-life elimination: Terminal: 24 hours

Excretion: Feces (~80%); urine (<1% as unchanged drug)

Dosage Note: Doses are often capped at 2 mg; however, this may reduce the efficacy of the therapy and may not be advisable. Refer to individual protocols; orders for single doses >2.5 mg or >5 mg/treatment cycle should be verified with the specific treatment regimen and/or an experienced oncologist prior to dispensing. I.V.:

Children ≤10 kg or BSA <1 m²: Initial therapy: 0.05 mg/kg once weekly then titrate dose

Children >10 kg or BSA ≥1 m²: 1-2 mg/m², may repeat once weekly for 3-6 weeks; maximum single dose: 2 mg

Neuroblastoma: I.V. continuous infusion with doxorubicin: 1 mg/m²/day for 72 hours

Adults: 0.4-1.4 mg/m², may repeat every week **or**

0.4-0.5 mg/day continuous infusion for 4 days every 4 weeks **or**

0.25-0.5 mg/m²/day for 5 days every 4 weeks

Dosing adjustment in renal impairment: No adjustment is necessary in patients with renal impairment.

Dosing adjustment in hepatic impairment:

The FDA-approved labeling recommends the following guidelines: Serum bilirubin >3 mg/dL: Administer 50% of normal dose

The following guidelines have been used by some clinicians:

Serum bilirubin 1.5-3 mg/dL or AST 60-180 units: Administer 50% of dose

Serum bilirubin 3-5 mg/dL: Administer 25% of dose

Serum bilirubin >5 mg/dL or AST >180 units: Avoid use

Floyd, 2006: Serum bilirubin 1.5-3 mg/dL or ALT/AST 2-3 times ULN or alkaline phosphatase elevated: Administer 50% of dose

Combination Regimens

Brain tumors:

8 in 1 (Brain Tumors) *on page 1141*

COPE *on page 1182*

MOP *on page 1249*

MOPP (Medulloblastoma) *on page 1253*

PCV *on page 1268*

POC *on page 1271*

Breast cancer: CMFVP (Cooper Regimen, VPCMF) *on page 1178*

Gestational trophoblastic tumor:

CHAMOCA (Modified Bagshawe Regimen) *on page 1170*

CHAMOMA (Bagshawe Regimen) *on page 1172*

EMA/CO *on page 1199*

Head and neck cancer: CABO *on page 1157*

Leukemia, acute lymphocytic:

DVP *on page 1196*

Hyper-CVAD + Imatinib *on page 1229*

Hyper-CVAD (Leukemia, Acute Lymphocytic) *on page 1231*

Larson Regimen *on page 1242*

Linker Protocol *on page 1243*

MTX/6-MP/VP (Maintenance) *on page 1254*

POMP *on page 1273*

PVA (POG 8602) *on page 1273*

PVDA *on page 1276*

VAD/CVAD *on page 1287*

Leukemia, chronic lymphocytic: CVP (Leukemia) *on page 1184*

Lung cancer (small cell): CAVE *on page 1163*

(Continued)

VinCRIStine *(Continued)*

CO *on page 1180*
CV *on page 1184*
VAC (Retinoblastoma) *on page 1286*
Rhabdomyosarcoma:
 CEV *on page 1168*
 VAC Pulse *on page 1286*
 VAC (Rhabdomyosarcoma) *on page 1286*
Sarcoma:
 CYVADIC *on page 1187*
 VAC Alternating With IE (Ewing's Sarcoma) *on page 1285*
Wilms' tumor:
 AAV (DD) *on page 1142*
 ACAV (J) *on page 1143*
 AV (EE) *on page 1147*
 AV (K) *on page 1148*
 AV (L) *on page 1148*
 AV (Wilms' Tumor) *on page 1148*
 AVD *on page 1147*
 EE *on page 1198*
 EE-4A *on page 1198*

Administration FATAL IF GIVEN INTRATHECALLY.

I.V.: Usually administered as short (10-15 minutes) infusion (preferred) or as slow (1-2 minutes) push; 24-hour continuous infusions are occasionally used

Intralesional injection has been reported for Kaposi's sarcoma.

Monitoring Parameters Serum electrolytes (sodium), hepatic function tests, neurologic examination, CBC, serum uric acid

Patient Information This medication can only be administered by infusion, usually on a cyclic basis. Maintain adequate hydration (2-3 L/day of fluids unless instructed to restrict fluid intake) and nutrition (small frequent meals will help). You will most likely lose your hair (reversible after therapy); experience constipation (request medication); or feel weak or lethargic (use caution when driving or engaging in tasks requiring alertness until response to drug is known). Use good oral care to reduce incidence of mouth sores. You will be more susceptible to infection; avoid crowds or exposure to infection. Report pain, numbness, or tingling in fingers or toes (use care to prevent injury); alterations in mental status (eg, confusion, insomnia, headaches, jaw pain, loss of vision); signs of infection (eg, fever, chills, sore throat, burning urination, fatigue); unusual bleeding (eg, tarry stools, easy bruising, or blood in stool, urine, or mouth); unresolved mouth sores; skin rash or itching; nausea; vomiting; abdominal pain; bloating; or difficulty breathing. Contraceptive measures are recommended during therapy.

Emetic Potential Very low (<10%)

Vesicant Yes; moderate. See Management of Drug Extravasations *on page 1301*.

Dosage Forms Excipient information presented when available (limited, particularly for generics); consult specific product labeling.

Injection, solution, as sulfate: 1 mg/mL (1 mL, 2 mL)

References

Ahn YS, Harrington WJ, Mylvaganam R, et al, "Slow Infusion of Vinca Alkaloids in the Treatment of Idiopathic Thrombocytopenic Purpura," *Ann Intern Med*, 1984, 100(2):192-6.

Aronoff GR, Bennett WM, Berns JS, et al, *Drug Prescribing in Renal Failure: Dosing Guidelines for Adults and Children*, 5th ed. Philadelphia, PA: American College of Physicians; 2007, p 102, 174.

Bermudez M, Fuster JL, Llinares E, et al, "Itraconazole-Related Increased Vincristine Neurotoxicity: Case Report and Review of Literature," *J Pediatr Hematol Oncol*, 2005, 27(7):389-92.

Bohme A, Ganser A, and Hoelzer D, "Aggravation of Vincristine-Induced Neurotoxicity by Itraconazole in the Treatment of Adult ALL," *Ann Hematol*, 1995, 71(6):311-2.

Camplejohn RS, "A Critical Review of the Use of Vincristine (VCR) as a Tumour Cell Synchronizing Agent in Cancer Therapy," *Cell Tissue Kinet*, 1980, 13(3):327-35.

Floyd J, Mirza I, Sachs B, et al, "Hepatotoxicity of Chemotherapy," *Semin Oncol*, 2006, 33(1):50-67.

Joel S, "The Comparative Clinical Pharmacology of Vincristine and Vindesine: Does Vindesine Offer Any Advantage in Clinical Use?" *Cancer Treat Rev*, 1996, 21(6):513-25.

Legha SS, "Vincristine Neurotoxicity. Pathophysiology and Management," *Med Toxicol*, 1986, 1(6):421-7.

McCune JS and Lindley C, "Appropriateness of Maximum-Dose Guidelines for Vincristine," *Am J Health Syst Pharm*, 1997, 54(15):1755-8.

Tajti J, Somogyi I, and Szilard J, "Treatment of Chronic Pain Syndromes With Transcutaneous Iontophoresis of Vinca Alkaloids, With Special Regard to Postherpetic Neuralgia," *Acta Med Hung*, 1989, 46(1):3-12.

♦ **Vincristine Sulfate** *see* VinCRIStine *on page 1099*

Vindesine (VIN de seen)

Medication Safety Issues

High alert medication: The Institute for Safe Medication Practices (ISMP) includes this medication among its list of drugs which have a heightened risk of causing significant patient harm when used in error.

Related Information

Investigational Drug Service *on page 1379*
Management of Drug Extravasations *on page 1301*
Safe Handling of Hazardous Drugs *on page 1382*

Index Terms DAVA; Deacetyl Vinblastine Carboxamide; Desacetyl Vinblastine Amide Sulfate; DVA; Eldisine Lilly 99094; Lilly CT-3231; NSC-245467; Vindesine Sulfate

Generic Available No

Pharmacologic Category Antineoplastic Agent, Vinca Alkaloid

Unlabeled/Investigational Use Investigational: Management of acute lymphocytic leukemia, chronic myelogenous leukemia; breast, head, neck, and lung cancers; lymphomas (Hodgkin's and non-Hodgkin's)

Restrictions Not available in U.S./Investigational

Lactation Breast-feeding is not recommended.

Labeled Contraindications Hypersensitivity to vindesine, vinca alkaloids, or any component of the formulation

Warnings/Precautions Hazardous agent - use appropriate precautions for handling and disposal. Vindesine should be used cautiously, if at all, in patients with impaired hepatic function or neurologic problems. **Intrathecal administration may be fatal**. Vindesine has been reported to be cross-resistance with vincristine.

Adverse Reactions

>10%:

Central nervous system: Pyrexia, malaise (up to 60%)

Dermatologic: Alopecia (6% to 92%)

Gastrointestinal: Mild nausea and vomiting (7% to 27%), constipation (10% to 17%) - related to the neurotoxicity

Hematologic: Leukopenia (50%) and thrombocytopenia (14% to 26%), may be dose limiting; thrombocytosis (20% to 28%)

Nadir: 6-12 days

Recovery: Days 14-18

Neuromuscular & skeletal: Paresthesia (40% to 70%); loss of deep tendon reflexes (35% to 60%, may be dose limiting); myalgia (up to 60%)

(Continued)

Vindesine *(Continued)*

1% to 10%:
Dermatologic: Rashes
Gastrointestinal: Loss of taste
Hematologic: Anemia
Local: Phlebitis
Neuromuscular & skeletal: Facial paralysis

<1%: Acute chest pain, ECG changes, paralytic ileus, jaw pain, photophobia

Storage/Stability Reconstituted solutions are stable for 30 days under refrigeration (2°C to 8°C/36°F to 46°F). Solutions diluted in dextrose or saline for I.V. infusion are stable for 24 hours at room temperature (15°C to 30°C/59°F to 86°F). **The drug will precipitate at pH >6.**

Reconstitution The powder is reconstituted to a concentration of 1 mg/mL.

Mechanism of Action Vindesine is a semisynthetic vinca alkaloid, having a mechanism of action similar to the other vinca derivatives. It arrests cell division in metaphase through inhibition of microtubular formation of the mitotic spindle. The drug is cell-cycle specific for the S phase.

Pharmacodynamics/Kinetics

Distribution: V_d: 8 L/kg; minimal distribution to adipose tissue or CNS
Metabolism: Hepatic
Half-life elimination:
Triphasic; Alpha: 2 minutes; Beta: 1 hour
Terminal: 24 hours
Excretion: Feces; urine (~3% to 25% of dose as unchanged drug)

Dosage Refer to individual protocols. I.V.: Adults:
3-4 mg/m^2/week **or**
1-2 mg/m^2 days 1 and 2 every 2 weeks **or**
1-2 mg/m^2 days 1-5 (continuous infusion) every 2-4 weeks **or**
1-2 mg/m^2 days 1-5 every 3-4 weeks

Dosage adjustment in hepatic impairment: Dosage reductions of 50% to 75% have been suggested for "severe" hepatic dysfunction; however, specific guidelines have not been published.

Combination Regimens

Breast cancer: VM *on page 1292*
Lymphoma, Hodgkin's disease: CAD/MOPP/ABV *on page 1157*

Administration Usually administered as a rapid I.V. push (2-3 minutes) or short (15-20 minutes) infusion; 24-hour continuous infusions are occasionally used.

Patient Information Hair loss is common but usually reversible. Report any loss of sensation or tingling in hands or feet, constipation, fever, sore throat, bruising, or bleeding.

Vesicant Yes; see Management of Drug Extravasations *on page 1301*.

Dosage Forms Excipient information presented when available (limited, particularly for generics); consult specific product labeling.
Injection, powder for reconstitution: 5 mg

References

Dancey J and Steward WP, "The Role of Vindesine in Oncology - Recommendations After 10 Years' Experience," *Anticancer Drugs*, 1995, 6(5):625-36.
Joel S, "The Comparative Clinical Pharmacology of Vincristine and Vindesine: Does Vindesine Offer Any Advantage in Clinical Use?" *Cancer Treat Rev*, 1996, 21(6):513-25.
Rhomberg W, Eiter H, Soltesz E, et al, "Long-Term Application of Vindesine: Toxicity and Tolerance," *J Cancer Res Clin Oncol*, 1990, 116(6):651-3.
Sorenson JB and Hansen HH, "Is There a Role for Vindesine in the Treatment of Nonsmall Cell Lung Cancer?" *Invest New Drugs*, 1993, 11(2-3):103-33.

♦ **Vindesine Sulfate** *see* Vindesine *on page 1105*

Vinorelbine (vi NOR el been)

Medication Safety Issues

Sound-alike/look-alike issues:

Vinorelbine may be confused with vinBLAStine

High alert medication: The Institute for Safe Medication Practices (ISMP) includes this medication among its list of drugs which have a heightened risk of causing significant patient harm when used in error.

Related Information

Management of Drug Extravasations *on page 1301*

Safe Handling of Hazardous Drugs *on page 1382*

U.S. Brand Names Navelbine®

Index Terms Dihydroxydeoxynorvinkaleukoblastine; NVB; Vinorelbine Tartrate

Generic Available Yes

Canadian Brand Names Navelbine®; Vinorelbine Injection, USP; Vinorelbine Tartrate for Injection

Pharmacologic Category Antineoplastic Agent, Natural Source (Plant) Derivative; Antineoplastic Agent, Vinca Alkaloid

Use Treatment of nonsmall-cell lung cancer

Unlabeled/Investigational Use Treatment of breast cancer, ovarian carcinoma, Hodgkin's disease, non-Hodgkin's lymphoma

Pregnancy Risk Factor D

Lactation Excretion in breast milk unknown/contraindicated

Labeled Contraindications For I.V. use only; **I.T. use may result in death**; hypersensitivity to vinorelbine or any component of the formulation; pregnancy

Warnings/Precautions Hazardous agent - use appropriate precautions for handling and disposal. Avoid extravasation; dosage modification required in patients with impaired liver function and neurotoxicity. Frequently monitor patients for myelosuppression both during and after therapy. **[U.S. Boxed Warnings]: Granulocytopenia is dose limiting. Intrathecal administration may result in death.** Use with caution in patients with cachexia or ulcerated skin.

Acute shortness of breath and severe bronchospasm have been reported, most commonly when administered with mitomycin. Fatal cases of interstitial pulmonary changes and ARDS have also been reported. May cause severe constipation (grade 3-4), paralytic ileus, intestinal obstruction, necrosis, and/or perforation. **[U.S. Boxed Warning]: Should be administered under the supervision of an experienced cancer chemotherapy physician.**

Adverse Reactions

>10%:

Central nervous system: Fatigue (27%)

Dermatologic: Alopecia (12%)

Gastrointestinal: Nausea (44%, severe <2%) and vomiting (20%) are most common and are easily controlled with standard antiemetics; constipation (35%), diarrhea (17%)

Emetic potential: Moderate (30% to 60%)

Hematologic: May cause severe bone marrow suppression and is the dose-limiting toxicity of vinorelbine; severe granulocytopenia (90%) may occur following the administration of vinorelbine; leukopenia (92%), anemia (83%)

Myelosuppressive:

WBC: Moderate - severe

Onset: 4-7 days

(Continued)

Vinorelbine *(Continued)*

Nadir: 7-10 days

Recovery: 14-21 days

Hepatic: AST (67%) increased, total bilirubin increased (13%)

Local: Injection site reaction (28%), injection site pain (16%)

Neuromuscular & skeletal: Weakness (36%), peripheral neuropathy (20% to 25%)

1% to 10%:

Cardiovascular: Chest pain (5%)

Gastrointestinal: Paralytic ileus (1%)

Hematologic: Thrombocytopenia (5%)

Local: Phlebitis (7%)

Neuromuscular & skeletal: Mild-to-moderate peripheral neuropathy manifested by paresthesia and hyperesthesia, loss of deep tendon reflexes (<5%); myalgia (<5%), arthralgia (<5%), jaw pain (<5%)

Respiratory: Dyspnea (3% to 7%)

<1%: Hemorrhagic cystitis, severe peripheral neuropathy (generally reversible), syndrome of inappropriate ADH secretion

Postmarketing and/or case reports: Angioedema, headache, DVT, flushing, hyper-/hypotension, vasodilation, tachycardia, hyponatremia, abdominal pain, dysphagia, esophagitis, mucositis, back pain, gait instability, muscle weakness, anaphylaxis, tumor pain, pancreatitis, pneumonia, pulmonary edema, pulmonary embolus, radiation recall (dermatitis, esophagitis)

Overdosage/Toxicology Symptoms of overdose include bone marrow suppression, mental depression, paresthesia, loss of deep tendon reflexes, and neurotoxicity. There are no antidotes for vinorelbine. Treatment is supportive and symptomatic, including fluid restriction or hypertonic saline (3% sodium chloride) for drug-induced secretion of inappropriate antidiuretic hormone (SIADH).

Drug Interactions

Cytochrome P450 Effect: Substrate of CYP2D6 (minor), 3A4 (major); **Inhibits** CYP2D6 (weak), 3A4 (weak)

Increased Effect/Toxicity: Previous or simultaneous use with mitomycin-C has resulted in acute shortness of breath and severe bronchospasm within minutes or several hours after vinca alkaloid injection and may occur up to 2 weeks after the dose of mitomycin. CYP3A4 inhibitors may increase the levels/effects of vinorelbine; example inhibitors include azole antifungals, clarithromycin, diclofenac, doxycycline, erythromycin, imatinib, isoniazid, nefazodone, nicardipine, propofol, protease inhibitors, quinidine, telithromycin, and verapamil. Incidence of granulocytopenia is significantly higher in cisplatin/vinorelbine combination therapy than with single-agent vinorelbine.

Decreased Effect: CYP3A4 inducers may decrease the levels/effects of vinorelbine; example inducers include aminoglutethimide, carbamazepine, nafcillin, nevirapine, phenobarbital, phenytoin, and rifamycins.

Ethanol/Nutrition/Herb Interactions Herb/Nutraceutical: St John's wort may decrease vinorelbine levels.

Storage/Stability Store intact vials under refrigeration (2°C to 8°C). Protect from light. Vials are stable at room temperature for up to 72 hours. Dilutions in D$_5$W or NS are stable for 24 hours at room temperature.

Reconstitution Dilute in 10-50 mL D$_5$W or NS.

Compatibility Stable in D$_5$1/2NS, D$_5$W, LR, NS, 1/2NS.

Y-site administration: Compatible: Amikacin, aztreonam, bleomycin, bumetanide, buprenorphine, butorphanol, calcium gluconate, carboplatin, carmustine, cefotaxime, ceftazidime, ceftizoxime, chlorpromazine, cimetidine, cisplatin, clindamycin, cyclophosphamide, cytarabine, dacarbazine, dactinomycin, daunorubicin, dexamethasone sodium phosphate, diphenhydramine, doxorubicin, doxorubicin liposome, doxycycline, droperidol, enalaprilat, etoposide, famotidine, filgrastim, floxuridine, fluconazole, fludarabine, gatifloxacin, gemcitabine, gentamicin, granisetron, haloperidol, hydrocortisone sodium phosphate, hydrocortisone sodium succinate, hydromorphone, hydroxyzine, idarubicin, ifosfamide, imipenem/cilastatin, lorazepam, mannitol, mechlorethamine, melphalan, meperidine, mesna, methotrexate, metoclopramide, metronidazole, minocycline, mitoxantrone, morphine, nalbuphine, netilmicin, ondansetron, plicamycin, streptozocin, teniposide, ticarcillin, ticarcillin/clavulanate, tobramycin, vancomycin, vinblastine, vincristine, zidovudine. **Incompatible:** Acyclovir, allopurinol, aminophylline, amphotericin B, amphotericin B cholesteryl sulfate complex, ampicillin, cefazolin, cefoperazone, cefotetan, ceftriaxone, cefuroxime, co-trimoxazole, fluorouracil, furosemide, ganciclovir, methylprednisolone sodium succinate, mitomycin, piperacillin, sodium bicarbonate, thiotepa. **Variable (consult detailed reference):** Heparin.

Mechanism of Action Semisynthetic vinca alkaloid which binds to tubulin and inhibits microtubule formation, therefore, arresting the cell at metaphase by disrupting the formation of the mitotic spindle; it is specific for the M and S phases. Vinorelbine may also interfere with nucleic acid and protein synthesis by blocking glutamic acid utilization.

Pharmacodynamics/Kinetics

Absorption: Unreliable; must be given I.V.

Distribution: V_d: 25.4-40.1 L/kg; binds extensively to human platelets and lymphocytes (79.6% to 91.2%)

Protein binding: 80% to 90%

Metabolism: Extensively hepatic to two metabolites, deacetylvinorelbine (active) and vinorelbine N-oxide

Bioavailability: Oral: 26% to 45%

Half-life elimination: Triphasic; Terminal: 27.7-43.6 hours

Excretion: Feces (46%); urine (18%, 10% to 12% as unchanged drug)

Clearance: Plasma: Mean: 0.97-1.26 L/hour/kg

Dosage Refer to individual protocols.

Adults: I.V.:

Single-agent therapy: 30 mg/m^2 every 7 days

Combination therapy with cisplatin: 25 mg/m^2 every 7 days (with cisplatin 100 mg/m^2 every 4 weeks); **Alternatively:** 30 mg/m^2 in combination with cisplatin 120 mg/m^2 on days 1 and 29, then every 6 weeks

Dosage adjustment in hematological toxicity: Granulocyte counts should be ≥1000 cells/mm^3 prior to the administration of vinorelbine. Adjustments in the dosage of vinorelbine should be based on granulocyte counts obtained on the day of treatment as follows:

Granulocytes ≥1500 cells/mm^3 on day of treatment: Administer 100% of starting dose

Granulocytes 1000-1499 cells/mm^3 on day of treatment: Administer 50% of starting dose

Granulocytes <1000 cells/mm^3 on day of treatment: Do not administer. Repeat granulocyte count in one week; if 3 consecutive doses are held because granulocyte count is <1000 cells/mm^3, discontinue vinorelbine.

For patients who, during treatment, have experienced fever and/or sepsis while granulocytopenic or had 2 consecutive weekly doses held due to granulocytopenia, subsequent doses of vinorelbine should be:

75% of starting dose for granulocytes ≥1500 cells/mm^3

37.5% of starting dose for granulocytes 1000-1499 cells/mm^3

(Continued)

Vinorelbine *(Continued)*

Dosage adjustment in renal impairment: No adjustment is necessary.

Dosing adjustment in hepatic impairment: The FDA-approved labeling guidelines are as follows: Vinorelbine should be administered with caution in patients with hepatic insufficiency. In patients who develop hyperbilirubinemia during treatment with vinorelbine, the dose should be adjusted for total bilirubin as follows:

Serum bilirubin ≤2 mg/dL: Administer 100% of dose

Serum bilirubin 2.1-3 mg/dL: Administer 50% of dose

Serum bilirubin >3 mg/dL: Administer 25% of dose

Dosing adjustment in patients with concurrent hematologic toxicity and hepatic impairment: Administer the lower of the doses determined from the adjustment recommendations.

Combination Regimens

Breast cancer:

Paclitaxel-Vinorelbine *on page 1266*

VD *on page 1289*

Vinorelbine-Trastuzumab *on page 1290*

Cervical cancer: Cisplatin-Vinorelbine *on page 1177*

Leukemia, acute lymphocytic: TVTG *on page 1285*

Leukemia, acute myeloid: TVTG *on page 1285*

Lung cancer (nonsmall cell):

Gemcitabine-Vinorelbine *on page 1228*

VC *on page 1288*

Vinorelbine-Gemcitabine *on page 1289*

Prostate cancer: Estramustine + Vinorelbine *on page 1209*

Administration FATAL IF GIVEN INTRATHECALLY. Administer as a direct intravenous push or rapid bolus, over 6-10 minutes (up to 30 minutes). Longer infusions may increase the risk of pain and phlebitis. Intravenous doses should be followed by 150-250 mL of saline or dextrose to reduce the incidence of phlebitis and inflammation.

Monitoring Parameters CBC with differential and platelet count, hepatic function tests

Patient Information This medication can only be administered by infusion, usually on a cyclic basis. Maintain adequate hydration (2-3 L/day of fluids unless instructed to restrict fluid intake) and nutrition (small frequent meals will help). You will most likely lose your hair (reversible after therapy); experience nausea or vomiting (request medication); or feel weak or lethargic (use caution when driving or engaging in tasks requiring alertness until response to drug is known). Use good oral care to reduce incidence of mouth sores. You will be more susceptible to infection; avoid crowds or exposure to infection. Report weakness, skeletal pain, or tremors; signs of infection (eg, fever, chills, sore throat, burning urination, fatigue); unusual bleeding (eg, tarry stools, easy bruising, blood in stool, urine, or mouth); numbness, pain, or tingling of fingers or toes; unresolved mouth sores; skin rash or itching; uncontrolled nausea, vomiting, or abdominal pain; or difficulty breathing. The drug may cause permanent sterility and may cause birth defects. Contraceptive measures are recommended during therapy. The drug is excreted in breast milk, therefore, an alternative form of feeding your baby should be used.

Emetic Potential Moderate (30% to 60%)

Vesicant Yes; moderate. See Management of Drug Extravasations *on page 1301.*

Dosage Forms Excipient information presented when available (limited, particularly for generics); consult specific product labeling.

Injection, solution [preservative free]: 10 mg/mL (1 mL, 5 mL)

References

Budman DR, "Vinorelbine (Navelbine®): A Third-Generation Vinca Alkaloid," *Cancer Invest*, 1997, 15(5):475-90.

Johnson SA, Harper P, Hortobagyi GN, et al, "Vinorelbine: An Overview," *Cancer Treat Rev*, 1996, 22(2):127-42.

Jones SF and Burris HA 3d, "Vinorelbine: A New Antineoplastic Drug for the Treatment of Nonsmall Cell Lung Cancer," *Ann Pharmacother*, 1996, 30(5):501-6.

LeVeque D and Jehl F, "Clinical Pharmacokinetics of Vinorelbine," *Clin Pharmacokinet*, 1996, 31(3):184-97.

Toso C and Lindley C, "Vinorelbine: A Novel Vinca Alkaloid," *Am J Health Syst Pharm*, 1995, 52(12):1287-304.

+ **Vinorelbine Injection, USP (Can)** *see* Vinorelbine *on page 1107*
+ **Vinorelbine Tartrate** *see* Vinorelbine *on page 1107*
+ **Vinorelbine Tartrate for Injection (Can)** *see* Vinorelbine *on page 1107*
+ **Vistaril®** *see* HydrOXYzine *on page 564*
+ **Vitamin K₁** *see* Phytonadione *on page 895*
+ **Vitrase®** *see* Hyaluronidase *on page 543*
+ **Vitrasert®** *see* Ganciclovir *on page 492*
+ **Vivaglobin®** *see* Immune Globulin (Subcutaneous) *on page 603*
+ **VLB** *see* VinBLAStine *on page 1095*
+ **VM-26** *see* Teniposide *on page 1018*

Voriconazole (vor i KOE na zole)

U.S. Brand Names VFEND®

Index Terms UK109496

Generic Available No

Canadian Brand Names VFEND®

Pharmacologic Category Antifungal Agent, Oral; Antifungal Agent, Parenteral

Use Treatment of invasive aspergillosis; treatment of esophageal candidiasis; treatment of candidemia (in non-neutropenic patients); treatment of disseminated *Candida* infections of the skin and viscera; treatment of serious fungal infections caused by *Scedosporium apiospermum* and *Fusarium* spp (including *Fusarium solani*) in patients intolerant of, or refractory to, other therapy

Pregnancy Risk Factor D

Lactation Excretion in breast milk unknown/not recommended

Labeled Contraindications Hypersensitivity to voriconazole or any component of the formulation (cross-reaction with other azole antifungal agents may occur but has not been established, use caution); coadministration of CYP3A4 substrates which may lead to QT$_c$ prolongation (cisapride, pimozide, or quinidine); coadministration with barbiturates (long acting), carbamazepine, efavirenz (with standard [eg, not adjusted] voriconazole and efavirenz doses), ergot alkaloids, rifampin, rifabutin, ritonavir (≥800 mg/day), and sirolimus; pregnancy (unless risk:benefit justifies use)

Warnings/Precautions Visual changes are commonly associated with treatment. Patients should be warned to avoid tasks which depend on vision, including operating machinery or driving. Changes are reversible on discontinuation following brief exposure/treatment regimens (≤28 days).

Serious hepatic reactions (including hepatitis, cholestasis, and fulminant hepatic failure) have occurred during treatment, primarily in patients with serious concomitant medical conditions. However, hepatotoxicity has occurred in patients with no identifiable risk factors. Use caution in patients with pre-existing hepatic impairment (dose adjustment required).
(Continued)

Voriconazole *(Continued)*

Voriconazole tablets contain lactose; avoid administration in hereditary galactose intolerance, Lapp lactase deficiency, or glucose-galactose malabsorption. Suspension contains sucrose; use caution with fructose intolerance, sucrose-isomaltase deficiency, or glucose-galactose malabsorption. Avoid/limit use of intravenous formulation in patients with renal impairment; intravenous formulation contains excipient sulfobutyl ether beta-cyclodextrin (SBECD), which may accumulate in renal insufficiency. Infusion-related reactions may occur with intravenous dosing. Consider discontinuation of infusion if reaction is severe.

Use caution in patients with an increased risk of arrhythmia (concurrent QT_c-prolonging drugs, hypokalemia, cardiomyopathy, or prior cardiotoxic therapy). Correct electrolyte abnormalities (low levels of calcium, magnesium, and potassium) before initiating therapy. Use caution in patients receiving concurrent non-nucleoside reverse transcriptase inhibitors (efavirenz is contraindicated).

Safety and efficacy have not been established in children <12 years of age.

Adverse Reactions

>10%:

Central nervous system: Hallucinations (4% to 12%; auditory and/or visual and likely serum concentration-dependent)

Ocular: Visual changes (dose dependent - photophobia, color changes, increased or decreased visual acuity, or blurred vision occur in ~21%)

2% to 10%:

Cardiovascular: Tachycardia (up to 2%), hyper-/hypotension (2%), vasodilation (2%)

Central nervous system: Fever (up to 6%), chills (up to 4%), headache (up to 3%), hallucinations (up to 3%)

Dermatologic: Rash (up to 7%)

Endocrine & metabolic: Hypokalemia (up to 2%)

Gastrointestinal: Nausea (1% to 5%), vomiting (1% to 4%), abdominal pain (2%)

Hepatic: Alkaline phosphatase increased (4% to 5%), AST increased (2% to 4%), ALT increased (2% to 3%), cholestatic jaundice (1% to 2%)

Ocular: Photophobia (2% to 3%)

<2% (Limited to important or life-threatening): Acute tubular necrosis, adrenal cortical insufficiency, agranulocytosis, allergic reaction, anaphylactoid reaction, anemia (aplastic, macrocytic, megaloblastic, or microcytic), angioedema, anorexia, ataxia, atrial arrhythmia, atrial fibrillation, AV block, bigeminy, bone marrow depression, bone necrosis, bradycardia, brain edema, bundle branch block, cardiac arrest, cerebral hemorrhage, cholecystitis, cholelithiasis, chromatopsia, color blindness, coma, CHF, convulsion, creatinine increased, delirium, dementia, depersonalization, depression, diarrhea, DIC, discoid lupus erythematosus, dizziness, duodenal ulcer perforation, dyspnea, encephalopathy, eosinophilia, erythema multiforme, exfoliative dermatitis, extrapyramidal symptoms, fixed drug eruption, gastrointestinal hemorrhage, grand mal seizure, Guillain-Barré syndrome, hematemesis, hemolytic anemia, hepatic coma, hepatic failure, hepatitis, hyperbilirubinemia, hypomagnesemia, intestinal perforation, intracranial hypertension, kidney dysfunction, leukopenia, liver enlarged, lung edema, myasthenia, MI, neuropathy, night blindness, optic atrophy, optic neuritis, pancreatitis, pancytopenia, papilledema, paresthesia, peripheral edema, photosensitivity, pruritus, psychosis, pulmonary embolus, QT interval prolongation, renal failure (acute), respiratory

distress syndrome, sepsis, spleen enlarged, Stevens-Johnson syndrome, suicidal ideation, supraventricular tachycardia, syncope, thrombotic thrombocytopenic purpura, toxic epidermal necrolysis, ventricular arrhythmia, ventricular fibrillation, ventricular tachycardia, thrombocytopenia, torsade de pointes, vertigo, visual field defect, xerostomia

Overdosage/Toxicology Visual changes may occur; one patient had photophobia for 10 minutes. Treatment is symptom-directed and supportive. Following intravenous overdose, toxicity from the vehicle, SBECD, may also occur. Both voriconazole and the intravenous vehicle may be eliminated via hemodialysis.

Drug Interactions

Cytochrome P450 Effect: Substrate of CYP2C9 (major), 2C19 (major), 3A4 (minor); **Inhibits** CYP2C9 (weak), 2C19 (weak), 3A4 (moderate)

Increased Effect/Toxicity: Voriconazole increases serum levels/effects of efavirenz, ergot alkaloids, pimozide, quinidine, rifabutin, and sirolimus; concurrent use is contraindicated (adjusted doses of efavirenz and voriconazole may be used together). Voriconazole increases serum levels/effects of benzodiazepines (metabolized by oxidation; eg, alprazolam, diazepam, triazolam, midazolam), buspirone, busulfan, calcium channel blockers (eg, felodipine, nifedipine, verapamil), cisapride, CYP2C9 substrates, CYP3A4 substrates, cyclosporine, HMG-CoA reductase inhibitors (except pravastatin and fluvastatin), methadone, omeprazole, phenytoin, tacrolimus, warfarin, and vinca alkaloids. Voriconazole may increase the levels of ethinyl estradiol and/or norethindrone; conversely, hormonal contraceptive agents may increase the levels/effects of voriconazole. Use with QT_c-prolonging agents may increase risk of malignant arrhythmia.

Decreased Effect: Barbiturates (phenobarbital, secobarbital), carbamazepine, efavirenz, rifampin, and ritonavir (≥800 mg/day) decrease serum levels/effects of voriconazole; concurrent use is contraindicated. Use caution with smaller doses (<800 mg/day) of ritonavir. CYP2C9 inducers, CYP2C19 inducers, and phenytoin decrease serum levels/effects of voriconazole.

Ethanol/Nutrition/Herb Interactions

Food: May decrease voriconazole absorption. Voriconazole should be taken 1 hour before or 1 hour after a meal.

Herb/Nutraceutical: St John's wort may decrease voriconazole levels.

Storage/Stability

Powder for injection: Store at 15°C to 30°C (59°F to 86°F). Reconstituted solutions are stable for up to 24 hours under refrigeration at 2°C to 8°C (36°F to 46°F).

Powder for oral suspension: Store at 2°C to 8°C (36°F to 46°F). Reconstituted oral suspension may be stored at 15°C to 30°C (59°F to 86°F).

Tablets: Store at 15°C to 30°C (59°F to 86°F).

Reconstitution

Powder for injection: Reconstitute 200 mg vial with 19 mL of sterile water for injection (use of automated syringe is not recommended). Resultant solution (20 mL) has a concentration of 10 mg/mL. Prior to infusion, must dilute to 0.5-5 mg/mL with NS, LR, D_5WLR, $D_5W^1/_2NS$, D_5W, D_5W with KCl 20 mEq, $^1/_2NS$, or D_5WNS. Do not dilute with 4.2% sodium bicarbonate infusion.

Powder for oral suspension: Add 46 mL of water to the bottle to make 40 mg/mL suspension. Discard unused portion after 14 days.

Compatibility Stable in NS, LR, D_5WLR, $D_5W^1/_2NS$, D_5W, D_5W with KCl 20 mEq, $^1/_2NS$, or D_5WNS. Do not infuse **concomitantly** into same line or (Continued)

Voriconazole *(Continued)*

cannula with other drug infusions, including TPN. May be infused simultaneously with TPN through a separate I.V. line.

Incompatible: Do not infuse simultaneously with blood products.

Mechanism of Action Interferes with fungal cytochrome P450 activity, decreasing ergosterol synthesis (principal sterol in fungal cell membrane) and inhibiting fungal cell membrane formation.

Pharmacodynamics/Kinetics

Absorption: Well absorbed after oral administration; administration of crushed tablets is considered bioequivalent to whole tablets

Distribution: V_d: 4.6 L/kg

Protein binding: 58%

Metabolism: Hepatic, via CYP2C19 (major pathway) and CYP2C9 and CYP3A4 (less significant); saturable (may demonstrate nonlinearity)

Bioavailability: 96%

Half-life elimination: Variable, dose-dependent

Time to peak: Oral: 1-2 hours; 0.5 hours (crushed tablet)

Excretion: Urine (as inactive metabolites)

Dosage

Usual dosage ranges:

Children <12 years: Dosage not established

Children ≥12 years and Adults:

Oral: 100-300 mg every 12 hours

I.V.: 6 mg/kg every 12 hours for 2 doses; followed by maintenance dose of 4 mg/kg every 12 hours

Indication-specific dosing: Children ≥12 years and Adults:

Aspergillosis (invasive), scedosporiosis, fusariosis: I.V.: Initial: Loading dose: 6 mg/kg every 12 hours for 2 doses; followed by maintenance dose of 4 mg/kg every 12 hours

Candidemia and other deep tissue *Candida* infections: I.V.: Initial: Loading dose 6 mg/kg every 12 hours for 2 doses; followed by maintenance dose of 3-4 mg/kg every 12 hours

Endophthalmitis, fungal: I.V.: 6 mg/kg every 12 hours for 2 doses, then 200 mg orally twice daily

Esophageal candidiasis: Oral:

Patients <40 kg: 100 mg every 12 hours; maximum: 300 mg/day

Patients ≥40 kg: 200 mg every 12 hours; maximum: 600 mg/day

Note: Treatment should continue for a minimum of 14 days, and for at least 7 days following resolution of symptoms.

Conversion to oral dosing:

Patients <40 kg: 100 mg every 12 hours; increase to 150 mg every 12 hours in patients who fail to respond adequately

Patients ≥40 kg: 200 mg every 12 hours; increase to 300 mg every 12 hours in patients who fail to respond adequately

Dosage adjustment in patients unable to tolerate treatment:

I.V.: Dose may be reduced to 3 mg/kg every 12 hours

Oral: Dose may be reduced in 50 mg increments to a minimum dosage of 200 mg every 12 hours in patients weighing ≥40 kg (100 mg every 12 hours in patients <40 kg)

Dosage adjustment in patients receiving concomitant CYP450 enzyme inducers or substrates:

Cyclosporine: Reduce cyclosporine dose by $1/2$ and monitor closely.

Efavirenz: Oral: Increase maintenance dose of voriconazole to 400 mg every 12 hours and reduce efavirenz dose to 300 mg once daily

Phenytoin:

I.V.: Increase maintenance dosage to 5 mg/kg every 12 hours

Oral: Increase dose to 400 mg every 12 hours in patients ≥40 kg (200 mg every 12 hours in patients <40 kg)

Dosage adjustment in renal impairment: In patients with Cl_{cr} <50 mL/ minute, accumulation of the intravenous vehicle (SBECD) occurs. After initial loading dose, oral voriconazole should be administered to these patients, unless an assessment of the benefit:risk to the patient justifies the use of I.V. voriconazole. Monitor serum creatinine and change to oral voriconazole therapy when possible.

Hemodialysis: Oral dosage adjustment not required; I.V. dosing not recommended since SBECD vehicle is cleared at half the rate of voriconazole and may accumulate

Dosage adjustment in hepatic impairment:

Mild-to-moderate hepatic dysfunction (Child-Pugh Class A and B): Following standard loading dose, reduce maintenance dosage by 50%

Severe hepatic impairment: Should only be used if benefit outweighs risk; monitor closely for toxicity

Administration

Oral: Administer 1 hour before or 1 hour after a meal.

I.V.: Infuse over 1-2 hours (rate not to exceed 3 mg/kg/hour). Do not infuse concomitantly into same line or cannula with other drug infusions, including TPN.

Monitoring Parameters Hepatic function at initiation and during course of treatment; visual function if treatment course continues >28 days; renal function

Dietary Considerations Oral: Should be taken 1 hour before or 1 hour after a meal. Voriconazole tablets contain lactose; avoid administration in hereditary galactose intolerance, Lapp lactase deficiency, or glucose-galactose malabsorption. Suspension contains sucrose; use caution with fructose intolerance, sucrose-isomaltase deficiency, or glucose-galactose malabsorption.

Dosage Forms Excipient information presented when available (limited, particularly for generics); consult specific product labeling.

Injection, powder for reconstitution: 200 mg [contains SBECD 3200 mg]

Powder for oral suspension: 200 mg/5 mL (70 mL) [contains sodium benzoate and sucrose; orange flavor]

Tablet: 50 mg, 200 mg [contains lactose]

References

Breit SM, Hariprasad SM, Mieler WF, et al, "Management of Endogenous Fungal Endophthalmitis With Voriconazole and Caspofungin," *Am J Ophthalmol*, 2005, 139(1):135-40.

Dodds-Ashley ES, Zaas AK, Fang AF, et al, "Comparative Pharmacokinetics of Voriconazole Administered Orally as Either Crushed or Whole Tablets," *Antimicrob Agents Chemother*, 2007, 51(3):877-80.

Durand ML, Kim IK, D'Amico DJ, et al, "Successful Treatment of Fusarium Endophthalmitis with Voriconazole and Aspergillus Endophthalmitis With Voriconazole Plus Caspofungin," *Am J Ophthalmol*, 2005, 140(3):552-4.

Hariprasad SM, Mieler WF, Holz ER, et al, "Determination of Vitreous, Aqueous, and Plasma Concentration of Orally Administered Voriconazole in Humans," *Arch Ophthalmol*, 2004, 122(1):42-7.

Herbrecht R, Denning DW, Patterson TF, et al, "Voriconazole Versus Amphotericin B for Primary Therapy of Invasive Aspergillosis," *N Engl J Med*, 2002, 347(6):408-15.

Walsh TJ, Pappas P, Winston DJ et al, "Voriconazole Compared with Liposomal Amphotericin B for Empirical Antifungal Therapy in Patients with Neutropenia and Persistent Fever," *N Engl J Med*, 2002, 346(4):225-34.

Zonios DI, Gea-Banacloche J, Childs R et al, "Hallucinations During Voriconazole Use," Abstract M-1172; 47th Interscience Conference on Antimicrobial Agents and Chemotherapy, Chicago, Illinois, September, 2007.

Vorinostat (vor IN oh stat)

Medication Safety Issues

High alert medication: The Institute for Safe Medication Practices (ISMP) includes this medication among its list of drugs which have a heightened risk of causing significant patient harm when used in error.

U.S. Brand Names Zolinza™

Index Terms NSC-701852; SAHA; Suberoylanilide Hydroxamic Acid

Generic Available No

Pharmacologic Category Antineoplastic Agent, Histone Deacetylase Inhibitor

Use Treatment of relapsed or refractory cutaneous T-cell lymphoma (CTCL)

Pregnancy Risk Factor D

Lactation Excretion in breast milk unknown/not recommended

Labeled Contraindications Hypersensitivity to vorinostat or any component of the formulation

Warnings/Precautions Hazardous agent - use appropriate precautions for handling and disposal. Pulmonary embolism and deep vein thrombosis (DVT) have been reported; monitor. Use caution in patients with a history of thrombotic events. Dose-related thrombocytopenia and/or anemia may occur. QT_c prolongation has been observed; a baseline and periodic 12-lead ECG should be obtained. Correct electrolyte abnormalities prior to treatment and monitor and correct potassium, calcium, and magnesium levels during therapy. Use caution in patients with a history of QT_c prolongation or with medications known to prolong the QT interval. May cause hyperglycemia; monitor and use with caution in diabetics; may require diet and/or therapy modifications. Safety and efficacy in children have not been established.

Adverse Reactions

>10%:

Cardiovascular: Peripheral edema (13%)

Central nervous system: Fatigue (52% to 73%), chills (16%), dizziness (15%), headache (12%), fever (11%)

Dermatologic: Alopecia (19%), pruritus (12%)

Endocrine & metabolic: Hyperglycemia (8% to 69%; grade 3: 5%), dehydration (16%)

Gastrointestinal: Diarrhea (49% to 52%), nausea (41% to 49%), taste perversion (28% to 46%), xerostomia (16% to 35%), weight loss (21% to 27%), anorexia (22% to 24%), vomiting (15% to 24%), appetite decreased (14% to 22%), constipation (15%)

Hematologic: Thrombocytopenia (26% to 54%; grades 3/4: 6% to 19%), anemia (2% to 14%; grades 3/4: 2% to 3%)

Neuromuscular & skeletal: Muscle spasm (20%)

Renal: Proteinuria (51%), creatinine increased (16% to 47%)

Respiratory: Dyspnea (34%), cough (11%), upper respiratory infection (11%)

1% to 10%:

Cardiovascular: QT_c prolongation (3% to 6%)

Dermatologic: Squamous cell carcinoma (4%)

Respiratory: Pulmonary embolism (5%)

<1%, postmarketing, and/or case reports: Angioneurotic edema, blurred vision, chest pain, cholecystitis, creatine phosphokinase (CPK) increased, DVT, enterococcal infection, exfoliative dermatitis, gastrointestinal hemorrhage, hemoptysis, hypertension, hypocalcemia, hypokalemia, hyponatremia, hypophosphatemia, infection, lethargy, leukopenia, MI,

neutropenia, pneumonia, renal failure, sepsis, spinal cord injury, strepto-coccal bacteremia, stroke (ischemic), syncope, T-cell lymphoma, transami-nases increased, tumor hemorrhage, ureteric obstruction, ureteropelvic junction obstruction, urinary retention, vasculitis, weakness

Overdosage/Toxicology Treatment is symptom-directed and supportive. The benefit of dialysis is unknown.

Drug Interactions

Increased Effect/Toxicity:

Concomitant QT_c prolonging agents may increase the risk of arrhythmia. Valproic acid may enhance thrombocytopenia or gastrointestinal bleeding. Vorinostat may enhance the anticoagulant effect of warfarin.

Storage/Stability Store at 15°C to 30°C (59°F to 86°F).

Mechanism of Action Inhibition of histone deacetylase enzymes, HDAC1, HDAC2, HDAC3, and HDAC6, which catalyze acetyl group removal from protein lysine residues (including histones and transcription factors). Inhibi-tion of histone deacetylase results in accumulation of acetyl groups, leading to alterations in chromatin structure and transcription factor activation causing termination of cell growth leading to cell death.

Pharmacodynamics/Kinetics

Protein binding: ~71%

Metabolism: Glucuronidated and hydrolyzed (followed by beta-oxidation) to inactive metabolites

Bioavailability: Fasting: ~43%

Half-life elimination: ~2 hours

Time to peak, plasma: With high-fat meal: ~4 hours

Excretion: Urine: 52% (<1% as unchanged drug, ~52% as inactive metabo-lites)

Dosage Oral: Adults: Cutaneous T-cell lymphoma: 400 mg once daily

Dosage adjustment for intolerance: Reduce dose to 300 mg once daily; may further reduce to 300 mg daily for 5 consecutive days per week

In clinical trials, **dose reductions** were instituted for the following adverse events: Increased serum creatinine, decreased appetite, hypokalemia, leukopenia, nausea, neutropenia, thrombocytopenia, and vomiting. Vori-nostat was **discontinued** for the following adverse events: Anemia, angioneurotic edema, weakness, chest pain, exfoliative dermatitis, DVT, ischemic stroke, lethargy, pulmonary embolism, and spinal cord injury.

Dosage adjustment in renal impairment: Not studied, however, based on the minimal renal elimination, adjustment may not be required.

Dosage adjustment in hepatic impairment: Not studied minimal.

Administration Administer with food. Do not open, crush, or chew capsules.

Monitoring Parameters Baseline, then periodic 12-lead ECG; baseline, then every other week serum electrolytes (including calcium, magnesium and potassium), CBC with differential, serum creatinine and blood glucose for 2 months, then monthly

Dietary Considerations Take with food.

Patient Information Do not take any new prescription or over-the-counter medications, or herbal products during therapy without consulting prescriber. Take exactly as directed. Maintain adequate hydration (2 L/day of fluids) unless instructed to restrict fluid intake. You will be required to have regularly scheduled laboratory tests while on this medication. You may experience headache, dizziness, or fatigue (use caution when driving or engaging in tasks requiring alertness until response to drug in known); loss of appetite, nausea or vomiting (food, small, frequent meals, chewing gum, or sucking lozenges may help); or diarrhea (buttermilk, boiled milk, or yogurt may reduce diarrhea); loss of hair (will resolve when therapy is discontinued); (Continued)

Vorinostat *(Continued)*

muscle spasm. Report chest pain, swelling of extremities, or weight gain >5 lb; cough, respiratory difficulty, or wheezing; persistent fatigue or weakness; easy bruising or unusual bleeding (eg, tarry stools, blood in vomitus, stool, urine, or mouth).

Emetic Potential Low (10% to 30%)

Dosage Forms Excipient information presented when available (limited, particularly for generics); consult specific product labeling.

Capsule:

Zolinza™: 100 mg

References

Duvic M, Talpur R, Ni X, et al, "Phase II Trial of Oral Vorinostat (Suberoylanilide Hydroxamic Acid, SAHA) for Refractory Cutaneous T-Cell Lymphoma (CTCL)," *Blood*, 2007, 109(1):31-9.

Kelly WK, O'Connor OA, Krug LM, et al, "Phase I Study of an Oral Histone Deacetylase Inhibitor, Suberoylanilide Hydroxamic Acid, in Patients With Advanced Cancer," *J Clin Oncol*, 2005, 23(17):3923-31.

O'Connor OA, Heaney ML, Schwartz L, et al, "Clinical Experience With Intravenous and Oral Formulations of the Novel Histone Deacetylase Inhibitor Suberoylanilide Hydroxamic Acid in Patients With Advanced Hematologic Malignancies," *J Clin Oncol*, 2006, 24(1):166-73.

- ◆ **VP-16** *see* Etoposide *on page 402*
- ◆ **VP-16-213** *see* Etoposide *on page 402*
- ◆ **Vumon®** *see* Teniposide *on page 1018*
- ◆ **Westcort®** *see* Hydrocortisone *on page 545*
- ◆ **Winpred™ (Can)** *see* PredniSONE *on page 919*
- ◆ **WinRho® SDF** *see* Rhₒ(D) Immune Globulin *on page 948*
- ◆ **WR-2721** *see* Amifostine *on page 53*
- ◆ **WR-139007** *see* Dacarbazine *on page 280*
- ◆ **WR-139013** *see* Chlorambucil *on page 205*
- ◆ **WR-139021** *see* Carmustine *on page 178*
- ◆ **Xeloda®** *see* Capecitabine *on page 168*
- ◆ **Xolegel™** *see* Ketoconazole *on page 649*
- ◆ **Y-90 Ibritumomab** *see* Ibritumomab *on page 570*
- ◆ **Y-90 Zevalin** *see* Ibritumomab *on page 570*
- ◆ **YM-08310** *see* Amifostine *on page 53*
- ◆ **Z4942** *see* Ifosfamide *on page 579*
- ◆ **Zanosar®** *see* Streptozocin *on page 979*
- ◆ **ZD1033** *see* Anastrozole *on page 89*
- ◆ **ZD1694** *see* Raltitrexed *on page 943*
- ◆ **ZD1839** *see* Gefitinib *on page 496*
- ◆ **Zenapax®** *see* Daclizumab *on page 284*
- ◆ **Zeneca 182,780** *see* Fulvestrant *on page 482*
- ◆ **Zevalin®** *see* Ibritumomab *on page 570*

Ziconotide *(zi KOE no tide)*

Medication Safety Issues

High alert medication: The Institute for Safe Medication Practices (ISMP) includes this medication among its list of drugs which have a heightened risk of causing significant patient harm when used in error.

U.S. Brand Names Prialt®

Generic Available No

Pharmacologic Category Analgesic, Nonopioid; Calcium Channel Blocker, N-Type

Use Management of severe chronic pain in patients requiring intrathecal (I.T.) therapy and who are intolerant or refractory to other therapies

Pregnancy Risk Factor C

Lactation Excretion in breast milk unknown/not recommended

Labeled Contraindications Hypersensitivity to ziconotide or any component of the formulation; history of psychosis; I.V. administration

I.T. administration is contraindicated in patients with infection at the injection site, uncontrolled bleeding, or spinal canal obstruction that impairs CSF circulation

Warnings/Precautions [U.S Boxed Warning]: Severe psychiatric symptoms and neurological impairment have been reported; interrupt or discontinue therapy if cognitive impairment, hallucinations, mood changes, or changes in consciousness occur. May cause or worsen depression and/or risk of suicide. Cognitive impairment may appear gradually during treatment and is generally reversible after discontinuation (may take up to 2 weeks for cognitive effects to reverse). Use caution in the elderly; may experience a higher incidence of confusion. Patients should be instructed to use caution in performing tasks which require alertness (eg, operating machinery or driving). May have additive effects with opiates or other CNS-depressant medications; may potentiate opioid-induced decreased GI motility; does not interact with opioid receptors or potentiate opiate-induced respiratory depression. Will not prevent or relieve symptoms associated with opiate withdrawal and opiates should not be abruptly discontinued. Unlike opioids, ziconotide therapy can be interrupted abruptly or discontinued without evidence of withdrawal.

Meningitis may occur with use of I.T. pumps; monitor for signs and symptoms of meningitis; treatment of meningitis may require removal of system and discontinuation of intrathecal therapy. Elevated serum creatine kinase can occur, particularly during the first 2 months of therapy; consider dose reduction or discontinuing if combined with new neuromuscular symptoms (myalgias, myasthenia, muscle cramps, weakness) or reduction in physical activity. Safety and efficacy have not been established with renal or hepatic dysfunction, or in pediatric patients. Should not be used in combination with intrathecal opiates.

Adverse Reactions

>10%:

Central nervous system: Dizziness (46%), confusion (15% to 33%), memory impairment (7% to 22%), somnolence (17%), ataxia (14%), speech disorder (14%), headache (13%), aphasia (12%), hallucination (12%; including auditory and visual)

Gastrointestinal: Nausea (40%), diarrhea (18%), vomiting (16%)

Neuromuscular & skeletal: Creatine kinase increased (40%; ≥3 times ULN; 11%), weakness (18%), gait disturbances (14%)

Ocular: Blurred vision (12%)

2% to 10%:

Cardiovascular: Hypotension, peripheral edema, postural hypotension

Central nervous system: Abnormal thinking (8%), amnesia (8%), anxiety (8%), vertigo (7%), insomnia (6%), fever (5%), paranoid reaction (3%), delirium (2%), hostility (2%), stupor (2%), agitation, attention disturbance, balance impaired, burning sensation, coordination abnormal, depression, disorientation, fatigue, fever, hypoesthesia, irritability, lethargy, mental impairment, mood disorder, nervousness, pain, sedation

Dermatologic: Pruritus (7%)

Gastrointestinal: Anorexia (6%), taste perversion (5%), abdominal pain, appetite decreased, constipation, xerostomia

(Continued)

Ziconotide *(Continued)*

Genitourinary: Urinary retention (9%), dysuria, urinary hesitance

Neuromuscular & skeletal: Dysarthria (7%), paresthesia (7%), rigors (7%), tremor (7%), muscle spasm (6%), limb pain (5%), areflexia, muscle cramp, muscle weakness, myalgia

Ocular: Nystagmus (8%), diplopia, visual disturbance

Respiratory: Sinusitis (5%)

Miscellaneous: Diaphoresis (5%)

<2%, postmarketing, and/or case reports: Acute renal failure, aspiration pneumonia (<1%), atrial fibrillation, cerebral vascular accident, ECG abnormalities, incoherence, loss of consciousness, mania, meningitis, myoclonus, psychosis (1%), psychotic disorder, respiratory distress, rhabdomyolysis, seizure (clonic and grand mal), sepsis, suicidal ideation, suicide attempt (<1%)

Overdosage/Toxicology Exaggerated pharmacological effects, including ataxia, confusion, dizziness, garbled speech, hypotension, nausea, nystagmus, sedation, spinal myoclonus, stupor, unresponsiveness, vomiting, and word-finding difficulty, are reported at doses >19.2 mcg/day. Respiratory depression was not observed. (Inadvertent intravenous or epidural administration may cause hypotension.) In case of overdose, ziconotide can be discontinued temporarily or withdrawn; additional treatment should be symptom-directed and supportive. Opioid antagonists are not effective. Most patients recover within 24 hours of discontinuing ziconotide therapy.

Drug Interactions

Increased Effect/Toxicity: Ziconotide may enhance the adverse/toxic effects of other CNS depressants.

Ethanol/Nutrition/Herb Interactions Ethanol: Avoid ethanol (may increase CNS adverse effects).

Storage/Stability Prior to use, store vials at 2°C to 8°C (36°F to 46°F). Once diluted, may be stored at 2°C to 8°C (36°F to 46°F) for 24 hours; refrigerate during transit. Do not freeze. Protect from light.

When using the Medtronic SynchroMed® EL or SynchroMed® II Infusion System, solutions expire as follows:

25 mcg/mL: Undiluted:

Initial fill: Use within 14 days.

Refill: Use within 84 days.

100 mcg/mL:

Undiluted: Refill: Use within 84 days.

Diluted: Refill: Use within 40 days.

Reconstitution Preservative free NS should be used when dilution is needed.

CADD-Micro® ambulatory infusion pump: Initial fill: Dilute to final concentration of 5 mcg/mL.

Medtronic SynchroMed® EL or SynchroMed® II infusion system: Prior to initial fill, rinse internal pump surfaces with 2 mL ziconotide (25 mcg/mL), repeat twice. Only the 25 mcg/mL concentration (undiluted) should be used for initial pump fill.

Mechanism of Action Ziconotide selectively binds to N-type voltage-sensitive calcium channels located on the nociceptive afferent nerves of the dorsal horn in the spinal cord. This binding is thought to block N-type calcium channels, leading to a blockade of excitatory neurotransmitter release and reducing sensitivity to painful stimuli.

Pharmacodynamics/Kinetics

Distribution: I.T.: V_d: ~140 mL

Protein binding: ~50%

Metabolism: Metabolized via endopeptidases and exopeptidases present on multiple organs including kidney, liver, lung; degraded to peptide fragments and free amino acids

Half-life elimination: I.V.: 1-1.6 hours (plasma); I.T.: 2.9-6.5 hours (CSF)

Excretion: I.V.: Urine (<1%)

Dosage I.T.:

Adults: Chronic pain: Initial dose: ≤2.4 mcg/day (0.1 mcg/hour)

Dose may be titrated by ≤2.4 mcg/day (0.1 mcg/hour) at intervals ≤2-3 times/week to a maximum dose of 19.2 mcg/day (0.8 mcg/hour) by day 21; average dose at day 21: 6.9 mcg/day (0.29 mcg/hour). A faster titration should be used only if the urgent need for analgesia outweighs the possible risk to patient safety.

Dosage adjustment for toxicity:

Cognitive impairment: Reduce dose or discontinue. Effects are generally reversible within 3-15 days of discontinuation.

Reduced level of consciousness: Discontinue until event resolves.

CK elevation with neuromuscular symptoms: Consider dose reduction or discontinuation.

Elderly: Refer to adult dosing; use with caution.

Administration Not for I.V. administration. For I.T. administration only using Medtronic SynchroMed® EL, SynchroMed® II Infusion System, or CADD-Micro® ambulatory infusion pump.

Medtronic SynchroMed® EL or SynchroMed® II Infusion Systems:

Naive pump priming (first time use with ziconotide): Use 2 mL of undiluted ziconotide 25 mcg/mL solution to rinse the internal surfaces of the pump; repeat twice for a total of 3 rinses

Initial pump fill: Use only undiluted 25 mcg/mL solution and fill pump after priming. Following the initial fill only, adsorption on internal device surfaces will occur, requiring the use of the undiluted solution and refill within 14 days.

Pump refills: Contents should be emptied prior to refill. Subsequent pump refills should occur at least every 40 days if using diluted solution or at least every 84 days if using undiluted solution.

CADD-Micro® ambulatory infusion pump: Refer to manufacturers' manual for initial fill and refill instructions

Monitoring Parameters Monitor for psychiatric or neurological impairment; signs and symptoms of meningitis or other infection; serum CPK (every other week for first month then monthly); pain relief

Special Geriatric Considerations Manufacturer reports that in all trials there was a higher incidence of confusion in the elderly compared to younger adults.

Dosage Forms Excipient information presented when available (limited, particularly for generics); consult specific product labeling.

Injection, solution, as acetate [preservative free]:

Prialt®: 25 mcg/mL (20 mL); 100 mcg/mL (1 mL, 2 mL, 5 mL)

References

Jain KK, "An Evaluation of Intrathecal Ziconotide for the Treatment of Chronic Pain," *Expert Opin Investig Drugs*, 2000, 9(10):2403-10.

Miljanich GP, "Ziconotide: Neuronal Calcium Channel Blocker for Treating Severe Chronic Pain," *Curr Med Chem*, 2004, 11(23):3029-40.

Staats PS, Yearwood T, Charapata SG, et al, "Intrathecal Ziconotide in the Treatment of Refractory Pain in Patients With Cancer or AIDS: A Randomized Controlled Trial," *JAMA*, 2004, 291(1):63-70.

Wermeling D, Drass M, Ellis D, et al, "Pharmacokinetics and Pharmacodynamics of Intrathecal Ziconotide in Chronic Pain Patients," *J Clin Pharmacol*, 2003, 43(6):624-36.

◆ **Zinecard®** *see* Dexrazoxane *on page 338*

◆ **ZM-182,780** *see* Fulvestrant *on page 482*

♦ **Zofran®** *see Ondansetron on page 837*

♦ **Zofran® ODT** *see Ondansetron on page 837*

♦ **Zoladex®** *see Goserelin on page 520*

♦ **Zoladex® LA (Can)** *see Goserelin on page 520*

♦ **Zoledronate** *see Zoledronic Acid on page 1122*

Zoledronic Acid (zoe le DRON ik AS id)

Related Information
Investigational Drug Service *on page 1379*

U.S. Brand Names Reclast®; Zometa®

Index Terms CGP-42446; NSC-721517; Zoledronate

Generic Available No

Canadian Brand Names Aclasta®; Zometa®

Pharmacologic Category Antidote; Bisphosphonate Derivative

Use Treatment of hypercalcemia of malignancy, multiple myeloma, bone metastases of solid tumors, Paget's disease of bone, postmenopausal osteoporosis

Unlabeled/Investigational Use Prevention of bone loss associated with aromatase inhibitor therapy in postmenopausal women with breast cancer; prevention of bone loss associated with androgen deprivation therapy in prostate cancer

Pregnancy Risk Factor D

Lactation Excretion in breast milk unknown/contraindicated

Labeled Contraindications Hypersensitivity to zoledronic acid, other bisphosphonates, or any component of the formulation; pregnancy; breast-feeding; hypocalcemia (Reclast®)

Warnings/Precautions Bisphosphonate therapy has been associated with osteonecrosis, primarily of the jaw; this has been observed mostly in cancer patients, but also in patients with postmenopausal osteoporosis and other diagnoses. Dental exams and preventative dentistry should be performed prior to placing patients with risk factors on chronic bisphosphonate therapy. Invasive dental procedures should be avoided during treatment.

Infrequently, severe (and occasionally debilitating) bone, joint, and/or muscle pain have been reported during bisphosphonate treatment. The onset of pain ranged from a single day to several months. Symptoms usually resolve upon discontinuation. Some patients experienced recurrence when rechallenged with same drug or another bisphosphonate; avoid use in patients with a history of these symptoms in association with bisphosphonate therapy.

May cause hypocalcemia in patients with Paget's disease, in whom the pretreatment rate of bone turnover may be greatly elevated. Hypocalcemia must be corrected before initiation of therapy in patients with Paget's disease and postmenopausal osteoporosis. Ensure adequate calcium and vitamin D intake during therapy. Use caution in patients with disturbances of calcium and mineral metabolism (eg, hypoparathyroidism, thyroid surgery, malabsorption syndromes).

Adequate hydration is required during treatment (urine output ~2 L/day); avoid overhydration, especially in patients with heart failure.

Reclast®: Use is not recommended in patients with severe renal impairment (Cl_{cr} <35 mL/minute). When used in the treatment of Paget's disease significant renal deterioration has not been observed with the usual 5 mg dose administered over at least 15 minutes.

Zometa®: Use caution in renal dysfunction; dosage adjustment required. In cancer patients, renal toxicity has been reported with doses >4 mg or infusions administered over 15 minutes. Risk factors for renal deterioration include pre-existing renal insufficiency and repeated doses of zoledronic acid and other bisphosphonates. Dehydration and the use of other nephrotoxic drugs which may contribute to renal deterioration should be identified and managed. Use is not recommended in patients with severe renal impairment (serum creatinine >3 mg/dL) and bone metastases (limited data); use in patients with hypercalcemia of malignancy and severe renal impairment should only be done if the benefits outweigh the risks. Renal function should be assessed prior to treatment; if decreased after treatment, additional treatments should be withheld until renal function returns to within 10% of baseline. Diuretics should not be used before correcting hypovolemia. Renal deterioration, resulting in renal failure and dialysis has occurred in patients treated with zoledronic acid after single and multiple infusions at recommended doses of 4 mg over 15 minutes.

Dehydration and concurrent use of other nephrotoxic drugs may increase the risk for renal impairment. Use caution in patients with aspirin-sensitive asthma (may cause bronchoconstriction), hepatic dysfunction, and the elderly. Women of childbearing age should be advised against becoming pregnant. Safety and efficacy in pediatric patients have not been established.

Adverse Reactions Note: An acute reaction (eg, arthralgia, fever, flu-like symptoms, myalgia) may occur within the first 3 days following infusion; usually resolves within 3-4 days of onset, although may take up to 14 days to resolve.

Zometa®:
>10%:
  Cardiovascular: Leg edema (5% to 21%), hypotension (11%)
  Central nervous system: Fatigue (39%), fever (32% to 44%), headache (5% to 19%), dizziness (18%), insomnia (15% to 16%), anxiety (11% to 14%), depression (14%), agitation (13%), confusion (7% to 13%), hypoesthesia (12%)
  Dermatologic: Alopecia (12%), dermatitis (11%)
  Endocrine & metabolic: Dehydration (5% to 14%), hypophosphatemia (12% to 13%), hypokalemia (12%), hypomagnesemia (11%)
  Gastrointestinal: Nausea (29% to 46%), constipation (27% to 31%), vomiting (14% to 32%), diarrhea (17% to 24%), anorexia (9% to 22%), abdominal pain (14% to 16%), weight loss (16%), appetite decreased (13%)
  Genitourinary: Urinary tract infection (12% to 14%)
  Hematologic: Anemia (22% to 33%), neutropenia (12%)
  Neuromuscular & skeletal: Bone pain (55%), weakness (5% to 24%), myalgia (23%), arthralgia (5% to 21%), back pain (15%), paresthesia (15%), limb pain (14%), skeletal pain (12%), rigors (11%)
  Renal: Renal deterioration (8% to 17%; up to 40% in patients with abnormal baseline creatinine)
  Respiratory: Dyspnea (22% to 27%), cough (12% to 22%)
  Miscellaneous: Cancer progression (16%), moniliasis (12%)
1% to 10%:
  Cardiovascular: Chest pain (5% to 10%)
  Central nervous system: Somnolence (5% to 10%)
  Endocrine & metabolic: Hypocalcemia (1% to 10%), hypermagnesemia (2%)
(Continued)

1123

Zoledronic Acid *(Continued)*

Gastrointestinal: Dysphagia (5% to 10%), dyspepsia (10%), mucositis (5% to 10%), stomatitis (8%), sore throat (8%)

Hematologic: Thrombocytopenia (5% to 10%), pancytopenia (5% to 10%), granulocytopenia (5% to 10%)

Renal: Serum creatinine increased (grades 3/4: 2%)

Respiratory: Pleural effusion, upper respiratory tract infection (10%)

Miscellaneous: Metastases (5% to 10%), nonspecific infection (5% to 10%)

Reclast®:

>10%:

Cardiovascular: Hypertension (13%)

Central nervous system: Fever (9% to 18%), headache (11% to 12%)

Neuromuscular & skeletal: Arthralgia (9% to 24%), myalgia (7% to 12%), limb pain (11%)

Miscellaneous: Flu-like syndrome (7% to 11%)

1% to 10%:

Cardiovascular: Peripheral edema (3% to 5%), atrial fibrillation (2% to 3%)

Central nervous system: Dizziness (8% to 9%), fatigue (5% to 8%), chills (5%), lethargy (5%), pain (3% to 5%), malaise (2%)

Dermatologic: Rash (3%)

Endocrine & metabolic: Hypocalcemia (≤3%)

Gastrointestinal: Nausea (9%), constipation (6%), diarrhea (6%), dyspepsia (4% to 5%), vomiting (2% to 5%), abdominal pain (1% to 5%), abdominal distension (2%), anorexia (2%)

Neuromuscular & skeletal: Bone pain (6% to 9%), rigors (8%), shoulder pain (7%), weakness (2% to 5%), back pain (4%), muscle spasm (4%), muscle stiffness (2%), paresthesia (2%)

Renal: Serum creatinine increased (2%)

Respiratory: Dyspnea (5%)

Zometa® and/or Reclast®: <1%, postmarketing, and/or case reports: Allergic reaction, anaphylactic reaction/shock, angioneurotic edema, arrhythmia, blurred vision, bradycardia, bronchoconstriction, conjunctivitis, diaphoresis, episcleritis; flu-like syndrome (fever, chills, flushing, bone pain, arthralgia, myalgia); hematuria, hyperesthesia, hyperkalemia, hypernatremia, hypersensitivity, hypertension; injection site reaction (eg, itching, pain, redness); irisitis, joint and/or muscle pain, muscle cramps, osteonecrosis (primarily of the jaws), proteinuria, pruritus, rash, renal failure, renal impairment, taste perversion, tremor, urticaria, uveitis, weight gain, xerostomia

Overdosage/Toxicology Clinically-significant renal impairment, hypocalcemia, hypophosphatemia, and hypomagnesemia may occur. Zometa® doses >4 mg or Reclast® doses >5 mg and infusion times <15 minutes are associated with a risk of renal toxicity. Treatment is symptom-directed and supportive.

Drug Interactions

Increased Effect/Toxicity: Aminoglycosides may enhance the hypocalcemic effect of zoledronic acid. NSAIDs may enhance the gastrointestinal adverse/toxic effects (increased incidence of GI ulcers) of bisphosphonate derivatives. Bisphosphonate derivatives may enhance the hypocalcemic effect of phosphate supplements. Thalidomide may enhance the adverse/toxic effect(s) of zoledronic acid.

Storage/Stability

Reclast®: Store at room temperature of 15°C to 30°C (59°F to 86°F). After opening, stable for 24 hours at 2°C to 8°C (36°F to 46°F).

Zometa®: Store vials at 15°C to 30°C (59°F to 86°F). Solutions for infusion may be stored for 24 hours at 15°C to 30°C (59°F to 86°F). Infusion of solution must be completed within 24 hours.

Reconstitution Zometa®: Dilute solution for injection in 100 mL NS or D₅W prior to administration.

Compatibility Incompatible with calcium-containing solutions (eg, LR).

Mechanism of Action A bisphosphonate which inhibits bone resorption via actions on osteoclasts or on osteoclast precursors; inhibits osteoclastic activity and skeletal calcium release induced by tumors. Decreases serum calcium and phosphorus, and increases their elimination. In osteoporosis, zoledronic acid inhibits osteoclast-mediated resorption, therefore reducing bone turnover.

Pharmacodynamics/Kinetics

Distribution: Binds to bone

Protein binding: ~22%

Half-life elimination: Triphasic; Terminal: 146 hours

Excretion: Urine (39% ± 16% as unchanged drug) within 24 hours; feces (<3%)

Dosage I.V.: Adults:

Hypercalcemia of malignancy (albumin-corrected serum calcium ≥12 mg/dL) (Zometa®): 4 mg (maximum) given as a single dose. Wait at least 7 days before considering retreatment. Dosage adjustment may be needed in patients with decreased renal function following treatment.

Multiple myeloma or metastatic bone lesions from solid tumors (Zometa®): 4 mg every 3-4 weeks

Note: Patients should receive a daily calcium supplement and multivitamin containing vitamin D

Paget's disease (Reclast®, Aclasta® [not available in U.S.]): 5 mg infused over at least 15 minutes. **Note:** Data concerning retreatment is not available, but may be considered. Patients should receive a daily calcium supplement and multivitamin containing vitamin D.

Postmenopausal osteoporosis (Reclast®): 5 mg every 12 months

Prevention of aromatase inhibitor-induced bone loss in breast cancer (unlabeled use): 4 mg every 6 months

Prevention of androgen deprivation-induced bone loss in nonmetastatic prostate cancer (unlabeled use): 4 mg every 3-12 months

Dosage adjustment in renal impairment (at treatment initiation):

Reclast®: Cl_{cr} <35 mL/minute: Not recommended

Zometa®: Multiple myeloma and bone metastases:

Cl_{cr} >60 mL/minute: 4 mg

Cl_{cr} 50-60 mL/minute: 3.5 mg

Cl_{cr} 40-49 mL/minute: 3.3 mg

Cl_{cr} 30-39 mL/minute: 3 mg

Cl_{cr} <30 mL/minute: Not recommended

Zometa®: Hypercalcemia of malignancy:

Mild-to-moderate impairment: No adjustment necessary

Severe impairment (serum creatinine >4.5 mg/dL): Evaluate risk versus benefit

Aclasta® [not available in U.S.]: Cl_{cr} >30 mL/minute: No adjustment recommended

Dosage adjustment for renal toxicity (during treatment):

Hypercalcemia of malignancy: Evidence of renal deterioration: Evaluate risk versus benefit.

(Continued)

Zoledronic Acid (Continued)

Multiple myeloma and bone metastases: Evidence of renal deterioration: Withhold dose until renal function returns to within 10% of baseline: renal deterioration defined as follows:

Normal baseline creatinine: Increase of 0.5 mg/dL

Abnormal baseline creatinine: Increase of 1 mg/dL

Reinitiate dose at the same dose administered prior to treatment interruption.

Dosage adjustment in hepatic impairment: Specific guidelines are not available.

Administration Infuse over 15-30 minutes; do not infuse over <15 minutes. Infuse in a line separate from other medications. Patients should be appropriately hydrated prior to treatment.

Reclast®: If refrigerated, allow to reach room temperature prior to administration.

Monitoring Parameters Prior to initiation of therapy, dental exam and preventative dentistry for patients at risk for osteonecrosis

Reclast®: Alkaline phosphatase, serum creatinine, calcium and mineral (phosphorus and magnesium) levels

Zometa®: Serum creatinine prior to each dose; serum electrolytes, phosphate, magnesium, and hemoglobin/hematocrit should be evaluated regularly. Monitor serum calcium to assess response and avoid overtreatment.

Test Interactions Bisphosphonates may interfere with diagnostic imaging agents such as technetium-99m-diphosphonate in bone scans.

Dietary Considerations

Multiple myeloma or metastatic bone lesions from solid tumors: Take daily calcium supplement (500 mg) and daily multivitamin (with 400 int. units vitamin D).

Postmenopausal osteoporosis: Ensure adequate calcium and vitamin D supplementation. Postmenopausal women generally require calcium 1200 mg/day and vitamin D 400-800 int. units/day.

Paget's disease: Take calcium 1500 mg/day and vitamin D 800 units/day, particularly during the first 2 weeks after administration.

Patient Information This medication can only be administered intravenously. Avoid food high in calcium or vitamins during infusion or for 2-3 hours after completion. You may experience some nausea or vomiting (small frequent meals, good mouth care, sucking lozenges, or chewing gum may help) or recurrent bone pain (consult prescriber for analgesic). Report unusual muscle twitching or spasms, severe diarrhea/constipation, acute bone pain, or other persistent adverse effects.

Special Geriatric Considerations This drug requires adequate hydration and adjustments for creatinine clearance for its use. Elderly are often volume depleted secondary to drugs and a blunted thirst reflex. See disease related concerns in Dosage: Renal Impairment.

Emetic Potential Very low (<10%)

Vesicant No

Dosage Forms Excipient information presented when available (limited, particularly for generics); consult specific product labeling. [CAN] = Canadian brand name

Infusion, solution [premixed]:

Aclasta® [CAN]: 5 mg (100 mL) [not available in U.S.]

Reclast®: 5 mg (100 mL)

Injection, solution:

Zometa®: 4 mg/5 mL (5 mL) [as monohydrate 4.264 mg]

References

American Dental Association Council on Scientific Affairs, "Dental Management of Patients Receiving Oral Bisphosphonate Therapy," *JADA*, 2006, 137(8):1144-50. Available at http://www.ada.org/prof/resources/pubs/jada/reports/report bisphosphonate.pdf

Black DM, Delmas PD, Eastell R, et al, "Once-Yearly Zoledronic Acid for Treatment of Postmenopausal Osteoporosis," *New Engl J Med*, 2007, 356(18):1809-22.

Body JJ, "Clinical Research Update: Zoledronate," *Cancer*, 1997, 80(Suppl):1699-701.

Brufsky A, Harker WG, Beck JT, et al, "Zoledronic Acid Inhibits Adjuvant Letrozole-Induced Bone Loss in Postmenopausal Women With Early Breast Cancer," *J Clin Oncol* 2007, 25(7):829-36.

Coleman RE and Seaman JJ, "The Role of Zoledronic Acid in Cancer: Clinical Studies in the Treatment and Prevention of Bone Metastases," *Semin Oncol*, 2001, 28(2 Suppl 6):11-6.

Durie BG, Katz M, and Crowley J, "Osteonecrosis of the Jaw and Bisphosphonates," *N Engl J Med*, 2005, 353(1):99-102.

Gatti D and Adami S, "New Bisphosphonates in the Treatment of Bone Diseases," *Drugs Aging*, 1999, 15(4):285-96.

Green JR, "Preclinical Pharmacology of Zoledronic Acid," *Semin Oncol*, 2002, 29(6 Suppl 21):3-11.

Li EC and Davis LE, "Zoledronic Acid: A New Parenteral Bisphosphonate," *Clin Ther*, 2003, 25(11):2669-708.

Lipton A, Small E, Saad F, et al, "The New Bisphosphonate, Zometa (Zoledronic Acid), Decreases Skeletal Complications in Both Osteolytic and Osteoblastic Lesions: A Comparison to Pamidronate," *Cancer Invest*, 2002, 20(Suppl 2):45-54.

Maerevoet M, Martin C, and Duck L, "Osteonecrosis of the Jaw and Bisphosphonates," *N Engl J Med*, 2005, 353(1):99-102.

Major P, "The Use of Zoledronic Acid, a Novel, Highly Potent Bisphosphonate, for the Treatment of Hypercalcemia of Malignancy," *Oncologist*, 2002, 7(6):481-91.

Major PP and Coleman RE, "Zoledronic Acid in the Treatment of Hypercalcemia of Malignancy: Results of the International Clinical Development Program," *Semin Oncol*, 2001, 28(2 Suppl 6):17-24.

McMahon RE, Bouquot JE, Glueck CJ, et al, "Osteonecrosis: A Multifactorial Etiology," *J Oral Maxillofac Surg*, 2004, 62(7):904-5.

Michaelson MD, Kaufman DS, Lee H, et al, "Randomized Controlled Trial of Annual Zoledronic Acid to Prevent Gonadotropin-Releasing Hormone Agonist-Induced Bone Loss in Men With Prostate Cancer," *J Clin Oncol*, 2007, 25(9):1038-42.

Perry CM and Figgitt DP, "Zoledronic Acid: A Review of its Use in Patients With Advanced Cancer," *Drugs*, 2004, 64(11):1197-211.

Reid IR, Miller P, Lyles K, et al, "Comparison of a Single Infusion of Zoledronic Acid With Risedronate for Paget's Disease," *N Engl J Med*, 2005, 353(9):898-908.

Ruggiero S, Gralow J, Marx RE, et al, "Practical Guidelines for the Prevention, Diagnosis, and Treatment of Osteonecrosis of the Jaw in Patients With Cancer," *J Clin Oncol*, 2006, 2(1):7-14.

Smith MR, Eastham J, Gleason DM, et al, "Randomized Controlled Trial of Zoledronic Acid to Prevent Bone Loss in Men Receiving Androgen Deprivation Therapy for Nonmetastatic Prostate Cancer," *J Urol*, 2003, 169(6):2008-12.

Tarassoff P and Csermak K, "Avascular Necrosis of the Jaws: Risk Factors in Metastatic Cancer Patients," *J Oral Maxillofac Surg*, 2003, 61(10):1238-9.

Theriault RL, "Zoledronic Acid (Zometa) Use in Bone Disease," *Expert Rev Anticancer Ther*, 2003, 3(2):157-66.

Wellington K and Goa KL, "Zoledronic Acid: A Review of its Use in the Management of Bone Metastases and Hypercalcaemia of Malignancy," *Drugs*, 2003, 63(4):417-37.

CHEMOTHERAPY REGIMEN INDEX

CHEMOTHERAPY REGIMEN INDEX

EYE

Retinoblastoma

GASTROINTESTINAL

Biliary Adenocarcinoma

Colorectal Cancer

CHEMOTHERAPY REGIMEN INDEX *(Continued)*

Esophageal Cancer

Gastric Cancer

Hepatoblastoma

Pancreatic Cancer

GENITOURINARY

Bladder Cancer

Prostate Cancer

CHEMOTHERAPY REGIMEN INDEX *(Continued)*

CHEMOTHERAPY REGIMEN INDEX *(Continued)*

CHEMOTHERAPY REGIMEN INDEX *(Continued)*

SKIN

Melanoma

ALPHABETICAL LISTING OF CHEMOTHERAPY REGIMENS

5 + 2

Index Terms Cytarabine-Daunorubicin (5 + 2); Daunorubicin-Cytarabine (5 + 2)

Use Leukemia, acute myeloid (induction)

Regimen

Cytarabine: I.V.: 100-200 mg/m^2/day continuous infusion days 1 to 5
[total dose/cycle = 500-1000 mg/m^2]

with

Daunorubicin: I.V.: 45 mg/m^2/day days 1 and 2
[total dose/cycle = 90 mg/m^2]

References

Rai KR, Holland JF, Glidewell OJ, et al, "Treatment of Acute Myelocytic Leukemia: A Study by Cancer and Leukemia Group B," *Blood*, 1981, 58(6):1203-12.

7 + 3 (Daunorubicin)

Index Terms Cytarabine-Daunorubicin (7 + 3)

Use Leukemia, acute myeloid (induction)

Regimen

Cytarabine: I.V.: 100 mg/m^2/day continuous infusion days 1 to 7
[total dose/cycle = 700 mg/m^2]

Daunorubicin: I.V.: 45 mg/m^2/day days 1 to 3
[total dose/cycle = 135 mg/m^2]

Administer one cycle only

References

Dilman RO, Davis RB, Green MR, et al, "A Comparative Study of Two Different Doses of Cytarabine for Acute Myeloid Leukemia: A Phase III Trial of Cancer and Leukemia Group B," *Blood*, 1991, 78(10):2520-6.

Preisler H, Davis RB, Kirschner J, et al, "Comparison of Three Remission Induction Regimens and Two Postinduction Strategies for the Treatment of Acute Nonlymphocytic Leukemia: A Cancer and Leukemia Group B Study," *Blood*, 1987, 69(5):1441-9.

Rai KR, Holland JF, Glidewell OJ, et al, "Treatment of Acute Myelocytic Leukemia: A Study by Cancer and Leukemia Group B," *Blood*, 1981, 58(6):1203-12.

Vogler WR, Velez-Garcia E, Weiner RS, et al, "A Phase III Trial Comparing Idarubicin and Daunorubicin in Combination With Cytarabine in Acute Myelogenous Leukemia: A Southeastern Cancer Study Group Study," *J Clin Oncol*, 1992, 10(7):1103-11.

Yates J, Glidewell O, Wiernik P, et al, "Cytosine Arabinoside With Daunorubicin or Adriamycin® for Therapy of Acute Myelocytic Leukemia: A CALGB Study," *Blood*, 1982, 60(2):454-62.

Yates JW, Wallace HJ Jr, Ellison RR, et al, "Cytosine Arabinoside (NSC-63878) and Daunorubicin (NSC-83142) Therapy in Acute Nonlymphocytic Leukemia," *Cancer Chemother Rep*, 1973, 57(4):485-8.

7 + 3 (Idarubicin)

Index Terms Cytarabine-Idarubicin (7 + 3)

Use Leukemia, acute myeloid (induction)

Regimen

Cytarabine: I.V.: 100-200 mg/m^2/day continuous infusion days 1 to 7
[total dose/cycle = 700 - 1400 mg/m^2]

Idarubicin: I.V.: 12 mg/m^2/day days 1 to 3
[total dose/cycle = 36 mg/m^2]

Administer one cycle only

References

Vogler WR, Velez-Garcia E, Weiner RS, et al, "A Phase III Trial Comparing Idarubicin and Daunorubicin in Combination With Cytarabine in Acute Myelogenous Leukemia: A Southeastern Cancer Study Group Study," *J Clin Oncol*, 1992, 10(7):1103-11.

7 + 3 (Mitoxantrone)

Index Terms Cytarabine-Mitoxantrone (7 + 3)

Use Leukemia, acute myeloid (induction)

Regimen

Cytarabine: I.V.: 100-200 mg/m^2/day continuous infusion days 1 to 7
[total dose/cycle = 700-1400 mg/m^2]

Mitoxantrone: I.V.: 12 mg/m^2/day days 1 to 3
[total dose/cycle = 36 mg/m^2]

Administer one cycle only

References

Arlin Z, Case DC Jr, Moore J, et al, "Randomized Multicenter Trial of Cytosine Arabinoside With Mitoxantrone or Daunorubicin in Previously Untreated Adult Patients With Acute Nonlymphocytic Leukemia (ANLL)," Lederle Cooperative Group, *Leukemia*, 1990, 4(3):177-83.

7 + 3 + 7

Index Terms Cytarabine-Daunorubicin-Etoposide (7 + 3 + 7)

Use Leukemia, acute myeloid

Regimen

Cytarabine: I.V.: 100 mg/m^2/day continuous infusion days 1 to 7
[total dose/cycle = 700 mg/m^2]

Daunorubicin: I.V.: 50 mg/m^2/day days 1 to 3
[total dose/cycle = 150 mg/m^2]

Etoposide: I.V.: 75 mg/m^2/day days 1 to 7
[total dose/cycle = 525 mg/m^2]

Repeat cycle every 21 days; up to 3 cycles may be given based on individual response

References

Bishop JF, Lowenthal RM, Joshua D, et al, "Etoposide in Acute Nonlymphocytic Leukemia," Australian Leukemia Study Group, *Blood*, 1990, 75(1):27-32.

8 in 1 (Brain Tumors)

Use Brain tumors

Regimen NOTE: Multiple variations are listed below.

Variation 1:

Methylprednisolone: I.V.: 300 mg/m^2 every 6 hours day 1 (3 doses)
[total dose/cycle = 900 mg/m^2]

Vincristine: I.V.: 1.5 mg/m^2 (maximum 2 mg) day 1

Lomustine: Oral: 75 mg/m^2 day 1

Procarbazine: Oral: 75 mg/m^2 day 1; 1 hour after methylprednisolone and vincristine

Hydroxyurea: Oral: 3000 mg/m^2 day 1; 2 hours after methylprednisolone and vincristine

Cisplatin: I.V.: 90 mg/m^2 day 1; 3 hours after methylprednisolone and vincristine

Cytarabine: I.V.: 300 mg/m^2 day 1; 9 hours after methylprednisolone and vincristine

Dacarbazine: I.V.: 150 mg/m^2 day 1; 12 hours after methylprednisolone and vincristine

Repeat cycle every 14 days

Variation 2:

Methylprednisolone: I.V.: 300 mg/m^2 every 6 hours day 1 (3 doses)
[total dose/cycle = 900 mg/m^2]

Vincristine: I.V.: 1.5 mg/m^2 (maximum 2 mg) day 1

Lomustine: Oral: 75 mg/m^2 day 1

Procarbazine: Oral: 75 mg/m^2 day 1; 1 hour after methylprednisolone and vincristine

Hydroxyurea: Oral: 3000 mg/m^2 day 1; 2 hours after methylprednisolone and vincristine

(Continued)

8 in 1 (Brain Tumors) *(Continued)*

Cisplatin: I.V.: 60 mg/m² day 1; 3 hours after methylprednisolone and vincristine

Cytarabine: I.V.: 300 mg/m² day 1; 9 hours after methylprednisolone and vincristine

Cyclophosphamide: I.V.: 300 mg/m² day 1; 12 hours after methylprednisolone and vincristine

Repeat cycle every 14 days

References

Pendergrass TW, Milstein JM, Geyer JR, et al, "Eight Drugs in One Day Chemotherapy for Brain Tumors: Experience in 107 Children and Rationale for Preradiation Chemotherapy," *J Clin Oncol*, 1987, 5(8):1221-31.

8 in 1 (Retinoblastoma)

Use Retinoblastoma

Regimen

Vincristine: I.V.: 1.5 mg/m² day 1

Methylprednisolone: I.V.: 300 mg/m² day 1

Lomustine: Oral: 75 mg/m² day 1

Procarbazine: Oral: 75 mg/m² day 1

Hydroxyurea: Oral: 1500 mg/m² day 1

Cisplatin: I.V.: 60 mg/m² day 1

Cytarabine: I.V.: 300 mg/m² day 1

Repeat cycle every 28 days

References

Doz F, Khelfaoui F, Mosseri V, et al, "The Role of Chemotherapy in Orbital Involvement of Retinoblastoma. The Experience of a Single Institution With 33 Patients," *Cancer*, 1994, 74(2):722-32.

AAV (DD)

Use Wilms' tumor

Regimen

Dactinomycin: I.V.: 15 mcg/kg/day days 1 to 5 of weeks 0, 13, 26, 39, 52, and 65

[total dose/cycle = 450 mcg/kg]

Doxorubicin: I.V.: 20 mg/m²/day days 1 to 3 of weeks 6, 19, 32, 45, and 58

[total dose/cycle = 300 mg/m²]

Vincristine: I.V.: 1.5 mg/m² day 1 of weeks 0-10, 13, 14, 26, 27, 39, 40, 52, 53, 65, and 66

[total dose/cycle = 31.5 mg/m²]

References

D'Angio GJ, Breslow N, Beckwith JB, et al, "Treatment of Wilms' Tumor. Results of the Third National Wilms' Tumor Study," *Cancer*, 1989, 64(2):349-60.

ABVD

Use Lymphoma, Hodgkin's disease

Regimen

Doxorubicin: I.V.: 25 mg/m²/day days 1 and 15

[total dose/cycle = 50 mg/m²]

Bleomycin: I.V.: 10 units/m²/day days 1 and 15

[total dose/cycle = 20 units/m²]

Vinblastine: I.V.: 6 mg/m²/day days 1 and 15

[total dose/cycle = 12 mg/m²]

Dacarbazine: I.V.: 375 mg/m²/day days 1 and 15

[total dose/cycle = 750 mg/m²]

Repeat cycle every 28 days

References

Bonadonna G, Zucali R, DeLena M, et al, "Combined Chemotherapy (MOPP or ABVD) - Radiotherapy Approach in Advanced Hodgkin's Disease," *Cancer Treat Rep*, 1977, 61(5):769-77.

Canellos GP, Anderson JR, Propert KJ, et al, "Chemotherapy of Advanced Hodgkin's Disease With MOPP, ABVD, or MOPP Alternating With ABVD," *N Engl J Med*, 1992, 327(21):1478-84.

AC

Use Breast cancer

Regimen NOTE: Multiple variations are listed below.

Variation 1: AC (conventional):

Doxorubicin: I.V.: 60 mg/m^2 day 1

[total dose/cycle = 60 mg/m^2]

Cyclophosphamide: I.V.: 600 mg/m^2 day 1

[total dose/cycle = 600 mg/m^2]

Repeat cycle every 21 days

Variation 2:

Cyclophosphamide: Oral: 200 mg/m^2/day days 3 to 6

[total dose/cycle = 800 mg/m^2]

Doxorubicin: I.V.: 40 mg/m^2 day 1

[total dose/cycle = 40 mg/m^2]

Repeat cycle every 3 weeks for 3 cycles, then every 4 weeks

References

Variation 1:

Fisher B, Brown AM, Dimitrov NV, et al, "Two Months of Doxorubicin-Cyclophosphamide With and Without Interval Reinduction Therapy Compared With 6 Months of Cyclophosphamide, Methotrexate, and Fluorouracil in Positive-Node Breast Cancer Patients With Tamoxifen-Nonresponsive Tumors: Results From the National Surgical Adjuvant Breast and Bowel Project B-15," *J Clin Oncol*, 1990, 8(9):1483-96.

Variation 2:

Jones SE, Durie BG, and Salmon SE, "Combination Chemotherapy With Adriamycin and Cyclophosphamide for Advanced Breast Cancer," *Cancer*, 1975, 36(1):90-7.

ACAV (J)

Use Wilms' tumor

Regimen

Dactinomycin: I.V.: 15 mcg/kg/day days 1 to 5 of weeks 0, 13, 26, 39, 52, and 65

[total dose/cycle = 450 mcg/kg]

Cyclophosphamide: I.V.: 10 mg/kg/day days 1 to 3 of weeks 0, 6, 13, 19, 26, 32, 39, 45, 52, 58, and 65

[total dose/cycle = 330 mg/kg]

Doxorubicin: I.V.: 20 mg/m^2/day days 1 to 3 of weeks 6, 19, 32, 45, and 58

[total dose/cycle = 300 mg/m^2]

Vincristine: I.V.: 1.5 mg/m^2 day 1 of weeks 0-10, 13, 14, 19, 20, 26, 27, 32, 33, 39, 40, 45, 52, 53, 56, 57, 65, and 66

[total dose/cycle = 42 mg/m^2]

References

D'Angio GJ, Breslow N, Beckwith JB, et al, "Treatment of Wilms' Tumor. Results of the Third National Wilms' Tumor Study," *Cancer*, 1989, 64(2):349-60.

AC/Paclitaxel (Sequential)

Use Breast cancer

Regimen

Variation 1: AC + Paclitaxel (conventional):

Doxorubicin: I.V.: 60 mg/m^2 day 1

[total dose/cycle = 60 mg/m^2]

(Continued)

AC/Paclitaxel (Sequential) *(Continued)*

Cyclophosphamide: I.V.: 600 mg/m^2 day 1
[total dose/cycle = 600 mg/m^2]
Repeat cycle every 21 days for 4 cycles
followed by
Paclitaxel: I.V.: 175 mg/m^2 day 1
[total dose/cycle = 175 mg/m^2]
Repeat cycle every 21 days for 4 cycles
Variation 2: AC + Paclitaxel (dose dense):
Doxorubicin: I.V.: 60 mg/m^2 day 1
[total dose/cycle = 60 mg/m^2]
Cyclophosphamide: I.V.: 600 mg/m^2 day 1
[total dose/cycle = 600 mg/m^2]
Filgrastim: SubQ: 5 mcg/kg/day days 3 to 10
[total dose/cycle = 40 mcg/kg]
Repeat cycle every 14 days for 4 cycles
followed by
Paclitaxel: I.V.: 175 mg/m^2 day 1
[total dose/cycle = 175 mg/m^2]
Filgrastim: SubQ: 5 mcg/kg/day days 3 to 10
[total dose/cycle = 40 mcg/kg]
Repeat cycle every 14 days for 4 cycles

References

Variation 1:
Henderson IC, Berry DA, Demetri GD, et al, "Improved Outcomes From Adding Sequential Paclitaxel but not From Escalating Doxorubicin Dose in an Adjuvant Chemotherapy Regimen for Patients With Node-Positive Primary Breast Cancer," *J Clin Oncol*, 2003, 21(6):976-83.
Variation 2:
Citron ML, Berry DA, Cirrincione C, et al, "Randomized Trial of Dose-Dense Versus Conventionally Scheduled and Sequential Versus Concurrent Combination Chemotherapy as Postoperative Adjuvant Treatment of Node-Positive Primary Breast Cancer: First Report of Intergroup Trial C9741/Cancer Leukemia Group B Trial 9741," *J Clin Oncol*, 2003, 21(8):1431-9.

AC-Paclitaxel-Trastuzumab

Use Breast cancer
Regimen NOTE: Multiple variations are listed below.
Variation 1:
Doxorubicin: I.V.: 60 mg/m^2 day 1
[total dose/cycle = 60 mg/m^2]
Cyclophosphamide: I.V.: 600 mg/m^2 day 1
[total dose/cycle = 600 mg/m^2]
Repeat cycle every 21 days for 4 cycles
followed by
Paclitaxel: I.V.: 175 mg/m^2 day 1
[total dose/cycle = 175 mg/m^2]
Trastuzumab: I.V.: 4 mg/kg (loading dose) day 1 (cycle 1 only)
[total dose/cycle = 4 mg/kg]
followed by I.V.: 2 mg/kg/day days 8 and 15 (cycle 1)
[total dose/cycle = 4 mg/kg]
then I.V.: 2 mg/kg/day days 1, 8, and 15 (cycles 2, 3, and 4)
[total dose/cycle = 6 mg/kg]
Repeat cycle every 21 days for 4 cycles
followed by
Trastuzumab: I.V.: 2 mg/kg weekly for 40 weeks
Variation 2:
Doxorubicin: I.V.: 60 mg/m^2 day 1
[total dose/cycle = 60 mg/m^2]

Cyclophosphamide: I.V.: 600 mg/m² day 1
  [total dose/cycle = 600 mg/m²]
Repeat cycle every 21 days for 4 cycles
followed by
Paclitaxel: I.V.: 80 mg/m² day 1 week 13
  [total dose/cycle = 80 mg/m²]
Trastuzumab: I.V.: 4 mg/kg (loading dose) day 1 week 13 only
  [total dose/cycle = 4 mg/kg]
followed by
Paclitaxel: I.V.: 80 mg/m² weekly
  [total dose/cycle = 80 mg/m²]
Trastuzumab: I.V.: 2 mg/kg /weekly
  [total dose/cycle = 2 mg/kg]
Repeat cycle every week for 11 cycles
followed by
Trastuzumab: I.V.: 2 mg/kg /weekly for 40 weeks

References

Romond EH, Perez EA, Bryant J, et al, "Trastuzumab Plus Adjuvant Chemotherapy for Operable HER2-Positive Breast Cancer," *N Engl J Med*, 2005, 353(16):1673-84.

AD

Use Soft tissue sarcoma
Regimen
Doxorubicin: I.V.: 60 mg/m²/day day 1
  [total dose/cycle = 60 mg/m²]
Dacarbazine: I.V.: 250 mg/m²/day days 1 to 5
  [total dose/cycle = 1250 mg/m²]
Repeat cycle every 21 days

References

Borden EC, Amato DA, Rosenbaum C, et al, "IRandomized Comparison of Three Adriamycin Regimens for Metastatic Soft Tissue Sarcomas," *J Clin Oncol*, 1987, 5(6):840-50.

AI

Use Soft tissue sarcoma
Regimen NOTE: Multiple variations are listed below.
Variation 1:
  Doxorubicin: I.V.: 25 mg/m²/day continuous infusion days 1, 2, and 3
    [total dose/cycle = 75 mg/m²]
  Ifosfamide: I.V.: 2 g/m²/day days 1 to 5
    [total dose/cycle = 10 g/m²]
  Mesna: I.V.: 400 mg/m² day 1
    followed by I.V.: 1200 mg/m²/day continuous infusion days 1 to 5
      [total dose/cycle = 6400 mg/m²]
  Repeat cycle every 3 weeks
Variation 2:
  Doxorubicin: I.V.: 30 mg/m²/day continuous infusion days 1, 2, and 3
    [total dose/cycle = 90 mg/m²]
  Ifosfamide: I.V.: 2.5 g/m² /day days 1 to 4
    [total dose/cycle = 10 g/m²]
  Mesna: I.V.: 500 mg/m² day 1
    followed by I.V.: 1500 mg/m²/day continuous infusion days 1 to 4
      [total dose/cycle = 6500 mg/m²]
  Filgrastim: SubQ: 5 mcg/kg/day days 5 through ANC recovery
  Repeat cycle every 3 weeks

References

Patel SR, Vadhan-Raj S, Burgess MA, et al, "Results of Two Consecutive Trials of Dose-Intensive Chemotherapy With Doxorubicin and Ifosfamide in Patients With Sarcomas," *Am J Clin Oncol*, 1998, 21(3):317-21.

♦ **AlinC 14** *see* PVA (POG 8602) *on page 1273*

AP

Use Endometrial cancer

Regimen
Doxorubicin: I.V.: 60 mg/m² day 1
  [total dose/cycle = 60 mg/m²]
Cisplatin: I.V.: 60 mg/m² day 1
  [total dose/cycle = 60 mg/m²]
Repeat cycle every 21-28 days

References
Barrett RJ, Blessing JA, Homesley HD, et al, "Circadian-Timed Combination Doxorubicin-Cisplatin Chemotherapy for Advanced Endometrial Carcinoma. A Phase II Study of the Gynecologic Oncology Group," *Am J Clin Oncol*, 1993, 16(6):494-6.

AT

Use Breast cancer

Regimen NOTE: Multiple variations are listed below.
Variation 1:
  Doxorubicin: I.V.: 50 mg/m² day 1
    [total dose/cycle = 50 mg/m²]
  Docetaxel: I.V.: 75 mg/m² day 1
    [total dose/cycle = 75 mg/m²]
  Repeat cycle every 3 weeks
Variation 2:
  Doxorubicin: I.V.: 60 mg/m² day 1
    [total dose/cycle = 60 mg/m²]
  Docetaxel: I.V.: 60 mg/m²
    [total dose/cycle = 60 mg/m²]
  Repeat cycle every 3 weeks
Variation 3:
  Doxorubicin: I.V.: 50 mg/m² day 1
    [total dose/cycle = 50 mg/m²]
  Docetaxel: I.V.: 75 mg/m² day 1
    [total dose/cycle = 75 mg/m²]
  Repeat cycle every 14 days
Variation 4:
  Doxorubicin: I.V.: 50 mg/m² day 1
    [total dose/cycle = 50 mg/m²]
  Docetaxel: I.V.: 60 mg/m² day 1
    [total dose/cycle = 60 mg/m²]
  Repeat cycle every 3 weeks
Variation 5:
  Doxorubicin: I.V.: 50 mg/m² day 1
    [total dose/cycle = 50 mg/m²]
  Docetaxel: I.V.: 60 mg/m² day 1
    [total dose/cycle = 60 mg/m²]
  Repeat cycle every 3-4 weeks
Variation 6:
  Doxorubicin: I.V.: 56 mg/m² day 1
    [total dose/cycle = 56 mg/m²]
  Docetaxel: I.V.: 75 mg/m² day 1
    [total dose/cycle = 75 mg/m²]
  Repeat cycle every 3 weeks

Variation 7:
Doxorubicin: I.V.: 50 mg/m² day 1
[total dose/cycle = 50 mg/m²]
Docetaxel: I.V.: 75 mg/m² day 2
[total dose/cycle = 75 mg/m²]
Repeat cycle every 4 weeks

References

Variation 1:

von Minckwitz G, Costa SD, Eiermann W, et al, "Maximized Reduction of Primary Breast Tumor Size Using Preoperative Chemotherapy With Doxorubicin and Docetaxel," *J Clin Oncol*, 1999, 17(7):1999-2005.

Variation 2:

Dieras V, "Docetaxel in Combination With Doxorubicin: A Phase I Dose-Finding Study," *Oncology (Williston Park)*, 1997, 11(6 Suppl 6):17-20.

Variation 3:

von Minckwitz G, Costa SD, Raab G, et al, "Dose-Dense Doxorubicin, Docetaxel, and Granulocyte Colony-Stimulating Factor Support With or Without Tamoxifen as Preoperative Therapy in Patients With Operable Carcinoma of the Breast: A Randomized, Controlled, Open Phase IIB Study," *J Clin Oncol*, 2001, 19(15):3506-15.

Variation 4:

Muthalib A, Darwis I, Prayogo N, et al, "Preliminary Results of Multicenter Phase II Trial of Docetaxel (Taxotere) in Combination With Doxorubicin as First-Line Chemotherapy in Indonesian Patients With Advanced or Metastatic Breast Cancer," *Gan To Kagaku Ryoho*, 2000, 27(Suppl 2):498-504.

Variation 5:

Aihara T, Takatsuka Y, Itoh K, et al, "Phase II Study of Concurrent Administration of Doxorubicin and Docetaxel as First-Line Chemotherapy for Metastatic Breast Cancer," *Oncology*, 2003, 64(2):124-30.

Variation 6:

Miller KD, McCaskill-Stevens W, Sisk J, et al, "Combination Versus Sequential Doxorubicin and Docetaxel as Primary Chemotherapy for Breast Cancer: A Randomized Pilot Trial of the Hoosier Oncology Group," *J Clin Oncol*, 1999, 17(10):3033-7.

Variation 7:

Palmeri S, Leonardi V, Tamburo De Bella M, et al, "Doxorubicin-Docetaxel Sequential Schedule: Results of Front-Line Treatment in Advanced Breast Cancer," *Oncology*, 2002, 63(3):205-12.

♦ **ATC** *see* TAC *on page 1279*

AVD

Use Wilms' tumor

Regimen

Dactinomycin: I.V.: 15 mcg/kg/day days 1 to 5 of weeks 0, 13, 26, 39, 52, and 65
[total dose/cycle = 450 mcg/kg]
Doxorubicin: I.V.: 60 mg/m²/day day 1 of weeks 6, 19, 32, 45, and 58
[total dose/cycle = 300 mg/m²]
Vincristine: I.V.: 1.5 mg/m² day 1 of weeks 1 to 8, 13, 14, 26, 27, 39, 40, 52, 53, 65, and 66
[total dose/cycle = 27 mg/m²]

References

Green DM, Breslow NE, Evans I, et al, "Treatment of Children With Stage IV Favorable Histology Wilms Tumor: A Report From the National Wilms' Tumor Study Group," *Med Pediatr Oncol*, 1996, 26(3):147-52.

AV (EE)

Use Wilms' tumor

Regimen

Dactinomycin: I.V.: 15 mcg/kg/day days 1 to 5 of weeks 0, 5, 13, and 26
[total dose/cycle = 300 mcg/kg]
Vincristine: I.V.: 1.5 mg/m²/dose day 1 of weeks 1 to 10, and days 1 and 5 of weeks 13 and 26
[total dose/cycle = 21 mg/m²]
(Continued)

AV (EE) *(Continued)*

References
D'Angio GJ, Breslow N, Beckwith JB, et al, "Treatment of Wilms' Tumor. Results of the Third National Wilms' Tumor Study," *Cancer*, 1989, 64(2):349-60.

AV (K)
Use Wilms' tumor
Regimen
Dactinomycin: I.V.: 15 mcg/kg/day days 1 to 5 of weeks 0, 5, 13, 22, 31, 40, 49, and 58
[total dose/cycle = 600 mcg/kg]
Vincristine: I.V.: 1.5 mg/m^2/dose day 1 of weeks 0-10, 15-20, 24-29, 33-38, 42-47, 51-56, and 60-65
[total dose/cycle = 70.5 mg/m^2]

References
D'Angio GJ, Breslow N, Beckwith JB, et al, "Treatment of Wilms' Tumor. Results of the Third National Wilms' Tumor Study," *Cancer*, 1989, 64(2):349-60.

AV (L)
Use Wilms' tumor
Regimen
Dactinomycin: I.V.: 15 mcg/kg/day days 1 to 5 of weeks 0 and 5
[total dose/cycle = 150 mcg/kg]
Vincristine: I.V.: 1.5 mg/m^2 day 1 of weeks 0-10
[total dose/cycle = 16.5 mg/m^2]

References
D'Angio GJ, Breslow N, Beckwith JB, et al, "Treatment of Wilms' Tumor. Results of the Third National Wilms' Tumor Study," *Cancer*, 1989, 64(2):349-60.

AV (Wilms' Tumor)
Use Wilms' tumor
Regimen
Dactinomycin: I.V.: 15 mcg/kg/day days 1 to 5 of weeks 0, 13, 26, 39, 52, and 65
[total dose/cycle = 450 mcg/kg]
Vincristine: I.V.: 1.5 mg/m^2/dose day 1 of weeks 1 to 8, 13, 14, 26, 27, 39, 40, 52, 53, 65, and 66
[total dose/cycle = 27 mg/m^2]

References
Green DM, Breslow NE, Evans I, et al, "Treatment of Children With Stage IV Favorable Histology Wilms' Tumor: A Report From the National Wilms Tumor Study Group," *Med Pediatr Oncol*, 1996, 26(3):147-52.

♦ **Baby Brain I** *see* COPE *on page 1182*

BEACOPP
Use Lymphoma, Hodgkin's disease
Regimen
Bleomycin: I.V.: 10 units/m^2 day 8
[total dose/cycle = 10 units/m^2]
Etoposide: I.V.: 100 mg/m^2/day days 1, 2 and 3
[total dose/cycle = 300 mg/m^2]
Doxorubicin: I.V.: 25 mg/m^2 day 1
[total dose/cycle = 25 mg/m^2]
Cyclophosphamide: I.V.: 650 mg/m^2 day 1
[total dose/cycle = 650 mg/m^2]
Vincristine: I.V.: 1.4 mg/m^2 (maximum 2 mg) day 8
[total dose/cycle = 1.4 mg/m^2; maximum 2 mg]

Procarbazine: Oral: 100 mg/m^2/day days 1 to 7
[total dose/cycle = 700 mg/m^2]
Prednisone: Oral: 40 mg/m^2/day days 1 to 14
[total dose/cycle = 560 mg/m^2]
Repeat cycle every 21 days

References
Diehl V, Franklin J, Hasenclever D, et al, "BEACOPP, a New Dose-Escalated and Accelerated Regimen, Is at Least as Effective as COPP/ABVD in Patients With Advanced-Stage Hodgkin's Lymphoma: Interim Report From a Trial of the German Hodgkin's Lymphoma Study Group," *J Clin Oncol*, 1998, 16(12):3810-21.

BEP (Ovarian Cancer)

Use Ovarian cancer

Regimen

Bleomycin: I.V.: 20 units/m^2 (maximum 30 units) day 1
[total dose/cycle = 20 units/m^2]
Etoposide: I.V.: 75 mg/m^2/day days 1 to 5
[total dose/cycle = 375 mg/m^2]
or 75 mg/m^2/day days 1 to 4 (if received prior radiation therapy)
[total dose/cycle = 300 mg/m^2]
Cisplatin: I.V.: 20 mg/m^2/day days 1 to 5
[total dose/cycle = 100 mg/m^2]
Repeat cycle every 3 weeks for 4 cycles

References
Homesley HD, Bundy BN, Hurteau JA, et al, "Bleomycin, Etoposide, and Cisplatin Combination Therapy of Ovarian Granulosa Cell Tumors and Other Stromal Malignancies: A Gynecologic Oncology Group Study," *Gynecol Oncol*, 1999, 72(2):131-7.

BEP (Ovarian Cancer, Testicular Cancer)

Use Ovarian cancer; testicular cancer

Regimen

Bleomycin: I.V.: 30 units/day days 2, 9, and 16
[total dose/cycle = 90 units]
Etoposide: I.V.: 100 mg/m^2/day days 1 to 5
[total dose/cycle = 500 mg/m^2]
or 120 mg/m^2/day days 1 to 3
[total dose/cycle = 360 mg/m^2]
Cisplatin: I.V.: 20 mg/m^2/day days 1 to 5
[total dose/cycle = 100 mg/m^2]
Repeat cycle every 21 days

References
Horwich A, Sleijfer DT, Fossa SD, et al, "Randomized Trial of Bleomycin, Etoposide, and Cisplatin Compared With Bleomycin, Etoposide, and Carboplatin in Good-Prognosis Metastatic Nonseminomatous Germ Cell Cancer: A Multiinstitutional Medical Research Council/European Organization for Research and Treatment of Cancer Trial," *J Clin Oncol*, 1997, 15(5):1844-52.

Nichols CR, Catalano PJ, Crawford ED, et al, "Randomized Comparison of Cisplatin and Etoposide and Either Bleomycin or Ifosfamide in Treatment of Advanced Disseminated Germ Cell Tumors: An Eastern Cooperative Oncology Group, Southwest Oncology Group, and Cancer and Leukemia Group B Study," *J Clin Oncol*, 1998, 16(4):1287-93.

Williams S, Blessing JA, Liao SY, et al, "Adjuvant Therapy of Ovarian Germ Cell Tumors With Cisplatin, Etoposide, and Bleomycin: A Trial of the Gynecologic Oncology Group," *J Clin Oncol*, 1994, 12(4):701-6.

BEP (Testicular Cancer)

Use Testicular cancer

Regimen NOTE: Multiple variations are listed on next page.
(Continued)

BEP (Testicular Cancer) *(Continued)*

Variation 1:
Bleomycin: I.V.: 30 units/day days 2, 9, and 16
[total dose/cycle = 90 units]
Etoposide: I.V.: 100 mg/m^2/day days 1 to 5
[total dose/cycle = 500 mg/m^2]
Cisplatin: I.V.: 20 mg/m^2/day days 1 to 5
[total dose/cycle = 100 mg/m^2]
Repeat cycle every 21 days

Variation 2:
Bleomycin: I.V.: 30 units once weekly
[total dose/cycle = 90 units]
Etoposide: I.V.: 120 mg/m^2/day days 1, 3, and 5
[total dose/cycle = 360 mg/m^2]
Cisplatin: I.V.: 20 mg/m^2/day days 1 to 5
[total dose/cycle = 100 mg/m^2]
Repeat cycle every 21 days

Variation 3:
Bleomycin: I.V.: 30 units/day days 1, 8, and 15
[total dose/cycle = 90 units]
Etoposide: I.V.: 165 mg/m^2/day days 1 to 3
[total dose/cycle = 495 mg/m^2]
Cisplatin: I.V.: 50 mg/m^2/day days 1 and 2
[total dose/cycle = 100 mg/m^2]
Repeat cycle every 21 days

References

Variation 1:
Williams SD, Birch R, Einhorn LH, et al, "Treatment of Disseminated Germ-Cell Tumors With Cisplatin, Bleomycin, and Either Vinblastine or Etoposide," *N Engl J Med*, 1987, 316(23):1435-40.

Variation 2:
de Wit R, Stoter G, Sleijfer DT, et al, "Four Cycles of BEP vs Four Cycles of VIP in Patients With Intermediate-Prognosis Metastatic Testicular Nonseminoma: A Randomized Study of the EORTC Genitourinary Tract Cancer Cooperative Group. European Organization for Research and Treatment of Cancer," *Br J Cancer*, 1998, 78(6):828-32.

Variation 3:
de Wit R, Roberts JT, Wilkinson PM, et al, "Equivalence of Three or Four Cycles of Bleomycin, Etoposide, and Cisplatin Chemotherapy and of a 3- or 5-Day Schedule in Good-Prognosis Germ Cell Cancer: A Randomized Study of the European Organization for Research and Treatment of Cancer Genitourinary Tract Cancer Cooperative Group and the Medical Research Council," *J Clin Oncol*, 2001, 19(6):1629-40.

Bevacizumab-Capecitabine

Index Terms Capecitabine-Bevacizumab

Use Breast cancer

Regimen

Capecitabine: Oral: 1250 mg/m^2 twice daily days 1 to 14
[total dose/cycle = 35,000 mg/m^2]
Bevacizumab: I.V.: 15 mg/kg/day day 1
[total dose/cycle = 15 mg/kg]
Repeat cycle every 21 days for up to 35 cycles

References

Miller KD, Chap LI, Holmes FA, et al, "Randomized Phase III Trial of Capecitabine Compared With Bevacizumab Plus Capecitabine in Patients With Previously Treated Metastatic Breast Cancer," *J Clin Oncol*, 2005, 23(4):792-9.

Bevacizumab-Fluorouracil-Leucovorin

Index Terms Fluorouracil-Leucovorin-Bevacizumab

Use Colorectal cancer

Regimen

Bevacizumab: I.V.: 5 mg/kg/day days 1, 15, 29, and 43
[total dose/cycle = 20 mg/kg]

Leucovorin: I.V.: 500 mg/m²/day days 1, 8, 15, 22, 29, and 36
[total dose/cycle = 3000 mg/m²]

Fluorouracil: I.V.: 500 mg/m²/day days 1, 8, 15, 22, 29, and 36
[total dose/cycle = 3000 mg/m²]

Repeat cycle every 56 days

References

Kabbinavar FF, Schulz J, McCleod M, et al, "Addition of Bevacizumab to Bolus Fluorouracil and Leucovorin in First-Line Metastatic Colorectal Cancer: Results of a Randomized Phase II Trial," *J Clin Oncol*, 2005, 23(16):3697-705.

Bevacizumab-Interferon Alfa-2a

Index Terms Interferon Alfa 2a-Bevacizumab

Use Renal cell cancer

Regimen

Interferon Alfa-2a: SubQ: 9 million units 3 times/week
[total dose/cycle = 54 million units]

Bevacizumab: I.V.: 10 mg/kg/day day 1
[total dose/cycle = 10 mg/kg]

Repeat cycle every 14 days for up to 1 year or until disease progression

References

Escudier B, Koralewski P, Pluzanska A, et al, "A Randomized, Controlled, Double-Blind Phase III Study (AVOREN) of Bevacizumab/Interferon-α2a vs Placebo/Interferon-α2a as First-Line Therapy in Metastatic Renal Cell Carcinoma," *J Clin Oncol*, 2007, 25(18S):3 [abstract from 2007 ASCO Annual Meeting Proceedings, Part I]

Bevacizumab-Irinotecan-Fluorouracil-Leucovorin

Index Terms Irinotecan-Fluorouracil-Leucovorin-Bevacizumab

Use Colorectal cancer

Regimen

Bevacizumab: I.V.: 5 mg/kg/day days 1, 15, and 29
[total dose/cycle = 15 mg/kg]

Irinotecan: I.V.: 125 mg/m²/day days 1, 8, 15, and 22
[total dose/cycle = 500 mg/m²]

Fluorouracil: I.V.: 500 mg/m²/day days 1, 8, 15, and 22
[total dose/cycle = 2000 mg/m²]

Leucovorin: I.V.: 20 mg/m²/day days 1, 8, 15, and 22
[total dose/cycle = 80 mg/m²]

Repeat cycle every 42 days

References

Hurwitz H, Fehrenbacher L, Novotny W, et al, "Bevacizumab Plus Irinotecan, Fluorouracil, and Leucovorin for Metastatic Colorectal Cancer," *N Engl J Med*, 2004, 350(23):2335-42.

Bevacizumab-Irinotecan (Glioblastoma)

Index Terms Irinotecan-Bevacizumab (Glioblastoma)

Use Brain tumors

Regimen Note: Patients receiving concurrent antiepileptic enzyme-inducing drugs received an increased dose of irinotecan (340 mg/m²/dose).

Bevacizumab: I.V.: 10 mg/kg day 1
[total dose/cycle = 10 mg/kg]
(Continued)

Bevacizumab-Irinotecan (Glioblastoma) *(Continued)*

Irinotecan: I.V.: 125 mg/m² day 1
   [total dose/cycle = 125 mg/m²]
Repeat cycle every 14 days

References
Vredenburgh JJ, Desjardins A, Herndon JE 2nd, et al, "Bevacizumab Plus Irinotecan in Recurrent Glioblastoma Multiforme," *J Clin Oncol*, 2007, 25(30):4722-9.

Bevacizumab-Oxaliplatin-Fluorouracil-Leucovorin

Index Terms Bevacizumab-Oxaliplatin-Leucovorin-Fluorouracil; Oxaliplatin-Fluorouracil-Leucovorin-Bevacizumab

Use Colorectal cancer

Regimen

Bevacizumab: I.V.: 10 mg/kg day 1
   [total dose/cycle = 10 mg/kg]
Oxaliplatin: I.V.: 85 mg/m² day 1
   [total dose/cycle = 85 mg/m²]
Leucovorin: I.V.: 200 mg/m²/day days 1 and 2
   [total dose/cycle = 400 mg/m²]
Fluorouracil: I.V. bolus: 400 mg/m²/day days 1 and 2
  followed by I.V.: 600 mg/m² continuous infusion over 22 hours days 1 and 2
   [total dose/cycle = 2000 mg/m²]
Repeat cycle every 14 days

References
Giantonio BJ, Catalano PJ, Meropol NJ, et al, "Bevacizumab in Combination With Oxaliplatin, Fluorouracil, and Leucovorin (FOLFOX4) for Previously Treated Metastatic Colorectal Cancer: Results From the Eastern Cooperative Oncology Group Study E3200," *J Clin Oncol*, 2007, 25(12):1539-44.

♦ **Bevacizumab-Oxaliplatin-Leucovorin-Fluorouracil** *see* Bevacizumab-Oxaliplatin-Fluorouracil-Leucovorin *on page 1152*

♦ **Bevacizumab-Paclitaxel** *see* Paclitaxel-Bevacizumab *on page 1263*

♦ **BI** *see* Bicalutamide + LHRH-A *on page 1152*

Bicalutamide + LHRH-A

Index Terms BI; BZ

Use Prostate cancer

Regimen

Bicalutamide: Oral: 50 mg/day
   [total dose/cycle = 50 mg]
  with
Goserelin acetate: SubQ: 3.6 mg day 1
   [total dose/cycle = 3.6 mg]
  or
Leuprolide depot: I.M.: 7.5 mg day 1
   [total dose/cycle = 7.5 mg]
Repeat cycle every 28 days

References
Schellhammer PF, Sharifi R, Block NL, et al, "A Controlled Trial of Bicalutamide Versus Flutamide, Each in Combination With Luteinizing Hormone-Releasing Hormone Analogue Therapy, in Patients With Advanced Prostate Cancer. Casodex Combination Study Group." *Urology*, 1995, 45(5):745-52.

BIP

Use Cervical cancer

Regimen

Bleomycin: I.V.: 30 units continuous infusion day 1
   [total dose/cycle = 30 units]

Cisplatin: I.V.: 50 mg/m² day 2
[total dose/cycle = 50 mg/m²]

Ifosfamide: I.V.: 5 g/m² continuous infusion day 2
[total dose/cycle = 5 g/m²]

Mesna: I.V.: 6 g/m² continuous infusion over 36 hours day 2 (start with ifosfamide)
[total dose/cycle = 6 g/m²]

Repeat cycle every 21 days

References

Buxton EJ, Meanwell CA, Hilton C, et al, "Combination Bleomycin, Ifosfamide, and Cisplatin Chemotherapy in Cervical Cancer," *J Natl Cancer Inst*, 1989, 81(5):359-61.

BOLD

Use Melanoma

Regimen

Dacarbazine: I.V.: 200 mg/m²/day days 1 to 5
[total dose/cycle = 1000 mg/m²]

Vincristine: I.V.: 1 mg/m²/day days 1 and 4
[total dose/cycle = 2 mg/m²]

Bleomycin: I.V.: 15 units/day days 2 and 5
[total dose/cycle = 30 units]

Lomustine: Oral: 80 mg day 1
[total dose/cycle = 80 mg]

Repeat cycle every 4 weeks

References

Nathan FE, Berd D, Sato T, et al, "BOLD + Interferon in the Treatment of Metastatic Uveal Melanoma: First Report of Active Systemic Therapy," *J Exp Clin Cancer Res*, 1997, 16(2):201-8.

Punt CJ, van Herpen CM, Janasen RL, et al, "Chemoimmunotherapy With Bleomycin, Vincristine, Lomustine, Dacarbazine (BOLD) Plus Interferon Alpha for Metastatic Melanoma: A Multicentre Phase II Study," *Br J Cancer*, 1997, 76(2):266-9.

BOLD + Interferon

Use Melanoma

Regimen NOTE: Multiple variations are listed below.

Variation 1:

Bleomycin: I.V.: 15 units/day days 2 and 5
[total dose/cycle = 30 units]

Vincristine: I.V.: 1 mg/m²/day days 1 and 4
[total dose/cycle = 2 mg/m²]

Lomustine: Oral: 80 mg day 1
[total dose/cycle = 80 mg]

Dacarbazine: I.V.: 200 mg/m²/day days 1 to 5
[total dose/cycle = 1000 mg/m²]

Interferon Alfa-2b: SubQ: 3 million units/day days 8 to 49 (cycles 1 and 2)
[total dose through day 49 = 126 million units]
followed by SubQ: 6 million units 3 times/week (beginning day 50 and subsequent cycles)
[total dose/cycle = 72 million units]

Repeat cycle every 4 weeks

Variation 2:

Bleomycin: I.V.: 30 units day 1
[total dose/cycle = 30 units]

Vincristine: I.V.: 2 mg day 1
[total dose/cycle = 2 mg]

(Continued)

BOLD + Interferon *(Continued)*

Lomustine: Oral: 80 mg day 1
[total dose/cycle = 80 mg]

Dacarbazine: I.V.: 700 mg/m² day 1
[total dose/cycle = 700 mg/m²]

Interferon Alfa-2b: SubQ: 3 million units 3 times/week
[total dose/cycle = 36 million units]

Repeat cycle every 4 weeks

Variation 3:

Bleomycin: I.V.: 15 units/day days 2 and 5
[total dose/cycle = 30 units]

Vincristine: I.V.: 1-2 mg/day days 1 and 4
[total dose/cycle = 2-4 mg]

Lomustine: Oral: 80 mg day 1
[total dose/cycle = 80 mg]

Dacarbazine: I.V.: 200 mg/m²/day days 1 to 5
[total dose/cycle = 1000 mg/m²]

Interferon Alfa-2b: SubQ: 6 million units 3 times/week, for 6 doses, starting day 8
[total dose/cycle = 36 million units]

Repeat cycle every 4 weeks

Variation 4:

Bleomycin: I.V.: 15 units/day days 2 and 5
[total dose/cycle = 30 units]

Vincristine: I.V.: 1 mg/m²/day (maximum 2 mg/dose) days 1 and 4
[total dose/cycle = 2 mg/m²]

Lomustine: Oral: 80 mg day 1
[total dose/cycle = 80 mg]

Dacarbazine: I.V.: 200 mg/m²/day days 1 to 5
[total dose/cycle = 1000 mg/m²]

Interferon Alfa-2b: SubQ: 3 million units/day days 8, 10, 12, 15, 17, and 19
[total dose/cycle = 18 million units]

Repeat cycle every 4 weeks

References

Variation 1:
Pyrhonen S, Hahka-Kemppinen M, and Muhonen T, "A Promising Interferon Plus Four-Drug Chemotherapy Regimen for Metastatic Melanoma," *J Clin Oncol*, 1992, 10(12):1919-26.
Variation 2:
Vuoristo MS, Grohn P, Kumpulainen E, et al, "Treatment of Patients With Metastatic Melanoma With a One Day Regimen of Dacarbazine, Vincristine, Bleomycin, and Lomustine Plus Interferon Alfa," *Eur J Cancer*, 1994, 30A(3):420.
Variation 3:
Vuoristo M, Grohn P, Kellokumpu-Lehtinen P, et al, "Intermittent Interferon and Polychemotherapy in Metastatic Melanoma," *J Cancer Res Clin Oncol*, 1995, 121(3):175-80.
Variation 4:
Nathan FE, Berd D, Sato T, et al, "BOLD + Interferon in the Treatment of Metastatic Uveal Melanoma: First Report of Active Systemic Therapy," *J Exp Clin Cancer Res*, 1997, 16(2):201-8.

BOLD (Melanoma)

Use Melanoma

Regimen NOTE: Multiple variations are listed below.

Variation 1:

Bleomycin: SubQ: 7.5 units/day days 1 and 4 (cycle 1 only)
followed by SubQ: 15 units/day days 1 and 4 (subsequent cycles)
[total dose/cycle = 45 units; maximum total dose (all cycles) = 400 units]

Vincristine: I.V.: 1 mg/m²/day days 1 and 5
[total dose/cycle = 2 mg/m²]

Lomustine: Oral: 80 mg/m^2 (maximum 150 mg/dose) day 1
[total dose/cycle = 80 mg/m^2]

Dacarbazine: I.V.: 200 mg/m^2/day (maximum 400 mg/dose) days 1 to 5
[total dose/cycle = 1000 mg/m^2; maximum 2000 mg]

Repeat cycle every 4-6 weeks

Variation 2:

Bleomycin: I.V.: 15 units/day days 1 and 4
[total dose/cycle = 30 units]

Vincristine: I.V.: 1 mg/m^2/day days 1 and 5
[total dose/cycle = 2 mg/m^2]

Lomustine: Oral: 80 mg/m^2 (maximum 150 mg/dose) day 1
[total dose/cycle = 80 mg/m^2]

Dacarbazine: I.V.: 200 mg/m^2/day days 1 to 5
[total dose/cycle = 1000 mg/m^2]

Repeat cycle every 4 weeks

Variation 3:

Bleomycin: I.V.: 15 units/day days 1 and 4
[total dose/cycle = 30 units]

Vincristine: I.V.: 1 mg/m^2 day 1
[total dose/cycle = 1 mg/m^2]

Lomustine: Oral: 80 mg/m^2 day 3 (odd numbered cycles)
[total dose/cycle = 80 mg/m^2; every other cycle]

Dacarbazine: I.V.: 200 mg/m^2/day days 1 to 5
[total dose/cycle = 1000 mg/m^2]

Repeat cycle every 4 weeks

References

Variation 1:

Seigler HF, Lucas VS, Pickett NJ, et al, "DTIC, CCNU, Bleomycin and Vincristine (BOLD) in Metastatic Melanoma," *Cancer*, 1980, 46(11):2346-8.

Variation 2:

York RM and Foltz AT, "Bleomycin, Vincristine, Lomustine, and DTIC Chemotherapy for Metastatic Melanoma," *Cancer*, 1988, 61(11):2183-6.

Variation 3:

Lakhani S, Selby P, Bliss JM, et al, "Chemotherapy for Malignant Melanoma: Combinations and High Doses Produce More Responses Without Survival Benefit," *Br J Cancer*, 1990, 61(2):330-4.

Bortezomib-Doxorubicin (Liposomal)

Index Terms Doxorubicin (Liposomal)-Bortezomib

Use Multiple myeloma

Regimen

Bortezomib: I.V.: 1.3 mg/m^2/day days 1, 4, 8, and 11
[total dose/cycle = 5.2 mg/m^2]

Doxorubicin (liposomal): I.V.: 30 mg/m^2 day 4
[total dose/cycle = 30 mg/m^2]

Repeat cycle every 21 days for up to 8 cycles

References

Biehn SE, Moore DT, Voorhees PM, et al, "Extended Follow-Up of Outcome Measures in Multiple Myeloma Patients Treated on a Phase I Study With Bortezomib and Pegylated Liposomal Doxorubicin," *Ann Hematol*, 2007, 86(3):211-6.

Orlowski RZ, Nagler A, Sonneveld P, et al, "Randomized Phase III Study of Pegylated Liposomal Doxorubicin Plus Bortezomib Compared With Bortezomib Alone in Relapsed or Refractory Multiple Myeloma: Combination Therapy Improves Time to Progression," *J Clin Oncol*, 2007, 25(25):3892-901.

Orlowski RZ, Voorhees PM, Garcia RA, et al, "Phase 1 Trial of the Proteasome Inhibitor Bortezomib and Pegylated Liposomal Doxorubicin in Patients With Advanced Hematologic Malignancies," *Blood*, 2005, 105(8):3058-65.

Bortezomib-Melphalan-Prednisone

Index Terms Melphalan-Prednisone-Bortezomib; VMP

Use Multiple myeloma

Regimen

Bortezomib: I.V.: 1-1.3 mg/m²/day days 1, 4, 8, 11, 22, 25, 29, and 32
  [total dose/cycle = 8-10.4 mg/m²]
Melphalan: Oral: 9 mg/m²/day days 1 to 4
  [total dose/cycle = 36 mg/m²]
Prednisone: Oral: 60 mg/m²/day days 1 to 4
  [total dose/cycle = 240 mg/m²]
Repeat cycle every 42 days for 4 cycles
followed by
Bortezomib: I.V.: 1-1.3 mg/m²/day days 1, 8, 15, and 22
  [total dose/cycle = 4-5.2 mg/m²]
Melphalan: Oral: 9 mg/m²/day days 1 to 4
  [total dose/cycle = 36 mg/m²]
Prednisone: Oral: 60 mg/m²/day days 1 to 4
  [total dose/cycle = 240 mg/m²]
Repeat cycle every 35 days for 5 cycles

References

Mateos MV, Hernández JM, Hernández MT, et al, "Bortezomib Plus Melphalan and Prednisone in Elderly Untreated Patients With Multiple Myeloma: Results of a Multicenter Phase 1/2 Study," *Blood*, 2006, 108(7):2165-72.

Bortezomib-Melphalan-Prednisone-Thalidomide

Index Terms Melphalan-Prednisone-Bortezomib-Thalidomide; VMPT

Use Multiple myeloma

Regimen

Bortezomib: I.V.: 1-1.3 mg/m²/day days 1, 4, 15, and 22
  [total dose/cycle = 4-5.2 mg/m²]
Melphalan: Oral: 6 mg/m²/day days 1 to 5
  [total dose/cycle = 30 mg/m²]
Prednisone: Oral: 60 mg/m²/day days 1 to 5
  [total dose/cycle = 300 mg/m²]
Thalidomide: Oral: 50 mg/day days 1 to 35
  [total dose/cycle = 1750 mg]
Repeat cycle every 35 days for 6 cycles

References

Palumbo A, Ambrosini MT, Benevolo G, et al, "Bortezomib, Melphalan, Prednisone, and Thalidomide for Relapsed Multiple Myeloma," *Blood*, 2007, 109(7):2767-72.

♦ **BZ** *see* Bicalutamide + LHRH-A *on page 1152*

CA

Use Leukemia, acute myeloid

Regimen

Cytarabine: I.V.: 3000 mg/m² every 12 hours days 1 and 2 (4 doses)
  [total dose/cycle = 12,000 mg/m²]
Asparaginase: I.M.: 6000 units/m² at hour 42
  [total dose/cycle = 6000 units/m²]
Repeat cycle every 7 days for 2 or 3 cycles

References

Capizzi RL, Davis R, Powell B, et al, "Synergy Between High-Dose Cytarabine and Asparaginase in the Treatment of Adults With Refractory and Relapsed Acute Myelogenous Leukemia: A Cancer and Leukemia Group B Study," *J Clin Oncol*, 1988, 6(3):499-508.

CABO

Use Head and neck cancer

Regimen

Cisplatin: I.V.: 50 mg/m² day 4
[total dose/cycle = 50 mg/m²]
Methotrexate: I.V.: 40 mg/m²/day days 1 and 15
[total dose/cycle = 80 mg/m²]
Bleomycin: I.V.: 10 units/day days 1, 8, and 15
[total dose/cycle = 30 units]
Vincristine: I.V.: 2 mg/day days 1, 8, and 15
[total dose/cycle = 6 mg]
Repeat cycle every 21 days

References

Clavel M, Vermorken JB, Cognetti F, et al, "Randomized Comparison of Cisplatin, Methotrexate, Bleomycin, and Vincristine (CABO) Versus Cisplatin and 5-Fluorouracil (CF) Versus Cisplatin in Recurrent or Metastatic Squamous Cell Carcinoma of the Head and Neck. A Phase III Study of the EORTC Head and Neck Cancer Cooperative Group," *Ann Oncol*, 1994, 5(6):521-6.

CAD/MOPP/ABV

Use Lymphoma, Hodgkin's disease

Regimen

CAD:

Lomustine: Oral: 100 mg/m² day 1
[total dose/cycle = 100 mg/m²]
Melphalan: Oral: 6 mg/m²/day days 1 to 4
[total dose/cycle = 24 mg/m²]
Vindesine: I.V.: 3 mg/m²/day day 1 and 8
[total dose/cycle = 6 mg/m²]

MOPP:

Mechlorethamine: I.V.: 6 mg/m²/day days 1 and 8
[total dose/cycle = 12 mg/m²]
Vincristine: I.V.: 1.4 mg/m²/day days 1 and 8
[total dose/cycle = 2.8 mg/m²]
Procarbazine: Oral: 100 mg/m²/day days 1 to 14
[total dose/cycle = 1400 mg/m²]
Prednisone: Oral: 40 mg/m²/day days 1 to 14
[total dose/cycle = 560 mg/m²]

ABV:

Doxorubicin: I.V.: 25 mg/m²/day days 1 and 14
[total dose/cycle = 50 mg/m²]
Bleomycin: SubQ: 6 units/m²/day days 1 and 14
[total dose/cycle = 12 units/m²]
Vinblastine: I.V.: 2 mg/m² continuous infusion days 4 to 12 and 18 to 26
[total dose/cycle = 36 mg/m²]

CAD is administered first, then MOPP begins on day 29 or day 37 following CAD. ABV is administered on day 29 following MOPP; CAD recycles on day 29 following ABV.

References

Straus DJ, Myers J, Koziner B, et al, "Combination Chemotherapy for the Treatment of Hodgkin's Disease in Relapse. Results With Lomustine (CCNU), Melphalan (Alkeran), and Vindesine (DVA) Alone (CAD) and in Alternation With MOPP and Doxorubicin (Adriamycin), Bleomycin, and Vinblastine (ABV)," *Cancer Chemother Pharmacol*, 1983, 11(2):80-5.

CAF

Use Breast cancer

Regimen NOTE: Multiple variations are listed on next page.
(Continued)

CAF (Continued)

Variation 1:
Cyclophosphamide: Oral: 100 mg/m^2/day days 1 to 14
[total dose/cycle = 1400 mg/m^2]
Doxorubicin: I.V.: 30 mg/m^2/day days 1 and 8
[total dose/cycle = 60 mg/m^2]
Fluorouracil: I.V.: 500 mg/m^2/day days 1 and 8
[total dose/cycle = 1000 mg/m^2]
Repeat cycle every 28 days
Variation 2:
Cyclophosphamide: Oral: 100 mg/m^2/day days 1 to 14
[total dose/cycle = 1400 mg/m^2]
Doxorubicin: I.V.: 25 mg/m^2/day days 1 and 8
[total dose/cycle = 50 mg/m^2]
Fluorouracil: I.V.: 500 mg/m^2/day days 1 and 8
[total dose/cycle = 1000 mg/m^2]
Repeat cycle every 28 days

References

Variation 1:
Bull JM, Tormey DC, Li SH, et al, "A Randomized Comparative Trial of Adriamycin® Versus Methotrexate in Combination Drug Therapy," *Cancer*, 1978, 41(5):1649-57.
Variation 2:
Aisner J, Weinberg V, Perloff M, et al, "Chemotherapy Versus Chemoimmunotherapy (CAF v CAFVP v CMF each +/- MER) for Metastatic Carcinoma of the Breast," *J Clin Oncol*, 1987, 5(10):1523-33.

♦ **CAF-IV** see FAC on page 1210

CAP

Use Bladder cancer
Regimen
Cyclophosphamide: I.V.: 400 mg/m^2 day 1
[total dose = 400 mg/m^2]
Doxorubicin: I.V.: 40 mg/m^2 day 1
[total dose = 40 mg/m^2]
Cisplatin: I.V.: 60 mg/m^2 day 1
[total dose = 60 mg/m^2]
Repeat cycle every 21 days

References

Eagan RT, Frytak S, Creagan ET, et al, "Phase II Study of Cyclophosphamide, Adriamycin, and Cis-Dichlorodiammineplatinum (II) by Infusion in Patients With Adenocarcinoma and Large Cell Carcinoma of the Lung," *Cancer Treat Rep*, 1979, 63(9-10):1589-91.

♦ **Capacitabine-Ixabepilone** see Ixabepilone-Capecitabine on page 1242
♦ **Capecitabine-Bevacizumab** see Bevacizumab-Capecitabine on page 1150

Capecitabine + Docetaxel (Breast Cancer)

Use Breast cancer
Regimen NOTE: Multiple variations are listed below.
Variation 1:
Capecitabine: Oral: 1250 mg/m^2 twice daily days 1 to 14
[total dose/cycle = 35,000 mg/m^2]
Docetaxel: I.V.: 75 mg/m^2 day 1
[total dose/cycle = 75 mg/m^2]
Repeat cycle every 3 weeks
Variation 2:
Capecitabine: Oral: 1000 mg/m^2 twice daily days 2 to 15
[total dose/cycle = 28,000 mg/m^2]

Docetaxel: I.V.: 75 mg/m² day 1
[total dose/cycle = 75 mg/m²]
Repeat cycle every 3 weeks
Variation 3:
Capecitabine: Oral: 937.5 mg/m² twice daily days 2 to 15
[total dose/cycle = 26,250 mg/m²]
Docetaxel: I.V.: 60 mg/m² day 1
[total dose/cycle = 60 mg/m²]
Repeat cycle every 3 weeks

References
Variation 1:
O'Shaughnessy J, Miles D, Vukelja S, et al, "Superior Survival With Capecitabine Plus Docetaxel Combination Therapy in Anthracycline-Pretreated Patients With Advanced Breast Cancer: Phase III Trial Results," *J Clin Oncol*, 2002, 20(12):2812-23.
Variation 2:
Lebowitz PF, Eng-Wong J, Swain SM, et al, "A Phase II Trial of Neoadjuvant Docetaxel and Capecitabine for Locally Advanced Breast Cancer," *Clin Cancer Res*, 2004, 10(20):6764-9.
Variation 3:
Lebowitz PF, Eng-Wong J, Swain SM, et al, "A Phase II Trial of Neoadjuvant Docetaxel and Capecitabine for Locally Advanced Breast Cancer," *Clin Cancer Res*, 2004, 10(20):6764-9.

Capecitabine + Docetaxel (Gastric Cancer)

Use Gastric cancer

Regimen NOTE: Multiple variations are listed below
Variation 1:
Capecitabine: Oral: 1000 mg/m² twice daily days 1 to 14
[total dose/cycle = 28,000 mg/m²]
Docetaxel: I.V.: 75 mg/m² day 1
[total dose/cycle = 75 mg/m²]
Repeat cycle every 3 weeks
Variation 2:
Capecitabine: Oral: 1000 mg/m² twice daily days 1 to 14
[total dose/cycle = 28,000 mg/m²]
Docetaxel: I.V.: 36 mg/m² days 1 and 8
[total dose/cycle = 72 mg/m²]
Repeat cycle every 3 weeks

References
Variation 1:
Kim JG, Sohn SK, Kim DH, et al, "Phase II Study of Docetaxel and Capecitabine in Patients With Metastatic or Recurrent Gastric Cancer," *Oncology*, 2005, 68(2-3):190-5.
Variation 2:
Chun JH, Kim HK, Lee JS, et al, "Weekly Docetaxel in Combination With Capecitabine in Patients With Metastatic Gastric Cancer," *Am J Clin Oncol*, 2005, 28(2):188-94.

Capecitabine + Docetaxel (Nonsmall Cell Lung Cancer)

Use Lung cancer, nonsmall cell

Regimen NOTE: Multiple variations are listed below
Variation 1:
Capecitabine: Oral: 1000 mg/m² twice daily days 1 to 14
[total dose/cycle = 28,000 mg/m²]
Docetaxel: I.V.: 36 mg/m² days 1 and 8
[total dose/cycle = 72 mg/m²]
Repeat cycle every 3 weeks
Variation 2:
Capecitabine: Oral: 625 mg/m² twice daily days 5 to 18
[total dose/cycle = 17,500 mg/m²]
Docetaxel: I.V.: 36 mg/m² days 1, 8, and 15
[total dose/cycle = 108 mg/m²]
Repeat cycle every 4 weeks
(Continued)

Capecitabine + Docetaxel (Nonsmall Cell Lung Cancer) *(Continued)*

References

Variation 1:
Han JY, Lee DH, Kim HY, et al, "A Phase II Study of Weekly Docetaxel Plus Capecitabine for Patients With Advanced Nonsmall Cell Lung Carcinoma," *Cancer*, 2003, 98(9):1918-24.

Variation 2:
Kindwall-Keller T, Otterson GA, Young D, et al, "Phase II Evaluation of Docetaxel-Modulated Capecitabine in Previously Treated Patients With Non-Small Cell Lung Cancer," *Clin Cancer Res*, 2005, 11(5):1870-6.

Capecitabine + Lapatinib

Index Terms Lapatinib-Capecitabine

Use Breast cancer

Regimen

Capecitabine: Oral: 1000 mg/m^2 twice daily days 1 to 14
  [total dose/cycle = 28,000 mg/m^2]
Lapatinib: Oral: 1250 mg/day days 1 to 21
  [total dose/cycle = 26,250 mg]
Repeat cycle every 3 weeks

References

Geyer CE, Forster J, Lindquist D, et al, "Lapatinib Plus Capecitabine for HER2-Positive Advanced Breast Cancer," *N Engl J Med*, 2006, 355(26):2733-43.

Capecitabine-Trastuzumab

Index Terms Trastuzumab-Capecitabine

Use Breast cancer

Regimen NOTE: Multiple variations are listed below.

Variation 1:

Cycle 1:

Capecitabine: Oral: 1250 mg/m^2 twice daily days 1 to 14
  [total dose/cycle 1 = 35,000 mg/m^2]
Trastuzumab: I.V.: 4 mg/kg (loading dose) day 1 cycle 1
  followed by I.V.: 2 mg/kg/day days 8 and 15 cycle 1
  [total dose/cycle 1 = 8 mg/kg]
Treatment cycle is 21 days

Subsequent cycles:

Capecitabine: Oral: 1250 mg/m^2 twice daily days 1 to 14
  [total dose/cycle = 35,000 mg/m^2]
Trastuzumab: I.V.: 2 mg/kg/day days 1, 8, and 15
  [total dose/cycle = 6 mg/kg]
Repeat cycle every 21 days

Variation 2:

Cycle 1:

Capecitabine: Oral: 1250 mg/m^2 twice daily days 1 to 14
  [total dose/cycle 1 = 35,000 mg/m^2]
Trastuzumab: I.V.: 8 mg/kg (loading dose) day 1 cycle 1
  [total dose/cycle 1 = 8 mg/kg]
Treatment cycle is 21 days

Subsequent cycles:

Capecitabine: Oral: 1250 mg/m^2 twice daily days 1 to 14
  [total dose/cycle = 35,000 mg/m^2]
Trastuzumab: I.V.: 6 mg/kg day 1
  [total dose/cycle = 6 mg/kg]
Repeat cycle every 21 days

References

Variation 1:

Schaller G, Fuchs I, Gonsch T, et al, "Phase II Study of Capecitabine Plus Trastuzumab in Human Epidermal Growth Factor Receptor 2 Overexpressing Metastatic Breast Cancer Pretreated With Anthracyclines or Taxanes," *J Clin Oncol*, 2007, 25(22):3246-50.

Variation 2:

Bartsch R, Wenzel C, Altorjai G, et al, "Capecitabine and Trastuzumab in Heavily Pretreated Metastatic Breast Cancer," *J Clin Oncol*, 2007, 25(25):3853-8.

Carboplatin-Cetuximab

Index Terms Cetuximab-Carboplatin

Use Head and neck cancer

Regimen

Cycle 1:

Cetuximab: I.V.: 400 mg/m^2 (loading dose) day 1 (week 1, cycle 1 only)

[total loading dose = 400 mg/m^2]

followed by I.V.: 250 mg/m^2/day days 8 and 15

[total dose/cycle 1 = 900 mg/m^2]

Carboplatin: I.V.: AUC 5 day 1

[total dose/cycle = AUC = 5]

Treatment cycle is 3 weeks

Subsequent cycles:

Cetuximab: I.V.: 250 mg/m^2/day days 1, 8, and 15

[total dose/cycle = 750 mg/m^2]

Carboplatin: I.V.: AUC 5 day 1

[total dose/cycle = AUC = 5]

Repeat cycle every 3 weeks

References

Chan AT, Hsu MM, Goh BC, et al, "Multicenter, Phase II Study of Cetuximab in Combination With Carboplatin in Patients With Recurrent or Metastatic Nasopharyngeal Carcinoma," *J Clin Oncol*, 2005, 23(15):3568-76.

♦ **Carboplatin-Paclitaxel (Bladder Cancer)** see Paclitaxel-Carboplatin (Bladder Cancer) on page 1264

Carbo-Tax (Adenocarcinoma)

Index Terms Paclitaxel-Carboplatin (Adenocarcinoma)

Use Adenocarcinoma, unknown primary

Regimen

Paclitaxel: I.V.: 135 mg/m^2 infused over 24 hours day 1,

[total dose = 135 mg/m^2]

followed by

Carboplatin: I.V.: Target AUC 7.5

[total dose = AUC = 7.5]

Repeat cycle every 21 days

References

Sulkes A, Uziely B, Isacson R, et al, "Combination Chemotherapy in Metastatic Tumors of Unknown Origin. 5-Fluorouracil, Adriamycin®, and Mitomycin C for Adenocarcinomas and Adriamycin®, Vinblastine and Mitomycin C for Anaplastic Carcinomas," *Isr J Med Sci*, 1988, 24(9-10):604-10.

Carbo-Tax (Nonsmall Cell Lung Cancer)

Index Terms Paclitaxel-Carboplatin (Nonsmall Cell Lung Cancer)

Use Lung cancer, nonsmall cell

Regimen

Paclitaxel: I.V.: 135-215 mg/m^2 infused over 24 hours day 1

[total dose/cycle = 135-215 mg/m^2]

or I.V.: 175 mg/m^2 infused over 3 hours day 1

[total dose/cycle = 175 mg/m^2]

(Continued)

Carbo-Tax (Nonsmall Cell Lung Cancer) *(Continued)*

followed by
Carboplatin: I.V.: Target AUC 7.5
  [total dose/cycle = AUC = 7.5]
Repeat cycle every 21 days

References
Langer CJ, Leighton JC, Comis RL, et al, "Paclitaxel By 24- or 1-hour Infusion in Combination With Carboplatin in Advanced Nonsmall-Cell Lung Cancer: The Fox Chase Cancer Center Experience," *Semin Oncol*, 1995, 22(4 Suppl 9):18-29.

Carbo-Tax (Ovarian Cancer)

Index Terms Paclitaxel-Carboplatin (Ovarian Cancer)
Use Ovarian cancer
Regimen NOTE: Multiple variations are listed below.
  Variation 1:
    Paclitaxel: I.V.: 135 mg/m² infused over 24 hours day 1
      [total dose/cycle = 135 mg/m²]
        or I.V.: 175 mg/m² infused over 3 hours day 1
          [total dose/cycle = 175 mg/m²]
    followed by
    Carboplatin: I.V.: Target AUC 5
      [total dose/cycle = AUC = 5]
    Repeat cycle every 21 days
  Variation 2:
    Paclitaxel: I.V.: 175 mg/m² day 1
      [total dose/cycle = 175 mg/m²]
    Carboplatin: I.V.: AUC 7.5 day 1
      [total dose/cycle = AUC = 7.5]
    Repeat cycle every 21 days
  Variation 3:
    Paclitaxel: I.V.: 185 mg/m² day 1
      [total dose/cycle = 185 mg/m²]
    Carboplatin: I.V.: AUC 6 day 1
      [total dose/cycle = AUC = 6]
    Repeat cycle every 21 days

References
Variation 1:
Ozols RF, "Carboplatin and Paclitaxel in Ovarian Cancer," *Semin Oncol*, 1995, 22(3 Suppl 6):78-83.
Ozols RF, "Update of the NCCN Ovarian Cancer Practice Guidelines," *Oncology (Huntingt)*, 1997, 11(11A):95-105.
Variation 2:
Ozols RF, "Combination Regimens of Paclitaxel and the Platinum Drugs as First-Line Regimens for Ovarian Cancer," *Semin Oncol*, 1995, 22(6 Suppl 15):1-6.
Variation 3:
Meerpohl HG, du Bois A, Kuhnle H, et al, "Paclitaxel Combined With Carboplatin in the First-Line Treatment of Advanced Ovarian Cancer," *Semin Oncol*, 1995, 22(6 Suppl 15):7-12.

CaT (Nonsmall Cell Lung Cancer)

Use Lung cancer, nonsmall cell
Regimen NOTE: Multiple variations are listed below.
  Variation 1:
    Paclitaxel: I.V.: 175 mg/m² day 1
      [total dose/cycle = 175 mg/m²]
        or 135 mg/m² continuous infusion day 1
          [total dose/cycle = 135 mg/m²]

Carboplatin: I.V.: AUC 7.5 day 1 or 2
[total dose/cycle = AUC = 7.5]
Repeat cycle every 21 days
Variation 2:
Paclitaxel: I.V.: 225 mg/m² day 1
[total dose/cycle = 225 mg/m²]
Carboplatin: I.V.: AUC 6 day 1
[total dose/cycle = AUC = 6]
Repeat cycle every 21 days

References
Variation 1:
Langer CJ, Leighton JC, Comis RL, et al, "Paclitaxel by 24- or 1-Hour Infusion in Combination With Carboplatin in Advanced Nonsmall-Cell Lung Cancer: The Fox Chase Cancer Center Experience," *Semin Oncol*, 1995, 22(4 Suppl 9):18-29.
Variation 2:
Schiller JH, Harrington D, Belani CP, et al, "Comparison of Four Chemotherapy Regimens for Advanced Nonsmall-Cell Lung Cancer," *N Engl J Med*, 2002, 346(2):92-8.

CaT (Ovarian Cancer)
Use Ovarian cancer
Regimen
Paclitaxel: I.V.: 175 mg/m² day 1
[total dose/cycle = 175 mg/m²]
or 135 mg/m² continuous infusion day 1
[total dose/cycle = 135 mg/m²]
Carboplatin: I.V.: AUC 7.5 day 1 or 2
[total dose/cycle = AUC = 7.5]
Repeat cycle every 21 days

References
Bookman MA, McGuire WP 3rd, Kilpatrick D, et al, "Carboplatin and Paclitaxel in Ovarian Carcinoma: A Phase I Study of the Gynecologic Oncology Group," *J Clin Oncol*, 1996, 14(6):1895-902.

CAVE
Use Lung cancer, small cell
Regimen
Cyclophosphamide: I.V.: 750 mg/m² day 1
[total dose/cycle = 750 mg/m²]
Doxorubicin: I.V.: 50 mg/m² day 1
[total dose/cycle = 50 mg/m²]
Vincristine: I.V.: 1.4 mg/m² (maximum 2 mg) day 1
[total dose/cycle = 1.4 mg/m²]
Etoposide: I.V.: 60-100 mg/m²/day days 1 to 3
[total dose/cycle = 180-300 mg/m²]
Repeat cycle every 21 days

References
Jett JR, Everson L, Therneau TM, et al, "Treatment of Limited-Stage Small-Cell Lung Cancer With Cyclophosphamide, Doxorubicin, and Vincristine With Or Without Etoposide: A Randomized Trial of the North Central Cancer Treatment Group," *J Clin Oncol*, 1990, 8(1):33-8.
Sufarlan AW and Zainudin BM, "Combination Chemotherapy for Small Cell Lung Cancer," *Med J Malaysia*, 1993, 48(2):166-70.

CAV-P/VP
Use Neuroblastoma
Regimen
Course 1, 2, 4, and 6:
Cyclophosphamide: I.V.: 70 mg/kg/day days 1 and 2
[total dose/cycle = 140 mg/kg]
(Continued)

CAV-P/VP *(Continued)*

Doxorubicin: I.V.: 25 mg/m^2/day continuous infusion days 1 to 3
[total dose/cycle = 75 mg/m^2]
Vincristine: I.V.: 0.033 mg/kg/day continuous infusion days 1 to 3
[total dose/cycle = 0.099 mg/kg]
Vincristine: I.V.: 1.5 mg/m^2 day 9
[total dose/cycle = 1.5 mg/m^2]
Course 3, 5, and 7:
Etoposide: I.V.: 200 mg/m^2/day days 1 to 3
[total dose/cycle = 600 mg/m^2]
Cisplatin: I.V.: 50 mg/m^2/day days 1 to 4
[total dose/cycle = 200 mg/m^2]

References

Kushner BH, LaQuaglia MP, Bonilla MA, et al, "Highly Effective Induction Therapy for Stage 4 Neuroblastoma in Children Over 1 Year of Age," *J Clin Oncol*, 1994, 12(12):2607-13.

CC

Use Ovarian cancer
Regimen
Carboplatin: I.V.: Target AUC 5-7.5 day 1
[total dose/cycle = AUC = 5-7.5]
Cyclophosphamide: I.V.: 600 mg/m^2 day 1
[total dose/cycle = 600 mg/m^2]
Repeat cycle every 28 days

References

Alberts DS, Green S, Hannigan EV, et al, "Improved Therapeutic Index of Carboplatin Plus Cyclophosphamide Versus Cisplatin Plus Cyclophosphamide: Final Report by the Southwest Oncology Group of a Phase III Randomized Trial in Stages III and IV Ovarian Cancer," *J Clin Oncol*, 1992, 10(5):706-17.

Swenerton K, Jeffrey J, Stuart G, et al, "Cisplatin-Cyclophosphamide Versus Carboplatin-Cyclophosphamide in Advanced Ovarian Cancer: A Randomized Phase III Study of the National Cancer Institute of Canada Clinical Trials Group," *J Clin Oncol*, 1992, 10(5):718-26.

CCCDE (Retinoblastoma)

Use Retinoblastoma
Regimen
Cyclophosphamide: I.V.: 150 mg/m^2/day days 1 to 7
[total dose/cycle = 1050 mg/m^2]
Cyclophosphamide: Oral: 150 mg/m^2/day days 22 to 28 and 43 to 49
[total dose/cycle = 2100 mg/m^2]
Doxorubicin: I.V.: 35 mg/m^2/day days 10 and 52
[total dose/cycle = 70 mg/m^2]
Cisplatin: I.V.: 90 mg/m^2/day days 8, 50, and 71
[total dose/cycle = 270 mg/m^2]
Etoposide: I.V.: 150 mg/m$_2$/day continuous infusion days 29 to 31 and 73 to 75
[total dose/cycle = 900 mg/m^2]

References

Advani SH, Rao SR, Iyer RS, et al, "Pilot Study of Sequential Combination Chemotherapy in Advanced and Recurrent Retinoblastoma," *Med Pediatr Oncol*, 1994, 22(2):125-8.

CCDDT (Neuroblastoma)

Use Neuroblastoma
Regimen
Cyclophosphamide: I.V.: 40 mg/kg/day days 1 and 2
[total dose/cycle = 80 mg/kg]
Cisplatin: I.V.: 20 mg/m^2/day days 1 to 5
[total dose/cycle = 100 mg/m^2]

Teniposide: I.V.: 100 mg/m^2 day 7
[total dose/cycle = 100 mg/m^2]
Doxorubicin: I.V.: 60 mg/m^2 day 1
[total dose/cycle = 60 mg/m^2]
Dacarbazine: I.V.: 250 mg/m^2/day days 1 to 5
[total dose/cycle = 1250 mg/m^2]
Repeat cycle every 21-28 days

References

Ikeda K, Nakagawara A, Yano H, et al, "Improved Survival Rates in Children Over 1 Year of Age With Stage III or IV Neuroblastoma Following an Intensive Chemotherapeutic Regimen," *J Pediatr Surg*, 1989, 24(2):189-93.

CCDT (Melanoma)

Use Melanoma

Regimen

Dacarbazine: I.V.: 220 mg/m^2/day days 1 to 3, every 21 to 28 days
[total dose/cycle = 660 mg/m^2]
Carmustine: I.V.: 150 mg/m^2 day 1, every 42 to 56 days
[total dose/cycle = 150 mg/m^2]
Cisplatin: I.V.: 25 mg/m^2/day days 1 to 3, every 21 to 28 days
[total dose/cycle = 75 mg/m^2]
Tamoxifen: Oral: 20 mg/day (use of tamoxifen is optional)

References

Del Prete SA, Maurer LH, O'Donnell J, et al, "Combination Chemotherapy With Cisplatin, Carmustine, Dacarbazine, and Tamoxifen in Metastatic Melanoma," *Cancer Treat Rep*, 1984, 68(11):1403-5.

Rusthoven JJ, Quirt IC, Iscoe NA, et al, "Randomized, Double-Blind, Placebo-Controlled Trial Comparing the Response Rates of Carmustine, Dacarbazine, and Cisplatin With and Without Tamoxifen in Patients With Metastatic Melanoma. National Cancer Institute of Canada Clinical Trials Group," *J Clin Oncol*, 1996, 14(7):2083-90.

CCT (Neuroblastoma)

Use Neuroblastoma

Regimen

Cyclophosphamide: I.V.: 40 mg/kg/day days 1 and 2
[total dose/cycle = 80 mg/kg]
Cisplatin: I.V.: 20 mg/m^2/day days 22 to 26
[total dose/cycle = 100 mg/m^2]
Teniposide: I.V.: 100 mg/m^2 day 28
[total dose/cycle = 100 mg/m^2]
Repeat every 42 days for 3 cycles

References

Ikeda K, Nakagawara A, Yano H, et al, "Improved Survival Rates in Children Over 1 Year of Age With Stage III or IV Neuroblastoma Following an Intensive Chemotherapeutic Regimen," *J Pediatr Surg*, 1989, 24(2):189-93.

CDDP/VP-16

Use Brain tumors

Regimen

Cisplatin: I.V.: 90 mg/m^2 day 1
[total dose/cycle = 90 mg/m^2]
Etoposide: I.V.: 150 mg/m^2/day days 3 and 4
[total dose/cycle = 300 mg/m^2]
Repeat cycle every 21 days
(Continued)

CDDP/VP-16 (Continued)

References
Kovnar EH, Kellie SJ, Horowitz ME, et al, "Preirradiation Cisplatin and Etoposide in the Treatment of High-Risk Medulloblastoma and Other Malignant Embryonal Tumors of the Central Nervous System: A Phase II Study," *J Clin Oncol*, 1990, 8(2):330-6.

CE-CAdO

Use Neuroblastoma

Regimen

Carboplatin: I.V.: 160 mg/m^2/day days 1 to 5
[total dose/cycle = 800 mg/m^2]
Etoposide: I.V.: 100 mg/m^2/day days 1 to 5
[total dose/cycle = 500 mg/m^2]

or

Carboplatin: I.V.: 200 mg/m^2/day days 1 to 3
[total dose/cycle = 600 mg/m^2]
Etoposide: I.V.: 150 mg/m^2/day days 1 to 3
[total dose/cycle = 450 mg/m^2]

and

Cyclophosphamide: I.V.: 300 mg/m^2/day days 1 to 5
[total dose/cycle = 1500 mg/m^2]
Doxorubicin: I.V.: 60 mg/m^2 day 5
[total dose/cycle = 60 mg/m^2]
Vincristine: I.V.: 1.5 mg/m^2/day days 1 and 5
[total dose/cycle = 3 mg/m^2]
Repeat cycle every 21 days

References
Rubie H, Michon J, Plantaz D, et al, "Unresectable Localized Neuroblastoma: Improved Survival After Primary Chemotherapy Including Carboplatin-Etoposide. Neuroblastoma Study Group of the Societe Francaise d'Oncologie Pediatrique (SFOP)," *Br J Cancer*, 1998, 77(12):2310-7.

CEF

Use Breast cancer

Regimen

Cyclophosphamide: Oral: 75 mg/m^2/day days 1 to 14
[total dose/cycle = 1050 mg/m^2]
Epirubicin: I.V.: 60 mg/m^2/day days 1 and 8
[total dose/cycle = 120 mg/m^2]
Fluorouracil: I.V.: 500 mg/m^2/day days 1 and 8
[total dose/cycle = 1000 mg/m^2]
Repeat cycle every 28 days

References
Levine MN, Bramwell VH, Pritchard KI, et al, "Randomized Trial of Intensive Cyclophosphamide, Epirubicin, and Fluorouracil Chemotherapy Compared With Cyclophosphamide, Methotrexate, and Fluorouracil in Premenopausal Women With Node-Positive Breast Cancer, National Cancer Institute of Canada Clinical Trials Group," *J Clin Oncol*, 1998, 16(8):2651-8.

CE (Neuroblastoma)

Use Neuroblastoma

Regimen

Carboplatin: I.V.: 500 mg/m^2/day days 1 and 2
[total dose/cycle = 1000 mg/m^2]
Etoposide: I.V.: 100 mg/m^2/day days 1 to 3
[total dose/cycle = 300 mg/m^2]
Repeat cycle every 21-28 days

References

Alvarado CS, Kretschmar C, Joshi VV, et al, "Chemotherapy for Patients With Recurrent or Refractory Neuroblastoma: A POG Phase II Study," *J Pediatr Hematol Oncol*, 1997, 19(1):62-7.

CEPP(B)

Use Lymphoma, non-Hodgkin's

Regimen

Cyclophosphamide: I.V.: 600-650 mg/m²/day days 1 and 8
[total dose/cycle = 1200-1300 mg/m²]
Etoposide: I.V.: 70-85 mg/m²/day days 1 to 3
[total dose/cycle = 210-255 mg/m²]
Procarbazine: Oral: 60 mg/m²/day days 1 to 10
[total dose/cycle = 600 mg/m²]
Prednisone: Oral: 60 mg/m²/day days 1 to 10
[total dose/cycle = 600 mg/m²]
Bleomycin: I.V.: 15 units/m²/day days 1 and 15 (Bleomycin is sometimes omitted)
[total dose/cycle = 30 units/m²]
Repeat cycle every 28 days

References

Chao NJ, Rosenberg SA, and Horning SJ, "CEPP(B): An Effective and Well-Tolerated Regimen in Poor-Risk, Aggressive Non-Hodgkin's Lymphoma," *Blood*, 1990, 76(7):1293-8.

CE (Retinoblastoma)

Use Retinoblastoma

Regimen

Etoposide: I.V.: 100 mg/m²/day days 1 to 5
[total dose/cycle = 500 mg/m²]
Carboplatin: I.V.: 160 mg/m²/day days 1 to 5
[total dose/cycle = 800 mg/m²]
Repeat cycle every 21 days

References

Doz F, Neuenschwander S, Plantaz D, et al, "Etoposide and Carboplatin in Extraocular Retinoblastoma: A Study by the Societe Francaise d'Oncologie Pediatrique," *J Clin Oncol*, 1995, 13(4):902-9.

- **Cetuximab-Carboplatin** *see* Carboplatin-Cetuximab *on page 1161*
- **Cetuximab-Cisplatin** *see* Cisplatin-Cetuximab *on page 1175*

Cetuximab-Irinotecan

Index Terms Irinotecan-Cetuximab

Use Colorectal cancer

Regimen NOTE: Multiple variations are listed below.

Variation 1:
Cycle 1:
Cetuximab: I.V.: 400 mg/m² (loading dose) day 1 (week 1, cycle 1 only)
[total loading dose = 400 mg/m²]
followed by I.V.: 250 mg/m²/day days 8, 15, 22, 29, and 36
[total dose/cycle 1 = 1650 mg/m²]
Irinotecan: I.V.: 125 mg/m²/day days 1, 8, 15, and 22
[total dose/cycle = 500 mg/m²]
Subsequent cycles:
Cetuximab: I.V.: 250 mg/m²/day days 1, 8, 15, 22, 29, and 36
[total dose/cycle = 1500 mg/m²]
Irinotecan: I.V.: 125 mg/m²/day days 1, 8, 15, and 22
[total dose/cycle = 500 mg/m²]
Repeat cycle every 42 days
(Continued)

Cetuximab-Irinotecan *(Continued)*

Variation 2:
Cycle 1:
Cetuximab: I.V.: 400 mg/m² (loading dose) day 1 (week 1, cycle 1 only)
   [total loading dose = 400 mg/m²]
     followed by I.V.: 250 mg/m²/day days 8 and 15 (cycle 1)
     [total dose/cycle 1 = 900 mg/m²]
Irinotecan: I.V.: 350 mg/m² day 1
   [total dose/cycle = 350 mg/m²]
Subsequent cycles:
Cetuximab: I.V.: 250 mg/m²/day days 1, 8, and 15
   [total dose/cycle = 750 mg/m²]
Irinotecan: I.V.: 350 mg/m² day 1
   [total dose/cycle = 350 mg/m²]
Repeat cycle every 21 days

References

Cunningham D, Humblet Y, Siena S, et al, "Cetuximab Monotherapy and Cetuximab Plus Irinotecan in Irinotecan-Refractory Metastatic Colorectal Cancer," *N Engl J Med*, 2004, 351(4):337-45.

CEV

Use Rhabdomyosarcoma

Regimen

Carboplatin: I.V.: 500 mg/m² day 1
   [total dose/cycle = 500 mg/m²]
Epirubicin: I.V.: 150 mg/m² day 1
   [total dose/cycle = 150 mg/m²]
Vincristine: I.V.: 1.5 mg/m²/day days 1 and 7
   [total dose/cycle = 3 mg/m²]
Repeat cycle every 21 days

References

Frascella E, Pritchard-Jones K, Modak S, et al, "Response of Previously Untreated Metastatic Rhabdomyosarcoma to Combination Chemotherapy With Carboplatin, Epirubicin and Vincristine," *Eur J Cancer*, 1996, 32A(5):821-5.

CF

Use Head and neck cancer

Regimen NOTE: Multiple variations are listed below.

Variation 1:
Cisplatin: I.V.: 100 mg/m² day 1
   [total dose/cycle = 100 mg/m²]
Fluorouracil: I.V.: 1000 mg/m²/day continuous infusion days 1 to 4
   [total dose/cycle = 4000 mg/m²]
Repeat cycle every 3 or 4 weeks

Variation 2:
Cisplatin: I.V.: 100 mg/m² day 1
   [total dose/cycle = 100 mg/m²]
Fluorouracil: I.V.: 1000 mg/m²/day continuous infusion days 1 to 5
   [total dose/cycle = 5000 mg/m²]
Repeat cycle every 3 or 4 weeks

Variation 3:
Cisplatin: I.V.: 60 mg/m² day 1
   [total dose/cycle = 60 mg/m²]
Fluorouracil: I.V.: 800 mg/m²/day continuous infusion days 1 to 5
   [total dose/cycle = 4000 mg/m²]
Repeat cycle every 14 days

Variation 4:
  Cisplatin: I.V.: 20 mg/m^2/day days 1 to 5
    [total dose/cycle = 100 mg/m^2]
  Fluorouracil: I.V.: 200 mg/m^2/day days 1 to 5
    [total dose/cycle = 1000 mg/m^2]
  Repeat cycle every 3 weeks
Variation 5:
  Cisplatin: I.V.: 80 mg/m^2 continuous infusion day 1
    [total dose/cycle = 80 mg/m^2]
  Fluorouracil: I.V.: 800 mg/m^2/day continuous infusion days 2 to 6
    [total dose/cycle = 4000 mg/m^2]
  Repeat cycle every 3 weeks
Variation 6:
  Cisplatin: I.V.: 75 mg/m^2 day 1
    [total dose/cycle = 75 mg/m^2]
  Fluorouracil: I.V.: 1000 mg/m^2/day continuous infusion days 1 to 4
    [total dose/cycle = 4000 mg/m^2]
  Repeat cycle every 4 weeks
Variation 7:
  Cisplatin: I.V.: 120 mg/m^2 day 1
    [total dose/cycle = 120 mg/m^2]
  Fluorouracil: I.V.: 1000 mg/m^2/day continuous infusion days 1 to 5
    [total dose/cycle = 5000 mg/m^2]
  Repeat cycle every 3 weeks
Variation 8:
  Cisplatin: I.V.: 25 mg/m^2/day continuous infusion days 1 to 4
    [total dose/cycle = 100 mg/m^2]
  Fluorouracil: I.V.: 1000 mg/m^2/day days 1 to 4
    [total dose/cycle = 4000 mg/m^2]
  Repeat cycle every 3 weeks
Variation 9:
  Fluorouracil: I.V.: 350 mg/m^2/day continuous infusion days 1 to 5
    [total dose/cycle = 1750 mg/m^2]
  Cisplatin: I.V.: 50 mg/m^2 day 6
    [total dose/cycle = 50 mg/m^2]
  Repeat cycle every 3 weeks
Variation 10:
  Cisplatin: I.V.: 5 mg/m^2/day continuous infusion days 1 to 14
    [total dose/cycle = 70 mg/m^2]
  Fluorouracil: I.V.: 200 mg/m^2/day continuous infusion days 1 to 14
    [total dose/cycle = 2800 mg/m^2]
  With concurrent radiation therapy, cycle does not repeat

References
Variation 1:
Kish J, Drelichman A, Jacobs J, et al, "Clinical Trial of Cisplatin and 5-FU Infusion as Initial Treatment for Advanced Squamous Cell Carcinoma of the Head and Neck," *Cancer Treat Rep*, 1982, 66(3):471-4.
Mercier RJ, Neal GD, Mattox DE, et al, "Cisplatin and 5-Fluorouracil Chemotherapy in Advanced or Recurrent Squamous Cell Carcinoma of the Head and Neck," *Cancer*, 1987, 60(11):2609-12.
Variation 2:
Rooney M, Kish J, Jacobs J, et al, "Improved Complete Response Rate and Survival in Advanced Head and Neck Cancer After Three-Course Induction Therapy With 120-Hour 5-FU Infusion and Cisplatin," *Cancer*, 1985, 55(5):1123-8.
Dasmahapatra KS, Citrin P, Hill GJ, et al, "A Prospective Evaluation of 5-Fluorouracil Plus Cisplatin in Advanced Squamous-Cell Cancer of the Head and Neck," *J Clin Oncol*, 1985, 3(11):1486-9.
(Continued)

CF *(Continued)*

Variation 3:
Taylor SG 4th, Murthy AK, Showel JL, et al, "Improved Control in Advanced Head and Neck Cancer With Simultaneous Radiation and Cisplatin/5-FU Chemotherapy," *Cancer Treat Rep*, 1985, 69(9):933-9.

Variation 4:
Merlano M, Tatarek R, Grimaldi A, et al, "Phase I-II Trial With Cisplatin and 5-FU in Recurrent Head and Neck Cancer: An Effective Outpatient Schedule," *Cancer Treat Rep*, 1985, 69(9):961-4.

Variation 5:
Amrein PC and Weitzman SA, "Treatment of Squamous-Cell Carcinoma of the Head and Neck With Cisplatin and 5-Fluorouracil," *J Clin Oncol*, 1985, 3(12):1632-9.

Variation 6:
Adelstein DJ, Li Y, Adams GL, et al, "An Intergroup Phase III Comparison of Standard Radiation and Two Schedules of Concurrent Chemoradiotherapy in Patients With Unresectable Squamous Cell Head and Neck Cancer," *J Clin Oncol*, 2003, 21(1):92-8.

Adelstein DJ, Sharan VM, Earle AS, et al, "Chemoradiotherapy as Initial Management in Patients With Squamous Cell Carcinoma of the Head and Neck," *Cancer Treat Rep*, 1986, 70(6):761-7.

Variation 7:
Paredes J, Hong WK, Felder TB, et al, "Prospective Randomized Trial of High-Dose Cisplatin and Fluorouracil Infusion With or Without Sodium Diethyldithiocarbamate in Recurrent and/or Metastatic Squamous Cell Carcinoma of the Head and Neck," *J Clin Oncol*, 1988, 6(6):955-62.

Variation 8:
Bernal AG, Cruz JJ, Sanchez P, et al, "Four-Day Continuous Infusion of Cisplatin and 5-Fluorouracil in Head and Neck Cancer," *Cancer*, 1989, 63(10):1927-30.

Variation 9:
Denham JW and Abbott RL, "Concurrent Cisplatin, Infusional Fluorouracil, and Conventionally Fractionated Radiation Therapy in Head and Neck Cancer: Dose-Limiting Mucosal Toxicity," *J Clin Oncol*, 1991, 9(3):458-63.

Variation 10:
Arcangeli G, Saracino B, Danesi DT, et al, "Accelerated Hyperfractionated Radiotherapy and Concurrent Protracted Venous Infusion Chemotherapy in Locally-Advanced Head and Neck Cancer," *Am J Clin Oncol*, 2002, 25(5):431-7.

♦ **CFM** *see* CNF *on page 1179*

CFP

Use Breast cancer

Regimen

Cyclophosphamide: I.V.: 150 mg/m²/day days 1 to 5
[total dose/cycle = 750 mg/m²]

Fluorouracil: I.V.: 300 mg/m²/day days 1 to 5
[total dose/cycle = 1500 mg/m²]

Prednisone: Oral: 30 mg/day days 1 to 14 (cycle 1 only)
followed by Oral: 20 mg/day days 15 to 21 (cycle 1 only)
followed by Oral: 10 mg daily thereafter as maintenance
[total dose/cycle = 700 mg in cycle 1; 350 mg in subsequent cycles]

Repeat cycle every 35 days

References

Marschke RF Jr, Ingle JN, Schaid DJ, et al, "Randomized Clinical Trial of CFP Versus CMFP in Women With Metastatic Breast Cancer," *Cancer*, 1989, 63(10):1931-7.

CHAMOCA (Modified Bagshawe Regimen)

Use Gestational trophoblastic tumor

Regimen NOTE: Multiple variations are listed below.

Variation 1:

Hydroxyurea: Oral: 500 mg every 6 hours, for 4 doses, day 1 (start at 6 AM)
[total dose/cycle = 2000 mg]

Dactinomycin: I.V.: 0.2 mg/day days 1 to 3 (give at 7 PM)
followed by I.V.: 0.5 mg/day days 4 and 5 (give at 7 PM)
[total dose/cycle = 1.6 mg]

Cyclophosphamide: I.V.: 500 mg/m^2/day days 3 and 8 (give at 7 PM)
  [total dose/cycle = 1000 mg/m^2]
Vincristine: I.V.: 1 mg/m^2 (maximum 2 mg) day 2 (give at 7 AM)
  [total dose/cycle = 1 mg/m^2; maximum 2 mg]
Methotrexate: I.V. bolus: 100 mg/m^2 day 2 (give at 7 PM)
  followed by I.V.: 200 mg/m^2 continuous infusion over 12 hours day 2
  [total dose/cycle = 300 mg/m^2]
Leucovorin: I.M.: 14 mg every 6 hours, for 6 doses, days 3 to 5 (begin at 7
  PM on day 3; start 24 hours after the start of methotrexate)
  [total dose/cycle = 84 mg]
Doxorubicin: I.V.: 30 mg/m^2 day 8 (give at 7 PM)
  [total dose/cycle = 30 mg/m^2]
Repeat cycle every 18 days or as toxicity permits (cycle may be repeated
  10 days after last treatment)
Variation 2:
  Hydroxyurea: Oral: 500 mg every 12 hours, for 4 doses, days 1 and 2
    (usually started in early morning)
    [total dose/cycle = 2000 mg]
  Dactinomycin: I.V.: 10 mcg/kg/day days 5, 6, and 7
    [total dose/cycle = 30 mcg/kg]
  Vincristine: I.V.: 1 mg/m^2 day 3
    [total dose/cycle = 1 mg/m^2]
  Methotrexate: I.V. bolus: 100 mg/m^2 day 3
    followed by I.V.: 200 mg/m^2 continuous infusion over 12 hours day 3
    [total dose/cycle = 300 mg/m^2]
  Leucovorin: I.M.: 10 mg/m^2 every 12 hours, for 4 doses, days 4 and 5 (start
    24 hours after the start of methotrexate)
    [total dose/cycle = 40 mg/m^2]
  Cyclophosphamide: I.V.: 600 mg/m^2 day 5
    [total dose/cycle = 600 mg/m^2]
  Doxorubicin: I.V.: 30 mg/m^2 day 10
    [total dose/cycle = 30 mg/m^2]
  Repeat cycle every 3 weeks
Variation 3:
  Hydroxyurea: Oral: 500 mg every 12 hours, for 4 doses, days 1 and 2
    (usually started in early morning)
    [total dose/cycle = 2000 mg/m^2]
  Vincristine: I.V.: 1 mg/m^2 day 3
    [total dose/cycle = 1 mg/m^2]
  Methotrexate: I.V. bolus: 100 mg/m^2 day 3
    followed by I.V.: 200 mg/m^2 continuous infusion over 12 hours day 3
    [total dose/cycle = 300 mg/m^2]
  Leucovorin: I.M.: 14 mg every 6 hours, for 6 doses, days 4, 5, and 6 (start
    24 hours after start of methotrexate)
    [total dose/cycle = 84 mg]
  Dactinomycin: I.V.: 0.2 mg/day days 2, 3, and 4
    followed by I.V.: 0.5 mg/day days 5 and 6
    [total dose/cycle = 1.6 mg]
  Cyclophosphamide: I.V.: 500 mg/m^2 day 4
    [total dose/cycle = 500 mg/m^2]
  Doxorubicin: I.V.: 30 mg/m^2 day 9
    [total dose/cycle = 30 mg/m^2]
  Melphalan: I.V.: 6 mg/m^2 day 9
    [total dose/cycle = 6 mg/m^2]
  Repeat cycle approximately every 3 weeks
(Continued)

CHAMOCA (Modified Bagshawe Regimen)
(Continued)
Variation 4:

Hydroxyurea: Oral: 500 mg 4 times/day, for 4 doses, day 1
[total dose/cycle = 2000 mg/m^2]

Vincristine: I.V.: 1 mg/m^2 day 2
[total dose/cycle = 1 mg/m^2]

Methotrexate: I.V. bolus: 100 mg/m^2 day 2
followed by I.V.: 200 mg/m^2 continuous infusion over 12 hours day 2
[total dose/cycle = 300 mg/m^2]

Leucovorin: I.M.: 14 mg every 6 hours, for 6 doses, days 3, 4, and 5 (start 24 hours after the start of methotrexate)
[total dose/cycle = 84 mg]

Dactinomycin: I.V.: 0.2 mg days 1, 2, and 3, then 0.5 mg days 4 and 5
[total dose/cycle = 1.6 mg]

Cyclophosphamide: I.V.: 500 mg/m^2 day 3
[total dose/cycle = 500 mg/m^2]

Cyclophosphamide: I.V.: 300 mg/m^2 on day 8
[total dose/cycle = 300 mg/m^2]

Doxorubicin: I.V.: 30 mg/m^2 day 8
[total dose/cycle = 30 mg/m^2]

Repeat cycle approximately every 3 weeks

References
Variation 1:
Weed JC Jr, Barnard DE, Currie JL, et al, "Chemotherapy With the Modified Bagshawe Protocol for Poor Prognosis Metastatic Trophoblastic Disease," *Obstet Gynecol*, 1982, 59(3):377-80.
Variation 2:
Wong LC, Choo YC, and Ma HK, "Modified Bagshawe's Regimen in High-Risk Gestational Trophoblastic Disease," *Gynecol Oncol*, 1986, 23(1):87-93.
Variation 3:
Surwit EA, Suciu TN, Schmidt HJ, et al,"A New Combination Chemotherapy for Resistant Trophoblastic Disease," *Gynecol Oncol*, 1979, 8(1):110-8.
Variation 4:
Surwit EA and Hammond CB, "Treatment of Metastatic Trophoblastic Disease With Poor Prognosis," *Obstet Gynecol*, 1980, 55(5):565-70.

CHAMOMA (Bagshawe Regimen)
Use Gestational trophoblastic tumor
Regimen

Hydroxyurea: Oral: 500 mg every 12 hours, for 4 doses, days 1 and 2
[total dose/cycle = 2000 mg]

Vincristine: I.V.: 1 mg/m^2 day 3
[total dose/cycle = 1 mg/m^2]

Methotrexate: I.V. bolus: 100 mg/m^2 day 3
followed by I.V.: 200 mg/m^2 continuous infusion over 12 hours day 3
[total dose/cycle = 300 mg/m^2]

Leucovorin: I.M.: 12 mg/m^2 every 12 hours, for 4 doses, days 4 and 5 (start 12 hours after the end of methotrexate infusion)
[total dose/cycle = 48 mg/m^2]

Dactinomycin: I.V.: 10 mcg/kg/day days 5, 6, and 7
[total dose/cycle = 30 mcg/kg]

Cyclophosphamide: I.V.: 600 mg/m^2 day 5
[total dose/cycle = 600 mg/m^2]

Doxorubicin: I.V.: 30 mg/m^2 day 10
[total dose/cycle = 30 mg/m^2]

Melphalan: I.V.: 6 mg/m² day 10
[total dose/cycle = 6 mg/m²]
Repeat cycle approximately every 3 weeks

References
Bagshawe KD, "Treatment of Trophoblastic Tumors," *Ann Acad Med Singapore*, 1976, 5:273-9.

CHL + PRED

Use Leukemia, chronic lymphocytic

Regimen
Chlorambucil: Oral: 0.4 mg/kg/day for 1 day every other week; increase initial dose of 0.4 mg/kg by 0.1 mg/kg every 2 weeks until toxicity or disease control is achieved
Prednisone: Oral: 100 mg/day for 2 days every other week

References
Han T, Ezdinli EZ, Shimaoka K, et al, "Chlorambucil vs Combined Chlorambucil-Corticosteroid Therapy in Chronic Lymphocytic Leukemia," *Cancer*, 1973,31(3):502-8.

ChIVPP

Use Lymphoma, Hodgkin's disease

Regimen
Chlorambucil: Oral: 6 mg/m²/day (maximum 10 mg) days 1 to 14
[total dose/cycle = 84 mg/m²]
Vinblastine: I.V.: 6 mg/m²/day (maximum 10 mg) days 1 and 8
[total dose/cycle = 12 mg/m²]
Procarbazine: Oral: 100 mg/m²/day (maximum 150 mg) days 1 to 14
[total dose/cycle = 1400 mg/m²]
Prednisone: Oral: 40-50 mg/day days 1 to 14
[total dose/cycle = 560-700 mg]
Repeat cycle every 28 days

References
Selby P, Patel P, Milan S, et al, "ChIVPP Combination Chemotherapy for Hodgkin's Disease: Long-Term Results," *Br J Cancer*, 1990, 62(2):279-85.

CHOP

Use Lymphoma, non-Hodgkin's

Regimen NOTE: Multiple variations are listed below.
Variation 1:
Cyclophosphamide: I.V.: 750 mg/m² day 1
[total dose/cycle = 750 mg/m²]
Doxorubicin: I.V.: 50 mg/m² day 1
[total dose/cycle = 50 mg/m²]
Vincristine: I.V.: 1.4 mg/m² (maximum 2 mg) day 1
[total dose/cycle = 1.4 mg/m²]
Prednisone: Oral: 100 mg/day days 1 to 5
[total dose/cycle = 500 mg]
or 50 mg/m²/day days 1 to 5
[total dose/cycle = 250 mg/m²]
or 100 mg/m²/day days 1 to 5
[total dose/cycle = 500 mg/m²]
Repeat cycle every 21 days
Variation 2:
Cyclophosphamide: I.V.: 750 mg/m² day 1
[total dose/cycle = 750 mg/m²]
Doxorubicin: I.V.: 50 mg/m² day 1
[total dose/cycle = 50 mg/m²]
Vincristine: I.V.: 2 mg day 1
[total dose/cycle = 2 mg]
(Continued)

CHOP (Continued)

    Prednisone: Oral: 75 mg/day days 1 to 5
       [total dose/cycle = 375 mg]
    Repeat cycle every 21 days
  Variation 3:
    Cyclophosphamide: I.V.: 750 mg/m²/day days 1 and 8
       [total dose/cycle = 1500 mg/m²]
    Doxorubicin: I.V.: 25 mg/m²/day days 1 and 8
       [total dose/cycle = 50 mg/m²]
    Vincristine: I.V.: 1.4 mg/m²/day (maximum 2 mg) days 1 and 8
       [total dose/cycle = 2.8 mg/m²]
    Prednisone: Oral: 50 mg/m²/day days 1 to 8
       [total dose/cycle = 400 mg/m²]
    Repeat cycle every 28 days
  Variation 4 - "mini-CHOP":
    Cyclophosphamide: I.V.: 250 mg/m²/day days 1, 8, and 15
       [total dose/cycle = 750 mg/m²]
    Doxorubicin: I.V.: 16.7 mg/m²/day days 1, 8, and 15
       [total dose/cycle = 50.1 mg/m²]
    Vincristine: I.V.: 0.67 mg/m²/day days 1, 8, and 15
       [total dose/cycle = 2.01 mg]
    Prednisone: Oral: 75 mg/day days 1 to 5
       [total dose/cycle = 375 mg]
    Repeat cycle every 21 days

References

Variation 1:
Bezwoda W, Rastogi RB, Erazo Valla A, et al, "Long-Term Results of a Multicentre Randomised, Comparative Phase III Trial of CHOP Versus CNOP Regimens in Patients With Intermediate- and High-Grade Non-Hodgkin's Lymphomas, Novantrone International Study Group," *Eur J Cancer*, 1995, 31A(6):903-11.

McKelvey EM, Gottlieb JA, Wilson HE, et al, "Hydroxyldaunomycin (Adriamycin®) Combination Chemotherapy in Malignant Lymphoma," *Cancer*, 1976, 38(4):1484-93.

Miller TP, Dahlberg S, Cassady JR, et al, "Chemotherapy Alone Compared With Chemotherapy Plus Radiotherapy for Localized Intermediate- and High-Grade Non-Hodgkin's Lymphoma," *N Engl J Med*, 1998, 339(1):21-6.

Variation 2 and 4:
Meyer RM, Browman GP, Samosh ML, et al, "Randomized Phase II Comparison of Standard CHOP With Weekly CHOP in Elderly Patients With Non-Hodgkin's Lymphoma," *J Clin Oncol*, 1995, 13(9):2386-93.

Variation 3:
Linch DC, Vaughan Hudson B, Hancock BW, et al, "A Randomised Comparison of a Third-Generation Regimen (PACEBOM) With a Standard Regimen (CHOP) in Patients With Histologically Aggressive Non-Hodgkin's Lymphoma: A British National Lymphoma Investigation Report," *Br J Cancer*, 1996, 74(2):318-22.

♦ **CHOP-Rituximab** see Rituximab-CHOP on page 1278

CI (Neuroblastoma)

Use Neuroblastoma

Regimen

  Ifosfamide: I.V.: 1500 mg/m²/day days 1, 2, and 3
    [total dose/cycle = 4500 mg/m²]
  Mesna: I.V.: 500 mg/m² every 3 hours, for 3 doses each day, days 1, 2, and 3
    [total dose/cycle = 4500 mg/m²]
  Carboplatin: I.V.: 400 mg/m² day 4
    [total dose/cycle = 400 mg/m²]
  Repeat cycle every 21-28 days

References

Alvarado CS, Kretschmar C, Joshi VV, et al, "Chemotherapy for Patients With Recurrent or Refractory Neuroblastoma: A POG Phase II Study," *J Pediatr Hematol Oncol*, 1997, 19(1):62-7.

CISCA

Use Bladder cancer

Regimen

Cyclophosphamide: I.V.: 650 mg/m² day 1

[total dose = 650 mg/m²]

Doxorubicin: I.V.: 50 mg/m² day 1

[total dose = 50 mg/m²]

Cisplatin: I.V.: 100 mg/m² day 2

[total dose = 100 mg/m²]

Repeat cycle every 21-28 days

References

Sternberg JJ, Bracken RB, Handel PB, et al, "Combination Chemotherapy (CISCA) for Advanced Urinary Tract Carcinoma. A Preliminary Report," *JAMA*, 1977, 238(21):2282-7.

Cisplatin-Cetuximab

Index Terms Cetuximab-Cisplatin

Use Head and neck cancer

Regimen NOTE: Multiple variations are listed below.

Variation 1:

Cycle 1:

Cetuximab: I.V.: 400 mg/m² (loading dose) day 1 (week 1, cycle 1 only)

[total loading dose = 400 mg/m²]

followed by I.V.: 250 mg/m²/day days 8, 15, and 22

[total dose/cycle 1 = 1150 mg/m²]

Cisplatin: I.V.: 100 mg/m² day 1

[total dose/cycle = 100 mg/m²]

Treatment cycle is 4 weeks

Subsequent cycles:

Cetuximab: I.V.: 250 mg/m²/day days 1, 8, 15, and 22

[total dose/cycle = 1000 mg/m²]

Cisplatin: I.V.: 100 mg/m² day 1

[total dose/cycle = 100 mg/m²]

Repeat cycle every 4 weeks

Variation 2:

Cycle 1:

Cetuximab: I.V.: 400 mg/m² (loading dose) day 1 (week 1, cycle 1 only)

[total loading dose = 400 mg/m²]

followed by I.V.: 250 mg/m²/day days 8 and 15

[total dose/cycle 1 = 900 mg/m²]

Cisplatin: I.V.: 75-100 mg/m² day 1

[total dose/cycle = 75-100 mg/m²]

Treatment cycle is 3 weeks

Subsequent cycles:

Cetuximab: I.V.: 250 mg/m²/day days 1, 8, and 15

[total dose/cycle = 750 mg/m²]

Cisplatin: I.V.: 75-100 mg/m² day 1

[total dose/cycle = 75-100 mg/m²]

Repeat cycle every 3 weeks

(Continued)

Cisplatin-Cetuximab *(Continued)*

References

Variation 1:

Burtness B, Goldwasser MA, Flood W, et al, "Phase III Randomized Trial of Cisplatin Plus Placebo Compared With Cisplatin Plus Cetuximab in Metastatic/Recurrent Head and Neck Cancer: An Eastern Cooperative Oncology Group Study," *J Clin Oncol*, 2005, 23(34):8646-54.

Variation 2:

Herbst RS, Arquette M, Shin DM, et al, "Phase II Multicenter Study of the Epidermal Growth Factor Receptor Antibody Cetuximab and Cisplatin for Recurrent and Refractory Aquamous Cell Carcinoma of the Head and Neck," *J Clin Oncol*, 2005, 23(24):5578-87.

Cisplatin-Docetaxel

Use Bladder cancer

Regimen

Cisplatin: I.V.: 30 mg/m^2 day 1

[total dose/cycle = 30 mg/m^2]

Docetaxel: I.V.: 40 mg/m^2 day 4

[total dose/cycle = 40 mg/m^2]

Repeat cycle weekly for 8 weeks

References

Varveris H, Delakas D, Anezinis P, et al, "Concurrent Platinum and Docetaxel Chemotherapy and External Radical Radiotherapy in Patients With Invasive Transitional Cell Bladder Carcinoma. A Preliminary Report of Tolerance and Local Control," *Anticancer Res*, 1997, 17(6D):4771-80.

Cisplatin-Fluorouracil

Use Cervical cancer

Regimen NOTE: Multiple variations are listed below.

Variation 1:

Cisplatin: I.V.: 75 mg/m^2 day 1

[total dose/cycle = 75 mg/m^2]

Fluorouracil: I.V.: 1000 mg/m^2/day continuous infusion days 1 to 4 (96 hours)

[total dose/cycle = 4000 mg/m^2]

Repeat cycle every 21 days

Variation 2:

Cisplatin: I.V.: 50 mg/m^2 day 1 starting 4 hours before radiotherapy

[total dose/cycle = 50 mg/m^2]

Fluorouracil: I.V.: 1000 mg/m^2/day continuous infusion days 2 to 5 (96 hours)

[total dose/cycle = 4000 mg/m^2]

Repeat cycle every 28 days

References

Variation 1:

Morris M, Eifel PJ, Lu J, et al, "Pelvic Radiation With Concurrent Chemotherapy Compared With Pelvic and Para-aortic Radiation for High-Risk Cervical Cancer," *N Engl J Med*, 1999, 340(15):1137-43.

Variation 2:

Whitney CW, Sause W, Bundy BN, et al, "Randomized Comparison of Fluorouracil Plus Cisplatin Versus Hydroxyurea as an Adjunct to Radiation Therapy in Stage IIB-IVA Carcinoma of the Cervix With Negative Para-aortic Lymph Nodes: A Gynecologic Oncology Group and Southwest Oncology Group Study," *J Clin Oncol*, 1999, 17(5):1339-48.

♦ **Cisplatin-Ifosfamide-Paclitaxel** *see* Paclitaxel-Ifosfamide-Cisplatin *on page 1265*

Cisplatin-Pemetrexed

Index Terms Pemetrexed-Cisplatin

Use Malignant pleural mesothelioma

Regimen

Pemetrexed: I.V.: 500 mg/m² infused over 10 minutes day 1
[total dose/cycle = 500 mg/m²]

Cisplatin: I.V.: 75 mg/m² infused over 2 hours (start 30 minutes after pemetrexed)
[total dose/cycle = 75 mg/m²]

Repeat cycle every 21 days

References

Vogelzang NJ, Rusthoven JJ, Symanowski J, et al, "Phase III Study of Pemetrexed in Combination With Cisplatin Versus Cisplatin Alone in Patients With Malignant Pleural Mesothelioma," *J Clin Oncol*, 2003, 21(14):2636-44.

♦ **Cisplatin-Topotecan (Oral)** *see* Topotecan (Oral)-Cisplatin *on page 1282*

Cisplatin-Vinorelbine

Use Cervical cancer

Regimen

Cisplatin: I.V.: 80 mg/m² day 1
[total dose/cycle = 80 mg/m²]

Vinorelbine: I.V.: 25 mg/m²/day days 1 and 8
[total dose/cycle = 50 mg/m²]

Repeat cycle every 21 days

References

Pignata S, Silvestro G, Ferrari E, et al, "Phase II Study of Cisplatin and Vinorelbine as First-Line Chemotherapy in Patients With Carcinoma of the Uterine Cervix," *J Clin Oncol*, 1999, 17(3):756-60.

CMF

Use Breast cancer

Regimen NOTE: Multiple variations are listed below.

Variation 1:

Methotrexate: I.V.: 40 mg/m²/day days 1 and 8
[total dose/cycle = 80 mg/m²]

Fluorouracil: I.V.: 600 mg/m²/day days 1 and 8
[total dose/cycle = 1200 mg/m²]

Cyclophosphamide: Oral: 100 mg/m²/day days 1 to 14
[total dose/cycle = 1400 mg/m²]

Repeat cycle every 28 days

Variation 2 (>60 years of age):

Methotrexate: I.V.: 30 mg/m²/day days 1 and 8
[total dose/cycle = 60 mg/m²]

Fluorouracil: I.V.: 400 mg/m²/day days 1 and 8
[total dose/cycle = 800 mg/m²]

Cyclophosphamide: Oral: 100 mg/m²/day days 1 to 14
[total dose/cycle = 1400 mg/m²]

Repeat cycle every 28 days

References

Variations 1 and 2:
Bonadonna G, Brusamolino E, Valagussa P, et al, "Combination Chemotherapy as an Adjuvant Treatment in Operable Breast Cancer," *N Engl J Med*, 1976, 294(8):405-10.
Canellos GP, Pocock SJ, Taylor SG III, et al, "Combination Chemotherapy for Metastatic Breast Carcinoma, Prospective Comparison of Multiple Drug Therapy With L-Phenylalanine Mustard," *Cancer*, 1976, 38(5):1882-6.

CMF-IV

Use Breast cancer

Regimen

Cyclophosphamide: I.V.: 600 mg/m² day 1
[total dose/cycle = 600 mg/m²]

(Continued)

CMF-IV *(Continued)*

Methotrexate: I.V.: 40 mg/m^2 day 1

[total dose/cycle = 40 mg/m^2]

Fluorouracil: I.V.: 600 mg/m^2 day 1

[total dose/cycle = 600 mg/m^2]

Repeat cycle every 21 or 28 days

References

Bonadonna G, Veronesi U, Brambilla C, et al, "Primary Chemotherapy to Avoid Mastectomy in Tumors With Diameters of Three Centimeters or More," *J Natl Cancer Inst*, 1990, 82(19):1539-45.

Tannock IF, Boyd NF, DeBoer G, et al, "A Randomized Trial of Two Dose Levels of Cyclophosphamide, Methotrexate, and Fluorouracil Chemotherapy for Patients With Metastatic Breast Cancer," *J Clin Oncol*, 1988, 6(9):1377-87.

CMFP

Use Breast cancer

Regimen

Cyclophosphamide: Oral: 100 mg/m^2/day days 1 to 14

[total dose = 1400 mg/m^2]

Methotrexate: I.V.: 30 or 40 mg/m^2/day days 1 and 8

[total dose = 60 or 80 mg/m^2]

Fluorouracil: I.V.: 400 or 600 mg/m^2/day days 1 and 8

[total dose = 800 or 1200 mg/m^2]

Prednisone: Oral: 40 mg/m^2/day days 1 to 14

[total dose = 560 mg/m^2]

Repeat cycle every 28 days

References

Marschke RF Jr, Ingle JN, Schaid DJ, et al, "Randomized Clinical Trial of CFP Versus CMFP in Women With Metastatic Breast Cancer," *Cancer*, 1989, 63(10):1931-7.

CMFVP (Cooper Regimen, VPCMF)

Use Breast cancer

Regimen

Cyclophosphamide: Oral: 2 mg/kg/day days 1 to 252

[total dose/cycle = 504 mg/kg]

Methotrexate: I.V.: 0.7 mg/kg day 1, weeks 1 to 8, 10, 12, 14, 16, 18, 20, 22, 24, 26, 28, 30, 32, 34, and 36

[total dose/cycle = 15.4 mg/kg]

Fluorouracil: I.V.: 12 mg/kg day 1, weeks 1 to 8, 10, 12, 14, 16, 18, 20, 22, 24, 26, 28, 30, 32, 34, and 36

[total dose/cycle = 264 mg/kg]

Vincristine: I.V.: 0.035 mg/kg (maximum 2 mg) day 1, weeks 1 to 5, 8, 12, 16, 20, 24, 28, 32, and 36

[total dose/cycle = 0.455 mg/kg]

Prednisone: Oral: 0.75 mg/kg/day days 1 to 10, taper off over next 40 days

Administer one cycle only

References

Cooper RG, Holland JF, and Glidewell O, "Adjuvant Chemotherapy of Breast Cancer," *Cancer*, 1979, 44(3):793-8.

♦ **C MOPP** *see* COPP *on page 1183*

CMV

Use Bladder cancer
Regimen
Cisplatin: I.V.: 100 mg/m² infused over 4 hours (start at least 12 hours after methotrexate) day 2
[total dose = 100 mg/m²]
Methotrexate: I.V.: 30 mg/m²/day days 1 and 8
[total dose = 60 mg/m²]
Vinblastine: I.V.: 4 mg/m²/day days 1 and 8
[total dose = 8 mg/m²]
Repeat cycle every 21 days
References
Harker WG, Meyers FJ, Freiha FS, et al, "Cisplatin, Methotrexate, and Vinblastine (CMV): An Effective Chemotherapy Regimen for Metastatic Transitional Cell Carcinoma of the Urinary Tract. A Northern California Oncology Group Study," *J Clin Oncol*, 1985, 3(11):1463-70.

CNF

Index Terms CFM; FNC
Use Breast cancer
Regimen NOTE: Multiple variations are listed below.
Variation 1:
Cyclophosphamide: I.V.: 500 mg/m² day 1
[total dose/cycle = 500 mg/m²]
Mitoxantrone: I.V.: 10 mg/m² day 1
[total dose/cycle = 10 mg/m²]
Fluorouracil: I.V.: 500 mg/m² day 1
[total dose/cycle = 500 mg/m²]
Repeat cycle every 21 days
Variation 2:
Cyclophosphamide: I.V.: 500-600 mg/m² day 1
[total dose/cycle = 500-600 mg/m²]
Fluorouracil: I.V.: 500-600 mg/m² day 1
[total dose/cycle = 500-600 mg/m²]
Mitoxantrone: I.V.: 10-12 mg/m² day 1
[total dose/cycle = 10-12 mg/m²]
Repeat cycle every 21 days
References
Variation 1:
Bennett JM, Muss HB, Doroshow JH, et al, "A Randomized Multicenter Trial Comparing Mitixantrone, Cyclophosphamide, and Fluorouracil With Doxorubicin, Cyclophosphamide, and Fluorouracil in the Therapy of Metastatic Breast Carcinoma," *J Clin Oncol*, 1988, 6(10):1611-20.
Variation 2:
Alonso MC, Tabernero JM, Ojeda B, "A Phase III Randomized Trial of Cyclophosphamide, Mitoxantrone, and 5-Fluorouracil (CNF) Versus Cyclophosphamide, Adriamycin®, and 5-Fluorouracil (CAF) in Patients With Metastatic Breast Cancer," *Breast Cancer Res Treat*, 1995, 34(1):15-24.
Casciato DA and Lowitz BB, eds, *Manual of Clinical Oncology*, 3rd ed, Boston, MA: Little, Brown, 1995, 596.

CNOP

Use Lymphoma, non-Hodgkin's
Regimen
Cyclophosphamide: I.V.: 750 mg/m² day 1
[total dose/cycle = 750 mg/m²]
Mitoxantrone: I.V.: 10 mg/m² day 1
[total dose/cycle = 10 mg/m²]
Vincristine: I.V.: 1.4 mg/m² day 1
[total dose/cycle = 1.4 mg/m²]
(Continued)

CNOP *(Continued)*

Prednisone: Oral: 50 mg/m²/day days 1 to 5
   [total dose/cycle = 250 mg/m²]
Repeat cycle every 21 days

References

Pavlovsky S, Santarelli MT, Erazo A, et al, "Results of a Randomized Study of Previously Untreated Intermediate and High Grade Lymphoma Using CHOP Versus CNOP," *Ann Oncol*, 1992, 3(3):205-9.

CO

Use Retinoblastoma

Regimen

Cyclophosphamide: I.V.: 10 mg/kg/day days 1 to 3
   [total dose/cycle = 30 mg/kg]
Vincristine: I.V.: 1.5 mg/m² day 1
   [total dose/cycle = 1.5 mg/m²]
Repeat cycle every 21 days

References

Doz F, Khelfaoui F, Mosseri V, et al, "The Role of Chemotherapy in Orbital Involvement of Retinoblastoma. The Experience of a Single Institution With 33 Patients," *Cancer*, 1994, 74(2):722-32.

CODOX-M

Use Lymphoma, non-Hodgkin's

Regimen

Cytarabine: I.T.: 70 mg/day days 1 and 3
   [total dose/cycle = 140 mg]
Cyclophosphamide: I.V.: 800 mg/m² day 1, then 200 mg/m²/day days 2 to 5
   [total dose/cycle = 1600 mg/m²]
Vincristine: I.V.: 1.5 mg/m²/day days 1 and 8 (cycle 1); days 1, 8, and 15 (cycle 3)
   [total dose/cycle = 3-4.5 mg/m²]
Doxorubicin: I.V.: 40 mg/m² day 1
   [total dose/cycle = 40 mg/m²]
Methotrexate:
   I.T.: 12 mg day 15
      [total dose/cycle = 12 mg]
   I.V.: 1200 mg/m² loading dose then 240 mg/m²/hour for 23 hours day 10
      [total dose/cycle = 6720 mg/m²]
Leucovorin: I.V.: 192 mg/m² day 11 then 12 mg/m² every 6 hours until methotrexate level <5 X 10⁻⁸M (begin 36 hours after the start of methotrexate infusion)
Sargramostim: SubQ: 7.5 mcg/kg/day day 13 until ANC >1000 cells/mm³
Repeat cycle when ANC >1000 cells/mm³

References

Magrath I, Adde M, Shad A, et al, "Adults and Children With Small Non-Cleaved-Cell Lymphoma Have a Similar Excellent Outcome When Treated With the Same Chemotherapy Regimen," *J Clin Oncol*, 1996, 14(3):925-34.

CODOX-M/IVAC

Use Lymphoma, non-Hodgkin's (Burkitt's)

Regimen

CODOX-M

Cyclophosphamide: I.V.: 800 mg/m²/day days 1 and 2
   [total dose/cycle = 1600 mg/m²]
Vincristine: I.V.: 1.4 mg/m²/day (maximum 2 mg) days 1 and 10
   [total dose/cycle = 2.8 mg/m²; maximum 4 mg/cycle]

Doxorubicin: I.V.: 50 mg/m² day 1
[total dose/cycle = 50 mg/m²]
Methotrexate: I.V.: 3 g/m² day 10
[total dose/cycle = 3 g/m²]
Leucovorin: I.V.: 200 mg/m² day 11
followed by Oral, I.V.: 15 mg/m² every 6 hours until methotrexate level
<0.1 Mmol/L
Cytarabine: I.T.: 50 mg/day days 1 and 3
[total dose/cycle = 100 mg]
Methotrexate: I.T.: 12 mg day 1
[total dose/cycle = 12 mg]
Filgrastim: SubQ: Dose not specified, days 3 to 8 and day 12 until ANC
>1000 cells/mm³
Cycle alternates with IVAC (cycles begin when ANC >1000 cells/mm³)
Note: Hydrocortisone 50 mg may be added to intrathecal therapy to reduce
the incidence of side effects/chemical arachnoiditis.
IVAC
Ifosfamide: I.V.: 1500 mg/m²/day days 1 to 5
[total dose/cycle = 7500 mg/m²]
Mesna: I.V.: 1500 mg/m²/day (in divided doses) days 1 to 5
[total dose/cycle = 7500 mg/m²]
Etoposide: I.V.: 60 mg/m²/day days 1 to 5
[total dose/cycle = 300 mg/m²]
Cytarabine: I.V.: 2 g/m² every 12 hours, for 4 doses, days 1 and 2
[total dose/cycle = 8 g/m²]
Methotrexate: I.T.: 12 mg day 5
[total dose/cycle = 12 mg]
Filgrastim: SubQ: Dose not specified, day 6 until ANC >1000 cells/mm³
Cycle alternates with CODOX-M (cycles begin when ANC >1000 cells/
mm³)
Note: Hydrocortisone 50 mg may be added to intrathecal therapy to reduce
the incidence of side effects/chemical arachnoiditis.
References

Lacasce A, Howard O, Lib S, et al, "Modified Magrath Regimens for Adults With Burkitt and
Burkitt-Like Lymphomas: Preserved Efficacy With Decreased Toxicity," *Leuk Lymphoma*,
2004, 45(4):761-7.

COMLA

Use Lymphoma, non-Hodgkin's
Regimen
Cyclophosphamide: I.V.: 1500 mg/m² day 1
[total dose/cycle = 1500 mg/m²]
Vincristine: I.V.: 1.4 mg/m²/day (maximum 2 mg) days 1, 8, and 15
[total dose/cycle = 4.2 mg/m²]
Methotrexate: I.V.: 120 mg/m²/day days 22, 29, 36, 43, 50, 57, 64, and 71
[total dose/cycle = 960 mg/m²]
Leucovorin: Oral: 25 mg/m² every 6 hours for 4 doses (beginning 24 hours
after each methotrexate dose)
[total dose/cycle = 800 mg/m²]
Cytarabine: I.V.: 300 mg/m²/day days 22, 29, 36, 43, 50, 57, 64, and 71
[total dose/cycle = 2400 mg/m²]
Repeat cycle every 85 days
References

Sweet DL, Golomb HM, Ultmann JE, et al, "Cyclophosphamide, Vincristine, Methotrexate With
Leucovorin Rescue, and Cytarabine (COMLA) Combination Sequential Chemotherapy for
Advanced Diffuse Histiocytic Lymphoma," *Ann Intern Med*, 1980, 92(6):785-90.

COMP

Use Lymphoma, Hodgkin's disease; lymphoma, non-Hodgkin's disease

Regimen

Cyclophosphamide: I.V.: 1200 mg/m² day 1, cycle 1
  [total dose/cycle = 1200 mg/m²]
    followed by I.V.: 1000 mg/m² day 1 on subsequent cycles
    [total dose/cycle = 1000 mg/m²]
Vincristine: I.V.: 2 mg/m²/day (maximum 2 mg) days 3, 10, 17, 24, cycle 1
  [total dose/cycle = 8 mg/m²]
    followed by I.V.: 1.5 mg/m²/day days 1 and 4, on subsequent cycles
    [total dose/cycle = 3 mg/m²]
Methotrexate: I.V.: 300 mg/m² day 12
  [total dose/cycle = 300 mg/m²]
Prednisone: Oral: 60 mg/m²/day (maximum 60 mg) days 3 to 30 then taper
  over next 7 days, cycle 1
  [total dose/cycle = 1680 mg/m² + taper over next 7 days]
    followed by Oral: 60 mg/m² (maximum 60 mg) days 1 to 5, on
    subsequent cycles
    [total dose/cycle = 300 mg/m²]
Maintenance cycles repeat every 28 days

References

Anderson JR, Wilson JF, Jenkin DT, et al, "Childhood Non-Hodgkin's Lymphoma. The Results of a Randomized Therapeutic Trial Comparing a 4-Drug Regimen (COMP) With a 10-Drug Regimen (LSA2-L2)." *N Engl J Med*, 1983, 308(10):559-65.

COP-BLAM

Use Lymphoma, non-Hodgkin's

Regimen

Cyclophosphamide: I.V.: 400 mg/m² day 1
  [total dose/cycle = 400 mg/m²]
Vincristine: I.V.: 1 mg/m² day 1
  [total dose/cycle = 1 mg/m²]
Prednisone: Oral: 40 mg/m²/day days 1 to 10
  [total dose/cycle = 400 mg/m²]
Bleomycin: I.V.: 15 mg day 14
  [total dose/cycle = 15 mg]
Doxorubicin: I.V.: 40 mg/m² day 1
  [total dose/cycle = 40 mg/m²]
Procarbazine: Oral: 100 mg/m²/day days 1 to 10
  [total dose/cycle = 1000 mg/m²]

References

Salles G, Shipp MA, and Coiffier B, "Chemotherapy of Non-Hodgkin's Aggressive Lymphomas," *Semin Hematol*, 1994, 31(1):46-69.
Urba WJ, Duffey PL, and Longo DL, "Treatment of Patients With Aggressive Lymphomas: An Overview," *J Natl Cancer Inst Monogr*, 1990, (10):29-37.

COPE

Index Terms Baby Brain I

Use Brain tumors

Regimen

Cycle A:
  Vincristine: I.V.: 0.065 mg/kg/day (maximum 1.5 mg) days 1 and 8
    [total dose/cycle = 0.13 mg/kg]
  Cyclophosphamide: I.V.: 65 mg/kg day 1
    [total dose/cycle = 65 mg/kg]

Cycle B:
Cisplatin: I.V.: 4 mg/kg day 1
[total dose/cycle = 4 mg/kg]
Etoposide: I.V.: 6.5 mg/kg/day days 3 and 4
[total dose/cycle = 13 mg/kg]
Repeat cycle every 28 days in the following sequence: AABAAB

References

Duffner PK, Horowitz ME, Krischer JP, et al "Postoperative Chemotherapy and Delayed Radiation in Children Less Than Three Years of Age With Malignant Brain Tumors," *N Engl J Med*, 1993, 328(24):1725-31.

COPP

Index Terms C MOPP

Use Lymphoma, non-Hodgkin's

Regimen

Cyclophosphamide: I.V.: 450-650 mg/m^2/day days 1 and 8
[total dose/cycle = 900-1300 mg/m^2]
Vincristine: I.V.: 1.4-2 mg/m^2/day (maximum 2 mg) days 1 and 8
[total dose/cycle = 2.8-4 mg/m^2]
Procarbazine: Oral: 100 mg/m^2/day days 1 to 14
[total dose/cycle = 1400 mg/m^2]
Prednisone: Oral: 40 mg/m^2/day days 1 to 14
[total dose/cycle = 560 mg/m^2]
Repeat cycle every 3-4 weeks

References

Brereton HD, Young RC, Longo DL, et al, "A Comparison Between Combination Chemotherapy and Total Body Irradiation Plus Combination Chemotherapy in Non-Hodgkin's Lymphoma," *Cancer*, 1979, 43(6):2227-31.

CP (Leukemia)

Use Leukemia, chronic lymphocytic

Regimen

Chlorambucil: Oral: 30 mg/m^2 day 1
[total dose/cycle = 30 mg/m^2]
Prednisone: Oral: 80 mg/day days 1 to 5
[total dose/cycle = 400 mg]
Repeat cycle every 14 days

References

Raphael B, Anderson JW, Silber R, et al, "Comparison of Chlorambucil and Prednisone Versus Cyclophosphamide, Vincristine, and Prednisone as Initial Treatment for Chronic Lymphocytic Leukemia: Long-Term Follow-up of an Eastern Cooperative Oncology Group Randomized Clinical Trial," *J Clin Oncol*, 1991, 9(5):770-6.

CP (Ovarian Cancer)

Use Ovarian cancer

Regimen

Cyclophosphamide: I.V.: 750 mg/m^2 day 1
[total dose/cycle = 750 mg/m^2]
Cisplatin: I.V.: 75 mg/m^2 day 1
[total dose/cycle = 75 mg/m^2]
Repeat cycle every 21 days

References

Hainsworth JD, Grosh WW, Burnett LS, et al, "Advanced Ovarian Cancer: Long-Term Results of Treatment With Intensive Cisplatin-Based Chemotherapy of Brief Duration," *Ann Intern Med*, 1988, 108(2):165-70.

Neijt JP, ten Bokkel Huinink WW, van der Burg ME, et al, "Randomized Trial Comparing Two Combination Chemotherapy Regimens (CHAP-5 v CP) in Advanced Ovarian Carcinoma," *J Clin Oncol*, 1987, 5(8):1157-68.

(Continued)

CP (Ovarian Cancer) (Continued)

Omura GA, Brady MF, Homesley HD, et al, "Long-Term Follow-up and Prognostic Factor Analysis in Advanced Ovarian Carcinoma: The Gynecologic Oncology Group Experience," *J Clin Oncol*, 1991, 9(7):1138-50.

CT

Use Ovarian cancer
Regimen
  Cisplatin: I.V.: 75 mg/m^2 day 2
    [total dose/cycle = 75 mg/m^2]
  Paclitaxel: I.V.: 135 mg/m^2 continuous infusion day 1
    [total dose/cycle = 135 mg/m^2]
  Repeat cycle every 21 days
References
McGuire WP, Hoskins WJ, Brady MF, et al, "Cyclophosphamide and Cisplatin Compared With Paclitaxel and Cisplatin in Patients With Stage III and Stage IV Ovarian Cancer," *N Engl J Med*, 1996, 334(1):1-6.

CV

Use Retinoblastoma
Regimen
  Cyclophosphamide: I.V.: 300 mg/m^2
    [total dose/cycle = 300 mg/m^2]
  Vincristine: I.V.: 1.5 mg/m^2
    [total dose/cycle = 1.5 mg/m^2]
  Repeat weekly for 6 weeks
  followed by
  Cyclophosphamide: I.V.: 200 mg/m^2
    [total dose/cycle = 200 mg/m^2]
  Vincristine: I.V.: 1.5 mg/m^2
    [total dose/cycle = 1.5 mg/m^2]
  Repeat weekly for 42 weeks
References
Zelter M, Damel A, Gonzalez G, et al, "A Prospective Study on the Treatment of Retinoblastoma in 72 Patients," *Cancer*, 1991, 68(8):1685-90.

CVD

Use Melanoma
Regimen
  Cisplatin: I.V.: 20 mg/m^2/day days 2 to 5
    [total dose/cycle = 80 mg/m^2]
  Vinblastine: I.V.: 1.6 mg/m^2/day days 1 to 5
    [total dose/cycle = 8 mg/m^2]
  Dacarbazine: I.V.: 800 mg/m^2 day 1
    [total dose/cycle = 800 mg/m^2]
  Repeat cycle every 21 days
References
Legha SS, Ring S, Papadopoulos N, et al, "A Prospective Evaluation of a Triple-Drug Regimen Containing Cisplatin, Vinblastine, and Dacarbazine (CVD) for Metastatic Melanoma," *Cancer*, 1989, 64(10):2024-9.

CVP (Leukemia)

Use Leukemia, chronic lymphocytic
Regimen NOTE: Multiple variations are listed below.
  Variation 1:
    Cyclophosphamide: Oral: 400 or 300 mg/m^2/day days 1 to 5
      [total dose/cycle = 2000 or 1500 mg/m^2]

Vincristine: I.V.: 1.4 mg/m² (maximum 2 mg) day 1
[total dose/cycle = 1.4 mg/m²]
Prednisone: Oral: 100 mg/m²/day days 1 to 5
[total dose/cycle = 500 mg/m²]
Repeat cycle every 21 days
Variation 2:
Cyclophosphamide: I.V.: 800 mg/m² day 1
[total dose/cycle = 800 mg/m²]
Vincristine: I.V.: 1.4 mg/m² (maximum 2 mg) day 1
[total dose/cycle = 1.4 mg/m²]
Prednisone: Oral: 100 mg/m²/day days 1 to 5
[total dose/cycle = 500 mg/m²]
Repeat cycle every 21 days

References

Variation 1:
Bagley CM, DeVita VT, Berard CW, et al, "Advanced Lymphosarcoma: Intensive Cyclical Combination Chemotherapy With Cyclophosphamide, Vincristine, and Prednisone," *Ann Int Med*, 1972, 76(2):227-34.
Raphael B, Anderson JW, Silber R, et al, "Comparison of Chlorambucil and Prednisone Versus Cyclophosphamide, Vincristine, and Prednisone as Initial Treatment for Chronic Lymphocytic Leukemia: Long-Term Follow-up of an Eastern Cooperative Oncology Group Randomized Clinical Trial," *J Clin Oncol*, 1991, 9(5):770-6.
Variation 2:
Oken MM and Kaplan ME, "Combination Chemotherapy With Cyclophosphamide, Vincristine, and Prednisone in the Treatment of Refractory Chronic Lymphocytic Leukemia," *Cancer Treat Rep*, 1979, 63(3):441-7.

CVP (Lymphoma, non-Hodgkin's)

Use Lymphoma, non-Hodgkin's

Regimen

Cyclophosphamide: Oral: 400 mg/m²/day days 1 to 5
[total dose/cycle = 2000 mg/m²]
Vincristine: I.V.: 1.4 mg/m² day 1
[total dose/cycle = 1.4 mg/m²]
Prednisone: Oral: 100 mg/m²/day days 1 to 5
[total dose/cycle = 500 mg/m²]
Repeat cycle every 21 days

References

Bagley CM Jr, Devita VT Jr, Berard CW, et al, "Advanced Lymphosarcoma: Intensive Cyclical Combination Chemotherapy With Cyclophosphamide, Vincristine, and Prednisone," *Ann Intern Med*, 1972, 76(2):227-34.
Portlock CS, Rosenberg SA, Glatstein E, et al, "Treatment of Advanced Non-Hodgkin's Lymphomas With Favorable Histologies: Preliminary Results of a Prospective Trial," *Blood*, 1976, 47(5):747-56.

♦ **CVP-R** *see* R-CVP *on page 1276*

Cyclophosphamide + Doxorubicin

Use Prostate cancer

Regimen

Doxorubicin: I.V.: 40 mg/m² day 1
[total dose/cycle = 40 mg/m²]
Cyclophosphamide: I.V.: 800-2000 mg/m² day 1
[total dose/cycle = 800-2000 mg/m²]
Filgrastim: SubQ: 5 mcg/kg/day days 2 to 10 (or until ANC >10,000 cells/μL)
[total dose/cycle = 45 mcg/kg or until ANC >10,000 cells/μL]
Repeat cycle every 21 days
(Continued)

Cyclophosphamide + Doxorubicin *(Continued)*

References
Small EJ, Srinivas S, Egan B, et al, "Doxorubicin and Dose-Escalated Cyclophosphamide With Granulocyte Colony-Stimulating Factor for the Treatment of Hormone-Resistant Prostate Cancer," *J Clin Oncol*, 1996, 14(5):1617-25.

Cyclophosphamide + Estramustine

Use Prostate cancer

Regimen
Cyclophosphamide: Oral: 2 mg/kg/day days 1 to 14
[total dose/cycle = 28 mg/kg]
Estramustine: Oral: 10 mg/kg/day days 1 to 14
[total dose/cycle = 140 mg/kg]
Repeat cycle every 28 days

References
Bracarda S, Tonato M, Rosi P, "Oral Estramustine and Cyclophosphamide in Patients With Metastatic Hormone Refractory Prostate Carcinoma: A Phase II Study," *Cancer*, 2000, 88(6):1438-44.

Cyclophosphamide + Etoposide

Use Prostate cancer

Regimen
Cyclophosphamide: Oral: 100 mg/day days 1 to 14
[total dose/cycle = 1400 mg]
Etoposide: Oral: 50 mg/day days 1 to 14
[total dose/cycle = 700 mg]
Repeat cycle every 28 days

References
Maulard-Durdux C, Dufour B, Hennequin C, et al, "Phase II Study of the Oral Cyclophosphamide and Oral Etoposide Combination in Hormone-Refractory Prostate Carcinoma Patients," *Cancer*, 1996, 77(6):1144-8.

♦ **Cyclophosphamide-Fludarabine** *see* Fludarabine-Cyclophosphamide (FC) *on page 1216*

Cyclophosphamide + Vincristine + Dexamethasone

Use Prostate cancer

Regimen
Cyclophosphamide: Oral: 250 mg/day days 1 to 14
[total dose/cycle = 3500 mg]
Vincristine: I.V.: 1 mg/day days 1, 8, and 15
[total dose/cycle = 3 mg]
Dexamethasone: Oral: 0.75 mg twice daily days 1 to 14
[total dose/cycle = 21 mg]
Repeat cycle every 28 days

References
Daliani DD, Assikis V, Tu SM, et al, "Phase II Trial of Cyclophosphamide, Vincristine, and Dexamethasone in the Treatment of Androgen-Independent Prostate Carcinoma," *Cancer*, 2003, 97(3):561-7.

♦ **Cytarabine-Daunorubicin (5 + 2)** *see* 5 + 2 *on page 1140*
♦ **Cytarabine-Daunorubicin (7 + 3)** *see* 7 + 3 (Daunorubicin) *on page 1140*
♦ **Cytarabine-Daunorubicin-Etoposide (7 + 3 + 7)** *see* 7 + 3 + 7 *on page 1141*
♦ **Cytarabine-Idarubicin (7 + 3)** *see* 7 + 3 (Idarubicin) *on page 1140*
♦ **Cytarabine-Mitoxantrone (7 + 3)** *see* 7 + 3 (Mitoxantrone) *on page 1140*

CYVADIC
Use Sarcoma
Regimen
Cyclophosphamide: I.V.: 500 mg/m² day 1
[total dose/cycle = 500 mg/m²]
Vincristine: I.V.: 1.4 mg/m²/day days 1 and 5
[total dose/cycle = 2.8 mg/m²]
Doxorubicin: I.V.: 50 mg/m² day 1
[total dose/cycle = 50 mg/m²]
Dacarbazine: I.V.: 250 mg/m²/day days 1 to 5
[total dose/cycle = 1250 mg/m²]
Repeat cycle every 21 days
References
Pinedo HM, Bramwell VH, Mouridsen HT, et al, "Cyvadic in Advanced Soft Tissue Sarcoma: A Randomized Study Comparing Two Schedules. A Study of the EORTC Soft Tissue and Bone Sarcoma Group," *Cancer*, 1984, 53(9):1825-32.

DA
Use Leukemia, acute myeloid (induction)
Regimen Induction:
Daunorubicin: I.V.: 45 mg/m²/day days 1 to 3
[total dose/cycle = 135 mg/m²]
Cytarabine: I.V.: 100 mg/m²/day continuous infusion days 1 to 7
[total dose/cycle = 700 mg/m²]
References
Rai KR, Holland JF, Glidewell OJ, et al, "Treatment of Acute Myelocytic Leukemia: A Study by Cancer and Leukemia Group B," *Blood*, 1981, 58(6):1203-12.
Yates J, Glidewell O, Wiernik P, et al, "Cytosine Arabinoside With Daunorubicin or Adriamycin for Therapy of Acute Myelocytic Leukemia: A CALGB Study," *Blood*, 1982, 60(2):454-62.

Dacarbazine-Carboplatin-Aldesleukin-Interferon
Use Melanoma
Regimen
Dacarbazine: I.V.: 750 mg/m²/day days 1 and 22
[total dose/cycle = 1500 mg/m²]
Carboplatin: I.V.: 400 mg/m²/day days 1 and 22
[total dose/cycle = 800 mg/m²]
Aldesleukin: SubQ: 4,800,000 units every 8 hours days 36 and 57
[total dose/cycle = 28,800,000 units]
then 4,800,000 units every 12 hours days 37 and 58
[total dose/cycle = 19,200,000 units]
then 4,800,000 units/day days 38 to 40, 43 to 47, 50 to 54, 59 to 61, 65 to 68, 71 to 75
[total dose/cycle = 120,000,000 units]
Interferon alpha-2a: SubQ: 6,000,000 units days 38, 40, 43, 45, 47, 50, 52, 54, 59, 61, 64, 66, 68, 71, 73, and 75
[total dose/cycle = 96,000,000 units]
Repeat cycle every 78 days for 3 cycles
References
Ron IG, Mordish Y, Eisenthal A, et al, "A Phase II Study of Combined Administration of Dacarbazine and Carboplatin With Home Therapy of Recombinant Interleukin-2 and Interferon-Alpha 2a in Patients With Advanced Malignant Melanoma," *Cancer Immunol Immunother*, 1994, 38(6):379-84.

Dartmouth Regimen
Use Melanoma
Regimen NOTE: Multiple variations are listed on next page.
(Continued)

Dartmouth Regimen *(Continued)*

Variation 1:

Cisplatin: I.V.: 25 mg/m²/day days 1 to 3
[total dose/cycle = 75 mg/m²]

Dacarbazine: I.V.: 220 mg/m²/day days 1 to 3
[total dose/cycle = 660 mg/m²]

Carmustine: I.V.: 150 mg/m² day 1 (every other cycle)
[total dose/cycle = 150 mg/m²; every other cycle]

Tamoxifen: Oral: 10 mg twice daily (begin 1 week before chemotherapy)
[total dose/cycle = 420 mg]

Repeat cycle every 21 days

Variation 2:

Carmustine: I.V.: 150 mg/m² day 1
[total dose/cycle = 150 mg/m²]

Cisplatin: I.V.: 25 mg/m²/day days 1, 2, 3, 22, 23, and 24
[total dose/cycle = 150 mg/m²]

Dacarbazine: I.V.: 220 mg/m²/day days 1, 2, 3, 22, 23, and 24
[total dose/cycle = 1320 mg/m²]

Tamoxifen: Oral: 10 mg twice daily days 1 to 42
[total dose/cycle = 840 mg]

Repeat cycle every 42 days

Variation 3:

Carmustine: I.V.: 150 mg/m² day 1
[total dose/cycle = 150 mg/m²]

Cisplatin: I.V.: 25 mg/m²/day days 1, 2, 3, 22, 23, and 24
[total dose/cycle = 150 mg/m²]

Dacarbazine: I.V.: 220 mg/m²/day days 1, 2, 3, 22, 23, and 24
[total dose/cycle = 1320 mg/m²]

Tamoxifen: Oral: 160 mg/day days -6 to 0 (cycle 1 only)
[total dose/cycle = 1120 mg]
followed by Oral: 40 mg/day days 1 to 42
[total dose/cycle = 1680 mg]

Repeat cycle every 42 days

Variation 4:

Carmustine: I.V.: 150 mg/m² day 1
[total dose/cycle = 150 mg/m²]

Cisplatin: I.V.: 25 mg/m²/day days 1, 2, 3, 29, 30, and 31
[total dose/cycle = 150 mg/m²]

Dacarbazine: I.V.: 220 mg/m²/day days 1, 2, 3, 29, 30, and 31
[total dose/cycle = 1320 mg/m²]

Tamoxifen: Oral: 10-20 mg twice daily days 1 to 56
[total dose/cycle = 1120-2240 mg]

Repeat cycle every 56 days

References

Variation 1:

Chapman PB, Einhorn LH, Meyers ML, et al, "Phase III Multicenter Randomized Trial of the Dartmouth Regimen Versus Dacarbazine in Patients With Metastatic Melanoma," *J Clin Oncol*, 1999, 17(9):2745-51.

Gause BL, Sharfman WH, Janik JE, et al, "A Phase II Study of Carboplatin, Interferon-Alpha, and Tamoxifen for Patients With Metastatic Melanoma," *Cancer Invest*, 1998, 16(6):374-80.

McClay EF, Berd D, and Mastrangelo MJ, "The Dartmouth Regimen: Gone or Going Strong?," *Cancer Invest*, 1998, 16(6):421-3.

Variation 2

Del Prete SA, Maurer LH, O'Donnell J, et al, "Combination Chemotherapy With Cisplatin, Carmustine, Dacarbazine, and Tamoxifen in Metastatic Melanoma," *Cancer Treat Rep*, 1984, 68(11):1403-5.

Variation 3:

Rusthoven JJ, Quirt IC, Iscoe NA, et al, "Randomized, Double-Blind, Placebo-Controlled Trial Comparing the Response Rates of Carmustine, Dacarbazine, and Cisplatin With and Without Tamoxifen in Patients With Metastatic Melanoma," *J Clin Oncol*, 1996, 14(7):2083-90.

Variation 4:

McClay EF, Mastrangelo MJ, Berd D, et al, "Effective Combination Chemo/Hormonal Therapy for Malignant Melanoma: Experience With Three Consecutive Trials," *Int J Cancer*, 1992, 50(4):553-6.

DAT

Use Leukemia, acute myeloid (induction)

Regimen Induction:

Daunorubicin: I.V. bolus: 45 mg/m²/day days 1 to 3

[total dose/cycle = 135 mg/m²]

Cytarabine: I.V. bolus: 200 mg/m²

[total dose/cycle = 200 mg/m²]

Thioguanine: Oral: 100 mg/m²/day days 1 to 7

[total dose/cycle = 700 mg/m²]

References

Gale RP and Cline MJ, "High Remission-Induction Rate in Acute Myeloid Leukaemia," *Lancet*, 1977, 1(8010):497-9.

♦ **Daunorubicin-Cytarabine (5 + 2)** *see* 5 + 2 *on page 1140*

DAV

Use Leukemia, acute myeloid

Regimen

Daunorubicin: I.V.: 60 mg/m²/day days 3 to 5

[total dose/cycle = 180 mg/m²]

Cytarabine I.V.: 100 mg/m²/day continuous infusion days 1 and 2

[total dose/cycle = 200 mg/m²]

followed by I.V.: 100 mg/m² over 30 minutes every 12 hours days 3 to 8 (12 doses)

[total dose/cycle = 1200 mg/m²]

Etoposide: I.V.: 150 mg/m²/day days 6 to 8

[total dose/cycle = 450 mg/m²]

Administer one cycle only

References

Creutzig U, Ritter J, and Schellong G, "Identification of Two Risk Groups in Childhood Acute Myelogenous Leukemia After Therapy Intensification in Study AML-BFM-83 as Compared With Study AML-BFM-78, AML-BFM Study Group," *Blood*, 1990, 75(10):1932-40.

♦ **DCF** *see* Docetaxel-Cisplatin-Fluorouracil (Gastric Cancer) *on page 1190*

Decitabine (Low Dose)

Use Myelodysplastic syndrome; leukemia, chronic myelogenous

Regimen

Decitabine: I.V.: 20 mg/m²/day days 1 to 5

[total dose/cycle = 100 mg/m²]

Repeat cycle every 28 days for at least 3 cycles

References

Kantarjian H, Oki Y, Garcia-Manero G, et al, "Results of a Randomized Study of 3 Schedules of Low-Dose Decitabine in Higher-Risk Myelodysplastic Syndrome and Chronic Myelomonocytic Leukemia," *Blood*, 2007, 109(1):52-7.

♦ **Dexamethasone-Lenalidomide** *see* Lenalidomide-Dexamethasone *on page 1243*

♦ **Dexamethasone (Low Dose)-Lenalidomide** *see* Lenalidomide-Dexamethasone (Low Dose) *on page 1243*

♦ **Dexamethasone-Thalidomide** see Thalidomide-Dexamethasone on page 1280

DHAP

Use Lymphoma, non-Hodgkin's

Regimen NOTE: Multiple variations are listed below.

Variation 1:

Dexamethasone: I.V. or Oral: 40 mg/day days 1 to 4
  [total dose/cycle = 160 mg]

Cisplatin: I.V.: 100 mg/m² day 1
  [total dose/cycle = 100 mg/m²]

Cytarabine: I.V.: 2000 mg/m² every 12 hours for 2 doses day 2 (begins at the end of the cisplatin infusion)
  [total dose/cycle = 4000 mg/m²]

Repeat cycle every 3-4 weeks for 6-10 cycles (salvage therapy) or 1-2 cycles (mobilization prior to high-dose therapy with peripheral hematopoietic progenitor cell support)

Variation 2:

Dexamethasone: I.V. or Oral: 40 mg/day days 1 to 4
  [total dose/cycle = 160 mg]

Oxaliplatin: I.V.: 130 mg/m² day 1
  [total dose/cycle = 130 mg/m²]

Cytarabine: I.V.: 2000 mg/m² every 12 hours for 2 doses day 2
  [total dose/cycle = 4000 mg/m²]

Repeat cycle every 3 weeks

References

Variation 1:
Velasquez WS, Cabanillas F, Salvador P, et al, "Effective Salvage Therapy for Lymphoma With Cisplatin in Combination With High-Dose Ara-C and Dexamethasone (DHAP)," *Blood*, 1988, 71(1):117-22.

Variation 2:
Chau I, Webb A, Cunningham D, et al, "An Oxaliplatin-Based Chemotherapy in Patients With Relapsed or Refractory Intermediate and High-Grade Non-Hodgkin's Lymphoma," *Br J Haematol*, 2001, 115(4):786-92.

Docetaxel-Cisplatin

Use Lung cancer, nonsmall cell

Regimen

Docetaxel: I.V.: 75 mg/m² day 1
  [total dose/cycle = 75 mg/m²]

Cisplatin: I.V.: 75 mg/m² day 1
  [total dose/cycle = 75 mg/m²]

Repeat cycle every 21 days

References

Zalcberg J, Millward M, Bishop J, et al, "Phase II Study of Docetaxel and Cisplatin in Advanced Nonsmall-Cell Lung Cancer," *J Clin Oncol*, 1998, 16(5):1948-53.

Docetaxel-Cisplatin-Fluorouracil (Gastric Cancer)

Index Terms DCF

Use Gastric cancer

Regimen

Docetaxel: I.V.: 75 mg/m² day 1
  [total dose/cycle = 75 mg/m²]

Cisplatin: I.V.: 75 mg/m² day 1
  [total dose/cycle = 75 mg/m²]

Fluorouracil: I.V.: 750 mg/m²/day continuous infusion days 1 to 5
  [total dose/cycle = 3750 mg/m²]

Repeat cycle every 21 days

References

Ajani JA, Fodor MB, Tjulandin SA, et al, "Phase II Multi-Institutional Randomized Trial of Docetaxel Plus Cisplatin With or Without Fluorouracil in Patients With Untreated, Advanced Gastric, or Gastroesophageal Adenocarcinoma," *J Clin Oncol*, 2005, 23(24):5660-7.

Docetaxel-Cisplatin-Fluorouracil (Head and Neck Cancer)

Index Terms TPF

Use Head and neck cancer

Regimen NOTE: Multiple variations are listed below.

Variation 1:

Docetaxel: I.V.: 75 mg/m² day 1

[total dose/cycle = 75 mg/m²]

Cisplatin: I.V.: 75 mg/m² day 1

[total dose/cycle = 75 mg/m²]

Fluorouracil: I.V.: 750 mg/m²/day continuous infusion days 1 to 5

[total dose/cycle = 3750 mg/m²]

Repeat cycle every 21 days for 4 cycles

Variation 2:

Docetaxel: I.V.: 75 mg/m² day 1

[total dose/cycle = 75 mg/m²]

Cisplatin: I.V.: 75-100 mg/m² day 1

[total dose/cycle = 75-100 mg/m²]

Fluorouracil: I.V.: 1000 mg/m²/day continuous infusion days 1 to 4

[total dose/cycle = 4000 mg/m²]

Repeat cycle every 21 days for total of 3 cycles

References

Variation 1:

Schrijvers D, van Herpen C, Kerger J, et al, "Docetaxel, Cisplatin and 5-Fluorouracil in Patients With Locally Advanced Unresectable Head and Neck Cancer: A Phase I-II Feasibility Study," *Ann Oncol*, 2004, 15(4):638-45.

Vermorken JB, Remenar E, van Herpen C, et al, "Cisplatin, Fluorouracil, and Docetaxel in Unresectable Head and Neck Cancer," *N Engl J Med*, 2007, 357(17):1695-1704.

Variation 2:

Posner MR, Glisson B, Frenette G, et al, "Multicenter Phase I-II Trial of Docetaxel, Cisplatin, and Fluorouracil Induction Chemotherapy for Patients With Locally Advanced Squamous Cell Cancer of the Head and Neck," *J Clin Oncol*, 2001, 19(4):1096-104.

Posner MR, Hershock DM, Blajman CR, et al, "Cisplatin and Fluorouracil Alone or With Docetaxel in Head and Neck Cancer," *N Engl J Med*, 2007, 357(17):1705-15.

Docetaxel-Cyclophosphamide (TC)

Index Terms TC

Use Breast cancer

Regimen

Docetaxel: I.V.: 75 mg/m² day 1

[total dose/cycle = 75 mg/m²]

Cyclophosphamide: I.V.: 600 mg/m² day 1

[total dose/cycle = 600 mg/m²]

Repeat cycle every 21 days for 4 cycles

References

Jones SE, Savin MA, Holmes FA, et al, "Phase III Trial Comparing Doxorubicin Plus Cyclophosphamide With Docetaxel Plus Cyclophosphamide as Adjuvant Therapy for Operable Breast Cancer," *J Clin Oncol*, 2006, 24(34):5381-7.

Docetaxel-Prednisone

Use Prostate cancer

Regimen

Docetaxel: I.V.: 75 mg/m² day 1
[total dose/cycle = 75 mg/m²]
Prednisone: Oral: 5 mg twice daily
[total dose/cycle = 210 mg]
Repeat cycle every 21 days for up to 10 cycles

References
Dagher R, Li N, Abraham S, et al, "Approval Summary: Docetaxel in Combination With Prednisone for the Treatment of Androgen-Independent Hormone-Refractory Prostate Cancer," *Clin Cancer Res*, 2004, 10(24):8147-51.
Tannock IF, de Wit R, Berry WR, et al, "Docetaxel Plus Prednisone or Mitoxantrone Plus Prednisone for Advanced Prostate Cancer," *N Engl J Med*, 2004, 351(15):1502-12

Docetaxel-Thalidomide

Use Prostate cancer

Regimen

Docetaxel: I.V.: 30 mg/m²/day days 1, 8, and 15
[total dose/cycle = 90 mg/m²]
Thalidomide: Oral: 200 mg daily (at bedtime)
[total dose/cycle = 5600 mg]
Repeat cycle every 28 days

References
Dahut WL, Gulley JL, Arlen PM, et al, "Randomized Phase II Trial of Docetaxel Plus Thalidomide in Androgen-Independent Prostate Cancer," *J Clin Oncol*, 2004, 22(13):2532-9.

Docetaxel-Trastuzumab

Index Terms Trastuzumab-Docetaxel

Use Breast cancer

Regimen

Cycle 1:
Docetaxel: I.V.: 100 mg/m² day 1
[total dose/cycle 1 = 100 mg/m²]
Trastuzumab: I.V.: 4 mg/kg (loading dose) day 1 cycle 1
followed by I.V.: 2 mg/kg/day days 8 and 15 cycle 1
[total dose/cycle 1 = 8 mg/kg]
Treatment cycle is 21 days
Subsequent cycles:
Docetaxel: I.V.: 100 mg/m² day 1
[total dose/cycle = 100 mg/m²]
Trastuzumab: I.V.: 2 mg/kg/day days 1, 8, and 15
[total dose/cycle = 6 mg/kg]
Repeat cycle every 21 days for a total of at least 6 cycles (continue weekly
trastuzumab until disease progression)

References
Marty M, Cognetti F, Maraninchi D, et al, "Randomized Phase II Trial of the Efficacy and Safety of Trastuzumab Combined With Docetaxel in Patients With Human Epidermal Growth Factor Receptor 2-Positive Metastatic Breast Cancer Administered as First-Line Treatment: The M77001 Study Group," *J Clin Oncol*, 2005, 23(19):4265-74.

Docetaxel-Trastuzumab-Carboplatin

Index Terms Trastuzumab-Docetaxel-Carboplatin

Use Breast cancer

Regimen

Cycle 1:
Trastuzumab: I.V.: 4 mg/kg (loading dose) day 1 cycle 1

followed by I.V.: 2 mg/kg/day days 8 and 15 cycle 1
[total dose/cycle 1 = 8 mg/kg]
Docetaxel: I.V.: 75 mg/m^2 day 2
[total dose/cycle 1 = 75 mg/m^2]
Carboplatin: I.V.: AUC 6 day 2
[total dose/cycle 1 = AUC = 6]
Treatment cycle is 21 days
Subsequent cycles:
Trastuzumab: I.V.: 2 mg/kg/day days 1, 8, and 15
[total dose/cycle = 6 mg/kg]
Docetaxel: I.V.: 75 mg/m^2 day 1
[total dose/cycle 1 = 75 mg/m^2]
Carboplatin: I.V.: AUC 6 day 1
[total dose/cycle = AUC = 6]
Repeat cycle every 21 days for a total of ~6 cycles (continue weekly
trastuzumab for 1 year after chemotherapy, or until disease progression
or unacceptable toxicity)

References

Pegram MD, Pienkowski T, Northfelt DW, et al, "Results of Two Open-Label, Multicenter Phase
II Studies of Docetaxel, Platinum Salts, and Trastuzumab in HER2-Positive Advanced Breast
Cancer," *J Natl Cancer Inst*, 2004, 96(10):759-69.

Docetaxel-Trastuzumab-Cisplatin

Index Terms Trastuzumab-Docetaxel-Cisplatin
Use Breast cancer
Regimen
Cycle 1:
Trastuzumab: I.V.: 4 mg/kg (loading dose) day 1 cycle 1
followed by I.V.: 2 mg/kg/day days 8 and 15 cycle 1
[total dose/cycle 1 = 8 mg/kg]
Docetaxel: I.V.: 75 mg/m^2 day 2
[total dose/cycle 1 = 75 mg/m^2]
Cisplatin: I.V.: 75 mg/m^2 day 2
[total dose/cycle 1 = 75 mg/m^2]
Treatment cycle is 21 days
Subsequent cycles:
Trastuzumab: I.V.: 2 mg/kg/day days 1, 8, and 15
[total dose/cycle = 6 mg/kg]
Docetaxel: I.V.: 75 mg/m^2 day 1
[total dose/cycle 1 = 75 mg/m^2]
Cisplatin: I.V.: 75 mg/m^2 day 1
[total dose/cycle = 75 mg/m^2]
Repeat cycle every 21 days for a total of ~6 cycles (continue weekly
trastuzumab for 1 year after chemotherapy, or until disease progression
or unacceptable toxicity)

References

Pegram MD, Pienkowski T, Northfelt DW, et al, "Results of Two Open-Label, Multicenter Phase
II Studies of Docetaxel, Platinum Salts, and Trastuzumab in HER2-Positive Advanced Breast
Cancer," *J Natl Cancer Inst*, 2004, 96(10):759-69.

Docetaxel-Trastuzumab-FEC

Index Terms Trastuzumab-Docetaxel-FEC
Use Breast cancer
Regimen
Cycle 1:
Trastuzumab: I.V.: 4 mg/kg (loading dose) day 1 cycle 1
followed by I.V.: 2 mg/kg/day days 8 and 15 cycle 1
[total dose/cycle 1 = 8 mg/kg]
(Continued)

Docetaxel-Trastuzumab-FEC *(Continued)*

Docetaxel: I.V.: 100 mg/m² day 1
[total dose/cycle 1 = 100 mg/m²]
Treatment cycle is 21 days
Cycles 2 and 3:
Trastuzumab: I.V.: 2 mg/kg/day days 1, 8, and 15
[total dose/cycle = 6 mg/kg]
Docetaxel: I.V.: 100 mg/m² day 1
[total dose/cycle = 100 mg/m²]
Treatment cycle is 21 days
Cycles 4, 5, and 6 (FEC):
Fluorouracil: I.V.: 600 mg/m² day 1
[total dose/cycle = 600 mg/m²]
Epirubicin: I.V.: 60 mg/m² day 1
[total dose/cycle = 60 mg/m²]
Cyclophosphamide: I.V.: 600 mg/m² day 1
[total dose/cycle = 600 mg/m²]
Repeat FEC cycle every 21 days for total of 3 cycles

References
Joensuu H, Kellokumpu-Lehtinen PL, Bono P, et al, "Adjuvant Docetaxel or Vinorelbine With or Without Trastuzumab for Breast Cancer," *N Engl J Med*, 2006, 354(8):809-20.

Docetaxel (Weekly)

Use Prostate cancer
Regimen
Docetaxel: I.V.: 40 mg/m² days 1, 8, and 15
[total dose/cycle = 120 mg/m²]
Repeat cycle every 4 weeks

References
Joshua AM, Nordman I, Venkataswaran R, et al, "Weekly Docetaxel as Second Line Treatment After Mitozantrone for Androgen-Independent Prostate Cancer," *Intern Med J*, 2005, 35(8):468-72.

Docetaxel (Weekly)-Trastuzumab

Index Terms Trastuzumab-Docetaxel (Weekly)
Use Breast cancer
Regimen
Cycle 1:
Docetaxel: I.V.: 35 mg/m²/day days 1, 8, and 15
[total dose/cycle 1 = 105 mg/m²]
Trastuzumab: I.V.: 4 mg/kg (loading dose) day 0 cycle 1
followed by I.V.: 2 mg/kg/day days 8 and 15 cycle 1
[total dose/cycle 1 = 8 mg/kg]
Treatment cycle is 28 days
Subsequent cycles:
Docetaxel: I.V.: 35 mg/m²/day days 1, 8, and 15
[total dose/cycle = 105 mg/m²]
Trastuzumab: I.V.: 2 mg/kg/day days 1, 8, and 15
[total dose/cycle = 6 mg/kg]
Repeat cycle every 28 days

References
Esteva FJ, Valero V, Booser D, et al, "Phase II Study of Weekly Docetaxel and Trastuzumab for Patients With HER-2-Overexpressing Metastatic Breast Cancer," *J Clin Oncol*, 2002, 20(7):1800-8.

Dox-CMF (Sequential)

Use Breast cancer

Regimen

Doxorubicin: I.V.: 75 mg/m² day 1
[total dose/cycle = 75 mg/m²]
Repeat cycle every 21 days for 4 cycles
followed by (after completing Cycle 4)
Cyclophosphamide: I.V.: 600 mg/m² day 1
[total dose/cycle = 600 mg/m²]
Methotrexate: I.V.: 40 mg/m² day 1
[total dose/cycle = 40 mg/m²]
Fluorouracil: I.V.: 600 mg/m² day 1
[total dose/cycle = 600 mg/m²]
Repeat cycle every 21 days for 8 cycles

References

Bonadonna G, Zambetti M, Velagussa P, "Sequential or Alternating Doxorubicin and CMF Regimens in Breast Cancer With More Than Three Positive Nodes. Ten-Year Results," *JAMA*, 1995, 273(7):542-7.

Doxorubicin + Ketoconazole

Use Prostate cancer

Regimen

Doxorubicin: I.V.: 20 mg/m² continuous infusion day 1
[total dose/cycle = 20 mg/m²]
Ketoconazole: Oral: 400 mg 3 times/day days 1 to 7
[total dose/cycle = 8400 mg]
Repeat cycle every 7 days

References

Sella A, Kilbourn R, Amato R, et al, "Phase II Study of Ketoconazole Combined With Weekly Doxorubicin in Patients With Androgen-Independent Prostate Cancer," *J Clin Oncol*, 1994, 12(4):683-8.

Doxorubicin + Ketoconazole/Estramustine + Vinblastine

Use Prostate cancer

Regimen

Doxorubicin: I.V.: 20 mg/m²/day days 1, 15, and 29
[total dose/cycle = 60 mg/m²]
Ketoconazole: Oral: 400 mg 3 times/day days 1 to 7, 15 to 21, and 29 to 35
[total dose/cycle = 25,200 mg]
Estramustine: Oral: 140 mg 3 times/day days 8 to 14, 22 to 28, and 36 to 42
[total dose/cycle = 8820 mg]
Vinblastine: I.V.: 5 mg/m²/day days 8, 22, and 36
[total dose/cycle = 15 mg/m²]
Repeat cycle every 8 weeks

References

Ellerhorst JA, Tu SM, Amato RJ, et al, "Phase II Trial of Alternating Weekly Chemohormonal Therapy for Patients With Androgen-Independent Prostate Cancer," *Clin Cancer Res*, 1997, 3(12 Pt 1):2371-6.

♦ **Doxorubicin (Liposomal)-Bortezomib** *see* Bortezomib-Doxorubicin (Liposomal) *on page 1155*

Doxorubicin (Liposomal)-Vincristine-Dexamethasone

Index Terms DVD

Use Multiple myeloma

Regimen NOTE: Multiple variations are listed on next page.
(Continued)

Doxorubicin (Liposomal)-Vincristine-Dexamethasone
(Continued)

Variation 1:

Doxorubicin, liposomal: I.V.: 40 mg/m^2 day 1
   [total dose/cycle = 40 mg/m^2]

Vincristine: I.V.: 2 mg day 1
   [total dose/cycle = 2 mg]

Dexamethasone: Oral or I.V.: 40 mg/day days 1 to 4
   [total dose/cycle = 160 mg]

Repeat cycle every 4 weeks

Variation 2:

Doxorubicin, liposomal: I.V.: 40 mg/m^2 day 1
   [total dose/cycle = 40 mg/m^2]

Vincristine: I.V.: 1.4 mg/m^2 (maximum 2 mg) day 1
   [total dose/cycle = 1.4 mg/m^2; maximum 2 mg]

Dexamethasone: Oral: 40 mg/day days 1 to 4
   [total dose/cycle = 160 mg]

Repeat cycle every 4 weeks

References

Variation 1:

Hussein MA, Wood L, Hsi E, et al, "A Phase II Trial of Pegylated Liposomal Doxorubicin, Vincristine, and Reduced-Dose Dexamethasone Combination Therapy in Newly Diagnosed Multiple Myeloma Patients," *Cancer*, 2002, 95(10):2160-8.

Variation 2:

Rifkin RM, Gregory SA, Mohrbacher A, et al, "Pegylated Liposomal Doxorubicin, Vincristine, and Dexamethasone Provide Significant Reduction in Toxicity Compared With Doxorubicin, Vincristine, and Dexamethasone in Patients With Newly Diagnosed Multiple Myeloma: A Phase III Multicenter Randomized Trial," *Cancer*, 2006, 106(4):848-58.

DTPACE

Use Multiple myeloma

Regimen

Dexamethasone: Oral: 40 mg/day days 1 to 4
   [total dose/cycle = 160 mg]

Thalidomide: Oral: 400 mg/day
   [total dose/cycle = 11,200 - 16,800 mg]

Cisplatin: I.V.: 10 mg/m^2/day continuous infusion days 1 to 4
   [total dose/cycle = 40 mg/m^2]

Doxorubicin: I.V.: 10 mg/m^2/day continuous infusion days 1 to 4
   [total dose/cycle = 40 mg/m^2]

Cyclophosphamide: I.V.: 400 mg/m^2 continuous infusion days 1 to 4
   [total dose/cycle = 1600 mg/m^2]

Etoposide: I.V.: 40 mg/m^2 continuous infusion days 1 to 4
   [total dose/cycle = 160 mg/m^2]

Repeat cycle every 4-6 weeks

References

Lee CK, Barlogie B, Munshi N, et al, "DTPACE: An Effective, Novel Combination Chemotherapy With Thalidomide for Previously Treated Patients With Myeloma," *J Clin Oncol*, 2003, 21(14):2732-9.

♦ **DVd** *see* Doxorubicin (Liposomal)-Vincristine-Dexamethasone *on page 1195*

DVP

Use Leukemia, acute lymphocytic

Regimen Induction:

Daunorubicin: I.V.: 25 mg/m^2/day days 1, 8, and 15
   [total dose/cycle = 75 mg/m^2]

Vincristine: I.V.: 1.5 mg/m²/day (maximum 2 mg) days 1, 8, 15, and 22
[total dose/cycle = 6 mg/m²]

Prednisone: Oral: 60 mg/m²/day days 1 to 28 then taper over next 14 days
[total dose/cycle = 1680 mg/m² + taper over next 14 days]

Administer single cycle; used in conjunction with intrathecal chemotherapy

References

Belasco JB, Luery N, and Scher C, "Multiagent Chemotherapy in Relapsed Acute Lymphoblastic Leukemia in Children," *Cancer*, 1990, 66(12):2492-7.

EAP

Use Gastric cancer

Regimen

Etoposide: I.V.: 120 mg/m²/day days 4, 5, and 6
[total dose/cycle = 360 mg/m²]

Doxorubicin: I.V.: 20 mg/m²/day days 1 and 7
[total dose/cycle = 40 mg/m²]

Cisplatin: I.V.: 40 mg/m²/day days 2 and 8
[total dose/cycle = 80 mg/m²]

Repeat cycle every 22-28 days

References

Preusser P, Wilke H, Achterrath W, et al, "Phase II Study With the Combination Etoposide, Doxorubicin, and Cisplatin in Advanced Measurable Gastric Cancer," *J Clin Oncol*, 1989, 7(9):1310-17.

Wilke H, Preusser P, Fink U, et al, "New Developments in the Treatment of Gastric Carcinoma," *Semin Oncol*, 1990, 17(1 Suppl 2):61-70.

Wilke H, Preusser P, Fink U, et al, "Preoperative Chemotherapy in Locally Advanced and Nonresectable Gastric Cancer: A Phase II Study With Etoposide, Doxorubicin, and Cisplatin," *J Clin Oncol*, 1989, 7(9):1318-26.

ECF

Use Gastric cancer

Regimen

Epirubicin: I.V.: 50 mg/m² day 1
[total dose/cycle = 50 mg/m²]

Cisplatin: I.V.: 60 mg/m² day 1
[total dose/cycle = 60 mg/m²]

Repeat cycle every 3 weeks

Fluorouracil: I.V.: 200 mg/m²/day continuous infusion for up to 6 months
[total dose/cycle = 36,000 mg/m²]

References

Webb A, Cunningham D, Scarffe JH, et al, "Randomized Trial Comparing Epirubicin, Cisplatin, and Fluorouracil Versus Fluorouracil, Doxorubicin, and Methotrexate in Advanced Esophago-gastric Cancer," *J Clin Oncol*, 1997, 15(1):261-7.

EC (Nonsmall Cell Lung Cancer)

Use Lung cancer, nonsmall cell

Regimen

Etoposide: I.V.: 120 mg/m²/day days 1 to 3
[total dose/cycle = 360 mg/m²]

Carboplatin: I.V.: AUC 6 day 1
[total dose/cycle = AUC = 6]

Repeat cycle every 21-28 days

References

Birch R, Weaver CH, Hainsworth JD, et al, "A Randomized Study of Etoposide and Carboplatin With or Without Paclitaxel in the Treatment of Small Cell Lung Cancer," *Semin Oncol*, 1997, 24(4 Suppl 12):S12-135, 137.

EC (Small Cell Lung Cancer)

Use Lung cancer, small cell

Regimen NOTE: Multiple variations are listed below.

Variation 1:

Etoposide: I.V.: 100-120 mg/m²/day days 1 to 3
[total dose/cycle = 300-360 mg/m²]

Carboplatin: I.V.: 325-400 mg/m² day 1
[total dose/cycle = 325-400 mg/m²]

Repeat cycle every 28 days

Variation 2:

Etoposide: I.V.: 120 mg/m²/day days 1 to 3
[total dose/cycle = 360 mg/m²]

Carboplatin: I.V.: AUC 6 day 1
[total dose/cycle = AUC = 6]

Repeat cycle every 21-28 days

References

Variation 1:

Kosmidis PA, Samantas E, Fountzilas G, et al, "Cisplatin/Etoposide Versus Carboplatin/Etoposide Chemotherapy and Irradiation in Small Cell Lung Cancer: A Randomized Phase III Study. Hellenic Cooperative Oncology Group for Lung Cancer Trials," *Semin Oncol,* 1994, 1(3 Suppl 6):23-30.

Variation 2:

Birch R, Weaver CH, Hainsworth JD, et al, "A Randomized Study of Etoposide and Carboplatin With or Without Paclitaxel in the Treatment of Small Cell Lung Cancer," *Semin Oncol,* 1997, 24(4 Suppl 12):135, 137.

EE

Use Wilms' tumor

Regimen

Dactinomycin: I.V.: 15 mcg/kg/day days 1 to 5 of weeks 0, 5, 13, and 24
[total dose/cycle = 300 mcg/kg]

Vincristine: I.V.: 1.5 mg/m² day 1 of weeks 1-10, 13, 14, 24, and 25
[total dose/cycle = 21 mg/m²]

References

Green DM, Breslow NE, Beckwith JB, et al, "Effect of Duration of Treatment on Treatment Outcome and Cost of Treatment for Wilms' Tumor: A Report From the National Wilms' Tumor Study Group," *J Clin Oncol,* 16(12):3744-51.

EE-4A

Use Wilms' tumor

Regimen

Dactinomycin: I.V.: 45 mcg/kg day 1 of weeks 0, 3, 6, 9, 12, 15, and 18
[total dose/cycle = 315 mcg/kg]

Vincristine: I.V.: 2 mg/m² day 1 of weeks 1-10, 12, 15, and 18
[total dose/cycle = 26 mg/m²]

References

Green DM, Breslow NE, Beckwith JB, et al, "Effect of Duration of Treatment on Treatment Outcome and Cost of Treatment for Wilms' Tumor: A Report From the National Wilms' Tumor Study Group," *J Clin Oncol,* 16(12):3744-51.

EFP

Use Gastric cancer

Regimen NOTE: Multiple variations are listed below.

Variation 1:

Etoposide: I.V.: 90 mg/m²/day days 1, 3, and 5
[total dose/cycle = 270 mg/m²]

Fluorouracil: I.V.: 900 mg/m²/day (20-hour infusion) days 1 to 5
[total dose/cycle = 4500 mg/m²]

1198

Cisplatin: I.V.: 20 mg/m^2/day days 1 to 5
  [total dose/cycle = 100 mg/m^2]
Repeat cycle every 24-28 days
Variation 2:
  Etoposide: I.V.: 100 mg/m^2/day days 1, 3, and 5
    [total dose/cycle = 300 mg/m^2]
  Fluorouracil: I.V.: 800 mg/m^2/day (12-hour infusion) days 1 to 5
    [total dose/cycle = 4000 mg/m^2]
  Cisplatin: I.V.: 20 mg/m^2/day days 1 to 5
    [total dose/cycle = 100 mg/m^2]
  Repeat cycle every 3 weeks

References

Variation 1:
Ajani JA, Roth JA, Ryan B, et al, "Evaluation of Pre- and Postoperative Chemotherapy for Resectable Adenocarcinoma of the Esophagus or Gastroesophageal Junction," *J Clin Oncol*, 1990, 8(7):1231-8.

Variation 2:
Ryoo BY, Kang YK, Im YH, et al, "Adjuvant (Cisplatin, Etoposide, and 5-Fluorouracil) Chemotherapy After Curative Resection of Gastric Adenocarcinomas Involving the Esophagogastric Junction," *Am J Clin Oncol*, 1999, 22(3):253-7.

ELF

Use Gastric cancer

Regimen

Leucovorin calcium: I.V.: 300 mg/m^2/day days 1, 2, and 3
  [total dose/cycle = 900 mg/m^2]
followed by
Etoposide: I.V.: 120 mg/m^2/day days 1, 2, and 3
  [total dose/cycle = 360 mg/m^2]
followed by
Fluorouracil: I.V.: 500 mg/m^2/day days 1, 2, and 3
  [total dose/cycle = 1500 mg/m^2]
Repeat cycle every 21-28 days

References

Wilke H, Preusser P, Fink U, et al, "New Developments in the Treatment of Gastric Carcinoma," *Semin Oncol*, 1990, 17(1 Suppl 2):61-70.

EMA 86

Use Leukemia, acute myeloid

Regimen

Mitoxantrone: I.V.: 12 mg/m^2/day days 1 to 3
  [total dose/cycle = 36 mg/m^2]
Etoposide: I.V.: 200 mg/m^2/day continuous infusion days 8 to 10
  [total dose/cycle = 600 mg/m^2]
Cytarabine: I.V.: 500 mg/m^2/day continuous infusion days 1 to 3 and 8 to 10
  [total dose/cycle = 3000 mg/m^2]
Administer one cycle only

References

Archimbaud E, Fenaux P, Reiffers J, et al, "Granulocyte-Macrophage Colony-Stimulating Factor in Association to Timed-Sequential Chemotherapy With Mitoxantrone, Etoposide, and Cytarabine for Refractory Acute Myelogenous Leukemia," *Leukemia*, 1993, 7(3):372-7.

EMA/CO

Use Gestational trophoblastic tumor

Regimen NOTE: Multiple variations are listed below.

Variation 1:
  Etoposide: I.V.: 100 mg/m^2/day days 1 and 2
    [total dose/cycle = 200 mg/m^2]
(Continued)

EMA/CO *(Continued)*

Methotrexate: I.V.: 300 mg/m² continuous infusion over 12 hours day 1
  [total dose/cycle = 300 mg/m²]
Dactinomycin: I.V. push: 0.5 mg/day days 1 and 2
  [total dose/cycle = 1 mg]
Leucovorin: Oral, I.M.: 15 mg twice daily for 2 days (start 24 hours after the
  start of methotrexate) days 2 and 3
  [total dose/cycle = 60 mg]
Alternate weekly with:
Cyclophosphamide: I.V.: 600 mg/m² day 1
  [total dose/cycle = 600 mg/m²]
Vincristine: I.V. push: 0.8 mg/m² (maximum 2 mg) day 1
  [total dose/cycle = 0.8 mg/m²]
Repeat cycle every 2 weeks
Variation 2:
  Dactinomycin: I.V.: 0.5 mg/day days 1 and 2
    [total dose/cycle = 1 mg]
  Etoposide: I.V.: 100 mg/m²/day days 1 and 2
    [total dose/cycle = 200 mg/m²]
  Methotrexate: I.V. bolus: 100 mg/m² then 200 mg/m² continuous infusion
    over 12 hours day 1
    [total dose/cycle = 300 mg/m²]
  Leucovorin: Oral, I.M.: 15 mg every 12 hours for 4 doses (start 24 hours
    after methotrexate) days 2 and 3
    [total dose/cycle = 60 mg]
  Vincristine: I.V.: 1 mg/m² day 8
    [total dose/cycle = 1 mg/m²]
  Cyclophosphamide: I.V.: 600 mg/m² day 8
    [total dose/cycle = 600 mg/m²]
  Repeat cycle every 2 weeks
Variation 3:
  Dactinomycin: I.V.: 0.5 mg/day days 1 and 2
    [total dose/cycle = 1 mg]
  Etoposide: I.V.: 100 mg/m²/day days 1 and 2
    [total dose/cycle = 200 mg/m²]
  Methotrexate: I.V.: 300 mg/m² continuous infusion over 12 hours day 1
    [total dose/cycle = 300 mg/m²]
  Leucovorin: Oral, I.M.: 15 mg every 12 hours for 4 doses (start 24 hours
    after start of methotrexate) days 2 and 3
    [total dose/cycle = 60 mg]
  Vincristine: I.V.: 1 mg/m² day 8
    [total dose/cycle = 1 mg/m²]
  Cyclophosphamide: I.V.: 600 mg/m² day 8
    [total dose/cycle = 600 mg/m²]
  Repeat cycle every 2 weeks
Variation 4:
  Dactinomycin: I.V.: 0.35 mg/m²/day days 1 and 2
    [total dose/cycle = 0.7 mg/m²]
  Etoposide: I.V.: 100 mg/m²/day days 1 and 2
    [total dose/cycle = 200 mg/m²]
  Methotrexate: I.V. bolus: 100 mg/m² then 200 mg/m² continuous infusion
    over 12 hours day 1
    [total dose/cycle = 300 mg/m²]
  Leucovorin: Oral, I.M.: 15 mg every 12 hours for 4 doses (start 24 hours
    after start of methotrexate) days 2 and 3
    [total dose/cycle = 60 mg]

Vincristine: I.V.: 1 mg/m^2 day 8
[total dose/cycle = 1 mg/m^2]
Cyclophosphamide: I.V.: 600 mg/m^2 day 8
[total dose/cycle = 600 mg/m^2]
Repeat cycle every 2 weeks

Variation 5 (patients with brain metastases):
Dactinomycin: I.V.: 0.5 mg/day days 1 and 2
[total dose/cycle = 1 mg]
Etoposide:I.V.: 100 mg/m^2/day days 1 and 2
[total dose/cycle = 200 mg/m^2]
Methotrexate: I.V.: 1 g/m^2 continuous infusion over 12 hours day 1
[total dose/cycle = 1 g/m^2]
Leucovorin: I.M.: 20 mg/m^2 every 6 hours for 12 doses (start 24 hours after start of methotrexate) days 2, 3 and 4
[total dose/cycle = 240 mg/m^2]
Vincristine: I.V.: 1 mg/m^2 day 8
[total dose/cycle = 1 mg/m^2]
Cyclophosphamide: I.V.: 600 mg/m^2 day 8
[total dose/cycle = 600 mg/m^2]
Repeat cycle every 2 weeks

Variation 6 (patients with brain metastases):
Dactinomycin: I.V.: 0.5 mg/day days 1 and 2
[total dose/cycle = 1 mg]
Etoposide: I.V.: 100 mg/m^2/day days 1 and 2
[total dose/cycle = 200 mg/m^2]
Methotrexate: I.V.: 1 g/m^2 continuous infusion over 12 hours day 1
[total dose/cycle = 1 g/m^2]
Leucovorin: Oral, I.M.: 30 mg/m^2 every 12 hours for 6 doses (start 32 hours after start of methotrexate) days 2, 3, and 4
[total dose/cycle = 180 mg/m^2]
Vincristine: I.V.: 1 mg/m^2 day 8
[total dose/cycle = 1 mg/m^2]
Cyclophosphamide: I.V.: 600 mg/m^2 day 8
[total dose/cycle = 600 mg/m^2]
Repeat cycle every 2 weeks

Variation 7:
Dactinomycin: I.V.: 0.5 mg/day days 1 and 2
[total dose/cycle = 1 mg]
Etoposide: I.V.: 100 mg/m^2/day days 1 and 2
[total dose/cycle = 200 mg/m^2]
Methotrexate: I.V.: 1 g/m^2 continuous infusion over 24 hours day 1
[total dose/cycle = 1 g/m^2]
Leucovorin: Oral, I.M.: 15 mg every 8 hours for 9 doses (start 32 hours after start of methotrexate) days 2, 3, and 4
[total dose/cycle = 135 mg/m^2]
Vincristine: I.V.: 1 mg/m^2 day 8
[total dose/cycle = 1 mg/m^2]
Cyclophosphamide: I.V.: 600 mg/m^2 day 8
[total dose/cycle = 600 mg/m^2]
Repeat cycle every 2 weeks

Variation 8 (patients with lung metastases):
Dactinomycin: I.V.: 0.5 mg/day days 1 and 2
[total dose/cycle = 1 mg]
Etoposide: I.V.: 100 mg/m^2/day days 1 and 2
[total dose/cycle = 200 mg/m^2]

(Continued)

EMA/CO *(Continued)*

Methotrexate: I.V. bolus: 100 mg/m² then 200 mg/m² continuous infusion over 12 hours day 1

[total dose/cycle = 300 mg/m²]

Leucovorin: Oral, I.M.: 15 mg every 12 hours for 4 doses (start 24 hours after start of methotrexate) days 2 and 3

[total dose/cycle = 60 mg]

Vincristine: I.V.: 1 mg/m² day 8

[total dose/cycle = 1 mg/m²]

Cyclophosphamide: I.V.: 600 mg/m² day 8

[total dose/cycle = 600 mg/m²]

Methotrexate: I.T.: 10 mg day 1 (every other cycle)

[total dose/cycle = 10 mg, every other cycle]

Repeat cycle every 2 weeks

Variation 9 (patients with lung metastases):

Dactinomycin: I.V.: 0.5 mg/day days 1 and 2

[total dose/cycle = 1 mg]

Etoposide: I.V.: 100 mg/m²/day days 1 and 2

[total dose/cycle = 200 mg/m²]

Methotrexate: I.V. bolus: 100 mg/m² then 200 mg/m² continuous infusion over 12 hours day 1

[total dose/cycle = 300 mg/m²]

Leucovorin: Oral, I.M.: 15 mg every 12 hours for 4 doses (start 24 hours after start of methotrexate) days 2 and 3

[total dose/cycle = 60 mg]

Vincristine: I.V.: 1 mg/m² day 8

[total dose/cycle = 1 mg/m²]

Cyclophosphamide: I.V.: 600 mg/m² day 8

[total dose/cycle = 600 mg/m²]

Methotrexate: I.T.: 12.5 mg day 8

[total dose/cycle = 12.5 mg]

Repeat cycle every 2 weeks

References

Variation 1:
Bagshawe KD, "High-Risk Metastatic Trophoblastic Disease," *Obstet Gynecol Clin North Am*, 1988, 15(3):531-43.

Variation 2:
Newlands ES, Bagshawe KD, Begent RH, et al, "Developments in Chemotherapy for Medium- and High-Risk Patients With Gestational Trophoblastic Tumours (1979-1984)," *Br J Obstet Gynaecol*, 1986, 93(1):63-9.

Variation 3:
Newlands ES, Bagshawe KD, Begent RH, et al, "Results With the EMA/CO (Etoposide, Methotrexate, Actinomycin D, Cyclophosphamide, Vincristine) Regimen in High-Risk Gestational Trophoblastic Tumours, 1979 to 1989," *J Obstet Gynaecol*, 1991, 98(6):550-7.

Variation 4:
Soper JT, Evans AC, Clarke-Pearson DL, et al, "Alternating Weekly Chemotherapy With Etoposide-Methotrexate-Dactinomycin/Cyclophosphamide-Vincristine for High-Risk Gestational Trophoblastic Disease," *Obstet Gynecol*, 1994, 83(1):113-7.

Variation 5:
Bolis G, Bonazzi C, Landoni F, et al, "EMA/CO Regimen in High-Risk Gestational Trophoblastic Tumor (GTT)," *Gynecol Oncol*, 1988, 31(3):439-44.

Variation 6:
Schink JC, Singh Dk, Rademaker AW, et al, "Etoposide, Methotrexate, Actinomycin-D, Cyclophosphamide, and Vincristine for the Treatment of Metastatic, High-Risk Gestational Trophoblastic Disease," *Obstet Gynecol*, 1992, 80(5):817-20.

Variation 7:
Newlands ES, Bagshawe KD, Begent RH, et al, "Results With the EMA/CO (Etoposide, Methotrexate, Actinomycin D, Cyclophosphamide, Vincristine) Regimen in High-Risk Gestational Trophoblastic Tumours, 1979 to 1989," *Br J Obstet Gynaecol*, 1991, 98(6):550-7.

Variation 8:

Bolis G, Bonazzi C, Landoni F, et al, "EMA/CO Regimen in High-Risk Gestational Trophoblastic Tumor (GTT),"*Gynecol Oncol*, 1988, 31(3):439-44.

Variation 9:

Newlands ES, Bagshawe KD, Begent RH, et al, "Developments in Chemotherapy for Medium- and High-Risk Patients With Gestational Trophoblastic Tumours (1979-1984)," *Br J Obstet Gynaecol*, 1986, 93(1):63-9.

♦ **EMA/EP** *see EP/EMA on page 1203*

EP (Adenocarcinoma)

Use Adenocarcinoma, unknown primary

Regimen

Cisplatin: I.V.: 60-100 mg/m² day 1

[total dose = 60-100 mg/m²]

Etoposide: I.V.: 80-100 mg/m²/day days 1 to 3

[total dose = 240-300 mg/m²]

Repeat cycle every 21 days

References

Sulkes A, Uziely B, Isacson R, et al, "Combination Chemotherapy in Metastatic Tumors of Unknown Origin. 5-Fluorouracil, Adriamycin® and Mitomycin C for Adenocarcinomas and Adriamycin®, Vinblastine, and Mitomycin C for Anaplastic Carcinomas," *Isr J Med Sci*, 1988, 24(9-10):604-10.

EP/EMA

Index Terms EMA/EP

Use Gestational trophoblastic tumor

Regimen NOTE: Multiple variations are listed below.

Variation 1:

Etoposide: I.V.: 150 mg/m² day 1

[total dose/cycle = 150 mg/m²]

Cisplatin: I.V.: 25 mg/m² infused over 4 hours for 3 consecutive doses, day 1

[total dose/cycle = 75 mg/m²]

Alternate weekly with:

Etoposide: I.V.: 100 mg/m² day 1

[total dose/cycle = 100 mg/m²]

Methotrexate: I.V.: 300 mg/m² infused over 12 hours day 1

[total dose/cycle = 300 mg/m²]

Dactinomycin: I.V. push: 0.5 mg day 1

[total dose/cycle = 0.5 mg]

Leucovorin: Oral, I.M.: 15 mg twice daily for 2 days (start 24 hours after the start of methotrexate) days 2 and 3

[total dose/cycle = 60 mg]

Variation 2:

Dactinomycin: I.V.: 0.5 mg/day days 1 and 2

[total dose/cycle = 1 mg]

Etoposide: I.V.: 100 mg/m²/day days 1 and 2

[total dose/cycle = 200 mg/m²]

Methotrexate: I.V.: 300 mg/m² continuous infusion over 12 hours day 1

[total dose/cycle = 300 mg/m²]

Leucovorin: Oral, I.M.: 15 mg every 12 hours for 4 doses (start 24 hours after start of methotrexate) days 2 and 3

[total dose/cycle = 60 mg]

Etoposide: I.V.: 150 mg/m² day 8

[total dose/cycle = 150 mg/m²]

Cisplatin: I.V.: 75 mg/m² day 8

[total dose/cycle = 75 mg/m²]

Repeat cycle every 2 weeks

(Continued)

EP/EMA (Continued)

References
Variation 1:

Newlands ES, Bower M, Holden L, et al, "Management of Resistant Gestational Trophoblastic Tumors," *J Reprod Med*, 1998, 43(2):111-8.

Variation 2:

Newlands ES, Bagshawe KD, Begent RH, et al, "Results With the EMA/CO (Etoposide, Methotrexate, Actinomycin D, Cyclophosphamide, Vincristine) Regimen in High Risk Gestational Trophoblastic Tumours, 1979 to 1989," *J Obstet Gynaecol*, 1991, 98(6):550-7.

EP (Nonsmall Cell Lung Cancer)

Use Lung cancer, nonsmall cell

Regimen

Etoposide: I.V.: 80-120 mg/m^2/day days 1 to 3

[total dose/cycle = 240-360 mg/m^2]

Cisplatin: I.V.: 80-100 mg/m^2 day 1

[total dose/cycle = 80-100 mg/m^2]

Repeat cycle every 21-28 days

References
Goldhirsch A, Joss RA, Cavalli F, et al, "Cis-Dichlorodiammineplatinum (II) and VP 16-213 Combination Chemotherapy for Nonsmall-Cell Lung Cancer," *Med Pediatr Oncol*, 1981, 9(3):205-8.

EPOCH

Use Lymphoma, non-Hodgkin's

Regimen

Etoposide: I.V.: 50 mg/m^2/day continuous infusion days 1 to 4

[total dose/cycle = 200 mg/m^2]

Vincristine: I.V.: 0.4 mg/m^2/day continuous infusion days 1 to 4

[total dose/cycle = 1.6 mg/m^2]

Doxorubicin: I.V.: 10 mg/m^2/day continuous infusion days 1 to 4

[total dose/cycle = 40 mg/m^2]

Cyclophosphamide: I.V.: 750 mg/m^2 day 6

[total dose/cycle = 750 mg/m^2]

Prednisone: Oral: 60 mg/m^2/day days 1 to 6

[total dose/cycle = 360 mg/m^2]

Repeat cycle every 21 days

References
Wilson WH, Bryant G, Bates S, et al, "EPOCH Chemotherapy: Toxicity and Efficacy in Relapsed and Refractory Non-Hodgkin's Lymphoma," *J Clin Oncol*, 1993, 11(8):1573-82.

EP/PE

Use Lung cancer, nonsmall cell

Regimen

Etoposide: I.V.: 120 mg/m^2/day days 1 to 3

[total dose/cycle = 360 mg/m^2]

Cisplatin: I.V.: 60-120 mg/m^2 day 1

[total dose/cycle = 60-120 mg/m^2]

Repeat cycle every 21-28 days

References
Weick JK, Crowley J, Natale RB, et al, "A Randomized Trial of Five Cisplatin-Containing Treatments in Patients With Metastatic Nonsmall-Cell Lung Cancer: A Southwest Oncology Group Study," *J Clin Oncol*, 1991, 9(7):1157-62.

EP (Small Cell Lung Cancer)

Use Lung cancer, small cell

Regimen NOTE: Multiple variations are listed below.

Variation 1:

Etoposide: I.V.: 100 mg/m²/day days 1 to 3

[total dose/cycle = 300 mg/m²]

Cisplatin: I.V.: 100 mg/m² day 1

[total dose/cycle = 100 mg/m²]

Repeat cycle every 21 days

Variation 2:

Etoposide: I.V.: 80 mg/m²/day days 1 to 3

[total dose/cycle = 240 mg/m²]

Cisplatin: I.V.: 80 mg/m² day 1

[total dose/cycle = 80 mg/m²]

Repeat cycle every 21-28 days

References

Variation 1:

Goodman GE, Crowley JJ, Blasko JC, et al, "Treatment of Limited Small-Cell Lung Cancer With Etoposide and Cisplatin Alternating With Vincristine, Doxorubicin, and Cyclophosphamide Versus Concurrent Etoposide, Vincristine, Doxorubicin, and Cyclophosphamide and Chest Radiotherapy: A Southwest Oncology Group Study," *J Clin Oncol*, 1990, 8(1):39-47.

Variation 2:

Perng RP, Chen YM, Ming-Liu J, et al, "Gemcitabine Versus the Combination of Cisplatin and Etoposide in Patients With Inoperable Nonsmall Cell Lung Cancer in a Phase II Randomized Study," *J Clin Oncol*, 1997, 15(5):2097-102.

EP (Testicular Cancer)

Use Testicular cancer

Regimen NOTE: Multiple variations are listed below.

Variation 1:

Etoposide: I.V.: 100 mg/m²/day days 1 to 5

[total dose/cycle = 500 mg/m²]

Cisplatin: I.V.: 20 mg/m²/day days 1 to 5

[total dose/cycle = 100 mg/m²]

Repeat cycle every 21 days

Variation 2:

Etoposide: I.V.: 120 mg/m²/day days 1 to 3

[total dose/cycle = 360 mg/m²]

Cisplatin: I.V.: 20 mg/m²/day days 1 to 5

[total dose/cycle = 100 mg/m²]

Repeat cycle every 3 or 4 weeks

Variation 3:

Etoposide: I.V.: 120 mg/m²/day days 1, 3, and 5

[total dose/cycle = 360 mg/m²]

Cisplatin: I.V.: 20 mg/m²/day days 1 to 5

[total dose/cycle = 100 mg/m²]

Repeat cycle every 3 weeks

References

Variation 1:

Hainsworth JD, Williams SD, Einhorn LH, et al, "Successful Treatment of Resistant Germinal Neoplasms With VP-16 and Cisplatin: Results of a Southeastern Cancer Study Group Trial," *J Clin Oncol*, 1985, 3(5):666-71.

Variation 2:

Peckham MJ, Horwich A, Blackmore C, et al, "Etoposide and Cisplatin With or Without Bleomycin as First-Line Chemotherapy for Patients With Small-Volume Metastases of Testicular Nonseminoma," *Cancer Treat Rep*, 1985, 69(5):483-8.

(Continued)

EP (Testicular Cancer) (Continued)

Variation 3:
de Wit R, Stoter G, Kaye SB, et al, "Importance of Bleomycin in Combination Chemotherapy for Good-Prognosis Testicular Nonseminoma: A Randomized Study of the European Organization for Research and Treatment of Cancer Genitourinary Tract Cancer Cooperative Group," *J Clin Oncol*, 1997, 15(5):1837-43.

♦ **Erlotinib-Gemcitabine** see Gemcitabine-Erlotinib on page 1227

ESHAP

Use Lymphoma, non-Hodgkin's

Regimen NOTE: Multiple variations are listed below.

Variation 1:
Etoposide: I.V.: 40 mg/m²/day days 1 to 4
[total dose/cycle = 160 mg/m²]
Methylprednisolone: I.V.: 250-500 mg/day days 1 to 5
[total dose/cycle = 1250-2500 mg]
Cytarabine: I.V.: 2000 mg/m² day 5
[total dose/cycle = 2000 mg/m²]
Cisplatin: I.V.: 25 mg/m²/day continuous infusion days 1 to 4
[total dose/cycle = 100 mg/m²]
Repeat cycle every 21-28 days

Variation 2:
Etoposide: I.V.: 40 mg/m²/day days 1 to 4
[total dose/cycle = 160 mg/m²]
Methylprednisolone: I.V.: 500 mg/day days 1 to 5
[total dose/cycle = 2500 mg]
Cytarabine: I.V.: 2000 mg/m² day 5
[total dose/cycle = 2000 mg/m²]
Cisplatin: I.V.: 25 mg/m²/day continuous infusion days 1 to 4
[total dose/cycle = 100 mg/m²]
Repeat cycle every 21-28 days

Variation 3:
Etoposide: I.V.: 60 mg/m²/day days 1 to 4
[total dose/cycle = 240 mg/m²]
Methylprednisolone: I.V.: 500 mg/day days 1 to 4
[total dose/cycle = 2000 mg]
Cytarabine: I.V.: 2000 mg/m² day 5
[total dose/cycle = 2000 mg/m²]
Cisplatin: I.V.: 25 mg/m²/day continuous infusion days 1 to 4
[total dose/cycle = 100 mg/m²]
Repeat cycle every 21 days

References

Variation 1:
Velasquez WF, McLaughlin P, Tucker S, et al, "ESHAP - An Effective Chemotherapy Regimen in Refractory and Relapsing Lymphoma: A 4-Year Follow-up Study," *J Clin Oncol*, 1994, 12(6):1169-76.
Variation 2:
Wang WS, Chiou TJ, Liu JH, et al, "ESHAP as Salvage Therapy for Refractory Non-Hodgkin's Lymphoma: Taiwan Experience," *Jpn J Clin Oncol*, 1999, 29(1):33-7.
Variation 3:
Rodriguez MA, Cabanillas FC, Velasquez W, et al, "Results of a Salvage Treatment Program for Relapsing Lymphoma: MINE Consolidated With ESHAP," *J Clin Oncol*, 1995, 13(7):1734-41.

Estramustine + Docetaxel

Use Prostate cancer

Regimen NOTE: Multiple variations are listed on next page.

Variation 1:
    Docetaxel: I.V.: 20-80 mg/m² day 2
        [total dose/cycle = 20-80 mg/m²]
    Estramustine: Oral: 280 mg 3 times/day days 1 to 5
        [total dose/cycle = 4200 mg]
    Repeat cycle every 21 days
Variation 2:
    Docetaxel: I.V.: 20-80 mg/m² day 2
        [total dose/cycle = 20-80 mg/m²]
    Estramustine: Oral: 14 mg/kg/day days 1 to 21
        [total dose/cycle = 294 mg/kg]
    Repeat cycle every 21 days
Variation 3:
    Docetaxel: I.V.: 35 mg/m²/day days 2 and 9
        [total dose/cycle = 70 mg/m²]
    Estramustine: Oral: 420 mg 3 times/day for 4 doses, then 280 mg 3 times/
        day for 5 doses days 1, 2, 3, 8, 9, and 10
        [total dose/cycle = 6160 mg]
    Repeat cycle every 21 days
Variation 4:
    Docetaxel: I.V.: 60 mg/m² day 2 cycle 1
        [total dose/cycle = 60 mg/m²]
        followed by I.V.: 60-70 mg/m² day 2 (subsequent cycles)
        [total dose/cycle = 60-70 mg/m²]
    Estramustine: Oral: 280 mg 3 times/day days 1 to 5
        [total dose/cycle = 4200 mg]
    Repeat cycle every 21 days for up to 12 cycles

References

Variation 1:
Petrylak DP, Macarthur RB, O'Connor J, et al, "Phase I Trial of Docetaxel With Estramustine in Androgen-Independent Prostate Cancer," *J Clin Oncol*, 1999, 17(3):958-67.
Variation 2:
Kreis W, Budman DR, Fetten J, et al, "Phase I Trial of The Combination of Daily Estramustine Phosphate and Intermittent Docetaxel in Patients With Metastatic Hormone Refractory Prostate Carcinoma," *Ann Oncol*, 1999, 10(1):33-8.
Variation 3:
Sitka Copur M, Ledakis P, Lynch J, et al, "Weekly Docetaxel and Estramustine in Patients With Hormone-Refractory Prostate Cancer," *Semin Oncol*, 2001, 28(4 Suppl 15):16-21.
Variation 4:
Petrylak DP, Tangen CM, Hussain MH, et al, "Docetaxel and Estramustine Compared With Mitoxantrone and Prednisone for Advanced Refractory Prostate Cancer," *N Engl J Med*, 2004, 351(15):1513-20.

Estramustine + Docetaxel + Calcitriol

Use Prostate cancer
Regimen
Cycle 1:
    Calcitriol: Oral: 60 mcg (in divided doses) day 1
        [total dose/cycle = 60 mcg]
    Estramustine: Oral: 280 mg 3 times/day days 1 to 5
        [total dose/cycle = 4200 mg]
    Docetaxel: I.V.: 60 mg/m² day 2
        [total dose/cycle = 60 mg/m²]
    Treatment is 21 days
Subsequent cycles:
    Calcitriol: Oral: 60 mcg (in divided doses) day 1
        [total dose/cycle = 60 mcg]
(Continued)

Estramustine + Docetaxel + Calcitriol *(Continued)*

Estramustine: Oral: 280 mg 3 times/day days 1 to 5
[total dose/cycle = 4200 mg]
Docetaxel: I.V.: 70 mg/m² day 2
[total dose/cycle = 70 mg/m²]
Repeat cycle every 21 days for up to 12 cycles

References
Tiffany NM, Ryan CW, Garzotto M, et al, "High Dose Pulse Calcitriol, Docetaxel and Estramustine for Androgen Independent Prostate Cancer: A Phase I/II Study," *J Urol*, 2005, 174(3):888-92.

Estramustine + Docetaxel + Carboplatin

Use Prostate cancer

Regimen
Docetaxel: I.V.: 70 mg/m² day 2
[total dose/cycle = 70 mg/m²]
Estramustine: Oral: 280 mg 3 times/day days 1 to 5
[total dose/cycle = 4200 mg]
Carboplatin: I.V.: Target AUC 5 day 2
[total dose/cycle = AUC = 5]
Repeat cycle every 3 weeks

References
Oh WK, Halabi S, Kelly WK, et al, "A Phase II Study of Estramustine, Docetaxel, and Carboplatin (EDC) with G-CSF Support in Men With Hormone Refractory Prostate Cancer: CALGB 99813," *Proc Am Soc Clin Oncol*, 2002, 21:195a.
Oh WK, Halabi S, Kelly WK, et al, "A Phase II Study of Estramustine, Docetaxel, and Carboplatin With Granulocyte-Colony-Stimulating Factor Support in Patients With Hormone-Refractory Prostate Carcinoma: Cancer and Leukemia Group B 99813," *Cancer*, 2003, 98(12):2592-8.

Estramustine + Docetaxel + Hydrocortisone

Use Prostate cancer

Regimen
Docetaxel: I.V.: 70 mg/m² day 2
[total dose/cycle = 70 mg/m²]
Estramustine: Oral: 10 mg/kg/day days 1 to 5
[total dose/cycle = 50 mg/kg]
Hydrocortisone: Oral: 40 mg daily
[total dose/cycle = 840 mg]
Repeat cycle every 3 weeks

References
Savarese DM, Halabi S, Hars V, et al, "Phase II Study of Docetaxel, Estramustine, and Low-Dose Hydrocortisone in Men With Hormone-Refractory Prostate Cancer: A Final Report of CALGB 9780. Cancer and Leukemia Group B," *J Clin Oncol*, 2001, 19(9):2509-16.

Estramustine + Docetaxel + Prednisone

Use Prostate cancer

Regimen
Estramustine: Oral: 280 mg 3 times/day days 1 to 5 and days 7 to 11
[total dose/cycle = 8400 mg]
Docetaxel: I.V.: 70 mg/m² day 2
[total dose/cycle = 70 mg/m²]
Prednisone: Oral: 10 mg daily
[total dose/cycle = 210 mg]
Repeat cycle every 21 days for up to 6 cycles

References
Boehmer A, Anastasiadis AG, Feyerabend S, et al, "Docetaxel, Estramustine and Prednisone for Hormone-Refractory Prostate Cancer: A Single-Center Experience," *Anticancer Res*, 2005, 25(6C):4481-6.

Estramustine + Etoposide

Use Prostate cancer

Regimen NOTE: Multiple variations are listed below.

Variation 1:

Estramustine: Oral: 15 mg/kg/day days 1 to 21
[total dose/cycle = 315 mg/kg]

Etoposide: Oral: 50 mg/m^2/day days 1 to 21
[total dose/cycle = 1050 mg/m^2]

Repeat cycle every 4 weeks

Variation 2:

Estramustine: Oral: 10 mg/kg/day days 1 to 21
[total dose/cycle = 210 mg/kg]

Etoposide: Oral: 50 mg/m^2/day days 1 to 21
[total dose/cycle = 1050 mg/m^2]

Repeat cycle every 4 weeks

Variation 3:

Estramustine: Oral: 140 mg 3 times/day days 1 to 21
[total dose/cycle = 8820 mg]

Etoposide: Oral: 50 mg/m^2/day days 1 to 21
[total dose/cycle = 1050 mg/m^2]

Repeat cycle every 4 weeks

References

Variation 1:

Pienta KJ, Redman B, Hussain M, et al, "Phase II Evaluation of Oral Estramustine and Oral Etoposide in Hormone-Refractory Adenocarcinoma of the Prostate," *J Clin Oncol*, 1994, 12(10):2005-12.

Variation 2:

Pienta KJ, Redman BG, Bandekar R, et al, "A Phase II Trial of Oral Estramustine and Oral Etoposide in Hormone Refractory Prostate Cancer," *Urology*, 1997, 50(3):401-6; discussion 406-7.

Variation 3:

Dimopoulos MA, Panopoulos C, Bamia C, et al, "Oral Estramustine and Oral Etoposide for Hormone-Refractory Prostate Cancer," *Urology*, 1997, 50(5):754-8.

♦ **Estramustine + Vinblastine** see EV on page 1210

Estramustine + Vinorelbine

Use Prostate cancer

Regimen NOTE: Multiple variations are listed below.

Variation 1:

Estramustine: Oral: 140 mg 3 times/day days 1 to 14
[total dose/cycle = 5880 mg]

Vinorelbine: I.V.: 25 mg/m^2/day days 1 and 8
[total dose/cycle = 50 mg/m^2]

Repeat cycle every 21 days

Variation 2:

Estramustine: Oral: 280 mg 3 times/day days 1-3
[total dose/cycle = 2520 mg/m^2]

Vinorelbine: I.V.: 15 or 20 mg/m^2 day 2
[total dose/cycle = 15 or 20 mg/m^2]

Repeat cycle weekly for 8 weeks, then every other week

References

Variation 1:

Smith MR, Kaufman D, Oh W, et al, "Vinorelbine and Estramustine in Androgen-Independent Metastatic Prostate Cancer: A Phase II Study," *Cancer*, 2000, 89(8):1824-8.

Variation 2:

Sweeney CJ, Monaco FJ, Jung SH, et al, "A Phase II Hoosier Oncology Group Study of Vinorelbine and Estramustine Phosphate in Hormone-Refractory Prostate Cancer," *Ann Oncol*, 2002, 13(3):435-40.

EV

Index Terms Estramustine + Vinblastine

Use Prostate cancer

Regimen NOTE: Multiple variations are listed below.

Variation 1:

Estramustine: Oral: 10 mg/kg/day days 1 to 42
  [total dose/cycle = 420 mg/kg]

Vinblastine: I.V.: 4 mg/m²/day days 1, 8, 15, 22, 29, and 36
  [total dose/cycle = 24 mg/m²]

Repeat cycle every 8 weeks

Variation 2:

Estramustine: Oral: 600 mg/m²/day days 1 to 42
  [total dose/cycle = 25,200 mg/m²]

Vinblastine: I.V.: 4 mg/m²/day days 1, 8, 15, 22, 29, and 36
  [total dose/cycle = 24 mg/m²]

Repeat cycle every 8 weeks

References

Variation 1:
Seidman AD, Scher HI, Petrylak D, et al, "Estramustine and Vinblastine: Use of Prostate Specific Antigen as a Clinical Trial Endpoint for Hormone Refractory Prostatic Cancer," *J Urol*, 1992, 147(3 Pt 2):931-4.
Variation 2:
Hudes GR, Greenberg R, Krigel RL, et al, "Phase II Study of Estramustine and Vinblastine, Two Microtubule Inhibitors, in Hormone-Refractory Prostate Cancer," *J Clin Oncol*, 1992, 10(11):1754-61.

EVA

Use Lymphoma, Hodgkin's disease

Regimen

Etoposide: I.V.: 100 mg/m²/day days 1 to 3
  [total dose/cycle = 300 mg/m²]

Vinblastine: I.V.: 6 mg/m² day 1
  [total dose/cycle = 6 mg/m²]

Doxorubicin: I.V.: 50 mg/m² day 1
  [total dose/cycle = 50 mg/m²]

Repeat cycle every 28 days

References

Canellos GP, Petroni GR, Barcos M, et al, "Etoposide, Vinblastine, and Doxorubicin: An Active Regimen for the Treatment of Hodgkin's Disease in Relapse Following MOPP. Cancer and Leukemia Group B," *J Clin Oncol*, 1995, 13(8):2005-11.

♦ **F-CL** *see Fluorouracil-Leucovorin on page 1218*

FAC

Index Terms CAF-IV; IVCAF

Use Breast cancer

Regimen NOTE: Multiple variations are listed below.

Variation 1:

Fluorouracil: I.V.: 500 mg/m²/day days 1 and 8
  [total dose/cycle = 1000 mg/m²]
    or 500 mg/m² day 1
    [total dose/cycle = 500 mg/m²]

Doxorubicin: I.V.: 50 mg/m² day 1
  [total dose/cycle = 50 mg/m²]

Cyclophosphamide: I.V.: 500 mg/m² day 1
  [total dose/cycle = 500 mg/m²]

Repeat cycle every 21-28 days

Variation 2:
   Fluorouracil: I.V.: 200 mg/m²/day days 1 to 3
      [total dose/cycle = 600 mg/m²]
   Doxorubicin: I.V.: 40 mg/m² day 1
      [total dose/cycle = 40 mg/m²]
   Cyclophosphamide: I.V.: 400 mg/m² day 1
      [total dose/cycle = 400 mg/m²]
   Repeat cycle every 28 days
Variation 3:
   Fluorouracil: I.V.: 400 mg/m²/day days 1 and 8
      [total dose/cycle = 800 mg/m²]
   Doxorubicin: I.V.: 40 mg/m² day 1
      [total dose/cycle = 40 mg/m²]
   Cyclophosphamide: I.V.: 400 mg/m² day 1
      [total dose/cycle = 400 mg/m²]
   Repeat cycle every 28 days
Variation 4:
   Fluorouracil: I.V.: 600 mg/m²/day days 1 and 8
      [total dose/cycle = 1200 mg/m²]
   Doxorubicin: I.V.: 60 mg/m² day 1
      [total dose/cycle = 60 mg/m²]
   Cyclophosphamide: I.V.: 600 mg/m² day 1
      [total dose/cycle = 600 mg/m²]
   Repeat cycle every 28 days
Variation 5:
   Fluorouracil: I.V.: 300 mg/m²/day days 1 and 8
      [total dose/cycle = 600 mg/m²]
   Doxorubicin: I.V.: 30 mg/m² day 1
      [total dose/cycle = 30 mg/m²]
   Cyclophosphamide: I.V.: 300 mg/m² day 1
      [total dose/cycle = 300 mg/m²]
   Repeat cycle every 28 days

References

Variation 1:

Smalley RV, Carpenter J, Bartolucci A, et al, "A Comparison of Cyclophosphamide, Adriamycin®, 5-Fluorouracil (CAF), and Cyclophosphamide, Methotrexate, 5-Fluorouracil, Vincristine, Prednisone (CMFVP) in Patients With Metastatic Breast Cancer: A Southeastern Cancer Study Group Project," *Cancer*, 1977, 40(2):625-32.

Swenerton KD, Legha SS, Smith T, et al, "Prognostic Factors in Metastatic Breast Cancer Treated With Combination Chemotherapy," *Cancer Res*, 1979, 39(5):1552-62.

Variation 2:

Nemoto T, Horton J, Simon R, et al, "Comparison of Four-Combination Chemotherapy Programs in Metastatic Breast Cancer: Comparison of Multiple Drug Therapy With Cytoxan, 5-FU, and Prednisone, Versus Cytoxan and Adriamycin, Versus Cytoxan, 5-FU, and Adriamycin, Versus Cytoxan, 5-FU, and Prednisone Alternation With Cytoxan and Adriamycin," *Cancer*, 1982, 49(10):1988-93.

Variation 3-5:

Wood WC, Budman DR, Korzun AH, et al, "Dose and Dose Intensity of Adjuvant Chemotherapy for State II, Node-Positive Breast Carcinoma," *N Engl J Med*, 1994, 330(18):1253-9.

FAM

Use Gastric cancer; pancreatic cancer
Regimen NOTE: Multiple variations are listed below
   Variation 1:
      Fluorouracil: I.V.: 600 mg/m²/day days 1, 8, 29, and 36
         [total dose/cycle = 2400 mg/m²]
      Doxorubicin: I.V.: 30 mg/m²/day days 1 and 29
         [total dose/cycle = 60 mg/m²]
(Continued)

FAM *(Continued)*

Mitomycin: I.V.: 10 mg/m² day 1
[total dose/cycle = 10 mg/m²]
Repeat cycle every 8 weeks

Variation 2:
Fluorouracil: I.V.: 600 mg/m²/day days 29 to 32
[total dose/cycle = 2400 mg/m²]
Doxorubicin: I.V.: 50 mg/m² day 1
[total dose/cycle = 50 mg/m²]
Mitomycin: I.V.: 10 mg/m² day 3
[total dose/cycle = 10 mg/m²]
Repeat cycle every 8 weeks

Variation 3:
Fluorouracil: I.V.: 500 mg/m²/day days 1, 8, 21, and 28
[total dose/cycle = 2000 mg/m²]
Doxorubicin: I.V.: 30 mg/m²/day days 1 and 21
[total dose/cycle = 60 mg/m²]
Mitomycin: I.V.: 10 mg/m² day 1
[total dose/cycle = 10 mg/m²]
Repeat cycle every 6 weeks

Variation 4:
Fluorouracil: I.V.: 275 mg/m²/day days 1 to 5 and 36 to 40
[total dose/cycle = 2750 mg/m²]
Doxorubicin: I.V.: 30 mg/m²/day days 1 and 36
[total dose/cycle = 60 mg/m²]
Mitomycin: I.V.: 10 mg/m² day 1
[total dose/cycle = 10 mg/m²]
Repeat cycle every 10 weeks

Variation 5:
Fluorouracil: I.V.: 600 mg/m²/day days 1, 8, 22, and 29
[total dose/cycle = 2400 mg/m²]
Doxorubicin: I.V.: 30 mg/m²/day days 1 and 22
[total dose/cycle = 60 mg/m²]
Mitomycin: I.V.: 10 mg/m² day 1
[total dose/cycle = 10 mg/m²]
Repeat cycle every 6 weeks

References

Variation 1:

Cullinan SA, Moertel CG, Fleming TR, et al, "A Comparison of Three Chemotherapeutic Regimens in the Treatment of Advanced Pancreatic and Gastric Carcinoma. Fluorouracil vs Fluorouracil and Doxorubicin vs Fluorouracil, Doxorubicin, and Mitomycin," *JAMA*, 1985, 253(14):2061-7.

Preusser P, Achterrath W, Wilke H, et al, "Chemotherapy of Gastric Cancer," *Cancer Treat Rev*, 1988, 15(4):257-77.

Variation 2:

Panettiere FJ, Haas C, McDonald B, et al, "Drug Combinations in the Treatment of Gastric Adenocarcinoma: A Randomized Southwest Oncology Group Study," *J Clin Oncol*, 1984, 2(5):420-4.

Variation 3:

Bitran JD, Desser RK, Kozloff MF, et al, "Treatment of Metastatic Pancreatic and Gastric Adenocarcinomas With 5-Fluorouracil, Adriamycin, and Mitomycin C (FAM)," *Cancer Treat Rep*, 1979, 63(11-12):2049-51.

Variation 4:

"A Comparative Clinical Assessment of Combination Chemotherapy in the Management of Advanced Gastric Carcinoma: The Gastrointestinal Tumor Study Group," *Cancer*, 1982, 49(7):1362-6.

Variation 5:

Haim N, Epelbaum R, Cohen Y, et al, "Further Studies on the Treatment of Advanced Gastric Cancer by 5-Fluorouracil, Adriamycin (Doxorubicin), and Mitomycin C (Modified FAM)," *Cancer*, 1984, 54(9):1999-2002.

FAMe

Use Gastric cancer

Regimen

Fluorouracil: I.V.: 325 mg/m²/day days 1 to 5 and days 36 to 40
  [total dose/cycle = 3250 mg/m²]
Doxorubicin: I.V.: 40 mg/m² day 1 and day 36
  [total dose/cycle = 80 mg/m²]
Lomustine: Oral: 110 mg/m² day 1
  [total dose/cycle = 110 mg/m²]
Repeat cycle every 10 weeks

References

Cullinan SA, Moertel CG, Wieand HS, et al, "Controlled Evaluation of Three Drug Combination Regimens Versus Fluorouracil Alone for the Therapy of Advanced Gastric Cancer. North Central Cancer Treatment Group," *J Clin Oncol*, 1994, 12(2):412-6.

FAMTX

Use Gastric cancer

Regimen NOTE: Multiple variations are listed below.

Variation 1:

Methotrexate: I.V.: 1500 mg/m² day 1
  [total dose/cycle = 1500 mg/m²]
Fluorouracil: I.V.: 1500 mg/m² (1 hour after methotrexate) day 1
  [total dose/cycle = 1500 mg/m²]
Leucovorin: Oral: 15 mg/m² every 6 hours for 48 hours (start 24 hours after methotrexate) day 2
  [total dose/cycle = 120 mg/m²]
Doxorubicin: I.V.: 30 mg/m² day 15
  [total dose/cycle = 30 mg/m²]
Repeat cycle every 28 days

Variation 2:

Methotrexate: I.V.: 1500 mg/m² day 1
  [total dose/cycle = 1500 mg/m²]
Fluorouracil: I.V.: 1500 mg/m² (1 hour after methotrexate) day 1
  [total dose/cycle = 1500 mg/m²]
Leucovorin: Oral: 30 mg/m² every 6 hours for 8 doses (start 24 hours after methotrexate)
  [total dose/cycle = 240 mg/m²]
    followed by Oral: 30 mg/m² every 6 hours for 8 more doses if 24-hour methotrexate level ≥2.5 mol/L
    [total cumulative dose/cycle = 480 mg/m²]
Doxorubicin: I.V.: 30 mg/m² day 15
  [total dose/cycle = 30 mg/m²]
Repeat cycle every 28 days

Variation 3:

Methotrexate: I.V.: 1000 mg/m² day 1
  [total dose/cycle = 1000 mg/m²]
Fluorouracil: I.V.: 1500 mg/m² (1 hour after methotrexate) day 1
  [total dose/cycle = 1500 mg/m²]
Leucovorin: Oral: 15 mg every 6 hours for 8 doses (start 24 hours after methotrexate)
  [total dose/cycle = 120 mg/m²]
Doxorubicin: I.V.: 30 mg/m² day 15
  [total dose/cycle = 30 mg/m²]
Repeat cycle every 28 days

(Continued)

FAMTX *(Continued)*

References

Variation 1:
Kelsen D, Atiq O, Salz L, et al, "FAMTX (Fluorouracil, Methotrexate, Adriamycin®) Is as Effective and Less Toxic Than EAP (Etoposide, Adriamycin®, Cisplatin): A Random Assignment Trial in Gastric Cancer," *Proc Am Soc Clin Oncol*, 1991, 10:137.

Variation 2:
Wils J, Bleiberg H, Dalesio O, et al, "An EORTC Gastrointestinal Group Evaluation of the Combination of Sequential Methotrexate and 5-Fluorouracil, Combined With Adriamycin in Advanced Measurable Gastric Cancer," *J Clin Oncol*, 1986, 4(12):1799-803.

Variation 3:
Murad AM, Santiago FF, Petroianu A, et al, "Modified Therapy With 5-Fluorouracil, Doxorubicin, and Methotrexate in Advanced Gastric Cancer," *Cancer*, 1993, 72(1):37-41.

FAP

Use Gastric cancer

Regimen

Fluorouracil: I.V.: 300 mg/m^2/day days 1 to 5
  [total dose/cycle = 1500 mg/m^2]
Doxorubicin: I.V.: 40 mg/m^2 day 1
  [total dose/cycle = 40 mg/m^2]
Cisplatin: I.V.: 60 mg/m^2 day 1
  [total dose/cycle = 60 mg/m^2]
Repeat cycle every 5 weeks

References

Cullinan SA, Moertel CG, Wieand HS, et al, "Controlled Evaluation of Three Drug Combination Regimens Versus Fluorouracil Alone for the Therapy of Advanced Gastric Cancer. North Central Cancer Treatment Group," *J Clin Oncol*, 1994, 12(2):412-6.

♦ **FC** *see* Fludarabine-Cyclophosphamide (FC) *on page 1216*

FEC

Use Breast cancer

Regimen

Fluorouracil: I.V.: 500 mg/m^2 day 1
  [total dose/cycle = 500 mg/m^2]
Cyclophosphamide: I.V.: 500 mg/m^2 day 1
  [total dose/cycle = 500 mg/m^2]
Epirubicin: I.V.: 100 mg/m^2 day 1
  [total dose/cycle = 100 mg/m^2]
Repeat cycle every 21 days

References

Bonneterre J, Roché H, Bremond A, et al, "Results of a Randomized Trial of Adjuvant Chemotherapy With FEC 50 vs FEC 100 in High Risk Node-Positive Breast Cancer Patients," *Proc Am Soc Clin Oncol*, 1998, 17:124a (abstract 473).

FIS-HAM

Use Leukemia, acute lymphocytic; leukemia, acute myeloid

Regimen

Fludarabine: I.V.: 15 mg/m^2/day every 12 hours days 1, 2, 8, and 9
  [total dose/cycle = 120 mg/m^2]
Cytarabine: I.V.: 750 mg/m^2/day every 3 hours days 1, 2, 8, and 9
  [total dose/cycle = 24,000 mg/m^2]
Mitoxantrone: I.V.: 10 mg/m^2/day days 3, 4, 10, and 11
  [total dose/cycle = 40 mg/m^2]

References

Kern W, Schleyer E, Braess J, et al, "Efficacy of Fludarabine, Intermittent Sequential High-Dose Cytosine Arabinoside, and Mitoxantrone (FIS-HAM) Salvage Therapy in Highly Resistant Acute Leukemias," *Ann Hematol*, 2001, 80(6):334-9.

FL

Index Terms Flutamide + Leuprolide

Use Prostate cancer

Regimen NOTE: Multiple variations are listed below.

Variation 1:

Flutamide: Oral: 250 mg every 8 hours

[total dose/cycle = 21,000 mg]

Leuprolide acetate: SubQ: 1 mg/day

[total dose/cycle = 28 mg]

Repeat cycle every 28 days

Variation 2:

Flutamide: Oral: 250 mg every 8 hours

[total dose/cycle = 67,500 mg]

Leuprolide acetate depot: I.M.: 22.5 mg day 1

[total dose/cycle = 22.5 mg]

Repeat cycle every 3 months

References

Variation 1: Crawford ED, Eisenberger MA, McLeod DG, et al, "A Controlled Trial of Leuprolide With and Without Flutamide in Prostatic Carcinoma," *N Engl J Med*, 1989, 17:321(7):419-24.

Variation 2: McLeod DG, Schellhammer PF, Vogelzang NJ, et al, "Exploratory Analysis on the Effect of Race on Clinical Outcome in Patients With Advanced Prostate Cancer Receiving Bicalutamide or Flutamide, Each in Combination With LHRH Analogues. The Casodex Combination Study Group." *Prostate*, 1999, 1:40(4):218-24.

FLAG

Use Leukemia, acute myeloid

Regimen

Fludarabine: I.V.: 30 mg/m^2/day days 1 to 5

[total dose/cycle = 150 mg/m^2]

Cytarabine: I.V.: 2 g/m^2/day days 1 to 5 (3.5 hours after end of fludarabine infusion)

[total dose/cycle = 10 g/m^2]

Filgrastim: SubQ: 5 mcg/kg day 1

followed by SubQ: 300 mcg daily until ANC >500-1000 cells/mcL postnadir

[total dose/cycle = 40-7800 mcg/kg]

Repeat cycle every 3-4 weeks

References

Clavio M, Carrara P, Miglino M, et al, "High Efficacy of Fludarabine-Containing Therapy (FLAG-FLANG) in Poor Risk Acute Myeloid Leukemia," *Haematologica*, 1996, 81(6):513-20.

FLAG-IDA

Use Leukemia, acute myeloid

Regimen

Fludarabine: I.V.: 30 mg/m^2/day days 1 to 5

[total dose/cycle = 150 mg/m^2]

Cytarabine: I.V.: 2 g/m^2/day days 1 to 5

[total dose/cycle = 10 g/m^2]

Idarubicin: I.V.: 10 mg/m^2/day days 1, 2, and 3

[total dose/cycle = 30 mg/m^2]

Filgrastim: 5 mcg/kg from day 6 until neutrophil recovery

Administer one cycle only

References

Pastore D, Specchia G, Carluccio P, et al, "FLAG-IDA in the Treatment of Refractory/Relapsed Acute Myeloid Leukemia: Single-Center Experience," *Ann Hematol*, 2003, 82(4):231-5.

♦ **Flox** *see* FLOX (Nordic FLOX) *on page 1216*

FLOX (Nordic FLOX)

Index Terms Flox

Use Colorectal cancer

Regimen

Oxaliplatin: I.V.: 85 mg/m² day 1
  [total dose/cycle = 85 mg/m²]
Fluorouracil: I.V.: 500 mg/m²/day days 1 and 2
  [total dose/cycle = 1000 mg/m²]
Leucovorin: I.V.: 60 mg/m²/day days 1 and 2
  [total dose/cycle = 120 mg/m²]
Repeat cycle every 2 weeks

References

Sorbye H and Dahl O, "Nordic 5-Fluorouracil/Leucovorin Bolus Schedule Combined With Oxaliplatin (Nordic FLOX) as First-Line Treatment of Metastatic Colorectal Cancer," *Acta Oncol*, 2003, 42(8):827-31.

Fludarabine-Cyclophosphamide (FC)

Index Terms Cyclophosphamide-Fludarabine; FC

Use Leukemia, chronic lymphocytic

Regimen NOTE: Multiple variations are listed below.

Variation 1:
  Fludarabine: I.V.: 25 mg/m²/day days 1, 2, and 3
    [total dose/cycle = 75 mg/m²]
  Cyclophosphamide: I.V.: 250 mg/m²/day days 1, 2, and 3
    [total dose/cycle = 750 mg/m²]
  Repeat cycle every 4 weeks for up to 6 cycles

Variation 2:
  Fludarabine: I.V.: 30 mg/m²/day days 1, 2, and 3
    [total dose/cycle = 90 mg/m²]
  Cyclophosphamide: I.V.: 250 mg/m²/day days 1, 2, and 3
    [total dose/cycle = 750 mg/m²]
  Repeat cycle every 4 weeks for up to 6 cycles

Variation 3:
  Cyclophosphamide: I.V.: 600 mg/m² day 1 only
    [total dose/cycle = 600 mg/m²]
  Fludarabine: I.V.: 20 mg/m²/day days 1 to 5
    [total dose/cycle = 100 mg/m²]
  Repeat cycle every 4 weeks for up to 6 cycles

Variation 4:
  Fludarabine: I.V.: 30 mg/m²/day days 1, 2, and 3
    [total dose/cycle = 90 mg/m²]
  Cyclophosphamide: I.V.: 300 mg/m²/day days 1, 2, and 3
    [total dose/cycle = 900 mg/m²]
  Repeat cycle every 4 weeks for up to 6 cycles

Variation 5:
  Fludarabine: I.V.: 30 mg/m²/day days 1, 2, and 3
    [total dose/cycle = 90 mg/m²]
  Cyclophosphamide: I.V.: 300 mg/m²/day days 1, 2, and 3
    [total dose/cycle = 900 mg/m²]
  Repeat cycle every 4-6 weeks for up to 6 cycles

References

Variation 1:
Catovsky D, Richards S, Matutes E, et al, "Assessment of Fludarabine Plus Cyclophosphamide for Patients With Chronic Lymphocytic Leukaemia (The LRF CLL4 Trial): A Randomised Controlled Trial," *Lancet*, 2007, 370(9583):230-9.

O'Brien S, Moore JO, Boyd TE, et al, "Randomized Phase III Trial of Fludarabine Plus Cyclo-phosphamide With or Without Oblimersen Sodium (Bcl-2 Antisense) in Patients With Relapsed or Refractory Chronic Lymphocytic Leukemia," *J Clin Oncol*, 2007, 25(9):1114-20.

Variation 2:

Eichhorst BF, Busch R, Obwandner T, et al, "Health-Related Quality of Life in Younger Patients With Chronic Lymphocytic Leukemia Treated With Fludarabine Plus Cyclophosphamide or Fludarabine Alone for First-Line Therapy: A Study by the German CLL Study Group," *J Clin Oncol*, 2007, 25(13):1722-31.

Variation 3:

Flinn IW, Neuberg DS, Grever MR, et al, "Phase III Trial of Fludarabine Plus Cyclophosphamide Compared With Fludarabine for Patients With Previously Untreated Chronic Lymphocytic Leukemia: US Intergroup Trial E2997," *J Clin Oncol*, 2007, 25(7):793-8.

Variation 4:

Wierda W, O'Brien S, Faderl S, et al, "A Retrospective Comparison of Three Sequential Groups of Patients With Recurrent/Refractory Chronic Lymphocytic Leukemia Treated With Fludarabine-Based Regimens," *Cancer*, 2006, 106(2):337-45.

Variation 5:

O'Brien SM, Kantarjian HM, Cortes J, et al, "Results of the Fludarabine and Cyclophosphamide Combination Regimen in Chronic Lymphocytic Leukemia," *J Clin Oncol*, 2001, 19(5):1414-20.

Fludarabine-Cyclophosphamide-Rituximab

Use Leukemia, chronic lymphocytic

Regimen

Cycle 1:

Rituximab: I.V.: 375 mg/m^2 day 1

[total dose/cycle = 375 mg/m^2]

Fludarabine: I.V.: 25 mg/m^2/day days 2, 3, and 4

[total dose/cycle = 75 mg/m^2]

Cyclophosphamide: I.V.: 250 mg/m^2/day days 2, 3, and 4

[total dose/cycle = 750 mg/m^2]

Treatment cycle is 4 weeks

Cycles 2-6:

Rituximab: I.V.: 500 mg/m^2 day 1

[total dose/cycle = 500 mg/m^2]

Fludarabine: I.V.: 25 mg/m^2/day days 1, 2, and 3

[total dose/cycle = 75 mg/m^2]

Cyclophosphamide: I.V.: 250 mg/m^2/day days 1, 2, and 3

[total dose/cycle = 750 mg/m^2]

Repeat cycle every 4 weeks

References

Keating MJ, O'Brien S, Albitar M, et al, "Early Results of a Chemoimmunotherapy Regimen of Fludarabine, Cyclophosphamide, and Rituximab as Initial Therapy for Chronic Lymphocytic Leukemia," *J Clin Oncol*, 2005, 23(18):4079-88.

Fludarabine-Rituximab

Use Leukemia, chronic lymphocytic

Regimen

Rituximab: I.V.: 375 mg/m^2/day days 1 and 4 (cycle 1); day 1 (cycles 2-6)

Fludarabine: I.V.: 25 mg/m^2/day days 1 to 5

Repeat cycle every 4 weeks

References

Byrd JC, Peterson BL, Morrison VA, et al, "Randomized Phase 2 Study of Fludarabine With Concurrent vs Sequential Treatment With Rituximab in Symptomatic, Untreated Patients With B-Cell Chronic Lymphocytic Leukemia: Results From Cancer and Leukemia Group B 9712 (CALGB 9712)," *Blood*, 2003, 101(1):6-14.

Fluorouracil + Carboplatin

Use Head and neck cancer

Regimen NOTE: Multiple variations are listed on next page.

(Continued)

Fluorouracil + Carboplatin *(Continued)*

Variation 1:
    Fluorouracil: I.V.: 600 mg/m^2/day continuous infusion days 1 to 4
      [total dose/cycle = 2400 mg/m^2]
    Carboplatin: I.V.: 70 mg/m^2/day days 1 to 4
      [total dose/cycle = 280 mg/m^2]
    Repeat cycle every 3 weeks for 3 cycles

Variation 2:
    Carboplatin: I.V.: 400 mg/m^2 day 1
      [total dose/cycle = 400 mg/m^2]
    Fluorouracil: I.V.: 1000 mg/m^2/day continuous infusion days 1 to 4
      [total dose/cycle = 4000 mg/m^2]
    Repeat cycle every 28 days

References

Variation 1:
Denis F, Garaud P, Bardet E, et al, "Final Results of the 94-01 French Head and Neck Oncology and Radiotherapy Group Randomized Trial Comparing Radiotherapy Alone With Concomitant Radiochemotherapy in Advanced-Stage Oropharynx Carcinoma," *J Clin Oncol*, 2004, 22(1):69-76.

Variation 2:
Gregoire V, Beauduin M, Humblet Y, et al, "A Phase I-II Trial of Induction Chemotherapy With Carboplatin and Fluorouracil in Locally Advanced Head and Neck Squamous Cell Carcinoma: A Report From the UCL-Oncology Group, Belgium," *J Clin Oncol*, 1991, 9(8):1385-92.

Fluorouracil-Leucovorin

Index Terms F-CL; FU/Leucovorin; FU-LV

Use Colorectal cancer

Regimen NOTE: Multiple variations are listed below.

Variation 1 (Mayo Regimen):
    Fluorouracil: I.V.: 425 mg/m^2/day days 1 to 5
      [total dose/cycle = 2125 mg/m^2]
    Leucovorin: I.V.: 20 mg/m^2/day days 1 to 5
      [total dose/cycle = 100 mg/m^2]
    Repeat cycle every 28 days

Variation 2:
    Fluorouracil: I.V.: 400 mg/m^2/day days 1 to 5
      [total dose/cycle = 2000 mg/m^2]
    Leucovorin: I.V.: 20 mg/m^2/day days 1 to 5
      [total dose/cycle = 100 mg/m^2]
    Repeat cycle every 28 days

Variation 3:
    Fluorouracil: I.V.: 500 mg/m^2 day 1
      [total dose/cycle = 500 mg/m^2]
    Leucovorin: I.V.: 20 mg/m^2 (2-hour infusion) day 1
      [total dose/cycle = 20 mg/m^2]
      or 500 mg/m^2 (2-hour infusion) day 1
        [total dose/cycle = 500 mg/m^2]
    Repeat cycle weekly

Variation 4:
    Fluorouracil: I.V.: 600 mg/m^2 weekly for 6 weeks
      [total dose/cycle = 3600 mg/m^2]
    Leucovorin: I.V.: 500 mg/m^2 (3-hour infusion) weekly for 6 weeks
      [total dose/cycle = 3000 mg/m^2]
    Repeat cycle every 8 weeks

Variation 5:
    Fluorouracil: I.V.: 600 mg/m^2 weekly for 6 weeks
      [total dose/cycle = 3600 mg/m^2]

Leucovorin: I.V.: 500 mg/m^2 weekly for 6 weeks
[total dose/cycle = 3000 mg/m^2]
Repeat cycle every 8 weeks

Variation 6:
Fluorouracil: I.V.: 600 mg/m^2 weekly
[total dose/cycle = 600 mg/m^2]
Leucovorin: I.V.: 500 mg/m^2 (2-hour infusion) weekly
[total dose/cycle = 500 mg/m^2]
Repeat cycle weekly

Variation 7:
Fluorouracil: I.V.: 2600 mg/m^2 continuous infusion day 1
[total dose/cycle = 2600 mg/m^2]
Leucovorin: I.V.: 500 mg/m^2 continuous infusion day 1
[total dose/cycle = 500 mg/m^2]
Repeat cycle weekly

Variation 8:
Fluorouracil: I.V.: 2600 mg/m^2 continuous infusion day 1
[total dose/cycle = 2600 mg/m^2]
Leucovorin: I.V.: 300 mg/m^2 (maximum 500 mg) continuous infusion day 1
[total dose/cycle = 300 mg/m^2; maximum 500 mg]
Repeat cycle weekly

Variation 9:
Fluorouracil: I.V.: 2600 mg/m^2 continuous infusion once weekly for 6 weeks
[total dose/cycle = 15,600 mg/m^2]
Leucovorin: I.V.: 500 mg/m^2 weekly for 6 weeks
[total dose/cycle = 3000 mg/m^2]
Repeat cycle every 8 weeks

Variation 10:
Fluorouracil: I.V.: 2300 mg/m^2 continuous infusion day 1
[total dose/cycle = 2300 mg/m^2]
Leucovorin: I.V.: 50 mg/m^2 continuous infusion day 1
[total dose/cycle = 50 mg/m^2]
Repeat cycle weekly

Variation 11:
Fluorouracil: I.V.: 200 mg/m^2/day continuous infusion days 1 to 14
[total dose/cycle = 2800 mg/m^2]
Leucovorin: I.V.: 5 mg/m^2/day continuous infusion days 1 to 14
[total dose/cycle = 70 mg/m^2]
Repeat cycle every 28 days

Variation 12:
Cycle 1:
Fluorouracil: I.V.: 200 mg/m^2/day continuous infusion for 4 weeks
[total dose/cycle = 5600 mg/m^2]
Leucovorin: I.V.: 20 mg/m^2/day days 1, 8, 15, 22
[total dose/cycle = 80 mg/m^2]
Treatment cycle is 6 weeks
Subsequent cycles (starting week 7):
Fluorouracil: 200 mg/m^2 continuous infusion days 1 to 21
[total dose/cycle = 4200 mg/m^2]
Leucovorin: I.V.: 20 mg/m^2/day days 1, 8, and 15
[total dose/cycle = 60 mg/m^2]
Repeat cycle every 4 weeks
(Continued)

Fluorouracil-Leucovorin *(Continued)*

References

Variation 1:
Poon MA, O'Connell MJ, Moertel CG, et al, "Biochemical Modulation of Fluorouracil: Evidence of Significant Improvement of Survival and Quality of Life in Patients With Advanced Colorectal Carcinoma," *J Clin Oncol*, 1989, 7(10):1407-18.

Variation 2:
Borner MM, Castiglione M, Bacchi M, et al "The Impact of Adding Low-Dose Leucovorin to Monthly 5-Fluorouracil in Advanced Colorectal Carcinoma: Results of a Phase III Trial. Swiss Group for Clinical Cancer Research (SAKK)," *Ann Oncol*, 1998, 9(5):535-41.

Variation 3:
Jager E, Heike M, Bernhard H, et al, "Weekly High-Dose Leucovorin Versus Low-Dose Leucovorin Combined With Fluorouracil in Advanced Colorectal Cancer: Results of a Randomized Multicenter Trial. Study Group for Palliative Treatment of Metastatic Colorectal Cancer Study Protocol 1," *J Clin Oncol*, 1996, 14(8):2274-9.

Variation 4:
Leichman CG, Fleming TR, Muggia FM, et al, "Phase II Study of Fluorouracil and Its Modulation in Advanced Colorectal Cancer: A Southwest Oncology Group Study," *J Clin Oncol*, 1995, 13(6):1303-11.

Variation 5:
Buroker TR, O'Connell MJ, Wieand HS, et al, "Randomized Comparison of Two Schedules of Fluorouracil and Leucovorin in the Treatment of Advanced Colorectal Cancer," *J Clin Oncol*, 1994, 12(1):14-20.

Variation 6:
Nobile MT, Rosso R, Sertoli MR, et al, "Randomised Comparison of Weekly Bolus 5-Fluorouracil With or Without Leucovorin in Metastatic Colorectal Carcinoma," *Eur J Cancer*, 1992, 28A(11):1823-7.

Variation 7:
Ardalan B, Chua L, Tian EM, et al, "A Phase II Study of Weekly 24-Hour Infusion With High-Dose Fluorouracil With Leucovorin in Colorectal Carcinoma," *J Clin Oncol*, 1991, 9(4):625-30.

Variation 8:
Yeh KH, Cheng AL, Lin MT, et al, "A Phase II Study of Weekly 24-Hour Infusion of High-Dose 5-Fluorouracil and Leucovorin (HDFL) in the Treatment of Recurrent or Metastatic Colorectal Cancers," *Anticancer Res*, 1997, 17(5B):3867-72.

Variation 9:
Kohne CH, Schoffski P, Wilke H, et al, "Effective Biomodulation by Leucovorin of High-Dose Infusion Fluorouracil Given as a Weekly 24-Hour Infusion: Results of a Randomized Trial in Patients With Advanced Colorectal Cancer," *J Clin Oncol*, 1998, 16(2):418-26.

Variation 10:
Haas NB, Schilder RJ, Nash S, et al, "A Phase II Trial of Weekly Infusional 5-Fluorouracil in Combination With Low-Dose Leucovorin in Patients With Advanced Colorectal Cancer," *Invest New Drugs*, 1995, 13(3):229-33.

Variation 11:
Falcone A, Allegrini G, Lencioni M, et al, "Protracted Continuous Infusion of 5-Fluorouracil and Low-Dose Leucovorin in Patients With Metastatic Colorectal Cancer Resistant to 5-Fluorouracil Bolus-Based Chemotherapy: A Phase II Study," *Cancer Chemother Pharmacol*, 1999, 44(2):159-63.

Variation 12:
Leichman CG, Leichman L, Spears CP, et al, "Prolonged Continuous Infusion of Fluorouracil With Weekly Bolus Leucovorin: A Phase II Study in Patients With Disseminated Colorectal Cancer," *J Natl Cancer Inst*, 1993, 85(1):41-4.

♦ **Fluorouracil-Leucovorin-Bevacizumab** *see* Bevacizumab-Fluorouracil-Leucovorin *on page 1151*

♦ **Fluorouracil-Leucovorin-Irinotecan** *see* FU-LV-CPT-11 *on page 1223*

Fluorouracil-Leucovorin-Irinotecan (Saltz Regimen)

Index Terms FU-LV-CPT-11 (Saltz Regimen); Irinotecan-Fluorouracil-Leucovorin (Saltz Regimen); Saltz Regimen

Use Colorectal cancer

Regimen

Fluorouracil: I.V.: 500 mg/m^2/day days 1, 8, 15, and 22
[total dose/cycle = 2000 mg/m^2]

Leucovorin: I.V.: 20 mg/m^2/day days 1, 8, 15, and 22
[total dose/cycle = 80 mg/m^2]
Irinotecan: I.V.: 125 mg/m^2/day days 1, 8, 15, and 22
[total dose/cycle = 500 mg/m^2]
Repeat cycle every 42 days

References

Saltz LB, Cox JV, Blanke C, et al, "Irinotecan Plus Fluorouracil and Leucovorin for Metastatic Colorectal Cancer, Irinotecan Study Group," *N Engl J Med*, 2000, 343(13):905-14.

♦ **Flutamide + Goserelin** see FZ on page 1224
♦ **Flutamide + Leuprolide** see FL on page 1215
♦ **FNC** see CNF on page 1179

FOIL

Use Colorectal cancer

Regimen

Irinotecan: I.V.: 175 mg/m^2 day 1
[total dose/cycle = 175 mg/m^2]
Oxaliplatin: I.V.: 100 mg/m^2 day 1
[total dose/cycle = 100 mg/m^2]
Leucovorin: I.V.: 200 mg/m^2 day 1
[total dose/cycle = 200 mg/m^2]
Fluorouracil: I.V.: 3800 mg/m^2/day continuous infusion days 1 and 2
[total dose/cycle = 7600 mg/m^2]
Repeat cycle every 14 days

References

Falcone A, Masi G, Allegrini G, et al, "Biweekly Chemotherapy With Oxaliplatin, Irinotecan, Infusional Fluorouracil, and Leucovorin: A Pilot Study in Patients With Metastatic Colorectal Cancer," *J Clin Oncol*, 2002, 20(19):4006-14.

FOLFOX 1

Use Colorectal cancer

Regimen

Oxaliplatin: I.V.: 130 mg/m^2 day 1 (every other cycle)
[total dose/cycle = 130 mg/m^2]
Leucovorin: I.V.: 500 mg/m^2/day days 1 and 2
[total dose/cycle = 1000 mg/m^2]
Fluorouracil: I.V.: 1.5-2 g/m^2/day continuous infusion days 1 and 2
[total dose/cycle = 3-4 g/m^2]
Repeat cycle every 14 days

References

de Gramont A, Tournigand C, Louvet C, et al, "Oxaliplatin, Folinic Acid, and 5-Fluorouracil (Folfox) in Pretreated Patients With Metastatic Advanced Cancer, The GERCOD," *Rev Med Interne*, 1997, 18(10):769-75.

FOLFOX 2

Use Colorectal cancer

Regimen

Oxaliplatin: I.V.: 100 mg/m^2 day 1
[total dose/cycle = 100 mg/m^2]
Leucovorin: I.V.: 500 mg/m^2/day days 1 and 2
[total dose/cycle = 1000 mg/m^2]
Fluorouracil: I.V.: 1.5-2 g/m^2/day continuous infusion days 1 and 2
[total dose/cycle = 3-4 g/m^2]
Repeat cycle every 14 days

References

de Gramont A, Vignoud J, Tournigand C, et al, "Oxaliplatin With High-Dose Leucovorin and 5-Fluorouracil 48-Hour Continuous Infusion in Pretreated Metastatic Colorectal Cancer," *Eur J Cancer*, 1997, 33(2):214-9.

FOLFOX 3

Use Colorectal cancer

Regimen

Oxaliplatin: I.V.: 85 mg/m² day 1
  [total dose/cycle = 85 mg/m²]

Leucovorin: I.V.: 500 mg/m²/day days 1 and 2
  [total dose/cycle = 1000 mg/m²]

Fluorouracil: I.V.: 1.5-2 g/m²/day continuous infusion days 1 and 2
  [total dose/cycle = 3-4 g/m²]

Repeat cycle every 14 days

References

de Gramont A, Tournigand C, Louvet C, et al, "Oxaliplatin, Folinic Acid, and 5-Fluorouracil (Folfox) in Pretreated Patients With Metastatic Advanced Cancer, The GERCOD," *Rev Med Interne*, 1997, 18(10):769-75.

FOLFOX 4

Use Colorectal cancer

Regimen

Oxaliplatin: I.V.: 85 mg/m² day 1
  [total dose/cycle = 85 mg/m²]

Leucovorin: I.V.: 200 mg/m²/day days 1 and 2
  [total dose/cycle = 400 mg/m²]

Fluorouracil: I.V. bolus: 400 mg/m²/day days 1 and 2
  [total dose/cycle = 800 mg/m²]
    followed by I.V.: 600 mg/m² continuous infusion (over 22 hours) days 1 and 2
    [total dose/cycle = 1200 mg/m²]

Note: Bolus fluorouracil and continuous infusion are both given on each day.

Repeat cycle every 14 days

References

André T, Bensmaine MA, Louvet C, et al, "Multicenter Phase II Study of Bimonthly High-Dose Leucovorin, Fluorouracil Infusion, and Oxaliplatin for Metastatic Colorectal Cancer Resistant to the Same Leucovorin and Fluorouracil Regimen," *J Clin Oncol*, 1999, 17(11):3560-8.

FOLFOX 6

Use Colorectal cancer

Regimen

Oxaliplatin: I.V.: 100 mg/m² day 1
  [total dose/cycle = 100 mg/m²]

Leucovorin: I.V.: 400 mg/m² day 1
  [total dose/cycle = 400 mg/m²]

Fluorouracil: I.V. bolus: 400 mg/m² day 1
  [total dose/cycle = 400 mg/m²]
    followed by I.V.: 2.4-3 g/m² continuous infusion (46 hours) extending over days 1 and 2
    [total dose/cycle = 2.4-3 g/m²]

Repeat cycle every 14 days

References

Maindrault-Goebel F, Louvet C, Andre T, et al, "Oxaliplatin Added to the Simplified Bimonthly Leucovorin and 5-Fluorouracil Regimen as Second-Line Therapy for Metastatic Colorectal Cancer (FOLFOX6), GERCOR," *Eur J Cancer*, 1999, 35(9):1338-42.

FOLFOX 7

Use Colorectal cancer

Regimen

Oxaliplatin: I.V.: 130 mg/m² day 1
  [total dose/cycle = 130 mg/m²]

Leucovorin: I.V.: 400 mg/m² day 1
[total dose/cycle = 400 mg/m²]
Fluorouracil: I.V. bolus: 400 mg/m² day 1
[total dose/cycle = 400 mg/m²]
followed by I.V.: 2.4 g/m² continuous infusion (46 hours) extending over days 1 and 2
[total dose/cycle = 2.4 g/m²]
Repeat cycle every 14 days

References
Maindrault-Goebel F, de Gramont A, Louvet C, et al, "High-Dose Intensity Oxaliplatin Added to the Simplified Bimonthly Leucovorin and 5-Fluorouracil Regimen as Second-Line Therapy for Metastatic Colorectal Cancer (FOLFOX 7)," *Eur J Cancer*, 2001, 37(8):1000-5.

♦ **FU-LV** see Fluorouracil-Leucovorin on page 1218
♦ **FU-LV-CPT-11 (Saltz Regimen)** see Fluorouracil-Leucovorin-Irinotecan (Saltz Regimen) on page 1220

FU HURT

Use Head and neck cancer
Regimen
Hydroxyurea: Oral: 1000 mg every 12 hours for 11 doses days 0 to 5
Fluorouracil: I.V.: 800 mg/m²/day continuous infusion (start AM after admission) days 1 to 5
Paclitaxel: I.V.: 5-25 mg/m²/day continuous infusion days 1 to 5
Filgrastim: SubQ: 5 mcg/kg/day days 6 to 12 (start ≥12 hours after completion of fluorouracil infusion)
5-7 cycles may be administered

References
"Induction Chemotherapy Plus Radiation Compared With Surgery Plus Radiation in Patients With Advanced Laryngeal Cancer. The Department of Veterans Affairs Laryngeal Cancer Study Group," *N Engl J Med*, 1991, 324(24):1685-90.

♦ **FU/Leucovorin** see Fluorouracil-Leucovorin on page 1218

FU-LV-CPT-11

Index Terms Fluorouracil-Leucovorin-Irinotecan; Irinotecan-Fluorouracil-Leucovorin
Use Colorectal cancer
Regimen NOTE: Multiple variations are listed below.
Variation 1:
Irinotecan: I.V.: 350 mg/m² day 1
[total dose/cycle = 350 mg/m²]
Leucovorin: I.V.: 20 mg/m²/day days 22 to 26
[total dose/cycle = 100 mg/m²]
Fluorouracil: I.V.: 425 mg/m²/day days 22 to 26
[total dose/cycle = 2125 mg/m²]
Repeat cycle every 6 weeks
Variation 2:
Irinotecan: I.V.: 80 mg/m² day 1
[total dose/cycle = 80 mg/m²]
Fluorouracil: I.V.: 2300 mg/m² continuous infusion day 1
[total dose/cycle = 2300 mg/m²]
Leucovorin: I.V.: 500 mg/m² day 1
[total dose/cycle = 500 mg/m²]
Repeat cycle weekly
or
Irinotecan: I.V.: 180 mg/m² day 1
[total dose/cycle = 180 mg/m²]
(Continued)

FU-LV-CPT-11 *(Continued)*

Leucovorin: I.V.: 200 mg/m^2/day days 1 and 2
[total dose/cycle = 400 mg/m^2]
Fluorouracil: I.V.: 400 mg/m^2/day days 1 and 2
[total dose/cycle = 800 mg/m^2]
followed by I.V.: 600 mg/m^2/day continuous infusion days 1 and 2
[total dose/cycle = 1200 mg/m^2]
Repeat cycle every 2 weeks
Variation 3:
Irinotecan: I.V.: 175 mg/m^2 day 1
[total dose/cycle = 175 mg/m^2]
Leucovorin: I.V.: 250 mg/m^2 day 2
[total dose/cycle = 250 mg/m^2]
Fluorouracil: I.V.: 950 mg/m^2 day 2
[total dose/cycle = 950 mg/m^2]
or
Irinotecan: I.V.: 200 mg/m^2 day 1
[total dose/cycle = 200 mg/m^2]
Leucovorin: I.V.: 250 mg/m^2 day 2
[total dose/cycle = 250 mg/m^2]
Fluorouracil: I.V.: 850 mg/m^2 day 2
[total dose/cycle = 850 mg/m^2]
Repeat cycle every other week

References

Variation 1:
Van Cutsem E, Pozzo C, Starkhammar H, et al, "A Phase II Study of Irinotecan Alternated With Five Days Bolus of 5-Fluorouracil and Leucovorin in First-Line Chemotherapy of Metastatic Colorectal Cancer," *Ann Oncol*, 1998, 9(11):1199-204.
Variation 2:
Douillard JY, Cunningham D, Roth AD, et al, "Irinotecan Combined With Fluorouracil Compared With Fluorouracil Alone as First-Line Treatment for Metastatic Colorectal Cancer: A Multicentre Randomised Trial," *Lancet*, 2000, 355(9209):1041-7.
Variation 3:
Comella P, Casaretti F, De Vita F, et al, "Concurrent Irinotecan and 5-Fluorouracil Plus Levo-Folinic Acid Given Every Other Week in the First-Line Management of Advanced Colorectal Carcinoma: A Phase I Study of the Southern Italy Cooperative Oncology Group," *Ann Oncol*, 1999, 10(8):915-21.

FUP

Use Gastric cancer

Regimen
Fluorouracil: I.V.: 1000 mg/m^2/day continuous infusion days 1 to 5
[total dose/cycle = 5000 mg/m^2]
Cisplatin: I.V.: 100 mg/m^2 day 2
[total dose/cycle = 100 mg/m^2]
Repeat cycle every 28 days

References

Vanhoefer U, Rougier P, Wilke H, et al, "Final Results of a Randomized Phase III Trial of Sequential High-Dose Methotrexate, Fluorouracil, and Doxorubicin Versus Etoposide, Leucovorin, and Fluorouracil Versus Infusional Fluorouracil and Cisplatin in Advanced Gastric Cancer: A Trial of the European Organization for Research and Treatment of Cancer Gastrointestinal Tract Cancer Cooperative Group," *J Clin Oncol*, 2000, 18(14):2648-57.

FZ

Index Terms Flutamide + Goserelin
Use Prostate cancer
Regimen NOTE: Multiple variations are listed on next page.

Variation 1:
Flutamide: Oral: 250 mg every 8 hours
[total dose/cycle = 21,000 mg]
Goserelin acetate: SubQ: 3.6 mg day 1
[total dose/cycle = 3.6 mg]
Repeat cycle every 28 days
Variation 2:
Flutamide: Oral: 250 mg every 8 hours
[total dose/cycle = 67,500 mg]
Goserelin acetate: SubQ: 10.8 mg day 1
[total dose/cycle = 10.8 mg]
Repeat cycle every 3 months

References

McLeod DG, Schellhammer PF, Vogelzang NJ, et al, "Exploratory Analysis on the Effect of Race on Clinical Outcome in Patients With Advanced Prostate Cancer Receiving Bicalutamide or Flutamide, Each in Combination With LHRH Analogues. The Casodex Combination Study Group," *Prostate*, 1999, 40(4):218-24.

GC

Use Lung cancer, nonsmall cell
Regimen
Gemcitabine: I.V.: 1000 mg/m^2/day days 1, 8, and 15
[total dose/cycle = 3000 mg/m^2]
Cisplatin: I.V.: 100 mg/m^2 day 1 **or** 2 **or** 15
[total dose/cycle = 100 mg/m^2]
Repeat cycle every 28 days for 2-6 cycles

References

Comella P, Frasci G, Panza N, et al, "Randomized Trial Comparing Cisplatin, Gemcitabine, and Vinorelbine With Either Cisplatin and Gemcitabine or Cisplatin and Vinorelbine in Advanced Nonsmall-Cell Lung Cancer: Interim Analysis of a Phase III Trial of the Southern Italy Cooperative Oncology Group," *J Clin Oncol*, 2000, 18(7):1451-7.

Sandler AB, Nemunaitis J, Denham C, et al, "Phase III Trial of Gemcitabine Plus Cisplatin Versus Cisplatin Alone in Patients With Locally Advanced or Metastatic Nonsmall-Cell Lung Cancer," *J Clin Oncol*, 2000, 18(1):122-30.

Gemcitabine-Capecitabine

Use Biliary adenocarcinoma; pancreatic cancer
Regimen
Gemcitabine: I.V.: 1000 mg/m^2/day days 1 and 8
[total dose/cycle = 2000 mg/m^2]
Capecitabine: Oral: 650 mg/m^2 twice daily days 1 to 14
[total dose/cycle = 18,200 mg/m^2]
Repeat cycle every 21 days

References

Hess V, Salzberg M, Borner M, et al, "Combining Capecitabine and Gemcitabine in Patients With Advanced Pancreatic Carcinoma: A Phase I/II Trial," *J Clin Oncol*, 2003, 21(1):66-8.

Knox JJ, Hedley D, Oza A, et al, "Combining Gemcitabine and Capecitabine in Patients With Advanced Biliary Cancer: A Phase II Trial," *J Clin Oncol*, 2005, 23(10):2332-8.

Gemcitabine-Carboplatin (Bladder Cancer)

Use Bladder cancer
Regimen
Gemcitabine: I.V.: 1000 mg/m^2/day days 1 and 8
[total dose/cycle = 2000 mg/m^2]
Carboplatin: I.V.: AUC 5 day 1
[total dose/cycle = AUC = 5]
Repeat cycle every 21 days for up to 6 cycles
(Continued)

Gemcitabine-Carboplatin (Bladder Cancer)

(Continued)

References

Bamias A, Moulopoulos LA, Koutras A, et al, "The Combination of Gemcitabine and Carboplatin as First-Line Treatment in Patients With Advanced Urothelial Carcinoma. A Phase II Study of the Hellenic Cooperative Oncology Group," *Cancer*, 2006, 106(2):297-303.

Gemcitabine-Carboplatin (Nonsmall Cell Lung Cancer)

Use Lung cancer, nonsmall cell

Regimen

Gemcitabine: I.V.: 1000 or 1100 mg/m^2/day days 1 and 8

[total dose/cycle = 2000 or 2200 mg/m^2]

Carboplatin: I.V.: AUC 5 day 8

[total dose/cycle = AUC = 5]

Repeat cycle every 28 days

References

Iaffaioli RV, Tortoriello A, Facchini G, et al, "Phase I-II Study of Gemcitabine and Carboplatin in Stage IIIB-IV Nonsmall-Cell Lung Cancer," *J Clin Oncol*, 1999, 17(3):921-6.

Gemcitabine-Carboplatin (Ovarian Cancer)

Use Ovarian cancer

Regimen

Gemcitabine: I.V.: 1000 mg/m^2/day days 1 and 8

[total dose/cycle = 2000 mg/m^2]

Carboplatin: I.V.: AUC 4 day 1

[total dose/cycle = AUC = 4]

Repeat cycle every 21 days for 6-10 cycles

References

Pfisterer J, Plante M, Vergote I, et al, "Gemcitabine Plus Carboplatin Compared With Carboplatin in Patients With Platinum-Sensitive Recurrent Ovarian Cancer: An Intergroup Trial of the AGO-OVAR, the NCIC CTG, and the EORTC GCG," *J Clin Oncol*, 2006, 24(29):4699-707.

Gemcitabine-Cisplatin (Bladder Cancer)

Use Bladder cancer

Regimen

Gemcitabine: I.V.: 1000 mg/m^2/day days 1, 8, and 15

[total dose/cycle = 3000 mg/m^2]

Cisplatin: I.V.: 70 mg/m^2 day 2

[total dose/cycle = 70 mg/m^2]

Repeat cycle every 28 days for 6 cycles

References

von der Maase H, Hansen SW, Roberts JT, et al, "Gemcitabine and Cisplatin Versus Methotrexate, Vinblastine, Doxorubicin, and Cisplatin in Advanced or Metastatic Bladder Cancer: Results of a Large, Randomized, Multinational, Multicenter, Phase III Study," *J Clin Oncol*, 2000, 18(17):3068-77.

Gemcitabine-Cisplatin (Lung Cancer)

Use Lung cancer, nonsmall cell

Regimen NOTE: Multiple variations are listed below.

Variation 1:

Gemcitabine: I.V.: 1000-1200 mg/m^2/day days 1, 8, and 15

[total dose/cycle = 3000-3600 mg/m^2]

Cisplatin: I.V.: 100 mg/m^2 day 2 **or** 15

[total dose/cycle = 100 mg/m^2]

Repeat cycle every 28 days

Variation 2:

Gemcitabine: I.V.: 1000-1200 mg/m²/day days 1, 8, and 15
[total dose/cycle = 3000-3600 mg/m²]

Cisplatin: I.V.: 100 mg/m² day 1 **or** 2 **or** 15
[total dose/cycle = 100 mg/m²]

Repeat cycle every 28 days

References

Variation 1:

Abratt RP, Bezwoda WR, Goedhals L, et al, "Weekly Gemcitabine With Monthly Cisplatin: Effective Chemotherapy for Advanced Nonsmall-Cell Lung Cancer," *J Clin Oncol*, 1997, 15(2):744-9.

Crino L, Scagliotti G, Marangolo M, et al, "Cisplatin-Gemcitabine Combination in Advanced Nonsmall-Cell Lung Cancer: A Phase II Study," *J Clin Oncol*, 1997, 15(1):297-303.

Variation 2:

Anton A, Diaz-Fernandez N, Gonzalez Larriba JL, et al, "Phase II Trial Assessing the Combination of Gemcitabine and Cisplatin in Advanced Non-Small Cell Lung Cancer (NSCLC)," *Lung Cancer*, 1998, 22(2):139-48.

Gemcitabine-Docetaxel (Bladder Cancer)

Use Bladder cancer

Regimen

Docetaxel: I.V.: 40 mg/m²/day days 1 and 8
[total dose/cycle = 80 mg/m²]

Gemcitabine: 800 mg/m²/day days 1 and 8
[total dose/cycle = 1600 mg/m²]

Repeat cycle every 21 days for up to 6 cycles

References

Dreicer R, Manola J, Schneider DJ, et al, "Phase II Trial of Gemcitabine and Docetaxel in Patients With Advanced Carcinoma of the Urothelium: A Trial of the Eastern Cooperative Oncology Group," *Cancer*, 2003, 97(11):2743-7.

Gemcitabine-Docetaxel (Sarcoma)

Use Osteosarcoma; soft tissue sarcoma

Regimen

Gemcitabine: I.V.: 675 mg/m²/day days 1 and 8
[total dose/cycle = 1350 mg/m²]

Docetaxel: I.V.: 100 mg/m² day 8
[total dose/cycle = 100 mg/m²]

Repeat cycle every 21 days

References

Leu KM, Ostruszka LJ, Shewach D, et al, "Laboratory and Clinical Evidence of Synergistic Cytotoxicity of Sequential Treatment With Gemcitabine Followed by Docetaxel in the Treatment of Sarcoma," *J Clin Oncol*, 2004, 22(9):1706-12.

Gemcitabine-Erlotinib

Index Terms Erlotinib-Gemcitabine

Use Pancreatic cancer

Regimen

Cycle 1:

Gemcitabine: I.V.: 1000 mg/m²/day days 1, 8, 15, 22, 29, 36, and 43 (cycle 1 only)
[total dose/cycle 1 = 7000 mg/m²]

Erlotinib: Oral: 100 mg once daily days 1 to 56
[total dose/cycle 1 = 5600 mg]

Treatment cycle is 56 days

Subsequent cycles:

Gemcitabine: I.V.: 1000 mg/m²/day days 1, 8, and 15
[total dose/cycle = 3000 mg/m²]

(Continued)

Gemcitabine-Erlotinib *(Continued)*

Erlotinib: Oral: 100 mg once daily days 1 to 28
[total dose/cycle = 2800 mg]
Repeat cycle every 28 days

References
Moore MJ, Goldstein D, Hamm J, et al, "Erlotinib Plus Gemcitabine Compared With Gemcitabine Alone in Patients With Advanced Pancreatic Cancer: A Phase III Trial of the National Cancer Institute of Canada Clinical Trials Group," *J Clin Oncol*, 2007, 25(15):1960-6.

Gemcitabine-Irinotecan

Index Terms Irinotecan-Gemcitabine

Use Pancreatic cancer

Regimen
Gemcitabine: I.V.: 1000 mg/m^2/day days 1 and 8
[total dose/cycle = 2000 mg/m^2]
Irinotecan: I.V.: 100 mg/m^2/day days 1 and 8
[total dose/cycle = 200 mg/m^2]
Repeat cycle 21 days

References
Rocha Lima CM, Savarese D, Bruckner H, et al, "Irinotecan Plus Gemcitabine Induces Both Radiographic and CA 19-9 Tumor Marker Responses in Patients With Previously Untreated Advanced Pancreatic Cancer," *J Clin Oncol*, 2002, 20(5):1182-91.

Gemcitabine-Paclitaxel

Use Ovarian cancer

Regimen
Paclitaxel: I.V.: 80 mg/m^2 infused over 60 minutes days 1, 8, and 15
[total dose/cycle = 240 mg/m^2]
Gemcitabine: I.V.: 1000 mg/m^2/day (start at end of paclitaxel infusion) days 1, 8, and 15
[total dose/cycle = 3000 mg/m^2]
Repeat cycle every 4 weeks

References
Garcia AA, O'Meara A, Bahador A, et al, "Phase II Study of Gemcitabine and Weekly Paclitaxel in Recurrent Platinum-Resistant Ovarian Cancer," *Gynecol Oncol*, 2004, 93(2):493-8.

♦ **Gemcitabine-Paclitaxel** *see* Paclitaxel-Gemcitabine *on page 1265*

Gemcitabine-Vinorelbine

Use Lung cancer, nonsmall cell

Regimen NOTE: Multiple variations are listed below.
Variation 1:
Gemcitabine: I.V.: 1200 mg/m^2/day days 1 and 8
[total dose/cycle = 2400 mg/m^2]
Vinorelbine: I.V.: 30 mg/m^2/day days 1 and 8
[total dose/cycle = 60 mg/m^2]
Repeat cycle every 21 days for 6 cycles
Variation 2:
Gemcitabine: I.V.: 1000 mg/m^2/day days 1, 8, and 15
[total dose/cycle = 3000 mg/m^2]
Vinorelbine: I.V.: 20 mg/m^2/day days 1, 8, and 15
[total dose/cycle = 60 mg/m^2]
Repeat cycle every 28 days for 6 cycles

References
Variation 1 and 2:
Frasci G, Lorusso V, Panza N, et al, "Gemcitabine Plus Vinorelbine vs Vinorelbine Alone in Elderly Patients With Advanced Nonsmall Cell Lung Cancer," *J Clin Oncol*, 2000, 18(13):2529-36.

Hainsworth JD, Burris HA 3rd, Litchy S, et al, "Gemcitabine and Vinorelbine in the Second-Line Treatment of Nonsmall Cell Lung Carcinoma Patients: A Minnie Pearl Cancer Research Network Phase II Trial," *Cancer*, 2000, 88(6):1353-8.

GEMOX

Use Biliary adenocarcinoma

Regimen

Gemcitabine: I.V.: 1000 mg/m^2 day 1
[total dose/cycle = 1000 mg/m^2]
Oxaliplatin: I.V.: 100 mg/m^2 day 2
[total dose/cycle = 100 mg/m^2]
Repeat cycle every 2 weeks

References

Andre T, Tournigand C, Rosmorduc O, et al, "Gemcitabine Combined With Oxaliplatin (GEMOX) in Advanced Biliary Tract Adenocarcinoma: A GERCOR Study," *Ann Oncol*, 2004, 15(9):1339-43.

HDMTX

Use Osteosarcoma

Regimen

Methotrexate: I.V.: 12 g/m^2/week for 2-12 weeks
[total dose/cycle = 24-144 g/m^2]
Leucovorin calcium rescue: Oral, I.V.: 15 mg/m^2 every 6 hours (beginning 30 hours after the beginning of the 4-hour methotrexate infusion) for 10 doses; **serum methotrexate levels must be monitored**
[total dose/cycle = 150 mg/m^2]

References

Camitta BM and Holcenberg JS, "Safety of Delayed Leucovorin "Rescue" Following High-Dose Methotrexate in Children," *Med Pediatr Oncol*, 1978, 5(1):55-9.

HIPE-IVAD

Use Neuroblastoma

Regimen

Cisplatin: I.V.: 40 mg/m^2/day days 1 to 5
[total dose/cycle = 200 mg/m^2]
Etoposide: I.V.: 100 mg/m^2/day days 1 to 5
[total dose/cycle = 500 mg/m^2]
Ifosfamide: I.V.: 3 g/m^2/day days 21 to 23
[total dose/cycle = 9 g/m^2]
Mesna: I.V.: 3 g/m^2/day continuous infusion days 21 to 23
[total dose/cycle = 9 g/m^2]
Vincristine: I.V.: 1.5 mg/m^2 day 21
[total dose/cycle = 1.5 mg/m^2]
Doxorubicin: I.V.: 60 mg/m^2 day 23
[total dose/cycle = 60 mg/m^2]
Repeat cycle every 28 days

References

Pinkerton CR, Zucker JM, Hartmann O, et al, "Short Duration, High Dose, Alternating Chemotherapy in Metastatic Neuroblastoma. (ENSG 3C Induction Regimen). The European Neuroblastoma Study Group," *Br J Cancer*, 1990, 62(2):319-23.

Hyper-CVAD + Imatinib

Use Leukemia, acute lymphocytic

Regimen

Cycle A: (Cycles 1, 3, 5, and 7)
Imatinib: Oral: 400 mg/day days 1 to 14
[total dose/cycle = 5600 mg]
(Continued)

Hyper-CVAD + Imatinib *(Continued)*

Cyclophosphamide: I.V.: 300 mg/m² every 12 hours, for 6 doses, days 1, 2, and 3
[total dose/cycle = 1800 mg/m²]

Mesna: I.V.: 600 mg/m²/day continuous infusion days 1, 2, and 3
[total dose/cycle = 1800 mg/m²]

Vincristine: I.V.: 2 mg/day days 4 and 11
[total dose/cycle = 4 mg]

Doxorubicin: I.V.: 50 mg/m²/day continuous infusion day 4
[total dose/cycle = 50 mg/m²]

Dexamethasone: Oral, I.V.: 40 mg/day days 1, 2, 3, 4, 11, 12, 13, and 14
[total dose/cycle = 320 mg]

Cycle B: (Cycles 2, 4, 6, and 8)

Imatinib: Oral: 400 mg/day days 1 to 14
[total dose/cycle = 5600 mg]

Methotrexate: I.V.: 1 g/m²/day continuous infusion day 1
[total dose/cycle = 1 g/m²]

Leucovorin: I.V.: 50 mg then 15 mg every 6 hours, for 8 doses (start 12 hours after the end of the methotrexate infusion)
[total dose/cycle = 170 mg]

Cytarabine: I.V.: 3 g/m² every 12 hours for 4 doses, days 2 and 3
[total dose/cycle = 12 g/m²]

Repeat every 6 weeks in the following sequence: ABABABAB

CNS Prophylaxis

Methotrexate: I.T.: 12 mg/day day 2
[total dose/cycle = 12 mg/day]

or 6 mg into Ommaya day 2
[total dose/cycle = 6 mg/day]

Cytarabine: I.T.: 100 mg/day day 7 or 8
[total dose/cycle = 100 mg/day]

Repeat cycle every 3 weeks for 3 or 4 cycles

Maintenance (POMP)

Imatinib: Oral: 600 mg/day
[total dose/cycle = 18,000 mg]

Vincristine: I.V.: 2 mg/day day 1
[total dose/cycle = 2 mg]

Prednisone: Oral: 200 mg/day days 1 to 5
[total dose/cycle = 1000 mg/m²]

Repeat cycle every month (except months 6 and 13) for 13 months

Intensification

Imatinib: Oral: 400 mg/day days 1 to 14
[total dose/cycle = 5600 mg]

Cyclophosphamide: I.V.: 300 mg/m² every 12 hours, for 6 doses, days 1, 2, and 3
[total dose/cycle = 1800 mg/m²]

Mesna: I.V.: 600 mg/m²/day continuous infusion days 1, 2, and 3
[total dose/cycle = 1800 mg/m²]

Vincristine: I.V.: 2 mg/day days 4 and 11
[total dose/cycle = 4 mg]

Doxorubicin: 50 mg/m²/day continuous infusion day 4
[total dose/cycle = 50 mg/m²]

Dexamethasone: I.V. or Oral: 40 mg/day days 1, 2, 3, 4, 11, 12, 13, and 14
[total dose/cycle = 320 mg]

Cycle is given in months 6 and 13 during maintenance

References

Thomas DA, Faderl S, Cortes J, et al, "Treatment of Philadelphia Chromosome-Positive Acute Lymphocytic Leukemia With Hyper-CVAD and Imatinib Mesylate," *Blood*, 2004, 103(12):4396-407.

Hyper-CVAD (Leukemia, Acute Lymphocytic)

Use

Leukemia, acute lymphocytic

Regimen NOTE: Multiple variations are listed below.

Variation 1:

Cycle A: (Cycles 1, 3, 5, and 7)

Cyclophosphamide: I.V.: 300 mg/m^2 every 12 hours, for 6 doses, days 1, 2, and 3

[total dose/cycle = 1800 mg/m^2]

Mesna: I.V.: 1200 mg/m^2/day continuous infusion days 1, 2, and 3

[total dose/cycle = 3600 mg/m^2]

Vincristine: I.V.: 2 mg/day days 4 and 11

[total dose/cycle = 4 mg]

Doxorubicin: I.V.: 50 mg/m^2 day 4

[total dose/cycle = 50 mg/m^2]

Dexamethasone: (route not specified): 40 mg/day days 1, 2, 3, 4, 11, 12, 13, and 14

[total dose/cycle = 320 mg]

Cycle B: (Cycles 2, 4, 6, and 8)

Methotrexate: I.V.: 1 g/m^2 continuous infusion day 1

[total dose/cycle = 1g/m^2]

Leucovorin: (route not specified): 15 mg every 6 hours, for 8 doses (start 12 hours after end of methotrexate infusion)

[total dose/cycle = 120 mg]

Cytarabine: I.V.: 3 g/m^2 every 12 hours, for 4 doses, days 2 and 3

[total dose/cycle = 12 g/m^2]

Methylprednisolone: I.V.: 50 mg twice daily, for 6 doses, days 1, 2, and 3

[total dose/cycle = 300 mg/m^2]

Repeat every 6 weeks in the following sequence: ABABABAB

CNS Prophylaxis

Methotrexate: I.T.: 12 mg/day day 2

[total dose/cycle = 12 mg]

or 6 mg/day into Ommaya day 2

[total dose/cycle = 6 mg]

Cytarabine: I.T: 100 mg day 8

[total dose/cycle = 100 mg]

Repeat cycle every 3 weeks

Maintenance (POMP)

Mercaptopurine: Oral: 50 mg 3 times/day

[total dose/cycle = 4200-4650 mg]

Vincristine: I.V.: 2 mg day 1

[total dose/cycle = 2 mg]

Methotrexate: Oral: 20 mg/m^2/day days 1, 8, 15, and 22

[total dose/cycle = 80 mg/m^2]

Prednisone: Oral: 200 mg/day days 1 to 5

[total dose/cycle = 1000 mg/m^2]

or

Mercaptopurine: I.V.: 1 g/m^2/day days 1 to 5

[total dose/cycle = 5 g/m^2]

Vincristine: I.V.: 2 mg day 1

[total dose/cycle = 2 mg]

(Continued)

Hyper-CVAD (Leukemia, Acute Lymphocytic)
(Continued)

    Methotrexate: I.V.: 10 mg/m^2/day days 1 to 5
      [total dose/cycle = 50 mg/m^2]
    Prednisone: Oral: 200 mg/day days 1 to 5
      [total dose/cycle = 1000 mg/m^2]
    Repeat cycles every month for 2 years
Variation 2:
  Cycle A: (Cycles 1, 3, 5, and 7)
    Cyclophosphamide: I.V.: 300 mg/m^2 every 12 hours, for 6 doses, days 1, 2, and 3
      [total dose/cycle = 1800 mg/m^2]
    Mesna: I.V.: 600 mg/m^2/day continuous infusion days 1, 2, and 3
      [total dose/cycle = 1800 mg/m^2]
    Vincristine: I.V.: 2 mg/day days 4 and 11
      [total dose/cycle = 4 mg]
    Doxorubicin: I.V.: 50 mg/m^2 day 4
      [total dose/cycle = 50 mg/m^2]
    Dexamethasone: Oral, I.V.: 40 mg/day days 1, 2, 3, 4, 11, 12, 13, and 14
      [total dose/cycle = 320 mg]
  Cycle B: (Cycles 2, 4, 6, and 8)
    Methotrexate: I.V.: 1 g/m^2 continuous infusion day 1
      [total dose/cycle = 1 g/m^2]
    Leucovorin: I.V.: 50 mg (start 12 hours after end of methotrexate infusion)
      followed by I.V.: 15 mg every 6 hours, for 8 doses
        [total dose/cycle = 170 mg]
    Cytarabine: I.V.: 3 g/m^2 every 12 hours, for 4 doses, days 2 and 3
      [total dose/cycle = 12 g/m^2]
    Repeat every 6 weeks in the following sequence: ABABABAB
  CNS Prophylaxis
    Methotrexate: I.T.: 12 mg day 2
      [total dose/cycle = 12 mg]
      or 6 mg into Ommaya day 2
      [total dose/cycle = 6 mg]
    Cytarabine: I.T.: 100 mg day 7
      [total dose/cycle = 100 mg]
    Repeat cycle every 3 weeks
Variation 3:
  Cycle A: (Cycles 1, 3, 5, and 7)
    Cyclophosphamide: I.V.: 300 mg/m^2 every 12 hours, for 6 doses, days 1, 2, and 3
      [total dose/cycle = 1800 mg/m^2]
    Mesna: I.V.: 600 mg/m^2/day continuous infusion days 1, 2, and 3
      [total dose/cycle = 1800 mg/m^2]
    Vincristine: I.V.: 2 mg/day days 4 and 11
      [total dose/cycle = 4 mg]
    Doxorubicin: I.V.: 50 mg/m^2 continuous infusion day 4
      [total dose/cycle = 50 mg/m^2]
    Dexamethasone: Oral, I.V.: 40 mg/day days 1, 2, 3, 4, 11, 12, 13, and 14
      [total dose/cycle = 320 mg]
  Cycle B: (Cycles 2, 4, 6, and 8)
    Methotrexate: I.V.: 200 mg/m^2 day 1
      followed by I.V.: 800 mg/m^2 continuous infusion day 1
        [total dose/cycle = 1 g/m^2]

Leucovorin: I.V.: 50 mg (start 12 hours after end of methotrexate infusion)
followed by I.V.: 15 mg every 6 hours, for 8 doses
[total dose/cycle = 170 mg/m²]
Cytarabine: I.V.: 3 g/m² every 12 hours, for 4 doses, days 2 and 3
[total dose/cycle = 12 g/m²]
Repeat every 6 weeks in the following sequence: ABABABAB

CNS Prophylaxis
Methotrexate: I.T.: 12 mg day 2
[total dose/cycle = 12 mg]
or 6 mg into Ommaya day 2
[total dose/cycle = 6 mg]
Cytarabine: I.T.: 100 mg day 7 **or** 8
[total dose/cycle = 100 mg]
Repeat cycles every 3 weeks for 6 or 8 cycles

Maintenance (POMP)
Mercaptopurine: Oral: 50 mg 3 times/day
[total dose/cycle = 4200-4650 mg]
Vincristine: I.V.: 2 mg day 1
[total dose/cycle = 2 mg]
Methotrexate: Oral, I V: 20 mg/m²/ day days 1, 8, 15, and 22
[total dose/cycle = 80 mg/m²]
Prednisone: Oral: 200 mg/day days 1 to 5
[total dose/cycle = 1000 mg/m²]
or
Mercaptopurine: I.V.: 1 g/m²/day days 1 to 5
[total dose/cycle = 5 g/m²]
Vincristine: I.V.: 2 mg day 1
[total dose/cycle = 2 mg]
Methotrexate: I.V.: 10 mg/m² /day days 1 to 5
[total dose/cycle = 50 mg/m²]
Prednisone: Oral: 200 mg/day days 1 to 5
[total dose/cycle = 1000 mg]
Repeat cycles every month (except months 7 and 11 or 9 and 12) for 2 years

Intensification
Etoposide: I.V.: 100 mg/m²/day days 1 to 5
[total dose/cycle = 500 mg/m²]
Pegaspargase: I.V.: 2500 units/m² day 1
[total dose/cycle = 2500 units/m²]
Given during months 9 and 12 of maintenance
or
Methotrexate: I.V.: 100 mg/m²/day days 1, 8, 15, and 22
[total dose/cycle = 400 mg/m²]
Asparaginase: I.V.: 20,000 units/day days 2, 9, 16, and 23
[total dose/cycle = 80,000 units]
Given during months 7 and 11 of maintenance

Variation 4:
Cycle A: (Cycles 1, 3, 5, and 7)
Cyclophosphamide: I.V.: 300 mg/m² every 12 hours, for 6 doses, days 1, 2, and 3
[total dose/cycle = 1800 mg/m²]
Mesna: I.V.: 600 mg/m²/day continuous infusion days 1, 2, and 3
[total dose/cycle = 1800 mg/m²]
Vincristine: I.V.: 2 mg/day days 4 and 11
[total dose/cycle = 4 mg]
(Continued)

Hyper-CVAD (Leukemia, Acute Lymphocytic)
(Continued)

Doxorubicin: I.V.: 50 mg/m^{2}day 4
[total dose/cycle = 50 mg/m^2]

Dexamethasone: (route not specified): 40 mg/day days 1, 2, 3, 4, 11, 12, 13, and 14
[total dose/cycle = 320 mg]

Cycle B: (Cycles 2, 4, 6, and 8)

Methotrexate: I.V.: 200 mg/m^2 day 1
followed by I.V.: 800 mg/m^2 continuous infusion day 1
[total dose/cycle = 1 g/m^2]

Leucovorin: (route not specified): 15 mg every 6 hours, for 8 doses (start 24 hours after end of methotrexate infusion)
[total dose/cycle = 120 mg]

Cytarabine: I.V.: 3 g/m^2 every 12 hours, for 4 doses, days 2 and 3
[total dose/cycle = 12 g/m^2]

Repeat every 6 weeks in the following sequence: ABABABAB

CNS Prophylaxis

Methotrexate: I.T.: 12 mg day 2
[total dose/cycle = 12 mg]

Cytarabine: I.T.: 100 mg day 8
[total dose/cycle = 100 mg]

Repeat cycle every 3 weeks for 4 or 8 cycles

Maintenance (POMP)

Mercaptopurine: Oral: 50 mg 3 times/day
[total dose/cycle = 4200-4650 mg]

Vincristine: I.V.: 2 mg day 1
[total dose/cycle = 2 mg]

Methotrexate: Oral: 20 mg/m^2/day days 1, 8, 15, and 22
[total dose/cycle = 80 mg/m^2]

Prednisone: Oral: 200 mg/day days 1 to 5
[total dose/cycle = 1000 mg/m^2]

or

Mercaptopurine: I.V.: 1 g/m^2/day days 1 to 5
[total dose/cycle = 5 g/m^2]

Vincristine: I.V.: 2 mg day 1
[total dose/cycle = 2 mg]

Methotrexate: I.V.: 10 mg/m^2/day days 1 to 5
[total dose/cycle = 50 mg/m^2]

Prednisone: Oral: 200 mg/day days 1 to 5
[total dose/cycle = 1000 mg/m^2]

or

Interferon alfa: SubQ: 5 million units/m^2 daily
[total dose/cycle = 140-155 million units/m^2]

Cytarabine: SubQ: 10 mg daily
[total dose/cycle = 280-310 mg]

Repeat cycles every month for 2 years

Variation 5:

Cycle A: (Cycles 1, 4, 6, and 8)

Cyclophosphamide: I.V.: 300 mg/m^2 every 12 hours, for 6 doses, days 1, 2, and 3
[total dose/cycle = 1800 mg/m^2]

Mesna: I.V.: 600 mg/m^2/day continuous infusion days 1, 2, and 3
[total dose/cycle = 1800 mg/m^2]

Vincristine: I.V.: 2 mg/day days 4 and 11
  [total dose/cycle = 4 mg]
Doxorubicin: I.V.: 50 mg/m^2 continuous infusion day 4
  [total dose/cycle = 50 mg/m^2]
Dexamethasone: Oral, I.V.: 40 mg/day days 1, 2, 3, 4, 11, 12, 13, and 14
  [total dose/cycle = 320 mg]
Cycle B: (Cycles 3, 5, 7, and 9)
  Methotrexate: I.V.: 200 mg/m^2 day 1
    followed by I.V.: 800 mg/m^2/day continuous infusion day 1
    [total dose/cycle = 1 g/m^2]
  Leucovorin: I.V.: 50 mg (start 12 hours after end of methotrexate infusion)
    followed by I.V.: 15 mg every 6 hours, for 8 doses
    [total dose/cycle = 170 mg]
  Cytarabine: I.V.: 3 g/m^2 every 12 hours, for 4 doses, days 2 and 3
    [total dose/cycle = 12 g/m^2]
Cycle C: Liposomal Daunorubicin/cytarabine (Cycle 2):
  Daunorubicin, liposomal: I.V.: 150 mg/m^2/day days 1 and 2
    [total dose/cycle = 300 mg/m^2]
  Cytarabine: I.V.: 1.5 g/m^2/day continuous infusion days 1 and 2
    [total dose/cycle = 3 g/m^2]
  Prednisone: Oral: 200 mg/day days 1 to 5
    [total dose/cycle = 1000 mg]
  Administer in the following sequence: ACBABABA (Cycle C does not repeat)
CNS Prophylaxis
  Methotrexate: I.T.: 12 mg day 2
    [total dose/cycle = 12 mg]
  or 6 mg into Ommaya day 2
    [total dose/cycle = 6 mg]
  Cytarabine: I.T.: 100 mg days 7 **or** 8
    [total dose/cycle = 100 mg]
  Repeat cycle every 3 weeks for 6 or 8 cycles
Maintenance (POMP)
  Mercaptopurine: I.V.: 1 g/m^2/day days 1 to 5
    [total dose/cycle = 5 g/m^2]
  Vincristine: I.V.: 2 mg day 1
    [total dose/cycle = 2 mg]
  Methotrexate: I.V.: 10 mg/m^2/day days 1 to 5
    [total dose/cycle = 50 mg/m^2]
  Prednisone: Oral: 200 mg/day days 1 to 5
    [total dose/cycle = 1000 mg]
  Repeat cycles monthly, except months 6, 7, 18, and 19 for 3 years
Intensification
  Methotrexate: I.V.: 100 mg/m^2/day days 1, 8, 15, and 22
    [total dose/cycle = 400 mg/m^2]
  Asparaginase: I.V.: 20,000 units/day days 2, 9, 16, and 23
    [total dose/cycle = 80,000 units]
  Given during months 6 and 18 of maintenance
  Cyclophosphamide: I.V.: 300 mg/m^2 every 12 hours, for 6 doses, days 1, 2, and 3
    [total dose/cycle = 1800 mg/m^2]
  Mesna: I.V.: 600 mg/m^2/day continuous infusion days 1, 2, and 3
    [total dose/cycle = 1800 mg/m^2]
  Vincristine: I.V.: 2 mg/day days 4 and 11
    [total dose/cycle = 4 mg]
(Continued)

Hyper-CVAD (Leukemia, Acute Lymphocytic)
(Continued)

Doxorubicin: I.V.: 50 mg/m²/day continuous infusion day 4
[total dose/cycle = 50 mg/m²]

Dexamethasone: Oral, I.V.: 40 mg/day days 1, 2, 3, 4, 11, 12, 13, and 14
[total dose/cycle = 320 mg]

Given during months 7 and 19 of maintenance

References

Variation 1:

Kantarjian H, Thomas D, O'Brien S, et al, "Long-Term Follow-Up Results of Hyperfractionated Cyclophosphamide, Vincristine, Doxorubicin, and Dexamethasone (Hyper-CVAD), A Dose-Intensive Regimen, in Adult Acute Lymphocytic Leukemia," *Cancer*, 2004, 101(12):2788-2801.

Variation 2:

Thomas DA, Cortes J, O'Brien S, et al, "Hyper-CVAD Program in Burkitt's-Type Adult Acute Lymphoblastic Leukemia," *J Clin Oncol*, 1999, 17(8):2461-70.

Variation 3:

Thomas DA, O'Brien S, Cortes J, et al, "Outcome With the Hyper-CVAD Regimens in Lympho-blastic Lymphoma," *Blood*, 2004, 104(6):1624-30.

Variation 4:

Kantarjian HM, O'Brien S, Smith TL, et al, "Results of Treatment With Hyper-CVAD, A Dose-Intensive Regimen, in Adult Acute Lymphocytic Leukemia," *J Clin Oncol*, 2000, 18(3): 547-61.

Variation 5:

Thomas DA, O'Brien S, Cortes J, et al, "Outcome With the Hyper-CVAD Regimens in Lympho-blastic Lymphoma," *Blood*, 2004, 104(6):1624-30.

Hyper-CVAD (Lymphoma, non-Hodgkin's)

Use Lymphoma, non-Hodgkin's

Regimen

Cycle A: (Cycles 1, 3, 5, and 7)

Cyclophosphamide: I.V.: 300 mg/m² every 12 hours, for 6 doses, days 1, 2, and 3
[total dose/cycle = 1800 mg/m²]

Vincristine: I.V.: 2 mg/day days 4 and 11
[total dose/cycle = 4 mg]

Doxorubicin: I.V.: 25 mg/m²/day continuous infusion days 4 and 5
[total dose/cycle = 50 mg/m²]

Dexamethasone: Oral, I.V.: 40 mg/day days 1, 2, 3, 4, 11, 12, 13, and 14
[total dose/cycle = 320 mg]

Cycle B: (Cycles 2, 4, 6, and 8)

Methotrexate: I.V.: 200 mg/m² day 1

followed by I.V.: 800 mg/m² continuous infusion day 1
[total dose/cycle = 1 g/m²]

Leucovorin: Oral: 50 mg

followed by Oral: 15 mg every 6 hours, for 8 doses (start 24 hours after end of methotrexate infusion)
[total dose/cycle = 170 mg]

Cytarabine: I.V.: 3 g/m² every 12 hours, for 4 doses, days 2 and 3
[total dose/cycle = 12 g/m²]

Repeat every 6 weeks in the following sequence: ABABABAB

References

Khouri IF, Romaguera J, Kantarjian H, et al, "Hyper-CVAD and High-Dose Methotrexate/Cytara-bine Followed by Stem-Cell Transplantation: An Active Regimen for Aggressive Mantle-Cell Lymphoma," *J Clin Oncol*, 1998, 16(12):3803-9.

Hyper-CVAD (Multiple Myeloma)

Use Multiple myeloma
Regimen

Cyclophosphamide: I.V.: 300 mg/m² every 12 hours, for 6 doses, days 1, 2, and 3
[total dose/cycle = 1800 mg/m²]

Mesna: I.V.: 600 mg/m²/day continuous infusion days 1, 2, and 3
[total dose/cycle = 1800 mg/m²]

Doxorubicin: I.V.: 25 mg/m²/day continuous infusion days 4 and 5
[total dose/cycle = 50 mg/m²]

Vincristine: I.V.: 1 mg/day continuous infusion days 4 and 5
followed by I.V.: 2 mg day 11
[total dose/cycle = 4 mg]

Dexamethasone: Oral, I.V.: 20 mg/m²/day days 1 to 5 and 11 to 14
[total dose/cycle = 180 mg/m²]

Repeat cycle once if ≥50% reduction in myeloma protein
Maintenance

Cyclophosphamide: Oral: 125 mg/m² every 12 hours, for 10 doses, days 1 to 5
[total dose/cycle = 1250 mg/m²]

Dexamethasone: Oral: 20 mg/m²/day days 1 to 5
[total dose/cycle = 100 mg/m²]

Repeat maintenance cycle every 5 weeks
References

Dimopoulos MA, Weber D, Kantarjian H, et al, "HyperCVAD for VAD-Resistant Multiple Myeloma," *Am J Hematol*, 1996, 52(2):77-81.

Hyper-CVAD + Rituximab

Use Lymphona, non-Hodgkin's (Mantle cell)
Regimen

Cycle A: (Cycles 1, 3, 5 [and 7, if needed])

Rituximab: I.V.: 375 mg/m² day 1
[total dose/cycle = 375 mg/m²]

Cyclophosphamide: I.V.: 300 mg/m² every 12 hours, for 6 doses, days 2, 3, and 4
[total dose/cycle = 1800 mg/m²]

Mesna: I.V.: 600 mg/m² continuous infusion days 2, 3, and 4
[total dose/cycle = 1800 mg/m²]

Vincristine: I.V.: 1.4 mg/m² (maximum 2 mg) days 5 and 12
[total dose/cycle = 2.8 mg/m²; maximum 4 mg]

Doxorubicin: I.V.: 16.7 mg/m² continuous infusion days 5, 6, and 7
[total dose/cycle = 50.1 mg/m²]

Dexamethasone: Oral, I.V.: 40 mg/day days 2, 3, 4, 5, 12, 13, 14, and 15
[total dose/cycle = 320 mg]

Cycle B: (Cycles 2, 4, 6 [and 8, if needed])

Rituximab: I.V.: 375 mg/m² day 1
[total dose/cycle = 375 mg/m²]

Methotrexate: I.V.: 200 mg/m² day 2
followed by I.V.: 800 mg/m² continuous infusion day 2
[total dose/cycle = 1000 mg/m²]

Leucovorin: Oral: 50 mg (start 12 hours after the end of the methotrexate infusion)
followed by Oral: 15 mg every 6 hours, for 8 doses
[total dose/cycle = 170 mg]

Cytarabine: I.V.: 3 g/m² every 12 hours, for 4 doses, day 3 and 4
[total dose/cycle = 12 g/m²]

Repeat every 6 weeks in the following sequence: ABABABAB
(Continued)

Hyper-CVAD + Rituximab *(Continued)*

References
Romaguera JE, Fayad L, Rodriguez MA, et al, "High Rate of Durable Remissions After Treatment of Newly Diagnosed Aggressive Mantle-Cell Lymphoma With Rituximab Plus Hyper-CVAD Alternating With Rituximab Plus High-Dose Methotrexate and Cytarabine," *J Clin Oncol*, 2005, 23(28):7013-23.

♦ **ICE (Leukemia)** *see* Idarubicin, Cytarabine, Etoposide (ICE Protocol) *on page 1239*

ICE (Lymphoma, non-Hodgkin's)
Use Lymphoma, non-Hodgkin's
Regimen
Etoposide: I.V.: 100 mg/m^2/day days 1 to 3
   [total dose/cycle = 300 mg/m^2]
Carboplatin: I.V.: AUC 5 (maximum 800 mg) day 2
   [total dose/cycle = AUC = 5]
Ifosfamide: I.V.: 5000 mg/m^2 continuous infusion day 2
   [total dose/cycle = 5000 mg/m^2]
Mesna: I.V.: 5000 mg/m^2 continuous infusion day 2
   [total dose/cycle = 5000 mg/m^2]
Filgrastim: SubQ: 5 mcg/kg/day days 5 through 12 (cycles 1 and 2 only)
   [total dose/cycle = 40 mcg/kg]
     followed by SubQ: 10 mcg/kg/day day 5 through completion of leukapheresis (cycle 3 only)
Repeat cycle every 2 weeks for 3 cycles

References
Moskowitz CH, Bertino JR, Glassman JR, et al, "Ifosfamide, Carboplatin, and Etoposide: A Highly Effective Cytoreduction and Peripheral-Blood Progenitor-Cell Mobilization Regimen for Transplant-Eligible Patients With Non-Hodgkin's Lymphoma," *J Clin Oncol*, 1999, 17(12):3776-85.

ICE (Sarcoma)
Use Osteosarcoma; soft tissue sarcoma
Regimen
Ifosfamide: I.V.: 1500 mg/m^2/day days 1 to 3
   [total dose/cycle = 4500 mg/m^2]
Carboplatin: I.V.: 300-635 mg/m^2 day 3
   [total dose/cycle = 300-635 mg/m^2]
Etoposide: I.V.: 100 mg/m^2/day days 1 to 3
   [total dose/cycle = 300 mg/m^2]
Mesna: I.V.: 500 mg/m^2 prior to each ifosfamide, and every 3 hours for 2 more doses/day days 1 to 3
   [total dose/cycle = 4500 mg/m^2]
Repeat cycle every 21-28 days

References
Kung FH, Desai SJ, Dickerman JD, et al, "Ifosfamide/Carboplatin/Etoposide (ICE) for Recurrent Malignant Solid Tumors of Childhood: A Pediatric Oncology Group Phase I/II Study," *J Pediatr Hematol Oncol*, 1995, 17(3):265-9.

ICE-T
Use Soft tissue sarcoma; breast cancer
Regimen
Ifosfamide: I.V.: 1250 mg/m^2/day days 1, 2, and 3
   [total dose/cycle = 3750 mg/m^2]
Carboplatin: I.V.: 300 mg/m^2 day 1
   [total dose/cycle = 300 mg/m^2]

Etoposide: I.V.: 80 mg/m^2/day days 1, 2, and 3
[total dose/cycle = 240 mg/m^2]
Paclitaxel: I.V.: 175 mg/m^2 day 4
[total dose/cycle = 175 mg/m^2]
Mesna: I.V.: 250 mg prior to ifosfamide days 1, 2, and 3
followed by: Oral: 500 mg at 4 and 8 hours after ifosfamide days 1, 2, and 3
[total dose/cycle = I.V. 750 mg; Oral: 3000 mg]
or
Mesna: I.V.: 1250 mg/m^2/day over 6 hours, days 1, 2, and 3
[total dose/cycle = 3750 mg/m^2]
Repeat cycle every 28 days

References

Chang AY, Boros L, Garrow GC, et al, "Ifosfamide, Carboplatin, Etoposide, and Paclitaxel Chemotherapy: A Dose-Escalation Study," *Semin Oncol*, 1996, 23(3 Suppl 6):74-7.

Idarubicin, Cytarabine, Etoposide (ICE Protocol)

Index Terms ICE (Leukemia)

Use Leukemia, acute myeloid

Regimen

Idarubicin: I.V.: 6 mg/m^2/day days 1 to 5
[total dose/cycle = 30 mg/m^2]
Cytarabine: I.V.: 600 mg/m^2/day days 1 to 5
[total dose/cycle = 3000 mg/m^2]
Etoposide: I.V.: 150 mg/m^2/day days 1 to 3
[total dose/cycle = 450 mg/m^2]
Administer one cycle only

References

Carella AM, Carlier P, Pungolino E, et al, "Idarubicin in Combination With Intermediate-Dose Cytarabine and VP-16 in the Treatment of Refractory or Rapidly Relapsed Patients With Acute Myeloid Leukemia," *Leukemia*, 1993, 7(2):196-9.

Idarubicin, Cytarabine, Etoposide (IDA-Based BF12)

Use Leukemia, acute myeloid

Regimen Induction:

Idarubicin: I.V.: 5 mg/m^2/day days 1 to 5
[total dose/cycle = 25 mg/m^2]
Cytarabine: I.V.: 2000 mg/m^2 every 12 hours days 1 to 5 (10 doses)
[total dose/cycle = 20,000 mg/m^2]
Etoposide: I.V.: 100 mg/m^2/day days 1 to 5
[total dose/cycle = 500 mg/m^2]
Second cycle may be given based on individual response; time between cycles not specified

References

Mehta J, Powles R, Singhal S, et al, "Idarubicin, High-Dose Cytarabine, and Etoposide for Induction of Remission in Acute Leukemia," *Semin Hematol*, 1996, 33(4 Suppl 3):18-23.

IE

Use Soft tissue sarcoma

Regimen

Etoposide: I.V.: 100 mg/m^2/day days 1 to 3
[total dose/cycle = 300 mg/m^2]
Ifosfamide: I.V.: 2500 mg/m^2/day days 1 to 3
[total dose/cycle = 7500 mg/m^2]
Mesna: I.V.: 500 mg/m^2 prior to ifosfamide, after ifosfamide, and every 4 hours for 3 more doses (total of 5 doses/day) days 1, 2, and 3
[total dose/cycle = 7500 mg/m^2]
Repeat cycle every 28 days
(Continued)

IE *(Continued)*

References

Edmonson JH, Buckner JC, Long HJ, et al, "Phase II Study of Ifosfamide-Etoposide-Mesna in Adults With Advanced Nonosseous Sarcomas," *J Natl Cancer Inst*, 1989, 81(11):863-6.

IL-2 + IFN
Use Melanoma

Regimen

Cisplatin: I.V.: 20 mg/m^2/day days 1 to 4
  [total dose/cycle = 80 mg/m^2]
Vinblastine: I.V.: 1.6 mg/m^2/day days 1 to 4
  [total dose/cycle = 6.4 mg/m^2]
Dacarbazine: I.V.: 800 mg/m^2 day 1
  [total dose/cycle = 800 mg/m^2]
Aldesleukin: I.V.: 9 million units/m^2/day continuous infusion days 1 to 4
  [total dose/cycle = 36 million units/m^2]
Interferon alfa-2b: SubQ: 5 million units/m^2/day days 1 to 5, 7, 9, 11, and 13
  [total dose/cycle = 45 million units/m^2]
Repeat cycle every 21 days

References

McDermott DF, Mier JW, Lawrence DP, et al, "A Phase II Pilot Trial of Concurrent Biochemotherapy With Cisplatin, Vinblastine, Dacarbazine, Interleukin 2, and Interferon Alpha-2B in Patients With Metastatic Melanoma," *Clin Cancer Res*, 2000, 6(6):2201-8.

IMVP-16
Use Lymphoma, non-Hodgkin's

Regimen

Ifosfamide: I.V.: 4 g/m^2 continuous infusion over 24 hours day 1
  [total dose/cycle = 4 g/m^2]
Mesna: I.V.: 800 mg/m^2 bolus prior to ifosfamide, then 4 g/m^2 continuous infusion over 12 hours concurrent with ifosfamide, then 2.4 g/m^2 continuous infusion over 12 hours after ifosfamide infusion day 1
  [total dose/cycle = 7.2 g/m^2]
Methotrexate: I.V.: 30 mg/m^2/day days 3 and 10
  [total dose/cycle = 60 mg/m^2]
Etoposide: I.V.: 100 mg/m^2/day days 1 to 3
  [total dose/cycle = 300 mg/m^2]
Repeat cycle every 21-28 days

References

Cabanillas F, Hagemeister FB, Bodey GP, et al, "IMVP-16: An Effective Regimen for Patients With Lymphoma Who Have Relapsed After Initial Combination Chemotherapy," *Blood*, 1982, 60(3):693-7.

♦ **Interferon Alfa 2a-Bevacizumab** *see* Bevacizumab-Interferon Alfa-2a *on page 1151*

Interleukin 2-Interferon Alfa-2
Use Renal cell cancer

Regimen

Weeks 1 and 4:
  Aldesleukin: SubQ: 20 million units/m^2 3 times weekly
    [total dose/cycle = 120 million units/m^2]
  Interferon Alfa-2: SubQ: 6 million units/m^2 once weekly
    [total dose/cycle = 12 million units/m^2]
Weeks 2, 3, 5, and 6:
  Aldesleukin: SubQ: 5 million units/m^2 3 times weekly
    [total dose/cycle = 60 million units/m^2]

Interferon Alfa-2: SubQ: 6 million units/m² 3 times weekly
[total dose/cycle = 72 million units/m²]
Repeat cycle every 56 days

References
Atzpodien J, Kirchner H, Hanninen EL, et al, "European Studies of Interleukin-2 in Metastatic Renal Cell Carcinoma," *Semin Oncol*, 1993, 20(6 Suppl 9):22-6.

Interleukin 2-Interferon Alfa-2-Fluorouracil

Use Renal cell cancer
Regimen
Weeks 1 and 4:
Aldesleukin: SubQ: 20 million units/m² 3 times weekly
[total dose/cycle = 120 million units/m²]
Interferon Alfa-2: SubQ: 6 million units/m² once weekly
[total dose/cycle = 12 million units/m²]
Weeks 2 and 3:
Aldesleukin: SubQ: 5 million units/m² 3 times weekly
[total dose/cycle = 30 million units/m²]
Weeks 5-8:
Interferon Alfa-2: SubQ: 9 million units/m² 3 times weekly
[total dose/cycle = 108 million units/m²]
Fluorouracil: I.V.: 750 mg/m² once weekly
[total dose/cycle = 3000 mg/m²]
Repeat cycle every 56 days

References
Atzpodien J, Kirchner H, Hanninen EL, et al, "European Studies of Interleukin-2 In Metastatic Renal Cell Carcinoma," *Semin Oncol*, 1993, 20(6 Suppl 9):22-6.

IPA

Use Hepatoblastoma
Regimen
Ifosfamide: I.V.: 500 mg/m² day 1
[total dose/cycle = 500 mg/m²]
followed by I.V.: 1000 mg/m²/day continuous infusion days 1 to 3
[total dose/cycle = 3000 mg/m²]
Cisplatin: I.V.: 20 mg/m²/day days 4 to 8
[total dose/cycle = 100 mg/m²]
Doxorubicin: I.V.: 30 mg/m²/day continuous infusion days 9 and 10
[total dose/cycle = 60 mg/m²]
Repeat cycle every 21 days

References
von Schweinitz D, Byrd DJ, Hecker H, et al, "Efficiency and Toxicity of Ifosfamide, Cisplatin, and Doxorubicin in the Treatment of Childhood Hepatoblastoma. Study Committee of the Cooperative Paediatric Liver Tumour Study HB89 of the German Society for Paediatric Oncology and Haematology," *Eur J Cancer*, 1997, 33(8):1243-9.

- **Irinotecan-Bevacizumab (Glioblastoma)** *see* Bevacizumab-Irinotecan (Glioblastoma) *on page 1151*
- **Irinotecan-Cetuximab** *see* Cetuximab-Irinotecan *on page 1167*

Irinotecan-Cisplatin

Use Esophageal cancer
Regimen
Cisplatin: I.V.: 30 mg/m²/day days 1, 8, 15, and 22
[total dose/cycle = 120 mg/m²]
Irinotecan: I.V.: 65 mg/m²/day days 1, 8, 15, and 22
[total dose/cycle = 260 mg/m²]
Repeat cycle every 6 weeks
(Continued)

Irinotecan-Cisplatin *(Continued)*

References

Ilson DH, Saltz L, Enzinger P, et al, "Phase II Trial of Weekly Irinotecan Plus Cisplatin in Advanced Esophageal Cancer," *J Clin Oncol*, 1999, 17(10):3270-5.

♦ **Irinotecan-Fluorouracil-Leucovorin** *see FU-LV-CPT-11 on page 1223*

♦ **Irinotecan-Fluorouracil-Leucovorin-Bevacizumab** *see* Bevacizumab-Irinotecan-Fluorouracil-Leucovorin *on page 1151*

♦ **Irinotecan-Fluorouracil-Leucovorin (Saltz Regimen)** *see Fluorouracil-Leucovorin-Irinotecan (Saltz Regimen) on page 1220*

♦ **Irinotecan-Gemcitabine** *see Gemcitabine-Irinotecan on page 1228*

IVAC

Use Lymphoma, non-Hodgkin's

Regimen

Ifosfamide: I.V.: 1500 mg/m^2/day days 1 to 5
  [total dose/cycle = 7500 mg/m^2]
Etoposide: I.V.: 60 mg/m^2/day days 1 to 5
  [total dose/cycle = 300 mg/m^2]
Cytarabine: I.V.: 2 g/m^2 every 12 hours days 1 and 2
  [total dose/cycle = 8 g/m^2]
Mesna: I.V.: 360 mg/m^2 every 3 hours days 1 to 5
  [total dose/cycle = 14,400 mg/m^2]
Methotrexate: I.T.: 12 mg day 5
Sargramostim: SubQ: 7.5 mcg/kg day 7 until ANC >1000 cells/mm^3
Repeat when ANC >1000 cells/mm^3

References

Magrath I, Adde M, Shad A, et al, "Adults and Children With Small Non-Cleaved-Cell Lymphoma Have a Similar Excellent Outcome When Treated With the Same Chemotherapy Regimen," *J Clin Oncol*, 1996, 14(3):925-34.

♦ **IVCAF** *see FAC on page 1210*

Ixabepilone-Capecitabine

Index Terms Capacitabine-Ixabepilone

Use Breast cancer

Regimen

Capecitabine: Oral: 1000 mg/m^2 twice daily days 1 to 14
  [total dose/cycle = 28,000 mg/m^2]
Ixabepilone: I.V.: 40 mg/m^2 day 1
  [total dose/cycle = 40 mg/m^2]
Repeat cycle every 3 weeks

References

Vahdat LT, Thomas E, Li R, et al, "Phase III Trial of Ixabepilone Plus Capecitabine Compared to Capecitabine Alone in Patients With Metastatic Breast Cancer (MBC) Previously Treated or Resistant to an Anthracycline and Resistant to Taxanes," *J Clin Onc*, 2007, 25(18S):1006 [abstract from 2007 Proceedings of ASCO Annual Meeting].

♦ **Lapatinib-Capecitabine** *see Capecitabine + Lapatinib on page 1160*

Larson Regimen

Use Leukemia, acute lymphocytic

Regimen

Cyclophosphamide: I.V.: 1200 mg/m^2 day 1
  [total dose/cycle = 1200 mg/m^2]
Daunorubicin: I.V.: 45 mg/m^2/day days 1 to 3
  [total dose/cycle = 135 mg/m^2]

Vincristine: I.V.: 2 mg/day days 1, 8, 15, and 22
[total dose/cycle = 8 mg]
Prednisone: Oral or I.V.: 60 mg/m^2/day days 1 to 21
[total dose/cycle = 1260 mg/m^2]
Asparaginase: SubQ: 6000 units/m^2/day days 5, 8, 11, 15, 18, and 22
[total dose/cycle = 36,000 units/m^2]
Administer one cycle only

References

Larson RA, Dodge RK, Burns CP, et al, "A Five-Drug Remission Induction Regimen With Intensive Consolidation for Adults With Acute Lymphoblastic Leukemia: Cancer and Leukemia Group B Study 8811," *Blood*, 1995, 85(8):2025-37.

Lenalidomide-Dexamethasone

Index Terms Dexamethasone-Lenalidomide

Use Multiple myeloma

Regimen

Lenalidomide: Oral: 25 mg/day days 1 to 21
[total dose/cycle = 525 mg]
Dexamethasone: Oral: 40 mg/day days 1 to 4, 9 to 12, and 17 to 20 (cycles 1, 2, 3, and 4)
[total dose/cycle = 480 mg]
Dexamethasone: Oral 40 mg/day days 1 to 4 (cycle 5 and beyond)
[total dose/cycle = 160 mg]
Repeat cycle every 28 days

References

Dimopoulos M, Spencer A, Attal M, et al, "Lenalidomide Plus Dexamethasone for Relapsed or Refractory Multiple Myeloma," *N Engl J Med*, 2007, 357(21):2123-32.

Rajkumar SV, Hayman SR, Lacy MQ, et al, "Combination Therapy With Lenalidomide Plus Dexamethasone (Rev/Dex) for Newly Diagnosed Myeloma," *Blood*, 2005, 106(13):4050-3.

Weber DM, Chen C, Niesvizky R, et al, "Lenalidomide Plus Dexamethasone for Relapsed Multiple Myeloma in North America," *N Engl J Med*, 2007, 357(21):2133-42.

Lenalidomide-Dexamethasone (Low Dose)

Index Terms Dexamethasone (Low Dose)-Lenalidomide

Use Multiple myeloma

Regimen

Lenalidomide: Oral: 25 mg/day days 1 to 21
[total dose/cycle = 525 mg]
Dexamethasone: Oral: 40 mg/day days 1, 8, 15, and 22
[total dose/cycle = 160 mg]
Repeat cycle every 28 days

References

Rajkumar SV, Jacobus S, Callander N, et al, "A Randomized Phase III Trial of Lenalidomide Plus High-Dose Dexamethasone Versus Lenalidomide Plus Low-Dose Dexamethasone in Newly Diagnosed Multiple Myeloma (E4A03): A Trial Coordinated by the Eastern Cooperative Oncology Group," *Blood*, 2006, 108(11), ASH Abstract 799.

Rajkumar SV, Jacobus S, Callander N, et al, "Phase III Trial of Lenalidomide Plus High-Dose Dexamethasone Versus Lenalidomide Plus Low-Dose Dexamethasone in Newly Diagnosed Multiple Myeloma (E4A03): A Trial Coordinated by the Eastern Cooperative Oncology Group, *J Clin Onc*, 2007, 25(18S), ASCO Abstract LBA8025.

Linker Protocol

Use Leukemia, acute lymphocytic

Regimen

Remission induction:

Daunorubicin: I.V.: 50 mg/m^2/day days 1 to 3
[total dose/cycle = 150 mg/m^2]

(Continued)

Linker Protocol *(Continued)*

Vincristine: I.V.: 2 mg/day days 1, 8, 15, and 22
[total dose/cycle = 8 mg]
Prednisone: Oral: 60 mg/m²/day days 1 to 28
[total dose/cycle = 1680 mg/m²]
Asparaginase: I.M.: 6000 units/m²/day days 17 to 28
[total dose/cycle = 72,000 units/m²]

If residual leukemia in bone marrow on day 14:
Daunorubicin: I.V.: 50 mg/m² day 15
[total dose/cycle = 50 mg/m²]

If residual leukemia in bone marrow on day 28:
Daunorubicin: I.V.: 50 mg/m²/day days 29 and 30
[total dose/cycle = 100 mg/m²]
Vincristine: I.V.: 2 mg/day days 29 and 36
[total dose/cycle = 4 mg]
Prednisone: Oral: 60 mg/m²/day days 29 to 42
[total dose/cycle = 840 mg/m²]
Asparaginase: I.M.: 6000 units/m²/day days 29 to 35
[total dose/cycle = 42,000 units/m²]

Consolidation therapy:
Treatment A (cycles 1, 3, 5, and 7)
Daunorubicin: I.V.: 50 mg/m²/day days 1 and 2
[total dose/cycle = 100 mg/m²]
Vincristine: I.V.: 2 mg/day days 1 and 8
[total dose/cycle = 4 mg]
Prednisone: Oral: 60 mg/m²/day days 1 to 14
[total dose/cycle = 840 mg/m²]
Asparaginase: I.M.: 12,000 units/m²/day days 2, 4, 7, 9, 11, and 14
[total dose/cycle = 72,000 units/m²]
Treatment B (cycles 2, 4, 6, and 8)
Teniposide: I.V.: 165 mg/m²/day days 1, 4, 8, and 11
[total dose/cycle = 660 mg/m²]
Cytarabine: I.V.: 300 mg/m²/day days 1, 4, 8, and 11
[total dose/cycle = 1200 mg/m²]
Treatment C (cycle 9)
Methotrexate: I.V.: 690 mg/m² continuous infusion day 1 (over 42 hours)
[total dose/cycle = 690 mg/m²]
Leucovorin: I.V.: 15 mg/m² every 6 hours for 12 doses (start at end of
methotrexate infusion)
[total dose/cycle = 180 mg/m²]
Administer remission induction regimen for one cycle only. Repeat consolidation cycle every 28 days.

References
Linker CA, Levitt LJ, O'Donnell M, et al, "Treatment of Adult Acute Lymphoblastic Leukemia With
Intensive Cyclical Chemotherapy: A Follow-up Report," *Blood*, 1991 78(11):2814-22.

LOPP

Use Lymphoma, Hodgkin's disease
Regimen
Chlorambucil: Oral: 10 mg/day days 1 to 10
[total dose/cycle = 100 mg/m²]
Vincristine: I.V.: 1.4 mg/m²/day (maximum 2 mg) days 1 and 8
[total dose/cycle = 2.8 mg/m²]
Procarbazine: Oral: 100 mg/m²/day days 1 to 10
[total dose/cycle = 1000 mg/m²]

Prednisone: Oral: 25 mg/m²/day (maximum 60 mg) days 1 to 14
[total dose/cycle = 350 mg/m²]
or
Prednisolone: Oral: 25 mg/m²/day (maximum 60 mg) days 1 to 14
[total dose/cycle = 350 mg/m²]
Repeat cycle every 28 days

References

Hancock BW, "Randomised Study of MOPP (Mustine, Oncovin, Procarbazine, Prednisone) Against LOPP (Leukeran Substituted for Mustine) in Advanced Hodgkin's Disease. British National Lymphoma Investigation," *Radiother Oncol*, 1986, 7(3):215-21.

M-2

Use Multiple myeloma

Regimen

Vincristine: I.V.: 0.03 mg/kg (maximum 2 mg) day 1
[total dose/cycle = 0.03 mg/kg]
Carmustine: I.V.: 0.5-1 mg/kg day 1
[total dose/cycle = 0.5-1 mg/kg]
Cyclophosphamide: I.V.: 10 mg/kg day 1
[total dose/cycle = 10 mg/kg]
Melphalan: Oral: 0.25 mg/kg/day days 1 to 4
[total dose/cycle = 1 mg/kg]
    or 0.1 mg/kg/day days 1 to 7 or 1 to 10
[total dose/cycle = 0.7 or 1 mg/kg]
Prednisone: Oral: 1 mg/kg/day days 1 to 7
[total dose/cycle = 7 mg/kg]
Repeat cycle every 35-42 days

References

Case DC Jr, Lee DJ 3rd, and Clarkson BD, "Improved Survival Times in Multiple Myeloma Treated With Melphalan, Prednisone, Cyclophosphamide, Vincristine, and BCNU: M-2 Protocol," *Am J Med*, 1977, 63(6):897-903.

MACOP-B

Use Lymphoma, non-Hodgkin's

Regimen

Methotrexate: I.V. bolus: 100 mg/m² weeks 2, 6, 10
followed by I.V.: 300 mg/m² over 4 hours weeks 2, 6, and 10
[total dose/cycle = 1200 mg/m²]
Doxorubicin: I.V.: 50 mg/m² weeks 1, 3, 5, 7, 9, and 11
[total dose/cycle = 300 mg/m²]
Cyclophosphamide: I.V.: 350 mg/m² weeks 1, 3, 5, 7, 9, and 11
[total dose/cycle = 2100 mg/m²]
Vincristine: I.V.: 1.4 mg/m² (maximum 2 mg) weeks 2, 4, 6, 8, 10, and 12
[total dose/cycle = 8.4 mg/m²; maximum 12 mg]
Bleomycin: I.V.: 10 units/m² weeks 4, 8, and 12
[total dose/cycle = 30 units/m²]
Prednisone: Oral: 75 mg/day for 12 weeks, then taper over 2 weeks
Leucovorin calcium: Oral: 15 mg/m² every 6 hours, for 6 doses (beginning 24 hours after methotrexate) weeks 2, 6, and 10
[total dose/cycle = 270 mg/m²]
Administer one cycle

References

Klimo P and Conors JM, "MACOP-B Chemotherapy for the Treatment of Diffuse Large-Cell Lymphoma," *Ann Intern Med*, 1985, 102(5):596-602.

MAID

Use Soft tissue sarcoma

Regimen

Mesna: I.V.: 2500 mg/m²/day continuous infusion days 1 to 4
[total dose/cycle = 10,000 mg/m²]
Doxorubicin: I.V.: 20 mg/m²/day continuous infusion days 1 to 3
[total dose/cycle = 60 mg/m²]
Ifosfamide: I.V.: 2500 mg/m²/day continuous infusion days 1 to 3
[total dose/cycle = 7500 mg/m²]
Dacarbazine: I.V.: 300 mg/m²/day continuous infusion days 1 to 3
[total dose/cycle = 900 mg/m²]
Repeat cycle every 21-28 days

References

Elias A, Ryan L, Sulkes A, et al, "Response to Mesna, Doxorubicin, Ifosfamide, and Dacarbazine in 108 Patients With Metastatic or Unresectable Sarcoma and No Prior Chemotherapy," *J Clin Oncol*, 1989, 7(9):1208-16.

m-BACOD

Use Lymphoma, non-Hodgkin's

Regimen

Methotrexate: I.V.: 200 mg/m²/day days 8 and 15
[total dose/cycle = 400 mg/m²]
Leucovorin calcium: Oral: 10 mg/m² every 6 hours for 8 doses (beginning 24 hours after each methotrexate dose) days 9 and 16
[total dose/cycle = 160 mg/m²]
Bleomycin: I.V.: 4 units/m² day 1
[total dose/cycle = 4 units/m²]
Doxorubicin: I.V.: 45 mg/m² day 1
[total dose/cycle = 45 mg/m²]
Cyclophosphamide: I.V.: 600 mg/m² day 1
[total dose/cycle = 600 mg/m²]
Vincristine: I.V.: 1 mg/m² day 1
[total dose/cycle = 1 mg/m²]
Dexamethasone: Oral: 6 mg/m²/day days 1 to 5
[total dose/cycle = 30 mg/m²]
Repeat cycle every 21 days

References

Salles G, Shipp MA, and Coiffier B, "Chemotherapy of Non-Hodgkin's Aggressive Lymphomas," *Semin Hematol*, 1994, 31(1):46-69.

Urba WJ, Duffey PL, and Longo DL, "Treatment of Patients With Aggressive Lymphomas: An Overview," *J Natl Cancer Inst Monogr*, 1990, (10):29-37.

♦ **Melphalan-Prednisone-Bortezomib** *see* Bortezomib-Melphalan-Prednisone *on page 1156*

♦ **Melphalan-Prednisone-Bortezomib-Thalidomide** *see* Bortezomib-Melphalan-Prednisone-Thalidomide *on page 1156*

Melphalan-Prednisone-Thalidomide

Use Multiple myeloma

Regimen

Melphalan: Oral: 4 mg/m²/day days 1 to 7
[total dose/cycle = 28 mg/m²]
Prednisone: Oral: 40 mg/m²/day days 1 to 7
[total dose/cycle = 280 mg/m²]
Thalidomide: Oral: 100 mg/day days 1 to 28
[total dose/cycle = 2800 mg]

Repeat cycle every 28 days for 6 cycles
followed by
Thalidomide: Oral: 100 mg daily (as maintenance)
References
Palumbo A, Bertola A, Musto P, et al, "Oral Melphalan, Prednisone, and Thalidomide for Newly Diagnosed Patients With Myeloma," *Cancer*, 2005, 104(7):1428-33.
Palumbo A, Bringhen S, Caravita T, et al, "Oral Melphalan and Prednisone Chemotherapy Plus Thalidomide Compared With Melphalan and Prednisone Alone in Elderly Patients With Multiple Myeloma: Randomised Controlled Trial," *Lancet*, 2006, 367(9513):825-31.

MF

Use Breast cancer
Regimen
Methotrexate: I.V. 100 mg/m²/day days 1 and 8
[total dose/cycle = 200 mg/m²]
Fluorouracil: I.V.: 600 mg/m²/day (start 1 hour after methotrexate) days 1 and 8
[total dose/cycle = 1200 mg/m²]
Leucovorin: Oral, I.V.: 10 mg/m² every 6 hours for 6 doses (start 24 hours after methotrexate)
[total dose/cycle = 60 mg/m²]
Repeat cycle every 28 days for 12 cycles
References
Fisher B, Dignam J, Mamounas EP, et al, "Sequential Methotrexate and Fluorouracil for the Treatment of Node-Negative Breast Cancer Patients With Estrogen Receptor-Negative Tumors: Eight-Year Results from National Surgical Adjuvant Breast and Bowel Project (NSABP) B-13 and First Report of Findings from NSABP B-19 Comparing Methotrexate and Fluorouracil With Conventional Cyclophosphamide, Methotrexate, and Fluorouracil," *J Clin Oncol*, 1996, 14(7):1982-92.

MINE

Use Lymphoma, non-Hodgkin's
Regimen
Mesna: I.V.: 1.33 g/m²/day concurrent with ifosfamide dose, then 500 mg orally (4 hours after each ifosfamide infusion) days 1 to 3
[total dose/cycle = 3.99 g/m²/1500 mg]
Ifosfamide: I.V.: 1.33 g/m²/day days 1 to 3
[total dose/cycle = 3.99 g/m²]
Mitoxantrone: I.V.: 8 mg/m² day 1
[total dose/cycle = 8 mg/m²]
Etoposide: I.V.: 65 mg/m²/day days 1 to 3
[total dose/cycle = 195 mg/m²]
Repeat cycle every 28 days
References
Rodriguez-Monge EJ and Cabanillas F, "Long-Term Follow-up of Platinum-Based Lymphoma Salvage Regimens. The M.D. Anderson Cancer Center Experience," *Hematol Oncol Clin North Am*, 1997, 11(5):937-47.

MINE-ESHAP

Use Lymphoma, non-Hodgkin's
Regimen
Mesna: I.V.: 1.33 g/m² concurrent with ifosfamide dose, then 500 mg orally (4 hours after ifosfamide) days 1 to 3
[total dose/cycle = 4 g/m²/1500 mg]
Ifosfamide: I.V.: 1.33 g/m²/day days 1 to 3
[total dose/cycle = 4 g/m²]
Mitoxantrone: I.V.: 8 mg/m² day 1
[total dose/cycle = 8 mg/m²]
(Continued)

MINE-ESHAP *(Continued)*

Etoposide: I.V.: 65 mg/m²/day days 1 to 3
[total dose/cycle = 195 mg/m²]
Repeat cycle every 21 days for 6 cycles, followed by 3-6 cycles of ESHAP

References
Rodriguez MA, Cabanillas FC, Velasquez W, et al, "Results of a Salvage Treatment Program for Relapsing Lymphoma: MINE Consolidated With ESHAP," *J Clin Oncol*, 1995, 13(7):1734-41.

mini-BEAM

Use Lymphoma, Hodgkin's disease

Regimen

Carmustine: I.V.: 60 mg/m² day 1
[total dose/cycle = 60 mg/m²]
Etoposide: I.V.: 75 mg/m²/day days 2 to 5
[total dose/cycle = 300 mg/m²]
Cytarabine: I.V.: 100 mg/m² every 12 hours days 2 to 5 (8 doses)
[total dose/cycle = 800 mg/m²]
Melphalan: I.V.: 30 mg/m² day 6
[total dose/cycle = 30 mg/m²]
Repeat cycle every 4-6 weeks

References
Colwill R, Crump M, Couture F, et al, "Mini-BEAM as Salvage Therapy for Relapsed or Refractory Hodgkin's Disease Before Intensive Therapy and Autologous Bone Marrow Transplantation," *J Clin Oncol*, 1995, 13(2):396-402.

Mitomycin-Vinblastine

Index Terms MV

Use Breast cancer

Regimen

Mitomycin: I.V.: 20 mg/m² day 1
[total dose/cycle = 20 mg/m²]
Vinblastine: I.V.: 0.15 mg/kg/day days 1 and 21
[total dose/cycle = 0.3 mg/kg]
Repeat cycle every 6-8 weeks

References
Konits PH, Aisner J, van Echo DA, et al, "Mitomycin C and Vinblastine Chemotherapy for Advanced Breast Cancer," *Cancer*, 1981, 48(6):1295-8.

Mitoxantrone + Hydrocortisone

Use Prostate cancer

Regimen

Mitoxantrone: I.V.: 14 mg/m² day 1
[total dose/cycle = 14 mg/m²]
Hydrocortisone: Oral: 40 mg daily
[total dose/cycle = 840 mg]
Repeat cycle every 3 weeks

References
Kantoff PW, Halabi S, Conaway M, et al, "Hydrocortisone With or Without Mitoxantrone in Men With Hormone-Refractory Prostate Cancer: Results of the Cancer and Leukemia Group B 9182 Study," *J Clin Oncol*, 1999, 17(8):2506-13.

♦ **Mitoxantrone + Prednisone** *see* MP (Prostate Cancer) *on page 1254*

MOP

Use Brain tumors

Regimen

Mechlorethamine: I.V.: 6 mg/m^2/day days 1 and 8
   [total dose/cycle = 12 mg/m^2]
Vincristine: I.V.: 1.5 mg/m^2/day (maximum 2 mg) days 1 and 8
   [total dose/cycle = 3 mg/m^2]
Procarbazine: Oral: 100 mg/m^2/day days 1 to 14
   [total dose/cycle = 1400 mg/m^2]
Repeat cycle every 28 days

References
Kretschmar CS, Tarbell NJ, Kupsky W, et al, "Preirradiation Chemotherapy for Infants and Children With Medulloblastoma: A Preliminary Report," *J Neurosurg*, 1989, 71(6):820-5.

MOPP/ABVD

Use Lymphoma, Hodgkin's disease

Regimen NOTE: Multiple variations are listed below.
Variation 1:
   Mechlorethamine: I.V.: 6 mg/m^2/day days 1 and 8
      [total dose/cycle = 12 mg/m^2]
   Vincristine: I.V.: 1.4 mg/m^2/day (maximum 2 mg) days 1 and 8
      [total dose/cycle = 2.8 mg/m^2]
   Procarbazine: I.V.: 100 mg/m^2/day days 1 to 14
      [total dose/cycle = 1400 mg/m^2]
   Prednisone: Oral: 40 mg/m^2/day days 1 to 14 (during cycles 1, 4, 7, and 10 only)
      [total dose/cycle = 560 mg/m^2]
   Doxorubicin: I.V.: 25 mg/m^2/day days 29 and 43
      [total dose/cycle = 50 mg/m^2]
   Bleomycin: I.V.: 10 units/m^2/day days 29 and 43
      [total dose/cycle = 20 units/m^2]
   Vinblastine: I.V.: 6 mg/m^2/day days 29 and 43
      [total dose/cycle = 12 mg/m^2]
   Dacarbazine: I.V.: 375 mg/m^2/day days 29 and 43
      [total dose/cycle = 750 mg/m^2]
   Repeat cycle every 56 days
Variation 2:
   Mechlorethamine: I.V.: 6 mg/m^2/day days 1 and 8
      [total dose/cycle = 12 mg/m^2]
   Vincristine: I.V.: 1.4 mg/m^2/day (maximum 2 mg) days 1 and 8
      [total dose/cycle = 2.8 mg/m^2]
   Procarbazine: I.V.: 100 mg/m^2/day days 1 to 14
      [total dose/cycle = 1400 mg/m^2]
   Prednisone: Oral: 40 mg/m^2/day days 1 to 14 (during cycles 1 and 7 only)
      [total dose/cycle = 560 mg/m^2]
   Doxorubicin: I.V.: 25 mg/m^2/day days 29 and 43
      [total dose/cycle = 50 mg/m^2]
   Bleomycin: I.V.: 10 units/m^2/day days 29 and 43
      [total dose/cycle = 20 units/m^2]
   Vinblastine: I.V.: 6 mg/m^2/day days 29 and 43
      [total dose/cycle = 12 mg/m^2]
(Continued)

MOPP/ABVD *(Continued)*

 Dacarbazine: I.V.: 375 mg/m²/day days 29 and 43
  [total dose/cycle = 750 mg/m²]
 Repeat cycle every 56 days
Variation 3:
 Mechlorethamine: I.V.: 6 mg/m²/day days 1 and 8
  [total dose/cycle = 12 mg/m²]
 Vincristine: I.V.: 1.4 mg/m²/day (maximum 2 mg) days 1 and 8
  [total dose/cycle = 2.8 mg/m²]
 Procarbazine: I.V.: 100 mg/m²/day days 1 to 14
  [total dose/cycle = 1400 mg/m²]
 Prednisone: Oral: 40 mg/m²/day days 1 to 14 (every cycle)
  [total dose/cycle = 560 mg/m²]
 Doxorubicin: I.V.: 25 mg/m²/day days 29 and 43
  [total dose/cycle = 50 mg/m²]
 Bleomycin: I.V.: 10 units/m²/day days 29 and 43
  [total dose/cycle = 20 units/m²]
 Vinblastine: I.V.: 6 mg/m²/day days 29 and 43
  [total dose/cycle = 12 mg/m²]
 Dacarbazine: I.V.: 375 mg/m²/day days 29 and 43
  [total dose/cycle = 750 mg/m²]
 Repeat cycle every 56 days
Variation 4:
 MOPP Regimen:
 Mechlorethamine: I.V.: 6 mg/m²/day days 1 and 8
  [total dose/cycle = 12 mg/m²]
 Vincristine: I.V.: 1.4 mg/m²/day (maximum 2 mg) days 1 and 8
  [total dose/cycle = 2.8 mg/m²]
 Procarbazine: I.V.: 100 mg/m²/day days 1 to 14
  [total dose/cycle = 1400 mg/m²]
 Prednisone: Oral: 25 mg/m²/day days 1 to 14
  [total dose/cycle = 350 mg/m²]
 ABVD Regimen:
 Doxorubicin: I.V.: 25 mg/m²/day days 1 and 15
  [total dose/cycle = 50 mg/m²]
 Bleomycin: I.V.: 6 units/m²/day days 1 and 15
  [total dose/cycle = 12 units/m²]
 Vinblastine: I.V.: 6 mg/m²/day days 1 and 15
  [total dose/cycle = 12 mg/m²]
 Dacarbazine: I.V.: 250 mg/m²/day days 1 and 15
  [total dose/cycle = 500 mg/m²]
 Each regimen cycle is 28 days. Administer regimens in alternating fashion
  as follows: 2 cycles of MOPP alternating with 2 cycles of ABVD for a total
  of 8 cycles
Variation 5 (pediatrics):
 Mechlorethamine: I.V.: 6 mg/m²/day days 1 and 8
  [total dose/cycle = 12 mg/m²]
 Vincristine: I.V.: 1.4 mg/m²/day days 1 and 8
  [total dose/cycle = 2.8 mg/m²]
 Procarbazine: Oral: 100 mg/m²/day days 1 to 14
  [total dose/cycle = 1400 mg/m²]
 Prednisone: Oral: 40 mg/m²/day days 1 to 14
  [total dose/cycle = 560 mg/m²]
 Doxorubicin: I.V.: 25 mg/m²/day days 29 and 42
  [total dose/cycle = 50 mg/m²]

Bleomycin: I.V.: 10 units/m² /day days 29 and 42
[total dose/cycle = 20 units/m²]
Vinblastine: I.V.: 6 mg/m² /day days 29 and 42
[total dose/cycle = 12 mg/m²]
Dacarbazine: I.V.: 150 mg/m² /day days 29 to 33
[total dose/cycle = 750 mg/m²]
Repeat cycle every 56 days for 4 cycles
Variation 6 (pediatrics):
Mechlorethamine: I.V.: 6 mg/m² /day days 1 and 8
[total dose/cycle = 12 mg/m²]
Vincristine: I.V.: 1.4 mg/m² /day days 1 and 8
[total dose/cycle = 2.8 mg/m²]
Procarbazine: Oral: 100 mg/m² /day days 1 to 14
[total dose/cycle = 1400 mg/m²]
Prednisone: Oral: 40 mg/m² /day days 1 to 14
[total dose/cycle = 560 mg/m²]
Doxorubicin: I.V.: 25 mg/m² /day days 29 and 42
[total dose/cycle = 50 mg/m²]
Bleomycin: I.V.: 10 units/m² /day days 29 and 42
[total dose/cycle = 20 units/m²]
Vinblastine: I.V.: 6 mg/m² /day days 29 and 42
[total dose/cycle = 12 mg/m²]
Dacarbazine: I.V.: 375 mg/m² /day days 29 and 43
[total dose/cycle = 750 mg/m²]
Repeat cycle every 56 days for 4 cycles

References
Variation 1:
Bonadonna G, Valagussa P, and Santoro A, "Alternating Noncross-Resistant Combination Chemotherapy or MOPP in State IV Hodgkin's Disease. A Report of 8-Year Results," *Ann Int Med*, 1986, 104(6):739-46.
Variation 2:
Canellos, GP, Anderson JR, Propert KJ, et al, "Chemotherapy of Advanced Hodgkin's Disease With MOPP, ABVD, or MOPP Alternating With ABVD," *N Engl J Med*, 1992, 327(21):1478-84.
Variation 3:
Glick JH, Young ML, Harrington D, et al, "MOPP/ABV Hybrid Chemotherapy for Advanced Hodgkin's Disease Significantly Improves Failure-Free and Overall Survival. The 8-Year Results of the Intergroup Trial," *J Clin Oncol* 1998, 16(1):19-26.
Variation 4:
Somers R, Carde P, Henry-Amar M, et al, "A Randomized Study in State IIIB and IV Hodgkin's Disease Comparing Eight Courses of MOPP Versus an Alternation of MOPP With ABVD. A European Organization for Research and Treatment of Cancer Lymphoma Cooperative Group and Groupe Pierre-et-Marie-Curie Controlled Clinical Trial," *J Clin Oncol*, 1994, 12(2):279-87.
Variation 5 (pediatrics):
Weiner MA, Leventhal BG, Marcus R, et al, "Intensive Chemotherapy and Low-Dose Radiotherapy for the Treatment of Advanced-Stage Hodgkin's Disease in Pediatric Patients. A Pediatric Oncology Group Study," *J Clin Oncol*, 1991, 9(9):1591-8.
Variation 6 (pediatrics):
Weiner MA, Leventhal B, Brecher ML, et al, "Randomized Study of Intensive MOPP-ABVD With or Without Low-Dose Total-Nodal Radiation Therapy in the Treatment of Stages IIB, IIIA2, IIIB, and IV Hodgkin's Disease in Pediatric Patients. A Pediatric Oncology Group Study," *J Clin Oncol*, 1997, 15(8):2769-79.

MOPP/ABV Hybrid
Use Lymphoma, Hodgkin's disease
Regimen
Mechlorethamine: I.V.: 6 mg/m² day 1
[total dose/cycle = 6 mg/m²]
Vincristine: I.V.: 1.4 mg/m² (maximum 2 mg) day 1
[total dose/cycle = 1.4 mg/m²]
(Continued)

MOPP/ABV Hybrid *(Continued)*

Procarbazine: Oral: 100 mg/m^2/day days 1 to 7
  [total dose/cycle = 700 mg/m^2]
Prednisone: Oral: 40 mg/m^2/day days 1 to 14
  [total dose/cycle = 560 mg/m^2]
Doxorubicin: I.V.: 35 mg/m^2 day 8
  [total dose/cycle = 35 mg/m^2]
Bleomycin: I.V.: 10 units/m^2 day 8
  [total dose/cycle = 10 units/m^2]
Vinblastine: I.V.: 6 mg/m^2 day 8
  [total dose/cycle = 6 mg/m^2]
Repeat cycle every 28 days

References
Klimo P and Connors JM, "MOPP/ABV Hybrid Program: Combination Chemotherapy Based on Early Introduction of Seven Effective Drugs for Advanced Hodgkin's Disease," *J Clin Oncol*, 1985, 3(9):1174-82.

MOPP (Lymphoma, Hodgkin's Disease)

Use Lymphoma, Hodgkin's disease

Regimen NOTE: Multiple variations are listed below.

Variation 1:
  Mechlorethamine: I.V.: 6 mg/m^2/day days 1 and 8
    [total dose/cycle = 12 mg/m^2]
  Vincristine: I.V.: 1.4 mg/m^2/day days 1 and 8
    [total dose/cycle = 2.8 mg/m^2]
  Procarbazine: Oral: 100 mg/m^2/day days 1 to 14
    [total dose/cycle = 1400 mg/m^2]
  Prednisone: Oral: 40 mg/m^2/day days 1 to 14 (cycles 1 and 4)
    [total dose/cycle = 560 mg/m^2]
  Repeat cycle every 28 days for 6-8 cycles

Variation 2:
  Mechlorethamine: I.V.: 6 mg/m^2/day (maximum 15 mg) days 1 and 8
    [total dose/cycle = 12 mg/m^2]
  Vincristine: I.V.: 1.4 mg/m^2/day (maximum 2 mg) days 1 and 8
    [total dose/cycle = 2.8 mg/m^2]
  Procarbazine: Oral: 100 mg/m^2/day days 1 to 10
    [total dose/cycle = 1000 mg/m^2]
  Prednisone: Oral: 25 mg/m^2/day (maximum 60 mg) days 1 to 14
    [total dose/cycle = 350 mg/m^2]
  or
  Prednisolone: Oral: 25 mg/m^2/day (maximum 60 mg) days 1 to 14
    [total dose/cycle = 350 mg/m^2]
  Repeat cycle every 28 days

Variation 3:
  Mechlorethamine: I.V.: 6 mg/m^2/day days 1 and 8
    [total dose/cycle = 12 mg/m^2]
  Vincristine: I.V.: 1.4 mg/m^2/day days 1 and 8
    [total dose/cycle = 2.8 mg/m^2]
  Procarbazine: Oral: 50 mg day 1, 100 mg day 2, 100 mg/m^2/day days 3 to 14
    [total dose/cycle = 150 mg / 1200 mg/m^2]
  Prednisone: Oral: 40 mg/m^2/day days 1 to 14
    [total dose/cycle = 560 mg/m^2]
  Repeat cycle every 28 days

Variation 4:
  Mechlorethamine: I.V.: 6 mg/m^2/day days 1 and 8
    [total dose/cycle = 12 mg/m^2]

Vincristine: I.V.: 1.4 mg/m²/day days 1 and 8
[total dose/cycle = 2.8 mg/m²]
Procarbazine: Oral: 50 mg day 1, 100 mg day 2, 100 mg/m²/day days 3 to 10
[total dose/cycle = 150 mg / 800 mg/m²]
Prednisone: Oral: 40 mg/m²/day days 1 to 14
[total dose/cycle = 560 mg/m²]
Repeat cycle every 28 days
Variation 5:
Mechlorethamine: I.V.: 6 mg/m²/day days 1 and 8
[total dose/cycle = 12 mg/m²]
Vincristine: I.V.: 1.4 mg/m²/day days 1 and 8
[total dose/cycle = 2.8 mg/m²]
Procarbazine: Oral: 50 mg/m² day 1, then 100 mg/m²/day days 2 to 14
[total dose/cycle = 1350 mg/m²]
Prednisone: Oral: 40 mg/m²/day days 1 to 14
[total dose/cycle = 560 mg/m²]
Repeat cycle every 28 days

References

Variation 1:
Devita VT Jr, Serpick AA, and Carbone PP, "Combination Chemotherapy in the Treatment of Advanced Hodgkin's Disease," *Ann Intern Med*, 1970, 73(6):881-95.
Variation 2:
Hancock BW, "Randomised Study Of MOPP (Mustine, Oncovin, Procarbazine, Prednisone) Against LOPP (Leukeran Substituted for Mustine) in Advanced Hodgkin's Disease. British National Lymphoma Investigation," *Radiother Oncol*, 1986, 7(3):215-21.
Variation 3:
Nissen NI, Pajak TF, Glidewell O, et al, "A Comparative Study of a BCNU Containing 4-Drug Program Versus MOPP Versus 3-Drug Combinations in Advanced Hodgkin's Disease: A Cooperative Study by the Cancer and Leukemia Group B," *Cancer*, 1979, 43(1):31-40.
Variation 4:
Huguley CM Jr, Durant JR, Moores RR, et al, "A Comparison of Nitrogen Mustard, Vincristine, Procarbazine, and Prednisone (MOPP) vs Nitrogen Mustard In Advanced Hodgkin's Disease," *Cancer*, 1975, 36(4):1227-40.
Variation 5:
Bakemeier RF, Anderson JR, Costello W, et al, "BCVPP Chemotherapy for Advanced Hodgkin's Disease: Evidence for Greater Duration of Complete Remission, Greater Survival, and Less Toxicity Than With a MOPP Regimen. Results of the Eastern Cooperative Oncology Group Study," *Ann Intern Med*, 1984, 101(4):447-56.

MOPP (Medulloblastoma)

Use Brain tumors

Regimen

Mechlorethamine: I.V.: 3 mg/m²/day days 1 and 8
[total dose/cycle = 6 mg/m²]
Vincristine: I.V.: 1.4 mg/m²/day (maximum 2 mg) days 1 and 8
[total dose/cycle = 2.8 mg/m²]
Prednisone: Oral: 40 mg/m²/day days 1 to 10
[total dose/cycle = 400 mg/m²]
Procarbazine: Oral: 50 mg day 1
[total dose/cycle = 50 mg]
followed by Oral: 100 mg day 2
[total dose/cycle = 100 mg]
followed by Oral: 100 mg/m²/day days 3 to 10
[total dose/cycle = 800 mg/m²]
Repeat cycle every 28 days

References

Krischer JP, Ragab AH, Kun L, et al, "Nitrogen Mustard, Vincristine, Procarbazine, and Prednisone as Adjuvant Chemotherapy in the Treatment of Medulloblastoma. A Pediatric Oncology Group Study," *J Neurosurg*, 1991, 74(6):905-9.

MP (Multiple Myeloma)
Use Multiple myeloma
Regimen
Melphalan: Oral: 8-10 mg/m²/day days 1 to 4
  [total dose/cycle = 32-40 mg/m²]
Prednisone: Oral: 40-60 mg/m²/day days 1 to 4
  [total dose/cycle = 160-240 mg/m²]
Repeat cycle every 28-42 days
References
Belch A, Shelley W, Bergsagel D, et al, "A Randomized Trial of Maintenance Versus No Maintenance Melphalan and Prednisone in Responding Multiple Myeloma Patients," *Br J Cancer*, 1988, 57(1):94-9.

MP (Prostate Cancer)
Index Terms Mitoxantrone + Prednisone
Use Prostate cancer
Regimen
Mitoxantrone: I.V.: 12 mg/m² day 1
  [total dose/cycle = 12 mg/m²]
Prednisone: Oral: 5 mg twice daily
  [total dose/cycle = 210 mg/m²]
Repeat cycle every 21 days
References
Moore MJ, Osoba D, Murphy K, et al, "Use of Palliative Endpoints to Evaluate the Effects of Mitoxantrone and Low-Dose Prednisone in Patients With Hormonally Resistant Prostate Cancer," *J Clin Oncol*, 1994, 12(4):689-94.

MTX/6-MP/VP (Maintenance)
Use Leukemia, acute lymphocytic
Regimen
Methotrexate: Oral: 20 mg/m² weekly
  [total dose/cycle = 80 mg/m²]
Mercaptopurine: Oral: 75 mg/m²/day
  [total dose/cycle = 2250 mg/m²]
Vincristine: I.V.: 1.5 mg/m² day 1
  [total dose/cycle = 1.5 mg/m²]
Prednisone: Oral: 40 mg/m²/day days 1 to 5
  [total dose/cycle = 200 mg/m²]
Repeat monthly for 2-3 years
References
Bleyer WA, Sather HN, Nickerson HJ, et al, "Monthly Pulses of Vincristine and Prednisone Prevent Bone Marrow and Testicular Relapse in Low-Risk Childhood Acute Lymphoblastic Leukemia: A Report of the CCG-161 Study by the Childrens Cancer Study Group," *J Clin Oncol*, 1991, 9(6):1012-21.

MTX-CDDPAdr
Use Osteosarcoma
Regimen
Cisplatin: I.V.: 75 mg/m² day 1 of cycles 1-7, then 120 mg/m² for cycles 8-10
Doxorubicin: I.V.: 25 mg/m²/day days 1 to 3 of cycles 1 to 7
Methotrexate: I.V.: 12 g/m²/day days 21 and 28
Leucovorin calcium rescue: I.V.: 20 mg/m² every 3 hours (beginning 16 hours after completion of methotrexate) for 8 doses, then orally every 6 hours for 8 doses
References
Meyers PA, Heller G, Healey J, et al, "Chemotherapy for Nonmetastatic Osteogenic Sarcoma: The Memorial Sloan-Kettering Experience," *J Clin Oncol*, 1992, 10(1):5-15.

MV

Use Leukemia, acute myeloid

Regimen Induction:

Mitoxantrone: I.V.: 10 mg/m²/day days 1 to 5

[total dose/cycle = 50 mg/m²]

Etoposide: I.V.: 100 mg/m²/day days 1 to 5

[total dose/cycle = 500 mg/m²]

Second cycle may be given based on individual response; time between cycles not specified

References

Ho AD, Lipp T, Ehninger G, et al, "Combination of Mitoxantrone and Etoposide in Refractory Acute Myelogenous Leukemia an Active and Well-Tolerated Regimen," *J Clin Oncol*, 1988, 6(2):213-17.

♦ **MV** see Mitomycin-Vinblastine *on page 1248*

M-VAC (Bladder Cancer)

Use Bladder cancer

Regimen NOTE: Multiple variations are listed below.

Variation 1:

Methotrexate: I.V.: 30 mg/m²/day days 1, 15, and 22

[total dose/cycle = 90 mg/m²]

Vinblastine: I.V.: 3 mg/m²/day days 2, 15, and 22

[total dose/cycle = 9 mg/m²]

Doxorubicin: I.V.: 30 mg/m² day 2

[total dose/cycle = 30 mg/m²]

Cisplatin: I.V.: 70 mg/m² day 2

[total dose/cycle = 70 mg/m²]

Repeat cycle every 4 weeks

Variation 2:

Methotrexate: I.V.: 40 or 50 mg/m²/day days 1, 15, and 22

[total dose/cycle = 120 or 150 mg/m²]

Vinblastine: I.V.: 4 or 5 mg/m²/day days 2, 15, and 22

[total dose/cycle = 12 or 15 mg/m²]

Doxorubicin: I.V.: 40 or 50 mg/m² day 2

[total dose/cycle = 40 or 50 mg/m²]

Cisplatin: I.V.: 100 mg/m² day 2

[total dose/cycle = 100 mg/m²]

Repeat cycle every 4 weeks

Variation 3:

Methotrexate: I.V.: 30 mg/m²/day days 1, 15, and 22

[total dose/cycle = 90 mg/m²]

Vinblastine: I.V.: 3 mg/m²/day day 2

[total dose/cycle = 3 mg/m²]

Doxorubicin: I.V.: 30 mg/m² day 2

[total dose/cycle = 30 mg/m²]

Cisplatin: I.V.: 70 mg/m² day 2

[total dose/cycle = 70 mg/m²]

Repeat cycle every 4 weeks

Variation 4:

Methotrexate: I.V.: 60 mg/m² day 1

[total dose/cycle = 60 mg/m²]

followed by I.V.: 30 mg/m² day 16

[total dose/cycle = 30 mg/m²]

Vinblastine: I.V.: 4 mg/m²/day days 2 and 16

[total dose/cycle = 8 mg/m²]

(Continued)

M-VAC (Bladder Cancer) *(Continued)*

Doxorubicin: I.V.: 60 mg/m^2 day 2
   [total dose/cycle = 60 mg/m^2]
Cisplatin: I.V.: 100 mg/m^2 day 2
   [total dose/cycle = 100 mg/m^2]
Repeat cycle every 23 days

Variation 5:
  Methotrexate: I.V.: 30 mg/m^2/day days 1, 16, and 23
    [total dose/cycle = 90 mg/m^2]
  Vinblastine: I.V.: 4 mg/m^2/day days 1, 16, and 23
    [total dose/cycle = 12 mg/m^2]
  Doxorubicin: I.V.: 60 mg/m^2 day 2
    [total dose/cycle = 60 mg/m^2]
  Cisplatin: I.V.: 100 mg/m^2 day 2
    [total dose/cycle = 100 mg/m^2]
  Repeat cycle every 23 days

Variation 6:
  Methotrexate: I.V.: 30 or 35 mg/m^2 day 1
    [total dose/cycle = 30 or 35 mg/m^2]
  Vinblastine: I.V.: 3 or 3.5 mg/m^2 day 2
    [total dose/cycle = 3 or 3.5 mg/m^2]
  Doxorubicin: I.V.: 30 or 35 mg/m^2 day 2
    [total dose/cycle = 30 or 35 mg/m^2]
  Cisplatin: I.V.: 70 or 80 mg/m^2 day 2
    [total dose/cycle = 70 or 80 mg/m^2]
  Repeat cycle every 2 weeks

Variation 7:
  Methotrexate: I.V.: 30 mg/m^2 day 1
    [total dose/cycle = 30 mg/m^2]
  Vinblastine: I.V.: 3 mg/m^2 day 2
    [total dose/cycle = 3 mg/m^2]
  Doxorubicin: I.V.: 30 mg/m^2 day 2
    [total dose/cycle = 30 mg/m^2]
  Cisplatin: I.V.: 70 mg/m^2 day 2
    [total dose/cycle = 70 mg/m^2]
  Repeat cycle every 14 days

Variation 8:
  Methotrexate: I.V.: 30 mg/m^2/day days 1, 15, and 22
    [total dose/cycle = 90 mg/m^2]
  Vinblastine: I.V.: 3 mg/m^2/day days 1, 15, and 22
    [total dose/cycle = 9 mg/m^2]
  Doxorubicin: I.V.: 45 mg/m^2 day 2
    [total dose/cycle = 45 mg/m^2]
  Cisplatin: I.V.: 70 mg/m^2 day 2
    [total dose/cycle = 70 mg/m^2]
  Repeat cycle every 4 weeks

Variation 9:
  Methotrexate: I.V.: 40 mg/m^2/day days 1 and 15
    [total dose/cycle = 80 mg/m^2]
  Vinblastine: I.V.: 4 mg/m^2/day days 1, 16, and 23
    [total dose/cycle = 12 mg/m^2]
  Doxorubicin: I.V.: 60 mg/m^2 day 2
    [total dose/cycle = 60 mg/m^2]
  Cisplatin: I.V.: 100 mg/m^2 day 2
    [total dose/cycle = 100 mg/m^2]
  Repeat cycle every 23 days

Variation 10:

Methotrexate: I.V.: 30 mg/m²/day days 1, 15, and 22
[total dose/cycle = 90 mg/m²]

Vinblastine: I.V.: 3 mg/m²/day days 1, 16, and 22
[total dose/cycle = 9 mg/m²]

Doxorubicin: I.V.: 30 mg/m² day 1
[total dose/cycle = 30 mg/m²]

Cisplatin: I.V.: 70 mg/m² day 1
[total dose/cycle = 70 mg/m²]

Repeat cycle every 4 weeks

Variation 11:

Methotrexate: I.V.: 30 mg/m²/day days 1, 15, and 22
[total dose/cycle = 90 mg/m²]

Vinblastine: I.V.: 3 mg/m²/day days 2, 15, and 22
[total dose/cycle = 9 mg/m²]

Doxorubicin: I.V.: 30 mg/m² day 2
[total dose/cycle = 30 mg/m²]

Cisplatin: I.V.: 70 mg/m² day 2
[total dose/cycle = 70 mg/m²]

Leucovorin: Oral: 15 mg every 6 hours for 4 doses, days 2, 16, and 23
[total dose/cycle = 180 mg]

Repeat cycle every 4 weeks

Variation 12:

Methotrexate: I.V.: 30 mg/m²/day days 1 and 15
[total dose/cycle = 60 mg/m²]

Vinblastine: I.V.: 3 mg/m²/day days 2 and 15
[total dose/cycle = 6 mg/m²]

Doxorubicin: I.V.: 30 or 40 mg/m² day 3
[total dose/cycle = 30 or 40 mg/m²]

Cisplatin: I.V.: 70 mg/m² day 2
[total dose/cycle = 70 mg/m²]

Repeat cycle every 4 weeks

Variation 13:

Methotrexate: I.V.: 30 mg/m²/day days 1 and 15
[total dose/cycle = 60 mg/m²]

Vinblastine: I.V.: 3 mg/m²/day days 2 and 15
[total dose/cycle = 6 mg/m²]

Doxorubicin: I.V.: 30 or 40 mg/m² day 2
[total dose/cycle = 30 or 40 mg/m²]

Cisplatin: I.V.: 70 mg/m² day 2
[total dose/cycle = 70 mg/m²]

Repeat cycle every 4 weeks

References

Variation 1:

Sternberg CN, Yagoda A, Scher HI, et al, "Preliminary Results of M-VAC (Methotrexate, Vinblastine, Doxorubicin, and Cisplatin) for Transitional Cell Carcinoma of the Urothelium," *J Urol*, 1985, 133(3):403-7.

Variation 2:

Loehrer PJ Sr, Elson P, Dreicer R, et al, "Escalated Dosages of Methotrexate, Vinblastine, Doxorubicin, and Cisplatin Plus Recombinant Human Granulocyte Colony-Stimulating Factor in Advanced Urothelial Carcinoma: An Eastern Cooperative Oncology Group Trial," *J Clin Oncol*, 1994, 12(3):483-8.

Variation 3:

Loehrer PJ Sr, Einhorn LH, Elson PJ, et al, "A Randomized Comparison of Cisplatin Alone or in Combination With Methotrexate, Vinblastine, and Doxorubicin in Patients With Metastatic Urothelial Carcinoma: A Cooperative Group Study," *J Clin Oncol*, 1992, 10(7):1066-73.

(Continued)

M-VAC (Bladder Cancer) *(Continued)*

Variation 4:

Logothetis CJ, Finn LD, Smith T, et al, "Escalated MVAC With or Without Recombinant Human Granulocyte-Macrophage Colony-Stimulating Factor for the Initial Treatment of Advanced Malignant Urothelial Tumors: Results of a Randomized Trial," *J Clin Oncol*, 1995, 13(9):2272-7.

Variation 5:

Logothetis CJ, Dexeus FH, Sella A, et al, "Escalated Therapy for Refractory Urothelial Tumors: Methotrexate-Vinblastine-Doxorubicin-Cisplatin Plus Unglycosylated Recombinant Human Granulocyte-Macrophage Colony-Stimulating Factor," *J Natl Cancer Inst*, 1990, 82(8):667-72.

Variation 6:

Sternberg CN, de Mulder PH, van Oosterom AT, et al, "Escalated M-VAC Chemotherapy and Recombinant Human Granulocyte-Macrophage Colony Stimulating Factor (rhGM-CSF) in Patients With Advanced Urothelial Tract Tumors," *Ann Oncol*, 1993, 4(5):403-7.

Variation 7:

Sternberg CN, de Mulder PH, Schornagel JH, et al, "Randomized Phase III Trial of High-Dose-Intensity Methotrexate, Vinblastine, Doxorubicin, and Cisplatin (M-VAC) Chemotherapy and Recombinant Human Granulocyte Colony-Stimulating Factor Versus Classic M-VAC in Advanced Urothelial Tract Tumors: European Organization for Research and Treatment of Cancer Protocol no. 30924," *J Clin Oncol*, 2001, 19(10):2638-46.

Variation 8 and 9:

Seidman AD, Scher HI, Gabrilove JL, et al, "Dose-Intensification of MVAC With Recombinant Granulocyte Colony-Stimulating Factor as Initial Therapy in Advanced Urothelial Cancer," *J Clin Oncol*, 1993, 11(3):408-14.

Variation 10:

Bamias A, Aravantinos G, Deliveliotis C, et al, "Docetaxel and Cisplatin With Granulocyte Colony-Stimulating Factor (G-CSF) Versus M-VAC With G-CSF in Advanced Urothelial Carcinoma: A Multicenter, Randomized, Phase III Study From the Hellenic Cooperative Oncology Group," *J Clin Oncol*, 2004, 22(2):220-8.

Variation 11:

Simon SD and Srougi M, "Neoadjuvant M-VAC Chemotherapy and Partial Cystectomy for Treatment of Locally Invasive Transitional Cell Carcinoma of the Bladder," *Prog Clin Biol Res*, 1990, 353:169-74.

Variation 12:

Farah R, Chodak GW, Vogelzang NJ, et al, "Curative Radiotherapy Following Chemotherapy for Invasive Bladder Carcinoma (A Preliminary Report)," *Int J Radiat Oncol Biol Phys*, 1991, 20(3):413-7.

Variation 13:

Vogelzang NJ, Moormeier JA, Awan AM, et al, "Methotrexate, Vinblastine, Doxorubicin, and Cisplatin Followed by Radiotherapy or Surgery for Muscle Invasive Bladder Cancer: The University of Chicago Experience," *J Urol*, 1993, 149(4):753-7.

M-VAC (Breast Cancer)

Use Breast cancer

Regimen

Methotrexate: I.V.: 30 mg/m^2/day days 1, 15, and 22

[total dose/cycle = 90 mg/m^2]

Vinblastine: I.V.: 3 mg/m^2/day days 2, 15, and 22

[total dose/cycle = 9 mg/m^2]

Doxorubicin: I.V.: 30 mg/m^2 day 2

[total dose/cycle = 30 mg/m^2]

Cisplatin: I.V.: 70 mg/m^2 day 2

[total dose/cycle = 70 mg/m^2]

Leucovorin: Oral: 10 mg every 6 hours for 6 doses days 2, 16, and 23

[total dose/cycle = 180 mg]

Repeat cycle every 4 weeks

References

Morrell LE, Lee YJ, Hurley J, et al, "A Phase II Trial of Neoadjuvant Methotrexate, Vinblastine, Doxorubicin, and Cisplatin in the Treatment of Patients With Locally Advanced Breast Carcinoma," *Cancer*, 1998, 82(3):503-11.

M-VAC (Cervical Cancer)
Use Cervical cancer
Regimen
Methotrexate: I.V.: 30 mg/m²/day days 1, 15, and 22
[total dose/cycle = 90 mg/m²]
Vinblastine: I.V.: 3 mg/m²/day days 2, 15, and 22
[total dose/cycle = 9 mg/m²]
Doxorubicin: I.V.: 30 mg/m² day 2
[total dose/cycle = 30 mg/m²]
Cisplatin: I.V.: 70 mg/m² day 2
[total dose/cycle = 70 mg/m²]
Repeat cycle every 4 weeks
References
Wilson TO, "Neoadjuvant MVAC (Methotrexate, Vinblastine, Doxorubicin, Cisplatin) Chemotherapy for Locally Advanced or Metastatic Cervical and Vaginal Cancer," *Adjuvant Therapy of Cancer VII*, Salmon SE, ed, Philadelphia, PA: J B Lipincott Co, 1997, 366-71.

M-VAC (Endometrial Cancer)
Use Endometrial cancer
Regimen
Methotrexate: I.V.: 30 mg/m²/day days 1, 15, and 22
[total dose/cycle = 90 mg/m²]
Vinblastine: I.V.: 3 mg/m²/day days 2, 15, and 22
[total dose/cycle = 9 mg/m²]
Doxorubicin: I.V.: 30 mg/m²/day day 2
[total dose/cycle = 30 mg/m²]
Cisplatin: I.V.: 70 mg/m²/day day 2
[total dose/cycle = 70 mg/m²]
Repeat cycle every 4 weeks
References
Long HJ 3rd, Langdon RM Jr, Cha SS, et al, "Phase II Trial of Methotrexate, Vinblastine, Doxorubicin, and Cisplatin in Advanced/Recurrent Endometrial Carcinoma," *Gynecol Oncol*, 1995, 58(2):240-3.

M-VAC (Head and Neck Cancer)
Use Head and neck cancer
Regimen
Methotrexate: I.V.: 30 mg/m²/day days 1, 15, and 22
[total dose/cycle = 90 mg/m²]
Vinblastine: I.V.: 3 mg/m²/day days 2, 15, and 22
[total dose/cycle = 9 mg/m²]
Doxorubicin: I.V.: 30 mg/m² day 2
[total dose/cycle = 30 mg/m²]
Cisplatin: I.V.: 70 mg/m² day 2
[total dose/cycle = 70 mg/m²]
Repeat cycle every 4 weeks
References
Okuno SH, Mailliard JA, Suman VJ, et al, "Phase II Study of Methotrexate, Vinblastine, Doxorubicin, and Cisplatin in Patients With Squamous Cell Carcinoma of the Upper Respiratory or Alimentary Passages of the Head and Neck," *Cancer*, 2002, 94(8):2224-31.

MVPP
Use Lymphoma, Hodgkin's disease
Regimen
Mechlorethamine: I.V.: 6 mg/m²/day days 1 and 8
[total dose/cycle = 12 mg/m²]
Vinblastine: I.V.: 4 mg/m²/day days 1 and 8
[total dose/cycle = 8 mg/m²]
(Continued)

MVPP *(Continued)*

Procarbazine: Oral: 100 mg/m^2/day days 1 to 14
  [total dose/cycle = 1400 mg/m^2]
Prednisone: Oral: 40 mg/m^2/day days 1 to 14
  [total dose/cycle = 560 mg/m^2]
Repeat cycle every 4-6 weeks

References

Cooper MR, Pajak TF, Nissen NI, et al, "A New Effective Four-Drug Combination of CCNU (1-[2-Chloroethyl]-3-Cyclohexyl-1-Nitrosourea) (NSC-79038), Vinblastine, Prednisone, and Procarbazine for the Treatment of Advanced Hodgkin's Disease," *Cancer*, 1980, 46(4):654-62.

N4SE Protocol

Use Neuroblastoma

Regimen

Vincristine: I.V.: 0.05 mg/kg/day days 1 and 2
  [total dose/cycle = 0.1 mg/kg]
Doxorubicin: I.V.: 15 mg/m^2/day days 1 and 2
  [total dose/cycle = 30 mg/m^2]
Cyclophosphamide: I.V.: 30 mg/kg/day days 1 and 2
  [total dose/cycle = 60 mg/kg]
Fluorouracil: I.V.: 1 mg/kg/day days 3, 8, and 9
  [total dose/cycle = 3 mg/kg]
Cytarabine: I.V.: 3 mg/kg/day days 3, 8, and 9
  [total dose/cycle = 9 mg/kg]
Hydroxyurea: Oral: 40 mg/kg/day days 3, 8, and 9
  [total dose/cycle = 120 mg/kg]
Repeat cycle every 21-28 days

References

Kushner BH and Helson L, "Coordinated Use of Sequentially Escalated Cyclophosphamide and Cell-Cycle-Specific Chemotherapy (N4SE Protocol) for Advanced Neuroblastoma: Experience With 100 Patients," *J Clin Oncol*, 1987, 5(11):1746-51.

N6 Protocol

Use Neuroblastoma

Regimen

Course 1, 2, 4, and 6:
  Cyclophosphamide: I.V.: 70 mg/kg/day days 1 and 2
    [total dose/cycle = 140 mg/kg]
  Doxorubicin: I.V.: 25 mg/m^2/day continuous infusion days 1 to 3
    [total dose/cycle = 75 mg/m^2]
  Vincristine: I.V.: 0.033 mg/kg/day continuous infusion days 1 to 3
    [total dose/cycle = 0.099 mg/kg]
  Vincristine: I.V.: 1.5 mg/m^2 day 9
    [total dose/cycle = 1.5 mg/m^2]
Course 3, 5, and 7:
  Etoposide: I.V.: 200 mg/m^2/day days 1 to 3
    [total dose/cycle = 600 mg/m^2]
  Cisplatin: I.V.: 50 mg/m^2/day days 1 to 4
    [total dose/cycle = 200 mg/m^2]

References

Kushner BH, LaQuaglia MP, Bonilla MA, et al, "Highly Effective Induction Therapy for Stage 4 Neuroblastoma in Children Over 1 Year of Age," *J Clin Oncol*, 1994, 12(12):2607-13.

NFL

Use Breast cancer

Regimen NOTE: Multiple variations are listed below.

Variation 1:

Mitoxantrone: I.V.: 12 mg/m^2 day 1

[total dose/cycle = 12 mg/m^2]

Fluorouracil: I.V.: 350 mg/m^2/day days 1 to 3

[total dose/cycle = 1050 mg/m^2]

Leucovorin: I.V.: 300 mg/m^2/day days 1 to 3

[total dose/cycle = 900 mg/m^2]

Repeat cycle every 21 days

Variation 2:

Mitoxantrone: I.V.: 10 mg/m^2 day 1

[total dose/cycle = 10 mg/m^2]

Fluorouracil: I.V.: 1000 mg/m^2/day continuous infusion days 1 to 3

[total dose/cycle = 3000 mg/m^2]

Leucovorin: I.V.: 100 mg/m^2/day days 1 to 3

[total dose/cycle = 300 mg/m^2]

Repeat cycle every 21 days

References

Variation 1:

Hainsworth JD, Andrews MB, Johnson DH, et al, "Mitoxantrone, Fluorouracil, and High-Dose Leucovorin: An Effective, Well-Tolerated Regimen for Metastatic Breast Cancer," *J Clin Oncol*, 1991, 9(10):1731-5.

Variation 2:

Jones SE, Mennel RG, Brooks B, et al, "Phase II Study of Mitoxantrone, Leucovorin, and Infusional Fluorouracil for Treatment of Metastatic Breast Cancer," *J Clin Oncol*, 1991, 9(10):1736-9.

OPA

Use Lymphoma, Hodgkin's disease

Regimen

Vincristine: I.V.: 1.5 mg/m^2/day (maximum 2 mg) days 1, 8, and 15

[total dose/cycle = 4.5 mg/m^2]

Prednisone: Oral: 60 mg/m^2/day days 1 to 15 in 3 divided doses

[total dose/cycle = 900 mg/m^2]

Doxorubicin: I.V.: 40 mg/m^2/day days 1 and 15

[total dose/cycle = 80 mg/m^2]

Second cycle may be given based on individual response; time between cycles not specified

References

Schellong G, Riepenhausen M, Creutzig U, et al, "Low Risk of Secondary Leukemias After Chemotherapy Without Mechlorethamine in Childhood Hodgkin's Disease. German-Austrian Pediatric Hodgkin's Disease Group," *J Clin Oncol*, 1997, 15(6):2247-53.

OPEC

Use Neuroblastoma

Regimen

Vincristine: I.V.: 1.5 mg/m^2 day 1

[total dose/cycle = 1.5 mg/m^2]

Cyclophosphamide: I.V.: 600 mg/m^2 day 1

[total dose/cycle = 600 mg/m^2]

Cisplatin: I.V.: 100 mg/m^2 day 2

[total dose/cycle = 100 mg/m^2]

Teniposide: I.V.: 150 mg/m^2 day 4

[total dose/cycle = 150 mg/m^2]

Repeat cycle every 21 days

(Continued)

OPEC (Continued)

References
Shafford EA, Rogers DW, Pritchard J, et al, "Advanced Neuroblastoma: Improved Response Rate Using a Multiagent Regimen (OPEC) Including Sequential Cisplatin and VM-26," *J Clin Oncol*, 1984, 2(7):742-7.

OPEC-D

Use Neuroblastoma

Regimen

Vincristine: I.V.: 1.5 mg/m^2 day 1
  [total dose/cycle = 1.5 mg/m^2]
Cyclophosphamide: I.V.: 600 mg/m^2 day 1
  [total dose/cycle = 600 mg/m^2]
Doxorubicin: I.V.: 40 mg/m^2 day 1
  [total dose/cycle = 40 mg/m^2]
Cisplatin: I.V.: 100 mg/m^2 day 2
  [total dose/cycle = 100 mg/m^2]
Teniposide: I.V.: 150 mg/m^2 day 4
  [total dose/cycle = 150 mg/m^2]
Repeat cycle every 21 days

References
Shafford EA, Rogers DW, Pritchard J, et al, "Advanced Neuroblastoma: Improved Response Rate Using a Multiagent Regimen (OPEC) Including Sequential Cisplatin and VM-26," *J Clin Oncol*, 1984, 2(7):742-7.

OPPA

Use Lymphoma, Hodgkin's disease

Regimen

Vincristine: I.V.: 1.5 mg/m^2/day (maximum 2 mg) days 1, 8, and 15
  [total dose/cycle = 4.5 mg/m^2]
Prednisone: Oral: 60 mg/m^2/day days 1 to 15 in 3 divided doses
  [total dose/cycle = 900 mg/m^2]
Doxorubicin: I.V.: 40 mg/m^2/day days 1 and 15
  [total dose/cycle = 80 mg/m^2]
Procarbazine: Oral: 100 mg/m^2/day days 1 to 15 in 2 or 3 divided doses
  [total dose/cycle = 1500 mg/m^2]
Second cycle may be given based on individual response; time between cycles not specified

References
Schellong G, Riepenhausen M, Creutzig U, et al, "Low Risk of Secondary Leukemias After Chemotherapy Without Mechlorethamine in Childhood Hodgkin's Disease. German-Austrian Pediatric Hodgkin's Disease Group," *J Clin Oncol*, 1997, 15(6):2247-53.

♦ **Oxaliplatin-Capecitabine** *see* XelOx *on page 1293*

♦ **Oxaliplatin-Fluorouracil-Leucovorin-Bevacizumab** *see*
  Bevacizumab-Oxaliplatin-Fluorouracil-Leucovorin *on page 1152*

PAC (CAP)

Use Ovarian cancer

Regimen

Cisplatin: I.V.: 50 mg/m^2 day 1
  [total dose/cycle = 50 mg/m^2]
Doxorubicin: I.V.: 50 mg/m^2 day 1
  [total dose/cycle = 50 mg/m^2]
Cyclophosphamide: I.V.: 1000 mg/m^2 day 1
  [total dose/cycle = 1000 mg/m^2]
Repeat cycle every 21 days for 8 cycles

References

Omura GA, Bundy BN, Berek JS, et al, "Randomized Trial of Cyclophosphamide Plus Cisplatin With or Without Doxorubicin in Ovarian Carcinoma: A Gynecologic Oncology Group Study," *J Clin Oncol*, 1989, 7(4):457-65.

PA-CI

Use Hepatoblastoma

Regimen NOTE: Multiple variations are listed below.

Variation 1:

Cisplatin: I.V.: 90 mg/m² day 1

[total dose/cycle = 90 mg/m²]

Doxorubicin: I.V.: 20 mg/m²/day continuous infusion days 2 to 5

[total dose/cycle = 80 mg/m²]

Repeat cycle every 21 days

Variation 2:

Cisplatin: I.V.: 20 mg/m²/day days 1 to 4

[total dose/cycle = 80 mg/m²]

Doxorubicin: I.V.: 100 mg/m² continuous infusion day 1

[total dose/cycle = 100 mg/m²]

Repeat cycle every 21-28 days

References

Variation 1:

Ortega JA, Douglass EC, Feusner JH, et al, "Randomized Comparison of Cisplatin/Vincristine/ Fluorouracil and Cisplatin/Continuous Infusion Doxorubicin for Treatment of Pediatric Hepatoblastoma: A Report From the Children's Cancer Group and the Pediatric Oncology Group," *J Clin Oncol*, 2000, 18(14):2665-75.

Variation 2:

Ortega JA, Krailo MD, Haas JE, et al, "Effective Treatment of Unresectable or Metastatic Hepatoblastoma With Cisplatin and Continuous Infusion Doxorubicin Chemotherapy: A Report From the Childrens Cancer Study Group," *J Clin Oncol*, 1991, 9(12):2167-76.

Paclitaxel-Bevacizumab

Index Terms Bevacizumab-Paclitaxel

Use Breast cancer

Regimen

Paclitaxel: I.V.: 90 mg/m²/day days 1, 8, and 15

[total dose/cycle = 270 mg/m²]

Bevacizumab: I.V.: 10 mg/kg/day days 1 and 15

[total dose/cycle = 20 mg/kg]

Repeat cycle every 28 days for up to 18 cycles

References

Miller KD, "E2100: A Phase III Trial of Paclitaxel Versus Paclitaxel/Bevacizumab for Metastatic Breast Cancer," *Clin Breast Cancer*, 2003, 3(6):421-2.

♦ **Paclitaxel-Carboplatin (Adenocarcinoma)** *see* Carbo-Tax (Adenocarcinoma) *on page 1161*

Paclitaxel-Carboplatin-Bevacizumab

Use Lung cancer, nonsquamous, nonsmall cell

Regimen

Paclitaxel: I.V.: 200 mg/m² infused over 3 hours day 1

[total dose/cycle = 200 mg/m²]

followed by

Carboplatin: I.V.: Target AUC 6 day 1

[total dose/cycle = AUC = 6]

followed by

Bevacizumab: I.V.: 15 mg/kg day 1

[total dose/cycle = 15 mg/kg]

Repeat cycle every 21 days for 6 cycles

(Continued)

Paclitaxel-Carboplatin-Bevacizumab *(Continued)*

References
Johnson DH, Fehrenbacher L, Novotny WF, "Randomized Phase II Trial Comparing Bevacizumab Plus Carboplatin and Paclitaxel With Carboplatin and Paclitaxel Alone in Previously Untreated Locally Advanced or Metastatic Nonsmall-Cell Lung Cancer," *J Clin Oncol*, 2004, 22(11):2184-91.

Sandler A, Gray R, Perry MC, et al, "Paclitaxel-Carboplatin Alone or With Bevacizumab for Nonsmall-Cell Lung Cancer," *N Engl J Med*, 2006, 355(24):2542-50.

Paclitaxel-Carboplatin (Bladder Cancer)
Index Terms Carboplatin-Paclitaxel (Bladder Cancer); PC (Bladder Cancer)
Use Bladder cancer
Regimen
Paclitaxel: I.V.: 200 mg/m^2 or 225 mg/m^2 day 1
[total dose/cycle = 200 or 225 mg/m^2]
Carboplatin: I.V.: AUC 5-6 day 1
[total dose/cycle = AUC = 5-6]
Repeat cycle every 21 days
References
Vaughn DJ, Malkowicz SB, Zoltick B, et al, "Paclitaxel Plus Carboplatin in Advanced Carcinoma of the Urothelium: An Active and Tolerable Outpatient Regimen," *J Clin Oncol*, 1998, 16(1):255-60.

Paclitaxel-Carboplatin-Etoposide
Use Adenocarcinoma, unknown primary
Regimen
Paclitaxel: I.V.: 200 mg/m^2 infused over 1 hour day 1
[total dose/cycle = 200 mg/m^2]
followed by
Carboplatin: I.V.: Target AUC 6
[total dose = AUC = 6]
Etoposide: Oral: 50 mg/day days 1, 3, 5, 7, and 9
and Oral: 100 mg/day days 2, 4, 6, 8, and 10
[total dose/cycle = 750 mg]
Repeat cycle every 21 days
References
Hainsworth JD, Erland JB, Kalman LA, et al, "Carcinoma of Unknown Primary Site: Treatment With 1-Hour Paclitaxel, Carboplatin, and Extended-Schedule Etoposide," *J Clin Oncol*, 1997, 15(6):2385-93.

Paclitaxel-Carboplatin-Gemcitabine
Use Bladder cancer
Regimen
Paclitaxel: I.V.: 200 mg/m^2 day 1
[total dose/cycle = 200 mg/m^2]
Gemcitabine: I.V.: 1000 mg/m^2/day days 1 and 8
[total dose/cycle = 2000 mg/m^2]
Carboplatin: I.V.: AUC 5 day 1
[total dose/cycle = AUC = 5]
Repeat cycle every 21 days
References
Hainsworth JD, Meluch AA, Litchy S, et al, "Paclitaxel, Carboplatin, and Gemcitabine in the Treatment of Patients With Advanced Transitional Cell Carcinoma of the Urothelium," *Cancer*, 2005, 103(11):2298-303

♦ **Paclitaxel-Carboplatin (Nonsmall Cell Lung Cancer)** *see* Carbo-Tax (Nonsmall Cell Lung Cancer) *on page 1161*

♦ **Paclitaxel-Carboplatin (Ovarian Cancer)** *see* Carbo-Tax (Ovarian Cancer) *on page 1162*

♦ **Paclitaxel + Estramustine** *see* PE *on page 1269*

Paclitaxel + Estramustine + Carboplatin

Use Prostate cancer

Regimen

Paclitaxel: I.V.: 100 mg/m^2 day 3 each week
[total dose/cycle = 400 mg/m^2]
Estramustine: Oral: 10 mg/kg/day days 1 to 5 each week
[total dose/cycle = 200 mg/kg]
Carboplatin: I.V.: Target AUC 6 day 3
[total dose/cycle = AUC = 6]
Repeat cycle every 28 days

References

Kelly WK, Curley T, Slovin S, et al, "Paclitaxel, Estramustine Phosphate, and Carboplatin in Patients With Advanced Prostate Cancer," *J Clin Oncol*, 2001, 19(1):44-53.

Paclitaxel + Estramustine + Etoposide

Use Prostate cancer

Regimen

Paclitaxel: I.V.: 135 mg/m^2 day 2
[total dose/cycle = 135 mg/m^2]
Estramustine: Oral: 280 mg 3 times/day days 1 to 14
[total dose/cycle = 11,760 mg]
Etoposide: Oral: 100 mg/day days 1 to 14
[total dose/cycle = 1400 mg]
Repeat cycle every 21 days

References

Smith DC, Esper P, Strawderman M, et al, "Phase II Trial of Oral Estramustine, Oral Etoposide, and Intravenous Paclitaxel in Hormone-Refractory Prostate Cancer," *J Clin Oncol*, 1999, 17(6):1664-71.

Paclitaxel-Gemcitabine

Index Terms Gemcitabine-Paclitaxel

Use Bladder cancer

Regimen

Paclitaxel: I.V.: 200 mg/m^2 day 1
[total dose/cycle = 200 mg/m^2]
Gemcitabine: I.V.: 1000 mg/m^2/day days 1, 8, and 15
[total dose/cycle = 3000 mg/m^2]
Repeat cycle every 21 days for a maximum of 6 cycles

References

Meluch AA, Greco FA, Burris HA 3rd, et al, "Paclitaxel and Gemcitabine Chemotherapy for Advanced Transitional-Cell Carcinoma of the Urothelial Tract: A Phase II Trial of the Minnie Pearl Cancer Research Network," *J Clin Oncol*, 2001, 19(12):3018-24.

Paclitaxel-Ifosfamide-Cisplatin

Index Terms Cisplatin-Ifosfamide-Paclitaxel

Use Testicular cancer

Regimen

Paclitaxel: I.V.: 250 mg/m^2 continuous infusion day 1
[total dose/cycle = 250 mg/m^2]
Ifosfamide: I.V.: 1500 mg/m^2/day days 2 to 5
[total dose/cycle = 6000 mg/m^2]
Cisplatin: I.V.: 25 mg/m^2/day days 2 to 5
[total dose/cycle = 100 mg/m^2]
(Continued)

Paclitaxel-Ifosfamide-Cisplatin *(Continued)*

Mesna: I.V.: 500 mg/m² prior to ifosfamide and every 4 hours for 2 doses, days 2 to 5

[total dose/cycle = 6000 mg/m²]

Repeat cycle every 21 days for 4 cycles

References

Kondagunta GV, Bacik J, Donadio A, et al, "Combination of Paclitaxel, Ifosfamide, and Cisplatin is an Effective Second-Line Therapy for Patients With Relapsed Testicular Germ Cell Tumors," *J Clin Oncol*, 2005, 23(27):6549-55.

Paclitaxel-Vinorelbine

Use Breast cancer

Regimen NOTE: Multiple variations are listed below.

Variation 1:

Paclitaxel: I.V.: 135 mg/m² day 1

[total dose/cycle = 135 mg/m²]

Vinorelbine: I.V.: 30 mg/m² day 1

[total dose/cycle = 30 mg/m²]

Repeat cycle every 21 days

Variation 2:

Paclitaxel: I.V.: 150 mg/m² day 1

[total dose/cycle = 150 mg/m²]

Vinorelbine: I.V.: 25 mg/m² day 1

[total dose/cycle = 25 mg/m²]

Repeat cycle every 21 days

Variation 3:

Paclitaxel: I.V.: 135 mg/m² day 1

[total dose/cycle = 135 mg/m²]

Vinorelbine: I.V.: 30 mg/m²/day days 1 and 8

[total dose/cycle = 60 mg/m²]

Repeat cycle every 28 days

References

Variation 1:
Martin M, Lluch A, Casado A, et al, "Paclitaxel Plus Vinorelbine: An Active Regimen in Metastatic Breast Cancer Patients With Prior Anthracycline Exposure," *Ann Oncol*, 2000, 11(1):85-9.

Variation 2:
Vici P, Amodio A, Di Lauro L, et al, "First-Line Chemotherapy With Vinorelbine and Paclitaxel As Simultaneous Infusion in Advanced Breast Cancer," *Oncology*, 2000, 58(1):3-7.

Variation 3:
Romero Acuna LR, Langhi M, Perez J, et al, "Vinorelbine and Paclitaxel as First-Line Chemotherapy in Metastatic Breast Cancer," *J Clin Oncol*, 1999, 17(1):74-81.

♦ **PC (Bladder Cancer)** *see* Paclitaxel-Carboplatin (Bladder Cancer) *on page 1264*

PCE

Use Adenocarcinoma, unknown primary

Regimen

Paclitaxel: I.V.: 200 mg/m² day 1

[total dose/cycle = 200 mg/m²]

Carboplatin: I.V.: AUC = 6 day 1

[total dose/cycle = AUC = 6]

Etoposide: Oral: 50 mg/day days 1, 3, 5, 7, and 9

and Oral: 100 mg/day days 2, 4, 6, 8, and 10

[total dose/cycle = 750 mg]

Repeat cycle every 3 weeks

References

Greco FA, Burris HA 3rd, Erland JB, et al, "Carcinoma of Unknown Primary Site," *Cancer*, 2000, 89(12):2655-60.

PC (Nonsmall Cell Lung Cancer)

Use Lung cancer, nonsmall cell

Regimen NOTE: Multiple variations are listed below.

Variation 1:

Paclitaxel: I.V.: 175-225 mg/m^2 day 1

[total dose/cycle = 175-225 mg/m^2]

Carboplatin: I.V.: Target AUC 5-7 day 1

[total dose/cycle = AUC = 5-7]

Repeat cycle every 21 days for 2-8 cycles

Variation 2:

Paclitaxel: I.V.: 175 mg/m^2 day 1

[total dose/cycle = 175 mg/m^2]

Cisplatin: I.V.: 80 mg/m^2 day 1

[total dose/cycle = 80 mg/m^2]

Repeat cycle every 21 days

Variation 3:

Paclitaxel: I.V.: 135 mg/m^2 continuous infusion day 1

[total dose/cycle = 135 mg/m^2]

Carboplatin: I.V.: AUC 7.5 day 2

[total dose/cycle = AUC = 7.5]

Repeat cycle every 21 days

Variation 4:

Paclitaxel: I.V.: 135 mg/m^2 continuous infusion day 1

[total dose/cycle = 135 mg/m^2]

Cisplatin: I.V.: 75 mg/m^2 day 2

[total dose/cycle = 75 mg/m^2]

Repeat cycle every 21 days

References

Variation 1:

Hainsworth JD, Urba WJ, Hon JK, et al, "One-Hour Paclitaxel Plus Carboplatin in the Treatment of Advanced Nonsmall-Cell Lung Cancer: Results of a Multicentre, Phase II Trial," *Eur J Cancer*, 1998, 34(5):654-8.

Helsing M, Thaning L, Sederholm C, et al, "Treatment With Paclitaxel 1-h Infusion and Carboplatin of Patients With Advanced Nonsmall-Cell Lung Cancer: A Phase II Multicentre Trial. Joint Lung Cancer Study Group," *Lung Cancer*, 1999, 24(2):107-13.

Kosmidis PA, Mylonakis N, Fountzilas G, et al, "Paclitaxel and Carboplatin in Inoperable Nonsmall-Cell Lung Cancer: A Phase II Study," *Ann Oncol*, 1997, 8(7):697-9.

Laohavinij S, Maoleekoonpairoj S, Cheirsilpa A, et al, "Phase II Study of Paclitaxel and Carboplatin for Advanced Nonsmall Cell Lung Cancer," *Lung Cancer*, 1999, 26(3):175-85.

Variation 2:

Giaccone G, Splinter TA, Debruyne C, et al, "Randomized Study of Paclitaxel-Cisplatin Versus Cisplatin-Teniposide in Patients With Advanced Nonsmall-Cell Lung Cancer. The European Organization for Research and Treatment of Cancer Lung Cancer Cooperative Group," *J Clin Oncol*, 1998, 16(6):2133-41.

Variation 3:

Langer CJ, Leighton JC, Comis RL, et al, "Paclitaxel by 24- or 1-Hour Infusion in Combination With Carboplatin in Advanced Nonsmall Cell Lung Cancer: The Fox Chase Cancer Center Experience," *Semin Oncol*, 1995, 22(4 Suppl 9):18-29.

Variation 4:

Schiller JH, Harrington D, Belani CP, et al, "Comparison of Four Chemotherapy Regimens for Advanced Nonsmall-Cell Lung Cancer," *N Engl J Med*, 2002, 346(2):92-8.

PCR

Index Terms Pentostatin-Cyclophosphamide-Rituximab

Use Leukemia, chronic lymphocytic

Regimen NOTE: Multiple variations are listed on next page.

(Continued)

PCR *(Continued)*

Variation 1:
  Cycle 1:
    Cyclophosphamide: I.V.: 600 mg/m^2 day 1
      [total dose/cycle = 600 mg/m^2]
    Pentostatin: I.V.: 4 mg/m^2 day 1
      [total dose/cycle = 4 mg/m^2]
    Treatment cycle is 3 weeks
  Cycles 2-6:
    Cyclophosphamide: I.V.: 600 mg/m^2 day 1
      [total dose/cycle = 600 mg/m^2]
    Pentostatin: I.V.: 4 mg/m^2 day 1
      [total dose/cycle = 4 mg/m^2]
    Rituximab: I.V.: 375 mg/m^2 day 1
      [total dose/cycle = 375 mg/m^2]
    Repeat cycle every 3 weeks
Variation 2:
  Cycle 1:
    Pentostatin: I.V.: 2 mg/m^2 day 1
      [total dose/cycle = 2 mg/m^2]
    Cyclophosphamide: I.V.: 600 mg/m^2 day 1
      [total dose/cycle = 600 mg/m^2]
    Rituximab: I.V.: 100 mg/m^2 day 1 only
      followed by I.V.: 375 mg/m^2/day days 3 and 5 only
      [total dose/cycle 1 = 850 mg/m^2]
    Treatment cycle is 3 weeks
  Cycles 2-6:
    Pentostatin: I.V.: 2 mg/m^2 day 1
      [total dose/cycle = 2 mg/m^2]
    Cyclophosphamide: I.V.: 600 mg/m^2 day 1
      [total dose/cycle = 600 mg/m^2]
    Rituximab: I.V.: 375 mg/m^2 day 1
      [total dose/cycle = 375 mg/m^2]
    Repeat cycle every 3 weeks

References

Variation 1:
Lamanna N, Kalaycio M, Maslak P, et al, "Pentostatin, Cyclophosphamide, and Rituximab Is an Active, Well-Tolerated Regimen for Patients With Previously Treated Chronic Lymphocytic Leukemia," *J Clin Oncol*, 2006, 24(10):1575-81.
Variation 2:
Kay NE, Geyer SM, Call TG, et al, "Combination Chemoimmunotherapy With Pentostatin, Cyclophosphamide, and Rituximab Shows Significant Clinical Activity With Low Accompanying Toxicity in Previously Untreated B Chronic Lymphocytic Leukemia," *Blood*, 2007, 109(2):405-11.

PCV

Use Brain tumors

Regimen
  Lomustine: Oral: 110 mg/m^2 day 1
    [total dose/cycle = 110 mg/m^2]
  Procarbazine: Oral: 60 mg/m^2/day days 8 to 21
    [total dose/cycle = 840 mg/m^2]
  Vincristine: I.V.: 1.4 mg/m^2/day (maximum 2 mg) days 8 and 29
    [total dose/cycle = 2.8 mg/m^2; maximum 4 mg]
  Repeat cycle every 6-8 weeks

References

Levin VA, Silver P, Hannigan J, et al, "Superiority of Postradiotherapy Adjuvant Chemotherapy With CCNU, Procarbazine, and Vincristine (PCV) Over BCNU for Anaplastic Gliomas: NCOG 6G61 Final Report," *Int J Radiat Oncol Biol Phys*, 1990, 18(2):321-4.

van den Bent MJ, Carpentier AF, Brandes AA, et al, "Adjuvant Procarbazine, Lomustine, and Vincristine Improves Progression-Free Survival but not Overall Survival in Newly Diagnosed Anaplastic Oligodendrogliomas and Oligoastrocytomas: A Randomized European Organisation for Research and Treatment of Cancer Phase III Trial," *J Clin Oncol*, 2006, 24(18):2715-22.

PE

Index Terms Paclitaxel + Estramustine

Use Prostate cancer

Regimen NOTE: Multiple variations are listed below.

Variation 1:

Paclitaxel: I.V.: 30-35 mg/m^2/day continuous infusion (given in 2-3 divided doses daily) either days 1 to 4 or days 2 to 5
[total dose/cycle = 120-140 mg/m^2]

Estramustine: Oral: 600 mg/m^2/day days 1 to 21
[total dose/cycle = 12,600 mg/m^2]

Repeat cycle every 21 days

Variation 2:

Paclitaxel: I.V. 60-107 mg/m^2 infused over 3 hours weekly for 6 weeks
[total dose/cycle = 360-642 mg/m^2]

Estramustine: Oral: 280 mg twice daily 3 days/week for 6 weeks
[total dose/cycle = 3360 mg]

Repeat cycle every 8 weeks

Variation 3:

Paclitaxel: I.V. 150 mg/m^2/day days 2, 9, and 16
[total dose/cycle = 450 mg/m^2]

Estramustine: Oral: 280 mg 3 times/day days 1, 2, 3, 8, 9, 10, 15, 16, and 17
[total dose/week = 7560 mg/m^2]

Repeat cycle every 4 weeks

Variation 4:

Paclitaxel: I.V.: 100 mg/m^2/day days 2, 9, and 16
[total dose/cycle = 300 mg/m^2]

Estramustine: Oral: 280 mg 3 times/day days 1, 2, 3, 8, 9, 10, 15, 16, and 17
[total dose/cycle = 7560 mg]

Repeat cycle every 4 weeks

References

Variation 1:

Hudes GR, Nathan FE, Khater C, et al, "Paclitaxel Plus Estramustine in Metastatic Hormone-Refractory Prostate Cancer," *Semin Oncol*, 1995, 22(5 Suppl 12):41-5.

Hudes GR, Nathan F, Khater C, et al, "Phase II Trial of 96-Hour Paclitaxel Plus Oral Estramustine Phosphate in Metastatic Hormone-Refractory Prostate Cancer," *J Clin Oncol*, 1997, 15(9):3156-63.

Variation 2:

Haas N, Roth B, Garay C, et al, "Phase I Trial of Weekly Paclitaxel Plus Oral Estramustine Phosphate in Patients With Hormone-Refractory Prostate Cancer," *Urology*, 2001, 58(1):59-64

Variation 3:

Vaishampayan U, Fontana J, Du W, et al, "An Active Regimen of Weekly Paclitaxel and Estramustine in Metastatic Androgen-Independent Prostate Cancer," *Urology*, 2002, 60(6):1050-4.

Variation 4:

Berry W, Gregurich M, Dakhil S, et al, "Phase II Randomized Trial of Weekly Paclitaxel With or Without Estramustine Phosphate in Patients With Symptomatic, Hormone-Refractory Metastatic Carcinoma of the Prostate." *Proc Am Soc Clin Oncol*, 2001, 20:175a.

PE-CAdO

Use Neuroblastoma

Regimen

Cisplatin: I.V.: 100 mg/m² day 1
[total dose/cycle = 100 mg/m²]
Teniposide: I.V.: 160 mg/m² day 3
[total dose/cycle = 160 mg/m²]

alternating with

Cyclophosphamide: I.V.: 300 mg/m²/day days 1 to 5
[total dose/cycle = 1500 mg/m²]
Doxorubicin: I.V.: 60 mg/m² day 5
[total dose/cycle = 60 mg/m²]
Vincristine: I.V.: 1.5 mg/m²/day days 1 and 5
[total dose/cycle = 3 mg/m²]
Repeat cycle every 21 days

References

Bernard JL, Philip T, Zucker JM, et al, "Sequential Cisplatin/VM-26 and Vincristine/Cyclophosphamide/Doxorubicin in Metastatic Neuroblastoma: An Effective Alternating Non-Cross-Resistant Regimen?" *J Clin Oncol*, 1987, 5(12):1952-9.

Pemetrexed (Bladder Cancer)

Use Bladder cancer

Regimen

Pemetrexed: I.V.: 500 mg/m² infused over 10 minutes day 1
[total dose/cycle = 500 mg/m²]
Repeat cycle every 21 days

References

Sweeney CJ, Roth BJ, Kabbinavar FF, et al, "Phase II Study of Pemetrexed for Second-Line Treatment of Transitional Cell Cancer of the Urothelium," *J Clin Oncol*, 2006, 24(21):3451-7.

♦ **Pemetrexed-Cisplatin** *see* Cisplatin-Pemetrexed *on page 1176*

Pentostatin-Cyclophosphamide

Use Leukemia, chronic lymphocytic

Regimen

Cyclophosphamide: I.V.: 600 mg/m² day 1
[total dose/cycle = 600 mg/m²]
Pentostatin: I.V.: 4 mg/m² day 1
[total dose/cycle = 4 mg/m²]
Repeat cycle every 3 weeks for up to 6 cycles

References

Weiss MA, Maslak PG, Jurcic JG, et al, "Pentostatin and Cyclophosphamide: An Effective New Regimen in Previously Treated Patients With Chronic Lymphocytic Leukemia," *J Clin Oncol*, 2003, 21(7):1278-84.

♦ **Pentostatin-Cyclophosphamide-Rituximab** *see* PCR *on page 1267*

PFL (Colorectal Cancer)

Use Colorectal cancer

Regimen

Cisplatin: I.V.: 25 mg/m²/day continuous infusion days 1 to 5
[total dose/cycle = 125 mg/m²]
Fluorouracil: I.V.: 800 mg/m²/day continuous infusion days 2 to 5
[total dose/cycle = 3200 mg/m²]
Leucovorin calcium: I.V.: 500 mg/m²/day continuous infusion days 1 to 5
[total dose/cycle = 2500 mg/m²]
Repeat cycle every 28 days

References

Dreyfuss AI, Clark JR, Wright JE, et al, "Continuous Infusion High-Dose Leucovorin With 5-Fluorouracil and Cisplatin for Untreated Stage IV Carcinoma of the Head and Neck," *Ann Intern Med*, 1990, 112(3):167-72.

PFL (Head and Neck Cancer)

Use Head and neck cancer

Regimen NOTE: Multiple variations are listed below.

Variation 1:

Cisplatin: I.V.: 25 mg/m^2/day continuous infusion days 1 to 5
[total dose/cycle = 125 mg/m^2]

Fluorouracil: I.V.: 800 mg/m^2/day continuous infusion days 2 to 6
[total dose/cycle = 4000 mg/m^2]

Leucovorin: I.V.: 500 mg/m^2/day continuous infusion days 1 to 6
[total dose/cycle = 3000 mg/m^2]

Repeat cycle every 28 days

Variation 2:

Cisplatin: I.V.: 100 mg/m^2 day 1
[total dose/cycle = 100 mg/m^2]

Fluorouracil: I.V.: 600-1000 mg/m^2/day continuous infusion days 1 to 5
[total dose/cycle = 3000-5000 mg/m^2]

Leucovorin: Oral: 50 mg/m^2 every 4-6 hours days 1 to 6
[total dose/cycle = 1200-1800 mg/m^2]

Repeat cycle every 21 days

References

Variation 1:

Dreyfuss AI, Clark JR, Wright JE, et al, "Continuous Infusion High-Dose Leucovorin With 5-Fluorouracil and Cisplatin for Untreated Stage IV Carcinoma of the Head and Neck," *Ann Intern Med*, 1990, 112(3):167-72.

Variation 2:

Vokes EE, Schilsky RL, Weichselbaum RR, et al, "Cisplatin, 5-Fluorouracil, and High-Dose Oral Leucovorin for Advanced Head and Neck Cancer," *Cancer*, 1989, 63(6 Suppl):1048-53.

PFL + IFN

Use Head and neck cancer

Regimen

Cisplatin: I.V.: 100 mg/m^2 day 1
[total dose/cycle = 100 mg/m^2]

Fluorouracil: I.V.: 640 mg/m^2/day continuous infusion days 1 to 5
[total dose/cycle = 3200 mg/m^2]

Leucovorin calcium: Oral: 100 mg every 4 hours days 1 to 5
[total dose/cycle = 3000 mg/m^2]

Interferon alfa-2b: SubQ: 2 x 10^6 units/m^2 days 1 to 6
[total dose/cycle = 12 x 10^6 units/m^2]

References

Brockstein BE, Weichselbaum RW, and Vokes EE, "Concomitant and Rapidly Alternating Chemoradiotherapy for Head and Neck Cancer," *Advances in Oncology*, 1998, 14:8-15.

Kies MS, Haraf DJ, Athanasiadis I, et al, "Induction Chemotherapy Followed by Concurrent Chemoradiation for Advanced Head and Neck Cancer: Improved Disease Control And Survival," *J Clin Oncol*, 1998, 16(8):2715-21.

POC

Use Brain tumors

Regimen

Prednisone: Oral: 40 mg/m^2/day days 1 to 14
[total dose/cycle = 560 mg/m^2]

Vincristine: I.V.: 1.5 mg/m^2/day (maximum 2 mg) days 1, 8, and 15
[total dose/cycle = 4.5 mg/m^2]

(Continued)

POC (Continued)

Lomustine: Oral: 100 mg/m² day 1

[total dose/cycle = 100 mg/m²]

Repeat cycle every 6 weeks

References

Finlay JL, Boyett JM, Yates AJ, et al, "Randomized Phase III Trial in Childhood High-Grade Astrocytoma Comparing Vincristine, Lomustine, and Prednisone With the Eight-Drugs-In-1-Day Regimen. Childrens Cancer Group," *J Clin Oncol*, 1995, 13(1):112-23.

POG-8651

Use Osteosarcoma

Regimen

(Surgery at week 10)

Methotrexate: I.V.: 12 g/m² weeks 0, 1, 5, 6, 13, 14, 18, 19, 23, 24, 37, and 38

[total dose/cycle = 144 g/m²]

Leucovorin: (route not specified): 15 mg every 6 hours for 10 doses, weeks 0, 1, 5, 6, 13, 14, 18, 19, 23, 24, 37, and 38

[total dose/cycle = 1800 mg]

Doxorubicin: I.V.: 37.5 mg/m²/day days 1 and weeks 2, 7, 25, and 28 and 30 mg/m² days 1, 2, and 3, week 20

[total dose/cycle = 390 mg/m²]

Cisplatin: I.V.: 60 mg/m²/day days 1 and 2, weeks 2, 7, 25, and 28

[total dose/cycle = 480 mg/m²]

Cyclophosphamide: I.V.: 600 mg/m²/day days 1, 2, and 3, weeks 15, 31, 34, 39, and 42

[total dose/cycle = 9000 mg/m²]

Bleomycin: I.V.: 15 units/m²/day days 1, 2, and 3, weeks 15, 31, 34, 39, and 42

[total dose/cycle = 225 units/m²]

Dactinomycin: I.V.: 0.6 mg/m²/day days 1, 2, and 3, weeks 15, 31, 34, 39, and 42

[total dose/cycle = 9 mg/m²]

or

(Surgery at week 0)

Methotrexate: 12 g/m² weeks 3, 4, 8, 9, 13, 14, 18, 19, 23, 24, 37, and 38

[total dose/cycle = 144 g/m²]

Leucovorin: (route not specified): 15 mg every 6 hours for 10 doses, weeks 3, 4, 8, 9, 13, 14, 18, 19, 23, 24, 37, and 38

[total dose/cycle = 1800 mg]

Doxorubicin: I.V.: 37.5 mg/m²/day days 1 and 2, weeks 5, 10, 25, and 28 and 30 mg/m² days 1, 2, and 3, week 20

[total dose/cycle = 390 mg/m²]

Cisplatin: I.V.: 60 mg/m²/day days 1 and 2, weeks 5, 10, 25, and 28

[total dose/cycle = 480 mg/m²]

Cyclophosphamide: I.V.: 600 mg/m²/day days 1, 2, and 3, weeks 15, 31, 34, 39, and 42

[total dose/cycle = 9000 mg/m²]

Bleomycin: I.V.: 15 units/m²/day days 1, 2, and 3, weeks 15, 31, 34, 39, and 42

[total dose/cycle = 225 units/m²]

Dactinomycin: I.V.: 0.6 mg/m²/day days 1, 2, and 3, weeks 15, 31, 34, 39, and 42

[total dose/cycle = 9 mg/m²]

References
Goorin AM, Schwartzentruber DJ, Devidas M, et al, "Presurgical Chemotherapy Compared With Immediate Surgery and Adjuvant Chemotherapy for Nonmetastatic Osteosarcoma: Pediatric Oncology Group Study POG-8651," *J Clin Oncol*, 2003, 21(8):1574-80.

POMP
Use Leukemia, acute lymphocytic
Regimen Maintenance:
  Mercaptopurine: Oral: 50 mg 3 times/day
    [total dose/cycle = 4200-4650 mg]
  Methotrexate: Oral: 20 mg/m^2 once weekly
    [total dose/cycle = 80 mg/m^2]
  Vincristine: I.V.: 2 mg day 1
    [total dose/cycle = 2 mg]
  Prednisone: Oral: 200 mg/day days 1 to 5
    [total dose/cycle = 1000 mg]
  Repeat cycle monthly for 2 years

References
Kantarjian HM, O'Brien S, Smith TL, et al, "Results of Treatment With Hyper-CVAD, a Dose-Intensive Regimen, in Adult Acute Lymphocytic Leukemia," *J Clin Oncol*, 2000, 18(3):547-61.

Pro-MACE-CytaBOM
Use Lymphoma, non-Hodgkin's
Regimen
  Prednisone: Oral: 60 mg/m^2/day days 1 to 14
    [total dose/cycle = 840 mg/m^2]
  Doxorubicin: I.V.: 25 mg/m^2 day 1
    [total dose/cycle = 25 mg/m^2]
  Cyclophosphamide: I.V.: 650 mg/m^2 day 1
    [total dose/cycle = 650 mg/m^2]
  Etoposide: I.V.: 120 mg/m^2 day 1
    [total dose/cycle = 120 mg/m^2]
  Cytarabine: I.V.: 300 mg/m^2 day 8
    [total dose/cycle = 300 mg/m^2]
  Bleomycin: I.V.: 5 units/m^2 day 8
    [total dose/cycle = 5 units/m^2]
  Vincristine: I.V.: 1.4 mg/m^2 (maximum 2 mg) day 8
    [total dose/cycle = 1.4 mg/m^2]
  Methotrexate: I.V.: 120 mg/m^2 day 8
    [total dose/cycle = 120 mg/m^2]
  Leucovorin: Oral: 25 mg/m^2 every 6 hours for 4 doses (start 24 hours after methotrexate dose) day 9
    [total dose/cycle = 100 mg/m^2]
  Repeat cycle every 21 days

References
Longo DL, DeVita VT Jr, Duffey PL, et al, "Superiority of ProMACE-CytaBOM Over ProMACE-MOPP in the Treatment of Advanced Diffuse Aggressive Lymphoma: Results of a Prospective Randomized Trial," *J Clin Oncol*, 1991, 9(1):25-38.

PVA (POG 8602)
Index Terms AlinC 14
Use Leukemia, acute lymphocytic
Regimen
  Induction:
  Prednisone: Oral: 40 mg/m^2/day (maximum 60 mg) days 0 to 28 (given in 3 divided doses)
    [total dose/cycle = 1160 mg/m^2]
(Continued)

PVA (POG 8602) *(Continued)*

    Vincristine: I.V.: 1.5 mg/m^2/day (maximum 2 mg) days 0, 7, 14, and 21
      [total dose/cycle = 6 mg/m^2; maximum 8 mg]

    Asparaginase: I.M.: 6000 units/m^2 3 times per week for 2 weeks
      [total dose/cycle = 36,000 units/m^2]

    Intrathecal therapy (triple): Days 0 and 22

    Leucovorin: route and dose not specified: single dose 24 hours after every
      intrathecal treatment days 1 and 23

    Administer one cycle only

CNS consolidation:

    Mercaptopurine: Oral: 75 mg/m^2/day days 29 to 43
      [total dose/cycle = 1125 mg/m^2]

    Intrathecal therapy (triple): Days 29 and 36

    Leucovorin: route and dose not specified: single dose 24 hours after every
      intrathecal treatment days 30 and 37

    Administer one cycle only

Intensification:

Regimen A:

    Methotrexate: I.V.: 1000 mg/m^2 continuous infusion over 24 hours day 1
      [total dose/cycle = 1000 mg/m^2]

    Cytarabine: I.V.: 1000 mg/m^2 continuous infusion over 24 hours day 1
      (start 12 hours after start of methotrexate)
      [total dose/cycle = 1000 mg/m^2]

    Leucovorin: I.M., I.V., or Oral: 30 mg/m^2 at 24 and 36 hours after the start
      of methotrexate
      [total dose/cycle = 60 mg/m^2]

      followed by I.M., I.V., or Oral: 3 mg/m^2 at 48, 60, and 72 hours after
        the start of methotrexate
        [total dose/cycle = 9 mg/m^2]

    Repeat cycle every 3 weeks for 6 cycles (administered weeks 7, 10, 13,
      16, 19, and 22)

    Intrathecal therapy (triple): Weeks 9, 12, 15, and 18

    Leucovorin: route and dose not specified: single dose 24 hours after every
      intrathecal treatment weeks 9, 12, 15, and 18

or

Regimen B:

    Methotrexate: I.V.: 1000 mg/m^2 continuous infusion over 24 hours day 1
      [total dose/cycle = 1000 mg/m^2]

    Cytarabine: I.V.: 1000 mg/m^2 continuous infusion over 24 hours day 1
      (start 12 hours after methotrexate)
      [total dose/cycle = 1000 mg/m^2]

    Leucovorin: I.M., I.V., or Oral: 30 mg/m^2 at 24 and 36 hours after the start
      of methotrexate
      [total dose/cycle = 60 mg/m^2]

      followed by I.M., I.V., or Oral: 3 mg/m^2 at 48, 60, and 72 hours after
        the start of methotrexate
        [total dose/cycle = 9 mg/m^2]

    Repeat cycle every 12 weeks for 6 cycles (administer weeks 7, 19, 31, 43,
      55, and 67)

    Intrathecal therapy (triple): Weeks 9, 12, 15, and 18

    Leucovorin: route and dose not specified: single dose 24 hours after every
      intrathecal treatment weeks 9, 12, 15, and 18

Maintenance:
Regimen A:
Methotrexate: I.M.: 20 mg/m² weekly, weeks 25 to 156
  [total dose/cycle = 2640 mg/m²]
Mercaptopurine: Oral: 75 mg/m² daily, weeks 25 to 156
  [total dose/cycle = 69,300 mg/m²]
Intrathecal therapy (triple): Every 8 weeks, weeks 26 through 105
Leucovorin: route and dose not specified: single dose 24 hours after every
  intrathecal treatment weeks 26 through 105
Prednisone: Oral: 40 mg/m²/day (maximum 60 mg) days 1 to 7 (given in 3
  divided doses), weeks 8, 17, 25, 41, 57, 73, 89, and 105
  [total dose/cycle = 2240 mg/m²; maximum 3360 mg]
Vincristine: I.V.: 1.5 mg/m²/day (maximum 2 mg) day 1, weeks 8, 9, 17, 18,
  25, 26, 41, 42, 57, 58, 73, 74, 89, 90, 105, and 106
  [total dose/cycle = 24 mg/m²; maximum 32 mg]
or
Regimen B:
Methotrexate: I.M.: 20 mg/m² weekly, weeks 22-28, 34-40, 46-52, and 58-64
  [total dose/cycle = 560 mg/m²]
Mercaptopurine: Oral: 75 mg/m² daily for 7 weeks, weeks 22-28, 34-40,
  46-52, and 58-64
  [total dose/cycle = 14700 mg/m²]
followed by
Methotrexate: I.M.: 20 mg/m² weekly, weeks 70 to 156
  [total dose/cycle = 1720 mg/m²]
Mercaptopurine: Oral: 75 mg/m² daily, weeks 70 to 156
  [total dose/cycle = 45,150 mg/m²]
Intrathecal therapy (triple): Every 8 weeks, weeks 26 through 105
Leucovorin: route and dose not specified: single dose 24 hours after every
  intrathecal treatment weeks 26 through 105
Prednisone: Oral: 40 mg/m²/day (maximum 60 mg) days 1 to 7 (given in 3
  divided doses), weeks 8, 17, 25, 41, 57, 73, 89, and 105
  [total dose/cycle = 2240 mg/m²]
Vincristine: I.V.: 1.5 mg/m²/day (maximum 2 mg) day 1, weeks 8, 9, 17, 18,
  25, 26, 41, 42, 57, 58, 73, 74, 89, 90, 105, and 106
  [total dose/cycle = 24 mg/m²; maximum 32 mg]

References

Land VJ, Shuster JJ, Crist WM, et al, "Comparison of Two Schedules of Intermediate-Dose
  Methotrexate and Cytarabine Consolidation Therapy for Childhood B-Precursor Cell Acute
  Lymphoblastic Leukemia: A Pediatric Oncology Group Study," *J Clin Oncol*, 1994,
  12(9):1939-45.

PVB

Use Testicular cancer
Regimen NOTE: Multiple variations are listed below.
  Variation 1:
  Cisplatin: I.V.: 20 mg/m²/day days 1 to 5
    [total dose/cycle = 100 mg/m²]
  Vinblastine: I.V.: 0.2 mg/kg/day days 1 and 2
    [total dose/cycle = 0.4 mg/kg]
  Bleomycin: I.V.: 30 units/day days 2, 9, and 16
    [total dose/cycle = 90 units]
  Repeat cycle every 3 weeks
  Variation 2:
  Cisplatin: I.V.: 20 mg/m²/day days 1 to 5
    [total dose/cycle = 100 mg/m²]
(Continued)

PVB *(Continued)*

    Vinblastine: I.V.: 0.15 mg/kg/day days 1 and 2
      [total dose/cycle = 0.3 mg/kg]
    Bleomycin: I.V.: 30 units/day days 2, 9, and 16
      [total dose/cycle = 90 units]
    Repeat cycle every 3 weeks
  Variation 3:
    Cisplatin: I.V.: 20 mg/m^2/day days 1 to 5
      [total dose/cycle = 100 mg/m^2]
    Vinblastine: I.V.: 6 mg/m^2/day days 1 and 2
      [total dose/cycle = 12 mg/m^2]
    Bleomycin: I.M.: 30 units/day days 2, 9, and 16
      [total dose/cycle = 90 units]
    Repeat cycle every 3 weeks

References

Variation 1:
Einhorn LH and Donohue J, "Cis-Diamminedichloroplatinum, Vinblastine, and Bleomycin Combination Chemotherapy in Disseminated Testicular Cancer," *Ann Intern Med*, 1977, 87(3):293-8.
Variation 2:
Williams SD, Birch R, Einhorn LH, et al, "Treatment of Disseminated Germ-Cell Tumors With Cisplatin, Bleomycin, and Either Vinblastine or Etoposide," *N Engl J Med*, 1987, 316(23):1435-40.
Variation 3:
Bodrogi I, Baki M, Horti J, et al, "Vinblastine, Cisplatin, and Bleomycin Treatment of Advanced Nonseminomatous Testicular Tumors," *Neoplasma*, 1990, 37(4):445-50.

♦ **PVB** *see* VBP *on page 1288*

PVDA

Use Leukemia, acute lymphocytic
Regimen Induction:
  Prednisone: Oral: 60 mg/m^2/day days 1 to 28
    [total dose/cycle = 1680 mg/m^2]
  Vincristine: I.V.: 1.5 mg/m^2/day days 1, 8, 15, and 22
    [total dose/cycle = 6 mg/m^2]
  Daunorubicin: I.V.: 25 mg/m^2/day days 1, 8, 15, and 22
    [total dose/cycle = 100 mg/m^2]
  Asparaginase: I.M., SubQ, or I.V.: 5000 units/m^2/day days 1 to 14
    [total dose/cycle = 70,000 units/m^2]
  Administer one cycle only; used in conjunction with intrathecal chemotherapy

References

Hoelzer D, Thiel E, Loffler H, et al, "Intensified Therapy in Acute Lymphoblastic and Acute Undifferentiated Leukemia in Adults," *Blood*, 1984, 64(1):38-47.

♦ **R-CHOP** *see* Rituximab-CHOP *on page 1278*

R-CVP

Index Terms CVP-R
Use Lymphoma, non-Hodgkin's
Regimen
  Rituximab: I.V.: 375 mg/m^2 day 1
    [total dose/cycle = 375 mg/m^2]
  Cyclophosphamide: I.V.: 750 mg/m^2 day 1
    [total dose/cycle = 750 mg/m^2]
  Vincristine: I.V.: 1.4 mg/m^2 day 1
    [total dose/cycle = 1.4 mg/m^2]

Prednisone: Oral: 40 mg/m^2/day days 1 to 5
[total dose/cycle = 200 mg/m^2]
Repeat cycle every 21 days

References

Marcus R, Imrie K, Belch A, et al, "CVP Chemotherapy Plus Rituximab Compared With CVP as First-Line Treatment for Advanced Follicular Lymphoma," *Blood*, 2005, 105(4):1417-23.

Regimen A1

Use Neuroblastoma

Regimen

Cyclophosphamide: I.V.: 1.2 g/m^2 day 1
[total dose/cycle = 1.2 g/m^2]
Vincristine: I.V.: 1.5 mg/m^2 day 1
[total dose/cycle = 1.5 mg/m^2]
Doxorubicin: I.V.: 40 mg/m^2 day 3
[total dose/cycle = 40 mg/m^2]
Cisplatin: I.V.: 90 mg/m^2 day 5
[total dose/cycle = 90 mg/m^2]
Repeat cycle every 28 days

References

Kaneko M, Nishihira H, Mugishima H, et al, "Stratification of Treatment of Stage 4 Neuroblastoma Patients Based on N-myc Amplification Status. Study Group of Japan for Treatment of Advanced Neuroblastoma, Tokyo, Japan," *Med Pediatr Oncol*, 1998, 31(1):1-7.

Regimen A2

Index Terms Regimen new A1

Use Neuroblastoma

Regimen

Cyclophosphamide: I.V.: 1.2 g/m^2 day 1
[total dose/cycle = 1.2 g/m^2]
Etoposide: I.V.: 100 mg/m^2/day days 1 to 5
[total dose/cycle = 500 mg/m^2]
Doxorubicin: I.V.: 40 mg/m^2 day 3
[total dose/cycle = 40 mg/m^2]
Cisplatin: I.V.: 90 mg/m^2 day 5
[total dose/cycle = 90 mg/m^2]
Repeat cycle every 28 days

References

Kaneko M, Nishihira H, Mugishima H, et al, "Stratification of Treatment of Stage 4 Neuroblastoma Patients Based on N-myc Amplification Status. Study Group of Japan for Treatment of Advanced Neuroblastoma, Tokyo, Japan," *Med Pediatr Oncol*, 1998, 31(1):1-7.

♦ **Regimen new A1** see Regimen A2 *on page 1277*
♦ **R-ICE** see RICE *on page 1277*

RICE

Index Terms Rituximab-ICE; R-ICE

Use Lymphoma, non-Hodgkin's

Regimen

Rituximab: I.V.: 375 mg/m^2/day days -2 and 1 (cycle 1)
[total dose/cycle = 750 mg/m^2]
Rituximab: I.V.: 375 mg/m^2 day 1 (cycles 2 and 3)
[total dose/cycle = 375 mg/m^2]
Etoposide: I.V.: 100 mg/m^2 days 3 to 5
[total dose/cycle = 300 mg/m^2]
Carboplatin: I.V.: AUC = 5 (maximum 800 mg) day 4
[total dose/cycle = AUC = 5]

(Continued)

RICE *(Continued)*

Ifosfamide: I.V.: 5000 mg/m² continuous infusion day 4
[total dose/cycle = 5000 mg/m²]
Mesna: I.V.: 5000 mg/m² continuous infusion day 4
[total dose/cycle = 5000 mg/m²]
Filgrastim: SubQ: 5 mcg/kg/day days 7 to 14 (cycles 1 and 2)
[total dose/cycle = 40 mcg/kg]
Filgrastim: SubQ: 10 mcg/kg/day days 7 to 14 (cycle 3)
[total dose/cycle = 80 mcg/kg]
Repeat cycle every 2 weeks

References
Kewalramani T, Zelenetz AD, Nimer SD, et al, "Rituximab and ICE as Second-Line Therapy before Autologous Stem Cell Transplantation for Relapsed or Primary Refractory Diffuse Large B-Cell Lymphoma," *Blood*, 2004, 103(10):3684-8.

Rituximab-CHOP

Index Terms CHOP-Rituximab; R-CHOP
Use Lymphoma, non-Hodgkin's
Regimen
Rituximab: I.V.: 375 mg/m² day 1
[total dose/cycle = 375 mg/m²]
Cyclophosphamide: I.V.: 750 mg/m² day 1
[total dose/cycle = 750 mg/m²]
Doxorubicin: I.V.: 50 mg/m² day 1
[total dose/cycle = 50 mg/m²]
Vincristine: I.V.: 1.4 mg/m² (maximum 2 mg) day 1
[total dose/cycle = 1.4 mg/m²; maximum 2 mg]
Prednisone: Oral: 40 mg/m²/day days 1 to 5
[total dose/cycle = 200 mg/m²]
Repeat cycle every 21 days

References
Coiffier B, Lepage E, Briere J, et al, "CHOP Chemotherapy Plus Rituximab Compared With CHOP Alone in Elderly Patients With Diffuse Large-B-Cell Lymphoma," *N Engl J Med*, 2002, 346(4):235-42.

♦ **Rituximab-ICE** *see RICE on page 1277*
♦ **Saltz Regimen** *see Fluorouracil-Leucovorin-Irinotecan (Saltz Regimen) on page 1220*

Stanford V

Use Lymphoma, Hodgkin's disease
Regimen
Mechlorethamine: I.V.: 6 mg/m² day 1
[total dose/cycle = 6 mg/m²]
Doxorubicin: I.V.: 25 mg/m²/day days 1 and 15
[total dose/cycle = 50 mg/m²]
Vinblastine: I.V.: 6 mg/m²/day days 1 and 15
[total dose/cycle = 12 mg/m²]
Vincristine: I.V.: 1.4 mg/m²/day (maximum 2 mg) days 8 and 22
[total dose/cycle = 2.8 mg/m²; maximum 4 mg]
Bleomycin: I.V.: 5 units/m²/day days 8 and 22
[total dose/cycle = 10 units/m²]
Etoposide: I.V.: 60 mg/m²/day days 15 and 16
[total dose/cycle = 120 mg/m²]
Prednisone: Oral: 40 mg/m² every other day for 9 weeks
followed by tapering of dose by 10 mg every other day, beginning at week 10
Repeat cycle every 28 days for 3 cycles

References

Bartlett NL, Rosenberg SA, Hoppe RT, et al, "Brief Chemotherapy, Stanford V, and Adjuvant Radiotherapy for Bulky or Advanced-Stage Hodgkin's Disease: A Preliminary Report," *J Clin Oncol*, 1995, 13(5):1080-8.

TAC

Index Terms ATC

Use Breast cancer

Regimen NOTE: Multiple variations are listed below.

Variation 1:

Docetaxel: I.V.: 75 mg/m^2 day 1
[total dose/cycle = 75 mg/m^2]

Doxorubicin: I.V.: 50 mg/m^2 day 1
[total dose/cycle = 50 mg/m^2]

Cyclophosphamide: I.V.: 500 mg/m^2 day 1
[total dose/cycle = 500 mg/m^2]

Repeat cycle every 3 weeks

Variation 2:

Docetaxel: I.V.: 60 mg/m^2 day 1
[total dose/cycle = 60 mg/m^2]

Doxorubicin: I.V.: 60 mg/m^2 day 1
[total dose/cycle = 60 mg/m^2]

Cyclophosphamide: I.V.: 600 mg/m^2 day 1
[total dose/cycle = 600 mg/m^2]

Repeat cycle every 3 weeks

References

Variation 1:

Martin M, Pienkowski T, Mackey J, et al, "Adjuvant Docetaxel for Node-Positive Breast Cancer," *N Engl J Med*, 2005, 352(22):2302-13.

Nabholtz JM, Smylie M, Mackey JR, et al, "Docetaxel/Doxorubicin/Cyclophosphamide in the Treatment of Metastatic Breast Cancer," *Oncology (Williston Park)*, 1997, 11(6 Suppl 6):25-7.

Variation 2:

Smith RE, Anderson SJ, Brown A, et al,"Phase II Trial of Doxorubicin/Docetaxel/Cyclophosphamide for Locally Advanced and Metastatic Breast Cancer: Results From NSABP Trial BP-58," *Clin Breast Cancer*, 2002, 3(5):333-40.

TAD

Use Leukemia, acute myeloid

Regimen

Daunorubicin: I.V.: 60 mg/m^2/day days 3 to 5
[total dose/cycle = 180 mg/m^2]

Cytarabine: I.V.: 100 mg/m^2/day continuous infusion days 1 and 2
[total dose/cycle = 200 mg/m^2]

followed by I.V.: 100 mg/m^2/day over 30 minutes every 12 hours days 3 to 8
[total dose/cycle = 1200 mg/m^2]

Thioguanine: Oral: 100 mg/m^2/day every 12 hours days 3 to 9
[total dose/cycle = 1400 mg/m^2]

Administer one cycle only

References

Buchner T, Hiddemann W, Wormann B, et al, "Double Inductions Strategy for Acute Myeloid Leukemia: The Effect of High-Dose Cytarabine With Mitoxantrone Instead of Standard-Dose Cytarabine With Daunorubicin and 6-Thioguanine: A Randomized Trial by the German AML Cooperative Group," *Blood*, 1999, 93(12):4116-24.

Tamoxifen-Epirubicin

Use Breast cancer

Regimen

Tamoxifen: Oral: 20 mg daily
[total dose/cycle = 560 mg]
Epirubicin: I.V.: 50 mg/m^2/day days 1 and 8
[total dose/cycle = 100 mg/m^2]
Repeat epirubicin cycle every 28 days for 6 cycles; continue tamoxifen for 4
years

References

Wils JA, Bliss JM, Marty M, et al, "Epirubicin Plus Tamoxifen Versus Tamoxifen Alone in Node-Positive Postmenopausal Patients With Breast Cancer: A Randomized Trial of the International Collaborative Cancer Group." *J Clin Oncol*, 1999, 17(7):1988-98.

♦ **TC** *see* Docetaxel-Cyclophosphamide (TC) *on page 1191*

TCF

Use Esophageal cancer

Regimen

Paclitaxel: I.V.: 175 mg/m^2 day 1
[total dose/cycle = 175 mg/m^2]
Cisplatin: I.V.: 20 mg/m^2/day days 1 to 5 for Cycles 1, 2, and 3
[total dose/cycle = 100 mg/m^2]
then 15 mg/m^2/day days 1 to 5
[total dose/cycle = 75 mg/m^2]
Fluorouracil: I.V.: 750 mg/m^2/day continuous infusion days 1 to 5
[total dose/cycle = 3750 mg/m^2]
Repeat cycle every 28 days

References

Ilson DH, Ajani J, Bhalla K, et al, "Phase II Trial of Paclitaxel, Fluorouracil, and Cisplatin in Patients With Advanced Carcinoma of the Esophagus," *J Clin Oncol*, 1998, 16(5):1826-34.

TEX (Capecitabine + Docetaxel + Epirubicin)

Use Breast cancer

Regimen

Capecitabine: Oral: 1000 mg/m^2 twice daily days 1 to 14
[total dose/cycle = 28,000 mg/m^2]
Docetaxel: I.V.: 75 mg/m^2 day 1
[total dose/cycle = 75 mg/m^2]
Epirubicin: I.V.: 75 mg/m^2 day 1
[total dose/cycle = 75 mg/m^2]
Repeat cycle every 3 weeks

References

Venturini M, Durando A, Garrone O, et al, "Capecitabine in Combination With Docetaxel and Epirubicin in Patients With Previously Untreated, Advanced Breast Carcinoma," *Cancer*, 2003, 97(5):1174-80.

Thalidomide-Dexamethasone

Index Terms Dexamethasone-Thalidomide

Use Multiple myeloma

Regimen Note: Multiple variations are listed below.

Variation 1:
Thalidomide: Oral: 100 mg/day days 1 to 28
[total dose/cycle = 2800 mg]
Dexamethasone: Oral: 40 mg/day days 1 to 4
[total dose/cycle = 160 mg]
Repeat cycle every 28 days

Variation 2:

Thalidomide: Oral: 200 mg/day days 1 to 14 cycle 1
followed by Oral: 400 mg/day days 15 to 28 cycle 1
[total dose/cycle = 8400 mg]
Thalidomide: Oral: 400 mg/day days 1 to 28 (subsequent cycles)
[total dose/cycle = 11,200 mg]
Dexamethasone: Oral: 20 mg/m^2/day days 1 to 4, 9 to 12, and 17 to 20
cycle 1 (subsequent cycles)
[total dose/cycle = 240 mg/m^2]
Dexamethasone: Oral 20 mg/m^2/day days 1 to 4 (subsequent cycles)
[total dose/cycle = 80 mg/m^2]
Repeat cycle every 28 days

Variation 3:

Thalidomide: Oral: 100 mg/day days 1 to 7, 150 mg/day days 8 to 14, 200
mg/day days 15 to 21, 250 mg/day days 22 to 28, and 300 mg/day days
29 to 35 (cycle 1)
[total dose/cycle = 7000 mg]
Thalidomide: Oral: 300 mg/day days 1 to 35 (subsequent cycles)
[total dose/cycle = 10,500 mg]
Dexamethasone: Oral: 20 mg/m^2/day days 1 to 4, 9 to 12, and 17 to 20
[total dose/cycle = 240 mg/m^2]
Repeat cycle every 35 days

Variation 4:

Thalidomide: Oral: 200 mg/day days 1 to 28
[total dose/cycle = 5600 mg]
Dexamethasone: Oral: 40 mg/day days 1 to 4, 9 to 12, and 17 to 20 (odd
cycles)
[total dose/cycle = 480 mg]
Dexamethasone: Oral: 40 mg/day days 1 to 4 (even cycles)
[total dose/cycle = 160 mg]
Repeat cycle every 28 days

References

Variation 1:
Palumbo A, Giaccone L, Bertola A, et al, "Low-Dose Thalidomide Plus Dexamethasone Is an
Effective Salvage Therapy for Advanced Myeloma," *Haematologica*, 2001, 86(4):399-403.
Variation 2:
Dimopoulos MA, Zervas K, Kouvatseas G, et al, "Thalidomide and Dexamethasone Combination
for Refractory Multiple Myeloma," *Ann Oncol*, 2001, 12(7):991-5.
Variation 3:
Alexanian R, Weber D, Giralt S, et al, "Consolidation Therapy of Multiple Myeloma With Thalido-
mide-Dexamethasone After Intensive Chemotherapy," *Ann Oncol*, 2002, 13(7):1116-9.
Variation 4:
Rajkumar SV, Hayman S, Gertz MA, et al, "Combination Therapy With Thalidomide Plus Dexa-
methasone for Newly Diagnosed Myeloma," *J Clin Oncol*, 2002, 20(21):4319-23.

TIP

Use Esophageal cancer; head and neck cancer

Regimen

Paclitaxel: I.V.: 175 mg/m^2 day 1
[total dose/cycle = 175 mg/m^2]
Ifosfamide: I.V.: 1000 mg/m^2/day days 1 to 3
[total dose/cycle = 3000 mg/m^2]
Mesna: I.V.: 400 mg/m^2/day before ifosfamide days 1 to 3
plus I.V.: 200 mg/m^2 4 hours after ifosfamide days 1 to 3
[total dose/cycle = 1800 mg/m^2]
Cisplatin: I.V.: 60 mg/m^2 day 1
[total dose/cycle = 60 mg/m^2]
Repeat cycle every 21-28 days
(Continued)

TIP *(Continued)*

References

Shin DM, Glisson BS, Khuri FR, et al, "Phase II Trial of Paclitaxel, Ifosfamide, and Cisplatin in Patients With Recurrent Head and Neck Squamous Cell Carcinoma," *J Clin Oncol*, 1998, 16(4):1325-30.

Topotecan-Cisplatin

Use Cervical cancer

Regimen Note: Body surface area capped at 2 m^2 maximum

Topotecan: I.V.: 0.75 mg/m^2/day days 1, 2, and 3

[total dose/cycle = 2.25 mg/m^2]

Cisplatin: I.V.: 50 mg/m^2/day day 1 only

[total dose/cycle = 50 mg/m^2]

Repeat cycle every 21 days

References

Long HJ 3rd, Bundy BN, Grendys EC Jr, et al, "Randomized Phase III Trial of Cisplatin With or Without Topotecan in Carcinoma of the Uterine Cervix: A Gynecologic Oncology Group Study," *J Clin Oncol*, 2005, 23(21):4626-33.

Topotecan (Oral)

Use Lung cancer, nonsmall cell; lung cancer, small cell; ovarian cancer

Regimen

Topotecan: Oral: 2.3 mg/m^2/day days 1 to 5

[total dose/cycle = 11.5 mg/m^2]

Repeat cycle every 21 days

References

Clarke-Pearson DL, Van Le L, Iveson T, et al, "Oral Topotecan as Single-Agent Second-Line Chemotherapy in Patients With Advanced Ovarian Cancer," *J Clin Oncol*, 2001, 19(19):3967-75.

Eckardt JR, von Pawel J, Pujol JL, et al, "Phase III Study of Oral Compared With Intravenous Topotecan as Second-Line Therapy in Small-Cell Lung Cancer," *J Clin Oncol*, 2007, 25(15):2086-92.

O'Brien ME, Ciuleanu TE, Tsekov H, et al, "Phase III Trial Comparing Supportive Care Alone With Supportive Care With Oral Topotecan in Patients With Relapsed Small-Cell Lung Cancer," *J Clin Oncol*, 2006, 24(34):5441-7.

Ramlau R, Gervais R, Krzakowski M, et al, "Phase III Study Comparing Oral Topotecan to Intravenous Docetaxel in Patients With Pretreated Advanced Non-Small-Cell Lung Cancer," *J Clin Oncol*, 2006, 24(18):2800-7.

White SC, Cheeseman S, Thatcher N, et al, "Phase II Study of Oral Topotecan in Advanced Non-Small Cell Lung Cancer," *Clin Cancer Res*, 2000, 6(3):868-73.

Topotecan (Oral)-Cisplatin

Index Terms Cisplatin-Topotecan (Oral)

Use Lung cancer, small cell

Regimen

Topotecan: Oral: 1.7 mg/m^2/day days 1 to 5

[total dose/cycle = 8.5 mg/m^2]

Cisplatin: I.V.: 60 mg/m^2 day 5 only

[total dose/cycle = 60 mg/m^2]

Repeat cycle every 21 days for 4 cycles (or for 2 cycles beyond best response)

References

Eckardt JR, von Pawel J, Papai Z, et al, "Open-Label, Multicenter, Randomized, Phase III Study Comparing Oral Topotecan/Cisplatin Versus Etoposide/Cisplatin as Treatment for Chemo-therapy-Naive Patients With Extensive-Disease Small-Cell Lung Cancer," *J Clin Oncol*, 2006, 24(13):2044-51.

Topotecan (Weekly)

Use Ovarian cancer; lung cancer, small cell

Regimen

Topotecan: I.V.: 4 mg/m^2/day days 1, 8, and 15
[total dose/cycle = 12 mg/m^2]
Repeat cycle every 28 days

References

Homesley HD, Hall DJ, Martin DA, et al, "A Dose-Escalating Study of Weekly Bolus Topotecan in Previously Treated Ovarian Cancer Patients," *Gynecol Oncol*, 2001, 83(2):394-9.

Levy T, Inbar M, Menczer J, et al, "Phase II Study of Weekly Topotecan in Patients With Recurrent or Persistent Epithelial Ovarian Cancer," *Gynecol Oncol*, 2004, 95(3):686-90.

Shah C, Ready N, Perry M, et al, "A Multi-Center Phase II Study of Weekly Topotecan as Second-Line Therapy for Small Cell Lung Cancer," *Lung Cancer*, 2007, 57(1):84-8.

♦ **TPF** see Docetaxel-Cisplatin-Fluorouracil (Head and Neck Cancer) on page 1191

♦ **Trastuzumab-Capecitabine** see Capecitabine-Trastuzumab on page 1160

♦ **Trastuzumab-Docetaxel** see Docetaxel-Trastuzumab on page 1192

♦ **Trastuzumab-Docetaxel-Carboplatin** see Docetaxel-Trastuzumab-Carboplatin on page 1192

♦ **Trastuzumab-Docetaxel-Cisplatin** see Docetaxel-Trastuzumab-Cisplatin on page 1193

♦ **Trastuzumab-Docetaxel-FEC** see Docetaxel-Trastuzumab-FEC on page 1193

♦ **Trastuzumab-Docetaxel (Weekly)** see Docetaxel (Weekly)-Trastuzumab on page 1194

Trastuzumab-Paclitaxel

Use Breast cancer

Regimen

Paclitaxel: I.V.: 175 mg/m^2 day 1
[total dose/cycle = 175 mg/m^2]
Trastuzumab: I.V.: 4 mg/kg (loading dose) day 1 cycle 1
[total dose/cycle = 4 mg/kg]
Trastuzumab: I.V.: 2 mg/kg/day days 8 and 15 cycle 1
[total dose/cycle = 4 mg/kg]
followed by I.V.: 2 mg/kg/day days 1, 8, and 15 (subsequent cycles)
[total dose/cycle = 6 mg/kg]
Repeat cycle every 21 days for at least 6 cycles

References

Slamon DJ, Leyland-Jones B, Shak S, et al, "Use of Chemotherapy Plus a Monoclonal Antibody Against HER2 for Metastatic Breast Cancer That Overexpresses HER2," *N Engl J Med*, 2001, 344(11):783-92.

♦ **Trastuzumab-Vinorelbine** see Vinorelbine-Trastuzumab on page 1290

Tretinoin-Idarubicin

Use Leukemia, acute promyelocytic

Regimen NOTE: Multiple variations are listed below.

Induction:
Variation 1:
Tretinoin: Oral: 45 mg/m^2/day day 1 up to 90 days
[total dose/cycle = up to 4050 mg/m^2]
≤20 years: 25 mg/m^2/day day 1 up to 90 days
[total dose/cycle = up to 2250 mg/m^2]
Idarubicin: I.V.: 12 mg/m^2/day days 2, 4, 6, and 8
[total dose/cycle = 48 mg/m^2]
(Continued)

Tretinoin-Idarubicin *(Continued)*

Consolidation:
Course 1:
  Idarubicin: I.V.: 5 mg/m^2/day days 1 to 4
    [total dose/cycle = 20 mg/m^2]
  or
  Idarubicin: I.V.: 7 mg/m^2/day days 1 to 4
    [total dose/cycle = 28 mg/m^2]
  Tretinoin: Oral: 45 mg/m^2/day days 1 to 15
    [total dose/cycle = 675 mg/m^2]
Course 2:
  Mitoxantrone: I.V.: 10 mg/m^2/day days 1 to 5
    [total dose/cycle = 50 mg/m^2]
  or
  Mitoxantrone: I.V.: 10 mg/m^2/day days 1 to 5
    [total dose/cycle = 50 mg/m^2]
  Tretinoin: Oral: 45 mg/m^2/day days 1 to 15
    [total dose/cycle = 675 mg/m^2]
Course 3:
  Idarubicin: I.V.: 12 mg/m^2 on day 1
    [total dose/cycle = 12 mg/m^2]
  or
  Idarubicin: I.V.: 12 mg/m^2/day on days 1 and 2
    [total dose/cycle = 24 mg/m^2]
  Tretinoin: Oral: 45 mg/m^2/day days 1 to 15
    [total dose/cycle = 675 mg/m^2]
  Administer courses sequentially at 1-month intervals for 3 months
Maintenance:
  Mercaptopurine: Oral: 50 mg/m^2 daily
    [total dose/cycle = 4500 mg/m^2 (90 days)]
  Methotrexate: I.M.: 15 mg/m^2 weekly
    [total dose/cycle = 180 mg/m^2]
  Tretinoin: Oral: 45 mg/m^2/day days 1 to 15
    [total dose/cycle = 675 mg/m^2]
  Repeat cycle every 3 months for 2 years
Variation 2:
Induction:
  Tretinoin: Oral: 45 mg/m^2/day day 1 up to 90 days
    [total dose/cycle = up to 4050 mg/m^2]
  <15 years: 25 mg/m^2/day day 1 up to 90 days
    [total dose/cycle = up to 2250 mg/m^2]
  Idarubicin: I.V.: 12 mg/m^2/day days 2, 4, 6, and 8
    [total dose/cycle = 48 mg/m^2]
Consolidation:
Course 1:
  Idarubicin: I.V.: 5 mg/m^2/day days 1 to 4
    [total dose/cycle = 20 mg/m^2]
Course 2:
  Mitoxantrone: I.V.: 10 mg/m^2/day days 1 to 5
    [total dose/cycle = 50 mg/m^2]
Course 3:
  Idarubicin: I.V.: 12 mg/m^2 day 1
    [total dose/cycle = 12 mg/m^2]
  Administer courses sequentially at 1-month intervals for 3 months

Maintenance:
Mercaptopurine: Oral: 90 mg/m² daily
[total dose/cycle = 8100 mg/m²]
Methotrexate: I.M.: 15 mg/m² weekly
[total dose/cycle = 180 mg/m²]
Tretinoin: Oral: 45 mg/m²/day days 1 to 15
[total dose/cycle = 675 mg/m²]
Repeat cycle every 3 months for 2 years

References

Variation 1: Sanz MA, Martin G, Gonzalez M, et al, "Risk-Adapted Treatment of Acute Promyelocytic Leukemia With All-Trans-Retinoic Acid and Anthracycline Monochemotherapy: A Multicenter Study by the PETHEMA Group," *Blood*, 2004, 103(4):1237-43.

Variation 2: Sanz MA, Martin G, Rayon C, et al, "A Modified AIDA Protocol With Anthracycline-Based Consolidation Results in High Antileukemic Efficacy and Reduced Toxicity in Newly Diagnosed PML/RARalpha-Positive Acute Promyelocytic Leukemia," *Blood* 1999, 94(9):3015-21.

TVTG

Use Leukemia, acute lymphocytic; leukemia, acute myeloid
Regimen
Topotecan: I.V.: 1 mg/m²/day continuous infusion days 1 to 5
[total dose/cycle = 5 mg/m²]
Vinorelbine: I.V.: 20 mg/m²/day days 0, 7, 14, and 21
[total dose/cycle = 80 mg/m²]
Thiotepa: I.V.: 15 mg/m² day 2
Gemcitabine: I.V.: 3600 mg/m² day 7
Dexamethasone: Oral or I.V.: 45 mg/m²/day days 7 to 14 (given in 3 divided doses)
[total dose/cycle = 315 mg/m²]
Repeat cycle when ANC >500 cells/mcL and platelet count >75,000 cells/mcL

References

Kolb EA and Steinherz PG, "A New Multidrug Reinduction Protocol With Topotecan, Vinorelbine, Thiotepa, Dexamethasone, and Gemcitabine for Relapsed or Refractory Acute Leukemia," *Leukemia*, 2003, 17(10):1967-72.

VAC Alternating With IE (Ewing's Sarcoma)

Use Ewing's sarcoma
Regimen
Cycle A: (Odd numbered cycles)
Cyclophosphamide: I.V.: 1200 mg/m² day 1 (followed by mesna; dose not specified)
[total dose/cycle = 1200 mg/m²]
Vincristine: I.V.: 2 mg/m² (maximum: 2 mg) day 1
[total dose/cycle = 2 mg/m²; maximum 2 mg]
Doxorubicin: I.V.: 75 mg/m² day 1, for 5 cycles (maximum cumulative dose: 375 mg/m²)
[total dose/cycle = 75 mg/m²; maximum cumulative dose: 375 mg/m²]
Dactinomycin: I.V.: 1.25 mg/m² day 1, begin cycle 11 (after reaching maximum cumulative doxorubicin dose)
[total dose/cycle = 1.25 mg/m²]
Cycle B: (Even numbered cycles)
Ifosfamide: I.V.: 1800 mg/m²/day days 1 to 5 (given with mesna)
[total dose/cycle = 9000 mg/m²]
Etoposide: I.V.: 100 mg/m²/day days 1 to 5
[total dose/cycle = 500 mg/m²]
(Continued)

VAC Alternating With IE (Ewing's Sarcoma)
(Continued)

Alternate Cycles A and B, administering a cycle every 3 weeks (alternating in the following sequence: ABABAB) for 17 cycles

References

Grier HE, Krailo MD, Tarbell NJ, et al, "Addition of Ifosfamide and Etoposide to Standard Chemotherapy for Ewing's Sarcoma and Primitive Neuroectodermal Tumor of Bone," *N Engl J Med*, 2003, 348(8):694-701.

VAC Pulse

Use Rhabdomyosarcoma

Regimen

Vincristine: I.V.: 2 mg/m^2/dose (maximum 2 mg/dose) every 7 days, for 12 weeks

Dactinomycin: I.V.: 0.015 mg/kg/day (maximum 0.5 mg/day) days 1 to 5, every 3 months for 5 courses

Cyclophosphamide: Oral, I.V.: 10 mg/kg/day for 7 days, repeat every 6 weeks

References

Wilbur JR, Sutow WW, Sullivan MP, et al, "Chemotherapy of Sarcomas," *Cancer*, 1975, 36(2):765-9.

VAC (Retinoblastoma)

Use Retinoblastoma

Regimen

Vincristine: I.V.: 1.5 mg/m^2 day 1
[total dose/cycle = 1.5 mg/m^2]

Dactinomycin: I.V.: 0.015 mg/kg/day days 1 to 5
[total dose/cycle = 0.075 mg/kg]

Cyclophosphamide: I.V.: 200 mg/m^2/day days 1 to 5
[total dose/cycle = 1000 mg/m^2]

References

Doz F, Khelfaoui F, Mosseri V, et al, "The Role of Chemotherapy in Orbital Involvement of Retinoblastoma. The Experience of a Single Institution With 33 Patients," *Cancer*, 1994, 74(2):722-32.

VAC (Rhabdomyosarcoma)

Use Rhabdomyosarcoma

Regimen

Induction (weeks 1 to 17):

Vincristine: I.V. push: 1.5 mg/m^2 (maximum 2 mg) day 1 of weeks 1 to 13, then one dose at week 17

Dactinomycin: I.V. push: 0.015 mg/kg/day (maximum 0.5 mg) days 1 to 5 of weeks 1, 4, 7, and 17

Cyclophosphamide: I.V.: 2.2 g/m^2 day 1 of weeks 1, 4, 7, 10, 13, and 17

Continuation (weeks 21 to 44):

Vincristine: I.V. push: 1.5 mg/m^2 (maximum 2 mg) day 1 of weeks 21 to 26, 30 to 35, and 39 to 44

Dactinomycin: I.V. push: 0.015 mg/kg/day (maximum 0.5 mg) days 1 to 5 of weeks 21, 24, 30, 33, 39, and 42

Cyclophosphamide: I.V.: 2.2 g/m^2 day 1 of weeks 21, 24, 30, 33, 39, and 42

References

Baker KS, Anderson JR, Link MP, et al, "Benefit of Intensified Therapy for Patients With Local or Regional Embryonal Rhabdomyosarcoma: Results From the Intergroup Rhabdomyosarcoma Study IV," *J Clin Oncol*, 2000, 18(12):2427-34.

VAD

Use Multiple myeloma

Regimen

Vincristine: I.V.: 0.4 mg/day continuous infusion days 1 to 4
[total dose/cycle = 1.6 mg]

Doxorubicin: I.V.: 9 mg/m²/day continuous infusion days 1 to 4
[total dose/cycle = 36 mg/m²]

Dexamethasone: Oral: 40 mg/day days 1 to 4, 9 to 12, and 17 to 20
[total dose/cycle = 480 mg]

Repeat cycle every 28-35 days

References

Barlogie B, Smith L, and Alexanian R, "Effective Treatment of Advanced Multiple Myeloma Refractory to Alkylating Agents," *N Engl J Med*, 1984, 310(21):1353-6.

VAD/CVAD

Use Leukemia, acute lymphocytic

Regimen Induction cycle:

Vincristine: I.V.: 0.4 mg/day continuous infusion days 1 to 4 and 24 to 27
[total dose/cycle = 3.2 mg]

Doxorubicin: I.V.: 12 mg/m²/day continuous infusion days 1 to 4 and 24 to 27
[total dose/cycle = 96 mg/m²]

Dexamethasone: Oral: 40 mg/day days 1 to 4, 9 to 12, 17 to 20, 24 to 27, 32 to 35, and 40 to 43
[total dose/cycle = 960 mg]

Cyclophosphamide: I.V.: 1 g/m² day 24
[total dose/cycle = 1 g/m²]

Administer one cycle only

References

Kantarjian H, Walters RS, Keating MJ, et al, "Results of the Vincristine, Doxorubicin, and Dexamethasone Regimen in Adults With Standard and High-Risk Acute Lymphocytic Leukemia," *J Clin Oncol*, 1990, 8(6):994-1004.

VATH

Use Breast cancer

Regimen

Vinblastine: I.V.: 4.5 mg/m² day 1
[total dose/cycle = 4.5 mg/m²]

Doxorubicin: I.V.: 45 mg/m² day 1
[total dose/cycle = 45 mg/m²]

Thiotepa: I.V.: 12 mg/m² day 1
[total dose/cycle = 12 mg/m²]

Fluoxymesterone: Oral: 10 mg 3 times/day days 1 to 21
[total dose/cycle = 630 mg]

Repeat cycle every 21 days

References

Hart RD, Perloff M, and Holland JF, "One-Day VATH (Vinblastine, Adriamycin®, Thiotepa, and Halotestin®) Therapy for Advanced Breast Cancer Refractory to Chemotherapy," *Cancer*, 1981, 48(7):1522-7.

VBAP

Use Multiple myeloma

Regimen

Vincristine: I.V.: 1 mg day 1
[total dose/cycle = 1 mg]

Carmustine: I.V.: 30 mg/m² day 1
[total dose/cycle = 30 mg/m²]

(Continued)

VBAP *(Continued)*

Doxorubicin: I.V.: 30 mg/m^2 day 1
[total dose/cycle = 30 mg/m^2]
Prednisone: Oral: 100 mg/day days 1 to 4
[total dose/cycle = 400 mg]
Repeat cycle every 21 days

References

Bonnet J, Alexanian R, Salmon S, et al, "Vincristine, BCNU, Doxorubicin, and Prednisone (VBAP) Combination in the Treatment of Relapsing or Resistant Multiple Myeloma: A Southwest Oncology Group Study," *Cancer Treat Rep*, 1982, 66(6):1267-71.

VBMCP

Use Multiple myeloma

Regimen

Vincristine: I.V.: 1.2 mg/m^2 (maximum 2 mg) day 1
[total dose/cycle = 1.2 mg/m^2; maximum 2 mg]
Carmustine: I.V.: 20 mg/m^2 day 1
[total dose/cycle = 20 mg/m^2]
Melphalan: Oral: 8 mg/m^2/day days 1 to 4
[total dose/cycle = 32 mg/m^2]
Cyclophosphamide: I.V.: 400 mg/m^2 day 1
[total dose/cycle = 400 mg/m^2]
Prednisone: Oral: 40 mg/m^2/day days 1 to 7 (all cycles)
[total dose/cycle = 280 mg/m^2]
followed by Oral: 20 mg/m^2/day days 8 to 14 (first 3 cycles only)
[total dose/cycle = 140 mg/m^2]
Repeat cycle every 35 days

References

Oken MM, Harrington DP, Abramson N, et al, "Comparison of Melphalan and Prednisone With Vincristine, Carmustine, Melphalan, Cyclophosphamide, and Prednisone in the Treatment of Multiple Myeloma: Results of Eastern Cooperative Oncology Group Study E2479," *Cancer*, 1997, 79(8):1561-7.

VBP

Index Terms PVB

Use Testicular cancer

Regimen

Vinblastine: I.V.: 0.15 mg/kg/day days 1 and 2
[total dose/cycle = 0.3 mg/kg]
Bleomycin: I.V.: 30 units/day days 2, 9, and 16
[total dose/cycle = 90 units]
Cisplatin: I.V.: 20 mg/m^2/day days 1 to 5
[total dose/cycle = 100 mg/m^2]
Repeat cycle every 21 days for 4 cycles

References

Williams SD, Birch R, Einhorn LH, et al, "Treatment of Disseminated Germ-Cell Tumors With Cisplatin, Bleomycin, and Either Vinblastine or Etoposide," *N Engl J Med*, 1987, 316(23):1435-40.

VC

Index Terms Vinorelbine-Cis

Use Lung cancer, nonsmall cell

Regimen NOTE: Multiple variations are listed below.
Variation 1:
Vinorelbine: I.V.: 25 mg/m^2/day days 1, 8, 15, and 22
[total dose/cycle = 100 mg/m^2]

Cisplatin: I.V.: 100 mg/m² day 1
[total dose/cycle = 100 mg/m²]
Repeat cycle every 28 days
Variation 2:
Vinorelbine: I.V.: 30 mg/m² weekly
Cisplatin: I.V.: 120 mg/m²/day days 1 and 29, then once every 6 weeks

References

Variation 1:

Kelly K, Crowley J, Bunn PA Jr, et al, "Randomized Phase III Trial of Paclitaxel Plus Carboplatin Versus Vinorelbine Plus Cisplatin in the Treatment of Patients With Advanced Nonsmall-Cell Lung Cancer: A Southwest Oncology Group Trial," *J Clin Oncol*, 2001, 19(13):3210-8.

Wozniak AJ, Crowley JJ, Balcerzak SP, et al, "Randomized Trial Comparing Cisplatin With Cisplatin Plus Vinorelbine in the Treatment of Advanced Nonsmall-Cell Lung Cancer: A Southwest Oncology Group Study," *J Clin Oncol*, 1998, 16(7):2459-65.

Variation 2:

Le Chevalier T, Brisgand D, Douillard JY, et al, "Randomized Study of Vinorelbine and Cisplatin Versus Vindesine and Cisplatin Versus Vinorelbine Alone in Advanced Nonsmall-Cell Lung Cancer: Results of a European Multicenter Trial Including 612 Patients," *J Clin Oncol*, 1994, 12(2):360-7.

Le Chevalier T, Pujol JL, Douillard JY, et al, "A Three-Arm Trial of Vinorelbine (Navelbine) Plus Cisplatin, Vindesine Plus Cisplatin, and Single-Agent Vinorelbine in the Treatment of Nonsmall Cell Lung Cancer: An Expanded Analysis," *Semin Oncol*, 1994, 21(5 Suppl 10):28-33; discussion 33-4.

VCAP

Use Multiple myeloma

Regimen

Vincristine: I.V.: 1 mg/m² (maximum 1.5 mg) day 1
[total dose/cycle = 1 mg/m²]
Cyclophosphamide: Oral: 125 mg/m²/day days 1 to 4
[total dose/cycle = 500 mg/m²]
Doxorubicin: I.V.: 30 mg/m² day 1
[total dose/cycle = 30 mg/m²]
Prednisone: Oral: 60 mg/m²/day days 1 to 4
[total dose/cycle = 240 mg/m²]
Repeat cycle every 21 days for 6-12 months

References

Salmon SE, Haut A, Bonnet JD, et al, "Alternating Combination Chemotherapy and Levamisole Improves Survival in Multiple Myeloma: A Southwest Oncology Group Study," *J Clin Oncol*, 1983, 1(8):453-61.

VD

Use Breast cancer

Regimen

Vinorelbine: I.V.: 25 mg/m²/day days 1 and 8
[total dose/cycle = 50 mg/m²]
Doxorubicin: I.V.: 50 mg/m² day 1
[total dose/cycle = 50 mg/m²]
Repeat cycle every 3 weeks

References

Spielmann M, Dorval T, Turpin F, et al, "Phase II Trial of Vinorelbine/Doxorubicin as First-Line Therapy of Advanced Breast Cancer," *J Clin Oncol*, 1994 12(9):1764-70.

♦ **Vinorelbine-Cis** see VC on page 1288

Vinorelbine-Gemcitabine

Use Lung cancer, nonsmall cell

Regimen

Vinorelbine: I.V.: 20 mg/m²/day days 1, 8, and 15
[total dose/cycle = 60 mg/m²]
(Continued)

Vinorelbine-Gemcitabine *(Continued)*

Gemcitabine: I.V.: 800 mg/m²/day days 1, 8, and 15
[total dose/cycle = 2400 mg/m²]
Repeat cycle every 28 days

References
Chen YM, Perng RP, Yang KY, et al, "A Multicenter Phase II Trial of Vinorelbine Plus Gemcitabine in Previously Untreated Inoperable (Stage IIIB/IV) Nonsmall Cell Lung Cancer," *Chest*, 2000, 117(6):1583-9.

Vinorelbine-Trastuzumab

Index Terms Trastuzumab-Vinorelbine

Use Breast cancer

Regimen

Week 1:

Trastuzumab: I.V.: 4 mg/kg (loading dose) day 1 week 1
[total dose/week 1 = 4 mg/kg]
Vinorelbine: I.V.: 25 mg/m² day 1
[total dose/week 1 = 25 mg/m²]

Subsequent weeks:

Trastuzumab: I.V.: 2 mg/kg (loading dose) day 1
[total dose/week = 2 mg/kg]
Vinorelbine: I.V.: 25 mg/m² day 1
[total dose/week = 25 mg/m²]
Repeat weekly

References
Burstein HJ, Kuter I, Campos SM, et al, "Clinical Activity of Trastuzumab and Vinorelbine in Women With HER2-Overexpressing Metastatic Breast Cancer," *J Clin Oncol*, 2001, 19(10):2722-30.

VIP (Etoposide) (Testicular Cancer)

Use Testicular cancer

Regimen NOTE: Multiple variations are listed below.

Variation 1:

Etoposide: I.V.: 75 mg/m²/day days 1 to 5
[total dose/cycle = 375 mg/m²]
Ifosfamide: I.V.: 1200 mg/m²/day days 1 to 5
[total dose/cycle = 6000 mg/m²]
Cisplatin: I.V.: 20 mg/m²/day days 1 to 5
[total dose/cycle = 100 mg/m²]
Mesna: I.V.: 400 mg day 1 only
followed by I.V.: 1200 mg/day continuous infusion days 1 to 5
[total dose/cycle = 6400 mg]
Repeat cycle every 21 days for 4 cycles

Variation 2:

Etoposide: I.V.: 100 mg/m²/day days 1 to 5
[total dose/cycle = 500 mg/m²]
Ifosfamide: I.V.: 1200 mg/m²/day days 1 to 5
[total dose/cycle = 6000 mg/m²]
Cisplatin: I.V.: 20 mg/m²/day days 1 to 5
[total dose/cycle = 100 mg/m²]
Mesna: I.V.: 200 mg/m² every 4 hours, for 3 doses each day, days 1, 2, and 3
[total dose/cycle = 1800 mg/m²]
Repeat cycle every 21 days

Variation 3:

Ifosfamide: I.V.: 2500 mg/m²/day days 1 and 2
[total dose/cycle = 5000 mg/m²]

Mesna: I.V.: 2400 mg/m^2/day days 1 and 2
    [total dose/cycle = 4800 mg/m^2]
Etoposide: I.V.: 100 mg/m^2/day days 3, 4, and 5
    [total dose/cycle = 300 mg/m^2]
Cisplatin: I.V.: 40 mg/m^2/day days 3, 4, and 5
    [total dose/cycle = 120 mg/m^2]
Repeat cycle every 21 days

Variation 4:
Etoposide: I.V.: 75 mg/m^2/day days 1 to 5
    [total dose/cycle = 375 mg/m^2]
Ifosfamide: I.V.: 1200 mg/m^2/day days 1 to 5
    [total dose/cycle = 6000 mg/m^2]
Cisplatin: I.V.: 20 mg/m^2/day days 1 to 5
    [total dose/cycle = 100 mg/m^2]
Mesna: I.V.: 120 mg/m^2 day 1 only
    followed by I.V.: 1200 mg/m^2/day continuous infusion days 1 to 5
    [total dose/cycle = 6120 mg/m^2]
Repeat cycle every 21 days for 4 cycles

References

Variation 1:
Loehrer PJ Sr, Lauer R, Roth BJ, et al, "Salvage Therapy in Recurrent Germ Cell Cancer: Ifosfamide and Cisplatin Plus Either Vinblastine or Etoposide," *Ann Intern Med*, 1988, 109(7):540-6.

Variation 2:
Harstrick A, Schmoll HJ, Wilke H, et al, "Cisplatin, Etoposide, and Ifosfamide Salvage Therapy for Refractory or Relapsing Germ Cell Carcinoma," *J Clin Oncol*, 1991, 9(9):1549-55.

Variation 3:
Pizzocaro G, Salvioni R, Piva L, et al, "Modified Cisplatin, Etoposide (or Vinblastine) and Ifosfamide Salvage Therapy for Male Germ-Cell Tumors. Long-Term Results," *Ann Oncol*, 1992, 3(3):211-6.

Variation 4:
Nichols CR, Catalano PJ, Crawford ED, et al, "Randomized Comparison of Cisplatin and Etoposide and Either Bleomycin or Ifosfamide in Treatment of Advanced Disseminated Germ Cell Tumors: An Eastern Cooperative Oncology Group, Southwest Oncology Group, and Cancer and Leukemia Group B Study," *J Clin Oncol*, 1998, 16(4):1287-93.

VIP (Small Cell Lung Cancer)

Use Lung cancer, small cell

Regimen

Etoposide: I.V.: 75 mg/m^2/day days 1 to 4
    [total dose/cycle = 300 mg/m^2]
Ifosfamide: I.V.: 1200 mg/m^2/day days 1 to 4
    [total dose/cycle = 4800 mg/m^2]
Cisplatin: I.V.: 20 mg/m^2/day days 1 to 4
    [total dose/cycle = 80 mg/m^2]
Mesna: I.V.: 300 mg/m^2 day 1 only
    followed by I.V.: 1200 mg/m^2/day continuous infusion days 1 to 4
    [total dose/cycle = 5100 mg/m^2]
Repeat cycle every 21 days

References

Loehrer PJ Sr, Ansari R, Gonin R, et al, "Cisplatin Plus Etoposide With and Without Ifosfamide in Extensive Small-Cell Lung Cancer: A Hoosier Oncology Group Study," *J Clin Oncol*, 1995, 13(10):2594-9.

VIP (Vinblastine) (Testicular Cancer)

Use Testicular cancer

Regimen NOTE: Multiple variations are listed below.

Variation 1:
Vinblastine: I.V.: 0.11 mg/kg/day days 1 and 2
    [total dose/cycle = 0.22 mg/kg]
(Continued)

VIP (Vinblastine) (Testicular Cancer) *(Continued)*

Ifosfamide: I.V.: 1200 mg/m^2/day days 1 to 5
[total dose/cycle = 6000 mg/m^2]
Cisplatin: I.V.: 20 mg/m^2/day days 1 to 5
[total dose/cycle = 100 mg/m^2]
Mesna: I.V.: 400 mg day 1
followed by I.V.: 1200 mg/day continuous infusion days 1 to 5
[total dose/cycle = 6400 mg]
Repeat cycle every 21 days for 4 cycles
Variation 2:
Vinblastine: I.V.: 6 mg/m^2/day days 1 and 2
[total dose/cycle = 12 mg/m^2]
Ifosfamide: I.V.: 1500 mg/m^2/day days 1 to 5
[total dose/cycle = 7500 mg/m^2]
Cisplatin: I.V.: 20 mg/m^2/day days 1 to 5
[total dose/cycle = 100 mg/m^2]
Mesna: I.V.: 300 mg/m^2 3 times/day days 1 to 5
[total dose/cycle = 4500 mg/m^2]
Repeat cycle every 21 days for 4 cycles

References

Variation 1:
Loehrer PJ Sr, Lauer R, Roth BJ, et al, "Salvage Therapy in Recurrent Germ Cell Cancer: Ifosfamide and Cisplatin Plus Either Vinblastine or Etoposide," *Ann Intern Med*, 1988, 109(7):540-6.
Variation 2:
Clemm C, Hartenstein R, Willich N, et al, "Vinblastine-Ifosfamide-Cisplatin Treatment of Bulky Seminoma," *Cancer*, 1986, 58(10):2203-7.

VM

Use Breast cancer
Regimen
Variation 1:
Mitomycin: I.V.: 10 mg/m^2 days 1 and 28, for 2 cycles
[total dose/cycle = 20 mg/m^2]
followed by I.V.: 10 mg/m^2 day 1 only for subsequent cycles
[total dose/cycle = 10 mg/m^2]
Vinblastine: I.V.: 5 mg/m^2/day days 1, 14, 28, and 42, for 2 cycles
[total dose/cycle = 20 mg/m^2]
followed by I.V.: 5 mg/m^2/day days 1 and 21
[total dose/cycle = 10 mg/m^2]
Repeat cycle every 6-8 weeks
Variation 2:
Mitomycin: I.V.: 10 mg/m^2/day days 1 and 28, for 2 cycles
[total dose/cycle = 20 mg/m^2]
followed by I.V.: 10 mg/m^2 day 1 only for subsequent cycles
[total dose/cycle = 10 mg/m^2]
Vindesine: I.V.: 2 mg/m^2/day days 1, 14, 28, and 42, for 2 cycles
[total dose/cycle = 8 mg/m^2]
followed by I.V.: 2 mg/m^2/ day days 1 and 21 for subsequent cycles
[total dose/cycle = 4 mg/m^2]
Repeat cycle every 6-8 weeks

References

Garewal HS, Brooks RJ, Jones SE, et al, "Treatment of Advanced Breast Cancer With Mitomycin C Combined With Vinblastine or Vindesine," *J Clin Oncol*, 1983, 1(12):772-5.

♦ **VMP** *see* Bortezomib-Melphalan-Prednisone *on page 1156*

♦ **VMPT** *see* Bortezomib-Melphalan-Prednisone-Thalidomide *on page 1156*

VP (Small Cell Lung Cancer)
Use Lung cancer, small cell
Regimen
Etoposide: I.V.: 100 mg/m²/day days 1 to 4
[total dose/cycle = 400 mg/m²]
Cisplatin: I.V.: 20 mg/m²/day days 1 to 4
[total dose/cycle = 80 mg/m²]
Repeat cycle every 21 days
References
Loehrer PJ Sr, Ansari R, Gonin R, et al, "Cisplatin Plus Etoposide With and Without Ifosfamide in Extensive Small Cell Lung Cancer: A Hoosier Oncology Group Study," *J Clin Oncol*, 1995, 13(10):2594-9.

V-TAD
Use Leukemia, acute myeloid
Regimen Induction:
Etoposide: I.V.: 50 mg/m²/day days 1 to 3
[total dose/cycle = 150 mg/m²]
Thioguanine: Oral: 75 mg/m²/day every 12 hours days 1 to 5
[total dose/cycle = 750 mg/m²]
Daunorubicin: I.V.: 20 mg/m²/day days 1 and 2
[total dose/cycle = 40 mg/m²]
Cytarabine: I.V.: 75 mg/m²/day continuous infusion days 1 to 5
[total dose/cycle = 375 mg/m²]
Up to 3 cycles may be given based on individual response; time between cycles not specified
References
Bigelow CL, Kopecky K, Files JC, et al, "Treatment of Acute Myelogenous Leukemia in Patients Over 50 Years of Age With V-TAD: A Southwest Oncology Group Study," *Am J Hematol*, 1995, 48(4):228-32.

XelOx
Index Terms Oxaliplatin-Capecitabine
Use Colorectal cancer
Regimen Note: Multiple variations are listed below.
Variation 1:
Oxaliplatin: I.V.: 130 mg/m² day 1
[total dose/cycle = 130 mg/m²]
Capecitabine: Oral: 2500 mg/m²/day days 1 to 14
[total dose/cycle = 35,000 mg/m²]
Repeat cycle every 21 days
Variation 2:
Oxaliplatin: I.V.: 85 mg/m² day 1
[total dose/cycle = 85 mg/m²]
Capecitabine: Oral: 3500 mg/m²/day days 1 to 7
[total dose/cycle = 24,500 mg/m²]
Repeat cycle every 14 days
Variation 3:
Oxaliplatin: I.V.: 50-80 mg/m²/day days 1, 8, 22, and 29
[total dose/cycle = 200-320 mg/m²]
Capecitabine: Oral: 1650 mg/m²/day days 1 to 14 and 22 to 35
[total dose/cycle = 46,200 mg/m²]
Variation 4:
Oxaliplatin: I.V.: 70 mg/m²/day days 1 and 8
[total dose/cycle = 140 mg/m²]
(Continued)

XeloX *(Continued)*

Capecitabine: Oral: 2000 mg/m^2/day days 1 to 14
[total dose/cycle = 28,000 mg/m^2]
Repeat cycle every 21 days

Variation 5:
Oxaliplatin: I.V.: 120 mg/m^2 day 1
[total dose/cycle = 120 mg/m^2]
Capecitabine: Oral: 2500 mg/m^2/day days 1 to 14
[total dose/cycle = 35,000 mg/m^2]
Repeat cycle every 21 days

Variation 6:
Oxaliplatin: I.V.: 85 mg/m^2 day 1
[total dose/cycle = 85 mg/m^2]
Capecitabine: Oral: 2500 mg/m^2/day days 1 to 7
[total dose/cycle = 17,500 mg/m^2]
or Capecitabine: Oral: 3000 mg/m^2/day days 1 to 7
[total dose/cycle = 21,000 mg/m^2]
or Capecitabine: Oral: 3500 mg/m^2/day days 1 to 7
[total dose/cycle = 24,500 mg/m^2]
or Capecitabine: Oral: 4000 mg/m^2/day days 1 to 7
[total dose/cycle = 28,000 mg/m^2]
Repeat cycle every 14 days

References

Variation 1:
Borner MM, Dietrich D, Stupp R, et al, "Phase II Study of Capecitabine and Oxaliplatin in First- and Second-Line Treatment of Advanced or Metastatic Colorectal Cancer," *J Clin Oncol*, 2002, 20(7):1759-66.

Variation 2:
Scheithauer W, Kornek GV, Raderer M, et al, "Randomized Multicenter Phase II Trial of Two Different Schedules of Capecitabine Plus Oxaliplatin as First-Line Treatment in Advanced Colorectal Cancer," *J Clin Oncol*, 2003, 21(7):1307-12.

Variation 3:
Rodel C, Grabenbauer GG, Papadopoulos T, et al, "Phase I/II Trial of Capecitabine, Oxaliplatin, and Radiation for Rectal Cancer," *J Clin Oncol*, 2003, 21(16):3098-104.

Variation 4:
Jordan K, Grothey A, Kellner O, et al, "Randomized Phase II Trial of Capecitabine Plus Irinotecan vs Capecitabine Plus Oxaliplatin as First-Line Therapy in Advanced Colorectal Cancer (ACRC): Results of an Interim Analysis," *Proc Annu Meet Am Soc Clin Oncol*, 2002, 21:2225.

Variation 5:
Zeuli M, Nardoni C, Pino MS, et al, "Phase II Study of Capecitabine and Oxaliplatin as First-Line Treatment in Advanced Colorectal Cancer," *Ann Oncol*, 2003, 14(9):1378-82.

Variation 6:
Scheithauer W, Kornek GV, Raderer M, et al, "Intermittent Weekly High-Dose Capecitabine in Combination With Oxaliplatin: A Phase I/II Study in First-Line Treatment of Patients With Advanced Colorectal Cancer," *Ann Oncol*, 2002, 13(10):1583-9.

SPECIAL TOPICS

CHEMOTHERAPY AND PREGNANCY

INTRODUCTION

The occurrence of cancer and pregnancy at the same time is reportedly rare. The cancers most often described in pregnancy women include breast cancer, cervical cancer, hematologic cancers, melanoma, ovarian cancer, thyroid cancer, and colorectal cancer. There is no apparent link between these malignancies and pregnancy; rather, these cancers are those most common in women of childbearing age. Obviously, the decision to continue or terminate a pregnancy encompasses a host of factors, including the effects of chemotherapy on the fetus.

EFFECTS OF CHEMOTHERAPY

As a rapidly proliferating tissue, the fetus would be expected to be a target for cytotoxic agents. Exposure to cytotoxic drugs during the first week of pregnancy is thought to present an "all or none" phenomenon – that is, spontaneous abortion or a normal fetus. Exposure during the remainder of the first trimester can lead to spontaneous abortion or to teratogenicity. Teratogenicity (ie, congenital abnormalities) occurs at this time, as this is the period of organ development. Indeed, teratogenicity is thought to be negligible when cytotoxic agents are given in the second and third trimesters. However, during the second and third trimesters, cytotoxic agents can interfere with fetal growth and functional development (eg, low birth weight, intrauterine growth retardation). To avoid potential complications from neutropenia and thrombocytopenia, delivery should be avoided during the maternal nadir (usually 2 to 3 weeks after treatment). It is also recommended not to administer chemotherapy beyond 35 weeks of gestation so that delivery does not occur prior to the marrow recovery. Neutropenia and thrombocytopenia at term are of concern for both the mother and the infant.

In addition to the timing of chemotherapy, the occurrence of an adverse outcome of pregnancy is influenced by the particular class of cytotoxic agent, as well as the dose. The literature suggests that antimetabolites, and in particular, methotrexate, are the most likely teratogens. The "aminopterin syndrome" of congenital abnormalities is characterized by dysostosis (delay in ossification of the bones of the skull), hypertelorism (a wide nasal bridge), anomalies of the external ears, and micrognathia (smallness of the jaws). Interestingly, a recent review noted no congenital abnormalities among fetuses exposed to low-dose methotrexate used in mothers with rheumatologic disorders. Methotrexate was used before or during the first trimester in 15 of 16 pregnancies described; six spontaneous abortions occurred, and none of the live births displayed congenital abnormalities. This would seem to underscore the influence of degree of exposure (ie, dose). Numerous case reports document successful pregnancies with no teratogenicity when chemotherapy was administered after the first trimester. Alkylating agents are reported to be "safer" than antimetabolites, and the vinca alkaloids are reportedly the "safest" even during the first trimester. If treatment during the first trimester is essential, consideration should be given to the use of a single-agent, followed up by a multi-agent regimen after 12 weeks.

Long-term complications following *in utero* exposure to cytotoxic drugs might include abnormal physical and/or mental development, carcinogenesis, and teratogenicity in subsequent generation(s). Children exposed to anthracyclines in utero may require long term monitoring for potential cardiotoxic effects. Some adverse long-term outcomes have been described, but there are few systematic long-term follow-up studies.

In addition to concerns of fetal exposure to chemotherapy agents, treatment interruptions may also have an effect on the pregnant cancer patient. Case reports of women with chronic myeloid leukemia on imatinib therapy report that some women in hematologic or cytogenic response with therapy interruptions for pregnancy failed to respond to imatinib upon treatment reinitiation after pregnancy completion.

CONCLUSION

Given the toxicity associated with most cytotoxic drugs, the likelihood of adverse outcomes of pregnancy seems lower than one might expect, especially after the first trimester. In addition to the effects of chemotherapy on the fetus, multiple other factors (eg, ability to stage cancer in the pregnant female; interactions, if any, of pregnancy and a particular cancer; prognosis) must be considered in the pregnant cancer patient.

Selected Readings

Ault P, Kantarjian H, O'Brien S, et al, "Pregnancy Among Patients With Chronic Myeloid Leukemia Treated With Imatinib," *J Clin Oncol*, 2006, 24(7):1204-8.

Caligiuri MA, "Leukemia and Pregnancy: Treatment and Outcome," *Adv Oncol*, 1992, 8:10-7.

Cardonick E and Iacobucci A, "Use of Chemotherapy During Human Pregnancy," *Lancet Oncol*, 2004, 5(5): 283-91.

Fisher PM and Hancock BW, "Hodgkin's Disease in the Pregnant Patient," *Br J Hosp Med*, 1996, 56(10):529-32.

Leslie KK, "Chemotherapy and Pregnancy," *Clin Obstet Gynecol*, 2002, 45(1):153-64.

National Comprehensive Cancer Network® (NCCN), "NCCN Clinical Practice Guidelines in Oncology™: Breast Cancer," V.2.2006. Available at http://www.nccn.org/professionals/physician_gls/PDF/breast.pdf.

Ring AE, Smith IE, Jones A, et al, "Chemotherapy for Breast Cancer During Pregnancy: An 18-Year Experience From Five London Teaching Hospitals," *J Clin Oncol*, 2005, 23(18):4192-7.

Shapiro CL and Mayer RJ, "Breast Cancer During Pregnancy," *Adv Oncol*, 1992, 8:25-9.

Ward FT and Weiss RB, "Managing Lymphoma During Pregnancy," *Adv Oncol*, 1992, 8:18-22.

FERTILITY AND CANCER THERAPY

Antineoplastic therapy (chemotherapy, radiation, surgery) or cancer itself may affect fertility and/or sexual function in both men and women. They may also effect pregnancy outcomes, neonatal development or pubertal development and gonadal function in children. These effects on fertility may be temporary or permanent; and are dependent on a variety of factors including: Intensity of therapy; duration of therapy; age; gender.

Antineoplastic Agents Associated With Sterility

Women	Men
Alkylating agents	Alkylating agents
Busulfan	Busulfan
Chlorambucil	Chlorambucil
Cyclophosphamide	Cisplatin
Mechlorethamine	Cyclophosphamide
Melphalan	Mechlorethamine
Procarbazine	Nitrosoureas
	Procarbazine

FEMALES

Females are born with a set number of ova that are arrested in the meiotic prophase stage. Following sexual maturation, growth of these oocytes is stimulated by follicle stimulating hormone (FSH). Each follicle produces estrogen, which inhibits the secretion of FSH and luteinizing hormone (LH). In midcycle, estrogen levels rise and a surge of LH and increased release of FSH cause the follicle to swell and induce ovulation. After release of the ovum, the corpus luteum is formed which secretes progesterone, estrogen, and inhibin. LH, FSH, and inhibin act as negative feedback to the hypothalamus and pituitary to decrease secretion of LH and FSH. If fertilization does not occur, progesterone levels decrease, the corpus luteum involutes, and the cycle begins again.

Antineoplastic drugs may stop the development of follicles or may damage oocytes. Prepubertal gonads may be more resistant than postpubertal gonads, possibly due to a larger number of follicles as compared to ovaries in older patients. Gonadal destruction causes clinical findings associated with estrogen deficiency such as amenorrhea, endometrial hypoplasia, vaginal atrophy and dryness, and hot flashes. FSH levels are elevated and estrogen levels decreased. The onset and duration of symptoms is dose- and age-related. Younger patients are able to tolerate higher doses of chemotherapy before symptoms develop and have a higher likelihood of the return of menses when therapy is stopped.

Radiation therapy can cause ovarian damage, but the ovaries are more radioresistant than the testes and can tolerate higher doses of radiation. The effect on the ovaries depends on the age of the patient, the number of remaining oocytes at the time of radiation, and the exposure dose and field.

Irradiation fields that do not include the pelvis generally do not cause infertility as evidenced by follow-up of Hodgkin's disease patients who received nodal irradiation.

For women, there is little available to protect against gonadal damage, and few options for preservation of ova. Although cryopreservation of ova is possible, it is experimental and has a low success rate. Standard *in vitro* fertilization and freezing of the embryo is another alternative, but there is little data to support this and it brings up many ethical issues. Other experimental approaches to preserving ovarian function that have been suggested include diminishing ovarian function during the period of treatment by use of gonadotropin-releasing hormone (GnRH) agonists or oral contraceptives; and implantation of cryopreserved ovarian cortical strips after chemotherapy.

MALES

Seminiferous tubules make up 75% of testicular mass. Their epithelium is composed of two cell types: Spermatogenic cells and Sertoli cells. Sertoli cells help regulate the release of mature spermatozoa. In males, gonadotropin-releasing hormone (GnRH) causes the release of FSH and LH from the anterior pituitary. LH stimulates Leydig cells in the testis to produce testosterone, which in turn has a negative feedback on the secretion of LH. FSH stimulates Sertoli cells that assist in spermatogenesis. Spermatogenesis occurs constantly. It takes about 64-90 days to progress from spermatogonia stem-cell mitosis to spermatocytes, spermatids, and finally spermatozoa.

Antineoplastic drugs and radiation destroy epithelial germ cells in a dose-dependent fashion. This damage results in increased FSH levels, decreased testosterone levels, oligospermia, or azoospermia. Spermatogenesis is more susceptible than testosterone production; and postpubertal testes are more susceptible to damage than prepubertal testes. Azoospermia may or may not be reversible. When it does recover, return of spermatogenesis may take up to 49 months.

Effects of radiation therapy on the testes are dependent on the dose, stage of development of the germ cell, and pubertal stage of the patient. Spermatogonia are the most sensitive to radiation damage, followed in decreasing sensitivity by spermatocytes and spermatids. Prepubertal boys may have oligo- or azoospermia once they reach sexual maturation. They may also have delayed sexual maturation due to destruction of Leydig cells and thus decreased testosterone production.

Surgery can affect male sexuality and fertility. Surgery for testicular cancer includes orchiectomy and retroperitoneal lymph node resection which has resulted in decreased semen volume, erectile dysfunction, and low sexual desire. Prostate cancer surgery can also produce erectile dysfunction and changes in semen volume or ejaculatory problems.

Interestingly, patients with testicular cancer may be at increased risk for fertility problems before treatment is started. Patients with testicular cancer are more likely to have impaired semen quality even before orchiectomy, and may have lower semen counts than would be expected following orchiectomy. This could be due to abnormal pathology in the contralateral testis. There is some evidence to suggest that exposure to abnormal hormone levels during development (eg, high progesterone levels associated with morning sickness) may be at risk for developing testicular cancer.

FERTILITY AND CANCER THERAPY *(Continued)*

In men, cryopreservation of sperm is a viable alternative and should be offered. Advances in *in vitro* fertilization using intracytoplasmic sperm injection may be helpful. There has also been some work done looking at suppressing spermatogenesis and Leydig cell function using LHRH analogues with either antiandrogens or testosterone to protect against chemotherapy-induced damage. Finally, cooling of the testes during radiation therapy has shown some promising results.

OUTCOMES OF PREGNANCY

Most studies of parents who have been treated for childhood cancer with chemotherapy, radiation therapy, or both suggest these individuals are not at increased risk of having children with congenital or chromosomal anomalies. However, one report of patients treated for Wilms' Tumor did suggest a trend toward increased risk of congenital malformations, fetal malposition, or early labor in previously irradiated women.

Available data do not show increased risk of miscarriage, fetal demise, or birth weight following chemotherapy. One small study of pregnancy outcome found no significant differences between patients who had received chemotherapy and controls. The same investigators also compared pregnancy outcome in the partners of male survivors of childhood cancer to outcome in the partners of their male siblings. The percent of live births in the male cancer survivors' partners was higher than among female cancer survivors, but was significantly lower than in the partners of male siblings. Rate of miscarriage, stillbirth, and birthweight distribution was similar in both cases and controls. In women who have received pelvic irradiation complications such as preterm labor and delivery, low birth weight, and placenta accrete have been reported.

Generally, there is no increased risk of cancer in the offspring of cancer survivors. Nor, with the possible exception of gestational trophoblastic disease, does pregnancy seem to affect the risk of cancer recurrence.

Selected Readings

Bahadur G, "Fertility Issues for Cancer Patients," *Mol Cell Endocrinol*, 2000, 169(1-2):117-22.

Goldman S and Johnson FL, "Effects of Chemotherapy and Irradiation on the Gonads," *Endocrinol Metab Clin North Am*, 1993, 22(3):617-29.

Gulati SC and Van Poznak C, "Pregnancy After Bone Marrow Transplantation," *J Clin Oncol*, 1998, 16(5):1978-85.

Kwon JS and Case AM, "Effects of Cancer Treatment on Reproduction and Fertility," *J Obstet Gynaecol Can*, 2002, 24(8):619-27.

Petersen PM, Giwercman A, Skakkebaek NE, et al, "Gonadal Function in Men With Testicular Cancer," *Sem Oncol*, 1998, 25(2):224-33.

Pont J and Albrecht W, "Fertility After Chemotherapy for Testicular Cancer," *Fertil Steril*, 1997, 68:1-5.

Shahin MS and Puscheck E, "Reproductive Sequelae of Cancer Treatment," *Obstet Gynecol Clin North Am*, 1998, 25(2):423-33.

MANAGEMENT OF DRUG EXTRAVASATIONS

Vesicant: An agent that causes tissue destruction.

Irritant: An agent that causes aching, tightness, and phlebitis with or without inflammation.

Extravasation: Unintentional leakage of fluid out of a blood vessel into surrounding tissue.

Vesicant extravasation: Leakage of a drug that causes pain, necrosis, or tissue sloughing.

Delayed extravasation: Symptoms occur 48 hours, or later, after drug administration.

Flare: Local, nonpainful, possibly allergic reaction often accompanied by reddening along the vein.

A potential, and potentially highly morbid, complication of drug therapy is soft tissue damage caused by leakage of the drug solution out of the vein. A variety of complications, including erythema, ulceration, pain, tissue sloughing, and necrosis are possible. This problem is not unique to antineoplastic therapy; a variety of drugs have been reported to cause tissue damage if extravasated. See table.

Vesicant Agents

Hyperosmotic Agents (>280 mOsmol/L)	Ischemia Inducers	Direct Cellular Toxins	
		Nonantineoplastic Agents	Antineoplastic Agents
Calcium chloride (>10%)	Aminophylline	Chlordiazepoxide	Amsacrine[1]
Calcium gluconate	Dobutamine	Diazepam	Dactinomycin
Calcium gluceptate	Dopamine	Digoxin	Daunorubicin
Contrast media	Epinephrine	Ethanol	Doxorubicin
Crystalline amino acids (4.25%)	Esmolol	Nafcillin	Epirubicin
Dextrose (>10%)	Metaraminol	Nitroglycerin	Esorubicin[1]
Mannitol (>5%)	Metoprolol	Phenytoin	Idarubicin
Potassium acetate (>2 mEq/mL)	Norepinephrine	Propylene glycol	Mechlorethamine
Potassium chloride (>2 mEq/mL)	Phenylephrine	Sodium thiopental	Mitomycin
Sodium bicarbonate (≥8.4%)	Vasopressin	Tetracycline	Streptozocin (?)
Sodium chloride (>1%)			Valrubicin
Thiopentone			Vinblastine
Urea (30%)			Vincristine
			Vindesine[1]
			Vinorelbine

[1]In addition to the known vesicants, a number of other antineoplastic agents, not generally considered to be vesicants, have been associated with isolated reports of tissue damage following extravasation.

MANAGEMENT OF DRUG EXTRAVASATIONS
(Continued)

Agents Associated With Occasional Extravasation Reactions

Aclarubicin[1]	Floxuridine
Arsenic trioxide	Fluorouracil
Bleomycin	Gemcitabine
Carboplatin ≥10 mg/mL	Gemtuzumab
Carmustine	Ifosfamide
Cisplatin	Irinotecan
Cyclophosphamide	Menogaril[1]
Dacarbazine	Mitoxantrone
Daunorubicin citrate	Oxaliplatin
(liposomal)	Paclitaxel
Dexrazoxane	Promethazine
Docetaxel	Teniposide
Doxorubicin (liposomal)	Topotecan
Etoposide	

[1]Not commercially available in the U.S.

The actual incidence of drug extravasations is unknown. Some of the uncertainty stems from varying definitions of incidence. Incidence rates have been reported based on total number of drug doses administered, number of vesicant doses administered, number of treatments, number of patients treated with vesicants, and total number of patients treated. Most estimates place the incidence of extravasations with cytotoxic agents in the range of 1% to 7%.

The optimal treatment of drug extravasations is uncertain. A variety of antidotes have been proposed; however, objective clinical evidence to support these recommendations frequently is not available. There are no well done randomized prospective trials of potential treatments. Controlled clinical trials are not feasible, limiting efforts to identify optimal management of these reactions. Extant reports are based on animal models, anecdotal cases, and/or small uncontrolled series of patients. Many of the existing reports, both animal and human, used more than one therapeutic intervention simultaneously, adding to the difficulty of identifying the efficacy of any single approach.

The best "treatment" for extravasation reactions is prevention. Although it is not possible to prevent all accidents, a few simple precautions can minimize the risk to the patient. The vein used should be a large, intact vessel with good blood flow. To minimize the risk of dislodging the catheter, veins in the hands and in the vicinity of joints (eg, antecubital) should be avoided. Veins in the forearm (ie, basilic, cephalic, and median antebrachial) are usually good options for peripheral infusions. Prior to drug administration, the patency of the I.V. line should be verified. The line should be flushed with 5-10 mL of a saline or dextrose solution and the drug(s) infused through the side of a free-flowing isotonic saline or dextrose infusion.

A frequently recommended precaution against drug extravasation is the use of a central venous catheter. Use of a central line has several advantages, including high patient satisfaction, reliable venous access, high flow rates, and rapid dilution of the drug. A wide variety of devices are readily available. Many institutions encourage or require use of a vascular access device for administration of vesicant agents.

Despite their benefit, central lines are not an absolute solution. Vascular access devices are subject to a number of complications. The catheter tip may not be properly positioned in the superior vena cava/right atrium, or may migrate out of position. Additionally, these catheters require routine care to maintain patency and avoid infections. Finally, extravasation of drugs from venous access devices is possible. Misplacement/migration of the catheter tip, improper placement of the needle in accessing injection ports, and cuts, punctures, or rupture of the catheter itself have all been reported. Reports of extravasation from central catheters range from 0.3% to 50% and are similar to extravasation rates reported from peripheral lines.

When a drug extravasation does occur, a variety of immediate actions have been recommended. Although there is considerable uncertainty regarding the value of some potential treatments, a few initial steps seem to be generally accepted.

1. **Stop the infusion.** At the first suspicion of infiltration, the drug infusion should be stopped. If infiltration is not certain, the line can be tested by attempting to aspirate blood, and careful infusion of a few milliliters of saline or dextrose solution.

2. **Do NOT remove the catheter/needle.** The infiltrated catheter should not be removed immediately. It should be left in place to facilitate aspiration of fluid from the extravasation site, and, if appropriate, administration of an antidote directly into the extravasation site.

3. **Aspirate fluid.** To the extent possible, the extravasated drug solution should be removed from the subcutaneous tissues.

4. **Do NOT flush the line.** Flooding the infiltration site with saline or dextrose in an attempt to dilute the drug solution generally is not recommended. Rather than minimizing damage, such a procedure may have the opposite effect by distributing the vesicant solution over a wider area.

5. **Remove the catheter/needle.** If an antidote is not going to be injected into the extravasation site, the infiltrated catheter should be removed. If an antidote is to be injected into the area, it should be injected through the catheter to ensure delivery of the antidote to the infiltration site. When this has been accomplished, the catheter should then be removed.

Two issues for which there is less consensus are the application of heat or cold, and the use of various antidotes. A variety of recommendations exist for each of these concerns; however, there is no consensus concerning the proper approach.

Cold. Intermittent cooling of the area of infiltration results in vasoconstriction, which tends to restrict the spread of the drug. It may also inhibit the local effects of some drugs (eg, anthracyclines). Application of cold is usually recommended as immediate treatment for most drug extravasations, except

MANAGEMENT OF DRUG EXTRAVASATIONS
(Continued)

the vinca alkaloids. In one report of antineoplastic drug extravasation treatment, almost 90% of the extravasations treated only with topical cold required no further therapy.

The largest single published series of antineoplastic drug extravasations was 175 patients reported by Larson in 1985. This series includes some of the more commonly used vesicants, including the anthracyclines, mechlorethamine, mitomycin, and the vinca alkaloids. For 119 patients, local application of cold (15 minutes four times a day for 3 days) and close observation was the sole treatment. The remaining 56 patients received a variety of antidotes. In 89% of the patients treated with cold alone, the extravasation resolved without further treatment. Of the patients treated by other methods, only 53% resolved without further treatment.

Helpful as it may be, Larson's report does have some limitations. Agents such as the epipodophyllotoxins and taxanes which are occasionally associated with soft tissue damage were not included, nor were extravasations of nonantineoplastic agents mentioned. The report included infiltrations of the vinca alkaloids, even though the literature recommends use of heat to treat these. Also, except for doxorubicin extravasations in the group treated with ice and observation, responses for the individual drugs were not indicated. In this group, 72% of the doxorubicin extravasations resolved completely.

Heat. Application of heat results in a localized vasodilation and increased blood flow. Increased circulation is believed to facilitate removal of the drug from the area of infiltration. The data supporting use of heat are less convincing than for cold. One report of the application of heat for nonantineoplastic drug extravasations suggested application of heat increased the risk of skin maceration and necrosis. Most data are from animal studies with relatively few human case reports. Animal models indicate application of heat exacerbates the damage from anthracycline extravasations. No large series of extravasations managed with the application of heat has been published. Heat is generally recommended for treatment for vinca alkaloid extravasations; a few reports recommend it for treatment of amino acid solutions, aminophylline, calcium, contrast media, dextrose, mannitol, nafcillin, paclitaxel, phenytoin, podophyllotoxin, potassium and vinca alkaloid infiltrations. There are conflicting reports on the initial management of paclitaxel infiltrations.

For some agents, such as cisplatin, epipodophyllotoxins, mechlorethamine, and paclitaxel, there are conflicting recommendations. Some reports recommend application of cold, others recommend heat. At least one report suggests neither cold nor heat is effective for paclitaxel extravasations.

ANTIDOTES

A very wide variety of agents have been reported as possible antidotes for extravasated drugs, with no consensus on their proper use. For a number of reasons, evaluation of the various reports is difficult.

1. Mechanism of action. For many drugs, the underlying mechanism responsible for the tissue damage is not certain. For some of the antidotes, the purported mechanism of action of the antidote is also unclear.

2. Controlled trials. Prospective, randomized controlled trials are not practical. Information concerning treatment of extravasations is based almost exclusively on animal models, anecdotal reports, and small, uncontrolled studies.

3. Outcome definitions. Published reports use a number of different end-points and outcomes to define efficacy of a given treatment.

4. Confounding factors. A number of confounding factors exist which make assessment of various antidotes difficult. Among these are:

   a. *Response to nonpharmacologic therapy.* Application of heat or cold alone, especially the latter, appears to have a significant protective effect.

   b. *Multiple therapies.* A number of reports used more than one therapeutic modality to treat drug extravasations. In many cases, cold or heat is applied along with the antidote. In some cases, more than one antidote is used, sometimes in conjunction with heat or cold. Use of multiple approaches further complicates the determination of the possible effect of a particular antidote, or the additive effect of various combinations.

   c. *Variable applications.* For some proposed antidotes, a wide variety of different doses, concentrations, methods of application, and duration of therapy have been reported, making determination of the optimal treatment regimen difficult.

Agents Used as Antidotes

Albumin	Iron dextran
Antihistamines	Isoproterenol
Antioxidants	Nitroglycerin paste
Beta-adrenergics	Phentolamine
Carnitine	Radical dimer
Corticosteroids[1]	Saline
Dexrazoxane	Sodium bicarbonate
Dextranomer	Sodium hypochlorite
Dimethyl sulfoxide	Sodium thiosulfate[1]
Dopamine	Terbutaline
Fluorescein	Vitamin E
Hyaluronidase[1]	

[1]Listed in the package insert of at least one agent.

MANAGEMENT OF DRUG EXTRAVASATIONS
(Continued)

Sodium bicarbonate. An 8.4% solution of sodium bicarbonate was briefly recommended for treatment of anthracycline extravasations. The recommendation was based on a case report of its use in a single patient. The proposed mechanism of action was that the high pH of the bicarbonate solution would break the glycosidic bond of the anthracycline, thereby inactivating it. Follow-up studies in a variety of animal models failed to confirm the original report. Also, the concentrated sodium bicarbonate may itself be a vesicant. See the Vesicant Agents table *on page 1301.* At present, most reviews and guidelines discourage its use for treating extravasations.

Corticosteroids. Steroids are most commonly used to treat anthracycline extravasations. Hydrocortisone is the steroid most frequently recommended, although dexamethasone has also been used. It is suggested that steroids reduce local inflammation from the extravasated drug. Such activity has not been confirmed, nor has it been demonstrated that the tissue damage from drug infiltrations is the result of an inflammatory process. Interpretation of steroid efficacy is complicated by the multiple doses, routes of administration, duration of therapy, and outcome measurements used. Reports of animal trials offer little additional information, being plagued by many of the limitations of the clinical case reports. The official labeling of only one of the three suppliers of doxorubicin includes a steroid as part of the treatment for drug extravasations. The product labeling from two doxorubicin suppliers (as well as the suppliers of daunorubicin, idarubicin, and liposome-encapsulated daunorubicin and doxorubicin) do not mention corticosteroids to treat drug infiltrations. Most reports question the efficacy of steroids for treatment of drug extravasations; they are not recommended by most guidelines.

Dexrazoxane. Dexrazoxane, a derivative of EDTA, is an intracellular chelating agent often used as a cardioprotective agent in patients receiving anthracycline therapy. It is believed that the cardioprotective effect of dexrazoxane is a result by chelating iron following intracellular hydrolysis. Dexrazoxane is not an effective chelator itself, but is hydrolyzed intracellularly to an open-ring chelator form, which complexes with iron, other heavy metals, and doxorubicin complexes to inhibit the generation of free radicals. It has been postulated that dexrazoxane's chelating effect, or its ability to inhibit topoisomerase II may be useful in preventing tissue damage from anthracycline infiltrations. Several case reports and two small (n = 23, n = 57), uncontrolled, open-labeled studies report dexrazoxane effective in preventing tissue damage following anthracycline extravasation.

Although localized cooling was permitted (except within 15 minutes of dexrazoxane infusion) in the trials, the number of patients in which this was used was not reported. Dexrazoxane was required to start within 6 hours of the drug extravasation. In two small (n = 23, n = 57) studies, 54 of the 80 patients were assessed for efficacy. In 53 patients, dexrazoxane appeared to be effective. One-third of the patients in the two studies were not assessed for efficacy, leaving the actual efficacy rate of dexrazoxane uncertain. Use of dexrazoxane was also associated with a variety of side effects, including fever, fatigue, reactions at the dexrazoxane injection site, nausea, vomiting, diarrhea, mucositis, myelosuppression, increased bilirubin and hepatic trans-aminases, and increased serum creatinine. What proportion of these toxici-ties were attributable to the dexrazoxane, and what was a result of the primary antineoplastic therapy was not clear. Dexrazoxane received approval by the Food and Drug Administration (FDA) in 2007 for treatment of anthra-cycline extravasations.

Dimethyl sulfoxide (DMSO). A number of reports have suggested applica-tion of DMSO is an effective treatment for infiltrations of a number of different drugs. It is believed DMSO's protective effect is due to its ability to act as a free radical scavenger (one theory suggests tissue damage from vesicants, particularly anthracyclines, is due to formation of hydroxyl free radicals). Results in animal models have been equivocal, with some reports indicating DMSO is beneficial, and some showing little or no effect. Clinical reports of its use are extremely difficult to interpret due to variations in DMSO concentra-tion, number of applications/day, duration of therapy, and concomitant treat-ments. A number of different treatments, including cold, steroids, vitamin E, and sodium bicarbonate have been used in conjunction with DMSO. Also, most reports that suggest DMSO is effective in preventing tissue damage used DMSO concentrations >90% which is not available for clinical use in the United States.

A further complication to interpretation of DMSO's efficacy is that some series included infiltrations of agents not generally considered to be vesicants. The largest clinical series included infiltrations in 75 patients, but only 31 of the extravasations involved vesicants (doxorubicin, epirubicin, or mitomycin). The remaining incidents involved drugs not usually associated with tissue damage (cisplatin, ifosfamide, and mitoxantrone). Application of 99% DMSO for 7 days and cold for 3 days resulted in a 93.5% success rate in the patients with vesicant extravasations. Only two patients (6.5%) had complications requiring further therapy. Whether the addition of DMSO represented a real improvement over cold alone is difficult to assess.

Hyaluronidase. Hyaluronidase is an enzyme that destroys hyaluronic acid, an essential component of connective tissue. This results in increased permeability of the tissue, facilitating diffusion and absorption of fluids. It is postulated that increasing the diffusion of extravasated fluids results in more rapid absorption, thereby limiting tissue damage. In individual case reports, hyaluronidase has been reported effective in preventing tissue damage from a wide variety of agents, including amino acid solutions, aminophylline, calcium, contrast media, dextrose, mannitol, nafcillin, phenytoin, potassium and vinca alkaloids. Other reports suggest it might also be useful in managing extravasations of epipodophyllotoxins and taxanes, although not all guide-lines recommend its use for these agents.

Phentolamine. Phentolamine is an alpha$_1$-adrenergic antagonist which produces peripheral vasodilation. It has been reported to reduce tissue necrosis following extravasation of pressor (vasoconstrictor) agents such as dobutamine, dopamine, epinephrine, and norepinephrine.

Sodium thiosulfate. A freshly prepared $1/6$M ($\sim$4%) solution of sodium thio-sulfate has been recommended for treatment of mechlorethamine and cisplatin infiltrations. A 2% solution has been recommended for doxorubicin, epirubicin, mitomycin, and vinblastine extravasations. This recommendation

MANAGEMENT OF DRUG EXTRAVASATIONS
(Continued)

is based on *in vitro* data demonstrating an interaction between sodium thiosulfate and cisplatin, dacarbazine, and mechlorethamine and very limited animal data on thiosulfate's ability to inactivate dacarbazine and mechlorethamine. At present, no clinical reports of its efficacy for treating cisplatin or dacarbazine extravasations have been published. Since cisplatin and dacarbazine are generally not considered to be vesicants, the use of thiosulfate to treat infiltrations of these drugs may not be required.

The use of sodium thiosulfate to treat mechlorethamine infiltrations is based almost exclusively on the *in vitro* and animal data. A single case report of successful thiosulfate treatment of an accidental intramuscular mechlorethamine injection has been published. Thus far, no reports of thiosulfate treatment of mechlorethamine infiltrations have been published.

One study of thiosulfate therapy of antineoplastic drug extravasations has been published. In a series of 63 patients with extravasation of doxorubicin, epirubicin, mitomycin, or vinblastine, 31 were treated with subcutaneous hydrocortisone and topical dexamethasone. The remaining 32 patients received subcutaneous injection of a 2% thiosulfate solution in addition to the subcutaneous and topical steroids. No patient in either group developed skin ulceration or required surgery, but the patients who received the thiosulfate healed in about half the time as the patients who received only the steroid therapy.

Reported Treatment Regimens for Drug Extravasations

Treatment	Dose	Route	Duration	Concomitant Therapy	Used to Treat	Preparation	Administration
Cold[1]	15 min qid	Topical	3-4 days	None	All agents[2]	N/A	N/A
Heat[1]	15 min on; 15 min off	Topical	1 day	None	Vinca alkaloids	N/A	N/A
Heat	NS	Topical	NS	None	Epipodophyllotoxins, taxanes[3]	N/A	N/A
Dexrazoxane	1000 mg/m² 500 mg/m²	I.V.	Days 1 and 2 Day 3	Cold[4]	Daunorubicin, doxorubicin, epirubicin, idarubicin	NS	NS
Dexamethasone	4 mg	SubQ, I.D.	One time	Cold	Daunorubicin, doxorubicin	NS	Inject into several sites surrounding the area of extravasation.
Dimethyl sulfoxide[5]	50%-99% q2-4h	Topical	3 days	Dexamethasone 8 mg I.D.	Doxorubicin	N/A	N/A
Dimethyl sulfoxide[5]	70% q3-4h	Topical	10 days	Sodium bicarbonate SubQ, dexamethasone 4 mg SubQ	Daunorubicin	N/A	N/A
Dimethyl sulfoxide[5]	90% q12h	Topical	2 days	Vitamin E 10% topical	Doxorubicin, esorubicin, mitomycin	N/A	N/A

MANAGEMENT OF DRUG EXTRAVASATIONS
(Continued)

Reported Treatment Regimens for Drug Extravasations *(continued)*

Treatment	Dose	Route	Duration	Concomitant Therapy	Used to Treat	Preparation	Administration
Dimethyl sulfoxide[5]	99% q8h for up to 1 week	Topical	1 week	Cold for 3 days	Doxorubicin, mitomycin, mitoxantrone	N/A	Apply 4 drops/10 cm² of skin surface over an area twice the size of the extravasation; allow to air dry without dressings.
Dimethyl sulfoxide[5]	99% q2-4h	Topical	3 days	None	Doxorubicin	N/A	N/A
Dimethyl sulfoxide[5]	99% q6-24h	Topical	14 days	None	Doxorubicin, daunorubicin	N/A	N/A
Dimethyl sulfoxide[5]	99% q6-12h	Topical	1-5 weeks	None	Mitomycin	N/A	N/A
Hyaluronidase[1]	15 units	SubQ	One time	Heat	Amino acid solutions, aminophylline, calcium, contrast media⁶, dextrose, mannitol, nafcillin, phenytoin, potassium, vinca alkaloids	Reconstitute vial with NS to a concentration of 150 units/mL. Dilute 0.1 mL (15 units) with 0.9 mL NS for a final concentration of 15 units/mL	4-5 injections (0.2 mL) into area of extravasation

Reported Treatment Regimens for Drug Extravasations *(continued)*

Treatment	Dose	Route	Duration	Concomitant Therapy	Used to Treat	Preparation	Administration
Hyaluronidase[1]	150 units	SubQ	One time	Heat	Amino acid solutions, aminophylline, calcium, contrast media[6], dextrose, mannitol, nafcillin, phenytoin, potassium, vinca alkaloids	Reconstitute with 1 mL NS	5-10 injections (0.5-1 mL) into area of extravasation
Hyaluronidase[1]	250 units	SubQ	One time	None	Amino acid solutions, aminophylline, calcium, contrast media[6], dextrose, mannitol, nafcillin, phenytoin, potassium, vinca alkaloids	Reconstitute with 6 mL NS	Inject directly through the original needle; **OR** 6 SubQ injections into area of extravasation.
Hydrocortisone	50-200 mg	I.V.; SubQ; I.D.	NS	Cold	All agents *except vinca alkaloids*	NS	Inject into several sites surrounding the area of extravasation.
Hydrocortisone	500 mg	SubQ	One time	Betamethasone and gentamicin ointment q12h for 2 days, then qd	Doxorubicin, epirubicin, vinblastine, mitomycin	500 mg in 10 mL NS	Inject at 1 cm intervals around the area of extravasation.

MANAGEMENT OF DRUG EXTRAVASATIONS
(Continued)

Reported Treatment Regimens for Drug Extravasations *(continued)*

Treatment	Dose	Route	Duration	Concomitant Therapy	Used to Treat	Preparation	Administration
Nitroglycerin paste	NS	Topical	NS	NS	Vasopressors (dobutamine, dopamine, epinephrine, norepinephrine, phenylephrine)	N/A	N/A
Phentolamine	5 mg	SubQ	1 day	None	Vasopressors (dobutamine, dopamine, epinephrine, norepinephrine, phenylephrine)	Mix 5 mg with 9 mL NS	Inject a small amount into area of extravasation. Blanching should reverse immediately. If blanching should recur, additional injections may be needed.
Sodium thiosulfate[1,6]	2%	SubQ	One time	Hydrocortisone 500 mg SubQ, betamethasone and gentamicin ointment q12h for 2 days, then qd	Doxorubicin, epirubicin, vinblastine, mitomycin	NS	Inject at 1 cm intervals around the area of extravasation.
Sodium thiosulfate[1]	⅙ M (~4%)	I.V., SubQ	One time	Ice or heat	Mechlorethamine, cisplatin	Mix 4 mL of 10% sodium thiosulfate with 6 mL sterile water	Inject 2 mL for each 1 mg of mechlorethamine or 100 mg cisplatin

Reported Treatment Regimens for Drug Extravasations (continued)

Treatment	Dose	Route	Duration	Concomitant Therapy	Used to Treat	Preparation	Administration
Terbutaline	1 mg	SubQ	NS	NS	Vasopressors (dobutamine, dopamine, epinephrine, norepinephrine, phenylephrine)	NS	NS

N/A = Not applicable; NS = Not specified; I.V. = Intravenous; SubQ = Subcutaneous; I.D. = Intradermal.

[1]Listed in the package insert of at least one product.

[2]Most guidelines discourage application of cold to treat infiltrations of vinca alkaloids. Some reports discourage its use to treat infiltrations of epipodophyllotoxins and/or taxanes.

[3]There are conflicting data on the efficacy of heat or cold for infiltrations of epipodophyllotoxins and taxanes. Each approach has been reported to be effective, harmful, and of no discernable effect.

[4]Remove cooling 15 minutes prior to dexrazoxane infusion.

[5]DMSO concentrations >50% are not available for human use in the U.S.

[6]Large extravasations only.

MANAGEMENT OF DRUG EXTRAVASATIONS
(Continued)

Selected Readings

Bertelli G, "Prevention and Management of Extravasation of Cytotoxic Drugs," *Drug Saf*, 1995, 12(4):245-55.

Boyle DM and Engelking C, "Vesicant Extravasation: Myths and Realities," *Oncol Nurs Forum*, 1995, 22(1):57-67.

Kurul S, Saip P, and Aydin T, "Totally Implantable Venous-Access Ports: Local Problems and Extravasation Injury," *Lancet Oncol*, 2002, 3(11):684-92.

Larson DL, "What Is the Appropriate Management of Tissue Extravasation by Antitumor Agents?," *Plast Reconstr Surg*, 1985, 75(3):397-405.

Larson DL, "Treatment of Tissue Extravasation by Antitumor Agents," *Cancer*, 1982, 49(9):1796-9.

Larson DL, "Alterations in Wound Healing Secondary to Infusion Injury," *Clin Plast Surg*, 1990, 17(3):509-17.

MacCara ME, "Extravasation: A Hazard of Intravenous Therapy," *Drug Intell Clin Pharm*, 1983, 17(10):713-7.

Mouridsen HT, Langer SW, Buter J, et al, "Treatment of Anthracycline Extravasation With Savene (Dexrazoxane): Results From Two Prospective Clinical Multicentre Studies," *Ann Oncol*, 2007, 18(3):546-50.

Schrijvers DL, "Extravasation: A Dreaded Complication of Chemotherapy," *Ann Oncol*, 2003, 14 Suppl 3:iii26-30.

Schulmeister L and Camp-Sorrell D, "Chemotherapy Extravasation From Implanted Ports," *Oncol Nurs Forum*, 2000, 27(3):531-8.

MANAGEMENT OF INFECTIONS

Certain oncology patients are at increased risk of morbidity and mortality from infectious complications secondary to disease- or treatment-related loss of immunity (see table). Impaired immunity is associated with malignancies that arise from hematologic cells and lymphoid tissues. Iatrogenic reasons for impaired immunity include splenectomy during staging of Hodgkin's disease and repeated courses of chemotherapy or radiation. Patients undergoing allogeneic bone marrow (stem cell) transplantation are at great risk for infectious complications because they generally have a hematologic malignancy, receive intensive chemotherapy prior to the bone marrow transplant, and require chronic immunosuppression to prevent graft-versus-host disease.

Disease-Related Risks for Infections

Cancer	Corresponding Normal Cell	Infectious Risk
Hodgkin's disease	Lymphoid?	Encapsulated bacteria; *Pneumocystis pneumoniae*; herpes simplex virus and varicella zoster virus; extensive chemotherapy/radiation
Non-Hodgkin's lymphoma	B cells (90%) T cells (10%)	*Pneumocystis pneumoniae*; herpes simplex virus and varicella zoster virus; extensive chemotherapy/radiation
Acute lymphoblastic leukemia	B cells (90%) T cells (10%)	Extensive chemotherapy/radiation
Acute myelogenous leukemia	Myelogenous cell	Extensive chemotherapy/radiation
Chronic lymphocytic leukemia	B cells (90%) T cells (10%)	Atypical infections secondary to chronic immune impairment with indolent course of disease

Treatment-related neutropenia increases the risk of developing infection. The likelihood of morbidity or mortality from infection increases as the depth and duration of neutropenia increase. An absolute neutrophil count (ANC) <500 cells/μL blood increases the risk of infectious complications. In fact, patients are considered "high-risk" neutropenics when the ANC is ≤100 cells/μL blood for ≥7 days. The ANC is calculated as follows.

$$ANC = WBC \times [(\% \text{ segmented neutrophils} + \% \text{ band neutrophils}) / 100]$$

The most frequent source of opportunistic pathogens is the patient or close human contacts. Common causes of gram-positive bacterial infections include *Staphylococcus aureus*, *Staphylococcus epidermidis*, *Streptococcus pneumoniae*, *Streptococcus pyogenes*, *Streptococcus viridans*, *Enterococcus faecalis*, *Enterococcus faecium*, and *Corynebacterium* spp. Common causes of gram-negative bacterial infections include *Escherichia coli*, *Klebsiella pneumoniae*, and *Pseudomonas* spp. *Candida albicans* generally colonizes mucous membranes of the gastrointestinal and urogenital tract. Environmental sources of opportunistic pathogens include the surface of fresh fruits and vegetables (bacteria), dried foliage, tobacco, marijuana leaves (*Aspergillus* spp); recent construction or renovation (*Aspergillus* spp);

MANAGEMENT OF INFECTIONS (Continued)

and tap water (*Legionella* spp). Rarely, viruses can be transmitted by blood products (packed red blood cells, platelets, stem cells) or plasma-derived products (intravenous immune globulin).

Thorough and frequent handwashing reduces the risk of transmitting opportunistic pathogens to neutropenic patients. In addition, limitation of the number of visitations and personal contacts also reduces opportunity for transmission of opportunistic pathogens. Additional preventive measures which are generally implemented to reduce the risk of infection in patients at greatest risk (eg, allogeneic bone marrow transplant patients) include hospital room-specific instrumentation, HEPA filtration of patient rooms or nursing units, total room clean following discharge, low microbial diets, and diligent mouth care. HEPA filtration involves circulation of room air through a filter 8-12 times per hour to remove small airborne particles. Low microbial diets prohibit ingestion of fresh fruits and vegetables, or undercooked meat. Diligent mouth care requires swishing and expectoration of mouthwash 4-6 times daily. Mouthwashes may be 0.9% NaCl or dilute bicarbonate solution (sodium bicarbonate 50 mEq/L in sterile water), because the greatest utility of mouth care is to remove oral debris and thereby prohibit microbial growth. However, chlorhexidine 0.12% may also be used as a mouthwash.

Selective gut decontamination using co-trimoxazole or a fluoroquinolone is used to reduce gram-negative colonization in patient undergoing intensive chemotherapy. Selective gut decontamination allows continued colonization of the lower gastrointestinal tract with anaerobic bacteria, which reduces the possibility of fungal overgrowth. High-risk patients undergoing treatment with intensive chemotherapy, such as allogeneic bone marrow transplant recipients, or patients with acute myelogenous leukemia undergoing induction chemotherapy, may also receive prophylactic acyclovir and fluconazole. Allogeneic bone marrow transplant recipients at risk for cytomegalovirus infection may receive prophylactic ganciclovir following engraftment.

Fever is frequently the only sign of infection in the neutropenic patient. Febrile neutropenic patients are empirically managed for presumed infection. Fever is defined as single oral temperature exceeding 38.3°C (101°F), or oral temperature 38°C (100.4°F) for at least 60 minutes. Evaluation of the febrile neutropenic patient should include history and physical examination, chest radiograph, blood cultures drawn from the central venous line (all ports), blood cultures drawn by peripheral venipuncture, specimens of urine and diarrheal stool, plus additional specimens as indicated by history and physical examination. Blood cultures must be drawn prior to initiation of antibiotics to increase the likelihood of acquiring a positive culture; although, blood cultures generally remain negative due to the small inoculum of microbes needed to cause infection in the neutropenic host and due to the early initiation of broad spectrum antibacterials. Empiric treatment with aggressive intravenous doses of broad spectrum, bactericidal antibiotics should be initiated as soon as possible after blood cultures have been collected. Choice of therapy greatly depends on the clinical status of the patient (ie, high vs. low risk), as well as the presumed origin of infection based on clinical presentation. Antibiotics should be infused through alternating central venous line ports.

Vancomycin is no longer recommended as a routine component of initial empiric therapy in the neutropenic patient due to concerns of emerging resistant organisms. Vancomycin should only be considered for patients considered high-risk for serious gram-positive infections. These include patients with a history of quinolone or trimethoprim/sulfamethoxazole prophylaxis, colonization with methicillin-resistant *S. aureus*, or penicillin/ cephalosporin-resistant *S. pneumoniae*, obvious central venous line involvement, hypotension, sepsis (in the absence of a causative pathogen), or are otherwise clinically unstable. Severe mucositis was previously considered a risk factor necessitating vancomycin usage; however, monotherapy with cefepime, imipenem, or piperacillin/tazobactam provide excellent coverage of viridans streptococcal infection in this setting. Vancomycin should be used in combination with a bactericidal agent with activity against gram-negative organisms, including *Pseudomonas* spp (eg, ceftazidime or aztreonam for penicillin-allergic patients). To minimize the development of resistant organisms, treatment with vancomycin should be discontinued in 2-3 days if resistant gram-positive organisms have not been identified. If history or cultures suggest vancomycin-resistant organisms (eg, enterococci), treatment options include linezolid, daptomycin, or quinupristin/ dalfopristin.

When criteria for use of vancomycin are not met, the patient may receive monotherapy (eg, ceftazidime, cefepime, or carbapenem), or dual therapy (aminoglycoside plus and antipseudomonal beta lactam or aztreonam for penicillin allergic patients) should be initiated. The choice for monotherapy versus dual therapy is determined by the patient's history and physical examination. The effect of antimicrobial therapy should be assessed in 72 hours or as indicated by the patient's clinical status.

The low-risk febrile neutropenic patient who defervesces within 72 hours following appropriate antibiotic therapy and is free of signs and symptoms of infection, may be converted to oral antibiotics (second generation cephalosporin or quinolone). Criteria for considering a patient high risk and continuing intravenous antibiotics include signs and symptoms of sepsis at presentation, additional signs of infection such as pneumonia or endocarditis, moderate-to-severe mucositis, dermal or mucosal loss of integrity, impending invasive procedure(s), or impending immunosuppressive therapy. If the patient remains febrile despite 72 hours of broad spectrum antibiotic coverage, the selection of antibiotics can be changed or additional antibiotics can be started. Vancomycin can be discontinued in patients who are clinically stable. Additional antibiotics should be added to patients who appear acutely ill from infection or are at high risk for infectious complications. The choice of antibiotic, which is dependent on current antimicrobial therapy in addition to the patient's history and physical examination, may include vancomycin, second gram-negative agent, amphotericin B, or antianaerobic agent. Treatment with amphotericin B should be started for patients with persistent fevers despite 5-7 days of appropriate empiric antibiotic therapy. Atypical pathogens, including invasive *Legionella pneumoniae*, molds (*Aspergillus* spp, *Fusarium* spp, mucormycoses), and viruses (cytomegalovirus [CMV], adenovirus, herpes simplex), should be considered in the chronically immunosuppressed patient. Appropriate empiric treatment for suspected viral infection would include acyclovir, but valacyclovir or famciclovir are reasonable alternatives. Treatment with ganciclovir, valganciclovir, or foscarnet is recommended if there is concern for CMV. Positive cultures and

MANAGEMENT OF INFECTIONS *(Continued)*

antibiotic sensitivity reports may streamline therapy in the stable patient. However, the high-risk patient may continue receiving broad spectrum antibacterials because the finding of a specific pathogen does not exclude the possibility of additional infecting organisms in the neutropenic patient. Caspofungin has replaced amphotericin B as the antifungal drug of choice for treatment of candidal fungal infection in the neutropenic patient. Prolonged and persistent neutropenia is a risk factor for invasive aspergillosis and voriconazole is the recommended first-line option. Central venous line removal is done judiciously due to the ongoing need for intravenous fluids, drugs, and blood products in the neutropenic and thrombocytopenic patient, and the risk of infection or bleeding with insertion of a new central venous line. Empiric antibiotics should be continued until the patient is afebrile and clinically stable. Empiric antibiotics can be discontinued after 7 days in the low-risk neutropenic patient. One may consider discontinuation of empiric antibiotics in the high-risk neutropenic patient following 5-7 days without fever. Antibiotics should be continued until neutrophil recovery for patients with ANC >100 cells/μL, severe mucositis, or signs and symptoms of sepsis. Four to 5 days following resolution of neutropenia, discontinuation of antibiotics may be considered in the low-risk, neutropenic, clinically stable patient with persistent fevers. With close observation and follow-up, antibiotics may be discontinued after 2 weeks of therapy in the clinically stable patient with persistent fever and persistent neutropenia.

Colony stimulating factors, which reduce the duration of neutropenia, are helpful in reducing hospital admission for neutropenic fevers in patients with a history of febrile neutropenia or prolonged neutropenia following outpatient chemotherapy.

Selected Readings

Hughes WT, Armstrong D, Bodey GP, et al, "1997 Guidelines for the Use of Antimicrobial Agents in Neutropenic Patients With Unexplained Fever," *Clin Infect Dis*, 1997, 25:551-73.

Maki DG, Alvarado CJ, Hassemer CA, et al, "Relation of the Inanimate Hospital Environment to Endemic Nosocomial Infection," *N Engl J Med*, 1982, 307(25):1562-5.

National Comprehensive Cancer Network® (NCCN), "NCCN Clinical Practice Guidelines in Oncology™ - Fever and Neutropenia," V.1.2006, available at http://www.nccn.org.

Pizzo PA, Hathorn JW, Hiemenz J, et al, "A Randomized Trial Comparing Ceftazidime Alone With Combination Antibiotic Therapy in Cancer Patients With Fever and Neutropenia," *N Engl J Med*, 1986, 315(9):552-8.

MANAGEMENT OF
NAUSEA AND VOMITING

Nausea: The feeling or sensation of an imminent desire to vomit.

Vomiting: The forceful upward expulsion of gastric contents.

Retching: Rhythmic, labored, spasmodic respiratory movements involving the diaphragm, chest wall, and abdominal muscles.

Nausea and vomiting are common side effects of many antineoplastic agents and are among the effects about which patients having the greatest concern. Uncontrolled nausea and vomiting can have a significant impact on a patient's overall therapy and response to treatment. In addition to the deleterious effect on the patient's attitude and quality of life, nausea and vomiting can cause significant, potentially fatal, complications. Uncontrolled nausea and vomiting can result in dehydration, electrolyte imbalances, weight loss, and malnutrition. Prolonged vomiting and retching can cause esophageal and/or gastric ruptures (Mallory-Weiss tears, Boerhaave's syndrome) and bleeding. Patients with poorly-controlled nausea or vomiting often require interruptions or delays in therapy. This can also lead to development of anticipatory nausea and vomiting, the patient's loss of confidence in the overall therapy, noncompliance, and refusal of further therapy.

Table 1. Causes of Nausea or Vomiting

Abdominal Emergencies
- Appendicitis
- Cholecystitis
- GI obstruction
- Peritonitis

Acute Systemic Infections
- Bacterial
- Parasitic
- Viral

Cardiovascular Disorders
- Congestive heart failure
- Hypotension
- Myocardial infarction
- Syncope

CNS Disorders
- Increased intracranial pressure
- Mènière's disease
- Otitis interna

Drugs
- Antibiotics
- Antineoplastics
- Aspirin
- Cardiac glycosides
- Levodopa
- Nonsteroidal anti-inflammatory agents
- Opiates
- Quinidine
- Steroids
- Theophylline

Endocrine Disorders
- Adrenal insufficiency
- Diabetes mellitus

Gastrointestinal Disorders

Pregnancy

Psychogenic Stimuli

Uremia

MANAGEMENT OF NAUSEA AND VOMITING
(Continued)

Emesis is controlled by a complex system, centering on the vomiting (or emetic) center in the medulla, and the chemoreceptor trigger zone (CTZ) located in the area postrema in the fourth ventricle of the brain. A network of various neuroreceptors, located throughout the gastrointestinal tract and CNS, processes signals to and from the emetic center and CTZ. When stimulated by impulses from visceral afferents, vestibular or limbic systems, cerebral cortex, or chemoreceptor trigger zone, the emetic center transmits signals that initiate the vomiting cascade. These impulses from the emetic center stimulate the salivary, vasomotor, respiratory centers, and cranial nerves, and initiate the vomiting reflex. Activation of the vomiting center appears to be crucial to initiation of vomiting. Elimination of the vomiting center, or failure to stimulate it, completely eliminates vomiting.

Receptors for a large number of different neurotransmitters, including dopamine, serotonin, acetylcholine, histamine, opiates, and benzodiazepines, are involved in the vomiting reflex. Blockade of one or more of these receptors is the basic mechanism of action of most antiemetic agents. Most drug-induced nausea, including that provoked by the antineoplastic drugs, appears to be caused by activation of the emetic center by impulses from the peripheral afferents and/or the CTZ. Blockade of these impulses is a primary focus of antiemetic therapy.

Patterns of Drug-Induced Nausea / Vomiting

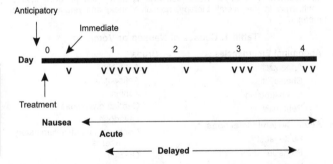

Nausea and vomiting caused by cytotoxic therapy generally falls into one of three categories: Immediate, acute, or delayed. While not drug-induced *per se*, a fourth syndrome, anticipatory nausea and vomiting, is also a relatively common complication of antineoplastic therapy. Immediate nausea or vomiting occurs within the first 30-120 minutes of drug administration. Acute nausea or vomiting is seen within the first 24 hours of drug administration. These two syndromes are often grouped together under the term acute nausea or vomiting. Delayed nausea or vomiting usually begins after the first 24 hours of drug administration; however, it may occur as early as 16 to 18 hours after drug administration, overlapping with acute nausea or vomiting. In some cases, onset of nausea or vomiting may be delayed for as long as 3-5 days. Even in the absence of actual emesis, patients may experience varying degrees of nausea, often accompanied by anorexia.

Table 2 describes the emetogenic potential of many of the antineoplastic agents. Several factors affect the emetic potential of these agents. For some drugs, such as cyclophosphamide or methotrexate, the dose given has a significant effect on the drug's emetogenicity. Higher doses of these agents are much more emetogenic than low doses. The method of administration can also affect the incidence of nausea. Cytarabine, when given as a continuous infusion, is generally moderately emetogenic; higher doses given as short infusions usually produce a much higher incidence and severity of nausea and vomiting.

Table 2. Emetogenic Potential of Antineoplastic Agents

Very High (>90%)

Cisplatin	Didemnin-B	Satraplatin
Cytarabine (>2 g)	Mechlorethamine	Streptozocin
Dacarbazine	Pixantrone	

High (60% to 90%)

Aldesleukin	Dactinomycin	Irinotecan
Amifostine	Denileukin diftitox	Lomustine
Arsenic trioxide	Elsamitrucin	Melphalan (I.V.)
Busulfan (high dose)	Epirubicin	Mitomycin
Carmustine	Etoposide	Oxaliplatin
Clofarabine	Gemcitabine	Pemetrexed
Cyclophosphamide (>1 g)	Gemtuzumab ozogamicin	Procarbazine Toremifene
Cytarabine (>1 g/m^2)	Hydroxyurea	Tretinoin

Moderate (30% to 60%)

Alemtuzumab	Dexrazoxane	Mitoguazone
Altretamine	Diazequone	Mitotane
Aminocamptothecin	Docetaxel	Mitoxantrone
Amonafide	Doxorubicin	PALA
Amsacrine	Epirubicin	Pegaspargase
Asparaginase	Estramustine	Pentostatin
Azacitidine	Floxuridine	Plicamycin
Bortezomib	Flutamide	Procarbazine
Capecitabine	Fulvestrant	Raltitrexed
Carboplatin	Gefitinib	Temozolomide
Cetuximab	Ibritumomab	Teniposide
Cladribine	Idarubicin	Tomudex
Cyclophosphamide (<1 g)	Ifosfamide	Tomitumomab Tositumomab
Cytarabine (≥1 g/m^2)	Imatinib	Trastuzumab
Cytarabine (liposomal)	Interferons	UFT
Daunorubicin	Interleukin-6	Vinblastine
Daunorubicin (liposomal)	Methotrexate (>250 mg/m^2)	Vinorelbine
Decitabine		

MANAGEMENT OF NAUSEA AND VOMITING
(Continued)

Low (10% to 30%)

Abarelix
BCG vaccine
Bexarotene
Cetuximab
Cytarabine
  (≤200 mg/m^2)
Dasatinib
Doxorubicin (liposomal)
Etoposide
Etoposide phosphate
Exemestane
Floxuridine
Fluorouracil
Flutamide

Fulvestrant
Gefitinib
Gemcitabine
Ixabepilone
Lapatinib
Lenalidomide
Letrozole
Levamisole
Methotrexate
  (<250 mg/m^2)
Nelarabine
Nilotinib
Nilutamide
Paclitaxel

Panitumumab
Pemetrexed
Porfimer
Rituximab
Sorafenib
Steroids
Sunitinib
Suramin
Tamoxifen
Temsirolimus
Thioguanine
Topotecan
Vindesine
Vorinostat

Very Low (<10%)

Alitretinoin
Aminoglutethimide
Anastrozole
Androgens
Bevacizumab
Bicalutamide
Bleomycin
Busulfan (low dose)
Chlorambucil

Cladribine
Estrogens
Fludarabine
Goserelin
Homoharringtonine
Leucovorin
Leuprolide
Megestrol
Melphalan (oral)

Mercaptopurine
Mesna
Paclitaxel (protein
  bound)
Thalidomide
Thiotepa
Triptorelin
Valrubicin
Vincristine

Drugs With a High Incidence But Low Severity of Nausea / Vomiting

Amonafide
Arsenic trioxide
Carboplatin
Cyclophosphamide (<1 g)
Dexrazoxane
Docetaxel
Gemcitabine

Hydroxyurea
Interferons
Mitoguazone
Mitoxantrone
Pixantrone
Tretinoin
Vinblastine

Drugs With a Low Incidence But High Severity of Nausea / Vomiting

Lomustine
Methotrexate (high dose)

Semustine

DELAYED NAUSEA AND VOMITING

The problem of delayed nausea and vomiting become obvious as effective antiemetics and combination antiemetic regimens were developed to control acute nausea or vomiting. Although it is most commonly associated with cisplatin, delayed nausea may also be seen in patients receiving mitomycin, cyclophosphamide, or ifosfamide. The nausea or vomiting generally begins within 48-72 hours after chemotherapy administration, but may be seen as early as 16-18 hours after drug administration, or as late as 4 or 5 days. The nausea or vomiting usually resolves over 2 or 3 days. The exact cause of this effect is not clear; however, it is believed to have a separate mechanism from acute nausea or vomiting. Gastritis, tissue destruction, electrolyte fluctuations, or effects on the central or peripheral nervous system have all been postulated as possible mechanisms for delayed nausea.

Appropriate therapy for delayed nausea and vomiting remains problematic. Current information supports early prophylactic therapy with a steroid or steroid/dopamine antagonist combination as the most effective therapy for delayed nausea and vomiting. In patients refractory to a steroid/dopamine antagonist regimen, a neurokinin receptor antagonist (aprepitant), may be added. A meta-analysis of serotonin antagonist trials found prolonged (>24 hours) use of these agents was of no benefit. A steroid and neurokinin antagonist, or steroid, neurokinin antagonist and dopamine antagonist combination is recommended for follow-up therapy. The current approach to delayed nausea and vomiting tends to favor a scheduled, prophylactic regimen of dexamethasone, or a dexamethasone/aprepitant or dopamine antagonist combination, beginning 16-24 hours after administration of the chemotherapy, and continuing for 2-5 days. This approach is more advantageous than intermittent intervention with a 5-HT$_3$ antagonist.

Olanzapine is a thienobenzodiazepine antipsychotic that blocks multiple receptors associated with nausea or vomiting, including dopamine, histamine, muscarinic, and serotonin receptors. A few small trials have reported olanzapine effective (in combination with a steroid and 5-HT$_3$-antagonist) for prevention of delayed nausea and vomiting.

BREAKTHROUGH NAUSEA AND VOMITING

Continuing the same regimen that failed to prevent vomiting usually is not desirable. There is little evidence that breakthrough vomiting may respond to an additional dose(s) of a serotonin blocker. A scheduled regimen of "conventional" antiemetics is probably more effective than intermittent administration of a 5-HT$_3$ antagonist. Merely increasing the dose of the serotonin antagonist may not be an option either. The currently available serotonin antagonists have relatively flat dose/response curves. Dose response studies have demonstrated that granisetron's efficacy seems to reach a plateau at 10 mcg/kg. There appears to be no difference in efficacy between granisetron doses of 10 mcg/kg and 40 mcg/kg. A few small studies suggest higher doses of granisetron (3 mg I.V. or 40-240 mcg/kg) may be effective in treating breakthrough nausea; however, none of these reports found the improvement to be statistically significant. A similar limitation exists for dolasetron, ondansetron, and palonosetron. A number of reports suggests that ondansetron doses between 20-32 mg have comparable efficacy in preventing nausea induced by a variety of antineoplastic drugs. Daily doses >32 mg seem to provide no increase in response. Data are also lacking on the value of using a different serotonin antagonist to treat nausea or vomiting resulting from the failure of the initial serotonin antagonist regimen.

Likewise, there is minimal information regarding the appropriate prophylactic antiemetic regimen for subsequent chemotherapy cycles, both in patients who responded well during the initial treatment cycle, and in patients who do not respond well to the initial serotonin antagonist/steroid regimen. Several reports suggest the efficacy of the initial antiemetic regimen diminishes over time. Patients often experience gradual increased incidences of nausea and vomiting during subsequent treatment cycles. A number of possible alternatives exist,

MANAGEMENT OF NAUSEA AND VOMITING
(Continued)

including switching to another serotonin antagonist, switching to a nonserotonin modulating antiemetic, adding a nonserotonin blocking antiemetic to the original regimen, and altering the schedule of drug administration. The addition of a neurokinin receptor antagonist (eg, aprepitant) to the previous serotonin antagonist/steroid regimen is recommended. One study suggests that the addition of low-dose propofol to the steroid/serotonin antagonist may be useful.

Table 3. Classification of Antiemetic Agents

Antihistamines	Diphenhydramine, hydroxyzine, promethazine
Anticholinergics	Scopolamine
Benzodiazepines	Diazepam, lorazepam
Butyrophenones	Droperidol, haloperidol
Cannabinoids	Dronabinol, nabilone
Corticosteroids	Dexamethasone, methylprednisolone
Neurokinin antagonists	Aprepitant, ezlopitant,[1] vofopitant,[1] L-758298,[1] CP-122721[1]
Phenothiazines	Chlorpromazine, perphenazine, prochlorperazine, thiethylperazine,[1] triflupromazine, (promethazine)
Serotonin antagonists	Dolasetron, granisetron, ondansetron, palonosetron, tropisetron[1]
Substituted benzamides	Metoclopramide, trimethobenzamide
Theinobenzodiazepines	Olanzapine

[1]Not commercially available in the United States.

Table 4. Site of Action of Antiemetic Agents

Emetic center	Antihistamines, anticholinergics, serotonin antagonists, thienobenzodiazepines(?)
Chemoreceptor trigger zone (CTZ)	Benzamides, butyrophenones, phenothiazines, thienobenzodiazepines(?)
Cerebral cortex	Antihistamines, benzodiazepines, cannabinoids, (corticosteroids), neurokinin antagonists(?), thienobenzodiazepines(?)
Peripheral	Metoclopramide, neurokinin antagonists, serotonin antagonists, thienobenzodiazepines(?)
Unknown	Corticosteroids

Table 5. Equitherapeutic Serotonin Antagonist Doses

Drug	Oral	I.V.
Dolasetron	100-200 mg	1.8 mg/kg or 100 mg
Granisetron	2 mg	10 mcg/kg or 1 mg
Ondansetron	8-24 mg	8-10 mg
Palonosetron	–	0.25 mg

Anticholinergics. Alkaloids (eg, atropine and scopolamine) exhibit some antiemetic activity, primarily postoperative nausea and vomiting, and motion sickness. The apparent mechanism of action is blockage of central muscarinic receptors. Toxicities such as sedation, restlessness, blurred vision, and dry mouth limit the systemic use of these agents. Transdermal application of scopolamine is sometimes helpful as an adjunct in delayed nausea, or in treating prolonged mild nausea seen occasionally. The recent lack of availability of the transdermal scopolamine formulation effectively precludes use of this drug for chemotherapy-induced nausea.

Antihistamines. The antihistamines block H_1 receptors both centrally and in the middle ear. A number of drugs in this class are effective against motion sickness and labyrinth disorders; but only diphenhydramine, hydroxyzine, and promethazine seem to have any activity against chemotherapy-induced nausea or vomiting. The major toxicities seen with these drugs are drowsiness, sedation, and dry mouth. These agents are most commonly used to enhance the efficacy of combination antiemetic regimens, although hydroxyzine or promethazine are occasionally used to treat mild-to-moderate nausea in patients who cannot tolerate, or are refractory to, other antiemetics. Diphenhydramine is frequently used in combination with dopamine antagonists to prevent extrapyramidal reactions often seen with those agents.

Benzodiazepines. The exact antiemetic mechanism or location of action of the benzodiazepines is unclear. An inhibitory effect on the vomiting center, anxiolytic activity, and general CNS depression have all been postulated. Possible sites of action include the limbic system, vomiting center, cerebrum, and brain stem. The most common side effects include sedation, drowsiness, and amnesia. Lorazepam is the most commonly used benzodiazepine, but midazolam and diazepam have also been used. As single agents, the benzodiazepines have only mild antiemetic activity. Benzodiazepines are commonly used as adjuncts to conventional antiemetics in the prophylaxis and treatment of acute nausea and vomiting. In this setting, the anterograde amnesia induced by the benzodiazepine is usually considered a desired therapeutic effect rather than an adverse reaction. The benzodiazepines are also highly effective in the prevention of anticipatory nausea and vomiting, possibly due to their anxiolytic effect.

Butyrophenones. A group of dopamine antagonists that is occasionally useful in treating chemotherapy-induced nausea and vomiting is the butyrophenones. Both haloperidol and droperidol have been reported to have antiemetic activity against moderate-to-highly emetogenic chemotherapy. Droperidol has been associated with cardiovascular toxicities, particularly QT prolongation and torsade de points, which have limited the use of this drug. One trial comparing ondansetron and droperidol, found no difference in the incidence or severity of QT_c interval changes between the two drugs. As with most other antiemetics, the optimum response to the butyrophenones is seen in multidrug regimens. Like other dopamine blockers, extrapyramidal reactions, restlessness, sedation, and hypotension are relatively common side effects.

Cannabinoids. Proper evaluation of the antiemetic activity of cannabinoid derivatives has been hindered by social and political stigmas associated with marijuana use. Tetrahydrocannabinol, levonantradol, and nabilone are all reported to be effective in treating chemotherapy-induced nausea and vomiting. The specific site and mechanism of activity is unclear. Inhibition of endorphins in the emetic center, suppression of prostaglandin synthesis, and inhibition of medullary activity through an unspecified cortical action have all been postulated. Cannabinoids can inhibit buildup of cyclic adenosine

MANAGEMENT OF NAUSEA AND VOMITING
(Continued)

monophosphate, and cannabinoid receptors have been identified in the hippocampus, hypothalamus, and cortex. What role, if any, these have in the control of nausea and vomiting is not known. Cannabinoids seem to be most effective against mild-to-moderately emetogenic chemotherapy. Blurred vision, hypotension, and tachycardia, and a number of CNS complications, including euphoria, dysphoria, hallucinations, and sedation are seen with cannabinoid therapy. Cannabinoids are not often used as initial antiemetic therapy, but do offer an alternative in patients unable to tolerate, or who are refractory to, other antiemetic agents.

Corticosteroids. The mechanism of antiemetic activity for the steroids is unknown, although alterations of cell permeability and inhibition of prostaglandin activity have been postulated. In spite of this uncertainty, corticosteroids, particularly dexamethasone, are frequent components of combination antiemetic regimens for high-to-moderately emetogenic chemotherapy. As a single agent, dexamethasone appears to be equal to, or more effective than, 5-HT$_3$ antagonists for delayed nausea and vomiting. For patients in whom a corticosteroid is not clearly contraindicated, these agents are an important component of antiemetic therapy.

Neurokinin-1 (NK$_1$) Receptor Antagonists. Neurokinin, or substance P, antagonists are the latest class of antiemetics. Substance P is a tachykinin (neurokinin) located in neurons of the central and peripheral nervous system. It is associated with a variety of functions, including emesis, depression, inflammatory pain and inflammatory/immune responses in asthma, and other diseases. Substance P's activity is mediated by the NK$_1$ receptor, a G-protein receptor coupled to the inositol phosphate signal pathway. Blocking this receptor is a mechanism to treat conditions mediated at least in part by substance P. Several neurokinin receptor antagonists, including aprepitant (MK-869, L-754030), its prodrug L-758298, ezlopitant (CJ-11974), vofopitant (GR-205171), and CP-122721 have been studied, but aprepitant is the only one that has been approved for marketing.

NK$_1$ antagonists are effective in preventing cisplatin-induced nausea and vomiting, when used in conjunction with a serotonin antagonist and steroid. Addition of a neurokinin antagonist to a serotonin (5-HT$_3$) antagonist and steroid combination increases control of acute nausea by 10% to 15%, and control of delayed nausea by 20% to 30%. Most studies indicate the neurokinin receptors are less effective then serotonin antagonists, particularly for prevention of acute nausea within the first 8-12 hours. However, the neurokinin antagonists appear to be more effective than serotonin antagonists in preventing delayed nausea (days 2-5). Current guidelines recommend aprepitant as initial therapy for highly emetogenic regimens or moderately emetogenic regimens that contain both doxorubicin and cyclophosphamide.

Phenothiazines. Phenothiazines were the first class of drugs accepted as antiemetic therapy for antineoplastic chemotherapy. Blockade of dopamine (D$_2$) receptors in the area postrema (chemoreceptor trigger zone and vomiting center) appears to be their primary mechanism of action. A number of different drugs, including chlorpromazine, perphenazine, prochlorperazine, promethazine, and thiethylperazine (no longer marketed in the United States), have antiemetic activity. Common toxicities such as extrapyramidal reactions, restlessness, sedation, and hypotension limit the use of these drugs. In generally tolerated doses, the phenothiazines are most effective against mild-to-moderate nausea or vomiting, but have little impact on emesis from highly emetogenic agents such as dacarbazine or cisplatin. Higher doses of these agents may have increased activity, but the increased incidence and severity of side effects usually prohibits their use. Since the serotonin antagonists became available, use of the phenothiazines generally has been limited to prevention of nausea from mildly emetogenic chemotherapy, treatment of breakthrough nausea or vomiting in patients refractory to a serotonin blocker, or in association with dexamethasone to treat delayed nausea.

Serotonin (5-HT$_3$) Antagonists. A major advance in antiemetic therapy was the introduction of the serotonin (5-HT$_3$) antagonists. The high efficacy rate of these agents in preventing acute nausea and vomiting, coupled with their low incidence of side effects, has made them the preferred choice in this setting. The major limitation to their use has been economic. The high cost of serotonin antagonists has resulted in many institutions placing severe limitations on their use. Most comparisons have shown that a serotonin antagonist/steroid combination is significantly better than either agent alone. For prevention of acute nausea and vomiting caused by highly emetogenic antineoplastic regimens, a serotonin antagonist/steroid combination usually represents the most effective antiemetic therapy. Since there seems to be little difference in efficacy or toxicity among the available serotonin antagonists, selection of a specific agent is a matter of institutional or prescriber preference.

Generally, toxicities (headache, constipation, diarrhea) with these agents has been minimal. However, one trial comparing ondansetron and droperidol found in the incidence or severity of QT$_c$ interval changes to be the same with both drugs. Clinicians should be aware of the possibility of QT$_c$ prolongation with the serotonin (5-HT$_3$) antagonist; QT$_c$ prolongation and/or ECG abnormalities have been observed with dolasetron, granisetron, ondansetron, and palonosetron.

In spite of their popularity, the serotonin antagonists are not the complete solution to treatment-induced emesis. Some trials have found no difference in efficacy between serotonin antagonist-based regimens and previously used combinations, leaving toxicity, convenience, and economic issues as the discriminating factors in drug selection. Two particular questions concerning serotonin antagonist use remain unanswered: appropriate second-line therapy for treatment failures, and use in noncisplatin regimens.

Like any medication, serotonin antagonists are not 100% effective. Approximately 40% to 60% of patients receiving serotonin antagonist monotherapy will experience some nausea, or have at least one episode of vomiting. Addition of a steroid to the regimen reduces the failure rate significantly, with some trials reporting only 10% to 15% of patients failing the initial therapy. Regardless of the initial antiemetic therapy, some patients will experience one or more episodes of vomiting following administration of the cytotoxic therapy. Choice of a salvage antiemetic regimen for these patients is problematic. Controlled trials of the serotonin antagonists have focused primarily on prevention of nausea or vomiting. Only a few small uncontrolled reports relate to their utility as salvage therapy to terminate vomiting once it begins.

Most studies in patients receiving chemotherapy over several consecutive days suggest the serotonin antagonists have their greatest protective effect in the initial 24 hours, and possibly the initial 16-18 hours, of a chemotherapy cycle. These factors further limit the usefulness of serotonin antagonists in patients who experience nausea or vomiting following prophylactic antiemetic therapy with one of these agents.

MANAGEMENT OF NAUSEA AND VOMITING
(Continued)

Substituted Benzamides. Metoclopramide is the most commonly used antiemetic drug in this category. Prior to introduction of the 5-HT$_3$ antagonists, high-dose (2-3 mg/kg) metoclopramide was the preferred drug for prevention of nausea or vomiting from highly emetogenic chemotherapy. Metoclopramide's ability to block central and peripheral dopamine receptors was believed to be the mechanism of it's antiemetic activity. Recognition that high doses also blocked serotonin receptors led to identification of the role serotonin inhibition has in preventing nausea or vomiting, and, ultimately, to development of the 5-HT$_3$ antagonists. Like the phenothiazines, use of metoclopramide is complicated by extrapyramidal reactions, restlessness, sedation, and hypotension. Diarrhea is also a significant side effect, especially with the high doses used for antiemetic therapy. Also like the phenothiazines, the current use of metoclopramide is generally limited to prevention of nausea from mild-to-moderately emetogenic chemotherapy, treatment of breakthrough nausea or vomiting, or to treat delayed nausea.

REPRESENTATIVE ANTIEMETIC REGIMENS

HIGHLY EMETOGENIC CHEMOTHERAPY

Aprepitant 125 mg P.O. day 1 and 80 mg P.O. days 2 and 3, dexamethasone 8-12 mg P.O. or I.V. + a serotonin antagonist daily 15-30 minutes before treatment on each day of chemotherapy

Recommended serotonin antagonist regimens:
Dolasetron 100-200 mg P.O. once daily
Dolasetron 1.8 mg/kg I.V. once daily
Dolasetron 100 mg I.V. once daily
Granisetron 2 mg P.O. once daily
Granisetron 1 mg P.O. q12h
Granisetron 10 mcg/kg I.V. once daily
Granisetron 1 mg I.V. once daily
Ondansetron 0.45 mg/kg I.V. once daily
Ondansetron 8-16 mg I.V. once daily
Ondansetron 8-10 mg I.V. q8h
Ondansetron 16-24 mg P.O. q12-24h
Palonosetron 0.25 mg I.V. day 1 of each cycle
(doses should not be given more than once weekly)

For continuous infusion therapy, carboplatin and high-dose (>1 g/m^2) cyclophosphamide regimens, the following regimen may be preferred:

Aprepitant 125 mg P.O. day 1 and 80 mg P.O. days 2 and 3, dexamethasone 8-12 mg P.O. or I.V. + a serotonin antagonist every 12 hours

Recommended serotonin antagonist regimens:
Granisetron 1 mg P.O.
Granisetron 10 mcg/kg I.V.
Ondansetron 8-16 mg I.V.
Ondansetron 16-24 mg P.O.
Palonosetron 0.25 mg I.V. day 1 of each cycle
(doses should not be given more than once weekly)

Refractory patients: Add:
Aprepitant 125 mg P.O. 30-60 minutes before treatment, then
Aprepitant 80 mg P.O. days 2 and 3

MODERATELY EMETOGENIC CHEMOTHERAPY

Dexamethasone 10 mg P.O. or I.V. + a serotonin antagonist daily 15-30 minutes before treatment on each day of chemotherapy

Recommended serotonin antagonist regimens:

Ondansetron 8-24 mg P.O. once daily

Ondansetron 8 mg P.O. q12h

Ondansetron 8-10 mg I.V. once daily

For continuous infusion therapy, the following regimen may be preferred:

Dexamethasone 4 mg P.O. or I.V. + ondansetron 8 mg P.O. or I.V. q12h on each day of chemotherapy

MILDLY EMETOGENIC CHEMOTHERAPY

All agents are given 15-30 minutes before treatment and may be repeated every 4-6 hours, if necessary. With the exceptions of dexamethasone (given over 5-15 minutes) and droperidol (given by I.V. push), intravenous doses should be given over 30 minutes.

Dexamethasone 4 mg P.O./I.V./I.M.

Droperidol 1.25-5 mg I.M./I.V. push

Haloperidol 2 mg P.O./I.V./I.M.

Metoclopramide 20-40 mg P.O./I.V./I.M.

Prochlorperazine 10-20 mg P.O./I.V./I.M.

DELAYED NAUSEA AND VOMITING

Dexamethasone + a dopamine, neurokinin, or serotonin antagonist ± olanzapine. Therapy should start within 12-24 hours of administration of the emetogenic chemotherapy.

Recommended **dexamethasone** regimens:

8 mg P.O. q12h for 2 days, then 4 mg P.O. q12h for 2 days

or

20 mg P.O. 1 hour before chemotherapy; 10 mg P.O. 12 hours after chemotherapy, then 8 mg P.O. q12h for 4 doses, then 4 mg P.O. q12h for 4 doses

Recommended dopamine/neurokinin/serotonin antagonist regimens:

Droperidol 1.25-2.5 mg I.V./I.M. q4h for 2-4 days

Metoclopramide 0.5 mg/kg P.O. q6h for 2-4 days

Ondansetron 8 mg P.O. q8h for 2-4 days

Prochlorperazine 10 mg P.O. q6h for 2-4 days

Aprepitant 125 mg P.O. day 1, 80 mg P.O. days 2 and 3

Recommended **olanzapine** regimens:

5 mg P.O. daily for 2 days before antineoplastic therapy, then 10 mg P.O. daily for 3-8 days, beginning the day of antineoplastic therapy

or

10 mg P.O. daily for 3-5 days, beginning the day of antineoplastic therapy

MANAGEMENT OF NAUSEA AND VOMITING
(Continued)

GENERAL PRINCIPLES FOR MANAGING NAUSEA AND VOMITING

1. **Prophylaxis is *MUCH* better than treatment of actual vomiting**. For agents with a moderate-to-high (30% to 100%) incidence of nausea, patients should be pretreated with an antiemetic. Depending on the antiemetic agent(s) and route(s) of administration, pretreatment may range from 1 hour to 5 minutes prior to administration of the antineoplastic agent(s).

2. **Doses and intervals of the antiemetic regimen need to be individualized for each patient**. "PRN" regimens should **not** be used. A fixed schedule of drug administration is preferable.

3. **If a patient has had no nausea for 24 hours** while on their scheduled antiemetic regimen, **it is usually possible to switch to a "PRN" regimen**. The patient should be advised to resume the fixed schedule *at the FIRST sign of recurrent nausea*, and continue it until they have had at least 24 hours without nausea.

4. **Titrate antiemetic dose to patient tolerance**.

5. In most cases, **combination regimens are required for optimum control of nausea**. Do not be afraid to use two or more agents, *from different pharmacologic categories*, to achieve optimal results.

6. To the extent possible, **avoid duplication of agents from the same pharmacologic category**.

7. **Anticipatory nausea and vomiting can often be minimized if the patient receives effective prophylaxis against nausea from the first cycle of therapy**.

8. **If anticipatory nausea does develop, an anxiolytic agent is usually the drug of choice**.

9. **"If it's not broken – DON'T fix it!"** Regardless of your own preferences, if the patient's current antiemetic regimen is working, don't change it.

10. **For moderately emetogenic regimens, a steroid and dopamine blocker** (eg, metoclopramide, prochlorperazine) **may be the most cost-effective regimen**.

11. **For highly and moderately emetogenic regimens containing doxorubicin and cyclophosphamide, a steroid, neurokinin antagonist** (eg, aprepitant) **and serotonin receptor blocker** (eg, dolasetron, granisetron, ondansetron) **combination is recommended**.

12. Although most nausea or vomiting develops within the first 24 hours after treatment, **delayed reactions (1-7 days after chemotherapy) are not uncommon**.

13. **Other antiemetics, such as cannabinoids, antihistamines, or anticholinergics) have limited use as initial therapy**. They are best used in combination with more effective agents (steroids, dopamine, or serotonin blockers); or, as second- or third-line therapy.

14. **Serotonin and neurokinin blockers are most effective in scheduled prophylactic regimens**; rather than in "PRN" regimens to chase existing vomiting.

15. **Serotonin and neurokinin antagonists have limited efficacy in stopping nausea or vomiting once it has begun**. A dopamine blocker may be more effective.

16. **The serotonin antagonists have a "ceiling" dose**, above which there is little or no added antiemetic effect.

17. **Serotonin antagonists are most effective within the first 24-48 hours**. Most studies of multiple day dosing show a sharp decline in the efficacy of the serotonin antagonists after the second or third day.

18. **Neurokinin antagonists are not very effective as single agents**, and should only be used in combination with a serotonin antagonist and steroid.

Selected References

Aapro M, "5-HT$_3$-Receptor Antagonists in the Management of Nausea and Vomiting in Cancer and Cancer Treatment," *Oncology*, 2005, 69(2):97-109.

Geling O and Eichler HG, "Should 5-Hydroxytryptamine-3 Receptor Antagonists Be Administered Beyond 24 Hours After Chemotherapy to Prevent Delayed Emesis? Systematic Re-evaluation of Clinical Evidence and Drug Cost Implications," *J Clin Oncol*, 2005, 23(6):1289-94.

Graves T, "Emesis as a Complication of Cancer Chemotherapy: Pathophysiology, Importance, and Treatment," *Pharmacotherapy*, 1992, 12(4):337-45.

Grunberg SM and Hesketh PJ, "Control of Chemotherapy-Induced Emesis," *N Engl J Med*, 1993, 329(24):1790-6.

Hesketh PJ, Kris MG, Grunberg SM, et al, "Proposal for Classifying the Acute Emetogenicity of Cancer Chemotherapy," *J Clin Oncol*, 1997, 15(1):103-9.

Hesketh PJ, Van Belle S, Aapro M, et al, "Differential Involvement of Neurotransmitters Through the Time Course of Cisplatin-Induced Emesis as Revealed by Therapy With Specific Receptor Antagonists," *Eur J Cancer*, 2003, 39(8):1074-80.

Holdsworth MT, "Ethical Issues Regarding Study Designs Used in Serotonin-Antagonist Drug Development," *Ann Pharmacother*, 1996, 30(10):1182-4.

Horiot JC, "Antiemetic Therapy in Cancer: An Update," *Expert Opin Pharmacother*, 2005, 6(10):1713-23.

Jordan K, Schmoll HJ, and Aapro MS, "Comparative Activity of Antiemetic Drugs," *Crit Rev Oncol Hematol*, 2007, 61(2):162-75.

Kris MG, Hesketh PJ, Somerfield MR, et al, "American Society of Clinical Oncology Guideline for Antiemetics in Oncology: Update 2006," *J Clin Oncol*, 2006, 24(18):2932-47.

Multinational Association of Supportive Care in Cancer, "Antiemetic Consensus Guidelines," Available at http://www.mascc.org/media/Resource_centers/MASCC_Guidelines_Update.pdf. Accessed September 10, 2007.

National Comprehensive Cancer Network® (NCCN), "NCCN Clinical Practice Guidelines in Oncology™ – Antiemesis," V.1.2007. Available at http://www.nccn.org/professionals/physician_gls/PDF/antiemesis.pdf. Accessed September 10, 2007

Navari RM, "Prevention of Emesis From Multiple-Day and High-Dose Chemotherapy Regimens," *J Natl Compr Canc Netw*, 2007, 5(1):51-9.

Oo TH and Hesketh PJ, "Drug Insight: New Antiemetics in the Management of Chemotherapy-Induced Nausea and Vomiting," *Nat Clin Pract Oncol*, 2005, 2(4):196-201.

ORAL MUCOSITIS / STOMATITIS

Also known as mucosal barrier injury, mucositis and stomatitis are general terms for the erythema, edema, desquamation, and ulceration of the gastrointestinal tract caused by many antineoplastic drugs and external beam radiation therapy (radiotherapy). Stomatitis refers to the finding of mucositis in the mouth or oropharynx. Gastrointestinal complications of mucositis include pain, xerostomia, bloating, diarrhea, malabsorption, and dysmotility. Airway compromise can develop from severe tissue damage and inflammation. Mucositis is defined as severe (grade 3-4) when the pain and anatomic damage prevent adequate oral hydration and oral nutrition, or airway compromise is evident (Table 1). Severe mucositis increases the risk of infectious complications. Moreover, some opportunistic infections, such as herpesvirus, cause and exacerbate mucositis. In addition, severe and prolonged mucositis contributes to anticancer treatment dosage reductions and delays, and increases the cost of therapy.

Table 1. National Cancer Institute (NCI) Common Toxicity Criteria Grading for Mucositis

Grade 0	Grade 1	Grade 2	Grade 3	Grade 4
No signs or symptoms	Painless ulcers, erythema, or mild soreness in the absence of lesions	Painful erythema, edema, or ulcers, but can eat or swallow	Painful erythema, edema, or ulcers requiring I.V. hydration	Severe ulceration or requires parenteral or enteral nutritional support or prophylatic intubation

The severity of chemotherapy-associated mucositis is related to drug selection, increased dose, combination versus single agent chemotherapy, extended infusion of cell cycle-specific chemotherapy drugs, concurrent radiotherapy, and female gender. The frequency of severe mucositis for patients undergoing standard dose therapy and high dose therapy is 5% to 40% and 60% to 100%, respectively. Major organ impairment that prolongs the clearance of anticancer treatments can increase the likelihood and severity of mucositis. Patients with Down syndrome or carriers of the methylenetetrahydrofolate reductase *677 TT* genotype have an increased risk of severe mucositis following methotrexate administration. The severity of mucositis secondary to radiotherapy is related to the anatomic site of radiation exposure, radiation dose, and dosage fractionation. Grade 3-4 mucositis occurs in more than 50% of patients undergoing radiotherapy to the head and neck, abdomen, or pelvis. Table 2 lists various anticancer treatments associated with severe mucositis. The duration and severity of regimen-related mucositis can be increased by concurrent infections from opportunistic bacterial or viral pathogens affecting the gastrointestinal tract. Moreover, graft-versus-host disease can worsen regimen-related mucositis following allogeneic hematopoietic stem cell transplantation.

Table 2. Standard Dose Regimens Associated With Grade 3-4 Mucositis

Occurring in ≥30% of Patients	Occurring in ≥10% of Patients
Anthracycline + docetaxel + fluorouracil	Anthracycline + cyclophosphamide
Taxane + radiotherapy	Anthracycline + taxane
Docetaxel + fluorouracil	Anthracycline + cyclophosphamide + docetaxel
Paclitaxel + fluorouracil + radiotherapy	Anthracycline + cyclophosphamide + paclitaxel
Taxane + platinum + radiotherapy	Anthracycline + docetaxel + platinum
Taxane + platinum + fluorouracil	Capecitabine + docetaxel
Oxaliplatin + radiotherapy	Docetaxel
Platinum + taxane + radiotherapy	Platinum + radiotherapy
Fluorouracil CIV[1] + platinum + radiotherapy	Platinum + gemcitabine + taxane
Fluorouracil + leucovorin + taxane	Platinum + taxane + irinotecan
Irinotecan	Platinum + methotrexate + leucovorin
Irinotecan + fluorouracil + radiotherapy	Fluorouracil CIV[1]
Irinotecan + fluorouracil + leucovorin	Fluorouracil CIV[1] + radiotherapy
Irinotecan + fluorouracil + leucovorin + platinum	Fluorouracil CIV[1] + platinum
	Fluorouracil + leucovorin
	Fluorouracil + leucovorin + mitomycin
	Irinotecan + taxane

[1]CIV, continuous intravenous infusion; adapted from Sonis ST, Elting LS, Keefe D, et al, "Perspectives on Cancer Therapy-Induced Mucosal Injury: Pathogenesis, Measurement, Epidemiology, and Consequences for Patients," *Cancer*, 2004, 100(9 Suppl):1995-2025.

Good oral hygiene is an essential constituent of routine supportive care for stomatitis and mucositis. Regular, gentle brushing with a soft toothbrush or cotton swab several times a day is helpful in removing dental plaque. Rinsing the mouth with a saline/bicarbonate solution helps remove debris and increases the pH, slowing the growth of oral flora. Use of mouthwashes containing alcohol may be painful or may dry the oral mucosa; phenol may promote mucosal ulceration.

Palifermin is a recombinant human keratinocyte growth factor that works in a receptor-mediated manner to reduce the duration and severity of mucositis by promoting epithelial cell proliferation, differentiation, and migration. Palifermin is indicated to decrease the incidence and duration of severe oral mucositis in patients with hematologic malignancies receiving myelotoxic therapy requiring hematopoietic stem cell support. Studies evaluating the efficacy and safety of palifermin for reduction of mucositis in other patient groups undergoing treatment (radiation therapy and chemotherapy) for solid tumors are ongoing. Precautions from the manufacturer include the lack of safety and efficacy data in patients with solid tumors. The effect of palifermin on tumor growth in patients has not been established; however, palifermin promotes *in vitro* and *in vivo* epithelial tumor growth in experimental models. Clinical trials suggest that amifostine pretreatment reduces pharyngeal and esophageal mucositis in patients receiving radiotherapy or the combination of chemotherapy and radiotherapy to the head and neck. Amifostine has been studied for reduction of chemotherapy-associated mucositis; however, the

ORAL MUCOSITIS / STOMATITIS *(Continued)*

findings are equivocal. Supplementation with oral glutamine throughout chemotherapy administration may reduce the rate of clinically significant or severe mucositis. Regular gum chewing by pediatric patients to promote salivation as a means for preventing chemotherapy-induced mucositis did not reduce the rate of severe stomatitis following administration of intensive treatment regimens. However, the frequency of grades 1-4 stomatitis was significantly reduced with gum chewing five times daily with lower intensity chemotherapy regimens. In the multivariate analysis, the risk of oral mucositis was related only to the type of chemotherapy regimen used. Additional pharmaceutical agents and interventions that have been employed to reduce the duration and severity of mucositis, but lack sufficient evidence to support routine use, include allopurinol-cryotherapy, celecoxib, chlorhexidine, doxepin rinse, histamine gel, pilocarpine, sargramostim, vitamin E, and zinc sulfate.

Cryotherapy reduces oral mucositis associated with intravenous bolus administration of fluorouracil, methotrexate, and high-dose melphalan. Cryotherapy requires that the patient hold ice in their mouth for 30-60 minutes before and following chemotherapy administration. Cryotherapy purportedly reduces local oromucosal blood flow and consequently reduces chemotherapy exposure to the effected area. Patient tolerance limits the duration of cryotherapy treatments and reduces the utility of cryotherapy for chemotherapy with prolonged systemic clearance or drugs administered by protracted continuous infusion.

Therapy of stomatitis consists primarily of symptomatic support.

Pain control is a crucial part of stomatitis therapy. In addition to making the patient more comfortable, adequate pain control allows the patient to communicate and eat normally, thereby improving quality of life and reducing nutritional complications. Narcotic analgesia is frequently required for management of moderate-to-severe pain from mucositis. Topical application of local anesthetics is the most common approach to management of mild-to-moderate pain from stomatitis. Local application of cold sometimes provides adequate relief. Diphenhydramine has been used, but may cause drying of local tissues and sedation. Most products also contain significant amounts of alcohol which can exacerbate symptomatology. Local anesthetics (eg, benzocaine, lidocaine, tetracaine) are more potent than diphenhydramine, and are not associated with significant drying of local tissues. However, the numbing effect of these agents can impair swallowing. In addition, most of these products are unpalatable, and some are relatively expensive. The following table lists some of the commonly used agents.

Table 3. Various Mouth Care Products

Product	Concentration(s)	Dosage
Anesthetics		
Benzocaine	5% to 20%	1-5 mL; swish and expectorate q4-6h
Diphenhydramine	12.5 mg/5 mL	5 mL; swish and expectorate (or swallow) q4-6h
Lidocaine	1%	5 mL; swish and expectorate (or swallow) q2-3h
Antimicrobials		
Amphotericin B	100 mg/mL	1 mL qid; swish in mouth as long as possible; swallow or expectorate
Chlorhexidine gluconate	0.12%	15 mL q4-6h; swish and expectorate
Clotrimazole	10 mg	1 troche tid (prophylaxis) One 5 times/day for 14 days (treatment)
Nystatin	100,000 units/mL	5 mL; swish and expectorate (or swallow) q4-6h
	100,000 units (vaginal tablet)	1 q4-6h (dissolve in mouth)
Mouth Rinses		
Sodium bicarbonate (8.4 g/50 mEq/ 0.9% NaCl [1000 mL] mixture)	0.5 mEq/10 mL	5-15 mL q3-4h
Sodium chloride	0.9%	5-15 mL q3-4h

Many institutions and prescribers use locally compounded anesthetic formulations for treatment of stomatitis pain. Although the exact formulae vary tremendously, the general rubric includes a local anesthetic to which one or more of the following are added: A second anesthetic, aluminum hydroxide/magnesium hydroxide suspension, diphenhydramine, hydrocortisone, kaolin/pectin suspension, sucralfate suspension, nystatin, tetracycline, and/or water. Controlled trials comparing various formulations with each other, or with the various individual ingredients are not available. However, these products often form the mainstay of symptomatic treatment for stomatitis. Examples of recipes for a few such formulations are found in Table 4.

Sucralfate is basic aluminum sucrose sulfate, a sulfate disaccharide, used primarily as an antiulcer agent. The activity of sucralfate appears to be local, rather than systemic. The drug forms a viscous material that adheres to the surface of gastric and duodenal ulcers, forming a protective barrier over the ulcer. Protected from the activity of gastric enzymes and acid, ulcers are able to heal naturally. This local activity stimulated investigation of sucralfate as a treatment for oral ulcers. A number of groups have studied sucralfate as a therapy for various oral ulcerative conditions with equivocal results. Although the results published to date do not demonstrate a real advantage to sucralfate therapy, some patients may benefit from its use. Sucralfate is commercially available as a tablet (1 g) or suspension (1 g/10 mL). When placed into water, the tablet readily absorbs the fluid and forms a gelatinous suspension.

ORAL MUCOSITIS / STOMATITIS *(Continued)*

Table 4. Examples of Extemporaneously Compounded Oral Stomatitis Products

Anesthetics

Diphenhydramine syrup 5 mL + lidocaine 2% 10 mL + aluminum/magnesium hydroxide suspension 15 mL (Maalox®/Mylanta®) (may also be referred to as "BMX")

Diphenhydramine elixir 5 mL + lidocaine 2% 5 mL + aluminum/magnesium hydroxide suspension 5 mL (Maalox®/Mylanta®) (may also be referred to as "BMX")

Lidocaine 2% 45 mL + diphenhydramine elixir 30 mL + sodium bicarbonate 8.4 g + 0.9% sodium chloride qs 1000 mL

Xerostomia often accompanies stomatitis, particularly in patients who have received radiation to the neck and lower jaw. The condition can result in severe pain, dysphagia, malnutrition, and secondary infections. Subcutaneous or intravenous push administration of amifostine 200 mg/m^2 15-30 minutes prior to radiotherapy of the head and neck reduces acute and chronic xerostomia. Clinical trials suggest that amifostine pretreatment reduces pharyngeal and esophageal mucositis in patients receiving radiotherapy to the head and neck. The dose of amifostine for reduction of radiation-associated xerostomia and mucositis can be standardized to 500 mg in 0.9% sodium chloride 2.5 mL. Benzydamine oral rinse (not available in the United States), which has local anesthetic and anti-inflammatory properties, may be used for the prevention of radiation-induced mucositis in head and neck cancer patients. Artificial saliva substitutes can provide symptomatic relief from dry mouth and throat discomfort following chemotherapy and radiotherapy. Saliva substitutes, which generally contain a mixture of electrolytes, sugars(s), and carboxymethylcellulose, are available without a prescription.

In spite of good oral hygiene, some patients develop oral infections. This is particularly common in the patient with additional sources of immunosuppression, such as severe neutropenia, treatment with exogenous immunosuppressions, or disease-related immune impairment. One organism most commonly seen in such infections is *Candida albicans*. Topical treatment with nystatin or clotrimazole is usually sufficient to control these infections. Such treatments are usually well tolerated and produce minimal systemic effects. Nystatin 400,000-600,000 units (4-6 mL) four times a day, swished in the mouth for at least 2 minutes, then swallowed is recommended. Alternatively, nystatin vaginal tablets can be used orally. Clotrimazole 10 mg five times a day is another effective treatment for these infections. Troches are placed under the tongue or in a buccal cavity and allowed to dissolve. In some patients, clotrimazole used three times a day is an effective prophylaxis against oral *Candida* infections. Patients with significant xerostomia may have trouble dissolving the nystatin or clotrimazole tablets, and may require an artificial saliva product to moisten the mouth. Oral or intravenous administration of fluconazole 100-200 mg daily may be necessary for treatment of microbiologically documented or presumed oromucosal candidiasis in the patient with moderate-to-severe mucositis extending proximally beyond the mouth or the patient with additional sources of immune suppression.

Fluconazole should be continued for at least 2 weeks, and until microbiologic and clinical evidence of infectious disease have resolved and the patient's immune recovery is considered adequate. Alternative systemic antifungal agents that can be considered for treatment of oromucosal and esophageal candidiasis include caspofungin, itraconazole, posaconazole, voriconazole, and amphotericin B products.

Herpes simplex virus is another common pathogen causing oral and other gastrointestinal infections in the patient with moderate-to-severe mucositis. The risk for oral Herpes simplex infection is greatest in patients with an additional source of immune compromise. Systemic treatment with acyclovir, famciclovir, or valacyclovir is required for oromucosal or gastrointestinal Herpes simplex infection. Alternative systemic antiviral agents for treatment of resistant Herpes simplex infections include ganciclovir, valganciclovir, and foscarnet.

Nondepolarizing neuromuscular blockade should be used for the patient with severe mucositis requiring intubation to support the airway. One case report describes succinylcholine-induced hyperkalemia in a patient with severe mucositis following treatment chemotherapy.

Selected Readings

Aisa Y, Mori T, Kudo M, et al, "Oral Cryotherapy for the Prevention of High-Dose Melphalan-Induced Stomatitis in Allogeneic Hematopoietic Stem Cell Transplant Recipients," *Support Care Cancer*, 2005, 13(4):266-9.

Al-Khafaji AH, Dewhirst WE, Cornell CJ Jr, et al, "Succinylcholine-Induced Hyperkalemia in a Patient With Mucositis Secondary to Chemotherapy," *Crit Care Med*, 2001, 29(6):1274-6.

Alterio D, Jereczek-Fossa BA, Zuccotti GF, et al, "Tetracaine Oral Gel in Patients Treated With Radiotherapy for Head-and-Neck Cancer: Final Results of a Phase II Study," *Int J Radiat Oncol Biol Phys*, 2006, 64(2):392-5.

Aquino VM, Harvey AR, Garvin JH, et al, "A Double-Blind Randomized Placebo-Controlled Study of Oral Glutamine in the Prevention of Mucositis in Children Undergoing Hematopoietic Stem Cell Transplantation: A Pediatric Blood and Marrow Transplant Consortium Study," *Bone Marrow Transplant*, 2005, 36(7):611-6.

Awidi A, Homsi U, Kakail RI, et al, "Double-Blind, Placebo-Controlled Cross-Over Study of Oral Pilocarpine for the Prevention of Chemotherapy-Induced Oral Mucositis in Adult Patients With Cancer," *Eur J Cancer*, 2001, 37(16):2010-4.

Berger A, Henderson M, Nadoolman W, et al, "Oral Capsaicin Provides Temporary Relief for Oral Mucositis Pain Secondary to Chemotherapy/Radiation Therapy," *J Pain Symptom Manage*, 1995, 10(3):243-8.

Cerchietti LC, Navigante AH, Lutteral MA, et al, "Double-Blinded, Placebo-Controlled Trial on Intravenous L-Alanyl-L-Glutamine in the Incidence of Oral Mucositis Following Chemoradiotherapy in Patients With Head-and-Neck Cancer," *Int J Radiat Oncol Biol Phys*, 2006, 65(5):1330-7.

Chan A and Ignoffo RJ, "Survey of Topical Oral Solutions for the Treatment of Chemo-Induced Oral Mucositis," *J Oncol Pharm Pract*, 2005, 11(4):139-43.

Chiara S, Nobile MT, Vincenti M, et al, "Sucralfate in the Treatment of Chemotherapy-Induced Stomatitis: A Double-Blind, Placebo-Controlled Pilot Study," *Anticancer Res*, 2001, 21(5):3707-10.

Choi K, Lee SS, Oh SJ, et al, "The Effect of Oral Glutamine on 5-Fluorouracil/Leucovorin-Induced Mucositis/Stomatitis Assessed by Intestinal Permeability Test," *Clin Nutr*, 2007, 26(1):57-62.

Dodd MJ, Miaskowski C, Greenspan D, et al, "Radiation-Induced Mucositis: A Randomized Clinical Trial of Micronized Sucralfate Versus Salt & Soda Mouthwashes," *Cancer Invest*, 2003, 21(1):21-33.

Elad S, Ackerstein A, Bitan M, et al, "A Prospective, Double-Blind Phase II Study Evaluating the Safety and Efficacy of a Topical Histamine Gel for the Prophylaxis of Oral Mucositis in Patients Post Hematopoietic Stem Cell Transplantation," *Bone Marrow Transplant*, 2006, 37(8):757-62.

ORAL MUCOSITIS / STOMATITIS *(Continued)*

El-Housseiny AA, Saleh SM, El-Masry AA, et al, "The Effectiveness of Vitamin "E" in the Treatment of Oral Mucositis in Children Receiving Chemotherapy," *J Clin Pediatr Dent*, 2007, 31(3):167-70.

Epstein JB, Epstein JD, Epstein MS, et al, "Oral Doxepin Rinse: The Analgesic Effect and Duration of Pain Reduction in Patients With Oral Mucositis Due to Cancer Therapy," *Anesth Analg*, 2006, 103(2):465-70.

Epstein JB, Silverman S Jr, Paggiarino DA, et al, "Benzydamine HCl for Prophylaxis of Radiation-Induced Oral Mucositis: Results From a Multicenter, Randomized, Double-Blind, Placebo-Controlled Clinical Trial," *Cancer*, 2001, 92(4):875-85.

Ertekin MV, Koc M, Karslioglu I, et al, "Zinc Sulfate in the Prevention of Radiation-Induced Oropharyngeal Mucositis: A Prospective, Placebo-Controlled, Randomized Study," *Int J Radiat Oncol Biol Phys*, 2004, 58(1):167-74.

Franzen L, Henriksson R, Littbrand B, et al, "Effects of Sucralfate on Mucositis During and Following Radiotherapy of Malignancies in the Head and Neck Region, A Double-Blind Placebo-Controlled Study" *Acta Oncol*, 1995, 34(2):219-23.

Gandemer V, Le Deley MC, Dollfus C, et al, "Multicenter Randomized Trial of Chewing Gum for Preventing Oral Mucositis in Children Receiving Chemotherapy," *J Pediatr Hematol Oncol*, 2007, 29(2):86-94.

Garre ML, Relling MV, Kalwinsky D, et al, "Pharmacokinetics and Toxicity of Methotrexate in Children with Down Syndrome and Acute Lymphocytic Leukemia," *J Pediatr*, 1987, 111(4):606-12.

Gori E, Arpinati M, Bonifazi F, et al, "Cryotherapy in the Prevention of Oral Mucositis in Patients Receiving Low-Dose Methotrexate Following Myeloablative Allogeneic Stem Cell Transplantation: A Prospective Randomized Study of the Gruppo Italiano Trapianto Di Midollo Osseo Nurses Group," *Bone Marrow Transplant*, 2007, 39(6):347-52.

Huang EY, Leung SW, Wang CJ, et al, "Oral Glutamine to Alleviate Radiation-Induced Oral Mucositis: A Pilot Randomized Trial," *Int J Radiat Oncol Biol Phys*, 2000, 46(3):535-9.

Javle MM, Cao S, Durrani FA, et al, "Celecoxib and Mucosal Protection: Translation From an Animal Model to a Phase I Clinical Trial of Celecoxib, Irinotecan, and 5-Fluorouracil," *Clin Cancer Res*, 2007, 13(3):965-71.

Keefe DM, Schubert MM, Elting LS, et al, "Updated Clinical Practice Guidelines for the Prevention and Treatment of Mucositis," *Cancer*, 2007, 109(5):820-31.

Lilleby K, Garcia P, Gooley T, et al, "A Prospective, Randomized Study of Cryotherapy During Administration of High-Dose Melphalan to Decrease the Severity and Duration of Oral Mucositis in Patients With Multiple Myeloma Undergoing Autologous Peripheral Blood Stem Cell Transplantation," *Bone Marrow Transplant*, 2006, 37(11):1031-5.

Lin LC, Que J, Lin LK, et al, "Zinc Supplementation to Improve Mucositis and Dermatitis in Patients After Radiotherapy for Head-and-Neck Cancers: A Double-Blind, Randomized Study," *Int J Radiat Oncol Biol Phys*, 2006, 65(3):745-50.

Makkonen TA, Bostrom P, Vilja P, et al, "Sucralfate Mouth Washing in the Prevention of Radiation-Induced Mucositis: A Placebo-Controlled Double-Blind Randomized Study," *Int J Radiat Oncol Biol Phys*, 1994, 30:177-82.

McAleese JJ, Bishop KM, A'Hern R, et al, "Randomized Phase II Study of GM-CSF to Reduce Mucositis Caused by Accelerated Radiotherapy of Laryngeal Cancer," *Br J Radiol*, 2006, 79(943):608-13.

Mori T, Yamazaki R, Aisa Y, et al, "Brief Oral Cryotherapy for the Prevention of High-Dose Melphalan-Induced Stomatitis in Allogeneic Hematopoietic Stem Cell Transplant Recipients," *Support Care Cancer*, 2006, 14(4):392-5.

"National Cancer Institute Common Terminology Criteria for Adverse Events (CTCAE) version 3," Available at: http://www.fda.gov/cder/cancer/toxicityframe.htm. Last accessed August 9, 2007.

Okuno SH, Woodhouse CO, Loprinzi CL, et al, "Phase III Controlled Evaluation of Glutamine for Decreasing Stomatitis in Patients Receiving Fluorouracil (5-FU)-Based Chemotherapy," *Am J Clin Oncol*, 1999, 22(3):258-61.

Peterson DE, Jones JB, and Petit RG 2nd, "Randomized, Placebo-Controlled Trial of Saforis for Prevention and Treatment of Oral Mucositis in Breast Cancer Patients Receiving Anthracycline-Based Chemotherapy," *Cancer*, 2007, 109(2):322-31.

Pfeiffer P, Madsen EL, Hansen O, et al, "Effect of Prophylactic Sucralfate Suspension on Stomatitis Induced by Cancer Chemotherapy: A Randomized, Double-Blind Cross-Over Study," *Acta Oncol*, 1990, 29(2):171-3.

Pitten FA, Kiefer T, Buth C, et al, "Do Cancer Patients With Chemotherapy-Induced Leukopenia Benefit From an Antiseptic Chlorhexidine-Based Oral Rinse? A Double-Blind, Block-Randomized, Controlled Study," *J Hosp Infect*, 2003, 53(4):283-91.

Potting CM, Uitterhoeve R, Op Reimer WS, et al, "The Effectiveness of Commonly Used Mouthwashes for the Prevention of Chemotherapy-Induced Oral Mucositis: A Systematic Review," *Eur J Cancer Care (Engl)*, 2006, 15(5):431-9.

Quintiliani R, Owens NJ, Quercia RA, et al, "Treatment and Prevention of Oropharyngeal Candidiasis," *Am J Med*, 1984, 77(4D):44-8.

Rattan J, Schneider M, Arber N, et al, "Sucralfate Suspension as a Treatment of Recurrent Aphthous Stomatitis," *J Intern Med*, 1994, 236(3):341-3.

Rossi A, Rosati G, Colarusso D, et al, "Subcutaneous Granulocyte-Macrophage Colony-Stimulating Factor in Mucositis Induced by an Adjuvant 5-Fluorouracil Plus Leuco-vorin Regimen. A Phase II Study and Review of the Literature," *Oncology*, 2003, 64(4):353-60.

Ryu JK, Swann S, LeVeque F, et al, "The Impact of Concurrent Granulocyte Macro-phage-Colony Stimulating Factor on Radiation-Induced Mucositis in Head and Neck Cancer Patients: A Double-Blind Placebo-Controlled Prospective Phase III Study by Radi-ation Therapy Oncology Group 9901," *Int J Radiat Oncol Biol Phys*, 2007, 67(3):643-50.

Saarilahti K, Kajanti M, Joensuu T, et al, "Comparison of Granulocyte-Macrophage Colony-Stimulating Factor and Sucralfate Mouthwashes in the Prevention of Radia-tion-Induced Mucositis: A Double-Blind Prospective Randomized Phase III Study," *Int J Radiat Oncol Biol Phys*, 2002, 54(2):479-85.

Scarantino C, LeVeque F, Swann RS, et al, "Effect of Pilocarpine During Radiation Therapy: Results of RTOG 97-09, a Phase III Randomized Study in Head and Neck Cancer Patients," *J Support Oncol*, 2006, 4(5):252-8.

Sonis ST, Elting LS, Keefe D, et al, "Perspectives on Cancer Therapy-Induced Mucosal Injury: Pathogenesis, Measurement, Epidemiology, and Consequences for Patients," *Cancer*, 2004, 100 (9 Suppl):1995-2025.

Stokman MA, Wachters FM, Koopmans P, et al, "Outcome of Local Application of Amifostine (WR-1065) on Epirubicin-Induced Oral Mucositis. A Phase II Study," *Anticancer Res*, 2004, 24(5B):3263-7.

Sung L, Tomlinson GA, Greenberg ML, et al, "Serial Controlled N-of-1 Trials of Topical Vitamin E as Prophylaxis for Chemotherapy-Induced Oral Mucositis in Paediatric Patients," *Eur J Cancer*, 2007, 43(8):1269-75.

Ulrich CM, Yasui Y, Storb R, et al, "Pharmacogenetics of Methotrexate: Toxicity Among Marrow Transplantation Patients Varies With the Methylenetetrahydrofolate Reductase C677T Polymorphism," *Blood*, 2001, 98(1):231-4.

Vokurka S, Bystricka E, Koza V, et al, "Higher Incidence of Chemotherapy Induced Oral Mucositis in Females: A Supplement of Multivariate Analysis to a Randomized Multicentre Study," *Support Care Cancer*, 2006, 14(9):974-6.

Yokomizo H, Yoshimatsu K, Hashimoto M, et al, "Prophylactic Efficacy of Allopurinol Ice Ball for Leucovorin/5-Fluorouracil Therapy-Induced Stomatitis, "*Anticancer Res*, 2004, 24(2C):1131-4.

TUMOR LYSIS SYNDROME

INTRODUCTION

Tumor lysis syndrome (TLS) is a potentially life threatening disorder that is characterized as an acute metabolic disturbance resulting from the rapid destruction of tumor cells. Destruction of tumor cells releases cellular break-down products (nucleic acids, anions, cations, peptides) that overwhelm the body's normal mechanisms for their utilization, excretion, and elimination. Signs and symptoms of TLS often develop within 72 hours of beginning cytotoxic chemotherapy in patients with newly diagnosed acute leukemias or lymphoproliferative malignancies (Burkitt's and non-Burkitt's lymphomas). However, TLS can occur spontaneously in malignant diseases with vigorous cell turnover. Although most commonly reported in patients with hematologic and lymphoid malignancies, TLS has also been reported with solid tumors such as breast cancer, colon cancer, melanoma, ovarian cancer, prostate cancer, small cell lung cancer, and testicular cancer. Case reports of acute TLS attributed to administration of a corticosteroid, rituximab, and zoledronic acid in patients with treatment-sensitive tumors are reported in the medical literature. Additional treatment and diagnostic procedures attributed with causing tumor lysis syndrome include total body irradiation, splenic irradiation, staging laparotomy, laparoscopic splenectomy preceded by splenic artery embolization, and radiofrequency interstitial thermal ablation of metastatic hepatic lesions. Metabolic abnormalities associated with acute TLS include hyperphosphatemia, hyperkalemia, hyperuricemia, azotemia, hypocalcemia, and metabolic acidosis. Cardiac arrhythmias, seizures, and major organ failure can occur in severe cases of TLS. Hyperkalemia, hyperuricemia, and hypocalcemia can produce cardiac arrhythmias, tetany, and sudden death. Acute renal failure can occur due to precipitation of uric acid and calcium phosphate in the renal tubules.

PREDISPOSING FACTORS

1. Bulky disease; leukemia with high white blood cell count

2. Acute myelogenous leukemia with history of chronic myelomonocytic leukemia

3. Marked sensitivity of the tumor to a particular treatment modality

4. Male gender

5. Renal impairment, including pre-existing volume depletion

6. Elevated pretreatment lactic dehydrogenase serum levels

7. Elevated pretreatment uric acid serum levels independent of renal impairment

CLINICAL FEATURES AND TREATMENT

General Principles

Prevention and early management of TLS are aimed at decreasing the risk of morbidity and mortality from cardiac arrhythmias, seizures, and organ failure. Vigorous hydration with intravenous 0.9% sodium chloride or crystalloid fluids (up to 3 liters/m^2/24 hours) to maintain urine output of at least 100 mL/hour, with or without administration of loop or osmotic diuretics, is the cornerstone of the initial management for acute or potential TLS. Addition of sodium bicarbonate to the intravenous fluid for alkalinization of the urine to pH 7.1-7.5 increases the solubility of uric acid, although it may also increase the tendency for calcium phosphate nephrocalcinosis. Allopurinol in doses of 300-600 mg/day should be given to decrease endogenous uric acid production.

Rasburicase is administered for rapid reduction of uric acid levels. Rasburicase, which is a recombinant form of urate oxidase produced in *Saccharomyces cerevisiae*, catalyzes the degradation of uric acid to allantoin which is more soluble and readily excreted by the kidneys. Rasburicase is reserved for patients at great risk for severe tumor lysis syndrome and patient's with elevated uric acid levels and signs of moderate-to-severe renal impairment or other major organ dysfunction. The major risks associated with administration of rasburicase include anaphylaxis, hypersensitivity reactions, methemoglobinemia, and hemolysis. This product is contraindicated in patients with glucose-6-phosphate dehydrogenase deficiency due to an elevated risk of hemolysis. An additional concern with rasburicase administration is the development of neutralizing antibodies. This phenomenon was observed in 64% of 28 normal, healthy volunteers studied; the effect of neutralizing antibodies on the efficacy of this product with repeated usage is unknown.

Rasburicase is approved for use in pediatric patients, with the labeled dose of 0.15-0.2 mg/kg/dose daily for a period of five days beginning 4-24 hours prior to the initiation of chemotherapy administration. However, due to the costs and risks of therapy plus the immediate and measureable effects of rasburicase, some centers administer a single dose which is repeated daily as warranted by plasma uric acid levels. Weight-based (0.15-0.2 mg/kg/dose) and set-dose (1.5-6 mg/dose) rasburicase dosing in adult patients is reported in the clinical literature. Rasburicase will degrade uric acid *in vitro* when stored at room temperature. Consequently, to prevent artifactually low rasburicase levels, plasma samples must be collected in prechilled tubes, then immediately placed in an ice water bath until centrifuged at 4°C. Plasma must be analyzed within four hours of collection.

Clinical features and treatment for specific metabolic disorders are discussed in the following sections.

Hyperuricemia

Cytolysis during TLS releases purine and pyrimidine nucleotides into the bloodstream and extracellular tissues. Oxidation of the purines hypoxanthine and xanthine yields uric acid, which can precipitate in the renal tubules and cause oliguric renal failure. A high concentration of uric acid and an acidic urine pH promote uric acid crystalization and renotubular precipitation. Maintenance of urine flow and urinary alkalinization are utilized to reduce purine precipitation and preserve renal function. Allopurinol blocks the endogenous production of uric acid by inhibiting the enzyme xanthine oxidase, which oxidizes hypoxanthine and xanthine to uric acid. Allopurinol is used prophylactically during the early management of TLS. Rasburicase decreases existing uric acid concentrations by conversion of this molecule to the inactive and soluble metabolite allantoin, which is readily excreted by the kidneys.

TUMOR LYSIS SYNDROME *(Continued)*

Hyperkalemia

Potassium is primarily an intracellular ion that is released during massive cellular breakdown. Increasing levels of serum potassium can be dangerous, leading to cardiac arrhythmias or sudden death, especially in the presence of hypocalcemia (see following discussion). Standard treatments to remove potassium from the blood stream and extracellular fluids should be initiated as warranted by the patient's serum potassium level and electrocardiographic abnormalities. Potassium intake from nutritional sources and intravenous solutions should be restricted in patients with TLS. Pharmaceutical measures routinely used to manage hyperkalemia in patients with TLS include volume expansion with forced diuresis, administration of glucose with insulin, and the cation exchange product sodium polystyrene sulfonate (Kayexalate®). Textbook algorithms for management of hyperkalemia include instructions for administration of calcium as a cardioprotective measure; however this is **not** a standard intervention in the setting of TLS. Calcium administration must be done judiciously in the patient with TLS because it can precipitate as calcium phosphate in highly perfused tissues.

Hyperphosphatemia and Hypocalcemia

The release of intracellular inorganic phosphate following massive cellular breakdown sets into motion several important clinical features. Serum phosphate levels will quickly exceed the threshold for normal renal excretion, with phosphate excretion becoming limited by the glomerular filtration rate. Any azotemia that develops during therapy will hinder phosphate excretion. Treatment includes the use of aluminum hydroxide orally to reduce phosphate levels and hemodialysis or hemofiltration, if necessary. High phosphate levels will also cause reciprocal hypocalcemia. Although generally asymptomatic, hypocalcemia may cause neuromuscular irritation, tetany, and cardiac dysrhythmias. Symptomatic patients may receive calcium gluconate 10%, 10 mL intravenously to increase serum calcium levels. Unfortunately, despite hypocalcemia, the solubility product of calcium and phosphate may be exceeded in acute TLS, resulting in tissue calcification and organ failure.

Hemodialysis / Hemofiltration

Due to the unpredictability of TLS, intermittent hemodialysis, continuous arteriovenous hemodialysis, or continuous veno-venous hemodiafiltration may be needed and can be life-saving. Hemodialysis or hemofiltration may be used to control and maintain fluid volume and/or to remove uric acid, phosphate, and potassium from serum. Intermittent hemodialysis, continuous arteriovenous hemodialysis, or continuous veno-venous hemodiafiltration should be considered as warranted by the severity of serum chemistry abnormalities, major organ dysfunction, and the patient's response to pharmaceutical treatments.

Selected Readings

Agha-Razii M, Amyot SL, Pichette V, et al, "Continuous Veno-Venous Hemodiafiltration for the Treatment of Spontaneous Tumor Lysis Syndrome Complicated by Acute Renal Failure and Severe Hyperuricemia," Clin Nephrol, 2000, 54(1):59-63.

Arnold TM, Reuter JP, Delman BS, et al, "Use of Single-Dose Rasburicase in an Obese Female," Ann Pharmacother, 2004, 38(9):1428-31.

Barry BD, Kell MR, and Redmond HP, "Tumor Lysis Syndrome Following Endoscopic Radiofrequency Interstitial Thermal Ablation of Colorectal Liver Metastases," Surg Endosc, 2002, 16(7):1109.

Cairo MS and Bishop M, "Tumour Lysis Syndrome: New Therapeutic Strategies and Classification," Br J Haematol, 2004, 127(1):3-11.

Chen SW, Hwang WS, Tsao CJ, et al, "Hydroxyurea and Splenic Irradiation-Induced Tumour Lysis Syndrome: A Case Report and Review of the Literature," J Clin Pharm Ther, 2005, 30(6):623-5.

Coiffier B, Mounier N, Bologna S, et al, "Efficacy and Safety of Rasburicase (Recombinant Urate Oxidase) for the Prevention and Treatment of Hyperuricemia During Induction Chemotherapy of Aggressive Non-Hodgkin's Lymphoma: Results of the GRAAL1 (Groupe d'Etude Des Lymphomes De l'Adulte Trial on Rasburicase Activity in Adult Lymphoma) Study," J Clin Oncol, 2003, 21(23):4402-9.

Duzova A, Cetin M, M, Gümrük F, et al, "Acute Tumour Lysis Syndrome Following a Single-Dose Corticosteroid in Children With Acute Lymphoblastic Leukaemia," Eur J Haematol, 2001, 66(6):404-7.

Gemici C, "Tumour Lysis Syndrome in Solid Tumours," Clin Oncol (R Coll Radiol), 2006, 18(10):773-80.

Habib GS and Saliba WR, "Tumor Lysis Syndrome After Hydrocortisone Treatment in Metastatic Melanoma: A Case Report and Review of the Literature," Am J Med Sci, 2002, 323(3):155-7.

Hutcherson DA, Gammon DC, Bhatt MS, et al, "Reduced-Dose Rasburicase in the Treatment of Adults With Hyperuricemia Associated With Malignancy," Pharmacotherapy, 2006, 26(2):242-7.

Jabr FI, "Acute Tumor Lysis Syndrome Induced by Rituximab in Diffuse Large B-Cell Lymphoma," Int J Hematol, 2005, 82(4):312-4.

Kurt M, Onal IK, Elkiran T, et al, "Acute Tumor Lysis Syndrome Triggered by Zoledronic Acid in a Patient With Metastatic Lung Adenocarcinoma," Med Oncol, 2005, 22(2):203-6.

Lee MH, Cheng KI, Jang RC, et al, "Tumour Lysis Syndrome Developing During an Operation," Anaesthesia, 2007, 62(1):85-7.

Lee AC, Li CH, So KT, et al, "Treatment of Impending Tumor Lysis With Single-Dose Rasburicase," Ann Pharmacother, 2003, 37(11):1614-7.

Leibowitz AB, Adamsky C, Gabrilove J, et al, "Intraoperative Acute Tumor Lysis Syndrome During Laparoscopic Splenectomy Preceded by Splenic Artery Embolization," Surg Laparosc Endosc Percutan Tech, 2007, 17(3):210-1.

Lerza R, Botta M, Barsotti B, et al, "Dexamethasone-Induced Acute Tumor Lysis Syndrome in a T-Cell Malignant Lymphoma," Leuk Lymphoma, 2002, 43(5):1129-32.

Linck D, Basara N, Tran V, et al, "Peracute Onset of Severe Tumor Lysis Syndrome Immediately After 4 Gy Fractionated TBI as Part of Reduced Intensity Preparative Regimen in a Patient With T-ALL With High Tumor Burden," Bone Marrow Transplant, 2003, 31(10):935-7.

Liu CY, Sims-McCallum RP, and Schiffer CA, "A Single Dose of Rasburicase is Sufficient for the Treatment of Hyperuricemia in Patients Receiving Chemotherapy," Leuk Res, 2005, 29(4):463-5.

Mato AR, Riccio BE, Qin L, et al, "A Predictive Model for the Detection of Tumor Lysis Syndrome During AML Induction Therapy," Leuk Lymphoma, 2006, 47(5):877-83.

McDonnell AM, Lenz KL, Frei-Lahr DA, et al, "Single-Dose Rasburicase 6 Mg in the Management of Tumor Lysis Syndrome in Adults," Pharmacotherapy, 2006, 26(6):806-12.

Oztop I, Demirkan B, Yaren A, et al, "Rapid Tumor Lysis Syndrome in a Patient With Metastatic Colon Cancer as a Complication of Treatment With 5-Fluorouracil/Leucoverin and Irinotecan," Tumori, 2004, 90(5):514-6.

Riccio B, Mato A, Olson EM, et al, "Spontaneous Tumor Lysis Syndrome in Acute Myeloid Leukemia: Two Cases and a Review of the Literature," Cancer Biol Ther, 2006, 5(12):1614-7.

Rostom AY, El-Hussainy G, Kandil A, et al, "Tumor Lysis Syndrome Following Hemi-Body Irradiation for Metastatic Breast Cancer," Ann Oncol, 2000, 11(10):1349-51.

TUMOR LYSIS SYNDROME *(Continued)*

Schelling JR, Ghandour FZ, Strickland TJ, et al, "Management of Tumor Lysis Syndrome With Standard Continuous Arteriovenous Hemodialysis: Case Report and a Review of the Literature," *Ren Fail*, 1998, 20(4):635-44.

Sorscher SM, "Tumor Lysis Syndrome Following Docetaxel Therapy for Extensive Metastatic Prostate Cancer," *Cancer Chemother Pharmacol*, 2004, 54(2):191-2.

Theodorou D, Lagoudianakis E, Pattas M, et al, "Pretreatment Tumor Lysis Syndrome Associated With Bulky Retroperitoneal Tumors. Recognition is the Mainstay of Therapy," *Tumori*, 2006, 92(6):540-1.

Tiu RV, Mountantonakis SE, Dunbar AJ, et al, "Tumor Lysis Syndrome," *Semin Thromb Hemost*, 2007, 33(4):397-407.

Trifilio S, Gordon L, Singhal S, et al, "Reduced-Dose Rasburicase (Recombinant Xanthine Oxidase) in Adult Cancer Patients With Hyperuricemia," *Bone Marrow Transplant*, 2006, 37(11):997-1001.

Yahata T, Nishikawa N, Aoki Y, et al, "Tumor Lysis Syndrome Associated With Weekly Paclitaxel Treatment in a Case With Ovarian Cancer," *Gynecol Oncol*, 2006, 103(2):752-4.

Yim BT, Sims-McCallum RP, and Chong PH, "Rasburicase for the Treatment and Prevention of Hyperuricemia," *Ann Pharmacother*, 2003, 37(7-8):1047-54.

Zigrossi P, Brustia M, Bobbio F, et al, "Flare and Tumor Lysis Syndrome With Atypical Features After Letrozole Therapy in Advanced Breast Cancer. A Case Report," *Ann Ital Med Int*, 2001, 16(2):112-7.

CHRONIC PAIN MANAGEMENT (CANCER)

DEFINITION AND INCIDENCE

Pain is defined by the International Society for the Study of Pain as "an unpleasant sensory and emotional experience associated with actual or potential tissue damage, or described in terms of such damage". The reported incidence of pain in cancer patients varies with the method used to determine the presence of pain, and the type and stage of cancer. It is estimated that 51% of patients with various stages of cancer experience pain, and patients with advanced disease are more likely to have severe pain. Pain in cancer patients may be due to the disease itself (eg, metastatic bone disease, visceral involvement); it may be secondary to some treatments (eg, painful neuropathy from vincristine or paclitaxel, or postoperative pain); it may result from complications associated with cancer (eg, postherpetic neuralgia); or it may have been present prior to the diagnosis of cancer and be unrelated to cancer (eg, arthritis). Most often, treatment guidelines and discussions are directed against chronic pain associated with progressive disease.

NONOPIOID ANALGESICS

The World Health Organization recommends a stepwise approach to the management of cancer pain (see figure).

WHO Three-Step Analgesic Ladder

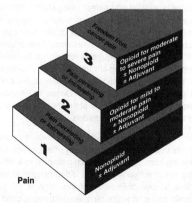

This approach recommends that the choice of therapy match the severity of pain (ie, strong opioids for moderate to severe pain). Nonopioids for (mild) cancer pain include acetaminophen, nonsteroidal anti-inflammatory drugs (NSAIDs), and aspirin. All of these have a ceiling above which increasing the dose will not enhance pain relief and will increase the likelihood of side effects. Although nonopioid analgesics are traditionally WHO step 1 products,

CHRONIC PAIN MANAGEMENT (CANCER) *(Continued)*

they do have a role in the management of moderate-to-severe cancer pain. One blinded, placebo-controlled study reports that acetaminophen added to a strong opioid regimen in cancer patients improves pain control and well being.

Acetaminophen is commonly used for the management of mild-to-moderate pain. The manufacturer recommends a maximum daily dose of acetaminophen 4000 mg per 24-hours to reduce the risk of hepatotoxicity. Concerns regarding the use of NSAIDs in chronic cancer pain include the reversible inhibition of platelet aggregation, and the potential for gastropathy and nephrotoxicity. Aspirin is frequently avoided because of the potential for gastropathy and inhibition of platelet aggregation. Platelets exposed to aspirin become acetylated and permanently impaired. Celecoxib and nonacetylated salicylates, such as choline salicylate and magnesium salicylate, do not inhibit platelet aggregation.

OPIOID ANALGESICS

Opioid analgesic therapy should be initiated when adequate doses of nonopioid analgesics provide inadequate pain control or they are poorly tolerated.

Opioid analgesics for severe, persistent pain should be given "around-the-clock", not on an "as needed" or "PRN" basis. It is easier to prevent pain from recurring than to treat it once it has recurred. Titration of opioids to pain relief is easiest and safest using short-acting drugs (average duration of pain relief of 4 hours) or a continuous parenteral infusion. Once adequate pain relief is achieved, the 24-hour opioid dose can be given as a long-acting preparation (eg, sustained release morphine or oxycodone, transdermal fentanyl). In fact, opioid requirements can be increased in a similar manner for patients with worsening chronic pain daily. Medication for breakthrough pain, a transient worsening of otherwise stable pain in a patient taking an opioid, should always be available. Doses for breakthrough pain (ie, rescue doses) are commonly 5% to 15% of the 24-hour opioid dose, and may be administered every 1-2 hours as needed.

The oral route of administration for opioids analgesics is preferred whenever possible. All opioids undergo a high first-pass effect, which must be considered when converting from one route of administration to another. The parenteral to oral ratios for effectiveness of the different opioids vary from 1:2 to 1:6. The parenteral to oral dose ratio for morphine is 1:3 and 1:6 for the treatment of chronic pain and acute pain, respectively. Opioid equianalgesic doses are listed in the table that follows. Dose titration of opioid analgesics is based on pain control and patient tolerance. There is no maximum dosage for administration of opioid analgesics. Unlike the nonopioid analgesics, no ceiling on effectiveness of opioids has been identified and tolerance develops to most of the medication-related adverse effects.

Table 1. Opioid Analgesics

Drug	Route of Administration	Approx Equianalgesic Dose (mg)	Approx Duration[1] (h)
Codeine	I.M., I.V.	120	4-6
	Oral	200	
Fentanyl[2]	I.V.	0.1	0.5-2
Hydrocodone	Oral	20	4-6
Hydromorphone	I.M., I.V., SubQ	1.5	2-5
	Oral, rectal	7.5	
Meperidine	I.M., I.V., SubQ	75	2-4
	Oral	300	
Methadone	I.M., I.V., SubQ	5	6-12
	Oral	10	
Morphine	I.M., I.V., SubQ	10	3-4[3]
	Oral, rectal	30	
Oxycodone	Oral	20	4-6[3]

[1]Parenteral or immediate-release products.

[2]Transdermal fentanyl conversion presented in separate table that follows.

[3]Duration for sustained release dosage forms is 8-12 hours (MS Contin®, Oramorph SR®), 24 hours (Kadian®), 12 hours (Oxycontin®).

Meperidine is not recommended for chronic use. This is because of the potential for accumulation of a neurotoxic metabolite, normeperidine (see following information). Meperidine administration is best reserved for incident pain (ie, before a painful manipulation or procedure).

Tolerance is characterized by the requirement for a higher dose of opioid in order to produce the same effect previously seen with a lower dose. Tolerance develops to many side effects of opioids: respiratory depression, sedation, nausea, and vomiting. Tolerance does not usually develop to constipation. When a given dose of opioid is not effective, for whatever reason, and if side effects are tolerable, the dose can be increased. Physical dependence occurs with regular use of opioids, but is only of clinical importance if the opioid is abruptly discontinued or an opioid antagonist (eg, naloxone) administered, in which cases a withdrawal syndrome can be seen. Opioids should be tapered in patients whose pain improves. Signs and symptoms of withdrawal can be reduced by maintaining at least 25% of the previous day's opioid dose. The opioid can be discontinued when the total daily dose is the equivalent of 10-15 mg of intramuscular morphine. Psychological dependence is defined as a "pattern of compulsive drug use characterized by a continued craving for an opioid and the need to use the opioid for effects other than pain relief." Unlike tolerance and physical dependence, psychological dependence is a characteristic of the patient, and is a function of environmental, social, economic, and personality factors. Psychological dependence, or addiction, can develop in patients requiring management of chronic pain; however, this is **not** a valid reason to undertreat pain.

CHRONIC PAIN MANAGEMENT (CANCER) *(Continued)*

The most troublesome side effect associated with chronic opioid use is constipation, and, as noted above, tolerance to constipation does not occur. Regular use of stimulant laxatives is often required.

Tolerance does develop to opioid-induced respiratory depression, allowing safe dose escalation. In the event of an acute overdose, or in the case of respiratory depression not responding to supportive measures, naloxone can be used. Naloxone administration is reserved for serious situations because it precipitates withdrawal symptoms and the prompt return of pain in patients physically dependent on opioids. Other side effects of naloxone administration include nausea, vomiting, sedation, sweating, itching, dry mouth, and tremulousness. Initiate naloxone therapy with low doses (0.1-0.2 mg) repeated and increased as warranted by respiratory rate and patient comfort. Nalmefene should be avoided due to the longer duration of action relative to that of naloxone, and the risk of prolonged rebound pain. Naltrexone is only available as an oral formulation, which limits its utility for acute reversal of opioid toxicity. Tolerance develops to nausea and vomiting, and these effects are more likely to occur when opioid therapy is initiated. Phenothiazines can be used to treat nausea and vomiting. Dimenhydrinate or meclizine can also be used to treat this side effect. Tolerance usually develops to sedation. For those patients in whom persistent or profound sedation limits opioid dose escalation and therefore pain relief, the use of stimulants (eg, dextroamphetamine, methylphenidate) should be considered. Sweating and itching are thought to be due to histamine release. Morphine and meperidine are notable for causing histamine release. Switching to another opioid should be considered for patients with intolerable sweating or itching. Seizures associated with opioids are generally attributed to accumulation of neurotoxic metabolites or large overdoses that presumably cause hypoxia. Normeperidine, a metabolite of meperidine that can accumulate with frequent repeated doses or in patients with renal insufficiency, is the most well known of these neurotoxic metabolites. Two weak opioid antagonists associated with seizures are tramadol and propoxyphene; these products are not recommended for management of chronic cancer pain. Distinct from seizures, myoclonic jerks may be seen with the use of high doses of opioids. Occasional reports indicate that they may also be seen with relatively lower doses. Benzodiazepines have been suggested to control this side effect.

Opioid-induced hyperalgesia (OIH) should be suspected when analgesic efficacy is inexplicably lost or when generalized or worsening pain develops during aggressive opioid titration. OIH is a rare consequence of opioid therapy in cancer patients, and most often seen with aggressive morphine titration. The underlying mechanism is thought to be related to inhibition of glycinergic activity at the level of the spinal cord by phenanthrene-type opioids that promotes a strychnine-like excitatory effect. Additional biochemical mechanisms implicated in OIH include upregulation of intracellular phosphokinase C which activates the NMDA receptor system, and intraspinal dynorphin-mediated substance P and glutamate release. In the scenario of OIH, continued dose escalation aggravates pain which then improves with dose reduction. Management of OIH includes dose reduction or interruption of treatment with the offending agent. Replacing a phenanthrene derivative to a piperidine-type opioid, such as fentanyl or methadone, is recommended.

As previously noted, the oral route of administration for opioids is generally preferred. When oral administration is not possible, several other routes are available (see Table 1). When patients suddenly become unable to take medication by mouth, opioids intended for oral administration have been administered rectally or vaginally. Morphine and hydromorphone are also available in rectal suppositories. The recommended rectal dose is the same as the oral dose. Continuous subcutaneous or intravenous infusions administered with an infusion control device are useful when oral administration is impossible. Continuous parenteral infusion of opioids provides more consistent pain relief and patient tolerance compared to intermittent injections which result in peaks and valleys of pain relief or side effects. Continuous infusions also allow for quick titration of opioid in patients with uncontrolled pain. Patient-controlled analgesia provides a continuous infusion of opioid with a capacity for patient-administered bolus injections for breakthrough pain. This is not unlike the concept of regularly scheduled sustained release oral opioid with immediate release tablets for breakthrough, as previously discussed. Assessment of the use of breakthrough doses, whether oral or parenteral, provides a basis for adjusting the dose/rate of the underlying opioid. Transdermal fentanyl is another alternative, long-acting, analgesic for patients unable to take oral opioids. Transdermal fentanyl should be avoided when initiating chronic analgia in opioid-naive patients to reduce the risk of profound respiratory depression. As is the case with sustained release oral opioids, it is preferable to titrate to pain relief using short-acting drugs, and then switch to transdermal fentanyl. The manufacturer recommends equianalgesic conversion to the fentanyl patch as presented in the table below. This schema represents a conservative conversion from an oral or parenteral opioid to the fentanyl transdermal system, so the tabulated information should **not** be used to convert from fentanyl transdermal to an oral or parenteral opioid analgesic.

Table 2. Dosing Conversion Guidelines

Current Analgesic	Daily Dosage (mg/day)			
Morphine (oral)	60-134	135-224	225-314	315-404
Morphine (parenteral)	10-22	23-37	38-52	53-67
Hydromorphone (oral)	8-17	17.1-28	28.1-39	39.1-51
Hydromorphone (parenteral)	1.5-3.4	3.5-5.6	5.7-7.9	8-10
Oxycodone (oral)	30-67	67.5-112	112.5-157	157.5-202
Meperidine (parenteral)	75-165	166-278	279-390	391-503
Fentanyl transdermal recommended dose	**25 mcg/h**	**50 mcg/h**	**75 mcg/h**	**100 mcg/h**

CHRONIC PAIN MANAGEMENT (CANCER) *(Continued)*

One method for switching transdermal fentanyl and oral methadone is described by using the transdermal fentanyl:oral methadone conversion factor of 1:20 (daily dose:daily dose) to change patients (n=31) with inadequate pain control from one product to another (Mercadante, 2005). Oral methadone was administered in divided doses every eight hours. Fentanyl patches were removed when the first dose of methadone was administered. Conversely, for patients transitioning to transdermal fentanyl, the patch was applied with administration of the last methadone dose. This method was used successfully in 24 of 31 patients (78%) with improved pain control reported within 24 hours of product conversion and acceptable patient tolerance. Inadequate symptom control (6 patients) and adverse effects (1 patient) were the reasons for unsuccessful switching in seven patients. Using this conversion ratio, treatment with transdermal fentanyl 200 mcg/hour is switched to oral methadone 96 mg daily administered in divided doses as 30 mg every eight hours.

A similar method has been described which calculates the appropriate methodone dose using two steps (Benitez-Rosario, 2004). First, the patients daily transdermal fentanyl dose is coverted to the equivalent oral morphine dose using a ratio of fentanyl:oral morphine of 1:100. The resultant value is converted to the equivalent daily dose of oral methadone using the ratio of oral morphine:oral methadone ratio of 5:1 or 10:1. The calculated methadone dose is divided for administration every 8-12 hours beginning 8-24 hours following removal of the transdermal fentanyl system. Using this method, a patient with adequate pain control from transdermal fentanyl 100 mcg/hour would be receiving a daily dose of fentanyl 2.4 mg every 24 hours, which converts to oral morphine 240 mg per 24-hour, which converts to oral methadone 24-48 mg per 24 hours. So, 8-24 hours after removing the fentanyl patch, a dosage of oral methadone 15 mg administered every 8 or 12 hours can be started.

Intraspinal administration of opioids should be reserved for patients in whom systemic administration of opioids results in unacceptable or unmanageable toxicity. Epidural morphine is 5-10 times more potent than parenteral morphine, and intrathecal morphine is 10 times more potent than epidural morphine. Bupivacaine, clonidine, and ketamine have been added to epidural morphine infusions to enhance effectiveness.

Partial opioid agonists (eg, buprenorphine) or agonist-antagonists (eg, pentazocine, butorphanol, dezocine, nalbuphine) are generally not recommended for use in chronic cancer pain management. They have a ceiling for analgesic effectiveness, above which side effects are much more likely to increase, and they may precipitate withdrawal in patients receiving opioid agonists (eg, morphine). Naloxone may not be effective in reversing respiratory depression caused by buprenorphine.

Tramadol is a synthetic opioid that inhibits the neuronal reuptake of norepinephrine and serotonin. This product is indicated for the management of moderate pain. Its use is limited by the risk of seizures which have occurred in patients taking the usual and recommended dosage. Abrupt discontinuation of tramadol can precipitate withdrawal symptoms, such as tremors, sweating, diarrhea, upper respiratory symptoms, and rarely, hallucinations. Propoxyphene is another weak opioid not generally recommended for chronic cancer pain.

ADJUVANT ANALGESICS

Adjuvant analgesics are frequently used in addition to, rather than instead of, opioid analgesics. Adjuvants are often drugs that have primary indications other than pain, but may provide pain relief in certain situations. NSAIDs are commonly used for pain due to bone metastases (see individual NSAID monographs). Gabapentin and pregabalin are commonly used as adjunctive therapy for neuropathic pain. Additional drugs that have been used for this purpose include tricyclic antidepressants (eg, amitriptyline, nortriptyline), anticonvulsants (eg, carbamazepine), corticosteroids, and antiarrhythmics (eg, topical lidocaine). Methadone and ketamine are thought to improve neuropathic pain through blockade of the N-methyl-D-aspartate (NMDA) receptor. Neuropathic pain, often characterized by sharp, shooting, lancinating sensations, may result from nerve compression, infiltration, or destruction by tumor or from other associated conditions (eg, postherpetic neuralgia). Pain relief is usually not complete and, as is the case with NSAIDs in bone pain, these drugs are generally used in addition to opioids. Baclofen has also been used as an adjuvant analgesic for various types of neuropathic pain. Stronium-89 is a radiopharmaceutical that is reported to decrease the need for analgesics in patients with osteoblastic bone metastases. Prostate cancer is the most frequent malignancy associated with painful osteoblastic lesions. The bisphosphonates pamidronate and zoledronic acid are used to decrease pain and adverse skeletal events in patients with multiple myeloma and breast cancer. Calcitonin has also been used as an adjunct to analgesia in cancer pain. Capsaicin is a topically applied adjuvant analgesic that depletes substance P, a "painful" neurotransmitter. Capsaicin is recommended for use in postherpetic neuralgia and other painful neuropathies.

Selected Readings

American Pain Society, *Principles of Analgesic Use in the Treatment of Acute Pain and Chronic Cancer Pain*, 3rd ed, Skokie, IL: American Pain Society, 1992.

Axelrod DJ and Reville B, "Using Methadone to Treat Opioid-Induced Hyperalgesia and Refractory Pain," *J Opioid Manag*, 2007, 3(2):113-4.

Benitez-Rosario MA, Feria M, Salinas-Martin A, et al, "Opioid Switching From Transdermal Fentanyl to Oral Methadone in Patients With Cancer Pain," *Cancer*, 2004, 101(12):2866-73.

Benrath J, Scharbert G, Gustorff B, et al, "Long-Term Intrathecal S(+)-Ketamine in a Patient With Cancer-Related Neuropathic Pain," *Br J Anaesth*, 2005, 95(2):247-9.

Berenson JR, Lichtenstein A, Porter L, et al, "Efficacy of Pamidronate in Reducing Skeletal Events in Patients With Advanced Multiple Myeloma. Myeloma Aredia Study Group," *N Engl J Med*, 1996, 334(8):488-93.

Cordell GA and Araujo OE, "Capsaicin: Identification, Nomenclature, and Pharmacotherapy," *Ann Pharmacother*, 1993, 27(3):330-6.

Davis MP, Shaiova LA, and Angst MS, "When Opioids Cause Pain," *J Clin Oncol*, 2007, 25(28):4497-8.

Elsner F, Radbruch L, Loick G, et al, "Intravenous Versus Subcutaneous Morphine Titration in Patients With Persisting Exacerbation of Cancer Pain," *J Palliat Med*, 2005, 8(4):743-50.

Foley KM, "The Treatment of Cancer Pain," *N Engl J Med*, 1985, 313(2):84-95.

Fromm GH, "Baclofen as an Adjuvant Analgesic," *J Pain Symptom Manage*, 1994, 9(8):500-9.

Hojsted J and Sjogren P, "Addiction to Opioids in Chronic Pain Patients: A Literature Review," *Eur J Pain*, 2007, 11(5):490-518.

Holdsworth MT, Adams VR, Chavez CM, et al, "Continuous Midazolam Infusion for the Management of Morphine-Induced Myoclonus," *Ann Pharmacother*, 1995, 29(1):25-9.

Jackson KC 2nd, "Pharmacotherapy for Neuropathic Pain," *Pain Pract*, 2006, 6(1):27-33.

Jacox A, Carr DB, Payne R, et al, "Management of Cancer Pain," *Clinical Practice Guideline No. 9, AHCPR Publication No. 94-0592*, Rockville, MD: Agency for Health Care Policy and

CHRONIC PAIN MANAGEMENT (CANCER) *(Continued)*

Research, U.S. Department of Health and Human Services, Public Health Service, March 1994.

Laizure SC, "Considerations in Morphine Therapy," *Am J Hosp Pharm*, 1994, 51(16):2042-3.

Levy MH, "Pharmacologic Treatment of Cancer Pain," *N Engl J Med*, 1996, 335(15):1124-32.

Lossignol DA, Obiols-Portis M, and Body JJ, "Successful Use of Ketamine for Intractable Cancer Pain," *Support Care Cancer*, 2005, 13(3):188-93.

Mercadante SL, Berchovich M, Casuccio A, et al, "A Prospective Randomized Study of Corticosteroids as Adjuvant Drugs to Opioids in Advanced Cancer Patients," *Am J Hosp Palliat Care*, 2007, 24(1):13-9.

Mercadante S, Ferrera P, Villari P, et al, "Rapid Switching Between Transdermal Fentanyl and Methadone in Cancer Patients," *J Clin Oncol*, 2005, 23(22):5229-34.

Portenoy RK and Hagen NA, "Breakthrough Pain: Definition, Prevalence, and Characteristics," *Pain*, 1990, 41(3):273-81.

Potter JM, Reid DB, Shaw RJ, et al, "Myoclonus Associated With Treatment With High Doses of Morphine: The Role of Supplemental Drugs," *BMJ*, 1989, 299(6692):150-3.

Robinson RG, Preston DF, Baxter KG, et al, "Clinical Experience With Strontium-89 in Prostatic and Breast Cancer Patients," *Semin Oncol*, 1993, 20(3 Suppl 2):44-8.

Rodriguez RF, Castillo JM, Del Pilar Castillo M, et al, "Codeine/Acetaminophen and Hydrocodone/Acetaminophen Combination Tablets for the Management of Chronic Cancer Pain in Adults: A 23-Day, Prospective, Double-Blind, Randomized, Parallel-Group Study," *Clin Ther*, 2007, 29(4):581-7.

Stearns L, Boortz-Marx R, Du Pen S, et al, "Intrathecal Drug Delivery for the Management of Cancer Pain: A Multidisciplinary Consensus of Best Clinical Practices," *J Support Oncol*, 2005, 3(6):399-408.

Stockler M, Vardy J, Pillai A, et al, "Acetaminophen (Paracetamol) Improves Pain and Well-Being in People With Advanced Cancer Already Receiving a Strong Opioid Regimen: A Randomized, Double-Blind, Placebo-Controlled Cross-Over Trial," *J Clin Oncol*, 2004, 22(16):3389-94.

Szeto HH, Inturrisi CE, Houde R, et al, "Accumulation of Normeperidine, an Active Metabolite of Meperidine, in Patients With Renal Failure of Cancer," *Ann Intern Med*, 1977, 86(6):738-41.

Tsavaris N, Kopterides P, Kosmas C, et al, "Analgesic Activity of High-Dose Intravenous Calcitonin in Cancer Patients With Bone Metastases," *Oncol Rep*, 2006, 16(4):871-5.

Vranken JH, van der Vegt MH, Kal JE, et al, "Treatment of Neuropathic Cancer Pain With Continuous Intrathecal Administration of S +-Ketamine," *Acta Anaesthesiol Scand*, 2004, 48(2):249-52.

Wellington K and Goa KL, "Zoledronic Acid: A Review of Its Use in the Management of Bone Metastases and Hypercalcaemia of Malignancy," *Drugs*, 2003, 63(4):417-37.

Yucel A, Ozyalcin S, Koknel Talu G, et al, "The Effect of Venlafaxine on Ongoing and Experimentally Induced Pain in Neuropathic Pain Patients: A Double Blind, Placebo Controlled Study," *Eur J Pain*, 2005, 9(4):407-16.

COMMON TOXICITY CRITERIA

Selected Common Toxicity Criteria

Toxicity	Grade 0	Grade 1	Grade 2	Grade 3	Grade 4
Hematologic					
Leukocytes (WBC)	WNL	3×10^9/L to <LLN	2 to <3×10^9/L	1 to <2×10^9/L	<1×10^9/L
Neutrophils (ANC)	WNL	1.5×10^9/L to <LLN	1 to <1.5×10^9/L	0.5 to <1×10^9/L	<0.5×10^9/L
Lymphocytes	WNL	0.8×10^9/L to <LLN	0.5 to <0.8×10^9/L	0.2 to <0.5×10^9/L	<0.2×10^9/L
Anemia (Hgb)	WNL	10 g/dL to <LLN	8 to <10 g/dL	6.5 to <8 g/dL	<6.5 g/dL
Platelets	WNL	75×10^9/L to <LLN	50 to <75×10^9/L	25 to <50×10^9/L	<25×10^9/L
Hemorrhage	None	Mild, no transfusion		Transfusion indicated	Major intervention required
Cardiovascular					
Hypotension	None	Changes, no treatment required	Brief treatment required	Sustained treatment required, resolves	Shock
Hypertension	None	Increase by >20 mm Hg or to >150/100 mm Hg, treatment not required	Recurrent/persistent grade 1 level, minor treatment required	More intensive treatment required	Hypertensive crisis
Pericardial effusion	None	Asymptomatic effusion		Physiologic consequences	Life-threatening consequences
Syncope	Absent			Present	Life-threatening consequences
Thrombosis/ embolism	None		DVT, intervention not indicated	DVT, intervention indicated	Pulmonary embolism/ life-threatening thrombus

COMMON TOXICITY CRITERIA *(Continued)*

Selected Common Toxicity Criteria *(continued)*

Toxicity	Grade 0	Grade 1	Grade 2	Grade 3	Grade 4
Dermatologic					
Rash (acne/acneiform)	None	Intervention not indicated	Intervention indicated	Pain, disfigurement, ulceration	
Rash (desquamation)	None	Macular or papular eruption	Erythema w/pruritus affecting <50% of BSA	Severe erythema/desquamation covering ≥50% of BSA	Generalized exfoliative or ulcerative dermatitis
Rash (erythema multiforme)	None		Scattered eruption	Severe eruption	Life-threatening eruption
Hand-foot syndrome	None	Minimal skin changes w/o pain	Skin changes or pain not interfering w/ADL	Skin changes/pain; interferes w/ADL	
Alopecia	None	Thinning/patchy	Complete		
Gastrointestinal					
Nausea	None	Loss of appetite/able to eat	Oral intake decreased/no weight loss	Inadequate intake/I.V. fluids required	Life-threatening consequences
Vomiting	None	1 episode/24 h	2-5 episodes/24 h	≥6 episodes/24 h, I.V. fluid required	Life-threatening consequences
Diarrhea	None	<4 stools/day increase over baseline	4-6 stools/day increase over baseline	≥7 stools/day increase/I.V. fluids required	Life-threatening consequences
Mucositis/stomatitis	None	Mucosal erythema	Patchy ulcerations	Confluent ulceration, bleeding	Tissue necrosis/bleeding; life-threatening
GI bleeding	None	Mild, intervention not indicated	Symptomatic, mild intervention indicated	Transfusion required, intervention indicated	Life-threatening consequences
Amylase elevation	None	>ULN to 1.5 x ULN	>1.5 to 2 x ULN	>2 to 5 x ULN	>5 x ULN
Lipase elevation	None	>ULN to 1.5 x ULN	>1.5 to 2 x ULN	>2 to 5 x ULN	>5 x ULN

Selected Common Toxicity Criteria *(continued)*

Toxicity	Grade 0	Grade 1	Grade 2	Grade 3	Grade 4
Hepatic					
Alkaline phosphatase elevation	WNL	>ULN to 2.5 x ULN	>2.5 to 5 x ULN	>5 to 20 x ULN	>20 x ULN
AST elevation	WNL	>ULN to 2.5 x ULN	>2.5 to 5 x ULN	>5 to 20 x ULN	>20 x ULN
ALT elevation	WNL	>ULN to 2.5 x ULN	>2.5 to 5 x ULN	>5 to 20 x ULN	>20 x ULN
Hyperbilirubinemia	WNL	>ULN to 1.5 x ULN	>1.5 to 3 x ULN	>3 to 10 x ULN	>10 x ULN
Ascites	None	Asymptomatic	Symptomatic, diuretics required	Symptomatic, procedure required	Life-threatening consequences
Veno-occlusive disease	None	Mild	Moderate	Severe	Life-threatening
Metabolic					
Hyperglycemia	WNL	>ULN to 160 mg/dL	>160 to 250 mg/dL	>250 to 500 mg/dL	>500 mg/dL
Hypoglycemia	WNL	55 to <LLN mg/dL	40 to <55 mg/dL	30 to <40 mg/dL	<30 mg/dL
Hypocalcemia	WNL	8 to <LLN mg/dL	7 to <8 mg/dL	6 to <7 mg/dL	<6 mg/dL
Hypokalemia	WNL	3 to <LLN mmol/L	—	2.5 to <3 mmol/L	<2.5 mmol/L
Hypomagnesemia	WNL	1.2 to <LLN mg/dL	0.9 to <1.2 mg/dL	0.7 to <0.9 mg/dL	<0.7 mg/dL
Hypophosphatemia	WNL	2.5 to <LLN mg/dL	2 to <2.5 mg/dL	1 to <2 mg/dL	<1 mg/dL
Renal / Genitourinary					
Hematuria	None	Minimal or microscopic	Symptomatic, minor intervention required	Transfusion required, intervention indicated	Life-threatening consequences
Hypoalbuminemia	WNL	3 g/dL to <LLN	2 to <3 g/dL	<2 g/dL	
Serum creatinine elevation	WNL	>ULN to 1.5 x ULN	>1.5 to 3 x ULN	>3 to 6 x ULN	>6 x ULN

1355

CANCER-RELATED COMPLICATIONS

COMMON TOXICITY CRITERIA *(Continued)*

Selected Common Toxicity Criteria *(continued)*

Toxicity	Grade 0	Grade 1	Grade 2	Grade 3	Grade 4
Respiratory					
Dyspnea	None	Mild dyspnea on exertion	Dyspnea on exertion	Dyspnea at ADL	Dyspnea at rest/ ventilator support indicated
Epistaxis	None	Mild, no transfusion	Symptomatic	Transfusion required, intervention indicated	Life-threatening consequences
Pleural effusion	None	Asymptomatic	Symptomatic, intervention required	Symptomatic, oxygen, or thoracentesis required	Life-threatening
CNS / Neurologic					
Fatigue/weakness	None	Mild fatigue over baseline	Moderate, some difficulty w/ADL	Severe, interferes w/ ADL	Disabling
Neuropathy, motor	Normal	Asymptomatic, weakness on exam	Symptomatic weakness, mild difficulty w/function	Weakness, interferes w/ADL	Life-threatening/ disabling
Neuropathy, sensory	Normal	Paresthesia/deep tendon reflex loss	Paresthesia/sensory loss, interferes w/ function	Sensory loss/ paresthesia; interferes w/ADL	Disabling

Selected Common Toxicity Criteria *(continued)*

Toxicity	Grade 0	Grade 1	Grade 2	Grade 3	Grade 4
			Miscellaneous		
Allergy/ hypersensitivity	None	Transient rash, drug fever <38°C	Urticaria, dyspnea, drug fever ≥38°C	Bronchospasm/ parenteral treatment required	Anaphylaxis
Fever	None	38°C to 39°C (100.4°F to 102.2°F)	>39°C to 40°C (102.3°F to 104°F)	>40°C (104°F) for ≤24 h	>40°C (104°F) for >24 h
Infection w/o neutropenia	None		Localized, local intervention indicated	I.V. antimicrobials indicated	Life-threatening sepsis
Neutropenic fever	None			Present	Life-threatening sepsis

ADL = activities of daily living; WNL = within normal limits; LLN = lower limits of normal; ULN = upper limits of normal.

Adapted from the NCI Common Toxicity Criteria (http://ctep.cancer.gov/forms/CTCAEv3.pdf).

HYPERCALCEMIA

INTRODUCTION

Hyperparathyroidism and cancer are the most frequent causes of hypercalcemia. In cancer patients, hypercalcemia is the most frequently occurring life-threatening metabolic disorder. The incidence varies with the specific type of cancer; the highest incidence is seen in multiple myeloma and breast cancer. The etiology of cancer-associated hypercalcemia is multifactorial. The immediate cause is increased bone resorption. Bone resorption is stimulated by mediators released from tumor cells. The most common mediator of osteoclastic bone resorption, in patients with and without bone metastases, is thought to be parathyroid hormone-related protein (PTH-RP). PTH-RP mimics some, but not all, of the effects of parathyroid hormone. Other mediators or presumed mediators of bone resorption include vitamin D_3, prostaglandins, and a variety of cytokines. Hypercalcemia leads to polyuria and resultant volume depletion and decreased glomerular filtration rate. Attempts by the kidney to increase intravascular volume by increasing proximal tubular reabsorption of water and sodium are accompanied by increased tubular reabsorption of calcium. This perpetuates the hypercalcemia. The median survival for cancer patients with hypercalcemia who are not receiving chemotherapy is reported to be 30 days. Treatment of hypercalcemia, however, can lead to improvement of symptoms (eg, confusion, constipation, malaise, nausea, vomiting, polyuria, polydipsia). Although treatment of the underlying malignancy may correct hypercalcemia, the late and/or refractory stage of cancer at which hypercalcemia occurs often precludes successful antitumor therapy.

TREATMENT

The urgency with which cancer-associated hypercalcemia is approached/treated is determined by the presence/severity of symptoms and the level of calcium. Most guidelines suggest that serum calcium be corrected for albumin in order to estimate the level of ionized (free or active) calcium. Although ionized calcium may in fact not be accurately estimated by the formulae that correct for albumin [eg, corrected Ca^{++} = measured Ca^{++} (mg/dL) + 0.8 mg/dL for each g albumin <4 g/dL, corrected Ca^{++} = measured Ca^{++} (mg/dL) - albumin (g/dL) + 4.0], many studies of treatments for hypercalcemia have used corrected rather than total calcium in determining study entry and/or endpoints.

Several treatments exist for the management of hypercalcemia. They have not all been compared to each other, or have not been compared at doses that reflect clinical usage, etc. Thus, treatment remains somewhat empiric.

0.9% NaCl

Sodium chloride provides replacement of intravascular volume. Following rehydration, proximal tubular reabsorption of sodium, and therefore calcium, will decrease. Further, other treatments for hypercalcemia require prior volume replacement in order to minimize toxicities. Sodium chloride can lower serum calcium by approximately 2 mg/dL. The rate of administration of sodium chloride depends on the degree of dehydration, the degree of hypercalcemia, and the cardiovascular status of the patient. Even if normocalcemia is achieved, without further treatment calcium will rise again. In many studies, rehydration has been continued for 48 hours before adding another calcium-lowering agent. In hospitalized patients, sodium chloride can be continued while other agents are administered.

Furosemide

The major use of furosemide in the management of cancer-associated hypercalcemia is to prevent/treat fluid overload in order to facilitate the administration of sodium chloride for volume replacement. Although high doses of furosemide (eg, 100 mg) have been used to promote calcium excretion, such high doses require the use of strict monitoring of input and output and replacement of fluid and electrolytes. The possibility of further dehydration and worsening of hypercalcemia with furosemide should be considered.

Bisphosphonates

Bisphosphonates bind to hydroxyapatite in bone and inhibit osteoclastic bone resorption. Pamidronate is reported to bring calcium to thenomocalcemic range in 70% to 100% of patients. Although there appears to be a dose-response relationship, it is not clear that 90 mg is clinically superior to 60 mg. It is recommended that use of pamidronate be weighed carefully in patients with serum creatinine ≥3 mg/dL. This is primarily because of lack of data in this population. Rehydration usually precedes administration of pamidronate, and elevated creatinine values are often corrected. Side effects of pamidronate are mild and include fever and infusion site reactions such as phlebitis. Etidronate is reported to bring calcium to the normocalcemic range in 40% to 100% of patients. Etidronate is generally thought to be less potent as a calcium-lowering agent than pamidronate. The usual dose of etidronate is 7.5 mg/kg/day for 3 days. Like pamidronate, etidronate is not recommended for use in patients with serum creatinine >5 mg/dL. Also, like pamidronate, etidronate is generally given after rehydration. Side effects of etidronate include occasional mild elevations in creatinine and a metallic taste. Because of the multiple daily dose regimens of etidronate, pamidronate is more convenient for outpatient administration. Oral etidronate has been used to maintain normocalcemia with minimal clinical benefit.

Calcitonin

Calcitonin inhibits bone resorption and enhances urinary excretion of calcium. It is the fastest acting of the agents used to treat hypercalcemia and may be given safely before rehydration is complete. The usual dose of calcitonin is 4 units/kg every 12 hours. Side effects are mild and infrequent and include nausea, abdominal cramps, and flushing. Calcitonin lowers serum calcium by approximately 2 mg/dL. As is the case for saline hydration, this may or may not result in normocalcemia. However, rebound hypercalcemia develops quickly (within days), limiting the usefulness of calcitonin in the treatment of hypercalcemia.

HYPERCALCEMIA *(Continued)*

Gallium Nitrate

Gallium decreases serum calcium by adsorbing to hydroxyapatite and inhibiting bone resorption. It is given as a continuous infusion at a dose of 200 mg/m^2/day for 5 days. Gallium is reported to result in normocalcemia in 75% of patients. Nephrotoxicity has been seen with the use of gallium. Although nephrotoxicity reportedly occurs with doses higher than those used to treat hypercalcemia, it has been noted in patients treated for hypercalcemia. Nephrotoxicity may be potentiated by other nephrotoxic drugs. Gallium should not be used in patients with serum creatinine >2.5 mg/dL. Because of the potential for nephrotoxicity and the inconvenient dosing schedule relative to other agents, gallium should not be considered a first-line treatment for hypercalcemia.

Miscellaneous

Other agents have been evaluated or used to treat hypercalcemia. Cisplatin is known to lower serum calcium and may be effective in hypercalcemia independent of tumor response. Amifostine has been associated with hypocalcemia and was effective in lowering serum calcium in at least one report. Intravenous alendronate as well as other bisphosphonates not available in the United States have also been reported to be effective in the management of hypercalcemia.

Drug	Usual Dose	Onset of Effect (h)	Duration of Effect
Calcitonin	4 units/kg q12h	3	Median 1 day (1-6)
Etidronate	7.5 mg/kg/d x 3 d	24-48	Median 5 days (2-30)
Gallium	200 mg/m^{2}d x 5 d	24-48	Median 6 days
NaCl	2-5 L/24 h	24-48	Transient
Pamidronate	60 or 90 mg	24-48	Median 10 days (1-30)
Plicamycin	25 mcg/kg	12	3-21 days

Selected Readings

Bilezikian JP, "Management of Acute Hypercalcemia," *N Engl J Med*, 1992, 326(18):1196-203.

Glover DJ, Shaw L, Glick JH, et al, "Treatment of Hypercalcemia in Parathyroid Cancer With WR-2721, S-2-(3-Aminopropylamino)Ethyl-Phosphorothioic Acid," *Ann Intern Med*, 1985, 103(1):55-7.

Lad TE, Mishoulam HM, Shevrin DH, et al, "Treatment of Cancer-Associated Hypercalcemia With Cisplatin," *Arch Intern Med*, 1987, 147(2):329-32.

Ladenson JH, Lewis JW, and Boyd JC, "Failure of Total Calcium Corrected for Protein, Albumin, and pH to Correctly Assess Free Calcium Status," *J Clin Endocrinol Metab*, 1978, 46:986-93.

Nakashima L, "Guidelines for the Treatment of Hypercalcemia Associated With Malignancy," *J Oncol Pharm Pract*, 1997, 3:31-7.

Nussbaum SR, Warrell RP Jr, Rude R, et al, "Dose-Response Study of Alendronate Sodium for the Treatment of Cancer-Associated Hypercalcemia," *J Clin Oncol*, 1993, 11(8):1618-23.

Nussbaum SR, Younger J, Vandepol CJ, et al, "Single-Dose Intravenous Therapy With Pamidronate for the Treatment of Hypercalcemia of Malignancy: Comparison of 30-, 60-, and 90-mg Dosages," *Am J Med*, 1993, 95(3):297-304.

Perlia CP, Gubisch NJ, Wolter J, et al, "Mithramycin Treatment of Hypercalcemia," *Cancer*, 1970, 25:389-94.

Ralston SH, Gallacher SJ, Patel U, et al, "Cancer-Associated Hypercalcemia: Morbidity and Mortality. Clinical Experience in 126 Treated Patients," *Ann Intern Med*, 1990, 112(7):499-504.

Ringenberg QS and Ritch PS, "Efficacy of Oral Administration of Etidronate Disodium in Maintaining Normal Serum Calcium Levels in Previously Hypercalcemic Cancer Patients," *Clin Ther*, 1987, 9(3):318-25.

Schaiff RA, Hall TG, and Bar RS, "Medical Treatment of Hypercalcemia," *Clin Pharm*, 1989, 8(2):108-21.

Shemerdiak WP, Kukreja SC, Lad TE, et al, "Evaluation of Routine Ionized Calcium Determination in Cancer Patients," *Clin Chem*, 1981, 27:1621-2.

Shevrin DH, Bressler LR, McGuire WP, et al, "Treatment of Cancer-Associated Hypercalcemia With Mithramycin and Oral Etidronate Disodium," *Clin Pharm*, 1985, 4(2):204-5.

Stewart AF, "Clinical Practice. Hypercalcemia Associated With Cancer, "*N Engl J Med*, 2005, 352(4):373-9.

Thiebaud D, Jaeger PH, Jacquet AF, et al, "Dose-Response in the Treatment of Hypercalcemia of Malignancy by a Single Infusion of the Bisphosphonate AHPrBP," *J Clin Oncol*, 1988, 6(5):762-8.

Warrell RP, "Metabolic Emergencies: Hypercalcemia", *Cancer: Principles and Practice of Oncology*, 5th ed, DeVita, Hellman, and Rosenberg, eds, Lippincott-Raven, 1997, 2486-93.

Warrell RP Jr, Israel R, Frisone M, et al, "Gallium Nitrate for Acute Treatment of Cancer-Related Hypercalcemia. A Randomized, Double-Blind Comparison to Calcitonin," *Ann Intern Med*, 1988, 108(5):699-74.

MALIGNANT EFFUSIONS

Malignant effusions occur when fluid accumulates in the pleural space secondary to direct extension of a tumor or because of metastatic dissemination. Carcinoma of the breast, carcinoma of the lung, and lymphomas account for two-thirds of malignant effusions but they are also found with gastric or ovarian carcinomas. A malignant effusion may be the presenting sign of cancer, but most often it is a complication of a diagnosed malignancy.

PATHOPHYSIOLOGY

The pleura is a thin membrane that covers the lungs and chest wall. It is composed of the visceral pleura (covering the surface of the lungs) and the parietal pleura (covering the thoracic cavity). The space between the visceral pleura and parietal pleura is the pleural space. Normally, pleural fluid production is <100 mL/day. Movement of fluid within the pleural space is governed by hydrostatic and oncotic pressures and follows Starling's law of transcapillary exchange. Hydrostatic pressure in the parietal capillaries is higher, causing a net movement into the pleural space. Reabsorption of the fluid occurs primarily through lymphatics on the parietal surface and less importantly via lymphatics on the visceral surface. Changes in pleural fluid production, reabsorption, or both produce a pleural effusion.

Malignancies can cause an imbalance within the pleural space in several ways. Pleural implantation of malignant cells can cause an inflammatory response that increases capillary permeability and increases the net filtration of fluid into the pleural space. Obstruction of lymphatic channels and changes in pleural fluid protein content can impair reabsorption of fluid. Any of these changes can result in a net accumulation of fluid.

Normally, pleural fluid is produced through a passive process and the ion content is similar to serum concentrations while the protein content is <2%. The resulting fluid is transudative. Neoplastic processes, which increase capillary permeability and obstruct lymphatic drainage, often produce an exudative pleural fluid with an increased protein and cell content. Typically, the characteristics of the exudative fluid include increased protein content, glucose level lower than the serum, variable number of identifiable tumor cells, and an absence of eosinophils.

CLINICAL SYMPTOMS

Many patients with pleural effusions are asymptomatic. The most common symptom is dyspnea, often in conjunction with cough, chest pain, and tachypnea. Symptoms are often related not to the amount of fluid present, but to the rate of fluid accumulation. A diagnosis often begins with a chest x-ray, which will demonstrate fluid accumulation on the PA and lateral decubitus film. Physical findings include dullness to percussion, decreased breath sounds, decreased diaphragmatic excursion, and possible contralateral tracheal deviation.

TREATMENT

The goal of treatment is to provide a cost-efficient, effective therapy that provides symptomatic relief with the least amount of discomfort to the patient. Not all patients with pleural effusions need to be treated. Some patients with effusions are asymptomatic and may not require treatment until symptoms develop. Patients with a life expectancy of less than 1 month might only require oxygen, narcotics, and possibly thoracentesis. Patients with tumors highly sensitive to chemotherapy may have resolution of the effusion with systemic treatment of the tumor.

LOCAL THERAPY

1. Thoracentesis is utilized frequently for symptomatic patients, but it is ineffective for any long-term control of the effusion. Recurrence is frequent, and repeated procedures carry a risk of increased complications such as pneumothorax.

2. Tube thoracostomy (chest tube) is effective in controlling a malignant effusion for a short period of time. Its 30-day success rate is approximately 70%. However, it is ineffective in the long-term control of effusions. It is most useful in draining the fluid from the pleural space prior to instilling a sclerosing agent.

3. Pleurectomy involves stripping the parietal and visceral pleura and it carries a high mortality and morbidity rate as compared to less invasive procedures.

4. Pleuroperitoneal shunts are used to manually pump fluid from the pleural space into the peritoneal cavity. The pumps must be manually operated daily and are prone to blockage by the high protein content of the fluid.

PLEURODESIS

Pleurodesis, or sclerosis, should be considered in symptomatic patients who have symptomatic relief from thoracentesis with complete lung re-expansion and a life expectancy of weeks to months. Sclerosing agents act by causing an inflammatory response in the pleura, which resolves to cause adhesions of the visceral and parietal pleura, resulting in obliteration of the pleural space. Sclerosing agents are administered via a thoracostomy tube following adequate drainage (<100 mL/day). Factors affecting the success of the agent include uniform distribution in the pleural space, the presence of loculations that interfere with distribution, and the dose of the selected drug.

GENERAL METHOD OF ADMINISTRATION

Fluid is drained via a chest tube until the production is <100 mL/day. The patient is premedicated with a parenteral narcotic. Since pleurodesis is associated with pleuritic chest pain, instillation of 10-25 mL of 1% lidocaine (3-4 mg/kg) is recommended 10-15 minutes prior to the sclerosing agent. The sclerosing agent is instilled through the chest tube and the tube is clamped for 30 minutes to 2 hours with frequent repositioning of the patient to assure uniform distribution, although this repositioning is controversial. Then the tube is unclamped, reconnected to water-seal suction until production is <100-150 mL/day, and the chest tube is removed.

MALIGNANT EFFUSIONS (Continued)

DRUGS

1. Doxycycline and minocycline: Tetracycline was one of the most widely used sclerosing agents with a success rate of 30% to 80%. It was inexpensive, caused few side effects, and was moderately effective. However, it was removed from the market in the mid-1990s and an effective replacement has been sought. In three noncomparative studies, doxycycline 500-1000 mg mixed in 50-100 mL NS, was found to be moderately effective in controlling effusions but generally required 1-4 instillations to achieve results similar to tetracycline. Comparative studies are needed to confirm these results. Minocycline has only been studied in two small noncomparative trials with good results. It is inexpensive and may offer an alternative to tetracycline but larger comparative trials are needed to fully assess its usefulness.

2. Bleomycin 30-180 units in 100 mL of 0.9% sodium chloride or dextrose 5% in water has been studied and found to be an effective agent in controlling malignant effusions. Because of a lack of increased efficacy at doses >60 units, some authors have recommended limiting the dose to 60 units or 1 unit/kg body weight. Also, report of 2 deaths in elderly patients who may have had decreased clearance of the drug has prompted the recommendation to limit the dose to 40 units/m^2 in the elderly. Although 40% to 50% of the dose may enter the systemic circulation, toxicity is generally low. Adverse effects include nausea, vomiting, diarrhea, febrile reactions, and chest pain. Myelosuppression has not been clinically important but is theoretically a potential side effect. A disadvantage is the high cost of therapy due to the cost of the drug.

3. Talc is one of the oldest and most effective treatments for malignant effusions. Its use is somewhat controversial because of the costs associated with preparation and administration. Although the talc itself is relatively inexpensive, in the past the talc (asbestos-free only) had to be sterilized (ethylene oxide gas, dry heat, or irradiation) and was administered via a thoracostomy tube while the patient was under general anesthesia. The talc (5-10 g) was either insufflated or instilled as a slurry. Talc sclerosis is associated with pain, hypotension, fever, and adult respiratory distress syndrome as well as complications of general anesthesia. The cost of sterilization, use of the operating room, and anesthesia drive the costs of this therapy up, despite its nearly 100% efficacy. Use of small-bore pigtail catheters for sclerosis in the ambulatory setting, insertion of chest tubes under local anesthesia, and the recent availability of an aerosolized talc product may make this an attractive alternative.

OTHER AGENTS

A number of other agents including aldesleukin, doxorubicin, mitoxantrone, cisplatin, cytarabine, interferon, aldesleukin-2, *Cornybacterium parvum*, fluorouracil, mechlorethamine, methylprednisone acetate, and quinacrine have been used with varying degrees of success in small numbers of patients. Routine use cannot be recommended although some have shown promising results.

COMPLICATIONS

Management of malignant effusions is associated with several complications. Pain from insertion of the chest tube or instillation of the sclerosing agent should be pretreated with parenteral narcotics. Traction pneumothorax results from repeated attempts to re-expand the lung. Cough is caused by lung re-expansion and is self-limiting. Fluid loculation is associated with drainage and pleurodesis. Lysis of adhesions may be necessary prior to pleurodesis. Empyema (purulent fluid) formation from contamination or bronchopulmonary communication should be treated with appropriate antibiotics.

CHOICE OF THERAPY

Although there have been many clinical trials documenting the efficacy of a number of agents for sclerosis, comparing efficacy is difficult. Flaws in the studies, such as different eligibility criteria, the use of concomitant therapies, and the lack of uniform response criteria make the task of choosing a therapy almost impossible. Talc is the least expensive and most effective therapy, but the cost of instillation under general anesthesia drives up hospital costs. The use of local anesthesia to insert chest tubes, the use of small-bore pigtail catheters, and the availability of aerosolized talc may provide alternatives in the future. Bleomycin is effective, requires one instillation allowing the chest tube to be removed earlier, and is well tolerated but is quite expensive. Doxycycline or minocycline may be alternatives but the lack of good dosing information and the small number of clinical trials make these agents alternatives to talc or bleomycin.

Selected Readings

Andrew CO and Gora ML, "Pleural Effusions: Pathophysiology and Management," *Ann Pharmcother*, 1994, 28:894-902.

Belani CP, Pajeau TS, and Bennett CL, "Treating Malignant Pleural Effusions Cost Consciously," *Chest*, 1998, 113:78S-85S.

Grossi F, Pennucci MC, Tixi L, et al, "Management of Malignant Pleural Effusions," *Drugs*, 1998, 55:47-58.

Hausheer FH and Yarbro JW, "Diagnosis and Treatment of Malignant Pleural Effusion," *Semin Oncol*, 1985, 12:54-75.

Putnam JB Jr., "Malignant Pleural Effusions," *Surg Clin North Am*, 2002, 82(4):867-83.

Walker-Renard PB, Vaughan LM, and Salm SA, "Chemical Pleurodesis for Malignant Pleural Effusions," *Ann Intern Med*, 1994, 120:56-64.

HEMATOPOIETIC STEM CELL TRANSPLANTATION

Hematopoietic stem cell transplantation (SCT) involves the infusion of hematopoietic stem and progenitor cells into a patient in order to treat nonmalignant, hematologic and immunologic diseases, and a number of malignant diseases. Hematopoietic stem cells are immature cells that mature and differentiate into the various functional myeloid (eg, neutrophils, monocytes, macrophages, megakaryocytes, erythrocytes) and lymphoid cells (eg, T lymphocytes, B lymphocytes, natural killer cells) of the hematopoietic system. Hematopoietic stem cells are transplanted in order to replace diseased hematopoietic cells, reduce the duration of pancytopenia following administration of high dose chemotherapy, or to generate antitumor immunity in cancer patients. Allogeneic stem cell transplants require donation of stem cells from a healthy donor; whereas, autologous transplantation uses stem cells previously collected from the patient undergoing treatment. Allogeneic stem cell transplants are further classified as related transplants (donor and recipient are siblings), unrelated transplants (donor and recipient are not related), or syngeneic transplants (donor and recipient are identical twins). Immunologic likeness of the donor and recipient is determined by comparison of the genotype and phenotype of donor and recipient class I and class II major histocompatibility (MHC) antigens. MHC Class I antigens (HLA-A, HLA-B, HLA-C) are present on all nucleated cells in the body and provide a means for the immune system to differentiate self versus nonself. MHC Class II proteins (HLA-DP, HLA-DQ, HLA-DR) are present on antigen presenting cells, such as macrophages, dendritic cells, B lymphocytes, and activated endothelial cells, and are critical in initiation and maintenance of long-lasting immunity and tolerance.

Classification of stem cell transplants according to the intensity of the pretransplant preparative regimen differentiates myeloablative versus nonmyeloablative regimens. Myeloablative chemotherapy regimens administer the highest possible dose of chemotherapy, with the doses limited by regimen-related nonhematologic toxicity. The goal of the myeloablative regimen is to achieve the maximum anticancer effect and complete immunosuppression through the effects of the high dose cytotoxic agents. The goal of the nonmyeloablative preparative regimen is to inhibit the recipient immune system adequately to allow engraftment of the donated hematopoietic cells. Complete donor engraftment following nonmyeloablative transplantation typically occurs after a period of mixed chimerism and is associated with antitumor effect mediated by donor immune cells. Less regimen-related morbidity occurs following treatment with nonmyeloablative preparative regimens in comparison to myeloablative preparative regimens.

Terms that are synonymous with hematopoietic stem cell transplantation include stem cell transplantation, bone marrow transplantation, peripheral blood cell transplantation, and peripheral blood cell rescue. The following table lists clinical uses for allogeneic and autologous myeloablative hematopoietic stem cell transplantation.

Condition	Allogeneic	Autologous
Acute lymphocytic leukemia (ALL)	+	+
Acute myelogenous leukemia (AML)	+	+
Myelodysplastic syndrome	+	-
Chronic lymphocytic leukemia (CLL)	+	-
Chronic myelogenous leukemia (CML)	+	-
Non-Hodgkin's lymphoma (NHL)	+	+
Hodgkin's lymphoma	+	+
Multiple myeloma (MM)	+	+
Severe aplastic anemia (SAA)	+	-
Sickle cell disease (SCD)	+	-
Congenital immunodeficiency syndromes	+	-
Adult autoimmune disorders (eg, scleroderma, multiple sclerosis, rheumatoid arthritis)	-	+
Germ cell/testicular cancer	-	+
Neuroblastoma	-	+
Congenital hematopoietic disorders	+	-
Inborn errors of metabolism	+	-
Paroxysmal nocturnal hemoglobinuria	+	-
Thalassemia major	+	-
Wiskott-Aldrich syndrome	+	-

SOURCES, COLLECTION, AND PROCESSING OF HEMATOPOIETIC PROGENITOR CELLS

Peripheral blood is generally the site for obtaining the hematopoietic progenitor cells for transplantation. The hematopoietic stem and progenitor cells are removed via leukapheresis, which is easily done in an ambulatory setting and requires no anesthesia. Cells collected for autologous transplantation are processed and can be either used immediately or cryopreserved for future use. Cells collected for allogeneic transplantation are generally processed and infused immediately; however, cells for allogeneic transplantation have been frozen and stored prior to transplantation. Leukapheresis involves the processing of approximately 10 L of peripheral blood over a 2- to 6-hour period. The usual goal is a product containing at least 2×10^6/kg, ideally 5×10^6/kg of recipient weight of CD34$^+$ cells, which closely correlate with the content of stem and progenitor cells collected. This may be accomplished by 1 or several leukaphereses. Patients may require calcium supplementation during leukapheresis due to the citrate anticoagulant used during the procedure. Common medical risks to the allogeneic donor of peripheral hematopoietic stem cells include adverse effects from treatment with a colony-stimulating factor (bone pain) and adverse events associated with leukapheresis (acute hypocalcemia, catheter-related discomfort). Although no long-term toxicity has been reported in donors treated with colony-stimulating factors, rare serious toxicity such as splenic rupture can occur and the donor must be screened carefully prior to donation.

HEMATOPOIETIC STEM CELL TRANSPLANTATION
(Continued)

The peripheral blood concentration of hematopoietic stem cells and progenitor cells must be increased to facilitate successful collection. This process is known as peripheral progenitor cell mobilization. After administration of chemotherapy, colony-stimulating factors, or a combination of the two agents, the numbers of circulating early and late progenitor cells becomes greatly increased. A colony-stimulating factor, such as filgrastim or sargramostim, is used for this purpose in the healthy allogeneic donor. For the autologous donor, a colony-stimulating factor is administered alone or prescribed following chemotherapy. Mobilization of hematopoietic progenitor cells can be more difficult in patients with hematologic malignancies, or a history of extensive treatment with chemotherapy and radiation. The following table provides the dosage and schedule for some of the more commonly used mobilization regimens. Selection of the chemotherapy for mobilization in the autologous donor is primarily based on the type of cancer being treated. Most recently, the CXCR4 analogue AMD3100 has been studied in difficult to mobilize patients with some promise. Cytokines such as stem cell factor (SCF), interleukin-3 (IL-3), and PIXY 321 have been used investigationally for mobilization of progenitor cells without success.

Mobilization Agent	Dosage and Duration
Filgrastim (G-CSF)	10 mcg/kg/day SubQ for 5-7 days or until target WBC; dose escalation to 16-32 mcg/kg/day has been used to improve inadequate mobilization
Sargramostim (GM-CSF)	250 mg/m²/day SubQ for 5-7 days or until target WBC
Etoposide (VP-16)	2 g/m² I.V. over 2 hours followed in 24 hours by G-CSF or GM-CSF until target WBC
Cyclophosphamide	4 g/m² (range of 1.5-7 g/m²) I.V. over 2 hours followed at 24 hours by G-CSF 5-10 mcg/kg/day until target WBC; higher doses are also used (7 g/m²)
Cytarabine plus etoposide	2 g/m² I.V. q12h x 8 doses + 40 mg/kg VP-16 over 4 days then G-CSF 10 mcg/kg/day from day 14 until cells collected

Historically, the bone marrow was the primary source of hematopoietic stem cells for transplantation and it still represents an equivalent, if not better stem cell source in the setting of allogeneic transplantation. The bone marrow contains populations of hematopoietic cells ranging from the pluripotent stem cell, early progenitor cells, and later, more differentiated progenitor cells that all exist within and are supported by the bone marrow stroma (matrix composed of connective tissue, reticuloendothelial cells, adipose cells). Compared to blood, the concentration of T-lymphocytes is significantly lower in the marrow. Bone marrow can be harvested by removing an adequate volume of marrow (approximately 10 mL/kg) from the posterior iliac crests of the donor or patient. This is generally done in an operating room and requires general or local anesthesia. Bone marrow collected for autologous transplantation is processed in a cryopreservation laboratory and frozen until the day of transplantation. Common medical risks to the donor of bone marrow include the risks of undergoing anesthesia, and transient moderate pain in the area of cell harvesting. Severe anemia can also develop. The frequency of life-threatening complications, which have included thromboembolic disorders, aspiration pneumonia, and cardiac dysrhythmias, is ≤0.3%. Hematopoietic engraftment (normalization of the peripheral white blood cell count) occurs earlier following peripheral stem cell transplantation than following bone marrow transplantation. However, chronic graft versus host disease (GVHD) risk is lower with bone marrow.

Umbilical cord blood (UCB) is another source of hematopoietic progenitor cells. The product, which is harvested from the placenta and umbilical cord immediately after birth, can be processed and transplanted or frozen for future use. The product obtained from UCB contains a high proportion of pluripotent stem cells, and natural killer cells, and a low proportion of mature lymphocytes. The time to engraftment is generally longer following UCB transplantation than following hematopoietic stem cell transplantation when peripheral blood or bone marrow is harvested and infused. Moreover, UCB transplantation is generally reserved for children and small adults because the number of stem cells that can be collected from cord blood may be inadequate to support timely engraftment for larger patients. The risk for severe GVHD is lower with UCB even when HLA matching is not perfect. The process of harvesting UCB does not present a medical risk to the donor, because the actual collection of cells is done after the placenta is extruded as part of the birthing process.

The hematopoietic progenitor cells may be treated prior to transplantation to eradicate tumor cell contamination in the product following autologous donation or reduce the number of T lymphocytes that may promote graft-versus-host disease in an allogeneic recipient. The term purging refers to the removal of tumor cells by various techniques such as binding to specific monoclonal antibodies or incubation with cytotoxic drugs, such as 4-hydroperoxycyclophosphamide, that spare the immature stem cells. *Ex vivo* T lymphocyte reduction, also known as T-cell depletion, is generally achieved using monoclonal antibodies directed against surface proteins expressed on T lymphocytes. An alternative to purging or T lymphocyte depletion is the application of positive selection techniques, which remove the CD34+ cells (CD34 is a marker for the hematopoietic stem and progenitor cells) for use and discards the remaining cells. Engraftment is generally delayed following transplantation of hematopoietic progenitor cells that have undergone *ex vivo* purging, T-cell depletion, or positive selection of CD34+ cells.

AUTOLOGOUS MYELOABLATIVE TRANSPLANTATION

Chemotherapy selection for this type of SCT is based on three important principles:

1. Certain drugs such as alkylating agents and etoposide exhibit steep dose-response curves when used to treat susceptible malignancies. Therefore, when the dose-limiting adverse effect of these drugs is myelosuppression, high doses can be administered with hematopoietic stem cell rescue to achieve high response rates.

HEMATOPOIETIC STEM CELL TRANSPLANTATION
(Continued)

2. High doses of chemotherapy with nonoverlapping major organ toxicity can be combined without compromising dose.

3. Cryopreserved bone marrow and/or blood progenitor cells can rescue the patient from the myeloablative effects of the high-dose chemotherapy.

Administration of filgrastim or sargramostim following reinfusion of the autologous hematopoietic progenitor cells can significantly shorten the duration of neutropenia associated with myeloablative chemotherapy (refer to filgrastim or sargramostim monographs for dosing, etc). The hematopoietic recovery period following SCT is generally 1-2 weeks, which is shorter than that for bone marrow or UCB transplants which require 2-4 weeks. The monocytes and neutrophils engraft first followed by the platelets about a week later. The most common complications associated with autologous SCT are febrile neutropenia, serum electrolyte abnormalities, infection, bleeding, gastrointestinal toxicities (mucositis, nausea, vomiting, and diarrhea), and less commonly, other organ toxicities that are related to the specific chemotherapy administered. The following table lists commonly used chemotherapy agents with their dose-limiting toxicities in SCT.

Chemotherapy	Standard Dose	Maximum SCT Dose as Single Agent	Maximum SCT Dose in Combination	Dose-Limiting Toxicity
Busulfan (oral)	4 mg/d	16 mg/kg	16 mg/kg	GI, liver (VOD), CNS (seizure), pulmonary
Busulfan (I.V.)		12 mg/kg	12 mg/kg	GI, liver (VOD), CNS (seizure), pulmonary
Carboplatin	400 mg/m^2	2000 mg/m^2	1800 mg/m^2	Liver, renal
Carmustine	200 mg/m^2	800 mg/m^2	600 mg/m^2	Liver, pulmonary
Cisplatin	75-100 mg/m^2	180-200 mg/m^2	165-200 (in BEP) mg/m^2	Renal, neuropathy
Cyclophosphamide	50 mg/kg or 600-1875 mg/m^2	200 mg/kg or 7.5 g/m^2	200 mg/kg or 7.5 g/m^2	Cardiac, hemorrhagic cystitis, liver (VOD)
Etoposide	360 mg/m^2	2400 mg/m^2	2400 mg/m^2	GI, hypotension
Ifosfamide	5 g/m^2	18 g/m^2	16 g/m^2	CNS, renal
Melphalan	40 mg/m^2	220 mg/m^2	140-180 mg/m^2	GI
Mitoxantrone	12 mg/m^2/d x 3	90 mg/m^2	60-80 mg/m^2	GI, cardiac
Thiotepa	30-50 mg/m^2	1500 mg/m^2	900 mg/m^2	CNS, GI

ALLOGENEIC MYELOABLATIVE TRANSPLANTATION

The principle behind allogeneic myeloablative hematopoietic stem cell transplantation is that hematological disease can be cured by complete marrow ablation with profound immunosuppression so that the donor cells can engraft and successfully replace the patient's diseased hematopoietic system. Post-transplant immunosuppressive therapy is essential for successful engraftment of donor cells and prevention of graft versus host disease (GVHD). Preparative regimens for allogeneic transplantation are based on the need for both marrow ablation and immunosuppression. The most commonly used regimens are listed below.

Acronym	Chemotherapy Drugs (Total Dose)	Dosages and Scheduling
BuCy	Busulfan (12-16 mg/kg)	0.875-1 mg/kg/dose P.O. q6h x 16 doses; or 1 mg/kg/dose P.O. q6h x 12 doses; or 0.8 mg/kg I.V. q6h x 16 doses
	Cyclophosphamide (120 mg/kg)	60 mg/kg/dose I.V. q24h x 2 doses
FTBI/Cy, or CyTBI	Fractionated total body irradiation	1200-1500 cGy divided bid over 3-5 days
	Cyclophosphamide (120-200 mg/kg)	50 mg/kg/dose I.V. q24h x 4 doses or 60 mg/kg/dose I.V. q24h x 2 doses
Bu/Mel	Busulfan (16 mg/kg)	1 mg/kg/dose P.O. q6h x 16 doses
	Melphalan (135-140 mg/m^2)	45 mg/m^2/dose I.V. q24h x 3, or 140 mg/m^2 once
FTBI/Mel	Fractionated total body irradiation	1200-1500 cGy divided bid over 3-5 days
	Melphalan (135-140 mg/m^2)	45 mg/m^2/dose I.V. q24h x 2, or 70 mg/m^2/dose I.V. q24h x 2; or 140 mg/m^2 once
CyATG	Cyclophosphamide (200 mg/kg)	50 mg/kg/dose I.V. q24h x 4
	Lymphocyte immune globulin (90-160 mg/kg)	30-40 mg/kg/dose I.V. q24-48h x 3-4 doses

Lymphocyte immune globulin or antithymocyte globulin is included in the preparative regimen for patients with severe aplastic anemia. Lymphocyte immune globulin or antithymocyte globulin is often added to the preparative regimen for allogeneic transplants when the donor and recipient are immunologically mismatched or unrelated, and for umbilical cord blood transplants. This added immunosuppression improves engraftment and may decrease acute GVHD.

Graft versus host disease (GVHD) is an immune-mediated reaction initiated by donor T-cell recognition of recipient tissues as nonself. GVHD which occurs before 100 days post-transplant is called acute GVHD, and after this time it is called chronic GVHD. Acute GVHD primarily affects the skin, gastrointestinal tract, and liver. It is graded based on extent of organ involvement from grade I (mild) to grade IV (life-threatening). Chronic GVHD affects the skin, gastrointestinal tract, liver, and other organs and tissues including the lungs, lacrimal glands, and connective tissue. Chronic GVHD is generally graded as limited or extensive disease. Mortality from this toxicity ranges from 10% to 30%. There is a strong positive correlation between development of acute or chronic GVHD and decreased risk of malignancy recurrence due to associated graft vs malignancy effect.

Given the high morbidity and mortality associated with severe GVHD, post-transplant care is directed to prevent this complication. A combination of 2-3 immunosuppressants is used to prevent GVHD. The selection of prophylactic immunosuppressants used is based on the degree of risk for GVHD and the risk of malignant relapse. In general, as the depth and duration of immunosuppression increase so does the risk of malignant relapse, and infectious disease. Commonly used prophylactic

HEMATOPOIETIC STEM CELL TRANSPLANTATION
(Continued)

immunosuppressants include cyclosporine or tacrolimus plus methotrexate, with addition of a methylprednisolone for patients at high risk for GVHD.

GVHD Prophylactic Agents	Usual Dose and Schedule
Cyclosporine	2.5-4 mg/kg/day I.V. continuous infusion or divided q12h over 2-6 hours. Dose adjust according to toxicity and blood concentrations. Convert to oral dose when appropriate.
Tacrolimus	0.03 mg/kg/day continuous infusion. Adjust dose according to toxicity and blood concentrations. Convert to oral dose when appropriate.
Methotrexate	15 mg/m^2/day on day + 1, 10 mg/m^2 on days +3, +6, and +11; give I.V. push, or "mini methotrexate" 5 mg/m^2/day IVP on days +1, +3, +6
Methylprednisolone	Variable; 0.5-1 mg/kg/day divided q6-12h then taper. May start +1 up to +7; increase dose for acute GVHD reactions.
Mycophenolate mofetil	1 g/dose I.V. or P.O. q12h; or 15 mg/kg/dose I.V. or P.O. q12h

Initial treatment of GVHD includes addition of a corticosteroid or a dosage increase of ongoing corticosteroid treatment. Additional agents used for the treatment of steroid-refractory acute GVHD include lymphocyte immune globulin or antithymocyte globulin, interleukin-2 receptor antagonists (basiliximab, daclizumab), tumor necrosis factor antagonists (etanercept, infliximab), sirolimus, pentostatin, and muromonab CD3. Additional agents used for the treatment of steroid-refractory chronic GVHD include thalidomide, pentostatin, PUVA (8-methoxypsoralen plus UV-A radiation), rituximab, and sirolimus.

Veno-occlusive disease (VOD) of the liver, also known as sinusoidal obstruction syndrome (SOS) may occur as a result of the pretransplant conditioning regimen. Patients with pre-existing liver disease, malignant involvement of the liver, and those previously treated with gemtuzumab ozogamicin are at increased risk for this complication. VOD, which usually presents within the first three weeks after transplant, results from obstruction of blood flow in the small hepatic veins. Signs and symptoms include right upper quadrant pain, hepatomegaly, weight gain, ascites, hyperbilirubinemia, and thrombocytopenia. Treatment options include supportive care, alteplase (has a high incidence of bleeding complications), antithrombin III, and defibrotide (an investigational antithrombotic agent with no system effect on coagulation). Low-dose heparin or ursodiol have been used for VOD prophylaxis.

Allogeneic stem cell transplantation is associated with a wide range of infectious complications that occur during identifiable time periods after the transplant. The early period of neutropenia is most commonly associated with bacterial infections, fungal infections (*Candida* species), and possibly herpes simplex virus (HSV) reactivation. *Pneumocystis pneumoniae* (PCP) risk increases with duration of immunosuppressive therapy. Other life-threatening infections typically occurring 2-3 months post-transplant include aspergillosis and CMV (disseminated or pneumonitis). Other serious atypical viral and fungal infections can also be seen at this later time.

Prophylaxis for certain infections is routine while others are treated when they are diagnosed. Trimethoprim-sulfamethoxazole is given during the preparative regimen as a selective gut decontaminant, and then restarted after hematopoietic recovery on a 2-3 times weekly schedule as PCP prophylaxis. The major concern with this drug is the myelosuppressive effect. Fluoroquinolones may be used as selective gut decontamination. Fungal prophylaxis is routinely given as well. This consists of either a daily low dose amphotericin B (0.15-0.25 mg/kg) or fluconazole 100-400 mg daily. Inhalation amphotericin B can also be used to decrease risk of pulmonary aspergillosis. Acyclovir is routinely used to prevent HSV reinfection. The role of acyclovir for prevention of CMV infection is controversial. Some centers routinely prescribe acyclovir immediately following the transplant for prevention of CMV or HSV infection. After cellular recovery, the patient may be switched to ganciclovir therapy. Ganciclovir is not used earlier due to the risk of graft failure. The role of antibacterial prophylaxis or gut decontamination varies with transplant centers but is often used in some form.

Hematopoietic growth factors (filgrastim or sargramostim) are usually administered after infusion of allogeneic donor blood cells. The doses range from 5-10 mcg/kg/day and administration is begun either on day 0 or +1 or may be delayed up to 6 days post cell infusion. The colony stimulating factors are discontinued when neutrophil recovery reaches some target number (5000-10,000/μL has been used).

NONMYELOABLATIVE TRANSPLANTS

Nonmyeloablative hematopoietic stem cell transplants are a new and largely investigational approach to the treatment of malignant and nonmalignant diseases. Clinical trials and case series describe use of nonmyeloablative hematopoietic stem cell transplantation for the following diseases: Congenital immunodeficiency syndromes, acute myelogenous leukemia, myelodysplastic syndrome, acute lymphocytic leukemia, multiple myeloma, non-Hodgkin's lymphoma, Hodgkin's disease, sickle cell disease, renal cell carcinoma, and various advanced solid tumors. Most of the published studies and case series report use of this procedure in patients with relapsed or refractory disease, elderly patients, or those unable to tolerate myeloablative preparative regimens.

The theory supporting nonmyeloablative transplantation is that nonmyeloablative, but sufficiently immunosuppressive conditioning regimens, can lead to a state of mixed chimerism in the recipient, which gradually converts to full donor chimerism. Even the chimeric engraftment will support a graft-versus-malignancy effect. The preparative regimens used for nonmyeloablative hematopoietic stem cell transplantation, which are termed "reduced-intensity preparative regimens", induce profound immunosuppression without total obliteration of the recipient's bone marrow. This supports chimeric engraftment, which involves engraftment of transplanted allogeneic hematopoietic progenitor cells in the presence of recipient hematopoietic cells. Complete donor engraftment, also known as 100% donor chimerism, occurs when all of the detectable hematopoietic cells are of donor origin. Complete donor chimerism occurring within 30-90 days following transplantation is generally associated with disease response. Because antitumor effects of nonmyeloablative allogeneic transplants appear somewhat late, 2-3

HEMATOPOIETIC STEM CELL TRANSPLANTATION
(Continued)

months after the procedure, patients with active or poorly controlled malignancies do not appear to be good candidates for this type of transplantation.

The preparative regimens used for nonmyeloablative hematopoietic stem cell transplantation are associated with less regimen-related toxicity than myeloablative preparative regimens. This provides the impetus for studying use of nonmyeloablative hematopoietic stem cell transplantation in patients unable to tolerate the myeloablative preparative regimens, such as the elderly, or patients with an extensive history of chemotherapy treatment, impaired major organ function, or comorbid conditions. Examples of reduced-intensity preparative regimens are listed in the following table.

Acronym	Chemotherapy Drugs (Total Dose)	Dosages and Scheduling
Flu/ATG	Lymphocyte immune globulin 40 mg/kg (Atgam®)	10 mg/kg/day I.V. on 4 consecutive days
	Antithymoglobulin 10 mg/kg (Thymoglobulin®)	2.5 mg/kg/day I.V. on 4 consecutive days
	Fludarabine 125 mg/m²	25 mg/m²/day I.V.on 5 consecutive days
FC-ATG	Fludarabine 125 mg/m²	25 mg/m²/day I.V. on days -6 to -2
	Cyclophosphamide 120 mg/kg	60 mg/kg/day I.V. on days -3 and -2
	Lymphocyte immune globulin 60 mg/kg (Atgam®)	20 mg/kg/day I.V. on 3 consecutive days
TBI/Flu	Total body irradiation 4 Gy	2 Gy/day on days -8 and -7
	Fludarabine 125 mg/m²	25 mg/m²/day I.V. on days -6 to -2
Flu/Mel/ATG	Fludarabine 125 mg/m²	25 mg/m²/day I.V. on days -6 to -2
	Melphalan 140-180 mg/m²	70-90 mg/m²/day I.V. on days -3 and -2
	Lymphocyte immune globulin 120 mg/kg (Atgam®)	30 mg/kg/day I.V. on days -4 to -1
Bu/Flu/ATG	Busulfan 8 mg/kg	1 mg/kg/dose P.O. q6h X8 doses on days -6 and -5
	Fludarabine 125 mg/m²	25 mg/m²/day I.V. on days -6 to -2
	Antithymocyte globulin (Fresnius) 10 mg/kg	2.5 mg/kg/day I.V. on 4 consecutive days
Cy/Flu/TBI	Cyclophosphamide 50 mg/kg	50 mg/kg I.V. on day -6
	Fludarabine 200 mg/m²	40 mg/m²/day I.V. on days -6 to -2
	TBI 200 cGy	TBI 200 cGy on day -1

GVHD prophylaxis generally includes cyclosporine or tacrolimus plus mycophenolate mofetil. Treatment of moderate-to-severe GVHD is similar to the approach taken for treatment of GVHD following myeloablative allogeneic hematopoietic stem cell transplantation. Most complications following nonmyeloablative hematopoietic stem cell transplantation are related to GVHD and the immunosuppression required for treatment of GVHD. Infectious complications from Cytomegalovirus, herpes virus, candidiasis, aspergillosis, and other atypical infections are common.

Selected Readings

Bacigalupo A, "Second EBMT Workshop on Reduced Intensity Allogeneic Hemopoietic Stem Cell Transplants (RI-HSCT)," *Bone Marrow Transplant*, 2002, 29:191-5.

Barker JN, Weisdorf DJ, DeFor TE, et al, "Rapid and Complete Donor Chimerism in Adult Recipients of Unrelated Donor Umbilical Cord Blood Transplantation After Reduced-Intensity Conditioning," *Blood*, 2003, 102(5):1915-9.

Cairo MS and Wagner JE, "Placental and/or Umbilical Cord Blood: An Alternative Source of Hematopoietic Stem Cells for Transplantation," *Blood*, 1997, 90:4665-78.

Champlin R, Khouri I, Anderlini P, et al, "Nonmyeloablative Preparative Regimens for Allogeneic Hematopoietic Transplantation," *Bone Marrow Transplant*, 2001, 27 Suppl 2:S13-22.

Copelan EA, "Hematopoietic Stem-Cell Transplantation," *N Engl J Med*, 2006, 354(17):1813-26.

Ho VT and Soiffer RJ, "The History and Future of T-Cell Depletion as Graft-Versus-Host Disease Prophylaxis for Allogeneic Hematopoietic Stem Cell Transplantation," *Blood*, 2001, 98:3192-204.

Klingebiel T and Schlegel PG, "GVHD: Overview on Pathophysiology, Incidence, Clinical and Biological Features," *Bone Marrow Transplant*, 1998, 21 (Suppl 2):S45-9.

Kumar S, DeLeve LD, Kamath PS, et al, "Hepatic Veno-Occlusive Disease (Sinusoidal Obstruction Syndrome) After Hematopoietic Stem Cell Transplantation," *Mayo Clin Proc*, 2003, (78):589-98.

Mogul MJ, "Unrelated Cord Blood Transplantation Vs Matched Unrelated Donor Bone Marrow Transplantation: The Risks and Benefits of Each Choice," *Bone Marrow Transplant*, 2000, 25 (Suppl 2):S58-60.

Pegram AA and Kennedy LD, "Prevention and Treatment of Veno-Occlusive Disease," *Ann Pharmacother*, 2001, 35(7-8):935-42.

Rowe JM, Ciobanu N, Ascensao J, et al, "Recommended Guidelines for the Management of Autologous and Allogeneic Bone Marrow Transplantation. A Report From the Eastern Cooperative Oncology Group (ECOG)," *Ann Intern Med*, 1994, 120:143-58.

Stiff P, "Mucositis Associated With Stem Cell Transplantation: Current Status and Innovative Approaches to Management," *Bone Marrow Transplant* , 2001, 27 (Suppl 2):S3-S11.

Storb R, Deeg HJ, Whitehead J, et al, "Methotrexate and Cyclosporine Compared With Cyclosporine Alone for Prophylaxis of Acute Graft Versus Host Disease After Marrow Transplantation for Leukemia," *N Engl J Med*, 1986, 314:729-35.

Vogelsang GB and Arai S, "Mycophenolate Mofetil for the Prevention and Treatment of Graft-Versus-Host Disease Following Stem Cell Transplantation: Preliminary Findings," *Bone Marrow Transplant*, 2001, 27:1255-62.

DRUG DEVELOPMENT PROCESS

DRUG SYNTHESIS

A rational and empiric approach is used in the discovery of drugs. Compounds may be selected which inhibit certain molecular targets. These compounds may be modified based on target inhibitor interactions. Increasingly, natural products are being studied as suitable compounds for anticancer therapy through molecular target screenings. Another screening technique is the use of human tumor cell lines, which have known characteristics with respect to drug response, growth factor dependence, oncogene expression, and other factors. The response patterns of these compounds is then compared against other agents.

PRECLINICAL PHARMACOLOGY

Studies in mice, rats, and dogs are conducted to provide pharmacokinetic and pharmacologic information prior to testing in humans. Pharmacokinetic studies provide a rationale for dose escalation in humans. Simultaneously, drug formulation studies begin, looking at solubility issues and drug delivery systems. Animal toxicology studies must occur before testing in humans. Initially, acute toxicity in mice is studied to determine the LD 10, the dose that is lethal to 10% of the mice. Then, organ-specific toxicity is studied in rodents. Toxicology studies must use the same drug schedule that will be utilized in humans.

INVESTIGATIONAL NEW DRUG (IND) APPLICATION (FDA 1571)

An IND must be submitted prior to clinical trials. It contains all of the preclinical data, proposed clinical protocol, investigator's brochure, and manufacturing information. There is a waiting period of 30 days after submission, after which clinical trials may start unless the FDA asks for changes. Emergency Use or Compassionate IND makes investigational drugs available before IND submission. This is used only for life-saving therapy in refractory patients. Treatment IND (group C drugs) makes investigational drugs available for use under an approved protocol before a new drug application is approved.

An institutional review board (IRB) must approve all phases of clinical drug trials. The purpose of an IRB is to review clinical trials to assure that patients will not be exposed to unnecessary risks and that there is a scientific basis for the research protocol.

PHASE I STUDIES

A protocol for drug administration that will be used in the Phase I trial is required in the IND. Additionally, an informed consent document is required. The purpose of the Phase I study is to characterize pharmacology, pharmacokinetics, pharmacodynamics, maximum tolerated dose (MTD), drug-related toxicity, and dose-limiting toxicity (DLT). Unlike other Phase I trials in normal human subjects, patients with advanced cancer refractory to treatment and with normal organ function, are utilized for Phase I oncology studies. The most common Phase I oncology study involves a new cytotoxic drug at a starting dose $1/10$ the LD10 dose in the most sensitive animal model. The dose is increased in a stepwise fashion until the DLT is reached in >33% of a patient cohort. The dose at which <33% of patients have DLT is utilized in Phase II studies.

PHASE II STUDIES

Phase II trials look at drug safety and efficacy in a group of patients with a disease the drug is intended to treat. Data is collected on adverse effects and response to the therapy, although tumor response is not the objective. The starting dose is the safest dose found in Phase I trials as detailed above.

PHASE III STUDIES

Phase III studies involve a larger number of patients with a particular tumor. Patients are randomized to the new treatment or the current standard of care. A placebo arm is used for Phase III analysis of novel treatments for which there is no comparable standard of care. Data is collected on efficacy, safety, drug interactions, affect on survival curve, etc. As was the case with gemcitabine in pancreatic cancer, a clinical benefit response may be an endpoint that is measured.

NEW DRUG APPLICATION (NDA)

All of the data collected from these trials is collated and submitted as a New Drug Application (NDA). The FDA has 60 days after an NDA filing to reject the NDA due to gross deficiencies. It then has 180 days (sometimes longer) to complete a full review.

PHASE IV STUDIES

Phase IV studies are postmarketing studies which look at a drug's performance in a clinical setting. An IND is not necessary unless the drug is being studied for an indication not present in the package labeling. Phase IV studies are large, multicenter studies that study a drug's use for a specific labeled indication. These studies may provide valuable information on long-term effects of the drug and potential adverse reactions that were not well documented in the limited number of patients in preclinical trials. In addition, restrictions on eligibility criteria will be less strict than in preclinical trials, providing information on efficacy and safety in a wide population.

ACCELERATED NDA REVIEW

In order to decrease the approval process for drugs with significant therapeutic gains, the FDA has instituted some short-track approval mechanisms. The FDA and sponsor may begin meeting as soon as Phase I trials are completed. NDA approval may be based on expanded Phase II trials. Parallel tracks may collect data from open-label noncontrolled studies as well as Phase II studies. Preclinical data from Europe and Japan may be submitted in some cases. Using surrogate endpoints, which may improve the patient's quality of life but do not show measurable disease improvement, may accelerate the approval process especially in diseases with little treatment options.

The FDA, whose purpose is to regulate drug development and manufacturing, and sales and marketing, oversees this entire process. The IND

DRUG DEVELOPMENT PROCESS *(Continued)*

requires FDA approval before the drug is tested in humans. The NDA is reviewed and approved, often with the help of advisory committees composed of non-FDA members. Postmarketing surveillance which includes voluntary reporting of adverse drug reactions and drug recalls are also of great interest to the FDA. It is important to recognize that this entire approval process is constantly changing to help both patients and investigators.

Selected Readings

Dunsworth T, "Drug Regulatory Process," *Pharmacotherapy Self-Assessment Program*, 2nd ed, Carter BL, Angaran DM, Lake KD, et al, eds, Kansas City, KS: American College of Clinical Pharmacy, 1996.

Grever MR and Chabner BA, "Cancer Drug Discovery and Development," *Cancer: Principles & Practice of Oncology*, 5th ed, DeVita VT, Hellman S, Rosenberg SA, eds, Philadelphia, PA: Lippincott-Raven Publishers, 1997.

Simon RM, "Design and Analysis of Clinical Trials," *Cancer: Principles & Practice of Oncology*, 5th ed, DeVita VT, Hellman S, Rosenberg SA, eds, Philadelphia, PA: Lippincott-Raven Publishers, 1997.

INVESTIGATIONAL DRUG SERVICE

An Investigational Drug Service (IDS) is an organized pharmacy-based service that controls the inventory, preparation, and dispensation of investigational drugs. Investigational drugs are administered only to patients who have, in an informed manner, signed a consent form to participate in the particular study using these investigational drugs. A patient formally enrolled to participate in a clinical study is known as a "subject". Investigational drugs used in this manner are frequently new drugs undergoing Phase I, Phase II, or Phase III evaluation prior to FDA approval for a medical purpose. However, investigational drugs can be commercially available drugs used under the direction of a protocol for a nonlabeled indication or as a supportive measure for a new drug. An IDS should be under the direction of an appropriately trained pharmacist with technical support as appropriate for the workload.

A study protocol is the document describing the scientific background providing the basis for doing the study, specific study objectives and endpoints, treatments and tests done as part of the study, study drug information, statistical methodology, means for assurance of patient confidentiality, and the subject consent form. Some studies provide an Investigator's Drug Brochure, which presents very detailed and comprehensive study drug information. Each study is assigned a unique study number, eg, SWOG 9923, that is frequently a truncation of the year of study development and its position within a series of studies. Study protocols and Investigator's Drug Brochures are confidential, and frequently proprietary documents. Prior to study activation at an institution, it must be approved by the institutional investigational review board. All departments needed to provide personnel or resources for study implementation should review the protocol prior to study implementation to ensure that study activities can reasonably be supported with available resources. The IDS pharmacist should scrutinize each study protocol prior to study activation to determine the impact of study implementation on pharmacy department personnel and resources.

Investigational drug inventory must be stored at the appropriate conditions, and separate from commercial drug inventory. An ongoing drug-specific inventory must be maintained for all investigational drugs housed within a pharmacy. Some studies will require lot number-specific, or subject-specific inventory for study drugs. Minimal inventory documentation should include study identification number, study drug dosage form and lot number, study drug expiration date or date of preparation, transaction date, transaction type (receipt, dispensation, return, waste), and current number of dosage forms available. Although it may be kept separately from individual study drug inventories, the pharmacy must maintain an ongoing refrigerator, freezer, and ambient temperature log for study drug storage facilities. All inventory records should be kept in a secure and accessible location by the pharmacy, even after study closure. In addition, study drug should be shipped directly to the Pharmacy Department rather than the Principal Investigator's office. This will ensure that the Pharmacy Department has shipping receipts and shipment invoices to verify receipt of the packaged contents. This will also reduce the possibility of prolonged study drug storage at inappropriate conditions, such as the institutional loading dock.

INVESTIGATIONAL DRUG SERVICE   *(Continued)*

Study drug preparation should be described in the protocol or Investigator's Drug Brochure. Unfortunately, extensive admixture stability and compatibility information is not available for many injectable study drugs. Subsequently, these may have to be prepared on a dose-by-dose basis. Departmental inservices to acquaint professional and technical personnel with each new study are helpful tools for increasing staff familiarity with new studies and study drug preparation. Pharmacy department personnel should have 24-hour access to information about study drug preparation. Ideally, this is in the form of an easy-to-read and readily accessible fast facts sheet. Study protocols and Investigator's Drug Brochures should also be available to Pharmacy Department personnel around the clock for questions that arise outside of standard business hours. The Investigational Drug Service must develop a plan such that study drug doses are labeled in the manner directed by the study, are consistent with institutional policies and procedures, and are in accordance with state and federal regulations.

Study drug doses prepared for administration within a hospital or clinic should be dispensed directly to the study or institutional nurse for delivery to the patient's bedside, or placed directly into the subject's medication bin for delivery to the nursing unit. Generally, study drug doses should not be intermixed with standard medication doses transported via the routine intra-institutional delivery system. Although the risk of inadvertent misplacement of a study drug dose may be low, the consequences can have ethical and legal implications. As an example, a study drug dose inadvertently transported to the wrong nursing unit may be mistakenly administered to a patient with a name similar to that of the actual study subject. In other words, the study drug dose could be administered to a person who did not consent to receive an investigational drug.

Pharmacy support of blinded studies can involve additional responsibilities and challenges. Pharmacy-related activities may include randomization (treatment assignment) of subjects when the Principal Investigator and other study personnel are blinded to the study treatment. Randomization for treatment assignment can be done for some studies by simply following a list of treatment assignments sequentially for consecutive subjects. However, randomization for some multicenter studies may require contacting a central randomization center with provision of patient-specific information. When pharmacy activities include randomization, it is important for the Investigational Drug Service to ensure that a workable plan is in place prior to study activation. Moreover, labeling of blinded study drug doses can be challenging since the traditional role of pharmacy labeling is to provide a completely clear description of the dosage form. In contrast, to maintain a study blind, the specific contents of a study dosage form must be omitted from the pharmacy label. Several approaches have been taken to balance study methods with institutional and legislative requirements. As an example, for a blinded study, protocol #9872, evaluating the efficacy of fluconazole 200 mg versus placebo (0.9% NaCl 100 mL), the following labeling techniques can be utilized to identify the dosage form: "fluconazole 200 mg or placebo", "fluconazole study drug", "protocol #9872 study drug". Nursing personnel should be consulted regarding the proposed labeling of blinded study drug to ensure that the labeling used is compatible with medication administration records maintained by nursing staff.

The Investigational Drug Service determines fair charges for Pharmacy Department personnel time and resources utilized in the support of study activities. As a rule, routine pharmacy charges to the patient's bill, cannot be generated for investigational new drugs, or study drugs provided free-of-charge by the study sponsor. The Investigation Drug Service must charge the study funds. This is generally achieved at the institutional level by generating charges to the local Principal Investigator or Clinical Trials Office.

SAFE HANDLING OF HAZARDOUS DRUGS

Due to their inherent toxicity, particularly mutagenicity and carcinogenicity, there is concern about the risks of long-term, low level exposure to a number of drugs, particularly antineoplastic agents. The possible risk to healthcare providers who are responsible for preparation and administration of such agents has been a subject of much debate, but few definite answers. Despite years of research and literally thousands of publications on the topic, there is

- no definitive evidence of a causal relationship between prolonged exposure to low levels of antineoplastic agents in the workplace and development of malignancies.

- no evidence of health problems among healthcare personnel who handle hazardous drugs that are not antineoplastic agents.

- no evidence documenting an actual increase in the incidence of malignant diseases among healthcare workers who handle hazardous agents.

- no estimate of "safe" or "nonhazardous" exposure level.

- no agreement on the definition of a hazardous drug or which drugs are hazardous (see Tables 1 and 2).

- *no conclusive evidence that exposure is not hazardous.*

In the absence of convincing evidence that healthcare personnel are not at risk, prudence requires the presumption that there is some degree of risk and employees should employ appropriate protective measures when handling hazardous agents. While usually considered as applicable primarily to handling antineoplastic agents, or in oncology clinics, these principles should be applied to *all hazardous agents throughout the entire institution.*

The potential for many antineoplastic agents to cause secondary malignancies in patients was identified in the 1960s and 1970s. Coupled with evidence of some drugs' carcinogenicity in animals, this information raised the question of possible adverse effects from prolonged low level exposure. In the late 1970s and 1980s, a large number of anecdotal reports of various side effects and adverse reactions in nurses, pharmacists, and pharmacy technicians involved in the preparation and administration of antineoplastic therapy began to appear in the literature. These were followed by reports of increased urine mutagenicity, chromosome abnormalities, changes in immune function, and detectable blood or urine drug levels in personnel who routinely handled antineoplastic agents. As a result of these concerns, a number of groups issued guidelines intended to minimize exposure to antineoplastic agents in the workplace. By the end of the 1980s, a variety of organizations, including the Occupational Safety and Health Administration (OSHA), American Society of Hospital (now Health-System) Pharmacists (ASHP), the National Institutes of Health (NIH), and the National Study Commission on Cytotoxic Exposure had all issued documents addressing the proper handling of cytotoxic agents by healthcare personnel. Most of the early guidelines acknowledged the paucity and low quality of the available data, and recommended further research to define the actual risks.

During the remainder of the 1980s and 1990s, a number of studies and reports attempting to delineate the nature of the risk, and the appropriate safety measures to be taken were published. The vast majority of these were uncontrolled trials involving very small numbers of individuals, usually at a single institution. One analysis of 63 studies published between 1979 and 1996 concluded the methods used were not "sufficiently reliable or reproducible for routine monitoring of exposure in the workplace." It also noted that only 45% of the biological studies were positive for exposure. Forty-eight percent showed no exposure, and 7% were equivocal. Seventeen percent of the urine analysis studies were also negative. The studies reviewed included many that are cited by the various safety guidelines to support common protective measures such as biologic safety cabinets (BSCs), gloves, and gowns.

The nature and magnitude of the risk has never been properly delineated. Due to the nature of the problem, there has never been a large scale, prospective controlled trial to determine the efficacy of the various protective measures employed. As a result, there is no known threshold of safety for exposure to these agents; nor have any reliable monitoring techniques to assess exposure been developed. Most guidelines are therefore based on an assumption of "zero tolerance" – any exposure is hazardous, and must be avoided. Achieving the appropriate balance between necessary protection for personnel who must work with these agents and over-reaction to the threat remains a challenge.

Simply defining hazardous agents and identifying effective protective measures remains a problem. There is no agreement among various agencies as to the definition of a hazardous agent or which agents should be classified as hazardous. The Environmental Protection Agency (EPA), National Institute for Occupational Safety and Health (NIOSH), and American Society of Health-System Pharmacists (ASHP) all have guidelines for handling hazardous agents, but there is little agreement, and considerable variation among these guidelines. The EPA lists 723 chemicals as hazardous. Only eight are antineoplastic agents; an additional 16 non-antineoplastic agents are listed as hazardous. NIOSH has 136 drugs on its "sample" list of which 52 are nonantineoplastic agents (see Tables 1 and 2). There are over 85 agents listed in the American Society of Health-System Pharmacists AHFS Category 10:00, which is one of the NIOSH criteria for listing a drug as "hazardous." Some manufacturers also recommend special precautions for handling specific drugs (see Table 2).

SAFE HANDLING OF HAZARDOUS DRUGS *(Continued)*

Table 1. Criteria for Defining Hazardous Agents

EPA	NIOSH	ASHP
Meets one of the following criteria: Ignitability: Create fire under certain conditions or are spontaneously combustible and have a flash point <600°C Corrosivity: Acids or bases (pH ≤2 or ≥12.5) capable of corroding metal containers Reactivity: Unstable under "normal" conditions; can cause explosions, toxic fumes, gases, or vapors when mixed with water Toxicity characteristic: When disposed of on land, contaminated liquid may drain or leach from the waste and pollute ground water	Manufacturer suggests use of special techniques in handling administration, or disposal Genotoxic Carcinogenic Teratogenic, developmental toxicity, or reproductive toxicant	Genotoxic Carcinogenic Teratogenic or impairs fertility Causes serious organ or other toxic manifestation at low doses
OR	Toxic to an organ system at low doses	
Appears on one of the following lists: F: Wastes from certain common or industrial manufacturing processes from nonspecific sources K: Wastes from certain specific industries from specific sources P: Wastes from pure or commercial grade formulations of certain specific unused chemicals U: Wastes from pure or commercial grade formulations of certain specific unused chemicals	New drugs with structural and toxicity profiles similar to existing hazardous drugs	

Table 2. Drugs Listed as Hazardous

EPA

Antineoplastic

Arsenic trioxide
Chlorambucil
Cyclophosphamide
Daunomycin

Melphalan
Mitomycin
Streptozocin
Uracil mustard

Nonantineoplastic

Chloral hydrate
Chloroform
Dichlorodifluoromethane
Diethylstilbestrol
Epinephrine
Formaldehyde
Hexachlorophene
Lindane
Mercury
Nicotine
Nitroglycerin
Paraldehyde

Phenacetin
Phenol
Phenteramine
Physostigmine
Physostigmine salicylate
Reserpine
Resorcinol
Saccharin
Selenium sulfide
Trichloromonofluoromethane
Warfarin

NIOSH

Antineoplastic

Aldesleukin
Alemtuzumab
Altretamine
Amsacrine
Anastrozole
Arsenic trioxide
Asparaginase
Azacitidine
Bexarotene
Bicalutamide
Bleomycin
Busulfan
Capecitabine
Carboplatin
Carmustine
Chlorambucil
Cisplatin
Cladribine
Cyclophosphamide
Cytarabine
Dacarbazine
Dactinomycin
Daunorubicin HCl
Denileukin

Docetaxel
Doxorubicin
Epirubicin
Estramustine
Etoposide
Exemestane
Floxuridine
Fludarabine
Fluorouracil
Flutamide
Fulvestrant
Gemcitabine
Gemtuzumab ozogamicin
Goserelin
Hydroxyurea
Ibritumomab
Idarubicin
Ifosfamide
Imatinib
Interferon alfa-2a
Interferon alfa-2b
Interferon alfa-n1
Interferon alfa-n3
Irinotecan

SAFE HANDLING OF HAZARDOUS DRUGS *(Continued)*

Letrozole
Leuprolide
Lomustine
Mechlorethamine
Melphalan
Mercaptopurine
Methotrexate
Mitomycin
Mitotane
Mitoxantrone
Nilutamide
Oxaliplatin
Paclitaxel
Pegaspargase
Pentostatin
Perphosphamide
Pipobroman
Piritrexim isethionate
Plicamycin
Prednimustine

Procarbazine
Raltitrexed
Streptozocin
Tamoxifen
Temozolomide
Teniposide
Thalidomide
Thioguanine
Thiotepa
Topotecan
Toremifene
Tositumomab
Trimetrexate
Triptorelin
Uracil mustard
Valrubicin
Vinblastine
Vincristine
Vindesine
Vinorelbine

Nonantineoplastic

Alitretinoin
Azathioprine
BCG vaccine
Cetrorelix acetate
Chloramphenicol
Choriogonadotropin alfa
Cidofovir
Colchicine
Cyclosporine
Dienestrol
Diethylstilbestrol
Dinoprostone
Dutasteride
Ergonovine/methylergonovine
Estradiol
Estrogen-progestin combinations
Estrogens, conjugated
Estrogens, esterified
Estrone
Estropipate
Finasteride
Fluoxymesterone
Ganciclovir
Ganirelix acetate

Gonadotropin, chorionic
Leflunomide
Megestrol
Menotropins
Methyltestosterone
Mifepristone
Mycophenolate
Nafarelin
Oxytocin
Pentamidine
Podofilox
Podophyllum resin
Progesterone
Progestins
Raloxifene
Ribavirin
Tacrolimus
Testolactone
Testosterone
Tretinoin
Trifluridine
Valganciclovir
Vidarabine
Zidovudine

Reference: National Institute for Occupational Safety and Health (NIOSH), "Preventing Occupational Exposure to Antineoplastic and Other Hazardous Drugs in Health Care Settings," Available at: http://www.cdc.gov/niosh/docs/ 2004-165/2004-165d.html#o. Last accessed October 1, 2007

Product Labeling
(not on EPA or NIOSH lists)
Antineoplastic

Bortezomib

Clofarabine

Cytarabine liposomal

Dasatinib

Daunorubicin citrate (liposomal)

Decitabine

Dexrazoxane

Doxorubicin liposomal

Ixabepilone

Nelarabine

Paclitaxel protein bound

Pemetrexed

Vorinostat

Table 3. Sample Listing of Teratogenic Agents

Pregnancy Risk Factor X

Antineoplastic

Abarelix

Bexarotene

Bicalutamide

Goserelin

Lenalidomide

Leuprolide

Methotrexate

Sodium iodide I^{131}

Thalidomide

Tositumomab

Nonantineoplastic

Acetohydroxamic acid

Acitretin

Alprostadil

Atorvastatin

Bosentan

Carboprost tromethamine

Cetrorelix

Chorionic gonadotropin (recombinant)

Clomiphene

Danazol

Dihydroergotamine

Ergonovine

Ergotamine

Estazolam

Estradiol

Estrogens (conjugated A/synthetic)

Estrogens (conjugated/equine)

Estrogens (esterified)

Estropipate

Finasteride

Fluoxymesterone

Flurazepam

Fluvastatin

Follitropins

Ganirelix

Histrelin

Isotretinoin

Leflunomide

Levonorgestrel

Lovastatin

Lutropin alfa

Medroxyprogesterone

Megestrol

Menotropins

Methyltestosterone

Mifepristone

Miglustat

Misoprostol

Nafarelin

Nandrolone

Norethindrone

Norgestrel

Oxymetholone

Oxytocin

Podophyllum resin

Pravastatin

Quinine

Raloxifene

Ribavirin

Rosuvastatin

Simvastatin

Stanozolol

Tazarotene

Temazepam

Testosterone

Triazolam

Triptorelin

Warfarin

SAFE HANDLING OF HAZARDOUS DRUGS *(Continued)*

Pregnancy Risk Factor D

Antineoplastic

Alitretinoin
Altretamine
Aminoglutethimide
Anastrozole
Arsenic trioxide
Azacitidine
Bleomycin
Bortezomib
Busulfan
Capecitabine
Carboplatin
Carmustine
Chlorambucil
Cisplatin
Cladribine
Clofarabine
Cyclophosphamide
Cytarabine
Cytarabine (liposomal)
Dactinomycin
Dasatinib
Daunorubicin citrate (liposomal)
Daunorubicin hydrochloride
Decitabine
Dexrazoxane
Docetaxel
Doxorubicin
Doxorubicin (liposomal)
Epirubicin
Erlotinib
Etoposide
Etoposide phosphate
Exemestane
Floxuridine
Fludarabine
Fluorouracil
Flutamide
Fulvestrant
Gefitinib
Gemcitabine

Gemtuzumab ozogamicin
Hydroxyurea
Ibritumomab
Idarubicin
Ifosfamide
Imatinib
Irinotecan
Ixabepilone
Lapatinib
Letrozole
Lomustine
Mechlorethamine
Melphalan
Mercaptopurine
Mitomycin
Mitoxantrone
Nelarabine
Nilotinib
Oxaliplatin
Paclitaxel
Paclitaxel (protein bound)
Pemetrexed
Pentostatin
Procarbazine
Sorafenib
Streptozocin
Sunitinib
Tamoxifen
Temozolomide
Temsirolimus
Teniposide
Thioguanine
Thiotepa
Topotecan
Toremifene
Tretinoin
Vinblastine
Vincristine
Vinorelbine
Vorinostat

Nonantineoplastic

Alprazolam
Amiodarone
Amitriptyline & chlordiazepoxide
Amitriptyline & perphenazine
Amobarbital

Anthrax vaccine
Aspirin & codeine
Aspirin & dipyridamole
Aspirin & meprobamate
Atenolol

Atenolol & chlorthalidone	Paroxetine
Azathioprine	Penicillamine
Butabarbital	Perindopril erbumine
Clidinium & chlordiazepoxide	Phenobarbital
Demeclocycline	Potassium iodide
Doxycycline	Primidone
Efavirenz	Propoxyphene
Fosphenytoin	Propylthiouracil
Hydrocodone & aspirin	Secobarbital
Meprobamate	Streptomycin
Methimazole	Tetracycline
Minocycline	Tigecycline
Mycophenolate	Tolbutamide
Nicotine	Valproic acid & derivatives
Orphenadrine, aspirin & caffeine	Voriconazole
Oxycodone & aspirin	Zoledronic acid
Pamidronate	

In addition to the differences among the available guidelines, some criteria are extremely vague or broad, adding to the uncertainty. The NIOSH criterion "Acutely toxic to an organ system" could be applied to almost any drug. ASHP's "Causes serious organ or other toxic manifestation at low doses" could also apply to a large number of drugs not commonly considered "hazardous" to persons handling them. The NIOSH and ASHP criterion of "teratogenic" would apply to more than 60 agents, if only pregnancy risk category X is considered. If risk category D is also included in this definition, the list of hazardous agents increases (see Table 3). It should be noted however, that many estrogens are category X due to the fact that they are not indicated for use in pregnancy.

The EPA standard "Appears on one of the following lists" seems to be particularly subjective. Drugs appear on, and are removed from, the EPA lists in what appears a purely arbitrary manner. For example, cisplatin and dexamethasone have appeared on previous lists, but are not on the current one. Daunomycin and cyclophosphamide are listed as hazardous; other anthracyclines and ifosfamide are not. Inquiries to EPA have failed to identify why these changes were made; or why one drug in a class is considered hazardous, but other agents in that category are not.

Analysis of the problem has not completely clarified the risks. Rather, previously accepted practices are subject to question. A 1992 report on exposure of healthcare personnel to hazardous agents suggested that the standard biologic safety cabinets recommended for use when compounding hazardous drugs may not provide the desired level of protection. There is evidence suggesting rather than forming particles or aerosol droplets that could be trapped in a standard HEPA filter, some antineoplastic agents vaporize, yielding particles that cannot be trapped in the filter. This potential for vaporization may be a partial explanation for reports indicating detectable contamination of work surfaces in, and near, hazardous drug preparation areas. This information has led some institutions to begin investigating use of isolator cabinets and sealed preparation systems as replacements for the biologic cabinets.

SAFE HANDLING OF HAZARDOUS DRUGS *(Continued)*

A 1996 review of 64 studies of workplace exposure to cytotoxic drugs noted numerous methodologic flaws in study design and procedures. The report concluded the methods used to assess exposure in these studies were too nonspecific and insensitive to be reliable measures of exposure. One disturbing aspect of this is the fact that the studies and procedures found to be not sensitive enough to assess routine levels of exposure were the ones used as the basis for development of existing safety guidelines.

Several studies have found containers have detectable amounts of drug residue on them when they arrive in the pharmacy. These reports raise the concern that exposure may be a hazard originating at least partially outside the pharmacy; and that additional procedures for decontaminating drug containers upon arrival at the pharmacy may be necessary.

Guidelines and institutional policies for minimizing exposure to hazardous materials have been based on the presumption that environmental exposure to hazardous drugs occurs through three mechanisms:

- **inhalation** of drug dust or aerosolized droplets
- **absorption** through the skin
- **ingestion** of contaminated food or drink

Accordingly, the existing recommendations are heavily weighted toward the use of physical barriers as the primary means of reducing exposure. Among the commonly employed precautions are:

- **Separation:** Hazardous agents are often prepared in a limited number of areas which are separated, to the extent possible, from other drug preparation areas. Almost all institutions have a separate biologic safety cabinet reserved solely for the preparation of antineoplastic agents. Many institutions have a separate "oncology" drug preparation area or satellite pharmacy.

- **Biologic safety cabinets:** Use of a Class IIA or B biologic safety cabinet for the preparation of hazardous agents. Recent reports have questioned the efficacy of these cabinets, and some institutions have adopted the use of Isolator™ systems or special closed preparation systems for compounding hazardous agents.

- **Protective clothing:** Another almost universal precaution is the use of protective gloves, gowns, and eye protection while handling antineoplastic agents. If drug preparation is performed in a biologic safety cabinet equipped with a glass front, many institutions dispense with the requirement for wearing safety goggles.

- **Self-contained preparation systems:** Self-contained or "closed system" devices have been recommended to minimize workplace contamination. Similar systems have been incorporated into the packaging of injectable antibiotics for some time, but are not useful with other hazardous agents, such as antineoplastics, which are usually ordered in precise, individualized doses. Systems for preparation of hazardous agents are available. These are multicomponent systems that minimize aerosolization and spilling of drug solutions in the workplace. The PhaSeal® system is the prevalent system in the U.S. This system incorporates a double membrane enclosing an injection cannula. Several studies have documented decreased environmental contamination with the system. However there are some limitations to the system, most notably that it may not fit all sizes or types of vials, can not be used with drugs that are packaged in ampuls, and may leak if not attached perfectly.

- Several other safety systems for handling hazardous agents are available, including Genie™ vial access system, Tevadaptor™ system, Texium™ adaptor, and SmartSite® needleless valve system. Less information about the efficacy of these newer systems is available, nor have any direct comparisons among the various systems been published.

- **Training:** Some of the early reports attributed lower, or undetectable, levels of exposure to hazardous drugs to the experience level, or skill at aseptic technique, of the individual worker. Many institutions require some degree of training before personnel are allowed to handle hazardous agents. Although most of the published guidelines recommend personnel who handle hazardous agents have "appropriate" training and experience, none specify what should be included in such a program. Accordingly, the exact nature and length of the required training programs vary widely among institutions.

- **Monitoring:** Appropriate physical parameters for assessing exposure to hazardous drugs are not available. Although some institutions require periodic health monitoring, the definition of what constitutes an appropriate screening program, or how to interpret test results is completely unknown. Attempts to monitor the existence of hazardous materials in the work area have been slightly more successful. Assessment of airborne drug levels and surface contamination, in preparation cabinets, "secure" work areas and areas outside the hazardous drug area has been reported. Additionally, techniques for using ultraviolet light to detect occult drug spills, and assess individual's handling technique have been reported. Most of these techniques have not been developed sufficiently to be used in routine practice, and are still limited to the research setting.

- **Decontamination:** Drug containers should be examined upon their arrival at the pharmacy. Containers that show signs of damage should be handled carefully, and may require quarantine and decontamination before being placed in stock. Consideration should be given to the possible need to quarantine and decontaminate all containers of hazardous agents as a routine precaution.

- **Spills:** Assess spill to determine magnitude and limit access to area of spill. Spill kits are available to assist in clean up. Wear appropriate personal protective equipment (PPE), including protective gloves (2 pair), gown, and mask during spill cleanup. If spill contains broken glass fragments, place in container that will not puncture. Use spill pads to absorb liquids and use damp pads to absorb powders. Gradually work from areas that are less contaminated to areas of higher contamination. After contaminate is removed, rinse the area with water, clean with detergent, sodium hypochlorite and neutralizer. Place all contaminated materials, including PPE, in disposal bags and dispose of as hazardous waste (do not remove inner gloves until disposal bags are sealed, then dispose of inner gloves by sealing in a sealable bag). Wash hands using soap and water. For spills occurring in a BSC or isolator, wear gloves, remove broken glass (place in container that will not puncture), thoroughly clean and decontaminate, including drain/spillage trough. If the BSC or isolator results in

SAFE HANDLING OF HAZARDOUS DRUGS *(Continued)*

contamination of the HEPA-filter, suspend use until the HEPA-filter has been replaced.

- **Transporting hazardous drugs:** Hazardous drugs should be transported in properly labeled, sealable bags. Individuals involved in transporting hazardous drugs should be educated on procedures for handling spills.

- **Noninjectable hazardous drugs:** Should be properly labeled. Hazardous capsules and tablets should NOT be counted using automatic counting machines; separate, dedicated trays should be used for counting and appropriate gloves (2 pairs are recommended) should be worn during handling. Equipment used during handling should be properly decontaminated with water saturated gauze, detergent, sodium hypochlorite, and neutralizer (properly contain and dispose of decontamination supplies). Use liquid formulations if possible; avoid opening capsules or crushing tablets. When compounding, use a ventilated cabinet and wear proper protective gloves and gowns. Decontaminate, clean, and/or dispose of all equipment and supplies used during compounding and dispense in appropriate container so as to prevent spills. Any unused hazardous substances should be disposed of properly.

Selected Readings

American Society of Hospital Pharmacists, "ASHP Guidelines on Handling Hazardous Drugs," 2006, 63(12):1172-93.

Baker ES and Connor TH, "Monitoring Occupational Exposure to Cancer Chemotherapy Drugs," *Am J Health Syst Pharm*, 1996, 53(22):2713-23.

Bos RP and Sessink PJ, "Biomonitoring of Occupational Exposures to Cytostatic Anticancer Drugs," *Rev Environ Health*, 1997, 12(1):43-58.

Connor TH, "Permeability of Nitrile Rubber, Latex, Polyurethane, and Neoprene Gloves to 18 Antineoplastic Drugs," *Am J Health Syst Pharm*, 1999, 56(23):2450-3.

Connor TH, Anderson RW, Sessink PJ, et al, "Surface Contamination With Antineoplastic Agents in Six Cancer Treatment Centers in Canada and the United States," *Am J Health Syst Pharm*, 1999, 56(14):1427-32.

Connor TH and McDiarmid MA, "Preventing Occupational Exposures to Antineoplastic Drugs in Health Care Settings," *CA Cancer J Clin*, 2006, 56(6):354-65.

Connor TH, Sessink PJ, Harrison BR, et al, "Surface Contamination of Chemotherapy Drug Vials and Evaluation of New Vial-Cleaning Techniques: Results of Three Studies," *Am J Health Syst Pharm*, 2005, 62(5):475-84.

"Preventing Occupational Exposure to Antineoplastic and Other Hazardous Drugs in Health Care Settings," Available at http://www.cdc.gov/niosh/docs/2004-165. Accessed February 6, 2005.

Sessink PJ, Anzion RB, Van den Broek PH, et al, "Detection of Contamination With Antineoplastic Agents in a Hospital Pharmacy Department," *Pharm Weekbl Sci*, 1992, 14(1):16-22.

Sessink PJ, Boer KA, Scheefhals AP, et al, "Occupational Exposure to Antineoplastic Agents at Several Departments in a Hospital. Environmental Contamination and Excretion of Cyclophosphamide and Ifosfamide in Urine of Exposed Workers," *Int Arch Occup Environ Health*, 1992, 64(2):105-12.

Sessink PJ and Bos RP, "Drugs Hazardous to Healthcare Workers. Evaluation of Methods for Monitoring Occupational Exposure to Cytostatic Drugs," *Drug Saf*, 1999, 20(4):347-59.

Solimando DA Jr and Wilson JP, "Demonstration of Skin Fluorescence Following Exposure to Doxorubicin," *Cancer Nurs*, 1983, 6(4):313-5.

Sorsa M and Anderson D, "Monitoring of Occupational Exposure to Cytostatic Anticancer Agents," *Mutat Res*, 1996, 355(1-2):253-61.

Wilson JP and Solimando DA Jr, "Aseptic Technique as a Safety Precaution in the Preparation of Antineoplastic Agents," *Hospital Pharmacy*, 1981, 16(11):575-81.

APPENDIX TABLE OF CONTENTS

MILLIEQUIVALENT AND MILLIMOLE CALCULATIONS AND CONVERSIONS

DEFINITIONS AND CALCULATIONS

Definitions

mole	=	gram molecular weight of a substance (aka molar weight)
millimole (mM)	=	milligram molecular weight of a substance (a millimole is 1/1000 of a mole)
equivalent weight	=	gram weight of a substance which will combine with or replace 1 gram (1 mole) of hydrogen; an equivalent weight can be determined by dividing the molar weight of a substance by its ionic valence
milliequivalent (mEq)	=	milligram weight of a substance which will combine with or replace 1 milligram (1 millimole) of hydrogen (a milliequivalent is 1/1000 of an equivalent)

Calculations

moles	=	$\dfrac{\text{weight of a substance (grams)}}{\text{molecular weight of that substance (grams)}}$
millimoles	=	$\dfrac{\text{weight of a substance (milligrams)}}{\text{molecular weight of that substance (milligrams)}}$
equivalents	=	moles x valence of ion
milliequivalents	=	millimoles x valence of ion
moles	=	$\dfrac{\text{equivalents}}{\text{valence of ion}}$
millimoles	=	$\dfrac{\text{milliequivalents}}{\text{valence of ion}}$
millimoles	=	moles x 1000
milliequivalents	=	equivalents x 1000

Note: Use of equivalents and milliequivalents is valid only for those substances which have fixed ionic valences (eg, sodium, potassium, calcium, chlorine, magnesium bromine, etc). For substances with variable ionic valences (eg, phosphorous), a reliable equivalent value cannot be determined. In these instances, one should calculate millimoles (which are fixed and reliable) rather than milliequivalents.

MILLIEQUIVALENT CONVERSIONS

To convert mg/100 mL to mEq/L the following formula may be used:

$$\frac{(\text{mg/100 mL}) \times 10 \times \text{valence}}{\text{atomic weight}} = \text{mEq/L}$$

To convert mEq/L to mg/100 mL the following formula may be used:

$$\frac{(\text{mEq/L}) \times \text{atomic weight}}{10 \times \text{valence}} = \text{mg/100 mL}$$

To convert mEq/L to volume of percent of a gas the following formula may be used:

$$\frac{(mEq/L) \times 22.4}{10} = \text{volume percent}$$

Valences and Atomic Weights of Selected Ions

Substance	Electrolyte	Valence	Molecular Wt
Calcium	Ca^{++}	2	40
Chloride	Cl^-	1	35.5
Magnesium	Mg^{++}	2	24
Phosphate	HPO_4^{--} (80%)	1.8	96[1]
pH = 7.4	$H_2PO_4^-$ (20%)	1.8	96[1]
Potassium	K^+	1	39
Sodium	Na^+	1	23
Sulfate	SO_4^{--}	2	96[1]

[1]The molecular weight of phosphorus only is 31, and sulfur only is 32.

Approximate Milliequivalents — Weights of Selected Ions

Salt	mEq/g Salt	mg Salt/mEq
Calcium carbonate [$CaCO_3$]	20	50
Calcium chloride [$CaCl_2 \bullet 2H_2O$]	14	74
Calcium gluceptate [$Ca(C_7H_{13}O_8)_2$]	4	245
Calcium gluconate [$Ca(C_6H_{11}O_7)_2 \bullet H_2O$]	5	224
Calcium lactate [$Ca(C_3H_5O_3)_2 \bullet 5H_2O$]	7	154
Magnesium gluconate [$Mg(C_6H_{11}O_7)_2 \bullet H_2O$]	5	216
Magnesium oxide [MgO]	50	20
Magnesium sulfate [$MgSO_4$]	17	60
Magnesium sulfate [$MgSO_4 \bullet 7H_2O$]	8	123
Potassium acetate [$K(C_2H_3O_2)$]	10	98
Potassium chloride [KCl]	13	75
Potassium citrate [$K_3(C_6H_5O_7) \bullet H_2O$]	9	108
Potassium iodide [KI]	6	166
Sodium acetate [$Na(C_2H_3O_2)$]	12	82
Sodium acetate [$Na(C_2H_3O_2) \bullet 3H_2O$]	7	136
Sodium bicarbonate [$NaHCO_3$]	12	84
Sodium chloride [$NaCl$]	17	58
Sodium citrate [$Na_3(C_6H_5O_7) \bullet 2H_2O$]	10	98
Sodium iodine [NaI]	7	150
Sodium lactate [$Na(C_3H_5O_3)$]	9	112
Zinc sulfate [$ZnSO_4 \bullet 7H_2O$]	7	144

CORRECTED SODIUM

Corrected Na^+ = measured Na^+ + [1.5 x (glucose – 150 divided by 100)]

Note: Do not correct for glucose <150.

MILLIEQUIVALENT AND MILLIMOLE CALCULATIONS AND CONVERSIONS *(Continued)*

WATER DEFICIT

Water deficit = 0.6 x body weight [1 − (140 divided by Na^+)]

Note: Body weight is estimated weight in kg when fully hydrated; **Na^+** is serum or plasma sodium. Use corrected Na^+ if necessary. Consult medical references for recommendations for replacement of deficit.

TOTAL SERUM CALCIUM CORRECTED FOR ALBUMIN LEVEL

[(Normal albumin − patient's albumin) x 0.8] + patient's measured total calcium

ACID-BASE ASSESSMENT

Henderson-Hasselbalch Equation

$$pH = 6.1 + \log (HCO_3^- / (0.03) (pCO_2))$$

Alveolar Gas Equation

PIO_2 = FiO_2 x (total atmospheric pressure − vapor pressure of H_2O at 37°C)

= FiO_2 x (760 mm Hg − 47 mm Hg)

PAO_2 = PIO_2 − $PACO_2$ / R

Alveolar/arterial oxygen gradient = PAO_2 − PaO_2

Normal ranges:

	Children	15-20 mm Hg
	Adults	20-25 mm Hg

where:

PIO_2	=	oxygen partial pressure of inspired gas (mm Hg) (150 mm Hg in room air at sea level)
FiO_2	=	fractional pressure of oxygen in inspired gas (0.21 in room air)
PAO_2	=	alveolar oxygen partial pressure
$PACO_2$	=	alveolar carbon dioxide partial pressure
PaO_2	=	arterial oxygen partial pressure
R	=	respiratory exchange quotient (typically 0.8, increases with high carbohydrate diet, decreases with high fat diet)

Acid-Base Disorders

Acute metabolic acidosis:
$PaCO_2$ expected = 1.5 (HCO_3^-) + 8 ± 2 **or**
Expected decrease in $PaCO_2$ = 1.3 (1-1.5) x decrease in HCO_3^-

Acute metabolic alkalosis:
Expected increase in $PaCO_2$ = 0.6 (0.5-1) x increase in HCO_3^-

Acute respiratory acidosis (<6 h duration):
For every $PaCO_2$ increase of 10 mm Hg, HCO_3 increases by 1 mEq/L

Chronic respiratory acidosis (>6 h duration):
For every $PaCO_2$ increase of 10 mm Hg, HCO_3 increases by 4 mEq/L

Acute respiratory alkalosis (<6 h duration):

For every $PaCO_2$ decrease of 10 mm Hg, HCO_3 decreases by 2 mEq/L

Chronic respiratory alkalosis (>6 h duration):

For every $PaCO_2$ decrease of 10 mm Hg, HCO_3 increases by 5 mEq/L

ACID-BASE EQUATION

H^+ (in mEq/L) = (24 x $PaCO_2$) divided by HCO_3^-

Aa GRADIENT

Aa gradient $[(713)(FiO_2 - (PaCO_2$ divided by 0.8))] – PaO_2

Aa gradient	=	alveolar-arterial oxygen gradient
FiO_2	=	inspired oxygen (expressed as a fraction)
$PaCO_2$	=	arterial partial pressure carbon dioxide (mm Hg)
PaO_2	=	arterial partial pressure oxygen (mm Hg)

OSMOLALITY

Definition: The summed concentrations of all osmotically active solute particles.

Predicted serum osmolality =

$$mOsm/L = (2 \times serum\ Na^{++}) + \frac{serum\ glucose}{18} + \frac{BUN}{2.8}$$

The normal range of serum osmolality is 285-295 mOsm/L.

Calculated Osm

Note: Osm is a term used to reconcile osmolality and osmolarity

Osmol gap = measured Osm – calculated Osm

0 to +10: Normal
>10: Abnormal
<0: Probable lab or calculation error

Drugs Causing Osmolar Gap

(by freezing-point depression, gap is >10 mOsm)

Ethanol	Isopropanol (acetone)
Ethylene glycol	Mannitol
Glycerol	Methanol
Hypermagnesemia (>9.5 mEq/L)	Sorbitol
Iodine (questionable)	

MILLIEQUIVALENT AND MILLIMOLE CALCULATIONS AND CONVERSIONS *(Continued)*

BICARBONATE DEFICIT

HCO_3^- deficit = (0.4 x wt in kg) x (HCO_3^- desired − HCO_3^- measured)

Note: In clinical practice, the calculated quantity may differ markedly from the actual amount of bicarbonate needed or that which may be safely administered.

ANION GAP

Definition: The difference in concentration between unmeasured cation and anion equivalents in serum.

Anion gap = Na^+ − (Cl^- + HCO_3^-)
(The normal anion gap is 10-14 mEq/L)

Differential Diagnosis of Increased Anion Gap Acidosis

Organic anions

Lactate (sepsis, hypovolemia, seizures, large tumor burden)
Pyruvate
Uremia
Ketoacidosis (β-hydroxybutyrate and acetoacetate)
Amino acids and their metabolites
Other organic acids

Inorganic anions

Hyperphosphatemia
Sulfates
Nitrates

Differential Diagnosis of Decreased Anion Gap

Organic cations

Hypergammaglobulinemia

Inorganic cations

Hyperkalemia
Hypercalcemia
Hypermagnesemia

Medications and toxins

Lithium

Hypoalbuminemia

RETICULOCYTE INDEX

(% retic divided by 2) x (patient's Hct divided by normal Hct) **or**
(% retic divided by 2) x (patient's Hgb divided by normal Hgb)

Normal index: 1.0
Good marrow response: 2.0-6.0

BODY SURFACE AREA

Body Surface Area (BSA) – Adults and Pediatric

$$BSA\ (m^2) = \frac{kg^{0.425} \times cm^{0.725} \times 71.84}{10,000}$$

or

$$log\ BSA\ (m^2) = \frac{(log\ kg \times 0.425) + (log\ cm \times 0.725) + 1.8564}{10,000}$$

DuBois D and DuBois EF, "A Formula to Estimate the Approximate Surface Area if Height and Weight Be Known," *Arch Intern Med*, 1916, 17:863-71.

$$BSA\ (m^2) = \sqrt{\frac{ht\ (in) \times wt\ (lb)}{3131}} \quad \textbf{or} \quad BSA\ (m^2) = \sqrt{\frac{ht\ (cm) \times wt\ (kg)}{3600}}$$

Lam TK and Leung DT, "More on Simplified Calculation of Body-Surface Area," *N Engl J Med*, 1988, 318(17):1130 (letter).

Mosteller RD, "Simplified Calculation of Body Surface Area," *N Engl J Med*, 1987, 317:1098 (letter).

Ideal Body Weight

Men:	50 kg + 2.3 kg/inch >5 ft
Women:	45 kg + 2.3 kg/in >5 ft

Devine BJ, "Gentamicin Therapy," *Drug Intelligence and Clinical Pharmacy*, 1974, 8:650-5.

or

Men:	51.65 kg + 1.85 kg/in >5 ft
Women:	48.67 kg + 1.7 kg/in >5 ft

Robinson JD, Lupkiewicz SM, Palenik L, et al, "Determination of Ideal Body Weight for Drug Dosage Calculations," *Am J Hosp Pharm*, 1983, 40(6): 1016-9.

Adjusted Body Weight

Adjusted wt (kg) = actual weight (kg) – 0.4 [actual wt (kg) – ideal weight (kg)]

Notari EE, "Biopharmaceuticals and Clinical Pharmacokinetics," New York, Basel, 1987, 380.

Area Under the Curve (AUC) for Carboplatin Dosing

Carboplatin (mg) = desired AUC x (25 + GFR)

GFR = creatinine clearance (measured or estimated)

Calvert AH, Newell DR, Gumbrell LA, et al, "Carboplatin Dosage: Prospective Evaluation of a Simple Formula Based on Renal Function," *J Clin Oncol*, 1989, 7(11):1748-56.

CREATININE CLEARANCE ESTIMATING METHODS IN PATIENTS WITH STABLE RENAL FUNCTION

These formulas provide an acceptable estimate of the patient's creatinine clearance **except** in the following instances.

- Patient's serum creatinine is changing rapidly (either up or down).
- Patients are markedly emaciated.

In above situations, certain assumptions have to be made.

- In patients with rapidly rising serum creatinine (ie, >0.5-0.7 mg/dL/day), it is best to assume that the patient's creatinine clearance is probably <10 mL/minute.
- In emaciated patients, although their actual creatinine clearance is less than their calculated creatinine clearance (because of decreased creatinine production), it is not possible to easily predict how much less.

Infants

Estimation of creatinine clearance using serum creatinine and body length (to be used when an adequate timed specimen cannot be obtained). **Note:** This formula may not provide an accurate estimation of creatinine clearance for infants younger than 6 months of age and for patients with severe starvation or muscle wasting.

$$Cl_{cr} = K \times L/S_{cr}$$

where:

Cl_{cr}	=	creatinine clearance in mL/minute/1.73 m²
K	=	constant of proportionality that is age specific

Age	K
Low birth weight ≤1 y	0.33
Full-term ≤1 y	0.45
2-12 y	0.55
13-21 y female	0.55
13-21 y male	0.70

L	=	length in cm
S_{cr}	=	serum creatinine concentration in mg/dL

Reference

Schwartz GJ, Brion LP, and Spitzer A, "The Use of Plasma Creatinine Concentration for Estimating Glomerular Filtration Rate in Infants, Children and Adolescents," *Pediatr Clin North Am*, 1987, 34(3):571-90.

Children (1-18 years)

<u>Method 1</u>: (Traub SL and Johnson CE, *Am J Hosp Pharm*, 1980, 37(2):195-201)

$$Cl_{cr} = \frac{0.48 \times (\text{height})}{S_{cr}}$$

where:

Cl_{cr}	=	creatinine clearance in mL/min/1.73 m²
S_{cr}	=	serum creatinine in mg/dL
Height	=	height in cm

Method 2: Nomogram (Traub SL and Johnson CE, *Am J Hosp Pharm*, 1980, 37(2):195-201)

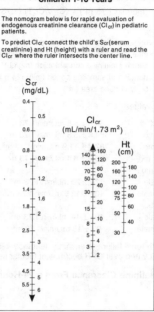

Children 1-18 Years

The nomogram below is for rapid evaluation of endogenous creatinine clearance (Cl_{cr}) in pediatric patients.

To predict Cl_{cr} connect the child's S_{cr}(serum creatinine) and Ht (height) with a ruler and read the Cl_{cr} where the ruler intersects the center line.

Adults (18 years and older)

Method 1: (Cockroft DW and Gault MH, *Nephron*, 1976, 16:31-41)

Estimated creatinine clearance (Cl_{cr}) (mL/min):

$$\text{Male} = \frac{(140 - \text{age}) \times \text{BW (kg)}}{72 \times S_{cr}}$$

$$\text{Female} = \text{male} \times 0.85$$

Note: Use of actual body weight (BW) in obese patients (and possibly patients with ascites) may significantly overestimate creatinine clearance. Some clinicians prefer to use an adjusted ideal body weight (IBW) in such cases [eg, IBW + 0.4(ABW-IBW)], especially when calculating dosages for aminoglycoside antibiotics.

Method 2: (Jelliffe RW, *Ann Intern Med*, 1973, 79:604)

Estimated creatinine clearance (Cl_{cr}) (mL/min/1.73 m²):

$$\text{Male} = \frac{98 - 0.8 \ (\text{age} - 20)}{S_{cr}}$$

$$\text{Female} = \text{male} \times 0.90$$

RENAL FUNCTION TESTS

Endogenous Creatinine Clearance vs Age (timed collection)

Creatinine clearance (mL/min/1.73 m^2) = (Cr_uV/Cr_sT) (1.73/A)

where:

Cr_u	=	urine creatinine concentration (mg/dL)
V	=	total urine collected during sampling period (mL)
Cr_s	=	serum creatinine concentration (mg/dL)
T	=	duration of sampling period (min) (24 h = 1440 min)
A	=	body surface area (m^2)

Age-specific normal values

5-7 d	50.6 ± 5.8 mL/min/1.73 m^2
1-2 mo	64.6 ± 5.8 mL/min/1.73 m^2
5-8 mo	87.7 ± 11.9 mL/min/1.73 m^2
9-12 mo	86.9 ± 8.4 mL/min/1.73 m^2
≥18 mo	
male	124 ± 26 mL/min/1.73 m^2
female	109 ± 13.5 mL/min/1.73 m^2
Adults	
male	105 ± 14 mL/min/1.73 m^2
female	95 ± 18 mL/min/1.73 m^2

Note: In patients with renal failure (creatinine clearance <25 mL/min), creatinine clearance may be elevated over GFR because of tubular secretion of creatinine.

Calculation of Creatinine Clearance From a 24-Hour Urine Collection

Equation 1:

$$Cl_{cr} = \frac{U \times V}{P}$$

where:

Cl_{cr}	=	creatinine clearance
U	=	urine concentration of creatinine
V	=	total urine volume in the collection
P	=	plasma creatinine concentration

Equation 2:

$$Cl_{cr} = \frac{(\text{total urine volume [mL]}) \times (\text{urine Cr concentration [mg/dL]})}{(\text{serum creatinine [mg/dL]}) \times (\text{time of urine collection [minutes]})}$$

Occasionally, a patient will have a 12- or 24-hour urine collection done for direct calculation of creatinine clearance. Although a urine collection for 24 hours is best, it is difficult to do since many urine collections occur for a much shorter period. A 24-hour urine collection is the desired duration of urine collection because the urine excretion of creatinine is diurnal and thus the measured creatinine clearance will vary throughout the day as the creatinine in the urine varies. When the urine collection is less than 24 hours, the total excreted creatinine will be affected by the time of the day during which the collection is performed. A 24-hour urine collection is sufficient to be able to accurately average the diurnal creatinine excretion variations. If a patient has 24 hours of urine collected for creatinine clearance, equation 1 can be used for calculating the creatinine clearance. To use equation 1 to calculate the creatinine clearance, it will be necessary to know the duration of urine collection, the urine collection volume, the urine creatinine concentration, and the serum creatinine value that reflects the urine collection period. In most cases, a serum creatinine concentration is drawn anytime during the day, but it is best to have the value drawn halfway through the collection period.

Amylase:Creatinine Clearance Ratio

$$\frac{Amylase_u \times creatinine_p}{Amylase_p \times creatinine_u} \times 100$$

u = urine; p = plasma

Serum BUN:Serum Creatinine Ratio

Serum BUN (mg/dL:serum creatinine (mg/dL))

Normal BUN:creatinine ratio is 10-15

BUN:creatinine ratio >20 suggests prerenal azotemia (also seen with high urea-generation states such as GI bleeding)

BUN:creatinine ratio <5 may be seen with disorders affecting urea biosynthesis such as urea cycle enzyme deficiencies and with hepatitis.

Fractional Sodium Excretion

Fractional sodium secretion (FENa) = $Na_uCr_s/Na_sCr_u \times 100\%$

where:

Na_u = urine sodium (mEq/L)
Na_s = serum sodium (mEq/L)
Cr_u = urine creatinine (mg/dL)
Cr_s = serum creatinine (mg/dL)

FENa <1% suggests prerenal failure
FENa >2% suggest intrinsic renal failure
(for newborns, normal FENa is approximately 2.5%)

Note: Disease states associated with a falsely elevated FENa include severe volume depletion (>10%), early acute tubular necrosis, and volume depletion in chronic renal disease. Disorders associated with a lowered FENa include acute glomerulonephritis, hemoglobinuric or myoglobinuric renal failure, nonoliguric acute tubular necrosis, and acute urinary tract obstruction. In addition, FENa may be <1% in patients with acute renal failure **and** a second condition predisposing to sodium retention (eg, burns, congestive heart failure, nephrotic syndrome).

Urine Calcium:Urine Creatinine Ratio (spot sample)

Urine calcium (mg/dL): urine creatinine (mg/dL)

Normal values <0.21 (mean values 0.08 males, 0.06 females)

Premature infants show wide variability of calcium:creatinine ratio, and tend to have lower thresholds for calcium loss than older children. Prematures without nephrolithiasis had mean Ca:Cr ratio of 0.75 ± 0.76. Infants with nephrolithiasis had mean Ca:Cr ratio of 1.32 ± 1.03 (Jacinto JS, Modanlou HD, Crade M, et al, "Renal Calcification Incidence in Very Low Birth Weight Infants," *Pediatrics*, 1988, 81:31.)

RENAL FUNCTION TESTS *(Continued)*

Urine Protein:Urine Creatinine Ratio (spot sample)

P_u/Cr_u	Total Protein Excretion $(mg/m^2/d)$
0.1	80
1	800
10	8000

where:

P_u = urine protein concentration (mg/dL)
Cr_u = urine creatinine concentration (mg/dL)

INTRAVENOUS IMMUNE GLOBULIN PRODUCT COMPARISON

Brand Name	FDA-Approved Indications	Labeled Contraindications	IgA Content	Half-life	pH	Osmolarity	Recommended Infusion Rates	Additional Comments
Carimune® NF Panglobulin® NF	Primary immunodeficiency; ITP	IgA deficiency with IgA antibody; severe systemic reaction to human immune globulins	Trace amounts	3 weeks	6.4-6.8	3% solution in NS: 498 mOsmol/kg 6% solution in NS: 690 mOsmol/kg 9% solution in NS: 882 mOsmol/kg 12% solution in NS: 1074 mOsmol/kg	Initial (3% solution): 0.5-1 mL/min Maximum (3% solution): 2 mg/kg/min	Contains sucrose
Flebogamma®	Primary immunodeficiency	IgA deficiency with IgA antibody; anaphylactic reactions to blood or blood derived products	<50 mcg/mL	30-45 days	5-6	240-350 mOsmol/L	Initial (5% solution): 0.01 mL/kg/min (0.5 mg/kg/min) Maximum (5% solution): 0.1 mL/kg/min (5 mg/kg/min) Maximum in patients with renal dysfunction (5% solution): 0.06 mL/kg/min (3 mg/kg/min)	Contains sorbitol
Gammagard Liquid	Primary immunodeficiency	IgA deficiency, history of anaphylaxis with immune globulin	37 mcg/mL	35 days	4.6-5.1	240-300 mOsmol/kg	Initial (10% solution): 0.5 mL/kg/h (0.8 mg/kg/min) Maximum (10% solution): 5 mL/kg/h (8.9 mg/kg/min); <2 mL/kg/h (3.3 mg/kg/min) in patients at risk for renal impairment or thrombosis	

(continued)

INTRAVENOUS IMMUNE GLOBULIN PRODUCT COMPARISON *(Continued)*

Brand Name	FDA-Approved Indications	Labeled Contraindications	IgA Content	Half-life	pH	Osmolarity	Recommended Infusion Rates	Additional Comments
Gammagard SD	Primary immunodeficiency, ITP, CLL prophylaxis, Kawasaki syndrome	IgA deficiency	≤2.2 mcg/mL	~23-53 days	6.4-7.2		Initial (5% solution): 0.5 mL/kg/h Maximum (5% solution): 4 mL/kg/h Maximum concentration for infusion: 10%	Contains glucose
Gammar®-P I.V.	Primary immunodeficiency	IgA deficiency; history of anaphylaxis with immune globulin or albumin		34-40 days	6.4-7.2		Initial: 0.01-0.02 mL/kg/min Maximum: 0.06 mL/kg/min Maximum concentration for infusion: 5%	Contains sucrose
Gamunex®	Primary immunodeficiency, ITP	IgA deficiency with IgA antibody; history of anaphylaxis with immune globulin	46 mcg/mL	35 days	4-4.5	258 mOsmol/kg	Initial (10% solution): 0.01 mL/kg/min Maximum (10% solution): 0.08 mL/kg/min Maximum concentration for infusion: 10%	
Octagam®	Primary immunodeficiency	IgA deficiency with IgA antibody	≤200 mcg/mL	Immuno-deficiency: 40 days	5.1-6	310-380 mOsmol/kg	Initial: 30 mg/kg/h Maximum: <200 mg/kg/h Maximum concentration for infusion: 5%	Contains maltose

(continued)

Brand Name	FDA-Approved Indications	Labeled Contraindications	IgA Content	Half-life	pH	Osmolarity	Recommended Infusion Rates	Additional Comments
Polygam® S/D	Primary immunodeficiency, ITP, CLL, Kawasaki syndrome	IgA deficiency	≤2.2 mcg/mL	~38 days	6.4–7.2		Initial: 0.5 mL/kg/h Maximum: 4 mL/kg/h Maximum concentration for infusion: 10%	Contains glucose

Carimune® NF prescribing information, ZLB Behring LLC, Kankakee, IL, January 2005.

Flebogamma® 5% prescribing information, Grifols Biologicals, Inc, Los Angeles, CA, September 2004.

Gammagard Liquid prescribing information, Baxter Healthcare Corporation, Westlake Village, CA, April 2005.

Gammagard S/D prescribing information, Baxter Healthcare Corporation, Westlake Village, CA, January 2005.

Gammar®-P I.V. prescribing information, ZLB Behring LLC, Kankakee, IL, August 2004.

Gamunex® prescribing information, Talecris Biotherapeutics, Inc, Research Triangle Park, NC, November 2005.

Octagam® prescribing information, Octapharma USA, Inc, Centreville, VA, March 2007.

Polygam® S/D prescribing information, Baxter Healthcare Corporation, Westlake Village, CA, January 2005.

REFERENCE VALUES FOR ADULTS

Automated Chemistry (CHEMISTRY A)

Test	Values	Remarks
SERUM / PLASMA		
Acetone	Negative	
Albumin	3.2-5 g/dL	
Alcohol, ethyl	Negative	
Aldolase	1.2-7.6 IU/L	
Ammonia	20-70 mcg/dL	Specimen to be placed on ice as soon as collected.
Amylase	30-110 units/L	
Bilirubin, direct	0-0.3 mg/dL	
Bilirubin, total	0.1-1.2 mg/dL	
Calcium	8.6-10.3 mg/dL	
Calcium, ionized	2.24-2.46 mEq/L	
Chloride	95-108 mEq/L	
Cholesterol, total	≤200 mg/dL	Fasted blood required – normal value affected by dietary habits. This reference range is for a general adult population.
HDL cholesterol	40-60 mg/dL	Fasted blood required – normal value affected by dietary habits.
LDL cholesterol	<160 mg/dL	If triglyceride is >400 mg/dL, LDL cannot be calculated accurately (Friedewald equation). Target LDL-C depends on patient's risk factors.
CO_2	23-30 mEq/L	
Creatine kinase (CK) isoenzymes		
CK-BB	0%	
CK-MB (cardiac)	0%-3.9%	
CK-MM (muscle)	96%-100%	
CK-MB levels must be both ≥4% and 10 IU/L to meet diagnostic criteria for CK-MB positive result consistent with myocardial injury.		
Creatine phosphokinase (CPK)	8-150 IU/L	
Creatinine	0.5-1.4 mg/dL	
Ferritin	13-300 ng/mL	
Folate	3.6-20 ng/dL	
GGT (gamma-glutamyltranspeptidase)		
male	11-63 IU/L	
female	8-35 IU/L	
GLDH	To be determined	
Glucose (preprandial)	<115 mg/dL	Goals different for diabetics.
Glucose, fasting	60-110 mg/dL	Goals different for diabetics.
Glucose, nonfasting (2-h postprandial)	<120 mg/dL	Goals different for diabetics.
Hemoglobin A_{1c}	<8	
Hemoglobin, plasma free	<2.5 mg/100 mL	

Automated Chemistry (CHEMISTRY A) *(continued)*

Test	Values	Remarks
Hemoglobin, total glycosolated (Hb A₁)	4%-8%	
Iron	65-150 mcg/dL	
Iron binding capacity, total (TIBC)	250-420 mcg/dL	
Lactic acid	0.7-2.1 mEq/L	Specimen to be kept on ice and sent to lab as soon as possible.
Lactate dehydrogenase (LDH)	56-194 IU/L	
Lactate dehydrogenase (LDH) isoenzymes		
LD₁	20%-34%	
LD₂	29%-41%	
LD₃	15%-25%	
LD₄	1%-12%	
LD₅	1%-15%	

Flipped LD_1/LD_2 ratios (>1 may be consistent with myocardial injury) particularly when considered in combination with a recent CK-MB positive result.

Test	Values	Remarks
Lipase	23-208 units/L	
Magnesium	1.6-2.5 mg/dL	Increased by slight hemolysis.
Osmolality	289-308 mOsm/kg	
Phosphatase, alkaline		
adults 25-60 y	33-131 IU/L	
adults 61 y or older	51-153 IU/L	
infancy-adolescence	Values range up to 3-5 times higher than adults	
Phosphate, inorganic	2.8-4.2 mg/dL	
Potassium	3.5-5.2 mEq/L	Increased by slight hemolysis.
Prealbumin	>15 mg/dL	
Protein, total	6.5-7.9 g/dL	
SGOT (AST)	<35 IU/L (20-48)	
SGPT (ALT) (10-35)	<35 IU/L	
Sodium	134-149 mEq/L	
Transferrin	>200 mg/dL	
Triglycerides	45-155 mg/dL	Fasted blood required.
Troponin I	<1.5 ng/mL	
Urea nitrogen (BUN)	7-20 mg/dL	
Uric acid		
male	2-8 mg/dL	
female	2-7.5 mg/dL	

REFERENCE VALUES FOR ADULTS *(Continued)*

Automated Chemistry (CHEMISTRY A) *(continued)*

Test	Values	Remarks
CEREBROSPINAL FLUID		
Glucose	50-70 mg/dL	
Protein		
adults and children	15-45 mg/dL	CSF obtained by lumbar puncture.
newborn infants	60-90 mg/dL	
On CSF obtained by cisternal puncture: About 25 mg/dL		
On CSF obtained by ventricular puncture: About 10 mg/dL		
Note: Bloody specimen gives erroneously high value due to contamination with blood proteins		
URINE		
(24-hour specimen is required for all these tests unless specified)		
Amylase	32-641 units/L	The value is in units/L and **not** calculated for total volume.
Amylase, fluid (random samples)		Interpretation of value left for physician, depends on the nature of fluid.
Calcium	Depends upon dietary intake	
Creatine		
male	150 mg/24 h	Higher value on children and during pregnancy.
female	250 mg/24 h	
Creatinine	1000-2000 mg/24 h	
Creatinine clearance (endogenous)		
male	85-125 mL/min	A blood sample must accompany urine specimen.
female	75-115 mL/min	
Glucose	1 g/24 h	
5-hydroxyindoleacetic acid	2-8 mg/24 h	
Iron	0.15 mg/24 h	Acid washed container required.
Magnesium	146-209 mg/24 h	
Osmolality	500-800 mOsm/kg	With normal fluid intake.
Oxalate	10-40 mg/24 h	
Phosphate	400-1300 mg/24 h	
Potassium	25-120 mEq/24 h	Varies with diet; the interpretation of urine electrolytes and osmolality should be left for the physician.
Sodium	40-220 mEq/24 h	
Porphobilinogen, qualitative	Negative	
Porphyrins, qualitative	Negative	
Proteins	0.05-0.1 g/24 h	
Salicylate	Negative	
Urea clearance	60-95 mL/min	A blood sample must accompany specimen.

Automated Chemistry (CHEMISTRY A) *(continued)*

Test	Values	Remarks
Urea N	10-40 g/24 h	Dependent on protein intake.
Uric acid	250-750 mg/24 h	Dependent on diet and therapy.
Urobilinogen	0.5-3.5 mg/24 h	For qualitative determination on random urine, send sample to urinalysis section in Hematology Lab.
Xylose absorption test		
children	16%-33% of ingested xylose	
FECES		
Fat, 3-day collection	<5 g/d	Value depends on fat intake of 100 g/d for 3 days preceding and during collection.
GASTRIC ACIDITY		
Acidity, total, 12 h	10-60 mEq/L	Titrated at pH 7.

REFERENCE VALUES FOR ADULTS *(Continued)*

Blood Gases

	Arterial	Capillary	Venous
pH	7.35-7.45	7.35-7.45	7.32-7.42
pCO_2 (mm Hg)	35-45	35-45	38-52
pO_2 (mm Hg)	70-100	60-80	24-48
HCO_3 (mEq/L)	19-25	19-25	19-25
TCO_2 (mEq/L)	19-29	19-29	23-33
O_2 saturation (%)	90-95	90-95	40-70
Base excess (mEq/L)	-5 to +5	-5 to +5	-5 to +5

HEMATOLOGY

Complete Blood Count

Age	Hgb (g/dL)	Hct (%)	RBC (mill/mm³)	RDW
0-3 d	15.0-20.0	45-61	4.0-5.9	<18
1-2 wk	12.5-18.5	39-57	3.6-5.5	<17
1-6 mo	10.0-13.0	29-42	3.1-4.3	<16.5
7 mo to 2 y	10.5-13.0	33-38	3.7-4.9	<16
2-5 y	11.5-13.0	34-39	3.9-5.0	<15
5-8 y	11.5-14.5	35-42	4.0-4.9	<15
13-18 y	12.0-15.2	36-47	4.5-5.1	<14.5
Adult male	13.5-16.5	41-50	4.5-5.5	<14.5
Adult female	12.0-15.0	36-44	4.0-4.9	<14.5

Age	MCV (fL)	MCH (pg)	MCHC (%)	Plts (x 10³/mm³)
0-3 d	95-115	31-37	29-37	250-450
1-2 wk	86-110	28-36	28-38	250-450
1-6 mo	74-96	25-35	30-36	300-700
7 mo to 2 y	70-84	23-30	31-37	250-600
2-5 y	75-87	24-30	31-37	250-550
5-8 y	77-95	25-33	31-37	250-550
13-18 y	78-96	25-35	31-37	150-450
Adult male	80-100	26-34	31-37	150-450
Adult female	80-100	26-34	31-37	150-450

WBC and Differential

Age	WBC (x 10³/mm³)	Segs	Bands	Lymphs	Monos
0-3 d	9.0-35.0	32-62	10-18	19-29	5-7
1-2 wk	5.0-20.0	14-34	6-14	36-45	6-10
1-6 mo	6.0-17.5	13-33	4-12	41-71	4-7
7 mo to 2 y	6.0-17.0	15-35	5-11	45-76	3-6
2-5 y	5.5-15.5	23-45	5-11	35-65	3-6
5-8 y	5.0-14.5	32-54	5-11	28-48	3-6
13-18 y	4.5-13.0	34-64	5-11	25-45	3-6
Adults	4.5-11.0	35-66	5-11	24-44	3-6

Age	Eosinophils	Basophils	Atypical Lymphs	No. of NRBCs
0-3 d	0-2	0-1	0-8	0-2
1-2 wk	0-2	0-1	0-8	0
1-6 mo	0-3	0-1	0-8	0
7 mo to 2 y	0-3	0-1	0-8	0
2-5 y	0-3	0-1	0-8	0
5-8 y	0-3	0-1	0-8	0
13-18 y	0-3	0-1	0-8	0
Adults	0-3	0-1	0-8	0

Segs = segmented neutrophils.
Bands = band neutrophils.
Lymphs = lymphocytes.
Monos = monocytes.

Erythrocyte Sedimentation Rates and Reticulocyte Counts

Sedimentation rate, Westergren	Children	0-20 mm/hour
	Adult male	0-15 mm/hour
	Adult female	0-20 mm/hour
Sedimentation rate, Wintrobe	Children	0-13 mm/hour
	Adult male	0-10 mm/hour
	Adult female	0-15 mm/hour
Reticulocyte count	Newborns	2%-6%
	1-6 mo	0%-2.8%
	Adults	0.5%-1.5%

PHARMACOLOGIC CATEGORY INDEX

NOTES

NOTES

NOTES

Other Products Offered by Lexi-Comp®

Anesthesiology & Critical Care Drug Handbook

Designed for anesthesiologists, critical care practitioners, and all healthcare professionals involved in the care of surgical or ICU patients.

Includes: Comprehensive drug information to ensure the appropriate clinical management of patients; Intensivist and Anesthesiologist perspective; Over 2000 medications most commonly used in the preoperative and critical care setting; and Special Topics/Issues section with frequently encountered patient conditions

Clinician's Guide to Diagnosis

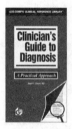

A reference with a practical approach to commonly-encountered symptoms, designed to follow the logical thought process of a seasoned clinician.

Includes: Evidence-based, easy-to-find answers to the questions that commonly arise in the symptom evaluation process; Over 35 algorithms that provide parallel references to the information in each chapter

Clinician's Guide to Internal Medicine

Quick access to essential information covering diagnosis, treatment, and management of commonly-encountered patient conditions in Internal Medicine.

Includes: Practical approaches ideal for point-of-care use; Algorithms to establish a diagnosis and select the appropriate therapy; and Tables to summarize diagnostic and therapeutic strategies

Other Products Offered by Lexi-Comp®

Clinician's Guide to Laboratory Medicine

A resource providing a logical step-by-step process from an abnormal lab test to diagnosis. This two-book set provides you with a full size guide and a portable pocket version for convenient referencing.

Includes: 137 chapters; 700 charts, tables, and algorithms; and sections such as neurology, infectious diseases, and obstetrics/gynecology

Drug Information Handbook

This easy-to-use drug reference is for the pharmacist, physician, or other healthcare professional requiring fast access to comprehensive drug information.

Over 1400 drug monographs are detailed with up to 33 fields of information per monograph. A valuable appendix includes hundreds of charts and reviews of special topics such as guidelines for treatment and therapy recommendations. A pharmacologic category index is also provided.

Published in cooperation with APhA. *Drug Information Handbook with International Trade Names Index* also available.

Drug Information Handbook for Advanced Practice Nursing

Designed to assist the Advanced Practice Nurse with prescribing, monitoring, and educating patients.

Includes: Over 4800 generic and brand names, cross-referenced by page number; Drug names and important Nursing fields highlighted in RED; Labeled and investigational indications; Adult, Geriatric, and Pediatric dosing; and Up to 58 fields including critical information on Patient Education and Physical Assessment

Other Products Offered by Lexi-Comp®

Drug Information Handbook for Nursing

Designed for registered professional nurses and upper-division nursing students requiring dosing, administration, monitoring, and patient education information.
Includes: Over 4800 generic and brand drug names cross-referenced by page number; Drug names and Nursing fields in RED; Fields of information include: Nursing Actions: Physical Assessment, and Patient Education; and Administration: I.V. Detail, Storage, Reconstitution, and Compatibility; and Labeled and investigational indications

Drug Information Handbook for Perioperative Nursing

Designed especially for perioperative nurses, Registered Nurses practicing in operative and interventional procedure settings, and upper-division nursing students seeking a distinctive reference for dosing, administration, monitoring, and patient education criteria for perioperative patient care environments.

Includes: Up to 40 fields per monograph including Medication Safety data; Adult, Pediatric, and Geriatric Dosing guidelines; and information on each phase of the perioperative encounter, with emphasis on special situations central to perioperative patient care

Drug Information Handbook for Psychiatry

Designed for any healthcare professional requiring quick access to comprehensive drug information as it relates to mental health issues.

Includes: Detailed drug monographs for psychotropic, nonpsychotropic, and herbal medications; Special fields such as Mental Health Comment (useful clinical pearls), Medication Safety Issues, Effects on Mental Status, and Effects on Psychiatric Treatment

To order call Customer Service at 1-866-397-3433 or go to www.lexi.com.
Outside of the U.S. call: 330-650-6506 or www.lexi.com

Other Products Offered by Lexi-Comp®

Geriatric Dosage Handbook

Designed for any healthcare professional managing geriatric patients.

Includes: Complete adult and geriatric dosing; Special geriatric considerations; Up to 36 key fields of information in each monograph including Medication Safety Issues; and Extensive information on drug interactions as well as dosing for patients with renal/hepatic impairment.

Laboratory Test Handbook

An invaluable source of information for anyone interested in diagnostic laboratory testing. Includes: 960 tests; Up to 25 fields per test; Extensive cross-referencing; Over 12,000 references; and Key Word Index: test result, disease, organ system and syndrome. Clinicians, nurse practitioners, residents, nurses, and students will appreciate the Concise version of the *Laboratory Test Handbook* for its convenience as a quick reference. This abridged version includes 876 tests.

Pediatric Dosage Handbook

This book is designed for any healthcare professional requiring quick access to comprehensive pediatric drug information. Each monograph contains multiple field of content, including usual dosage by age group, indication and route of administration. Drug interactions, adverse reactions, extemporaneous preparations, pharmacodynamics/pharma-cokinetics data, and medication safety issue are covered.
Pediatric Dosage Handbook with International Trade Names Index also available.

To order call Customer Service at 1-866-397-3433 or go to www.lexi.com.
Outside of the U.S. call: 330-650-6506 or www.lexi.com

Other Products Offered by Lexi-Comp®

Pharmacogenomics Handbook

Ideal for any healthcare professional or student wishing to gain insight into the emerging field of pharmacogenomics. Includes: Information concerning key genetic variations that may influence drug disposition and/or sensitivity; brief introductions to fundamental concepts in genetics and genomics. A foundation for all clinicians who will be called on to integrate rapidly-expanding genomic knowledge into the management of drug therapy.

Pharmacology Companion Guides

Our Pharmacology Companion Guide series supplies the best of Lexi-Comp's comparative charts, therapy guidelines, and supplemental data. Ideal for healthcare providers who require a quick reference resource for the key appendix information found in the *Drug Information Handbook* and *Pediatric Dosage Handbook*. An excellent companion to our PDA software.

Rating Scales for Mental Health

Ideal for clinicians as well as administrators, this book provides an overview of over 100 recommended rating scales for mental assessment.

Includes: Rating scales for conditions such as General Anxiety, Social/Family Functioning, Eating Disorders, and Sleep Disorders; and Monograph format covering such topics as Overview of Scale, General Applications, Psychometric Properties, and References

To order call Customer Service at 1-866-397-3433 or go to www.lexi.com.
Outside of the U.S. call: 330-650-6506 or www.lexi.com